BaseBall america®
2009 ALMANAC

BASEBALL AMERICA INC. · DURHAM, N.C.

BaseBall america
2009 ALMANAC

A COMPREHENSIVE REVIEW OF THE 2008 SEASON, FEATURING STATISTICS AND COMMENTARY

Editor
WILL LINGO

Assistant Editors
BEN BADLER, KARY BOOHER, JIM CALLIS, J.J. COOPER, MATT EDDY, AARON FITT, JOSH LEVENTHAL, JOHN MANUEL, NATHAN RODE, JIM SHONERD

Contributing Writer
JOHN PERROTTO

Photo Editor
NATHAN RODE

Editorial Assistants
JESSE BURKHART, BRYAN CHMIELEWSKI, MIKE EHRLICH, CONOR GLASSEY, AUSTIN MALONEY

Design & Production
SARA HIATT, LINWOOD WEBB

Jacket Photo
B.J. UPTON BY CLIFF WELCH

BaseBall america

PRESIDENT/PUBLISHER: LEE FOLGER
EDITORS IN CHIEF: WILL LINGO, JOHN MANUEL
EXECUTIVE EDITOR: JIM CALLIS
DESIGN & PRODUCTION DIRECTOR: SARA HIATT

DISTRIBUTED BY SIMON & SCHUSTER
ISBN-13: 978-1-932391-23-7

STATISTICS COMPILED AND PROVIDED BY MAJOR LEAGUE BASEBALL ADVANCED MEDIA.

BaseballAmerica.com

EDITOR'S NOTE: Major league statistics are based on final, unofficial 2008 averages. >> The organization statistics, which begin on page 43, include all players who participated in at least one game during the 2008 season. >> Pitchers' batting statistics are not included, nor are the pitching statistics of field players who pitched in less than two games. >> For players who played with more than one team in the same league, the player's cumulative statistics appear on the line immediately after the player's statistics with each team. >> Innings pitched have been rounded off to the nearest full inning.

TABLE OF CONTENTS

Rays players celebrate their American League championship win over the Red Sox

CLIFF WELCH

MAJOR LEAGUES

Rays overcome long odds to realize goal

BY JOHN PERROTTO

Scott Kazmir surveyed the field one day during a Rays workout early in spring training and the idea, seemingly preposterous at the time, hit him. So when a reporter happened to approach the Tampa Bay lefthander later that day, Kazmir spoke his mind.

"I think this team can make the playoffs," Kazmir said with a straight face.

The idea of the Rays making the postseason seemed almost impossible. Though the franchise dropped the "devil" from its original Devil Rays moniker during the offseason—and changed its logo and uniforms—this was still a club that had lost at least 91 games in each of its first 10 years of existence. They had finished out of last place in the American League East only once since joining the league in 1998.

Yet, Kazmir was ultimately proven to be a prophet. In one of the great turnaround stories in baseball history, the Rays went from having the worst record in the major leagues at 66-96, in 2007, to winning the AL East title with a 97-65 record. Impressively, they finished ahead of the two most powerful franchises in the game, the Red Sox and the Yankees.

"I knew we had something here," Kazmir said. "I knew we had the depth. I knew we had the pitching. I knew we had everything. We just had to put it together, and we did."

Only one team in the major leagues, the AL West-champion Angels, won more games in the regular season. They also established a club record for victories in finishing at 100-62.

The Rays were a loose group with a roster of rising young stars, led by black-rimmed glasses-wearing manager Joe Maddon, whom Kazmir referred to as "the coolest manager in baseball." They also were a determined group, intent on changing their image as a franchise.

"It's so special how we've come together," Maddon said. "The way we've changed here so dramatically is remarkable. We went from being down to being the most unified team out there."

When the Rays arrived in spring training, they each found a T-shirt in their lockers emblazoned with the seemingly nonsensical equation 9=8. It would become their slogan throughout a magical season.

Third-year manager Joe Maddon's fuzzy math unified a talented, young Rays club

CLIFF WELCH

"Primarily, it means that if we played hard for nine innings every day that we could be one of the eight teams going to the playoffs when the season ended," Maddon said. "There was also a second meaning. I felt if we got nine more wins because of better offense, nine more wins because of better defense and nine more wins because of better pitching that we would be at least in the thick of the pennant race, if not in the playoffs."

Maddon's math meant he was hoping for 93 wins. The Rays went four better.

"When we first got those T-shirts, everyone just kind of rolled their eyes," Rays righthander James Shields said. "Joe is the man with a million slogans and we all kind of got a chuckle out of it, but he was serious. He really believed we had enough talent and could show enough improvement to make the playoffs. In fact, I'm sure he had more confidence in that than anyone in the clubhouse when spring training began, but he got all of us to believe and then the impossible happened."

Plenty Of Divisional Drama

The Rays weren't the only surprise division winners in the American League. In a season in which the defending AL Central-champion Indians were expected to compete with the Tigers for top honors, the White Sox and Twins were supposed to battle for third place. After all, the Tigers had made a blockbuster trade for third baseman Miguel Cabrera and lefthander Dontrelle Willis in the offseason and began the year with the third-highest payroll in the game at $137 million.

Yet, it was the White Sox and Twins who wound up tied for first place with identical 88-74 marks—even though the White Sox needed to win a makeup game with the Tigers a day after the regular season ended to reach those 88 wins. The Twins and White Sox then squared off in a one-game playoff at Chicago's U.S. Cellular Field, which the White Sox won 1-0.

White Sox lefthander John Danks pitched eight innings of two-hit ball on three days' rest while DH Jim Thome hit a 461-foot home run to center field in the seventh inning off rookie righthander Nick Blackburn for the game's lone run. Meanwhile, center fielder Ken Griffey Jr. prevented the Twins from scoring when he threw out Michael Cuddyer at home plate as he tried to score from third base following Brendan Harris' fly out.

Losing in the 163rd game was tough to swallow for the Twins.

"You never want to see a six-month season boil down to one game, but that's what happened," first baseman Justin Morneau said. "It hurts to have the season end this way."

The Angels, though, didn't have any painful regular-season moments, as they won the AL West by 21 games over the Rangers. In fact, the Angels

clinched their fourth division title in five years on Sept. 10, with 17 games remaining in the regular season.

For the first time since 1997, neither the Red Sox nor Yankees won the AL East, as the upstart Rays ended that streak. However, the Red Sox won the wild card with a 95-67 record. The Yankees, on the other hand, missed the playoffs for the first time since 1993, their 13-year postseason streak snapped with an 89-73 mark that put them eight games behind the Rays and six behind the Red Sox.

The Yankees, though, saw their string of playoff appearances coincide with having a new manager. Joe Girardi replaced Joe Torre at the end of the 2007 season. Adding insult to injury, the Yankees' failed to qualify for the postseason despite having a $209 million payroll, the sport's largest.

"It basically boils down to we weren't good enough," Yankees shortstop Derek Jeter said. "That's the only way you can put it. Our team didn't play well enough the whole season in order to get where we needed to be. It's a huge disappointment. That's pretty much all you can say."

In the National League, a quarter-century of disappointment ended when the Brewers won the wild card on the final day of the regular season for their first postseason berth since 1982. The Brewers struggled during the season's final month, costing manager Ned Yost his job in a stunning development on Sept. 15—even though his team still held the wild card lead. The firing came on the heels of the Brewers' losing four straight games at the Phillies.

Third-base coach Dale Sveum was promoted to interim manager and guided the Brewers to the playoffs when they beat the NL Central-cham-

FROM WORST TO FIRST: THE 2008 TAMPA BAY RAYS

Not only did the Rays jump from the cellar in 2007 to win the AL East in 2008—becoming the ninth team ever to accomplish the feat—but they also narrowly missed becoming the most-improved worst-to-first team in baseball history. Tampa Bay increased its win total by 31 games in '08, falling just four games short of the Diamondbacks' remarkable 35-win improvement in 1999. Those D'backs, though, didn't have to contend with the Red Sox and Yankees to win their division, the NL West, as they finished 14 games ahead of the Giants.

It's also interesting to note that all six of the '90s teams to go from worst-to-first squandered the premium draft pick they had coming to them in year No. 2. The Giants, at least, were able to trade Jason Grilli for Livan Hernandez in 1999. The outlook is more positive for the Cubs, Diamondbacks and Rays, as their premium picks all rank among the top prospects in the minors.

Team	Year 1	Year 2	Wins	Result	Premium Pick (Overall)
1990-91 Twins	74-88	95-67	+21	Defeated Braves in World Series, 4-3	David McCarty, 1b (3)
1990-91 Braves	65-97	94-68	+29	Lost to Twins in World Series, 4-3	Mike Kelly, of (2)
1992-93 Phillies	70-92	97-65	+27	Lost to Blue Jays in World Series, 4-2	Wayne Gomes, rhp (4)
1996-97 Giants	68-94	90-72	+22	Lost to Marlins in NLDS, 3-0	Jason Grilli, rhp (4)
1997-98 Padres	76-86	98-64	+22	Lost to Yankees in World Series, 4-0	Sean Burroughs, 3b (9)
1998-99 Diamondbacks	65-97	100-62	+35	Lost to Mets in NLDS, 3-1	Corey Myers, ss (4)
2006-07 Cubs	66-96	85-77	+19	Lost to Diamondbacks in NLDS, 3-0	Josh Vitters, 3b (3)
2006-07 Diamondbacks	76-86	90-72	+14	Lost to Rockies in NLCS, 4-0	Jarrod Parker, rhp (9)
2007-08 Rays	66-96	97-65	+31	Lost to Phillies in World Series, 4-1	Tim Beckham, ss (1)

pion Cubs 3-1 on Sept. 28. Brewers lefthander C.C. Sabathia, acquired in a July trade with the Indians, pitched a complete-game four-hitter in his third straight start on three days' rest and left fielder Ryan Braun broke a 1-1 tie with a two-run home run in the eighth inning to give Milwaukee a 90-72 record.

The Mets, on the other hand, did not find a way, marking two straight years in which they disqualified themselves from playoff play on the final day of the season. Their 4-2 loss to the Marlins combined with the Brewers' win knocked New York out of the wild card race. The Mets, who finished 89-73, also surrendered a 3½-game lead to the Phillies in the NL East with 17 games remaining. Just one year earlier, the Mets had squandered a seven-game lead in the final 17 games to finish second to Philadelphia.

"We failed. We failed as a team," Mets third baseman David Wright said. "There are no pointing fingers. There are no excuses. We didn't get the job done."

The Dodgers, during Torre's first season as manager on the West Coast, were able to get it done in the NL West, winning the division title by two games. However, their 84-78 record was the worst of the eight playoff teams. Torre was able to keep the Dodgers afloat during an injury-plagued season, and Los Angeles showed resiliency in overtaking the Diamondbacks, who held a 4½-game lead on Aug. 29. The Dodgers notably received a late-season boost with the trade-deadline acquisition of left fielder Manny Ramirez from the Red Sox in a three-team trade that also included the Pirates.

"Anytime a manager thinks that he's responsible for something that players do, he's a little deluded," said Torre, who led the Yankees to the postseason in each of his 12 seasons as their manager. "I just try to get everybody thinking and going in the same direction and being on the same page. That's my job, trying to put out fires here and there. My job is to keep people focused.

"I never envisioned myself at 68 years old going somewhere new to start over. I'm glad I did it."

Lou Piniella also started over as a manager with the Cubs at age 64 in 2007. Chicago won the NL Central that season, and then repeated in 2008, finishing with the best record in the league at 97-65, seven games ahead of the Brewers.

The Phillies charged past the Mets for the second straight season in winning consecutive division titles for the first time since capturing three straight NL East crowns from 1976 to 1978. The Phillies finished at 92-70, three game in front.

"Determination always beats talent," Phillies

CHRIS PROCTOR

John Danks' eight shutout innings in game No. 163 pushed Chicago to the playoffs

shortstop Jimmy Rollins said. "When you have both like we do, it's a tough combination to stop."

Trading Places

Sabathia and Ramirez both made huge impacts on their new teams, propelling the Brewers and Dodgers to the playoffs. But they were just two of a number of big-name players who were traded during the season.

The Brewers acquired Sabathia from the Indians on July 7 in exchange for four minor leaguers, headed by outfielder Matt LaPorta, the seventh overall pick in 2007. Even though Sabathia had won the AL Cy Young award the previous season, the Indians felt they had no chance to re-sign him as a free agent and decided to restock their farm system. Sabathia went on to go 11-2, 1.65 in 17 starts for Milwaukee, pitching seven complete games and three shutouts, both league-leading totals.

Ramirez was the hitting equivalent of Sabathia after the Dodgers acquired him seconds before the July 31 deadline for making non-waiver trades. The Red Sox got left fielder Jason Bay from the Pirates, who, in turn, received two young players each from Boston and the Dodgers.

Ramirez had fallen out of favor with the Red Sox after pushing traveling secretary Jack McCormick to the ground before a game in Houston following

Big arm, bigger heart

BY TOM HAUDRICOURT

GEORGE GOJKOVICH

Brewers lefthander C.C. Sabathia

MILWAUKEE

"We're going for it."

With that proclamation, Brewers general manager Doug Melvin announced one of the biggest trades in franchise history on July 7.

As it turned out, it would evolve into one of the best in-season acquisitions in major league history.

The small-revenue Brewers stunned the baseball world by trading for lefthander C.C. Sabathia—the top pitcher on the trade market and one coveted by many large-revenue franchises, including the Yankees, Dodgers and Phillies. How often does a team get the chance to acquire a reigning Cy Young award winner?

The Brewers served notice that it was playoffs or bust after waiting since 1982 to play October baseball. And they figured Sabathia was just the pitcher to get them over the hump.

They were right: He went 11-2, 1.65 in 17 starts for the Brewers and 17-10, 2.70 in 35 starts overall, covering 253 innings. Most impressive of all, Sabathia overcame a rocky start with the Indians to win our Major League Player of the Year award.

The 6-foot-7, 311-pound Sabathia is a very large man. The Brewers soon learned there was more to him than sheer physical size.

"We didn't realize at the time that his heart is as big as he is," Melvin said. "We knew he was one of the best pitchers in baseball. We

learned later how good of a person he is."

Sabathia's impact on the Brewers was immediate. He donned a Brewers uniform for the first time one day after the trade and went out in a fishbowl atmosphere at Miller Park to beat the Rockies.

The winning never stopped.

Sabathia pitched complete games in his next three outings, including a brilliant three-hit shutout in St. Louis in which he needed only 106 pitches to finish off the Cardinals. He went 4-0, 1.82 in five July starts to earn National League pitcher of the month honors.

Beyond Sabathia's excellence as a pitcher, his new teammates soon learned he also is an outstanding individual. Laid-back and understated, the soft-spoken giant was a seamless fit into an already close clubhouse.

During the dark days of September, when little seemed to go right, the Brewers often would take consolation by saying, "Tomorrow we've got C.C. pitching."

"It's probably the greatest two-and-a-half-month performance you've ever seen from a professional athlete, in any sport," Brewers interim manager Dale Sveum said.

The easygoing Sabathia took it all in stride. He never seemed to think he was doing anything special, never considered himself more important than any other player wearing "Brewers" across his chest.

"I'd be lying if I didn't say this was one of the better times of my career and my life, coming here and meeting these guys and making some new friends," Sabathia said.

Thanks to Sabathia, the Brewers had the best time they've had since 1982.

PREVIOUS 10 WINNERS

1998: Mark McGwire, 1b, Cardinals
1999: Pedro Martinez, rhp, Red Sox
2000: Alex Rodriguez, ss, Mariners
2001: Barry Bonds, of, Giants
2002: Alex Rodriguez, ss, Rangers
2003: Barry Bonds, of, Giants
2004: Barry Bonds, of, Giants
2005: Albert Pujols, 1b, Cardinals
2006: Johan Santana, lhp, Twins
2007: Alex Rodriguez, 3b, Yankees

Full list: BaseballAmerica.com/awards

a dispute over a request for tickets. In late July, he threatened to sit out the remainder of the season with a knee injury if the Red Sox did not trade him. The Red Sox forced Ramirez to have MRIs on both knees that revealed no structural damage.

Ramirez, who hit his 500th career home run on May 31, went on to hit .396/.489/.743 with 17 home runs and 53 RBIs in 53 games for the Dodgers. Bay also did well for the Red Sox, batting .293/.370/.527 with nine homers and 37 RBIs in 49 games.

The Red Sox also made the playoffs, and they were glad to be rid of the quirky Ramirez.

"I make it a point not to say anything bad about players when they are on our team, so I'm not going to say anything bad about a player who is no longer with us," Francona said. "I just leave it at this: The last couple of months of the season were the most fun I had in my five years as manager of the Red Sox."

While the Angels likely would have won the AL West without first baseman Mark Teixeira, acquiring the switch-hitting slugger from the Braves in a July 29 trade for first baseman Casey Kotchman surely did not hurt the cause. Teixeira hit .358/.449/.632 with 13 home runs and 43 RBIs in 54 games for the Angels.

Like Ramirez, two other probable Hall of Famers also changed teams after reaching significant milestones earlier in the season. Griffey, 38, was traded to the White Sox from the Reds on July 31, and 42-year-old righthander Greg Maddux was dealt from the Padres to the Dodgers on Aug. 19. However,

Manny Ramirez hit 17 homers in 53 games to propel the Dodgers to the division title

neither Griffey nor Maddux made a significant impact on their new teams reaching the playoffs.

Limited Instant Replay

Commissioner Bud Selig is certainly not big on technology. In fact, the 74-year-old commissioner, who readily admits he is old-fashioned and loves the human element involved in baseball, likes to tell the story about how he has a computer on the desk in his office but doesn't know how to turn it on.

AMERICAN LEAGUE STANDINGS

EAST	W	L	PCT	GB	Manager	General Manager	Attendance	Average	Last Penn.
Tampa Bay Rays	97	65	.599	—	Joe Maddon	Andrew Friedman	1,811,986	22,370	2008
*Boston Red Sox	95	67	.586	2	Terry Francona	Theo Epstein	3,048,250	37,633	2007
New York Yankees	89	73	.549	8	Joe Girardi	Brian Cashman	4,298,655	53,070	2003
Toronto Blue Jays	86	76	.531	11	J. Gibbons/C. Gaston	J.P. Ricciardi	2,399,786	29,627	1993
Baltimore Orioles	68	93	.422	28½	Dave Trembley	Andy MacPhail	1,950,075	25,001	1983
CENTRAL	W	L	PCT	GB	Manager	General Manager	Attendance	Average	Last Penn.
Chicago White Sox	89	74	.546	—	Ozzie Guillen	Ken Williams	2,500,648	30,872	2005
Minnesota Twins	88	75	.540	1	Ron Gardenhire	Bill Smith	2,302,431	28,425	1991
Cleveland Indians	81	81	.500	7½	Eric Wedge	Mark Shapiro	2,169,760	27,122	1997
Kansas City Royals	75	87	.463	13½	Trey Hillman	Dayton Moore	1,578,922	19,986	1985
Detroit Tigers	74	88	.457	14½	Jim Leyland	Dave Dombrowski	3,202,645	39,539	2006
WEST	W	L	PCT	GB	Manager	General Manager	Attendance	Average	Last Penn.
Los Angeles Angels	100	62	.617	—	Mike Scioscia	Bill Stoneman	3,336,747	41,194	2002
Texas Rangers	79	83	.488	21	Ron Washington	Jon Daniels	1,945,677	24,321	None
Oakland Athletics	75	86	.466	24½	Bob Geren	Billy Beane	1,665,256	20,559	1990
Seattle Mariners	61	101	.377	39	J. McLaren/J. Riggleman	B. Bavasi/L. Pelekoudas	2,329,702	28,762	None

*Won wild card

PLAYOFFS—Division Series: Tampa Bay defeated Chicago 3-1 and Boston defeated Los Angeles 3-1 in best-of-five series.
Championship Series: Tampa Bay defeated Boston 4-3 in a best-of-seven series.

However, Selig finally decided to give in to technology late in the season after umpires missed a number of home run calls in May and June. Begrudgingly, Selig signed off on the idea of umpires being able to use the aid of television instant replay to determine boundary calls on potential home runs, specifically in instances in which it's unclear whether a fly ball went over the fence or whether a ball is fair or foul. Replay can also be employed to aid in making fan interference calls on potential homers.

"Like everything else in life, there are times that you have to make an adjustment," Selig said. "My opposition to unlimited instant replay is still very much in play. I really think that the game has prospered for well over a century now doing things the way we did it.

"I believe that because of the configuration of the ballparks, both new and old, that calling home runs is really much more difficult than it once was. I don't believe in the use of instant replay for other things.

"Anytime you try to change anything in baseball, it's both emotional and difficult. There has been some concern that, if you start here, look what it's going to lead to. Not as long as I'm the commissioner."

Replay went into use on Aug. 28 and was used five times in the final month of the season.

Major League Baseball became the last of the four major professional sports leagues to adopt replay to help officials. The NFL first used video in 1986 and was followed by the NHL in 1991 and NBA in 2002. General managers had voted 25-5 following the 2007 season to recommend using the technol-

ogy and the players' and umpires' unions signed off on the idea following in-season negotiations.

MLB set up the system so that video from available broadcast feeds is collected at the office of MLB Advanced Media in New York. There, a technician and either an umpire supervisor or a retired umpire monitors the video. That video can then be examined during a game at the discretion of the umpire crew chief, at which point all the umpires leave the field so that technicians at MLBAM can show them the video. The crew chief makes the final call, overturning the decision only if there is "clear and convincing evidence."

Of the five times home runs were reviewed, two were overturned. The first test of the system came Sept. 3 when Yankees third baseman Alex Rodriguez hit a drive against the Rays at Tropicana Field in St. Petersburg that went over the left-field foul pole and struck one of the catwalks that support the building's roof. It was ruled a home run in real time.

The umpires, at the request of Maddon, gathered behind the pitcher's mound and crew chief Charlie Reliford then led his crew to the review room where they determined after watching replays from four angles that the call should stand.

"We all believed it was a home run, but since the technology is in place we made the decision to use the technology and go look at the replays," Reliford said. "The process worked exactly like they trained us it would go. Technically, it's up to the crew chief but when the ship sinks, everyone drowns. We operate as a crew, we do everything as a crew and

NATIONAL LEAGUE STANDINGS

EAST	W	L	PCT	GB	Manager	General Manager	Attendance	Average	Last Penn.
Philadelphia Phillies	92	70	.568	—	Charlie Manuel	Pat Gillick	3,422,583	42,254	2008
New York Mets	89	73	.549	3	W. Randolph/J. Manuel	Omar Minaya	4,042,045	51,165	2000
Florida Marlins	84	77	.522	7½	Fredi Gonzalez	Larry Beinfest	1,335,076	16,688	2003
Atlanta Braves	72	90	.444	20	Bobby Cox	Frank Wren	2,532,834	31,270	1999
Washington Nationals	59	102	.366	32½	Manny Acta	Jim Bowden	2,320,400	29,005	None
CENTRAL	W	L	PCT	GB	Manager	General Manager	Attendance	Average	Last Penn.
Chicago Cubs	97	64	.602	—	Lou Piniella	Jim Hendry	3,300,200	40,743	1945
*Milwaukee Brewers	90	72	.556	7½	N. Yost/D. Svuem	Doug Melvin	3,068,458	37,882	^1982
Houston Astros	86	75	.534	11	Cecil Cooper	Ed Wade	2,779,487	34,744	2005
St. Louis Cardinals	86	76	.531	11½	Tony La Russa	John Mozeliak	3,432,917	42,382	2006
Cincinnati Reds	74	88	.457	23½	Dusty Baker	W. Krivsky/W. Jocketty	2,058,632	25,415	1990
Pittsburgh Pirates	67	95	.414	30½	John Russell	Neal Huntington	1,609,076	20,113	1979
WEST	W	L	PCT	GB	Manager	General Manager	Attendance	Average	Last Penn.
Los Angeles Dodgers	84	78	.519	—	Joe Torre	Ned Colletti	3,730,553	46,056	1988
Arizona Diamondbacks	82	80	.506	2	Bob Melvin	Josh Byrnes	2,509,924	30,987	2001
Colorado Rockies	74	88	.457	10	Clint Hurdle	Dan O'Dowd	2,650,218	33,128	2007
San Francisco Giants	72	90	.444	12	Bruce Bochy	Brian Sabean	2,863,837	35,356	2002
San Diego Padres	63	99	.389	21	Bud Black	Kevin Towers	2,427,535	29,970	1998

*Won wild card. ^American League franchise, 1969-1997

PLAYOFFS—Division Series: Philadelphia defeated Milwaukee 3-1 and Los Angeles defeated Chicago 3-0 in best-of-five series.
Championship Series: Philadelphia defeated Los Angeles 4-1 in a best-of-seven series.

we make decisions as a crew. If it comes down to a split decision, then the crew chief is going to have to decide which decision is most likely correct."

Selig also considered banning the use of maple bats after they began shattering on a regular basis, sending shrapnel flying toward players in the field, personnel in the dugout and even fans in the stands. The scariest moment came during an April 15 game when Pirates center fielder Nate McLouth's bat broke during a game against the Dodgers at Dodger Stadium. A jagged piece of the bat struck Pirates hitting coach Don Long in the face, resulting in a large cut along with nerve damage that resulted in partial paralysis in his cheek. Long had been looking down as he was writing something in a notebook.

MLB formed a safety and health advisory committee, which included executives from the commissioner's office, general managers, players and representatives of the union, to study the issue.

The committee gathered every broken bat in the major leagues from July 2 through Sept. 7 and compiled information about each, including its manufacturer, the model, the dimensions, the point of the game when it was broken, the area where wood fragments landed and video footage from MLB.com. MLB also retained the USDA Forest Service's Products Laboratory, the wood-testing agency Timberco, Inc., Harvard professor Carl Morris and the University of Massachusetts-Lowell professor James Sherwood to analyze the data and develop tests.

The End Of A (Yankees) Era

While baseball was saying hello to instant replay, it said goodbye to Yankee Stadium, which opened long before the invention of television and was one of the most hallowed venues in all of sports. The Yankees closed the 85-year-old cathedral in the Bronx on Sept. 21 with a 7-3 win against the Orioles.

It was an unforgettable night at the House That Ruth Built as scores of Yankees stars returned and dotted the field during pre-game ceremonies before Julia Ruth Stevens, 92-year-old daughter of Babe Ruth, threw out the ceremonial first pitch. Jeter, the team captain, received a thunderous ovation upon being lifted from the game by Girardi with two outs in the bottom of the ninth. He then addressed the crowd following the game.

"Take the memories from this stadium, add it to the next memories that come with the new Yankee Stadium and continue to pass them on from generation to generation," Jeter said. "We just want to take this moment to salute you, the greatest fans in the world."

Before the Yankees got ready to move into a palatial new ballpark just across the street, the players

took one lap around the field and waved their caps to the fans as Frank Sinatra's "New York, New York" blared over the sound system one final time.

Yankee Stadium opened in 1923 after being built at the cost of $2.5 million, and the Yankees won the

This catcher is a keeper

Cubs catcher Geovany Soto tapped into his power potential in the PCL in 2007

DENNIS WIERZBICKI

BY KARY BOOHER

The call would come in occasionally from the minor leagues, from a kid catcher in Des Moines who wasn't so much interested in job openings but rather in pocket-collecting a pointer or two.

To Cubs catcher Geovany Soto, then biding his time at Triple-A Iowa, phoning veteran Henry Blanco offered another creative avenue to improve his skills.

Surely Blanco would have the answers on how better to block those quirky pitches tailing away and in the dirt, or perhaps offer insight into motivational tactics designed to prop up a struggling pitcher. That's all Soto wanted—answers and nothing more.

"To be honest with you," Soto said before baseball's playoffs got under way, "I wouldn't be doing the stuff I'm doing without him. He's like my backbone."

The Cubs probably could say the same now of Soto, the 2008 Baseball America Rookie of the Year.

The 25-year-old backstop crafted a remarkable freshman season in the majors as he steadied one of the game's top pitching staffs while doubling as a fearsome weapon within the lineup.

That he held down the fort for a Cubs team that won the National League Central with an NL-best 97 victories and earned the respect of veteran manager Lou Piniella was all the more impressive.

"I don't see anybody else that's had the year or the impact that he's had on a baseball team," Piniella said. "The pitchers like throwing to him. They respect him. He does a real nice job of calling a baseball game."

The twist? Soto's career path hardly led anyone to believe he would deliver like this.

An 11th-round pick in 2001 out of the American Military Academy in Puerto Rico, Soto converted from the corner infield to catching in 2003 at high Class A Daytona.

At the time, the Cubs had not developed a catcher with staying power since Joe Girardi (1989) and Rick Wilkins (1991) and that June exhausted third- and fourth-round picks on college catchers Jake Fox and Tony Richie.

"Offensively," Rangers farm director and former Cubs catching instructor Scott Servais said, "I'd be lying if I predicted he would hit with the power he has."

Before a breakout 2007 at Triple-A Iowa—he hit .353/.424/.652 with 26 home runs—Soto slowly progressed. From 2003 to 2006, he never hit better than .272 or delivered more than nine home runs or drove in more than 48 runs in any season.

Along the way, Soto found confidence.

"I think I'm a little more aggressive in my defense and the mental part of it," he said. "I feel comfortable going out there and talking with the guys and trying to come up with the best plan for the game."

Contributing: Bruce Miles,
The Daily Herald in Arlington Heights, Ill.

PREVIOUS 10 WINNERS

1998: Kerry Wood, rhp, Cubs
1999: Carlos Beltran, of, Royals
2000: Rafael Furcal, ss/2b, Braves
2001: Albert Pujols, of/3b/1b, Cardinals
2002: Eric Hinske, 3b, Blue Jays
2003: Brandon Webb, rhp, Diamondbacks
2004: Khalil Greene, ss, Padres
2005: Huston Street, rhp, Athletics
2006: Justin Verlander, rhp, Tigers
2007: Ryan Braun, 3b, Brewers

Full list: BaseballAmerica.com/awards

TOP 20 ROOKIES

RK	BATTER, POS, TEAM	AVG	OBP	SLG	AB	R	H	2B	3B	HR	RBI	SB	CS	BB	SO
1.	Geovany Soto, c, Cubs	.285	.364	.504	494	66	141	35	2	23	86	0	1	62	121
2.	Evan Longoria, 3b, Rays	.272	.343	.531	448	67	122	31	2	27	85	7	0	46	122
3.	Joey Votto, 1b, Reds	.297	.368	.506	526	69	156	32	3	24	84	7	5	59	102
5.	Alexei Ramirez, 2b, White Sox	.290	.317	.475	480	65	139	22	2	21	77	13	9	18	61
6.	Mike Aviles, ss, Royals	.325	.354	.480	419	68	136	27	4	10	51	8	3	18	58
8.	Denard Span, of, Twins	.294	.387	.432	347	70	102	16	7	6	47	18	7	50	60
11.	Chris Davis, 1b/3b, Rangers	.285	.331	.549	295	51	84	23	2	17	55	1	2	20	88
16.	Jacoby Ellsbury, of, Red Sox	.280	.336	.394	554	98	155	22	7	9	47	50	11	41	80
19.	Jay Bruce, of, Reds	.254	.314	.453	413	63	105	17	1	21	52	4	6	33	110

RK	PITCHER, POS, TEAM	W	L	ERA	G	GS	CG	SV	IP	H	BB	SO	HR	G/F	AVG
4.	Jair Jurrjens, rhp, Braves	13	10	3.68	31	31	0	0	188	188	70	139	11	1.83	.260
7.	Joba Chamberlain, rhp, Yankees	4	3	2.60	42	12	0	0	100	87	39	118	5	1.55	.233
9.	Brad Ziegler, rhp, Athletics	3	0	1.06	47	0	0	11	60	47	22	30	2	3.44	.236
10.	Armando Galarraga, rhp, Tigers	13	7	3.73	30	28	0	0	179	152	61	126	28	1.18	.226
12.	Hiroki Kuroda, rhp, Dodgers	9	10	3.73	31	31	2	0	183	181	42	116	13	1.85	.253
13.	Nick Blackburn, rhp, Twins	11	11	4.05	33	33	0	0	193	224	39	96	23	1.35	.292
14.	Jose Arredondo, rhp, Angels	10	2	1.62	52	0	0	0	61	42	22	55	3	1.72	.190
15.	Chris Volstad, rhp, Marlins	6	4	2.88	15	14	0	0	84	76	36	52	3	1.97	.240
17.	John Lannan, lhp, Nationals	9	15	3.91	31	31	0	0	182	172	72	117	23	2.03	.252
18.	Clayton Kershaw, lhp, Dodgers	5	5	4.26	22	21	0	0	108	109	52	100	11	1.64	.265
20.	Greg Smith, lhp, Athletics	7	16	4.16	32	32	2	0	190	169	87	111	21	0.78	.243

first of their record 26 World Series titles that year. The Yankees went 3,934-2,312 (.630) in the first sports venue ever to be called a stadium.

Yankee Stadium underwent a major renovation in the mid-1970s that made it look vastly different from the park that was home to such icons as Ruth, Lou Gehrig, Joe DiMaggio and Mickey Mantle. However, it was the same field and the same grounds, which gave it a feel like no other park in baseball.

"I think what really made Yankee Stadium unique were the people more than the actual stadium," former Yankees star center fielder Bernie Williams said. "People talk a lot about the magic and the aura, but what really made the stadium were the fans. Concrete doesn't talk back to you. Chairs don't talk back to you. It's the people who are there, who root for you day in and day out. That's what makes this place magical."

New York also said goodbye to Shea Stadium, home of the Mets since 1964. The park hosted its last game on Sept. 28, the Mets' season-ending loss to the Marlins. Therefore, Mets fans weren't in a festive mood as such former greats as Tom Seaver, Mike Piazza, Willie Mays, Dwight Gooden and Darryl Strawberry took part in post-game festivities to mark the closing of the 42-year-old facility, which played host to four World Series.

The Mets will move in 2009 to Citi Field, just beyond the center-field fence from Shea Stadium.

Meanwhile, $611 million Nationals Park opened in Washington on March 30 with President George W. Bush throwing out the ceremonial first pitch.

The Nationals christened their new home, which replaced dilapidated Robert F. Kennedy Memorial Stadium, with a dramatic 3-2 victory against the Braves, with third baseman Ryan Zimmerman hitting a game-winning solo home run with two outs in the bottom of the ninth inning.

Nationals Park, the exterior of which was made of glass and stone, unlike many other ballparks of recent vintage, included a view of the U.S. Capitol beyond the left-field fence and the Washington Momentum from patches of the upper deck. However, the new digs did not keep the Nationals from finishing 60-102 for the worst record in the major leagues.

Record Setters

The Angels had the best record in the major leagues and closer Francisco Rodriguez played a major role by setting a major league record with 62 saves. That easily surpassed the old mark of 57 set by Bobby Thigpen with the 1990 White Sox.

Rodriguez set the record by closing out a 5-2 win against the Mariners on Sept. 13 at Angel Stadium, pitching a scoreless ninth inning while working around a double and a walk. He struck out Mariners left fielder Raul Ibanez swinging for the final out then lifted his head and arms skyward while sinking to his knees.

After he was mobbed on the mound by his teammates, Rodriguez ran over toward the first-base dugout and blew kisses to his young daughters in the stands. He then walked toward the third-base dugout and doffed his cap to the crowd.

It also was an unbelievable year for Athletics rookie righthanded reliever Brad Ziegler, a 28-year-old who made his major league debut on May 3 after spending five seasons in the Oakland farm system following his release by the Phillies in 2004. Ziegler began his career by pitching 39 scoreless innings, easily breaking the record of 25 for the start of a career set by George McQuillan with the 1907 Phillies.

The submarine-style throwing Ziegler's streak spanned 29 games until the Rays finally broke through for a run on Aug. 14 on center fielder B.J. Upton's RBI double.

Red Sox lefthander Jon Lester and Cubs righthander Carlos Zambrano also had amazing moments by throwing the first no-hitters of their careers. Lester threw his on May 19 against the Royals at home in Fenway Park, while Zambrano's no-hitter came on Sept. 14 against the Astros. The gem was the first ever thrown at a neutral site as it came at Milwaukee's Miller Park after Hurricane Ike forced the game to be moved from Houston.

Lester's no-hitter continued an amazing start to the 24-year-old's career. He survived a bout with cancer in 2006 and then started and won the World Series clincher against the Rockies in 2007. Lester struck out nine, including Alberto Callaspo to end his no-hitter, while walking two and committing an error on a pickoff throw.

It was also Lester's first career complete game in his 37th start. He threw a career-high 130 pitches.

"You don't feel tired in that situation," Lester said. "You've got so much adrenaline going that all you're thinking about is finishing the game. I definitely didn't want to come out."

Zambrano's no-hitter, the first by a Cubs pitcher since Milt Pappas in 1972, came after he had his previous turn in the rotation skipped because of a sore shoulder. Zambrano struck out 10, including Darin Erstad swinging to end the game, while walking one and hitting a batter.

"I felt confused when I got the last out because it didn't seem like it was real," Zambrano said. "I couldn't believe it. It's a great feeling, though, a feeling you can't even begin to describe. There's nothing like it."

There are few things in baseball like an unassisted triple play, but Indians second baseman Asdrubal Cabrera performed the feat for the 14th time in major league history against the Blue Jays in the second game of a doubleheader on May 12 at Progressive Field in Cleveland. Cabrera made a diving catch of a line drive by Lyle Overbay and, because the runners on first and second were running with the pitch, he simply touched second base to double off Kevin Mench and then tagged Marco

NATIONAL LEAGUE: BEST TOOLS

A Baseball America survey of American League managers, conducted at midseason 2008, ranked players with the best tools:

BEST HITTER
1. Albert Pujols, Cardinals
2. Chipper Jones, Braves
3. Lance Berkman, Astros

BEST CONTROL
1. Dan Haren, Diamondbacks
2. Greg Maddux, Padres
3. Cole Hamels, Phillies

BEST POWER
1. Ryan Howard, Phillies
2. Albert Pujols, Cardinals
3. Adam Dunn, Reds

BEST PICKOFF MOVE
1. Doug Davis, Diamondbacks
2. Jamie Moyer, Phillies
3. Aaron Cook, Rockies

BEST BUNTER
1. Juan Pierre, Dodgers
2. Willy Taveras, Rockies
3. Cristian Guzman, Nationals

BEST RELIEVER
1. Brad Lidge, Phillies
2. Brian Wilson, Giants
3. Kerry Wood, Cubs

BEST STRIKE-ZONE JUDGMENT
1. Todd Helton, Rockies
2. Albert Pujols, Cardinals
3. Chipper Jones, Braves

BEST DEFENSIVE C
1. Yadier Molina, Cardinals
2. Russell Martin, Dodgers
3. Bengie Molina, Giants

BEST HIT-AND-RUN ARTIST
1. Ryan Theriot, Cubs
2. Bengie Molina, Giants
3. Jack Wilson, Pirates

BEST DEFENSIVE 1B
1. Derrek Lee, Cubs
2. Albert Pujols, Cardinals
3. Todd Helton, Rockies

BEST BASERUNNER
1. Juan Pierre, Dodgers
2. Jimmy Rollins, Phillies
3. Jose Reyes, Mets

BEST DEFENSIVE 2B
1. Orlando Hudson, D'backs
2. Brandon Phillips, Reds
3. Chase Utley, Phillies

FASTEST BASERUNNER
1. Jose Reyes, Mets
2. Willy Taveras, Rockies
3. Juan Pierre, Dodgers

BEST DEFENSIVE 3B
1. David Wright, Mets
2. Aramis Ramirez, Cubs
3. Ryan Zimmerman, Nationals

MOST EXCITING PLAYER
1. Hanley Ramirez, Marlins
2. Jose Reyes, Mets
3. Albert Pujols, Cardinals

BEST DEFENSIVE SS
1. Jimmy Rollins, Phillies
2. Jack Wilson, Pirates
3. Rafael Furcal, Dodgers

BEST PITCHER
1. Brandon Webb, D'backs
2. Tim Lincecum, Giants
3. Carlos Zambrano, Cubs

BEST INFIELD ARM
1. Jose Reyes, Mets
2. Rafael Furcal, Dodgers
3. Hanley Ramirez, Marlins

BEST FASTBALL
1. Tim Lincecum, Giants
2. Ben Sheets, Brewers
3. Edinson Volquez, Reds

BEST DFENSIVE OF
1. Carlos Beltran, Mets
2. Mike Cameron, Brewers
3. Shane Victorino, Phillies

BEST CURVEBALL
1. Ben Sheets, Brewers
2. Tim Lincecum, Giants
3. Cole Hamels, Phillies

BEST OUTFIELD ARM
1. Rick Ankiel, Cardinals
2. Jeff Francoeur, Braves
3. Matt Kemp, Dodgers

BEST SLIDER
1. Jake Peavy, Padres
2. Brad Lidge, Phillies
3. John Smoltz, Braves

BEST MANAGER
1. Bobby Cox, Braves
2. Tony La Russa, Cardinals
3. Lou Piniella, Cubs

BEST CHANGEUP
1. Johan Santana, Mets
2. Cole Hamels, Phillies
3. Edinson Volquez, Reds

Scutaro as he was going from first to second.

The Giants' Omar Vizquel also had a special moment on May 25 when he set the major league record for career games at shortstop with his 2,587th appearance at the position in the second game of a doubleheader against the Marlins at Dolphin Stadium. Hall of Famer Luis Aparicio, a native of Venezuela like Vizquel, had previously held the record.

"Aparicio has always been the biggest baseball name in Venezuela," Vizquel said. "Just to talk about him was like a fantasy."

The Red Sox also made history by selling out their 456th consecutive home game on Sept. 8 against the Rays, a streak that dated back to May 15, 2003, and reached 469 by the end of the season. The old record was 455 by the Indians from June 12, 1995, to April 2, 2001, at what was then known as Jacobs Field.

Career Achievement

While Griffey, Ramirez and Maddux ended their seasons with other clubs, they joined exclusive clubs before being traded. Griffey became the sixth player to hit 600 home runs, Ramirez became the 24th player to reach 500 and Maddux became the ninth pitcher to win 350 games.

Griffey hit No. 600 off Marlins lefty Mark Hendrickson on June 9 at Dolphin Stadium, joining Barry Bonds, Hank Aaron, Ruth, Mays and Sammy Sosa as the only sluggers to reach that plateau.

"I don't think I touched any of the bases," Griffey said. "I sort of floated around."

Ramirez added to his gaudy total by hitting his 500th homer on May 10 off Orioles righthander Chad Bradford in Baltimore. Ramirez struggled to get to the milestone, hitting just three home runs in his previous 34 games.

Maddux notched win No. 350 on May 10 as he allowed one unearned run in six innings of a 3-2 victory against the Rockies at Petco Park in San Diego. Maddux, in his typically understated fashion, downplayed reaching yet another major milestone in his career.

"It was kind of cool," he said.

A number of other players also reached significant career milestones.

■ Braves third baseman Chipper Jones hit his 400th home run on June 5 against Marlins righthander Ricky Nolasco.

■ Jeter collected his 2,500th hit, a single off Orioles righthander Radhames Liz on Aug. 22.

■ Braves righthander John Smoltz notched his 3,000th strikeout, getting Nationals second baseman Felipe Lopez swinging on April 22.

Power Outage

Home runs in 2008 dropped to their lowest level in 15 years. An average of 2.01 home runs

CONTINUED ON PAGE 19

ALL-TIME ACHIEVEMENTS

Active players in bold. *Bats/Throws lefthanded. #Switch-hitter.

500 HOME RUNS

Manny Ramirez was the sole player to join the 500-home run club in 2008, though Gary Sheffield came very close to joining him. He stalled at 499. In addition to Sheffield, Carlos Delgado (469) and Chipper Jones (408) are the only active players with more than 400 homers. Because they received no contract offers, Barry Bonds and Sammy Sosa did not have the opportunity to build on their totals.

1.	Barry Bonds*	762		13.	Mike Schmidt	548
2.	Hank Aaron	755		14.	**Jim Thome***	541
3.	Babe Ruth*	714		15.	Mickey Mantle#	536
4.	Willie Mays	660		16.	Jimmie Foxx	534
5.	**Ken Griffey***	611		17.	Manny Ramirez	527
6.	Sammy Sosa	609		18.	Willie McCovey*	521
7.	Frank Robinson	586			**Frank Thomas**	521
8.	Mark McGwire	583			Ted Williams*	521
9.	Harmon Killebrew	573		21.	Ernie Banks	512
10.	Rafael Palmeiro*	569			Eddie Mathews*	512
11.	Reggie Jackson*	563		23.	Mel Ott*	511
12.	**Alex Rodriguez**	553		24.	Eddie Murray#	504

350 WINS

Who says baseball will never see another 300-game winner? The ageless Greg Maddux *just* sneaked past the inactive (though not officially retired) Roger Clemens to record win No. 355 and move into sole possession of eighth place all time. How remarkable is this milestone? Well, consider that Warren Spahn, who retired in 1965, is the only 350-game winner—besides Maddux and Clemens—to pitch after World War II. Active pitchers Randy Johnson (295) and Mike Mussina (270) figure to keep plugging away at 300.

1.	Cy Young	511		6.	Warren Spahn*	363
2.	Walter Johnson	417		7.	Kid Nichols	361
3.	Pete Alexander	373		8.	**Greg Maddux**	355
	Christy Mathewson	373		9.	Roger Clemens	354
5.	Pud Galvin	364				

3,000 STRIKEOUTS

With a 173-strikeout season, Randy Johnson passed Roger Clemens on the all-time list and inched closer to Nolan Ryan's record. At the rate of 200 strikeouts per season, the 45-year-old Johnson would need to pitch for 4½ more seasons to catch Ryan. John Smoltz recorded his 3,000th strikeout in 2008, and Pedro Martinez padded his total, but both veteran hurlers struggled to stay healthy.

1.	Nolan Ryan	5,714		9.	Walter Johnson	3,509
2.	**Randy Johnson***	4,789		10.	**Greg Maddux**	3,371
3.	Roger Clemens	4,672		11.	Phil Niekro	3,342
4.	Steve Carlton*	4,136		12.	Fergie Jenkins	3,192
5.	Bert Blyleven	3,701		13.	Bob Gibson	3,117
6.	Tom Seaver	3,640			**Pedro Martinez**	3,117
7.	Don Sutton	3,574		15.	**Curt Schilling**	3,116
8.	Gaylord Perry	3,534		16.	**John Smoltz**	3,011

ORGANIZATION OF THE YEAR

Rays shine through for first time

BY BILL BALLEW

Next up: Pigs fly and hell freezes over. The list of life's impossibilities decreased by one when the Rays went from last place in the American League East to the World Series. They joined the 1991 Braves as the only teams in major league history to reach the playoffs one season after having baseball's worst record.

Sporting the majors' second-lowest Opening Day payroll ($43.8 million) and its third-youngest roster, Tampa Bay entered the campaign never having won more than 70 games in a season and finishing out of last place just once in 10 seasons.

Fittingly, their sudden jump to 97 wins and the AL pennant was accomplished through player development.

After some missteps in the early days of the franchise, the Rays have built primarily from within. Their World Series roster featured nine one-time first-round picks, including B.J. Upton and Evan Longoria, who went in the top three picks, and Matt Garza and Scott Kazmir, acquired in trades for veterans.

The grow-your-own approach isn't expected to end any time soon. Postseason hero David Price, the No. 1 overall pick in 2007, will carve out a significant role for himself in 2009, and he headlines the pitching that overflows throughout the system.

In fact, despite the Rays' long-held philosophy of building through the farm system, they never have been more oriented toward devel-

Evan Longoria's emergence as a rookie helped push the Rays into the playoffs

CLIFF WELCH

oping young players. In each of the past two drafts, for example, Tampa Bay has selected several of the youngest players eligible.

The organization also is more driven than ever in developing international players after building facilities in the Dominican Republic and Venezuela in the past two years.

It's obvious that the entire organization, from top to bottom, has more planning and vision than at any time in its first dozen years. President Matt Silverman and general manager Andrew Friedman have displayed a Midas touch with nearly every move they have made, ranging from dropping "Devil" from the team nickname to displaying the proper patience for rising prospects to making the correct decisions in terms of adding major league talent.

Gone are the days when physical ability trumped everything, with strong mental makeup now the most desired trait for any Ray, on the field or off.

There's no reason why the Rays shouldn't remain contenders for the foreseeable future. This team was built for the long haul with a plethora of talented young players, and their sudden surge in 2008 was no fluke.

PREVIOUS 10 WINNERS

1998: New York Yankees
1999: Oakland Athletics
2000: Chicago White Sox
2001: Houston Astros
2002: Minnesota Twins
2003: Florida Marlins
2004: Minnesota Twins
2005: Atlanta Braves
2006: Los Angeles Dodgers
2007: Colorado Rockies

Full list: BaseballAmerica.com/awards

CONTINUED FROM PAGE 17

were hit in '08, down from 2.04 in 2007 and the lowest since 1.78 in 1993. Home runs peaked at 2.34 per game in 2000.

Numerous theories abounded as to why home runs were on the decline, but the consensus was that a reduction in players' use of performance-enhancing drugs was the most likely reason. MLB began its drug-testing program in 2002 and gradually increased the frequency of tests and toughened the penalties for using the illegal drugs.

"I think the steroid testing has something to do with it," Angels center fielder Torii Hunter said. "If there were any guys who were taking it, they're not taking it anymore. I'd say it's a small percentage, but it's still going to have an impact."

Cabrera led the AL with 37 home runs, the fewest for a league leader since Fred McGriff had 35 for the 1992 Padres to pace the NL. It was also the lowest total for an AL leader since McGriff hit 36 for the 1989 Blue Jays. Meanwhile, Phillies first baseman Ryan Howard hit 48 home runs to top the NL and lead the major leagues for the second time in three years.

Another indication that offense was on the wane was Red Sox second baseman Dustin Pedroia's AL-leading 118 runs scored, the lowest figure to top the AL in a non-shortened season since Tony Phillips scored 114 runs for the 1992 Tigers. Furthermore, Alex Rodriguez's AL-leading .573 slugging percentage was the lowest to top the AL since Ruben Sierra had a .543 mark for the 1989 Rangers.

Rangers center fielder Josh Hamilton's 130 RBIs and 331 total bases were the lowest AL-leading figures since Albert Belle's 129 for the 1993 Indians and Kirby Puckett's 313 for the 1992 Twins.

Teixeira thought a possible composition in the baseballs had something to do with less scoring.

ACTIVE HITS LEADERS

Derek Jeter reached the 2,500-hit plateau at age 34, meaning he's practically a lock to make it to 3,000. Alex Rodriguez, his Yankees teammate, is just 131 hits behind, but he's a year younger. This list does not include players who do not play in 2008.

1.	Ken Griffey*	2,680	6.	Derek Jeter	2,535
2.	Omar Vizquel#	2,657	7.	Frank Thomas	2,468
3.	Gary Sheffield	2,615	8.	Jeff Kent	2,461
4.	Ivan Rodriguez	2,605	9.	Alex Rodriguez	2,404
5.	Luis Gonzalez*	2,591	10.	Manny Ramirez	2,392

"It doesn't seem like the ball is jumping off the bat as much," he said. "I can feel the ball being a little softer. I can feel the seams being a little raised and the leather not being as tight."

Howard led the NL with 146 RBIs and Cardinals first baseman Albert Pujols was tops in slugging with a .653 percentage. Chipper Jones won his first batting title with a career-high .364 average, finishing seven points ahead of Pujols. Jones came up shy of Mantle's single-season record for a switch-hitter, which he established by hitting .365 for the 1967 Yankees.

Twins catcher Joe Mauer won his second AL batting title in three seasons by hitting .328, two points in front of Pedroia. Meanwhile, Pedroia shared the AL lead in hits with Mariners center fielder Ichiro Suzuki as both had 213. Suzuki tied a major league record with his eighth straight 200-hit season, matching Wee Willie Keeler's run from 1894 to 1901. Mets shortstop Jose Reyes paced the NL with 204 hits.

Diamondbacks third baseman Mark Reynolds set a dubious big league record by striking out 204 times. That surpassed the old record of 199 set by Howard a year earlier.

Astros closer Jose Valverde paced the NL with 44 saves, a full 18 behind Rodriguez, the AL leader.

Diamondbacks righthander Brandon Webb and Indians lefthander Cliff Lee led their leagues in wins with 22, while Lee also topped the AL with a 2.54 ERA. Mets lefthander Johan Santana's 2.53 ERA led the NL and gave him three such titles in his career along with the two he won in the AL.

The Pirates did not have a pitcher win at least 10 games for the first time since 1890, one of the reasons why they went 67-95 and tied a major league record with their 16th consecutive losing season, matching the mark set by the 1933-48 Phillies.

Giants righthander Tim Lincecum struck out 265 to lead the NL, while the Blue Jays righthander A.J. Burnett paced the AL with 231 whiffs.

SINGLE SEASON STRIKEOUTS

Diamondbacks third baseman Mark Reynolds established a major league seasonal record with 204 strikeouts, while Athletics DH Jack Cust set a new AL standard with 199 whiffs. The future is bright for Reynolds, a second-year player, who figures to challenge for strikeout supremacy as long as he holds a regular job. Try as he may, Phillies first baseman Ryan Howard can't seem to get over the hump. He stalled at 199 strikeouts in each of the past two seasons.

1.	Mark Reynolds	204	2008	6. Adam Dunn*	194	2006
2.	Ryan Howard*	199	2007	7. Bobby Bonds	189	1970
	Ryan Howard*	199	2008	8. Jose Hernandez	188	2002
4.	Jack Cust*	197	2008	9. Bobby Bonds	187	1969
5.	Adam Dunn*	195	2004	Preston Wilson	187	2000

Mitchell Report Fallout

MLB continued to toughen its drug policy by

Albert Pujols led all batters in slugging, but narrowly missed his second batting title

Roy Halladay won 20 games for the second time, while striking out a career-high 206

First Team

POS	PLAYER, TEAM	AVG	OBP	SLG	AB	R	H	2B	3B	HR	RBI	SB	CS	BB	SO
C	Joe Mauer, Twins	.328	.413	.451	536	98	176	31	4	9	85	1	1	84	50
1B	Albert Pujols, Cardinals	.357	.462	.653	524	100	187	44	0	37	116	7	3	104	54
2B	Chase Utley, Phillies	.292	.380	.535	607	113	177	41	4	33	104	14	2	64	104
3B	Chipper Jones, Braves	.364	.470	.574	439	82	160	24	1	22	75	4	0	90	61
SS	Hanley Ramirez, Marlins	.301	.400	.540	589	125	177	34	4	33	67	35	12	92	122
LF	Manny Ramirez, Red Sox/Dodgers	.332	.430	.601	552	102	183	36	1	37	121	3	0	87	124
CF	Grady Sizemore, Indians	.268	.374	.502	634	101	170	39	5	33	90	38	5	98	130
RF	Ryan Ludwick, Cardinals	.299	.375	.591	538	104	161	40	3	37	113	4	4	62	146
DH	Lance Berkman, Astros	.312	.420	.567	554	114	173	46	4	29	106	18	4	99	108

POS	PITCHER, TEAM	W	L	ERA	G	GS	CG	SV	IP	H	BB	SO	HR	G/F	AVG
SP	Roy Halladay, Blue Jays	20	11	2.78	34	33	9	0	246	220	39	206	18	2.08	.237
SP	Cliff Lee, Indians	22	3	2.54	31	31	4	0	223	214	34	170	12	1.38	.253
SP	Tim Lincecum, Giants	18	5	2.62	34	33	2	0	227	182	84	265	11	1.30	.221
SP	C.C. Sabathia, Indians/Brewers	17	10	2.70	35	35	10	0	253	223	59	251	19	1.49	.237
RP	Brad Lidge, Phillies	2	0	1.95	72	0	0	41	69	50	35	92	2	1.42	.198

Second Team

POS	PLAYER, TEAM	AVG	OBP	SLG	AB	R	H	2B	3B	HR	RBI	SB	CS	BB	SO
C	Brian McCann, Braves	.301	.373	.523	509	68	153	42	1	23	87	5	0	57	64
1B	Mark Teixeira, Braves/Angels	.308	.410	.552	574	102	177	41	0	33	121	2	0	97	93
2B	Dustin Pedroia, Red Sox	.326	.376	.493	653	118	213	54	2	17	83	20	1	50	52
3B	Alex Rodriguez, Yankees	.302	.392	.573	510	104	154	33	0	35	103	18	3	65	117
SS	Jose Reyes, Mets	.297	.358	.475	688	113	204	37	19	16	68	56	15	66	82
LF	Matt Holliday, Rockies	.321	.409	.538	539	107	173	38	2	25	88	28	2	74	104
CF	Carlos Beltran, Mets	.284	.376	.500	606	116	172	40	5	27	112	25	3	92	96
RF	Nick Markakis, Orioles	.306	.406	.491	595	106	182	48	1	20	87	10	7	99	113
DH	David Wright, Mets	.302	.390	.534	626	115	189	42	2	33	124	15	5	94	118

POS	PITCHER, TEAM	W	L	ERA	G	GS	CG	SV	IP	H	BB	SO	HR	G/F	AVG
SP	Cole Hamels, Phillies	14	10	3.09	33	33	2	0	227	193	53	196	28	1.05	.227
SP	Ervin Santana, Angels	16	7	3.49	32	32	2	0	219	198	47	214	23	0.98	.237
SP	Johan Santana, Mets	16	7	2.53	34	34	3	0	234	206	63	206	23	1.08	.232
SP	Brandon Webb, Diamondbacks	22	7	3.30	34	34	3	0	227	206	65	183	13	3.22	.242
RP	Mariano Rivera, Yankees	6	5	1.40	64	0	0	39	71	41	6	77	4	1.73	.165

EXECUTIVE OF THE YEAR

The Red Sox aren't exactly spendthrifts when it comes to investing in major league talent, but if not for general manager Theo Epstein and Boston's scouting and player-development staffs, the club might still be looking up at the Yankees in the AL East.

Theo Epstein

On the job since 2003, Epstein oversaw the drafts that yielded impact talents like closer Jonathan Papelbon (2003), second baseman Dustin Pedroia (2004), shortstop Jed Lowrie and center fielder Jacoby Ellsbury (both 2005) and righthander Justin Masterson (2006). Boston's playoff run in 2008 could not have been accomplished without their contributions.

PREVIOUS 10 WINNERS

1998: Doug Melvin, Rangers	**2003:** Brian Sabean, Giants
1999: Jim Bowden, Reds	**2004:** Terry Ryan, Twins
2000: Walt Jocketty, Cardinals	**2005:** Mark Shapiro, Indians
2001: Pat Gillick, Mariners	**2006:** Dave Dombrowski, Tigers
2002: Billy Beane, Athletics	**2007:** Jack Zduriencik, Brewers

Full list: BaseballAmerica.com/awards

MANAGER OF THE YEAR

Though the Twins fell one game short of making the playoffs, it wasn't for a lack of ingenuity on the part of manager Ron Gardenhire.

The seventh-year skipper already had won four AL Central division titles with the Twins, but what

Ron Gardenhire

made the 2008 run so unique was that the club went 88-75 even while placing much of its faith in largely untested youngsters.

Offseason trades of Johan Santana and Matt Garza gutted the pitching staff, but a host of young arms, like Nick Blackburn and Scott Baker, stepped to the forefront. Carlos Gomez and Denard Span fueled the offense.

PREVIOUS 10 WINNERS

1998: Larry Dierker, Astros	**2003:** Jack McKeon, Marlins
1999: Jimy Williams, Red Sox	**2004:** Bobby Cox, Braves
2000: Dusty Baker, Giants	**2005:** Ozzie Guillen, White Sox
2001: Lou Piniella, Mariners	**2006:** Jim Leyland, Tigers
2002: Mike Scioscia, Angels	**2007:** Terry Francona, Red Sox

Full list: BaseballAmerica.com/awards

---

implementing tougher testing rules that increased the frequency of tests and the authority of the program's independent administrator. The 30 club owners unanimously passed the proposal and the Brewers' Mark Attanasio said it was important for MLB to prove to its customers that the players are not gaining an illegal edge.

"I talk to fans and they want to see it clean," Attanasio said. "They want to know that what they're seeing out there is legitimate, especially in the historical context. The fans want to see that when they compare players of this generation to prior generations, that the performance is legitimate."

As part of the agreement, all players implicated in the Mitchell Report on performance-enhancing drugs use in baseball that was released the previous December were given amnesty. Thus, Royals right fielder Jose Guillen and Orioles left fielder Jay Gibbons were spared 15-game suspensions for admitting they used human growth hormone.

"It is time for the game to move forward," Selig said. "There is little to be gained at this point in debating dated misconduct and enduring numer-

ous disciplinary proceedings."

The agreement also ensured there would never be any other independent reports on performance-enhancing drugs, as both sides agreed to keep players' names private until discipline is imposed in any future probes. The sides also agreed to allow players to be given allegations and evidence against them before submitting to any investigatory interviews.

MLB and the union also agreed to recommendations made in the Mitchell Report, most notably hiring an independent administrator for the program and imposing certification standards for strength and conditioning coaches.

Managing Change

Four managerial changes were carried out during the season and two general managers were fired. However, the strangest case clearly involved the Brewers' ousting of Yost on Sept. 15—even though his team still held the lead in the NL wild card race. Sveum led the Brewers to a 7-5 record the rest of the way after they had lost 11 of their final 14 games under Yost, who compiled a 457-502 record in six seasons.

"Ned didn't have all the answers to what was going on those last two weeks before we made the move, and I'm not sure I had all the answers," Brewers GM Doug Melvin said. "I wasn't sure if firing Ned was the right answer, either, but we did get it turned around at the end."

With his team struggling at 34-35, the Mets' Willie Randolph was the first manager to be fired, getting the axe on June 16, following a 9-6 win against the Angles in Anaheim. Randolph's firing was announced in a press release e-mailed at 3:15 a.m. Eastern time. Bench coach Jerry Manuel replaced Randolph, who went 302-253 in four seasons. Speculation had swirled around Randolph in the weeks preceding his firing, but the timing of the dismissal still puzzled many observers.

Three days later, the Mariners fired John McLaren following a 25-47 start. McLaren was jettisoned three days after general manager Bill Bavasi was fired in his fifth year on the job. Bench coach Jim Riggleman finished the season as manager and assistant GM Lee Pelekoudas finished out the year as the GM. Little could save the 61-101 Mariners, who became the first team in history to lose at least 100 games with a payroll of at least $100 million. Their payroll actually was estimated at $117 million.

The Blue Jays decided to use an old approach when they fired John Gibbons as manager on June 20 and replaced him with Cito Gaston, a special assistant to the president and chief executive. Gaston led the Blue Jays to World Series titles in 1992 and 1993 but had not managed since being fired in 1997. Gibbons was 305-305 in four seasons.

Gaston did have a positive impact judging by the Blue Jays' in-season improvement. Toronto overcame a 35-39 start to finish at 86-76.

Joining Bavasi in the GM unemployment line was the Reds' Wayne Krivsky, who was let go on April 23, just 21 games into his third season at the helm. Cincinnati got off to a 9-12 start. Walt Jocketty, a special assistant to Krivsky who had spent the previous 12 seasons at the helm of the Cardinals, took over as the Reds' GM.

The Reds endured their eighth consecutive losing season, finishing at 74-88.

Two other organizations underwent changes at the top. Brothers Hal and Hank Steinbrenner took over as co-chairmen of the Yankees when their father George, one of the most famous owners in professional sports, decided to step down.

Peter Magowan decided to retire after 16 seasons as the Giants' managing general partner, handing the reins over to Bill Neukom. Magowan put together a group that bought the Giants from Bob Lurie follow-

ing the 1992 season, preventing the franchise from moving to St. Petersburg, Fla., and stabilizing it by signing Bonds as a free agent that winter and opening scenic AT&T Park in 2000. Neukom joined the Giants' ownership group in 1995 and was Microsoft's chief legal counsel for 25 years.

Early Retirement?

A number of big-name players retired in 2008, though many of them did so involuntarily as they were not offered contracts as free agents. Chief among them were Sosa and Piazza.

Sosa also retired in 2006 when he did not receive any major league contract offers as a free agent, but he returned in 2007 with the Rangers and hit his 600th career home run. Sosa, though, generated no interest after that and retired again with 609 home runs in his 18-year career. He is the only player to hit at least 60 home runs in three different seasons, connecting for 66 in 1998, 63 in 1999 and 64 in 2001, all with the Cubs.

Piazza's 16-year career, primarily spent with the Dodgers and Mets, wound up coming to an end with the Athletics in 2007. He hit more home runs than any catcher in baseball history, finishing with a total of 427.

Catcher Mike Lieberthal, who finished his 14-year career in a backup role with the Dodgers in 2007, also did not play in 2008. He spent all but his final season with the Phillies, hitting 150 home runs.

Second baseman Bret Boone decided to retire after failing to make the Nationals' Opening Day roster. Boone hit 252 home runs in a 14-year career spent primarily with the Mariners and Reds.

Tigers closer Todd Jones, plagued by arm injuries throughout the second half of the season, called it quits after 16 seasons. He compiled 319 career saves.

While Bonds, the game's all-time home run leader, never officially announced his retirement, he also did not play in 2008 after being shunned on the free agent market. His agent, Jeff Borris, considered filing collusion charges against the owners based on the fact Bonds hit 28 home runs in 340 at-bats and led the major leagues with a .480 on-base percentage with the Giants in 2007.

However, many teams claimed they shied away from Bonds because the 43-year-old left fielder's availability was in question as he faced a potential prison term. Bonds was charged with 15 felony counts in May alleging he lied to a grand jury in 2003 when he denied knowingly using performance-enhancing drugs and also alleging that he hampered the federal government's doping inves-

CONTINUED ON PAGE 24

AL wins 12th straight game

The Rangers' Michael Young ended the 15-inning marathon with a sacrifice fly

ED WOLFSTEIN

The All-Star Game made a final appearance at Yankee Stadium in 2008 and it was as if the Midsummer Classic could not bear to say goodbye to the House That Ruth Built.

It took until the bottom of the 15th, tying the record for longest All-Star Game in terms of innings that was set in 1967, before Rangers shortstop Michael Young's sacrifice fly scored Twins first baseman Justin Morneau with the winning run to give the American League its 12th straight victory, 4-3 over the National League as the Midsummer Classic returned to New York for the first time since 1977.

The game took four hours and 40 minutes and Yankee Stadium, in its final season, was nearly half-empty by the time Morneau slid home at 1:37 a.m local time. Both teams had exhausted their pitching staffs and Red Sox outfielder J.D. Drew and Mets third baseman David Wright were set to take the mound if the game had been extended to a 16th inning.

Drew, even without having to make the first pitching appearance of his 11-year career, captured Most Valuable Player honors as his two-run home run in the seventh off the Reds' Edinson Volquez tied the game at 2-2 and his walk in the 15th off losing pitcher Brad Lidge of the Phillies helped spark the winning rally.

"I was kind of looking forward to pitching," Drew said. "I used to have a good knuckleball when I was a kid."

Rays lefthander Scott Kazmir, the AL's 12th pitcher, got credit for the win.

The NL might not even have been in a position to win had Rockies righthander Aaron Cook not provided three scoreless innings of relief from the 10th through 12th innings.

Morneau scored the winning run a night after winning the Home Run Derby, even though he played second fiddle to Rangers center fielder Josh Hamilton in that event. Morneau topped Hamilton 5-3 in the final. However, Hamilton was clearly worn out after hitting a record 28 homers in the first round, surpassing the mark of 24 set by Bobby Abreu in 2005 in Detroit.

—John Perrotto

JULY 15 IN NEW YORK

American League 4, National League 3

NATIONAL	AB	R	H	BI	AMERICAN	AB	R	H	BI
Ramirez, ss	3	1	2	0	Suzuki, rf	3	0	1	0
Tejada, ss	3	1	2	0	Drew, rf	4	1	2	2
Utley, 2b	3	0	1	0	Jeter, ss	3	0	1	0
Uggla, 2b	4	0	0	0	Young, ss	4	0	1	1
Berkman, 1b	2	0	0	1	Hamilton, cf-lf	3	0	1	0
Gonzalez, 1b	3	0	1	1	Quentin, lf	4	0	0	0
Pujols, dh	3	0	2	0	Rodriguez, 3b	2	0	0	0
Wright, ph-dh	3	0	1	0	Crede, 3b	1	0	0	0
Jones, 3b	3	0	1	0	Guillen, ph-3b	3	0	1	0
Ramirez, 3b	0	0	0	0	Ramirez, lf	2	0	0	0
Guzman, pr-3b	3	0	0	0	Sizemore, cf	5	1	1	0
Holliday, rf	3	1	1	1	Bradley, dh	2	0	0	0
Hart, rf	3	0	0	0	Longoria, ph-dh	4	0	1	1
Braun, lf	3	0	0	0	Youkilis, 1b	2	0	0	0
Ludwick, lf	2	0	0	0	Morneau, 1b	4	2	2	0
Fukudome, cf	2	0	0	0	Mauer, c	1	0	1	0
McLouth, cf	4	0	1	0	Kinsler, pr-2b	5	0	1	0
Soto, c	2	0	0	0	Pedroia, 2b	1	0	0	0
Martin, c	3	0	1	0	Varitek, c	0	0	0	0
McCann, c	0	0	0	0	Navarro, ph-c	4	0	1	0
Totals	52	3	13	3	**Totals**	57	4	14	4

National	000 011 010	000 000—3	
American	000 000 210	000 001—4	

LOB—National 11, American 17. **2B**—Morneau, Longoria, Guillen. **HR**—Holliday, Drew. **GIDP**—Jeter, Uggla. **SF**—Berkman, Gonzalez, Young. **SB**—Tejada, Drew, Sizemore, Jeter, Hamilton, Bradley, Kinsler. **CS**—Guzman, Kinsler. **PO**—Bradley. **E**—Ramirez, Uggla 3, Navarro.

NATIONAL	IP	H	R	ER	BB	SO	AMERICAN	IP	H	R	ER	BB	SO
Sheets	2	1	0	0	2	3	Lee	2	1	0	0	0	3
Zambrano	2	1	0	0	0	1	Saunders	1	0	0	0	0	0
Haren	2	2	0	0	1	2	Halladay	1	1	0	0	0	1
Volquez BS	1	2	2	2	0	2	Santana	1	1	1	1	0	2
Wilson	⅔	0	0	0	0	1	Duchscherer	1	3	1	1	0	1
Wagner BS	⅓	2	1	1	0	0	Nathan	1	0	0	0	0	1
Dempster	1	0	0	0	0	3	Papelbon	1	1	1	0	0	2
Cook	3	4	0	0	0	3	Rodriguez	⅓	0	0	0	0	1
Marmol	1	0	0	0	0	2	Rivera	1⅔	2	0	0	0	2
Webb	1	0	0	0	0	2	Soria	1⅓	2	0	0	2	2
Lidge L	⅔	2	1	1	1	0	Sherrill	2⅓	2	0	0	1	0
							Kazmir W	1	0	0	0	1	1

Umpires: HP—Derryl Cousins. **1B**—Ed Rapuano. **2B**—Tom Hallion. **3B**—Mark Wegner. **LF**—Greg Gibson. **RF**—Phil Cuzzi.
T—4:50. **A**—55,632.

tigation. A federal grand jury indicted Bonds with 14 counts of making false declarations to a grand jury and one count of obstruction of justice.

Goose Lands In Cooperstown

Righthanded reliever Rich "Goose" Gossage and manager Dick Williams headed up the Hall of Fame class of 2008 in Cooperstown that also included four posthumous inductees: former Dodgers owner Walter O'Malley, former Pirates owner Barney Dreyfuss, former commissioner Bowie Kuhn and former manager Billy Southworth.

Elected by the Baseball Writers Association of America in his ninth time on the ballot, Gossage went 124-107 with 310 saves and a 3.01 ERA during a 22-year career with the White Sox (1972-76), Pirates (1977), Yankees (1978-83, 1989), Padres (1984-87), Cubs (1988), Giants (1989), Rangers (1991), Athletics (1992-93) and Mariners (1994).

Gossage was one of the most intimidating relievers in baseball history and said he learned to be more menacing after his older brother called him a sissy and challenged him to throw harder during a backyard game of catch as a youngster.

Williams, who was elected by the Hall's reconstituted Veterans Committee along with the other four inductees, compiled a 1,571-1,451 record in 22 seasons with the Red Sox (1967-69), Athletics (1971-73), Angels (1974-76), Expos (1977-81), Padres (1982-85) and Mariners (1986-88). He won two World Series with the A's and two other pennants ('67 Red Sox, '84 Padres).

Larry Whiteside, a pioneering black journalist who worked primarily for the Boston Globe, was awarded the J.G. Taylor Spink Award, and longtime Mariners broadcaster Dave Niehaus received the Ford C. Frick Award.

Hall president Dale Petroskey resigned in March after the Hall's executive committee said it found he "failed to exercise proper fiduciary responsibility and other business judgments that were not in the best interest of the National Baseball Hall of Fame and Museum." Jeff Idelson, the Hall's vice president for education and communications, replaced Petroskey.

MLB decided to end the Hall of Fame game, which had been played since 1940, citing scheduling difficulties in holding an in-season exhibition game. The Cubs and Padres were rained out on June 16, in what would have been the final game. Maddux was sorry to see the tradition end.

"The game is a good thing," Maddux said. "When you look at the schedules in spring training,

you're like, 'Oh, that's a day we don't want to go.' But once you're here, you're kind of glad you're here. For me, it's a great place to spend an off day."

Spring Training Changes

The Dodgers ended another long spring training journey when they played their final exhibition game at Holman Stadium at the Dodgertown complex in Vero Beach, Fla. The Dodgers had trained at the picturesque former naval air station since 1948 and the last Grapefruit League game, a 12-10 loss to the Astros, was an emotional affair.

"We're going to leave, but we're not leaving our memories," said former Dodgers manager and Hall of Famer Tommy Lasorda.

The Dodgers will move into a new complex in Glendale, Ariz., in 2009 that they will share with the White Sox. Also playing their last game in Florida was the Indians, who said goodbye to Winter Haven on their way to Goodyear, Ariz., where they will share a complex with the Reds, who announced they will leave their spring training base in Sarasota, Fla., once the lease expires in 2009.

Another historic spring training venue also hosted its last game when the Reds beat the Rays 6-3 on March 28 at Al Lang Field in St. Petersburg, Fla. The scenic waterfront ballpark played host to Grapefruit League games for eight decades and was the site of more spring training games than any other venue. However, the Rays decided to move their spring training headquarters to Port Charlotte, Fla., in 2009 and hope to eventually build a retractable-roof stadium on the site of Al Lang.

The American Pastime?

Finally, some rather jarring news came from Southern England in 2008 that threatened to destroy the idea that baseball is an American creation.

Julian Pooley, the manager of the Surrey History Centre, said he had authenticated a reference to baseball in a diary by English lawyer William Bray dating to 1755. That would have been nearly 50 years before the previous first known reference to baseball.

Bray, who was believed to be 18 at the time, wrote that he played the game with both men and women on the day after Easter, a traditional holiday in England. Baseball has always been thought to be an American invention, with the first recorded game occurring in Hoboken, N.J., in 1846, with roots in the British games of rounders and cricket.

Furthermore, Pooley said there is a reference to baseball that came earlier than Bray's in a fictional book by British author John Newberry called "A Little Pretty Pocket-Book." The exact year that the book was published is unclear.

MAJOR LEAGUE DEBUTS

ARIZONA DIAMONDBACKS
Name	Date
D'Antona, Jamie	July 22
Romero, Alex	April 2
Rosales, Leo	June 15
Scherzer, Max	April 29
Whitesell, Josh	Sept. 2

ATLANTA BRAVES
Name	Date
Blanco, Gregor	March 30
Bueno, Francisley	Aug. 13
Lillibridge, Brent	April 26
Morton, Charlie	June 14
Parr, James	Sept. 4
Perry, Jason	July 4

BALTIMORE ORIOLES
Name	Date
Bierd, Randor	April 2
Castillo, Alberto	April 28
McCrory, Bob	April 30
Mickolio, Kam	Aug. 20
Miller, Jim	Sept. 1
Montanez, Lou	April 28
Santos, Omir	Sept. 5
Simon, Alfredo	Sept. 6
Torres, Eider	April 26
Waters, Chris	Aug. 5

BOSTON RED SOX
Name	Date
Bowden, Michael	Aug. 30
Carter, Chris	June 5
Kottaras, George	Sept. 13
Lowrie, Jed	April 15
Masterson, Justin	April 24
Smith, Chris	June 21
Van Every, Jonathan	May 14
Velazquez, Gil	Sept. 25
Zink, Charlie	Aug. 12

CHICAGO CUBS
Name	Date
Fukudome, Kosuke	March 31
Hoffpauir, Micah	May 18
McGehee, Casey	Sept. 2
Samardzija, Jeff	July 25

CHICAGO WHITE SOX
Name	Date
Bourgeois, Jason	Sept. 9
Getz, Chris	April 28
Ramirez, Alexei	March 31
Richard, Clayton	July 23
Russell, Adam	June 17

CINCINNATI REDS
Name	Date
Bruce, Jay	May 27
Castillo, Wilkin	Sept. 2
Cueto, Johnny	April 3
Dickerson, Chris	Aug. 12
Herrera, Danny	June 3
Janish, Paul	May 14
Ramirez, Ramon	Aug. 30
Roenicke, Josh	Sept. 13
Rosales, Adam	Aug. 9
Thompson, Daryl	June 21

CLEVELAND INDIANS
Name	Date
Aubrey, Michael	May 17
Kobayashi, Masahide	April 2
Lewis, Scott	Sept. 10
Rundles, Rich	Sept. 3

COLORADO ROCKIES
Name	Date
Bernier, Doug	June 17
Bowers, Cedrick	July 2
Fowler, Dexter	Sept. 2
Herrera, Jonathan	April 30
Nix, Jayson	April 1
Register, Steven	Aug. 4
Reynolds, Greg	May 11

DETROIT TIGERS
Name	Date
Bonine, Eddie	June 14
Dolsi, Freddy	May 6
Hollimon, Michael	June 9
Joyce, Matt	May 5

FLORIDA MARLINS
Name	Date
Badenhop, Burke	April 9
Baker, John	July 9
Delgado, Jesus	Sept. 17
Miller, Jai	June 22
Sanchez, Gaby	Sept. 17
Tucker, Ryan	June 8
Volstad, Chris	July 6

HOUSTON ASTROS
Name	Date
Maysonet, Edwin	Sept. 7
Saccomanno, Mark	Sept. 8
Wright, Wesley	March 31

KANSAS CITY ROYALS
Name	Date
Aviles, Mike	May 29
Ka'aihue, Kila	Sept. 4
Lowery, Devon	Sept. 5
Rosa, Carlos	June 14
Tupman, Mat	May 18
Yabuta, Yasuhiko	April 5

LOS ANGELES ANGELS
Name	Date
Adenhart, Nick	May 1
Arredondo, Jose	May 14
Jepsen, Kevin	Sept. 8
O'Day, Darren	March 31
Rodriguez, Sean	April 19
Sandoval, Freddy	Sept. 8
Serrano, Alex	April 16
Wilson, Bobby	April 28

LOS ANGELES DODGERS
Name	Date
DeWitt, Blake	March 31
Elbert, Scott	Aug. 29
Ellis, A.J.	Sept. 15
Kershaw, Clayton	May 25
Kuroda, Hiroki	April 4
Maza, Luis	May 14
McDonald, James	Sept. 17
Troncoso, Ramon	April 1
Wade, Cory	April 24

MILWAUKEE BREWERS
Name	Date
DiFelice, Mark	May 18
Dillard, Tim	May 23
Escobar, Alcides	Sept. 3
Gamel, Mat	Sept. 3
Iribarren, Hernan	April 12
Nelson, Brad	Sept. 1
Salome, Angel	Sept. 3

MINNESOTA TWINS
Name	Date
Bass, Brian	April 1
Korecky, Bobby	April 26
Macri, Matt	May 24
Mijares, Jose	Sept. 13
Pridie, Jason	Sept. 3
Ruiz, Randy	Aug. 1
Span, Denard	April 6
Tolbert, Matt	April 1

NEW YORK METS
Name	Date
Evans, Nick	May 24
Kunz, Eddie	Aug. 3
Murphy, Daniel	Aug. 2
Niese, Jonathon	Sept. 2
Parnell, Bobby	Sept. 15
Reyes, Argenis	July 3

NEW YORK YANKEES
Name	Date
Aceves, Alfredo	Aug. 31
Cervelli, Francisco	Sept. 18
Christian, Justin	June 24
Coke, Phil	Sept. 1
Gardner, Brett	June 30
Miranda, Juan	Sept. 18
Patterson, Scott	June 1

OAKLAND ATHLETICS
Name	Date
Baisley, Jeff	Sept. 9
Bankston, Wes	July 2
Conrad, Brooks	July 21
Cunningham, Aaron	Aug. 31
Gonzalez, Carlos	May 30
Gonzalez, Gio	Aug. 6
Gray, Jeff	Sept. 8
Hernandez, Fernando	April 9
Outman, Josh	Sept. 2
Pennington, Cliff	Aug. 12
Petit, Gregorio	May 18
Smith, Greg	April 9
Ziegler, Brad	May 31

PHILADELPHIA PHILLIES
Name	Date
Carpenter, Andrew	Aug. 27
Cervenak, Mike	July 11
Golson, Greg	Sept. 3
Harman, Brad	April 22
Marson, Lou	Sept. 28
Swindle, R.J.	July 7

PITTSBURGH PIRATES
Name	Date
Barthmaier, Jimmy	June 27
Bixler, Brian	April 6
Chavez, Jesse	Aug. 27
Cruz, Luis	Sept. 2
Herrera, Yoslan	July 12
Meek, Evan	April 2
Salas, Marino	May 13

ST. LOUIS CARDINALS
Name	Date
Barton, Brian	April 1
Boggs, Mitchell	June 6
Garcia, Jaime	July 11
Mather, Joe	May 30
McClellan, Kyle	April 1
Motte, Jason	Sept. 3
Parisi, Mike	May 5
Perez, Chris	May 16
Stavinoha, Nick	June 22
Washington, Rico	April 1
Worrell, Mark	June 3

SAN DIEGO PADRES
Name	Date
Antonelli, Matt	Sept. 1
Carlin, Luke	May 10
Crabbe, Callix	April 3
Ekstrom, Mike	Sept. 10
Geer, Josh	Aug. 30
Gonzalez, Edgar	May 12
Guevara, Carlos	June 2
Hayhurst, Dirk	Aug. 23
Hundley, Nick	July 4
Kazmar, Sean	Aug. 13
LeBlanc, Wade	Sept. 3
Reineke, Chad	Aug. 16
Venable, Will	Aug. 29
Wells, Jared	May 24

SAN FRANCISCO GIANTS
Name	Date
Bocock, Brian	March 31
Bowker, John	April 12
Burriss, Emmanuel	April 20
Denker, Travis	May 21
Espineli, Geno	July 20
Gillaspie, Conor	Sept. 9
Hinshaw, Alex	May 15
Holm, Steve	April 4
Horwitz, Brian	May 30
Matos, Osiris	July 3
Ochoa, Ivan	July 12
Palmer, Matt	Aug. 16
Rohlinger, Ryan	Aug. 13
Romo, Sergio	June 26
Sandoval, Pablo	Aug. 14
Timpner, Clay	April 8

SEATTLE MARINERS
Name	Date
Hulett, Tug	July 12
LaHair, Bryan	July 18
Thomas, Justin	Sept. 1
Tuiasosopo, Matt	Sept. 5
Valbuena, Luis	Sept. 2

TAMPA BAY RAYS
Name	Date
Brignac, Reid	July 4
Jaso, John	Sept. 6
Johnson, Elliot	April 5
Longoria, Evan	April 12
Niemann, Jeff	April 13
Perez, Fernando	Sept. 5
Price, David	Sept. 14
Talbot, Mitch	Sept. 15

TEXAS RANGERS
Name	Date
Boggs, Brandon	April 29
Davis, Chris	June 26
Duran, German	April 17
Fukumori, Kazuo	March 31
Gordon, Brian	Sept. 17
Harrison, Matt	July 8
Hunter, Tommy	Aug. 1
Hurley, Eric	June 12
Madrigal, Warner	July 2
Mathis, Doug	May 12
Ramirez, Max	June 22
Teagarden, Taylor	July 18

TORONTO BLUE JAYS
Name	Date
Carlson, Jesse	April 10
Diaz, Robinzon	April 23
Purcey, David	April 18
Richmond, Scott	July 30
Snider, Travis	Aug. 29
Wells, Randy	April 5

WASHINGTON NATIONALS
Name	Date
Balester, Collin	July 1
Bernadina, Roger	June 29
Estrada, Marco	Aug. 20
Hinckley, Mike	Sept. 2
Manning, Charlie	May 24
Martis, Shairon	Sept. 4
Mock, Garrett	June 8
Montz, Luke	Sept. 4
Shell, Steven	June 22

Reds outfielder Jay Bruce hit 21 home runs after being called up on May 27

CHRIS PROCTOR

CLUB BATTING

	AVG	G	AB	R	H	2B	3B	HR	RBI	BB	SO	SB	CS	OBP	SLG
Texas	.283	162	5728	901	1619	376	35	194	867	595	1207	81	25	.354	.462
Boston	.280	162	5596	845	1565	353	33	173	807	646	1068	120	35	.358	.447
Minnesota	.279	163	5641	829	1572	298	49	111	791	529	979	102	42	.340	.408
Detroit	.271	162	5641	821	1529	293	41	200	780	572	1076	63	31	.340	.444
New York	.271	162	5572	789	1512	289	20	180	758	535	1015	118	39	.342	.427
Kansas City	.269	162	5608	691	1507	303	28	120	650	392	1005	79	38	.320	.397
Los Angeles	.268	162	5540	765	1486	274	25	159	721	481	987	129	48	.330	.413
Baltimore	.267	161	5559	782	1486	322	30	172	750	533	990	81	37	.333	.429
Seattle	.265	162	5643	671	1498	285	20	124	631	417	890	90	32	.318	.389
Toronto	.264	162	5503	714	1453	303	32	126	681	521	938	80	27	.331	.399
Chicago	.263	163	5553	811	1458	296	13	235	785	540	1016	67	34	.332	.448
Cleveland	.262	162	5543	805	1455	339	22	171	772	560	1213	77	29	.339	.424
Tampa Bay	.260	162	5541	774	1443	284	37	180	735	626	1224	142	50	.340	.422
Oakland	.242	161	5451	646	1318	270	23	125	610	574	1226	88	21	.318	.369

CLUB PITCHING

	ERA	G	CG	SHO	SV	IP	H	R	ER	HR	BB	SO	AVG
Toronto	3.49	162	15	13	44	1447	1330	610	561	134	467	1184	.244
Tampa Bay	3.82	162	7	12	52	1458	1349	671	618	166	526	1143	.246
Los Angeles	4.00	162	7	10	66	1451	1455	697	644	160	457	1106	.261
Boston	4.01	162	5	16	47	1446	1369	694	645	147	548	1185	.250
Oakland	4.01	161	4	7	33	1435	1364	690	640	135	576	1061	.253
Chicago	4.11	163	4	10	34	1458	1471	729	658	156	460	1147	.261
Minnesota	4.18	163	5	10	42	1459	1568	745	675	183	406	995	.274
New York	4.28	162	1	11	42	1442	1478	727	685	143	489	1141	.266
Cleveland	4.46	162	10	13	31	1437	1530	761	711	170	444	986	.273
Kansas City	4.50	162	2	8	44	1446	1473	781	720	159	515	1085	.264
Seattle	4.73	162	4	4	36	1435	1544	811	754	161	626	1016	.276
Detroit	4.91	162	1	2	34	1445	1541	857	786	172	644	991	.274
Baltimore	5.15	161	4	4	35	1422	1538	869	810	184	687	922	.277
Texas	5.37	162	6	8	36	1442	1647	967	860	176	625	963	.288

CLUB FIELDING

	PCT	PO	A	E	DP		PCT	PO	A	E	DP
Boston	.986	4339	1597	85	149	Oakland	.984	4305	1573	98	169
New York	.986	4325	1586	83	141	Seattle	.984	4306	1654	99	160
Toronto	.986	4340	1699	84	137	Baltimore	.983	4266	1661	100	163
Cleveland	.985	4311	1689	94	182	Chicago	.983	4373	1730	108	155
Los Angeles	.985	4354	1646	91	159	Minnesota	.982	4377	1682	108	168
Tampa Bay	.985	4373	1495	90	153	Detroit	.981	4335	1634	113	172
Kansas City	.984	4337	1548	96	159	Texas	.978	4326	1676	132	191

INDIVIDUAL BATTING LEADERS *(MINIMUM 3.1 PA/TEAM GAME)*

	AVG	G	AB	R	H	2B	3B	HR	RBI	BB	SO	SB
Mauer, Joe, Minnesota	.328	146	536	98	176	31	4	9	85	84	50	1
Pedroia, Dustin, Boston	.326	157	653	118	213	54	2	17	83	50	52	20
Bradley, Milton, Texas	.321	126	414	78	133	32	1	22	77	80	112	5
Kinsler, Ian, Texas	.319	121	518	102	165	41	4	18	71	45	67	26
Ordonez, Magglio, Detroit	.317	146	561	72	178	32	2	21	103	52	76	1
Youkilis, Kevin, Boston	.312	145	538	91	168	43	4	29	115	62	108	3
Suzuki, Ichiro, Seattle	.310	162	686	103	213	20	7	6	42	51	65	43
DeJesus, David, Kansas City	.307	135	518	70	159	25	7	12	73	46	71	11
Polanco, Placido, Detroit	.307	141	580	90	178	34	3	8	58	35	43	7
Markakis, Nick, Baltimore	.306	157	595	106	182	48	1	20	87	99	113	10

INDIVIDUAL PITCHING LEADERS *(MINIMUM 1 IP/TEAM GAME)*

	W	L	ERA	G	GS	CG	SHO	SV	IP	H	R	ER	BB	SO
Lee, Cliff, Cleveland	22	3	2.54	31	31	4	2	0	223	214	68	63	34	170
Halladay, Roy, Toronto	20	11	2.78	34	33	9	2	0	246	220	88	76	39	206
Matsuzaka, Daisuke, Boston	18	3	2.90	29	29	0	0	0	168	128	58	54	94	154
Lester, Jon, Boston	16	6	3.21	33	33	2	2	0	210	202	78	75	66	152
Danks, John, Chicago	12	9	3.32	33	33	0	0	0	195	182	74	72	57	159
Mussina, Mike, New York	20	9	3.37	34	34	0	0	0	200	214	85	75	31	150
Saunders, Joe, Los Angeles	17	7	3.41	31	31	1	0	0	198	187	82	75	53	103
Hernandez, Felix, Seattle	9	11	3.45	31	31	2	0	0	201	198	85	77	80	175
Baker, Scott, Minnesota	11	4	3.45	28	28	0	0	0	172	161	66	66	42	141
Greinke, Zack, Kansas City	13	10	3.47	32	32	1	0	0	202	202	87	78	56	183

AWARD WINNERS

Selected by Baseball Writers Association of America

MOST VALUABLE PLAYER

Player	1st	2nd	3rd	Total
Dustin Pedroia, Bos.	16	6	4	317
Justin Morneau, Minn.	7	7	6	257
Kevin Youkilis, Bos.	2	4	4	201
Joe Mauer, Minn.	2	8	1	188
Carlos Quentin, Chi.	—	1	4	160
Francisco Rodriguez, L.A.	1	2	6	143
Josh Hamilton, Texas	—	—	2	112
Alex Rodriguez, N.Y.	—	—	—	45
Carlos Pena, T.B.	—	—	1	44
Grady Sizemore, Cle.	—	—	—	42
Evan Longoria, T.B.	—	—	—	38
Cliff Lee, Cle.	—	—	—	24
Miguel Cabrera, Det.	—	—	—	17
Vladimir Guerrero, L.A.	—	—	—	16
Jermaine Dye, Chi.	—	—	—	14
Aubrey Huff, Bal.	—	—	—	12
Milton Bradley, Texas	—	—	—	9
Jason Bartlett, T.B.	—	—	—	6
Mike Mussina, N.Y.	—	—	—	3
Raul Ibanez, Sea.	—	—	—	1
Ian Kinsler, Texas	—	—	—	1
Ichiro Suzuki, Sea.	—	—	—	1
Mark Teixeira, L.A.	—	—	—	1

CY YOUNG AWARD

Pitchers	1st	2nd	3rd	Total
Cliff Lee, Cle.	24	4	—	132
Roy Halladay, Tor.	4	15	6	71
Francisco Rodriguez, L.A.	—	7	11	32
Daisuke Matsuzaka, Bos.	—	2	4	10
Mariano Rivera, N.Y.	—	—	3	3
Mike Mussina, N.Y.	—	—	2	2
Ervin Santana, L.A.	—	—	2	2

ROOKIE OF THE YEAR

Player	1st	2nd	3rd	Total
Evan Longoria, T.B.	28	—	—	140
Alexei Ramirez, Chi.	—	18	5	59
Jacoby Ellsbury, Bos.	—	7	5	26
Mike Aviles, K.C.	—	2	3	9
Armando Galarraga, Det.	—	—	9	9
Joey Devine, Oak.	—	1	—	3
Denard Span, Minn.	—	—	3	3
Nick Blackburn, Minn.	—	—	1	1
Joba Chamberlain, N.Y.	—	—	1	1
Brad Ziegler, Oak.	—	—	1	1

MANAGER OF THE YEAR

Managers	1st	2nd	3rd	Total
Joe Maddon, T.B.	27	1	—	138
Ron Gardenhire, Minn.	1	15	8	58
Mike Scioscia, L.A.	—	12	9	45
Terry Francona, Bos.	—	—	6	6
Ozzie Guillen, Chi.	—	—	3	3
Cito Gaston, Tor.	—	—	2	2

GOLD GLOVE AWARDS

Selected by AL managers

C—Joe Mauer, Minnesota. 1B—Carlos Pena, Tampa Bay. 2B—Dustin Pedroia, Boston. 3B—Adrian Beltre, Seattle. SS—Michael Young, Texas. OF—Torii Hunter, Los Angeles; Grady Sizemore, Cleveland; Ichiro Suzuki, Seattle. P—Mike Mussina, New York.

SILVER SLUGGER AWARDS

Selected by AL managers, coaches

C—Joe Mauer, Minnesota. 1B—Justin Morneau, Minnesota. 2B—Dustin Pedroia, Boston. 3B—Alex Rodriguez, New York. SS—Derek Jeter, New York. OF—Josh Hamilton, Texas; Carlos Quentin, Chicago; Grady Sizemore, Cleveland. DH—Aubrey Huff, Baltimore.

DEPARTMENT LEADERS

BATTING

GAMES
Morneau, Justin, Twins	163
Ibanez, Raul, Mariners	162
Suzuki, Ichiro, Mariners	162
Cabrera, Orlando, White Sox	161
Cabrera, Miguel, Tigers	160

AT-BATS
Suzuki, Ichiro, Mariners	686
Cabrera, Orlando, White Sox	661
Pedroia, Dustin, Red Sox	653
Young, Michael, Rangers	645
Lopez, Jose, Mariners	644

RUNS
Pedroia, Dustin, Red Sox	118
Granderson, Curtis, Tigers	112
Roberts, Brian, Orioles	107
Markakis, Nick, Orioles	106
Peralta, Jhonny, Indians	104

HITS
Pedroia, Dustin, Red Sox	213
Suzuki, Ichiro, Mariners	213
Lopez, Jose, Mariners	191
Hamilton, Josh, Rangers	190
Morneau, Justin, Twins	187

TOTAL BASES
Cabrera, Miguel, Tigers	331
Hamilton, Josh, Rangers	331
Huff, Aubrey, Orioles	330
Pedroia, Dustin, Red Sox	322
Dye, Jermaine, White Sox	319

DOUBLES
Pedroia, Dustin, Red Sox	54
Roberts, Brian, Orioles	51
Huff, Aubrey, Orioles	48
Markakis, Nick, Orioles	48
Morneau, Justin, Twins	47
Rios, Alex, Blue Jays	47

TRIPLES
Granderson, Curtis, Tigers	13
Crawford, Carl, Rays	10
Iwamura, Akinori, Rays	9
Rios, Alex, Blue Jays	8
Roberts, Brian, Orioles	8

EXTRA-BASE HITS
Huff, Aubrey, Orioles	82
Dye, Jermaine, White Sox	77
Sizemore, Grady, Indians	77
Youkilis, Kevin, Red Sox	76
Cabrera, Miguel, Tigers	75

HOME RUNS
Cabrera, Miguel, Tigers	37
Quentin, Carlos, White Sox	36
Rodriguez, Alex, Yankees	35
Dye, Jermaine, White Sox	34
Thome, Jim, White Sox	34

RUNS BATTED IN
Hamilton, Josh, Rangers	130
Morneau, Justin, Twins	129
Cabrera, Miguel, Tigers	127
Youkilis, Kevin, Red Sox	115
Ibanez, Raul, Mariners	110

SACRIFICES
Casilla, Alexi, Twins	13
Cabrera, Asdrubal, Indians	11
Carroll, Jamey, Indians	10
Gathright, Joey, Royals	10
2 players	9

Miguel Cabrera

RONNIE ALLEN

SACRIFICE FLIES
Mauer, Joe, Twins	11
Morneau, Justin, Twins	10
8 players	9

HIT BY PITCHES
Giambi, Jason, Yankees	22
Quentin, Carlos, White Sox	20
Garko, Ryan, Indians	15
Rodriguez, Alex, Yankees	14
2 players	12

WALKS
Cust, Jack, Athletics	111
Markakis, Nick, Orioles	99
Sizemore, Grady, Indians	98
Upton, B.J., Rays	97
Pena, Carlos, Rays	96

INTENTIONAL WALKS
Guerrero, Vladimir, Angels	16
Morneau, Justin, Twins	16
Sizemore, Grady, Indians	14

Cliff Lee

ED WOLFSTEIN

Bradley, Milton, Rangers	13
2 players	12

STOLEN BASES
Ellsbury, Jacoby, Red Sox	50
Upton, B.J., Rays	44
Suzuki, Ichiro, Mariners	43
Roberts, Brian, Orioles	40
Sizemore, Grady, Indians	38

CAUGHT STEALING
Upton, B.J., Rays	16
Figgins, Chone, Angels	13
Abreu, Bobby, Yankees	11
Ellsbury, Jacoby, Red Sox	11
Gomez, Carlos, Twins	11

STOLEN BASE PERCENTAGE
Pedroia, Dustin, Red Sox	95.2%
Kinsler, Ian, Rangers	92.9%
Suzuki, Ichiro, Mariners	91.5%
Sizemore, Grady, Indians	88.4%
Rodriguez, Alex, Yankees	85.7%

STRIKEOUTS
Cust, Jack, Athletics	197
Pena, Carlos, Rays	166
Thome, Jim, White Sox	147
Gomez, Carlos, Twins	142
Swisher, Nick, White Sox	135

TOUGHEST TO STRIKE OUT
(At-bats per strikeout)
Polanco, Placido, Tigers	13.49
Betancourt, Y., Mariners	13.31
Pedroia, Dustin, Red Sox	12.56
Mauer, Joe, Twins	10.72
Suzuki, Ichiro, Mariners	10.55

GROUNDED INTO DOUBLE PLAYS
Guerrero, Vladimir, Angels	27
Ordonez, Magglio, Tigers	27
Peralta, Jhonny, Indians	26
Jeter, Derek, Yankees	24
Overbay, Lyle, Blue Jays	24

MULTIPLE-HIT GAMES
Pedroia, Dustin, Red Sox	61
Hamilton, Josh, Rangers	59
Suzuki, Ichiro, Mariners	58
Abreu, Bobby, Yankees	57
2 players	54

ON-BASE PERCENTAGE
Bradley, Milton, Rangers	.436
Mauer, Joe, Twins	.413
Markakis, Nick, Orioles	.406
Quentin, Carlos, White Sox	.394
Rodriguez, Alex, Yankees	.392

SLUGGING PERCENTAGE
Rodriguez, Alex, Yankees	.573
Quentin, Carlos, White Sox	.571
Youkilis, Kevin, Red Sox	.569
Bradley, Milton, Rangers	.563
Huff, Aubrey, Orioles	.552

ON-BASE PLUS SLUGGING
Bradley, Milton, Rangers	.999
Rodriguez, Alex, Yankees	.965
Quentin, Carlos, White Sox	.965
Youkilis, Kevin, Red Sox	.959
Huff, Aubrey, Orioles	.912

PITCHING

WINS
Lee, Cliff, Indians	22
Halladay, Roy, Blue Jays	20

Mussina, Mike, Yankees	20
Burnett, A.J., Blue Jays	18
Matsuzaka, Daisuke, Red Sox	18

LOSSES

Verlander, Justin, Tigers	17
Bannister, Brian, Royals	16
Smith, Greg, Athletics	16
Vazquez, Javier, White Sox	16
Silva, Carlos, Mariners	15

GAMES

Guerrier, Matt, Twins	76
Rodriguez, Francisco, Angels	76
Reyes, Dennys, Twins	75
Wright, Jamey, Rangers	75
Thornton, Matt, White Sox	74

GAMES STARTED

Buehrle, Mark, White Sox	34
Burnett, A.J., Blue Jays	34
Meche, Gil, Royals	34
Mussina, Mike, Yankees	34
9 players	33

COMPLETE GAMES

Halladay, Roy, Blue Jays	9
Lee, Cliff, Indians	4
6 players	3

SHUTOUTS

Garza, Matt, Rays	2
Halladay, Roy, Blue Jays	2
Lee, Cliff, Indians	2
Lester, Jon, Red Sox	2
Litsch, Jesse, Blue Jays	2
Sabathia, CC, Indians	2
Shields, James, Rays	2
Slowey, Kevin, Twins	2

SAVES

Rodriguez, Francisco, Angels	62
Soria, Joakim, Royals	42
Papelbon, Jonathan, Red Sox	41
Nathan, Joe, Twins	39
Rivera, Mariano, Yankees	39

INNINGS PITCHED

Halladay, Roy, Blue Jays	246.0
Lee, Cliff, Indians	223.1
Burnett, A.J., Blue Jays	221.1
Santana, Ervin, Angels	219.0
Buehrle, Mark, White Sox	218.2

Matt Garza

CLIFF WELCH

HITS ALLOWED

Buehrle, Mark, White Sox	240
Garland, Jon, Angels	237
Pettitte, Andy, Yankees	233
Blackburn, Nick, Twins	224
2 players	220

RUNS ALLOWED

Bannister, Brian, Royals	127
Robertson, Nate, Tigers	124
Verlander, Justin, Tigers	119
Rogers, Kenny, Tigers	118
Garland, Jon, Angels	116

EARNED RUNS ALLOWED

Robertson, Nate, Tigers	119
Bannister, Brian, Royals	117
Rogers, Kenny, Tigers	110
Silva, Carlos, Mariners	110
2 players	108

HOME RUNS ALLOWED

Byrd, Paul, Indians/Red Sox	31
Floyd, Gavin, White Sox	30
Bannister, Brian, Royals	29
Galarraga, Armando, Tigers	28
3 players	26

WALKS

Matsuzaka, Daisuke, Red Sox	94
Cabrera, Daniel, Orioles	90
Smith, Greg, Athletics	87
Verlander, Justin, Tigers	87
Burnett, A.J., Blue Jays	86

WALKS PER NINE INNINGS

Lee, Cliff, Indians	1.37
Mussina, Mike, Yankees	1.39
Halladay, Roy, Blue Jays	1.43
Shields, James, Rays	1.67
Byrd, Paul, Indians/Red Sox	1.70

HIT BATSMEN

Cabrera, Daniel, Orioles	18
Padilla, Vicente, Rangers	15
Verlander, Justin, Tigers	14

Wakefield, Tim, Red Sox	13
3 players	12

STRIKEOUTS

Burnett, A.J., Blue Jays	231
Santana, Ervin, Angels	214
Halladay, Roy, Blue Jays	206
Vazquez, Javier, White Sox	200
Greinke, Zack, Royals	183
Meche, Gil, Royals	183

STRIKEOUTS PER NINE INNINGS

Burnett, A.J., Blue Jays	9.39
Beckett, Josh, Red Sox	8.88
Santana, Ervin, Angels	8.79
Vazquez, Javier, White Sox	8.64
Matsuzaka, D., Red Sox	8.27

STRIKEOUTS PER NINE INNINGS (RELIEVERS)

Dotel, Octavio, White Sox	12.36
Thornton, Matt, White Sox	10.29
Perez, Rafael, Indians	10.14
Rodriguez, F., Angels	10.14
Papelbon, J., Red Sox	10.00

PICKOFFS

Smith, Greg, Athletics	15
Pettitte, Andy, Yankees	9
Braden, Dallas, Athletics	7
Buehrle, Mark, White Sox	7
Danks, John, White Sox	6

WILD PITCHES

Cabrera, Daniel, Orioles	15
Padilla, Vicente, Rangers	12
Wakefield, Tim, Red Sox	12
Burnett, A.J., Blue Jays	11
Dickey, R.A., Mariners	11

OPPONENT AVERAGE

Matsuzaka, D., Red Sox	.211
Galarraga, Armando, Tigers	.226
Wakefield, Tim, Red Sox	.228
Halladay, Roy, Blue Jays	.237
Santana, Ervin, Angels	.237

WORST ERA

Robertson, Nate, Tigers	6.35
Bannister, Brian, Royals	5.76
Rogers, Kenny, Tigers	5.70
Cabrera, Daniel, Orioles	5.25
Millwood, Kevin, Rangers	5.07

FIELDING

PITCHER

FPCT	Nine players tied with	1.000
PO	Halladay, Roy, Blue Jays	33
A	Rogers, Kenny, Tigers	50
E	Burnett, A.J., Blue Jays	7
TC	Rogers, Kenny, Tigers	77
DP	Rogers, Kenny, Tigers	11

CATCHER

FPCT	Mauer, Joe, Twins	.997
PO	Suzuki, Kurt, Athletics	927
A	Rodriguez, Ivan, Tigers/Yankees	58
E	Mathis, Jeff, Angels	13
TC	Suzuki, Kurt, Athletics	986
DP	Navarro, Dioner, Rays	10
PB	Cash, Kevin, Red Sox	14
CS%	Molina, Jose, Yankees	44%

FIRST BASE

FPCT	Pena, Carlos, Rays	.998
PO	Overbay, Lyle, Blue Jays	1316

	Morneau, Justin, Twins	1316
A	Overbay, Lyle, Blue Jays	155
E	Barton, Daric, Athletics	13
TC	Overbay, Lyle, Blue Jays	1476
DP	Morneau, Justin, Twins	149

SECOND BASE

FPCT	Ellis, Mark, Athletics	.993
PO	Polanco, Placido, Tigers	323
A	Cano, Robinson, Yankees	482
E	Kinsler, Ian, Rangers	18
TC	Cano, Robinson, Yankees	800
DP	Kinsler, Ian, Rangers	123

THIRD BASE

FPCT	Rodriguez, Alex, Yankees	.970
PO	Gordon, Alex, Royals	112
A	Beltre, Adrian, Mariners	272
E	Crede, Joe, White Sox	20
TC	Beltre, Adrian, Mariners	386
DP	Mora, Melvin, Orioles	28

SHORTSTOP

FPCT	Young, Michael, Rangers	.984
PO	Cabrera, Orlando, White Sox	242
A	Cabrera, Orlando, White Sox	472
E	Betancourt, Yuniesky, Mariners	21
TC	Cabrera, Orlando, White Sox	730
DP	Young, Michael, Rangers	113

OUTFIELD

FPCT	Hunter, Torii, Angels	1.000
PO	Gomez, Carlos, Twins	436
A	Markakis, Nick, Orioles	17
E	Matthews, Gary, Angels	8
	Young, Delmon, Twins	8
	Gomez, Carlos, Twins	8
TC	Gomez, Carlos, Twins	453
DP	Hamilton, Josh, Rangers	5
	Upton, B.J., Rays	5
	Cuddyer, Michael, Twins	5

CLUB BATTING

	AVG	G	AB	R	H	2B	3B	HR	RBI	BB	SO	SB	CS	OBP	SLG
St. Louis	.281	162	5636	779	1585	283	26	174	744	577	985	73	32	.350	.433
Chicago	.278	161	5588	855	1552	329	21	184	811	636	1186	87	34	.354	.443
Atlanta	.270	162	5604	753	1514	316	33	130	721	618	1023	58	27	.345	.408
New York	.266	162	5606	799	1491	274	38	172	751	619	1024	138	36	.340	.420
Los Angeles	.264	162	5506	700	1455	271	29	137	659	543	1032	126	43	.333	.399
Colorado	.263	162	5557	747	1462	310	28	160	714	570	1209	141	37	.336	.415
Houston	.263	161	5451	712	1432	284	22	167	684	449	1051	114	52	.323	.415
San Francisco	.262	162	5543	640	1452	311	37	94	606	452	1044	108	46	.321	.382
Pittsburgh	.258	162	5628	735	1454	314	21	153	705	474	1039	57	19	.320	.403
Philadelphia	.255	162	5509	799	1407	291	36	214	762	586	1117	136	25	.332	.438
Florida	.254	161	5499	770	1397	302	28	208	741	543	1371	76	28	.326	.433
Milwaukee	.253	162	5535	750	1398	324	35	198	722	550	1203	108	38	.325	.431
Arizona	.251	162	5409	720	1355	318	47	159	683	587	1287	58	23	.327	.415
Washington	.251	161	5491	641	1376	269	26	117	608	534	1095	81	43	.323	.373
San Diego	.250	162	5568	637	1390	264	27	154	615	518	1259	36	17	.317	.390
Cincinnati	.247	162	5465	704	1351	269	24	187	677	560	1125	85	47	.321	.408

CLUB PITCHING

	ERA	G	CG	SHO	SV	IP	H	R	ER	HR	BB	SO	AVG
Los Angeles	3.68	162	5	11	35	1447	1381	648	591	123	480	1205	.251
Chicago	3.87	161	2	8	44	1451	1329	671	624	160	548	1264	.242
Milwaukee	3.87	162	12	10	45	1456	1415	689	623	175	528	1110	.256
Philadelphia	3.89	162	4	11	47	1450	1444	680	625	160	533	1081	.260
Arizona	3.99	162	6	9	39	1435	1403	706	635	147	451	1229	.256
New York	4.07	162	5	12	43	1464	1415	715	662	163	590	1181	.254
St. Louis	4.20	162	2	7	42	1454	1517	725	677	163	496	957	.270
San Francisco	4.38	162	4	12	41	1442	1416	759	701	147	652	1240	.258
Houston	4.39	161	4	13	48	1425	1453	743	691	197	492	1095	.264
San Diego	4.41	162	3	6	30	1458	1466	764	714	165	561	1100	.263
Florida	4.44	161	2	8	36	1435	1421	767	707	161	586	1127	.258
Atlanta	4.47	162	2	7	26	1441	1439	778	714	156	586	1076	.263
Cincinnati	4.55	162	2	6	34	1442	1542	800	729	201	557	1227	.275
Washington	4.66	161	2	8	28	1434	1496	825	742	190	588	1063	.270
Colorado	4.77	162	3	8	36	1446	1547	822	766	148	562	1041	.276
Pittsburgh	5.10	162	3	7	34	1455	1631	884	822	176	657	963	.286

CLUB FIELDING

	PCT	PO	A	E	DP		PCT	PO	A	E	DP
Houston	.989	4276	1596	67	142	Atlanta	.983	4322	1791	107	149
New York	.986	4393	1552	83	126	Chicago	.983	4352	1445	99	118
San Diego	.986	4375	1626	85	149	Pittsburgh	.983	4365	1830	107	179
St. Louis	.986	4362	1817	85	156	San Francisco	.983	4326	1393	96	129
Colorado	.985	4338	1816	96	176	Arizona	.981	4304	1565	113	137
Philadelphia	.985	4349	1698	90	142	Cincinnati	.981	4327	1567	114	156
Los Angeles	.984	4342	1795	101	138	Florida	.980	4306	1501	117	122
Milwaukee	.984	4367	1698	101	160	Washington	.980	4302	1578	123	143

INDIVIDUAL BATTING LEADERS (MINIMUM 3.1 PA/TEAM GAME)

	AVG	G	AB	R	H	2B	3B	HR	RBI	BB	SO	SB
Jones, Chipper, Atlanta	.364	128	439	82	160	24	1	22	75	90	61	4
Pujols, Albert, St. Louis	.357	148	524	100	187	44	0	37	116	104	54	7
Holliday, Matt, Colorado	.321	139	539	107	173	38	2	25	88	74	104	28
Guzman, Cristian, Washington	.316	138	579	77	183	35	5	9	55	23	57	6
Berkman, Lance, Houston	.312	159	554	114	173	46	4	29	106	99	108	18
Theriot, Ryan, Chicago	.307	149	580	85	178	19	4	1	38	73	58	22
Winn, Randy, San Francisco	.306	155	598	84	183	38	2	10	64	59	88	25
Giles, Brian, San Diego	.306	147	559	81	171	40	4	12	63	87	52	2
Ethier, Andre, Los Angeles	.305	141	525	90	160	38	5	20	77	59	88	6
Wright, David, New York	.302	160	626	115	189	42	2	33	124	94	118	15

INDIVIDUAL PITCHING LEADERS (MINIMUM 1 IP/TEAM GAME)

	W	L	ERA	G	GS	CG	SHO	SV	IP	H	R	ER	BB	SO
Santana, Johan, New York	16	7	2.53	34	34	3	2	0	234	206	74	66	63	206
Lincecum, Tim, San Francisco	18	5	2.62	34	33	2	1	0	227	182	72	66	84	265
Peavy, Jake, San Diego	10	11	2.85	27	27	1	0	0	174	146	57	55	59	166
Dempster, Ryan, Chicago	17	6	2.96	33	33	1	0	0	207	174	75	68	76	187
Hamels, Cole, Philadelphia	14	10	3.09	33	33	2	2	0	227	193	89	78	53	196
Sheets, Ben, Milwaukee	13	9	3.09	31	31	5	3	0	198	181	74	68	47	158
Billingsley, Chad, Los Angeles	16	10	3.14	35	32	1	1	0	201	188	76	70	80	201
Volquez, Edinson, Cincinnati	17	6	3.21	33	32	0	0	0	196	167	82	70	93	206
Lowe, Derek, Los Angeles	14	11	3.24	34	34	1	0	0	211	194	84	76	45	147
Webb, Brandon, Arizona	22	7	3.30	34	34	3	1	0	227	206	95	83	65	183

AWARD WINNERS

Selected by Baseball Writers Association of America

MOST VALUABLE PLAYER

Player	1st	2nd	3rd	Total
Albert Pujols, St.L	18	10	2	369
Ryan Howard, Phil.	12	8	6	308
Ryan Braun, Mil.	—	2	3	139
Manny Ramirez, L.A.	—	2	4	138
Lance Berkman, Hou.	—	2	4	126
C.C. Sabathia, Mil.	—	4	5	121
David Wright, N.Y.	—	2	1	115
Brad Lidge, Phil.	2	—	2	104
Carlos Delgado, N.Y.	—	—	5	96
Aramis Ramirez, Chi.	—	—	—	66
Hanley Ramirez, Fla.	—	—	—	55
Chipper Jones, Atl.	—	1	—	44
Geovany Soto, Chi.	—	—	—	41
Johan Santana, N.Y.	—	1	—	30
Chase Utley, Phil.	—	—	—	30
Ryan Ludwick, St.L	—	—	—	17
Brandon Webb, Ari.	—	—	—	14
Adrian Gonzalez, S.D.	—	—	—	13
Matt Holliday, Col.	—	—	—	13
Prince Fielder, Mil.	—	—	—	11
Derrek Lee, Chi.	—	—	—	10
Carlos Beltran, N.Y.	—	—	—	10
Tim Lincecum, S.F.	—	—	—	9
Jose Reyes, N.Y.	—	—	—	3
Jose Valverde, Hou.	—	—	—	3
Stephen Drew, Ari.	—	—	—	2
Nate McLouth, Pit.	—	—	—	1

CY YOUNG AWARD

Pitchers	1st	2nd	3rd	Total
Tim Lincecum, S.F.	23	7	1	137
Brandon Webb, Ari.	4	15	8	73
Johan Santana, N.Y.	4	8	11	55
Brad Lidge, Phil.	—	1	7	10
C.C. Sabathia, Mil.	1	1	1	9
Ryan Dempster, Chi.	—	—	4	4

ROOKIE OF THE YEAR

Player	1st	2nd	3rd	Total
Geovany Soto, Chi.	31	1	—	158
Joey Votto, Cin.	1	21	8	76
Jair Jurrjens, Atl.	—	6	16	34
Edinson Volquez, Cin.*	—	3	—	9
Jay Bruce, Cin.	—	—	7	7
Kosuke Fukudome, Chi.	—	—	1	1

*Volquez received votes despite not being rookie-eligible.

MANAGER OF THE YEAR

Managers	1st	2nd	3rd	Total
Lou Piniella, Chi.	15	8	4	103
Charlie Manuel, Phil.	8	6	9	67
Fredi Gonzalez, Fla.	5	6	5	48
Joe Torre, L.A.	3	8	6	45
Tony La Russa, St.L	1	1	3	11
Jerry Manuel, N.Y.	—	3	1	10
Cecil Cooper, Hou.	—	—	3	3
Dale Sveum, Mil.	—	—	1	1

GOLD GLOVE AWARDS

Selected by NL managers

C—Yadier Molina, St.L. 1B—Adrian Gonzalez, S.D. 2B—Brandon Phillips, Cin. 3B—David Wright, N.Y. SS—Jimmy Rollins, Phil. OF—Carlos Beltran, N.Y.; Nate McLouth, Pit.; Shane Victorino, Phil. P—Greg Maddux, L.A.

SILVER SLUGGER AWARDS

Selected by NL managers, coaches

C—Brian McCann, Atl. 1B—Albert Pujols, St.L. 2B—Chase Utley, Phil. 3B—David Wright, N.Y. SS—Hanley Ramirez, Fla. OF—Ryan Braun, Mil.; Matt Holliday, Col.; Ryan Ludwick, St.L. P—Carlos Zambrano, Chi.

BATTING

GAMES

Gonzalez, Adrian, Padres	162
Howard, Ryan, Phillies	162
Beltran, Carlos, Mets	161
Loney, James, Dodgers	161
2 players	160

AT-BATS

Reyes, Jose, Mets	688
Tejada, Miguel, Astros	632
Cantu, Jorge, Marlins	628
Wright, David, Mets	626
Young, Chris, Diamondbacks	625

RUNS

Ramirez, Hanley, Marlins	125
Beltran, Carlos, Mets	116
Wright, David, Mets	115
Berkman, Lance, Astros	114
McLouth, Nate, Pirates	113
Utley, Chase, Phillies	113
Reyes, Jose, Mets	113

HITS

Reyes, Jose, Mets	204
Wright, David, Mets	189
Pujols, Albert, Cardinals	187
Winn, Randy, Giants	183
Guzman, Cristian, Nationals	183

TOTAL BASES

Pujols, Albert, Cardinals	342
Braun, Ryan, Brewers	338
Wright, David, Mets	334
Howard, Ryan, Phillies	331
Reyes, Jose, Mets	327

DOUBLES

Berkman, Lance, Astros	46
McLouth, Nate, Pirates	46
Hart, Corey, Brewers	45
Pujols, Albert, Cardinals	44
Ramirez, Aramis, Cubs	44
Drew, Stephen, D'backs	44

TRIPLES

Reyes, Jose, Mets	19
Drew, Stephen, D'backs	11
Lewis, Fred, Giants	11
Rollins, Jimmy, Phillies	9
Victorino, Shane, Phillies	8

EXTRA-BASE HITS

Braun, Ryan, Brewers	83
Pujols, Albert, Cardinals	81
Ludwick, Ryan, Cardinals	80
Berkman, Lance, Astros	79
Howard, Ryan, Phillies	78
Utley, Chase, Phillies	78

HOME RUNS

Howard, Ryan, Phillies	48
Dunn, Adam, Reds/D'backs	40
Delgado, Carlos, Mets	38
Braun, Ryan, Brewers	37
Ludwick, Ryan, Cardinals	37
Pujols, Albert, Cardinals	37

RUNS BATTED IN

Howard, Ryan, Phillies	146
Wright, David, Mets	124
Gonzalez, Adrian, Padres	119
Pujols, Albert, Cardinals	116
Delgado, Carlos, Mets	115

SACRIFICES

Dempster, Ryan, Cubs	19

Ryan Howard

Cook, Aaron, Rockies	16	Kouzmanoff, Kevin, Padres	15
Taveras, Willy, Rockies	15	5 players	14
3 players	13		

SACRIFICE FLIES

Molina, Bengie, Giants	11
Wright, David, Mets	11
Atkins, Garrett, Rockies	10
Fielder, Prince, Brewers	10
2 players	9

HIT BY PITCHES

Utley, Chase, Phillies	27

WALKS

Dunn, Adam, Reds/D'backs	122
Pujols, Albert, Cardinals	104
Burrell, Pat, Phillies	102
Berkman, Lance, Astros	99
Wright, David, Mets	94

INTENTIONAL WALKS

Pujols, Albert, Cardinals	34
Delgado, Carlos, Mets	19

Fielder, Prince, Brewers	19
Berkman, Lance, Astros	18
Gonzalez, Adrian, Padres	18

STOLEN BASES

Taveras, Willy, Rockies	68
Reyes, Jose, Mets	56
Rollins, Jimmy, Phillies	47
Bourn, Michael, Astros	41
Pierre, Juan, Dodgers	40

CAUGHT STEALING

Reyes, Jose, Mets	15
Theriot, Ryan, Cubs	13
Pierre, Juan, Dodgers	12
Ramirez, Hanley, Marlins	12
2 players	11

STOLEN BASE PERCENTAGE

Werth, Jayson, Phillies	95.2%
Rollins, Jimmy, Phillies	94.0%
Holliday, Matt, Rockies	93.3%
Winn, Randy, Giants	92.6%
Taveras, Willy, Rockies	90.7%

STRIKEOUTS

Reynolds, Mark, D'backs	204
Howard, Ryan, Phillies	199
Uggla, Dan, Marlins	171
Young, Chris, Diamondbacks	165
Dunn, Adam, Reds/D'backs	164

TOUGHEST TO STRIKE OUT
(AT-BATS PER STRIKEOUT)

Keppinger, Jeff, Reds	19.13
Molina, Bengie, Giants	13.95
Kendall, Jason, Brewers	11.47
Giles, Brian, Padres	10.75
Guzman, C., Nationals	10.16

GROUNDED INTO DOUBLE PLAYS

Tejada, Miguel, Astros	32
Lee, Derrek, Cubs	27
Loney, James, Dodgers	25
Escobar, Yunel, Braves	24
Gonzalez, Adrian, Padres	24

MULTIPLE-HIT GAMES

Reyes, Jose, Mets	64
Theriot, Ryan, Cubs	58
Guzman, Cristian, Nationals	57
Pujols, Albert, Cardinals	56
Drew, Stephen, D'backs	53

ON-BASE PERCENTAGE

Jones, Chipper, Braves	.470
Pujols, Albert, Cardinals	.462
Berkman, Lance, Astros	.420
Holliday, Matt, Rockies	.409
Ramirez, Hanley, Marlins	.400

SLUGGING PERCENTAGE

Pujols, Albert, Cardinals	.653
Ludwick, Ryan, Cardinals	.591
Jones, Chipper, Braves	.574
Berkman, Lance, Astros	.567
Braun, Ryan, Brewers	.553

ON-BASE PLUS SLUGGING

Pujols, Albert, Cardinals	1.115
Jones, Chipper, Braves	1.044
Berkman, Lance, Astros	.987
Ludwick, Ryan, Cardinals	.966
Holliday, Matt, Rockies	.947

PITCHING

WINS

Webb, Brandon, D'backs	22

Tim Lincecum

Lincecum, Tim, Giants 18
Dempster, Ryan, Cubs 17
Lilly, Ted, Cubs 17
Oswalt, Roy, Astros 17
Volquez, Edinson, Reds 17

LOSSES
Harang, Aaron, Reds 17
Zito, Barry, Giants 17
Lannan, John, Nationals 15
5 players 14

GAMES
Feliciano, Pedro, Mets 86
Ohman, Will, Braves 83
Marmol, Carlos, Cubs 82
Smith, Joe, Mets 82
Ayala, Luis, Nationals/Mets 81
Romero, J.C., Phillies 81

GAMES STARTED
Arroyo, Bronson, Reds 34
Cain, Matt, Giants 34
Jimenez, Ubaldo, Rockies 34
Lilly, Ted, Cubs 34
Lowe, Derek, Dodgers 34
Perez, Oliver, Mets 34
Santana, Johan, Mets 34
Webb, Brandon, D'backs 34

COMPLETE GAMES
Sabathia, C.C., Brewers 7
Sheets, Ben, Brewers 5
Oswalt, Roy, Astros 3
Santana, Johan, Mets 3
Webb, Brandon, D'backs 3

SHUTOUTS
Sabathia, C.C., Brewers 3
Sheets, Ben, Brewers 3
4 players 2

SAVES
Valverde, Jose, Astros 44
Lidge, Brad, Phillies 41
Wilson, Brian, Giants 41
Cordero, Francisco, Reds 34
Wood, Kerry, Cubs 34

INNINGS PITCHED
Santana, Johan, Mets 234.1
Hamels, Cole, Phillies 227.1
Lincecum, Tim, Giants 227.0

Hanley Ramirez
MORRIS FOSTOFF

Webb, Brandon, D'backs 226.2
Cain, Matt, Giants 217.2

HITS ALLOWED
Cook, Aaron, Rockies 236
Duke, Zach, Pirates 230
Arroyo, Bronson, Reds 219
Looper, Braden, Cardinals 216
Lohse, Kyle, Cardinals 211

RUNS ALLOWED
Arroyo, Bronson, Reds 116
Zito, Barry, Giants 115
Backe, Brandon, Astros 114
Duke, Zach, Pirates 111
2 players 110

EARNED RUNS ALLOWED
Backe, Brandon, Astros 112
Arroyo, Bronson, Reds 106
Zito, Barry, Giants 103
Redding, Tim, Nationals 100

2 players 99
HOME RUNS ALLOWED
Backe, Brandon, Astros 36
Harang, Aaron, Reds 35
Lilly, Ted, Cubs 32
Olsen, Scott, Marlins 30
Suppan, Jeff, Brewers 30

WALKS
Perez, Oliver, Mets 105
Jimenez, Ubaldo, Rockies 103
Zito, Barry, Giants 102
Volquez, Edinson, Reds 93
Cain, Matt, Giants 91

WALKS PER NINE INNINGS
Maddux, G., Padres/Dodgers 1.39
Haren, Dan, Diamondbacks 1.67
Nolasco, Ricky, Marlins 1.78
Lowe, Derek, Dodgers 1.92
Oswalt, Roy, Astros 2.03

HIT BATSMEN
Cueto, Johnny, Reds 14
Kendrick, Kyle, Phillies 14
Volquez, Edinson, Reds 14
Pelfrey, Mike, Mets 13
3 players 12

STRIKEOUTS
Lincecum, Tim, Giants 265
Haren, Dan, Diamondbacks 206
Santana, Johan, Mets 206
Volquez, Edinson, Reds 206
Billingsley, Chad, Dodgers 201

STRIKEOUTS PER NINE INNINGS
Lincecum, Tim, Giants 10.51
Volquez, Edinson, Reds 9.46
Billingsley, Chad, Dodgers 9.01
Peavy, Jake, Padres 8.60
Haren, Dan, Diamondbacks 8.58

STRIKEOUTS PER NINE INNINGS (RELIEVERS)
Lidge, Brad, Phillies 11.94
Marmol, Carlos, Cubs 11.75
Broxton, J., Dodgers 11.48
Wood, Kerry, Cubs 11.40
Kuo, Hong-Chih, Dodgers 11.16

PICKOFFS
Lilly, Ted, Cubs 5
5 players 4

WILD PITCHES
Lincecum, Tim, Giants 17
Parra, Manny, Brewers 17
Jimenez, Ubaldo, Rockies 16
De La Rosa, Jorge, Rockies 14
Haren, Dan, Diamondbacks 11

OPPONENT AVERAGE
Lincecum, Tim, Giants .221
Hamels, Cole, Phillies .227
Dempster, Ryan, Cubs .227
Peavy, Jake, Padres .229
Volquez, Edinson, Reds .232

WORST ERA
Backe, Brandon, Astros 6.05
Snell, Ian, Pirates 5.42
Zito, Barry, Giants 5.15
Suppan, Jeff, Brewers 4.96
Redding, Tim, Nationals 4.95

FIELDING

PITCHER
FPCT 13 players tied with 1.000
PO Oswalt, Roy, Astros 24
A Maddux, Greg, Padres/Dodgers 57
E Campillo, Jorge, Braves 5
TC Maddux, Greg, Padres/Dodgers 77
DP Park, Chan Ho, Dodgers 5

CATCHER
FPCT Snyder, Chris, Diamondbacks 1.000
PO Martin, Russell, Dodgers 1042
A Kendall, Jason, Brewers 94
E Martin, Russell, Dodgers 11
TC Kendall, Jason, Brewers 1125
DP Kendall, Jason, Brewers 13
PB Doumit, Ryan, Pirates 9
   Bako, Paul, Reds 9
CS% Kendall, Jason, Brewers 43%

FIRST BASE
FPCT Berkman, Lance, Astros .996
PO Howard, Ryan, Phillies 1408
A Votto, Joey, Reds 136
E Howard, Ryan, Phillies 19
TC Howard, Ryan, Phillies 1528
DP Fielder, Prince, Brewers 132

SECOND BASE
FPCT Phillips, Brandon, Reds .990
PO Utley, Chase, Phillies 340
A Utley, Chase, Phillies 463
E Weeks, Rickie, Brewers 15
TC Utley, Chase, Phillies 816
DP Sanchez, Freddy, Pirates 104

THIRD BASE
FPCT Glaus, Troy, Cardinals .982
PO Kouzmanoff, Kevin, Padres 128
A Wright, David, Mets 286
E Reynolds, Mark, Diamondbacks 34
TC Wright, David, Mets 416
   Kouzmanoff, Kevin, Padres 416
DP Kouzmanoff, Kevin, Padres 34

SHORTSTOP
FPCT Rollins, Jimmy, Phillies .988
PO Ramirez, Hanley, Marlins 236
A Tejada, Miguel, Astros 442
E Ramirez, Hanley, Marlins 22
TC Reyes, Jose, Mets 660
DP Tejada, Miguel, Astros 97

OUTFIELD
FPCT Braun, Ryan, Brewers 1.000
     Andre Ethier, Dodgers
PO Beltran, Carlos, Mets 418
A Pence, Hunter, Astros 16
   Kemp, Matt, Dodgers 16
E Upton, Justin, Diamondbacks 11
   Bruce, Jay, Reds 11
TC Beltran, Carlos, Mets 429
DP Soriano, Alfonso, Cubs 5
   Nady, Xavier, Pirates 5

Phillies' frantic finish ends in World Series win

BY JOHN PERROTTO

Everyone knows how the Red Sox reversed the curse in 2004 in winning their first World Series in 86 years and how the White Sox ended an 88-year drought the following October.

Of course, the Cubs have set the gold standard for losing. The 2008 season came and went without a World Series title, running that drought to an even 100 years.

However, for sheer volume of losing, nobody beats the Phillies. While they won a World Series as recently as 1980, it was their only title in the franchise's first 125 years and no other professional sports team can lay claim to having suffered more than 10,000 regular-season losses.

Thus, it was understandable why the frozen crowd at Citizens Bank Park went into a frenzy when the Phillies wrapped up their second title by beating the upstart Rays in five games in the 2008 World Series. Nothing stirred the fans more than when slugging first baseman Ryan Howard grabbed the public address microphone following the trophy presentation and bellowed:

"Losers no more. Nobody can call us losers now. We're winners, Philadelphia. We're winners."

The Phillies' win ended a stretch of 25 years in which the nation's sixth most-populous city had gone without a major sports championship. With all due respect to the Soul, winners of the 2008 ArenaBowl, the last Philadelphia team to win a title that mattered was the 76ers, who, led by Julius Erving, defeated the Lakers in the 1983 NBA Finals.

"The thing I'll always remember from this is standing there in the infield with two outs in the ninth inning and just listening to the crowd," Howard said. "It was amazing. We have great fans and they always make a lot of noise, but I never heard anything like this. It was like they were letting 25 years of frustration out all at once."

The Phillies came into the World Series as underdogs to the Rays, who made the postseason for the first time following one of the most stunning reversals in baseball history. The Rays won the American League East with a 97-65 record and then

CLIFF WELCH

Cole Hamels allowed four runs on 10 hits in 13 innings to win World Series MVP honors

beat the White Sox in four games in the AL Division Series and the Red Sox in seven games in the AL Championship Series.

The Phillies, who were swept by the Rockies in the 2007 National League Division Series, vowed to go deeper into the postseason after winning their second straight NL East crown. The Phillies rolled to their first NL pennant since 1993, losing just two games in the NL playoffs in dispatching with the Brewers in four games in the NLDS and the Dodgers in five games in the NL Championship Series.

The Phillies continued their roll in the World Series, winning the final three games on their home field as a Fall Classic failed to go past five games for a record fifth consecutive year. The Phillies went 11-3 in the postseason after winning 14 of their final 17 regular-season games, meaning they went 25-6 in their last 31 games during a time of the year in which victories are at a premium.

"My philosophy of baseball has always been excellence over success because if you strive for excellence then success will take care of itself," Phillies manager Charlie Manuel said. "The key is taking it day by day and trying to win that day's games. The whole postseason, we just looked at it like we needed to win three out of five, four out of seven and four out of seven. If you do it that way, all of a sudden you look up and you're 25-6 or whatever."

The Phillies' clinching victory was even more dramatic because it was spread out over three days when Game Five became the first suspended game in World Series history. Commissioner Bud Selig stopped the game in the middle of the sixth after the Rays scored a run in the top half of the inning in a heavy downpour to tie the score at 2-2. Play was not resumed until two nights later because of inclement weather, though by that time Phillies ace lefthander Cole Hamels, who had thrown 75 pitches, was forced out of action.

"It was the longest day of my life," Phillies right fielder Jayson Werth said. "If anyone else in this clubhouse tells you anything differently, then they aren't leveling with you. We were all ready to win the series and then the plug got pulled."

Once play resumed, the dire predictions about the Phillies losing their edge were proven false as pinch-hitter Geoff Jenkins led off the bottom of the sixth with a two-out double and scored on a bloop single by Werth to snap the tie.

Though Rocco Baldelli's leadoff homer in the seventh tied the game for the Rays, the Phillies pushed across the go-ahead run in the bottom of the seventh inning when Pat Burrell led off with a double off losing pitcher J.P. Howell. Pinch-runner Eric Bruntlett then moved to third on Shane Victorino's groundout before scoring when Pedro Feliz grounded a single to center field through a drawn-in infield off Chad Bradford.

The Series featured four close games, three of which were decided by one run. A fourth was decided by two runs, and only the outcome of Game Four, which Philadelphia won 10-2, was out of reach. Eventually, Game Five was put in the hands of closer Brad Lidge, who went a perfect 41-for-41 in saves during the regular season. He entered in the ninth inning to replace winning pitcher J.C. Romero to protect the 4-3 lead. Lidge gave up a one-out, broken-bat single to Dioner Navarro, after which pinch-runner Fernando Perez promptly stole second base, but Perez was stranded there as pinch-hitter Ben Zobrist lined out to right and pinch-hitter Eric Hinske struck out swinging.

"I'd gotten a couple of sliders up earlier in the inning and Navarro hit one for a single and Zobrist hit one hard for an out," Lidge said. "Once I got to two strikes on Hinske, I knew it was time to keep the slider low, really try to bury it. I saw him swing over it and I just kind of froze for a second. Then, the gravity of the situation hit me and I nearly blacked out until I felt all my teammates jumping on top of me."

Though Hamels did not figure in the Game Five decision, he was named the World Series MVP. The 24-year-old won Game One and went 1-0, 2.77 in two starts, allowing four runs and 10 hits in 13 innings with two walks and eight strikeouts. For the postseason, he was 4-0, 1.80 in five starts, giving up seven runs on 23 hits in 35 innings. He walked nine and struck out 30.

Hamels also was MVP of the NLCS and became the fifth player to win two postseason MVP awards in the same year, joining Willie Stargell of the 1979 Pirates, Darrell Porter of the 1982 Cardinals, Orel Hershiser of the 1988 Dodgers and Livan Hernandez of the 1997 Marlins.

Youth Is Served

As it turned out, young pitchers swept the postseason MVP awards. Rays 24-year-old righthander Matt Garza took the honor in Tampa Bay's ALCS victory over the Red Sox by going 2-0, 1.38 and winning a tense Game Seven by a slim 3-1 margin.

However, the Rays' winning ways stopped in the World Series as they never seemed to get any traction. Even that could not dampen the enthusiasm of manager Joe Maddon, who walked out of Citizens Bank Park with a smile on his face after Game Five.

"Very few people in this country or throughout the baseball world would have even guessed that we would get here," Maddon said. "I'm very proud of our guys as a group because they really did a truly remarkable job. We made a powerful statement, and I view this as just the beginning. I think we validated and created the Ray way of playing baseball."

However, the Phillies were too much in the end, and even the youthful Hamels understood the magnitude of his team's victory on the psyche of a city's sports fans.

"I think it will really hit us when we come back here when we're all old and retired and the fans still give us a standing ovation, just like they do to all the guys that played on the 1980 World Series team," Hamels said. "We've had the chance to witness that. Knowing that and seeing the city and the excitement that has been there from the first game of the season this year throughout the multiple sellouts in the regular season and, then, of course, the playoff excitement was just really huge. I really think the fans could taste it as much as we could. And that taste, now that we've won it, is very sweet."

Not Enough Drama

As it had been in 2007, the ALCS turned out to be the most dramatic of the seven playoff matchups. The Red Sox required seven games to knock off the Indians in 2007, but the tables were turned in 2008 with Boston falling to Tampa Bay in seven games.

Red Sox righthander Daisuke Matsuzaka rolled to a 2-0 victory in Game One with seven shut-out innings at Tropicana Field, but the Rays answered in Game Two by outlasting Boston in 11 innings. As it neared 1 a.m. in the East, the Rays pushed across the winning run when pinch-run-ner Fernando Perez dashed home on a B.J. Upton sacrifice fly to medium right field. The Rays won the game 9-8 and continued to score runs in bunches in Games Three, Four and Five. Tampa Bay took Games Three and Four in Boston by scores of 9-1 and 13-4 to pull within one win of the World Series.

In Game Five, the Rays jumped out to an early 7-0 lead, but relievers Grant Balfour and Dan Wheeler combined to give the lead back in the seventh and eighth innings. Among the barrage were two home runs, including a crushing three-run shot by Red

AMERICAN LEAGUE CHAMPIONS, 1901–2008

	PENNANT	PCT		PENNANT	PCT		PENNANT	PCT		PENNANT	PCT
1901	Chicago	.610	1918	Boston	.595	1935	Detroit	.616	1952	New York	.617
1902	Philadelphia	.610	1919	Chicago	.629	1936	New York	.667	1953	New York	.656
1903	Boston	.659	1920	Cleveland	.636	1937	New York	.662	1954	Cleveland	.721
1904	Boston	.617	1921	New York	.641	1938	New York	.651	1955	New York	.623
1905	Philadelphia	.622	1922	New York	.610	1939	New York	.702	1956	New York	.630
1906	Chicago	.616	1923	New York	.645	1940	Detroit	.584	1957	New York	.636
1907	Detroit	.613	1924	Washington	.597	1941	New York	.656	1958	New York	.597
1908	Detroit	.588	1925	Washington	.636	1942	New York	.669	1959	Chicago	.610
1909	Detroit	.645	1926	New York	.591	1943	New York	.636	1960	New York	.630
1910	Philadelphia	.680	1927	New York	.714	1944	St. Louis	.578	1961	New York	.673
1911	Philadelphia	.669	1928	New York	.656	1945	Detroit	.575	1962	New York	.593
1912	Boston	.691	1929	Philadelphia	.693	1946	Boston	.675	1963	New York	.646
1913	Philadelphia	.627	1930	Philadelphia	.662	1947	New York	.630	1964	New York	.611
1914	Philadelphia	.651	1931	Philadelphia	.704	1948	Cleveland	.626	1965	Minnesota	.630
1915	Boston	.669	1932	New York	.695	1949	New York	.630	1966	Baltimore	.606
1916	Boston	.591	1933	Washington	.651	1950	New York	.636	1967	Boston	.568
1917	Chicago	.649	1934	Detroit	.656	1951	New York	.636	1968	Detroit	.636

DIVISION ERA (1969-1993)
*Won pennant. ^ Won first half; defeated Milwaukee 3-2 in playoff. ^^ Won first half, defeated Kansas City 3-0.

	EAST	PCT	WEST	PCT	LCS		EAST	PCT	WEST	PCT	LCS
1969	Baltimore*	.673	Minnesota	.599	3-0						
1970	Baltimore*	.667	Minnesota	.605	3-0						
1971	Baltimore*	.639	Oakland	.627	3-0						
1972	Detroit	.551	Oakland*	.600	3-2						
1973	Baltimore	.599	Oakland*	.580	3-2						
1974	Baltimore	.562	Oakland*	.556	3-1						
1975	Boston*	.594	Oakland	.605	3-0						
1976	New York*	.610	Kansas City	.556	3-2						
1977	New York*	.617	Kansas City	.630	3-2						
1978	New York*	.613	Kansas City	.568	3-1						
1979	Baltimore*	.642	California	.543	3-1						
1980	New York*^	.636	Kansas City*	.599	3-0						
1981	New York*^	.607	Oakland^^	.587	3-0						

	EAST	PCT	WEST	PCT	LCS
	Milwaukee	.585	Kansas City	.566	
1982	Milwaukee*	.586	California	.574	3-2
1983	Baltimore*	.605	Chicago	.611	3-1
1984	Detroit*	.642	Kansas City	.519	3-0
1985	Toronto	.615	Kansas City*	.562	4-3
1986	Boston*	.590	California	.568	4-3
1987	Detroit	.605	Minnesota*	.525	4-1
1988	Boston	.549	Oakland*	.642	4-0
1989	Toronto	.549	Oakland*	.611	4-1
1990	Boston	.543	Oakland*	.636	4-0
1991	Toronto	.562	Minnesota*	.586	4-1
1992	Toronto*	.593	Oakland	.593	4-2
1993	Toronto*	.586	Chicago	.580	4-2

WILD CARD ERA (1994—2008)
*Won pennant. † Lost ALCS.

	EAST	PCT	CENTRAL	PCT	WEST	PCT	WILD CARD	PCT	LCS
1994	New York	.619	Chicago	.593	Texas	.456	None		
1995	Boston	.597	Cleveland*	.694	Seattle†	.545	New York (E)	.549	4-2
1996	New York*	.568	Cleveland	.615	Texas	.556	Baltimore (E)†	.543	4-1
1997	Baltimore†	.605	Cleveland*	.534	Seattle	.556	New York (E)	.593	4-2
1998	New York*	.704	Cleveland†	.549	Texas	.543	Boston (E)	.568	4-2
1999	New York*	.605	Cleveland	.599	Texas	.586	Boston (E)†	.580	4-1
2000	New York*	.540	Chicago	.586	Oakland	.565	Seattle (W)†	.562	4-2
2001	New York*	.594	Cleveland	.562	Seattle†	.716	Oakland (W)	.630	4-1
2002	New York	.640	Minnesota†	.584	Oakland	.636	Anaheim (W)*	.611	4-1
2003	New York*	.623	Minnesota	.556	Oakland	.593	Boston (E)†	.586	4-3
2004	New York†	.623	Minnesota	.568	Anaheim	.568	Boston (E)*	.605	4-3
2005	New York	.586	Chicago*	.611	Los Angeles†	.586	Boston (E)	.586	4-1
2006	New York	.599	Minnesota	.593	Oakland†	.574	Detroit (C)*	.586	4-0
2007	Boston*	.593	Cleveland†	.593	Los Angeles	.580	New York (E)	.580	4-3
2008	Tampa Bay*	.599	Chicago	.546	Los Angeles	.617	Boston (E)†	.586	4-3

Sox DH David Ortiz in the seventh inning.

Howell completed the bullpen collapse in the bottom of the ninth when he surrendered the walk-off hit to Boston right fielder J.D. Drew, whose single scored Kevin Youkilis, who had reached on a two-out error, from second base. Boston won the game 8-7 and rolled to a 4-2 victory in Game Six. The stage was set for Game Seven.

Garza throttled the Red Sox' lineup in the deciding game, striking out nine batters in seven innings, while allowing just two hits and a lone solo home run, to punch Tampa Bay's ticket to the

World Series.

To reach the ALCS, the Red Sox upended the 100-win Angels in four games in the ALDS. The Rays handled the White Sox in four games in the other ALDS matchup, winning the franchise's first-ever playoff series in its first-ever appearance.

The Phillies took care of the Brewers in four games to win the NLDS, and then defeated the Dodgers in five games to win the pennant in convincing fashion. The Dodgers, in turn, swept 97-win Chicago in their NLDS matchup, outscoring the favored Cubs by a margin of 20-8.

NATIONAL LEAGUE CHAMPIONS, 1901-2008

	PENNANT	PCT		PENNANT	PCT		PENNANT	PCT		PENNANT	PCT
1901	Pittsburgh	.647	1918	Chicago	.651	1935	Chicago	.649	1952	Brooklyn	.627
1902	Pittsburgh	.741	1919	Cincinnati	.686	1936	New York	.597	1953	Brooklyn	.682
1903	Pittsburgh	.650	1920	Brooklyn	.604	1937	New York	.625	1954	New York	.630
1904	New York	.693	1921	New York	.614	1938	Chicago	.586	1955	Brooklyn	.641
1905	New York	.686	1922	New York	.604	1939	Cincinnati	.630	1956	Brooklyn	.604
1906	Chicago	.763	1923	New York	.621	1940	Cincinnati	.654	1957	Milwaukee	.617
1907	Chicago	.704	1924	New York	.608	1941	Brooklyn	.649	1958	Milwaukee	.597
1908	Chicago	.643	1925	Pittsburgh	.621	1942	St. Louis	.688	1959	Los Angeles	.564
1909	Pittsburgh	.724	1926	St. Louis	.578	1943	St. Louis	.682	1960	Pittsburgh	.617
1910	Chicago	.675	1927	Pittsburgh	.610	1944	St. Louis	.682	1961	Cincinnati	.604
1911	New York	.647	1928	St. Louis	.617	1945	Chicago	.636	1962	San Francisco	.624
1912	New York	.682	1929	Chicago	.645	1946	St. Louis	.628	1963	Los Angeles	.611
1913	New York	.664	1930	St. Louis	.597	1947	Brooklyn	.610	1964	St. Louis	.574
1914	Boston	.614	1931	St. Louis	.656	1948	Boston	.595	1965	Los Angeles	.599
1915	Philadelphia	.592	1932	Chicago	.584	1949	Brooklyn	.630	1966	Los Angeles	.586
1916	Brooklyn	.610	1933	New York	.599	1950	Philadelphia	.591	1967	St. Louis	.627
1917	New York	.636	1934	St. Louis	.621	1951	New York	.624	1968	St. Louis	.599

DIVISION ERA (1969-1993)
*Won pennant. ^ Won first half; defeated Milwaukee 3-2 in playoff. ^^ Won first half, defeated Kansas City 3-0.

	EAST	PCT	WEST	PCT	LCS		EAST	PCT	WEST	PCT	LCS
1969	New York*	.617	Atlanta	.574	3-0		Philadelphia	.618	Houston	.623	
1970	Pittsburgh	.549	Cincinnati*	.630	3-0	1982	St. Louis*	.568	Atlanta	.549	3-0
1971	Pittsburgh*	.599	San Francisco	.556	3-1	1983	Philadelphia*	.556	Los Angeles	.562	3-1
1972	Pittsburgh	.619	Cincinnati*	.617	3-2	1984	Chicago	.596	San Diego*	.568	3-2
1973	New York*	.509	Cincinnati	.611	3-2	1985	St. Louis*	.623	Los Angeles	.586	4-2
1974	Pittsburgh	.543	Los Angeles*	.630	3-1	1986	New York*	.667	Houston	.593	4-2
1975	Pittsburgh	.571	Cincinnati*	.667	3-0	1987	St. Louis*	.586	San Francisco	.556	4-3
1976	Philadelphia	.623	Cincinnati*	.630	3-0	1988	New York	.625	Los Angeles*	.584	4-3
1977	Philadelphia	.623	Los Angeles*	.605	3-1	1989	Chicago	.571	San Francisco*	.568	4-1
1978	Philadelphia	.556	Los Angeles*	.586	3-1	1990	Pittsburgh	.586	Cincinnati*	.562	4-2
1979	Pittsburgh*	.605	Cincinnati	.559	3-0	1991	Pittsburgh	.605	Atlanta*	.580	4-3
1980	Philadelphia*	.562	Houston	.571	3-2	1992	Pittsburgh	.593	Atlanta*	.605	4-3
1981	Montreal^	.566	Los Angeles*^^	.632	3-2	1993	Philadelphia*	.599	Atlanta	.642	4-2

WILD CARD ERA (1994—2008)
*Won pennant. † Lost ALCS.

	EAST	PCT	CENTRAL	PCT	WEST	PCT	WILD CARD	PCT	LCS
1994	Montreal	.649	Cincinnati	.593	Los Angeles	.509	None		
1995	Atlanta*	.625	Cincinnati†	.590	Los Angeles	.542	Colorado (W)	.535	4-2
1996	Atlanta*	.593	St. Louis†	.543	San Diego	.562	Los Angeles (W)	.556	4-3
1997	Atlanta†	.623	Houston	.519	San Francisco	.556	Florida (E)*	.568	4-2
1998	Atlanta†	.654	Houston	.630	San Diego*	.605	Chicago (C)	.552	4-2
1999	Atlanta*	.636	Houston	.599	Arizona	.617	New York (E)†	.595	4-2
2000	Atlanta	.586	St. Louis†	.586	San Francisco	.599	New York (E)*	.580	4-1
2001	Atlanta†	.543	Houston	.574	Arizona*	.568	St. Louis (C)	.574	4-1
2002	Atlanta	.631	St. Louis†	.599	Arizona	.605	San Francisco (W)*	.590	4-1
2003	Atlanta	.623	Chicago†	.543	San Francisco	.621	Florida (E)*	.562	4-3
2004	Atlanta	.593	St. Louis*	.648	Los Angeles	.574	Houston (C)†	.568	4-3
2005	Atlanta	.556	St. Louis†	.617	San Diego	.506	Houston (C)*	.549	4-2
2006	New York†	.599	St. Louis*	.516	San Diego	.543	Los Angeles (W)	.543	4-3
2007	Philadelphia	.549	Chicago	.525	Arizona†	.556	Colorado (W)*	.552	4-0
2008	Philadelphia*	.568	Chicago	.602	Los Angeles†	.519	Milwaukee (C)	.556	4-1

Year	Winner	Loser	Result
1903	Boston (AL)	Pittsburgh (NL)	5-3
1904	NO SERIES		
1905	New York (NL)	Philadelphia (AL)	4-1
1906	Chicago (AL)	Chicago (NL)	4-2
1907	Chicago (NL)	Detroit (AL)	4-0
1908	Chicago (NL)	Detroit (AL)	4-1
1909	Pittsburgh (NL)	Detroit (AL)	4-3
1910	Philadelphia (AL)	Chicago (NL)	4-1
1911	Philadelphia (AL)	New York (NL)	4-2
1912	Boston (AL)	New York (NL)	4-3-1
1913	Philadelphia (AL)	New York (NL)	4-1
1914	Boston (NL)	Philadelphia (AL)	4-0
1915	Boston (AL)	Philadelphia (AL)	4-1
1916	Boston (AL)	Brooklyn (NL)	4-1
1917	Chicago (AL)	New York (NL)	4-2
1918	Boston (AL)	Chicago (NL)	4-2
1919	Cincinnati (NL)	Chicago (AL)	5-3
1920	Cleveland (AL)	Brooklyn (NL)	5-2
1921	New York (NL)	New York (AL)	5-3
1922	New York (NL)	New York (AL)	4-0
1923	New York (AL)	New York (NL)	4-2
1924	Washington (AL)	New York (NL)	4-3
1925	Pittsburgh (NL)	Washington (AL)	4-3
1926	St. Louis (NL)	New York (AL)	4-3
1927	New York (AL)	Pittsburgh (NL)	4-0
1928	New York (AL)	St. Louis (NL)	4-0
1929	Philadelphia (AL)	Chicago (NL)	4-1
1930	Philadelphia (AL)	St. Louis (NL)	4-2
1931	St. Louis (NL)	Philadelphia (AL)	4-3
1932	New York (AL)	Chicago (NL)	4-0
1933	New York (NL)	Washington (AL)	4-1
1934	St. Louis (NL)	Detroit (AL)	4-3
1935	Detroit (AL)	Chicago (NL)	4-2
1936	New York (AL)	New York (NL)	4-2
1937	New York (AL)	New York (NL)	4-1
1938	New York (AL)	Chicago (NL)	4-0
1939	New York (AL)	Cincinnati (NL)	4-0
1940	Cincinnati (NL)	Detroit (AL)	4-3
1941	New York (AL)	Brooklyn (NL)	4-1
1942	St. Louis (NL)	New York (AL)	4-1
1943	New York (AL)	St. Louis (NL)	4-1
1944	St. Louis (NL)	St. Louis (AL)	4-2
1945	Detroit (AL)	Chicago (NL)	4-3
1946	St. Louis (NL)	Boston (AL)	4-3
1947	New York (AL)	Brooklyn (NL)	4-3
1948	Cleveland (AL)	Boston (NL)	4-2
1949	New York (AL)	Brooklyn (NL)	4-1
1950	New York (AL)	Philadelphia (NL)	4-0
1951	New York (AL)	New York (NL)	4-2
1952	New York (AL)	Brooklyn (NL)	4-3
1953	New York (AL)	Brooklyn (NL)	4-2
1954	New York (NL)	Cleveland (AL)	4-0
1955	Brooklyn (NL)	New York (AL)	4-3
1956	New York (AL)	Brooklyn (NL)	4-3
1957	Milwaukee (NL)	New York (AL)	4-3
1958	New York (AL)	Milwaukee (NL)	4-3
1959	Los Angeles (NL)	Chicago (AL)	4-2
1960	Pittsburgh (NL)	New York (AL)	4-3
1961	New York (AL)	Cincinnati (NL)	4-1
1962	New York (AL)	San Francisco (NL)	4-3
1963	Los Angeles (NL)	New York (AL)	4-0
1964	St. Louis (NL)	New York (AL)	4-3

Brad Lidge saved Game Five of the Series, the Phillies' second win in 126 years

Year	Winner	Loser	Result
1965	Los Angeles (NL)	Minnesota (AL)	4-3
1966	Baltimore (AL)	Los Angeles (NL)	4-0
1967	St. Louis (NL)	Boston (AL)	4-3
1968	Detroit (AL)	St. Louis (NL)	4-3
1969	New York (NL)	Baltimore (AL)	4-1
1970	Baltimore (AL)	Cincinnati (NL)	4-1
1971	Pittsburgh (NL)	Baltimore (AL)	4-3
1972	Oakland (AL)	Cincinnati (NL)	4-3
1973	Oakland (AL)	New York (NL)	4-3
1974	Oakland (AL)	Los Angeles (NL)	4-1
1975	Cincinnati (NL)	Boston (AL)	4-3
1976	Cincinnati (NL)	New York (AL)	4-0
1977	New York (AL)	Los Angeles (NL)	4-2
1978	New York (AL)	Los Angeles (NL)	4-2
1979	Pittsburgh (NL)	Baltimore (AL)	4-3
1980	Philadelphia (NL)	Kansas City (AL)	4-2
1981	Los Angeles (NL)	New York (AL)	4-2
1982	St. Louis (NL)	Milwaukee (AL)	4-3
1983	Baltimore (AL)	Philadelphia (NL)	4-1
1984	Detroit (AL)	San Diego (NL)	4-1
1985	Kansas City (AL)	St. Louis (NL)	4-3
1986	New York (NL)	Boston (AL)	4-3
1987	Minnesota (AL)	St. Louis (NL)	4-3
1988	Los Angeles (NL)	Oakland (AL)	4-1
1989	Oakland (AL)	San Francisco (NL)	4-0
1990	Cincinnati (NL)	Oakland (AL)	4-0
1991	Minnesota (AL)	Atlanta (NL)	4-3
1992	Toronto (AL)	Atlanta (NL)	4-2
1993	Toronto (AL)	Philadelphia (NL)	4-2
1994	NO SERIES		
1995	Atlanta (NL)	Cleveland (AL)	4-2
1996	New York (AL)	Atlanta (NL)	4-2
1997	Florida (NL)	Cleveland (AL)	4-3
1998	New York (AL)	San Diego (NL)	4-0
1999	New York (AL)	Atlanta (NL)	4-0
2000	New York (AL)	New York (NL)	4-1
2001	Arizona (NL)	New York (AL)	4-3
2002	Anaheim (AL)	San Francisco (NL)	4-3
2003	Florida (NL)	New York (AL)	4-2
2004	Boston (AL)	St. Louis (NL)	4-0
2005	Chicago (AL)	Houston (NL)	4-0
2006	St. Louis (NL)	Detroit (AL)	4-1
2007	Boston (AL)	Colorado (NL)	4-0
2008	Philadelphia (NL)	Tampa Bay (AL)	4-1

WORLD SERIES BOX SCORES

GAME ONE *OCTOBER 22, 2008*

PHILADELPHIA PHILLIES 3, TAMPA BAY RAYS 2

PHILADELPHIA	AB	R	H	BI	BB	SO	TAMPA BAY	AB	R	H	BI	BB	SO
Rollins, ss	5	0	0	0	0	2	Iwamura, 2b	4	0	3	1	0	0
Werth, rf	4	1	2	0	1	1	Upton, cf	4	0	0	0	0	1
Utley, 2b	4	1	2	2	1	0	Pena, 1b	4	0	0	0	0	1
Howard, 1b	4	0	0	0	1	3	Longoria, 3b	4	0	0	0	0	3
Burrell, lf	3	0	0	0	1	2	Crawford, lf	4	1	1	1	0	0
a-Bruntlett, pr-lf	1	0	0	0	0	0	Aybar, dh	3	0	0	0	0	1
Victorino, cf	4	1	2	0	0	1	Navarro, c	3	0	0	0	0	2
Feliz, 3b	3	0	2	0	1	0	Zobrist, rf	3	0	1	0	0	0
Coste, dh	4	0	0	0	0	0	Bartlett, ss	1	1	0	0	2	0
Ruiz, c	3	0	0	1	1	0							
TOTALS	**35**	**3**	**8**	**3**	**6**	**9**	**TOTALS**	**30**	**2**	**5**	**2**	**2**	**8**

Philadelphia **200 100 000—3**
Tampa Bay **000 001 100—2**

a-Ran for Burrell in the 7th.

LOB—Phillies 11, Rays 3. **2B**—Werth 2 (2), Iwamura (1). **HR**—Utley (1), Crawford (1). **SB**—Utley 2 (2), Werth (1), Bartlett (1). **PO**—Pena. **E**—Howard (1), Pena (1). **A**—Upton.

PHILADELPHIA	IP	H	R	ER	BB	SO	TAMPA BAY	IP	H	R	ER	BB	SO
Hamels W	7	5	2	2	2	5	Kazmir L	6	6	3	3	4	4
Madson	1	0	0	0	0	1	Howell	⅔	1	0	0	1	2
Lidge S	1	0	0	0	0	2	Balfour	1⅔	1	0	0	1	2
							Miller	⅓	0	0	0	0	1
							Wheeler	⅓	0	0	0	0	0

Pickoff: Hamels (Pena at 1st base). **WP**—Howell. **IBB**—Utley (by Balfour).

T—3:23. **A**—40,783.

GAME TWO *OCTOBER 23, 2008*

TAMPA BAY RAYS 4, PHILADELPHIA PHILLIES 2

PHILADELPHIA	AB	R	H	BI	BB	SO	TAMPA BAY	AB	R	H	BI	BB	SO
Rollins, ss	5	0	0	0	0	1	Iwamura, 2b	3	1	0	0	1	0
Werth, rf	5	0	1	0	0	2	Upton, cf	4	1	2	1	0	0
Utley, 2b	4	0	0	0	1	1	Pena, 1b	3	0	0	1	1	1
Howard, 1b	5	0	2	0	0	1	Longoria, 3b	4	0	0	1	0	1
Burrell, lf	3	0	0	0	1	1	Crawford, lf	4	0	0	0	0	0
Victorino, cf	4	0	2	0	0	0	Floyd, dh	3	1	1	0	0	0
Dobbs, dh	3	0	1	0	0	2	Navarro, c	3	1	2	0	0	0
a-Bruntlett, ph-dh	1	1	1	1	0	0	Baldelli, rf	2	0	0	0	1	1
Feliz, 3b	4	0	0	0	0	0	Bartlett, ss	2	0	2	1	0	0
Ruiz, c	2	1	2	0	2	0							
TOTALS	**36**	**2**	**9**	**1**	**4**	**8**	**TOTALS**	**28**	**4**	**7**	**4**	**3**	**3**

Philadelphia **000 000 011—2**
Tampa Bay **210 100 00x—4**

a-Homered for Dobbs in the 8th.

LOB—Phillies 11, Rays 4. **2B**—Howard (1), Ruiz 2 (2). **HR**—Bruntlett (1). **S**—Bartlett. **SB**—Ruiz (1). **E**—Werth (1), Ruiz (1), Longoria (1). **A**—Werth, Baldelli.

PHILADELPHIA	IP	H	R	ER	BB	SO	TAMPA BAY	IP	H	R	ER	BB	SO
Myers L	7	7	4	3	3	2	Shields W	5⅔	7	0	0	2	4
Romero	1	0	0	0	0	1	Wheeler	1	0	0	0	1	2
							Price	2⅓	2	2	1	1	2

WP—Shields.

T—3:05. **A**—40,843.

GAME THREE *OCTOBER 25, 2008*

PHILADELPHIA PHILLIES 5, TAMPA BAY RAYS 4

TAMPA BAY	AB	R	H	BI	BB	SO	PHILADELPHIA	AB	R	H	BI	BB	SO
Iwamura, 2b	4	0	0	0	0	2	Rollins, ss	4	1	2	0	0	0
Upton, cf	4	1	2	0	0	1	Werth, rf	2	0	1	0	2	0
Pena, 1b	3	0	0	0	1	2	Utley, 2b	4	1	1	2	0	1
Longoria, 3b	4	0	0	0	0	2	Howard, 1b	4	1	1	1	0	2
Crawford, lf	4	2	2	0	0	0	Burrell, lf	3	0	0	0	0	2
Navarro, c	4	1	2	0	0	1	Bruntlett, lf	0	1	0	0	0	0
Gross, rf	3	0	0	2	0	0	Victorino, cf	3	0	0	0	1	1
Balfour, p	0	0	0	0	0	0	Feliz, 3b	3	0	0	0	0	2
Bartlett, ss	4	0	0	1	0	0	c-Dobbs, ph	0	0	0	0	1	0
Garza, p	2	0	0	0	0	0	Ruiz, c	3	1	2	2	1	0
a-Aybar, ph	0	0	0	0	1	0	Moyer, p	2	0	0	0	0	1
Bradford, p	0	0	0	0	0	0	Durbin, p	0	0	0	0	0	0
Howell, p	0	0	0	0	0	0	Eyre, p	0	0	0	0	0	0
Zobrist, rf	0	0	0	0	0	0	b-Jenkins, ph	1	0	0	0	0	0
							Madson, p	0	0	0	0	0	0
							Romero, p	0	0	0	0	0	0
TOTALS	**32**	**4**	**6**	**3**	**2**	**8**	**TOTALS**	**29**	**5**	**7**	**5**	**5**	**9**

Tampa Bay **010 000 210—4**
Philadelphia **110 002 001—5**

a-Walked for Garza in the 7th. b-Grounded out for Eyre in the 7th. c-Intentionally walked for Feliz in the 9th.

LOB—Rays 4, Phillies 6. **2B**—Crawford (1), Navarro (1). **HR**—Ruiz (1), Utley (2), Howard (1). **SF**—Gross. **SB**—Upton 3 (3), Crawford (1), Werth (2). **PO**—Werth. **E**—Navarro (1), Ruiz (2).

TAMPA BAY	IP	H	R	ER	BB	SO	PHILADELPHIA	IP	H	R	ER	BB	SO
Garza	6	6	4	4	2	7	Moyer	6⅓	5	3	3	1	5
Bradford	1	0	0	0	1	0	Durbin	⅓	0	0	0	1	0
Howell L	1	0	1	1	0	2	Eyre	⅓	0	0	0	0	1
Balfour	0	1	0	0	2	0	Madson BS	⅔	1	1	1	0	1
							Romero W	1⅓	0	0	0	0	1

Bradford pitched to 1 batter in the 8th.
Howell pitched to 1 batter in the 9th.
Balfour pitched to 3 batters in the 9th.

Pickoff: Howell (Werth at 2nd base). **WP**—Garza, Balfour. **IBB**—Victorino (by Balfour), Dobbs (by Balfour). **HBP**—Bruntlett (by Howell).

T—3:41 (1:31 delay). **A**—45,900.

GAME FOUR *OCTOBER 26, 2008*

PHILADELPHIA PHILLIES 10, TAMPA BAY RAYS 2

TAMPA BAY	AB	R	H	BI	BB	SO	PHILADELPHIA	AB	R	H	BI	BB	SO
Iwamura, 2b	4	0	0	0	0	0	Rollins, ss	5	3	3	0	0	0
Upton, cf	4	0	0	0	0	2	Werth, rf	4	2	2	2	1	0
Pena, 1b	3	0	0	0	1	2	Utley, 2b	3	2	0	0	2	2
Longoria, 3b	4	0	0	0	0	3	Howard, 1b	4	2	3	5	1	0
Crawford, lf	3	1	1	1	0	1	Burrell, lf	3	0	0	1	1	0
Navarro, c	4	0	1	0	0	1	Bruntlett, lf	1	0	0	0	0	0
Zobrist, rf	3	0	0	0	1	0	Victorino, cf	5	0	0	0	0	0
Bartlett, ss	4	0	0	0	0	2	Feliz, 3b	4	0	2	1	0	0
Sonnanstine, p	1	0	1	0	0	0	Ruiz, c	4	0	1	0	0	0
a-Hinske, ph	1	1	1	1	0	0	Blanton, p	3	1	1	1	0	1
Jackson, p	0	0	0	0	0	0	Durbin, p	0	0	0	0	0	0
b-Aybar, ph	1	0	1	0	0	0	Eyre, p	0	0	0	0	0	0
Wheeler, p	0	0	0	0	0	0	Madson, p	0	0	0	0	0	0
Miller, p	0	0	0	0	0	0	c-Stairs, ph	1	0	0	0	0	1
d-Baldelli, ph	1	0	0	0	0	1	Romero, p	0	0	0	0	0	0
TOTALS	**33**	**2**	**5**	**2**	**2**	**12**	**TOTALS**	**37**	**10**	**12**	**10**	**5**	**4**

Tampa Bay **000 110 000—2**
Philadelphia **101 310 04x—10**

a-Homered for Sonnanstine in the 5th. b-Singled for Jackson in the 7th. c-Struck out for Madson in the 8th. d-Struck out for Miller in the 9th.

LOB—Rays 7, Phillies 8. **2B**—Rollins 2 (2), Werth (3). **HR**—Crawford (2), Hinske (1), Howard 2 (3), Blanton (1), Werth (1). **E**—Iwamura 2 (2), Romero (1).

TAMPA BAY	IP	H	R	ER	BB	SO	PHILADELPHIA	IP	H	R	ER	BB	SO
Sonnanstine L	4	6	5	3	3	2	Blanton W	6	4	2	2	2	7
Jackson	2	2	1	1	1	1	Durbin	⅓	1	0	0	0	0
Wheeler	1⅓	3	2	2	0	1	Eyre	⅓	0	0	0	0	0
Miller	⅔	1	2	2	1	0	Madson	1⅓	0	0	0	0	3
							Romero	1	0	0	0	0	2

Blanton pitched to 1 batter in the 7th.
IBB—Howard (by Jackson). **HBP**—Crawford (by Blanton).
T—3:08. **A**—45,903.

GAME FIVE *OCTOBER 27, 2008*

(Suspended and completed on October 29)

PHILADELPHIA PHILLIES 4, TAMPA BAY RAYS 3

TAMPA BAY	AB	R	H	BI	BB	SO	PHILADELPHIA	AB	R	H	BI	BB	SO
Iwamura, 2b	4	0	2	0	0	1	Rollins, ss	3	0	0	0	1	0
Crawford, lf	4	0	1	0	0	0	Werth, rf	3	1	2	1	2	1
Upton, cf	4	1	1	0	0	0	Utley, 2b	3	1	0	0	1	1
Pena, 1b	4	1	2	1	0	0	Howard, 1b	4	0	0	1	3	0
Price, p	0	0	0	0	0	0	Burrell, lf	2	0	1	0	2	0
Longoria, 3b	4	0	1	1	0	0	b-Bruntlett, pr-lf	0	1	0	0	0	0
Navarro, c	3	0	1	0	1	1	Victorino, cf	4	0	1	2	0	1
c-Perez, pr	0	0	0	0	0	0	Feliz, 3b	4	0	2	1	0	1
Baldelli, rf	3	1	1	1	0	0	Ruiz, c	4	0	1	0	0	0
d-Zobrist, ph	1	0	0	0	0	0	Hamels, p	2	0	0	0	0	1
Bartlett, ss	3	0	1	0	0	0	a-Jenkins, ph	1	1	1	0	0	0
e-Hinske, ph	1	0	0	0	0	1	Madson, p	0	0	0	0	0	0
Kazmir, p	2	0	0	0	0	2	Romero, p	1	0	0	0	0	0
Balfour, p	0	0	0	0	0	0	Lidge, p	0	0	0	0	0	0
Howell, p	0	0	0	0	0	0							
Bradford, p	0	0	0	0	0	0							
Aybar, 1b	0	0	0	0	0	0							
TOTALS	**33**	**3**	**10**	**3**	**1**	**5**	**TOTALS**	**31**	**4**	**8**	**4**	**7**	**8**

Tampa Bay	000	101	100—3
Philadelphia	200	001	10x—4

a-Doubled for Hamels in the 6th. b-Ran for Burrell in the 7th. c-Ran for Navarro in the 9th. d-Lined out for Baldelli in the 9th. e-Struck out for Bartlett in the 9th.

LOB—Rays 5, Phillies 12. **2B**—Pena (1), Jenkins (1), Burrell (1). **HR**—Baldelli (1). **S**—Howell, Rollins. **SB**—Perez (1), Upton (4), Werth (3), Utley (3). **E**—Rollins (1). **PB**—Ruiz (1).

TAMPA BAY	IP	H	R	ER	BB	SO	PHILADELPHIA	IP	H	R	ER	BB	SO
Kazmir	4	4	2	2	6	5	Hamels	6	5	2	2	1	3
Balfour	1⅓	2	1	1	0	0	Madson	⅔	2	1	1	0	1
Howell L	⅔	1	1	1	0	1	Romero W	1⅓	2	0	0	0	0
Bradford	1	1	0	0	0	0	Lidge S	1	1	0	0	0	1
Price	1	0	0	0	1	2							

Kazmir pitched to 2 batters in the 5th.
Howell pitched to 1 batter in the 7th.
HBP—Utley (by Kazmir).
T—3:28 (:30 delay). **A**—45,940.

2008 WORLD SERIES

PHILADELPHIA

Player, Pos	AVG	G	AB	R	H	2B	3B	HR	RBI	BB	SO	SB
Joe Blanton, p	.333	1	3	1	1	0	0	1	1	0	1	0
Eric Bruntlett, lf	.333	5	3	3	1	0	0	1	1	0	0	0
Pat Burrell, lf	.071	5	14	0	1	1	0	0	1	5	5	0
Chris Coste, dh	.000	1	4	0	0	0	0	0	0	0	0	0
Greg Dobbs, dh	.333	2	3	0	1	0	0	0	0	1	2	0
Chad Durbin, p	.000	2	0	0	0	0	0	0	0	0	0	0
Scott Eyre, p	.000	2	0	0	0	0	0	0	0	0	0	0
Pedro Feliz, 3b	.333	5	18	0	6	0	0	0	2	1	3	0
Cole Hamels, p	.000	1	2	0	0	0	0	0	0	0	1	0
Ryan Howard, 1b	.286	5	21	3	6	1	0	3	6	3	9	0
Geoff Jenkins, ph	.500	2	2	1	1	1	0	0	0	0	0	0
Brad Lidge, p	.000	1	0	0	0	0	0	0	0	0	0	0
Ryan Madson, p	.000	3	0	0	0	0	0	0	0	0	0	0
Jamie Moyer, p	.000	1	2	0	0	0	0	0	0	0	1	0
Jimmy Rollins, ss	.227	5	22	4	5	2	0	0	0	1	3	0
J.C. Romero, p	.000	3	1	0	0	0	0	0	0	0	0	0
Carlos Ruiz, c	.375	5	16	2	6	2	0	1	3	4	0	1
Matt Stairs, ph	.000	1	1	0	0	0	0	0	0	0	1	0
Chase Utley, 2b	.167	5	18	5	3	0	0	2	4	5	5	3
Shane Victorino, cf	.250	5	20	1	5	0	0	0	2	1	3	0
Jayson Werth, rf	.444	5	18	4	8	3	0	1	3	6	4	3
Totals	**.262**	**5**	**168**	**24**	**44**	**10**	**0**	**9**	**23**	**27**	**38**	**7**

Pitcher	W	L	ERA	G	GS	SV	IP	H	R	ER	BB	SO
Joe Blanton	1	0	3.00	1	1	0	6.0	4	2	2	2	7
Chad Durbin	0	0	0.00	2	0	0	0.2	1	0	0	1	0
Scott Eyre	0	0	0.00	2	0	0	0.2	0	0	0	0	1
Cole Hamels	1	0	2.77	2	2	0	13.0	10	4	4	3	8
Brad Lidge	0	0	0.00	2	0	2	2.0	1	0	0	0	3
Ryan Madson	0	0	4.91	4	0	0	3.2	3	2	2	0	6
Jamie Moyer	0	0	4.26	1	1	0	6.1	5	3	3	1	5
Brett Myers	0	1	3.86	1	1	0	7.0	7	4	3	3	2
J.C. Romero	2	0	0.00	4	0	0	4.2	2	0	0	4	4
Totals	**4**	**1**	**2.86**	**5**	**5**		**244.0**	**33**	**15**	**14**	**10**	**36**

TAMPA BAY

Player, Pos	AVG	G	AB	R	H	2B	3B	HR	RBI	BB	SO	SB
Willy Aybar, 1b	.250	4	4	0	1	0	0	0	0	1	1	0
Jason Baldelli, rf	.167	3	6	1	1	0	0	1	1	1	2	0
Grant Balfour, p	.000	2	0	0	0	0	0	0	0	0	0	0
Jason Bartlett, ss	.214	5	14	1	3	0	0	0	2	2	2	1
Chad Bradford, p	.000	2	0	0	0	0	0	0	0	0	0	0
Carl Crawford, lf	.263	5	19	4	5	1	0	2	2	0	1	1
Cliff Floyd, dh	.333	1	3	1	1	0	0	0	0	0	0	0
Matt Garza, p	.000	1	2	0	0	0	0	0	0	0	0	0
Gabe Gross, rf	.000	1	3	0	0	0	0	0	2	0	0	0
Eric Hinske, ph	.500	2	2	1	1	0	0	1	1	0	1	0
J.P. Howell, p	.000	2	0	0	0	0	0	0	0	0	0	0
Akinori Iwamura, 2b	.263	5	19	1	5	1	0	0	1	1	3	0
Edwin Jackson, p	.000	1	0	0	0	0	0	0	0	0	0	0
Scott Kazmir, p	.000	1	2	0	0	0	0	0	0	0	2	0
Evan Longoria, 3b	.050	5	20	0	1	0	0	0	2	0	9	0
Trever Miller, p	.000	1	0	0	0	0	0	0	0	0	0	0
Dioner Navarro, c	.353	5	17	2	6	1	0	0	0	1	5	0
Carlos Pena, 1b	.118	5	17	1	2	1	0	0	2	3	6	0
Fernando Perez, pr	.000	1	0	0	0	0	0	0	0	0	0	1
David Price, p	.000	1	0	0	0	0	0	0	0	0	0	0
Andy Sonnanstine, p	1.000	1	1	0	1	0	0	0	0	0	0	0
B.J. Upton, cf	.250	5	20	3	5	0	0	1	0	4	4	4
Dan Wheeler, p	.000	1	0	0	0	0	0	0	0	0	0	0
Ben Zobrist, rf	.143	4	7	0	1	0	0	0	0	1	0	0
Totals	**.212**	**5**	**156**	**15**	**33**	**4**	**0**	**4**	**14**	**10**	**36**	**7**

Pitcher	W	L	ERA	G	GS	SV	IP	H	R	ER	BB	SO
Grant Balfour	0	0	3.00	3	0	0	3.0	4	1	1	3	2
Chad Bradford	0	0	0.00	2	0	0	2.0	1	0	0	1	0
Matt Garza	0	0	6.00	1	1	0	6.0	6	4	4	2	7
J.P. Howell	0	2	7.71	3	0	0	2.1	2	2	2	1	5
Edwin Jackson	0	0	4.50	1	0	0	2.0	2	1	1	1	1
Scott Kazmir	0	1	4.50	2	2	0	10.0	10	5	5	10	9
Trever Miller	0	0	18.00	1	0	0	1.0	1	2	2	1	1
David Price	0	0	2.70	2	0	0	3.1	2	1	1	2	4
James Shields	1	0	0.00	1	1	0	5.2	7	0	0	2	4
Andy Sonnanstine	0	1	6.75	1	1	0	4.0	6	5	3	3	2
Dan Wheeler	0	0	6.75	3	0	0	2.2	3	2	2	1	3
Totals	**1**	**4**	**4.50**	**5**	**5**		**042.0**	**44**	**24**	**21**	**27**	**38**

E—Howard, Werth, Ruiz (2), Romero, Rollins, Pena, Longoria, Navarro, Iwamura (2). **DP**—Philadelphia 6, Tampa Bay 4. **LOB**—Philadelphia 48, Tampa Bay 23. **SB**—Utley (3), Werth (3), Ruiz, Upton (4), Bartlett, Crawford, Perez. **CS**—Rollins, Pena. **S**—Rollins, Bartlett, Howell. **SF**—Gross. **HBP**—Bruntlett (Howell), Crawford (Blanton), Utley (by Kazmir). **IBB**—Utley (Balfour), Victorino (Balfour), Dobbs (Balfour), Howard (Jackson). **WP**—Howell, Shields, Garza, Balfour. **PB**—Ruiz. **BK**—None.

SCORE BY INNINGS

Philadelphia	611	413	152—24
Tampa Bay	220	421	310—15

AMERICAN LEAGUE DIVISION SERIES
BOSTON VS. LOS ANGELES *COMPOSITE BOX*

BOSTON

Player, Pos	AVG	G	AB	R	H	2B	3B	HR	RBI	BB	SO	SB
Jason Bay, lf	.412	4	17	3	7	2	0	2	5	2	4	0
Kevin Cash, c	.000	1	0	0	0	0	0	0	0	0	0	0
Alex Cora, ss	250	2	4	1	1	1	0	0	0	1	1	0
Coco Crisp, cf	.250	2	4	2	1	0	0	0	0	1	0	1
J.D.Drew, rf	.286	4	14	2	4	1	0	1	3	0	4	0
Jacoby Ellsbury, cf	.333	4	18	2	6	3	0	0	6	2	2	3
Mark Kotsay, 1b	.333	3	10	1	3	0	0	0	0	0	1	0
Mike Lowell, 3b	.000	2	8	0	0	0	0	0	0	1	3	0
Jed Lowrie, ss	.364	3	11	2	4	0	0	0	1	1	3	0
David Ortiz, dh	.235	4	17	1	4	1	0	0	1	3	4	0
Dustin Pedroia, 2b	059	4	17	0	1	1	0	0	1	2	2	0
David Ross, c	.000	1	0	0	0	0	0	0	0	0	0	0
Jason Varitek, c	.214	4	14	2	3	0	0	0	0	0	1	0
Kevin Youkilis, 1b	.222	4	18	2	4	1	0	0	1	2	3	0
Totals	**.250**	**4**	**152**	**18**	**38**	**10**	**0**	**3**	**18**	**15**	**28**	**4**

Pitcher	W	L	ERA	G	GS	SV	IP	H	R	ER	BB	SO
Josh Beckett	0	0	7.20	1	1	0	5.0	9	4	4	4	6
Manny Delcarmen	1	0	0.00	2	0	0	2.1	1	0	0	0	1
Jon Lester	1	0	0.00	2	2	0	14.0	10	1	0	3	11
Javier Lopez	0	1	9.00	1	0	0	1.0	3	1	1	0	1
Justin Masterson	0	0	2.25	4	0	0	4.0	6	2	1	3	3
Daisuke Matsuzaka	0	0	5.40	1	1	0	5.0	8	3	3	3	5
Hideke Okajima	0	0	6.75	3	0	0	2.2	3	2	2	1	0
Jonathan Papelbon	1	0	0.00	3	0	1	5.0	2	0	0	1	7
Totals	**3**	**1**	**2.54**	**4**	**4**	**1**	**39.0**	**42**	**13**	**11**	**15**	**34**

LOS ANGELES

Player, Pos	AVG	G	AB	R	H	2B	3B	HR	RBI	BB	SO	SB
Garret Anderson, lf	.158	4	19	1	3	0	0	0	0	1	4	0
Erick Aybar, ss	.111	4	18	0	2	0	0	0	1	0	2	0
Chone Figgins, 3b	.333	4	21	2	7	1	1	0	1	0	6	1
Vladimir Guerrero, rf	.467	4	15	2	7	1	0	0	4	1	1	0
Torii Hunter, cf	.389	4	18	0	7	0	0	0	5	1	3	0
Howie Kendrick, 2b	.118	4	17	0	2	0	0	0	0	0	7	0
Jeff Mathis, c	.500	1	2	0	1	0	0	0	1	0	1	0
Gary Matthews, rf	.000	3	5	0	0	0	0	0	0	0	2	0
Kendry Morales, ph	.500	4	4	0	2	1	0	0	0	0	0	0
Mike Napoli, c	.250	4	12	3	3	0	0	2	4	2	3	0
Juan Rivera, rf	.125	3	8	1	1	0	0	0	1	3	2	0
Mark Teixeira, 1b	.467	4	15	4	7	0	0	1	4	3	0	0
Reggie Willits, rf	.000	3	0	0	0	0	0	0	0	0	0	0
Totals	**.273**	**4**	**154**	**13**	**42**	**3**	**1**	**2**	**14**	**15**	**34**	**2**

Pitcher	W	L	ERA	G	GS	SV	IP	H	R	ER	BB	SO
Jose Arredondo	0	0	0.00	3	0	0	3.2	2	0	0	2	4
John Lackey	0	1	2.63	2	2	0	13.2	11	4	4	4	6
Darren Oliver	0	0	0.00	2	0	0	1.1	0	0	0	1	1
Francisco Rodriguez	0	1	7.71	2	0	0	2.1	5	2	2	2	2
Ervin Santana	0	0	8.44	1	1	0	5.1	8	5	5	0	3
Joe Saunders	0	0	7.71	1	1	0	4.2	5	4	4	4	2
Scot Shields	0	1	4.76	4	0	0	5.2	6	3	3	1	7
Jered Weaver	1	0	0.00	1	0	0	2.0	1	0	0	1	3
Totals	**1**	**3**	**4.19**	**4**	**4**	**0**	**38.2**	**38**	**18**	**18**	**15**	**28**

SCORE BY INNINGS

Boston	430 132 005 000—18	
Los Angeles	203 102 130 001—13	

E—Aybar, Hunter, Matthews, Figgins, Lowrie. **DP**—Boston 0, Anaheim 4. **LOB**—Boston 36, Anaheim 43. **SB**—Ellsbury 3, Crisp, Figgins, Guerrero. **CS**—Ellsbury, Willits. **S**—Kendrick 2, Varitek. **SF**—Teixeira. **HBP**—Lowrie (Lackey), Pedroia (Saunders), Napoli (Delcarmen). **IBB**—None. **WP**—None. **PB**—Varitek. **BK**—None.

CHICAGO VS. TAMPA BAY

CHICAGO

Player, Pos	AVG	G	AB	R	H	2B	3B	HR	RBI	BB	SO	SB
Brian Anderson, cf	.000	3	5	1	0	0	0	0	0	0	4	1
Orlando Cabrera, ss	.125	4	16	1	2	0	0	0	0	0	3	0
Jermaine Dye, rf	.375	4	16	1	6	1	0	1	1	1	3	0

Angels first baseman Mark Teixeira went 7-for-15 (.467) in his first 15 playoff at-bats

	AVG	G	AB	R	H	2B	3B	HR	RBI	BB	SO	SB
Ken Griffey Jr, cf	.200	3	10	1	2	0	0	0	1	5	0	
Paul Konerko, 1b	.313	4	16	3	5	0	0	2	2	1	1	0
A.J. Pierzynski, c	.385	4	13	1	5	1	0	0	1	2	1	0
Alexi Ramirez, 2b	.250	4	12	1	3	0	0	0	2	1	1	0
Nick Swisher, lf	.250	3	4	1	1	0	0	0	0	2	1	0
Jim Thome, dh	.125	4	16	1	2	1	0	0	1	1	3	0
Juan Uribe, 2b	.167	4	12	0	2	0	0	0	1	0	5	1
Dewayne Wise, cf	.286	3	7	2	2	1	0	1	5	1	2	1
Totals	**.236**	**4**	**127**	**13**	**30**	**4**	**0**	**4**	**13**	**10**	**29**	**3**

Pitcher	W	L	ERA	G	GS	SV	IP	H	R	ER	BB	SO
Mark Buehrle	0	1	6.43	1	1	0	7.0	10	5	5	0	3
John Danks	1	0	4.05	1	1	0	6.2	7	3	3	3	7
Octavio Dotel	0	0	13.50	4	0	0	1.1	2	2	2	0	3
Gavin Floyd	0	1	12.00	1	1	0	3.0	5	4	4	2	4
Bobby Jenks	0	0	0.00	1	0	1	1.0	1	0	0	0	1
Scott Linebrink	0	0	0.00	1	0	0	1.0	1	0	0	1	1
Clayton Richard	0	0	1.42	2	0	0	6.1	5	1	1	3	6
Matt Thornton	0	0	0.00	3	0	0	3.1	2	0	0	2	2
Javier Vazquez	0	1	12.46	1	1	0	4.1	8	6	6	1	6
Totals	**1**	**3**	**5.56**	**4**	**4**	**1**	**34.0**	**41**	**21**	**21**	**12**	**33**

TAMPA BAY

Player, Pos	AVG	G	AB	R	H	2B	3B	HR	RBI	BB	SO	SB
Willy Aybar, 1b	.273	4	11	2	3	1	0	0	1	0	2	0
Jason Baldelli, rf	.125	3	8	2	1	0	0	0	1	1	0	0
Jason Bartlett, ss	.286	4	14	3	4	1	0	0	0	1	3	0
Carl Crawford, lf	.214	4	14	2	3	0	0	0	2	2	2	3
Cliff Floyd, dh	.200	2	5	1	1	1	0	0	1	0	3	0
Gabe Gross, rf	.167	3	6	0	1	0	0	0	0	2	2	1
Akinori Iwamura, 2b	.389	4	18	3	7	1	1	1	4	1	4	0
Evan Longoria, 3b	.267	4	15	2	4	0	0	2	3	2	6	1
Dioner Navarro, c	.400	4	15	1	6	3	0	0	3	1	2	0
Carlos Pena, 1b	.500	3	10	0	5	0	0	0	2	1	4	2
Fernando Perez, rf	.250	1	4	0	1	0	0	0	0	0	0	0
B.J. Upton, cf	.278	4	18	5	5	0	1	3	4	1	5	0
Totals	**.297**	**4**	**138**	**21**	**41**	**7**	**2**	**6**	**21**	**12**	**33**	**7**

Pitcher	W	L	ERA	G	GS	SV	IP	H	R	ER	BB	SO
Grant Balfour	0	0	0.00	3	0	0	3.1	2	0	0	1	4
Chad Bradford	0	0	0.00	2	0	0	3.0	1	0	0	0	0
Matt Garza	0	1	7.50	1	1	0	6.0	7	5	5	4	4
J.P. Howell	0	0	0.00	3	0	0	4.1	2	0	0	0	6
Scott Kazmir	1	0	3.38	1	1	0	5.1	8	2	2	2	4
Trever Miller	0	0	0.00	1	0	0	0.0	0	0	0	1	0
James Shields	1	0	4.26	1	1	0	6.1	6	3	3	1	4
Andy Sonnanstine	1	0	3.18	1	1	0	5.2	3	2	2	1	4

Dan Wheeler	0	0	9.00	1	0	1	1.0	1	1	1	0	1
Totals	3	1	3.34	4	4	1	35.0	30	13	13	10	29

SCORE BY INNINGS

Chicago	204 402 001—13
Tampa Bay	134 250 330—21

E—Ramirez. DP—Chicago 2, Tampa Bay 3. LOB—Chicago 25, Tampa Bay 29. SB—Crawford 3, Gross, Longoria, Pena 2, Anderson, Uribe, Wise. CS—Pierzynski, Pena. S—Uribe, Anderson, Aybar. SF—Aybar, Ramirez 2. HBP—Pierzynski (Shields), Cabrera (Kazmir). IBB—Upton (Thornton), Pena (Linebrink). WP—Garza, Dotel. PB—Pierzynski. BK—None.

NATIONAL LEAGUE DIVISION SERIES
LOS ANGELES VS. CHICAGO

LOS ANGELES

Player, Pos	AVG	G	AB	R	H	2B	3B	HR	RBI	BB	SO	SB
Angel Berroa, 2b	1.000	3	1	0	1	0	0	0	0	0	0	0
Chad Billingsley, p	.000	1	3	0	0	0	0	0	0	0	1	0
Casey Blake, 3b	.273	3	11	2	3	0	0	0	2	0	1	0
Jonathan Broxton, p	.000	3	0	0	0	0	0	0	0	0	0	0
Blake DeWitt, 2b	.273	3	11	2	3	2	0	0	1	0	2	0
Andre Ethier, rf	.100	3	10	2	1	0	0	0	0	4	4	0
Rafael Furcal, ss	.333	3	12	4	4	0	0	0	2	3	2	0
Matt Kemp, cf	.154	3	13	0	2	2	0	0	1	0	5	0
Jeff Kent, ph	.000	1	1	0	0	0	0	0	0	0	0	0
Hiroki Kuroda, p	.000	1	3	0	0	0	0	0	0	0	2	0
James Loney, 1b	.214	3	14	2	3	1	0	1	6	2	0	0
Derek Lowe, p	.000	1	1	0	0	0	0	0	0	0	2	0
Greg Maddux, p	.000	1	0	0	0	0	0	0	0	0	0	0
Russell Martin, c	.308	3	13	4	4	3	0	1	5	5	3	0
Juan Pierre, lf	.000	1	1	1	0	0	0	0	0	0	0	0
Manny Ramirez, lf	.500	3	10	5	5	0	0	2	3	4	3	0
Takashi Saito, p	.000	1	0	0	0	0	0	0	0	0	0	0
Cory Wade, p	.000	3	0	0	0	0	0	0	0	0	0	0
Totals	.250	3	104	20	26	8	0	4	20	14	25	0

Pitcher	W	L	ERA	G	GS	SV	IP	H	R	ER	BB	SO
Chad Billingsley	1	0	1.35	1	1	0	6.2	5	1	1	1	7
Jonathan Broxton	0	0	0.00	3	0	1	3.1	0	0	0	2	5
Hiroki Kuroda	1	0	0.00	1	1	0	6.1	6	0	0	2	4
Derek Lowe	1	0	3.00	1	1	0	6.0	7	2	2	1	6
Greg Maddux	0	0	0.00	1	0	0	1.0	1	0	0	0	0
Takashi Saito	0	0	—	1	0	0	0.3	2	2	0	0	0
Cory Wade	0	0	2.45	3	0	0	3.2	3	1	1	0	2
Totals	3	0	2.00	3	3	1	27.0	25	6	6	6	24

CHICAGO

Player, Pos	AVG	G	AB	R	H	2B	3B	HR	RBI	BB	SO	SB
Ronny Cedeno, pr	.000	1	0	0	0	0	0	0	0	0	0	1
Neal Cotts, p	.000	2	0	0	0	0	0	0	0	0	0	0
Mark DeRosa, 2b	.333	3	12	2	4	2	0	1	4	0	1	0
Ryan Dempster, p	.500	1	2	0	1	0	0	0	0	0	1	0
Jim Edmonds, cf	.200	3	10	1	2	1	0	0	1	0	2	0
Mike Fontenot, 2b	.333	3	6	2	0	0	0	0	0	0	0	0
Kosuke Fukudome, rf	.100	3	10	0	1	0	0	0	0	0	4	0
Rich Harden, p	.000	1	2	0	0	0	0	0	0	0	1	0
Derek Lee, 1b	.545	3	11	2	6	3	0	0	0	1	2	0
Sean Marshall, p	.000	2	0	0	0	0	0	0	0	0	0	0
Jason Marquis, p	.000	1	0	0	0	0	0	0	0	0	0	0
Carlos Marmol, p	.000	2	0	0	0	0	0	0	0	0	0	0
Felix Pie, ph	.000	1	0	0	0	0	0	0	0	0	1	0
Aramis Ramirez, 3b	.182	3	11	1	2	1	0	0	0	1	2	0
Jeff Samardzija, p	.000	1	0	0	0	0	0	0	0	0	0	0
Alfonso Soriano, lf	.071	3	14	0	1	0	0	0	0	0	4	0
Geovany Soto, c	.182	3	11	0	2	1	0	0	0	1	3	0
Ryan Theriot, ss	.273	3	11	0	3	0	0	0	0	1	3	0
Daryle Ward, ph	.333	3	3	0	1	0	0	0	1	0	1	0
Kerry Wood, p	.000	1	0	0	0	0	0	0	0	0	0	0
Carlos Zambrano, p	.000	1	1	0	0	0	0	0	0	0	1	0
Totals	.240	3	104	6	25	8	0	1	6	6	24	1

PITCHER	W	L	ERA	G	GS	SV	IP	H	R	ER	BB	SO
Neal Cotts	0	0	0.00	2	0	0	1.2	1	0	0	1	3
Ryan Dempster	0	1	7.71	1	1	0	4.2	4	4	4	7	2

CHRIS PROCTOR

Not even trade acquisition Rich Harden could spare the Cubs from another sweep

Rich Harden	0	1	6.23	1	1	0	4.1	5	3	3	3	4
Sean Marshall	0	0	2.70	2	0	0	3.1	2	1	1	1	5
Jason Marquis	0	0	9.00	1	0	0	1.0	1	1	1	0	1
Carlos Marmol	0	0	6.75	2	0	0	2.2	3	2	2	0	3
Jeff Samardzija	0	0	9.00	1	0	0	1.0	2	1	1	0	0
Kerry Wood	0	0	0.00	1	0	0	1.0	2	1	0	0	0
Carlos Zambrano	0	1	4.26	1	1	0	6.1	6	7	3	2	7
Totals	0	3	5.19	3	3	0	26.0	26	20	15	14	25

SCORE BY INNINGS

Los Angeles	250 060 232—20
Chicago	020 000 112—6

E—Blake, Edmonds, DeRosa, Lee, Ramirez, Theriot, Harden. DP—Los Angeles 3, Chicago 3. LOB—Los Angeles 22, Chicago 23. SB—Cedeno. CS—None. S—Berroa. SF—None. HBP—Blake (Zambrano). IBB—Ramirez (Harden 2), Theriot (Kuroda). WP—Billingsley, Wade. PB—None. BK—None.

MILWAUKEE VS. PHILADELPHIA

MILWAUKEE

Player, Pos	AVG	G	AB	R	H	2B	3B	HR	RBI	BB	SO	SB
Ryan Braun, lf	.313	4	16	0	5	2	0	0	2	0	4	0
Dave Bush, p	.000	1	1	0	0	0	0	0	0	0	0	0
Mike Cameron, cf	.154	4	13	3	2	0	0	0	0	3	4	0
Craig Counsell, 3b	.167	4	12	0	2	0	0	0	1	0	3	0
Ray Durham, 2b	.125	3	8	2	1	0	0	0	0	1	2	0
Prince Fielder, 1b	.071	4	14	1	1	0	0	1	2	2	5	0
Eric Gagne, p	.000	2	0	0	0	0	0	0	0	0	0	0
Yovani Gallardo, p	.000	2	1	0	0	0	0	0	0	0	0	0
Tony Gwynn, ph	.333	3	3	0	1	0	0	0	0	0	1	0
Bill Hall, 3b	.250	3	8	1	2	0	0	0	0	1	3	0
J.J. Hardy, ss	.429	4	14	2	6	1	0	0	2	2	0	0
Corey Hart, rf	.231	4	13	0	3	0	0	0	0	1	3	0
Jason Kendall, c	.142	4	14	0	2	0	0	0	1	0	2	0
Seth McClung, p	.000	1	0	0	0	0	0	0	0	0	0	0
Guillermo Mota, p	.000	2	0	0	0	0	0	0	0	0	0	0
Brad Nelson, ph	.000	2	2	0	0	0	0	0	0	0	2	0
Manny Parra, p	.000	2	0	0	0	0	0	0	0	0	0	0
CC Sabathia, p	.000	2	2	0	0	0	0	0	0	1	0	0
Mitch Stetter, p	.000	3	0	0	0	0	0	0	0	0	0	0
Jeff Suppan, p	.000	1	0	0	0	0	0	0	0	0	0	0
Salomon Torres, p	.000	2	0	0	0	0	0	0	0	0	0	0
Carlos Villanueva, p	1.000	2	1	0	1	0	0	0	0	0	0	0
Rickie Weeks, 2b	.000	3	4	0	0	0	0	0	0	0	2	0
Totals	.206	4	126	9	26	3	0	1	8	10	32	0

Pitcher	W	L	ERA	G	GS	SV	IP	H	R	ER	BB	SO
Dave Bush	1	0	1.69	1	1	0	5.1	5	1	1	0	3
Eric Gagne	0	0	0.00	2	0	0	2.0	1	0	0	0	1
Yovani Gallardo	0	1	0.00	2	1	0	7.0	4	3	0	5	4
Seth McClung	0	0	0.00	1	0	0	2.0	2	0	0	3	1
Guillermo Mota	0	0	5.40	2	0	0	1.2	2	1	1	0	0
Manny Parra	0	0	0.00	2	0	0	2.1	2	0	0	1	3
CC Sabathia	0	1	12.27	1	1	0	3.2	6	5	5	4	5
Mitch Stetter	0	0	0.00	3	0	0	1.1	0	0	0	0	2
Jeff Suppan	0	1	15.00	1	1	0	3.0	6	5	5	2	3
Salomon Torres	0	0	0.00	2	0	1	2.0	4	0	0	0	1
Carlos Villanueva	0	0	0.00	2	0	0	3.2	0	0	0	0	3
Totals	1	3	3.18	4	4	1	34.0	32	15	12	15	26

PHILADELPHIA

Player, Pos	AVG	G	AB	R	H	2B	3B	HR	RBI	BB	SO	SB
Joe Blanton, p	.000	1	3	0	0	0	0	0	0	0	3	0
Eric Bruntlett, lf	1.000	3	1	0	1	0	0	0	0	0	0	0
Pat Burrell, lf	.250	4	12	2	3	0	0	2	4	2	1	0
Clay Condrey, p	.000	1	0	0	0	0	0	0	0	0	0	0
Greg Dobbs, 3b	.600	3	5	0	3	0	0	0	0	0	1	0
Chad Durbin, p	.000	1	0	0	0	0	0	0	0	0	0	0
Scott Eyre, p	.000	1	0	0	0	0	0	0	0	0	0	0
Pedro Feliz, 3b	.231	4	13	1	3	1	0	0	1	0	1	0
Cole Hamels, p	.000	1	2	1	0	0	0	0	0	0	2	0
Ryan Howard, 1b	.182	4	11	1	2	1	0	0	1	5	5	0
Geoff Jenkins, rf	.000	1	1	0	0	0	0	0	0	0	0	0
Brad Lidge, p	.000	3	0	0	0	0	0	0	0	0	0	0
Ryan Madson, p	.000	3	0	0	0	0	0	0	0	0	0	0
Jamie Moyer, p	.000	1	1	0	0	0	0	0	0	0	0	0
Brett Myers, p	.500	1	2	1	1	0	0	0	0	1	0	0
Jimmy Rollins, ss	.375	4	16	2	6	2	0	1	1	1	2	1
J.C. Romero, p	.000	1	0	0	0	0	0	0	0	0	0	0
Carlos Ruiz, c	.071	4	14	1	1	0	0	0	0	1	1	0
Matt Stairs, ph	.000	2	2	0	0	0	0	0	0	0	0	0
Chase Utley, 2b	.133	4	15	1	2	1	0	0	2	2	4	0
Shane Victorino, cf	.357	4	14	2	5	3	0	1	5	3	0	3
Jayson Werth, rf	.313	4	16	3	5	3	1	1	1	0	6	1
Totals	.250	4	128	15	32	11	1	5	15	15	26	5

Pitcher	W	L	ERA	G	GS	SV	IP	H	R	ER	BB	SO
Joe Blanton	1	0	1.50	1	1	0	6.0	5	1	1	0	7
Clay Condrey	0	0	9.00	1	0	0	1.0	1	1	1	2	1
Chad Durbin	0	0	0.00	1	0	0	0.2	3	0	0	0	1
Scott Eyre	0	0	9.00	1	0	0	1.0	3	1	1	0	1
Cole Hamels	1	0	0.00	1	1	0	8.0	2	0	0	1	9
Brad Lidge	0	0	3.00	3	0	2	3.0	3	1	1	1	4
Ryan Madson	0	0	2.25	3	0	0	4.0	3	1	1	0	2
Jamie Moyer	0	1	4.50	1	1	0	4.0	4	2	2	3	3
Brett Myers	1	0	2.57	1	1	0	7.0	2	2	2	3	4
J.C. Romero	0	0	0.00	1	0	0	1.0	0	0	0	0	0
Totals	3	1	2.31	4	4	2	35.0	26	9	9	10	32

SCORE BY INNINGS

Milwaukee	300	010	311—9
Philadelphia	157	001	010—15

E—Weeks, Utley, Rollins. DP—Milwaukee 5, Philadelphia 1. LOB—Milwaukee 28, Philadelphia 27. SB—Victorino 3, Rollins, Werth. CS—Rollins. S—Hamels, Bush, Hart. SF—Fielder, Braun. HBP—Hart (Myers), Cameron (Condrey). IBB—Howard 3 (Gallardo, McClung, Suppan), Victorino (Sabathia), Fielder 2 (Myers, Condrey). WP—Lidge, Moyer, Suppan. PB—None. BK—None.

AMERICAN LEAGUE CHAMPIONSHIP SERIES
BOSTON VS. TAMPA BAY

BOSTON

Player, Pos	AVG	G	AB	R	H	2B	3B	HR	RBI	BB	SO	SB
Jason Bay, lf	.292	7	24	3	7	1	0	1	4	7	8	0
Sean Casey, ph	.000	2	2	0	0	0	0	0	0	0	2	0
Kevin Cash, c	.333	3	3	1	1	0	0	0	1	0	1	0
Alex Cora, ss	.143	2	7	0	1	0	0	0	0	0	1	0
Coco Crisp, cf	.450	5	20	2	9	2	0	0	1	4	3	0
J.D. Drew, rf	.250	7	24	1	6	1	0	1	3	4	6	0

Kevin Youkilis hit .333 with two homers and three doubles in a seven-game ALCS

KEN BABBITT

Player, Pos	AVG	G	AB	R	H	2B	3B	HR	RBI	BB	SO	SB
Jacoby Ellsbury, cf	.000	4	14	0	0	0	0	0	0	1	3	0
Mark Kotsay, 1b	.233	7	30	1	7	3	0	0	0	0	4	0
Jed Lowrie, ss	.111	6	18	2	2	1	0	0	1	4	4	0
David Ortiz, dh	.154	7	26	3	4	1	1	1	4	6	9	0
Dustin Pedroia, 2b	.346	7	26	9	9	1	0	3	5	5	3	2
Jason Varitek, c	.050	6	20	2	1	0	0	1	1	2	8	0
Kevin Youkilis, 3b	.333	7	30	4	10	3	0	2	6	2	4	0
Totals	.234	7	244	28	57	13	1	10	27	35	56	2

Pitcher	W	L	ERA	G	GS	SV	IP	H	R	ER	BB	SO
Josh Beckett	1	0	9.64	2	2	0	9.1	13	10	10	2	8
Paul Byrd	0	0	10.80	1	0	0	3.1	5	4	4	0	2
Manny Delcarmen	0	0	31.50	3	0	0	2.0	3	7	7	5	2
Jon Lester	0	2	4.97	2	2	0	12.2	14	8	7	2	15
Javier Lopez	0	0	0.00	2	0	0	1.2	3	0	0	0	0
Justin Masterson	1	0	1.59	5	0	0	5.2	4	1	1	2	6
Daisuke Matsuzaka	1	0	4.09	2	2	0	11.0	9	5	5	6	11
Hideki Okajima	0	0	0.00	5	0	0	7.1	1	0	0	1	5
Jonathan Papelbon	0	0	0.00	4	0	2	5.1	1	0	0	1	6
Mike Timlin	0	1	10.12	2	0	0	2.2	2	3	3	4	0
Tim Wakefield	0	1	16.87	1	1	0	2.2	6	5	5	2	2
Totals	3	4	5.94	7	7	2	63.2	61	43	42	25	57

TAMPA BAY

Player, Pos	AVG	G	AB	R	H	2B	3B	HR	RBI	BB	SO	SB
Willy Aybar, dh	.421	6	19	3	8	1	0	2	6	0	3	0
Rocco Baldelli, rf	.333	2	6	1	2	0	0	1	4	1	3	0
Jason Bartlett, ss	.217	7	23	4	5	0	1	1	1	1	5	1
Carl Crawford, lf	.345	7	29	3	10	2	1	0	4	1	7	3
Cliff Floyd, dh	.200	4	10	1	2	0	0	1	1	0	4	0
Gabe Gross, rf	.000	6	10	0	0	0	0	0	0	1	5	1
Akinori Iwamura, 2b	.207	7	29	4	6	2	0	0	0	5	5	2
Evan Longoria, 3b	.259	7	27	8	7	3	0	4	8	3	5	0
Dioner Navarro, c	.192	7	26	1	5	0	0	0	2	2	4	0
Carlos Pena, 1b	.269	7	26	8	7	1	0	3	6	6	7	1
Fernando Perez, rf	.000	3	5	2	0	0	0	0	0	0	2	0
B.J. Upton, cf	.321	7	28	8	9	1	0	4	11	4	7	2
Ben Zobrist, rf	.000	3	4	0	0	0	0	0	0	1	0	0
Totals	.252	7	242	43	61	10	2	16	43	25	57	10

Pitcher	W	L	ERA	G	GS	SV	IP	H	R	ER	BB	SO
Grant Balfour	0	0	19.29	4	0	0	2.1	5	5	5	4	1
Chad Bradford	0	0	3.00	0	0	0	3.0	4	1	1	2	1
Matt Garza	2	0	1.38	2	2	0	13.0	8	2	2	6	14
J.P. Howell	0	1	3.38	6	0	0	5.1	5	2	2	3	6

	W	L	ERA	G	GS	SV	IP	H	R	ER	BB	SO
Edwin Jackson	0	0	0.00	2	0	0	2.1	0	0	0	2	4
Scott Kazmir	0	0	4.35	2	2	0	10.1	8	5	5	6	9
Trever Miller	0	0	0.00	3	0	0	0.2	1	0	0	1	1
David Price	1	0	0.00	3	0	1	2.1	0	0	0	2	4
James Shields	0	2	3.46	2	2	0	13.0	15	6	5	5	9
Andy Sonnanstine	1	0	3.68	1	1	0	7.1	6	4	3	1	2
Dan Wheeler	0	0	5.40	3	0	0	5.0	5	3	3	3	5
Totals	4	3	3.62	7	7	1	64.2	57	28	26	35	56

SCORE BY INNINGS

Boston	313	412	671	00	—28
Tampa Bay	81(11)	265	351	01	—43

E—Longoria 3, Upton, Bartlett 2. **DP**—Boston 6, Tampa Bay 6. **LOB**—Boston 63, Tampa Bay 36. **SB**—Pedroia 2, Crawford 3, Gross, Bartlett, Iwamura 2, Pena, Upton 2. **CS**—Navarro, Pedroia. **S**—None. **SF**—Lowrie, Ellsbury, Upton. **HBP**—Drew (Balfour), Varitek (Kazmir), Bartlett 2 (Beckett, Masterson), Bay (Howell), Pedroia (Garza). **IBB**—Iwamura (Timlin), Bay (Howell) Pena (Papelbon), Ortiz (Bradford). **WP**—Matsuzaka, Wheeler, Kazmir. **PB**—Varitek, Navarro. **BK**—None.

NATIONAL LEAGUE CHAMPIONSHIP SERIES
LOS ANGELES VS. PHILADELPHIA

LOS ANGELES

Player, Pos	AVG	G	AB	R	H	2B	3B	HR	RBI	BB	SO	SB
Joe Beimel, p	.000	3	0	0	0	0	0	0	0	0	0	0
Angel Berroa, 2b	.000	2	1	0	0	0	0	0	0	0	0	0
Chad Billingsley, p	.000	2	1	0	0	0	0	0	0	0	0	0
Casey Blake, 3b	.263	5	19	2	5	0	0	1	2	2	4	0
Jonathan Broxton, p	.000	2	0	0	0	0	0	0	0	0	0	0
Blake DeWitt, 2b	.077	5	13	0	1	0	1	0	5	1	4	0
Andre Ethier, rf	.227	5	22	4	5	1	0	0	0	1	6	0
Rafael Furcal, ss	.211	5	19	5	4	0	0	1	1	3	2	0
Nomar Garciaparra, 3b	.429	4	7	0	3	0	0	0	1	1	2	0
Matt Kemp, cf	.333	5	15	1	5	1	0	0	0	4	4	0
Jeff Kent, 2b	.000	5	8	0	0	0	0	0	0	0	4	0
Clayton Kershaw, p	.000	2	0	0	0	0	0	0	0	0	0	0
Hong-Chih Kuo, p	.000	3	0	0	0	0	0	0	0	0	0	0
Hiroki Kuroda, p	.000	1	3	0	0	0	0	0	0	0	1	0
James Loney, 1b	.438	5	16	0	7	2	0	0	2	3	5	0
Derek Lowe, p	.250	2	4	0	1	0	0	0	0	0	2	0
Greg Maddux, p	.000	2	0	0	0	0	0	0	0	0	0	0
Russell Martin, c	.118	5	17	3	2	0	0	0	1	3	7	1
James McDonald, p	.000	2	1	0	0	0	0	0	0	0	0	0
Pablo Ozuna, ph	.000	1	1	0	0	0	0	0	0	0	0	0
Chan Ho Park, p	.000	4	0	0	0	0	0	0	0	0	0	0
Juan Pierre, cf	.667	1	3	1	2	1	0	0	0	0	0	0
Manny Ramirez, lf	.533	5	15	4	8	2	0	2	7	7	1	0
Cory Wade, p	.000	4	0	0	0	0	0	0	0	0	0	0
Totals	.261	5	165	20	43	7	1	4	19	25	42	1

Pitcher	W	L	ERA	G	GS	SV	IP	H	R	ER	BB	SO
Joe Beimel	0	0	0.00	3	0	0	0.2	0	0	0	2	0
Chad Billingsley	0	2	18.00	2	2	0	5.0	12	11	10	7	9
Jonathan Broxton	0	0	3.86	2	0	0	2.1	3	1	1	1	2
Clayton Kershaw	0	0	4.50	2	0	0	2.0	1	1	1	2	1
Hong-Chih Kuo	0	0	3.00	3	0	0	3.0	2	1	1	0	3
Hiroki Kuroda	1	0	3.00	1	1	0	6.0	5	2	2	1	3
Derek Lowe	0	1	3.48	2	2	0	10.1	12	5	4	2	6
Greg Maddux	0	0	0.00	2	0	0	3.0	3	2	0	1	3
James McDonald	0	0	0.00	2	0	0	5.1	3	0	0	2	7
Chan Ho Park	0	0	0.00	4	0	0	1.2	1	0	0	1	1
Cory Wade	0	1	4.91	4	0	0	3.2	3	2	2	0	2
Totals	1	4	4.40	5	5	0	43.0	45	25	21	19	37

PHILADELPHIA

Player, Pos	AVG	G	AB	R	H	2B	3B	HR	RBI	BB	SO	SB
Joe Blanton, p	.000	1	2	0	0	0	0	0	0	0	2	0
Eric Bruntlett, lf	.000	4	2	0	0	0	0	0	0	1	0	0
Pat Burrell, lf	.333	5	18	1	6	0	0	1	3	1	7	0
Clay Condrey, p	.000	1	0	0	0	0	0	0	0	0	0	0
Chris Coste, c	1.000	1	1	0	1	0	0	0	0	0	0	0
Greg Dobbs, 3b	.500	3	6	2	3	1	0	0	0	1	1	0
Chad Durbin, p	.000	3	0	0	0	0	0	0	0	0	0	0
Scott Eyre, p	.000	2	0	0	0	0	0	0	0	0	0	0
Pedro Feliz, 3b	.154	5	13	0	2	0	0	0	1	1	2	0
Cole Hamels, p	.200	2	5	0	1	0	0	0	0	0	2	0
J.A. Happ, p	.000	1	0	0	0	0	0	0	0	0	0	0
Ryan Howard, 1b	.300	5	20	4	6	1	0	0	2	3	2	0
Geoff Jenkins, ph	.000	2	1	0	0	0	0	0	0	0	0	0
Brad Lidge, p	.000	4	0	0	0	0	0	0	0	0	0	0
Ryan Madson, p	.000	4	0	0	0	0	0	0	0	0	0	0
Jamie Moyer, p	.000	1	0	0	0	0	0	0	0	0	0	0
Brett Myers, p	1.000	1	3	2	3	0	0	0	3	0	0	0
Jimmy Rollins, ss	.143	5	21	4	3	0	0	1	1	2	8	2
J.C. Romero, p	.000	3	0	0	0	0	0	0	0	0	0	0
Carlos Ruiz, c	.313	5	16	3	5	1	0	0	1	1	0	0
Matt Stairs, ph	1.000	1	1	1	1	0	0	1	2	0	0	0
So Taguchi, ph	.000	4	4	0	0	0	0	0	0	0	1	0
Chase Utley, 2b	.353	5	17	4	6	2	0	1	3	6	5	0
Shane Victorino, cf	.222	5	18	2	4	0	1	1	6	2	1	0
Jayson Werth, rf	.190	5	21	2	4	1	0	0	1	0	7	0
Totals	.266	5	169	25	45	6	1	5	22	19	37	2

Pitcher	W	L	ERA	G	GS	SV	IP	H	R	ER	BB	SO
Joe Blanton	0	0	5.40	1	1	0	5.0	7	3	3	4	4
Clay Condrey	0	0	0.00	1	0	0	0.2	0	0	0	1	0
Chad Durbin	0	0	4.50	3	0	0	2.0	3	2	1	2	2
Scott Eyre	0	0	0.00	2	0	0	1.1	0	0	0	1	0
Cole Hamels	2	0	1.93	2	2	0	14.0	11	3	3	5	13
J.A. Happ	0	0	3.00	1	0	0	3.0	4	1	1	2	2
Brad Lidge	0	0	0.00	4	0	3	4.1	2	0	0	2	6
Ryan Madson	1	0	0.00	4	0	0	5.0	4	0	0	1	4
Jamie Moyer	0	1	40.50	1	1	0	1.1	6	6	6	0	2
Brett Myers	1	0	9.00	1	1	0	5.0	6	5	5	4	6
J.C. Romero	0	0	0.00	3	0	0	2.1	0	0	0	3	3
Totals	4	1	3.89	5	5	3	44.0	43	20	19	25	42

SCORE BY INNINGS

Los Angeles	721	523	000	—20	
Philadelphia	356	024	140	—25	

E—Furcal 4, Kemp, Dobbs, Howard. **DP**—Los Angeles 5, Philadelphia 8. **LOB**—Los Angeles 43, Philadelphia 35. **SB**—Martin, Rollins 2. **CS**—Utley, Kemp, Bruntlett, Pierre. **S**—Victorino, Furcal, Kuo. **SF**—DeWitt. **HBP**—Martin 2 (Moyer, Durbin). **IBB**—Dobbs (Billingsley), Blake (Myers), Ramirez 2 (Blanton, Eyre), Loney (Blanton), Victorino 2 (Billingsley, Maddux). **WP**—Myers, Lidge, Park, Billingsley. **PB**—Ruiz. **BK**—None.

Dodgers righthander Chad Billingsley was touched for 11 runs in five NLCS innings

LARRY GOREN

ORGANIZATION STATISTICS

Arizona Diamondbacks

BY JACK MAGRUDER

The Diamondbacks led or were tied atop the National League West for 153 consecutive days in 2008 but could not sustain it through a dreary September, failing to defend their division title. Despite the disappointing stretch run, the team did take another step forward in the organization's big-picture plan to win with youth.

Righthander Brandon Webb had a career-high 22 victories and with newcomer Dan Haren gave Arizona arguably the best 1-2 starting punch in the NL. Stephen Drew scaled historic heights by becoming the third shortstop in major league history—and first in the NL—to have at least 40 doubles, 10 triples and 20 home runs in the same season.

But after taking the NL West lead on April 6, the Diamondbacks gave it back to the Dodgers on Sept. 6 during a disastrous stretch in which they were 4-14 and lost five straight games to Los Angeles.

Webb was arguably the NL's best pitcher, yet he struggled during the stretch run. The 29-year-old went 11 starts without a loss before dropping three consecutive games in late August and early September, including two against Los Angeles, in which he lasted just 14 innings and gave up 19 earned runs.

The real culprit was not pitching, though: the Diamondbacks led the major leagues with 95 quality starts and had a 3.98 ERA, seventh-best in the majors. Arizona was just 10th in the NL in runs despite playing in one of the most hitter-friendly parks in the majors. Even the Aug. 11 addition of big bopper Adam Dunn did little to end the offensive woes and did not match the boost that Manny Ramirez provided in Los Angeles.

"We need to be better at run-scoring," general manager Josh Byrnes said. "It puts demands on our pitching. I do think our core group is very good. We have young, talented players who can be here for a while."

Part of the problem was injuries. Outfielder Eric Byrnes, who in 2007 became the 11th player in major league history to have at least 20 homers and 50 stolen bases in the same season, suffered a right hamstring injury in a spring training footrace with teammate Chris Young and was never healthy. He was finally forced out of the lineup for good in late June. Gold Glove second baseman and sparkplug

Orlando Hudson suffered a season-ending wrist injury in August.

Drew's spectacular season was the best but not the only step forward by a young, core group. that includes first baseman/outfielder Conor Jackson, outfielders Young and Justin Upton, catcher Chris Snyder and infielder Mark Reynolds.

PLAYERS OF THE YEAR

MAJOR LEAGUE: BRANDON WEBB, RHP

Webb challenged for yet another Cy Young Award in firing his way to a 22-7, 3.30 season. He owned the NL's most wins, ranked 10th in ERA, pitched three complete games and struck out 183 in 226 innings, the fourth-most total in the senior circuit.

MINOR LEAGUE: JARROD PARKER, RHP

A first-round pick in 2007 out of Norwell, Ind., Parker was a standout in his first full season. The 19-year-old righthander finished 12-5, 3.44 at low Class A South Bend. His line included 117 strikeouts and 33 walks in almost 118 innings.

PAUL GIERHART

ORGANIZATION LEADERS

BATTING		*Minimum 250 at-bats
*AVG	D'Antona, Jamie, Tucson	.365
R	Frey, Evan, South Bend/Visalia	98
H	Frey, Evan, South Bend/Visalia	169
TB	Whitesell, Josh, Tucson	270
2B	Clifford, Peter, Visalia	41
3B	Raines, Tim, Tucson	13
HR	Whitesell, Josh, Tucson	26
RBI	Whitesell, Josh, Tucson	110
BB	Mee, Michael, South Bend/Visalia	84
SO	Whitesell, Josh, Tucson	136
SB	Ciriaco, Pedro, Visalia	40
*OBP	Whitesell, Josh, Tucson	.425
*SLG	D'Antona, Jamie, Tucson	.604

PITCHING		†Minimum 75 innings
W	Valdez, Cesar, Visalia/Mobile	13
	Beltre, Christian, South Bend	13
L	Brown, Brooks, Mobile	15
†ERA	Augenstein, Bryan, South Bend/Visalia	2.74
G	Mahon, Reid, Mobile/Tucson	52
GS	Enright, Barry, Visalia	29
SV	Mahon, Reid, Mobile/Tucson	24
IP	Enright, Barry, Visalia	164
BB	Vasquez, Esmerling, Tucson	73
SO	Enright, Barry, Visalia	143
†AVG	Beck, Chad, South Bend/Visalia	.230

2008 PERFORMANCE

General Manager: Josh Byrnes. **Farm Director:** A.J. Hinch. **Scouting Director:** Tom Allison.

Class	Team	League	W	L	PCT	Finish*	Manager	Affiliate Since
Majors	Arizona	National	82	80	.506	9th (16)	Bob Melvin	—
Triple-A	Tucson Sidewinders	Pacific Coast	60	82	.423	15th (16)	Bill Plummer	1998
Double-A	Mobile BayBears	Southern	58	79	.423	10th (10)	Hector De La Cruz	2007
High A	Visalia Oaks	California	67	72	.482	7th (10)	Mike Bell	2007
Low A	South Bend Silver Hawks	Midwest	76	63	.547	2nd (14)	Mark Haley	1997
Short-season	Yakima Bears	Northwest	28	48	.368	8th (8)	Bob Didier	2001
Rookie	Missoula Osprey	Pioneer	21	54	.280	8th (8)	Audo Vicente	1999
Overall 2008 Minor League Record			310	417	.426	29th		

* Finish in overall standings (No. of teams in league). ^League champion.

ORGANIZATION STATISTICS

ARIZONA DIAMONDBACKS

NATIONAL LEAGUE

Batting	B-T	HT	WT	DOB	AVG	vLH	vRH	G	AB	R	H	2B	3B	HR	RBI	BB	HBP	SH	SF	SO	SB	CS	SLG	OBP
Bonifacio, Emilio	B-R	5-10	195	4-23-85	.167	.000	.200	8	12	3	2	1	0	0	2	0	0	0	0	5	1	0	.250	.167
2-team total (41 Washington)					.243	—	—	49	169	29	41	6	5	0	14	14	0	0	3	46	7	4	.337	.296
Burke, Chris	R-R	5-11	195	3-11-80	.194	.209	.177	86	165	20	32	5	1	2	12	27	2	2	3	33	5	0	.273	.310
Byrnes, Eric	R-R	6-2	215	2-16-76	.209	.258	.188	52	206	28	43	13	1	6	23	16	2	0	0	36	4	4	.369	.272
Clark, Tony	B-R	6-7	245	6-15-72	.206	.318	.146	38	63	7	13	2	0	2	13	12	1	0	1	23	0	0	.333	.338
2-team total (70 San Diego)					.225	—	—	108	151	12	34	5	0	3	24	31	1	0	1	55	0	0	.318	.359
D'Antona, Jamie	R-R	6-2	220	5-12-82	.176	.200	.143	18	17	2	3	0	0	1	2	0	0	0	4	0	0	.176	.263
Drew, Stephen	L-R	6-0	185	3-16-83	.291	.267	.300	152	611	91	178	44	11	21	67	41	1	3	7	109	3	3	.502	.333
Dunn, Adam	L-R	6-6	275	11-9-79	.243	.179	.267	44	144	21	35	9	0	8	26	24	1	0	0	44	1	0	.472	.417
2-team total (114 Cincinnati)					.236	—	—	158	517	79	122	23	0	40	100	122	7	0	5	164	2	1	.513	.386
Eckstein, David	R-R	5-7	175	1-20-75	.219	.167	.231	18	64	5	14	3	0	1	4	7	1	0	1	5	0	0	.313	.301
Hammock, Robby	R-R	5-10	185	5-13-77	.190	.158	.217	18	42	4	8	1	0	0	2	5	1	0	0	9	0	0	.214	.292
Hudson, Orlando	B-R	6-0	190	12-12-77	.305	.269	.321	107	407	54	124	29	3	8	41	40	2	3	3	62	4	1	.450	.367
Jackson, Conor	R-R	6-2	215	5-7-82	.300	.315	.295	144	540	87	162	31	6	12	75	59	9	1	3	61	10	2	.446	.376
Montero, Miguel	L-R	5-11	190	7-9-83	.255	.286	.250	70	184	24	47	16	1	5	18	19	2	1	1	49	0	0	.435	.330
Ojeda, Augie	B-R	5-9	175	12-20-74	.242	.250	.240	105	231	27	56	9	2	0	17	26	10	4	1	24	0	0	.299	.343
Reynolds, Mark	R-R	6-2	220	8-3-83	.239	.279	.226	152	539	87	129	28	3	28	97	64	3	1	6	204	11	2	.458	.320
Romero, Alex	L-R	6-0	200	9-9-83	.230	.174	.241	78	135	13	31	8	2	1	13	12	3	1	2	20	4	0	.341	.250
Salazar, Jeff	L-L	6-0	195	11-24-80	.211	.300	.203	90	128	17	27	5	3	2	12	21	2	1	0	41	0	2	.344	.331
Snyder, Chris	R-R	6-4	245	2-12-81	.237	.250	.231	115	334	47	79	22	1	16	64	56	4	5	5	101	0	0	.452	.348
Tracy, Chad	L-R	6-2	215	5-22-80	.267	.243	.271	88	273	25	73	16	0	8	39	16	1	0	2	49	0	0	.414	.308
Upton, Justin	R-R	6-2	205	8-25-87	.250	.253	.249	108	356	52	89	19	6	15	42	54	4	0	3	121	1	4	.463	.353
Whitesell, Josh	L-L	6-1	225	4-14-82	.286	—	.286	7	7	1	2	0	0	1	1	1	0	0	2	0	0	.714	.444
Young, Chris	R-R	6-2	200	9-5-83	.248	.285	.236	160	625	85	155	42	7	22	85	62	1	6	5	165	14	5	.443	.315

Pitching	B-T	HT	WT	DOB	W	L	ERA	G	GS	CG	SV	IP	H	R	ER	HR	BB	SO	AVG	vLH	vRH	K/9	BB/9
Buckner, Billy	R-R	6-2	215	8-27-83	1	0	3.21	10	0	0	0	14	16	5	5	3	4	11	.296	.231	.357	7.07	2.57
Cruz, Juan	R-R	6-2	145	10-15-78	4	0	2.61	57	0	0	0	52	34	17	15	5	31	71	.192	.159	.221	12.37	5.40
Davis, Doug	L-L	6-4	215	9-21-75	6	8	4.32	26	26	0	0	146	160	76	70	13	64	112	.282	.321	.269	6.90	3.95
Gonzalez, Edgar	R-R	6-2	210	2-23-83	1	3	6.00	17	6	0	0	48	58	34	32	8	21	32	.302	.259	.336	6.00	3.94
Haren, Dan	R-R	6-5	215	9-17-80	16	8	3.33	33	33	1	0	216	204	86	80	19	40	206	.247	.241	.253	8.58	1.67
Johnson, Randy	R-L	6-10	225	9-10-63	11	10	3.91	30	30	2	0	184	184	92	80	24	44	173	.260	.215	.267	8.46	2.15
Ledezma, Wil	L-L	6-4	210	1-21-81	0	0	0.00	3	0	0	0	4	3	0	0	0	3	4	.143	.400	.000	9.00	6.75
2-team total (25 San Diego)					0	2	4.17	28	6	0	0	58	51	29	27	4	41	53	—	—	—	8.18	6.33
Lyon, Brandon	R-R	6-1	195	8-10-79	3	5	4.70	61	0	0	26	59	75	34	31	7	13	44	.301	.278	.321	6.67	1.97
Medders, Brandon	R-R	6-1	200	1-26-80	1	0	4.58	18	0	0	0	20	17	11	10	2	11	8	.236	.286	.205	3.66	5.03
Owings, Micah	R-R	6-5	220	9-28-82	6	9	5.93	22	18	0	0	105	104	73	69	14	41	87	.256	.268	.242	7.48	3.53
Peguero, Jailen	R-R	6-0	185	1-14-81	0	0	4.82	7	0	0	0	9	9	6	5	0	4	5	.281	.444	.217	4.82	3.86
Pena, Tony	R-R	6-2	220	1-9-82	3	2	4.33	72	0	0	3	73	80	38	35	5	17	52	.281	.296	.267	6.44	2.11
Petit, Yusmeiro	R-R	6-0	255	11-22-84	3	5	4.31	19	8	0	0	56	45	29	27	12	14	42	.216	.231	.205	6.71	2.24
Qualls, Chad	R-R	6-5	220	8-17-78	4	8	2.81	77	0	0	9	74	61	29	23	4	18	71	.224	.220	.229	8.67	2.20
Rauch, Jon	R-R	6-11	290	9-27-78	0	6	6.56	26	0	0	1	23	27	18	17	6	9	22	.303	.313	.293	8.49	3.47
2-team total (48 Washington)					4	8	4.14	74	0	0	18	72	69	36	33	11	16	66	—	—	—	8.29	2.01
Robertson, Connor	R-R	6-2	220	9-10-81	0	1	5.14	6	0	0	0	7	8	4	4	1	2	2	.286	.250	.300	2.57	2.57
Rosales, Leo	R-R	6-0	205	5-28-81	1	1	4.20	27	0	0	0	30	32	15	14	2	15	18	.271	.286	.263	5.40	4.50
Scherzer, Max	R-R	6-3	215	7-27-84	0	4	3.05	16	7	0	0	56	48	24	19	5	21	66	.234	.319	.167	10.61	3.38
Slaten, Doug	L-L	6-5	215	2-4-80	0	3	4.73	45	0	0	0	32	33	20	17	4	14	20	.260	.232	.282	5.57	3.90
Webb, Brandon	R-R	6-2	230	5-9-79	22	7	3.30	34	34	3	0	227	206	95	83	13	65	183	.242	.265	.219	7.27	2.58

Fielding

Catcher	PCT	G	PO	A	E	DP	PB
Hammock	1.000	15	92	3	0	0	0
Montero	.989	53	352	23	4	2	0
Snyder	1.000	112	777	70	0	5	7

First Base	PCT	G	PO	A	E	DP
Burke	1.000	9	67	4	0	6
Clark	.988	25	148	14	2	15

	PCT	G	PO	A	E	DP
D'Antona	1.000	2	7	2	0	2
Dunn	.977	19	123	7	3	14
Jackson	.993	68	533	30	4	34
Reynolds	.500	1	1	0	1	0
Tracy	.993	65	528	26	4	49
Whitesell	1.000	1	7	0	0	0

Second Base	PCT	G	PO	A	E	DP
Burke	1.000	18	21	34	0	7
Eckstein	1.000	18	30	65	0	14
Hudson	.982	105	200	284	9	60
Ojeda	1.000	44	70	92	0	26

Third Base	PCT	G	PO	A	E	DP
Burke	1.000	4	2	5	0	0

Ojeda	1.000	28	6	32	0	3		Ojeda	.949	22	17	39	3	6
Reynolds	.904	150	82	240	34	23		**Outfield**	**PCT**	**G**	**PO**	**A**	**E**	**DP**
Tracy	1.000	2	2	2	0	0		Bonifacio	1.000	3	1	0	0	0
Shortstop	**PCT**	**G**	**PO**	**A**	**E**	**DP**		Burke	1.000	26	52	1	0	0
Burke	.857	2	4	1	2			Byrnes	.988	51	78	1	1	0
Drew	.976	151	190	378	14	85		Dunn	.980	31	48	0	1	0

Jackson	.981	77	146	5	3	3
Romero	.980	52	48	1	1	0
Salazar	1.000	47	36	3	0	0
Upton	.943	101	175	6	11	2
Young	.993	159	393	5	3	2

TUCSON SIDEWINDERS   TRIPLE-A

PACIFIC COAST LEAGUE

Batting	B-T	HT	WT	DOB	AVG	vLH	vRH	G	AB	R	H	2B	3B	HR	RBI	BB	HBP	SH	SF	SO	SB	CS	SLG	OBP
Avlas, Phil	R-R	5-11	183	12-17-82	.294	.284	.299	91	221	29	65	14	0	2	28	17	0	5	6	32	4	1	.385	.336
Bonifacio, Emilio	B-R	5-10	195	4-23-85	.302	.240	.326	85	367	49	111	18	5	1	29	27	0	6	2	64	17	8	.387	.348
Brito, Javier	R-R	6-1	245	3-25-83	.170	.188	.162	18	53	8	9	3	0	2	8	11	0	0	0	15	0	0	.340	.313
Castillo, Wilkin	B-R	6-0	200	6-1-84	.254	.196	.272	104	386	40	98	18	2	6	47	24	6	6	3	54	4	1	.358	.305
Curreri, Frank	L-R	6-4	210	12-4-82	.267	.636	.229	43	116	13	31	4	0	0	9	16	0	3	1	20	2	1	.302	.353
D'Antona, Jamie	R-R	6-2	220	5-12-82	.365	.354	.369	110	419	69	153	35	1	21	79	30	1	0	4	64	1	0	.604	.405
Hammock, Robby	R-R	5-10	185	5-13-77	.240	.220	.246	62	217	29	52	6	2	5	27	18	1	3	3	47	1	0	.355	.297
Kelly, Don	L-R	6-4	210	2-15-80	.275	.272	.276	124	436	61	120	24	5	8	55	32	2	4	5	42	2	1	.408	.324
Krynzel, Dave	L-L	6-1	185	11-7-81	.250	—	.250	4	4	1	1	0	0	0	1	2	1	0	0	1	0	0	.250	.571
Mercado, Richard	R-R	6-0	205	5-23-83	.111	.250	.071	10	18	4	2	0	0	0	3	0	0	0	0	4	0	0	.111	.238
Merchan, Jesus	R-R	6-0	185	3-26-81	.339	.387	.323	114	436	50	148	23	5	4	72	18	11	3	9	44	2	2	.443	.373
Montero, Miguel	L-R	5-11	190	7-9-83	.281	.200	.353	11	32	3	9	2	0	1	5	5	1	0	0	3	0	0	.438	.395
Morgan, Matt	R-R	6-2	195	8-10-81	.257	.205	.274	47	152	16	39	9	1	1	10	10	0	3	0	27	1	0	.349	.302
Nixon, Trot	L-L	6-2	210	4-11-74	.309	.209	.341	58	181	39	56	15	0	10	31	40	1	0	0	25	1	0	.558	.437
2-team total (10 New Orleans)					.306	—		68	222	48	68	16	0	14	44	48	1	0	0	34	2	0	.568	.432
Oeltjen, Trent	L-L	6-1	190	2-28-83	.317	.333	.312	127	442	75	140	28	10	6	60	24	10	4	11	68	15	7	.466	.357
Raines Jr., Tim	B-R	5-10	190	8-31-79	.311	.345	.297	128	502	96	156	30	13	18	78	26	3	5	4	96	28	8	.530	.346
Romero, Alex	L-R	6-0	200	9-9-83	.281	.250	.349	41	173	28	56	9	2	3	19	11	1	1	0	19	4	3	.451	.368
Salazar, Jeff	L-L	6-0	195	11-24-80	.364	.308	.384	24	99	29	36	6	3	4	18	14	0	1	1	14	3	0	.606	.439
Tracy, Chad	L-R	6-2	215	5-22-80	.306	.364	.259	12	49	5	15	2	0	6	1	0	0	0	0	4	0	0	.347	.320
Upton, Justin	R-R	6-2	205	8-25-87	.279	.333	.261	15	61	13	17	3	1	3	10	7	0	0	0	26	2	0	.508	.353
Whitesell, Josh	L-L	6-1	225	4-14-82	.328	.289	.343	127	475	86	156	36	0	26	110	74	8	0	3	136	1	2	.568	.425

Pitching	B-T	HT	WT	DOB	W	L	ERA	G	GS	CG	SV	IP	H	R	ER	HR	BB	SO	AVG	vLH	vRH	K/9	BB/9
Buckner, Billy	R-R	6-2	215	8-27-83	5	10	4.95	21	20	0	0	116	136	74	64	9	43	69	.296	.313	.281	5.34	3.33
Coutlangus, Jon	L-L	6-1	185	10-21-80	0	2	12.71	5	0	0	0	6	7	8	8	1	7	6	.318	.000	.389	9.53	11.12
Cruz, Juan	R-R	6-2	145	10-15-78	0	0	3.00	2	2	0	0	3	3	1	1	0	0	4	.250	.250	.200	12.00	0.00
Davis, Doug	R-L	6-4	215	9-21-75	1	1	3.72	2	2	0	0	10	10	4	4	0	3	6	.256	.333	.233	5.59	2.79
Ellis, Josh	R-R	6-1	190	8-7-84	0	0	0.00	2	0	0	0	3	1	0	0	0	0	4	.111	.000	.500	12.00	0.00
Evans, Cody	R-R	6-5	190	9-3-83	1	0	1.08	4	0	0	0	8	7	2	1	1	3	6	.250	.125	.300	6.48	3.24
Fruto, Emiliano	R-R	6-3	230	6-6-84	6	6	5.26	49	4	0	2	89	88	58	52	19	59	102	.257	.266	.250	10.31	5.97
Glant, Dustin	R-R	6-2	200	7-20-81	3	3	7.51	40	1	0	0	74	107	70	62	7	43	58	.340	.424	.284	7.02	5.21
Goocher, Clint	L-L	6-2	195	6-15-82	0	2	10.80	9	0	0	0	12	13	14	14	2	7	13	.271	.211	.310	10.03	5.40
Green, Matthew	R-R	6-4	200	1-5-82	0	0	5.06	1	1	0	0	5	8	3	3	1	3	3	.348	.400	.250	5.06	5.06
Gutierrez, Juan	R-R	6-2	210	7-14-83	5	11	6.09	25	22	0	0	117	152	94	79	11	44	87	.318	.324	.314	6.71	3.39
Johnson, Randy	R-L	6-10	225	9-10-63	0	1	7.20	2	2	0	0	10	11	8	8	1	3	8	.282	.538	.154	7.20	2.70
Kinsey, Chris	R-R	6-3	230	10-18-82	0	2	7.89	12	2	0	0	22	30	25	19	4	17	12	.326	.390	.275	4.98	7.06
MacLane, Evan	L-L	6-2	185	11-4-82	7	8	4.96	30	25	0	0	152	184	91	84	21	31	83	.303	.314	.299	4.90	1.83
Mahon, Reid	R-R	6-3	215	6-1-83	0	2	5.25	19	0	0	6	24	22	15	14	3	14	18	.242	.250	.235	6.75	5.25
Medders, Brandon	R-R	6-1	200	1-26-80	1	2	7.45	26	0	0	0	39	45	35	32	4	24	33	.287	.271	.299	7.68	5.59
Owings, Micah	R-R	6-5	220	9-28-82	0	0	4.09	2	2	0	0	11	8	5	5	3	6	9	.205	.188	.217	7.36	4.91
Peguero, Jailen	R-R	6-0	185	1-4-81	6	4	4.22	51	0	0	5	70	71	41	33	5	40	68	.261	.336	.210	8.70	5.12
Petit, Yusmeiro	R-R	6-0	255	11-22-84	3	3	4.80	11	11	0	0	60	64	34	32	7	8	67	.270	.250	.285	10.05	1.20
Robertson, Connor	R-R	6-2	220	9-10-81	7	4	5.02	47	0	0	1	72	69	45	40	7	30	72	.259	.271	.252	9.04	3.77
Rosales, Leo	R-R	6-0	205	5-28-81	2	2	4.46	29	0	0	9	36	39	22	18	5	14	28	.275	.309	.243	6.94	3.47
Scherzer, Max	R-R	6-3	215	7-27-84	1	1	2.72	13	10	0	0	53	35	19	16	2	22	79	.182	.266	.124	13.42	3.74
Shappi, A.J.	R-R	6-2	195	10-16-82	2	5	6.02	19	8	0	0	55	81	44	37	11	15	39	.342	.369	.321	6.34	2.44
Slaten, Doug	L-L	6-5	215	2-4-80	0	0	4.05	6	0	0	0	7	6	3	3	1	4	9	.250	.250	.250	12.15	5.40
Summers, Houston	R-R	5-10	180	8-20-87	0	1	21.00	1	1	0	0	3	7	7	7	1	5	6	.438	.250	.500	18.00	15.00
Torra, Matt	R-R	6-3	225	6-29-84	5	5	4.71	14	13	0	0	78	97	49	41	13	19	46	.301	.363	.263	5.29	2.18
Urquidez, Jason	R-R	6-0	177	9-12-82	1	0	2.35	5	0	0	0	8	5	3	2	0	5	7	.179	.273	.118	8.22	5.87
Vasquez, Esmerling	R-R	6-1	175	11-7-83	3	6	6.72	24	15	0	0	83	79	64	62	11	73	57	.262	.281	.249	6.18	7.92
Woody, Abe	R-R	6-0	200	11-9-82	1	1	7.45	10	0	0	0	19	31	16	16	2	15	12	.392	.455	.348	5.59	6.98
Zepeda, Bayron	L-L	5-10	185	8-29-87	0	0	0.00	1	0	0	0	1	0	0	0	0	0	1	.000	.000	.000	9.00	0.00

Fielding

Catcher	PCT	G	PO	A	E	DP	PB
Castillo	.992	51	333	38	3	4	9
Curreri	1.000	23	154	7	0	1	1
D'Antona	1.000	3	14	2	0	0	0
Hammock	.992	32	224	16	2	2	1
Mercado	1.000	6	29	1	0	0	0
Montero	1.000	6	14	1	0	0	0
Morgan	.992	39	214	23	2	2	1

First Base	PCT	G	PO	A	E	DP
Brito	.941	2	15	1	1	1

Curreri	.979	8	44	3	1	6
D'Antona	.965	15	104	6	4	11
Hammock	1.000	2	12	1	0	2
Kelly	1.000	1	2	0	0	0
Tracy	.977	4	37	5	1	5
Whitesell	.989	117	886	82	11	101

Second Base	PCT	G	PO	A	E	DP
Avlas	.500	1	0	2	2	0
Bonifacio	.978	73	141	211	8	44
Castillo	.875	4	5	9	2	0

Kelly	.982	63	142	182	6	44
Merchan	.882	3	7	8	2	2
Morgan	1.000	6	9	14	0	3

Third Base	PCT	G	PO	A	E	DP
Castillo	.923	41	27	69	8	11
D'Antona	.904	78	57	103	17	14
Hammock	.926	12	9	16	2	1
Kelly	.977	23	16	27	1	4
Merchan	—	2	0	0	0	0
Tracy	.917	6	1	10	1	1

Shortstop	PCT	G	PO	A	E	DP
Bonifacio	.857	3	4	2	1	0
Castillo	.920	6	10	13	2	3
Kelly	.896	34	37	58	11	14
Merchan	.957	107	175	297	21	81

Outfield	PCT	G	PO	A	E	DP
Avlas	.979	62	92	1	2	0

Bonifacio	.958	12	22	1	1	0
Brito	.900	10	18	0	2	0
Castillo	1.000	7	5	1	0	0
Curreri	1.000	4	7	0	0	0
Hammock	1.000	16	31	2	0	0
Kelly	1.000	6	8	0	0	0
Krynzel	1.000	1	1	0	0	0
Merchan	1.000	1	2	0	0	0

Morgan	1.000	2	5	0	0	0
Nixon	.970	38	63	1	2	1
Oeltjen	.985	117	246	10	4	3
Raines Jr.	.996	116	234	4	1	0
Romero	.989	40	91	1	1	2
Salazar	1.000	16	35	0	0	0
Upton	.900	14	18	0	2	0

MOBILE BAYBEARS   DOUBLE-A
SOUTHERN LEAGUE

Batting	B-T	HT	WT	DOB	AVG	vLH	vRH	G	AB	R	H	2B	3B	HR	RBI	BB	HBP	SH	SF	SO	SB	CS	SLG	OBP
Brito, Javier	R-R	6-1	245	3-25-83	.269	.300	.248	63	193	33	52	11	0	12	42	35	2	0	1	40	1	0	.513	.385
Burgess, Brandon	B-R	6-3	222	2-24-83	.200	.186	.205	72	175	19	35	12	0	5	27	11	18	0	2	69	3	2	.354	.311
Byrne, Bryan	L-R	6-3	200	4-30-84	.303	.288	.312	121	416	64	126	27	0	9	54	66	7	0	2	70	1	3	.433	.405
Curreri, Frank	L-R	6-4	210	12-4-82	.251	.230	.262	69	219	21	55	17	0	5	32	33	2	1	3	35	1	0	.397	.350
Hankerd, Cyle	R-R	6-3	215	1-24-85	.245	.235	.251	125	436	35	107	17	3	5	52	21	9	0	4	67	2	6	.333	.291
Hester, John	R-R	6-3	220	9-14-83	.268	.337	.240	92	306	38	82	26	2	11	49	16	2	0	7	78	3	2	.474	.302
Mercado, Orlando	R-R	5-10	213	3-13-85	.227	.309	.183	71	194	22	44	6	0	2	23	39	2	0	3	28	0	2	.289	.357
Nicolas, Cesar	R-R	6-4	230	4-17-82	.260	.236	.274	97	296	38	77	23	0	7	43	55	10	0	3	60	1	2	.409	.390
Parra, Gerardo	L-L	5-11	195	5-6-87	.275	.216	.310	73	265	35	73	14	6	4	33	24	5	3	5	34	16	9	.419	.341
Rahl, Chris	R-R	5-10	185	12-5-83	.216	.239	.202	116	421	47	91	25	2	6	25	26	2	0	1	115	18	12	.338	.264
Reyes, Guillermo	B-R	5-9	177	12-29-81	.251	.213	.270	95	279	42	70	8	2	1	15	30	1	6	2	44	3	5	.305	.324
Ryal, Rusty	R-R	6-2	195	3-16-83	.274	.287	.267	128	460	65	126	22	4	16	66	35	9	0	5	96	4	4	.443	.334
Sanchez, Yunesky	B-R	6-2	212	5-3-84	.296	.253	.320	122	494	61	146	20	3	0	22	23	5	1	0	41	8	13	.348	.333
Thomson, Greg	L-L	6-1	205	6-13-84	.207	.125	.234	50	164	23	34	7	1	1	13	16	5	1	0	37	3	3	.280	.297

Pitching	B-T	HT	WT	DOB	W	L	ERA	G	GS	CG	SV	IP	H	R	ER	HR	BB	SO	AVG	vLH	vRH	K/9	BB/9
Ambriz, Hector	L-R	6-2	235	5-24-84	5	13	4.89	27	26	2	0	153	155	91	83	22	47	118	.262	.268	.256	6.96	2.77
Barnette, Tony	R-R	6-1	192	11-9-83	11	7	3.87	27	27	0	0	154	143	70	66	17	42	133	.246	.231	.259	7.79	2.46
Bongiovanni, Vince	R-R	6-5	215	1-11-83	3	3	4.40	42	0	0	3	61	65	33	30	6	36	49	.284	.297	.273	7.19	5.28
Brown, Brooks	L-R	6-3	210	6-20-85	6	15	4.18	26	26	0	0	144	152	69	67	8	67	112	.278	.279	.278	6.98	4.18
Cory, Forrest	R-L	6-3	205	10-13-83	3	2	5.53	37	0	0	1	68	83	44	42	7	27	36	.304	.207	.354	4.74	3.56
Elliott, Matt	R-R	6-0	175	4-6-84	0	1	5.29	13	0	0	0	17	19	11	10	2	12	19	.297	.296	.297	10.06	6.35
Evans, Cody	R-R	6-5	190	9-3-83	4	8	4.77	29	5	0	0	66	69	39	35	8	25	38	.278	.250	.301	5.18	3.41
Green, Matthew	R-R	6-4	200	1-5-82	3	2	5.77	16	8	0	0	48	59	36	31	9	15	39	.296	.262	.322	7.26	2.79
Howard, Adam	R-R	6-4	200	8-16-83	7	8	5.14	28	20	0	0	117	140	80	67	16	49	79	.299	.306	.293	6.06	3.76
Mahon, Reid	R-R	6-3	215	6-1-83	0	0	3.07	33	0	0	18	41	45	19	14	5	10	33	.274	.278	.270	7.24	2.20
Marte, Jose	R-R	6-5	185	9-4-83	4	2	4.38	36	0	0	7	49	50	28	24	6	24	37	.259	.265	.255	6.75	4.38
Rosen, Mark	L-L	5-10	235	6-30-84	0	0	4.76	9	0	0	0	11	11	11	6	1	14	7	.268	.500	.148	5.56	11.12
Shappi, A.J.	R-R	6-2	195	10-16-82	0	1	1.53	19	0	0	1	29	25	8	5	1	4	27	.223	.143	.286	8.28	1.23
Torra, Matt	R-R	6-3	225	6-29-84	5	5	2.85	13	13	1	0	79	91	33	25	5	12	50	.285	.265	.302	5.70	1.37
Urquidez, Jason	R-R	6-0	177	9-12-82	2	1	4.32	13	0	0	0	25	23	12	12	3	9	30	.245	.227	.260	10.80	3.24
Valdez, Cesar	R-R	6-2	200	3-17-85	3	5	4.06	12	12	0	0	64	63	30	29	2	23	60	.261	.284	.247	8.39	3.22
Woody, Abe	R-R	6-0	200	11-9-82	1	6	3.16	35	0	0	3	51	43	21	18	1	21	39	.239	.209	.266	6.84	3.68

Fielding

Catcher	PCT	G	PO	A	E	DP	PB
Curreri	.988	13	73	7	1	0	1
Hester	.988	78	525	47	7	6	5
Mercado	.989	54	337	24	4	3	2

First Base	PCT	G	PO	A	E	DP
Brito	1.000	11	81	6	0	8
Burgess	.973	10	68	4	2	9
Byrne	.989	110	844	82	10	95
Curreri	1.000	7	40	6	0	2
Nicolas	1.000	6	52	4	0	7

Second Base	PCT	G	PO	A	E	DP
Reyes	.969	33	41	85	4	17
Ryal	.984	97	202	287	8	68
Sanchez	.987	16	30	44	1	9

Third Base	PCT	G	PO	A	E	DP
Burgess	.861	31	21	41	10	7
Byrne	1.000	6	5	6	0	0
Nicolas	.939	79	53	115	11	12
Reyes	1.000	6	5	12	0	2
Ryal	.965	28	15	40	2	4

Shortstop	PCT	G	PO	A	E	DP
Reyes	.952	42	46	94	7	21
Sanchez	.969	100	156	277	14	62

Outfield	PCT	G	PO	A	E	DP
Brito	1.000	33	50	1	0	1
Burgess	1.000	6	8	0	0	0
Curreri	.972	41	66	4	2	0
Hankerd	.987	115	221	8	3	4
Parra	.960	72	157	10	7	4
Rahl	.985	112	250	8	4	2
Thomson	.980	41	96	2	2	0

VISALIA OAKS   HIGH CLASS A
CALIFORNIA LEAGUE

Batting	B-T	HT	WT	DOB	AVG	vLH	vRH	G	AB	R	H	2B	3B	HR	RBI	BB	HBP	SH	SF	SO	SB	CS	SLG	OBP
Batten, Jo Jo	R-R	5-11	180	12-14-84	.248	.288	.227	58	214	24	53	12	1	1	15	22	1	0	2	39	5	3	.327	.318
Brashear, Justin	L-R	6-2	215	1-19-85	.195	.250	.177	26	82	11	16	5	0	1	8	17	0	0	0	27	1	0	.293	.333
Byrnes, Eric	R-R	6-2	215	2-16-76	.083	.333	.000	3	12	1	1	0	0	0	0	1	0	0	4	0	0	.083	.214
Ciriaco, Pedro	R-R	6-0	150	9-27-85	.310	.313	.308	124	520	85	161	26	5	5	61	18	6	7	11	89	40	9	.408	.333
Clifford, Pete	L-R	6-0	195	12-20-83	.282	.269	.286	131	476	81	134	41	5	11	75	75	8	0	5	126	11	8	.458	.385
Easley, Ed	R-R	6-0	200	12-21-85	.247	.264	.239	118	453	52	112	20	1	6	53	42	3	0	4	106	1	1	.336	.313
Ferrer, Manuel	R-R	5-9	201	2-15-85	.213	.194	.220	97	320	25	68	4	1	1	22	37	12	1	3	82	2	6	.241	.315
Frey, Evan	L-L	6-0	170	6-7-86	.297	.296	.297	56	229	44	68	5	5	3	18	37	3	1	2	46	17	5	.402	.399
Hallberg, Mark	R-R	5-11	170	12-9-85	.283	.303	.276	69	272	42	77	10	2	3	30	33	3	3	3	28	5	2	.368	.357
Jones, Tyler	L-L	6-0	176	12-29-83	.226	.174	.236	41	133	15	30	4	2	4	17	11	1	3	1	26	6	3	.376	.288
Mee, Mike	L-R	6-0	190	10-14-83	.267	.211	.290	39	131	18	35	8	0	2	21	26	2	0	1	24	0	1	.374	.394
Mena, Steve	R-R	6-2	230	1-24-85	.203	.237	.188	102	370	41	75	14	2	5	45	25	6	0	3	103	1	5	.292	.262
Mercado, Richard	R-R	6-0	220	5-23-83	.228	.139	.269	32	114	6	26	6	0	0	13	10	1	0	2	23	0	1	.281	.291

Name	B-T	HT	WT	DOB	AVG	vLH	vRH	G	AB	R	H	2B	3B	HR	RBI	BB	HBP	SH	SF	SO	SB	CS	SLG	OBP
Miller, Brad	R-R	6-5	220	6-25-83	.178	.145	.192	59	213	18	38	10	1	5	22	5	1	0	2	47	0	0	.305	.199
Musselman, Bill	R-R	6-2	210	11-1-84	.154	.143	.158	9	26	3	4	0	0	0	1	4	0	0	1	9	0	1	.154	.258
Parra, Gerardo	L-L	5-11	195	5-6-87	.301	.317	.294	50	196	26	59	8	4	2	19	23	3	1	1	31	12	4	.413	.381
Schmidt, Konrad	R-R	6-0	225	8-2-84	.329	.273	.352	40	152	21	50	10	1	1	19	3	4	0	1	26	0	0	.428	.356
Side, Joey	R-R	6-1	180	12-4-83	.281	.236	.301	44	178	22	50	7	1	2	26	6	1	0	3	51	4	1	.365	.303
Snyder, Chris	R-R	6-4	245	2-12-81	.400	.500	.333	1	5	1	2	0	0	1	4	0	0	0	0	2	0	0	1.000	.400
Sosa, Ricardo	R-R	6-1	213	5-24-84	.265	.286	.257	103	396	50	105	26	1	13	74	21	10	0	2	65	5	5	.434	.317
Thomson, Greg	L-L	6-1	205	6-13-84	.264	.308	.246	68	261	37	69	16	2	6	31	17	4	0	0	40	8	4	.410	.319

Pitching	B-T	HT	WT	DOB	W	L	ERA	G	GS	CG	SV	IP	H	R	ER	HR	BB	SO	AVG	vLH	vRH	K/9	BB/9
Augenstein, Bryan	R-R	6-5	225	7-11-86	2	4	3.89	9	9	0	0	44	57	26	19	5	5	30	.318	.333	.303	6.14	1.02
Beck, Chad	R-R	6-4	251	1-17-85	6	5	3.98	25	15	0	1	95	86	45	42	8	25	89	.239	.227	.251	8.43	2.37
Buck, Dallas	R-R	6-2	195	11-11-84	0	1	0.00	1	1	0	0	5	3	3	0	1	1	4	.167	.000	.333	7.20	1.80
Christianson, Chase	R-R	6-5	220	12-11-84	5	6	5.95	35	16	0	1	115	146	83	76	14	31	67	.309	.265	.350	5.24	2.43
Ellis, Josh	R-R	6-1	190	8-7-84	2	3	2.40	39	0	0	7	64	50	23	17	3	19	63	.210	.228	.194	8.91	2.69
Enright, Barry	R-R	6-3	220	3-30-86	12	8	4.44	29	29	0	0	164	185	88	81	17	35	143	.281	.320	.239	7.83	1.92
Evans, Cody	R-R	6-5	190	9-3-83	1	0	4.00	6	0	0	1	9	10	4	4	1	3	7	.278	.160	.545	7.00	3.00
Maine, Scott	L-L	6-3	195	2-2-85	3	2	3.19	32	0	0	5	48	48	20	17	4	21	53	.262	.235	.284	9.94	3.94
Marte, Jose	R-R	6-5	185	9-4-83	1	0	1.93	9	0	0	3	14	13	4	3	0	4	15	.250	.214	.292	9.64	2.57
Newby, Kyler	R-R	6-4	225	2-22-85	4	3	2.69	46	0	0	16	67	49	23	20	4	30	86	.199	.165	.232	11.55	4.03
Perez, Jorge	R-R	5-11	167	1-16-86	2	2	6.34	38	0	0	0	60	72	43	42	5	19	48	.293	.291	.295	7.24	2.87
Roemer, Wes	R-R	6-0	205	10-7-86	7	12	4.59	28	28	1	0	163	199	95	83	25	33	122	.308	.291	.330	6.75	1.83
Romero, Eddie	L-L	5-10	206	11-7-85	7	12	4.48	25	24	0	0	121	154	73	60	17	26	84	.310	.298	.315	6.27	1.94
Scribner, Evan	R-R	6-3	190	7-19-85	0	1	1.86	5	0	0	1	10	5	2	2	1	2	10	.147	.176	.118	9.31	1.86
2-team total (20 Lake Elsinore)					2	2	2.45	25	0	0	2	33	19	9	9	4	5	41	—	—	—	11.18	1.36
Stange, Daniel	R-R	6-3	185	12-22-85	1	2	3.95	11	0	0	0	14	10	6	6	2	6	14	.204	.318	.111	9.22	3.95
Urquidez, Jason	R-R	6-0	177	9-12-82	1	1	2.86	21	0	0	0	35	26	15	11	2	11	35	.197	.188	.206	9.09	2.86
Valdez, Cesar	R-R	6-2	200	3-17-85	10	3	2.53	15	15	1	0	96	88	36	27	5	16	80	.238	.248	.227	7.50	1.50
Wright, Kyle	R-R	6-3	170	4-27-83	3	5	4.16	36	2	0	0	71	87	38	33	7	14	46	.304	.327	.276	5.80	1.77

Fielding

Catcher	PCT	G	PO	A	E	DP	PB
Brashear	.986	8	62	9	1	0	2
Easley	.984	94	671	74	12	1	23
Mercado	.991	16	100	8	1	1	0
Musselman	1.000	7	51	4	0	2	0
Schmidt	1.000	17	139	10	0	0	6
Snyder	1.000	1	8	0	0	0	0

First Base	PCT	G	PO	A	E	DP
Brashear	.950	6	53	4	3	4
Easley	.982	12	102	9	2	7
Mee	.986	32	255	18	4	23
Mena	.983	24	209	23	4	18
Mercado	.987	8	74	4	1	7
Miller	.992	59	535	51	5	48

Sosa 1.000 1 8 1 0 1

Second Base	PCT	G	PO	A	E	DP
Ciriaco	.985	38	62	141	3	30
Ferrer	.963	73	107	203	12	40
Hallberg	.974	18	24	50	2	3
Mena	.963	14	26	53	3	4

Third Base	PCT	G	PO	A	E	DP
Ferrer	.905	19	8	30	4	2
Hallberg	.917	4	2	9	1	1
Mena	.877	27	14	43	8	4
Sosa	.925	95	61	137	16	10

Shortstop	PCT	G	PO	A	E	DP
Ciriaco	.949	87	124	250	20	44

Ferrer .962 7 12 13 1 6
Hallberg .955 48 82 129 10 32

Outfield	PCT	G	PO	A	E	DP
Batten	.939	51	101	6	7	2
Byrnes	1.000	2	5	0	0	0
Clifford	.971	110	197	7	6	2
Frey	.977	56	120	9	3	0
Jones	.988	38	78	1	1	1
Mee	1.000	6	9	0	0	0
Mena	.936	25	39	5	3	0
Parra	.966	49	109	3	4	0
Side	.968	18	29	1	1	0
Thomson	.965	65	131	6	5	3

SOUTH BEND SILVER HAWKS — LOW CLASS A

MIDWEST LEAGUE

Batting	B-T	HT	WT	DOB	AVG	vLH	vRH	G	AB	R	H	2B	3B	HR	RBI	BB	HBP	SH	SF	SO	SB	CS	SLG	OBP
Batten, Jo Jo	R-R	5-11	180	12-14-84	.247	.250	.245	49	170	31	42	8	0	6	21	19	1	2	0	32	1	3	.400	.326
Bustamante, Gerard	R-R	5-8	184	6-10-86	.200	.182	.207	15	40	4	8	2	0	0	3	4	0	0	0	7	0	0	.250	.273
Conner, Clayton	R-R	6-3	210	10-8-86	.170	.222	.151	26	100	13	17	5	3	3	12	4	2	0	0	23	1	0	.370	.217
Coughlin, Sean	L-R	6-1	215	5-14-85	.240	.246	.237	103	363	50	87	24	0	15	81	56	6	0	12	73	0	0	.430	.341
Cowgill, Collin	R-L	5-9	195	5-22-86	.249	.242	.252	50	201	31	50	13	1	1	17	25	5	0	0	61	1	0	.358	.346
Frey, Evan	L-L	6-0	170	6-7-86	.327	.366	.308	75	309	54	101	16	6	0	29	39	1	0	3	38	20	6	.417	.401
Hanke, Aaron	R-R	6-0	195	12-3-84	.236	.309	.200	47	165	26	39	11	1	7	23	18	0	0	2	41	2	0	.442	.308
Harbin, Taylor	R-R	5-9	175	2-13-86	.276	.260	.283	133	548	70	151	40	3	12	85	26	8	0	7	78	3	4	.414	.314
Linton, Ollie	L-L	5-8	160	4-7-86	.277	.256	.287	34	137	25	38	2	1	0	10	19	4	2	0	32	6	4	.307	.381
Mee, Mike	R-R	6-0	190	10-14-83	.299	.245	.327	87	318	47	95	12	1	2	38	58	1	0	2	39	2	1	.362	.406
Musselman, Bill	R-R	6-2	210	11-1-84	.160	.192	.143	22	75	7	12	3	0	1	5	5	1	1	0	25	0	0	.240	.222
Oxendine, Matthew	R-R	6-0	187	10-13-83	.264	.268	.262	103	360	41	95	19	0	2	40	39	2	1	4	84	5	5	.333	.336
Principe, Jimmy	R-R	6-2	185	3-11-86	.153	.214	.123	24	85	5	13	4	0	0	8	6	1	0	2	18	1	2	.200	.213
Ramirez, Ramon	R-R	6-2	170	2-22-86	.224	.155	.249	89	321	33	72	17	0	3	31	23	3	0	2	60	1	3	.277	.281
Rumler, Eli	R-R	5-8	185	12-30-84	.226	.267	.205	113	399	54	90	18	0	3	31	49	18	3	3	87	2	8	.293	.335
Schmidt, Konrad	R-R	6-0	225	8-2-84	.259	.260	.259	62	216	21	56	10	0	2	18	20	4	1	3	41	3	3	.333	.329
Smith, Anthony	L-L	6-1	205	3-28-85	.212	.286	.192	10	33	3	7	1	0	0	6	0	0	0	0	8	0	0	.242	.333
Urena, Ariel	R-R	5-11	170	1-29-86	.171	.136	.188	21	70	7	12	1	0	0	4	1	0	0	0	26	2	0	.186	.227
Walker, Derrick	R-R	6-0	215	10-10-85	.266	.241	.248	113	391	61	104	22	4	9	48	44	23	0	4	108	7	3	.391	.353
Wheeless, Chance	L-L	6-5	220	9-28-84	.191	.148	.217	86	288	30	55	12	0	9	41	45	1	0	4	83	1	0	.326	.299
White, Ryne	L-L	5-11	205	10-17-86	.358	.318	.387	12	53	6	19	6	0	0	13	4	0	0	0	10	0	0	.472	.404

Pitching	B-T	HT	WT	DOB	W	L	ERA	G	GS	CG	SV	IP	H	R	ER	HR	BB	SO	AVG	vLH	vRH	K/9	BB/9
Augenstein, Bryan	R-R	6-5	225	7-11-86	5	1	2.16	13	13	0	0	87	73	21	21	2	9	69	.224	.195	.257	7.11	0.93
Beck, Chad	R-R	6-4	251	1-17-85	2	0	2.04	7	0	0	0	18	13	7	4	0	3	19	.186	.125	.237	9.68	1.53
Beltre, Cristian	R-R	6-1	195	5-10-85	13	8	3.53	26	26	3	0	155	160	73	61	11	24	108	.266	.245	.292	6.26	1.39
Blake, J.J.	L-L	6-4	205	10-17-84	0	2	9.35	11	0	0	0	17	19	18	18	3	13	10	.271	.250	.280	5.19	6.75
Buck, Dallas	R-R	6-2	195	11-11-84	1	4	3.94	9	8	1	0	46	44	28	20	5	10	25	.250	.298	.195	4.73	1.97
Collmenter, Josh	R-R	6-4	235	2-7-86	12	8	3.41	27	27	0	0	145	126	62	55	8	47	123	.230	.212	.250	7.62	2.91

Pitching	B-T	HT	WT	DOB	W	L	ERA	G	GS	CG	SV	IP	H	R	ER	HR	BB	SO	AVG	vLH	vRH	K/9	BB/9
Davis, Ty	R-R	6-6	225	9-11-84	1	1	14.29	6	0	0	0	6	10	10	9	1	7	0	.385	.467	.273	0.00	11.12
Dietz, Jeff	R-R	6-3	215	1-28-86	1	2	2.18	33	0	0	4	54	41	17	13	2	13	49	.212	.287	.141	8.22	2.18
Fournier, Daniel	R-R	6-4	205	5-19-85	0	3	6.94	28	0	0	2	58	76	50	45	2	39	35	.323	.306	.342	5.40	6.02
Harrington, Ian	L-L	6-1	190	4-23-85	0	0	3.72	5	0	0	0	10	10	4	4	1	3	5	.278	.167	.300	4.66	2.79
Henry, Bryan	R-R	6-3	205	2-15-85	4	6	3.10	35	6	0	1	90	76	37	31	11	18	51	.226	.227	.226	5.10	1.80
Layne, Tom	L-L	6-3	185	11-2-84	6	5	3.44	35	13	0	0	115	107	48	44	3	43	71	.247	.243	.248	5.56	3.37
McAnaney, Pat	R-R	6-3	185	3-11-86	2	1	1.50	4	4	0	0	18	11	4	3	1	5	12	.177	.222	.159	6.00	2.50
Norberto, Jordan	L-L	6-0	195	12-8-86	5	7	5.31	31	18	0	0	102	108	72	60	15	56	109	.276	.237	.292	9.65	4.96
Ortega, Alvaro	R-R	5-11	192	1-22-86	0	1	5.87	3	0	0	0	8	11	5	5	1	6	5	.344	.316	.385	5.87	7.04
Parker, Jarrod	R-R	6-1	180	11-24-88	12	5	3.44	24	24	0	0	118	113	56	45	8	33	117	.251	.243	.261	8.95	2.52
Schlereth, Daniel	L-L	6-0	210	5-9-86	1	0	2.00	7	0	0	0	9	3	2	2	0	4	14	.103	.111	.100	14.00	4.00
Scribner, Evan	R-R	6-3	190	7-19-85	2	3	1.57	23	0	0	8	34	23	7	6	0	8	52	.185	.210	.161	13.63	2.10
Shaw, Bryan	R-R	6-1	210	11-8-87	0	1	4.03	11	0	0	0	22	18	12	10	0	6	16	.217	.233	.200	6.45	2.42
Spottiswood, Billy	R-R	6-3	208	4-24-85	5	5	2.11	44	0	0	13	64	52	18	15	1	16	58	.217	.218	.216	8.16	2.25
Stange, Daniel	R-R	6-3	185	12-22-85	1	0	1.59	11	0	0	1	17	11	3	3	0	1	17	.183	.200	.167	9.00	0.53
Zavada, Clay	L-L	6-1	195	6-28-84	3	1	0.51	24	0	0	8	35	6	2	2	1	5	54	.056	.028	.069	13.75	1.27

Fielding

Catcher	PCT	G	PO	A	E	DP	PB
Bustamante	.989	14	86	4	1	1	3
Coughlin	.990	71	536	35	6	4	7
Musselman	.994	19	140	19	1	1	2
Schmidt	.993	39	278	16	2	1	4

First Base	PCT	G	PO	A	E	DP
Mee	.993	45	386	30	3	25
Ramirez	1.000	8	64	1	0	5
Wheeless	.982	76	654	58	13	63
White	1.000	11	90	8	0	8

Second Base	PCT	G	PO	A	E	DP
Harbin	.983	87	153	240	7	51

	PCT	G	PO	A	E	DP
Oxendine	.954	30	50	94	7	20
Rumler	.977	24	30	56	2	10

Third Base	PCT	G	PO	A	E	DP
Conner	.811	12	9	21	7	0
Ramirez	.930	67	42	118	12	7
Rumler	.959	63	39	123	7	11

Shortstop	PCT	G	PO	A	E	DP
Harbin	.937	43	74	120	13	25
Oxendine	.953	71	102	182	14	35
Rumler	.951	26	34	64	5	15

Outfield	PCT	G	PO	A	E	DP
Batten	.988	39	75	5	1	2

	PCT	G	PO	A	E	DP
Cowgill	.989	47	84	3	1	0
Frey	.989	72	174	1	2	1
Hanke	.957	40	64	3	3	0
Linton	1.000	31	76	1	0	1
Mee	1.000	37	61	1	0	0
Principe	1.000	22	32	2	0	0
Smith	.895	8	15	2	2	0
Urena	.977	19	43	0	1	0
Walker	.969	103	186	4	6	0
Wheeless	1.000	1	3	0	0	0

YAKIMA BEARS — SHORT-SEASON
NORTHWEST LEAGUE

Batting	B-T	HT	WT	DOB	AVG	vLH	vRH	G	AB	R	H	2B	3B	HR	RBI	BB	HBP	SH	SF	SO	SB	CS	SLG	OBP
Ayers, Joe	R-R	6-0	190	9-26-84	.143	.129	.149	31	98	5	14	4	2	0	8	10	2	0	0	34	5	1	.224	.236
Babineau, Ryan	R-R	6-2	205	12-13-86	.231	.222	.234	43	147	14	34	10	0	1	13	29	3	0	0	34	7	3	.320	.369
Bordes, Greg	R-R	5-9	160	6-3-85	.197	.176	.204	49	147	22	29	3	0	0	15	20	1	3	2	40	1	4	.218	.294
Bustamante, Gerard	R-R	5-8	184	6-10-86	.218	.158	.250	22	55	1	12	3	1	0	7	9	0	0	1	10	0	0	.309	.323
Castillo, Ramon	R-R	5-11	190	9-6-88	.222	.179	.247	42	153	13	34	7	1	2	22	4	6	0	2	24	1	2	.320	.267
Cooper, David	L-R	5-8	170	6-18-85	.252	.269	.247	67	234	45	59	4	2	0	16	66	3	5	1	55	19	9	.286	.421
Cowgill, Collin	R-L	5-9	195	5-22-86	.304	.333	.295	20	79	21	24	3	1	11	28	12	3	1	0	17	5	0	.785	.415
Davis, Chris	R-R	6-0	200	9-22-86	.000	.000	.000	5	10	1	0	0	0	0	0	4	1	0	0	1	0	0	.000	.333
Duffy, Brendan	L-L	6-1	180	5-22-85	.274	.345	.259	53	164	33	45	5	4	1	11	28	15	2	1	45	17	5	.372	.423
Estevez, Victor	R-R	5-11	183	9-8-88	.125	.000	.200	2	8	0	1	1	0	0	1	0	0	0	0	5	0	0	.250	.125
Fie, Andrew	R-R	6-3	205	10-25-87	.178	.212	.166	68	259	20	46	6	5	4	25	8	2	0	2	71	9	5	.286	.207
Marte, Alfredo	R-R	6-1	170	3-31-89	.251	.152	.284	70	267	37	67	18	0	1	27	24	6	6	2	44	19	5	.330	.324
Parker, Justin	R-R	6-1	190	3-14-87	.210	.190	.216	51	181	20	38	7	4	0	14	23	2	0	0	49	12	2	.293	.306
Pimentel, Johan	R-R	5-11	175	7-13-89	.185	.167	.189	36	108	7	20	4	0	0	6	5	0	2	0	25	1	2	.222	.221
Principe, Jimmy	R-R	6-2	185	3-11-86	.273	.211	.286	31	110	21	30	7	1	0	6	17	3	1	1	28	4	3	.355	.382
Rodriguez, Daniel	R-R	6-2	205	1-20-87	.080	.083	.077	10	25	4	2	0	0	0	1	11	2	0	1	14	1	1	.080	.385
Rodriguez, Roberto	L-L	6-0	156	3-22-89	.183	.100	.203	47	153	15	28	5	1	1	11	18	3	7	0	52	2	3	.248	.282
Smith, Anthony	L-L	6-1	205	3-28-85	.241	.206	.247	59	220	27	53	11	2	5	31	21	1	0	3	40	7	1	.377	.306
Urena, Ariel	R-R	5-11	170	1-29-86	.109	.190	.059	16	55	5	6	0	0	1	3	3	2	2	0	21	1	0	.164	.183

Pitching	B-T	HT	WT	DOB	W	L	ERA	G	GS	CG	SV	IP	H	R	ER	HR	BB	SO	AVG	vLH	vRH	K/9	BB/9
Baez, Santo	R-R	6-1	155	12-16-88	0	2	5.56	15	1	0	0	23	30	17	14	1	15	18	.326	.515	.220	7.15	5.96
Brea, Ariel	L-L	5-10	155	5-14-88	1	2	4.35	8	0	0	0	10	8	5		0	12	6	.278	.250	.286	5.23	10.45
Cespedes, Jesus	R-R	6-2	200	12-24-88	0	0	9.19	11	0	0	0	16	18	17	16	0	14	12	.286	.238	.310	6.89	8.04
Cook, Ryan	R-R	6-3	200	6-30-87	2	4	4.64	7	7	0	0	33	37	25	17	4	11	23	.272	.333	.239	6.27	3.00
Dollar, Ben	R-R	6-4	225	9-19-86	1	1	3.38	10	0	0	0	13	12	5		2	10	9	.245	.333	.194	6.07	6.75
Durst, Jason	R-R	6-2	200	8-28-87	0	1	7.20	25	0	0	3	35	48	32	28	4	15	27	.336	.370	.320	6.94	3.86
Gautier, Joseph	L-L	5-10	165	12-31-87	0	1	6.00	3	2	0	0	6	11	4	4	0	4	4	.423	.500	.400	6.00	6.00
Harrington, Ian	L-L	6-1	190	4-23-85	6	6	4.12	16	15	0	0	79	95	42	36	7	13	43	.300	.342	.286	4.92	1.49
Hose, T.J.	R-R	5-10	185	4-15-86	4	5	4.48	15	15	0	0	78	82	46	39	5	20	57	.270	.302	.246	6.55	2.30
McAnaney, Pat	R-L	6-3	185	3-11-86	2	1	0.55	9	6	0	0	33	22	2	2	0	13	38	.191	.269	.169	10.47	3.58
Meaker, Jordan	R-R	6-6	220	9-22-86	1	1	1.47	26	0	0	6	37	24	13	6	2	21	35	.186	.226	.158	8.59	5.15
Miley, Wade	L-L	6-2	190	11-13-86	1	1	4.91	7	0	0	0	11	11	6	6	0	5	11	.250	.455	.182	9.00	4.09
Moorhouse, Brett	R-R	6-2	190	6-28-87	0	1	13.50	2	0	0	0	3	5	4	4	0	2	1	.455	.500	.400	3.38	6.75
Morgan, Sean	R-R	6-3	215	1-15-86	1	3	4.76	13	5	0	0	34	30	22	18	3	24	26	.244	.257	.239	6.88	6.35
Rosario, Amado	R-R	5-11	160	12-17-87	2	2	4.40	15	2	0	0	31	39	22	15	1	22	22	.310	.447	.250	6.46	6.46
Summers, Houston	R-R	5-10	180	8-20-87	5	7	5.29	14	14	0	0	78	77	52	46	7	45	34	.253	.290	.223	3.91	5.17
Suss, Clayton	R-R	6-2	190	10-8-88	0	0	8.31	13	0	0	0	13	20	14	12	1	4	7	.351	.381	.333	4.85	2.77
Taveras, Ricardo	R-R	6-2	210	10-17-87	0	5	5.63	17	9	0	0	56	50	40	35	4	49	37	.236	.259	.220	5.95	7.88
Vasquez, Daniel	R-R	6-0	195	3-4-86	0	2	3.95	27	0	0	4	41	34	18	18	4	21	40	.225	.211	.238	8.78	4.61
Woodall, Bryan	R-R	6-1	200	10-24-86	2	5	3.72	27	0	0	4	36	32	16	15	3	15	40	.235	.271	.216	9.91	3.72

Fielding

Catcher	PCT	G	PO	A	E	DP	PB
Babineau	.987	28	193	27	3	5	7
Bustamante	.965	20	96	13	4	2	8
Davis	1.000	3	14	2	0	0	2
Pimentel	.991	36	189	27	2	3	9

First Base	PCT	G	PO	A	E	DP
Castillo	.985	24	178	16	3	17
Fie	1.000	2	11	1	0	1
Smith	.981	55	478	30	10	42

Second Base	PCT	G	PO	A	E	DP
Ayers	.957	18	38	51	4	14

	PCT	G	PO	A	E	DP
Bordes	.974	42	85	104	5	28
Cooper	.973	19	35	36	2	13

Third Base	PCT	G	PO	A	E	DP
Ayers	.792	7	6	13	5	1
Estevez	—	1	0	0	0	0
Fie	.898	63	47	164	24	16
Parker	.917	7	4	18	2	3

Shortstop	PCT	G	PO	A	E	DP
Bordes	1.000	8	10	12	0	4
Cooper	.939	49	81	150	15	25
Parker	.925	24	51	60	9	16

Outfield	PCT	G	PO	A	E	DP
Ayers	.923	6	10	2	1	0
Cowgill	1.000	19	47	1	0	0
Duffy	.990	49	93	7	1	1
Marte	.965	61	106	3	4	0
Principe	.981	31	51	0	1	0
D. Rodriguez	1.000	6	8	0	0	0
R. Rodriguez	.990	46	94	1	1	1
Smith	1.000	1	1	0	0	0
Urena	.955	16	41	1	2	0

MISSOULA OSPREY   ROOKIE

PIONEER LEAGUE

Batting	B-T	HT	WT	DOB	AVG	vLH	vRH	G	AB	R	H	2B	3B	HR	RBI	BB	HBP	SH	SF	SO	SB	CS	SLG	OBP
Asencio, Isaias	R-R	6-0	169	12-31-87	.293	.288	.296	58	215	34	63	10	5	9	36	6	5	1	2	53	3	1	.512	.325
Canelo, Adonys	B-R	5-11	165	1-23-89	.500	.000	.500	2	4	3	2	1	0	0	3	0	1	0	0	0	0	0	.750	.600
Corniel, Jorge	R-R	5-8	180	1-4-88	.154	.222	.118	14	52	3	8	0	0	1	3	1	0	0	1	12	0	0	.212	.167
Davis, Chris	R-R	6-0	200	9-22-86	.282	.333	.255	27	78	7	22	3	2	1	7	13	3	1	1	10	0	1	.410	.400
Diaz, Alberto	R-R	6-1	180	9-3-88	.275	.282	.272	70	291	51	80	10	7	8	37	22	2	4	3	62	9	5	.440	.327
Elmore, Jake	R-R	5-10	180	6-15-87	.296	.286	.301	53	179	38	53	15	3	3	22	26	4	3	4	36	9	8	.464	.390
Estevez, Victor	R-R	5-11	183	9-8-88	.277	.308	.258	31	101	12	28	5	1	3	12	10	3	2	0	30	4	1	.436	.360
Gomez, Nelson	R-R	6-1	210	10-21-86	.276	.230	.298	59	225	29	62	12	0	10	45	17	5	0	3	48	0	1	.462	.336
Greene, Kyle	L-R	6-2	200	5-26-86	.302	.338	.286	52	212	33	64	14	0	5	26	10	7	0	2	59	1	1	.439	.351
Hilario, Rafael	R-R	5-10	175	1-28-88	.222	.278	.200	42	126	13	28	5	2	1	17	16	4	0	1	30	4	3	.317	.327
Kauffman, Dan	L-L	6-2	225	1-1-87	.000	—	.000	3	7	1	0	0	0	0	0	3	0	0	0	3	0	0	.000	.300
Linton, Ollie	L-L	5-8	160	4-7-86	.246	.375	.178	16	69	17	17	1	1	1	9	6	2	1	0	16	8	3	.333	.325
Musselman, Bill	R-R	6-2	210	11-1-84	.242	.143	.269	10	33	6	8	3	1	1	6	2	0	0	0	11	0	0	.485	.286
Navarro, Reynaldo	B-R	5-10	175	12-22-89	.258	.391	.201	72	291	42	75	17	7	2	31	25	4	1	2	77	17	9	.385	.323
Perez, Rossmel	B-R	5-10	180	8-26-89	.243	.184	.264	43	144	15	35	8	0	0	11	16	1	1	0	13	0	0	.299	.323
Stone, Bobby	L-L	6-2	205	11-14-89	.213	.213	.213	64	225	28	48	10	2	7	27	24	0	0	6	64	0	3	.369	.289
White, Ryne	L-L	5-11	205	10-17-86	.274	.299	.261	58	234	40	64	13	1	7	38	26	2	0	2	41	1	1	.427	.348
Worthington, Tyrell	R-R	6-0	190	8-2-88	.143	.289	.080	39	126	12	18	3	1	0	6	18	1	0	0	67	4	2	.183	.255

Pitching	B-T	HT	WT	DOB	W	L	ERA	G	GS	CG	SV	IP	H	R	ER	HR	BB	SO	AVG	vLH	vRH	K/9	BB/9
Baez, Santo	R-R	6-1	155	12-16-88	0	1	6.75	2	2	0	0	8	10	7	6	0	4	2	.303	.286	.308	2.25	4.50
Blake, Josh	L-L	6-4	205	10-17-84	0	1	9.00	3	0	0	0	7	10	7	7	2	6	4	.370	.500	.316	5.14	7.71
Burke, Brandon	R-R	6-3	200	9-15-85	0	2	5.53	16	0	0	0	28	38	22	17	5	9	28	.330	.346	.317	9.11	2.93
Capellan, Victor	R-R	6-2	195	7-24-89	0	1	6.18	15	0	0	0	28	36	22	19	5	13	22	.316	.225	.365	7.16	4.23
Eichhorn, Kevin	R-R	6-0	170	2-6-90	0	0	6.75	2	0	0	0	3	2	2	2	0	1	2	.222	.333	.167	6.75	3.38
Gautier, Joseph	L-L	5-10	165	12-31-87	0	0	10.13	1	1	0	0	3	5	3	3	1	2	4	.417	.600	.286	13.50	6.75
Harden, Trevor	B-R	6-2	215	9-1-87	1	3	1.91	12	6	0	2	42	34	14	9	2	11	64	.224	.239	.212	13.61	2.34
Mace, Justin	L-R	6-3	205	3-11-86	1	4	4.22	22	0	0	1	53	61	36	25	4	16	49	.280	.250	.297	8.27	2.70
Moorhouse, Brett	R-R	6-2	190	6-28-87	1	3	8.37	10	6	0	0	33	45	32	31	6	11	21	.326	.250	.372	5.67	2.97
Orosco Jr., Jesse	R-R	6-2	200	7-3-87	3	0	3.72	17	0	0	0	36	39	28	15	8	19	28	.273	.286	.264	6.94	4.71
Quezada, Rafael	R-R	6-3	180	11-21-86	2	8	8.17	16	15	0	0	68	85	64	62	11	36	53	.306	.277	.327	6.98	4.74
Reagan, Miles	R-R	6-2	200	11-16-90	0	4	7.31	17	5	0	0	32	31	30	26	2	33	38	.256	.273	.247	10.69	9.28
Reynolds, Brett	R-R	6-3	195	9-28-84	2	7	5.23	15	15	1	0	74	102	58	43	8	33	47	.342	.344	.341	5.72	4.01
Rodriguez, Pedro	R-R	6-0	190	6-20-89	1	4	5.68	18	0	0	2	32	34	23	20	5	13	28	.272	.286	.265	7.96	3.69
Rodriguez, Randy	L-L	6-0	155	1-6-88	2	6	8.10	19	0	0	0	53	89	60	48	9	19	27	.379	.415	.365	4.56	3.21
Schlereth, Daniel	L-L	6-0	210	5-9-86	0	0	0.00	3	0	0	0	3	1	0	0	2	6	.250	.000	.300	18.00	6.00
Shaw, Bryan	B-R	6-1	210	11-8-87	0	1	6.75	10	0	0	2	17	24	19	13	2	7	17	.316	.304	.321	8.83	3.63
Sinclair, Taylor	L-L	6-3	180	12-23-85	5	2	3.07	9	8	0	0	44	38	17	15	2	5	48	.226	.304	.197	9.82	1.02
Sosa, Kenny	L-L	6-0	167	3-26-87	2	3	6.02	17	3	0	1	40	44	28	27	3	25	35	.275	.279	.274	7.81	5.58
Suss, Clayton	R-R	6-2	190	10-2-88	0	1	10.61	5	1	0	0	9	19	15	11	4	5	4	.442	.647	.308	3.86	4.82
Zepeda, Bayron	L-L	5-10	185	8-29-87	1	3	4.97	20	4	0	0	42	56	35	23	6	9	37	.299	.314	.294	7.99	1.94

Fielding

Catcher	PCT	G	PO	A	E	DP	PB
Corniel	.969	6	55	8	2	1	3
Davis	.964	26	172	18	7	1	5
Gomez	1.000	1	1	0	0	0	0
Musselman	1.000	9	51	6	0	1	1
Perez	.985	40	296	39	5	7	4

First Base	PCT	G	PO	A	E	DP
Elmore	1.000	2	5	0	0	0
Estevez	.857	2	11	1	2	2
Gomez	.982	13	102	6	2	9
Greene	1.000	3	32	2	0	4
Kauffman	1.000	1	10	1	0	1

	PCT	G	PO	A	E	DP
Musselman	1.000	2	11	0	0	0
White	.990	55	465	41	5	40

Second Base	PCT	G	PO	A	E	DP
Elmore	.982	41	90	129	4	25
Estevez	1.000	4	8	6	0	4
Hilario	.947	33	55	88	8	17

Third Base	PCT	G	PO	A	E	DP
Estevez	.828	10	10	14	5	1
Gomez	.896	22	22	38	7	6
Greene	.947	43	36	89	7	9
Hilario	1.000	3	3	2	0	0
Perez	—	1	0	0	0	0

Shortstop	PCT	G	PO	A	E	DP
Elmore	.966	6	10	18	1	2
Navarro	.906	70	140	228	38	42

Outfield	PCT	G	PO	A	E	DP
Asencio	.966	55	80	6	3	1
Diaz	.940	69	116	9	8	3
Estevez	1.000	4	4	0	0	0
Gomez	.667	3	2	0	1	0
Linton	.941	16	31	1	2	0
Stone	.957	62	77	12	4	3
Worthington	.878	26	30	6	5	0

DSL DIAMONDBACKS   ROOKIE
DOMINICAN SUMMER LEAGUE

Batting	B-T	HT	WT	DOB	AVG	vLH	vRH	G	AB	R	H	2B	3B	HR	RBI	BB	HBP	SH	SF	SO	SB	CS	SLG	OBP
Acevedo, Edwin	R-R			10-30-88	.167	.200	.143	3	12	1	2	0	0	0	3	0	0	0	3	1	0	.167	.333
Arias, Pedro	R-R	6-1	195	9-8-88	.223	.318	.200	33	112	8	25	5	0	1	11	7	3	1	1	23	0	1	.295	.285
Brito, Luis	R-R	6-4	215	8-27-89	.220	.194	.226	51	164	20	36	12	0	2	19	23	2	0	0	64	2	1	.329	.323
Canelo, Adonys	B-R	5-11	165	1-23-89	.204	.167	.217	27	93	10	19	2	1	0	9	8	2	3	0	23	1	1	.247	.282
Felix, Ruben	R-R			8-28-88	.171	.167	.173	38	140	16	24	5	1	0	11	9	5	0	1	38	1	2	.221	.245
Garcia, Manuel	B-R	5-11	170	3-8-89	.243	.333	.235	13	37	6	9	2	1	0	2	6	0	0	0	4	0	2	.351	.349
Gomez, Raywilly	B-R	5-11	170	1-25-90	.317	.327	.314	63	230	33	73	12	5	0	25	37	5	0	1	21	8	4	.413	.421
Inciarte, Astolfo	L-L	5-8	170	2-9-88	.322	.344	.315	38	143	18	46	7	1	0	17	16	2	2	1	17	2	0	.385	.395
Javier, Kelvin				10-7-90	.219	.214	.220	39	137	16	30	7	1	0	15	15	4	0	5	50	2	3	.285	.304
Jimenez, Bernardino	R-R	6-1	160	8-7-90	.165	.032	.214	36	115	20	19	3	1	0	6	20	4	0	0	37	2	3	.209	.309
Jose, Jose	L-L			7-21-90	.179	.160	.185	67	234	29	42	8	3	6	23	22	4	0	3	121	1	5	.316	.259
Mejia, Yermis	B-R	6-0	165	1-5-90	.133	1.000	.071	7	15	2	2	1	0	0	3	4	2	0	0	6	0	0	.200	.381
Montilla, Gerson	R-R	5-10	168	11-13-89	.249	.300	.233	60	213	35	53	10	2	0	19	24	7	0	1	39	9	10	.315	.343
Noboa, Michael	R-R	5-8	160	6-21-87	.191	.133	.208	24	68	8	13	3	0	0	4	7	3	0	0	20	1	3	.235	.295
Sepulveda, Antonio	B-R	5-9	150	12-31-91	.237	.158	.257	24	93	13	22	3	1	0	2	13	2	2	0	26	5	4	.290	.343
Soriano, Domingo				10-29-89	.247	.214	.254	41	150	19	37	8	2	3	15	10	4	0	1	42	2	4	.387	.309
Taveras, Damil	B-R	6-0	185	2-5-89	.127	.172	.111	37	110	13	14	5	1	0	14	9	0	0	0	26	0	1	.191	.193
Zaballa, Henry	R-R	6-1	175	10-20-89	.271	.267	.273	69	258	27	70	6	3	3	37	25	7	0	5	46	12	3	.353	.346

Pitching	B-T	HT	WT	DOB	W	L	ERA	G	GS	CG	SV	IP	H	R	ER	HR	BB	SO	AVG	vLH	vRH	K/9	BB/9
Adino, Hector	R-R	5-11	155	6-14-88	2	1	7.36	14	1	0	0	26	30	21	21	3	16	15	.291	.346	.273	5.26	5.61
Batista, Jose	L-L	6-2	200	2-24-90	0	0	5.87	5	0	0	1	8	9	6	5	0	8	8	.300	.429	.261	9.39	9.39
Brea, Ariel	L-L	5-10	155	5-14-89	0	0	4.76	6	0	0	0	6	9	3	3	0	3	3	.391	.667	.350	4.76	4.76
Burgos, Enrique	R-R	6-4	200	11-23-90	2	0	3.92	10	10	0	0	41	35	19	18	2	26	41	.238	.341	.194	8.93	5.66
Camacho, Yiomar	R-R	6-1	172	2-24-90	2	4	4.39	16	8	0	0	53	44	34	26	0	27	46	.220	.246	.210	7.76	4.56
Cespedes, Jesus	R-R	6-2	200	12-24-88	0	0	1.23	4	0	0	1	7	5	1	1	0	2	8	.185	.000	.250	9.82	2.45
De Jesus, Cesse	R-R	5-11	155	5-16-90	1	1	2.13	17	0	0	5	25	18	10	6	0	7	17	.207	.241	.190	6.04	2.49
De La Rosa, Eury	L-L	5-9	150	2-24-90	1	2	2.11	13	2	0	2	43	38	18	10	2	7	56	.235	.353	.221	11.81	1.48
De Los Santos, Sammy	R-R			12-9-89	2	4	1.12	11	11	0	0	64	41	17	8	1	9	49	.181	.100	.224	6.85	1.26
Familia, Silio	L-L			5-30-90	0	0	5.19	4	0	0	0	9	9	7	5	2	6	5	.290	.500	.276	5.19	6.23
Gil, Manuel	R-R			3-17-91	3	6	4.01	12	11	0	0	43	39	25	19	2	19	31	.248	.268	.241	6.54	4.01
Gomez, Eduardo	R-R	6-0	165	12-31-89	0	1	6.89	10	0	0	0	16	17	14	12	0	6	8	.288	.421	.225	4.60	3.45
Gutierrez, Teo	R-R			5-23-90	0	1	5.23	6	0	0	1	10	15	8	6	0	2	9	.326	.385	.303	7.84	1.74
Leon, Danny	R-R	6-5	180	9-16-89	0	0	2.25	18	1	0	0	32	28	11	8	0	14	21	.239	.211	.253	5.91	3.94
Mariano, Ramon	B-L	6-1	187	11-1-87	2	3	2.12	18	0	0	0	47	49	18	11	0	8	51	.266	.333	.258	9.84	1.54
Martinez, Gustavo	R-R	6-2	162	3-13-90	3	4	3.62	12	11	0	0	50	39	28	20	1	20	33	.212	.143	.237	5.98	3.62
Pena, Miguel	R-R	6-0	160	9-18-90	1	4	8.17	9	9	0	0	25	32	32	23	3	16	18	.296	.294	.297	6.39	5.68
Rosario, Diogenes	R-R	6-0	170	9-1-88	4	7	3.45	20	4	0	2	60	51	31	23	3	15	45	.228	.195	.245	6.75	2.25
Rosario, Juan	R-R			4-3-91	0	0	7.90	12	0	0	0	14	19	12	12	0	9	8	.345	.133	.425	5.27	5.93
Santana, Frank	R-R	6-2	200	2-21-89	0	2	6.55	14	2	0	2	22	21	21	16	1	11	21	.244	.387	.164	8.59	4.50
Serrano, Ruben	R-R			5-21-89	2	5	7.17	16	0	0	0	21	25	24	17	0	10	12	.294	.192	.339	5.06	4.22

Fielding

Catcher	PCT	G	PO	A	E	DP	PB
Arias	.992	29	202	40	2	2	5
Felix	.985	33	233	28	4	5	11
Garcia	.990	11	89	11	1	1	0

First Base	PCT	G	PO	A	E	DP
Acevedo	.941	2	16	0	1	3
Arias	1.000	2	5	1	0	1
Brito	.971	43	339	23	11	23
Inciarte	.986	8	65	4	1	4
Montilla	.963	4	26	0	1	2
Taveras	.993	21	137	10	1	16
Zaballa	1.000	2	11	0	0	1

Second Base	PCT	G	PO	A	E	DP
Canelo	.875	16	32	31	9	3

	PCT	G	PO	A	E	DP
Gomez	.982	10	27	28	1	3
Mejia	.833	3	2	3	1	1
Montilla	.985	30	68	64	2	17
Noboa	.943	16	32	34	4	12
Sepulveda	.963	5	12	14	1	2

Third Base	PCT	G	PO	A	E	DP
Brito	—	1	0	0	0	0
Gomez	.858	50	61	114	29	15
Montilla	.968	17	20	40	2	5
Taveras	.913	10	3	18	2	0

Shortstop	PCT	G	PO	A	E	DP
Canelo	.838	9	11	20	6	3
Gomez	1.000	1	2	4	0	0
Jimenez	.892	36	47	101	18	16

	PCT	G	PO	A	E	DP
Mejia	.800	3	3	1	1	0
Montilla	.913	5	11	10	2	3
Sepulveda	.869	19	27	46	11	6

Outfield	PCT	G	PO	A	E	DP
Acevedo	.800	2	4	0	1	0
Brito	1.000	7	6	0	0	0
Inciarte	.963	19	24	2	1	0
Javier	.918	35	51	5	5	0
Jose	.901	58	94	15	12	5
Montilla	—	1	0	0	0	0
Rosario	1.000	3	6	0	0	0
Soriano	.923	39	66	6	6	1
Taveras	1.000	1	2	0	0	0
Zaballa	.991	58	102	11	1	2

DSL DIAMONDBACKS/REDS   ROOKIE
DOMINICAN SUMMER LEAGUE (A—ARIZONA; C—CINCINNATI; M—MINNESOTA)

Batting	B-T	HT	WT	DOB	AVG	vLH	vRH	G	AB	R	H	2B	3B	HR	RBI	BB	HBP	SH	SF	SO	SB	CS	SLG	OBP
Acevedo, Edwin (A)	R-R			10-30-88	.114	.091	.119	25	70	5	8	3	0	1	3	8	4	0	1	29	1	2	.200	.241
2-team total (3 Diamondbacks)					.122	—	—	28	82	6	10	3	0	1	3	11	4	0	1	32	2	2	.195	.255
Alegria, Jose (A)	R-R	6-1	200	11-5-90	.206	.276	.186	45	126	6	26	2	1	0	10	12	1	0	0	26	0	2	.238	.281
Canelo, Adonys (A)	B-R	5-11	165	1-23-89	.183	.133	.200	17	60	6	11	2	1	0	2	3	0	0	1	17	3	3	.250	.219
2-team total (27 Diamondbacks)					.196	—	—	44	153	16	30	4	2	0	11	11	2	3	1	40	4	4	.248	.257
Colmenares, Cesar (C)	R-R	6-1	165	6-28-90	.181	.227	.167	36	94	12	17	1	0	0	3	10	1	1	1	16	3	0	.191	.264
Estevez, Wilfrel (C)	R-R	6-0	177	8-11-90	.203	.171	.216	36	123	8	25	5	1	0	16	6	3	1	2	30	0	1	.260	.254
Inciarte, Astolfo (A)	L-L	5-8	170	2-9-88	.260	.158	.284	29	100	16	26	5	1	0	18	17	0	0	2	8	2	1	.330	.361
2-team total (38 Diamondbacks)					.296	—	—	67	243	34	72	12	2	0	35	33	2	2	3	25	4	1	.362	.381
Inciarte, Ender (A)	L-L			10-29-90	.300	.321	.293	62	227	36	68	7	0	0	18	27	2	3	1	35	22	6	.330	.377

Player	B-T	HT	WT	DOB	AVG	vLH	vRH	G	AB	R	H	2B	3B	HR	RBI	BB	HBP	SH	SF	SO	SB	CS	OBP	SLG
Jimenez, Bernard (A)	R-R	6-1	160	8-7-90	.143	.200	.130	10	28	6	4	0	0	0	2	6	2	0	0	8	3	0	.143	.333
2-team total (36 Diamondbacks)					.161	—	—	46	143	26	23	3	1	0	8	26	6	0	0	45	5	3	.196	.314
Logrono, Angel (C)	R-R	6-2	190	7-3-90	.187	.276	.164	46	139	13	26	4	0	1	15	11	3	0	1	39	2	2	.237	.260
Mejia, Yermis (A)	B-R	6-0	165	1-5-90	.071	.154	.034	17	42	3	3	1	0	0	0	3	7	0	1	16	1	1	.095	.204
2-team total (7 Diamondbacks)					.088	—	—	24	57	5	5	2	0	0	6	11	2	1	0	22	1	1	.123	.257
Meran, George (C)	R-R	5-10	158	12-5-89	.213	.200	.220	18	61	5	13	2	0	0	11	3	1	0	0	12	0	0	.246	.262
Noboa, Michael (A)	R-R	5-8	160	6-21-87	.244	.231	.246	24	78	13	19	2	1	0	7	22	3	3	0	15	6	2	.295	.427
2-team total (24 Diamondbacks)					.219	—	—	48	146	21	32	5	1	0	11	29	6	3	0	35	7	5	.267	.370
Ortuno, Jose (C)	R-R	6-1	185	12-23-90	.170	.333	.122	26	53	1	9	0	0	0	3	3	0	0	0	13	0	0	.170	.214
Perez, Jonathan (A)	R-R	6-0	205	9-14-90	.174	.188	.171	54	149	16	26	5	1	4	18	23	5	0	4	70	7	2	.302	.298
Quintero, Jose (C)	L-R	6-1	175	12-6-90	.150	.200	.133	16	40	12	6	3	0	0	1	16	1	1	0	9	3	4	.225	.404
Restrepo, Alberto (C)	R-R	5-9	160	6-8-88	.152	.120	.162	43	99	4	15	0	0	0	5	12	2	2	0	17	0	3	.152	.257
Rodriguez, Henry (C)	R-R	5-10	150	2-9-90	.337	.209	.377	46	181	25	61	8	3	1	18	20	2	2	2	14	16	6	.431	.405
Rondon, Victor (C)	B-R	6-3	180	3-19-91	.132	.125	.133	35	76	7	10	1	0	0	3	9	1	0	0	34	1	2	.145	.233
Santoni, Andres (C)	R-R	5-11	170	6-6-91	.126	.045	.154	45	87	6	11	2	0	0	7	13	2	0	0	38	3	1	.149	.255
Sepulveda, Antonio (A)	B-R	5-9	150	12-31-91	.218	.000	.279	18	55	4	12	0	2	0	5	11	1	2	0	19	5	1	.291	.358
2-team total (24 Diamondbacks)					.230	—	—	42	148	17	34	3	3	0	7	24	3	4	0	45	10	5	.291	.349
Sierra, Jefry (C)	R-R	5-10	165	4-16-90	.107	.118	.103	19	56	4	6	0	0	0	2	5	0	2	0	10	5	0	.107	.180
Soriano, Domingo (A)	R-R			10-29-89	.226	.182	.242	22	84	6	19	7	0	0	7	5	0	0	0	23	3	1	.310	.270
2-team total (41 Diamondbacks)					.239	—	—	63	234	25	56	15	2	3	22	15	4	0	1	65	5	5	.359	.295
Sujilio, Jose Ramon (C)	R-R	6-3	165	11-27-89	.140	.208	.120	42	107	7	15	3	2	0	4	6	5	0	0	49	4	1	.206	.220
Victor, Jose (C)	R-R	6-2	170	5-25-90	.154	.143	.157	55	130	19	20	5	2	0	7	37	11	1	0	49	8	2	.223	.382

Pitching	B-T	HT	WT	DOB	W	L	ERA	G	GS	CG	SV	IP	H	R	ER	HR	BB	SO	AVG	vLH	vRH	K/9	BB/9
Abreu, Rafael (C)	L-L	6-0	165	8-25-90	0		4.26	4	0	0	0	6	7	3	3	0	6	2	.292	—	.292	2.84	8.53
Adames, Jesus (C)	R-R	6-4	195	1-25-91	0	4	4.74	4	0	0	0	19	16	12	10	1	7	16	.222	.238	.216	7.58	3.32
Almonte, Ramon (C)	R-R	6-0	165	6-20-88	1	3	3.95	8	8	0	0	27	17	22	12	0	28	31	.183	.167	.188	10.21	9.22
Amador, Renny (C)	L-L	6-0	185	2-26-88	0	0	3.38	3	0	0	0	3	1	1	0	0	1	2	.100	.000	.100	6.75	33.75
Caceres, Alvaro (M)	L-L	6-0	165	5-4-86	1	1	3.50	10	0	0	0	18	15	14	7	0	12	19	.227	.333	.222	9.50	6.00
De La Rosa, Winfil (A)	R-R	6-3	190	11-17-87	0	1	8.36	7	1	0	0	14	21	15	13	0	8	12	.350	.500	.313	7.71	5.14
Delgado, Gustavo (A)	R-R	5-11	165	4-8-90	0	1	9.82	17	0	0	0	18	23	26	20	0	20	11	.315	.167	.388	5.40	9.82
Familia, Silio (A)	L-L			5-30-90	1	0	1.49	14	0	0	1	36	27	10	6	1	13	37	.211	.000	.235	9.17	3.22
2-team total (4 Diamondbacks)					1	0	2.20	18	0	0	1	45	36	17	11	3	19	42	—	—		8.40	3.80
Gonzalez, Gabriel (A)	R-R	6-2	170	5-27-91	2	2	3.40	11	9	0	0	42	35	20	16	2	11	37	.215	.180	.230	7.87	2.34
Gonzalez, Fernando (C)	R-R	6-3	175	5-19-89	0	3	4.81	12	3	0	0	24	18	29	13	1	33	22	.198	.160	.212	8.14	12.21
Gutierrez, Teo (A)	R-R			5-23-90	2	7	3.55	12	10	0	0	51	62	30	20	1	9	39	.292	.317	.283	6.93	1.60
2-team total (6 Diamondbacks)					2	8	3.84	18	10	0	1	61	77	38	26	1	11	48	—	—		7.08	1.62
Lujan, Mario (A)	R-R	6-2	180	11-7-90	1	3	5.36	23	0	0	1	40	50	29	24	0	18	27	.307	.340	.293	6.02	4.02
Mercedes, Elvin (C)	R-R	6-4	150	3-2-89	0	3	4.33	16	7	0	0	54	56	32	26	3	21	29	.275	.284	.270	4.83	3.50
Molina, Marcos (C)	R-R	6-1	185	4-4-88	0	3	8.20	20	3	0	0	37	45	51	34	0	45	24	.308	.425	.264	5.79	10.85
Navarro, Victor (C)	R-R	6-3	180	11-7-89	0	1	4.15	6	0	0	0	9	6	5	4	0	4	4	.200	.167	.222	4.15	4.15
Palencia, Juan (C)	R-R	5-11	150	6-20-90	1	5	7.86	17	1	0	1	26	32	29	23	3	24	26	.302	.229	.338	8.89	8.20
Pena, Miguel (A)	R-R	6-0	160	9-18-90	2	1	2.70	4	4	0	0	20	15	10	6	2	5	18	.195	.143	.214	8.10	2.25
2-team total (9 Diamondbacks)					3	5	5.76	13	13	0	0	45	47	42	29	5	21	36	—	—		7.15	4.17
Quezada, Radhames (A)	R-R	6-2	175	7-6-90	1	1	4.03	11	1	0	0	22	22	12	10	0	10	18	.265	.400	.207	7.25	4.03
Rosario, Juan (A)	R-R			4-3-91	0	0	9.00	5	0	0	0	7	6	8	7	0	7	4	.240	.167	.263	5.14	9.00
2-team total (12 Diamondbacks)					0	0	8.27	17	0	0	0	21	25	20	19	0	16	12	—	—		5.23	6.97
Santana, Diony (A)	L-L	6-0	150	1-15-91	0	6	5.90	11	4	0	0	29	28	19	19	0	22	32	.259	.231	.263	9.93	6.83
Santana, Frank (A)	R-R	6-2	200	2-21-89	0	0	0.00	1	0	0	0	1	0	0	0	0	0	0	.000	.000	.000	0.00	0.00
2-team total (14 Diamondbacks)					0	2	6.26	15	2	0	2	23	21	21	16	1	11	21	—	—		8.22	4.30
Santana, Eddy (M)	R-R	6-1	165	9-21-87	1	3	3.64	29	1	0	7	42	38	21	17	1	16	25	.232	.167	.264	5.36	3.43
Silvestre, Elvin (A)	R-R	6-1	166	10-8-89	2	5	4.91	13	12	0	0	59	65	45	32	1	37	49	.288	.384	.242	7.52	5.68
Tineo, Carlos (C)	R-R			3-12-91	0	2	9.00	10	2	0	0	12	14	14	12	0	16	10	.304	.188	.367	7.50	12.00

Fielding

Catcher

Catcher	PCT	G	PO	A	E	DP	PB
Alegria	.969	34	188	32	7	2	17
Ortuno	.963	21	98	7	4	0	5
Perez	1.000	1	3	0	0	0	1
Restrepo	.984	43	219	33	4	5	11
Santoni	1.000	1	5	1	0	0	0

First Base

First Base	PCT	G	PO	A	E	DP
Acevedo	.981	15	97	6	2	11
Estevez	1.000	1	6	0	0	0
A. Inciarte	.968	15	145	5	5	14
Logrono	.966	22	162	10	6	15
Ortuno	1.000	1	11	0	0	1
Perez	.982	26	214	7	4	21

Second Base

Second Base	PCT	G	PO	A	E	DP
Canelo	.936	10	23	21	3	6
Mejia	.906	10	11	18	3	3
Meran	—	1	0	0	0	0
Noboa	.945	23	42	61	6	13
Pena	1.000	1	2	5	0	0
Rodriguez	1.000	2	4	3	0	0
Santoni	.946	25	29	59	5	13
Sepulveda	.952	5	11	9	1	2
Sierra	1.000	2	4	2	0	0
Sujilio	.861	12	9	22	5	4

Third Base

Third Base	PCT	G	PO	A	E	DP
Mejia	1.000	2	2	1	0	0
Meran	.804	17	6	35	10	3
Perez	.830	26	22	51	15	4
Rodriguez	.919	21	25	43	6	5
Rondon	—	1	0	0	0	0
Santoni	1.000	4	2	5	0	2
Sierra	.000	1	0	0	1	0
Sujilio	.905	8	3	16	2	0
Victor	—	1	0	0	0	0

Shortstop

Shortstop	PCT	G	PO	A	E	DP
Canelo	.889	12	12	20	4	3
Jimenez	.917	9	12	32	4	7
Mejia	1.000	5	8	3	0	1
Rodriguez	.920	20	40	52	8	10
Santoni	1.000	1	1	1	0	0
Sepulveda	.872	14	23	45	10	6
Sierra	.875	17	22	55	11	13
Sujilio	1.000	4	3	5	0	2

Outfield

Outfield	PCT	G	PO	A	E	DP
Acevedo	1.000	1	3	0	0	0
Alegria	1.000	1	6	0	0	0
Colmenares	.951	25	37	2	2	1
Estevez	.952	31	37	3	2	1
A. Inciarte	.931	15	24	3	2	1
E. Inciarte	.985	62	124	5	2	0
Logrono	.857	10	6	0	1	0
Quintero	1.000	13	18	0	0	0
Rondon	.923	11	8	4	1	0
Soriano	.939	19	27	4	2	0
Sujilio	.333	3	1	0	2	0
Victor	.975	50	72	6	2	3

Atlanta Braves

BY BILL BALLEW

Afterwards 14 consecutive campaigns of postseason play, the Braves extended a less enviable string by failing to reach the playoffs for the third straight season.

There were moments when the on-field performance was as ugly as the days when John Smoltz and Tom Glavine were in their early 20s. The results, at least from a team perspective, were similar, as well, with the Braves posting their first 90-loss season since 1990.

Such results were not expected during spring training, not with Smoltz pitching as well as ever in his long and distinguished career and Glavine returning to the rotation after a five-year stint with the Mets. Yet neither hurler took the mound after June, with Smoltz having shoulder surgery and Glavine experiencing life on the disabled list for the first time before having elbow surgery in August. Making matters worse, fellow starter Tim Hudson also failed to finish the race and had Tommy John surgery in August, a procedure that will keep him out of action for at least the first half of the 2009 campaign.

"We entered the season believing we had solid depth in our rotation," first-year general manager Frank Wren said. "I don't think anyone could have envisioned what eventually took place."

The Braves also suffered setbacks in the bullpen. Closer Rafael Soriano and set-up man Peter Moylan missed most of the season, which created a shuttle system of arms between Triple-A Richmond and the big leagues. As a result, the Braves concluded the season ranked last in the National League with 26 saves and two complete games.

The offense, meanwhile, did not have enough power to overcome the lack of consistent pitching. The Braves were steady if not spectacular at the plate, thanks largely to third baseman Chipper Jones overcoming a variety of ailments and hitting .364/.470/.574 to win his first batting title.

First baseman Mark Teixeira was one of the few long-ball threats in the lineup, but when the season went south, the Braves decided to get what they could for him and dealt Teixeira to the Angels on July 29 for first baseman Casey Kotchman and righthander Stephen Marek.

For all that went wrong, there were some positives. Rookie righthander Jair Jurrjens (13-10, 3.68 in 188 innings) led the staff in wins, and 30-year-

old righthander Jorge Campillo went from being a non-roster invitee to a solid starter after joining the rotation on May 20. Second baseman Kelly Johnson used a torrid finish to score a team-high 86 runs, and Brian McCann solidified his status as one of the NL's premier catchers, topping the team with 23 home runs and 86 RBIs.

PLAYERS OF THE YEAR

MAJOR LEAGUE: CHIPPER JONES, 3B

Jones won the National League batting title, edging Albert Pujols. Jones hit .364/.470/.574 with 22 home runs, 22 doubles and 75 RBIs, and he secured the batting title by hitting .408 in September, his third month hitting better than .400.

MINOR LEAGUE: TOMMY HANSON, RHP

Hanson, a draft-and-follow signed ahead of the 2006 draft, stormed through the minors as he finished 11-5, 2.41 in 138 innings combined between high Class A Myrtle Beach and Double-A Mississippi. He struck out 163 and issued 52 walks.

RODGER WOOD

ORGANIZATION LEADERS

BATTING		*Minimum 250 at-bats
*AVG	Heyward, Jason, Rome/Myrtle Beach	.316
R	Mejia, Ernesto, Myrtle Beach	93
H	Anderson, Josh, Richmond	155
H	Freeman, Frederick, Rome	155
TB	Mejia, Ernesto, Myrtle Beach	262
2B	Mejia, Ernesto, Myrtle Beach	47
3B	Young, Matt, Mississippi	11
HR	Johnson, Cody, Rome	26
RBI	Freeman, Frederick, Rome	95
BB	Flowers, Tyler, Myrtle Beach	98
SO	Johnson, Cody, Rome	177
SB	Anderson, Josh, Richmond	42
*OBP	Flowers, Tyler, Myrtle Beach	.427
*SLG	Perry, Jason, Mississippi/Richmond	.534

PITCHING		†Minimum 75 innings
W	Diamond, Scott, Rome/Myrtle Beach	15
L	Locke, Jeffrey, Rome	12
†ERA	Hanson, Tommy, Myrtle Beach/Mississippi	2.41
G	Valdez, Luis, Mississippi	55
GS	Redmond, Todd, Mississippi	27
SV	Valdez, Luis, Mississippi	28
IP	Redmond, Todd, Mississippi	166
BB	Barrett, Eric, Rome	78
SO	Hanson, Tommy, Myrtle Beach/Mississippi	163
†AVG	Hanson, Tommy, Myrtle Beach/Mississippi	.175

2008 PERFORMANCE

General Manager: Frank Wren. **Farm Director:** Paul Snyder. **Scouting Director:** Roy Clark.

Class	Team	League	W	L	PCT	Finish*	Manager	Affiliate Since
Majors	Atlanta	National	72	90	.444	12th (16)	Bobby Cox	—
Triple-A	Richmond Braves	International	63	78	.447	13th (14)	Dave Brundage	1966
Double-A	Mississippi Braves	Southern	73	66	.525	^3rd (10)	Phillip Wellman	2005
High A	Myrtle Beach Pelicans	Carolina	89	51	.636	1st (8)	Rocket Wheeler	1999
Low A	Rome Braves	South Atlantic	56	81	.409	14th (16)	Randy Ingle	2003
Rookie	Danville Braves	Appalachian	35	32	.522	5th (10)	Paul Runge	1993
Rookie	GCL Braves	Gulf Coast	29	29	.500	9th (16)	Jesus Alfaro	1998
Overall 2008 Minor League Record			345	337	.506	12th		

* Finish in overall standings (No. of teams in league). ^League champion.

ORGANIZATION STATISTICS

ATLANTA BRAVES

NATIONAL LEAGUE

Batting	B-T	HT	WT	DOB	AVG	vLH	vRH	G	AB	R	H	2B	3B	HR	RBI	BB	HBP	SH	SF	SO	SB	CS	SLG	OBP
Anderson, Josh	L-R	6-2	195	8-10-82	.294	.200	.341	40	136	21	40	7	1	3	12	8	1	1	0	33	10	1	.426	.338
Blanco, Gregor	L-L	5-11	170	12-12-83	.251	.248	.252	144	430	52	108	14	4	1	38	74	6	6	3	99	13	5	.309	.366
Diaz, Matt	R-R	6-1	215	3-3-78	.244	.319	.159	43	135	9	33	2	0	2	14	3	1	0	1	32	4	2	.304	.264
Escobar, Yunel	R-R	6-2	200	11-2-82	.288	.262	.299	136	514	71	148	24	2	10	60	59	5	7	2	62	2	5	.401	.366
Francoeur, Jeff	R-R	6-4	220	1-8-84	.239	.210	.251	155	599	70	143	33	3	11	71	39	10	0	4	111	0	1	.359	.294
Gotay, Ruben	B-R	5-11	190	12-25-82	.235	.154	.263	88	102	10	24	5	0	2	8	13	0	2	0	32	1	1	.343	.322
Infante, Omar	R-R	6-0	180	12-26-81	.293	.325	.273	96	317	45	93	24	3	3	40	22	2	2	5	44	0	1	.416	.338
Johnson, Kelly	L-R	6-1	205	2-22-82	.287	.333	.270	150	547	86	157	39	6	12	69	52	2	9	4	113	11	6	.446	.349
Jones, Brandon	L-R	6-1	210	12-10-83	.267	.267	.267	41	116	16	31	10	1	1	17	7	1	3	1	28	1	0	.397	.312
Jones, Chipper	B-R	6-4	210	4-24-72	.364	.394	.349	128	439	82	160	24	1	22	75	90	1	0	4	61	4	0	.574	.470
Kotchman, Casey	L-L	6-3	215	2-22-83	.237	.237	.237	43	152	18	36	4	1	2	20	18	4	0	1	16	0	0	.316	.331
Kotsay, Mark	L-L	6-0	205	12-2-75	.289	.253	.305	88	318	39	92	17	3	6	37	25	0	1	1	34	2	3	.418	.340
Lillibridge, Brent	R-R	5-11	190	9-18-83	.200	.171	.222	29	80	9	16	6	1	1	8	3	1	1	0	23	2	0	.338	.238
McCann, Brian	L-R	6-3	230	2-20-84	.301	.299	.301	145	509	68	153	42	1	23	87	57	4	0	3	64	5	0	.523	.373
Miller, Corky	R-R	6-1	245	3-18-76	.083	.120	.057	31	60	4	5	0	0	1	5	5	0	1	1	15	0	0	.133	.152
Norton, Greg	B-R	6-1	205	7-6-72	.246	.163	.279	111	171	27	42	10	0	7	31	31	0	0	0	40	0	0	.427	.361
Pena, Brayan	B-R	5-11	210	1-7-82	.286	.333	.273	14	14	3	4	1	0	0	0	1	0	0	0	2	0	0	.357	.333
Perry, Jason	L-R	6-0	200	8-18-80	.118	.000	.154	4	17	0	2	0	1	0	1	0	0	0	0	4	0	0	.235	.118
Prado, Martin	R-R	6-1	190	10-27-83	.320	.283	.349	78	228	36	73	18	4	2	33	21	1	2	2	29	3	1	.461	.377
Sammons, Clint	R-R	6-0	200	5-15-83	.148	.176	.135	23	54	2	8	0	0	1	4	5	0	0	0	12	0	0	.204	.220
Teixeira, Mark	B-R	6-3	220	4-11-80	.283	.269	.291	103	381	63	108	27	0	20	78	65	3	0	2	70	0	0	.512	.390

Pitching	B-T	HT	WT	DOB	W	L	ERA	G	GS	CG	SV	IP	H	R	ER	HR	BB	SO	AVG	vLH	vRH	K/9	BB/9
Acosta, Manny	B-R	6-4	170	5-1-81	3	5	3.57	46	0	0	3	53	48	25	21	7	26	31	.247	.280	.218	5.26	4.42
Bennett, Jeff	R-R	6-3	200	6-10-80	3	7	3.70	72	4	0	3	97	86	44	40	5	47	68	.243	.269	.228	6.29	4.35
Boyer, Blaine	R-R	6-3	215	7-11-81	2	6	5.88	76	0	0	1	72	73	51	47	10	25	67	.262	.271	.256	8.38	3.13
Bueno, Francisley	L-L	5-11	200	3-5-81	0	0	7.71	1	0	0	0	2	5	2	2	1	1	1	.417	.000	.417	3.86	3.86
Campillo, Jorge	R-R	6-1	225	8-10-78	8	7	3.91	39	25	1	0	159	158	74	69	18	38	107	.262	.249	.274	6.07	2.16
Carlyle, Buddy	L-R	6-3	210	12-21-77	2	0	3.59	45	0	0	0	63	52	26	25	5	26	59	.228	.247	.215	8.47	3.73
DeSalvo, Matt	R-R	6-0	180	9-11-80	0	0	31.50	2	0	0	0	2	11	7	7	0	2	2	.688	.700	.667	9.00	9.00
Dessens, Elmer	R-R	5-11	200	1-13-71	0	1	22.50	4	0	0	0	4	10	10	10	1	4	2	.500	.500	.500	4.50	9.00
Glavine, Tom	L-L	6-0	205	3-25-66	2	4	5.54	13	13	0	0	63	67	40	39	11	37	37	.288	.290	.287	5.26	5.26
Gonzalez, Mike	R-L	6-2	215	5-23-78	0	3	4.28	36	0	0	14	34	26	21	16	6	14	44	.210	.209	.196	11.76	3.74
Hampton, Mike	R-L	5-10	195	9-9-72	3	4	4.85	13	13	0	0	78	83	45	42	10	28	38	.281	.339	.267	4.38	3.23
Hudson, Tim	R-R	6-1	170	7-14-75	11	7	3.17	23	22	1	0	142	125	53	50	11	40	85	.239	.255	.223	5.39	2.54
James, Chuck	L-L	6-0	190	11-9-81	2	5	9.10	7	7	0	0	30	36	30	30	10	20	22	.310	.148	.360	6.67	6.07
Julio, Jorge	R-R	6-1	225	3-3-79	3	0	0.73	12	0	0	0	12	9	1	1	0	8	19	.200	.192	.211	13.86	5.84
Jurrjens, Jair	R-R	6-1	200	1-29-86	13	10	3.68	31	31	0	0	188	188	87	77	11	70	139	.260	.261	.260	6.64	3.35
Morton, Charlie	R-R	6-4	190	10-12-83	4	8	6.15	16	15	0	0	75	80	56	51	9	41	48	.273	.306	.245	5.79	4.94
Moylan, Peter	R-R	6-2	200	12-2-78	0	1	1.59	7	0	0	1	6	5	1	1	1	1	5	.217	.273	.167	7.94	1.59
Nunez, Vladimir	R-R	6-4	240	3-15-75	1	2	3.86	23	0	0	0	33	32	14	14	0	19	24	.260	.211	.303	6.61	5.23
Ohman, Will	L-L	6-2	210	8-13-77	4	1	3.68	83	0	0	1	59	51	27	24	3	22	53	.230	.200	.256	8.13	3.38
Parr, James	R-R	6-1	185	2-27-86	1	0	4.84	5	5	0	0	22	29	13	12	4	9	14	.315	.304	.326	5.64	3.63
Resop, Chris	R-R	6-3	215	11-4-82	0	1	5.89	16	0	0	0	18	16	12	12	2	10	13	.239	.192	.268	6.38	4.91
Reyes, Jo-Jo	L-L	6-2	230	11-20-84	3	11	5.81	23	22	0	0	113	134	77	73	18	52	78	.301	.255	.313	6.21	4.14
Ridgway, Jeff	R-L	6-3	210	8-17-80	1	0	3.72	10	0	0	0	10	7	4	4	3	1	8	.194	.133	.238	7.45	0.93
Ring, Royce	L-L	6-0	220	12-21-80	2	1	8.46	42	0	0	0	22	32	25	21	2	10	16	.333	.264	.419	6.45	4.03
Smoltz, John	R-R	6-3	220	5-15-67	3	2	2.57	6	5	0	0	28	25	8	8	2	8	36	.229	.226	.234	11.57	2.57
Soriano, Rafael	R-R	6-1	220	12-19-79	0	1	2.57	14	0	0	3	14	7	5	4	1	9	16	.149	.222	.103	10.29	5.79
Stockman, Phil	R-R	6-8	250	1-25-80	0	0	0.00	6	0	0	0	7	2	0	0	0	4	9	.087	.000	.125	11.05	4.91
Tavarez, Julian	L-R	6-2	195	5-22-73	1	3	3.89	36	0	0	0	35	42	20	15	5	14	35	.296	.284	.307	9.09	3.63
2-team total (7 Milwaukee)					1	4	4.71	43	0	0	0	42	55	30	22	5	19	45	—	—	—	9.64	4.07

Fielding

Catcher	PCT	G	PO	A	E	DP	PB
McCann	.991	138	879	70	9	9	7
Miller	.980	29	129	18	3	0	4
Sammons	1.000	22	106	3	0	0	3

First Base	PCT	G	PO	A	E	DP
Kotchman	1.000	41	367	23	0	39
Norton	.974	10	73	2	2	6
Prado	.993	17	123	11	1	10
Teixeira	.998	102	963	65	2	85

Second Base	PCT	G	PO	A	E	DP
Gotay	1.000	3	3	10	0	2
Infante	1.000	10	14	19	0	6
Johnson	.980	144	262	425	14	89

	PCT	G	PO	A	E	DP
Prado	.967	17	33	55	3	7

Third Base	PCT	G	PO	A	E	DP
Gotay	.882	10	2	13	2	0
Infante	.944	32	13	55	4	6
C. Jones	.958	115	64	235	13	21
Lillibridge	1.000	1	0	1	0	0
Prado	.982	24	9	46	1	3

Shortstop	PCT	G	PO	A	E	DP
Escobar	.974	126	193	396	16	78
Infante	.935	20	27	45	5	12
Lillibridge	.943	23	39	61	6	13
Prado	.800	2	2	2	1	1

Outfield	PCT	G	PO	A	E	DP
Anderson	.970	35	64	1	2	0
Blanco	.991	137	222	7	2	0
Diaz	.984	37	59	2	1	1
Francoeur	.987	152	282	14	4	2
Infante	.980	36	48	0	1	0
B. Jones	1.000	34	53	2	0	0
Kotsay	1.000	84	173	3	0	1
Norton	1.000	25	29	0	0	0
Perry	1.000	4	13	0	0	0
Prado	1.000	3	7	0	0	0
Resop	—	1	0	0	0	0

RICHMOND BRAVES   TRIPLE-A
INTERNATIONAL LEAGUE

Batting	B-T	HT	WT	DOB	AVG	vLH	vRH	G	AB	R	H	2B	3B	HR	RBI	BB	HBP	SH	SF	SO	SB	CS	SLG	OBP
Anderson, Josh	L-R	6-2	195	8-10-82	.314	.338	.304	121	494	77	155	25	4	4	40	30	6	8	3	57	42	7	.405	.358
Arnold, Derrick	R-R	5-10	165	8-3-83	.248	.289	.231	48	149	9	37	7	0	1	10	5	0	2	0	35	5	2	.315	.273
Bennett, Paul	R-R	5-10	180	9-6-83	.333	.500	.167	5	12	2	4	1	0	0	1	0	0	0	0	4	0	0	.417	.385
Borchard, Joe	B-R	6-4	230	11-25-78	.274	.355	.244	33	117	16	32	5	2	4	12	13	0	0	0	29	3	2	.453	.346
Canizares, Barbaro	R-R	6-3	210	11-21-79	.300	.355	.278	134	504	56	151	28	0	13	67	43	1	0	5	69	1	0	.433	.353
Cruz, Enrique	R-R	6-1	205	11-21-81	.213	.167	.229	72	230	13	49	14	0	3	23	11	0	2	2	59	0	2	.313	.247
Diaz, Matt	R-R	6-1	215	3-3-78	.167	.125	.250	4	12	0	2	0	0	0	1	1	0	0	0	3	0	0	.167	.231
Fasano, Sal	R-R	6-2	225	8-10-71	.193	.211	.188	26	83	6	16	3	1	2	9	5	4	0	0	22	0	0	.325	.272
Gorecki, Reid	R-R	6-1	180	12-22-80	.538	.667	.500	4	13	2	7	0	0	0	1	2	0	0	0	4	1	1	.538	.600
Gotay, Ruben	B-R	5-11	190	12-25-82	.250	.000	.333	3	12	1	3	0	0	0	1	1	1	0	0	2	0	0	.250	.357
Hernandez, Diory	R-R	6-0	185	4-8-84	.288	.264	.296	120	459	46	132	23	3	5	53	20	2	4	5	73	7	5	.383	.317
Holt, J.C.	L-R	5-9	175	12-8-82	.215	.182	.228	26	79	11	17	1	0	0	7	14	0	4	0	21	7	1	.228	.333
Infante, Omar	R-R	6-0	180	12-26-81	.364	—	.364	3	11	3	4	1	0	0	3	1	0	0	0	1	0	0	.455	.417
Jones, Brandon	L-R	6-1	210	12-10-83	.260	.250	.265	95	346	44	90	24	1	8	52	46	0	0	4	76	9	6	.405	.343
Jurich, Mark	L-L	5-10	195	12-29-80	.229	.148	.256	30	109	13	25	9	0	1	9	5	0	1	0	24	0	0	.339	.263
Lillibridge, Brent	R-R	5-11	190	9-18-83	.220	.202	.227	90	355	46	78	18	7	4	39	33	6	5	4	90	23	7	.344	.294
Loadenthal, Carl	L-L	5-11	185	12-27-81	.278	.358	.250	68	209	25	58	3	0	0	13	21	3	6	1	53	19	6	.292	.350
Miller, Corky	R-R	6-1	245	3-18-76	.339	.400	.326	16	56	9	19	3	0	5	12	9	2	0	0	11	0	1	.661	.448
Perry, Jason	L-R	6-0	200	8-18-80	.246	.190	.265	66	228	38	56	10	1	10	25	25	11	0	1	65	5	0	.430	.347
Phillips, Jason	R-R	6-1	220	9-27-76	.275	.306	.262	35	120	14	33	7	0	4	15	7	1	1	1	14	0	1	.433	.318
Rozema, Mike	L-R	6-2	180	9-16-81	.286	1.000	.000	4	7	0	2	0	0	0	2	0	1	0	2	0	0	0	.286	.300
Sammons, Clint	R-R	6-0	200	5-15-83	.237	.279	.224	81	278	23	66	18	0	1	22	21	2	3	1	60	7	2	.333	.295
Serrano, Ray	R-R	5-8	221	1-19-81	.294	.200	.333	8	17	3	5	0	0	1	2	0	1	0	0	2	0	1	.471	.368
Spiezio, Scott	B-R	6-2	215	9-21-72	.333	.444	.250	5	21	2	7	2	0	0	5	0	0	0	0	3	0	0	.429	.318
Taylor, Reggie	L-R	6-1	180	1-12-77	.248	.323	.230	53	153	17	38	5	3	2	11	11	0	1	1	28	5	3	.359	.297
Thorman, Scott	L-R	6-3	235	1-6-82	.251	.218	.262	101	387	47	97	22	2	19	56	19	0	1	4	83	7	1	.465	.283
Timmons, Wes	R-R	6-0	190	7-12-79	.251	.283	.240	81	239	39	60	18	0	2	26	45	12	4	1	25	12	0	.351	.394

Pitching	B-T	HT	WT	DOB	W	L	ERA	G	GS	CG	SV	IP	H	R	ER	HR	BB	SO	AVG	vLH	vRH	K/9	BB/9
Acosta, Manny	B-R	6-4	170	5-1-81	0	0	0.00	4	3	0	0	4	4	0	0	0	2	4	.267	.333	.000	9.82	4.91
Basner, Ryan	R-R	6-3	230	7-15-81	2	2	8.02	25	1	0	0	46	61	41	41	8	21	33	.323	.404	.242	6.46	4.11
Bueno, Francisley	L-L	5-11	200	3-5-81	2	6	5.23	19	14	0	0	84	100	51	49	8	29	59	.297	.324	.283	6.30	3.09
Campillo, Jorge	R-R	6-1	225	8-10-78	0	0	0.00	1	1	0	0	4	5	0	0	0	0	4	.263	.273	.250	8.31	0.00
Carlyle, Buddy	L-R	6-3	210	12-21-77	0	0	7.04	2	2	0	0	8	11	7	6	0	3	7	.355	.278	.462	8.22	3.52
DeSalvo, Matt	R-R	6-0	180	9-11-80	2	11	4.87	34	8	0	0	92	98	58	50	7	55	91	.279	.293	.265	8.87	5.36
Gamble, Jerome	R-R	6-2	200	4-5-80	0	5	7.88	8	6	0	0	32	38	29	28	5	14	25	.292	.234	.377	7.03	3.94
Gonzalez, Mike	R-L	6-2	215	5-23-78	1	0	1.50	5	0	0	1	6	5	1	1	0	1	8	.227	.300	.167	12.00	1.50
Hampton, Mike	R-L	5-10	195	9-9-72	0	1	1.42	2	2	0	0	6	6	1	1	0	3	6	.250	.200	.286	8.53	4.26
James, Chuck	L-L	6-0	190	11-9-81	5	5	2.92	16	15	0	0	86	76	34	28	5	39	74	.237	.290	.210	7.71	4.07
Julio, Jorge	R-R	6-1	225	3-3-79	1	2	2.04	38	0	0	13	40	33	15	9	1	23	45	.231	.265	.183	10.21	5.22
Lawrence, Brian	R-R	6-0	195	5-14-76	6	6	5.55	16	15	0	0	86	113	55	53	4	19	54	.318	.332	.300	5.65	1.99
Lerew, Anthony	L-R	6-3	220	10-28-82	1	4	4.14	9	8	0	0	37	43	24	17	5	20	22	.295	.280	.321	5.35	4.86
Morton, Charlie	R-R	6-4	190	10-12-83	5	2	2.05	13	12	0	0	79	51	20	18	0	27	72	.181	.195	.167	8.20	3.08
Moss, Damian	R-L	6-0	185	11-24-76	5	9	3.92	41	15	0	0	96	105	57	42	8	62	86	.282	.250	.300	8.03	5.79
Nelson, Brad	R-R	6-3	200	1-5-82	2	3	6.06	20	5	0	1	36	50	27	24	3	12	26	.333	.301	.373	6.56	3.03
Nix, Michael	R-R	6-5	235	5-21-83	1	1	3.07	11	0	0	0	15	14	6	5	0	8	16	.246	.290	.192	9.82	4.91
Nunez, Vladimir	R-R	6-4	240	3-15-75	3	1	3.45	37	0	0	3	57	54	23	22	1	28	61	.251	.235	.265	9.58	4.40
Parr, James	R-R	6-1	185	2-27-86	5	3	3.23	10	9	0	0	56	49	20	20	4	14	44	.233	.268	.184	7.11	2.26
Resop, Chris	R-R	6-3	215	11-4-82	2	0	1.50	9	2	0	0	18	14	4	3	0	12	22	.212	.303	.121	11.00	6.00
Reyes, Jo-Jo	L-L	6-2	230	11-20-84	1	1	2.31	8	8	0	0	39	31	11	10	2	16	38	.218	.231	.211	8.77	3.69
Ridgway, Jeff	R-L	6-3	210	8-17-80	4	0	5.47	44	0	0	4	53	67	38	32	3	26	57	.315	.301	.323	9.74	4.44
Ring, Royce	L-L	6-0	220	12-21-80	0	1	3.00	11	0	0	0	9	5	3	3	0	7	7	.167	.238	.000	7.00	7.00
Rouwenhorst, Jonathon	L-L	6-1	180	9-25-79	9	10	5.27	41	14	1	1	113	140	76	66	9	44	78	.320	.265	.351	6.23	3.51
Schreiber, Zach	R-R	6-1	220	6-24-82	2	2	2.97	34	0	0	6	39	29	13	13	6	26	29	.209	.250	.177	6.64	5.95
Shibilo, Andy	R-R	6-7	220	9-16-76	1	1	6.37	32	0	0	1	41	53	30	29	3	29	39	.315	.321	.310	8.56	6.37

	B-T	HT	WT	DOB	W	L	ERA	G	GS	CG	SV	IP	H	R	ER	HR	BB	SO	AVG	vLH	vRH	K/9	BB/9
Stockman, Phil	R-R	6-8	250	1-25-80	1	1	2.10	19	0	0	2	30	15	7	7	3	18	26	.147	.133	.158	7.80	5.40
Williamson, Scott	R-R	6-0	195	2-17-76	2	1	6.61	15	1	0	0	16	18	12	12	3	5	20	.277	.308	.256	11.02	2.76

Fielding

Catcher
Catcher	PCT	G	PO	A	E	DP	PB
Fasano	.994	23	147	15	1	1	2
Miller	1.000	14	101	12	0	2	3
Phillips	.995	25	206	5	1	0	4
Sammons	.986	80	591	35	9	4	14
Serrano	1.000	3	20	2	0	0	0

First Base
First Base	PCT	G	PO	A	E	DP
Canizares	.987	66	502	40	7	50
Jurich	1.000	1	7	0	0	0
Miller	1.000	1	8	1	0	0
Phillips	1.000	4	38	1	0	4
Spiezio	1.000	1	9	0	0	1
Thorman	.990	75	534	58	6	58
Timmons	1.000	4	40	2	0	3

Second Base
Second Base	PCT	G	PO	A	E	DP
Arnold	.980	27	33	64	2	19
Bennett	1.000	4	7	13	0	1
Cruz	.938	21	25	51	5	7
Gotay	1.000	2	2	7	0	0
Hernandez	.969	52	106	146	8	39
Holt	.982	26	45	63	2	14
Rozema	1.000	2	1	1	0	0
Spiezio	1.000	1	1	2	0	0
Timmons	.949	19	30	45	4	10

Third Base
Third Base	PCT	G	PO	A	E	DP
Arnold	1.000	1	1	2	0	1
Cruz	.939	39	22	40	4	4
Gotay	1.000	1	2	2	0	0
Hernandez	.927	37	23	66	7	9
Rozema	1.000	1	1	2	0	0
Spiezio	1.000	2	1	1	0	0
Thorman	1.000	13	1	25	0	2
Timmons	.948	58	28	82	6	6

Shortstop
Shortstop	PCT	G	PO	A	E	DP
Arnold	.928	16	30	47	6	14
Cruz	1.000	6	3	5	0	1

	PCT	G	PO	A	E	DP
Hernandez	.993	31	59	89	1	23
Lillibridge	.953	90	141	242	19	46
Rozema	.833	1	5	0	1	0

Outfield
Outfield	PCT	G	PO	A	E	DP
Anderson	.987	119	293	8	4	2
Borchard	.964	30	51	2	2	0
Cruz	.857	3	5	1	1	0
Diaz	1.000	2	2	0	0	0
Gorecki	1.000	4	9	0	0	0
Infante	1.000	3	1	5	0	1
Jones	.979	88	178	5	4	1
Jurich	1.000	23	39	0	0	0
Loadenthal	.977	62	82	4	2	1
Perry	.981	57	99	3	2	1
Taylor	.971	42	66	2	2	0
Thorman	1.000	8	19	1	0	0

MISSISSIPPI BRAVES   DOUBLE-A

SOUTHERN LEAGUE

Batting	B-T	HT	WT	DOB	AVG	vLH	vRH	G	AB	R	H	2B	3B	HR	RBI	BB	HBP	SH	SF	SO	SB	CS	SLG	OBP
Arnold, Derrick	R-R	5-10	165	8-3-83	.151	.133	.158	18	53	4	8	1	2	0	4	6	2	0	2	15	1	0	.245	.254
Bennett, Paul	R-R	5-11	180	9-6-83	.182	.250	.148	48	132	13	24	4	1	0	10	10	3	1	0	39	1	1	.227	.255
Boscan, J.C.	R-R	6-2	215	12-26-79	.235	.159	.272	79	255	26	60	13	0	2	29	34	4	4	0	49	0	0	.310	.334
Britton, Phillip	R-R	6-0	180	9-25-84	.000	.000	.000	1	4	0	0	0	0	0	0	0	0	0	2	0	1	0	.000	.000
Cabrera, Willie	R-R	5-11	185	8-3-86	.269	.667	.217	9	26	4	7	1	1	0	2	2	0	0	0	3	0	2	.385	.321
Camarena, Jose	R-R	5-10	170	5-29-84	.244	.322	.214	62	213	17	52	9	0	3	25	11	1	3	0	47	1	1	.329	.284
Creek, Greg	L-R	6-3	225	8-29-82	.268	.277	.265	119	351	49	94	20	7	6	55	42	7	0	2	74	0	3	.416	.356
Davis, Quentin	L-R	5-10	170	3-7-83	.191	.196	.189	92	199	19	38	6	0	5	22	10	3	5	2	47	10	4	.296	.238
Diaz, Matt	R-R	6-1	215	3-3-78	.231	.300	.188	7	26	5	6	0	0	1	4	2	0	0	0	5	1	0	.346	.286
Francoeur, Jeff	R-R	6-4	220	1-8-84	.538	.833	.286	3	13	3	7	0	1	0	2	1	0	0	0	2	0	0	.692	.571
Gorecki, Reid	R-R	6-1	180	12-22-80	.292	.302	.285	63	240	51	70	9	0	10	43	31	1	2	1	47	16	4	.454	.377
Guzman, Javier	B-R	6-0	170	5-4-82	.253	.260	.250	108	387	50	98	15	4	4	35	19	8	12	4	49	8	4	.344	.299
Hernandez, Diory	R-R	6-0	185	4-8-84	.286	.267	.298	22	77	8	22	3	1	2	8	6	1	0	1	8	1	4	.429	.341
Hicks, Brandon	R-R	6-2	200	9-14-85	.241	.333	.194	16	54	9	13	3	1	1	7	7	1	1	1	17	0	0	.389	.333
Holt, J.C.	L-R	5-9	175	12-8-82	.285	.304	.275	96	393	54	112	17	9	3	45	39	2	3	2	68	22	11	.397	.351
Jurich, Mark	L-L	5-10	195	12-29-80	.219	.128	.255	46	137	14	30	8	1	3	18	15	1	0	2	39	0	1	.358	.297
Ka'aihue, Kala	R-R	6-2	230	3-29-85	.274	.281	.270	126	376	63	103	23	2	14	61	88	7	0	4	119	0	4	.457	.417
Kotsay, Mark	L-L	6-0	205	12-2-75	.333	.400	.308	5	18	4	6	1	0	1	0	0	0	0	0	4	0	0	.389	.368
Loadenthal, Carl	L-L	5-11	185	12-27-81	.227	.233	.224	26	97	8	22	3	0	1	2	6	0	2	0	20	4	2	.289	.272
Lundahl, Chad	R-R	6-2	190	8-18-84	1.000	1.000	.000	1	1	0	1	0	0	0	1	0	0	0	0	0	0	0	1.000	1.000
Marcial, Robert	R-R	5-10	170	4-21-84	.167	—	.167	4	6	1	1	0	0	0	0	0	0	0	0	1	0	0	.167	.286
Perry, Jason	L-R	6-0	200	8-18-80	.314	.245	.352	38	137	34	43	11	2	13	41	23	5	0	3	44	1	0	.708	.423
Pope, Van	R-R	6-0	200	2-26-84	.260	.239	.270	99	350	47	91	21	1	4	50	35	3	2	2	54	8	5	.360	.331
Prado, Martin	R-R	6-1	190	10-27-83	.263	.143	.333	5	19	2	5	2	0	0	3	3	0	0	0	2	0	0	.368	.364
Rozema, Mike	L-R	6-2	180	9-16-81	.182	.000	.333	4	11	1	2	0	1	0	1	0	0	0	0	1	0	0	.364	.182
Schafer, Jordan	L-L	6-1	200	9-4-86	.269	.196	.311	84	297	46	80	18	6	10	51	49	3	0	0	88	12	5	.471	.378
Serrano, Ray	R-R	5-8	221	1-19-81	.063	.250	.000	7	16	2	1	0	0	0	0	0	0	0	0	2	2	0	.063	.063
Young, Matt	L-R	5-8	175	10-3-82	.289	.250	.310	135	491	74	142	16	11	3	50	68	9	7	2	62	30	12	.385	.384

Pitching	B-T	HT	WT	DOB	W	L	ERA	G	GS	CG	SV	IP	H	R	ER	HR	BB	SO	AVG	vLH	vRH	K/9	BB/9
Basner, Ryan	R-R	6-3	230	7-15-81	2	0	5.56	14	0	0	0	23	26	18	14	5	10	14	.289	.375	.190	5.56	3.97
Bush, Paul	R-R	6-1	175	10-5-79	0	1	3.24	12	0	0	0	17	10	6	6	2	7	21	.175	.250	.156	11.34	3.78
Cuevas, Jairo	R-R	6-2	215	1-24-84	0	2	7.50	3	3	0	0	12	21	10	10	1	6	8	.382	.483	.269	6.00	4.50
Dumesnil, Bryan	R-L	6-3	210	9-19-83	2	1	4.41	15	0	0	1	16	15	8	8	1	10	14	.242	.214	.250	7.71	5.51
Evans, Dustin	R-R	6-3	200	9-24-84	1	5	10.91	8	7	0	0	31	55	39	38	2	18	21	.390	.400	.382	6.03	5.17
Gamble, Jerome	R-R	6-2	200	4-5-80	3	5	4.09	23	7	0	0	66	58	32	30	5	25	51	.235	.275	.203	6.95	3.41
Glavine, Tom	L-L	6-0	205	3-25-66	1	1	3.60	1	1	0	0	5	4	3	2	0	1	1	.222	—	.222	1.80	1.80
Gonzalez, Mike	R-L	6-2	215	5-23-78	0	0	0.00	4	0	0	0	5	7	0	0	0	0	4	.350	.500	.313	7.20	0.00
Gunderson, Kevin	R-L	5-10	165	9-16-84	2	2	4.74	36	0	0	3	44	46	23	23	2	14	22	.289	.204	.333	4.53	2.89
Hampton, Mike	R-L	5-10	195	9-9-72	0	0	3.86	2	2	0	0	7	7	3	3	1	1	6	.269	.500	.250	7.71	1.29
Hanson, Tommy	R-R	6-6	210	8-28-86	8	4	3.03	18	18	1	0	98	70	39	33	9	41	114	.197	.233	.166	10.47	3.77
Heath, Deunte	R-R	6-4	215	8-8-85	4	5	5.56	13	11	0	0	66	76	50	41	5	32	46	.284	.262	.303	6.24	4.34
Jung, Sung Ki	R-R	5-10	161	8-6-79	2	2	4.41	49	0	0	6	63	63	37	31	0	24	59	.253	.306	.226	8.38	3.41
Lyman, Jeff	R-R	6-3	215	1-14-87	0	0	0.00	1	1	0	0	5	2	0	0	0	2	3	.133	.125	.143	5.40	3.60
Marek, Stephen	L-R	6-2	200	9-3-83	1	2	3.21	10	0	0	1	14	12	5	5	1	6	11	.261	.182	.286	7.07	3.86
Medlen, Kris	B-R	5-10	175	10-7-85	7	8	3.52	36	17	0	1	120	121	47	47	8	27	120	.268	.236	.290	8.98	2.02
Nelson, Brad	R-R	6-3	200	1-5-82	1	0	4.47	23	1	0	1	46	53	30	23	2	14	30	.286	.295	.278	5.83	2.72

Nix, Michael	R-R	6-5	235	5-21-83	4	3	6.34	36	0	0	1	50	52	42	35	4	36	41	.271	.268	.273	7.43	6.52
Parr, James	R-R	6-1	185	2-27-86	8	4	3.69	18	17	0	0	95	87	40	39	9	37	81	.246	.217	.277	7.67	3.51
Payano, Nelson	L-L	6-2	180	11-13-82	3	2	3.95	27	0	0	0	43	41	22	19	1	22	36	.253	.288	.229	7.48	4.57
2-team total (14 West Tenn)					4	3	4.16	41	0	0	0	67	69	36	31	3	42	65	—	—	—	8.73	5.64
Redmond, Todd	R-R	6-3	210	5-17-85	13	5	3.52	28	27	0	0	166	164	72	65	17	33	133	.257	.288	.234	7.20	1.79
Sencion, Carlos	L-L	6-6	170	11-17-84	6	4	4.72	25	12	0	0	76	73	40	40	6	44	63	.255	.217	.267	7.43	5.19
Smith, Danny	L-L	6-5	250	9-9-83	1	7	6.16	14	12	0	0	61	81	45	42	5	34	47	.328	.383	.301	6.90	4.99
Smoltz, John	R-R	6-3	220	5-15-67	0	0	0.00	1	0	0	0	1	1	0	0	0	0	0	.250	.250	—	0.00	0.00
Soriano, Rafael	R-R	6-1	220	12-19-79	0	0	0.00	2	1	0	0	2	1	0	0	0	1	2	.167	.200	.000	9.00	4.50
Valdez, Luis	R-R	6-2	195	5-5-84	4	3	2.76	55	0	0	28	65	48	30	20	3	36	77	.208	.170	.240	10.61	4.96
Venters, Jonny	L-L	6-3	188	3-20-85	1	0	1.00	3	2	0	0	9	10	2	1	0	5	7	.270	.250	.276	7.00	5.00

Fielding

Catcher	PCT	G	PO	A	E	DP	PB
Boscan	.997	78	588	62	2	6	11
Britton	.875	1	7	0	1	0	0
Camarena	.994	61	449	34	3	6	8
Serrano	1.000	2	14	0	0	0	0

First Base	PCT	G	PO	A	E	DP
Bennett	1.000	2	10	1	0	2
Creek	.994	49	314	23	2	26
Ka'aihue	.987	97	727	85	11	77

Second Base	PCT	G	PO	A	E	DP
Arnold	1.000	2	1	2	0	0
Bennett	.986	19	33	40	1	5
Guzman	1.000	3	5	3	0	0
Hernandez	.976	11	16	24	1	7
Holt	.982	96	151	235	7	50
Marcial	1.000	1	4	1	0	0
Prado	1.000	2	6	5	0	2

	PCT	G	PO	A	E	DP
Rozema	1.000	2	3	3	0	1
Young	.947	10	19	17	2	6

Third Base	PCT	G	PO	A	E	DP
Arnold	1.000	6	3	10	0	0
Bennett	.947	8	6	12	1	2
Creek	.948	29	18	37	3	4
Hernandez	1.000	1	1	0	0	0
Pope	.949	98	73	169	13	15
Prado	1.000	1	1	0	0	0
Rozema	1.000	1	0	1	0	0

Shortstop	PCT	G	PO	A	E	DP
Arnold	.962	8	10	15	1	6
Bennett	.875	8	10	11	3	3
Guzman	.942	102	152	235	24	45
Hernandez	.920	10	15	31	4	3
Hicks	.986	16	25	45	1	8
Holt	1.000	1	0	1	0	0

	PCT	G	PO	A	E	DP
Prado	1.000	1	1	4	0	0

Outfield	PCT	G	PO	A	E	DP
Arnold	1.000	1	3	0	0	0
Cabrera	1.000	7	13	0	0	0
Creek	—	1	0	0	0	0
Davis	.983	56	113	1	2	0
Diaz	1.000	6	7	0	0	0
Francoeur	1.000	3	8	0	0	0
Gorecki	.969	59	123	4	4	1
Jurich	1.000	32	50	4	0	0
Kotsay	1.000	3	1	0	0	0
Loadenthal	1.000	26	59	3	0	0
Perry	.988	38	75	5	1	1
Prado	1.000	1	2	1	0	0
Schafer	1.000	82	164	6	0	1
Young	.989	123	251	9	3	4

MYRTLE BEACH PELICANS

HIGH CLASS A

CAROLINA LEAGUE

Batting	B-T	HT	WT	DOB	AVG	vLH	vRH	G	AB	R	H	2B	3B	HR	RBI	BB	HBP	SH	SF	SO	SB	CS	SLG	OBP
Alvarez, Roberto	R-R	5-11	190	8-30-83	.107	.000	.120	7	28	3	3	1	0	0	1	2	0	0	0	6	0	0	.143	.167
Anderson, Chris	R-R	6-0	210	10-27-85	.000	.000	.000	1	3	0	0	0	0	0	0	0	0	0	0	0	0	0	.000	.000
Arnold, Derrick	R-R	5-10	165	8-3-83	.290	.500	.276	9	31	2	9	2	1	0	1	4	0	0	0	8	2	1	.419	.371
Bennett, Paul	R-R	5-11	180	9-6-83	.189	.250	.182	12	37	2	7	1	0	0	3	2	0	1	0	13	1	1	.216	.231
Britton, Phillip	R-R	6-0	180	9-25-84	.246	.255	.244	84	297	30	73	10	1	6	26	11	3	3	3	42	5	2	.347	.277
Cabrera, Willie	R-R	5-11	185	8-3-86	.290	.295	.289	116	469	86	136	32	3	16	78	35	7	0	5	51	6	3	.473	.345
Campbell, Eric	R-R	6-0	195	8-6-85	.255	.279	.246	88	330	56	84	15	1	19	67	50	7	0	3	58	4	1	.479	.362
Flowers, Tyler	R-R	6-4	245	1-24-86	.288	.312	.281	122	413	72	119	32	1	17	88	98	5	0	4	102	8	7	.494	.427
Gress, Randy	R-R	6-3	180	12-6-84	.169	.250	.155	27	83	6	14	4	0	1	9	3	1	0	0	29	0	1	.253	.207
Hernandez, Gorkys	R-R	6-0	175	9-7-87	.264	.257	.266	100	406	75	107	23	6	5	42	48	6	4	3	79	20	4	.387	.348
Heyward, Jason	L-L	6-4	220	8-9-89	.182	.167	.188	7	22	3	4	2	0	0	4	2	0	0	1	4	0	0	.273	.240
Hicks, Brandon	R-R	6-2	200	9-14-85	.234	.258	.225	93	342	68	80	23	2	19	56	45	8	3	2	122	14	3	.480	.335
Jones, Travis	R-R	5-9	190	11-10-85	.248	.254	.246	128	463	81	115	29	3	16	78	77	6	2	2	107	17	8	.428	.361
Lee, C.J.	R-R	6-3	195	8-12-84	.250	—	.250	1	4	0	1	0	0	0	0	0	0	0	0	2	0	0	.250	.250
Lundahl, Chad	R-R	6-2	190	8-18-84	.224	.133	.256	19	58	6	13	1	0	1	9	1	0	1	0	12	1	1	.293	.237
Marcial, Robert	R-R	5-10	170	4-21-84	.262	.286	.254	53	145	22	38	9	1	0	15	20	3	4	1	28	4	3	.345	.361
Mejia, Ernesto	R-R	6-6	190	12-2-85	.274	.325	.259	131	519	93	142	47	5	21	93	28	13	0	5	139	2	4	.505	.324
Owings, Jon	R-R	6-4	195	4-4-85	.275	.260	.280	123	425	65	117	29	5	16	62	37	5	2	6	95	9	5	.480	.336
Powell, Brandon	L-R	6-0	191	8-15-80	.225	.111	.258	33	120	16	27	5	0	3	11	10	2	0	0	31	4	1	.350	.295
Rodriguez, Concepcion	R-R	6-2	170	9-19-86	.280	.289	.277	108	379	56	106	26	5	11	56	33	4	2	4	66	9	6	.462	.340
Silva, Yohan	B-R	5-11	175	1-30-85	.211	.226	.203	31	95	20	20	6	1	1	6	11	1	0	1	22	2	1	.326	.296
White, Will	B-R	5-10	170	9-4-85	.222	.000	.286	3	9	2	2	0	1	0	0	1	0	1	0	3	1	0	.444	.300

Pitching	B-T	HT	WT	DOB	W	L	ERA	G	GS	CG	SV	IP	H	R	ER	HR	BB	SO	AVG	vLH	vRH	K/9	BB/9
Bennett, Jeff	R-R	6-3	200	6-10-80	0	0	0.00	4	4	0	0	4	3	0	0	0	0	3	.231	.000	.300	6.75	0.00
Broadway, Mike	R-R	6-5	190	3-30-87	2	2	3.40	22	0	0	2	50	37	23	19	3	21	33	.199	.198	.200	5.90	3.75
Butts, Brett	R-R	6-1	190	4-24-86	3	4	4.16	36	2	0	10	76	62	40	35	9	24	66	.220	.193	.245	7.85	2.85
Chapman, Jaye	R-R	6-0	180	5-22-87	4	2	3.34	13	1	0	0	30	30	13	11	3	12	25	.259	.240	.273	7.58	3.64
Cofield, Kyle	R-R	6-5	190	1-23-87	8	10	3.26	24	22	0	0	116	113	54	42	2	66	80	.260	.289	.241	6.21	5.12
Diamond, Scott	L-L	6-3	190	7-30-86	12	2	2.79	17	15	1	0	100	95	42	31	6	28	85	.245	.190	.261	7.65	2.52
Dumesnil, Bryan	R-L	6-3	210	9-19-83	3	0	1.18	32	0	0	12	38	24	11	5	1	20	53	.175	.103	.204	12.55	4.74
Evans, Dustin	R-R	6-3	200	9-24-84	2	2	2.45	6	0	0	0	11	8	6	3	1	2	9	.195	.111	.261	7.36	1.64
Fellman, Nick	L-R	6-3	190	8-29-85	4	4	3.67	44	0	0	8	54	55	31	22	8	21	51	.263	.324	.230	8.50	3.50
Gearrin, Cory	R-R	6-3	200	4-14-86	3	1	5.32	17	0	0	0	24	19	14	14	2	21	36	.218	.194	.235	13.69	7.99
Glavine, Tom	L-L	6-0	205	3-25-66	0	0	2.25	1	1	0	0	4	3	1	1	0	1	4	.214	.500	.100	9.00	2.25
Gunderson, Kevin	R-L	5-10	165	9-16-84	1	0	1.04	15	0	0	10	17	13	3	2	0	6	20	.197	.143	.222	10.38	3.12
Hampton, Mike	R-L	5-10	195	9-9-72	0	0	0.00	1	1	0	0	5	5	0	0	0	0	6	.278	.000	.333	10.80	0.00
Hanson, Tommy	R-R	6-6	210	8-28-86	3	1	0.90	7	7	0	0	40	15	6	4	0	11	49	.116	.135	.104	11.03	2.48
Heath, Deunte	R-R	6-4	215	8-8-85	9	3	3.11	14	14	1	0	84	78	40	29	5	41	53	.247	.231	.256	5.68	4.39

Name	B-T	HT	WT	DOB	W	L	ERA	G	GS	CG	SV	IP	H	R	ER	HR	BB	SO	AVG	vLH	vRH	K/9	BB/9
Hyde, Lee	R-L	6-2	185	2-14-85	1	0	0.00	2	0	0	0	2	1	1	0	0	2	0	.200	.500	.000	0.00	9.00
Kimbrel, Craig	R-R	5-11	205	5-28-88	0	0	0.00	2	0	0	0	4	5	0	0	0	1	3	.385	.667	.143	7.36	2.45
Lopez, Gonzalo	R-R	6-2	175	10-6-83	2	3	6.32	16	9	0	0	47	48	35	33	7	26	47	.265	.284	.254	9.00	4.98
Lyman, Jeff	R-R	6-3	215	1-14-87	3	6	4.59	32	7	0	0	84	75	50	43	5	46	82	.240	.242	.238	8.75	4.91
Reynoso, Ryne	L-R	6-2	215	3-15-85	10	6	3.36	27	26	0	0	131	121	58	49	16	37	105	.247	.234	.259	7.20	2.54
Rivas, Carlos	L-L	6-3	160	1-3-85	6	4	5.20	25	7	1	0	73	75	54	42	8	32	54	.263	.282	.257	6.69	3.96
Rohrbough, Cole	L-L	6-3	205	5-23-87	2	2	3.41	5	5	1	0	32	27	16	12	0	8	28	.233	.130	.258	7.96	2.27
Sencion, Carlos	L-L	6-6	170	11-17-84	0	0	1.50	3	0	0	0	12	5	2	2	0	4	15	.132	.000	.152	11.25	3.00
Tejeda, Ferdin	R-R	6-0	185	9-15-82	2	1	2.43	28	0	0	4	41	33	13	11	3	9	29	.220	.181	.256	6.42	1.99
Venters, Jonny	L-L	6-3	188	3-20-85	1	2	4.08	5	3	0	1	18	21	12	8	0	7	7	.300	.133	.345	3.57	3.57
Villa, Kelvin	L-L	5-10	170	12-14-85	2	1	5.52	9	1	0	0	15	18	11	9	2	9	13	.305	.300	.308	7.98	5.52
Vines, Chris	R-R	6-5	215	2-26-85	4	1	3.98	20	13	0	2	86	86	44	38	6	21	77	.258	.227	.285	8.06	2.20
Wilson, Tyler	L-L	6-1	210	7-11-86	2	1	3.24	24	0	0	2	33	27	16	12	1	17	46	.218	.231	.212	12.42	4.59

Fielding

Catcher	PCT	G	PO	A	E	DP	PB
Anderson	1.000	1	9	0	0	0	0
Britton	.993	58	404	54	3	2	7
Flowers	.984	86	681	76	12	5	11
Lundahl	.882	4	7	8	2	0	
Marcial	.935	15	17	41	4	5	
White	1.000	2	5	12	0	2	
Hicks	.955	91	131	249	18	44	
Lundahl	.925	13	16	21	3	3	
Marcial	.956	23	30	56	4	6	

First Base	PCT	G	PO	A	E	DP
Alvarez	1.000	1	5	0	0	0
Bennett	.974	3	36	2	1	4
Flowers	.833	1	4	1	1	0
Gress	1.000	8	49	7	0	4
Marcial	1.000	1	5	0	0	1
Mejia	.980	127	1061	93	23	79
Powell	1.000	1	9	1	0	2

Second Base	PCT	G	PO	A	E	DP
Gress	1.000	1	3	1	0	0
Jones	.963	124	184	316	19	58

Third Base	PCT	G	PO	A	E	DP
Arnold	1.000	5	3	10	0	0
Bennett	1.000	6	4	3	0	0
Campbell	.938	84	61	167	15	16
Gress	.900	3	2	7	1	1
Lundahl	1.000	2	3	2	0	1
Marcial	.872	14	13	28	6	4
Powell	.892	31	28	55	10	6

Shortstop	PCT	G	PO	A	E	DP
Arnold	.885	5	11	12	3	1
Bennett	.500	2	2	1	3	0
Gress	.887	16	23	32	7	7

Outfield	PCT	G	PO	A	E	DP
Alvarez	1.000	3	3	1	0	0
Cabrera	.972	103	131	8	4	1
Hernandez	.981	93	247	10	5	2
Heyward	1.000	5	8	0	0	0
Lee	—	1	0	0	0	0
Marcial	1.000	2	1	0	0	0
Owings	.972	96	166	6	5	1
Rodriguez	.989	96	170	4	2	2
Silva	.987	31	70	4	1	1
White	1.000	1	2	1	0	1

ROME BRAVES   LOW CLASS A
SOUTH ATLANTIC LEAGUE

Batting	B-T	HT	WT	DOB	AVG	vLH	vRH	G	AB	R	H	2B	3B	HR	RBI	BB	HBP	SH	SF	SO	SB	CS	SLG	OBP
Anderson, Chris	R-R	6-0	210	10-27-85	.221	.286	.206	27	77	5	17	6	0	0	6	11	0	1	0	36	0	0	.299	.318
Berres, David	L-R	6-1	185	12-16-86	.241	.205	.248	77	249	25	60	7	0	1	21	42	2	2	1	56	6	5	.281	.354
Coe, Adam	R-R	6-0	190	6-7-88	.255	.250	.256	105	392	42	100	28	1	7	45	15	6	5	1	96	6	7	.385	.292
Dominguez, Javier	B-R	6-1	150	7-14-85	.207	.152	.224	39	140	10	29	4	1	1	8	11	2	0	0	33	6	4	.271	.275
Fisher, Michael	B-R	6-2	188	3-22-85	.253	.177	.274	123	446	50	113	20	2	4	38	31	7	6	1	94	10	7	.334	.311
Freeman, Freddie	L-R	6-5	220	9-12-89	.316	.245	.334	130	491	70	155	33	7	18	95	46	3	0	7	74	15	3	.521	.378
Gilmore, Jon	R-R	6-3	195	8-23-88	.186	.280	.156	27	102	6	19	1	0	0	4	2	0	0	0	16	1	0	.196	.202
Gress, Randy	R-R	6-3	180	12-6-84	.100	.118	.091	19	50	2	5	2	0	0	3	2	0	0	1	16	1	0	.140	.132
Heyward, Jason	L-L	6-4	220	8-9-89	.323	.351	.315	120	449	88	145	27	6	11	52	49	3	0	7	74	15	3	.483	.388
Johnson, Benji	R-R	6-1	195	7-17-86	.218	.205	.221	69	243	26	53	7	0	4	17	19	0	1	4	50	3	1	.296	.271
Johnson, Cody	L-R	6-2	195	8-18-88	.252	.239	.255	127	468	62	118	26	1	26	89	40	0	0	6	177	8	3	.479	.307
Kennelly, Matt	R-R	6-1	180	3-21-89	.457	.600	.400	10	35	4	16	5	0	0	10	2	1	2	2	8	0	0	.600	.475
Kramer, Matt	R-R	6-3	215	5-7-86	.286	.000	.667	2	7	0	2	0	0	0	0	0	0	0	0	2	0	0	.286	.286
Lee, C.J.	R-R	6-3	195	8-12-84	.235	.343	.206	95	332	37	78	16	4	2	27	19	3	0	1	82	10	9	.325	.282
Lundahl, Chad	R-R	6-2	190	8-18-84	.248	.288	.238	68	254	25	63	14	1	4	27	5	1	5	2	39	1	1	.358	.263
Miles, Cole	R-R	5-8	165	3-24-87	.239	.188	.246	118	443	58	106	9	5	1	15	35	1	13	0	74	28	8	.289	.296
Rodriguez, Concepcion	R-R	6-2	170	9-19-86	.267	.300	.260	19	60	8	16	2	0	3	13	12	0	3		16	1	2	.450	.373
Shehan, Chris	R-R	6-0	205	5-5-87	.357	.250	.400	4	14	2	5	1	1	0	5	0	2	0	0	1	3	0	.571	.438
Shults, Stephen	R-R	6-2	190	12-27-86	.204	.167	.209	15	49	4	10	1	0	3	6	1	0	0	0	13	0	0	.408	.220
Silva, Yohan	B-R	5-11	175	1-30-85	.204	.250	.200	19	54	11	11	4	0	2	4	16	1	0	0	13	2	1	.389	.394
Sime, Samuel	R-R	6-2	180	4-20-87	.211	.204	.213	76	261	33	55	10	1	4	20	11	1	1	2	57	10	2	.303	.244
Sumoza, Luis	R-R	6-0	170	7-15-88	.211	.500	.176	5	19	3	4	2	0	0	3	2	0	0	0	4	0	0	.316	.286

Pitching	B-T	HT	WT	DOB	W	L	ERA	G	GS	CG	SV	IP	H	R	ER	HR	BB	SO	AVG	vLH	vRH	K/9	BB/9
Barrett, Eric	L-L	6-3	180	12-19-86	1	7	5.85	24	14	0	0	85	80	65	55	7	78	92	.244	.190	.261	9.78	8.29
Beck, Casey	R-R	6-1	215	3-28-87	1	4	4.75	30	0	0	0	42	41	26	22	2	27	38	.255	.305	.225	8.21	5.83
Broadway, Mike	R-R	6-5	190	3-30-87	0	3	4.96	15	0	0	0	33	43	28	18	2	6	21	.309	.358	.279	5.79	1.65
Bullard, Adam	R-R	6-6	225	2-10-87	0	1	11.88	4	0	0	0	8	15	11	11	0	6	3	.415	.313	.480	3.24	6.48
Castro, Yeliar	R-R	6-3	180	12-3-87	5	6	4.98	34	5	0	1	72	72	49	40	4	39	77	.260	.271	.252	9.58	4.85
Chapman, Jaye	R-R	6-0	180	5-22-87	0	0	3.72	8	0	0	0	19	21	8	8	1	8	14	.276	.323	.244	6.52	3.72
Clemens, Paul	R-R	6-4	170	2-14-88	0	1	9.00	1	1	0	0	4	7	5	4	0	2	0	.412	.500	.333	0.00	4.50
Cordier, Erik	R-R	6-3	214	2-25-86	1	2	5.18	9	9	0	0	40	51	25	23	3	21	31	.317	.379	.274	6.98	4.73
Diamond, Scott	L-L	6-3	190	7-30-86	3	1	3.08	9	9	0	0	53	47	20	18	2	11	38	.240	.273	.227	6.49	1.88
Evarts, Steve	L-L	6-3	180	10-13-87	2	1	1.50	3	3	0	0	18	15	5	3	0	1	14	.234	.091	.264	7.00	0.50
Figueroa, Steven	R-R	6-0	215	5-1-88	1	0	11.12	3	0	0	0	6	7	7	7	1	5	2	.304	.500	.200	3.18	7.94
Gearrin, Cory	R-R	6-3	200	4-14-86	3	2	2.82	19	0	0	1	22	19	11	7	1	15	36	.218	.333	.125	14.51	6.04
Gonzalez, Raul	R-R	6-2	155	7-12-85	0	0	12.79	3	0	0	0	6	12	9	9	2	4	0	.462	.286	.526	0.00	5.68
Hampton, Mike	R-L	5-10	195	9-9-72	0	0	9.00	1	1	0	0	3	8	4	3	0	0	5	.444	.750	.357	15.00	0.00
Kimbrel, Craig	R-R	5-11	205	5-28-88	2	0	0.71	10	0	0	0	4	13	6	1	0	4	26	.140	.111	.160	18.47	2.84
Ladd, Tim	L-L	6-3	175	11-26-88	1	0	6.23	4	0	0	0	3	6	5	4	2	3	6	.250	.250	.250	6.23	8.31
Locke, Jeff	L-L	6-2	180	11-20-87	5	12	4.06	25	24	1	0	140	150	75	63	6	38	113	.269	.303	.256	7.28	2.45
Lopez, Rodrigo	R-R	6-1	185	12-14-75	0	1	40.50	1	1	0	0	2	8	9	9	2	2	1	.615	.500	.667	4.50	9.00

	B-T	HT	WT	DOB	W	L	ERA	G	GS	CG	SV	IP	H	R	ER	HR	BB	SO	AVG	vLH	vRH	K/9	BB/9
Mehlich, Michael	R-R	6-2	180	9-5-87	2	3	3.02	21	2	0	1	51	48	20	17	2	16	57	.249	.333	.195	10.13	2.84
Ortegano, Jose	L-L	6-1	145	8-5-87	2	5	4.62	17	15	0	0	86	90	49	44	2	25	83	.275	.266	.278	8.72	2.63
Osuna, Edgar	L-L	6-1	165	11-25-87	10	5	3.38	30	14	2	5	125	122	53	47	9	31	135	.253	.286	.243	9.69	2.23
Palica, Tommy	L-L	6-3	215	7-21-87	6	7	3.68	36	1	0	8	66	51	30	27	3	24	83	.210	.281	.184	11.32	3.27
Pruneda, Benino	R-R	5-9	170	8-8-88	4	4	2.83	41	0	0	3	57	53	19	18	2	23	73	.243	.246	.242	11.46	3.61
Reid, Rico	R-R	5-11	220	9-24-88	0	0	18.00	2	0	0	0	3	6	6	6	1	4	2	.429	.500	.400	6.00	12.00
Rivas, Carlos	L-L	6-3	160	1-3-85	0	0	1.02	9	0	0	1	18	14	3	2	1	9	18	.219	.267	.204	9.17	4.58
Rodgers, Chad	L-L	6-3	185	11-23-87	2	10	4.53	20	16	0	0	91	96	54	46	5	28	77	.267	.292	.258	7.59	2.76
Rohrbough, Cole	L-L	6-3	205	5-23-87	3	4	4.94	13	12	0	0	58	55	37	32	3	31	76	.248	.327	.224	11.73	4.78
Smoltz, John	R-R	6-3	220	5-15-67	0	0	0.00	2	1	0	0	3	1	0	0	0	0	4	.091	.000	.167	12.00	0.00
Sullivan, Richard	L-L	6-3	235	4-14-87	2	2	2.80	8	8	0	0	35	40	15	11	0	4	27	.282	.294	.278	6.88	1.02
Thompson, Jacob	R-R	6-6	215	11-19-86	0	0	1.80	1	1	0	0	5	3	1	1	1	1	3	.158	.000	.231	5.40	1.80
Timms, Matt	R-R	6-6	220	1-18-87	1	1	7.50	9	0	0	1	18	17	15	15	1	20	21	.250	.344	.167	10.50	10.00

Fielding

Catcher	PCT	G	PO	A	E	DP	PB
Anderson	.990	27	172	24	2	3	6
Dominguez	.992	37	346	34	3	1	16
B. Johnson	.989	64	505	49	6	5	12
Kennelly	.991	10	100	7	1	0	0
Kramer	1.000	2	26	2	0	1	0
Lundahl	.900	1	6	3	1	1	0

First Base	PCT	G	PO	A	E	DP
Coe	1.000	5	31	2	0	1
Freeman	.988	122	1055	63	14	85
Gress	1.000	6	26	2	0	0
Lundahl	1.000	14	72	6	0	5
Shults	1.000	1	4	0	0	0

Second Base	PCT	G	PO	A	E	DP
Coe	.970	19	21	43	2	4

	PCT	G	PO	A	E	DP
Fisher	.934	23	39	46	6	10
Gress	1.000	1	2	5	0	1
Lundahl	.900	3	5	13	2	6
Miles	.976	96	124	245	9	41
Sime	—	1	0	0	0	0

Third Base	PCT	G	PO	A	E	DP
Coe	.925	55	25	98	10	11
Gilmore	.891	24	12	45	7	4
Shults	1.000	1	1	2	0	0
Sime	.899	60	40	94	15	3

Shortstop	PCT	G	PO	A	E	DP
Fisher	.935	74	102	202	21	35
Gress	.917	9	16	28	4	5
Lundahl	.938	52	68	129	13	22
Miles	1.000	4	4	6	0	2

Sime	.800	2	1	3	1	0

Outfield	PCT	G	PO	A	E	DP
Berres	1.000	72	129	7	0	3
Dominguez	1.000	2	4	0	0	0
Heyward	.961	104	215	9	9	2
C. Johnson	.946	109	117	5	7	0
Lee	.963	93	180	4	7	0
Lundahl	—	1	0	0	0	0
Miles	1.000	9	7	0	0	0
Rodriguez	1.000	13	14	1	0	0
Shehan	1.000	2	2	0	0	0
Shults	1.000	7	5	0	0	0
Silva	1.000	18	28	2	0	1
Sumoza	1.000	4	10	0	0	0

DANVILLE BRAVES   ROOKIE
APPALACHIAN LEAGUE

Batting	B-T	HT	WT	DOB	AVG	vLH	vRH	G	AB	R	H	2B	3B	HR	RBI	BB	HBP	SH	SF	SO	SB	CS	SLG	OBP
Anderson, Chris	R-R	6-0	210	10-27-85	.100	—	.100	5	10	1	1	1	0	0	2	3	0	0	0	4	0	0	.200	.308
Berres, David	L-R	6-1	185	12-16-86	.300	.000	.316	6	20	4	6	0	0	1	5	6	0	1	0	4	0	1	.450	.462
Campusano, Albaro	R-R	5-11	200	12-14-86	.291	.400	.262	50	189	27	55	9	3	0	19	22	2	2	0	28	5	2	.370	.371
Elkerson, Mike	R-R	6-2	195	10-2-85	.228	.150	.247	29	101	18	23	7	1	1	11	8	3	0	1	35	0	1	.347	.301
Fuller, Chais	R-R	5-11	190	8-11-84	.295	.324	.288	49	173	26	51	17	1	3	20	11	7	5	3	35	1	1	.457	.356
Gilmore, Jon	R-R	6-3	195	8-23-88	.337	.489	.305	67	258	27	87	23	0	4	31	13	1	0	5	41	0	3	.473	.365
Gress, Randy	R-R	6-3	180	12-6-84	.417	.333	.429	8	24	8	10	4	1	0	5	1	0	0	0	8	1	1	.667	.440
Kennelly, Matt	R-R	6-1	180	3-21-89	.246	.133	.270	44	167	14	41	9	0	4	25	8	0	1	1	37	0	2	.371	.278
Miles, Kuyaunnis	L-R	5-11	175	5-15-87	.225	.385	.197	26	89	10	20	2	1	1	8	3	1	0	2	32	2	0	.303	.253
Moody, Shayne	R-R	6-0	200	10-24-84	.272	.140	.303	58	228	29	62	11	1	0	15	21	4	3	0	40	0	4	.329	.344
Parra, Camilo	R-R	6-3	170	11-9-86	.208	.368	.151	20	72	6	15	3	0	0	6	4	2	1	0	33	1	1	.250	.269
Redden, Ray	R-R	6-2	200	1-3-84	.185	.600	.091	11	27	0	5	0	0	0	1	3	0	0	0	6	0	0	.185	.267
Rodriguez, Gerardo	R-R	6-1	195	10-20-87	.253	.179	.269	58	221	31	56	11	3	13	49	17	3	0	4	67	1	1	.507	.310
Shehan, Chris	R-R	6-0	205	5-5-87	.277	.200	.292	65	235	34	65	11	3	5	22	22	6	1	3	53	6	2	.413	.350
Shults, Stephen	R-R	6-2	190	12-27-86	.375	1.000	.286	2	8	1	3	0	0	1	2	1	0	0	0	3	0	0	.750	.444
Sucre, Jesus	R-R	6-0	200	4-30-88	.182	.172	.184	44	154	14	28	2	0	3	15	7	1	1	0	24	1	1	.253	.222
Ware, L.V.	R-R	5-10	185	3-18-87	.272	.340	.255	65	243	42	66	11	6	3	33	11	10	0	5	57	13	1	.403	.323
White, Will	B-R	5-10	170	9-4-85	.241	.286	.235	28	58	13	14	2	0	0	2	6	6	1	0	17	6	1	.276	.371

Pitching	B-T	HT	WT	DOB	W	L	ERA	G	GS	CG	SV	IP	H	R	ER	HR	BB	SO	AVG	vLH	vRH	K/9	BB/9
Beachey, Brandon	R-R	6-2	210	9-3-86	2	0	2.25	6	0	0	0	12	12	5	3	1	2	16	.261	.222	.286	12.00	1.50
Bullard, Adam	R-R	6-6	225	2-10-87	1	1	4.09	11	0	0	0	22	26	15	10	1	7	24	.286	.185	.328	9.82	2.86
Clemens, Paul	R-R	6-4	170	2-14-88	3	3	3.39	12	8	0	1	58	57	33	22	6	18	57	.252	.207	.278	8.79	2.78
Delgado, Randall	R-R	6-3	165	2-9-90	3	8	3.13	14	14	0	0	69	63	32	24	5	30	81	.249	.250	.248	10.57	3.91
Figueroa, Steven	R-R	6-0	215	5-1-88	0	0	0.00	2	0	0	0	1	6	6	0	0	7	4	.261	.143	.313	9.95	2.84
Francis, David	R-R	6-1	200	2-8-88	5	3	2.35	11	8	0	0	54	38	18	14	2	17	69	.203	.233	.184	11.57	2.85
Himpsl, Derick	L-L	6-4	240	6-4-86	0	1	6.86	15	0	0	0	20	21	19	15	0	23	26	.269	.350	.241	11.90	10.53
Hodges, Casey	R-R	6-2	195	3-29-85	4	5	2.47	12	12	1	0	69	57	25	19	3	16	56	.225	.235	.219	7.27	2.08
Hoover, J.J.	R-R	6-3	215	8-13-87	1	0	0.00	2	0	0	0	5	4	0	0	1	6	.235	.250	.222	11.57	1.93
Kent, Steve	L-L	6-0	170	5-8-89	0	3	3.68	12	3	0	0	29	25	13	12	1	9	31	.231	.303	.200	9.51	2.76
Kimbrel, Craig	R-R	5-11	205	5-28-88	1	2	0.47	12	0	0	6	19	6	1	1	0	10	27	.076	.111	.051	12.79	4.74
Ladd, Tim	L-L	5-11	175	11-2-85	0	1	4.91	8	2	0	0	18	19	12	10	1	12	14	.264	.250	.268	6.87	5.89
McMillan, Clayton	L-L	6-3	180	9-19-86	0	2	2.42	18	0	0	5	22	21	8	6	1	9	32	.239	.227	.242	12.90	3.63
Paulino, Angelo	R-R	6-4	190	12-15-86	2	2	3.38	15	7	0	1	48	39	23	18	2	18	60	.217	.234	.204	11.25	3.38
Railsback, Cody	R-R	6-4	175	6-3-87	5	1	4.70	14	1	0	1	38	49	27	20	4	11	41	.295	.282	.305	9.63	2.58
Reid, Rico	R-R	5-11	220	9-24-88	0	1	2.45	11	1	0	0	22	20	7	6	2	10	22	.235	.222	.245	9.00	4.09
Rojas, Junior	R-R	6-2	210	4-8-87	0	0	1.59	2	0	0	0	6	5	1	1	1	1	5	.091	.222	7.94	1.59	
Small, Matt	R-R	6-3	185	12-29-87	1	2	2.55	13	0	0	6	18	13	5	5	1	6	27	.200	.160	.225	13.75	3.06
Sullivan, Richard	L-L	6-3	235	4-14-87	2	1	1.40	4	4	0	0	19	10	4	3	1	0	22	.149	.143	.150	10.24	0.00
Teheran, Julio	R-R	6-2	150	1-27-91	1	2	6.60	6	6	0	0	15	18	12	11	2	4	17	.305	.310	.300	10.20	2.40
Thompson, Jacob	R-R	6-6	215	11-19-86	0	0	1.93	2	1	0	0	5	5	1	1	0	1	5	.211	.111	.300	9.64	1.93
Timms, Matt	R-R	6-6	220	1-18-87	1	1	2.45	7	0	0	0	11	11	3	3	0	2	18	.262	.333	.222	14.73	1.64

Fielding

Catcher	PCT	G	PO	A	E	DP	PB
Anderson	1.000	4	22	3	0	0	0
Kennelly	.997	29	256	45	1	3	2
Redden	.978	7	38	6	1	0	1
Sucre	.992	34	331	36	3	2	6

First Base	PCT	G	PO	A	E	DP
Fuller	.990	11	96	4	1	9
Rodriguez	.978	58	455	29	11	38

Second Base	PCT	G	PO	A	E	DP
Campusano	.979	47	78	108	4	24

	PCT	G	PO	A	E	DP
Fuller	.980	12	24	25	1	5
Gress	.935	6	16	13	2	5
Moody	1.000	1	1	1	0	0
White	.909	8	8	12	2	0

Third Base	PCT	G	PO	A	E	DP
Fuller	.875	7	4	10	2	0
Gilmore	.896	62	33	96	15	6

Shortstop	PCT	G	PO	A	E	DP
Fuller	.887	17	19	44	8	8
Gress	1.000	2	2	8	0	3

	PCT	G	PO	A	E	DP
Moody	.928	49	50	130	14	22

Outfield	PCT	G	PO	A	E	DP
Berres	1.000	6	7	3	0	1
Elkerson	1.000	21	11	2	0	1
Fuller	—	1	0	0	0	0
Miles	.969	22	31	0	1	0
Parra	.933	18	27	1	2	1
Shehan	.975	64	77	1	2	1
Ware	.977	65	122	6	3	1
White	1.000	13	16	1	0	0

GCL BRAVES   ROOKIE

GULF COAST LEAGUE

Batting	B-T	HT	WT	DOB	AVG	vLH	vRH	G	AB	R	H	2B	3B	HR	RBI	BB	HBP	SH	SF	SO	SB	CS	SLG	OBP
Adair, Travis	L-R	5-10	175	12-23-87	.289	.236	.310	51	197	27	57	6	2	0	20	19	1	4	0	42	10	3	.340	.355
Barnett, Tyler	L-R	5-9	175	2-22-86	.181	.167	.186	33	94	10	17	2	1	0	4	7	1	0	1	26	1	2	.223	.243
Brooks, Robert	R-R	6-1	180	5-29-88	.329	.413	.294	47	155	30	51	7	5	3	20	15	12	0	1	27	12	1	.497	.426
Culver, Calvin	R-R	6-2	220	10-7-88	.252	.214	.265	58	218	24	55	14	4	2	25	13	0	0	2	35	4	2	.381	.292
Elorriaga-Matra, Daniel	R-R	6-0	185	12-28-88	.350	.250	.375	17	60	11	21	5	0	1	11	1	1	0	1	6	1	0	.483	.365
Feliz, Anthony	R-R	6-2	195	10-7-87	.278	.340	.247	48	144	17	40	9	0	2	14	1	3	0	0	23	6	1	.382	.297
Hanson, Jake	R-R	6-0	180	11-20-89	.246	.295	.228	54	171	36	42	6	0	3	17	26	8	0	0	51	6	1	.333	.371
Henry, Rashod	R-R	5-11	175	8-26-88	.163	.167	.161	23	49	4	8	0	2	0	8	3	2	1	0	11	5	3	.245	.241
Hiller, Layton	R-R	6-3	220	5-18-88	.203	.256	.181	44	133	13	27	7	1	5	18	10	8	0	1	36	1	0	.383	.296
Johnson, Benji	R-R	6-1	195	7-17-86	.333	.000	.500	1	3	0	1	1	0	0	0	0	0	0	0	1	0	0	.667	.333
Kramer, Matt	R-R	6-3	215	5-7-86	.207	.400	.167	13	29	3	6	2	0	1	4	2	1	0	1	2	0	0	.379	.273
Maddox, Chad	R-R	5-11	190	4-5-86	.252	.250	.252	44	151	19	38	16	0	4	22	4	4	1	1	27	2	1	.437	.288
Marval, Osman	B-R	6-1	185	11-26-86	.213	.200	.217	36	75	9	16	2	1	0	5	6	2	1	0	12	1	0	.267	.289
Parra, Camilo	R-R	6-3	170	11-9-86	.255	.250	.257	31	94	18	24	3	0	3	11	3	2	1	1	24	6	1	.383	.290
Redden, Ray	R-R	6-2	200	1-3-84	.000	.000	.000	3	4	0	0	0	0	0	0	1	0	0	0	2	0	0	.000	.200
Schlehuber, Braeden	R-R	6-3	190	1-7-88	.268	.324	.244	41	123	18	33	4	0	0	11	10	8	0	1	27	7	2	.301	.359
Shimabukuro, Ryohei	L-R	6-0	205	9-1-89	.253	.222	.263	47	150	14	38	6	0	1	19	8	4	0	1	18	0	0	.313	.307
Silva, Yohan	B-R	5-11	175	1-30-85	.143	.000	.200	3	7	1	1	1	0	0	0	2	0	0	0	3	1	0	.286	.333
Voelkel, Ryan	R-R	6-6	235	2-6-88	.194	.150	.214	33	62	6	12	2	0	2	10	5	4	0	1	20	0	3	.323	.307

Pitching	B-T	HT	WT	DOB	W	L	ERA	G	GS	CG	SV	IP	H	R	ER	HR	BB	SO	AVG	vLH	vRH	K/9	BB/9
Avilan, Luis	L-L	6-2	165	7-19-89	2	0	2.58	10	4	0	0	38	31	14	11	2	15	49	.217	.286	.205	11.50	3.52
Barrett, Eric	L-L	6-3	180	12-19-86	0	0	0.00	1	0	0	0	1	0	0	0	0	0	1	.000	.000	.000	9.00	0.00
Bush, Paul	R-R	6-1	175	10-5-79	0	1	1.74	5	3	0	0	10	5	3	2	0	2	13	.135	.091	.154	11.32	1.74
Clemens, Paul	R-R	6-4	170	2-14-88	1	0	0.00	1	0	0	0	3	1	0	0	0	0	2	.111	1.000	.000	6.00	0.00
Cordier, Erik	R-R	6-2	214	2-25-86	0	0	0.00	3	2	0	0	5	4	0	0	0	1	5	.211	.000	.222	9.00	1.80
Cuevas, Jairo	R-R	6-2	215	1-24-84	1	0	2.00	4	3	0	0	9	7	2	2	0	5	5	.226	.000	.318	5.00	5.00
Delgado, Dimaster	L-L	6-2	180	3-3-89	5	1	4.31	11	3	0	0	40	51	22	19	2	9	39	.297	.341	.282	8.85	2.04
DeVall, Brett	R-L	6-3	215	1-8-90	0	0	0.93	4	3	0	0	10	4	1	1	0	2	7	.125	.167	.115	6.52	1.86
Evans, Dustin	R-R	6-3	200	9-24-84	0	0	3.00	2	1	0	0	3	3	1	1	0	1	2	.300	.000	.375	6.00	3.00
Farrell, Kyle	R-R	6-4	210	5-6-89	0	1	4.58	10	6	0	0	35	43	22	18	1	17	28	.293	.273	.304	7.13	4.33
Gustafson, Tim	R-R	6-3	185	12-29-84	0	1	3.60	3	3	0	0	5	5	4	2	0	2	3	.238	.167	.267	5.40	3.60
Hampton, Mike	R-L	5-10	195	9-9-72	0	0	0.00	2	2	0	0	6	4	0	0	0	0	4	.182	.000	.200	6.35	0.00
Hung, Chen-En	R-R	6-1	188		4	1	2.30	14	0	0	0	27	23	14	7	3	14	26	.223	.286	.191	8.56	4.61
Hyde, Lee	R-L	6-2	185	2-14-85	0	1	4.32	6	3	0	0	8	4	5	4	0	7	11	.138	.100	.158	11.88	7.56
Lagua, Eligio	R-R	6-4	180	3-29-87	0	1	4.12	16	0	0	4	20	18	10	9	1	10	24	.243	.258	.233	10.98	4.58
Lerew, Anthony	L-R	6-3	220	10-28-82	0	1	5.40	5	5	0	0	12	11	9	7	0	6	8	.234	.125	.290	6.17	4.63
Lopez, Daniel	R-R	6-1	185	5-16-87	2	4	2.57	18	0	0	3	28	31	13	8	1	13	26	.277	.240	.287	8.36	4.18
Lopez, Rodrigo	R-R	6-1	185	12-14-75	0	0	0.00	2	2	0	0	3	2	0	0	0	0	4	.182	.250	.000	12.00	0.00
Murillo, Eliezer	R-R	6-4	200	10-21-88	0	3	5.06	16	0	0	2	21	22	14	12	0	13	16	.272	.440	.196	6.75	5.48
Oberholtzer, Brett	L-L	6-2	190	7-1-89	4	1	2.89	10	0	0	0	37	34	16	12	1	10	32	.241	.250	.238	7.71	2.41
Ortegano, Jose	L-L	6-1	145	8-5-87	0	0	0.00	2	2	0	0	3	1	0	0	0	0	4	.100	.250	.000	12.00	0.00
Rasmus, Cory	R-R	6-1	220	11-6-87	0	0	0.00	4	1	0	0	6	4	4	0	1	1	9	.174	.273	.083	14.29	1.59
Reid, Rico	R-R	5-11	220	9-24-88	0	1	1.00	4	0	0	0	9	7	1	1	2	8		.237	.143	.292	8.00	2.00
Rodriguez, Santos	L-L	6-5	180	1-2-88	1	2	2.79	14	0	0	5	29	16	12	9	0	13	45	.155	.217	.138	13.97	4.03
Santiago, Jose	R-R	6-4	180	8-1-81	0	0	4.91	6	4	0	0	11	10	6	6	0	3	11	.227	.250	.208	9.00	2.45
Schreiber, Zach	R-R	6-1	220	6-24-82	0	0	0.00	1	0	0	0	1	0	0	0	0	0	0	.000	.000	.000	0.00	0.00
Spruill, Zeke	B-R	6-4	184	9-11-89	7	1	2.93	10	3	0	0	40	42	16	13	1	8	32	.268	.259	.272	7.20	1.80
Stovall, Tyler	L-L	6-1	180	12-27-89	1	1	6.30	7	3	0	0	20	20	15	14	1	14	29	.250	.294	.238	13.05	6.30
Surinach, Julio	R-R	6-1	157	7-29-88	2	2	6.28	10	1	0	0	29	35	27	20	2	20	28	.294	.256	.313	8.79	6.28
Tejeda, Ferdin	R-R	6-1	185	9-15-82	0	1	1.80	3	0	0	0	5	2	2	1	0	0	4	.111	.000	.182	7.20	0.00
Venters, Jonny	L-L	6-3	188	3-20-85	0	0	4.70	4	4	0	0	8	10	6	4	1	2	10	.313	.333	.304	11.74	2.35
Wohlever, T.J.	L-L	5-11	200	1-10-87	1	0	2.53	10	0	0	0	11	8	3	3	0	16	6	.211	.143	.226	5.06	13.50

Fielding

Catcher	PCT	G	PO	A	E	DP	PB
Elorriaga-Matra	.990	12	94	5	1	1	0
Johnson	.875	1	7	0	1	0	0
Kramer	.976	12	77	6	2	0	4

	PCT	G	PO	A	E	DP	PB
Marval	1.000	19	82	10	0	1	4
Redden	1.000	1	1	0	0	0	0
Schlehuber	.992	36	244	17	2	0	5

First Base	PCT	G	PO	A	E	DP
Marval	1.000	3	3	0	0	0
Shimabukuro	.986	43	261	17	4	21
Voelkel	.990	32	188	11	2	16

Second Base	PCT	G	PO	A	E	DP
Adair	1.000	5	7	6	0	2
Barnett	.968	17	29	31	2	4
Brooks	.930	42	60	99	12	16
Redden	1.000	1	0	1	0	0
Schlehuber	—	1	0	0	0	0

Third Base	PCT	G	PO	A	E	DP
Adair	1.000	1	2	0	0	0

	PCT	G	PO	A	E	DP
Hanson	.842	53	24	93	22	7
Marval	1.000	8	4	7	0	0

Shortstop	PCT	G	PO	A	E	DP
Adair	.872	44	53	110	24	20
Barnett	.883	15	24	29	7	7
Brooks	.667	2	2	4	3	1

Outfield	PCT	G	PO	A	E	DP
Culver	.991	55	108	5	1	0
Feliz	.956	46	62	3	3	0
Henry	1.000	3	2	0	0	0
Hiller	1.000	28	32	2	0	0
Maddox	.981	37	52	0	1	0
Parra	.946	28	33	2	2	1
Silva	1.000	3	2	0	0	0

DSL BRAVES

ROOKIE

DOMINICAN SUMMER LEAGUE

Batting	B-T	HT	WT	DOB	AVG	vLH	vRH	G	AB	R	H	2B	3B	HR	RBI	BB	HBP	SH	SF	SO	SB	CS	SLG	OBP
Alcantara, Aris	R-R	6-2	170	5-5-90	.231	.125	.246	20	65	15	15	4	0	1	3	7	3	1	0	15	1	0	.338	.333
Arias, Yuliecer	R-R	6-1	170	5-17-89	.241	.250	.239	42	141	22	34	7	1	0	21	14	5	2	0	26	4	1	.305	.331
Betancourt, Christian	R-R	6-2	175	9-2-91	.267	.273	.266	34	116	12	31	6	3	0	17	11	1	0	3	25	1	0	.371	.328
Blanco, Elys	B-R	5-11	160	4-8-89	.304	.214	.323	51	158	41	48	7	5	0	24	45	7	1	1	34	24	8	.411	.474
Cadette, Victor	R-R	6-0	180	12-6-90	.236	.289	.224	51	203	25	48	12	1	2	17	9	2	0	1	41	4	3	.335	.274
Contreras, Luis	L-L	6-0	170	3-31-91	.254	.292	.246	46	138	26	35	4	3	0	22	18	3	2	2	25	2	2	.326	.348
Cordero, Tomy	R-R	5-11	175	11-21-90	.243	.381	.224	46	173	40	42	11	3	1	33	32	5	0	1	55	20	2	.358	.374
De Los Santos, Ramon	R-R	6-0	190	12-26-89	.224	.111	.241	21	67	11	15	1	0	1	8	6	0	0	0	16	0	0	.284	.288
Epifano, Erick	R-R	6-1	160	3-31-90	.255	.313	.244	32	94	18	24	2	1	0	9	12	0	1	0	18	3	0	.298	.340
Falcon, Daniel	R-R	6-1	220	12-27-88	.296	.263	.305	45	179	42	53	8	3	9	40	18	4	0	2	41	9	1	.525	.369
Garibaldi, Abdiel	B-R	6-1	185	2-8-89	.230	.333	.212	21	61	16	14	4	1	0	7	12	6	1	1	12	0	0	.328	.400
Guzman, Luis	R-R	6-2	195	4-17-90	.286	.000	.333	4	7	2	2	0	0	0	1	1	1	0	0	2	0	0	.286	.444
Linares, Donell	R-R	6-0	190	10-28-83	.266	.333	.250	21	79	16	21	6	0	2	11	12	3	0	3	7	0	1	.418	.371
Marte, Felix	R-R	6-1	180	11-14-90	.146	.000	.156	21	48	9	7	2	1	1	6	7	1	0	1	19	0	0	.292	.263
Nunez, Anthony	R-R	6-3	205	2-2-90	.160	.143	.163	19	50	4	8	0	0	0	3	8	0	1	0	15	0	0	.160	.276
Ochoa, Emilio	R-R	6-0	185	9-18-89	.243	.222	.250	15	37	5	9	1	0	0	7	1	3	1	0	10	1	1	.270	.317
Odreman, Alberto	R-R	6-3	210	3-12-89	.286	.355	.275	58	213	38	61	13	1	10	41	32	8	0	1	52	0	1	.498	.398
Puello, Ramon	R-R	6-3	195	8-31-88	.240	.241	.240	53	200	25	48	11	2	1	22	5	4	1	1	49	2	2	.330	.271
Ramos, Abdiel	R-R	6-3	195	8-6-91	.205	.273	.194	26	78	10	16	2	0	0	5	9	2	0	0	24	0	2	.231	.303
Rivera, Wilson	R-R	6-1	195	10-30-89	.245	.056	.286	31	102	18	25	5	0	1	15	11	2	1	0	33	2	0	.324	.330
Sanchez, Edison	R-R	6-4	195	11-1-90	.121	.190	.105	37	107	24	13	3	1	1	12	25	9	3	0	45	1	0	.196	.333
Theran, Miguel	R-R	5-10	175	1-5-90	.000	.000	.000	3	7	0	0	0	0	0	0	1	0	0	0	5	0	0	.000	.125
Vizcaya, Johnder	R-R	6-0	180	2-18-89	.300	.000	.316	12	40	5	12	0	4	0	7	2	0	0	0	8	1	0	.500	.417

Pitching	B-T	HT	WT	DOB	W	L	ERA	G	GS	CG	SV	IP	H	R	ER	HR	BB	SO	AVG	vLH	vRH	K/9	BB/9
Alvarez, Danilo	R-R	6-0	210	1-14-90	3	2	2.90	7	4	0	0	31	24	15	10	1	9	28	.205	.200	.207	8.13	2.61
Cervantes, Hugo	R-R	6-2	195	10-6-90	0	0	9.00	1	0	0	0	1	0	1	1	0	3	0	.000	.000	.000	0.00	27.00
De Leon, Melquin	R-R	6-4	185	12-25-88	5	3	4.06	20	7	0	3	62	52	32	28	3	28	64	.228	.354	.178	9.29	4.06
de Luna, Luis	R-R	6-4	200	6-10-89	3	2	6.23	15	13	0	0	61	68	46	42	1	29	50	.285	.369	.239	7.42	4.30
Escobar, Reidy	R-R	6-4	170	11-27-89	3	3	5.45	21	0	0	1	38	32	28	23	0	24	33	.215	.106	.265	7.82	5.68
Estevez, Wilton	R-R	6-1	175	5-30-87	1	1	2.77	7	0	0	0	13	12	5	4	0	7	7	.240	.350	.167	4.85	4.85
Javier, Rafael	R-R	6-4	205	9-20-88	2	2	4.22	18	9	0	0	49	42	28	23	1	23	47	.225	.194	.240	8.63	4.22
Martinez, Luis	L-L	6-2	165	2-5-91	0	1	6.00	3	1	0	0	3	4	4	2	0	2	3	.267	.000	.308	9.00	6.00
Milander, Garlton	R-R	6-0	175	11-2-89	2	3	9.97	18	0	0	0	22	36	32	24	2	25	10	.367	.387	.358	4.15	10.38
Mirabal, Leiberth	L-L	6-0	180	11-5-89	0	2	6.21	17	1	0	0	33	44	26	23	0	12	25	.317	.267	.323	6.75	3.24
Mora, Edison	R-R	6-1	195	10-20-88	6	5	1.76	24	2	0	2	61	50	23	12	0	11	42	.214	.221	.211	6.16	1.61
Pacheco, Ronan	L-L	6-6	170	7-29-88	2	3	3.86	14	11	0	0	54	46	31	23	0	38	48	.247	.250	.247	8.05	6.37
Paulino, Jorge	R-R	6-2	200	7-8-89	1	1	10.80	8	5	0	0	12	10	15	14	0	23	16	.238	.250	.233	12.34	17.74
Roman, Milton	R-R	6-1	175	5-16-89	1	1	3.43	20	0	0	4	39	32	22	15	1	20	28	.224	.224	.223	6.41	4.58
Soriano, Rafael	R-R	6-1	220	12-19-79	0	1	0.00	2	0	0	2	3	1	0	0	0	2	3	.333	.333	.333	9.00	0.00
Torres, Carlos	R-R	6-2	205	5-13-90	0	3	8.33	18	2	0	1	27	33	28	25	0	16	13	.300	.286	.307	4.33	5.33
Vargas, Isaac	L-L	6-2	170	4-27-89	1	3	7.17	22	3	0	0	43	39	39	34	2	31	39	.248	.167	.263	8.23	6.54
Vega, Manuel	R-R	6-2	195	9-14-89	2	4	4.64	13	10	0	0	54	47	33	28	2	25	30	.229	.321	.197	4.97	4.14

Fielding

Catcher	PCT	G	PO	A	E	DP	PB
Betancourt	.976	32	207	36	6	1	14
De Los Santos	.973	21	133	9	4	0	4
Garibaldi	1.000	10	45	10	0	0	4
Guzman	1.000	3	14	1	0	0	3
Nunez	1.000	19	111	20	0	0	0

First Base	PCT	G	PO	A	E	DP
Falcon	.990	10	91	7	1	6
Garibaldi	1.000	7	41	5	0	2
Linares	1.000	2	25	1	0	1
Odreman	.994	54	445	26	3	24

Second Base	PCT	G	PO	A	E	DP
Blanco	.937	20	41	48	6	7
Cordero	.950	42	88	101	10	13

	PCT	G	PO	A	E	DP
Epifano	.933	12	21	21	3	3
Marte	.667	1	1	1	1	1
Sanchez	.000	1	0	0	1	0
Theran	1.000	2	3	3	0	1
Vizcaya	.900	2	5	4	1	1

Third Base	PCT	G	PO	A	E	DP
Cordero	1.000	1	1	1	0	0
Epifano	—	1	0	0	0	0
Falcon	.930	14	15	38	4	2
Linares	.982	13	17	39	1	3
Marte	.857	2	2	4	1	0
Sanchez	.945	35	40	80	7	6
Vizcaya	.853	9	10	19	5	2

Shortstop	PCT	G	PO	A	E	DP
Cadette	.887	48	77	128	26	13
Epifano	.947	22	31	41	4	2
Marte	.735	9	10	15	9	1

Outfield	PCT	G	PO	A	E	DP
Alcantara	.969	19	27	4	1	0
Arias	.967	42	57	1	2	0
Contreras	.949	45	72	2	4	0
Falcon	1.000	13	20	2	0	1
Linares	1.000	5	5	0	0	0
Ochoa	.900	14	9	0	1	0
Puello	.948	48	52	3	3	1
Ramos	.800	20	19	1	5	0
Rivera	.962	30	47	3	2	0

Baltimore Orioles

BY ROCH KUBATKO

Without the Rays to cushion their annual plunge down the American League East standings, the Orioles concluded their season with a loud thud. They hit bottom in a variety of ways, most notably with their first last-place finish since 1988.

That's 11 straight losing seasons for the Orioles, who dropped 11 of their last 12 games and 28 of their last 34. Almost forgotten is the promise that the first four-plus months held for a team that was supposed to be rebuilding. The Orioles had a .500

winning percentage on July 8 and were 60-63 on Aug. 17. But they went 8-30 the rest of the way to finish 68-93.

A familiar lack of depth, especially in the rotation and bullpen, proved to be the club's undoing. The Orioles' 5.13 ERA ranked 13th in the league, and they led the AL in walks allowed.

Releasing ineffective veteran Steve Trachsel and losing former No. 1 pick Adam Loewen to injury began the downfall, and it kept getting worse. Young replacements weren't ready for the challenge, and castoffs didn't fare much better.

Unfortunately for the Orioles, changing divisions isn't an option. They were 22-50 vs. the East, 46-43 vs. everyone else.

"Our guys fought it out pretty good for three quarters of the season, and that last round took some of the fun of this season away for me," team president Andy MacPhail said. "We just don't have the depth yet to go round three with top teams."

On the plus side, Aubrey Huff recovered from sports hernia surgery and posted one of the finest seasons of his career, batting .304/.360/.552 with 48 doubles, 32 homers and 108 RBIs. He picked up the offensive slack following the Miguel Tejada trade and led the offense along with Nick Markakis, who batted .306/.406/.491 with 48 doubles, 20 homers and 87 RBIs, and played Gold Glove-caliber defense in right field.

In his first season as closer, George Sherrill saved 31 games. Jim Johnson emerged as a set-up guy after spending most of his professional career as a starter. But Johnson eventually went down with an injury, further depleting a bullpen that also lost Sherrill, Matt Albers and Dennis Sarfate.

Down on the farm, Double-A Bowie reached the Eastern League playoffs for the first time since 1997 and won its division for the first time in

PLAYERS OF THE YEAR

MAJOR LEAGUE: BRIAN ROBERTS, 2B

Roberts was a bright spot for the Orioles in hitting .296/.378/.450 with nine home runs, a career-high 51 doubles and 57 RBIs. His 40 steals were fourth in the American League, while his doubles ranked second and his 107 runs scored were third.

MINOR LEAGUE: MATT WIETERS, C

The 2007 first-round pick dominated at high Class A Frederick and then at Double-A Bowie, batting a combined .355/.454/.600 with 27 home runs, 22 doubles and 91 RBIs and was Baseball America's Minor League Player of the Year.

RODGER WOOD

ORGANIZATION LEADERS

BATTING		*Minimum 250 at-bats
*AVG	Wieters, Matt, Frederick/Bowie	.355
R	Montanez, Lou, Bowie	90
H	Wieters, Matt, Frederick/Bowie	155
TB	Montanez, Lou, Bowie	271
2B	Salazar, Oscar, Norfolk	42
3B	Terrero, Luis, Norfolk	8
HR	Wieters, Matt, Frederick/Bowie	27
RBI	Montanez, Lou, Bowie	97
BB	Wieters, Matt, Frederick/Bowie	82
SO	Costanzo, Mike, Norfolk	159
SB	Angle, Matthew, Delmarva	37
*OBP	Wieters, Matt, Frederick/Bowie	.454
*SLG	Montanez, Lou, Bowie	.601

PITCHING		†Minimum 75 innings
W	Bergesen, Bradley, Frederick/Bowie	16
L	Erbe, Brandon, Frederick	12
†ERA	Gleason, Sean, Delmarva	2.63
G	Manon, Julio, Bowie	56
G	Miller, Jim, Bowie, Norfolk	56
GS	Erbe, Brandon, Frederick	28
GS	Tillman, Chris, Bowie	28
SV	Manon, Julio, Bowie	32
IP	Bergesen, Bradley, Frederick/Bowie	165
BB	Noel, Luis, Delmarva	73
SO	Hernandez, David, Bowie	166
†AVG	Arrieta, Jake, Frederick	.199

franchise history (though the Baysox lost in the first round). Outfielder Lou Montanez won the league's triple crown. Catcher Matt Wieters was named Baseball America's Minor League Player of the Year after hitting .345/.448/.576 with 15 homers at high Class A Frederick, and .365/.460/625 with 12 homers at Bowie.

2008 PERFORMANCE

General Manager: Andy MacPhail. **Farm Director:** David Stockstill. **Scouting Director:** Joe Jordan.

Class	Team	League	W	L	PCT	Finish*	Manager	Affiliate Since
Majors	Baltimore	American	68	93	.422	13th (14)	Dave Trembley	—
Triple-A	Norfolk Tides	International	64	78	.451	11th (14)	Gary Allenson	2007
Double-A	Bowie Baysox	Eastern	84	58	.592	2nd (12)	Brad Komminsk	1993
High A	Frederick Keys	Carolina	63	76	.453	6th (8)	T. Thompson/R. Hebner	1989
Low A	Delmarva Shorebirds	South Atlantic	78	61	.561	5th (16)	Ramon Sambo	1997
Short-season	Aberdeen IronBirds	New York-Penn	36	39	.480	9th (14)	Gary Kendall	2002
Rookie	Bluefield Orioles	Appalachian	29	36	.446	8th (10)	Orlando Gomez	1958
Rookie	GCL Orioles	Gulf Coast	14	41	.255	16th (16)	Jesus Alfaro	2008
Overall 2008 Minor League Record			368	419	.468	23rd		

* Finish in overall standings (No. of teams in league). ^League champion.

ORGANIZATION STATISTICS

BALTIMORE ORIOLES

AMERICAN LEAGUE

Batting	B-T	HT	WT	DOB	AVG	vLH	vRH	G	AB	R	H	2B	3B	HR	RBI	BB	HBP	SH	SF	SO	SB	CS	SLG	OBP
Bynum Jr., Freddie	L-R	6-1	190	3-15-80	.179	.118	.189	40	112	13	20	3	1	0	8	5	1	3	0	31	2	3	.223	.220
Castro, Juan	R-R	5-11	190	6-20-72	.205	.208	.204	54	151	15	31	6	0	2	16	10	1	2	2	26	0	0	.285	.256
Cintron, Alex	B-R	6-1	205	12-17-78	.286	.250	.301	61	133	12	38	5	1	1	10	7	0	4	0	15	0	2	.361	.321
Fahey, Brandon	L-R	6-2	160	1-18-81	.226	.200	.235	58	106	8	24	9	2	0	12	3	1	2	1	25	0	0	.349	.252
Hernandez, Luis	B-R	5-10	180	6-26-84	.241	.200	.250	36	79	9	19	1	0	0	3	7	0	3	2	11	2	0	.253	.295
Hernandez, Ramon	R-R	6-0	235	5-20-76	.257	.283	.245	133	463	49	119	22	1	15	65	32	5	1	6	62	0	0	.406	.308
Huff, Aubrey	L-R	6-4	235	12-20-76	.304	.270	.321	154	598	96	182	48	2	32	108	53	3	0	7	89	4	0	.552	.360
Jones, Adam	R-R	6-2	210	8-1-85	.270	.256	.275	132	477	61	129	21	7	9	57	23	7	2	5	108	10	3	.400	.311
Markakis, Nick	L-L	6-2	195	11-17-83	.306	.297	.310	157	595	106	182	48	1	20	87	99	2	0	1	113	10	7	.491	.406
Millar, Kevin	R-R	6-0	215	9-24-71	.234	.238	.232	145	531	73	124	25	0	20	72	71	2	0	6	93	0	1	.394	.323
Montanez, Lou	R-R	6-2	200	12-15-81	.295	.283	.305	38	112	18	33	6	1	3	14	4	0	0	1	20	0	0	.446	.316
Moore, Scott	L-R	6-2	195	11-17-83	.125	—	.125	4	8	1	1	0	0	1	1	1	0	0	0	3	0	0	.500	.222
Mora, Melvin	R-R	5-11	200	2-2-72	.285	.314	.272	135	513	77	146	29	2	23	104	37	11	3	6	70	3	7	.483	.342
Payton, Jay	R-R	5-10	205	11-22-72	.243	.248	.240	127	338	41	82	10	2	7	41	22	1	2	0	53	8	1	.346	.291
Quiroz, Guillermo	R-R	6-1	200	11-29-81	.187	.200	.183	56	134	12	25	5	0	2	14	12	1	1	0	34	0	0	.269	.259
Roberts, Brian	B-R	5-9	175	10-9-77	.296	.313	.289	155	611	107	181	51	8	9	57	82	2	3	6	104	40	10	.450	.378
Salazar, Oscar	R-R	6-0	195	6-27-78	.284	.211	.349	34	81	13	23	3	0	5	15	12	0	0	1	13	0	1	.506	.372
Santos, Omir	R-R	6-0	200	4-29-81	.100	.000	.100	11	10	0	1	0	0	0	0	0	0	0	0	2	0	0	.100	.100
Scott, Luke	L-R	6-0	210	6-25-78	.257	.215	.269	148	475	67	122	29	2	23	65	53	5	0	3	102	2	2	.472	.336
Torres, Eider	B-R	5-9	175	1-16-83	.222	.333	.167	8	9	2	2	0	0	0	0	0	0	0	0	2	0	0	.222	.222

Pitching	B-T	HT	WT	DOB	W	L	ERA	G	GS	CG	SV	IP	H	R	ER	HR	BB	SO	AVG	vLH	vRH	K/9	BB/9
Albers, Matt	L-R	6-0	205	1-20-83	3	3	3.49	28	3	0	0	49	43	21	19	4	22	26	.240	.163	.312	4.78	4.04
Aquino, Greg	R-R	6-1	190	1-11-78	0	0	12.54	9	0	0	0	9	17	13	13	1	9	9	.415	.333	.478	8.68	8.68
Bass, Brian	R-R	6-2	215	1-6-82	1	0	4.71	5	4	0	0	21	14	13	11	1	9	13	.192	.152	.259	5.57	3.86
2-team total (44 Minnesota)					4	4	4.84	49	4	0	1	89	98	55	48	12	31	45	—	—	—	4.53	3.12
Bierd, Randor	R-R	6-4	190	3-14-84	0	2	4.91	29	0	0	0	37	48	21	20	3	19	25	.316	.333	.301	6.14	4.66
Bradford, Chad	R-R	6-5	205	9-14-74	3	3	2.45	47	0	0	0	40	41	17	11	2	7	13	.279	.311	.265	2.90	1.56
2-team total (21 Tampa Bay)					4	4	2.12	68	0	0	0	59	59	24	15	3	15	17	—	—	—	2.58	2.28
Bukvich, Ryan	R-R	6-2	250	5-13-78	0	0	6.75	4	0	0	0	5	9	4	4	2	6	5	.375	.600	.214	8.44	10.13
Burres, Brian	L-L	6-1	180	4-8-81	7	10	6.04	31	22	0	0	130	165	90	87	17	50	63	.311	.321	.306	4.37	3.47
Cabrera, Daniel	R-R	6-9	270	5-28-81	8	10	5.25	30	30	2	0	180	199	109	105	24	90	95	.286	.308	.259	4.75	4.50
Cabrera, Fernando	R-R	6-4	220	11-16-81	2	1	5.40	22	0	0	0	28	32	18	17	9	17	31	.283	.304	.269	9.85	5.40
Castillo, Alberto	L-L	6-3	200	7-5-75	1	0	3.81	28	0	0	0	26	27	11	11	3	10	23	.260	.256	.262	7.96	3.46
Cherry, Rocky	R-R	6-5	225	8-19-79	0	3	6.35	18	0	0	1	17	15	15	12	3	16	15	.231	.167	.268	7.94	8.47
Cormier, Lance	R-R	6-1	200	8-19-80	3	3	4.02	45	1	0	1	72	78	36	32	4	34	46	.279	.240	.308	5.78	4.27
Guthrie, Jeremy	R-R	6-1	195	4-8-79	10	12	3.63	30	30	1	0	191	176	82	77	24	58	120	.242	.241	.243	5.66	2.74
Johnson, Jim	R-R	6-5	230	6-27-83	2	4	2.23	54	0	0	1	69	54	18	17	0	28	38	.219	.227	.212	4.98	3.67
Liz, Radhames	R-R	6-2	185	10-6-83	6	6	6.72	17	17	0	0	84	99	67	63	16	51	57	.296	.318	.269	6.08	5.44
Loewen, Adam	L-L	6-5	235	4-9-84	0	2	8.02	7	4	0	0	21	25	19	19	5	18	14	.305	.296	.309	5.91	7.59
McCrory, Bob	R-R	6-1	205	5-3-82	0	0	15.63	8	0	0	0	6	10	12	11	0	8	5	.370	.294	.500	7.11	11.37
Mickolio, Kam	R-R	6-9	255	5-10-84	0	1	5.87	9	0	0	0	8	5	5	5	0	4	8	.267	.214	.313	9.39	4.70
Miller, Jim	R-R	6-1	200	4-28-82	0	2	1.17	8	0	0	1	8	9	3	1	0	5	8	.290	.333	.250	9.39	5.87
Olson, Garrett	R-L	6-1	195	10-18-83	9	10	6.65	26	26	0	0	133	168	100	98	17	62	83	.309	.310	.309	5.63	4.21
Sarfate, Dennis	R-R	6-4	225	4-9-81	4	3	4.74	57	4	0	0	80	62	47	42	8	62	86	.218	.198	.234	9.72	7.00
Sherrill, George	L-L	6-0	230	4-19-77	3	5	4.73	57	0	0	31	53	47	28	28	6	33	58	.234	.190	.254	9.79	5.57
Simon, Alfredo	R-R	6-4	230	5-8-81	0	0	6.23	4	1	0	0	13	16	10	9	4	2	8	.296	.243	.412	5.54	1.38
Trachsel, Steve	R-R	6-4	205	10-31-70	2	5	8.39	10	8	0	0	40	53	41	37	10	27	16	.321	.244	.398	3.63	6.13
Walker, Jamie	L-L	6-2	195	7-1-71	1	3	6.87	59	0	0	0	38	53	31	29	12	11	24	.325	.304	.352	5.68	2.61
Waters, Chris	L-L	6-0	170	8-17-80	3	5	5.01	11	11	1	0	65	70	38	36	9	29	33	.273	.303	.263	4.59	4.04

Fielding

Catcher	PCT	G	PO	A	E	DP	PB
R. Hernandez	.988	127	714	45	9	8	10
Quiroz	.996	54	229	17	1	3	5
Santos	1.000	9	19	0	0	0	0

First Base	PCT	G	PO	A	E	DP
Cintron	1.000	2	3	1	0	1
R. Hernandez	1.000	2	11	0	0	0
Huff	1.000	24	177	16	0	16
Millar	.995	130	1099	110	6	128
Salazar	1.000	10	79	5	0	5

Second Base	PCT	G	PO	A	E	DP
Bynum Jr.	—	1	0	0	0	0
Cintron	1.000	7	4	4	0	1
Fahey	1.000	10	10	11	0	8
L. Hernandez	1.000	5	3	9	0	2
Moore	1.000	1	2	2	0	0
Roberts	.989	154	289	441	8	110
Torres	1.000	1	1	2	0	0

Third Base	PCT	G	PO	A	E	DP
Castro	1.000	4	1	0	0	0
Cintron	.875	8	1	6	1	0
Huff	.967	33	23	64	3	4
Moore	1.000	1	0	2	0	0
Mora	.960	124	85	252	14	28
Salazar	1.000	7	3	10	0	3

Shortstop	PCT	G	PO	A	E	DP
Bynum Jr.	.965	37	56	81	5	28
Castro	.977	54	72	136	5	22
Cintron	.953	45	50	92	7	21
Fahey	.963	46	43	87	5	19
L. Hernandez	.977	30	52	75	3	19
Mora	—	1	0	0	0	0
Salazar	—	1	0	0	0	0
Torres	.700	5	2	5	3	1

Outfield	PCT	G	PO	A	E	DP
Jones	.991	129	336	4	3	1
Markakis	.991	156	327	17	3	3
Montanez	.947	33	35	1	2	0
Payton	1.000	108	239	8	0	1
Scott	.990	106	200	3	2	1

NORFOLK TIDES　　　　　　　　　　　TRIPLE-A
INTERNATIONAL LEAGUE

Batting	B-T	HT	WT	DOB	AVG	vLH	vRH	G	AB	R	H	2B	3B	HR	RBI	BB	HBP	SH	SF	SO	SB	CS	SLG	OBP
Boucher, Sebastien	L-R	6-0	190	10-19-81	.282	.276	.286	22	71	14	20	2	1	0	5	7	2	1	0	22	3	1	.338	.363
Brown, Travis	R-R	5-11	180	8-1-80	.111	.000	.250	7	18	2	2	0	0	0	0	1	0	0	0	3	0	1	.111	.158
Bynum Jr., Freddie	L-R	6-1	190	3-15-80	.246	.243	.247	37	130	15	32	4	3	0	15	20	0	3	2	39	8	1	.323	.342
Cintron, Alex	B-R	6-1	205	12-17-78	.288	.250	.316	16	66	9	19	1	0	2	10	2	2	1	0	11	0	0	.394	.329
Costanzo, Mike	L-R	6-3	215	9-9-83	.261	.257	.263	129	483	56	126	28	2	11	63	52	1	0	2	159	2	2	.395	.333
Davis, Ben	B-R	6-4	215	3-10-77	.172	.219	.125	20	64	2	11	2	0	1	2	0	1	0	0	17	0	0	.250	.185
Fahey, Brandon	L-R	6-2	160	1-18-81	.252	.257	.250	64	222	26	56	7	0	1	23	21	1	2	2	47	1	4	.297	.317
Fiorentino, Jeff	L-R	6-1	185	4-14-83	.268	.196	.291	68	228	25	61	12	1	2	25	34	1	1	3	52	7	3	.355	.361
Heintz, Chris	R-R	6-1	205	8-6-74	.250	.241	.255	46	164	11	41	6	1	2	19	11	1	3	2	21	1	0	.335	.298
Hernandez, Luis	B-R	5-10	180	6-26-84	.185	.161	.196	57	205	18	38	7	0	0	11	8	0	3	0	27	2	2	.220	.216
McCoy, Mike	R-R	5-9	171	4-2-81	.276	.339	.237	53	152	25	42	6	1	2	16	19	0	4	1	27	6	3	.368	.355
Moore, Scott	L-R	6-2	195	11-17-83	.247	.229	.258	78	287	41	71	21	2	7	44	23	8	0	0	67	3	0	.408	.321
Redman, Tike	L-L	5-11	175	3-10-77	.292	.301	.287	116	463	77	135	19	4	3	36	48	4	8	4	50	13	12	.369	.360
Roberson, Chris	B-R	6-2	180	8-23-79	.279	.263	.288	123	437	52	122	14	2	6	57	38	3	3	4	64	20	17	.362	.338
Salazar, Oscar	R-R	6-0	195	6-27-78	.316	.427	.259	112	443	73	140	42	3	13	85	42	0	0	6	56	8	2	.512	.371
Santos, Omir	R-R	6-0	200	4-29-81	.269	.333	.240	84	297	31	80	13	0	1	36	20	8	3	4	57	1	2	.323	.328
Stern, Adam	L-R	5-11	185	2-12-80	.221	.167	.250	38	122	16	27	5	1	1	8	5	1	3	2	23	6	2	.303	.254
Tarnow, Josh	R-R	6-0	180	11-4-84	.000	—	.000	1	1	0	0	0	0	0	0	0	0	0	0	0	0	0	.000	.000
Terrero, Luis	R-R	6-3	205	5-18-80	.274	.293	.264	129	497	73	136	31	8	13	88	43	9	1	5	118	13	11	.447	.339
Torres, Eider	R-R	5-9	175	1-16-83	.307	.329	.294	115	473	69	145	20	6	1	34	38	1	10	3	60	28	11	.381	.357

Pitching	B-T	HT	WT	DOB	W	L	ERA	G	GS	CG	SV	IP	H	R	ER	HR	BB	SO	AVG	vLH	vRH	K/9	BB/9
Anderson, Craig	L-L	6-3	185	10-30-80	7	9	6.51	26	20	0	0	113	164	92	82	21	24	75	.346	.370	.333	5.96	1.91
Aquino, Greg	R-R	6-1	190	1-11-78	2	2	2.45	23	0	0	9	26	23	10	7	2	6	29	.240	.283	.200	10.17	2.10
Bukvich, Ryan	R-R	6-2	250	5-13-78	8	4	4.54	34	9	0	1	85	82	49	43	4	54	60	.255	.287	.221	6.33	5.70
Burres, Brian	L-L	6-1	180	4-8-81	1	0	0.82	4	1	0	0	11	9	1	1	0	11		.214	.133	.259	9.00	0.82
Cabrera, Fernando	R-R	6-4	220	11-16-81	0	0	0.69	11	0	0	0	13	11	1	1	0	7	13	.229	.190	.259	9.00	4.85
Castillo, Alberto	L-L	6-3	200	7-5-75	3	1	2.05	19	0	0	0	26	16	6	6	2	6	26	.172	.093	.240	8.89	2.05
Cherry, Rocky	R-R	6-5	225	8-19-79	0	1	2.89	28	0	0	0	37	35	15	12	3	9	37	.252	.282	.221	8.92	2.17
Chiasson, Scott	R-R	6-3	205	8-14-77	0	0	3.38	10	0	0	1	11	8	4	4	1	3	10	.200	.150	.250	8.44	2.53
Clark, Zach	R-R	6-0	195	7-11-83	1	2	5.40	4	4	0	0	18	23	13	11		6	11	.315	.304	.333	5.40	2.95
Cormier, Lance	R-R	6-1	200	8-19-80	1	1	0.96	9	0	0	0	19	12	4	2	0	5	12	.182	.091	.273	5.79	2.41
Deza, Fredy	R-R	6-2	175	12-11-82	1	1	2.25	6	0	0	0	8	5	4	2	1	5	16	.167	.214	.125	18.00	5.63
Doyne, Cory	R-R	6-2	240	8-13-81	0	0	3.68	4	0	0	0	7	6	3	3	1	2	8	.250	.250	.250	9.82	2.45
Johnson, Jim	R-R	6-5	230	6-27-83	0	1	5.25	1	1	0	0	4	2	1	1	0	1	2	.143	.111	.200	4.50	2.25
Keisler, Randy	L-L	6-3	200	2-24-76	2	3	5.25	9	0	0	0	48	69	37	28	4	25	24	.343	.377	.323	4.50	4.69
Knotts, Gary	R-R	6-4	215	2-12-77	0	2	3.18	4	1	0	0	11	8	5	4	0	8	12	.190	.150	.227	9.53	6.35
2-team total (35 Lehigh Valley)					2	7	5.08	39	11	0	0	103	117	65	58	12	52	98	—	—	—	8.59	4.56
Leicester, Jon	R-R	6-3	220	2-7-79	3	8	5.26	39	13	0	1	106	125	75	62	14	40	95	.290	.298	.282	8.07	3.40
Liz, Radhames	R-R	6-2	185	10-6-83	3	7	3.62	15	15	1	0	87	77	42	35	6	32	85	.240	.269	.211	8.79	3.31
McCrory, Bob	R-R	6-1	205	5-3-82	2	3	3.80	35	1	0	5	45	41	22	19	1	24	35	.250	.260	.242	7.00	4.80
Mickolio, Kam	R-R	6-9	255	5-10-84	1	0	1.80	17	0	0	2	15	10	3	3	0	4	9	.173	.209	.125	10.35	4.05
Miller, Jim	R-R	6-1	200	4-28-82	3	5	3.09	49	0	0	10	67	50	26	23	4	22	79	.205	.218	.194	10.61	2.96
Mitchell, Andy	R-R	6-3	205	9-10-78	12	8	4.29	32	21	0	0	138	136	75	66	12	58	71	.260	.279	.239	4.62	3.77
Novoa, Roberto	R-R	6-3	200	8-15-79	3	2	4.73	35	0	0	2	53	64	32	28	4	26	42	.308	.297	.318	7.09	4.39
Olson, Garrett	R-L	6-1	195	10-18-83	1	2	2.97	7	7	0	0	36	35	14	12	1	16	39	.261	.310	.239	9.66	3.96
Penn, Hayden	R-R	6-3	200	10-13-84	6	7	4.79	21	21	0	0	100	110	59	53	14	35	65	.281	.264	.297	5.87	3.16
Romero, Felix	R-R	6-1	192	6-18-80	0	0	2.16	5	1	0	0	8	5	3	2	0	6	6	.179	.200	.154	6.48	6.48
Simon, Alfredo	R-R	6-4	230	5-8-81	0	1	7.11	1	1	0	0	5	9	4	4	1	2	5	.429	.444	.417	9.64	3.86
Waters, Chris	L-L	6-0	170	8-17-80	3	6	5.70	18	16	1	0	90	97	62	57	10	43	72	.279	.210	.317	7.20	4.30
Yan, Esteban	R-R	6-4	255	6-22-75	1	2	5.70	37	1	0	0	47	51	35	30	3	15	55	.266	.255	.276	10.46	2.85

Fielding

Catcher	PCT	G	PO	A	E	DP	PB
Costanzo	1.000	5	22	2	0	0	2
Davis	.986	20	128	12	2	2	6
Heintz	.993	40	284	18	2	4	8
Santos	.997	81	612	53	2	6	4

First Base	PCT	G	PO	A	E	DP
Costanzo	.971	34	267	35	9	23
Fahey	1.000	1	7	1	0	0
Fiorentino	.947	2	16	2	1	0
Heintz	1.000	7	51	0	0	6
Moore	.976	17	110	12	3	11
Salazar	.991	84	690	42	7	68
Santos	1.000	1	15	1	0	1

Second Base	PCT	G	PO	A	E	DP
Brown	1.000	1	1	3	0	1
Bynum Jr.	.950	3	8	11	1	3
Cintron	1.000	1	1	2	0	0

	PCT	G	PO	A	E	DP
Fahey	.930	11	20	20	3	5
McCoy	.992	29	44	84	1	20
Moore	1.000	3	1	6	0	0
Salazar	1.000	1	2	3	0	1
Torres	.990	99	155	258	4	51

Third Base	PCT	G	PO	A	E	DP
Brown	1.000	2	1	1	0	0
Bynum Jr.	.900	17	6	30	4	4
Costanzo	.929	73	49	121	13	13
Fahey	.692	5	2	7	4	0
McCoy	.923	8	2	10	1	3
Moore	.931	39	28	53	6	4
Salazar	1.000	6	4	9	0	2

Shortstop	PCT	G	PO	A	E	DP
Brown	.889	4	6	2	1	0
Bynum Jr.	.900	4	8	10	2	4
Cintron	1.000	15	25	33	0	4

	PCT	G	PO	A	E	DP
Fahey	.956	41	71	101	8	28
Hernandez	.972	54	78	134	6	25
McCoy	.944	13	20	31	3	7
Moore	.909	3	2	8	1	0
Torres	.940	11	17	30	3	6

Outfield	PCT	G	PO	A	E	DP
Boucher	.947	19	34	2	2	0
Bynum Jr.	.857	4	5	1	1	0
Fahey	.917	6	11	0	1	0
Fiorentino	.993	64	139	6	1	1
McCoy	1.000	4	11	0	0	0
Redman	.984	89	178	2	3	0
Roberson	.976	116	257	22	7	6
Salazar	1.000	1	2	0	0	0
Stern	.985	35	66	1	1	1
Terrero	.937	97	186	8	13	2

BOWIE BAYSOX DOUBLE-A
EASTERN LEAGUE

Batting	B-T	HT	WT	DOB	AVG	vLH	vRH	G	AB	R	H	2B	3B	HR	RBI	BB	HBP	SH	SF	SO	SB	CS	SLG	OBP
Boucher, Sebastien	L-R	6-0	190	10-19-81	.267	.196	.285	75	258	47	69	14	3	10	29	32	3	3	0	65	5	6	.461	.355
Brown, Travis	R-R	5-11	180	8-1-80	.173	.182	.163	35	98	9	17	1	1	0	11	9	0	1	0	24	0	1	.204	.241
Bynum Jr., Freddie	L-R	6-1	190	3-15-80	.350	.111	.545	6	20	4	7	1	1	1	3	1	0	1	0	3	0	1	.650	.381
Cintron, Alex	B-R	6-1	205	12-17-78	.333	.000	.500	3	9	0	3	0	0	0	0	0	0	0	0	2	0	0	.333	.400
Davis, Ben	B-R	6-4	215	3-10-77	.227	.226	.227	24	97	10	22	6	1	2	13	5	1	0	0	15	0	0	.371	.272
Davis, Blake	L-R	5-11	160	12-22-83	.284	.313	.271	132	457	57	130	22	7	4	53	26	3	7	4	80	8	7	.389	.324
Dillon, Zach	L-R	5-10	210	5-18-83	.278	.250	.286	12	36	5	10	1	0	0	6	4	3	1	0	1	0	0	.306	.341
Finan, Ryan	L-R	6-5	220	1-5-82	.257	.200	.275	107	377	58	97	21	1	11	54	48	7	0	6	85	0	0	.406	.347
Jones, Kennard	L-L	5-11	185	9-8-81	.257	.357	.214	40	140	19	36	6	2	1	16	15	0	2	3	21	6	2	.350	.323
Montanez, Lou	R-R	6-2	200	12-15-81	.335	.331	.337	116	451	90	151	32	5	26	97	36	6	0	8	63	4	4	.601	.385
Nettles, Jeff	R-R	6-2	200	8-20-78	.253	.262	.249	134	510	74	129	25	0	24	78	44	4	0	4	84	0	1	.443	.315
Peterson, Brian	R-R	6-2	225	10-22-78	.243	.320	.213	51	177	17	43	9	0	2	20	15	3	1	1	27	0	1	.328	.311
Pierce, Mike	R-R	6-1	225	4-19-84	.133	.125	.143	5	15	3	2	0	0	0	3	1	0	1	0	7	0	1	.333	.300
Reimold, Nolan	R-R	6-4	207	10-12-83	.284	.264	.292	139	507	87	144	29	3	25	84	63	8	0	8	82	7	3	.501	.367
Rodriguez, Mike	L-L	5-10	180	10-15-80	.256	.313	.233	99	395	48	101	18	5	4	53	28	1	5	3	72	11	1	.357	.304
Rojas, Carlos	R-R	6-1	175	1-11-84	.247	.231	.256	120	441	74	109	13	1	2	38	49	9	7	3	76	1	3	.295	.333
Torrealba, Steve	R-R	6-0	220	2-24-78	.283	.279	.286	37	120	16	34	8	0	8	26	13	1	0	0	22	1	0	.550	.358
Tucker, Jonathan	R-R	5-7	170	7-2-83	.278	.317	.257	118	418	74	116	27	4	7	47	49	4	4	2	64	8	7	.411	.357
Valichka, Brian	R-R	6-3	200	8-21-83	.067	.000	.111	7	15	1	1	0	0	0	2	3	0	0	0	4	0	0	.267	.222
Wieters, Matt	B-R	6-5	215	5-21-86	.365	.393	.354	42	208	41	76	14	2	12	51	38	1	0	3	29	1	0	.625	.460

Pitching	B-T	HT	WT	DOB	W	L	ERA	G	GS	CG	SV	IP	H	R	ER	HR	BB	SO	AVG	vLH	vRH	K/9	BB/9
Anderson, Craig	L-L	6-3	185	10-30-80	0	0	5.87	3	3	0	0	15	12	10	10	5	1	8	.211	.300	.162	4.70	0.59
Aquino, Greg	R-R	6-1	190	1-11-78	0	0	0.00	1	0	0	0	1	2	0	0	0	0	1	.400	.667	.000	9.00	0.00
Bergesen, Brad	L-R	6-2	205	9-25-85	15	6	3.22	24	23	3	0	148	143	59	53	11	27	72	.253	.304	.208	4.38	1.64
Berken, Jason	R-R	6-0	175	11-27-83	12	4	3.58	26	25	2	0	146	141	69	58	9	38	125	.255	.232	.273	7.72	2.35
Bierd, Randor	R-R	6-4	190	3-14-84	0	0	4.50	5	1	0	0	6	7	3	3	0	3	9	.304	.333	.286	13.50	4.50
Burch, Jason	R-R	6-5	215	10-15-82	3	2	3.77	21	0	0	0	31	37	16	13	3	12	26	.301	.333	.280	7.55	3.48
2-team total (10 New Hampshire)					3	3	4.37	31	0	0	0	45	59	25	22	4	16	42	—	—		8.34	3.18
Casadiego, Gerardo	R-R	6-0	180	12-19-80	5	3	3.18	55	0	0	1	71	66	34	25	3	30	55	.248	.198	.274	7.00	3.82
Cherry, Rocky	R-R	6-5	225	8-19-79	0	0	0.00	2	0	0	0	2	1	0	0	0	2	3	.143	.000	.500	13.50	9.00
Clark, Zach	R-R	6-0	195	7-11-83	4	2	3.60	10	10	0	0	60	57	27	24	6	13	25	.248	.252	.244	3.75	1.95
Hernandez, David	R-R	6-3	215	5-13-85	10	4	2.68	27	27	0	0	141	112	53	42	10	71	166	.217	.218	.217	10.60	4.53
Keefer, Ryan	L-R	6-3	225	8-10-81	2	4	4.80	39	0	0	1	66	60	42	35	10	38	59	.247	.296	.214	8.09	5.21
Lewis Jr., Rommie	L-L	6-5	200	9-2-82	1	6	3.41	38	5	0	0	66	81	29	25	4	26	63	.308	.373	.278	8.59	3.55
Loewen, Adam	L-L	6-5	235	4-9-84	1	0	1.35	6	0	0	0	7	3	1	1		2	6	.280	.500	.238	8.10	2.70
Lonsberry, Dan	R-R	6-4	200	7-6-83	0	2	13.50	3	0	0	0	5	5	7	7	0	5	1	.278	.250	.300	1.93	9.64
Manon, Julio	R-R	6-0	180	10-6-73	2	7	3.39	56	0	0	32	64	35	27	24	4	27	80	.162	.176	.153	11.31	3.82
Mickolio, Kam	R-R	6-9	255	5-10-84	2	1	4.70	28	0	0	1	38	39	21	20	2	22	40	.262	.276	.253	9.39	5.17
Miller, Jim	R-R	6-1	200	4-28-82	0	1	3.46	7	0	0	0	13	11	5	5	1	5	17	.229	.200	.242	11.77	3.46
Perez, Wilfredo	L-L	6-0	145	8-12-84	0	2	2.31	16	0	0	1	23	16	6	6	1	8	23	.195	.227	.183	8.87	3.09
Ray, Chris	R-R	6-3	225	1-12-82	0	0	0.00	1	0	0	0	1	0	0	0	0	0	2	.000	.000		18.00	0.00
Romero, Felix	R-R	6-1	192	6-18-80	8	3	3.39	40	0	0	1	77	66	33	29	8	19	100	.228	.258	.206	11.69	2.22
Schmidt, Kyle	R-R	6-3	220	8-25-83	0	2	6.55	5	5	0	0	22	23	17	16	1	15	19	.299	.348	.226	7.77	6.14
Spoone, Chorye	R-R	6-1	215	9-16-85	3	3	4.57	9	9	0	0	41	40	23	21	4	27	32	.252	.305	.220	6.97	5.88
Thall, Chad	L-L	6-4	220	8-2-85	0	0	3.63	15	0	0	0	22	26	10	9	2	4	11	.286	.172	.339	4.43	1.61
Tillman, Chris	R-R	6-5	195	4-15-88	11	4	3.18	28	28	0	0	136	115	53	48	10	65	154	.227	.232	.223	10.22	4.31
Walker, Jamie	L-L	6-2	195	7-1-71	0	0	27.00	1	0	0	0	1	5	3	3	1	0	0	.833	1.000	.500	0.00	0.00
Waters, Chris	L-L	6-0	170	8-17-80	5	0	1.69	6	6	0	0	32	20	6	6	2	8	22	.179	.105	.194	6.19	2.25

Fielding

Catcher	PCT	G	PO	A	E	DP	PB
Davis	1.000	23	193	9	0	1	12
Dillon	1.000	7	49	3	0	0	1
Peterson	.981	45	338	28	7	7	7
Pierce	.970	5	31	1	1	1	0
Torrealba	1.000	14	101	12	0	1	3
Valichka	1.000	7	40	4	0	1	0
Wieters	.993	44	388	23	3	3	0

First Base	PCT	G	PO	A	E	DP
Dillon	1.000	1	3	0	0	0
Finan	.993	103	837	56	6	77
Nettles	.990	36	293	15	3	29
Peterson	1.000	2	19	1	0	2

	PCT	G	PO	A	E	DP
Rojas	1.000	1	1	0	0	0
Torrealba	.944	3	16	1	1	3

Second Base	PCT	G	PO	A	E	DP
Brown	.929	3	7	6	1	3
Rojas	.988	112	179	316	6	67
Tucker	.976	31	55	68	3	16

Third Base	PCT	G	PO	A	E	DP
Brown	.922	16	11	36	4	4
Nettles	.924	91	64	154	18	15
Tucker	.914	40	23	62	8	6

Shortstop	PCT	G	PO	A	E	DP
Brown	1.000	8	9	22	0	5

	PCT	G	PO	A	E	DP
Bynum Jr.	1.000	4	8	11	0	4
Cintron	1.000	3	0	2	0	0
Davis	.960	124	177	309	20	68
Rojas	1.000	7	11	14	0	2

Outfield	PCT	G	PO	A	E	DP
Boucher	.975	59	114	2	3	0
Jones	.981	26	50	1	1	1
Montanez	.980	106	190	8	4	1
Reimold	.983	133	229	3	4	1
Rodriguez	.976	83	158	4	4	2
Tucker	1.000	27	49	2	0	0

FREDERICK KEYS   HIGH CLASS A

CAROLINA LEAGUE

Batting	B-T	HT	WT	DOB	AVG	vLH	vRH	G	AB	R	H	2B	3B	HR	RBI	BB	HBP	SH	SF	SO	SB	CS	SLG	OBP
Abreu, Miguel	R-R	6-0	190	11-14-84	.275	.302	.265	116	429	55	118	24	1	6	43	15	4	10	3	44	21	10	.378	.304
Amador, Chris	R-R	5-10	167	12-14-82	.241	.234	.243	112	424	63	102	21	5	9	62	29	9	4	1	90	15	7	.377	.302
Andrews, Bobby	R-R	6-0	200	12-23-83	.222	.207	.227	48	117	22	26	1	1	1	6	18	2	2	1	26	4	4	.274	.333
Cintron, Alex	B-R	6-1	205	12-17-78	.600	—	.600	2	5	2	3	0	0	1	2	0	0	0	0	1	0	0	1.200	.600
Davison, Todd	R-R	5-10	175	10-7-83	.258	.247	.263	83	248	35	64	10	0	1	19	34	3	5	3	52	7	6	.310	.351
Dillon, Zach	L-R	5-10	210	5-18-83	.195	.000	.211	14	41	8	8	2	0	1	9	8	0	0	4	1	0	0	.317	.302
Figueroa, Daniel	R-R	5-11	182	2-19-83	.239	.255	.233	104	364	66	87	12	1	2	29	65	10	9	2	98	33	7	.294	.367
Johnson, Justin	L-R	6-1	180	11-7-82	.250	.250	.250	52	132	23	33	7	1	4	16	16	4	3	0	28	4	4	.409	.349
McCarthy, Ryan	R-R	6-3	195	9-4-82	.242	.212	.258	56	198	24	48	9	3	5	23	19	2	0	0	38	2	3	.394	.315
McCoy, Mike	R-R	5-9	171	4-2-81	.600	.500	.667	1	5	1	3	0	0	0	1	0	0	0	0	1	0	1	.600	.600
Pierce, Mike	R-R	6-1	225	4-19-84	.159	.143	.165	57	170	19	27	10	0	4	15	12	0	2	1	76	2	0	.288	.213
Rowell, Bill	L-R	6-5	205	9-10-88	.248	.187	.268	111	375	39	93	24	0	7	50	36	1	1	1	104	1	4	.368	.315
Snyder, Brandon	R-R	6-2	210	11-23-86	.315	.286	.325	116	435	70	137	33	2	13	80	29	4	1	7	83	3	2	.490	.358
Tripp, Brandon	L-R	6-2	200	4-2-85	.236	.212	.242	123	428	49	101	20	0	17	69	33	6	2	6	145	10	3	.402	.296
Valichka, Brian	R-R	6-3	200	8-21-83	.455	.333	.500	4	11	2	5	2	0	0	2	0	2	1	0	2	0	0	.636	.538
Vinyard, Chris	R-R	6-4	230	12-15-85	.240	.217	.248	123	430	44	103	16	0	16	65	56	3	0	2	102	1	5	.388	.330
White, Jason	L-R	6-1	175	6-7-84	.238	.200	.247	63	214	27	51	8	1	1	17	17	5	7	1	53	10	4	.299	.308
Wieters, Matt	B-R	6-5	230	5-21-86	.345	.391	.327	69	229	48	79	8	0	15	40	44	2	1	4	47	1	2	.576	.448
Winterling, Paul	R-R	6-3	220	7-31-83	.223	.282	.199	87	269	30	60	8	2	5	24	32	3	2	0	90	9	6	.323	.313

Pitching	B-T	HT	WT	DOB	W	L	ERA	G	GS	CG	SV	IP	H	R	ER	HR	BB	SO	AVG	vLH	vRH	K/9	BB/9
Aquino, Greg	R-R	6-1	190	1-11-78	0	0	0.00	1	0	0	0	1	1	0	0	0	0	2	.250	.500	.000	18.00	0.00
Arrieta, Jake	R-R	6-4	225	3-6-86	6	5	2.87	20	20	0	0	113	80	44	36	7	51	120	.199	.257	.165	9.56	4.06
Barajas, Jose	R-R	6-4	190	2-25-88	0	0	6.75	2	0	0	0	4	4	3	3	0	2	1	.267	.500	.000	2.25	4.50
Bascom, Tim	R-R	6-1	205	1-4-85	6	5	5.78	19	19	0	0	95	115	67	61	15	46	74	.303	.277	.320	7.01	4.36
Beato, Pedro	R-R	6-6	230	10-27-86	4	10	5.85	19	19	0	0	97	119	74	63	11	33	51	.306	.371	.269	4.73	3.06
Bergesen, Brad	L-R	6-2	205	9-25-85	1	1	2.08	4	3	0	0	17	15	6	4	2	6	15	.227	.281	.176	7.79	3.12
Bierd, Randor	R-R	6-4	190	3-14-84	0	0	0.00	3	0	0	0	3	0	0	0	0	2	7	.000	.000	.000	21.00	6.00
Bordes, Brett	L-L	5-10	175	11-30-83	0	1	9.00	16	1	0	0	16	21	16	16	0	19	11	.350	.438	.318	6.19	10.69
Burch, Jason	R-R	6-5	215	10-15-82	1	1	1.64	10	0	0	5	11	8	2	2	1	1	9	.200	.182	.207	7.36	0.82
Clark, Zach	R-R	6-0	195	7-11-83	2	2	3.25	12	4	0	1	28	23	13	10	4	5	11	.223	.258	.208	3.58	1.63
Deza, Fredy	R-R	6-2	175	12-11-82	0	2	4.74	12	0	0	4	25	19	15	13	1	8	18	.209	.240	.197	6.57	2.92
Doyne, Cory	R-R	6-2	240	8-13-81	0	0	0.00	3	0	0	0	4	2	0	0	0	4	1	.133	.000	.250	8.31	0.00
Erbe, Brandon	R-R	6-4	180	12-25-87	10	12	4.30	28	28	2	0	151	120	82	72	21	50	151	.216	.228	.208	9.02	2.99
Loewen, Adam	L-L	6-5	235	4-9-84	0	0	0.00	3	1	0	0	3	1	0	0	0	0	5	1.000	.333	.000	15.00	0.00
Martinez, J.P.	R-R	6-2	205	6-8-82	1	0	5.17	35	0	0	4	54	50	31	31	5	35	56	.239	.234	.242	9.33	5.83
Mattaliano, Mick	R-R	6-3	200	1-17-85	0	0	6.43	5	0	0	1	7	10	6	5	0	3	4	.333	.308	.353	5.14	3.86
Miller, Aubrey	R-R	6-4	215	9-22-80	1	0	4.91	1	1	0	0	4	6	2	2	1	1	2	.375	.333	.429	4.91	2.45
Moore, Jeff	R-R	6-1	195	3-26-83	5	3	3.63	36	3	0	0	62	55	31	25	8	23	54	.234	.320	.174	7.84	3.34
Moreland, Kenny	R-R	5-11	185	4-2-86	0	1	9.00	1	0	0	0	2	2	2	2	0	1	3	.286	.400	.000	13.50	4.50
Mueller, Scott	R-R	6-3	175	6-9-86	1	1	5.73	14	0	0	2	22	27	14	14	2	14	16	.314	.368	.271	6.55	5.73
Neigebauer, Robert	R-R	6-4	220	3-6-84	0	1	9.00	2	0	0	0	3	6	3	3	1	4	4	.353	.375	.333	12.00	12.00
Ouellette, Ryan	R-R	5-11	185	10-4-85	5	7	5.22	43	0	0	1	69	75	50	40	4	45	37	.281	.309	.265	4.83	5.87
Parker, Brian	R-R	6-4	195	8-21-85	0	0	5.40	4	0	0	0	5	9	5	3	0	2	6	.391	.571	.313	10.80	3.60
Perez, Wilfredo	L-L	6-0	145	8-12-84	2	4	2.88	26	0	0	2	56	44	21	18	5	30	69	.218	.240	.199	11.02	4.79
Ray, Chris	R-R	6-3	225	1-12-82	0	0	18.00	1	0	0	0	1	3	2	2	1	0	1	.500	.000	.600	9.00	0.00
Renshaw, Jake	R-R	6-3	215	4-29-86	9	11	5.11	27	25	0	0	136	143	82	77	16	57	96	.274	.272	.276	6.37	3.78
Rodriguez, Ryan	L-L	6-4	233	7-10-84	5	3	3.10	47	0	0	4	70	63	35	24	4	28	41	.236	.179	.259	5.30	3.62
Schmidt, Kyle	R-R	6-3	220	8-25-83	4	4	3.57	23	14	0	1	98	86	49	39	9	41	77	.233	.259	.216	7.05	3.75
Thall, Chad	L-L	6-4	220	8-2-85	1	0	2.70	30	1	0	9	43	36	16	13	3	15	44	.226	.119	.265	9.14	3.12
Walker, Jamie	L-L	6-2	195	7-1-71	0	0	0.00	1	0	0	0	1	1	0	0	0	0	0	.250	—	.250	0.00	0.00

Fielding

Catcher	PCT	G	PO	A	E	DP	PB
Dillon	.980	5	45	5	1	0	4
Johnson	.976	38	258	24	7	2	9
Pierce	.982	54	349	37	7	6	7
Valichka	1.000	4	24	5	0	0	0
Wieters	.985	49	346	42	6	5	3

First Base	PCT	G	PO	A	E	DP
Davison	1.000	2	4	1	0	1
Johnson	1.000	2	9	0	0	0
McCarthy	1.000	2	7	2	0	1
Snyder	.986	83	701	53	11	55
Vinyard	.990	55	466	31	5	34
Winterling	1.000	3	18	1	0	1

Second Base	PCT	G	PO	A	E	DP
Abreu	.969	114	206	324	17	68
Amador	1.000	11	20	25	0	2
Davison	.966	17	22	35	2	3
McCoy	—	1	0	0	0	0

Third Base	PCT	G	PO	A	E	DP
Amador	1.000	2	2	4	0	1
Davison	.908	32	17	52	7	4
Rowell	.925	104	62	211	22	19
Snyder	.933	6	5	9	1	1
White	1.000	2	2	7	0	2

Shortstop	PCT	G	PO	A	E	DP
Amador	.935	14	23	35	4	9

	PCT	G	PO	A	E	DP
Cintron	1.000	2	2	3	0	1
Davison	.929	18	24	41	5	12
McCarthy	.949	51	59	129	10	19
White	.979	60	87	148	5	23

Outfield	PCT	G	PO	A	E	DP
Amador	.975	82	110	5	3	4
Andrews	1.000	36	63	3	0	2
Burch	—	1	0	0	0	0
Davison	.867	9	13	0	2	0
Figueroa	.988	103	244	9	3	5
Johnson	1.000	6	4	0	0	0
Tripp	.981	120	190	12	4	2
Winterling	.973	80	137	5	4	0

DELMARVA SHOREBIRDS
SOUTH ATLANTIC LEAGUE
LOW CLASS A

Batting	B-T	HT	WT	DOB	AVG	vLH	vRH	G	AB	R	H	2B	3B	HR	RBI	BB	HBP	SH	SF	SO	SB	CS	SLG	OBP
Adams, Ryan	R-R	6-0	195	4-21-87	.308	.344	.299	119	448	68	138	26	5	11	57	36	6	6	1	109	12	5	.462	.367
Angle, Matt	L-R	5-10	175	9-10-85	.287	.262	.294	126	478	82	137	22	5	4	35	71	7	7	3	86	37	11	.379	.385
Cash, David	B-R	6-3	180	11-22-85	.258	.273	.255	17	62	7	16	4	1	1	9	4	0	1	0	10	5	0	.403	.303
Castillo, Victor	B-R	5-11	180	9-12-84	.231	.261	.223	39	117	11	27	4	0	4	12	8	0	1	2	29	0	2	.368	.276
Crancer, Wally	L-R	6-0	215	7-7-84	.287	.195	.302	83	286	34	82	20	3	6	39	28	4	3	1	55	1	2	.441	.357
Figueroa, Paco	R-R	5-11	180	2-19-83	.314	.467	.282	22	86	12	27	4	0	0	8	8	1	0	3	16	4	1	.360	.367
Florimon Jr., Pedro	B-R	6-2	165	12-10-86	.223	.333	.195	81	269	28	60	18	1	0	19	27	3	3	3	97	13	2	.297	.298
Henson, Tyler	R-R	6-1	190	12-15-87	.265	.260	.266	127	502	71	133	25	3	11	62	25	9	3	2	121	20	3	.392	.310
Lester, Calvin	B-R	6-1	180	12-23-84	.074	.000	.095	18	27	5	2	0	1	0	5	0	3	0	8	3	1	.148	.219
Mahoney, Joe	L-L	6-7	255	2-1-87	.222	.190	.230	31	95	352	37	78	22	1	7	61	24	4	1	6	96	2	0	.349	.275
Martinez, Anthony	R-R	6-3	240	12-19-83	.258	.284	.251	115	423	54	109	27	1	11	54	38	1	0	6	113	3	1	.404	.316
Monaghan, Brendan	R-R	6-2	190	4-11-85	.197	.296	.173	47	137	14	27	6	0	1	14	18	2	2	1	38	4	3	.263	.297
Nowicki, Joe	L-L	6-2	210	11-12-82	.276	.217	.293	130	492	74	136	36	6	19	78	46	8	0	4	142	14	4	.490	.345
Pope, Kieron	R-R	6-1	195	10-3-86	.232	.247	.228	107	383	50	89	18	2	12	45	21	17	0	0	139	7	3	.384	.302
Silveren, Pedro	R-R	6-0	160	9-2-84	.267	.333	.262	16	45	7	12	3	0	0	8	3	0	0	0	7	0	0	.333	.313
Stephen, Jedidiah	R-R	6-2	195	4-30-84	.040	.000	.043	7	25	2	1	0	0	0	1	1	0	0	0	13	0	0	.040	.111
Tucker, Matt	B-R	6-2	185	6-5-83	.286	.278	.289	77	255	43	73	18	2	3	33	29	5	2	2	54	6	6	.408	.368
Valichka, Brian	R-R	6-3	200	8-21-83	.272	.381	.239	30	92	12	25	5	1	1	12	10	4	0	0	23	1	1	.380	.368
White, Jason	L-R	6-1	175	6-7-84	.253	.292	.246	49	150	22	38	4	1	0	15	20	4	3	1	47	8	4	.293	.354
Widlansky, Robbie	L-R	6-2	210	11-6-84	.222	.167	.231	12	45	3	10	3	1	0	2	2	0	0	0	6	0	0	.333	.255
Wolf, Jordan	R-R	6-1	195	5-5-85	.750	1.000	.667	2	4	0	3	0	1	0	1	2	1	0	0	1	1	.250	.857

Pitching	B-T	HT	WT	DOB	W	L	ERA	G	GS	CG	SV	IP	H	R	ER	HR	BB	SO	AVG	vLH	vRH	K/9	BB/9
Aquino, Greg	R-R	6-1	190	1-11-78	0	0	0.00	1	0	0	0	1	0	0	0	0	0	1	.000	.000	.000	9.00	0.00
Bordes, Brett	L-L	5-10	175	11-30-83	2	1	2.70	25	0	0	2	33	27	11	10	2	17	34	.214	.179	.230	9.18	4.59
Britton, Zach	L-L	6-2	172	12-22-87	12	7	3.12	27	27	1	0	147	118	68	51	9	49	114	.219	.166	.239	6.96	2.99
Butler, Tony	L-L	6-7	220	11-18-87	3	4	4.42	12	11	0	0	55	59	31	27	7	11	44	.273	.377	.239	7.20	1.80
Clark, Zach	R-R	6-0	195	7-11-83	1	2	4.11	6	1	0	1	15	15	8	7	2	4	8	.234	.091	.310	4.70	2.35
Esposito, Joe	L-R	5-11	220	5-15-85	2	0	4.86	8	0	0	0	17	16	11	9	1	7	26	.235	.214	.250	14.04	3.78
Flagello, Cliff	R-R	5-10	200	1-3-85	5	3	2.29	39	0	0	3	83	54	26	21	2	39	82	.185	.208	.169	8.93	4.25
Gleason, Sean	L-R	6-0	190	8-21-85	12	3	2.63	30	21	2	0	151	124	54	44	3	46	108	.228	.234	.224	6.45	2.75
Mariotti, John	L-R	6-0	225	8-19-84	3	2	3.74	8	6	0	0	34	27	18	14	2	7	26	.213	.255	.181	6.95	1.87
Mathews, Shane	R-R	6-3	210	3-28-85	0	2	4.29	28	0	0	1	50	48	32	24	1	29	34	.255	.306	.224	6.08	5.19
Mattaliano, Mick	R-R	6-3	200	1-17-85	2	2	1.24	41	0	0	27	44	25	12	6	1	18	16	.167	.194	.148	3.71	1.24
McCurry, Cole	L-L	6-2	180	9-25-85	2	6	6.51	13	12	0	0	57	67	45	41	7	17	54	.282	.262	.289	8.58	2.70
Miller, Aubrey	R-R	6-4	215	9-22-83	3	5	4.48	26	2	0	0	66	73	41	33	6	15	53	.275	.327	.237	7.19	2.04
Moore, Jeff	R-R	6-1	195	3-26-83	0	1	5.40	5	0	0	0	10	11	7	6	3	1	8	.275	.250	.286	7.20	0.90
Mueller, Scott	R-R	6-3	175	6-9-86	0	1	8.16	11	0	0	0	14	13	14	13	5	14	14	.228	.231	.226	8.79	9.42
Neigebauer, Robert	R-R	6-4	220	3-6-84	4	4	4.06	16	5	1	1	51	44	28	23	4	23	37	.230	.250	.216	6.53	4.06
Nery, Nathan	R-L	6-4	212	8-25-85	7	3	3.39	15	15	0	0	82	74	35	31	5	22	59	.242	.266	.236	6.45	2.40
Noel, Luis	R-R	6-1	175	9-29-87	10	8	3.96	27	27	0	0	139	124	70	61	13	73	116	.238	.224	.249	7.53	4.74
Odom, Aaron	L-L	6-0	165	9-24-84	1	2	6.33	7	2	0	0	21	30	16	15	4	8	22	.326	.143	.406	9.28	3.38
Parker, Brian	R-R	6-4	195	8-21-85	7	5	3.64	35	0	0	2	67	62	42	27	4	23	70	.236	.309	.195	9.45	3.10
Ray, Chris	R-R	6-3	225	1-12-82	0	0	0.00	1	0	0	0	1	1	0	0	0	1	2	.333	.333	.000	18.00	10.00
Salberg, Chris	R-L	6-1	185	5-8-84	1	4	4.08	10	10	0	0	53	52	28	24	3	21	46	.251	.236	.257	7.81	3.57
Schindling, Andy	R-R	6-2	175	8-15-86	1	1	3.60	7	0	0	1	15	13	6	6	2	9	8	.241	.318	.188	4.80	5.40
Williamson, Hank	R-R	6-5	233	11-1-85	0	0	0.00	3	0	0	2	6	6	2	0	0	0	8	.231	.000	.333	11.37	0.00

Fielding

Catcher	PCT	G	PO	A	E	DP	PB
Castillo	.986	38	261	31	4	5	5
Crancer	.984	38	225	26	4	1	22
Monaghan	.977	47	309	31	8	4	2
Valichka	.985	30	175	17	3	0	6
Wolf	1.000	2	20	4	0	1	0

First Base	PCT	G	PO	A	E	DP
Crancer	1.000	5	17	1	0	2
Mahoney	.996	49	430	33	2	39
Martinez	.987	93	889	58	12	58
Tucker	1.000	2	2	1	0	0

Second Base	PCT	G	PO	A	E	DP
Adams	.905	96	150	289	46	46
Figueroa	.976	7	13	28	1	4
Florimon Jr.	1.000	1	0	2	0	0
Silveren	.947	9	13	23	2	1
Stephen	1.000	2	3	3	0	0

Tucker	.962	16	31	45	3	9
White	.983	12	22	37	1	6

Third Base	PCT	G	PO	A	E	DP
Adams	.800	1	1	3	1	0
Henson	.917	120	71	250	29	19
Silveren	.000	3	0	0	1	0
Stephen	.833	4	1	9	2	2
Tucker	.912	14	8	23	3	0
White	1.000	2	1	5	0	1

Shortstop	PCT	G	PO	A	E	DP
Adams	.839	7	11	15	5	2
Florimon Jr.	.945	80	112	251	21	45
Henson	1.000	1	0	8	0	0
Tucker	.890	21	28	53	10	11
White	.948	33	39	88	7	18

Outfield	PCT	G	PO	A	E	DP
Angle	.996	126	247	9	1	2
Cash	.966	16	27	1	1	0

Crancer	.946	28	50	3	3	1
Lester	.889	15	16	0	2	0
Mahoney	1.000	7	5	1	0	0
Nowicki	.971	130	228	4	7	1
Pope	.982	79	108	3	2	0
Silveren	—	1	0	0	0	0
Stephen	—	1	0	0	0	0
Tucker	.970	19	30	2	1	1
Widlansky	1.000	12	10	1	0	0

ABERDEEN IRONBIRDS   SHORT-SEASON

NEW YORK-PENN LEAGUE

Batting	B-T	HT	WT	DOB	AVG	vLH	vRH	G	AB	R	H	2B	3B	HR	RBI	BB	HBP	SH	SF	SO	SB	CS	SLG	OBP
Altenhof, Jason	L-R	5-9	165	8-20-86	.207	.000	.261	14	29	7	6	1	1	0	1	4	0	0	0	7	1	0	.310	.303
Baxter, T.J.	L-R	6-1	208	12-13-85	.279	.268	.282	52	183	25	51	8	2	2	25	17	2	0	2	65	4	1	.377	.343
Bent, Brian	R-R	6-2	210	9-11-85	.164	.231	.128	22	73	5	12	3	0	0	4	4	2	0	0	28	0	0	.205	.228
Binick, Kraig	R-L	5-10	180	2-10-85	.253	.268	.248	39	146	23	37	4	3	2	22	10	1	4	2	25	3	2	.363	.302
Bonevacia, Arthur	B-R	5-9	160	5-16-88	.160	.154	.167	8	25	3	4	0	0	0	3	1	2	1	1	6	0	1	.160	.241
Chmiel, Paul	L-R	6-5	200	5-17-87	.233	.258	.225	39	133	11	31	12	0	0	14	17	3	0	1	43	0	0	.323	.331
Durakis, Chad	R-R	6-1	210	9-3-85	.211	.238	.203	29	90	7	19	8	0	0	9	4	6	0	1	20	1	1	.300	.287
Edwards, Tom	L-R	6-2	200	10-15-85	.219	.259	.211	47	155	19	34	8	0	0	11	12	0	2	0	57	0	0	.271	.275
Ellis, Lee	R-R	6-1	213	7-22-84	.210	.212	.209	36	119	10	25	7	0	0	9	13	0	1	0	40	3	1	.269	.288
Figueroa, Paco	R-R	5-11	180	2-19-83	.267	.556	.143	10	30	6	8	2	0	0	2	6	0	1	0	1	2	0	.333	.389
Hudson, Kyle	L-L	5-11	175	1-7-87	.216	.143	.233	11	37	5	8	1	0	0	5	8	0	1	0	12	4	3	.243	.356
Joseph, Caleb	R-R	6-3	180	6-18-86	.261	.290	.249	63	238	34	62	19	0	8	34	15	2	2	6	56	2	0	.441	.303
Julius, Jacob	L-L	6-5	185	3-13-86	.231	.200	.241	61	225	30	52	14	1	6	31	20	8	1	2	56	5	3	.382	.314
Kolodny, Tyler	R-R	6-2	210	3-9-88	.240	.238	.241	72	250	38	60	9	4	10	38	34	15	3	1	83	9	6	.428	.363
Lester, Calvin	B-R	6-1	180	12-23-83	.234	.302	.209	60	192	31	45	2	3	0	12	26	2	2	1	58	19	4	.276	.330
Miclat, Greg	B-R	5-9	180	7-23-87	.291	.375	.256	16	55	9	16	2	0	0	6	8	1	4	0	13	3	2	.327	.391
Perlozzo, Eric	R-R	5-9	175	9-7-84	.241	.288	.217	51	158	18	38	4	0	1	8	10	1	1	1	31	0	1	.285	.288
Rosa, Garabez	R-R	6-2	166	10-12-89	.250	.200	.267	6	20	2	5	0	0	0	2	0	0	0	0	11	0	1	.250	.318
Stephen, Jedidiah	R-R	6-2	195	4-30-84	.243	.170	.275	46	173	24	42	9	1	8	29	12	1	1	0	55	3	2	.445	.296
Widlansky, Robbie	L-R	6-2	210	11-6-84	.279	.188	.323	43	147	23	41	10	1	4	29	11	3	0	1	26	2	0	.442	.340

Pitching	B-T	HT	WT	DOB	W	L	ERA	G	GS	CG	SV	IP	H	R	ER	HR	BB	SO	AVG	vLH	vRH	K/9	BB/9
Albers, Matt	L-R	6-0	205	1-20-83	0	0	0.00	2	0	0	0	2	1	0	0	0	1	4	.143	.333	.000	18.00	4.50
Allar, Brent	R-R	6-3	230	3-1-85	0	0	0.00	3	0	0	0	2	0	0	0	0	4	.000	.000	.000	15.43	7.71
Aquino, Greg	R-R	6-1	190	1-11-78	0	0	0.00	1	0	0	0	1	0	0	0	0	2	.000	—	.000	18.00	0.00
Cooney, Brandon	R-R	6-6	240	8-2-85	1	3	3.81	28	0	0	10	26	24	13	11	3	9	38	.242	.257	.234	13.15	3.12
Deza, Fredy	R-R	6-2	175	12-11-82	1	0	0.00	7	0	0	4	8	6	2	0	0	1	8	.194	.250	.158	9.00	1.13
Doyne, Cory	R-R	6-2	240	8-13-81	0	1	8.44	6	0	0	0	5	6	6	5	0	4	10	.273	.250	.286	16.88	6.75
Drake, Oliver	R-R	6-4	210	1-18-87	0	0	0.87	5	0	0	1	10	9	3	1	1	1	13	.214	.250	.200	11.32	0.87
Egan, Pat	R-R	6-8	225	10-25-84	5	6	3.24	14	14	0	0	78	77	35	28	5	20	72	.254	.276	.237	8.34	2.32
Esposito, Joe	L-R	5-11	220	5-15-85	1	2	2.03	16	0	0	1	27	21	8	6	0	11	31	.226	.286	.190	10.46	3.71
Haughian, Nick	L-L	6-0	205	1-1-87	0	2	9.60	9	1	0	0	15	20	17	16	2	18	11	.333	.286	.348	6.60	10.80
Kirbis, Tony	R-R	6-2	220	2-16-85	2	4	3.73	20	0	0	0	31	33	17	13	1	16	27	.277	.286	.273	7.76	4.60
Lebron, Luis	R-R	6-1	172	3-15-85	0	0	6.52	10	0	0	0	10	11	7	7	0	12	11	.314	.200	.400	10.24	11.17
McCrory, Bob	R-R	6-5	225	5-3-82	0	0	18.00	1	0	0	0	1	1	2	2	0	2	2	.250	1.000	.000	18.00	18.00
McCurry, Cole	L-L	6-2	180	9-25-85	8	3	2.76	15	15	2	0	82	67	31	25	5	22	75	.219	.227	.216	8.27	2.42
Moore, Marcus	R-R	6-4	180	6-1-84	0	0	0.00	1	0	0	0	2	2	2	0	0	0	0	.250	.500	.167	0.00	0.00
Moreau, Nathan	L-L	6-4	222	9-15-86	1	2	5.70	10	7	0	0	36	34	25	23	4	9	48	.246	.326	.211	11.89	2.23
Mueller, Scott	R-R	6-3	175	6-9-86	0	1	—	1	0	0	0	0	2	0	0	0	0	0	.667	.000	.667	—	—
O'Shea, Ryan	L-R	6-1	200	5-29-86	2	1	3.00	16	0	0	3	33	21	13	11	2	15	31	.181	.182	.181	8.45	4.09
Odom, Aaron	L-L	6-0	165	9-24-84	3	6	4.18	14	14	0	0	71	72	51	33	4	33	63	.250	.241	.252	7.99	4.18
Procner, Stephen	R-R	6-2	200	12-27-84	0	2	4.50	15	3	0	0	36	38	22	18	5	11	23	.268	.324	.248	5.75	2.75
Ray, Chris	R-R	6-3	225	1-12-82	0	0	0.00	3	0	0	0	3	4	0	0	0	0	5	.308	.400	.250	15.00	0.00
Salberg, Chris	R-L	6-1	185	5-8-84	3	1	2.17	6	6	0	0	29	25	9	7	0	10	35	.227	.320	.200	10.86	3.10
Schindling, Andy	R-R	6-2	175	8-15-86	1	1	2.55	10	0	0	0	18	15	6	5	1	5	15	.231	.280	.200	7.64	2.55
Smith, Jacob	L-L	6-4	210	10-1-85	1	1	6.66	11	4	0	0	24	37	22	18	1	15	18	.352	.276	.382	6.66	5.55
Spooneybarger, Tim	R-R	6-3	205	10-21-79	0	0	3.68	6	0	0	0	7	9	4	3	0	4	12	.290	.154	.389	14.73	4.91
Tamba, Josh	L-R	6-2	200	11-15-84	0	1	13.50	1	0	0	0	1	1	1	1	0	2	2	.333	.000	1.000	27.00	27.00
Williamson, Hank	R-R	6-5	231	11-1-85	0	1	4.76	17	0	0	0	23	19	14	12	3	5	34	.218	.231	.213	13.50	1.99
Zagone, Rick	L-L	6-4	215	9-30-86	7	1	2.89	15	11	0	0	65	57	22	21	2	14	79	.236	.234	.236	10.88	1.93

Fielding

Catcher	PCT	G	PO	A	E	DP	PB
Bent	.990	22	191	10	2	3	7
Durakis	1.000	9	82	3	0	0	
Joseph	.986	45	388	40	6	6	6

First Base	PCT	G	PO	A	E	DP
Baxter	.974	28	209	17	6	20
Chmiel	.997	36	285	21	1	17
Edwards	1.000	1	4	1	0	0

Joseph	.946	7	46	7	3	2
Julius	1.000	2	14	0	0	1
Widlansky	1.000	3	22	1	0	2

Second Base	PCT	G	PO	A	E	DP
Altenhof	1.000	3	3	7	0	0
Edwards	.901	22	39	43	9	9
Figueroa	.933	4	5	9	1	2
Miclat	1.000	1	2	4	0	1

Perlozzo	.969	48	67	123	6	17
Stephen	1.000	3	6	10	0	1

Third Base	PCT	G	PO	A	E	DP
Baxter	.667	1	1	1	1	0
Edwards	1.000	1	1	0	0	0
Kolodny	.905	71	50	121	18	6
Stephen	1.000	3	1	6	0	1

Shortstop	PCT	G	PO	A	E	DP
Altenhof	.865	10	15	17	5	3
Edwards	.924	23	34	51	7	8
Miclat	.977	8	12	30	1	5
Rosa	.889	5	13	19	4	4
Stephen	.930	34	55	91	11	19

Outfield	PCT	G	PO	A	E	DP
Baxter	.500	3	1	1	2	0
Binick	1.000	27	48	2	0	1
Bonevacia	1.000	8	11	0	0	0
Ellis	.979	34	45	1	1	0
Hudson	.944	11	17	0	1	0

Joseph	1.000	3	2	0	0	0
Julius	1.000	58	96	0	0	0
Lester	.991	58	105	3	1	0
Perlozzo	—	1	0	0	0	0
Widlansky	1.000	33	39	4	0	0

BLUEFIELD ORIOLES   ROOKIE
APPALACHIAN LEAGUE

Batting	B-T	HT	WT	DOB	AVG	vLH	vRH	G	AB	R	H	2B	3B	HR	RBI	BB	HBP	SH	SF	SO	SB	CS	SLG	OBP
Bernardo, Luis	R-R	6-0	170	1-16-88	.197	.237	.179	40	122	7	24	1	0	1	8	5	3	3	1	17	1	1	.230	.244
Black, Dustin	R-R	6-0	205	12-8-86	.128	.071	.160	14	39	3	5	0	0	0	2	8	2	0	1	14	0	0	.128	.300
Bonevacia, Arthur	B-R	5-9	160	5-16-88	.256	.238	.263	30	78	12	20	1	0	1	8	10	0	5	0	30	1	4	.308	.341
Britton, Buck	L-R	6-1	163	5-16-86	.289	.158	.308	47	149	19	43	5	0	0	14	20	1	3	2	20	3	1	.322	.372
Cardona, Rodolfo	R-R	5-10	155	11-27-86	.283	.356	.256	49	166	25	47	10	0	3	28	22	2	2	1	40	4	4	.398	.372
Carolus, Levi	R-R	6-0	160	9-22-87	.275	.244	.287	49	167	21	46	8	1	7	29	10	2	3	0	55	6	2	.461	.324
Conley, Brian	L-R	6-2	195	5-7-86	.248	.276	.240	38	133	25	33	5	3	2	10	19	3	0	0	17	3	3	.376	.355
D'Oleo, Richard	L-L	6-2	165	5-5-86	.216	.333	.199	52	162	25	35	5	2	3	19	25	0	1	0	34	7	5	.327	.319
Heller, Danny	L-L	6-3	210	1-11-87	.159	.000	.171	17	44	4	7	3	0	0	3	8	1	0	0	12	0	0	.227	.302
Pehrson, Preston	L-R	6-2	215	9-25-84	.192	.400	.176	37	73	11	14	3	0	2	6	11	2	0	1	20	0	1	.315	.310
Polanco, Elvin	B-L	6-3	190	3-3-87	.311	.254	.333	62	219	36	68	16	1	10	42	19	1	0	2	45	3	0	.530	.365
Ray, Nick	L-L	6-0	185	11-5-85	.225	.240	.222	46	142	18	32	7	1	0	12	19	3	1	2	54	3	4	.289	.325
Rook, Jason	L-R	6-1	200	8-28-87	.232	.118	.269	45	138	19	32	4	2	1	8	17	0	3	1	47	7	2	.312	.314
Stevens, Bobby	R-R	6-0	190	3-30-87	.213	.216	.212	49	150	29	32	5	1	1	12	9	23	2	1	48	13	4	.280	.350
Tarnow, Josh	R-R	6-0	180	11-4-84	.183	.133	.200	22	60	4	11	3	0	0	8	8	1	0	1	24	0	0	.233	.286
Welty, Ronnie	R-R	6-2	190	1-19-88	.314	.339	.304	55	207	26	65	13	2	3	34	9	7	2	1	49	6	3	.440	.362
West, Lance	R-R	6-2	215	11-8-87	.210	.172	.231	29	81	14	17	5	0	5	17	5	6	0	0	35	0	1	.457	.304

Pitching	B-T	HT	WT	DOB	W	L	ERA	G	GS	CG	SV	IP	H	R	ER	HR	BB	SO	AVG	vLH	vRH	K/9	BB/9
Allen, Colin	R-R	6-1	175	10-14-86	3	2	2.31	14	11	0	0	62	59	25	16	2	20	64	.239	.194	.271	9.24	2.89
Barajas, Jose	R-R	6-4	190	2-25-88	1	0	2.75	17	0	0	7	20	15	8	6	0	3	26	.205	.360	.125	11.90	1.37
Basta, Samuel	L-L	6-0	165	2-21-86	0	0	13.50	5	0	0	0	9	12	13	13	1	16	3	.353	.500	.292	3.12	16.62
Drake, Oliver	R-R	6-4	210	1-13-87	1	0	0.77	7	0	0	0	12	7	2	1	1	2	11	.167	.000	.241	8.49	1.54
Eastham, Dan	R-R	6-2	200	12-30-84	1	4	9.45	12	0	0	0	20	26	24	21	1	18	18	.329	.333	.327	8.10	8.10
Faiola, Josh	R-R	6-3	200	10-3-83	1	1	3.94	13	0	0	0	32	26	20	14	1	14	37	.220	.214	.222	10.41	3.94
Gamboa, Eddie	R-R	6-2	195	12-21-84	1	7	3.63	12	12	1	0	62	64	31	25	6	14	41	.264	.275	.259	5.95	2.03
Garcia, Adolfito	R-R	6-2	170	1-31-85	0	0	—	1	0	0	0	1	2	2	0	2	1	.500	1.000	.000	—	—
Gurka, Jason	L-L	6-0	170	1-10-88	0	0	9.00	2	0	0	0	3	5	3	3	1	0	5	.357	.333	.375	15.00	0.00
Kantakevich, Pat	R-R	6-2	198	8-11-86	3	0	1.29	14	0	0	3	21	9	5	3	0	8	18	.127	.185	.091	7.71	3.43
Keating, Travis	R-R	6-6	205	9-16-85	2	1	3.45	13	0	0	2	29	29	17	11	1	7	23	.250	.314	.222	7.22	2.20
Moreland, Kenny	R-R	5-11	185	4-24-86	6	4	2.93	13	13	0	0	68	70	22	22	5	6	65	.266	.256	.273	8.65	0.80
Orman, Conrad	L-L	6-2	180	5-1-87	0	1	20.86	7	0	0	0	7	18	17	16	2	2	7	.425	.375	.438	8.59	2.45
Phelps, Thomas	R-R	6-2	215	10-12-87	2	2	4.75	10	4	0	0	30	41	17	16	3	9	17	.331	.352	.314	5.04	2.67
Phillips, Chase	R-R	6-4	175	9-14-86	1	0	4.70	4	0	0	0	8	9	5	4	0	8	8	.310	.333	.294	9.39	9.39
Rivero, Raul	R-R	6-0	165	5-6-86	1	5	5.78	13	13	0	0	62	84	49	40	5	16	47	.317	.302	.324	6.79	2.31
Sexton, Tyler	L-L	6-4	205	7-24-85	3	5	4.19	12	12	1	0	54	65	36	25	1	17	42	.300	.303	.297	7.04	2.85
Sisk, Brian	L-L	5-10	200	8-21-85	3	1	3.74	13	0	0	0	22	34	18	9	3	6	10	.337	.414	.306	4.15	2.49
Touchatt, Kyle	R-R	6-2	200	11-22-84	0	3	4.31	13	0	0	0	31	37	20	15	1	13	26	.291	.275	.299	7.47	3.73

Fielding

Catcher	PCT	G	PO	A	E	DP	PB
Bernardo	.978	40	245	70	7	2	14
Black	.984	8	59	4	1	1	2
Pehrson	1.000	18	51	4	0	0	5
Tarnow	.980	12	86	11	2	3	1

First Base	PCT	G	PO	A	E	DP
Carolus	.882	3	14	1	2	3
Pehrson	.988	11	75	1	1	6
Polanco	.975	60	528	29	14	38
Tarnow	.917	2	11	0	1	1
West	—	1	0	0	0	0

Second Base	PCT	G	PO	A	E	DP
Britton	.969	43	83	106	6	28

Cardona	.959	21	28	65	4	11
Carolus	1.000	1	1	1	0	1
Stevens	.927	9	21	17	3	2

Third Base	PCT	G	PO	A	E	DP
Britton	1.000	1	0	2	0	0
Carolus	.876	43	33	94	18	10
Conley	.906	23	11	47	6	5
Stevens	—	1	0	0	0	0
Tarnow	1.000	2	2	6	0	1

Shortstop	PCT	G	PO	A	E	DP
Britton	—	1	0	0	0	0
Cardona	.930	30	29	77	8	7
Stevens	.923	40	57	134	16	32

Outfield	PCT	G	PO	A	E	DP
Bonevacia	.963	27	26	0	1	0
Carolus	—	1	0	0	0	0
Conley	1.000	15	20	3	0	0
D'Oleo	1.000	11	11	0	0	0
Heller	1.000	5	6	0	0	0
Ray	.939	44	59	3	4	1
Rook	.975	44	73	4	2	1
Welty	.952	55	78	1	4	1
West	.857	14	11	1	2	0

GCL ORIOLES   ROOKIE
GULF COAST LEAGUE

Batting	B-T	HT	WT	DOB	AVG	vLH	vRH	G	AB	R	H	2B	3B	HR	RBI	BB	HBP	SH	SF	SO	SB	CS	SLG	OBP
Avery, Xavier	L-L	5-11	180	1-1-90	.280	.267	.290	47	175	27	49	8	1	0	7	10	4	3	0	51	13	3	.337	.333
Binick, Kraig	R-L	5-10	180	2-10-85	.267	.600	.100	5	15	2	4	2	0	0	1	4	1	1	0	2	1	1	.400	.353
Casamayor, Omar	B-R	5-11	170	11-3-86	.281	.288	.275	40	128	12	36	8	1	0	16	9	3	3	0	17	2	4	.359	.343
Cintron, Edwin	B-R	5-11	175	6-29-90	.226	.103	.333	21	62	7	14	1	0	0	4	2	0	0	1	20	2	1	.242	.246
Dillon, Zach	L-R	5-10	210	5-18-83	.294	.250	.308	6	17	1	5	3	0	0	3	6	0	0	0	1	0	0	.471	.478

	B-T	HT	WT	DOB	AVG	vLH	vRH	G	AB	R	H	2B	3B	HR	RBI	BB	HBP	SH	SF	SO	SB	CS	SLG	OBP
Gianakas, Derek	R-R	5-10	185	4-7-86	.152	.000	.357	11	33	4	5	1	0	0	4	3	2	0	0	4	0	0	.182	.263
Gioioso, Mike	R-R	6-0	190	2-14-85	.200	.300	.150	27	60	10	12	1	0	1	7	13	4	1	1	12	1	0	.267	.372
Gonzalez, Grolmann	R-R	6-1	180	10-12-88	.222	.229	.218	36	90	11	20	1	0	0	8	12	5	1	3	21	1	1	.233	.336
Guerrero, Janensis	R-R	6-0	170	5-21-89	.154	.087	.207	19	52	4	8	2	1	0	0	1	0	0	0	11	0	0	.231	.170
Hoes, L.J.	R-R	6-1	181	3-5-90	.308	.261	.344	48	159	36	49	4	3	1	18	30	0	1	1	22	10	0	.390	.416
Kianes, Jose	B-L	6-2	182	5-1-87	.175	.300	.133	11	40	3	7	1	1	1	2	2	0	0	0	17	0	0	.325	.214
Martin, Justin	R-R	5-10	185	9-25-84	.239	.214	.256	28	71	7	17	1	0	0	6	4	1	1	2	9	1	1	.254	.282
Mejia, Francisco	R-R	6-1	150	2-27-86	.206	.214	.200	39	97	7	20	4	0	2	15	3	2	4	1	22	1	2	.309	.243
Meyer, Edinho	R-R	6-2	170	2-7-88	.317	.333	.304	42	139	17	44	9	0	3	17	12	4	1	1	30	0	0	.446	.385
Miclat, Greg	B-R	5-9	180	7-23-87	.500	.000	.667	1	4	1	2	1	0	0	1	0	0	0	0	2	0	0	.750	.500
Perez, Dennis	R-R	5-11	185	7-30-88	.213	.242	.196	34	89	6	19	5	0	0	11	10	0	0	1	11	2	1	.270	.290
Ramirez, Luis	L-L	6-3	170	4-24-88	.321	.268	.353	30	109	15	35	8	0	1	7	5	1	1	0	17	2	1	.422	.357
Ricardo, Dashenko	R-R	6-0	160	3-1-90	.169	.200	.148	39	136	8	23	4	0	0	8	4	1	1	0	33	0	0	.199	.199
Rivera, Larry	B-R	6-1	170	5-26-88	.242	.308	.200	14	33	4	8	1	0	0	4	3	1	2	0	9	4	1	.273	.324
Rosa, Garabez	R-R	6-2	166	10-12-89	.330	.342	.321	49	185	24	61	8	3	4	29	1	2	3	1	26	4	2	.470	.339
Santana, Javier	B-R	6-1	160	7-31-87	.238	.419	.132	31	84	6	20	2	0	0	6	8	1	2	2	22	2	0	.262	.305
Thomas, Corey	R-R	6-2	201	9-23-88	.286	.000	.500	2	7	0	2	0	0	0	1	0	0	0	0	4	0	0	.286	.375

Pitching	B-T	HT	WT	DOB	W	L	ERA	G	GS	CG	SV	IP	H	R	ER	HR	BB	SO	AVG	vLH	vRH	K/9	BB/9
Achil, Miguel	R-R	6-4	145	3-18-88	0	0	7.98	15	0	0	0	15	13	17	13	0	19	7	.224	.273	.160	4.30	11.66
Allar, Brent	R-R	6-3	230	3-1-85	0	0	0.00	4	0	0	0	4	6	3	0	0	2	5	.316	.455	.125	11.25	4.50
Almanzar, Jorge	R-R	6-2	160	7-25-86	2	4	4.75	12	3	1	1	30	33	21	16	1	20	29	.282	.262	.304	8.60	5.93
Anderson, Brian	R-R	6-4	215	3-6-86	1	1	5.51	15	0	0	0	16	16	11	10	0	13	9	.276	.265	.292	4.96	7.16
Beal, Jesse	B-R	6-6	210	7-12-90	0	1	5.14	5	0	0	0	7	9	4	4	0	1	8	.321	.083	.500	10.29	1.29
Beato, Pedro	R-R	6-6	230	10-27-86	0	0	2.53	2	2	0	0	11	10	3	3	1	1	3	.244	.143	.350	2.53	0.84
Bierd, Randor	R-R	6-4	190	3-14-84	0	1	4.50	3	0	0	0	4	3	3	2	0	2	5	.200	.400	.100	11.25	4.50
Bundy, Bobby	R-R	6-2	215	1-13-90	0	0	9.00	2	0	0	0	2	5	2	2	1	0	4	.455	.333	.600	18.00	0.00
Conklin, Andrew	R-R	6-2	215	7-8-87	0	0	7.98	11	0	0	0	15	20	15	13	0	21	6	.317	.344	.290	3.68	12.89
De La Cruz, Jario	R-R	6-3	183	7-15-87	0	2	3.00	10	2	0	0	21	18	9	7	0	9	27	.220	.171	.255	11.57	3.86
Doyne, Cory	R-R	6-2	240	8-13-81	0	0	0.00	4	0	0	0	4	2	0	0	0	1	5	.154	.000	.222	11.25	2.25
Frabizio, Vito	R-R			6-28-89	3	4	5.93	10	8	0	0	41	64	29	27	0	14	27	.356	.359	.352	5.93	3.07
Lebron, Luis	R-R	6-1	172	3-15-85	0	1	14.40	11	0	0	2	10	20	18	16	0	15	6	.426	.571	.308	5.40	13.50
Madrigal, Leonardo	L-L	6-3	140	1-12-87	0	3	6.04	16	0	0	0	22	18	21	15	1	28	15	.222	.115	.273	6.04	11.28
Moore, Justin	R-R	6-3	190	7-26-89	1	4	2.98	12	11	0	0	57	63	28	19	1	16	51	.279	.318	.244	8.01	2.51
Moore, Marcus	R-R	6-4	180	6-1-84	2	1	0.50	12	0	0	2	18	10	5	1	0	5	31	.156	.129	.182	15.50	2.50
Ray, Chris	R-R	6-3	225	1-12-82	0	0	0.00	3	3	0	0	3	3	0	0	0	0	3	.250	.200	.286	9.00	0.00
Reyes, Jean Carlos	R-R	6-1	150	6-22-87	0	5	3.04	17	0	0	2	27	23	11	9	0	14	28	.245	.292	.196	9.45	4.73
Tavarez, Daurin	R-R	6-6	160	2-8-89	2	7	4.83	12	12	0	0	50	64	35	27	2	17	28	.317	.370	.265	5.01	3.04
Taveras, Sam	R-R	6-3	180	1-4-88	2	4	3.60	11	10	0	0	35	40	25	14	1	19	33	.288	.310	.265	8.49	4.89

Fielding

Catcher	PCT	G	PO	A	E	DP	PB
Dillon	1.000	3	14	1	0	0	0
Guerrero	.977	19	115	11	3	1	8
Martin	.978	12	43	1	1	0	0
Perez	1.000	2	12	1	0	1	1
Ricardo	.977	32	182	26	5	4	18

First Base	PCT	G	PO	A	E	DP
Casamayor	1.000	5	23	1	0	4
Gonzalez	1.000	1	2	0	0	0
Kianes	.750	2	3	0	1	0
Martin	1.000	4	23	2	0	3
Meyer	.976	31	228	14	6	14
Perez	1.000	24	167	12	0	26

Second Base	PCT	G	PO	A	E	DP
Casamayor	.786	2	4	7	3	2

	PCT	G	PO	A	E	DP
Gioioso	.941	7	15	17	2	6
Hoes	.930	42	84	114	15	22
Santana	.923	8	18	18	3	6

Third Base	PCT	G	PO	A	E	DP
Casamayor	.963	30	18	60	3	2
Gioioso	.913	17	9	12	2	3
Hoes	1.000	1	0	1	0	0
Martin	1.000	1	1	1	0	1
Santana	.806	12	6	23	7	1
Thomas	1.000	2	1	5	0	0

Shortstop	PCT	G	PO	A	E	DP
Casamayor	.923	5	5	7	1	1
Gioioso	.500	1	0	1	1	0
Miclat	1.000	1	2	0	0	0
Rosa	.927	48	64	139	16	32

	PCT	G	PO	A	E	DP
Santana	.966	9	12	16	1	5

Outfield	PCT	G	PO	A	E	DP
Avery	.974	43	73	2	2	1
Binick	1.000	3	5	0	0	0
Cintron	.962	18	23	2	1	1
Gianakas	1.000	10	14	0	0	0
Gioioso	—					
Gonzalez	.886	29	33	6	5	1
Kianes	1.000	8	11	0	0	0
Martin	.750	2	3	0	1	0
Mejia	.983	39	53	4	1	3
Perez	1.000	1	4	0	0	0
Ramirez	.977	27	36	6	1	2
Rivera	1.000	12	21	2	0	1
Santana	1.000	4	3	0	0	0

DSL ORIOLES   ROOKIE

DOMINICAN SUMMER LEAGUE

Batting	B-T	HT	WT	DOB	AVG	vLH	vRH	G	AB	R	H	2B	3B	HR	RBI	BB	HBP	SH	SF	SO	SB	CS	SLG	OBP
Arias, Moises	R-R	6-6	205	2-3-89	.200	.100	.233	33	80	10	16	3	0	0	2	6	0	2	1	29	0	1	.238	.253
Calderon, David	R-R	6-1	180	1-30-90	.238	.176	.254	29	84	6	20	1	1	0	6	16	1	2	0	18	0	0	.274	.366
Cleofa, Rojean	R-R	5-11	176	9-11-90	.233	.258	.224	43	116	20	27	7	2	0	7	8	4	2	0	17	2	7	.328	.305
Feliz, Esteylin	L-R	6-1	190	9-24-88	.120	.143	.116	46	133	6	16	2	1	0	8	13	3	0	2	34	0	3	.150	.212
Guerrero, Janensis	R-R	6-0	170	5-21-89	.250	.000	.250	10	31	4	7	1	0	0	4	3	0	2	0	4	1	1	.258	.294
Melenciano, Jaynnertt	R-R	6-1	170	11-13-87	.239	.167	.257	56	176	23	42	6	3	0	18	17	10	3	2	41	12	3	.307	.337
Moranci, Gino	L-L	6-4	188	1-27-90	.213	.300	.202	32	94	8	20	4	1	0	5	9	2	1	0	29	1	0	.277	.295
Nivar, Jose	B-R	6-1	170	2-28-89	.249	.268	.244	58	221	20	55	10	1	0	24	13	5	0	1	51	4	6	.303	.304
Polanco, Joel	R-R	6-2	190	9-27-85	.296	.250	.302	44	98	9	29	6	1	0	8	11	4	2	1	7	1	1	.378	.386
Rivera, Larry	B-R	6-1	170	5-26-88	.216	.160	.230	40	125	20	27	6	2	2	18	17	7	2	1	26	10	4	.344	.340
Roson, Deibisson	R-R	6-4	210	8-12-89	.206	.167	.222	22	63	4	13	0	0	3	6	0	0	0	0	19	0	1	.206	.275
Serrata, Martin	B-R	6-1	170	11-3-88	.216	.106	.250	60	199	19	43	3	2	1	10	14	1	6	0	37	14	6	.266	.271
Tejeda, Anyi	R-R	6-3	173	1-19-89	.160	.211	.145	58	169	15	27	4	1	0	10	3	5	2	3	47	2	3	.195	.194

	B-T	HT	WT	DOB	AVG	vLH	vRH	AB	H															
Wilson, Octavio	R-R	6-2	162	10-11-89	.240	.257	.235	50	154	27	37	4	1	0	12	22	3	2	1	39	6	4	.279	.344
Wilson, Edwin	R-R	6-1	170	11-10-89	.214	.214	.214	66	201	21	43	8	0	1	17	19	6	2	3	45	2	3	.269	.297
Zorrilla, Alexander	R-R	6-1	169	5-16-91	.087	.000	.111	9	23	4	2	1	0	0	4	5	0	0	1	10	0	0	.130	.241

Pitching

	B-T	HT	WT	DOB	W	L	ERA	G	GS	CG	SV	IP	H	R	ER	HR	BB	SO	AVG	vLH	vRH	K/9	BB/9
Abad, Leonaldo	R-R	6-3	193	1-17-87	0	0	4.15	4	0	0	0	4	5	2	2	0	4	2	.294	.667	.214	4.15	8.31
Castillo, Yancarlos	R-R	6-2	175	1-7-91	4	0	3.14	15	8	0	0	49	46	27	17	1	33	35	.258	.217	.273	6.47	6.10
Cespedes, Angel	R-R	6-2	170	8-27-89	4	6	4.61	13	13	0	0	68	76	45	35	4	23	34	.283	.319	.264	4.48	3.03
Garcia, Rafael	R-R	6-3	170	9-15-89	0	1	4.19	11	0	0	0	19	20	13	9	2	4	4	.260	.095	.321	1.86	1.86
Jean, Samuel	L-L	6-1	175	6-22-89	2	3	5.04	16	6	0	0	50	45	31	28	0	25	45	.239	.308	.234	8.10	4.50
Jimenez, Enrico	L-L	6-3	195	2-7-89	1	4	5.04	16	8	0	0	45	46	36	25	0	40	35	.269	.333	.259	7.05	8.06
Mambru, Dionicio	R-R	6-1	180	4-8-89	0	4	3.78	17	6	0	0	50	28	27	21	1	41	62	.163	.250	.129	11.16	7.38
Nunez, Eduardo	R-R	6-2	170	11-29-89	0	4	4.60	29	0	0	11	31	21	18	16	1	15	28	.188	.269	.163	8.04	4.31
Nunez, Julio	R-R	6-5	200	11-30-88	3	8	4.56	12	9	0	0	49	57	33	25	2	17	26	.294	.289	.295	4.74	3.10
Princivil, William	R-R	6-2	180	4-12-90	0	6	6.56	15	6	0	0	36	42	31	26	0	21	27	.298	.256	.314	6.81	5.30
Ramirez, Eiri	R-R	6-0	173	2-2-88	3	4	2.44	15	8	0	0	59	41	24	16	0	26	43	.203	.220	.192	6.56	3.97
Reyes, Julio	R-R	6-3	180	8-30-90	0	1	8.82	12	0	0	0	16	21	21	16	1	22	13	.318	.318	.318	7.16	12.12
Rivera, Jorge	L-L	6-0	200	10-30-90	0	0	6.55	6	0	0	0	11	7	8	8	0	9	14	.194	.500	.156	11.45	7.36
Rodriguez, Mike	L-L	6-1	165	4-24-89	0	1	6.43	11	1	0	0	14	14	14	10	1	22	16	.250	.000	.264	10.29	14.14
Santana, Kelvin	R-R	6-4	190	4-15-90	0	0	5.02	10	0	0	0	14	14	10	8	0	16	9	.250	.350	.194	5.65	10.05
Sosa, Israel	L-L	6-2	180	6-6-89	0	3	11.05	14	4	0	0	22	29	30	27	0	23	21	.305	.364	.298	8.59	9.41
Sosa, Jose	R-R	6-4	190	4-2-87	0	2	9.43	18	0	0	0	21	27	28	22	0	18	14	.303	.476	.250	6.00	7.71
Suero, Ambiorix	R-R	6-1	165	2-2-91	0	1	9.53	6	1	0	0	6	3	6	6	0	11	7	.167	.286	.091	11.12	17.47

Fielding

Catcher	PCT	G	PO	A	E	DP	PB
Arias	1.000	1	3	1	0	0	0
Calderon	.983	28	151	21	3	1	6
Guerrero	1.000	10	77	8	0	0	2
Lapaix	.969	23	117	10	4	1	6
Polanco	.988	31	133	26	2	1	1

First Base	PCT	G	PO	A	E	DP
Arias	.978	26	166	10	4	12
Calderon	1.000	1	3	0	0	0
Moranci	.986	8	67	3	1	10
Polanco	.985	9	61	4	1	4
E. Wilson	.983	45	325	19	6	23

Second Base	PCT	G	PO	A	E	DP
Ciriaco	.967	64	166	186	12	39
Feliz	.952	4	7	13	1	3
O. Wilson	.889	3	3	5	1	0
Zorrilla	.857	3	2	4	1	1

Third Base	PCT	G	PO	A	E	DP
Feliz	.838	38	30	68	19	4
Jabalera	.978	11	8	36	1	1
Rivera	.833	3	3	7	2	0
Tejeda	.917	29	25	52	7	3
E. Wilson	.750	3	0	3	1	0
Zorrilla	1.000	1	1	0	0	0

Shortstop	PCT	G	PO	A	E	DP
Feliz	—	1	0	0	0	0
Tejeda	.939	31	37	86	8	9
O. Wilson	.886	43	57	106	21	22
Zorrilla	.720	6	9	9	7	2

Outfield	PCT	G	PO	A	E	DP
Arias	1.000	1	2	0	0	0
Cleofa	.955	33	63	1	3	0
Melenciano	.981	38	50	1	1	0
Moranci	1.000	7	6	1	0	0
Nivar	.928	54	95	8	8	5
Rivera	1.000	34	50	3	0	1
Roson	.909	8	8	2	1	0
Serrata	.975	49	74	4	2	1
E. Wilson	1.000	13	13	2	0	0

Boston Red Sox

BY ALEX SPEIER

Most teams that come within a single win of the World Series are left with heartache. But given the formidable circumstances that the 2008 Red Sox overcame to reach that point, they could be forgiven for expressing little remorse about falling just short of the Fall Classic.

It began before spring training, when righthander Curt Schilling found out he had a degenerative biceps condition that necessitated season-ending surgery. Josh Beckett landed on the disabled list in spring training with a back injury. The Sox began the regular season in Japan, and the intercontinental flight sidelined J.D. Drew. Injuries to key contributors remained a season-long constant: Beckett (back, elbow, oblique), Drew (back), Mike Lowell (thumb, oblique, hip), Daisuke Matsuzaka (shoulder) and David Ortiz (wrist) all missed at least three weeks.

While injuries left the team scrambling to round out its roster, so, too, did the unsettling saga of Manny Ramirez' eighth season in Boston. Ramirez received raves from coaches and players alike for his team-first attitude through May, when he launched his 500th career homer. But a dark swirl of events commenced in June, and just before the trade deadline the Sox made a three-way deal that sent Ramirez to the Dodgers and imported Jason Bay from the Pirates.

Still, the Sox managed to claim the wild card, then beat the Angels in the Division Series. They rose from the dead against the Rays with a historic comeback from a 7-0, seventh-inning deficit in Game Five of the American League Championship Series before finally falling in Game Seven.

In many ways, the Sox were a stronger organization than in 2007, when they won the World Series. The team's biggest contributors were largely homegrown, and its ability to withstand injuries was thanks to minor league depth.

The offensive engine was powered by first baseman (and sometimes third baseman) Kevin Youkilis and second baseman Dustin Pedroia.

Youkilis finished in the top six in the American League in average, on-base percentage, slugging, OPS, RBIs and extra-base hits. Pedroia became just the eighth second baseman to have at least a .325 average, 15 homers, 15 steals and 100 runs.

Meanwhile, a healthy Jon Lester emerged as one of the top pitchers in baseball. The 24-year-old

PLAYERS OF THE YEAR

MAJOR LEAGUE: JON LESTER, LHP

Lester blitzed through 2008 at breakneck speed and fired the Red Sox to the brink of the World Series. He pitched a no-hitter May 19 against the Royals, and his 3.21 ERA ranked fourth in the AL. He also went 1-2, 2.36 in 27 postseason innings.

MINOR LEAGUE: MICHAEL BOWDEN, RHP

A first-round supplemental pick in 2005, Bowden was 9-7, 2.62 with 130 strikeouts and 29 walks in 144 innings combined at Double-A Portland and Triple-A Pawtucket. He won his major league debut on Aug. 30 against the White Sox.

MIKE JANES

ORGANIZATION LEADERS

BATTING		*Minimum 250 at-bats
*AVG	Nava, Daniel, Lancaster	.341
R	Reddick, Josh, Greenville/Lanc./Portland	89
H	Thurston, Joe, Pawtucket	160
TB	Reddick, Josh, Greenville/Lanc./Portland	262
2B	Daeges, Zach, Portland	34
3B	Reddick, Josh, Greenville/Lanc./Portland	12
HR	Van Every, Jonathan, Pawtucket	26
RBI	Reddick, Josh, Greenville/Lanc./Portland	91
BB	Anderson, Lars, Lancaster/Portland	75
SO	Van Every, Jonathan, Pawtucket	157
SB	Lin, Che-Hsuan, Greenville	33
*OBP	Nava, Daniel, Lancaster	.424
*SLG	Bailey, Jeff, Pawtucket	.562
PITCHING		**†Minimum 75 innings**
W	Pauley, David, Pawtucket	14
	Zink, Charlie, Pawtucket	14
L	Richardson, Dustin, Portland	10
	Hansack, Devern, Pawtucket	10
	Beazley, Travis, Lancaster	10
†ERA	Bowden, Michael, Portland, Pawtucket	2.62
G	Switzer, Jon, Pawtucket	52
GS	Zink, Charlie, Pawtucket	28
SV	Ventura, Felix, Greenville	19
IP	Zink, Charlie, Pawtucket	174
BB	Martinez, Edgar, Pawtucket	58
SO	Doubront, Felix, Greenville, Lancaster	138
†AVG	Bowden, Michael, Portland, Pawtucket	.212

lefthander finished 16-6, 3.21 ERA, highlighted by a no-hitter against the Royals on May 19.

Righthander Justin Masterson emerged as a key contributor to the pitching staff. Jed Lowrie, meanwhile, played error-free defense at short and delivered quality at-bats throughout the year.

2008 PERFORMANCE

General Manager: Theo Epstein. **Farm Director:** Mike Hazen. **Scouting Director:** Jason McLeod.

Class	Team	League	W	L	PCT	Finish*	Manager	Affiliate Since
Majors	Boston	American	95	67	.586	3rd (14)	Terry Francona	—
Triple-A	Pawtucket Red Sox	International	85	58	.594	3rd (14)	Ron Johnson	1973
Double-A	Portland Sea Dogs	Eastern	74	66	.529	4th (12)	Arnie Beyeler	2003
High A	Lancaster JetHawks	California	76	64	.543	2nd (10)	Chad Epperson	2007
Low A	Greenville Drive	South Atlantic	70	69	.504	8th (16)	Kevin Boles	2005
Short-season	Lowell Spinners	New York-Penn	40	33	.548	5th (14)	Gary DiSarcina	1996
Rookie	GCL Red Sox	Gulf Coast	28	27	.509	8th (16)	Dave Tomlin	1993

Overall 2008 Minor League Record 373 347 9th

* Finish in overall standings (No. of teams in league). ^League champion.

ORGANIZATION STATISTICS

BOSTON RED SOX

AMERICAN LEAGUE

Batting	B-T	HT	WT	DOB	AVG	vLH	vRH	G	AB	R	H	2B	3B	HR	RBI	BB	HBP	SH	SF	SO	SB	CS	SLG	OBP
Bailey, Jeff	R-R	6-2	200	11-19-78	.280	.269	.292	27	50	10	14	1	1	2	6	9	0	0	0	17	0	0	.460	.390
Bay, Jason	R-R	6-2	205	9-20-78	.293	.362	.270	49	184	39	54	12	2	9	37	22	2	0	3	51	3	0	.527	.370
Carter, Chris	L-L	6-0	230	9-16-82	.333	1.000	.250	9	18	5	6	0	0	0	3	2	0	0	0	5	0	0	.333	.400
Casey, Sean	L-R	6-4	230	7-2-74	.322	.324	.321	69	199	14	64	14	0	0	17	17	2	0	0	25	1	0	.392	.381
Cash, Kevin	R-R	6-0	200	12-6-77	.225	.361	.179	61	142	11	32	7	0	3	15	18	0	0	2	50	0	0	.338	.309
Cora, Alex	L-R	6-0	200	10-18-75	.270	.286	.266	75	152	14	41	8	2	0	9	16	9	1	1	13	1	1	.349	.371
Crisp, Coco	B-R	6-0	180	11-1-79	.283	.295	.278	118	361	55	102	18	3	7	41	35	1	8	4	59	20	7	.407	.344
Drew, J.D.	L-R	6-1	200	11-20-75	.280	.284	.279	109	368	79	103	23	4	19	64	79	4	0	5	80	4	1	.519	.408
Ellsbury, Jacoby	L-L	6-1	185	9-11-83	.280	.295	.275	145	554	98	155	22	7	9	47	41	7	4	3	80	50	11	.394	.336
Kotsay, Mark	L-L	6-0	205	12-2-75	.226	.241	.218	22	84	6	19	8	1	0	12	7	0	0	0	11	0	1	.345	.286
Kottaras, George	L-R	6-0	185	5-16-83	.200	.500	.000	3	5	1	1	1	0	0	0	0	0	0	0	2	0	0	.400	.200
Lowell, Mike	R-R	6-3	210	2-24-74	.274	.318	.263	113	419	58	115	27	0	17	73	38	5	0	6	61	2	2	.461	.338
Lowrie, Jed	B-R	6-0	180	4-17-84	.258	.338	.222	81	260	34	67	25	3	2	46	35	1	2	8	68	1	0	.400	.339
Lugo, Julio	R-R	6-1	175	11-16-75	.268	.283	.264	82	261	27	70	13	0	1	22	34	4	3	5	51	12	4	.330	.355
Moss, Brandon	L-R	6-0	205	9-16-83	.295	.263	.305	34	78	7	23	5	1	1	6	6	0	0	2	25	1	1	.462	.337
Ortiz, David	L-L	6-4	230	11-18-75	.264	.221	.279	109	416	74	110	30	1	23	89	70	1	1	3	74	1	0	.507	.369
Pedroia, Dustin	R-R	5-9	180	8-17-83	.326	.313	.331	157	653	118	213	54	2	17	83	50	7	7	9	52	20	1	.493	.376
Ramirez, Manny	R-R	6-0	200	5-30-72	.299	.274	.305	100	365	66	109	22	1	20	68	52	8	0	0	86	1	0	.529	.398
Ross, David	R-R	6-2	240	3-19-77	.125	.000	.167	8	8	1	1	0	0	0	0	1	0	1	0	3	0	0	.125	.125
Thurston, Joe	L-R	5-11	190	9-29-79	.000	.000	.000	4	8	0	0	0	0	0	0	0	0	0	0	1	0	0	.000	.111
Van Every, Jonathan	L-L	6-1	190	11-27-79	.235	.333	.214	11	17	0	4	0	1	0	5	1	0	0	0	6	0	0	.353	.278
Varitek, Jason	B-R	6-2	230	4-11-72	.220	.284	.201	131	423	37	93	20	0	13	43	52	6	0	2	122	0	1	.359	.313
Velazquez, Gil	R-R	6-3	190	10-17-79	.125	.000	.143	3	8	0	1	0	0	0	0	0	0	0	0	0	0	0	.125	.125
Youkilis, Kevin	R-R	6-1	220	3-15-79	.312	.288	.318	145	538	91	168	43	4	29	115	62	12	0	9	108	3	5	.569	.390

Pitching	B-T	HT	WT	DOB	W	L	ERA	G	GS	CG	SV	IP	H	R	ER	HR	BB	SO	AVG	vLH	vRH	K/9	BB/9
Aardsma, David	R-R	6-4	205	12-27-81	4	2	5.55	47	0	0	0	49	49	32	30	4	35	49	.268	.289	.250	9.06	6.47
Beckett, Josh	R-R	6-5	220	5-15-80	12	10	4.03	27	27	1	0	174	173	80	78	18	34	172	.256	.260	.252	8.88	1.76
Bowden, Michael	R-R	6-3	215	9-9-86	1	0	3.60	1	1	0	0	5	7	2	2	0	1	3	.333	.222	.417	5.40	1.80
Buchholz, Clay	L-R	6-3	190	8-14-84	2	9	6.75	16	15	1	0	76	93	63	57	11	41	72	.299	.293	.305	8.53	4.86
Byrd, Paul	R-R	6-1	190	12-3-70	4	2	4.78	8	8	0	0	49	58	26	26	8	10	26	.297	.315	.282	4.78	1.84
2-team total (22 Cleveland)					11	12	4.60	30	30	1	0	180	204	96	92	31	34	82	—	—	—	4.10	1.70
Colon, Bartolo	R-R	5-11	245	5-24-73	4	2	3.92	7	7	0	0	39	44	23	17	5	10	27	.282	.309	.253	6.23	2.31
Corey, Bryan	R-R	6-0	175	10-21-73	0	0	10.50	7	0	0	0	6	11	7	7	1	3	4	.407	.250	.533	6.00	4.50
Delcarmen, Manny	R-R	6-2	205	2-16-82	1	2	3.27	73	0	0	2	74	55	28	27	5	28	72	.205	.190	.218	8.72	3.39
Hansack, Devern	R-R	6-2	185	2-5-78	1	0	4.05	4	0	0	0	7	6	5	3	0	1	5	.250	.308	.182	6.75	1.35
Hansen, Craig	R-R	6-6	230	11-15-83	1	3	5.58	32	0	0	0	2	31	29	23	19	2	23	.256	.240	.271	.219	7.34	6.75
Lester, Jon	L-L	6-2	190	1-7-84	16	6	3.21	33	33	2	0	210	202	78	75	14	66	152	.256	.217	.273	6.50	2.82
Lopez, Javier	L-L	6-4	220	7-11-77	2	0	2.43	70	0	0	0	59	53	18	16	4	27	38	.245	.182	.311	5.76	4.10
Masterson, Justin	R-R	6-6	250	3-22-85	6	5	3.16	36	9	0	0	88	68	31	31	10	40	68	.216	.238	.196	6.93	4.08
Matsuzaka, Daisuke	R-R	6-0	185	9-13-80	18	3	2.90	29	29	0	0	168	128	58	54	12	94	154	.211	.225	.195	8.27	5.05
Okajima, Hideki	L-L	6-1	195	12-25-75	3	2	2.61	64	0	0	1	62	49	18	18	6	23	60	.212	.184	.234	8.71	3.34
Papelbon, Jonathan	R-R	6-4	225	11-23-80	5	4	2.34	67	0	0	41	69	58	24	18	4	8	77	.223	.235	.210	10.00	1.04
Pauley, David	R-R	6-2	210	6-17-83	0	1	11.68	6	2	0	0	12	23	17	16	2	5	11	.383	.400	.367	8.03	3.65
Smith, Chris	R-R	6-2	200	4-9-81	1	0	7.85	12	0	0	0	18	18	16	16	6	7	13	.261	.200	.345	6.38	3.44
Snyder, Kyle	B-R	6-8	230	9-9-77	0	0	21.60	2	0	0	0	2	2	4	4	1	2	1	.333	.333	.333	5.40	10.80
Tavarez, Julian	L-R	6-2	195	5-22-73	0	1	6.39	9	0	0	0	13	18	12	9	0	6	9	.346	.478	.241	6.26	6.39
Timlin, Mike	R-R	6-4	210	3-10-66	4	4	5.66	47	0	0	1	49	60	32	31	9	20	32	.302	.337	.269	5.84	3.65
Wakefield, Tim	R-R	6-2	210	8-2-66	10	11	4.13	30	30	1	0	181	154	89	83	25	60	117	.228	.243	.218	5.82	2.98
Zink, Charlie	R-R	6-1	190	8-26-79	0	0	16.62	1	1	0	0	4	11	8	8	0	1	1	.458	.400	.500	2.08	2.08

Fielding

Catcher	PCT	G	PO	A	E	DP	PB
Cash	.987	57	280	26	4	5	14
Kottaras	1.000	2	5	0	0	0	0
Ross	1.000	8	23	0	0	0	0
Varitek	.996	131	903	42	4	7	4

First Base	PCT	G	PO	A	E	DP
Bailey	1.000	12	77	3	0	10
Casey	.991	45	331	13	3	25
Kotsay	.974	6	35	3	1	7
Moss	1.000	2	10	0	0	1
Youkilis	.996	125	923	87	4	92

Second Base	PCT	G	PO	A	E	DP
Cora	1.000	7	6	14	0	3
Lowrie	1.000	3	2	4	0	0

	PCT	G	PO	A	E	DP
Pedroia	.992	157	279	448	6	101
Velazquez	1.000	2	5	9	0	2

Third Base	PCT	G	PO	A	E	DP
Cash	1.000	4	1	1	0	0
Lowell	.967	110	80	217	10	20
Lowrie	.974	45	16	59	2	8
Youkilis	.969	36	23	70	3	5

Shortstop	PCT	G	PO	A	E	DP
Cora	.972	69	74	136	6	39
Lowrie	1.000	49	46	109	0	21
Lugo	.945	81	100	176	16	34
Velazquez	1.000	1	0	1	0	0

Outfield	PCT	G	PO	A	E	DP
Bailey	1.000	6	3	0	0	0

	PCT	G	PO	A	E	DP
Bay	.988	49	76	5	1	0
Carter	1.000	3	3	0	0	0
Crisp	.992	114	234	4	2	1
Drew	.979	106	184	6	4	1
Ellsbury	1.000	140	332	4	0	2
Kotsay	1.000	19	32	0	0	0
Lugo	—	1	0	0	0	0
Moss	1.000	23	36	2	0	0
Ramirez	.991	66	99	6	1	2
Thurston	1.000	4	5	0	0	0
Van Every	1.000	9	16	0	0	0
Youkilis	1.000	2	3	0	0	0

PAWTUCKET RED SOX   TRIPLE-A
INTERNATIONAL LEAGUE

Batting	B-T	HT	WT	DOB	AVG	vLH	vRH	G	AB	R	H	2B	3B	HR	RBI	BB	HBP	SH	SF	SO	SB	CS	SLG	OBP
Bailey, Jeff	R-R	6-2	200	11-19-78	.301	.325	.292	109	418	88	126	28	3	25	75	62	12	0	2	90	5	2	.562	.405
Brown, Dusty	R-R	6-0	180	6-19-82	.290	.337	.269	84	297	39	86	14	2	12	55	40	6	0	7	81	0	0	.471	.377
Carter, Chris	L-L	6-0	230	9-16-82	.300	.291	.304	121	470	65	141	25	2	24	81	41	4	0	7	84	0	0	.515	.356
Casey, Sean	L-R	6-4	230	7-2-74	.500	.667	.333	2	6	3	3	1	0	0	0	1	0	0	0	1	0	0	.667	.571
Cora, Alex	L-R	6-0	200	10-18-75	.273	.500	.143	3	11	2	3	0	0	0	0	0	0	0	0	2	0	0	.273	.273
Corsaletti, Jeff	L-R	6-0	190	2-22-83	.232	.250	.225	44	151	23	35	11	2	2	13	18	2	0	1	35	1	1	.371	.320
Danielson, Sean	R-R	5-8	165	8-6-82	.246	.298	.215	83	252	30	62	8	3	1	21	23	1	4	0	75	19	3	.313	.312
Ginter, Keith	R-R	5-10	195	5-5-76	.250	.311	.224	123	444	49	111	21	0	7	54	55	14	1	6	91	5	1	.345	.347
Granadillo, Tony	R-R	5-10	165	8-10-84	.000	.000	.000	1	2	0	0	0	0	0	0	0	0	0	0	1	0	0	.000	.000
Kielty, Bobby	R-R	6-1	225	8-5-76	.228	.333	.191	28	92	9	21	4	1	3	18	17	1	0	2	26	0	0	.391	.348
2-team total (16 Rochester)					.224	—		44	147	18	33	7	1	5	26	30	1	0	3	42	0	1	.388	.354
Kottaras, George	L-R	6-0	185	5-16-83	.243	.246	.242	107	395	63	96	18	0	22	65	64	1	0	2	110	0	0	.456	.348
Lane, Jason	L-L	6-2	220	12-22-76	.208	.300	.152	13	53	10	11	4	0	2	9	8	0	1	0	14	0	0	.396	.306
2-team total (97 Scranton/W-B)					.233	—		110	400	64	93	23	3	18	60	58	7	0	6	84	3	3	.440	.335
Lowell, Mike	R-R	6-3	210	2-24-74	.231	.000	.250	3	13	0	3	0	0	0	3	0	0	0	1	1	0	0	.231	.214
Lowrie, Jed	B-R	6-0	180	4-17-84	.268	.250	.277	53	198	35	53	14	2	5	32	31	0	0	5	43	1	0	.434	.359
Madera, Sandy	R-R	6-2	176	8-11-80	.292	.378	.250	35	113	18	33	8	0	6	25	14	2	0	2	25	0	0	.522	.374
Moss, Brandon	L-R	6-0	205	9-16-83	.282	.268	.287	43	163	29	46	8	4	8	30	16	1	0	2	47	2	0	.528	.346
Natale, Jeff	R-R	5-9	180	8-24-82	.280	.367	.231	25	82	12	23	2	1	3	11	11	7	0	0	11	0	0	.439	.410
Ortiz, David	L-L	6-4	230	11-18-75	.333	.000	.375	3	9	1	3	0	0	0	3	5	3	0	0	2	0	0	1.333	.500
Pritz, Bryan	R-R	5-10	180	5-5-82	.264	.263	.264	28	91	11	24	8	0	0	7	0	0	0	0	17	0	1	.352	.316
Ross, David	R-R	6-2	240	3-19-77	.250	.182	.294	6	28	4	7	1	0	1	3	1	0	0	0	7	0	0	.393	.276
2-team total (9 Louisville)					.207	—		15	58	8	12	2	1	2	5	4	0	0	1	19	0		.379	.254
Spann, Chad	R-R	6-1	195	10-25-83	.185	.241	.159	56	184	21	34	5	0	3	20	12	1	1	2	53	1	1	.261	.236
Thurston, Joe	L-R	5-11	190	9-29-79	.316	.346	.302	126	507	83	160	28	5	11	64	35	11	14	8	75	19	11	.456	.367
Van Every, Jonathan	L-L	6-1	190	11-27-79	.263	.250	.269	119	380	84	100	15	3	26	70	54	4	3	1	157	6	1	.524	.360
Velazquez, Gil	R-R	6-3	190	10-17-79	.260	.267	.258	101	350	54	91	17	4	10	46	22	5	5	4	73	3	3	.417	.310
Wilson, Josh	R-R	6-1	170	3-26-81	.223	.270	.200	27	112	16	25	6	0	2	10	5	5	0	0	23	2	0	.330	.287
2-team total (97 Indianapolis)					.262	—		124	405	44	106	24	1	7	42	29	14	8	3	71	13	5	.378	.330

Pitching	B-T	HT	WT	DOB	W	L	ERA	G	GS	CG	SV	IP	H	R	ER	HR	BB	SO	AVG	vLH	vRH	K/9	BB/9
Aardsma, David	R-R	6-4	205	12-27-81	0	0	0.00	2	0	0	0	2	1	0	0	0	2	2	.000	.000	.000	9.00	9.00
Alvarez, Abe	L-L	6-2	190	10-17-82	2	1	6.46	13	1	0	0	15	16	13	11	0	2	11	8	.258	.174	.308	4.70	6.46
Asencio, Miguel	R-R	6-2	240	9-29-80	0	0	3.38	8	0	0	0	16	10	8	6	1	4	10	.179	.241	.111	5.63	2.25
Bowden, Michael	R-R	6-3	215	9-9-86	0	3	3.38	7	6	0	0	40	40	16	15	5	5	29	.261	.250	.274	6.53	1.13
Buchholz, Clay	R-R	6-3	190	8-14-84	4	2	2.47	9	9	0	0	44	36	13	12	3	17	43	.232	.289	.167	8.86	3.50
Colon, Bartolo	R-R	5-11	245	5-24-73	3	1	2.27	9	9	0	0	32	23	9	8	2	6	21	.197	.200	.192	5.97	1.71
Corey, Bryan	R-R	6-0	175	10-21-73	0	0	0.00	5	0	0	1	5	4	0	0	0	1	5	.211	.111	.300	9.00	1.80
Gronkiewicz, Lee	R-R	5-11	185	8-21-78	0	0	0.79	11	0	0	5	11	6	1	1	1	2	11	.154	.250	.111	8.74	1.59
Hansack, Devern	R-R	6-2	185	2-5-78	6	10	4.08	25	25	2	0	139	123	68	63	16	41	128	.237	.257	.217	8.29	2.65
Hansen, Craig	R-R	6-6	220	11-15-83	1	0	1.62	11	0	0	0	17	6	4	3	0	5	17	.107	.118	.103	9.18	2.70
2-team total (2 Indianapolis)					1	0	2.41	13	0	0	0	19	10	6	5	0	6	19	—	—	—	9.16	2.89
Holdzkom, Lincoln	R-R	6-5	245	3-23-82	6	5	5.33	36	0	0	0	51	57	33	30	1	33	29	.297	.281	.311	5.15	5.86
Hull, Eric	R-R	5-11	185	12-3-79	2	3	4.12	40	1	0	0	55	66	26	25	2	21	64	.297	.360	.234	10.54	3.46
Jones, Hunter	L-L	6-4	235	1-10-84	7	2	3.02	35	0	0	8	51	55	20	17	3	14	50	.274	.384	.191	8.88	2.49
Kolb, Dan	R-R	6-4	210	3-29-75	0	0	2.92	9	0	0	0	12	18	7	4	1	4	5	.327	.429	.293	3.65	2.92
Martinez, Edgar	R-R	6-0	220	10-23-81	0	3	3.89	33	16	0	2	113	95	53	49	15	58	87	.230	.235	.226	6.91	4.61
Masterson, Justin	R-R	6-6	250	3-22-85	1	0	2.89	4	1	0	0	9	6	4	3	1	1	8	.194	.235	.143	7.71	0.96
Matsuzaka, Daisuke	R-R	6-0	185	9-13-80	1	1	3.60	1	1	0	0	5	4	2	2	0	1	5	.222	.214	.250	9.00	1.80
McBeth, Marcus	R-R	6-2	195	8-23-80	1	0	2.57	4	0	0	0	7	3	2	2	1	1	11	.136	.167	.100	14.14	1.29
2-team total (24 Louisville)					2	1	5.40	28	0	0	2	32	26	21	19	7	16	31	—	—	—	8.81	4.55
Pauley, David	R-R	6-2	210	6-17-83	14	4	3.55	25	25	0	0	147	147	66	58	10	41	103	.263	.295	.227	6.31	2.51
Smith, Chris	R-R	6-2	200	4-9-81	1	5	3.19	37	4	0	15	59	54	23	21	6	11	52	.242	.238	.246	7.89	1.67
Snyder, Kyle	B-R	6-8	230	9-9-77	1	4	5.26	14	7	0	1	38	34	23	22	5	12	30	.234	.244	.224	7.17	2.87

	B-T	HT	WT	DOB	W	L	ERA	G	GS	CG	SV	IP	H	R	ER	HR	BB	SO	AVG	vLH	vRH	K/9	BB/9
Switzer, Jon	L-L	6-3	210	8-13-79	5	1	4.40	52	1	0	3	76	85	40	37	12	19	65	.285	.240	.316	7.73	2.26
Tejera, Michael	L-L	5-10	195	10-18-76	3	6	5.10	34	8	0	2	78	76	45	44	12	33	47	.266	.267	.265	5.45	3.82
Timlin, Mike	R-R	6-4	210	3-10-66	0	0	0.00	5	1	0	0	5	2	0	0	0	0	4	.118	.222	.000	7.20	0.00
Vaquedano, Jose	R-R	6-4	167	7-9-81	4	1	4.95	30	0	0	1	40	49	22	22	4	26	24	.302	.410	.202	5.40	5.85
Vaughan, Beau	B-R	6-4	230	6-4-81	1	1	3.18	7	0	0	1	11	14	6	4	2	6	14	.326	.455	.190	11.12	4.76
Zink, Charlie	R-R	6-1	190	8-26-79	14	6	2.84	28	28	2	0	174	144	73	55	13	49	106	.223	.212	.234	5.47	2.53

Fielding

Catcher	PCT	G	PO	A	E	DP	PB
Brown	.985	70	481	44	8	3	12
Kottaras	.996	70	513	21	2	3	10
Ross	1.000	3	24	2	0	0	1

First Base	PCT	G	PO	A	E	DP
Bailey	.994	68	487	37	3	48
Casey	1.000	1	4	0	0	0
Lane	1.000	1	14	2	0	1
Madera	.976	16	116	4	3	16
Moss	.991	36	318	17	3	30
Natale	1.000	13	85	5	0	9
Spann	.976	16	118	6	3	14
Velazquez	1.000	4	37	2	0	2

Second Base	PCT	G	PO	A	E	DP
Cora	1.000	2	1	5	0	1
Ginter	1.000	22	30	54	0	10
Lowrie	1.000	2	4	10	0	3
Natale	1.000	8	10	13	0	3
Thurston	.981	99	194	279	9	76
Velazquez	.986	15	30	40	1	6
Wilson	.957	4	11	11	1	5

Third Base	PCT	G	PO	A	E	DP
Ginter	.963	97	78	180	10	13
Lowell	.750	1	0	3	1	1
Lowrie	1.000	2	0	2	0	0
Spann	.966	38	26	60	3	5
Velazquez	.889	9	5	11	2	2
Wilson	.833	2	1	4	1	0

Shortstop	PCT	G	PO	A	E	DP
Cora	1.000	1	1	1	0	0
Ginter	1.000	6	5	15	0	4
Lowrie	.961	48	62	112	7	21
Thurston	1.000	1	1	1	0	0
Velazquez	.975	70	112	195	8	51
Wilson	.953	21	40	41	4	13

Outfield	PCT	G	PO	A	E	DP
Bailey	.978	34	43	1	1	0
Carter	.971	76	135	1	4	0
Corsaletti	.986	44	68	0	1	0
Danielson	.989	80	166	13	2	4
Kielty	.980	25	46	2	1	0
Lane	1.000	11	15	1	0	0
Moss	1.000	5	9	0	0	0
Pritz	.974	26	37	1	1	0
Thurston	1.000	30	52	3	0	1
Van Every	1.000	119	299	7	0	4
Velazquez	1.000	4	8	0	0	0

PORTLAND SEA DOGS — DOUBLE-A

EASTERN LEAGUE

Batting	B-T	HT	WT	DOB	AVG	vLH	vRH	G	AB	R	H	2B	3B	HR	RBI	BB	HBP	SH	SF	SO	SB	CS	SLG	OBP
Anderson, Lars	L-L	6-4	215	9-25-87	.316	.225	.355	41	133	27	42	13	0	5	30	29	0	0	1	43	1	0	.526	.436
Apodaca, Juan	R-R	5-11	180	7-15-86	.278	.429	.182	6	18	3	5	0	0	1	1	1	0	1	4	0	0		.278	.333
Bates, Aaron	R-R	6-4	232	3-10-84	.276	.245	.291	124	457	61	126	29	2	11	68	50	18	0	5	114	0	0	.420	.366
Bell, Bubba	L-R	6-0	195	10-9-82	.285	.291	.282	79	312	50	89	15	3	13	49	39	1	0	3	61	3	1	.478	.363
Corsaletti, Jeff	L-R	6-0	190	2-22-83	.312	.344	.272	78	295	60	92	20	4	12	50	53	3	0	4	58	7	1	.529	.417
Daeges, Zach	L-R	6-4	225	11-16-83	.307	.309	.306	108	394	63	121	34	3	6	63	72	3	0	7	72	3	2	.454	.412
Danielson, Sean	B-R	5-8	165	8-6-82	.309	.276	.323	22	94	15	29	5	1	0	2	10	0	1	0	19	6	1	.383	.375
Diaz, Argenis	R-R	5-11	155	2-12-87	.288	.171	.337	39	139	20	40	8	2	2	23	10	1	1	2	30	0	1	.417	.336
Granadillo, Tony	R-R	5-10	165	8-10-84	.232	.245	.226	98	349	51	81	20	5	5	43	55	5	0	3	75	1	1	.338	.342
Hall, Mickey	L-L	6-1	195	5-20-85	.232	.265	.217	82	263	48	61	16	2	13	35	37	4	0	2	101	4	1	.456	.333
Jimenez, Jorge	R-R	6-1	190	9-12-84	.270	.233	.285	55	211	23	57	12	2	3	22	8	3	0	1	29	1	1	.389	.305
Johnson, Jay	R-R	6-2	185	12-9-84	.256	.200	.273	12	43	8	11	2	0	0	7	0	0	0	3	0	1		.302	.340
Khoury, Ryan	R-R	5-10	180	3-19-84	.284	.289	.282	85	299	45	85	20	2	4	40	44	5	0	2	66	4	3	.405	.383
Madera, Sandy	R-R	6-2	176	8-11-80	.291	.206	.346	44	172	22	50	9	1	7	29	12	3	0	2	19	1	0	.477	.344
Natale, Jeff	R-R	5-9	180	8-24-82	.241	.667	.192	9	29	4	7	2	0	1	4	6	2	0	1	1	2	1	.414	.395
Negron, Kris	R-R	6-0	180	2-1-86	.143	.333	.000	4	7	0	1	1	0	0	0	1	0	1	0	2	0	0	.286	.250
Ortiz, David	L-L	6-4	230	11-18-75	.250	—	.250	3	8	2	2	0	0	0	1	2	0	0	0	1	0	0	.250	.400
Otness, John	R-R	5-11	200	9-15-81	.263	.297	.249	69	251	35	66	14	1	2	33	26	10	0	6	32	0	3	.351	.348
Pinckney, Andrew	L-R	6-1	205	4-7-82	.271	.309	.250	57	221	27	60	12	1	5	37	9	1	1	2	48	1	1	.403	.300
2-team total (58 New Hampshire)					.273	—	.250	115	406	50	111	28	2	9	50	29	2	2	4	95	2	3	.419	.322
Pritz, Bryan	R-R	5-10	180	5-5-82	.240	.235	.241	27	96	14	23	6	0	1	6	12	0	0	0	14	2	0	.333	.324
Reddick, Josh	L-R	6-2	180	2-19-87	.214	.226	.209	34	117	22	25	4	2	6	25	12	1	1	1	25	3	1	.436	.290
Stanley, Jered	R-R	6-3	220	9-18-84	.130	.000	.188	8	23	3	3	0	0	1	3	3	0	0	0	11	0	0	.261	.231
Suarez, Iggy	R-R	5-11	165	5-3-81	.242	.266	.233	124	442	57	107	23	0	5	50	41	1	2	2	88	15	5	.328	.307
Wagner, Mark	R-R	6-1	205	6-11-84	.219	.229	.215	94	342	44	75	19	0	10	48	38	6	1	6	78	0	0	.363	.304

Pitching	B-T	HT	WT	DOB	W	L	ERA	G	GS	CG	SV	IP	H	R	ER	HR	BB	SO	AVG	vLH	vRH	K/9	BB/9
Asencio, Miguel	R-R	6-2	240	9-29-80	2	4	5.50	33	0	0	0	56	58	35	34	2	30	38	.265	.284	.250	6.14	4.85
Bard, Daniel	R-R	6-4	195	6-25-85	4	1	1.99	31	0	0	5	50	30	14	11	3	26	64	.173	.167	.178	11.60	4.71
Bowden, Michael	R-R	6-3	215	9-9-86	9	4	2.33	19	19	0	0	104	72	31	27	5	24	101	.192	.198	.186	8.71	2.07
Buchholz, Clay	R-R	6-3	190	8-14-84	1	0	1.80	2	2	0	0	15	7	4	3	0	1	18	.137	.136	.138	10.80	0.60
Fernandes, Kyle	L-L	6-0	190	9-12-85	1	0	0.00	1	0	0	0	2	1	0	0	0	1	2	.000	.000	.000	9.00	4.50
Gassner, Dave	R-L	6-2	190	12-14-78	8	5	5.82	16	15	0	0	82	108	61	53	11	15	32	.319	.263	.335	3.51	1.65
Goodson, Matt	R-R	6-3	195	9-26-82	4	4	5.46	14	14	0	0	59	67	39	36	9	31	41	.285	.311	.257	6.22	4.70
Haigwood, Daniel	R-L	6-2	200	11-19-83	2	3	3.36	38	3	0	1	67	55	29	25	6	42	70	.224	.182	.244	9.40	5.64
Hottovy, Tommy	L-L	6-1	195	7-9-81	1	0	5.00	2	2	0	0	9	9	7	5	2	2	4	.250	.455	.160	4.00	2.00
Jackson, Kyle	R-R	6-3	200	4-9-83	5	3	6.47	28	11	0	0	81	87	60	58	9	44	55	.275	.289	.262	6.14	4.91
James, Michael	R-R	6-1	185	6-2-81	5	4	3.77	46	0	0	2	76	66	36	32	6	29	66	.228	.257	.201	7.78	3.42
Johnson, Kris	L-L	6-4	170	10-14-84	8	9	3.63	27	27	0	0	136	147	70	55	5	56	108	.277	.257	.284	7.13	3.70
Jones, Hunter	L-L	6-4	235	1-10-83	0	1	1.19	13	0	0	4	23	21	3	3	0	4	26	.241	.273	.222	10.32	1.59
Large, T.J.	R-R	6-4	185	5-28-83	0	2	5.88	22	0	0	1	34	37	22	22	3	23	37	.272	.234	.306	9.89	6.15
Lawson, Ryne	L-R	6-2	180	6-21-85	1	1	4.06	6	6	0	0	31	28	18	14	1	17	17	.241	.255	.231	4.94	4.94
Lentz, Richie	R-R	6-2	210	8-6-84	2	3	3.75	16	0	0	1	24	22	11	10	2	13	35	.237	.279	.200	13.13	4.88
Masterson, Justin	R-R	6-6	250	3-22-85	1	3	4.23	8	8	0	0	38	37	22	18	0	16	37	.248	.221	.278	8.69	3.76
Mills, Adam	R-R	5-11	190	11-19-84	0	5	4.00	11	11	0	0	63	67	30	28	2	8	38	.272	.262	.283	5.43	1.14

Rhoades, Chad	R-R	5-10	175	3-10-83	5	3	5.14	41	0	0	2	61	71	38	35	6	28	65	.281	.327	.245	9.54	4.11
Richardson, Dustin	L-L	6-5	195	1-9-84	7	10	6.33	22	22	0	0	107	108	76	75	17	51	114	.267	.193	.297	9.62	4.30
Vaquedano, Jose	R-R	6-4	167	7-9-81	4	0	0.41	13	0	0	0	22	12	2	1	1	4	17	.160	.189	.132	6.95	1.64
Vasquez, Carlos	L-L	6-3	230	12-6-82	2	1	8.39	19	0	0	1	25	40	24	23	1	23	18	.388	.419	.375	6.57	8.39
Vaughan, Beau	B-R	6-4	230	6-4-81	2	1	2.12	39	0	0	16	47	34	15	11	1	18	55	.209	.232	.191	10.61	3.47

Fielding

Catcher	PCT	G	PO	A	E	DP	PB
Apodaca	.980	6	50	0	1	0	1
Otness	.986	52	397	27	6	4	1
Wagner	.997	84	629	60	2	8	13

First Base	PCT	G	PO	A	E	DP
Anderson	.985	22	188	11	3	23
Bates	.987	94	720	57	10	57
Jimenez	1.000	2	5	0	0	0
Madera	.987	11	74	1	1	6
Otness	.986	9	67	2	1	10
Pinckney	1.000	8	50	4	0	7

Second Base	PCT	G	PO	A	E	DP
Granadillo	.982	89	170	208	7	53

Khoury	.950	30	55	78	7	20
Natale	1.000	5	6	8	0	0
Negron	.909	3	4	6	1	0
Suarez	.964	19	29	52	3	12

Third Base	PCT	G	PO	A	E	DP
Granadillo	.889	3	2	6	1	0
Jimenez	.902	52	38	73	12	9
Khoury	.959	43	28	66	4	1
Pinckney	.907	38	37	70	11	5
Suarez	.944	9	3	14	1	1

Shortstop	PCT	G	PO	A	E	DP
Diaz	.963	37	55	100	6	23
Khoury	.935	12	14	29	3	5

Suarez	.960	94	139	223	15	49

Outfield	PCT	G	PO	A	E	DP
Bell	.976	76	160	4	4	1
Corsaletti	.979	74	134	4	3	0
Daeges	.979	102	182	7	4	1
Danielson	1.000	22	25	1	0	0
Hall	.988	77	160	4	2	2
Johnson	1.000	11	22	0	0	0
Khoury	1.000	1	2	0	0	0
Pritz	1.000	26	44	1	0	0
Reddick	.960	33	67	5	3	2
Stanley	1.000	6	11	1	0	0
Suarez	1.000	4	8	0	0	0

LANCASTER JETHAWKS   HIGH CLASS A

CALIFORNIA LEAGUE

Batting	B-T	HT	WT	DOB	AVG	vLH	vRH	G	AB	R	H	2B	3B	HR	RBI	BB	HBP	SH	SF	SO	SB	CS	SLG	OBP
Anderson, Lars	L-L	6-4	215	9-25-87	.317	.395	.286	77	306	58	97	19	1	13	50	46	3	0	3	64	0	0	.513	.408
Blackmon, Dennis	R-R	6-2	205	11-18-82	.286	.219	.318	29	98	14	28	4	0	3	17	14	0	0	3	27	0	0	.418	.365
Chiang, Chih-Hsien	L-R	6-2	170	2-21-88	.303	.317	.298	83	320	47	97	19	2	9	59	18	1	0	5	52	2	1	.459	.337
Diaz, Argenis	R-R	5-11	155	2-12-87	.281	.269	.286	71	256	31	72	9	6	0	29	20	1	0	5	60	3	2	.363	.330
Engel, Reid	L-R	6-3	190	5-7-87	.248	.280	.235	77	306	41	76	10	2	10	40	18	4	2	2	78	2	1	.392	.297
Exposito, Luis	R-R	6-3	210	1-20-87	.301	.319	.292	55	226	31	68	13	2	10	37	9	2	0	2	47	0	1	.509	.331
Farkes, Zak	R-R	5-11	190	5-30-83	.251	.268	.245	88	319	47	80	20	2	10	48	28	7	0	5	72	4	1	.420	.320
Hall, Mickey	L-L	6-1	195	5-20-85	.216	.273	.192	12	37	8	8	1	0	1	2	8	0	0	1	10	3	0	.324	.348
Jimenez, Jorge	L-R	6-1	210	9-12-84	.352	.433	.325	70	267	47	94	20	1	4	42	26	8	0	3	31	1	0	.479	.421
Jones, Michael	L-R	6-3	220	6-14-85	.275	.321	.254	44	178	23	49	10	1	6	28	15	3	0	0	33	0	0	.444	.342
Kalish, Ryan	L-L	6-1	205	3-28-88	.233	.320	.188	18	73	6	17	6	0	2	14	8	0	0	1	23	1	0	.397	.305
Keowen, Kade	R-R	6-5	215	4-18-86	.063	.000	.111	4	16	1	1	0	0	0	0	0	0	0	0	9	0	0	.063	.063
Kielty, Bobby	B-R	6-1	225	8-5-76	.250	.250	.250	3	8	1	2	2	0	0	3	4	1	0	0	5	0	0	.500	.538
Lara, Christian	B-R	5-11	150	4-11-85	.375	.000	.375	2	8	4	3	1	0	1	2	3	0	0	0	2	0	0	.875	.545
2-team total (104 Inland Empire)					.256	—	—	106	359	50	92	17	8	1	43	39	1	8	3	100	10	2	.357	.328
Nava, Daniel	B-L	5-10	200	2-22-83	.341	.269	.370	85	323	54	110	27	1	10	59	43	7	2	4	70	4	3	.523	.424
Navarro, Yamaico	R-R	5-11	170	10-31-87	.348	.328	.360	42	181	33	63	13	2	4	23	12	2	0	1	30	3	2	.508	.393
Negron, Kris	R-R	6-0	180	2-1-86	.328	.444	.275	33	116	23	38	8	3	7	19	5	6	1	3	25	6	1	.629	.377
Place, Jason	R-R	6-3	205	5-8-88	.246	.241	.248	114	484	88	119	25	4	19	65	44	9	0	1	147	5	5	.432	.320
Reddick, Josh	L-R	6-2	180	2-19-87	.343	.352	.339	76	312	60	107	11	8	17	57	17	0	0	2	49	9	1	.593	.375
Reza, Aaron	R-R	5-7	180	6-25-85	.258	.230	.269	101	349	51	90	15	4	6	36	39	10	0	2	70	3	0	.375	.348
Segovia, Luis	B-R	5-10	150	7-19-86	.259	.298	.240	50	147	18	38	7	2	0	12	4	2	0	1	43	4	3	.333	.286
Sheely, Matt	R-R	5-9	160	8-30-86	.218	.185	.230	68	206	28	45	4	5	0	12	19	3	0	1	49	8	0	.286	.293
Still, Jon	R-R	6-2	210	11-16-84	.265	.235	.278	122	456	82	121	30	3	22	83	65	9	0	7	111	0	0	.489	.363

Pitching	B-T	HT	WT	DOB	W	L	ERA	G	GS	CG	SV	IP	H	R	ER	HR	BB	SO	AVG	vLH	vRH	K/9	BB/9
Bajoczky, Tony	R-R	6-0	170	9-24-84	5	4	4.73	21	19	0	0	110	147	64	58	12	13	67	.326	.322	.330	5.47	1.06
Beazley, Travis	R-R	6-0	175	6-17-83	7	10	4.68	27	27	0	0	140	164	92	73	9	31	121	.285	.241	.332	7.76	1.99
Blackey, Jason	R-R	6-4	206	4-11-83	8	4	3.65	35	0	0	7	62	57	29	25	11	17	56	.242	.244	.239	8.17	2.48
Cox, Bryce	R-R	6-4	205	8-10-84	2	2	5.80	27	0	0	1	45	57	34	29	8	10	34	.298	.358	.240	6.80	2.00
Doubront, Felix	L-L	6-2	166	10-23-87	1	1	3.86	3	3	0	0	14	15	6	6	1	4	20	.278	.316	.257	12.86	2.57
Fernandes, Kyle	L-L	6-0	190	9-12-85	0	1	1.99	9	0	0	1	23	18	5	5	1	3	25	.220	.276	.189	9.93	1.19
Garcia, Felipe	R-R	5-11	165	9-20-82	1	0	4.60	12	0	0	0	16	21	9	8	1	5	15	.328	.250	.389	8.62	2.87
James, Jimmy	R-R	6-2	175	10-16-84	2	1	5.85	4	4	0	0	20	26	14	13	2	5	16	.317	.270	.356	7.20	2.25
Jones, Chris	R-R	6-3	205	6-9-84	7	9	6.09	26	26	0	0	127	168	92	86	17	24	108	.331	.314	.329	7.65	1.70
Large, T.J.	R-R	6-4	185	5-28-83	2	1	3.16	27	0	0	9	37	38	15	13	3	14	38	.252	.197	.300	9.24	3.41
Lentz, Richie	R-R	6-2	210	8-6-84	4	3	2.87	28	0	0	1	53	32	20	17	3	30	77	.174	.195	.155	12.99	5.06
Lonergan, Scott	B-R	6-4	220	12-11-83	0	0	5.84	6	0	0	0	12	11	10	8	1	7	4	.250	.304	.190	2.92	5.11
Loop, Derrick	R-L	6-3	220	12-11-83	6	0	3.04	17	5	0	1	53	58	22	18	2	21	43	.280	.244	.302	7.26	3.54
Maxwell, Blake	R-R	6-5	255	8-1-84	5	9	3.32	37	15	0	1	133	138	62	49	7	19	67	.267	.284	.250	4.53	1.29
McAllister, Cody	R-R	6-2	190	3-21-84	4	2	3.31	31	0	0	5	54	40	30	20	5	16	52	.198	.240	.153	8.61	2.65
Mills, Adam	R-R	5-11	190	11-19-84	7	4	4.43	15	15	0	0	81	95	42	40	5	15	43	.287	.315	.259	4.76	1.66
Molldrem, Craig	R-R	6-6	205	9-17-81	1	1	4.26	14	0	0	0	25	31	19	12	2	6	27	.292	.333	.259	9.59	2.13
Papelbon, Josh	R-R	6-1	210	6-24-83	4	3	4.46	39	0	0	1	71	66	44	35	6	27	59	.245	.292	.201	7.51	3.44
Province, Chris	R-R	6-3	220	12-20-85	5	3	6.26	16	16	0	0	78	111	68	54	8	31	40	.331	.349	.317	4.64	2.90
Russ, James	R-R	6-4	210	10-24-80	0	4	7.82	8	6	0	0	25	38	23	22	4	16	14	.355	.420	.298	4.97	5.68
Steinocher, Brian	R-R	6-1	190	8-1-84	3	2	4.25	16	4	0	2	42	37	22	20	4	15	20	.239	.269	.194	4.25	3.19
Vasquez, Carlos	L-R	6-3	230	12-6-82	2	0	3.12	8	0	0	0	17	16	8	6	0	3	18	.235	.318	.196	9.35	1.56

Fielding

Catcher	PCT	G	PO	A	E	DP	PB
Blackmon	.995	25	167	16	1	1	4
Exposito	.989	44	319	39	4	3	4
Farkes	1.000	7	34	6	0	0	1
Still	.983	69	447	24	8	1	2

First Base	PCT	G	PO	A	E	DP
Anderson	.991	71	616	56	6	65
Farkes	.987	9	71	3	1	4
Jimenez	.981	15	141	17	3	16
Jones	.990	36	337	40	4	25
Still	.975	11	108	9	3	5

Second Base	PCT	G	PO	A	E	DP
Chiang	.944	60	100	184	17	38
Farkes	—	1	0	0	0	0

	PCT	G	PO	A	E	DP
Lara	1.000	1	0	2	0	0
Negron	.972	23	29	75	3	8
Reza	.987	43	76	155	3	37
Segovia	.981	24	39	66	2	13

Third Base	PCT	G	PO	A	E	DP
Farkes	.851	44	34	92	22	7
Jimenez	.920	51	39	88	11	11
Reza	.981	38	25	76	2	4
Segovia	.872	14	12	22	5	5

Shortstop	PCT	G	PO	A	E	DP
Diaz	.949	71	116	200	17	52
Lara	.857	1	3	3	1	0
Navarro	.955	42	80	110	9	24
Reza	.968	21	39	52	3	16

	PCT	G	PO	A	E	DP
Segovia	.929	10	9	17	2	4

Outfield	PCT	G	PO	A	E	DP
Engel	.951	72	111	6	6	1
Hall	.947	9	18	0	1	0
Kalish	.966	18	27	1	1	0
Keowen	1.000	3	4	0	0	0
Kielty	1.000	2	3	0	0	0
Nava	.965	75	128	10	5	1
Negron	.917	10	33	0	3	0
Place	.960	112	233	7	10	3
Reddick	.970	70	115	15	4	4
Segovia	—	1	0	0	0	0
Sheely	.936	61	98	4	7	0

GREENVILLE DRIVE   LOW CLASS A
SOUTH ATLANTIC LEAGUE

Batting	B-T	HT	WT	DOB	AVG	vLH	vRH	G	AB	R	H	2B	3B	HR	RBI	BB	HBP	SH	SF	SO	SB	CS	SLG	OBP
Almanzar, Michael	R-R	6-3	190	12-2-90	.207	.125	.224	35	140	12	29	5	2	2	11	5	1	0	1	39	0	1	.314	.238
Apodaca, Juan	R-R	5-11	180	7-15-86	.217	.300	.194	16	46	5	10	1	0	0	4	7	2	0	0	11	0	0	.239	.345
Arambarris, Manuel	R-R	6-0	178	8-25-85	.209	.212	.208	91	330	32	69	12	1	8	40	12	6	0	0	49	2	0	.324	.250
Cabreja, Rafael	L-R	5-9	170	4-14-87	.160	.182	.154	15	50	10	8	2	0	1	6	16	1	1	0	13	1	1	.260	.373
Cooney, Matt	R-R	5-11	215	12-26-85	.146	.067	.192	12	41	3	6	1	0	0	3	1	0	0	0	17	0	0	.171	.222
DiBenedetto, Tom	R-R	6-1	192	11-3-85	.256	.083	.323	14	43	7	11	1	0	0	6	4	1	0	0	11	0	0	.279	.360
Exposito, Luis	R-R	6-3	210	1-20-87	.283	.357	.252	49	191	34	54	8	1	11	31	12	1	0	0	42	1	1	.508	.328
Fernandez-Oliva, Carlos	B-R	6-1	175	9-23-86	.280	.211	.302	40	164	16	46	10	0	0	15	9	1	0	1	35	0	3	.341	.320
Gilardo, Peter	R-R	6-0	205	11-19-85	.138	.000	.174	10	29	2	4	1	0	0	6	2	0	1	0	10	0	0	.172	.316
Jones, Michael	L-R	6-3	220	6-14-85	.317	.250	.339	86	331	49	105	22	1	7	52	35	1	0	4	68	2	0	.453	.380
Kalish, Ryan	L-L	6-1	205	3-28-88	.281	.270	.284	96	360	51	101	16	1	3	32	53	4	0	3	76	18	4	.356	.376
Lin, Che-Hsuan	R-R	6-0	180	9-21-88	.249	.258	.245	91	362	60	90	13	6	5	37	43	9	0	1	62	33	7	.359	.342
Mailman, David	L-L	6-2	180	10-7-88	.249	.154	.280	115	426	55	106	21	3	8	51	50	1	0	1	94	15	7	.369	.328
Marks, David	L-R	6-0	190	3-23-87	.227	.206	.234	81	273	42	62	18	2	10	35	42	3	0	1	102	2	3	.418	.335
Navarro, Yamaico	R-R	5-11	170	10-31-87	.280	.329	.265	83	325	46	91	14	4	7	54	29	3	0	4	73	3	2	.412	.341
Negron, Kris	R-R	6-0	180	2-16-86	.244	.310	.225	92	311	50	76	15	5	1	27	31	10	6	4	48	25	5	.334	.329
Penprase, Zach	R-R	6-2	180	2-16-85	.235	.269	.222	26	98	9	23	4	1	0	8	10	0	1	0	30	2	1	.296	.306
Reddick, Josh	L-R	6-2	180	2-19-87	.340	.286	.348	14	53	7	18	4	2	0	9	5	0	0	0	8	2	1	.491	.397
Reza, Aaron	R-R	5-7	180	6-25-85	.353	.333	.359	16	51	12	18	7	0	3	11	4	4	0	0	9	0	0	.667	.441
Rizzo, Anthony	L-L	6-3	220	8-8-89	.373	.353	.379	21	83	9	31	6	0	0	11	3	1	0	0	15	0	0	.446	.402
Sanchez, Maykol	R-R	5-11	176	5-30-88	.000	—	.000	1	1	0	0	0	0	0	0	0	0	0	0	0	0	0	.000	.000
Stanley, Jered	R-R	6-0	220	9-18-84	.270	.261	.273	77	285	39	77	16	2	17	54	28	9	0	1	97	3	0	.519	.353
Tejeda, Oscar	R-R	6-1	177	12-26-89	.261	.247	.265	97	372	44	97	18	1	4	38	20	2	0	2	76	11	5	.347	.301
Vazquez, Will	R-R	6-2	190	2-22-85	.226	.268	.214	59	186	20	42	14	0	1	15	17	1	0	1	48	0	1	.317	.293
Weeden, Ty	R-R	6-2	220	9-26-87	.225	.239	.220	53	187	26	42	12	0	8	32	22	4	0	0	63	1	0	.417	.319

Pitching	B-T	HT	WT	DOB	W	L	ERA	G	GS	CG	SV	IP	H	R	ER	HR	BB	SO	AVG	vLH	vRH	K/9	BB/9
Alvarez, Jose	L-L	5-11	150	5-6-89	8	9	5.70	24	19	0	0	107	118	74	68	15	37	86	.281	.307	.273	7.21	3.10
Bailey, Austin	B-R	6-1	195	10-10-88	0	0	3.86	1	1	0	0	5	2	2	2	1	3		.222	.250	.200	5.79	1.93
Bard, Daniel	R-R	6-4	195	6-25-85	1	0	0.64	15	0	0	0	28	12	2	2	1	4	43	.129	.171	.096	13.82	1.29
Buller, Daniel	R-L	6-0	205	12-25-84	0	0	54.00	1	0	0	0	1	6	6	6	0	1	2	.667	.000	.857	18.00	0.00
Capellan, Jose	L-L	6-2	170	7-18-86	3	6	4.65	15	15	0	0	70	96	44	36	7	15	54	.330	.313	.336	6.98	1.94
Colvin, Ryan	L-R	6-2	165	4-12-87	1	2	7.36	8	3	0	1	22	27	19	18	2	9	22	.300	.306	.296	9.00	3.68
Cox, Bryce	R-R	6-4	205	8-10-84	1	0	1.50	14	0	0	0	24	21	6	4	0	3	23	.228	.158	.278	8.63	1.13
Craft, Jordan	R-R	6-3	200	6-5-85	0	5	7.29	17	0	0	1	33	38	28	27	3	16	24	.295	.327	.270	6.48	4.32
Doubront, Felix	L-L	6-2	166	10-23-87	12	8	3.67	23	23	0	0	115	115	53	47	9	24	118	.260	.294	.248	9.21	1.87
Fernandes, Kyle	L-L	6-0	190	9-12-85	3	1	4.47	24	0	0	1	58	62	30	29	2	19	54	.272	.230	.292	8.33	2.93
Foster, Kyle	R-R	6-0	220	6-4-85	3	1	5.12	18	0	0	0	32	44	22	18	1	11	20	.341	.333	.345	5.68	3.13
Garcia, Javier	R-R	6-5	207	1-5-84	3	1	5.06	25	0	0	2	43	53	26	24	5	13	45	.312	.393	.272	9.49	2.74
Guerra, Joseph	R-R	5-11	178	9-4-86	0	2	6.57	8	0	0	1	12	11	9	9	1	6	10	.250	.353	.185	7.30	4.38
Hagadone, Nick	L-L	6-5	230	1-1-86	1	1	0.00	3	3	0	0	10	5	3	0	0	6	12	.135	.200	.091	10.80	5.40
Huntzinger, Brock	R-R	6-3	200	7-2-88	2	3	7.09	6	6	0	0	27	34	23	21	12	6	11	.304	.348	.273	3.71	2.03
Kehrt, Jeremy	R-R	6-2	190	12-21-85	0	0	9.00	1	0	0	0	2	4	2	2	0	3	3	.400	.000	.667	13.50	13.50
Latimer, Will	L-L	6-3	190	12-4-85	0	0	0.00	1	0	0	0	2	2	0	0	0	0	0	.286	.000		0.00	0.00
Lawson, Ryne	L-R	6-2	180	6-21-85	4	3	3.40	30	5	0	4	79	63	38	30	1	34	56	.220	.238	.205	6.35	3.86
Matsuo, Terumasa	R-R	5-11	176	1-18-82	7	5	4.12	27	27	0	0	138	130	74	63	16	51	135	.256	.240	.268	8.83	3.33
McClain, Lance	R-L	6-1	175	3-26-87	1	0	2.57	12	0	0	3	28	26	11	8	0	7	19	.255	.324	.221	6.11	2.25
Miller, Ryne	R-R	6-4	230	9-25-85	2	3	5.68	29	0	0	4	51	63	39	32	7	23	44	.300	.378	.242	7.82	4.09
Portice, Eammon	R-R	6-2	185	6-18-85	4	4	3.64	18	11	0	0	72	62	43	29	8	26	80	.226	.265	.199	10.05	3.27
Povich, Chad	R-R	6-0	185	6-13-86	8	7	3.92	34	15	0	2	126	115	60	55	11	34	110	.240	.277	.214	7.84	2.42
Province, Chris	R-R	6-3	220	1-20-85	6	3	2.86	11	11	0	0	57	54	22	18	2	8	34	.245	.277	.218	5.40	1.27
Rozier, Michael	L-L	6-5	210	7-4-85	0	1	7.58	11	0	0	0	19	20	20	16	1	19	21	.267	.350	.236	9.95	9.00
Ventura, Felix	R-R	5-11	165	4-27-84	2	4	2.91	49	0	0	19	65	47	27	21	2	32	58	.201	.222	.185	8.03	4.43

Fielding

Catcher	PCT	G	PO	A	E	DP	PB
Apodaca	.992	14	118	6	1	0	3
Cooney	.962	6	48	3	2	0	1
Exposito	.994	33	276	32	2	4	7
Gilardo	.985	9	61	5	1	1	3
Vazquez	.997	40	303	27	1	3	5
Weeden	.984	39	280	35	5	4	9

First Base	PCT	G	PO	A	E	DP
Arambarris	.992	15	117	9	1	15
Cooney	.857	1	6	0	1	1
Fernandez-Oliva	.993	33	251	19	2	20
Jones	.980	64	580	46	13	46
Rizzo	.988	19	155	9	2	9
Stanley	.917	1	10	1	1	1
Vazquez	1.000	9	78	7	0	5

Second Base	PCT	G	PO	A	E	DP
DiBenedetto	.957	10	19	26	2	4
Navarro	1.000	11	24	32	0	7
Negron	.980	82	162	228	8	48
Penprase	.964	24	53	55	4	13
Reza	.979	13	16	31	1	4
Vazquez	1.000	4	1	5	0	0

Third Base	PCT	G	PO	A	E	DP
Almanzar	.898	33	27	70	11	8
Arambarris	.938	72	29	151	12	9
DiBenedetto	.714	3	1	4	2	0
Navarro	1.000	10	11	24	0	6
Negron	.929	3	4	9	1	3
Reza	1.000	3	0	4	0	1
Tejeda	.930	17	11	29	3	2
Vazquez	.889	5	1	7	1	1

Shortstop	PCT	G	PO	A	E	DP
Navarro	.951	61	87	148	12	21
Negron	1.000	4	3	12	0	1
Penprase	.900	2	3	6	1	0
Tejeda	.924	76	100	168	22	34

Outfield	PCT	G	PO	A	E	DP
Cabreja	.962	15	24	1	1	0
Fernandez-Oliva	1.000	4	8	0	0	0
Kalish	.985	91	189	9	3	1
Lin	.961	88	193	6	8	2
Mailman	.967	110	181	21	7	6
Marks	.891	49	53	4	7	1
Negron	1.000	6	8	1	0	0
Reddick	.944	13	15	2	1	0
Stanley	.971	51	96	4	3	0

LOWELL SPINNERS   SHORT-SEASON

NEW YORK-PENN LEAGUE

Batting	B-T	HT	WT	DOB	AVG	vLH	vRH	G	AB	R	H	2B	3B	HR	RBI	BB	HBP	SH	SF	SO	SB	CS	SLG	OBP
Bermudez, Ronald	R-R	6-1	165	6-6-88	.201	.250	.180	57	214	24	43	9	3	3	17	11	2	0	2	47	4	2	.313	.245
Blocker, Darren	R-R	6-0	200	2-23-87	.205	.185	.216	24	78	9	16	2	2	0	9	6	0	1	0	24	1	3	.282	.262
Brooks, Deshaun	R-R	6-4	230	10-25-84	.248	.195	.276	34	117	9	29	5	0	2	15	7	0	0	0	37	0	0	.342	.290
Burgos, Ricardo	L-R	5-10	170	6-23-87	.198	.212	.193	41	121	24	24	8	1	4	22	29	0	0	4	47	3	2	.380	.344
Cabreja, Rafael	L-R	5-9	170	4-14-87	.255	.296	.239	27	94	13	24	5	3	2	10	16	2	0	0	19	3	3	.436	.375
Cooney, Matt	R-R	5-11	215	12-26-85	.071	.000	.100	13	28	0	2	0	0	0	0	4	3	1	0	2	11	0	.071	.176
Dening, Mitch	L-R	6-1	165	8-17-88	.321	.352	.308	62	240	35	77	13	7	3	20	18	3	1	0	50	9	7	.471	.375
Dent, Ryan	R-R	6-0	190	3-15-89	.154	.186	.137	58	201	33	31	7	2	6	21	29	3	2	3	87	17	4	.299	.267
Federowicz, Tim	R-R	5-10	213	8-5-87	.244	.250	.242	36	127	14	31	6	0	1	15	19	0	0	2	24	10	3	.315	.338
Fernandez-Oliva, Carlos	B-R	6-1	175	9-23-86	.234	.267	.219	23	94	8	22	5	0	1	8	5	0	0	0	26	2	2	.319	.273
Gentile, Zach	L-R	5-8	165	11-1-86	.222	.184	.237	40	135	13	30	3	1	0	13	8	1	1	0	17	2	4	.259	.271
Gibson, Derrik	R-R	6-1	170	12-5-89	.086	.000	.103	14	35	4	3	0	0	0	3	6	1	0	1	11	2	0	.086	.233
Gil, Rafael	R-R	6-0	165	10-3-85	.140	.250	.086	25	86	7	12	2	0	1	7	4	0	0	0	25	1	0	.198	.178
Hee, Jonathan	R-R	6-0	180	8-11-85	.196	.333	.139	47	143	19	28	6	0	0	9	29	4	1	0	26	4	3	.238	.347
Hissey, Pete	L-L	6-1	180	1-17-90	.265	.200	.292	9	34	3	9	0	0	0	2	5	0	0	0	11	6	0	.265	.359
Kelly, Casey	R-R	6-3	194	10-4-89	.344	.500	.292	9	32	5	11	5	1	0	4	0	0	0	0	8	0	1	.563	.344
Keowen, Kade	R-R	6-5	215	4-18-86	.241	.269	.224	38	137	15	33	7	2	0	13	9	0	0	0	43	2	3	.321	.288
Khoury, Ryan	R-R	5-10	180	3-19-84	.313	.400	.273	5	16	2	5	1	0	0	2	5	1	0	1	8	1	1	.375	.478
Kielty, Bobby	B-R	6-1	225	8-5-76	.250	.250	.500	2	8	2	3	0	1	0	3	0	0	1	2	0	0	.625	.333
Lavarnway, Ryan	R-R	6-4	225	8-7-87	.211	.318	.163	22	71	10	15	5	0	2	9	8	3	0	0	18	0	0	.366	.317
Middlebrooks, Will	R-R	6-4	200	9-9-88	.254	.327	.227	59	209	21	53	17	2	1	21	12	2	1	2	73	10	0	.368	.298
Natale, Jeff	R-R	5-9	180	8-24-82	.333	.200	.417	11	39	11	13	6	0	1	6	9	0	0	1	3	2	0	.564	.449
Pichardo, Wilfred	B-R	5-9	146	10-21-89	.286	.000	.333	3	7	2	2	0	0	0	0	0	0	0	0	1	1	.286	.286
Sumoza, Luis	R-R	6-0	170	7-15-88	.301	.364	.275	51	193	31	58	15	0	11	38	21	0	0	2	59	9	6	.549	.366

Pitching	B-T	HT	WT	DOB	W	L	ERA	G	GS	CG	SV	IP	H	R	ER	HR	BB	SO	AVG	vLH	vRH	K/9	BB/9
Britton, Drake	L-L	6-2	200	5-22-89	1	2	4.28	8	7	0	0	34	30	18	16	3	16	26	.234	.278	.227	6.95	4.28
Buller, Daniel	R-L	6-0	205	12-25-84	0	0	4.74	13	0	0	0	25	25	13	13	1	13	21	.255	.346	.222	7.66	4.74
Castillo, Yeiper	R-R	6-3	158	9-6-88	3	6	4.19	15	11	0	0	58	46	32	27	6	29	62	.215	.176	.240	9.62	4.50
Fife, Stephen	R-R	6-3	210	10-4-86	1	1	2.33	14	0	0	2	39	28	14	10	1	11	41	.196	.173	.209	9.54	2.56
Garrison, Seth	B-R	6-5	220	8-13-85	2	1	1.45	22	0	0	9	31	20	6	5	1	4	26	.189	.130	.233	7.55	1.16
Goodson, Matt	R-R	6-3	195	9-26-82	0	0	33.75	1	1	0	0	1	5	5	5	1	1	1	.556	.000	.556	6.75	6.75
Guerra, Joseph	R-R	5-11	178	9-4-86	0	1	6.75	1	0	0	0	3	3	2	2	1	3	2	.300	.250	.333	6.75	10.13
Hale, Alex	R-R	6-0	215	2-9-86	0	2	2.35	8	0	0	0	8	7	3	2	1	5	7	.233	.083	.333	8.22	5.87
Herold, Mitch	L-L	6-0	200	6-18-86	3	1	2.57	17	0	0	1	28	20	9	8	2	14	26	.198	.200	.197	8.36	4.50
Huntzinger, Brock	R-R	6-3	200	7-2-88	5	0	0.64	8	8	1	0	42	25	3	3	1	7	32	.168	.196	.153	6.86	1.50
Kehrt, Jeremy	R-R	6-2	190	12-21-85	0	0	9.00	1	0	0	0	2	4	2	2	1	0	1	.444	.250	.600	4.50	0.00
Lee, Michael	R-R	6-7	220	11-18-86	0	0	12.00	4	0	0	0	6	7	8	8	1	3	11	.280	.357	.182	16.50	4.50
Lin, Wang-Yi	R-R	6-2	192	6-28-88	0	0	13.50	1	1	0	0	3	4	4	4	0	2	1	.333	.000	.500	3.38	6.75
Lonergan, Scott	B-R	6-4	200	12-6-83	0	0	31.50	2	0	0	0	2	6	7	7	1	2	1	.600	1.000	.429	4.50	9.00
McClain, Lance	R-L	6-1	175	3-20-86	0	3	3.80	10	1	0	1	21	15	10	9	2	7	20	.192	.111	.217	8.44	2.95
Neuman, Dennis	R-R	5-11	185	10-18-89	2	1	7.20	8	0	0	0	15	20	12	12	2	3	12	.317	.321	.314	7.20	1.80
Pimentel, Stolmy	R-R	6-3	186	2-1-90	5	2	3.14	13	11	0	0	63	51	25	22	7	17	61	.224	.271	.196	8.71	2.43
Price, Bryan	R-R	6-4	210	11-13-86	1	3	3.83	12	9	0	0	40	47	22	17	2	10	43	.281	.299	.267	9.67	2.25
Rhoades, Chad	R-R	5-10	175	3-10-83	0	0	1.50	4	1	0	0	6	5	1	1	0	2	11	.238	.300	.182	16.50	3.00
Richardson, Dustin	L-L	6-5	195	1-9-84	0	1	9.00	2	2	0	0	5	8	5	5	2	4	4	.333	.167	.389	7.20	3.60
Rodriguez, Jorge	R-R	6-1	160	3-11-85	0	0	2.91	11	0	0	1	22	21	8	7	1	12	22	.253	.375	.176	9.14	4.98
Romero, Robert	R-R	5-10	190	3-28-85	0	1	1.50	5	0	0	0	6	3	1	1	0	2	2	.163	.167	.150	3.00	3.00
Rosario, Charlie	R-R	5-10	158	7-23-88	2	2	3.63	17	0	0	2	45	48	21	18	4	12	33	.274	.348	.229	6.65	2.42
Snyder, Kyle	B-R	6-8	230	9-9-77	0	0	0.00	1	1	0	0	2	1	2	0	0	0	0	.111	.000	.250	3.86	0.00
Strickland, Hunter	R-R	6-5	200	9-24-88	5	3	3.18	15	10	0	0	71	67	32	25	5	17	59	.249	.222	.261	7.51	2.17
Tomoleoni, Michael	L-L			7-30-85	1	1	8.03	9	0	0	1	12	11	11	11	0	20	7	.234	.313	.194	5.11	14.59

	B-T	HT	WT	DOB	W	L	ERA	G	GS	CG	SV	IP	H	R	ER	HR	BB	SO	AVG	vLH	vRH	K/9	BB/9
Weiland, Kyle	L-R	6-4	195	9-12-86	3	3	1.50	15	10	0	0	60	36	17	10	1	10	68	.166	.141	.184	10.20	1.50
Zerpa, Armando	L-L	5-11	175	2-13-87	1	1	5.87	5	0	0	0	8	9	5	5	0	3	9	.290	.222	.318	10.57	3.52

Fielding

Catcher	PCT	G	PO	A	E	DP	PB
Cooney	.976	13	73	8	2	2	2
Federowicz	.993	29	240	34	2	3	3
Gil	.996	25	205	17	1	4	3
Lavarnway	1.000	10	84	11	0	2	1

First Base	PCT	G	PO	A	E	DP
Blocker	.957	4	20	2	1	2
Brooks	.988	22	154	9	2	12
Burgos	.993	31	248	28	2	14
Fernandez-Oliva	.987	20	143	10	2	11
Hee	1.000	2	9	0	0	2

Second Base	PCT	G	PO	A	E	DP
Dent	.958	5	12	11	1	4
Gentile	.961	32	56	66	5	14

	PCT	G	PO	A	E	DP
Gibson	1.000	6	3	12	0	2
Hee	.978	29	52	82	3	9
Khoury	1.000	2	6	7	0	0
Natale	.964	6	14	13	1	2

Third Base	PCT	G	PO	A	E	DP
Blocker	.897	12	8	18	3	0
Gibson	.600	3	0	3	2	0
Hee	.875	4	0	7	1	0
Khoury	1.000	2	2	2	0	0
Middlebrooks	.927	55	32	82	9	4

Shortstop	PCT	G	PO	A	E	DP
Dent	.946	52	77	135	12	22
Gibson	.929	4	3	10	1	0
Hee	.953	12	12	29	2	6

	PCT	G	PO	A	E	DP
Kelly	.938	9	10	20	2	4
Khoury	.750	1	1	2	1	1

Outfield	PCT	G	PO	A	E	DP
Bermudez	.994	55	155	0	1	0
Cabreja	1.000	12	24	2	0	0
Dening	.977	60	121	4	3	1
Fernandez-Oliva	.750	4	2	1	1	0
Gentile	1.000	7	5	3	0	0
Hee	1.000	1	2	0	0	0
Hissey	.882	9	15	0	2	0
Keowen	.980	33	45	3	1	0
Kielty	1.000	2	7	0	0	0
Pichardo	1.000	3	5	0	0	0
Sumoza	.957	44	83	6	4	2

GCL RED SOX
ROOKIE
GULF COAST LEAGUE

Batting	B-T	HT	WT	DOB	AVG	vLH	vRH	G	AB	R	H	2B	3B	HR	RBI	BB	HBP	SH	SF	SO	SB	CS	SLG	OBP
Almanzar, Michael	R-R	6-3	190	12-2-90	.348	.348	.348	23	89	16	31	6	1	1	11	8	2	0	0	15	3	3	.472	.414
Apodaca, Juan	R-R	5-11	180	7-15-86	.400	—	.400	2	5	1	2	0	0	0	2	0	2	0	0	3	1	0	.400	.571
Blair, Carson	R-R	6-1	190	10-18-89	.409	.250	.600	6	22	2	9	1	0	1	9	0	0	0	1	5	0	0	.591	.391
Cabreja, Rafael	L-R	5-9	170	4-14-87	.357	.667	.273	4	14	4	5	2	0	0	5	0	0	0	0	3	0	0	.500	.357
Chen, Chia-Chu	L-R	5-10	175	4-7-89	.255	.256	.256	18	51	2	13	4	0	0	4	6	0	0	0	14	0	0	.333	.333
DiBenedetto, Tom	R-R	6-1	192	11-3-85	.259	.200	.273	11	27	4	7	2	0	0	2	8	2	0	1	6	1	0	.333	.447
Feliz, Roberto	R-R	6-1	180	12-30-87	.232	.190	.250	40	142	16	33	6	1	7	25	13	4	0	1	39	5	0	.437	.313
Frezza, Andrew	R-R	5-9	199	5-16-86	.263	.235	.274	36	118	19	31	7	2	1	8	8	1	1	0	26	10	0	.381	.315
Garcia, Joantoni	R-R	5-11	165	9-9-90	.253	.220	.267	46	146	19	37	8	0	1	11	17	0	2	3	34	5	0	.329	.325
Gibson, Derrik	R-R	6-1	170	12-5-89	.309	.296	.313	27	94	15	29	6	1	0	9	14	3	1	1	18	14	0	.394	.411
Gilardo, Peter	R-R	6-0	205	11-19-85	.294	.000	.333	8	17	5	5	1	0	0	2	4	1	0	0	5	2	0	.353	.455
Hissey, Pete	L-L	6-1	180	1-17-90	.238	.333	.167	6	21	6	5	1	0	0	4	3	1	0	0	4	3	0	.286	.385
Huang, Chih-Hsiang	R-L	6-1	165	11-18-87	.248	.260	.241	42	133	16	33	12	0	2	14	20	1	0	3	38	1	0	.383	.344
Kelly, Casey	R-R	6-3	194	10-4-89	.173	.172	.174	27	98	10	17	5	0	1	9	6	2	0	3	34	1	0	.255	.229
Lora, Eddie	B-L	6-2	215	3-21-89	.000	.000	.000	10	32	1	0	0	0	0	0	2	1	0	0	12	0	0	.000	.086
Moanaroa, Moko	L-L	5-11	200	12-22-89	.111	.000	.174	11	36	4	4	1	0	0	3	4	0	0	0	11	0	0	.139	.200
Natale, Jeff	R-R	5-9	180	8-24-82	.167	.000	.200	3	6	2	1	0	0	0	1	2	0	0	1	0	0	0	.167	.333
Peterson, Bryan	L-R	6-3	190	3-21-90	.277	.167	.308	38	137	20	38	7	3	1	24	18	1	0	2	31	7	2	.394	.361
Pichardo, Wilfred	B-R	5-9	146	10-21-89	.297	.361	.270	52	202	36	60	4	2	0	11	18	1	4	0	47	42	9	.337	.357
Ramos, Roberto	B-R	5-10	160	9-4-88	.261	.300	.250	18	46	3	12	4	0	0	5	3	0	3	0	10	2	1	.348	.306
Roque, Kenneth	L-R	5-11	162	9-20-89	.236	.208	.244	37	106	6	25	5	1	1	12	11	1	2	0	28	4	3	.330	.314
Sanchez, Maykol	R-R	5-11	176	5-30-88	.205	.182	.214	18	39	3	8	2	0	0	5	4	3	0	1	7	0	0	.256	.319
Vazquez, Christian	R-R	5-9	195	8-21-90	.190	.118	.220	21	58	7	11	1	0	0	5	6	0	1	0	17	0	0	.207	.266
Yockey, Tyler	L-L	6-1	196	10-16-89	.163	.045	.200	27	92	7	15	4	0	1	10	4	0	0	0	42	2	0	.239	.198

Pitching	B-T	HT	WT	DOB	W	L	ERA	G	GS	CG	SV	IP	H	R	ER	HR	BB	SO	AVG	vLH	vRH	K/9	BB/9
Batista, Anatanaer	R-R	5-10	150	2-2-89	5	1	5.82	13	0	0	1	22	23	17	14	2	4	22	.267	.333	.213	9.14	1.66
Cabral, Cesar	L-L	6-3	175	2-11-89	1	1	5.59	11	9	0	0	48	55	37	30	3	15	51	.282	.227	.298	9.50	2.79
Clay, Caleb	R-R	6-2	180	2-15-88	0	0	0.00	2	2	0	0	3	4	0	0	0	1	2	.333	.000	.667	6.75	3.38
Colvin, Ryan	R-R	6-2	165	4-12-87	0	0	7.71	2	0	0	0	2	6	4	2	0	0	2	.429	.286	.571	7.71	0.00
Hudson, Jennell	R-R	6-4	185	1-20-90	0	0	5.40	10	0	0	0	15	15	11	9	1	11	11	.263	.250	.276	6.60	6.60
Huijer, Swen	R-R	6-9	205	11-7-90	3	1	2.81	8	1	0	0	16	15	5	5	1	0	4	.246	.250	.243	2.25	0.00
Jimenez, Manuel	R-R	5-11	177	1-6-87	1	1	4.43	10	0	0	0	20	18	11	10	1	9	8	.243	.296	.213	3.54	3.98
Kehrt, Jeremy	R-R	6-2	190	12-21-85	3	2	2.84	11	8	0	1	51	46	19	16	2	7	44	.243	.306	.192	7.82	1.24
Lennox, Michael	R-R	6-4	195	8-25-89	2	3	3.94	8	0	0	0	16	18	8	7	3	2	10	.273	.200	.333	5.63	1.13
Lin, Wang-Yi	R-R	6-2	192	6-28-88	0	2	4.63	11	9	0	0	45	50	30	23	4	11	36	.284	.238	.323	7.25	2.22
Lonergan, Scott	B-R	6-4	200	12-6-83	0	0	3.00	2	2	0	0	3	3	1	1	0	0	2	.273	.400	.167	6.00	0.00
Marin, Leandro	R-R	5-11	165	11-9-88	1	1	3.95	13	0	0	2	14	13	6	6	1	5	16	.245	.211	.265	10.54	3.29
Mercadante, Dustin	R-R	6-7	230	10-24-88	0	0	1.42	15	0	0	8	19	13	4	3	1	5	12	.194	.114	.281	5.68	2.37
Neuman, Dennis	R-R	5-11	185	10-18-89	0	0	0.00	9	0	0	0	3	11	6	0	0	0	2	10	.167	.182	.160	8.44	1.69
Perez, Pedro	R-R	6-4	170	5-3-88	1	2	4.68	12	6	0	1	42	50	25	22	1	10	33	.286	.203	.347	7.02	2.13
Portice, Eammon	R-R	6-2	185	6-18-85	0	0	0.00	2	1	0	0	3	2	0	0	0	2	1	.222	.500	.143	3.00	6.00
Pressly, Ryan	R-R	6-3	175	12-15-88	1	3	3.79	10	9	0	0	40	41	18	17	2	21	34	.277	.238	.306	7.59	4.69
Rodriguez, Jorge	R-R	6-1	160	3-11-85	4	1	2.76	8	0	0	0	16	9	7	5	1	10	13	.153	.143	.158	7.16	5.51
Rozier, Michael	L-L	6-5	210	7-4-85	1	1	7.15	5	0	0	0	11	13	9	9	1	6	14	.289	.286	.290	11.12	4.76
Ruiz, Pete	R-R	6-3	205	8-21-87	2	1	5.09	9	3	0	0	23	27	16	13	1	9	15	.290	.220	.346	5.87	3.52
Snyder, Kyle	R-R	6-8	230	9-9-77	0	0	3.38	6	3	0	0	11	8	4	4	1	1	12	.205	.316	.100	10.13	0.84
Tomoleoni, Michael	L-L			7-30-85	0	0	0.00	1	0	0	0	2	0	0	0	0	2	0	.000	.000	.000	0.00	10.80
Wasielewski, Richie	L-L	6-4	240	9-23-89	0	1	7.20	3	2	0	0	5	7	5	4	0	2	2	.318	.200	.353	3.60	3.60
Zerpa, Armando	L-L	5-11	175	2-13-87	2	1	2.57	8	0	0	0	14	12	5	4	1	3	9	.231	.167	.250	5.79	1.93

Fielding

Catcher	PCT	G	PO	A	E	DP	PB
Apodaca	1.000	2	13	2	0	0	0
Chen	.989	18	77	13	1	1	3
Gilardo	1.000	8	39	3	0	0	2
Sanchez	.970	18	85	12	3	2	1
Vazquez	.981	21	141	18	3	2	5

First Base	PCT	G	PO	A	E	DP
DiBenedetto	1.000	3	34	0	0	1
Frezza	1.000	1	2	0	0	0
Garcia	1.000	1	6	2	0	1
Huang	.992	38	372	21	3	23
Lora	.966	9	77	8	3	7
Yockey	.966	6	57	0	2	5

Second Base	PCT	G	PO	A	E	DP
DiBenedetto	1.000	3	6	5	0	0

Garcia	1.000	12	13	31	0	2
Gibson	.920	5	9	14	2	1
Natale	1.000	3	7	4	0	1
Ramos	1.000	1	1	3	0	0
Roque	.938	35	55	82	9	21

Third Base	PCT	G	PO	A	E	DP
Almanzar	.973	23	18	53	2	3
Blair	.923	6	2	10	1	1
DiBenedetto	.800	1	3	1	1	0
Garcia	.921	12	12	23	3	2
Gibson	1.000	14	4	34	0	2

Shortstop	PCT	G	PO	A	E	DP
DiBenedetto	1.000	3	2	5	0	0
Garcia	.965	21	35	104	5	18
Gibson	.909	5	9	11	2	2

Huang	1.000	1	3	2	0	2
Kelly	.938	22	27	64	6	8
Ramos	1.000	7	4	25	0	1
Roque	1.000	1	1	1	0	1

Outfield	PCT	G	PO	A	E	DP
Cabreja	1.000	4	4	1	0	1
Feliz	.949	34	36	1	2	1
Frezza	1.000	28	28	4	0	1
Hissey	1.000	4	5	0	0	0
Moanaroa	1.000	4	4	0	0	0
Peterson	.959	34	46	1	2	0
Pichardo	.917	41	66	0	6	0
Ramos	1.000	7	8	1	0	0
Yockey	1.000	17	17	1	0	0

DSL RED SOX   ROOKIE

DOMINICAN SUMMER LEAGUE

Batting	B-T	HT	WT	DOB	AVG	vLH	vRH	G	AB	R	H	2B	3B	HR	RBI	BB	HBP	SH	SF	SO	SB	CS	SLG	OBP
Bonifacio, Juan	R-R	6-2	168	12-7-88	.275	.171	.297	60	193	37	53	9	5	4	34	37	10	1	4	60	13	6	.435	.410
Chourio, Pedro	R-R	6-2	211	3-13-90	.237	.267	.230	65	232	38	55	11	6	5	35	29	12	0	4	71	0	0	.401	.347
De La Rosa, Christopher	R-R	5-9	185	5-10-89	.219	.143	.239	42	137	25	30	10	2	1	16	24	11	1	0	47	7	3	.343	.378
Escobar, Leonel	R-R	5-10	175	9-4-90	.280	.324	.267	47	150	29	42	6	0	0	11	19	10	3	0	24	3	0	.320	.397
Espinoza, Rafael	B-R	5-7	150	10-12-90	.237	.111	.267	65	236	40	56	9	8	0	28	50	13	3	1	65	14	5	.343	.397
Garcia, Jose	R-R			4-23-91	.216	.163	.228	60	232	37	50	4	2	3	27	28	4	5	2	80	17	7	.289	.308
Gonzalez, Pedro	L-L	6-0	185	3-17-90	.176	.220	.161	50	165	20	29	6	2	3	26	28	3	0	2	53	11	5	.291	.303
Gutierrez, Javier	R-R	6-0	170	8-26-90	.230	.308	.215	65	230	38	53	14	2	3	29	40	10	2	3	60	7	2	.348	.364
Lora, Eddie	B-L	6-2	215	3-21-89	.300	.316	.297	53	120	21	36	6	1	5	26	34	1	0	1	38	0	1	.492	.455
Menses, Heiker	R-R	5-9	160	7-1-91	.220	.125	.241	43	132	20	29	1	2	0	16	29	4	1	0	44	9	3	.258	.376
Pinto, Derwin	R-R	5-10	196	2-20-90	.188	.143	.197	29	80	11	15	4	0	0	11	21	4	0	0	21	2	1	.238	.381
Rojas, Jesus	R-R	5-10	180	4-21-90	.258	.500	.241	11	31	2	8	0	0	3	1	2	1	0	0	.258	.273
Sanchez, Felix	B-R	6-0	165	6-2-90	.244	.167	.269	41	123	23	30	2	2	0	13	24	3	2	0	35	12	3	.293	.380
Urena, Lewis	R-R	5-8	145	5-6-91	.224	.244	.219	56	201	29	45	7	5	0	20	33	4	5	1	48	17	5	.308	.343

Pitching	B-T	HT	WT	DOB	W	L	ERA	G	GS	CG	SV	IP	H	R	ER	HR	SO	AVG	vLH	vRH	K/9	BB/9
Bastardo, Luis	R-R	6-1	165	5-14-90	0	1	3.70	14	1	0	4	24	20	11	10	1	13	13	.227	.368	.188	4.81	4.81
Consuegra, Randy	R-R	6-2	211	10-14-89	0	0	0.00	3	0	0	4	2	0	0	0	0	2	.154	.200	.125	4.50	0.00
De La Cruz, Victor	R-R	6-0	168	10-10-88	3	0	1.25	11	0	0	3	36	23	6	5	1	12	37	.183	.216	.169	9.25	3.00
Dilon, Danny	R-R	6-1	170	7-30-89	3	3	2.96	12	10	1	2	46	41	17	15	1	18	29	.236	.234	.236	5.72	3.55
Garcia, Samuel	R-R	5-10	150	11-6-90	1	0	9.39	6	0	0	0	8	6	8	8	0	8	3	.214	.400	.174	3.52	9.39
Jimenez, Javier	R-R	6-3	143	7-28-89	3	3	2.83	13	13	0	0	54	40	23	17	0	29	30	.206	.265	.186	5.00	4.83
Juan, Ronaldo	R-R	6-1	170	1-15-90	2	2	11.74	7	1	0	0	15	21	24	20	1	14	4	.328	.400	.295	2.35	8.22
Lastreto, Nestor	L-L	6-0	160	9-28-89	5	0	1.72	15	3	1	2	52	46	13	10	2	15	41	.237	.389	.222	7.05	2.58
Lopez, Edwin	L-L	6-1	165	12-11-87	2	3	3.31	17	0	0	4	33	29	15	12	1	11	40	.234	.143	.245	11.02	3.03
Machiz, Darlin	R-R	6-4	187	9-5-88	2	0	3.10	7	0	0	0	20	13	9	7	0	19	13	.186	.238	.163	5.75	8.41
Mateo, Alexander	R-R	5-11	165	4-10-91	0	0	13.50	5	0	0	0	9	19	17	13	0	12	3	.442	.400	.455	3.12	12.46
Mendez, Roman	R-R	6-2	180	7-25-90	3	1	2.65	11	11	0	0	51	43	19	15	1	16	46	.222	.200	.230	8.12	2.82
Perez, Israel	L-L	6-1	175	1-13-91	0	1	11.25	6	0	0	0	12	17	19	15	1	23	15	.340	.500	.310	11.25	17.25
Reyes, Ernesto	L-L	6-0	190	7-31-90	2	2	5.09	16	0	0	2	23	21	13	13	2	10	17	.253	.500	.227	6.65	3.91
Rivera, Manuel	L-L	6-0	170	9-1-89	4	3	2.24	13	13	0	0	52	40	21	13	1	19	58	.214	.059	.229	9.97	3.27
Rodriguez, Juan	R-R	6-5	165	12-12-88	2	1	3.03	16	0	0	2	30	14	13	10	0	27	25	.140	.087	.156	7.58	8.19
Ulloa, Brandon	R-R	6-2	170	2-9-89	1	2	4.15	11	4	0	1	35	31	26	16	1	17	36	.237	.229	.240	9.35	4.41
Vellette, Raynel	R-R	6-2	165	6-10-91	4	3	3.44	14	10	0	0	55	40	23	21	0	23	45	.204	.191	.208	7.36	3.76

Fielding

Catcher	PCT	G	PO	A	E	DP	PB
Escobar	.986	46	321	43	5	0	3
Pinto	.984	19	116	11	2	1	2
Rojas	1.000	11	63	13	0	0	1

First Base	PCT	G	PO	A	E	DP
Chourio	.988	17	154	7	2	16
Gonzalez	.979	20	182	4	4	16
Lora	.983	34	316	23	6	16

Second Base	PCT	G	PO	A	E	DP
Espinoza	.946	47	89	102	11	21

Menses	1.000	16	39	35	0	8
Urena	.979	12	25	21	1	3

Third Base	PCT	G	PO	A	E	DP
Chourio	.928	32	38	65	8	3
Menses	.938	15	13	32	3	2
Urena	.942	28	27	71	6	4

Shortstop	PCT	G	PO	A	E	DP
Espinoza	.821	7	10	13	5	4
Garcia	.930	57	68	184	19	24
Menses	.971	7	7	26	1	5

Outfield	PCT	G	PO	A	E	DP
Bonifacio	1.000	55	92	6	0	1
De La Rosa	.929	42	76	2	6	1
Gonzalez	.926	16	25	0	2	0
Gutierrez	.988	55	73	6	1	1
Sanchez	1.000	37	49	2	0	1
Urena	.944	17	33	1	2	0

Chicago Cubs

BY JEFF VORVA

Four days of agony trumped six months of ecstasy.

It was a regular season full of glory when the Cubs won a National League-best 97 games. They qualified for the postseason for the second year in a row, the first time that had happened since 1906-1908.

The team's flagship radio station constantly played a sound bite of legend Ron Santo bellowing, "This is THE YEAR!" And when the team won 44 come-from-behind victories and Carlos Zambrano threw the first Cubs no-hitter since 1972, who was going to argue with the man?

The way the Cubs played during the regular season, it looked good that on the 100th anniversary of their last World Series title, they were going to win it all again.

Then the National League Division Series hit. And hit hard. Unlike the Cubs. For the second straight season, the Cubs bowed out in three games, and that left a bitter taste in their fans' mouths as the Dodgers outscored them 20-6.

It was tough for fans to stomach. The Cubs had a team-record eight players named to the National League all-star team and won their most games at home (55) since 1935.

For his part, general manager Jim Hendry believed he built a team that would not only dominate in the regular season but was built for a playoff run as well. His addition of pitcher Rich Harden in July, just one day after Milwaukee made a big bang trading for C.C. Sabathia, showed the GM meant business.

But in the end, feeble hitting by some of their stars (.071 from Alfonso Soriano, .182 from Aramis Ramirez, .182 from Geovany Soto and .100 from Kosuke Fukudome) did the Cubs in during the short series against the Dodgers.

The good news for the Cubs is that much of the team that won 97 games should be in tact for 2009. Any team with a nucleus of Soriano, Ramirez, Derrek Lee, Soto, Carlos Zambrano, Ted Lilly, Jason Marquis, Kerry Wood, Carlos Marmol and Harden should be a contender.

There is also the potential of prospect Jeff Samardzija. The former Notre Dame wide receiver impressed during the regular season (1-0, a 2.28 ERA in 26 relief appearances) and should be poised to challenge for a job in the rotation.

PLAYERS OF THE YEAR

MAJOR LEAGUE: RYAN DEMPSTER, RHP

Dempster made a successful transition from closer to the rotation, his first year as a full-time starter since 2003. He went on to finish 17-6, 2.96, the fourth-best ERA in the National League, with 187 strikeouts and 76 walks in nearly 207 innings.

MINOR LEAGUE: MICAH HOFFPAUIR, 1B

Hoffpauir, drafted in the 13th round in 2002, enjoyed a solid season at Triple-A Iowa as he hit .362/.393/.752 with 25 home runs and 100 RBIs, both career highs. And he compiled the numbers despite missing April because of an oblique strain.

ORGANIZATION LEADERS

BATTING		*Minimum 250 at-bats
*AVG	Lalli, Blake, Peoria/Tenn./Daytona	.326
R	Scales, Bobby, Iowa	94
H	McGehee, Casey, Iowa	147
TB	Fox, Jake, Iowa/Tennessee	281
2B	Rosa, Jovan, Peoria	43
3B	Colvin, Tyler, Tennessee	11
HR	Fox, Jake, Iowa/Tennessee	31
RBI	Fox, Jake, Iowa/Tennessee	105
BB	Adduci, James, Daytona	63
SO	Rosa, Jovan, Peoria	127
SB	Torres, Andres, Iowa	29
*OBP	Scales, Bobby, Iowa	.415
*SLG	Fox, Jake, Iowa/Tennessee	.556

PITCHING		†Minimum 75 innings
W	Atkins, Mitch, Tennessee/Iowa	17
L	Burns, Mike, Iowa	12
†ERA	Chen, Hung-Wen, Peoria/Daytona	3.38
G	Lambert, Casey, Daytona/Tennessee	55
GS	Veal, Donald, Tennessee	29
SV	Vento, Stephen, Peoria	14
IP	Atkins, Mitch, Tennessee/Iowa	164
BB	Veal, Donald, Tennessee	81
SO	Atkins, Mitch, Tennessee/Iowa	132
†AVG	Carrillo, Marco, Daytona/Tennessee	.223

Another wild card could be Fukudome, who was red hot at the plate in April and May but hit just .217 after the all-star break.

In the minors, first baseman/outfielder Micah Hoffpauir hit 25 homers and 100 RBIs in 71 games for Triple-A Iowa and .342/.400/.534 in 33 major league games and the Cubs are eager to see if he can keep that up in 2009.

General Manager: Jim Hendry. **Farm Director:** Oneri Fleita. **Scouting Director:** Tim Wilken.

Class	Team	League	W	L	PCT	Finish*	Manager	Affiliate Since
Majors	Chicago	National	97	64	.602	1st (16)	Lou Piniella	—
Triple-A	Iowa Cubs	Pacific Coast	83	59	.585	1st (16)	Pat Listach	1981
Double-A	Tennessee Smokies	Southern	63	77	.446	9th (10)	Buddy Bailey	2007
High A	Daytona Cubs	Florida State	73	59	.553	^3rd (12)	Jody Davis	1993
Low A	Peoria Chiefs	Midwest	60	78	.435	12th (14)	Ryne Sandberg	2005
Short-season	Boise Hawks	Northwest	43	33	.566	2nd (8)	Tom Beyers	2001
Rookie	AZL Cubs	Arizona	31	24	.564	5th (9)	Franklin Font	1997

Overall 2008 Minor League Record 352 370 .488 16th

* Finish in overall standings (No. of teams in league). ^League champion.

ORGANIZATION STATISTICS

CHICAGO CUBS

NATIONAL LEAGUE

Batting	B-T	HT	WT	DOB	AVG	vLH	vRH	G	AB	R	H	2B	3B	HR	RBI	BB	HBP	SH	SF	SO	SB	CS	SLG	OBP
Blanco, Henry	R-R	5-11	220	8-29-71	.292	.316	.270	58	120	15	35	3	0	3	12	6	0	2	0	22	0	0	.392	.325
Cedeno, Ronny	R-R	6-0	180	2-2-83	.269	.257	.282	99	216	36	58	12	0	2	28	18	1	1	0	41	4	1	.352	.328
DeRosa, Mark	R-R	6-1	205	2-26-75	.285	.310	.275	149	505	103	144	30	3	21	87	69	9	2	8	106	6	0	.481	.376
Edmonds, Jim	L-L	6-1	210	6-27-70	.256	.161	.269	85	250	47	64	17	2	19	49	45	1	0	2	58	0	1	.568	.369
2-team total (26 San Diego)					.235	—	—	111	340	53	80	19	2	20	55	55	2	1	3	82	2	2	.479	.343
Fontenot, Mike	L-R	5-8	170	6-9-80	.305	.333	.302	119	243	42	74	22	1	9	40	34	3	3	1	51	2	0	.514	.395
Fukudome, Kosuke	L-R	6-0	185	4-26-77	.257	.276	.251	150	501	79	129	25	3	10	58	81	1	2	5	104	12	4	.379	.359
Hill, Koyie	B-R	6-0	190	3-9-79	.095	.333	.056	10	21	0	2	1	0	0	1	0	0	1	0	12	0	0	.143	.095
Hoffpauir, Micah	L-L	6-3	215	3-1-80	.342	.273	.355	33	73	14	25	8	0	2	8	6	1	0	0	24	1	0	.534	.400
Johnson, Reed	R-R	5-10	180	12-8-76	.303	.333	.280	109	333	52	101	21	0	6	50	19	12	5	5	68	5	6	.420	.358
Lee, Derrek	R-R	6-5	245	9-6-75	.291	.306	.286	155	623	93	181	41	3	20	90	71	0	0	4	119	8	2	.462	.361
McGehee, Casey	R-R	6-1	195	10-12-82	.167	.125	.188	9	24	1	4	1	0	0	5	0	0	0	1	8	0	0	.208	.160
Murton, Matt	R-R	6-1	220	10-3-81	.250	.167	.318	19	40	2	10	2	0	0	6	1	1	0	0	5	0	0	.300	.286
Patterson, Eric	L-R	5-11	170	4-8-83	.237	.500	.222	13	38	5	9	1	0	1	7	5	0	0	1	12	2	1	.342	.318
Pie, Felix	L-L	6-2	170	2-8-85	.241	.091	.264	43	83	9	20	2	1	1	10	7	2	0	1	29	3	0	.325	.312
Ramirez, Aramis	R-R	6-1	215	6-25-78	.289	.239	.305	149	554	97	160	44	1	27	111	74	11	0	6	94	2	2	.518	.380
Soriano, Alfonso	R-R	6-1	180	1-7-76	.280	.351	.252	109	453	76	127	27	0	29	75	43	3	0	4	103	19	3	.532	.344
Soto, Geovany	R-R	6-1	225	1-20-83	.285	.312	.276	141	494	66	141	35	2	23	86	62	2	0	5	121	0	1	.504	.364
Theriot, Ryan	R-R	5-11	175	12-7-79	.307	.305	.308	149	580	85	178	19	4	1	38	73	3	4	1	58	22	13	.359	.387
Ward, Daryle	L-L	6-2	240	6-27-75	.216	.200	.217	89	102	8	22	2	0	4	17	16	0	0	1	24	0	0	.402	.319

Pitching	B-T	HT	WT	DOB	W	L	ERA	G	GS	CG	SV	IP	H	R	ER	HR	BB	SO	AVG	vLH	vRH	K/9	BB/9
Ascanio, Jose	R-R	6-0	170	5-2-85	0	0	7.94	6	0	0	0	6	8	5	5	1	4	3	.348	.300	.385	4.76	6.35
Cotts, Neal	L-L	6-1	200	3-25-80	0	2	4.29	50	0	0	0	36	38	18	17	7	13	43	.266	.269	.263	10.85	3.28
Dempster, Ryan	R-R	6-2	215	5-3-77	17	6	2.96	33	33	1	0	207	174	75	68	14	76	187	.227	.243	.213	8.14	3.31
Eyre, Scott	L-L	6-1	220	5-30-72	2	0	7.15	19	0	0	0	11	15	9	9	1	4	14	.326	.259	.421	11.12	3.18
2-team total (19 Philadelphia)					5	0	4.21	38	0	0	0	26	23	12	12	2	7	32	—	—	—	11.22	2.45
Gallagher, Sean	R-R	6-2	235	12-30-85	3	4	4.45	12	10	0	0	59	58	31	29	6	22	49	.256	.248	.264	7.52	3.38
Gaudin, Chad	R-R	5-10	190	3-24-83	4	2	6.26	24	0	0	0	27	29	21	19	5	10	27	.271	.300	.254	8.89	3.29
Guzman, Angel	R-R	6-3	200	12-14-81	0	0	5.59	6	1	0	0	10	10	6	6	1	4	10	.256	.263	.250	9.31	3.72
Harden, Rich	L-R	6-1	195	11-30-81	5	1	1.77	12	12	0	0	71	39	17	14	6	30	89	.157	.167	.148	11.28	3.80
Hart, Kevin	R-R	6-4	220	12-29-82	2	2	6.51	21	0	0	0	28	39	24	20	2	18	23	.325	.367	.296	7.48	5.86
Hill, Rich	L-L	6-5	205	3-11-80	1	0	4.12	5	5	0	0	20	13	9	9	2	18	15	.191	.154	.200	6.86	8.24
Howry, Bob	R-R	6-5	220	8-4-73	7	5	5.35	72	0	0	1	71	90	44	42	13	13	59	.309	.328	.297	7.51	1.66
Lieber, Jon	R-R	6-2	240	4-2-70	2	3	4.05	26	1	0	0	47	59	24	21	10	6	27	.306	.368	.272	5.21	1.16
Lilly, Ted	L-L	6-1	190	1-4-76	17	9	4.09	34	34	0	0	205	187	96	93	32	64	184	.239	.307	.219	8.09	2.81
Marmol, Carlos	R-R	6-2	180	10-14-82	2	4	2.68	82	0	0	7	87	40	30	26	10	41	114	.135	.182	.098	11.75	4.23
Marquis, Jason	L-R	6-1	210	8-21-78	11	9	4.53	29	28	0	0	167	172	87	84	15	70	91	.267	.244	.287	4.90	3.77
Marshall, Sean	L-L	6-7	215	8-30-82	3	5	3.86	34	7	0	1	65	60	28	28	9	23	58	.245	.269	.236	7.99	3.17
Pignatiello, Carmen	R-L	6-0	205	9-12-82	0	0	13.50	2	0	0	0	1	2	1	1	0	2	0	.500	.000	.500	0.00	27.00
Samardzija, Jeff	R-R	6-5	220	1-23-85	1	0	2.28	26	0	0	1	28	24	12	7	0	15	25	.226	.167	.276	8.13	4.88
Wells, Randy	R-R	6-5	235	8-28-82	0	0	0.00	3	0	0	0	4	0	0	0	0	2	1	.000	.000	.000	2.08	4.15
Wood, Kerry	R-R	6-5	210	6-16-77	5	4	3.26	65	0	0	34	66	54	24	24	3	18	84	.219	.209	.227	11.40	2.44
Wuertz, Michael	R-R	6-3	205	12-15-78	1	1	3.63	45	0	0	0	45	44	23	18	4	20	30	.267	.230	.288	6.04	4.03
Zambrano, Carlos	B-R	6-5	255	6-1-81	14	6	3.91	30	30	1	0	189	172	85	82	18	72	130	.241	.235	.247	6.20	3.43

Fielding

Catcher	PCT	G	PO	A	E	DP	PB
Blanco	.992	45	235	15	2	2	3
Hill	.976	9	40	1	1	0	0
Soto	.995	136	1011	55	5	9	5

First Base	PCT	G	PO	A	E	DP
Blanco	1.000	1	3	0	0	0
DeRosa	1.000	1	2	0	0	0

Hoffpauir	.974	6	37	1	1	3
Lee	.993	153	1193	110	9	98
Ward	1.000	13	54	4	0	4

Second Base	PCT	G	PO	A	E	DP
Cedeno	.985	43	60	75	2	19
DeRosa	.976	95	143	185	8	32
Fontenot	.996	82	101	143	1	27

Patterson	1.000	2	3	0	0	0
Soriano	1.000	1	0	2	0	0

Third Base	PCT	G	PO	A	E	DP
Cedeno	1.000	7	1	1	0	0
DeRosa	.944	22	6	28	2	2
McGehee	1.000	6	3	13	0	3
Ramirez	.945	147	83	225	18	17

Shortstop	PCT	G	PO	A	E	DP
Cedeno	.968	27	41	50	3	10
DeRosa	1.000	1	0	1	0	0
Fontenot	—	1	0	0	0	0
Theriot	.975	149	207	341	14	69

Outfield	PCT	G	PO	A	E	DP
Cedeno	—	2	0	0	0	0
DeRosa	.991	59	111	0	1	0
Edmonds	.973	77	179	0	5	0
Fukudome	.981	143	255	6	5	0
Hoffpauir	.923	12	12	0	1	0

Johnson	.995	99	183	3	1	1
Murton	1.000	12	14	0	0	0
Patterson	.824	9	13	1	3	0
Pie	1.000	40	61	1	0	0
Soriano	.975	108	186	10	5	5
Ward	1.000	9	11	0	0	0

IOWA CUBS — TRIPLE-A

PACIFIC COAST LEAGUE

Batting	B-T	HT	WT	DOB	AVG	vLH	vRH	G	AB	R	H	2B	3B	HR	RBI	BB	HBP	SH	SF	SO	SB	CS	SLG	OBP
Blanco, Andres	B-R	5-10	190	4-11-84	.285	.260	.293	102	298	30	85	8	2	1	36	15	5	9	3	31	9	3	.336	.327
Broussard, Ben	L-L	6-2	230	9-24-76	.267	.250	.275	16	60	14	16	2	0	3	13	7	0	0	2	16	0	0	.450	.333
Castillo, Welington	R-R	6-0	200	4-24-87	.200	.200	—	1	5	0	1	0	0	0	1	0	0	0	0	1	0	0	.200	.200
Closser, J.D.	B-R	5-10	200	1-15-80	.333	.500	.300	5	12	1	4	1	0	0	0	0	0	0	0	4	0	0	.417	.333
2-team total (17 Portland)					.172	—	—	22	58	4	10	2	0	1	5	7	0	2	0	17	0	0	.259	.262
Coles, Corey	L-L	6-2	180	1-30-82	.360	.000	.375	11	25	5	9	1	0	0	2	3	1	0	0	1	1	0	.400	.448
Craig, Matt	B-R	6-2	200	4-16-81	.276	.353	.226	36	87	13	24	6	0	5	12	7	1	0	0	16	1	0	.517	.337
Dubois, Jason	R-R	6-4	230	3-26-79	.307	.247	.342	76	238	62	73	10	0	25	56	29	8	0	1	67	1	1	.664	.399
Figueroa, Luis	B-R	5-9	165	2-16-74	.300	.301	.300	112	370	59	111	18	1	2	46	33	1	10	5	30	1	2	.370	.355
Fox, Jake	R-R	6-0	210	7-20-82	.222	.333	.184	29	117	17	26	10	1	6	26	2	1	0	0	31	3	0	.479	.242
Fuld, Sam	L-L	5-10	185	11-20-81	.222	.389	.156	20	63	11	14	3	0	1	4	8	0	5	0	12	3	2	.317	.310
Garcia, Jesse	R-R	5-10	170	9-24-73	.273	.167	.400	5	11	0	3	0	0	0	1	0	0	0	0	3	0	0	.273	.333
Hill, Koyie	B-R	6-0	190	3-9-79	.275	.316	.264	113	364	56	100	24	2	17	64	40	3	3	2	77	3	2	.492	.350
Hoffpauir, Micah	L-L	6-3	215	3-1-80	.362	.307	.381	71	290	63	105	34	2	25	100	17	1	0	5	46	2	0	.752	.393
Kroeger, Josh	L-L	6-3	230	8-31-82	.307	.273	.316	123	430	73	132	38	3	15	69	43	4	0	3	82	12	3	.514	.373
McGehee, Casey	R-R	6-1	195	10-12-82	.296	.287	.299	133	497	68	147	30	0	12	92	40	3	0	10	89	0	3	.429	.345
2-team total (32 Sacramento)					.290	—	—	86	321	45	93	23	3	2	28	42	4	1	2	40	7	3	.399	.377
Murton, Matt	R-R	6-1	220	10-3-81	.298	.352	.277	54	191	26	57	11	1	1	15	29	3	1	1	20	4	2	.382	.397
Patterson, Eric	L-R	5-11	170	4-8-83	.320	.304	.325	52	203	33	65	16	3	6	28	12	1	2	2	45	11	0	.517	.358
2-team total (25 Sacramento)					.324	—	—	77	312	51	101	24	5	10	47	21	2	5	4	73	19	2	.529	.366
Pie, Felix	L-L	6-2	170	2-8-85	.287	.245	.303	85	335	57	96	20	5	10	55	23	3	5	2	54	11	7	.466	.336
Richie, Tony	R-R	6-1	215	2-9-82	.267	.281	.259	61	172	15	46	13	0	3	23	6	2	1	3	28	1	0	.395	.295
Samson, Nate	R-R	6-0	170	8-19-87	.222	.250	.200	2	9	0	2	0	0	0	0	0	0	0	0	2	0	0	.222	.222
Scales, Bobby	B-R	6-0	185	10-4-77	.320	.315	.323	121	387	94	124	20	2	15	59	59	5	4	2	90	7	5	.499	.415
Simokaitis, Joe	L-L	6-1	200	12-27-82	.667	.000	1.000	2	3	1	2	0	0	0	0	0	0	0	0	1	0	0	.667	.667
Soriano, Alfonso	R-R	6-1	180	1-7-76	.333	.333	—	1	3	0	1	0	0	0	0	0	0	0	0	0	0	0	.333	.333
Spears, Nate	L-R	5-11	165	5-3-85	.278	.000	.417	5	18	5	5	1	0	0	1	3	0	0	0	1	0	0	.333	.381
Torres, Andres	B-R	5-10	190	1-26-78	.306	.316	.301	118	409	91	125	27	10	11	51	55	4	8	3	103	29	4	.501	.391
Ward, Daryle	L-L	6-2	240	6-27-75	.500	.333	.571	3	10	3	5	0	0	0	1	0	0	0	0	1	0	0	.500	.545

Pitching	B-T	HT	WT	DOB	W	L	ERA	G	GS	CG	SV	IP	H	R	ER	HR	BB	SO	AVG	vLH	vRH	K/9	BB/9
Ascanio, Jose	R-R	6-0	170	5-2-85	2	1	5.10	40	0	0	11	55	54	35	31	10	23	58	.254	.259	.250	9.55	3.79
Atkins, Mitch	R-R	6-3	220	10-1-85	8	1	4.47	10	10	0	0	54	48	29	27	11	23	44	.236	.264	.216	7.29	3.81
Berg, Justin	R-R	6-3	230	6-7-84	4	6	5.68	27	16	0	0	90	91	64	57	11	48	49	.269	.284	.256	4.88	4.78
Brower, Jim	R-R	6-3	215	12-29-72	2	1	4.26	17	0	0	5	19	25	11	9	2	11	11	.329	.269	.360	5.21	5.21
2-team total (2 Round Rock)					2	1	3.68	19	0	0	6	22	29	14	9	2	11	16	—	—		6.55	4.50
Burns, Mike	R-R	6-1	210	7-14-78	8	12	4.67	37	14	0	2	133	150	77	69	18	24	101	.288	.303	.277	6.83	1.62
Carrasco, Hector	R-R	6-2	235	10-22-69	5	6	3.86	42	1	0	1	68	62	31	29	9	25	60	.257	.293	.235	7.98	3.33
Cavazos, Andy	R-R	6-3	230	1-5-81	2	1	5.88	26	0	0	1	34	29	23	22	4	23	28	.236	.130	.299	7.49	6.15
Cotts, Neal	L-L	6-1	200	3-25-80	2	0	2.00	19	0	0	3	27	23	7	6	0	10	33	.232	.206	.246	11.00	3.33
Estrada, Jesse	R-R	6-8	260	10-27-83	3	0	5.36	22	0	0	0	47	54	30	28	5	13	46	.287	.348	.232	8.81	2.49
Eyre, Scott	L-L	6-1	220	5-30-72	0	0	9.00	1	0	0	0	1	2	1	1	0	0	2	.400	.000	.667	18.00	0.00
Gallagher, Sean	R-R	6-2	235	12-30-85	2	2	3.10	5	5	0	0	29	21	11	10	2	9	30	.196	.162	.214	9.31	2.79
Garcia, Dumas	R-R	6-2	165	7-7-83	0	0	9.00	3	0	0	0	4	5	4	4	1	3	6	.294	.143	.400	13.50	6.75
Guzman, Angel	R-R	6-3	200	12-14-81	1	0	1.00	4	1	0	0	9	7	1	1	0	3	12	.233	.000	.333	12.00	3.00
Hart, Kevin	R-R	6-4	220	12-29-82	4	2	2.81	26	10	0	5	58	38	19	18	3	20	63	.187	.204	.173	9.83	3.12
Henderson, Jim	L-R	6-5	190	10-21-82	0	0	15.00	1	0	0	0	3	2	5	5	1	5	4	.182	.200	.167	12.00	15.00
Hill, Rich	L-L	6-5	205	3-11-80	2	4	5.88	7	7	0	0	26	22	19	17	4	28	32	.234	.263	.227	11.08	9.69
Holliman, Mark	R-R	6-0	195	9-19-83	1	1	5.16	5	5	0	0	23	25	14	13	1	12	14	.281	.250	.306	5.56	4.76
Jones, Geoffrey	L-L	6-5	245	8-10-79	2	1	8.44	10	0	0	1	16	20	17	15	2	9	14	.308	.231	.337	7.88	5.06
Keisler, Randy	L-L	6-3	200	2-24-76	4	6	3.14	12	11	0	0	66	65	25	23	4	26	65	.258	.143	.281	8.86	3.55
Marshall, Sean	L-L	6-7	220	8-30-82	1	1	3.41	7	7	0	0	32	26	13	12	2	6	25	.220	.292	.202	7.11	1.71
Mateo, Juan	R-R	6-2	220	12-17-82	1	0	11.81	4	0	0	0	5	11	9	7	1	2	4	.393	.417	.375	6.75	3.38
Mathes, J.R.	L-L	6-3	205	11-9-81	9	5	4.29	27	22	1	0	141	156	75	67	16	32	73	.281	.232	.295	4.67	2.05
Parker, Blake	R-R	6-3	225	6-19-85	0	0	6.00	2	0	0	0	3	1	2	2	1	2	3	.091	.000	.250	9.00	6.00
Pignatiello, Carmen	R-L	6-0	205	9-12-82	0	1	7.94	45	0	0	0	40	52	35	35	6	19	35	.315	.182	.404	7.94	4.31
Reinhard, Greg	R-R	6-2	215	8-11-83	2	0	3.24	8	1	0	0	17	12	10	6	1	12	20	.207	.200	.214	10.80	6.48
Samardzija, Jeff	R-R	6-5	220	1-23-85	4	1	3.13	6	6	1	0	37	32	13	13	5	16	40	.241	.212	.259	9.64	3.86
Shaver, Chris	L-L	6-7	250	8-21-81	0	0	9.00	3	0	0	0	4	9	4	4	0	3	3	.429	.667	.389	6.75	6.75
Stanford, Jason	L-L	6-1	210	1-23-77	3	1	5.06	7	7	0	0	37	42	23	21	4	16	29	.282	.194	.305	6.99	3.86
Walrond, Les	L-L	6-3	205	11-7-76	1	1	6.55	7	0	0	0	11	20	11	8	1	5	14	.377	.556	.341	11.45	4.09
Wells, Randy	R-R	6-5	235	8-28-82	10	4	4.02	27	19	0	0	119	127	64	53	15	34	102	.268	.283	.257	7.74	2.58
Wuertz, Michael	R-R	6-3	205	12-15-78	0	1	3.60	17	0	0	4	20	13	8	8	2	14	29	.186	.250	.143	13.05	6.30

Fielding

Catcher	PCT	G	PO	A	E	DP	PB
Castillo	1.000	1	7	0	0	0	0
Closser	1.000	3	26	3	0	1	0
Hill	.991	94	644	51	6	9	3
McGehee	.982	17	98	9	2	2	1
Richie	.997	38	307	16	1	3	2

First Base	PCT	G	PO	A	E	DP
Broussard	1.000	2	12	2	0	3
Closser	1.000	2	1	1	0	0
Craig	.990	17	96	0	1	11
Dubois	.991	29	203	9	2	20
Fox	.987	26	206	16	3	11
Garcia	1.000	1	2	0	0	0
Hill	.929	3	26	0	2	1
Hoffpauir	.996	61	483	21	2	50
Kroeger	.917	2	11	0	1	1
McGehee	1.000	8	37	0	0	5
Richie	1.000	1	6	2	0	2
Scales	1.000	12	106	6	0	8

	PCT	G	PO	A	E	DP
Ward	.957	3	22	0	1	4

Second Base	PCT	G	PO	A	E	DP
Blanco	1.000	2	0	4	0	1
Figueroa	.969	34	52	74	4	20
Garcia	—	1	0	0	0	0
McGehee	1.000	2	0	3	0	1
Patterson	.977	47	83	132	5	25
Scales	.968	70	145	162	10	47
Spears	1.000	5	13	14	0	6

Third Base	PCT	G	PO	A	E	DP
Blanco	.875	1	2	5	1	0
Craig	.941	9	3	13	1	0
Figueroa	.972	23	10	25	1	4
Fox	—	1	0	0	0	0
Garcia	1.000	1	2	4	0	0
McGehee	.962	115	78	222	12	25
Scales	.879	15	9	20	4	3

Shortstop	PCT	G	PO	A	E	DP
Blanco	.942	94	115	240	22	48
Figueroa	.970	67	79	176	8	45
Samson	.800	1	3	1	1	0
Simokaitis	—	1	0	0	0	0

Outfield	PCT	G	PO	A	E	DP
Broussard	.857	13	12	0	2	0
Coles	1.000	8	9	1	0	0
Dubois	1.000	35	46	4	0	1
Fox	1.000	3	3	0	0	0
Fuld	1.000	18	30	2	0	1
Hoffpauir	1.000	16	21	0	0	0
Kroeger	.978	110	174	5	4	0
Murton	.972	49	65	4	2	1
Patterson	.833	4	5	0	1	0
Pie	.964	84	180	5	7	1
Scales	.923	10	10	2	1	1
Soriano	1.000	1	1	0	0	0
Torres	.990	104	190	12	2	4

TENNESSEE SMOKIES DOUBLE-A

SOUTHERN LEAGUE

Batting	B-T	HT	WT	DOB	AVG	vLH	vRH	G	AB	R	H	2B	3B	HR	RBI	BB	HBP	SH	SF	SO	SB	CS	SLG	OBP
Broussard, Ben	L-L	6-2	230	9-24-76	.222	.000	.333	2	9	3	2	0	0	1	2	0	1	0	0	1	0	0	.556	.300
Camp, Matt	L-R	6-0	175	5-29-84	.261	.260	.262	133	482	70	126	11	4	2	37	49	5	10	0	55	23	8	.313	.336
Castillo, Welington	R-R	6-0	200	4-24-87	.298	.453	.224	57	198	25	59	11	0	4	24	14	6	2	0	50	0	0	.414	.362
Chirinos, Robinson	R-R	6-1	185	4-5-84	.243	.268	.226	38	103	12	25	7	3	0	8	10	0	2	2	18	0	0	.369	.304
Clevenger, Steve	L-R	6-0	185	4-5-86	.247	.269	.238	29	89	5	22	5	1	1	15	10	0	2	3	10	0	0	.360	.314
Coles, Corey	L-L	6-2	180	1-30-82	.154	.143	.158	10	26	2	4	0	0	0	3	5	0	1	0	9	0	0	.154	.290
Colvin, Tyler	L-L	6-3	190	9-5-85	.256	.260	.253	137	540	68	138	27	11	14	80	44	4	5	9	101	7	4	.424	.312
Craig, Matt	B-R	6-2	190	4-16-81	.333	.302	.348	42	135	30	45	9	0	5	23	39	3	0	0	27	1	0	.511	.492
Deeds, Doug	L-L	6-2	190	6-2-81	.325	.319	.327	122	416	73	135	37	3	12	58	43	3	3	3	100	8	1	.514	.389
Fox, Jake	R-R	6-0	210	7-20-82	.307	.282	.319	105	388	76	119	29	1	25	79	46	17	0	8	73	4	2	.580	.397
Fuld, Sam	L-L	5-10	185	11-20-81	.271	.311	.254	85	339	48	92	16	3	5	48	50	3	1	4	40	7	8	.381	.366
Harvey, Ryan	R-R	6-5	240	8-30-84	.216	.261	.185	36	111	8	24	7	0	3	15	7	3	1	2	39	1	1	.360	.276
Lalli, Blake	L-R	6-1	210	5-12-83	.286	.150	.340	22	70	9	20	5	0	3	14	4	0	0	0	18	0	0	.486	.324
Lansford, Josh	R-R	6-2	200	7-31-84	.236	.306	.192	48	161	14	38	15	0	1	16	6	1	4	0	23	0	1	.348	.268
Made, Jose	R-R	5-8	175	10-23-85	.077	.167	.000	10	13	0	1	0	0	0	0	0	0	0	0	8	0	0	.077	.077
Matulia, Matt	B-R	6-0	185	5-24-84	.224	.241	.215	93	250	41	56	7	1	2	33	42	5	4	3	57	4	3	.284	.343
Muyco, Jake	R-R	6-0	190	9-16-84	.190	.125	.231	8	21	1	4	0	0	0	3	0	0	0	0	9	0	0	.190	.292
Reed, Mark	L-R	5-11	175	4-13-86	.317	.333	.313	18	63	9	20	3	1	1	11	4	0	1	0	15	0	0	.444	.358
Reynolds, Kyle	L-R	6-2	190	9-1-83	.244	.269	.235	111	357	39	87	21	1	11	48	29	1	2	6	93	2	3	.401	.298
Robinson, Chris	R-R	6-0	200	5-12-84	.214	.222	.210	49	159	13	34	5	0	1	19	12	4	1	1	39	0	1	.264	.284
Salas, Issmael	R-R	5-9	200	7-25-82	.227	.226	.229	23	66	8	15	4	0	0	3	6	0	3	0	5	3	0	.288	.292
Simokaitis, Joe	R-R	6-1	200	12-27-82	.183	.207	.167	60	142	22	26	6	0	2	15	27	3	6	1	39	0	1	.268	.324
Spears, Nate	L-R	5-11	165	5-3-85	.299	.344	.285	115	384	71	115	22	5	7	51	58	6	19	6	72	6	5	.438	.394

Pitching	B-T	HT	WT	DOB	W	L	ERA	G	GS	CG	SV	IP	H	R	ER	HR	BB	SO	AVG	vLH	vRH	K/9	BB/9
Atkins, Mitch	R-R	6-3	220	10-1-85	9	6	3.76	18	18	0	0	110	107	58	46	14	27	88	.250	.263	.241	7.20	2.21
Avery, Matt	R-R	6-0	230	9-7-83	4	2	4.45	32	1	0	1	67	66	40	33	10	35	52	.251	.288	.226	7.02	4.72
Berg, Justin	R-R	6-3	230	6-7-84	0	3	3.49	5	5	0	0	28	29	14	11	1	11	10	.264	.261	.266	3.18	3.49
Campusano, Edward	L-L	6-4	175	7-14-82	3	3	6.34	34	0	0	1	50	50	37	35	10	29	44	.267	.250	.273	7.97	5.26
Caridad, Esmailin	R-R	5-10	195	10-28-83	7	3	3.16	14	14	0	0	83	67	31	29	15	21	50	.218	.230	.210	5.44	2.29
Carrillo, Marco	R-R	5-11	200	2-1-87	2	2	7.03	5	4	0	0	24	32	24	19	4	10	22	.314	.298	.327	8.14	3.70
Ceda, Jose	R-R	6-4	275	1-28-87	2	1	2.08	22	0	0	9	30	26	8	7	2	14	42	.234	.410	.139	12.46	4.15
Cooper, Michael	R-R	6-6	230	1-29-84	1	3	5.91	22	0	0	7	21	24	15	14	1	15	9	.279	.382	.212	3.80	6.33
Cova, Rafael	R-R	6-2	170	3-5-82	0	0	0.00	1	0	0	0	1	1	2	0	1	0	0	.200	.000	.333	0.00	0.00
Downs, Darin	R-L	6-3	190	12-26-84	0	2	6.56	22	0	0	0	23	32	19	17	1	16	17	.323	.271	.373	6.56	6.17
Estrada, Jesse	R-R	6-8	260	10-27-83	4	3	4.71	17	0	0	1	29	31	17	15	5	10	16	.274	.211	.307	5.02	3.14
Eyre, Scott	L-L	6-1	225	5-30-72	0	0	0.00	3	0	0	0	3	1	0	0	0	1	3	.100	.000	.125	9.00	3.00
Garcia, Dumas	R-R	6-2	165	7-7-83	2	2	2.89	30	0	0	2	44	32	16	14	3	23	36	.205	.194	.213	7.42	4.74
Guzman, Angel	R-R	6-3	200	12-14-81	0	0	0.00	1	1	0	0	3	3	0	0	0	0	2	.273	.500	.000	6.00	0.00
Hart, Kevin	R-R	6-4	220	12-29-82	0	0	3.00	1	1	0	0	3	2	1	1	0	2	3	.200	.143	.333	9.00	6.00
Henderson, Jim	L-R	6-5	190	10-21-82	0	1	0.00	5	0	0	1	6	5	1	0	0	1	4	.217	.571	.063	5.68	1.42
Holliman, Mark	R-R	6-0	195	9-19-83	3	4	4.50	26	13	0	0	86	96	50	43	14	54	78	.294	.331	.267	8.16	5.65
Johnson, Grant	R-R	6-6	220	5-26-83	2	5	5.55	21	9	0	0	60	68	41	37	6	26	32	.300	.258	.331	4.80	3.90
Lambert, Casey	L-L	5-11	175	12-11-85	1	2	2.70	24	0	0	1	27	29	10	8	0	11	21	.287	.441	.209	7.09	3.71
Maestri, Alessandro	R-R	6-1	180	6-1-85	0	1	6.55	2	2	0	0	11	14	8	8	2	3	10	.318	.300	.323	8.18	2.45
Mateo, Juan	R-R	6-2	220	12-17-82	0	0	24.00	2	0	0	0	3	9	8	8	2	3	3	.500	.444	.556	9.00	9.00
Reinhard, Greg	L-R	6-2	215	8-11-83	3	4	4.17	37	0	0	4	69	62	33	32	7	29	68	.240	.234	.244	8.87	3.78
Roquet, Rocky	R-R	6-2	215	11-6-82	4	2	3.70	39	0	0	3	49	40	23	20	3	20	54	.231	.201	.207	9.99	4.99
Russell, James	L-L	6-4	205	1-8-86	4	8	6.36	18	17	0	0	86	111	64	61	18	25	62	.315	.313	.316	6.46	2.61
Samardzija, Jeff	R-R	6-5	220	1-23-85	3	5	4.86	16	15	0	0	76	71	43	41	6	42	44	.252	.237	.262	5.21	4.97
Shaver, Chris	L-L	6-7	250	8-21-81	2	1	3.42	17	0	0	0	24	24	10	9	1	5	31	.269	.269	.283	4.18	1.90
Veal, Donnie	L-L	6-4	215	9-18-84	5	10	4.52	29	29	0	0	145	150	89	73	19	81	123	.276	.216	.292	7.62	5.02
Watson, Tanner	R-R	6-3	210	6-14-82	1	3	5.65	17	10	0	0	57	77	40	36	6	23	34	.325	.326	.324	5.34	3.61

Fielding

Catcher	PCT	G	PO	A	E	DP	PB
Castillo	.995	49	333	29	2	2	13
Clevenger	.983	18	104	10	2	0	1
Lalli	.984	9	56	4	1	1	1
Matulia	1.000	1	1	0	0	0	0
Muyco	.964	8	50	4	2	1	1
Reed	.969	16	119	8	4	0	0
Robinson	.988	47	284	50	4	4	3

First Base	PCT	G	PO	A	E	DP
Clevenger	.980	7	46	4	1	8
Craig	.990	33	288	16	3	37
Deeds	.982	20	148	19	3	18
Fox	.990	49	375	38	4	30
Lalli	1.000	8	66	4	0	3
Matulia	1.000	3	19	3	0	2
Reed	1.000	1	1	0	0	0
Reynolds	.995	27	180	11	1	21
Salas	1.000	5	40	2	0	5

Spears	1.000	1	2	0	0	0

Second Base	PCT	G	PO	A	E	DP
Chirinos	1.000	4	11	9	0	4
Made	1.000	2	3	1	0	1
Matulia	.969	28	49	44	3	13
Reed	—	1	0	0	0	0
Salas	.969	8	14	17	1	3
Simokaitis	.941	5	3	13	1	2
Spears	.979	110	238	287	11	66

Third Base	PCT	G	PO	A	E	DP
Chirinos	.911	21	15	26	4	2
Fox	1.000	2	1	3	0	0
Lansford	.930	45	32	88	9	9
Matulia	.951	21	14	25	2	2
Reynolds	.886	66	26	106	17	8
Salas	1.000	5	2	2	0	0
Simokaitis	1.000	3	0	1	0	0

Shortstop	PCT	G	PO	A	E	DP
Camp	.966	85	122	195	11	38
Chirinos	1.000	10	12	23	0	9
Made	.875	4	1	6	1	1
Matulia	.962	33	46	80	5	20
Simokaitis	.939	32	47	107	10	23
Spears	1.000	1	0	1	0	1

Outfield	PCT	G	PO	A	E	DP
Broussard	1.000	2	4	0	0	0
Camp	.970	49	91	6	3	2
Coles	.957	10	22	0	1	0
Colvin	.993	132	274	7	2	1
Deeds	.983	93	168	5	3	1
Fox	.983	35	55	2	1	0
Fuld	.979	83	182	8	4	3
Harvey	1.000	25	49	0	0	0
Salas	1.000	5	4	0	0	0
Simokaitis	1.000	5	6	2	0	0

DAYTONA CUBS

HIGH CLASS A

FLORIDA STATE LEAGUE

Batting	B-T	HT	WT	DOB	AVG	vLH	vRH	G	AB	R	H	2B	3B	HR	RBI	BB	HBP	SH	SF	SO	SB	CS	SLG	OBP
Adduci, James	L-L	6-2	185	5-15-85	.290	.277	.296	123	458	81	133	19	3	3	48	63	5	10	3	96	26	8	.365	.380
Barney, Darwin	R-R	5-10	175	11-8-85	.262	.286	.252	123	409	46	107	22	4	3	51	38	3	4	5	58	8	3	.357	.325
Canzler, Russ	R-R	6-2	215	4-11-86	.273	.342	.237	98	326	47	89	22	2	12	59	27	1	3	4	70	7	4	.463	.327
Carter, Yusuf	R-R	6-2	205	2-6-85	.233	.238	.231	83	279	55	65	18	1	13	40	27	2	2	3	69	16	4	.444	.302
Castillo, Welington	R-R	6-0	200	4-24-87	.273	.350	.235	33	121	15	33	8	0	0	12	4	1	0	1	23	1	0	.339	.299
Chirinos, Robinson	R-R	6-1	185	6-5-84	.283	.286	.282	37	120	22	34	4	2	5	18	26	6	3	1	21	3	1	.475	.431
Clevenger, Steve	L-R	6-0	185	4-5-86	.313	.295	.323	84	284	36	89	20	0	2	39	39	1	1	4	41	7	3	.405	.393
Harvey, Ryan	R-R	6-5	240	8-30-84	.228	.172	.250	59	202	25	46	9	0	10	31	22	4	1	2	75	1	3	.421	.313
Lalli, Blake	L-R	6-1	210	5-12-83	.343	.226	.370	78	283	30	97	29	0	7	49	19	3	1	3	34	0	0	.519	.386
Lansford, Josh	R-R	6-2	220	7-31-84	.249	.286	.236	61	217	22	54	10	0	1	17	12	3	7	0	35	1	4	.309	.297
Made, Jose	R-R	5-8	175	10-23-85	.056	.000	.083	9	18	3	1	0	0	0	0	1	0	1	0	4	0	0	.056	.105
Malone, Ryne	L-R	5-11	180	1-6-85	.000	.000	.000	1	4	0	0	0	0	0	0	0	0	0	0	3	0	0	.000	.000
Matulia, Matt	B-R	6-0	185	5-24-84	.317	.333	.314	14	41	7	13	1	0	1	7	4	2	2	1	7	4	1	.415	.396
Mercedes, Mario	R-R	5-10	160	11-22-86	.000	.000	.000	5	8	0	0	0	0	0	0	0	0	0	1	0	0	0	.000	.111
Mota, Jonathan	R-R	6-0	180	6-1-87	.260	.264	.258	91	323	46	84	17	2	4	34	26	4	9	3	59	6	6	.362	.320
Reed, Mark	L-R	5-11	175	4-13-86	.256	.185	.275	48	129	15	33	5	2	1	11	17	0	2	0	38	2	4	.349	.342
Rundle, Drew	L-L	6-4	180	11-5-87	.000	.000	—	3	5	0	0	0	0	0	0	0	0	0	0	2	0	0	.000	.000
Smith, Marquez	R-R	5-10	210	3-20-85	.237	.217	.254	38	131	16	31	10	1	3	17	12	3	0	0	29	0	0	.397	.315
Thomas Jr., Tony	R-R	5-10	180	7-10-86	.266	.206	.286	113	443	62	118	30	4	7	43	34	3	9	4	113	22	10	.400	.320
Wright, Ty	R-R	6-0	200	2-26-85	.300	.345	.283	113	426	60	128	21	1	8	72	41	7	4	2	71	7	2	.411	.370
Wyatt, Jonathan	R-R	5-10	180	9-6-84	.230	.172	.241	55	191	29	44	6	3	3	20	33	1	5	1	32	3	4	.340	.345

Pitching	B-T	HT	WT	DOB	W	L	ERA	G	GS	CG	SV	IP	H	R	ER	HR	BB	SO	AVG	vLH	vRH	K/9	BB/9
Avery, Matt	R-R	6-6	230	9-7-83	1	1	1.17	5	0	0	2	8	6	2	1	1	4	8	.222	.300	.176	9.39	4.70
Blackford, Todd	L-R	6-4	205	6-10-85	7	1	2.40	26	0	0	1	45	40	17	12	0	19	31	.241	.232	.247	6.20	3.80
Campusano, Edward	L-L	6-4	175	7-14-82	2	0	0.59	9	0	0	0	15	8	1	1	0	5	18	.151	.040	.250	10.57	2.93
Caridad, Esmailin	R-R	5-10	195	10-28-83	6	4	4.41	14	13	0	0	69	64	35	34	3	17	38	.252	.248	.255	4.93	2.21
Carrillo, Marco	R-R	5-11	200	2-1-87	7	6	2.88	23	17	0	0	116	82	42	37	9	33	71	.200	.218	.188	5.52	2.57
Cashner, Andrew	R-R	6-6	185	9-11-86	0	1	13.50	1	1	0	0	3	4	4	4	0	4	1	.364	.400	.333	3.38	13.50
Ceda, Jose	R-R	6-4	275	1-28-87	2	2	4.80	15	12	0	0	54	41	29	29	4	28	53	.212	.272	.170	8.78	4.64
Chen, Hung-Wen	R-R	5-11	195	2-3-86	2	1	3.65	12	10	0	0	57	49	25	23	9	13	42	.230	.277	.200	6.67	2.06
Coleman, Joe	L-R	6-1	180	7-3-87	1	0	0.00	1	1	0	0	5	4	1	0	0	2	2	.222	.333	.167	3.60	3.60
Cooper, Michael	R-R	6-6	230	1-29-84	2	0	4.18	20	0	0	2	28	32	13	13	2	12	16	.291	.320	.267	5.14	3.86
Downs, Darin	R-L	6-3	190	12-26-84	2	0	2.89	17	0	0	0	28	29	11	9	0	13	25	.261	.387	.213	8.04	4.18
2-team total (10 Vero Beach)					2	3	4.22	27	1	0	0	49	53	26	23	1	22	49	—	—		9.00	4.04
Estrada, Jesse	R-R	6-8	260	10-27-83	0	0	9.00	1	0	0	0	1	1	1	1	0	1	0	.250	.000	.500	9.00	9.00
Eyre, Scott	L-L	6-1	220	5-30-72	0	0	13.50	3	1	0	0	1	3	5	4	0	1	2	.417	.429	.400	6.75	3.38
Garcia, Dumas	R-R	6-2	165	7-7-83	3	0	2.33	19	0	0	5	27	13	7	7	0	10	22	.143	.077	.169	7.33	3.33
Guzman, Angel	R-R	6-3	200	12-14-81	0	0	3.60	2	2	0	0	5	4	4	2	0	1	6	.235	.333	.182	10.80	1.80
Harben, Adam	R-R	6-5	210	8-19-83	3	6	5.37	23	7	0	0	59	57	42	35	0	56	53	.268	.291	.252	8.13	8.59
Hill, Rich	L-L	6-5	205	3-11-80	1	2	8.03	3	3	0	0	12	12	11	11	0	11	14	.267	.400	.229	10.22	8.03
Jackson, Jay	R-R	6-1	195	10-27-87	2	0	1.59	4	3	0	0	17	11	4	3	0	7	21	.183	.231	.147	11.12	3.71
Johnson, Grant	R-R	6-6	220	5-26-83	0	2	4.74	7	5	0	0	19	22	11	10	3	5	13	.297	.207	.356	6.16	2.37
Lambert, Casey	L-L	5-11	175	12-11-85	1	3	2.88	31	0	0	11	44	39	15	13	3	11	39	.257	.246	.263	8.43	2.43
Latham, Jordan	R-R	6-1	180	9-25-86	1	0	2.16	11	0	0	0	17	15	4	4	1	8	12	.234	.370	.135	6.48	4.32
Maestri, Alessandro	R-R	5-11	180	6-1-85	5	3	3.69	15	14	0	0	78	72	39	32	5	27	66	.248	.248	.248	7.62	3.12
Mateo, Marcos	R-R	6-1	160	4-18-84	4	3	3.57	25	16	0	0	88	87	42	35	6	29	65	.257	.320	.208	6.62	2.95
Meyers, Ryan	L-R	6-5	195	7-17-85	0	2	6.30	6	0	0	0	10	11	8	7	1	6	6	.289	.273	.296	5.40	5.40
Muldowney, Billy	R-R	6-1	215	8-9-84	3	2	2.98	11	11	0	0	54	47	19	18	7	13	39	.235	.260	.220	6.46	2.15
Papelbon, Jeremy	R-L	6-1	205	6-24-83	2	1	2.57	38	4	0	2	74	64	24	21	2	25	51	.237	.250	.230	6.23	3.05
Parker, Blake	R-R	6-3	225	6-19-85	1	2	3.38	20	0	0	9	21	17	8	8	0	10	21	.221	.179	.245	8.86	4.22
Petrick, Billy	R-R	6-6	240	4-29-84	1	2	4.09	8	0	0	0	11	11	7	5	2	3	7	.256	.429	.172	5.73	2.45
Phelps, Michael	R-R	6-4	190	5-26-84	2	1	5.56	28	0	0	1	34	26	23	21	5	27	29	.218	.308	.175	7.68	7.15

	B-T	HT	WT	DOB	W	L	ERA	G	GS	CG	SV	IP	H	R	ER	HR	BB	SO	AVG	vLH	vRH	K/9	BB/9
Roquet, Rocky	R-R	6-2	215	11-6-82	0	0	1.74	7	0	0	0	10	7	2	2	0	3	9	.189	.143	.217	7.84	2.61
Ruhlman, Jayson	L-L	6-1	180	8-17-84	8	6	2.84	45	0	0	0	67	60	23	21	4	34	58	.245	.250	.242	7.83	4.59
Russell, James	L-L	6-4	205	1-8-86	2	2	3.51	8	8	0	0	41	36	18	16	4	13	24	.243	.310	.217	5.27	2.85
Sasser, Dustin	L-L	6-0	200	9-13-85	1	3	4.50	20	1	0	0	30	30	18	15	3	21	18	.261	.216	.282	5.40	6.30
Schlitter, Brian	R-R	6-5	240	12-21-85	0	1	2.16	7	0	0	3	8	9	2	2	0	3	9	.281	.200	.318	9.72	3.24
2-team total (34 Clearwater)					4	4	2.21	41	0	0	9	57	48	15	14	1	24	67	—	—	—	10.58	3.79

Fielding

Catcher	PCT	G	PO	A	E	DP	PB
Castillo	.968	30	158	24	6	3	8
Chirinos	.992	18	117	13	1	1	2
Clevenger	.993	43	251	25	2	2	3
Lalli	.987	10	66	12	1	1	0
Mercedes	1.000	5	19	2	0	0	
Perez	1.000	3	3	0	0	0	
Reed	.994	41	275	33	2	6	4

First Base	PCT	G	PO	A	E	DP
Canzler	.995	75	620	30	3	65
Clevenger	.996	32	241	13	1	21
Lalli	.982	37	313	18	6	32
Reed	1.000	4	4	0	0	0

Second Base	PCT	G	PO	A	E	DP
Chirinos	.982	11	18	37	1	5

Made	1.000	4	5	9	0	3
Matulia	1.000	5	6	6	0	1
Mota	.985	13	25	39	1	12
Thomas Jr.	.989	105	228	320	6	73

Third Base	PCT	G	PO	A	E	DP
Chirinos	.857	5	2	10	2	1
Lansford	.921	60	41	122	14	14
Made	.727	3	1	7	3	0
Matulia	1.000	3	1	3	0	0
Mota	.946	45	34	106	8	11
Smith	.938	21	19	42	4	3

Shortstop	PCT	G	PO	A	E	DP
Barney	.963	121	193	351	21	72
Chirinos	.900	3	4	5	1	3
Matulia	1.000	1	3	5	0	2

Mota	.929	13	23	29	4	7

Outfield	PCT	G	PO	A	E	DP
Adduci	.977	116	242	10	6	2
Canzler	.950	14	19	0	1	0
Carter	.957	67	130	2	6	1
Harvey	.978	54	83	8	2	4
Matulia	1.000	4	1	0	0	0
Mota	1.000	9	15	0	0	0
Reed	.667	1	2	0	1	0
Ruhlman	1.000	1	1	0	0	0
Rundle	1.000	3	2	0	0	0
Wright	.987	90	142	13	2	3
Wyatt	.985	53	127	4	2	2

PEORIA CHIEFS   LOW CLASS A

MIDWEST LEAGUE

Batting	B-T	HT	WT	DOB	AVG	vLH	vRH	G	AB	R	H	2B	3B	HR	RBI	BB	HBP	SH	SF	SO	SB	CS	SLG	OBP
Andersen, Cliff	L-L	6-2	185	7-24-87	.221	.182	.234	106	366	30	81	13	3	3	21	33	12	5	1	118	10	5	.298	.306
Bautista, Luis	R-R	6-4	240	9-19-84	.313	.292	.321	89	326	40	102	25	1	13	50	21	5	4	3	64	5	2	.515	.361
Burke, Kyler	L-L	6-3	205	4-20-88	.206	.158	.226	35	131	12	27	5	1	2	8	11	2	0	0	34	3	0	.305	.278
Donaldson, Josh	R-R	6-1	215	12-8-85	.217	.286	.202	63	235	27	51	13	0	6	23	17	2	0	0	41	7	1	.349	.276
Flores, Luis	R-R	5-10	195	11-2-86	.189	.167	.200	33	106	6	20	1	1	1	13	12	4	2	2	19	1	3	.245	.290
Gonzalez, Marwin	B-R	6-1	186	3-14-89	.224	.323	.188	33	116	6	26	7	0	0	9	3	0	1	2	15	1	1	.284	.240
Guyer, Brandon	R-R	6-1	210	1-28-86	.269	.234	.283	88	327	55	88	27	3	14	38	19	13	1	3	63	22	7	.498	.331
Guzman, Gian	R-R	6-2	180	5-26-89	.202	.273	.179	33	89	11	18	3	1	2	5	6	1	3	1	11	0	2	.326	.258
Harrison, Josh	R-R	5-8	175	7-8-87	.262	.214	.288	31	122	15	32	4	1	1	4	3	1	0	0	11	6	2	.336	.286
Johnson, Leon	L-L	6-1	185	6-11-85	.220	.152	.247	32	118	6	26	3	0	0	9	12	3	3	0	18	9	6	.246	.308
Johnston, Dylan	L-R	6-0	180	3-25-87	.288	.289	.287	78	271	39	78	17	1	15	50	22	4	0	1	87	4	8	.524	.349
Lalli, Blake	L-R	6-1	210	5-12-83	.283	.111	.324	12	46	5	13	4	0	1	7	2	0	0	1	9	0	0	.435	.306
Lara, Elvis	R-R	5-11	160	11-19-86	.266	.356	.223	84	278	31	74	5	1	2	29	12	2	7	3	42	18	13	.313	.298
Made, Jose	R-R	5-8	175	10-23-85	.069	.091	.056	8	29	5	2	1	0	0	1	3	2	0	0	7	0	0	.103	.206
Mercedes, Mario	R-R	5-10	160	11-22-86	.218	.125	.270	52	179	11	39	8	0	0	18	9	1	4	1	17	1	1	.263	.258
Mota, Jonathan	R-R	6-0	180	6-1-87	.227	.000	.250	8	22	0	5	2	0	0	5	0	0	0	0	5	0	0	.318	.370
Opitz, Jake	L-R	6-0	180	7-28-86	.142	.250	.099	42	127	13	18	6	0	0	1	8	3	2	0	25	3	1	.189	.210
Rea, Jeffrey	L-R	5-8	160	7-10-84	.000	—	.000	2	5	0	0	0	0	0	0	1	0	1	0	0	0	0	.000	.167
Ridling, Rebel	R-R	6-4	230	5-22-86	.200	.210	.194	45	165	21	33	7	0	10	35	8	5	0	2	50	1	0	.424	.256
Rosa, Jovan	R-R	6-2	180	10-26-87	.293	.331	.279	128	481	58	141	43	4	7	81	40	7	3	5	127	3	2	.443	.353
Rundle, Drew	L-L	6-4	180	11-5-87	.164	.000	.190	21	67	9	11	5	0	2	4	6	3	2	0	22	6	1	.328	.263
Samson, Nate	R-R	6-0	170	8-19-87	.293	.320	.283	128	481	69	141	17	2	3	42	40	16	22	2	49	15	11	.356	.365
Smith, Marquez	R-R	5-10	210	3-20-85	.295	.329	.285	84	315	55	93	17	4	14	49	35	5	1	4	65	1	3	.508	.370
Sung, Min	B-R	5-9	180	7-8-82	.000	—	.000	3	4	0	0	0	0	0	0	1	0	0	0	1	0	0	.000	.200
Vitters, Josh	R-R	6-3	200	8-27-89	.214	.250	.200	4	14	1	3	3	0	0	1	0	0	0	0	6	0	0	.429	.214
Wyatt, Jonathan	L-R	5-10	180	9-6-84	.277	.259	.282	61	235	36	65	8	1	6	21	19	2	5	2	43	15	5	.396	.333

Pitching	B-T	HT	WT	DOB	W	L	ERA	G	GS	CG	SV	IP	H	R	ER	HR	BB	SO	AVG	vLH	vRH	K/9	BB/9
Acosta, Ryan	R-R	6-2	170	11-4-88	1	1	4.19	8	8	0	0	34	45	25	16	7	9	25	.306	.352	.263	6.55	2.36
Ashwood, Zach	B-L	6-4	202	5-20-86	6	10	6.24	32	7	0	0	84	105	62	58	18	31	63	.313	.366	.292	6.78	3.33
Blackford, Todd	L-R	6-4	205	6-10-85	1	1	2.60	9	0	0	0	17	16	7	5	0	6	.239	.172	.260	3.12	4.67
Cabrera, Alberto	R-R	6-4	170	10-25-88	4	6	5.71	12	11	0	0	52	55	39	33	7	30	37	.281	.244	.311	6.40	5.19
Castillo, Julio	R-R	6-3	212	10-6-87	0	2	2.86	6	3	0	0	22	24	12	7	0	8	10	.286	.231	.333	4.09	3.27
Chen, Hung-Wen	R-R	5-11	195	2-3-86	2	4	3.15	17	12	0	0	71	67	25	25	3	12	44	.251	.259	.245	5.55	1.51
Coleman, Joe	L-R	6-1	180	7-3-87	2	2	2.70	5	5	0	0	23	25	11	7	1	4	18	.272	.245	.302	6.94	1.54
Eyre, Scott	L-L	6-1	220	5-30-72	0	0	11.57	2	1	0	0	2	3	3	3	.500	.333	.667	11.57	0.00
Hernandez, Robert	R-R	6-2	165	10-7-88	2	4	5.14	17	15	1	0	77	79	51	44	10	27	60	.269	.306	.226	7.01	3.16
Jackson, Jay	R-R	6-1	195	10-27-87	2	2	3.00	6	1	0	0	24	22	8	8	3	5	37	.253	.235	.278	13.88	1.88
Kreier, Kevin	R-R	6-4	195	8-31-87	5	10	4.42	21	18	0	0	94	122	56	46	6	21	58	.319	.357	.284	5.57	2.02
Latham, Jordan	R-R	6-1	180	9-25-86	2	1	1.93	31	0	0	3	61	47	23	13	3	17	59	.212	.253	.179	8.75	2.52
Lieber, Jon	L-R	6-2	240	4-2-70	0	1	3.86	3	1	0	0	7	8	4	3	1	0	6	.286	.294	.273	7.71	0.00
Mateo, Marcos	R-R	6-1	160	4-18-84	1	0	1.20	8	0	0	1	15	4	3	2	1	7	20	.085	.160	.000	12.00	4.20
Mueller, Jon	R-R	6-4	180	5-12-84	0	1	5.35	21	0	0	1	39	42	28	23	7	15	34	.276	.211	.333	7.91	3.49
Muldowney, Billy	R-R	6-1	215	8-9-84	1	0	2.61	7	0	0	0	31	17	10	9	2	10	25	.152	.178	.134	7.26	2.90
Muller, John	L-R	6-2	200	7-28-84	1	1	4.64	11	0	0	0	21	18	11	11	3	9	21	.220	.220	.220	8.86	3.80
Muschko, Craig	R-R	6-2	192	8-17-85	4	3	4.32	42	0	0	6	83	98	44	40	4	11	69	.294	.351	.247	7.45	1.19
Parker, Blake	R-R	6-3	225	6-19-85	3	0	1.33	23	0	0	3	47	32	8	7	2	18	51	.193	.222	.170	9.70	3.42
Pina, Jose	R-R	6-2	155	11-21-85	0	5	5.27	11	8	0	1	27	40	19	16	1	6	22	.336	.411	.270	7.24	1.98
Rhee, Dae-Eun	L-R	6-2	190	3-23-89	4	1	1.80	10	10	0	0	40	28	13	8	0	16	33	.194	.238	.160	7.43	3.60
Santana, Audy	R-R	6-3	160	11-10-86	1	7	4.83	32	14	0	1	86	86	50	46	8	33	60	.263	.223	.296	6.30	3.47

	B-T	HT	WT	DOB	W	L	ERA	G	GS	CG	SV	IP	H	R	ER	HR	BB	SO	AVG	vLH	vRH	K/9	BB/9
Sasser, Dustin	L-L	6-0	200	9-13-85	1	4	1.53	20	0	0	4	35	28	10	6	0	15	24	.224	.250	.213	6.11	3.82
Siegfried, Chris	L-L	6-5	195	12-12-85	5	7	6.30	31	14	0	0	96	121	72	67	14	33	47	.316	.246	.346	4.42	3.10
Vento, Stephen	R-R	6-3	210	3-28-86	7	5	3.38	48	0	0	14	72	79	40	27	8	20	59	.275	.293	.262	7.38	2.50
Whitlock, Josh	R-R	6-1	195	3-12-86	1	2	5.66	6	4	0	0	21	18	17	13	2	7	10	.237	.237	.237	4.35	3.05

Fielding

Catcher	PCT	G	PO	A	E	DP	PB
Bautista	.986	9	64	5	1	0	0
Donaldson	.981	52	359	59	8	4	6
Flores	1.000	33	203	28	0	2	2
Lalli	1.000	1	5	1	0	0	0
Mercedes	.983	47	292	50	6	2	7

First Base	PCT	G	PO	A	E	DP
Bautista	.986	46	395	34	6	40
Burke	1.000	4	26	1	0	2
Guzman	1.000	1	1	0	0	0
Johnston	.968	3	29	1	1	4
Lalli	.950	4	35	3	2	3
Opitz	1.000	1	1	0	0	0
Ridling	.989	29	256	17	3	18
Rosa	.985	57	495	28	8	49

Second Base	PCT	G	PO	A	E	DP
Gonzalez	.966	17	41	44	3	13
Guzman	.972	25	44	61	3	14
Harrison	.952	24	35	64	5	8
Lara	.981	13	16	35	1	7
Made	.939	6	16	15	2	5
Mota	.833	3	2	3	1	0
Opitz	.979	26	46	92	3	16
Rea	1.000	2	3	1	0	1
Samson	.952	14	27	53	4	10
Smith	.983	22	41	72	2	16

Third Base	PCT	G	PO	A	E	DP
Bautista	.900	3	4	5	1	1
Guzman	.750	2	1	2	1	1
Mota	—	1	0	0	0	0
Rosa	.889	71	59	109	21	14
Smith	.934	64	41	115	11	14
Vitters	.800	3	3	5	2	2

Shortstop	PCT	G	PO	A	E	DP
Gonzalez	.920	16	31	49	7	8
Guzman	.917	5	9	13	2	3
Mota	.929	3	9	4	1	5
Opitz	.833	4	8	7	3	1
Samson	.954	114	174	339	25	60

Outfield	PCT	G	PO	A	E	DP
Andersen	.980	98	195	4	4	0
Burke	.955	30	59	5	3	2
Guyer	.976	80	154	10	4	3
Harrison	.714	4	5	0	2	0
Johnson	.983	32	52	5	1	0
Johnston	.954	50	77	6	4	1
Lara	.986	39	64	6	1	0
Mota	1.000	2	1	0	0	0
Opitz	.889	6	8	0	1	0
Ridling	1.000	7	12	0	0	0
Rundle	1.000	20	41	0	0	0
Sung	1.000	2	1	0	0	0
Wyatt	.978	60	130	6	3	1

BOISE HAWKS   SHORT-SEASON

NORTHWEST LEAGUE

Batting	B-T	HT	WT	DOB	AVG	vLH	vRH	G	AB	R	H	2B	3B	HR	RBI	BB	HBP	SH	SF	SO	SB	CS	SLG	OBP
Brenly, Michael	R-R	6-3	210	10-14-86	.325	.400	.297	39	126	24	41	10	0	1	18	14	2	3	1	28	2	0	.429	.399
Burke, Kyler	L-L	6-3	205	4-20-88	.261	.156	.298	67	245	46	64	18	2	7	41	28	2	0	5	70	6	3	.437	.336
Calvert, Kurt	L-L	5-9	170	7-5-85	.216	.235	.212	55	204	33	44	8	0	1	11	29	4	4	2	32	13	4	.270	.322
Campana, Tony	L-L	5-8	160	5-30-86	.000	.000	.000	1	3	0	0	0	0	0	0	1	0	0	0	1	0	0	.000	.400
Flaherty, Ryan	L-R	6-3	200	7-27-86	.297	.380	.272	56	219	39	65	19	2	8	26	24	1	1	0	51	4	2	.511	.369
Flores, Luis	R-R	5-10	195	11-2-86	.167	.143	.176	9	24	1	4	1	0	0	3	0	1	0	1	5	0	1	.208	.259
Gonzalez, Marwin	B-R	6-1	186	3-14-89	.279	.242	.292	65	244	29	68	15	3	0	43	13	2	6	2	36	15	7	.365	.318
Harrison, Josh	R-R	5-8	175	7-8-87	.351	.261	.374	33	114	27	40	11	2	1	25	23	3	1	3	12	12	6	.509	.462
Hoorelbeke, Sean	R-R	6-0	220	5-26-85	.281	.211	.311	35	128	19	36	10	0	1	18	23	2	0	1	38	1	4	.383	.396
Keedy, Ryan	L-R	6-3	220	8-15-85	.333	.339	.332	70	252	34	84	15	1	3	40	35	3	1	1	58	2	3	.437	.419
Kemp, Dwayne	B-R	5-8	160	2-24-88	.200	.130	.238	25	65	11	13	4	0	1	6	3	1	2	0	23	1	0	.308	.246
Macias, David	B-R	5-9	185	3-7-86	.228	.250	.218	54	184	22	42	9	1	0	16	22	2	4	1	34	4	2	.288	.316
Mahoney, Pat	R-R		0	12-26-85	.077	.125	.000	8	13	0	1	0	0	0	1	0	1	0	0	1	0	0	.077	.143
Opitz, Jake	L-R	6-0	180	12-28-86	.250	.333	.214	15	40	6	10	0	2	2	3	8	0	0	0	8	0	0	.500	.375
Perez, Carlos	R-R	6-1	180	10-18-87	.285	.226	.299	42	158	16	45	11	0	1	19	11	3	2	0	16	3	2	.373	.343
Ridling, Rebel	R-R	6-4	230	5-22-86	.366	.368	.365	19	71	11	26	8	0	4	19	5	2	0	2	18	0	1	.648	.413
Rundle, Drew	L-L	6-4	180	11-5-88	.292	.269	.300	53	192	45	56	22	3	8	36	30	2	6	0	62	6	4	.563	.393
Sommer, Luke	L-L	6-3	190	6-22-85	.000	.000	—	1	1	0	0	0	0	0	0	0	0	0	0	0	0	0	.000	.000
Sontag, Ryan	L-L	5-10	195	9-13-85	.218	.154	.238	38	110	16	24	3	2	0	17	16	1	5	2	36	5	0	.282	.318
Vitters, Josh	R-R	6-3	200	8-27-89	.328	.365	.316	61	259	38	85	25	2	5	37	13	3	0	2	45	1	3	.498	.365

Pitching	B-T	HT	WT	DOB	W	L	ERA	G	GS	CG	SV	IP	H	R	ER	HR	BB	SO	AVG	vLH	vRH	K/9	BB/9
Beliveau, Jeff	L-L	6-1	197	1-17-87	2	1	2.60	13	7	0	0	35	25	12	10	1	28	51	.202	.250	.182	13.24	7.27
Bristow, Justin	R-R	6-4	220	3-6-87	2	1	9.00	5	3	0	0	12	15	12	12	3	5	14	.306	.333	.280	10.50	3.75
Bunton, Michael	L-L	6-3	195	10-23-85	0	0	12.71	8	0	0	0	11	17	16	16	2	7	12	.327	.211	.394	9.53	5.56
Cales, David	R-R	5-11	200	7-27-87	3	0	1.84	8	0	0	1	15	11	4	3	1	4	15	.204	.278	.167	9.20	2.45
Camacaro, Israel	R-R	6-3	185	4-6-85	0	1	6.31	11	4	0	0	36	38	29	25	2	19	24	.277	.277	.278	6.06	4.79
Carpenter, Chris	R-R	6-4	215	12-26-85	4	2	4.22	10	6	0	0	32	32	21	15	2	22	24	.258	.185	.314	6.75	6.19
Cashner, Andrew	R-R	6-6	185	9-11-86	1	1	4.96	6	4	0	0	16	19	12	9	1	19	16	.302	.370	.250	8.82	10.47
Coleman, Joe	L-R	6-1	190	7-3-87	1	1	4.05	7	4	0	0	27	27	13	12	4	7	24	.257	.200	.300	8.10	2.36
de Leon, Manolin	R-R	6-0	175	11-23-86	0	0	3.38	2	0	0	0	3	4	1	1	0	1	3	.333	.000	.444	10.13	3.38
Hamren, Erik	R-R	6-1	195	8-21-86	1	0	4.32	6	0	0	0	8	16	5	4	0	6	6	.421	.462	.400	6.48	6.48
Hatley, Marcus	R-R	6-5	190	3-26-88	1	3	5.71	12	6	0	0	35	46	25	22	3	21	30	.317	.408	.271	7.79	5.45
Hempy, Arik	R-L	6-4	245	7-19-84	0	0	2.25	7	0	0	0	8	8	3	2	0	7	6	.296	.600	.227	6.75	7.88
Jackson, Jay	R-R	6-1	195	10-27-87	0	0	5.00	3	1	0	0	9	7	5	5	1	1	14	.212	.211	.214	14.00	1.00
Leverton, James	R-L	6-2	185	5-13-86	1	3	4.61	15	10	0	0	55	50	30	28	1	27	38	.250	.298	.231	6.26	4.45
McDaniel, Dan	R-R	6-3	220	4-18-88	2	1	1.67	20	0	0	7	32	14	6	6	1	17	45	.128	.167	.110	12.53	4.73
Mejia, Tommy	R-R	6-1	200	7-2-86	3	2	5.04	16	0	0	2	25	35	19	14	3	15	16	.315	.238	.362	5.76	5.40
Muller, John	L-R	6-2	200	7-28-84	2	0	1.50	14	0	0	8	18	12	3	3	0	7	21	.185	.308	.103	10.50	3.50
O'Donnell, Bubba	R-R	6-2	210	2-17-86	6	3	3.97	25	0	0	2	45	49	24	20	3	20	36	.287	.387	.229	7.15	3.97
Pawelek, Mark	L-L	6-3	190	8-18-86	2	2	6.20	13	2	0	0	25	25	21	17	0	19	21	.272	.217	.290	7.66	6.93
Perconte, Mike	R-R	6-4	170	3-18-86	2	1	4.85	19	4	0	2	52	52	34	28	7	15	49	.264	.294	.248	8.48	2.60
Pina, Jose	R-R	6-2	150	11-2-85	0	1	1.50	3	3	0	0	6	4	1	1	0	2	8	.182	.125	.214	12.00	3.00
Redmond, Cedric	R-R	6-3	180	8-30-88	0	0	6.00	2	0	0	0	3	3	2	2	0	2	2	.250	.250	.250	6.00	6.00
Searle, Ryan	R-R	6-0	190	6-22-89	1	2	1.03	6	5	0	0	26	18	7	3	0	10	19	.189	.250	.153	6.49	3.42
Shafer, Aaron	L-R	6-5	185	12-2-86	2	2	3.09	8	7	0	0	32	25	13	11	3	5	24	.231	.184	.264	6.75	1.41
Tolentino, Harol	R-L	6-4	165	11-8-88	3	3	5.52	17	5	0	0	44	43	29	24	7	33	23	.265	.283	.255	4.70	6.75
Whitlock, Josh	R-R	6-1	195	3-12-86	0	1	4.31	9	5	0	0	31	28	20	15	4	14	31	.246	.244	.246	8.90	4.02

Fielding

Catcher	PCT	G	PO	A	E	DP	PB
Brenly	.983	30	210	19	4	1	4
Flores	.971	7	59	9	2	1	2
Mahoney	1.000	3	19	2	0	0	1
Perez	.984	42	324	38	6	7	3

First Base	PCT	G	PO	A	E	DP
Brenly	1.000	2	18	1	0	0
Burke	1.000	1	2	0	0	0
Hoorelbeke	.988	8	76	7	1	7
Keedy	.988	61	533	46	7	55
Ridling	.985	7	59	5	1	5

Second Base	PCT	G	PO	A	E	DP
Calvert	1.000	1	1	2	0	0
Gonzalez	.975	30	64	93	4	20
Harrison	.991	23	36	80	1	8
Kemp	.964	13	20	34	2	4
Macias	1.000	4	5	8	0	4
Opitz	.941	12	19	29	3	4

Third Base	PCT	G	PO	A	E	DP
Gonzalez	.905	11	4	15	2	2
Macias	.913	11	9	12	2	1
Vitters	.915	57	40	111	14	14

Shortstop	PCT	G	PO	A	E	DP
Flaherty	.935	52	78	154	16	30
Gonzalez	.957	26	50	85	6	15
Opitz	—	1	0	0	0	0

Outfield	PCT	G	PO	A	E	DP
Burke	.977	65	120	10	3	4
Calvert	.960	53	69	3	3	1
Campana	1.000	1	2	0	0	0
Harrison	.500	3	1	0	1	0
Macias	1.000	38	41	2	0	0
Rundle	.976	50	80	3	2	0
Sontag	.978	29	41	4	1	1

AZL CUBS   ROOKIE
ARIZONA LEAGUE

Batting	B-T	HT	WT	DOB	AVG	vLH	vRH	G	AB	R	H	2B	3B	HR	RBI	BB	HBP	SH	SF	SO	SB	CS	SLG	OBP
Calvert, Kurt	L-L	5-9	170	7-5-85	.286	.167	.333	5	21	5	6	1	0	0	3	3	1	0	0	2	1	2	.333	.400
Campana, Tony	L-L	5-8	160	5-30-86	.277	.133	.309	24	83	17	23	0	0	0	10	8	0	1	1	14	22	2	.277	.337
Castro, Starlin	R-R	6-1	160	3-24-90	.311	.263	.331	51	196	33	61	11	5	3	22	14	3	1	1	33	6	5	.464	.364
Cerda, Matt	L-R	5-9	165	6-20-90	.253	.171	.277	42	154	29	39	5	1	2	15	21	0	1	1	25	2	0	.338	.341
Chirinos, Robinson	R-R	6-1	185	6-5-84	.462	.333	.500	4	13	5	6	1	1	0	3	6	0	0	0	2	1	0	.692	.632
Contreras, John	R-R	6-0	185	4-17-86	.283	.342	.264	44	159	36	45	12	4	9	38	16	5	1	2	34	3	0	.579	.363
Guevara, Jose	R-R	6-1	180	3-17-88	.261	.167	.294	22	46	7	12	4	0	0	4	7	3	0	0	18	0	0	.348	.393
Hoorelbeke, Sean	R-R	6-0	220	5-26-85	.388	.273	.431	23	80	21	31	9	1	5	21	15	0	0	1	18	4	1	.713	.479
Jones, Jericho	R-R	6-5	215	7-21-87	.340	.356	.333	43	159	29	54	7	6	5	30	10	3	0	0	41	2	1	.553	.390
Jost, Bryan	L-L	6-4	205	3-25-86	.266	.143	.301	35	94	19	25	5	1	0	10	20	0	0	1	29	1	0	.340	.391
Kemp, Dwayne	B-R	5-8	160	2-24-88	.304	.286	.313	7	23	6	7	4	1	0	3	2	1	0	0	3	2	0	.565	.407
Lake, Junior	R-R	6-3	175	3-27-90	.286	.389	.258	47	168	24	48	4	6	2	23	13	1	0	3	42	12	2	.417	.335
Matheus, George	R-R	6-0	170	7-20-88	.252	.250	.253	35	103	17	26	2	2	0	15	6	4	1	1	18	2	1	.311	.316
Perez, Nelson	R-R	6-3	215	11-16-87	.305	.316	.302	39	154	33	47	7	10	9	37	8	2	1	3	35	3	3	.656	.341
Pie, Felix	L-L	6-2	170	2-8-85	.667	—	.667	1	3	3	2	0	0	0	1	5	1	0	0	0	0	0	1.667	.750
Reed, Mark	L-R	5-11	175	4-13-86	.125	.200	.000	4	8	0	1	0	0	0	0	1	0	0	0	3	0	0	.125	.222
Soriano, Alfonso	R-R	6-1	180	1-7-76	.000	—	.000	1	2	1	0	0	0	0	0	0	0	0	0	1	0	0	.000	.333
Sosa, Alvaro	L-R	6-0	181	6-7-86	.214	.200	.218	36	103	12	22	6	2	0	11	11	0	0	1	19	3	3	.311	.287
Soto, Kevin	R-R	6-1	170	10-12-88	.256	.107	.301	37	121	16	31	4	1	0	19	8	2	2	0	25	8	1	.306	.313
Watkins, Logan	L-R	5-11	170	8-29-89	.325	.278	.339	27	80	15	26	3	0	0	14	20	2	3	2	19	2	0	.363	.462
Willis, TeWayne	R-R	5-9	165	10-29-84	.196	.148	.212	41	112	23	22	1	0	0	12	21	7	2	6	24	10	5	.205	.342

Pitching	B-T	HT	WT	DOB	W	L	ERA	G	GS	CG	SV	IP	H	R	ER	HR	BB	SO	AVG	vLH	vRH	K/9	BB/9
Acosta, Francisco	R-R	6-4	170	8-7-88	0	0	0.82	7	0	0	0	11	10	4	1	0	7	9	.238	.214	.250	7.36	5.73
Acosta, Ryan	R-R	6-2	170	11-4-88	0	0	6.23	3	0	0	0	4	4	3	3	1	1	5	.250	.750	.083	10.38	2.08
Allen, Eric	R-R	6-3	195	2-22-85	2	1	5.21	14	0	0	0	19	25	15	11	1	14	16	.325	.385	.294	7.58	6.63
Antigua, Jeffry	R-L	6-1	170	6-23-90	2	3	3.05	14	6	0	0	41	42	22	14	2	16	32	.258	.308	.248	6.97	3.48
Beliveau, Jeff	L-L	6-1	197	1-17-87	0	0	13.50	1	1	0	0	1	1	1	1	0	1	1	.333	.000	.333	13.50	13.50
Bristow, Justin	R-R	6-4	220	3-6-87	0	0	9.00	1	0	0	0	1	1	1	1	0	1	1	.250	.000	.333	9.00	9.00
Cales, David	R-R	5-11	200	7-27-87	0	1	5.87	6	1	0	0	8	9	6	5	1	3	11	.273	.417	.190	12.91	3.52
Carmona, Rogelino	R-R	6-3	210	8-30-89	0	0	8.31	4	0	0	0	9	13	8	8	1	2	3	.351	.222	.393	3.12	2.08
Carpenter, Chris	R-R	6-4	215	12-26-85	0	0	18.00	1	1	0	0	1	2	2	2	0	1	1	.500	—	.500	9.00	9.00
Cashner, Andrew	R-R	6-6	185	9-11-86	0	0	0.00	1	1	0	0	1	1	1	0	0	0	2	.333	—	.333	18.00	0.00
de Leon, Manolin	R-R	6-0	175	11-23-86	1	0	2.45	15	0	0	6	22	29	7	6	1	4	22	.330	.222	.377	9.00	1.64
Eyre, Scott	L-L	6-1	220	5-30-72	0	0	0.00	1	0	0	0	1	0	0	0	0	0	1	.000	—	.000	0.00	9.00
Gonzalez, Yohan	R-R	6-4	170	4-15-90	5	1	1.96	14	0	0	0	37	30	10	8	0	13	21	.226	.270	.208	5.15	3.19
Hamren, Erik	R-R	6-1	195	8-21-86	1	1	5.87	7	2	0	2	8	8	5	5	0	4	5	.296	.429	.250	5.87	4.70
Hill, Rich	L-L	6-5	205	3-11-80	1	1	2.89	3	3	0	0	9	5	5	3	0	5	11	.161	.286	.125	10.61	4.82
Huseby, Chris	R-R	6-7	220	1-11-88	1	1	7.20	9	7	0	0	15	15	15	12	0	17	8	.263	.294	.250	4.80	10.20
Kopach, Kitt	L-R	6-2	195	2-14-85	0	0	4.15	9	4	0	0	13	10	7	6	1	7	12	.217	.083	.265	8.31	4.85
Lieber, Jon	L-R	6-2	240	4-2-70	0	0	0.00	1	1	0	0	3	4	0	0	0	1	6	.364	.500	.333	3.00	0.00
Martinez, Oswaldo	R-R	6-0	180	9-25-88	2	2	7.85	14	3	0	0	18	27	19	16	4	10	16	.338	.091	.431	7.85	4.91
Matchulat, Toby	R-R	6-5	195	2-7-89	0	1	11.57	14	3	0	0	19	17	28	24	0	29	21	.233	.333	.200	10.13	13.98
McDaniel, Dan	R-R	6-3	220	4-18-88	0	0	0.00	2	0	0	0	2	3	0	0	0	1	3	.375	.000	.500	11.57	3.86
Mitchell, Tarlandas	R-R	5-8	190	3-9-90	0	1	4.86	11	0	0	1	17	11	13	9	0	16	19	.186	.200	.179	10.26	8.64
Nunez, Dionis	R-R	6-4	170	9-28-88	3	3	6.95	13	5	0	0	34	42	31	26	1	19	20	.311	.289	.320	5.35	5.08
Pena, Julio	R-R	6-3	185	3-1-89	5	1	3.16	13	1	0	1	43	35	20	15	1	10	32	.224	.214	.228	6.75	2.11
Redmond, Cedric	R-R	6-3	180	8-30-88	1	0	2.95	12	3	0	0	21	12	8	7	2	6	25	.158	.000	.194	10.55	2.53
Rojas, Carlos	R-R	6-1	170	5-22-90	2	1	4.57	18	0	0	3	22	14	11	11	0	12	13	.179	.190	.175	5.40	4.98
Searle, Ryan	R-R	6-0	190	6-22-89	1	0	1.13	2	1	0	0	8	3	1	1	0	0	9	.107	.167	.091	10.13	0.00
Severino, Jose	R-R	5-11	165	8-13-89	0	0	13.50	4	0	0	0	5	12	10	8	1	1	2	.444	.417	.467	3.38	1.69
Shafer, Aaron	L-R	6-5	185	12-2-86	0	0	0.00	1	0	0	0	1	0	0	0	0	0	1	.000	.000	.000	9.00	9.00
Sierra, Miguel	R-R	6-5	170	7-28-88	2	4	5.28	14	5	0	1	44	57	31	26	4	13	25	.315	.345	.302	5.08	2.64
Suarez, Larry	R-R	6-4	245	12-20-89	0	2	2.78	10	7	0	0	23	17	9	7	1	9	19	.213	.208	.214	7.54	3.57

Fielding

Catcher	PCT	G	PO	A	E	DP	PB
Cerda	.989	13	79	10	1	0	7
Chirinos	1.000	2	12	4	0	1	1
Guevara	.990	17	81	14	1	0	6
Reed	1.000	2	6	2	0	1	0
Sosa	.958	35	186	40	10	1	9

First Base	PCT	G	PO	A	E	DP
Contreras	.989	11	84	5	1	8
Guevara	1.000	1	2	1	0	1
Hoorelbeke	.994	17	154	8	1	15
Jones	.974	8	74	2	2	4
Jost	1.000	26	223	8	0	21

Second Base	PCT	G	PO	A	E	DP
Castro	.949	20	38	73	6	13

	PCT	G	PO	A	E	DP
Cerda	.889	2	1	7	1	1
Kemp	.931	6	11	16	2	6
Lake	.917	2	8	3	1	0
Matheus	.969	14	26	37	2	9
Watkins	.952	16	22	38	3	12

Third Base	PCT	G	PO	A	E	DP
Castro	.909	5	1	9	1	0
Chirinos	1.000	1	0	2	0	0
Contreras	.914	32	29	67	9	6
Lake	.828	9	8	16	5	4
Matheus	.944	11	10	24	2	1

Shortstop	PCT	G	PO	A	E	DP
Castro	.955	21	32	75	5	11
Lake	.922	33	52	114	14	23

	PCT	G	PO	A	E	DP
Matheus	.941	5	5	11	1	4

Outfield	PCT	G	PO	A	E	DP
Calvert	1.000	5	15	2	0	1
Campana	.980	24	46	3	1	1
Castro	—	1	0	0	0	0
Jones	.968	31	30	0	1	0
Jost	1.000	4	2	0	0	0
Perez	.930	38	49	4	4	0
Pie	—	1	0	0	0	0
Soto	.937	36	56	3	4	2
Watkins	1.000	5	9	1	0	0
Willis	.891	36	39	2	5	0

DSL CUBS 1 — ROOKIE

DOMINICAN SUMMER LEAGUE

Batting	B-T	HT	WT	DOB	AVG	vLH	vRH	G	AB	R	H	2B	3B	HR	RBI	BB	HBP	SH	SF	SO	SB	CS	SLG	OBP
Avila, Jose	R-R	6-0	175	5-18-89	.000	.000	.000	3	5	1	0	0	0	0	0	1	1	0	0	2	0	0	.000	.286
Bautista, Robert	B-R	6-1	165	8-20-88	.189	.196	.187	65	217	34	41	3	4	2	28	30	4	10	3	56	12	5	.267	.295
Bonilla, Ramon	B-R	6-0	160	4-8-88	.249	.304	.231	62	193	29	48	7	3	1	26	16	7	7	0	24	10	6	.332	.329
Camarena, Melvin	R-R	6-4	210	10-12-89	.228	.188	.237	57	167	24	38	8	3	0	18	8	4	2	3	55	12	5	.311	.275
Damian, Alejandro	R-R	6-2	190	6-17-90	.270	.182	.291	55	174	36	47	7	2	1	13	33	8	0	0	61	6	7	.351	.409
Gonzalez, Miguel	R-R	6-0	180	10-30-89	.125	.111	.128	18	56	5	7	0	0	0	4	3	1	0	0	10	1	0	.125	.183
Guzman, Francisco	L-L	6-1	160	4-12-88	.299	.364	.277	57	174	35	52	2	3	0	16	16	2	5	2	30	18	8	.345	.361
Hernandez, Albert	R-R	6-1	170	2-25-89	.324	.293	.333	56	170	33	55	12	4	1	26	19	7	0	4	25	6	4	.459	.405
Medina, Juan	R-R	6-1	185	6-13-86	.300	.208	.327	63	210	30	63	9	4	2	34	22	3	1	2	24	12	8	.410	.371
Medina, Pedro	R-R	6-2	170	6-15-90	.000	—	.000	4	6	3	0	0	0	0	0	0	0	1	0	2	1	0	.000	.000
Mejia, Alexander	B-R	6-0	179	1-18-86	.299	.233	.315	62	224	36	67	12	10	7	43	22	10	0	4	25	13	6	.536	.381
Parra, Ricardo	R-R	6-0	180	5-30-91	.179	.455	.071	15	39	4	7	0	0	0	4	3	3	1	0	9	1	0	.179	.289
Perez, Melido	L-R	5-10	160	10-22-90	.000	.000	.000	6	13	2	0	0	0	0	0	0	0	0	0	8	0	0	.000	.000
Pierre, Nelson	B-R	6-0	160	12-23-87	.222	.122	.248	61	198	32	44	6	4	1	23	16	1	6	2	41	32	4	.308	.281
Quezada, Andres	B-R	5-11	170	3-15-86	.000	.000	.000	3	2	1	0	0	0	0	0	1	0	0	1	0	0	0	.000	.333
Valdez, Jose	B-R	6-1	170	9-5-87	.231	.295	.210	58	182	38	42	0	3	0	14	17	9	3	0	35	26	9	.264	.327
Vigay, Jose	R-R	5-10	185	12-10-88	.268	.500	.256	13	41	9	11	3	1	0	2	4	2	0	0	11	3	2	.390	.362

Pitching	B-T	HT	WT	DOB	W	L	ERA	G	GS	CG	SV	IP	H	R	ER	HR	BB	SO	AVG	vLH	vRH	K/9	BB/9
Carmona, Rogelino	R-R	6-3	210	8-30-89	1	1	2.16	9	0	0	0	17	14	6	4	0	8	19	.222	.222	.222	10.26	4.32
Castillo, Julio	R-R	6-3	212	10-6-87	1	0	0.00	4	4	0	0	18	7	0	0	0	5	13	.111	.095	.119	6.50	2.50
Coletto, Miguel	B-R	6-0	185	2-4-87	1	3	3.29	16	2	0	2	27	23	17	10	0	23	28	.310	.197	.222	9.22	7.57
Encarnacion, Diego	R-R	6-2	190	3-4-90	2	0	2.72	14	6	0	0	43	30	14	13	2	17	42	.200	.200	.200	8.79	3.56
Florentino, Arturo	R-R	6-4	170	1-3-85	6	1	3.43	30	0	0	9	42	36	20	16	3	8	32	.229	.255	.217	6.86	1.71
Galvez, Carlos	L-L	6-1	170	4-26-90	1	2	2.52	16	0	0	1	25	21	10	7	1	16	19	.239	.250	.238	6.84	5.76
Infante, Edilmar	R-R	5-11	180	12-19-87	5	3	2.66	15	15	0	0	81	76	31	24	3	12	53	.243	.245	.242	5.86	1.33
Mayora, Hector	R-R	6-1	178	6-22-89	2	2	1.89	9	7	0	0	33	30	18	7	0	14	34	.224	.333	.188	9.18	3.78
Mota, Pacheco	R-R	6-4	200	7-13-90	1	0	6.48	5	0	0	0	8	9	6	6	0	3	2	.281	.200	.318	2.16	3.24
Perez, Marcos	L-R	6-1	175	1-1-90	6	1	1.38	13	13	0	0	65	53	17	10	1	9	52	.221	.177	.242	7.16	1.24
Pichardo, Roderick	R-R	5-10	180	9-24-90	5	2	2.41	17	7	0	0	52	41	20	14	2	19	43	.222	.217	.224	7.39	3.27
Pineda, Francory	R-R	6-1	180	5-25-89	0	0	3.78	9	0	0	0	17	17	10	7	0	6	8	.258	.333	.229	4.32	3.24
Reyes, Roeldwin	R-R	6-1	160	5-14-89	0	1	2.84	10	0	0	1	19	19	13	6	1	8	14	.247	.250	.245	6.63	3.79
Rodriguez, Santo	L-R	6-1	185	9-29-89	3	2	4.36	18	0	0	3	33	30	23	16	1	14	20	.242	.300	.214	5.45	3.82
Rodriguez, Jhon	R-R	6-0	185	7-18-90	1	0	0.00	7	1	0	0	14	6	3	0	1	3	13	.146	.125	.152	8.56	1.98
Rosario, Jose	R-R	6-1	180	8-29-90	1	0	5.06	4	0	0	0	5	6	3	3	1	4	3	.273	.167	.313	5.06	6.75
Ruiz, Adner	L-L	6-1	180	4-1-89	4	2	1.91	14	7	0	0	47	29	17	10	1	21	48	.177	.190	.175	9.19	4.02
Severino, Jose	R-R	5-11	165	8-13-89	1	0	2.38	3	2	0	0	11	9	3	3	1	1	7	.231	.250	.217	5.56	0.79
Tineo, Jose	R-R	5-10	170	8-29-90	1	1	3.94	10	2	0	0	16	10	8	7	0	15	21	.179	.200	.171	11.81	8.44
Vasquez, Melvin	L-L	5-11	180	5-13-88	1	1	2.13	5	1	0	1	13	15	5	3	0	0	10	.300	.200	.311	7.11	0.00

Fielding

Catcher	PCT	G	PO	A	E	DP	PB
Gonzalez	1.000	8	61	5	0	0	3
J. Medina	.978	53	314	42	8	2	8
Mejia	1.000	1	7	1	0	0	0
Parra	.982	15	96	14	2	2	4
Vigay	1.000	10	51	6	0	1	3

First Base	PCT	G	PO	A	E	DP
Camarena	.960	5	23	1	1	0
Gonzalez	1.000	1	0	0	0	0
Guzman	1.000	1	1	1	0	0
Hernandez	.969	4	29	2	1	3
J. Medina	.981	15	95	8	2	0
Mejia	.981	54	449	22	9	35
Pena	1.000	9	63	1	0	5

Second Base	PCT	G	PO	A	E	DP
Avila	.889	2	3	5	1	0
Bautista	1.000	5	8	6	0	3
Bonilla	.964	42	84	106	7	28
Mejia	1.000	3	2	2	0	0
Perez	1.000	2	3	5	0	0
Pierre	.941	28	66	61	8	13
Vigay	1.000	1	0	1	0	0

Third Base	PCT	G	PO	A	E	DP
Avila	—	1	0	0	0	0
Bautista	.833	2	1	4	1	1
Bonilla	.909	9	1	9	1	1
Mejia	1.000	3	1	3	0	1
Pena	.880	47	23	72	13	5
Pierre	.897	31	22	56	9	8

Shortstop	PCT	G	PO	A	E	DP
Bautista	.903	57	75	177	27	30
Bonilla	.958	9	15	31	2	5
Pena	1.000	1	0	4	0	0
Pierre	.800	8	3	17	5	1

Outfield	PCT	G	PO	A	E	DP
Bonilla	1.000	2	1	0	0	0
Camarena	.946	43	33	2	2	1
Damian	1.000	38	49	5	0	1
Guzman	.970	55	61	4	2	1
Hernandez	.964	38	51	3	2	1
P. Medina	1.000	3	3	0	0	0
Mejia	1.000	10	10	1	0	1
Pierre	1.000	1	1	0	0	0
Valdez	.982	58	102	10	2	2

DOMINICAN SUMMER LEAGUE

Batting	B-T	HT	WT	DOB	AVG	vLH	vRH	G	AB	R	H	2B	3B	HR	RBI	BB	HBP	SH	SF	SO	SB	CS	SLG	OBP
Andrades, Luis	R-R	5-11	170	4-29-88	.184	.216	.172	55	179	30	33	4	2	0	19	29	8	4	0	75	7	5	.229	.324
Bieneme, Vismeldy	B-R	5-10	160	3-19-90	.246	.409	.193	59	179	38	44	5	7	0	16	41	5	3	2	63	36	8	.352	.396
Gonzalez, Miguel	R-R	6-0	180	10-30-89	.063	.000	.077	4	16	1	1	0	1	0	2	0	0	0	0	6	0	0	.188	.063
2-team total (18 Cubs 1)					.111	—	—	22	72	6	8	0	1	0	6	3	1	0	0	16	1	0	.139	.158
Guzman, Justino	R-R	6-2	190	4-19-88	.207	.400	.167	9	29	3	6	1	1	0	2	6	1	0	1	14	0	0	.310	.351
Liria, Yamel	R-R	5-11	190	11-5-89	.160	.304	.117	35	100	11	16	6	1	1	7	12	9	0	1	34	0	0	.270	.303
Medina, Pedro	R-R	6-2	170	6-15-90	.199	.214	.193	50	161	26	32	6	3	0	17	28	3	4	1	52	12	7	.273	.326
2-team total (4 Cubs 1)					.192	—	—	54	167	29	32	6	3	0	17	28	3	5	1	54	13	7	.263	.317
Montecino, Jose	B-R	5-11	175	7-31-90	.164	.071	.191	22	61	12	10	1	0	0	2	14	0	2	0	21	5	0	.180	.320
Morales, Carlos	R-R	6-2	145	3-14-89	.284	.269	.288	64	243	36	69	11	5	2	32	20	7	0	2	63	18	5	.395	.353
Morelli, Jesus	R-R	6-3	180	4-25-90	.317	.289	.325	56	189	39	60	11	3	5	38	34	7	1	4	37	13	8	.487	.432
Parra, Ricardo	R-R	6-0	180	5-30-91	.238	.500	.211	6	21	2	5	0	0	0	2	0	0	0	0	5	0	0	.238	.304
2-team total (15 Cubs 1)					.200	—	—	21	60	6	12	0	0	0	4	5	3	1	0	14	1	0	.200	.294
Pestana, Manuel	R-R	6-0	150	3-9-90	.279	.111	.322	59	219	44	61	9	2	0	22	34	7	2	2	29	14	10	.338	.389
Ramirez, Pedro	R-R	6-1	185	9-9-87	.233	.208	.240	62	227	21	53	15	1	3	25	22	2	0	1	34	2	2	.348	.306
Robles, Gregorio	B-R	6-1	170	3-4-91	.230	.250	.224	45	135	13	31	5	3	1	13	14	3	0	0	41	5	3	.333	.316
Romero, Carlos	R-R	6-1	180	5-28-90	.264	.237	.271	53	178	20	47	10	1	2	23	21	5	3	0	34	1	6	.365	.358
Salazar, Miguel	R-R	6-1	150	1-19-89	.262	.255	.263	65	237	33	62	5	2	1	28	25	4	5	5	23	13	3	.312	.336
Vigay, Jose	R-R	5-10	185	12-10-88	.215	.071	.255	18	65	7	14	2	2	0	7	5	1	0	0	20	3	0	.308	.282
2-team total (13 Cubs 1)					.236	—	—	31	106	9	25	4	2	1	16	9	3	0	0	31	6	2	.340	.314

Pitching	B-T	HT	WT	DOB	W	L	ERA	G	GS	CG	SV	IP	H	R	ER	HR	BB	SO	AVG	vLH	vRH	K/9	BB/9
Acosta, Francisco	R-R	6-4	170	8-7-88	0	2	6.00	2	2	0	0	6	6	9	4	0	3	9	.222	.333	.167	13.50	4.50
Bremon, Jane	R-R	6-3	180	10-27-90	2	0	4.71	18	0	0	0	21	21	17	11	0	18	16	.259	.211	.274	6.86	7.71
Cabrera, Yeison	R-R	6-1	165	8-2-88	0	0	0.00	1	0	0	0	1	0	0	0	1	1		.000	.000	.000	9.00	9.00
Figueroa, Eduardo	R-R	6-1	185	11-30-88	5	6	4.22	14	12	0	0	60	54	36	28	2	23	46	.239	.193	.254	6.94	3.47
Garcia, Ramon	R-R	6-2	170	8-2-91	2	6	5.61	13	11	0	0	51	63	43	32	5	13	45	.297	.311	.291	7.89	2.28
Lebron, Jesse	R-R	6-0	165	9-11-89	1	0	8.40	13	0	0	0	15	10	21	14	1	32	9	.182	.167	.186	5.40	19.20
Liria, Luis	B-R	6-2	170	1-15-90	1	3	4.10	15	9	0	2	53	46	39	24	3	26	45	.234	.339	.188	7.69	4.44
Mayora, Hector	R-R	6-1	178	6-22-89	2	0	0.90	4	4	0	0	20	17	4	2	1	4	26	.230	.227	.231	11.70	1.80
2-team total (9 Cubs 1)					4	2	1.52	13	11	0	0	53	47	22	9	1	18	60	—	—	—	10.13	3.04
Mejia, Roneidy	R-R	6-3	180	5-14-90	2	1	2.61	18	0	0	4	31	33	14	9	1	14	24	.275	.167	.311	6.97	4.06
Mota, Pacheco	R-R	6-4	200	7-13-90	0	1	9.64	3	0	0	0	5	4	6	5	0	5	4	.250	.333	.231	7.71	9.64
2-team total (5 Cubs 1)					1	1	7.62	8	0	0	0	13	13	12	11	0	8	6	—	—	—	4.15	5.54
Navarro, Reinaldo	R-R	6-1	170	12-22-88	3	0	3.80	17	0	0	0	45	33	23	19	2	22	33	.202	.149	.224	6.60	4.40
Pena, Enyelberth	R-R	6-2	175	9-8-90	2	4	5.61	21	0	0	0	34	38	25	21	3	24	15	.288	.231	.312	4.01	6.42
Peralta, Starlin	R-R	6-4	180	11-11-90	4	4	6.92	15	8	0	0	40	50	36	31	1	24	33	.314	.342	.306	7.36	5.36
Pineda, George	R-R	6-3	175	7-19-88	1	3	3.60	21	3	0	6	35	30	17	14	1	16	41	.238	.235	.239	10.54	4.11
Reyes, Ramon	B-R	6-3	185	1-2-89	2	3	1.99	15	14	0	0	68	55	23	15	3	18	79	.217	.221	.215	10.46	2.38
Reyes, Roeldwin	R-R	6-1	160	5-14-89	0	0	0.00	1	0	0	0	1	1	0	0	0	1	1	.250	.000	.333	9.00	9.00
2-team total (10 Cubs 1)					0	1	2.70	11	0	0	1	20	20	13	6	1	9	15	—	—	—	6.75	4.05
Rosario, Braulio	R-R	6-3	175	9-21-89	1	0	4.73	7	0	0	0	13	12	8	7	0	3	6	.250	.143	.294	4.05	2.03
Sanchez, Julio	L-R	6-4	185	12-6-88	0	2	11.01	17	2	0	0	25	28	33	31	1	33	17	.304	.346	.288	6.04	11.72
Tineo, Jose	R-R	5-10	170	8-29-90	0	2	6.38	7	5	0	0	24	24	22	17	1	15	25	.253	.179	.284	9.38	5.63
2-team total (10 Cubs 1)					1	3	5.40	17	7	0	0	40	34	30	24	1	30	46	—	—	—	10.35	6.75
Veras, Yubrany	B-R	6-6	220	1-4-91	0	1	7.24	18	0	0	0	27	28	28	22	3	27	16	.272	.250	.280	5.27	8.89

Fielding

Catcher	PCT	G	PO	A	E	DP	PB
L. Liria	1.000	1	11	3	0	0	2
Y. Liria	.987	30	199	37	3	3	4
Parra	.978	4	40	4	1	0	3
Romero	.975	29	197	35	6	1	9
Vigay	.967	12	79	9	3	1	14

First Base	PCT	G	PO	A	E	DP
Guzman	.986	8	70	0	1	3
Medina	.975	13	109	7	3	17
Ramirez	.992	31	235	10	2	14
Robles	1.000	2	3	0	0	0
Romero	.973	22	176	7	5	18
Salazar	1.000	2	4	0	0	0
Vigay	1.000	3	21	0	0	0

Second Base	PCT	G	PO	A	E	DP
Bieneme	.956	45	98	117	10	26
Montecino	.939	12	25	37	4	6
Morales	1.000	2	3	7	0	1
Pestana	1.000	1	1	0	0	0
Salazar	.962	13	19	31	2	3

Third Base	PCT	G	PO	A	E	DP
Bieneme	1.000	2	0	1	0	0
Morales	1.000	4	2	14	0	0
Ramirez	.913	31	19	54	7	1
Salazar	.900	41	41	76	13	14

Shortstop	PCT	G	PO	A	E	DP
Bieneme	.893	6	9	16	3	1
Morales	.896	57	114	187	35	29

	PCT	G	PO	A	E	DP
Morelli	.857	1	3	3	1	0
Ramirez	—	1	0	0	0	0
Salazar	.945	12	20	32	3	9

Outfield	PCT	G	PO	A	E	DP
Andrades	.925	42	45	4	4	0
Guzman	—	2	0	0	0	0
Medina	.927	33	47	4	4	0
Montecino	1.000	1	2	0	0	0
Morales	1.000	1	6	0	0	0
Morelli	.946	43	44	9	3	1
Pestana	.973	54	98	11	3	1
Robles	.941	39	45	3	3	1
Romero	1.000	3	3	0	0	0

ORGANIZATION STATISTICS

Chicago White Sox

BY PHIL ROGERS

No team ever feels good about losing in the first round of the playoffs. That is no one's ultimate goal. But if ever a team had a right to feel proud of itself after a first-round exit, it was the 2008 White Sox.

They weren't picked to win the American League Central—few even picked the White Sox to finish near the top of the division—and they wound up winning a race with the Twins that extended all the way to a 163rd game. They were ousted in the AL Division Series by the Rays, but only after they had

won four elimination games.

Hanging on by a thread, Chicago beat the Indians in the final scheduled game and then the Tigers in the makeup of a rained-out, regular season game. Those victories got the White Sox into a one-game playoff against Minnesota, and John Danks pitched them to a 1-0 victory. They fell into an early hole at Tampa Bay but beat the Rays in Game Three before finally losing a game they had to win.

After going 72-90 in 2007, when they were off in all regards, the Sox delivered a major league-high 235 home runs and got good work from a rotation built around Mark Buehrle and youngsters Gavin Floyd and John Danks. They finished at 89-74 to raise Guillen's mark as their manager to 433-378. No one played a bigger role for the White Sox than left fielder Carlos Quentin. After being acquired from the Diamondbacks during the offseason for first baseman Chris Carter, he finished second in the AL with 36 home runs, losing his lead to Miguel Cabrera while missing the last three weeks with a self-inflicted injury. He broke his hand slapping his bat in frustration after missing a Cliff Lee pitch, and the Sox missed Quentin down the stretch. Jermaine Dye and Jim Thome each hit 34 homers.

The White Sox were also forced to improvise at third base, as Joe Crede's surgically repaired back allowed him to play only 97 games. But despite those losses the Sox took advantage of disappointing starts by Cleveland and Detroit to make the playoffs for the third time in nine seasons.

Along with Quentin, the White Sox got a big boost from Cuban newcomer Alexei Ramirez, who signed over the winter and earned a starting job at second base. He hit .290/.317/.475 with 21 homers and 77 RBIs despite early struggles that resulted in a .138 April average.

PLAYERS OF THE YEAR

MAJOR LEAGUE: JOHN DANKS, RHP

Talk about a steady hand. Danks finished 12-9, 3.32, with his ERA ranking fifth in the American League. He was at his best late in the year and fired the White Sox into the playoffs with eight scoreless innings against the Twins in the regular season finale.

MINOR LEAGUE: BRANDON ALLEN, 1B

A former Texas high schooler drafted in the fifth round in 2005, Allen had a breakthrough season. He batted .278/.367/.555 with 29 home runs, 32 doubles and 75 RBIs combined at high Class A Winston-Salem and Double-A Birmingham.

ORGANIZATION LEADERS

BATTING		*Minimum 250 at-bats
*AVG	Getz, Chris, Charlotte	.302
R	Allen, Brandon, Winston-Salem/Birmingham	87
H	Bourgeois, Jason, Charlotte	146
TB	Allen, Brandon, Winston-Salem/Birmingham	262
2B	Shelby, John, Winston-Salem	37
3B	Orlando, Paulo, Winston-Salem	12
HR	Eldred, Brad, Charlotte	35
RBI	Eldred, Brad, Charlotte	100
BB	Cook, David, Birmingham/Charlotte	93
SO	Eldred, Brad, Charlotte	144
SB	Shelby, John, Winston-Salem	33
*OBP	Cook, David, Birmingham/Charlotte	.410
*SLG	Allen, Brandon, Winston-Salem/Birmingham	.555

PITCHING		†Minimum 75 innings
W	Maxwell, Levi, Winston-Salem/Kannapolis	15
L	Haeger, Charlie, Charlotte	13
†ERA	Richard, Clayton, Birmingham/Charlotte	2.47
G	Torres, Joseph, Birmingham	59
GS	Cassel, Justin, Birmingham	28
SV	Link, Jon, Birmingham	35
IP	Haeger, Charlie, Charlotte	178
BB	Haeger, Charlie, Charlotte	77
SO	Luis, Santo, Winston-Salem/Kannapolis	135
†AVG	Richard, Clayton, Birmingham/Charlotte	.212

Lefthander Clayton Richard, who started the season at Double-A Birmingham, rose through the ranks to assume the fifth starter's spot after Jose Contreras was lost to a ruptured Achilles tendon. He had been invited to join Team USA for the Beijing Olympics after going 12-6, 2.47 in 20 starts between Birmingham and Triple-A Charlotte.

General Manager: Kenny Williams. **Farm Director:** Buddy Bell. **Scouting Director:** Doug Laumann.

Class	Team	League	W	L	PCT	Finish*	Manager	Affiliate Since
Majors	Chicago	American	89	74	.546	5th (14)	Ozzie Guillen	—
Triple-A	Charlotte Knights	International	63	78	.447	12th (14)	Marc Bombard	1999
Double-A	Birmingham Barons	Southern	74	63	.540	2nd (10)	Carlos Subero	1986
High A	Winston-Salem Warthogs	Carolina	71	68	.511	4th (8)	Tim Blackwell	1997
Low A	Kannapolis Intimidators	South Atlantic	67	68	.496	9th (16)	Chris Jones	2001
Rookie	Bristol White Sox	Appalachian	34	30	.531	4th (10)	Bobby Thigpen	1995
Rookie	Great Falls Voyagers	Pioneer	39	37	.513	^4th (8)	Chris Cron	2003
Overall 2008 Minor League Record			348	344	.503	14th		

* Finish in overall standings (No. of teams in league). ^League champion.

ORGANIZATION STATISTICS

CHICAGO WHITE SOX
AMERICAN LEAGUE

Batting	B-T	HT	WT	DOB	AVG	vLH	vRH	G	AB	R	H	2B	3B	HR	RBI	BB	HBP	SH	SF	SO	SB	CS	SLG	OBP
Anderson, Brian	R-R	6-2	220	3-11-82	.232	.225	.238	109	181	24	42	13	0	8	26	10	0	2	0	45	5	1	.436	.272
Bourgeois, Jason	R-R	5-9	190	1-4-82	.333	.000	.333	6	3	0	1	0	0	0	0	0	0	0	0	0	0	0	.667	.333
Cabrera, Orlando	R-R	5-9	185	11-2-74	.281	.273	.284	161	661	93	186	33	1	8	57	56	1	3	9	71	19	6	.371	.334
Crede, Joe	R-R	6-2	230	4-26-78	.248	.122	.289	97	335	41	83	18	1	17	55	30	4	0	4	45	0	3	.460	.314
Dye, Jermaine	R-R	6-5	245	1-28-74	.292	.285	.294	154	590	96	172	41	2	34	96	44	6	0	5	104	3	2	.541	.344
Fields, Josh	R-R	6-1	220	12-14-82	.156	.273	.095	14	32	3	5	1	0	0	2	3	0	0	0	17	0	0	.188	.229
Getz, Chris	L-R	6-0	185	8-30-83	.286	.500	.200	10	7	2	2	0	0	0	1	0	0	0	0	1	1	1	.286	.286
Griffey Jr., Ken	L-L	6-3	230	11-21-69	.260	.178	.302	41	131	16	34	10	0	3	18	17	1	0	1	25	0	0	.405	.347
Hall, Toby	R-R	6-2	255	10-21-75	.260	.377	.176	41	127	7	33	3	0	2	7	6	2	1	0	19	0	0	.331	.304
Konerko, Paul	R-R	6-2	220	3-5-76	.240	.236	.241	122	438	59	105	19	1	22	62	65	7	0	4	80	2	0	.438	.344
Owens, Jerry	L-L	6-3	195	2-16-81	.250	.333	.231	12	16	1	4	0	0	0	1	0	0	1	0	4	2	1	.250	.250
Ozuna, Pablo	R-R	5-11	200	8-25-74	.281	.391	.220	32	64	5	18	3	0	0	6	2	1	2	0	3	0	2	.328	.313
Phillips, Paul	R-R	5-11	205	4-15-77	.000	—	.000	4	2	0	0	0	0	0	0	0	0	0	0	1	0	0	.000	.000
Pierzynski, A.J.	L-R	6-4	240	12-30-76	.281	.286	.279	134	534	66	150	31	1	13	60	19	8	3	6	71	1	0	.416	.312
Quentin, Carlos	R-R	6-2	220	8-28-82	.288	.246	.303	130	480	96	138	26	1	36	100	66	20	0	3	80	7	3	.571	.394
Ramirez, Alexei	R-R	6-3	185	9-22-81	.290	.272	.281	136	480	65	139	22	2	21	77	18	3	4	4	61	13	9	.475	.317
Swisher, Nick	B-L	6-0	215	11-25-80	.219	.197	.227	153	497	86	109	21	1	24	69	82	4	1	4	135	3	3	.410	.332
Thome, Jim	R-R	6-3	255	8-27-70	.245	.233	.249	149	503	93	123	28	0	34	90	91	4	0	4	147	1	0	.503	.362
Uribe, Juan	R-R	6-0	225	3-22-79	.247	.254	.245	101	324	38	80	22	1	7	40	22	1	5	1	64	1	3	.386	.296
Wise, Dewayne	L-L	6-1	195	2-24-78	.248	.143	.261	57	129	20	32	4	2	6	18	8	1	3	2	32	9	0	.450	.293

Pitching	B-T	HT	WT	DOB	W	L	ERA	G	GS	CG	SV	IP	H	R	ER	HR	BB	SO	AVG	vLH	vRH	K/9	BB/9
Broadway, Lance	R-R	6-3	190	8-20-83	1	0	7.07	7	1	0	0	14	20	11	11	4	5	7	.328	.308	.343	4.50	3.21
Buehrle, Mark	L-L	6-2	230	3-23-79	15	12	3.79	34	34	1	0	219	240	106	92	22	52	140	.281	.293	.277	5.76	2.14
Carrasco, D.J.	R-R	6-1	215	4-12-77	1	0	3.96	31	0	0	0	39	30	17	17	2	14	30	.219	.186	.244	6.98	3.26
Contreras, Jose	R-R	6-4	255	12-6-71	7	6	4.54	20	20	1	0	121	130	64	61	12	35	70	.272	.286	.258	5.21	2.60
Danks, John	L-L	6-1	200	4-15-85	12	9	3.32	33	33	0	0	195	182	74	72	15	57	159	.246	.264	.240	7.34	2.63
Dotel, Octavio	R-R	6-0	215	11-25-73	4	4	3.76	72	0	0	1	67	52	34	28	12	29	92	.208	.240	.194	12.30	3.90
Floyd, Gavin	R-R	6-5	230	1-27-83	17	8	3.84	33	33	1	0	206	190	107	88	30	70	145	.241	.259	.226	6.32	3.05
Jenks, Bobby	R-R	6-3	275	3-14-81	3	1	2.63	57	0	0	30	62	51	18	18	3	17	38	.230	.219	.241	5.55	2.48
Linebrink, Scott	R-R	6-2	215	8-4-76	2	2	3.69	50	0	0	1	46	41	20	19	8	9	40	.234	.200	.263	7.77	1.75
Loaiza, Esteban	R-R	6-2	230	12-31-71	0	0	3.00	3	0	0	0	3	3	2	1	0	1	1	.231	.500	.000	3.00	0.00
Logan, Boone	R-L	6-5	210	8-13-84	2	3	5.95	55	0	0	0	42	57	31	28	7	14	42	.317	.291	.351	8.93	2.98
MacDougal, Mike	B-R	6-4	175	3-5-77	0	0	2.12	16	0	0	0	17	16	4	4	0	12	12	.250	.350	.205	6.35	6.35
Masset, Nick	R-R	6-4	235	5-17-82	1	0	4.63	32	1	0	1	45	55	26	23	4	21	32	.313	.279	.330	6.45	4.23
Ramirez, Horacio	L-L	6-1	220	11-24-79	0	3	7.62	17	0	0	0	13	24	11	11	0	8	2	.393	.500	.314	1.38	5.54
2-team total (15 Kansas City)					1	4	4.34	32	0	0	0	37	45	20	18	1	9	13	—	—	—	3.13	2.17
Richard, Clayton	L-L	6-5	240	9-12-83	2	5	6.04	13	8	0	0	48	61	37	32	5	13	29	.303	.274	.320	5.48	2.45
Russell, Adam	R-R	6-8	250	4-14-83	4	0	5.19	22	0	0	0	26	30	15	15	1	10	22	.291	.292	.291	7.62	3.46
Thornton, Matt	L-L	6-5	245	9-15-76	5	3	2.67	74	0	0	1	67	48	20	20	5	19	77	.196	.170	.218	10.29	2.54
Vazquez, Javier	R-R	6-2	210	7-25-76	12	16	4.67	33	33	1	0	208	214	113	108	25	61	200	.263	.259	.266	8.64	2.64
Wassermann, Ehren	B-R	6-0	185	12-6-80	1	2	7.78	24	0	0	0	20	27	19	17	0	14	9	.333	.364	.322	4.12	6.41

Fielding

Catcher	PCT	G	PO	A	E	DP	PB
Hall	.992	37	231	15	2	0	1
Phillips	1.000	4	7	0	0	0	0
Pierzynski	.991	131	913	54	9	8	5

First Base	PCT	G	PO	A	E	DP
Konerko	.994	116	1010	75	7	94
Swisher	.996	71	447	32	2	52

Second Base	PCT	G	PO	A	E	DP
Bourgeois	—	1	0	0	0	0
Getz	1.000	7	6	9	0	1
Ozuna	.955	10	10	11	1	0

	PCT	G	PO	A	E	DP
Ramirez	.981	121	237	327	11	71
Uribe	.996	52	104	124	1	34

Third Base	PCT	G	PO	A	E	DP
Crede	.930	97	57	207	20	22
Fields	.917	12	6	16	2	3
Ozuna	.902	16	8	29	4	4
Ramirez	1.000	1	0	1	0	0
Uribe	.960	57	41	125	7	10

Shortstop	PCT	G	PO	A	E	DP
Cabrera	.978	161	242	472	16	101
Ramirez	.958	16	8	15	1	4

	PCT	G	PO	A	E	DP
Uribe	1.000	4	2	2	0	0

Outfield	PCT	G	PO	A	E	DP
Anderson	1.000	98	105	0	0	0
Dye	.996	151	266	5	1	0
Griffey Jr.	1.000	33	63	1	0	1
Owens	1.000	10	7	0	0	0
Quentin	.971	130	228	5	7	2
Ramirez	.944	11	16	1	1	0
Swisher	.975	97	194	3	5	0
Wise	.974	46	72	2	2	0

INTERNATIONAL LEAGUE

Batting	B-T	HT	WT	DOB	AVG	vLH	vRH	G	AB	R	H	2B	3B	HR	RBI	BB	HBP	SH	SF	SO	SB	CS	SLG	OBP
Armstrong, Cole	L-R	6-3	220	8-24-83	.275	.118	.327	35	138	12	38	12	0	2	17	5	2	0	0	27	0	0	.406	.310
Blasi, Nick	R-R	5-10	200	9-23-81	.218	.235	.205	36	124	18	27	4	0	2	11	12	1	3	1	31	2	1	.298	.290
Bourgeois, Jason	R-R	5-9	190	1-4-82	.286	.308	.277	127	510	83	146	23	5	9	48	33	5	9	2	65	30	11	.404	.335
Castillo, Javier	R-R	6-2	220	8-29-83	.287	.344	.261	28	101	12	29	7	1	0	18	8	0	0	4	23	1	2	.376	.327
Colina, Javier	R-R	6-1	200	2-15-79	.380	.409	.368	26	79	12	30	4	1	3	8	4	1	1	2	15	0	0	.570	.407
Collaro, Tom	R-R	6-4	216	4-4-83	.242	.152	.333	19	66	12	16	2	0	5	9	8	0	0	0	24	0	0	.500	.324
Cook, David	R-R	5-11	205	7-21-81	.259	.275	.252	65	228	32	59	11	2	7	26	31	2	0	1	65	6	0	.417	.351
Cortez, Fernando	L-R	6-1	190	8-10-81	.262	.231	.273	104	355	27	93	12	2	4	35	16	2	6	2	33	10	5	.341	.296
Crede, Joe	R-R	6-2	230	4-26-78	.125	—	.125	5	16	0	2	0	0	0	0	0	0	0	0	3	0	0	.125	.125
DaVanon, Jeff	B-R	6-0	200	12-8-73	.079	.083	.077	11	38	4	3	0	0	1	3	6	0	0	1	12	1	0	.158	.200
Dawkins, Gookie	R-R	6-0		5-12-79	.093	.050	.130	12	43	0	4	2	0	0	2	2	0	0	0	17	1	0	.140	.133
2-team total (6 Lehigh Valley)					.123	—		18	57	1	7	4	0	0	4	4	0	0	0	23	2	0	.193	.180
Eldred, Brad	R-R	6-5	275	7-12-80	.244	.227	.251	114	427	62	104	22	1	35	100	28	11	0	3	144	3	3	.546	.305
Fields, Josh	R-R	6-1	220	12-14-82	.246	.266	.239	75	276	41	68	15	3	10	35	37	3	1	1	98	8	2	.431	.341
Getz, Chris	L-R	6-0	185	8-30-83	.302	.319	.293	111	404	60	122	24	1	11	52	41	3	4	5	53	11	4	.448	.366
Guillen, Oney	R-R	5-9	155	1-25-86	.333	—	.333	1	3	1	1	1	0	0	0	0	0	0	0	1	0	0	.667	.333
Hall, Noah	R-R	5-11	205	6-9-77	.292	.409	.192	15	48	4	14	1	0	1	6	8	0	0	0	6	1	1	.375	.393
Huffman, Royce	R-R	6-0	205	1-11-77	.259	.265	.256	106	370	46	96	26	0	10	43	40	7	0	4	92	4	4	.411	.340
Konerko, Paul	R-R	6-2	220	3-5-76	.455	.000	.455	4	11	3	5	2	0	0	3	6	0	0	1	1	0	0	.636	.611
Liefer, Jeff	L-R	6-4	220	8-17-74	.224	.292	.209	40	134	15	30	9	0	3	16	19	0	0	1	39	1	0	.358	.318
Lucy, Donny	R-R	6-2	205	8-8-82	.279	.273	.281	12	43	6	12	2	0	2	6	2	1	0	0	12	1	0	.465	.326
Owens, Jerry	L-L	6-3	195	2-16-81	.276	.317	.255	89	351	39	97	11	0	1	21	38	2	5	5	56	30	13	.316	.346
Phillips, Paul	R-R	5-11	205	4-15-77	.269	.295	.255	73	253	22	68	15	0	2	17	17	1	3	0	32	0	0	.352	.317
Price, Jared	R-R	6-1	230	3-18-82	.099	.120	.087	22	71	4	7	3	0	1	4	0	0	0	0	33	0	0	.183	.147
Richar, Danny	L-R	6-1	195	6-9-83	.262	.253	.268	62	248	35	65	12	1	9	39	20	2	0	1	45	11	2	.427	.321
2-team total (29 Louisville)					.260	—	—	91	362	51	94	21	3	11	55	31	3	1	3	71	14	5	.425	.321
Rouse, Mike	L-R	6-0	190	4-25-80	.234	.143	.268	24	77	12	18	1	0	3	10	3	9	5	1	18	2	0	.364	.302
2-team total (89 Lehigh Valley)					.247	—	—	113	393	42	97	18	0	5	38	19	5	12	2	85	7	3	.331	.289
Smith, Ryan	R-R	5-11	220	6-20-79	.000	.000	.000	2	5	1	0	0	0	0	0	0	0	1	0	2	0	0	.000	.167
Tyner, Jason	L-L	6-1	180	4-23-77	.290	.200	.305	21	69	8	20	3	0	0	4	8	1	1	0	6	3	1	.333	.372
2-team total (76 Buffalo)					.248	—	—	97	307	39	76	12	0	1	18	36	4	10	1	26	11	1	.296	.333
Uribe, Juan	R-R	6-0	225	3-22-79	.182	.000	.200	3	11	0	2	0	0	0	2	0	0	0	0	3	0	0	.182	.182
Valido, Robert	R-R	6-2	210	5-16-85	.042	.000	.045	7	24	0	1	1	0	0	0	2	0	0	1	11	0	0	.083	.040
Wise, Dewayne	L-L	6-1	195	2-24-78	.319	.298	.328	55	191	39	61	14	3	9	23	22	5	3	1	32	15	7	.565	.402

Pitching	B-T	HT	WT	DOB	W	L	ERA	G	GS	CG	SV	IP	H	R	ER	HR	BB	SO	AVG	vLH	vRH	K/9	BB/9
Anderson, Matt	R-R	6-4	200	8-17-76	0	0	5.60	15	0	0	0	18	16	11	11	2	8	15	.235	.257	.212	7.64	4.08
Babula, Shaun	B-L	5-11	183	5-21-77	0	0	7.71	3	0	0	0	5	6	4	4	1	4	2	.316	.300	.333	3.86	7.71
Bell, Rob	R-R	6-3	205	1-17-77	1	5	8.03	12	6	0	0	37	52	34	33	5	10	26	.347	.321	.375	6.32	2.43
Broadway, Lance	R-R	6-3	205	8-20-83	11	7	4.66	24	23	1	0	145	166	87	75	24	44	101	.292	.317	.262	6.27	2.73
Carrasco, D.J.	R-R	6-1	215	4-12-77	2	1	2.88	8	1	0	1	25	24	9	8	0	7	24	.258	.392	.095	8.64	2.52
Childers, Jason	R-R	6-0	160	1-13-75	4	2	1.22	50	0	0	17	59	34	10	8	2	13	61	.167	.177	.156	9.31	1.98
Contreras, Jose	R-R	6-4	255	12-6-71	0	0	5.40	1	1	0	0	5	4	3	3	0	3	4	.250	.250	—	7.20	5.40
Day, Dewon	R-R	6-4	210	9-29-80	0	3	4.56	21	0	0	0	24	29	14	12	3	6	25	.290	.356	.236	9.51	2.28
Egbert, Jack	L-R	6-3	220	5-12-83	4	12	4.65	24	22	1	0	130	133	80	67	15	41	117	.263	.275	.249	8.12	2.85
German, Franklyn	R-R	6-7	260	1-20-80	1	1	4.26	5	0	0	0	6	6	7	3	1	6	9	.231	.308	.154	12.79	8.53
2-team total (24 Indianapolis)					2	2	3.71	29	0	0	0	34	30	19	14	4	23	31	—	—	—	8.21	6.09
Haeger, Charlie	R-R	6-1	220	9-19-83	10	13	4.45	28	25	3	0	178	167	96	88	13	77	117	.251	.267	.233	5.92	3.89
King, Ray	L-L	6-0	250	1-15-74	0	0	3.86	4	0	0	0	5	6	2	2	1	1	5	.316	.167	.571	9.64	1.93
Loaiza, Esteban	R-R	6-2	230	12-31-71	0	2	6.55	5	5	0	0	11	18	9	8	2	0	5	.375	.471	.143	4.09	0.00
Logan, Boone	R-L	6-5	210	8-13-84	0	1	6.00	5	0	0	0	9	10	8	6	2	6	7	.294	.364	.261	7.00	6.00
MacDougal, Mike	B-R	6-4	175	3-5-77	4	3	3.83	38	2	0	4	49	48	22	21	2	30	65	.250	.279	.216	11.86	5.47
Ohka, Tomo	B-R	6-1	200	3-18-76	5	11	4.18	28	20	1	0	136	146	71	63	23	35	112	.274	.284	.263	7.43	2.32
2-team total (7 Buffalo)					0	8	8.49	21	0	0	2	30	48	28	28	7	17	34	—	—	—	10.31	5.16
Richard, Clayton	L-L	6-5	240	9-12-83	6	6	2.45	7	7	1	0	44	33	12	12	3	4	33	.204	.250	.176	6.75	0.82
Rodriguez, Derek	R-R	6-1	195	5-17-83	0	1	3.19	20	1	0	1	37	24	16	13	5	15	44	.179	.139	.226	10.80	3.68
Russell, Adam	R-R	6-8	250	4-14-83	3	2	2.89	25	0	0	0	37	28	13	12	3	19	28	.203	.211	.194	6.75	4.58
Sauerbeck, Scott	R-L	6-3	200	11-9-71	1	2	4.37	31	0	0	0	23	15	16	11	1	26	26	.179	.224	.114	10.32	10.32
2-team total (4 Louisville)					1	3	5.06	35	0	0	0	27	21	20	15	2	30	31	—	—	—	10.46	10.13
Torres, Carlos	R-R	6-2	195	10-22-82	0	0	4.58	8	1	0	0	20	23	10	10	2	11	19	.295	.250	.342	8.69	5.03
Wassermann, Ehren	B-R	6-0	185	12-6-80	0	0	1.15	32	0	0	7	39	29	6	5	1	13	42	.212	.183	.242	9.69	3.00
Whisler, Wes	L-L	6-5	240	4-7-83	12	10	3.81	27	27	1	0	156	175	86	66	12	45	71	.281	.318	.261	4.10	2.60
Winkelsas, Joe	R-R	6-3	188	9-14-73	0	0	3.60	3	0	0	0	5	3	2	2	1	2	5	.167	.250	.100	9.00	3.60

Fielding

Catcher	PCT	G	PO	A	E	DP	PB
Armstrong	.997	35	283	15	1	1	8
Lucy	1.000	12	80	6	0	0	4
Phillips	.991	73	519	52	5	3	15
Price	.992	21	123	9	1	1	6
Smith	1.000	2	7	1	0	1	2

First Base	PCT	G	PO	A	E	DP
Colina	1.000	1	5	0	0	2
Cortez	1.000	1	1	0	0	0
Eldred	.986	81	679	45	10	51
Huffman	.996	50	476	23	2	36
Konerko	1.000	3	33	3	0	1
Liefer	1.000	8	69	5	0	6
Price	1.000	1	5	0	0	0

ORGANIZATION STATISTICS

Second Base	PCT	G	PO	A	E	DP
Bourgeois	.976	19	31	50	2	9
Colina	1.000	6	6	10	0	2
Cortez	.975	8	15	24	1	5
Getz	.990	61	108	201	3	41
Guillen	1.000	1	0	4	0	0
Richar	.954	47	70	117	9	20
Uribe	.800	2	1	3	1	0

Third Base	PCT	G	PO	A	E	DP
Castillo	.929	26	13	65	6	3
Colina	.970	17	11	21	1	0
Cortez	.950	9	6	13	1	0
Crede	.933	5	2	12	1	2

	PCT	G	PO	A	E	DP
Dawkins	.900	6	1	8	1	0
Fields	.933	59	42	112	11	9
Getz	.929	6	0	13	1	1
Huffman	.837	21	10	26	7	1

Shortstop	PCT	G	PO	A	E	DP
Colina	—	1	0	0	0	0
Cortez	.957	73	127	206	15	48
Dawkins	.955	6	5	16	1	1
Getz	.950	27	34	61	5	9
Richar	.923	8	11	13	2	5
Rouse	.981	23	32	71	2	16
Uribe	1.000	1	4	3	0	0
Valido	.973	7	9	27	1	4

Outfield	PCT	G	PO	A	E	DP
Blasi	.967	34	56	2	2	0
Bourgeois	.979	106	184	7	4	4
Collaro	.938	7	15	0	1	0
Cook	.949	64	92	2	5	0
Cortez	.963	17	26	0	1	0
DaVanon	1.000	11	16	0	0	0
Eldred	.962	14	23	2	1	1
Getz	.931	15	27	0	2	0
Hall	1.000	5	7	0	0	0
Owens	1.000	88	200	4	0	0
Tyner	1.000	21	27	1	0	1
Wise	1.000	51	95	5	0	0

BIRMINGHAM BARONS   DOUBLE-A

SOUTHERN LEAGUE

Batting	B-T	HT	WT	DOB	AVG	vLH	vRH	G	AB	R	H	2B	3B	HR	RBI	BB	HBP	SH	SF	SO	SB	CS	SLG	OBP
Allen, Brandon	L-R	6-2	235	2-12-86	.275	.211	.313	41	153	30	42	6	2	14	31	19	1	0	0	41	3	1	.614	.358
Armstrong, Cole	L-R	6-3	220	8-24-83	.252	.241	.256	64	218	27	55	17	0	6	31	10	3	2	1	31	0	1	.413	.293
Castillo, Javier	R-R	6-2	220	8-29-83	.289	.331	.268	102	388	60	112	20	9	8	58	42	0	0	5	85	3	0	.448	.354
Colina, Javier	R-R	6-1	200	2-15-79	.216	.346	.171	27	102	11	22	5	1	3	14	7	1	0	0	14	2	0	.373	.273
Collaro, Tom	R-R	6-4	216	4-4-83	.235	.258	.222	23	85	8	20	7	0	1	12	6	1	0	0	21	0	0	.353	.293
2-team total (38 Chattanooga)					.202	—	—	61	173	18	35	11	1	3	27	14	2	0	6	55	0	0	.329	.262
Cook, David	R-R	5-11	205	7-21-81	.313	.279	.327	63	208	44	65	15	2	12	30	62	1	0	3	47	8	7	.577	.467
Cruz, Lee	R-R	6-2	205	6-13-83	.274	.259	.281	54	197	25	54	13	1	10	27	12	4	1	1	40	0	3	.503	.327
Gartrell, Stefan	R-R	6-3	230	1-14-84	.254	.323	.223	122	409	54	104	22	2	14	52	45	6	2	4	106	7	1	.421	.334
Hall, Noah	R-R	5-11	205	6-9-77	.226	.147	.280	26	84	9	19	6	0	0	12	14	2	2	0	5	1	1	.298	.350
2-team total (15 West Tenn)					.252	—	—	41	127	15	32	11	0	1	19	21	3	4	0	15	3	2	.362	.371
Hollis, Eric	R-R	6-3	220	9-26-82	.213	.129	.254	31	94	13	20	1	0	0	5	3	0	0	0	16	0	2	.223	.237
Hudson, Robert	R-R	6-0	170	8-31-83	.250	.260	.246	93	320	28	80	18	0	1	28	18	1	9	0	55	10	6	.316	.292
Lang, C.J.	R-R	5-8	170	4-12-84	.241	.370	.173	28	79	17	19	4	0	1	10	13	2	1	2	7	1	1	.329	.354
Mercedes, Victor	B-R	5-11	190	4-15-79	.272	.213	.296	104	416	57	113	29	3	12	59	16	3	7	2	75	11	10	.442	.302
Nanita, Ricardo	L-L	6-0	205	6-12-81	.286	.321	.270	111	412	52	118	22	2	9	51	37	5	8	2	56	14	9	.415	.351
Negron, Miguel	L-L	6-1	190	8-22-82	.299	.324	.287	126	479	72	143	17	5	7	57	63	2	5	2	60	25	16	.399	.381
Persichina, Joe	L-R	6-0	190	12-14-84	.286	.333	.267	7	21	2	6	2	0	0	2	0	0	0	0	4	0	0	.381	.286
Price, Jared	R-R	6-1	230	3-18-82	.196	.222	.184	37	112	11	22	0	0	5	7	12	4	2	0	40	0	0	.330	.297
Ricks, Adam	B-R	5-10	190	9-24-82	.000	—	.000	1	0	0	0	0	0	0	0	0	0	0	0	0	0	0	.000	.000
San Pedro, Erick	R-R	6-0	205	10-5-83	.198	.174	.207	28	81	7	16	4	0	0	5	6	0	1	0	31	0	0	.247	.253
Schnurstein, Micah	R-R	6-1	220	7-18-84	.218	.253	.203	86	293	38	64	11	1	4	20	20	5	1	3	53	8	1	.304	.277
Thon, Freddie	L-L	6-0	215	4-9-84	.107	.143	.095	8	28	1	3	2	0	0	2	2	0	0	0	2	0	0	.179	.167
Valido, Robert	R-R	6-2	210	5-16-85	.222	.230	.219	112	383	36	85	9	6	3	27	20	4	5	1	80	18	10	.300	.267

Pitching	B-T	HT	WT	DOB	W	L	ERA	G	GS	CG	SV	IP	H	R	ER	HR	BB	SO	AVG	vLH	vRH	K/9	BB/9
Babula, Shaun	B-L	5-11	183	5-21-77	2	0	5.29	22	0	0	0	34	40	22	20	2	13	24	.292	.189	.330	6.35	3.44
Cassel, Justin	R-R	6-2	215	9-25-84	10	4	3.11	28	28	0	0	165	171	76	57	7	57	104	.271	.268	.273	5.67	3.11
Day, Dewon	R-R	6-4	210	9-29-80	1	1	6.61	14	13	0	0	48	51	37	35	3	28	35	.277	.301	.257	6.61	5.29
Egbert, Jack	L-R	6-3	220	5-12-83	0	0	2.25	1	1	0	0	4	5	1	1	0	1	4	.313	.250	.375	9.00	2.25
Harrell, Lucas	R-R	6-2	205	6-3-85	3	3	3.46	11	10	0	0	55	56	30	21	3	19	34	.272	.271	.273	5.60	3.13
Hernandez, Fernando	R-R	5-11	190	7-31-84	6	5	4.66	41	0	0	0	58	60	32	30	2	29	47	.274	.320	.238	7.29	4.50
Jenks, Bobby	R-R	6-3	275	3-14-81	0	0	0.00	1	1	0	0	1	0	0	0	0	0	3	.000	.000	.000	27.00	0.00
Link, Jon	R-R	6-1	210	3-23-84	5	4	3.02	56	0	0	35	57	48	21	19	3	27	66	.223	.208	.235	10.48	4.29
Loaiza, Esteban	R-R	6-2	230	12-31-71	0	0	0.00	3	1	0	0	3	1	0	0	0	0	3	.150	.133	.200	4.50	1.50
Lujan, John	R-R	6-1	210	5-10-84	3	2	3.43	50	0	0	4	76	64	29	29	6	39	51	.231	.255	.216	6.04	4.62
McCulloch, Kyle	R-R	6-3	190	3-20-85	8	11	4.65	28	27	0	0	157	188	91	81	9	60	85	.306	.347	.273	4.88	3.45
O'Malley, Ryan	R-L	6-1	205	4-9-80	4	3	5.32	20	6	0	0	64	100	43	38	3	16	46	.365	.306	.386	6.44	2.24
Omogrosso, Brian	R-R	6-4	230	4-26-84	2	3	3.69	17	5	0	1	39	32	19	16	2	25	26	.230	.262	.203	6.00	5.77
Poreda, Aaron	L-L	6-6	240	10-1-86	3	4	2.98	15	15	1	0	88	81	34	29	5	22	72	.249	.280	.240	7.39	2.26
Richard, Clayton	L-L	6-5	240	9-12-83	6	6	2.47	13	13	1	0	84	66	29	23	2	16	53	.217	.213	.219	5.70	1.72
Rodriguez, Derek	R-R	6-1	195	5-17-83	5	1	3.38	29	0	0	1	43	30	17	16	2	18	44	.203	.185	.217	9.28	3.80
Rote, Ryan	R-R	6-4	235	8-8-82	1	1	4.39	23	0	0	0	27	25	13	13	3	20	25	.263	.300	.236	8.44	6.75
Santeliz, Clevelan	R-R	6-0	190	9-1-86	0	1	4.41	10	0	0	0	16	14	8	8	2	8	6	.246	.200	.281	3.31	4.41
Texeira, Kanekoa	R-R	6-0	210	2-6-86	3	2	2.01	15	0	0	1	22	18	5	5	2	7	24	.225	.189	.256	9.67	2.82
Torres, Carlos	R-R	6-2	195	10-22-82	9	5	3.20	21	17	0	0	101	86	40	36	4	29	93	.234	.248	.222	8.26	2.58
Torres, Joe	L-L	6-2	195	9-3-82	3	1	2.68	59	0	0	0	50	29	15	15	2	31	58	.164	.189	.146	10.37	5.54
Winkelsas, Joe	R-R	6-3	188	9-14-73	0	1	10.80	4	0	0	1	5	7	6	6	0	3	3	.333	.111	.500	5.40	5.40
Zaleski, Matthew	R-R	6-1	190	12-2-81	0	0	0.00	5	0	0	0	9	7	1	0	0	1	3	.219	.143	.278	3.12	1.04

Fielding

Catcher	PCT	G	PO	A	E	DP	PB
Armstrong	.990	59	370	29	4	2	1
Hollis	.995	30	187	19	1	3	3
Price	.996	36	230	21	1	4	8
Ricks	1.000	1	1	1	0	0	0
San Pedro	.988	25	148	16	2	1	5

First Base	PCT	G	PO	A	E	DP
Allen	.994	39	337	24	2	44
Castillo	1.000	9	84	5	0	7
Colina	1.000	7	58	2	0	9
Hollis	1.000	1	2	0	0	0
Nanita	1.000	2	0	1	0	0
Schnurstein	.992	85	709	68	6	87
Thon	.960	2	24	0	1	2

Second Base	PCT	G	PO	A	E	DP
Hudson	.989	54	117	161	3	42
Lang	1.000	5	11	23	0	4

Mercedes	.970	79	170 256	13	66
Persichina	1.000	4	7 13	0	5

Third Base	PCT	G	PO	A	E	DP
Castillo	.950	87	60	151	11	20
Colina	.976	16	7	34	1	4
Hudson	.913	12	4	17	2	3
Lang	.917	11	6	16	2	2
Mercedes	.929	16	10	29	3	3
Persichina	1.000	3	3	8	0	1

Schnurstein	—	2	0	0	0	0

Shortstop	PCT	G	PO	A	E	DP
Hudson	.983	22	38	79	2	18
Lang	1.000	4	2	2	0	0
Mercedes	.950	5	5	14	1	2
Valido	.950	111	195	316	27	82

Outfield	PCT	G	PO	A	E	DP
Cook	.973	57	108	2	3	2

Cruz	1.000	30	30	0	0	0
Gartrell	.947	97	170	7	10	3
Hall	1.000	7	9	0	0	0
Hudson	.900	9	8	1	1	0
Lang	1.000	4	5	0	0	0
Nanita	.984	98	180	9	3	3
Negron	.984	125	233	7	4	1

WINSTON-SALEM WARTHOGS   HIGH CLASS A
CAROLINA LEAGUE

Batting	B-T	HT	WT	DOB	AVG	vLH	vRH	G	AB	R	H	2B	3B	HR	RBI	BB	HBP	SH	SF	SO	SB	CS	SLG	OBP
Allen, Brandon	L-R	6-2	235	2-12-86	.279	.264	.284	89	319	57	89	26	4	15	44	41	6	0	0	83	14	3	.527	.372
Bonvechio, Brett	L-R	6-1	190	11-13-82	.241	.206	.252	40	141	16	34	12	0	2	20	12	2	0	3	35	1	0	.369	.304
Colina, Javier	R-R	6-1	200	2-15-79	.306	.339	.293	59	216	34	66	22	1	3	22	22	2	0	1	22	10	5	.458	.373
Cruz, Lee	R-R	6-2	205	6-13-83	.196	.234	.184	56	194	16	38	16	0	2	22	12	2	2	2	49	1	1	.309	.248
Fields, Josh	R-R	6-1	220	12-14-82	.333	.333	.333	4	9	1	3	1	0	1	5	0	0	0	2	0	1	.444	.571
Gaines, Ronnie	R-R	6-1	185	9-8-83	.295	.318	.282	18	61	12	18	8	2	0	5	5	2	1	1	15	3	1	.492	.362
Gomes, Anderson	R-R	6-1	215	3-12-85	.196	.105	.230	42	138	10	27	7	0	4	14	17	1	1	0	39	4	0	.333	.288
Harris, Estee	R-R	6-0	180	1-8-85	.282	.214	.302	52	181	27	51	13	2	6	26	15	2	2	0	63	8	4	.475	.343
Hernandez, Francisco	B-R	5-10	180	2-4-86	.245	.289	.224	79	241	28	59	15	0	6	31	32	3	10	2	33	2	2	.382	.338
Killian, Billy	L-R	6-0	210	6-12-86	.206	.200	.207	47	131	13	27	7	0	0	6	1	3	4	1	23	3	2	.260	.228
Lang, C.J.	R-R	5-8	170	4-12-84	.255	.246	.259	65	204	25	52	14	1	2	19	23	3	3	1	28	9	3	.363	.338
Miranda, Sergio	B-R	5-9	180	3-5-87	.209	.184	.222	39	110	11	23	5	2	0	12	7	0	1	3	15	5	5	.291	.250
Mollenhauer, Dale	L-R	5-10	170	6-26-86	.262	.120	.295	37	130	14	34	5	3	0	11	5	0	6	1	21	4	1	.346	.287
Orlando, Paulo	R-R	6-3	185	11-1-85	.262	.287	.252	112	451	73	118	15	12	9	42	22	9	5	2	97	28	9	.408	.308
2-team total (18 Wilmington)					.261	—	—	130	522	84	136	20	14	12	51	30	9	7	3	116	29	13	.421	.310
Paiml, Greg	R-R	6-0	185	8-3-84	.271	.269	.271	92	329	41	89	19	5	3	28	19	0	5	0	88	6	3	.386	.310
Persichina, Joe	R-R	6-0	190	12-14-84	.275	.282	.273	52	167	18	46	5	3	1	22	18	2	2	2	25	10	5	.359	.349
Retherford, C.J.	R-R	5-10	190	8-14-85	.295	.382	.263	130	461	66	136	28	1	16	71	37	6	7	8	78	11	6	.464	.350
Ricks, Adam	B-R	5-10	190	9-24-82	.217	.216	.217	52	120	15	26	7	0	1	15	30	2	5	0	26	4	1	.300	.382
Sanchez, Salvador	S-6	220	9-13-85	.241	.286	.224	115	427	54	103	22	4	5	58	24	3	4	3	99	24	15	.347	.284
Shelby, John	R-R	5-10	185	8-6-85	.295	.293	.296	114	447	81	132	37	7	15	80	22	4	5	4	98	33	5	.510	.331
Thon, Freddie	L-L	6-2	215	4-9-84	.264	.231	.275	27	106	13	28	6	0	3	15	1	2	0	0	10	1	4	.406	.284

Pitching	B-T	HT	WT	DOB	W	L	ERA	G	GS	CG	SV	IP	H	R	ER	HR	BB	SO	AVG	vLH	vRH	K/9	BB/9
Albritton, Dan	R-R	6-0	200	11-10-84	0	0	0.00	1	0	0	0	4	0	0	0	0	1	6	.000	.000	.000	13.50	2.25
Brooks, Richard	R-R	6-3	185	7-18-84	4	3	3.40	45	2	0	0	85	85	37	32	4	29	94	.266	.271	.265	9.99	3.08
Carter, Anthony	L-R	6-3	180	4-4-86	6	5	4.90	17	16	0	0	83	91	49	45	11	30	41	.278	.285	.274	4.46	3.27
Chirino, Israel	L-L	6-1	200	11-8-83	1	1	13.50	13	0	0	1	19	29	31	28	2	20	17	.377	.450	.351	8.20	9.64
Davis, Matt	R-R	6-2	205	11-19-81	4	2	5.57	38	1	0	4	63	63	43	39	7	24	47	.257	.258	.257	6.71	3.43
Dubee, Michael	R-R	6-3	185	1-12-86	5	7	4.37	30	13	1	1	103	103	57	50	12	37	90	.263	.287	.247	7.86	3.23
Ely, John	R-R	6-1	200	5-17-86	10	12	4.71	27	27	0	0	145	142	83	76	18	46	134	.259	.262	.257	8.30	2.85
Jenks, Bobby	R-R	6-3	275	3-14-81	0	0	9.00	1	1	0	0	1	3	1	1	0	0	0	.600	.750	.000	0.00	0.00
Jones, Nathan	R-R	6-5	190	1-28-86	0	0	3.38	2	0	0	0	3	1	1	1	0	2	1	.111	.333	.000	3.38	6.75
Long, Matthew	R-R	6-5	225	2-23-84	7	11	4.47	28	21	1	0	129	136	80	64	9	40	116	.270	.310	.242	8.09	2.79
Luis, Santo	R-R	6-4	200	1-27-84	0	0	31.50	1	0	0	0	2	10	9	7	1	1	2	.625	.667	.571	9.00	4.50
Mabee, Henry	R-R	6-4	230	7-10-85	3	1	4.50	27	0	0	3	40	39	22	20	1	12	34	.253	.309	.222	7.65	2.70
Maxwell, Levi	R-R	6-2	200	12-22-84	0	1	6.32	4	3	0	0	16	17	12	11	1	11	10	.274	.438	.217	5.74	6.32
Perez, Wander	L-L	6-3	160	1-5-85	1	0	2.70	21	0	0	0	17	12	5	5	1	11	11	.194	.219	.167	5.94	5.94
Poreda, Aaron	L-L	6-6	240	10-1-86	5	5	3.31	12	12	1	0	73	67	31	27	1	18	46	.238	.154	.257	5.65	2.21
Rasner, Jacob	R-R	6-4	210	12-4-86	5	7	3.29	29	18	0	0	107	113	49	39	2	48	88	.274	.253	.288	7.43	4.05
Rodriguez, Noe	L-L	6-0	170	8-12-84	0	0	7.50	10	0	0	0	12	14	10	10	1	6	11	.304	.333	.290	8.25	4.50
Rote, Ryan	R-R	6-4	235	8-8-82	4	2	3.64	25	0	0	4	30	28	15	12	1	18	25	.259	.262	.258	7.58	5.46
Santeliz, Clevelan	R-R	6-0	190	9-5-86	3	6	4.90	15	15	0	0	68	55	47	37	8	48	60	.224	.206	.239	7.94	6.35
Spurgeon, Steven	R-R	6-4	230	8-22-83	3	2	5.58	29	1	0	0	60	69	48	37	9	27	47	.284	.348	.247	7.09	4.07
Texeira, Kanekoa	R-R	6-0	210	2-6-86	3	1	0.93	36	0	0	20	39	28	10	4	0	14	36	.194	.231	.174	8.38	3.26
Zaleski, Matthew	R-R	6-1	190	12-2-81	7	2	2.93	35	9	0	6	101	90	39	33	10	36	72	.237	.235	.238	6.39	3.20

Fielding

Catcher	PCT	G	PO	A	E	DP	PB
Hernandez	.993	74	514	66	4	5	5
Killian	.990	42	267	34	3	3	12
Ricks	.992	38	212	32	2	2	12

First Base	PCT	G	PO	A	E	DP
Allen	.985	85	761	76	13	66
Bonvechio	.973	15	97	12	3	12
Colina	1.000	9	78	4	0	2
Hernandez	1.000	1	2	0	0	0
Persichina	.978	13	84	7	2	4
Ricks	1.000	1	1	1	0	0
Thon	.987	25	221	10	3	16

Second Base	PCT	G	PO	A	E	DP
Colina	.983	40	69	101	3	20
Lang	.975	43	82	117	5	21
Miranda	1.000	7	6	14	0	2
Mollenhauer	.969	36	69	87	5	17
Paiml	1.000	1	1	0	0	0
Persichina	.972	24	34	71	3	7
Retherford	1.000	2	1	6	0	1
Ricks	—	1	0	0	0	0

Third Base	PCT	G	PO	A	E	DP
Bonvechio	.857	5	1	5	1	0
Colina	.933	9	6	8	1	3

Fields	1.000	3	0	5	0	1
Miranda	1.000	3	1	1	0	0
Persichina	.889	6	4	12	2	0
Retherford	.933	122	76	256	24	21
Ricks	—	1	0	0	0	0

Shortstop	PCT	G	PO	A	E	DP
Lang	.936	23	43	59	7	10
Miranda	.973	28	34	75	3	12
Paiml	.947	90	131	263	22	49
Persichina	.909	2	3	7	1	1
Ricks	—	1	0	0	0	0

Outfield	PCT	G	PO	A	E	DP
Cruz	.946	44	52	1	3	0
Gaines	1.000	16	26	0	0	0
Gomes	.926	32	47	3	4	0
Harris	.952	31	40	0	2	0
Orlando	.978	109	215	7	5	2
Persichina	1.000	4	1	0	0	0
Ricks	1.000	1	1	0	0	0
Sanchez	.967	104	193	10	7	7
Shelby	.979	89	134	8	3	0

KANNAPOLIS INTIMIDATORS   LOW CLASS A

SOUTH ATLANTIC LEAGUE

Batting	B-T	HT	WT	DOB	AVG	vLH	vRH	G	AB	R	H	2B	3B	HR	RBI	BB	HBP	SH	SF	SO	SB	CS	SLG	OBP
Beckham, Gordon	R-R	6-0	185	9-16-86	.310	.222	.350	14	58	11	18	2	0	3	8	5	0	0	0	7	0	1	.500	.365
Castillo, Jorge	L-R	6-2	225	9-26-86	.394	.333	.404	16	66	6	26	4	0	0	14	2	1	0	2	6	0	0	.455	.408
Cruz, Lee	R-R	6-2	205	6-13-83	.050	.143	.000	5	20	1	1	1	0	0	3	1	0	0	0	4	1	0	.100	.095
Curtis, John	L-R	6-2	210	11-22-84	.210	.077	.239	67	219	15	46	9	1	3	19	23	6	3	1	72	2	1	.301	.301
Damas, Nick	R-R	6-2	185	4-11-85	.118	.000	.143	6	17	1	2	0	0	1	2	0	0	0	0	5	0	0	.294	.118
Danks, Jordan	L-R	6-5	205	8-7-86	.325	.308	.333	10	40	10	13	4	1	2	7	4	1	0	0	14	1	0	.625	.400
Escobar, Eduardo	B-R	5-10	150	1-5-89	.267	.200	.292	60	243	37	65	6	1	0	22	13	0	8	2	65	4	3	.300	.302
Estill, Lyndon	R-R	6-3	215	3-29-87	.197	.160	.216	21	76	9	15	4	0	0	9	7	0	0	0	37	2	0	.250	.265
Fischer, Lee	R-R	6-4	170	7-31-86	.000	.000	.000	4	11	1	0	0	0	0	0	0	0	0	0	1	0	0	.000	.000
Fleisher, Mark	R-R	6-4	235	9-18-83	.300	.326	.289	78	307	45	92	28	1	14	67	24	6	0	6	70	0	2	.534	.356
Gaines, Ronnie	R-R	6-1	185	9-8-83	.250	.318	.217	19	68	11	17	5	0	3	9	3	2	0	0	17	3	1	.456	.301
Gallagher, Jimmy	L-L	6-1	195	9-3-85	.267	.271	.266	123	483	76	129	30	5	14	65	27	3	1	4	75	10	3	.437	.308
Gomes, Anderson	R-R	6-1	215	3-12-85	.667	.667	.000	1	3	0	2	1	0	0	2	0	0	0	0	1	0	0	1.000	.667
Grace, Michael	R-R	6-1	220	4-27-84	.200	.136	.233	20	65	4	13	2	0	0	5	5	2	1	0	15	3	1	.231	.278
Greene, Justin	R-R	6-0	185	10-10-85	.250	.429	.190	7	28	6	7	1	1	0	1	0	1	0	1	4	1	0	.357	.267
Guillen, Oney	R-R	5-9	155	1-25-86	.182	.158	.200	17	44	4	8	0	0	0	3	7	0	3	0	14	0	2	.182	.294
Inouye, Matt	R-R	5-10	190	5-20-84	.271	.321	.240	58	203	31	55	13	0	6	26	14	6	2	3	36	4	3	.424	.332
Johnson, Logan	L-R	5-9	175	11-22-83	.283	.250	.296	78	283	44	80	14	0	12	44	27	12	0	3	55	3	1	.459	.366
Jordan, Danny	R-R	6-0	190	5-9-86	.235	.370	.146	22	68	6	16	1	0	3	9	7	0	0	1	19	1	0	.382	.303
Mahin, Nick	R-R	6-2	230	8-19-85	.152	.227	.114	21	66	13	10	3	0	0	5	9	2	1	0	25	2	2	.197	.273
Marrero, Christian	L-L	6-1	185	7-30-86	.273	.305	.261	124	436	53	119	29	5	10	61	54	6	1	8	89	11	5	.431	.355
Martinez, Jose	R-R	6-5	170	7-25-88	.306	.378	.273	39	144	19	44	5	0	2	18	12	0	0	0	26	7	5	.382	.359
Mead, Andrew	R-R	6-1	190	4-17-84	.143	.133	.146	21	63	9	9	2	0	2	8	2	1	1	0	21	6	3	.270	.257
Miranda, Sergio	R-R	5-9	180	3-5-87	.306	.258	.327	65	216	31	66	9	0	2	35	23	4	7	0	26	7	2	.375	.383
Mollenhauer, Dale	L-R	5-10	170	6-26-86	.293	.318	.282	90	348	46	102	29	5	2	35	24	1	6	3	57	19	2	.422	.338
Morales, Sergio	R-R	6-1	190	12-17-87	.224	.242	.216	112	401	62	90	24	2	6	27	50	2	0	3	132	18	2	.339	.311
Morel, Brent	R-R	6-1	220	4-21-87	.297	.275	.303	45	172	26	51	6	2	6	24	16	2	0	2	28	5	2	.459	.359
Paiml, Greg	R-R	6-0	185	8-3-84	.211	.229	.205	37	123	9	26	4	1	0	5	5	0	2	2	37	2	0	.260	.238
Persichina, Joe	L-R	6-0	190	12-14-84	.214	.206	.216	41	145	18	31	7	0	0	8	7	3	0	1	31	2	1	.262	.263
Ricks, Adam	B-R	5-10	190	9-24-82	.000	—	.000	1	1	0	0	0	0	0	0	0	0	0	0	0	0	0	.000	.500
Sierra, Luis	R-R	5-11	150	7-23-87	.174	.100	.194	26	92	9	16	1	1	2	4	3	0	1	3	13	4	1	.272	.216

Pitching	B-T	HT	WT	DOB	W	L	ERA	G	GS	CG	SV	IP	H	R	ER	HR	BB	SO	AVG	vLH	vRH	K/9	BB/9
Albritton, Dan	R-R	6-0	200	11-10-84	0	0	7.18	10	0	0	0	26	36	22	21	8	8	26	.321	.304	.333	8.89	2.73
Bowling, Adam	R-R	6-4	180	1-16-84	4	1	3.67	26	1	0	1	56	58	24	23	7	9	55	.265	.298	.244	8.79	1.44
Burdie, Charls	R-R	6-1	185	9-8-85	0	0	2.20	13	0	0	1	16	9	4	4	0	8	17	.161	.100	.194	9.37	4.41
Carter, Anthony	L-R	6-3	180	4-4-86	5	2	2.77	11	11	0	0	62	47	22	19	5	11	66	.213	.162	.259	9.63	1.61
Corley, Tyson	R-R	6-6	200	1-26-86	0	5	3.42	36	0	0	2	50	37	21	19	0	19	48	.202	.270	.167	8.64	3.42
Harrell, Lucas	B-R	6-2	205	6-3-85	1	1	5.91	3	3	0	0	11	13	7	7	0	4	7	.302	.150	.435	5.91	3.38
Hunt, Leroy	R-R	6-6	240	11-28-87	3	7	2.74	37	0	0	7	46	32	17	14	2	31	45	.190	.167	.206	8.80	6.07
Infante, Gregory	R-R	6-2	185	7-10-87	1	2	6.59	4	3	0	0	14	16	12	10	0	12	11	.286	.294	.282	7.24	7.90
Jones, Nathan	R-R	6-5	190	1-28-86	1	7	6.83	18	10	1	0	57	63	45	43	8	35	71	.281	.198	.338	11.28	5.56
Leesman, Charlie	L-L	6-4	210	3-10-87	0	0	0.00	1	1	0	0	5	3	1	0	0	2	5	.188	.250	.167	9.64	3.86
Lowe, Johnnie	R-R	6-5	220	3-21-85	5	7	4.10	22	16	0	0	99	105	58	45	4	27	80	.269	.272	.267	7.30	2.46
Luis, Santo	R-R	6-4	200	1-27-84	6	3	3.20	41	2	0	4	90	73	35	32	3	28	133	.218	.230	.209	13.30	2.80
Mabee, Henry	R-R	6-4	230	7-10-85	0	1	1.33	28	0	0	17	41	31	9	6	0	18	41	.207	.228	.194	9.07	3.98
Maxwell, Levi	R-R	6-2	180	12-22-84	15	5	3.47	26	17	2	1	125	102	51	48	13	29	105	.227	.211	.237	7.58	2.09
Moreno, Juan	R-R	6-3	176	11-29-86	1	4	7.23	6	5	0	0	24	35	22	19	6	9	11	.354	.404	.308	4.18	3.42
Perez, Wander	L-L	6-3	160	1-5-85	0	0	4.73	30	0	0	1	32	33	18	17	3	18	43	.258	.164	.329	11.97	5.01
Rice, Jason	R-R	6-0	190	5-13-86	8	8	4.44	24	23	1	1	116	128	65	57	5	40	109	.278	.253	.294	8.48	3.11
Santiago, Hector	R-L	6-0	210	12-16-87	5	1	4.06	38	0	0	1	64	57	37	29	1	44	83	.241	.293	.213	11.61	6.16
Shirek, Charlie	R-R	6-3	205	10-25-85	6	6	3.54	22	21	0	0	112	112	52	44	8	25	82	.249	.257	.244	6.59	2.01
Skogley, Kevin	L-L	6-6	203	9-24-84	0	1	7.79	4	4	0	0	17	24	15	15	1	12	21	.338	.348	.333	10.90	6.23
Socolovich, Miguel	R-R	6-1	155	7-24-86	6	6	4.68	21	18	0	0	90	86	53	47	12	33	72	.253	.285	.233	7.17	3.29
Spurgeon, Steven	R-R	6-4	230	8-22-83	0	1	1.50	5	0	0	0	6	3	3	1	0	4	4	.158	.125	.182	6.00	6.00
Stephenson, Eric	R-L	6-4	200	9-3-82	0	3	5.56	13	0	0	1	11	11	7	7	1	8	10	.250	.176	.296	7.94	6.35

Fielding

Catcher	PCT	G	PO	A	E	DP	PB
Curtis	.991	67	594	34	6	5	16
Inouye	.978	54	421	34	10	3	7
Jordan	.971	16	130	3	4	0	5
Marrero	.990	56	444	40	5	40	
Persichina	1.000	12	87	12	0	13	
Persichina	.950	6	11	8	1	2	
Sierra	1.000	2	2	2	0	0	

First Base	PCT	G	PO	A	E	DP
Castillo	1.000	4	32	6	0	7
Fleisher	.988	62	544	29	7	43
Grace	1.000	2	16	1	0	2

Second Base	PCT	G	PO	A	E	DP
Escobar	.984	12	26	34	1	15
Fischer	1.000	1	0	1	0	0
Guillen	.940	13	19	28	3	6
Miranda	.935	23	29	58	6	8
Mollenhauer	.976	87	134	225	9	49

Third Base	PCT	G	PO	A	E	DP
Castillo	1.000	1	1	2	0	0
Grace	1.000	3	3	3	0	0
Johnson	.944	52	38	96	8	9
Miranda	.957	9	6	16	1	2
Morel	.947	45	26	82	6	9

Persichina	.931	22	17 37	4	3
Sierra	.917	7	3 8	1	1

Shortstop	PCT	G	PO	A	E	DP
Beckham	.958	13	26	43	3	15
Escobar	.957	48	65	133	9	17
Fischer	.875	2	1	6	1	1
Miranda	.949	22	30	64	5	11
Mollenhauer	1.000	3	2	9	0	2
Paiml	.951	36	50	105	8	23

Sierra	.966	16	21 36	2	11

Outfield	PCT	G	PO	A	E	DP
Cruz	—	2	0	0	0	0
Damas	1.000	4	5	0	0	0
Danks	1.000	10	12	0	0	0
Estill	1.000	20	34	0	0	1
Gaines	.917	10	11	0	1	0
Gallagher	.985	115	186	11	3	1
Gomes	1.000	1	1	0	0	0

Greene	.917	6	10	1 1	0
Inouye	1.000	1	3	0 0	0
Mahin	.895	11	17	0 2	0
Marrero	.971	66	96	4 3	1
Martinez	.986	38	66	3 1	1
Mead	1.000	18	28	1 0	0
Morales	.974	110	180	7 5	1
Persichina	1.000	3	5	0 0	0

BRISTOL WHITE SOX
APPALACHIAN LEAGUE

ROOKIE

Batting	B-T	HT	WT	DOB	AVG	vLH	vRH	G	AB	R	H	2B	3B	HR	RBI	BB	HBP	SH	SF	SO	SB	CS	SLG	OBP
Buckridge, Shaydron	R-R	5-10	170	5-12-88	.220	.200	.226	14	41	5	9	1	0	0	6	5	2	2	1	10	0	0	.244	.327
Castillo, Jorge	L-R	6-2	225	9-26-86	.365	.259	.386	43	167	18	61	11	2	1	25	11	4	0	3	21	0	1	.473	.411
Damas, Nick	R-R	6-2	185	4-11-85	.250	—	.250	1	4	1	1	1	0	0	0	0	0	0	0	2	0	0	.500	.250
Dubler, Kevin	L-R	6-1	200	2-18-87	.238	.286	.230	31	101	14	24	3	0	1	15	11	2	1	3	16	1	0	.297	.316
Garcia, Drew	B-R	6-1	175	4-22-86	.299	.342	.290	61	231	39	69	11	1	8	37	10	5	0	3	43	2	1	.459	.337
Gilbert, Kenny	L-L	6-2	185	2-6-89	.272	.444	.250	43	162	25	44	11	0	4	31	6	1	1	0	43	3	1	.414	.302
Greene, Justin	R-R	6-0	185	10-10-85	.274	.294	.270	49	186	42	51	9	5	2	15	18	6	2	0	46	26	8	.409	.357
Kateon, John	R-R	6-0	190	8-4-84	.291	.125	.329	27	86	16	25	1	0	2	12	9	1	3	2	23	0	1	.372	.357
Kendall, Jordan	R-R	6-0	195	2-20-87	.319	.171	.353	48	185	35	59	9	3	3	26	9	5	0	2	34	20	15	.449	.363
Larson, Zack	R-R	6-4	230	10-15-86	.250	.000	.333	1	4	1	1	0	0	0	0	0	0	0	0	3	0	0	.250	.250
Matthews, Jedon	R-R	6-2	190	12-7-87	.300	.278	.306	27	80	18	24	5	1	2	12	9	0	1	0	33	4	3	.463	.371
Santos, Orlando	R-R	6-0	187	12-10-86	.259	.444	.236	22	81	13	21	6	0	1	8	3	3	2	0	22	1	2	.370	.310
Short, Brandon	R-R	6-1	175	9-9-88	.273	.469	.232	49	183	30	50	13	2	1	23	16	8	1	0	37	14	7	.383	.357
Sierra, Luis	L-R	5-11	150	7-23-87	.167	.000	.176	5	18	1	3	0	0	0	1	4	0	1	0	4	0	0	.167	.318
Silverio, Juan	R-R	6-1	175	4-18-91	.228	.167	.240	59	215	31	49	8	0	4	35	8	4	3	3	56	3	1	.321	.265
Tavarez, Misael	R-R	6-5	190	12-6-87	.193	.154	.205	32	114	19	22	6	0	3	8	6	1	2	0	54	2	1	.325	.240
Vargas, Hancer	B-R	5-11	174	12-5-88	.241	.133	.254	42	137	18	33	4	1	0	18	9	3	5	3	19	9	5	.285	.296
Vargas, Jose	R-R	6-3	225	12-15-87	.232	.280	.223	42	155	17	36	8	2	6	27	4	1	1	4	43	2	2	.426	.255

Pitching	B-T	HT	WT	DOB	W	L	ERA	G	GS	CG	SV	IP	H	R	ER	HR	BB	SO	AVG	vLH	vRH	K/9	BB/9
Asselin, Kevin	L-R	6-1	180	2-16-85	0	1	1.31	16	0	0	9	21	15	5	3	2	7	23	.200	.182	.208	10.02	3.05
Buriff, Shane	R-L	6-2	205	5-22-86	3	1	5.60	9	0	0	0	18	18	14	11	1	8	21	.254	.185	.295	10.70	4.08
Dawson, Chad	R-R	6-4	200	3-6-86	0	1	2.70	10	0	0	0	10	7	4	3	1	11	6	.200	.118	.278	5.40	9.90
DeFoor, Brent	R-R	6-2	175	1-9-86	1	0	2.76	11	0	0	4	16	15	5	5	2	3	22	.254	.238	.263	12.12	1.65
Doyle, Terry	R-R	6-4	225	11-2-85	1	2	1.88	10	0	0	0	24	27	11	5	0	3	27	.278		.283	10.13	1.13
Gouvea, Murillo	R-R	6-2	190	9-15-88	4	1	7.28	12	5	0	1	38	49	37	31	3	14	34	.302	.242	.344	7.98	3.29
Graffy, Brett	R-R	6-2	185	3-12-87	1	4	3.29	10	2	0	1	27	25	13	10	3	8	28	.236	.346	.200	9.22	2.63
Harrell, Lucas	B-R	6-2	205	6-3-85	0	0	3.00	1	1	0	0	3	3	1	1	0	1	5	.273	.000	.429	15.00	3.00
Infante, Gregory	R-R	6-2	185	7-10-87	4	3	2.66	13	12	0	0	74	63	26	22	4	19	57	.232	.167	.262	6.90	2.30
Johnson, Garrett	L-L	6-10	205	9-2-87	4	4	4.13	12	11	0	0	52	57	28	24	5	23	63	.275	.135	.306	10.83	3.96
Jones, Nathan	R-R	6-5	190	1-28-86	1	0	1.35	4	1	0	0	7	6	4	1	0	2	12	.222	.273	.188	16.20	2.70
Kuehn, Justin	R-R	6-2	190	6-9-87	1	0	1.80	11	0	0	2	25	14	6	5	1	9	25	.165	.158	.167	9.00	3.24
Leesman, Charlie	L-L	6-4	210	3-10-87	0	0	0.00	2	0	0	1	5	5	0	0	0	1	6	.263	.000	.357	10.13	1.69
Lin, Po-Yu	R-R	6-0	221	9-16-86	1	2	2.56	6	5	0	0	32	30	12	9	3	11	25	.246	.184	.288	7.11	3.13
Lucas, Michael	R-R	6-3	200	7-18-85	1	2	6.14	10	0	0	0	22	29	16	15	0	7	18	.312	.324	.304	7.36	2.86
Martinez, Joucer	R-R	6-2	160	2-3-86	4	3	4.11	12	12	0	0	57	55	28	26	5	21	41	.253	.231	.263	6.47	3.32
Moreno, Juan	R-R	6-3	176	11-29-86	0	1	1.86	5	0	0	1	10	9	4	2	2	0	10	.237	.429	.194	9.31	0.00
Mota, Willy	R-R	6-1	165	10-25-85	0	1	8.53	4	0	0	0	6	6	8	6	7	9	16	.200		.143	12.79	9.95
Paniagua, Onarkys	R-R	6-3	170	1-26-86	5	2	3.97	11	11	1	0	59	69	31	26	5	12	47	.289	.277	.297	7.17	1.83
Puls, Dan	R-L	6-7	200	1-30-86	1	0	2.95	9	0	0	0	18	15	7	6	1	5	19	.231	.273	.209	9.33	2.45
Remenowsky, Dan	R-R	6-5	245	4-7-86	0	0	0.00	1	0	0	0	2	1	0	0	0	2	1	.143	.000	.250	9.00	0.00
Upchurch, Steven	R-R	6-4	180	9-14-89	2	2	3.26	7	4	0	0	30	23	13	11	4	10	28	.209	.370	.157	8.31	2.97

Fielding

Catcher	PCT	G	PO	A	E	DP	PB
Buckridge	.974	14	103	10	3	0	4
Dubler	.979	29	216	18	5	2	1
Larson	1.000	1	11	1	0	0	2
Santos	.978	21	187	36	5	5	10

First Base	PCT	G	PO	A	E	DP
Castillo	.994	41	329	27	2	41
Matthews	1.000	2	13	0	0	1
Vargas	1.000	1	8	1	0	1
Vargas	.996	25	207	16	1	20

Second Base	PCT	G	PO	A	E	DP
Garcia	.980	58	113	178	6	41
Kateon	.889	2	3	5	1	1
Sierra	1.000	1	1	3	0	1
Silverio	.857	2	3	3	1	1
Vargas	1.000	2	7	10	0	5

Third Base	PCT	G	PO	A	E	DP
Kateon	.927	15	9	29	3	1
Matthews	.667	6	1	5	3	1
Sierra	.900	4	3	6	1	2
Vargas	.919	34	24	67	8	8
Vargas	.867	9	8	18	4	4

Shortstop	PCT	G	PO	A	E	DP
Garcia	1.000	4	2	6	0	1
Kateon	.933	4	7	7	1	1
Silverio	.911	58	86	160	24	42

Outfield	PCT	G	PO	A	E	DP
Damas	.667	1	2	0	1	0
Gilbert	.972	24	34	1	1	0
Greene	.946	47	86	2	5	0
Kendall	.930	47	69	11	6	4
Matthews	1.000	4	5	0	0	0
Short	.974	47	70	4	2	0
Tavarez	.909	28	27	3	3	0

GREAT FALLS VOYAGERS   ROOKIE

PIONEER LEAGUE

Batting	B-T	HT	WT	DOB	AVG	vLH	vRH	G	AB	R	H	2B	3B	HR	RBI	BB	HBP	SH	SF	SO	SB	CS	SLG	OBP
Avila, Jesus	R-L	6-0	165	11-26-88	.271	.274	.270	66	247	27	67	7	2	1	27	9	2	6	2	27	4	3	.328	.300
Celis, Johny	L-R	6-0	165	3-26-86	.283	.229	.306	71	240	36	68	22	1	5	39	41	4	0	2	51	1	2	.446	.394
Cheatham, Jordan	L-L	5-10	185	11-2-87	.264	.283	.259	65	231	35	61	9	0	1	27	35	2	4	2	64	20	8	.316	.363
Damas, Nick	R-R	6-2	185	4-11-85	.203	.214	.196	30	74	10	15	3	0	1	6	7	1	0	0	10	5	1	.284	.280
Escobar, Eduardo	B-R	5-10	150	1-5-89	.417	.375	.438	6	24	6	10	2	1	1	4	2	1	0	1	3	1	1	.708	.464
Estill, Lyndon	R-R	6-3	215	3-29-87	.226	.191	.237	56	186	31	42	5	3	8	24	35	7	3	0	87	9	3	.414	.368
Fischer, Lee	R-R	6-4	170	7-31-86	.206	.224	.195	45	131	22	27	4	0	0	12	9	10	7	0	23	3	3	.237	.307
Gerst, Kent	L-R	5-10	170	2-6-88	.275	.246	.287	55	204	36	56	10	4	5	26	26	2	1	1	63	15	7	.436	.361
Grace, Michael	R-R	6-1	220	4-27-84	.287	.344	.257	67	265	48	76	11	2	13	54	25	2	1	3	84	8	3	.491	.349
Guillen, Oney	R-R	5-9	155	1-25-86	.000	.000	.000	2	6	0	0	0	0	0	0	1	0	0	0	2	0	0	.000	.143
Jordan, Danny	R-R	6-0	190	5-9-86	.213	.091	.267	35	108	14	23	10	0	2	16	10	3	1	0	47	0	0	.361	.298
Kuhn, Tyler	L-R	5-10	185	9-9-86	.375	.395	.365	62	256	51	96	23	9	3	46	21	1	2	0	35	7	3	.570	.424
Larson, Zack	R-R	6-4	230	10-15-86	.220	.143	.263	25	59	6	13	2	0	0	5	2	2	2	1	18	0	0	.254	.266
Mahin, Nick	R-R	6-2	230	8-19-85	.318	.250	.357	5	22	3	7	0	0	1	5	1	0	0	0	5	2	0	.455	.348
Morel, Brent	R-R	6-1	220	4-21-87	.375	.400	.367	15	64	11	24	0	2	0	3	6	1	0	0	7	7	0	.438	.437
Shelton, Kyle	R-R	6-0	184	5-15-86	.292	.347	.261	51	209	29	61	12	1	5	33	12	3	1	1	49	5	1	.431	.338
Sierra, Luis	L-R	5-11	150	7-20-87	.329	.421	.302	26	82	19	27	4	0	2	12	14	1	5	0	10	2	0	.451	.433
Thennis, Doug	R-R	6-2	195	2-19-86	.221	.275	.190	58	190	25	42	14	0	4	21	21	6	1	1	69	2	3	.358	.317
Williams Jr., Kenny	B-R	6-0	180	5-22-86	.114	.000	.174	11	35	6	4	2	1	0	4	6	2	2	0	11	2	1	.229	.279

Pitching	B-T	HT	WT	DOB	W	L	ERA	G	GS	CG	SV	IP	H	R	ER	HR	BB	SO	AVG	vLH	vRH	K/9	BB/9
Albritton, Dan	R-R	6-0	200	11-10-84	2	2	3.52	24	0	0	1	46	48	21	18	5	10	63	.264	.338	.216	12.33	1.96
Allen, Cody	R-R	6-2	190	9-19-86	4	6	5.01	15	15	0	0	74	87	54	41	8	22	60	.285	.281	.288	7.33	2.69
Billeaud, Josh	R-R	6-3	210	3-22-87	3	2	4.34	19	8	0	0	1	56	65	33	27	4	16	32	.289	.314	.273	5.14	2.57
Burdie, Charlis	R-R	6-1	185	9-8-85	2	0	0.00	6	0	0	0	11	3	0	0	0	4	22	.083	.000	.100	18.00	3.27
Carter, Dexter	R-R	6-6	195	2-5-87	6	1	2.23	15	12	0	0	69	44	23	17	3	25	89	.179	.168	.186	11.67	3.28
Griffith, Nevin	R-R	6-2	165	3-23-89	0	0	2.13	3	3	0	0	13	13	6	3	0	5	12	.245	.455	.190	8.53	3.55
Hudson, Dan	R-R	6-4	220	3-9-87	5	4	3.36	14	14	0	0	70	52	30	26	6	22	90	.202	.210	.197	11.63	2.84
Lechuga, Enrique	L-L	6-0	180	6-6-86	0	2	4.36	22	0	0	0	33	31	20	16	3	12	33	.252	.308	.226	9.00	3.27
Lin, Po-Yu	R-R	6-0	221	9-16-86	1	0	4.50	6	1	0	0	14	15	7	7	1	0	16	.294	.278	.303	10.29	0.00
Morales, Ronnie	L-L	6-3	195	1-22-85	3	5	3.67	28	0	0	3	42	45	24	17	3	18	41	.269	.154	.305	8.86	3.89
O'Neil, Drew	R-R	6-3	200	11-8-85	2	2	6.97	25	0	0	1	31	29	25	24	1	22	40	.252	.282	.237	11.61	6.39
Remenowsky, Dan	R-R	6-5	245	4-7-86	4	0	0.48	11	0	0	3	19	17	2	1	0	6	18	.239	.115	.311	8.68	2.89
Rojas, Wilmer	L-L	6-0	163	10-12-86	0	0	13.21	13	0	0	0	16	32	24	23	3	13	15	.427	.385	.449	8.62	7.47
Rosario, Frank	R-R	6-2	162	10-31-85	0	5	7.14	14	8	0	0	40	54	33	32	8	14	27	.325	.357	.302	6.02	3.12
Sauer, Stephen	R-R	6-2	185	8-13-86	3	2	3.41	19	0	0	5	29	19	13	11	3	7	27	.178	.167	.185	8.38	2.17
Skogley, Kevin	L-L	6-6	203	9-24-84	4	5	4.98	15	15	0	0	87	95	54	48	6	22	88	.274	.222	.285	9.14	2.28
Strauss, Ryan	R-R	6-2	200	10-21-85	0	1	7.59	8	0	0	0	11	13	9	9	1	2	9	.310	.310	.308	7.59	1.69
Wickswat, Matt	L-L	6-2	210	8-4-86	0	0	2.63	9	0	0	0	14	9	9	4	0	11	15	.180	.125	.206	9.88	7.24

Fielding

Catcher	PCT	G	PO	A	E	DP	PB
Grace	.982	34	249	30	5	1	10
Jordan	.986	31	256	20	4	0	7
Larson	.989	25	166	16	2	1	3

First Base	PCT	G	PO	A	E	DP
Celis	.967	3	24	5	1	2
Grace	.979	19	133	10	3	13
Jordan	—	1	0	0	0	0
Mahin	1.000	2	26	0	0	0
Shelton	.983	21	163	10	3	17
Thennis	.984	41	351	19	6	21

Second Base	PCT	G	PO	A	E	DP
Avila	.978	52	83	138	5	27
Fischer	.973	23	34	75	3	15
Guillen	1.000	2	2	4	0	3
Kuhn	.929	4	5	8	1	1

Third Base	PCT	G	PO	A	E	DP
Avila	.893	12	7	18	3	5
Kuhn	—	1	0	0	0	0
Morel	.920	15	17	29	4	3
Shelton	.870	34	17	50	10	1
Sierra	.839	17	7	19	5	4
Thennis	.600	3	1	2	2	0

Shortstop	PCT	G	PO	A	E	DP
Escobar	.974	6	13	25	1	6
Fischer	.952	21	27	53	4	11
Kuhn	.936	48	73	147	15	29
Sierra	.960	7	6	18	1	0

Outfield	PCT	G	PO	A	E	DP
Celis	.923	32	35	1	3	0
Cheatham	.977	60	82	2	2	0
Damas	1.000	27	23	4	0	0
Estill	.950	51	71	5	4	3
Gerst	.972	53	67	3	2	1
Thennis	1.000	13	17	1	0	1
Williams Jr.	1.000	8	13	0	0	0

DSL WHITE SOX 1   ROOKIE

DOMINICAN SUMMER LEAGUE

Batting	B-T	HT	WT	DOB	AVG	vLH	vRH	G	AB	R	H	2B	3B	HR	RBI	BB	HBP	SH	SF	SO	SB	CS	SLG	OBP
Acuna, Hector	B-R	6-2	200	8-26-88	.194	.167	.196	22	62	7	12	4	0	0	9	10	2	0	1	15	1	0	.258	.320
Acuna, Luis	B-R	6-0	160	4-17-85	.225	.194	.233	52	169	18	38	6	0	2	21	12	1	0	4	42	2	0	.296	.274
Aguasvivas, Nestor	R-R	6-1	187	9-19-87	.235	1.000	.188	6	17	1	4	2	0	0	4	0	1	0	1	3	0	0	.353	.263
Brazoban, Rafael	R-R	6-1	200	12-12-87	.111	.200	.077	15	18	2	2	0	0	0	0	5	1	0	0	9	1	0	.111	.333
Ferreiras, Angel	R-R	6-1	184	8-12-88	.275	.318	.266	67	251	39	69	16	3	3	33	32	6	2	1	56	10	2	.398	.369
Garabito, Alder	R-R	5-11	180	8-6-87	.228	.000	.245	23	57	10	13	4	1	0	13	13	2	0	1	13	0	0	.333	.384
Garcia, Miguel	R-R	6-1	150	5-16-90	.089	.000	.103	19	45	3	4	0	0	0	1	1	0	1	0	4	1	0	.089	.109
Gonzalez, Miguel	R-R	6-0	200	6-5-91	.500	—	.500	2	2	0	1	1	0	0	0	0	0	0	0	0	0	0	1.000	.500
Lora, Ronald	R-R	6-1	180	3-31-89	.250	.195	.262	66	228	32	57	12	0	2	26	22	2	3	0	59	11	2	.329	.321
Lugo, Antoni	R-R	6-1	187	6-16-88	.232	.290	.218	47	155	17	36	7	0	2	16	13	4	3	1	25	1	1	.316	.306
Marte, Abrahan	R-R	6-2	205	8-6-87	.159	.125	.167	12	44	7	7	2	0	0	6	2	2	0	0	8	1	0	.205	.229
Marte, Victor	R-R	6-0	180	9-15-89	.150	.200	.133	5	20	1	3	1	0	0	3	1	1	0	0	9	0	0	.200	.227

	B-T	HT	WT	DOB	AVG	vLH	vRH	G	AB	R	H	2B	3B	HR	RBI	BB	HBP	SH	SF	SO	SB	CS	SLG	OBP
Mercedes, Daurys	R-R	6-1	165	2-26-90	.170	.111	.184	13	47	4	8	4	0	0	5	6	2	0	0	13	1	2	.255	.291
Pascual, Oliver	R-R	5-10	170	11-13-89	.147	.143	.148	16	34	6	5	2	0	0	2	4	2	0	0	11	1	1	.206	.275
Patino, Jeffer	R-R	5-10	163	10-8-88	.327	.258	.343	47	168	34	55	15	2	3	28	26	6	4	2	23	3	5	.494	.431
Peguero, Anneury	R-R	6-0	180	4-6-87	.200	.154	.211	50	135	29	27	4	0	1	13	28	2	0	1	25	11	3	.252	.343
Pimentel, Francisco	R-R		195	11-13-87	.042	.000	.050	8	24	2	1	1	0	0	0	3	0	0	0	9	0	0	.083	.148
Puentes, Jerry	R-R	6-1		7-18-91	.261	.250	.265	46	180	24	47	3	2	0	19	22	2	4	1	24	7	4	.300	.346
Ramos, Luis	R-R	6-3	185	6-19-88	.270	.500	.207	11	37	3	10	3	0	0	4	3	1	0	0	10	3	0	.351	.341
Reyes, Rafi	R-R	6-2	195	7-31-91	.167	.222	.154	13	48	6	8	1	0	0	3	1	1	0	0	14	3	0	.188	.200
Trujillo, Rather	R-R	6-0	185	2-23-89	.286	.200	.306	44	154	42	44	6	2	0	12	33	19	2	1	30	17	10	.351	.464
Vega, Juan	R-R	6-1	165	3-9-89	.294	.341	.282	51	197	33	58	10	1	1	35	9	15	2	4	26	10	3	.371	.364
Williams, Ariel	R-R	5-11	155	11-13-88	.316	.300	.319	19	57	12	18	1	1	0	6	12	1	0	0	12	11	3	.368	.443
Yepez, Daniel	R-R	6-1	190	5-6-91	.192	.103	.217	56	177	22	34	6	1	0	16	11	11	4	2	37	1	0	.237	.279

Pitching	B-T	HT	WT	DOB	W	L	ERA	G	GS	CG	SV	IP	H	R	ER	HR	BB	SO	AVG	vLH	vRH	K/9	BB/9
Almonte, Juan	R-R	5-11	180	8-19-85	0	0	3.86	2	0	0	0	2	1	1	1	0	1	3	.125	.000	.167	11.57	3.86
Arias, Emenejildo	L-L	6-3	179	11-23-86	0	0	2.92	8	0	0	1	12	10	8	4	0	4	9	.204	.000	.208	6.57	2.92
Bremon, Tony	R-R	6-1	165	12-5-87	6	2	2.33	9	8	1	1	58	47	19	15	1	4	48	.217	.271	.190	7.45	0.62
Bruno, Keuri	R-R	6-0	180	1-20-87	0	0	3.60	3	0	0	0	5	3	2	2	1	6	4	.214	.200	.222	7.20	10.80
Cueva, Jorge	R-R	6-3	205	3-24-89	0	0	2.25	3	0	0	1	4	3	1	1	0	4	4	.214	.400	.111	9.00	9.00
Eusebio, Hector	R-R	6-5	215	11-1-87	1	4	3.95	20	0	0	7	41	42	21	18	0	18	41	.259	.325	.238	9.00	3.95
Jean, Dominque	R-R	6-2	170	11-24-88	0	0	0.00	5	0	0	0	10	7	2	0	0	5	8	.200	.444	.115	7.20	4.50
Juma, Ronny	L-L	6-2	182	10-26-88	0	0	3.48	8	0	0	0	10	11	4	4	0	7	5	.275	.167	.294	4.35	6.10
Marte, Luis	R-R	6-1	190	12-15-86	0	2	3.91	15	0	0	3	25	32	17	11	1	8	16	.314	.353	.294	5.68	2.84
Medina, Aneuris	L-L	6-2	175	5-21-87	6	3	1.99	11	10	0	0	59	35	21	13	1	16	63	.163	.095	.171	9.66	2.45
Mercedes, Raffy	R-R	6-1	185	12-17-88	2	1	2.58	11	7	0	0	38	29	16	11	0	8	30	.200	.139	.220	7.04	1.88
Payano, Luis	R-R	6-1	176	3-31-87	0	1	4.71	10	4	0	0	21	25	14	11	2	7	19	.291	.313	.278	8.14	3.00
Rienzo, Andre	R-R	6-3	160	6-5-88	3	0	0.96	3	3	0	0	19	15	3	2	0	3	22	.214	.214	.214	10.61	1.45
Rodriguez, Yovan	R-R	6-0	180	7-12-86	2	2	2.65	9	6	0	0	34	27	18	10	0	13	22	.211	.268	.184	5.82	3.44
Rojas, Juan	R-R	5-11	174	11-2-83	3	4	1.91	20	4	1	6	66	59	19	14	2	11	77	.233	.319	.185	10.50	1.50
Rosario, Jose	R-R	6-1	198	8-30-88	4	2	4.11	21	2	0	4	50	55	28	23	4	25	45	.281	.240	.306	8.05	4.47
Tejada, Silvio	R-R	6-6	190	9-6-88	0	1	8.10	4	0	0	0	7	8	7	6	0	5	9	.286	.571	.190	12.15	6.75
Zabala, Carlos	L-L	6-2	180	11-4-85	7	3	1.83	15	13	0	0	88	72	31	18	2	17	91	.222	.308	.205	9.27	1.73

Fielding

Catcher	PCT	G	PO	A	E	DP	PB
Garabito	.991	17	112	4	1	0	8
Gonzalez	1.000	2	5	0	0	0	1
Pascual	.976	9	35	5	1	0	3
Pimentel	1.000	4	35	3	0	0	0
Yepez	.979	54	383	32	9	0	16

First Base	PCT	G	PO	A	E	DP
Acuna	.981	19	149	4	3	13
Acuna	.989	31	260	12	3	21
Ferreiras	.952	4	35	5	2	3
Garcia	1.000	1	1	0	0	1
Lugo	.971	14	96	6	3	9
Marte	.962	9	74	1	3	5
Pimentel	1.000	1	2	1	0	0
Yepez	1.000	3	18	3	0	1

Second Base	PCT	G	PO	A	E	DP
Acuna	1.000	1	1	0	0	0
Garcia	—	1	0	0	0	0
Marte	1.000	2	5	6	0	1
Patino	.962	46	82	123	8	24
Peguero	.933	8	11	17	2	3
Williams	.944	17	22	46	4	6

Third Base	PCT	G	PO	A	E	DP
Acuna	.822	16	11	26	8	2
Garcia	.946	15	6	29	2	1
Lugo	.891	34	18	64	10	3
Peguero	.906	24	23	35	6	5

Shortstop	PCT	G	PO	A	E	DP
Garcia	.778	2	3	4	2	1
Mercedes	.906	13	20	28	5	6

	PCT	G	PO	A	E	DP
Peguero	.921	13	25	33	5	8
Puentes	.944	46	75	127	12	22

Outfield	PCT	G	PO	A	E	DP
Acuna	—	1	0	0	0	0
Acuna	1.000	2	1	0	0	0
Brazoban	1.000	6	6	0	0	0
Ferreiras	.957	54	105	6	5	0
Lora	.945	41	50	2	3	0
Peguero	1.000	4	2	0	0	0
Ramos	.923	9	11	1	1	0
Reyes	.913	13	19	2	2	1
Rodriguez	.667	1	2	0	1	0
Trujillo	.949	41	71	4	4	2
Vega	.962	50	70	6	3	1

DSL WHITE SOX 2 — ROOKIE

DOMINICAN SUMMER LEAGUE

Batting	B-T	HT	WT	DOB	AVG	vLH	vRH	G	AB	R	H	2B	3B	HR	RBI	BB	HBP	SH	SF	SO	SB	CS	SLG	OBP
Acuna, Hector	B-R	6-2	200	8-26-88	.290	.258	.301	38	124	16	36	7	0	0	18	16	3	0	2	25	1	1	.347	.379
2-team total (22 White Sox 1)					.258	—	—	60	186	23	48	11	0	0	27	26	5	0	3	40	2	1	.317	.359
Alcala, Julio	R-R	6-0	165	12-24-90	.239	.182	.258	55	176	23	42	6	4	0	17	25	7	6	3	23	6	3	.318	.351
Cabrera, Raldy	R-R	6-0	180	9-25-89	.246	.176	.274	45	118	19	29	2	2	0	12	11	4	1	0	38	5	6	.297	.331
De La Cruz, Edgar	R-R	6-0	190	7-24-89	.000	.000	.000	4	7	0	0	0	0	0	0	1	0	0	0	4	0	0	.000	.125
Garcia, Miguel	R-R	6-1	150	5-16-90	.220	.154	.239	23	59	4	13	1	1	0	6	3	0	4	0	8	1	4	.271	.258
2-team total (19 White Sox 1)					.163	—	—	42	104	7	17	1	1	0	7	4	0	5	0	12	2	4	.192	.194
Gonzalez, Miguel	R-R	6-0	200	6-5-91	.291	.161	.327	43	141	25	41	9	1	0	23	16	7	2	1	18	8	1	.369	.388
2-team total (2 White Sox 1)					.294	—	—	45	143	25	42	10	1	0	23	16	7	2	1	18	8	1	.378	.389
Ladera, Kevin	R-R	6-0	155	6-2-89	.178	.136	.191	56	185	27	33	1	0	0	13	33	6	7	1	29	8	4	.184	.320
Marte, Abrahan	R-R	6-2	205	8-6-87	.310	.333	.302	37	87	13	27	5	0	1	16	10	3	0	1	13	2	0	.402	.396
2-team total (12 White Sox 1)					.260	—	—	49	131	20	34	7	0	1	22	12	5	0	1	21	3	0	.336	.342
Mercedes, Daurys	R-R	6-1	165	2-26-90	.221	.135	.253	45	136	13	30	3	2	1	17	11	4	5	0	49	3	1	.294	.298
2-team total (13 White Sox 1)					.208	—	—	58	183	17	38	7	2	1	22	17	6	5	0	62	4	3	.284	.296
Parra, Carlos	L-R	6-0	188	2-24-90	.296	.286	.298	46	115	20	34	6	1	0	19	29	5	1	0	22	5	1	.365	.456
Pascual, Oliver	R-R	5-10	170	11-13-89	.143	.000	.333	3	7	0	1	0	0	0	0	1	0	0	0	3	0	0	.143	.250
2-team total (16 White Sox 1)					.146	—	—	19	41	6	6	2	0	0	2	5	2	0	0	14	1	1	.195	.271
Puentes, Jerry	R-R	6-1	170	7-18-91	.400	.444	.385	9	35	10	14	2	1	0	7	1	0	3	0	6	2	0	.514	.417
2-team total (46 White Sox 1)					.284	—	—	55	215	34	61	5	3	0	26	23	2	7	1	30	9	4	.335	.357
Ramos, Luis	R-R	6-3	185	6-19-88	.282	.341	.264	53	181	28	51	7	1	2	31	14	4	0	1	21	12	2	.365	.345
2-team total (11 White Sox 1)					.280	—	—	64	218	31	61	10	1	2	35	17	5	0	1	31	15	2	.362	.344

ORGANIZATION STATISTICS

	B-T	HT	WT	DOB	AVG	vLH	vRH	G	AB	R	H	2B	3B	HR	RBI	BB	SB	CS	HP	SO			OBP	SLG
Reyes, Rafi	R-R	6-2	195	7-31-91	.183	.118	.204	51	208	25	38	7	1	4	13	11	7	0	1	79	9	6	.284	.247
2-team total (13 White Sox 1)					.180	—	—	64	256	31	46	8	1	4	16	12	8	0	1	93	12	6	.266	.238
Robles, Abraham	R-R	6-2	170	3-15-90	.184	.205	.177	54	163	21	30	4	2	2	20	19	2	3	0	39	3	3	.270	.277
Rosales, Yeikler	R-R	6-1	180	6-5-88	.211	.125	.239	46	95	9	20	2	2	0	10	18	4	1	0	31	0	4	.274	.359
Sanchez, Leopoldo	R-R	6-1	180	6-5-91	.209	.167	.223	58	172	18	36	2	0	0	15	33	4	0	2	33	5	1	.221	.346
Trujillo, Rather	R-R	6-0	185	2-23-89	.320	.333	.316	13	50	15	16	3	2	1	8	6	4	4	0	4	6	1	.520	.433
2-team total (44 White Sox 1)					.294	—	—	57	204	57	60	9	4	1	20	39	23	6	1	34	23	11	.392	.457
Vega, Juan	R-R	6-1	165	3-9-89	.239	.182	.257	12	46	5	11	2	0	1	10	3	1	0	2	14	6	0	.348	.288
2-team total (51 White Sox 1)					.284	—	—	63	243	38	69	12	1	2	45	12	16	2	6	30	16	3	.366	.350
Williams, Ariel	R-R	5-11	155	11-13-88	.290	.267	.298	19	62	10	18	2	3	1	5	2	0	0	0	16	3	3	.468	.313
2-team total (19 White Sox 1)					.303	—	—	38	119	22	36	3	4	1	11	14	1	0	0	28	14	6	.420	.381

Pitching	B-T	HT	WT	DOB	W	L	ERA	G	GS	CG	SV	IP	H	R	ER	HR	BB	SO	AVG	vLH	vRH	K/9	BB/9
Aguilera, Hector	R-R	6-3	185	3-26-90	3	3	3.46	13	9	0	1	42	51	31	16	2	23	25	.307	.350	.294	5.40	4.97
Arias, Emenejildo	L-L	6-3	179	11-23-86	0	0	3.71	7	0	0	2	17	21	12	7	1	7	15	.288	.250	.292	7.94	3.71
2-team total (8 White Sox 1)					0	0	3.38	15	0	0	3	29	31	20	11	1	11	24	—	—	—	7.36	3.38
Bremon, Tony	R-R	6-1	165	12-5-87	1	1	2.08	3	2	0	0	13	10	5	3	1	4	17	.213	.313	.161	11.77	2.77
2-team total (9 White Sox 1)					7	3	2.28	12	10	1	1	71	57	24	18	2	8	65	—	—	—	8.24	1.01
Bruno, Keuri	R-R	6-0	180	1-20-87	2	1	4.61	12	3	0	1	41	47	28	21	1	26	37	.280	.302	.270	8.12	5.71
2-team total (3 White Sox 1)					2	1	4.50	15	3	0	1	46	50	30	23	2	32	41	—	—	—	8.02	6.26
Calixto, Tiago	R-R	6-4	180	5-6-89	0	3	7.16	8	3	0	0	16	15	15	13	1	19	7	.259	.389	.200	3.86	10.47
Carrillo, Marco	R-R	5-10	155	4-3-89	6	2	4.41	21	0	0	2	49	36	30	24	1	39	44	.213	.171	.224	8.08	7.16
Cueva, Jorge	R-R	6-3	205	3-24-89	1	2	7.47	15	0	0	2	37	59	42	31	1	16	30	.349	.400	.333	7.23	3.86
2-team total (3 White Sox 1)					1	2	6.97	18	0	0	3	41	62	43	32	1	20	34	—	—	—	7.40	4.35
Duque, Jean	R-R	6-3	190	7-17-89	1	4	3.43	15	9	0	1	58	46	30	22	2	35	60	.220	.254	.205	9.36	5.46
Eusebio, Hector	R-R	6-5	215	11-1-87	1	2	1.35	5	0	0	1	13	11	4	2	0	5	18	.204	.143	.225	12.15	3.38
2-team total (20 White Sox 1)					2	6	3.31	25	0	0	8	54	53	25	20	0	23	59	—	—	—	9.77	3.81
Jean, Dominque	R-R	6-2	170	11-24-88	0	5	7.20	16	7	0	1	45	49	46	36	1	46	41	.280	.316	.263	8.20	9.20
2-team total (5 White Sox 1)					0	5	5.89	21	7	0	1	55	56	48	36	1	51	49	—	—	—	8.02	8.35
Juma, Ronny	L-L	6-2	182	10-26-88	1	1	6.17	4	0	0	0	12	10	8	8	0	8	9	.250	.167	.265	6.94	6.17
2-team total (8 White Sox 1)					1	1	4.91	12	0	0	0	22	21	12	12	0	15	14	—	—	—	5.73	6.14
Marte, Luis	R-R	6-1	190	12-15-86	0	0	2.89	4	0	0	2	9	14	4	3	0	2	7	.350	.222	.387	6.75	1.93
2-team total (15 White Sox 1)					0	2	3.63	19	0	0	5	35	46	21	14	1	10	23	—	—	—	5.97	2.60
Merejildo, Jose	R-R	6-1	185	3-19-86	5	3	3.39	14	11	1	0	77	81	47	29	4	35	53	.269	.237	.284	6.19	4.09
Mota, Arismendy	R-R	6-2	165	2-16-87	1	7	4.48	16	14	1	0	68	70	45	34	3	41	66	.267	.258	.270	8.69	5.40
Ortega, Yorvix	R-R	5-11	175	8-1-89	1	7	6.66	17	2	0	3	49	52	41	36	3	24	44	.283	.259	.292	9.25	8.14
Rienzo, Andre	R-R	6-3	160	6-5-88	2	1	1.64	5	4	0	0	22	17	5	4	0	6	22	.218	.136	.250	9.00	2.45
2-team total (3 White Sox 1)					5	1	1.33	8	7	0	0	41	32	8	6	0	9	44	—	—	—	9.74	1.99
Ruiz, Diogenes	R-R	6-2	185	10-1-88	0	2	6.17	11	2	0	0	23	24	21	16	1	18	16	.276	.286	.273	6.17	6.94
Tejada, Silvio	R-R	6-6	190	9-6-88	0	1	9.82	12	4	0	0	29	26	35	32	2	37	20	.243	.261	.238	6.14	11.35
2-team total (4 White Sox 1)					0	2	9.50	16	4	0	0	36	34	42	38	2	42	29	—	—	—	7.25	10.50

Fielding

Catcher	PCT	G	PO	A	E	DP	PB
Del Valle	.980	37	265	22	6	1	16
Gonzalez	.965	30	179	39	8	2	13
Parra	.990	12	88	13	1	0	4
Pascual	.944	2	17	0	1	0	2

First Base	PCT	G	PO	A	E	DP
Acuna	.989	35	266	14	3	24
De La Cruz	1.000	4	24	0	0	2
Del Valle	1.000	3	23	0	0	3
Garcia	1.000	3	18	1	0	0
Marte	1.000	4	19	0	0	2
Parra	.978	24	167	7	4	17
Ramos	1.000	1	1	0	0	0
Robles	.980	16	96	2	2	5

Second Base	PCT	G	PO	A	E	DP
Alcala	.964	11	23	30	2	6
Cabrera	—	1	0	0	0	0
Garcia	.900	5	5	4	1	1
Ladera	.971	41	92	111	6	24
Mercedes	.333	2	0	1	2	1
Robles	.818	2	4	5	2	2
Williams	.926	18	39	36	6	7

Third Base	PCT	G	PO	A	E	DP
Garcia	.879	13	10	19	4	2
Ladera	.957	9	8	14	1	0
Marte	—	1	0	0	0	0
Robles	.875	6	6	15	3	3
Sanchez	.907	56	40	96	14	9

Shortstop	PCT	G	PO	A	E	DP
Ladera	.962	11	6	19	1	1
Mercedes	.912	42	64	133	19	27
Puentes	.889	9	12	36	6	4
Robles	.897	19	34	53	10	10

Outfield	PCT	G	PO	A	E	DP
Alcala	.889	32	45	3	6	0
Cabrera	.927	40	46	5	4	1
Garcia	—	1	0	0	0	0
Marte	—	2	0	0	0	0
Ramos	.881	51	69	5	10	0
Reyes	.929	50	85	7	7	1
Robles	1.000	2	1	0	0	0
Rosales	1.000	43	43	8	0	2
Trujillo	1.000	13	30	3	0	0
Vega	1.000	12	13	2	0	0

Cincinnati Reds

BY JOHN FAY

The Reds made a $46 million bet before the 2008 season that they could compete in the National League Central when they signed closer Francisco Cordero to a four-year deal.

Cordero was the big offseason acquisition. But the Reds upgraded the rotation by trading Josh Hamilton to the Rangers for Edinson Volquez. They added lefthander Jeremy Affeldt to the bullpen. They brought in Corey Patterson and Josh Fogg in late-spring moves.

The additional players—which pushed the payroll to a franchise-record $74.1 million—along  with the hiring of manager Dusty Baker had hopes high.

But it didn't work out.

Ken Griffey Jr., coming off a 30-home run, 93-RBI season in 2007, struggled at the plate. Shortstop Alex Gonzalez got hurt in the spring training and didn't play an inning. No. 1 starter Aaron Harang went from winning 16 games in 2007 to winning six. Fogg, and whomever the Reds put in the No. 5 spot, struggled. Patterson spent the year hovering around the .200 mark.

There were some bright spots for the Reds. Joey Votto hit .297 with 24 home runs and 84 RBIs. Volquez went 17-6, 3.21 in his first full year in the majors. Jay Bruce put up respectable numbers (.254 with 21 home runs) at 21 years old.

The struggles brought changes within the front office, however. General manager Wayne Krivsky was fired on April 23 after an 8-12 start. Former St. Louis GM Walt Jocketty, hired in January as a consultant, was moved to the GM role. CEO Bob Castellini said at the press conference announcing the move, "We're not going to lose anymore."

Well, the Reds did lose a lot more after Krivsky's firing. They went 65-76 the rest of the way. The 74-88 record—a two-game improvement over 2007—was the franchise's eighth straight losing season. You have to go back to the 1950s to find a similar streak of futility for the franchise.

But the Reds are clearly a team headed in a different direction. There were signs of that when Bruce, BA's 2007 Minor League Player of the Year, was called up on May 27 and installed as the center fielder. It became clearer when the club traded Griffey to the White Sox in a deadline deal. It was crystal clear when Adam Dunn was traded to the Diamondbacks 11 days later.

Ten Reds made their big league debuts in 2008:

righthanders Johnny Cueto, Daryl Thompson, Ramon Ramirez and Josh Roenicke; lefthander Daniel Ray Herrera; infielders Paul Janish and Adam Rosales; outfielders Bruce and Chris Dickerson; and utilityman Wilkin Castillo. And the team will continue to build around its young core.

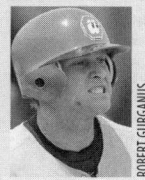
ORGANIZATION LEADERS

BATTING		*Minimum 250 at-bats
*AVG	Valaika, Chris, Sarasota/Chattanooga	.317
R	Heisey, Chris, Sarasota/Chattanooga	88
H	Valaika, Chris, Sarasota/Chattanooga	163
TB	Francisco, Juan, Sarasota	256
2B	Heisey, Chris, Sarasota/Chattanooga	37
3B	Dickerson, Chris, Louisville	9
3B	Anderson, Drew T., Louisville	9
HR	Francisco, Juan, Sarasota	23
RBI	Francisco, Juan, Sarasota	92
BB	Gutierrez, Tonys, Chattanooga	68
SO	Waring, Brandon, Dayton	156
SB	Stubbs, Drew, Sarasota/Chatt./Louisville	33
*OBP	Gutierrez, Tonys, Chattanooga	.396
*SLG	Dorn, Daniel, Sarasota/Chattanooga	.537

PITCHING		†Minimum 75 innings
W	Pettyjohn, Adam, Louisville	15
L	Wood, Travis, Sarasota/Chattanooga	13
†ERA	Thompson, Daryl, Chatt./Sarasota/Louisville	2.79
G	Adkins, Jon, Louisville	57
G	Roenicke, Josh, Chattanooga/Louisville	57
G	Herrera, Daniel Ray, Chattanooga/Louisville	57
GS	Pettyjohn, Adam, Louisville	28
SV	Adkins, Jon, Louisville	30
IP	Pettyjohn, Adam, Louisville	174
BB	Wood, Travis, Sarasota/Chattanooga	69
SO	Ramirez, Ramon, Chattanooga/Louisville	145
†AVG	Ramirez, Ramon, Chattanooga/Louisville	.222

General Manager: Wayne Krivsky/Walt Jocketty . **Farm Director:** Terry Reynolds. **Scouting Director:** Chris Buckley.

Class	Team	League	W	L	PCT	Finish*	Manager	Affiliate Since
Majors	Cincinnati	National	74	88	.457	10th (16)	Dusty Baker	—
Triple-A	Louisville Bats	International	88	56	.611	1st (14)	Rick Sweet	2000
Double-A	Chattanooga Lookouts	Southern	67	72	.482	8th (10)	Mike Goff	1988
High A	Sarasota Reds	Florida State	60	78	.435	10th (12)	Joe Ayrault	2005
Low A	Dayton Dragons	Midwest	66	72	.478	11th (14)	Donnie Scott	2000
Rookie	Billings Mustangs	Pioneer	42	32	.568	2nd (8)	Julio Garcia	1974
Rookie	GCL Reds	Gulf Coast	25	31	.446	14th (16)	Pat Kelly	1999
Overall 2008 Minor League Record			348	383	.476	19th		

* Finish in overall standings (No. of teams in league). ^League champion.

ORGANIZATION STATISTICS

CINCINNATI REDS
NATIONAL LEAGUE

Batting	B-T	HT	WT	DOB	AVG	vLH	vRH	G	AB	R	H	2B	3B	HR	RBI	BB	HBP	SH	SF	SO	SB	CS	SLG	OBP
Bako, Paul	L-R	6-2	205	6-20-72	.217	.197	.224	99	299	30	65	11	2	6	35	34	1	3	1	90	0	2	.328	.299
Bruce, Jay	L-L	6-3	205	4-3-87	.254	.190	.286	108	413	63	105	17	1	21	52	33	4	0	2	110	4	6	.453	.314
Cabrera, Jolbert	R-R	6-1	215	12-8-72	.252	.238	.260	48	115	17	29	6	1	3	12	8	2	0	1	29	2	0	.400	.310
Castillo, Wilkin	B-R	6-0	200	6-1-84	.281	.200	.296	18	32	6	9	1	0	0	1	1	0	1	0	5	0	0	.313	.303
Castro, Juan	R-R	5-11	190	6-20-72	.000	.000	.000	7	10	1	0	0	0	0	0	1	0	0	0	0	0	0	.000	.091
Dickerson, Chris	L-L	6-3	225	4-10-82	.304	.286	.309	31	102	20	31	9	2	6	15	17	2	1	0	35	5	3	.608	.413
Dunn, Adam	L-R	6-6	275	11-9-79	.233	.200	.248	114	373	58	87	14	0	32	74	80	6	0	5	120	1	1	.528	.373
2-team total (44 Arizona)					.236	—	—	158	517	79	122	23	0	40	100	122	7	0	5	164	2	1	.513	.386
Encarnacion, Edwin	R-R	6-1	215	1-7-83	.251	.292	.235	146	506	75	127	29	1	26	68	61	10	0	5	102	1	0	.466	.340
Freel, Ryan	R-R	5-10	185	3-8-76	.298	.339	.261	48	131	17	39	8	0	0	10	8	1	2	1	18	6	4	.359	.340
Griffey Jr., Ken	L-L	6-3	230	11-21-69	.245	.212	.261	102	359	51	88	20	1	15	53	61	2	0	3	64	0	1	.432	.355
Hairston Jr., Jerry	R-R	5-10	185	5-29-76	.326	.345	.316	80	261	47	85	20	2	6	36	23	3	8	2	36	15	3	.487	.384
Hanigan, Ryan	R-R	6-0	195	8-16-80	.271	.237	.298	31	85	9	23	2	0	2	9	10	3	0	0	9	0	0	.365	.367
Hatteberg, Scott	L-R	6-1	210	12-14-69	.173	.100	.190	34	52	3	9	3	0	0	7	7	0	0	2	7	0	1	.231	.262
Hopper, Norris	R-R	5-10	210	3-24-79	.200	.269	.125	26	50	3	10	0	0	0	1	5	1	2	0	6	1	0	.200	.286
Janish, Paul	R-R	6-2	190	10-12-82	.188	.323	.102	38	80	5	15	2	0	1	6	7	2	0	0	18	0	0	.250	.270
Keppinger, Jeff	R-R	6-0	180	4-21-80	.266	.360	.225	121	459	45	122	24	2	3	43	30	2	6	5	24	3	1	.346	.310
Patterson, Corey	L-R	5-9	175	8-13-79	.205	.188	.209	135	366	46	75	17	2	10	34	16	1	5	4	57	14	9	.344	.238
Phillips, Andy	R-R	6-0	210	4-6-77	.233	.256	.206	52	73	11	17	3	0	3	10	6	1	0	0	14	0	0	.397	.300
2-team total (4 New York)					.231	—	—	56	78	12	18	3	0	3	10	6	1	0	0	14	0	0	.385	.294
Phillips, Brandon	R-R	6-0	195	6-28-81	.261	.296	.247	141	559	80	146	24	7	21	78	39	5	0	6	93	23	10	.442	.312
Richar, Danny	L-R	6-1	195	6-9-83	.222	.000	.229	16	36	4	8	2	0	0	3	0	0	1	0	9	1	0	.278	.222
Rosales, Adam	R-R	6-1	195	5-20-83	.207	.273	.167	18	29	0	6	1	0	0	2	1	0	0	0	4	1	0	.241	.233
Ross, David	R-R	6-2	240	3-19-77	.231	.213	.247	52	134	17	31	9	0	3	13	32	1	5	1	36	0	1	.366	.381
Valentin, Javier	B-R	5-10	215	9-19-75	.256	.182	.271	94	129	10	33	8	0	4	18	14	0	0	1	27	0	0	.411	.326
Votto, Joey	L-R	6-3	220	9-10-83	.297	.292	.299	151	526	69	156	32	3	24	84	59	2	0	2	102	7	5	.506	.368

Pitching	B-T	HT	WT	DOB	W	L	ERA	G	GS	CG	SV	IP	H	R	ER	HR	BB	SO	AVG	vLH	vRH	K/9	BB/9
Adkins, Jon	L-R	6-0	210	8-30-77	1	0	2.45	4	0	0	0	4	4	1	1	1	3	3	.333	.250	.375	7.36	7.36
Affeldt, Jeremy	L-L	6-4	225	6-6-79	1	1	3.33	74	0	0	0	78	78	36	29	9	25	80	.260	.269	.255	9.19	2.87
Arroyo, Bronson	R-R	6-5	195	2-24-77	15	11	4.77	34	34	1	0	200	219	116	106	29	68	163	.281	.314	.254	7.33	3.06
Bailey, Homer	R-R	6-4	205	5-3-86	0	6	7.93	8	8	0	0	36	50	36	32	8	17	18	.378	.305	.423	4.46	4.21
Belisle, Matt	R-R	6-3	230	6-6-80	1	4	7.28	6	6	0	0	30	47	27	24	4	6	14	.353	.296	.419	4.25	1.82
Bray, Bill	L-L	6-3	220	6-5-83	2	2	2.87	63	0	0	0	47	50	19	15	4	24	54	.269	.260	.274	10.34	4.60
Burton, Jared	R-R	6-5	230	6-2-81	5	1	3.22	54	0	0	0	59	56	24	21	6	25	58	.249	.247	.250	8.90	3.84
Coffey, Todd	R-R	6-5	240	9-9-80	0	1	6.05	17	0	0	0	19	25	13	13	4	6	8	.321	.259	.353	3.72	2.79
2-team total (9 Milwaukee)					1	0	4.39	26	0	0	0	27	31	13	13	4	8	15	—	—	—	5.06	2.70
Cordero, Francisco	R-R	6-3	240	5-11-75	5	4	3.33	72	0	0	34	70	61	28	26	6	38	78	.235	.212	.252	9.98	4.86
Cueto, Johnny	R-R	5-10	185	2-15-86	9	14	4.81	31	31	0	0	174	178	101	93	29	68	158	.266	.249	.275	8.17	3.52
Fogg, Josh	R-R	6-0	205	12-13-76	2	7	7.58	22	14	0	0	78	97	69	66	17	27	45	.302	.299	.305	5.17	3.10
Harang, Aaron	R-R	6-7	275	5-9-78	6	17	4.78	30	29	1	0	184	205	104	98	35	50	153	.284	.298	.274	7.47	2.44
Herrera, Danny Ray	L-L	5-7	145	10-21-84	0	0	7.36	7	0	0	0	7	16	6	6	1	3	8	.333	.000	.455	9.82	3.68
Lincoln, Mike	R-R	6-2	215	4-10-75	2	5	4.48	64	0	0	0	70	66	37	35	10	24	57	.250	.225	.268	7.29	3.07
Majewski, Gary	R-R	6-1	220	2-26-80	1	0	6.53	37	0	0	0	40	61	31	29	6	15	27	.363	.348	.373	6.08	3.38
Masset, Nick	R-R	6-4	235	5-17-82	1	0	2.08	10	0	0	0	17	16	6	4	3	5	11	.254	.217	.275	5.71	2.60
Mercker, Kent	L-L	6-2	205	2-1-68	1	0	3.29	15	0	0	0	14	13	5	5	1	8	6	.265	.333	.226	3.95	5.27
Pettyjohn, Adam	R-L	6-3	200	6-11-77	0	1	20.25	3	1	0	0	4	11	9	9	2	2	1	.478	.000	.524	2.25	4.50
Ramirez, Ramon	R-R	5-10	170	9-16-82	1	1	2.67	5	4	0	0	27	17	8	8	3	11	21	.183	.297	.107	7.00	3.67
Roenicke, Josh	R-R	6-0	200	8-4-82	0	0	9.00	5	0	0	0	3	6	3	3	0	2	6	.400	.600	.300	18.00	6.00
Thompson, Daryl	R-R	6-0	180	11-2-85	0	2	6.91	3	3	0	0	14	20	11	11	3	7	6	.328	.308	.343	3.77	4.40
Volquez, Edinson	R-R	6-0	200	7-3-83	17	6	3.21	33	32	0	0	196	167	82	70	14	93	206	.232	.249	.214	9.46	4.27
Weathers, David	R-R	6-3	235	9-25-69	4	6	3.25	72	0	0	0	69	76	27	25	6	30	46	.276	.245	.296	5.97	3.89

Fielding

Catcher	PCT	G	PO	A	E	DP	PB
Bako	.993	96	679	39	5	7	9
Hanigan	.995	30	186	19	1	4	1
Ross	.992	46	323	29	3	4	6
Valentin	1.000	17	67	5	0	0	1

First Base	PCT	G	PO	A	E	DP
Hatteberg	.987	16	69	6	1	3
Keppinger	1.000	3	15	1	0	0
A. Phillips	.972	4	35	0	1	3
Valentin	1.000	11	75	4	0	10
Votto	.991	144	1050	136	11	119

Second Base	PCT	G	PO	A	E	DP
Cabrera	1.000	3	4	6	0	3
Castillo	1.000	2	5	2	0	2
Castro	1.000	2	1	2	0	0
Freel	1.000	3	4	5	0	1
Hairston Jr.	1.000	7	11	17	0	5
Keppinger	1.000	3	5	5	0	2
A. Phillips	1.000	6	5	8	0	3
B. Phillips	.990	140	298	401	7	85
Richar	.966	10	12	16	1	4
Rosales	1.000	2	6	6	0	4

Third Base	PCT	G	PO	A	E	DP
Cabrera	1.000	3	1	2	0	0
Castro	1.000	1	0	4	0	0
Encarnacion	.930	143	91	216	23	23
Freel	.889	4	4	4	1	0
Hairston Jr.	—	1	0	0	0	0
Keppinger	1.000	10	3	18	0	2
A. Phillips	.917	8	1	10	1	2
Rosales	1.000	4	2	1	0	1
Valentin	—	4	0	0	0	0

Shortstop	PCT	G	PO	A	E	DP
Cabrera	1.000	9	7	14	0	5
Castro	1.000	3	1	4	0	0
Hairston Jr.	.970	34	61	68	4	18
Janish	.973	36	31	78	3	13
Keppinger	.980	108	145	246	8	72
Richar	1.000	1	1	1	0	0

Outfield	PCT	G	PO	A	E	DP
Bruce	.955	105	223	8	11	4
Cabrera	.960	20	22	2	1	0
Castillo	1.000	5	6	0	0	0
Dickerson	1.000	28	48	0	0	0
Dunn	.966	110	191	5	7	1
Freel	1.000	34	55	1	0	0
Griffey Jr.	.970	90	156	7	5	0
Hairston Jr.	.982	42	54	1	1	0
Hopper	1.000	18	23	0	0	0
Patterson	.988	124	242	3	3	1

LOUISVILLE BATS   TRIPLE-A
INTERNATIONAL LEAGUE

Batting	B-T	HT	WT	DOB	AVG	vLH	vRH	G	AB	R	H	2B	3B	HR	RBI	BB	HBP	SH	SF	SO	SB	CS	SLG	OBP
Anderson, Drew M.	B-R	5-9	170	2-2-83	.154	.333	.100	8	13	0	2	0	0	0	1	1	0	0	1	5	1	0	.154	.200
Anderson, Drew T.	L-R	6-2	200	6-9-81	.290	.318	.282	108	404	54	117	28	9	8	71	21	7	5	4	100	4	6	.463	.333
Barker, Kevin	L-L	6-1	200	7-26-75	.258	.239	.264	114	399	73	103	22	0	21	77	55	4	0	10	98	0	1	.471	.346
Bolivar, Luis	R-R	6-0	180	2-15-81	.262	.243	.268	104	298	46	78	15	4	7	39	11	7	9	4	76	18	1	.409	.317
Bruce, Jay	L-L	6-3	205	4-3-87	.364	.389	.354	49	184	34	67	9	5	10	37	12	0	0	5	45	8	1	.630	.393
Cabrera, Jolbert	R-R	6-1	215	12-8-72	.288	.281	.291	57	215	26	62	16	5	4	30	13	6	1	4	39	5	3	.465	.340
Castillo, Wilkin	B-R	6-0	200	6-1-84	.190	.000	.216	11	42	2	8	0	0	0	1	0	0	0	5	1	2	.190	.209
Colina, Alvin	R-R	6-3	210	12-26-81	.256	.296	.243	65	227	25	58	8	2	8	54	17	5	0	5	68	2	1	.414	.315
Cumberland, Shaun	L-R	6-2	185	8-1-84	.274	.310	.266	48	168	18	46	9	3	1	13	12	0	4	1	50	6	0	.381	.320
Dickerson, Chris	L-L	6-3	225	4-10-82	.287	.247	.300	97	349	65	100	16	9	11	53	54	3	5	3	102	26	7	.479	.384
Gil, Jerry	R-R	6-3	200	10-14-82	.162	.070	.207	33	130	13	21	6	0	2	13	4	2	0	1	39	4	0	.254	.197
Green, Andy	R-R	5-10	180	7-7-77	.233	.241	.230	71	262	43	61	15	2	5	19	30	4	4	1	43	4	3	.363	.320
Griffin, Michael	R-R	5-10	195	10-1-83	.271	.279	.269	89	310	28	84	20	3	3	32	11	4	3	2	72	6	5	.384	.303
Hairston Jr., Jerry	R-R	5-10	185	5-29-76	.380	.429	.362	20	79	11	30	8	2	4	19	3	1	1	1	9	1	1	.684	.405
Hanigan, Ryan	R-R	6-0	195	8-16-80	.324	.343	.317	75	272	37	88	14	0	4	35	25	8	2	4	39	1	0	.419	.392
Herr, Aaron	R-R	6-0	210	3-7-81	.134	.294	.080	18	67	10	9	2	1	2	4	8	0	0	0	22	0	0	.284	.183
2-team total (65 Buffalo)					.221	—	—	83	308	37	68	9	4	11	40	15	3	1	1	97	1	0	.383	.263
Hopper, Norris	R-R	5-10	210	3-24-79	.294	.222	.375	4	17	3	5	1	0	0	0	0	0	1	0	4	0	0	.353	.294
Janish, Paul	R-R	6-2	190	10-12-82	.252	.293	.237	92	318	45	80	20	1	7	42	26	9	10	2	71	2	0	.387	.324
Keppinger, Jeff	R-R	6-0	180	4-21-80	.500	.417	.600	6	22	3	11	2	0	1	2	2	0	1	0	1	0	0	.727	.542
Kroski, Chris	L-R	6-2	220	5-17-82	.300	.000	.375	3	10	0	3	0	0	0	0	0	0	0	0	4	0	0	.300	.300
Mackowiak, Rob	L-R	5-11	190	6-20-76	.255	.167	.274	49	141	31	36	2	1	5	15	37	5	1	0	42	4	1	.390	.426
Patterson, Corey	L-R	5-9	175	8-13-79	.409	.545	.273	5	22	3	9	2	0	0	5	0	0			5	1	1	.500	.435
Phillips, Andy	R-R	6-0	210	4-6-77	.315	.372	.291	40	146	27	46	9	1	5	22	20	1	0	3	19	2	0	.493	.394
Richar, Danny	R-L	6-1	195	6-9-83	.254	.316	.242	29	114	16	29	9	2	2	16	11	1	1	2	26	3	3	.421	.320
2-team total (62 Charlotte)					.260	—	—	91	362	51	94	21	3	11	55	31	3	1	3	71	14	5	.425	.321
Rosales, Adam	R-R	6-1	195	5-20-83	.287	.218	.311	117	432	70	124	29	7	11	58	22	14	1	4	82	7	1	.463	.339
Ross, David	R-R	6-2	240	3-19-77	.167	.143	.174	9	30	4	5	1	1	1	2	3	0	0	1	12	0	0	.367	.235
2-team total (6 Pawtucket)					.207	—	—	15	58	8	12	2	1	2	5	4	0	0	1	19	0	0	.379	.254
Stubbs, Drew	R-R	6-4	200	10-4-84	.293	.444	.273	19	75	14	22	4	2	2	10	6	1	2	0	20	3	0	.480	.354
Szymanski, B.J.	R-R	6-5	210	10-1-82	.156	.111	.185	22	45	4	7	0	0	1	6	3	1	1	2	16	1	0	.222	.216
Tatum, Craig	R-R	6-0	225	3-18-83	.179	.400	.103	10	39	1	7	0	0	0	4	0	0	1	0	16	0	0	.179	.175

Pitching	B-T	HT	WT	DOB	W	L	ERA	G	GS	CG	SV	IP	H	R	ER	HR	BB	SO	AVG	vLH	vRH	K/9	BB/9
Adkins, Jon	L-R	6-0	210	8-30-77	1	3	3.48	57	0	0	30	62	62	26	24	5	13	39	.261	.264	.257	5.66	1.89
Bailey, Homer	R-R	6-4	205	5-3-86	4	7	4.77	19	19	0	0	111	118	62	59	10	46	96	.281	.278	.286	7.76	3.72
Belisle, Matt	R-R	6-3	230	6-6-80	5	1	4.26	26	1	0	4	38	43	22	18	1	11	27	.281	.329	.234	6.39	2.61
Bray, Bill	L-L	6-3	220	6-5-83	0	0	3.00	9	0	0	1	9	6	3	3	1	5	15	.182	.071	.263	15.00	5.00
Brower, Jim	R-R	6-3	215	12-29-72	0	1	2.88	17	0	0	2	25	27	13	8	1	11	28	.267	.261	.273	10.08	3.96
Burton, Jared	R-R	6-5	230	6-2-81	0	0	4.50	2	1	0	0	2	1	1	1	0	2	1	.167	.000	.200	4.50	9.00
Coffey, Todd	R-R	6-5	240	9-9-80	3	3	4.35	34	0	0	2	39	49	23	19	4	15	43	.299	.333	.274	9.84	3.43
Fisher, Carlos	R-R	6-3	215	2-22-83	5	0	1.04	14	0	0	0	17	14	2	2	0	9	21	.215	.152	.281	10.90	4.67
Fogg, Josh	R-R	6-0	205	12-13-76	1	1	1.59	2	2	1	0	17	14	4	3	0	3	12	.233	.364	.158	6.35	1.59
Harang, Aaron	R-R	6-7	275	5-9-78	1	0	0.00	1	1	0	0	6	5	0	0	0	6	2	.238	.214	.286	9.00	0.00
Herrera, Danny Ray	L-L	5-7	145	10-21-84	4	4	2.78	47	0	0	6	55	47	20	17	4	10	50	.227	.194	.254	8.18	1.64
Jukich, Ben	L-L	6-4	190	10-17-82	1	1	4.37	4	3	0	0	23	30	14	11	2	4	15	.309	.400	.258	5.96	1.59
Lehr, Justin	R-R	6-2	205	8-3-77	6	2	2.10	16	8	0	1	64	51	15	15	5	11	41	.223	.188	.259	5.74	1.54
Livingston, Bobby	L-L	6-3	205	9-3-82	4	4	4.98	9	9	0	0	56	63	33	31	6	17	35	.289	.299	.284	5.63	2.73
Majewski, Gary	R-R	6-1	220	2-26-80	2	1	3.76	22	0	0	3	26	27	11	11	2	7	22	.270	.283	.259	7.52	2.39
Mallett, Justin	R-R	6-6	210	11-11-81	6	4	4.50	25	14	0	0	100	96	51	50	9	37	70	.259	.307	.202	6.30	3.33
Maloney, Matt	L-L	6-4	220	1-16-84	11	5	4.68	25	25	2	0	140	143	75	73	18	39	132	.264	.238	.273	8.47	2.50

ORGANIZATION STATISTICS

Name	B-T	HT	WT	DOB	W	L	ERA	G	GS	CG	SV	IP	H	R	ER	HR	BB	SO	AVG	vLH	vRH	K/9	BB/9
Manuel, Robert	R-R	6-3	197	7-9-83	0	0	0.00	1	0	0	0	2	2	0	0	0	0	0	.250	.167	.500	0.00	0.00
McBeth, Marcus	R-R	6-2	195	8-23-80	1	1	6.20	24	0	0	2	25	23	19	17	6	15	20	.245	.271	.217	7.30	5.47
2-team total (4 Pawtucket)					2	1	5.40	28	0	0	2	32	26	21	19	7	16	31	—	—	—	8.81	4.55
Mercker, Kent	L-L	6-2	205	2-1-68	0	1	5.40	2	1	0	0	2	2	1	1	0	1	0	.286	.000	.500	0.00	5.40
Ondrusek, Logan	R-R	6-7	205	2-13-85	0	0	0.00	1	0	0	0	1	1	0	0	0	0	2 1	.250	1.000	.000	6.75	13.50
Pelland, Tyler	R-L	6-0	210	10-9-83	1	2	4.06	36	0	0	1	44	39	20	20	4	28	51	.241	.246	.237	10.35	5.68
Pettyjohn, Adam	R-L	6-3	200	6-11-77	15	6	4.59	28	28	0	0	174	188	97	89	20	43	95	.279	.286	.275	4.90	2.22
Ramirez, Ramon	R-R	5-10	170	9-16-82	4	5	3.08	19	15	0	1	99	76	37	34	8	42	93	.215	.225	.200	8.43	3.81
Roenicke, Josh	R-R	6-3	200	8-4-82	2	0	2.54	35	0	0	3	39	34	11	11	2	14	43	.234	.270	.207	9.92	3.23
Sauerbeck, Scott	R-L	6-3	200	11-9-71	0	1	9.00	4	0	0	0	4	6	4	4	1	4	5	.353	.429	.300	11.25	9.00
2-team total (31 Charlotte)					1	3	5.06	35	0	0	0	27	21	20	15	2	30	31	—	—	—	10.46	10.13
Shearn, Tom	R-R	6-4	230	8-28-77	6	2	4.53	10	10	0	0	58	60	29	29	8	15	31	.269	.214	.340	4.84	2.34
2-team total (6 Rochester)					7	4	4.80	16	16	1	0	86	98	47	46	12	22	57	—	—	—	5.94	2.29
Stone, Ricky	R-R	6-1	195	2-28-75	0	0	12.00	3	0	0	0	3	5	4	4	2	0	0	.357	.167	.500	0.00	0.00
Thompson, Daryl	R-R	6-0	180	11-2-85	5	0	2.76	7	7	0	0	46	39	15	14	4	9	33	.232	.232	.233	6.50	1.77
Vazquez, Camilo	L-L	5-11	205	10-3-83	0	1	5.40	2	0	0	0	2	4	1	1	0	0	1	.444	.400	.500	5.40	0.00
Weathers, David	R-R	6-3	235	9-25-69	0	0	0.00	1	0	0	0	1	0	0	0	0	0	1	.000	.000	.000	9.00	0.00

Fielding

Catcher	PCT	G	PO	A	E	DP	PB
Castillo	1.000	3	22	4	0	0	0
Colina	.986	53	333	32	5	9	2
Hanigan	.992	71	550	52	5	5	0
Kroski	1.000	3	21	1	0	0	0
Ross	1.000	6	46	5	0	0	0
Tatum	1.000	10	79	6	0	1	0

First Base	PCT	G	PO	A	E	DP
Barker	.996	97	832	80	4	69
Bolivar	.965	10	78	5	3	6
Cabrera	1.000	12	86	3	0	8
Hanigan	1.000	1	2	0	0	0
Phillips	1.000	16	116	9	0	8
Rosales	.994	19	155	17	1	17

Second Base	PCT	G	PO	A	E	DP
D.M. Anderson	.833	4	6	4	2	2
Bolivar	.981	15	19	32	1	8
Castillo	1.000	1	1	0	0	0
Green	.984	66	133	172	5	37
Griffin	.975	28	45	70	3	19
Hairston Jr.	1.000	1	2	4	0	0

	PCT	G	PO	A	E	DP
Herr	.929	14	18	34	4	3
Janish	1.000	1	2	2	0	1
Phillips	1.000	2	5	4	0	1
Richar	.973	23	39	70	3	14
Rosales	1.000	9	12	27	0	5

Third Base	PCT	G	PO	A	E	DP
Bolivar	.917	35	37	51	8	10
Cabrera	.933	16	15	27	3	3
Castillo	.933	7	3	11	1	1
Gil	1.000	2	3	3	0	2
Green	.667	1	1	1	1	0
Griffin	.938	21	9	21	2	2
Hairston Jr.	.800	2	0	4	1	0
Keppinger	1.000	2	0	4	0	0
Phillips	.971	14	10	24	1	1
Rosales	.942	66	46	117	10	7

Shortstop	PCT	G	PO	A	E	DP
Bolivar	.941	31	41	70	7	15
Hairston Jr.	.903	7	10	18	3	4
Janish	.971	90	154	248	12	53
Keppinger	1.000	1	1	1	0	0
Richar	.950	5	7	12	1	5
Rosales	.990	25	29	69	1	10

Outfield	PCT	G	PO	A	E	DP
D. T. Anderson	.994	96	157	6	1	2
Bolivar	1.000	9	7	0	0	0
Bruce	.990	46	101	3	1	0
Cabrera	.969	18	29	2	1	0
Castillo	—	1	0	0	0	0
Cumberland	.976	45	82	1	2	0
Dickerson	.985	91	191	5	3	2
Gil	1.000	24	45	1	0	0
Green	1.000	2	2	0	0	0
Griffin	1.000	42	54	5	0	0
Hairston Jr.	1.000	11	20	0	0	0
Hopper	1.000	4	7	0	0	0
Mackowiak	.984	39	60	1	1	0
Patterson	1.000	4	12	0	0	0
Stubbs	.980	18	48	1	1	0
Szymanski	.952	18	19	1	1	0

CHATTANOOGA LOOKOUTS   DOUBLE-A
SOUTHERN LEAGUE

Batting	B-T	HT	WT	DOB	AVG	vLH	vRH	G	AB	R	H	2B	3B	HR	RBI	BB	HBP	SH	SF	SO	SB	CS	SLG	OBP
Anderson, Drew M.	B-R	5-9	170	2-2-81	.262	.205	.289	78	225	35	59	15	1	5	26	23	0	4	2	35	4	0	.404	.328
Bolivar, Luis	R-R	6-0	180	2-15-81	.306	.400	.255	18	72	13	22	5	0	3	9	9	1	1	1	15	4	3	.500	.386
Castro, Jose	B-R	5-11	172	11-5-86	.235	.367	.132	24	68	6	16	4	1	0	7	4	1	4	0	4	0	1	.324	.288
Collaro, Tom	R-R	6-4	216	4-4-83	.170	.207	.153	38	88	10	15	4	1	2	15	8	1	0	6	34	0	0	.307	.233
2-team total (23 Birmingham)					.202	—	—	61	173	18	35	11	1	3	27	14	2	0	6	55	0	0	.329	.262
Cumberland, Shaun	L-R	6-2	185	8-1-84	.295	.228	.313	81	268	57	79	11	4	8	28	36	2	2	1	52	13	6	.455	.381
DeJesus, Michael	L-R	5-8	173	7-16-83	.270	.238	.274	67	178	32	48	9	0	2	16	32	2	1	2	30	2	1	.354	.383
Denove, Christopher	R-R	6-1	200	12-9-82	.245	.200	.260	53	163	11	40	12	0	0	14	20	2	4	3	30	1	2	.319	.330
Dorn, Daniel	L-L	6-2	190	7-20-84	.277	.235	.290	98	336	64	93	21	2	21	60	42	7	1	2	84	1	0	.539	.367
Eymann, Eric	R-R	6-2	191	2-9-84	.299	.291	.302	125	445	62	133	31	3	8	71	25	6	6	3	65	5	4	.436	.342
Gil, Jerry	R-R	6-3	200	10-14-82	.182	.214	.171	14	55	4	10	6	0	2	11	1	0	0	1	21	1	0	.400	.193
Griffin, Michael	R-R	5-10	195	10-1-83	.289	.286	.290	38	142	18	41	12	2	1	9	9	5	0	0	15	7	3	.423	.353
Gutierrez, Tonys	L-L	6-1	220	8-18-83	.283	.287	.281	127	414	71	117	23	1	7	60	68	12	3	4	75	8	12	.394	.396
Heisey, Chris	R-R	6-0	200	12-14-84	.316	.364	.298	19	79	11	25	6	1	2	10	3	0	0	0	15	5	0	.494	.341
Henry, Sean	R-R	5-10	180	8-18-85	.285	.285	.286	113	396	66	113	22	6	11	62	42	8	3	5	75	16	7	.455	.361
Kroski, Chris	L-R	6-2	220	5-17-82	.059	.000	.077	6	17	0	1	0	0	0	0	2	1	1	0	1	0	0	.059	.150
Rodriguez, Eddy	R-R	6-0	205	12-1-85	.240	.167	.263	7	25	4	6	1	0	2	7	2	1	0	0	8	0	0	.520	.321
Strait, Cody	R-R	6-1	180	5-28-83	.257	.257	.256	73	226	32	58	17	3	5	19	14	2	1	1	55	4	3	.425	.305
Stubbs, Drew	R-R	6-4	200	10-4-84	.315	.250	.333	26	92	12	29	8	0	0	9	11	2	1	0	21	3	1	.402	.400
Szymanski, B.J.	R-R	6-5	210	10-1-82	.234	.247	.225	77	231	25	54	9	1	9	34	11	2	1	1	90	4	1	.398	.273
Tatum, Craig	R-R	6-0	225	3-18-83	.253	.317	.227	86	293	31	74	18	1	8	57	26	2	1	6	59	1	1	.403	.312
Tordi, Justin	R-R	6-1	180	4-9-84	.000	.000	.000	4	5	0	0	0	0	0	0	0	0	1	0	1	0	0	.000	.000
Turner, Justin	R-R	5-11	180	11-23-84	.289	.372	.253	78	280	45	81	14	1	8	42	33	1	3	6	54	2	1	.432	.359
Valaika, Chris	R-R	6-1	180	8-14-85	.301	.343	.284	97	379	58	114	19	1	11	50	28	3	5	2	74	7	4	.443	.352

Pitching	B-T	HT	WT	DOB	W	L	ERA	G	GS	CG	SV	IP	H	R	ER	HR	BB	SO	AVG	vLH	vRH	K/9	BB/9
Avery, James	R-R	6-0	216	6-10-84	7	8	4.89	24	24	0	0	131	151	80	71	15	45	93	.293	.283	.300	6.41	3.10
Belisle, Matt	R-R	6-3	230	6-6-80	1	0	2.00	1	1	1	0	9	7	3	2	0	0	3	.206	.067	.316	3.00	0.00
DeJesus, Misael	R-R	6-2	235	11-5-84	0	1	13.50	1	1	0	0	5	6	7	7	1	4	4	.316	.400	.222	7.71	7.71
Fisher, Carlos	R-R	6-3	215	2-22-83	1	5	3.73	36	0	0	8	51	52	28	21	3	20	46	.259	.278	.246	8.17	3.55

Pitcher	T	HT	WT	DOB	W	L	ERA	G	GS	CG	SV	IP	H	R	ER	HR	BB	SO	AVG	vLH	vRH	K/9	BB/9
Geronimo, Ramon	R-R	6-0	185	10-8-83	1	2	3.75	17	0	0	2	24	21	12	10	1	11	27	.228	.273	.188	10.13	4.13
Herrera, Danny Ray	L-L	5-7	145	10-21-84	3	0	2.55	10	0	0	0	18	12	6	5	0	7	10	.211	.286	.167	5.09	3.57
Hrynio, Mike	R-R	6-2	220	11-18-82	3	1	5.50	39	0	0	0	54	55	44	33	8	32	46	.266	.333	.227	7.67	5.33
James, Justin	R-R	6-3	215	9-13-81	0	2	7.36	12	0	0	0	15	21	17	12	2	8	10	.328	.410	.200	6.14	4.91
Jeffords, Jeff	R-R	6-1	200	11-4-84	0	1	—	1	0	0	0	0	0	2	3	3	0	0	1	.667	1.000	.500	
Jukich, Ben	L-L	6-4	190	10-17-82	10	4	3.82	23	23	1	0	139	147	68	59	6	54	111	.281	.278	.282	7.19	3.50
Lecure, Sam	R-R	6-0	192	5-4-84	9	7	3.42	27	27	0	0	155	147	61	59	12	58	128	.251	.243	.259	7.42	3.36
Lutz, Derrik	R-R	6-0	210	4-22-85	2	2	5.01	52	0	0	3	50	63	34	28	2	27	43	.303	.366	.262	7.69	4.83
Mallett, Justin	R-R	6-6	210	11-11-81	0	1	4.50	5	1	0	0	8	6	4	4	2	3	7	.207	.200	.214	7.88	3.38
Manuel, Robert	R-R	6-3	197	7-9-83	5	3	1.40	47	0	0	3	77	47	16	12	2	15	92	.172	.129	.197	10.75	1.75
Medina, Ruben	R-R	5-11	157	7-29-86	0	0	10.13	1	0	0	0	3	3	3	3	1	0	3	.273	.250	.333	10.13	0.00
Ramirez, Ramon	R-R	5-10	170	9-16-82	2	3	4.70	11	9	0	0	46	41	29	24	6	15	52	.237	.193	.278	10.17	2.93
Roenicke, Josh	R-R	6-3	200	8-4-82	4	2	3.27	22	0	0	10	22	21	10	8	2	12	28	.253	.216	.283	11.45	4.91
Smith, Jordan	R-R	6-3	206	2-4-86	2	6	5.40	11	11	0	0	55	72	42	33	6	17	42	.316	.364	.279	6.87	2.78
Tabor, Lee	L-L	6-2	175	12-17-84	1	1	5.40	36	0	0	0	42	54	27	25	3	20	32	.321	.295	.336	6.91	4.32
Thompson, Daryl	R-R	6-0	180	11-2-85	3	2	1.76	10	10	0	0	61	44	19	12	2	14	56	.208	.220	.196	8.22	2.05
Valentine, Joe	R-R	6-2	210	12-24-79	1	0	3.29	11	0	0	4	14	14	7	5	1	6	11	.259	.296	.222	7.24	3.95
Vazquez, Camilo	L-L	5-11	205	10-3-83	3	3	6.05	8	8	0	0	39	51	30	26	11	19	31	.309	.259	.333	7.22	4.42
Viola, Pedro	L-L	6-1	185	6-29-83	4	7	4.48	52	7	0	2	82	88	50	41	6	36	84	.278	.288	.272	9.18	3.94
Watson, Sean	R-R	6-2	215	7-24-85	1	2	4.37	31	0	0	3	35	27	18	17	1	28	45	.214	.211	.216	11.57	7.20
Wood, Travis	R-L	5-11	166	2-6-87	4	9	7.09	17	17	0	0	80	91	67	63	9	48	58	.289	.361	.263	6.53	5.40

Fielding

Catcher	PCT	G	PO	A	E	DP	PB
Denove	.993	52	401	27	3	5	0
Kroski	1.000	6	39	4	0	0	0
Rodriguez	.957	7	41	3	2	0	0
Tatum	.990	79	616	55	7	11	4

First Base	PCT	G	PO	A	E	DP
Bolivar	.941	3	12	4	1	1
Dorn	.994	22	158	9	1	12
Eymann	1.000	6	26	2	0	5
Gutierrez	.990	121	859	96	10	81
Tordi	1.000	1	4	0	0	2

Second Base	PCT	G	PO	A	E	DP
Anderson	.981	38	68	89	3	19
Bolivar	.980	11	16	32	1	6
DeJesus	.951	21	28	49	4	4
Eymann	—	1	0	0	0	0

	PCT	G	PO	A	E	DP
Griffin	1.000	5	9	7	0	0
Henry	1.000	1	3	0	0	0
Turner	.975	73	142	165	8	47

Third Base	PCT	G	PO	A	E	DP
Anderson	.903	14	4	24	3	0
Bolivar	.867	5	3	10	2	3
DeJesus	1.000	5	4	13	0	1
Eymann	.926	90	54	159	17	15
Gil	.750	5	5	7	4	0
Griffin	.924	27	18	43	5	4
Tordi	.000	2	0	0	1	0
Turner	1.000	2	3	6	0	0

Shortstop	PCT	G	PO	A	E	DP
Bolivar	1.000	2	1	0	0	0
Castro	.909	23	18	32	5	8
Eymann	.936	28	33	55	6	6

	PCT	G	PO	A	E	DP
Gil	1.000	1	0	1	0	0
Valaika	.952	95	152	266	21	57

Outfield	PCT	G	PO	A	E	DP
Anderson	1.000	7	8	0	0	0
Collaro	.958	15	21	2	1	1
Cumberland	.953	75	138	4	7	0
DeJesus	.882	16	14	1	2	0
Dorn	.991	63	106	9	1	2
Gil	.957	9	21	1	1	0
Griffin	1.000	2	2	1	0	1
Heisey	.978	19	43	1	1	0
Henry	.965	102	156	9	6	2
Hrynio	1.000	1	1	0	0	0
Strait	.962	62	122	6	5	1
Stubbs	1.000	25	70	3	0	0
Szymanski	.940	62	108	2	7	2

SARASOTA REDS   HIGH CLASS A

FLORIDA STATE LEAGUE

Batting	B-T	HT	WT	DOB	AVG	vLH	vRH	G	AB	R	H	2B	3B	HR	RBI	BB	HBP	SH	SF	SO	SB	CS	SLG	OBP
Alonso, Yonder	L-R	6-2	215	4-8-87	.316	.125	.455	6	19	1	6	1	0	0	2	5	0	0	1	5	0	0	.368	.440
Bartles, Brett	R-R	6-1	180	8-20-86	.250	1.000	.000	2	4	0	1	1	0	0	1	0	0	0	0	2	0	0	.500	.250
Castro, Jose	B-R	5-11	172	11-5-86	.238	.228	.242	91	357	31	85	12	3	1	15	9	8	4	0	31	2	3	.297	.273
Contreras, Efrain	R-R	6-1	165	2-6-87	.167	.333	.095	11	30	2	5	1	0	1	4	1	0	0	0	5	0	0	.300	.194
DeJesus, Michael	L-R	5-8	173	7-16-83	.246	.310	.232	42	167	20	41	5	2	1	17	19	0	1	3	35	2	2	.317	.317
Denove, Christopher	R-R	6-1	200	12-9-82	.286	—	.286	6	14	1	4	1	0	0	2	3	0	1	0	1	0	0	.357	.412
Dorn, Daniel	L-L	6-2	190	7-20-84	.250	.400	.200	5	20	3	5	2	0	1	3	1	0	0	0	8	0	0	.500	.286
Esquer, Anthony	R-R	6-1	215	9-3-84	.167	.000	.211	7	24	1	4	0	0	0	2	0	0	0	0	1	0	0	.167	.167
Francisco, Juan	L-R	6-2	180	6-24-87	.277	.264	.281	127	516	71	143	34	5	23	92	19	2	0	4	123	1	2	.496	.303
Frazier, Todd	R-R	6-3	215	2-12-86	.281	.370	.252	100	366	62	103	20	3	12	54	41	4	0	3	84	8	4	.451	.357
Gil, Jerry	R-R	6-3	200	10-14-82	.000	—	.000	1	1	0	0	0	0	0	0	0	0	0	0	0	0	0	.000	.000
Hale, Darrick	L-R	5-10	175	5-25-85	.286	.000	.400	3	7	0	2	1	0	0	1	0	0	0	0	3	0	0	.429	.375
Heisey, Chris	R-R	6-0	200	12-14-84	.287	.381	.260	117	436	77	125	31	7	7	51	57	11	8	3	69	27	2	.438	.381
Henry, Sean	R-R	5-10	180	8-18-85	.293	.300	.290	10	41	6	12	3	1	0	7	3	2	0	0	7	4	0	.415	.370
Hopper, Norris	R-R	5-10	210	3-24-79	.286	.000	.333	2	7	3	2	0	0	0	2	0	0	0	0	0	0	0	.286	.444
Kahaulelio, Jacob	R-R	5-10	195	6-7-85	.262	.345	.221	48	168	29	44	9	2	3	17	16	2	1	0	26	1	0	.393	.333
Kainer, Carson	R-R	6-1	210	10-27-84	.260	.290	.249	98	361	42	94	20	1	2	38	14	4	2	4	67	3	2	.338	.292
Keppinger, Jeff	R-R	6-0	180	4-21-80	.286	.000	.400	2	7	1	2	0	0	0	0	0	0	0	0	0	0	0	.286	.286
Long, Jake	R-R	6-1	180	4-17-86	.222	.190	.231	32	99	5	22	4	0	0	7	6	0	0	1	29	0	0	.263	.264
Louwsma, Jason	R-R	6-2	210	9-9-83	.226	.218	.229	112	420	25	95	12	0	5	43	16	2	1	2	82	1	1	.290	.257
Parker, Logan	L-L	6-3	215	7-18-84	.301	.161	.339	38	143	16	43	10	0	6	24	13	1	0	1	32	0	1	.497	.361
Perales, Daniel	L-L	5-10	176	3-18-85	.206	.189	.209	68	238	23	49	16	4	3	18	20	1	2	3	64	4	1	.345	.267
Puckett, Cody	R-R	5-10	180	4-3-87	.000	.000	.000	2	7	0	0	0	0	0	0	0	0	0	0	2	0	0	.000	.000
Rodriguez, Eddy	R-R	6-0	205	12-1-85	.201	.196	.202	70	229	20	46	5	1	5	20	14	3	1	1	63	0	0	.297	.255
Rodriguez, Yuber	R-R	6-0	200	11-17-83	.221	.161	.247	33	104	11	23	6	0	0	5	8	0	0	1	33	1	0	.279	.274
Ross, David	R-R	6-2	240	3-19-77	.182	.000	.500	4	11	2	2	0	0	0	1	3	0	0	1	4	0	0	.182	.333
Soto, Luis	B-R	5-11	179	12-7-85	.162	.125	.172	14	37	5	6	2	0	0	2	4	0	0	0	11	1	1	.216	.262
Stubbs, Drew	R-R	6-4	200	10-4-84	.261	.333	.237	86	303	49	79	21	4	5	38	50	2	0	3	82	27	8	.406	.366
Tordi, Justin	R-R	6-1	208	4-9-84	.223	.327	.190	64	202	12	45	9	0	1	18	23	3	4	2	47	0	0	.282	.309
Turner, Justin	R-R	5-11	180	11-23-84	.316	.379	.299	33	136	23	43	8	1	0	11	12	3	0	0	19	3	1	.390	.384

	B-T	HT	WT	DOB	AVG	vLH	vRH	G	AB	R	H	2B	3B	HR	RBI	BB	HBP	SH	SF	SO	SB	CS	SLG	OBP
Valaika, Chris	R-R	6-1	180	8-14-85	.363	.393	.355	32	135	20	49	9	0	7	31	7	1	0	2	28	2	0	.585	.393
Waller, Todd	R-R	6-1	195	4-26-87	.000	.000	.000	6	14	1	0	0	0	0	0	0	3	0	0	5	0	0	.000	.176

Pitching	B-T	HT	WT	DOB	W	L	ERA	G	GS	CG	SV	IP	H	R	ER	HR	BB	SO	AVG	vLH	vRH	K/9	BB/9
Beal, Josh	R-R	6-2	220	10-21-87	0	0	4.50	1	0	0	0	2	2	1	1	0	0	1	.250	.500	.167	4.50	0.00
Belisle, Matt	R-R	6-3	230	6-6-80	1	0	0.00	1	1	0	0	9	2	0	0	0	0	3	.071	.000	.133	3.12	0.00
Buck, Dallas	R-R	6-2	195	11-11-84	0	1	4.15	3	3	0	0	13	9	6	6	0	4	9	.191	.143	.212	6.23	2.77
Carroll, Scott	R-R	6-5	210	9-24-84	6	5	3.51	14	12	0	0	82	90	38	32	2	21	58	.290	.252	.317	6.37	2.30
DeJesus, Misael	R-R	6-2	235	11-5-84	5	5	3.64	34	12	0	0	99	84	42	40	9	41	110	.227	.262	.204	10.00	3.73
Del Rosario, Enerio	R-R	6-2	165	10-16-85	1	4	6.09	13	6	0	0	44	57	31	30	2	23	32	.318	.333	.308	6.50	4.67
Fogg, Josh	R-R	6-0	205	12-13-76	1	0	3.32	3	3	0	0	19	24	7	7	1	3	14	.312	.400	.238	6.63	1.42
Geronimo, Ramon	R-R	6-0	185	10-8-83	0	0	0.87	36	0	0	11	41	22	6	4	0	11	48	.152	.218	.111	10.45	2.40
Gonzalez, Aguido	L-L	5-10	185	9-19-86	1	0	0.00	2	0	0	0	4	2	1	0	0	4	1	.154	.000	.200	2.25	9.00
Gonzalez, Rafael	R-R	6-1	232	3-21-86	5	12	6.44	24	22	0	0	102	130	86	73	19	45	75	.307	.310	.305	6.62	3.97
Guerrero, Daniel	R-R	6-1	190	7-21-85	3	6	7.48	13	13	0	0	65	83	59	54	17	19	48	.313	.325	.305	6.65	2.63
Gunter, Kevin	R-R	6-3	210	11-5-83	0	0	13.50	2	0	0	0	3	7	5	5	0	2	6	.412	.400	.417	16.20	5.40
2-team total (3 Jupiter)					0	0	10.57	5	0	0	0	8	13	9	9	1	5	9	—	—	—	10.57	5.87
Howell, Blaine	L-L	5-11	210	10-2-88	0	0	0.00	1	0	0	0	2	1	0	0	0	1	1	.143	—	.143	4.50	4.50
James, Justin	R-R	6-3	215	9-13-81	1	1	1.56	7	3	0	0	17	6	3	3	1	5	11	.103	.143	.081	5.71	2.60
Klinker, Matt	R-R	6-5	220	10-8-84	2	2	5.50	6	6	0	0	34	41	21	21	5	11	28	.306	.268	.333	7.34	2.88
Krebs, Joseph	L-L	6-0	200	9-14-84	1	2	4.03	19	0	0	0	29	30	14	13	2	9	26	.275	.115	.325	8.07	2.79
Livingston, Bobby	L-L	6-3	205	9-3-82	3	1	2.03	4	4	1	0	27	27	7	6	0	4	18	.273	.185	.306	6.07	1.35
Manuel, Robert	R-R	6-3	197	7-9-83	1	0	0.00	4	0	0	0	8	5	1	0	0	3	11	.172	.111	.200	12.91	3.52
Medina, Ruben	R-R	5-11	157	7-29-86	2	7	3.33	37	0	0	0	54	56	25	20	1	26	35	.271	.341	.224	5.83	4.33
Ondrusek, Logan	R-R	6-7	205	2-13-85	1	7	4.97	40	3	0	1	80	93	47	44	5	32	58	.284	.391	.211	6.55	3.62
Otterness, Steven	L-L	6-4	210	10-30-84	0	0	2.37	11	0	0	0	19	19	7	5	0	12	18	.257	.348	.216	8.53	5.68
Rafael, Juan	R-R	6-2	165	12-4-85	0	0	11.57	1	0	0	0	2	7	3	3	0	2	0	.583	.750	.500	0.00	7.71
Rhoden, Tyler	R-R	6-3	222	12-23-84	0	0	3.86	2	0	0	0	2	3	1	1	0	1	1	.333	.333	.333	3.86	3.86
Santana, Hector	R-R	6-1	186	2-4-88	0	0	0.00	2	0	0	0	2	0	0	0	0	0	0	.000	.000	.000	9.00	0.00
Smit, Alexander	L-L	6-3	215	10-2-85	8	7	3.87	21	21	0	0	112	98	53	48	9	56	94	.242	.241	.242	7.58	4.51
Smith, Jordan	R-R	6-3	206	2-4-86	7	2	2.55	10	10	0	0	67	61	23	19	2	7	44	.241	.230	.252	5.91	0.94
Stewart, Zach	R-R	6-2	205	9-28-86	0	2	1.62	13	0	0	2	17	16	5	3	0	11	23	.262	.280	.250	12.42	5.94
Tabor, Lee	L-L	6-2	175	12-17-84	0	1	2.45	14	0	0	0	18	12	6	5	1	6	14	.190	.150	.209	6.87	2.95
Thompson, Daryl	R-R	6-0	180	11-2-85	0	2	6.89	3	3	0	0	16	20	12	12	2	7	7	.339	.250	.385	4.02	4.02
Valiquette, Philippe	L-L	6-0	175	2-14-87	2	2	3.92	31	0	0	2	39	45	18	17	4	18	33	.294	.275	.304	7.62	4.15
Vazquez, Camilo	L-L	5-11	205	10-3-83	5	2	4.20	23	7	0	1	64	67	35	30	4	29	51	.277	.222	.291	7.13	4.06
Watson, Sean	R-R	6-2	215	7-24-85	0	1	4.50	22	0	0	10	20	19	10	10	4	14	30	.247	.281	.222	13.50	6.30
Wood, Travis	R-L	5-11	166	2-6-87	3	4	2.70	9	9	0	0	47	39	18	14	2	21	41	.222	.167	.239	7.91	4.05
Young, Terrell	R-R	6-3	175	8-7-85	1	2	2.41	25	0	0	2	34	31	13	9	0	13	26	.237	.233	.239	6.95	3.48
Zeffiro, Dan	R-R	6-3	175	8-13-85	0	0	6.75	3	0	0	0	4	8	4	3	0	0	1	.444	.333	.500	2.25	0.00

Fielding

Catcher	PCT	G	PO	A	E	DP	PB
Denove	1.000	6	35	1	0	0	1
Esquer	.963	7	48	4	2	0	2
Long	.986	31	209	8	3	0	11
E. Rodriguez	.980	70	478	53	11	3	10
Ross	1.000	4	28	4	0	0	0
Tordi	.994	25	156	10	1	0	6
Waller	1.000	6	33	0	0	0	2

First Base	PCT	G	PO	A	E	DP
Alonso	1.000	4	36	3	0	6
Dorn	1.000	1	5	0	0	0
Frazier	.980	16	133	16	3	13
Kainer	1.000	1	6	0	0	0
Louwsma	.990	83	681	43	7	69
Parker	.988	27	231	20	3	30
Tordi	1.000	7	57	5	0	6

Second Base	PCT	G	PO	A	E	DP
Bartles	1.000	1	2	2	0	1

	PCT	G	PO	A	E	DP	PB
Castro	.970	39	75	119	6	32	
DeJesus	.989	21	35	59	1	12	
Hale	1.000	3	4	11	0	2	
Kahaulelio	.988	38	74	87	2	22	
Puckett	1.000	1	1	0	0	0	
Tordi	.978	10	21	23	1	5	
Turner	.992	29	47	77	1	20	

Third Base	PCT	G	PO	A	E	DP
Francisco	.937	105	80	173	17	20
Frazier	.933	11	7	21	2	3
Keppinger	—	1	0	0	0	0
Louwsma	.968	9	7	23	1	4
Tordi	.923	13	5	31	3	3

Shortstop	PCT	G	PO	A	E	DP
Castro	.934	49	69	128	14	27
Frazier	.981	55	104	159	5	44
Tordi	.972	8	13	22	1	6
Valaika	.971	28	42	90	4	17

Outfield	PCT	G	PO	A	E	DP
Contreras	.929	10	13	0	1	0
DeJesus	1.000	3	4	0	0	0
Dorn	1.000	4	5	1	0	0
Francisco	1.000	3	5	1	0	0
Frazier	1.000	6	11	1	0	0
Gressick	1.000	3	4	0	0	0
Heisey	.986	116	275	14	4	4
Henry	.895	9	16	1	2	1
Hopper	1.000	2	3	1	0	0
Kainer	.978	78	128	3	3	0
Louwsma	1.000	2	4	0	0	0
Perales	.969	65	121	6	4	0
Y. Rodriguez	.939	22	29	2	2	0
Soto	1.000	9	13	0	0	0
Stubbs	.968	84	179	3	6	1

DAYTON DRAGONS
LOW CLASS A
MIDWEST LEAGUE

Batting	B-T	HT	WT	DOB	AVG	vLH	vRH	G	AB	R	H	2B	3B	HR	RBI	BB	HBP	SH	SF	SO	SB	CS	SLG	OBP
Bartles, Brett	R-R	6-1	180	8-20-86	.186	.091	.219	14	43	3	8	0	0	1	3	6	0	1	0	12	0	0	.256	.286
Bour, Jason	R-R	6-3	215	7-2-86	.231	.210	.245	70	247	22	57	16	2	7	28	10	3	1	3	70	0	1	.397	.266
Cabrera, Angel	R-R	6-0	185	10-14-85	.263	.292	.248	65	217	20	57	12	1	3	22	17	5	2	0	48	3	4	.369	.331
Cabrera, Jolbert	R-R	6-1	215	12-8-72	.364	.111	.538	6	22	3	8	1	1	0	4	1	1	0	0	4	0	0	.500	.417
Cozart, Zack	R-R	6-1	185	8-12-85	.280	.282	.279	109	418	57	117	20	6	14	49	24	10	6	6	77	3	3	.457	.330
Esquer, Anthony	R-R	6-1	215	9-3-84	.000	.000	.000	1	3	0	0	0	0	0	0	1	0	0	0	1	0	0	.000	.250
Feiner, Kevyn	R-R	6-1	170	6-11-87	.235	.242	.230	78	268	31	63	9	2	1	22	15	4	1	3	57	8	3	.295	.283
Frazier, Todd	R-R	6-3	215	2-12-86	.321	.414	.289	30	112	25	36	10	0	7	20	15	0	0	0	28	4	2	.598	.402
Jones, Keltavious	L-L	5-9	170	9-21-85	.251	.181	.271	100	367	64	92	12	5	5	25	42	4	3	2	77	16	4	.351	.333
Kahaulelio, Jacob	R-R	5-10	195	6-7-85	.244	.294	.211	32	127	16	31	8	1	1	14	8	4	1	2	24	5	0	.346	.305

Batting	B-T	HT	WT	DOB	AVG	vLH	vRH	G	AB	R	H	2B	3B	HR	RBI	BB	HBP	SH	SF	SO	SB	CS	SLG	OBP
Long, Jake	R-R	6-1	180	4-17-86	.288	.154	.326	17	59	7	17	4	0	0	9	5	0	0	0	17	0	1	.356	.344
McKennon, Michael	L-L	6-3	210	3-31-85	.246	.221	.255	100	357	37	88	20	5	9	34	15	8	3	5	82	3	4	.406	.288
Meade, Frank	R-R	6-1	215	9-27-85	.125	.333	.000	3	8	0	1	0	0	0	1	0	0	0	0	2	0	0	.125	.125
Menchaca, Brandon	R-R	5-11	195	4-15-85	.176	.211	.150	71	256	28	45	8	4	5	25	17	4	0	1	80	5	3	.297	.237
Mesoraco, Devin	R-R	6-1	200	6-19-88	.261	.252	.266	83	306	29	80	13	1	9	42	20	4	0	4	64	2	3	.399	.311
Parker, Logan	L-L	6-3	215	7-18-84	.267	.185	.298	55	195	34	52	13	2	9	37	24	1	0	2	45	2	1	.492	.347
Perales, Daniel	L-L	5-10	176	3-18-85	.231	.091	.286	11	39	2	9	3	1	1	6	3	0	0	0	12	1	1	.436	.286
Phipps, Denis	R-R	6-2	177	7-22-85	.255	.230	.268	124	474	57	121	19	4	7	57	34	4	0	6	113	10	10	.357	.307
Reed, Justin	L-R	5-11	179	11-29-87	.239	.191	.257	118	410	64	98	14	6	11	36	38	5	6	1	137	18	9	.383	.311
Sosa, Humberto	R-R	5-11	195	10-13-85	.000	.000	.000	3	7	0	0	0	0	0	0	1	0	0	0	3	0	0	.000	.125
Soto, Neftali	R-R	6-2	180	2-28-89	.326	.345	.313	52	218	26	71	15	1	7	36	7	2	0	6	36	1	1	.500	.343
Waring, Brandon	R-R	6-4	195	1-2-86	.270	.314	.247	119	441	63	119	23	2	20	71	43	12	0	7	156	1	0	.467	.346

Pitching	B-T	HT	WT	DOB	W	L	ERA	G	GS	CG	SV	IP	H	R	ER	HR	BB	SO	AVG	vLH	vRH	K/9	BB/9
Arias, Henry	R-R	6-3	201	1-6-85	1	1	5.81	21	0	0	1	31	35	21	20	1	21	29	.282	.318	.241	8.42	6.10
2-team total (18 Burlington)					3	4	4.76	39	0	0	3	64	67	37	34	4	39	59	—	—	—	8.25	5.46
Arneson, Jamie	L-L	6-5	195	11-5-85	0	3	9.22	15	7	0	0	41	58	45	42	7	37	34	.341	.362	.333	7.46	8.12
Bowman, Drew	R-L	6-4	190	11-8-85	0	1	2.45	2	2	0	0	4	5	4	1	0	1	5	.313	.400	.273	12.27	2.45
Carroll, Scott	R-R	6-5	210	9-24-84	1	2	3.75	9	9	0	0	48	50	22	20	2	16	24	.269	.235	.307	4.50	3.00
Conatser, Derrick	R-R	6-3	180	12-4-85	2	3	4.67	27	0	0	1	54	56	30	28	2	20	26	.264	.292	.236	4.33	3.33
Del Rosario, Enerio	R-R	6-2	165	10-16-85	5	2	1.16	19	9	1	5	70	52	19	9	3	11	49	.208	.218	.197	6.30	1.41
Gonzalez, Aguido	L-L	5-10	185	9-19-86	1	0	1.77	15	0	0	6	20	12	4	4	0	7	21	.169	.250	.137	9.30	3.10
Guerrero, Daniel	R-R	6-1	190	7-21-85	2	5	7.92	13	10	0	1	50	73	45	44	9	15	31	.340	.352	.327	5.58	2.70
Gunter, Kevin	R-R	6-3	210	11-5-83	0	0	6.00	4	0	0	0	6	6	4	4	0	4	3	.273	.286	.267	4.50	6.00
Horst, Jeremy	L-L	6-4	220	10-1-85	8	2	2.38	36	10	0	4	102	74	30	27	3	33	110	.202	.247	.185	9.71	2.91
Jeffords, Jeff	R-R	6-1	200	11-4-84	3	6	3.39	40	0	0	6	77	65	33	29	3	39	86	.227	.255	.199	10.05	4.56
Klinker, Matt	R-R	6-5	220	10-8-84	6	4	3.26	19	18	0	0	105	98	43	38	5	27	76	.251	.288	.217	6.51	2.31
Krebs, Joseph	L-L	6-0	200	9-14-84	6	2	2.25	26	0	0	6	40	38	11	10	3	14	33	.250	.111	.327	7.43	3.15
Lotzkar, Kyle	R-R	6-2	200	10-24-89	2	3	3.58	10	10	0	0	38	29	19	15	2	24	50	.215	.224	.206	11.95	5.73
Medina, Ruben	R-R	5-11	157	7-29-86	1	1	2.45	7	0	0	1	11	8	5	3	0	4	6	.195	.240	.125	4.91	3.27
Mercker, Kent	L-L	6-2	205	2-1-68	0	0	0.00	1	0	0	0	1	0	0	0	0	0	1	.000	.000	.000	9.00	0.00
Montano, Luis	R-R	6-0	180	3-20-85	12	8	4.02	26	26	0	0	137	136	77	61	17	34	97	.250	.300	.199	6.39	2.24
Otterness, Steven	L-L	6-4	210	10-30-84	0	0	10.03	8	0	0	0	12	17	13	13	2	12	7	.340	.308	.351	5.40	9.26
Partch, Curtis	R-R	6-5	200	2-13-87	5	11	5.00	33	17	0	1	112	118	76	62	6	42	74	.267	.320	.220	5.96	3.39
Rafael, Juan	R-R	6-2	165	12-4-85	3	3	5.17	13	5	0	0	56	55	34	32	8	28	49	.258	.252	.265	7.92	4.53
Ravin, Josh	R-R	6-4	195	1-21-88	2	8	7.19	14	14	0	0	56	55	49	45	9	50	47	.261	.267	.250	7.51	7.99
Rhoden, Tyler	R-R	6-3	222	12-23-84	3	1	4.99	28	0	0	2	49	54	33	27	3	32	29	.283	.240	.333	5.36	5.92
Stewart, Zach	R-R	6-2	205	9-28-86	1	2	0.55	11	0	0	3	16	10	2	1	0	3	13	.175	.185	.167	7.16	1.65
Thurman, Mace	R-R	6-1	180	4-5-87	1	0	5.40	7	0	0	1	17	12	10	10	1	10	27	.197	.200	.195	14.58	5.40
Valiquette, Philippe	L-L	6-0	175	2-14-87	0	1	3.12	16	0	0	1	26	25	11	9	2	10	32	.250	.313	.221	11.08	3.46
Weathers, David	R-R	6-3	235	9-25-69	0	0	0.00	2	1	0	0	2	0	0	0	0	0	3	.000	.000	.000	13.50	0.00
Young, Terrell	R-R	6-3	175	8-7-85	1	3	3.51	18	0	0	1	26	25	11	10	1	15	21	.266	.186	.333	7.36	5.26

Fielding

Catcher	PCT	G	PO	A	E	DP	PB
Bour	.987	54	360	30	5	2	4
Esquer	.923	1	10	2	1	0	0
Long	1.000	12	79	7	0	0	3
Meade	1.000	2	5	0	0	0	0
Mesoraco	.985	72	547	37	9	2	15
Sosa	1.000	1	2	1	0	0	0

First Base	PCT	G	PO	A	E	DP
Bour	1.000	1	9	1	0	0
J. Cabrera	1.000	2	10	1	0	1
Frazier	1.000	4	34	8	0	1
McKennon	.991	84	715	47	7	56
Parker	.993	35	273	18	2	25
Sosa	.900	2	9	0	1	2
Soto	1.000	2	10	1	0	2
Waring	.983	13	106	9	2	5

Second Base	PCT	G	PO	A	E	DP
Bartles	.900	1	2	7	1	2
A. Cabrera	.960	34	69	98	7	18
J. Cabrera	1.000	2	5	2	0	0
Cozart	1.000	1	3	4	0	0
Feiner	.938	71	120	183	20	31
Kahaulelio	.980	30	59	90	3	17

Third Base	PCT	G	PO	A	E	DP
Bartles	.900	5	1	8	1	0
A. Cabrera	1.000	12	12	19	0	3
Frazier	.875	3	2	5	1	0
Gressick	1.000	2	0	3	0	0
Soto	.910	29	16	55	7	4
Waring	.935	90	46	155	14	12

Shortstop	PCT	G	PO	A	E	DP
A. Cabrera	.925	16	19	30	4	5

	PCT	G	PO	A	E	DP
Cozart	.978	102	181	271	10	51
Feiner	1.000	4	2	7	0	3
Frazier	.933	16	34	49	6	8
Soto	.882	4	4	11	2	1

Outfield	PCT	G	PO	A	E	DP
Bartles	1.000	2	4	0	0	0
A. Cabrera	1.000	1	3	0	0	0
J. Cabrera	1.000	2	2	0	0	0
Frazier	1.000	2	4	0	0	0
Gressick	1.000	15	19	2	0	0
Jones	.954	79	139	6	7	0
Menchaca	.971	70	128	6	4	0
Perales	1.000	10	19	0	0	0
Phipps	.965	122	236	13	9	4
Reed	.989	118	246	12	3	5

GCL REDS

GULF COAST LEAGUE

ROOKIE

Batting	B-T	HT	WT	DOB	AVG	vLH	vRH	G	AB	R	H	2B	3B	HR	RBI	BB	HBP	SH	SF	SO	SB	CS	SLG	OBP
Bowe, Theodis	L-R	5-9	160	8-5-90	.200	.087	.232	31	105	16	21	2	1	0	6	12	1	1	0	29	6	0	.238	.288
Cech, Petr	L-R	5-10	185	10-13-87	.235	.000	.242	14	34	7	8	1	0	0	1	4	0	0	0	3	1	0	.265	.316
Coddington, Kevin	R-R	6-4	205	7-21-87	.275	.348	.253	31	102	11	28	6	0	0	7	10	4	1	0	19	0	0	.333	.362
Conner, Sean	L-R	6-2	198	7-24-88	.218	.182	.225	41	142	15	31	8	1	3	19	19	1	0	3	42	2	1	.352	.309
Contreras, Efrain	R-R	6-1	165	2-6-87	.271	.250	.278	37	129	19	35	11	1	1	30	10	8	2	4	20	3	0	.395	.351
Gregorius, Mariekson	L-R	6-1	160	2-18-90	.155	.000	.185	31	97	6	15	0	0	0	9	10	1	1	0	10	2	1	.155	.241
Hale, Darrick	L-R	5-10	175	5-25-86	.240	.000	.273	15	50	4	12	2	1	0	2	8	0	0	0	15	0	0	.320	.345
Kuo, Yen-Wen	L-R	5-10	165	10-25-88	.281	.188	.300	25	96	13	27	5	0	0	15	7	1	1	3	14	0	1	.333	.327
Lutz, Donald	L-R	6-4	230	2-6-89	.250	.278	.244	34	108	22	27	9	0	1	19	9	2	0	1	21	4	1	.361	.317
Oliveras, Alexis	L-R	6-0	180	3-29-89	.279	.238	.286	39	154	28	43	5	4	1	16	14	2	0	1	45	3	5	.383	.345

					AVG	vLH	vRH	G	AB	R	H	2B	3B	HR	RBI	BB	HBP	SH	SF	SO	SB	CS	SLG	OBP
Pfister, Frank	R-R	6-1	205	8-25-86	.236	.167	.250	38	140	20	33	8	0	0	14	7	3	0	3	16	0	1	.293	.281
Pimentel, Mauricio	B-R	6-0	165	12-11-88	.268	.250	.273	37	123	18	33	5	2	1	19	19	1	1	3	32	5	5	.366	.363
Puckett, Cody	R-R	5-10	180	4-3-87	.269	.188	.294	18	67	11	18	1	0	2	10	10	1	0	0	19	6	1	.373	.372
Pullen, Brodie	R-R	6-0	195	10-26-88	.192	.118	.214	23	73	5	14	4	0	0	7	12	0	0	0	23	1	0	.247	.306
Rimes, Eli	L-L	6-0	210	6-7-85	.195	.125	.212	15	41	2	8	1	0	0	3	6	0	1	0	11	0	0	.220	.298
Sosa, Humberto	R-R	5-11	195	10-13-85	.304	.240	.316	42	158	17	48	10	0	3	22	14	0	0	0	34	0	0	.424	.360
Vasquez, Samuel	R-R	6-0	175	2-6-87	.259	.243	.264	46	166	22	43	9	4	2	15	2	3	0	0	39	8	0	.398	.281
Waller, Todd	R-R	6-1	195	4-26-87	.157	.000	.211	17	51	6	8	2	0	0	6	6	4	0	0	18	0	0	.196	.295

Pitching	B-T	HT	WT	DOB	W	L	ERA	G	GS	CG	SV	IP	H	R	ER	HR	BB	SO	AVG	vLH	vRH	K/9	BB/9
Bohana, Michael	R-R	6-1	190	10-14-85	0	4	4.35	10	0	0	1	10	14	9	5	0	4	10	.326	.278	.360	8.71	3.48
Bowman, Drew	R-L	6-4	190	11-8-85	1	0	4.85	4	4	0	0	13	16	8	7	0	3	14	.308	.111	.349	9.69	2.08
Calderon, Hugo	R-R	6-1	170	9-19-87	2	0	3.63	14	0	0	0	17	18	8	7	0	12	10	.273	.370	.205	5.19	6.23
Ceballos, Rafael	R-R	6-2	190	3-17-89	3	1	7.63	13	0	0	1	15	23	15	13	3	8	7	.338	.310	.359	4.11	4.70
Chiu, Tzu-Kai	L-L	6-0	220	9-14-87	0	0	2.25	2	1	0	0	4	5	2	1	1	2	2	.333	.250	.364	4.50	4.50
Cline, Tyler	R-R	6-2	215	6-24-90	0	3	9.72	5	5	0	0	8	11	9	9	1	7	10	.314	.353	.278	10.80	7.56
De La Rosa, Rafael	L-R	6-0	180	5-12-88	0	0	5.93	4	2	0	0	14	19	9	9	2	4	13	.306	.000	.322	8.56	2.63
Dombrowski, Greg	R-R	5-11	170	3-30-86	0	0	2.25	4	0	0	0	4	5	1	1	0	1	6	.294	.429	.200	13.50	2.25
Gardner, Bryan	L-L	5-11	190	10-8-86	0	1	4.50	18	0	0	1	22	22	12	11	2	11	25	.262	.294	.254	10.23	4.50
Henry, Michael	R-R	6-3	205	9-1-89	1	1	7.76	12	5	0	0	31	35	33	27	1	26	25	.276	.292	.266	7.18	7.47
Hildenbrandt, Evan	L-R	6-2	190	2-13-89	4	2	2.67	11	11	0	0	57	49	19	17	5	16	56	.228	.205	.244	8.79	2.51
Howell, Blaine	L-L	5-11	210	10-2-88	1	0	1.59	8	0	0	0	11	11	5	2	0	5	16	.244	.111	.278	12.71	3.97
James, Justin	R-R	6-3	215	9-13-81	0	0	1.80	3	1	0	0	5	4	2	1	0	0	5	.235	.167	.273	9.00	0.00
Livingston, Bobby	L-L	6-3	205	9-3-82	0	1	4.05	2	2	0	0	7	10	5	3	0	3	5	.345	.333	.350	6.75	4.05
Machuca, Luis	R-R	6-1	190	3-16-88	1	3	6.48	4	4	0	0	17	23	12	12	1	4	7	.343	.276	.395	3.78	2.16
Maloney, Matt	L-L	6-4	220	1-16-84	1	0	0.00	1	0	0	0	6	1	0	0	0	0	9	.056	.000	.063	14.29	0.00
Panerati, Luca	L-L	6-2	167	12-2-89	1	0	2.84	10	0	0	0	19	18	7	6	0	3	8	.250	.261	.245	3.79	1.42
Pizziconi, Matteo	L-L	6-2	172	10-30-89	3	0	0.70	15	0	0	0	26	18	3	2	0	11	15	.212	.368	.167	5.26	3.86
Rafael, Juan	R-R	6-2	165	12-4-85	1	3	1.63	6	5	0	0	28	26	9	5	0	9	29	.243	.241	.245	9.43	2.93
Rodriguez, Efrain	R-R	6-2	175	11-22-89	0	2	5.47	8	5	0	0	26	38	18	16	1	9	11	.362	.423	.302	3.76	3.08
Rodriguez, Raul	R-R	6-3	190	10-16-90	0	0	1.04	8	0	0	0	9	8	2	1	0	4	4	.242	.200	.278	4.15	4.15
Santana, Hector	R-R	6-1	186	2-4-88	1	2	3.63	14	2	0	2	22	29	12	9	0	4	19	.305	.395	.231	7.66	1.61
Snowden, Shea	L-L	6-1	150	10-6-88	3	3	1.50	7	5	0	0	36	28	12	6	0	10	29	.212	.088	.255	7.25	2.50
Thompson, Daryl	R-R	6-0	180	11-2-85	0	0	0.00	1	0	0	0	4	2	1	0	0	3	.133	.167	.111	6.75	0.00
Torcise, David	L-L	6-1	185	8-22-85	1	0	1.48	17	0	0	1	24	19	4	4	1	5	20	.221	.176	.232	7.40	1.85
Villarreal, Pedro	R-R	6-1	215	12-9-87	0	1	7.71	2	0	0	0	2	6	5	2	0	2	3	.400	.286	.500	11.57	7.71
Vinyard, Jeremy	R-R	6-1	165	8-10-88	1	0	3.00	10	0	0	0	12	17	6	4	1	5	12	.333	.211	.406	9.00	3.75
Walker, Justin	L-L	6-5	200	11-3-86	0	0	3.38	3	0	0	0	3	5	1	1	0	2	1	.455	.250	.571	3.38	6.75

Fielding

Catcher	PCT	G	PO	A	E	DP	PB
Bowe	—	1	0	0	0	0	
Cech	.949	12	52	4	3	0	4
Coddington	.979	31	206	26	5	4	6
Sosa	.950	4	17	2	1	0	1
Waller	.976	17	114	10	3	0	1

First Base	PCT	G	PO	A	E	DP
Lutz	.963	14	104	1	4	9
Rimes	.970	8	62	3	2	6
Sosa	.994	37	301	20	2	20

Second Base	PCT	G	PO	A	E	DP
Hale	1.000	6	10	11	0	2
Kuo	1.000	6	5	13	0	2
Pimentel	.957	35	73	84	7	22
Puckett	.915	12	23	31	5	3

Third Base	PCT	G	PO	A	E	DP
Pfister	.963	37	33	71	4	11
Pullen	.877	21	15	35	7	2
Sosa	—	1	0	0	0	0

Shortstop	PCT	G	PO	A	E	DP
Gregorius	.910	31	37	85	12	11

Hale	.938	9	12	33	3	8
Kuo	.928	15	23	41	5	7
Puckett	.917	3	5	6	1	1

Outfield	PCT	G	PO	A	E	DP
Bowe	.976	23	39	1	1	0
Conner	.954	31	60	2	3	0
Contreras	.986	37	68	1	1	1
Lutz	1.000	3	2	0	0	0
Oliveras	1.000	33	60	4	0	0
Vasquez	.957	46	84	4	4	1

BILLINGS MUSTANGS   ROOKIE

PIONEER LEAGUE

Batting	B-T	HT	WT	DOB	AVG	vLH	vRH	G	AB	R	H	2B	3B	HR	RBI	BB	HBP	SH	SF	SO	SB	CS	SLG	OBP
Bartles, Brett	R-R	6-1	180	8-20-86	.257	.364	.194	38	148	21	38	7	0	2	19	13	3	0	1	39	2	0	.345	.327
Brown, Tony	L-L	6-0	190	1-26-88	.283	.253	.297	65	258	55	73	14	3	12	47	18	11	0	1	85	2	2	.500	.354
Buchholz, Alex	R-R	6-0	185	9-30-87	.396	.353	.410	34	134	31	53	15	2	3	26	16	3	0	0	25	3	2	.604	.471
Coddington, Kevin	R-R	6-4	205	7-21-87	.300	.000	.375	3	10	3	3	1	0	0	0	0	0	0	0	2	0	0	.400	.300
Day, Kyle	L-R	5-11	200	7-13-86	.268	.190	.286	31	112	18	30	10	1	1	11	11	6	0	1	25	0	0	.402	.362
Gualdron, Jose	R-R	5-11	165	7-18-87	.282	.250	.295	46	156	25	44	12	2	2	17	15	1	1	0	30	3	2	.423	.349
Konstanty, Mike	R-R	6-4	225	4-17-86	.253	.288	.237	52	198	30	50	14	2	10	43	22	4	0	8	53	0	3	.495	.328
McMurray, Chris	R-R	6-1	195	10-12-86	.234	.250	.228	25	77	9	18	2	1	0	13	7	1	0	0	16	1	0	.286	.306
Meade, Frank	R-R	6-1	215	9-27-85	.200	.250	.182	6	15	4	3	2	1	0	4	6	1	0	1	4	0	0	.467	.435
Means, Andrew	R-R	6-1	195	9-11-86	.231	.259	.219	22	91	16	21	1	1	3	16	4	1	1	0	15	6	0	.363	.271
Mendez, Carlos	R-R	6-0	175	9-15-86	.250	.232	.256	57	216	27	54	12	0	2	33	19	6	0	0	27	3	3	.333	.328
Puckett, Cody	R-R	5-10	180	4-3-87	.287	.361	.256	33	122	22	35	7	1	6	19	22	2	0	1	30	2	5	.508	.401
Rojas, Miguel	R-R	5-9	160	2-24-89	.183	.131	.204	61	208	27	38	8	1	1	21	14	4	2	0	35	3	1	.245	.248
Sappelt, David	R-R	5-9	195	1-2-87	.299	.316	.292	62	254	47	76	19	5	7	35	21	1	2	1	45	6	3	.496	.354
Soto, Neftali	R-R	6-2	180	2-28-89	.388	.556	.327	15	67	12	26	10	1	4	11	4	0	0	0	10	1	0	.746	.423
Stiffler, Matt	L-L	6-0	175	3-9-86	.225	.304	.197	26	89	18	20	8	0	1	15	19	0	0	2	23	3	3	.348	.361
Stovall, Tyler	R-R	6-1	215	10-19-85	.333	.383	.310	38	147	32	49	10	3	1	16	14	2	0	2	33	2	1	.463	.394
Wideman, Jordan	R-R	5-11	200	3-14-89	.254	.140	.308	38	134	19	34	9	0	1	22	9	4	0	3	24	0	0	.343	.313
Wiley, Byron	L-L	6-1	200	12-12-86	.328	.314	.333	39	137	29	45	17	5	5	37	24	1	0	2	49	3	1	.635	.427

Pitching	B-T	HT	WT	DOB	W	L	ERA	G	GS	CG	SV	IP	H	R	ER	HR	BB	SO	AVG	vLH	vRH	K/9	BB/9
Arneson, Jamie	L-L	6-5	195	11-5-85	6	3	4.65	15	15	0	0	72	73	46	37	5	42	60	.262	.278	.258	7.53	5.27
Astorga, Leonardo	R-R	6-2	175	3-25-86	4	1	2.98	11	11	0	0	51	52	28	17	2	11	40	.265	.255	.278	7.01	1.93
Beal, Josh	R-R	6-2	220	10-21-87	1	2	2.60	22	0	0	0	28	24	9	8	1	9	43	.224	.250	.209	13.99	2.93
Bohana, Michael	R-R	6-1	190	10-14-85	0	0	2.81	10	0	0	2	16	21	6	5	0	3	18	.313	.208	.372	10.13	1.69
Bowman, Drew	R-L	6-4	190	11-8-85	2	4	5.56	7	7	0	0	34	41	26	21	4	23	23	.301	.423	.273	6.09	6.09
Castro, Oscar	R-R	6-2	165	3-29-89	4	2	4.14	13	13	0	0	67	69	34	31	2	18	52	.265	.278	.254	6.95	2.41
Freeman, Justin	R-R	6-1	170	10-22-86	3	2	3.95	17	1	0	0	41	42	24	18	4	9	48	.261	.234	.278	10.54	1.98
Garcia, Enrique	R-R	6-4	227	11-14-86	3	1	5.72	9	4	0	0	28	35	21	18	5	16	20	.315	.280	.344	6.35	5.08
Gardner, Bryan	L-L	5-11	190	10-8-86	0	1	81.00	2	0	0	0	1	5	6	6	0	3	1	.833	.750	1.000	13.50	40.50
Gonzalez, Aguido	L-L	5-10	185	9-19-86	2	0	0.00	10	0	0	4	12	5	0	0	0	5	23	.125	.154	.111	16.78	3.65
Hildenbrandt, Evan	L-R	6-2	190	2-13-89	0	1	5.00	3	1	0	0	9	9	5	5	1	4	7	.250	.267	.238	7.00	4.00
Hotchkiss, Jordan	R-R	6-4	210	4-3-86	1	3	4.01	22	0	0	3	34	31	21	15	1	15	30	.244	.304	.197	8.02	4.01
Hudgens, Will	R-R	6-3	220	1-24-85	3	0	10.45	5	0	0	0	10	14	12	12	2	2	7	.326	.231	.471	6.10	1.74
Janke, Lance	R-R	6-2	190	10-8-85	1	2	5.60	11	11	0	0	45	55	36	28	2	12	35	.294	.297	.292	7.00	2.40
Linebaugh, Randall	R-R	6-0	170	10-2-85	1	2	2.45	17	0	0	5	18	16	5	5	2	6	25	.239	.294	.182	12.27	2.95
Martinez, Junior	R-R	6-0	210	4-30-86	1	0	6.67	19	0	0	0	30	34	23	22	4	26	24	.296	.279	.306	7.28	7.89
Otterness, Steven	L-L	6-4	210	10-30-84	2	1	4.26	13	0	0	3	19	16	9	9	2	9	21	.222	.194	.244	9.95	4.26
Ravin, Josh	R-R	6-4	195	1-21-88	0	1	10.50	4	1	0	0	12	13	14	14	4	9	12	.271	.304	.240	9.00	6.75
Rice, Brandon	R-R	6-4	210	1-11-88	2	2	6.41	15	0	0	0	27	40	22	19	4	11	10	.348	.255	.433	3.38	3.71
Santana, Hector	R-R	6-1	186	2-4-88	0	0	1.35	3	0	0	0	7	5	1	1	0	2	4	.208	.300	.143	5.40	2.70
Shunick, Clayton	R-R	6-1	175	9-10-86	1	4	8.45	10	10	0	0	38	54	37	36	7	7	38	.321	.310	.330	8.92	1.64
Thurman, Mace	L-L	6-1	180	4-5-87	1	0	0.54	9	0	0	0	17	8	1	1	1	4	18	.143	.261	.061	9.72	2.16
Torcise, David	L-L	6-1	185	8-22-85	0	0	3.38	3	0	0	0	5	5	3	2	0	1	1	.278	.500	.214	1.69	1.69
Zeffiro, Dan	R-R	6-3	175	8-13-85	2	0	4.31	14	0	0	0	31	30	17	15	3	11	25	.256	.232	.279	7.18	3.16

Fielding

Catcher	PCT	G	PO	A	E	DP	PB
Coddington	.929	3	12	1	1	0	0
Day	.990	12	94	5	1	1	4
McMurray	.984	25	166	20	3	3	2
Meade	1.000	3	17	2	0	0	1
Wideman	.985	38	303	35	5	1	3

First Base	PCT	G	PO	A	E	DP
Bartles	1.000	23	212	17	0	17
Gualdron	1.000	1	7	0	0	1
Konstanty	.981	44	384	33	8	36
Mendez	.981	5	46	7	1	2
Stiffler	1.000	1	10	0	0	0

Second Base	PCT	G	PO	A	E	DP
Bartles	.667	1	0	2	1	1
Buchholz	.968	31	51	102	5	17
Gualdron	.972	24	41	63	3	9
Mendez	.833	2	1	4	1	1
Puckett	.947	20	46	62	6	16

Third Base	PCT	G	PO	A	E	DP
Bartles	.846	8	2	9	2	1
Gualdron	1.000	7	2	7	0	0
Mendez	.926	51	25	88	9	12
Soto	.889	11	7	17	3	1

Shortstop	PCT	G	PO	A	E	DP
Buchholz	1.000	2	1	2	0	1
Gualdron	.892	14	28	38	8	11
Rojas	.963	61	94	163	10	34

Outfield	PCT	G	PO	A	E	DP
Brown	.882	54	71	4	10	0
Day	1.000	7	10	0	0	0
Konstanty	1.000	7	12	0	0	0
Means	1.000	9	14	1	0	0
Sappelt	.992	62	120	3	1	1
Stiffler	.973	23	32	4	1	1
Stovall	1.000	29	38	2	0	0
Wiley	.897	36	57	4	7	0

DSL REDS

DOMINICAN SUMMER LEAGUE

ROOKIE

Batting	B-T	HT	WT	DOB	AVG	vLH	vRH	G	AB	R	H	2B	3B	HR	RBI	BB	HBP	SH	SF	SO	SB	CS	SLG	OBP
Candelario, Alexander	R-R	5-11	169	6-17-91	.279	.174	.301	43	136	27	38	9	1	3	18	23	7	0	1	31	7	4	.426	.407
Chacoa, Miguel	B-R	5-11	165	11-27-88	.321	.267	.333	52	165	30	53	6	1	0	27	28	3	5	0	13	13	8	.370	.429
Duran, Juan	R-R	6-5	190	9-2-91	.215	.160	.227	41	135	15	29	3	4	1	14	24	2	1	1	47	8	5	.319	.340
Estevez, Wilfrel	R-R	6-0	177	8-11-90	.227	.111	.257	15	44	3	10	2	1	0	5	2	1	3	0	10	0	0	.318	.260
2-team total (36 Diamondbacks/Reds)					.210	—	—	51	167	11	35	7	2	0	21	8	4	2	5	40	0	1	.275	.255
Felipe, Ayeudi	R-R	6-1	175	3-12-90	.212	.158	.234	21	66	12	14	5	3	2	11	3	3	0	1	18	2	2	.470	.274
Figueroa, Carlos	R-R	6-1	175	10-12-89	.222	.231	.220	20	54	8	12	1	0	0	5	9	1	1	1	10	0	0	.241	.338
Gonzalez, Argenis	R-R	6-1	190	3-30-87	.258	.345	.238	49	155	25	40	12	0	0	19	22	10	1	0	21	3	2	.335	.385
Guerrero, Sergio	R-R	6-0	179	11-13-87	.240	.244	.239	56	204	28	49	15	4	4	29	22	4	1	2	41	7	4	.412	.323
Hernandez, David	R-R	6-1	155	3-24-87	.257	.311	.243	62	214	44	55	15	1	0	22	36	5	3	0	34	21	8	.336	.376
Lopez, Frederman	L-L	6-1	185	1-11-90	.167	.000	.200	23	66	9	11	3	1	1	7	6	0	0	1	21	1	0	.288	.225
Martinez, Mario	R-R	6-1	165	12-5-87	.279	.211	.294	62	201	27	56	13	1	0	22	10	8	5	2	20	6	4	.353	.335
Meran, George	R-R	5-10	158	12-5-89	.244	.125	.310	18	45	6	11	3	1	0	3	1	1	2	0	11	0	2	.356	.277
2-team total (18 Diamondbacks/Reds)					.226	—	—	36	106	11	24	5	1	0	14	4	2	2	0	23	0	2	.292	.268
Moreno, Michael	R-R	6-3	200	10-21-87	.213	.300	.189	17	47	3	10	1	0	0	3	3	2	0	1	13	0	0	.234	.283
Ortuno, Jose	R-R	6-1	185	12-23-90	.375	.667	.200	3	8	2	3	0	1	0	1	1	1	0	0	1	0	0	.625	.500
2-team total (26 Diamondbacks/Reds)					.197	—	—	29	61	3	12	0	1	0	4	4	1	0	0	14	0	0	.230	.258
Quintero, Jose	L-R	6-1	175	12-6-90	.188	.115	.214	34	96	16	18	3	0	0	8	16	4	1	2	27	4	1	.219	.322
2-team total (16 Diamondbacks/Reds)					.176	—	—	50	136	28	24	6	0	0	9	32	5	2	2	36	7	5	.221	.349
Rodriguez, Cristobal	R-R	5-11	165	11-1-89	.197	.236	.184	64	229	34	45	15	2	3	16	15	9	4	1	70	5	3	.319	.272
Rodriguez, Henry	B-R	5-10	150	2-9-90	.240	.300	.225	13	50	5	12	1	0	0	3	7	0	0	1	9	5	1	.260	.328
2-team total (46 Diamondbacks/Reds)					.316	—	—	59	231	30	73	9	3	1	21	27	2	2	3	23	21	7	.394	.388
Rodriguez, Miguel	R-R	6-0	199	2-4-87	.314	.277	.323	66	239	34	75	24	2	3	40	26	11	0	3	45	5	2	.469	.401
Sierra, Jefry	R-R	5-10	165	4-16-90	.250	.133	.297	22	52	5	13	0	1	0	2	0	0	0	2	12	2	3	.288	.278
2-team total (19 Diamondbacks/Reds)					.176	—	—	41	108	9	19	0	1	0	5	7	0	4	0	22	7	3	.194	.226
Vicioso, Danny	R-R	6-0	190	10-27-88	.204	.000	.274	32	98	9	20	1	0	1	11	4	3	0	0	18	2	0	.245	.257

Pitching	B-T	HT	WT	DOB	W	L	ERA	G	GS	CG	SV	IP	H	R	ER	HR	BB	SO	AVG	vLH	vRH	K/9	BB/9
Adames, Jesus	R-R	6-4	195	1-25-91	2	1	3.23	11	8	0	0	39	29	18	14	1	26	28	.215	.186	.237	6.46	6.00
2-team total (4 Diamondbacks/Reds)					2	5	3.72	15	12	0	0	58	45	30	24	2	33	44	—	—	—	6.83	5.12

Player	B-T	HT	WT	DOB	W	L	ERA	G	GS	CG	SV	IP	H	R	ER	HR	BB	SO	AVG	vLH	vRH	SO/9	BB/9
Albino, Reinaldo	R-R	6-2	165	3-16-89	2	4	5.35	16	5	0	1	39	51	24	23	2	20	34	.336	.358	.323	7.91	4.66
Almonte, Ramon	R-R	6-0	165	6-20-88	0	1	11.05	6	2	0	0	7	7	10	9	0	13	9	.269	.182	.333	11.05	15.95
2-team total (8 Diamondbacks/Reds)					1	4	5.45	14	10	0	0	35	24	32	21	0	41	40	—	—	—	10.38	10.64
Aquino, Juan	R-R	6-1	175	12-27-87	7	2	1.27	12	11	0	0	64	49	19	9	2	10	63	.202	.287	.154	8.91	1.41
Calderon, Hugo	R-R	6-1	170	9-19-87	1	1	4.66	8	0	0	1	10	9	5	5	0	3	8	.265	.111	.320	7.45	2.79
Contreras, Carlos	R-R	6-0	165	1-8-91	0	1	8.64	17	0	0	0	17	14	21	16	0	30	17	.241	.227	.250	9.18	16.20
Corcino, Daniel	R-R	5-11	165	8-26-90	6	2	5.29	23	0	0	0	34	37	28	20	2	14	26	.280	.190	.322	6.88	3.71
Correa, Jonathan	R-R	6-1	168	9-13-90	2	1	1.19	4	4	0	0	23	17	4	3	0	8	20	.215	.273	.193	7.94	3.18
De La Rosa, Rafael	L-L	6-0	180	5-12-88	3	3	2.10	12	11	0	0	60	43	20	14	0	23	37	.205	.136	.213	5.55	3.45
Gerson, Starlin	R-R	6-4	175	8-26-88	2	4	3.30	23	1	0	2	44	41	25	16	2	14	37	.247	.203	.275	7.63	2.89
Infante, Ezequiel	L-L	5-10	152	8-31-88	3	0	0.19	26	0	0	14	47	32	5	1	1	9	31	.199	.125	.207	5.94	1.72
Machuca, Luis	R-R	6-1	190	3-16-88	4	2	3.03	12	11	0	0	59	67	29	20	1	8	46	.286	.299	.281	6.98	1.21
Marizan, Jose	L-L	6-1	170	2-7-88	2	5	2.66	13	12	1	0	61	53	22	18	2	20	55	.238	.385	.218	8.11	2.95
Martinez, Porfirio	R-R	5-10	175	11-29-89	0	1	4.24	15	0	0	0	23	21	17	11	1	16	20	.247	.273	.238	7.71	6.17
Martinez, Daniel	L-L	6-2	170	6-4-90	3	1	2.00	16	5	0	0	45	29	16	10	0	22	32	.191	.150	.197	6.40	4.40
Palencia, Juan	R-R	5-11	150	6-20-90	0	0	6.23	5	0	0	0	4	7	3	3	0	1	1	.350	.167	.429	2.08	2.08
2-team total (17 Diamondbacks/Reds)					1	5	7.63	22	1	0	1	31	39	32	26	3	25	27	—	—	—	7.92	7.34
Quezada, Radhames	R-R	6-2	175	7-6-90	0	0	16.20	5	0	0	0	5	7	10	9	0	7	4	.304	.400	.278	7.20	12.60
2-team total (11 Diamondbacks/Reds)					1	6	6.26	16	1	0	0	27	29	22	19	0	17	22	—	—	—	7.24	5.60
Rodriguez, Ramon	R-R	6-2	182	2-14-88	2	0	2.45	18	0	0	0	29	27	16	8	0	11	23	.239	.229	.244	7.06	3.38
Tineo, Carlos	R-R			3-12-91	1	1	8.64	7	0	0	0	8	5	8	8	0	11	6	.185	.222	.167	6.48	11.88
2-team total (10 Diamondbacks/Reds)					1	3	8.85	17	2	0	0	20	19	22	20	0	27	16	—	—	—	7.08	11.95

Fielding

Catcher	PCT	G	PO	A	E	DP	PB
Figueroa	.958	16	106	9	5	0	4
Gonzalez	.978	41	253	53	7	2	13
Ortuno	.944	3	16	1	1	0	2
Vicioso	.993	21	136	16	1	1	5

First Base	PCT	G	PO	A	E	DP
Chacoa	1.000	4	18	1	0	3
Figueroa	1.000	4	36	4	0	2
Gonzalez	1.000	5	52	3	0	3
Hernandez	1.000	7	64	1	0	6
Martinez	1.000	1	4	0	0	0
M. Rodriguez	.982	50	429	9	8	38
Vicioso	.983	8	53	5	1	9

Second Base	PCT	G	PO	A	E	DP
Candelario	.974	15	35	41	2	10
Chacoa	.953	23	42	60	5	13
Hernandez	.976	5	18	22	1	6
Meran	.947	9	18	18	2	4
C. Rodriguez	1.000	3	5	7	0	1
H. Rodriguez	.967	11	26	33	2	9
Sierra	.917	14	20	35	5	4

Third Base	PCT	G	PO	A	E	DP
Candelario	.700	4	3	4	3	0
Chacoa	.868	12	18	28	7	4
Hernandez	.904	42	45	96	15	12
Meran	.750	7	0	6	2	1
C. Rodriguez	.933	5	3	11	1	1
M. Rodriguez	.909	6	6	14	2	2

Shortstop	PCT	G	PO	A	E	DP
Candelario	.833	2	0	5	1	0
Chacoa	.902	11	17	29	5	6
Hernandez	1.000	3	10	6	0	3
C. Rodriguez	.922	58	85	152	20	30
Sierra	.800	1	2	2	1	0

Outfield	PCT	G	PO	A	E	DP
Duran	.882	31	30	0	4	0
Estevez	1.000	15	15	1	0	0
Felipe	.903	19	27	1	3	1
Guerrero	.944	56	80	4	5	1
Lopez	.929	16	12	1	1	0
Martinez	.975	60	112	5	3	1
Moreno	.900	7	9	0	1	0
Quintero	.941	30	30	2	2	0

DSL DIAMONDBACKS/REDS   *ROOKIE*

DOMINICAN SUMMER LEAGUE

STATISTICS FOR THIS TEAM ARE ON PAGE 51.

Cleveland Indians

BY STEPHANIE STORM

Even an amazing Cliff Lee was not enough to help the Indians overcome a bevy of injuries to key players that ultimately prompted general manager Mark Shapiro to trade reigning American League Cy Young Award winner, and free agent-to-be, C.C. Sabathia to the Brewers in July. By then, the Indians had fallen out of post-season contention.

Certainly one player couldn't begin to overcome the volume of injuries that plagued the team from  the start: DH Travis Hafner (right shoulder), catcher Victor Martinez (right elbow and left hamstring), starting pitchers Jake Westbrook (right elbow) and Fausto Carmona (left hip) and closer Joe Borowski (left triceps).

"We lost (the players) who batted second, third and fourth from 2007," Indians manager Eric Wedge said. "We lost our closer, our bullpen went south and we lost two starters—that's tough to overcome."

So the lefthanded Lee was a huge bright spot in an otherwise forgettable season that saw the Tribe go from one win away from the World Series in 2007 to unloading proven major league players for young prospects just a year later.

Sure, the Indians ultimately finished a respectable 81-81, good for third place in the American League Central. But that's only after regrouping in a pressure-less second half after dumping expensive components in Sabathia, clubhouse leader and versatile outfielder Casey Blake, and savvy veteran righthander Paul Byrd.

But while the Indians' brass held open tryouts at several positions for the 2009 season through much of the summer, Lee (who was nearly traded in the offseason after an ineffective 2007 campaign) continued to pile up wins en route to becoming Cleveland's first 20-game winner in 34 years.

The 30-year-old cruised to a 22-3 mark with a tidy 2.54 ERA, allowing just 63 earned runs over 223 innings in which he also struck out a team-high 170 batters and walked only 34. Lee went 5-0, 0.96 in April and was strong in August with a 5-0, 1.86 mark.

Meanwhile, centerfielder Grady Sizemore recorded another solid season, becoming only the Indians' second 30-30 man in history with 33 home runs and 38 stolen bases to go along with a

PLAYERS OF THE YEAR

MAJOR LEAGUE: CLIFF LEE, RHP

Lee put himself back among the best pitchers in the American League just one year after he looked headed for oblivion. He finished 22-3, 2.54, leading the AL in wins and ERA. He also finished with 170 stikeouts in 223 innings for the 81-81 Indians.

MINOR LEAGUE: DAVID HUFF, LHP

Huff, a first-round pick in 2006 out of UCLA, took a major step toward the majors. Or, more accurately, two steps. He opened at Double-A Akron and finished at Triple-A Buffalo, going a combined 11-5, 2.52 with 143 strikeouts in 146 innings .

RODGER WOOD

ORGANIZATION LEADERS

BATTING		*Minimum 250 at-bats
*AVG	Brown, Matthew, Lake County	.308
R	Pena, Roman, Lake County/Kinston	80
H	Hodges, Wes, Akron	146
TB	Mills, Beau, Kinston	244
2B	Mills, Beau, Kinston	34
3B	Rodriguez, Josh, Akron	10
HR	Mills, Beau, Kinston	21
RBI	Hodges, Wes, Akron	97
BB	Rodriguez, Josh, Akron	77
SO	Snyder, Brad, Buffalo	123
SB	Montero, Lucas, Lake County/Kinston	60
*OBP	Gimenez, Chris, Akron/Buffalo	.421
*SLG	Mills, Beau, Kinston	.506

PITCHING		†Minimum 75 innings
W	Smith, Carlton, Kinston	12
	Martin, J.D., Buffalo/Akron	12
	De La Cruz, Kelvin, Akron/Lake Co./Kinston	12
	Judy, Josh, Lake County/Kinston	12
L	Dixon, Kevin, Akron	11
ERA	Huff, David, Akron/Buffalo	2.52
G	Newsom, Randy, Buffalo/Akron	56
GS	Wright, Steven, Kinston/Akron	28
SV	Newsom, Randy, Buffalo/Akron	30
IP	Dixon, Kevin, Akron	157
BB	Archer, Christopher, Lake County	84
SO	Rondon, Hector, Kinston	145
†AVG	Huff, David, Akron/Buffalo	.209

.268 batting average.

Below the majors, the Indians signed Taiwanese righthander Chen-Chang Lee and, in trades, acquired outfielders Matt LaPorta and Michael Brantley and catcher Carlos Santana, who should be key pieces in coming seasons.

2008 PERFORMANCE

General Manager: Mark Shapiro. **Farm Director:** Ross Atkins. **Scouting Director:** Brad Grant.

Class	Team	League	W	L	PCT	Finish*	Manager	Affiliate Since
Majors	Cleveland	American	81	81	.500	8th (14)	Eric Wedge	—
Triple-A	Buffalo Bisons	International	66	77	.462	10th (14)	Torey Lovullo	1995
Double-A	Akron Aeros	Eastern	80	62	.563	3rd (12)	Mike Sarbaugh	1997
High A	Kinston Indians	Carolina	72	66	.522	3rd (8)	Chris Tremie	1987
Low A	Lake County Captains	South Atlantic	75	65	.536	7th (16)	Aaron Holbert	2003
Short-season	Mahoning Valley Scrappers	New York-Penn	31	44	.413	12th (14)	Travis Fryman	1999
Rookie	GCL Indians	Gulf Coast	27	29	.482	11th (16)	Rouglas Odor	2006
Overall 2008 Minor League Record			351	343	.506	13th		

* Finish in overall standings (No. of teams in league). ^League champion.

ORGANIZATION STATISTICS

CLEVELAND INDIANS

AMERICAN LEAGUE

Batting	B-T	HT	WT	DOB	AVG	vLH	vRH	G	AB	R	H	2B	3B	HR	RBI	BB	HBP	SH	SF	SO	SB	CS	SLG	OBP
Aubrey, Michael	L-L	6-0	195	4-15-82	.200	.000	.209	15	45	2	9	0	0	2	3	5	0	0	0	5	0	0	.333	.280
Barfield, Josh	R-R	6-0	190	12-17-82	.182	.182	.182	12	33	3	6	1	0	0	2	0	0	0	0	10	0	0	.212	.182
Blake, Casey	R-R	6-2	210	8-23-73	.289	.313	.283	94	325	46	94	24	0	11	58	33	7	1	2	68	2	0	.465	.365
Cabrera, Asdrubal	B-R	6-0	170	11-13-85	.259	.349	.230	114	352	48	91	20	0	6	47	46	4	11	5	77	4	4	.366	.346
Carroll, Jamey	R-R	5-9	170	2-18-74	.277	.261	.284	113	347	60	96	13	4	1	36	34	9	10	2	65	7	3	.346	.355
Choo, Shin-Soo	L-L	5-11	200	7-13-82	.309	.286	.317	94	317	68	98	28	3	14	66	44	5	0	4	78	4	3	.549	.397
Dellucci, David	L-L	5-11	205	10-31-73	.238	.000	.251	113	336	41	80	19	2	11	47	24	11	0	4	76	3	2	.405	.307
Fasano, Sal	R-R	6-2	225	8-10-71	.261	.235	.276	15	46	5	12	4	0	0	6	3	3	1	1	17	0	0	.348	.340
Francisco, Ben	R-R	6-1	190	10-23-81	.266	.269	.265	121	447	65	119	32	0	15	54	40	6	2	4	86	4	3	.438	.332
Garko, Ryan	R-R	6-2	225	1-2-81	.273	.315	.259	141	495	61	135	21	1	14	90	45	15	0	8	86	0	0	.404	.346
Gonzalez, Andy	R-R	6-3	205	12-15-81	.208	.231	.182	10	24	3	5	0	0	1	2	6	0	0	0	5	1	0	.333	.367
Gutierrez, Franklin	R-R	6-2	190	2-21-83	.248	.252	.246	134	399	54	99	26	2	8	41	27	8	4	2	87	9	3	.383	.307
Hafner, Travis	L-R	6-3	240	6-3-77	.197	.220	.189	57	198	21	39	10	0	5	24	27	5	0	3	55	1	1	.323	.305
Marte, Andy	R-R	6-1	205	10-21-83	.221	.293	.198	80	235	21	52	11	3	3	17	14	1	7	0	52	1	2	.315	.268
Martinez, Victor	B-R	6-2	210	12-23-78	.278	.339	.260	73	266	30	74	17	0	2	35	24	1	0	3	32	0	0	.365	.337
Michaels, Jason	R-R	6-0	205	5-4-76	.207	.125	.265	21	58	3	12	4	0	0	9	4	1	1	3	13	1	1	.276	.258
Peralta, Jhonny	R-R	6-1	210	5-28-82	.276	.247	.285	154	605	104	167	42	4	23	89	48	4	2	5	126	3	1	.473	.331
Shoppach, Kelly	R-R	6-0	220	4-29-80	.261	.304	.246	112	352	67	92	27	0	21	55	36	11	3	1	133	0	0	.517	.348
Sizemore III, Grady	L-L	6-2	200	8-2-82	.268	.224	.286	157	634	101	170	39	5	33	90	98	11	0	2	130	38	5	.502	.374
Tyner, Jason	L-L	6-1	180	4-23-77	.000	—	.000	1	2	0	0	0	0	0	0	0	1	0	0	0	0	0	.000	.333
Velandia, Jorge	R-R	5-9	190	1-12-75	.375	.000	.600	7	8	1	3	1	0	0	1	0	0	0	0	2	0	0	.500	.444
2-team total (3 Toronto)					.200	—	—	10	15	1	3	1	0	0	1	0	0	0	0	4	0	0	.267	.250

Pitching	B-T	HT	WT	DOB	W	L	ERA	G	GS	CG	SV	IP	H	R	ER	HR	BB	SO	AVG	vLH	vRH	K/9	BB/9
Bauer, Rick	R-R	6-6	225	1-10-77	0	0	13.50	4	0	0	0	6	10	9	9	1	3	4	.370	.250	.467	6.00	4.50
Betancourt, Rafael	R-R	6-2	200	4-29-75	3	4	5.07	69	0	0	4	71	76	41	40	11	25	64	.276	.252	.295	8.11	3.17
Borowski, Joe	R-R	6-2	215	5-4-71	1	3	7.56	18	0	0	6	17	24	14	14	4	8	9	.333	.333	.333	4.86	4.32
Breslow, Craig	L-L	6-0	185	8-8-80	0	0	3.24	7	0	0	0	8	10	3	3	1	5	7	.286	.400	.240	7.56	5.40
2-team total (42 Minnesota)					0	2	1.91	49	0	0	1	47	34	12	10	1	19	39	—	—	—	7.47	3.64
Bullington, Bryan	R-R	6-4	220	9-30-80	0	2	4.91	3	2	0	0	15	15	9	8	4	2	12	.268	.333	.192	7.36	1.23
Byrd, Paul	R-R	6-1	190	12-3-70	7	10	4.53	22	22	1	0	131	146	70	66	23	24	56	.282	.317	.244	3.85	1.65
2-team total (8 Boston)					11	12	4.60	30	30	1	0	180	204	96	92	31	34	82	—	—	—	4.10	1.70
Carmona, Fausto	R-R	6-4	230	12-7-83	8	7	5.44	22	22	1	0	121	126	80	73	7	70	58	.271	.303	.230	4.33	5.22
Donnelly, Brendan	R-R	6-3	250	7-4-71	1	0	8.56	15	0	0	0	14	20	13	13	2	10	8	.357	.286	.400	5.27	6.59
Elarton, Scott	R-R	6-8	240	2-23-76	0	1	3.52	8	0	0	0	15	16	7	6	0	9	15	.262	.280	.250	8.80	5.28
Ginter, Matt	R-R	6-1	220	12-24-77	1	3	5.14	4	4	0	0	21	25	12	12	3	12	12	.301	.308	.290	5.14	1.29
Jackson, Zach	L-L	6-5	220	5-13-83	2	3	5.60	9	9	0	0	55	64	36	34	7	14	30	.292	.365	.263	4.94	2.30
Julio, Jorge	R-R	6-1	225	3-3-79	0	0	5.60	15	0	0	0	18	18	11	11	3	11	15	.277	.310	.250	7.64	5.60
Kobayashi, Masahide	R-R	6-0	195	5-24-74	4	5	4.53	57	0	0	6	56	65	30	28	8	14	35	.286	.280	.292	5.66	2.26
Laffey, Aaron	L-L	6-0	180	4-15-85	5	7	4.23	16	16	0	0	94	103	52	44	10	31	43	.281	.244	.292	4.13	2.98
Lee, Cliff	L-L	6-3	190	8-30-78	22	3	2.54	31	31	4	0	223	214	68	63	12	34	170	.253	.272	.245	6.85	1.37
Lewis, Jensen	R-R	6-3	210	5-16-84	0	4	3.82	51	0	0	13	66	68	29	28	8	27	52	.266	.267	.264	7.09	3.68
Lewis, Scott	B-L	6-0	195	9-26-83	4	0	2.63	4	4	0	0	24	20	9	7	4	6	15	.222	.130	.254	5.63	2.25
Mastny, Tom	R-R	6-6	225	2-4-81	2	2	10.80	14	1	0	0	20	28	24	24	6	11	19	.318	.326	.310	8.55	4.95
Meloan, Jonathan	R-R	6-3	230	7-11-84	0	0	0.00	2	0	0	0	2	0	0	0	0	1	2	.000	.000	.000	9.00	4.50
Mujica, Edward	R-R	6-2	215	5-10-84	3	2	6.75	33	0	0	0	39	46	29	29	5	10	27	.301	.277	.318	6.28	2.33
Perez, Rafael	L-L	6-3	195	5-15-82	4	4	3.54	73	0	0	2	76	67	32	30	8	23	86	.234	.222	.243	10.14	2.71
Reyes, Anthony	R-R	6-2	230	10-16-81	2	1	1.83	6	6	0	0	34	31	7	7	2	12	15	.242	.257	.222	3.93	3.15
Rincon, Juan	R-R	5-11	210	1-23-79	1	1	5.60	23	0	0	0	27	34	18	17	3	8	19	.304	.300	.306	6.26	2.63
2-team total (24 Minnesota)					3	3	5.86	47	0	0	0	55	67	39	36	8	24	39	—	—	—	6.34	3.90
Rundles, Rich	L-L	6-5	210	6-3-81	0	0	1.80	5	0	0	0	5	5	1	1	0	3	6	.263	.167	.429	10.80	5.40
Sabathia, C.C.	L-L	6-7	290	7-21-80	6	8	3.83	18	18	3	0	122	117	54	52	13	34	123	.252	.211	.269	9.05	2.50

	B-T	HT	WT	DOB	W	L	ERA	G	GS	CG	SV	IP	H	R	ER	HR	BB	SO	AVG	vLH	vRH	K/9	BB/9
Slocum, Brian	R-R	6-3	210	3-27-81	0	0	27.00	2	0	0	0	2	8	6	6	2	0	1	.615	.571	.667	4.50	0.00
Sowers, Jeremy	L-L	6-1	180	5-17-83	4	9	5.58	22	22	0	0	121	141	84	75	18	39	64	.291	.258	.303	4.76	2.90
Westbrook, Jake	R-R	6-3	215	9-29-77	1	2	3.12	5	5	1	0	35	33	13	12	5	7	19	.256	.238	.273	4.93	1.82

Fielder

Catcher	PCT	G	PO	A	E	DP	PB
Fasano	.982	15	102	9	2	1	3
Martinez	.991	55	328	16	3	1	2
Shoppach	.989	110	586	34	7	2	8

First Base	PCT	G	PO	A	E	DP
Aubrey	1.000	12	99	6	0	14
Blake	.995	27	171	10	1	20
Fasano	—	1	0	0	0	0
Garko	.996	121	1039	80	4	123
Gonzalez	.951	7	39	0	2	4
Marte	1.000	1	2	1	0	1
Martinez	.989	10	82	4	1	9

Second Base	PCT	G	PO	A	E	DP
Barfield	1.000	9	26	24	0	9
Cabrera	.994	94	202	281	3	83
Carroll	.990	74	105	192	3	46
Velandia	1.000	1	3	4	0	1

Third Base	PCT	G	PO	A	E	DP
Blake	.938	77	39	141	12	15
Carroll	.918	43	12	55	6	5
Gonzalez	.667	2	1	1	1	1
Marte	.971	76	43	155	6	19
Peralta	1.000	1	1	2	0	1

Shortstop	PCT	G	PO	A	E	DP
Blake	1.000	1	0	1	0	0

	PCT	G	PO	A	E	DP
Cabrera	.951	20	38	59	5	17
Peralta	.979	146	217	427	14	104
Velandia	1.000	2	1	4	0	2

Outfield	PCT	G	PO	A	E	DP
Carroll	—	1	0	0	0	0
Choo	.985	75	128	4	2	0
Dellucci	1.000	56	75	1	0	0
Francisco	.981	104	196	12	4	3
Gutierrez	.989	119	268	5	3	0
Michaels	.976	20	38	3	1	0
Sizemore III	.995	151	382	2	2	1
Tyner	—	1	0	0	0	0

BUFFALO BISONS

TRIPLE-A

INTERNATIONAL LEAGUE

Batting	B-T	HT	WT	DOB	AVG	vLH	vRH	G	AB	R	H	2B	3B	HR	RBI	BB	HBP	SH	SF	SO	SB	CS	SLG	OBP
Aubrey, Michael	L-L	6-0	195	4-15-82	.281	.273	.285	72	285	29	80	18	0	7	37	16	5	1	2	40	0	0	.418	.328
Barfield, Josh	R-R	6-0	190	12-17-82	.251	.247	.252	73	299	30	75	18	1	5	23	15	1	2		58	9	5	.368	.292
Brown, Jordan	L-L	6-0	205	12-18-83	.281	.199	.323	109	420	52	118	30	3	7	51	35	2	0	3	67	3	3	.417	.337
Cabrera, Asdrubal	B-R	6-0	170	11-13-85	.326	.306	.337	34	141	25	46	7	1	4	13	7	4	0	0	25	2	2	.475	.375
Camacaro, Armando	R-R	5-11	215	4-6-79	.111	.250	.071	8	18	0	2	0	0	0	0	1	0	1	0	5	0	0	.111	.158
Cannizaro, Andy	R-R	5-10	170	12-19-78	.321	.323	.321	25	84	15	27	4	0	3	14	7	0	0	0	7	0	0	.476	.374
2-team total (51 Durham)					.267	—	—	76	255	31	68	12	0	4	28	24	2	5	3	25	1	0	.361	.331
Choo, Shin-Soo	L-L	5-11	200	7-13-82	.262	.467	.148	12	42	1	11	2	0	1	3	5	2	0	0	14	1	3	.381	.367
Cooper, Jason	L-R	6-2	215	12-6-80	.247	.291	.222	102	304	38	75	19	4	9	45	46	8	0	4	63	2	5	.424	.356
Crowe, Trevor	B-R	6-0	190	11-17-83	.274	.302	.258	35	146	25	40	12	2	5	13	15	2	1	0	43	5	2	.486	.350
de la Cruz, Chris	B-R	6-0	160	5-3-82	.156	.176	.143	19	45	5	7	0	0	0	4	3	1	1	0	8	0	1	.156	.224
Diaz, Walter	R-R	6-0	180	11-13-85	.069	.125	.048	8	29	1	2	0	0	0	1	0	0	0	0	11	0	0	.069	.100
Ensberg, Morgan	R-R	6-2	210	8-26-75	.189	.246	.153	52	159	24	30	9	0	5	23	31	1	4	1	43	1	1	.340	.323
Francisco, Ben	R-R	6-1	190	10-23-81	.228	.240	.224	24	92	9	21	3	1	1	6	11	0	0	1	25	3	0	.315	.308
Gimenez, Chris	R-R	6-2	190	12-27-82	.272	.292	.262	54	195	23	53	9	1	3	19	23	4	3	4	60	2	1	.374	.354
Gonzalez, Andy	R-R	6-3	205	12-15-81	.242	.311	.219	83	289	37	70	13	0	7	35	39	6	2	4	71	2	2	.360	.340
Graffanino, Tony	R-R	6-1	190	6-6-72	.315	.304	.318	25	89	8	28	7	1	0	6	8	2	1	0	11	0	1	.416	.384
Haad, Yamid	R-R	6-2	220	9-2-77	.167	.133	.179	40	108	9	18	3	0	1	6	8	2	0	2	28	0	0	.222	.233
Hafner, Travis	R-R	6-3	240	6-3-77	.318	.375	.167	7	22	4	7	3	0	0	4	3	0	0	0	4	0	0	.455	.400
Head, Jerad	R-R	6-1	205	11-15-82	.286	1.000	.167	3	7	1	2	1	0	0	1	0	0	0	0	1	0	0	.857	.375
Herr, Aaron	R-R	6-0	210	3-7-81	.245	.222	.258	65	241	27	59	7	3	9	32	11	3	1	1	75	1	0	.411	.285
2-team total (18 Louisville)					.221	—	—	83	308	37	68	9	4	11	40	15	3	1	1	97	1	0	.383	.263
Linden, Todd	B-R	6-3	220	6-30-80	.278	.268	.284	90	324	51	90	20	1	14	50	52	5	2	0	101	3	2	.475	.386
Martinez, Victor	B-R	6-2	210	12-23-78	.300	.364	.222	6	20	2	6	2	0	0	2	4	0	0	1	4	0	0	.400	.400
Mulhern, Ryan	R-R	6-2	205	11-29-80	.250	.197	.279	58	200	30	50	11	0	7	26	26	0	0	1	63	0	0	.410	.335
2-team total (35 Indianapolis)					.234	—	—	93	316	45	74	15	0	13	42	36	4	0	1	96	0	1	.405	.319
Sandoval, Danny	B-R	5-11	205	4-7-79	.247	.250	.245	43	150	15	37	6	0	1	13	14	0	4	1	21	6	1	.307	.309
2-team total (79 Syracuse)					.280	—	—	122	465	53	130	20	0	8	48	30	1	7	1	64	9	4	.374	.324
Sardinha, Bronson	L-R	6-1	220	4-6-83	.300	.417	.222	12	30	4	9	0	0	2	5	4	0	1	0	6	0	1	.500	.382
Snyder, Brad	L-L	6-3	200	5-25-82	.246	.205	.263	115	411	52	101	28	5	12	61	27	4	1	3	123	7	3	.426	.297
Toregas, Wyatt	R-R	5-11	200	12-2-82	.219	.283	.193	50	155	15	34	8	0	2	25	15	3	5	0	32	2	0	.310	.301
Tyner, Jason	L-L	6-1	180	4-23-77	.235	.190	.258	76	238	31	56	9	0	1	14	28	3	9	1	20	8	0	.286	.322
2-team total (21 Charlotte)					.248	—	—	97	307	39	76	12	0	1	18	36	4	10	1	26	11	1	.296	.333
Velandia, Jorge	R-R	5-9	190	1-12-75	.209	.169	.227	52	206	18	43	3	0	0	18	30	4	4	0	49	2	0	.223	.291
2-team total (28 Syracuse)					.233	—	—	80	300	34	70	5	1	3	20	34	5	5	0	67	2	0	.287	.322

Pitching	B-T	HT	WT	DOB	W	L	ERA	G	GS	CG	SV	IP	H	R	ER	HR	BB	SO	AVG	vLH	vRH	K/9	BB/9
Bauer, Rick	R-R	6-6	225	1-10-77	0	0	1.54	22	0	0	15	23	17	4	4	0	10	30	.200	.233	.167	11.57	3.86
2-team total (12 Syracuse)					0	0	2.08	34	0	0	18	35	27	11	8	1	17	43	—	—		11.16	4.41
Bullington, Bryan	R-R	6-4	220	9-30-80	1	3	4.75	10	8	0	1	53	65	34	28	7	13	47	.302	.307	.297	7.98	2.21
2-team total (15 Indianapolis)					5	9	5.20	25	23	0	1	128	155	88	74	15	38	107	—	—		7.52	2.67
Buzachero, Bubbie	R-R	5-11	180	6-13-81	3	4	3.14	40	2	0	10	66	61	28	23	7	20	51	.248	.288	.215	6.95	2.73
Donnelly, Brendan	R-R	6-3	250	7-4-71	0	1	0.50	6	0	0	0	6	5	1	1	1	1	5	.217	.455	.000	7.50	1.50
Elarton, Scott	R-R	6-8	240	2-23-76	1	2	2.45	15	0	0	0	26	21	9	7	2	7	18	.223	.217	.229	6.31	2.45
Ginter, Matt	R-R	6-1	220	12-24-77	6	6	4.14	18	17	0	0	100	109	57	46	10	32	65	.275	.315	.235	5.85	2.88
Halama, John	L-L	6-5	215	2-22-72	8	6	4.60	16	16	2	0	108	123	62	55	13	19	42	.303	.329	.269	3.51	1.59
Harris, Jeff	R-R	6-1	190	7-4-74	3	5	5.01	18	11	0	1	79	96	48	44	14	18	55	.303	.348	.255	6.27	2.05
Herrmann, Frank	L-R	6-4	220	5-30-84	0	2	1.38	2	2	0	0	13	11	3	2	1	6	14	.239	.188	.267	9.69	4.15
Huff, David	L-L	6-2	190	8-22-84	6	4	3.01	16	16	0	0	81	68	31	27	8	15	81	.224	.215	.231	9.04	1.67
Jackson, Zach	L-L	6-5	220	5-13-83	3	1	4.05	8	4	0	0	27	25	13	12	3	5	20	.243	.351	.182	6.75	1.69
Laffey, Aaron	L-L	6-0	180	4-15-85	6	2	4.38	11	11	0	0	62	72	33	30	2	18	47	.291	.269	.302	6.86	2.63

	B-T	HT	WT	DOB	W	L	ERA	G	GS	CG	SV	IP	H	R	ER	HR	BB	SO	AVG	vLH	vRH	K/9	BB/9
Larrison, Preston	R-R	6-4	235	11-19-80	1	2	3.60	19	0	0	1	25	31	11	10	1	6	22	.307	.308	.306	7.92	2.16
2-team total (29 Toledo)					3	4	3.43	48	0	0	1	60	60	25	23	4	21	41	—	—	—	6.12	3.13
Lewis, Jensen	R-R	6-3	210	5-16-84	1	2	3.60	11	0	0	1	20	16	11	8	2	8	18	.219	.250	.189	8.10	3.60
Lewis, Scott	B-L	6-0	195	9-26-83	2	2	2.63	4	4	1	0	24	19	8	7	2	4	21	.221	.333	.161	7.88	1.50
Martin, J.D.	R-R	6-4	195	1-2-83	1	0	1.80	4	1	0	0	10	6	2	2	2	2	8	.171	.125	.211	7.20	1.80
Mastny, Tom	R-R	6-6	225	2-4-81	2	2	1.78	28	0	0	0	35	26	10	7	1	12	43	.206	.242	.172	10.95	3.06
Meloan, Jon	R-R	6-3	230	7-11-84	0	1	4.30	12	0	0	0	15	12	8	7	1	9	12	.235	.269	.200	7.36	5.52
Miller, Adam	R-R	6-4	200	11-26-84	0	1	1.88	6	6	0	0	29	26	9	6	0	12	20	.239	.212	.279	6.28	3.77
Mujica, Edward	R-R	6-2	215	5-10-84	0	2	4.15	18	0	0	4	26	29	14	12	2	10	27	.284	.250	.326	9.35	3.46
Newsom, Randy	R-R	6-2	200	5-6-82	0	1	1.86	9	0	0	1	10	9	4	2	0	6	6	.231	.455	.143	5.59	5.59
Perez, Oneli	R-R	6-2	200	5-26-83	0	0	7.11	7	0	0	2	13	20	10	10	2	8	15	.377	.560	.214	10.66	5.68
2-team total (14 Charlotte)					0	1	8.49	21	0	0	2	30	48	28	28	7	17	34	—	—	—	10.31	5.16
Reichert, Dan	R-R	6-3	175	7-12-76	1	3	4.40	8	8	0	0	43	52	25	21	3	15	29	.286	.363	.209	6.07	3.14
2-team total (1 Indianapolis)					1	4	4.40	9	9	0	0	47	57	30	23	3	17	31	—	—	—	5.94	3.26
Reyes, Anthony	R-R	6-2	230	10-16-81	2	0	2.77	2	2	0	0	13	10	4	4	3	4	8	.208	.176	.286	5.54	2.77
Rincon, Juan	R-R	5-11	210	1-23-79	0	1	6.75	4	0	0	0	5	11	7	4	1	3	4	.379	.417	.353	6.75	5.06
Rundles, Rich	L-L	6-5	210	6-3-81	5	4	2.91	55	0	0	4	53	40	18	17	3	24	60	.205	.165	.250	10.25	4.10
Santos, Reid	L-L	6-1	170	8-24-82	2	2	7.20	16	0	0	0	25	42	21	20	3	9	24	.378	.382	.377	8.64	3.24
Slocum, Brian	R-R	6-3	210	3-27-81	3	7	4.85	30	11	0	1	85	83	50	46	12	42	81	.253	.224	.286	8.54	4.43
Smith, Sean	R-R	6-4	195	10-13-83	0	1	4.00	4	4	0	0	18	14	8	8	1	10	20	.222	.286	.143	10.00	5.00
Sowers, Jeremy	L-L	6-0	180	5-17-83	4	3	2.08	10	10	1	0	61	56	16	14	4	17	43	.251	.240	.257	6.38	2.52
Stanford, Jason	L-L	6-1	210	1-23-77	1	3	3.90	6	5	0	0	28	34	17	12	2	11	12	.315	.313	.317	3.90	3.58
2-team total (5 Columbus)					3	5	6.00	11	8	0	0	42	53	35	28	5	20	24	—	—	—	5.14	4.29
Stevens, Jeff	R-R	6-2	205	9-5-83	0	3	3.94	19	0	0	5	30	19	14	13	3	16	44	.181	.188	.175	13.35	4.85
Tomlin, Josh	R-R	6-1	195	10-19-84	1	0	3.86	1	1	0	0	7	6	3	3	2	1	3	.250	.333	.167	3.86	1.29
Weaver, Jeff	R-R	6-5	200	8-22-76	2	2	6.07	13	4	0	0	30	38	21	20	7	10	22	.311	.338	.275	6.67	3.03

Fielding

Catcher	PCT	G	PO	A	E	DP	PB
Camacaro	.981	7	47	4	1	0	2
Gimenez	.986	51	405	22	6	4	4
Haad	.996	38	223	22	1	4	5
Martinez	1.000	4	22	1	0	0	0
Toregas	.990	50	361	19	4	3	4

	PCT	G	PO	A	E	DP
de la Cruz	1.000	13	14	30	0	3
Ensberg	1.000	1	1	0	0	0
Gonzalez	.972	26	45	60	3	10
Graffanino	1.000	9	16	25	0	9
Head	—	0	0	0	0	0
Velandia	1.000	12	20	42	0	11

	PCT	G	PO	A	E	DP
Cannizaro	1.000	11	19	24	0	12
de la Cruz	.800	3	2	2	1	1
Diaz	.897	8	13	22	4	7
Gonzalez	.898	15	19	25	5	7
Graffanino	1.000	3	1	2	0	0
Sandoval	.957	43	65	113	8	30
Velandia	.953	41	59	124	9	30

First Base	PCT	G	PO	A	E	DP
Aubrey	.987	34	265	28	4	36
Brown	.989	87	698	54	8	74
Gonzalez	1.000	16	53	4	0	5
Graffanino	1.000	3	34	0	0	3
Haad	1.000	2	10	0	0	0
Mulhern	.991	14	102	5	1	13

Second Base	PCT	G	PO	A	E	DP
Barfield	.984	71	157	204	6	58
Cabrera	.952	6	6	14	1	5
Cannizaro	.955	15	19	44	3	12

Third Base	PCT	G	PO	A	E	DP
de la Cruz	1.000	1	0	2	0	0
Ensberg	.890	51	27	94	15	8
Gimenez	.667	3	1	3	2	0
Gonzalez	.923	17	16	20	3	2
Graffanino	.871	10	12	15	4	3
Head	.750	2	0	3	1	0
Herr	.892	63	49	100	18	12
Velandia	1.000	2	0	4	0	0

Shortstop	PCT	G	PO	A	E	DP
Cabrera	.924	29	44	66	9	13

Outfield	PCT	G	PO	A	E	DP
Choo	1.000	8	13	1	0	0
Cooper	.993	86	147	1	1	0
Crowe	.982	35	53	1	1	0
Francisco	.976	23	41	0	1	0
Gonzalez	1.000	16	31	1	0	0
Linden	.987	80	147	3	2	3
Sardinha	1.000	11	16	2	0	1
Snyder	.985	114	263	5	4	0
Tyner	1.000	68	131	4	0	1

AKRON AEROS

DOUBLE-A

EASTERN LEAGUE

Batting	B-T	HT	WT	DOB	AVG	vLH	vRH	G	AB	R	H	2B	3B	HR	RBI	BB	HBP	SH	SF	SO	SB	CS	SLG	OBP
Aubrey, Michael	L-L	6-0	195	4-15-82	.282	.217	.300	25	103	14	29	10	1	2	16	8	0	0	1	12	0	0	.456	.330
Barfield, Josh	R-R	6-0	190	12-17-82	.000	.000	.000	2	4	0	0	0	0	0	0	0	0	0	0	2	0	0	.000	.000
Camacaro, Armando	R-R	5-11	215	4-6-79	.233	.263	.222	22	73	8	17	3	0	4	14	5	0	0	1	11	4	1	.438	.282
Chaves, Brandon	B-R	6-3	181	8-5-79	.198	.191	.200	80	247	25	49	2	3	2	16	30	2	3	3	47	11	4	.255	.287
Constanza, Jose	B-L	5-9	150	9-1-83	.278	.217	.301	95	338	44	94	12	6	0	34	28	2	5	3	42	23	6	.349	.334
Crowe, Trevor	B-R	6-0	190	11-17-83	.323	.275	.349	49	198	45	64	16	2	4	28	27	1	1	2	29	13	5	.485	.404
de la Cruz, Chris	B-R	6-0	160	5-3-82	.140	.125	.143	14	50	5	7	0	0	1	6	6	0	0	0	10	0	0	.200	.232
Espino, Damaso	R-R	6-1	210	5-8-83	.275	.303	.261	31	102	6	28	3	0	0	11	10	1	0	1	12	0	0	.304	.342
Gimenez, Chris	R-R	6-2	220	12-27-82	.339	.309	.352	55	177	46	60	15	1	6	26	52	1	1	2	33	0	1	.537	.487
Goleski, Ryan	R-R	6-3	215	3-19-82	.249	.282	.232	99	338	48	84	17	4	12	37	40	4	0	2	98	2	2	.429	.333
Head, Stephen	L-L	6-3	220	1-13-84	.290	.322	.276	106	404	50	117	24	2	13	49	24	0	0	6	75	1	1	.455	.325
Head, Jerad	R-R	6-1	205	11-15-82	.143	.250	.000	2	7	0	1	0	0	0	1	0	0	0	2	0	0	.143	.250
Hodges, Wes	R-R	6-2	180	9-14-84	.290	.263	.300	133	504	70	146	29	3	18	97	52	5	0	12	105	3	1	.466	.354
LaPorta, Matt	R-R	6-2	210	1-8-85	.233	.267	.222	17	60	6	14	1	0	2	8	4	2	0	1	12	0	0	.350	.299
Martinez, Victor	B-R	6-2	210	12-23-78	.333	.500	.000	2	6	1	2	0	0	1	1	1	0	0	0	2	0	0	.833	.429
Panther, Nathan	L-L	6-2	180	7-12-81	.248	.257	.246	91	294	44	73	16	2	7	27	45	0	5	3	59	4	0	.388	.345
Pickens, Doug	R-R	6-0	190	6-19-85	.250	.000	.333	1	4	0	1	0	0	0	0	0	0	0	0	0	0	0	.250	.250
Pinckney, Brandon	R-R	5-10	165	4-12-82	.280	.325	.254	90	322	40	90	15	1	6	36	13	4	4	2	47	2	1	.388	.314
Rodriguez, Josh	R-R	6-0	185	12-18-84	.241	.205	.255	137	532	75	128	22	10	7	49	77	0	9	3	122	12	6	.359	.335
Santana, Carlos	B-R	5-11	188	4-8-86	.125	.000	.250	2	8	1	1	0	0	0	1	2	0	0	0	2	0	0	.500	.125
Sardinha, Bronson	L-R	6-1	220	4-6-83	.271	.268	.272	88	340	45	92	17	4	6	46	39	2	2	4	66	3	2	.397	.345
Toregas, Wyatt	R-R	5-11	200	12-2-82	.296	.400	.256	47	162	22	48	9	0	12	35	17	6	0	3	20	0	1	.574	.371
Whitney, Matt	R-R	6-2	210	2-19-84	.268	.302	.254	129	463	57	124	29	2	10	58	59	6	0	3	93	0	0	.404	.356

Pitching	B-T	HT	WT	DOB	W	L	ERA	G	GS	CG	SV	IP	H	R	ER	HR	BB	SO	AVG	vLH	vRH	K/9	BB/9
Borowski, Joe	R-R	6-2	215	5-4-71	0	0	0.00	1	0	0	0	1	1	0	0	0	0	1	.250	—	.250	9.00	0.00

	B-T	HT	WT	DOB	W	L	ERA	G	GS	CG	SV	IP	H	R	ER	HR	BB	SO	AVG	vLH	vRH	K/9	BB/9
Burton, T.J.	L-R	6-3	185	7-30-83	2	2	3.90	29	0	0	0	30	41	17	13	1	14	23	.323	.346	.307	6.90	4.20
Buzachero, Bubbie	R-R	5-11	180	6-13-81	0	0	3.38	5	0	0	1	5	8	4	2	0	4	6	.333	.500	.214	10.13	6.75
Carmona, Fausto	R-R	6-4	230	12-7-83	1	0	1.80	1	1	0	0	5	9	1	1	0	0	2	.429	.500	.364	3.60	0.00
De La Cruz, Kelvin	L-L	6-5	187	1-8-88	1	0	7.20	1	1	0	0	5	4	4	4	1	3	4	.222	.000	.222	7.20	5.40
Deters, James	R-R	6-4	180	6-4-83	0	3	6.91	10	4	0	0	29	43	25	22	2	14	13	.355	.385	.341	4.08	4.40
Dixon, Kevin	R-R	6-3	225	12-16-83	9	11	4.41	27	26	0	1	157	159	87	77	17	48	113	.262	.270	.257	6.48	2.75
Edell, Ryan	L-L	6-1	215	7-6-83	7	8	3.80	26	26	0	0	144	146	68	61	14	21	99	.258	.262	.256	6.17	1.31
Herrmann, Frank	L-R	6-4	220	5-30-84	11	6	4.10	23	23	0	0	132	142	70	60	9	36	86	.275	.256	.290	5.88	2.46
Huff, David	L-L	6-2	190	8-22-84	5	1	1.92	11	10	1	0	66	44	17	14	5	14	62	.189	.111	.212	8.50	1.92
Lewis, Scott	B-L	6-0	195	9-26-83	6	2	2.33	13	13	0	0	73	62	22	19	2	9	61	.224	.197	.232	7.49	1.10
Lofgren, Chuck	L-L	6-3	205	1-29-86	2	6	5.99	28	15	0	0	86	93	59	57	9	52	72	.278	.286	.275	7.56	5.46
Martin, J.D.	R-R	6-4	195	1-2-83	11	3	2.49	31	8	0	0	80	73	25	22	5	19	71	.249	.178	.297	8.02	2.15
Montero, Joanniel	R-R	6-5	200	2-2-86	0	0	15.43	1	0	0	0	2	6	4	4	1	1	1	.500	.333	.667	3.86	3.86
Newsom, Randy	R-R	6-2	200	5-6-82	5	1	3.00	47	0	0	29	45	43	17	15	2	29	28	.259	.277	.248	5.60	5.80
Nottingham, Shawn	L-L	6-1	190	1-22-85	0	2	7.09	19	0	0	0	33	40	29	26	5	16	33	.301	.280	.313	9.00	4.36
Perdomo, Luis	R-R	6-0	170	4-27-84	2	0	3.52	9	0	0	1	15	12	6	6	1	7	17	.218	.263	.194	9.98	4.11
Roehl, Scott	R-R	6-1	195	8-19-81	1	2	2.54	40	0	0	7	50	38	20	14	2	19	53	.207	.203	.208	9.60	3.44
Santos, Reid	L-L	6-1	170	8-24-82	2	1	3.78	29	0	0	2	52	43	22	22	5	13	45	.223	.118	.280	7.74	2.24
Sipp, Tony	L-L	6-0	190	7-12-83	0	3	3.74	16	0	0	1	22	19	12	9	4	7	32	.235	.182	.254	13.29	2.91
Stevens, Jeff	R-R	6-2	205	9-5-83	5	1	2.51	17	0	0	1	29	19	8	8	2	11	37	.188	.179	.194	11.62	3.45
Stiller, Erik	R-R	6-5	210	7-10-84	6	5	4.13	35	0	0	0	57	47	28	26	5	21	55	.228	.280	.198	8.74	3.34
Tseng, Sung-Wei	R-R	5-10	195	12-28-84	0	0	8.80	9	0	0	0	15	21	15	15	3	6	12	.328	.440	.256	7.04	3.52
Wagner, Neil	R-R	6-0	195	1-1-84	0	2	3.60	7	0	0	0	10	10	5	4	1	4	11	.256	.300	.241	9.90	3.60
Westbrook, Jake	R-R	6-3	215	9-29-77	0	0	0.00	1	1	0	0	6	3	0	0	0	4	2	.167	.000	.375	3.00	6.00
Wright, Steven	R-R	6-2	210	9-30-84	4	3	4.30	14	14	0	0	75	80	38	36	14	17	58	.268	.230	.295	6.93	2.03

Fielding

Catcher	PCT	G	PO	A	E	DP	PB
Camacaro	.993	22	128	11	1	1	4
Espino	1.000	30	191	13	0	0	6
Gimenez	.990	48	360	21	4	2	4
Pickens	.889	1	8	0	1	0	0
Santana	1.000	1	12	0	0	0	0
Toregas	1.000	43	335	18	0	1	2

First Base	PCT	G	PO	A	E	DP
Aubrey	.993	16	124	18	1	11
Gimenez	1.000	4	20	6	0	4
S. Head	.996	56	447	35	2	54
Whitney	.997	68	533	42	2	51

Second Base	PCT	G	PO	A	E	DP
Barfield	1.000	2	2	2	0	1

	PCT	G	PO	A	E	DP
Chaves	1.000	13	22	40	0	8
de la Cruz	.974	8	13	24	1	7
Pinckney	.975	61	93	137	6	43
Rodriguez	.986	62	116	168	4	38

Third Base	PCT	G	PO	A	E	DP
Chaves	1.000	4	2	3	0	0
de la Cruz	1.000	5	0	7	0	0
Gimenez	—	1	0	0	0	0
Hodges	.899	125	58	190	28	16
Pinckney	.833	6	0	5	1	1
Whitney	1.000	3	1	2	0	1

Shortstop	PCT	G	PO	A	E	DP
Chaves	.986	52	73	143	3	34
Pinckney	.973	21	24	47	2	10

	PCT	G	PO	A	E	DP
Rodriguez	.955	74	129	207	16	49

Outfield	PCT	G	PO	A	E	DP
Chaves	1.000	7	20	0	0	0
Constanza	.984	90	178	5	3	2
Crowe	.990	40	94	4	1	0
Gimenez	1.000	2	2	0	0	0
Goleski	.969	69	121	5	4	1
J. Head	1.000	2	2	0	0	0
S. Head	.989	42	86	2	1	1
LaPorta	.968	15	29	1	1	0
Panther	.967	88	171	5	6	1
Sardinha	.979	81	181	5	4	0

KINSTON INDIANS

HIGH CLASS A

CAROLINA LEAGUE

Batting	B-T	HT	WT	DOB	AVG	vLH	vRH	G	AB	R	H	2B	3B	HR	RBI	BB	HBP	SH	SF	SO	SB	CS	SLG	OBP
Arnal, Cristo	R-R	6-0	180	9-17-85	.198	.185	.203	36	106	7	21	3	0	0	8	5	0	6	0	19	3	2	.226	.234
Camacaro, Armando	R-R	5-11	215	4-6-79	.286	.500	.200	2	7	0	2	0	0	0	2	1	0	0	0	1	0	0	.286	.375
Castillo, Alex	R-R	6-2	195	11-29-85	.226	.309	.205	78	265	28	60	17	2	8	44	15	2	2	2	76	4	4	.396	.271
Cumberbatch, Cirilo	R-R	6-0	205	7-11-86	.236	.282	.218	105	365	45	86	14	0	2	43	29	6	3	5	68	7	5	.290	.299
Davis, Adam	B-R	5-9	190	10-15-84	.203	.250	.183	37	148	22	30	5	1	4	16	15	2	2	1	26	5	2	.331	.283
de la Cruz, Chris	B-R	6-0	160	5-3-82	.316	.250	.250	11	38	4	12	2	0	0	14	8	0	0	0	8	1	1	.368	.435
Denham, Jason	L-L	6-0	190	5-1-86	.265	.303	.258	65	211	30	56	8	0	5	31	33	1	2	3	35	17	2	.374	.363
Drennen, John	L-L	5-11	195	8-26-86	.235	.273	.223	117	460	71	108	27	1	3	39	46	7	3	1	73	5	5	.317	.313
Goedert, Jared	R-R	6-2	200	5-25-85	.255	.254	.255	126	467	75	119	23	1	10	74	57	5	3	9	77	1	1	.373	.336
Goleski, Ryan	R-R	6-3	215	3-19-82	.211	.250	.182	6	19	3	4	1	0	1	1	4	1	0	0	2	0	0	.421	.375
Head, Jerad	R-R	6-1	205	11-15-82	.238	.282	.225	92	307	53	73	17	4	11	46	25	12	2	2	58	14	6	.427	.318
Infante, Jansy	B-R	6-1	170	2-27-86	.294	.286	.300	7	17	1	5	1	1	0	1	2	0	0	0	3	1	0	.471	.368
Juhl, Brian	R-R	6-0	205	9-22-85	.240	.233	.242	41	121	18	29	5	1	3	21	19	5	3	0	36	0	0	.372	.366
Martin, Todd	L-L	6-3	230	6-25-83	.209	.286	.174	21	67	6	14	4	0	0	6	11	0	1	0	12	0	0	.269	.321
Martinez, Richard	R-R	6-0	186	6-19-87	.182	.333	.125	4	11	0	2	0	0	0	0	3	0	0	0	2	0	0	.182	.357
McBride, Matt	R-R	6-2	215	3-23-85	.179	.333	.125	17	67	9	12	2	0	0	5	7	1	0	1	9	0	0	.299	.263
Mills, Beau	L-R	6-2	220	8-15-86	.293	.321	.281	125	482	78	141	34	3	21	90	54	10	3		105	2	3	.506	.373
Montero, Lucas	B-R	5-11	180	10-18-84	.246	.293	.226	32	134	26	33	3	1	1	13	17	0	5	0	20	13	2	.306	.331
Pena, Roman	L-L	6-0	190	9-2-86	.148	.000	.151	16	54	10	8	3	0	2	6	8	1	0	1	18	0	1	.315	.266
Rivero, Carlos	R-R	6-3	210	5-20-88	.282	.275	.285	108	411	46	116	27	1	8	64	36	3	2	3	84	1	2	.411	.342
Romero, Niuman	B-R	6-1	200	1-24-85	.296	.250	.310	108	395	64	117	22	1	6	53	34	2	4	5	55	10	4	.403	.351
Santana, Carlos	B-R	5-11	188	4-8-86	.352	.406	.329	29	105	34	37	5	1	6	19	20	0	0	1	24	3	0	.590	.452
Weglarz, Nick	L-L	6-3	245	12-16-87	.272	.296	.262	106	375	66	102	15	0	14	51	40	4	0	9	71	5	1	.456	.396

Pitching	B-T	HT	WT	DOB	W	L	ERA	G	GS	CG	SV	IP	H	R	ER	HR	BB	SO	AVG	vLH	vRH	K/9	BB/9
Cevette, Dan	L-L	6-3	195	10-19-83	3	1	7.11	17	0	0	0	19	27	19	15	5	10	31	.338	.435	.298	14.68	4.74
De La Cruz, Kelvin	L-L	6-5	187	1-8-88	3	2	6.44	8	8	0	0	29	35	22	21	1	25	36	.292	.263	.297	11.05	7.67
Deters, James	R-R	6-4	180	6-4-83	4	2	3.12	20	3	1	1	49	44	20	17	4	9	30	.244	.161	.288	5.51	1.65
Donnelly, Brendan	R-R	6-3	250	7-4-71	0	0	0.00	2	0	0	0	2	1	0	0	0	0	2	.143	.000	.200	9.00	0.00

Name	B-T	HT	WT	DOB	W	L	ERA	G	GS	CG	SV	IP	H	R	ER	HR	BB	SO	AVG	vLH	vRH	K/9	BB/9
Espino, Paolo	R-R	5-10	190	1-10-87	0	2	8.49	7	6	0	0	30	39	31	28	5	11	20	.312	.364	.271	6.07	3.34
Finocchi, Mike	R-R	6-0	190	4-28-85	1	1	6.52	22	0	0	0	29	36	21	21	9	19	15	.305	.257	.325	4.66	5.90
Gomez, Jeanmar	R-R	6-4	190	2-10-88	5	9	4.55	27	27	0	0	138	154	76	70	14	46	110	.283	.285	.282	7.16	2.99
Harris, Jeff	R-R	6-1	190	7-4-74	1	0	2.70	1	0	0	0	3	4	1	1	1	2	2	.308	—	.308	5.40	5.40
Herrmann, Frank	L-R	6-4	220	5-30-84	0	0	11.81	1	1	0	0	5	8	7	7	1	1	4	.333	.200	.368	6.75	1.69
Judy, Josh	R-R	6-4	200	2-9-86	0	0	1.93	7	0	0	0	14	12	3	3	0	1	17	.226	.176	.250	10.93	0.64
Landis, Kyle	R-R	6-1	185	5-30-86	0	2	10.64	7	0	0	0	11	16	13	13	2	6	9	.333	.417	.306	7.36	4.91
Meyer, Matt	L-L	6-4	220	1-17-85	4	2	4.23	42	0	0	1	55	48	27	26	2	29	61	.245	.283	.231	9.92	4.72
Montero, Joanniel	R-R	6-5	200	2-2-86	0	0	5.40	3	0	0	1	5	6	3	3	2	1	2	.300	.286	.308	3.60	1.80
Nottingham, Shawn	L-L	6-1	190	1-22-85	3	4	4.58	14	14	0	0	71	76	43	36	4	26	70	.273	.195	.287	8.92	3.31
Perdomo, Luis	R-R	6-0	170	4-27-84	3	1	0.92	31	0	0	18	39	19	6	4	0	17	43	.146	.208	.104	9.92	3.92
Pestano, Vinnie	R-R	6-0	205	2-20-85	1	2	4.00	25	0	0	9	27	23	13	12	1	11	27	.219	.182	.236	9.00	3.67
Pontius, Mike	R-R	6-2	235	10-26-87	4	1	6.26	25	0	0	0	42	42	34	29	4	39	42	.261	.246	.271	9.07	8.42
Rodrigues, Mark	R-R	6-2	165	4-6-83	0	0	0.00	2	0	0	0	2	2	0	0	0	0	0	.222	.000	.222	0.00	0.00
Rondon, Hector	R-R	6-3	180	2-26-88	11	6	3.60	27	27	0	0	145	130	63	58	12	42	145	.239	.238	.239	9.00	2.61
Sipp, Tony	L-L	6-0	190	7-12-83	0	0	1.13	5	0	0	0	8	4	2	1	0	3	10	.148	.154	.143	11.25	3.38
Smith, Carlton	L-R	6-2	205	1-23-86	12	6	4.37	26	26	0	0	146	143	91	71	12	33	81	.249	.292	.221	4.98	2.03
Stiller, Erik	R-R	6-5	210	7-10-84	1	0	2.79	9	0	0	0	19	15	13	6	1	9	27	.205	.231	.191	12.57	4.19
Taylor, Heath	L-L	6-0	215	5-26-86	2	2	4.79	10	0	0	0	21	16	13	11	2	17	21	.225	.273	.204	9.15	7.40
Tomlin, Josh	R-R	6-1	195	10-19-84	9	5	2.98	40	9	1	3	103	82	40	34	10	16	109	.222	.225	.220	9.56	1.40
Tseng, Sung-Wei	R-R	5-10	195	12-28-84	0	8	5.27	30	3	0	1	55	60	40	32	9	27	44	.282	.303	.270	7.24	4.45
Wagner, Neil	R-R	6-0	195	1-1-84	3	6	4.50	41	0	0	3	62	67	34	31	1	21	81	.275	.303	.258	11.76	3.05
Wright, Steven	R-R	6-2	210	9-30-84	2	4	2.99	14	14	1	0	72	59	30	24	6	17	61	.225	.178	.250	7.59	2.12

Fielding

Catcher	PCT	G	PO	A	E	DP	PB
Camacaro	1.000	2	16	1	0	0	0
Castillo	.987	69	566	49	8	5	17
Davis	1.000	4	31	10	0	1	4
Juhl	.993	40	265	25	2	2	7
Martinez	.971	3	32	2	1	0	0
McBride	1.000	1	14	0	0	0	0
Santana	.986	25	189	26	3	2	4

First Base	PCT	G	PO	A	E	DP
Head	.979	18	124	14	3	10
Martin	.980	13	96	3	2	3
Mills	.992	99	861	47	7	66
Romero	.992	13	115	5	1	8

Second Base	PCT	G	PO	A	E	DP
Arnal	.986	35	51	85	2	15
Davis	.992	24	53	79	1	16
de la Cruz	.935	7	15	14	2	2
Goedert	1.000	23	43	65	0	11
Head	.850	5	4	13	3	2
Romero	.990	52	90	112	2	19

Third Base	PCT	G	PO	A	E	DP
Goedert	.930	95	54	198	19	16
Head	.847	24	16	34	9	2
Infante	1.000	5	1	8	0	0
Mills	.900	8	6	12	2	0
Romero	.962	11	7	18	1	1

Shortstop	PCT	G	PO	A	E	DP
Arnal	1.000	1	0	1	0	0
de la Cruz	1.000	2	3	5	0	0
Rivero	.948	104	141	294	24	59
Romero	.963	35	41	90	5	9

Outfield	PCT	G	PO	A	E	DP
Cumberbatch	.975	92	146	7	4	2
Davis	1.000	4	7	0	0	0
Denham	.977	58	122	6	3	4
Drennen	.972	104	166	8	5	3
Goleski	1.000	6	10	0	0	0
Head	.926	31	49	1	4	1
Martin	1.000	3	4	2	0	0
Montero	.970	32	62	3	2	0
Pena	1.000	16	36	0	0	0
Weglarz	.950	77	113	2	6	1

LAKE COUNTY CAPTAINS   LOW CLASS A

SOUTH ATLANTIC LEAGUE

Batting	B-T	HT	WT	DOB	AVG	vLH	vRH	G	AB	R	H	2B	3B	HR	RBI	BB	HBP	SH	SF	SO	SB	CS	SLG	OBP
Arnal, Cristo	R-R	6-0	180	9-17-85	.294	.375	.269	10	34	5	10	0	1	1	2	3	0	0	0	4	0	0	.441	.351
Brown, Matt	L-R	6-1	183	2-21-85	.308	.287	.314	122	451	64	139	26	3	8	75	35	2	1	6	62	3	4	.432	.356
Davis, Adam	B-R	5-9	190	10-15-84	.196	.226	.184	57	194	26	38	9	1	3	17	31	0	1	0	41	7	4	.299	.307
Hehr, Jeff	R-R	6-0	180	7-27-85	.240	.256	.236	106	366	50	88	25	1	3	41	23	5	2	5	73	4	2	.339	.291
Hernandez, Ramon	R-R	6-1	170	8-25-86	.429	—	.429	4	7	0	3	0	0	0	1	0	0	1	0	0	0	1	.429	.429
Infante, Jansy	B-R	6-1	170	2-27-86	.125	.200	.109	19	56	2	7	2	0	0	3	2	0	2	0	4	0	1	.161	.155
Martin, Todd	L-L	6-3	230	6-25-83	.333	.600	.290	10	36	4	12	3	0	3	9	1	0	0	1	13	0	0	.667	.342
Martinez, Richard	R-R	6-0	186	6-19-87	.304	.256	.323	44	135	18	41	5	0	5	13	25	0	0	0	29	1	1	.452	.413
McBride, Matt	R-R	6-2	215	5-23-85	.308	.364	.286	11	39	6	12	4	0	1	7	5	0	0	0	5	0	0	.487	.386
Montero, Lucas	B-R	5-11	180	10-18-84	.264	.328	.247	83	273	53	72	10	2	8	36	41	5	7	0	56	47	11	.403	.370
Nash, Chris	R-R	6-4	230	2-22-87	.230	.200	.238	74	270	26	62	15	1	5	38	22	4	1	4	82	2	1	.348	.293
Pena, Roman	L-L	6-0	190	9-2-86	.275	.247	.282	113	426	70	117	26	2	11	66	33	3	1	4	104	14	6	.423	.328
Pickens, Doug	R-R	6-0	190	6-19-85	.235	.206	.243	47	149	14	35	6	0	1	18	28	1	0	2	19	1	1	.295	.356
Realini, Dustin	R-R	6-2	200	5-14-84	.289	.297	.287	70	235	32	68	14	0	4	41	43	12	0	3	58	3	3	.400	.420
Rivas, Ronald	R-R	6-2	184	1-16-88	.291	.213	.313	81	275	26	80	11	5	0	27	17	3	5	2	63	4	2	.367	.337
Sanchez, Karexon	B-R	5-11	175	8-22-87	.246	.240	.248	116	414	71	102	22	5	12	60	38	11	5	5	118	12	8	.411	.323
Thompson, Mark	R-R	5-9	165	11-26-84	.236	.200	.245	121	416	63	98	20	3	5	46	37	17	10	4	77	19	4	.334	.321
Valadez, Michael	R-R	6-1	220	5-31-86	.242	.115	.274	40	132	18	32	5	1	1	14	8	5	0	1	26	1	1	.318	.308
Valdes, Juan	B-R	6-0	150	6-22-85	.241	.167	.278	16	54	8	13	1	1	2	15	3	1	2	2	11	0	1	.407	.283
White, Matt	B-R	5-10	190	4-21-85	.215	.264	.203	129	455	78	98	14	4	4	40	62	4	5	11	116	32	11	.290	.312
Willard, Matt	R-R	5-11	177	12-31-85	.184	.273	.160	39	103	13	19	1	1	1	8	6	2	1	1	30	1	1	.243	.241

Pitching	B-T	HT	WT	DOB	W	L	ERA	G	GS	CG	SV	IP	H	R	ER	HR	BB	SO	AVG	vLH	vRH	K/9	BB/9
Archer, Chris	R-R	6-2	165	9-26-88	4	8	4.29	27	27	0	0	115	92	64	55	8	84	106	.220	.225	.215	8.27	6.55
Berger, Eric	L-L	6-2	205	4-22-86	0	0	2.08	2	1	0	0	4	3	1	1	0	2	4	.176	.333	.091	8.31	4.15
Borowski, Joe	R-R	6-2	215	5-4-71	0	0	0.00	1	1	0	0	1	0	0	0	0	0	0	.000	.000	.000	0.00	0.00
Bryson, Rob	R-R	6-1	200	12-11-87	0	1	2.19	7	0	0	0	12	6	6	3	1	6	11	.140	.267	.071	8.03	4.38
2-team total (22 West Virginia)					3	3	3.88	29	5	0	5	67	49	37	29	4	26	84	—	—	—	11.23	3.48
Campfield, Gary	R-R	6-1	200	5-29-84	7	4	2.98	44	0	0	0	66	48	31	22	6	35	58	.198	.267	.159	7.87	4.75

	B-T	HT	WT	DOB	W	L	ERA	G	GS	CG	SV	IP	H	R	ER	HR	BB	SO	AVG	vLH	vRH	K/9	BB/9
Carmona, Fausto	R-R	6-4	230	12-7-83	0	0	0.00	1	1	0	0	4	1	0	0	0	0	3	.077	.000	.200	6.75	0.00
Cawiezell, Dallas	R-R	6-6	255	9-4-85	3	8	3.60	40	0	0	2	55	52	23	22	6	16	54	.246	.205	.273	8.84	2.62
De La Cruz, Kelvin	L-L	6-5	187	1-8-88	8	4	1.69	18	18	1	0	96	71	23	18	2	34	96	.207	.198	.210	9.03	3.20
Espino, Paolo	R-R	5-10	190	1-10-87	2	0	3.16	19	0	0	1	37	35	13	13	4	12	48	.252	.241	.259	11.68	2.92
Frias, Santo	R-R	6-3	189	12-8-87	1	1	6.94	5	5	0	0	23	26	22	18	8	12	20	.277	.289	.265	7.71	4.63
Gaub, John	R-L	6-2	200	4-28-85	1	1	3.38	34	0	0	2	64	44	30	24	3	32	100	.195	.181	.201	14.06	4.50
Holt, Jonathan	L-R	6-2	210	3-10-86	4	6	3.20	41	6	0	1	76	80	33	27	7	7	68	.263	.220	.290	8.05	0.83
Judy, Josh	R-R	6-4	200	2-9-86	12	1	3.51	35	0	0	1	74	60	38	29	6	25	80	.223	.284	.181	9.69	3.03
Landis, Kyle	R-R	6-1	185	5-30-86	2	1	1.97	38	1	0	6	59	47	14	13	5	20	73	.218	.217	.218	11.07	3.03
Mahalic, Joey	R-R	6-3	205	11-28-88	7	6	4.19	20	18	0	0	101	103	56	47	9	31	73	.265	.316	.233	6.50	2.76
Martinez, Anillins	L-L	6-2	176	4-6-87	0	0	27.00	2	0	0	0	2	8	7	7	0	6	2	.533	.500	.545	7.71	23.14
Miller, Ryan	L-L	6-0	195	12-14-86	8	7	3.72	26	24	0	0	126	123	61	52	13	74	113	.258	.219	.273	8.09	5.30
Montero, Joanniel	R-R	6-5	200	2-2-86	4	7	5.05	24	10	0	0	71	80	41	40	12	12	54	.284	.291	.279	6.81	1.51
Morris, Ryan	L-L	6-3	175	1-10-88	9	7	3.76	27	27	0	0	134	116	63	56	6	57	101	.238	.231	.240	6.78	3.83
Pestano, Vinnie	R-R	6-0	205	2-20-85	1	1	1.55	29	0	0	1	29	20	5	5	1	13	23	.231	.275	.206	7.14	4.03
Pontius, Mike	R-R	6-2	235	10-26-87	1	1	0.82	16	0	0	2	33	16	4	3	0	15	39	.144	.151	.138	10.64	4.09
Rieck, Garrett	L-L	6-2	175	9-4-85	1	1	4.61	10	0	0	0	14	14	7	7	2	5	13	.259	.250	.263	8.56	3.29
Westbrook, Jake	R-R	6-3	215	9-29-77	0	0	2.45	1	1	0	0	4	3	1	1	0	1	4	.231	.000	.429	9.82	2.45

Fielding

Catcher	PCT	G	PO	A	E	DP	PB
Davis	.998	49	367	44	1	8	16
Martinez	.987	13	87	16	1	0	1
McBride	1.000	2	21	1	0	0	1
Pickens	.989	45	342	33	4	2	6
Valadez	.994	39	313	39	2	6	4

First Base	PCT	G	PO	A	E	DP
Arnal	1.000	2	15	2	0	2
Hehr	.988	20	155	10	2	15
Martin	1.000	5	27	1	0	3
Martinez	1.000	21	161	11	0	14
Nash	.996	53	473	16	2	41
Realini	.997	46	362	33	1	32

Second Base	PCT	G	PO	A	E	DP
Arnal	.969	6	9	22	1	5
Hehr	.973	7	15	21	1	5
Infante	.727	3	2	6	3	2
Sanchez	.954	68	139	171	15	37
Thompson	.977	40	70	100	4	17
Willard	.898	19	28	51	9	12

Third Base	PCT	G	PO	A	E	DP
Arnal	.500	2	2	0	2	0
Hehr	.918	61	38	118	14	12
Infante	.909	14	4	26	3	3
Rivas	.917	24	14	41	5	2
Sanchez	.901	42	31	60	10	5
Willard	.500	1	0	1	1	0

Shortstop	PCT	G	PO	A	E	DP
Infante	—	1	0	0	0	0
Rivas	.959	56	80	153	10	29
Thompson	.955	77	90	228	15	51
Willard	.917	11	12	21	3	2

Outfield	PCT	G	PO	A	E	DP
Brown	.966	111	185	11	7	4
Davis	1.000	4	6	0	0	0
Hernandez	1.000	3	3	0	0	0
Martin	—	1	0	0	0	0
Montero	.966	56	80	4	3	1
Pena	.967	100	165	13	6	3
Realini	1.000	16	22	2	0	1
Valdes	.962	15	22	3	1	0
White	.986	122	200	11	3	3

MAHONING VALLEY SCRAPPERS   SHORT-SEASON

NEW YORK-PENN LEAGUE

Batting	B-T	HT	WT	DOB	AVG	vLH	vRH	G	AB	R	H	2B	3B	HR	RBI	BB	HBP	SH	SF	SO	SB	CS	SLG	OBP
Alcombrack, Robert	R-R	6-0	205	6-10-88	.248	.229	.256	49	165	19	41	11	0	1	13	16	2	1	0	52	0	0	.333	.322
Armstrong, Corteze	L-L	5-11	180	6-9-84	.122	.059	.132	43	123	13	15	1	2	0	10	22	3	2	1	40	3	0	.163	.268
Blair, Ryan	L-R	6-2	185	4-6-86	.235	.208	.242	66	247	34	58	8	1	2	22	25	3	3	2	62	5	1	.300	.310
Booker, Zach	R-R	6-0	220	4-24-85	.227	.259	.214	31	97	12	22	6	1	1	18	10	3	0	2	24	0	0	.340	.313
Chisenhall, Lonnie	L-L	6-1	200	10-4-88	.290	.258	.299	68	276	38	80	20	3	5	45	24	4	1	0	32	7	2	.438	.355
Diaz, Walter	R-R	6-0	180	11-13-85	.237	.208	.247	32	97	15	23	4	0	0	12	18	1	2	1	19	0	0	.278	.359
Fedroff, Tim	L-R	5-11	220	2-4-87	.319	.360	.303	23	91	12	29	6	1	0	12	10	0	0	1	20	1	1	.407	.382
Hernandez, Ramon	R-R	6-1	170	8-25-86	.223	.205	.232	39	121	19	27	4	1	2	15	12	3	0	2	29	3	0	.322	.304
Infante, Jansy	B-R	6-1	170	2-27-86	.400	.333	.429	3	10	0	4	0	0	0	2	0	0	0	0	1	0	0	.400	.400
Phelps, Cord	B-R	6-2	200	1-23-87	.312	.324	.308	35	141	24	44	10	2	2	21	15	0	0	1	22	4	3	.454	.376
Pickens, Doug	R-R	6-0	190	6-19-85	.226	.375	.191	24	84	13	19	4	0	1	7	9	4	0	0	18	2	0	.310	.330
Realini, Dustin	R-R	6-2	200	5-14-84	.231	.000	.250	4	13	2	3	0	0	0	1	2	1	0	1	5	0	0	.231	.353
Rodriguez, Jason	L-R	6-0	195	12-6-85	.217	.000	.278	6	23	1	5	0	0	0	2	1	0	0	0	2	0	0	.217	.250
Simpson, Brock	L-R	6-3	210	11-15-85	.294	.220	.315	60	218	32	64	11	2	2	24	28	1	0	2	24	0	3	.390	.373
Tice, Jeremie	L-R	6-1	225	9-25-86	.274	.203	.304	63	237	36	65	11	4	5	36	28	1	0	3	64	2	2	.418	.349
Valadez, Michael	R-R	6-1	220	5-31-86	.271	.417	.234	18	59	9	16	2	0	0	3	2	1	1	1	11	0	0	.305	.302
Valdes, Juan	B-R	6-0	150	6-22-85	.256	.242	.261	39	125	17	32	8	1	2	25	27	0	2	1	25	3	3	.384	.386
Velasquez, Isaias	R-R	5-11	155	5-7-88	.281	.177	.285	64	242	40	68	10	1	1	18	31	3	5	1	42	7	4	.343	.368
Webb, Donnie	B-R	5-11	190	4-30-86	.218	.195	.231	51	174	24	38	3	1	3	17	21	2	2	3	42	6	3	.276	.305

Pitching	B-T	HT	WT	DOB	W	L	ERA	G	GS	CG	SV	IP	H	R	ER	HR	BB	SO	AVG	vLH	vRH	K/9	BB/9
Arias, Carlos	R-R	6-2	178	7-4-85	1	2	3.41	22	0	0	0	29	30	13	11	3	14	38	.268	.281	.263	11.79	4.34
Berger, Eric	L-L	6-2	205	4-22-86	2	0	2.12	8	8	0	0	34	26	11	8	2	9	41	.203	.265	.181	10.85	2.38
Burns, Eddie	R-R	6-8	225	9-11-85	0	0	2.70	3	2	0	0	10	6	4	3	1	4	12	.176	.333	.091	10.80	3.60
Creps, Austin	R-R	6-2	175	2-23-85	2	3	4.88	16	0	0	0	28	32	22	15	2	16	16	.288	.243	.311	5.20	5.20
Fonseca, Guido	R-R	6-0	260	9-15-85	0	1	7.27	3	3	0	0	9	12	8	7	1	2	7	.324	.400	.296	7.27	2.08
Grening, Brian	R-R	5-11	200	6-10-85	1	0	4.09	19	0	0	2	33	39	19	15	2	14	38	.279	.229	.295	10.36	3.82
Haley III, Trey	R-R	6-3	180	6-21-90	0	1	54.00	2	1	0	0	1	4	8	6	1	6	1	.571	.000	.571	6.75	40.50
Hinkle, Brad	R-R	6-10	220	10-13-84	1	1	3.54	19	6	0	2	48	45	22	19	6	14	56	.238	.242	.236	10.43	2.61
Langwell, Matt	R-R	6-3	220	5-6-86	1	4	7.47	12	7	0	0	31	52	27	26	6	11	20	.369	.395	.357	5.74	3.16
Martinez, Anillins	L-L	6-2	176	4-6-87	0	0	3.43	16	0	0	0	33	14	12	9	1	21	32	.126	.208	.103	8.64	5.67
McGuire, Mike	R-R	6-7	240	6-29-86	3	5	4.05	21	0	0	1	40	36	23	18	0	16	47	.231	.275	.210	10.58	3.60
Mead, Kaimi	L-L	5-11	195	8-19-85	5	8	5.52	15	15	0	0	62	76	48	38	3	24	40	.299	.231	.317	5.81	3.48
Morales, Daniel	R-R	6-3	230	1-28-85	2	0	2.67	21	0	0	5	27	17	9	8	1	9	27	.181	.286	.136	9.00	3.00
Putnam, Zach	R-R	6-2	225	7-3-87	0	1	3.72	3	3	0	0	10	7	5	4	0	5	8	.206	.200	.207	7.45	4.66

Ramirez, Wilfredo	L-L	6-4	210	11-24-87	2	0	3.77	17	0	0	3	29	34	14	12	3	5	23	.288	.219	.314	7.22	1.57
Rieck, Garrett	L-L	6-2	175	9-4-85	1	2	1.26	11	0	0	0	14	11	3	2	0	3	17	.208	.273	.190	10.67	1.88
Roberts, David	L-R	6-3	215	10-29-86	1	1	6.11	21	0	0	0	35	34	25	24	5	12	32	.248	.262	.242	8.15	3.06
Rodrigues, Mark	R-R	6-2	165	4-6-83	0	2	2.66	17	0	0	0	24	25	12	7	0	10	16	.269	.257	.276	6.08	3.80
Taylor, Heath	L-L	6-0	215	5-26-86	0	0	0.00	3	0	0	0	4	1	0	0	0	3	6	.091	.000	.100	14.73	7.36
Turek, Travis	R-R	6-1	170	9-2-87	0	2	10.45	6	0	0	0	10	17	16	12	2	6	7	.340	.500	.265	6.10	5.23
Young, Russell	L-L	6-4	205	11-27-85	6	3	3.38	15	15	0	0	67	65	32	25	4	14	62	.246	.362	.214	8.37	1.89
Zocchi, Peter	R-R	5-11	195	6-19-85	3	5	4.91	15	15	0	0	70	88	39	38	5	17	57	.297	.326	.286	7.36	2.20

Fielding

Catcher	PCT	G	PO	A	E	DP	PB
Alcombrack	.981	32	237	23	5	1	6
Booker	.959	11	69	2	3	0	0
Pickens	.978	24	174	7	4	1	1
Valadez	.978	17	125	6	3	0	2

First Base	PCT	G	PO	A	E	DP
Alcombrack	.982	13	103	5	2	6
Booker	1.000	16	135	5	0	10
Realini	1.000	1	4	0	0	3
Simpson	.980	47	368	17	8	31

Second Base	PCT	G	PO	A	E	DP
Diaz	.900	7	4	14	2	1

	PCT	G	PO	A	E	DP
Phelps	.955	26	50	55	5	14
Rodriguez	.964	5	7	20	1	3
Velasquez	.950	39	93	114	11	26

Third Base	PCT	G	PO	A	E	DP
Alcombrack	1.000	1	0	1	0	0
Diaz	1.000	13	8	11	0	1
Infante	.667	1	1	1	1	0
Realini	1.000	1	0	2	0	0
Rodriguez	.250	1	1	0	3	0
Tice	.852	58	20	89	19	2
Velasquez	.824	5	3	11	3	1

Shortstop	PCT	G	PO	A	E	DP
Chisenhall	.929	58	62	146	16	28
Diaz	.893	11	13	37	6	10
Velasquez	.851	10	14	26	7	5

Outfield	PCT	G	PO	A	E	DP
Armstrong	.978	33	42	3	1	0
Blair	.953	61	120	2	6	0
Fedroff	.940	23	47	0	3	0
Hernandez	.953	32	61	0	3	0
Simpson	1.000	5	5	0	0	0
Valdes	1.000	34	80	1	0	0
Webb	.987	44	74	3	1	0

GCL INDIANS   ROOKIE

GULF COAST LEAGUE

Batting	B-T	HT	WT	DOB	AVG	vLH	vRH	G	AB	R	H	2B	3B	HR	RBI	BB	HBP	SH	SF	SO	SB	CS	SLG	OBP
Abraham, Adam	R-R	6-0	210	3-27-87	.214	.200	.222	40	131	21	28	7	0	5	22	17	3	0	2	29	1	0	.382	.314
Abreu, Abner	R-R	6-3	170	10-24-89	.251	.257	.248	51	199	32	50	16	4	11	37	9	2	0	1	52	4	1	.538	.289
Allman, John	R-R	6-2	220	4-18-85	.315	.280	.333	27	73	14	23	3	0	2	10	12	3	1	1	22	3	0	.438	.427
Aponte, Juan	R-R	6-0	185	3-2-88	.183	.136	.204	24	71	4	13	6	0	0	10	8	1	1	1	17	0	0	.268	.272
Basabe, Lurvin	B-R	5-8	179	9-23-89	.165	.125	.186	35	91	14	15	1	1	1	10	11	2	3	1	22	9	1	.231	.267
Camargo, Jose	R-R	6-0	175	9-6-89	.239	.176	.276	31	92	12	22	5	0	1	9	11	2	1	2	26	1	3	.326	.327
Chen, Chun-Hsiu	R-R	6-1	200	11-1-88	.261	.345	.183	38	115	11	30	4	2	3	15	13	0	0	0	29	1	1	.409	.336
Cid, Delvi	R-R	6-2	170	7-19-89	.299	.286	.306	35	127	17	38	3	0	0	11	17	1	2	1	28	14	3	.323	.384
Diaz, Walter	R-R	6-0	180	11-13-85	.421	.250	.467	5	19	2	8	2	0	0	1	3	0	0	0	7	2	0	.526	.500
Fontanez, Kevin	R-R	5-11	170	6-21-90	.256	.212	.281	26	90	9	23	4	0	1	8	13	1	1	1	16	2	3	.333	.352
Greenwell, Bo	L-L	6-0	185	10-15-88	.263	.219	.292	46	160	18	42	8	3	2	14	23	1	0	0	17	4	4	.388	.359
Martin, Todd	L-L	6-3	230	6-25-83	.400	.400	.400	5	15	1	6	0	0	0	1	0	1	0	0	2	0	0	.400	.438
McBride, Matt	R-R	6-2	215	5-23-85	.380	.636	.308	17	50	13	19	7	1	2	9	6	4	0	0	5	3	0	.680	.483
Montero, Moises	R-R	6-0	210	11-4-89	.042	.000	.077	9	24	2	1	0	0	0	2	3	1	1	0	10	0	1	.042	.179
Nash, Chris	R-R	6-4	230	2-22-87	.250	.000	1.000	2	4	1	1	0	0	0	0	1	1	0	0	1	0	0	.250	.400
Phelps, Cord	B-R	6-2	200	1-23-87	.000	.000	.000	1	3	0	0	0	0	0	0	1	0	0	1	2	0	0	.000	.000
Recknagel, Nate	R-R	6-2	220	4-29-86	.750	1.000	.667	1	4	0	3	1	0	0	0	0	0	0	0	1	0	0	1.000	.750
Rodriguez, Angel	L-L	6-0	176	7-10-87	.259	.286	.245	41	143	20	37	6	0	3	16	17	3	2	1	19	10	1	.364	.348
Rucker, Kevin	R-R	6-1	185	9-14-89	.210	.213	.207	39	105	19	22	4	0	2	9	16	0	1	0	44	5	2	.305	.314
Smit, Jason	R-R	6-0	165	10-27-89	.236	.278	.216	23	55	10	13	3	1	1	8	3	0	0	0	18	2	0	.382	.364
Vera, Rafael	R-R	6-1	180	11-21-87	.257	.279	.241	38	148	19	38	6	0	3	19	14	2	0	2	32	9	1	.358	.325
Willard, Matt	R-R	5-11	177	12-31-85	.155	.188	.128	22	71	8	11	2	2	1	7	7	0	2	0	24	1	3	.282	.231

Pitching	B-T	HT	WT	DOB	W	L	ERA	G	GS	CG	SV	IP	H	R	ER	HR	BB	SO	AVG	vLH	vRH	K/9	BB/9
Cook, Clayton	R-R	6-3	175	7-23-90	1	2	2.52	11	6	0	0	25	20	11	7	2	8	26	.217	.190	.225	9.36	2.88
Diaz, Juan	R-R	6-2	170	3-13-87	0	1	3.77	11	0	0	0	14	15	9	6	2	6	14	.268	.350	.222	8.79	3.77
Donnelly, Brendan	R-R	6-3	250	7-4-71	0	1	13.50	3	2	0	0	3	7	4	4	0	0	1	.500	.571	.429	3.38	0.00
Fonseca, Guido	R-R	6-0	260	9-15-85	1	0	3.00	8	0	0	1	12	10	9	4	1	4	11	.208	.143	.235	8.25	3.00
Haley III, Trey	R-R	6-3	180	6-21-90	0	0	0.00	1	1	0	0	1	0	0	0	0	1	0	.000	.000	.000	9.00	9.00
Jesus, Candido	L-L	6-1	170	10-5-85	1	2	10.29	12	0	0	0	14	20	20	16	2	14	23	.317	.417	.294	14.79	9.00
Jimenez, Jose	R-R	6-3	190	11-5-85	3	1	4.30	15	0	0	5	15	11	9	7	1	5	15	.208	.105	.265	9.20	3.07
Jones, Chris	R-R	6-2	165	9-19-88	3	4	3.10	11	10	0	0	52	44	19	18	4	20	36	.233	.135	.264	6.19	3.44
McFarland, T.J.	L-L	6-3	190	6-8-89	3	4	5.07	12	10	0	0	55	70	38	31	3	15	38	.314	.333	.308	6.22	2.45
Mendez, Sandy	R-R	6-3	183	10-9-85	0	1	5.19	12	0	0	2	17	15	11	10	1	3	20	.231	.261	.214	10.38	1.56
Moncrief, Carlos	L-R	6-1	210	11-3-88	0	0	13.50	9	0	0	0	4	9	9	1	0	4	4	.346	.455	.267	6.00	15.00
Montero, Denny	R-R	6-4	200	4-29-88	1	0	2.57	14	0	0	2	21	18	14	6	0	19	18	.231	.321	.180	7.71	8.14
Perez, Alexander	R-R	6-2	156	7-24-89	2	4	4.26	10	9	0	0	51	37	24	24	5	16	49	.204	.280	.176	8.70	2.84
Popham, Marty	R-R	6-6	235	8-4-87	1	1	0.78	14	0	0	1	23	15	7	2	0	5	25	.179	.229	.143	9.78	1.96
Reust, Jacob	R-R	6-1	185	1-25-90	0	0	0.00	1	0	0	0	1	0	0	0	0	0	0	.000	.000	.000	0.00	0.00
Salazar, Danny	R-R	6-0	180	1-11-90	4	2	2.87	11	11	0	0	53	46	19	17	5	13	43	.231	.245	.219	7.26	2.19
Sipp, Tony	L-L	6-0	190	7-12-83	0	0	0.00	3	1	0	0	4	0	0	0	0	1	5	.000	.000	.000	9.00	2.25
Smith, Steve	R-R	6-0	195	10-27-85	1	1	2.59	16	2	0	2	24	16	7	7	1	5	30	.186	.083	.226	11.10	1.85
Solano, Luis	R-R	5-11	160	1-27-87	0	1	5.73	10	0	0	0	11	18	9	7	2	5	9	.383	.500	.343	7.36	4.09
Soto, Franklin	R-R	6-2	170	9-18-89	2	0	5.95	11	1	0	0	20	25	14	13	3	12	21	.256	.300	.241	9.61	5.49
Taylor, Heath	R-R	6-0	215	5-26-86	0	0	0.00	2	0	0	0	2	0	0	0	0	1	4	.000	.000	.000	18.00	4.50
Turek, Travis	R-R	6-1	170	9-2-87	1	1	0.75	13	0	0	1	12	6	4	1	0	1	7	.146	.133	.154	5.25	0.75
Urena, Jose	L-L	6-2	186	3-14-88	3	1	4.02	11	2	0	0	31	41	21	14	3	7	22	.325	.333	.323	6.32	2.01

Fielding

Catcher	PCT	G	PO	A	E	DP	PB
Aponte	.984	19	111	9	2	1	4
Chen	.982	31	199	21	4	0	7
McBride	.976	6	38	2	1	0	0
Montero	.972	9	63	6	2	0	2
Vera	1.000	1	5	0	0	0	0

First Base	PCT	G	PO	A	E	DP
Abraham	.987	37	293	19	4	34
Aponte	1.000	2	18	1	0	1
Chen	1.000	1	2	0	0	1
Martin	1.000	3	10	1	0	2
Nash	1.000	1	4	0	0	1
Vera	.993	17	129	4	1	9

Second Base	PCT	G	PO	A	E	DP
Basabe	.947	30	42	65	6	15
Camargo	.879	6	10	19	4	3
Fontanez	1.000	10	15	24	0	9
Phelps	1.000	1	3	4	0	2
Smit	.833	4	7	3	2	1
Vera	.979	11	23	24	1	6
Willard	—	1	0	0	0	0

Third Base	PCT	G	PO	A	E	DP
Abreu	.856	49	30	77	18	13
Camargo	1.000	2	2	1	0	0
Vera	.850	5	2	15	3	0
Willard	.833	2	0	5	1	0

Shortstop	PCT	G	PO	A	E	DP
Camargo	.885	21	37	55	12	15
Diaz	.920	5	12	11	2	1
Fontanez	.971	16	27	39	2	9
Smit	1.000	1	0	0	0	0
Vera	1.000	1	3	2	0	1
Willard	.949	16	17	39	3	8

Outfield	PCT	G	PO	A	E	DP
Allman	1.000	25	33	0	0	0
Cid	.968	34	59	1	2	1
Greenwell	.968	43	61	0	2	0
Rodriguez	.972	37	66	4	2	1
Rucker	.984	34	60	2	1	1
Smit	1.000	5	5	0	0	0

DSL INDIANS   ROOKIE

DOMINICAN SUMMER LEAGUE

Batting	B-T	HT	WT	DOB	AVG	vLH	vRH	G	AB	R	H	2B	3B	HR	RBI	BB	HBP	SH	SF	SO	SB	CS	SLG	OBP
Aguilar, Jesus	R-R	6-3	241	6-30-90	.209	.268	.196	68	235	23	49	12	0	4	45	23	6	1	9	29	4	3	.311	.286
Avila, Agustin	B-R	5-10	167	6-3-90	.181	.119	.195	67	216	29	39	4	4	0	16	35	6	3	2	66	20	10	.236	.309
Brito, Jesus	R-R	6-1	160	12-25-87	.239	.227	.242	68	230	45	55	5	1	1	19	44	1	6	3	32	20	5	.283	.360
Cabrera, Jose	R-R	6-3	185	2-17-91	.262	.263	.262	30	84	10	22	1	2	0	7	10	4	0	1	25	7	11	.321	.364
Diaz, Kelvin	R-R	5-11	184	1-20-87	.305	.286	.309	56	197	34	60	15	4	5	44	13	11	0	5	34	11	3	.497	.372
Fermin, Joly	R-R	5-11	162	2-18-91	.162	.256	.140	64	210	28	34	7	2	2	19	21	2	2	1	61	11	7	.243	.244
Fernandez, Yileiviu	R-R	6-0	189	1-5-91	.222	.167	.235	24	63	10	14	2	0	0	3	8	3	0	0	24	0	0	.254	.338
Izaguirre, Nelson	R-R	5-11	175	3-31-90	.170	.250	.151	41	106	11	18	3	0	0	5	14	3	0	0	18	4	2	.198	.285
Martinez, Argenis	B-R	5-11	160	4-8-90	.265	.211	.277	58	204	46	54	6	5	0	15	32	5	4	1	40	32	6	.343	.376
Moreno, Henry	R-R	6-0	219	12-17-90	.202	.167	.208	31	84	5	17	3	0	0	5	5	4	1	0	18	0	1	.238	.280
Petit, Rolando	R-R	6-2	205	4-27-90	.217	.184	.225	59	189	23	41	7	2	1	27	33	2	1	4	64	7	2	.291	.333
Quintero, Rafael	R-R	6-1	145	9-3-87	.000	—	.000	1	0	0	0	0	0	0	0	0	0	0	0	0	0	0	.000	.000
Read, Darling	R-R	6-1	190	5-29-88	.281	.277	.282	70	249	41	70	19	4	13	47	23	7	0	4	79	25	9	.546	.353
Vinicio, Roman	R-R	5-11	170	5-23-87	.160	.222	.145	48	144	13	23	3	0	3	17	15	5	2	3	39	3	2	.243	.257

Pitching	B-T	HT	WT	DOB	W	L	ERA	G	GS	CG	SV	IP	H	R	ER	HR	BB	SO	AVG	vLH	vRH	K/9	BB/9
Araujo, Elvis	L-L	6-6	215	7-15-91	4	2	1.89	14	14	0	0	57	46	20	12	0	23	37	.230	.286	.223	5.84	3.63
Campos, Jose	R-R	6-4	207	8-18-90	4	3	3.32	15	13	0	0	62	62	30	23	2	21	28	.267	.183	.304	4.04	3.03
Cespedes, Ramon	R-R	6-2	174	11-1-90	2	3	2.29	17	0	0	0	35	22	14	9	1	11	21	.171	.159	.176	5.35	2.80
Flores, Fernando	R-R	6-3	230	11-11-90	0	3	3.86	9	8	0	0	26	29	14	11	0	13	18	.293	.364	.273	6.31	4.56
Flores, Jose	R-R	6-3	185	6-4-89	2	1	2.79	19	1	0	2	39	29	16	12	0	17	30	.207	.242	.196	6.98	3.96
Guerrero, Harold	L-L	6-3	215	5-21-90	0	7	5.58	17	7	0	0	40	53	42	25	0	24	38	.308	.400	.299	8.48	5.36
Jimenez, Francisco	L-L	5-11	164	10-2-88	4	1	2.84	19	7	0	1	63	62	27	20	1	15	67	.256	.323	.246	9.52	2.13
Montano, Francisco	R-R	6-1	175	6-4-89	2	1	6.35	15	0	0	1	23	25	20	16	3	7	8	.281	.421	.243	3.18	2.78
Munoz, Oswell	R-R	6-5	179	11-22-90	0	1	1.65	9	2	0	0	16	14	4	3	0	1	16	.226	.190	.244	8.82	0.55
Pena, Jose	R-R	6-4	192	6-23-87	0	1	1.69	23	0	0	16	27	19	5	5	0	7	30	.200	.241	.182	10.13	2.36
Pinales, Wady	R-R	6-5	224	12-4-89	0	1	7.04	11	0	0	0	15	15	16	12	3	14	11	.246	.350	.195	6.46	8.22
Quintero, Jesus	R-R	6-2	165	5-16-89	1	2	2.96	18	4	0	1	46	38	21	15	1	22	48	.233	.216	.241	9.46	4.34
Salazar, Yobanis	R-R	6-2	199	4-27-89	2	0	1.80	8	0	0	0	10	7	3	2	0	11	7	.194	.444	.111	6.30	9.90
Torres, Alexander	L-L	5-11	170	1-8-90	5	1	5.18	20	0	0	0	24	23	18	14	1	23	28	.250	.250	.250	10.36	8.51
Valera, Francisco	R-R	6-1	170	10-19-89	6	1	3.16	14	14	0	0	68	66	33	24	3	19	50	.255	.256	.254	6.59	2.50
Virgen, Carlos	R-R	6-4	170	2-4-91	1	0	5.40	6	0	0	0	8	5	5	5	0	5	10	.172	.375	.095	10.80	5.40

Fielding

Catcher	PCT	G	PO	A	E	DP	PB
Fernandez	.889	10	40	0	5	0	2
Izaguirre	.968	33	186	24	7	2	5
Moreno	.973	7	33	3	1	0	1
Petit	.975	38	239	33	7	3	13

First Base	PCT	G	PO	A	E	DP
Aguilar	.987	56	474	42	7	43
Brito	1.000	1	4	0	0	2
Cabrera	1.000	1	2	0	0	1
Diaz	.933	5	39	3	3	4
Fernandez	.938	2	15	0	1	1
Izaguirre	1.000	2	12	1	0	1
Moreno	1.000	7	39	3	0	2

	PCT	G	PO	A	E	DP
Petit	.977	5	41	2	1	6
Vinicio	.923	2	12	0	1	3

Second Base	PCT	G	PO	A	E	DP
Avila	.933	23	43	55	7	11
Brito	.875	2	2	5	1	1
Fermin	.800	2	4	4	2	1
Izaguirre	1.000	1	1	0	0	0
Martinez	.984	47	111	140	4	32

Third Base	PCT	G	PO	A	E	DP
Brito	.500	1	1	0	1	0
Diaz	.922	39	49	104	13	13
Vinicio	.894	32	30	63	11	6

Shortstop	PCT	G	PO	A	E	DP
Fermin	.902	60	89	178	29	28
Martinez	.929	7	3	23	2	4
Vinicio	.818	4	6	12	4	2

Outfield	PCT	G	PO	A	E	DP
Aguilar	.952	16	18	2	1	1
Avila	.962	37	46	4	2	0
Brito	.983	65	109	9	2	4
Cabrera	.929	25	36	3	3	1
Izaguirre	1.000	1	1	0	0	0
Moreno	—	1	0	0	0	0
Read	.944	70	94	8	6	0
Vinicio	1.000	6	5	0	0	0

Colorado Rockies

BY JACK ETKIN

Faced with lofty expectations for the first time in their history, the reigning National League champion Rockies stumbled early and suffered an embarrassing fall.

They limped along all season, never hopelessly out of the race in the lackluster NL West but never a serious contender. The Rockies last saw .500 on April 20 yet were within five games of first place as late as Sept. 5. However, they finished 10 games out in third place with a 74-88 record.

Clint Hurdle let just one coach go after his first five seasons as Rockies manager. But bench coach Jamie Quirk, hitting coach Alan Cockrell and third-base coach Mike Gallego were fired after the 2008 debacle, and bullpen coach Rick Mathews was reassigned.

The Rockies never won more than five straight games, a reflection of their inconsistent starters. They paid a heavy price for shunning any major rotation acquisitions in the offseason, believing instead young pitchers who contributed in 2007 would continue to progress.

"We were a little less aggressive," general manager Dan O'Dowd said. "We tried to find someone who was more of a swing guy than a true starter. We felt after the way Franklin (Morales) pitched in the final two months, and with what we saw with Jason Hirsh, that we didn't want to take away any chance they had to flourish."

A strained rotator cuff kept Hirsh from pitching for the Rockies until September. Morales went 1-2, 6.39 in five starts, allowing 28 hits and 17 walks in 25 innings before being sent to Triple-A Colorado Springs in late April. Rather than being recalled in September, Morales was sent to the instructional league to work on delivery issues.

Colorado's starters went 54-61 and ranked 12th in the NL in innings (910) and 15th in ERA (5.14). Aaron Cook had a breakout season, going 16-9, 3.96. Ubaldo Jimenez was 2-8, 4.71 at the end of June but finished 12-12, 3.99. But Jeff Francis, a 17-game winner in 2007 tailed off to 4-10, 5.01. He was troubled by shoulder inflammation that ended his season Sept. 12.

Offensively, the Rockies spun their wheels. Their run production tumbled from 860 in 2007 to 747, which ranked eighth in the league. The team batting average fell from .280 to .263. Their .256 average with runners in scoring position was

MAJOR LEAGUE: MATT HOLLIDAY, LF

Holliday hit .321/.409/.538 with 25 home runs, 38 doubles and 88 RBIs. His home runs tied Brad Hawpe for the team lead, and his doubles led the team, while his 88 RBIs finished second among all Rockies. He also stole 28 bases in 30 attempts.

MINOR LEAGUE: JHOULYS CHACIN, RHP

Four years after signing out of Venezuela, Chacin led all minor leaguers with 18 victories, to go along with a razor-thin 2.03 ERA. He also posted 160 strikeouts in 178 innings between low Class A Asheville and high Class A Modesto.

RODGER WOOD

ORGANIZATION LEADERS

BATTING		*Minimum 250 at-bats
*AVG	Miller, Matt, Tulsa/Colorado Springs	.341
R	Miller, Matt, Tulsa/Colorado Springs	98
H	Miller, Matt, Tulsa/Colorado Springs	181
TB	Koshansky, Joe, Colorado Springs	274
2B	Holcomb, Darin, Asheville	46
3B	Fowler, Dexter, Tulsa	9
HR	Koshansky, Joe, Colorado Springs	31
RBI	Koshansky, Joe, Colorado Springs	121
BB	Fowler, Dexter, Tulsa	65
BB	Holcomb, Darin, Asheville	65
SO	Rike, Brian, Asheville	161
SB	Cabrera, Everth, Asheville	73
*OBP	Fowler, Dexter, Tulsa	.431
*SLG	Koshansky, Joe, Colorado Springs	.600

PITCHING		†Minimum 75 innings
W	Chacin, Jhoulys, Asheville/Modesto	18
L	Johnson, Alan, Tulsa	14
†ERA	Chacin, Jhoulys, Asheville/Modesto	2.03
G	Daley, Matt, Tulsa/Colorado Springs	63
GS	Chacin, Jhoulys, Asheville/Modesto	28
GS	Johnson, Alan, Tulsa	28
SV	Taylor, Randall, Asheville	32
IP	Weiser, Keith, Modesto/Tulsa	180
BB	Graham, Connor, Asheville	83
SO	Chacin, Jhoulys, Asheville/Modesto	160
SO	Riordan, Cory, Asheville	160
†AVG	Graham, Connor, Asheville	.189

11th in the league.

First baseman Todd Helton was hindered by a bulging disk that whittled his on-base plus slugging percentage to .779, limited him to two pinch-hitting appearances after July 2 and ultimately required surgery in early October.

2008 PERFORMANCE

General Manager: Dan O'Dowd. **Farm Director:** Marc Gustafson. **Scouting Director:** Bill Schmidt.

Class	Team	League	W	L	PCT	Finish*	Manager	Affiliate Since
Majors	Colorado	National	74	88	.457	11th (16)	Clint Hurdle	—
Triple-A	Colorado Springs Sky Sox	Pacific Coast	71	72	.497	8th (16)	Tom Runnells	1993
Double-A	Tulsa Drillers	Texas	58	82	.414	7th (8)	Stu Cole	2003
High A	Modesto Nuts	California	70	69	.504	5th (10)	Jerry Weinstein	2005
Low A	Asheville Tourists	South Atlantic	83	56	.597	2nd (16)	Joe Mikulik	1994
Short-season	Tri-City Dust Devils	Northwest	36	40	.474	5th (8)	Fred Ocasio	2001
Rookie	Casper Ghosts	Pioneer	36	37	.493	5th (8)	Tony Diaz	2001
Overall 2008 Minor League Record			354	356	.499	15th		

* Finish in overall standings (No. of teams in league). ^League champion.

ORGANIZATION STATISTICS

COLORADO ROCKIES

NATIONAL LEAGUE

Batting	B-T	HT	WT	DOB	AVG	vLH	vRH	G	AB	R	H	2B	3B	HR	RBI	BB	HBP	SH	SF	SO	SB	CS	SLG	OBP
Atkins, Garrett	R-R	6-3	215	12-12-79	.286	.357	.265	155	611	86	175	32	3	21	99	40	3	0	10	100	1	1	.452	.328
Baker, Jeff	R-R	6-2	210	6-21-81	.268	.290	.256	104	299	55	80	22	1	12	48	26	1	1	6	85	4	0	.468	.322
Barmes, Clint	R-R	6-0	210	3-6-79	.290	.307	.283	107	393	47	114	25	6	11	44	17	2	4	1	69	13	4	.468	.322
Bellorin, Edwin	R-R	5-9	225	2-21-82	.333	.000	.500	3	3	0	1	0	0	0	0	0	0	0	0	0	0	0	.333	.333
Bernier, Doug	R-R	5-11	175	6-24-80	.000	.000	.000	2	4	0	0	0	0	0	0	0	0	0	0	1	0	0	.000	.000
Fowler, Dexter	B-R	6-4	175	3-22-86	.154	.364	.000	13	26	3	4	0	0	0	0	1	0	0	5	0	1	.154	.185
Hawpe, Brad	L-L	6-3	205	6-22-79	.283	.282	.283	138	488	69	138	24	3	25	85	76	3	0	2	134	2	2	.498	.381
Helton, Todd	L-L	6-2	210	8-20-73	.264	.246	.270	83	299	39	79	16	0	7	29	61	1	0	0	50	0	0	.388	.391
Herrera, Jonathan	B-R	5-9	150	11-3-84	.230	.200	.244	28	61	5	14	1	1	0	3	4	0	1	0	10	1	1	.279	.277
Holliday, Matt	R-R	6-4	235	1-15-80	.321	.293	.329	139	539	107	173	38	2	25	88	74	8	0	2	104	28	2	.538	.409
Iannetta, Chris	R-R	6-0	225	4-8-83	.264	.275	.261	104	333	50	88	22	2	18	65	56	14	2	2	92	0	0	.505	.390
Koshansky, Joe	L-L	6-4	225	5-26-82	.211	.250	.206	18	38	5	8	3	0	3	8	1	1	0	0	17	0	0	.526	.250
Melhuse, Adam	B-R	6-2	210	3-27-72	.100	—	.100	7	10	2	1	1	0	0	1	0	0	0	0	4	0	0	.200	.100
Nix, Jayson	R-R	5-11	185	8-26-82	.125	.000	.179	22	56	2	7	2	0	0	2	7	1	1	0	17	1	0	.161	.234
Podsednik, Scott	L-L	6-2	190	3-18-76	.253	.167	.264	93	162	22	41	8	1	1	15	16	1	1	1	28	12	4	.333	.322
Quintanilla, Omar	L-R	5-9	190	10-24-81	.238	.209	.246	81	210	28	50	17	0	2	15	15	0	8	1	46	0	0	.348	.288
Smith, Seth	L-L	6-3	215	9-30-82	.259	.000	.289	67	108	13	28	7	0	4	15	15	0	0	0	23	1	0	.435	.350
Spilborghs, Ryan	R-R	6-1	190	9-5-79	.313	.326	.306	89	233	38	73	14	2	6	36	38	1	0	3	41	7	4	.468	.407
Stewart, Ian	L-R	6-3	205	4-5-85	.259	.370	.231	81	266	33	69	18	2	10	41	30	7	0	1	94	1	1	.455	.349
Sullivan, Cory	L-L	6-0	180	8-20-79	.217	.250	.211	18	23	3	5	0	1	0	4	1	0	0	0	5	1	0	.304	.250
Taveras, Willy	R-R	6-0	160	12-25-81	.251	.266	.245	133	479	64	120	15	2	1	26	36	5	15	3	79	68	7	.296	.308
Torrealba, Yorvit	R-R	5-11	200	7-19-78	.246	.279	.231	70	236	19	58	17	0	6	31	12	5	5	3	44	0	4	.394	.293
Tulowitzki, Troy	R-R	6-3	205	10-10-84	.263	.330	.242	101	377	48	99	24	2	8	46	38	2	2	2	56	1	5	.401	.332

Pitching	B-T	HT	WT	DOB	W	L	ERA	G	GS	CG	SV	IP	H	R	ER	HR	BB	SO	AVG	vLH	vRH	K/9	BB/9
Arias, Alberto	R-R	5-11	155	10-14-83	0	0	2.63	12	0	0	0	14	12	4	4	1	4	5	.235	.278	.212	3.29	2.63
2-team total (3 Houston)					1	1	4.15	15	2	0	0	22	23	10	10	1	10	13	—	—	—	5.40	4.15
Bowers, Cedrick	B-L	6-2	220	2-10-78	0	0	13.50	5	0	0	0	7	11	10	10	2	5	5	.423	.571	.368	6.75	6.75
Bowie, Micah	L-L	6-4	220	11-10-74	0	1	9.00	10	0	0	0	8	11	8	8	1	3	5	.333	.308	.350	5.63	3.38
Buchholz, Taylor	R-R	6-4	220	10-13-81	6	6	2.17	63	0	0	1	66	45	23	16	5	18	56	.188	.198	.180	7.60	2.44
Capellan, Jose	R-R	6-4	235	1-13-81	0	0	4.50	1	0	0	0	2	3	1	1	0	0	2	.333	.333	.333	9.00	0.00
Cook, Aaron	R-R	6-3	215	2-8-79	16	9	3.96	32	32	2	0	211	236	102	93	13	48	96	.287	.297	.276	4.09	2.04
Corpas, Manny	R-R	6-3	170	12-3-82	3	4	4.52	76	0	0	4	80	93	41	40	7	23	50	.296	.285	.308	5.65	2.60
De La Rosa, Jorge	L-L	6-1	210	4-5-81	10	8	4.92	28	23	0	0	130	128	77	71	13	62	128	.262	.289	.253	8.86	4.29
de los Santos, Valerio	L-L	6-2	210	10-6-72	0	0	5.63	2	2	0	0	8	6	5	5	1	11	10	.207	.444	.100	11.25	12.38
Francis, Jeff	L-L	6-5	205	1-8-81	4	10	5.01	24	24	0	0	144	164	84	80	21	49	94	.286	.248	.295	5.89	3.07
Fuentes, Brian	L-L	6-4	230	8-9-75	1	5	2.73	67	0	0	30	63	47	22	19	3	22	82	.205	.184	.211	11.78	3.16
Grilli, Jason	R-R	6-5	225	11-11-76	3	2	2.93	51	0	0	1	61	55	22	20	1	31	59	.241	.240	.242	8.66	4.55
Herges, Matt	L-R	6-0	200	4-1-70	3	4	5.04	58	0	0	0	64	79	40	36	5	24	46	.304	.280	.326	6.44	3.36
Hernandez, Livan	R-R	6-2	245	2-20-75	3	3	8.03	8	8	0	0	40	58	36	36	7	14	13	.345	.336	.361	2.90	3.12
Hirsh, Jason	R-R	6-8	250	2-20-82	0	0	8.31	4	1	0	0	9	15	10	8	3	4	6	.357	.450	.273	6.23	4.15
Jimenez, Ubaldo	R-R	6-4	200	1-22-84	12	12	3.99	34	34	1	0	199	182	97	88	11	103	172	.245	.248	.241	7.79	4.67
Morales, Franklin	L-L	6-0	170	1-24-86	1	2	6.39	5	5	0	0	25	28	18	18	2	17	9	.286	.200	.295	3.20	6.04
Morillo, Juan	R-R	6-3	190	11-5-83	0	0	0.00	1	0	0	0	1	1	0	0	0	0	0	.250	.500	.000	0.00	0.00
Newman, Josh	L-L	6-1	200	6-11-82	0	0	9.35	8	0	0	0	9	15	9	9	3	6	6	.366	.333	.375	6.23	6.23
Redman, Mark	L-L	6-5	245	1-5-74	2	5	7.54	10	9	0	0	45	61	40	38	7	16	20	.324	.283	.338	3.97	3.18
Register, Steven	R-R	6-1	180	5-16-83	0	0	9.00	10	0	0	0	10	13	10	10	4	6	8	.310	.375	.222	7.20	5.40
Reynolds, Greg	R-R	6-7	225	7-3-85	2	8	8.13	14	13	0	0	62	83	58	56	14	26	22	.322	.344	.299	3.19	3.77
Rusch, Glendon	L-L	6-1	225	11-7-74	4	3	4.78	23	9	0	0	64	72	35	34	8	14	43	.285	.238	.306	6.05	1.97
2-team total (12 San Diego)					5	5	5.16	35	9	0	0	84	94	50	48	10	25	55	—	—	—	5.92	2.69
Speier, Ryan	R-R	6-7	210	7-24-79	2	1	4.06	43	0	0	0	51	52	23	23	3	18	33	.272	.272	.273	5.82	3.18
Vizcaino, Luis	R-R	5-11	210	8-6-74	1	3	5.28	43	0	0	0	46	48	28	27	10	19	49	.267	.372	.170	9.59	3.72
Wells, Kip	R-R	6-3	205	4-21-77	1	2	5.27	15	2	0	0	27	29	19	16	3	19	22	.282	.265	.296	7.24	6.26

Fielding

Catcher	PCT	G	PO	A	E	DP	PB
Bellorin	1.000	2	4	0	0	0	
Iannetta	1.000	100	606	51	0	4	6
Melhuse	1.000	4	17	5	0	0	
Torrealba	.996	67	433	26	2	4	4

First Base	PCT	G	PO	A	E	DP
Atkins	.990	61	551	23	6	55
Baker	1.000	22	143	5	0	14
Helton	.997	81	830	57	3	79
Koshansky	.987	11	71	6	1	8

Second Base	PCT	G	PO	A	E	DP
Atkins	1.000	1	3	5	0	2
Baker	.981	49	71	131	4	31
Barmes	.978	61	91	178	6	35

	PCT	G	PO	A	E	DP	PB
Bernier	1.000	2	5	2	0	0	
Herrera	.976	21	34	48	2	13	
Nix	1.000	20	27	61	0	9	
Quintanilla	.991	40	40	72	1	24	
Stewart	.982	12	16	38	1	5	

Third Base	PCT	G	PO	A	E	DP
Atkins	.964	94	47	197	9	21
Baker	1.000	9	5	17	0	4
Barmes	.917	13	1	10	1	2
Iannetta	1.000	1	1	1	0	0
Stewart	.944	65	40	127	10	15

Shortstop	PCT	G	PO	A	E	DP
Barmes	.983	36	57	113	3	30
Herrera	1.000	2	2	4	0	0

	PCT	G	PO	A	E	DP
Quintanilla	.979	39	42	100	3	20
Tulowitzki	.984	101	190	311	8	70

Outfield	PCT	G	PO	A	E	DP
Baker	.667	3	2	0	1	0
Barmes	1.000	1	2	0	0	0
Fowler	1.000	9	12	1	0	1
Hawpe	.956	133	186	9	9	0
Holliday	.988	139	240	9	3	3
Podsednik	.970	45	63	1	2	0
Smith	.977	28	42	1	1	0
Spilborghs	.981	57	101	0	2	0
Sullivan	1.000	11	4	0	0	0
Taveras	.976	124	282	6	7	2

COLORADO SPRINGS SKY SOX
TRIPLE-A
PACIFIC COAST LEAGUE

Batting	B-T	HT	WT	DOB	AVG	vLH	vRH	G	AB	R	H	2B	3B	HR	RBI	BB	HBP	SH	SF	SO	SB	CS	SLG	OBP
Barker, Sean	R-R	6-3	220	5-26-80	.240	.252	.236	115	362	56	87	26	4	2	48	23	5	3	2	103	12	4	.351	.293
Barmes, Clint	R-R	6-0	210	3-6-79	.278	—	.278	5	18	2	5	0	0	0	3	1	1	0	0	1	0	0	.278	.350
Bellorin, Edwin	R-R	5-9	225	2-21-82	.293	.321	.283	87	335	28	98	27	3	5	65	15	3	2	1	43	1	1	.436	.328
Bernier, Doug	R-R	5-11	175	6-24-80	.255	.244	.259	110	337	58	86	10	4	9	42	64	8	5	4	79	1	2	.389	.383
Castro, Juan	R-R	5-11	190	6-20-72	.300	.222	.317	18	50	8	15	2	0	1	3	4	0	0	0	7	0	0	.400	.352
Colonel, Christian	R-R	6-2	210	12-25-81	.308	.348	.297	117	429	72	132	33	2	12	65	34	2	0	2	65	7	5	.478	.360
Cornejo, Eduardo	L-R	5-10	180	11-19-81	.250	.222	.257	22	44	5	11	1	0	0	5	8	0	1	1	4	0	1	.273	.358
2-team total (3 Sacramento)					.222	—		25	54	5	12	1	0	0	6	8	0	1	1	6	0	2	.241	.317
Cota, Humberto	R-R	5-11	225	2-7-79	.319	.292	.333	37	138	23	44	12	0	4	26	6	0	1	2	23	0	1	.493	.342
Dragicevich, Jeff	R-R	6-2	200	8-1-82	.306	.500	.269	18	62	8	19	4	0	2	7	5	1	1	0	13	1	2	.468	.368
Frey, Chris	L-L	6-1	180	8-11-83	.290	.284	.291	127	421	50	122	25	5	3	42	22	0	5	3	53	12	4	.394	.323
Guarno, Rick	R-R	6-0	185	8-16-82	.237	.105	.269	24	97	14	23	7	2	1	10	0	1	1	2	17	1	1	.381	.240
Hawpe, Brad	L-L	6-3	205	6-22-79	.091	.000	.143	3	11	1	1	0	0	0	1	0	0	0	0	4	0	0	.091	.167
Herrera, Jonathan	B-R	5-9	150	11-3-84	.310	.316	.307	66	226	40	70	7	0	3	31	19	2	2	1	30	15	2	.381	.367
Holliday, Matt	R-R	6-4	235	1-15-80	.600	—	.600	3	10	4	6	1	0	1	3	1	0	0	0	3	0	0	1.000	.636
Koshansky, Joe	L-L	6-4	225	5-26-82	.300	.302	.299	122	457	90	137	36	4	31	121	60	3	0	6	158	1	0	.600	.380
McCoy, Mike	R-R	5-9	171	4-2-81	.343	.323	.349	39	140	32	48	7	2	4	27	15	0	1	6	20	7	1	.507	.391
Melhuse, Adam	B-R	6-2	210	3-27-72	.311	.214	.329	32	90	14	28	7	0	3	16	15	1	0	1	22	0	0	.489	.411
Miller, Matt	R-R	6-2	210	12-26-82	.331	.308	.337	33	124	26	41	14	0	0	20	15	3	0	2	16	2	0	.444	.410
Mohr, Dustan	R-R	6-1	210	6-19-76	.149	.333	.105	19	47	5	7	4	0	2	4	2	0	0	0	11	0	0	.362	.184
Nazario, Radames	R-R	6-0	166	11-14-87	.000	.000	.000	4	3	0	0	0	0	0	0	0	0	0	0	3	0	0	.000	.250
Nix, Jayson	R-R	5-11	185	8-26-82	.303	.294	.305	67	264	63	80	21	2	17	51	27	5	3	4	64	11	5	.591	.373
Perez, Kenny	B-R	6-2	190	9-28-81	.338	.400	.327	51	133	23	45	13	1	1	20	16	0	2	16	2	0		.474	.404
Podsednik, Scott	L-L	6-2	190	3-18-76	.438	.000	.500	4	16	2	7	0	0	0	3	3	0	0	0	3	0	0	.438	.526
Quintanilla, Omar	L-R	5-9	190	10-24-81	.329	.313	.341	20	73	18	24	4	0	1	8	16	1	0	1	11	3	0	.425	.451
Reyes, Leonardo	R-R	6-0	165	8-2-88	.000	—	.000	2	0	0	0	0	0	0	0	0	0	0	0	0	0	0	.000	.000
Smith, Seth	L-L	6-3	215	9-30-82	.323	.284	.337	68	248	55	80	16	2	10	53	46	3	0	6	46	11	0	.524	.426
Spilborghs, Ryan	R-R	6-1	190	9-5-79	.300	.375	.273	11	30	9	9	1	0	1	4	5	0	0	1	6	0	1	.433	.389
Stewart, Ian	L-R	6-2	205	4-5-85	.280	.316	.264	69	257	65	72	15	6	19	57	34	5	0	2	66	7	2	.607	.372
Sullivan, Cory	L-L	6-0	180	8-20-79	.320	.280	.331	94	381	70	122	32	3	7	47	31	3	1	3	63	13	7	.475	.373
Tulowitzki, Troy	R-R	6-3	205	10-10-84	.429	—	.429	2	7	2	3	1	0	0	0	0	0	0	0	1	0	0	.571	.500

Pitching	B-T	HT	WT	DOB	W	L	ERA	G	GS	CG	SV	IP	H	R	ER	HR	BB	SO	AVG	vLH	vRH	K/9	BB/9
Arias, Alberto	R-R	5-11	155	10-14-83	3	4	4.73	30	0	0	0	46	50	25	24	3	16	41	.287	.290	.286	8.08	3.15
2-team total (8 Round Rock)					4	4	3.63	38	0	0	1	69	71	29	28	3	21	56	—	—	—	7.27	2.73
Bowers, Cedrick	B-L	6-2	220	2-10-78	6	1	3.74	35	2	0	1	65	50	28	27	5	43	74	.213	.258	.197	10.25	5.95
Bowie, Micah	L-L	6-4	220	11-10-74	0	1	7.36	9	0	0	0	7	12	8	6	1	4	8	.353	.385	.333	9.82	4.91
2-team total (11 Round Rock)					1	1	6.55	20	0	0	0	22	34	21	16	3	12	23	—	—	—	9.41	4.91
Capellan, Jose	R-R	6-4	235	1-13-81	2	0	3.94	3	3	0	0	16	12	7	7	2	5	11	.203	.167	.241	6.19	2.81
2-team total (6 Omaha)					4	1	4.05	9	8	0	0	53	47	24	24	5	19	31	—	—	—	5.23	3.21
Daley, Matt	R-R	6-2	175	6-23-82	4	5	3.75	60	0	0	1	62	56	27	26	6	33	61	.241	.233	.247	8.81	4.76
de los Santos, Valerio	L-L	6-2	210	10-6-72	4	5	5.63	23	8	0	0	78	89	55	49	13	28	66	.288	.269	.296	7.58	3.22
George, Chris	L-L	6-2	185	9-16-79	0	4	5.13	27	0	0	1	33	39	20	19	1	18	23	.291	.321	.272	6.21	4.86
Hall, Josh	R-R	6-2	190	12-16-80	2	2	3.96	4	4	0	0	25	25	11	11	5	8	15	.263	.279	.250	5.40	2.88
Herges, Matt	L-R	6-0	210	4-1-70	0	0	4.50	2	0	0	0	2	2	1	1	0	1	1	.250	.500	.000	4.50	0.00
Hirsh, Jason	R-R	6-8	250	2-20-82	4	4	5.80	18	17	0	0	99	115	66	64	16	52	51	.293	.318	.271	4.62	4.71
Koronka, John	L-L	6-1	180	7-3-80	5	7	4.79	13	12	0	0	68	87	42	36	6	35	29	.315	.320	.313	3.86	4.66
Morales, Franklin	L-L	6-0	170	1-24-86	10	5	5.47	21	21	0	0	110	108	72	67	14	82	83	.268	.302	.257	6.77	6.69
Morillo, Juan	R-R	6-3	190	11-5-83	1	0	5.28	52	0	0	0	60	53	38	35	3	56	55	.244	.233	.252	8.30	8.45
Newman, Josh	L-L	6-1	200	6-11-82	1	1	2.45	20	0	0	1	22	16	9	6	1	9	18	.200	.167	.214	7.36	3.68
2-team total (7 Omaha)					1	2	3.68	27	2	0	1	44	39	22	18	1	22	40	—	—	—	8.18	4.50
Redman, Mark	L-L	6-5	245	1-5-74	8	5	5.29	18	12	0	0	85	96	53	50	5	22	51	.290	.304	.286	5.40	2.33
Register, Steven	R-R	6-1	180	5-16-83	5	3	3.36	56	0	0	16	59	57	25	22	4	19	52	.253	.260	.248	7.93	2.90
Reynolds, Greg	R-R	6-7	225	7-3-85	1	3	4.26	13	13	0	0	63	84	38	30	4	22	37	.328	.350	.308	5.26	3.13

Player	B-T	HT	WT	DOB	W	L	ERA	G	GS	CG	SV	IP	H	R	ER	HR	BB	SO	AVG	vLH	vRH	K/9	BB/9
Rusch, Glendon	L-L	6-1	225	11-7-74	1	2	4.61	7	7	0	0	41	48	21	21	4	13	24	.304	.222	.328	5.27	2.85
Smith, Sean	R-R	6-4	195	10-13-83	6	7	5.87	18	16	0	0	97	101	70	63	16	49	67	.268	.283	.257	6.24	4.56
Speier, Ryan	R-R	6-7	210	7-24-79	1	0	2.03	11	0	0	5	13	10	3	3	1	4	9	.208	.200	.217	6.07	2.70
Towers, Josh	R-R	6-1	190	2-26-77	6	7	6.27	31	15	0	0	116	156	83	81	12	29	79	.322	.304	.339	6.11	2.24
Valdez, Edward	R-R	6-1	190	2-8-80	1	0	9.95	4	0	0	6	12	7	7	2	1	10		.387	.545	.300	14.21	1.42
Villarreal, Oscar	L-R	6-0	215	11-22-81	0	1	6.23	3	3	0	0	13	17	11	9	1	7	7	.333	.250	.387	4.85	4.85
2-team total (5 Tacoma)					1	1	5.56	8	3	0	1	23	24	18	14	3	11	18	—	—	—	7.15	4.37
Vizcaino, Luis	R-R	5-11	210	8-6-74	0	0	0.00	4	0	0	0	4	1	0	0	0	4	0	.077	.125	.000	9.00	0.00
Wells, Kip	R-R	6-3	205	4-21-77	0	3	8.84	4	4	0	0	18	32	25	18	4	6	15	.386	.452	.346	7.36	2.95
Zambrano, Victor	B-R	6-0	205	8-6-75	0	6	9.45	14	6	0	0	40	62	52	42	7	30	36	.367	.364	.370	8.10	6.75

Fielding

Catcher

Player	PCT	G	PO	A	E	DP	PB
Bellorin	.998	82	527	44	1	8	2
Cota	.995	31	201	18	1	3	1
Guarno	.974	21	143	8	4	2	1
Melhuse	.990	16	91	7	1	2	2
Nazario	—	1	0	0	0	0	
Nix	.981	64	132	179	6	55	
Perez	.933	5	3	11	1	2	
Quintanilla	1.000	6	10	9	0	0	
Stewart	1.000	2	1	0	0	0	
Herrera	.970	31	42	89	4	25	
McCoy	.967	6	8	21	1	3	
Perez	1.000	2	4	4	0	0	
Quintanilla	.951	14	21	37	3	10	
Tulowitzki	1.000	2	3	8	0	2	

First Base

Player	PCT	G	PO	A	E	DP
Bernier	1.000	1	1	0	0	0
Colonel	.987	20	141	10	2	17
Koshansky	.990	119	1041	76	11	135
Melhuse	.978	6	40	4	1	2
Perez	1.000	5	45	2	0	6

Second Base

Player	PCT	G	PO	A	E	DP
Barmes	.857	3	3	3	1	1
Bernier	1.000	13	24	44	0	15
Castro	1.000	4	4	6	0	2
Colonel	1.000	4	9	10	0	1
Cornejo	.833	3	1	4	1	0
Herrera	1.000	29	54	74	0	24
McCoy	.961	26	63	83	6	33

Third Base

Player	PCT	G	PO	A	E	DP
Bernier	1.000	9	4	14	0	0
Colonel	.943	32	26	57	5	10
Cornejo	1.000	10	5	18	0	2
Dragicevich	.946	18	16	37	3	5
McCoy	1.000	2	1	1	0	0
Nix	.833	2	2	3	1	0
Perez	.906	27	16	32	5	2
Stewart	.914	64	33	137	16	18

Shortstop

Player	PCT	G	PO	A	E	DP
Barmes	1.000	1	2	1	0	1
Bernier	.983	84	135	275	7	75
Castro	.912	11	7	24	3	5
Cornejo	.952	5	7	13	1	1

Outfield

Player	PCT	G	PO	A	E	DP
Barker	.989	94	171	7	2	2
Bernier	—	1	0	0	0	0
Colonel	.975	50	75	3	2	0
Frey	.978	115	214	5	5	2
Hawpe	1.000	3	4	0	0	0
Holliday	1.000	3	2	0	0	0
McCoy	1.000	2	2	0	0	0
Miller	.957	32	41	4	2	1
Mohr	.800	3	4	0	1	0
Podsednik	1.000	3	4	0	0	0
Smith	.975	65	112	7	3	1
Spilborghs	1.000	8	15	1	0	0
Sullivan	.979	91	177	7	4	1

TULSA DRILLERS   DOUBLE-A
TEXAS LEAGUE

Batting	B-T	HT	WT	DOB	AVG	vLH	vRH	G	AB	R	H	2B	3B	HR	RBI	BB	HBP	SH	SF	SO	SB	CS	SLG	OBP
Blanco, Tony	R-R	6-2	200	11-10-81	.323	.394	.307	103	390	59	126	34	0	23	88	31	13	0	7	74	6	2	.587	.385
Carte, Daniel	R-R	6-0	190	5-18-84	.273	.273	.272	112	422	53	115	16	0	10	59	22	7	4	4	113	4	8	.382	.316
Cates, Gary	R-R	5-7	155	7-3-81	.333	.250	.366	16	57	6	19	4	0	0	4	0	1	1	0	2	0	0	.404	.345
Collaro, Tom	R-R	6-4	216	4-4-83	.159	.231	.140	19	63	5	10	3	0	0	2	4	0	0	0	27	1	0	.206	.209
Cornejo, Eduardo	L-R	5-10	180	11-19-81	.286	.267	.290	60	175	19	50	6	0	1	19	30	1	1	0	31	2	3	.337	.393
Dragicevich, Jeff	R-R	6-2	200	8-1-82	.272	.217	.288	95	272	33	74	9	2	9	42	52	3	5	4	78	1	3	.419	.390
Esposito, Brian	R-R	6-1	205	2-24-79	.206	.140	.223	68	247	27	51	2	1	5	26	8	4	5	2	46	4	1	.283	.241
Fowler, Dexter	B-R	6-4	175	3-22-86	.335	.405	.318	108	421	92	141	31	9	9	64	65	8	3		89	20	8	.515	.431
Guarno, Rick	R-R	6-0	185	8-16-82	.290	.292	.289	27	100	15	29	3	0	5	15	3	6	1	2	21	0	1	.470	.342
Kindel, Jeff	L-L	6-3	205	9-1-83	.289	.310	.284	133	506	60	146	25	1	11	73	53	5	2	4	94	4	2	.407	.359
Miller, Matt	R-R	6-2	210	12-26-82	.344	.342	.344	106	407	72	140	21	0	10	87	44	4	0	6	45	4	2	.469	.408
Nelson, Chris	R-R	5-11	175	9-3-85	.237	.140	.258	73	283	38	67	18	2	3	42	35	4	2	5	69	6	1	.346	.324
Nelson, Justin	L-L	6-3	205	4-23-83	.247	.172	.263	114	364	61	90	19	4	20	54	49	7	0	0	117	1	5	.486	.348
Parrish, David	R-R	6-3	220	6-13-79	.212	.429	.154	9	33	4	7	1	0	1	2	1	0	1	0	4	0	0	.333	.235
2-team total (12 San Antonio)					.172	—	—	21	58	6	10	2	0	2	3	12	1	1	0	9	0	0	.310	.324
Sardinha, Duke	R-R	6-0	200	12-9-80	.176	.235	.158	28	74	4	13	3	0	1	4	2	2	0	0	22	0	0	.257	.218
Tulowitzki, Troy	R-R	6-3	205	10-10-84	.333	.250	.353	5	21	5	7	0	0	2	3	3	0	0	0	1	0	0	.619	.417
Wilson, Neil	R-R	6-1	190	12-7-83	.259	.310	.248	45	158	17	41	8	0	6	14	9	1	2	0	23	0	1	.424	.304
Wimberly, Corey	B-R	5-8	180	10-26-83	.291	.272	.296	108	388	65	113	17	2	0	26	41	9	9	2	45	59	16	.345	.370
Young Jr., Eric	B-R	5-10	180	5-25-85	.290	.272	.296	105	403	74	117	24	4	3	33	61	6	6	0	77	46	16	.392	.391

Pitching	B-T	HT	WT	DOB	W	L	ERA	G	GS	CG	SV	IP	H	R	ER	HR	BB	SO	AVG	vLH	vRH	K/9	BB/9
Bright, Adam	L-L	5-11	175	8-11-84	3	8	4.41	47	0	0	0	49	56	29	24	4	13	37	.293	.234	.323	6.80	2.39
Cedeno, Xavier	L-L	6-1	165	8-26-86	7	7	4.12	19	19	0	0	103	126	66	47	10	37	52	.300	.364	.288	4.56	3.24
Clarke, Darren	R-R	6-8	235	3-18-81	2	2	5.40	29	0	0	1	30	34	21	18	6	23	24	.288	.233	.320	7.20	6.90
Daley, Matt	R-R	6-2	175	6-23-82	0	0	2.25	3	0	0	0	4	5	1	1	0	1	4	.294	.667	.214	9.00	2.25
Francis, Jeff	L-L	6-5	205	1-8-81	1	0	0.63	3	3	0	0	14	12	1	1	0	2	19	.231	.250	.229	11.93	1.26
Fultz, Aaron	L-L	6-0	210	9-4-73	0	2	18.00	2	0	0	0	1	2	2	2	0	2	0	.400	.500	.333	18.00	0.00
George, Jon	R-R	6-4	220	7-6-84	0	2	5.98	25	1	0	0	41	47	32	27	9	8	19	.290	.222	.316	4.20	1.77
Gonzalez, Luis E.	L-L	6-0	205	2-27-83	0	1	10.47	15	0	0	0	16	23	23	19	2	20	9	.333	.417	.316	4.96	11.02
Grube, Jarrett	R-R	6-4	220	11-5-81	4	3	4.26	49	0	0	0	68	70	34	32	11	33	46	.269	.337	.237	6.12	4.39
Hall, Josh	R-R	6-2	190	12-16-80	1	2	7.97	4	4	0	0	20	31	21	18	1	12	12	.365	.379	.357	5.31	5.31
Hynick, Brandon	R-R	6-3	205	3-7-85	10	7	4.44	27	27	0	0	172	183	93	85	27	31	97	.270	.261	.274	5.07	1.62
Johnson, Alan	R-R	6-1	180	8-24-83	4	14	5.23	28	28	0	0	176	217	121	102	19	55	92	.312	.338	.296	4.71	2.82
Johnston, Andrew	R-R	6-5	205	4-20-84	0	0	5.06	15	0	0	0	16	20	10	9	1	5	22	.333	.478	.220	2.81	3.94
Lo, Ching-Lung	R-R	6-6	190	8-20-85	8	8	5.25	19	18	1	0	98	102	69	57	16	23	49	.267	.194	.304	4.52	2.12
Mattheus, Ryan	R-R	6-3	215	11-10-83	2	5	3.28	58	0	0	17	58	50	27	21	5	27	56	.245	.318	.210	8.74	4.21
McClellan, Zach	R-R	6-5	190	11-25-78	0	0	4.50	2	0	0	0	2	3	1	1	0	0	0	.333	.000	.429	0.00	0.00
Ritchie, Todd	R-R	6-3	205	11-7-71	0	1	12.71	1	1	0	0	6	8	8	8	2	5	1	.348	.250	.400	1.59	7.94

	B-T	HT	WT	DOB	W	L	ERA	G	GS	CG	SV	IP	H	R	ER	HR	BB	SO	AVG	vLH	vRH	K/9	BB/9
Roe, Chaz	R-R	6-5	180	10-9-86	5	4	4.27	16	16	1	0	105	98	57	50	15	34	70	.248	.265	.236	5.98	2.91
Santiago, Tomas	R-R	6-4	210	10-30-81	4	8	4.42	32	17	0	0	106	112	62	52	11	52	82	.275	.316	.255	6.96	4.42
Strop, Pedro	R-R	6-0	160	6-13-85	0	0	2.57	7	0	0	3	7	6	2	2	0	4	7	.231	.125	.278	9.00	5.14
Valdez, Edward	R-R	6-1	190	2-8-80	4	4	4.12	46	0	0	2	68	67	38	31	3	24	61	.261	.250	.266	8.11	3.19
Weathers, Casey	R-R	6-1	200	6-10-85	2	1	3.05	44	0	0	2	44	34	18	15	1	28	54	.210	.319	.165	10.96	5.68
Weiser, Keith	R-L	6-2	190	9-21-84	1	2	3.60	5	5	0	0	35	37	17	14	2	6	13	.285	.343	.263	3.34	1.54
Wells, Kip	R-R	6-3	205	4-21-77	0	0	2.70	1	1	0	0	7	6	2	2	0	1	8	.240	.444	.125	10.80	1.35

Fielding

Catcher	PCT	G	PO	A	E	DP	PB
Esposito	.993	66	407	42	3	7	10
Guarno	.968	23	126	24	5	1	0
Parrish	.980	9	43	5	1	0	1
Wilson	.986	44	257	17	4	3	4

First Base	PCT	G	PO	A	E	DP
Blanco	1.000	1	12	1	0	1
Dragicevich	1.000	9	69	5	0	8
Kindel	.992	128	1206	87	10	124
Sardinha	.987	8	70	4	1	13

Second Base	PCT	G	PO	A	E	DP
Cates	.958	5	12	11	1	4
Cornejo	1.000	4	11	6	0	3

	PCT	G	PO	A	E	DP
Dragicevich	1.000	3	8	6	0	1
Sardinha	.833	2	0	5	1	0
Wimberly	.967	43	90	116	7	38
Young Jr.	.974	95	231	303	14	79

Third Base	PCT	G	PO	A	E	DP
Blanco	.849	62	34	129	29	15
Cates	.963	9	6	20	1	1
Cornejo	.939	19	19	43	4	4
Dragicevich	.940	46	24	118	9	11
Sardinha	1.000	1	0	1	0	1
Wimberly	.891	15	5	36	5	5

Shortstop	PCT	G	PO	A	E	DP
Cornejo	.977	21	27	57	2	15

	PCT	G	PO	A	E	DP
Dragicevich	.922	21	24	59	7	7
C. Nelson	.930	72	104	217	24	52
Tulowitzki	1.000	4	9	9	0	3
Wimberly	.941	33	51	109	10	23

Outfield	PCT	G	PO	A	E	DP
Blanco	.957	16	21	1	1	0
Carte	.990	102	187	11	2	4
Collaro	1.000	15	20	1	0	0
Fowler	.978	106	255	8	6	1
Miller	.993	90	138	5	1	0
J. Nelson	.966	89	163	7	6	0
Wimberly	.960	13	23	1	1	0
Young Jr.	1.000	5	7	0	0	0

MODESTO NUTS

HIGH CLASS A

CALIFORNIA LEAGUE

Batting	B-T	HT	WT	DOB	AVG	vLH	vRH	G	AB	R	H	2B	3B	HR	RBI	BB	HBP	SH	SF	SO	SB	CS	SLG	OBP
Becktel, Travis	R-R	6-1	205	4-3-83	.243	.277	.226	67	202	26	49	12	5	3	24	13	3	5	0	56	11	2	.396	.298
Berglund, Bret	R-R	6-4	210	12-9-82	.214	.200	.222	4	14	4	3	0	0	0	1	0	0	0	0	5	3	0	.214	.214
Blanco, Tony	R-R	6-2	200	11-10-81	.550	1.000	.471	5	20	5	11	2	1	1	3	0	1	0	0	1	1	0	.900	.571
Bowden, Johnny	R-R	6-3	205	8-15-84	.125	.125	.125	11	32	5	4	1	0	0	4	0	1	1	0	12	0	2	.156	.216
Cabrera, Angel	R-R	6-0	185	10-14-85	.242	.222	.250	9	33	6	8	2	0	2	4	2	0	1	0	7	3	1	.485	.286
Cox, Jay	L-R	6-0	200	10-30-84	.250	.200	.264	99	360	43	90	28	4	7	48	21	1	4	2	112	1	5	.408	.292
Ferrante, Victor	R-R	6-3	220	12-6-84	.248	.310	.226	117	431	55	107	19	5	11	62	46	8	1	3	111	9	2	.392	.330
Garcia, Lino	R-R	6-3	192	10-12-83	.311	.316	.309	20	74	11	23	5	0	3	11	8	0	1	1	20	2	0	.500	.373
Garner, Cole	R-R	6-2	210	12-15-84	.318	.391	.281	50	192	27	61	14	2	2	17	9	4	1	0	51	7	5	.443	.361
Gomez, Hector	R-R	6-1	157	3-5-88	.333	—	.333	1	3	0	1	0	0	0	0	0	0	2	0	0	0	0	.333	.333
Guerrero, James	R-R	5-7	175	6-8-84	.333	.000	.400	5	6	2	2	0	1	0	1	3	0	0	0	2	0	0	.667	.556
Haley, Nick	L-R	5-11	185	5-25-84	.243	.229	.246	101	338	48	82	14	2	1	33	52	6	11	3	78	14	8	.305	.351
Jackson, Anthony	B-R	5-8	175	6-17-84	.298	.280	.304	107	430	71	128	21	7	1	39	29	15	4	3	85	39	9	.386	.361
Mayora, Daniel	R-R	5-11	145	7-27-85	.288	.296	.285	127	486	65	140	34	5	7	55	44	12	11	3	100	8	8	.422	.360
McKenry, Michael	R-R	5-10	200	3-4-85	.258	.211	.275	111	400	59	103	28	1	18	75	55	10	5	2	101	2	4	.468	.360
Nazario, Radames	R-R	6-0	166	6-14-87	.241	.333	.231	10	29	4	7	3	0	0	3	1	2	1	0	6	0	0	.345	.281
Nelson, Chris	R-R	5-11	175	9-3-85	.167	.222	.143	8	30	2	5	1	0	1	5	2	0	0	0	8	0	2	.300	.219
Paulk, Mike	L-L	6-2	195	4-23-84	.310	.288	.317	132	510	81	158	28	3	8	66	63	3	2	8	79	8	5	.424	.384
Repec, Matt	R-R	6-1	190	8-30-83	.248	.248	.247	112	400	43	99	18	2	10	57	31	3	6	3	115	2	2	.378	.304
Reyes, Leonardo	R-R	6-0	165	8-2-88	.167	.000	.167	2	6	1	1	0	0	1	1	2	1	0	0	1	1	0	.667	.444
Robledo, Nelson	R-R	6-1	180	6-13-84	.186	.108	.221	66	210	17	39	5	0	1	16	24	2	3	3	62	0	0	.224	.272
Simmons, Thomas	L-L	6-1	187	6-14-84	.271	.333	.262	24	70	11	19	3	0	2	9	2	2	0	0	19	1	0	.400	.311
Strickland, Geoff	B-R	5-10	180	7-1-84	.221	.261	.213	43	131	15	29	9	1	2	11	19	0	4	1	48	14	2	.351	.318
Tulowitzki, Troy	R-R	6-3	205	10-10-84	.333	1.000	.273	5	12	3	4	3	0	1	5	0	0	1		2	0	0	.583	.500
Van Kooten, Jason	R-R	6-0	170	9-1-84	.245	.258	.240	101	343	41	84	24	2	4	32	16	6	4	2	76	20	6	.362	.289

Pitching	B-T	HT	WT	DOB	W	L	ERA	G	GS	CG	SV	IP	H	R	ER	HR	BB	SO	AVG	vLH	vRH	K/9	BB/9
Baumgardner, Tommy	L-L	6-2	220	10-15-83	2	1	3.80	49	0	0	1	64	67	33	27	6	21	41	.268	.297	.245	5.77	2.95
Burok, James	R-R	6-3	220	11-16-82	0	1	7.50	18	1	0	0	24	29	20	20	5	12	23	.299	.229	.367	8.63	4.50
Chacin, Jhoulys	R-R	6-1	168	1-7-88	8	2	2.31	12	12	0	0	66	61	20	17	3	12	62	.247	.224	.274	8.41	1.63
Chambliss, Austin	L-R	6-2	185	2-19-87	0	0	0.00	1	0	0	0	1	0	0	0	0	0	0	.000	.000	.000	0.00	0.00
Durden, Brandon	R-L	6-3	215	7-20-84	4	2	5.79	29	8	0	0	78	101	56	50	9	18	43	.316	.311	.319	4.98	2.09
Ferrer, Simon	B-R	5-10	175	6-24-80	8	11	5.62	29	27	0	0	146	172	96	91	14	61	72	.302	.310	.295	4.45	3.77
George, Jon	R-R	6-4	220	7-6-84	1	1	3.18	11	0	0	1	17	16	7	6	1	2	12	.250	.290	.212	6.35	1.06
Graham, Andy	R-R	6-4	210	6-29-84	4	4	4.10	47	0	0	0	68	79	38	31	8	19	64	.290	.321	.262	8.47	2.51
Harris, William	R-R	6-4	225	8-28-84	3	5	2.77	49	0	0	3	62	51	20	19	4	20	70	.221	.212	.228	10.22	2.92
Jarrett, Sean	R-R	6-5	210	4-26-83	0	0	3.00	2	0	0	0	3	2	1	1	0	1	2	.182	.500	.111	6.00	3.00
Johnston, Andrew	R-R	6-5	205	4-20-84	3	1	2.03	38	0	0	24	40	30	14	9	1	14	58	.209	.254	.169	6.30	3.38
Lindsay, Shane	R-R	6-1	205	1-25-85	2	3	3.99	10	10	0	0	47	33	29	21	1	34	56	.194	.153	.224	10.65	6.46
Malone, Chris	R-R	6-4	215	6-28-83	2	4	4.04	27	1	0	3	56	62	30	25	3	14	39	.288	.276	.299	6.31	2.26
Patton, David	R-R	6-3	175	5-18-84	4	5	3.54	50	0	0	4	74	74	31	29	8	28	87	.260	.281	.242	10.63	3.42
Ritchie, Todd	R-R	6-3	205	11-7-71	3	0	3.18	4	3	0	0	17	14	6	6	0	3	9	.233	.282	.143	4.76	1.59
Rodriguez, Aneury	R-R	6-3	180	12-13-87	9	10	3.74	27	27	2	0	156	148	78	65	12	40	139	.251	.289	.213	8.00	2.30
Roe, Chaz	R-R	6-5	180	10-9-86	2	1	5.49	3	3	0	0	20	24	17	12	1	3	16	.290	.258	.291	7.32	1.37
Rogers, Esmil	R-R	6-1	150	8-14-85	9	7	3.95	25	25	0	0	144	146	73	63	9	45	116	.264	.262	.267	7.27	2.82
Simons, Zach	L-R	6-3	200	5-23-85	1	0	2.70	7	0	0	0	13	12	5	4	1	9	14	.255	.304	.208	9.45	6.07
Weiser, Keith	R-L	6-2	190	9-21-84	7	10	3.05	22	22	1	0	145	146	59	49	5	19	75	.263	.268	.260	4.67	1.18

Fielding

Catcher	PCT	G	PO	A	E	DP	PB
Bowden	1.000	8	48	6	0	0	4
McKenry	.986	97	701	63	11	8	10
Robledo	.989	39	253	18	3	2	5

First Base	PCT	G	PO	A	E	DP
Paulk	.995	120	1041	74	6	88
Repec	1.000	6	38	7	0	2
Robledo	1.000	17	116	12	0	13
Strickland	1.000	1	2	0	0	0

Second Base	PCT	G	PO	A	E	DP
Cabrera	1.000	2	3	7	0	2
Haley	.971	33	52	117	5	21
Jackson	1.000	3	1	5	0	1
Mayora	.949	40	66	119	10	19
Nazario	1.000	1	1	2	0	0
Repec	.000	1	0	0	1	0

	PCT	G	PO	A	E	DP
Strickland	.963	22	42	62	4	11
Van Kooten	.966	50	81	118	7	22

Third Base	PCT	G	PO	A	E	DP
Blanco	.500	3	1	1	2	0
Haley	.960	42	28	68	4	7
Repec	.947	95	52	143	11	12
Strickland	.800	3	2	2	1	0
Van Kooten	1.000	1	0	3	0	0

Shortstop	PCT	G	PO	A	E	DP
Cabrera	.900	4	4	5	1	0
Gomez	.714	1	3	2	2	0
Guerrero	.933	3	5	9	1	1
Mayora	.924	89	140	223	30	44
Nazario	1.000	8	16	28	0	6
Nelson	.929	5	13	13	2	4
Strickland	.962	8	10	15	1	5

	PCT	G	PO	A	E	DP
Tulowitzki	.882	3	1	14	2	2
Van Kooten	.943	29	53	79	8	14

Outfield	PCT	G	PO	A	E	DP
Becktel	.984	64	114	7	2	0
Berglund	1.000	4	3	0	0	0
Cox	.981	78	152	5	3	2
Ferrante	.984	103	166	13	3	3
Garcia	1.000	20	43	1	0	0
Garner	.973	35	66	6	2	0
Haley	1.000	3	3	1	0	0
Jackson	.975	106	262	10	7	4
Paulk	1.000	10	15	1	0	0
Reyes	.750	2	3	0	1	0
Robledo	—	1	0	0	0	0
Simmons	1.000	12	15	0	0	0
Strickland	1.000	6	6	0	0	0

ASHEVILLE TOURISTS   *LOW CLASS A*
SOUTH ATLANTIC LEAGUE

Batting	B-T	HT	WT	DOB	AVG	vLH	vRH	G	AB	R	H	2B	3B	HR	RBI	BB	HBP	SH	SF	SO	SB	CS	SLG	OBP
Aguailar, Brian	L-R	5-11	185	4-29-84	.164	.176	.158	16	55	9	9	1	0	0	2	5	1	0	0	16	1	0	.182	.246
Bowman, Bo	L-L	6-2	200	9-22-84	.325	.333	.324	31	126	15	41	7	1	2	16	9	1	0	0	19	5	2	.444	.375
Cabrera, Everth	R-R	5-8	160	11-17-86	.284	.309	.274	121	479	80	136	25	6	6	38	51	8	10	2	101	73	16	.399	.361
Christensen, David	R-R	6-1	195	2-11-88	.227	.194	.240	94	335	44	76	21	1	11	46	23	6	0	1	130	12	3	.394	.288
Clark, Kevin	L-L	6-0	195	12-10-85	.262	.216	.280	112	397	60	104	23	1	17	76	54	3	1	9	136	22	6	.453	.348
Cunningham, Jeff	R-R	6-3	220	3-22-86	.257	.245	.262	109	404	63	104	23	2	18	78	47	3	0	1	134	6	6	.458	.338
Davis, Lars	L-R	6-3	205	11-7-85	.250	.217	.260	81	296	29	74	10	3	5	27	15	3	2	2	77	8	5	.355	.291
Holcomb, Darin	R-R	5-11	205	12-7-85	.318	.316	.319	137	509	89	162	46	0	14	102	65	8	1	5	60	6	5	.491	.400
Lapin, Brian	R-R	6-6	230	5-24-85	.209	.130	.234	55	191	25	40	7	3	6	23	12	3	0	2	44	1	1	.372	.264
Mitchell, Mike	R-R	5-11	185	8-24-85	.300	.380	.270	127	500	93	150	24	5	4	45	37	15	17	1	118	55	9	.392	.365
Nagy, Spence	B-R	5-11	185	6-14-85	.147	.333	.107	12	34	6	5	2	0	1	2	2	0	0	1	5	4	0	.294	.189
Rike, Brian	L-L	6-2	200	12-13-85	.247	.218	.257	120	445	67	110	13	2	15	75	62	7	1	4	161	13	7	.387	.346
Schaeffer, Warren	R-R	6-0	180	1-28-85	.226	.203	.235	92	287	38	65	16	1	3	33	20	4	5	3	63	6	2	.321	.283
Seabury, Beau	R-R	6-1	190	6-13-85	.176	.184	.174	51	170	18	30	7	0	1	14	11	1	3	2	56	3	2	.235	.228
Velazquez, Helder	R-R	6-3	165	10-14-88	.234	.280	.218	117	448	57	105	29	2	9	49	15	5	5	1	94	12	13	.368	.267

Pitching	B-T	HT	WT	DOB	W	L	ERA	G	GS	CG	SV	IP	H	R	ER	HR	BB	SO	AVG	vLH	vRH	K/9	BB/9
Baker, Craig	R-R	6-2	210	1-31-85	7	5	2.22	52	0	0	6	57	49	16	14	5	11	70	.228	.205	.239	11.12	1.75
Billings, Bruce	R-R	6-0	200	11-18-85	9	11	4.13	27	27	2	0	161	163	85	74	11	42	144	.258	.253	.261	8.03	2.34
Chacin, Jhoulys	R-R	6-1	168	1-7-88	10	1	1.86	16	16	2	0	111	82	30	23	3	30	98	.205	.232	.186	7.92	2.43
Escalona, Edgmer	R-R	6-4	175	10-6-86	6	2	3.22	44	0	0	1	78	71	32	28	9	18	79	.242	.333	.187	9.08	2.07
Fabian, Robinson	R-R	6-3	152	2-10-86	4	6	5.38	17	13	0	0	72	89	54	43	10	22	59	.301	.325	.282	7.38	2.75
Friedrich, Christian	R-L	6-3	210	7-8-87	0	1	7.50	3	3	0	0	12	14	10	10	2	7	15	.269	.211	.303	11.25	5.25
Graham, Connor	R-R	6-6	235	12-30-85	12	6	2.26	26	26	2	0	147	99	50	37	3	83	138	.189	.163	.206	8.43	5.07
Groves, Andy	R-R	6-2	210	10-6-84	0	0	9.22	13	0	0	0	14	19	14	14	1	15	8	.358	.389	.343	5.27	9.88
Katz, Ethan	R-R	6-5	210	7-4-83	0	0	3.00	14	0	0	0	15	18	5	5	2	2	13	.300	.318	.289	7.80	1.20
Kuo, Sheng-An	R-R	6-2	190	1-1-86	9	7	5.16	24	21	0	0	113	132	83	65	15	65	79	.293	.286	.300	6.27	5.16
Lindsay, Shane	R-R	6-1	205	1-25-85	1	2	5.55	6	0	0	0	24	30	16	15	1	12	26	.306	.286	.317	9.62	4.44
Reynolds, Matt	L-L	6-5	240	10-2-84	6	2	2.53	42	0	0	2	57	49	19	16	4	14	53	.226	.192	.245	8.37	2.21
Riordan, Cory	R-R	6-4	200	5-25-86	8	9	3.65	26	25	2	0	168	185	91	68	18	29	160	.274	.315	.248	8.59	1.56
Rodriguez, Craig	L-L	6-4	210	6-27-85	4	3	2.59	42	0	0	1	59	51	19	17	2	22	61	.232	.247	.224	9.31	3.36
Speier, Ryan	R-R	6-7	210	7-24-79	0	0	10.80	2	0	0	0	2	1	2	2	0	2	3	.167	.333	.000	16.20	10.80
Taylor, Don	R-R	6-1	185	5-23-85	3	1	3.91	52	0	0	32	51	50	24	22	7	16	55	.262	.314	.231	9.77	2.84
Williamson, Joey	R-R	6-2	210	1-28-86	4	0	3.04	35	2	0	1	83	67	32	28	6	32	89	.220	.252	.199	9.65	3.47

Fielding

Catcher	PCT	G	PO	A	E	DP	PB
Aguailar	.983	14	104	13	2	0	1
Davis	.990	75	639	63	7	6	5
Seabury	.998	51	407	45	1	7	5

First Base	PCT	G	PO	A	E	DP
Bowman	.974	21	171	15	5	19
Cunningham	.982	102	851	74	17	76
Nagy	.967	4	27	2	1	3
Schaeffer	.991	17	103	9	1	15

Second Base	PCT	G	PO	A	E	DP
Cabrera	.959	84	160	239	17	44
Holcomb	1.000	1	3	2	0	1

	PCT	G	PO	A	E	DP
Nagy	.944	2	11	6	1	3
Schaeffer	.988	38	78	93	2	24
Velazquez	.967	18	40	48	3	10

Third Base	PCT	G	PO	A	E	DP
Cunningham	1.000	1	0	1	0	0
Holcomb	.941	117	69	218	18	22
Nagy	.667	4	5	3	4	1
Schaeffer	.956	23	11	32	2	3
Velazquez	.750	1	0	3	1	0

Shortstop	PCT	G	PO	A	E	DP
Cabrera	.945	34	50	104	9	18
Nagy	.833	1	2	3	1	1

	PCT	G	PO	A	E	DP
Schaeffer	.969	15	25	37	2	7
Velazquez	.921	90	132	243	32	50

Outfield	PCT	G	PO	A	E	DP
Bowman	1.000	2	1	0	0	0
Christensen	.950	37	55	2	3	0
Clark	.970	105	156	4	5	2
Lapin	.958	34	46	0	2	0
Mitchell	.976	127	236	9	6	4
Rike	.966	116	184	17	7	2

ORGANIZATION STATISTICS

TRI-CITY DUST DEVILS

TRI-CITY DUST DEVILS

SHORT-SEASON

NORTHWEST LEAGUE

Batting	B-T	HT	WT	DOB	AVG	vLH	vRH	G	AB	R	H	2B	3B	HR	RBI	BB	HBP	SH	SF	SO	SB	CS	SLG	OBP
Agustin, Jhaysson	R-R	6-0	170	3-16-85	.211	.000	.276	11	38	3	8	3	0	0	4	4	0	0	1	14	0	0	.289	.279
Banda, Josh	R-R	6-2	205	9-7-85	.218	.231	.214	16	55	3	12	2	0	3	11	2	0	0	1	15	0	2	.418	.241
Blackmon, Charlie	L-L	6-2	185	7-1-86	.338	.386	.323	68	290	42	98	21	5	2	33	16	10	3	2	37	13	7	.466	.390
Bowden, Johnny	R-R	6-3	205	8-15-84	.276	.259	.280	36	134	21	37	7	2	4	18	15	2	1	2	36	1	0	.448	.353
Bowman, Bo	L-L	6-2	200	9-22-84	.338	.200	.362	21	68	17	23	2	1	5	13	9	1	0	2	14	3	3	.618	.413
Field, Thomas	R-R	5-9	175	2-22-87	.247	.250	.246	56	182	34	45	8	2	5	32	42	6	1	1	34	10	6	.396	.403
Goff, Andy	R-R	5-11	180	9-2-85	.095	.167	.067	7	21	2	2	1	0	1	1	3	1	1	0	3	0	1	.286	.240
Kinzler, Derek	L-R	6-0	176	11-27-84	.262	.263	.262	17	61	5	16	3	0	0	8	4	2	1	2	15	2	1	.311	.319
Lembeck, Chad	R-R	6-2	195	11-2-84	.146	.100	.167	30	96	15	14	5	1	3	5	7	3	2	0	36	2	1	.313	.226
Melhuse, Adam	B-R	6-2	210	3-27-72	.083	.200	.000	5	12	1	1	1	0	0	1	2	1	0	0	5	0	0	.167	.267
Nazario, Radames	R-R	6-0	166	6-14-87	.241	.188	.254	24	79	12	19	4	0	1	6	10	0	1	3	13	1	1	.329	.315
Pacheco, Jordan	R-R	6-1	190	1-30-86	.280	.269	.284	54	214	25	60	8	3	1	35	26	6	1	4	20	3	3	.360	.368
Peisel, Ryan	R-R	6-3	195	6-14-86	.208	.290	.186	39	144	11	30	8	2	0	12	16	2	1	1	43	1	3	.292	.294
Rauch, Austin	R-R	6-3	210	3-30-88	.200	.184	.204	49	180	26	36	7	1	4	17	26	1	1	6	60	0	2	.317	.303
Reyes, Leonardo	R-R	6-0	165	8-2-88	.245	.310	.223	59	237	28	58	14	2	4	30	20	2	4	1	55	5	3	.371	.308
Robinson, Scott	R-R	6-0	185	7-6-88	.268	.281	.262	59	228	38	61	8	3	6	25	18	7	2	1	49	15	6	.408	.339
Rose, Patrick	R-R	5-11	180	10-2-85	.274	.286	.269	60	223	30	61	6	5	3	27	34	6	5	1	56	12	3	.386	.383
Simmons, Thomas	L-L	6-1	187	6-14-84	.211	.750	.067	5	19	1	4	2	0	1	7	2	0	0	2	6	0	0	.474	.261
Sims, James	R-R	6-0	200	4-11-86	.183	.190	.179	16	60	12	11	3	2	0	5	5	1	0	1	22	3	0	.300	.254
Vasami, Chris	R-R	6-4	230	3-7-85	.252	.212	.267	34	119	15	30	5	1	2	16	7	4	2	1	27	0	3	.361	.313
Wetzel, Erik	R-R	6-1	180	12-25-86	.271	.250	.280	38	140	19	38	8	0	0	14	20	2	8	1	29	6	2	.329	.368

Pitching	B-T	HT	WT	DOB	W	L	ERA	G	GS	CG	SV	IP	H	R	ER	HR	BB	SO	AVG	vLH	vRH	K/9	BB/9
Aristil, Jonnathan	R-R	6-1	160	11-30-86	3	1	2.91	15	15	0	0	77	72	31	25	1	30	54	.249	.273	.229	6.28	3.49
Chambliss, Austin	L-R	6-2	185	2-19-87	1	0	2.27	28	0	0	13	32	25	11	8	0	8	34	.212	.102	.290	9.66	2.27
Coffey, Drew	R-R	6-1	185	11-2-85	0	0	2.25	7	0	0	0	8	5	2	2	0	6	10	.167	.143	.174	11.25	6.75
Durst, Kenny	B-L	6-0	195	10-1-85	4	5	3.80	15	12	0	0	64	63	34	27	5	13	61	.257	.328	.235	8.58	1.83
Frazier, Parker	R-R	6-5	159	11-11-88	5	5	3.83	15	15	0	0	87	94	41	37	3	20	47	.281	.301	.267	4.86	2.07
Friedrich, Christian	R-L	6-3	210	7-8-87	2	1	3.25	8	8	0	0	36	31	16	13	2	8	50	.228	.286	.202	12.50	2.00
Groves, Andy	R-R	6-2	210	10-6-84	1	0	7.36	10	0	0	0	11	18	9	9	1	10	11	.367	.471	.313	9.00	8.18
Jarrett, Sean	R-R	6-5	210	4-26-83	2	3	3.21	22	0	0	0	28	29	15	10	0	9	41	.248	.317	.211	13.18	2.89
Katz, Ethan	R-R	6-0	210	7-4-83	0	1	1.08	8	0	0	0	8	2	2	1	1	2	9	.074	.182	.000	9.72	2.16
Kuo, Sheng-An	R-R	6-2	190	1-1-86	1	2	5.40	3	3	0	0	13	14	8	8	0	3	17	.259	.217	.290	11.48	2.03
Luna, Carlos	R-R	5-11	175	10-5-86	3	3	1.98	26	0	0	2	36	28	13	8	1	18	37	.211	.228	.197	9.17	4.46
Marbry, Michael	R-R	6-3	185	9-3-84	2	2	2.01	20	0	0	0	31	33	12	7	1	10	21	.268	.262	.272	6.03	2.87
McAtee, Brad	R-R	6-5	215	3-15-87	3	4	5.86	13	8	0	0	35	27	28	23	0	45	33	.225	.265	.197	8.41	11.46
McClellan, Zach	R-R	6-5	190	11-25-78	0	0	0.00	4	0	0	0	4	0	0	0	0	1	3	.000	.000	.000	6.75	2.25
Miller, Brandon	L-L	6-2	195	11-24-84	3	3	3.81	18	0	0	0	26	34	17	11	0	11	14	.330	.353	.319	4.85	3.81
Murphy, J.R.	R-R	6-4	210	2-23-86	1	3	3.67	22	0	0	0	34	23	16	14	2	14	45	.185	.170	.195	11.80	3.67
Nicasio, Juan	R-R	6-3	190	8-31-86	2	4	4.50	12	12	0	0	54	46	30	27	1	19	61	.229	.222	.233	10.17	3.17
Parker, David	R-R	6-0	180	12-5-82	1	2	2.66	15	0	0	0	20	14	7	6	1	13	16	.194	.267	.143	7.08	5.75
Paschal, Bobby	L-L	6-2	190	4-3-84	1	7	7.41	16	0	0	0	17	21	14	14	2	17	17	.323	.333	.318	9.00	9.00
Scurry, Rod	R-R	6-7	190	2-1-86	0	1	6.10	15	0	0	0	21	21	14	14	1	7	12	.266	.268	.263	5.23	3.05
Sullivan, Josh	R-R	6-4	215	7-5-84	0	1	3.38	3	3	0	0	11	12	4	4	0	5	8	.286	.400	.222	6.75	4.22
Trice, Tyler	R-R	6-4	205	5-16-86	1	1	4.07	20	0	0	1	24	31	18	11	0	5	18	.295	.239	.339	6.66	1.85

Fielding

Catcher	PCT	G	PO	A	E	DP	PB
Agustin	.938	2	15	0	1	0	1
Bowden	.992	30	233	27	2	1	2
Melhuse	1.000	2	11	0	0	0	0
Pacheco	.980	44	363	33	8	0	21

First Base	PCT	G	PO	A	E	DP
Agustin	.987	8	71	5	1	9
Bowman	.952	2	19	1	1	0
Rauch	.991	49	410	29	4	35
Vasami	.977	19	153	16	4	12

Second Base	PCT	G	PO	A	E	DP
Field	.909	10	17	23	4	5

Goff	1.000	2	4	5	0	0
Kinzler	.962	17	26	49	3	8
Rose	.957	17	29	59	4	10
Wetzel	.962	30	60	90	6	22

Third Base	PCT	G	PO	A	E	DP
Nazario	1.000	3	4	4	0	1
Peisel	.928	38	25	65	7	7
Rose	.851	24	20	43	11	2
Vasami	.759	13	6	16	7	1

Shortstop	PCT	G	PO	A	E	DP
Field	.925	46	64	120	15	24
Goff	.895	5	2	15	2	0

Nazario	.972	21	43	63	3	8
Rose	.714	2	2	3	2	2
Wetzel	.966	7	13	15	1	4

Outfield	PCT	G	PO	A	E	DP
Banda	1.000	9	10	0	0	0
Blackmon	.965	52	103	7	4	4
Bowman	1.000	8	13	1	0	0
Lembeck	.981	27	50	2	1	0
Reyes	.944	59	81	4	5	0
Robinson	.991	59	110	6	1	0
Sims	.967	16	29	0	1	0

CASPER GHOSTS

ROOKIE

PIONEER LEAGUE

Batting	B-T	HT	WT	DOB	AVG	vLH	vRH	G	AB	R	H	2B	3B	HR	RBI	BB	HBP	SH	SF	SO	SB	CS	SLG	OBP
Cesario, Jimmy	R-L	6-0	200	10-15-85	.333	.423	.288	22	78	15	26	4	1	1	9	3	5	0	0	12	3	2	.449	.395
Cleary, Delta	B-R	6-3	180	8-14-89	.276	.243	.294	27	105	22	29	2	1	3	9	6	1	2	0	19	4	0	.400	.321
Feinberg, Alex	R-R	6-0	185	4-29-86	.304	.239	.356	49	158	27	48	6	0	0	17	28	4	0	0	24	6	3	.342	.421
Goff, Andy	R-R	5-11	180	9-2-85	.179	.143	.190	13	28	4	5	0	0	0	4	5	1	2	1	8	0	1	.179	.314
Gomez, Leuris	R-R	6-0	170	10-20-86	.237	.214	.250	14	38	3	9	2	0	0	3	2	0	4	0	15	2	1	.289	.275
Gonzalez, Jose	R-R	6-1	165	6-23-87	.279	.077	.405	26	68	12	19	7	0	2	14	12	3	0	0	18	1	3	.471	.410
Gonzalez, Maikol	R-R	5-10	175	3-25-86	.358	.432	.310	25	95	17	34	7	2	0	13	12	0	3	0	13	5	2	.474	.430

ORGANIZATION STATISTICS

Name	B-T	HT	WT	DOB	AVG	vLH	vRH	G	AB	R	H	2B	3B	HR	RBI	BB	HBP	SH	SF	SO	SB	CS	SLG	OBP
Jacobsen, Chad	R-R	6-1	210	4-3-86	.243	.288	.210	40	140	10	34	6	0	3	23	20	1	0	0	34	0	1	.350	.342
Lowe, Shane	B-R	6-3	184	8-14-87	.189	.163	.206	37	111	14	21	2	3	2	6	14	0	1	1	47	4	5	.315	.278
Martinez, Carlos	R-R	5-11	182	9-22-88	.284	.337	.255	65	250	41	71	14	3	2	27	21	5	4	1	54	21	8	.388	.350
Massey, Tyler	L-L	6-0	205	7-21-89	.257	.238	.265	19	70	7	18	4	0	1	5	1	1	0	0	18	5	3	.357	.278
Mesa, Eliezer	R-R	5-11	180	11-24-88	.226	.211	.236	41	146	17	33	4	2	2	19	6	3	2	3	36	3	2	.322	.266
Murry, Zack	L-R	6-0	185	6-12-87	.260	.233	.270	44	154	17	40	8	2	1	15	8	4	2	1	24	6	4	.357	.311
Nina, Angelys	R-R	5-11	165	11-16-88	.228	.129	.292	24	79	10	18	4	0	1	6	9	0	0	0	14	1	1	.316	.307
Roling, Kiel	R-R	6-3	240	1-23-87	.344	.381	.326	18	64	10	22	7	0	4	17	8	0	0	0	11	0	0	.641	.417
Rosario, Wilin	R-R	5-11	180	2-23-89	.316	.307	.321	66	263	48	83	15	3	12	49	24	1	0	3	57	4	3	.532	.371
Sandoval, Orlando	R-R	6-0	185	1-22-86	.324	.269	.356	66	253	39	82	15	3	4	35	9	4	0	1	62	8	2	.455	.356
Simmons, Thomas	L-L	6-1	187	6-14-84	.349	.240	.397	24	83	12	29	9	3	2	22	7	2	0	0	20	3	0	.602	.413
Sims, James	R-R	6-0	200	4-11-86	.302	.357	.274	32	126	22	38	7	4	3	19	11	1	0	1	39	10	5	.492	.360
Valdez, Nick	R-R	5-11	212	5-26-86	.257	.297	.235	31	105	16	27	4	1	6	14	11	1	0	2	21	3	2	.486	.328
Zuanich, Mike	R-L	6-4	225	7-10-86	.185	.097	.240	30	41	10	15	6	1	0	8	16	1	0	0	29	0	0	.284	.327

Pitching	B-T	HT	WT	DOB	W	L	ERA	G	GS	CG	SV	IP	H	R	ER	HR	BB	SO	AVG	vLH	vRH	K/9	BB/9
Baugh, Matt	L-L	6-1	190	1-25-86	3	2	5.50	12	9	0	0	52	71	35	32	7	9	40	.324	.189	.352	6.88	1.55
Bennigson, Craig	R-L	6-2	215	3-21-87	0	0	10.13	2	1	0	0	3	5	3	3			3	.500	.500	.500	10.13	10.13
Cabrera, Edwar	L-L	6-0	160	10-20-87	0	4	7.80	9	5	0	0	30	38	29	26	7	15	38	.304	.175	.365	11.40	4.50
Deratt, Alan	R-R	6-5	225	11-6-85	2	2	3.94	15	1	0	0	30	24	15	13	1	13	39	.214	.109	.288	11.83	3.94
Dill, Brandon	R-R	6-1	195	12-5-84	3	1	2.92	13	0	0	0	25	20	8	8	3	7	24	.227	.189	.255	8.76	2.55
Duarte, Marco	R-R	6-2	185	8-19-86	5	6	5.86	14	13	0	0	66	87	51	43	9	12	67	.311	.372	.264	9.14	1.64
Fischer, Jeff	R-R	6-5	200	12-2-85	4	7	4.86	15	15	1	0	83	83	50	45	9	15	85	.253	.260	.247	9.18	1.62
Froneberger, Isaiah	L-L	5-8	200	6-23-89	0	0	4.08	25	0	0	2	29	28	13	13	1	17	41	.262	.226	.276	12.87	5.34
Hollingsworth, Ethan	R-R	6-2	200	5-4-87	4	7	6.10	14	13	0	0	59	80	49	40	7	16	55	.325	.293	.354	8.39	2.44
Houston, Dan	R-R	6-3	205	10-24-86	6	4	4.17	14	14	1	0	69	61	39	32	10	20	68	.229	.195	.263	8.87	2.61
Jorgenson, Adam	R-R	6-0	185	9-10-85	2	1	1.24	23	0	0	4	29	17	4	4	0	4	43	.163	.174	.155	13.34	1.24
Lopez, Ronny	R-R	6-2	185	8-12-86	1	0	4.45	18	1	0	0	30	25	17	15	1	7	23	.227	.222	.230	6.82	2.08
Marrero, Andres	R-R	6-1	190	7-8-88	2	0	6.86	15	0	0	0	28	28	19	16	2	7	24	.301	.211	.364	10.29	3.00
Rodriguez, Juan	B-R	6-2	186	9-15-88	1	0	7.71	16	0	0	1	21	29	20	18	1	9	15	.319	.436	.231	6.43	3.86
Rose, Chad	R-R	6-2	200	2-17-88	1	1	5.87	18	0	0	0	23	19	15	15	2	12	32	.218	.167	.246	12.52	4.70
Schaler, Eric	R-R	6-4	210	3-5-84	0	1	15.43	12	0	0	0	12	18	22	20	1	18	12	.340	.227	.419	9.26	13.89
Schnaitmann, Nick	R-R	6-6	190	11-16-89	0	0	0.00	2	0	0	0	2	3	0	0	0	1	2	.375	.200	.667	9.00	4.50
Silano, Yull	R-R	6-2	165	5-13-86	0	0	2.25	1	1	0	0	4	4	1	1	0	3	2	.286	.143	.429	4.50	6.75
Walker, Kyle	L-L	6-0	190	6-9-87	1	0	5.14	19	0	0	0	21	20	16	12	2	14	28	.238	.304	.213	12.00	6.00
Yacko, Kurt	R-R	5-11	180	8-22-87	1	1	4.44	24	0	0	11	26	25	17	13	5	9	43	.229	.268	.206	14.70	3.08

Fielding

Catcher	PCT	G	PO	A	E	DP	PB
J. Gonzalez	.984	18	112	8	2	2	6
Rosario	.994	50	462	38	3	3	14
Valdez	1.000	11	106	5	0	0	6

First Base	PCT	G	PO	A	E	DP
J. Gonzalez	1.000	7	43	5	0	2
Jacobsen	.980	30	233	14	5	18
Roling	.986	16	135	8	2	10
Valdez	1.000	8	54	5	0	7
Zuanich	.993	24	126	7	1	11

Second Base	PCT	G	PO	A	E	DP
Cesario	.955	4	10	11	1	2
Feinberg	1.000	16	17	32	0	6
Goff	.750	1	0	3	1	0

	PCT	G	PO	A	E	DP
M. Gonzalez	.957	18	21	46	3	9
Murry	.953	33	33	90	6	11
Nina	.917	8	10	12	2	3

Third Base	PCT	G	PO	A	E	DP
Cesario	.773	9	6	11	5	1
Feinberg	.949	33	15	59	4	5
Goff	.818	6	9	2	1	
Gomez	.968	12	13	17	1	1
J. Gonzalez	.333	1	0	1	2	0
M. Gonzalez	.929	5	3	10	1	0
Murry	.857	3	1	5	1	0
Nina	.897	15	9	17	3	0

Shortstop	PCT	G	PO	A	E	DP
Goff	.923	6	6	18	2	3

	PCT	G	PO	A	E	DP
M. Gonzalez	1.000	2	3	5	0	1
Martinez	.917	65	113	164	25	29
Nina	.938	3	7	8	1	3

Outfield	PCT	G	PO	A	E	DP
Cesario	1.000	5	9	0	0	0
Cleary	.941	24	29	3	2	0
Lowe	.930	32	39	1	3	0
Massey	.900	17	25	2	3	0
Mesa	.983	38	57	1	1	0
Sandoval	.941	65	109	2	7	1
Simmons	.875	10	14	0	2	0
Sims	.957	28	43	1	2	0
Zuanich	1.000	9	15	0	0	0

DSL ROCKIES   ROOKIE

DOMINICAN SUMMER LEAGUE

Batting	B-T	HT	WT	DOB	AVG	vLH	vRH	G	AB	R	H	2B	3B	HR	RBI	BB	HBP	SH	SF	SO	SB	CS	SLG	OBP
Adames, Cristhian	B-R	6-0	160	7-26-91	.262	.311	.244	51	168	22	44	5	0	0	18	2	3	1		26	7	8	.292	.339
Castillo, Engels	R-R	6-3	194	7-25-90	.292	.294	.292	28	89	8	26	1	0	0	6	6	8	3	1	19	4	0	.303	.385
Charles, Moises	R-R	5-11	168	12-1-88	.316	.290	.322	51	177	25	56	6	3	0	23	16	4	2	1	31	14	8	.384	.384
Crousset, Juan	L-L	5-11	193	4-30-90	.320	.286	.330	64	259	35	83	10	5	4	42	21	4	2	3	40	16	4	.444	.376
De Jesus, Kelvin	R-R	5-9	167	11-22-88	.301	.360	.286	38	123	16	37	7	0	0	14	17	3	2	2	16	4	6	.358	.393
De La Cruz, Robert	R-R	5-11	189	10-10-89	.291	.154	.333	48	165	17	48	8	0	1	22	16	4	1	2	32	6	1	.358	.364
De Leon, Miguel	R-R	6-2	195	8-5-91	.223	.276	.211	45	157	11	35	4	1	0	10	12	4	3	2	46	0	1	.261	.291
Fernandez, Raul	R-R	6-2	180	6-22-90	.221	.067	.264	21	68	5	15	3	0	0	6	4	0	1	0	12	2	0	.265	.264
Gonzalez, Maikol	R-R	5-10	175	3-25-86	1.000	—	1.000	1	2	0	2	0	0	0	0	0	0	0	0	0	0	0	1.000	1.000
Ortega, Rafael	L-R	5-11	160	5-15-91	.277	.340	.255	52	188	38	52	4	2	1	11	20	2	6	2	20	17	3	.335	.349
Perez, Miguel	B-R	6-0	156	9-9-88	.205	.219	.200	36	117	20	24	4	4	0	7	15	2	3	0	20	7	3	.308	.306
Ramirez, Michael	R-R	5-10	169	4-27-90	.316	.393	.284	27	95	6	30	4	0	0	10	2	1	0	1	13	2	0	.358	.333
Reyes, Gabriel	R-R	6-0	166	4-28-91	.267	.271	.265	51	195	22	52	7	1	0	23	19	1	13	0	33	7	7	.313	.335
Rogers, John	R-R	6-2	189	12-13-89	.198	.333	.141	43	111	15	22	5	1	4	13	15	9	1	0	40	8	4	.369	.341
Sosa, Francisco	R-R	6-4	180	2-27-90	.203	.275	.183	57	182	18	37	6	1	3	13	15	7	2	1	55	10	9	.297	.288
Soto, Jose	R-R	6-1	145	12-30-90	.035	.063	.024	24	57	6	2	0	0	0	0	4	0	0	0	14	0	0	.035	.098
Valdez, Fausto	R-R	6-2	220	5-9-88	.233	.100	.273	26	86	11	20	5	0	1	9	7	1	3	3	25	2	1	.326	.289
Valera, Smit	R-R	6-1	168	7-14-90	.218	.238	.212	56	193	14	42	2	0	0	9	11	1	2	2	37	10	7	.228	.261

Pitching

Pitching	B-T	HT	WT	DOB	W	L	ERA	G	GS	CG	SV	IP	H	R	ER	HR	BB	SO	AVG	vLH	vRH	K/9	BB/9
Brazoban, Gustavo	R-R	6-3	159	8-13-91	1	4	3.89	14	8	0	0	37	37	20	16	2	19	27	.264	.236	.282	6.57	4.62
Cabrera, Edwar	L-L	6-0	160	10-20-87	5	1	0.92	8	8	0	0	49	26	8	5	1	18	75	.158	.286	.139	13.87	3.33
Campos, Albert	R-R	6-4	222	2-4-91	0	1	1.56	15	4	0	0	35	28	18	6	0	12	27	.219	.262	.198	7.01	3.12
De Los Santos, Joel	R-R	6-2	170	5-2-90	0	1	6.46	12	0	0	0	15	15	13	11	1	15	7	.273	.238	.294	4.11	8.80
Dominguez, Felito	R-R	5-9	179	3-2-86	4	3	2.05	36	0	0	16	48	46	16	11	1	7	39	.249	.235	.254	7.26	1.30
Garcia, Joan	L-L	6-2	158	3-26-89	1	0	0.84	6	0	0	0	11	6	1	1	1	3	4	.167	.000	.207	3.38	2.53
Gonzalez, Juan	R-R	6-2	206	4-5-90	5	2	2.30	13	13	1	0	78	58	26	20	1	10	53	.207	.218	.200	6.09	1.15
Gonzalez, Nelson	R-R	6-1	168	2-15-90	4	6	3.05	16	7	0	0	62	51	27	21	3	9	54	.223	.191	.244	7.84	1.31
Hernandez, Jefri	R-R	6-1	170	4-27-91	1	1	4.37	15	4	0	0	35	32	24	17	1	10	22	.239	.154	.293	5.66	2.57
Mayo, Vianney	R-R	6-2	165	4-6-90	2	4	6.69	15	4	0	0	38	35	31	28	1	21	44	.245	.265	.239	10.51	5.02
Mendez, Luis	R-R	6-1	165	11-12-89	0	0	10.66	10	0	0	0	13	14	16	15	0	11	9	.264	.167	.293	6.39	7.82
Morillo, Scarly	R-R	6-1	175	6-17-89	0	1	1.80	5	1	0	0	5	4	9	1	0	5	3	.182	.000	.211	5.40	9.00
Pacheco, Anthony	R-R	6-1	160	10-6-89	2	4	4.42	20	4	0	0	37	36	24	18	2	14	27	.254	.216	.275	6.63	3.44
Sacramento, Lowin	R-R	6-6	203	9-4-87	1	1	3.22	14	0	0	0	22	30	11	8	1	9	12	.323	.433	.270	4.84	3.63
Sanchez, Danny	R-R	6-2	173	12-28-89	0	0	7.71	11	0	0	0	16	24	18	14	0	8	5	.338	.389	.321	2.76	4.41
Sanchez, Miguel	R-R	6-2	190	6-12-90	2	0	0.83	19	3	0	0	43	18	14	4	0	16	30	.122	.135	.116	6.23	3.32
Santana, Argenis	R-R	6-1	190	11-14-90	2	3	4.60	16	4	0	0	31	29	26	16	1	23	24	.232	.238	.229	6.89	6.61
Suarez, Rafael	R-R	6-0	200	5-14-89	1	3	8.44	5	4	0	0	16	19	19	15	1	8	23	.279	.400	.245	12.94	4.50
Vargas, Jonathan	L-L	6-2	150	5-29-89	1	2	1.71	7	6	0	0	26	16	10	5	0	15	30	.172	.000	.184	10.25	5.13

Fielding

Catcher	PCT	G	PO	A	E	DP	PB
De Jesus	.979	38	242	38	6	3	8
Fernandez	.980	20	132	14	3	0	4
Ramirez	.983	23	158	18	3	0	5

First Base	PCT	G	PO	A	E	DP
Crousset	.961	36	300	21	13	27
De Leon	.961	14	119	5	5	7
Perez	1.000	1	10	0	0	0
Valdez	.992	25	227	12	2	18

Second Base	PCT	G	PO	A	E	DP
Perez	.953	31	86	76	8	20
Reyes	.953	29	54	67	6	8
Soto	.929	4	6	7	1	2
Valera	.955	15	29	34	3	6

Third Base	PCT	G	PO	A	E	DP
De Leon	.757	24	17	36	17	5
Perez	.909	2	5	5	1	1
Reyes	.846	16	12	32	8	3
Soto	.894	17	9	33	5	1
Valera	.817	24	16	33	11	3

Shortstop	PCT	G	PO	A	E	DP
Adames	.936	49	66	152	15	23
Reyes	.806	10	23	27	12	6
Valera	.919	20	26	53	7	7

Outfield	PCT	G	PO	A	E	DP
Castillo	.920	16	22	1	2	0
Charles	.976	46	76	4	2	0
Crousset	.915	28	41	2	4	0
De La Cruz	.893	27	24	1	3	1
Ortega	.931	35	52	2	4	0
Rogers	.971	30	31	2	1	2
Sosa	.975	51	76	3	2	1

Detroit Tigers

BY JON PAUL MOROSI

When the season began, there was talk of a 1,000-run offense, 11 prior all-stars and World Series tickets. When it ended, the Tigers were in last place.

With a payroll in excess of $130 million, the Tigers became the most expensive team in baseball history to finish with a losing record.

Detroit started 0-7 and did not move above .500 until late June. In the end, Jim Leyland's team was doomed by injuries, poor performance and a balky bullpen. "This hasn't been disappointing—this has been unbelievably disappointing," Leyland said near the end of the season. "We're embarrassed, and we should be."

The flop was unforeseen, given that team president and general manager Dave Dombrowski spent the offseason upgrading a roster that won 183 games over the previous two years.

Less than 24 hours after the 2007 World Series, Dombrowski acquired veteran shortstop Edgar Renteria from the Braves for righthander Jair Jurrjens and outfielder Gorkys Hernandez.

It appeared that Renteria, who batted .332 in his final season with the Braves, would be the only significant everyday player added to the Tigers' lineup. Then they struck a blockbuster deal in which they sent six prospects to the Marlins for third baseman Miguel Cabrera and lefthander Dontrelle Willis. In between, Dombrowski acquired outfielder Jacque Jones from the Cubs.

The moves were followed by long-term contract extensions for Willis and fellow lefthander Nate Robertson. By Opening Day, the payroll was roughly $40 million higher than it had been the season before. But the results were dismal.

Jones batted .165/.244/.253 and was released in May. Renteria's diminished range weakened the defense, and he did not produce enough offensively to compensate. He hit .270, the second-lowest average of his career. Willis did not win a single game. He battled control issues that forced him to spend roughly three months in the minor leagues. He finished the year 0-2, 9.38. Robertson went 7-11, 6.35 and was dropped from the rotation in August.

Cabrera struggled in April and May before a torrid second half left him with the sort of numbers the Tigers expected: .292/.349/.537, with a league-leading 37 home runs and 127 RBIs.

PLAYERS OF THE YEAR

MAJOR LEAGUE: MIGUEL CABRERA, 1B

Traded from the Marlins before the 2008 season, Cabrera delivered for an otherwise disappointing Tigers team. He led the American League in home runs (37) and finished third in RBIs (127), while also finishing fifth in extra-base hits (75).

MINOR LEAGUE: RICK PORCELLO, RHP

A year before he was a New Jersey high schooler, but in 2008 the 19-year-old Porcello was atop the high Class A Florida State League with a 2.66 ERA. The Tigers' 2007 first-round pick was 8-6 overall with 72 strikeouts and 33 walks in 125 innings.

CLIFF WELCH

ORGANIZATION LEADERS

BATTING		*Minimum 250 at-bats
*AVG	Rhymes, Will, Erie/Toledo	.307
R	Guzman, Freddy, Erie/Toledo	101
H	Rhymes, Will, Erie/Toledo	166
TB	Hessman, Mike, Toledo	240
2B	Perez, Timo, Toledo	30
3B	Guzman, Freddy, Erie/Toledo	15
HR	Hessman, Mike, Toledo	34
RBI	Strieby, Ryan, Lakeland	94
BB	Skelton, James, Lakeland/Erie	83
SO	Laster, Jeramy, Lakeland	200
SB	Guzman, Freddy, Erie/Toledo	71
*OBP	Skelton, James, Lakeland/Erie	.456
*SLG	Hessman, Mike, Toledo	.602

PITCHING		†Minimum 75 innings
W	Kibler, Jon, West Michigan	14
L	Bazardo, Yorman, Toledo	13
	Gagnier, Lauren, Toledo/Erie/W. Mich./Lakeland	13
†ERA	Kibler, Jon, West Michigan	1.75
G	Fien, Casey, Erie/Toledo	52
GS	Three tied with	27
SV	Neal, Blaine, Toledo	26
IP	French, Lucas, Erie	170
BB	Below, Duane, Lakeland	70
SO	Below, Duane, Lakeland	126
	Gagnier, Lauren, Toledo/Erie/W. Mich./Lakeland	126
	Kibler, Jon, West Michigan	126
†AVG	Kibler, Jon, West Michigan	.190

Another bright spot was rookie pitcher Armando Galarraga, who was acquired in a low-profile trade with the Rangers prior to spring training and ended up winning 13 games. If the bullpen—a weak link all year—had pitched better behind him, Galarraga could have easily won 16 games.

2008 PERFORMANCE

General Manager: Dave Dombrowski. **Farm Director:** Dan Lunetta. **Scouting Director:** David Chadd.

Class	Team	League	W	L	PCT	Finish*	Manager	Affiliate Since
Majors	Detroit	American	74	88	.457	12th (14)	Jim Leyland	—
Triple-A	Toledo Mud Hens	International	75	69	.521	4th (14)	Larry Parrish	1987
Double-A	Erie Seawolves	Eastern	68	74	.479	8th (12)	Tom Brookens	2001
High A	Lakeland Tigers	Florida State	67	70	.489	7th (12)	Andy Barkett	1967
Low A	West Michigan Whitecaps	Midwest	72	65	.526	5th (14)	Joe DePastino	1997
Short-season	Oneonta Tigers	New York-Penn	33	31	.446	10th (14)	Ryan Newman	1999
Rookie	GCL Tigers	Gulf Coast	27	31	.466	12th (16)	Basilio Cabrera	1995
Overall 2008 Minor League Record			342	422	.448	26th		

*Finish in overall standings (No. of teams in league). ^League champion.

ORGANIZATION STATISTICS

DETROIT TIGERS

AMERICAN LEAGUE

Batting	B-T	HT	WT	DOB	AVG	vLH	vRH	G	AB	R	H	2B	3B	HR	RBI	BB	HBP	SH	SF	SO	SB	CS	SLG	OBP
Cabrera, Miguel	R-R	6-4	240	4-18-83	.292	.311	.286	160	616	85	180	36	2	37	127	56	3	0	9	126	1	0	.537	.349
Clevlen, Brent	R-R	6-2	190	10-27-83	.208	.100	.286	11	24	4	5	0	0	1	3	0	1	0	0	8	0	0	.208	.296
Granderson, Curtis	L-R	6-1	185	3-16-81	.280	.259	.288	141	553	112	155	26	13	22	66	71	3	1	1	111	12	4	.494	.365
Guillen, Carlos	B-R	6-1	215	9-30-75	.286	.287	.285	113	420	68	120	29	2	10	54	60	3	2	4	67	9	3	.436	.376
Hessman, Mike	R-R	6-5	215	3-5-78	.296	.231	.357	12	27	6	8	1	0	5	7	2	2	0	0	9	0	0	.889	.387
Hollimon, Michael	B-R	6-1	185	6-14-82	.261	.000	.273	11	23	4	6	2	1	1	2	1	0	0	1	6	0	0	.565	.280
Inge, Brandon	R-R	5-11	190	5-19-77	.205	.232	.196	113	347	41	71	16	4	11	51	43	8	5	4	94	4	3	.369	.303
Jones, Jacque	L-L	5-10	200	4-25-75	.165	.000	.173	24	79	10	13	2	1	1	5	8	1	0	2	18	0	1	.253	.244
Joyce, Matt	L-R	6-2	185	8-3-84	.252	.227	.255	92	242	40	61	16	3	12	33	31	2	0	2	65	0	2	.492	.339
Larish, Jeff	L-R	6-2	200	10-11-82	.260	.250	.260	42	104	12	27	6	0	2	16	7	0	0	0	34	2	2	.375	.306
Ordonez, Magglio	R-R	6-0	215	1-28-74	.317	.328	.314	146	561	72	178	32	2	21	103	53	3	0	6	76	1	5	.494	.376
Polanco, Placido	R-R	5-10	195	10-10-75	.307	.321	.301	141	580	90	178	34	3	8	58	35	6	4	4	43	7	1	.417	.350
Raburn, Ryan	R-R	6-0	185	4-17-81	.236	.238	.235	92	182	26	43	10	1	4	20	16	0	1	0	49	3	1	.368	.298
Renteria, Edgar	R-R	6-1	200	8-7-75	.270	.366	.239	138	503	69	136	22	2	10	55	37	0	2	5	64	6	3	.382	.317
Rodriguez, Ivan	R-R	5-9	190	11-30-71	.295	.293	.295	82	302	33	89	16	3	5	32	19	2	3	2	52	6	1	.417	.338
2-team total (33 New York)					.276	—	—	115	398	44	110	20	3	7	35	23	3	3	2	67	10	1	.394	.319
Ryan, Dusty	R-R	6-4	230	9-2-84	.318	.429	.267	15	44	6	14	2	0	2	7	5	0	0	1	13	0	0	.500	.380
Santiago, Ramon	B-R	5-11	175	8-31-79	.282	.320	.273	58	124	30	35	6	2	4	18	22	5	5	0	17	1	0	.460	.411
Sardinha, Dane	R-R	6-0	215	4-8-79	.159	.000	.189	17	44	2	7	0	1	0	3	4	0	1	0	11	0	0	.205	.229
Sheffield, Gary	R-R	6-0	215	11-18-68	.225	.239	.220	114	418	52	94	16	0	19	57	58	5	0	1	83	9	2	.400	.326
Thames, Marcus	R-R	6-2	220	3-6-77	.241	.234	.245	103	316	50	76	12	0	25	56	24	0	0	2	95	0	3	.516	.292
Thomas, Clete	L-R	5-11	195	11-14-83	.284	.368	.268	40	116	7	33	9	1	1	9	14	1	2	0	26	2	0	.405	.366

Pitching	B-T	HT	WT	DOB	W	L	ERA	G	GS	CG	SV	IP	H	R	ER	HR	BB	SO	AVG	vLH	vRH	K/9	BB/9
Bautista, Denny	R-R	6-5	190	8-23-80	0	1	3.32	16	0	0	0	19	15	7	7	1	14	10	.231	.143	.273	4.74	6.63
Bazardo, Yorman	R-R	6-2	220	7-11-84	0	0	24.00	3	0	0	3	7	8	8	0	5	3	.500	.500	.500	9.00	15.00
Beltran, Francis	R-R	6-6	255	11-29-79	1	0	4.85	11	0	0	0	13	13	7	7	3	6	9	.260	.176	.303	6.23	4.15
Bonderman, Jeremy	R-R	6-2	220	10-28-82	3	4	4.29	12	12	0	0	71	75	39	34	9	36	44	.273	.291	.255	5.55	4.54
Bonine, Eddie	R-R	6-2	220	6-6-81	2	1	5.40	5	5	0	0	27	36	19	16	3	5	9	.333	.340	.328	3.04	1.69
Cruceta, Francisco	R-R	6-2	215	7-4-81	0	1	5.40	13	0	0	0	12	13	8	7	2	10	11	.295	.350	.250	8.49	7.71
Dolsi, Freddy	R-R	6-0	160	1-9-83	1	5	3.97	42	0	0	2	48	50	21	21	3	28	29	.267	.364	.215	5.48	5.29
Farnsworth, Kyle	R-R	6-4	235	4-14-76	1	1	6.75	16	0	0	0	16	27	14	12	4	5	18	.380	.276	.452	10.13	2.81
2-team total (45 New York)					2	3	4.48	61	0	0	1	60	70	32	30	15	22	61	—	—	—	9.10	3.28
Fossum, Casey	L-L	6-1	160	1-6-78	3	1	5.66	31	0	0	0	41	44	26	26	4	18	28	.278	.243	.310	6.10	3.92
Galarraga, Armando	R-R	6-4	180	1-15-82	13	7	3.73	30	28	0	0	179	152	83	74	28	61	126	.226	.267	.174	6.35	3.07
Garcia, Freddy	R-R	6-4	240	10-6-75	1	1	4.20	3	3	0	0	15	11	8	7	3	6	12	.204	.100	.265	7.20	3.60
Glover, Gary	R-R	6-5	225	12-3-76	1	1	4.43	18	0	0	0	20	22	11	10	4	4	15	.272	.276	.269	6.64	1.77
2-team total (29 Tampa Bay)					2	3	5.30	47	0	0	0	54	64	33	32	7	22	37	—	—	—	6.13	3.64
Grilli, Jason	R-R	6-5	225	11-11-76	0	1	3.29	9	0	0	0	14	12	5	5	1	7	10	.235	.214	.243	6.59	4.61
Jones, Todd	L-R	6-3	230	4-24-68	4	4	4.97	45	0	0	18	42	50	30	23	5	18	14	.298	.289	.304	3.02	3.89
Lambert, Chris	R-R	6-1	205	3-8-83	1	2	5.66	8	3	0	0	21	31	18	13	3	7	15	.337	.372	.306	6.53	3.05
Lopez, Aquilino	R-R	6-3	185	4-21-75	4	1	3.55	48	0	0	0	79	86	33	31	9	22	61	.277	.298	.265	6.98	2.52
Miner, Zach	R-R	6-3	200	3-12-82	8	5	4.27	45	13	0	0	118	118	60	56	10	46	62	.262	.269	.256	4.73	3.51
Rapada, Clay	R-L	6-5	200	3-9-81	3	0	4.22	25	0	0	0	21	19	11	10	0	14	15	.244	.237	.250	6.33	5.91
Robertson, Nate	R-L	6-2	225	9-3-77	7	11	6.35	32	28	0	0	169	218	124	119	26	62	108	.315	.323	.311	5.76	3.31
Rodney, Fernando	R-R	5-11	220	3-18-77	0	6	4.91	38	0	0	13	40	34	22	22	3	30	49	.224	.256	.186	10.93	6.69
Rogers, Kenny	L-L	6-1	190	11-10-64	9	13	5.70	30	30	0	0	174	212	118	110	22	71	82	.309	.293	.315	4.25	3.68
Seay, Bobby	L-L	6-2	235	6-20-78	1	2	4.47	60	0	0	0	56	59	28	28	4	25	58	.278	.303	.252	9.27	3.99
Verlander, Justin	R-R	6-5	200	2-20-83	11	17	4.84	33	33	1	0	201	195	119	108	18	87	163	.254	.254	.254	7.30	3.90
Willis, Dontrelle	L-L	6-4	225	1-12-82	0	2	9.38	8	7	0	0	24	18	25	25	4	35	18	.209	.125	.242	6.75	13.13
Zumaya, Joel	R-R	6-3	210	11-9-84	0	2	3.47	21	0	0	1	23	24	13	9	3	22	22	.264	.161	.317	8.49	8.49

Fielding

Catcher	PCT	G	PO	A	E	DP	PB
Inge	1.000	60	370	33	0	4	11
Rodriguez	.992	81	447	44	4	8	4
Ryan	1.000	15	99	5	0	0	1
Sardinha	.992	17	109	8	1	1	0

First Base	PCT	G	PO	A	E	DP
Cabrera	.992	143	1117	73	9	116
Guillen	.987	24	142	11	2	22
Larish	1.000	8	41	3	0	9
Thames	1.000	9	34	1	0	10

Second Base	PCT	G	PO	A	E	DP
Hollimon	1.000	2	3	2	0	0
Polanco	.989	141	323	374	8	100
Raburn	.924	16	27	34	5	12
Santiago	1.000	21	30	36	0	13

Third Base	PCT	G	PO	A	E	DP
Cabrera	.900	14	15	30	5	4
Guillen	.949	89	68	195	14	15
Hessman	.964	12	7	20	1	3
Hollimon	1.000	2	1	0	0	0
Inge	.992	51	38	80	1	14
Larish	.931	12	10	17	2	1
Raburn	.880	18	8	14	3	1
Santiago	.714	6	2	3	2	0

Shortstop	PCT	G	PO	A	E	DP
Hollimon	.929	6	1	12	1	2

	PCT	G	PO	A	E	DP
Renteria	.972	138	197	365	16	91
Santiago	.975	33	45	70	3	15

Outfield	PCT	G	PO	A	E	DP
Clevlen	1.000	11	23	1	0	0
Granderson	.989	140	366	5	4	1
Guillen	1.000	2	6	0	0	0
Inge	1.000	13	26	2	0	0
Jones	.975	23	38	1	1	0
Joyce	.972	84	136	2	4	0
Ordonez	.979	135	220	8	5	0
Raburn	.970	57	63	2	2	0
Sheffield	1.000	6	13	0	0	0
Thames	.963	80	128	3	5	1
Thomas	.958	40	88	4	4	1

TOLEDO MUD HENS

INTERNATIONAL LEAGUE

TRIPLE-A

Batting	B-T	HT	WT	DOB	AVG	vLH	vRH	G	AB	R	H	2B	3B	HR	RBI	BB	HBP	SH	SF	SO	SB	CS	SLG	OBP
Almonte, Erick	R-R	6-2	180	2-1-78	.258	.321	.234	113	395	50	102	27	1	10	50	55	1	1	2	71	3	2	.408	.349
Casanova, Adrian	R-R	6-1	210	5-6-83	.200	—	.200	3	10	1	2	0	0	0	0	0	0	0	0	1	0	0	.200	.200
Clevlen, Brent	R-R	6-2	190	10-27-83	.279	.250	.287	126	476	75	133	23	7	22	82	54	6	1	3	166	7	2	.496	.358
Cosme, Caonabo	R-R	6-2	160	3-18-79	.353	.429	.300	5	17	3	6	1	0	2	3	1	0	0	1	5	0	0	.765	.368
Frazier, Jeff	R-R	6-3	195	8-10-82	.250	.000	.273	3	12	0	3	0	0	0	1	0	0	0	0	3	0	0	.250	.250
Granderson, Curtis	L-R	6-1	185	3-16-81	.333	.000	.429	2	9	1	3	1	0	0	0	0	0	0	0	1	0	0	.444	.333
Guzman, Freddy	B-R	5-10	165	1-20-81	.270	.305	.260	101	397	74	107	16	9	3	41	35	2	3	4	42	56	6	.378	.329
Hessman, Mike	R-R	6-5	215	3-5-78	.271	.221	.284	108	399	83	108	20	5	34	72	59	10	0	5	140	3	4	.602	.374
Hollimon, Michael	B-R	6-1	185	6-14-82	.211	.160	.228	91	331	56	70	16	4	15	33	45	2	3	4	109	7	3	.420	.306
Inge, Brandon	R-R	5-11	190	5-19-77	.300	.000	.375	3	10	2	3	0	0	1	4	2	0	0	0	2	0	0	.600	.417
Joyce, Matt	L-R	6-2	185	8-3-84	.270	.217	.286	56	200	36	54	13	2	13	41	24	2	0	1	62	2	3	.550	.352
Kirkland, Kody	R-R	6-4	200	6-9-83	.229	.214	.233	34	118	15	27	7	2	3	9	12	1	0	1	39	4	1	.398	.303
Larish, Jeff	L-R	6-2	200	10-11-82	.250	.243	.253	103	384	49	96	20	2	21	64	50	4	0	2	109	0	1	.477	.341
Leon, Maxwell	B-R	5-11	190	6-27-84	.275	.243	.286	50	149	16	41	2	2	0	12	17	0	4	2	33	8	2	.315	.345
Mateo, Henry	B-R	6-0	175	10-14-76	.228	.158	.263	13	57	5	13	4	0	1	3	0	1	2	0	9	1	0	.351	.241
Melian, Jackson	R-R	6-2	205	1-7-80	.227	.294	.192	45	150	16	34	8	0	4	16	7	0	2	0	27	3	2	.360	.261
Perez, Timo	L-L	5-9	180	4-8-75	.302	.319	.297	112	427	56	129	30	2	13	63	48	4	4	5	43	19	6	.473	.374
Raburn, Ryan	R-R	6-0	185	4-17-81	.316	.250	.333	5	19	6	6	2	0	2	6	4	0	0	0	5	0	0	.737	.435
Ramirez, Wilkin	R-R	6-2	190	10-25-85	.083	.000	.107	11	36	2	3	1	0	0	0	1	1	0	0	11	1	0	.111	.132
Rhymes, William	L-R	5-9	155	4-1-83	.320	1.000	.292	6	25	5	8	0	1	0	2	2	0	0	0	4	0	0	.400	.370
Roberson, Ryan	R-R	6-5	240	8-1-83	.240	.000	.240	7	25	2	6	2	0	0	1	0	0	0	0	7	0	0	.320	.240
Ryan, Dusty	R-R	6-4	220	9-24-84	.315	.400	.293	20	73	12	23	7	2	2	13	6	1	0	1	27	0	0	.548	.370
Santiago, Ramon	B-R	5-11	175	8-31-79	.214	.000	.240	8	28	3	6	2	0	0	3	2	2	1	0	7	0	0	.286	.313
Sardinha, Dane	R-R	6-0	215	4-8-79	.202	.289	.179	54	183	19	37	9	0	6	18	8	1	4	1	59	1	0	.350	.248
Seguignol, Fernando	B-R	6-5	257	1-19-75	.286	.320	.271	24	84	13	24	4	1	3	15	10	1	0	0	23	0	0	.464	.368
St. Pierre, Max	R-R	6-0	175	4-17-80	.213	.211	.214	42	150	10	32	4	0	2	16	4	0	4	1	21	0	0	.280	.232
Thomas, Clete	L-R	5-11	195	11-14-83	.247	.220	.258	76	291	44	72	18	2	9	45	37	1	3	1	88	29	11	.416	.333
Trzesniak, Nick	R-R	6-0	210	11-19-80	.224	.250	.213	32	107	8	24	5	0	3	16	4	2	2	1	38	0	0	.355	.263
Wathan, Derek	B-R	6-3	190	12-13-76	.212	.173	.221	81	283	28	60	6	3	3	27	11	1	6	1	54	8	4	.286	.243
Worth, Danny	R-R	6-1	185	9-30-85	.500	—	.500	1	2	0	1	0	0	0	0	0	0	0	0	0	0	0	.500	.500

Pitching	B-T	HT	WT	DOB	W	L	ERA	G	GS	CG	SV	IP	H	R	ER	HR	BB	SO	AVG	vLH	vRH	K/9	BB/9
Bautista, Denny	R-R	6-5	190	8-23-80	0	1	0.00	5	0	0	0	6	2	1	0	0	3	7	.095	.111	.083	9.95	4.26
Bazardo, Yorman	R-R	6-2	220	7-11-84	4	13	6.72	25	22	0	0	130	177	100	97	19	44	75	.340	.357	.325	5.19	3.05
Beltran, Francis	R-R	6-6	255	11-29-79	3	5	4.70	37	0	0	3	44	44	24	23	5	11	38	.257	.257	.258	7.77	2.25
Bonine, Eddie	R-R	6-5	220	6-6-81	12	4	4.15	17	17	1	0	106	107	53	49	10	18	69	.262	.272	.252	5.84	1.52
Connolly, Jon	R-L	6-0	205	8-24-83	0	3	5.06	4	4	0	0	21	26	15	12	2	7	12	.292	.333	.277	5.06	2.95
Cruceta, Francisco	R-R	6-2	215	7-4-81	2	3	4.22	32	0	0	3	43	39	21	20	0	24	61	.247	.233	.259	12.87	5.06
Dolsi, Freddy	R-R	6-0	160	1-9-83	0	0	1.00	4	0	0	1	9	5	1	1	0	3	7	.167	.133	.200	7.00	3.00
Fien, Casey	R-R	6-2	195	10-21-83	2	0	2.40	12	0	0	1	15	14	4	4	2	4	17	.246	.214	.276	10.20	2.40
Fossum, Casey	L-L	6-1	160	1-6-78	3	0	1.96	11	4	0	0	46	21	11	10	4	19	48	.138	.118	.149	9.39	3.72
Fultz, Aaron	L-L	6-0	210	9-4-73	0	1	1.59	4	0	0	0	6	1	1	1	0	4	4	.304	.125	.400	6.35	6.35
Gagnier, Lauren	R-R	6-2	210	2-28-85	3	5	5.66	7	7	0	0	35	38	24	22	3	22	32	.286	.294	.277	8.23	5.66
Galarraga, Armando	R-R	6-4	180	1-15-82	2	0	2.25	2	2	0	0	12	7	3	3	1	1	11	.163	.217	.100	8.25	0.75
Garcia, Freddy	R-R	6-4	240	10-6-75	0	0	0.00	1	1	0	0	3	2	0	0	0	0	4	.200	.000	.400	12.00	0.00
Glover, Gary	R-R	6-5	225	12-3-76	0	0	0.00	3	0	0	1	4	3	0	0	0	0	4	.214	.286	.143	9.00	0.00
Johnson, Jeremy	R-R	6-3	170	7-19-82	5	3	4.96	23	10	0	1	82	100	50	45	9	29	59	.294	.292	.297	6.50	3.20
Lambert, Chris	R-R	6-1	205	3-8-83	12	8	3.50	26	26	3	0	149	143	69	58	7	48	124	.253	.241	.264	7.47	2.89
Larrison, Preston	R-R	6-4	235	11-19-80	2	2	3.31	29	0	0	0	35	29	14	13	3	15	19	.240	.277	.216	4.84	3.82
2-team total (19 Buffalo)					3	4	3.43	48	0	0	1	60	60	25	23	4	21	41	—	—		6.12	3.13
Lopez, Aquilino	R-R	6-3	185	4-21-75	0	0	2.45	3	2	0	0	11	5	3	3	1	0	14	.132	.222	.050	11.45	0.00
Martinez, Anastacio	R-R	6-2	180	11-3-78	2	7	5.29	32	13	0	1	97	112	71	57	13	45	71	.292	.298	.286	6.59	4.18
McBride, Macay	L-L	5-11	210	10-24-82	0	0	0.00	1	1	0	0	1	1	0	0	0	0	0	.000	.250		0.00	0.00
Miner, Zach	R-R	6-3	200	3-12-82	0	1	3.38	4	2	0	0	11	11	4	4	0	3	15	.268	.231	.286	12.66	2.53
Neal, Blaine	L-R	6-5	240	4-6-78	1	0	1.21	38	0	0	26	37	29	8	5	3	12	39	.207	.219	.197	9.40	2.89

ORGANIZATION STATISTICS

					W	L	ERA	G	GS	CG	SV	IP	H	R	ER	HR	BB	SO	AVG	vLH	vRH	K/9	BB/9
Ostlund, Ian	R-L	6-1	200	10-17-78	3	0	2.45	44	0	0	0	70	62	19	19	6	17	77	.234	.255	.221	9.95	2.20
Rapada, Clay	R-L	6-5	200	3-9-81	0	1	2.31	28	0	0	2	35	32	10	9	2	14	45	.244	.207	.274	11.57	3.60
Righter, Matthew	R-R	6-5	195	8-7-81	0	0	6.75	2	0	0	0	3	6	2	2	0	1	0	.500	.429	.600	0.00	3.38
Rodney, Fernando	R-R	5-11	220	3-18-77	1	0	6.75	4	0	0	0	5	3	4	4	1	5	8	.158	.167	.154	13.50	8.44
Rogers, Brian	R-R	6-4	190	7-17-82	0	1	7.65	16	0	0	0	20	28	20	17	3	12	25	.333	.324	.340	11.25	5.40
2-team total (10 Indianapolis)					0	2	4.98	26	0	0	0	34	42	27	19	4	16	38	—	—	—	9.96	4.19
Rusch, Matt	R-R	5-11	180	5-20-83	3	0	4.24	26	0	0	0	40	44	20	19	7	13	33	.277	.284	.272	7.36	2.90
Vasquez, Virgil	R-R	6-3	205	6-7-82	12	12	4.81	27	27	2	0	159	179	91	85	27	37	115	.283	.287	.279	6.51	2.09
Willis, Dontrelle	L-L	6-4	225	1-12-82	3	1	4.45	6	6	0	0	28	34	16	14	2	14	20	.298	.227	.343	6.35	4.45
Zumaya, Joel	R-R	6-3	210	11-9-84	0	0	2.25	4	0	0	0	4	5	3	1	0	2	4	.278	.300	.250	9.00	4.50

Fielding

Catcher	PCT	G	PO	A	E	DP	PB
Casanova	1.000	3	25	4	0	0	0
Inge	1.000	2	7	1	0	0	1
Ryan	.993	17	124	12	1	2	2
Sardinha	.986	53	378	32	6	6	2
St. Pierre	.994	42	329	31	2	3	7
Trzesniak	1.000	32	227	23	0	4	2

First Base	PCT	G	PO	A	E	DP
Almonte	.920	3	20	3	2	3
Kirkland	.988	10	75	9	1	7
Larish	.992	95	816	70	7	76
Roberson	.980	6	45	4	1	2
Sardinha	—	1	0	0	0	0
Seguignol	.972	14	97	6	3	10
Wathan	.989	21	176	11	2	15

Second Base	PCT	G	PO	A	E	DP
Almonte	.975	28	49	68	3	16

	PCT	G	PO	A	E	DP
Cosme	.941	3	6	10	1	5
Hollimon	.978	75	129	183	7	44
Leon	1.000	6	7	18	0	4
Mateo	.962	12	20	31	2	2
Rhymes	1.000	6	10	14	0	2
Wathan	.972	18	31	39	2	6

Third Base	PCT	G	PO	A	E	DP
Almonte	1.000	12	7	25	0	4
Hessman	.982	104	81	189	5	16
Inge	1.000	1	0	1	0	0
Kirkland	.926	23	16	47	5	4
Larish	.900	9	6	12	2	2
Leon	1.000	1	0	1	0	0

Shortstop	PCT	G	PO	A	E	DP
Almonte	.973	51	60	156	6	32
Hessman	.875	5	2	12	2	3
Hollimon	.911	14	10	31	4	4

	PCT	G	PO	A	E	DP
Leon	.954	38	54	91	7	17
Santiago	.971	8	15	19	1	9
Wathan	.956	35	59	114	8	19
Worth	1.000	1	0	1	0	0

Outfield	PCT	G	PO	A	E	DP
Clevlen	.967	119	227	9	8	1
Frazier	1.000	3	6	0	0	0
Granderson	1.000	2	2	0	0	0
Guzman	1.000	74	126	6	0	1
Joyce	1.000	54	114	6	0	0
Leon	1.000	3	6	0	0	0
Melian	.984	31	56	6	1	2
Perez	.979	59	89	6	2	1
Raburn	1.000	5	12	0	0	0
Ramirez	.875	10	7	0	1	0
Thomas	.974	74	177	9	5	1
Wathan	1.000	4	8	0	0	0

ERIE SEAWOLVES   DOUBLE-A

EASTERN LEAGUE

Batting	B-T	HT	WT	DOB	AVG	vLH	vRH	G	AB	R	H	2B	3B	HR	RBI	BB	HBP	SH	SF	SO	SB	CS	SLG	OBP
Casanova, Adrian	R-R	6-1	210	5-6-83	.250	.143	.308	7	20	1	5	0	0	0	0	0	0	1	0	7	0	0	.250	.250
Cosme, Caonabo	R-R	6-2	160	3-18-79	.248	.156	.283	47	165	20	41	4	1	2	12	7	0	2	0	49	0	0	.321	.279
Cotto, Pedro	L-L	5-11	175	5-26-82	.255	.190	.270	36	110	10	28	4	2	2	16	8	3	1	0	17	0	3	.382	.322
De Leon, Santo	R-R	6-2	175	11-1-83	.278	.239	.293	44	169	25	47	11	1	7	25	7	0	1	1	27	1	1	.479	.305
Douglas, Brandon	R-R	6-0	185	8-27-85	.263	.500	.235	5	19	2	5	0	0	1	2	0	0	0	0	2	1	1	.421	.263
Flores, Angel	R-R	6-0	200	8-16-86	.000	—	.000	2	1	0	0	0	0	0	0	0	0	0	0	0	0	0	.000	.000
Frazier, Jeff	R-R	6-3	195	8-10-82	.303	.291	.307	116	446	55	135	22	1	6	55	31	3	1	3	51	1	1	.397	.350
Guzman, Freddy	B-R	5-10	165	1-20-81	.281	.273	.283	30	121	27	34	2	6	2	19	16	1	1	3	14	15	5	.446	.362
Justice, Justin	L-L	6-0	180	2-19-85	.153	.120	.159	48	157	15	24	5	1	3	16	14	1	1	2	41	1	1	.255	.224
Kirkland, Kody	R-R	6-4	200	6-9-83	.244	.309	.221	78	258	33	63	7	4	7	40	29	7	5	6	80	5	1	.384	.330
Kunkel, Jeffrey	B-R	5-11	190	3-11-83	.192	.125	.222	16	52	3	10	3	0	1	5	2	0	0	1	18	0	0	.308	.218
Leon, Maxwell	B-R	5-11	190	6-27-84	.313	.250	.330	44	147	24	46	5	1	0	17	30	2	1	2	41	8	5	.361	.431
McIntyre, Nick	B-R	5-11	185	3-11-81	.182	.000	.235	9	22	3	4	1	0	0	0	2	0	1	0	3	1	0	.227	.250
Ott, Louis	R-R	6-0	185	2-22-85	.238	.500	.000	7	21	0	5	1	0	0	1	3	0	0	0	7	0	0	.286	.333
Ramirez, Wilkin	R-R	6-2	190	10-25-85	.303	.298	.304	110	433	74	131	24	7	19	73	43	5	0	1	138	26	12	.522	.371
Rhymes, William	L-R	5-9	155	4-1-83	.306	.351	.291	131	516	76	158	21	7	3	60	44	3	10	3	66	17	6	.391	.362
Roberson, Ryan	R-R	6-5	240	8-1-83	.289	.308	.282	117	440	75	127	19	1	25	86	34	7	0	4	120	7	4	.507	.346
Roof, Shawn	R-R	5-10	175	8-3-84	.234	.257	.225	42	124	15	29	3	0	0	8	11	4	4	1	23	1	0	.258	.314
Ryan, Dusty	R-R	6-4	220	9-24-84	.253	.262	.250	82	296	46	75	17	2	15	50	38	2	0	2	95	2	1	.476	.340
Scram, Deik	L-R	6-2	180	2-1-84	.253	.218	.264	131	482	70	122	24	4	13	69	57	5	2	6	127	14	3	.400	.335
Skelton, James	L-R	5-11	165	10-28-85	.294	.391	.258	24	85	22	25	2	0	2	11	19	1	0	1	23	1	1	.388	.425
St. Pierre, Max	R-R	6-0	175	4-17-80	.250	.229	.256	44	156	22	39	9	0	6	31	16	3	0	0	23	0	1	.423	.331
Tucker, Joseph	R-R	5-11	170	1-25-84	.167	.167	.167	9	18	4	3	0	0	1	2	0	0	0	0	5	0	0	.333	.167
Wells, Casper	R-R	6-2	210	11-23-84	.289	.262	.301	75	270	60	78	18	6	17	53	30	9	2	2	66	8	3	.589	.376
Worth, Danny	R-R	6-1	185	9-30-85	.254	.253	.255	79	295	44	75	18	3	5	33	32	3	4	2	59	8	0	.386	.331

Pitching	B-T	HT	WT	DOB	W	L	ERA	G	GS	CG	SV	IP	H	R	ER	HR	BB	SO	AVG	vLH	vRH	K/9	BB/9
Bonine, Eddie	R-R	6-5	220	6-6-81	0	1	2.45	1	1	0	0	4	4	2	1	0	2	1	.286	.250	.300	2.45	4.91
Castro, Angel	R-R	5-11	200	11-14-82	2	2	3.30	26	0	0	2	44	31	19	16	3	19	33	.203	.169	.223	6.80	3.92
Cedeno, Juan	L-L	6-1	165	8-19-83	3	2	4.64	28	4	0	1	54	57	29	28	2	26	26	.277	.254	.289	4.31	4.31
Christensen, Daniel	L-L	6-1	210	8-10-83	7	10	4.14	27	27	2	0	159	169	90	73	17	58	98	.275	.274	.275	5.56	3.29
Connolly, Jon	R-L	6-0	205	8-24-83	0	5	6.50	8	8	0	0	46	63	40	33	6	15	16	.330	.367	.317	3.15	2.96
Darrow, Rudy	R-R	5-10	180	2-11-84	1	1	2.63	14	0	0	6	14	13	7	4	0	8	14	.241	.346	.143	9.22	5.27
Dolsi, Freddy	R-R	6-0	160	1-9-83	0	0	0.00	3	0	0	2	3	1	0	0	0	1	1	.111	.200	.000	3.00	3.00
Drucker, Scot	R-R	6-1	192	5-30-82	0	0	3.75	9	0	0	0	12	11	5	5	0	6	7	.244	.333	.200	5.25	4.50
Fien, Casey	R-R	6-2	195	10-21-83	3	3	2.96	40	0	0	12	46	38	16	15	5	12	42	.226	.246	.215	8.28	2.36
French, Lucas	L-L	6-4	220	9-3-85	9	11	4.02	27	26	3	0	170	195	92	76	16	60	88	.292	.313	.285	4.66	3.18
Fritz, Ben	R-R	6-4	238	3-29-81	3	5	6.40	18	14	0	0	84	116	69	60	13	29	45	.325	.301	.345	4.80	3.09
Gagnier, Lauren	R-R	6-2	210	2-28-85	2	2	12.91	4	4	0	0	15	25	23	22	3	8	9	.362	.229	.500	5.28	4.70
Jensen, Brett	R-R	6-7	190	11-29-83	1	0	4.00	10	0	0	1	9	10	4	4	1	1	6	.286	.267	.300	6.00	1.00
Kite, Josh	L-L	6-2	190	3-2-82	3	0	0.75	9	0	0	2	12	5	1	1	0	7	11	.135	.000	.185	8.25	5.25

Name	B-T	HT	WT	DOB	W	L	ERA	G	GS	CG	SV	IP	H	R	ER	HR	BB	SO	AVG	vLH	vRH	K/9	BB/9
Kown, Andrew	L-R	6-7	210	10-7-82	5	9	5.38	17	16	1	0	94	111	62	56	16	34	42	.295	.280	.307	4.04	3.27
2-team total (2 Harrisburg)					5	9	6.00	19	16	1	0	96	119	70	64	18	37	43	—	—	—	4.03	3.47
Marte, Luis	R-R	5-11	170	8-26-86	4	4	5.05	10	10	0	0	57	57	35	32	8	26	32	.264	.242	.280	5.05	4.11
Martinez, Anastacio	R-R	6-2	180	11-3-78	0	0	0.00	3	0	0	0	2	1	0	0	0	1	1	.111	.167	.000	3.86	3.86
Moscoso, Guillermo	R-R	6-1	160	11-14-83	3	1	3.12	6	6	0	0	35	24	17	12	4	8	50	.196	.187		12.98	2.08
Perez, Marcelo	R-R	6-0	200	10-10-80	1	1	5.90	30	0	0	2	40	48	29	26	8	25	27	.293	.268	.306	6.13	5.67
Rainwater, Josh	R-R	6-1	220	4-9-85	10	7	4.09	24	23	0	0	132	135	75	60	7	64	78	.271	.320	.238	5.32	4.36
Righter, Matthew	R-R	6-5	195	8-7-81	1	1	5.51	16	3	0	0	33	32	23	20	4	22	9	.254	.286	.234	2.48	6.06
Rusch, Matt	R-R	5-11	180	5-20-83	1	1	5.45	22	0	0	1	33	39	21	20	5	8	30	.291	.250	.311	8.18	2.18
Tomey, Anthony	R-R	6-4	245	8-17-81	3	4	4.93	23	0	0	0	35	34	20	19	3	21	39	.264	.313	.235	10.13	5.45
Wise, Brendan	L-R	6-2	190	1-9-86	2	1	3.30	30	0	0	3	44	43	18	16	4	14	20	.267	.298	.250	4.12	2.89
Witt, Derek	R-R	6-1	180	12-31-83	0	0	0.00	1	0	0	0	1	1	0	0	0	0	1	.250	.000	.333	9.00	0.00
Zell, Danny	L-L	6-5	210	11-27-81	4	2	4.74	47	0	0	1	49	58	31	26	5	14	37	.294	.260	.317	6.75	2.55

Fielding

Catcher	PCT	G	PO	A	E	DP	PB
Casanova	.977	7	38	5	1	1	2
Flores	1.000	2	2	0	0	0	0
Kunkel	.989	15	88	2	1	0	1
Ott	1.000	1	1	0	0	0	0
Ryan	.984	66	338	41	6	7	11
Skelton	.977	23	154	16	4	4	5
St. Pierre	.980	36	160	32	4	3	1

First Base	PCT	G	PO	A	E	DP
Cosme	.991	13	102	11	1	11
Cotto	1.000	6	51	1	0	8
Leon	.966	8	50	6	2	6
McIntyre	1.000	1	2	0	0	0
Roberson	.988	111	973	59	13	126
Ryan	.984	7	59	2	1	5
Tucker	1.000	2	7	2	0	1

Second Base	PCT	G	PO	A	E	DP
Cosme	.974	16	29	46	2	15

	PCT	G	PO	A	E	DP
Leon	.969	6	18	13	1	8
McIntyre	1.000	2	2	7	0	1
Ott	1.000	1	3	3	0	0
Rhymes	.972	113	236	310	16	86
Roof	.937	12	34	40	5	10

Third Base	PCT	G	PO	A	E	DP
Cosme	.778	4	1	6	2	1
De Leon	.933	44	35	105	10	11
Kirkland	.929	73	56	181	18	18
Leon	.946	16	20	33	3	5
McIntyre	.833	2	1	4	1	0
Ott	1.000	1	1	3	0	0
Ramirez	1.000	2	1	13	0	1
Rhymes	1.000	1	0	3	0	1

Shortstop	PCT	G	PO	A	E	DP
Cosme	.933	13	18	38	4	11
Douglas	.970	5	10	22	1	8
Kirkland	1.000	1	2	3	0	1

	PCT	G	PO	A	E	DP
Leon	.800	1	1	3	1	0
McIntyre	.857	1	2	4	1	1
Rhymes	.926	16	18	32	4	12
Roof	.952	30	44	76	6	17
Worth	.955	79	141	241	18	65

Outfield	PCT	G	PO	A	E	DP
Cotto	.947	18	36	0	2	0
Frazier	.930	34	52	1	4	0
Guzman	.974	26	75	1	2	0
Justice	.981	43	102	3	2	1
Leon	1.000	10	18	2	0	0
Ott	1.000	3	3	1	0	0
Ramirez	.979	101	181	7	4	0
Scram	.970	122	280	12	9	3
Tucker	1.000	4	13	0	0	0
Wells	.961	74	163	11	7	2

LAKELAND FLYING TIGERS

HIGH CLASS A

FLORIDA STATE LEAGUE

Batting	B-T	HT	WT	DOB	AVG	vLH	vRH	G	AB	R	H	2B	3B	HR	RBI	BB	HBP	SH	SF	SO	SB	CS	SLG	OBP
Bertram, Michael	L-R	6-2	220	2-25-84	.285	.261	.296	102	372	51	106	21	4	8	55	27	6	0	4	69	2	2	.427	.340
Boesch, Brennan	L-L	6-6	210	4-12-85	.249	.192	.269	111	417	46	104	17	8	7	64	36	3	0	5	90	3	5	.379	.310
Casanova, Adrian	R-R	6-1	210	5-6-83	.167	.500	.125	5	18	0	3	0	0	0	2	0	0	0	0	3	0	0	.167	.167
Cotto, Pedro	L-L	5-11	175	5-26-82	.185	.217	.179	40	130	13	24	4	1	3	10	11	2	2	2	15	1	1	.300	.255
De Leon, Santo	R-R	6-2	175	11-1-83	.291	.302	.289	46	179	19	52	11	0	4	18	4	0	0	1	30	2	0	.419	.304
Frost, Adam	R-R	5-11	165	10-13-86	.241	.250	.235	9	29	6	7	2	1	2	4	2	1	0	0	4	0	1	.586	.313
Guzman, Joaquin	B-R	6-0	170	9-22-86	.000	—	—	1	0	0	0	0	0	0	0	0	0	0	0	0	0	0	.000	.000
Iorg, Cale	R-R	6-2	190	9-6-85	.251	.267	.248	99	383	61	96	15	7	10	47	35	11	0	2	111	22	11	.405	.329
Jaime, Carmelo	B-R	5-9	170	7-16-85	.195	.176	.207	37	128	12	25	2	0	0	8	15	0	2	1	29	1	6	.211	.278
Justice, Justin	L-L	6-0	180	2-19-85	.298	.246	.306	76	282	46	84	18	5	10	37	29	1	0	1	77	3	9	.504	.364
Kunkel, Jeffrey	B-R	5-11	200	3-11-83	.237	.275	.221	53	173	14	41	8	0	1	21	12	2	2	3	30	1	1	.301	.289
Laster, Jeramy	R-R	6-1	185	4-5-85	.204	.213	.197	129	481	68	98	22	4	24	64	40	4	1	5	200	11	10	.416	.268
Lennerton, Jordan	L-L	6-2	230	2-16-86	.179	.083	.205	18	56	9	10	2	0	1	8	14	0	0	1	18	0	0	.268	.338
Nunez, Gustavo	B-R	5-10	148	2-8-88	.245	.308	.222	45	147	14	36	4	0	0	15	11	2	3	1	29	1	3	.272	.304
Ott, Louis	B-R	6-0	185	2-22-85	.255	.203	.273	93	322	42	82	10	3	2	29	46	2	7	2	76	5	5	.323	.349
Roof, Shawn	R-R	5-10	175	8-3-84	.261	.244	.269	48	153	21	40	8	0	0	16	20	5	4	0	26	3	5	.314	.365
Salas, Luis	R-R	6-0	172	1-2-89	.267	.250	.273	6	15	0	4	1	1	0	4	4	0	0	0	5	1	1	.467	.421
Sheffield, Gary	R-R	6-0	215	11-18-68	.154	.000	.182	5	13	7	2	0	0	2	2	6	0	0	0	1	0	0	.615	.421
Sizemore, Scott	R-R	6-0	185	1-4-85	.286	.344	.261	53	203	32	58	11	1	4	20	24	3	1	3	44	14	3	.409	.365
Skelton, James	L-R	5-11	165	10-28-85	.307	.275	.314	63	212	43	65	8	2	3	23	64	1	4	1	50	14	5	.406	.468
Strieby, Ryan	R-R	6-5	235	8-9-85	.278	.255	.287	112	421	65	117	19	7	29	94	46	5	1	5	101	0	1	.563	.352
Thomas, Devin	B-R	5-11	195	2-22-85	.171	.233	.153	41	117	17	20	2	1	3	11	16	3	1	0	37	4	2	.282	.287
Timm, Brandon	R-R	6-2	200	12-4-84	.239	.280	.224	93	314	36	75	7	4	4	30	36	2	4	1	94	12	5	.325	.320

Pitching	B-T	HT	WT	DOB	W	L	ERA	G	GS	CG	SV	IP	H	R	ER	HR	BB	SO	AVG	vLH	vRH	K/9	BB/9
Below, Duane	L-L	6-2	205	11-15-85	8	7	4.45	27	26	0	0	133	144	75	66	10	70	126	.280	.273	.282	8.50	4.72
Benitez, Gabriel	R-R	6-5	165	3-1-83	0	1	3.75	7	1	0	0	12	8	5	5	2	10	6	.195	.176	.208	4.50	7.50
Brackman, Mark	R-R	6-7	230	3-23-85	0	3	10.50	6	1	0	0	12	23	15	14	2	6	5	.411	.313	.450	3.75	4.50
Castro, Angel	R-R	5-11	200	11-14-82	2	1	2.80	21	0	0	5	35	39	12	11	1	11	19	.293	.333	.268	4.84	2.80
Cedeno, Juan	L-L	6-1	165	8-19-83	0	0	4.00	6	0	0	5	5	1	1	0	1	4	.208	.167	.222	5.68	1.42	
Clelland, Ed	L-L	6-0	165	6-27-82	1	0	4.70	13	0	0	2	15	21	8	8	2	5	11	.344	.200	.415	6.46	2.93
Dolsi, Freddy	R-R	6-0	160	1-9-83	0	1	6.14	9	0	0	5	7	7	5	5	1	3	11	.241	.308	.188	13.50	3.68
Figaro, Alfredo	R-R	6-0	173	7-7-84	0	5	4.91	6	5	1	0	29	37	22	16	2	12	23	.311	.278	.338	7.06	3.68
Gagnier, Lauren	R-R	6-2	210	2-28-85	0	0	3.86	2	2	0	0	12	10	7	5	1	4	6	.227	.118	.296	4.63	3.09
Garcia, Freddy	R-R	6-4	240	10-6-75	0	0	0.00	1	1	0	0	2	3	0	0	0	1	1	.375	.000	.750	4.50	4.50
Garcia, Ramon	L-R	6-2	165	10-30-84	4	4	4.57	30	6	0	1	83	99	56	42	11	24	56	.289	.382	.257	6.10	2.61
Marte, Luis	R-R	5-11	170	8-26-86	3	2	1.98	7	7	0	0	41	29	11	9	1	11	41	.196	.192	.200	9.00	2.41

Martin, Nick	L-L	6-3	190	3-5-80	2	3	4.06	33	0	0	1	38	38	18	17	5	22	28	.260	.226	.286	6.69	5.26
Mieses, Santo	R-R	5-11	185	4-15-85	0	0	7.20	3	0	0	0	5	7	5	4	0	7	3	.318	.222	.385	5.40	12.60
Moscoso, Guillermo	R-R	6-1	160	11-14-83	2	3	2.42	15	6	0	1	52	36	16	14	4	13	72	.196	.242	.169	12.46	2.25
Nickerson, Jonah	R-R	6-1	200	3-9-85	12	4	3.99	27	26	1	1	147	138	82	65	13	43	114	.246	.239	.251	7.00	2.64
O'Brien, Matt	R-R	6-3	215	8-10-82	5	8	4.95	21	18	1	0	107	128	71	59	12	22	46	.298	.308	.292	3.86	1.84
Oliveros, Lester	R-R	5-11	178	5-28-88	1	1	4.22	5	0	0	0	11	12	8	5	0	9	3	.293	.333	.276	2.53	7.59
Pearson, Kyle	R-R	6-1	200	10-8-84	1	1	6.52	7	0	0	0	10	14	10	7	1	5	4	.326	.300	.333	3.72	4.66
Perry, Ryan	R-R	6-4	200	2-13-87	1	2	3.86	12	0	0	4	12	15	6	5	0	7	12	.300	.421	.226	9.26	5.40
Porcello, Rick	R-R	6-5	200	12-27-88	8	6	2.66	24	24	0	0	125	116	51	37	7	33	72	.244	.230	.253	5.18	2.38
Satterwhite, Cody	R-R	6-4	205	1-27-87	0	0	4.42	17	0	0	2	18	16	10	9	0	12	22	.232	.115	.302	10.80	5.89
Sborz, Jay	R-R	6-4	210	1-24-85	3	2	2.87	40	0	0	7	53	44	22	17	3	25	48	.223	.200	.236	8.10	4.22
Simons, Zach	L-R	6-3	200	5-23-85	5	2	2.36	39	0	0	2	53	29	15	14	2	30	61	.166	.109	.192	10.29	5.06
Tata, Jordan	R-R	6-6	220	9-20-81	1	3	9.67	11	6	0	0	27	28	32	29	5	26	20	.283	.275	.288	6.67	8.67
Weinhardt, Robbie	R-R	6-2	205	12-8-85	3	1	2.04	21	0	0	4	35	19	11	8	1	11	44	.162	.136	.178	11.21	2.80
Willis, Dontrelle	L-L	6-4	225	1-12-82	0	3	4.50	6	5	0	0	28	30	15	14	2	11	18	.278	.212	.307	5.79	3.54
Wise, Brendan	L-R	6-2	190	1-9-86	1	3	4.64	18	0	0	1	21	24	12	11	0	11	9	.300	.333	.283	3.80	4.64
Witt, Derek	R-R	6-1	180	12-31-83	4	4	3.53	45	3	0	0	71	72	33	28	0	34	44	.261	.320	.229	5.55	4.29
Zumaya, Joel	R-R	6-3	210	11-9-84	0	0	0.00	2	0	0	0	3	1	0	0	0	1	2	.100	.250	.000	6.00	3.00

Fielding

Catcher	PCT	G	PO	A	E	DP	PB
Casanova	.976	4	38	3	1	0	1
Kunkel	.992	53	350	32	3	3	8
Ott	1.000	1	1	0	0	0	
Skelton	.987	54	361	31	5	1	7
Thomas	.957	31	193	7	9	3	5

First Base	PCT	G	PO	A	E	DP
Bertram	.996	28	245	15	1	22
Cotto	.875	1	7	0	1	1
Lennerton	.987	18	141	10	2	20
Strieby	.992	92	801	67	7	77

Second Base	PCT	G	PO	A	E	DP
Frost	.905	6	8	11	2	2
Jaime	.978	30	59	74	3	16

Nunez	.933	13	20	36	4	8
Ott	.973	24	45	63	3	14
Roof	.970	18	36	60	3	12
Sizemore	.970	51	91	167	8	38

Third Base	PCT	G	PO	A	E	DP
Bertram	.921	57	32	96	11	7
De Leon	.930	44	21	85	8	3
Ott	.903	28	15	41	6	1
Roof	.839	15	2	24	5	2

Shortstop	PCT	G	PO	A	E	DP
De Leon	—	1	0	0	0	0
Frost	.750	1	2	1	1	1
Guzman	—	1	0	0	0	0
Iorg	.960	94	153	278	18	68

Jaime	.857	3	3	9	2	2
Nunez	.938	31	28	77	7	14
Ott	1.000	2	6	4	0	1
Roof	.923	10	17	31	4	10

Outfield	PCT	G	PO	A	E	DP
Boesch	.968	104	176	3	6	0
Cotto	1.000	33	72	1	0	0
Jaime	1.000	2	2	0	0	0
Justice	.987	70	145	6	2	1
Laster	.975	120	310	6	8	2
Nunez	1.000	1	1	0	0	0
Ott	1.000	9	14	0	0	0
Salas	1.000	4	15	0	0	0
Timm	.956	81	121	8	6	2

WEST MICHIGAN WHITECAPS — LOW CLASS A

MIDWEST LEAGUE

Batting	B-T	HT	WT	DOB	AVG	vLH	vRH	G	AB	R	H	2B	3B	HR	RBI	BB	HBP	SH	SF	SO	SB	CS	SLG	OBP
Avila, Alex	L-R	5-11	210	1-29-87	.305	.253	.333	58	213	21	65	14	0	1	22	27	1	1	2	41	0	1	.385	.383
Bourquin, Ron	L-R	6-3	205	4-29-85	.235	.183	.253	118	409	49	96	22	1	3	46	66	2	1	7	93	6	6	.315	.339
Bowen, Joseph	B-R	6-1	190	9-25-87	.176	.211	.164	22	74	4	13	2	0	0	6	12	0	0	0	27	0	0	.203	.291
Carlson, Christopher	R-R	6-4	230	1-7-84	.277	.278	.276	94	358	37	99	17	3	10	49	29	5	0	6	71	1	1	.425	.334
Casanova, Adrian	R-R	6-1	210	5-6-83	.193	.192	.194	29	88	6	17	1	0	1	9	10	2	1	3	30	1	1	.239	.282
Ciriaco, Audy	R-R	6-3	195	6-16-87	.240	.264	.227	107	417	47	100	12	5	7	50	16	2	5	4	68	12	6	.343	.269
Dirks, Andy	L-L	6-0	195	1-24-86	.100	.250	.000	3	10	0	1	0	0	0	2	1	0	0	0	2	0	0	.100	.182
Douglas, Brandon	R-R	6-0	185	8-27-85	.436	.429	.438	9	39	5	17	3	0	1	8	1	1	0	0	2	0	0	.590	.463
Flores, Angel	R-R	6-0	200	8-16-86	.180	.250	.141	26	89	5	16	1	0	0	8	8	0	0	2	18	0	0	.191	.242
Granderson, Curtis	L-R	6-1	185	3-16-81	.364	.200	.500	3	11	1	4	0	2	0	1	1	0	0	0	2	0	0	.727	.417
Guzman, Joaquin	B-R	6-0	170	9-22-86	.182	.250	.143	4	11	2	2	0	0	0	1	1	0	0	0	2	0	0	.182	.250
Henry, Justin	L-R	6-3	180	4-30-85	.295	.290	.297	120	475	74	140	24	2	1	46	44	3	7	3	36	27	7	.360	.356
Kaiser, Kody	B-R	5-9	185	4-6-85	.260	.307	.238	110	392	55	102	24	6	11	57	45	4	5	0	114	30	6	.436	.342
McBratney Jr., Mark	R-R	5-10	175	12-26-84	.186	.417	.149	24	86	9	16	4	2	0	5	8	1	0	1	24	0	3	.279	.260
Middleton, Cory	R-R	6-1	185	10-3-85	.194	.135	.220	76	247	33	48	9	0	6	25	24	6	0	2	61	2	1	.304	.280
Newton, Jordan	R-R	5-10	195	8-29-85	.267	.278	.263	95	363	48	97	21	10	7	48	20	5	4	5	97	8	2	.438	.310
Ordonez, Magglio	R-R	6-0	215	1-28-74	.250	—	.250	1	4	1	1	0	0	0	0	0	0	0	0	0	0	0	.250	.250
Parrott, Hayden	R-R	195	4-11-88	.200	.250	.171	16	55	2	11	0	1	1	6	2	0	0	0	16	0	1	.291	.228
Peter, Kyle	L-R	6-2	185	2-4-86	.263	.213	.285	103	396	64	104	11	1	0	34	57	5	2	5	80	42	12	.295	.359
Stein, Keith	L-R	5-10	185	10-17-85	.093	.200	.061	13	43	3	4	0	0	1	6	6	1	0	1	12	0	0	.163	.216
Tomas, Roger	B-R	5-8	185	4-17-86	.310	.276	.328	58	210	28	65	1	2	1	20	17	2	5	3	32	6	4	.348	.362
Tucker, Joseph	R-R	5-11	170	1-25-84	.286	.272	.292	96	367	46	105	17	1	3	42	22	13	3	8	48	5	8	.362	.341
Wells, Casper	R-R	6-2	210	11-23-84	.240	.412	.172	50	179	30	43	7	0	10	26	22	9	0	1	39	17	5	.447	.351
White, Christopher	B-R	5-11	170	11-12-87	.284	.385	.229	23	74	11	21	8	0	2	5	5	0	0	0	13	5	0	.473	.329

Pitching	B-T	HT	WT	DOB	W	L	ERA	G	GS	CG	SV	IP	H	R	ER	HR	BB	SO	AVG	vLH	vRH	K/9	BB/9
Cedano, Kelvin	R-R	6-0	175	11-3-85	2	1	5.35	25	0	0	0	37	41	25	22	5	31	41	.295	.328	.268	9.97	7.54
Darrow, Rudy	R-R	5-10	180	2-11-84	4	2	1.85	33	0	0	4	49	39	13	10	1	15	43	.213	.250	.176	7.95	2.77
Figaro, Alfredo	R-R	6-0	173	7-7-84	12	2	2.05	19	19	2	0	123	99	35	28	0	30	96	.218	.248	.185	7.02	2.20
Fuhrman, Aaron	L-L	6-0	185	4-2-88	0	1	4.22	3	2	0	0	11	18	7	5	1	3	11	.367	.000	.429	9.28	2.53
Gagnier, Lauren	R-R	6-2	210	2-28-85	1	8	4.42	14	14	0	0	75	71	48	37	4	33	79	.248	.274	.217	9.44	3.94
Garcia, Ramon	L-L	6-2	165	10-30-84	4	3	2.81	7	7	1	0	48	43	16	15	3	5	38	.235	.394	.200	7.13	0.94
Garcia, Wilton	R-R	6-1	165	4-12-85	9	4	4.40	47	0	0	1	74	65	41	36	5	28	54	.236	.278	.208	6.60	3.42
Green, Scott	R-R	6-7	240	8-10-85	1	2	3.57	15	0	0	2	18	14	9	7	1	5	15	.219	.250	.194	7.64	2.55
Hamilton, Joey	R-R	6-3	220	12-25-88	0	5	5.01	9	6	0	0	32	34	25	18	2	28	22	.286	.348	.208	6.12	7.79
Hess, Andrew	R-R	6-4	210	11-6-84	2	3	3.19	33	6	0	1	85	77	42	30	6	36	64	.238	.270	.213	6.80	3.83

	B-T	HT	WT	DOB	W	L	ERA	G	GS	CG	SV	IP	H	R	ER	HR	BB	SO	AVG	vLH	vRH	K/9	BB/9
Hoffman, Matt	L-L	6-2	195	11-18-88	0	2	4.60	5	2	0	0	16	19	10	8	1	14	20	.284	.556	.184	11.49	8.04
Jacobson, Brett	R-R	6-6	205	11-9-86	2	2	1.52	21	0	0	1	30	26	7	5	0	5	31	.236	.203	.275	9.40	1.52
Kibler, Jon	L-L	6-5	210	8-10-86	14	5	1.75	23	23	2	0	154	103	39	30	4	32	126	.190	.197	.187	7.35	1.87
Krol, Noah	B-R	6-2	185	6-6-84	4	3	3.93	47	0	0	15	50	39	28	22	2	28	49	.214	.202	.227	8.76	5.01
Mieses, Santo	R-R	5-11	185	4-15-85	1	3	4.74	17	0	0	0	25	24	14	13	4	12	20	.258	.279	.240	7.30	4.38
Miguelez, Manny	L-L	6-2	200	11-16-85	5	6	4.39	29	19	2	0	123	125	70	60	7	55	86	.263	.276	.258	6.29	4.02
Nardozzi, Paul	R-R	6-0	200	3-14-85	5	5	3.95	32	11	0	0	93	105	51	41	9	30	76	.282	.319	.247	7.33	2.89
Perdomo, Orlando	R-R	6-0	160	5-3-84	0	0	3.52	9	0	0	0	15	21	10	6	2	3	6	.344	.333	.350	3.52	1.76
Robles, Mauricio	L-L	5-10	160	3-5-89	5	3	2.66	23	16	0	0	91	54	27	27	2	54	79	.176	.187	.173	7.78	5.32
Villareal, Brayan	R-R	5-10	140	5-10-87	0	1	16.20	1	1	0	0	3	7	7	6	1	1	0	.438	.333	.500	0.00	2.70
Weber, Thad	R-R	6-2	200	9-28-84	1	4	2.56	11	11	0	0	56	46	20	16	3	11	49	.219	.226	.214	7.83	1.76

Fielding

Catcher	PCT	G	PO	A	E	DP	PB
Avila	.991	42	313	30	3	1	4
Bowen	1.000	22	185	13	0	0	4
Casanova	.995	29	180	15	1	0	1
Flores	.989	26	169	14	2	1	2
Newton	.962	21	157	19	7	2	2

First Base	PCT	G	PO	A	E	DP
Bourquin	.990	40	380	15	4	40
Carlson	.986	76	635	53	10	58
Middleton	1.000	5	59	4	0	7
Tucker	.994	19	143	12	1	11

Second Base	PCT	G	PO	A	E	DP
Guzman	1.000	1	2	1	0	0
Henry	.966	115	213	332	19	78

	PCT	G	PO	A	E	DP
Kaiser	.923	3	1	11	1	2
Tomas	.938	4	5	10	1	4
Tucker	.987	17	35	40	1	10
Third Base						
Bourquin	.916	57	54	98	14	6
Guzman	.667	2	1	3	2	0
Kaiser	.917	15	11	22	3	2
Middleton	.921	21	22	48	6	5
Tomas	.953	42	27	75	5	10
Tucker	1.000	4	0	6	0	1
Shortstop						
Ciriaco	.920	107	134	335	41	69
Douglas	.974	8	20	18	1	4
Guzman	—	1	0	0	0	0

	PCT	G	PO	A	E	DP
Tomas	1.000	11	18	24	0	4
Tucker	.905	12	15	23	4	7
Outfield						
Dirks	1.000	2	3	0	0	0
Granderson	1.000	3	6	0	0	0
Kaiser	.985	76	128	6	2	2
McBratney Jr.	1.000	24	32	2	0	1
Middleton	1.000	26	36	2	0	0
Newton	.983	56	109	5	2	0
Parrott	1.000	11	15	0	0	0
Peter	.984	101	235	10	4	2
Stein	.950	13	18	1	1	0
Tucker	.961	39	69	5	3	3
Wells	.990	48	92	8	1	3
White	1.000	22	34	1	0	0

ONEONTA TIGERS

SHORT-SEASON

NEW YORK-PENN LEAGUE

Batting	B-T	HT	WT	DOB	AVG	vLH	vRH	G	AB	R	H	2B	3B	HR	RBI	BB	HBP	SH	SF	SO	SB	CS	SLG	OBP
Arlet, Luis	R-R	5-11	174	11-8-84	.175	.190	.171	35	97	9	17	3	2	0	5	5	1	1	34	1	0	.247	.221
Bowen, Joseph	B-R	6-1	190	9-25-87	.192	.184	.195	40	120	15	23	6	1	0	9	22	1	2	0	41	2	1	.258	.322
Douglas, Brandon	R-R	6-0	185	8-27-85	.312	.310	.313	47	189	33	59	5	5	1	12	10	1	1	0	19	13	1	.407	.350
Flores, Angel	R-R	6-0	200	8-16-86	.267	.300	.250	9	30	2	8	1	0	1	2	5	0	0	0	6	0	0	.400	.371
Gosse, Mike	L-R	5-7	165	5-30-86	.277	.254	.285	63	231	27	64	9	2	1	35	16	0	2	4	17	1	3	.346	.319
Guez, Ben	R-R	5-10	170	1-24-87	.223	.197	.232	70	256	43	57	14	4	5	25	33	8	3	5	57	16	5	.367	.325
Guzman, Joaquin	B-R	6-0	170	9-22-86	.240	.333	.188	12	50	7	12	4	1	0	4	6	0	0	0	7	0	1	.360	.321
Harryman, Eric	R-R	5-10	170	10-26-84	.194	.156	.212	34	98	12	19	3	0	4	13	6	1	2	1	21	1	1	.347	.245
Lamont, Wade	L-R	6-2	230	6-25-84	.255	.333	.228	34	106	8	27	9	0	0	9	12	2	0	0	36	0	0	.340	.342
Nowlin, Billy	R-R	6-1	210	12-16-86	.236	.208	.246	49	178	19	42	5	0	6	26	10	4	0	3	27	1	1	.365	.287
Parrott, Hayden	R-R	6-1	195	4-11-88	.224	.235	.217	35	134	18	30	2	1	3	19	8	3	1	1	31	0	1	.321	.281
Pounds, Bryan	R-R	6-0	195	10-4-85	.217	.246	.207	61	221	20	48	9	3	2	28	20	4	1	3	60	2	0	.312	.290
Ramirez, Carlos	R-R	5-11	190	9-1-85	.219	.235	.213	52	192	21	42	7	3	3	23	13	1	1	1	45	1	0	.333	.271
Stein, Keith	L-R	5-10	185	10-17-85	.253	.192	.284	40	154	16	39	10	2	1	17	11	0	0	1	26	2	0	.364	.301
Weber, Tyler	R-R	6-3	220	2-25-86	.186	.242	.163	33	113	8	21	7	0	0	6	3	1	1	1	37	0	0	.248	.212
White, Christopher	B-R	5-11	170	11-12-87	.230	.158	.247	31	100	12	23	2	0	0	11	12	0	1	0	17	6	1	.290	.313
Workman, Josh	L-R	6-1	200	11-4-85	.304	.000	.333	7	23	2	7	2	1	0	4	2	1	0	0	2	0	0	.478	.385
Wyatt, Brent	B-R	5-10	185	1-25-85	.305	.291	.310	55	197	25	60	11	3	0	14	25	8	4	1	41	5	4	.391	.403

Pitching	B-T	HT	WT	DOB	W	L	ERA	G	GS	CG	SV	IP	H	R	ER	HR	BB	SO	AVG	vLH	vRH	K/9	BB/9
Brackman, Mark	R-R	6-7	230	3-23-85	4	3	3.88	20	2	0	0	46	51	28	20	2	12	48	.273	.306	.252	9.32	2.33
Cassavecchia, Nick	R-R	6-0	185	12-18-85	0	1	3.60	3	0	0	0	5	5	2	2	0	3	8	.263	.600	.143	14.40	5.40
Conn, Tyler	L-L	6-1	180	11-9-85	0	0	3.27	17	0	0	1	22	19	8	8	0	12	18	.241	.240	.241	7.36	4.91
De Leon, Darwin	L-L	6-0	150	9-15-88	6	3	4.20	13	12	0	0	56	48	28	26	2	30	42	.233	.200	.242	6.79	4.85
DeLucia, Dan	L-L	6-4	220	6-1-85	2	2	1.95	15	3	0	1	37	31	11	8	1	13	32	.220	.282	.196	7.78	3.16
Feeney, Trevor	R-R	6-1	185	6-4-86	3	6	3.25	15	13	0	0	72	69	36	26	3	21	64	.244	.294	.215	8.00	2.63
Finefrock, Sean	R-R	6-5	200	2-11-87	0	0	14.00	6	0	0	0	9	18	14	14	0	4	11	.409	.300	.500	11.00	4.00
Fuhrman, Aaron	L-L	6-0	185	4-2-88	3	3	4.17	12	1	0	1	37	36	17	17	2	12	42	.252	.205	.269	10.31	2.95
Gayhart, Jared	L-R	6-3	195	10-29-86	0	1	11.57	3	0	0	0	2	5	3	3	0	7	4	.222	.000	.286	15.43	27.00
Gil, Luis	R-R	6-1	170	2-12-84	0	0	5.40	16	0	0	0	25	26	16	15	3	6	10	.271	.342	.224	3.60	2.16
Gilman, Steve	R-R	6-1	194	10-1-85	0	0	3.38	13	0	0	0	21	18	10	8	0	11	18	.234	.353	.140	7.59	4.64
Hoffman, Matt	L-L	6-2	195	11-18-88	3	5	3.05	12	10	0	0	56	49	24	19	1	24	44	.237	.291	.217	7.07	3.86
Mieses, Santo	R-R	5-11	185	4-15-85	1	0	3.21	9	0	0	0	14	12	6	5	0	5	22	.222	.292	.167	14.14	3.21
Oliveros, Lester	R-R	5-11	178	5-28-88	1	2	1.74	15	0	0	4	21	15	4	4	1	6	34	.197	.120	.235	14.81	2.61
Perdomo, Orlando	R-R	6-0	160	5-3-84	0	0	0.00	2	0	0	0	3	1	0	0	0	3	4	.000	.000	.000	13.50	10.13
Putkonen, Luke	R-R	6-6	225	5-10-86	2	1	3.65	6	6	0	0	25	24	10	10	1	8	17	.270	.344	.228	6.20	2.92
Shawler, Anthony	R-R	6-3	188	5-16-87	2	3	1.76	22	1	0	3	51	34	12	10	0	18	54	.180	.261	.133	9.53	3.18
Sorensen, Mark	R-R	6-3	205	2-21-86	3	3	3.66	13	12	0	0	59	77	29	24	2	13	39	.316	.276	.342	5.95	1.98
Stohr, Tyler	L-R	6-2	210	9-19-86	0	1	3.98	21	0	0	12	20	17	10	9	0	15	24	.224	.294	.167	10.62	6.64
Stokes, David	R-R	6-8	245	7-19-86	3	7	5.74	14	14	0	0	64	90	53	41	9	22	43	.335	.374	.309	6.02	3.08

Fielding

Catcher	PCT	G	PO	A	E	DP	PB
Bowen	.990	40	281	26	3	4	1
Flores	1.000	8	47	7	0	0	0
Weber	.993	32	267	11	2	1	3

First Base	PCT	G	PO	A	E	DP
Harryman	1.000	1	7	0	0	1
Lamont	.977	20	166	6	4	14
Nowlin	.966	11	78	8	3	8
Ramirez	.982	47	366	17	7	46

Second Base	PCT	G	PO	A	E	DP
Gosse	.955	62	97	159	12	50

	PCT	G	PO	A	E	DP
Harryman	.969	15	25	38	2	7
Wyatt	1.000	1	2	4	0	0

Third Base	PCT	G	PO	A	E	DP
Bowen	1.000	1	0	1	0	0
Guzman	.625	4	1	4	3	0
Harryman	.783	11	4	14	5	0
Pounds	.867	61	39	117	24	13

Shortstop	PCT	G	PO	A	E	DP
Douglas	.904	45	70	127	21	36
Guzman	.951	8	14	25	2	4
Harryman	.952	5	10	10	1	3

	PCT	G	PO	A	E	DP
Wyatt	.961	18	28	70	4	19

Outfield	PCT	G	PO	A	E	DP
Arlet	1.000	26	37	4	0	0
Guez	.974	70	143	8	4	1
Nowlin	1.000	1	4	0	0	0
Parrott	.896	31	41	2	5	0
Stein	.972	39	64	5	2	3
White	.953	30	59	2	3	0
Workman	1.000	3	7	1	0	0
Wyatt	.943	30	49	1	3	0

GCL TIGERS   ROOKIE

GULF COAST LEAGUE

Batting	B-T	HT	WT	DOB	AVG	vLH	vRH	G	AB	R	H	2B	3B	HR	RBI	BB	HBP	SH	SF	SO	SB	CS	SLG	OBP
Anderson, Brett	R-R	6-3	185	9-3-90	.178	.262	.132	39	118	7	21	3	0	0	6	3	1	0	0	32	0	2	.203	.205
Carrithers, Alden	L-R	5-9	165	11-14-84	.316	.324	.312	39	114	21	36	5	1	2	17	28	6	1	3	19	16	1	.430	.464
Dirks, Andy	L-L	6-0	195	1-24-86	.412	.421	.400	10	34	10	14	3	2	0	7	3	0	0	1	6	2	0	.618	.447
Dlugach, Brent	R-R	6-4	195	3-3-83	.200	.000	.250	7	15	2	3	2	0	0	2	2	0	0	1	4	0	0	.333	.278
Douglas, Brandon	R-R	6-0	185	8-27-85	.333	.429	.300	7	27	7	9	2	0	1	5	3	0	0	1	2	3	0	.519	.387
Espinoza, Alexis	R-R	6-1	180	12-20-88	.266	.205	.300	39	124	14	33	6	0	3	11	2	1	1	2	33	7	1	.387	.279
Frost, Adam	R-R	5-11	165	10-13-86	.277	.278	.276	32	112	13	31	8	0	2	15	6	3	2	1	18	3	0	.402	.328
Grullon, Luis	R-R	6-3	200	9-12-87	.186	.250	.152	27	70	5	13	4	0	0	6	1	4	0	2	28	0	0	.243	.234
Harrigan, Brandon	R-R	6-1	220	1-26-85	.218	.182	.241	29	87	8	19	5	1	0	5	6	0	0	1	18	1	0	.299	.299
Hernandez, Keith	R-R	5-11	212	8-13-84	.178	.194	.169	32	90	5	16	0	0	0	5	14	4	0	0	25	2	0	.211	.315
Jaime, Carmelo	B-R	5-9	170	7-16-85	.267	.222	.333	6	15	4	4	1	1	0	1	2	1	1	1	2	2	2	.467	.368
Lehrman, Derek	L-R	6-1	205	12-11-84	.210	.200	.215	40	124	15	26	11	0	2	17	12	3	1	1	30	0	0	.347	.293
Lennerton, Jordan	L-L	6-2	230	2-16-86	.243	.205	.263	36	115	11	28	9	1	1	22	18	1	0	1	36	2	1	.365	.348
Nowlin, Billy	R-R	6-1	210	12-16-86	.286	.333	.278	6	21	2	6	2	0	1	5	2	0	0	0	7	0	0	.524	.348
Nunez, Gustavo	B-R	5-10	148	2-8-88	.200	.353	.087	13	40	5	8	3	0	0	5	2	0	0	1	6	1	1	.275	.233
Palacios, Luis	R-R	5-10	162	7-7-89	.245	.360	.186	43	147	15	36	13	0	3	17	12	4	2	0	37	0	0	.395	.319
Salas, Luis	R-R	6-0	172	1-2-89	.253	.208	.278	45	150	17	38	8	1	4	11	16	3	0	2	58	4	1	.400	.333
Tang, Chao-Ting	L-R	5-11	176	10-12-87	.222	.227	.220	38	126	13	28	7	2	1	15	9	2	0	2	29	3	1	.333	.281
Taylor, Londell	R-R	6-2	200	9-13-88	.205	.175	.222	35	112	20	23	6	1	2	11	12	2	0	0	32	9	0	.330	.294
Vaughn, D'Andre	R-R	5-11	190	9-7-88	.109	.207	.063	30	92	12	10	1	1	0	6	14	1	0	0	32	3	0	.141	.234
Workman, Josh	L-R	6-1	200	11-4-85	.268	.278	.263	18	56	17	15	1	1	2	8	6	7	0	1	15	4	2	.429	.400

Pitching	B-T	HT	WT	DOB	W	L	ERA	G	GS	CG	SV	IP	H	R	ER	HR	BB	SO	AVG	vLH	vRH	K/9	BB/9
Broberg, Eric	R-R	6-3	225	12-25-87	1	1	4.32	9	0	0	0	8	7	4	4	1	6	11	.226	.214	.235	11.88	6.48
Carvajal, Dario	R-R	6-1	165	4-17-85	0	1	5.48	15	1	0	1	21	20	16	13	1	18	18	.241	.136	.279	7.59	7.59
Cassavecchia, Nick	R-R	6-0	185	12-18-85	2	1	0.99	20	0	0	9	27	19	3	3	0	6	32	.192	.211	.180	10.54	1.98
Crosby, Casey	R-L	6-5	200	9-17-88	0	0	0.00	3	3	0	0	5	4	1	0	0	3	2	.211	.500	.176	3.86	5.79
Duran, Darlin	L-L	6-0	160	3-3-89	1	4	6.95	12	6	0	0	34	29	27	26	3	21	22	.236	.100	.262	5.88	5.61
Gayhart, Jared	L-R	6-3	195	10-29-86	1	0	4.82	10	0	0	2	9	11	6	5	0	6	6	.333	.167	.370	5.79	5.79
Hamilton, Joey	R-R	6-3	200	12-25-88	5	1	1.86	9	7	0	0	39	27	12	8	1	13	42	.186	.205	.179	9.78	3.03
Lackey, Hayden	R-R	6-1	175	9-27-85	0	0	4.84	14	0	0	1	22	30	19	12	2	2	18	.316	.308	.319	7.25	0.81
Larez, Victor	R-R	6-3	160	5-28-87	5	3	3.67	13	10	0	0	56	63	33	23	4	10	54	.274	.274	.274	8.63	1.60
Marte, Luis	R-R	5-11	170	8-26-86	0	1	3.60	1	1	0	0	5	5	2	2	0	0	5	.238	.200	.333	9.00	0.00
Mieses, Santo	R-R	5-11	185	4-15-85	1	0	4.15	3	0	0	0	4	5	2	2	0	0	5	.333	.200	.400	10.38	0.00
Perdomo, Orlando	R-R	6-0	160	5-3-84	0	0	3.52	6	0	0	0	8	9	3	3	1	3	5	.310	.417	.235	5.87	3.52
Perry, Ryan	R-R	6-4	200	2-13-87	0	0	0.00	2	0	0	0	2	0	0	0	0	0	4	.000	.000	.000	18.00	0.00
Sanz, Luis	R-R	6-1	173	11-19-87	5	3	3.66	11	9	0	0	52	41	26	21	4	19	48	.223	.232	.219	8.36	3.31
Satterwhite, Cody	R-R	6-4	205	1-27-87	0	0	0.00	3	0	0	1	2	4	0	0	0	1	2	.400	.000	.444	7.71	3.86
Tata, Jordan	R-R	6-6	220	9-20-81	1	2	2.83	6	6	0	0	29	24	11	9	1	18	18	.231	.130	.310	5.65	5.65
Todd, Jade	R-L	6-2	190	3-22-90	3	1	2.34	12	5	0	0	42	35	15	11	2	18	48	.226	.121	.254	10.20	3.83
Villareal, Brayan	R-R	5-10	140	5-10-87	1	5	3.65	11	6	1	0	37	26	19	15	0	11	37	.197	.288	.138	9.00	2.68
Waite, Robb	R-R	6-3	210	1-9-87	1	3	4.67	17	0	0	2	27	27	15	14	1	12	25	.252	.237	.261	8.33	4.00
Weber, Thad	R-R	6-2	200	9-28-84	0	0	0.00	2	1	0	0	4	1	0	0	0	0	9	.077	.000	.200	20.25	0.00
Weinhardt, Robbie	R-R	6-2	205	12-8-85	0	0	0.00	3	0	0	0	6	6	3	0	0	2	4	.261	.000	.353	6.35	3.18
Zumaya, Richard	R-R	6-0	180	11-10-89	0	5	6.61	13	4	0	0	33	43	30	24	2	14	25	.309	.270	.342	6.89	3.86

Fielding

Catcher	PCT	G	PO	A	E	DP	PB
Harrigan	.943	25	157	8	10	0	3
Hernandez	.988	32	217	24	3	3	6
Lehrman	1.000	9	56	7	0	0	0
Nowlin	1.000	1	6	0	0	0	1

First Base	PCT	G	PO	A	E	DP
Grullon	.977	14	76	9	2	6
Lehrman	.982	21	162	5	3	17
Lennerton	.992	29	241	10	2	18
Nowlin	1.000	1	9	0	0	0
Vaughn	1.000	1	1	1	0	0

Second Base	PCT	G	PO	A	E	DP
Carrithers	1.000	39	55	100	0	21
Frost	1.000	7	8	13	0	1
Jaime	1.000	6	7	11	0	2
Nunez	1.000	1	3	2	0	1
Palacios	.976	12	15	25	1	6
Workman	1.000	2	2	1	0	1

Third Base	PCT	G	PO	A	E	DP
Anderson	.820	36	21	61	18	8
Douglas	.905	5	6	13	2	0
Frost	.815	11	5	17	5	1

	PCT	G	PO	A	E	DP
Grullon	.769	6	4	6	3	1
Palacios	.947	5	3	15	1	0

Shortstop	PCT	G	PO	A	E	DP
Anderson	1.000	3	6	10	0	2
Dlugach	1.000	7	5	16	0	0
Douglas	1.000	1	1	2	0	0
Frost	.951	16	23	35	3	7
Nunez	.897	13	20	41	7	9
Palacios	.980	26	32	65	2	15

Outfield	PCT	G	PO	A	E	DP
Dirks	1.000	8	14	0	0	0

| Espinoza | .964 | 34 | 50 | 3 | 2 | 2 | Tang | .940 | 34 | 44 | 3 | 3 | 0 | Vaughn | 1.000 | 23 | 25 | 2 | 0 | 1 |
| Salas | .986 | 45 | 69 | 2 | 1 | 0 | Taylor | .972 | 26 | 32 | 3 | 1 | 0 | Workman | 1.000 | 11 | 17 | 0 | 0 | 0 |

DSL TIGERS   ROOKIE
DOMINICAN SUMMER LEAGUE

Batting	B-T	HT	WT	DOB	AVG	vLH	vRH	G	AB	R	H	2B	3B	HR	RBI	BB	HBP	SH	SF	SO	SB	CS	SLG	OBP
Aguasvivas, Juaner	R-R	6-3	225	9-15-89	.254	.325	.236	53	197	31	50	8	0	6	19	19	7	0	1	66	0	0	.386	.339
Castillo, Luis	R-R	5-11	160	5-15-89	.245	.244	.246	57	212	29	52	5	1	1	13	26	3	3	1	24	14	6	.292	.335
Dionicio, Victor	L-L	6-1	180	2-10-90	.208	.037	.242	51	159	16	33	7	1	0	10	23	1	0	1	62	3	3	.264	.310
Figueroa, Robinson	R-R	6-0	160	3-11-90	.149	.108	.161	65	174	20	26	5	3	2	15	17	6	1	3	58	7	3	.247	.245
Gonzalez, Domingo	R-R	6-1	175	3-10-91	.134	.176	.123	51	172	15	23	4	2	2	19	17	2	3	0	53	2	1	.215	.220
Guzman, Raynolds	R-R	6-0	185	3-16-90	.254	.323	.229	36	114	11	29	6	0	0	16	9	5	0	2	20	0	2	.307	.331
Heredia, Santos	B-L	5-8	170	10-15-89	.272	.233	.283	45	136	32	37	4	5	0	13	19	6	2	0	26	16	7	.375	.385
Marte, Ernesto	R-R	6-2	190	9-11-89	.129	.063	.143	32	93	10	12	4	0	0	7	11	4	0	1	51	0	0	.172	.248
Olivo, Ricardo	R-R	6-0	179	11-5-90	.219	.227	.217	42	137	14	30	6	0	2	16	13	6	0	0	35	0	1	.307	.314
Ortiz, Samuel	R-R	5-11	155	6-12-91	.217	.281	.200	47	152	15	33	7	1	0	15	16	10	0	1	49	4	2	.276	.330
Rijo, Samir	B-R	6-2	205	6-26-90	.216	.240	.210	64	231	36	50	8	0	5	18	21	10	3	6	54	1	5	.316	.309
Rodriguez, Julio	R-R	6-2	200	3-8-89	.261	.310	.250	48	153	21	40	10	1	0	28	14	9	0	4	15	6	2	.340	.350
Soto, Elvin	L-R	6-2	190	5-6-89	.231	.188	.241	58	169	32	39	11	1	7	29	44	9	2	2	53	5	1	.432	.411

Pitching	B-T	HT	WT	DOB	W	L	ERA	G	GS	CG	SV	IP	H	R	ER	HR	BB	SO	AVG	vLH	vRH	K/9	BB/9
Acosta, Alvin	R-R	6-2	170	6-12-90	1	3	5.45	10	6	0	0	33	36	30	20	2	13	31	.275	.318	.253	8.45	3.55
Calderon, Yinio	R-R	6-4	170	11-16-90	0	3	4.55	18	1	0	1	32	21	24	16	1	34	30	.193	.316	.167	8.53	9.66
De La Cruz, Sandy	R-R	6-1	180	6-11-87	1	2	2.84	11	0	0	2	13	13	5	4	0	5	11	.260	.231	.270	7.82	3.55
Del Orbe, Emmaneul	R-R	6-3	188	12-20-90	2	4	7.65	21	3	0	0	40	45	44	34	3	33	37	.285	.343	.268	8.33	7.43
Diaz, Robert	L-L	6-2	180	2-12-89	3	2	4.11	16	14	0	0	66	57	36	30	4	32	90	.230	.071	.239	12.34	4.39
Guichardo, Rayni	L-L	6-1	165	8-13-91	3	5	3.90	16	13	0	0	62	56	34	27	2	20	79	.235	.250	.234	11.41	2.89
Herrera, Gabriel	R-R	6-0	190	5-8-86	4	3	3.15	26	0	0	8	40	41	17	14	4	24	57	.275	.414	.242	12.83	5.40
Lebron, Ramon	R-R	6-1	180	2-1-89	2	4	4.31	16	9	0	1	48	40	27	23	4	27	51	.225	.341	.190	9.56	5.06
Martinez, Jose	R-T	6-2	170	1-26-89	0	0	4.50	7	0	0	0	14	12	11	7	0	8	11	.218	.143	.244	7.07	5.14
Medina, Kelvin	L-L	6-4	147	7-30-90	0	5	5.87	20	2	0	0	23	23	21	15	3	28	28	.258	.333	.253	10.96	10.96
Melo, Carlos	R-R	6-3	180	2-27-91	3	3	5.14	14	13	0	0	49	47	33	28	2	20	61	.251	.324	.233	11.20	3.67
Mercedes, Melvin	R-R	6-3	190	11-2-90	2	2	3.19	24	0	0	6	37	28	19	13	1	24	33	.207	.172	.217	8.10	5.89
Moreno, Crucito	R-R	6-3	175	5-3-88	0	0	7.20	4	0	0	0	10	11	11	8	0	7	8	.282	.154	.346	7.20	6.30
Nunez, Marcos	R-R	6-5	210	7-10-89	4	2	1.78	18	10	0	0	76	57	21	15	1	20	69	.210	.274	.190	8.17	2.37
Ortiz, Vladimir	R-R	6-2	186	3-24-89	3	3	3.61	25	0	0	0	42	36	21	17	2	17	47	.232	.306	.210	9.99	3.61

Fielding

Catcher	PCT	G	PO	A	E	DP	PB
Guzman	.975	19	164	28	5	0	2
Olivo	.972	24	183	29	6	1	9
Rodriguez	.989	34	315	48	4	3	8

First Base	PCT	G	PO	A	E	DP
Aguasvivas	.969	51	361	14	12	36
Marte	.980	13	92	4	2	13
Rijo	1.000	12	69	2	0	10
Rodriguez	1.000	1	1	0	0	0

Second Base	PCT	G	PO	A	E	DP
Heredia	.964	30	61	46	4	15
Nunez	.961	42	90	81	7	27
Ortiz	.846	6	5	6	2	3

Third Base	PCT	G	PO	A	E	DP
Gonzalez	.851	22	14	43	10	3
Guzman	—	1	0	0	0	0
Marte	.500	5	1	0	1	0
Olivo	.500	2	0	1	1	0
Soto	.891	52	49	122	21	20

Shortstop	PCT	G	PO	A	E	DP
Gonzalez	.893	35	54	71	15	19
Ortiz	.856	43	40	85	21	14
Outfield	PCT	G	PO	A	E	DP
Castillo	.991	56	100	5	1	1
Dionicio	.879	50	54	4	8	2
Figueroa	.981	63	99	7	2	2
Heredia	.500	3	1	1	2	0
Rijo	.896	56	63	6	8	1

VSL TIGERS   ROOKIE
VENEZUELAN SUMMER LEAGUE

Batting	B-T	HT	WT	DOB	AVG	vLH	vRH	G	AB	R	H	2B	3B	HR	RBI	BB	HBP	SH	SF	SO	SB	CS	SLG	OBP
De Los Santos, Wondy	B-R	5-9	154	1-3-90	.301	.370	.279	58	186	28	56	9	3	1	15	15	2	5	2	20	10	5	.398	.356
Espinoza, Ivan	R-R	6-0	165	1-16-89	.263	.273	.260	68	247	29	65	6	0	0	18	19	6	6	0	44	7	7	.287	.331
Garcia, Avisail	R-R	6-3	190	6-12-91	.298	.375	.275	63	245	33	73	12	2	7	34	15	2	0	1	39	7	5	.449	.342
Gomez, Gilbert	R-R	6-0	165	4-30-90	.254	.333	.241	31	67	12	17	2	0	3	8	6	4	1	0	23	0	0	.418	.351
Gomez, Oscar	R-R	5-11	155	3-25-91	.111	.118	.109	36	81	10	9	2	1	0	6	4	2	0	0	30	1	2	.160	.172
Guanipa, Dick	R-R	6-0	180	6-20-90	.214	.111	.242	17	42	2	9	0	0	0	1	10	1	0	0	17	0	0	.214	.377
Hoyer, Wilfredo	R-R	6-1	180	5-14-91	.172	.091	.214	25	64	3	11	1	0	0	6	5	1	1	0	29	0	0	.188	.243
Leiva, Raul	B-R	6-2	185	1-30-90	.300	.304	.299	32	100	3	30	7	0	0	9	4	1	0	1	8	1	0	.370	.330
Martinez, Francisco	R-R	6-1	180	9-1-90	.321	.200	.360	68	249	32	80	4	0	1	23	28	2	1	0	28	20	10	.349	.394
Moreno, Alexander	R-R	6-4	185	4-1-90	.238	.227	.241	60	202	16	48	7	1	3	17	13	5	0	1	55	3	4	.327	.299
Perez, Hernan	R-R	6-0	160	3-26-91	.226	.213	.230	68	265	38	60	8	4	1	22	16	4	3	3	35	4	4	.298	.278
Reina, Adolfo	R-R	6-1	190	1-22-90	.260	.279	.255	54	208	24	54	12	0	5	28	10	3	0	2	28	1	2	.389	.300
Sanz, Luis	R-R	5-10	165	2-23-91	.251	.341	.229	58	207	21	52	13	1	2	25	17	4	1	1	23	3	2	.353	.319
Torrealba, Ronald	R-R	5-11	145	6-1-90	.177	.222	.162	55	147	13	26	7	0	0	7	21	9	6	0	24	1	6	.224	.316

Pitching	B-T	HT	WT	DOB	W	L	ERA	G	GS	CG	SV	IP	H	R	ER	HR	BB	SO	AVG	vLH	vRH	K/9	BB/9
Aguirre, Gino	R-R	6-2	155	9-12-90	2	4	4.71	10	10	0	0	36	42	25	19	4	13	28	.288	.257	.297	6.94	3.22
Alvarez, Carlos	R-R	6-1	175	1-15-91	0	3	3.46	13	0	0	0	26	25	18	10	2	21	25	.250	.261	.247	8.65	7.27
Carreno, Josue	R-R	6-1	170	6-26-91	2	2	2.82	12	12	0	0	54	35	18	17	2	15	39	.185	.250	.172	6.46	2.48
Celis, Fernando	R-R	6-1	165	3-27-89	1	5	5.40	14	2	0	0	30	44	22	18	3	16	15	.376	.320	.391	4.50	4.80
Diaz, Jose	R-R	6-0	160	4-20-90	3	5	2.29	14	14	0	0	83	51	32	21	6	20	47	.173	.184	.169	5.12	2.18
Gonzalez, Eduardo	R-R	6-3	152	11-2-88	3	7	4.73	13	13	0	0	59	62	38	31	4	30	27	.273	.205	.290	4.12	4.58

Lozano, Juan	L-L	6-0	175	9-14-89	0	0	6.14	7	2	0	0	7	5	7	5	1	7	6	.167	.000	.172	7.36	8.59
Mendoza, Clemente	R-R	6-0	170	7-24-90	3	5	2.51	21	0	0	2	47	35	22	13	3	14	37	.201	.152	.213	7.14	2.70
Ortega, Jose	R-R	5-11	165	10-12-88	1	1	2.20	23	0	0	5	45	43	18	11	5	15	27	.256	.250	.257	5.40	3.00
Palacios, Wilsen	R-R	6-3	180	12-15-89	2	3	1.52	16	1	0	2	41	39	14	7	1	15	36	.252	.233	.256	7.84	3.27
Penalver, Frank	R-R	6-0	150	1-19-91	1	2	3.19	16	0	0	0	37	37	16	13	1	19	17	.276	.290	.272	4.17	4.66
Rondon, Bruce	R-R	6-2	190	12-9-90	2	6	3.58	13	13	1	0	55	48	36	22	0	20	34	.225	.250	.217	5.53	3.25
Siso, Jose	L-L	5-11	155	3-22-89	0	0	5.45	16	2	0	0	35	32	27	21	3	14	39	.241	.000	.242	10.13	3.63
Torrealba, Michael	R-R	5-11	150	11-19-89	4	1	2.06	20	0	0	4	48	28	17	11	3	21	62	.169	.190	.161	11.63	3.94

Fielding

Catcher	PCT	G	PO	A	E	DP	PB
G. Gomez	.923	18	64	8	6	0	6
Hoyer	.932	12	59	10	5	0	3
Leiva	.992	17	103	21	1	2	3
Reina	.988	12	64	15	1	0	4
Sanz	.989	27	150	22	2	2	6
Martinez	.983	12	110	4	2	8	
Reina	.967	15	115	3	4	14	
Sanz	.990	31	280	16	3	21	
Torrealba	1.000	1	1	0	0	0	

First Base	PCT	G	PO	A	E	DP
G. Gomez	.889	2	7	1	1	0
O. Gomez	1.000	6	35	1	0	3
Guanipa	1.000	6	51	1	0	4
Hoyer	1.000	1	2	0	0	0
Leiva	1.000	8	87	7	0	4

Second Base	PCT	G	PO	A	E	DP
De Los Santos	.865	11	15	17	5	6
O. Gomez	.862	11	12	13	4	6
Reina	.972	8	17	18	1	3
Torrealba	.972	49	97	114	6	26

Third Base	PCT	G	PO	A	E	DP
O. Gomez	.333	1	0	1	2	0
Martinez	.889	51	45	155	25	10
Reina	.927	19	17	59	6	9

Shortstop	PCT	G	PO	A	E	DP
Perez	.935	67	88	231	22	33
Torrealba	1.000	4	1	8	0	1

Outfield	PCT	G	PO	A	E	DP
De Los Santos	.935	39	64	8	5	2
Espinoza	.947	67	138	6	8	0
Garcia	.924	61	91	6	8	0
O. Gomez	1.000	2	3	1	0	1
Martinez	—	1	0	0	0	0
Moreno	.973	43	64	9	2	0
Torrealba	1.000	2	3	1	0	0

Florida Marlins

BY MIKE BERARDINO

For the bulk of their short, strange history, the Marlins' performance typically has been inversely proportional to the preseason expectations they have faced.

With the single notable exception of 1997, when the store-bought champions were supposed to be good and managed to deliver, the Marlins tend to thrive when dismissed and wilt when exalted.

That pattern held again in 2008, which they entered without franchise stalwarts Miguel Cabrera and Dontrelle Willis after an offseason trade sent them to the Tigers for a package of prospects.

Saddled with the sport's lowest payroll ($22 million) and widely predicted to finish fourth at best and lose 90-plus games, the Marlins rallied under second-year manager Fredi Gonzalez to post the third-highest win total (84) in their existence.

They held at least a share of first place for 42 days. before finishing third in the rugged National League East, 7½ games behind the eventual World Series-champion Phillies. The Marlins missed the wild card by just 5½ games despite a flawed formula that relied too heavily on the home run, an injury marred rotation and shaky defense.

Andrew Miller, the big lefty who highlighted the Cabrera/Willis deal, had an uneven first season with the Marlins, finishing up in the bullpen after missing more than a month in the second half with patellar tendinitis.

However, Cameron Maybin, the electric center fielder who joined Miller in that same trade, was an eye-popping revelation once he was recalled for the season's final 10 days. The center fielder job almost certainly belongs to Maybin in 2009.

Their top rookie was another first-round pick, righthander Chris Volstad. Summoned from Double-A at the start of July, Volstad won his first two outings and generally wowed the league with his heavy sinker and impressive maturity.

Hard-throwing righthander Ryan Tucker beat Volstad to the majors, but he was shipped back to the minors, where he trained as a short reliever.

Shortstop Hanley Ramirez was signed to a six-year, $70-million extension in May, then went out and made the NL all-star team for the first time.

Josh Johnson (elbow) and Anibal Sanchez (shoulder) returned at midseason from major

surgeries and had varying degrees of success in recapturing their rookie form of 2006. Johnson's path was smoother than that of the No-Hit Kid.

Third baseman Dallas McPherson, the former Angel, led the minors with 42 home runs at Triple-A Albuquerque.

PLAYERS OF THE YEAR

MAJOR LEAGUE: HANLEY RAMIREZ, SS

Ramirez, a 24-year-old from the Dominican, emerged as the Marlins' offensive sparkplug as the shortstop hit .301/.400/.540 with 33 home runs, 34 doubles and 67 RBIs. His home runs led the team, and he also stole 35 bases in 47 attempts.

MINOR LEAGUE: MIKE STANTON, OF

Stanton, 18 and a second-round pick out of Sherman Oaks, Calif., in 2007, was the catalyst at low Class A Greensboro. He hit .293/.381/.511, leading the South Atlantic League in home runs (39) and ranking second in RBIs (97).

RODGER WOOD

ORGANIZATION LEADERS

BATTING		*Minimum 250 at-bats
*AVG	Morrison, Logan, Jupiter	.332
R	Raynor, John, Carolina	104
H	Morrison, Logan, Jupiter	162
TB	Stanton, Michael, Greensboro	286
2B	Sanchez, Gaby, Carolina	42
3B	Maybin, Cameron, Carolina	8
HR	McPherson, Dallas, Albuquerque	42
RBI	McPherson, Dallas, Albuquerque	98
BB	McPherson, Dallas, Albuquerque	76
SO	McPherson, Dallas, Albuquerque	168
SB	Raynor, John, Carolina	48
*OBP	Sanchez, Gaby, Carolina	.404
*SLG	McPherson, Dallas, Albuquerque	.618

PITCHING		†Minimum 75 innings
W	De La Cruz, Eulogio, Albuquerque	13
W	Taylor, Graham, Jupiter/Carolina	13
L	Keppel, Bob, Albuquerque	11
L	Trahern, Dallas, Jupiter/Albuquerque	11
†ERA	Taylor, Graham, Jupiter/Carolina	3.4
G	Villafuerte, Brandon, Albuquerque	62
GS	Five tied with	27
SV	Mendez, Adalberto, Jupiter	29
IP	Taylor, Graham, Jupiter/Carolina	164
BB	Seddon, Chris, Albuquerque	69
SO	Seddon, Chris, Albuquerque	126
†AVG	De La Cruz, Eulogio, Albuquerque	.253

General Manager: Michael Hill. **Farm Director:** Brian Chattin. **Scouting Director:** Stan Meek.

Class	Team	League	W	L	PCT	Finish*	Manager	Affiliate Since
Majors	Florida	National	84	77	.522	7th (16)	Fredi Gonzalez	—
Triple-A	Albuquerque Isotopes	Pacific Coast	68	75	.476	10th (16)	Dean Treanor	2003
Double-A	Carolina Mudcats	Southern	80	60	.571	1st (10)	Matt Raleigh	2003
High A	Jupiter Hammerheads	Florida State	74	64	.536	5th (12)	Brandon Hyde	2002
Low A	Greensboro Grasshoppers	South Atlantic	66	72	.478	11th (16)	Edwin Rodriguez	2002
Short-season	Jamestown Jammers	New York-Penn	47	29	.618	3rd (14)	Darin Everson	2002
Rookie	GCL Marlins	Gulf Coast	30	24	.556	5th (16)	Steve Watson	1992
Overall 2008 Minor League Record			365	324	.530	6th		

* Finish in overall standings (No. of teams in league). ^League champion.

ORGANIZATION STATISTICS

FLORIDA MARLINS

NATIONAL LEAGUE

Batting	B-T	HT	WT	DOB	AVG	vLH	vRH	G	AB	R	H	2B	3B	HR	RBI	BB	HBP	SH	SF	SO	SB	CS	SLG	OBP
Amezaga, Alfredo	B-R	5-10	180	1-16-78	.264	.254	.266	125	311	41	82	13	5	3	32	19	3	4	0	47	8	2	.367	.312
Andino, Robert	R-R	6-0	170	4-25-84	.206	.250	.186	44	63	7	13	2	0	2	9	4	0	1	0	23	0	0	.333	.254
Baker, John	L-R	6-1	210	1-20-81	.299	.213	.327	61	197	32	59	14	0	5	32	30	2	1	3	48	0	0	.447	.392
Cantu, Jorge	R-R	6-3	200	1-30-82	.277	.293	.272	155	628	92	174	41	0	29	95	40	10	0	7	111	6	2	.481	.327
Carroll, Brett	R-R	6-0	190	10-3-82	.059	.000	.125	26	17	5	1	0	1	0	1	1	0	0	0	6	0	0	.176	.111
Gonzalez, Luis	L-R	6-2	210	9-3-67	.261	.239	.267	136	341	30	89	26	1	8	47	41	0	0	5	43	1	2	.413	.336
Helms, Wes	R-R	6-4	220	5-12-76	.243	.258	.234	132	251	28	61	11	0	5	31	17	5	0	5	65	0	0	.347	.299
Hermida, Jeremy	L-R	6-3	210	1-30-84	.249	.240	.252	142	502	74	125	22	3	17	61	48	7	1	1	138	6	1	.406	.323
Hoover, Paul	R-R	6-1	210	4-14-76	.200	.286	.154	13	40	1	8	1	0	0	2	2	0	0	0	17	0	0	.225	.238
Jacobs, Mike	L-R	6-3	215	10-30-80	.247	.218	.257	141	477	67	118	27	2	32	93	36	1	0	5	119	1	0	.514	.299
Jones, Jacque	L-L	5-10	200	4-25-75	.108	.000	.154	18	37	5	4	0	0	0	2	6	0	0	1	8	0	0	.108	.227
Lo Duca, Paul	R-R	5-9	215	4-12-72	.294	.300	.286	21	34	3	10	2	0	0	3	6	0	0	0	2	0	0	.353	.400
2-team total (46 Washington)					.243	—	—	67	173	16	42	9	0	0	15	15	5	0	0	11	1	0	.295	.321
Maybin, Cameron	R-R	6-4	205	4-4-87	.500	.375	.542	8	32	9	16	2	0	0	2	3	0	1	0	8	4	0	.563	.543
McPherson, Dallas	L-R	6-4	235	7-23-80	.182	.000	.250	11	11	3	2	2	0	0	4	0	0	0	0	5	0	0	.364	.400
Miller, Jai	R-R	6-4	195	1-17-85	.000	—	.000	1	1	0	0	0	0	0	0	0	0	0	0	1	0	0	.000	.000
Rabelo, Mike	B-R	6-1	210	1-17-80	.202	.222	.198	34	109	9	22	1	0	3	16	8	1	1	3	25	0	1	.294	.256
Ramirez, Hanley	R-R	6-3	200	12-23-83	.301	.258	.313	153	589	125	177	34	4	33	67	92	8	0	4	122	35	12	.540	.400
Ross, Cody	R-L	5-9	205	12-23-80	.260	.285	.249	145	461	59	120	29	5	22	73	33	7	0	5	116	6	1	.488	.316
Sanchez, Gaby	R-R	6-2	225	9-2-83	.375	.000	.429	5	8	0	3	2	0	0	1	0	0	0	0	2	0	0	.625	.375
Treanor, Matt	R-R	6-0	210	3-3-76	.238	.197	.255	65	206	18	49	7	0	2	23	18	3	5	2	53	1	0	.301	.306
Uggla, Dan	R-R	5-11	200	3-11-80	.260	.191	.283	146	531	97	138	37	1	32	92	77	8	0	3	171	5	5	.514	.360
Willingham, Josh	R-R	6-2	215	2-17-79	.254	.242	.258	102	351	54	89	21	5	15	51	48	14	1	2	82	3	2	.470	.364
Wood, Jason	R-R	6-1	170	12-16-69	.000	.000	.000	3	2	0	0	0	0	0	0	1	0	0	0	1	0	0	.000	.333

Pitching	B-T	HT	WT	DOB	W	L	ERA	G	GS	CG	SV	IP	H	R	ER	HR	BB	SO	AVG	vLH	vRH	K/9	BB/9
Badenhop, Burke	R-R	6-5	220	2-8-83	2	3	6.08	13	8	0	0	47	55	34	32	7	21	35	.289	.298	.281	6.65	3.99
De La Cruz, Eulogio	R-R	5-11	175	3-12-84	0	0	18.00	6	1	0	0	9	15	20	18	2	11	4	.375	.400	.350	4.00	11.00
Delgado, Jesus	R-R	6-1	200	4-19-84	0	0	4.50	2	0	0	0	2	1	1	1	0	3	0	.167	.000	.250	0.00	13.50
Gardner, Lee	R-R	6-0	220	1-16-75	0	0	10.80	7	0	0	0	7	14	8	8	2	4	4	.424	.412	.438	5.40	5.40
Gregg, Kevin	R-R	6-6	240	6-20-78	7	8	3.41	72	0	0	29	69	51	30	26	3	37	58	.203	.181	.222	7.60	4.85
Hendrickson, Mark	L-L	6-9	240	6-23-74	7	8	5.45	36	19	0	0	134	148	87	81	17	48	81	.283	.248	.296	5.45	3.23
Johnson, Josh	L-R	6-7	230	1-31-84	7	1	3.61	14	14	1	0	87	91	36	35	7	27	77	.275	.288	.259	7.94	2.78
Kensing, Logan	R-R	6-1	185	7-3-82	3	1	4.23	48	0	0	0	55	50	26	26	7	33	55	.234	.208	.259	8.95	5.37
Lindstrom, Matt	R-R	6-4	210	2-11-80	3	3	3.14	66	0	0	5	57	57	21	20	1	26	43	.270	.324	.214	6.75	4.08
Miller, Andrew	L-L	6-6	210	5-21-85	6	10	5.87	29	20	0	0	107	120	78	70	7	56	89	.289	.226	.307	7.46	4.70
Miller, Justin	R-R	6-2	200	8-27-77	4	2	4.24	46	0	0	0	47	46	26	22	4	20	43	.258	.310	.224	8.29	3.86
Nelson, Joe	R-R	6-1	200	10-25-74	3	1	2.00	59	0	0	1	54	42	16	12	5	22	60	.207	.227	.189	10.00	3.67
Nolasco, Ricky	R-R	6-2	220	12-13-82	15	8	3.52	34	32	1	0	212	192	88	83	28	42	186	.239	.238	.239	7.88	1.78
Olsen, Scott	L-L	6-5	215	1-12-84	8	11	4.20	33	33	0	0	202	195	106	94	30	69	113	.253	.187	.266	5.04	3.08
Pinto, Renyel	L-L	6-4	215	7-8-82	2	5	4.45	67	0	0	0	65	52	33	32	9	39	56	.226	.264	.203	7.79	5.43
Rhodes Jr., Arthur	L-L	6-2	210	10-24-69	2	0	0.68	25	0	0	1	13	11	1	1	0	3	14	.220	.103	.381	9.45	2.03
Sanchez, Anibal	R-R	6-0	180	2-27-84	2	5	5.57	10	10	0	0	52	54	35	32	7	27	50	.267	.340	.188	8.71	4.70
Tankersley, Taylor	L-L	6-1	220	3-7-83	0	1	8.15	25	0	0	0	18	22	16	16	6	8	13	.297	.360	.265	6.62	4.08
Tucker, Ryan	R-R	6-2	190	12-6-86	2	3	8.27	13	6	0	0	37	46	34	34	8	23	28	.305	.342	.264	6.81	5.59
Vanden Hurk, Rick	R-R	6-5	195	5-22-85	1	1	7.71	4	4	0	0	14	20	12	12	1	10	20	.333	.300	.367	12.86	6.43
Volstad, Chris	R-R	6-8	225	9-23-86	6	4	2.88	15	14	0	0	84	76	30	27	3	36	52	.240	.243	.236	5.55	3.84
Waechter, Doug	R-R	6-4	210	1-28-81	4	2	3.69	48	0	0	0	63	63	29	26	7	21	46	.254	.303	.216	6.54	2.98

Fielding

Catcher	PCT	G	PO	A	E	DP	PB
Baker	.991	59	402	22	4	0	3
Hoover	1.000	13	84	8	0	0	2
Lo Duca	.962	6	49	1	2	0	0
Rabelo	.995	32	179	11	1	1	3
Treanor	.984	65	453	29	8	3	2

First Base	PCT	G	PO	A	E	DP
Cantu	.993	66	260	14	2	23
Helms	.990	42	185	13	2	19
Jacobs	.988	119	825	62	11	67
Lo Duca	1.000	1	1	0	0	0
Sanchez	1.000	3	13	1	0	1

Second Base	PCT	G	PO	A	E	DP
Amezaga	.974	10	19	18	1	3
Andino	.968	15	30	31	2	7
Uggla	.981	144	297	390	13	82

Third Base	PCT	G	PO	A	E	DP
Amezaga	1.000	15	2	5	0	0
Andino	—	1	0	0	0	0
Cantu	.937	129	83	214	20	21
Helms	.989	60	31	63	1	3
McPherson	1.000	2	0	1	0	0

Shortstop	PCT	G	PO	A	E	DP
Amezaga	1.000	19	22	31	0	3
Andino	1.000	4	0	2	0	0
Ramirez	.967	150	236	401	22	89

Outfield	PCT	G	PO	A	E	DP
Amezaga	.993	79	144	6	1	1
Andino	1.000	1	2	0	0	0
Carroll	1.000	15	13	2	0	0
Gonzalez	.971	85	135	1	4	0
Helms	—	1	0	0	0	0
Hermida	.982	132	266	4	5	0
Jones	1.000	11	20	0	0	0
Maybin	1.000	8	23	0	0	0
Miller	—	1	0	0	0	0
Ross	.997	133	301	8	1	2
Willingham	1.000	98	166	7	0	0

ALBUQUERQUE ISOTOPES

TRIPLE-A

PACIFIC COAST LEAGUE

Batting	B-T	HT	WT	DOB	AVG	vLH	vRH	G	AB	R	H	2B	3B	HR	RBI	BB	HBP	SH	SF	SO	SB	CS	SLG	OBP
Andino, Robert	R-R	6-0	170	4-25-84	.287	.196	.319	43	181	28	52	14	3	6	26	18	2	2	1	31	9	5	.497	.356
Baker, John	L-R	6-1	210	1-20-81	.321	.382	.297	59	193	35	62	14	1	6	31	24	2	0	2	34	1	2	.497	.398
Barnwell, Chris	R-R	5-10	180	3-1-79	.276	.359	.250	94	330	50	91	20	1	6	42	40	8	4	4	49	16	3	.397	.364
Beattie, Andrew	B-R	5-10	175	2-28-78	.296	.301	.295	129	442	72	131	26	4	11	60	40	1	2	6	87	13	4	.448	.352
Bozied, Tagg	R-R	6-3	215	7-24-79	.306	.321	.300	123	425	86	130	28	3	26	80	50	5	0	4	76	7	2	.569	.382
Brinkley, Dante	R-R	5-11	180	8-21-81	.220	.133	.239	33	82	13	18	5	0	2	9	12	1	1	0	28	3	0	.354	.326
Carroll, Brett	R-R	6-0	190	10-3-82	.418	.467	.404	18	67	18	28	5	0	9	23	8	0	0	0	18	1	1	.896	.480
Concepcion, Alberto	R-R	6-1	220	4-18-81	.298	.231	.324	19	47	9	14	1	1	1	9	6	2	0	0	13	0	1	.426	.400
Gall, John	R-R	6-0	195	4-2-78	.312	.350	.301	98	359	49	112	29	0	12	76	31	4	1	4	50	8	4	.493	.369
Gomez, Alexis	L-L	6-2	180	8-8-78	.234	.167	.246	23	77	12	18	5	1	4	12	8	0	1	1	18	5	2	.481	.302
Hayes, Brett	R-R	6-1	200	2-13-84	.293	.370	.270	37	116	21	34	3	1	5	17	4	3	2	1	23	1	1	.466	.331
Hoover, Paul	R-R	6-1	210	4-14-76	.251	.146	.284	50	175	27	44	8	0	6	19	14	3	0	1	44	1	1	.400	.316
Lambin, Chase	B-R	6-2	195	7-7-79	.300	.347	.285	114	307	55	92	15	5	14	54	36	4	0	2	83	2	1	.518	.378
Lo Duca, Paul	R-R	5-9	215	4-12-72	.423	.800	.333	7	26	5	11	1	0	0	7	5	0	0	0	4	0	0	.462	.516
Lombard, George	L-R	6-0	210	9-14-75	.407	.000	.550	9	27	9	11	2	1	2	9	1	0	0	0	9	0	0	.778	.429
2-team total (13 Las Vegas)					.257	—	—	22	70	15	18	4	1	3	13	8	1	0	0	23	2	1	.471	.342
Mayorson, Manuel	R-R	5-10	185	3-10-83	.275	.429	.216	12	51	7	14	4	0	1	10	4	0	1	1	10	2	2	.412	.321
McPherson, Dallas	L-R	6-4	235	7-23-80	.275	.231	.288	127	448	94	123	22	3	42	98	76	2	0	4	168	14	6	.618	.379
Miller, Jai	R-R	6-4	195	1-17-85	.267	.265	.268	117	434	67	116	22	5	19	56	52	5	2	5	133	20	6	.472	.349
Mitchell, Lee	R-R	6-1	200	4-21-82	.238	.143	.286	12	21	4	5	2	0	1	4	0	0	0	0	6	0	0	.333	.360
Murphy, Tommy	B-R	5-11	200	8-27-79	.321	.262	.338	45	187	35	60	9	1	4	22	18	0	4	0	28	23	4	.444	.380
Psomas, Grant	R-R	6-3	210	9-2-82	.500	.667	.417	7	18	5	9	1	0	3	7	2	0	0	1	2	0	0	1.056	.524
Rabelo, Mike	B-R	6-1	210	1-17-80	.241	.167	.261	9	29	2	7	1	0	1	2	1	0	0	0	8	0	0	.379	.267
Randel, Kevin	L-R	6-1	180	6-11-81	.320	.167	.368	7	25	4	8	1	0	1	4	2	0	0	0	7	0	0	.480	.370
Reed, Eric	L-L	6-0	170	12-2-80	.118	.000	.154	4	17	2	2	0	0	0	1	0	0	0	0	4	1	1	.118	.118
Ryan, Michael	L-R	6-0	190	7-6-77	.321	.296	.329	33	109	15	35	7	2	9	27	7	0	1	1	26	1	0	.670	.359
Scott Jr., Lorenzo	L-L	6-3	210	3-1-82	.323	.286	.333	38	133	25	43	6	1	3	13	18	1	0	1	41	15	7	.451	.405
Wood, Jason	R-R	6-1	170	12-16-69	.269	.297	.257	105	346	53	93	14	0	4	42	27	6	2	3	59	3	0	.344	.330

Pitching	B-T	HT	WT	DOB	W	L	ERA	G	GS	CG	SV	IP	H	R	ER	HR	BB	SO	AVG	vLH	vRH	K/9	BB/9
Barone, Daniel	R-R	6-2	185	4-24-83	1	5	6.61	9	9	1	0	48	62	37	35	9	8	40	.315	.310	.320	7.55	1.51
Baugh, Kenny	R-R	6-4	190	2-5-79	3	1	5.65	15	3	0	0	37	44	24	23	6	19	24	.299	.378	.219	5.89	4.66
Carvajal, Marcos	R-R	6-4	175	8-19-84	1	2	6.92	24	2	0	0	53	66	47	41	8	42	38	.310	.333	.288	6.41	7.09
Corcoran, Tim	R-R	6-2	205	4-15-78	0	0	4.50	3	2	0	0	14	19	7	7	2	4	10	.328	.276	.379	6.43	2.57
De La Cruz, Eulogio	R-R	5-11	175	3-12-84	13	8	4.34	25	25	0	0	147	139	85	71	13	60	118	.253	.263	.245	7.21	3.67
Delgado, Jesus	R-R	6-1	200	4-19-84	0	0	11.81	6	0	0	0	11	17	14	14	2	4	6	.362	.231	.524	5.06	3.38
Glen, Willie	R-R	6-1	185	10-30-77	0	1	27.00	1	1	0	0	2	5	6	6	0	3	1	.455	.500	.444	4.50	13.50
Gwynn, Marc	R-R	6-3	215	11-4-77	1	0	4.09	36	0	0	5	44	44	27	20	4	17	37	.267	.279	.258	7.53	3.48
Hernandez, Gaby	R-R	6-3	215	5-21-86	2	8	7.24	13	13	0	0	65	94	59	52	14	26	54	.335	.299	.373	7.52	3.62
Kensing, Logan	R-R	6-1	185	7-3-82	1	0	6.39	13	0	0	3	13	8	10	9	3	12	17	.174	.167	.179	12.08	8.53
Keppel, Bob	R-R	6-5	205	6-11-82	9	11	5.99	28	27	1	0	159	208	120	106	26	57	85	.323	.316	.330	4.80	3.22
Lindstrom, Matt	R-R	6-4	200	2-11-80	0	0	9.00	3	0	0	0	4	5	4	4	1	4	4	.294	.333	.200	9.00	2.25
Martinez, Carlos	R-R	6-3	200	5-26-82	2	2	3.07	10	0	0	0	15	10	5	5	3	4	19	.189	.263	.147	11.66	2.45
McCurdy, Nick	R-R	6-3	185	1-24-80	0	0	0.00	1	0	0	0	1	0	0	0	0	1	0	.200	—	.200	9.00	0.00
Michalak, Chris	L-L	6-2	195	1-4-71	0	3	5.40	9	3	0	0	22	29	22	13	5	12	10	.322	.391	.299	4.15	4.98
Miller, Justin	R-R	6-2	200	8-27-77	0	0	40.50	1	0	0	0	1	4	3	3	1	0	1	.667	.000	.800	13.50	0.00
Mobley, Chris	R-R	5-11	170	8-16-83	0	0	27.00	5	0	0	0	4	16	12	12	0	3	2	.640	.750	.538	4.50	6.75
Nelson, Joe	R-R	6-0	200	10-25-74	1	1	2.10	19	0	0	11	26	17	6	6	1	6	36	.187	.275	.118	12.62	2.10
Nestor, Scott	R-R	6-4	225	8-20-84	1	1	7.44	55	0	0	0	62	54	51	51	9	49	64	.234	.274	.200	9.34	7.15
Santos, Jarrett	R-R	6-4	215	8-18-81	0	1	11.74	4	0	0	0	8	12	10	10	2	3	1	.375	.182	.476	1.17	3.52
Seddon, Chris	L-L	6-3	220	10-13-83	10	9	5.09	28	27	2	0	152	170	95	86	23	69	126	.291	.230	.309	7.46	4.09
Tankersley, Taylor	L-L	6-1	210	3-7-83	2	1	1.71	29	0	0	0	32	32	8	6	2	17	28	.271	.244	.288	7.96	4.83
Trahern, Dallas	R-R	6-3	190	11-29-85	5	11	6.16	21	21	0	0	111	141	87	76	20	45	71	.315	.310	.320	5.76	3.65
Vanden Hurk, Rick	R-R	6-5	195	5-22-85	2	1	4.08	4	4	0	0	18	13	11	8	3	11	21	.200	.138	.250	10.70	5.60
Villafuerte, Brandon	R-R	5-11	195	12-17-75	7	3	3.50	62	1	0	7	64	68	30	25	5	25	57	.278	.320	.246	7.97	3.50
Waechter, Doug	R-R	6-4	210	1-28-81	1	0	4.22	2	2	0	0	11	17	5	5	3	2	4	.362	.385	.333	3.38	1.69

ORGANIZATION STATISTICS

Williams, Randy	L-L	6-3	195	9-18-75	0	2	4.33	33	0	0	1	27	28	14	13	3	14	34	.272	.240	.302	11.33	4.67
Wolf, Ross	R-R	6-0	180	10-18-82	5	2	3.92	38	0	0	1	39	47	19	17	4	15	20	.309	.270	.337	4.62	3.46

Fielding

Catcher	PCT	G	PO	A	E	DP	PB
Baker	.992	50	333	33	3	3	3
Concepcion	.975	10	72	7	2	0	0
Hayes	.991	34	209	17	2	2	4
Hoover	.986	46	308	35	5	1	5
Lo Duca	1.000	3	29	4	0	1	0
Rabelo	.977	7	40	2	1	0	0

First Base	PCT	G	PO	A	E	DP
Baker	1.000	1	11	1	0	0
Bozied	.993	87	716	48	5	83
Concepcion	.917	2	19	3	2	2
Gall	1.000	7	35	1	0	3
McPherson	.992	14	119	13	1	9
Psomas	1.000	4	34	2	0	5
Wood	.997	42	351	22	1	46

Second Base	PCT	G	PO	A	E	DP
Andino	1.000	1	5	5	0	3

Barnwell	1.000	13	26	37	0	10
Beattie	.978	104	208	283	11	75
Lambin	.969	32	45	78	4	23
Randel	1.000	7	14	22	0	6
Wood	1.000	1	1	0	0	0

Third Base	PCT	G	PO	A	E	DP
Beattie	1.000	3	3	5	0	1
Bozied	.857	2	2	4	1	1
Lambin	1.000	2	1	2	0	1
McPherson	.941	108	68	203	17	20
Mitchell	1.000	4	3	4	0	1
Psomas	1.000	1	1	2	0	0
Wood	.987	32	16	59	1	7

Shortstop	PCT	G	PO	A	E	DP
Andino	.969	42	51	139	6	33
Barnwell	.978	78	135	258	9	68
Lambin	.878	11	7	36	6	8

Mayorson	1.000	12	17	36	0	9
Wood	1.000	2	2	6	0	1

Outfield	PCT	G	PO	A	E	DP
Beattie	1.000	14	22	0	0	0
Bozied	1.000	29	31	0	0	0
Brinkley	1.000	29	41	2	0	1
Carroll	1.000	17	35	3	0	2
Gall	.983	78	109	8	2	1
Gomez	.966	20	26	2	1	0
Hoover	—	1	0	0	0	0
Lambin	.966	38	52	4	2	0
Lombard	1.000	7	14	0	0	0
Miller	.962	117	216	9	9	1
Murphy	.939	45	87	6	6	1
Reed	1.000	4	7	0	0	0
Ryan	.930	28	39	1	3	0
Scott Jr.	.978	36	87	2	2	0

CAROLINA MUDCATS

DOUBLE-A

SOUTHERN LEAGUE

Batting	B-T	HT	WT	DOB	AVG	vLH	vRH	G	AB	R	H	2B	3B	HR	RBI	BB	HBP	SH	SF	SO	SB	CS	SLG	OBP
Brinkley, Dante	R-R	5-11	180	8-21-81	.231	.351	.186	43	134	27	31	8	1	3	15	21	5	0	1	43	1	3	.373	.354
Coghlan, Chris	L-R	6-1	195	6-18-85	.298	.301	.297	132	483	83	144	32	5	7	74	67	12	2	1	65	34	10	.429	.396
Concepcion, Alberto	R-R	6-1	220	4-18-81	.265	.444	.198	61	166	25	44	10	0	4	26	21	5	1	2	29	1	1	.398	.361
Cousins, Scott	L-L	6-2	190	1-22-85	.264	.176	.284	27	91	15	24	7	1	1	9	10	2	0	0	28	4	1	.396	.350
Davis, Brad	R-R	6-2	185	12-29-82	.205	.235	.193	81	249	30	51	15	1	6	28	35	3	5	4	57	0	2	.345	.306
de la Cruz, Chris	B-R	6-0	160	5-3-82	.360	.353	.362	26	75	9	27	7	0	2	12	17	0	0	0	11	0	2	.533	.478
Hayes, Brett	R-R	6-1	200	2-13-84	.232	.143	.265	54	181	19	42	8	0	6	18	10	1	1	1	43	1	4	.376	.275
Jenkins, Andrew	R-R	6-0	205	7-23-83	.259	.288	.251	110	347	37	90	16	1	8	53	19	4	1	1	66	2	3	.380	.305
Maybin, Cameron	R-R	6-4	205	4-4-87	.277	.287	.273	108	390	73	108	15	8	13	49	60	3	3	3	124	21	7	.456	.375
Mayorson, Manuel	R-R	5-10	185	3-10-83	.319	.317	.320	108	373	47	119	31	1	3	39	29	6	10	8	20	21	13	.416	.370
Mitchell, Lee	R-R	6-1	200	4-21-82	.238	.272	.225	93	303	32	72	21	2	6	51	60	4	2	8	81	4	3	.380	.363
Ontiveros, Emilio	R-R	5-11	170	1-2-85	.000	.000	—	1	2	0	0	0	0	0	0	0	0	0	0	1	0	0	.000	.000
Perez, Smelin	B-R	5-10	150	8-26-85	.125	.083	.139	17	48	2	6	1	1	0	3	3	0	3	1	16	1	0	.188	.173
Petersen, Bryan	L-R	6-0	200	4-9-86	.351	.400	.333	12	37	5	13	2	0	1	10	5	0	0	2	6	1	2	.486	.409
Psomas, Grant	R-R	6-3	210	9-2-82	.144	.212	.115	51	111	13	16	5	3	2	14	19	1	0	0	44	1	1	.297	.275
Purdom, John	R-R	6-2	230	5-28-81	.143	.000	.167	2	7	0	1	0	0	0	0	1	0	0	0	2	0	0	.143	.250
Randel, Kevin	L-R	6-1	180	6-11-81	.333	.500	.300	4	12	0	4	0	0	0	1	0	0	0	0	2	0	0	.333	.385
Raynor, John	R-R	6-2	185	1-4-84	.312	.356	.290	126	452	104	141	29	6	13	51	62	11	1	8	122	48	11	.489	.402
Roberts, Daron	R-R	6-0	215	2-25-83	.122	.083	.138	13	41	4	5	2	0	1	1	1	1	0	0	14	1	0	.244	.163
Sanchez, Gaby	R-R	6-2	225	9-2-83	.314	.374	.287	133	478	70	150	42	1	17	92	69	6	0	4	70	17	8	.513	.404
Scott Jr., Lorenzo	L-L	6-3	210	3-1-82	.273	.290	.260	52	132	25	36	4	3	4	17	26	0	0	4	45	15	1	.439	.392
Willingham, Josh	R-R	6-2	215	2-17-79	.231	.333	.143	8	26	6	6	2	0	0	5	2	2	0	0	5	0	0	.308	.333

Pitching	B-T	HT	WT	DOB	W	L	ERA	G	GS	CG	SV	IP	H	R	ER	HR	BB	SO	AVG	vLH	vRH	K/9	BB/9
Alvarez, Carlos	L-L	5-9	160	3-31-85	0	0	18.00	1	0	0	0	1	2	2	2	0	1	0	.500	1.000	.333	0.00	9.00
Badenhop, Burke	R-R	6-5	220	2-8-83	1	0	0.00	1	1	0	0	6	6	1	0	0	0	3	.240	.200	.267	4.26	0.00
Barone, Daniel	R-R	6-2	185	4-24-83	3	1	2.38	7	6	0	0	34	30	11	9	1	12	18	.236	.246	.229	4.76	3.18
Corcoran, Tim	R-R	6-2	205	4-15-78	4	2	4.54	13	7	0	0	42	42	25	21	2	12	42	.261	.250	.271	9.07	2.59
Delgado, Jesus	R-R	6-1	200	4-19-84	5	2	3.45	42	0	0	1	57	46	27	22	2	31	52	.229	.256	.207	8.16	4.87
Doolittle, Todd	R-R	5-10	175	11-1-82	5	3	3.27	36	0	0	8	44	38	20	16	3	20	61	.229	.214	.240	12.48	4.09
Glen, Willie	R-R	6-1	185	10-30-77	9	4	2.01	24	17	0	0	94	59	26	21	6	36	87	.180	.186	.176	8.33	3.45
Gogal, Jeff	R-L	6-2	195	6-10-82	6	2	2.93	47	0	0	1	58	55	29	19	6	24	62	.244	.231	.252	9.57	3.70
Hernandez, Gaby	R-R	6-3	215	5-21-86	3	0	4.30	4	4	0	0	23	21	11	11	3	4	17	.226	.235	.236	6.65	1.57
2-team total (6 West Tenn)					4	1	4.72	10	10	0	0	55	59	30	29	6	19	40	—	—	—	6.51	3.09
Johnson, Josh	L-R	6-7	230	1-31-84	1	1	3.32	3	3	0	0	19	22	9	7	0	3	14	.289	.235	.333	6.63	1.42
Lamacchia, Marc	R-R	6-1	190	3-27-82	0	2	9.49	4	3	0	0	12	18	14	13	1	5	7	.346	.250	.389	5.11	3.65
Marceaux, Jacob	R-R	6-1	190	2-14-84	4	1	4.42	45	0	0	2	59	49	37	29	4	43	45	.222	.241	.209	6.86	6.56
Martinez, Carlos	R-R	6-3	200	5-26-82	2	2	4.70	35	0	0	3	38	38	22	20	5	16	33	.271	.404	.181	7.75	3.76
McCall, Derell	R-R	6-2	230	9-20-81	1	4	5.60	8	6	0	0	35	39	26	22	3	14	25	.269	.333	.220	6.37	3.57
McCurdy, Nick	R-R	6-3	185	1-24-80	1	0	3.38	2	2	0	0	8	3	3	3	0	1	6	.276	.231	.313	6.75	1.13
Miller, Andrew	L-L	6-6	210	5-21-85	0	0	3.18	1	1	0	0	6	2	2	2	0	4	6	.118	.200	.000	9.53	6.35
Mobley, Chris	R-R	5-11	170	8-16-83	5	3	2.93	53	0	0	28	58	48	22	19	4	16	70	.224	.298	.177	10.80	2.47
Sanchez, Anibal	R-R	6-0	180	2-27-84	1	0	3.46	2	2	1	0	13	12	5	5	0	5	16	.250	.280	.231	3.46	3.46
Santos, Jarrett	R-R	6-4	215	8-18-81	5	1	3.14	29	4	0	0	57	59	22	20	3	13	32	.273	.278	.269	5.02	2.04
Sinkbeil, Brett	R-R	6-3	190	12-26-84	5	9	5.02	26	26	1	0	143	172	84	80	12	51	66	.306	.313	.300	4.14	3.20
Taylor, Graham	L-L	6-3	225	5-25-84	2	1	3.04	5	5	0	0	24	29	11	8	4	8	15	.312	.171	.397	5.70	3.04
Thompson, Aaron	L-L	6-3	195	2-28-87	2	5	5.62	16	16	0	0	82	111	61	51	9	40	53	.331	.337	.329	5.84	4.41
Tucker, Ryan	R-R	6-2	190	12-6-86	5	3	1.58	25	12	0	0	91	64	17	16	2	37	74	.195	.220	.171	7.32	3.66
Vanden Hurk, Rick	R-R	6-5	195	5-22-85	3	3	4.23	10	10	0	0	55	49	32	26	8	19	55	.240	.227	.250	8.95	3.09

	B-T	HT	WT	DOB	W	L	ERA	G	GS	CG	SV	IP	H	R	ER	HR	BB	SO	AVG	vLH	vRH	K/9	BB/9
Volstad, Chris	R-R	6-8	225	9-23-86	4	4	3.36	15	15	1	0	91	86	37	34	0	30	56	.251	.248	.254	5.54	2.97
Wood, Tim	R-R	6-1	185	11-16-82	2	1	5.75	12	0	0	0	20	20	14	13	2	6	15	.250	.292	.188	6.64	2.66
Yourkin, Matt	R-L	6-3	225	7-4-81	2	5	6.08	35	0	0	0	47	59	35	32	5	26	42	.316	.321	.313	7.99	4.94

Fielding

Catcher	PCT	G	PO	A	E	DP	PB
Concepcion	1.000	8	63	3	0	0	2
Davis	.982	75	543	44	11	9	3
Hayes	.988	49	308	30	4	3	7
Jenkins	1.000	12	69	10	0	2	0
Purdom	1.000	1	9	0	0	0	0

First Base	PCT	G	PO	A	E	DP
Concepcion	.993	33	269	31	2	21
Hayes	1.000	1	8	0	0	0
Jenkins	.993	38	274	22	2	27
Psomas	.992	14	114	8	1	6
Sanchez	.991	69	612	52	6	58

Second Base	PCT	G	PO	A	E	DP
Coghlan	.968	117	220	317	18	79
de la Cruz	1.000	4	7	10	0	2

Mayorson	1.000	4	4	8	0	1
Mitchell	.955	16	24	39	3	4
Ontiveros	1.000	1	0	2	0	0
Randel	.917	3	5	6	1	1

Third Base	PCT	G	PO	A	E	DP
Coghlan	.844	10	7	20	5	1
de la Cruz	.909	3	1	9	1	3
Mitchell	.943	66	35	129	10	13
Psomas	.917	6	2	9	1	0
Sanchez	.938	62	53	128	12	9

Shortstop	PCT	G	PO	A	E	DP
de la Cruz	.968	16	20	40	2	4
Mayorson	.967	103	145	268	14	64
Mitchell	.970	11	15	17	1	3
Perez	.891	11	14	27	5	4

Psomas	.970	10	8	24	1	3

Outfield	PCT	G	PO	A	E	DP
Brinkley	.985	37	62	2	1	1
Cousins	.971	24	30	4	1	1
Harvey	.958	59	87	5	4	1
Jenkins	.953	33	36	5	2	0
Maybin	.983	102	230	6	4	3
Perez	.750	2	3	0	1	0
Petersen	1.000	10	19	0	0	0
Psomas	1.000	5	6	0	0	0
Raynor	.966	120	185	11	7	2
Roberts	.944	11	17	0	1	0
Scott Jr.	.957	39	63	4	3	1
Willingham	.875	7	7	0	1	0

JUPITER HAMMERHEADS HIGH CLASS A

FLORIDA STATE LEAGUE

Batting	B-T	HT	WT	DOB	AVG	vLH	vRH	G	AB	R	H	2B	3B	HR	RBI	BB	HBP	SH	SF	SO	SB	CS	SLG	OBP
Blackwood, Jacob	R-R	6-0	195	9-14-85	.208	.228	.202	92	317	30	66	10	3	4	29	21	4	0	2	39	5	1	.297	.265
Brinkley, Dante	R-R	5-11	180	8-21-81	.254	.304	.227	22	67	11	17	1	0	1	9	6	4	0	0	22	3	1	.313	.351
Burns, Greg	L-L	6-2	185	11-7-86	.244	.225	.251	121	377	55	92	12	5	3	28	61	1	5	0	143	34	12	.326	.351
Carroll, Brett	R-R	6-0	190	10-3-82	.169	.161	.175	18	71	10	12	2	0	2	6	6	0	1	0	22	1	0	.282	.231
Ceballos, Jose	R-R	6-0	190	12-27-89	.000	.000	—	1	1	0	0	0	0	0	0	0	0	0	0	0	0	0	.000	.000
Cousins, Scott	L-L	6-2	190	1-22-85	.304	.259	.323	49	191	35	58	9	2	9	29	20	0	0	0	47	11	3	.513	.370
Curry, Ryan	R-R	5-10	185	4-18-85	.200	.167	.214	5	20	1	4	1	0	0	4	0	0	1	0	2	0	0	.250	.200
Dunn, Chris	R-R	5-10	180	3-8-84	.253	.220	.274	55	154	20	39	2	1	0	11	9	1	1	2	26	4	1	.279	.295
Guerrero, James	R-R	5-7	175	6-8-84	.167	.121	.185	35	114	16	19	4	1	1	6	23	2	2	1	26	4	1	.246	.314
Hatcher, Chris	R-R	6-2	190	1-12-85	.178	.154	.190	63	202	22	36	12	0	6	28	23	6	1	3	78	3	1	.327	.278
Hermida, Jeremy	L-R	6-3	210	1-30-84	.333	.250	.364	5	15	6	5	1	0	1	1	4	0	0	0	3	0	0	.600	.474
Manzanillo, Ernesto	R-R	5-11	165	12-24-88	.500	1.000	.333	1	4	2	2	0	0	0	0	0	0	0	0	1	0	0	.500	.500
Martinez, Guillermo	R-R	6-0	180	10-5-84	.201	.234	.183	61	184	12	37	5	0	0	16	17	2	2	0	50	4	3	.228	.276
McDougall, Spike	R-R	6-3	180	2-7-84	.248	.280	.234	104	355	51	88	19	2	10	59	42	2	0	5	117	6	2	.397	.327
Morrison, Logan	L-L	6-2	215	8-25-87	.332	.291	.350	130	488	71	162	38	1	13	74	57	4	0	6	80	9	3	.494	.402
Nelson, Dan	B-R	5-11	180	2-12-84	.129	.000	.182	10	31	5	4	2	0	0	4	3	0	0	1	7	1	0	.194	.200
2-team total (20 Palm Beach)					.165	—	—	30	85	9	14	5	0	0	15	13	0	0	2	18	2	0	.224	.270
Ontiveros, Emilio	R-R	5-11	170	1-2-85	.200	.250	.182	7	15	2	3	0	0	0	1	1	1	1	1	4	0	0	.200	.278
Perez, Smelin	B-R	5-10	150	8-26-85	.285	.293	.281	87	323	39	92	12	4	2	30	29	2	4	4	63	9	4	.365	.344
Petersen, Bryan	L-R	6-0	190	4-9-86	.265	.262	.266	40	155	23	41	5	0	3	12	15	3	1	1	29	7	1	.355	.339
Psomas, Grant	R-R	6-3	210	9-2-82	.169	.182	.167	20	83	6	14	6	0	1	5	7	0	0	0	27	0	0	.277	.233
Purdom, John	R-R	6-2	230	5-28-81	.230	.277	.211	65	217	21	50	14	0	6	29	20	2	1	4	32	2	0	.378	.296
Rabelo, Mike	B-R	6-1	180	1-17-80	.200	.200	.200	8	30	2	6	2	0	0	1	2	0	0	0	8	0	0	.267	.250
Randel, Kevin	L-R	6-1	180	6-11-81	.298	.245	.320	93	326	59	97	23	4	15	62	49	4	1	4	84	3	2	.531	.392
Roberts, Daron	R-R	6-0	215	2-25-83	.271	.283	.266	88	339	54	92	19	4	12	57	12	8	1	4	80	15	5	.457	.309
Septimo, Agustin	L-R	5-11	170	5-27-84	.229	.207	.235	38	131	16	30	3	2	1	18	8	0	3	1	30	4	3	.305	.271
Spanos, Vasili	R-R	6-1	225	2-25-81	.271	.257	.278	80	292	41	79	24	1	7	41	27	12	0	3	52	1	1	.432	.353
Thieme, Konrad	R-R	6-3	205	2-15-85	.000	—	.000	2	1	0	0	0	0	0	0	1	0	0	0	1	0	0	.000	.500
Treanor, Matt	R-R	6-0	210	3-3-76	.313	.250	.333	5	16	7	5	1	0	1	5	6	0	0	1	3	0	0	.563	.478
Webb, Justin	R-R	6-1	175	11-5-82	.256	.273	.250	13	39	3	10	2	1	0	2	1	2	1	0	9	1	0	.359	.310

Pitching	B-T	HT	WT	DOB	W	L	ERA	G	GS	CG	SV	IP	H	R	ER	HR	BB	SO	AVG	vLH	vRH	K/9	BB/9
Allison, Jeff	R-R	6-2	195	11-7-84	9	8	5.22	26	25	0	0	121	122	85	70	12	57	69	.260	.316	.228	5.15	4.25
Alvarez, Carlos	L-L	5-9	160	3-31-85	1	1	2.70	25	0	0	0	33	27	11	10	1	12	25	.229	.286	.205	6.75	3.24
Buente, Jay	R-R	6-3	185	9-28-83	5	1	3.00	40	0	0	1	60	49	22	20	4	27	63	.220	.256	.197	9.45	4.05
Campbell, Adam	R-R	6-1	215	9-21-84	0	0	1.80	4	0	0	0	5	7	2	1	0	2	1	.350	.333	.357	1.80	3.60
Corcoran, Tim	R-R	6-2	205	4-15-78	0	0	13.50	3	0	0	0	3	7	5	5	0	0	4	.438	.455	.400	10.80	0.00
Fernandez, Kenny	R-R	6-2	170	2-19-87	0	0	—	1	0	0	0	1	0	0	0	0	1	0	1.000	—	1.000	—	—
Gunter, Kevin	R-R	6-3	210	11-5-83	0	0	8.31	3	0	0	0	4	6	4	4	1	3	3	.333	.286	.364	6.23	6.23
2-team total (2 Sarasota)					0	0	10.57	5	0	0	0	8	13	9	9	1	5	9	—	—	—	10.57	5.87
Johnson, Josh	L-R	6-2	230	1-31-84	0	0	5.06	1	1	0	0	5	6	3	3	1	2	2	.273	.273	.273	3.38	3.38
Jones, Blake	R-R	6-5	220	4-15-81	1	0	1.17	6	0	0	0	8	9	1	1	1	7	5	.290	.364	.250	5.87	8.22
Kaminska, Kyle	L-R	6-4	180	10-5-88	0	1	7.00	2	2	0	0	9	7	9	7	1	2	11	.212	.200	.222	11.00	2.00
Koehler, Kurt	R-R	6-1	190	9-5-84	0	1	6.30	22	0	0	0	30	39	28	21	6	9	18	.315	.282	.329	5.40	2.70
Lamacchia, Marc	R-R	6-1	190	3-27-82	0	2	4.05	12	0	0	0	13	9	6	6	0	3	16	.191	.167	.207	10.80	2.03
Leroux, Christopher	L-R	6-6	210	4-14-84	6	7	3.65	57	0	0	1	74	60	37	30	6	26	78	.225	.270	.207	9.49	3.16
Madden, Corey	R-R	6-1	195	3-30-84	1	0	0.79	8	0	0	0	11	6	1	1	0	1	12	.162	.444	.071	9.53	0.79
Martinez, Cristhian	R-R	6-1	180	3-6-82	2	7	3.79	20	19	1	0	109	117	56	46	7	16	78	.273	.248	.288	6.42	1.32
McCall, Derell	R-R	6-2	230	9-22-81	8	3	3.83	24	14	0	0	96	93	46	41	4	31	60	.258	.252	.262	5.61	2.90
Mendez, Adalberto	R-R	6-2	160	2-22-82	3	7	3.47	57	0	0	29	57	46	25	22	3	24	59	.215	.179	.235	9.32	3.79

	B-T	HT	WT	DOB	W	L	ERA	G	GS	CG	SV	IP	H	R	ER	HR	BB	SO	AVG	vLH	vRH	K/9	BB/9
Miller, Colby	R-R	6-2	190	3-19-82	0	1	6.75	6	0	0	0	9	15	13	7	1	7	5	.341	.316	.360	4.82	6.75
Miller, Justin	R-R	6-2	200	8-27-77	1	0	0.00	3	0	0	0	3	2	0	0	0	1	3	.182	.333	.125	9.00	3.00
Miller, Andrew	L-L	6-6	210	5-21-85	1	0	0.71	4	2	0	0	13	10	1	1	1	1	11	.217	.429	.179	7.82	0.71
Ramirez, Andy	R-R	6-1	164	10-10-87	0	0	0.00	2	0	0	0	3	3	0	0	0	1		.300	.000	.333	3.00	3.00
Sanchez, Anibal	R-R	6-0	180	2-27-84	0	1	1.80	2	2	0	0	10	7	2	2	0	4	9	.194	.182	.200	8.10	3.60
Santos, Jarrett	R-R	6-4	215	8-18-81	4	3	2.82	13	4	0	0	38	34	14	12	2	7	20	.239	.200	.264	4.70	1.64
Stone, Brad	R-R	6-3	190	5-20-84	2	4	3.96	32	1	0	1	52	55	24	23	3	13	35	.276	.290	.269	6.02	2.24
Taylor, Graham	L-L	6-3	225	5-25-84	11	6	3.46	23	22	1	0	140	147	59	54	7	25	95	.268	.278	.263	6.09	1.60
Trahern, Dallas	R-R	6-3	190	11-29-85	0	0	1.80	1	1	0	0	5	6	3	1	0	1	2	.300	.167	.357	3.60	1.80
Villanueva, Elih	R-R	6-2	235	7-26-86	1	0	0.77	4	2	0	0	12	7	1	1	0	4	12	.167	.154	.172	9.26	3.09
Waechter, Doug	R-R	6-4	210	1-28-81	0	0	5.40	2	0	0	0	2	3	3	1	0	0	2	.333	.333	.333	10.80	0.00
West, Sean	L-L	6-8		6-15-86	6	5	2.41	21	20	0	0	101	79	33	27	3	60	92	.224	.198	.232	8.23	5.36
Winters, Kyle	R-R	6-4	190	4-22-87	6	4	3.68	22	21	0	0	110	100	52	45	6	50	65	.242	.250	.238	5.32	4.09
Wolf, Ross	R-R	6-0	180	10-18-82	0	0	2.25	3	0	0	1	4	3	1	1	0	1	7	.214	.500	.100	15.75	2.25
Wood, Tim	R-R	6-1	185	11-16-82	5	2	1.80	27	1	0	1	40	25	10	8	1	15	22	.182	.115	.224	4.95	3.38
Yourkin, Matt	R-L	6-3	225	7-4-81	1	0	2.93	13	1	0	0	15	18	5	5	0	4	17	.295	.238	.325	9.98	2.35

Fielding

Catcher	PCT	G	PO	A	E	DP	PB
Hatcher	.981	63	429	44	9	1	7
Purdom	.988	61	369	42	5	7	7
Rabelo	1.000	5	27	4	0	0	0
Thieme	1.000	2	7	0	0	0	0
Treanor	1.000	4	20	2	0	0	0
Webb	1.000	11	63	9	0	0	1

First Base	PCT	G	PO	A	E	DP
McDougall	1.000	3	17	6	0	2
Morrison	.990	118	1075	67	12	90
Psomas	1.000	1	8	1	0	1
Purdom	1.000	2	9	0	0	1
Randel	.911	4	38	3	4	5
Spanos	.991	11	99	7	1	12

Second Base	PCT	G	PO	A	E	DP
Curry	1.000	5	12	19	0	4
Guerrero	.978	35	65	113	4	19

	PCT	G	PO	A	E	DP
Manzanillo	1.000	1	1	2	0	1
Martinez	1.000	5	6	9	0	3
McDougall	1.000	1	0	1	0	0
Nelson	.977	10	13	30	1	6
Perez	.983	39	68	103	3	32
Randel	.992	52	108	142	2	12

Third Base	PCT	G	PO	A	E	DP
Blackwood	.932	87	42	177	16	17
Martinez	.833	5	2	8	2	1
Perez	.923	6	1	11	1	0
Psomas	1.000	4	1	7	0	1
Randel	1.000	4	5	0	0	0
Spanos	.953	39	27	74	5	10
Webb	1.000	1	0	3	0	0

Shortstop	PCT	G	PO	A	E	DP
Cousins	—	1	0	0	0	0
Martinez	.953	50	55	148	10	23

	PCT	G	PO	A	E	DP
Ontiveros	.969	7	11	20	1	2
Perez	.913	42	64	103	16	26
Psomas	.981	10	25	27	1	11
Septimo	.949	37	71	117	10	24

Outfield	PCT	G	PO	A	E	DP
Brinkley	1.000	16	24	1	0	0
Burns	.989	116	246	13	3	1
Carroll	1.000	11	22	1	0	0
Cousins	.933	43	82	1	6	0
Dunn	.988	47	79	5	1	2
Hermida	.750	5	6	0	2	0
McDougall	.973	84	139	5	4	2
Petersen	1.000	38	72	3	0	0
Psomas	1.000	3	4	0	0	0
Roberts	.949	67	109	3	6	0

GREENSBORO GRASSHOPPERS   LOW CLASS A
SOUTH ATLANTIC LEAGUE

Batting	B-T	HT	WT	DOB	AVG	vLH	vRH	G	AB	R	H	2B	3B	HR	RBI	BB	HBP	SH	SF	SO	SB	CS	SLG	OBP
Anetsberger, Ryan	R-R	6-2	210	7-22-85	.265	.315	.245	69	257	33	68	16	0	3	28	27	10	0	0	49	2	3	.362	.357
Belcher, Tyler	R-R	5-11	215	7-22-85	.256	.193	.285	52	180	22	46	11	1	2	15	2	3	2	0	32	0	1	.361	.276
Ceballos, Jose	R-R	6-0	190	12-27-89	.200	.000	.235	6	20	4	4	1	0	1	5	1	0	0	1	7	0	0	.400	.227
Curry, Ryan	R-R	5-10	185	4-18-85	.264	.237	.274	116	459	69	121	26	2	10	47	38	5	3	1	78	6	2	.394	.326
Dominguez, Matt	R-R	6-2	180	8-28-89	.296	.272	.304	88	345	59	102	16	0	18	70	28	5	0	3	68	0	1	.499	.354
Garcia, Daniel	R-R	6-0	165	12-27-87	.215	.224	.212	72	279	34	60	8	0	7	25	21	3	3	2	66	3	0	.319	.275
Hickman, Tom	L-L	6-0	180	4-18-88	.231	.274	.219	101	338	45	78	18	2	15	59	49	7	1	3	103	1	0	.429	.338
Howard, Adam	R-R	6-2	195	10-3-85	.183	.156	.193	33	115	15	21	3	0	2	5	5	7	0	0	31	0	1	.261	.230
Jacobs, Justin	R-R	6-1	180	7-31-88	.230	.257	.218	74	235	34	54	12	1	8	27	23	3	2	1	57	4	1	.391	.305
Langley, Torre	R-R	5-9	175	10-9-87	.209	.203	.211	71	258	31	54	11	3	6	32	14	0	2	1	45	0	0	.345	.249
Lasater, Ben	R-R	6-3	195	5-25-84	.229	.150	.245	33	118	15	27	3	0	7	24	10	4	0	2	32	0	0	.432	.306
Lechelt, Lonnie	R-R	6-1	195	10-17-85	.200	.167	.211	6	25	0	5	0	0	0	2	0	0	0	0	14	1	0	.200	.200
Martinez, Osvaldo	R-R	5-10	170	5-7-88	.296	.219	.317	85	304	44	90	11	3	6	29	13	4	8	2	46	5	5	.411	.331
Mense, Hunter	L-L	5-11	185	8-30-84	.289	.186	.315	111	432	65	125	25	1	13	56	31	8	1	2	90	5	4	.442	.347
Ontiveros, Emilio	R-R	5-11	170	1-2-85	.270	.295	.259	77	267	37	72	6	0	3	29	21	5	11	1	47	0	2	.326	.333
Petersen, Bryan	L-R	6-0	200	4-9-86	.301	.274	.309	79	296	60	89	10	2	19	58	38	4	1	6	74	15	6	.541	.381
Schultz, Brian	L-L	6-0	200	10-19-84	.244	.313	.230	25	90	9	22	6	0	1	10	9	3	1	1	24	2	0	.344	.330
Smith, Jameson	L-R	5-11	190	10-9-86	.234	.088	.263	69	209	25	49	9	0	1	13	32	2	5	1	55	0	0	.292	.340
Stanton, Mike	R-R	6-5	205	11-8-89	.293	.270	.301	125	468	89	137	26	3	39	97	58	11	0	3	153	4	2	.611	.381

Pitching	B-T	HT	WT	DOB	W	L	ERA	G	GS	CG	SV	IP	H	R	ER	HR	BB	SO	AVG	vLH	vRH	K/9	BB/9
Alexander, Stu	R-R	6-5	210	10-25-84	11	8	4.00	25	23	0	0	126	139	69	56	11	38	89	.286	.304	.272	6.36	2.71
Andrelczyk, Pete	R-R	6-1	185	11-10-85	1	4	6.12	19	0	0	1	25	31	17	17	1	12	29	.310	.333	.295	10.44	4.32
Basurto, Eric	R-R	6-3	200	4-17-86	1	2	1.64	25	0	0	0	44	38	15	8	1	26	36	.225	.276	.183	7.36	5.32
Battisto, A.J.	R-R	6-0	193	9-30-83	8	1	1.55	49	0	0	4	81	62	17	14	3	11	101	.204	.179	.221	11.18	1.22
Bodishbaugh, Chris	R-R	6-3	190	10-24	1	2	10.29	12	0	0	0	21	36	24	24	3	9	10	.371	.305	.474	4.29	3.86
Caminero, Arquimedes	R-R	6-4	185	6-16-87	0	0	3.00	1	0	0	0	3	2	3	1	0		3	.182	.000	.182	9.00	0.00
Campbell, Adam	R-R	6-1	215	9-21-84	1	1	7.04	6	0	0	0	8	8	10	6	1	6	7	.276	.333	.235	8.22	7.04
Cishek, Steven	R-R	6-6	200	6-18-86	3	5	4.66	50	0	0	2	75	69	40	39	8	34	75	.246	.239	.252	8.96	4.06
Correa, Hector	R-R	6-3	165	3-18-88	0	1	6.30	4	0	0	0	10	15	8	7	1	1	9	.326	.316	.333	8.10	0.90
Czyz, Donald	R-R	6-2	200	9-16-83	0	0	2.35	19	0	0	3	31	25	11	8	3	6	37	.217	.212	.222	10.86	1.76
Durand, Brett	R-R	6-2	200	5-19-86	10	6	5.53	29	27	1	0	143	180	102	88	22	21	95	.303	.286	.317	5.97	1.32
Evans, Bryan	R-R	6-3	205	2-25-87	2	5	7.48	10	9	0	0	43	69	38	36	9	9	25	.361	.360	.362	5.19	1.87
Gunter, Kevin	R-R	6-3	210	11-5-83	1	2	4.14	24	0	0	0	37	36	22	17	3	23	29	.261	.260	.261	7.05	5.59
Haar, Jeremiah	L-R	6-2	190	12-29-84	0	2	5.60	8	4	0	0	27	39	20	17	2	11	10	.345	.415	.283	3.29	3.62

Name	B-T	HT	WT	DOB	W	L	ERA	G	GS	CG	SV	IP	H	R	ER	HR	BB	SO	AVG	vLH	vRH	K/9	BB/9
Harvey, Kris	R-R	6-2	195	1-5-84	0	2	7.50	4	0	0	0	6	10	8	5	0	7	2	.400	.286	.444	3.00	10.50
Johnson, Josh	L-R	6-7	230	1-31-84	0	1	3.60	1	1	0	0	5	8	2	2	0	0	7	.364	.200	.412	12.60	0.00
Kaminska, Kyle	L-R	6-4	180	10-5-88	5	7	6.54	18	17	0	0	85	122	67	62	13	14	82	.332	.347	.318	8.65	1.48
Madden, Corey	R-R	6-1	195	3-30-84	5	0	1.09	42	0	0	4	58	36	8	7	3	19	92	.177	.213	.149	14.28	2.95
Mallory, Matt	R-R	6-3	220	3-4-85	0	2	2.45	24	4	0	0	48	54	21	13	3	10	30	.276	.265	.287	5.66	1.89
Martinez, Cristhian	R-R	6-1	160	3-6-82	4	1	4.67	8	8	0	0	44	44	24	23	2	9	14	.256	.247	.263	2.84	1.83
McCurdy, Nick	R-R	6-3	185	1-24-80	0	0	2.00	7	0	0	3	9	11	3	2	0	1	11	.297	.294	.300	11.00	1.00
Miller, Colby	R-R	6-2	190	3-19-82	1	6	6.49	9	8	0	0	43	53	33	31	9	14	31	.298	.325	.274	6.49	2.93
Parcell, Garrett	R-R	6-5	220	7-12-84	0	2	3.49	29	0	0	17	28	27	13	11	2	8	26	.255	.196	.300	8.26	2.54
Phillips, Shawn	R-R	6-1	195	12-19-82	1	0	0.00	3	0	0	0	7	2	0	0	0	0	6	.080	.125	.059	7.71	0.00
Rosario, Jose	R-R	6-0	170	2-16-86	0	1	8.10	2	2	0	0	10	8	9	9	1	6	13	.216	.333	.105	11.70	5.40
Rosario, Sandy	R-R	6-1	170	8-22-85	0	0	13.50	1	1	0	0	2	3	4	3	0	3	4	.375	—	.375	18.00	13.50
Sanabia, Alejandro	R-R	6-1	165	9-8-88	5	5	4.93	19	19	0	0	97	106	60	53	11	25	75	.273	.267	.278	6.98	2.33
Stone, Brad	R-R	6-3	190	5-20-84	3	0	1.89	11	0	0	0	19	11	4	4	0	4	15	.164	.308	.073	7.11	1.89
Voss, Jay	L-L	6-4	195	4-22-87	3	6	6.39	26	11	0	0	69	106	56	49	8	24	55	.355	.409	.332	7.17	3.13

Fielding

Catcher	PCT	G	PO	A	E	DP	PB
Belcher	.980	38	279	20	6	2	6
Ceballos	1.000	6	47	7	0	0	2
Langley	.989	65	434	34	5	1	7
Smith	.962	42	265	16	11	2	2

First Base	PCT	G	PO	A	E	DP
Anetsberger	.990	54	486	27	5	39
Belcher	.991	12	97	10	1	7
Curry	1.000	1	7	0	0	0
Howard	.971	11	96	6	3	5
Jacobs	1.000	2	7	0	0	0
Lasater	.981	5	48	4	1	3
Martinez	1.000	1	7	0	0	0
Mense	.985	56	433	18	7	39

	PCT	G	PO	A	E	DP
Smith	.989	10	79	7	1	6

Second Base	PCT	G	PO	A	E	DP
Curry	.982	89	171	271	8	55
Garcia	.951	46	70	165	12	25
Lechelt	1.000	2	2	11	0	1
Ontiveros	1.000	2	2	4	0	0

Third Base	PCT	G	PO	A	E	DP
Anetsberger	.600	6	3	6	6	0
Curry	.923	3	1	11	1	1
Dominguez	.948	88	65	152	12	21
Howard	.895	6	6	11	2	0
Lasater	.871	27	9	45	8	5
Ontiveros	.929	12	8	18	2	1

Shortstop	PCT	G	PO	A	E	DP
Anetsberger	1.000	1	0	2	0	0
Curry	.846	3	2	9	2	0
Lechelt	.941	3	5	11	1	2
Martinez	.922	73	104	229	28	36
Ontiveros	.966	60	76	177	9	32

Outfield	PCT	G	PO	A	E	DP
Hickman	.957	95	149	7	7	2
Howard	.875	10	14	0	2	0
Jacobs	.942	68	106	8	7	2
Mense	.919	41	66	2	6	0
Petersen	.964	79	153	7	6	2
Schultz	.936	25	42	2	3	0
Stanton	.978	107	219	6	5	1

JAMESTOWN JAMMERS — SHORT-SEASON

NEW YORK-PENN LEAGUE

Batting	B-T	HT	WT	DOB	AVG	vLH	vRH	G	AB	R	H	2B	3B	HR	RBI	BB	HBP	SH	SF	SO	SB	CS	SLG	OBP
Banks, Ernie	R-R	6-4	220	5-14-86	.300	.176	.333	67	243	41	73	13	1	6	51	27	3	0	0	52	0	1	.436	.377
Bass, Justin	R-R	6-0	205	12-12-85	.253	.224	.262	64	190	31	48	17	1	6	22	20	6	6	1	50	6	3	.447	.341
Fermin, Miguel	R-R	6-0	165	2-11-85	.347	.242	.386	65	242	54	84	13	2	17	47	9	3	1	3	43	6	1	.628	.374
Gran, Paul	R-R	5-11	182	4-7-86	.322	.448	.289	70	276	52	89	14	3	6	39	23	8	0	5	56	13	3	.460	.387
Lasater, Ben	R-R	6-3	195	5-25-84	.324	.340	.318	59	207	29	67	12	0	9	41	22	4	2	2	55	2	0	.512	.396
Lechelt, Lonnie	R-R	6-1	195	10-17-85	.196	.207	.192	40	107	24	21	5	1	4	11	8	2	0	1	52	8	0	.374	.263
MacDonald, Mitch	L-R	5-11	185	6-8-87	.245	.000	.264	39	98	11	24	3	1	3	7	12	0	0	0	33	0	0	.388	.327
Martinez, Felix	R-R	6-2	200	8-16-84	.196	.188	.200	24	51	7	10	4	0	1	5	3	0	0	1	19	1	0	.333	.236
Mattison, Kevin	L-L	6-0	180	9-20-85	.250	.270	.244	70	268	48	67	10	6	4	20	37	2	1	1	71	14	4	.377	.344
Pasek, Mike	R-R	5-9	160	9-8-89	.000	.000	.000	1	4	0	0	0	0	0	0	0	0	0	0	1	0	0	.000	.000
Rojas, Jesus	R-R	6-1	170	7-16-86	.128	.091	.139	23	47	4	6	1	0	0	3	7	0	0	0	16	0	1	.149	.241
Schultz, Brian	L-L	6-0	200	10-15-84	.214	.000	.231	5	14	2	3	0	0	0	1	0	0	0	0	6	0	0	.214	.214
Staples, Joel	R-R	6-2	205	5-26-87	.293	.257	.307	70	246	39	72	13	2	6	31	28	0	2	1	69	9	4	.435	.364
Synan, Jeremy	L-R	6-0	193	7-14-86	.297	.226	.319	67	266	37	79	21	5	3	35	23	2	0	1	61	4	2	.447	.356
Taylor, Robert	R-R	6-2	215	10-10-85	.224	.320	.195	38	107	12	24	3	1	5	18	10	1	0	2	32	0	1	.411	.292
Thieme, Konrad	R-R	6-3	205	2-15-85	.250	.200	.275	2	60	9	15	6	0	2	11	5	1	1	0	20	0	1	.450	.318
Turner, Brandon	L-R	6-1	185	2-15-87	.331	.400	.317	44	151	13	50	7	0	2	32	9	2	2	2	30	1	0	.417	.372
White, Ray	R-R	5-8	160	6-25-87	.139	.125	.143	29	36	7	5	1	0	0	2	5	0	1	1	18	1	0	.167	.238

Pitching	B-T	HT	WT	DOB	W	L	ERA	G	GS	CG	SV	IP	H	R	ER	HR	BB	SO	AVG	vLH	vRH	K/9	BB/9
Andrelczyk, Pete	R-R	6-1	185	11-10-85	0	0	0.00	7	0	0	4	8	4	0	0	0	0	10	.143	.182	.118	10.80	0.00
Bodishbaugh, Chris	R-R	6-3	190	10-2-84	1	0	2.40	11	0	0	0	15	15	4	4	1	7	18	.250	.267	.244	10.80	4.20
Caminero, Arquimedes	R-R	6-4	185	6-16-87	1	0	4.91	6	0	0	0	7	8	4	4	0	3	8	.276	.300	.263	9.82	3.68
Campbell, Adam	R-R	6-1	215	9-21-84	3	0	0.93	15	0	0	1	29	25	9	3	1	5	40	.219	.213		12.41	1.55
Clothier, Drew	L-L	6-2	180	2-18-86	2	0	4.05	10	0	0	0	20	17	10	9	1	8	24	.227	.143	.259	10.80	3.60
Crawford, Skyler	R-R	6-1	175	4-20-88	1	3	7.03	14	13	0	0	56	81	48	44	4	24	51	.343	.356	.336	8.15	3.83
Dorn, Johnny	R-R	6-3	210	8-4-85	3	2	2.95	16	16	0	0	76	60	29	25	4	23	63	.212	.207	.215	7.43	2.71
Evans, Bryan	R-R	6-3	205	2-25-87	1	3	5.11	3	3	0	0	12	15	7	7	1	3	7	.294	.333	.273	5.11	2.19
Gooch, Wayman	R-R	6-3	185	10-22-87	2	0	8.13	19	0	0	1	34	48	32	31	2	20	31	.329	.364	.314	8.13	5.24
Hand, Brad	L-L	6-2	185	3-20-90	1	2	3.00	3	3	0	0	15	11	6	5	0	10	12	.208	.222	.205	7.20	6.00
Jennings, Dan	L-L	6-3	190	4-17-87	1	4	3.53	13	13	0	0	59	79	31	23	2	18	62	.321	.323	.321	9.51	2.76
Koehler, Tom	R-R	6-3	235	6-29-86	5	5	3.68	15	13	0	0	66	66	33	27	0	29	58	.261	.270	.254	7.91	3.95
Korpi, Wade	R-R	6-3	190	3-10-86	5	1	5.08	15	2	0	0	37	32	16	14	0	16	41	.239	.273	.222	9.88	3.86
Loomis, Andy	L-L	5-10	175	11-25-85	5	3	3.31	12	0	0	0	33	36	17	12	4	10	46	.275	.171	.313	12.67	2.76
Martin, Kedrick	L-L	6-1	170	1-28-87	0	0	4.28	20	0	0	0	34	27	17	16	2	23	38	.220	.242	.211	10.06	6.15
Ramirez, Andy	R-R	6-1	164	10-16-87	3	4	6.09	14	12	0	0	58	70	45	39	7	24	38	.299	.371	.273	5.93	3.75
Todd, Brandon	R-R	6-1	205	4-5-85	3	2	2.25	25	0	0	12	32	26	11	8	1	14	43	.218	.225	.215	12.09	3.94
Vieira, Matt	L-L	6-1	185	8-9-85	2	0	4.11	9	0	0	0	15	20	8	7	0	3	15	.317	.353	.304	8.80	1.76
Villanueva, Elih	R-R	6-2	235	7-26-86	2	1	1.89	5	1	0	0	19	15	6	4	0	5	20	.205	.121	.275	9.47	2.37
Yecker, Jared	R-R	6-6	210	12-8-86	2	1	0.91	21	0	0	9	30	9	3	3	1	9	36	.090	.071	.103	10.92	2.73

Fielding

Catcher	PCT	G	PO	A	E	DP	PB
Fermin	.988	59	461	46	6	0	7
Taylor	1.000	12	76	5	0	0	3
Thieme	1.000	15	108	5	0	1	2

First Base	PCT	G	PO	A	E	DP
Banks	.994	43	333	25	2	34
Lasater	1.000	31	234	15	0	24
MacDonald	1.000	8	35	3	0	0
Rojas	1.000	4	10	1	0	1
Taylor	.941	3	16	0	1	3

Second Base	PCT	G	PO	A	E	DP
Gran	.969	19	23	39	2	8

	PCT	G	PO	A	E	DP
Lechelt	.924	24	28	45	6	12
Pasek	1.000	1	2	5	0	1
Turner	.964	43	66	93	6	20
White	1.000	4	5	5	0	2

Third Base	PCT	G	PO	A	E	DP
Gran	.919	46	33	80	10	7
Lasater	.759	23	13	31	14	4
Rojas	.854	17	8	33	7	3

Shortstop	PCT	G	PO	A	E	DP
Gran	.970	8	12	20	1	3
Lechelt	1.000	2	2	5	0	2
Staples	.925	70	81	203	23	43

	PCT	G	PO	A	E	DP
Turner	1.000	2	0	1	0	0

Outfield	PCT	G	PO	A	E	DP
Bass	.972	62	95	8	3	3
Lasater	1.000	1	1	0	0	0
Lechelt	1.000	11	12	0	0	0
Martinez	1.000	20	14	0	0	0
Mattison	.951	68	148	7	8	2
Schultz	1.000	4	7	0	0	0
Synan	.970	66	95	1	3	0
Taylor	1.000	6	4	0	0	0
White	1.000	14	12	0	0	0

GCL MARLINS   ROOKIE
GULF COAST LEAGUE

Batting	B-T	HT	WT	DOB	AVG	vLH	vRH	G	AB	R	H	2B	3B	HR	RBI	BB	HBP	SH	SF	SO	SB	CS	SLG	OBP
Arias, Rene	R-R	6-0	182	6-22-87	.281	.375	.265	21	57	11	16	4	0	0	8	5	1	2	1	7	1	0	.351	.344
Asencio, Ramon	L-L	6-4	185	6-4-87	.291	.200	.322	32	79	18	23	3	4	3	14	9	6	1	2	30	4	3	.544	.396
Carroll, Brett	R-R	6-0	190	10-3-82	.250	.000	.286	2	8	1	2	1	0	0	0	1	0	0	0	1	0	0	.375	.333
Castillo, Nestor	B-R	6-2	176	10-24-89	.230	.250	.227	39	113	15	26	2	1	0	12	13	1	4	1	30	3	3	.265	.313
Ceballos, Jose	R-R	6-0	190	12-27-89	.258	.214	.266	27	93	9	24	3	2	0	15	4	4	0	2	25	1	0	.333	.311
Cousins, Scott	L-L	6-2	190	1-22-85	.000	.000	.000	2	6	0	0	0	0	0	0	0	0	0	0	5	0	0	.000	.000
Escalona, Raul	R-R	5-10	184	2-21-88	.250	.250	.250	8	20	2	5	0	0	0	2	4	0	0	0	2	0	1	.250	.375
Galloway, Isaac	R-R	6-2	190	10-10-89	.286	.297	.284	48	199	29	57	13	5	1	23	4	2	3	3	33	4	2	.417	.303
Lokken, Matt	R-R	6-4	200	9-18-89	.000	—	.000	1	2	0	0	0	0	0	0	0	0	0	0	0	0	0	.000	.000
Lombard, George	L-R	6-0	210	9-14-75	.091	.000	.100	3	11	2	1	1	0	0	0	1	0	0	0	5	0	0	.182	.231
Manzanillo, Ernesto	R-R	5-11	165	12-24-88	.347	.208	.383	40	118	21	41	6	6	2	21	25	0	0	2	29	11	6	.551	.455
Mercedes, Luis	R-R	5-10	165	4-16-89	.250	.333	.200	8	8	2	2	0	0	0	2	0	0	1	0	1	0	0	.250	.250
Moore, Zach	L-R	6-4	205	8-6-88	.284	.222	.299	32	95	13	27	4	0	0	12	11	1	1	2	16	7	3	.326	.358
Orton, Ricky	L-R	6-4	225	9-7-86	.246	.120	.274	43	138	20	34	6	2	1	19	22	0	0	0	27	1	0	.341	.350
Pasek, Mike	R-R	5-9	160	9-8-89	.202	.167	.211	37	119	19	24	4	1	0	15	7	7	0	2	24	2	1	.252	.281
Paulino, Carlos	R-R	6-0	167	9-24-89	.152	.333	.140	17	46	5	7	3	1	0	2	1	2	0	0	3	1	0	.261	.204
Peacock, Jason	R-R	6-0	225	9-22-85	.289	.188	.311	27	90	9	26	4	0	0	9	8	0	1	0	20	0	1	.333	.347
Pertusati, Danny	R-R	6-1	185	4-27-90	.295	.273	.301	46	176	33	52	7	2	2	23	12	5	1	5	22	4	6	.392	.348
Schultz, Brian	L-L	6-0	200	10-15-84	.380	.250	.407	22	71	15	27	4	3	1	15	12	1	1	0	11	3	4	.563	.476
Skipworth, Kyle	L-R	6-3	195	3-1-90	.208	.161	.219	43	159	22	33	6	0	5	21	13	0	1	3	46	2	2	.340	.263
Torres, Jose	R-R	6-0	170	10-22-90	.252	.267	.250	36	107	10	27	3	0	0	12	9	4	2	1	13	1	1	.280	.331

Pitching	B-T	HT	WT	DOB	W	L	ERA	G	GS	CG	SV	IP	H	R	ER	HR	BB	SO	AVG	vLH	vRH	K/9	BB/9
Badenhop, Burke	R-R	6-5	220	2-8-83	0	0	0.00	1	1	0	0	3	1	0	0	0	0	2	.100	.200	.000	6.00	0.00
Barrow, Brandon	L-L	6-4	195	4-18-89	2	4	5.46	14	4	0	1	28	32	19	17	2	17	28	.291	.200	.311	9.00	5.46
Beato, Benito	R-R	6-2	190	3-21-85	0	0	1.69	4	0	0	1	5	3	1	1	0	1	6	.176	.333	.091	10.13	1.69
Brewer, Blake	R-R	6-5	177	3-2-90	3	1	2.16	7	4	0	0	25	15	6	6	0	13	32	.172	.270	.100	11.52	4.68
Caminero, Arquimedes	R-R	6-4	185	6-16-87	0	1	1.56	14	0	0	3	17	9	5	3	0	11	20	.158	.160	.156	10.38	5.71
Correa, Hector	R-R	6-3	165	3-18-88	0	0	13.50	1	1	0	0	3	5	4	4	0	2	2	.357	.500	.300	6.75	6.75
Doolittle, Todd	R-R	5-10	175	11-1-82	0	0	0.00	2	0	0	0	2	1	0	0	0	0	2	.167	.167	.000	9.00	0.00
Fernandez, Kenny	R-R	6-2	170	2-19-87	3	0	1.50	15	3	0	0	30	25	6	5	1	6	21	.234	.200	.254	6.30	1.80
Franco, Juan	R-R	6-3	185	11-9-87	3	1	5.66	13	0	0	0	21	18	13	13	1	12	12	.228	.308	.189	5.23	5.23
Hand, Brad	L-L	6-2	185	3-20-90	2	0	2.48	9	7	0	0	33	25	16	9	0	11	34	.212	.217	.211	9.37	3.03
Harvey, Kris	R-R	6-2	195	1-5-84	1	0	6.23	4	0	0	0	4	3	3	3	1	3	5	.200	.000	.231	10.38	6.23
Hernandez, Ricardo	L-L	5-10	152	1-23-88	0	1	2.70	15	1	0	2	23	16	8	7	1	10	27	.186	.250	.176	10.41	3.86
Johnson, Graham	R-R	6-6	215	10-13-89	0	0	5.40	3	2	0	0	5	6	3	3	1	0	8	.286	.357	.143	14.40	0.00
Jones, Blake	R-R	6-5	220	4-15-81	0	0	4.15	9	0	0	0	9	8	4	4	0	1	9	.250	.273	.238	9.35	1.04
Koehler, Kurt	R-R	6-1	190	9-5-84	0	0	2.25	2	0	0	0	4	4	1	1	0	1	4	.250	.200	.333	9.00	2.25
Lamacchia, Marc	R-R	6-1	190	3-27-82	0	0	0.00	2	0	0	1	2	2	0	0	0	0	3	.222	.500	.143	11.57	0.00
Marinez, Jhan	R-R	6-1	165	8-12-88	1	1	6.11	12	1	0	1	18	21	14	12	0	14	18	.296	.333	.268	9.17	7.13
Matos, Wilson	R-R	6-2	180	4-10-88	1	2	3.71	14	1	0	2	27	23	16	11	0	12	27	.228	.222	.231	9.11	4.05
Miller, Andrew	L-L	6-6	210	5-21-85	0	1	18.00	1	1	0	0	2	2	2	2	1	0	1	.400	.000	.500	9.00	9.00
Miller, Justin	R-R	6-2	200	8-27-77	0	0	9.00	1	0	0	0	1	2	1	1	0	0	2	.333	.000	1.000	18.00	0.00
Olmos, Edgar	L-L	6-5	180	4-12-90	0	0	0.00	1	1	0	0	2	2	0	0	0	0	5	.250	.000	.286	27.00	0.00
Paulauskas, Andrew	R-R	6-3	185	4-7-89	0	2	17.10	6	3	0	0	10	20	21	19	1	8	10	.408	.412	.406	9.00	7.20
Petersen, Curtis	R-R	6-3	180	8-28-89	0	2	9.64	5	4	0	0	14	19	16	15	0	13	9	.352	.286	.375	5.79	8.36
Prieto, Daniel	L-L	6-0	195	4-22-88	1	2	7.89	9	4	0	0	22	32	20	19	0	10	13	.348	.240	.388	5.40	4.15
Rosario, Jose	R-R	6-0	170	2-16-86	3	0	4.54	11	10	0	0	40	36	22	20	4	16	39	.238	.242	.235	8.85	3.63
Sanchez, Anibal	R-R	6-0	180	2-27-84	1	0	3.60	1	1	0	0	5	4	2	2	0	1	5	.211		.125	7.20	1.80
Shafer, Chris	R-R	6-2	245	5-16-89	5	1	4.18	14	1	0	1	32	33	19	15	1	12	31	.264	.325	.235	8.63	3.34
Thompson, Aaron	L-L	6-3	195	2-28-87	0	2	2.00	2	2	0	0	9	8	2	2	0	1	9	.242	.500	.226	9.00	1.00
Villanueva, Elih	R-R	6-2	235	7-26-86	0	3	3.00	2	1	0	0	6	4	2	2	0	0	9	.200	.167	.214	13.50	0.00
Waechter, Doug	R-R	6-4	210	1-28-81	0	0	0.00	1	1	0	0	1	0	0	0	0	0	2	.250	.000	.333	18.00	0.00

Fielding

Catcher	PCT	G	PO	A	E	DP	PB
Arias	.923	3	12	0	1	0	0
Ceballos	.991	14	107	4	1	0	3
Paulino	.982	16	94	13	2	0	3
Skipworth	.989	30	236	26	3	1	7

First Base	PCT	G	PO	A	E	DP
Arias	1.000	1	1	0	0	0
Asencio	—	1	0	0	0	0
Escalona	1.000	5	27	1	0	4
Orton	.992	32	235	14	2	21
Peacock	.984	23	178	11	3	11

Second Base	PCT	G	PO	A	E	DP
Manzanillo	.800	2	1	3	1	1

Mercedes	1.000	5	2	3	0	1
Pasek	.947	7	7	11	1	3
Paulino	1.000	1	0	1	0	0
Pertusati	.950	46	71	119	10	27
Torres	1.000	1	0	2	0	0

Third Base	PCT	G	PO	A	E	DP
Arias	1.000	1	1	0	0	0
Manzanillo	.827	20	4	39	9	0
Mercedes	.750	2	2	1	1	0
Orton	.958	9	9	14	1	0
Pasek	.897	26	13	39	6	1

Shortstop	PCT	G	PO	A	E	DP
Manzanillo	.938	16	21	55	5	10

Mercedes	—	1	0	0	0	0
Pasek	.933	5	5	9	1	2
Torres	.956	35	61	91	7	22

Outfield	PCT	G	PO	A	E	DP
Arias	.833	7	5	0	1	0
Asencio	.889	30	30	2	4	0
Carroll	1.000	1	3	0	0	0
Castillo	.981	37	48	3	1	0
Cousins	1.000	2	5	0	0	0
Galloway	.966	48	83	2	3	0
Lombard	1.000	2	3	0	0	0
Moore	.952	29	38	2	2	0
Schultz	.944	19	16	1	1	0

DSL MARLINS

ROOKIE

DOMINICAN SUMMER LEAGUE

Batting	B-T	HT	WT	DOB	AVG	vLH	vRH	G	AB	R	H	2B	3B	HR	RBI	BB	HBP	SH	SF	SO	SB	CS	SLG	OBP
Bautista, Samuel	L-R	6-1	148	12-12-88	.218	.143	.234	56	202	34	44	5	5	5	27	21	5	3	1	61	11	3	.366	.306
Bonifacio, Joan	R-R	6-1	173	3-6-90	.180	.174	.182	30	89	13	16	3	0	0	3	17	1	0	0	39	1	1	.213	.318
Brito, Welington	R-R	6-5	200	5-13-89	.059	.000	.067	7	17	1	1	1	0	0	0	0	1	0	0	6	0	0	.118	.111
Calzado, Jose	R-R	5-11	135	3-2-88	.245	.204	.259	59	184	27	45	6	2	0	13	28	5	4	0	36	15	11	.299	.359
Diaz, Aury	R-R	6-1	155	5-29-90	.269	.378	.244	61	238	49	64	11	2	0	21	34	5	1	1	39	8	1	.332	.371
Geronimo, Jose	R-R	5-11	150	6-30-90	.052	.083	.043	19	58	3	3	0	0	0	5	0	5	1	2	19	0	0	.052	.123
Gimenez, Wilfredo	R-R	6-0	180	12-18-90	.265	.333	.245	54	211	27	56	11	2	1	19	18	5	0	2	14	1	2	.351	.335
Gomez, Raul	L-R	6-0	180	2-23-89	.171	.136	.182	56	187	18	32	6	0	1	16	18	3	1	2	41	2	2	.219	.252
Indriago, Javier	R-R	6-0	180	8-31-90	.040	.000	.053	10	25	0	1	0	0	0	0	4	0	0	0	12	0	1	.040	.172
Martinez, Juancito	R-R	6-1	170	6-10-89	.192	.143	.205	44	99	21	19	3	0	0	5	24	3	1	1	35	13	2	.222	.362
Martinez, Julio	R-R	6-1	145	3-5-91	.200	.300	.167	31	80	7	16	4	0	1	6	7	1	0	0	21	4	1	.288	.273
Mercedes, Luis	R-R	5-10	165	4-16-89	.280	.171	.320	42	132	17	37	8	1	0	19	30	3	4	3	19	14	7	.356	.417
Osuna, Hector	B-R	6-1	170	10-17-90	.245	.100	.285	54	184	18	45	9	2	1	25	14	4	0	5	31	3	1	.332	.304
Ozuna, Marcell	R-R	6-2	190	11-12-90	.279	.208	.297	63	233	33	65	14	0	6	43	23	0	0	7	61	8	1	.416	.335
Peralta, Rony	L-R	6-0	160	8-19-90	.250	.109	.288	65	216	37	54	6	4	1	21	44	6	1	1	49	7	6	.329	.390
Rodriguez, Jesus	R-R	6-1	175	1-11-90	.150	.105	.160	34	113	11	17	4	1	0	12	17	1	0	0	36	3	1	.204	.267
Urena, Maicol	R-R	6-0	165	11-11-90	.200	.143	.211	13	45	4	9	2	0	0	3	4	1	0	1	13	2	1	.244	.275

Pitching	B-T	HT	WT	DOB	W	L	ERA	G	GS	CG	SV	IP	H	R	ER	HR	BB	SO	AVG	vLH	vRH	K/9	BB/9
Buret, Alfredo	R-R	6-1	160	8-22-87	6	3	2.34	15	15	1	0	96	67	35	25	1	27	68	.190	.211	.185	6.35	2.52
Chirinos, Luis	R-R	6-2	170	4-22-90	7	2	2.84	13	10	0	0	67	58	26	21	0	20	55	.226	.186	.241	7.43	2.70
Estevez, Alvaro	R-R	6-2	180	3-15-89	4	5	4.79	17	3	0	3	41	35	26	22	0	24	34	.238	.229	.241	7.40	5.23
Ferreira, Kelvin	L-L	6-0	156	10-31-90	0	1	1.40	15	0	0	3	19	15	4	3	1	10	20	.217	1.000	.194	9.31	4.66
Garcia, Michael	R-R			3-25-91	0	1	3.34	15	0	0	2	35	39	14	13	2	13	38	.289	.200	.320	9.77	3.34
Gil, Daniel	R-R	6-5	184	3-28-90	3	3	2.87	11	6	0	1	47	37	19	15	2	16	41	.219	.237	.209	7.85	3.06
Gonzalez, Saul	R-R	6-1	182	9-19-88	4	1	1.76	13	1	0	0	72	45	21	14	1	27	70	.179	.258	.151	8.79	3.39
Jimenez, Oliver	R-R			9-29-89	0	0	8.10	5	0	0	0	7	6	8	6	0	8	2	.222	.333	.190	2.70	10.80
Lopez, Jose	L-L	6-0	165	11-11-90	2	3	4.95	13	5	0	0	36	32	22	20	0	25	37	.242	.286	.240	9.17	6.19
Manzueta, Jheyson	R-R	6-2	162	12-5-89	0	2	16.20	6	3	0	0	8	18	15	0	17	7	.324	.294	.350	7.56	18.36
Oviedo, Grabiel	R-R	6-4	187	10-30-89	0	0	6.75	7	0	0	0	9	12	15	7	0	12	5	.293	.200	.323	4.82	11.57
Rodriguez, Jose	R-R	6-1	195	9-24-90	1	2	3.72	10	1	0	1	19	10	8	8	0	14	20	.159	.059	.196	9.31	6.52
Rojas, Wilfredo	R-R	6-2	150	8-31-89	1	5	5.27	23	0	0	6	41	40	27	24	1	18	29	.265	.318	.243	6.37	3.95
Salom, Brahian	R-R	6-3	180	7-26-89	0	2	4.32	6	5	0	0	25	19	17	12	1	16	21	.216	.400	.162	7.56	5.76
Solano, Aneurys	R-R	6-1	180	11-18-88	0	4	8.83	12	2	0	0	17	14	22	17	1	22	26	.209	.385	.167	13.50	11.42
Soto, Juan	R-R			10-23-90	0	1	6.00	8	0	0	0	12	14	10	8	0	11	11	.304	.182	.343	8.25	8.25
Tamares, Joel	R-R			8-13-90	5	1	3.86	15	6	0	0	44	39	27	19	0	27	36	.231	.244	.227	7.31	5.48

Fielding

Catcher	PCT	G	PO	A	E	DP	PB
Geronimo	.992	16	117	9	1	1	7
Gimenez	.960	47	354	51	17	1	6
Jimenez	1.000	1	6	0	0	0	0
Osuna	.978	10	79	8	2	2	2

First Base	PCT	G	PO	A	E	DP
Brito	1.000	6	42	0	1	0
Calzado	.967	9	55	3	2	3
Diaz	.981	7	50	2	1	6
Gomez	.985	44	371	11	6	29
Gonzalez	1.000	1	11	0	0	0
Osuna	.972	17	132	8	4	12
Ozuna	1.000	1	2	0	0	0

Peralta	—	1	0	0	0	0

Second Base	PCT	G	PO	A	E	DP
Calzado	.938	8	14	16	2	3
Diaz	.952	47	100	139	12	25
Mercedes	1.000	19	38	71	0	16

Third Base	PCT	G	PO	A	E	DP
Calzado	.929	34	25	67	7	3
Diaz	.811	11	10	20	7	3
Gomez	1.000	1	1	0	0	0
Mercedes	.947	23	14	40	3	3
Osuna	.903	9	7	21	3	2

Shortstop	PCT	G	PO	A	E	DP
Calzado	.922	12	16	31	4	5

Peralta	.914	61	86	201	27	36

Outfield	PCT	G	PO	A	E	DP
Bautista	.950	52	90	6	5	2
Bonifacio	.900	18	17	1	2	0
Gomez	.923	4	12	0	1	0
Indriago	1.000	5	7	1	0	1
Juan Martinez	.964	39	51	2	2	1
Julio Martinez	.947	26	35	1	2	0
Ozuna	.964	62	100	7	4	1
Jesus Rodriguez	.870	24	16	4	3	1
Jose Rodriguez	1.000	1	1	0	0	0
Urena	1.000	4	2	0	0	0

Houston Astros

BY BRIAN MCTAGGART

Despite another typical late-season charge to get back in the playoff race when nearly everyone counted them out, the Astros found themselves out of the playoffs for the third consecutive year—their longest postseason drought since 1994-96.

The Astros, who won just 73 games in 2007, rebounded to go 86-75 in 2008 and finished in third place in the National League Central behind division winner Chicago and NL wild card representative Milwaukee.

It was the seventh time in the last eight years and 14th time in 16 years the Astros finished with a winning record, and their 13½-game improvement was the third-best in baseball.

That's because the Astros posted the best record in the NL after the All-Star break, going 42-24 in the second half and remained in contention until the 159th game of the season.

"Obviously, we're not pleased with the end result with regard to not making the postseason, but we're pleased with the performance of the club the second half of the season," general manager Ed Wade said.

The Astros were carried early in the season by Lance Berkman, who had a record-breaking May and started at first base for the NL in the All-Star Game. Despite slumping in the second half, he still led the club in hitting (.312), home runs (29), doubles (46), runs (114) and RBIs (106).

While Berkman led the way early, Carlos Lee took over in the middle of the season and was en route to an MVP-caliber year before a broken finger ended his season Aug. 9. When he got injured, Lee led the league with 100 RBIs.

Ty Wigginton, who moved to left field from third base when Lee was injured, carried the club in August by hitting 12 homers, and the Astros rode the pitching of Roy Oswalt and Jose Valverde down the stretch.

Oswalt set a franchise record by throwing 32⅓ consecutive scoreless innings to finish 17-10, 3.54 after an 0-3 start, and Valverde led the league in saves for the second year in a row with a franchise record-tying 44.

The Astros had won eight consecutive games heading into a Sept. 12-14 showdown with the Cubs scheduled for Minute Maid Park, but the series was postponed because of Hurricane Ike and moved to Miller Park in Milwaukee.

The Cubs held the Astros to one hit in a span of two games. The Astros got to within two games of the wild-card lead after being no-hit by Carlos Zambrano on Sept. 14, but couldn't recover.

PLAYERS OF THE YEAR

MAJOR LEAGUE: LANCE BERKMAN, 1B

Berkman challenged for National League MVP honors as he finished fifth in batting (.312), tied for first in doubles (460), and also was third in OBP (.420) and fourth in slugging (.567). He also had 29 home runs and drove in 106 runs, both team highs.

MINOR LEAGUE: DREW SUTTON, INF

Sutton, 25, enjoyed a breakout season at Double-A Corpus Christi as he led the Astros minor leaguers in average (.317), runs scored (102), hits (165), walks (76), doubles (39) and on-base percentage (.408). He also cracked 20 home runs.

JOHN WILLIAMSON

ORGANIZATION LEADERS

BATTING		*Minimum 250 at-bats
*AVG	Sutton, Drew, Corpus Christi	.317
R	Sutton, Drew, Corpus Christi	102
H	Sutton, Drew, Corpus Christi	165
TB	Saccomanno, Mark, Round Rock	275
2B	Sutton, Drew, Corpus Christi	39
3B	DeLome, Collin, Lexington/Salem	9
HR	Saccomanno, Mark, Round Rock	27
RBI	Ori, Mark, Salem	89
BB	Sutton, Drew, Corpus Christi	76
SO	DeLome, Collin, Lexington/Salem	128
SB	Corrado, Craig, Lexington	43
*OBP	Sutton, Drew, Corpus Christi	.408
*SLG	Sadler, Ray, Corpus Christi/Round Rock	.527

PITCHING		†Minimum 75 innings
W	Trinidad, Polin, Salem/Corpus Christi	10
	Arguello, Douglas, Salem	10
L	Bass, Corey, Salem	15
†ERA	Trinidad, Polin, Salem/Corpus Christi	3.14
G	Diaz, Raymar, Salem	55
GS	Muecke, Josh, Round Rock	29
SV	Salamida, Christopher, Salem/Corpus Christi	12
	Pacella, Jay, Lexington/Salem	12
IP	Trinidad, Polin, Salem/Corpus Christi	169
BB	Severino, Sergio, Lexington/Salem	72
SO	Cespedes, Leandro, Lexington	137
†AVG	Arguello, Douglas, Salem	.236

2008 PERFORMANCE

General Manager: Ed Wade. **Farm Director:** Ricky Bennett. **Scouting Director:** Bobby Heck.

Class	Team	League	W	L	PCT	Finish*	Manager	Affiliate Since
Majors	Houston	National	86	76	.534	5th (16)	Cecil Cooper	—
Triple-A	Round Rock Express	Pacific Coast	64	79	.448	13th (16)	Dave Clark	2005
Double-A	Corpus Christi Hooks	Texas	55	85	.393	8th (8)	Luis Pujols	2005
High A	Salem Avalanche	Carolina	56	84	.400	8th (8)	Jim Pankovits	2003
Low A	Lexington Legends	South Atlantic	45	93	.326	16th (16)	Gregg Langbehn	2001
Short-season	Tri-City Valley Cats	New York-Penn	28	45	.384	13th (14)	Pete Rancont	2001
Rookie	Greeneville Astros	Appalachian	30	36	.455	7th (10)	Rodney Linares	2004
Overall 2008 Minor League Record			278	462	.376	30th		

* Finish in overall standings (No. of teams in league). ^League champion.

ORGANIZATION STATISTICS

HOUSTON ASTROS

NATIONAL LEAGUE

Batting	B-T	HT	WT	DOB	AVG	vLH	vRH	G	AB	R	H	2B	3B	HR	RBI	BB	HBP	SH	SF	SO	SB	CS	SLG	OBP
Abercrombie, Reggie	R-R	6-3	215	7-15-81	.309	.353	.238	34	55	10	17	5	0	2	5	1	2	1	1	23	5	2	.509	.339
Ausmus, Brad	R-R	5-11	190	4-14-69	.218	.277	.192	81	216	15	47	8	0	3	24	25	2	6	1	41	0	2	.296	.303
Berkman, Lance	B-L	6-1	220	2-10-76	.312	.276	.327	159	554	114	173	46	4	29	106	99	7	0	5	108	18	4	.567	.420
Blum, Geoff	R-R	6-3	205	4-26-73	.240	.229	.242	114	325	36	78	14	1	14	53	21	3	0	7	54	1	2	.418	.287
Bourn, Michael	L-R	5-11	180	12-27-82	.229	.190	.242	138	467	57	107	10	4	5	29	37	2	1	7	111	41	10	.300	.288
Castillo, Jose	R-R	6-1	220	3-19-81	.281	.286	.278	15	32	4	9	1	0	0	2	2	0	0	1	10	0	0	.313	.314
2-team total (112 San Francisco)					.246	—		127	426	46	105	29	4	6	37	27	1	0	1	81	2	2	.376	.292
Cruz, Jose	B-R	6-0	210	4-19-74	.122	.150	.103	38	49	6	6	1	0	0	1	11	0	0	0	9	0	0	.143	.283
Erstad, Darin	L-L	6-2	220	6-4-74	.276	.243	.286	140	322	49	89	16	0	4	31	14	2	2	2	68	2	3	.363	.309
House, J.R.	R-R	6-0	210	11-11-79	.000	.000	.000	3	3	0	0	0	0	0	0	0	0	0	0	1	0	0	.000	.000
Lee, Carlos	R-R	6-2	240	6-20-76	.314	.330	.309	115	436	61	137	27	0	28	100	37	3	0	5	49	4	1	.569	.368
Loretta, Mark	R-R	6-0	185	8-14-71	.280	.330	.250	101	261	27	73	15	0	4	38	29	2	0	5	30	0	0	.383	.350
Matsui, Kazuo	B-R	5-10	185	10-23-75	.293	.291	.294	96	375	58	110	26	3	6	33	37	0	7	3	53	20	5	.427	.354
Maysonet, Edwin	R-R	6-1	180	10-17-81	.143	.000	.167	7	7	0	1	0	0	0	0	0	0	0	0	2	0	0	.143	.143
Newhan, David	L-R	5-10	185	9-7-73	.260	.286	.258	64	104	11	27	5	2	2	12	6	0	0	1	28	1	0	.404	.297
Pence, Hunter	R-R	6-4	210	4-13-83	.269	.250	.275	157	595	78	160	34	4	25	83	40	4	0	3	124	11	10	.466	.318
Perez, Tomas	B-R	5-11	185	12-29-73	.200	.000	.222	8	10	0	2	0	0	0	0	0	0	0	0	2	0	0	.200	.200
Quintero, Humberto	R-R	5-9	215	8-2-79	.226	.273	.215	59	168	16	38	6	0	2	12	6	4	5	0	34	0	0	.298	.270
Saccomanno, Mark	R-R	6-3	210	4-30-80	.200	.000	.286	10	10	1	2	1	0	1	2	0	0	0	0	3	0	0	.600	.200
Tejada, Miguel	R-R	5-9	215	5-25-74	.283	.282	.284	158	632	92	179	38	3	13	66	24	6	1	3	72	7	7	.415	.314
Towles, J.R.	R-R	6-2	190	2-11-84	.137	.222	.118	54	146	10	20	5	0	4	16	16	6	3	0	40	0	0	.253	.250
Wigginton, Ty	R-R	6-0	225	10-11-77	.285	.340	.265	111	386	50	110	22	1	23	58	32	8	0	3	69	4	6	.526	.350

Pitching	B-T	HT	WT	DOB	W	L	ERA	G	GS	CG	SV	IP	H	R	ER	HR	BB	SO	AVG	vLH	vRH	K/9	BB/9
Arias, Alberto	R-R	5-11	155	10-14-83	1	1	6.75	3	2	0	0	8	11	6	6	0	6	8	.344	.444	.214	9.00	6.75
2-team total (12 Colorado)					1	1	4.15	15	2	0	0	22	23	10	10	1	10	13	—	—	—	5.40	4.15
Backe, Brandon	R-R	6-0	195	4-5-78	9	14	6.05	31	31	0	0	167	202	114	112	36	77	127	.302	.304	.301	6.86	4.16
Borkowski, Dave	R-R	6-1	230	2-7-77	0	2	7.50	26	0	0	0	36	54	30	30	9	14	24	.348	.339	.355	6.00	3.50
Brocail, Doug	R-R	6-5	250	5-16-67	7	5	3.93	72	0	0	2	69	63	30	30	8	21	64	.242	.305	.200	8.39	2.75
Byrdak, Tim	L-L	5-11	195	10-31-73	2	1	3.90	59	0	0	0	55	45	24	24	10	29	47	.222	.135	.289	7.64	4.72
Cassel, Jack	R-R	6-2	190	8-8-80	1	1	5.64	9	3	0	0	30	38	21	19	5	8	14	.311	.333	.297	4.15	2.37
Chacon, Shawn	R-R	6-3	220	12-23-77	2	3	5.04	15	15	0	0	86	88	52	48	16	41	53	.270	.270	.270	5.51	4.31
Geary, Geoff	R-R	6-0	180	8-26-76	2	3	2.53	55	0	0	0	64	45	18	18	3	28	45	.197	.220	.182	6.33	3.94
Hawkins, LaTroy	R-R	6-5	215	12-21-72	2	0	0.43	24	0	0	1	21	11	3	1	0	5	25	.151	.206	.103	10.71	2.14
Hernandez, Runelvys	R-R	6-1	250	4-27-78	0	3	8.38	4	4	0	0	19	32	19	18	4	11	15	.372	.364	.377	6.98	5.12
Moehler, Brian	R-R	6-3	235	12-31-71	11	8	4.56	31	26	0	0	150	166	79	76	20	36	82	.279	.307	.255	4.92	2.16
Nieve, Fernando	R-R	6-0	195	7-15-82	0	1	8.44	11	0	0	0	11	17	10	10	2	2	12	.362	.636	.278	10.13	1.69
Oswalt, Roy	R-R	6-0	185	8-29-77	17	10	3.54	32	32	3	0	209	199	89	82	23	47	165	.253	.262	.243	7.12	2.03
Paronto, Chad	R-R	6-5	250	7-28-75	0	1	4.35	6	0	0	0	10	11	5	5	2	4	4	.289	.200	.348	3.48	1.74
Rodriguez, Wandy	R-L	5-11	180	1-18-79	9	7	3.54	25	25	0	0	137	136	65	54	14	44	131	.256	.282	.248	8.58	2.88
Sampson, Chris	R-R	6-1	190	5-23-78	6	4	4.22	54	11	0	0	117	118	60	55	8	23	61	.266	.273	.261	4.68	1.76
Valverde, Jose	R-R	6-4	255	3-24-79	6	3	3.38	74	0	0	44	72	62	27	27	5	18	83	.231	.190	.252	10.38	2.48
Villarreal, Oscar	L-R	6-0	215	11-22-81	1	3	5.02	35	0	0	0	38	42	25	21	12	17	21	.286	.258	.306	5.02	4.06
Wolf, Randy	L-L	5-10	200	8-22-76	6	2	3.57	12	12	1	0	71	68	31	28	7	24	57	.255	.250	.256	7.26	3.06
2-team total (21 San Diego)					12	12	4.30	33	33	1	0	190	191	100	91	21	71	162	—	—	—	7.66	3.36
Wright, Wesley	R-L	5-11	160	1-28-85	4	3	5.01	71	0	0	1	56	45	34	31	8	34	57	.214	.207	.220	9.22	5.50

ORGANIZATION STATISTICS

Fielding

Catcher	PCT	G	PO	A	E	DP	PB
Ausmus	.996	77	428	33	2	4	4
Quintero	.998	59	373	26	1	3	1
Towles	.994	53	312	13	2	1	3

First Base	PCT	G	PO	A	E	DP
Ausmus	1.000	2	5	0	0	0
Berkman	.996	152	1240	132	5	122
Blum	1.000	5	17	1	0	1
Erstad	1.000	12	71	2	0	4
Loretta	1.000	2	14	0	0	0
Saccomanno	1.000	2	6	0	0	0

Second Base	PCT	G	PO	A	E	DP
Ausmus	—	1	0	0	0	0
Blum	1.000	8	9	17	0	2

	PCT	G	PO	A	E	DP
Castillo	1.000	3	5	4	0	1
Loretta	.995	46	85	119	1	28
Matsui	.971	94	190	219	12	56
Maysonet	1.000	3	2	0	0	0
Newhan	.986	28	33	39	1	11
Perez	1.000	5	2	2	0	2

Third Base	PCT	G	PO	A	E	DP
Ausmus	.000	1	0	0	1	0
Blum	.979	75	43	144	4	8
Castillo	1.000	7	6	11	0	0
Loretta	.974	17	7	31	1	1
Perez	—	1	0	0	0	0
Wigginton	.969	82	46	144	6	11

Shortstop	PCT	G	PO	A	E	DP
Blum	1.000	4	2	7	0	0
Loretta	.913	5	3	18	2	3
Maysonet	.857	4	0	6	1	0
Tejada	.983	157	187	442	11	97

Outfield	PCT	G	PO	A	E	DP
Abercrombie	1.000	22	36	2	0	1
Bourn	.984	130	291	9	5	2
Cruz	1.000	15	18	0	0	0
Erstad	1.000	88	146	2	0	1
Lee	.995	110	187	4	1	0
Newhan		2	0	6	0	0
Pence	.997	156	340	16	1	4
Wigginton	1.000	30	46	2	0	0

ROUND ROCK EXPRESS   TRIPLE-A

PACIFIC COAST LEAGUE

Batting	B-T	HT	WT	DOB	AVG	vLH	vRH	G	AB	R	H	2B	3B	HR	RBI	BB	HBP	SH	SF	SO	SB	CS	SLG	OBP
Abercrombie, Reggie	R-R	6-3	215	7-15-81	.273	.300	.265	78	289	37	79	14	2	12	36	9	1	0	1	93	17	9	.460	.297
Ash, Jonny	L-R	5-9	185	9-11-82	.224	.200	.227	73	152	16	34	6	0	0	2	22	1	5	0	17	1	3	.263	.326
Diaz, Victor	R-R	6-0	210	12-10-81	.296	.368	.269	22	71	4	21	2	0	1	7	12	0	1	0	19	2	1	.366	.398
2-team total (107 Tacoma)					.282	—	—	129	485	69	137	40	0	25	107	61	6	1	4	168	9	3	.520	.367
Gorneault, Nick	R-R	6-3	220	4-19-79	.257	.270	.251	120	370	59	95	18	1	19	56	46	3	1	1	96	8	7	.465	.343
House, J.R.	R-R	6-0	210	11-11-79	.306	.349	.290	127	454	63	139	25	0	18	60	53	2	0	4	52	1	2	.480	.378
Johnson, Chris	R-R	6-3	200	10-1-84	.218	.161	.243	30	101	10	22	2	1	1	9	5	0	0	1	25	0	0	.287	.252
Johnson, Josh	R-R	6-0	205	11-3-82	.400	.333	.500	2	5	1	2	1	0	0	2	0	0	0	0	1	0	0	.600	.400
Klassen, Danny	R-R	6-0	190	9-22-75	.219	.229	.214	37	105	9	23	3	1	1	15	16	2	1	0	25	0	2	.295	.333
Lopez, Jose	R-R	5-11	195	3-8-85	.000	.000	—	2	4	0	0	0	0	0	0	0	0	0	0	0	0	0	.000	.000
Majewski, Val	L-L	6-2	220	6-19-81	.266	.200	.278	36	94	16	25	5	1	5	14	16	1	0	0	14	1	2	.500	.378
Manzella, Tommy	R-R	6-2	190	4-16-83	.219	.205	.227	61	228	19	50	15	1	0	15	17	0	2	0	39	0	4	.294	.273
Matsui, Kazuo	B-R	5-10	185	10-23-75	.182	—	.182	3	11	1	2	1	0	1	1	1	0	0	0	2	0	0	.545	.250
Maysonet, Edwin	R-R	6-1	180	10-17-81	.271	.246	.281	117	406	59	110	24	1	6	34	44	4	6	6	70	4	3	.379	.343
Melian, Jackson	R-R	6-2	205	1-7-80	.160	.125	.176	8	25	3	4	0	0	2	3	0	0	0	0	8	0		.400	.160
Newhan, David	L-R	5-10	185	9-7-73	.308	.226	.323	60	198	39	61	14	2	9	36	14	1	2	1	33	8	2	.535	.355
Niekro, Lance	R-R	6-3	225	1-29-79	.212	.286	.200	17	52	5	11	2	0	1	2	6	0	0	0	7	1	0	.308	.293
Paul, Josh	R-R	6-1	210	5-19-75	.121	.154	.111	28	58	4	7	1	0	1	6	9	1	2	0	15	0	0	.190	.250
Paz, Richard	R-R	5-8	180	7-30-77	.217	.111	.286	18	46	8	10	4	0	0	4	8	0	3	0	7	2	0	.304	.333
Perez, Tomas	B-R	5-11	185	12-29-73	.275	.221	.295	79	306	32	84	15	5	1	25	22	1	4	6	44	1	6	.366	.319
Quintero, Humberto	R-R	5-9	215	8-2-79	.237	.233	.239	32	118	13	28	2	2	3	18	5	1	0	0	15	0	2	.364	.274
Ramirez, Yordany	R-R	6-0	190	7-31-84	.231	.283	.212	124	432	50	100	23	3	12	52	11	5	1	8	65	19	9	.382	.254
Saccomanno, Mark	R-R	6-3	210	4-30-80	.297	.260	.312	137	528	83	157	33	2	27	84	35	1	1	6	94	4	3	.521	.339
Sadler, Ray	R-R	6-1	200	9-19-80	.267	.321	.243	93	345	49	92	22	3	21	59	21	4	0	1	86	5	1	.530	.315
Santangelo, Lou	R-R	6-1	200	3-16-83	.205	.167	.222	13	39	6	8	0	0	3	6	4	0	0	0	14	0	0	.436	.279
Towles, J.R.	R-R	6-2	190	2-11-84	.304	.393	.252	48	168	28	51	8	2	7	28	13	6	3	2	31	4	3	.500	.370
Wigginton, Ty	R-R	6-0	225	10-11-77	.111	.000	.125	3	9	1	1	0	1	0	1	2	2	0	0	3	0	1	.333	.385

Pitching	B-T	HT	WT	DOB	W	L	ERA	G	GS	CG	SV	IP	H	R	ER	HR	BB	SO	AVG	vLH	vRH	K/9	BB/9
Arias, Alberto	R-R	5-11	155	10-14-83	1	0	1.52	8	3	0	1	24	21	4	4	0	5	15	.236	.282	.200	5.70	1.90
2-team total (30 Colorado Springs)					4	4	3.63	38	3	0	1	69	71	29	28	3	21	56	—	—	—	7.27	2.73
Borkowski, Dave	R-R	6-1	230	2-7-77	2	2	2.43	27	1	0	2	41	40	12	11	3	7	26	.263	.242	.278	5.75	1.55
Bowie, Micah	L-L	6-4	220	11-10-74	1	0	6.14	11	0	0	0	15	22	13	10	2	8	15	.349	.296	.389	9.20	4.91
2-team total (9 Colorado Springs)					1	1	6.55	20	0	0	0	22	34	21	16	3	12	23	—	—	—	9.41	4.91
Brower, Jim	R-R	6-3	215	12-29-72	0	0	0.00	2	0	0	1	3	4	3	0	0	0	5	.286	.250	.300	15.00	0.00
2-team total (17 Iowa)					2	1	3.68	19	0	0	6	22	29	14	9	2	11	16	—	—	—	6.55	4.50
Byrdak, Tim	L-L	5-11	195	10-31-73	0	0	3.68	7	0	0	0	7	8	3	3	0	0	8	.267	.133	.400	12.27	0.00
Cassel, Jack	R-R	6-2	190	8-8-80	9	5	3.69	19	17	0	0	107	113	46	44	10	30	72	.274	.294	.255	6.04	2.52
Chiavacci, Ron	R-R	6-0	240	9-5-77	5	5	6.48	14	13	1	0	74	97	56	53	16	30	60	.328	.352	.310	7.33	3.67
Douglass, Chance	R-R	6-1	200	2-24-84	2	1	3.24	6	3	0	0	25	19	11	9	4	10	15	.221	.257	.196	5.40	3.60
Gervacio, Samuel	R-R	6-0	170	1-10-85	1	0	2.25	3	0	0	0	8	6	2	2	0	3	14	.207	.273	.167	15.75	3.38
Gothreaux, Jared	R-R	6-0	200	1-27-80	1	5	5.66	15	2	0	0	41	60	30	26	4	10	21	.349	.345	.352	4.57	2.18
Hernandez, Runelvys	R-R	6-1	250	4-27-78	8	8	4.91	24	23	1	0	125	120	72	68	18	43	95	.255	.261	.250	6.86	3.10
Hines, Carlos	R-R	6-3	190	9-26-80	2	1	5.53	21	0	0	1	28	39	19	17	2	12	23	.308	.349	.261	7.48	3.90
Houston, Ryan	R-R	6-4	230	9-22-79	1	1	7.54	39	0	0	1	45	54	40	38	9	25	36	.293	.231	.340	7.15	4.96
King, Ray	L-L	6-0	250	1-15-74	2	1	2.25	32	0	0	5	32	23	10	8	1	14	23	.197	.107	.279	6.47	3.94
Middleton, Kyle	R-R	6-0	225	6-13-80	1	2	5.13	11	4	0	1	33	33	21	19	4	8	20	.264	.271	.250	5.40	2.16
Miller, Josh	R-R	6-1	200	2-7-79	8	8	5.41	28	21	2	1	148	186	94	89	30	19	74	.309	.300	.317	4.50	1.16
Muecke, Josh	L-L	6-3	195	1-9-82	8	13	4.89	29	29	0	0	166	169	101	90	23	64	107	.266	.233	.274	5.81	3.48
Nieve, Fernando	R-R	6-0	195	7-15-82	2	5	5.72	36	7	0	6	72	87	50	46	13	27	63	.297	.310	.285	7.84	3.36
Oyervidez, Jose	R-R	5-11	195	2-18-82	0	1	9.00	1	1	0	0	3	4	3	3	1	3	1	.308	.000	.364	3.00	9.00
Paronto, Chad	R-R	6-5	250	7-28-75	0	2	3.08	35	0	0	3	53	61	19	18	2	14	57	.290	.302	.281	9.74	2.39
Paulino, Felipe	R-R	6-2	180	10-5-83	0	0	0.00	1	0	0	0	1	1	0	0	0	1	3	.333	.000	.500	13.50	13.50
Randolph, Stephen	L-L	6-2	205	5-1-74	0	1	1.23	11	0	0	2	15	8	2	2	1	11	21	.160	.158	.161	12.89	6.75
Regilio, Nick	R-R	6-2	190	9-4-78	4	4	3.00	50	0	0	9	60	58	21	20	7	31	59	.258	.276	.242	8.85	4.65

Pitcher	B-T	HT	WT	DOB	W	L	ERA	G	GS	CG	SV	IP	H	R	ER	HR	BB	SO	AVG	vLH	vRH	K/9	BB/9
Reineke, Chad	R-R	6-6	210	4-9-82	5	9	4.41	20	19	1	0	112	112	62	55	15	35	100	.255	.290	.219	8.01	2.80
2-team total (3 Portland)					5	10	4.37	23	22	1	0	130	129	70	63	20	41	113	—	—	—	7.84	2.85
Sosa, Jorge	R-R	6-2	220	4-28-77	1	2	4.15	17	0	0	2	22	20	11	10	5	8	24	.238	.206	.260	9.97	3.32
2-team total (10 Tacoma)					2	2	3.96	27	0	0	4	36	34	17	16	5	21	36	—	—	—	8.92	5.20

Fielding

Catcher	PCT	G	PO	A	E	DP	PB
House	1.000	45	294	18	0	1	4
J. Johnson	1.000	1	10	2	0	0	0
Lopez	1.000	1	6	0	0	0	0
Paul	.975	18	109	7	3	2	0
Quintero	.973	30	190	24	6	2	2
Santangelo	.976	11	76	4	2	0	0
Towles	.991	47	301	19	3	4	1

First Base	PCT	G	PO	A	E	DP
House	.995	73	582	47	3	53
Majewski	1.000	10	85	6	0	7
Niekro	.977	15	117	8	3	10
Perez	1.000	1	3	0	0	1
Quintero	1.000	2	19	1	0	1
Saccomanno	.989	53	407	28	5	51

Second Base	PCT	G	PO	A	E	DP
Ash	.969	36	45	80	4	18
Klassen	1.000	12	15	27	0	4
Matsui	1.000	3	5	10	0	5
Maysonet	.975	42	77	120	5	37
Newhan	.989	21	36	54	1	12
Paz	1.000	9	14	21	0	5
Perez	.966	31	63	79	5	16

Third Base	PCT	G	PO	A	E	DP
House	—	1	0	0	0	0
C. Johnson	.949	28	19	55	4	9
Klassen	1.000	2	2	4	0	0
Newhan	.667	3	0	2	1	0
Paz	1.000	1	1	1	0	0
Perez	.976	34	22	59	2	5
Saccomanno	.907	79	48	138	19	10

	PCT	G	PO	A	E	DP
Wigginton	1.000	3	2	6	0	1

Shortstop	PCT	G	PO	A	E	DP
Klassen	.946	12	10	25	2	5
Manzella	.989	61	81	189	3	42
Maysonet	.969	65	75	177	8	37
Perez	.957	13	27	40	3	9

Outfield	PCT	G	PO	A	E	DP
Abercrombie	.964	77	153	8	6	4
Diaz	.955	17	20	1	1	0
Gorneault	.995	103	196	7	1	1
Majewski	1.000	11	14	1	0	1
Maysonet	1.000	3	5	0	0	0
Melian	.923	6	12	0	1	0
Newhan	1.000	23	32	1	0	0
Ramirez	.994	118	334	17	2	3
Sadler	.990	87	192	7	2	2

CORPUS CHRISTI HOOKS DOUBLE-A
TEXAS LEAGUE

Batting	B-T	HT	WT	DOB	AVG	vLH	vRH	G	AB	R	H	2B	3B	HR	RBI	BB	HBP	SH	SF	SO	SB	CS	SLG	OBP
Ash, Jonny	L-R	5-9	185	9-11-82	.260	.100	.291	32	123	16	32	5	1	0	9	17	2	1	2	4	1	0	.317	.354
Ball, Jarred	B-R	6-0	185	4-18-83	.259	.250	.261	52	170	30	44	11	5	1	16	25	2	1	0	48	14	2	.400	.360
Bogusevic, Brian	L-L	6-3	215	2-18-84	.371	.357	.373	42	124	21	46	10	2	3	20	16	1	4	0	24	8	1	.556	.447
Cosby, Rob	R-R	6-1	215	4-2-81	.222	.213	.224	102	369	35	82	21	2	10	48	14	2	0	3	48	2	0	.371	.253
Einertson, Mitch	R-R	5-10	178	4-4-86	.262	.293	.256	105	382	51	100	26	2	11	62	26	4	0	4	88	5	3	.427	.313
Fixler, Jon	R-R	6-1	205	6-13-86	.143	.000	.167	3	7	3	1	0	0	0	0	1	0	1	0	4	0	0	.143	.222
Goethals, Jim	R-R	5-10	195	7-12-82	.071	.000	.083	6	14	4	1	0	0	0	2	5	0	1	0	6	0	0	.071	.316
Hart, Billy	R-R	6-2	215	11-2-82	.260	.351	.240	96	319	51	83	23	1	7	39	41	3	2	1	64	9	8	.404	.349
Iorg, Eli	R-R	6-2	215	3-14-83	.268	.296	.263	127	459	53	123	21	5	11	59	23	5	2	4	112	21	9	.407	.308
Johnson, Chris	R-R	6-3	220	10-1-84	.324	.265	.335	84	330	43	107	24	0	12	58	20	3	1	4	61	5	0	.506	.364
Lopez, Jose	R-R	5-11	195	3-8-85	.222	.368	.196	39	126	12	28	2	0	2	10	5	1	2	1	31	0	0	.286	.256
Majewski, Val	L-L	6-2	220	6-19-81	.333	.429	.308	16	66	11	22	6	0	3	10	3	0	0	0	9	0	1	.561	.362
Manzella, Tommy	R-R	6-2	190	4-16-83	.299	.314	.296	54	224	27	67	11	5	4	34	17	1	3	4	35	4	4	.446	.346
Matsui, Kazuo	B-R	5-10	185	10-23-75	.429	—	.429	2	7	1	3	3	0	0	0	0	0	1	0	1	0	0	.857	.429
Paz, Richard	R-R	5-8	180	7-30-77	.287	.375	.267	67	216	22	62	8	2	4	32	47	5	2	3	32	0	0	.398	.421
Quintero, Humberto	R-R	5-9	215	8-2-79	.250	.333	.222	3	12	0	3	2	0	0	3	0	0	0	0	0	0	0	.417	.250
Rosales, Orlando	R-R	5-8	180	4-9-84	.217	.125	.224	32	106	13	23	4	0	1	5	5	1	1	0	17	0	2	.283	.259
Sadler, Ray	R-R	6-1	200	9-19-80	.290	.444	.258	33	107	24	31	6	3	4	19	10	4	0	2	20	1	2	.514	.366
Santangelo, Lou	R-R	6-1	200	3-16-83	.241	.213	.245	96	349	32	84	11	0	8	39	26	0	2	1	86	1	0	.341	.293
Sheldon, Ole	R-R	6-4	225	11-25-82	.282	.305	.277	114	373	60	105	15	2	13	55	58	6	1	4	71	3	1	.437	.383
Sutil, Wladimir	R-R	5-10	155	10-31-84	.259	.333	.247	93	316	44	82	13	0	0	24	16	3	8	3	32	22	4	.301	.299
Sutton, Drew	R-B	6-3	190	6-30-83	.317	.287	.323	133	520	102	165	39	4	20	69	76	6	1	3	98	20	7	.523	.408
Van Ostrand, Jimmy	R-R	6-4	210	8-7-84	.160	.000	.222	9	25	1	4	2	0	0	4	3	0	0	0	6	0	0	.240	.250

Pitching	B-T	HT	WT	DOB	W	L	ERA	G	GS	CG	SV	IP	H	R	ER	HR	BB	SO	AVG	vLH	vRH	K/9	BB/9
Blazek, Chris	L-L	6-0	195	3-2-84	4	4	4.52	47	0	0	2	70	67	38	35	8	28	84	.253	.351	.215	10.85	3.62
Douglass, Chance	R-R	6-1	200	2-24-84	4	10	5.09	22	22	0	0	124	144	77	70	19	44	69	.301	.333	.282	5.02	3.20
Englebrook, Evan	R-R	6-8	225	4-28-82	2	2	3.90	34	2	0	4	55	54	26	24	3	25	33	.257	.260	.255	5.37	4.07
Estrada, Paul	R-R	6-1	220	9-10-82	2	1	7.88	9	0	0	0	8	12	7	7	2	5	3	.364	.350	.385	3.38	5.63
Fairchild, Tip	R-R	6-2	200	12-5-83	2	8	8.80	22	10	0	1	61	78	62	60	10	31	45	.308	.273	.327	6.60	4.55
Gervacio, Samuel	R-R	6-0	170	1-10-85	2	5	4.13	47	0	0	5	65	69	36	30	8	26	82	.275	.253	.285	11.30	3.58
Gordon, Brian	L-R	6-0	205	8-16-78	0	0	4.50	1	0	0	0	2	2	1	1	1	1	2	.286	.333	.250	4.50	4.50
2-team total (15 Frisco)					2	0	0.38	16	0	0	3	24	11	2	1	1	5	19	—	—	—	7.13	1.88
Hall, Bo	R-R	6-0	187	9-5-80	2	1	10.90	8	0	0	0	17	29	21	21	9	5	13	.367	.258	.438	6.75	2.60
Hudspeth, Casey	R-R	6-0	165	10-1-84	4	5	5.40	10	9	0	0	55	57	35	33	4	28	36	.269	.305	.239	5.89	4.58
James, Brad	R-R	6-2	200	6-19-84	6	6	4.45	18	18	0	0	93	107	52	46	9	35	45	.300	.405	.239	4.35	3.39
McKeller, Ryan	R-R	6-5	220	7-8-83	4	6	5.89	45	0	0	1	70	88	50	46	10	36	71	.299	.312	.292	9.09	4.61
Melendez, German	R-R	5-9		9-13-80	1	0	3.63	10	0	0	1	17	11	8	7	1	11	14	.183	.300	.125	7.27	5.71
Middleton, Kyle	R-R	6-4	225	6-13-80	0	0	4.50	6	0	0	3	6	6	3	3	1	0	5	.261	.000	.286	7.50	0.00
Norris, Bud	R-R	6-0	195	3-2-85	3	8	4.05	19	19	0	0	80	89	42	36	9	35	84	.286	.286	.286	9.45	3.49
Oyervidez, Jose	R-R	5-11	195	2-18-82	1	2	6.26	42	0	0	3	73	91	58	51	5	38	54	.306	.313	.303	6.63	4.66
Perez, Sergio	R-R	6-3	230	12-5-84	2	3	2.30	7	5	0	0	27	30	8	7	3	8	18	.283	.216	.319	5.93	2.63
Rodriguez, Wandy	R-L	5-11	180	1-18-79	1	1	1.50	1	1	0	0	6	4	1	1	1	0	1	.190	.000	.235	0.00	1.50
Salamida, Chris	L-L	6-0	180	5-7-84	0	2	5.52	11	0	0	1	15	22	11	9	0	5	4	.333	.286	.356	2.45	3.07
Thompson, Ryan	R-R	6-4	220	8-6-82	1	3	5.65	19	0	0	0	37	40	24	23	6	9	39	.274	.286	.268	9.57	2.21
Trinidad, Polin	L-L	6-3	170	11-19-84	6	3	3.61	18	18	0	0	107	109	47	43	13	21	75	.263	.309	.249	6.29	1.76
Van Hekken, Andy	R-L	6-3	185	7-31-79	6	3	3.19	11	11	0	0	68	82	30	24	6	10	56	.298	.262	.310	7.45	1.33
Walker, Sean	R-R	6-1	175	10-31-82	1	6	7.24	26	8	0	0	87	125	76	70	5	33	50	.341	.379	.323	5.17	3.41

Fielding

Catcher	PCT	G	PO	A	E	DP	PB
Fixler	1.000	3	19	1	0	0	0
Goethals	1.000	5	29	5	0	0	0
Lopez	.977	37	236	16	6	4	3
Quintero	1.000	3	30	6	0	0	0
Santangelo	.991	96	636	54	6	8	8

First Base	PCT	G	PO	A	E	DP
Cosby	.994	60	490	24	3	53
Sheldon	.996	89	739	49	3	95
Van Ostrand	.900	1	6	3	1	0

Second Base	PCT	G	PO	A	E	DP
Ash	.991	23	49	63	1	14
Cosby	.933	4	5	9	1	3

	PCT	G	PO	A	E	DP
Matsui	1.000	2	3	6	0	1
Paz	.974	18	33	43	2	13
Sutil	1.000	4	12	10	0	3
Sutton	.968	99	201	283	16	85

Third Base	PCT	G	PO	A	E	DP
Ash	1.000	9	3	6	0	0
Cosby	.964	24	13	41	2	4
Johnson	.909	82	48	182	23	17
Paz	.868	16	14	32	7	6
Sutton	.896	15	12	31	5	2

Shortstop	PCT	G	PO	A	E	DP
Manzella	.984	53	95	156	4	42
Sutil	.973	80	119	245	10	65

	PCT	G	PO	A	E	DP
Sutton	.906	14	20	28	5	11

Outfield	PCT	G	PO	A	E	DP
Ball	1.000	45	100	3	0	2
Bogusevic	1.000	31	67	1	0	0
Einertson	.958	97	172	10	8	4
Hart	.975	75	111	5	3	1
Iorg	.982	118	268	8	5	1
Majewski	1.000	14	20	1	0	0
Rosales	.962	29	50	0	2	0
Sadler	.975	24	35	4	1	1
Sutil	1.000	5	5	0	0	0
Van Ostrand	.875	5	7	0	1	0

SALEM AVALANCHE

HIGH CLASS A

CAROLINA LEAGUE

Batting	B-T	HT	WT	DOB	AVG	vLH	vRH	G	AB	R	H	2B	3B	HR	RBI	BB	HBP	SH	SF	SO	SB	CS	SLG	OBP
Bogusevic, Brian	L-L	6-3	215	2-18-84	.217	.222	.214	8	23	4	5	2	0	1	6	4	1	0	0	1	1	0	.435	.357
Buchanan, Greg	B-R	5-11	180	11-16-83	.240	.282	.230	114	383	51	92	18	5	0	39	31	2	5	5	74	10	2	.313	.297
Carkeek, Kevin	R-R	6-3	200	10-20-84	.222	.250	.213	44	126	13	28	6	0	1	12	11	3	4	2	30	0	1	.294	.296
Clemens, Koby	R-R	5-11	193	12-4-86	.268	.253	.272	109	388	54	104	29	5	7	52	61	4	0	5	99	1	4	.423	.369
DeLome, Collin	L-R	6-2	195	12-18-85	.232	.188	.239	68	237	40	55	14	3	10	35	17	9	1	3	57	7	2	.443	.305
Florentino, Jhon	R-R	6-0	155	8-22-83	.290	.265	.295	117	452	58	131	24	6	4	48	24	6	2	5	74	14	8	.396	.331
Goethals, Jim	R-R	5-10	195	7-12-82	.250	.250	.250	7	16	3	4	0	0	0	4	0	0	0	0	6	0	0	.250	.400
Iacono, Sal	R-R	5-9	190	3-4-85	.250	.000	.333	8	16	3	4	2	0	0	2	3	0	1	1	4	0	0	.375	.350
Mena, Roberto	R-R	6-0	185	1-17-85	.213	.220	.211	76	240	31	51	10	2	0	15	13	1	4	3	48	4	5	.271	.253
Moresi, Nick	R-R	6-4	180	11-22-84	.218	.219	.217	55	170	20	37	8	0	2	15	14	4	1	4	48	5	4	.300	.286
Ori, Mark	L-R	6-4	225	12-16-83	.304	.313	.302	131	497	73	151	36	2	11	89	49	10	0	6	92	4	1	.451	.374
Parraz, Jordan	R-R	6-3	210	10-8-84	.289	.299	.287	114	425	82	123	31	3	6	42	64	14	0	1	79	21	10	.419	.399
Quintero, Cesar	R-R	5-11	165	1-7-83	.224	.239	.220	115	392	44	88	15	3	7	46	26	2	7	4	105	13	5	.332	.274
Reed, Ryan	L-L	6-4	210	12-19-83	.196	.182	.200	14	51	3	10	3	1	0	2	1	0	1	0	19	0	0	.294	.212
Rosales, Orlando	R-R	5-8	180	4-9-84	.216	.217	.215	64	232	18	50	18	0	0	27	21	2	0	3	31	2	5	.293	.283
Sutil, Wladimir	R-R	5-10	155	10-31-84	.268	.176	.292	21	82	15	22	6	0	0	5	2	1	1	0	13	6	2	.341	.294
Sweet, Travis	R-R	6-0	190	4-17-86	.150	.083	.159	33	100	9	15	3	0	1	9	6	0	2	3	25	1	2	.210	.193
Tellam, Justin	R-R	6-3	190	11-20-84	.195	.235	.185	26	82	8	16	5	1	2	11	9	0	1	2	18	1	0	.354	.269
Torres, Tim	R-R	6-2	180	11-12-83	.272	.351	.252	127	475	67	129	36	4	9	62	62	2	3	3	97	12	6	.421	.356
Van Ostrand, Jimmy	R-R	6-4	210	8-7-84	.292	.343	.280	97	363	41	106	28	1	7	64	30	8	1	4	45	1	3	.433	.356

Pitching	B-T	HT	WT	DOB	W	L	ERA	G	GS	CG	SV	IP	H	R	ER	HR	BB	SO	AVG	vLH	vRH	K/9	BB/9
Abreu, Erick	R-R	6-1	170	8-9-83	7	6	3.98	35	19	0	1	131	141	64	58	12	33	92	.280	.292	.272	6.32	2.27
Appell, Josh	L-L	6-1	195	6-23-83	1	2	5.96	44	0	0	0	54	62	39	36	4	38	48	.294	.279	.300	7.95	6.29
Arguello, Douglas	L-L	6-3	190	11-21-84	10	6	3.30	27	25	2	0	142	119	59	52	5	69	90	.236	.258	.231	5.70	4.37
Bass, Corey	R-R	6-3	210	2-8-85	4	15	6.70	27	27	0	0	129	166	110	96	11	47	48	.313	.320	.308	3.35	3.28
Diaz, Raymar	R-R	6-7	190	11-13-83	3	4	5.12	55	0	0	1	83	91	50	47	9	30	52	.293	.294	.292	5.66	3.27
Dominguez, Jason	R-R	6-3	193	12-17-85	5	4	3.81	52	0	0	5	80	74	39	34	3	23	47	.246	.337	.198	5.27	2.58
Hallberg, Bryan	R-R	6-0	185	4-23-85	5	8	2.68	49	1	0	6	81	59	28	24	5	33	66	.206	.162	.230	7.36	3.68
Hudspeth, Casey	R-R	6-0	165	10-1-84	4	7	3.96	17	17	0	0	100	104	53	44	4	29	49	.266	.270	.264	4.41	2.61
Pacella, Jay	R-R	6-6	212	12-26-83	0	2	3.38	8	0	0	0	13	12	9	5	2	5	17	.231	.167	.265	11.48	3.38
Powell, Jordan	R-R	6-2	205	4-14-85	0	1	5.56	9	0	0	0	11	17	11	7	0	4	5	.340	.304	.370	3.97	3.18
Qualben, David	L-L	6-3	200	7-29-85	3	11	5.46	35	8	0	0	84	93	67	51	9	48	57	.287	.354	.264	6.11	5.14
Salamida, Chris	L-L	6-0	180	5-7-84	4	2	5.75	36	2	0	11	67	78	47	43	11	14	45	.302	.229	.330	6.01	1.87
Santo, Joel	R-R	6-3	194	6-4-84	0	3	5.70	26	4	0	0	47	51	33	30	3	35	31	.279	.325	.240	5.89	6.65
Severino, Sergio	L-L	5-11	150	9-1-84	1	6	7.66	17	17	0	0	67	85	63	57	7	48	38	.318	.279	.326	5.10	6.45
Trinidad, Polin	L-L	6-3	170	11-19-84	4	2	2.32	10	10	0	0	62	46	18	16	2	11	34	.202	.262	.188	4.94	1.60
Wagler, Chad	R-R	6-1	185	9-11-83	5	4	3.66	13	10	0	0	59	61	28	24	3	11	22	.262	.247	.271	3.36	1.68
Walker, Sean	R-R	6-1	175	10-31-82	0	1	2.81	13	0	0	3	16	12	7	5	1	4	19	.197	.219	.172	10.69	2.25

Fielding

Catcher	PCT	G	PO	A	E	DP	PB
Carkeek	.965	35	198	22	8	1	8
Clemens	.984	76	429	51	8	3	10
Goethals	.882	7	28	2	4	1	2
Iacono	.960	6	23	1	1	0	1
Tellam	.983	22	102	13	2	1	5

First Base	PCT	G	PO	A	E	DP
Carkeek	1.000	4	6	0	0	0
Ori	.990	100	932	76	10	92
Torres	1.000	4	21	0	0	1
Van Ostrand	.982	40	344	28	7	38

Second Base	PCT	G	PO	A	E	DP
Buchanan	.979	112	214	288	11	77

	PCT	G	PO	A	E	DP
Mena	.969	24	36	57	3	10
Sutil	.962	4	14	11	1	6
Torres	.975	7	20	19	1	8

Third Base	PCT	G	PO	A	E	DP
Clemens	—	1	0	0	0	0
Florentino	.938	114	84	233	21	19
Iacono	—	1	0	0	0	0
Mena	.918	19	16	40	5	4
Sutil	.958	6	6	17	1	1
Torres	1.000	4	0	8	0	2

Shortstop	PCT	G	PO	A	E	DP
Mena	.945	34	41	97	8	20
Sutil	.909	8	21	29	5	8

	PCT	G	PO	A	E	DP
Torres	.970	109	180	366	17	71

Outfield	PCT	G	PO	A	E	DP
Bogusevic	.909	8	9	1	1	0
DeLome	.949	54	69	5	4	1
Moresi	1.000	49	117	2	0	0
Parraz	.983	105	231	6	4	3
Quintero	.983	103	220	11	4	4
Reed	.900	11	18	0	2	0
Rosales	.979	56	132	7	3	1
Sweet	.984	27	61	1	1	0
Torres	1.000	4	6	0	0	0
Van Ostrand	1.000	25	27	1	0	0

SOUTH ATLANTIC LEAGUE

Batting	B-T	HT	WT	DOB	AVG	vLH	vRH	G	AB	R	H	2B	3B	HR	RBI	BB	HBP	SH	SF	SO	SB	CS	SLG	OBP
Barnes, Brandon	R-R	6-2	210	5-15-86	.241	.269	.232	87	311	27	75	19	1	2	19	18	2	3	2	96	7	3	.328	.285
Brown, Bryan	R-R	5-10	170	8-3-85	.159	.121	.169	52	157	11	25	3	0	0	12	17	0	5	1	41	2	2	.178	.240
Brown, Steve	R-R	6-0	180	9-3-86	.212	.173	.223	102	340	46	72	13	3	10	31	22	9	3	1	98	15	6	.356	.277
Carkeek, Kevin	R-R	6-3	200	10-20-84	.186	.333	.147	13	43	5	8	2	0	1	3	7	0	0	0	7	0	0	.302	.300
Corrado, Craig	R-R	6-2	185	9-10-84	.275	.254	.283	126	505	60	139	26	1	3	43	24	6	9	2	92	43	5	.349	.315
Cusick, Matt	L-R	5-10	190	5-5-86	.285	.239	.300	94	351	55	100	23	6	9	38	40	1	4	4	43	8	1	.462	.356
DeLome, Collin	L-R	6-2	195	12-18-85	.261	.100	.307	61	226	41	59	9	6	12	36	18	6	0	2	71	7	2	.513	.329
Dixon, Russell	L-R	6-2	205	8-28-85	.237	.149	.264	118	405	42	96	20	3	3	33	48	7	3	4	120	15	4	.323	.325
Everett, Cat	R-R	6-1	190	10-5-85	.203	.140	.221	71	231	23	47	6	0	0	14	23	3	7	2	60	2	0	.229	.282
Fixler, Jon	R-R	6-1	205	6-13-86	.248	.197	.265	80	270	21	67	13	2	8	50	16	14	3	5	82	1	1	.400	.318
Henson, Julian	R-R	5-10	190	4-10-87	.250	.250	.250	10	32	6	8	1	0	1	3	2	0	0	0	7	0	0	.375	.351
Jackson, Chris	R-R	5-11	185	12-30-86	.244	.286	.224	23	86	10	21	2	2	1	7	6	2	0	0	24	6	2	.349	.309
Melton, Joe	R-R	6-2	215	7-14-84	.265	.333	.240	10	34	4	9	3	0	0	4	3	0	0	1	10	1	0	.353	.316
Mena, Roberto	R-R	6-0	185	1-17-85	.190	.167	.200	17	63	6	12	4	0	1	7	0	0	0	1	13	0	0	.302	.188
Miller, Kyle	R-R	6-1	200	9-1-86	.234	.211	.244	32	128	14	30	6	0	7	24	8	1	0	0	50	1	2	.445	.285
Moresi, Nick	R-R	6-4	180	11-22-84	.224	.318	.190	24	85	12	19	3	2	2	11	4	0	0	0	26	1	1	.376	.258
Pellegrini, Brian	R-R	6-1	240	10-3-84	.226	.235	.223	87	310	50	70	13	5	21	69	36	14	0	2	95	13	1	.503	.331
Priday, Jacob	R-R	6-1	220	10-2-85	.221	.200	.228	24	77	6	17	5	1	1	9	8	3	0	1	38	0	0	.351	.315
Ramirez, Ronald	R-R	5-11	165	1-30-86	.216	.243	.209	58	190	19	41	14	0	0	8	14	0	1	2	39	2	1	.289	.267
Sapp, Max	L-R	6-2	220	2-21-88	.200	.170	.208	74	255	24	51	12	0	4	29	30	1	0	5	77	0	1	.294	.282
Taylor, Eric	R-R	6-3	195	7-29-85	.255	.229	.263	132	483	67	123	22	1	9	56	48	10	5	4	91	27	3	.360	.332

Pitching	B-T	HT	WT	DOB	W	L	ERA	G	GS	CG	SV	IP	H	R	ER	HR	BB	SO	AVG	vLH	vRH	K/9	BB/9
Abad, Fernando	L-L	6-2	170	12-17-85	2	7	3.30	45	0	0	3	76	78	31	28	9	13	94	.259	.292	.244	11.08	1.53
Adams, Colt	R-R	6-5	220	5-23-85	1	3	8.77	7	7	0	0	26	48	29	25	2	3	17	.380	.408	.596	5.96	1.05
Bello, Anthony	L-L	6-2	200	10-9-85	7	7	4.17	23	23	0	0	117	121	63	54	5	18	80	.261	.181	.288	6.17	2.93
Cespedes, Leandro	R-R	5-11	160	4-19-87	4	6	4.02	28	27	0	0	130	138	73	58	19	45	137	.267	.244	.287	9.48	3.12
Duran, Jose	R-R	6-1	175	5-1-85	2	1	1.66	8	0	0	1	22	12	7	4	0	9	19	.156	.161	.152	7.89	3.74
Icenogle, Jeff	L-L	6-2	205	5-30-84	3	10	4.58	23	22	0	0	106	113	58	54	10	45	116	.278	.284	.276	9.85	3.82
Kelly, Reid	R-R	6-1	182	10-31-86	3	3	3.41	35	0	0	4	71	68	34	27	6	28	72	.246	.280	.227	9.08	3.53
Koons, Mike	R-R	6-2	205	9-18-85	1	4	5.85	39	0	0	2	65	88	54	42	4	19	57	.314	.343	.297	7.93	2.64
Ladeuth, Carlos	R-R	5-11	180	6-13-84	6	11	4.15	32	13	0	0	117	132	65	54	16	35	107	.289	.289	.289	8.23	2.69
Leonhardt, Jacob	R-R	6-5	220	9-27-84	4	14	5.56	30	20	0	1	123	165	97	76	13	38	69	.324	.343	.310	5.05	2.78
Pacella, Jay	R-R	6-6	212	12-26-83	1	4	3.02	38	0	0	12	60	54	24	20	4	21	73	.236	.288	.192	11.01	3.17
Pardo, Luis	R-R	6-5	230	7-14-85	1	9	5.57	16	12	0	0	63	86	47	39	8	30	45	.326	.346	.312	6.43	4.29
Powell, Jordan	R-R	6-2	205	4-14-85	1	7	3.52	34	0	0	5	69	86	35	27	4	23	49	.305	.357	.271	6.39	3.00
Qualben, David	L-L	6-3	200	7-29-85	0	0	1.74	3	0	0	0	10	10	4	2	0	3	8	.263	.286	.258	6.97	2.61
Robinson, Brett	R-R	6-0	185	1-23-85	4	1	6.02	40	0	0	0	64	88	49	43	11	23	44	.319	.252	.364	6.16	3.22
Severino, Sergio	L-L	5-11	150	9-1-84	3	3	2.66	10	9	0	0	51	34	16	15	2	24	54	.186	.214	.177	9.59	4.26
Tilghman, Jack	R-R	6-2	205	5-19-87	1	0	2.70	9	0	0	0	13	14	7	4	0	9	5	.298	.267	.313	3.38	6.07
Vessella, Tom	R-L	6-6	205	10-12-85	1	3	6.83	6	5	0	0	29	38	22	22	6	6	13	.319	.231	.363	4.03	1.86

Fielding

Catcher	PCT	G	PO	A	E	DP	PB
Carkeek	1.000	9	69	8	0	0	2
Fixler	.982	64	479	62	10	3	9
Henson	.959	10	64	6	3	0	1
Melton	1.000	7	43	2	0	0	1
Miller	1.000	1	2	0	0	0	
Sapp	.991	54	384	42	4	4	9

First Base	PCT	G	PO	A	E	DP
Carkeek	1.000	3	20	1	0	4
Fixler	1.000	3	21	0	0	2
Miller	.969	7	60	3	2	5
Taylor	.992	127	1082	76	9	96

Second Base	PCT	G	PO	A	E	DP
B. Brown	.959	12	15	32	2	5
Corrado	.947	63	122	166	16	42
Cusick	.965	47	80	111	7	21
Mena	1.000	4	4	7	0	0
Ramirez	.975	17	26	53	2	9
Taylor	—	1	0	0	0	0

Third Base	PCT	G	PO	A	E	DP
B. Brown	.882	15	11	19	4	1
Corrado	.807	46	23	48	17	2
Cusick	.929	44	35	70	8	13
Jackson	.929	14	11	15	2	2
Mena	.867	7	4	9	2	0
Miller	.909	20	13	27	4	2

Shortstop	PCT	G	PO	A	E	DP
B. Brown	.930	21	32	48	6	14
Everett	.952	71	94	204	15	42
Jackson	.962	6	10	15	1	1
Mena	.931	6	11	16	2	5
Ramirez	.892	40	60	114	21	23

Outfield	PCT	G	PO	A	E	DP
Barnes	.972	80	160	11	5	3
S. Brown	.982	94	211	6	4	2
DeLome	.971	52	100	2	3	0
Dixon	.963	85	149	5	6	1
Moresi	.949	24	37	0	2	0
Pellegrini	.991	80	105	4	1	0
Priday	.769	9	10	0	3	0

TRI-CITY VALLEYCATS   SHORT-SEASON

NEW YORK-PENN LEAGUE

Batting	B-T	HT	WT	DOB	AVG	vLH	vRH	G	AB	R	H	2B	3B	HR	RBI	BB	HBP	SH	SF	SO	SB	CS	SLG	OBP
Castro, Jason	L-R	6-3	210	6-18-87	.275	.378	.238	39	138	10	38	9	0	2	12	22	2	0	0	32	0	2	.384	.383
Diaz, Mike	L-R	5-10	160	4-11-87	.282	.176	.308	48	177	29	50	10	2	5	22	11	2	1	0	34	6	3	.446	.332
Disher, Phil	R-R	6-2	215	6-17-85	.304	.300	.305	71	280	40	85	20	3	13	56	33	3	0	2	71	1	0	.536	.381
Flores, David	R-R	6-2	220	10-13-86	.266	.315	.250	56	218	34	58	17	0	11	37	12	5	1	0	35	5	0	.495	.319
Gaston, Jon	L-R	6-0	210	11-13-86	.193	.204	.190	62	207	18	40	11	1	2	25	25	4	0	0	65	0	2	.285	.292
Gonzalez, Pedro	L-R	5-11	180	10-29-86	.333	.000	.333	5	15	4	5	0	0	0	1	2	0	1	0	4	0	0	.333	.412
Henson, Julian	R-R	5-10	190	4-10-87	.172	.286	.140	18	64	5	11	2	0	0	6	7	1	1	1	26	0	0	.203	.260
Hulett, Jeff	R-R	6-0	185	11-16-87	.194	.207	.189	33	103	14	20	2	1	1	10	11	1	0	3	39	1	0	.262	.271
Jackson, Chris	R-R	5-11	185	12-30-86	.257	.208	.280	22	74	13	19	3	1	1	9	5	3	3	1	22	2	0	.365	.325

	B-T	HT	WT	DOB	AVG	vLH	vRH	G	AB	R	H	2B	3B	HR	RBI	BB	HBP	SH	SF	SO	SB	CS	SLG	OBP
Meier, Danny	R-R	6-3	205	10-28-85	.200	.205	.199	58	180	20	36	5	3	7	27	11	6	5	1	82	2	4	.378	.268
Pestana, Reinaldo	R-R	6-1	180	5-24-87	.146	.200	.127	29	96	7	14	2	0	0	6	2	3	0	1	33	0	1	.167	.186
Priday, Jacob	R-R	6-1	220	10-2-85	.200	.400	.150	8	25	2	5	1	0	0	2	5	2	0	0	11	0	0	.240	.375
Ramirez, Ronald	R-R	5-11	165	1-30-86	.178	.231	.162	49	169	19	30	3	0	3	11	10	3	4	1	54	5	4	.249	.235
Rosario, Ebert	R-R	6-3	165	5-27-87	.071	.000	.091	4	14	1	1	0	0	0	1	1	1	0	1	6	0	0	.071	.176
Shuck, J.B.	L-L	5-11	185	6-18-87	.300	.268	.313	65	263	51	79	12	5	4	24	35	2	2	1	34	8	6	.430	.385
Simunic, Andy	R-R	6-0	170	8-7-85	.234	.326	.203	53	184	20	43	2	1	0	14	21	2	0	1	49	4	3	.255	.317
Steele, T.J.	R-R	6-3	185	9-21-86	.283	.297	.279	40	159	18	45	8	1	3	21	6	3	1	1	51	6	1	.403	.320
Williams, Marques	R-R	6-0	185	10-24-85	.213	.184	.223	46	150	17	32	6	2	0	10	6	3	0	0	40	2	5	.280	.258

Pitching	B-T	HT	WT	DOB	W	L	ERA	G	GS	CG	SV	IP	H	R	ER	HR	BB	SO	AVG	vLH	vRH	K/9	BB/9
Bono, Robert	R-R	6-2	175	12-12-88	0	4	4.68	15	15	0	0	75	97	53	39	7	11	46	.311	.356	.270	5.52	1.32
Ciriaco, Eduin	L-L	6-0	175	10-26-85	2	0	2.65	16	0	0	0	37	22	13	11	3	20	47	.164	.077	.185	11.33	4.82
Duncan, David	L-L	6-9	230	6-1-86	3	4	4.88	14	14	0	0	55	60	37	30	5	9	45	.269	.273	.268	7.32	1.46
Duran, Jose	R-R	6-1	175	5-1-85	3	1	3.10	13	0	0	0	29	28	12	10	3	11	22	.243	.313	.217	6.83	3.41
Godfrey, Kyle	R-R	6-4	200	2-6-86	1	4	6.90	19	0	0	0	30	35	27	23	3	19	32	.278	.275	.279	9.60	5.70
Greenwalt, Kyle	R-R	6-0	200	9-29-88	1	0	1.50	2	1	0	0	6	3	1	1	0	2	5	.143	.286	.071	7.50	3.00
Hacker, Mike	L-L	5-9	175	11-6-85	1	3	2.73	23	0	0	5	26	17	14	8	0	17	27	.187	.130	.206	9.23	5.81
Hicks, Chris	R-R	6-4	205	2-17-87	0	0	3.38	6	0	0	0	8	3	3	3	1	3	13	.111	.333	.048	14.63	3.38
Holloway, Jarred	R-L	6-3	218	8-28-88	0	5	4.07	13	13	0	0	49	48	31	22	2	27	37	.270	.310	.262	6.84	4.99
Lehr, Chase	R-R	6-3	170	10-9-87	0	1	6.52	7	0	0	0	10	10	12	7	1	12	4	.256	.182	.286	3.72	11.17
Lyles, Jordan	R-R	6-4	185	10-19-90	0	0	6.35	2	2	0	0	6	7	5	4	2	7	4	.292	.500	.250	6.35	11.12
Meszaros, Danny	R-R	6-0	170	9-6-85	1	3	4.44	12	0	0	1	26	21	14	13	0	2 8	46	.212	.313	.164	15.72	2.73
Miller, David	L-R	6-10	210	9-29-84	3	2	3.51	18	0	0	0	41	33	17	16	2	23	30	.217	.333	.177	6.59	5.05
Mowdy, Ashton	R-R	6-0	185	6-21-86	4	3	4.10	21	2	0	1	42	39	21	19	5	21	48	.242	.333	.192	10.37	4.54
Noguera, Antonio	L-L	6-3	194	2-26-88	2	8	7.59	15	13	0	0	53	77	56	45	7	21	24	.328	.222	.347	4.05	3.54
Rivers, Kirkland	L-L	6-1	180	1-6-86	1	2	5.25	19	0	0	3	36	38	24	21	3	21	49	.273	.367	.248	12.25	5.25
Rummel, Philip	R-R	6-5	235	6-26-85	3	2	2.84	21	0	0	0	38	39	18	12	1	9	31	.271	.228	.299	7.34	2.13
Wabick, Brian	R-R	6-0	180	8-3-87	2	1	2.14	11	0	0	2	21	18	5	5	0	1	23	.222	.200	.239	9.86	0.43
Wolf, Shane	L-L	6-3	225	9-10-86	1	2	4.19	13	13	0	0	58	65	27	27	3	12	48	.280	.364	.254	7.45	1.86

Fielding

Catcher	PCT	G	PO	A	E	DP	PB
Castro	.982	27	199	21	4	0	6
Gonzalez	.957	5	39	6	2	0	0
Henson	.967	16	111	8	4	1	4
Pestana	.985	29	222	38	4	2	5

First Base	PCT	G	PO	A	E	DP
Disher	.973	66	556	29	16	48
Meier	.981	12	94	7	2	6

Second Base	PCT	G	PO	A	E	DP
Diaz	.919	29	48	76	11	14

Ramirez	1.000	2	7	3	0	1
Simunic	.984	46	98	142	4	28

Third Base	PCT	G	PO	A	E	DP
Flores	.873	49	29	95	18	6
Jackson	.972	12	12	23	1	3
Meier	.744	12	9	20	10	1
Rosario	.800	3	3	9	3	3

Shortstop	PCT	G	PO	A	E	DP
Hulett	.835	24	31	60	18	13
Jackson	.741	4	6	14	7	1

Ramirez	.926	48	72	129	16	21

Outfield	PCT	G	PO	A	E	DP
Gaston	1.000	45	92	5	0	1
Hulett	—	1	0	0	0	0
Meier	1.000	35	57	5	0	1
Priday	1.000	4	6	1	0	0
Shuck	.981	63	94	8	2	0
Simunic	1.000	7	8	2	0	0
Steele	.983	37	57	2	1	0
Williams	.938	42	58	2	4	0

GREENEVILLE ASTROS   ROOKIE
APPALACHIAN LEAGUE

Batting	B-T	HT	WT	DOB	AVG	vLH	vRH	G	AB	R	H	2B	3B	HR	RBI	BB	HBP	SH	SF	SO	SB	CS	SLG	OBP
Almonte, Frank	R-R	6-2	190	1-24-89	.271	.275	.270	53	199	23	54	10	3	5	30	10	5	0	0	67	0	3	.427	.322
Altuve, Jose	R-R	5-5	148	5-6-90	.284	.278	.285	40	141	26	40	9	3	2	21	8	0	2	1	26	8	2	.433	.320
Austin, Jay	L-L	5-11	170	8-10-90	.198	.162	.206	55	212	31	42	4	2	0	14	19	4	0	0	69	14	6	.236	.277
Bonfante, Ricardo	R-R	5-9	140	10-21-88	.261	.308	.256	43	138	19	36	6	2	0	12	6	1	1	1	14	10	3	.333	.295
Cartwright, Albert	R-R	5-10	180	10-31-87	.306	.370	.287	39	121	23	37	2	2	3	17	15	7	0	1	32	13	4	.430	.410
De Leon, Jorge	R-R	6-0	168	8-15-87	.235	.276	.219	32	102	16	24	6	3	0	14	6	3	0	0	24	1	2	.363	.297
Garcia, Rene	R-R	6-1	172	3-21-90	.295	.273	.303	18	44	4	13	1	0	1	6	3	0	0	0	3	0	0	.386	.340
Gonzalez, Pedro	L-R	5-11	180	10-29-86	.253	.250	.253	26	87	5	22	2	0	0	8	6	0	1	0	18	0	0	.276	.301
Hernandez, Federico	R-R	6-0	170	2-9-88	.298	.440	.258	36	114	14	34	8	0	3	17	8	1	1	1	19	0	0	.447	.347
Hinze, Kody	R-R	6-0	225	7-29-87	.269	.243	.275	55	197	29	53	13	0	8	32	34	1	0	3	46	1	1	.457	.374
Infante, Wilton	R-R	6-1	175	8-11-87	.185	.300	.171	34	92	9	17	1	0	0	5	8	2	0	0	19	3	4	.196	.265
Metroka, Nathan	R-R	6-2	220	8-30-86	.327	.313	.330	33	113	14	37	8	3	3	17	11	0	0	0	37	1	4	.531	.387
Miller, Kyle	R-R	6-0	200	9-1-86	.274	.400	.263	19	62	3	17	2	1	1	13	6	0	0	1	9	0	0	.387	.333
Mojica, Carlos	R-R	6-0	190	6-7-88	.302	.667	.243	16	43	8	13	0	0	0	3	2	4	1	0	15	0	0	.302	.388
Montas, Dionel	R-R	6-2	200	5-17-87	.168	.222	.147	29	95	12	16	3	0	3	8	10	2	0	1	34	0	2	.295	.259
Rosario, Ebert	R-R	6-3	165	5-27-87	.304	.241	.317	47	168	23	51	6	2	3	18	13	3	1	2	24	4	2	.411	.360
Tello, Renzo	R-R	6-1	155	6-30-87	.288	.226	.303	44	153	25	44	9	2	3	25	12	3	0	2	37	4	1	.431	.347
Torrence, Devon	R-R	6-0	190	5-8-89	.151	.130	.156	34	119	15	18	2	0	0	2	19	0	1	0	53	2	3	.168	.266
Turner, Chris	R-R	5-11	185	10-21-88		.000	.219	14	39	6	7	1	0	0	3	2	1	0	0	18	0	0	.205	.238

Pitching	B-T	HT	WT	DOB	W	L	ERA	G	GS	CG	SV	IP	H	R	ER	HR	BB	SO	AVG	vLH	vRH	K/9	BB/9
Castillo, Jeiler	R-R	6-0	155	10-26-87	0	3	5.66	13	0	0	0	21	23	20	13	2	21	18	.274	.375	.233	7.84	9.15
Cruz, Luis	L-L	5-9	170	9-10-90	1	1	2.28	7	7	0	0	24	20	7	6	2	7	19	.227	.308	.213	7.23	2.66
Dinelli, David	R-R	6-3	215	3-14-87	2	2	6.97	13	0	0	1	31	40	26	24	4	28	18	.313	.286	.326	5.23	8.13
Dydalewicz, Brad	L-L	6-1	180	3-24-90	0	2	2.70	4	4	0	0	10	7	3	3	1	6	20	.206	.333	.194	5.40	2.70
Greenwalt, Kyle	R-R	6-0	200	9-29-88	6	4	3.14	13	13	0	0	72	77	27	25	2	14	53	.274	.308	.254	6.66	1.76
Grimmett, Zach	R-R	6-3	185	2-5-90	1	2	5.40	13	0	0	0	32	41	23	19	3	6	18	.318	.341	.306	5.12	1.71
Lazu, Carlos	R-L	6-0	185	2-4-86	0	0	5.40	3	0	0	0	3	6	3	2	0	2	5	.375	.000	.429	13.50	5.40

Name	B-T	HT	WT	DOB	W	L	ERA	G	GS	CG	SV	IP	H	R	ER	HR	BB	SO	AVG	vLH	vRH	K/9	BB/9
Leon, Arcenio	R-R	6-1	162	9-22-86	3	1	3.33	15	2	0	0	49	55	34	18	2	19	42	.285	.357	.244	7.77	3.51
Lucati, Andrea	R-R	6-3	247	1-17-90	0	0	5.14	7	0	0	0	7	7	4	4	0	7	12	.259	.273	.250	15.43	9.00
Lyles, Jordan	R-R	6-4	185	10-19-90	3	3	3.99	13	13	0	0	50	44	26	22	4	10	64	.228	.247	.210	11.60	1.81
Ortiz, Wander	R-R	5-11	159	2-10-87	1	6	5.79	14	1	0	0	42	55	32	27	2	7	33	.320	.311	.323	7.07	1.50
Pettus, Nate	R-R	6-1	200	10-9-88	2	2	4.91	16	0	0	4	22	26	17	12	1	11	18	.283	.286	.281	7.36	4.50
Pitkin, Colton	R-L	6-3	210	8-10-89	2	2	3.07	17	0	0	4	44	40	15	15	2	20	45	.240	.302	.218	9.20	4.09
Romero, Joel	R-R	6-0	180	7-25-88	1	1	4.82	7	0	0	0	9	6	7	5	1	6	7	.171	.154	.182	6.75	5.79
Seaton, Ross	L-R	6-4	190	9-18-89	0	0	13.50	3	3	0	0	4	8	7	6	1	2	4	.381	.429	.357	9.00	4.50
Trinidad, Jose	R-R	5-11	150	7-13-87	3	2	2.73	10	10	0	0	56	57	23	17	0	6	40	.251	.250	.252	6.43	0.96
Urckfitz, Pat	L-L	6-3	190	7-21-88	1	0	1.40	15	0	0	3	19	13	8	3	1	9	23	.191	.176	.196	10.71	4.19
Villar, Henry	R-R	5-11	150	5-24-87	3	6	4.41	13	13	0	0	65	69	32	32	6	12	65	.272	.309	.243	8.95	1.65
Wabick, Brian	R-R	6-0	180	8-3-87	1	1	3.93	10	0	0	5	18	22	8	8	2	5	16	.319	.269	.349	7.85	2.45

Fielding

Catcher	PCT	G	PO	A	E	DP	PB
Garcia	.955	6	40	2	2	0	0
Gonzalez	.995	26	168	21	1	3	2
Hernandez	.983	28	196	34	4	1	5
Mojica	.964	16	98	8	4	2	4

First Base	PCT	G	PO	A	E	DP
Hinze	.986	54	483	21	7	49
Metroka	1.000	6	33	0	0	1
Miller	1.000	10	81	0	0	7

Second Base	PCT	G	PO	A	E	DP
Altuve	.948	38	89	110	11	25
Cartwright	.936	29	60	87	10	21

Third Base	PCT	G	PO	A	E	DP
Altuve	—	1	0	0	0	0
Miller	.700	2	3	4	3	0
Montas	.886	23	7	55	8	4
Rosario	.889	45	26	94	15	9

Shortstop	PCT	G	PO	A	E	DP
Bonfante	.951	41	55	120	9	25

De Leon	.905	32	38	76	12	12

Outfield	PCT	G	PO	A	E	DP
Almonte	.978	34	42	2	1	0
Austin	.925	54	108	3	9	1
Infante	.929	32	49	3	4	2
Metroka	1.000	20	35	2	0	0
Tello	.963	44	48	4	2	0
Torrence	.918	24	43	2	4	1
Turner	1.000	9	10	1	0	0

DSL ASTROS
ROOKIE

DOMINICAN SUMMER LEAGUE

Batting	B-T	HT	WT	DOB	AVG	vLH	vRH	G	AB	R	H	2B	3B	HR	RBI	BB	HBP	SH	SF	SO	SB	CS	SLG	OBP
Alcantara, Carlos	R-R	6-4	210	2-16-90	.141	.231	.127	30	92	4	13	2	0	0	6	17	4	0	2	42	1	0	.163	.296
Arrendell, Miguel	L-R	6-0	165	3-26-88	.284	.289	.282	57	194	37	55	6	2	0	14	57	6	1	0	30	20	6	.335	.459
Bryan, Luis	R-R	6-2	165	11-26-90	.154	.136	.157	44	156	13	24	3	1	0	8	11	3	1	1	25	4	3	.186	.222
Feliz, Pedro	B-R	6-0	150	12-5-90	.248	.211	.255	39	125	21	31	4	0	0	15	31	0	1	1	28	6	6	.280	.395
Fulgencio, Lonny	R-R	5-11	175	2-14-90	.232	.385	.192	37	125	22	29	4	0	2	9	22	3	2	1	41	9	8	.312	.358
Heredia, Ricardo	R-R	6-2	170	3-1-89	.258	.250	.260	43	155	13	40	6	0	2	18	6	4	0	1	38	7	1	.335	.301
Hirland, Cristian	R-R	6-1	180	5-30-91	.243	.125	.276	30	37	5	9	4	0	0	5	0	1	0	0	8	0	0	.351	.263
King, Emilio	R-R	6-1	180	8-17-89	.202	.100	.226	33	104	12	21	2	1	1	8	10	4	0	0	18	2	2	.269	.297
Mejia, Jhoan	R-R	6-3	190	12-25-88	.198	.154	.212	30	111	13	22	5	0	0	8	5	0	0	1	12	2	0	.243	.282
Moronta, Cristian	R-R	5-10	185	12-5-89	.211	.125	.233	19	38	4	8	2	1	0	4	1	0	1	0	7	2	0	.316	.231
Perez, Rainier	R-R	6-1	185	8-19-90	.082	.100	.078	40	122	10	10	1	1	1	6	20	1	0	0	63	8	1	.131	.217
Ramos, Eudy	L-L	6-2	210	1-5-91	.142	.192	.130	38	134	8	19	5	0	0	17	7	0	1		43	2	2	.179	.270
Reyes, Carlos	R-R	6-0	180	12-5-87	.239	.279	.230	67	243	27	58	8	2	1	29	31	3	1	0	65	21	7	.300	.332
Rodriguez, Amilkin	B-R	6-2	190	3-13-88	.238	.344	.212	54	164	27	39	5	1	2	16	28	0	1	0	40	15	4	.317	.349
Rodriguez, Hector	R-R	5-11	150	8-8-89	.214	.158	.226	32	103	11	22	0	0	6	10	2	1	0	29	4	2	.214	.296
Santana, Jose	R-R	6-2	185	3-2-89	.289	.563	.235	33	97	19	28	4	0	0	11	4	0	0	26	9	2	.330	.434
Valdez, Pedro	R-R	6-2	180	9-17-89	.137	.130	.139	39	124	9	17	7	0	2	14	11	1	1	1	59	3	0	.242	.212
Vargas, Jose	R-R	6-1	200	4-30-91	.236	.143	.252	43	144	13	34	4	1	0	11	15	7	0	0	37	0	0	.278	.337

Pitching	B-T	HT	WT	DOB	W	L	ERA	G	GS	CG	SV	IP	H	R	ER	HR	BB	SO	AVG	vLH	vRH	K/9	BB/9
Batista, Ricardo	L-L	6-1	170	8-19-91	1	2	8.06	13	4	0	0	26	30	34	23	1	24	20	.280	.091	.302	7.01	8.42
Bautista, Reyes	L-L	6-1	170	10-6-90	1	1	3.75	7	0	0	0	12	9	10	5	0	10	10	.205	.333	.195	7.50	7.50
Belliard, Joan	R-R	6-2	185	3-3-89	2	1	2.78	17	0	0	2	36	30	15	11	1	7	32	.221	.345	.187	8.07	1.77
Cisnero, Jose	R-R	6-3	185	4-11-89	0	3	3.10	16	6	0	2	29	18	15	10	0	11	34	.180	.242	.149	10.55	3.41
De La Cruz, Leonel	R-R	6-2	160	10-3-90	2	0	5.74	8	0	0	0	16	22	14	10	4	9	6	.314	.318	.313	3.45	5.17
De Leon, Noel	R-R	6-5	176	7-6-88	0	3	5.58	11	0	0	0	31	37	26	19	1	14	14	.303	.444	.263	4.11	4.11
Espinal, Martin	R-R	6-0	195	11-3-86	2	7	2.53	14	14	0	0	75	61	33	21	4	16	62	.214	.161	.240	7.47	1.93
Estrella, Joel	R-R	6-2	160	1-20-90	1	1	3.51	13	5	0	0	33	26	17	13	0	15	26	.215	.174	.224	7.02	4.05
Feliz, Rafael	R-R	6-0	180	9-21-89	0	1	7.82	9	0	0	0	13	18	11	0	1	13	8	.327	.261	.375	5.68	9.24
Gil, Carlos	R-R	6-4	175	4-19-90	0	5	7.82	15	6	0	1	38	53	44	33	1	24	25	.317	.286	.331	5.92	5.68
Gonzalez, Angel	L-L	6-0	160	8-12-88	2	4	2.95	12	12	0	0	58	48	31	19	0	25	59	.218	.130	.228	9.16	3.88
Luna, Rafael	L-L	6-0	175	1-20-90	0	5	3.96	13	7	0	0	39	40	23	17	0	19	28	.265	.286	.264	6.52	4.42
Mojica, Juan	R-R	6-4	190	2-13-89	2	7	2.96	14	9	1	0	52	45	33	17	2	18	40	.231	.226	.232	6.97	3.14
Pio, Rafael	R-R	6-3	210	1-9-88	1	4	4.96	22	1	0	1	49	42	32	27	3	26	35	.228	.265	.215	6.43	4.78
Vargas, Radaulin	L-L	6-2	160	5-22-89	5	3	3.02	18	7	0	0	60	53	27	20	3	18	64	.240	.167	.249	9.65	2.72

Fielding

Catcher	PCT	G	PO	A	E	DP	PB
Hirland	.937	10	65	9	5	1	2
King	.972	23	168	7	5	2	3
Moronta	.892	18	49	9	7	0	1
Vargas	.968	31	214	30	8	0	10

First Base	PCT	G	PO	A	E	DP
Alcantara	.959	14	92	1	4	12
Mejia	.979	5	46	1	1	3
Ramos	.988	37	316	14	4	32

A. Rodriguez	.973	23	138	5	4	13

Second Base	PCT	G	PO	A	E	DP
Arrendell	.956	40	115	102	10	25
Feliz	.976	9	17	24	1	7
Fulgencio	.877	15	33	38	10	8
H. Rodriguez	.980	8	16	32	1	8

Third Base	PCT	G	PO	A	E	DP
Arrendell	.804	17	14	31	11	1
Feliz	.824	5	3	11	3	0

Mejia	.887	23	30	56	11	8
A. Rodriguez	.787	27	19	55	20	10
H. Rodriguez	1.000	3	1	1	0	0

Shortstop	PCT	G	PO	A	E	DP
Arrendell	1.000	1	3	5	0	2
Bryan	.859	44	68	127	32	17
Feliz	.977	13	12	30	1	7
H. Rodriguez	.910	18	25	56	8	13

Outfield	PCT	G	PO	A	E	DP
Heredia	.938	41	55	5	4	2
Perez	.902	39	54	1	6	0

Reyes	.955	67	140	8	7	2
A. Rodriguez	1.000	1	2	0	0	0
Santana	.945	33	48	4	3	0

Valdez	.964	39	50	4	2	0

VSL ASTROS — ROOKIE

VENEZUELAN SUMMER LEAGUE

Batting	B-T	HT	WT	DOB	AVG	vLH	vRH	G	AB	R	H	2B	3B	HR	RBI	BB	HBP	SH	SF	SO	SB	CS	SLG	OBP
Alvarez, Luis	R-R	5-11	198	2-28-90	.333	.316	.337	61	207	44	69	17	0	7	33	32	11	2	3	32	4	2	.517	.443
Baldee, Jan	R-R	6-2	170	12-8-90	.070	.077	.067	13	43	0	3	0	0	0	1	1	2	1	0	19	1	0	.070	.130
Blanco, Robert	R-R	5-11	177	4-18-89	.245	.357	.205	39	106	12	26	4	0	1	11	10	4	1	0	15	3	0	.311	.333
Figueroa, Oscar	R-R	5-11	154	1-10-88	.268	.291	.261	64	235	40	63	13	2	5	33	34	6	4	2	24	9	3	.404	.372
Garcia, Ricardo	R-R	5-9	142	1-20-89	.317	.333	.311	48	142	37	45	12	3	0	21	29	7	2	1	17	11	4	.444	.453
Lopez, Jose	R-R	5-11	172	5-8-90	.236	.220	.240	62	229	33	54	8	0	0	26	20	4	5	3	40	3	2	.271	.305
Lopez, Raymer	R-R	5-10	145	3-31-91	.280	.294	.276	38	157	25	44	1	1	1	20	10	9	2	1	33	4	4	.318	.356
Nieves, Angel	R-R	5-11	175	7-11-90	.277	.356	.252	52	184	22	51	10	0	2	23	6	5	7	1	21	4	2	.364	.316
Parra, Wilder	R-R	6-0	175	3-2-91	.234	.240	.233	32	111	6	26	3	1	1	12	4	1	2	0	27	0	0	.306	.267
Rojas, Saul	R-R	5-11	182	5-3-91	.240	.429	.209	16	50	5	12	1	0	0	2	3	1	0	0	17	0	1	.260	.296
Santana, Nestor	R-R	6-0	190	5-30-90	.255	.295	.243	59	196	28	50	7	0	1	29	22	6	2	3	41	6	2	.306	.344
Sumoza, Luis	R-R	5-10	186	6-9-89	.182	.125	.198	47	148	27	27	7	0	1	16	38	2	1	0	35	9	2	.250	.356
Torres, Julio	R-R	5-11	166	7-28-90	.267	.317	.253	56	191	36	51	9	2	3	26	30	5	3	0	55	10	2	.382	.381
Valdes, Joseph	R-R	6-1	197	7-17-90	.242	.278	.234	32	95	9	23	4	0	1	14	18	2	0	1	13	1	1	.316	.371

Pitching	B-T	HT	WT	DOB	W	L	ERA	G	GS	CG	SV	IP	H	R	ER	HR	BB	SO	AVG	vLH	vRH	K/9	BB/9
Baso, Xavier	R-R	6-0	182	12-1-91	1	2	3.42	15	0	0	2	24	28	15	9	0	5	8	.292	.310	.284	3.04	1.90
Castellano, Julio	L-L	6-2	170	6-11-87	2	4	5.26	15	0	0	2	38	44	26	22	1	20	24	.297	.500	.286	5.73	4.78
De Leon, Elias	L-L	5-11	177	7-8-90	3	1	1.24	14	1	0	2	36	31	10	5	1	5	24	.226	.500	.214	5.94	1.24
Del Rio, Danilo	R-R	5-11	179	9-28-90	0	0	3.13	10	4	0	1	23	23	13	8	3	8	11	.267	.250	.274	4.30	3.13
Diaz, Dayan	R-R	5-10	156	2-10-89	2	2	1.85	13	8	0	2	49	42	14	10	2	5	36	.233	.302	.212	6.66	0.92
Farias, Rafael	R-R	6-3	160	9-27-89	1	1	5.01	11	3	0	0	23	25	22	13	0	5	16	.253	.276	.243	6.17	1.93
Garcia, Gabriel de Jesus	L-L	5-11	142	5-11-89	3	3	3.46	14	7	0	0	55	67	36	21	3	7	45	.302	.111	.310	7.41	1.15
Gomez, Pedro	R-R	6-3	204	5-10-91	2	2	2.40	13	6	0	1	49	51	22	13	6	8	14	.267	.234	.278	2.59	1.48
Iturralde, Roliner	R-R	5-11	167	11-23-90	2	2	1.77	14	0	0	1	20	12	7	4	1	5	10	.174	.412	.096	4.43	2.21
Martinez, David	R-R	6-2	180	8-8-87	4	3	4.75	13	7	0	0	53	65	37	28	2	13	41	.291	.268	.299	6.96	2.21
Mendoza, Ricardo	R-R	6-0	162	6-28-89	1	0	4.24	10	0	0	1	17	18	8	8	1	7	10	.273	.263	.277	5.29	3.71
Moreno, Robert	R-R	5-11	169	9-20-89	2	4	4.18	18	0	0	3	24	29	16	11	1	12	12	.312	.400	.279	4.56	4.56
Paracuto, Erick	L-L	5-9	181	1-14-90	2	0	4.82	7	0	0	0	9	8	10	5	2	8	7	.216	.000	.229	6.75	7.71
Perez, German	L-L	5-11	147	9-21-89	1	1	3.86	9	3	0	1	26	28	12	11	1	9	13	.275	.500	.270	4.56	3.16
Perez, Yuri	R-R	5-11	148	8-8-90	4	4	2.68	12	11	0	0	57	43	22	17	2	19	28	.209	.265	.191	4.42	3.00
Pina, Wladimir	R-R	6-2	197	10-9-89	0	1	4.22	5	4	0	0	11	16	11	5	0	11	4	.340	.333	.342	3.38	9.28
Quevedo, Carlos	R-R	6-1	222	9-30-89	4	2	1.98	14	14	0	0	68	56	19	15	2	11	53	.224	.218	.226	6.98	1.45
Ulloa, Gilberto	L-L	5-11	182	4-28-89	3	1	7.00	13	0	0	1	18	29	15	14	1	9	9	.372	.500	.368	4.50	4.50

Fielding

Catcher	PCT	G	PO	A	E	DP	PB
Alvarez	.990	15	82	14	1	2	6
Genoves	.980	27	123	25	3	4	6
Parra	.981	21	84	18	2	1	10
Rojas	.985	9	59	6	1	0	0
Valdes	1.000	6	20	3	0	0	1

First Base	PCT	G	PO	A	E	DP
Alvarez	.983	29	264	18	5	30
Figueroa	.977	5	42	1	1	5
Genoves	.965	25	208	12	8	14
Sumoza	1.000	7	56	5	0	7
Valdes	1.000	9	68	6	0	4

Second Base	PCT	G	PO	A	E	DP
Figueroa	.917	8	13	20	3	4
Garcia	1.000	1	5	3	0	2
R. Lopez	.931	34	87	76	12	18
Santana	1.000	1	4	4	0	4
Sumoza	.961	27	72	74	6	15

Third Base	PCT	G	PO	A	E	DP
Alvarez	.871	18	11	43	8	3
Figueroa	.882	13	19	41	8	5
Nieves	.907	32	27	71	10	5
Sumoza	.915	11	10	33	4	3

Shortstop	PCT	G	PO	A	E	DP
Baldee	.720	13	16	20	14	4

	PCT	G	PO	A	E	DP
Figueroa	.929	37	68	127	15	23
R. Lopez	.955	3	4	17	1	1
Nieves	.893	20	38	70	13	14

Outfield	PCT	G	PO	A	E	DP
Blanco	.964	39	51	2	2	1
Figueroa	1.000	3	5	0	0	0
J. Lopez	.982	61	109	3	2	1
R. Lopez	1.000	1	1	0	0	0
Santana	.940	57	91	3	6	1
Sumoza	.875	3	6	1	1	0
Torres	.920	56	109	6	10	3
Valdes	1.000	4	4	1	0	0

Kansas City Royals

BY ALAN ESKEW

If the Royals played all season like they did in September, they would have been playing in October.

The Royals won a major league-best 18 games in September, which allowed them to escape the American League Central basement for the first time since 2003. Their 75 victories under first-year manager Trey Hillman were their most since going 83-79 in 2003— their only winning record since 1994.

The Royals, who have not been in the playoffs since winning the 1985 World Series, were doomed by two horrible stretches this year. The Royals lost 12 straight in May and then dropped 18 of 21 during an August slide.

"The way we finished, I think we had more highs than lows," Hillman said. "It was a positive ending and hopefully provides more hope going into next year. With six more wins than we had last year and finishing in a different place (not last), that's a big deal for me, for our organization."

The Royals went from 27 back in 2007 to 13 out in 2008.

Righthanders Gil Meche and Zack Greinke provided the Royals with solid No. 1 and 2 starters. Meche led the club by going 14-13, 3.98. Greinke was 13-10 with a staff-best 3.47 ERA. They each finished with 183 strikeouts.

Joakim Soria developed into one of the most consistent closers in his sophomore season. Soria went 42 for 45 in save situations, had a 1.60 ERA and held opposing hitters to a .169 average.

Brian Bannister, who was the No. 3 starter, digressed from fnishing third in the AL rookie of the year balloting, ending 9-16, 5.76 ERA in 2008. Kyle Davies won his final three starts, including wins over the division-leading White Sox and Twins, to finish 9-7, 4.06 in 21 starts and could be a boost to the rotation next season.

However a lack offense again plagued the Royals and ultimately cost hitting coach Mike Barnett his job. He was replaced by former Royal Kevin Seitzer after the season. The Royals improved only slightly after finishing last in home runs and RBIs in the AL last year, as they finished second to last in home runs (120) and 12th in RBIs (650). They did jump from 11th to sixth this season with a .269 team batting average, yet scored fewer runs because their on-base percentage declined.

Among offseason changes, Royals general manager Dayton Moore dismissed longtime scouting director Deric Ladnier, promoting farm director J.J. Picollo to oversee the draft.

PLAYERS OF THE YEAR

MAJOR LEAGUE: ZACK GREINKE, RHP

If the Royals ever return to the playoffs, they know Greinke will be a key. He furthered his reputation in 2008 as he finished 13-10, 3.47 with 183 strikeouts against 56 walks in 202 innings. His ERA was 10th-best in the American League.

MINOR LEAGUE: KILA KAAIHUE, 1B

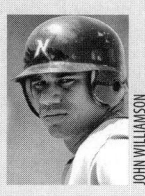

After two years in the Double-A Texas League, Kaaihue proved the third time was a charm as he became the circuit's MVP. He hit .313/.457/.629 with 37 home runs and 99 RBIs between Double-A and Triple-A before receiving a September callup.

JOHN WILLIAMSON

ORGANIZATION LEADERS

BATTING		*Minimum 250 at-bats
*AVG	Maier, Mitch, Omaha	.316
R	Ka'aihue, Kila, NW Arkansas/Omaha	91
H	Ortiz, Adrian, Burlington (MWL)/Wilmington	162
TB	Ka'aihue, Kila, NW Arkansas/Omaha	252
2B	Richardson, Juan, NW Arkansas	36
3B	Lough, David, Burlington (MWL)	11
HR	Ka'aihue, Kila, NW Arkansas/Omaha	37
RBI	Ka'aihue, Kila, NW Arkansas/Omaha	100
BB	Ka'aihue, Kila, NW Arkansas/Omaha	104
SO	Lubanski, Chris, Omaha	130
SB	Robinson, Derrick, Wilmington	62
*OBP	Ka'aihue, Kila, NW Arkansas/Omaha	.456
*SLG	Ka'aihue, Kila, NW Arkansas/Omaha	.628

PITCHING		†Minimum 75 innings
W	Hartsock, Aaron, NW Arkansas/Wilmington	12
	Caldera, Alexander, Burlington (MWL)	12
L	Lumsden, Tyler, Omaha	13
	Pimentel, Julio Cesar, Northwest Arkansas	13
	Mildren, Paul, Omaha/Wilmington/NW Arkansas	13
†ERA	Caldera, Alexander, Burlington (MWL)	2.89
G	Chambliss, Tyler, Wilmington	49
GS	Pimentel, Julio Cesar, Northwest Arkansas	28
	Wood, Blake, Wilmington/NW Arkansas	28
SV	Chambliss, Tyler, Wilmington	24
IP	Cegarra, Edward, Burlington (MWL)/Wilmington	160
BB	Lumsden, Tyler, Omaha	62
SO	Wood, Blake, Wilmington/NW Arkansas	139
†AVG	Cortes, Dan, Northwest Arkansas	.241

2008 PERFORMANCE

General Manager: Dayton Moore. **Farm Director:** J.J. Picollo. **Scouting Director:** Daric Ladnier.

Class	Team	League	W	L	PCT	Finish*	Manager	Affiliate Since
Majors	Kansas City	American	75	87	.463	11th (14)	Trey Hillman	—
Triple-A	Omaha Royals	Pacific Coast	63	81	.438	14th (16)	Mike Jirschele	1969
Double-A	NW Arkansas Naturals	Texas	75	65	.536	4th (8)	Brian Poldberg	2008
High A	Wilmington Blue Rocks	Carolina	69	71	.493	5th (8)	Darryl Kennedy	2007
Low A	Burlington Bees	Midwest	73	65	.529	^4th (14)	Brian Rupp	2001
Rookie	Idaho Falls Chukars	Pioneer	33	43	.434	7th (8)	Jim Gabella	2001
Rookie	Burlington Royals	Appalachian	24	41	.369	10th (10)	Tony Tijerina	2007
Rookie	AZL Royals	Arizona	23	33	.411	6th (9)	Julio Bruno	2008
Overall 2008 Minor League Record			360	455	.442	27th		

* Finish in overall standings (No. of teams in league). ^League champion.

ORGANIZATION STATISTICS

KANSAS CITY ROYALS

AMERICAN LEAGUE

Batting	B-T	HT	WT	DOB	AVG	vLH	vRH	G	AB	R	H	2B	3B	HR	RBI	BB	HBP	SH	SF	SO	SB	CS	SLG	OBP
Aviles, Mike	R-R	5-9	195	3-13-81	.325	.348	.313	102	419	68	136	27	4	10	51	18	2	0	2	58	8	3	.480	.354
Buck, John	R-R	6-3	220	7-7-80	.224	.236	.219	109	370	48	83	23	1	9	48	38	6	0	4	96	0	3	.365	.304
Butler, Billy	R-R	6-1	240	4-18-86	.275	.340	.244	124	443	44	122	22	0	11	55	33	0	0	2	57	0	1	.400	.324
Callaspo, Alberto	B-R	5-9	180	4-19-83	.305	.333	.291	74	213	21	65	8	3	0	16	19	0	1	1	14	2	1	.371	.361
DeJesus, David	L-L	6-0	190	12-20-79	.307	.302	.310	135	518	70	159	25	7	12	73	46	5	4	4	71	11	8	.452	.366
Gathright, Joey	L-R	5-10	185	4-27-81	.254	.250	.256	105	279	41	71	3	1	0	22	20	4	10	2	40	21	4	.272	.311
German, Esteban	R-R	5-9	195	1-26-78	.245	.255	.236	89	216	30	53	14	3	0	22	18	1	4	3	42	7	3	.338	.303
Gload, Ross	L-L	6-1	190	4-5-76	.273	.263	.277	122	388	46	106	18	1	3	37	23	3	1	3	39	3	4	.348	.317
Gordon, Alex	L-R	6-1	220	2-10-84	.260	.234	.273	134	493	72	128	35	1	16	59	66	6	1	5	120	9	2	.432	.351
Grudzielanek, Mark	R-R	6-0	200	6-30-70	.299	.395	.265	86	331	36	99	24	0	3	24	19	5	3	2	41	2	1	.399	.345
Guillen, Jose	R-R	6-0	210	5-17-76	.264	.305	.248	153	598	66	158	42	1	20	97	23	9	0	3	106	2	1	.438	.300
Ka'aihue, Kila	L-R	6-3	230	3-29-84	.286	.500	.263	12	21	4	6	0	0	1	1	3	0	0	0	2	0	0	.429	.375
Maier, Mitch	L-R	6-2	205	6-30-82	.286	.273	.293	34	91	9	26	1	1	0	9	2	2	2	0	18	0	2	.319	.316
Olivo, Miguel	R-R	6-0	210	7-15-78	.255	.262	.251	84	306	29	78	22	0	12	41	7	3	0	1	82	7	0	.444	.278
Pena, Tony	R-R	6-2	180	3-23-81	.169	.243	.135	95	225	22	38	4	1	1	14	6	0	2	2	49	3	1	.209	.189
Shealy, Ryan	R-R	6-5	240	8-29-79	.301	.273	.325	20	73	12	22	1	0	7	20	5	1	0	0	19	0	0	.603	.354
Smith, Jason	L-R	6-3	200	7-24-77	.214	.167	.227	22	28	6	6	2	0	0	1	0	0	0	0	12	0	1	.286	.214
Teahen, Mark	L-R	6-3	210	9-6-81	.255	.262	.252	149	572	66	146	31	4	15	59	46	3	0	2	131	4	3	.402	.313
Tupman, Matt	L-R	5-11	185	11-25-79	1.000	—	1.000	1	1	0	1	0	0	0	0	0	0	0	0	0	0	0	1.000	1.000

Pitching	B-T	HT	WT	DOB	W	L	ERA	G	GS	CG	SV	IP	H	R	ER	HR	BB	SO	AVG	vLH	vRH	K/9	BB/9
Bale, John	L-L	6-4	220	5-22-74	0	3	4.39	13	3	0	0	27	29	13	13	1	6	14	.293	.275	.305	4.73	2.03
Bannister, Brian	R-R	6-2	210	2-28-81	9	16	5.76	32	32	1	0	183	215	127	117	29	58	113	.294	.313	.274	5.57	2.86
Davies, Kyle	R-R	6-2	205	9-9-83	9	7	4.06	21	21	0	0	113	121	57	51	10	43	71	.276	.251	.300	5.65	3.42
Duckworth, Brandon	R-R	6-1	215	1-23-76	3	3	4.50	7	7	0	0	38	38	20	19	2	19	20	.266	.299	.237	4.74	4.50
Fulchino, Jeff	R-R	6-5	250	11-26-79	0	1	9.00	12	0	0	0	14	21	15	14	2	8	12	.339	.364	.310	7.71	5.14
Gobble, Jimmy	L-L	6-2	200	7-19-81	0	2	8.81	39	0	0	1	32	39	31	31	5	23	27	.293	.200	.382	7.67	6.54
Greinke, Zack	R-R	6-2	185	10-21-83	13	10	3.47	32	32	1	0	202	202	87	78	21	56	183	.257	.287	.232	8.14	2.49
Hochevar, Luke	R-R	6-5	205	9-15-83	6	12	5.51	22	22	0	0	129	143	84	79	12	47	72	.280	.314	.244	5.02	3.28
Lowery, Devon	L-R	6-1	195	3-24-83	0	0	10.38	5	0	0	0	4	6	5	5	2	2	6	.316	.444	.200	12.46	4.15
Mahay, Ron	L-L	6-2	190	6-28-71	5	0	3.48	57	0	0	0	65	61	27	25	6	29	49	.252	.255	.250	6.82	4.04
Meche, Gil	R-R	6-3	220	9-8-78	14	11	3.98	34	34	0	0	210	204	98	93	19	73	183	.255	.238	.273	7.83	3.12
Musser, Neal	L-L	6-1	235	8-25-80	0	0	0.00	1	0	0	0	1	0	0	0	0	1	0	.000	.000	.000	0.00	9.00
Newman, Josh	L-L	6-1	200	6-11-82	0	0	7.71	4	0	0	0	7	10	9	6	1	6	2	.357	.231	.467	2.57	7.71
Nomo, Hideo	R-R	6-2	220	8-31-68	0	0	18.69	3	0	0	0	4	10	9	9	3	4	3	.455	.167	.800	6.23	8.31
Nunez, Leo	R-R	6-1	175	8-14-83	4	1	2.98	45	0	0	0	48	45	19	16	2	15	26	.249	.272	.230	4.84	2.79
Peralta, Joel	R-R	5-11	180	3-23-76	1	2	5.98	40	0	0	0	53	56	37	35	15	14	38	.275	.247	.294	6.49	2.39
Ramirez, Horacio	L-L	6-1	220	11-24-79	1	1	2.59	15	0	0	0	24	21	9	7	1	1	11	.228	.235	.224	4.07	0.37
2-team total (17 Chicago)					1	4	4.34	32	0	0	0	37	45	20	18	1	9	13	—	—	—	3.13	2.17
Ramirez, Ramon	R-R	5-11	190	8-31-81	3	2	2.64	71	0	0	1	72	57	23	21	2	31	70	.222	.300	.153	8.79	3.89
Rosa, Carlos	R-R	6-1	185	9-21-84	0	0	2.70	2	0	0	0	3	3	1	1	0	0	3	.250	.333	.167	8.10	0.00
Soria, Joakim	R-R	6-3	185	5-18-84	2	3	1.60	63	0	0	42	67	39	13	12	5	19	66	.169	.167	.171	8.82	2.54
Tejeda, Robinson	R-R	6-3	230	3-24-82	2	2	3.20	25	1	0	0	39	22	17	14	3	19	41	.163	.215	.114	9.38	4.35
2-team total (4 Texas)					2	2	3.97	29	1	0	0	45	27	23	20	4	24	45	—	—	—	8.93	4.76
Tomko, Brett	R-R	6-4	220	4-7-73	2	7	6.97	16	10	0	0	61	80	49	47	11	13	40	.314	.311	.317	5.93	1.93
Wells, Kip	R-R	6-3	205	4-21-77	0	1	8.71	10	0	0	0	10	10	10	10	1	11	9	.263	.267	.261	7.84	9.58
Yabuta, Yasuhiko	R-R	6-2	185	6-19-73	1	3	4.78	31	0	0	0	38	41	21	20	6	17	25	.275	.185	.345	5.97	4.06

Fielding

Catcher	PCT	G	PO	A	E	DP	PB
Buck	.990	107	751	24	8	6	4
Olivo	.988	58	378	32	5	6	4
Tupman	—	1	0	0	0	0	0

First Base	PCT	G	PO	A	E	DP
Butler	.992	34	233	9	2	27
Gload	.995	111	837	43	4	86
Ka'aihue	1.000	4	12	1	0	2
Shealy	.988	20	155	12	2	18

	PCT	G	PO	A	E	DP
Smith	1.000	1	2	0	0	0
Teahen	.993	14	130	10	1	13
Second Base	PCT	G	PO	A	E	DP
Aviles	1.000	28	26	33	0	5

Callaspo	1.000	46	74 119	0	36
German	.975	35	41 77	3	19
Grudzielanek	.990	85	135 257	4	58
Smith	1.000	9	5 16	0	2

Third Base	PCT	G	PO	A	E	DP
Aviles	1.000	7	3	3	0	0
Callaspo	1.000	1	1	5	0	1
German	1.000	6	2	5	0	2
Gordon	.955	133	112	230	16	21

Smith	1.000	5	5	1	0 0
Teahen	.933	19	18 24	3	3

Shortstop	PCT	G	PO	A	E	DP
Aviles	.974	91	141	238	10	65
Callaspo	.960	18	18	30	2	8
German	.857	3	2	4	1	0
Pena	.966	94	74	180	9	35

Outfield	PCT	G	PO	A	E	DP
Callaspo	—	3	0	0	0	0

DeJesus	.997	134	310	3	1 1
Gathright	.995	103	199	5	1 0
German	.964	39	54	0	2 0
Gload	1.000	11	21	0	0 0
Guillen	.982	109	204	10	4 2
Maier	.986	34	71	0	1 0
Smith	—	1	0	0	0 0
Teahen	.993	119	260	7	2 3

OMAHA ROYALS

PACIFIC COAST LEAGUE

Batting	B-T	HT	WT	DOB	AVG	vLH	vRH	G	AB	R	H	2B	3B	HR	RBI	BB	HBP	SH	SF	SO	SB	CS	SLG	OBP
Aviles, Mike	R-R	5-9	195	3-13-81	.336	.346	.333	51	214	42	72	21	6	10	42	11	1	0	1	23	3	0	.631	.370
Balduf, Todd	B-R	6-2	200	7-6-84	.000	—	.000	1	1	0	0	0	0	0	0	0	0	0	0	1	0	0	.000	.000
Berroa, Angel	R-R	6-0	195	1-27-78	.291	.255	.304	51	189	34	55	13	0	10	27	8	2	0	2	25	4	2	.519	.323
Bigler, Brett	L-L	6-1	185	10-16-84	.333	.500	.263	17	54	8	18	4	0	1	8	1	1	1	1	11	1	1	.463	.413
Buchanan, Brian	R-R	6-4	230	7-21-73	.228	.281	.208	64	232	36	53	11	1	8	34	15	4	0	3	54	1	1	.388	.283
Butler, Billy	R-R	6-1	240	4-18-86	.337	.385	.330	26	101	18	34	6	1	5	13	14	0	0	0	7	0	0	.564	.417
Callaspo, Alberto	B-R	5-9	180	4-19-83	.188	.000	.214	4	16	5	3	0	0	0	1	0	0	0	0	4	0	0	.188	.235
Clark, Cody	R-R	6-2	170	9-14-81	.667	—	.667	1	3	1	2	0	1	1	0	0	0	0	0	0	0	02.333	.667
Costa, Shane	L-R	6-0	190	12-12-81	.295	.221	.321	75	292	42	86	21	0	10	42	28	1	3	4	39	11	2	.469	.354
Dawkins, Gookie	R-R	6-1	180	5-12-79	.266	.351	.244	68	278	34	74	16	1	9	32	18	1	0	3	78	3	2	.428	.310
Espino, Damaso	R-R	6-1	210	5-8-83	.167	.273	.120	13	36	4	6	0	0	0	5	1	1	0	6	0	0	.167	.286
Gathright, Joey	L-R	5-10	185	4-27-81	.152	.111	.167	9	33	3	5	0	0	0	1	2	0	0	1	1	0	0	.152	.222
Gutierrez, Jorge	R-R	5-10	185	7-23-85	.333	.500	.250	4	12	0	4	0	0	0	0	1	0	1	0	0	0	.333	.333
Hollins, Damon	R-L	5-11	180	6-12-74	.220	.266	.204	105	363	53	80	16	2	16	55	50	2	0	6	80	2	2	.408	.318
Huckaby, Ken	R-R	6-1	240	1-27-71	.222	.000	.286	10	36	3	8	0	0	0	1	0	0	1	0	7	1	0	.222	.222
Ka'aihue, Kila	L-L	6-3	230	3-29-84	.316	.314	.316	33	114	27	36	4	0	11	21	24	1	0	0	26	0	0	.640	.439
Labandeira, Josh	R-R	5-7	180	2-25-79	.210	.324	.147	28	105	7	22	2	0	2	12	5	1	2	0	19	0	0	.286	.252
Lubanski, Chris	L-L	6-3	210	3-24-85	.242	.159	.266	116	393	51	95	20	8	15	54	38	0	4	3	130	5	1	.448	.306
Lucas, Edward	R-R	6-3	205	5-21-82	.128	.083	.143	16	47	7	6	0	0	0	7	0	1	0	14	0	1	.128	.241
Maier, Mitch	L-R	6-2	205	6-30-82	.316	.315	.316	85	345	57	109	24	1	9	41	29	1	3	5	42	12	3	.470	.366
Matranga, Dave	R-R	6-0	185	1-8-77	.269	.240	.278	61	201	32	54	8	4	6	31	22	4	4	3	53	2	3	.438	.348
Pena, Brayan	B-R	5-11	210	1-7-82	.303	.405	.256	60	234	33	71	17	1	6	31	26	2	3	1	17	7	3	.462	.354
Sanchez, Angel	R-R	6-2	190	9-20-83	.221	.290	.200	38	131	13	29	7	1	1	13	9	1	0	5	20	1	1	.313	.271
Shealy, Ryan	R-R	6-5	240	8-29-79	.283	.250	.292	111	400	53	113	22	0	22	65	55	8	0	5	93	0	1	.502	.376
Smith, Jason	L-R	6-3	200	7-24-77	.253	.202	.267	110	423	52	107	20	7	20	62	23	1	6	6	128	3	1	.475	.289
Spann, Chad	R-R	6-1	195	10-25-83	.292	.300	.288	19	72	6	21	2	0	1	11	5	2	0	0	15	0	0	.361	.354
Stodolka, Mike	L-L	6-2	215	9-24-81	.286	.273	.290	75	227	32	65	12	0	5	21	27	2	2	1	42	0	1	.405	.366
Tupman, Matt	L-R	5-11	185	11-25-79	.229	.181	.245	81	288	36	66	10	1	4	34	22	2	4	4	44	0	1	.313	.285

Pitching	B-T	HT	WT	DOB	W	L	ERA	G	GS	CG	SV	IP	H	R	ER	HR	BB	SO	AVG	vLH	vRH	K/9	BB/9
Atencio, Greg	R-R	6-2	191	7-15-81	1	1	3.24	9	0	0	1	25	25	9	9	0	11	22	.284	.259	.295	7.92	3.96
Bale, John	L-L	6-4	220	5-22-74	0	3	10.80	10	7	0	0	12	17	14	14	3	5	8	.340	.500	.278	6.17	3.86
Bradley, Anthony	L-L	6-3	205	7-10-85	0	0	16.88	2	0	0	0	3	6	5	5	0	4	4	.462	.500	.444	13.50	13.50
Capellan, Jose	R-R	6-4	235	1-13-81	2	1	4.10	6	5	0	0	37	35	17	17	3	14	20	.255	.271	.239	4.82	3.38
2-team total (3 Colorado Springs)					4	1	4.05	9	8	0	0	53	47	24	24	5	19	31	—	—	—	5.23	3.21
Colon, Roman	R-R	6-6	225	8-13-79	5	5	4.64	23	10	0	1	95	109	51	49	15	27	62	.294	.271	.312	5.87	2.56
Davies, Kyle	R-R	6-2	205	9-9-83	6	2	2.03	11	11	0	0	58	47	22	13	4	21	38	.225	.263	.191	5.93	3.28
De La Rosa, Jorge	L-L	6-1	210	4-5-81	3	0	1.64	4	4	0	0	22	18	4	4	0	7	23	.217	.368	.172	9.41	2.86
Duckworth, Brandon	R-R	6-1	215	1-23-76	5	11	4.75	27	17	1	1	135	132	78	71	23	49	103	.256	.237	.270	6.88	3.27
Foster, John	L-L	6-0	200	5-17-78	0	1	11.74	5	0	0	0	8	12	10	10	3	6	5	.387	.400	.381	5.87	7.04
Fulchino, Jeff	R-R	6-5	250	11-26-79	3	4	4.84	25	5	0	5	61	71	38	33	5	27	53	.292	.278	.304	7.78	3.96
Giron, Roberto	R-R	6-2	195	3-24-76	3	5	5.86	20	0	0	1	43	41	31	28	13	17	39	.255	.197	.306	8.16	3.56
Gobble, Jimmy	L-L	6-3	200	7-19-81	1	1	5.65	8	4	0	0	14	16	9	9	1	9	16	.281	.154	.318	10.05	5.65
Hochevar, Luke	R-R	6-5	205	9-15-83	1	1	2.60	3	3	0	0	17	11	7	5	2	6	12	.180	.258	.100	6.23	3.12
Hughes, Dusty	L-L	5-10	187	6-29-82	3	2	5.04	12	11	0	0	55	65	32	31	8	25	36	.298	.302	.297	5.86	4.07
Lowery, Devon	L-R	6-1	195	3-24-83	1	1	2.12	31	0	0	5	59	48	19	14	4	30	43	.223	.203	.235	6.52	4.55
Lumsden, Tyler	L-L	6-4	215	5-9-83	3	13	7.21	28	18	0	1	107	138	93	86	15	62	44	.322	.297	.331	3.69	5.20
Maroth, Mike	L-L	6-0	190	8-17-77	0	2	12.91	3	3	0	0	8	12	11	11	3	5	4	.364	.400	.357	4.70	5.87
Mildren, Paul	R-L	6-1	195	5-31-84	0	0	2.70	4	0	0	0	3	2	1	1	1	4	3	.200	.333	.143	8.10	10.80
Musser, Neal	L-L	6-1	235	8-25-80	3	5	4.34	36	3	0	6	56	47	32	27	9	37	64	.221	.175	.240	10.29	5.95
Newman, Josh	L-L	6-1	200	6-11-82	0	1	4.91	7	2	0	0	22	23	13	12	1	13	22	.271	.292	.262	9.00	5.32
2-team total (20 Colorado Springs)					1	2	3.68	27	2	0	1	44	39	22	18	1	22	40	—	—	—	8.18	4.50
Nunez, Leo	R-R	6-1	175	8-14-83	0	0	6.75	4	0	0	0	4	7	3	3	1	1	3	.368	.364	.375	6.75	2.25
Peralta, Joel	R-R	5-11	190	3-23-76	1	0	0.00	10	0	0	2	19	9	0	0	0	6	19	.145	.100	.167	9.16	2.89
Ramirez, Horacio	L-L	6-1	220	11-24-79	1	1	1.42	3	3	0	0	19	13	5	3	2	3	8	.194	.235	.180	3.79	1.42
Richardson, Brett	R-R	6-3	195	3-2-88	0	0	11.57	3	0	0	1	2	6	3	3	0	1	2	.462	.500	.400	7.71	3.86
Rosa, Carlos	R-R	6-1	185	9-21-84	4	3	4.09	11	11	0	0	51	51	24	23	3	12	44	.267	.258	.275	7.82	2.13
Salmon, Brad	L-R	6-4	225	1-3-80	8	7	4.62	47	4	0	3	101	105	68	52	11	54	90	.266	.286	.252	7.99	4.80
Tsao, Chin-hui	R-R	6-1	210	6-2-81	0	1	5.56	7	0	0	1	11	10	7	7	0	6	9	.238	.375	.154	7.94	0.00
Wright, Matt	R-R	6-4	230	3-13-82	4	10	5.47	27	23	1	0	148	169	99	90	29	60	90	.289	.297	.284	5.47	3.65
Yabuta, Yasuhiko	R-R	6-2	185	6-19-73	4	3	5.36	20	0	0	3	40	46	24	24	3	16	33	.291	.282	.299	7.36	3.57

Fielding

Catcher	PCT	G	PO	A	E	DP	PB
Balduf	1.000	1	1	0	0	0	0
Clark	1.000	1	3	0	0	0	0
Espino	1.000	13	74	8	0	2	0
Huckaby	1.000	10	62	6	0	1	1
Pena	.994	44	300	14	2	2	1
Tupman	.992	78	483	38	4	1	14

First Base	PCT	G	PO	A	E	DP
Butler	1.000	21	194	6	0	23
Ka'aihue	.991	25	194	18	2	24
Shealy	.996	59	478	33	2	59
Smith	1.000	12	100	10	0	13
Stodolka	.990	35	286	15	3	38

Second Base	PCT	G	PO	A	E	DP
Aviles	.989	32	65	113	2	33
Berroa	1.000	17	30	37	0	9

Callaspo	1.000	4	6	10	0	5
Dawkins	1.000	5	10	17	0	3
Gutierrez	1.000	3	6	8	0	3
Labandeira	.984	24	45	76	2	21
Matranga	.994	32	70	109	1	29
Smith	.987	31	65	85	2	24

Third Base	PCT	G	PO	A	E	DP
Dawkins	.967	40	23	66	3	6
Labandeira	1.000	1	0	6	0	0
Lucas	.951	15	4	35	2	3
Matranga	.967	27	15	43	2	4
Pena	1.000	6	0	7	0	0
Smith	.934	40	32	95	9	13
Spann	.935	19	15	43	4	9

Shortstop	PCT	G	PO	A	E	DP
Aviles	.954	19	36	67	5	14

Outfield	PCT	G	PO	A	E	DP
Berroa	.967	35	49	99	5	31
Dawkins	.967	24	32	57	3	18
Gutierrez	—	1	0	0	0	0
Labandeira	.833	1	4	1	1	0
Sanchez	.971	38	52	113	5	32
Smith	.955	30	42	84	6	19

Outfield	PCT	G	PO	A	E	DP
Bigler	.950	16	36	2	2	0
Buchanan	1.000	4	5	0	0	0
Costa	.993	75	138	3	1	0
Gathright	1.000	9	21	1	0	0
Hollins	.983	95	167	10	3	2
Labandeira	1.000	2	6	0	0	0
Lubanski	.972	113	204	5	6	1
Maier	.988	85	240	7	3	1
Pena	.933	8	14	0	1	0
Stodolka	.947	31	51	3	3	1

NORTHWEST ARKANSAS NATURALS
DOUBLE-A
TEXAS LEAGUE

Batting	B-T	HT	WT	DOB	AVG	vLH	vRH	G	AB	R	H	2B	3B	HR	RBI	BB	HBP	SH	SF	SO	SB	CS	SLG	OBP
Aldridge, Cory	L-R	6-1	225	6-13-79	.269	.136	.290	49	167	23	45	6	1	10	40	25	0	1	2	37	2	4	.497	.361
Clark, Cody	R-R	6-2	170	9-14-81	.184	.250	.176	40	103	9	19	3	0	4	14	5	2	1	1	19	1	1	.330	.234
Donachie, Adam	R-R	6-1	235	3-3-84	.212	.162	.220	91	264	30	56	8	0	5	29	37	1	5	1	71	1	1	.299	.310
Duarte, Jose	R-R	5-10	165	3-7-85	.250	.238	.252	133	528	68	132	19	2	10	47	50	0	3	4	91	28	8	.350	.313
Falu, Irving	B-R	6-0	180	6-6-83	.301	.357	.291	101	362	57	109	11	2	5	42	38	0	4	1	31	11	9	.384	.367
Ka'aihue, Kila	L-R	6-3	230	3-29-84	.314	.238	.327	91	287	64	90	11	0	26	79	80	4	0	5	41	3	2	.624	.463
Lisson, Mario	R-R	6-2	210	5-31-84	.225	.151	.241	130	476	57	107	23	3	14	65	33	9	7	6	105	31	6	.374	.284
Lucas, Edward	R-R	6-3	205	5-21-82	.304	.200	.324	79	270	38	82	10	4	4	30	29	1	2	1	47	14	7	.415	.372
Maddox, Marc	R-R	5-11	185	9-16-83	.283	.300	.279	127	453	69	128	30	0	4	30	48	10	5	2	73	15	12	.375	.363
McFall, Brian	R-R	6-3	215	3-14-84	.241	.179	.253	106	348	42	84	16	2	18	61	39	9	3	5	103	7	6	.454	.329
Richardson, Juan	R-R	6-1	215	1-10-79	.296	.333	.289	133	494	90	146	36	2	16	82	54	7	0	4	93	2	5	.474	.370
Sanchez, Angel	R-R	6-2	190	9-20-83	.261	.353	.246	63	241	28	63	7	2	1	23	28	1	5	2	40	4	4	.320	.338
Suero, Ovandy	B-R	5-10	160	6-20-82	.253	.283	.248	98	328	39	83	12	5	2	24	19	5	9	2	61	42	16	.338	.302
Thibault, Kiel	R-R	6-0	200	3-2-84	.160	.235	.145	31	100	7	16	6	0	0	9	5	0	2	2	23	5	0	.220	.196
Valentin, Geraldo	R-R	6-0	184	9-8-82	.250	.241	.251	70	256	19	64	10	1	3	19	10	1	4	4	25	1	4	.332	.277

Pitching	B-T	HT	WT	DOB	W	L	ERA	G	GS	CG	SV	IP	H	R	ER	HR	BB	SO	AVG	vLH	vRH	K/9	BB/9
Atencio, Greg	R-R	6-2	191	7-15-81	3	3	3.81	27	0	0	3	54	44	29	23	4	25	63	.226	.233	.221	10.44	4.14
Bale, John	L-L	6-4	220	5-22-74	0	0	5.40	2	1	0	0	3	3	1	1	0	0	3	.429	.500	.400	16.20	0.00
Colon, Roman	R-R	6-6	225	8-13-79	2	0	5.29	10	0	0	1	17	18	10	10	1	4	8	.273	.333	.250	4.24	2.12
Cortes, Daniel	R-R	6-5	205	3-4-87	10	4	3.78	23	23	0	0	117	103	51	49	13	55	109	.241	.285	.213	8.41	4.24
Crist, Kyle	R-R	6-3	194	6-27-83	4	1	3.89	42	1	0	6	74	67	33	32	11	33	56	.245	.234	.253	6.81	4.01
De La Cruz, Julio	R-R	6-1	161	10-7-80	0	1	4.23	14	0	0	0	28	25	14	13	5	12	13	.255	.286	.238	4.23	3.90
de la Vara, Gilbert	L-L	5-11	160	10-4-84	3	0	2.76	21	0	0	2	33	23	12	10	0	15	21	.205	.136	.250	5.79	4.13
Fulchino, Jeff	R-R	6-5	250	11-26-79	0	0	5.40	2	0	0	1	3	3	2	2	0	1	6	.231	.500	.182	16.20	2.70
Green, Patrick	L-R	6-2	193	2-13-82	0	1	8.38	7	0	0	0	10	14	9	9	3	3	8	.341	.353	.333	7.45	2.79
Hamulack, Tim	R-L	6-2	220	11-14-76	0	1	1.96	18	0	0	6	23	13	5	5	2	1	23	.165	.182	.152	9.00	0.39
Hardy, Rowdy	L-L	6-4	170	10-26-82	6	11	4.97	28	27	0	0	156	195	97	86	14	31	87	.311	.275	.321	5.03	1.79
Hartsock, Aaron	R-R	6-3	200	1-17-84	0	0	2.25	1	0	0	1	4	1	1	1	0	0	5	.077	.000	.125	11.25	0.00
Hayes, Chris	R-R	6-1	195	2-5-83	5	2	1.64	40	0	0	12	66	49	14	12	4	13	39	.217	.216	.217	5.35	1.78
Hughes, Dusty	L-L	5-10	187	6-29-82	5	2	2.91	20	4	0	3	53	47	17	17	3	16	43	.247	.147	.269	7.35	2.73
Johnson, Blake	R-R	6-5	200	6-14-85	10	9	4.85	26	25	0	0	143	168	85	77	20	38	86	.296	.328	.274	5.41	2.39
Lowery, Devon	L-R	6-1	195	3-24-83	1	0	0.69	9	0	0	2	13	8	2	1	0	5	17	.167	.133	.182	11.77	3.46
Mildren, Paul	R-L	6-1	195	5-3-84	2	6	6.33	19	3	0	1	43	54	31	30	5	25	34	.310	.275	.321	7.17	5.27
Nicoll, Christopher	R-R	6-3	190	10-30-83	4	1	3.09	19	1	0	0	44	43	16	15	2	8	55	.259	.237	.271	11.34	1.65
Nunez, Leo	R-R	6-1	175	8-14-83	0	0	0.00	1	1	0	0	2	0	0	0	0	0	2	.000	.000	.000	9.00	0.00
Peterson, Matt	R-R	6-5	220	2-11-82	0	0	2.41	11	0	0	3	19	16	5	5	3	5	13	.232	.240	.227	6.27	2.41
Pimentel, Julio	R-R	6-1	190	12-14-85	7	13	5.38	28	28	0	0	157	193	103	94	17	52	115	.307	.303	.309	6.58	2.97
Plummer, Jarod	R-R	6-5	200	1-27-84	4	1	4.19	29	0	0	3	58	57	27	27	12	15	65	.256	.228	.271	10.09	2.33
Rosa, Carlos	R-R	6-1	185	9-21-84	4	2	1.20	8	8	0	0	45	30	8	6	2	7	42	.189	.213	.179	8.40	1.40
Wood, Blake	R-R	6-4	225	8-8-85	5	7	5.30	18	18	2	0	87	96	55	51	7	32	76	.283	.256	.309	7.89	3.32

Fielding

Catcher	PCT	G	PO	A	E	DP	PB
Clark	.992	39	239	24	2	3	2
Donachie	.989	90	570	84	7	9	3
Thibault	.995	27	198	11	1	0	3

First Base	PCT	G	PO	A	E	DP
Clark	1.000	1	6	0	0	0
Donachie	1.000	1	7	1	0	0
Ka'aihue	.988	70	617	38	8	66
Lucas	1.000	5	26	3	0	2

Richardson	.990	67	546	35	6	58
Valentin	1.000	3	28	1	0	4

Second Base	PCT	G	PO	A	E	DP
Falu	1.000	20	51	52	0	17
Lucas	.950	3	8	11	1	1
Maddox	.983	119	231	340	10	89

Third Base	PCT	G	PO	A	E	DP
Falu	1.000	12	12	15	0	2
Lisson	.947	68	48	150	11	16

Lucas	.937	47	24	80	7	5
Richardson	.982	20	18	38	1	4
Valentin	1.000	1	0	1	0	0

Shortstop	PCT	G	PO	A	E	DP
Falu	.978	21	30	59	2	10
Lisson	.958	60	97	176	12	52
Lucas	1.000	2	3	3	0	0
Sanchez	.963	61	80	207	11	4

Outfield	PCT	G	PO	A	E	DP								
Aldridge	.955	14	21	0	1	0
Duarte	.986	131	330	18	5	7

Falu	.972	45	65	4	2	1
Lucas	1.000	9	19	1	0	0
McFall	.989	99	170	8	2	2

Suero	.971	91	161	7	5	0
Valentin	.977	52	82	3	2	0

WILMINGTON BLUE ROCKS
CAROLINA LEAGUE

HIGH CLASS A

Batting	B-T	HT	WT	DOB	AVG	vLH	vRH	G	AB	R	H	2B	3B	HR	RBI	BB	HBP	SH	SF	SO	SB	CS	SLG	OBP
Balduf, Todd	B-R	6-2	200	7-6-84	.167	.200	.143	4	12	1	2	0	0	0	0	1	0	0	0	2	0	0	.167	.231
Bianchi, Jeff	R-R	6-0	175	10-5-86	.255	.264	.252	104	396	57	101	34	5	10	61	20	3	4	8	95	13	4	.442	.290
Bigler, Brett	L-L	6-1	185	10-16-84	.197	.143	.207	54	132	19	26	5	3	0	10	24	1	2	2	30	5	3	.280	.321
Correll, Brad	R-R	6-2	205	6-17-81	.277	.245	.289	52	191	34	53	18	0	8	28	26	1	0	1	35	1	2	.497	.365
Dickerson, Joseph	L-L	6-1	190	10-3-86	.297	.293	.298	87	310	39	92	10	10	5	45	31	9	2	1	48	24	14	.442	.376
Dyson, Jarrod	L-R	5-10	160	8-15-84	.260	.159	.289	93	288	40	75	8	0	2	24	32	2	8	1	60	39	9	.288	.337
Howell, Jeffrey	R-R	6-0	200	4-1-83	.259	.235	.269	85	286	30	74	18	0	6	44	24	4	0	2	54	1	3	.385	.323
Johnson, Joshua	B-R	5-11	170	1-11-86	.253	.314	.234	118	359	49	91	13	4	3	38	85	3	10	2	76	14	12	.337	.399
McConnell, Chris	R-R	5-11	175	12-18-85	.252	.246	.254	120	461	46	116	29	1	1	34	48	10	7	3	71	23	16	.325	.333
Mertins, Kurt	R-R	6-0	175	4-22-86	.282	.267	.287	118	425	60	120	27	7	3	46	36	10	2	2	91	28	5	.400	.351
Morizio, Matthew	L-R	6-3	215	12-14-83	.172	.067	.194	57	169	17	29	6	4	0	26	28	3	3	1	33	8	2	.254	.299
Orlando, Paulo	R-R	6-3	185	11-1-85	.254	.278	.245	18	71	11	18	5	2	3	9	8	0	2	1	19	1	4	.507	.325
2-team total (112 Winston-Salem)					.261	—	—	130	522	84	136	20	14	12	51	30	9	7	3	116	29	13	.421	.310
Ortiz, Adrian	L-R	6-0	172	1-14-87	.311	.231	.322	28	103	10	32	5	2	0	12	9	4	2	0	11	5	5	.398	.388
Perez, Wilver	R-R	5-11	165	8-28-83	.170	.194	.159	31	94	7	16	7	0	1	7	7	0	0	1	28	3	0	.277	.225
Robinson, Derrick	B-L	5-11	170	9-28-87	.245	.283	.231	124	497	69	122	22	8	0	34	51	2	3	3	97	62	17	.322	.316
Seratelli, Anthony	B-R	6-0	205	2-27-83	.230	.162	.247	110	357	49	82	16	7	8	51	41	2	0	6	101	17	6	.381	.308
Strait, Cody	R-R	6-1	180	5-28-83	.296	.239	.313	54	196	39	58	13	1	13	35	19	2	1	1	40	11	2	.571	.362
Vega, Miguel	R-R	6-2	220	7-31-85	.230	.160	.265	22	74	5	17	4	0	1	4	2	0	0	0	19	0	0	.324	.250
Wood, David	L-L	6-2	210	12-21-84	.156	.154	.157	37	128	9	20	4	0	0	12	4	0	2	2	34	3	1	.188	.179

Pitching	B-T	HT	WT	DOB	W	L	ERA	G	GS	CG	SV	IP	H	R	ER	HR	BB	SO	AVG	vLH	vRH	K/9	BB/9
Barrera, Henry	R-R	6-0	205	11-25-85	0	3	2.81	42	0	0	4	58	47	21	18	2	24	78	.224	.275	.199	12.17	3.75
Bradley, Anthony	L-L	6-3	205	7-10-85	0	0	3.00	3	0	0	0	3	3	1	1	0	3	4	.000	.000	.000	12.00	9.00
Cegarra, Edward	R-R	5-11	175	2-27-89	6	7	4.67	18	18	0	0	106	115	59	55	15	21	59	.280	.270	.287	5.01	1.78
Chambliss, Tyler	R-R	5-11	175	12-4-84	2	4	4.55	49	0	0	24	59	60	32	30	6	32	45	.264	.263	.265	6.83	4.85
Chavez, Chris	L-R	6-3	195	9-11-84	2	0	3.12	12	0	0	0	26	24	9	9	1	11	17	.240	.250	.233	5.88	3.81
de la Vara, Gilbert	L-L	5-11	160	10-4-84	3	3	3.65	24	1	0	2	44	33	18	18	1	12	31	.217	.132	.246	6.29	2.44
Godin, Jason	R-R	6-5	170	9-23-84	2	7	5.33	14	14	0	0	73	80	52	43	5	24	44	.282	.326	.262	5.45	2.97
Haltiwanger, Russell	R-R	6-2	180	4-21-84	4	1	3.83	35	0	0	1	56	60	29	24	2	29	40	.276	.192	.324	6.39	4.63
Hartsock, Aaron	R-R	6-3	190	1-17-84	12	5	3.46	42	0	0	1	78	75	33	30	4	22	58	.253	.238	.262	6.69	2.54
Holland, Greg	R-R	5-11	180	11-20-85	4	5	3.42	32	7	0	4	84	70	37	32	4	35	96	.226	.231	.222	10.25	3.74
Kniginyzky, Matthew	L-R	6-3	185	10-5-82	9	8	3.57	27	27	0	0	141	133	66	56	7	51	113	.250	.250	.250	7.21	3.26
Liotta, Ray	L-L	6-3	220	4-3-83	1	1	1.80	4	4	0	0	15	14	5	3	0	8	10	.250	.286	.238	6.00	4.80
Mildren, Paul	R-L	6-1	195	5-3-84	0	7	7.24	8	8	0	0	41	62	35	33	3	11	28	.354	.359	.353	6.15	2.41
Nicoll, Christopher	R-R	6-3	190	10-30-83	2	1	2.91	20	1	0	1	43	34	15	14	7	15	49	.217	.184	.231	10.18	3.12
Santiago, Mario	R-R	6-2	210	12-16-84	8	8	3.43	27	27	0	0	142	155	69	54	9	39	86	.280	.234	.307	5.46	2.48
Swaggerty, Ben	L-L	6-1	185	8-8-82	3	2	2.66	32	0	0	0	47	41	19	14	3	26	58	.237	.219	.248	11.03	4.94
Teaford, Everett	L-L	6-0	155	5-15-84	8	6	3.80	28	23	0	1	144	135	70	61	15	46	116	.246	.269	.238	7.23	2.87
Wood, Blake	R-R	6-4	225	8-8-85	3	2	2.67	10	10	0	0	57	32	17	17	3	15	63	.168	.207	.150	9.89	2.35

Fielding

Catcher	PCT	G	PO	A	E	DP	PB
Balduf	1.000	4	14	2	0	1	0
Howell	.988	85	600	69	8	4	10
Morizio	.983	57	363	54	7	7	10

First Base	PCT	G	PO	A	E	DP
Correll	.965	29	234	16	9	29
Perez	—	1	0	0	0	0
Seratelli	.997	67	614	34	2	55
Vega	1.000	18	124	11	0	17
Wood	.973	33	276	12	8	21

Second Base	PCT	G	PO	A	E	DP
Bianchi	.994	75	139	208	2	51

	PCT	G	PO	A	E	DP
Mertins	.977	61	89	166	6	44
Perez	1.000	3	6	9	0	2
Seratelli	.917	4	8	3	1	2

Third Base	PCT	G	PO	A	E	DP
Johnson	.956	104	66	172	11	17
Mertins	.929	33	16	62	6	6
Perez	.905	8	5	14	2	0

Shortstop	PCT	G	PO	A	E	DP
Bianchi	.917	12	21	34	5	12
Johnson	1.000	10	9	25	0	5
McConnell	.950	120	157	371	28	75
Mertins	.800	2	0	4	1	0

Outfield	PCT	G	PO	A	E	DP
Bigler	.966	51	79	7	3	2
Dickerson	.988	82	165	6	2	2
Dyson	.979	85	171	14	4	1
Orlando	.909	15	30	0	3	0
Ortiz	1.000	28	27	4	0	2
Perez	1.000	6	10	0	0	0
Robinson	.980	116	279	8	6	5
Seratelli	1.000	9	14	0	0	0
Strait	.975	45	74	4	2	1
Wood	—	1	0	0	0	0

BURLINGTON BEES
MIDWEST LEAGUE

LOW CLASS A

Batting	B-T	HT	WT	DOB	AVG	vLH	vRH	G	AB	R	H	2B	3B	HR	RBI	BB	HBP	SH	SF	SO	SB	CS	SLG	OBP
Balduf, Todd	B-R	6-2	200	7-6-84	.197	.235	.185	24	71	7	14	3	1	1	3	9	1	1	1	13	0	1	.310	.293
Billick, Joe	R-R	6-2	230	5-30-85	.240	.167	.281	21	50	9	12	5	0	0	3	9	3	2	0	12	0	0	.340	.387
Doscher, Nick	R-R	6-2	205	5-20-87	.091	.000	.111	9	22	3	2	1	0	0	7	0	0	0	8	1	0	.136	.310
Eigsti, Ryan	R-R	6-2	195	8-24-85	.218	.176	.228	91	331	33	72	18	1	9	35	20	18	2	5	104	1	2	.360	.294
Evangelho, Zach	L-R	5-10	185	4-11-85	.192	.158	.203	53	156	8	30	3	0	0	12	6	7	2	2	39	4	1	.212	.251
Francis, Nicholas	R-R	6-3	195	3-5-86	.265	.333	.247	31	113	14	30	6	3	2	17	10	3	1	2	35	3	0	.425	.336
Giavotella, Johnny	R-R	5-8	185	7-10-87	.299	.250	.313	68	278	50	83	18	2	4	26	25	1	3	3	34	10	7	.421	.355
Hayes, Shawn	L-R	6-4	220	11-5-84	.232	.182	.244	20	56	6	13	2	0	1	8	9	3	1	1	26	1	4	.321	.362

Batting	B-R/...	HT	WT	DOB	AVG	vLH	vRH	G	AB	R	H	2B	3B	HR	RBI	BB	HBP	SH	SF	SO	SB	CS	SLG	OBP
Jimenez, Antonio	B-R	6-2	157	4-20-87	.184	.257	.158	49	136	10	25	4	0	0	10	11	2	3	0	45	4	3	.213	.255
Lough, David	L-L	6-0	180	1-20-86	.268	.223	.282	126	488	76	131	21	11	16	62	35	10	8	2	70	12	11	.455	.329
Martin, Kyle	R-R	6-0	175	11-22-84	.316	.316	.316	56	190	26	60	13	1	9	28	17	1	0	1	40	2	2	.537	.373
Moustakas, Mike	L-R	6-0	195	9-11-88	.272	.239	.282	126	496	77	135	25	3	22	71	43	7	0	3	86	8	4	.468	.337
Ortiz, Adrian	L-R	6-0	172	1-14-87	.308	.319	.304	100	422	50	130	10	7	3	33	15	2	6	1	68	29	15	.386	.334
Perez, Alwin	L-R	6-0	150	4-4-87	.207	.179	.215	48	174	11	36	9	1	1	12	12	0	5	1	43	9	4	.287	.257
Rivera, Juan	B-R	6-0	150	3-17-87	.248	.276	.238	66	230	26	57	6	1	0	21	18	4	3	3	40	19	5	.283	.310
2-team total (10 Great Lakes)					.247	—		76	259	28	64	9	1	0	24	19	4	3	3	45	19	5	.290	.305
Robinson, Clint	L-L	6-4	225	2-16-85	.264	.242	.271	106	379	53	100	22	3	17	64	37	4	1	3	67	0	3	.472	.333
Taylor, Jason	R-R	6-0	210	1-14-88	.242	.248	.241	127	433	79	105	17	4	17	58	81	11	3	5	97	40	14	.418	.372
Tucker, Will	R-R	6-1	205	1-14-85	.184	.162	.191	42	147	14	27	7	3	2	13	4	1	1	5	39	2	4	.313	.204
Van Stratten, Nick	R-R	6-1	185	5-22-85	.345	.438	.297	40	139	22	48	13	2	1	18	12	2	0	2	20	5	3	.489	.400
Walton, Jamar	L-R	6-4	195	1-5-86	.266	.202	.287	98	357	43	95	20	2	7	49	21	1	0	4	86	6	5	.392	.305

Pitching	B-T	HT	WT	DOB	W	L	ERA	G	GS	CG	SV	IP	H	R	ER	HR	BB	SO	AVG	vLH	vRH	K/9	BB/9
Abreu, Juan	R-R	6-0	170	4-8-85	4		3.66	22	4	0	7	76	59	40	31	6	42	104	.214	.220	.209	12.26	4.95
Arias, Henry	R-R	6-3	201	1-6-85	2	3	3.78	18	0	0	2	33	32	16	14	3	18	30	.260	.245	.270	8.10	4.86
2-team total (21 Dayton)					3	4	4.76	39	0	0	3	64	67	37	34	4	39	59	—	—	—	8.25	5.46
Augustine, Joe	R-R	6-2	219	1-18-85	4	2	3.77	28	5	0	9	105	106	57	44	10	34	85	.256	.345	.195	7.29	2.91
Baldwin, Burke	R-L	6-5	215	5-28-85	1	2	7.18	17	0	0	0	26	36	23	21	7	13	16	.340	.233	.382	5.47	4.44
Bowden, Barry	R-R	6-1	205	11-9-84	0	0	0.00	2	0	0	0	5	2	0	0	0	0	7	.105	.000	.125	11.81	0.00
Bradley, Anthony	L-L	6-3	205	7-10-85	1	4	2.14	26	0	0	4	42	32	12	10	1	18	35	.225	.188	.236	7.50	3.86
Caldera, Alex	R-R	6-3	200	10-1-85	12	6	2.89	25	25	0	0	149	141	53	48	6	36	120	.255	.276	.238	7.23	2.17
Cegarra, Edward	R-R	5-11	174	2-27-89	4	2	2.67	9	8	0	1	54	46	18	16	4	5	53	.225	.193	.250	8.83	0.83
Chavez, Chris	L-R	6-3	195	9-11-84	6	1	2.77	21	0	0	4	39	41	13	12	0	7	39	.268	.193	.313	9.00	1.62
Cota, Luis	R-R	6-2	200	8-19-85	2	5	5.80	8	8	0	0	36	39	25	23	4	14	32	.287	.356	.253	8.07	3.53
Duffy, Danny	L-L	6-2	185	12-21-88	8	4	2.20	17	17	0	0	82	56	26	20	4	25	102	.193	.192	.194	11.24	2.76
Fisher, Brent	L-L	6-2	190	8-6-87	1	1	3.71	4	2	0	1	17	20	10	7	1	4	17	.282	.429	.246	9.00	2.12
Gutierrez, Danny	R-R	6-1	180	3-8-87	4	2	2.70	19	18	0	0	90	83	38	27	7	25	104	.246	.261	.235	10.40	2.50
Herrera, Kelvin	R-R	5-10	162	12-31-89	2	0	2.13	3	1	0	0	13	13	4	3	0	2	7	.265	.400	.206	4.97	1.42
Huber, Tim	L-L	5-10	190	2-1-86	0	1	10.50	4	0	0	0	6	10	7	7	1	5	3	.385	.364	.400	4.50	7.50
Liotta, Ray	L-L	6-3	220	4-3-83	1	1	2.81	3	3	0	0	16	13	5	5	2	4	14	.224	.300	.208	7.88	2.25
Lopez, Yensi	R-R	6-0	160	3-13-86	0	3	4.80	11	0	0	1	15	16	9	8	1	7	16	.262	.333	.179	9.60	4.20
Mitchell, Matt	R-R	6-2	205	3-31-89	8	8	3.47	25	21	0	0	117	116	55	45	9	25	77	.260	.245	.271	5.94	1.93
Paulino, Eduardo	R-R	5-11	176	9-29-85	5	4	3.68	19	17	1	0	100	103	44	41	9	19	80	.272	.302	.251	7.18	1.70
Peterson, Zach	B-R	6-1	165	11-6-84	3	3	3.13	30	4	0	5	78	74	27	27	7	20	82	.253	.220	.285	9.50	2.32
Peterson, Matt	R-R	6-5	220	2-11-82	0	0	5.79	6	0	0	0	9	13	7	6	1	1	7	.333	.235	.409	6.75	0.96
Raglione, Paul	R-R	6-5	195	1-15-87	2	0	6.06	19	0	0	1	36	39	27	24	3	11	18	.275	.275	.275	4.54	2.78
Rodriguez, Jacob	R-R	6-2	220	7-24-88	1	1	5.14	2	1	0	0	7	7	4	4	0	2	7	.280	.286	.278	9.00	2.57
Runion, Sam	R-R	6-4	220	11-9-88	2	5	5.75	9	5	0	0	41	54	35	26	7	9	11	.327	.323	.330	2.43	1.99
Sisk, Brandon	L-L	6-3	210	7-13-85	1	1	1.19	10	0	0	2	23	14	4	3	0	9	36	.175	.200	.169	14.29	3.57
Swaggerty, Ben	L-L	6-1	185	8-8-82	1	0	3.93	12	0	0	0	18	18	10	8	0	10	14	.261	.167	.294	6.87	4.91

Fielding

Catcher	PCT	G	PO	A	E	DP	PB
Balduf	1.000	22	166	25	0	2	3
Billick	.992	15	116	16	1	0	1
Doscher	.950	5	35	3	2	2	0
Eigsti	.989	103	801	88	10	5	12
Evangelho	1.000	1	1	1	0	0	0

First Base	PCT	G	PO	A	E	DP
Billick	1.000	1	1	0	0	0
Evangelho	1.000	1	2	0	0	0
Hayes	1.000	12	88	4	0	10
Jimenez	.984	25	161	18	3	14
Martin	1.000	6	43	3	0	4
Robinson	.987	53	425	26	6	27
Taylor	.986	54	452	26	7	44

Second Base	PCT	G	PO	A	E	DP
Evangelho	.992	29	48	70	1	14
Giavotella	.955	67	104	173	13	42
Jimenez	.923	6	13	11	2	4
Martin	.897	9	14	21	4	4
Perez	.935	35	47	68	8	9
Rivera	1.000	2	4	2	0	0

Third Base	PCT	G	PO	A	E	DP
Evangelho	.850	9	3	14	3	1
Jimenez	.857	3	4	2	1	0
Martin	.875	13	10	25	5	5
Moustakas	.942	59	36	126	10	13
Rivera	—	1	0	0	0	0
Taylor	.904	61	30	93	13	8

Shortstop	PCT	G	PO	A	E	DP
Evangelho	1.000	1	2	3	0	2
Jimenez	.824	8	4	10	3	1
Martin	.981	13	24	28	1	12
Moustakas	.956	57	96	166	12	28
Rivera	.943	63	87	146	14	23

Outfield	PCT	G	PO	A	E	DP
Evangelho	1.000	14	18	0	0	0
Francis	.966	31	54	3	2	0
Lough	.973	124	245	9	7	2
Ortiz	.984	99	224	18	4	4
Perez	—	2	0	0	0	0
Taylor	1.000	1	2	0	0	0
Tucker	.963	39	72	5	3	0
Van Stratten	.987	38	71	7	1	1
Walton	.965	82	136	3	5	2

IDAHO FALLS CHUKARS · ROOKIE

PIONEER LEAGUE

Batting	B-T	HT	WT	DOB	AVG	vLH	vRH	G	AB	R	H	2B	3B	HR	RBI	BB	HBP	SH	SF	SO	SB	CS	SLG	OBP
Alfaro, J.D.	R-R	5-9	170	4-28-88	.266	.293	.250	59	248	41	66	22	5	9	55	10	3	2	2	72	9	2	.504	.300
Billick, Joe	R-R	6-2	230	5-30-85	.000	.000	.000	4	7	0	0	0	0	0	0	1	1	0	0	1	1	0	.000	.111
Espinosa, Alberto	R-R	5-11	210	9-15-86	.216	.259	.199	56	199	21	43	10	2	1	18	16	1	1	2	45	1	1	.296	.275
Francis, Nicholas	R-R	6-3	195	3-5-86	.320	.389	.291	31	122	22	39	10	5	4	21	15	1	0	1	38	4	2	.582	.396
Garcia, Fernando	B-R	6-0	160	7-28-88	.238	.242	.236	54	189	20	45	8	2	1	18	17	3	6	0	44	21	8	.317	.311
Graterol, Ivan	R-R	6-0	170	2-14-89	.276	.257	.286	32	98	13	27	4	0	0	15	11	3	0	0	16	2	1	.316	.366
Griffin, Shawn	B-R	6-3	200	8-9-86	.249	.204	.274	69	257	44	64	15	3	5	30	38	1	0	2	83	14	5	.389	.346
Hosmer, Eric	L-L	6-4	215	10-24-89	.364	.167	.600	3	11	2	4	2	0	0	2	3	1	0	0	2	0	0	.545	.533
Jimenez, Antonio	B-R	6-2	157	4-20-87	.288	.337	.260	69	281	34	81	13	3	3	29	14	1	1	3	86	20	7	.388	.321
McCauley, Sean	R-R	6-2	170	5-13-89	.278	.327	.256	45	169	26	47	12	0	2	19	17	2	0	2	28	3	1	.385	.347

	B-T	HT	WT	DOB	AVG	vLH	vRH	G	AB	R	H	2B	3B	HR	RBI	BB	HBP	SH	SF	SO	SB	CS	SLG	OBP
Molina, Yeldrys	R-R	5-9	150	1-8-89	.289	.556	.207	11	38	6	11	4	1	0	4	5	0	1	1	7	5	1	.447	.364
Norris, Patrick	B-R	6-2	190	3-17-86	.263	.248	.273	67	259	58	68	13	2	1	18	44	0	2	3	67	33	6	.340	.366
Perez, Alwin	L-R	6-0	150	4-4-87	.244	.246	.243	55	205	21	50	14	2	2	35	22	3	2	2	72	11	8	.361	.323
Perez, Salvador	R-R	6-3	175	5-10-90	.395	.400	.391	12	43	7	17	3	1	1	6	2	0	0	1	5	0	1	.581	.413
Severino, Neder	R-R	6-2	205	2-9-88	.192	.178	.200	40	130	14	25	4	0	2	11	10	0	0	1	37	2	1	.269	.248
Testa, Carlo	L-R	6-3	218	12-16-86	.304	.362	.274	51	171	37	52	6	3	5	35	25	2	0	2	51	12	4	.462	.395
Van De Keere, Devery	L-R	6-2	210	1-29-85	.280	.167	.329	61	200	34	56	17	1	6	28	22	3	0	1	39	5	2	.465	.358

Pitching	B-T	HT	WT	DOB	W	L	ERA	G	GS	CG	SV	IP	H	R	ER	HR	BB	SO	AVG	vLH	vRH	K/9	BB/9
Beach, Colby	R-R	6-0	205	7-9-85	4	4	6.00	15	7	0	0	48	51	36	32	10	16	51	.263	.256	.268	9.56	3.00
Carver, Jesse	L-L	6-0	183	1-28-85	2	0	6.99	16	0	0	0	28	37	22	22	5	13	25	.330	.351	.320	7.94	4.13
Casey, Bryan	R-R	6-1	200	6-5-86	3	5	3.36	16	16	0	0	72	65	31	27	6	26	66	.242	.236	.245	8.21	3.24
Cota, Luis	R-R	6-2	200	8-19-85	1	1	3.55	6	6	0	0	25	24	15	10	1	16	21	.255	.273	.246	7.46	5.68
Foster, John	L-L	6-0	200	5-17-78	0	0	5.06	9	0	0	0	11	11	6	6	2	8	13	.262	.091	.323	10.97	6.75
Garcia, Justin	R-R	6-0	185	10-19-84	4	1	3.00	18	0	0	3	42	41	16	14	1	5	35	.252	.208	.270	7.50	1.07
Gilgenbach, Steve	L-L	6-2	215	2-12-86	0	1	9.59	20	0	0	0	25	33	31	30	27	3	25	26	.316	.343	.302	9.24	8.88
Hardy, Blaine	L-L	6-2	195	3-14-87	1	0	4.15	21	0	0	4	35	34	18	16	5	8	34	.256	.162	.292	8.83	2.08
Hodgson, Ivor	B-L	6-3	190	4-25-86	3	6	3.14	15	15	0	0	72	62	37	25	1	33	67	.233	.224	.236	8.41	4.14
Huber, Tim	L-L	5-10	190	2-1-86	1	0	3.38	13	0	0	3	24	19	9	9	3	13	18	.226	.238	.222	6.75	4.88
Miller, Steven	R-R	6-2	220	3-23-86	0	2	6.14	16	1	0	0	29	31	19	15	3	23	18	.229	.300	.189	7.36	9.41
Morgan, Ryan	R-R	6-1	190	1-29-87	0	4	6.70	15	11	0	0	43	54	36	32	7	34	32	.312	.290	.324	6.70	7.12
Novakowski, Gary	R-R	6-4	215	6-15-85	1	4	5.71	18	0	0	0	35	56	30	22	5	13	22	.357	.304	.386	5.71	3.38
Peterson, Matt	R-R	6-5	220	2-11-82	0	0	0.00	1	0	0	0	1	1	0	0	0	0	1	.250	.000	.333	9.00	0.00
Rada, Orlando	L-L	5-11	165	12-20-85	4	2	4.79	17	0	0	1	41	50	24	22	3	12	40	.301	.245	.327	8.71	2.61
Raglione, Paul	R-R	6-5	195	1-15-87	0	1	6.14	3	3	0	0	7	6	5	5	1	4	6	.222	.400	.118	7.36	4.91
Saito, Derrick	L-L	5-9	155	12-26-87	3	4	4.36	18	0	0	1	33	34	20	16	3	19	37	.272	.286	.268	10.09	5.18
Sisk, Brandon	L-L	6-3	210	7-13-85	0	0	2.45	4	2	0	0	11	8	5	3	1	4	9	.200	.286	.182	7.36	3.27
Thompson, James	R-R	6-3	195	8-15-87	3	3	3.99	22	0	0	3	29	28	15	13	0	18	39	.248	.341	.194	11.97	5.52
Toribio, Aneidy	L-L	6-1	172	5-21-88	3	5	4.67	16	15	0	0	62	69	44	32	7	33	68	.284	.154	.309	9.92	4.82

Fielding

Catcher	PCT	G	PO	A	E	DP	PB
Billick	1.000	3	12	2	0	0	0
Espinosa	1.000	2	4	1	0	0	0
Graterol	.995	22	156	25	1	4	7
McCauley	.983	45	353	44	7	7	7
S. Perez	.983	12	103	14	2	0	0

First Base	PCT	G	PO	A	E	DP
Espinosa	.981	52	419	37	9	55
Hosmer	1.000	1	10	0	0	0
Van De Keere	.966	30	215	11	8	20

Second Base	PCT	G	PO	A	E	DP
Garcia	.945	41	67	105	10	26
Molina	1.000	4	13	0	0	3
A. Perez	.975	32	57	96	4	31
Van De Keere	—	1	0	0	0	0

Third Base	PCT	G	PO	A	E	DP
Jimenez	.917	56	40	125	15	8
Van De Keere	.885	23	13	33	6	7

Shortstop	PCT	G	PO	A	E	DP
Alfaro	.943	57	87	161	15	43

Garcia	.905	5	5	14	2	4
Jimenez	.936	9	18	26	3	8
Molina	.848	6	10	18	5	3

Outfield	PCT	G	PO	A	E	DP
Francis	1.000	31	57	5	0	0
Griffin	.958	64	83	9	4	1
Norris	.993	67	136	9	1	2
A. Perez	1.000	7	9	0	0	0
Severino	.938	28	26	4	2	1
Testa	.974	43	74	1	2	0

BURLINGTON ROYALS

APPALACHIAN LEAGUE

ROOKIE

Batting	B-T	HT	WT	DOB	AVG	vLH	vRH	G	AB	R	H	2B	3B	HR	RBI	BB	HBP	SH	SF	SO	SB	CS	SLG	OBP
Aparicio, Julio	R-R	6-2	175	1-4-90	.252	.315	.232	57	218	32	55	8	1	2	27	15	3	0	2	66	7	4	.326	.307
Caldwell, Keven	L-L	5-11	170	3-29-88	.201	.108	.222	54	199	20	40	7	3	4	21	17	2	0	2	44	1	3	.327	.268
Cruz, Diego	L-L	6-0	175	11-13-87	.267	.212	.284	38	135	15	36	6	0	1	14	3	1	0	0	27	1	1	.333	.288
Cruz, Fernando	B-R	6-2	184	3-28-90	.237	.239	.237	53	198	19	47	9	0	0	14	3	3	0	0	43	3	3	.283	.260
Franco, Angel	B-R	5-10	152	5-23-90	.257	.220	.267	62	237	27	61	10	1	1	25	19	1	6	1	41	14	7	.321	.314
Gutierrez, Jorge	R-R	5-10	185	7-23-85	.233	.130	.258	38	120	15	28	2	0	0	11	10	2	1	2	20	6	4	.250	.299
Jose, Lifete	B-R	6-0	168	3-24-89	.182	.200	.174	11	33	2	6	1	0	0	3	1	0	0	1	14	0	1	.212	.270
McFadden, Warren	R-R	6-1	205	12-21-85	.212	.276	.190	32	113	14	24	3	1	2	7	13	2	0	0	24	2	0	.310	.305
Moctezuma, Miguel	R-R	5-10	190	1-14-87	.158	.217	.141	31	101	5	16	3	0	1	12	6	1	0	1	31	0	0	.218	.211
Molina, Yeldrys	R-R	5-9	150	1-8-89	.280	.294	.277	27	82	12	23	1	3	2	4	16	0	3	0	28	1	2	.439	.398
Morales, Jason	R-R	6-0	210	12-9-85	.187	.167	.194	35	123	16	23	4	1	1	9	13	3	2	1	32	1	1	.260	.279
Olson, Matt	L-R	6-1	210	5-17-85	.067	.000	.071	4	15	3	1	0	0	0	1	0	0	0	0	7	0	0	.067	.125
Perez, Salvador	R-R	6-3	175	5-10-90	.325	.222	.355	13	40	4	13	0	1	0	10	5	1	2	1	5	0	0	.375	.404
Reyes, Yenssi	R-R	5-10	182	10-23-87	.190	.182	.194	16	42	4	8	2	0	0	1	2	2	0	0	7	0	0	.238	.261
Richardson, Hilton	L-L	6-3	200	1-10-89	.229	.242	.227	54	205	36	47	7	5	1	16	17	2	4	1	61	10	7	.327	.293
Testa, Carlo	L-L	6-3	218	12-16-86	.188	.400	.091	7	16	1	3	2	0	0	1	4	0	0	0	5	1	0	.313	.350
Vittek, Josh	L-R	6-4	240	4-9-86	.297	.241	.310	42	155	24	46	7	1	8	34	10	2	0	1	57	0	1	.510	.345
Wood, David	L-R	6-2	210	12-21-84	.289	.433	.252	40	149	17	43	10	1	2	21	15	0	0	1	14	1	5	.409	.352

Pitching	B-T	HT	WT	DOB	W	L	ERA	G	GS	CG	SV	IP	H	R	ER	HR	BB	SO	AVG	vLH	vRH	K/9	BB/9
Bowden, Barry	R-R	6-1	205	11-9-84	3	2	1.86	20	0	0	7	29	21	7	6	2	12	40	.204	.086	.265	12.41	3.72
Bryant, Carson	R-R	6-2	180	6-6-86	0	4	4.62	13	5	0	0	37	41	23	19	5	10	42	.279	.255	.292	10.22	2.43
Colon, Roque	R-R	5-10	152	4-23-88	1	2	7.23	16	0	0	0	24	27	25	19	5	17	25	.278	.237	.305	9.51	6.46
De La Cruz, Giancarlo	R-R	6-0	166	9-23-89	3	5	5.69	13	8	0	0	49	55	33	31	7	13	44	.281	.172	.333	8.08	2.39
Farinas, Williams	R-R	6-0	175	1-5-87	1	0	7.91	15	0	0	0	19	24	19	17	6	13	22	.296	.286	.302	10.24	6.05
Fisher, Brent	L-L	6-2	190	8-6-87	0	1	6.43	2	1	0	0	7	9	6	5	0	2	8	.300	.167	.333	10.29	2.57
Flanagan, John	L-L	6-5	200	6-15-88	3	3	2.56	12	7	0	0	46	36	14	13	2	14	43	.216	.276	.203	8.47	2.76
Garrido, Santiago	R-R	6-0	178	10-4-89	0	2	3.86	6	3	0	0	19	19	11	8	1	6	13	.275	.300	.265	6.27	2.89
Halliman, Pernell	R-R	6-7	240	12-20-86	0	1	8.31	12	3	0	0	26	38	29	24	4	16	20	.339	.324	.346	6.92	5.54

Herrera, Kelvin	R-R	5-10	162	12-31-89	2	2	1.42	11	8	0	0	51	48	17	8	0	5	45	.254	.277	.242	7.99	0.89
Huber, Tim	L-L	5-10	190	2-1-86	0	0	18.00	3	0	0	0	3	8	6	6	1	2	4	.471	.333	.500	12.00	6.00
Hudnall, Jaeson	R-R	6-6	220	10-4-86	0	0	3.38	4	0	0	0	5	5	3	2	1	0	6	.238	.300	.182	10.13	0.00
Jorge, Victor	R-R	6-3	190	5-18-87	0	2	8.54	10	5	0	0	26	32	27	25	4	13	15	.314	.344	.300	5.13	4.44
Lehmann, Mike	B-R	6-2	190	5-3-89	4	4	3.43	13	9	0	0	58	57	30	22	4	16	42	.257	.235	.266	6.55	2.50
Marimon, Sugar Ray	R-R	6-1	168	9-30-88	0	2	11.08	6	3	0	0	13	19	17	16	2	10	12	.345	.333	.350	8.31	6.92
Mieles, Edwin	R-R	6-4	180	9-1-87	0	0	5.21	15	0	0	0	19	24	15	11	3	14	15	.293	.207	.340	7.11	6.63
Rodriguez, Jacob	R-R	6-2	220	7-24-88	2	2	3.51	11	0	0	0	1	33	27	15	13	0	12	48	.216	.224	.211	12.96	3.24
Runion, Sam	R-R	6-4	220	11-9-88	3	4	3.35	10	10	0	0	48	47	25	18	4	10	30	.253	.243	.259	5.59	1.86

Fielding

Catcher	PCT	G	PO	A	E	DP	PB
Franco	1.000	1	3	1	0	0	0
Moctezuma	.996	30	244	21	1	2	14
Perez	.986	9	58	13	1	2	2
Reyes	1.000	15	92	6	0	0	2
Vittek	.973	16	121	22	4	4	9

First Base	PCT	G	PO	A	E	DP
D. Cruz	.981	30	243	18	5	18
Gutierrez	.800	1	4	0	1	1
Morales	.978	9	87	3	2	10
Vittek	.980	6	50	0	1	4
Wood	.982	23	206	13	4	22

Second Base	PCT	G	PO	A	E	DP
Franco	.965	59	103	176	10	38
Gutierrez	1.000	6	13	14	0	4
Jose	1.000	2	3	5	0	1
Perez	1.000	1	0	2	0	0

Third Base	PCT	G	PO	A	E	DP
F. Cruz	.911	48	17	75	9	7
Franco	.750	2	0	3	1	0
Morales	.886	19	8	23	4	3

Shortstop	PCT	G	PO	A	E	DP
Gutierrez	.968	30	47	103	5	22
Jose	.829	8	11	18	6	3
Molina	.944	27	34	84	7	15

Outfield	PCT	G	PO	A	E	DP
Aparicio	.970	50	93	4	3	0
Caldwell	.929	51	73	6	6	2
McFadden	.980	29	46	2	1	1
Olson	1.000	3	2	0	0	0
Richardson	.944	50	83	2	5	1
Testa	.900	5	9	0	1	0
Wood	1.000	10	14	1	0	1

AZL ROYALS   ROOKIE

ARIZONA LEAGUE

Batting	B-T	HT	WT	DOB	AVG	vLH	vRH	G	AB	R	H	2B	3B	HR	RBI	BB	HBP	SH	SF	SO	SB	CS	SLG	OBP
Batista, Deivy	R-R	5-11	150	5-7-88	.317	.439	.275	49	161	37	51	12	2	3	21	15	2	0	0	32	9	9	.472	.382
Beltre, Geulin		6-0	180	10-27-90	.188	.222	.179	23	96	11	18	3	0	1	3	6	0	0	0	33	6	1	.250	.235
Bonilla, Jose	R-R	5-10	188	8-4-88	.357	.393	.345	34	112	20	40	9	3	5	24	5	4	0	0	22	5	0	.625	.405
Espinal, Yowill	R-R	6-0	180	4-1-91	.240	.216	.248	50	204	21	49	4	3	4	19	2	0	0	0	42	13	2	.348	.248
Fowler, Brandon	R-R	6-0	185	6-10-89	.273	.000	.333	7	11	3	3	0	0	0	1	4	0	0	1	4	1	0	.273	.438
Henriquez, Edwin	B-R	6-2	168	11-7-88	.179	.125	.194	46	156	20	28	5	1	0	10	6	3	1	0	30	4	6	.224	.224
Jacobo, Astin	R-R	6-0	167	12-15-88	.162	.077	.208	14	37	2	6	2	2	0	2	2	0	0	1	22	0	1	.324	.200
Jacobs, Nestor	R-R	5-11	169	3-8-88	.211	.000	.250	8	19	1	4	2	0	0	4	0	0	0	0	4	0	0	.316	.211
Jones, Travis	R-R	6-3	200	5-23-89	.188	.000	.250	5	16	1	3	0	0	0	1	3	0	0	0	7	0	0	.188	.316
Jose, Lifete	B-R	6-0	168	3-24-89	.261	.280	.254	30	92	11	24	3	1	2	17	10	2	2	1	31	6	4	.380	.343
Kuebler, Jake	R-R	6-5	190	9-3-89	.187	.217	.180	35	123	13	23	4	0	1	10	6	1	1	0	25	1	5	.244	.231
Llanos, Alex	R-R	6-1	160	9-21-90	.182	.178	.184	54	203	20	37	8	1	0	17	13	3	2	2	63	14	4	.232	.240
Mariano, Miguel	L-R	6-0	170	10-11-88	.103	.182	.088	24	68	7	7	2	0	0	7	10	0	1	2	39	2	2	.132	.213
Marte, Alexis	L-L	5-11	197	6-13-85	.209	.188	.213	36	91	10	19	2	2	1	11	14	3	0	0	17	1	2	.308	.333
Matos, Mauricio	R-R	6-0	185	9-10-90	.269	.385	.246	24	78	8	21	5	0	0	7	1	1	0	1	14	0	2	.333	.284
McFadden, Warren	R-R	6-1	205	12-21-85	.333	—	.333	1	3	0	1	0	0	0	0	0	0	0	0	2	0	0	.333	.333
Nilsen, Jamie	R-R	5-11	180	5-15-85	.273	.105	.328	31	77	10	21	4	1	3	15	7	5	2	1	15	5	2	.468	.367
Richardson, Hilton	L-L	6-3	200	1-10-89	.474	1.000	.412	5	19	3	9	1	0	1	2	1	0	0	0	4	0	1	.684	.500
Rodriguez, Derek	R-R	5-9	155	2-13-89	.213	.304	.183	39	94	13	20	3	0	1	6	16	1	2	0	31	6	3	.277	.333
Rosario, Luis	R-R	6-2	181	5-21-90	.279	.350	.258	52	172	26	48	8	1	2	13	27	1	2	0	44	7	11	.372	.380

Pitching	B-T	HT	WT	DOB	W	L	ERA	G	GS	CG	SV	IP	H	R	ER	HR	BB	SO	AVG	vLH	vRH	K/9	BB/9
Billo, Greg	R-R	6-4	180	7-15-90	0	1	5.65	7	4	0	1	14	21	9	9	1	8	13	.375	.471	.333	8.16	5.02
Bonilla, Ariel	R-R	6-2	170	7-10-88	0	1	6.06	7	0	0	1	16	23	15	11	2	8	9	.333	.208	.400	4.96	4.41
Cuevas, Gary	R-R	6-0	184	5-23-88	3	2	5.32	12	2	0	0	46	52	30	27	2	26	42	.287	.264	.297	8.28	5.12
Culver, Malcolm	R-R	6-2	185	2-9-90	0	0	0.00	1	1	0	0	2	1	0	0	0	0	0	.143	1.000	0.00	0.00	0.00
De La Cruz, Deivi	R-R	5-11	155	3-25-90	5	3	4.74	12	5	0	0	49	53	28	26	2	14	50	.277	.329	.248	9.12	2.55
De La Cruz, Julio	R-R	6-1	161	10-7-80	0	0	2.08	5	2	0	0	4	5	1	1	0	1	2	.313	.333	.300	4.15	2.08
Feickert, Casey	R-R	6-3	180	8-5-88	0	1	13.50	12	0	0	0	13	28	21	20	0	9	5	.452	.429	.463	3.38	6.07
Fisher, Brent	L-L	6-2	190	8-6-87	0	1	1.93	4	4	0	0	9	8	4	2	0	4	8	.229	.000	.267	7.71	3.86
Fortuna, Carlos	R-R	6-2	185	3-31-90	2	2	5.82	11	5	0	0	39	39	26	25	5	19	41	.267	.179	.322	9.54	4.42
Garrido, Santiago	R-R	6-0	178	10-4-89	0	1	5.49	7	0	0	0	20	20	15	12	0	9	8	.274	.250	.289	3.66	4.12
Hamulack, Tim	R-L	6-2	220	11-14-76	0	1	4.50	3	0	0	0	4	4	2	2	0	1	4	.286	.000	.333	9.00	2.25
Hentges, Chase	R-R	6-5	180	5-15-90	1	1	4.11	12	0	0	2	15	19	8	7	0	3	11	.317	.316	.317	6.46	1.76
Hodge Nielsen, Peter	R-R	6-2	210	6-15-89	0	4	9.79	11	6	0	0	30	47	43	33	0	31	14	.359	.409	.333	4.15	9.20
Liotta, Ray	L-L	6-3	220	4-3-83	0	0	0.96	4	3	0	0	9	7	1	1	0	1	10	.206	.167	.214	9.64	0.96
Martinez, Angel	R-R			4-18-85	0	1	7.71	10	1	0	0	14	22	17	12	3	7	14	.338	.261	.381	9.00	4.50
Montgomery, Mike	L-L	6-5	180	7-1-89	2	1	1.69	12	9	0	0	43	31	12	8	2	12	34	.211	.233	.205	7.17	2.53
Musser, Neal	L-L	6-1	235	8-25-80	0	1	3.38	3	3	0	0	3	3	1	1	0	0	6	.273	.250	.286	20.25	0.00
Perez, Leondy	R-R	6-1	175	6-19-90	1	2	2.53	12	1	0	1	43	38	19	12	2	16	46	.241	.171	.265	9.70	3.38
Peterson, Matt	R-R	6-5	220	2-11-82	0	0	5.40	2	1	0	0	2	4	2	1	0	0	3	.364	.000	.444	16.20	0.00
Richardson, Brett	R-R	6-3	195	3-2-88	0	0	1.37	14	0	0	4	20	18	7	3	0	3	9	.237	.190	.255	4.12	1.37
Ruhlman, Josh	L-L	6-0	160	5-3-86	2	2	3.00	11	0	0	2	15	17	8	5	0	2	19	.288	.211	.325	11.40	1.20
Sample, Tyler	L-R	6-7	245	6-27-89	0	5	9.00	10	8	0	0	27	30	36	27	0	29	39	.270	.360	.244	13.00	9.67
Sirrett, Onassis	R-R	5-11	170	12-15-88	3	2	3.05	12	1	0	1	41	45	21	14	1	6	28	.269	.282	.266	6.10	1.31
Smith, Jace	R-R	5-11	160	10-6-85	1	0	1.15	13	0	0	2	16	15	4	2	0	4	13	.254	.280	.235	7.47	2.30
Theis, Jake	R-R	6-6	220	4-8-90	0	0	—	1	0	0	0	0	4	1	1	0	0	0	1.000	1.000	1.000	—	—

Fielding

Catcher	PCT	G	PO	A	E	DP	PB
Bonilla	1.000	1	11	0	0	0	0
Bonilla	.986	32	229	44	4	4	16
Fowler	1.000	3	5	0	0	0	0
Jacobs	.952	8	19	1	1	0	4
Jones	1.000	5	41	6	0	1	2
Matos	.986	20	123	15	2	2	6

First Base	PCT	G	PO	A	E	DP
Batista	1.000	1	11	0	0	4
Henriquez	.985	36	309	14	5	31
Marte	.986	30	196	18	3	16

Second Base	PCT	G	PO	A	E	DP
Batista	.986	19	32	41	1	8
Culver	.962	7	10	15	1	7
Espinal	1.000	12	20	25	0	4
Henriquez	.900	4	6	3	1	2
Jose	.928	15	31	33	5	7
Marte	1.000	1	1	0	0	0
Nilsen	.920	14	21	25	4	11

Third Base	PCT	G	PO	A	E	DP
Batista	.971	12	5	28	1	2
Henriquez	1.000	8	7	10	0	2
Kuebler	.875	33	22	76	14	4
Nilsen	.875	6	3	11	2	0

Shortstop	PCT	G	PO	A	E	DP
Batista	1.000	13	10	27	0	3
Espinal	.884	37	48	89	18	27
Jose	.938	15	13	47	4	7

Outfield	PCT	G	PO	A	E	DP
Jacobo	.962	14	24	1	1	0
Llanos	.960	53	91	5	4	1
Mariano	.968	24	28	2	1	0
McFadden	1.000	1	2	0	0	0
Nilsen	—	1	0	0	0	0
Richardson	.909	5	9	1	1	0
Rodriguez	.953	39	57	4	3	2
Rosario	.967	52	79	8	3	2

DSL ROYALS

DOMINICAN SUMMER LEAGUE

ROOKIE

Batting	B-T	HT	WT	DOB	AVG	vLH	vRH	G	AB	R	H	2B	3B	HR	RBI	BB	HBP	SH	SF	SO	SB	CS	SLG	OBP
Alcantara, Ysmelin	R-R	6-2	180	5-13-90	.239	.333	.196	29	67	8	16	1	2	1	11	5	1	0	1	28	1	1	.358	.297
Alvarez, Jhonson	R-R	5-11	160	1-2-90	.205	.091	.250	20	39	8	8	0	0	0	2	8	1	0	0	10	0	1	.205	.354
Cabrera, Santos	R-R	5-10	170	1-28-90	.273	.387	.241	48	143	18	39	3	1	1	23	15	4	2	3	24	9	6	.329	.352
Carmona, Samuel	R-R	6-1	183	2-8-91	.220	.167	.234	21	59	8	13	2	0	0	5	10	2	0	0	19	0	0	.254	.352
Escobar, Edul	R-R	5-11	185	9-2-90	.250	.231	.258	43	128	17	32	4	1	1	18	21	4	1	1	32	1	1	.320	.370
Figueroa, Yunior	B-R	6-0	170	8-8-90	.304	.218	.331	61	224	42	68	14	0	2	27	16	3	4	0	29	6	1	.393	.358
Fortuna, Juan	R-R	5-11	185	1-12-89	.244	.241	.245	48	131	18	32	6	0	0	15	26	6	1	1	29	4	1	.290	.390
Lantigua, Roberto	B-R	5-10	142	3-5-90	.210	.172	.222	40	119	29	25	4	0	0	10	38	2	2	0	29	11	5	.244	.409
Mariano, Miguel	L-R	6-0	170	10-11-88	.275	.211	.289	33	109	15	30	7	5	2	21	26	1	0	0	30	6	5	.486	.419
Martinez, Adrian	R-R	6-1	158	1-12-91	.245	.208	.257	55	188	34	46	6	0	0	27	31	4	2	2	32	12	6	.277	.360
Moreno, Henry	R-R	6-2	162	6-6-89	.314	.189	.348	53	169	22	53	20	3	2	41	28	0	0	0	26	2	0	.503	.411
Pereira, Vicni	R-R	6-1	175	1-20-91	.179	.176	.179	52	151	20	27	5	1	0	15	23	2	0	1	49	4	0	.225	.294
Piterson, Luis	R-R	5-11	155	6-10-90	.256	.184	.275	50	180	29	46	9	0	0	31	18	5	5	1	20	11	2	.306	.338
Polonia, Juan	B-R	6-1	173	12-16-89	.190	.095	.215	41	100	25	19	2	2	0	4	15	3	4	0	39	15	4	.250	.314
Sanchez, Williams	R-R	6-1	185	11-12-89	.182	.235	.163	22	66	4	12	2	0	0	3	5	2	0	0	13	2	0	.212	.260
Soto, Victor	R-R	5-11	150	10-16-88	.295	.308	.291	58	173	37	51	10	3	0	33	26	8	3	1	31	31	7	.387	.409
Wilmore, Juan	B-R	6-1	175	5-27-89	.238	.167	.253	38	101	16	24	4	1	0	9	12	0	1	1	29	8	1	.297	.316

Pitching	B-T	HT	WT	DOB	W	L	ERA	G	GS	CG	SV	IP	H	R	ER	HR	BB	SO	AVG	vLH	vRH	K/9	BB/9
Amador, Ezequiel	R-R	6-1	154	7-26-88	2	5	4.42	17	8	0	3	55	61	38	27	2	35	48	.285	.291	.283	7.85	5.73
Avinazar, Willian	R-R	6-4	195	2-27-89	8	2	2.37	14	14	0	0	68	51	20	18	1	19	56	.216	.283	.200	7.38	2.50
Batista, Geronimo	R-R	6-3	180	6-10-90	5	2	3.75	17	0	0	3	36	32	20	15	2	15	26	.246	.324	.219	6.50	3.75
Breton, Roque	R-R	6-0	174	4-18-91	0	1	5.40	10	1	0	1	28	36	24	17	2	17	20	.310	.448	.264	6.35	5.40
Castillo, Domingo	R-R	6-1	160	9-23-87	0	1	2.92	6	1	0	0	12	9	10	4	0	12	12	.200	.133	.233	8.76	8.76
De La Rosa, Starling	L-L	6-5	159	9-19-87	1	4	4.74	17	1	0	2	25	17	15	13	0	27	32	.221	.300	.209	11.68	9.85
Garcia, Angel	R-R	6-1	160	6-19-89	2	2	1.57	20	1	0	2	34	23	12	6	1	25	37	.195	.250	.171	9.70	6.55
Garcia, Juan	R-R	6-1	196	3-27-89	0	5	3.82	13	2	0	3	31	31	19	13	0	14	23	.270	.321	.253	6.75	4.11
Gomez, Leo	R-R	6-1	204	1-11-91	0	2	5.68	6	5	0	0	19	24	12	12	1	9	10	.304	.333	.297	4.74	4.26
Gomez, Omar	L-L	6-2	190	1-26-89	5	0	2.88	13	1	0	0	34	27	16	11	0	27	34	.227	.273	.222	8.91	7.08
Nina, Aroni	R-R	6-4	160	4-9-90	0	0	6.00	7	0	0	0	12	11	11	8	1	12	10	.239	.091	.286	7.50	9.00
Nunez, Edgar	L-L	6-0	174	8-21-90	0	0	4.50	4	0	0	0	6	5	4	3	0	10	3	.238	.333	.200	4.50	15.00
Ramirez, Abraham	R-R	6-2	189	10-17-90	0	0	3.38	2	0	0	0	3	1	2	1	0	6	3	.125	.000	.143	10.13	20.25
Rodriguez, Freddy	R-R	6-3	188	12-1-90	3	3	2.59	15	7	0	1	63	57	26	18	3	14	32	.242	.277	.228	4.60	2.01
Rodriguez, Jonathan	R-R	6-1	165	12-13-88	0	1	2.92	10	1	0	1	25	27	10	8	0	6	17	.290	.316	.284	6.20	2.19
Santiago, Leonel	R-R	6-0	178	12-23-89	3	1	2.97	13	11	0	0	58	52	30	19	0	25	37	.232	.339	.194	5.77	3.90
Violi, Willer	R-R	6-1	165	5-29-90	2	3	4.75	10	8	0	0	36	39	29	19	1	16	33	.264	.356	.223	8.25	4.00
Yambati, Robinson	R-R	6-3	185	1-15-91	4	1	3.09	14	8	0	0	55	49	27	19	0	16	40	.236	.276	.220	6.51	2.60

Fielding

Catcher	PCT	G	PO	A	E	DP	PB
Alvarez	.972	11	31	4	1	1	0
Escobar	.968	36	239	31	9	4	15
Fortuna	.980	25	124	22	3	0	7
Moreno	.979	16	86	8	2	1	7

First Base	PCT	G	PO	A	E	DP
Alvarez	.921	5	34	1	3	3
Fortuna	.984	21	173	15	3	14
Moreno	1.000	20	142	6	0	16
Polonia	1.000	1	1	0	0	0
Soto	.985	39	303	21	5	33

Second Base	PCT	G	PO	A	E	DP
Figueroa	1.000	2	4	6	0	2
Lantigua	.958	25	56	57	5	15
Martinez	1.000	2	3	5	0	1
Piterson	.982	30	71	91	3	21
Soto	.923	6	12	12	2	0
Wilmore	1.000	16	34	44	0	12

Third Base	PCT	G	PO	A	E	DP
Carmona	.769	13	6	14	6	1
Figueroa	.938	46	26	110	9	11
Soto	.875	4	3	4	1	1
Wilmore	.838	24	4	27	6	2

Shortstop	PCT	G	PO	A	E	DP
Lantigua	.904	18	13	53	7	5
Martinez	.942	53	65	180	15	29
Piterson	.946	7	11	24	2	4

Outfield	PCT	G	PO	A	E	DP
Alcantara	.842	23	30	2	6	0
Cabrera	.944	46	48	3	3	0
Mariano	.984	31	58	4	1	2
Pereira	.983	48	54	4	1	2
Polonia	.964	35	49	4	2	2
Rosario	.971	43	60	6	2	2
Sanchez	.900	22	26	1	3	1

Los Angeles Angels

BY BILL SHAIKIN

The Angels had walked off the field for the final time this season—all but one of them.

Chone Figgins did not move. He stood alone at third base, hands on hips, staring across the diamond. The Red Sox were full of life, hopping atop each other. Figgins was a portrait in still life.

"I couldn't believe it," he said. "Once again, we're on their field, and they're celebrating.

"I'm just wondering: How does this keep happening?"

For the third time in five years, the Red Sox knocked the Angels out of the playoffs in the first round. Angels owners Arte Moreno refused to be consoled by the Angels' first 100-victory season. "You win those games because you want to have an opportunity to win a championship," Moreno said. "Let's put it this way: I hate to (bleeping) lose."

They are the Braves for a new generation, an unhappy label not easily removed. The Braves boast, and rightfully so, about 14 consecutive division championships. Their fans focus on one World Series victory. That's one for 14, a batting average of .071.

This was the Angels chance to stake their claim as an elite franchise, maybe their best chance, maybe the last chance before Mark Teixeira and closer Francisco Rodriguez cash in this winter.

They also are expected to discuss contract extensions with Vladimir Guerrero and Lackey.

After Lackey gave up two runs and lost Game One of the American League Division Series, he pointed the finger at his offense. After he gave up two runs and got a no decision in Game Four, he warned against that line of questioning.

"Don't stir the pot," he said.

If the season was a disappointment, it was not without distinction. The Angels led the major leagues in victories for the first time, including a 50-31 road record. They also won the American League West by 21 games, the largest margin in division history, and they clinched the division on Sept. 10, the earliest clinching date in division history.

In reflection, there was much to celebrate. Guerrero joined Lou Gehrig as the only players in major league history to hit 25 home runs and bat .300 for 11 consecutive seasons. Rodriguez set a

MAJOR LEAGUE: ERVIN SANTANA, RHP

Santana became a key figure for the 100-win Angels, finishing 16-7, 3.49 with the fourth-most innings (219) in the American League. He finished with a whopping 214 strikeouts against 47 walks. Eleven victories came away from Edison Field.

MINOR LEAGUE: BRANDON WOOD, SS

Wood solidified himself as the Angels' top prospect as he hit .296/.375/.595 with 31 home runs and 84 RBIs at Triple-A Salt Lake. He also was called up twice to the Angels, including a two-month stint, and hit five home runs with 13 RBIs in 150 at-bats.

BATTING		*Minimum 250 at-bats
*AVG	Sandoval, Freddy, Salt Lake	.335
R	Sandoval, Freddy, Salt Lake	92
H	Sandoval, Freddy, Salt Lake	176
TB	Trumbo, Mark, Rancho Cucamonga/Arkansas	286
2B	Sandoval, Freddy, Salt Lake	45
3B	Fuller, Clay, Cedar Rapids	13
HR	Trumbo, Mark, Rancho Cucamonga/Arkansas	32
RBI	Trumbo, Mark, Rancho Cucamonga/Arkansas	93
BB	Fuller, Clay, Cedar Rapids	68
SO	Phillips, P.J., Rancho Cucamonga	125
SO	Moore, Jeremy, Cedar Rapids	125
SB	Romine, Andrew, Cedar Rapids	62
*OBP	Nieves, Abel, Rancho Cucamonga	.409
*SLG	Wood, Brandon, Salt Lake	.595

PITCHING		†Minimum 75 innings
W	O'Sullivan, Sean, Rancho Cucamonga	16
L	Adenhart, Nick, Salt Lake	13
†ERA	Walden, Jordan, Cedar Rapids/R. Cucamonga	2.76
G	Browning, Barret, Rancho Cucamonga/Arkansas	57
GS	Mosebach, Robert, Arkansas	29
SV	McKiernan, Eddie, Cedar Rapids	22
IP	Mosebach, Robert, Arkansas	177
BB	Adenhart, Nick, Salt Lake	75
SO	Walden, Jordan, Cedar Rapids/R. Cucamonga	141
†AVG	Walden, Jordan, Cedar Rapids/R. Cucamonga	.213

major league record with 62 saves.

Ervin Santana and Joe Saunders, neither of whom was assured a spot in the starting rotation in spring training, joined Rodriguez in representing the Angels at the All-Star Game. Saunders went 17-7, 3.41, sixth in the league, and led the AL with a 2.55 road ERA.

General Manager: Tony Reagins. **Farm Director:** Abe Flores. **Scouting Director:** Eddie Bane.

Class	Team	League	W	L	PCT	Finish*	Manager	Affiliate Since
Majors	Los Angeles	American	100	62	.617	1st (14)	Mike Scoscia	—
Triple-A	Salt Lake Bees	Pacific Coast	84	60	.583	2nd (16)	Bobby Mitchell	2001
Double-A	Arkansas Travelers	Texas	62	78	.443	^6th (8)	Bobby Magallanes	2001
High A	R. Cucamonga Quakes	California	67	74	.475	8th (10)	Ever Magallanes	2001
Low A	Cedar Rapids Kernels	Midwest	72	66	.522	6th (14)	Keith Johnson	1993
Rookie	Orem Owlz	Pioneer	52	23	.693	1st (8)	Tom Kotchman	2001
Rookie	AZL Angels	Arizona	39	17	.696	1st (9)	Tyrone Boykin	2001
Overall 2008 Minor League Record			376	318	.542	4th		

* Finish in overall standings (No. of teams in league). ^League champion.

ORGANIZATION STATISTICS

LOS ANGELES ANGELS

AMERICAN LEAGUE

Batting	B-T	HT	WT	DOB	AVG	vLH	vRH	G	AB	R	H	2B	3B	HR	RBI	BB	HBP	SH	SF	SO	SB	CS	SLG	OBP
Anderson, Garret	L-L	6-3	225	6-30-72	.293	.290	.293	145	557	66	163	27	3	15	84	29	1	0	6	77	7	4	.433	.325
Aybar, Erick	B-R	5-10	170	1-14-84	.277	.286	.274	98	346	53	96	18	5	3	39	14	5	9	1	45	7	2	.384	.314
Brown, Matt	R-R	6-0	200	8-8-82	.053	.111	.000	11	19	0	1	1	0	0	3	1	0	0	0	10	0	0	.105	.100
Budde, Ryan	R-R	5-11	210	8-15-79	.000	.000	.000	8	2	0	0	0	0	0	0	0	0	1	0	0	0	0	.000	.000
Figgins, Chone	B-R	5-8	180	1-22-78	.276	.272	.277	116	453	72	125	14	1	1	22	62	3	2	0	80	34	13	.318	.367
Guerrero, Vladimir	R-R	6-3	235	2-9-76	.303	.286	.309	143	541	85	164	31	3	27	91	51	4	0	4	77	5	3	.521	.365
Hunter, Torii	R-R	6-2	225	7-18-75	.278	.304	.268	146	551	85	153	37	2	21	78	50	6	0	1	108	19	5	.466	.344
Izturis, Maicer	B-R	5-8	170	9-12-80	.269	.258	.272	79	290	44	78	14	2	3	37	26	1	2	2	27	11	2	.362	.329
Kendrick, Howie	R-R	5-10	200	7-12-83	.306	.300	.308	92	340	43	104	26	2	3	37	12	4	1	4	58	11	4	.421	.333
Kotchman, Casey	L-L	6-3	215	2-22-83	.287	.349	.269	100	373	47	107	24	0	12	54	18	5	0	2	23	2	1	.448	.327
Mathis, Jeff	R-R	6-0	200	3-31-83	.194	.224	.184	94	283	35	55	8	0	9	42	30	3	8	4	90	2	1	.318	.275
Matthews Jr., Gary	B-R	6-3	225	8-25-74	.242	.285	.223	127	426	53	103	19	3	8	46	45	4	0	2	95	8	3	.357	.319
Morales, Kendry	B-R	6-1	215	6-20-83	.213	.214	.213	27	61	7	13	2	0	3	8	4	1	0	0	7	0	1	.393	.273
Napoli, Mike	R-R	6-0	215	10-31-81	.273	.286	.270	78	227	39	62	9	1	20	49	35	5	1	6	70	7	3	.586	.374
Quinlan, Robb	R-R	6-1	215	3-17-77	.262	.282	.244	68	164	15	43	1	2	1	11	14	2	0	1	28	4	2	.311	.326
Rivera, Juan	R-R	6-2	225	7-3-78	.246	.233	.253	89	256	31	63	13	0	12	45	16	0	0	8	33	1	1	.438	.282
Rodriguez, Sean	R-R	6-1	185	4-26-85	.204	.178	.213	59	167	18	34	8	1	3	10	14	3	2	1	55	3	1	.317	.276
Sandoval, Freddy	B-R	6-1	200	8-16-82	.167	—	.167	6	6	0	1	0	0	0	0	1	0	0	0	0	0	0	.167	.286
Teixeira, Mark	B-R	6-3	220	4-11-80	.358	.369	.352	54	193	39	69	14	0	13	43	32	4	0	5	23	2	0	.632	.449
Willits, Reggie	B-R	5-11	185	5-30-81	.194	.200	.193	82	108	21	21	4	0	0	7	21	0	5	2	26	2	1	.231	.321
Wilson, Bobby	R-R	6-0	220	4-8-83	.167	.500	.000	7	6	0	1	0	0	0	1	1	0	0	0	3	0	0	.167	.286
Wood, Brandon	R-R	6-3	190	3-2-85	.200	.094	.229	55	150	12	30	4	0	5	13	4	1	1	1	43	4	0	.327	.224

Pitching	B-T	HT	WT	DOB	W	L	ERA	G	GS	CG	SV	IP	H	R	ER	HR	BB	SO	AVG	vLH	vRH	K/9	BB/9
Adenhart, Nick	R-R	6-3	185	8-24-86	1	0	9.00	3	3	0	0	12	18	12	12	0	13	4	.360	.300	.400	3.00	9.75
Arredondo, Jose	R-R	6-0	175	3-30-84	10	2	1.62	52	0	0	0	61	42	15	11	3	22	55	.190	.148	.236	8.11	3.25
Bootcheck, Chris	R-R	6-5	210	10-24-78	0	1	10.13	10	0	0	0	16	30	18	18	2	12	14	.385	.406	.370	7.88	6.75
Bulger, Jason	R-R	6-4	210	12-6-78	0	0	7.31	14	0	0	0	16	15	13	13	3	9	20	.242	.229	.259	11.25	5.06
Garland, Jon	R-R	6-6	210	9-27-79	14	8	4.90	32	32	1	0	197	237	116	107	23	59	90	.303	.300	.307	4.12	2.70
Jepsen, Kevin	R-R	6-3	215	7-26-84	0	1	4.32	9	0	0	0	8	8	5	4	0	4	7	.250	.235	.267	7.56	4.32
Lackey, John	R-R	6-6	245	10-23-78	12	5	3.75	24	24	3	0	163	161	71	68	26	40	130	.260	.221	.301	7.16	2.20
Loux, Shane	R-R	6-2	235	8-31-79	0	0	2.81	7	0	0	0	16	16	6	5	1	2	4	.262	.379	.156	2.25	1.13
Moseley, Dustin	R-R	6-4	215	12-26-81	2	4	6.79	12	10	0	0	50	70	38	38	6	20	37	.332	.366	.300	6.62	3.58
O'Day, Darren	R-R	6-4	225	10-22-82	0	1	4.57	30	0	0	0	43	49	24	22	2	14	29	.283	.275	.290	6.02	2.91
Oliver, Darren	R-L	6-2	200	10-6-70	7	1	2.88	54	0	0	0	72	67	24	23	5	16	48	.254	.229	.271	6.00	2.00
Rodriguez, Francisco	R-R	6-0	195	1-7-82	2	3	2.24	76	0	0	62	68	54	21	17	4	34	77	.216	.227	.205	10.14	4.48
Santana, Ervin	R-R	6-2	185	12-12-82	16	7	3.49	32	32	2	0	219	198	89	85	23	47	214	.237	.240	.234	8.79	1.93
Saunders, Joe	L-L	6-3	210	6-16-81	17	7	3.41	31	31	1	0	198	187	82	75	21	53	103	.253	.260	.250	4.68	2.41
Serrano, Alex	R-R	6-1	200	2-18-81	0	0	0.00	1	0	0	0	1	1	0	0	0	1	1	.250	.500	.000	9.00	0.00
Shields, Scot	R-R	6-1	180	7-22-75	6	4	2.70	64	0	0	4	63	56	29	19	6	29	64	.236	.209	.262	9.09	4.12
Speier, Justin	R-R	6-4	205	11-6-73	2	8	5.03	62	0	0	0	68	69	41	38	15	27	56	.261	.288	.240	7.41	3.57
Thompson, Rich	R-R	6-1	180	7-1-84	0	0	22.50	2	0	0	0	2	4	5	5	0	2	1	.400	.400	.400	4.50	9.00
Weaver, Jered	R-R	6-7	205	10-4-82	11	10	4.33	30	30	0	0	177	173	88	85	20	54	152	.254	.243	.266	7.74	2.75

Fielding

Catcher	PCT	G	PO	A	E	DP	PB
Budde	1.000	7	13	2	0	0	0
Mathis	.981	94	624	57	13	5	3
Napoli	.994	75	469	21	3	3	7
Wilson	1.000	7	15	1	0	0	0

Catcher	PCT	G	PO	A	E	DP	PB
Morales	1.000	6	30	3	0	7	
Quinlan	1.000	22	105	11	0	11	
Rivera	1.000	1	5	0	0	0	
Sandoval	—	1	0	0	0	0	
Teixeira	.994	51	431	34	3	45	

Catcher	PCT	G	PO	A	E	DP	PB
Brown	1.000	1	1	1	0	0	
Figgins	1.000	9	10	19	0	4	
Izturis	.982	23	49	61	2	15	
Kendrick	.991	92	155	287	4	67	
Rivera	—	1	0	0	0	0	
Rodriguez	.991	51	97	127	2	36	

First Base	PCT	G	PO	A	E	DP
Kotchman	.998	100	838	73	2	86

Second Base	PCT	G	PO	A	E	DP
Aybar	1.000	2	0	1	0	0

Third Base	PCT	G	PO	A	E	DP
Brown	.846	10	3	8	2	2
Figgins	.978	105	84	185	6	15
Izturis	1.000	5	1	7	0	0
Quinlan	.946	39	22	48	4	8
Rodriguez	—	1	0	0	0	0
Sandoval	1.000	1	0	3	0	0
Wood	.967	32	18	40	2	3

Shortstop	PCT	G	PO	A	E	DP
Aybar	.959	96	140	276	18	63
Izturis	.991	52	69	147	2	31
Rodriguez	1.000	4	5	12	0	2
Wood	.979	28	42	50	2	19

Outfield	PCT	G	PO	A	E	DP
Anderson	1.000	82	144	9	0	2

	PCT	G	PO	A	E	DP
Guerrero	.979	99	180	8	4	1
Hunter	1.000	137	350	4	0	0
Matthews Jr.	.963	106	200	6	8	0
Morales	1.000	12	19	0	0	0
Quinlan	1.000	6	2	0	0	0
Rivera	.966	59	81	4	3	1
Willits	1.000	57	46	0	0	0

SALT LAKE BEES   TRIPLE-A
PACIFIC COAST LEAGUE

Batting	B-T	HT	WT	DOB	AVG	vLH	vRH	G	AB	R	H	2B	3B	HR	RBI	BB	HBP	SH	SF	SO	SB	CS	SLG	OBP
Brown, Dee	L-R	6-0	235	3-27-78	.264	.230	.279	130	485	70	128	32	0	12	74	61	6	0	6	66	10	2	.404	.349
Brown, Matt	R-R	6-0	200	8-8-82	.320	.339	.312	97	400	75	128	33	4	21	67	32	3	0	2	80	4	2	.580	.373
Budde, Ryan	R-R	5-11	210	8-15-79	.202	.167	.218	48	173	16	35	8	2	2	23	10	3	0	0	47	3	0	.306	.258
Coon, Brad	L-L	6-0	175	12-11-82	.306	.378	.276	85	337	73	103	9	2	4	30	47	10	2	0	52	17	10	.380	.406
Czarniecki, Jordan	R-R	6-1	175	10-4-80	.252	.200	.264	32	111	13	28	5	2	3	10	6	3	3	0	19	1	0	.414	.308
Duff, Tim	R-R	6-2	210	6-26-81	.196	.231	.172	30	97	9	19	4	0	0	8	6	1	0	0	25	0	0	.237	.250
Evans, Terry	R-R	6-3	205	1-19-82	.270	.305	.252	46	174	31	47	12	0	4	21	20	2	0	4	60	6	5	.408	.345
Figgins, Chone	B-R	5-8	180	1-22-78	.200	.000	.250	3	10	2	2	0	0	0	2	0	0	0	0	3	0	0	.200	.333
Infante, Larry	L-R	5-10	160	4-4-85	.100	.000	.125	3	10	0	1	0	0	0	1	0	0	0	0	2	0	0	.100	.100
Johnson, Ben	R-R	5-11	195	10-17-81	.225	.308	.207	22	71	9	16	2	0	3	13	1	1	0	1	7	0	0	.380	.243
Kendrickk, Howie	R-R	5-10	200	7-12-83	.200	.200	—	2	5	0	1	0	0	0	1	0	0	0	0	1	0	0	.200	.200
Morales, Kendry	B-R	6-1	225	6-20-83	.341	.314	.353	78	317	46	108	19	0	15	64	19	1	0	3	43	1	3	.543	.376
Morrissey, Adam	R-R	5-11	170	6-8-81	.299	.229	.333	32	107	14	32	7	0	5	15	10	0	0	3	21	0	0	.505	.359
Patchett, Gary	R-R	6-2	180	9-25-78	.239	.271	.220	95	318	30	76	11	2	4	35	29	4	8	3	81	2	3	.324	.308
Pavkovich, Adam	R-R	6-2	185	12-31-81	.280	.246	.295	121	450	76	126	25	4	22	80	38	5	3	4	107	8	3	.500	.340
Rodriguez, Sean	R-R	6-1	215	4-26-85	.306	.344	.294	66	248	68	76	19	1	21	52	29	9	2	1	45	4	1	.645	.397
Rosario, Alberto	R-R	6-0	165	1-10-87	.333	—	.333	1	3	1	1	0	0	0	0	0	0	0	0	0	0	0	.333	.333
Sandoval, Freddy	B-R	6-1	200	8-16-82	.335	.319	.343	131	525	92	176	45	2	15	88	47	4	4	7	74	6	3	.514	.389
Smith, Coby	R-R	6-0	200	9-21-80	.195	.184	.203	42	123	12	24	3	1	0	8	13	3	1	1	21	3	1	.236	.286
Smith, Corey	R-R	6-1	200	4-15-82	.174	.000	.182	7	23	1	4	0	0	1	2	2	0	0	0	8	0	0	.304	.240
Thomas, Derrick	L-R	6-0	210	9-10-82	.000	—	.000	1	1	0	0	0	0	0	0	0	0	0	0	0	0	0	.000	.000
Walker, Chris	B-R	5-8	170	7-3-80	.257	.314	.229	78	319	45	82	11	6	1	27	17	1	5	3	58	14	10	.339	.294
Willits, Reggie	B-R	5-11	185	5-30-81	.378	.556	.321	10	37	7	14	2	1	0	4	4	0	0	1	6	1	1	.486	.452
Wilson, Bobby	R-R	6-0	220	4-8-83	.312	.257	.332	72	260	33	81	20	0	4	45	29	4	3	2	45	0	0	.435	.386
Wipke, Flint	R-R	6-0	195	1-22-83	.077	.143	.000	5	13	3	1	0	0	0	0	2	0	0	0	7	1	0	.077	.200
Wood, Brandon	R-R	6-3	190	3-2-85	.296	.230	.323	103	395	82	117	21	2	31	84	45	6	0	2	104	6	5	.595	.375

Pitching	B-T	HT	WT	DOB	W	L	ERA	G	GS	CG	SV	IP	H	R	ER	HR	BB	SO	AVG	vLH	vRH	K/9	BB/9
Adenhart, Nick	R-R	6-3	185	8-24-86	9	13	5.76	26	26	0	0	145	173	99	93	15	75	110	.306	.296	.314	6.81	4.64
Albano, Marco	R-R	5-11	215	8-26-83	0	0	0.00	1	0	0	0	1	1	0	0	0	1	1	.250	.500	.000	9.00	9.00
Alvarado, Carlo	R-R	6-4	210	1-24-78	7	5	4.27	26	23	1	0	131	123	69	62	14	64	131	.245	.273	.217	9.02	4.41
Armstrong, Chris	L-L	5-10	195	2-10-88	1	0	5.06	5	0	0	0	5	4	3	3	1	4	1	.211	.250	.200	1.69	6.75
Arredondo, Jose	R-R	6-0	175	3-30-84	1	1	2.12	15	0	0	0	17	12	10	4	4	4	15	.203	.240	.176	7.94	2.12
Austen, David	R-R	6-1	185	5-21-81	1	8	8.04	10	4	0	0	28	41	27	25	4	9	19	.342	.279	.407	6.11	2.89
Bonilla, Henry	R-R	6-0	190	8-16-78	5	2	4.67	51	1	0	3	71	70	45	37	11	33	64	.255	.238	.269	8.07	4.16
Bootcheck, Chris	R-R	6-5	210	10-24-78	0	0	2.86	19	0	0	1	28	29	12	9	2	17	34	.250	.245	.254	10.80	5.40
Bulger, Jason	R-R	6-4	210	12-6-78	0	0	0.63	37	0	0	16	43	25	3	3	0	22	75	.169	.149	.185	15.70	4.60
Davidson, Daniel	L-L	6-4	225	1-8-81	0	0	2.35	4	0	0	0	8	7	2	2	1	0	2	.250	.200	.278	2.35	0.00
Dinga, Milan	R-R	6-1	205	12-27-84	0	0	0.00	1	0	0	0	1	1	0	0	1	1	1	.250	.000	.333	9.00	9.00
Green, Nick	R-R	6-4	200	8-20-84	8	8	5.32	28	28	0	0	159	186	101	94	31	44	112	.292	.309	.279	6.34	2.49
Jepsen, Kevin	R-R	6-3	215	7-26-84	1	3	2.35	15	0	0	2	23	17	9	6	3	12	21	.213	.226	.204	8.22	4.70
Kennard, Jeff	R-R	6-2	195	7-26-81	4	3	6.55	42	0	0	0	56	72	50	41	11	28	38	.306	.325	.288	6.07	4.47
Loux, Shane	R-R	6-2	235	8-31-79	12	6	3.98	22	22	1	0	138	154	69	61	14	40	77	.283	.269	.292	5.02	2.61
Moseley, Dustin	R-R	6-4	215	12-26-81	7	10	6.94	20	20	0	0	117	150	93	90	23	34	83	.314	.325	.307	6.40	2.62
O'Day, Darren	R-R	6-4	225	10-22-82	2	2	3.27	21	0	0	7	33	29	13	12	3	7	30	.244	.271	.225	8.18	1.91
Olenberger, Kasey	R-R	6-4	235	3-18-78	4	6	4.81	36	13	0	0	116	118	69	62	18	53	81	.263	.277	.249	6.28	4.11
Ortega, Anthony	R-R	6-0	170	8-24-85	5	0	2.52	6	6	0	0	39	46	14	11	2	6	22	.282	.267	.299	5.03	1.37
Rodriguez, Rafael	R-R	6-1	175	9-24-84	2	0	6.28	9	0	0	0	14	20	12	10	2	6	8	.351	.333	.375	5.02	3.77
Serrano, Alex	R-R	6-1	200	2-18-81	2	0	6.50	14	0	0	0	18	26	13	13	7	5	12	.342	.278	.400	6.00	2.50
Shields, Scot	R-R	6-1	180	7-22-75	0	0	0.00	1	0	0	0	1	2	0	0	0	0	3	.400	.333	.500	27.00	0.00
Thompson, Rich	R-R	6-1	180	7-1-84	1	0	4.05	10	0	0	0	13	12	6	6	1	9	11	.240	.324	.063	7.43	6.07
Wilhite, Matt	R-R	6-1	185	7-3-81	7	0	4.71	47	0	0	0	63	75	37	33	9	16	58	.299	.360	.258	8.29	2.29

Fielding

Catcher	PCT	G	PO	A	E	DP	PB
Budde	.976	38	260	25	7	1	2
Duff	.979	30	204	26	5	0	7
Johnson	1.000	18	121	8	0	1	3
Rosario	1.000	1	5	0	0	0	0
Wilson	.995	62	401	41	2	6	1
Wipke	1.000	5	27	3	0	0	0

First Base	PCT	G	PO	A	E	DP
M. Brown	.985	40	354	29	6	28
Budde	.979	10	86	8	2	6
Johnson	1.000	2	19	0	0	2
Morales	.995	62	514	32	3	51
Sandoval	.980	24	187	12	4	29
Corey Smith	1.000	4	30	2	0	1
Wilson	1.000	8	77	6	0	6

Second Base	PCT	G	PO	A	E	DP
Kendrick	1.000	2	0	4	0	0
Morrissey	.977	11	18	25	1	7
Patchett	.981	48	72	140	4	37
Pavkovich	.975	15	27	50	2	7
Rodriguez	.984	55	88	165	4	38
Sandoval	.962	20	30	46	3	13

Third Base	PCT	G	PO	A	E	DP
M. Brown	.920	33	28	64	8	9
Figgins	1.000	3	0	7	0	0
Infante	.889	3	6	2	1	0
Morrissey	.909	9	2	8	1	0
Pavkovich	.906	13	9	20	3	1
Sandoval	.946	77	47	164	12	15
Wood	.902	14	11	26	4	5

Shortstop	PCT	G	PO	A	E	DP
Patchett	.985	47	51	149	3	28
Rodriguez	1.000	8	10	13	0	4
Wood	.957	90	140	213	16	57
Outfield	**PCT**	**G**	**PO**	**A**	**E**	**DP**
D. Brown	.990	52	97	1	1	0
Coon	.991	85	216	3	2	0
Czarniecki	1.000	31	47	2	0	1

	PCT	G	PO	A	E	DP
Evans	.972	43	64	6	2	1
Morales	1.000	8	8	0	0	0
Pavkovich	.970	94	180	11	6	4
Rodriguez	1.000	3	9	0	0	0
Sandoval	.667	1	2	0	1	0
Coby Smith	.975	37	78	1	2	0
Walker	.994	77	175	4	1	1
Willits	1.000	9	24	0	0	0

ARKANSAS TRAVELERS

DOUBLE-A

TEXAS LEAGUE

Batting	B-T	HT	WT	DOB	AVG	vLH	vRH	G	AB	R	H	2B	3B	HR	RBI	BB	HBP	SH	SF	SO	SB	CS	SLG	OBP
Collins, Michael	R-R	6-3	213	7-18-84	.264	.311	.254	67	250	45	66	18	2	5	37	15	21	2	5	37	8	5	.412	.351
Czarniecki, Jordan	R-R	6-1	175	10-4-80	.284	.370	.263	76	282	43	80	18	3	6	27	39	5	0	1	44	10	10	.433	.379
De Los Santos, Anel	R-R	6-0	190	6-19-88	.280	.000	.333	7	25	3	7	3	0	0	1	0	0	0	0	8	1	0	.400	.280
Duff, Tim	R-R	6-2	210	6-26-81	.217	.320	.195	41	138	8	30	4	0	2	14	10	2	1	2	40	3	1	.290	.276
Fuller, Cody	R-R	6-0	190	9-19-82	.205	.163	.220	54	166	17	34	5	1	4	11	7	3	5	2	28	3	5	.319	.247
Greenberg, Adam	L-R	5-9	180	2-21-81	.271	.182	.295	70	262	47	71	8	3	2	15	32	5	4	0	55	16	7	.347	.361
Hoorelbeke, Jesse	R-R	6-2	263	10-13-77	.154	.000	.167	4	13	1	2	0	0	0	1	2	0	0	0	6	1	0	.154	.267
Johnson, Ben	B-R	5-11	195	10-17-81	.262	.276	.258	106	409	55	107	19	1	20	77	17	16	1	6	80	6	5	.460	.313
Leahy, Ryan	R-R	5-10	180	7-8-81	.172	.178	.169	52	169	14	29	4	0	0	10	6	1	7	1	22	1	0	.195	.203
Morrissey, Adam	R-R	5-11	170	6-8-81	.280	.322	.269	78	286	28	80	15	0	9	34	23	5	1	3	72	2	2	.437	.341
Ortiz, Wilberto	R-R	5-10	180	1-30-85	.264	.154	.284	67	254	26	67	11	0	3	24	15	4	4	3	38	4	1	.343	.312
Peel, Aaron	R-R	6-1	190	2-8-83	.278	.000	.294	7	18	2	5	0	0	1	3	6	1	0	0	3	1	0	.444	.480
Pettit, Chris	R-R	6-0	190	8-15-84	.248	.174	.267	61	222	27	55	12	2	6	26	16	8	4	1	39	5	2	.401	.320
Remole, Clifton	L-L	6-0	205	10-24-82	.202	.000	.215	28	84	8	17	4	1	0	4	5	0	2	0	9	1	0	.274	.247
Renz, Jordan	R-R	6-3	225	7-21-83	.273	—	.273	3	11	1	3	1	0	0	2	0	0	0	0	4	0	0	.364	.333
Rosario, Anderson	R-R	6-0	170	3-2-85	.233	.250	.231	13	30	4	7	1	1	1	2	2	0	0	0	14	1	1	.433	.281
Smith, Coby	R-R	6-0	190	9-21-80	.275	.137	.321	61	207	31	57	12	1	2	16	23	7	7	2	31	11	4	.372	.364
Smith, Corey	R-R	6-1	200	4-15-82	.271	.276	.270	128	495	58	134	31	1	26	80	28	10	0	2	96	15	7	.495	.321
Statia, Hainley	B-R	5-10	160	1-19-86	.242	.250	.240	59	223	26	54	12	3	1	20	14	1	12	2	17	8	4	.336	.288
Stavisky, Brian	L-R	6-2	210	7-6-80	.312	.345	.305	86	314	56	98	18	0	16	51	48	5	1	3	62	12	3	.522	.408
Sutton, Nate	L-R	6-0	195	9-1-82	.276	.288	.274	118	453	58	125	12	6	7	44	27	2	6	3	68	19	10	.375	.318
Toussaint, Drew	R-R	6-2	175	10-24-82	.222	.391	.184	33	126	15	28	1	2	4	13	2	4	1	0	42	0	1	.357	.258
Trumbo, Mark	R-R	6-4	220	1-16-86	.276	.143	.316	32	123	13	34	7	1	6	25	7	0	2	2	29	1	2	.496	.311
Walker, Brian	L-R	6-0	215	7-17-85	.182	.091	.190	41	148	12	27	6	0	4	14	6	1	0	2	38	0	2	.304	.217
Wipke, Flint	R-R	6-0	195	1-22-83	.278	.364	.240	11	36	3	10	3	0	3	5	2	0	0	0	14	2	1	.611	.316

Pitching	B-T	HT	WT	DOB	W	L	ERA	G	GS	CG	SV	IP	H	R	ER	HR	BB	SO	AVG	vLH	vRH	K/9	BB/9
Albano, Marco	R-R	5-11	215	8-26-83	1	1	4.05	7	0	0	0	7	8	3	3	1	4	6	.296	.364	.250	8.10	5.40
Aldridge, Ryan	R-R	6-2	200	9-10-83	2	0	3.18	17	0	0	5	17	18	6	6	1	6	20	.273	.308	.250	10.59	3.18
Austen, David	R-R	6-1	185	5-21-81	2	3	4.50	10	6	0	0	42	52	23	21	5	4	20	.302	.222	.360	4.29	0.86
Brandt, Doug	L-L	6-0	205	10-23-84	2	4	6.30	42	1	0	0	60	71	52	42	10	34	54	.290	.250	.312	8.10	5.10
Browning, Barret	L-L	6-1	175	12-28-84	1	1	5.97	27	0	0	1	32	31	21	21	2	14	34	.263	.273	.257	9.66	3.98
Butcher, Brok	R-R	6-1	180	10-13-83	5	5	6.00	17	17	0	0	96	122	74	64	14	33	57	.314	.344	.298	5.34	3.09
Cook, Aaron	R-R	6-5	175	10-20-83	0	0	5.84	8	0	0	0	12	20	8	8	0	5	10	.377	.350	.394	7.30	3.65
Davidson, Daniel	L-L	6-4	225	1-8-81	1	0	2.93	20	6	0	0	46	35	15	15	3	15	44	.213	.173	.232	8.61	2.93
Denham, Dan	R-R	6-2	190	12-24-82	9	10	4.44	25	25	0	0	146	157	82	72	16	58	99	.279	.325	.254	6.10	3.58
Diaz, Amalio	R-R	6-2	170	9-10-86	3	4	4.40	10	10	0	0	57	62	31	28	5	27	38	.281	.347	.228	5.97	4.24
Edwards, Bill	R-R	6-3	185	3-26-81	0	2	4.62	19	1	0	0	39	40	24	20	4	28	32	.268	.250	.278	7.38	6.46
Ibanez, Yosandy	R-R	6-1	195	3-4-82	0	0	5.28	8	0	0	0	15	16	9	9	0	13	14	.271	.211	.300	8.22	7.63
Jepsen, Kevin	R-R	6-3	215	7-26-84	2	1	1.42	25	0	0	11	32	22	5	5	0	18	35	.198	.200	.198	9.95	5.12
Kennard, Jeff	R-R	6-2	195	7-26-81	0	1	3.86	5	0	0	0	7	9	3	3	0	4	6	.321	.300	.333	7.71	5.14
Marek, Stephen	L-R	6-2	200	9-3-83	2	6	3.66	34	0	0	3	47	39	20	19	2	21	57	.223	.250	.211	10.99	4.05
Mosebach, Robert	R-R	6-4	195	9-14-84	9	12	4.62	29	29	2	0	177	209	106	91	6	69	88	.305	.318	.298	4.47	3.50
Ortega, Anthony	R-R	6-0	170	8-24-85	9	7	3.73	22	22	1	0	135	124	65	56	11	49	83	.247	.275	.234	5.53	3.27
Rodriguez, Fernando	R-R	6-2	210	6-18-84	7	11	5.53	33	22	1	0	137	153	96	84	10	62	85	.289	.320	.272	5.60	4.08
Rodriguez, Francisco	R-R	6-1	195	2-26-83	5	5	3.82	50	0	0	2	75	76	41	32	9	33	69	.262	.207	.286	8.24	3.94
Rodriguez, Rafael	R-R	6-1	175	9-24-84	2	4	1.86	42	0	0	11	53	46	11	11	3	11	48	.237	.203	.256	8.10	1.86
Smith, Jesse	R-R	6-2	214	7-11-80	0	1	16.88	1	1	0	0	3	5	5	5	1	0	3	.385	.500	.333	10.13	0.00
Stertzbach, Von	R-R	6-2	190	5-15-81	0	0	6.48	4	0	0	0	8	9	6	6	0	6	5	.273	.286	.263	10.80	5.40

Fielding

Catcher	PCT	G	PO	A	E	DP	PB
De Los Santos	.974	7	32	6	1	0	3
Duff	.994	39	272	38	2	1	5
Johnson	.984	61	384	50	7	9	6
Walker	.990	29	180	18	2	2	0
Wipke	.987	11	64	11	1	1	3

First Base	PCT	G	PO	A	E	DP
Collins	.990	64	585	32	6	61
Hoorelbeke	1.000	1	9	0	0	0
Johnson	.987	17	139	11	2	11
Morrissey	1.000	3	31	4	0	3

	PCT	G	PO	A	E	DP
Remole	1.000	1	6	1	0	1
Corey Smith	.980	20	189	12	4	26
Stavisky	.987	8	71	6	1	4
Trumbo	.993	28	259	21	2	32

Second Base	PCT	G	PO	A	E	DP
Leahy	.974	20	47	64	3	20
Morrissey	.971	22	34	66	3	8
Sutton	.974	102	184	306	13	72

Third Base	PCT	G	PO	A	E	DP
Leahy	1.000	3	1	10	0	0
Morrissey	.968	38	18	74	3	8

	PCT	G	PO	A	E	DP
Ortiz	.857	10	8	16	4	4
Corey Smith	.920	90	53	199	22	18

Shortstop	PCT	G	PO	A	E	DP
Leahy	.976	30	38	83	3	18
Ortiz	.955	57	101	178	13	40
Statia	.976	59	99	189	7	38
Sutton	1.000	1	0	1	0	1

Outfield	PCT	G	PO	A	E	DP
Czarniecki	.988	75	155	4	2	0
Fuller	.992	53	112	6	1	1
Greenberg	.995	69	190	6	1	2

Johnson	1.000	14	23	3	0	0	Remole	1.000	27	29	2	0	0
Morrissey	.875	4	7	0	1	0	Renz	1.000	3	7	0	0	0
Peel	1.000	4	8	0	0	0	Rosario	.955	12	19	2	1	0
Pettit	.982	56	104	5	2	0	Coby Smith	.991	61	99	6	1	3

Stavisky	.984	39	56	5	1	0
Sutton	1.000	1	4	0	0	0
Toussaint	.962	24	48	3	2	1

RANCHO CUCAMONGA QUAKES　　　　　　　　　　　HIGH CLASS A

CALIFORNIA LEAGUE

Batting	B-T	HT	WT	DOB	AVG	vLH	vRH	G	AB	R	H	2B	3B	HR	RBI	BB	HBP	SH	SF	SO	SB	CS	SLG	OBP
Aybar, Erick	B-T	5-10	170	1-14-84	.400	.500	.333	3	10	2	4	1	0	0	3	0	0	0	0	2	0	0	.500	.400
Bourjos, Peter	R-R	6-1	175	3-31-87	.295	.276	.301	121	509	83	150	29	10	9	51	19	7	5	5	96	50	10	.444	.326
Bressoud, C.J.	R-R	6-2	200	5-12-85	.188	.222	.174	16	32	3	6	0	0	0	6	6	1	3	0	7	0	0	.188	.333
Brewer, Tadd	R-R	6-1	190	5-4-84	.173	.045	.220	25	81	8	14	2	1	1	7	5	0	4	0	19	0	1	.259	.221
Colmenares, Carlos	B-R	6-0	175	2-11-86	.100	.500	.000	5	10	2	1	0	0	0	0	2	1	0	0	0	0	0	.100	.308
Conger, Hank	B-R	6-0	205	1-29-88	.303	.250	.317	73	294	47	89	20	2	13	75	14	3	0	7	55	2	1	.517	.333
Fuller, Cody	B-R	6-0	190	9-19-82	.178	.273	.147	16	45	4	8	2	2	0	0	0	2	2	0	18	1	0	.311	.213
Infante, Larry	L-R	5-10	160	4-4-85	.274	.320	.259	111	390	45	107	24	0	2	38	31	4	7	2	79	10	6	.351	.333
Izturis, Maicer	B-R	5-8	170	9-12-80	.500	.500	—	1	2	0	1	0	0	0	0	0	0	0	0	1	0	0	.500	.500
Kendrick, Howie	R-R	5-10	200	7-12-83	.833	—	.833	2	6	3	5	0	0	2	0	0	0	0	0	0	0	1	.833	.833
Kiniry, Rian	L-R	5-10	160	12-12-86	.191	.231	.175	31	89	13	17	1	2	1	4	9	2	2	0	25	9	1	.281	.280
Mount, Ryan	L-R	6-0	175	8-17-86	.290	.312	.284	82	338	68	98	17	5	16	49	23	3	1	4	67	10	2	.512	.337
Napoli, Mike	R-R	6-0	215	10-31-81	.571	.667	.545	5	14	3	8	3	0	1	4	2	0	0	1	2	0	0	1.000	.588
Navarro, Efren	L-L	6-0	200	5-14-86	.349	.290	.367	35	129	13	45	9	0	2	18	19	0	0	2	20	0	3	.465	.427
Nieves, Abel	R-R	5-11	175	8-14-85	.318	.340	.309	101	336	46	107	24	2	4	54	53	0	4	2	74	4	3	.438	.409
Norman, Anthony	R-R	6-0	185	10-20-84	.257	.266	.254	118	374	77	96	16	9	15	44	66	10	5	1	76	36	6	.468	.381
Ortiz, Wilberto	R-R	5-10	180	1-30-85	.268	.274	.266	60	231	29	62	15	2	2	29	12	2	1	3	34	10	3	.377	.306
Perez, Darwin	B-R	5-10	160	7-27-89	.571	1.000	.250	4	7	2	4	3	0	0	1	1	0	1	0	1	0	0	1.000	.625
Phillips, P.J.	R-R	6-3	170	9-23-86	.276	.310	.265	130	485	68	134	22	11	8	55	24	4	3	5	125	35	9	.416	.313
Remole, Clifton	L-L	6-0	205	10-24-82	.203	.125	.222	22	79	5	16	3	1	0	7	4	0	0	2	5	0	2	.266	.235
Renz, Jordan	R-R	6-3	225	7-21-83	.250	1.000	.000	2	8	2	2	1	0	0	0	1	0	0	0	4	0	0	.375	.333
Rosario, Alberto	R-R	6-0	165	1-10-87	.218	.132	.256	42	124	11	27	5	0	0	16	8	0	0	2	18	3	1	.258	.261
Rosario, Anderson	R-R	6-0	170	3-2-85	.152	.200	.133	64	145	14	22	4	0	2	10	12	2	4	1	65	2	4	.221	.225
Rosenbaum, Chris	R-R	6-1	205	4-2-84	.000	—	.000	1	1	0	0	0	0	0	0	0	0	0	0	1	0	0	.000	.000
Toussaint, Drew	R-R	6-2	175	10-24-82	.324	.357	.313	84	324	44	105	14	6	13	58	13	6	2	4	65	6	6	.525	.357
Trumbo, Mark	R-R	6-4	220	1-16-86	.283	.275	.285	103	407	70	115	28	2	26	68	26	3	0	2	67	7	3	.553	.329
Villaescusa, Ivan	R-R	6-0	200	10-13-86	.000	.000	.000	4	8	1	0	0	0	0	1	0	0	0	0	2	0	0	.000	.111
Walker, Brian	L-R	6-0	215	7-17-85	.263	.343	.243	52	179	19	47	9	0	8	26	12	0	2	2	55	1	2	.447	.306
Willits, Reggie	B-R	5-11	185	5-30-81	.357	.333	.375	4	14	4	5	0	0	0	2	0	0	0	1	2	0	0	.357	.438
Wipke, Flint	R-R	6-0	195	1-22-83	.253	.324	.229	41	146	17	37	12	0	4	24	14	1	2	0	59	1	1	.418	.323

Pitching	B-T	HT	WT	DOB	W	L	ERA	G	GS	CG	SV	IP	H	R	ER	HR	BB	SO	AVG	vLH	vRH	K/9	BB/9
Albano, Marco	R-R	5-11	215	8-26-83	3	3	6.63	35	0	0	0	54	58	46	40	6	28	49	.279	.327	.234	8.12	4.64
Aldridge, Ryan	R-R	6-2	210	9-10-83	0	0	0.00	10	0	0	0	5	9	4	0	0	2	11	.125	.118	.133	10.61	1.93
Anton, Mike	L-L	6-0	195	4-3-85	6	5	5.51	15	15	0	0	82	101	53	50	8	34	58	.312	.298	.317	6.39	3.75
Arredondo, Felipe	R-R	6-4	225	10-4-86	1	2	8.04	21	0	0	0	31	42	29	28	4	9	22	.321	.341	.286	6.32	2.59
Bell, Trevor	L-R	6-2	180	10-12-86	6	8	4.22	36	12	2	0	100	106	60	47	8	39	80	.274	.285	.262	7.18	3.50
Bootcheck, Chris	R-R	6-5	210	10-24-78	1	0	4.66	6	0	0	0	10	9	7	5	0	6	10	.257	.320	.100	9.31	5.59
Brasier, Ryan	R-R	6-0	190	8-26-87	0	0	2.70	3	0	0	0	3	3	1	1	0	2	0	.300	.250	.333	0.00	5.40
Browning, Barret	L-L	6-1	175	12-28-84	2	1	4.01	30	0	0	6	34	35	16	15	2	16	39	.271	.203	.350	10.43	4.28
Cassevah, Bobby	R-R	6-3	195	9-11-85	2	3	3.79	44	0	0	1	71	67	33	30	1	40	52	.250	.244	.256	6.56	5.05
Chambers, Brian	R-R	6-2	202	8-14-85	1	4	6.53	21	0	0	0	30	37	25	22	1	19	18	.303	.304	.303	5.34	5.64
Cook, Aaron	R-R	6-5	175	10-20-83	2	0	3.49	23	0	0	3	28	34	15	11	0	15	17	.304	.276	.333	5.40	4.76
Diaz, Amalio	R-R	6-2	170	9-10-86	7	4	4.28	17	17	0	0	103	111	55	49	10	26	65	.275	.290	.258	5.68	2.27
Escobar, Kelvim	R-R	6-1	230	4-11-76	0	0	0.00	1	1	0	0	3	1	0	0	0	3	1	.100	.150	.000	12.00	0.00
Ford, A.J.	R-R	6-1	195	10-27-84	1	1	3.38	15	0	0	0	27	20	11	10	0	15	20	.206	.244	.179	6.75	5.06
Haynes, Jeremy	R-R	6-2	180	5-28-86	1	2	10.03	6	6	0	0	23	37	28	26	7	23	8	.370	.404	.340	3.09	8.87
Herndon, David	R-R	6-3	230	9-4-85	3	7	5.01	43	12	0	17	101	120	58	56	10	16	70	.301	.326	.271	6.26	1.43
Incinelli, Jared	R-R	6-4	200	4-12-83	0	0	5.60	8	0	0	0	18	14	12	11	2	9	17	.230	.286	.182	8.66	4.58
Lackey, John	R-R	6-6	245	10-23-78	0	0	4.00	3	3	0	0	9	8	4	4	1	2	11	.229	.364	.000	11.00	2.00
Leon, Sammy	R-R	6-0	160	5-19-85	1	2	7.97	15	2	0	1	20	29	22	18	3	18	23	.333	.366	.304	10.18	7.97
McRobbie, Alex	R-R	6-2	185	1-16-83	0	0	36.00	1	0	0	0	1	4	4	4	0	1	1	.571	.500	.600	9.00	9.00
Mendoza, Tommy	R-R	6-2	195	8-18-87	4	12	4.73	20	19	0	0	110	130	69	58	11	39	50	.298	.313	.279	4.08	3.18
Moseley, Dustin	R-R	6-4	215	12-26-81	0	0	0.00	1	1	0	0	4	3	0	0	0	2	6	.214	.167	.500	14.73	4.91
O'Sullivan, Sean	R-R	6-2	200	9-1-87	16	8	4.73	28	25	1	0	158	167	94	83	8	50	111	.268	.269	.267	6.32	2.85
Perez, Jose	R-R	6-2	180	9-14-87	0	0	0.00	1	1	0	0	4	1	0	0	0	0	3	.154	.000	.333	2.25	6.75
Pugliese, Nick	R-R	6-1	205	9-18-85	0	0	2.25	2	0	0	0	4	2	1	1	0	2	1	.143	.222	.000	4.50	0.00
Rembisz, Bryan	R-R	5-8	165	8-16-85	1	3	3.44	21	1	0	2	37	34	16	14	3	5	26	.245	.227	.260	6.38	1.23
Shearer, Kelly	L-L	6-3	200	4-8-85	0	2	6.35	7	0	0	0	11	12	9	8	2	11	10	.267	.182	.348	7.94	8.74
Torres, Alexander	L-L	5-10	160	12-8-87	3	2	3.91	10	10	0	0	53	52	26	23	1	29	62	.264	.339	.232	10.53	4.92
Towns, Jordan	R-R	6-2	220	9-21-85	1	5	6.12	16	7	0	0	43	55	38	29	5	17	34	.306	.269	.333	7.17	3.59
Walden, Jordan	R-R	6-5	220	11-16-87	5	2	4.04	9	9	0	0	49	42	30	22	4	24	50	.226	.283	.170	9.18	4.41

Fielding

Catcher	PCT	G	PO	A	E	DP	PB
Bressoud	.935	14	53	5	4	0	7
Conger	.986	10	66	2	1	0	0
Napoli	1.000	4	27	6	0	0	0
Al. Rosario	.989	41	248	26	3	0	4
Rosenbaum	1.000	1	3	0	0	1	1
Villaescusa	.944	3	14	3	1	0	1
Walker	.984	44	274	30	5	5	8
Wipke	.990	39	246	45	3	3	8

First Base	PCT	G	PO	A	E	DP
Navarro	1.000	34	324	33	0	21
Nieves	.965	10	78	4	3	7
Remole	1.000	2	17	2	0	2
Trumbo	.980	96	933	67	20	89

Second Base	PCT	G	PO	A	E	DP
Brewer	.965	16	19	36	2	6
Colmenares	1.000	2	1	7	0	1
Izturis	—	1	0	0	0	0
Kendrick	.857	2	3	3	1	1
Mount	.965	80	123	236	13	46
Nieves	.975	8	13	26	1	7
Ortiz	.994	37	53	110	1	25

Third Base	PCT	G	PO	A	E	DP
Brewer	.880	7	10	12	3	3
Colmenares	—	1	0	0	0	0
Infante	.965	91	62	186	9	20
Nieves	.968	41	20	70	3	3
Ortiz	.917	11	5	17	2	0

Shortstop	PCT	G	PO	A	E	DP
Aybar	1.000	3	6	3	0	2
Infante	.938	9	13	32	3	5
Ortiz	.971	9	6	27	1	4
Perez	.933	3	4	10	1	0
Phillips	.941	125	216	375	37	75

Outfield	PCT	G	PO	A	E	DP
Bourjos	.978	119	252	11	6	1
Colmenares	.000	1	0	0	1	0
Fuller	1.000	14	19	1	0	0
Infante	1.000	10	11	1	0	0
Kiniry	.959	27	45	2	2	0
Norman	.964	113	208	6	8	0
Ortiz	—	1	0	0	0	0
Phillips	.000	1	0	0	1	0
Remole	1.000	19	21	3	0	0
Renz	1.000	2	4	0	0	0
An. Rosario	.944	63	79	5	5	1
Toussaint	.966	78	137	5	5	1
Willits	1.000	3	6	0	0	0

CEDAR RAPIDS KERNELS
LOW CLASS A

MIDWEST LEAGUE

Batting	B-T	HT	WT	DOB	AVG	vLH	vRH	G	AB	R	H	2B	3B	HR	RBI	BB	HBP	SH	SF	SO	SB	CS	SLG	OBP
Amarista, Alexia	B-R	5-8	150	4-6-89	.000	—	.000	1	2	0	0	0	0	0	0	0	0	0	0	1	0	0	.000	.000
Bressoud, C.J.	R-R	6-2	200	5-12-85	.080	.000	.087	9	25	1	2	0	0	0	2	2	0	0	0	5	0	0	.080	.148
Brossman, Jay	R-R	6-2	210	1-17-85	.239	.305	.214	127	465	67	111	36	2	12	61	41	12	1	6	106	16	8	.402	.313
Castillo, Angel	R-R	6-3	190	6-7-89	.133	.000	.171	12	45	3	6	4	0	0	4	0	2	1	0	12	1	1	.222	.170
Collet, Cody	R-R	6-1	215	1-22-85	.091	.125	.071	9	22	0	2	0	0	0	3	5	0	0	2	9	0	1	.091	.241
Colmenares, Carlos	B-R	6-0	175	2-11-86	.213	.259	.194	32	89	16	19	3	0	2	12	13	4	0	2	24	7	2	.315	.333
Contreras, Ivan	R-R	5-9	155	1-3-87	.189	.208	.180	22	74	8	14	3	2	2	5	2	0	0	0	15	1	3	.365	.211
De Los Santos, Anel	R-R	6-0	190	6-19-88	.178	.234	.155	62	225	19	40	6	0	3	25	5	2	0	1	69	6	6	.244	.202
Estrella, Hector	R-R	5-11	175	12-22-84	.302	.323	.294	87	334	43	101	23	0	5	42	33	3	1	2	53	6	5	.416	.368
Fuller, Clay	B-R	6-2	190	6-17-87	.260	.301	.244	125	438	77	114	19	13	9	47	68	18	5	4	122	36	10	.425	.379
Giovanatto, Donato	R-R	6-1	195	10-20-84	.125	.250	.100	9	24	0	3	1	0	0	4	1	0	2	2	5	1	0	.167	.148
Golliner, David	R-R	6-2	205	3-18-86	.000	.000	.000	4	10	0	0	0	0	0	0	1	0	0	0	6	0	0	.000	.167
Gonzalez-Lopez, Jerry	R-R	5-9	175	10-30-85	.216	.197	.222	92	269	36	58	12	0	0	14	24	10	3	1	58	14	7	.260	.303
Gronkowski, Gordie	R-R	6-6	250	6-26-83	.219	.222	.218	56	201	18	44	12	4	2	18	18	2	1	1	61	3	3	.348	.288
Groth, Ryan	L-L	6-2	208	7-23-86	.224	.143	.250	20	85	11	19	3	2	3	10	3	1	0	0	22	4	4	.412	.258
Jacobo, Gabe	R-R	6-2	190	4-14-87	.320	.200	.376	34	125	15	40	12	1	3	24	2	3	0	3	25	5	0	.504	.338
Johnson, Tyler	R-R	6-2	220	11-2-85	.223	.269	.208	98	314	48	70	19	6	9	40	38	6	2	4	120	24	10	.408	.315
Moore, Jeremy	L-R	6-1	190	6-29-87	.240	.241	.240	96	362	47	87	11	12	17	48	21	2	2	2	125	28	10	.478	.284
Navarro, Efren	L-L	6-0	200	5-14-86	.269	.263	.271	94	331	37	89	18	0	2	45	42	4	2	6	66	7	7	.341	.352
Norman, Anthony	R-R	6-0	185	10-20-84	.333	.500	.000	1	3	0	1	0	0	0	0	0	1	0	0	0	0	0	.333	.333
Pardo, Braulio	B-R	5-11	180	10-10-86	.140	.000	.171	16	43	3	6	1	0	0	5	2	1	2	0	10	0	1	.163	.196
Perez, Julio	R-R	6-2	160	9-28-85	.267	.301	.253	111	412	54	110	27	2	15	75	17	6	4	4	101	23	10	.451	.303
Romine, Andrew	B-R	6-1	190	12-24-85	.260	.215	.281	126	461	79	120	21	4	2	34	55	9	12	6	76	62	18	.336	.347
Rosario, Alberto	R-R	6-0	165	1-10-87	.239	.400	.194	16	46	5	11	2	0	0	2	1	0	2	0	11	1	1	.283	.255
Rosenbaum, Chris	R-R	6-1	205	4-2-84	.248	.250	.247	36	109	12	27	7	0	0	10	7	4	0	0	16	1	0	.312	.317
Silversmith, Alex	R-R	6-2	210	10-22-85	.206	.200	.208	14	34	3	7	1	0	0	4	5	1	1	0	3	1	0	.235	.325

Pitching	B-T	HT	WT	DOB	W	L	ERA	G	GS	CG	SV	IP	H	R	ER	HR	BB	SO	AVG	vLH	vRH	K/9	BB/9
Anton, Mike	L-L	6-3	195	4-3-85	7	2	2.40	13	13	3	0	90	75	26	24	4	23	58	.234	.293	.208	5.80	2.30
Armstrong, Chris	L-L	5-10	195	2-10-88	0	4	7.85	29	0	0	0	29	42	26	25	3	27	24	.365	.268	.419	7.53	8.48
Bell, Trevor	L-R	6-2	180	10-12-86	1	0	2.12	3	2	1	0	17	13	4	4	0	4	13	.232	.208	.250	6.88	2.12
Brasier, Ryan	R-R	6-0	190	8-26-87	1	3	1.59	23	0	0	9	28	22	8	5	0	14	24	.210	.212	.208	7.62	4.45
Cabrera, Francis	R-R	6-1	184	5-27-87	1	1	3.07	11	0	0	0	15	5	6	5	0	14	17	.106	.158	.071	10.43	8.59
Calderon, Leonardo	L-L	5-11	170	7-31-86	3	0	1.59	19	0	0	1	34	19	6	6	2	16	39	.165	.146	.176	10.32	4.24
Carmona, Ismael	R-R	6-0	190	2-12-85	2	4	5.37	44	0	0	2	54	51	41	32	3	47	47	.244	.330	.165	7.88	7.88
Chambers, Brian	R-R	6-3	202	8-14-85	2	0	2.89	19	0	0	0	28	23	12	9	0	12	19	.228	.217	.236	6.11	3.86
Davitt, Michael	R-R	6-6	230	9-8-86	6	9	4.68	27	19	0	0	125	146	75	65	7	55	87	.305	.347	.270	6.26	3.96
Dinga, Milan	R-R	6-2	205	12-27-84	0	1	27.00	1	0	0	0	1	2	3	3	0	2	2	.400	.333	.500	18.00	18.00
Fish, Robert	L-L	6-3	225	1-19-88	10	4	4.85	28	28	0	0	143	138	87	77	12	68	138	.254	.222	.265	8.69	4.28
Ford, A.J.	R-R	6-1	195	10-27-84	2	1	2.49	15	0	0	0	22	15	7	6	1	12	24	.190	.167	.204	9.97	4.98
Haynes, Jeremy	R-R	6-2	180	5-28-86	2	1	2.67	5	5	0	0	27	19	8	8	0	20	13	.204	.186	.220	4.33	6.67
Howard, Cephas	R-R	6-5	240	9-5-84	0	1	3.24	6	0	0	0	8	5	3	3	0	4	8	.194	.200	.190	8.64	4.32
Jimenez, Esmerlin	R-R	6-2	184	8-1-84	6	7	3.64	29	14	1	0	114	107	53	46	8	47	87	.258	.287	.232	6.89	3.72
Kiely, Tim	R-R	6-1	190	8-26-85	5	1	2.00	21	0	0	2	36	35	8	8	1	8	33	.255	.306	.213	8.25	2.00
Leon, Sammy	R-R	6-0	160	5-19-85	3	1	4.50	24	0	0	0	38	41	25	19	3	17	34	.270	.322	.237	8.05	4.03
McKiernan, Eddie	R-R	5-11	160	3-21-89	1	5	3.73	50	0	0	22	63	60	30	26	6	16	56	.254	.262	.248	8.04	2.30
Perez, Jose	R-R	6-2	180	9-14-87	2	2	2.79	5	5	0	0	29	30	11	9	4	6	21	.278	.302	.255	6.52	1.86
Reckling, Trevor	L-L	6-2	205	5-22-89	10	7	3.37	26	26	1	0	152	137	64	57	8	59	128	.246	.238	.249	7.56	3.49
Tobin, Mason	R-R	6-4	220	7-8-87	2	3	3.13	8	1	0	0	37	29	13	13	2	18	18	.225	.306	.123	4.34	4.34
Towns, Jordan	R-R	6-2	220	9-21-85	2	1	3.12	14	0	0	2	26	20	10	9	0	8	9	.217	.244	.191	3.12	2.77
Walden, Jordan	R-R	6-5	220	11-16-87	4	6	2.18	18	18	1	0	107	80	32	26	3	32	91	.207	.238	.183	7.63	2.68

Fielding

Catcher	PCT	G	PO	A	E	DP	PB
Bressoud	1.000	4	28	3	0	0	0
De Los Santos	.982	62	414	67	9	11	12
Golliner	1.000	4	30	3	0	0	2
Pardo	1.000	16	118	12	0	1	5
Rosario	.983	16	99	19	2	5	1
Rosenbaum	.996	36	242	23	1	4	1
Silversmith	.978	13	81	6	2	2	1

First Base	PCT	G	PO	A	E	DP
Brossman	1.000	6	36	3	0	5
Gronkowski	1.000	15	126	9	0	10
Jacobo	1.000	32	280	19	0	30
Navarro	.990	89	855	62	9	68

Second Base	PCT	G	PO	A	E	DP
Colmenares	.935	6	12	17	2	7
Contreras	.943	21	30	70	6	9
Estrella	.991	73	146	184	3	44
Gonzalez-Lopez	.995	47	79	116	1	25

Third Base	PCT	G	PO	A	E	DP
Brossman	.927	106	53	190	19	20

	PCT	G	PO	A	E	DP
Colmenares	.978	17	13	32	1	2
Estrella	.917	4	1	10	1	0
Gonzalez-Lopez	.919	15	5	29	3	1
Gronkowski	—	1	0	0	0	0

Shortstop	PCT	G	PO	A	E	DP
Amarista	1.000	1	1	1	0	0
Brossman	—	1	0	0	0	0
Colmenares	1.000	3	4	5	0	2
Gonzalez-Lopez	.867	18	32	46	12	12
Romine	.959	121	200	380	25	76

Outfield	PCT	G	PO	A	E	DP
Amarista	—	1	0	0	0	0

	PCT	G	PO	A	E	DP
Castillo	1.000	11	22	1	0	0
Colmenares	1.000	1	1	0	0	0
Estrella	—	1	0	0	0	0
Fuller	.975	110	226	7	6	2
Giovanatto	1.000	7	9	1	0	0
Gonzalez-Lopez	1.000	10	8	0	0	0
Groth	.818	19	17	1	4	0
Johnson	.970	90	152	9	5	2
Moore	.978	80	124	11	3	3
Norman	1.000	1	2	0	0	0
Perez	.957	101	167	13	8	5

OREM OWLZ
ROOKIE
PIONEER LEAGUE

Batting	B-T	HT	WT	DOB	AVG	vLH	vRH	G	AB	R	H	2B	3B	HR	RBI	BB	HBP	SH	SF	SO	SB	CS	SLG	OBP
Auer, Tyson	R-R	6-0	188	10-24-85	.287	.422	.179	33	101	15	29	5	1	2	11	12	1	1	0	20	5	3	.416	.368
Bailey, Dwayne	B-R	6-2	200	8-11-86	.286	.278	.289	37	126	28	36	3	0	1	18	11	2	1	1	36	7	1	.333	.350
Brooks, Beau	L-R	6-1	200	8-3-87	.153	.136	.162	37	118	14	18	5	0	2	14	19	2	2	1	49	0	0	.246	.279
Castillo, Angel	R-R	6-3	190	6-7-89	.281	.245	.301	66	270	53	76	20	3	14	47	18	8	0	0	85	7	2	.533	.345
Champagnie, Marcel	R-R	5-11	170	10-18-85	.357	.333	.375	6	14	4	5	0	0	0	1	2	0	2	0	1	2	0	.357	.438
Colmenares, Carlos	B-R	6-0	175	2-11-86	.000	.000	.000	1	4	0	0	0	0	0	0	0	0	0	0	1	0	0	.000	.000
Contreras, Ivan	B-R	5-9	155	1-3-87	.286	.290	.284	62	234	52	67	12	5	0	24	28	1	2	3	59	14	3	.380	.361
Garcia, Chris	L-R	6-2	225	11-25-87	.318	.276	.351	20	66	11	21	2	2	1	10	8	1	0	0	11	0	0	.455	.400
Giovanatto, Donato	R-R	6-1	195	10-20-84	.309	.271	.331	63	236	47	73	14	2	9	38	19	11	0	2	48	1	2	.500	.384
Groth, Ryan	L-L	6-2	208	7-23-86	.286	.250	.299	33	119	16	34	7	5	5	25	2	3	1	1	40	4	1	.555	.312
Jacobo, Gabe	R-R	6-2	190	4-14-87	.327	.327	.327	36	150	27	49	16	2	7	32	9	1	2	3	22	1	0	.600	.372
Jimenez, Luis	R-R	6-1	170	1-18-88	.331	.317	.339	66	284	57	94	28	6	15	65	11	4	0	3	45	6	2	.630	.361
Kiniry, Rian	L-R	5-10	160	12-12-86	.262	.271	.258	48	172	32	45	5	0	0	19	16	3	6	3	32	7	7	.291	.330
Lopez, Roberto	R-R	6-0	195	10-1-85	.400	.409	.395	67	270	68	108	28	1	14	72	34	11	0	4	23	3	2	.667	.480
Pardo, Braulio	B-R	5-11	180	10-10-86	.195	.231	.179	13	41	2	8	3	0	0	3	2	0	0	0	17	0	0	.268	.233
Perez, Darwin	B-R	5-10	160	7-27-89	.280	.324	.252	67	261	59	73	11	7	3	27	44	2	8	0	63	14	2	.410	.388
Pippin, Trevor	L-L	6-3	190	12-3-86	.161	.125	.174	11	31	1	5	3	0	0	4	2	0	0	0	16	0	0	.258	.212
Rosario, Alberto	R-R	6-0	165	1-10-87	.236	.294	.211	14	55	5	13	1	0	0	9	1	1	0	0	13	0	0	.364	.263
Silversmith, Alex	R-R	6-2	210	10-22-85	.500	.500	.500	10	26	6	13	1	1	2	10	6	1	1	1	3	0	0	.846	.588
Townsend, Jon	R-R	6-0	190	9-24-84	.281	.238	.306	23	57	15	16	3	1	1	8	9	3	2	0	13	1	1	.421	.406
Villaescusa, Ivan	B-R	6-2	210	10-13-86	.345	.318	.361	15	58	7	20	5	0	0	13	1	0	1	0	17	0	0	.431	.356
Wing, Michael	R-R	6-1	180	10-25-88	.583	.500	.625	3	12	2	7	2	1	0	2	1	0	0	0	2	0	0	.917	.615

Pitching	B-T	HT	WT	DOB	W	L	ERA	G	GS	CG	SV	IP	H	R	ER	HR	BB	SO	AVG	vLH	vRH	K/9	BB/9
Boshiers, Buddy	L-L	6-3	205	5-9-88	5	0	2.68	13	12	0	0	50	43	24	15	1	22	43	.221	.276	.197	7.69	3.93
Cabrera, Francis	R-R	6-1	184	5-27-87	2	0	3.24	11	0	0	0	17	16	6	6	0	6	19	.250	.273	.238	10.26	3.24
Calderon, Leonardo	L-L	5-11	170	7-31-86	1	0	3.38	3	0	0	0	5	4	2	2	1	5	9	.200	.364	.000	15.19	8.44
Correa, Manuarys	R-R	6-3	170	1-5-89	2	0	6.20	5	4	0	0	20	32	16	14	3	5	17	.368	.400	.346	7.52	2.21
Dorado, Reyes	L-R	6-1	195	1-10-86	2	0	5.63	18	1	0	0	24	21	16	15	1	10	32	.228	.289	.185	12.00	3.75
Geltz, Steve	R-R	5-10	170	11-1-87	1	0	6.15	16	0	0	0	26	31	19	18	4	9	36	.295	.100	.415	12.30	3.08
Green, Lou	R-R	6-5	220	7-17-87	1	2	13.10	8	3	0	1	23	39	34	33	1	19	14	.402	.500	.344	5.56	7.54
Howard, Cephas	R-R	6-5	240	9-5-84	0	1	4.05	10	0	0	0	13	16	9	6	1	2	18	.271	.240	.294	12.15	1.35
Hurst, Kyle	R-R	6-4	230	8-23-85	0	2	19.29	3	1	0	0	5	13	13	10	1	5	5	.565	.643	.444	9.64	9.64
Keller, Josh	R-R	6-4	240	2-2-86	1	1	5.68	7	0	0	0	13	16	11	8	0	7	11	.302	.333	.281	7.82	4.97
Kiely, Tim	R-R	6-1	190	8-26-85	0	0	3.00	4	0	0	0	6	4	2	2	0	0	7	.182	.200	.167	10.50	0.00
Kohn, Michael	R-R	6-2	200	6-26-86	2	1	1.93	16	0	0	0	23	11	5	5	1	11	44	.134	.206	.083	16.97	4.24
Miller, Jayson	L-L	5-11	180	11-25-85	8	2	2.33	15	13	0	0	81	75	29	21	4	7	68	.241	.172	.259	7.56	0.78
Nabors, Kevin	R-R	6-3	210	8-12-85	3	2	3.94	18	0	0	1	30	31	14	13	2	17	34	.267	.275	.262	10.31	5.16
Perez, Jose	R-R	6-2	180	9-14-87	5	2	4.17	11	11	0	0	58	58	30	27	7	8	77	.251	.306	.211	11.88	1.23
Plefka, Jon	R-R	6-8	230	6-30-84	2	1	7.81	16	0	0	0	28	33	28	24	3	15	33	.289	.286	.292	10.73	4.88
Scholl, Chris	R-R	5-11	195	10-27-87	4	2	2.06	23	0	0	0	44	30	15	10	4	14	43	.195	.211	.181	8.86	2.89
Short, Baron	R-R	6-5	230	8-2-86	3	4	5.73	17	13	0	0	66	71	47	42	6	35	52	.276	.289	.269	7.09	4.77
Smith, Will	R-L	6-5	215	7-10-89	8	2	3.08	16	14	0	0	73	73	28	25	6	6	76	.253	.284	.243	9.37	0.74
Taylor, Drew	R-L	6-2	190	8-18-86	2	1	4.37	21	3	0	0	35	33	22	17	4	13	39	.248	.225	.258	10.03	3.34
Thorne, Jeremy	R-R	6-4	260	10-4-85	0	0	0.66	20	0	0	8	27	11	2	2	1	7	20	.121	.129	.117	6.59	2.30

Fielding

Catcher	PCT	G	PO	A	E	DP	PB
Brooks	.975	37	319	28	9	2	10
Pardo	.981	12	96	9	2	1	2
Rosario	1.000	14	112	23	0	1	5
Silversmith	.987	9	67	8	1	2	1
Villaescusa	.979	11	88	7	2	0	1

First Base	PCT	G	PO	A	E	DP
Bailey	1.000	3	35	1	0	1
Colmenares	—	1	0	0	0	0
Garcia	.926	10	59	4	5	6

Jacobo	.994	34	297	25	2	27
Lopez	.996	33	265	12	1	17

Second Base	PCT	G	PO	A	E	DP
Bailey	.987	16	27	49	1	15
Colmenares	1.000	1	4	1	0	1
Contreras	.958	61	107	166	12	26
Wing	1.000	1	3	1	0	0

Third Base	PCT	G	PO	A	E	DP
Bailey	.813	9	2	11	3	1
Jimenez	.909	46	36	94	13	6

Lopez	.667	6	1	9	5	2
Townsend	.897	21	15	20	4	1
Wing	—	1	0	0	0	0

Shortstop	PCT	G	PO	A	E	DP
Bailey	.974	9	12	26	1	6
Perez	.932	67	69	193	19	28
Wing	1.000	1	1	2	0	1

Outfield	PCT	G	PO	A	E	DP
Auer	.982	32	51	3	1	1
Castillo	.963	65	99	6	4	1

Champagnie	.929	4	13	0	1	0	Groth	.926	30	22	3	2	1	Lopez	.970	18	29	3	1	1
Giovanatto	1.000	39	47	5	0	0	Kiniry	.978	46	84	6	2	2	Pippin	1.000	9	10	3	0	0

AZL ANGELS   ROOKIE
ARIZONA LEAGUE

Batting	B-T	HT	WT	DOB	AVG	vLH	vRH	G	AB	R	H	2B	3B	HR	RBI	BB	HBP	SH	SF	SO	SB	CS	SLG	OBP
Alliman, Terrell	R-R	6-3	185	10-15-88	.339	.382	.329	45	180	36	61	17	5	1	39	12	2	0	2	44	8	3	.506	.383
Alvarez, Ricky	R-R	5-11	217	2-7-89	.273	.167	.289	13	44	6	12	3	1	0	6	1	1	2	0	7	3	2	.386	.304
Amarista, Alexia	B-R	5-8	150	4-6-89	.332	.289	.344	51	202	46	67	6	4	2	21	29	1	3	1	20	22	14	.431	.416
Bass, Justin	B-R	5-11	190	4-6-89	.383	.333	.396	37	60	13	23	4	0	0	10	6	1	1	0	12	2	2	.450	.448
Brannon, Nolan	L-R	6-0	185	7-5-85	.250	—	.250	3	4	1	1	1	0	0	2	1	0	0	0	0	0	0	.500	.400
Brooks, Beau	L-R	6-1	200	8-3-87	.182	.200	.176	8	22	4	4	0	1	0	3	3	0	3	0	6	1	0	.273	.280
Coon, Brad	L-L	6-0	175	12-11-82	.211	.333	.188	5	19	6	4	1	0	0	1	2	0	1	0	4	0	1	.263	.286
Crawford, Matt	B-R	6-0	165	5-9-86	.373	.364	.375	37	142	31	53	4	2	2	20	11	1	4	1	20	19	2	.472	.419
Evans, Terry	R-R	6-3	205	1-19-82	.417	—	.417	4	12	5	5	2	0	1	2	2	0	0	0	2	0	0	.833	.500
Farnsworth, Nick	L-L	6-2	210	6-17-89	.275	.273	.275	46	182	30	50	15	3	5	42	15	4	1	3	52	1	1	.473	.338
Fox, Chris	L-L	5-10	205	3-21-86	.346	.400	.333	17	52	15	18	5	2	0	9	12	4	0	0	11	9	1	.519	.500
Fuller, Cody	R-R	6-0	190	9-19-82	.267	.250	.273	4	15	1	4	0	2	0	2	3	0	1	0	3	2	0	.533	.389
Garcia, Chris	L-R	6-2	225	11-25-87	.412	.357	.426	20	68	12	28	5	0	1	14	13	1	1	0	13	2	0	.529	.512
Glaser, Ludwig	R-R	6-0	195	12-19-87	.222	.000	.250	11	36	2	8	1	0	0	5	5	0	1	2	5	0	0	.306	.302
Golliner, David	R-R	6-2	205	3-18-86	.286	.000	.326	14	49	7	14	3	0	0	6	2	1	0	0	12	0	0	.347	.327
Gomez, Rolando	L-R	5-7	145	6-18-89	.133	.000	.133	4	15	2	2	0	1	0	2	1	0	0	0	3	0	0	.267	.188
Mann, Tyler	L-R	6-2	195	7-21-89	.246	.286	.241	22	61	15	15	2	2	0	4	15	0	1	0	19	3	1	.344	.395
Morales, Kendry	B-R	6-1	225	6-20-83	.524	.333	.556	5	21	4	11	3	0	1	10	1	0	0	0	1	0	0	.810	.545
Peel, Aaron	R-R	6-1	190	2-8-83	.158	.222	.138	10	38	9	6	1	0	1	2	6	1	0	0	13	0	0	.263	.289
Pettit, Chris	R-R	6-0	190	8-15-84	.231	.250	.222	3	13	3	3	1	0	0	2	2	0	0	0	2	0	0	.308	.333
Ramos, Kevin	R-R	5-11	170	6-6-86	.319	.379	.304	40	141	35	45	8	7	1	34	8	0	3	3	21	9	5	.496	.349
Rickard, John	R-R	6-0	185	3-23-90	.096	.000	.109	20	52	5	5	0	0	0	5	12	1	1	1	14	1	1	.096	.273
Rosenbaum, Chris	R-R	6-1	205	4-2-84	.167	1.000	.000	3	6	1	1	0	0	0	1	1	0	0	0	0	0	0	.167	.286
Segura, Jean	R-L	5-11	155	3-17-90	.250	.400	.226	11	36	13	9	0	0	0	4	6	1	0	0	5	1	0	.250	.372
Sierra, Raddy	R-R	6-0	175	9-21-89	.298	.231	.308	33	104	18	31	3	3	0	17	11	3	1	1	27	7	4	.385	.378
Silversmith, Alex	R-R	6-2	210	10-22-85	.143	.250	.000	3	7	0	1	0	0	0	0	2	0	0	1	0	0	0	.143	.333
Sumi, Ikko	R-R	5-9	200	10-20-87	.241	.313	.211	22	54	11	13	1	0	0	7	8	2	4	1	16	2	1	.259	.354
Washington, Demetrius	R-R	6-0	185	7-13-89	.471	.500	.467	5	17	4	8	1	1	0	3	2	0	0	1	2	1	0	.647	.500
Wing, Michael	R-R	6-1	180	10-25-88	.267	.273	.266	34	116	14	31	4	3	2	22	11	1	1	1	20	2	2	.405	.333
Younger, Adam	R-R	6-2	207	8-25-85	.292	.211	.310	34	106	20	31	6	0	0	14	18	7	3	1	22	2	1	.349	.424

Pitching	B-T	HT	WT	DOB	W	L	ERA	G	GS	CG	SV	IP	H	R	ER	HR	BB	SO	AVG	vLH	vRH	K/9	BB/9
Almeida, Yeison	R-R	5-11	150	3-30-90	1	2	5.40	6	0	0	0	5	5	3	3	0	3	5	.250	.333	.235	9.00	5.40
Blanco, Josh	L-L	6-2	190	11-16-89	4	2	2.88	14	6	0	0	50	42	21	16	3	19	52	.228	.357	.205	9.36	3.42
Brasier, Ryan	R-R	6-0	190	8-26-87	1	0	3.86	4	0	0	1	5	3	2	2	0	1	2	.188	.000	.250	3.86	1.93
Chatwood, Tyler	R-R	5-11	175	12-16-89	1	2	3.08	11	11	0	0	38	25	15	13	1	36	48	.195	.310	.162	11.37	8.53
Correa, Manuarys	R-R	6-3	170	1-5-89	5	1	2.65	10	8	0	0	58	56	23	17	1	10	67	.249	.203	.267	10.46	1.56
Escobar, Kelvim	R-R	6-1	230	4-11-76	0	0	4.50	1	1	0	0	2	2	1	1	0	0	2	.286	.333	.250	9.00	0.00
Ferguson, Kevin	L-L	5-11	185	1-8-86	2	0	6.75	15	0	0	0	15	21	15	11	2	9	16	.333	.353	.326	9.82	5.52
Flores, Manuel	L-L	6-2	170	6-1-87	7	4	3.16	13	12	0	0	74	90	35	26	0	10	63	.294	.276	.300	7.66	1.22
Geltz, Steve	R-R	5-10	170	11-1-87	1	0	3.86	3	0	0	0	2	3	1	1	0	0	7	.300	.000	.300	27.00	0.00
Gonzalez, Abraham	R-R	5-11	175	12-13-86	2	0	2.70	17	0	0	1	20	12	8	6	3	6	16	.167	.136	.180	7.20	2.70
Green, Lou	R-R	6-5	220	7-17-87	1	1	4.00	6	4	0	0	27	32	13	12	0	6	34	.299	.176	.356	11.33	2.00
Hellweg, John	R-R	6-7	200	10-29-88	1	0	4.98	14	3	0	0	22	19	28	12	1	38	25	.224	.238	.219	10.38	15.78
Hurst, Kyle	R-R	6-4	230	8-23-85	3	0	1.83	13	4	1	0	34	23	9	7	3	5	40	.184	.086	.222	10.49	1.31
Keller, Josh	R-R	6-4	240	2-2-86	1	0	3.77	12	0	0	6	14	9	8	6		2	15	.173	.188	.167	9.42	1.26
Kenney, Mike	R-R	6-4	210	8-16-86	2	1	8.20	16	0	0	0	19	22	18	17	0	9	12	.306	.368	.283	5.79	4.34
McRobbie, Alex	R-R	6-2	185	1-16-83	0	0	0.00	3	0	0	0	3	1	0	0	0	0	2	.100	.333	.000	6.00	0.00
Molina, Robin	R-R	6-3	185	6-29-87	0	2	3.10	16	1	0	0	20	16	14	7	1	11	13	.211	.250	.196	5.75	4.87
Pugliese, Nick	R-R	6-1	205	9-18-85	1	1	1.21	17	0	0	0	22	17	6	3	0	5	21	.207	.292	.172	8.46	2.01
Serrano, Alex	R-R	6-1	200	2-18-81	1	1	2.84	10	2	0	1	13	11	6	4	0	0	7	.224	.250	.212	4.97	0.00
Shoemaker, Matt	R-R	6-2	225	9-27-86	1	0	4.50	3	0	0	1	4	6	2	2	0	0	4	.353	.250	.385	9.00	0.00
Thompson, Rich	R-R	6-1	180	7-1-84	0	0	3.00	7	0	0	2	9	6	3	3	0	2	13	.194	.000	.214	13.00	2.00
Thorne, Jeremy	R-R	6-4	260	10-4-85	0	0	3.00	2	0	0	0	3	2	1	1	0	0	2	.222	1.000	.125	6.00	0.00
Torres, Alexander	L-L	5-10	160	12-8-87	4	4	1.54	4	4	0	0	23	11	4	4	1	10	24	.153	.154	.153	9.26	3.86
Wilson, Brian	R-R	6-0	175	1-16-87	0	0	0.00	1	0	0	0	1	0	0	0	0	0	1	.000	—	.000	9.00	0.00

Fielding

Catcher	PCT	G	PO	A	E	DP	PB
Brooks	1.000	8	54	5	0	0	3
Golliner	.976	14	98	23	3	2	2
Rickard	.982	19	148	14	3	0	0
Rosenbaum	1.000	2	8	1	0	0	0
Silversmith	1.000	2	8	0	0	0	0
Sumi	.983	22	160	14	3	0	7

First Base	PCT	G	PO	A	E	DP
Farnsworth	.983	45	383	17	7	27
Garcia	1.000	2	15	1	0	0

	PCT	G	PO	A	E	DP
Mann	.963	11	99	5	4	5
Second Base	PCT	G	PO	A	E	DP
Amarista	.981	12	20	32	1	5
Bass	.964	6	14	13	1	4
Ramos	.976	31	35	87	3	18
Segura	.941	10	12	20	2	3
Wing	1.000	2	3	3	0	2

Third Base	PCT	G	PO	A	E	DP
Alliman	.804	18	8	33	10	1

	PCT	G	PO	A	E	DP
Alvarez	.842	8	5	11	3	0
Brannon	1.000	3	0	2	0	0
Glaser	.955	9	8	13	1	3
Wing	.909	23	15	45	6	5
Shortstop	PCT	G	PO	A	E	DP
Gomez	.815	4	7	15	5	0
Ramos	.930	11	12	28	3	1
Wing	.911	9	14	27	4	2
Younger	.944	34	48	104	9	17

Outfield	PCT	G	PO	A	E	DP
Alliman	.909	26	26	4	3	1
Amarista	1.000	40	60	3	0	1
Coon	1.000	5	7	0	0	0
Crawford	.982	37	53	2	1	0
Evans	1.000	2	0	1	0	0
Fox	1.000	17	23	2	0	0
Fuller	1.000	4	9	0	0	0
Morales	1.000	3	5	0	0	0
Peel	1.000	5	7	0	0	0
Pettit	1.000	3	8	0	0	0
Segura	1.000	1	1	0	0	0
Sierra	.980	30	48	1	1	0
Washington	1.000	5	9	1	0	0

DSL ANGELS   ROOKIE

DOMINICAN SUMMER LEAGUE

Batting	B-T	HT	WT	DOB	AVG	vLH	vRH	G	AB	R	H	2B	3B	HR	RBI	BB	HBP	SH	SF	SO	SB	CS	SLG	OBP
Adames, Waskal	R-R	5-11	195	2-28-89	.288	.310	.280	67	260	33	75	8	5	3	35	17	2	0	1	51	10	3	.392	.336
Almanzar, Jean	B-R	5-7	150	2-7-89	.267	.197	.294	69	273	50	73	8	4	0	22	28	0	6	1	26	10	5	.326	.334
Aybar, Jose	R-R	6-0	180	7-6-91	.197	.174	.209	22	66	11	13	2	0	0	7	6	4	0	0	20	3	0	.227	.303
Barrios, Emanuel	B-R	5-10	150	7-23-90	.199	.278	.175	54	156	24	31	6	1	0	18	28	5	9	1	36	11	3	.250	.337
Batista, Hamsem	L-L	6-2	195	7-12-90	.136	.083	.156	20	44	5	6	1	1	0	5	4	2	0	0	20	1	0	.205	.240
Batista, Lay	R-R	6-2	180	8-4-89	.197	.222	.189	35	117	18	23	4	2	1	15	15	1	1	2	27	2	3	.291	.289
Beltre, Elvin	R-R	6-0	180	5-13-89	.237	.262	.230	54	177	19	42	12	1	1	25	24	4	0	3	60	5	3	.333	.337
Diaz, Jairo	R-R	6-0	195	5-27-91	.184	.130	.200	31	98	12	18	3	0	1	7	11	1	2	1	33	1	1	.245	.270
Florian, Maximo	R-R	6-0	160	3-5-89	.000	.000	.000	3	3	0	0	0	0	0	0	2	0	0	0	1	0	0	.000	.400
Linares, Raul	R-R	5-11	160	10-4-90	.324	.200	.344	13	37	4	12	1	0	0	3	5	2	2	0	9	3	2	.351	.432
Lopez, Franklin	L-R	6-0	175	2-15-89	.259	.302	.244	54	174	18	45	7	1	0	17	20	4	3	2	27	4	3	.310	.345
Lugo, Carlos	R-R	6-0	190	11-20-89	.189	.250	.143	21	37	3	7	1	0	0	3	6	2	4	0	13	0	2	.216	.333
Martinez, Alejandro	R-R	6-3	180	2-24-88	.216	.279	.188	57	199	37	43	5	2	0	16	21	7	3	1	40	8	3	.261	.311
Martinez, Joaquin	R-R	6-1	195	6-1-90	.345	.471	.293	19	58	10	20	6	0	0	8	5	0	0	0	26	1	1	.448	.397
Molina, Manuel	R-R	6-3	215	1-4-89	.220	.149	.247	71	245	37	54	16	0	5	32	29	2	1	3	44	5	3	.347	.305
Rodriguez, Jose	R-R	6-4	190	3-10-90	.148	.200	.131	32	81	12	12	0	0	0	5	15	2	1	1	34	1	0	.148	.293
Soto, Eduardo	R-R	6-0	165	4-25-91	.323	.329	.320	67	248	44	80	19	3	4	48	24	6	1	1	51	19	6	.472	.394
Toribio, Pedro	R-R	5-10	158	7-21-90	.154	.250	.111	5	13	4	2	0	0	0	0	4	1	0	0	6	0	1	.154	.389

Pitching	B-T	HT	WT	DOB	W	L	ERA	G	GS	CG	SV	IP	H	R	ER	HR	BB	SO	AVG	vLH	vRH	K/9	BB/9
Arenas, Orangel	R-R	6-0	165	3-31-89	8	1	1.36	13	13	1	0	86	52	20	13	2	25	71	.173	.230	.150	7.43	2.62
Baez, Suammy	R-R	6-4	200	9-28-88	1	2	4.82	14	0	0	4	19	17	12	10	0	10	24	.254	.294	.240	11.57	4.82
Brujan, Eusebio	R-R	6-4	185	1-11-90	4	2	3.71	13	4	1	1	34	24	18	14	1	15	34	.189	.132	.213	9.00	3.97
Cruz, Junior	R-R	6-1	180	4-5-90	1	2	2.41	13	2	0	1	34	30	13	9	1	12	23	.238	.237	.239	6.15	3.21
De Los Santos, Cesar	R-R	6-1	160	1-10-91	1	2	9.58	7	0	0	0	10	16	16	11	2	11	7	.340	.267	.375	6.10	9.58
Feliz, Starlin	L-L	6-0	200	6-28-88	3	3	2.10	13	4	0	1	34	24	15	8	2	19	44	.198	.267	.189	11.53	4.98
Gomez, Jordany	R-R	6-3	180	9-1-90	0	1	4.15	11	0	0	1	17	20	14	8	1	10	9	.286	.444	.231	4.67	5.19
Lara, Luis	R-R	6-3	165	8-25-91	1	2	3.18	15	0	0	1	23	18	10	8	1	12	20	.214	.167	.241	7.94	4.76
Lopez, Baudilio	R-R	6-1	190	11-20-90	5	2	2.27	15	14	0	0	87	62	35	22	3	24	109	.197	.184	.201	11.23	2.47
Martinez Mesa, Fabio	R-R	6-3	190	10-29-89	6	1	1.53	13	13	1	0	76	55	17	13	1	32	93	.202	.245	.180	10.97	3.77
Nova, Erison	L-L	5-11	185	7-26-89	1	0	6.91	8	0	0	0	14	12	11	11	0	8	7	.226	.286	.217	4.40	5.02
Pena, Ariel	R-R	6-3	186	5-20-89	7	3	1.86	15	15	0	0	97	73	33	20	0	26	110	.208	.224	.203	10.24	2.42
Pichardo, Pedro	R-R	6-1	190	7-16-88	5	2	2.10	21	0	0	8	30	20	13	7	1	14	28	.189	.087	.217	8.40	4.20
Santos, Edward	R-R	6-2	220	10-22-89	2	0	3.68	11	0	0	1	15	16	9	6	0	9	10	.276	.250	.286	6.14	5.52
Toribio, Roberto	R-R	6-0	180	11-2-89	1	0	3.68	7	1	0	0	15	4	7	6	0	13	17	.083	.000	.125	10.43	7.98
Valdez, Carlos	L-L	6-0	170	9-30-90	0	0	6.00	1	1	0	0	3	3	2	2	0	2	3	.273	.000	.273	9.00	6.00

Fielding

Catcher	PCT	G	PO	A	E	DP	PB
Diaz	.918	8	60	7	6	0	8
Lopez	.992	53	420	65	4	1	9
Lugo	.964	20	119	16	5	1	7
Piron	.833	3	5	0	1	0	0

First Base	PCT	G	PO	A	E	DP
H. Batista	.818	2	8	1	2	0
Martinez	1.000	2	7	0	0	1
Molina	.982	71	581	26	11	42
Rodriguez	.958	4	23	0	1	3

Second Base	PCT	G	PO	A	E	DP
Barrios	1.000	10	28	24	0	5
Linares	.946	10	22	13	2	3
Martinez	.973	8	13	23	1	4
Soto	.927	42	84	94	14	18
Toribio	.955	5	9	12	1	2
Toribio	—	1	0	0	0	0

Third Base	PCT	G	PO	A	E	DP
H. Batista	.846	3	5	6	2	1
L. Batista	.857	31	14	58	12	4
Martinez	.886	37	20	58	10	5
Soto	.867	3	3	10	2	0

Shortstop	PCT	G	PO	A	E	DP
Adames	1.000	1	3	0	0	0
Almanzar	.953	68	109	198	15	30
Martinez	.952	5	8	12	1	3

Outfield	PCT	G	PO	A	E	DP
Adames	.942	65	123	6	8	2
Almanzar	1.000	1	2	0	0	0
Aybar	.857	19	11	1	2	0
Barrios	.958	41	45	1	2	0
H. Batista	1.000	6	0	1	0	0
Beltre	.939	54	74	3	5	1
Florian	.833	3	4	1	1	0
Martinez	.882	14	12	3	2	0
Piron	1.000	1	1	0	0	0
Rodriguez	.882	27	30	0	4	0

Los Angeles Dodgers

BY TONY JACKSON

The Dodgers took what would seem to have been a gigantic step forward in 2008, reaching the playoffs for the third time in five years and actually winning a series for the first time in two decades. But given the large number of potential free agent defections over the coming winter, there is a question as to whether the club can sustain its success.

The Dodgers aren't expected to re-sign second baseman Jeff Kent or infielders Nomar Garciaparra and Mark Sweeney. They also could lose left fielder Manny Ramirez, righthander Derek Lowe, third baseman Casey Blake, shortstop Rafael Furcal and reliever Joe Beimel.

But the good news for the Dodgers was that their core of young players—comprised primarily of righthander Chad Billingsley, lefthander Clayton Kershaw, reliever Jonathan Broxton, catcher Russell Martin, first baseman James Loney, second baseman Blake DeWitt, center fielder Matt Kemp and right fielder Andre Ethier—remains under control, and every one of those players gained an invaluable level of experience that should only help them.

The Dodgers were riding high in early May, when an eight-game winning streak helped them forge a 19-14 record. But Furcal, who was hitting .366 at the time, was scratched from the starting lineup with lower-back tightness on May 6. What no one knew at the time was that he wouldn't play again until late September, and for a while, the club seemed directionless without his presence at the top of the lineup.

From there, the Dodgers pretty much sputtered along until the all-star break, when they were three games under .500 and appeared to be going nowhere. They also had lost two-time all-star pitcher Brad Penny in early June with a shoulder problem that, for all practical purposes, would end his season.

However, the Dodgers acquired Blake a few days before the trading deadline. And then, in a development that would mark the first of two turning points in their season, they acquired Ramirez literally minutes before the deadline. He would end up batting .396/.489/.743 with 17 home runs and 53 RBIs in 53 games.

Then on Aug. 30 and Sept. 1, the Dodgers beat Arizona aces Dan Haren and Brandon Webb on consecutive days, kicking off an eight-game win-

ning streak that would include five victories over the Diamondbacks and vault the Dodgers into the National League West lead for good.

The Dodgers went on to sweep the heavily favored Cubs in the NL Division Series, but couldn't keep up the momentum in the NLCS against the Phillies.

2008 PERFORMANCE

General Manager: Ned Colletti. **Farm Director:** De Jon Watson. **Scouting Director:** Logan White.

Class	Team	League	W	L	PCT	Finish*	Manager	Affiliate Since
Majors	Los Angeles	National	84	78	.519	8th (16)	Joe Torre	—
Triple-A	Las Vegas 51s	Pacific Coast	74	69	.517	7th (16)	Lorenzo Bundy	2001
Double-A	Jacksonville Suns	Southern	68	72	.486	7th (10)	John Shoemaker	2002
High A	Inland Empire 66ers	California	68	73	.482	6th (10)	John Valentin	2007
Low A	Great Lakes Loons	Midwest	54	85	.388	14th (14)	Juan Bustabad	2007
Rookie	Ogden Raptors	Pioneer	42	33	.560	3rd (8)	Mike Brumley	2003
Rookie	GCL Dodgers	Gulf Coast	30	26	.536	6th (16)	Jeff Carter	2001
Overall 2008 Minor League Record			336	358	.484	17th		

* Finish in overall standings (No. of teams in league). ^League champion.

ORGANIZATION STATISTICS

LOS ANGELES DODGERS

NATIONAL LEAGUE

Batting	B-T	HT	WT	DOB	AVG	vLH	vRH	G	AB	R	H	2B	3B	HR	RBI	BB	HBP	SH	SF	SO	SB	CS	SLG	OBP
Ardoin, Danny	R-R	6-0	220	7-8-74	.235	.320	.154	24	51	3	12	1	0	1	4	2	1	0	0	10	1	0	.314	.278
Bennett Jr., Gary	R-R	6-0	210	4-17-72	.190	.167	.222	10	21	1	4	1	0	1	4	2	0	0	0	0	0	0	.381	.261
Berroa, Angel	R-R	6-0	195	1-27-78	.230	.219	.235	84	226	26	52	13	1	1	16	20	4	6	0	41	0	0	.310	.304
Blake, Casey	R-R	6-2	210	8-23-73	.251	.258	.248	58	211	25	53	12	1	10	23	16	4	0	2	52	1	0	.460	.313
Dewitt, Blake	L-R	5-11	175	8-20-85	.264	.286	.257	117	368	45	97	13	2	9	52	45	3	0	5	68	3	0	.383	.344
Ellis, A.J.	R-R	6-3	230	4-9-81	.000	—	.000	4	3	1	0	0	0	0	0	0	0	0	0	2	0	0	.000	.000
Ethier, Andre	L-L	6-2	210	4-10-82	.305	.243	.326	141	525	90	160	38	5	20	77	59	4	1	7	88	6	3	.510	.375
Furcal, Rafael	B-R	5-9	195	10-24-77	.357	.365	.352	36	143	34	51	12	2	5	16	20	1	0	0	17	8	3	.573	.439
Garciaparra, Nomar	R-R	6-0	190	7-23-73	.264	.339	.224	55	163	24	43	9	0	8	28	15	1	0	2	11	1	1	.466	.326
Hu, Chin-Lung	R-R	5-11	190	2-2-84	.181	.158	.186	65	116	16	21	2	2	0	9	11	0	0	0	23	2	0	.233	.252
Jones, Andruw	R-R	6-1	240	4-23-77	.158	.178	.147	75	209	21	33	8	1	3	14	27	1	0	1	76	0	1	.249	.256
Kemp, Matt	R-R	6-2	230	9-23-84	.290	.369	.260	155	606	93	176	38	5	18	76	46	1	1	3	153	35	11	.459	.340
Kent, Jeff	R-R	6-2	210	3-7-68	.280	.288	.276	121	440	42	123	23	1	12	59	25	7	0	2	52	0	1	.418	.327
LaRoche, Andy	R-R	6-1	225	9-13-83	.203	.176	.240	27	59	6	12	1	0	2	6	10	0	0	0	7	0	0	.322	.319
2-team total (49 Pittsburgh)					.166			76	223	17	37	5	0	5	18	24	2	2	1	37	2	0	.256	.252
Loney, James	L-L	6-3	220	5-7-84	.289	.249	.305	161	595	66	172	35	6	13	90	45	3	1	7	85	7	4	.434	.338
Martin, Russell	R-R	5-10	210	2-15-83	.280	.253	.291	155	553	87	155	25	0	13	69	90	5	0	2	83	18	6	.396	.385
Maza, Luis	R-R	5-9	180	6-22-80	.228	.286	.207	45	79	7	18	1	0	1	4	5	1	3	0	11	0	0	.278	.282
Ozuna, Pablo	R-R	5-11	200	8-25-74	.219	.375	.167	36	32	6	7	0	1	1	3	1	0	0	0	5	1	1	.375	.242
Pierre, Juan	L-L	5-11	180	8-14-77	.283	.346	.257	119	375	44	106	10	2	1	28	22	3	5	1	24	40	12	.328	.327
Ramirez, Manny	R-R	6-0	200	5-30-72	.396	.350	.417	53	187	36	74	14	0	17	53	35	3	0	4	38	2	0	.743	.489
Repko, Jason	R-R	5-11	190	12-27-80	.167	.400	.077	22	18	0	3	1	0	0	2	0	0	0	0	9	1	0	.222	.250
Sweeney, Mark	L-L	6-1	195	10-26-69	.130	.071	.141	98	92	2	12	3	0	0	5	15	0	0	1	28	0	0	.163	.250
Tiffee, Terry	B-R	6-3	215	4-21-79	.250	.000	.500	6	4	0	1	0	0	0	0	1	0	0	0	0	0	0	.250	.400
Young, Delwyn	B-R	5-10	210	6-21-82	.246	.231	.253	83	126	10	31	9	0	1	7	14	0	3	0	34	0	0	.341	.321

Pitching	B-T	HT	WT	DOB	W	L	ERA	G	GS	CG	SV	IP	H	R	ER	HR	BB	SO	AVG	vLH	vRH	K/9	BB/9
Beimel, Joe	L-L	6-3	215	4-19-77	5	1	2.02	71	0	0	0	49	50	11	11	0	21	32	.270	.278	.263	5.88	3.86
Billingsley, Chad	R-R	6-1	245	7-29-84	16	10	3.14	35	32	1	0	201	188	76	70	14	80	201	.248	.274	.225	9.01	3.59
Brazoban, Yhency	R-R	6-1	250	11-6-80	0	0	6.00	2	0	0	0	3	4	2	2	0	3	3	.308	.333	.286	9.00	9.00
Broxton, Jonathan	R-R	6-4	290	6-16-84	3	5	3.13	70	0	0	14	69	54	29	24	2	27	88	.217	.270	.181	11.48	3.52
Elbert, Scott	L-L	6-1	210	8-13-85	0	1	12.00	10	0	0	0	6	9	8	8	2	4	8	.346	.417	.286	12.00	6.00
Falkenborg, Brian	R-R	6-7	235	1-18-78	2	2	6.17	16	0	0	0	12	11	8	8	2	4	9	.250	.214	.267	6.94	3.09
2-team total (9 San Diego)					2	3	5.24	25	0	0	0	22	26	13	13	4	12	19	—	—	—	7.66	4.84
Johnson, Jason	R-R	6-6	225	10-27-73	1	2	5.22	16	2	0	0	29	32	19	17	5	12	20	.278	.300	.262	6.14	3.68
Kershaw, Clayton	L-L	6-3	220	3-19-88	5	5	4.26	22	21	0	0	108	109	51	51	11	52	100	.265	.250	.269	8.36	4.35
Kuo, Hong-Chih	L-L	6-1	235	7-23-81	5	3	2.14	42	3	0	1	80	60	21	19	4	21	96	.204	.202	.205	10.80	2.36
Kuroda, Hiroki	R-R	6-1	210	2-10-75	9	10	3.73	31	31	2	0	183	181	85	76	13	42	116	.253	.260	.246	5.69	2.06
Loaiza, Esteban	R-R	6-2	230	12-31-71	1	2	5.63	7	3	0	0	24	24	15	15	3	5	9	.255	.364	.197	3.38	1.88
Lowe, Derek	R-R	6-6	230	6-1-73	14	11	3.24	34	34	1	0	211	194	84	76	14	45	147	.246	.251	.240	6.27	1.92
Maddux, Greg	R-R	6-0	195	4-14-66	2	4	5.09	7	7	0	0	41	43	25	23	5	4	18	.276	.308	.231	3.98	0.89
2-team total (26 San Diego)					8	13	4.22	33	33	0	0	194	204	105	91	21	30	98	—	—	—	4.55	1.39
McDonald, James	L-R	6-5	195	10-19-84	0	0	0.00	4	0	0	0	5	1	0	0	0	1	2	.227	.118	.600	3.00	1.50
Park, Chan Ho	R-R	6-2	210	6-30-73	4	4	3.40	54	5	0	2	95	97	43	36	12	36	79	.264	.301	.237	7.46	3.40
Penny, Brad	R-R	6-4	260	5-24-78	6	9	6.27	19	17	0	0	95	112	68	66	13	42	51	.304	.328	.284	4.85	3.99
Proctor, Scott	R-R	6-1	195	1-2-77	3	6	6.05	41	0	0	0	39	41	30	26	7	24	46	.261	.263	.260	10.71	5.59
Saito, Takashi	R-R	6-2	215	2-14-70	4	4	2.49	45	0	0	18	47	40	14	13	1	16	60	.226	.244	.209	11.49	3.06
Stults, Eric	L-L	6-0	225	12-9-79	2	3	3.49	7	7	1	0	39	38	18	15	6	13	30	.252	.314	.233	6.98	3.03
Sturtze, Tanyon	R-R	6-5	230	10-12-70	0	0	0.00	3	0	0	0	2	1	0	0	0	1	1	.125	.000	.200	3.86	3.86
Troncoso, Ramon	R-R	6-2	200	2-16-83	1	1	4.26	32	0	0	0	38	37	19	18	2	12	38	.268	.254	.278	9.00	2.84
Wade, Cory	R-R	6-2	185	5-28-83	2	1	2.27	55	0	0	0	71	51	22	18	7	15	51	.202	.211	.194	6.43	1.89

Fielding

Catcher	PCT	G	PO	A	E	DP	PB
Ardoin	.993	24	126	11	1	4	2
Bennett	.979	10	43	3	1	0	1
Ellis	1.000	3	7	1	0	0	0
Martin	.990	149	1042	65	11	8	6

First Base	PCT	G	PO	A	E	DP
Blake	.964	2	27	0	1	2
Garciaparra	1.000	8	49	4	0	2
Kent	1.000	1	7	1	0	0
LaRoche	1.000	1	11	1	0	1
Loney	.991	158	1364	121	13	123
Sweeney	1.000	2	18	1	0	1

Second Base	PCT	G	PO	A	E	DP
Berroa	1.000	5	1	4	0	0
Blake	—	1	0	0	0	0
Dewitt	.981	27	41	62	2	9

	PCT	G	PO	A	E	DP
Hu	.977	30	15	28	1	4
Kent	.976	116	168	279	11	53
LaRoche	1.000	3	7	2	0	3
Maza	.974	35	30	45	2	13
Ozuna	1.000	27	17	32	0	4
Young	1.000	5	3	6	0	0

Third Base	PCT	G	PO	A	E	DP
Blake	.985	56	27	104	2	10
Dewitt	.969	95	58	193	8	19
Garciaparra	.920	11	2	21	2	0
LaRoche	.969	14	6	25	1	1
Martin	.885	11	2	21	3	3
Ozuna	—	1	0	0	0	0

Shortstop	PCT	G	PO	A	E	DP
Berroa	.975	79	91	219	8	39
Furcal	.972	36	46	92	4	17

	PCT	G	PO	A	E	DP
Garciaparra	.967	31	29	89	4	14
Hu	1.000	35	46	75	0	14
Maza	.967	16	23	35	2	6
Ozuna	1.000	4	0	4	0	0

Outfield	PCT	G	PO	A	E	DP
Ethier	.991	140	219	11	2	0
Jones	.993	66	133	1	1	0
Kemp	.991	151	306	16	3	3
Ozuna	—	2	0	0	0	0
Pierre	.981	93	153	1	3	1
Ramirez	.979	53	91	1	2	0
Repko	1.000	19	15	0	0	0
Sweeney	—	1	0	0	0	0
Tiffee	—	1	0	0	0	0
Young	1.000	23	24	4	0	1

LAS VEGAS 51S

PACIFIC COAST LEAGUE

TRIPLE-A

Batting	B-T	HT	WT	DOB	AVG	vLH	vRH	G	AB	R	H	2B	3B	HR	RBI	BB	HBP	SH	SF	SO	SB	CS	SLG	OBP
Ardoin, Danny	R-R	6-0	220	7-8-74	.303	.257	.328	29	99	14	30	6	0	4	16	8	3	3	1	24	0	0	.485	.369
Bennett, Gary	R-R	6-0	210	4-17-72	.400	—	.400	3	5	1	2	0	0	0	1	4	0	0	0	0	0	0	.400	.667
Chavez, Angel	R-R	6-0	205	7-22-81	.292	.293	.291	117	463	68	135	31	0	10	68	27	4	5	2	54	5	3	.423	.335
Dewitt, Blake	L-R	5-11	175	8-20-85	.306	.341	.286	27	111	16	34	4	2	4	18	10	1	1	1	14	1	0	.486	.366
Ellis, A.J.	R-R	6-3	230	4-9-81	.321	.297	.329	84	274	44	88	17	4	4	59	50	8	2	3	44	0	2	.456	.436
Erickson, Gorman	B-R	6-3	205	3-11-88	.000	—	.000	1	5	0	0	0	0	0	0	0	0	0	0	2	0	0	.000	.000
Furcal, Rafael	B-R	5-9	195	10-24-77	.333	—	.333	1	3	0	1	1	0	0	1	0	0	0	0	0	0	0	.667	.333
Garcia, Sergio	R-R	5-10	170	3-29-80	.289	.313	.284	28	90	14	26	4	2	0	15	12	1	0	0	8	1	0	.378	.379
Garciaparra, Nomar	R-R	6-0	190	7-23-73	.450	.000	.600	7	20	4	9	1	0	1	4	3	0	0	0	5	0	0	.650	.522
Green, Garett	R-R	5-11	190	2-24-85	.000	—	.000	1	4	0	0	0	0	0	0	0	0	0	1	1	0	0	.000	.000
Griffin, John-Ford	L-L	6-2	215	11-19-79	.310	.333	.305	94	319	56	99	19	4	14	67	36	5	0	3	60	1	1	.527	.386
Gulledge, Kelly	R-R	6-1	215	1-25-79	.000	.000	.000	7	18	1	0	0	0	0	1	2	0	0	0	8	0	0	.000	.100
Howard, Kevin	R-R	6-2	190	6-25-81	.257	.240	.260	60	179	19	46	11	0	3	27	29	0	3	0	23	1	4	.369	.361
2-team total (20 Tacoma)					.275	—	—	80	247	34	68	15	0	11	45	37	0	4	1	34	1	4	.470	.368
Hu, Chin-Lung	R-R	5-11	190	2-2-84	.295	.189	.350	41	156	21	46	5	3	1	15	7	0	4	1	19	2	0	.385	.323
Jacobs, Greg	L-L	5-9	195	10-9-76	.346	.000	.346	15	26	7	9	1	0	0	2	4	0	0	1	5	0	0	.385	.419
Jones, Andruw	R-R	6-1	240	4-23-77	.323	.182	.400	11	31	7	10	0	0	4	11	3	0	0	2	5	2	0	.710	.361
Jones, Mitch	R-R	6-2	215	10-15-77	.275	.286	.273	54	200	38	55	14	1	16	45	20	3	0	2	55	4	0	.595	.347
LaRoche, Andy	R-R	6-2	225	9-13-83	.293	.320	.286	39	123	35	36	3	0	5	28	37	2	0	4	14	2	1	.439	.452
Lindsey, John	R-R	6-2	245	1-30-77	.316	.333	.310	133	481	85	152	36	1	26	100	63	14	0	5	82	0	0	.557	.407
Lizarraga, Francisco	R-R	6-1	170	10-1-85	.310	.000	.317	16	42	7	13	3	0	0	6	8	0	2	0	11	0	0	.381	.420
Lombard, George	L-R	6-0	210	9-14-75	.163	.250	.129	13	43	6	7	2	0	1	4	7	1	0	0	14	2	1	.279	.294
2-team total (9 Albuquerque)					.257	—	—	22	70	15	18	4	1	3	13	8	1	0	0	23	2	1	.471	.342
Martinez, Ramon	R-R	6-0	190	10-10-72	.287	.286	.288	28	101	15	29	7	0	2	13	9	2	1	2	6	0	0	.416	.351
2-team total (25 New Orleans)					.289	—	—	53	187	23	54	8	0	2	18	21	3	2	4	17	1	1	.364	.363
Maza, Luis	R-R	5-9	180	6-22-80	.378	.408	.364	63	238	51	90	11	5	2	29	31	1	2	1	30	1	2	.492	.450
Paul, Xavier	L-R	6-0	195	2-25-85	.316	.250	.333	115	443	82	140	28	5	9	68	43	5	9	6	96	17	7	.463	.378
Pierre, Juan	L-L	5-11	180	8-14-77	.500	.333	.667	2	6	2	3	1	0	0	0	2	0	0	0	1	0	0	.667	.625
Poole, Lyndon	R-R	6-1	190	8-30-86	.000	—	.000	1	4	0	0	0	0	0	0	0	0	0	0	0	0	0	.000	.000
Repko, Jason	R-R	5-11	190	12-27-80	.283	.356	.258	121	459	89	130	26	7	12	50	50	18	4	4	108	20	6	.449	.373
Rivera, Rene	R-R	5-10	230	7-31-83	.271	.200	.295	37	118	12	32	7	0	4	12	11	1	0	1	20	0	1	.432	.336
Ruan, Wilkin	R-R	6-0	180	9-18-78	.341	.351	.338	86	211	28	72	8	5	0	17	8	1	4	2	20	4	3	.427	.365
Rundgren, Rex	R-R	6-1	170	11-20-80	.185	.321	.138	40	108	12	20	1	0	1	6	4	1	1	1	16	1	0	.222	.219
Sweeney, Mark	L-L	6-1	195	10-26-69	.250	.000	.286	4	16	2	4	0	0	0	0	1	0	0	0	2	0	0	.250	.294
Tiffee, Terry	B-R	6-3	215	4-21-79	.378	.370	.380	93	392	73	148	39	3	9	69	27	2	0	4	43	1	2	.561	.416
Young, Delwyn	R-B	5-10	210	6-30-82	.347	.308	.391	13	49	14	17	5	1	3	10	7	0	0	0	8	0	0	.673	.429

Pitching	B-T	HT	WT	DOB	W	L	ERA	G	GS	CG	SV	IP	H	R	ER	HR	BB	SO	AVG	vLH	vRH	K/9	BB/9
Akin, Brian	R-R	6-3	185	10-13-81	0	1	13.89	7	0	0	0	12	22	19	18	2	17	7	.407	.333	.436	5.40	13.11
Brazoban, Yhency	R-R	6-1	250	11-6-80	0	0	10.80	10	0	0	1	10	19	12	12	4	5	5	.396	.478	.320	4.50	4.50
Cyr, Eric	R-L	6-4	200	2-11-79	1	2	10.07	8	2	0	1	22	38	25	25	9	13	24	.373	.429	.343	9.67	5.24
2-team total (7 Tacoma)					2	2	9.00	15	3	0	1	33	50	33	33	10	20	38	—	—	—	10.36	5.45
DuBose, Eric	L-L	6-3	235	5-15-76	0	1	2.08	2	0	0	0	4	2	2	1	0	2	3	.143	.000	.182	6.23	4.15
Falkenborg, Brian	R-R	6-7	235	1-18-78	1	1	3.60	32	0	0	13	35	33	14	14	3	8	41	.244	.194	.294	10.54	2.06
Felix, Francisco	R-R	5-11	191	7-28-83	0	1	5.81	15	0	0	1	31	32	20	20	5	11	30	.262	.328	.197	8.71	3.19
Johnson, Jason	R-R	6-6	225	10-27-73	11	5	3.82	20	16	0	0	113	127	55	48	15	30	95	.285	.292	.277	7.57	2.39
Jones, Greg	R-R	6-2	205	11-15-76	3	3	4.71	28	0	0	0	42	45	25	22	7	33	39	.269	.286	.256	8.36	7.07
Koplove, Mike	R-R	6-0	160	8-30-76	2	1	3.46	41	0	0	9	55	43	22	21	5	18	46	.213	.242	.187	7.57	2.96
LaMura, B.J.	R-R	6-1	200	1-1-81	2	2	7.22	14	7	0	1	52	71	44	42	10	24	40	.324	.333	.317	6.88	4.13
McDonald, James	L-R	6-5	195	10-19-84	2	1	3.63	5	4	0	0	22	17	9	9	3	7	28	.200	.226	.185	11.28	2.82
Meloan, Jon	R-R	6-3	230	7-11-84	5	10	4.97	21	20	0	0	105	119	72	58	7	60	99	.289	.258	.318	8.49	5.14
Miller, Greg	L-L	6-6	220	11-3-84	2	3	7.71	48	0	0	0	54	56	53	46	3	63	53	.272	.264	.276	8.89	10.57

	B-T	HT	WT	DOB	W	L	ERA	G	GS	CG	SV	IP	H	R	ER	HR	BB	SO	AVG	vLH	vRH	K/9	BB/9
Myers, Mike	L-L	6-3	220	6-26-69	1	1	3.38	10	0	0	1	11	11	4	4	1	2	14	.268	.154	.321	11.81	1.69
Orenduff, Justin	R-R	6-4	205	5-27-83	3	7	6.55	31	21	0	1	110	142	85	80	25	66	95	.316	.325	.309	7.77	5.40
Penny, Brad	R-R	6-4	260	5-24-78	0	0	4.50	1	1	0	0	4	6	2	2	0	1	4	.353	.500	.333	9.00	2.25
Pinango, Miguel	R-R	6-1	190	1-20-83	5	9	5.16	27	24	0	0	136	165	82	78	20	38	93	.304	.358	.252	6.15	2.51
Pollok, Dwayne	R-R	6-3	195	11-12-80	10	5	4.61	40	8	0	4	105	121	62	54	11	20	63	.287	.317	.260	5.38	1.71
Proctor, Scott	R-R	6-1	195	1-2-77	1	0	0.00	2	0	0	0	3	2	0	0	0	0	5	.182	.000	.286	15.00	0.00
Riley, Matt	L-L	6-1	225	8-2-79	2	1	2.88	25	0	0	1	41	37	13	13	5	24	55	.250	.245	.253	12.17	5.31
Schmidt, Jason	R-R	6-4	210	1-29-73	0	1	7.30	5	5	0	0	12	19	13	10	3	8	5	.352	.360	.345	3.65	5.84
Sierra, Eduardo	R-R	6-3	185	4-15-82	0	0	4.91	7	0	0	0	11	10	7	6	1	7	6	.263	.313	.227	4.91	5.73
Stults, Eric	L-L	6-0	225	12-9-79	7	7	3.82	20	20	0	0	118	118	53	50	14	35	102	.258	.321	.239	7.80	2.68
Sturtze, Tanyon	R-R	6-5	230	10-12-70	1	1	4.13	21	0	0	5	28	25	15	13	4	12	23	.238	.277	.207	7.31	3.81
Totten, Heath	R-R	6-3	210	9-30-78	8	5	4.30	13	13	0	0	73	105	49	35	4	10	37	.343	.402	.302	4.54	1.23
Troncoso, Ramon	R-R	6-2	200	2-16-83	4	0	4.99	22	0	0	0	31	43	24	17	1	16	18	.336	.333	.338	5.28	4.70
Tuten, Brandon	R-R	6-2	185	10-4-85	0	0	7.71	2	0	0	0	2	4	2	2	0	2	0	.364	.500	.286	0.00	7.71
Williams, Jerome	R-R	6-3	240	12-4-81	2	2	2.08	10	2	0	0	26	23	7	6	2	9	21	.250	.242	.254	7.27	3.12

Fielding

Catcher	PCT	G	PO	A	E	DP	PB
Ardoin	.992	28	222	22	2	3	2
Bennett	1.000	3	11	0	0	0	1
Ellis	.996	83	616	54	3	6	6
Erickson	1.000	1	4	0	0	0	0
Gulledge	.968	5	26	4	1	0	2
Rivera	.991	32	199	14	2	4	5

First Base	PCT	G	PO	A	E	DP
Chavez	.976	8	39	2	1	5
Dewitt	1.000	2	7	0	0	0
Ellis	1.000	1	1	0	0	0
Jacobs	1.000	4	9	2	0	2
A. Jones	1.000	5	28	1	0	0
M. Jones	.974	17	142	8	4	19
LaRoche	.969	3	26	5	1	1
Lindsey	.991	98	713	53	7	61
Rivera	1.000	3	7	0	0	1
Sweeney	1.000	2	25	0	0	3
Tiffee	.976	29	190	15	5	17

Second Base	PCT	G	PO	A	E	DP
Chavez	.991	23	47	60	1	13
Dewitt	.969	22	44	51	3	11

	PCT	G	PO	A	E	DP
Garcia	.987	17	40	38	1	11
Green	1.000	1	3	0	0	0
Howard	.953	51	84	119	10	23
LaRoche	1.000	8	14	16	0	3
Lizarraga	1.000	4	9	10	0	3
Martinez	.980	14	21	29	1	5
Maza	.975	21	32	46	2	9
Rundgren	1.000	3	9	6	0	3
Tiffee	1.000	1	1	1	0	0

Third Base	PCT	G	PO	A	E	DP
Ardoin	—	1	0	0	0	0
Chavez	.972	57	33	104	4	13
Dewitt	1.000	5	2	11	0	1
Garciaparra	1.000	1	0	3	0	0
Howard	1.000	3	0	1	0	0
LaRoche	.934	26	17	54	5	4
Lizarraga	1.000	1	0	0	0	0
Martinez	1.000	1	0	3	0	1
Maza	.938	17	6	24	2	1
Tiffee	.918	53	42	92	12	8

Shortstop	PCT	G	PO	A	E	DP
Chavez	.957	43	57	98	7	20

	PCT	G	PO	A	E	DP
Furcal	—	1	0	0	0	0
Garcia	.960	11	13	35	2	6
Garciaparra	1.000	2	2	0	0	1
Hu	.966	41	49	120	6	14
Lizarraga	.938	11	18	27	3	5
Martinez	1.000	15	21	36	0	12
Maza	1.000	12	18	25	0	7
Rundgren	.931	31	37	84	9	19

Outfield	PCT	G	PO	A	E	DP
Griffin	.979	84	136	6	3	1
Jacobs	1.000	7	4	2	0	0
A. Jones	1.000	5	9	0	0	0
M. Jones	.947	40	52	2	3	0
Lindsey	1.000	1	2	0	0	0
Lombard	1.000	10	21	0	0	0
Maza	.969	22	28	3	1	0
Paul	.975	111	228	7	6	3
Pierre	1.000	2	2	0	0	0
Poole	1.000	1	3	0	0	0
Repko	.988	112	236	18	3	7
Ruan	.987	60	71	6	1	0
Tiffee	1.000	21	23	0	0	0
Young	1.000	13	26	2	0	1

JACKSONVILLE SUNS   DOUBLE-A
SOUTHERN LEAGUE

Batting	B-T	HT	WT	DOB	AVG	vLH	vRH	G	AB	R	H	2B	3B	HR	RBI	BB	HBP	SH	SF	SO	SB	CS	SLG	OBP
Bellhorn, Mark	B-R	6-1	205	8-23-74	.242	.333	.214	59	207	34	50	14	1	7	29	36	1	0	0	46	1	0	.420	.357
Berezay, Matt	B-R	5-11	185	11-15-83	.128	.154	.123	33	78	6	10	2	0	0	4	10	1	1	0	22	0	0	.154	.236
De Jesus, Ivan	R-R	5-11	182	5-1-87	.324	.304	.331	128	463	91	150	21	2	7	58	76	5	9	7	81	16	2	.423	.419
Godwin, Adam	R-R	5-11	170	12-13-82	.264	.283	.257	132	417	58	110	17	3	2	37	51	3	6	2	67	31	5	.333	.347
Gonzalez, Adolfo	R-R	5-11	160	6-13-85	.298	.333	.286	93	245	24	73	14	1	1	20	11	0	1	2	53	4	1	.376	.326
Gonzalez, Juan	R-R	6-0	165	2-23-82	.261	.280	.255	116	360	46	94	21	0	14	59	57	9	3	1	84	2	1	.436	.375
Gulledge, Kelly	R-R	6-1	215	1-25-79	.286	.364	.250	27	70	9	20	7	0	4	15	8	3	0	0	25	0	0	.557	.383
Gutierrez, Gabriel	R-R	5-11	190	11-24-83	.244	.231	.247	35	86	10	21	1	0	1	7	20	5	0	0	14	0	0	.291	.414
Hoffmann, Jamie	R-R	6-3	230	8-20-84	.278	.299	.270	133	478	64	133	20	3	10	71	54	2	4	6	73	28	9	.395	.350
Jacobs, Greg	L-L	5-9	195	10-9-76	.276	.327	.256	47	185	24	51	12	1	4	29	17	2	0	2	27	1	1	.416	.340
Justis, Shane	R-R	5-10	175	3-11-83	.266	.277	.262	117	338	47	90	17	2	2	37	40	8	3	1	48	9	8	.346	.357
Lambo, Andrew	L-L	6-3	190	8-11-88	.389	.417	.375	9	36	7	14	2	1	3	12	12	0	0	0	9	0	0	.750	.421
LaRoche, Andy	R-R	6-1	225	9-13-83	.318	.412	.000	6	22	5	7	1	0	0	1	3	0	0	0	6	1	0	.364	.400
Malek, Bobby	L-R	6-3	210	7-6-81	.211	.143	.220	28	57	12	12	2	0	0	6	6	1	1	0	17	0	0	.246	.281
May, Lucas	R-R	6-0	190	10-24-84	.230	.243	.224	107	392	54	90	27	1	13	54	32	7	2	8	112	6	1	.403	.294
Mitchell, Russell	R-R	6-1	182	2-15-85	.264	.309	.249	133	485	65	128	22	4	16	75	42	4	3	8	95	8	4	.425	.323
Rivera, Rene	R-R	5-10	230	7-31-83	.231	.226	.233	98	134	13	31	5	0	5	18	11	1	1	1	32	0	0	.381	.293
Rogowski, Ryan	L-L	6-2	200	1-26-84	.198	.083	.230	46	111	12	22	3	0	2	11	21	2	4	1	27	7	1	.279	.333
Tomlin, James	R-R	6-0	183	8-12-82	.313	.333	.306	108	383	59	120	31	2	2	35	36	5	9	1	47	14	6	.420	.379

Pitching	B-T	HT	WT	DOB	W	L	ERA	G	GS	CG	SV	IP	H	R	ER	HR	BB	SO	AVG	vLH	vRH	K/9	BB/9
Adkins, James	L-L	6-5	195	11-26-85	1	3	4.74	8	8	0	0	38	42	24	20	5	28	25	.269	.162	.303	5.92	6.63
Akin, Brian	R-R	6-3	185	10-13-81	2	7	5.83	25	0	0	1	42	49	33	27	4	38	37	.292	.328	.269	7.99	8.21
Allison, Clayton	R-R	6-5	235	10-10-85	1	0	4.50	5	0	0	1	6	9	4	3	1	4	4	.375	.364	.385	6.00	6.00
Alvarez, Mario	R-R	6-0	205	3-26-84	1	5	7.08	10	10	0	0	41	51	35	32	5	23	20	.321	.359	.295	4.43	5.09
Arias, Marlon	L-L	6-3	155	9-1-84	7	3	4.90	15	14	0	0	68	81	44	37	8	29	49	.292	.375	.263	6.49	3.84
Asadoorian, Rick	R-R	6-2	185	7-23-80	4	4	6.75	17	2	0	1	43	51	34	32	3	19	22	.291	.263	.313	4.64	4.01
Brazoban, Yhency	R-R	6-1	250	11-6-80	0	1	2.53	11	0	0	2	11	7	3	3	1	2	13	.175	.200	.160	10.97	1.69
Castillo, Jesus	R-R	6-1	195	5-31-84	7	4	3.24	23	23	0	0	114	123	51	41	7	33	76	.280	.255	.298	6.00	2.61
Cyr, Eric	R-L	6-4	200	2-11-79	1	0	1.50	2	2	0	0	12	8	2	2	0	6	11	.190	.125	.231	8.25	4.50

Name	B-T	HT	WT	DOB	W	L	ERA	G	GS	CG	SV	IP	H	R	ER	HR	BB	SO	AVG	vLH	vRH	K/9	BB/9
DuBose, Eric	L-L	6-3	235	5-15-76	1	1	2.95	4	3	1	0	18	16	7	6	1	14	23	.222	.231	.217	11.29	6.87
Elbert, Scott	L-L	6-1	210	8-13-85	4	1	2.40	25	1	0	0	41	22	14	11	2	20	46	.157	.143	.162	10.02	4.35
Ferreras, Luis	R-R	6-0	151	12-28-89	0	0	0.00	2	0	0	0	3	0	0	0	0	1	1	.000	.000	.000	3.00	3.00
Hammes, Zach	R-R	6-6	240	5-15-84	2	5	5.31	37	1	0	4	59	61	37	35	3	35	45	.265	.277	.259	6.83	5.31
Kershaw, Clayton	L-L	6-3	220	3-19-88	2	3	1.91	13	11	0	0	61	39	19	13	0	19	59	.179	.115	.204	8.66	2.79
LaMura, B.J.	R-R	6-1	200	1-1-81	2	2	3.86	7	6	0	0	35	35	18	15	5	10	33	.271	.361	.237	8.49	2.57
Leach, Brent	L-L	6-5	205	11-18-82	2	2	2.88	40	0	0	12	59	44	23	19	2	34	49	.215	.210	.217	7.43	5.16
Lindblom, Josh	R-R	6-5	220	6-15-87	0	0	3.60	1	1	0	0	5	5	2	2	0	1	4	.263	.455	.000	7.20	1.80
Mattison, Kieran	L-R	6-0	205	6-21-80	0	1	9.42	9	0	0	1	14	21	15	15	3	9	19	.344	.462	.257	11.93	5.65
McDonald, James	L-R	6-5	195	10-19-84	5	3	3.19	22	22	0	0	119	98	47	42	12	46	113	.227	.218	.235	8.57	3.49
Meque, Jacobo	L-L	6-2	175	10-1-83	2	1	3.55	25	0	0	5	33	26	14	13	1	13	39	.215	.222	.213	10.64	3.55
Muegge, Danny	L-R	6-5	180	3-6-81	0	5	4.82	23	7	0	1	65	77	40	35	4	19	35	.297	.368	.241	4.82	2.62
Rodriguez, Jesus	R-R	6-0	180	9-13-85	5	5	4.97	13	12	0	0	67	71	41	37	14	31	43	.282	.265	.296	5.78	4.16
Schlichting, Travis	R-R	6-4	190	10-19-84	6	4	3.77	33	0	0	6	60	58	31	25	4	18	49	.260	.272	.252	7.39	2.72
Sierra, Eduardo	R-R	6-3	185	4-15-82	5	2	4.82	36	0	0	8	47	33	28	25	4	32	44	.199	.222	.184	8.49	6.17
Sturtze, Tanyon	R-R	6-5	230	10-12-70	1	1	4.70	18	1	0	0	23	31	16	12	2	6	16	.310	.390	.254	6.26	2.35
Tomey, Anthony	R-R	6-4	245	8-17-81	2	1	4.91	16	0	0	0	29	25	18	16	6	15	33	.227	.200	.246	10.13	4.60
Wade, Cory	R-R	6-2	185	5-28-83	0	0	4.30	6	0	0	1	15	14	7	7	3	1	13	.255	.258	.250	7.98	0.61
White, Cody	L-L	6-3	185	2-27-85	4	6	6.12	16	16	0	0	85	103	61	58	10	40	49	.299	.330	.289	5.17	4.22
Wilson, Kyle	R-R	6-2	200	4-21-83	1	0	4.26	9	0	0	0	13	14	8	6	2	6	7	.280	.261	.296	4.97	4.26

Fielding

Catcher	PCT	G	PO	A	E	DP	PB
Gulledge	1.000	2	11	0	0	0	2
Gutierrez	1.000	31	183	13	0	2	3
May	.989	96	679	61	8	5	24
Rivera	.993	18	114	21	1	5	4

First Base	PCT	G	PO	A	E	DP
Bellhorn	.998	56	410	28	1	39
A. Gonzalez	.988	15	74	6	1	3
Gulledge	.986	9	61	10	1	4
Gutierrez	—	1	0	0	0	0
Hammes	1.000	1	1	0	0	0
Jacobs	.963	7	49	3	2	4
Justis	1.000	3	9	1	0	2
Lambo	.900	2	7	2	1	1
Mitchell	.997	52	366	22	1	43
Rivera	.987	21	137	13	2	9

Schlichting — 1 0 0 0 0

Second Base	PCT	G	PO	A	E	DP
Bellhorn	—	1	0	0	0	0
De Jesus	.973	37	75	106	5	15
A. Gonzalez	.974	28	46	68	3	15
J. Gonzalez	.971	53	86	112	6	24
Justis	.989	45	80	96	2	24

Third Base	PCT	G	PO	A	E	DP
Bellhorn	1.000	2	0	1	0	0
A. Gonzalez	.913	31	16	26	4	3
Gutierrez	1.000	1	0	1	0	0
Justis	.876	47	22	56	11	7
LaRoche	1.000	5	4	4	0	0
Mitchell	.938	88	54	141	13	15

Shortstop	PCT	G	PO	A	E	DP
De Jesus	.948	91	158	228	21	50
A. Gonzalez	1.000	5	4	11	0	1
J. Gonzalez	.947	50	85	111	11	23
Justis	1.000	3	2	2	0	1

Outfield	PCT	G	PO	A	E	DP
Berezay	.976	21	40	1	1	1
Godwin	.981	123	300	13	6	1
A. Gonzalez	—	1	0	0	0	0
Hoffmann	.971	125	228	10	7	3
Jacobs	.978	34	41	3	1	2
Justis	1.000	15	17	0	0	0
Lambo	1.000	7	12	1	0	1
Malek	.897	16	23	3	3	1
Rogowski	.982	37	52	2	1	0
Tomlin	.995	99	191	6	1	2

INLAND EMPIRE 66ERS

HIGH CLASS A

CALIFORNIA LEAGUE

Batting	B-T	HT	WT	DOB	AVG	vLH	vRH	G	AB	R	H	2B	3B	HR	RBI	BB	HBP	SH	SF	SO	SB	CS	SLG	OBP
Bell, Joshua	B-R	6-3	235	11-13-86	.273	.275	.272	51	187	34	51	12	2	6	21	31	0	0	2	56	4	2	.455	.373
Bennett Jr., Gary	R-R	6-0	210	4-17-72	.143	.500	.000	3	7	1	1	0	0	0	1	1	0	0	0	1	0	0	.143	.250
Berezay, Matt	B-R	5-11	185	11-15-83	.249	.261	.245	90	337	41	84	13	9	11	58	35	3	4	1	82	7	2	.439	.324
Fuller, Justin	L-R	6-1	175	7-10-83	.240	.280	.234	55	179	28	43	7	4	0	9	22	5	9	1	42	5	5	.324	.338
Gallagher, Austin	L-R	6-5	210	11-16-88	.293	.359	.276	78	307	36	90	33	1	5	55	29	1	0	7	73	1	4	.456	.349
Garabedian, Alex	R-R	6-2	210	8-26-85	.095	.000	.129	13	42	2	4	0	1	0	1	1	0	2	0	11	1	0	.143	.116
Giles, Thomas	L-L	6-0	190	8-28-83	.280	.250	.286	126	471	78	132	30	5	22	100	53	6	0	5	117	5	3	.505	.357
Gutierrez, Gabriel	R-R	5-11	190	11-24-83	.219	.158	.244	19	64	4	14	4	0	0	9	1	1	0	0	10	0	0	.281	.242
Herrera, Elian	B-R	5-11	190	2-1-85	.167	—	.167	4	6	0	1	0	0	0	0	0	0	0	0	3	0	0	.167	.167
Hunt, Bridger	R-R	6-0	185	7-24-85	.292	.304	.288	93	353	62	103	18	0	1	33	40	4	5	1	53	4	9	.351	.369
Ishibashi, Fuminasa	R-R	6-0	190	9-9-83	.000	—	.000	2	2	0	0	0	0	0	0	0	0	0	0	0	0	0	.000	.000
Lara, Christian	B-R	5-11	150	4-11-85	.254	.282	.245	104	351	46	89	16	8	0	41	36	1	8	3	98	10	2	.345	.322
2-team total (2 Lancaster)					.256	—		106	359	50	92	17	8	1	43	39	1	8	3	100	10	2	.357	.328
Lizarraga, Francisco	R-R	6-1	170	10-1-85	.158	.250	.147	13	38	2	6	0	1	0	4	4	1	4	0	10	0	0	.211	.256
Locke, Drew	R-R	6-1	205	2-28-83	.311	.277	.320	122	470	81	146	37	4	11	85	42	2	1	7	86	5	2	.477	.365
Lopez, Esteban	R-R	6-1	210	6-20-84	.241	.241	.241	43	141	17	34	8	0	1	13	13	2	0	1	42	0	1	.319	.312
Mathews, Brian	R-R	6-0	210	8-26-87	.200	.500	.125	10	30	2	6	0	0	0	2	10	0	1	0	7	0	1	.267	.400
Pedroza, Jaime	B-R	5-10	175	9-12-86	.290	.287	.291	128	479	78	139	31	7	9	57	33	8	9	6	120	25	11	.441	.342
Perez, Eduardo	B-R	6-1	175	8-30-84	.267	.298	.256	49	176	28	47	14	0	4	19	19	2	0	1	40	2	1	.415	.343
Robinson, Trayvon	B-R	5-10	175	9-1-87	.276	.311	.264	112	439	67	121	20	8	4	42	33	4	8	5	104	22	12	.385	.328
Rogowski, Ryan	L-L	6-2	200	1-26-84	.270	.289	.267	74	281	48	76	13	3	2	35	37	2	5	2	37	30	7	.359	.357
Santana, Carlos	B-R	5-11	188	4-8-86	.323	.341	.317	99	350	88	113	34	4	14	96	69	4	2	9	59	7	4	.563	.431
Van Slyke, Scott	R-R	6-5	195	7-24-86	.261	.317	.244	48	176	29	46	9	2	5	26	11	2	1	2	35	7	4	.420	.309

Pitching	B-T	HT	WT	DOB	W	L	ERA	G	GS	CG	SV	IP	H	R	ER	HR	BB	SO	AVG	vLH	vRH	K/9	BB/9
Adkins, James	L-L	6-5	195	11-26-85	5	8	5.34	19	18	0	0	88	106	64	52	6	38	75	.295	.294	.296	7.70	3.90
Bastardo, Alberto	L-L	6-0	160	4-6-84	5	8	5.19	30	21	0	0	132	152	89	76	9	51	109	.286	.280	.288	7.45	3.49
Brannon, Blake	R-R	6-2	225	3-5-85	0	0	4.70	7	0	0	0	8	8	4	4	1	5	5	.276	.364	.222	5.87	5.87
Cyr, Eric	R-L	6-4	200	2-11-79	1	2	3.79	3	3	0	0	19	17	8	8	0	3	17	.233	.250	.230	8.05	1.42
Felix, Francisco	R-R	5-11	191	7-28-83	5	3	3.31	25	0	0	2	49	35	20	18	2	21	50	.198	.145	.238	9.18	3.86
Garate, Victor	L-L	6-2	185	9-25-84	3	0	4.70	7	7	0	0	38	44	20	20	6	14	47	.289	.410	.248	11.03	3.29
Guerra, Javier	R-R	6-1	195	10-31-85	5	4	4.07	31	3	0	2	66	68	34	30	0	44	63	.262	.279	.246	8.55	5.97

Name	B-T	HT	WT	DOB	W	L	ERA	G	GS	CG	SV	IP	H	R	ER	HR	BB	SO	AVG	vLH	vRH	K/9	BB/9
Johnson, Steven	R-R	6-1	200	8-31-87	3	6	7.10	11	11	0	0	52	68	47	41	9	21	55	.318	.305	.333	9.52	3.63
Jones, Joe	R-R	6-5	210	11-16-82	3	3	5.60	30	3	0	2	82	95	54	51	6	28	31	.302	.329	.278	3.40	3.07
Koss, Paul	R-R	6-4	215	6-17-85	3	2	3.50	48	0	0	14	69	63	28	27	3	27	66	.239	.265	.219	8.57	3.50
Kutz, Given	R-R	6-3	215	11-5-84	0	1	4.43	10	0	0	1	20	24	15	10	2	6	16	.279	.267	.286	7.08	2.66
Leach, Brent	L-L	6-5	205	11-18-82	0	1	1.35	9	0	0	3	13	11	2	2	0	4	13	.239	.350	.154	8.78	2.70
Loaiza, Esteban	R-R	6-2	230	12-31-71	0	1	3.00	1	1	0	0	3	3	1	1	0	0	2	.273	.250	.333	6.00	0.00
Meque, Jacobo	L-L	6-2	175	10-1-83	1	0	2.40	14	0	0	7	15	12	4	4	0	12	19	.214	.200	.222	11.40	7.20
Pfeiffer, David	L-L	6-3	190	8-17-85	3	3	5.55	39	0	0	1	62	79	42	38	2	20	60	.309	.333	.292	8.76	2.92
Pratt, Jordan	R-R	6-3	195	5-17-85	4	3	4.83	42	1	0	2	69	49	38	37	2	67	80	.203	.205	.202	10.43	8.74
Proctor, Scott	R-R	6-1	195	1-2-77	0	0	13.50	1	0	0	0	1	3	1	1	0	0	1	.500	.500	.500	13.50	0.00
Rodriguez, Jesus	R-R	6-0	180	9-13-85	2	1	3.94	10	4	0	0	30	23	14	13	5	12	23	.213	.204	.222	6.98	3.64
Sartor, Matt	R-R	6-6	250	8-18-84	4	3	2.15	20	0	0	1	38	37	15	9	1	7	40	.257	.270	.247	9.56	1.67
Schmidt, Jason	R-R	6-4	210	1-29-73	0	0	3.48	4	4	0	0	10	8	5	4	0	4	9	.211	.136	.313	7.84	3.48
Sexton, Tim	R-R	6-6	185	6-10-87	5	12	6.04	28	26	0	0	142	184	105	95	17	36	92	.317	.329	.307	5.84	2.29
Tuten, Brandon	R-R	6-2	185	10-4-85	1	1	3.44	14	0	0	0	18	19	15	7	0	15	18	.268	.333	.211	8.84	7.36
Vasquez, Luis	R-R	6-4	155	4-3-86	0	0	4.74	8	1	0	0	19	14	10	10	1	14	8	.219	.179	.250	3.79	6.63
Wall, Josh	R-R	6-6	190	1-21-87	9	6	6.28	27	25	0	0	129	152	92	90	12	63	101	.297	.309	.287	7.05	4.40
White, Cody	L-L	6-3	185	2-27-85	6	3	3.28	12	10	0	0	60	58	28	22	4	23	45	.246	.272	.232	6.71	3.43
White, Garrett	L-L	6-5	235	5-22-84	0	2	8.05	18	0	0	0	19	25	19	17	6	15	16	.316	.385	.283	7.58	7.11
Williams, Jerome	R-R	6-3	240	12-4-81	0	1	6.30	3	3	0	0	10	13	7	7	1	6	8	.310	.308	.313	7.20	5.40
Withrow, Chris	R-R	6-3	195	4-1-89	0	0	4.50	4	0	0	0	4	2	2	2	0	6	1	.182	.333	.000	2.25	13.50

Fielding

Catcher	PCT	G	PO	A	E	DP	PB
Bennett Jr.	1.000	3	12	1	0	0	0
Garabedian	.989	11	78	8	1	1	1
Gutierrez	1.000	18	153	15	0	2	2
Ishibashi	—	1	0	0	0	0	0
Lopez	.981	41	282	26	6	3	3
Santana	.975	80	563	53	16	8	10

First Base	PCT	G	PO	A	E	DP
Gallagher	.962	21	144	8	6	12
Locke	.988	94	730	67	10	81
Lopez	1.000	1	7	1	0	2
Perez	.993	32	262	28	2	19
Santana	.833	2	4	1	1	1

Second Base	PCT	G	PO	A	E	DP
Fuller	.981	51	100	153	5	34
Hunt	.954	26	53	71	6	17

	PCT	G	PO	A	E	DP
Lara	.977	44	82	132	5	29
Lizarraga	1.000	6	9	18	0	1
Pedroza	.950	24	39	57	5	12
Santana	—	1	0	0	0	0

Third Base	PCT	G	PO	A	E	DP
Bell	.932	31	25	43	5	4
Gallagher	.921	57	37	79	10	11
Hunt	.889	6	1	7	1	0
Lara	.945	29	19	33	3	2
Lizarraga	1.000	1	0	3	0	0
Mathews	.931	10	9	18	2	4
Pedroza	1.000	1	2	2	0	0
Perez	.833	13	9	16	5	4
Santana	1.000	1	0	2	0	0

Shortstop	PCT	G	PO	A	E	DP
Fuller	1.000	2	1	4	0	0

	PCT	G	PO	A	E	DP
Hunt	1.000	3	2	5	0	1
Lara	.936	32	55	91	10	22
Lizarraga	.944	8	11	23	2	6
Pedroza	.957	104	140	237	17	51

Outfield	PCT	G	PO	A	E	DP
Berezay	.993	76	145	2	1	0
Giles	.984	97	172	8	3	2
Herrera	1.000	4	4	0	0	0
Hunt	.977	44	81	5	2	2
Lara	1.000	1	2	0	0	0
Locke	.846	11	11	0	2	0
Robinson	.977	106	253	6	6	1
Rogowski	.976	64	118	3	3	1
Santana	1.000	3	5	1	0	1
Van Slyke	.988	42	75	4	1	1

GREAT LAKES LOONS   LOW CLASS A

MIDWEST LEAGUE

Batting	B-T	HT	WT	DOB	AVG	vLH	vRH	G	AB	R	H	2B	3B	HR	RBI	BB	HBP	SH	SF	SO	SB	CS	SLG	OBP
Baez, Pedro	R-R	6-2	195	3-11-88	.178	.254	.139	59	185	23	33	10	1	1	16	17	0	6	3	45	3	1	.259	.244
Becker, Joseph	R-R	5-11	175	11-8-85	.195	.176	.207	41	133	14	26	5	0	0	3	11	3	0	5	35	3	0	.233	.262
Dalton, Parker	R-R	6-1	185	7-7-83	.231	.314	.181	83	273	25	63	17	2	2	22	18	6	5	0	82	8	2	.330	.293
Fuller, Justin	L-R	6-1	175	7-10-83	.277	.176	.333	16	47	8	13	3	0	0	4	10	2	1	2	7	2	3	.383	.410
Garabedian, Alex	R-R	6-2	210	8-26-85	.267	.338	.217	54	180	12	48	13	1	3	21	11	1	0	0	38	0	6	.400	.313
Garcia, Yosanddy	R-R	6-0	170	10-20-87	.136	.107	.158	25	66	5	9	3	0	1	2	1	1	3	0	30	1	2	.227	.162
Jansen, Kenley	B-R	6-2	220	9-30-87	.227	.218	.231	79	247	31	56	15	0	9	27	23	2	5	0	72	3	0	.397	.298
Kanaby, Erik	L-R	6-1	185	7-26-85	.272	.285	.266	122	448	56	122	9	3	0	25	56	0	6	3	54	26	19	.306	.351
Lambo, Andrew	L-L	6-3	190	8-11-88	.288	.317	.269	123	472	58	136	33	2	15	79	41	2	0	3	110	5	2	.462	.346
Lizarraga, Francisco	R-R	6-1	170	10-1-85	.191	.150	.212	51	173	13	33	2	0	2	10	8	1	5	0	35	1	5	.237	.231
Lopez, Esteban	R-R	6-1	210	6-20-84	.286	.500	.200	3	7	0	2	0	0	0	0	2	0	1	0	2	0	0	.286	.444
Mathews, Brian	R-R	6-0	210	8-26-87	.204	.267	.165	64	196	16	40	13	1	4	19	31	3	1	1	42	3	0	.342	.320
Mattingly, Preston	R-R	6-3	205	8-28-87	.224	.287	.194	92	335	37	75	14	3	6	24	16	2	1	1	108	11	4	.337	.263
Mier, Jessie	R-R	6-1	215	3-5-85	.278	.313	.263	14	54	5	15	3	0	0	5	0	0	0	0	10	0	0	.333	.278
Ortiz, Jaime	L-L	6-3	200	7-14-88	.217	.210	.220	97	336	36	73	18	1	13	48	33	3	1	0	86	2	1	.393	.293
Perez, Eduardo	R-R	6-3	185	8-30-84	.280	.263	.288	47	175	24	49	10	1	5	24	14	4	0	4	50	1	1	.434	.340
Rivera, Juan	B-R	6-0	150	3-17-87	.241	.353	.083	10	29	2	7	3	0	0	3	1	0	0	0	5	0	0	.345	.267
2-team total (66 Burlington)					.247	—		76	259	28	64	9	1	0	24	19	4	3	3	45	19	5	.290	.305
Rosario, Jovanny	B-R	5-9	160	4-12-85	.270	.181	.309	127	482	68	130	17	10	1	35	30	2	9	1	94	39	14	.353	.315
Silverio, Alfredo	R-R	6-1	185	5-6-87	.263	.265	.262	95	376	37	99	15	4	10	45	7	3	5	8	63	4	3	.404	.279
Van Slyke, Scott	R-R	6-5	195	7-24-86	.148	.273	.077	22	61	4	9	4	0	2	7	12	0	1	2	11	0	0	.213	.280
Vetters, Travis	R-R	6-2	190	9-11-83	.218	.256	.194	28	101	9	22	6	0	0	6	6	1	0	0	26	4	1	.277	.269

Pitching	B-T	HT	WT	DOB	W	L	ERA	G	GS	CG	SV	IP	H	R	ER	HR	BB	SO	AVG	vLH	vRH	K/9	BB/9
Aguasviva, Geison	L-L	6-2	166	8-3-87		2	8.38	2	2	0	0	19	34	21	18	1	6	20	.378	.375	.379	9.31	2.79
Blevins, Bobby	R-R	6-0	200	1-16-85	2	7	2.96	23	1	0	5	49	44	21	16	3	14	57	.239	.272	.214	10.54	2.59
Brannon, Blake	R-R	6-2	225	3-5-85	2	0	2.86	18	0	0	1	35	18	12	11	2	18	44	.153	.154	.152	11.42	4.67
Cedeno, Juan	L-L	6-1	185	8-19-83	0	1	4.22	6	6	0	0	32	45	18	15	3	7	18	.338	.340	.337	5.06	1.97
Diaz, Wilfredo	L-L	5-11	180	1-22-87	0	1	6.39	7	0	0	0	13	14	9	9	2	10	15	.286	.400	.256	10.66	7.11
Dutton, Johnathan	L-L	6-1	155	9-30-87	1	1	5.20	15	0	0	1	36	30	22	21	2	37	43	.226	.211	.232	10.65	9.17
Ferreras, Luis	R-R	6-0	151	12-28-89	1	0	8.53	7	0	0	0	13	20	12	12	1	10	3	.385	.318	.433	2.13	7.11

Name	B-T	HT	WT	DOB	W	L	ERA	G	GS	CG	SV	IP	H	R	ER	HR	BB	SO	AVG	vLH	vRH	K/9	BB/9
Garate, Victor	L-L	6-2	185	9-25-84	6	3	1.85	17	12	0	0	78	61	22	16	4	28	103	.215	.227	.211	11.94	3.24
Johnson, Steven	R-R	6-1	200	8-31-87	9	2	2.34	13	13	0	0	73	59	21	19	4	25	57	.223	.241	.203	7.03	3.08
Kutz, Given	R-R	6-3	215	11-5-84	5	6	4.09	23	18	0	1	106	110	51	48	9	18	81	.266	.276	.255	6.90	1.53
Lindblom, Josh	R-R	6-5	220	6-15-87	0	0	1.86	8	8	0	0	29	14	6	6	2	4	33	.137	.118	.157	10.24	1.24
Mattison, Kieran	L-R	6-0	205	6-21-80	1	0	0.00	1	1	0	0	6	7	0	0	0	2	3	.318	.143	.400	4.50	3.00
Melgarejo, Thomas	L-L	6-1	216	1-10-87	2	6	4.19	28	8	0	1	73	83	43	34	8	30	62	.280	.208	.306	7.64	3.70
Miller, Justin	R-R	6-3	190	8-2-87	4	11	3.99	27	25	0	0	140	132	76	62	6	74	82	.250	.255	.246	5.27	4.76
Morris, Bryan	L-R	6-3	200	3-28-87	2	4	3.20	17	17	1	0	82	74	34	29	5	31	72	.247	.216	.271	7.93	3.42
Ramirez, Miguel	R-R	5-11	180	7-15-83	2	9	4.29	43	0	0	20	50	56	30	24	3	32	47	.287	.309	.267	8.40	5.72
Rondon, Daigoro	R-R	6-2	163	11-4-86	4	11	6.96	21	11	0	0	74	113	64	57	7	28	82	.345	.389	.304	10.02	3.42
Sanfler, Miguel	L-L	5-11	165	10-5-84	2	4	3.95	38	0	0	2	80	66	42	35	2	41	77	.222	.189	.238	8.70	4.63
Sartor, Matt	R-R	6-6	250	8-18-84	4	2	3.83	25	0	0	4	52	41	23	22	6	17	66	.215	.292	.137	11.50	2.96
Smit, Kyle	R-R	6-3	165	10-14-87	1	4	6.55	16	12	0	0	58	68	47	42	6	36	44	.296	.310	.281	6.87	5.62
Stanke, Cal	R-R	5-10	175	3-15-85	2	0	3.60	7	0	0	1	15	14	9	6	0	8	11	.246	.333	.182	6.60	4.80
Thompson, Eric	R-R	6-6	210	4-4-88	0	1	4.85	4	0	0	0	13	11	8	7	3	5	7	.229	.273	.192	4.85	3.46
Tomey, Anthony	R-R	6-4	245	8-17-81	0	1	4.76	4	0	0	0	6	7	3	3	0	3	11	.292	.267	.333	17.47	4.76
Wade, Cory	R-R	6-2	185	5-28-83	0	0	0.00	1	1	0	0	1	1	0	0	0	0	0	.250	.500	.000	0.00	0.00
White, Garrett	L-L	6-5	235	5-22-84	3	3	3.67	15	4	0	2	54	45	24	22	5	16	55	.221	.294	.196	9.17	2.67
Zimmermann, Rob	R-R	6-5	245	11-17-81	1	4	4.06	18	0	0	0	31	36	18	14	1	6	26	.298	.370	.239	7.55	1.74

Fielding

Catcher	PCT	G	PO	A	E	DP	PB
Garabedian	.986	52	379	34	6	3	3
Jansen	.980	78	635	59	14	5	7
Lopez	1.000	3	29	1	0	1	1
Mier	.982	14	100	7	2	1	2

First Base	PCT	G	PO	A	E	DP
Lambo	1.000	6	36	2	0	1
Mathews	.987	42	277	27	4	13
Ortiz	.985	76	624	42	10	62
Perez	.996	26	221	18	1	16

Second Base	PCT	G	PO	A	E	DP
Dalton	.979	48	86	150	5	30

	PCT	G	PO	A	E	DP
Fuller	.800	1	2	2	1	0
Lizarraga	1.000	2	3	4	0	3
Mattingly	.967	82	149	202	12	40
Rivera	.974	7	14	24	1	7

Third Base	PCT	G	PO	A	E	DP
Baez	.934	59	38	90	9	8
Dalton	.964	10	7	20	1	0
Mathews	.900	19	12	42	6	0
Perez	.882	18	16	29	6	1
Taylor	.930	40	39	81	9	6

Shortstop	PCT	G	PO	A	E	DP
Becker	.973	41	70	107	5	22

	PCT	G	PO	A	E	DP
Dalton	.964	25	34	74	4	11
Fuller	.926	15	22	53	6	7
Lizarraga	.969	49	64	123	6	32
Taylor	.968	13	18	42	2	4

Outfield	PCT	G	PO	A	E	DP
Garcia	1.000	19	23	0	0	0
Kanaby	.972	75	132	8	4	2
Lambo	.950	101	130	3	7	0
Rosario	.974	99	186	5	5	1
Silverio	.959	90	150	12	7	5
Van Slyke	.956	19	43	0	2	0
Vetters	1.000	21	25	2	0	0

OGDEN RAPTORS — ROOKIE

PIONEER LEAGUE

Batting	B-T	HT	WT	DOB	AVG	vLH	vRH	G	AB	R	H	2B	3B	HR	RBI	BB	HBP	SH	SF	SO	SB	CS	SLG	OBP
Arp, Ryan	R-R	6-0	185	11-16-85	.278	.400	.231	13	18	1	5	2	0	0	1	4	0	0	0	6	0	0	.389	.409
Baez, Pedro	R-R	6-2	195	3-11-88	.267	.253	.276	61	247	37	66	20	1	12	50	18	1	0	2	69	2	2	.502	.317
Becker, Joseph	R-R	5-11	175	11-8-85	.255	.194	.280	30	106	20	27	5	1	0	7	9	3	1	0	36	0	0	.321	.331
Buss, Nick	L-R	6-0	180	12-15-86	.279	.361	.250	36	140	32	39	11	4	4	19	17	4	4	0	20	2	2	.500	.373
Calfee, Clay	L-R	6-6	220	6-2-86	.232	.283	.212	49	190	28	44	12	3	8	35	18	2	0	0	72	2	0	.453	.305
Casanova, Gabriel	R-R	6-1	190	7-29-84	.240	.255	.226	30	104	26	25	3	0	1	5	15	2	0	0	27	0	1	.298	.347
Caseres, Steven	L-R	6-4	220	3-26-87	.268	.212	.301	44	179	24	48	11	2	7	38	13	3	0	1	54	0	0	.469	.327
Collado, Keyter	R-R	5-11	178	6-8-86	.091	.000	.111	4	11	1	1	0	0	0	0	0	0	0	0	3	0	0	.091	.091
Delmonico, Tony	R-R	6-0	194	4-27-87	.340	.373	.322	35	141	38	48	20	0	11	39	18	8	0	0	28	0	0	.716	.443
Garcia, Yosanddy	R-R	6-0	170	10-20-87	.200	.000	.250	1	5	1	1	0	0	0	0	1	0	0	0	2	0	0	.400	.333
Gordon, Devaris	L-R	5-11	150	4-22-88	.331	.324	.333	60	251	45	83	13	3	2	27	16	2	2	3	29	18	5	.430	.371
Herrera, Elian	B-R	5-11	190	2-1-85	.298	.176	.344	33	124	28	37	12	1	5	27	16	2	1	1	32	5	0	.532	.385
Mier, Jessie	R-R	6-1	215	3-5-85	.265	.256	.273	28	98	21	26	6	0	1	7	18	5	0	0	15	0	1	.357	.405
Orr, Kyle	L-R	6-5	205	9-29-88	.225	.079	.267	45	173	22	39	12	1	5	24	14	1	0	1	66	0	0	.393	.286
Poole, Lyndon	R-R	6-1	190	8-30-86	.160	.182	.143	17	50	6	8	1	2	0	2	6	1	0	0	20	0	0	.260	.263
Ruggiano, Brian	R-R	6-0	175	6-9-86	.241	.233	.245	46	170	27	41	9	4	2	21	17	3	0	1	47	9	1	.376	.319
Russell, Kyle	L-L	6-5	190	6-27-86	.279	.277	.279	61	219	46	61	13	5	11	46	27	7	0	7	82	4	0	.534	.365
Vetters, Travis	R-R	6-2	190	9-11-83	.404	.436	.385	37	151	30	61	17	1	9	43	9	5	0	1	29	3	0	.709	.452
Wallach, Matt	L-R	6-2	190	2-17-86	.283	.323	.262	51	184	34	52	5	1	7	31	10	3	6	1	49	0	0	.571	.356
Yount, Austin	L-R	6-0	185	10-9-86	.301	.217	.322	33	113	15	34	10	1	1	21	15	4	0	2	29	0	3	.434	.396

Pitching	B-T	HT	WT	DOB	W	L	ERA	G	GS	CG	SV	IP	H	R	ER	HR	BB	SO	AVG	vLH	vRH	K/9	BB/9
Aguasviva, Geison	L-L	6-2	166	8-3-87	3	4	2.90	13	13	0	0	71	85	39	23	4	13	60	.287	.173	.311	7.57	1.64
Boothe, Robert	R-R	6-2	190	1-30-86	2	5	6.89	14	12	0	0	64	79	54	49	6	24	61	.302	.307	.298	8.58	3.38
Dutton, Johnathan	L-L	6-1	155	9-30-87	9	2	5.21	15	15	0	0	76	94	46	44	5	34	61	.314	.246	.331	7.22	4.03
Eovaldi, Nathan	R-R	6-3	195	2-13-90	0	0	0.00	1	0	0	0	3	1	0	0	0	0	2	.125	.000	.250	6.75	0.00
Garcia, Luis	R-R	6-2	175	1-30-87	3	0	2.40	21	2	0	9	30	22	14	8	1	17	37	.193	.163	.211	11.10	5.10
Perez, Eduardo	R-R	6-2	185	2-3-88	0	1	10.80	1	1	0	0	3	6	4	4	1	9	4	.462	.286	.667	10.80	24.30
Pimentel, Elisaul	R-R	6-2	170	7-10-88	0	1	6.75	2	0	0	0	4	5	3	3	0	2	2	.357	.333	.364	4.50	4.50
Prado, Marcel	R-R	6-4	226	11-22-87	1	1	4.86	21	0	0	2	37	39	25	20	1	25	40	.265	.262	.267	9.73	6.08
Redding, Jon Michael	R-R	6-1	195	11-16-87	0	4	5.17	13	9	0	0	31	39	26	18	4	11	36	.305	.345	.271	10.34	3.16
Roberts, Jordan	L-L	6-1	180	1-5-86	1	1	5.82	12	0	0	0	17	27	16	11	1	5	18	.333	.280	.357	9.53	2.65
Rondon, Daigoro	R-R	6-2	163	11-4-86	1	0	1.17	5	0	0	0	8	6	1	1	0	2	11	.207	.222	.200	12.91	2.35
Runnels, Jonathan	L-L	6-1	165	2-7-86	3	0	6.39	16	0	0	0	31	45	25	22	5	15	40	.336	.394	.317	11.61	4.35
Smit, Kyle	R-R	6-3	165	10-14-87	0	1	6.55	7	6	0	0	22	29	17	16	2	15	18	.319	.292	.349	7.36	6.14
Smith, Matt	R-R	6-6	195	11-2-86	3	0	4.56	13	0	0	1	24	21	13	12	3	6	22	.231	.132	.302	8.37	2.28
Smith, Steve	R-R	6-2	215	5-15-86	1	0	5.40	13	1	0	0	28	38	18	17	3	12	18	.330	.263	.364	5.72	3.81

	B-T	HT	WT	DOB	W	L	ERA	G	GS	CG	SV	IP	H	R	ER	HR	BB	SO	AVG	vLH	vRH	K/9	BB/9
Solano, Javier	R-R	6-0	177	3-31-90	2	3	9.47	18	0	0	0	38	50	44	40	7	24	36	.314	.303	.323	8.53	5.68
St. Clair, Cole	L-L	6-5	225	7-30-86	0	0	3.18	12	0	0	5	17	18	8	6	3	5	22	.261	.231	.268	11.65	2.65
Stanke, Cal	R-R	5-10	175	3-15-85	2	2	6.75	11	0	0	0	23	25	17	17	2	9	20	.269	.179	.308	7.94	3.57
Thompson, Eric	R-R	6-6	210	4-4-88	2	1	5.22	11	1	0	0	29	35	20	17	2	15	26	.289	.333	.271	7.98	4.60
Tuten, Brandon	R-R	6-2	185	10-4-85	0	3	10.38	6	0	0	0	9	15	13	10	1	6	11	.395	.357	.417	11.42	6.23
Vasquez, Luis	R-R	6-4	155	4-3-86	0	1	1.50	6	0	0	0	12	9	6	2	0	6	6	.220	.286	.185	4.50	4.50
Walter, Josh	R-R	6-4	250	4-5-85	0	0	10.06	14	0	0	0	17	28	19	19	3	7	18	.384	.500	.319	9.53	3.71
Watt, Michael	L-L	6-1	185	2-24-89	9	4	4.35	15	15	2	0	81	91	46	39	7	21	79	.281	.383	.258	8.81	2.34

Fielding

Catcher	PCT	G	PO	A	E	DP	PB
Arp	1.000	7	15	1	0	0	2
Collado	1.000	4	26	2	0	0	0
Mier	.996	27	229	24	1	3	4
Wallach	.986	44	371	45	6	4	10

First Base	PCT	G	PO	A	E	DP
Calfee	1.000	1	7	0	0	0
Casanova	.973	9	68	5	2	7
Caseres	.986	29	278	14	4	26
Herrera	1.000	1	6	0	0	0
Orr	.975	36	340	18	9	32

Second Base	PCT	G	PO	A	E	DP
Becker	.985	16	30	37	1	7
Casanova	.974	10	14	24	1	8

	PCT	G	PO	A	E	DP
Delmonico	.925	30	39	85	10	19
Herrera	.800	2	6	6	3	4
Ruggiano	.970	19	32	65	3	13
Yount	1.000	2	1	4	0	0

Third Base	PCT	G	PO	A	E	DP
Baez	.898	59	47	129	20	16
Becker	1.000	2	0	1	0	0
Casanova	1.000	1	0	1	0	0
Wallach	.923	3	4	8	1	1
Yount	.714	12	5	5	4	0

Shortstop	PCT	G	PO	A	E	DP
Baez	.750	1	0	3	1	0
Becker	.934	12	21	36	4	9
Casanova	.813	3	2	11	3	3

	PCT	G	PO	A	E	DP
Gordon	.922	59	97	186	24	38
Wallach	—	1	0	0	0	0

Outfield	PCT	G	PO	A	E	DP
Buss	.984	33	56	6	1	2
Calfee	.982	39	53	2	1	1
Casanova	—	1	0	0	0	0
Caseres	1.000	1	2	0	0	0
Garcia	1.000	1	1	1	0	1
Herrera	.973	28	34	2	1	0
Orr	1.000	1	1	0	0	0
Poole	1.000	16	26	2	0	0
Ruggiano	.967	25	26	3	1	0
Russell	.990	59	94	8	1	1
Vetters	1.000	32	60	3	0	1

GCL DODGERS   ROOKIE
GULF COAST LEAGUE

Batting	B-T	HT	WT	DOB	AVG	vLH	vRH	G	AB	R	H	2B	3B	HR	RBI	BB	HBP	SH	SF	SO	SB	CS	SLG	OBP
Bert, Joris	L-L	5-10	165	5-16-87	.250	.148	.317	28	68	11	17	2	1	0	6	16	3	0	0	19	3	4	.309	.414
Collado, Keyter	R-R	5-11	178	6-8-86	.288	.300	.281	19	52	5	15	3	0	0	5	7	2	1	0	7	0	1	.346	.393
Erickson, Gorman	R-R	6-3	205	3-11-88	.261	.314	.228	29	92	11	24	5	0	2	7	12	1	0	1	17	0	1	.380	.349
Garcia, Johan	R-R	6-0	170	9-6-86	.242	.245	.240	38	124	16	30	3	1	0	13	12	1	2	1	15	7	0	.282	.312
Garcia, Sergio	R-R	5-10	170	3-29-80	.167	.333	.000	2	6	1	1	0	0	0	0	0	0	1	0	0	1	0	.167	.286
Goulder, Albie	L-L	6-2	205	5-3-86	.229	.133	.273	34	96	13	22	4	0	1	6	16	5	0	2	27	2	0	.302	.361
Green, Garett	R-R	5-11	190	2-24-85	.253	.259	.250	37	95	14	24	4	2	1	13	17	5	1	4	18	2	2	.368	.380
Guerrero, Pedro	R-R	6-3	181	12-3-88	.263	.146	.343	32	118	17	31	7	0	2	13	8	2	2	2	33	2	3	.373	.315
Guzman, Johancy	R-R	5-10	155	4-20-87	.192	.375	.111	30	52	10	10	2	0	0	2	9	1	1	1	12	4	0	.231	.317
Howard, Kevin	L-R	6-2	190	6-25-81	.304	.375	.267	8	23	4	7	2	0	0	4	3	0	0	0	4	1	0	.391	.385
Jacobs, Chris	R-R	6-5	260	11-25-88	.271	.304	.250	43	144	23	39	5	2	3	26	24	2	0	1	35	1	2	.396	.380
Jean, Ramon	R-R	6-0	160	10-10-87	.279	.350	.239	33	111	20	31	7	0	4	16	9	2	3	0	27	10	2	.450	.344
Martinez, Ramon	R-R	6-0	190	10-10-72	.167	.000	.250	6	1	0	0	0	0	0	1	0	0	0	2	0	0	.167	.286
Mathews, Brian	R-R	6-0	210	8-26-87	.200	.143	.222	9	25	4	5	1	0	0	3	5	1	0	0	5	3	0	.240	.355
McGee, Lenell	R-R	6-2	185	8-10-88	.222	.167	.250	34	108	15	24	5	0	2	21	10	5	1	0	36	0	0	.324	.317
New, Jake	L-R	6-0	185	12-12-85	.236	.209	.254	35	110	14	26	5	0	0	8	13	3	1	0	17	6	0	.282	.333
Poole, Lyndon	R-R	6-1	190	8-30-86	.262	.111	.375	20	42	6	11	0	0	2	6	7	2	0	0	18	4	0	.405	.392
Ray, Melvin	R-R	6-4	205	4-23-89	.162	.200	.118	15	37	3	6	0	0	0	2	3	0	0	0	14	0	2	.162	.225
Sands, Jerry	R-R	6-4	210	9-28-87	.205	.245	.186	46	146	29	30	4	0	10	33	29	5	0	5	43	5	0	.438	.346
Sullivan, Shan	R-R	6-1	210	5-7-86	.065	.077	.061	18	46	4	3	1	0	1	3	4	4	0	0	16	1	0	.152	.204
Villalobos, Andrick	R-R	6-0	165	6-30-86	.224	.190	.245	25	70	8	16	2	0	0	3	8	2	0	1	14	2	0	.257	.299
Ynoa, Rafael	R-R	5-10	162	8-7-87	.306	.271	.329	43	124	24	38	5	1	0	16	21	1	6	1	21	7	4	.363	.408

Pitching	B-T	HT	WT	DOB	W	L	ERA	G	GS	CG	SV	IP	H	R	ER	HR	BB	SO	AVG	vLH	vRH	K/9	BB/9
Allison, Clayton	R-R	6-5	235	10-10-85	0	1	9.00	2	0	0	0	2	3	2	2	0	0	2	.375	.400	.333	9.00	0.00
Arias, Marlon	L-L	6-3	155	9-1-84	0	0	—	1	1	0	0	0	2	2	1	0	1	0	1.000	.000	1.000	—	4.50
Brazoban, Yhency	R-R	6-1	200	11-6-80	0	0	4.50	2	2	0	0	2	2	1	1	0	1	2	.222	.000	.400	9.00	4.50
Contreras, Edwin	R-R	6-2	165	9-17-88	5	0	2.30	11	9	1	0	55	44	18	14	3	12	34	.219	.279	.188	5.60	1.98
Danielson, Danny	R-R	6-4	220	12-12-88	0	0	5.59	9	0	0	0	10	11	6	6	0	4	8	.282	.364	.176	7.45	3.72
Eovaldi, Nathan	R-R	6-2	195	2-13-90	0	1	1.13	6	0	0	1	8	6	1	1	0	3	9	.207	.200	.214	10.13	3.38
Feliciano, Roberto	L-L	6-0	214	8-16-90	2	0	3.10	13	0	0	1	20	17	8	7	0	11	25	.230	.050	.296	11.07	4.87
Ferreras, Luis	R-R	6-0	151	12-28-89	0	1	0.75	7	0	0	2	12	7	1	1	0	2	9	.163	.154	.167	6.75	1.50
Frias, Carlos	R-R	6-4	170	11-13-89	1	2	3.82	11	3	0	0	31	25	14	13	0	13	19	.236	.311	.180	5.58	3.82
Fructuoso, Beyker	R-R	6-3	195	4-8-90	4	2	2.37	13	4	0	2	38	30	11	10	2	17	37	.229	.275	.200	8.76	4.03
Magill, Matt	R-R	6-3	175	11-10-89	1	3	3.34	11	3	0	0	30	30	16	11	2	9	25	.265	.273	.261	7.58	2.73
McCarter, Jacob	R-R	6-1	185	8-31-84	2	0	4.40	11	0	0	0	14	15	10	7	1	9	17	.268	.227	.294	10.67	5.65
Perez, Eduardo	R-R	6-2	185	2-3-88	4	2	2.91	11	9	0	0	53	44	19	17	3	14	48	.226	.311	.180	8.20	2.39
Pimentel, Elisaul	R-R	6-2	170	7-10-88	3	6	2.41	11	10	2	0	56	43	20	15	0	13	43	.212	.200	.224	6.91	2.09
Quintero, Fredy	R-R	6-3	180	12-29-87	3	1	4.03	12	1	0	2	29	33	16	13	2	6	22	.292	.409	.217	6.83	1.86
Santiago, Andres	R-R	6-2	190	10-26-89	1	1	4.00	4	4	0	0	18	22	10	8	1	8	8	.310	.293	.333	4.00	4.00
Smith, Steve	R-R	6-2	215	5-15-86	0	0	0.00	1	0	0	0	2	0	0	0	0	0	4	.000	.000	.000	18.00	0.00
Tavarez, Gari	R-R	6-0	170	10-26-87	2	5	5.03	10	5	0	0	34	40	25	19	2	15	17	.286	.247	.328	4.50	3.97
Webster, Carl	R-R	6-2	165	2-10-90	1	3	3.44	13	0	0	1	18	12	9	7	1	13	13	.197	.174	.211	6.38	8.35
Wilson, Kyle	R-R	6-2	200	4-21-83	1	0	0.90	6	5	0	0	10	8	1	1	0	3	4	.222	.200	.231	3.60	2.70

Fielding

Catcher	PCT	G	PO	A	E	DP	PB
Collado	.982	16	96	13	2	1	1
Erickson	.988	25	139	24	2	2	4
Villalobos	.986	23	113	23	2	0	1

First Base	PCT	G	PO	A	E	DP
Goulder	.994	20	148	12	1	9
Jacobs	.994	38	292	28	2	25
Mathews	1.000	3	3	1	0	0
Sullivan	1.000	2	4	0	0	0

Second Base	PCT	G	PO	A	E	DP
J. Garcia	1.000	7	5	10	0	1
Green	.857	7	7	11	3	2
Howard	1.000	8	6	15	0	0

	PCT	G	PO	A	E	DP	PB
Jean	.984	17	24	39	1	5	
Martinez	1.000	1	0	2	0	0	
Ray	1.000	1	1	1	0	1	
Ynoa	.955	26	40	66	5	7	

Third Base	PCT	G	PO	A	E	DP
J. Garcia	.969	14	9	22	1	1
Green	.972	18	10	25	1	2
Guerrero	1.000	7	7	13	0	1
Mathews	1.000	7	3	10	0	0
Sullivan	.935	15	9	20	2	1

Shortstop	PCT	G	PO	A	E	DP
J. Garcia	.915	12	14	29	4	6
Guerrero	.874	25	39	44	12	9

	PCT	G	PO	A	E	DP
Jean	.885	12	18	28	6	2
Martinez	1.000	1	3	6	0	2
Ynoa	1.000	9	13	16	0	3

Outfield	PCT	G	PO	A	E	DP
Bert	.965	23	52	3	2	1
Guzman	.976	20	39	1	1	0
McGee	1.000	31	41	4	0	2
New	.975	34	37	2	1	0
Poole	1.000	16	35	0	0	0
Ray	.917	11	11	0	1	0
Sands	.990	44	88	8	1	3

DSL DODGERS
DOMINICAN SUMMER LEAGUE
ROOKIE

Batting	B-T	HT	WT	DOB	AVG	vLH	vRH	G	AB	R	H	2B	3B	HR	RBI	BB	HBP	SH	SF	SO	SB	CS	SLG	OBP
Aguilar, Alexis	R-R	5-11	162	6-17-91	.211	.207	.212	41	128	11	27	1	0	0	8	10	3	7	1	23	8	1	.219	.282
Arias, Jose	R-R	6-3	200	10-15-88	.222	—	.222	5	9	0	2	1	0	0	0	0	0	0	0	3	0	0	.333	.222
Aviles, Adrian	L-L	6-1	155	4-7-89	.267	.282	.264	64	232	35	62	7	4	0	16	21	4	3	1	42	9	5	.332	.337
Aybar, Rafael	R-R	6-0	160	5-14-90	.224	.250	.218	44	107	20	24	1	1	1	7	17	2	0	0	26	8	1	.280	.341
Bens, Edward	R-R	6-1	189	1-15-89	.205	.300	.186	41	117	19	24	5	0	1	15	20	4	1	2	25	5	0	.274	.336
Castillo, Jerry	R-R	6-3	190	11-17-88	.285	.367	.263	56	144	20	41	5	1	0	16	6	12	2	2	29	16	7	.333	.360
Charles, Wilner	R-R	5-11	160	4-6-91	.268	.294	.259	34	71	6	19	1	1	0	8	7	3	1	1	18	7	3	.310	.354
Crispin, Alexis	R-R	6-1	172	10-15-89	.236	.353	.215	37	110	11	26	3	0	1	10	12	2	1	0	18	6	2	.291	.323
De La Cruz, Alexis	R-R	5-10	185	10-15-90	.231	.000	.273	20	26	3	6	0	0	0	2	3	1	0	0	5	0	0	.231	.333
Eusebio, Jean	R-R	6-1	195	6-5-89	.138	.000	.190	15	29	2	4	0	0	0	1	1	0	0	0	14	0	0	.138	.167
Franco, Bladimir	R-R	6-1	172	2-4-91	.169	.156	.173	66	213	29	36	9	0	5	13	31	5	1	0	94	3	4	.282	.289
Franco, Tito	R-R	6-0	170	7-31-91	.242	.152	.273	44	132	8	32	9	1	2	15	12	2	1	0	45	2	3	.371	.315
Lantigua, Erick	R-R	6-3	165	7-23-90	.247	.111	.291	53	146	15	36	8	0	1	9	19	21	3	2	42	1	0	.342	.349
Martinez, Yorniel	R-R	6-1	160	7-27-90	.228	.316	.206	52	193	26	44	3	1	1	21	19	1	3	1	40	12	12	.269	.299
Matos, Luis	R-R	6-0	190	12-20-88	.000	.000	.000	2	1	0	0	0	0	0	0	1	0	0	0	1	0	0	.000	.500
Morales, Enlly	R-R	5-11	168	9-13-89	.292	.222	.311	67	250	29	73	23	1	2	27	17	8	0	3	39	4	8	.416	.353
Sanchez, Jose	R-R	6-2	175	5-11-90	.182	.000	.250	5	11	0	2	0	0	0	2	0	0	0	0	4	0	0	.182	.182
Sucre, Marlon	R-R	6-2	160	3-12-90	.286	.324	.275	53	175	29	50	11	4	2	23	19	3	1	2	38	2	3	.429	.362
Tavarez, Pedro	R-R	6-0	198	6-28-87	.220	.146	.238	58	205	21	45	9	1	1	27	20	4	2	2	18	4	5	.288	.299

Pitching	B-T	HT	WT	DOB	W	L	ERA	G	GS	CG	SV	IP	H	R	ER	HR	BB	SO	AVG	vLH	vRH	K/9	BB/9
Antuan, Ernesto	R-R	6-0	162	10-6-89	1	1	2.37	11	1	0	1	19	10	7	5	0	8	16	.149	.105	.167	7.58	3.79
Beras, Leonel	L-L	5-11	143	5-7-91	0	1	2.18	13	0	0	0	21	19	11	5	0	15	18	.235	.250	.232	7.84	6.53
Brazoban, Yhency	R-R	6-1	250	11-6-80	0	0	0.00	2	2	0	0	2	2	0	0	0	0	1	.200	.000	.286	4.50	0.00
Castillo, Antonio	L-L	5-11	180	3-5-88	3	1	1.18	14	11	0	0	69	38	16	9	1	17	74	.160	.176	.158	9.70	2.23
Chery, Rogelito	R-R	5-10	171	12-12-89	3	3	6.00	19	0	0	1	30	36	26	20	2	16	29	.298	.308	.295	8.70	4.80
De Aza, Carlos	R-R	6-3	178	5-4-90	1	5	6.53	12	0	0	0	21	17	17	15	0	26	20	.233	.350	.189	8.71	11.32
De La Rosa, Rubby	R-R	6-1	160	3-4-89	1	4	1.71	12	12	0	0	47	34	18	9	0	21	51	.197	.188	.200	9.70	3.99
Dominguez, Jose	R-R	6-0	180	8-7-90	2	4	5.14	15	9	0	0	42	38	32	24	4	28	55	.235	.222	.239	11.79	6.00
Gomez, Gustavo	R-R	6-1	150	5-24-91	0	2	5.08	14	0	0	0	28	33	22	16	2	12	19	.295	.324	.282	6.04	3.81
Hanson, Yennifree	R-R	6-1	180	12-29-86	2	1	5.24	19	0	0	3	22	25	16	13	0	14	14	.284	.278	.286	5.64	5.64
Lima, Joel	R-R	6-0	165	8-7-89	2	2	2.52	17	1	0	2	39	34	14	11	1	5	33	.243	.200	.260	7.55	1.14
Lopez, Jhan	R-R	6-2	180	11-7-86	1	1	8.79	12	0	0	1	14	23	17	14	0	8	17	.359	.524	.279	10.67	5.02
Martinez, Geraldo	L-L	6-0	162	1-22-88	0	1	5.40	10	0	0	0	17	14	12	10	0	7	8	.230	.200	.232	4.32	3.78
Mendez, Irvit	R-R	6-0	206	4-11-90	0	0		1	0	0	0	0	1	4	4	0	5	0	1.000	.000	1.000		
Nunez, Jonady	R-R	6-1	185	11-27-89	0	6	3.57	13	8	0	0	45	38	25	18	2	23	30	.230	.225	.232	5.96	4.57
Tamares, Daniel	R-R	6-3	170	12-20-89	3	4	2.37	11	10	0	0	49	51	17	13	2	10	39	.267	.208	.290	7.11	1.82
Urriola, Marlon	R-R	6-2	165	7-1-88	1	4	5.04	13	9	0	0	50	56	32	28	2	24	47	.287	.262	.299	8.46	4.32

Fielding

Catcher	PCT	G	PO	A	E	DP	PB
Bens	.964	35	241	28	10	1	12
De La Cruz	.953	15	35	6	2	1	5
Eusebio	.981	13	47	6	1	0	7
Tavarez	.972	35	206	38	7	1	3

First Base	PCT	G	PO	A	E	DP
Arias	1.000	5	30	1	0	3
Castillo	.974	26	141	6	4	17
B. Franco	1.000	1	8	1	0	3
Lantigua	.996	30	236	6	1	14
Tavarez	.982	31	263	14	5	34

Second Base	PCT	G	PO	A	E	DP
Aguilar	1.000	6	6	10	0	2

	PCT	G	PO	A	E	DP
Aybar	.962	27	45	55	4	16
Charles	.973	19	32	41	2	14
Morales	.923	34	64	67	11	16

Third Base	PCT	G	PO	A	E	DP
B. Franco	.851	40	20	66	15	5
Lantigua	.935	19	14	44	4	3
Matos	1.000	1	1	0	0	0
Morales	.854	19	10	31	7	3

Shortstop	PCT	G	PO	A	E	DP
Aguilar	.942	34	43	88	8	20
Aybar	.947	9	17	19	2	4
Charles	1.000	1	0	1	0	0
Crispin	.897	37	45	121	19	19

Outfield	PCT	G	PO	A	E	DP
Aviles	.957	63	83	6	4	1
Castillo	.980	31	44	4	1	2
Charles	—	1	0	0	0	0
B. Franco	.917	22	21	1	2	0
T. Franco	.935	34	55	3	4	0
G. Martinez	1.000	2	2	1	0	0
Y. Martinez	.914	39	63	1	6	0
Sanchez	—	3	0	0	0	0
Sucre	.927	41	36	2	3	0

Milwaukee Brewers

BY TOM HAUDRICOURT

Playoffs or bust.

That was the Brewers' motto in 2008, after barely missing the year before while extending the franchise's postseason drought to a quarter of a century.

There was no looking back after the July trade with Cleveland for C.C. Sabathia, the reigning American League Cy Young Award winner. That stunning move, coming at the cost of top prospect Matt LaPorta and three other minor leaguers, showed how serious the Brewers were about playing October baseball.

With a full head of steam, the Brewers roared into September with an 80-56 record, easily the second-best in the league. At the time, there was no way to foresee the turbulence ahead.

With the offense slipping into a team-wide slump and the rotation faltering, the Brewers went 3-11 over the first two weeks of the month. Looking for a means to jump-start the team, management shocked baseball by firing manager Ned Yost with 12 games remaining, replacing him with third-base coach Dale Sveum

The Brewers continued to sputter for another week before a 6-1 finish, sparked by a series of late-inning home runs, secured the National League wild card berth. They bowed out in four games in the Division Series against Philadelphia, but making it to the playoffs for the first time since 1982 was reason to celebrate.

As expected, the 1-2 punch of left fielder Ryan Braun (37 homers, 106 RBIs) and first baseman Prince Fielder (34 homers, 102 RBIs) did most of the damage in an offense reliant on home runs. With a .253 team batting average and .325 on-base percentage, "small ball" went out the window.

The addition of Sabathia solidified a rotation thinned in the early going by a knee injury to Yovani Gallardo. Sabathia was everything the Brewers hoped for and more, going 11-2, 1.65 in 17 starts, with a league-leading seven complete games as well as three shutouts.

In an act of unselfishness, particularly with free agency looming, Sabathia made his last three starts on short rest. On the final day of the regular season, the big lefty pitched a four-hitter against the Cubs, propelling the Brewers into the postseason.

Many players stepped up along the way, including veteran reliever Salomon Torres. When Eric

PLAYERS OF THE YEAR

MAJOR LEAGUE: RYAN BRAUN, OF

Braun followed up his Rookie of the Year season by hitting .285/.335/.553 with 37 home runs, 39 doubles and 106 RBIs despite moving to left field from third base. He was fifth in the NL in slugging and led the circuit with 83 extra-base hits.

MINOR LEAGUE: ALICIDES ESCOBAR, SS

Signed out of Venezuela in 2003, Escobar opened at Double-A Huntsville and tore through the Southern League in 2008, batting .328/.363/.434 with 34 steals, 24 doubles, eight home runs and 76 RBIs. He also earned a September callup, playing nine games.

BRIAN BISSELL

ORGANIZATION LEADERS

BATTING		*Minimum 250 at-bats
*AVG	Salome, Angel, Huntsville	.360
R	Gamel, Mat, Huntsville/Nashville	99
H	Escobar, Alcides, Huntsville	179
TB	Gamel, Mat, Huntsville/Nashville	281
2B	Gillespie, Cole, Huntsville	38
	Gindl, Caleb, West Virginia	38
3B	Cain, Lorenzo, Nashville/Brevard Co./Huntsville	9
HR	Nix, Laynce, Nashville	23
RBI	Wilson, Steffan, West Virginia	100
BB	Gillespie, Cole, Huntsville	75
SO	Gindl, Caleb, West Virginia	144
SB	Ford, Darren, Brevard County	48
*OBP	Salome, Angel, Huntsville	.415
*SLG	Salome, Angel, Huntsville	.559

PITCHING		†Minimum 75 innings
W	Narron, Sam, Huntsville/Nashville	15
L	Narveson, Chris, Nashville	13
†ERA	Cody, Chris, West Virginia/Brevard County	1.81
G	Pena, Luis, Nashville	52
GS	Anundsen, Evan, West Virginia	28
SV	Sandoval, Juan, Huntsville	20
IP	Narron, Sam, Huntsville/Nashville	172
BB	Gulin, Lindsay, Nashville	73
BB	Axford, John, Brevard County	73
SO	Narveson, Chris, Nashville	125
†AVG	Cody, Chris, West Virginia/Brevard County	.213

Gagne faltered, Torres took over as closer in late May and converted 27 of 32 save opportunities the rest of the way.

Though Double-A Huntsville failed to make the playoffs, the Stars had one of the most talented teams in the minors, including third baseman Mat Gamel and shortstop Alcides Escobar.

General Manager: Doug Melvin. **Farm Director:** Reid Nichols. **Scouting Director:** Jack Zduriencik.

Class	Team	League	W	L	PCT	Finish*	Manager	Affiliate Since
Majors	Milwaukee	National	90	72	.556	3rd (16)	Ned Yost/Dale Sveum	—
Triple-A	Nashville Sounds	Pacific Coast	59	81	.421	16th (16)	Frank Kremblas	2005
Double-A	Huntsville Stars	Southern	73	67	.521	4th (10)	Don Money	1999
High A	Brevard County Manatees	Florida State	66	72	.478	8th (12)	Mike Guerrero	2005
Low A	West Virginia Power	South Atlantic	77	62	.554	6th (16)	Jeff Isom	2003
Rookie	Helena Brewers	Pioneer	35	41	.461	6th (8)	Rene Gonzales	2003
Rookie	AZL Brewers	Arizona	13	42	.236	9th (9)	Tony Diggs	2001
Overall 2008 Minor League Record			323	365	.469	22nd		

* Finish in overall standings (No. of teams in league). ^League champion.

ORGANIZATION STATISTICS

MILWAUKEE BREWERS
NATIONAL LEAGUE

Batting	B-T	HT	WT	DOB	AVG	vLH	vRH	G	AB	R	H	2B	3B	HR	RBI	BB	HBP	SH	SF	SO	SB	CS	SLG	OBP
Branyan, Russell	L-R	6-3	195	12-19-75	.250	.000	.280	50	132	24	33	8	0	12	20	19	0	0	1	42	1	0	.583	.342
Braun, Ryan	R-R	6-1	200	11-17-83	.285	.287	.284	151	611	92	174	39	7	37	106	42	6	0	4	129	14	4	.553	.335
Cameron, Mike	R-R	6-2	200	1-8-73	.243	.282	.231	120	444	69	108	25	2	25	70	54	6	1	3	142	17	5	.477	.331
Counsell, Craig	L-R	6-0	180	8-21-70	.226	.190	.229	110	248	31	56	14	1	1	14	46	5	1	2	42	3	1	.302	.355
Dillon, Joe	R-R	6-2	215	8-2-75	.213	.357	.128	56	75	13	16	3	0	1	6	13	1	1	0	21	1	0	.293	.337
Durham, Ray	B-R	5-8	205	11-30-71	.280	.333	.274	41	107	21	30	12	0	3	13	15	0	0	0	23	2	2	.477	.369
2-team total (87 San Francisco)					.289	—		128	370	64	107	35	0	6	45	53	2	0	1	72	8	4	.432	.380
Escobar, Alcides	R-R	6-1	175	12-16-86	.500	.667	.000	9	4	2	2	0	0	0	0	0	0	0	0	0	1	0	0	.500	.500
Fielder, Prince	L-R	5-11	270	5-9-84	.276	.239	.295	159	588	86	162	30	2	34	102	84	12	0	10	134	3	2	.507	.372
Gamel, Mat	L-R	6-0	195	7-26-85	.500	—	.500	2	2	0	1	1	0	0	0	0	0	0	0	1	0	0	1.000	.500
Gross, Gabe	L-R	6-3	220	10-21-79	.209	—	.209	16	43	6	9	3	0	0	2	10	0	0	1	7	2	0	.279	.352
Gwynn Jr., Tony	L-R	5-11	190	10-4-82	.190	1.000	.150	29	42	5	8	1	0	0	1	4	1	1	1	7	3	1	.214	.271
Hall, Bill	R-R	6-0	210	12-28-79	.225	.306	.174	128	404	50	91	22	1	15	55	37	3	1	3	124	5	6	.396	.293
Hardy, J.J.	R-R	6-2	190	8-19-82	.283	.304	.276	146	569	78	161	31	4	24	74	52	1	5	2	98	2	1	.478	.343
Hart, Corey	R-R	6-6	220	3-24-82	.268	.281	.263	157	612	76	164	45	6	20	91	27	5	4	9	109	23	7	.459	.300
Iribarren, Hernan	L-R	6-1	180	6-29-84	.143	.000	.154	12	14	1	2	1	0	0	1	1	0	0	0	3	0	0	.214	.200
Kapler, Gabe	R-R	6-2	190	7-31-75	.301	.354	.272	96	229	36	69	17	2	8	38	13	1	1	1	39	3	1	.498	.340
Kendall, Jason	R-R	6-0	205	6-26-74	.246	.250	.245	151	516	46	127	30	2	2	49	50	13	6	2	45	8	3	.324	.327
Lamb, Mike	L-R	6-1	205	8-9-75	.273	—	.273	11	11	2	3	0	0	0	0	0	0	0	0	1	0	0	.273	.273
Nelson, Brad	L-R	6-2	255	12-23-82	.286	.000	.333	9	7	0	2	2	0	0	1	0	0	0	0	1	0	0	.571	.375
Nix, Laynce	L-L	6-1	220	10-30-80	.083	.000	.091	10	12	1	1	0	0	0	0	1	0	0	0	3	0	0	.083	.154
Rivera, Mike	R-R	6-1	230	9-8-76	.306	.176	.356	21	62	8	19	5	0	1	14	6	1	0	0	10	2	0	.435	.377
Rottino, Vinny	R-R	6-1	205	4-7-80	.000	.000	—	1	1	0	0	0	0	0	0	0	0	0	0	0	0	0	.000	.000
Salome, Angel	R-R	5-7	200	6-8-86	.000	.000	.000	3	3	0	0	0	0	0	0	0	0	0	0	1	0	0	.000	.000
Weeks, Rickie	R-R	5-10	215	9-13-82	.234	.250	.227	129	475	89	111	22	7	14	46	66	14	1	4	115	19	5	.398	.342

Pitching	B-T	HT	WT	DOB	W	L	ERA	G	GS	CG	SV	IP	H	R	ER	HR	BB	SO	AVG	vLH	vRH	K/9	BB/9
Bush, Dave	R-R	6-2	205	11-9-79	9	10	4.18	31	29	0	0	185	163	92	86	29	48	109	.234	.244	.224	5.30	2.34
Coffey, Todd	R-R	6-5	240	9-9-80	1	0	0.00	9	0	0	0	7	6	0	0	0	2	7	.231	.500	.182	8.59	2.45
2-team total (17 Cincinnati)					1	0	4.39	26	0	0	0	27	31	13	13	4	8	15	—	—	—	5.06	2.70
DiFelice, Mark	R-R	6-2	190	8-23-76	1	0	2.84	15	0	0	0	19	17	7	6	4	4	20	.230	.333	.170	9.47	1.89
Dillard, Tim	R-R	6-4	215	7-19-83	0	0	4.40	13	0	0	0	14	17	12	7	2	6	5	.293	.269	.313	3.14	3.77
Gagne, Eric	R-R	6-0	240	1-7-76	4	3	5.44	50	0	0	10	46	46	28	28	11	22	38	.258	.241	.275	7.38	4.27
Gallardo, Yovani	R-R	6-2	220	2-27-86	0	0	1.88	4	4	0	0	24	22	5	5	3	8	20	.256	.324	.204	7.50	3.00
Jackson, Zach	L-L	6-5	220	5-13-83	0	0	4.91	2	0	0	0	4	5	2	2	0	2	1	.313	.167	.400	2.45	4.91
McClung, Seth	R-R	6-6	250	2-7-81	6	6	4.02	37	12	0	0	105	93	47	47	10	55	87	.243	.251	.235	7.43	4.70
Mota, Guillermo	R-R	6-6	210	7-25-73	5	6	4.11	58	0	0	1	57	52	28	26	7	28	50	.245	.287	.216	7.89	4.42
Parra, Manny	L-L	6-3	210	10-30-82	10	8	4.39	32	29	0	0	166	181	91	81	18	75	147	.278	.233	.288	7.97	4.07
Riske, David	R-R	6-2	180	10-23-76	1	2	5.31	45	0	0	2	42	47	25	25	6	25	27	.287	.359	.240	5.74	5.31
Sabathia, C.C.	L-L	6-7	290	7-21-80	11	2	1.65	17	17	7	0	131	106	31	24	6	25	128	.222	.198	.228	8.82	1.72
Sheets, Ben	R-R	6-1	225	7-18-78	13	9	3.09	31	31	5	0	198	181	74	68	17	47	158	.241	.256	.226	7.17	2.13
Shouse, Brian	L-L	5-10	195	9-26-68	5	1	2.81	69	0	0	2	51	46	19	16	5	14	33	.238	.180	.301	5.79	2.45
Stetter, Mitch	L-L	6-4	200	1-16-81	3	1	3.20	30	0	0	0	25	14	9	9	2	19	31	.165	.158	.170	11.01	6.75
Suppan, Jeff	R-R	6-2	235	1-2-75	10	10	4.96	31	31	0	0	178	207	110	98	30	67	90	.298	.288	.308	4.56	3.39
Tavarez, Julian	L-R	6-2	195	5-22-73	0	1	8.59	7	0	0	0	7	10	8	8		5	10	.371	.588	.167	12.27	6.14
2-team total (36 Atlanta)					1	4	4.71	43	0	0	0	42	55	30	22	5	19	45	—	—	—	9.64	4.07
Torres, Salomon	R-R	5-11	220	3-11-72	7	5	3.49	71	0	0	28	80	75	35	31	6	33	51	.253	.258	.250	5.74	3.71
Turnbow, Derrick	R-R	6-3	220	1-25-78	0	1	15.63	8	0	0	0	6	12	11	11	1	13	5	.414	.500	.353	7.11	18.47
Villanueva, Carlos	R-R	6-2	215	11-28-83	4	7	4.07	47	9	0	1	108	112	53	49	18	30	93	.266	.227	.300	7.73	2.49

Fielding

Catcher	PCT	G	PO	A	E	DP	PB
Kendall	.995	149	1025	94	6	13	4
Rivera	.976	17	112	11	3	2	1

First Base	PCT	G	PO	A	E	DP
Branyan	1.000	5	26	1	0	3
Dillon	1.000	4	25	3	0	4
Fielder	.988	155	1369	89	17	132
Nelson	1.000	2	1	0	0	0
Rivera	1.000	3	20	3	0	3

Second Base	PCT	G	PO	A	E	DP
Counsell	1.000	19	16	42	0	5
Dillon	.964	6	9	18	1	5
Durham	1.000	25	58	61	0	15
Hall	.905	6	3	16	2	1
Iribarren	1.000	2	1	3	0	1
Weeks	.975	120	256	333	15	84

Third Base	PCT	G	PO	A	E	DP
Branyan	.955	35	22	63	4	6
Counsell	.987	38	23	54	1	6
Dillon	1.000	1	0	2	0	0
Gamel	—	1	0	0	0	0
Hall	.939	113	69	193	17	24
Lamb	.667	1	0	2	1	0

Shortstop	PCT	G	PO	A	E	DP
Counsell	.981	24	30	73	2	13
Escobar	—	2	0	0	0	0
Hardy	.977	145	202	430	15	86

Outfield	PCT	G	PO	A	E	DP
Braun	1.000	149	275	9	0	0
Cameron	.997	119	293	3	1	0
Dillon	1.000	2	1	0	0	0
Gross	.971	14	33	1	1	1
Gwynn Jr.	1.000	10	15	0	0	0
Hart	.984	156	302	8	5	2
Iribarren	1.000	1	1	0	0	0
Kapler	.990	66	101	1	1	0
Nix	1.000	2	4	0	0	0

NASHVILLE SOUNDS   TRIPLE-A
PACIFIC COAST LEAGUE

Batting	B-T	HT	WT	DOB	AVG	vLH	vRH	G	AB	R	H	2B	3B	HR	RBI	BB	HBP	SH	SF	SO	SB	CS	SLG	OBP
Branyan, Russell	L-R	6-3	195	12-19-75	.359	.279	.391	45	153	24	55	15	0	12	36	25	1	0	0	49	4	1	.693	.453
Cain, Lorenzo	R-R	6-2	185	4-13-86	.158	.143	.167	6	19	0	3	0	0	0	2	3	0	0	0	6	0	0	.158	.273
Cameron, Mike	R-R	6-2	200	1-8-73	.200	.250	.143	4	15	4	3	0	0	1	2	3	0	0	0	4	0	0	.400	.333
Chavez, Ozzie	B-R	6-1	160	7-13-83	.223	.210	.228	87	251	19	56	6	3	3	29	17	1	5	3	49	5	1	.307	.272
Corporan, Carlos	B-R	6-3	210	1-7-84	.230	.250	.225	26	87	8	20	6	1	3	12	1	1	2	1	24	1	1	.425	.244
Crabbe, Callix	B-R	5-7	185	2-14-83	.270	.232	.284	69	204	32	55	9	3	1	18	40	1	5	4	41	9	5	.358	.386
Dillon, Joe	R-R	6-2	215	8-2-75	.263	.114	.315	46	171	35	45	8	1	5	23	29	3	0	3	30	1	2	.409	.374
Gamel, Mat	L-R	6-0	195	7-26-85	.238	.250	.235	5	21	3	5	0	0	1	3	2	0	0	0	10	0	0	.381	.304
Gibbons, Jay	L-L	6-0	195	3-2-77	.312	.269	.325	29	109	14	34	10	0	5	15	6	0	0	0	18	0	0	.541	.348
Gwynn Jr., Tony	L-R	5-11	190	10-4-82	.275	.202	.303	93	375	47	103	9	3	2	26	29	2	4	2	54	20	6	.331	.328
Heether, Adam	R-R	6-0	190	1-14-82	.272	.278	.270	124	390	70	106	31	2	11	51	64	10	1	6	89	11	1	.446	.383
Hopf, J.R.	L-R	6-1	205	11-4-82	.340	.429	.303	20	47	12	16	1	0	2	6	13	0	0	1	12	0	0	.489	.475
Iribarren, Hernan	L-R	6-1	180	6-29-84	.277	.254	.282	99	361	47	100	17	3	0	30	28	1	5	2	61	19	8	.341	.329
Katin, Brendan	R-R	6-1	235	1-28-83	.271	.230	.293	106	321	47	87	22	4	19	72	13	8	0	2	109	7	2	.542	.314
Munson, Eric	L-R	6-3	220	10-3-77	.165	.200	.145	27	85	7	14	5	0	1	12	14	2	0	1	24	0	1	.259	.294
Nelson, Brad	L-R	6-2	255	12-23-82	.286	.237	.303	132	475	78	136	36	1	18	78	73	1	0	4	77	13	8	.480	.380
Nix, Laynce	L-L	6-1	190	10-30-80	.284	.250	.295	103	380	63	108	22	3	23	60	36	2	0	2	88	5	3	.539	.348
Nunez, Abraham	B-R	5-11	200	3-16-76	.210	.320	.175	33	105	14	22	2	0	0	8	14	1	2	1	18	5	0	.229	.306
2-team total (72 New Orleans)					.211	—	—	105	323	40	68	6	0	4	28	56	3	5	1	56	9	1	.266	.332
Rottino, Vinny	R-R	6-1	205	4-7-80	.260	.310	.245	118	431	59	112	30	3	7	55	31	6	1	8	72	9	4	.392	.313
Sollmann, Steve	R-R	5-11	195	4-1-82	.210	.324	.128	31	81	13	17	1	1	2	10	10	1	1	2	19	4	0	.321	.298
Stocker, Mel	B-R	5-10	160	8-15-80	.276	.217	.287	64	145	24	40	7	0	0	12	12	2	3	1	21	18	1	.324	.338
Woodward, Chris	R-R	6-0	190	6-27-76	.291	.250	.303	71	234	26	68	13	1	5	23	23	3	2	1	28	3	1	.410	.341

Pitching	B-T	HT	WT	DOB	W	L	ERA	G	GS	CG	SV	IP	H	R	ER	HR	BB	SO	AVG	vLH	vRH	K/9	BB/9
Bateman, Joe	R-R	6-2	170	5-6-80	1	0	1.60	23	0	0	4	34	22	6	6	1	9	37	.190	.229	.173	9.89	2.41
Bray, Steve	R-R	6-1	195	12-22-80	1	5	6.41	25	1	0	0	39	39	32	28	11	21	38	.258	.299	.226	8.69	4.81
Bush, Dave	R-R	6-2	205	11-9-79	0	0	1.50	1	1	0	0	6	3	3	1	1	2	7	.136	.200	.083	10.50	3.00
Cate, Troy	L-L	6-1	220	10-21-80	1	2	4.76	11	4	0	0	28	25	15	15	3	10	17	.236	.208	.244	5.40	3.18
2-team total (12 Sacramento)					2	3	5.72	23	4	0	1	46	48	29	29	5	16	26	—	—	—	5.12	3.15
Choate, Randy	L-L	6-1	195	9-5-75	0	4	5.08	26	2	0	2	39	42	24	22	4	20	31	.271	.206	.289	7.15	4.62
DiFelice, Mark	R-R	6-2	190	8-23-76	5	1	3.22	13	12	0	0	64	50	25	23	5	8	65	.212	.212	.211	9.09	1.12
Dillard, Tim	R-R	6-4	215	7-19-83	6	1	1.99	37	0	0	2	63	57	21	14	5	28	55	.244	.253	.238	7.82	3.98
Gagne, Eric	R-R	6-0	240	1-7-76	0	0	10.80	2	2	0	0	2	2	2	2	0	1	3	.286	.000	.400	16.20	5.40
Gallardo, Yovani	R-R	6-2	220	2-27-86	1	0	5.17	3	3	1	0	16	20	9	9	2	5	18	.317	.320	.316	10.34	2.87
Gardner, Richie	R-R	6-2	205	2-1-82	6	5	5.18	30	17	0	1	120	140	80	69	17	65	84	.300	.354	.258	6.30	4.88
Gulin, Lindsay	L-L	6-2	175	11-2-76	7	7	3.54	26	23	1	0	137	111	59	54	16	73	120	.219	.252	.210	7.86	4.78
Hammond, Steve	R-L	6-2	205	4-30-82	4	4	7.41	4	4	0	0	17	24	14	14	6	15	20	.333	.316	.340	10.59	2.65
2-team total (9 Fresno)					5	7	6.07	13	12	0	0	67	86	46	45	13	22	54	—	—	—	7.29	2.97
Howard, Ben	R-R	6-2	220	1-15-79	2	6	4.73	31	2	0	1	59	66	34	31	5	22	41	.281	.237	.302	6.25	3.36
Jackson, Zach	L-L	6-5	220	5-13-83	1	5	7.85	22	6	0	0	57	81	54	50	10	18	34	.329	.308	.335	5.34	2.83
Narron, Sam	L-L	6-7	200	7-12-81	9	4	4.80	20	18	1	0	120	137	67	64	18	40	58	.293	.233	.307	4.35	3.00
Narveson, Chris	L-L	6-3	205	12-20-81	6	13	5.43	28	22	0	0	136	140	90	82	23	57	125	.265	.292	.257	8.27	3.77
Pena, Luis	R-R	6-5	200	1-10-83	2	3	6.93	52	0	0	15	49	54	40	38	4	47	49	.284	.319	.263	8.94	8.57
Ramirez, Erasmo	R-L	6-0	190	4-29-76	3	5	3.46	42	0	0	1	55	58	21	21	7	11	48	.282	.233	.301	7.90	1.81
Riske, David	R-R	6-2	180	10-23-76	0	0	0.00	1	1	0	0	1	0	0	0	0	0	1	.000	—	.000	27.00	0.00
Shiell, Jason	R-R	6-1	215	10-19-76	0	3	7.71	21	0	0	0	26	37	26	22	7	14	27	.333	.333	.333	9.47	4.91
Stetter, Mitch	L-L	6-0	200	1-16-81	3	3	2.48	28	0	0	0	29	21	10	8	2	7	30	.200	.194	.203	9.31	2.17
Torres, Melqui	R-R	6-2	205	5-27-77	0	0	5.00	7	0	0	0	9	6	5	5	1	6	8	.188	.118	.267	8.00	6.00
Turnbow, Derrick	R-R	6-3	220	1-25-78	2	1	10.50	18	4	0	0	18	17	21	21	0	41	28	.246	.227	.255	14.00	20.50
Ungs, Nic	R-R	6-1	220	9-3-79	2	3	7.49	8	7	0	0	34	42	29	28	7	10	27	.298	.294	.300	7.22	2.67
Weaver, Jeff	R-R	6-5	200	8-22-76	2	4	6.22	9	9	0	0	55	64	43	38	9	20	37	.299	.291	.306	6.05	3.27

Fielding

Catcher	PCT	G	PO	A	E	DP	PB
Corporan	.986	24	192	14	3	2	1
Hopf	.986	8	64	8	1	3	1
Munson	.968	9	55	5	2	1	3
Rottino	.991	101	709	51	7	8	16

First Base	PCT	G	PO	A	E	DP
Branyan	.962	3	23	2	1	1
Corporan	1.000	1	4	0	0	0
Dillon	1.000	3	21	5	0	1
Hopf	1.000	8	51	6	0	3
Munson	.992	12	110	7	1	13
Nelson	.992	103	841	51	7	86
Rottino	1.000	6	39	10	0	2
Sollmann	1.000	5	34	4	0	0
Woodward	1.000	7	53	5	0	7

Second Base	PCT	G	PO	A	E	DP
Chavez	.987	18	31	46	1	11
Crabbe	.970	35	72	87	5	23
Dillon	.941	8	13	19	2	5
Heether	1.000	6	9	11	0	4

	PCT	G	PO	A	E	DP
Iribarren	.992	29	58	66	1	9
Nunez	.960	24	43	53	4	19
Sollmann	1.000	15	36	35	0	16
Woodward	.970	23	46	51	3	16

Third Base	PCT	G	PO	A	E	DP
Branyan	.964	32	26	81	4	8
Chavez	1.000	5	2	7	0	2
Crabbe	.750	1	0	3	1	1
Dillon	.963	35	24	55	3	4
Gamel	.846	5	2	9	2	0
Heether	.953	49	30	92	6	1
Munson	.500	1	0	1	1	0
Nelson	.955	8	3	18	1	2
Nunez	1.000	2	1	5	0	0
Rottino	1.000	4	2	7	0	0
Woodward	.889	8	3	13	2	0

Shortstop	PCT	G	PO	A	E	DP
Chavez	.960	50	69	147	9	30
Crabbe	—	1	0	0	0	0
Heether	.957	53	61	164	10	36

	PCT	G	PO	A	E	DP
Nunez	.895	5	6	11	2	3
Sollmann	.833	2	2	3	1	3
Woodward	.977	34	38	89	3	19

Outfield	PCT	G	PO	A	E	DP
Branyan	1.000	2	2	0	0	0
Cain	1.000	5	12	0	0	0
Cameron	1.000	4	10	0	0	0
Crabbe	1.000	20	35	1	0	0
Dillon	1.000	1	1	0	0	0
Gibbons	.931	17	26	1	2	0
Gwynn Jr.	.973	93	210	5	6	0
Heether	1.000	12	15	0	0	0
Iribarren	1.000	66	100	7	0	2
Katin	.926	82	121	5	10	1
Nelson	1.000	7	10	0	0	0
Nix	.973	91	171	7	5	3
Rottino	1.000	7	10	1	0	0
Sollmann	1.000	7	6	2	0	0
Stocker	.985	41	66	1	1	0

HUNTSVILLE STARS

SOUTHERN LEAGUE

DOUBLE-A

Batting	B-T	HT	WT	DOB	AVG	vLH	vRH	G	AB	R	H	2B	3B	HR	RBI	BB	HBP	SH	SF	SO	SB	CS	SLG	OBP
Bell, Michael	R-R	6-0	185	3-30-85	.245	.282	.231	124	444	53	109	28	3	10	53	25	4	9	4	83	1	3	.390	.289
Brantley, Michael	L-L	6-2	180	5-15-87	.319	.286	.330	106	420	80	134	17	2	4	40	50	4	3	2	27	28	8	.398	.395
Cain, Lorenzo	R-R	6-2	185	4-13-86	.277	.255	.287	40	148	21	41	9	5	4	17	19	2	1	2	41	6	2	.486	.363
Chavez, Ozzie	B-R	6-1	160	7-13-83	.350	.500	.313	7	20	4	7	0	1	1	4	2	0	0	0	3	0	1	.600	.409
Corporan, Carlos	B-R	6-3	210	1-7-84	.265	.367	.229	34	113	14	30	8	0	3	15	14	3	5	0	15	1	1	.416	.362
Crew, Ryan	R-R	6-0	175	8-31-83	.197	.214	.191	38	61	13	12	3	0	0	2	9	0	1	0	8	0	0	.246	.300
De La Rosa, Anderson	R-R	6-0	190	8-1-84	.250	1.000	.143	2	8	0	2	0	0	0	1	1	0	0	0	2	0	0	.250	.333
Errecart, Chris	R-L	6-1	210	2-11-85	.247	.263	.241	104	360	57	89	22	1	15	46	33	10	4	4	109	1	2	.439	.324
Escobar, Alcides	R-R	6-1	175	12-16-86	.328	.374	.311	131	546	95	179	24	5	8	76	31	3	10	7	82	34	8	.434	.363
Gamel, Mat	L-R	6-0	195	7-26-85	.329	.353	.318	127	508	96	167	35	7	19	96	55	4	0	5	111	6	7	.537	.395
Garciaparra, Michael	R-R	6-1	165	4-2-83	.340	.500	.261	44	103	12	35	4	1	3	20	3	2	3	0	25	2	1	.485	.370
Gibbons, Jay	L-L	6-0	195	3-2-77	.273	.500	.222	5	11	0	3	0	0	0	2	3	0	0	1	2	0	0	.273	.400
Gillespie, Cole	R-R	6-1	205	6-20-84	.281	.298	.276	131	462	73	130	38	4	14	79	75	6	3	4	102	17	1	.472	.386
Hopf, J.R.	L-R	6-1	205	11-4-82	.170	.143	.175	16	47	4	8	2	0	0	3	4	0	1	0	16	0	0	.213	.235
Krause, Brent	R-R	6-3	215	11-2-81	.375	.667	.200	3	8	0	3	1	0	0	2	0	0	0	0	4	0	0	.500	.375
LaPorta, Matt	R-R	6-2	210	1-8-85	.288	.250	.301	84	302	56	87	23	2	20	66	45	15	0	4	63	2	1	.576	.402
Maldonado, Martin	R-R	6-1	190	8-16-86	.194	.192	.194	31	98	4	19	2	0	2	8	4	0	4	0	24	0	0	.276	.225
Parejo, Freddy	R-R	6-2	175	10-16-84	.275	.289	.270	103	334	39	92	12	3	2	33	9	6	12	3	59	13	4	.347	.304
Perez, Yohannis	R-R	6-0	190	10-11-82	.000	.000	.000	1	2	0	0	0	0	0	0	0	0	0	0	0	0	0	.000	.000
Rodriguez, Guilder	B-R	6-1	160	7-24-83	.246	.297	.232	72	175	29	43	2	0	0	5	20	0	9	1	24	12	2	.257	.321
Salome, Angel	R-R	5-7	200	6-8-86	.360	.378	.353	98	367	67	132	30	2	13	83	33	5	1	5	57	3	2	.559	.415

Pitching	B-T	HT	WT	DOB	W	L	ERA	G	GS	CG	SV	IP	H	R	ER	HR	BB	SO	AVG	vLH	vRH	K/9	BB/9
Aguilar, Omar	R-R	6-0	220	3-31-85	0	3	3.08	28	0	0	4	38	26	24	13	5	22	42	.191	.189	.193	9.95	5.21
Bateman, Joe	R-R	6-2	170	5-6-80	2	1	2.47	26	0	0	4	44	40	16	12	3	13	39	.244	.286	.213	8.04	2.68
Bray, Steve	R-R	6-1	195	12-22-80	1	3	4.29	21	0	0	1	36	40	18	17	4	7	34	.280	.387	.198	8.58	1.77
Cate, Troy	L-L	6-1	220	10-21-80	3	0	2.36	4	4	0	0	27	22	9	7	3	7	14	.218	.250	.200	4.73	2.36
Hammond, Steve	R-L	6-2	205	4-30-82	7	4	3.45	15	15	0	0	89	77	39	34	5	33	78	.234	.185	.253	7.92	3.35
Hand, Donovan	R-R	6-4	190	4-20-86	3	4	5.09	16	12	2	0	81	101	56	46	11	26	41	.312	.341	.292	4.54	2.88
Hinton, Robert	R-R	6-1	195	8-13-84	3	4	5.37	30	0	0	3	54	49	35	32	8	30	57	.246	.287	.214	9.56	5.03
Howard, Ben	R-R	6-2	220	1-15-79	0	1	6.75	4	0	0	0	7	8	6	5	0	4	2	.320	.333	.300	2.70	5.40
Jeffress, Jeremy	R-R	6-0	197	9-21-87	2	1	5.52	4	4	0	0	15	17	9	9	2	11	13	.298	.292	.303	7.98	6.75
Johnson, Dave	R-R	6-5	205	8-25-82	5	3	3.32	40	1	0	3	62	54	27	23	5	27	72	.233	.242	.226	10.40	3.90
Jones, Mike	R-R	6-2	220	4-23-83	1	6	6.09	18	12	0	0	58	54	39	39	11	45	32	.262	.197	.293	4.99	7.02
Miller, Derek	L-L	6-0	195	11-8-81	2	4	4.66	16	16	1	0	73	84	39	38	6	38	42	.294	.224	.319	5.15	4.66
Narron, Sam	L-L	6-7	200	7-12-81	6	1	2.77	8	8	2	0	52	44	19	16	3	12	20	.237	.197	.256	3.46	2.08
Periard, Alexandre	L-R	6-1	180	6-15-87	2	4	5.68	8	8	0	0	38	42	25	24	3	16	20	.288	.368	.218	4.74	3.79
Ryan, Patrick	R-R	6-0	200	5-31-83	5	5	2.52	39	0	0	6	64	62	26	18	3	29	38	.261	.196	.305	5.32	4.06
Sandoval, Juan	R-R	6-2	170	1-13-81	2	6	3.38	45	0	0	20	48	41	20	18	5	27	36	.234	.301	.186	6.75	5.06
Shanks, E.J.	R-R	6-5	230	4-8-82	0	0	6.75	14	0	0	0	20	24	17	15	0	15	10	.308	.367	.271	4.50	6.75
Shiell, Jason	R-R	6-1	215	10-19-76	3	3	3.58	18	0	0	0	28	29	15	11	2	18	22	.271	.288	.255	7.16	5.86
Stanczyk, Ben	R-R	6-2	210	9-26-82	0	1	10.24	6	0	0	0	10	13	11	11	2	7	4	.351	.222	.474	3.72	6.52
Torres, Melqui	R-R	6-2	205	5-27-77	0	0	2.45	3	0	0	0	4	2	1	1	0	3	3	.154	.286	.000	7.36	7.36
Tucker, Rusty	R-L	6-1	190	7-15-80	0	0	3.24	6	0	0	0	8	5	3	3	1	5	9	.172	.100	.211	9.72	5.40
Ungs, Nic	R-R	6-1	220	9-3-79	4	1	1.96	7	7	1	0	46	36	10	10	4	10	24	.221	.152	.286	4.70	1.96
Wahpepah, Josh	R-R	6-4	185	7-17-84	1	0	9.64	3	0	0	0	5	10	5	5	0	3	7	.400	.500	.353	13.50	5.79
Welch, David	R-L	6-4	215	6-2-83	11	4	3.90	27	27	1	0	148	145	69	64	23	51	95	.257	.290	.243	5.79	3.11
Wright, Brae	L-L	6-4	205	11-1-83	6	9	3.59	27	27	0	0	171	164	80	68	9	60	120	.258	.258	.258	6.33	3.16

Fielding

Catcher	PCT	G	PO	A	E	DP	PB
Corporan	.991	32	200	17	2	1	2
De La Rosa	1.000	2	17	1	0	1	0
Hopf	1.000	1	3	0	0	1	0
Maldonado	.995	29	190	25	1	2	3
Salome	.995	78	496	50	3	3	13

First Base	PCT	G	PO	A	E	DP
Brantley	.995	21	194	12	1	14
Errecart	.988	94	861	55	11	85
Garciaparra	1.000	10	91	5	0	4
Gibbons	1.000	1	11	0	0	1
Hopf	.993	13	124	9	1	16
LaPorta	.966	2	28	0	1	3
Rodriguez	1.000	5	28	1	0	1

Second Base	PCT	G	PO	A	E	DP
Bell	.959	116	203	333	23	70
Chavez	1.000	2	3	6	0	1
Crew	.947	5	9	9	1	2
Garciaparra	1.000	1	0	2	0	0
Perez	1.000	1	0	5	0	0
Rodriguez	.964	28	44	64	4	9

Third Base	PCT	G	PO	A	E	DP
Crew	1.000	2	0	2	0	0
Gamel	.918	126	89	245	30	27
Garciaparra	.667	4	0	8	4	0
Rodriguez	.957	9	7	15	1	1

Shortstop	PCT	G	PO	A	E	DP
Chavez	.923	3	5	7	1	2
Escobar	.971	125	231	429	20	94
Garciaparra	1.000	3	1	3	0	0
Perez	1.000	1	0	2	0	0
Rodriguez	.946	9	13	22	2	3

Outfield	PCT	G	PO	A	E	DP
Brantley	.994	83	167	9	1	1
Cain	1.000	40	75	3	0	2
Crew	1.000	4	2	0	0	0
Garciaparra	1.000	7	8	0	0	0
Gibbons	1.000	3	2	0	0	0
Gillespie	.977	129	198	10	5	0
Krause	1.000	3	6	1	0	0
LaPorta	.993	79	131	5	1	1
Parejo	.984	88	173	8	3	2
Rodriguez	.667	2	4	0	2	0

BREVARD COUNTY MANATEES   HIGH CLASS A

FLORIDA STATE LEAGUE

Batting	B-T	HT	WT	DOB	AVG	vLH	vRH	G	AB	R	H	2B	3B	HR	RBI	BB	HBP	SH	SF	SO	SB	CS	SLG	OBP
Bouchie, Andy	R-R	6-1	205	8-6-85	.197	.229	.191	73	239	15	47	6	0	4	17	25	1	3	4	47	0	0	.272	.271
Brewer, Brent	R-R	6-2	190	12-19-87	.251	.394	.201	76	275	36	69	17	2	2	25	25	2	4	2	57	15	5	.349	.316
Cain, Lorenzo	R-R	6-2	185	4-13-86	.287	.269	.291	80	317	50	91	22	4	7	41	29	7	1	2	68	19	4	.448	.358
Caufield, Chuck	R-R	6-1	180	7-6-83	.235	.324	.208	119	438	42	103	20	0	4	51	37	9	2	5	79	10	3	.308	.305
Chapman, Stephen	L-L	6-0	205	10-12-85	.202	.169	.209	89	312	40	63	12	7	12	31	33	3	2	4	112	11	2	.401	.281
Cline, Matt	R-R	5-10	180	10-18-85	.266	.211	.280	32	94	15	25	5	1	0	8	5	3	4	1	7	2	2	.340	.320
De La Rosa, Anderson	R-R	6-0	190	8-1-84	.230	.231	.230	24	74	8	17	3	0	2	13	1	2	2	2	17	0	0	.351	.253
Fermaint, Charlie	R-R	5-9	180	10-11-85	.212	.297	.191	122	452	48	96	22	1	6	46	36	7	2	6	99	27	10	.305	.277
Ford, Darren	R-R	5-11	195	10-1-85	.230	.288	.218	91	343	57	79	13	3	2	27	46	2	7	3	88	48	11	.303	.322
Green, Taylor	L-R	5-10	180	11-2-86	.289	.330	.279	114	418	46	121	19	0	15	73	61	4	3	4	59	4	2	.443	.382
Holmberg, Kenny	R-R	5-9	175	2-21-83	.218	.322	.190	91	280	24	61	8	1	0	24	51	10	0	2	56	1	1	.254	.356
Hopf, J.R.	R-R	6-1	205	11-4-82	.206	.214	.204	19	63	4	13	0	0	0	7	10	1	0	0	15	0	0	.254	.324
Houin, Scott	R-R	6-2	195	4-11-85	.105	.222	.083	25	57	5	6	4	0	0	2	6	3	1	0	23	2	1	.175	.227
Lucroy, Jonathan	R-R	6-0	195	6-13-86	.292	.259	.302	64	236	31	69	12	1	10	44	28	2	0	6	45	1	2	.479	.364
Maldonado, Martin	R-R	6-1	190	8-16-86	.266	.261	.268	34	94	8	25	8	0	0	9	8	5	2	1	17	3	1	.351	.352
Mojica, Jimmy	R-R	5-11	170	11-3-83	.231	.146	.251	76	208	33	48	5	2	4	21	35	3	3	2	41	4	3	.332	.347
Palmisano, Lou	R-R	6-0	200	9-16-82	.306	.368	.283	19	72	8	22	2	0	2	8	5	2	0	0	11	0	1	.417	.367
Perez, Yohannis	R-R	6-0	190	10-11-82	.240	.257	.235	106	346	37	83	11	5	2	27	18	7	3	1	67	1	4	.318	.290
Stocker, Mel	B-R	5-10	160	8-15-80	.323	.206	.355	40	155	27	50	7	3	0	7	10	3	3	1	17	19	6	.406	.373

Pitching	B-T	HT	WT	DOB	W	L	ERA	G	GS	CG	SV	IP	H	R	ER	HR	BB	SO	AVG	vLH	vRH	K/9	BB/9
Aguilar, Omar	R-R	6-0	220	3-31-85	3	0	0.35	19	0	0	13	26	13	2	1	0	10	25	.155	.207	.127	8.77	3.51
Axford, John	R-R	6-5	195	4-1-83	5	10	4.55	26	14	0	0	95	86	58	48	5	73	89	.246	.270	.227	8.43	6.92
Baron, Casey	L-L	6-2	185	11-29-84	4	2	3.45	47	0	0	4	70	84	33	27	3	16	53	.301	.347	.276	6.78	2.05
Braddock, Zach	L-L	6-4	230	8-23-87	4	7	5.51	21	11	0	0	65	55	44	40	7	42	80	.226	.188	.240	11.02	5.79
Bramhall, Bobby	L-L	5-10	190	7-13-85	5	4	2.51	34	9	0	1	111	91	37	31	5	32	106	.222	.246	.200	8.57	2.59
Butler, Joshua	R-R	6-5	195	12-11-84	2	8	5.36	20	20	0	0	82	86	53	49	10	40	63	.271	.285	.263	6.89	4.37
2-team total (3 Vero Beach)					2	10	5.53	23	23	0	0	99	104	66	61	11	45	73	—	—	—	6.61	4.08
Choate, Randy	L-L	6-1	195	9-5-75	0	0	0.00	1	1	0	0	1	0	0	0	0	0	1	.000	.000	.000	9.00	0.00
Cody, Chris	L-L	6-1	195	1-7-84	4	5	1.83	14	13	1	0	84	68	17	17	4	25	62	.227	.333	.188	6.67	2.69
Dickert, Reed	R-R	6-1	227	6-29-84	0	1	13.50	1	0	0	0	2	3	3	3	0	1	2	.333	.333	.333	9.00	4.50
Ellison, Derrick	L-L	6-2	195	9-6-78	1	0	2.70	10	0	0	1	20	22	8	6	0	13	21	.286	.333	.260	9.45	5.85
Ferguson, Shawn	R-R	6-2	205	1-12-83	3	1	6.31	26	0	0	3	36	49	29	25	2	20	14	.327	.400	.290	3.53	5.05
Hand, Donovan	R-R	6-4	190	4-20-86	4	2	2.31	10	9	0	0	58	49	15	15	3	10	36	.234	.264	.213	5.55	1.54
Hinton, Robert	R-R	6-1	195	8-13-84	0	0	0.00	5	0	0	0	7	2	0	0	0	1	3	.087	.000	.105	3.86	1.29
Jeffress, Jeremy	R-R	6-0	197	9-21-87	4	6	4.08	15	14	1	0	79	65	39	36	5	41	102	.226	.250	.212	11.57	4.65
Jones, Mike	R-R	6-4	220	4-23-83	0	0	4.50	8	7	0	0	18	15	10	9	1	14	11	.238	.227	.244	5.50	7.00
Lluberes, Rafael	L-L	6-4	215	9-21-84	2	3	5.32	34	6	0	0	68	74	47	40	5	48	68	.286	.232	.311	9.04	6.38
McClendon, Mike	R-R	6-5	215	4-3-85	7	6	4.19	46	5	0	10	88	103	50	41	6	15	61	.287	.344	.254	6.24	1.53
Miller, Derek	L-L	6-0	195	11-8-81	0	0	3.65	4	3	0	0	12	7	5	5	1	4	10	.167	.200	.148	7.30	2.92
Periard, Alexandre	L-R	6-1	180	6-15-87	9	6	3.51	19	18	1	0	113	114	52	44	6	30	76	.256	.252	.259	6.07	2.40
Ramlow, Mike	L-L	6-6	185	3-2-86	2	2	3.29	5	2	0	0	14	10	5	5	1	5	8	.204	.333	.147	5.23	3.29
Rivas, Amaury	R-R	6-2	189	12-20-85	1	2	4.20	7	6	0	0	30	35	16	14	2	11	20	.294	.365	.239	6.00	3.30
Shanks, E.J.	R-R	6-5	230	4-8-82	0	2	4.31	25	0	0	1	31	40	16	15	2	10	9	.305	.388	.256	2.59	2.87
Wahpepah, Josh	R-R	6-4	185	7-17-84	2	5	3.97	35	0	0	2	57	60	27	25	1	36	55	.270	.307	.246	8.74	5.72
Wendte, Travis	R-R	6-2	195	11-17-82	4	0	5.46	25	0	0	0	28	37	18	17	7	9	20	.308	.340	.288	6.43	2.89

Fielding

Catcher	PCT	G	PO	A	E	DP	PB
Bouchie	.989	44	340	26	4	2	10
De La Rosa	1.000	18	105	13	0	1	3
Lucroy	.992	48	343	34	3	4	7
Maldonado	.985	32	233	27	4	0	6

First Base	PCT	G	PO	A	E	DP
Bouchie	.981	8	47	4	1	5
Caufield	1.000	1	7	0	0	1
Chapman	.984	75	655	41	11	57
De La Rosa	1.000	1	5	1	0	1
Green	1.000	5	25	0	0	1
Holmberg	.989	31	242	21	3	33
Hopf	1.000	19	126	11	0	10
Maldonado	.800	2	4	0	1	1
Mojica	.981	6	50	2	1	2

Second Base	PCT	G	PO	A	E	DP
Cline	.964	12	19	34	2	6
Holmberg	.987	32	63	90	2	29
Mojica	.961	40	92	103	8	27
Perez	.974	58	113	151	7	34
Stocker	.947	5	9	9	1	1

Third Base	PCT	G	PO	A	E	DP
Brewer	.857	2	1	5	1	1
Cline	.769	6	1	9	3	0

	PCT	G	PO	A	E	DP
Green	.934	100	57	198	18	13
Holmberg	.904	24	10	37	5	3
Mojica	.813	10	3	10	3	4
Perez	1.000	4	1	2	0	0

Shortstop	PCT	G	PO	A	E	DP
Brewer	.941	70	101	202	19	32
Cline	.905	14	20	37	6	7
Mojica	.942	16	24	41	4	13
Perez	.949	45	68	136	11	29

Outfield	PCT	G	PO	A	E	DP
Cain	.987	76	146	8	2	2
Caufield	.971	79	124	11	4	3
Chapman	1.000	9	19	2	0	0
De La Rosa	1.000	4	7	1	0	0
Fermaint	.973	124	206	9	6	2
Ford	.988	86	161	3	2	1
Houin	1.000	18	29	1	0	0
Stocker	.986	34	67	1	1	1

WEST VIRGINIA POWER
SOUTH ATLANTIC LEAGUE
LOW CLASS A

Batting	B-T	HT	WT	DOB	AVG	vLH	vRH	G	AB	R	H	2B	3B	HR	RBI	BB	HBP	SH	SF	SO	SB	CS	SLG	OBP
Alonso, John	R-R	6-0	225	2-19-86	.194	.238	.171	18	62	7	12	3	0	3	8	5	2	0	0	19	0	0	.387	.275
Brewer, Brent	R-R	6-2	190	12-19-87	.213	.173	.230	47	174	25	37	13	2	0	17	18	2	2	0	54	16	4	.310	.294
Cline, Matt	R-R	5-10	180	10-18-85	.266	.308	.253	82	282	51	75	14	0	3	30	38	9	11	5	43	15	2	.348	.365
Crowell, Kurt	R-R	6-3	215	9-21-84	.217	.227	.213	19	69	6	15	2	0	2	11	1	0	0	0	20	0	1	.333	.229
De La Rosa, Anderson	R-R	6-0	190	8-1-84	.237	.250	.234	34	118	17	28	6	0	4	18	5	4	1	0	24	1	1	.390	.291
Farris, Eric	R-R	5-10	173	3-3-86	.293	.319	.284	103	454	73	133	21	4	3	54	24	5	4	5	50	32	10	.377	.332
Fonseca, David	R-R	6-0	180	8-28-86	.212	.211	.212	29	85	13	18	1	0	2	6	7	0	1	0	24	1	2	.294	.272
Fryer, Eric	R-R	6-2	215	8-26-85	.335	.370	.323	104	385	76	129	26	5	10	63	43	6	0	3	74	15	3	.506	.407
Gindl, Caleb	L-L	5-9	185	8-31-88	.307	.343	.294	137	508	86	156	38	4	13	81	63	5	0	2	144	14	5	.474	.388
Haydel, Lee	L-L	6-0	185	7-15-87	.295	.254	.308	131	522	68	154	21	8	0	50	32	2	10	2	107	34	17	.366	.337
Houin, Scott	R-R	6-0	195	4-11-85	.207	.321	.179	47	140	12	29	5	1	1	9	5	6	4	0	62	7	1	.279	.265
Lucroy, Jonathan	R-R	6-0	195	6-13-86	.310	.371	.288	65	239	45	74	16	1	10	33	30	3	0	2	39	8	1	.510	.391
Rindal, Curt	R-R	6-3	215	9-15-83	.262	.253	.265	112	393	48	103	24	1	9	58	31	10	0	6	77	3	6	.397	.327
Schafer, Logan	L-L	6-1	170	9-8-86	.276	.242	.294	43	181	25	50	13	2	0	20	8	1	3	3	42	3	8	.370	.306
Snijders, Ulrich	R-R	6-2	220	7-8-86	.200	.115	.220	45	135	22	27	6	1	4	19	20	0	1	0	55	0	1	.348	.303
Vass, Mike	R-R	6-1	210	4-19-85	.091	.100	.083	9	22	2	2	0	0	1	4	4	0	0	0	7	0	0	.227	.231
Wheeler, Zelous	R-R	5-10	220	1-16-87	.258	.248	.262	137	503	80	130	31	2	13	87	61	7	3	2	105	13	11	.406	.346
Wilson, Steffan	R-R	6-1	220	5-24-86	.289	.279	.292	131	485	91	140	27	5	19	100	46	2	2	4	98	4	5	.482	.350

Pitching	B-T	HT	WT	DOB	W	L	ERA	G	GS	CG	SV	IP	H	R	ER	HR	BB	SO	AVG	vLH	vRH	K/9	BB/9
Anundsen, Evan	R-R	6-3	200	5-17-88	12	8	4.28	28	28	0	0	145	158	80	69	8	38	102	.283	.340	.238	6.33	2.36
Bowman, Michael	R-R	6-2	195	5-2-87	3	1	3.58	8	4	0	0	28	23	14	11	1	15	19	.225	.222	.228	6.18	4.88
Braddock, Zach	L-L	6-4	230	8-23-87	0	0	0.00	2	2	0	0	6	1	0	0	3	13	.095	.000	.154	19.50	4.50	
Bryson, Rob	R-R	6-1	200	12-11-87	3	2	4.25	22	5	0	5	55	43	31	26	3	20	73	.209	.218	.202	11.95	3.27
2-team total (7 Lake County)					3	3	3.88	29	5	0	5	67	49	37	29	4	26	84	—	—		11.23	3.48
Cody, Chris	L-L	6-1	195	1-7-84	2	1	1.74	5	4	0	0	31	19	8	6	3	3	31	.174	.179	.173	9.00	0.87
Dickert, Reed	R-R	6-1	227	6-29-84	2	4	2.50	24	1	0	3	58	40	20	16	6	29	57	.198	.179	.210	8.90	4.53
Etheridge, Wes	R-R	6-1	185	8-12-84	0	1	5.14	20	0	0	4	35	32	21	20	3	9	29	.246	.207	.278	7.46	2.31
Frederickson, Evan	L-L	6-6	240	9-23-86	0	1	6.20	9	4	0	0	20	16	19	14	1	26	18	.229	.200	.233	7.97	11.51
Frerichs, Corey	R-R	5-11	200	5-7-86	6	9	2.82	40	0	0	10	73	57	35	23	7	41	92	.213	.224	.205	11.29	5.03
Garcia, Jose	R-R	6-4	175	5-25-88	3	2	5.90	29	0	0	0	50	53	33	33	5	31	41	.273	.373	.210	7.33	5.54
Lambertus, Pedro	R-R	6-3	190	6-4-88	1	2	5.12	24	0	0	1	39	38	28	22	3	24	27	.262	.280	.253	6.28	5.59
Luetge, Lucas	L-L	6-3	180	3-24-87	1	2	3.72	8	6	0	0	48	39	27	20	1	10	33	.252	.286	.240	8.17	2.48
Mercedes, Roque	B-R	6-3	185	9-28-86	5	5	4.30	30	13	0	3	113	112	59	54	14	27	111	.252	.289	.224	8.84	2.15
Merklinger, Daniel	L-L	6-1	195	11-19-85	7	9	5.75	25	23	0	0	97	97	66	62	8	42	98	.257	.281	.249	9.09	3.90
Pasma, Curtis	L-L	6-0	206	9-19-85	4	2	3.91	32	0	0	2	51	49	23	22	9	13	49	.257	.247	.263	8.70	2.31
Peralta, Wily	R-R	6-2	225	5-8-89	0	1	10.80	2	2	0	0	5	9	6	6	2	5	4	.316	.800	.143	5.40	5.40
Ramlow, Mike	L-L	6-6	185	3-2-86	6	3	2.59	31	6	0	8	90	75	32	26	5	10	68	.223	.209	.228	6.77	1.00
Rivas, Amaury	R-R	6-2	189	12-20-85	8	3	3.50	19	15	0	0	90	83	41	35	11	32	70	.239	.238	.241	7.00	3.20
Seidel, R.J.	R-R	6-5	200	9-3-87	9	5	4.51	26	25	0	0	122	135	72	61	10	45	81	.284	.272	.292	5.99	3.33
Sutton, Jared	R-R	6-2	210	5-4-83	1	0	3.00	4	0	0	0	9	5	3	3	1	2	5	.172	.250	.118	7.00	5.00
Tyson, Nicholas	R-R	6-3	185	1-13-88	2	2	8.74	16	1	0	0	34	60	36	33	4	7	26	.392	.393	.392	6.88	1.85
Wooten, Rob	R-R	6-1	208	7-21-85	1	0	2.38	10	0	0	4	23	14	6	6	0	4	30	.173	.192	.164	11.91	1.59

Fielding

Catcher	PCT	G	PO	A	E	DP	PB
De La Rosa	.991	25	198	25	2	0	7
Fryer	.962	39	276	31	12	4	5
Lucroy	.988	49	364	44	5	1	3
Snijders	1.000	36	217	19	0	1	3

First Base	PCT	G	PO	A	E	DP
Alonso	1.000	3	22	1	0	0
De La Rosa	1.000	1	4	0	0	0
Fryer	.900	1	9	0	1	0
Rindal	.992	81	688	50	6	58
Wilson	.989	60	519	32	6	41

Second Base	PCT	G	PO	A	E	DP
Farris	.961	92	164	277	18	50

	PCT	G	PO	A	E	DP
Fonseca	.972	17	23	47	2	8
Wheeler	.975	34	62	95	4	25

Third Base	PCT	G	PO	A	E	DP
Cline	.850	11	9	25	6	6
Wheeler	.954	91	61	189	12	12
Wilson	.936	43	18	70	6	5

Shortstop	PCT	G	PO	A	E	DP
Brewer	.931	47	68	133	15	27
Cline	.939	68	99	195	19	31
Farris	1.000	8	8	22	0	5
Fonseca	1.000	4	2	12	0	2
Wheeler	.935	14	12	31	3	2
Wilson	—	1	0	0	0	0

Outfield	PCT	G	PO	A	E	DP
Crowell	.920	16	22	1	2	0
De La Rosa	.857	4	6	0	1	0
Fryer	.988	55	78	3	1	3
Gindl	.978	135	257	8	6	2
Haydel	.971	129	229	6	7	2
Houin	.933	38	37	5	3	1
Schafer	.975	39	72	5	2	0
Vass	1.000	4	5	2	0	0
Wheeler	.900	3	8	1	1	0
Wilson	1.000	9	15	4	0	1

HELENA BREWERS

PIONEER LEAGUE

Batting	B-T	HT	WT	DOB	AVG	vLH	vRH	G	AB	R	H	2B	3B	HR	RBI	BB	HBP	SH	SF	SO	SB	CS	SLG	OBP
Alfonso, Derrick	R-R	6-0	210	7-6-85	.227	.316	.181	31	110	11	25	4	1	3	16	8	3	2	1	32	0	2	.364	.295
Braun, Steve	R-R	6-0	185	5-17-85	.175	.167	.182	25	80	8	14	2	1	1	6	4	0	1	0	20	3	1	.263	.214
Delaney, John	R-R	5-9	180	12-30-85	.262	.358	.207	75	302	63	79	12	5	9	33	51	5	0	1	78	2	1	.424	.376
Dennis, Chris	L-R	6-1	205	9-15-88	.253	.236	.261	63	229	40	58	7	2	12	40	43	3	0	1	73	6	1	.459	.377
Duran, Jose	R-R	5-11	190	11-27-86	.221	.100	.291	36	136	15	30	4	1	2	16	11	1	2	0	38	1	1	.309	.284
Dykstra, Cutter	R-R	5-11	180	6-29-89	.271	.231	.293	38	144	24	39	9	0	5	17	21	1	0	0	30	4	4	.438	.367
Fonseca, David	R-R	6-0	180	8-28-86	.262	.276	.254	49	210	24	55	11	0	5	22	8	3	0	2	60	3	5	.386	.296
Kemp, Corey	R-R	6-0	240	2-24-86	.253	.246	.255	53	198	24	50	9	0	3	28	21	8	3	2	40	0	2	.343	.345
Komatsu, Erik	L-L	5-10	190	10-1-87	.321	.330	.316	68	277	61	89	19	4	11	47	30	5	1	3	42	8	4	.538	.394
Marseco, Michael	R-R	5-9	145	1-7-87	.311	.320	.307	40	151	18	47	13	3	0	24	6	1	0	2	20	5	2	.437	.338
Miller, Erik	R-R	6-3	200	8-23-87	.257	.328	.163	37	101	18	26	3	1	0	7	7	3	2	1	26	6	4	.307	.321
Roberts, Michael	R-R	6-2	185	8-28-87	.270	.234	.287	36	141	26	38	7	1	3	23	14	2	1	1	34	3	1	.397	.342
Schafer, Logan	L-L	6-1	170	9-8-86	.240	.667	.182	8	25	4	6	0	1	2	8	5	0	0	1	4	1	0	.560	.355
Trejo, Edgar	R-R	6-3	200	7-28-89	.364	.500	.286	3	11	2	4	0	0	1	2	0	0	0	0	3	0	0	.636	.364
Vasquez, Miguel	B-R	6-1	185	11-25-86	.183	.222	.159	19	71	11	13	1	1	1	4	9	0	1	0	28	6	0	.268	.275
Vass, Mike	R-R	6-1	210	4-19-85	.242	.286	.219	43	161	22	39	4	3	7	28	18	2	1	3	34	1	2	.435	.321
Whiteside, Brett	R-R	6-2	210	3-29-88	.148	.083	.200	9	27	2	4	1	0	0	1	2	0	0	0	17	0	1	.185	.207

Pitching	B-T	HT	WT	DOB	W	L	ERA	G	GS	CG	SV	IP	H	R	ER	HR	BB	SO	AVG	vLH	vRH	K/9	BB/9
Adams, Cody	R-R	6-2	180	11-26-86	5	4	3.48	14	5	0	0	54	56	30	21	3	16	37	.273	.341	.219	6.13	2.65
Arnold, Adam	R-R	6-0	185	5-15-86	3	2	3.20	15	0	0	5	25	19	14	9	2	17	28	.207	.324	.127	9.95	6.04
Bowman, Michael	R-R	6-2	195	5-2-87	1	1	4.26	4	4	0	0	19	21	11	9	3	6	19	.269	.250	.283	9.00	2.84
Crespo, Jorge	R-R	6-2	195	2-3-87	0	0	8.53	3	0	0	1	6	7	12	6	1	7	5	.241	.200	.263	7.11	9.95
Frederickson, Evan	L-L	6-6	240	9-23-86	0	0	3.09	3	3	0	0	12	13	7	4	1	16	16	.289	.429	.226	12.34	3.86
Luetge, Lucas	L-L	6-3	180	3-24-87	4	0	0.00	5	1	0	0	14	5	2	0	0	5	13	.106	.286	.075	8.36	3.21
Manzanillo, Santo	R-R	6-0	175	12-20-88	0	1	9.28	13	6	0	1	32	41	35	33	3	26	27	.318	.321	.316	7.59	7.31
Meadows, Dan	L-L	6-5	235	11-3-87	2	2	5.45	12	6	0	0	40	43	26	24	6	15	38	.277	.286	.274	8.62	3.40
Nieves, Efrain	L-L	6-0	169	11-15-89	6	3	4.48	16	11	0	0	76	78	40	38	9	10	66	.264	.250	.268	7.78	1.18
Ohlmann, Liam	R-R	6-0	241	9-15-86	0	5	5.68	11	4	0	0	32	37	22	20	6	16	30	.291	.273	.306	8.53	4.55
Pascual, Rolando	B-R	6-6	245	2-8-89	0	1	17.80	9	0	0	0	15	18	30	29	3	22	8	.310	.250	.353	4.91	13.50
Peralta, Wily	R-R	6-2	225	5-8-89	1	1	3.07	15	2	0	2	29	23	14	10	4	8	36	.209	.261	.172	11.05	2.45
Rapoza, Brandon	R-R	6-2	220	11-14-85	0	1	1.04	13	0	0	1	26	14	3	3	1	9	16	.161	.200	.135	5.54	3.12
Ritchie, Brandon	L-L	6-4	230	12-10-86	1	3	6.87	15	9	0	1	55	84	52	42	3	21	49	.356	.391	.341	8.02	3.44
Salmon, Marcus	R-R	6-2	235	4-27-88	2	4	3.60	11	7	0	0	40	41	26	16	1	13	39	.253	.260	.247	8.78	2.93
Scarpetta, Cody	R-R	6-3	225	8-25-88	1	0	3.48	6	3	0	0	21	18	10	8	2	8	31	.237	.290	.200	13.50	3.48
Sherrill, Gerritt	R-R	6-5	210	9-4-87	1	9	4.71	21	0	0	3	36	29	21	19	3	21	46	.213	.245	.193	11.39	5.20
Tyson, Nicholas	R-R	6-3	185	1-13-88	1	3	3.48	13	5	0	1	44	52	19	17	1	7	42	.294	.345	.244	8.59	1.43
Watten, Trey	R-R	6-3	180	12-16-86	3	2	5.40	15	10	0	1	55	64	35	33	5	25	40	.292	.271	.306	6.55	4.09
Willinsky, Mark	R-R	6-4	250	3-14-87	3	1	4.86	15	0	0	0	33	31	19	18	5	24	35	.238	.196	.266	9.45	6.48
Wooten, Rob	R-R	6-1	208	7-21-85	0	0	0.00	4	0	0	2	9	10	0	0	0	2	14	.286	.200	.320	14.00	2.00

Fielding

Catcher	PCT	G	PO	A	E	DP	PB
Alfonso	.986	17	131	14	2	3	3
Kemp	.981	27	237	23	5	1	9
Roberts	.974	31	270	25	8	1	5
Whiteside	.933	2	12	2	1	0	1

First Base	PCT	G	PO	A	E	DP
Duran	1.000	1	11	2	0	1
Kjeldgaard	.989	75	744	55	9	55

Second Base	PCT	G	PO	A	E	DP
Braun	.989	19	24	67	1	8
Delaney	.933	3	5	9	1	0
Duran	.932	27	44	94	10	20

Third Base	PCT	G	PO	A	E	DP
Dykstra	—	1	0	0	0	0
Fonseca	.960	16	25	70	4	12
Vasquez	.961	13	20	29	2	6

Third Base	PCT	G	PO	A	E	DP
Delaney	.929	71	33	111	11	10
Fonseca	1.000	1	0	1	0	0
Kemp	.667	1	0	2	1	0
Schafer	—	1	0	0	0	0
Trejo	1.000	3	0	9	0	0

Shortstop	PCT	G	PO	A	E	DP
Braun	1.000	2	3	2	0	0
Fonseca	.956	32	52	99	7	14

	PCT	G	PO	A	E	DP
Marseco	.964	39	61	125	7	27
Vasquez	.964	6	8	19	1	4

Outfield	PCT	G	PO	A	E	DP
Delaney	—	1	0	0	0	0
Dennis	.974	57	70	4	2	2
Dykstra	.930	30	49	4	4	0
Komatsu	.977	67	124	6	3	0
Miller	.982	35	51	3	1	0
Schafer	.947	7	18	0	1	0
Vass	.956	38	41	2	2	0
Whiteside	1.000	5	6	0	0	0

AZL BREWERS

ARIZONA LEAGUE

Batting	B-T	HT	WT	DOB	AVG	vLH	vRH	G	AB	R	H	2B	3B	HR	RBI	BB	HBP	SH	SF	SO	SB	CS	SLG	OBP
Arias, Hitaniel	R-R	6-6	202	9-20-90	.174	.130	.183	40	132	10	23	5	1	3	17	16	3	2	1	50	2	0	.295	.276
Cequea, Allixon	R-R	6-1	175	6-16-90	.268	.212	.282	44	157	10	42	12	1	1	15	14	4	2	0	41	2	2	.376	.343
Drespling, Brandon	R-R	5-9	162	12-9-84	.176	.000	.200	12	34	4	6	0	0	0	2	1	0	0	7	4	0	.176	.243
Dykstra, Cutter	R-R	5-11	180	6-29-89	.269	.000	.333	10	26	5	7	0	0	0	5	1	0	0	7	0	1	.269	.406
Errecart, Chris	R-L	6-1	210	2-11-85	.000	—	.000	2	6	1	0	0	0	0	0	2	0	0	1	0	0	.000	.250
Garcia, Jose	R-R	6-3	195	3-5-91	.165	.103	.182	46	176	22	29	7	4	3	13	7	4	2	0	64	4	3	.301	.214
George, Carlos	R-R	6-2	165	2-6-89	.234	.097	.264	46	171	13	40	10	2	0	20	5	1	3	1	41	10	6	.316	.258
Miller, Erik	R-R	6-3	200	8-23-87	.000	.000	.000	3	11	0	0	0	0	0	0	0	0	0	7	0	0	.000	.000
Paciorek, Joey	R-R	6-2	225	9-20-88	.165	.100	.178	38	127	22	21	6	4	0	3	22	4	0	0	38	3	2	.276	.307
Palmisano, Lou	R-R	6-0	200	9-16-82	.276	.600	.208	8	29	4	8	2	1	0	1	5	0	0	4	1	0	.414	.382
Pena, Carlos	R-R	5-10	195	8-31-87	.171	.100	.194	19	41	4	7	3	0	0	4	4	0	1	0	8	1	0	.244	.244
Ramos, Pedro	L-L	6-3	218	8-31-89	.211	.100	.241	39	142	15	30	9	3	0	12	13	0	1	0	52	3	1	.317	.277

	B-T	HT	WT	DOB																				
Rangel, Jose	R-R	6-1	189	6-23-88	.191	.276	.171	49	152	14	29	5	2	0	8	18	5	2	0	41	16	4	.250	.297
Requena, Jonathan	R-R	5-11	215	3-25-89	.145	.125	.149	20	55	4	8	2	0	1	9	5	2	0	0	20	0	1	.236	.242
Robulack, Cameron	L-R	6-3	220	11-2-88	.229	.214	.235	28	96	5	22	2	0	0	10	8	0	0	1	21	0	2	.250	.286
Rodriguez, Orton	R-R	6-2	187	9-15-89	.182	.077	.214	21	55	6	10	2	0	0	7	4	1	1	0	14	0	0	.218	.250
Sanchez, Luis	R-R	5-11	185	7-3-89	.226	.250	.221	35	133	17	30	1	1	0	7	8	2	3	0	45	10	2	.248	.280
Snijders, Ulrich	R-R	6-2	220	7-8-86	.216	.167	.231	14	51	8	11	5	0	2	4	6	2	0	0	25	0	0	.431	.322
Vasquez, Miguel	B-R	6-1	185	11-25-86	.299	.385	.284	30	87	17	26	6	4	1	17	12	3	4	0	32	5	1	.494	.402
Zarraga, Shawn	R-R	6-2	215	1-21-89	.300	.471	.269	36	110	17	33	9	0	2	16	23	4	0	2	24	3	0	.436	.432

Pitching	B-T	HT	WT	DOB	W	L	ERA	G	GS	CG	SV	IP	H	R	ER	HR	BB	SO	AVG	vLH	vRH	K/9	BB/9
Billings, Blake	R-R	6-5	200	1-8-90	0	1	2.25	6	2	0	0	12	10	5	3	0	1	15	.213	.100	.243	11.25	0.75
Bucci, Nick	R-R	6-2	180	7-16-90	0	3	7.36	5	4	0	0	11	12	9	9	2	2	14	.273	.389	.192	11.45	1.64
Bueno, Kristian	L-L	6-2	195	12-10-88	0	4	6.69	14	4	0	0	39	41	37	29	0	32	33	.270	.173	.320	7.62	7.38
Crespo, Jorge	R-R	6-2	195	2-3-87	0	0	9.00	3	0	0	0	4	6	6	4	1	5	4	.316	.250	.364	9.00	11.25
Etheridge, Wes	R-R	6-1	185	8-12-84	0	0	0.00	1	0	0	0	1	0	0	0	0	0	1	.000	—	.000	9.00	0.00
Guerrero, Luis	R-R	6-0	170	6-20-90	2	4	4.60	14	7	0	1	43	43	30	22	1	21	40	.253	.277	.244	8.37	4.40
Hill, Shane	R-R	6-4	185	7-5-88	0	1	8.38	12	0	0	0	19	21	20	18	3	25	16	.280	.217	.308	7.45	11.64
Jeffers, Ben	R-R	6-1	200	8-30-87	2	2	8.13	14	1	0	0	28	33	30	25	1	20	37	.282	.219	.306	12.04	6.51
Krestalude, Damon	R-R	6-4	185	6-5-89	1	4	3.15	14	5	0	0	34	36	17	12	2	16	28	.263	.302	.245	7.34	4.19
Linares, Edwin	R-R	6-2	198	10-15-89	2	1	4.50	13	0	0	0	26	26	22	13	1	8	18	.252	.346	.221	6.23	2.77
Lintz, Seth	R-R	6-1	170	2-7-90	0	3	6.87	9	6	0	0	18	22	20	14	3	16	26	.289	.368	.263	12.76	7.85
McEwen, Bobby	R-R	6-0	185	8-25-84	0	1	6.60	8	0	0	1	15	14	15	11	0	12	18	.250	.333	.211	10.80	7.20
Meadows, Dan	L-L	6-5	235	11-3-87	0	1	0.00	3	0	0	0	8	5	3	0	0	3	4	.167	.000	.217	4.50	3.38
Miller, Gregory	R-R	6-3	213	2-8-87	0	1	9.30	13	3	0	0	20	28	25	21	1	20	24	.318	.400	.286	10.62	8.85
Morales, Joel	R-R	6-3	206	3-12-89	2	4	5.58	13	1	0	1	31	39	31	19	0	7	24	.300	.340	.277	7.04	2.05
Odorizzi, Jake	R-R	6-2	175	3-27-90	1	2	3.48	11	4	0	0	21	18	10	8	2	9	19	.220	.294	.167	8.27	3.92
Ohlmann, Liam	R-R	6-0	241	9-15-86	0	0	1.42	4	0	0	0	6	4	1	1	0	1	5	.174	.286	.125	7.11	1.42
Pascual, Rolando	B-R	6-6	245	2-8-89	0	1	3.60	5	2	0	0	10	7	5	4	0	10	8	.194	.200	.192	7.20	9.00
Rapoza, Brandon	R-R	6-2	220	11-14-85	0	2	4.22	8	0	0	1	11	10	8	5	0	6	9	.233	.353	.154	7.59	5.06
Rivero, Francisco	R-R	6-2	204	3-11-91	0	0	1.86	7	0	0	0	10	11	6	2	0	4	8	.282	.333	.259	7.45	3.72
Rosario, Adrian	R-R	6-4	180	9-30-89	1	3	4.20	11	5	0	0	41	47	29	19	1	13	28	.292	.341	.274	6.20	2.88
Salmon, Marcus	R-R	6-2	235	4-27-88	0	0	2.25	2	1	0	0	4	2	1	1	0	0	5	.143	.000	.222	11.25	0.00
Sanchez, Jose	R-R	6-1	178	10-4-88	0	1	5.40	15	0	0	1	22	21	21	13	0	15	11	.250	.227	.258	4.57	6.23
Scarpetta, Cody	R-R	6-3	225	8-25-88	1	0	0.57	6	5	0	0	16	8	1	1	0	8	27	.154	.313	.083	15.51	4.60
Wawrzasek, Stosh	R-R	6-0	225	8-30-90	0	3	6.94	6	5	0	0	12	15	11	9	0	7	12	.306	.300	.310	9.26	5.40

Fielding

Catcher	PCT	G	PO	A	E	DP	PB
Pena	1.000	8	15	1	0	0	1
Requena	.959	12	65	6	3	0	7
Rodriguez	.977	16	76	10	2	1	8
Snijders	.988	8	76	9	1	0	0
Zarraga	.983	28	208	26	4	1	8

First Base	PCT	G	PO	A	E	DP
Drespling	—	1	0	0	0	0
Errecart	1.000	1	5	0	0	0
Paciorek	1.000	1	2	0	0	0
Ramos	.978	34	291	19	7	19
Robulack	.949	20	155	12	9	22
Vasquez	.909	3	10	0	1	1

Second Base	PCT	G	PO	A	E	DP
Cequea	.940	24	43	66	7	16
George	.882	15	26	34	8	12
Pena	.833	6	4	11	3	1
Sanchez	.917	8	10	12	2	2
Vasquez	1.000	7	6	15	0	2

Third Base	PCT	G	PO	A	E	DP
Cequea	.911	18	10	41	5	6
Paciorek	.899	37	32	75	12	9
Requena	1.000	2	0	2	0	0
Vasquez	.923	3	5	7	1	1

Shortstop	PCT	G	PO	A	E	DP
Cequea	1.000	1	0	1	0	0
George	.805	31	50	70	29	16
Sanchez	.907	25	31	67	10	6
Vasquez	.750	1	1	2	1	1

Outfield	PCT	G	PO	A	E	DP
Arias	.882	39	42	3	6	0
Cequea	1.000	2	2	0	0	0
Drespling	.947	9	17	1	1	0
Dykstra	1.000	9	14	2	0	0
Garcia	.914	42	62	2	6	0
Miller	.857	3	6	0	1	0
Rangel	.938	49	88	3	6	3
Rodriguez	1.000	3	3	0	0	0
Sanchez	1.000	5	5	0	0	0
Vasquez	.962	16	22	3	1	1

Minnesota Twins

BY JOHN MILLEA

Minnesota's 2008 season began with lowered expectations for a variety of reasons. Most compelling were the subtractions: Torii Hunter left to sign with the Angels as a free agent and Johan Santana was traded to the Mets. Those moves, coupled with a roster that was pockmarked with questions, left the Twins in a puzzling position.

They had their stumbles during the season but, in the end, Minnesota missed capturing its fifth American League Central title in seven years by the width of a 1-0 loss to the White Sox in a one-game playoff. So as low as the preseason expectations were, the Twins had a season that far exceeded them.

The year began with six new starting position players, all except catcher Joe Mauer, first baseman Justin Morneau and right fielder Michael Cuddyer. That trio has become the veteran backbone of the lineup, but another team strength developed as the season progressed: a young rotation.

Righthanders Scott Baker, Nick Blackburn and Kevin Slowey and lefthanders Francisco Liriano and Glen Perkins, were solid throughout the campaign. No one performed to Santana standards, but the group was strong and reliable. One of the team's biggest weaknesses was middle relief, but closer Joe Nathan remains one of the best in the business. Getting to Nathan was often an adventure, and improving the middle relief corps will be one of the front office's biggest offseason challenges. One positive sign came in the form of reliever Jose Mijares, a September callup who was thrown to the lions, including 1½ innings in the playoff game.

The club's biggest offseason acquisition was outfielder Delmon Young, who came from Tampa Bay in a November trade. His numbers—10 home runs and 69 RBIs—weren't enough for a corner outfielder and he might be on the trading block.

The most valuable newcomers to the Minnesota lineup were players who were called up from the minor leagues after Opening Day, and their performances bode well for the future.

As Cuddyer battled injuries much of the season, outfielder Denard Span got the call and responded in spectacular fashion. He hit .294 with a .387 on-base percentage and 18 stolen bases. Span was quickly viewed as the successor to Hunter.

Carlos Gomez, who came in the Santana deal

from the Mets, joined the big league team during the season and provided the Twins with another speedster in the outfield. Alexi Casilla filled a gaping hole at second base in his first major league stint.

PLAYERS OF THE YEAR

MAJOR LEAGUE: JOE MAUER, C

Mauer enjoyed another fine season at the plate as the Twins catcher won the American League batting title after hitting .328. He also ranked second in on-base percentage (.571), just three hundredths of a point from winning that title as well.

MINOR LEAGUE: BEN REVERE, OF

It didn't take long for Revere to establish himself. A 2007 first-round pick, he hit 379/.433/.497 with 28 extra-base hits at low Class A Beloit in the Midwest League. His totals included 17 doubles, 10 triples, one home run and 44 steals in 57 attempts.

JOHN SPEAR

ORGANIZATION LEADERS

BATTING		*Minimum 250 at-bats
*AVG	Revere, Ben, Beloit	.379
R	Pridie, Jason, Rochester	84
H	Pridie, Jason, Rochester	151
H	Valencia, Danny, Fort Myers/New Britain	151
TB	Jones, Garrett, Rochester	255
2B	Valencia, Danny, Fort Myers/New Britain	37
3B	Pridie, Jason, Rochester	16
HR	Jones, Garrett, Rochester	23
RBI	Jones, Garrett, Rochester	92
BB	Parmelee, Chris, Beloit	52
BB	Robbins, Whitney, Fort Myers	52
SO	Pridie, Jason, Rochester	152
SB	Revere, Ben, Beloit	44
*OBP	Revere, Ben, Beloit	.433
*SLG	Ruiz, Randy, Rochester	.536

PITCHING		†Minimum 75 innings
W	Guerra, Deolis, Fort Myers	11
L	Tarsi, Michael, Beloit	11
	Duensing, Brian, Rochester	11
†ERA	McCardell, Michael, Beloit	2.86
G	Julianel, Ben, New Britain	56
GS	Four players tied with	27
SV	Korecky, Bobby, Rochester	26
	Julianel, Ben, New Britain	26
IP	Manship, Jeff, Fort Myers/New Britain	155
BB	Sosa, Oswaldo, New Britain/Fort Myers	75
SO	Bromberg, David, Beloit	177
†AVG	McCardell, Michael, Beloit	.219

General Manager: Bill Smith. **Farm Director:** Jim Rantz. **Scouting Director:** Deron Johnson.

Class	Team	League	W	L	PCT	Finish*	Manager	Affiliate Since
Majors	Minnesota	American	88	75	.540	6th (14)	Ron Gardenhire	—
Triple-A	Rochester Red Wings	International	74	70	.514	6th (14)	Stan Cliburn	2003
Double-A	New Britain Rock Cats	Eastern	64	77	.454	10th (12)	Bobby Cuellar	1995
High A	Fort Myers Miracle	Florida State	77	59	.566	2nd (12)	Jeff Smith	1993
Low A	Beloit Snappers	Midwest	71	67	.514	8th (14)	Nelson Prada	2005
Rookie	Elizabethton Twins	Appalachian	41	25	.621	^1st (10)	Ray Smith	1974
Rookie	GCL Twins	Gulf Coast	35	21	.625	2nd (16)	Jake Mauer	1989
Overall 2008 Minor League Record			362	319	.532	5th		

* Finish in overall standings (No. of teams in league). ^League champion.

ORGANIZATION STATISTICS

MINNESOTA TWINS

AMERICAN LEAGUE

Batting	B-T	HT	WT	DOB	AVG	vLH	vRH	G	AB	R	H	2B	3B	HR	RBI	BB	HBP	SH	SF	SO	SB	CS	SLG	OBP
Buscher, Brian	L-R	6-0	220	4-18-81	.294	.205	.316	70	218	29	64	9	0	4	47	19	0	0	7	42	0	2	.390	.340
Casilla, Alexi	B-R	5-9	180	7-20-84	.281	.264	.289	98	385	58	108	15	0	7	50	31	2	13	6	45	7	2	.374	.333
Clark, Howie	L-R	5-10	190	2-13-74	.250	.333	.200	4	8	0	2	2	0	0	1	0	0	0	0	2	0	0	.500	.250
Cuddyer, Michael	R-R	6-2	215	3-27-79	.249	.250	.249	71	249	30	62	13	4	3	36	25	5	0	0	40	5	1	.369	.330
Everett, Adam	R-R	6-0	180	2-5-77	.213	.310	.184	48	127	19	27	6	1	2	20	12	1	6	4	15	0	0	.323	.278
Gomez, Carlos	R-R	6-4	195	12-4-85	.258	.270	.254	153	577	79	149	24	7	7	59	25	7	3	2	142	33	11	.360	.296
Harris, Brendan	R-R	6-1	210	8-26-80	.265	.265	.265	130	434	57	115	29	3	7	49	39	4	7	6	98	1	1	.394	.327
Jorgensen, Ryan	R-R	6-2	220	5-4-79	.000	—	.000	2	1	0	0	0	0	0	0	0	0	0	0	0	0	0	.000	.000
Kubel, Jason	L-R	6-0	210	5-25-82	.272	.232	.283	141	463	74	126	22	5	20	78	47	0	0	7	91	0	1	.471	.335
Lamb, Mike	L-R	6-1	205	8-9-75	.233	.067	.257	81	236	20	55	12	3	1	32	17	0	0	8	32	0	1	.322	.276
Macri, Matt	R-R	6-2	215	5-29-82	.324	.375	.200	18	34	3	11	1	0	1	4	2	0	0	0	10	1	1	.441	.361
Mauer, Joe	L-R	6-5	230	4-19-83	.328	.361	.312	146	536	98	176	31	4	9	85	84	1	1	11	50	1	1	.451	.413
Monroe, Craig	R-R	6-1	215	2-27-77	.202	.138	.276	58	163	22	33	9	0	8	29	16	0	0	0	48	0	1	.405	.274
Morneau, Justin	L-R	6-4	230	5-15-81	.300	.284	.310	163	623	97	187	47	4	23	129	76	3	0	10	85	0	1	.499	.374
Pridie, Jason	R-R	6-1	200	10-9-83	.000	.000	.000	10	4	3	0	0	0	0	0	1	0	1	0	1	0	0	.000	.200
Punto, Nick	B-R	5-9	195	11-8-77	.284	.302	.274	99	338	43	96	19	4	2	28	32	0	5	2	57	15	6	.382	.344
Redmond, Mike	R-R	5-11	200	5-5-71	.287	.277	.297	38	129	14	37	6	0	0	12	5	2	0	1	11	0	0	.333	.321
Ruiz, Randy	R-R	6-3	235	10-19-77	.274	.273	.276	22	62	13	17	2	0	1	7	6	0	0	0	21	0	0	.355	.338
Span, Denard	L-L	6-0	205	2-27-84	.294	.283	.299	93	347	70	102	16	7	6	47	50	4	8	2	60	18	7	.432	.387
Tolbert, Matt	B-R	6-0	185	5-4-82	.283	.306	.273	41	113	18	32	6	3	0	6	7	0	2	1	19	7	1	.389	.322
Young, Delmon	R-R	6-3	200	9-14-85	.290	.300	.286	152	575	80	167	28	4	10	69	35	7	1	5	105	14	5	.405	.336

Pitching	B-T	HT	WT	DOB	W	L	ERA	G	GS	CG	SV	IP	H	R	ER	HR	BB	SO	AVG	vLH	vRH	K/9	BB/9
Baker, Scott	R-R	6-4	220	9-19-81	11	4	3.45	28	28	0	0	172	161	66	66	20	42	141	.247	.263	.230	7.36	2.19
Bass, Brian	R-R	6-2	215	1-6-82	3	4	4.87	44	0	0	1	68	84	42	37	11	22	32	.303	.279	.318	4.21	2.90
2-team total (5 Baltimore)					4	4	4.84	49	4	0	1	89	98	55	48	12	31	45	—	—	—	4.53	3.12
Blackburn, Nick	R-R	6-4	225	2-24-82	11	11	4.05	33	33	0	0	193	224	102	87	23	39	96	.292	.295	.289	4.47	1.82
Bonser, Boof	R-R	6-4	245	10-14-81	3	7	5.93	47	12	0	0	118	139	87	78	16	36	97	.285	.315	.260	7.38	2.74
Breslow, Craig	L-L	6-0	185	8-8-80	0	2	1.63	42	0	0	1	39	24	9	7	0	14	32	.180	.153	.213	7.45	3.26
2-team total (7 Cleveland)					0	2	1.91	49	0	0	1	47	34	12	10	1	19	39	—	—	—	7.47	3.64
Crain, Jesse	R-R	6-1	215	7-5-81	5	4	3.59	66	0	0	0	63	62	29	25	6	24	50	.257	.250	.261	7.18	3.45
Guardado, Eddie	R-L	6-0	225	10-2-70	1	1	7.71	9	0	0	0	7	12	6	6	1	2	5	.387	.400	.375	6.43	2.57
2-team total (55 Texas)					4	4	4.15	64	0	0	4	56	50	26	26	4	19	33	—	—	—	5.27	3.04
Guerrier, Matt	R-R	6-3	195	8-2-78	6	9	5.19	76	0	0	1	76	84	47	44	12	37	59	.275	.282	.272	6.96	4.36
Hernandez, Livan	R-R	6-2	245	2-20-75	10	8	5.48	23	23	2	0	140	199	93	85	18	29	54	.341	.341	.340	3.48	1.87
Humber, Philip	R-R	6-4	225	12-21-82	0	0	4.63	5	0	0	0	12	11	6	6	4	5	6	.250	.150	.333	4.63	3.86
Korecky, Bobby	R-R	5-11	185	9-16-79	2	0	4.58	16	0	0	0	18	19	9	9	2	8	6	.288	.310	.270	3.06	4.08
Liriano, Francisco	L-L	6-2	210	10-26-83	6	4	3.91	14	14	0	0	76	74	40	33	7	32	67	.254	.217	.266	7.93	3.79
Mijares, Jose	L-L	6-0	230	10-29-84	0	1	0.87	10	0	0	0	10	3	1	1	0	5	13	.088	.143	.050	4.35	0.00
Nathan, Joe	R-R	6-4	225	11-22-74	1	2	1.33	68	0	0	39	68	43	13	10	5	18	74	.179	.167	.192	9.84	2.39
Neshek, Pat	R-R	6-3	210	9-4-80	0	1	4.73	15	0	0	0	13	12	7	7	2	4	15	.240	.250	.233	10.13	2.70
Perkins, Glen	L-L	6-0	200	3-2-83	12	4	4.41	26	26	0	0	151	183	81	74	25	39	74	.301	.352	.288	4.41	2.32
Reyes, Dennys	R-L	6-3	250	4-19-77	3	0	2.33	75	0	0	0	46	40	12	12	4	15	39	.235	.202	.276	7.58	2.91
Rincon, Juan	R-R	5-11	210	1-23-79	2	2	6.11	24	0	0	0	28	33	21	19	5	16	20	.292	.348	.254	6.43	5.14
2-team total (23 Cleveland)					3	3	5.86	47	0	0	0	55	67	39	36	8	24	39	—	—	—	6.34	3.90
Slowey, Kevin	R-R	6-3	205	5-4-84	12	11	3.99	27	27	3	0	160	161	74	71	22	24	123	.260	.277	.246	6.90	1.35

Fielding

Catcher	PCT	G	PO	A	E	DP	PB
Jorgensen	1.000	2	1	0	0	0	0
Mauer	.997	139	831	52	3	1	4
Redmond	1.000	30	180	9	0	2	0

First Base	PCT	G	PO	A	E	DP
Buscher	1.000	6	13	0	0	1
Clark	1.000	2	3	1	0	0
Cuddyer	.958	2	22	1	1	5

Harris	1.000	2	1	1	0	0
Lamb	1.000	9	46	8	0	4
Macri	1.000	2	3	0	0	1
Morneau	.997	155	1316	89	4	149

Second Base	PCT	G	PO	A	E	DP
Buscher	—	1	0	0	0	0
Casilla	.974	95	196	247	12	71
Clark	1.000	1	0	2	0	1
Everett	—	1	0	0	0	0
Harris	.969	39	56	101	5	24
Macri	1.000	2	1	6	0	1
Punto	.985	26	54	79	2	18
Tolbert	.978	11	15	30	1	7

Third Base	PCT	G	PO	A	E	DP
Buscher	.938	64	37	113	10	9

	PCT	G	PO	A	E	DP
Clark	1.000	1	3	2	0	1
Harris	.971	34	18	48	2	4
Lamb	.970	55	41	88	4	8
Macri	.944	11	3	14	1	3
Punto	1.000	12	3	16	0	1
Tolbert	.892	17	9	24	4	4

Shortstop	PCT	G	PO	A	E	DP
Casilla	1.000	2	2	3	0	0
Everett	.967	44	61	145	7	30
Harris	.976	55	84	159	6	42
Punto	.973	61	103	187	8	46

	PCT	G	PO	A	E	DP
Tolbert	.976	14	14	26	1	4

Outfield	PCT	G	PO	A	E	DP
Cuddyer	.993	58	126	7	1	5
Gomez	.982	151	436	9	8	4
Kubel	.971	49	98	2	3	1
Monroe	1.000	11	18	1	0	1
Pridie	.750	6	3	0	1	0
Punto	1.000	3	1	0	0	0
Span	.983	92	226	6	4	2
Young	.973	151	282	11	8	2

ROCHESTER RED WINGS — TRIPLE-A
INTERNATIONAL LEAGUE

Batting	B-T	HT	WT	DOB	AVG	vLH	vRH	G	AB	R	H	2B	3B	HR	RBI	BB	HBP	SH	SF	SO	SB	CS	SLG	OBP
Basak, Chris	R-R	6-2	210	12-6-78	.260	.269	.255	56	173	20	45	11	0	6	17	15	1	2	1	38	5	7	.428	.321
2-team total (45 Scranton/W-B)					.257	—	—	101	319	36	82	20	2	6	28	20	3	3	4	64	11	7	.389	.303
Buscher, Brian	L-R	6-0	220	4-18-81	.319	.306	.327	53	185	27	59	12	0	8	30	20	7	0	2	21	1	2	.514	.402
Casilla, Alexi	B-R	5-9	180	7-20-84	.219	.194	.233	32	96	11	21	3	0	0	2	18	2	4	1	18	4	3	.250	.350
Christy, Jeff	R-R	6-1	205	4-13-84	.211	.235	.205	36	90	14	19	6	0	0	5	15	0	5	1	26	0	1	.278	.321
Clark, Howie	L-R	5-10	190	2-13-74	.293	.361	.271	93	338	50	99	17	6	6	48	25	2	1	5	30	2	1	.432	.341
Cuddyer, Michael	R-R	6-2	215	3-27-79	.300	.500	.167	4	10	3	3	2	0	0	1	3	0	0	0	3	0	0	.500	.462
Everett, Adam	R-R	6-0	180	2-5-77	.316	.250	.333	5	19	5	6	0	0	0	3	2	0	0	0	4	0	0	.316	.381
Hughes, Luke	R-R	6-0	190	8-2-84	.283	.306	.271	29	106	17	30	7	1	3	11	7	1	0	3	30	2	0	.453	.325
Jones, Garrett	L-L	6-4	245	6-21-81	.279	.225	.305	138	527	82	147	33	3	23	92	50	1	0	9	98	9	2	.484	.337
Jorgensen, Ryan	R-R	6-2	220	5-4-79	.247	.273	.240	65	198	27	49	12	0	8	25	18	2	5	2	54	0	0	.429	.314
Kielty, Bobby	B-R	6-1	225	8-5-76	.218	.261	.188	16	55	9	12	3	0	2	8	13	0	0	1	16	0	1	.382	.362
2-team total (28 Pawtucket)					.224			44	147	18	33	7	1	5	26	30	1	0	3	42	0	1	.388	.354
Knott, Jon	R-R	6-3	225	8-4-78	.182	.130	.219	17	55	7	10	2	0	1	3	9	0	0	0	15	0	0	.273	.297
2-team total (111 Lehigh Valley)					.251	—	—	128	462	61	116	30	2	20	68	52	7	1	2	111	2	1	.455	.335
Machado, Alejandro	B-R	6-0	185	4-26-82	.338	.370	.326	54	195	33	66	16	2	2	31	13	0	5	2	26	12	3	.472	.376
Macri, Matt	R-R	6-2	215	5-29-82	.259	.218	.278	89	313	35	81	24	4	11	48	26	5	3	3	84	2	2	.466	.323
McDonald, Darnell	R-R	5-11	210	11-17-78	.268	.286	.262	93	369	53	99	25	4	11	57	36	2	0	3	81	19	3	.447	.334
Molina, Felix	L-R	5-8	180	5-5-83	.000	.000	.000	3	2	1	0	0	0	0	0	0	0	0	0	2	0	0	.000	.000
Morales, Jose	B-R	5-11	190	2-20-83	.315	.327	.310	54	197	18	62	8	1	4	15	8	2	1	0	28	0	1	.426	.348
Peterson, Brock	R-R	6-3	215	11-20-83	.175	.067	.240	11	40	5	7	1	0	2	6	4	0	0	0	17	0	0	.350	.250
Plouffe, Trevor	R-R	6-1	175	6-15-86	.256	.322	.236	66	250	34	64	17	3	6	34	16	0	5	3	47	1	1	.420	.292
Pridie, Jason	L-R	6-1	200	10-9-83	.270	.245	.280	138	559	84	151	21	16	13	61	30	1	7	6	152	25	9	.435	.305
Ruiz, Randy	R-R	6-3	235	10-19-77	.320	.315	.321	111	416	58	133	33	3	17	68	23	11	0	6	116	1	2	.536	.366
Santos, Sergio	R-R	6-3	225	7-4-83	.242	.234	.245	86	297	44	72	24	0	5	43	16	1	0	5	59	4	1	.374	.279
2-team total (26 Syracuse)					.228	—	—	112	390	51	89	29	0	5	47	21	1	0	5	72	6	2	.341	.266
Span, Denard	L-L	6-0	205	2-27-84	.340	.174	.409	40	156	32	53	11	3	1	14	26	0	2	0	36	15	8	.481	.434
Watkins, Tommy	R-R	5-10	225	6-18-80	.219	.235	.212	76	233	32	51	9	3	1	18	25	2	5	0	31	5	4	.296	.300
Whiteside, Eli	R-R	6-2	215	10-22-79	.167	.063	.375	8	24	2	4	0	0	1	1	1	0	0	0	6	0	0	.292	.200

Pitching	B-T	HT	WT	DOB	W	L	ERA	G	GS	CG	SV	IP	H	R	ER	HR	BB	SO	AVG	vLH	vRH	K/9	BB/9
Barrett, Ricky	L-L	6-0	190	3-9-81	4	5	3.21	50	0	0	2	70	55	26	25	4	38	81	.218	.248	.199	10.41	4.89
Bass, Brian	R-R	6-2	215	1-6-82	1	0	4.00	2	2	0	0	9	8	5	4	1	4	6	.235	.357	.150	6.00	4.00
Cali, Carmen	L-L	5-10	210	11-2-78	5	1	4.52	50	2	0	2	66	77	41	33	5	25	49	.286	.258	.310	6.72	3.43
Daigle, Casey	R-R	6-6	240	4-4-81	1	5	3.78	44	1	0	1	69	61	37	29	9	34	65	.228	.212	.246	8.48	4.43
DePaula, Julio	R-R	6-0	180	12-31-82	3	5	5.70	51	5	0	2	77	86	51	49	11	41	65	.278	.294	.265	7.56	4.77
Duensing, Brian	L-L	5-11	210	2-22-83	5	11	4.28	25	24	0	0	139	150	75	66	16	34	77	.278	.279	.278	5.00	2.21
Gomez, Mariano	L-L	6-6	195	9-12-82	5	2	2.76	54	0	0	1	65	68	26	20	3	22	45	.265	.261	.267	6.20	3.03
Graves, Danny	R-R	6-0	200	8-7-73	4	6	6.30	25	16	0	1	84	116	65	59	10	27	32	.334	.399	.262	3.42	2.88
Humber, Philip	R-R	6-4	225	12-21-82	10	8	4.56	31	23	2	0	136	145	76	69	21	49	106	.273	.270	.275	7.00	3.23
Korecky, Bobby	R-R	5-11	185	9-16-79	6	5	2.91	53	0	0	26	74	66	26	24	3	22	71	.237	.286	.193	8.60	2.66
Lahey, Tim	R-R	6-6	250	2-7-82	5	5	5.43	48	1	0	8	63	69	41	38	7	23	53	.288	.378	.225	7.57	3.29
Liriano, Francisco	L-L	6-2	225	10-26-83	10	2	3.28	19	19	0	0	118	102	44	43	8	31	113	.231	.194	.248	8.62	2.36
Mulvey, Kevin	R-R	6-2	190	5-26-85	7	9	3.77	27	27	1	0	148	152	80	62	16	48	121	.265	.286	.242	7.36	2.92
Perkins, Glen	L-L	6-0	200	3-2-83	2	1	2.97	7	6	1	0	33	28	15	11	2	19	27	.220	.250	.209	7.29	5.13
Shearn, Tom	R-R	6-4	230	8-28-77	1	2	5.34	6	6	1	0	29	38	18	17	4	7	26	.314	.265	.377	8.16	2.20
2-team total (10 Louisville)					7	4	4.80	16	16	1	0	86	98	47	46	12	22	57	—	—	—	5.94	2.29
Slowey, Kevin	R-R	6-3	205	5-4-84	1	1	3.60	1	1	0	0	5	3	2	2	2	0	9	.167	.000	.500	16.20	3.60
Swarzak, Anthony	R-R	6-3	195	9-10-85	5	0	1.80	7	7	0	0	45	41	14	9	4	14	26	.243	.239	.247	5.20	2.80
Totten, Heath	R-R	6-3	210	9-30-78	0	2	5.79	16	4	0	0	28	35	20	18	3	9	21	.294	.269	.327	6.75	2.89

Fielding

Catcher	PCT	G	PO	A	E	DP	PB
Christy	.992	36	225	21	2	2	5
Jorgensen	.991	65	426	30	4	1	1
Morales	1.000	46	309	25	0	2	6
Whiteside	.970	8	61	3	2	0	0

First Base	PCT	G	PO	A	E	DP
Basak	1.000	6	55	2	0	8

Buscher	1.000	8	57	4	0	5
Jones	.988	71	519	44	7	55
Knott	1.000	1	8	1	0	2
Macri	.919	6	32	2	3	4
Peterson	.988	9	74	8	1	7
Ruiz	.973	40	335	27	10	36
Santos	.986	9	59	10	1	4

Second Base	PCT	G	PO	A	E	DP
Basak	.952	14	20	40	3	10
Casilla	.969	10	16	15	1	1
Clark	.975	37	67	90	4	19
Hughes	1.000	1	2	2	0	0
Machado	.982	26	55	54	2	16
Macri	.972	30	68	103	5	31

	PCT	G	PO	A	E	DP
Molina	1.000	1	1	2	0	1
Plouffe	.946	20	32	56	5	15
Watkins	.968	17	26	34	2	7

Third Base	PCT	G	PO	A	E	DP
Basak	.952	17	9	31	2	3
Buscher	.960	37	23	73	4	10
Hughes	.911	26	16	35	5	4
Macri	.865	16	10	35	7	5
Plouffe	.934	32	22	63	6	3
Santos	.923	15	6	18	2	0

	PCT	G	PO	A	E	DP
Watkins	.875	8	6	15	3	1

Shortstop	PCT	G	PO	A	E	DP
Basak	.938	20	24	37	4	5
Casilla	.957	27	31	59	4	17
Everett	.909	5	3	7	1	2
Macri	.945	35	52	86	8	24
Plouffe	1.000	12	16	37	0	6
Santos	.943	57	93	154	15	40
Watkins	—	1	0	0	0	0

Outfield	PCT	G	PO	A	E	DP
Clark	.961	49	93	6	4	0
Cuddyer	1.000	3	4	0	0	0
Jones	.989	49	89	4	1	1
Kielty	.973	16	35	1	1	0
Knott	1.000	13	29	1	0	0
McDonald	.983	93	165	6	3	2
Peterson	1.000	1	1	0	0	0
Pridie	.989	136	337	8	4	1
Span	.989	40	84	2	1	0
Watkins	1.000	43	81	5	0	3

NEW BRITAIN ROCK CATS

DOUBLE-A

EASTERN LEAGUE

Batting	B-T	HT	WT	DOB	AVG	vLH	vRH	G	AB	R	H	2B	3B	HR	RBI	BB	HBP	SH	SF	SO	SB	CS	SLG	OBP
Berg, Daniel	R-R	6-0	200	11-21-84	.255	.250	.257	15	47	7	12	3	0	0	2	3	2	3	0	18	0	0	.319	.327
Butera, Drew	R-R	6-1	211	8-9-83	.219	.269	.204	96	302	39	66	18	1	7	39	35	6	4	4	55	0	1	.354	.308
Christy, Jeff	R-R	6-1	205	4-13-84	.216	.136	.250	23	74	10	16	4	0	0	4	12	0	1	1	14	0	0	.270	.322
Dinkelman, Brian	L-R	5-11	195	11-10-83	.247	.140	.277	52	198	26	49	14	2	2	21	10	5	2	1	24	2	2	.369	.299
Gaetti, Joe	R-R	5-11	205	10-18-81	1.000	—	1.000	1	1	0	1	0	0	0	1	1	0	0	0	0	0	0	4.000	1.000
Gardenhire, Toby	B-R	6-0	170	9-11-82	.261	.291	.247	87	284	30	74	4	1	1	21	28	10	9	0	52	2	1	.292	.348
Hughes, Luke	R-R	6-0	190	8-2-84	.319	.405	.286	70	285	53	91	15	3	15	40	28	3	2	1	70	4	1	.551	.385
Lis, Erik	L-L	6-1	220	3-8-84	.277	.271	.279	105	405	49	112	36	3	11	51	27	0	0	5	93	1	1	.462	.318
Martin, Dustin	L-L	6-2	210	4-4-84	.290	.343	.270	133	510	68	148	34	8	10	72	49	5	4	5	125	22	11	.447	.355
Molina, Felix	L-R	5-8	180	5-5-83	.247	.132	.280	86	300	28	74	18	2	2	35	20	2	2	2	50	5	8	.340	.296
Moses, Matt	L-R	6-0	210	2-20-85	.230	.191	.242	105	387	42	89	21	2	3	35	35	1	3	3	69	7	4	.318	.293
Palacios, Rodolfo	R-R	5-10	205	6-26-85	.207	.310	.172	33	116	12	24	4	0	1	8	3	0	1	1	27	0	0	.267	.225
Peterson, Brock	R-R	6-3	215	11-20-83	.264	.228	.275	109	421	63	111	32	2	14	67	41	2	1	3	102	1	1	.449	.330
Plouffe, Trevor	R-R	6-1	175	6-15-86	.269	.294	.258	58	227	32	61	17	3	3	21	16	3	0	4	43	4	2	.410	.325
Roberts, Brandon	L-R	6-0	185	11-9-84	.200	.148	.221	28	95	8	19	2	0	1	7	8	1	1	0	18	2	0	.253	.269
Tolbert, Matt	B-R	6-0	185	5-4-82	.250	.167	.289	14	56	6	14	3	0	0	6	1	0	0	0	6	3	3	.304	.263
Tolleson, Steven	R-R	5-10	180	11-1-83	.300	.320	.292	93	343	54	103	28	1	9	50	44	3	4	3	74	12	6	.466	.382
Valencia, Danny	R-R	6-2	200	9-19-84	.289	.344	.273	69	266	40	77	18	2	10	32	18	1	0	2	70	2	1	.485	.334
Winfree, David	R-R	6-3	215	8-5-85	.252	.292	.237	126	453	59	114	27	3	19	87	41	5	0	3	87	2	3	.450	.319

Pitching	B-T	HT	WT	DOB	W	L	ERA	G	GS	CG	SV	IP	H	R	ER	HR	BB	SO	AVG	vLH	vRH	K/9	BB/9
Aselton, Kyle	R-R	6-5	215	2-28-83	8	6	4.24	38	14	0	1	110	113	59	52	7	60	86	.270	.228	.288	7.02	4.89
Delaney, Rob	L-R	6-3	225	9-8-84	2	1	1.05	23	0	0	5	34	20	4	4	2	7	38	.171	.261	.113	9.96	1.83
Gabino, Armando	R-R	6-3	215	8-31-83	6	5	3.10	49	0	0	3	81	84	28	28	6	31	61	.272	.349	.219	6.75	3.43
Graves, Danny	R-R	6-0	200	8-7-73	2	0	3.60	7	0	0	0	10	8	4	4	0	4	7	.222	.063	.350	6.30	3.60
Julianel, Ben	B-L	6-2	185	9-4-79	3	2	2.37	56	0	0	26	68	62	24	18	3	30	78	.235	.223	.241	10.27	3.95
Manship, Jeff	R-R	6-0	165	1-16-85	3	6	4.46	14	14	0	0	77	90	47	38	8	24	62	.292	.274	.311	7.28	2.82
Mata, Frank	R-R	6-0	168	3-11-84	1	1	7.20	23	0	0	1	30	36	26	24	7	18	22	.300	.326	.286	6.60	5.40
Mijares, Jose	L-L	6-0	230	10-29-84	1	1	2.93	11	0	0	2	15	16	5	5	2	7	17	.258	.217	.282	9.98	4.11
Miller, Jason	L-L	6-1	195	7-20-82	1	3	5.61	36	3	0	0	85	100	59	53	11	34	81	.292	.303	.285	8.58	3.60
Mullins, Ryan	L-L	6-6	180	11-13-83	9	4	4.31	30	24	1	0	148	169	87	71	18	59	99	.287	.204	.318	6.01	3.58
Pino, Yohan	R-R	6-3	158	12-26-83	7	7	4.54	26	18	0	0	109	115	58	55	16	37	76	.274	.310	.241	6.28	3.06
Rainville, Jay	R-R	6-3	230	10-16-85	9	9	5.78	24	24	0	0	123	143	84	79	22	44	83	.289	.235	.336	6.07	3.22
Sawatski, Jay	L-L	6-2	195	5-7-82	1	4	7.75	22	0	0	0	38	51	35	33	6	22	39	.315	.377	.277	9.16	5.17
Shinskie, David	R-R	6-4	205	5-4-84	0	0	2.57	4	0	0	1	7	6	2	2	0	0	5	.231	.167	.286	6.43	0.00
Simonitsch, Errol	L-L	6-4	230	8-24-82	1	4	9.96	6	6	0	0	28	49	32	31	5	12	17	.389	.357	.394	5.46	3.86
Sosa, Oswaldo	R-R	6-4	225	9-19-85	2	5	5.81	13	13	0	0	62	70	41	40	4	43	47	.294	.328	.262	6.82	6.24
Swarzak, Anthony	R-R	6-3	195	9-10-85	3	8	5.67	20	20	0	0	102	126	71	64	12	37	76	.304	.284	.320	6.73	3.28
Ward, Zach	R-R	6-3	250	1-14-84	5	6	3.77	46	5	0	1	93	95	45	39	4	51	81	.264	.293	.245	7.84	4.94

Fielding

Catcher	PCT	G	PO	A	E	DP	PB
Butera	.991	92	645	45	6	7	10
Christy	1.000	23	157	13	0	1	2
Palacios	.996	28	201	21	1	2	2

First Base	PCT	G	PO	A	E	DP
Berg	1.000	2	14	0	0	2
Butera	1.000	2	10	1	0	1
Gardenhire	.990	27	190	11	2	22
Lis	.995	25	192	14	1	26
Molina	1.000	2	13	0	0	0
Palacios	1.000	2	18	0	0	4
Peterson	.986	80	622	31	9	66
Valencia	1.000	2	9	0	0	4
Winfree	1.000	1	10	1	0	0

Second Base	PCT	G	PO	A	E	DP
Dinkelman	.960	38	81	87	7	29
Gardenhire	.857	3	6	6	2	4
Hughes	.956	18	24	41	3	3
Molina	.981	50	86	122	4	41
Moses	1.000	2	4	3	0	1
Tolbert	1.000	3	8	9	0	2
Tolleson	.982	33	60	101	3	27

Third Base	PCT	G	PO	A	E	DP
Gardenhire	.929	31	22	57	6	11
Hughes	.888	39	29	42	9	7
Molina	.500	1	0	1	1	0
Moses	.714	4	0	5	2	0
Plouffe	1.000	11	9	17	0	4
Tolbert	1.000	1	0	1	0	0
Valencia	.949	57	44	104	8	13

Shortstop	PCT	G	PO	A	E	DP
Dinkelman	1.000	7	15	23	0	6
Gardenhire	.959	26	47	69	5	21
Molina	.913	27	39	55	9	13
Plouffe	.961	44	62	109	7	26
Tolbert	1.000	9	12	20	0	2
Tolleson	.930	34	49	71	9	16

Outfield	PCT	G	PO	A	E	DP
Berg	1.000	12	12	1	0	0
Dinkelman	1.000	5	8	0	0	0
Gaetti	—	1	0	0	0	0
Hughes	1.000	8	21	1	0	1
Lis	.963	38	77	1	3	0
Martin	.994	128	316	15	2	1
Moses	.982	82	159	5	3	1
Peterson	.971	18	29	4	1	0
Roberts	1.000	19	41	0	0	0
Tolbert	1.000	1	2	0	0	0
Tolleson	1.000	17	46	2	0	1
Winfree	.991	104	210	6	2	1

FLORIDA STATE LEAGUE

Batting	B-T	HT	WT	DOB	AVG	vLH	vRH	G	AB	R	H	2B	3B	HR	RBI	BB	HBP	SH	SF	SO	SB	CS	SLG	OBP
Berg, Daniel	R-R	6-0	200	11-21-84	.279	.258	.288	67	222	39	62	8	2	6	22	32	5	2	1	49	2	2	.414	.381
De San Miguel, Allan	R-R	5-9	200	2-1-88	.123	.105	.130	24	65	5	8	1	1	1	5	8	1	2	2	21	0	0	.215	.224
Dinkelman, Brian	L-R	5-11	195	11-10-83	.293	.333	.279	63	232	44	68	18	2	2	19	33	8	1	0	28	10	1	.414	.399
Everett, Adam	R-R	6-0	180	2-5-77	.000	—	.000	2	8	0	0	0	0	0	0	0	0	0	0	2	0	0	.000	.000
Gardenhire, Toby	B-R	6-0	170	9-11-82	.333	.636	.214	15	39	2	13	2	0	0	4	1	1	0	0	5	0	0	.385	.366
Lehmann, Danny	R-R	5-11	186	9-5-85	.244	.250	.243	44	131	12	32	3	0	0	6	16	6	1	1	12	2	1	.267	.351
Olson, Garrett	R-R	6-2	200	3-10-85	.201	.207	.199	61	209	19	42	6	0	2	22	9	5	3	2	38	6	3	.258	.249
Ortiz, Yancarlos	R-R	5-9	150	9-15-84	.251	.256	.251	111	343	36	86	8	3	0	30	27	3	13	4	71	8	6	.292	.308
Ovalle, Edward	R-R	5-11	178	6-15-85	.284	.305	.277	127	447	61	127	14	11	7	62	34	16	5	7	112	17	9	.412	.351
Palacios, Rodolfo	R-R	5-10	205	6-26-85	.231	.160	.275	28	65	5	15	2	0	0	5	4	0	0	0	9	0	0	.262	.275
Portes, Juan	R-R	5-11	170	11-26-85	.270	.246	.278	124	456	68	123	21	0	12	54	29	9	1	11	83	13	6	.395	.319
Punto, Nick	B-R	5-9	195	11-8-77	.250	.000	.375	3	12	0	3	0	0	0	1	1	0	0	1	1	0	.250	.308
Ramos, Wilson	R-R	6-0	205	8-10-87	.288	.344	.266	126	452	50	130	23	2	13	78	37	6	0	5	103	0	1	.434	.346
Robbins, Whitney	L-R	6-0	205	9-25-84	.268	.200	.290	91	284	39	76	13	4	6	42	52	4	1	5	55	1	2	.405	.383
Roberts, Brandon	L-R	6-0	185	11-9-84	.409	1.000	.350	8	22	3	9	0	0	1	2	2	1	0	3	1	2	.409	.500
Santiesteban, Danny	R-R	6-2	195	2-17-85	.213	.202	.218	94	286	31	61	11	1	6	37	20	2	4	2	80	7	5	.322	.268
Singleton, Steven	L-R	5-11	189	9-12-85	.295	.293	.295	62	241	38	71	19	2	5	26	26	5	2	3	24	4	1	.452	.371
Solarte, Yangervis	S-R	5-11	176	7-7-87	.259	.216	.273	42	147	18	38	9	1	3	16	7	4	3	0	25	2	2	.395	.310
Tintor, Eli	R-R	6-2	190	12-24-84	.253	.273	.246	71	237	27	60	12	2	6	23	22	2	0	4	76	3	4	.397	.317
Tosoni, Rene	L-R	6-0	194	7-2-86	.300	.440	.270	42	140	27	42	7	3	1	19	21	6	1	2	30	3	5	.414	.408
Valencia, Danny	R-R	6-2	205	9-19-84	.336	.371	.323	60	220	35	74	19	3	5	44	27	0	0	4	43	2	2	.518	.402
Woodard, Johnny	L-R	6-4	208	9-15-84	.241	.158	.266	69	245	37	59	13	3	6	35	34	7	0	2	62	1	2	.392	.347

Pitching	B-T	HT	WT	DOB	W	L	ERA	G	GS	CG	SV	IP	H	R	ER	HR	BB	SO	AVG	vLH	vRH	K/9	BB/9
Allen, Michael	R-R	6-3	220	5-27-87	0	1	6.75	1	0	0	0	1	3	1	1	0	0	1	.429	—	.429	6.75	0.00
Baker, Scott	R-R	6-4	220	9-19-81	1	0	5.40	1	1	0	0	5	7	3	3	0	0	4	.304	.300	.308	7.20	0.00
Burnett, Alex	R-R	6-0	190	7-26-87	8	6	3.76	28	25	0	0	144	151	72	60	12	36	84	.269	.269	.269	5.26	2.26
Craig, Aaron	R-R	6-1	233	3-22-86	0	0	—	2	0	0	0	2	1	1	0	2	0	1.000	1.000	1.000		
Day, Zach	R-R	6-3	215	6-15-78	1	0	5.63	6	0	0	0	8	14	6	5	0	1	3	.389	.417	.375	3.38	1.13
Delaney, Rob	L-R	6-3	225	9-8-84	1	2	1.42	23	0	0	13	32	24	6	5	1	4	34	.207	.250	.184	9.66	1.14
Devries, Cole	R-R	6-2	185	2-12-85	10	9	2.93	24	23	1	0	135	138	51	44	8	38	105	.264	.304	.238	6.98	2.53
Erickson, Blair	R-R	6-1	212	10-28-84	3	0	2.63	32	0	0	1	41	22	12	12	1	21	50	.157	.122	.172	10.98	4.61
Fox, Matt	R-R	6-3	192	12-4-82	7	7	3.37	32	14	0	1	118	120	47	44	9	33	99	.268	.301	.249	7.57	2.52
Graves, Danny	R-R	6-0	200	8-7-73	0	0	6.00	4	0	0	0	6	6	4	4	0	1	5	.250	.300	.214	7.50	1.50
Guerra, Deolis	R-R	6-5	200	4-17-89	11	9	5.47	26	25	1	0	130	138	85	79	12	71	71	.272	.327	.230	4.92	4.92
Gutierrez, Carlos	R-R	6-3	205	9-22-86	3	1	2.10	16	0	0	1	26	23	7	6	0	7	19	.240	.319	.163	6.66	2.45
Hernandez, Danny	R-R	6-2	180	11-19-85	0	1	7.45	7	0	0	0	9	8	8	8	0	12	4	.242	.273	.227	3.72	11.17
Lahey, Tim	R-R	6-6	250	7-2-81	0	0	0.00	2	0	0	0	3	1	0	0	0	1	2	.111	.000	.167	6.00	3.00
Liriano, Francisco	L-L	6-2	225	10-26-83	0	1	6.75	1	1	0	0	5	6	4	4	0	2	8	.300	—	.300	13.50	3.38
Lobanov, Andrei	L-L	6-3	171	1-25-90	0	0	0.00	1	0	0	0	2	1	0	0	0	3	.143	.250	.000	13.50	4.50
Lugo, Jose	L-L	6-1	159	4-10-84	2	6	4.04	51	0	0	1	69	68	34	31	4	33	76	.254	.280	.240	9.91	4.30
Manship, Jeff	R-R	6-0	165	1-16-85	7	3	2.86	13	13	1	0	79	68	31	25	0	20	63	.231	.257	.208	7.21	2.29
Mata, Frank	R-R	6-0	168	3-11-84	1	0	1.93	11	0	0	0	14	10	4	3	0	4	15	.189	.263	.147	9.64	2.57
Mijares, Jose	L-L	6-0	230	10-29-84	0	0	2.61	5	0	0	0	10	7	3	3	0	3	8	.194	.182	.200	6.97	2.61
Rainville, Jay	R-R	6-3	230	10-16-85	1	1	2.87	3	2	0	0	16	13	7	5	1	3	13	.217	.217	.216	7.47	1.72
Reyes, Henry	L-L	6-7	183	5-10-85	1	1	1.93	2	1	0	0	5	2	1	1	0	4	3	.125	.000	.154	5.79	7.71
Robertson, Tyler	L-L	6-5	220	12-23-87	5	3	2.72	15	15	1	0	83	78	36	25	3	31	73	.247	.168	.284	7.95	3.38
Shinskie, David	R-R	6-4	205	5-4-84	0	0	7.11	5	0	0	0	6	12	8	5	0	2	4	.414	.313	.538	5.68	2.84
Simonitsch, Errol	L-L	6-4	230	8-24-82	1	0	0.00	1	0	0	0	1	0	0	0	0	0	1	.000	.000	.000	9.00	0.00
Slama, Anthony	R-R	6-3	207	1-6-84	4	1	1.01	51	0	0	25	71	43	12	8	0	24	110	.173	.200	.154	13.94	3.04
Slowey, Kevin	R-R	6-3	205	5-4-84	0	0	1.13	2	2	0	0	8	1	1	1	2	10	.040	.000	.077	11.25	2.25
Sosa, Oswaldo	R-R	6-4	225	9-19-85	2	2	5.44	17	6	0	0	43	46	32	26	0	32	33	.280	.286	.277	6.91	6.70
Steedley, Spencer	L-L	6-2	194	5-31-85	1	4	6.59	15	4	0	1	29	34	24	21	4	19	19	.304	.222	.342	5.97	5.97
Testa, Joe	L-L	5-10	175	12-18-85	1	0	4.91	4	2	0	0	15	14	8	8	1	7	13	.255	.208	.290	7.98	4.30
Vais, Danny	R-R	6-1	210	11-21-84	4	0	2.76	18	0	0	0	29	18	9	9	2	12	23	.176	.262	.117	7.06	3.68
Williams, Matthew	R-R	6-1	180	2-28-87	2	2	3.35	20	2	0	0	46	44	21	17	5	16	37	.260	.343	.202	7.29	3.15

Fielding

Catcher	PCT	G	PO	A	E	DP	PB
Berg	3	11	0	0	0	0	
De San Miguel	1.000	22	158	9	0	1	0
Lehmann	.978	35	236	31	6	1	2
Palacios	1.000	12	48	5	0	0	0
Ramos	.987	80	553	62	8	4	5

First Base	PCT	G	PO	A	E	DP
Berg	.990	36	270	16	3	23
Olson	1.000	4	37	3	0	4
Palacios	1.000	2	13	2	0	4
Robbins	.992	39	354	25	3	28
Woodard	.985	59	479	38	8	43

Second Base	PCT	G	PO	A	E	DP
Berg	1.000	3	4	4	0	1
Dinkelman	.985	56	113	148	4	29
Gardenhire	.944	3	5	12	1	2
Olson	1.000	7	9	12	0	5
Ortiz	1.000	1	1	6	0	0
Portes	.968	7	10	20	1	6
Singleton	.971	58	107	162	8	36
Solarte	.970	9	13	19	1	4

Third Base	PCT	G	PO	A	E	DP
Berg	1.000	5	5	6	0	1
Gardenhire	—	1	0	0	0	0
Olson	.957	25	11	34	2	2

	PCT	G	PO	A	E	DP
Ortiz	1.000	2	1	1	0	0
Portes	.932	38	23	46	5	5
Robbins	.889	14	9	15	3	0
Solarte	.920	9	2	21	2	1
Valencia	.956	53	26	105	6	11

Shortstop	PCT	G	PO	A	E	DP
Dinkelman	1.000	7	9	16	0	7
Everett	1.000	2	0	4	0	0
Gardenhire	.905	11	14	24	4	5
Olson	.986	18	22	50	1	10
Ortiz	.962	105	143	318	18	51
Portes	—	1	0	0	0	0
Punto	1.000	3	2	4	0	2

Solarte	1.000	1	1	3	0	1
Valencia	1.000	1	0	2	0	0
Outfield	**PCT**	**G**	**PO**	**A**	**E**	**DP**
Berg	.968	14	30	0	1	0
Lehmann	1.000	3	1	0	0	0

Olson	.923	10	23	1	2	0
Ovalle	.977	118	212	5	5	0
Portes	.947	72	119	5	7	1
Roberts	.833	5	5	0	1	0
Santiesteban	.991	87	208	10	2	1

Solarte	.920	17	23	0	2	0
Tintor	.993	69	148	3	1	0
Tosoni	.985	40	64	3	1	0

BELOIT SNAPPERS   *LOW CLASS A*

MIDWEST LEAGUE

Batting	B-T	HT	WT	DOB	AVG	vLH	vRH	G	AB	R	H	2B	3B	HR	RBI	BB	HBP	SH	SF	SO	SB	CS	SLG	OBP
Benson, Joe	R-R	6-2	211	3-5-88	.248	.259	.245	69	254	39	63	16	3	4	27	24	7	2	3	73	17	11	.382	.326
Brito, Jeanfred	R-R	5-9	160	12-21-87	.234	.209	.243	47	158	15	37	4	2	0	14	13	1	2	1	19	7	6	.285	.295
Casilla, Alexi	B-R	5-9	180	7-20-84	.571	.500	.667	2	7	2	4	0	0	0	1	2	0	0	0	1	0	1	.571	.667
Cates, Chris	R-R	5-3	145	4-15-85	.252	.296	.239	122	408	44	103	13	0	0	39	45	4	18	4	41	8	9	.284	.330
De Los Santos, Estarlin	B-R	5-10	165	1-20-87	.242	.246	.240	66	236	33	57	4	3	2	25	19	3	9	2	55	15	8	.309	.304
De San Miguel, Allan	R-R	5-9	200	2-1-88	.269	.214	.295	45	130	22	35	9	0	1	25	21	7	4	1	39	1	2	.362	.396
Dolenc, Mark	R-R	6-3	218	11-8-84	.260	.276	.253	119	389	77	101	9	8	3	41	41	6	13	2	120	31	8	.347	.338
Fernandez, Jair	R-R	6-1	170	12-10-86	.283	.269	.287	36	127	16	36	8	0	1	20	9	1	3	1	24	0	1	.370	.333
Kelly, Paul	R-R	6-0	185	10-19-86	.321	.125	.400	7	28	2	9	2	0	0	2	0	0	1	0	3	0	6	.393	.367
Lehmann, Danny	R-R	5-11	186	9-5-85	.240	.292	.225	31	104	13	25	4	3	0	6	9	2	2	0	15	0	2	.337	.313
Leveret, Rene	R-R	6-2	224	11-19-85	.286	.208	.318	49	182	26	52	9	0	3	34	17	2	0	1	37	2	1	.385	.351
Lewis, Ozzie	R-R	6-4	193	3-21-86	.218	.185	.229	60	211	27	46	10	1	4	23	24	0	0	2	67	7	3	.332	.295
Olson, Garrett	R-R	6-2	200	3-10-85	.247	.219	.257	65	247	32	61	11	2	5	37	17	2	6	3	30	10	6	.368	.297
Parmelee, Chris	L-L	6-2	223	2-24-88	.239	.250	.235	69	226	41	54	10	3	14	49	52	5	1	5	83	3	1	.496	.385
Petsch, Ben	R-R	6-2	205	9-3-84	.224	.238	.217	21	67	5	15	1	0	0	6	10	1	0	0	13	5	4	.239	.325
Revere, Ben	L-R	5-9	166	5-3-88	.379	.397	.375	83	340	51	129	17	10	1	43	27	5	2	0	31	44	13	.497	.433
Richardson, Juan	R-R	6-0	200	12-27-86	.206	.190	.214	36	126	12	26	3	0	0	10	10	1	0	1	21	4	3	.230	.268
Romero, Deibinson	R-R	6-0	193	9-24-86	.268	.265	.270	40	149	21	40	8	1	3	18	7	3	0	3	38	1	2	.396	.309
Santana, Ramon	R-R	5-9	152	6-20-86	.241	.230	.245	75	245	38	59	12	2	8	26	16	12	5	2	84	9	3	.404	.316
Santiago, Eric	R-R	5-8		7-10-87	.190	.200	.188	6	21	4	4	0	0	0	1	2	0	0	0	2	2	1	.190	.261
Schmiesing, Andrew	L-L	6-4	190	5-24-86	.230	.255	.220	52	178	15	41	6	0	0	22	18	1	4	3	41	3	3	.264	.300
Singleton, Steven	L-R	5-11	189	9-12-85	.302	.295	.305	65	235	37	71	6	2	6	32	13	5	3	3	29	2	6	.421	.348
Solarte, Yangervis	B-R	5-11	176	7-7-87	.218	.160	.247	41	147	16	32	4	0	0	13	7	4	2	3	13	7	2	.245	.293
Yersich, Gregory	R-R	6-0	225	10-7-86	.225	.256	.215	97	338	36	76	15	1	8	28	21	2	0	4	84	1	2	.346	.271

Pitching	B-T	HT	WT	DOB	W	L	ERA	G	GS	CG	SV	IP	H	R	ER	HR	BB	SO	AVG	vLH	vRH	K/9	BB/9
Allen, Michael	R-R	6-3	220	5-27-87	1	0	1.75	14	2	0	0	36	25	11	7	1	9	37	.188	.274	.083	9.25	2.25
Anderson, Chris	L-L	5-10	205	3-14-86	2	0	6.84	18	0	0	2	25	36	21	19	2	9	17	.343	.310	.355	6.12	3.24
Arias, Santos	R-R	5-11	162	3-17-87	5	6	3.27	30	15	1	4	110	106	48	40	6	29	91	.251	.268	.237	7.45	2.37
Berlind, Dan	R-R	6-7	215	12-3-87	4	4	4.47	11	10	0	0	52	53	30	26	2	27	37	.271	.291	.247	6.36	4.64
Bromberg, David	L-R	6-5	241	9-14-87	9	10	4.44	27	27	0	0	150	149	81	74	10	54	177	.262	.251	.273	10.62	3.24
Erickson, Blair	R-R	6-1	212	10-28-84	1	3	3.38	16	0	0	0	19	17	7	7	3	8	26	.258	.194	.314	12.54	3.86
Hernandez, Danny	R-R	6-2	180	11-19-85	0	2	7.98	26	0	0	0	29	21	27	26	10	25	26	.196	.160	.228	7.98	7.67
Hirschfeld, Steven	R-R	6-5	226	9-8-85	10	5	3.30	31	16	0	1	109	104	51	40	3	38	80	.252	.251	.252	6.61	3.14
Hunt, Shooter	R-R	6-3	200	8-16-86	1	4	5.46	7	7	0	0	31	26	21	19	2	27	34	.230	.250	.211	9.77	7.76
Kirwan, Brian	R-R	6-4	218	6-9-87	4	4	4.98	14	12	0	0	65	81	42	36	6	24	31	.309	.311	.307	4.29	3.32
Martin, Blake	L-L	6-2	195	6-19-86	1	2	3.18	20	0	0	2	28	24	11	10	1	13	40	.243	.224	.259	12.71	4.13
McCardell, Mike	R-R	6-5	220	4-13-85	9	4	2.86	22	21	1	0	135	110	51	43	10	25	139	.219	.215	.222	9.24	1.66
Nolte, Charles	R-R	6-3	200	3-19-86	4	3	2.05	44	0	0	1	70	63	26	16	1	35	75	.242	.292	.200	9.60	4.48
Reyes, Henry	L-L	6-7	183	5-10-85	3	3	5.04	17	8	0	0	61	62	38	34	11	23	49	.262	.232	.274	7.27	3.41
Rodgers, Dominique	R-R	6-2	211	1-21-85	0	0	2.61	6	0	0	0	10	10	3	3	1	3	10	.250	.222	.273	8.71	2.61
Steedley, Spencer	L-L	6-2	194	5-31-85	5	3	2.14	31	0	0	8	46	35	16	11	2	17	59	.208	.221	.200	11.46	3.30
Tarsi, Mike	R-L	6-8	185	8-11-86	6	11	5.13	34	20	3	1	132	168	89	75	12	34	113	.314	.255	.338	7.72	2.32
Tippett, Bradley	R-R	6-1	190	2-11-88	2	1	4.24	13	0	0	1	17	19	9	8	3	5	15	.288	.242	.333	7.94	2.65
Van Mil, Loek	R-R	7-1	232	9-15-84	2	2	3.22	28	0	0	3	45	36	21	16	5	25	42	.221	.197	.237	8.46	5.04
Williams, Matthew	R-R	6-1	180	2-28-87	2	0	2.09	23	0	0	7	39	29	11	9	2	12	42	.204	.186	.222	9.78	2.79

Fielding

Catcher	PCT	G	PO	A	E	DP	PB
Benson	—	1	0	0	0	0	0
De San Miguel	.979	40	302	28	7	3	1
Fernandez	.978	21	159	18	4	1	3
Lehmann	.981	27	230	31	5	1	3
Yersich	.971	59	455	55	15	8	4

First Base	PCT	G	PO	A	E	DP
De San Miguel	1.000	1	8	0	0	0
Leveret	.981	41	297	17	6	24
Olson	1.000	14	87	4	0	13
Parmelee	.987	46	353	24	5	29
Petsch	.941	3	28	4	2	3
Richardson	.986	7	66	2	1	6
Romero	.846	3	9	2	2	0
Singleton	1.000	1	5	0	0	0
Yersich	.982	33	267	12	5	18

Second Base	PCT	G	PO	A	E	DP
Brito	.949	30	49	63	6	15
Casilla	1.000	2	2	5	0	0
Cates	.986	16	25	45	1	12
De Los Santos	.984	26	61	62	2	13
Santana	.933	20	29	55	6	11
Santiago	1.000	3	5	6	0	2
Singleton	.954	46	93	114	10	22
Solarte	1.000	2	5	2	0	1

Third Base	PCT	G	PO	A	E	DP
Brito	1.000	1	1	1	0	0
Cates	.957	35	27	63	4	7
De San Miguel	.000	1	0	0	1	0
Olson	.919	38	35	67	8	9
Richardson	.929	28	19	46	5	3
Romero	.905	35	23	63	9	11
Santana	—	1	0	0	0	0

	PCT	G	PO	A	E	DP
Santiago	.750	1	1	2	1	1
Singleton	1.000	1	1	0	0	0
Solarte	.895	6	6	11	2	2

Shortstop	PCT	G	PO	A	E	DP
Brito	.750	2	0	3	1	0
Cates	.948	60	84	154	13	26
De Los Santos	.911	37	53	90	14	19
Kelly	.963	6	5	21	1	4
Olson	.962	17	25	26	2	9
Santana	.882	23	32	43	10	6
Singleton	—	1	0	0	0	0

Outfield	PCT	G	PO	A	E	DP
Benson	.977	69	115	14	3	2
Cates	1.000	2	1	0	0	0
De San Miguel	1.000	1	1	0	0	0
Dolenc	.950	114	199	11	11	4

Lewis	.921	47	55	3	5	1	Revere	.943	76	160	5	10	2	Williams	—	1	0	0	0	0	
Parmelee	.976	25	36	4	1	1	Schmiesing	.978	50	82	7	2	1								
Petsch	1.000	10	15	0	0	0	Solarte	.952	32	56	3	3	1								

ORGANIZATION STATISTICS

ELIZABETHTON TWINS ROOKIE

APPALACHIAN LEAGUE

Batting	B-T	HT	WT	DOB	AVG	vLH	vRH	G	AB	R	H	2B	3B	HR	RBI	BB	HBP	SH	SF	SO	SB	CS	SLG	OBP
Beresford, James	L-R	6-1	155	1-19-89	.246	.179	.258	55	179	26	44	5	1	0	23	25	2	5	0	35	1	4	.285	.345
Bigley, Evan	R-R	6-0	200	3-9-87	.300	.231	.316	53	213	45	64	13	3	14	47	13	8	0	2	43	2	2	.587	.360
Brito, Jeanfred	R-R	5-9	160	12-21-87	.261	.500	.211	11	46	11	12	3	0	0	2	2	0	0	0	7	2	0	.326	.292
De La Osa, Dominic	R-R	5-11	205	1-13-86	.263	.220	.272	59	236	50	62	13	0	6	32	37	10	0	1	65	8	3	.394	.384
Hanson, Nate	R-R	6-0	195	2-8-87	.215	.238	.208	29	93	21	20	6	0	2	8	15	4	0	0	31	0	0	.344	.348
Harrington, Michael	L-R	6-0	200	10-6-85	.266	.220	.277	63	241	40	64	18	0	9	44	30	4	0	1	56	0	1	.452	.355
Lanning, Jeff	R-R	6-0	210	1-1-87	.255	.111	.286	30	102	14	26	7	0	4	21	12	3	0	2	28	0	0	.441	.345
Leveret, Rene	R-R	6-2	224	11-19-85	.306	.300	.308	9	36	7	11	3	0	2	6	5	1	0	0	9	0	0	.556	.405
Morales, Angel	R-R	6-1	180	11-24-89	.301	.135	.342	54	183	33	55	12	1	15	28	26	9	0	0	72	7	2	.623	.413
Papasan, Nick	R-R	5-9	170	3-14-88	.389	.500	.382	10	36	7	14	3	0	1	5	1	0	0	0	9	0	1	.556	.405
Rams, Danny	R-R	6-2	205	12-19-88	.228	.296	.213	41	149	21	34	8	3	5	24	15	1	0	1	71	0	0	.423	.301
Richardson, Juan	R-R	6-0	200	12-27-86	.250	.286	.239	15	60	10	15	3	0	0	10	5	1	0	3	12	0	1	.300	.304
Romero, Nick	B-R	6-1	200	7-15-87	.274	.241	.280	48	197	34	54	10	1	7	32	17	4	0	4	57	0	1	.442	.338
Santiago, Eric	R-R	6-0	185	7-10-87	.111	.500	.000	2	9	1	1	0	0	0	0	0	0	0	0	2	0	0	.111	.111
Schmiesing, Andrew	L-L	6-4	190	5-24-86	.379	.750	.320	7	29	8	11	1	0	1	5	6	0	1	0	6	0	0	.517	.486
Severino, Adan	L-R	6-0	200	10-22-86	.243	.167	.253	32	103	18	25	5	1	2	10	18	2	0	0	25	4	2	.369	.366
Soto, Alexander	R-R	5-11	205	11-8-86	.276	.136	.309	31	116	23	32	10	0	10	26	9	3	0	0	40	0	0	.621	.344
Waltenbury, Jonathan	L-R	6-4	230	4-1-88	.319	.174	.350	63	263	49	84	22	3	10	45	27	1	0	2	46	0	2	.540	.382

Pitching	B-T	HT	WT	DOB	W	L	ERA	G	GS	CG	SV	IP	H	R	ER	HR	BB	SO	AVG	vLH	vRH	K/9	BB/9
Alcala, Omar	L-L	6-1	190	12-24-86	0	0	8.10	5	0	0	0	10	11	9	9	3	9	9	.275	.250	.281	8.10	8.10
Berlind, Dan	R-R	6-7	215	12-3-87	2	3	10.98	14	8	0	1	39	67	51	48	7	27	57	.372	.333	.393	13.04	6.18
Blevins, Steve	R-R	6-2	215	11-17-86	1	2	5.47	17	0	0	1	26	25	16	16	3	9	27	.240	.231	.244	9.23	3.08
Carr, Kyle	R-L	6-5	200	11-11-86	0	0	9.60	11	0	0	0	15	20	18	16	2	10	16	.317	.211	.364	9.60	6.00
Curry, Alex	R-R	6-1	170	12-29-87	0	2	11.81	3	3	0	0	11	21	18	14	2	4	8	.412	.357	.432	6.75	3.38
Eacott, Jarrad	L-L	5-11	190	8-2-88	1	0	1.17	5	0	0	0	8	2	1	1	0	4	9	.087	.000	.118	10.57	4.70
Fritz, Nathan	R-R	6-3	180	5-5-86	1	0	8.38	9	0	0	0	10	14	9	9	1	5	8	.350	.286	.385	7.45	4.66
Hamburger, Mark	R-R	6-4	195	2-5-87	1	2	4.17	27	0	0	13	37	35	19	17	2	13	40	.250	.311	.221	9.82	3.19
Hunt, Shooter	R-R	6-3	200	8-16-86	0	0	0.47	4	4	0	0	19	4	3	1	0	6	34	.066	.067	.065	16.11	2.84
Lanigan, Bobby	R-R	6-4	220	5-5-87	6	5	2.78	13	13	0	0	74	74	33	23	5	9	65	.250	.233	.259	7.87	1.09
Leavitt, Curtis	R-R	6-4	195	1-10-87	6	2	4.45	14	8	0	0	63	67	35	31	8	19	61	.276	.321	.255	8.76	2.73
Martin, Blake	L-L	6-2	195	6-19-86	0	0	2.25	2	0	0	0	4	3	1	1	0	0	5	.214	.500	.167	11.25	0.00
Martin, Lee	R-R	6-0	185	5-28-86	4	2	4.60	18	0	0	0	31	34	25	16	1	20	25	.281	.315	.254	7.18	5.74
Osterbrock, Dan	R-L	6-3	190	1-27-87	7	2	3.00	13	13	1	0	75	70	33	25	7	8	104	.240	.283	.232	12.48	0.96
Rondon, Danny	R-R	6-0	160	6-21-87	1	1	4.00	22	0	0	1	36	44	22	16	4	9	30	.301	.280	.313	7.50	2.25
Tippett, Bradley	R-R	6-1	190	2-11-88	8	3	2.55	14	14	1	0	74	70	31	21	5	9	63	.249	.253	.247	7.66	1.09
Wright, Thomas	B-R	6-3	210	1-28-88	4	0	3.20	18	3	0	0	45	42	18	16	2	20	34	.239	.130	.277	6.80	4.00

Fielding

Catcher	PCT	G	PO	A	E	DP	PB
Lanning	.988	18	151	15	2	3	2
Rams	1.000	22	201	26	0	0	11
Soto	.992	29	208	27	2	0	9

First Base	PCT	G	PO	A	E	DP
Leveret	.959	5	45	2	2	3
Rams	.967	7	55	3	2	2
Waltenbury	.985	56	509	23	8	48

Second Base	PCT	G	PO	A	E	DP
Beresford	1.000	2	4	7	0	1

	De La Osa	.953	53	100	141	12	35
	Papasan	.914	8	15	17	3	2
	Romero	.800	1	3	5	2	1
	Santiago	1.000	2	1	9	0	1

Third Base	PCT	G	PO	A	E	DP
Hanson	.946	26	16	54	4	7
Richardson	1.000	11	10	31	0	2
Romero	.933	29	22	48	5	2

Shortstop	PCT	G	PO	A	E	DP
Beresford	.917	53	70	184	23	32

	Brito	.943	9	11	22	2	4
	De La Osa	1.000	1	1	1	0	0
	Romero	.905	6	5	14	2	4

Outfield	PCT	G	PO	A	E	DP
Bigley	.917	52	62	4	6	1
Brito	.667	2	2	0	1	0
De La Osa	1.000	4	2	0	0	0
Harrington	.955	53	63	1	3	1
Morales	.962	53	97	4	4	0
Schmiesing	.889	7	8	0	1	0
Severino	.960	29	41	7	2	3

GCL TWINS ROOKIE

GULF COAST LEAGUE

Batting	B-T	HT	WT	DOB	AVG	vLH	vRH	G	AB	R	H	2B	3B	HR	RBI	BB	HBP	SH	SF	SO	SB	CS	SLG	OBP
Atherton, Tim	R-R	6-2	196	11-7-89	.375	.600	.273	5	16	4	6	2	0	0	4	3	2	0	0	3	0	0	.500	.524
Brown, Javier	R-R	6-0	180	6-24-87	.234	.077	.294	17	47	2	11	0	0	0	2	6	3	1	1	14	2	2	.234	.351
Choi, Hyeong-rok	R-R	5-11	189	8-23-89	.235	.167	.254	23	85	11	20	4	0	1	7	8	1	0	0	15	0	2	.318	.309
Choi, Hyun-wook	L-L	6-0	187	12-4-89	.297	.333	.283	23	64	6	19	1	0	1	7	3	0	2	2	6	1	0	.359	.319
Diaz, Andres	R-R	6-1	195	7-22-88	.246	.286	.237	32	114	23	28	8	0	3	9	12	1	0	0	18	1	0	.395	.323
Everett, Adam	R-R	6-0	180	2-5-77	.500	.500	.500	4	12	1	6	1	0	0	0	0	1	1	0	1	1	0	.583	.462
Goncalves, Jonathan	R-R	5-11	159	5-13-89	.261	.238	.269	31	88	19	23	4	1	0	10	17	2	1	2	16	7	1	.330	.385
Gonzales, Mike	L-R	6-6	245	6-16-88	.331	.241	.356	41	133	14	44	10	1	3	23	10	4	0	3	36	0	1	.489	.387
Hajtmar, Jakub	R-R	6-2	173	6-14-87	.247	.333	.224	33	85	7	21	3	0	0	2	5	1	5	0	20	5	2	.282	.297
Hanvi, Frederic	R-R	6-2	180	5-2-89	.500	—	.500	1	2	1	1	0	0	0	0	0	0	1	0	0	1	0	.500	.667
Hicks, Aaron	B-R	6-2	170	10-2-89	.318	.355	.310	45	173	32	55	10	4	4	27	28	0	1	2	32	12	2	.491	.409
Hidalgo, Anderson	R-R	5-9	172	9-5-88	.364	.222	.400	26	88	15	32	6	0	1	17	15	1	1	2	13	1	1	.466	.453
Jang, Jae-Hyung	R-R	5-11	191	10-16-86	.250	.231	.257	15	48	2	12	3	1	0	10	5	0	0	3	12	0	0	.354	.304

	B-T	HT	WT	DOB	AVG	vLH	vRH	G	AB	R	H	2B	3B	HR	RBI	BB	HBP	SH	SF	SO	SB	CS	SLG	OBP
Ladendorf, Tyler	R-R	6-0	185	3-7-88	.204	.222	.200	45	147	17	30	8	1	1	13	17	6	3	2	29	6	0	.293	.308
Lara, Herbert	B-R	5-10	154	6-29-88	.281	.258	.287	42	146	26	41	7	0	1	18	10	2	4	1	12	6	3	.349	.333
Lin, Wang-Wei	L-R	6-0	185	6-28-88	.100	—	.100	4	10	0	1	0	0	0	0	1	0	0	0	4	0	0	.100	.182
Ortiz, Danny	L-L	5-11	166	1-5-90	.274	.238	.285	48	186	22	51	11	5	2	27	11	5	1	2	30	4	0	.419	.328
Pinto, Josmil	R-R	5-11	184	3-31-89	.329	.280	.350	24	85	14	28	9	3	1	14	9	0	0	0	14	1	0	.541	.394
Roberts, Brandon	L-R	6-0	185	11-9-84	.286	1.000	.167	4	7	0	2	1	0	0	0	3	4	0	0	1	4	0	.429	.643
Rohlfing, Dan	R-R	6-0	185	2-12-89	.200	.200	.200	25	70	10	14	3	1	1	8	7	3	0	0	17	0	0	.314	.300
Sanchez, Henry	R-R	6-3	235	11-29-86	.050	.000	.059	7	20	1	1	1	0	0	0	3	0	0	0	14	0	0	.100	.174
Sanchez, Juan	R-R	5-11	167	1-16-87	.314	.182	.356	42	137	25	43	13	1	2	17	11	4	4	0	22	3	1	.467	.382
Tosoni, Rene	L-R	6-0	194	7-2-86	.667	—	.667	2	6	3	4	0	0	1	3	0	0	0	0	1	0	0	1.167	.667
Williams, Reggie	L-R	6-2	185	11-5-88	.286	.154	.310	23	84	12	24	7	3	0	13	9	1	1	1	10	1	1	.440	.358
Woodard, Johnny	L-R	6-4	208	9-15-84	.200	.000	.333	2	5	1	1	0	0	0	0	1	0	0	0	2	1	0	.200	.333

Pitching	B-T	HT	WT	DOB	W	L	ERA	G	GS	CG	SV	IP	H	R	ER	HR	BB	SO	AVG	vLH	vRH	K/9	BB/9
Biddle, Elliot	R-L	5-11	157	11-23-86	0	0	3.86	3	0	0	0	5	6	3	2	0	3	1	.316	.143	.417	1.93	5.79
Blevins, Steve	R-R	6-2	215	11-17-86	1	1	3.00	8	0	0	0	9	6	3	3	0	2	10	.182	.250	.143	10.00	2.00
Carr, Kyle	R-L	6-5	200	11-11-86	0	0	0.00	3	0	0	0	3	1	1	0	0	0	3	.091	.000	.143	9.00	0.00
Curry, Alex	R-R	6-1	170	12-29-87	2	0	1.46	6	5	0	0	25	15	4	4	1	3	23	.167	.170	.163	8.39	1.09
Garcia, Martire	L-L	5-11	150	3-1-90	2	2	2.91	11	11	0	0	53	45	25	17	3	22	53	.225	.196	.236	9.06	3.76
Guanchez, Wilmer	R-R	6-2	180	6-1-87	0	0	0.00	1	0	0	0	1	2	3	0	0	1	0	.333	.000	.400	18.00	9.00
Ibarra, Edgar	L-L	5-11	170	5-31-89	4	0	3.12	10	10	0	0	49	44	22	17	1	21	51	.235	.217	.241	9.37	3.86
Kirwan, Brian	R-R	6-4	218	6-9-87	0	0	0.00	1	0	0	0	1	0	0	0	0	0	2	.000	.000		18.00	0.00
Lobanov, Andrei	L-L	6-3	171	1-25-90	3	1	3.54	9	2	0	0	20	18	9	8	0	3	17	.237	.167	.259	7.52	1.33
Lobanov, Nick	R-L	6-0	195	3-26-89	0	0	6.97	7	0	0	0	10	8	9	8	0	8	8	.229	.100	.280	6.97	6.97
Mijares, Jean	L-L	5-11	149	1-10-88	0	3	5.13	13	5	0	0	33	32	22	19	0	20	30	.250	.321	.230	8.10	5.40
Mijares, Jose	L-L	6-0	230	10-29-84	2	1	2.45	7	0	0	0	11	10	3	3	0	1	16	.238	.125	.265	13.09	0.82
Mopas, Michael	L-L	6-1	170	12-23-87	2	1	2.45	12	1	0	1	22	17	9	6	0	12	14	.210	.150	.230	5.73	4.91
Mota, Kelvin	R-R	6-3	190	6-23-88	2	0	1.07	19	0	0	12	25	21	4	3	0	9	18	.223	.186	.255	6.39	3.20
Munoz, Miguel	R-R	6-2	182	8-4-88	5	2	3.04	11	10	0	0	53	56	19	18	0	10	51	.262	.224	.293	8.61	1.69
Nanney, Khol	R-R	6-2	185	10-29-84	4	2	3.12	10	0	0	0	17	18	7	6	0	4	8	.273	.300	.250	4.15	2.08
Pugh, Bruce	R-R	6-3	180	7-18-88	1	2	3.20	13	0	0	2	25	18	10	9	1	17	26	.202	.265	.164	9.24	6.04
Sanchez, Angelo	R-R	6-2	215	6-7-89	4	3	3.62	11	11	0	0	55	66	28	22	2	18	55	.307	.302	.311	9.05	2.96
Sawatski, Jay	L-L	6-2	195	5-7-82	0	0	4.50	2	0	0	0	2	5	2	1	0	0	1	.500	.500	.500	4.50	0.00
Testa, Joe	L-L	5-10	175	12-18-85	2	0	1.32	8	0	0	1	14	9	3	2	0	1	17	.191	.067	.250	11.20	0.66
Tonkin, Mike	R-R	6-7	215	11-19-89	0	1	3.27	6	1	0	0	11	10	4	4	0	3	8	.244	.192	.333	6.55	2.45
Weller, Blayne	R-R	6-5	220	1-30-90	0	0	0.00	1	0	0	0	1	2	0	0	0	0	1	.500	.500		9.00	0.00

Fielding

Catcher	PCT	G	PO	A	E	DP	PB
Hanvi	1.000	1	5	1	0	0	0
Jang	.984	14	114	11	2	0	4
Pinto	.968	24	189	23	7	2	2
Rohlfing	.986	22	124	16	2	3	3

First Base	PCT	G	PO	A	E	DP
Diaz	.974	23	179	5	5	15
Gonzales	.985	19	120	8	2	10
Hajtmar	.992	20	120	2	1	12
Rohlfing	1.000	3	14	1	0	1
H. Sanchez	.974	5	35	3	1	2
Woodard	1.000	2	13	0	0	0

Second Base	PCT	G	PO	A	E	DP
Brown	.953	11	15	26	2	4

	PCT	G	PO	A	E	DP
Choi	.968	17	24	36	2	8
Hajtmar	1.000	9	19	30	0	7
J. Sanchez	1.000	2	5	6	0	0
Williams	.905	19	35	51	9	11

Third Base	PCT	G	PO	A	E	DP
Choi	.944	6	2	15	1	2
Hidalgo	.897	19	18	34	6	1
Ladendorf	.952	8	4	16	1	0
J. Sanchez	.905	27	11	46	6	4
Williams	.667	1	0	2	1	0

Shortstop	PCT	G	PO	A	E	DP
Brown	.923	5	3	9	1	4
Everett	.909	4	3	7	1	0
Hajtmar	.714	2	2	3	2	1

	PCT	G	PO	A	E	DP
Ladendorf	.961	37	59	88	6	17
J. Sanchez	.977	13	12	30	1	5

Outfield	PCT	G	PO	A	E	DP
Atherton	1.000	4	9	0	0	0
Choi	1.000	19	19	1	0	0
Goncalves	.966	29	53	4	2	2
Hicks	.976	44	78	3	2	0
Lara	.984	39	56	4	1	2
Lin	1.000	2	4	0	0	0
Ortiz	.984	40	63	0	1	0
Roberts	1.000	4	4	0	0	0
Tosoni	.500	1	1	0	1	0

DSL TWINS

ROOKIE

DOMINICAN SUMMER LEAGUE

Batting	B-T	HT	WT	DOB	AVG	vLH	vRH	G	AB	R	H	2B	3B	HR	RBI	BB	HBP	SH	SF	SO	SB	CS	SLG	OBP
Arcia, Oswaldo	R-R	6-0	186	5-9-91	.293	.278	.297	61	229	38	67	12	4	4	36	16	2	0	1	27	8	7	.432	.343
Arias, Jhonatan	R-R	5-10	180	2-18-89	.248	.194	.264	50	141	11	35	6	0	0	15	15	1	0	2	24	3	2	.291	.321
Blanco, Juan	R-R	5-10	152	4-24-89	.264	.294	.253	39	125	15	33	4	3	0	17	4	2	2	1	18	5	3	.344	.295
Caro, Felix	R-R	6-0	186	3-20-90	.215	.189	.223	47	149	16	32	5	1	4	21	9	4	0	0	46	1	2	.342	.278
Franco, Yancarlo	R-S	5-9	145	8-29-88	.184	.143	.198	48	114	21	21	4	1	1	7	6	3	3	0	26	4	4	.263	.244
Galvan, Lesther	R-R	5-10	178	4-10-90	.224	.200	.227	14	49	12	11	3	0	1	11	9	0	0	0	12	3	2	.347	.345
Gil, Wilfy	R-R	6-2	180	11-10-89	.261	.258	.262	41	138	26	36	3	2	0	11	21	5	1	1	40	18	4	.312	.376
Gonzalez, Xavier	R-R	5-11	170	2-22-89	.154	.053	.196	23	65	4	10	1	0	0	10	3	0	0	2	0	2	4	.169	.295
Martinez, Yorby	B-R	6-0	170	1-12-89	.212	.179	.226	44	132	14	28	6	0	0	10	19	2	1	1	26	5	2	.258	.318
Mercedes, Jean Carlos	R-R	6-0	185	11-29-87	.223	.161	.244	39	121	20	27	4	1	2	15	18	5	1	0	33	2	2	.322	.347
Perez, Jairo	R-R	5-10	160	6-10-88	.330	.234	.381	48	136	38	54	16	1	4	36	20	12	1	5	24	8	4	.525	.437
Pina, Randy	R-R	6-0	189	5-1-91	.267	.000	.308	12	30	4	8	1	0	0	1	3	3	0	0	8	1	0	.300	.389
Rodriguez, Jairo	R-R	5-11	180	8-24-88	.236	.222	.240	42	140	17	33	4	0	2	14	13	0	0	0	16	2	2	.307	.301
Sanchez, Rafael	R-R	6-0	170	9-8-89	.182	.077	.226	15	44	2	8	2	0	0	2	6	0	0	0	26	0	1	.227	.280
Santana, Daniel	B-R	5-11	150	11-7-90	.274	.237	.283	51	190	37	52	6	10	1	27	20	2	3	4	38	15	4	.426	.343
Sierra, Eliel	R-R	5-10	162	1-21-86	.230	.192	.244	58	187	31	43	16	0	2	20	29	13	0	1	36	4	4	.348	.370
Soliman, Manuel	R-R	6-2	185	8-11-89	.211	.217	.209	58	185	26	39	11	2	1	26	30	5	0	3	39	2	1	.308	.332
Vasquez, Carlos	R-R	6-1	160	10-26-90	.119	.115	.121	31	84	13	10	1	0	0	9	17	4	1	0	24	3	1	.131	.295

Pitching	B-T	HT	WT	DOB	W	L	ERA	G	GS	CG	SV	IP	H	R	ER	HR	BB	SO	AVG	vLH	vRH	K/9	BB/9
Acosta, Ramon	R-R	6-0	166	1-21-87	5	0	0.00	9	9	1	0	55	26	6	0	0	9	35	.135	.161	.125	5.76	1.48
Alvarez, Edison	L-R	6-3	163	8-4-88	0	3	2.09	28	0	0	15	39	34	15	9	1	7	37	.233	.255	.222	8.61	1.63
Cardenas, Eliecer	R-R	6-2	177	1-30-88	5	1	1.57	14	11	0	0	69	56	15	12	2	11	59	.221	.212	.227	7.73	1.44
Carrillo, Carlos	R-R	6-4	180	11-25-89	0	2	7.36	15	0	0	0	26	40	25	21	1	12	23	.351	.485	.296	8.06	4.21
Ciurcina, Cesar	R-R	5-11	192	10-23-90	3	2	3.68	11	8	0	0	44	44	22	18	0	10	35	.262	.319	.240	7.16	2.05
Garcia, Jhon	R-R	6-1	200	5-19-87	3	0	2.31	6	0	0	0	12	10	3	3	0	1	13	.233	.143	.276	10.03	0.77
Germosen, Deivi	R-R	6-0	155	8-1-89	0	0	12.15	6	0	0	0	7	9	9	9	0	10	6	.321	.333	.318	8.10	13.50
Gonzalez, Jose	L-L	5-9	166	2-3-90	1	0	1.87	21	0	0	3	34	20	8	7	0	9	43	.167	.250	.150	11.50	2.41
Guerra, Pedro	R-R	6-0	180	1-9-90	8	2	2.45	14	14	0	0	84	75	31	23	4	12	75	.242	.228	.249	8.00	1.28
Reverol, Renzo	R-R	6-2	192	1-24-91	4	2	3.00	19	1	0	0	30	31	16	10	0	12	34	.263	.243	.272	10.20	3.60
Salcedo, Adrian	R-R	6-4	175	4-24-91	4	4	1.65	12	12	0	0	65	47	18	12	1	8	50	.198	.228	.184	6.89	1.10
Vargas, Lesmir	R-R	6-1	160	9-2-86	1	3	2.73	19	2	0	2	33	27	14	10	0	10	16	.229	.233	.227	4.36	2.73
Villaroel, Orlando	R-R	6-1	190	3-8-90	4	4	2.51	13	12	0	0	57	50	23	16	0	26	46	.237	.246	.232	7.22	4.08

Fielding

Catcher	PCT	G	PO	A	E	DP	PB
Arias	.970	49	298	52	11	0	4
Pina	1.000	10	63	8	0	0	2
Rodriguez	.980	21	123	21	3	1	2
Sanchez	.927	6	35	3	3	1	1

First Base	PCT	G	PO	A	E	DP
Caro	.958	17	110	4	5	7
Galvan	.952	2	20	0	1	1
Gonzalez	1.000	1	12	0	0	0
Martinez	1.000	1	1	0	0	0
Mercedes	.917	3	19	3	2	2
Perez	.991	23	226	5	2	12
Rodriguez	1.000	10	79	6	0	5
Sanchez	.941	4	30	2	2	4
Sierra	1.000	1	11	0	0	2
Soliman	1.000	22	158	17	0	14

Second Base	PCT	G	PO	A	E	DP
Blanco	1.000	13	18	28	0	4

	PCT	G	PO	A	E	DP
Franco	.912	7	12	19	3	6
Galvan	1.000	1	1	2	0	1
Gonzalez	1.000	15	32	38	0	8
Martinez	.923	12	22	26	4	4
Perez	.984	14	29	34	1	9
Santana	.979	9	20	27	1	7
Vasquez	.926	7	13	12	2	2

Third Base	PCT	G	PO	A	E	DP
Blanco	.833	4	4	6	2	1
Caro	.818	11	12	24	8	2
Franco	.957	8	3	19	1	1
Gonzalez	1.000	1	0	2	0	0
Martinez	.882	17	19	26	6	3
Perez	1.000	2	0	2	0	0
Soliman	.905	40	30	94	13	6
Vasquez	1.000	1	0	3	0	0

Shortstop	PCT	G	PO	A	E	DP
Blanco	1.000	4	7	9	0	2

	PCT	G	PO	A	E	DP
Franco	.857	2	2	4	1	0
Gonzalez	1.000	1	1	1	0	0
Martinez	.980	14	18	31	1	7
Santana	.920	35	56	94	13	13
Vasquez	.906	23	28	49	8	12

Outfield	PCT	G	PO	A	E	DP
Arcia	.971	60	89	10	3	0
Blanco	.931	17	26	1	2	0
Caro	.947	19	18	0	1	0
Franco	.966	27	27	1	1	0
Galvan	—	1	0	0	0	0
Gil	.873	41	60	2	9	0
Gonzalez	1.000	3	4	0	0	0
Martinez	1.000	3	4	0	0	0
Mercedes	1.000	5	4	0	0	0
Sierra	.988	56	73	7	1	2

New York Mets

BY ADAM RUBIN

The unfathomable happened again.

In 2007, the Mets squandered a seven-game lead with 17 to play. In 2008, they squandered a 3½-game division lead with 17 to play and again were eliminated from postseason contention on the regular season's final day.

The Mets, who entered game No. 162 tied with the Brewers for the wild-card lead, lost to the Marlins 4-2 in the final game in Shea Stadium's history. The Mets move into Citi Field in 2009.

Offseason acquisition Johan Santana nearly car-  ried the Mets into the postseason. The 29-year-old lefthander tossed a career-high 125 pitches on Sept. 23 to beat the Cubs, then came back on short rest in the season's second-to-last game and shut out the Marlins. Santana made that extraordinary performance despite pitching with a torn meniscus in his left knee that required surgery three days after the season.

The ace went 16-7 with a National League-best 2.53 ERA while logging 234⅓ innings, the most by a Mets pitcher since Frank Viola in 1990. Santana won his final nine decisions, with his final loss coming June 28 against the Yankees in a duel with Andy Pettitte. Santana might have been in the dialogue for the NL's Cy Young Award had seven leads turned over to the bullpen not resulted in no-decisions.

The lowlight of the Mets' season—at least off the field—came in the early morning hours of June 17 when general manager Omar Minaya fired manager Willie Randolph in a hotel room after a Mets win in Anaheim. The Mets were 34-35 and were tied for third place in the NL East, 6½ games behind the Phillies at the time of Randolph's dismissal.

The Mets also fired pitching coach Rick Peterson and first-base coach Tom Nieto. Bench coach Jerry Manuel, a former American League manager of the year with the White Sox, took over as interim manager and guided the Mets to a 55-38 record over the remainder of the season. Manuel was rewarded with a two-year contract, while Minaya signed a three-year extension through the 2012 season despite the Mets' second straight September swoon.

The Mets' bullpen proved to be the Achilles' heel, as the three primary cogs of the 2006 team that reached the NLCS all faltered. Billy Wagner, who blew seven saves, eventually required Tommy

John surgery that should sideline him for 2009 as well, while set-up men Aaron Heilman and Duaner Sanchez both underperformed. Minaya struck out trying to strike a deal at the non-waiver trading deadline, and his August acquisition of reliever Luis Ayala from the Nationals couldn't remedy the dreadful bullpen showing.

PLAYERS OF THE YEAR

MAJOR LEAGUE: JOHAN SANTANA, LHP

The Mets traded for Santana in the offseason and the former Twins stalwart delivered, by finishing 16-7 and winning the National League ERA title with a 2.53 mark. His 206 strikeouts also tied with two others for the second-best mark in the NL.

MINOR LEAGUE: JONATHAN NIESE, LHP

A seventh-round pick in 2005 out of high school, Niese opened the year at Double-A Binghamton, reached Triple-A New Orleans and then got three starts in the majors. In the minors, he was 11-8, 3.13 with 114 strikeouts and 58 walks in 164 innings.

STEVE MOORE

ORGANIZATION LEADERS

BATTING		*Minimum 250 at-bats
*AVG	Feliciano, Jesus, New Orleans	.308
R	Veloz, Greg, Savannah/St. Lucie	76
H	Feliciano, Jesus, New Orleans	157
TB	Aguila, Chris, New Orleans	235
2B	Stewart, Caleb, New Orleans/Binghamton	34
3B	Carrera, Ezequiel, St. Lucie	12
HR	Aguila, Chris, New Orleans	29
RBI	Pascucci, Valentino, New Orleans	81
BB	Carp, Mike, Binghamton	79
SO	Duda, Lucas, St. Lucie	129
SB	Veloz, Greg, Savannah/St. Lucie	29
*OBP	Pascucci, Valentino, New Orleans	.410
*SLG	Aguila, Chris, New Orleans	.560

PITCHING		†Minimum 75 innings
W	Sanchez, Jose, Binghamton	13
	Owen, Dylan, St. Lucie, Binghamton	13
L	Four players tied with	12
†ERA	Antonini, Michael, Savannah/St. Lucie/Bing.	2.77
G	Camacho, Eddie, Binghamton/New Orleans	51
GS	Niese, Jon, Binghamton/New Orleans	29
SV	Kunz, Eddie, Binghamton/New Orleans	27
IP	Niese, Jon, Binghamton/New Orleans	164
BB	Parnell, Bobby, Binghamton/New Orleans	66
SO	Niese, Jon, Binghamton/New Orleans	144
†AVG	Antonini, Michael, Savannah/St. Lucie/Bing.	.228

General Manager: Omar Minaya. **Farm Director:** Adam Wogan. **Scouting Director:** Rudy Terrasas.

Class	Team	League	W	L	PCT	Finish*	Manager(s)	Affiliate Since
Majors	New York	National	89	73	.549	4th (16)	W. Randolph/J. Manuel	—
Triple-A	New Orleans Zephyrs	Pacific Coast	66	75	.468	12th (16)	K. Oberkfell/M. Scott	2007
Double-A	Binghamton Mets	Eastern	73	69	.514	5th (12)	Mako Oliveras	1992
High A	St. Lucie Mets	Florida State	53	81	.396	12th (12)	Tim Teufel	1988
Low A	Savannah Sand Gnats	South Atlantic	61	76	.445	12th (16)	Donovan Mitchell	2007
Short-season	Brooklyn Cyclones	New York-Penn	45	30	.600	4th (14)	Edgar Alfonzo	2001
Rookie	Kingsport Mets	Appalachian	34	32	.515	6th (10)	Nick Leyva	1980
Rookie	GCL Mets	Gulf Coast	27	27	.500	10th (16)	---------	2004
Overall 2008 Minor League Record			359	434	.453	25th		

* Finish in overall standings (No. of teams in league). ^League champion.

ORGANIZATION STATISTICS

NEW YORK METS
NATIONAL LEAGUE

Batting	B-T	HT	WT	DOB	AVG	vLH	vRH	G	AB	R	H	2B	3B	HR	RBI	BB	HBP	SH	SF	SO	SB	CS	SLG	OBP
Aquila, Chris	R-R	5-11	200	2-23-79	.167	.167	.167	8	12	0	2	0	0	0	0	2	0	1	0	4	0	0	.167	.286
Alou, Moises	R-R	6-3	230	7-3-66	.347	.462	.306	15	49	4	17	2	0	0	9	2	2	0	1	4	1	1	.388	.389
Anderson, Marlon	L-R	5-11	200	1-6-74	.210	.000	.213	87	138	16	29	6	0	1	10	9	0	2	2	27	2	1	.275	.255
Beltran, Carlos	B-R	6-1	205	4-24-77	.284	.326	.266	161	606	116	172	40	5	27	112	92	1	1	6	96	25	3	.500	.376
Cancel, Robinson	R-R	6-0	190	5-4-76	.245	.429	.107	27	49	5	12	2	0	1	5	3	0	1	0	6	1	2	.347	.288
Casanova, Raul	B-R	6-0	230	8-23-72	.273	.333	.250	20	55	5	15	2	0	1	6	6	0	0	0	10	0	0	.364	.344
Castillo, Luis	B-R	5-11	190	9-12-75	.245	.211	.257	87	298	46	73	7	1	3	28	50	2	7	2	35	17	2	.305	.355
Castro, Ramon	R-R	6-3	260	3-1-76	.245	.277	.218	52	143	15	35	7	0	7	24	13	1	0	0	34	0	0	.441	.312
Chavez, Endy	L-L	6-0	170	2-7-78	.267	.194	.278	133	270	30	72	10	2	1	12	17	0	9	2	22	6	1	.330	.308
Church, Ryan	L-L	6-1	190	10-14-78	.276	.264	.282	90	319	54	88	14	1	12	49	33	3	1	3	83	2	3	.439	.346
Clark, Brady	R-R	6-2	200	4-18-73	.250	.167	.500	7	8	0	2	0	0	0	1	1	1	0	2	1	0	0	.250	.400
Delgado, Carlos	L-R	6-3	265	6-25-72	.271	.267	.273	159	598	96	162	32	1	38	115	72	8	0	8	124	1	1	.518	.353
Easley, Damion	R-R	5-11	195	11-11-69	.269	.287	.260	113	316	33	85	10	2	6	44	19	7	2	3	38	0	0	.370	.322
Evans, Nick	R-R	6-3	210	1-30-86	.257	.319	.135	50	109	18	28	10	0	2	9	7	1	0	2	24	0	0	.404	.303
Martinez, Ramon	R-R	6-0	190	10-10-72	.250	.000	.308	7	16	0	4	3	0	0	3	2	0	0	0	3	0	0	.438	.333
Molina, Gustavo	R-R	6-0	220	2-24-82	.143	.000	.200	2	7	1	1	0	0	0	1	0	0	0	0	1	0	0	.143	.250
Murphy, Daniel	L-R	6-3	210	4-1-85	.313	.400	.306	49	131	24	41	9	3	2	17	18	1	0	1	28	0	2	.473	.397
Nixon, Trot	L-L	6-2	210	4-11-74	.171	.000	.176	11	35	2	6	1	0	1	1	6	0	0	0	9	1	0	.286	.293
Nunez, Abraham	R-R	5-11	200	3-16-76	.000	—	.000	2	2	0	0	0	0	0	0	0	0	0	0	0	0	0	.000	.000
Pagan, Angel	B-R	6-2	195	7-2-81	.275	.250	.294	31	91	12	25	7	1	0	13	11	0	1	2	18	4	0	.374	.346
Phillips, Andy	R-R	6-0	210	4-6-77	.200	.000	.333	4	5	1	1	0	0	0	0	0	0	0	0	0	0	0	.200	.200
2-team total (52 Cincinnati)					.231			56	78	12	18	3	0	3	10	6	1	0	0	14	0	0	.385	.294
Reyes, Argenis	B-R	5-10	165	9-25-82	.218	.167	.233	49	110	13	24	0	0	1	3	4	2	5	0	20	2	0	.245	.259
Reyes, Jose	B-R	6-1	200	6-11-83	.297	.280	.303	159	688	113	204	37	19	16	68	66	1	5	3	82	56	15	.475	.358
Schneider, Brian	L-R	6-1	195	11-26-76	.257	.187	.277	110	335	30	86	10	0	9	38	42	1	4	2	53	0	0	.367	.339
Tatis, Fernando	R-R	5-11	195	1-1-75	.297	.311	.287	92	273	33	81	16	1	11	47	29	3	0	1	59	3	0	.484	.369
Wright, David	R-R	6-0	215	12-20-82	.302	.382	.275	160	626	115	189	42	2	33	124	94	4	0	11	118	15	5	.534	.390

Pitching	B-T	HT	WT	DOB	W	L	ERA	G	GS	CG	SV	IP	H	R	ER	HR	BB	SO	AVG	vLH	vRH	K/9	BB/9
Armas, Tony	R-R	225	4-29-78		1	0	7.56	3	1	0	0	8	11	7	7	2	1	6	.324	.412	.235	6.48	1.08
Ayala, Luis	R-R	6-1	200	1-12-78	1	2	5.50	19	0	0	9	18	23	12	11	3	2	14	.307	.324	.289	7.00	1.00
2-team total (62 Washington)					2	10	5.71	81	0	0	9	76	86	53	48	9	24	50				5.95	2.85
Feliciano, Pedro	L-L	5-10	190	8-25-76	3	4	4.05	86	0	0	2	53	57	24	24	7	26	50	.281	.210	.357	8.44	4.39
Figueroa, Nelson	R-R	6-1	205	5-18-74	3	3	4.57	16	6	0	0	45	48	26	23	3	26	36	.267	.371	.200	7.15	5.16
Heilman, Aaron	R-R	6-5	225	11-12-78	3	8	5.21	78	0	0	3	76	75	48	44	10	46	80	.258	.308	.222	9.47	5.45
Knight, Brandon	L-R	6-0	195	10-1-75	1	0	5.25	4	2	0	0	12	14	7	7	0	7	10	.298	.435	.167	7.50	5.25
Kunz, Eddie	R-R	6-5	265	4-8-86	0	0	13.50	4	0	0	0	3	5	4	4	1	1	1	.455	.500	.333	3.38	3.38
Maine, John	R-R	6-4	200	5-8-81	10	8	4.18	25	25	0	0	140	122	70	65	16	67	122	.234	.238	.229	7.84	4.31
Martinez, Pedro	R-R	5-11	195	10-25-71	5	6	5.61	20	20	0	0	109	127	70	68	19	44	87	.294	.304	.282	7.18	3.63
Muniz, Carlos	R-R	6-1	190	3-12-81	1	1	5.40	18	0	0	0	23	24	14	14	4	7	16	.267	.294	.250	6.17	2.70
Niese, Jonathon	L-L	6-4	215	10-27-86	1	1	7.07	3	3	0	0	14	20	11	11	2	8	11	.333	.353	.326	7.07	5.14
Parnell, Bobby	R-R	6-4	200	9-8-84	0	0	5.40	6	0	0	0	5	3	3	3	2	3	.176	.000	.273	5.40	3.60
Pelfrey, Mike	R-R	6-7	230	1-14-84	13	11	3.72	32	32	2	0	201	209	86	83	12	64	110	.276	.307	.245	4.93	2.87
Perez, Oliver	L-L	6-3	215	8-15-81	10	7	4.22	34	34	0	0	194	167	100	91	24	105	180	.234	.158	.258	8.35	4.87
Rincon, Ricardo	L-L	5-10	190	4-13-70	0	0	4.50	8	0	0	0	4	4	2	2	1	1	3	.267	.500	.000	6.75	2.25
Sanchez, Duaner	R-R	6-2	210	10-14-79	5	1	4.32	66	0	0	0	58	54	28	28	6	23	44	.238	.200	.268	6.79	3.55
Santana, Johan	L-L	6-0	210	3-13-79	16	7	2.53	34	34	3	0	234	206	74	66	23	63	206	.232	.247	.227	7.91	2.42
Schoeneweis, Scott	L-L	6-0	190	10-2-73	2	3	3.34	73	0	0	1	57	55	23	21	7	23	34	.259	.178	.333	5.40	3.65
Smith, Joe	R-R	6-2	210	3-22-84	6	3	3.55	82	0	0	0	63	51	28	25	4	31	52	.220	.320	.192	7.39	4.41
Sosa, Jorge	R-R	6-2	220	4-28-77	4	1	7.06	20	0	0	0	22	30	23	17	4	11	12	.323	.375	.295	4.98	4.57
Stokes, Brian	R-R	6-1	210	9-7-79	1	0	3.51	24	1	0	1	33	35	13	13	5	8	26	.280	.316	.250	7.02	2.16
Vargas, Claudio	R-R	6-4	240	6-19-78	3	2	4.62	11	4	0	0	37	33	20	19	4	11	20	.244	.323	.178	4.86	2.68
Wagner, Billy	L-L	5-11	205	7-25-71	0	1	2.30	45	0	0	27	47	32	17	12	4	10	52	.185	.220	.174	9.96	1.91
Wise, Matt	R-R	6-4	200	11-18-75	0	1	6.43	8	0	0	0	7	10	5	5	2	3	6	.323	.364	.300	7.71	3.86

Fielding

Catcher	PCT	G	PO	A	E	DP	PB
Cancel	1.000	15	81	1	0	0	1
Casanova	1.000	13	89	7	0	0	1
Castro	.987	47	286	19	4	2	1
Molina	1.000	2	19	0	0	0	0
Schneider	.994	109	741	41	5	3	4

First Base	PCT	G	PO	A	E	DP
Anderson	1.000	6	22	4	0	4
Delgado	.994	154	1237	105	8	106
Easley	1.000	4	25	1	0	1
Evans	1.000	3	7	0	0	3
Phillips	—	1	0	0	0	0
Tatis	.895	6	16	1	2	0

Second Base	PCT	G	PO	A	E	DP
Anderson	1.000	1	1	2	0	0
Castillo	.983	81	160	186	6	41
Easley	.983	64	128	160	5	38
Martinez	1.000	5	5	11	0	2
A. Reyes	1.000	27	48	59	0	17

Third Base	PCT	G	PO	A	E	DP
Easley	1.000	1	3	0	0	0
Tatis	1.000	4	2	2	0	0
Wright	.962	159	114	286	16	21

Shortstop	PCT	G	PO	A	E	DP
Easley	1.000	8	7	14	0	1
J. Reyes	.974	158	221	422	17	89

Outfield	PCT	G	PO	A	E	DP
Aguila	1.000	6	5	1	0	0
Alou	1.000	13	18	0	0	0
Anderson	.958	25	45	1	2	1
Beltran	.993	158	418	8	3	1
Chavez	.995	120	180	7	1	2
Church	.995	83	180	7	1	1
Clark	1.000	4	2	0	0	0
Easley	.667	7	2	0	1	0
Evans	1.000	28	37	2	0	0
Murphy	.962	32	50	1	2	1
Nixon	1.000	10	20	1	0	0
Pagan	.975	24	39	0	1	0
Phillips	1.000	2	1	0	0	0
Tatis	.981	71	102	2	2	0

NEW ORLEANS ZEPHYRS
TRIPLE-A
PACIFIC COAST LEAGUE

Batting	B-T	HT	WT	DOB	AVG	vLH	vRH	G	AB	R	H	2B	3B	HR	RBI	BB	HBP	SH	SF	SO	SB	CS	SLG	OBP
Abreu, Michel	R-R	6-3	255	1-2-79	.285	.241	.301	120	425	62	121	24	0	15	66	38	3	0	6	59	1	0	.447	.343
Aguila, Chris	R-R	5-11	200	2-23-79	.295	.330	.282	116	420	74	124	20	2	29	73	53	4	0	2	102	13	4	.560	.378
Cancel, Robinson	R-R	6-0	190	5-4-76	.346	.500	.310	15	52	8	18	4	1	1	8	4	1	1	1	5	1	0	.519	.397
Casanova, Raul	B-R	6-0	230	8-23-72	.295	.294	.295	44	156	18	46	12	0	4	23	11	1	0	0	29	0	0	.449	.345
Church, Ryan	L-L	6-1	190	10-14-78	.200	.000	.333	2	5	0	1	0	0	0	1	1	0	0	0	1	0	0	.400	.333
Clark, Brady	R-R	6-2	200	4-18-73	.304	.200	.385	6	23	3	7	1	0	0	1	3	0	0	0	1	0	0	.348	.385
Feliciano, Jesus	L-L	6-0	174	6-5-79	.308	.285	.316	139	509	70	157	21	4	3	55	41	8	4	5	57	12	14	.383	.366
Gonzalez, Raul	R-R	5-9	190	12-27-73	.279	.222	.302	17	61	5	17	4	0	1	8	3	0	0	0	9	0	0	.393	.313
Green, Andy	R-R	5-10	180	7-7-77	.331	.340	.328	52	178	35	59	10	2	8	28	38	3	3	4	36	3	1	.545	.448
Hernandez, Anderson	B-R	5-9	170	10-30-82	.203	.246	.186	125	479	57	97	21	7	5	36	38	1	3	2	95	11	8	.307	.262
Machado, Anderson	R-R	6-0	185	1-25-81	.226	.115	.263	76	212	27	48	12	2	4	21	35	0	4	2	49	3	0	.358	.333
Martinez, Ramon	R-R	6-0	190	10-10-72	.291	.381	.262	25	86	8	25	1	0	0	5	12	1	1	2	11	1	1	.302	.376
2-team total (28 Las Vegas)					.289	—	—	53	187	23	54	8	0	2	18	21	3	2	4	17	1	1	.364	.363
Mendez, Victor	B-R	5-11	205	6-28-80	.238	.278	.217	51	105	10	25	2	0	2	10	14	0	1	1	24	1	1	.314	.325
Molina, Gustavo	R-R	6-0	220	2-24-82	.206	.250	.188	74	228	22	47	7	0	7	27	16	5	0	1	56	0	0	.329	.272
Nickeas, Mike	R-R	6-0	210	2-13-83	.215	.242	.208	54	163	16	35	9	0	2	17	14	1	2	4	42	0	1	.307	.275
Nixon, Trot	L-L	6-2	210	4-11-74	.293	.273	.300	10	41	9	12	1	0	4	13	8	0	0	0	9	1	0	.610	.408
2-team total (58 Tucson)					.306	—	—	68	222	48	68	16	0	14	44	48	1	0	0	34	2	0	.568	.432
Nunez, Abraham	B-R	5-11	200	3-16-76	.211	.192	.217	72	218	26	46	4	0	4	20	42	2	3	0	38	4	1	.284	.344
2-team total (33 Nashville)					.211	—	—	105	323	40	68	6	0	4	28	56	3	5	1	56	9	1	.266	.332
Pascucci, Valentino	R-R	6-6	260	11-17-78	.290	.373	.262	114	396	72	115	23	0	27	81	77	5	0	3	109	4	1	.553	.410
Petersen, Joshua	R-R	6-3	215	4-15-83	.200	.400	.100	9	15	1	3	0	0	0	3	1	0	0	0	6	0	0	.200	.250
Reyes, Argenis	R-R	5-10	165	9-25-82	.283	.326	.266	81	311	41	88	11	1	0	22	31	1	7	3	47	13	6	.325	.347
Rodriguez, John	L-L	6-0	205	1-20-78	.288	.233	.305	43	125	21	36	6	1	4	20	17	5	1	0	28	0	0	.448	.395
Stewart, Caleb	R-R	6-2	230	6-11-82	.221	.211	.224	20	77	10	17	5	2	1	9	5	0	0	0	15	1	0	.377	.268
Tatis Jr., Fernando	R-R	5-11	190	1-1-75	.242	.182	.276	37	120	18	29	6	0	12	31	17	2	0	0	23	0	0	.592	.345
Valentin, Jose	B-R	5-10	190	10-12-69	.182	.111	.208	10	33	4	6	2	0	1	4	2	0	0	0	8	1	1	.333	.229
Wooten, Shawn	R-R	5-10	230	7-24-72	.152	.154	.150	16	33	4	5	1	0	1	2	4	0	0	0	7	0	0	.273	.243
2-team total (42 Portland)					.195	—	—	58	164	14	32	6	0	3	16	19	1	0	0	37	0	0	.287	.283

Pitching	B-T	HT	WT	DOB	W	L	ERA	G	GS	CG	SV	IP	H	R	ER	HR	BB	SO	AVG	vLH	vRH	K/9	BB/9
Armas, Tony	R-R	6-3	225	4-29-78	5	7	2.54	17	17	0	0	103	85	31	29	9	20	88	.227	.207	.238	7.71	1.75
Bostick II, Adam	L-L	6-1	235	3-17-83	2	2	6.04	11	10	0	0	45	48	30	30	6	20	30	.271	.340	.246	6.04	4.03
Brito, Eude	L-L	6-0	170	8-19-78	0	1	8.03	18	2	0	1	25	32	23	22	4	11	24	.317	.387	.286	8.76	4.01
Camacho, Eddie	L-L	6-1	195	9-17-82	1	0	5.00	14	0	0	0	18	15	11	10	5	7	10	.231	.188	.245	5.00	3.50
Collazo, Willie	L-L	5-9	170	11-7-79	4	9	4.05	37	16	0	2	136	134	66	61	18	35	71	.266	.252	.271	4.71	2.32
Diaz, Jose	R-R	6-3	230	4-13-80	1	5	5.69	12	7	0	0	39	31	31	29	8	33	36	.215	.218	.213	8.31	7.62
2-team total (15 Oklahoma)					2	6	6.32	27	7	0	2	57	46	43	40	10	47	52	—	—	—	8.21	7.42
Field, Nate	R-R	6-2	210	12-11-75	1	3	4.68	50	0	0	13	50	42	28	26	9	29	55	.220	.353	.146	9.90	5.22
Figueroa, Nelson	R-R	6-1	205	5-18-74	4	7	4.43	20	16	0	0	114	120	62	56	15	33	97	.275	.254	.293	7.68	2.61
Hoorelbeke, Casey	R-R	6-8	245	4-4-80	0	0	0.00	2	0	0	1	3	2	0	0	0	1	2	.222	.000	.333	0.00	2.70
Knight, Brandon	L-R	6-0	195	10-1-75	5	1	2.28	12	5	0	1	43	28	12	11	5	12	55	.185	.212	.172	11.42	2.49
Kunz, Eddie	R-R	6-5	265	4-8-86	0	1	7.94	6	0	0	0	6	9	5	5	1	6	5	.346	.214	.500	6.35	3.18
Lugo, Ruddy	B-R	6-0	210	5-22-80	7	12	5.36	24	24	1	0	134	137	84	80	18	51	105	.267	.232	.293	7.03	3.42
Maldonado, Ivan	R-R	6-4	230	6-7-80	4	5	4.07	47	0	0	3	66	73	31	30	6	39	65	.286	.277	.292	8.82	5.29
McNab, Tim	R-R	6-0	175	6-4-80	3	3	5.55	50	1	0	0	73	75	52	45	11	26	39	.263	.307	.234	4.81	3.21
Muniz, Carlos	R-R	6-1	190	3-12-81	2	4	3.93	33	0	0	9	37	30	16	16	5	14	31	.226	.241	.215	7.61	3.44
Niese, Jonathon	L-L	6-4	215	10-27-86	5	1	3.40	7	7	0	0	40	34	15	15	4	14	32	.231	.243	.227	7.26	3.18
Padilla, Juan	R-R	6-0	210	2-17-77	0	0	9.64	14	0	0	0	14	25	15	15	2	8	5	.417	.391	.432	3.21	5.14
Parnell, Bobby	R-R	6-4	200	9-8-84	2	2	6.64	5	4	0	0	20	25	16	15	0	9	23	.298	.313	.278	10.18	3.98
Paulk, Robert	R-R	5-11	175	3-14-81	0	0	3.38	4	0	0	0	5	10	3	2	0	4	2	.455	.500	.429	3.38	6.75
Rincon, Ricardo	L-L	5-10	190	4-13-70	0	0	0.00	1	0	0	0	1	0	0	0	0	0	1	.000	.000	.000	9.00	0.00
Sanchez, Duaner	R-R	6-2	210	10-14-79	0	0	0.00	2	0	0	0	2	0	0	0	0	1	1	.000	.000	.000	4.50	4.50
Santiago, Jose	R-R	6-3	225	11-5-74	5	2	5.38	43	2	0	1	87	116	57	52	17	15	45	.325	.309	.337	4.66	1.55
Stokes, Brian	R-R	6-1	210	9-7-79	10	8	4.41	23	22	1	0	131	124	74	64	7	48	97	.251	.226	.263	6.68	3.31
Vargas, Claudio	R-R	6-4	240	6-19-78	5	2	4.36	8	8	0	0	43	47	24	21	5	13	43	.280	.365	.213	8.93	2.70

Fielding

Catcher

Catcher	PCT	G	PO	A	E	DP	PB
Alen	1.000	1	1	0	0	0	0
Cancel	.988	13	80	5	1	0	2
Casanova	.969	22	150	6	5	2	3
Molina	.996	64	459	40	2	4	3
Nickeas	.984	48	290	22	5	2	6
Wooten	1.000	3	14	4	0	1	0

First Base

First Base	PCT	G	PO	A	E	DP
Abreu	.996	110	890	69	4	82
Cancel	1.000	1	7	0	0	0
Casanova	.977	12	80	6	2	10
Martinez	1.000	3	27	0	0	1
Molina	1.000	3	19	2	0	3
Pascucci	.973	22	166	15	5	14
Wooten	1.000	1	10	1	0	0

Second Base

Second Base	PCT	G	PO	A	E	DP
Green	.987	47	90	144	3	26
Hernandez	1.000	6	19	13	0	4
Machado	.875	6	11	10	3	2
Martinez	1.000	4	14	10	0	5
Nunez	1.000	6	11	11	0	4
Reyes	.989	78	173	198	4	50
Tatis Jr.	1.000	2	5	3	0	2

Third Base

Third Base	PCT	G	PO	A	E	DP
Green	.900	2	5	4	1	1
Machado	.932	50	22	101	9	8
Martinez	1.000	3	0	6	0	2
Molina	1.000	2	1	1	0	0
Murphy	.750	1	0	3	1	0
Nunez	.954	62	35	132	8	9
Petersen	1.000	2	0	9	0	0
Tatis Jr.	.963	26	27	52	3	5
Wooten	.833	3	1	9	2	0

Shortstop

Shortstop	PCT	G	PO	A	E	DP
Green	1.000	1	1	1	0	0
Hernandez	.970	117	158	294	14	57
Machado	.973	11	10	26	1	9
Martinez	1.000	14	20	42	0	5
Nunez	1.000	1	0	1	0	0
Reyes	1.000	2	2	7	0	2
Tatis Jr.	1.000	1	1	4	0	1

Outfield

Outfield	PCT	G	PO	A	E	DP
Aguila	.984	113	178	10	3	1
Church	1.000	2	4	0	0	0
Clark	.933	6	13	1	1	0
Feliciano	.994	133	329	9	2	2
Gonzalez	1.000	14	18	0	0	0
Martinez	1.000	2	1	0	0	0
Mendez	.964	24	27	0	1	0
Nickeas	—	1	0	0	0	0
Nixon	1.000	9	12	0	0	0
Nunez	1.000	2	2	0	0	0
Pascucci	.966	86	135	5	5	0
Petersen	1.000	3	4	0	0	0
Rodriguez	1.000	31	60	1	0	0
Stewart	.964	20	52	2	2	0
Tatis Jr.	1.000	5	6	0	0	0

BINGHAMTON METS

DOUBLE-A

EASTERN LEAGUE

Batting	B-T	HT	WT	DOB	AVG	vLH	vRH	G	AB	R	H	2B	3B	HR	RBI	BB	HBP	SH	SF	SO	SB	CS	SLG	OBP
Alou, Moises	R-R	6-3	230	7-3-66	.167	.333	.000	2	6	0	1	0	0	0	0	0	0	0	0	0	0	0	.167	.167
Arroyo, Rafael	R-R	5-9	170	10-26-82	.213	.300	.160	28	80	7	17	2	0	2	5	10	1	2	1	33	1	0	.313	.304
Bowman, Shawn	R-R	6-2	205	12-9-84	.248	.280	.239	29	113	12	28	7	0	2	10	2	1	1	2	35	3	1	.363	.263
Carp, Mike	L-R	6-2	215	6-30-86	.299	.268	.314	134	478	67	143	29	1	17	72	79	6	0	3	88	1	2	.471	.403
Castillo, Luis	R-R	5-11	190	9-12-75	.250	.250	.250	5	16	1	4	0	0	0	2	2	0	0	0	3	0	0	.250	.333
Church, Ryan	L-L	6-1	190	10-14-78	.000	.000	.000	2	8	0	0	0	0	0	0	0	0	0	0	2	0	0	.000	.000
Concepcion, Ambiorix	R-R	6-2	180	3-19-82	.241	.291	.222	126	456	56	110	22	3	12	54	18	6	2	4	110	24	6	.382	.277
Coronado, Jose	R-R	6-1	175	4-13-86	.260	.285	.249	139	507	56	132	24	0	1	39	57	2	12	4	79	9	3	.314	.335
Evans, Nick	R-R	6-3	210	1-30-86	.311	.366	.286	75	296	52	92	18	7	14	53	26	1	0	3	64	2	1	.561	.365
Garcia, Emmanuel	L-R	6-2	185	3-4-86	.243	.228	.249	104	367	51	89	12	2	4	40	34	2	11	4	83	17	9	.319	.307
Hill, Jamar	R-R	6-2	200	9-20-82	.071	.000	.083	6	14	1	1	0	0	0	1	0	0	0	0	8	0	0	.071	.235
Machado, Anderson	B-R	6-0	185	1-25-81	.200	.333	.161	14	40	4	8	2	0	1	6	7	0	1	0	11	0	0	.325	.319
Malo, Jonathan	R-R	6-1	175	9-29-83	.261	.278	.254	99	276	48	72	14	1	4	30	28	4	4	4	52	12	3	.362	.333
Manriquez, Salomon	R-R	6-1	200	9-15-82	.271	.213	.290	94	321	40	87	16	2	4	28	22	6	3	1	54	2	2	.371	.329
Martinez, Fernando	L-R	6-1	190	10-10-88	.287	.217	.317	86	352	48	101	19	4	8	43	27	3	0	3	73	6	2	.432	.340
Murphy, Daniel	L-R	6-3	210	4-1-85	.308	.298	.313	95	357	56	110	26	1	13	67	39	3	1	7	46	14	5	.496	.374
Nickeas, Mike	R-R	6-0	210	2-13-83	.196	.167	.205	17	51	2	10	1	0	1	4	7	0	0	1	7	0	0	.275	.288
Paniagua, Salvador	R-R	6-1	240	5-21-83	.248	.238	.254	45	113	16	28	7	0	7	19	4	1	0	0	37	1	0	.496	.280
Petersen, Joshua	R-R	6-3	215	4-15-83	.288	.254	.303	72	226	24	65	13	2	3	27	16	4	1	1	51	3	3	.403	.344
Ramos, Peeter	R-R	5-11	180	3-18-82	.207	.000	.273	10	29	2	6	0	0	0	3	0	0	0	0	5	2	3	.207	.281
Reed, Eric	L-L	6-0	170	12-2-80	.229	.105	.253	38	118	16	27	3	0	0	7	11	1	0	0	20	5	2	.254	.300
Smith, Matt	L-R	5-10	172	6-12-83	.500	.000	.000	4	2	0	1	0	0	0	0	0	0	0	0	0	0	0	.750	.500
Stewart, Caleb	R-R	6-2	230	6-11-82	.279	.218	.300	112	394	57	110	29	2	13	57	49	7	0	5	69	7	2	.462	.365

Pitching	B-T	HT	WT	DOB	W	L	ERA	G	GS	CG	SV	IP	H	R	ER	HR	BB	SO	AVG	vLH	vRH	K/9	BB/9
Abel, Nick	R-R	6-4	200	2-18-83	0	0	18.00	5	0	0	0	5	11	10	10	1	6	2	.478	.636	.333	3.60	10.80
Aguilar, Salvador	R-R	6-0	190	1-9-82	10	3	3.14	24	14	1	0	112	102	43	39	8	38	77	.242	.249	.236	6.21	3.06
Alfonzo, Edgar	L-L	5-10	170	12-14-84	2	2	4.26	28	0	0	0	38	43	21	18	7	14	32	.287	.255	.303	7.58	3.32
Antonini, Mike	R-L	6-0	190	8-6-85	1	3	3.74	8	8	0	0	46	43	19	19	10	16	32	.247	.324	.229	6.31	3.15
Brito, Eude	L-L	6-0	170	8-19-78	4	2	2.92	27	1	0	0	49	44	18	16	2	16	30	.247	.227	.259	5.47	2.92
2-team total (1 Harrisburg)					4	2	2.88	28	1	0	0	50	44	18	16	2	17	31	—	—		5.58	3.06
Brown, Eric	R-R	6-6	225	2-23-84	6	9	5.05	30	17	0	0	123	143	77	69	15	29	80	.289	.316	.267	5.85	2.12
Camacho, Eddie	L-L	6-1	195	9-17-82	4	3	2.48	37	0	0	0	62	54	27	17	3	24	43	.237	.333	.184	6.28	3.50
Gee, Dillon	R-R	6-1	195	4-28-86	0	0	1.33	4	4	0	0	27	18	4	4	1	5	20	.194	.154	.222	6.67	1.67
Hernandez, Orlando	R-R	6-2	220	10-11-69	0	1	18.00	1	1	0	0	1	2	2	2	0	2	1	.400	.500	.000	9.00	18.00
Hietpas, Joe	R-R	6-3	230	5-1-79	3	5	6.34	43	1	0	0	65	73	51	46	13	31	48	.272	.287	.263	6.61	4.27
Hoorelbeke, Casey	R-R	6-8	245	4-4-80	0	0	2.65	11	0	0	0	17	19	6	5	3	4	5	.311	.400	.250	2.65	2.12
Kunz, Eddie	R-R	6-5	265	4-8-86	1	4	2.79	44	0	0	27	48	39	19	15	0	25	43	.222	.253	.196	8.01	4.66
Lavigne, Tim	R-R	5-10	210	7-4-78	2	6	4.91	43	0	0	9	44	47	29	24	8	31	36	.278	.275	.280	7.36	6.34
Marte, German	R-R	6-1	180	4-29-85	0	0	5.79	19	0	0	2	28	35	18	18	4	13	24	.307	.311	.304	7.71	4.18
Niese, Jonathon	L-L	6-4	215	10-27-86	6	7	3.04	22	22	2	0	124	118	53	42	5	44	112	.253	.212	.264	8.11	3.18
Owen, Dylan	R-R	5-11	185	7-12-86	1	1	5.51	3	3	0	0	16	20	10	10	3	9	15	.299	.182	.356	8.27	4.96
Parnell, Bobby	R-R	6-4	200	9-8-84	10	6	4.30	24	24	0	0	128	126	66	61	14	57	91	.258	.242	.271	6.42	4.02
Paulk, Robert	R-R	5-11	175	3-14-81	1	0	10.89	16	0	0	0	21	35	25	25	2	16	9	.368	.370	.367	3.92	6.97
Quezada, Elvys	R-R	6-1	210	12-15-81	2	1	4.96	10	0	0	0	16	14	9	9	1	5	7	.233	.148	.303	3.86	2.76
Reyes, Al	R-R	6-1	230	4-10-70	0	0	0.00	5	0	0	1	5	4	0	0	2	1	2	.235	.250	.231	5.40	3.60
Rogers, Brian	R-R	6-4	190	7-17-82	0	0	0.00	4	0	0	1	4	3	0	0	0	2	2	.214	.250	.200	4.15	4.15
2-team total (7 Altoona)					2	0	0.47	11	0	0	1	19	12	1	1	0	5	15	—	—		6.98	2.33
Ruckle, Jacob	R-R	6-1	180	5-27-86	1	3	7.36	6	6	0	0	29	40	25	24	3	9	10	.331	.333	.328	3.07	2.76
Sanchez, Jose	R-R	6-0	170	5-12-84	13	7	3.83	29	20	0	0	153	160	71	65	11	44	118	.265	.278	.255	6.96	2.59
Stoner, Tobi	B-R	6-2	192	12-3-84	4	6	4.33	15	15	0	0	79	80	39	38	7	29	59	.267	.310	.228	6.72	3.30
Wagner, Billy	L-L	5-11	205	7-25-71	0	0	0.00	1	0	0	0	1	0	0	0	0	0	2	.000	—	.000	18.00	0.00

Fielding

Catcher	PCT	G	PO	A	E	DP	PB
Arroyo	.983	26	160	15	3	2	0
Manriquez	.988	86	542	44	7	3	14
Nickeas	1.000	16	94	9	0	1	2
Paniagua	.993	22	127	9	1	0	1

First Base	PCT	G	PO	A	E	DP
Bowman	1.000	1	6	0	0	0
Carp	.984	61	522	37	9	65
Evans	.998	55	497	30	1	45
Machado	1.000	2	23	0	0	3
Manriquez	.969	4	30	1	1	3
Murphy	.989	13	88	5	1	13
Paniagua	1.000	7	45	2	0	8
Petersen	1.000	13	98	8	0	10

Second Base	PCT	G	PO	A	E	DP
Castillo	.909	5	12	8	2	6
Coronado	1.000	2	7	10	0	2

Garcia	.972	76	156	261	12	50
Machado	1.000	2	5	3	0	1
Malo	.991	46	78	133	2	35
Murphy	.949	17	35	58	5	16
Ramos	1.000	5	11	19	0	7
Smith	1.000	1	3	4	0	1

Third Base	PCT	G	PO	A	E	DP
Bowman	.975	28	23	56	2	7
Evans	.786	5	1	10	3	2
Garcia	.931	13	8	19	2	3
Machado	1.000	1	1	2	0	0
Malo	.965	26	8	47	2	4
Murphy	.927	64	29	135	13	10
Petersen	.917	16	9	24	3	2

Shortstop	PCT	G	PO	A	E	DP
Coronado	.952	136	205	391	30	100
Garcia	.727	3	3	5	3	2

	PCT	G	PO	A	E	DP
Machado	1.000	3	4	6	0	1
Malo	1.000	1	0	5	0	1

Outfield	PCT	G	PO	A	E	DP
Alou	1.000	2	1	0	0	0
Carp	.972	52	69	1	2	0
Church	1.000	2	4	0	0	0
Concepcion	.953	119	231	15	12	3
Evans	.923	22	34	2	3	0
Hill	1.000	6	6	1	0	0
Machado	1.000	2	2	0	0	0
Malo	1.000	4	2	0	0	0
Martinez	1.000	83	197	3	0	0
Murphy	1.000	4	11	0	0	0
Petersen	.977	22	39	3	1	0
Reed	1.000	33	63	2	0	2
Stewart	1.000	100	167	4	0	0

ST. LUCIE METS

HIGH CLASS A

FLORIDA STATE LEAGUE

Batting	B-T	HT	WT	DOB	AVG	vLH	vRH	G	AB	R	H	2B	3B	HR	RBI	BB	HBP	SH	SF	SO	SB	CS	SLG	OBP
Abruzzo, Jordan	B-R	6-3	230	8-2-84	.303	.318	.295	19	66	7	20	4	0	2	8	2	1	0	0	7	1	0	.455	.333
Alen, Luis	R-R	6-1	175	4-16-85	.105	.100	.111	10	19	1	2	0	0	0	1	5	0	0	0	2	0	1	.105	.292
Alou, Moises	R-R	6-3	230	7-3-66	1.000	—	1.000	1	3	1	3	1	0	0	0	0	0	0	0	0	0	0	1.333	1.000
Anderson, Marlon	L-R	5-11	200	1-6-74	.231	.250	.200	4	13	0	3	0	0	0	1	0	0	0	0	3	0	0	.231	.286
Bowman, Shawn	R-R	6-2	205	12-9-84	.340	.517	.265	26	97	12	33	4	2	2	11	4	1	0	1	23	0	1	.485	.369
Burgamy, Brian	B-R	5-10	190	6-27-81	.300	.000	.391	8	30	8	9	2	0	0	2	6	1	0	1	9	0	0	.367	.421
Cancel, Robinson	R-R	6-0	190	5-4-76	.143	.400	.000	4	14	1	2	0	0	0	1	1	0	0	0	1	1	0	.143	.200
Carrera, Ezequiel	L-L	5-11	175	6-11-87	.263	.282	.254	114	430	61	113	11	12	7	29	46	9	6	3	86	28	9	.393	.344
Castillo, Luis	B-R	5-11	190	9-12-75	.067	.000	.143	5	15	1	1	0	0	0	0	4	0	1	0	0	0	0	.067	.263
Castro, Ramon	R-R	6-3	260	3-1-76	.350	.400	.333	7	20	6	7	1	0	2	5	3	0	0	1	2	0	0	.700	.417
Duda, Lucas	L-R	6-4	225	2-3-86	.263	.187	.298	133	483	58	127	26	3	11	66	66	7	0	3	129	2	7	.398	.358
Eigsti, Jacob	R-R	6-0	185	6-13-84	.200	.111	.294	12	35	3	7	0	0	0	0	2	1	1	0	4	0	1	.200	.263
Fournier, Chris	R-R	6-0	188	8-24-84	.278	.308	.300	14	36	8	10	0	1	2	5	7	0	0	0	9	0	0	.500	.395
Hernandez, Michael	R-R	6-0	195	12-18-83	.160	.250	.077	7	25	3	4	1	0	0	2	2	0	0	0	5	0	0	.200	.222
Hill, Jamar	R-R	6-3	200	9-20-82	.228	.250	.222	17	57	6	13	1	0	1	4	5	1	2	1	15	0	2	.298	.297
Holden, Joe	L-R	5-11	175	4-10-84	.259	.208	.272	42	116	6	30	3	0	1	11	13	0	0	2	23	4	2	.310	.328
Hubbert, B.J.	R-R	6-4	210	8-24-85	.250	.125	.270	18	56	5	14	4	0	1	7	1	0	0	0	22	2	2	.375	.263
Jacobs, Jason	R-R	6-1	212	12-9-83	.229	.228	.229	59	153	21	35	4	0	2	19	26	6	1	2	45	0	2	.294	.358
Maldonado, Brahiam	R-R	6-0	185	9-18-85	.232	.262	.218	75	272	18	63	11	0	5	30	15	5	1	0	76	6	1	.327	.284
McCraw, Sean	L-R	6-0	185	3-11-86	.143	.083	.154	28	77	2	11	1	0	0	2	10	1	1	0	18	1	0	.156	.250
Mendez, Victor	B-R	5-11	205	6-28-80	.283	.206	.316	34	113	19	32	9	0	4	17	11	2	0	2	22	4	4	.469	.352
Pagan, Angel	R-R	6-2	195	7-2-81	.000	—	.000	1	4	1	0	0	0	0	0	0	0	0	0	0	0	0	.000	.000
Paniagua, Salvador	R-R	6-1	240	5-21-83	.246	.438	.178	16	61	7	15	5	0	3	8	1	1	0	1	20	0	0	.475	.266
Pellot, Hector	R-R	5-11	184	2-8-87	.165	.333	.129	23	85	11	14	2	0	0	4	8	2	1	1	23	1	3	.188	.250
Petersen, Joshua	R-R	6-3	215	4-15-83	.220	.313	.176	14	50	5	11	1	1	0	4	2	1	0	0	8	0	0	.280	.264
Ramos, Peeter	R-R	5-11	180	3-18-82	.210	.290	.182	37	119	13	25	3	2	0	9	11	1	1	0	21	4	2	.269	.282
Richey, Brandon	R-R	6-0	180	4-27-86	.000	—	.000	1	0	1	0	0	0	0	0	0	0	0	0	0	0	0	.000	.000
Rivera, Luis	R-R	6-1	180	1-25-84	.222	.246	.219	61	198	22	44	5	1	1	15	8	0	2	1	22	1	1	.273	.251
Smith, Matt	L-R	5-10	172	6-12-83	.250	.250	.250	10	24	5	6	1	0	2	6	3	0	1	0	3		2	.542	.333
Tejada, Ruben	R-R	5-11	165	9-1-89	.229	.246	.219	131	497	55	114	19	4	2	37	41	5	8	4	77	8	5	.296	.293
Thole, Josh	L-R	6-1	190	10-28-86	.300	.333	.289	111	347	49	104	25	2	5	56	45	4	1	5	38	2	1	.427	.382
Valentin, Jose	B-R	5-10	190	10-12-69	.320	.286	.333	7	25	4	8	4	0	0	4	3	0	0	0	5	0	1	.480	.393
Veloz, Greg	B-R	6-1	175	6-3-88	.234	.222	.240	21	77	8	18	1	0	0	4	7	0	1	0	20	1	2	.247	.298
Ventura, Leivi	R-R	6-1	185	7-19-83	.226	.347	.173	47	159	17	36	7	0	7	20	10	1	1	1	40	0	2	.403	.275
Vogl, Will	R-R	5-9	175	12-10-83	.000	.000	.000	2	1	0	0	0	0	0	0	0	0	0	0	1	0	0	.000	.000
Voyles, J.R.	R-R	5-10	185	11-29-83	.216	.257	.198	41	139	16	30	3	0	4	13	17	0	2	1	30	0	3	.324	.299
Wabick, D.J.	L-R	6-2	185	5-30-84	.289	.256	.306	125	454	56	131	27	2	7	59	31	0	1	2	70	3	4	.403	.333

Pitching	B-T	HT	WT	DOB	W	L	ERA	G	GS	CG	SV	IP	H	R	ER	HR	BB	SO	AVG	vLH	vRH	K/9	BB/9
Abel, Nick	R-R	6-4	200	2-18-83	2	2	6.75	14	0	0	0	19	25	15	14	2	9	18	.321	.308	.327	8.68	4.34
Alfonzo, Edgar	L-L	5-10	170	12-14-84	0	0	3.93	19	0	0	1	18	18	10	8	2	10	16	.254	.250	.256	7.85	4.91
Antonini, Mike	R-L	6-0	190	8-6-85	4	0	1.84	7	7	1	0	44	34	10	9	3	7	33	.211	.190	.218	6.75	1.43
Bakker, Garry	R-R	6-2	208	3-28-83	0	3	18.00	5	1	0	0	7	17	14	14	3	5	4	.472	.417	.500	5.14	6.43
Bierd, Jose	R-R	6-2	155	5-8-85	0	0	19.29	2	0	0	0	2	3	5	5	0	4	0	.300	.250	.333	0.00	15.43
Burgos, Ambiorix	R-R	6-3	245	4-19-84	0	1	3.00	3	3	0	0	3	2	1	1	0	3	2	.167	.250	.125	6.00	9.00
Calero, Angel	L-L	6-3	190	9-25-86	1	1	7.07	4	0	0	0	14	18	11	11	3	7	10	.300	.368	.268	6.43	4.50
Carr, Nick	R-R	6-1	195	4-19-87	2	10	5.70	22	21	0	0	95	103	64	60	10	50	80	.282	.297	.272	7.61	4.75
Carrillo, Matias	L-L	6-3	224	12-13-86	0	1	5.25	5	0	0	0	12	13	7	7	1	5	8	.277	.176	.333	6.00	3.75
Castillo, Jonathan	R-R	5-10	194	12-27-83	0	0	18.90	3	0	0	0	3	11	7	7	0	2	3	.579	.714	.500	10.80	2.70
Cheney, Steven	R-R	6-5	200	7-3-86	0	1	6.75	9	0	0	0	13	23	11	10	2	4	9	.390	.667	.295	6.07	2.70
Cleto, Maikel	R-R	6-3	218	5-1-89	0	1	9.00	1	1	0	0	5	5	5	5	1	2	1	.278	.200	.308	1.80	3.60
Clyne, Stephen	B-R	6-2	215	9-22-84	1	3	5.92	27	0	0	2	38	36	30	25	3	15	23	.248	.326	.216	5.45	3.55
Frederick, Emary	R-R	6-0	180	1-17-84	2	5	4.50	35	0	0	7	50	35	27	25	5	22	51	.192	.193	.192	9.18	3.96

Name	B-T	HT	WT	DOB	W	L	ERA	G	GS	CG	SV	IP	H	R	ER	HR	BB	SO	AVG	vLH	vRH	K/9	BB/9
Gee, Dillon	R-R	6-1	195	4-28-86	8	6	3.25	21	21	0	0	127	117	49	46	6	19	94	.245	.316	.203	6.64	1.34
Guerra, Junior	R-R	5-11	213	1-16-85	0	0	0.00	4	0	0	0	4	0	0	0	0	1	4	.000	.000	.000	9.00	2.25
Hernandez, Orlando	R-R	6-2	220	10-11-69	0	0	3.38	2	2	0	0	11	6	4	4	1	2	11	.167	.133	.190	9.28	1.69
Hoorelbeke, Casey	R-R	6-8	245	4-4-80	1	4	4.89	23	0	0	1	39	49	24	21	3	12	17	.320	.281	.344	3.96	2.79
Marte, German	R-R	6-1	180	4-29-85	3	3	2.51	25	0	0	11	29	24	10	8	4	12	31	.233	.286	.206	9.73	3.77
Martinez, Pedro	R-R	5-11	195	10-25-71	0	1	3.00	1	1	0	0	6	4	2	2	0	0	6	.174	.400	.111	9.00	0.00
Merritt, Roydrick	L-L	6-0	170	9-22-85	0	0	5.87	6	0	0	0	9	7	5	5	1	6	4	.259	.125	.316	4.70	7.04
Morgan, Will	R-R	6-1	205	11-3-85	0	0	2.25	3	0	0	0	4	3	1	1	0	1	3	.214	.500	.167	6.75	2.25
Moviel, Scott	R-R	6-11	235	5-7-88	1	0	0.00	1	1	0	0	5	2	0	0	0	1	2	.133	.000	.182	3.60	1.80
Nall, Brandon	R-R	6-4	190	3-18-82	1	1	6.00	14	0	0	0	18	22	19	12	3	3	14	.293	.400	.222	7.00	1.50
Niesen, Eric	L-L	6-0	192	9-4-85	6	12	4.64	26	24	0	0	118	136	75	61	10	46	77	.286	.230	.305	5.86	3.50
Owen, Dylan	R-R	5-11	185	7-12-86	12	6	3.43	24	24	2	0	134	135	55	51	12	33	116	.265	.311	.240	7.81	2.22
Polanco, Julio	L-L	5-11	195	11-29-86	0	3	6.08	6	6	0	0	24	23	17	16	5	10	15	.250	.250	.250	5.70	3.80
Quezada, Elvys	R-R	6-1	210	12-15-81	2	0	2.23	16	0	0	0	32	29	10	8	2	8	21	.240	.245	.236	5.85	2.23
Ramirez, Edgar	R-R	6-4	250	11-30-83	1	1	4.75	14	1	0	0	30	32	18	16	3	8	27	.278	.400	.213	8.01	2.37
Sanchez, Duaner	R-R	6-2	210	10-14-79	0	0	4.50	3	0	0	0	4	6	2	2	0	2	6	.353	.250	.385	13.50	0.00
Santos, Arthur	R-R	6-0	180	2-20-82	0	0	0.00	4	0	0	0	5	6	0	0	0	2	2	.300	.250	.333	3.38	3.38
Stinson, Josh	R-R	6-4	210	3-14-88	0	2	6.14	7	2	0	0	15	17	12	10	0	5	14	.293	.556	.175	8.59	3.07
Stoner, Tobi	B-R	6-2	192	12-3-84	1	5	2.60	9	9	0	0	52	46	17	15	3	9	48	.238	.231	.243	8.31	1.56
Stronach, Tim	L-R	6-5	185	12-20-85	3	3	5.98	19	2	0	0	41	54	29	27	5	22	32	.320	.339	.309	7.08	4.87
Tomasiewicz, Kevin	L-L	6-2	225	9-17-83	0	1	7.20	5	0	0	0	5	10	4	4	0	3	2	.417	.455	.385	3.60	5.40
Vargas, Claudio	R-R	6-4	240	6-19-78	0	0	1.80	1	1	0	0	5	3	2	1	0	0	6	.188	.200	.182	10.80	0.00
Waechter, Nick	R-R	6-3	200	11-30-84	2	1	3.70	9	3	0	1	24	22	12	10	3	10	21	.237	.200	.259	7.77	3.70
Wesley, John	R-R	6-6	263	10-14-80	0	0	15.19	7	0	0	0	5	8	10	9	1	4	3	.348	.308	.400	5.06	6.75
Wise, Matt	R-R	6-4	200	11-18-75	0	0	0.00	3	0	0	0	4	0	0	0	0	0	6	.000	.000	.000	13.50	0.00

Fielding

Catcher	PCT	G	PO	A	E	DP	PB
Abruzzo	1.000	9	52	5	0	0	3
Alen	.962	9	46	5	2	0	1
Cancel	1.000	3	16	0	0	0	0
Castro	1.000	7	54	3	0	1	0
Jacobs	.981	27	143	8	3	1	7
McCraw	.988	25	151	14	2	1	3
Paniagua	1.000	1	7	0	0	0	0
Thole	.994	75	461	40	3	7	7

First Base	PCT	G	PO	A	E	DP
Duda	.992	118	964	69	8	92
Jacobs	1.000	2	12	2	0	1
Paniagua	1.000	3	25	2	0	2
Petersen	1.000	1	1	0	0	0
Rivera	1.000	2	5	0	0	1
Thole	.990	12	101	3	1	18
Ventura	1.000	3	14	1	0	1

Second Base	PCT	G	PO	A	E	DP
Castillo	.947	5	8	10	1	2
Pellot	.983	23	47	70	2	19
Ramos	.955	37	56	92	7	22

	PCT	G	PO	A	E	DP
Rivera	.947	34	70	92	9	22
Smith	.943	8	13	20	2	2
Veloz	.989	21	32	55	1	16
Voyles	.959	14	32	39	3	10

Third Base	PCT	G	PO	A	E	DP
Bowman	.964	26	22	59	3	3
Burgamy	1.000	1	1	0	0	0
Eigsti	.880	7	9	13	3	1
Jacobs	.857	15	7	23	5	2
Petersen	.900	5	3	6	1	2
Rivera	.969	17	14	17	1	2
Ventura	.915	44	33	85	11	8
Voyles	.868	26	10	36	7	3

Shortstop	PCT	G	PO	A	E	DP
Eigsti	1.000	2	0	5	0	0
Rivera	1.000	5	4	10	0	0
Tejada	.948	131	181	369	30	83
Valentin	1.000	1	1	2	0	0

Outfield	PCT	G	PO	A	E	DP
Alou	.500	1	1	0	1	0
Anderson	.800	2	4	0	1	0
Burgamy	1.000	6	16	0	0	0
Cancel	1.000	2	3	0	0	0
Carrera	.967	94	224	13	8	2
Duda	1.000	9	11	1	0	0
Fournier	.947	13	18	0	1	0
Hernandez	.944	7	15	2	1	0
Hill	.919	17	30	4	3	1
Holden	.971	36	64	4	2	0
Hubbert	1.000	17	46	1	0	0
Jacobs	1.000	1	3	0	0	0
Maldonado	.970	75	123	7	4	3
Mendez	1.000	31	61	6	0	4
Pagan	1.000	1	2	0	0	0
Petersen	1.000	2	1	1	0	0
Rivera	1.000	2	1	1	0	0
Valentin	—	2	0	0	0	0
Vogl	—	2	0	0	0	0
Wabick	.993	96	135	8	1	0

SAVANNAH SAND GNATS   LOW CLASS A
SOUTH ATLANTIC LEAGUE

Batting	B-T	HT	WT	DOB	AVG	vLH	vRH	G	AB	R	H	2B	3B	HR	RBI	BB	HBP	SH	SF	SO	SB	CS	SLG	OBP
Abruzzo, Jordan	B-R	6-3	230	8-2-84	.300	.385	.272	54	203	24	61	13	1	5	30	13	2	0	1	36	1	0	.448	.347
Bouchard, Matt	R-R	6-0	185	12-12-86	.215	.260	.202	62	223	34	48	11	4	3	20	15	2	5	0	51	5	6	.341	.271
Clark, Darren	L-L	6-0	188	7-21-84	.247	.176	.266	46	158	13	39	10	0	1	15	9	1	0	0	33	3	2	.329	.292
Craig, Casey	L-R	6-1	185	1-12-85	.288	.275	.293	95	361	50	104	16	3	5	49	33	3	5	7	69	24	7	.391	.347
Eigsti, Jacob	R-R	6-0	185	6-13-84	.253	.327	.211	43	150	17	38	5	3	1	10	11	1	1	0	25	3	0	.347	.309
Flores, Wilmer	R-R	6-3	175	8-6-91	.400	—	.400	1	5	1	2	0	0	0	0	0	0	0	0	2	0	0	.400	.400
Giarraputo, Nick	R-R	6-3	200	5-29-88	.242	.255	.238	56	198	21	48	12	0	3	34	3	1	1		48	2	0	.303	.301
Guzman, Carlos	L-R	6-3	195	5-24-86	.269	.207	.292	84	294	36	79	14	1	8	33	20	1	2	3	84	14	3	.405	.314
Henriquez, Ralph	B-R	6-1	190	4-7-87	.273	.250	.276	9	33	2	9	2	1	0	3	0	0	0		6	0	1	.394	.273
Hernandez, Michael	R-R	6-0	195	12-18-83	.394	.357	.421	9	33	9	13	2	1	0	4	2	0	0		5	0	0	.515	.429
Hubbert, B.J.	R-R	6-4	210	8-24-85	.194	.212	.185	40	98	17	19	5	1	3	13	14	4	1	1	45	3	1	.357	.316
Jimenez, Jose	R-R	6-2	185	5-9-87	.253	.241	.259	90	336	46	85	23	1	11	48	28	6	0	6	75	2	3	.426	.316
Kawal, Brandon	R-R	6-3	205	10-29-84	.250	.200	.500	3	12	1	3	1	0	0	0	0	0	0		3	0	0	.333	.250
Lagares, Juan	R-R	6-1	175	3-17-89	.254	.293	.236	46	181	14	46	9	0	2	17	8	1	4	3	28	3	4	.337	.285
Lucas III, Richard	R-R	6-1	205	11-2-88	.185	.184	.185	31	119	15	22	5	2	2	13	11	0	1	1	41	1	3	.311	.252
Maccani, Tony	R-R	6-3	191	9-24-84	.233	.250	.225	32	60	8	14	2	0	4	6	13	0	1	0	14	0	0	.267	.313
McCraw, Sean	L-R	6-0	185	3-11-86	.266	.214	.280	38	128	11	34	7	0	1	12	21	0	1	1	32	0	1	.336	.367
Nieves, Luis	R-R	5-11	160	12-15-88	.179	.250	.161	13	39	3	7	1	0	0	1	0	1	0		7	0	1	.205	.200
Parker, Michael	R-R	5-11	190	2-28-85	.198	.246	.179	67	212	21	42	11	1	3	28	15	1	2	2	42	2	0	.302	.252
Pena, Francisco	R-R	6-2	230	10-12-89	.264	.274	.261	105	397	34	105	22	3	6	41	25	1	0	3	95	0	0	.380	.308
Pena, Richard	R-R	6-2	175	8-15-87	.204	.213	.201	90	323	32	66	15	0	0	20	37	4	2	2	108	16	5	.251	.292
Reyes, Raul	L-L	6-0	195	12-30-86	.298	.333	.295	13	47	2	14	3	1	1	5	2	0	0	0	15	0	0	.468	.327
Rodriguez, Joaquin	R-R	6-4	180	10-29-84	.239	.247	.236	78	272	30	65	12	1	1	17	13	4	1	4	56	4	0	.301	.280
Stegall, Daniel	L-R	6-3	180	9-24-87	.196	.160	.207	32	107	13	21	4	1	0	9	6	2	0	0	33	2	2	.308	.252
Tatford, Jefferies	L-R	6-3	210	9-16-84	.276	.269	.278	30	105	14	29	8	0	2	12	14	4	0	0	31	0	1	.410	.382

	B-T	HT	WT	DOB	AVG	vLH	vRH	G	AB	R	H	2B	3B	HR	RBI	BB	HBP	SH	SF	SO	SB	CS	SLG	OBP
Veloz, Greg	B-R	6-1	175	6-3-88	.286	.244	.303	111	455	68	130	25	5	6	52	32	6	6	2	93	28	12	.402	.339
Vogl, Will	R-R	5-9	175	12-10-83	.129	.059	.214	9	31	0	4	0	0	0	2	0	0	1	1	10	1	0	.129	.125
Welch, Stefan	L-R	6-3	175	8-12-88	.263	.000	.294	5	19	4	5	1	0	1	3	2	1	0	0	5	0	0	.474	.364

Pitching	B-T	HT	WT	DOB	W	L	ERA	G	GS	CG	SV	IP	H	R	ER	HR	BB	SO	AVG	vLH	vRH	K/9	BB/9
Abel, Nick	R-R	6-4	200	2-18-83	3	1	1.16	14	0	0	5	23	16	5	3	0	8	15	.200	.206	.196	5.79	3.09
Antonini, Mike	R-L	6-0	190	8-6-85	4	4	2.71	13	13	0	0	73	63	29	22	2	16	61	.227	.292	.204	7.52	1.97
Beaulac, Eric	R-R	6-5	190	11-13-86	1	2	3.55	6	6	0	0	25	22	13	10	1	18	31	.239	.262	.220	11.01	6.39
Bierd, Jose	R-R	6-2	155	5-8-85	3	1	3.20	34	0	0	8	51	48	20	18	8	16	41	.247	.205	.273	7.28	2.84
Burns, Brad	R-R	6-4	182	5-28-86	0	4	8.10	8	1	0	0	17	20	18	15	3	16	17	.290	.167	.385	9.18	8.64
Calero, Angel	L-L	6-3	170	9-25-86	3	5	2.57	12	12	0	0	67	54	30	19	3	15	59	.220	.169	.237	7.96	2.03
Carr, Nick	R-R	6-1	195	4-19-87	1	2	3.33	4	4	0	0	24	22	11	9	0	4	16	.239	.323	.197	5.92	1.48
Cheney, Steven	R-R	6-5	200	7-3-86	1	0	2.25	16	0	0	2	28	24	9	7	0	3	38	.231	.235	.229	12.21	0.96
Cleto, Maikel	R-R	6-3	218	5-1-89	5	11	4.25	25	22	1	0	136	140	78	64	8	34	81	.268	.250	.280	5.37	2.26
Cohoon, Mark	L-L	6-2	195	9-15-87	2	2	3.82	7	7	0	0	33	29	17	14	2	18	21	.242	.250	.240	5.73	4.91
Cruz, Rhinel	R-R	6-2	205	11-1-86	2	5	5.04	15	0	0	1	30	27	20	17	4	14	33	.235	.311	.186	9.79	4.15
Guerra, Junior	R-R	5-11	213	1-16-85	1	1	1.75	10	0	0	2	26	14	6	5	3	2	34	.156	.167	.150	11.92	0.70
Holdzkom, John	R-R	6-7	225	10-19-87	2	3	5.89	20	5	0	0	47	45	40	31	1	45	56	.246	.221	.264	10.65	8.56
Houck, Mitch	L-L	6-1	200	5-26-87	0	0	2.25	2	0	0	0	4	7	3	1	0	2	2	.412	.600	.333	4.50	4.50
Lavorgna, Jason	R-R	5-9	190	3-4-86	1	2	5.63	15	0	0	0	24	28	19	15	2	16	17	.286	.333	.258	6.38	6.00
Moviel, Scott	R-R	6-11	235	5-7-88	9	8	4.43	24	24	0	0	120	128	75	59	9	36	82	.271	.280	.264	6.15	2.70
Neguilis, Jacobo	R-R	6-3	180	4-25-84	0	1	6.43	6	0	0	0	7	11	7	5	0	6	6	.367	.500	.300	7.71	7.71
Olivares, Manuel	R-R	6-0	170	5-20-86	3	1	3.08	15	1	0	1	38	34	14	13	1	9	42	.241	.268	.224	9.95	2.13
Olmsted, Michael	R-R	6-6	245	5-2-87	1	0	3.86	2	2	0	0	9	12	4	4	1	3	11	.293	.316	.273	10.61	2.89
Orta, Phillips	R-R	6-2	175	5-9-86	0	1	2.70	2	0	0	0	10	9	3	3	0	5	5	.231	.188	.261	4.50	4.50
Polanco, Julio	L-L	5-11	195	11-29-86	2	1	4.19	25	3	0	5	69	74	34	32	8	15	60	.272	.241	.286	7.86	1.97
Powers, Michael	R-R	6-3	180	4-7-86	0	1	2.25	3	0	0	1	4	2	1	1	1	2	1	.154	.000	.250	2.25	4.50
Puhl, Stephen	B-R	6-0	195	7-6-84	0	2	4.35	10	0	0	0	21	12	12	10	2	15	14	.171	.269	.114	6.10	6.53
Ramirez, Edgar	R-R	6-4	250	11-30-83	3	1	3.13	14	0	0	1	32	27	11	11	4	6	24	.223	.267	.197	6.82	1.71
Ramirez, Elvin	R-R	6-3	208	10-10-87	6	7	3.67	18	18	0	0	81	81	38	33	1	36	62	.257	.305	.225	6.89	4.00
Rosa, Wendy	R-R	6-0	170	8-26-86	0	0	6.55	9	0	0	1	11	10	8	8	0	8	13	.238	.176	.280	10.64	6.55
Rustich, Brant	R-R	6-6	230	1-23-85	3	4	3.62	20	8	0	0	50	42	26	20	1	16	48	.231	.225	.234	8.70	2.90
Stinson, Josh	R-R	6-4	200	3-14-88	3	6	3.52	21	6	0	3	72	78	36	28	7	32	46	.280	.267	.287	5.78	4.02
Stronach, Tim	L-R	6-5	185	12-20-85	0	0	2.25	1	1	0	0	4	2	1	1	0	2	1	.167	.000	.222	2.25	4.50
Vineyard, Nathan	L-L	6-2	200	10-3-88	0	2	14.63	2	2	0	0	8	13	13	13	1	6	3	.382	.545	.304	3.38	6.75
Waechter, Nick	R-R	6-3	200	11-30-84	2	0	2.91	21	0	0	3	53	43	17	17	4	10	59	.219	.241	.205	10.08	1.71

Fielding

Catcher	PCT	G	PO	A	E	DP	PB
Abruzzo	.977	17	114	12	3	1	3
Henriquez	1.000	4	22	2	0	0	1
Maccani	1.000	16	91	7	0	0	1
McCraw	.983	15	96	19	2	2	3
F. Pena	.991	92	685	76	7	5	28

First Base	PCT	G	PO	A	E	DP
Jimenez	.992	84	815	55	7	61
Rodriguez	.987	25	207	21	3	23
Tatford	.995	28	201	8	1	16
Welch	1.000	3	28	1	0	3

Second Base	PCT	G	PO	A	E	DP
Eigsti	.968	6	11	19	1	5
Nieves	1.000	1	2	2	0	1
Parker	.971	19	35	33	2	9

	PCT	G	PO	A	E	DP
Rodriguez	.750	2	2	1	1	1
Veloz	.965	109	184	311	18	65

Third Base	PCT	G	PO	A	E	DP
Eigsti	.926	24	22	53	6	6
Giarraputo	.929	52	28	89	9	6
Lucas III	.909	29	19	41	6	5
Parker	—	1	0	0	0	
Rodriguez	.928	34	25	65	7	6
Welch	1.000	3	4	3	0	0

Shortstop	PCT	G	PO	A	E	DP
Bouchard	.942	59	87	204	18	31
Eigsti	.983	14	15	42	1	8
Flores	1.000	1	1	3	0	0
Lagares	.932	45	61	116	13	16
Nieves	.882	11	16	29	6	7

	PCT	G	PO	A	E	DP
Rodriguez	.958	10	20	26	2	4

Outfield	PCT	G	PO	A	E	DP
Clark	.932	33	52	3	4	0
Craig	.988	88	159	5	2	1
Guzman	.969	83	147	10	5	4
Hernandez	.875	8	14	0	2	0
Hubbert	1.000	32	49	0	0	0
Kawal	1.000	3	6	0	0	0
Parker	.965	35	54	1	2	0
R. Pena	.953	89	153	8	8	0
Reyes	1.000	13	23	1	0	0
Stegall	.966	28	56	1	2	1
Vogl	1.000	9	23	1	0	1

BROOKLYN CYCLONES

SHORT-SEASON

NEW YORK-PENN LEAGUE

Batting	B-T	HT	WT	DOB	AVG	vLH	vRH	G	AB	R	H	2B	3B	HR	RBI	BB	HBP	SH	SF	SO	SB	CS	SLG	OBP
Abruzzo, Jordan	B-R	6-3	230	8-2-84	.275	.333	.255	49	182	22	50	9	0	7	21	8	1	0	0	27	0	0	.440	.309
Alen, Luis	R-R	6-1	175	4-16-85	.000	.000	.000	6	20	0	0	0	0	0	0	2	1	0	0	1	0	0	.000	.130
Bouchard, Matt	R-R	6-0	185	12-12-86	.294	.176	.353	13	51	5	15	3	0	0	3	5	1	0	0	13	2	0	.353	.368
Campbell, Eric	R-R	6-3	220	4-9-87	.260	.264	.259	66	215	27	56	9	0	4	28	28	6	4	2	41	1	2	.358	.359
Church, Ryan	L-L	6-1	190	10-14-78	.500	.500	—	2	6	1	3	1	0	0	1	0	0	0	0	2	0	0	.667	.500
Clark, Darren	L-L	6-0	188	7-21-84	.333	.000	.375	5	9	1	3	1	0	0	0	0	0	0	0	0	0	0	.444	.333
Cordido, Cesar	R-R	5-10	175	9-10-85	.225	.190	.240	24	71	6	16	2	0	0	4	3	0	1	1	12	0	0	.254	.253
Davis, Ike	L-L	6-5	195	3-22-87	.256	.317	.232	58	215	17	55	15	0	0	17	23	0	0	1	43	0	0	.326	.326
Doyle, Dock	L-R	6-0	200	3-24-86	.250	.333	.231	5	16	2	4	2	0	0	2	0	1	0	0	6	0	0	.375	.294
Eigsti, Jacob	R-R	6-0	185	6-13-84	.146	.143	.147	18	48	3	7	3	1	0	6	5	0	2	1	10	0	0	.250	.222
Fernandez, Rafael	L-L	6-1	171	8-3-88	.000	.000	.000	6	3	0	0	0	0	0	0	0	0	0	0	3	0	0	.000	.000
Flores, Wilmer	R-R	6-3	175	8-6-91	.267	.200	.300	8	30	3	8	1	0	0	1	1	0	1	0	7	0	0	.300	.290
Giarraputo, Nick	R-R	6-3	200	5-29-88	.167	—	.167	3	6	0	1	0	0	0	0	0	0	0	0	2	0	0	.167	.167
Havens, Reese	R-R	6-1	195	10-20-86	.247	.313	.232	23	85	13	21	6	2	3	11	11	1	0	0	27	3	1	.471	.340
Henriquez, Ralph	B-R	6-1	190	4-7-87	.210	.357	.167	20	62	4	13	3	0	0	1	4	1	0	0	15	1	1	.258	.269
Jacobs, Jason	R-R	6-1	212	12-9-83	.176	.333	.143	4	17	2	3	0	0	0	1	2	0	0	0	6	0	0	.176	.300
Jimenez, Jose	R-R	6-2	185	5-9-87	.212	.065	.257	36	132	11	28	4	0	4	16	6	0	3		42	1	3	.333	.272
Kawal, Brandon	R-R	6-3	215	10-29-84	.143	.000	.222	6	14	0	2	1	0	0	0	0	0	0	0	4	0	0	.214	.143
Lagares, Juan	R-R	6-1	175	3-17-89	.250	.227	.260	19	72	8	18	7	0	1	7	1	2	3	0	10	1	3	.389	.280
Lutz, Zach	R-R	6-1	220	6-3-86	.333	.296	.356	24	72	9	24	4	0	3	12	14	0	0	0	12	0	2	.514	.442

	B-T	HT	WT	DOB	AVG	vLH	vRH	G	AB	R	H	2B	3B	HR	RBI	BB	HBP	SH	SF	SO	SB	CS	SLG	OBP
Machado, Anderson	B-R	6-0	185	1-25-81	.333	1.000	.000	1	3	0	1	1	0	0	0	1	0	0	0	0	0	0	.667	.500
Medrano, Ignacio	R-R	6-2	160	7-17-86	.083	.000	.100	4	12	1	1	0	0	0	0	3	1	0	0	4	1	1	.083	.313
Murphy, Daniel	L-R	6-3	210	4-1-85	.500	.375	.667	3	14	1	7	0	0	0	2	0	0	0	2	0	0		.500	.500
Nieuwenhuis, Kirk	L-R	6-3	210	8-7-87	.277	.221	.295	74	285	34	79	15	5	3	29	29	3	0	2	70	11	7	.396	.348
Pagan, Angel	B-R	6-2	195	7-2-81	.308	1.000	.182	4	13	0	4	0	0	0	1	1	0	0	0	3	0	0	.308	.357
Parker, Michael	R-R	5-11	190	2-28-85	.071	.250	.000	4	14	0	1	0	0	0	0	0	0	0	0	6	0	0	.071	.071
Ratliff, Sean	L-L	6-3	185	2-24-87	.229	.325	.205	59	201	32	46	9	1	7	22	18	3	2	1	67	1	3	.388	.300
Richey, Brandon	R-R	6-0	180	4-27-86	.225	.286	.212	14	40	11	9	1	2	0	2	7	1	0	0	9	1	1	.350	.354
Satin, Josh	R-R	6-2	200	12-23-84	.280	.224	.309	45	143	21	40	10	2	4	13	16	0	4	1	28	0	1	.462	.350
Servidio, John	R-R	6-1	194	8-22-85	.239	.216	.248	40	138	17	33	9	2	3	17	8	3	4	1	37	0	2	.399	.293
Smith, Matt	L-R	5-10	172	6-12-83	.198	.286	.181	25	86	8	17	1	1	2	9	14	1	3	0	11	0	2	.302	.317
Suire, Kyle	B-R	5-11	200	8-22-85	.000	.000	.000	3	5	0	0	0	0	0	0	0	0	0	0	3	0	0	.000	.000
Tatford, Jefferies	L-R	6-3	210	9-16-84	.192	.250	.182	15	26	1	5	0	0	0	2	4	0	0	0	11	0	0	.192	.300
Vogl, Will	R-R	5-9	175	12-10-83	.222	.200	.231	13	36	5	8	1	1	1	4	4	1	1	0	12	0	0	.389	.317
Voyles, J.R.	R-R	5-10	185	11-29-83	.223	.292	.206	36	121	14	27	4	0	3	15	8	3	4	0	25	2	2	.331	.288
Williams, Seth	R-R	6-2	205	11-21-85	.295	.423	.231	24	78	5	23	5	1	2	14	5	1	1	1	20	0	1	.385	.341

Pitching

	B-T	HT	WT	DOB	W	L	ERA	G	GS	CG	SV	IP	H	R	ER	HR	BB	SO	AVG	vLH	vRH	K/9	BB/9
Beaulac, Eric	R-R	6-5	190	11-13-86	0	0	9.82	2	0	0	0	4	1	4	4	0	2	6	.091	.000	.200	14.73	4.91
Carrillo, Matias	L-L	6-3	224	12-13-86	1	0	2.45	15	0	0	0	33	29	10	9	2	16	37	.236	.188	.267	10.09	4.36
Clyne, Stephen	R-R	6-2	215	9-22-84	2	2	2.82	17	0	0	9	22	19	9	7	1	12	23	.244	.263	.237	9.27	4.84
Cruz, Rhinel	R-R	6-2	205	11-1-86	0	0	3.72	6	0	0	1	10	9	5	4	1	6	13	.243	.167	.280	12.10	5.59
Fuller, Jim	L-L	5-10	180	6-1-87	2	0	1.00	8	1	0	1	18	15	2	2	0	5	22	.238	.217	.250	11.00	2.50
Guerra, Junior	R-R	5-11	213	1-16-85	0	0	—	1	0	0	0	1	1	2	2	1	0	.500	.000	.500	—	11.94	—
Holt, Brad	R-R	6-4	194	10-13-86	5	3	1.87	14	14	0	0	72	43	18	15	3	33	96	.171	.115	.211	11.94	4.11
Johnson, Jimmy	L-L	6-0	195	11-24-85	5	0	1.25	23	0	0	1	36	20	5	5	0	11	41	.164	.176	.155	10.25	2.75
Kaplan, Jeff	R-R	6-0	190	7-9-85	3	2	3.45	15	4	0	2	47	37	19	18	1	17	39	.223	.230	.219	7.47	3.26
Lynn, Mike	R-R	5-10	170	10-11-84	0	1	5.79	4	0	0	0	5	7	5	3	0	3	5	.333	.222	.417	9.64	5.79
Martinez, Pedro P.	R-R	6-4	191	7-8-85	3	2	3.63	15	15	0	0	67	72	31	27	5	22	55	.277	.228	.308	7.39	2.96
Mejia, Jenrry	R-R	6-0	162	10-11-89	3	2	3.49	11	11	0	0	57	42	22	22	4	23	52	.209	.190	.221	8.26	3.65
Merritt, Roydrick	L-L	6-0	170	9-22-85	3	0	1.49	25	0	0	4	42	22	9	7	1	17	55	.150	.100	.175	11.69	3.61
Moore, Brandon	R-R	6-3	190	1-24-86	3	1	9.00	3	0	0	0	9	8	7	2	6	11	.300	.250	.333	14.14	7.71
Olivares, Manuel	R-R	6-0	170	5-22-86	0	2	4.02	6	2	0	0	16	20	9	7	1	7	11	.317	.276	.353	6.32	4.02
Rosa, Wendy	R-R	6-0	170	8-26-86	1	1	2.01	21	0	0	0	31	16	7	7	1	23	48	.150	.167	.143	13.79	6.61
Santana, Yury	R-R	6-0	190	8-15-82	2	4	2.45	27	0	0	13	26	19	11	7	3	13	37	.194	.156	.212	12.97	4.56
Schwinden, Chris	R-R	6-3	165	9-22-86	4	1	2.01	14	8	0	0	63	53	21	14	3	12	70	.233	.213	.252	10.05	1.72
Shaw, Scott	R-R	6-5	230		6	3	2.80	15	14	0	0	74	66	24	23	4	15	79	.238	.217	.253	9.61	1.82
Stronach, Tim	L-R	6-5	185	12-20-85	2	5	4.05	8	6	0	0	33	37	18	15	0	14	29	.285	.321	.260	7.83	3.78
Turgeon, Erik	R-R	6-0	170	3-25-87	0	1	2.76	11	0	0	1	16	14	6	5	1	5	23	.226	.292	.184	12.67	2.76

Fielding

Catcher	PCT	G	PO	A	E	DP	PB
Abruzzo	.993	38	369	35	3	3	4
Alen	1.000	5	47	9	0	0	0
Cordido	.996	23	202	20	1	1	3
Doyle	.857	1	6	0	1	0	1
Henriquez	.993	16	120	14	1	1	0

First Base	PCT	G	PO	A	E	DP
Campbell	.979	7	44	3	1	1
Davis	.998	57	462	29	1	43
Giarraputo	.923	3	10	2	1	3
Jacobs	1.000	1	8	1	0	1
Jimenez	.983	7	57	0	1	4
Tatford	1.000	7	38	2	0	4

Second Base	PCT	G	PO	A	E	DP
Campbell	1.000	2	0	2	0	0
Eigsti	1.000	3	5	9	0	3
Lutz	1.000	3	0	3	0	0
Medrano	1.000	4	9	9	0	4
Richey	1.000	8	14	18	0	3

		G	PO	A	E	DP
Satin	.989	44	59	114	2	20
Suire	.800	2	4	0	1	0
Voyles	.990	26	46	50	1	18

Third Base	PCT	G	PO	A	E	DP
Campbell	.949	40	16	58	4	5
Eigsti	1.000	2	1	0	0	0
Jimenez	.824	7	5	9	3	0
Lagares	.789	5	5	10	4	1
Lutz	.951	19	3	36	2	3
Richey	1.000	3	0	6	0	1
Satin	—	1	0	0	0	0
Tatford	1.000	2	1	1	0	0
Voyles	.833	11	4	11	3	2

Shortstop	PCT	G	PO	A	E	DP
Bouchard	.917	13	22	33	5	6
Eigsti	.980	14	18	32	1	6
Flores	.941	8	10	22	2	4
Havens	1.000	2	2	1	0	2
Lagares	.960	11	19	29	2	3

		G	PO	A	E	DP
Machado	.800	1	2	2	1	2
Richey	1.000	5	2	6	0	2
Satin	—	2	0	0	0	0
Smith	.970	25	32	64	3	18
Voyles	1.000	2	0	1	0	0

Outfield	PCT	G	PO	A	E	DP
Campbell	.962	19	24	1	1	0
Church	1.000	2	2	0	0	0
Clark	.857	5	6	0	1	0
Fernandez	1.000	6	2	0	0	0
Kawal	1.000	5	5	0	0	0
Medrano	—	1	0	0	0	0
Nieuwenhuis	.975	73	116	6	3	1
Pagan	1.000	4	4	1	0	0
Parker	—	3	0	0	0	0
Ratliff	1.000	58	97	7	0	3
Servidio	.971	39	64	3	2	0
Vogl	1.000	13	20	1	0	0
Williams	1.000	22	27	2	0	0

KINGSPORT METS

ROOKIE

APPALACHIAN LEAGUE

Batting	B-T	HT	WT	DOB	AVG	vLH	vRH	G	AB	R	H	2B	3B	HR	RBI	BB	HBP	SH	SF	SO	SB	CS	SLG	OBP
Alvarez, Imbewer	R-R	6-1	180	5-15-86	.189	.000	.234	29	95	16	18	4	0	1	7	3	5	0	1	29	2	1	.263	.250
Blaquiere, Jean Luc	R-R	6-0	196	2-27-86	.271	.286	.267	37	129	25	35	9	0	3	18	26	4	0	1	47	0	0	.411	.406
Del Campo, Rogelio	L-R	5-10	195	7-25-86	.237	.200	.242	10	38	3	9	0	0	1	5	1	0	0	1	5	1	1	.316	.256
Doyle, Dock	L-R	6-0	200	3-24-86	.308	.214	.317	41	159	27	49	11	1	0	20	22	0	0	1	24	1	1	.390	.390
Fernandez, Rafael	L-L	6-1	171	8-3-88	.259	.161	.274	57	228	43	59	10	5	4	31	24	1	1	0	69	4	4	.399	.332
Flores, Wilmer	R-R	6-3	175	8-6-91	.310	.294	.313	59	245	36	76	12	4	8	41	12	5	1	2	28	2	1	.490	.352
Garber, Justin	R-R	6-0	190	12-3-84	.266	.250	.268	28	94	17	25	3	2	1	6	7	4	1	1	18	3	0	.372	.340
Lucas III, Richard	R-R	6-1	205	11-2-88	.185	1.000	.154	7	27	2	5	1	0	1	3	3	0	0	0	10	0	0	.333	.267
Maat, Patrick	R-R	6-4	250	9-15-87	.000	.000	.000	2	6	0	0	0	0	0	0	1	0	0	0	2	0	0	.000	.000
McNulty, Doug	R-R	6-5	220	2-11-85	.201	.214	.199	49	179	18	36	7	2	6	26	8	5	0	1	39	0	1	.363	.254
Medrano, Ignacio	R-R	6-2	160	7-17-86	.239	.167	.362	17	70	15	23	6	1	0	8	6	1	0	2	15	2	2	.443	.380
Moras, Michael	R-R	6-1	200	9-11-85	.338	.300	.362	20	68	14	23	3	0	1	9	8	2	0	0	11	1	0	.426	.423
Satin, Josh	R-R	6-2	200	12-23-84	.583	—	.583	3	12	3	7	2	0	1	2	1	0	0	0	2	0	0	1.000	.615

Batting	B-T	HT	WT	DOB	AVG	vLH	vRH	G	AB	R	H	2B	3B	HR	RBI	BB	HBP	SH	SF	SO	SB	CS	SLG	OBP
Servidio, John	R-R	6-1	194	8-22-85	.000	—	.000	2	5	1	0	0	0	0	0	0	1	0	0	3	0	0	.000	.167
Stegall, Daniel	L-R	6-3	180	9-24-87	.295	.333	.288	30	122	16	36	6	0	3	13	13	1	0	1	26	1	1	.418	.365
Suire, Kyle	B-R	5-11	200	8-22-85	.297	.346	.288	48	182	34	54	19	0	9	36	16	5	0	0	28	3	2	.549	.369
Welch, Stefan	L-R	6-3	175	8-12-88	.281	.303	.277	63	253	33	71	14	8	4	34	11	3	0	2	40	4	0	.447	.316
Williams, Seth	R-R	6-2	205	11-21-85	.368	.500	.353	12	38	10	14	3	0	1	9	11	4	0	0	4	0	0	.526	.547
Zapata, Pedro	R-R	6-4	185	10-3-87	.221	.300	.209	58	226	24	50	4	1	0	15	8	3	1	0	56	12	2	.248	.257
Zavala, Gabriel	R-R	6-3	180	5-14-87	.250	.313	.240	33	120	18	30	13	1	4	18	3	4	0	1	48	0	2	.475	.289

Pitching	B-T	HT	WT	DOB	W	L	ERA	G	GS	CG	SV	IP	H	R	ER	HR	BB	SO	AVG	vLH	vRH	K/9	BB/9
Alvarez, Manuel	R-R	5-11	200	12-18-85	0	4	6.59	17	0	0	3	27	43	27	20	4	6	14	.352	.388	.329	4.61	1.98
Babin, Travis	R-R	6-1	205	12-2-86	0	1	5.74	15	0	0	1	27	34	17	17	2	9	27	.318	.359	.294	9.11	3.04
Batis, Raul	L-L	6-3	170	3-5-89	2	4	4.15	12	8	0	1	52	58	35	24	5	13	41	.278	.237	.287	7.10	2.25
Beaulac, Eric	R-R	6-5	190	11-13-86	1	0	1.89	6	2	0	1	19	15	5	4	1	6	23	.214	.280	.178	10.89	2.84
Burgos, Ambiorix	R-R	6-3	245	4-19-84	0	0	4.50	2	0	0	0	2	1	1	1	1	2	1	.286	.333	.000	4.50	9.00
Carson, Robert	L-L	6-3	220	1-23-89	2	3	1.76	6	6	0	0	31	29	12	6	1	18	21	.274	.158	.299	6.16	5.28
Cohoon, Mark	L-L	6-2	195	9-15-87	1	1	5.89	6	3	0	0	18	17	13	12	0	10	22	.239	.222	.242	10.80	4.91
Guerra, Junior	R-R	5-11	213	1-16-85	0	0	2.25	3	0	0	0	4	0	1	1	0	3	3	.000	.000	.000	6.75	6.75
Holdzkom, John	R-R	6-7	225	10-19-87	3	1	3.66	8	7	0	0	39	38	19	16	3	12	44	.257	.275	.247	10.07	2.75
Lavorgna, Jason	R-R	5-9	190	3-4-86	1	0	2.45	6	0	0	0	7	4	2	2	0	3	10	.154	.200	.143	12.27	3.68
Leduc, Guillaume	R-R	6-4	192	7-28-87	3	4	4.24	13	9	1	1	57	58	38	27	9	9	41	.264	.289	.246	6.44	1.41
McHugh, Collin	R-R	6-2	195	6-19-87	0	0	4.17	12	8	0	1	41	47	25	19	5	16	41	.285	.277	.290	9.00	3.51
Melendez, Oscar	R-R	6-0	170	9-15-86	4	3	5.94	13	11	0	0	50	61	44	33	6	22	42	.292	.275	.300	7.56	3.96
Moore, Brandon	R-R	6-3	190	1-24-86	2	0	0.90	6	0	0	0	20	12	2	2	0	8	22	.174	.167	.178	9.90	3.60
Olmsted, Michael	R-R	6-6	245	5-2-87	1	1	1.83	4	4	0	0	20	11	4	4	1	5	23	.164	.083	.209	10.53	2.29
Orta, Phillips	R-R	6-2	175	5-9-86	4	2	2.05	14	3	0	0	44	35	14	10	2	21	31	.222	.194	.240	6.34	4.30
Paredes, Thomas	R-R	6-3	170	6-3-88	0	0	16.20	2	0	0	0	2	4	3	3	0	2	0	.571	.500	.600	10.80	10.80
Powers, Michael	R-R	6-3	180	4-7-86	2	1	3.00	15	0	0	0	7	21	17	7	7	0	4	20	.236	.238	.235	8.57	1.71
Puhl, Stephen	B-R	6-0	195	7-6-84	3	0	2.40	8	0	0	0	15	8	5	4	1	7	20	.148	.111	.156	12.00	4.20
Rodriguez, Jorge	R-R	6-3	182	5-10-87	2	1	5.27	18	0	0	0	27	32	19	16	3	9	33	.286	.302	.275	10.87	2.96
Rosenbaum, Zach	R-R	6-4	190	4-25-87	2	4	6.25	14	3	0	1	36	45	33	25	4	15	41	.308	.350	.292	10.25	3.75
Turgeon, Erik	R-R	6-0	170	3-25-87	1	0	4.05	7	0	0	2	7	9	3	3	1	0	8	.310	.333	.300	10.80	0.00

Fielding

Catcher	PCT	G	PO	A	E	DP	PB
Blaquiere	.996	34	250	29	1	3	12
Del Campo	1.000	3	23	4	0	1	0
Doyle	.986	23	184	21	3	0	14
Moras	.982	7	53	2	1	0	1

First Base	PCT	G	PO	A	E	DP
McNulty	.990	44	380	33	4	47
Welch	1.000	22	177	14	0	20

Second Base	PCT	G	PO	A	E	DP
Alvarez	.964	6	17	10	1	3

	PCT	G	PO	A	E	DP
Medrano	.962	11	25	26	2	6
Satin	.923	3	3	9	1	2
Suire	.967	48	89	147	8	46

Third Base	PCT	G	PO	A	E	DP
Alvarez	.795	16	9	26	9	4
Lucas III	.786	7	1	10	3	0
Medrano	1.000	4	1	5	0	0
Welch	.943	41	38	94	8	15

Shortstop	PCT	G	PO	A	E	DP
Alvarez	.833	6	5	15	4	4

	PCT	G	PO	A	E	DP
Flores	.934	58	86	185	19	46
Medrano	.929	3	5	8	1	1

Outfield	PCT	G	PO	A	E	DP
Fernandez	.978	57	86	4	2	0
Garber	1.000	26	34	1	0	0
Servidio	—	1	0	0	0	0
Stegall	.953	25	35	6	2	0
Williams	1.000	8	17	1	0	0
Zapata	.974	58	107	4	3	1
Zavala	1.000	26	34	0	0	0

GCL METS — ROOKIE

GULF COAST LEAGUE

Batting	B-T	HT	WT	DOB	AVG	vLH	vRH	G	AB	R	H	2B	3B	HR	RBI	BB	HBP	SH	SF	SO	SB	CS	SLG	OBP
Alou, Moises	R-R	6-3	230	7-3-66	.667	—	.667	1	3	1	2	0	0	1	2	0	0	0	0	0	0	0	1.667	.667
Castillo, Luis	B-R	5-11	190	9-12-75	.000	.000	.000	3	5	0	0	0	0	0	0	3	0	0	0	0	0	0	.000	.375
Centeno, Juan	L-R	5-9	172	11-16-89	.220	.111	.240	23	59	10	13	1	0	0	1	8	2	2	0	8	0	0	.237	.333
Church, Ryan	L-L	6-1	190	10-14-78	.167	.000	.250	2	6	0	1	0	0	0	1	1	0	0	0	3	0	0	.167	.286
Clark, Darren	L-L	6-0	188	7-21-84	.357	.500	.346	10	28	1	10	1	0	0	2	3	0	0	1	4	0	0	.393	.406
Flagg, Jeff	R-R	6-5	234	11-7-85	.223	.333	.213	45	139	17	31	8	2	5	25	21	2	0	1	35	7	0	.417	.331
Gronauer, Kai	R-R	6-1	196	11-28-86	.356	.364	.353	16	45	4	16	1	0	0	10	2	2	1	0	6	1	0	.378	.408
Harris, Alonzo	R-R	6-0	170	1-16-89	.308	.280	.316	33	104	23	32	6	0	5	10	9	3	1	0	23	7	2	.510	.379
Hinojosa, Charlie	R-R	6-3	190	6-16-89	.226	.500	.204	19	53	6	12	3	0	1	6	1	0	0	0	10	0	0	.340	.241
Howe, Tyler	R-L	6-1	200	2-7-86	.306	.000	.344	14	36	4	11	5	0	0	6	4	5	0	0	13	0	0	.444	.444
Maat, Patrick	R-R	6-4	250	9-15-87	.250	.333	.200	4	8	0	2	1	0	0	2	0	0	0	0	2	0	0	.375	.400
Maldonado, Brahiam	R-R	6-0	188	9-18-85	.333	—	.333	5	18	4	6	3	0	0	3	2	0	0	0	1	1	0	.500	.400
Marte, Jefry	R-R	6-1	187	6-21-91	.325	.250	.338	44	154	29	50	14	3	4	24	13	7	1	2	30	2	0	.532	.398
Martinez, Fernando	L-R	6-1	190	10-10-88	.429	—	.429	4	14	2	6	1	1	0	0	0	1	0	0	2	0	0	.643	.467
Martinez, Ruben	R-R	6-1	190	7-15-86	.201	.200	.201	46	169	16	34	4	5	0	20	11	3	2	1	42	7	4	.284	.261
McCarney, Matthew	R-R	6-2	195	8-17-88	.107	.167	.091	10	28	1	3	1	0	0	5	1	5	0	1	6	0	1	.143	.257
McGonigle, Mark	R-R	6-3	205	8-6-85	.297	.261	.307	38	111	23	33	5	3	0	15	18	1	0	1	29	4	0	.396	.397
Mosquera, Jose	R-R	5-11	185	8-24-86	.000	—	.000	1	4	0	0	0	0	0	0	0	0	0	0	0	0	0	.000	.000
Nieves, Luis	R-R	5-11	160	12-15-88	.205	.176	.211	26	88	9	18	3	1	0	8	0	0	1	0	19	2	1	.261	.205
Nixon, Trot	L-L	6-2	210	4-11-74	.600	—	.600	3	10	1	6	2	0	0	1	0	0	0	0	0	0	0	.800	.636
Ortiz, Giovanni	R-R	6-5	233	5-11-88	.350	.400	.333	15	40	7	14	0	0	0	3	6	1	0	1	10	0	0	.350	.447
Pagan, Angel	B-R	6-2	195	7-2-81	.600	.500	.667	2	5	1	3	1	0	0	0	1	0	0	0	1	0	0	.800	.600
Puello, Cesar	R-R	6-2	195	4-1-91	.305	.294	.306	40	151	24	46	6	0	1	17	5	6	0	1	32	13	5	.364	.350
Ramos, Valentin	R-R	6-3	185	7-21-88	.214	.500	.167	6	14	3	3	0	0	0	3	0	0	0	1	5	1	0	.214	.267
Rodriguez, Javier	R-R	6-2	165	4-4-90	.193	.192	.193	38	135	17	26	3	0	1	20	10	3	1	3	27	0	2	.237	.258
Rodriguez, Orlando	R-R	6-2	185	11-23-88	.231	.000	.273	6	13	2	3	0	0	0	1	0	0	0	0	4	0	0	.231	.286
Tejada, Miguel	R-R	6-1	175	11-11-90	.220	.154	.230	29	100	8	22	3	0	0	7	6	0	0	0	37	2	1	.250	.275
Torres, Juan	R-R	6-1	180	10-7-88	.293	.300	.292	21	58	12	17	4	0	1	8	0	0	1	0	14	0	1	.414	.300
Valdespin, Jordany	L-R	5-10	150	12-23-87	.284	.304	.279	34	134	23	38	6	3	3	22	7	1	1	2	10	9	2	.440	.319

Pitching	B-T	HT	WT	DOB	W	L	ERA	G	GS	CG	SV	IP	H	R	ER	HR	BB	SO	AVG	vLH	vRH	K/9	BB/9
Aldama, Eduardo	R-R	6-1	175	12-23-89	1	5	4.75	12	9	0	0	47	48	36	25	1	13	42	.265	.244	.283	7.99	2.47
Allen, Kyle	R-R	6-3	195	2-12-90	1	1	2.12	11	5	0	2	34	24	13	8	1	10	45	.194	.123	.254	11.91	2.65
Bello, Julio	L-R	6-5	175	10-16-86	2	1	2.50	11	5	0	1	36	34	16	10	0	15	27	.258	.306	.214	6.75	3.75
Burgos, Ambiorix	R-R	6-3	245	4-19-84	0	0	5.40	3	1	0	0	5	6	3	3	0	0	8	.286	.300	.273	14.40	0.00
Carson, Robert	L-L	6-3	220	1-23-89	1	0	1.57	5	5	0	0	23	11	5	4	0	6	25	.143	.150	.140	9.78	2.35
Erickson, Tim	R-L	6-0	180	11-12-84	0	0	0.00	1	0	0	0	1	2	0	0	0	0	1	.500	.667	.000	9.00	0.00
Familia, Jeurys	R-R	6-3	185	10-10-89	2	2	2.79	11	11	0	0	52	46	20	16	2	13	38	.232	.191	.269	6.62	2.26
Feliz, Tony	R-R	6-4	205	11-3-85	0	0	4.15	2	0	0	0	4	3	3	2	0	4	6	.188	.200	.167	12.46	8.31
Goldberg, Jake	R-R	6-0	185	11-28-85	1	4	7.52	12	1	0	2	26	42	30	22	2	6	29	.347	.356	.342	9.91	2.05
Hebert, Mike	R-R	6-3	180	8-11-90	2	2	4.71	9	3	0	0	21	11	15	11	0	29	19	.162	.206	.118	8.14	12.43
Hernandez, Orlando	R-R	6-2	220	10-11-69	0	0	2.25	1	1	0	0	4	4	2	1	0	1	6	.222	.308	.000	13.50	2.25
Hilliard, Chris	L-L	6-0	175	10-26-87	1	0	2.87	10	0	0	0	16	18	6	5	0	2	17	.281	.333	.273	9.77	1.15
Hodge, Lachlan	L-L	6-2	185	2-3-89	0	1	8.10	11	5	0	0	30	29	29	27	3	26	33	.257	.050	.301	9.90	7.80
Houck, Mitch	L-L	6-1	200	5-26-87	2	2	1.08	6	0	0	1	8	4	2	1	0	3	7	.148	.000	.154	7.56	3.24
Lynn, Mike	R-R	5-10	170	10-11-84	0	0	0.00	1	0	0	0	1	0	0	0	0	2	1	.000	.000	.000	9.00	18.00
Martinez, PedroE	R-R	5-11	173	6-20-87	1	0	2.70	2	0	0	0	3	1	1	1	0	1	1	.111	.000	.125	2.70	2.70
Mejia, Jenrry	R-R	6-0	162	10-11-89	2	0	0.60	3	3	1	0	15	9	1	1	0	3	15	.164	.217	.125	9.00	1.80
Neguilis, Jacobo	R-R	6-3	180	4-25-84	0	1	9.64	4	0	0	0	5	10	9	5	1	3	4	.400	.571	.333	7.71	5.79
Olmsted, Michael	R-R	6-6	245	5-2-87	0	0	3.86	2	2	0	0	5	6	4	2	1	2	3	.333	.500	.125	5.79	3.86
Rojas, Luis	R-R	6-1	165	7-29-89	3	2	2.19	17	0	0	1	25	16	9	6	0	18	24	.190	.103	.236	8.76	6.57
Smith, Tim	R-R	6-0	195	6-25-86	2	1	4.02	8	1	0	0	16	16	10	7	0	6	16	.258	.333	.188	9.19	3.45
Valenzuela, Brian	L-L	5-10	155	10-21-89	0	1	18.00	1	1	0	0	1	1	2	2	0	2	0	.200	.000	.250	0.00	18.00
White, Johnathan	R-R	6-1	205	1-19-88	1	0	2.55	8	1	0	1	25	23	7	7	0	3	25	.256	.279	.234	9.12	1.09

Fielding

Catcher	PCT	G	PO	A	E	DP	PB
Centeno	.977	23	157	16	4	3	10
Gronauer	.977	16	123	7	3	0	2
Howe	1.000	14	107	11	0	2	1
Maat	1.000	3	19	2	0	0	0
Mosquera	1.000	1	6	0	0	0	0
O. Rodriguez	.976	6	38	2	1	0	2
Torres	1.000	4	8	1	0	0	1

First Base	PCT	G	PO	A	E	DP
Flagg	.986	44	335	14	5	40
Ortiz	.966	12	83	1	3	5
Puello	1.000	1	8	0	0	0
Torres	.917	1	10	1	1	2

Second Base	PCT	G	PO	A	E	DP
Castillo	1.000	2	1	1	0	1

Harris	.916	28	40	69	10	13
Hinojosa	1.000	1	1	5	0	0
Nieves	1.000	2	3	4	0	3
Ramos	—	1	0	0	0	0
Valdespin	.942	24	38	60	6	13

Third Base	PCT	G	PO	A	E	DP
Hinojosa	1.000	12	5	15	0	1
Marte	.821	40	24	63	19	9
Nieves	—	1	0	0	0	0
Ramos	.857	5	0	6	1	0
Torres	1.000	1	0	0	0	0

Shortstop	PCT	G	PO	A	E	DP
Nieves	.937	20	33	56	6	15
Ortiz	.750	1	2	1	1	0
Tejada	.908	29	50	69	12	16

Valdespin	1.000	6	12	13	0	5

Outfield	PCT	G	PO	A	E	DP
Alou	—	1	0	0	0	0
Clark	1.000	7	5	0	0	0
Maldonado	1.000	3	3	0	0	0
F. Martinez	.833	3	4	1	1	0
R. Martinez	.986	46	65	5	1	1
McCarney	1.000	4	3	0	0	0
McGonigle	1.000	33	30	4	0	1
Nixon	—	1	0	0	0	0
Pagan	1.000	2	2	0	0	0
Puello	.984	38	58	2	1	1
J. Rodriguez	.935	37	54	4	4	0

DSL METS

ROOKIE

DOMINICAN SUMMER LEAGUE

Batting	B-T	HT	WT	DOB	AVG	vLH	vRH	G	AB	R	H	2B	3B	HR	RBI	BB	HBP	SH	SF	SO	SB	CS	SLG	OBP
Castillo, Edwin	R-R	6-0	181	5-30-90	.220	.111	.250	41	123	11	27	7	3	1	11	19	3	1	1	36	3	0	.350	.336
Castillo, Jairo	R-R	6-2	190	1-9-89	.206	.105	.229	61	214	28	44	15	1	2	27	37	9	1	1	83	2	1	.313	.345
Concepcion, Julio	R-R	6-4	194	9-5-89	.285	.250	.293	65	267	43	76	16	2	3	40	24	9	0	2	52	7	2	.393	.361
De Leon, Jeyckol	R-R	6-2	185	7-25-90	.260	.364	.230	29	96	12	25	5	0	0	13	6	7	1	2	15	2	0	.313	.342
De Los Santos, Francisco	R-R	6-2	180	8-15-90	.333	.000	.333	2	3	5	1	0	0	0	3	5	2	0	1	1	4	0	.333	.727
Duncan, Dani	R-R	6-2	192	10-30-89	.194	.273	.174	55	165	28	32	7	1	4	20	24	5	2	0	70	9	4	.321	.314
Eusebio, Ramon	R-R	6-3	178	8-31-88	.230	.190	.240	62	217	32	50	5	1	0	26	22	8	2	1	37	4	3	.263	.323
Francisco, Jose	R-R	6-0	173	8-29-87	.202	.146	.215	60	218	50	44	3	0	0	14	40	7	5	3	50	39	8	.216	.340
Hiraldo, Wily	B-R	5-11	153	8-9-88	.252	.160	.277	39	119	21	30	0	2	1	18	24	3	2	0	28	6	3	.311	.390
Mejia, Humberto	R-R	6-1	195	10-13-90	.186	.174	.189	37	118	17	22	5	0	0	12	10	4	2	1	27	0	0	.229	.271
Moreno, Gerardo	R-R	5-10	152	6-16-89	.182	.038	.213	54	148	27	27	1	0	0	11	32	4	0	0	19	10	2	.189	.342
Perez, Andres	R-R	6-1	189	7-5-89	.261	.256	.264	64	241	33	63	8	4	1	40	22	2	0	1	45	1	0	.340	.327
Santana, Breydi	R-R	6-2	200	9-27-88	.212	.333	.185	15	33	3	7	1	0	0	3	7	1	0	0	10	0	0	.242	.366
Santos, Franklin	R-R	5-11	154	3-28-88	.248	.200	.258	62	230	48	57	11	2	0	34	42	9	2	1	31	27	10	.313	.383
Valdez, Amauris	R-R	5-11	194	8-24-88	.234	.333	.207	54	201	31	47	10	2	3	28	20	8	1	1	40	0	0	.348	.326

Pitching	B-T	HT	WT	DOB	W	L	ERA	G	GS	CG	SV	IP	H	R	ER	HR	BB	SO	AVG	vLH	vRH	K/9	BB/9
Almonte, Yohan	R-R	6-1	150	11-9-89	3	3	2.95	14	9	0	2	61	59	29	20	2	23	55	.254	.288	.241	8.11	3.39
Batista, Eudy	L-L	6-1	175	8-6-90	0	0	3.86	11	0	0	0	12	11	9	5	0	12	8	.262	.333	.250	6.17	9.26
Cabrera, Alan	R-R	6-3	205	3-9-87	1	0	5.40	4	0	0	0	3	4	2	2	0	4	2	.286	.500	.250	5.40	10.80
Camarena, Marcos	R-R	6-3	190	9-8-90	0	1	3.68	7	0	0	0	7	6	6	3	0	8	8	.222	.333	.133	9.82	9.82
Geremy, Leandro	R-R	6-4	208	10-4-86	1	2	3.58	14	0	0	1	28	25	16	11	0	13	17	.238	.296	.218	5.53	4.23
Germen, Gonzalez	R-R	6-1	175	9-23-87	5	2	1.34	15	14	0	0	74	41	21	11	0	15	70	.159	.151	.162	8.51	1.82
Guerrero, Rafael	R-R	5-11	183	3-23-89	0	0	4.50	4	0	0	0	8	4	4	4	0	9	4	.167	.200	.143	4.50	10.13
Martinez, PedroE	R-R	5-11	173	6-20-87	0	0	3.60	11	0	0	0	15	10	7	6	0	8	12	.196	.222	.190	7.20	4.80
Mendez, Ismael	L-L	6-1	184	5-13-86	6	1	1.07	15	14	0	0	76	38	16	9	2	29	62	.151	.276	.135	7.37	3.45
Mueses, Jose	L-L	6-3	170	12-17-80	0	0	7.71	7	0	0	0	7	5	7	6	0	8	4	.200	.000	.208	5.14	10.29
Paulino, Jhoan	R-R	6-2	175	4-25-88	0	0	8.62	8	3	0	0	16	14	20	15	2	14	16	.226	.278	.205	9.19	8.04
Pena, Wily	R-R	6-2	190	10-30-90	4	0	1.76	11	0	0	1	31	22	7	6	0	15	14	.204	.207	.203	4.11	4.40
Peralta, Victor	L-L	5-11	178	7-2-89	4	3	3.45	20	0	0	3	31	29	17	12	2	22	30	.244	.176	.255	8.62	6.32
Reyes, Edinson	R-R	6-0	181	8-9-90	2	0	1.74	4	1	0	0	10	4	2	2	0	7	9	.114	.000	.154	7.84	6.10
Rodriguez, Armando	R-R	6-2	185	1-28-88	4	4	2.63	15	13	0	0	72	48	28	21	0	22	81	.188	.173	.194	10.13	2.75

Rojas, Leonel	L-L	6-4	167	8-19-86	2	3	3.94	12	5	0	0	30	26	18	13	0	27	23	.232	.111	.243	6.98	8.19
Sanchez, Erigson	R-R	6-1	180	11-3-90	2	1	3.32	14	1	0	2	41	41	16	15	2	17	28	.273	.255	.282	6.20	3.76
Soriano, Derlin	R-R	6-2	184	12-6-89	5	0	3.94	15	0	0	2	30	24	15	13	0	20	21	.220	.407	.159	6.34	6.07
Taveras, Samuel	R-R	6-4	185	4-14-89	4	2	0.90	23	0	0	12	30	20	6	3	1	7	37	.189	.206	.181	11.10	2.10
Valentin, Jose	R-R	6-4	190	8-4-87	1	5	3.48	11	11	0	0	44	39	20	17	0	28	37	.235	.273	.221	7.57	5.73

Fielding

Catcher	PCT	G	PO	A	E	DP	PB
De Leon	1.000	2	6	0	0	0	0
Mejia	.981	27	186	26	4	2	6
Santana	1.000	5	6	0	0	0	0
Valdez	.987	50	345	42	5	2	11

First Base	PCT	G	PO	A	E	DP
E. Castillo	.954	14	100	4	5	5
J. Castillo	1.000	2	29	1	0	3
De Leon	.950	3	16	3	1	3
Eusebio	.986	61	538	32	8	57
Mejia	—	1	0	0	0	0

	PCT	G	PO	A	E	DP
Santana	—	1	0	0	0	0
Second Base	PCT	G	PO	A	E	DP
E. Castillo	.913	5	12	9	2	3
Hiraldo	.955	25	43	63	5	16
Moreno	.974	52	89	132	6	30
Third Base	PCT	G	PO	A	E	DP
E. Castillo	.914	12	6	26	3	3
J. Castillo	.864	59	54	131	29	8
Eusebio	.800	1	1	3	1	0
Shortstop	PCT	G	PO	A	E	DP
De Los Santos	1.000	2	5	5	0	1

	PCT	G	PO	A	E	DP
Eusebio	1.000	1	1	4	0	0
Hiraldo	.946	9	10	25	2	3
Sanchez	.750	1	0	3	1	0
Santos	.936	62	101	192	20	42
Outfield	PCT	G	PO	A	E	DP
E. Castillo	1.000	6	9	0	0	0
Concepcion	.939	64	75	2	5	0
Duncan	.970	52	91	7	3	3
Francisco	.975	59	109	7	3	0
Hiraldo	.500	1	0	1	1	0
Perez	1.000	38	54	3	0	1

VSL METS

VENEZUELAN SUMMER LEAGUE

ROOKIE

Batting	B-T	HT	WT	DOB	AVG	vLH	vRH	G	AB	R	H	2B	3B	HR	RBI	BB	HBP	SH	SF	SO	SB	CS	SLG	OBP
Alvarez, Hector	R-R	5-11	170	2-14-91	.224	.190	.232	40	116	14	26	7	0	1	14	15	6	1	2	37	1	1	.310	.338
Bellorin, Jose	R-R	6-0	160	12-14-90	.262	.172	.280	50	172	19	45	6	2	0	18	18	5	1	1	44	4	6	.320	.347
Cordero, Albert	R-R	5-11	175	1-14-90	.267	.333	.250	14	45	5	12	2	0	0	2	1	0	0	0	4	0	0	.311	.283
Decuba, Quintin	R-R	6-3	180	9-9-87	.263	.091	.296	42	137	15	36	3	2	7	25	13	1	0	1	42	1	0	.467	.329
Diaz, Cesar	R-R	6-0	172	12-7-88	.204	.174	.211	38	113	18	23	4	2	7	13	10	1	0	1	31	7	2	.327	.338
Diaz, Jose	B-R	6-2	190	7-26-89	.265	.281	.261	46	166	17	44	8	0	3	24	12	7	0	1	26	8	6	.367	.339
Hernandez, Luis	R-R	6-2	204	6-24-88	.180	.217	.172	46	139	12	25	2	1	2	11	8	2	2	33	0	0	.252	.275	
Marquez, Cesar	R-R	6-1	180	7-16-91	.129	.150	.123	35	85	2	11	3	0	0	7	8	2	1	0	23	1	3	.165	.221
Pirela, Adrian	R-R	6-0	205	12-23-88	.282	.265	.285	64	206	33	58	11	1	6	22	25	11	1	1	50	4	5	.432	.387
Ponce, Dimas	R-R	5-11	140	1-22-91	.188	.200	.185	31	64	7	12	0	0	4	12	3	1	1	13	1	7	.188	.338
Soto, Breiner	R-R	6-2	147	2-23-90	.228	.257	.223	63	219	32	50	10	6	3	13	10	3	0	6	83	11	7	.370	.277
Tijerina, Ismael	R-R	6-0	165	8-19-89	.214	.233	.210	53	154	16	33	2	1	0	12	13	1	4	3	18	5	6	.240	.275
Tovar, Wilfredo	R-R	5-10	150	8-11-91	.203	.176	.206	49	153	16	31	7	1	2	11	12	2	6	0	23	7	4	.301	.269
Van Gurp, Ray	R-R	5-11	165	1-2-89	.275	.267	.276	63	222	36	61	7	2	2	21	24	0	2	2	34	29	12	.351	.343
Vernouij, Marinus	R-R	6-3	215	1-30-89	.201	.289	.180	58	199	17	40	14	1	1	17	16	5	0	1	57	2	1	.296	.276

Pitching	B-T	HT	WT	DOB	W	L	ERA	G	GS	CG	SV	IP	H	R	ER	HR	BB	SO	AVG	vLH	vRH	K/9	BB/9
Aguilar, Victor	R-R	6-2	175	3-18-89	1	2	5.40	8	0	0	0	17	27	12	10	1	3	13	.370	.273	.412	7.02	1.62
Brito, Jose	R-R	5-11	170	4-28-91	1	1	3.67	11	6	0	0	42	41	22	17	0	18	11	.258	.324	.238	2.38	3.89
Burgos, Jhoan	R-R	6-4	226	9-1-85	1	1	0.42	9	0	0	3	21	11	2	1	0	6	22	.147	.200	.138	9.28	2.53
Carreno, Josmar	R-R	5-11	202	8-13-87	2	0	6.00	11	0	0	0	18	17	15	12	0	10	10	.258	.364	.236	5.00	5.00
Castro, Rafael	R-R	6-2	200	8-8-91	0	2	3.96	9	2	0	0	25	18	15	11	2	13	26	.194	.111	.213	9.36	4.68
Contreras, Yoel	R-L	6-3	180	1-1-86	0	0	2.45	2	0	0	0	4	4	3	1	0	3	1	.308	.000	.308	2.45	7.36
Cuan, Angel	L-L	5-11	150	5-29-89	1	8	3.13	14	14	0	0	72	71	36	25	2	11	74	.254	.067	.264	9.25	1.38
Delgado, Ruben	R-R	6-2	182	8-18-89	1	0	2.84	3	0	0	1	6	4	2	2	1	2	5	.211	.000	.235	7.11	2.84
Diaz, Roberto	R-R	6-0	170	4-25-90	0	2	14.21	5	0	0	0	6	10	11	10	0	9	2	.400	.400	.400	2.84	12.79
Duarte, Luis	R-R	6-1	180	8-7-87	1	2	2.55	4	2	1	0	18	21	6	5	1	3	12	.309	.333	.293	6.11	1.53
Galarraga, Luis	R-R	6-2	180	12-5-87	1	0	4.15	5	2	0	0	17	21	10	8	0	3	5	.313	.231	.333	2.60	1.56
Guerrero, Rafael	R-R	5-11	183	3-23-89	3	3	3.63	13	5	0	0	45	39	25	18	0	20	30	.238	.200	.248	6.04	4.03
Gutierrez, Dennis	R-R	6-2	180	12-24-88	1	1	3.60	4	4	0	0	15	23	8	6	0	0	9	.338	.200	.377	5.40	0.00
Hernandez, Jose	R-R	6-1	210	1-22-89	0	3	6.75	9	0	0	0	15	19	15	11	0	12	9	.317	.353	.302	5.52	7.36
Hernandez, Oralbis	R-R	6-1	175	12-4-87	2	1	5.00	12	1	0	0	36	52	26	20	2	8	25	.342	.313	.350	6.25	2.00
Montano, Elys	L-L	6-5	195	8-20-89	1	2	5.74	7	4	0	0	16	15	11	10	1	12	10	.242	.000	.250	5.74	6.89
Peralta, Ramiro	R-R	6-3	180	9-8-89	4	2	2.74	13	4	0	0	43	31	16	13	1	22	33	.214	.280	.200	6.96	4.64
Romero, Johan	R-R	5-11	200	12-13-89	1	7	4.11	23	0	0	10	35	41	26	16	2	14	19	.311	.310	.311	4.89	3.60
Sanchez, Yeyber	R-R	6-4	198	6-18-90	0	2	6.39	4	4	0	0	13	14	12	9	0	10	8	.275	.500	.244	5.68	7.11
Torres, Jhonathan	L-L	5-11	170	3-20-90	5	2	3.39	13	13	0	0	64	63	30	24	2	13	42	.274	.200	.276	5.94	1.84
Tovar, Orlando	L-L	6-3	213	3-26-88	0	1	1.54	8	8	0	0	41	34	9	7	1	10	52	.222	.000	.230	11.41	2.20

Fielding

Catcher	PCT	G	PO	A	E	DP	PB
Alvarez	.978	38	221	42	6	6	7
Cordero	.964	4	16	11	1	1	2
Decuba	1.000	2	2	0	0	0	1
Hernandez	.978	35	197	30	5	2	3

First Base	PCT	G	PO	A	E	DP
Decuba	.990	23	197	10	2	19
Gomez	1.000	1	8	0	0	0
Hernandez	.991	13	108	5	1	12
Pirela	.993	16	134	3	1	19
Vernouij	.995	22	193	12	1	21

Second Base	PCT	G	PO	A	E	DP
Alvarez	1.000	1	3	2	0	0
Bellorin	1.000	2	1	4	0	1

	PCT					
Ponce	.944	23	55	46	6	17
Tijerina	1.000	11	21	17	0	3
Tovar	1.000	1	0	2	0	1
Tovar	.964	16	33	48	3	13
Van Gurp	.970	27	64	67	4	20
Third Base	PCT	G	PO	A	E	DP
Bellorin	.857	3	0	6	1	2
Ponce	1.000	1	1	0	0	0
Tijerina	.888	39	18	69	11	7
Van Gurp	.923	19	15	45	5	5
Vernouij	.863	20	17	46	10	5
Shortstop	PCT	G	PO	A	E	DP
Bellorin	.914	44	61	151	20	29
Ponce	1.000	1	1	1	0	0

	PCT	G	PO	A	E	DP
Tijerina	.944	6	8	9	1	3
Tovar	.943	17	26	56	5	9
Van Gurp	.941	6	14	18	2	6
Outfield	PCT	G	PO	A	E	DP
Decuba	1.000	2	0	1	0	0
C. Diaz	.950	32	55	2	3	0
J. Diaz	.971	45	62	6	2	0
Marquez	.958	31	21	2	1	0
Pirela	.934	44	66	5	5	1
Soto	.949	62	125	6	7	1
Tovar	.917	8	10	1	1	0

New York Yankees

BY GEORGE KING

You never heard the "R" word roll off anybody's lips within the organization because how can a team rebuild with a $209 million payroll?

And how can you tell Alex Rodriguez, Derek Jeter, Mariano Rivera, Andy Pettitte, Johnny Damon, Bobby Abreu, Mike Mussina, Jason Giambi and Jorge Posada it was time to rebuild while they are in uniform?

Yet, from the moment Hal Steinbrenner and Brian Cashman refused to part with young pitchers who would fail miserably at the big league level for Johan Santana in December, there was a feel that the Yankees were willing to take a step back to make sure their future was better than it was on the eve of the 2008 season.

After watching the Yankees miss the postseason for the first time since 1993, Hank Steinbrenner still lamented not prodding his brother and Cashman harder to make the deal.

"I should have pushed the Santana thing," Hank Steinbrenner said two weeks after the nightmarish season ended with the Yankees in third place in the American League East, behind the Rays and Red Sox. "My dad wanted that."

To say that the Yankees' decision not to part with Phil Hughes, Ian Kennedy, Alan Horne or Jeff Marquez and Melky Cabrera for Santana was the only reason for the dismal season would be wrong.

Injuries, something every team deals with, also played a part. So did Robinson Cano hitting a disappointing .271/.305/.410 in the first season of a four-year, $30 million deal.

Righthander Chien-Ming Wang was 8-2, 4.07 on June 15 when he sprained his foot running the bases in Houston and lost for the season. Suddenly, a rotation that already had serious question marks lost a pitcher who had a combined 38 wins in 2006-2007.

Instead of making a deal for the best available veteran pitcher, the Yankees recalled journeyman righthander Dan Giese from Triple-A Scranton/Wilkes-Barre.

That was a strong indication the Yankees were married to the idea of not mortgaging the future for short-term gain.

Posada played in 51 games and had right

MAJOR LEAGUE: ALEX RODRIGUEZ, 3B

Coming off a career year, Rodriguez again put up strong numbers in the Bronx. He led the American League in slugging (.573), ranked fifth in on-base percentage (.392) and was third in home runs (35). He also drove in a team-best 103 runs.

MINOR LEAGUE: JESUS MONTERO, C

Signed out of Venezuela in 2006, Montero tore through low Class A Charleston in batting .326/.376/.491 with 17 home runs, 34 doubles and 87 RBIs. His 187 hits led the South Atlantic League, with his batting average finishing second.

BRIAN BISSELL

BATTING		*Minimum 250 at-bats
*AVG	Montero, Jesus, Charleston	.326
R	Montero, Jesus, Charleston	86
H	Montero, Jesus, Charleston	171
TB	Montero, Jesus, Charleston	258
2B	Gonzalez, Edwar, Tampa, Trenton	42
3B	Gardner, Brett, Scranton/Wilkes-Barre	11
HR	Laird, Brandon, Charleston	23
RBI	Montero, Jesus, Charleston	87
BB	Gardner, Brett, Scranton/Wilkes-Barre	70
SO	Fortenberry, Seth, Tampa	125
SB	Gardner, Brett, Scranton/Wilkes-Barre	37
*OBP	Gardner, Brett, Scranton/Wilkes-Barre	.414
*SLG	Laird, Brandon, Charleston	.498
PITCHING		**†Minimum 75 innings**
W	McAllister, Zach, Charleston/Tampa	14
	Igawa, Kei, Scranton/Wilkes-Barre	14
L	Nova, Ivan, Tampa	13
†ERA	McAllister, Zach, Charleston/Tampa	2.09
G	Ortiz, Jonathan, Charleston	57
GS	Jones, Jason, Scranton/Trenton	27
	Kontos, George, Trenton	27
SV	Ortiz, Jonathan, Charleston	33
IP	Jones, Jason, Scranton/Trenton	160
BB	Dunn, Michael, Tampa/Trenton	59
	Betances, Dellin, Charleston	59
SO	Kontos, George, Trenton	152
†AVG	Betances, Dellin, Charleston	.208

shoulder surgery in September. Joba Chamberlain missed three weeks with rotator cuff tendinitis. Rodriguez was out almost a month with a quad problem and Damon went on the DL for the first time in his career with a shoulder issue. Hideki Matsui missed considerable time as well.

General Manager: Brian Cashman. **Farm Director:** Mark Newman. **Scouting Director:** Damon Oppenheimer.

Class	Team	League	W	L	PCT	Finish*	Manager	Affiliate Since
Majors	New York	American	89	73	.549	4th (14)	Joe Girardi	—
Triple-A	Scranton/W-B Yankees	International	88	56	.611	^2nd (14)	Dave Miley	2007
Double-A	Trenton Thunder	Eastern	86	54	.614	^1st (12)	Tony Franklin	2003
High A	Tampa Yankees	Florida State	76	65	.526	6th (12)	Luis Sojo	1994
Low A	Charleston River Dogs	South Atlantic	80	59	.576	3rd (16)	Torre Tyson	2005
Short-season	Staten Island Yankees	New York-Penn	49	26	.653	1st (14)	Pat McMahon	1999
Rookie	GCL Yankees	Gulf Coast	31	27	.534	7th (16)	Jody Reed	1980
Overall 2008 Minor League Record			406	287	.586	1st		

* Finish in overall standings (No. of teams in league). ^League champion.

ORGANIZATION STATISTICS

NEW YORK YANKEES
AMERICAN LEAGUE

Batting	B-T	HT	WT	DOB	AVG	vLH	vRH	G	AB	R	H	2B	3B	HR	RBI	BB	HBP	SH	SF	SO	SB	CS	SLG	OBP
Abreu, Bobby	L-R	6-0	210	3-11-74	.296	.315	.287	156	609	100	180	39	4	20	100	73	1	0	1	109	22	11	.471	.371
Betemit, Wilson	B-R	6-3	230	11-2-81	.265	.233	.274	87	189	24	50	13	0	6	25	6	1	1	1	56	0	1	.429	.289
Cabrera, Melky	B-L	5-11	200	8-11-84	.249	.213	.265	129	414	42	103	12	1	8	37	29	3	4	3	58	9	2	.341	.301
Cano, Robinson	L-R	6-0	205	10-22-82	.271	.292	.263	159	597	70	162	35	3	14	72	26	5	1	5	65	2	4	.410	.305
Cervelli, Francisco	R-R	6-1	210	3-6-86	.000	—	.000	3	5	0	0	0	0	0	0	0	0	0	0	3	0	0	.000	.000
Christian, Justin	R-R	6-1	190	4-3-80	.250	.333	.077	24	40	6	10	3	0	0	6	3	0	0	0	4	7	1	.325	.302
Damon, Johnny	L-L	6-2	205	11-5-73	.303	.258	.321	143	555	95	168	27	5	17	71	64	1	2	1	82	29	8	.461	.375
Duncan, Shelley	R-R	6-5	225	9-29-79	.175	.225	.059	23	57	7	10	3	0	1	6	7	0	0	1	13	0	0	.281	.262
Ensberg, Morgan	R-R	6-2	210	8-26-75	.203	.167	.227	28	74	6	15	0	0	1	4	6	0	0	0	22	0	1	.243	.263
Gardner, Brett	L-L	5-10	180	8-24-83	.228	.125	.252	42	127	18	29	5	2	0	16	8	2	3	1	30	13	1	.299	.283
Giambi, Jason	L-R	6-3	235	1-8-71	.247	.231	.253	145	458	68	113	19	1	32	96	76	22	0	9	111	2	1	.502	.373
Gonzalez, Alberto	R-R	5-11	160	4-18-83	.173	.100	.219	28	52	4	9	2	0	0	1	4	0	2	0	8	0	0	.212	.232
Jeter, Derek	R-R	6-3	195	6-26-74	.300	.302	.300	150	596	88	179	25	3	11	69	52	9	7	4	85	11	5	.408	.363
Matsui, Hideki	L-R	6-2	210	6-12-74	.294	.315	.284	93	337	43	99	17	0	9	45	38	3	0	0	47	0	0	.424	.370
Miranda, Juan	L-L	6-0	220	4-25-83	.400	1.000	.333	5	10	2	4	1	0	0	1	2	1	0	1	4	0	0	.500	.500
Moeller, Chad	R-R	6-4	215	2-18-75	.231	.185	.250	41	91	13	21	6	0	1	9	7	4	0	1	18	0	0	.330	.311
Molina, Jose	R-R	6-2	235	6-3-75	.216	.188	.230	100	268	32	58	17	0	3	18	12	6	8	3	52	0	0	.313	.263
Nady, Xavier	R-R	6-2	215	11-14-78	.268	.203	.290	59	228	26	61	11	0	12	40	14	4	0	1	48	1	1	.474	.320
Posada, Jorge	B-R	6-2	215	8-17-71	.268	.255	.274	51	168	18	45	13	1	3	22	24	2	0	1	38	0	0	.411	.364
Ransom, Cody	R-R	6-2	190	2-17-76	.302	.214	.345	33	43	9	13	3	0	4	8	6	1	1	0	12	0	0	.651	.400
Rodriguez, Alex	R-R	6-3	225	7-27-75	.302	.263	.316	138	510	104	154	33	0	35	103	65	14	0	5	117	18	3	.573	.392
Rodriguez, Ivan	R-R	5-9	190	11-30-71	.219	.273	.203	33	96	11	21	4	0	2	3	4	1	0	0	15	4	0	.323	.257
2-team total (82 Detroit)					.276	—	—	115	398	44	110	20	3	7	35	23	3	3	2	67	10	1	.394	.319
Sexson, Richie	R-R	6-8	240	12-29-74	.250	.273	.167	22	28	2	7	1	0	1	6	6	0	0	1	10	0	0	.393	.371
2-team total (74 Seattle)					.221	—	—	96	280	29	62	9	0	12	36	43	0	0	4	86	1	0	.382	.321
Stewart, Chris	R-R	6-4	210	2-19-82	.000	.000	—	1	3	0	0	0	0	0	0	0	0	0	0	1	0	0	.000	.000

Pitching	B-T	HT	WT	DOB	W	L	ERA	G	GS	CG	SV	IP	H	R	ER	HR	BB	SO	AVG	vLH	vRH	K/9	BB/9
Aceves, Alfredo	R-R	6-3	220	12-8-82	1	0	2.40	6	4	0	0	30	25	8	8	4	10	16	.227	.238	.213	4.80	3.00
Albaladejo, Jonathan	R-R	6-5	260	10-30-82	0	1	3.95	7	0	0	0	14	15	6	6	1	6	13	.294	.304	.286	8.56	3.95
Britton, Chris	R-R	6-3	275	12-16-82	0	0	5.09	15	0	0	0	23	28	13	13	4	11	12	.301	.391	.213	4.70	4.30
Bruney, Brian	R-R	6-3	235	2-17-82	3	0	1.83	32	1	0	1	34	18	7	7	2	16	33	.153	.106	.183	8.65	4.19
Chamberlain, Joba	R-R	6-2	230	9-23-85	4	3	2.60	42	12	0	0	100	87	32	29	5	39	118	.233	.247	.219	10.58	3.50
Coke, Phil	L-L	6-1	210	7-19-82	1	0	0.61	12	0	0	0	15	8	1	1	0	2	14	.160	.207	.095	8.59	1.23
Farnsworth, Kyle	R-R	6-4	235	4-14-76	1	2	3.65	45	0	0	1	44	43	18	18	11	17	43	.264	.274	.256	8.73	3.45
2-team total (16 Detroit)					2	3	4.48	61	0	0	1	60	70	32	30	15	22	61	—	—	—	9.10	3.28
Giese, Dan	R-R	6-3	195	5-19-77	1	3	3.53	20	3	0	0	43	39	22	17	3	14	29	.232	.209	.260	6.02	2.91
Hawkins, LaTroy	R-R	6-5	215	12-21-72	1	1	5.71	33	0	0	0	41	42	26	26	3	17	23	.275	.338	.227	5.05	3.73
Hughes, Phil	R-R	6-5	230	6-24-86	0	4	6.62	8	8	0	0	34	43	26	25	3	15	23	.314	.333	.299	6.09	3.97
Igawa, Kei	L-L	6-1	210	7-13-79	0	1	13.50	2	1	0	0	4	13	6	6	0	0	0	.565	.000	.591	0.00	0.00
Kennedy, Ian	R-R	6-0	195	12-19-84	0	4	8.17	10	9	0	0	40	50	37	36	5	26	27	.309	.236	.397	6.13	5.90
Marte, Damaso	L-L	6-2	215	2-14-75	1	3	5.40	25	0	0	0	18	14	11	11	1	10	24	.206	.233	.184	11.78	4.91
Mussina, Mike	L-R	6-2	190	12-8-68	20	9	3.37	34	34	0	0	200	214	85	75	17	31	150	.278	.236	.317	6.74	1.39
Ohlendorf, Ross	R-R	6-4	235	8-8-82	1	1	6.53	25	0	0	0	40	50	31	29	7	19	36	.299	.349	.247	8.10	4.27
Patterson, Scott	R-R	6-6	230	6-20-79	0	0	6.75	1	0	0	0	1	1	1	1	0	2	2	.000	.000	.500	13.50	13.50
Pavano, Carl	R-R	6-5	240	1-8-76	4	2	5.77	7	7	0	0	34	41	23	22	5	10	15	.306	.324	.283	3.93	2.62
Pettitte, Andy	L-L	6-5	225	6-15-72	14	14	4.54	33	33	0	0	204	233	112	103	19	55	158	.290	.203	.325	6.97	2.43
Ponson, Sidney	R-R	6-1	260	11-2-76	4	4	5.85	16	15	0	0	80	99	53	52	11	32	33	.315	.363	.236	3.71	3.60
2-team total (9 Texas)					8	5	5.04	25	24	1	0	136	170	89	76	14	48	58	—	—	—	3.85	3.18
Ramirez, Edwar	R-R	6-3	165	3-28-81	5	1	3.90	55	0	0	1	55	44	25	24	7	24	63	.215	.229	.195	10.25	3.90
Rasner, Darrell	R-R	6-3	210	1-13-81	5	10	5.40	24	20	0	0	113	135	74	68	14	39	67	.293	.279	.312	5.32	3.10
Rivera, Mariano	R-R	6-2	185	11-29-69	6	5	1.40	64	0	0	39	71	41	11	11	4	6	77	.165	.147	.183	9.81	0.76
Robertson, David	R-R	5-11	180	4-9-85	4	0	5.34	25	0	0	0	30	29	18	18	3	15	36	.257	.259	.254	10.68	4.45
Sanchez, Humberto	R-R	6-6	270	5-28-83	0	0	4.50	2	0	0	0	2	1	1	1	0	2	1	.167	.000	.333	4.50	9.00
Traber, Billy	L-L	6-5	205	9-18-79	0	0	7.02	19	0	0	0	17	23	13	13	3	7	11	.324	.410	.219	5.94	3.78

Veras, Jose	R-R	6-5	235	10-20-80	5	3	3.59	60	0	0	0	58	52	23	23	7	29	63	.239	.217	.254	9.83	4.53
Wang, Chien-Ming	R-R	6-3	225	3-31-80	8	2	4.07	15	15	1	0	95	90	44	43	4	35	54	.249	.261	.238	5.12	3.32

Fielding

Catcher	PCT	G	PO	A	E	DP	PB
Cervelli	1.000	3	11	0	0	0	0
Moeller	.983	33	159	15	3	2	0
Molina	.996	97	634	52	3	6	7
Posada	.995	30	197	7	1	1	2
I. Rodriguez	.995	31	173	14	1	1	2
Stewart	1.000	1	8	0	0	0	0

First Base	PCT	G	PO	A	E	DP
Betemit	.995	36	191	13	1	23
Damon	1.000	1	1	0	0	0
Duncan	.972	16	98	5	3	8
Ensberg	1.000	7	38	0	0	1
Giambi	.990	113	870	36	9	77
Miranda	1.000	5	30	2	0	1
Moeller	1.000	2	4	0	0	1
Molina	—	1	0	0	0	0

Nady	1.000	3	3	1	0	0
Posada	1.000	7	25	0	0	2
Ransom	1.000	19	47	1	0	2
Sexson	1.000	19	78	8	0	6

Second Base	PCT	G	PO	A	E	DP
Betemit	.923	3	4	8	1	2
Cano	.984	159	305	482	13	103
Gonzalez	1.000	4	4	7	0	1
Ransom	.857	2	3	3	1	0

Third Base	PCT	G	PO	A	E	DP
Betemit	.893	21	4	21	3	4
Ensberg	.976	21	8	32	1	2
Gonzalez	.944	11	6	11	1	2
Moeller	—	3	0	0	0	0
Ransom	1.000	4	1	6	0	0
A. Rodriguez	.970	131	73	251	10	23

Shortstop	PCT	G	PO	A	E	DP
Betemit	1.000	14	10	19	0	5
Gonzalez	1.000	14	12	15	0	2
Jeter	.979	148	220	347	12	69
Ransom	.944	9	12	22	2	4

Outfield	PCT	G	PO	A	E	DP
Abreu	.993	150	270	10	2	3
Cabrera	.986	128	284	7	4	1
Christian	.944	17	16	1	1	0
Damon	.992	113	232	3	2	0
Duncan	1.000	4	4	0	0	0
Gardner	1.000	38	78	5	0	0
Matsui	.978	23	42	2	1	1
Nady	.980	52	97	2	2	0

SCRANTON/WILKES-BARRE YANKEES   TRIPLE-A

INTERNATIONAL LEAGUE

Batting	B-T	HT	WT	DOB	AVG	vLH	vRH	G	AB	R	H	2B	3B	HR	RBI	BB	HBP	SH	SF	SO	SB	CS	SLG	OBP
Basak, Chris	R-R	6-2	210	12-6-78	.253	.291	.231	45	146	16	37	9	2	0	11	5	2	1	3	26	6	0	.342	.282
2-team total (56 Rochester)					.257	—	—	101	319	36	82	20	2	6	28	20	3	3	4	64	11	7	.389	.303
Betemit, Wilson	B-R	6-3	230	11-2-81	.333	1.000	.280	8	27	5	9	4	0	1	5	6	0	0	0	7	0	0	.593	.455
Broussard, Ben	L-L	6-2	230	9-24-76	.276	.301	.263	64	239	44	66	18	1	13	46	18	9	0	1	45	1	0	.523	.348
Brown, Jason	R-R	6-2	200	5-22-74	.067	.000	.091	7	15	0	1	0	0	0	2	0	0	0	0	8	0	0	.067	.176
Cabrera, Melky	B-L	5-11	200	8-11-84	.333	.250	.394	15	57	8	19	2	0	5	8	6	0	0	1	9	1	3	.368	.409
Carson, Matt	R-R	6-2	200	7-1-81	.289	.333	.266	84	305	53	88	10	6	10	38	21	8	2	3	63	10	3	.459	.347
Castro, Bernie	B-R	5-10	170	7-14-79	.266	.314	.239	83	282	44	75	11	0	1	21	30	1	7	1	36	21	9	.316	.338
Christian, Justin	R-R	6-1	190	4-3-80	.306	.250	.330	74	268	48	82	17	1	6	45	20	4	0	5	34	22	4	.444	.357
Closser, J.D.	B-R	5-10	200	1-15-80	.248	.278	.239	50	149	17	37	7	0	4	19	23	1	0	0	28	0	1	.376	.353
Cox, Danny	L-R	6-1	180	7-10-86	.000	—	.000	1	1	0	0	0	0	0	0	0	0	0	0	1	0	0	.000	.000
Duncan, Eric	L-R	6-3	195	12-7-84	.233	.195	.248	120	437	47	102	23	1	11	60	37	3	0	4	113	6	4	.366	.295
Duncan, Shelley	R-R	6-5	225	9-29-79	.239	.233	.241	58	205	38	49	14	0	12	44	41	2	0	4	55	6	1	.483	.365
Gardner, Brett	L-L	5-10	180	8-24-83	.296	.327	.283	94	341	68	101	12	11	3	32	70	1	11	3	76	37	9	.422	.414
Gonzalez, Alberto	R-R	5-11	160	4-18-83	.250	.297	.226	47	188	23	47	8	0	4	23	16	3	2	4	30	4	2	.356	.313
2-team total (8 Columbus)					.258	—	—	55	221	25	57	11	0	5	29	16	4	2	4	35	4	2	.376	.314
Green, Nick	R-R	6-0	180	9-10-78	.233	.352	.177	112	391	41	91	15	2	12	50	26	4	6	4	102	3	2	.373	.285
Kunda, Chris	R-R	6-1	175	11-1-84	.333	.000	.500	2	3	0	1	0	0	0	2	1	0	0	0	0	0	0	.667	.500
Lane, Jason	R-L	6-2	220	12-22-76	.236	.224	.241	97	347	54	82	19	3	16	51	50	7	0	5	70	3	3	.447	.340
2-team total (13 Pawtucket)					.233	—	—	110	400	64	93	23	3	18	60	58	7	0	6	84	3	3	.440	.335
Miranda, Juan	L-L	6-0	220	4-25-83	.287	.195	.332	99	356	40	102	22	0	12	52	55	3	0	3	79	2	1	.449	.384
Moeller, Chad	R-R	6-4	215	2-18-75	.235	.103	.308	23	81	6	19	4	0	1	7	5	0	0	3	22	0	0	.321	.270
Nunez, Luis	R-R	5-11	160	11-21-86	.333	.500	.200	3	9	1	3	0	0	0	0	0	0	0	0	1	0	0	.333	.333
Porter, Greg	L-R	6-4	225	8-15-80	.261	.246	.266	72	245	27	64	15	0	2	19	18	1	0	1	55	3	2	.347	.313
2-team total (20 Columbus)					.255	—	—	92	318	32	81	17	0	3	23	24	1	0	1	73	4	2	.336	.308
Ransom, Cody	R-R	6-2	190	2-17-76	.255	.203	.277	116	423	69	108	24	3	22	71	50	4	2	1	115	9	5	.482	.338
Rodriguez, Eladio	R-R	5-11	190	4-4-79	.333	1.000	.000	1	3	1	1	0	0	0	2	0	0	0	0	1	0	0	.667	.600
Stewart, Chris	R-R	6-4	210	2-19-82	.279	.344	.246	86	272	32	76	19	0	2	24	28	3	5	1	38	2	1	.371	.352

Pitching	B-T	HT	WT	DOB	W	L	ERA	G	GS	CG	SV	IP	H	R	ER	HR	BB	SO	AVG	vLH	vRH	K/9	BB/9
Aceves, Alfredo	R-R	6-2	220	12-8-82	2	3	4.12	10	8	0	0	44	42	21	20	6	13	42	.250	.213	.291	8.66	2.68
Albaladejo, Jonathan	R-R	6-5	260	10-30-82	0	0	1.29	4	0	0	0	7	5	2	1	1	4	5	.192	.083	.286	6.43	5.14
Britton, Chris	R-R	6-3	275	12-16-82	3	1	2.28	21	0	0	0	28	28	7	7	2	7	26	.264	.341	.215	8.46	2.28
Bruney, Brian	R-R	6-3	235	2-17-82	0	0	3.68	7	1	0	0	7	7	4	3	0	7	7	.250	.294	.182	8.59	8.59
Coke, Phil	L-L	6-1	210	7-19-82	2	2	4.67	14	1	0	0	17	19	11	9	0	5	22	.271	.257	.286	11.42	2.60
Cox, J.B.	L-R	6-2	205	5-13-84	5	4	4.75	28	0	0	0	36	30	21	19	3	17	16	.234	.275	.186	4.00	4.25
Giese, Dan	R-R	6-3	195	5-19-77	4	2	1.98	13	10	1	0	59	43	16	13	2	14	51	.201	.149	.242	7.78	2.14
Hall, Bo	R-R	6-0	187	9-5-80	1	0	3.00	3	0	0	0	6	2	2	2	0	4	2	.095	.333	3.00	6.00
Henn, Sean	R-L	6-4	225	4-23-81	1	0	1.35	5	0	0	0	7	5	2	1	0	1	7	.208	.167	.250	9.45	1.35
Horne, Alan	R-R	6-4	195	1-5-83	2	5	5.63	8	8	0	0	32	35	25	20	2	22	24	.278	.328	.231	6.75	6.19
Hughes, Phil	R-R	6-5	230	6-24-86	1	0	5.90	6	6	0	0	29	34	19	19	3	9	31	.281	.331	.167	9.62	2.79
Igawa, Kei	L-L	6-1	210	7-13-79	14	6	3.45	26	24	2	0	156	141	65	60	15	45	117	.241	.277	.224	6.74	2.59
Jackson, Steven	R-R	6-5	215	3-15-82	3	0	3.17	34	1	0	4	48	44	18	17	2	19	54	.246	.227	.264	10.06	3.54
Jones, Jason	R-R	6-5	225	11-20-82	0	1	2.38	2	2	0	0	11	6	3	3	0	1	11	.150	.222	.000	8.74	0.79
Karstens, Jeff	R-R	6-3	185	9-24-82	6	4	3.80	12	12	0	0	69	66	31	29	8	15	55	.256	.266	.243	7.21	1.97
Kennedy, Ian	R-R	6-0	195	12-19-84	5	5	2.35	13	12	0	0	69	52	19	18	4	17	72	.206	.180	.243	9.39	2.22
Kroenke, Zach	R-L	6-3	210	4-21-84	1	0	0.00	1	0	0	0	2	1	0	0	0	2	0	.206	.214	.200	9.00	1.80
Marquez, Jeff	R-R	6-2	190	8-10-84	6	7	4.69	14	14	1	0	81	93	51	42	12	24	33	.300	.271	.329	3.68	2.68
McCutchen, Dan	R-R	6-2	195	9-26-82	4	4	3.58	11	11	2	0	70	73	32	28	10	11	58	.265	.259	.274	7.42	1.41
2-team total (8 Indianapolis)					7	9	4.03	19	19	2	0	118	122	57	53	22	18	99	—	—	—	7.53	1.37
Melancon, Mark	R-R	6-2	215	3-28-85	1	1	2.70	12	0	0	1	20	11	7	6	1	4	22	.162	.100	.211	9.90	1.80
Ohlendorf, Ross	R-R	6-4	235	8-8-82	1	4	4.03	5	5	0	0	22	28	11	10	0	5	25	.301	.327	.273	10.07	2.01
2-team total (7 Indianapolis)					5	4	3.65	12	12	0	0	69	74	29	28	7	13	65	—	—	—	8.48	1.70

ORGANIZATION STATISTICS

Name	B-T	HT	WT	DOB	W	L	ERA	G	GS	CG	SV	IP	H	R	ER	HR	BB	SO	AVG	vLH	vRH	K/9	BB/9
Patterson, Scott	R-R	6-6	230	6-20-79	2	1	3.80	42	0	0	5	47	47	22	20	7	13	54	.258	.289	.232	10.27	2.47
Phillips, Heath	L-L	6-3	200	3-24-82	3	4	5.50	35	4	0	0	56	67	39	34	5	22	43	.303	.268	.331	6.95	3.56
2-team total (9 Durham)					4	5	4.75	44	7	0	0	78	90	46	41	7	33	61	—	—	—	7.07	3.82
Ponson, Sidney	R-R	6-1	260	11-2-76	0	0	2.25	1	1	0	0	4	3	1	0	0	3	2	.214	.250	.167	4.50	6.75
Ramirez, Edwar	R-R	6-3	165	3-28-81	1	0	0.00	8	0	0	0	9	2	0	0	0	1	13	.069	.083	.059	13.00	1.00
Rasner, Darrell	R-R	6-3	210	1-13-81	4	0	0.87	5	5	0	0	31	18	4	3	0	6	27	.170	.246	.082	7.84	1.74
Robertson, David	R-R	5-11	180	4-9-85	4	0	2.06	21	0	0	1	35	20	11	8	1	17	51	.159	.180	.138	13.11	4.37
Strickland, Scott	R-R	5-11	215	4-26-76	4	0	3.53	52	0	0	12	66	50	28	26	7	27	72	.207	.236	.183	9.77	3.66
Traber, Billy	L-L	6-5	205	9-18-79	2	1	3.40	40	2	0	4	48	46	19	18	3	13	41	.250	.253	.247	7.74	2.45
Veras, Jose	R-R	6-5	235	10-20-80	0	0	1.38	13	0	0	9	13	8	3	2	1	4	21	.170	.190	.154	14.54	2.77
White, Steven	R-R	6-4	205	6-15-81	4	4	6.28	25	10	1	0	82	94	64	57	13	43	53	.284	.273	.295	5.84	4.74
Wright, Chase	L-L	6-2	205	2-8-83	2	1	2.41	6	6	0	0	37	27	12	10	1	9	19	.201	.182	.215	4.58	2.17
Zambrano, Victor	B-R	6-0	205	8-6-75	0	1	18.00	1	1	0	0	4	11	8	8	1	3	2	.524	.538	.500	4.50	6.75

Fielding

Catcher

Catcher	PCT	G	PO	A	E	DP	PB
Brown	1.000	7	36	2	0	0	0
Closser	.989	40	240	18	3	1	2
Moeller	1.000	23	202	9	0	2	1
Rodriguez	1.000	1	8	0	0	0	1
Stewart	.986	86	619	71	10	6	9

First Base

First Base	PCT	G	PO	A	E	DP
Betemit	.923	3	12	0	1	1
Broussard	.987	10	72	4	1	4
E. Duncan	1.000	25	200	5	0	17
S. Duncan	1.000	19	155	10	0	11
Lane	.990	12	90	6	1	4
Miranda	.993	78	617	48	5	51
Ransom	.968	4	28	2	1	2

Second Base

Second Base	PCT	G	PO	A	E	DP
Basak	.981	27	37	66	2	10
Betemit	1.000	1	2	0	0	0
Castro	.972	78	126	183	9	33
Gonzalez	.947	8	13	23	2	6
Green	.969	33	48	76	4	14
Nunez	.889	2	5	3	1	1
Ransom	1.000	5	14	16	0	3

Third Base

Third Base	PCT	G	PO	A	E	DP
Basak	1.000	15	10	21	0	1
Betemit	1.000	2	0	1	0	0
E. Duncan	.929	64	42	103	11	8
Gonzalez	.950	5	9	10	1	0
Green	.895	6	1	16	2	0
Kunda	1.000	2	0	1	0	0
Ransom	.959	59	37	102	6	7

Shortstop

Shortstop	PCT	G	PO	A	E	DP
Basak	1.000	2	4	3	0	2
Betemit	.875	1	3	4	1	2
Gonzalez	.948	33	33	76	6	15
Green	.948	63	80	159	13	25
Ransom	.973	49	58	119	5	20

Outfield

Outfield	PCT	G	PO	A	E	DP
Broussard	.957	34	45	0	2	0
Cabrera	1.000	15	32	0	0	0
Carson	1.000	83	176	10	0	3
Christian	.994	70	151	4	1	0
S. Duncan	.957	24	43	1	2	1
Gardner	1.000	93	225	7	0	1
Green	1.000	8	9	1	0	0
Lane	.987	80	143	5	2	1
Porter	.968	45	89	2	3	0

TRENTON THUNDER   DOUBLE-A
EASTERN LEAGUE

Batting	B-T	HT	WT	DOB	AVG	vLH	vRH	G	AB	R	H	2B	3B	HR	RBI	BB	HBP	SH	SF	SO	SB	CS	SLG	OBP
Carson, Matt	R-R	6-2	200	7-1-81	.277	.258	.284	27	112	17	31	7	4	5	26	9	0	1	0	20	1	1	.545	.331
Cervelli, Francisco	R-R	6-1	210	3-6-86	.315	.357	.305	21	73	8	23	5	0	0	8	11	4	0	0	14	0	0	.384	.432
Cooper, James	L-R	5-10	190	2-18-84	.232	.239	.230	52	168	13	39	5	1	0	17	22	3	0	1	28	3	3	.274	.330
Corona, Reegie	R-R	5-11	160	11-7-86	.274	.317	.255	129	457	72	125	27	3	3	39	51	1	7	4	78	24	4	.365	.345
Curtis, Colin	L-L	6-1	200	2-1-85	.255	.177	.287	132	495	68	126	20	3	10	71	55	3	2	7	86	6	3	.368	.329
Ehlers, Cody	L-L	5-11	190	4-16-82	.200	.207	.198	104	370	45	74	26	1	8	43	47	0	1	5	92	0	0	.341	.287
Gonzalez, Edwar	R-R	5-10	200	1-1-83	.295	.311	.289	104	396	58	117	31	0	14	67	20	5	0	5	74	8	5	.480	.333
Ibarra, Walter	B-R	5-11	180	11-1-87	.268	.238	.286	18	56	5	15	3	0	1	5	2	1	1	0	8	0	2	.375	.305
Jackson, Austin	R-R	6-1	185	2-1-87	.285	.293	.282	131	520	75	148	33	5	9	69	56	2	2	4	113	19	6	.419	.354
Malec, Chris	B-R	5-11	195	8-28-82	.291	.231	.316	119	405	65	118	28	3	5	52	68	12	0	2	57	0	2	.412	.407
Mendoza, Carlos	R-R	6-0	191	11-27-79	.280	.278	.282	30	75	10	21	5	1	0	13	14	1	2	1	15	1	1	.373	.396
Muich, Joseph	R-R	6-1	205	8-18-82	.218	.242	.211	45	142	7	31	4	0	0	10	11	2	1	1	42	0	0	.246	.282
Pena, Ramiro	B-R	5-11	160	7-18-85	.266	.269	.265	111	443	57	118	20	7	2	45	41	4	12	6	86	8	6	.357	.330
Pilittere, P.J.	R-R	6-0	215	11-23-81	.277	.336	.251	97	364	46	101	15	1	3	48	20	3	1	4	32	0	1	.349	.317
Rodriguez, Eladio	R-R	5-11	190	4-4-79	.190	.333	.083	6	21	2	4	3	0	0	2	0	0	0	0	6	0	0	.333	.190
Russo, Kevin	R-R	5-11	190	7-8-84	.307	.276	.322	71	267	46	82	17	3	2	33	33	2	3	3	42	8	3	.416	.363
Tabata, Jose	R-R	5-11	160	8-12-88	.248	.333	.213	79	294	40	73	9	0	3	36	26	7	1	4	49	10	2	.310	.320
2-team total (22 Altoona)					.272	—	—	101	383	56	104	15	2	6	49	34	7	1	4	67	18	2	.368	.339
Vechionacci, Marcos	B-R	6-2	170	8-7-86	.302	.250	.324	17	53	8	16	5	0	0	8	0	1	1	0	10	0	0	.396	.387

Pitching	B-T	HT	WT	DOB	W	L	ERA	G	GS	CG	SV	IP	H	R	ER	HR	BB	SO	AVG	vLH	vRH	K/9	BB/9
Aceves, Alfredo	R-R	6-3	220	12-8-82	2	2	1.80	7	7	1	0	50	37	10	10	3	6	35	.213	.217	.210	6.30	1.08
Arias, Wilkins	L-L	6-1	150	11-4-80	0	0	5.93	11	0	0	0	14	14	9	9	1	11	16	.269	.280	.259	10.54	7.24
Bruney, Brian	R-R	6-3	235	2-17-82	0	1	3.86	2	1	0	0	2	2	1	1	0	2	2	.250	.200	.333	7.71	7.71
Claggett, Anthony	B-R	6-2	185	7-15-84	4	2	2.15	29	0	0	9	59	52	17	14	1	30	55	.233	.195	.257	8.44	4.60
Coke, Phil	L-L	6-1	210	7-19-82	9	4	2.51	23	20	1	0	118	105	39	33	7	39	115	.239	.300	.216	8.75	2.97
Cox, J.B.	L-R	6-3	205	5-13-84	0	0	1.35	5	0	0	1	7	3	1	1	0	2	6	.130	.222	.071	8.10	2.70
Dunn, Mike	L-L	6-1	185	5-23-85	1	0	0.00	1	0	0	0	2	1	0	0	0	1	2	.167	1.000	.000	10.80	5.40
Garcia, Christian	R-R	6-4	220	8-24-85	0	0	3.38	1	0	0	0	5	4	2	2	0	6	2	.211	.143	.250	8.44	10.13
Gardner, Michael	R-R	6-0	190	5-23-81	3	5	3.60	33	3	0	5	53	53	38	33	7	41	50	.262	.198	.306	8.49	6.96
Hacker, Eric	B-R	6-1	215	3-26-83	7	4	2.76	17	17	0	0	91	83	33	28	3	28	84	.249	.257	.242	8.28	2.76
Hall, Bo	R-R	6-0	187	9-5-80	2	2	2.93	21	0	0	3	31	24	11	10	5	10	26	.216	.103	.278	7.63	2.93
Jackson, Steven	R-R	6-5	215	3-30-82	3	5	5.74	15	0	0	2	31	28	20	20	2	12	37	.247	.244	.248	10.63	3.45
Jones, Jason	R-R	6-5	225	11-20-82	13	7	3.33	25	25	1	0	149	146	64	55	11	49	91	.258	.227	.280	5.51	2.97
Kontos, George	R-R	6-3	215	6-12-85	6	11	3.68	27	27	0	0	152	134	76	62	14	57	152	.239	.273	.212	9.02	3.38
Kroenke, Zach	R-L	6-1	200	4-21-84	6	0	3.09	37	0	0	1	44	28	16	15	4	26	44	.187	.225	.152	9.07	5.36
Marquez, Jeff	R-R	6-2	190	8-10-84	1	1	2.93	3	3	0	0	15	12	5	5	0	7	12	.218	.176	.237	7.04	4.11
McCutchen, Dan	R-R	6-2	195	9-26-82	4	3	2.55	9	9	0	0	53	43	16	15	4	18	52	.219	.247	.198	8.83	3.06
Melancon, Mark	R-R	6-2	215	3-28-85	6	1	1.81	19	0	0	2	50	32	14	10	3	12	47	.183	.172	.189	8.52	2.17
Nunez, Jhonny	R-R	6-3	185	11-26-85	1	0	1.86	8	0	0	0	19	16	5	4	2	6	26	.229	.219	.237	12.10	2.79
2-team total (5 Harrisburg)					1	0	1.65	13	0	0	0	27	25	6	5	2	12	34	—	—	—	11.20	3.95

	B-T	HT	WT	DOB	W	L	ERA	G	GS	CG	SV	IP	H	R	ER	HR	BB	SO	AVG	vLH	vRH	K/9	BB/9
Pavano, Carl	R-R	6-5	240	1-8-76	1	1	3.86	3	3	0	0	14	14	6	6	3	3	13	.259	.304	.226	8.36	1.93
Perez, Oneli	R-R	6-2	200	5-26-83	2	2	3.48	17	1	0	0	31	21	15	12	3	13	42	.186	.125	.231	12.19	3.77
Robertson, David	R-R	5-11	180	4-9-85	0	0	0.96	9	0	0	2	19	8	2	2	0	6	26	.133	.190	.103	12.54	2.89
Sanchez, Humberto	R-R	6-6	270	5-28-83	0	0	9.00	1	1	0	0	1	2	1	1	0	0	2	.500	.000	1.000	18.00	0.00
Schmidt, Josh	R-R	6-4	175	11-14-82	1	1	3.09	8	0	0	0	12	11	7	4	2	7	8	.256	.154	.300	6.17	5.40
Stephens, Jason	R-R	6-5	200	10-10-84	0	0	3.38	1	1	0	0	5	3	2	2	1	2	9	.150	.182	.111	15.19	3.38
Valdez, Jose	R-R	6-4	186	1-22-83	1	0	2.22	17	0	0	4	24	17	7	6	4	7	23	.195	.316	.102	8.51	2.59
Whelan, Kevin	R-R	6-0	200	1-8-84	2	0	4.35	15	0	0	1	21	13	10	10	2	15	27	.176	.037	.255	11.76	6.53
White, Steven	R-R	6-4	205	6-15-81	0	1	5.59	3	3	0	0	10	8	8	6	1	5	10	.216	.333	.105	4.66	10.24
Wordekemper, Eric	R-R	6-1	200	8-8-83	3	2	3.93	33	1	0	6	50	59	25	22	6	26	46	.286	.288	.286	8.23	4.65
Wright, Chase	L-L	6-2	205	2-8-83	8	2	2.96	16	16	0	0	94	84	36	31	5	34	53	.240	.271	.224	5.06	3.24
Zambrano, Victor	B-R	6-0	205	8-6-75	2	0	0.75	2	2	0	0	12	7	1	1	1	2	11	.167	.300	.125	8.25	1.50

Fielding

Catcher	PCT	G	PO	A	E	DP	PB								
Cervelli	.994	16	146	9	1	3	1
Muich	.984	44	343	24	6	3	8
Pilittere	.992	80	605	41	5	3	3
Rodriguez	1.000	5	37	2	0	0	3

First Base	PCT	G	PO	A	E	DP
Ehlers	.991	99	803	69	8	94
Malec	.985	41	300	28	5	36
Mendoza	1.000	3	12	2	0	1
Pilittere	.968	5	26	4	1	3

Second Base	PCT	G	PO	A	E	DP
Corona	.994	99	206	268	3	68

	PCT	G	PO	A	E	DP
Ibarra	.952	9	21	19	2	6
Malec	1.000	1	5	3	0	1
Mendoza	.778	2	3	4	2	0
Russo	.988	33	67	101	2	25

Third Base	PCT	G	PO	A	E	DP
Ehlers	—	1	0	0	0	0
Gonzalez	1.000	1	1	0	0	0
Ibarra	.938	6	6	9	1	0
Malec	.926	77	30	145	14	18
Mendoza	.950	21	6	32	2	3
Muich	—	1	0	0	0	0
Russo	.904	27	13	53	7	5
Vechionacci	.914	17	6	26	3	4

Shortstop	PCT	G	PO	A	E	DP
Corona	.938	30	53	82	9	28
Ibarra	.857	3	3	3	1	0
Pena	.955	111	154	288	21	67

Outfield	PCT	G	PO	A	E	DP
Carson	.973	13	33	3	1	1
Cooper	1.000	38	64	0	0	0
Curtis	.973	117	209	7	6	1
Gonzalez	.987	70	140	8	2	1
Jackson	.987	113	217	7	3	1
Malec	.500	2	1	0	1	0
Russo	1.000	6	7	0	0	0
Tabata	.976	67	117	3	3	2

TAMPA YANKEES   HIGH CLASS A

FLORIDA STATE LEAGUE

Batting	B-T	HT	WT	DOB	AVG	vLH	vRH	G	AB	R	H	2B	3B	HR	RBI	BB	HBP	SH	SF	SO	SB	CS	SLG	OBP
Anson, Kyle	B-R	6-0	200	4-21-83	.241	.226	.246	68	224	27	54	11	1	4	25	44	1	2	1	35	1	3	.353	.367
Baker, Ryan J.	R-R	5-9	205	11-9-84	.143	.000	.250	2	7	0	1	0	0	0	0	0	0	0	0	1	0	0	.143	.143
Baker, Ryan M.	R-R	5-11	190	11-6-83	.000	.000	.000	1	2	0	0	0	0	0	0	0	0	0	0	1	0	0	.000	.000
Baldridge, Tommy	L-L	6-1	195	8-18-86	.253	.087	.327	26	75	13	19	3	0	0	6	12	1	0	1	13	2	0	.293	.360
Battle, Tim	R-R	6-2	185	9-10-85	.254	.257	.252	108	355	53	90	16	8	11	37	17	3	6	0	118	18	6	.437	.293
Blumenthal, Ben	R-R	6-2	210	4-24-83	.207	.250	.176	10	29	6	6	2	0	1	6	5	0	0	0	7	0	0	.379	.324
Calzado, Josue	R-R	6-1	160	11-6-85	.179	.227	.164	50	184	20	33	7	3	4	20	10	7	0	1	42	10	1	.315	.248
Cervelli, Francisco	R-R	6-1	210	3-6-86	.300	1.000	.222	3	10	2	3	0	0	0	1	0	1	0	0	3	0	0	.300	.364
Chavez, Brian	R-R	6-2	190	3-23-86	.000	.000	.000	1	3	0	0	0	0	0	0	0	0	0	0	1	0	0	.000	.000
Cooper, James	L-R	5-10	190	2-18-84	.311	.218	.339	66	241	32	75	15	1	1	22	19	15	1	3	25	7	3	.394	.392
Cox, Danny	L-R	6-1	180	7-10-86	.000	.000	.000	2	8	0	0	0	0	0	0	0	0	0	0	2	0	0	.000	.000
Cusick, Matt	L-R	5-10	190	5-5-86	.174	.125	.200	7	23	1	4	0	0	0	2	2	1	0	0	2	0	0	.174	.269
Fortenberry, Seth	L-L	6-2	175	9-1-83	.263	.239	.272	119	399	50	105	18	7	12	46	64	6	2	2	125	9	5	.434	.372
Gil, Jose	R-R	6-0	170	9-4-86	.240	.310	.204	73	246	17	59	17	0	1	25	14	4	4	2	41	8	4	.321	.289
Gomez, Roy	R-R	5-11	160	1-7-85	.091	.200	.000	3	11	0	1	1	0	0	0	0	0	0	0	3	0	0	.182	.091
Gonzalez, Edwar	R-R	5-10	200	1-1-83	.279	.158	.304	27	111	18	31	11	1	6	18	5	2	0	1	18	3	1	.559	.319
Henry, C.J.	R-R	6-3	205	5-31-86	.234	.217	.244	20	64	7	15	2	0	2	6	5	3	0	0	24	3	2	.359	.319
Hilligoss, Mitch	L-R	6-1	195	6-17-85	.241	.230	.246	121	456	47	110	23	0	1	31	31	0	7	4	61	17	9	.298	.287
Kreuzer, Josh	R-R	6-6	245	9-28-82	.235	.184	.252	45	149	17	35	8	0	2	19	22	5	0	1	39	3	1	.329	.350
Kunda, Chris	R-R	6-1	175	11-1-84	.145	.143	.146	45	131	10	19	3	0	0	12	9	1	1	3	35	1	3	.168	.201
Matsui, Hideki	L-R	6-2	210	6-12-74	.250	.333	.200	3	8	1	2	0	0	1	1	2	0	0	0	0	0	0	.625	.400
Nunez, Eduardo	R-R	6-0	155	6-15-87	.271	.269	.271	94	373	45	101	18	3	6	42	19	1	5	4	48	14	10	.383	.305
Nunez, Luis	R-R	5-11	160	11-21-86	.280	.301	.272	110	415	49	116	17	2	3	40	25	1	7	4	40	16	6	.352	.319
Perez, Andres	R-R	6-0	200	5-23-84	.269	.304	.254	86	316	38	85	20	2	8	44	18	3	2	2	58	8	6	.421	.313
Pruitt, Braedyn	L-R	6-2	205	3-23-85	.100	.000	.121	12	40	2	4	1	0	0	2	8	0	0	0	6	0	0	.125	.250
Rodriguez, Eladio	R-R	5-11	190	4-4-79	.095	.167	.000	7	21	3	2	0	0	0	2	0	0	0	0	9	0	1	.095	.174
Smith, Kevin	L-R	6-1	215	1-15-84	.290	.237	.309	124	445	51	129	35	1	5	62	32	2	0	4	93	7	5	.407	.337
Sublett, Damon	L-R	6-1	190	9-22-85	.263	.229	.272	42	160	22	42	6	3	2	11	24	2	1	1	44	3	1	.375	.364

Pitching	B-T	HT	WT	DOB	W	L	ERA	G	GS	CG	SV	IP	H	R	ER	HR	BB	SO	AVG	vLH	vRH	K/9	BB/9
Aceves, Alfredo	R-R	6-3	220	12-8-82	4	1	2.11	8	8	0	0	47	32	16	11	1	8	37	.188	.154	.203	7.09	1.53
Arias, Wilkins	L-L	6-1	150	11-4-80	4	0	2.61	29	0	0	1	48	46	16	14	1	14	64	.245	.148	.291	11.92	2.61
Artz, Stephen	R-R	6-2	200	4-23-84	1	2	3.05	13	0	0	0	21	23	10	7	2	2	6	.295	.278	.310	2.61	0.87
Bartleski, Philip	R-R	6-7	240	4-22-83	2	1	1.64	29	0	0	1	55	34	10	10	2	26	60	.179	.176	.181	9.82	4.25
Castillo, Noel	R-R	6-1	160	10-5-83	1	0	1.50	1	1	0	0	6	6	1	1	0	2	7	.250	.375	.188	10.50	3.00
Claggett, Anthony	B-R	6-2	185	7-15-84	0	0	3.00	1	0	0	0	3	4	1	1	0	3	3	.400	.333	.429	9.00	0.00
Cox, J.B.	L-R	6-3	205	5-13-84	0	0	3.00	6	0	0	1	6	8	2	2	0	2	2	.320	.286	.333	3.00	3.00
De La Rosa, Wilkins	L-L	6-1	185	2-21-85	2	1	1.10	3	3	0	0	16	12	4	2	0	5	15	.200	.200	.200	8.27	2.76
Duff, Grant	R-R	6-6	210	12-19-82	3	4	4.30	30	8	0	2	82	73	42	39	2	35	64	.243	.263	.231	7.05	3.86
Dunn, Mike	L-L	6-1	185	5-23-85	4	4	4.55	30	22	0	1	125	124	70	63	10	58	118	.266	.248	.273	8.52	4.19
Garcia, Christian	R-R	6-4	220	8-24-85	4	2	2.90	10	10	0	0	50	45	20	16	2	17	60	.241	.217	.260	10.87	3.08
Hacker, Eric	R-R	6-1	215	3-26-83	2	2	1.87	9	9	0	0	53	38	14	11	1	9	31	.205	.221	.191	5.26	1.53
Henn, Sean	R-L	6-4	225	4-23-81	0	0	0.00	3	0	0	0	4	5	0	0	0	1	5	.313	.000	.333	11.25	0.00
Hoover, Jesse	R-R	6-3	210	1-8-82	0	0	4.50	6	0	0	0	12	14	6	6	2	6	6	.292	.263	.310	4.50	4.50
Horne, Alan	R-R	6-4	195	1-5-83	0	1	23.14	3	3	0	0	7	21	18	18	4	5	6	.553	.550	.556	7.71	6.43
Hovis, Jonathan	R-R	5-11	185	12-27-83	2	1	1.14	21	0	0	10	24	13	3	3	2	3	24	.155	.148	.158	9.13	1.14

Name	B-T	HT	WT	DOB	W	L	ERA	G	GS	CG	SV	IP	H	R	ER	HR	BB	SO	AVG	vLH	vRH	K/9	BB/9
Kennedy, Ian	R-R	6-0	195	12-19-84	0	0	0.00	1	1	0	0	5	2	0	0	0	1	4	.118	.200	.000	7.20	1.80
Marte, Ronny	R-R	6-1	173	2-26-86	1	1	6.75	4	1	0	0	8	11	7	6	1	2	5	.314	.375	.263	5.63	2.25
McAllister, Zach	R-R	6-6	230	12-8-87	8	6	1.83	15	14	1	1	89	74	24	18	6	13	62	.225	.231	.220	6.29	1.32
Melancon, Mark	R-R	6-2	215	3-28-85	1	0	2.84	13	0	0	0	25	26	9	8	2	6	20	.265	.200	.302	7.11	2.13
Nova, Ivan	R-R	6-4	210	1-12-87	8	13	4.36	26	24	0	0	149	168	81	72	6	46	109	.294	.322	.275	6.60	2.78
Obradovich, Mike	R-R	6-0	185	9-26-85	0	0	0.00	1	0	0	0	1	0	0	0	0	0	3	.000	.000	.000	27.00	0.00
Perez, Kelvin	R-R	6-1	140	10-10-85	0	0	9.00	1	0	0	0	1	3	1	1	0	3	0	.500	.333	.667	0.00	27.00
Pope, Ryan	R-R	6-3	200	5-21-86	7	7	4.15	20	20	1	0	104	114	57	48	8	22	72	.281	.316	.260	6.23	1.90
Sanchez, Humberto	R-R	6-6	270	5-28-83	0	1	9.00	2	2	0	0	2	3	2	2	0	1	2	.333	.500	.000	9.00	4.50
Schmidt, Josh	R-R	6-4	175	11-14-82	0	2	2.41	30	0	0	16	37	30	10	10	1	14	41	.226	.346	.148	9.88	3.38
Selenes, Josue	R-R	6-0	180	10-8-85	1	1	2.84	4	0	0	1	6	5	2	2	0	3	5	.227	.571	.067	7.11	4.26
Semerano, Rob	R-R	6-1	185	7-18-81	4	1	5.09	22	0	0	0	35	50	26	20	2	11	19	.331	.300	.358	4.84	2.80
Solbach, Michael	R-R	6-3	185	7-31-85	0	0	4.50	1	1	0	0	2	1	1	1	0	0	0	.000	.000	.333	0.00	0.00
Soto, Edgar	L-L	5-11	175	12-28-84	3	3	4.34	30	2	0	1	64	77	42	31	3	34	61	.292	.325	.278	8.53	4.76
Stephens, Jason	R-R	6-5	200	10-10-84	3	5	4.47	11	8	0	0	48	69	30	24	0	18	33	.347	.373	.320	6.14	3.35
Valdez, Jose	R-R	6-4	186	1-22-83	6	2	2.75	27	0	0	3	36	30	13	11	4	9	32	.231	.295	.198	8.00	2.25
Whelan, Kevin	R-R	6-0	200	1-8-84	1	0	4.67	9	0	0	1	17	11	9	9	0	14	19	.186	.167	.200	9.87	7.27
Wordekemper, Eric	R-R	6-1	200	8-8-83	0	0	10.80	2	0	0	0	2	5	4	2	0	0	0	.455	.000	.625	0.00	0.00

Fielding

Catcher	PCT	G	PO	A	E	DP	PB
Anson	.990	65	457	47	5	2	13
R. J. Baker	1.000	2	12	2	0	0	0
R. M. Baker	1.000	1	4	1	0	0	0
Blumenthal	1.000	5	30	5	0	1	3
Cervelli	1.000	3	18	4	0	0	3
Gil	.992	60	425	51	4	5	6
Rodriguez	1.000	7	40	7	0	0	0

First Base	PCT	G	PO	A	E	DP
Blumenthal	1.000	2	11	1	0	2
Gil	1.000	8	61	6	0	4
Kreuzer	1.000	12	82	6	0	5
Kunda	—	1	0	0	0	0
L. Nunez	1.000	2	23	2	0	2
Pruitt	1.000	3	34	2	0	2

	PCT	G	PO	A	E	DP
Smith	.994	113	989	65	6	114

Second Base	PCT	G	PO	A	E	DP
Cox	1.000	1	3	1	0	0
Cusick	1.000	7	12	12	0	3
Gomez	1.000	3	4	7	0	0
Kunda	.970	35	63	96	5	20
L. Nunez	.973	62	119	169	8	55
Sublett	.937	39	65	114	12	25

Third Base	PCT	G	PO	A	E	DP
Cox	1.000	1	1	2	0	1
Hilligoss	.950	120	72	212	15	27
Kunda	1.000	2	0	4	0	2
L. Nunez	1.000	8	5	19	0	3
Pruitt	.913	8	8	13	2	1

Shortstop	PCT	G	PO	A	E	DP
Chavez	1.000	1	1	1	0	0
Kunda	.938	7	13	17	2	3
E. Nunez	.952	92	113	267	19	68
L. Nunez	.955	42	60	109	8	22

Outfield	PCT	G	PO	A	E	DP
Baldridge	1.000	25	35	3	0	0
Battle	.989	101	180	6	2	1
Calzado	.943	44	93	7	6	4
Cooper	1.000	47	74	5	0	0
Fortenberry	.993	117	271	1	2	0
Gonzalez	.955	12	19	2	1	0
Henry	1.000	16	26	0	0	0
L. Nunez	—	1	0	0	0	0
Perez	.990	55	92	3	1	1

CHARLESTON RIVERDOGS   LOW CLASS A
SOUTH ATLANTIC LEAGUE

Batting	B-T	HT	WT	DOB	AVG	vLH	vRH	G	AB	R	H	2B	3B	HR	RBI	BB	HBP	SH	SF	SO	SB	CS	SLG	OBP
Almonte, Abraham	B-R	5-9	205	6-27-89	.228	.183	.249	115	443	61	101	20	7	8	46	47	1	3	1	101	29	10	.359	.303
Angelini, Carmen	R-R	6-2	185	9-22-88	.236	.227	.240	134	474	64	112	14	1	4	46	42	4	1	3	99	17	6	.295	.302
Baisley, Brian	R-R	6-3	223	12-19-82	.252	.294	.235	33	115	20	29	10	0	5	15	9	4	0	2	33	0	0	.470	.323
Cox, Danny	L-R	6-1	180	7-10-86	.200	.500	.154	9	15	1	3	0	0	0	1	5	0	0	0	3	0	0	.200	.400
Cuello, Prilys	B-R	5-11	168	11-17-88	.239	.258	.230	31	92	10	22	3	1	1	9	9	1	0	0	27	3	3	.326	.314
Day, Larry	R-R	6-0	210	3-22-85	.067	.000	.111	7	15	4	1	1	0	0	2	1	2	0	1	3	0	0	.133	.211
Holiday, Taylor	R-R	5-11	190	4-21-84	.215	.300	.180	59	172	20	37	8	0	2	29	13	8	1	6	48	9	2	.297	.291
Hollingsworth, D.J.	L-L	5-9	175	5-28-85	.500	.000	.500	2	2	0	1	0	0	0	0	1	0	0	0	0	0	0	.500	.500
Ibarra, Walter	B-R	5-11	180	11-1-87	.198	.167	.213	27	91	13	18	6	1	1	13	6	0	0	0	16	1	0	.319	.247
Krum, Austin	L-L	6-0	190	1-19-86	.272	.272	.272	131	459	74	125	21	6	8	67	55	7	3	4	92	12	7	.397	.356
Laird, Brandon	R-R	6-1	215	9-11-87	.273	.257	.281	122	454	71	124	31	1	23	86	40	5	0	7	86	1	0	.498	.334
Montero, Jesus	R-R	6-4	225	11-28-89	.326	.306	.334	132	525	86	171	34	1	17	87	37	6	0	1	83	2	1	.491	.376
Morris, Matt	R-R	6-1	180	2-10-85	.129	.222	.091	15	31	3	4	2	0	0	1	2	2	1	0	13	1	1	.194	.229
Nutt, Jeff	L-R	5-11	200	4-22-85	.333	.000	.364	8	12	0	4	1	0	0	1	1	0	0	0	5	0	0	.417	.385
Odenreider, Chase	R-R	6-1	209	8-19-85	.061	.167	.037	12	33	3	2	0	0	1	2	3	1	0	0	8	1	0	.152	.162
Pruitt, Braedyn	L-R	6-2	205	3-23-85	.288	.750	.255	17	59	9	17	0	0	0	1	8	0	0	0	7	0	0	.288	.373
Romine, Austin	R-R	6-2	210	11-22-88	.300	.325	.289	104	407	66	122	24	1	10	49	25	3	0	1	56	3	0	.437	.344
Rufino, Wady	R-R	6-2	220	4-8-85	.259	.213	.292	31	112	18	29	6	0	5	20	8	4	0	1	27	0	0	.446	.328
Snyder, Justin	L-R	5-9	190	4-8-86	.288	.297	.283	132	504	77	145	33	3	7	59	68	2	4	6	95	7	1	.407	.371
Suttle, Bradley	B-R	6-2	215	1-24-86	.271	.237	.285	96	377	63	102	23	7	11	44	45	2	0	4	93	2	1	.456	.348
Weems, Chase	L-R	6-2	170	1-17-89	.143	.000	.250	5	7	1	1	0	0	0	4	1	0	0	0	2	0	0	.143	.250
Williams, Dave	R-R	6-3	210	8-15-84	.249	.261	.244	104	338	41	84	14	4	6	48	32	5	5	2	77	4	4	.367	.321

Pitching	B-T	HT	WT	DOB	W	L	ERA	G	GS	CG	SV	IP	H	R	ER	HR	BB	SO	AVG	vLH	vRH	K/9	BB/9
Artz, Stephen	R-R	6-2	200	4-23-84	3	0	4.02	16	0	0	0	31	44	17	14	2	5	28	.331	.294	.354	8.04	1.44
Asselin, Nick	R-R	6-0	200	1-19-85	0	0	7.71	1	0	0	0	2	3	2	2	0	0	2	.300	.250	.333	7.71	0.00
Betances, Dellin	R-R	6-8	245	3-23-88	9	4	3.67	22	22	0	0	115	87	57	47	9	59	135	.208	.165	.239	10.53	4.60
Castillo, Noel	R-R	6-1	160	10-5-83	7	8	3.90	25	21	1	0	127	115	64	55	6	44	119	.239	.210	.261	8.43	3.12
Chigges, Nick	R-R	6-0	195	9-23-84	0	0	3.18	4	0	0	0	6	4	2	2	0	3	4	.200	.250	.167	6.35	4.76
De La Rosa, Wilkins	L-L	6-1	185	2-21-85	7	3	2.29	29	8	0	0	90	60	31	23	2	39	110	.189	.182	.191	10.96	3.89
Erickson, Casey	R-R	6-3	187	8-28-85	1	1	6.23	3	0	0	0	4	7	3	3	2	0	5	.300	.500	.286	10.38	0.00
Heredia, Jairo	R-R	6-1	190	10-8-89	6	7	3.25	21	21	0	0	102	99	58	37	7	43	95	.249	.258	.242	8.36	3.78
Heyer, Craig	R-R	6-3	205	11-15-85	7	1	2.08	41	1	0	1	86	78	25	20	3	15	51	.237	.169	.281	5.32	1.56
Hoover, Jesse	R-R	6-3	210	1-8-82	4	3	3.44	30	0	0	0	55	52	26	21	2	25	44	.252	.282	.231	7.20	4.09
Hughes, Phil	R-R	6-5	230	6-24-86	2	0	0.00	2	0	0	0	7	3	0	0	0	2	6	.136	.125	.143	8.10	2.70
Kapala, Daniel	R-R	6-5	220	9-6-85	0	0	0.00	1	0	0	0	2	4	2	0	0	1	0	.400	.750	.167	0.00	5.40
McAllister, Zach	R-R	6-6	230	12-8-87	6	3	2.45	10	10	0	0	62	59	28	17	3	8	53	.245	.306	.203	7.65	1.16
Medina, Gabriel	R-R	6-5	235	2-17-84	0	0	5.29	25	0	0	0	48	59	34	28	4	16	30	.303	.296	.307	5.66	3.02

	B-T	HT	WT	DOB	W	L	ERA	G	GS	CG	SV	IP	H	R	ER	HR	BB	SO	AVG	vLH	vRH	K/9	BB/9
Olbrychowski, Adam	R-R	6-3	205	9-7-86	7	8	5.13	22	19	0	1	98	112	69	56	9	41	72	.288	.300	.278	6.59	3.75
Ortiz, Jonathan	R-R	5-10	170	10-29-85	4	2	2.03	57	0	0	33	62	48	21	14	2	13	87	.206	.242	.179	12.63	1.89
Pavano, Carl	R-R	6-5	240	1-8-76	0	0	1.80	2	2	0	0	5	6	1	1	0	1	6	.300	.333	.273	10.80	1.80
Pendleton, Lance	L-R	6-3	205	9-10-83	7	9	3.52	28	23	0	0	128	136	62	50	3	46	119	.270	.300	.249	8.37	3.23
Reyes, Angel	L-L	5-11	170	1-8-87	0	0	11.74	7	0	0	0	8	15	10	10	2	4	11	.385	.300	.414	12.91	4.70
Stephens, Jason	R-R	6-5	200	10-10-84	2	3	3.02	17	8	0	1	60	67	21	20	5	10	52	.279	.320	.248	7.84	1.51
Vacek, Chase	R-R	6-1	200	8-12-83	5	6	3.79	54	0	0	8	71	67	39	30	2	24	51	.249	.259	.242	6.43	3.03
Zink, Ryan	R-R	6-5	230	4-1-85	3	2	2.42	25	4	0	1	52	43	16	14	3	14	43	.224	.295	.175	7.44	2.42

Fielding

Catcher	PCT	G	PO	A	E	DP	PB
Baisley	1.000	10	73	1	0	0	2
Day	1.000	7	36	1	0	0	0
Montero	.993	71	529	55	4	3	11
Nutt	1.000	8	31	0	0	0	0
Romine	.988	54	428	53	6	0	18
Weems	1.000	5	18	2	0	0	1

First Base	PCT	G	PO	A	E	DP
Baisley	.995	19	190	11	1	13
Holiday	1.000	6	44	1	0	6
Laird	.993	88	765	48	6	66
Odenreider	.923	3	10	2	1	0
Pruitt	1.000	9	77	3	0	7
Rufino	.978	19	167	11	4	11
Snyder	1.000	3	23	2	0	3

Second Base	PCT	G	PO	A	E	DP
Cox	—	1	0	0	0	0
Cuello	.889	12	15	25	5	5
Ibarra	.974	7	18	20	1	7
Snyder	.961	124	216	393	25	77

Third Base	PCT	G	PO	A	E	DP
Cox	1.000	1	1	0	0	0
Ibarra	.917	5	1	10	1	1
Laird	.934	33	22	63	6	5
Odenreider	.750	1	0	3	1	1
Pruitt	1.000	8	4	11	0	0
Snyder	1.000	2	1	2	0	1
Suttle	.935	92	53	193	17	19

Shortstop	PCT	G	PO	A	E	DP
Angelini	.926	131	182	340	42	65

	PCT	G	PO	A	E	DP
Cox	.857	2	2	4	1	1
Ibarra	.941	7	8	24	2	4
Snyder	.778	2	5	2	2	1

Outfield	PCT	G	PO	A	E	DP
Almonte	.964	110	181	9	7	0
Cuello	.875	17	14	0	2	0
Holiday	.983	47	57	1	1	0
Hollingsworth	1.000	2	1	0	0	0
Ibarra	1.000	7	9	1	0	0
Krum	.958	130	220	8	10	3
Morris	.933	12	14	0	1	0
Odenreider	.750	3	3	0	1	0
Rufino	1.000	9	13	0	0	0
Snyder	—	1	0	0	0	0
Williams	.973	101	170	9	5	2

STATEN ISLAND YANKEES · SHORT-SEASON

NEW YORK-PENN LEAGUE

Batting	B-T	HT	WT	DOB	AVG	vLH	vRH	G	AB	R	H	2B	3B	HR	RBI	BB	HBP	SH	SF	SO	SB	CS	SLG	OBP
Abeita, Mitch	R-R	6-0	185	4-7-86	.250	.182	.273	53	172	21	43	10	2	1	19	25	3	1	1	45	0	0	.349	.353
Adams, David	R-R	6-2	190	5-15-87	.257	.277	.247	67	257	45	66	19	2	4	31	32	6	0	2	57	8	2	.393	.350
Baisley, Brian	R-R	6-3	223	12-19-82	.336	.246	.373	58	226	31	76	15	1	6	50	15	6	0	4	44	0	1	.491	.386
Blumenthal, Ben	R-R	6-2	210	4-24-83	.250	.143	.308	10	20	3	5	2	0	0	1	2	0	3	0	5	0	0	.350	.318
Brewer, Dan	R-R	6-0	185	7-19-87	.296	.275	.307	66	230	29	68	19	1	3	40	21	8	1	2	65	10	1	.426	.372
Castro, Kelvin	R-R	6-3	164	12-14-87	.000	.000	.000	9	26	2	0	0	0	0	1	1	0	1	0	11	0	0	.000	.037
Chavez, Brian	R-R	6-2	190	3-23-86	.276	.250	.286	9	29	3	8	3	0	0	4	0	0	0	0	11	0	0	.379	.276
Cuello, Prilys	B-R	5-11	168	11-17-88	.400	.000	.500	3	5	1	2	2	0	0	2	0	0	0	0	2	0	0	.800	.400
Gomez, Roy	R-R	5-11	160	1-7-85	.219	.333	.150	11	32	5	7	2	0	0	3	6	0	0	1	4	0	0	.281	.333
Grote, Taylor	L-R	6-2	195	12-5-88	.223	.222	.224	56	188	23	42	6	1	3	20	24	0	1	1	73	2	2	.314	.310
Hollingsworth, D.J.	L-L	5-9	175	5-28-85	.333	—	.333	5	9	2	3	0	0	0	1	0	1	1		2	1	0	.333	.300
Ibarra, Walter	B-R	5-11	180	11-1-87	.224	.208	.240	12	49	10	11	3	0	2	6	2	0	1	0	7	2	1	.408	.255
Kruml, Ray	L-R	5-11	175	8-5-85	.294	.175	.333	65	231	42	68	15	2	0	24	16	4	1	2	65	13	4	.377	.348
Lovett, Erik	L-L	6-1	180	8-22-85	.273	.167	.302	23	55	7	15	5	0	3	11	3	0	0	1	20	0	0	.527	.305
Lyon, Mike	R-R	6-2	220	8-13-86	.268	.329	.233	61	205	32	55	11	2	6	27	29	2	0	2	54	6	0	.429	.361
Maruszak, Addison	R-R	6-1	195	12-21-86	.317	.341	.310	44	167	30	53	9	2	6	25	14	1	1	1	25	5	1	.503	.372
Mesa, Melky	R-R	6-1	165	1-31-87	.221	.264	.188	46	122	19	27	5	2	7	23	4	1	1	0	38	4	1	.467	.252
Morris, Matt	R-R	6-1	180	2-10-85	.333	.500	.286	9	6	9	1	3	1	0	0	2	2	1	0	1	3	2	.444	.462
Nutt, Jeff	R-R	5-11	200	4-22-85	.000	.000	.000	2	3	1	0	0	0	0	0	1	0	0	0	1	0	0	.000	.250
Pruitt, Braedyn	L-R	6-2	205	3-23-85	.222	.152	.250	36	117	15	26	4	1	0	12	15	1	2	3	15	1	0	.274	.309
Rye, Jack	L-L	6-1	200	3-8-86	.276	.217	.298	49	170	26	47	10	1	2	17	18	0	1	2	31	3	3	.382	.342
Santamaria, Jahdiel	R-R	6-3	170	4-5-87	.250	.163	.296	50	124	23	31	8	2	0	13	11	1	2	1	24	3	3	.347	.314
Strausbaugh, Steven	R-R	5-9	200	11-4-85	.209	.100	.304	18	43	5	9	1	0	1	6	6	0	0	1	8	0	0	.302	.300
Vechionacci, Marcos	B-R	6-2	170	8-7-86	.440	.429	.444	7	25	2	11	1	0	0	7	0	0	0	0	2	0	0	.480	.440
Wilkes, Ryan	B-R	5-11	190	8-22-85	.227	.200	.235	8	22	2	5	0	0	0	1	4	0	0	1	8	0	0	.227	.333

Pitching	B-T	HT	WT	DOB	W	L	ERA	G	GS	CG	SV	IP	H	R	ER	HR	BB	SO	AVG	vLH	vRH	K/9	BB/9
Albaladejo, Jonathan	R-R	6-5	260	10-30-82	0	0	0.00	2	2	0	0	4	3	0	0	0	0	4	.214	.300	.000	9.00	0.00
Arbiso, Cory	R-R	6-3	185	4-21-86	0	2	4.18	8	7	0	0	28	33	17	13	2	4	20	.297	.321	.273	6.43	1.29
Asselin, Nick	R-R	6-0	200	1-19-85	1	1	4.07	14	1	0	0	24	20	11	11	2	2	22	.217	.132	.278	8.14	0.74
Bleich, Jeremy	L-L	6-2	195	6-18-87	0	0	6.00	1	1	0	0	3	2	2	2	1	0	4	.182	.333	.125	12.00	0.00
Braboy, Brandon	R-R	6-0	195	10-31-85	2	3	3.21	10	10	0	0	42	42	20	15	2	18	31	.263	.169	.326	6.64	3.86
Dennehy, Tim	L-L	6-1	195	9-22-86	2	1	3.68	16	0	0	0	22	24	12	9	1	5	16	.286	.351	.234	6.55	2.05
Erickson, Casey	R-R	6-3	187	8-28-85	5	1	2.76	16	15	0	0	75	82	31	23	2	17	77	.275	.360	.204	9.24	2.04
Gonell, Jacinto	R-R	6-1	165	9-9-83	4	1	4.05	17	0	0	0	27	21	12	12	1	14	23	.216	.286	.164	7.76	4.73
Greinke, Luke	R-R	6-1	195	6-14-86	0	4	4.01	9	9	0	0	34	31	20	15	2	17	26	.248	.237	.258	6.95	4.54
Kapala, Daniel	R-R	6-5	220	9-6-85	2	2	2.10	15	0	0	0	26	16	9	6	0	9	18	.180	.220	.146	6.31	3.16
Kiley, Jason	R-R	6-5	235	6-14-85	2	1	4.24	20	0	0	1	34	42	19	16	2	3	21	.294	.279	.305	5.56	0.79
Montgomery, Nick	R-R	6-2	218	8-28-84	1	1	4.33	9	0	0	0	35	40	25	17	5	9	17	.282	.320	.261	6.88	2.29
Noesi, Hector	R-R	6-2	174	1-26-87	1	1	3.00	5	5	0	0	24	20	12	8	5	7	31	.227	.257	.208	11.63	2.63
Obradovich, Mike	R-R	6-0	185	9-26-85	2	0	3.71	11	0	0	0	17	15	7	7	1	3	18	.234	.208	.250	9.53	1.59
Phelps, David	R-R	6-2	180	10-9-86	3	2	2.72	15	15	0	0	73	67	26	22	3	10	52	.245	.266	.230	6.44	2.23
Rulon, Brad	L-R	5-11	186	6-22-86	2	2	0.41	28	0	0	4	44	21	2	2	1	20	68	.142	.167	.125	13.91	4.09
Selenes, Josue	R-R	6-0	180	10-8-85	5	1	2.48	20	0	0	2	29	22	8	8	0	11	28	.216	.175	.242	8.69	3.41
Shafer, Jake	R-R	6-4	215	10-11-85	0	0	—	1	0	0	0	3	2	2	2	0	0	0	.000	.000	.000	—	—
Shetrone, Drew	R-R	6-2	185	9-18-84	2	2	2.41	22	0	0	0	41	39	19	11	2	10	46	.247	.279	.227	10.10	2.20
Shive, Andrew	R-R	6-6	260	11-5-85	9	2	1.96	22	1	0	0	46	42	15	10	0	17	50	.250	.301	.211	9.78	3.33
Venditte, Pat	R-R	6-1	180	6-30-85	1	0	0.83	30	0	0	23	33	13	5	3	2	10	42	.117	.089	.136	11.57	2.76

Fielding

Catcher

	PCT	G	PO	A	E	DP	PB
Abeita	.987	51	404	42	6	3	5
Baisley	.994	16	145	15	1	2	2
Blumenthal	.985	10	58	7	1	0	0
Nutt	.900	2	8	1	1	0	0
Strausbaugh	.958	6	17	6	1	1	1

First Base

	PCT	G	PO	A	E	DP
Baisley	.985	28	231	26	4	23
Lovett	.985	18	129	6	2	12
Pruitt	.986	9	66	4	1	6
Santamaria	.972	41	228	19	7	13

Second Base

	PCT	G	PO	A	E	DP
Adams	.975	67	113	194	8	41
Chavez	1.000	4	3	3	0	1
Gomez	1.000	2	2	5	0	0
Wilkes	1.000	6	4	16	0	1

Third Base

	PCT	G	PO	A	E	DP
Brewer	1.000	1	0	1	0	0
Chavez	1.000	2	0	3	0	0
Lyon	.896	52	3	89	14	8
Pruitt	.864	23	9	42	8	4
Vechionacci	.938	7	6	9	1	0

Shortstop

	PCT	G	PO	A	E	DP
Castro	.833	9	7	18	5	1
Chavez	.933	3	6	8	1	4
Gomez	.973	9	15	21	1	5
Ibarra	.911	12	21	30	5	7
Lyon	1.000	1	3	0	0	0
Maruszak	.969	43	69	121	6	26
Wilkes	.818	2	5	4	2	1

Outfield

	PCT	G	PO	A	E	DP
Brewer	.978	52	84	6	2	1
Grote	.944	48	66	2	4	0
Hollingsworth	1.000	3	7	1	0	0
Kruml	.950	64	93	2	5	1
Mesa	.981	43	47	4	1	0
Morris	1.000	4	3	0	0	0
Rye	.925	32	47	2	4	0
Santamaria	1.000	8	11	1	0	1

GCL YANKEES   ROOKIE

GULF COAST LEAGUE

Batting

Batting	B-T	HT	WT	DOB	AVG	vLH	vRH	G	AB	R	H	2B	3B	HR	RBI	BB	HBP	SH	SF	SO	SB	CS	SLG	OBP
Almonte, Zoilo	B-R	5-11	165	6-10-89	.239	.288	.215	57	180	24	43	7	1	5	20	13	2	1	4	35	3	0	.372	.291
Anson, Kyle	B-R	6-0	200	4-21-83	.111	.286	.000	7	18	0	2	0	0	2	3	1	0	0	5	0	0	.111	.273
Arcia, Francisco	B-R	6-0	155	9-14-89	.128	.250	.065	22	47	5	6	1	0	1	2	2	1	1	6	0	1	.213	.192
Baker, Ryan J.	R-R	5-9	205	11-9-84	.077	.000	.100	10	13	0	1	0	0	0	0	0	0	0	5	0	0	.077	.077
Baker, Ryan M.	R-R	5-11	190	11-6-83	.000	—	.000	1	1	0	0	0	0	0	0	0	0	0	0	0	0	.000	.000
Baldridge, Tommy	L-L	6-1	195	8-18-86	.288	.267	.294	19	66	10	19	4	0	2	10	10	1	0	0	16	1	0	.439	.390
Castro, Kelvin	R-R	6-3	164	12-14-87	.286	.333	.273	6	14	3	4	1	0	0	0	1	0	2	0	2	0	0	.357	.333
Cervelli, Francisco	R-R	6-1	210	3-6-86	.250	—	.250	3	8	0	2	1	0	0	0	0	0	0	1	0	0	.375	.250
Delaney, Mitch	L-R	6-2	215	4-14-89	.237	.208	.250	25	76	5	18	2	0	0	7	3	1	0	0	23	0	0	.263	.275
Dionicio, Andres	R-R	6-0	160	12-29-87	.200	.143	.250	5	15	0	3	0	1	0	2	0	0	0	2	0	0	.333	.200
Duncan, Shelley	R-R	6-5	225	9-29-79	.000	—	.000	2	7	0	0	0	0	0	0	1	0	0	3	0	0	.000	.125
French, Neall	R-R	6-3	210	8-5-83	.345	.296	.368	35	84	15	29	4	0	3	15	10	4	1	1	13	2	1	.500	.434
Gomez, Roy	R-R	5-11	160	1-7-85	.360	.125	.471	11	25	6	9	3	1	0	6	2	0	0	1	4	0	0	.560	.393
Gross, Chad	R-R	6-5	220	5-3-88	.238	.293	.216	46	143	16	34	7	0	2	20	6	4	0	1	45	5	1	.329	.286
Higashioka, Kyle	R-R	6-1	190	4-20-90	.261	.176	.310	18	46	5	12	1	0	1	3	2	1	0	1	8	0	0	.348	.300
Jones, Mike	R-R	6-5	200	9-9-86	.184	.083	.216	15	49	0	9	5	0	0	2	5	1	0	0	18	1	0	.286	.273
Joseph, Corban	L-R	6-0	168	10-28-88	.277	.235	.296	49	159	25	44	15	2	2	18	20	1	2	1	24	2	5	.434	.359
Landoni, Emerson	B-R	5-10	146	2-18-89	.310	.185	.356	36	100	15	31	2	2	1	8	9	2	1	0	18	2	1	.400	.378
Lassiter, Garrison	L-R	6-1	185	12-22-89	.261	.286	.250	6	23	2	6	0	0	2	1	0	0	0	6	1	0	.261	.292
Lucian, Spencer	R-R	6-2	205	10-4-85	.250	.238	.255	28	72	7	18	5	0	1	8	10	0	1	0	19	0	0	.361	.341
Paredes, Jimmy	B-R	6-1	178	11-25-88	.280	.311	.267	47	161	23	45	9	2	1	15	8	4	1	1	20	6	0	.379	.328
Pirela, Jose	B-R	5-11	191	11-21-89	.234	.255	.223	35	141	19	33	4	1	0	10	8	3	0	1	19	4	2	.277	.288
Ramirez, Alvaro	L-L	5-9	160	4-5-86	.238	.152	.278	39	105	14	25	4	1	2	9	7	1	0	2	15	4	3	.352	.287
Rufino, Wady	R-R	6-2	220	4-8-85	.176	.143	.200	5	17	2	3	0	0	0	0	0	0	0	0	2	1	0	.176	.176
Smith, Chris	L-L	6-0	190	1-11-90	.142	.094	.162	36	106	13	15	5	0	1	12	4	5	0	1	31	1	0	.217	.207
Tabares, Yunior	R-R	6-5	215	7-15-85	.146	.400	.116	19	48	5	7	2	0	1	3	3	0	0	13	0	0	.250	.241
Weems, Chase	L-R	6-2	170	1-17-89	.227	.250	.220	28	75	7	17	5	0	1	10	11	3	1	0	27	2	0	.333	.348

Pitching

Pitching	B-T	HT	WT	DOB	W	L	ERA	G	GS	CG	SV	IP	H	R	ER	HR	BB	SO	AVG	vLH	vRH	K/9	BB/9
Asselin, Nick	R-R	6-0	200	1-19-85	0	0	2.08	3	0	0	0	4	2	1	1	0	2	6	.133	.200	.100	12.46	4.15
Banuelos, Manuel	L-L	5-10	155	3-13-91	4	1	2.57	12	3	0	0	42	32	14	12	3	13	37	.208	.242	.198	7.93	2.79
Barreda, Manuel	R-R	5-11	165	10-8-88	0	0	2.65	6	2	0	1	17	15	6	5	1	8	14	.234	.333	.186	7.41	4.24
Batista, Israel	R-R	6-1	172	11-5-87	1	1	6.00	15	0	0	0	18	18	13	12	2	4	10	.261	.143	.313	5.00	2.00
Betances, Dellin	R-R	6-8	245	3-23-88	0	1	8.53	3	2	0	0	6	13	7	6	0	3	6	.406	.429	.400	8.53	4.26
Britton, Chris	R-R	6-3	275	12-16-82	0	0	0.00	2	2	0	0	3	0	0	0	0	0	3	.000	.000	.000	9.00	0.00
Bruney, Brian	R-R	6-3	235	2-17-82	0	1	2.25	3	2	0	0	4	3	1	1	0	2	6	.200	.333		11.50	4.50
Castillo, Francisco	R-R	6-2	195	10-3-86	0	0	6.35	4	1	0	0	6	5	4	4	0	9	4	.263	.333	.250	6.35	14.29
Flannery, Ryan	R-R	6-4	245	1-6-86	2	1	0.86	15	0	0	7	21	12	3	2	0	16		.164	.105	.185	6.86	0.00
Garcia, Christian	R-R	6-4	220	8-24-85	0	2	14.73	3	3	0	0	7	19	12	12	3	2	9	.487	.250	.548	11.05	2.45
Joy, Shawn	R-L	5-10	185	6-3-86	1	1	3.66	15	0	0	4	20	23	9	8	0	7	9	.303	.176	.339	4.12	3.20
Kapala, Daniel	R-R	6-5	220	9-6-85	0	0	0.00	1	0	0	1	1	0	0	0	0	0	0	.000	.000	.000	0.00	0.00
Kennedy, Ian	R-R	6-0	195	12-19-84	1	0	3.00	1	0	0	0	3	3	1	1	0	0	7	.250	.000		21.00	0.00
Marquez, Dickson	R-R	6-2	170	4-19-86	5	2	6.03	12	6	0	0	37	57	30	25	3	4	18	.350	.421	.328	4.34	0.96
Marquez, Jeff	R-R	6-2	190	8-10-84	1	0	5.40	2	1	0	0	7	10	4	4	0	1	6	.333	.444	.286	8.10	1.35
Marshall, Brett	R-R	6-0	195	3-22-90	0	0	3.00	3	3	0	0	6	2	1	0	0	2	8	.087	.143	.063	12.00	3.00
Marte, Ronny	R-R	6-1	173	2-26-86	3	1	2.60	14	1	0	1	28	25	13	8	1	5	26	.238	.333	.218	8.46	1.63
Martinez, Richard	R-R	6-1	194	7-19-88	0	3	4.50	6	0	0	0	14	16	10	7	2	4	11	.267	.286	.261	7.07	2.57
Noesi, Hector	R-R	6-2	174	1-26-87	2	1	3.65	9	2	0	0	25	23	11	10	2	3	24	.253	.255	.257	8.76	1.09
O'Brien, Mikey	R-R	5-11	185	3-3-90	1	1	5.00	6	2	0	0	18	26	14	10	1	4	14	.329	.448	.260	7.00	2.00
Obradovich, Mike	R-R	6-0	185	9-26-85	1	1	3.48	10	0	0	6	10	6	4	4	0	0	15	.158	.222	.138	13.06	0.00
Perez, Kelvin	R-R	6-1	140	10-10-85	0	2	4.08	8	1	0	0	18	15	8	8	0	7	19	.234	.188	.250	9.68	3.57
Pope, Ryan	R-R	6-3	200	5-21-86	0	0	6.43	2	1	0	0	7	7	5	5	1	1	4	.250	.111	.316	5.14	1.29
Preisendorfer, Clint	L-L	6-5	215	7-11-86	1	1	7.20	5	0	0	0	5	6	10	4	0	8	2	.250	.333	.222	3.60	14.40
Richardson, Matt	R-R	6-1	175	5-29-86	0	1	3.86	6	4	0	0	14	12	6	6	2	6	17	.231	.400	.162	10.93	3.86
Rondon, Francisco	L-L	6-1	160	4-19-88	2	1	3.22	9	4	0	0	36	31	17	13	4	13	34	.233	.281	.218	8.42	3.22
Sanchez, Humberto	R-R	6-6	270	5-28-83	0	1	2.31	12	9	0	0	12	9	4	3	0	4	15	.209	.000	.310	11.57	3.09
Solbach, Michael	R-R	6-3	185	7-31-85	0	0	0.00	4	0	0	5	5	0	0	0	2	6		.263	.333	.231	10.80	3.60
Tatis, Gabriel	R-R	6-0	180	5-18-85	1	2	3.71	11	0	0	0	17	20	16	7	1	12	18	.282	.200	.314	9.53	6.35

	B-T	HT	WT	DOB																				
Turley, Nik	L-L	6-7	195	9-11-89	2	1	1.13	4	1	0	0	8	6	1	1	0	0	13	.207	.600	.125	14.63	0.00
Vizcaino, Arodys	R-R	6-0	189	11-13-90	3	2	3.68	12	6	0	0	44	38	22	18	5	13	48	.222	.238	.217	9.82	2.66
Wright, Chase	L-L	6-2	205	2-8-83	0	0	0.00	2	0	0	0	1	4	3	2	0	0	1	6	.200	.000	.231	13.50	2.25
Zambrano, Victor	B-R	6-0	205	8-6-75	0	0	0.00	2	2	0	0	8	4	0	0	0	2	9	.154	.125	.167	10.13	2.25

Fielding

Catcher	PCT	G	PO	A	E	DP	PB
Anson	1.000	5	26	4	0	0	0
Arcia	.984	21	117	10	2	0	3
R.J. Baker	.941	8	14	2	1	0	0
R. M. Baker	1.000	1	3	1	0	0	0
Cervelli	1.000	2	8	6	0	0	0
Higashioka	1.000	15	114	3	0	0	2
Weems	.960	27	157	13	7	2	5

First Base	PCT	G	PO	A	E	DP
Delaney	.975	21	146	9	4	9
Dionicio	1.000	5	29	2	0	2
French	.990	27	186	8	2	10
Tabares	1.000	13	90	7	0	11

Second Base	PCT	G	PO	A	E	DP
Joseph	.953	44	77	84	8	20
Landoni	1.000	4	6	10	0	4
Lucian	.750	2	1	2	1	0
Pirela	1.000	10	24	20	0	2

Third Base	PCT	G	PO	A	E	DP
Gomez	.920	9	4	19	2	2
Landoni	.946	13	5	30	2	1
Lucian	.877	26	11	53	9	3
Paredes	.863	16	13	31	7	4

Shortstop	PCT	G	PO	A	E	DP
Castro	.947	6	4	14	1	1
Gomez	1.000	2	0	3	0	0

Landoni	.925	13	12	25	3	2
Lassiter	.846	6	9	13	4	3
Paredes	.872	8	12	29	6	4
Pirela	.973	25	39	71	3	13

Outfield	PCT	G	PO	A	E	DP
Almonte	.991	56	102	5	1	0
Baldridge	1.000	18	25	3	0	1
French	1.000	1	1	0	0	0
Gross	.985	44	60	5	1	1
Jones	1.000	7	9	0	0	0
Ramirez	.953	39	57	4	3	1
Rufino	.929	5	13	0	1	0
Smith	.913	21	20	1	2	0
Tabares	.857	6	6	0	1	0

DSL YANKEES 1   *ROOKIE*

DOMINICAN SUMMER LEAGUE

Batting	B-T	HT	WT	DOB	AVG	vLH	vRH	G	AB	R	H	2B	3B	HR	RBI	BB	HBP	SH	SF	SO	SB	CS	SLG	OBP
Acosta, Alberto	R-R	6-3	190	2-24-90	.234	.259	.230	57	192	24	45	9	0	4	31	24	6	0	0	51	1	0	.344	.338
Baez, Luigi	L-L	6-0	160	6-11-89	.301	.306	.300	57	196	29	59	12	4	4	36	44	2	0	0	32	2	4	.464	.434
Beard, Edwin	R-R	6-3	188	8-31-89	.211	.167	.219	19	38	14	8	2	1	1	1	3	1	0	0	13	3	1	.342	.423
Castillo, Ali	R-R	5-10	165	6-19-89	.288	.244	.297	68	243	42	70	10	4	1	36	27	7	2	0	25	8	10	.374	.375
Classe, Luis	L-L	5-11	140	6-23-88	.000	—	.000	2	8	0	0	0	0	0	0	0	0	0	0	1	0	0	.000	.000
De La Cruz, Aris	R-R	5-11	172	3-5-90	.343	.000	.400	16	35	8	12	2	0	1	3	4	1	0	0	13	3	0	.486	.425
de Morais, Moacyr	R-R	5-11	170	3-16-90	.087	.000	.095	21	46	12	4	3	0	0	3	23	4	2	0	20	3	0	.152	.425
Duran, Kelvin	L-L	5-11	165	11-10-90	.278	.500	.250	9	36	10	10	0	2	0	5	6	0	1	0	11	2	0	.389	.381
Lapaix, Arielkis	R-R	5-11	186	10-14-88	.330	.455	.299	29	109	21	36	7	1	3	16	7	3	0	0	30	3	2	.495	.387
Morillo, Ronald	R-R	5-11	155	1-15-90	.183	.226	.175	57	208	28	38	5	0	3	27	24	9	1	1	51	7	5	.250	.293
Parache, Luis	L-R	5-8	175	11-25-88	.290	.292	.290	69	272	47	79	16	6	4	43	28	4	1	4	30	7	2	.438	.360
Pena, Arturo	R-R				.279	.300	.274	34	104	19	29	8	0	0	9	16	2	0	1	7	6	3	.356	.382
Pena, Ramon	R-R	5-10	153	9-22-85	.222	.167	.238	9	27	4	6	2	0	0	3	0	1	0	0	6	0	0	.296	.300
Ramirez, John	L-R	6-1	180	9-27-89	.294	.444	.262	31	102	14	30	2	0	1	9	5	4	0	0	36	0	1	.343	.351
Rodriguez, Josue	R-R	6-0	165	10-2-90	.279	.167	.323	27	86	8	24	3	1	0	13	7	4	0	1	25	1	1	.337	.357
Romero, Yakensi	R-R	6-3	210	12-2-89	.243	.306	.229	56	202	26	49	13	2	3	29	17	9	0	0	47	0	0	.371	.329
Santana, Francisco	L-L	5-10	170	6-18-88	.307	.381	.290	52	225	41	69	10	8	6	38	27	1	0	3	38	19	2	.502	.379
Taveras, Damian	R-R	6-1	205	11-28-89	.229	.174	.238	43	166	34	38	9	2	1	19	19	7	0	0	38	4	2	.325	.333
Ventura, Nicolas	R-R	6-2	170	2-7-89	.279	.273	.280	23	86	15	24	5	1	1	8	3	5	1	1	17	5	3	.395	.337

Pitching	B-T	HT	WT	DOB	W	L	ERA	G	GS	CG	SV	IP	H	R	ER	HR	BB	SO	AVG	vLH	vRH	K/9	BB/9
Alvarez, Isaias	R-R	6-2	175	12-9-89	1	3	3.57	10	4	0	0	23	23	15	9	0	17	12	.274	.391	.230	4.76	6.75
Arias, Randy	R-R	6-0	160	11-13-89	1	0	6.30	7	2	0	0	20	24	16	14	2	11	7	.300	.273	.310	3.15	4.95
Bravo, Wilfi	R-R	6-2	180	2-26-89	2	2	2.36	18	1	0	7	46	39	17	12	0	17	30	.231	.237	.229	5.91	3.35
Diaz, Luilli	R-R	6-0	150	2-4-88	1	0	22.09	9	0	0	0	7	11	20	18	0	17	7	.344	.364	.333	8.59	20.86
Garce, Harold	R-R	6-4	205	11-28-85	0	7	7.65	17	8	0	0	38	26	45	32	2	84	32	.200	.156	.214	7.65	20.07
Gonzalez, Felipe	R-R	6-2	165	8-15-91	2	1	8.79	7	0	0	0	14	24	17	14	3	2	10	.369	.222	.426	6.28	1.26
Jimenez, Warlin	R-R	6-0	165	9-14-89	2	2	4.50	12	5	0	0	34	38	27	17	1	14	14	.277	.167	.301	3.71	3.71
Lopez, Juan	R-R	6-1	170	6-23-90	1	0	12.54	3	2	0	0	9	17	13	13	3	2	14	.405	.556	.364	13.50	1.93
Marcano, Juan	L-L	6-1	165	8-24-90	2	1	2.75	11	8	0	0	36	22	13	11	1	23	45	.179	.333	.167	11.25	5.75
Marte, Joel	R-R	5-11	195	1-18-88	1	4	3.02	15	9	0	0	54	51	37	18	0	26	41	.245	.263	.241	6.88	4.36
Martinez, Rafael	L-L	6-3	175	3-27-85	6	2	4.67	17	4	0	0	44	50	29	23	1	27	55	.279	.200	.284	11.17	5.48
Mejia, Edison	R-R	6-1	185	7-2-90	1	1	2.90	10	5	0	0	31	20	21	10	0	13	19	.174	.156	.181	5.52	3.77
Mojica, Deivi	R-R	6-1	185	3-19-91	1	4	5.45	12	6	0	0	38	61	32	23	3	11	24	.355	.340	.360	5.68	2.61
Moreta, Francis	R-L	6-1	160	8-27-86	6	0	3.75	20	1	0	1	50	57	28	21	2	24	27	.291	.222	.294	4.83	4.29
Mundo, Angel	R-R	6-1	150	11-13-89	0	0	3.42	10	3	0	1	24	19	10	9	1	9	11	.224	.211	.227	4.18	3.42
Ramirez, Jose	R-R	6-1	160	10-29-88	1	2	6.28	17	4	0	0	43	58	41	30	2	35	29	.331	.383	.313	6.07	7.33
Rodino, Manuel	R-R	6-3	190	3-7-90	2	1	6.00	18	2	0	1	36	46	28	24	2	24	23	.322	.324	.321	5.75	6.00
Rodriguez, Wilton	R-R	6-3	195	11-6-90	0	2	6.75	10	5	0	0	20	25	18	15	1	14	13	.316	.375	.302	5.85	6.30
Rojas, Gerald	R-R	6-1	145	2-19-91	2	1	2.45	9	0	0	1	18	19	6	5	0	3	11	.268	.235	.278	5.40	1.47
Varillas, Andres	L-L	6-1	170	4-19-88	0	2	36.00	3	1	0	0	2	2	8	8	0	8	3	.286	.000	.286	13.50	36.00

Fielding

Catcher	PCT	G	PO	A	E	DP	PB
Rodriguez	.978	21	115	17	3	4	12
Taveras	.965	37	251	28	10	3	18
Ventura	.961	17	106	18	5	1	7

First Base	PCT	G	PO	A	E	DP
Acosta	.961	26	212	8	9	24
Castillo	1.000	2	17	3	0	1
Morillo	.938	8	57	3	4	4
A. Pena	1.000	5	14	2	0	1
R. Pena	1.000	1	11	0	0	0

John Ramirez	.988	23	155	5	2	12
Jose Ramirez	1.000	3	22	1	0	2
Rodriguez	1.000	1	7	0	0	1
Romero	.991	13	103	4	1	5
Taveras	1.000	1	7	0	0	0
Ventura	.923	1	12	0	1	1

Second Base	PCT	G	PO	A	E	DP
De La Cruz	.500	2	0	2	2	0
Parache	.955	67	171	172	16	33
A. Pena	.800	4	2	10	3	1

R. Pena	1.000	1	2	1	0	0

Third Base	PCT	G	PO	A	E	DP
Castillo	.942	56	65	146	13	12
De La Cruz	.833	9	4	11	3	1
A. Pena	1.000	4	1	8	0	2
R. Pena	1.000	4	4	13	0	1

Shortstop	PCT	G	PO	A	E	DP
Acosta	.750	1	0	3	1	0
Castillo	.970	6	10	22	1	2
Morillo	.923	52	72	133	17	27

A. Pena	.973	16	19	52	2	4	Classe	1.000	2	3	0 0 0	Ramirez	1.000	1	1	0 0 0

A. Pena .973 16 19 52 2 4

Outfield PCT G PO A E DP
Acosta .977 30 40 2 1 1
Baez .969 21 30 1 1 0
Beard 1.000 6 10 1 0 0

Classe 1.000 2 3 0 0 0
de Morais 1.000 21 28 3 0 0
Duran 1.000 8 18 2 0 0
Lapaix .885 26 52 2 7 0
A. Pena .909 7 8 2 1 0

Ramirez 1.000 1 1 0 0 0
Rodriguez .778 6 7 0 2 0
Romero .901 43 66 7 8 3
Santana .986 52 135 6 2 2

DSL YANKEES 2 — ROOKIE

DOMINICAN SUMMER LEAGUE

Batting	B-T	HT	WT	DOB	AVG	vLH	vRH	G	AB	R	H	2B	3B	HR	RBI	BB	HBP	SH	SF	SO	SB	CS	SLG	OBP
Calderon, Ronny	L-R	5-9	155	12-6-87	.147	.333	.080	13	34	1	5	2	0	0	2	1	2	0	0	2	0	0	.206	.216
De La Rosa, Elio	R-R	6-0	185	4-18-91	.134	.107	.143	32	119	9	16	3	0	0	12	5	0	0	1	35	1	0	.160	.168
De Leon, Kelvin	R-R	6-2	180	10-29-90	.289	.289	.289	63	235	43	68	16	2	9	43	34	10	0	2	74	8	3	.489	.399
de Morais, Moacyr	R-R	5-11	170	3-16-90	.154	.000	.167	8	13	4	2	0	0	0	0	2	1	0	0	7	0	0	.154	.313
2-team total (21 Yankees 1)					.102	—	—	29	59	16	6	3	0	0	3	25	5	2	0	27	3	0	.153	.404
Herrera, Julian	R-R	6-0	145	3-30-87	.267	.333	.259	8	30	3	8	0	0	0	2	3	0	0	0	10	0	1	.267	.333
Lapaix, Arielkis	R-R	5-11	186	10-14-88	.220	.000	.241	19	59	10	13	2	1	0	7	12	2	0	0	22	3	1	.288	.370
2-team total (29 Yankees 1)					.292	—	—	48	168	31	49	9	2	3	23	19	5	0	0	52	6	3	.423	.380
Liccien, Jhorge	R-R	6-0	165	10-10-90	.274	.211	.288	56	215	39	59	14	0	3	22	15	1	0	0	33	5	3	.381	.325
Nunez, Reymond	R-R	6-4	210	9-25-90	.230	.205	.235	65	256	25	59	8	2	2	41	19	4	1	0	73	0	3	.301	.294
Palomo, Jesus	R-R	5-11	170	12-15-89	.215	.235	.211	37	93	19	20	6	1	1	6	17	7	0	0	31	1	2	.333	.376
Pena, Henry	L-R	6-0	180	10-26-90	.167	.065	.186	51	192	22	32	14	0	1	17	32	1	0	0	64	1	3	.255	.289
Perez, Nixton	R-R	5-11	165	7-16-88	.300	.318	.297	46	150	29	45	15	1	2	18	16	2	1	4	23	2	1	.453	.366
Ramirez, Alcibiades	B-R	5-11	165	1-27-89	.286	.000	.500	4	7	1	2	1	0	0	1	1	1	0	0	3	0	0	.429	.444
Rijo, Juan	R-R	6-2	155	5-8-86	.309	.276	.317	43	149	24	46	8	4	0	27	7	1	0	2	19	6	2	.416	.340
Rodriguez, Keny	R-R	6-1	170	2-25-90	.226	.240	.238	55	155	26	35	7	1	1	14	32	6	0	1	29	9	2	.303	.376
Sosa, Eduardo	L-L	5-11	155	3-14-91	.315	.293	.319	63	254	48	80	18	5	4	37	34	6	0	2	54	30	8	.472	.405
Toussen, Jose	L-L	5-11	166	11-13-89	.269	.275	.268	65	234	41	63	12	1	0	23	34	6	1	0	45	16	7	.329	.376
Urena, Carlos	R-R	6-1	183	11-17-89	.375	.000	.409	6	24	6	9	2	1	1	8	1	1	0	1	4	0	0	.667	.407

Pitching	B-T	HT	WT	DOB	W	L	ERA	G	GS	CG	SV	IP	H	R	ER	HR	BB	SO	AVG	vLH	vRH	K/9	BB/9
Alves, Maicon	R-R	5-11	165	3-27-90	1	0	2.30	13	0	0	0	16	10	6	4	1	2	17	.185	.357	.125	9.77	1.15
Arias, Justo	R-R	6-2	145	10-29-88	5	4	3.18	20	1	0	3	45	32	16	16	2	9	38	.193	.184	.197	7.54	1.79
Atacho, Alan	R-R	6-1	171	3-21-88	2	2	1.30	20	0	0	5	42	30	9	6	1	17	40	.204	.250	.182	8.64	3.67
Croussett, Melvin	L-L	6-1	168	12-28-88	2	0	0.64	17	0	0	9	28	12	2	2	1	9	47	.125	.222	.115	14.93	2.86
Cruz, Dawerd	R-R	6-1	170	12-7-88	1	0	4.11	11	0	0	0	15	15	8	7	0	8	9	.250	.313	.227	5.28	4.70
Cruz, Sheryssy	R-R	6-4	200	8-19-89	1	0	0.00	8	0	0	0	12	4	1	0	0	4	6	.108	.083	.120	4.50	3.00
Eusebio, Wilkinson	R-R	6-2	178	9-26-90	4	5	5.27	16	4	0	0	41	43	28	24	2	17	34	.283	.304	.274	7.46	3.73
Garcia, Charlyn	R-R	6-1	165	6-9-86	2	1	3.82	13	5	0	0	35	31	24	15	1	31	28	.237	.192	.248	7.13	7.90
Heredia, Juan	L-L	6-3	160	1-20-89	5	3	3.35	15	6	0	0	48	34	22	18	1	18	58	.193	.176	.195	10.80	3.35
Martinez, Alejandro	R-R	5-10	165	2-11-89	5	1	2.93	20	2	0	1	40	36	13	13	1	16	37	.247	.229	.255	8.33	3.60
Orozco, Elvin	R-R	6-1	195	10-24-88	5	1	3.83	17	5	0	1	42	39	19	18	2	8	46	.236	.200	.255	9.78	1.70
Quintana, Jose	L-L	6-0	170	1-24-89	3	2	1.96	15	12	0	0	55	36	17	12	0	24	76	.186	.231	.182	12.44	3.93
Reyes, Yobanny	R-R	6-0	165	11-29-88	2	0	5.64	14	0	0	1	22	20	15	14	2	20	17	.270	.294	.263	6.85	8.06
Sanchez, Pedro	L-L	6-0	160	9-8-84	1	1	1.93	6	0	0	0	9	11	2	2	1	2	7	.297	.143	.333	6.75	1.93
Sanit, Amaury	R-R	5-11	187	11-11-79	0	0	0.00	2	0	0	1	2	1	0	0	0	0	3	.143	.000	.200	9.00	0.00
Santos, Andres	L-L	6-2	189	11-8-86	3	2	1.85	13	9	0	0	49	29	13	10	0	16	49	.173	.000	.187	9.06	2.96
Tapia, Eric	L-L	6-1	193	9-6-87	1	0	4.58	11	7	0	0	37	32	20	19	0	17	30	.237	.111	.256	7.23	4.10
Tolentino, Israel	R-R	6-4	190	1-11-88	0	0	13.50	6	0	0	0	5	4	8	7	1	9	3	.222	.000	.222	5.79	17.36

Fielding

Catcher	PCT	G	PO	A	E	DP	PB
Calderon	.987	11	63	15	1	0	3
Liccien	.997	36	262	36	1	1	4
Palomo	.986	33	242	36	4	3	7
Ramirez	.957	4	20	2	1	0	4

First Base	PCT	G	PO	A	E	DP
Herrera	1.000	1	9	0	0	1
Nunez	.983	65	548	39	10	37
Palomo	.960	3	24	0	1	2
Perez	1.000	1	6	0	0	0
Rijo	1.000	1	9	0	0	2
Rojas	1.000	1	10	0	0	0

Second Base	PCT	G	PO	A	E	DP
Perez	1.000	10	19	13	0	3
Rijo	1.000	18	30	31	0	7
Rodriguez	.969	53	87	131	7	19

Third Base	PCT	G	PO	A	E	DP
De La Rosa	.866	32	19	65	13	4
Herrera	.786	6	5	6	3	0
Perez	.931	22	22	45	5	3
Rijo	.926	18	18	32	4	1
Toussen	1.000	1	0	2	0	0

Shortstop	PCT	G	PO	A	E	DP
Perez	1.000	1	2	4	0	0

Rijo	.900	5	8	10	2	1
Toussen	.931	64	123	148	20	25

Outfield	PCT	G	PO	A	E	DP
De Leon	.915	46	42	1	4	0
de Morais	.909	7	10	0	1	0
Lapaix	1.000	15	22	3	0	1
Pena	.964	42	49	5	2	1
Rijo	1.000	4	1	0	0	0
Rojas	.956	42	59	6	3	4
Sosa	.991	61	105	6	1	1
Urena	.900	6	8	1	1	0

Oakland Athletics

BY CASEY TEFERTILLER

Long before the season opened, Billy Beane faced a challenging decision.

He recognized that he could take a decent Athletics team into the 2008 season and hope for the fates to fall his way and the A's to somehow find a way to slip away with the American League West Division title. Or Beane figured he could blast the team apart and start over, risking the wrath of the fan base and assuring poor attendance totals.

So in November, the A's general manager called together his coven of advisers for the big talk. By then, they knew that third baseman Eric Chavez likely would not be ready to open the season, and they could see the Angels and Mariners both apparently on the rise. After a decade of success, the A's farm system short on depth had fallen in quality with few quick fixes on the way up.

Beane made the toughest call: 2008 would be a year of rebuilding, of tooling for the future.

Before the season began, Beane dealt away stars and fan favorites. He moved power-hitting outfielder Nick Swisher to the White Sox for lefthander Gio Gonzalez, righthander Fautino de los Santos and outfielder Ryan Sweeney. Center fielder Mark Kotsay was dealt to the Braves for righthanders Joey Devine and Jamie Richmond. And 2007 All-Star Game starter Dan Haren was sent to the Diamondbacks in an eight-player deal that landed the Athletics a core of talent, including outfielder Carlos Gonzalez, first baseman Chris Carter and lefthanders Brett Anderson, Dana Eveland and Greg Smith. In return, the Athletics gained a load of young players that Beane hoped would become the base of the future.

Then the season took an unexpected turn—the young A's started winning. At the end of June, they were eight games over .500 as a strong rotation, led by veterans Rich Harden and Joe Blanton, kept the A's close in games and close in the division.

However, Beane stayed the course and stuck with his plan. On July 8, he traded Harden and right-hander Chad Gaudin to the Cubs for four players and two weeks later traded Blanton to the Phillies in another prospect-laden deal. The Athletics lost 20 or 24 games after the Harden deal and reeled into third place, ahead of only the Mariners.

Brad Ziegler was a revelation out of the bullpen. The 28-year-old sidearmer set a big league record

ORGANIZATION STATISTICS

PLAYERS OF THE YEAR

MAJOR LEAGUE: JUSTIN DUCHSHERER, RHP

Duscsherer, a reliever the previous four years, made a nice transition to the rotation. He finished 10-8, 2.54 with 95 strikeouts and 34 walks in 142 innings. His ERA was second on the team, and he pitched a two-hitter on July 8 against Seattle.

MINOR LEAGUE: CHRIS CARTER, 1B/3B

A 15th-round pick in 2005, Carter was dealt twice in 11 days in December 2007 as he went from the White Sox to Diamondbacks and then to the Athletics. He hit .259/.361/.569 with 39 home runs, 32 doubles and 104 RBIs at high Class A Stockton.

BILL MITCHELL

ORGANIZATION LEADERS

BATTING		*Minimum 250 at-bats
*AVG	Guzman, Jesus, Sacramento/Midland	.345
R	Carter, Chris, Stockton	101
H	Doolittle, Sean, Stockton/Midland	153
TB	Carter, Chris, Stockton	288
2B	Doolittle, Sean, Stockton/Midland	40
3B	Sellers, Justin, Midland	8
HR	Carter, Chris, Stockton	39
RBI	Everidge, Tommy, Midland	115
BB	Pennington, Cliff, Midland/Sacramento	93
SO	Brown, Corey, Kane County/Stockton	168
SB	Donovan, Todd, Midland	37
*OBP	Pennington, Cliff, Midland/Sacramento	.404
*SLG	Carter, Chris, Stockton	.569

PITCHING		†Minimum 75 innings
W	Mazzaro, Vince, Midland/Sacramento	15
L	Richmond, Jamie, Kane County	11
†ERA	Cahill, Trevor, Stockton/Midland	2.61
G	Currin, Pat, Midland/Stockton	59
GS	Richmond, Jamie, Kane County	28
SV	Carignan, Andrew, Stockton/Midland	28
IP	Mazzaro, Vince, Midland/Sacramento	171
BB	Rodriguez, Henry, Stockton/Midland	84
SO	Rodriguez, Henry, Stockton/Midland	147
†AVG	Cahill, Trevor, Stockton, Midland	.179

for scoreless innings to start a career with 18—and kept on going. His run ended at 39 innings— the longest streak ever assembled by a pure reliever.

In the minors, the influx of talent led to a big season. Sacramento won the Triple-A championship, and Stockton won the high Class A California League title. Double-A Midland finished 75-65, and low Class A Kane County was 72-66.

General Manager: Billy Beane. **Farm Director:** Keith Lieppman. **Scouting Director:** Eric Kubota.

Class	Team	League	W	L	PCT	Finish*	Manager	Affiliate Since
Majors	Oakland	American	75	86	.466	10th (14)	Bob Geren	—
Triple-A	Sacramento River Cats	Pacific Coast	83	61	.576	^3rd (16)	Todd Steverson	2000
Double-A	Midland RockHounds	Texas	75	65	.536	3rd (8)	Webster Garrison	1999
High A	Stockton Ports	California	76	64	.543	^3rd (10)	Darren Bush	2005
Low A	Kane County Cougars	Midwest	72	66	.522	7th (14)	Aaron Nieckula	2003
Short-season	Vancouver Canadians	Northwest	34	42	.447	6th (8)	Rick Magnante	1979
Rookie	AZL Athletics	Arizona	21	35	.375	7th (9)	Ruben Escalera	1988
Overall 2008 Minor League Record			361	333	.520	8th		

* Finish in overall standings (No. of teams in league). ^League champion.

ORGANIZATION STATISTICS

OAKLAND ATHLETICS

AMERICAN LEAGUE

Batting	B-T	HT	WT	DOB	AVG	vLH	vRH	G	AB	R	H	2B	3B	HR	RBI	BB	HBP	SH	SF	SO	SB	CS	SLG	OBP
Baisley, Jeff	R-R	6-3	210	12-19-82	.256	.188	.296	14	43	1	11	1	0	0	5	4	0	0	0	7	0	0	.279	.319
Bankston, Wes	R-R	6-4	215	11-23-83	.203	.300	.154	17	59	4	12	3	0	1	4	2	1	0	1	15	0	0	.305	.238
Barton, Daric	L-R	6-0	225	8-16-85	.226	.273	.208	140	446	59	101	17	5	9	47	65	3	6	3	99	2	1	.348	.327
Bowen, Rob	B-R	6-3	225	2-24-81	.176	.167	.180	37	91	6	16	5	1	1	9	4	1	2	0	38	0	0	.286	.219
Brown, Emil	R-R	6-2	210	12-29-74	.244	.295	.211	117	402	48	98	14	2	13	59	27	5	0	4	65	4	2	.386	.297
Buck, Travis	L-R	6-2	225	11-18-83	.226	.196	.239	38	155	16	35	9	1	7	25	11	4	0	2	38	1	0	.432	.291
Chavez, Eric	L-R	6-1	220	12-7-77	.247	.333	.215	23	89	10	22	7	0	2	14	6	0	0	0	18	0	0	.393	.295
Conrad, Brooks	B-R	5-11	190	1-16-80	.158	.000	.176	6	19	0	3	1	0	0	2	0	0	0	0	9	0	0	.211	.158
Crosby, Bobby	R-R	6-3	205	1-12-80	.237	.222	.244	145	556	66	132	39	1	7	61	47	0	0	2	96	7	3	.349	.296
Cunningham, Aaron	R-R	5-11	195	4-24-86	.250	.208	.268	22	80	7	20	7	1	1	14	6	1	0	0	24	2	0	.400	.310
Cust, Jack	L-R	6-1	230	1-16-79	.231	.235	.229	148	481	77	111	19	0	33	77	111	2	0	4	197	0	0	.476	.375
Davis, Rajai	R-R	5-11	195	10-19-80	.260	.250	.267	101	196	28	51	5	4	3	19	7	1	2	1	34	25	6	.372	.288
Denorfia, Chris	R-R	6-0	195	7-15-80	.290	.241	.333	29	62	10	18	3	0	1	9	6	1	2	0	16	2	0	.387	.362
Ellis, Mark	R-R	5-11	190	6-6-77	.233	.176	.256	117	442	55	103	20	3	12	41	53	5	5	2	65	14	2	.373	.321
Fiorentino, Jeff	L-R	6-1	185	4-14-83	1.000	.000	1.000	2	1	0	1	0	0	0	1	0	0	0	0	0	0	0	1.000	1.000
Gonzalez, Carlos	L-L	6-1	200	10-17-85	.242	.188	.263	85	302	31	73	22	1	4	26	13	0	1	0	81	4	1	.361	.273
Hannahan, Jack	L-R	6-2	205	3-4-80	.218	.204	.223	143	436	48	95	27	0	9	47	55	2	3	5	131	2	0	.342	.305
Johnson, Dan	L-R	6-2	215	8-10-79	.000	—	.000	1	1	0	0	0	0	0	0	0	0	0	0	0	0	0	.000	.000
2-team total (10 Tampa Bay)					.192	—		11	26	3	5	0	0	2	4	3	0	0	0	7	0	0	.423	.276
Murphy, Donnie	R-R	5-10	185	3-10-83	.184	.196	.175	46	103	10	19	3	0	3	13	11	2	0	1	38	2	1	.301	.274
Murton, Matt	R-R	6-1	220	10-3-81	.100	.000	.125	9	30	1	3	1	0	0	2	1	0	0	0	7	0	0	.133	.129
Patterson, Eric	L-R	5-11	170	4-8-83	.174	.190	.169	30	92	11	16	3	0	0	8	12	0	0	0	24	8	0	.207	.269
Pennington, Cliff	B-R	5-11	185	6-15-84	.242	.289	.213	36	99	14	24	5	0	0	9	13	2	2	1	18	4	1	.293	.339
Petit, Gregorio	R-R	5-10	190	12-10-84	.348	.364	.333	14	23	4	8	2	0	0	2	0	0	0	0	9	0	0	.435	.400
Suzuki, Kurt	R-R	6-0	195	10-4-83	.279	.246	.291	148	530	54	148	25	1	7	42	44	11	2	1	69	2	3	.370	.346
Sweeney, Mike	R-R	6-3	225	7-22-73	.286	.321	.260	42	126	13	36	8	0	2	12	7	2	0	1	6	0	0	.397	.331
Sweeney, Ryan	L-L	6-4	215	2-20-85	.286	.216	.307	115	384	53	110	18	2	5	45	38	3	2	6	67	9	1	.383	.350
Thomas, Frank	R-R	6-5	275	5-27-68	.263	.220	.283	55	186	20	49	6	1	5	19	28	2	0	1	44	0	0	.387	.364
2-team total (16 Toronto)					.240	—		71	246	27	59	7	1	8	30	39	3	0	1	57	0	0	.374	.349

Pitching	B-T	HT	WT	DOB	W	L	ERA	G	GS	CG	SV	IP	H	R	ER	HR	BB	SO	AVG	vLH	vRH	K/9	BB/9
Blanton, Joe	R-R	6-3	255	12-11-80	5	12	4.96	20	20	0	0	127	145	74	70	12	35	62	.284	.247	.328	4.39	2.48
Blevins, Jerry	L-L	6-6	175	9-6-83	1	3	3.11	36	0	0	0	38	32	14	13	2	13	35	.230	.193	.256	8.36	3.11
Braden, Dallas	L-L	6-1	195	8-13-83	5	4	4.14	19	10	0	0	72	77	36	33	8	25	41	.284	.319	.272	5.15	3.14
Brown, Andrew	R-R	6-6	230	2-17-81	1	0	3.09	31	0	0	0	35	23	13	12	3	21	28	.187	.183	.190	7.20	5.40
Calero, Kiko	R-R	6-1	210	1-9-75	0	0	3.86	5	0	0	0	5	3	3	2	0	3	7	.176	.500	.000	13.50	5.79
Casilla, Santiago	R-R	6-0	200	7-25-80	2	1	3.93	51	0	0	2	50	60	22	22	5	20	43	.299	.308	.291	7.69	3.58
Devine, Joey	R-R	5-11	205	9-19-83	6	1	0.59	42	0	0	1	46	23	7	3	0	15	49	.150	.197	.120	9.66	2.96
DiNardo, Lenny	L-L	6-2	210	9-19-79	1	2	7.43	11	2	0	0	23	31	20	19	3	13	12	.316	.303	.323	4.70	5.09
Duchscherer, Justin	R-R	6-2	200	11-19-77	10	8	2.54	22	22	1	0	142	107	45	40	11	34	95	.210	.227	.188	6.04	2.16
Embree, Alan	L-L	6-2	190	1-23-70	2	5	4.96	70	0	0	0	62	59	36	34	8	30	57	.253	.232	.265	8.32	4.38
Eveland, Dana	L-L	6-0	240	10-29-83	9	9	4.34	29	29	1	0	168	172	82	81	10	77	118	.269	.248	.275	6.32	4.13
Foulke, Keith	R-R	6-0	210	10-19-72	0	3	4.06	31	0	0	1	31	28	14	14	7	13	23	.241	.200	.279	6.68	3.77
Gallagher, Sean	R-R	6-2	235	12-30-85	2	3	5.88	11	11	0	0	57	60	42	37	7	36	54	.270	.282	.253	8.58	5.72
Gaudin, Chad	R-R	5-10	190	3-24-83	5	3	3.59	26	6	0	0	63	63	29	25	6	17	44	.263	.264	.261	6.32	2.44
Gonzalez, Gio	R-L	5-11	185	9-19-85	1	4	7.68	10	7	0	0	34	32	34	29	9	25	34	.242	.194	.260	9.00	6.62
Gray, Jeff	R-R	6-2	210	11-19-81	0	0	7.71	5	0	0	0	5	8	4	4	1	1	4	.364	.444	.308	7.71	1.93
Harden, Rich	L-R	6-1	195	11-30-81	5	1	2.34	13	13	0	0	77	57	21	20	5	31	92	.206	.225	.187	10.75	3.62
Hernandez, Fernando	R-R	5-11	190	7-31-84	1	0	18.00	3	0	0	0	3	4	6	6	0	5	2	.308	.333	.250	6.00	15.00
Meyer, Dan	L-R	6-3	220	7-3-81	0	1	7.48	11	4	0	0	28	35	28	23	6	14	20	.304	.314	.300	6.51	4.55
Outman, Josh	L-L	6-1	185	9-14-84	1	2	4.56	6	4	0	0	26	34	14	13	1	8	19	.327	.217	.358	6.66	2.81
Saarloos, Kirk	R-R	6-0	180	5-23-79	1	0	5.47	8	1	0	0	26	37	17	16	2	4	12	.330	.385	.283	4.10	1.37
Smith, Greg	L-L	6-2	190	12-22-83	7	16	4.16	32	32	2	0	190	169	92	88	21	87	111	.243	.232	.247	5.25	4.11

	B-T	HT	WT	DOB																					
Street, Huston	R-R	6-0	200	8-2-83	7	5	3.73	63	0	0	18	70	58	29	29	6	27	69	.229	.200	.250	8.87	3.47
Ziegler, Brad	R-R	6-4	200	10-10-79	3	0	1.06	47	0	0	11	60	47	8	7	2	22	30	.236	.280	.198	4.53	3.32

Fielding

Catcher	PCT	G	PO	A	E	DP	PB
Bowen	.987	31	147	9	2	1	3
Suzuki	.994	141	927	53	6	4	5

First Base	PCT	G	PO	A	E	DP
Baisley	.974	4	37	1	1	3
Bankston	.991	13	104	6	1	10
Barton	.988	134	1021	73	13	128
Bowen	1.000	1	2	0	0	2
Brown	1.000	1	1	0	0	0
Hannahan	.978	10	82	5	2	7
M. Sweeney	1.000	13	89	11	0	9

Second Base	PCT	G	PO	A	E	DP
Conrad	1.000	2	4	3	0	1
Davis	—	1	0	0	0	0
Ellis	.993	115	228	336	4	88

Third Base	PCT	G	PO	A	E	DP
Murphy	1.000	10	12	20	0	3
Patterson	.960	20	48	49	4	15
Pennington	1.000	16	33	44	0	17
Petit	1.000	4	7	14	0	1
Baisley	1.000	1	6	14	0	1
Barton	1.000	1	1	1	0	1
Chavez	.978	15	12	32	1	4
Conrad	.833	4	1	4	1	1
Hannahan	.970	126	70	218	9	24
Murphy	.975	24	12	27	1	7
Pennington	.950	9	8	11	1	2

Shortstop	PCT	G	PO	A	E	DP
Crosby	.972	145	202	383	17	99
Murphy	.949	13	10	27	2	6

	PCT	G	PO	A	E	DP
Pennington	.867	10	10	16	4	5
Petit	.905	8	7	12	2	5

Outfield	PCT	G	PO	A	E	DP
Brown	.981	100	200	10	4	3
Buck	1.000	37	84	3	0	0
Cunningham	.941	20	47	1	3	0
Cust	.972	83	133	4	4	0
Davis	.993	84	147	4	1	2
Denorfia	1.000	24	37	1	0	0
Fiorentino	—	2	0	0	0	0
Gonzalez	.991	81	219	5	2	1
Murphy	—	1	0	0	0	0
Murton	1.000	7	27	1	0	1
Patterson	.938	8	15	0	1	0
R. Sweeney	.996	110	243	6	1	0

SACRAMENTO RIVER CATS   TRIPLE-A

PACIFIC COAST LEAGUE

Batting	B-T	HT	WT	DOB	AVG	vLH	vRH	G	AB	R	H	2B	3B	HR	RBI	BB	HBP	SH	SF	SO	SB	CS	SLG	OBP
Affronti, Michael	R-R	6-2	195	2-13-84	.367	.000	.440	9	30	5	11	3	0	0	3	0	0	0	0	4	0	0	.467	.367
Baisley, Jeff	R-R	6-3	210	12-19-82	.298	.205	.327	81	299	45	89	25	1	9	44	32	5	0	1	43	0	1	.478	.374
Bankston, Wes	R-R	6-4	215	11-23-83	.280	.229	.301	97	375	56	105	19	1	20	73	21	7	0	2	71	0	2	.496	.328
Barton, Daric	L-R	6-0	225	8-16-85	.194	.167	.231	8	31	4	6	0	0	1	3	2	0	0	0	0	0	0	.290	.242
Blasi, Nick	R-R	5-10	200	9-23-81	.236	.233	.238	30	106	13	25	3	0	2	8	4	0	0	0	23	3	1	.321	.264
2-team total (6 Tacoma)					.238	—	—	36	126	17	30	4	0	2	9	6	1	0	0	28	3	1	.317	.278
Buck, Travis	L-R	6-2	225	11-18-83	.296	.216	.318	45	169	28	50	8	2	2	17	25	3	0	0	34	4	1	.402	.396
Chavez, Eric	L-R	6-1	220	12-7-77	.367	.417	.333	9	30	7	11	3	0	2	3	3	0	0	0	7	0	0	.667	.424
Conrad, Brooks	B-R	5-11	190	1-16-80	.243	.174	.267	117	465	86	113	29	5	28	91	46	2	2	2	127	4	1	.508	.313
Cornejo, Eduardo	L-R	5-10	180	11-19-81	.100	.000	.143	3	10	0	1	0	0	0	1	0	0	0	0	2	0	1	.100	.100
2-team total (22 Colorado Springs)					.222	—	—	25	54	5	12	1	0	0	6	8	0	1	1	6	0	2	.241	.317
Cunningham, Aaron	R-R	5-11	195	4-24-86	.382	.467	.361	20	76	21	29	5	0	5	14	11	1	0	1	16	3	1	.645	.461
Denorfia, Chris	R-R	6-0	195	7-15-80	.302	.298	.303	45	189	34	57	13	1	2	20	12	0	2	1	31	5	4	.413	.342
Fiorentino, Jeff	L-R	6-1	185	4-14-83	.273	.143	.333	8	22	3	6	0	0	0	3	4	0	0	2	5	1	0	.273	.357
Gaetti, Joe	R-R	5-11	205	10-18-81	.263	.264	.263	55	190	34	50	11	1	14	33	21	3	0	0	65	2	0	.553	.346
Gonzalez, Carlos	L-L	6-1	200	10-17-85	.283	.300	.276	46	173	23	49	9	1	4	28	16	0	0	0	35	1	1	.416	.344
Guzman, Jesus	R-R	6-1	165	6-14-84	.237	.182	.250	15	59	5	14	2	0	2	9	4	0	1	1	13	0	2	.373	.281
Knoedler, Justin	R-R	6-2	215	7-17-80	.175	.255	.151	66	217	34	38	12	1	10	34	15	4	1	4	58	2	0	.378	.238
Linden, Todd	B-R	6-3	220	6-30-80	.333	.241	.388	23	78	13	26	7	0	3	12	14	2	0	0	22	1	0	.538	.447
Massaro, Michael	L-L	5-11	160	4-15-84	.280	.294	.273	15	50	5	14	3	1	0	5	4	0	3	0	9	0	0	.380	.333
Melillo, Kevin	L-R	5-11	195	5-14-82	.260	.206	.277	38	146	21	38	4	2	5	17	21	1	0	1	32	1	0	.418	.355
Murphy, Donnie	R-R	5-10	185	3-10-83	.270	.222	.292	36	141	25	38	10	2	11	27	8	2	1	1	46	1	0	.603	.316
Murton, Matt	R-R	6-1	220	10-3-81	.277	.200	.300	32	130	19	36	12	2	1	13	13	1	0	1	20	3	1	.423	.345
2-team total (54 Iowa)					.290	—	—	86	321	45	93	23	3	2	28	42	4	1	2	40	7	3	.399	.377
Padron, Raul	R-R	6-0	195	9-17-84	.118	.000	.143	6	17	1	2	1	0	0	3	1	0	0	0	6	0	0	.176	.167
Patterson, Eric	L-R	5-11	170	4-8-83	.330	.296	.341	25	109	18	36	8	2	4	19	9	1	3	2	28	8	2	.550	.380
2-team total (52 Iowa)					.324	—	—	77	312	51	101	24	5	10	47	21	2	5	4	73	19	2	.529	.366
Pennington, Cliff	B-R	5-11	185	6-15-84	.297	.303	.294	65	236	47	70	9	3	2	16	54	0	3	1	34	11	5	.386	.426
Petit, Gregorio	R-R	5-10	190	12-10-84	.269	.240	.279	79	308	39	83	14	3	1	35	23	1	7	0	60	3	5	.344	.322
Powell, Landon	B-R	6-3	250	3-19-82	.230	.276	.211	88	300	42	69	11	0	15	53	63	0	0	4	85	0	1	.417	.360
Putnam, Danny	L-L	5-10	200	9-17-82	.276	.298	.268	89	308	54	85	18	2	15	57	47	7	1	0	83	3	2	.494	.384
Robnett, Richie	L-L	5-9	215	9-17-83	.236	.190	.253	58	208	28	49	15	0	3	19	21	1	0	1	61	2	0	.351	.307
Rogowski, Casey	L-L	6-3	230	5-1-81	.277	.296	.270	117	415	67	115	22	3	14	64	52	1	2	3	111	16	3	.446	.357
Sweeney, Mike	R-R	6-3	225	7-22-73	.222	.000	.316	9	27	4	6	1	0	1	2	6	0	0	4	0	0	.370	.276
Sweeney, Ryan	L-L	6-4	215	2-20-85	.412	.333	.440	8	34	5	14	4	0	1	5	3	0	0	1	5	0	0	.618	.459

Pitching	B-T	HT	WT	DOB	W	L	ERA	G	GS	CG	SV	IP	H	R	ER	HR	BB	SO	AVG	vLH	vRH	K/9	BB/9
Blevins, Jerry	L-L	6-6	175	9-6-83	2	2	2.78	28	0	0	10	32	31	16	10	3	6	36	.244	.262	.235	10.02	1.67
Borrell, Danny	L-L	6-3	200	1-24-79	3	1	3.64	5	5	0	0	30	31	15	12	3	8	19	.277	.333	.250	5.76	2.43
Braden, Dallas	L-L	6-1	195	8-13-83	1	1	2.36	11	9	1	0	53	49	19	14	7	11	54	.246	.200	.262	9.11	1.86
Brown, Andrew	R-R	6-6	230	2-17-81	0	0	6.75	1	0	0	0	1	1	1	1	0	1	1	.250	1.000	.000	6.75	6.75
Calero, Kiko	R-R	6-1	210	1-9-75	1	4	4.00	8	0	0	0	9	8	4	4	1	10	10	.250	.333	.143	10.00	10.00
2-team total (18 Oklahoma)					2	8	6.53	26	0	0	1	30	32	22	22	5	22	31	—	—	—	9.20	6.53
Casilla, Santiago	R-R	6-0	200	7-25-80	0	0	3.38	2	2	0	0	3	3	1	1	0	1	5	.300	.200	.400	16.88	3.38
Cate, Troy	L-L	6-1	220	10-21-80	1	1	7.27	12	0	0	1	17	23	14	14	2	6	9	.324	.333	.317	4.67	3.12
2-team total (11 Nashville)					2	3	5.72	23	4	0	1	46	48	29	29	5	16	26	—	—	—	5.12	3.15
Devine, Joey	R-R	5-11	205	9-19-83	0	1	6.75	4	2	0	0	4	4	4	3	1	1	8	.235	.375	.111	18.00	2.25
DiNardo, Lenny	L-L	6-2	210	9-19-79	6	5	6.69	15	13	0	0	71	107	56	53	7	16	49	.352	.429	.323	6.18	2.02
Dowdy, Justin	L-L	6-1	175	8-13-83	0	3	3.75	3	2	0	0	12	9	6	5	1	12	9	.231	.267	.208	6.75	9.00
Duchscherer, Justin	R-R	6-2	200	11-19-77	0	1	6.75	1	1	0	0	3	5	2	2	0	0	1	.417	.250	.500	3.38	0.00

Eveland, Dana	L-L	6-0	240	10-29-83	3	0	2.57	3	3	0	0	21	23	9	6	2	4	21	.267	.278	.265	9.00	1.71
Farley, Chris	R-R	6-2	220	2-24-83	0	0	18.00	3	0	0	0	2	5	4	4	1	1	2	.500	.333	.571	9.00	4.50
Fernandez, Jason	R-R	6-2	175	1-8-85	0	1	13.50	2	1	0	0	4	9	6	6	0	3	5	.429	.556	.333	11.25	6.75
Foulke, Keith	R-R	6-0	210	10-19-72	0	0	12.79	4	1	0	0	6	12	9	9	3	0	7	.400	.167	.556	9.95	0.00
Garcia, Jose	R-R	5-11	165	1-7-85	0	0	6.75	1	0	0	0	1	1	1	1	1	1	2	.200	.333	.000	13.50	0.00
Gissell, Chris	R-R	6-5	210	1-4-78	7	3	3.43	25	12	0	1	81	79	33	31	10	19	67	.256	.259	.254	7.41	2.10
Glushon, Jason	R-R	6-2	195	5-26-85	0	0	7.11	3	1	0	0	6	8	6	5	3	4	1	.308	.250	.357	1.42	5.68
Godfrey, Graham	R-R	6-3	205	8-9-84	0	0	4.05	2	0	0	0	7	6	3	3	1	2	4	.261	.333	.235	5.40	2.70
Gonzalez, Gio	R-L	5-11	185	9-19-85	8	7	4.24	23	22	1	0	123	106	65	58	12	61	128	.233	.198	.246	9.37	4.46
Gray, Jeff	R-R	6-2	210	11-19-81	2	7	4.39	54	0	0	4	68	86	33	33	9	23	50	.313	.330	.301	6.65	3.06
Harden, Rich	L-R	6-1	195	11-30-81	0	0	2.45	1	1	0	0	4	3	1	1	0	0	4	.214	.143	.286	9.82	0.00
Kilby, Brad	L-L	6-1	235	2-19-83	7	2	3.47	51	0	0	2	70	51	33	27	9	26	66	.202	.163	.222	8.49	3.34
Knox, Brad	R-R	6-2	230	5-27-82	7	4	5.33	27	18	0	0	137	156	87	81	19	41	84	.286	.268	.305	5.53	2.70
Komine, Shane	R-R	5-9	180	10-18-80	0	0	7.20	4	0	0	0	5	5	4	4	1	3	5	.263	.182	.375	9.00	5.40
Marshall, Jay	L-L	6-5	205	2-25-83	3	5	6.16	37	0	0	2	38	55	26	26	3	20	21	.346	.270	.396	4.97	4.74
Mazzaro, Vin	R-R	6-2	190	9-27-86	3	3	6.15	6	5	0	0	34	49	26	23	3	9	27	.340	.358	.330	7.22	2.41
Meyer, Dan	R-L	6-3	220	7-3-81	10	5	4.48	22	20	0	0	123	113	65	61	10	52	109	.245	.264	.237	8.00	3.82
Outman, Josh	L-L	6-1	185	9-14-84	1	0	1.76	5	2	0	0	15	9	3	3	1	5	15	.167	.214	.150	8.80	2.93
Prinz, Bret	R-R	6-3	210	6-15-77	1	3	6.75	31	0	0	5	29	34	22	22	8	17	20	.306	.349	.279	6.14	5.22
Saarloos, Kirk	R-R	6-0	180	5-23-79	9	4	4.22	22	22	1	0	141	150	73	66	18	36	79	.272	.277	.266	5.05	2.30
Shafer, David	R-R	6-2	190	3-7-82	2	1	5.06	14	1	0	0	27	19	17	15	7	17	25	.196	.121	.234	8.44	5.74
Silva, Jesus	R-R	6-0	199	12-24-82	0	1	7.04	6	0	0	0	8	16	10	6	3	4	2	.400	.353	.435	2.35	4.70
Smith, Greg	L-L	6-2	190	12-22-83	0	1	3.00	1	1	0	0	6	6	2	2	0	1	4	.261	.222	.286	6.00	1.50
Wing, Ryan	L-L	6-2	190	2-1-82	2	1	2.33	47	0	0	0	54	44	16	14	2	26	47	.218	.272	.182	7.83	4.33
Ziegler, Brad	R-R	6-4	200	10-10-79	2	0	0.37	19	0	0	8	24	15	2	1	0	4	20	.174	.257	.118	7.40	1.48

Fielding

Catcher	PCT	G	PO	A	E	DP	PB
Knoedler	.985	56	357	32	6	4	6
Padron	1.000	5	34	3	0	0	0
Powell	.987	86	657	34	9	5	10

First Base	PCT	G	PO	A	E	DP
Bankston	.994	54	461	34	3	54
Barton	1.000	6	50	5	0	6
Knoedler	1.000	2	18	1	0	3
Padron	1.000	1	2	0	0	0
Rogowski	.996	83	683	46	3	77
M. Sweeney	1.000	3	12	1	0	3

Second Base	PCT	G	PO	A	E	DP
Affronti	1.000	5	10	9	0	4
Conrad	.985	53	98	161	4	50
Melillo	.978	36	78	99	4	22
Murphy	.934	11	23	34	4	7
Patterson	.980	21	43	56	2	15
Pennington	.962	15	37	38	3	9

	PCT	G	PO	A	E	DP
Petit	1.000	4	4	12	0	1
Third Base	PCT	G	PO	A	E	DP
Affronti	.800	3	1	7	2	1
Baisley	.938	77	66	162	15	17
Bankston	.850	8	6	11	3	1
Chavez	1.000	5	2	10	0	1
Conrad	.971	15	10	24	1	2
Cornejo	1.000	3	0	1	0	0
Guzman	.857	14	4	20	4	1
Knoedler	.750	3	1	5	2	1
Murphy	.963	11	6	20	1	2
Pennington	.818	3	1	8	2	2
Petit	1.000	1	0	4	0	0

Shortstop	PCT	G	PO	A	E	DP
Affronti	1.000	1	2	3	0	1
Conrad	.938	18	26	50	5	8
Murphy	1.000	11	11	21	0	5
Pennington	.965	46	72	151	8	33

	PCT	G	PO	A	E	DP
Petit	.952	68	115	203	16	55
Outfield	PCT	G	PO	A	E	DP
Blasi	.980	29	48	2	1	0
Buck	.987	42	73	2	1	1
Conrad	.971	16	33	0	1	0
Cunningham	.974	20	37	1	1	0
Denorfia	.982	45	102	5	2	3
Fiorentino	1.000	8	22	0	0	0
Gaetti	.976	42	79	2	2	1
Gonzalez	.978	44	87	3	2	1
Linden	1.000	19	30	3	0	0
Massaro	1.000	14	24	0	0	0
Murton	.967	29	56	2	2	1
Patterson	1.000	4	11	0	0	0
Putnam	.952	74	117	3	6	0
Robnett	.991	54	111	3	1	0
Rogowski	1.000	4	9	0	0	0
R. Sweeney	1.000	8	14	0	0	0

MIDLAND ROCKHOUNDS

DOUBLE-A

TEXAS LEAGUE

Batting	B-T	HT	WT	DOB	AVG	vLH	vRH	G	AB	R	H	2B	3B	HR	RBI	BB	HBP	SH	SF	SO	SB	CS	SLG	OBP
Affronti, Michael	R-R	6-2	195	2-13-84	.265	.263	.266	27	98	8	26	8	0	2	14	0	1	3	1	20	0	0	.408	.270
Blasi, Nick	R-R	5-10	200	9-23-81	.296	.500	.211	13	54	11	16	2	0	1	9	5	0	0	0	18	2	1	.389	.356
Cardenas, Adrian	L-R	6-0	185	10-10-87	.279	.200	.296	26	86	12	24	4	0	0	7	15	1	0	0	10	0	1	.326	.392
Cunningham, Aaron	R-R	5-11	195	4-24-86	.317	.359	.305	87	347	65	110	18	6	12	52	38	5	5	6	92	12	4	.507	.386
Donovan, Todd	R-R	6-1	180	8-12-78	.274	.393	.244	79	307	53	84	14	2	1	26	42	1	2	1	63	37	6	.342	.362
Doolittle, Sean	L-L	6-3	190	9-26-86	.254	.224	.263	51	201	25	51	15	0	4	30	17	0	0	1	54	1	1	.388	.311
Everidge, Tommy	R-R	6-1	215	4-20-83	.279	.364	.257	136	531	89	148	34	0	22	115	55	7	0	14	133	0	0	.467	.346
Gaetti, Joe	R-R	5-11	205	10-18-81	.316	.345	.304	24	98	19	31	6	1	3	18	10	1	0	1	26	0	0	.490	.382
Guzman, Jesus	R-R	6-1	165	6-14-84	.364	.279	.385	80	341	57	124	21	2	14	76	33	0	1	1	56	5	2	.560	.419
Herrera, Javier	R-R	5-10	205	4-9-85	.267	.298	.260	61	255	44	68	13	2	9	36	22	2	2	0	71	8	4	.439	.330
Klein, Adam	L-L	5-11	185	8-21-83	.313	.000	.333	7	16	6	5	0	0	0	1	5	0	0	0	2	1	1	.313	.476
Leslie, Myron	B-R	6-3	220	5-2-82	.248	.143	.270	108	367	47	91	18	0	10	43	51	3	0	1	94	2	3	.379	.344
Martinez, Frank	R-R	6-0	164	7-19-85	.260	.000	.325	14	50	7	13	1	1	1	5	3	0	2	1	6	1	0	.380	.296
Massaro, Michael	L-L	5-11	160	4-15-84	.268	.188	.288	24	82	10	22	5	0	0	4	4	0	4	0	14	1	5	.329	.302
Morris, Jed	L-R	5-11	200	3-4-80	.261	.125	.282	35	119	15	31	6	1	3	14	13	0	0	0	18	0	0	.403	.333
Myers, Casey	R-R	5-10	209	10-23-84	.237	.250	.233	12	38	7	9	3	0	1	6	8	0	0	1	5	0	0	.395	.362
Pennington, Cliff	B-R	5-11	185	6-15-84	.260	.302	.245	50	204	42	53	7	2	0	18	39	0	1	0	36	20	1	.314	.379
Putnam, Danny	L-L	5-10	200	9-17-82	.222	.000	.250	4	18	2	4	0	0	1	6	1	0	0	0	7	0	0	.389	.263
Recker, Anthony	R-R	6-2	240	8-29-83	.274	.340	.255	117	430	57	118	29	4	11	64	43	5	2	2	140	1	2	.437	.346
Robnett, Richie	L-L	5-9	215	9-17-83	.259	.273	.254	23	85	13	22	6	0	1	8	17	1	0	1	24	1	0	.365	.385
Sellers, Justin	R-R	5-10	160	2-1-86	.255	.212	.266	123	439	72	112	15	8	6	46	47	7	9	5	77	10	6	.367	.333
Snyder, Brian	L-L	5-10	200	3-17-82	.248	.326	.229	61	218	23	54	13	1	2	29	36	1	1	0	47	1	1	.344	.357
2-team total (14 San Antonio)					.234	—	—	75	252	27	59	16	1	3	35	43	1	1	0	62	2	1	.341	.348
Zeringue, Jon	R-R	6-2	215	3-29-83	.257	.266	.255	126	478	75	123	22	3	23	89	52	12	2	1	121	4	4	.460	.344

Pitching	B-T	HT	WT	DOB	W	L	ERA	G	GS	CG	SV	IP	H	R	ER	HR	BB	SO	AVG	vLH	vRH	K/9	BB/9
Anderson, Brett	L-L	6-4	215	2-1-88	2	1	2.61	6	6	0	0	31	27	10	9	3	9	38	.235	.206	.247	11.03	2.61
Bailey, Andrew	R-R	6-3	220	5-31-84	5	9	4.32	37	15	0	0	110	99	63	53	13	56	110	.240	.235	.243	8.97	4.57
Bell, Kristian	R-R	6-0	185	1-11-84	1	1	9.45	11	0	0	0	13	23	17	14	4	7	7	.383	.375	.386	4.73	4.73
Borrell, Danny	L-L	6-3	200	1-24-79	1	1	9.00	3	3	0	0	8	10	9	8	2	8	5	.323	.400	.286	5.63	9.00
Cahill, Trevor	R-R	6-3	195	3-1-88	6	1	2.19	7	6	0	0	37	24	15	9	2	19	33	.190	.229	.167	8.03	4.62
Carignan Jr., Andrew	R-R	5-11	205	7-23-86	3	3	2.22	46	0	0	24	53	36	15	13	4	39	67	.196	.229	.175	11.45	6.66
Currin, Patrick	R-R	6-0	188	5-12-84	4	3	6.80	28	0	0	1	46	61	37	35	7	15	34	.323	.333	.319	6.60	2.91
Dowdy, Justin	L-L	6-1	175	8-13-83	1	7	7.16	38	1	0	1	49	60	39	39	4	34	44	.300	.280	.307	8.08	6.24
Farley, Chris	R-R	6-2	220	2-24-83	2	2	4.01	33	1	0	1	61	55	36	27	5	33	59	.237	.231	.240	8.75	4.90
Fernandez, Jason	R-R	6-2	175	1-8-85	1	3	4.91	7	6	0	0	37	42	21	20	3	17	28	.294	.300	.289	6.87	4.17
Garcia, Jose	R-R	5-11	165	1-7-85	0	1	4.63	7	0	0	0	12	9	6	6	1	3	13	.225	.188	.250	10.03	2.31
Glushon, Jason	R-R	6-2	195	5-26-85	0	3	3.38	8	0	0	0	16	19	7	6	2	7	10	.317	.400	.289	5.63	3.94
Knox, Brad	R-R	6-2	230	5-27-82	0	1	5.59	2	2	0	0	10	13	9	6	0	4	9	.325	.375	.292	8.38	3.72
Lansford, Jared	R-R	6-2	190	10-22-86	3	1	0.70	15	0	0	5	26	20	2	2	0	9	19	.227	.162	.275	6.66	3.16
Madsen, Michael	R-R	6-0	160	11-29-82	2	0	2.25	2	2	0	0	12	7	4	3	2	3	6	.167	.211	.130	4.50	2.25
Marshall, Jay	L-L	6-5	205	2-25-83	1	0	0.84	20	0	0	1	32	23	4	3	1	7	21	.205	.135	.240	5.85	1.95
Mazzaro, Vin	R-R	6-2	190	9-27-86	12	3	1.90	22	22	0	0	137	115	40	29	3	36	104	.229	.244	.222	6.82	2.36
Michalak, Chris	L-L	6-2	195	1-4-71	0	0	4.82	10	0	0	0	9	8	8	5	3	7	9	.222	.067	.333	8.68	6.75
2-team total (16 Frisco)					1	1	5.22	26	0	0	0	29	30	23	17	6	17	17	—	—	—	5.22	5.22
Moore, Scott	R-R	6-1	210	12-4-83	1	1	10.67	5	3	0	0	14	20	18	17	2	17	15	.333	.450	.275	9.42	10.67
Murray, Justin	R-R	6-4	200	5-11-87	2	1	5.52	5	3	0	0	15	15	9	9	0	5	5	.278	.296	.259	3.07	3.07
Outman, Josh	L-L	6-1	185	9-14-84	1	0	4.26	4	4	0	0	13	13	7	6	1	3	5	.260	.167	.273	3.55	2.13
Rodriguez, Henry	R-R	6-1	175	2-25-87	2	7	7.46	14	9	0	0	41	51	39	34	1	44	43	.302	.309	.298	9.44	9.66
Rojas, Jose	R-R	5-11	195	3-2-83	2	5	5.44	31	0	0	1	41	38	27	25	5	29	44	.253	.152	.298	9.58	6.31
Shafer, David	R-R	6-2	190	3-7-82	0	1	1.52	20	1	0	1	30	22	8	5	1	21	20	.214	.111	.250	6.07	6.37
Sharpe, Steven	R-R	6-1	195	7-20-81	1	1	7.84	19	2	0	1	31	43	28	27	2	15	15	.331	.340	.325	4.35	4.35
Shipman, Andy	R-R	6-3	185	12-10-81	2	2	5.13	37	0	0	1	54	73	37	31	6	17	41	.338	.292	.358	6.79	2.82
Silva, Jesus	R-R	6-0	199	12-24-82	0	0	5.40	6	0	0	1	8	11	8	5	1	3	10	.297	.300	.296	10.80	3.24
Simmons, James	R-R	6-3	205	9-29-86	9	6	3.51	25	25	0	0	136	150	58	53	11	32	120	.282	.254	.302	7.94	2.12
Tyler, Scott	R-R	6-5	265	8-20-82	0	0	8.22	9	0	0	0	15	18	14	14	3	9	8	.290	.412	.244	4.70	5.28
Webb, Ryan	R-R	6-6	205	2-5-86	9	8	5.19	25	22	0	0	130	165	86	75	12	44	94	.310	.288	.322	6.51	3.05
Windsor, Jason	R-R	6-2	235	7-16-82	2	2	8.88	7	7	0	0	24	30	25	24	3	22	17	.316	.382	.279	6.29	8.14

Fielding

Catcher	PCT	G	PO	A	E	DP	PB
Morris	.995	22	171	10	1	1	6
Myers	.957	7	44	0	2	0	0
Recker	.986	115	861	78	13	8	20

First Base	PCT	G	PO	A	E	DP
Donovan	—	1	0	0	0	0
Doolittle	.987	42	350	40	5	38
Everidge	.994	87	744	71	5	88
Leslie	.983	8	54	5	1	6
Myers	1.000	2	11	0	0	3
Snyder	1.000	4	37	1	0	6

Second Base	PCT	G	PO	A	E	DP
Affronti	.929	19	39	53	7	12
Donovan	.889	3	5	3	1	0
Guzman	.948	31	66	79	8	25
Leslie	1.000	7	7	8	0	2

	PCT	G	PO	A	E	DP
Martinez	.769	3	4	6	3	0
Pennington	.943	17	33	50	5	15
Sellers	.986	60	131	159	4	54
Snyder	.914	8	15	17	3	4

Third Base	PCT	G	PO	A	E	DP
Everidge	.952	18	10	30	2	2
Guzman	.929	49	26	91	9	9
Leslie	.930	60	37	96	10	8
Martinez	1.000	1	0	4	0	0
Morris	1.000	3	1	1	0	0
Snyder	.933	24	8	34	3	4

Shortstop	PCT	G	PO	A	E	DP
Affronti	1.000	8	12	30	0	2
Cardenas	.984	26	39	81	2	22
Martinez	.966	11	24	33	2	10
Pennington	.967	34	61	114	6	33

	PCT	G	PO	A	E	DP
Sellers	.958	63	98	224	14	50

Outfield	PCT	G	PO	A	E	DP
Blasi	.947	12	16	2	1	2
Cunningham	.977	83	164	4	4	1
Donovan	1.000	68	139	0	0	0
Doolittle	.926	11	24	1	2	0
Gaetti	1.000	19	32	1	0	0
Herrera	.965	35	54	1	2	0
Klein	1.000	6	15	3	0	0
Leslie	.983	28	52	5	1	1
Massaro	.977	24	42	0	1	0
Morris	1.000	1	2	0	0	0
Putnam	1.000	3	4	0	0	0
Robnett	.969	23	29	2	1	1
Zeringue	.967	118	198	10	7	2

STOCKTON PORTS

HIGH CLASS A

CALIFORNIA LEAGUE

Batting	B-T	HT	WT	DOB	AVG	vLH	vRH	G	AB	R	H	2B	3B	HR	RBI	BB	HBP	SH	SF	SO	SB	CS	SLG	OBP
Affronti, Michael	R-R	6-2	195	2-13-84	.271	.329	.250	70	273	33	74	13	2	5	26	13	8	3	4	39	4	2	.388	.319
Arrieche, Carlos	R-R	5-10	190	3-30-85	.225	.200	.236	24	80	8	18	6	0	0	7	1	3	1	1	19	0	0	.300	.259
Brown, Corey	L-L	6-2	210	11-26-85	.260	.273	.255	49	196	34	51	9	0	16	34	17	1	0	0	72	4	1	.551	.322
Cardenas, Adrian	L-R	6-0	185	10-10-87	.278	.300	.269	15	72	11	20	1	0	1	10	1	0	0	1	14	1	0	.333	.297
Carter, Chris	R-R	6-4	210	12-18-86	.259	.254	.261	137	506	101	131	32	4	39	104	77	7	0	6	156	4	0	.569	.361
Cobb, Larry	R-R	5-9	179	7-10-85	.118	.000	.143	5	17	1	2	0	0	0	3	4	0	0	1	4	0	1	.118	.273
Denorfia, Chris	R-R	6-0	195	7-15-80	.333	.750	.000	3	9	3	3	0	0	0	0	0	0	0	0	1	0	1	.333	.333
Donaldson, Josh	R-R	6-1	215	12-8-85	.330	.305	.341	47	188	37	62	13	2	9	39	17	2	0	0	29	0	2	.564	.391
Doolittle, Sean	L-L	6-3	190	9-26-86	.305	.323	.298	86	334	64	102	25	3	18	61	46	0	0	4	99	7	3	.560	.385
Gilbert, Archie	R-R	5-8	180	7-8-83	.278	.288	.275	119	478	85	133	30	5	7	49	55	12	0	5	61	35	18	.406	.364
Horton, Josh	L-R	6-1	195	2-19-86	.277	.292	.271	118	477	63	132	24	4	3	42	49	4	1	4	87	2	6	.331	.346
Lawhorn, Darryl	L-R	6-1	180	12-18-82	.272	.231	.287	53	202	24	55	10	3	8	39	13	0	0	6	46	2	0	.470	.308
Martinez, Frank	B-R	6-0	164	7-19-85	.279	.298	.272	114	433	65	121	24	4	6	42	36	4	2	5	60	5	5	.395	.337
Massaro, Michael	L-L	5-11	160	4-15-84	.329	.315	.330	56	216	37	71	14	1	0	30	11	0	1	2	30	0	1	.403	.358
Mitchell, Jermaine	L-L	6-0	205	11-2-84	.244	.208	.260	114	422	55	103	20	3	10	49	54	7	3	2	116	23	6	.377	.338
Morris, Jed	L-R	5-11	200	3-4-80	.290	.280	.293	27	107	17	31	8	2	7	32	12	0	0	0	22	0	0	.598	.361

	B-T	HT	WT	DOB	AVG	vLH	vRH	G	AB	R	H	2B	3B	HR	RBI	BB	HBP	SH	SF	SO	SB	CS	SLG	OBP
Murphy, Donnie	R-R	5-10	185	3-10-83	.333	.333	—	1	3	1	1	1	0	0	0	0	0	0	0	2	0	0	.667	.333
Nunez, Juan	R-R	6-2	191	8-27-87	.042	.077	.000	11	24	2	1	0	0	0	0	5	0	0	0	9	1	0	.042	.207
Padron, Raul	L-R	6-0	195	9-17-84	.257	.274	.248	47	171	17	44	7	0	4	20	13	2	1	1	45	0	1	.368	.316
Robnett, Richie	L-L	5-9	215	9-17-83	.000	.000	.000	1	3	0	0	0	0	0	0	1	0	0	0	1	0	0	.000	.250
Rosendo, Gustavo	R-R	6-0	242	3-1-86	.187	.296	.141	26	91	6	17	1	0	1	6	1	0	1	0	16	0	0	.231	.196
Smith, Matt	R-R	5-11	215	1-30-86	.150	.000	.188	7	20	2	3	0	0	0	1	2	2	0	1	4	0	0	.150	.280
Spencer, Matt	L-L	6-4	225	1-27-86	.333	.354	.325	41	168	30	56	12	1	8	27	6	6	0	1	39	7	1	.560	.376
Sulentic, Matt	L-R	5-10	170	10-6-87	.309	.340	.297	95	343	52	106	24	4	9	55	30	3	3	2	91	7	2	.481	.368
Valdez, Alex	B-R	6-1	160	9-2-84	.169	.286	.140	21	71	5	12	1	0	0	5	2	1	0	3	17	1	2	.183	.195

Pitching	B-T	HT	WT	DOB	W	L	ERA	G	GS	CG	SV	IP	H	R	ER	HR	BB	SO	AVG	vLH	vRH	K/9	BB/9
Anderson, Brett	L-L	6-4	215	2-1-88	9	4	4.14	14	13	0	0	74	68	35	34	5	18	80	.238	.263	.229	9.73	2.19
Banwart, Travis	R-R	6-4	205	2-14-86	2	4	4.45	14	14	0	0	59	63	35	29	7	32	54	.268	.284	.256	8.28	4.91
Bell, Kristian	R-R	6-0	185	1-11-84	0	0	7.71	6	0	0	0	7	11	7	6	2	4	6	.355	.385	.333	7.71	5.14
Benacka, Mike	R-R	6-2	210	8-2-82	4	2	2.39	15	0	0	0	26	18	8	7	4	11	37	.200	.156	.224	12.65	3.76
Brown, Andrew	R-R	6-6	230	2-17-81	0	0	0.00	1	1	0	0	2	0	0	0	0	0	0	.000	.000	.000	0.00	0.00
Cahill, Trevor	R-R	6-3	195	3-1-88	5	4	2.78	14	13	0	0	87	52	29	27	3	31	103	.174	.150	.197	10.61	3.19
Carignan, Andrew	R-R	5-11	205	7-23-86	1	1	0.90	9	0	0	4	10	5	1	1	0	5	17	.147	.143	.150	15.30	4.50
Casilla, Santiago	R-R	6-0	200	7-25-80	0	0	0.00	1	1	0	0	1	0	0	0	0	2	0	.000	.000	.000	18.00	0.00
Currin, Patrick	R-R	6-0	188	5-12-84	0	1	3.40	31	1	0	7	45	53	19	17	3	13	40	.293	.288	.296	8.00	2.60
De Los Santos, Fautino	R-R	6-0	205	2-15-86	2	2	5.87	5	5	0	0	23	29	17	15	3	11	26	.309	.378	.245	10.17	4.30
Demel, Sam	R-R	6-0	200	10-23-85	5	2	3.36	54	0	0	18	67	61	31	25	5	32	90	.227	.286	.185	12.09	4.30
Dewing, Branden	L-L	6-0	165	1-1-84	1	1	4.86	35	0	0	1	54	64	40	29	3	30	26	.288	.322	.267	4.36	5.03
Farley, Chris	R-R	6-2	220	2-24-83	2	1	1.74	14	0	0	3	21	21	7	4	1	4	20	.256	.280	.246	8.71	1.74
Fernandez, Jason	R-R	6-2	175	1-8-85	9	5	3.36	19	18	0	0	110	104	53	41	9	51	77	.254	.303	.213	6.32	4.19
Foulke, Keith	R-R	6-0	210	10-19-72	0	0	4.50	1	0	0	0	2	2	1	1	0	1	0	.250	.000	.333	4.50	0.00
Fragoso, Jose	R-R	6-0	170	11-12-84	3	3	4.44	22	0	0	0	26	19	19	13	3	22	24	.194	.150	.224	8.20	7.52
Glushon, Jason	R-R	6-2	195	5-26-85	1	1	3.67	14	5	0	0	42	38	21	17	4	6	28	.239	.226	.247	6.05	1.30
Godfrey, Graham	R-R	6-3	205	8-9-84	5	5	5.10	29	24	0	0	134	157	90	76	14	37	119	.293	.338	.249	7.99	2.49
Gordon, Derrick	L-L	5-9	185	10-16-83	5	5	4.93	44	5	0	2	77	78	54	42	11	47	75	.262	.346	.216	8.80	5.52
Guzman, Jose	R-R	5-11	185	11-5-87	0	0	2.08	4	0	0	0	4	5	2	1	0	0	1	.294	.455	.000	2.08	0.00
Harden, Rich	L-R	6-1	195	11-30-81	1	0	0.00	1	1	0	0	1	0	0	0	1	0	1	.000	.000	.200	13.50	0.00
Heuser, James	L-L	6-5	215	3-30-84	9	3	4.53	48	6	0	1	95	98	59	48	8	61	103	.268	.298	.252	9.72	5.76
Italiano, Craig	R-R	6-4	209	7-22-86	1	4	9.90	14	5	0	0	30	44	37	33	7	26	33	.333	.288	.370	9.90	7.80
Lansford, Jared	R-R	6-2	190	10-22-86	2	6	4.41	31	2	0	3	63	62	33	31	4	20	75	.258	.330	.201	10.66	2.84
Leon, Arnold	R-R	5-11	190	9-6-88	0	0	2.86	20	0	0	2	28	25	12	9	1	9	28	.238	.233	.242	8.89	2.86
Mitchinson, Scott	R-R	6-3	185	12-28-84	1	0	1.69	2	2	0	0	11	5	2	2	0	1	9	.139	.308	.043	7.59	0.84
Moore, Scott	R-R	6-1	210	12-4-83	5	2	6.57	13	11	0	0	63	78	48	46	4	34	56	.308	.301	.314	8.00	4.86
Rodriguez, Henry	R-R	6-1	175	2-25-87	2	3	3.96	20	13	0	2	75	57	38	33	5	40	104	.208	.256	.166	12.48	4.80
Rojas, Jose	R-R	5-11	195	3-2-83	1	2	6.17	6	0	0	0	12	10	9	8	0	8	16	.233	.222	.240	12.34	6.17

Fielding

Catcher	PCT	G	PO	A	E	DP	PB
Donaldson	.978	42	366	27	9	4	12
Morris	.992	27	248	15	2	1	10
Nunez	.987	11	69	7	1	0	3
Padron	.984	35	283	27	5	2	6
Rosendo	.983	26	210	24	4	0	3
Smith	1.000	7	73	6	0	0	1

First Base	PCT	G	PO	A	E	DP
Carter	.974	41	349	25	10	39
Donaldson	.941	2	16	0	1	1
Doolittle	.993	65	534	42	4	46
Lawhorn	1.000	1	5	1	0	0
Padron	1.000	11	68	6	0	8
Spencer	.971	25	178	21	6	17

Second Base	PCT	G	PO	A	E	DP
Affronti	.975	62	103	167	7	31
Arrieche	1.000	2	3	2	0	0

	PCT	G	PO	A	E	DP
Cardenas	1.000	12	20	26	0	5
Cobb	.957	4	9	13	1	3
Lawhorn	1.000	2	1	1	0	0
Martinez	.966	58	109	178	10	39
Valdez	.933	4	8	6	1	0

Third Base	PCT	G	PO	A	E	DP
Arrieche	.833	8	5	5	2	1
Carter	.846	41	22	55	14	5
Donaldson	1.000	3	2	7	0	1
Lawhorn	.901	29	22	42	7	6
Martinez	.871	52	29	72	15	5
Morris	—	1	0	0	0	0
Valdez	.894	16	12	30	5	2

Shortstop	PCT	G	PO	A	E	DP
Affronti	.906	10	9	20	3	3
Arrieche	.932	13	19	36	4	7
Cardenas	1.000	3	1	11	0	0

	PCT	G	PO	A	E	DP
Horton	.959	117	171	300	20	74
Murphy	1.000	1	0	3	0	0

Outfield	PCT	G	PO	A	E	DP
Brown	.989	42	88	2	1	1
Carter	.909	14	10	0	1	0
Cobb	1.000	1	1	0	0	0
Denorfia	1.000	2	2	0	0	0
Doolittle	1.000	14	19	0	0	0
Gilbert	.990	107	185	8	2	2
Lawhorn	1.000	11	6	0	0	0
Massaro	.989	43	85	4	1	0
Mitchell	.958	104	203	2	9	0
Morris	1.000	1	3	0	0	0
Robnett	1.000	1	1	0	0	0
Spencer	.923	8	12	0	1	0
Sulentic	.975	80	113	6	3	2

KANE COUNTY COUGARS
LOW CLASS A
MIDWEST LEAGUE

Batting	B-T	HT	WT	DOB	AVG	vLH	vRH	G	AB	R	H	2B	3B	HR	RBI	BB	HBP	SH	SF	SO	SB	CS	SLG	OBP
Arrieche, Carlos	R-R	5-10	190	3-30-85	.230	.154	.250	19	61	2	14	4	0	0	4	0	0	1	0	11	0	1	.295	.230
Brown, Corey	L-L	6-2	210	11-26-85	.270	.230	.283	85	300	44	81	18	2	14	49	41	3	3	4	96	12	0	.483	.359
Christian, Jason	L-R	6-3	170	6-16-87	.320	.400	.300	6	25	3	8	1	0	0	1	0	0	0	0	6	0	0	.360	.320
Cobb, Larry	R-R	5-9	179	7-10-85	.273	.308	.262	107	406	57	111	25	2	13	70	44	11	0	11	80	19	6	.441	.352
Correa, Walter	R-R	6-1	200	7-6-87	.188	.111	.216	30	101	12	19	4	0	1	6	13	1	1	1	20	4	3	.257	.284
Dowling, Greg	L-L	6-3	231	11-15-83	.269	.252	.275	132	510	51	137	33	0	15	71	30	8	3	7	86	1	1	.422	.315
Frash, Justin	L-R	5-9	190	4-26-84	.281	.274	.283	72	274	34	77	10	0	1	24	27	0	4	0	58	2	1	.328	.346
Hamblin, Danny	R-R	6-1	200	2-10-85	.145	.000	.175	22	76	12	11	1	1	1	6	10	0	0	0	27	0	0	.224	.244
Hollingsworth, D.J.	L-L	5-9	175	5-28-85	.224	.273	.216	28	85	14	19	0	1	0	6	15	4	5	1	16	6	3	.247	.362
Johnson, Toddric	L-L	6-1	202	12-17-84	.281	.296	.275	109	413	55	116	24	5	13	74	42	5	3	7	81	11	4	.458	.349

	B-T	HT	WT	DOB	AVG	vLH	vRH	G	AB	R	H	2B	3B	HR	RBI	BB	HBP	SH	SF	SO	SB	CS	SLG	OBP
Johnston, Johnston	L-R	6-0	195	2-13-84	.228	.214	.230	36	114	21	26	4	0	1	11	21	2	1	3	38	11	4	.289	.350
Keough, Shane	B-R	6-3	196	9-11-86	.244	.303	.223	104	340	43	83	7	3	2	26	29	2	3	1	103	3	8	.300	.306
Klein, Adam	L-L	5-11	185	8-21-83	.271	.296	.259	79	266	61	72	13	2	1	26	68	2	5	5	60	18	7	.346	.416
Lissman, Michael	R-L	6-0	205	6-10-85	.203	.277	.176	54	172	16	35	7	1	2	13	20	3	4	0	34	1	2	.291	.297
Love, Dante	R-R	5-11	195	4-8-87	.161	.167	.160	9	31	4	5	2	0	0	2	2	1	0	0	7	0	0	.226	.235
Napoleon, Dusty	L-R	6-2	208	5-21-86	.205	.200	.205	16	44	3	9	1	0	0	3	9	1	0	1	12	0	1	.227	.345
Nunez, Juan	R-R	6-2	191	8-27-87	.333	.500	.267	7	21	3	7	0	0	0	1	2	1	1	0	5	0	0	.333	.417
Paramore, Petey	R-R	6-2	195	10-30-86	.225	.233	.222	31	102	14	23	8	0	1	14	22	1	1	0	30	0	0	.333	.368
Ray, Matt	B-R	5-9	179	1-28-84	.251	.165	.281	105	371	50	93	13	3	3	35	41	6	7	3	87	14	7	.326	.333
Richard, Michael	R-R	5-11	180	8-20-84	.287	.341	.266	85	321	56	92	9	2	2	42	41	4	5	5	35	35	7	.346	.369
Rosendo, Gustavo	R-R	6-0	242	3-1-86	.211	.294	.143	12	38	5	8	0	0	0	1	2	1	1	0	5	0	0	.211	.268
Smith, Jacob	R-R	6-0	214	6-5-83	.288	.292	.286	81	313	32	90	24	0	6	47	25	11	2	4	52	3	0	.422	.357
Smith, Matt	R-R	5-11	215	1-30-86	.232	.222	.237	18	56	8	13	6	1	2	8	10	1	0	0	19	1	1	.482	.358
Vitters, Christian	L-R	6-3	201	6-26-85	.257	.310	.238	33	113	16	29	4	0	2	15	13	2	1	5	28	2	1	.345	.331
Weeks, Jemile	B-R	5-10	175	1-26-87	.297	.346	.271	19	74	11	22	3	1	1	8	13	3	0	0	12	6	2	.405	.422

Pitching	B-T	HT	WT	DOB	W	L	ERA	G	GS	CG	SV	IP	H	R	ER	HR	BB	SO	AVG	vLH	vRH	K/9	BB/9
Banwart, Travis	R-R	6-4	205	2-14-86	2	3	2.38	7	7	1	0	42	39	15	11	0	11	41	.253	.350	.191	8.86	2.38
Capra, Anthony	L-L	6-1	200	4-3-87	4	3	4.22	10	10	0	0	49	48	25	23	3	22	39	.257	.171	.281	7.16	4.04
Deal, Scott	R-R	6-3	182	12-11-86	6	6	4.73	32	17	0	1	122	131	69	64	19	40	86	.274	.277	.272	6.36	2.96
Dewing, Branden	L-L	6-0	165	1-1-84	0	0	0.00	7	0	0	3	10	4	1	0	0	1	2	.118	.000	.222	1.74	0.87
Espinal, Leonardo	R-R	6-3	226	2-6-84	5	5	3.06	40	0	0	4	62	60	29	21	3	23	53	.253	.240	.263	7.74	3.36
Farley, Chris	R-R	6-2	220	2-24-83	0	0	0.00	2	0	0	0	4	1	0	0	0	1	2	.083	.167	.000	4.50	2.25
Fragoso, Jose	R-R	6-0	170	11-12-84	1	0	0.00	4	0	0	1	6	2	0	0	0	1	12	.105	.000	.154	19.06	1.59
Friend, Justin	R-R	6-1	200	6-21-86	5	5	3.84	42	0	0	11	63	59	34	27	6	32	78	.248	.268	.234	11.08	4.55
Glushon, Jason	R-R	6-2	195	5-26-85	1	0	2.96	9	0	0	1	24	24	10	8	3	2	15	.258	.243	.268	5.55	0.74
Hernandez, Carlos	L-L	5-11	155	3-4-87	5	0	2.29	7	6	0	0	35	30	9	9	1	7	29	.240	.273	.228	7.39	1.78
Hertzler, Bradley	R-L	6-1	210	4-11-86	2	5	5.26	24	4	0	0	63	70	45	37	5	13	49	.286	.351	.257	6.96	1.85
Hodsdon, Scott	R-R	6-1	185	5-31-85	5	8	2.93	25	23	0	0	120	134	60	39	7	23	86	.282	.309	.260	6.45	1.73
Hornbeck, Ben	R-L	6-5	180	7-22-87	1	0	2.25	3	0	0	0	4	3	1	1	0	1	5	.214	.000	.333	11.25	2.25
Hunter, Brett	R-R	6-4	215	6-27-87	0	0	5.40	2	0	0	0	2	0	1	1	0	2	1	.000	.000	.000	5.40	10.80
Italiano, Craig	R-R	6-4	209	7-22-86	1	0	1.16	14	14	0	0	70	43	16	9	2	35	79	.177	.135	.209	10.16	4.50
Kerfoot, Chad	R-R	6-0	185	4-1-85	8	1	2.35	34	2	0	4	73	64	27	19	5	15	34	.234	.202	.255	9.04	1.86
Lysander, Brent	R-R	6-7	210	4-5-85	1	3	4.53	24	1	0	0	52	70	37	26	5	18	27	.313	.303	.320	4.70	3.14
Mitchinson, Scott	R-R	6-1	185	12-28-84	5	3	1.74	14	13	0	0	78	60	21	15	1	11	78	.210	.206	.213	9.04	1.27
Moore, Scott	R-R	6-1	210	12-4-83	1	3	4.62	11	2	0	4	25	25	14	13	2	8	33	.255	.333	.180	11.72	2.84
Oakes, Earl	R-R	6-3	225	9-3-85	0	0	18.00	2	0	0	0	2	7	4	4	1	0	2	.538	.400	.625	9.00	0.00
Richmond, Jamie	R-R	6-3	190	3-23-86	7	11	4.79	28	28	1	0	163	175	99	87	16	27	98	.269	.295	.249	5.40	1.49
Ross, Tyson	R-R	6-5	215	4-22-87	0	1	4.66	6	4	0	0	19	16	11	10	1	5	16	.219	.240	.208	7.45	2.33
Sewell, Lance	L-L	6-3	195	6-17-86	5	5	2.88	26	6	0	2	78	61	33	25	7	28	78	.214	.338	.173	9.00	3.23
Tacker, Ryne	R-R	6-2	195	2-2-84	0	0	27.00	1	1	0	0	1	3	3	3	0	2	2	.600	.500	.667	18.00	18.00
Walters, Nick	L-L	6-2	175	9-30-85	1	4	3.81	41	0	0	5	52	47	27	22	4	36	55	.240	.183	.272	9.52	6.23

Fielding

Catcher	PCT	G	PO	A	E	DP	PB
Johnston	.994	33	291	18	2	3	13
Love	1.000	9	81	7	0	0	1
Napoleon	.965	9	49	6	2	0	3
Nunez	.971	7	32	1	1	0	0
Paramore	1.000	25	178	20	0	2	3
Rosendo	1.000	11	88	6	0	1	0
J. Smith	.988	33	220	23	3	1	2
M. Smith	.986	17	130	15	2	2	1

First Base	PCT	G	PO	A	E	DP
Correa	1.000	1	5	0	0	0
Dowling	.990	125	1074	77	12	86
Frash	1.000	2	9	2	0	1
Hamblin	1.000	2	9	0	0	1
Napoleon	1.000	3	21	1	0	1
J. Smith	.947	7	51	3	3	2
Vitters	1.000	2	9	0	0	0

Second Base	PCT	G	PO	A	E	DP
Arrieche	1.000	3	7	6	0	0
Christian	1.000	5	17	11	0	3
Cobb	.963	59	111	174	11	22
Correa	1.000	2	1	2	0	0
Ray	.966	55	99	156	9	29
Richard	1.000	1	0	1	0	1
Vitters	1.000	1	0	2	0	1
Weeks	.911	18	42	40	8	14

Third Base	PCT	G	PO	A	E	DP
Arrieche	.917	16	7	26	3	1
Cobb	.727	2	2	6	3	0
Correa	1.000	3	2	2	0	0
Frash	.953	57	44	117	8	13
Hamblin	.960	17	15	33	2	2
Ray	.857	18	14	46	10	8
Vitters	.916	30	27	49	7	4

Shortstop	PCT	G	PO	A	E	DP
Christian	.800	2	1	3	1	1
Cobb	1.000	1	1	1	0	1
Correa	.915	25	38	69	10	16
Ray	.922	32	40	78	10	10
Richard	.927	83	117	200	25	41
Vitters	1.000	1	2	2	0	2

Outfield	PCT	G	PO	A	E	DP
Brown	.980	74	148	2	3	0
Cobb	.982	44	105	5	2	1
Hollingsworth	1.000	26	48	0	0	0
Johnson	.978	97	171	10	4	3
Keough	.916	76	118	2	11	0
Klein	.976	68	113	8	3	0
Lissman	.959	39	46	1	2	1

VANCOUVER CANADIANS   SHORT-SEASON

NORTHWEST LEAGUE

Batting	B-T	HT	WT	DOB	AVG	vLH	vRH	G	AB	R	H	2B	3B	HR	RBI	BB	HBP	SH	SF	SO	SB	CS	SLG	OBP
Arrieche, Carlos	R-R	5-10	190	3-30-85	.125	.000	.167	7	16	1	2	0	0	0	1	1	2	0	0	2	0	1	.125	.263
Barfield, Jeremy	R-L	6-5	240	7-12-88	.271	.216	.285	69	251	28	68	17	0	3	41	26	1	2	1	42	5	3	.375	.341
Christian, Jason	L-R	6-3	170	6-16-87	.291	.291	.291	62	213	27	62	16	1	4	24	39	2	1	1	65	11	1	.432	.404
Coleman, Dusty	R-R	6-2	185	4-20-87	.319	.308	.322	19	72	13	23	8	1	0	6	4	0	2	0	26	1	0	.458	.355
Correa, Walter	R-R	6-1	200	7-17-86	.200	.300	.160	11	35	5	7	1	0	1	3	4	0	0		8	3	1	.314	.349
Gil, Leonardo	R-R	6-1	160	8-18-87	.208	.211	.208	25	72	5	15	3	0	1	8	10	3	1	2	29	1	1	.292	.322
Jernigan, Ryne	R-R	5-10	175	6-27-85	.111	.182	.088	16	45	0	5	1	0	0	1	5	0	4	0	9	0	1	.133	.200
LeVier, Mitch	L-L	5-11	185	1-12-88	.241	.256	.237	50	170	15	41	7	1	0	12	9	1	5	1	52	4	2	.294	.282
Lissman, Michael	R-L	6-0	205	6-10-85	.219	.171	.233	44	155	25	34	8	0	6	22	21	4	0	2	28	1	1	.387	.324

Batting	B-T	HT	WT	DOB	AVG	vLH	vRH	G	AB	R	H	2B	3B	HR	RBI	BB	HBP	SH	SF	SO	SB	CS	SLG	OBP
Love, Dante	R-R	5-11	195	4-8-87	.151	.179	.143	37	119	14	18	5	1	2	16	19	1	1	5	23	1	0	.261	.264
Luis, Marcos	R-R	5-11	180	11-27-85	.250	.242	.253	38	128	9	32	2	1	0	12	8	2	3	1	21	3	5	.281	.302
Macias, Lorenzo	R-R	6-2	188	8-17-85	.079	.125	.067	13	38	1	3	0	0	0	2	2	0	0	0	5	0	0	.079	.125
Napoleon, Dusty	L-R	6-2	208	5-21-86	.244	.231	.248	61	209	29	51	12	1	2	28	41	2	3	1	41	0	0	.340	.372
Nunez, Juan	R-R	6-2	191	8-27-87	.206	.200	.208	22	63	8	13	3	0	1	4	6	0	3	0	18	0	1	.302	.275
Pruitt, J.D.	R-R	5-9	195	3-11-85	.282	.444	.237	40	124	33	35	4	2	4	14	39	11	1	1	33	8	3	.444	.486
Rivera, Julio	R-R	5-11	178	7-20-87	.195	.333	.156	29	82	8	16	4	0	0	5	4	2	2	0	30	0	1	.244	.250
Rutherford, Rodney	R-R	5-10	185	6-7-85	.210	.222	.205	40	124	15	26	6	2	0	15	16	5	4	1	39	0	0	.290	.322
Thomas, David	B-R	5-11	180	7-29-86	.290	.333	.273	57	207	30	60	18	2	2	32	29	8	5	6	43	7	4	.425	.388
Tirado, Francisco	B-R	6-0	175	7-30-87	.211	.000	.238	51	166	22	35	8	0	0	12	16	0	4	0	43	3	2	.259	.280
Wentzell, Dan	L-L	6-3	200	5-16-85	.125	.000	.158	8	24	2	3	1	0	0	1	2	0	0	0	11	0	0	.167	.192
West, Jareck	R-R	5-10	210	4-30-85	.181	.267	.148	59	160	24	29	7	4	2	16	31	2	5	1	48	9	2	.313	.320

Pitching	B-T	HT	WT	DOB	W	L	ERA	G	GS	CG	SV	IP	H	R	ER	HR	BB	SO	AVG	vLH	vRH	K/9	BB/9
Barham, Trey	L-L	6-0	215	11-7-85	4	4	3.46	20	7	0	0	52	51	23	20	1	17	36	.262	.310	.241	6.23	2.94
Deaza, Inoel	R-R	6-2	180	5-10-86	0	0	7.11	4	0	0	0	6	8	5	5	2	2	6	.308	.222	.353	8.53	2.84
Figueroa, Pedro	L-L	6-1	164	11-23-85	2	5	3.93	15	15	0	0	69	62	37	30	3	32	77	.238	.236	.239	10.09	4.19
Fitts, Matt	R-R	6-1	205	9-14-85	1	1	2.86	18	1	0	0	35	32	12	11	1	9	22	.244	.208	.269	5.71	2.34
Garcia, Hector	R-R	6-3	160	10-22-85	2	4	4.46	12	6	0	0	36	33	22	18	1	27	22	.248	.196	.276	5.45	6.69
Gomez, Fabian	B-L	6-0	190	8-27-84	3	2	5.94	24	0	0	1	36	46	25	24	1	19	26	.324	.211	.365	6.44	4.71
Guzman, Jose	R-R	5-11	185	11-5-87	2	2	2.25	30	0	0	15	36	34	14	9	1	12	38	.245	.273	.226	9.50	3.00
Hart, Michael	R-R	6-1	210	2-9-87	0	2	2.52	15	6	0	1	36	26	11	10	1	10	40	.202	.172	.225	10.09	3.28
Haviland, Shawn	R-R	6-2	200	11-10-85	2	3	3.48	18	9	0	0	54	56	25	21	1	18	61	.262	.242	.276	10.10	2.98
Hernandez, Carlos	L-L	5-11	155	3-4-87	2	0	1.82	7	7	0	0	40	32	9	8	0	7	38	.221	.257	.209	8.62	1.59
Hertzler, Bradley	R-L	6-1	210	4-11-86	2	1	3.60	7	1	0	0	15	13	10	6	1	7	7	.241	.143	.303	4.20	4.20
Hornbeck, Ben	R-L	6-5	180	7-22-87	2	2	4.88	18	0	0	1	31	30	18	17	2	18	40	.256	.433	.195	11.49	5.17
LeBlanc Poirier, Mathieu	L-R	6-1	175	3-10-87	1	0	0.93	6	0	0	0	10	4	1	1	0	7	9	.129	.000	.235	8.38	6.52
Lee, Chad	R-R	6-4	210	12-20-85	0	0	9.95	5	0	0	0	6	10	10	7	0	10	3	.345	.385	.313	4.26	14.21
Lysander, Brent	R-R	6-7	210	4-5-85	1	0	7.94	2	0	0	0	6	7	5	5	0	3	0	.350	.000	.538	0.00	4.76
Morla, Ronny	R-R	6-4	180	5-19-88	2	6	4.88	16	16	0	0	76	87	50	41	4	33	77	.285	.288	.283	9.16	3.93
Smalley, Ken	R-R	6-2	195	7-25-87	5	1	3.07	20	0	0	1	29	19	11	10	2	12	34	.190	.167	.203	10.43	3.68
Tacker, Ryne	R-R	6-2	195	2-2-84	0	5	10.03	14	8	0	0	35	51	44	39	2	34	27	.342	.340	.344	6.94	8.74
Tejeda, Edgar	R-R	6-0	180	3-4-87	1	1	5.17	22	0	0	1	31	30	24	18	2	19	40	.246	.279	.228	11.49	5.46
Thomas, Daniel	R-R	6-2	200	2-10-86	2	1	2.41	13	0	0	0	19	11	5	5	0	9	20	.172	.190	.163	9.64	4.34
Villegas, Juan	R-R	6-0	170	1-20-87	0	1	2.70	2	0	0	3	5	3	1	1	1	3	.294	.600	.167	8.10	2.70

Fielding

Catcher	PCT	G	PO	A	E	DP	PB
Love	.993	33	249	33	2	5	8
Nunez	.984	22	167	21	3	0	5
Rivera	.978	29	196	26	5	1	10

First Base	PCT	G	PO	A	E	DP
Arrieche	.889	1	6	2	1	0
Correa	.977	4	41	2	1	5
Napoleon	.984	58	489	51	9	49
Thomas	.983	7	50	8	1	2
Tirado	1.000	2	11	1	0	1
Wentzell	.982	6	49	5	1	5

Second Base	PCT	G	PO	A	E	DP
Arrieche	—	1	0	0	0	0
Christian	1.000	3	5	6	0	1

	PCT	G	PO	A	E	DP
Correa	.938	3	10	5	1	1
Gil	.978	8	20	24	1	6
Jernigan	.968	15	25	36	2	7
Luis	.968	36	56	93	5	15
Tirado	.945	19	29	40	4	5
West	—	2	0	0	0	0

Third Base	PCT	G	PO	A	E	DP
Arrieche	.813	4	2	11	3	1
Correa	1.000	2	0	4	0	0
Gil	.914	16	7	25	3	1
Rutherford Jr.	.816	37	19	52	16	7
Tirado	.823	27	19	46	14	3

Shortstop	PCT	G	PO	A	E	DP
Christian	.930	53	84	155	18	35

	PCT	G	PO	A	E	DP
Coleman	.958	18	19	49	3	11
Correa	1.000	2	4	3	0	0
Gil	1.000	1	2	4	0	1
Tirado	.889	4	5	11	2	2

Outfield	PCT	G	PO	A	E	DP
Barfield	.955	68	101	6	5	1
LeVier	1.000	40	66	6	0	1
Lissman	1.000	5	4	1	0	0
Macias	1.000	9	8	0	0	0
Pruitt	1.000	24	29	2	0	0
Thomas	.986	43	71	1	1	1
Wentzell	—	1	0	0	0	0
West	.979	49	90	3	2	2

AZL ATHLETICS

ROOKIE

ARIZONA LEAGUE

Batting	B-T	HT	WT	DOB	AVG	vLH	vRH	G	AB	R	H	2B	3B	HR	RBI	BB	HBP	SH	SF	SO	SB	CS	SLG	OBP
Baisley, Jeff	R-R	6-3	210	12-19-82	.273	.000	.316	6	22	4	6	2	0	1	5	0	2	0	0	4	0	0	.500	.333
Berroa, Chris	R-R	6-1	175	2-3-89	.311	.333	.308	13	45	8	14	0	0	0	3	5	2	0	0	10	4	3	.311	.396
Buck, Travis	L-R	6-2	225	11-18-83	.667	.333	.750	4	15	4	10	2	0	1	6	1	0	0	0	3	0	0	1.000	.688
Coleman, Dusty	R-R	6-2	185	4-20-87	.222	.200	.227	7	27	4	6	0	0	1	5	2	1	0	0	10	1	1	.333	.300
Crisostomo, Jose	L-R	6-1	181	4-20-89	.308	.462	.286	28	104	17	32	5	3	0	9	13	0	0	1	24	8	6	.413	.381
Desme, Grant	R-R	6-2	205	4-4-86	.333	.000	.500	2	3	2	1	0	0	1	2	0	1	0	0	0	0	0	1.333	.500
Dixon, Rashun	R-R	6-2	200	8-27-90	.263	.192	.275	45	179	32	47	3	10	8	42	18	1	0	3	68	5	2	.525	.328
Gil, Leonardo	R-R	6-1	160	8-18-87	.235	.167	.254	23	81	10	19	6	0	1	10	12	2	1	2	19	2	0	.346	.340
Guzman, Jesus	R-R	6-1	165	6-14-84	.467	.000	.538	5	15	2	7	3	0	1	3	0	2	0	0	1	1	0	.867	.529
Hernandez, Franklin	R-R	6-3	165	4-19-87	.316	.394	.302	55	225	29	71	17	5	4	36	18	4	0	2	61	1	1	.489	.373
House, Tyreace	R-R	5-10	175	3-1-88	.263	.143	.282	29	99	25	26	1	0	0	10	18	1	1	1	22	12	1	.273	.378
Hudson, Herbert	R-R	6-0	185	9-13-85	.164	.375	.132	19	61	10	10	2	0	0	4	8	4	0	0	12	2	1	.197	.301
Jernigan, Ryne	R-R	5-10	175	6-27-85	.333	.222	.353	17	60	7	20	4	1	0	7	10	1	0	1	13	1	0	.433	.431
Leyja, Nino	R-R	5-10	170	10-2-90	.315	.300	.319	43	165	42	52	12	6	1	25	19	1	0	3	31	10	2	.479	.383
Made, Alcibiades	R-R	6-0	169	4-5-89	.198	.250	.186	28	86	12	17	3	0	1	6	5	1	1	0	25	1	0	.267	.250
Mercedes, Wilson	R-R	6-1	170	4-5-88	.169	.083	.186	22	71	10	12	3	0	2	8	9	0	1	1	21	3	0	.296	.259
Ortiz, Gabriel	R-R	6-1	215	11-7-85	.256	.133	.282	26	86	9	22	5	2	1	16	3	1	0	2	25	0	1	.395	.283
Paramore, Petey	B-R	6-2	195	10-30-86	.364	.600	.294	9	22	7	8	2	0	0	4	10	0	0	0	2	0	0	.455	.563

	B-T	HT	WT	DOB	AVG	vLH	vRH	G	AB	R	H	2B	3B	HR	RBI	BB	HBP	SH	SF	SO	SB	CS	SLG	OBP
Penaloza, Carmelo	R-R	6-0	165	3-1-87	.258	.200	.269	19	62	9	16	2	1	0	10	5	3	2	0	19	0	1	.323	.343
Rodriguez, Keyter	R-R	6-1	175	2-7-86	.265	.381	.234	30	98	9	26	4	1	2	11	2	5	2	0	20	0	1	.388	.314
Rodriguez, Raymond	R-R	6-2	191	8-11-89	.179	.000	.215	27	78	9	14	7	0	0	5	4	2	0	0	32	0	1	.269	.238
Rodriguez, Yunior	R-R	6-1	166	10-1-86	.247	.235	.250	28	81	12	20	3	0	0	6	6	3	2	1	11	0	1	.284	.319
Sierra, Angel	B-R	6-0	172	8-2-88	.234	.300	.222	21	64	13	15	1	1	0	3	11	0	0	0	21	12	2	.281	.347
Smith, Jacob	R-R	6-0	214	6-5-83	.100	.000	.111	3	10	2	1	1	0	0	0	2	0	0	0	1	0	0	.200	.250
Sosa, Wilfredo	R-R	6-2	175	10-24-88	.200	.000	.221	31	95	8	19	6	2	0	13	8	4	3	2	33	3	0	.305	.284
Soto, Ramon	R-R	6-2	190	11-3-87	.098	.000	.119	17	51	4	5	1	0	1	4	4	0	1	0	22	0	0	.176	.164
Sweeney, Ryan	L-L	6-4	215	2-20-85	.000	.000	.000	1	3	0	0	0	0	0	0	2	0	0	0	0	0	0	.000	.400
Thomas, David	B-R	5-11	180	7-29-86	.462	.333	.500	5	13	3	6	2	0	0	3	2	0	1	0	1	1	0	.615	.533

Pitching	B-T	HT	WT	DOB	W	L	ERA	G	GS	CG	SV	IP	H	R	ER	HR	BB	SO	AVG	vLH	vRH	K/9	BB/9
Adames, Joselito	R-R	6-3	190	10-26-88	0	3	8.31	14	3	0	0	30	45	39	28	0	17	20	.357	.442	.297	5.93	5.04
Delgado, Richard	R-R	6-1	177	5-15-86	0	0	6.00	14	0	0	5	18	25	12	12	2	10	17	.342	.250	.377	8.50	5.00
Doolittle, Ryan	R-R	6-3	185	3-25-88	2	3	4.44	14	7	0	0	47	50	28	23	2	10	36	.275	.362	.234	6.94	1.93
Ferreras, Ronald	R-R	6-1	180	2-8-87	1	4	4.37	14	0	0	1	23	21	15	11	0	14	22	.263	.250	.269	8.74	5.56
Foulke, Keith	R-R	6-0	210	10-19-72	0	0	0.00	1	1	0	0	1	1	0	0	0	1	1	.333	.000	.333	9.00	9.00
Garcia, Jose	R-R	5-11	165	1-7-85	0	0	0.00	3	3	0	0	6	2	0	0	0	1	5	.100	.000	.143	7.50	1.50
Hunter, Brett	R-R	6-4	215	6-27-87	0	0	0.00	1	1	0	0	1	1	0	0	0	0	2	.250	.500	.000	18.00	0.00
Joseph, Jonathan	R-R	6-1	180	5-17-88	1	1	4.56	16	0	0	4	24	30	17	12	1	11	37	.300	.154	.351	14.07	4.18
LeBlanc Poirier, Mathieu	L-R	6-1	175	3-10-87	0	1	7.89	11	2	0	0	22	34	23	19	1	6	18	.362	.286	.394	7.48	2.49
Lee, Chad	R-R	6-4	210	12-20-85	0	0	0.00	2	1	0	0	3	2	0	0	0	0	5	.200	.250	.167	15.00	0.00
Madsen, Michael	R-R	6-0	160	11-29-82	0	0	0.00	1	1	0	0	1	0	0	0	0	0	0	.000	.000	.000	0.00	0.00
Murray, Justin	R-R	6-4	200	5-11-87	0	1	1.69	3	1	0	0	11	6	5	2	1	2	7	.154	.154	.154	5.91	1.69
Oliveros, Jose	R-R	6-0	170	9-29-89	2	1	4.93	14	5	0	0	35	54	23	19	0	16	22	.353	.383	.333	5.71	4.15
Penalba, Ricardo	R-R	5-11	170	1-6-89	1	0	3.86	7	1	0	1	9	7	5	4	0	3	12	.219	.273	.190	11.57	2.89
Quinonez, Jose	R-R	6-1	186	3-12-88	1	0	10.57	8	0	0	0	8	10	10	9	0	6	5	.333	.556	.238	5.87	7.04
Ramirez, Anvioris	L-L	6-1	165	3-10-88	2	4	6.22	14	6	0	0	46	52	38	32	14	16	34	.281	.270	.284	6.60	3.11
Ramos, Julio	L-L	6-1	158	2-13-88	3	2	1.41	14	7	0	0	51	56	17	8	0	12	36	.279	.333	.269	6.35	2.12
Samuel, David	R-R	6-1	174	3-8-87	0	1	7.84	12	0	0	0	10	14	14	9	0	9	10	.292	.267	.303	8.71	7.84
Schultz, Patrick	R-R	6-3	215	9-25-85	4	3	5.24	14	7	0	0	45	43	33	26	0	25	30	.250	.306	.210	6.04	5.04
Sharpe, Steven	R-R	6-1	195	7-20-81	0	1	10.13	1	1	0	0	3	4	3	3	0	0	3	.364	.400	.333	10.13	0.00
Storey, Mickey	R-R	6-2	183	3-16-86	2	2	3.27	14	0	0	1	22	17	8	8	2	6	23	.210	.261	.190	9.41	2.45
Street, Juston	R-R	6-2	200	8-27-85	0	1	3.32	16	0	0	0	19	25	16	7	1	5	19	.313	.259	.340	9.00	2.37
Vidal, Pedro	R-R	6-3	194	7-31-87	1	0	2.95	14	5	0	0	40	30	21	13	5	10	32	.204	.191	.210	7.26	2.27
Villegas, Juan	R-R	6-0	170	1-20-87	1	1	10.80	6	0	0	0	7	13	8	8	0	4	8	.419	.333	.455	10.80	5.40
Windsor, Jason	R-R	6-2	235	7-16-82	0	1	7.36	4	4	0	0	11	15	13	9	2	5	9	.319	.267	.344	7.36	4.09

Fielding

Catcher	PCT	G	PO	A	E	DP	PB
Ortiz	.973	25	160	23	5	1	2
Paramore	1.000	5	23	3	0	0	2
Penaloza	.993	19	121	16	1	1	4
Smith	1.000	2	14	0	0	0	0
Soto	.975	16	106	10	3	1	1

First Base	PCT	G	PO	A	E	DP
Hernandez	.988	55	478	34	6	43
Ortiz	1.000	1	7	1	0	0

Second Base	PCT	G	PO	A	E	DP
Gil	.957	6	13	9	1	3
Guzman	1.000	1	2	2	0	0
House	1.000	1	2	3	0	1
Hudson	—	1	0	0	0	0
Jernigan	.929	13	18	34	4	4
Leyja	.873	11	24	24	7	5

	PCT	G	PO	A	E	DP
Mercedes	.923	4	3	9	1	0
Y. Rodriguez	.978	24	39	52	2	13
Sosa	1.000	1	2	3	0	2

Third Base	PCT	G	PO	A	E	DP
Baisley	.643	5	1	8	5	1
Gil	.920	7	5	18	2	2
Guzman	.833	2	1	4	1	0
Leyja	.750	2	1	2	1	0
Made	.794	24	8	42	13	3
Mercedes	.884	15	9	29	5	0
Y. Rodriguez	1.000	1	1	0	0	0
Sosa	.778	6	1	6	2	1

Shortstop	PCT	G	PO	A	E	DP
Coleman	.957	7	16	28	2	5
Gil	.898	10	17	36	6	3
Guzman	.750	2	1	2	1	0

	PCT	G	PO	A	E	DP
Leyja	.911	20	25	47	7	11
Made	1.000	1	0	1	0	0
Sosa	.912	24	28	55	8	9

Outfield	PCT	G	PO	A	E	DP
Berroa	.938	12	28	2	2	0
Buck	.667	3	2	0	1	0
Crisostomo	.929	23	34	5	3	0
Desme	—	2	0	0	0	0
Dixon	.978	41	89	1	2	0
House	.982	26	53	2	1	0
Hudson	.889	15	24	0	3	0
K. Rodriguez	.903	23	26	2	3	1
R. Rodriguez	.909	21	19	1	2	0
Sierra	.976	18	40	1	1	0
Soto	—	1	0	0	0	0
Thomas	.750	3	3	0	1	0

DSL ATHLETICS 1   ROOKIE

DOMINICAN SUMMER LEAGUE

Batting	B-T	HT	WT	DOB	AVG	vLH	vRH	G	AB	R	H	2B	3B	HR	RBI	BB	HBP	SH	SF	SO	SB	CS	SLG	OBP
Brazoban, Yeudy	R-R	6-1	185	9-9-88	.260	.167	.277	48	154	24	40	11	2	0	16	12	2	0	1	25	9	3	.357	.320
Chevalier, Edward	R-R	6-1	215	5-13-88	.182	.296	.161	58	176	19	32	1	0	0	15	30	8	3	2	39	1	1	.188	.324
Contreras, Franklin	R-R	6-2	165	6-10-90	.172	.087	.189	50	145	12	25	4	4	0	19	23	1	0	5	32	5	2	.255	.282
Crisostomo, Jose	L-R	6-1	181	4-20-89	.400	.000	.444	3	10	5	4	2	0	0	1	2	0	0	0	2	0	0	.600	.500
Cruzado, Fernando	R-R	6-2	210	10-25-89	.176	.091	.193	28	68	4	12	3	1	0	5	5	2	0	0	18	0	1	.250	.253
De La Cruz, Jonatan	R-R	6-0	160	5-28-88	.286	.257	.292	59	206	36	59	12	5	1	28	32	3	3	4	30	20	6	.408	.384
De Leon, Abraham	R-R	6-0	194	2-20-89	.245	.045	.282	56	139	21	34	5	1	0	13	32	5	2	1	18	10	4	.295	.401
Garabito, Yeis	R-R	6-2	170	1-28-90	.320	.158	.350	50	122	22	39	7	4	0	10	9	4	3	0	30	4	5	.443	.385
Ledezma, Diego	R-R	6-5	170	8-14-90	.211	—	.211	7	19	1	4	1	0	0	0	1	1	0	0	7	0	0	.263	.286
Lendor, Edgar	R-R	6-0	170	10-23-89	.132	.167	.125	19	38	3	5	0	0	0	5	2	0	0	0	16	2	0	.132	.267
Marte, Miguel	R-R	6-3	180	8-29-89	.194	.071	.214	43	98	13	19	4	0	1	15	13	2	0	1	23	0	0	.265	.298
Mercedes, Wilson	R-R	6-1	170	4-5-88	.100	.000	.111	4	10	2	1	0	0	0	1	2	0	0	1	3	0	0	.100	.231
Millan, Pedro	R-R	5-10	145	11-18-89	.114	.000	.129	27	35	7	4	0	0	0	1	5	3	1	0	11	2	0	.114	.279
Mota, Francis	R-R	6-2	187	10-26-88	.200	.300	.188	37	90	8	18	4	1	0	7	13	0	0	0	21	0	1	.267	.301

Name	B-T	HT	WT	DOB	AVG	vLH	vRH	G	AB	R	H	2B	3B	HR	RBI	BB	HBP	SH	SF	SO	SB	CS	SLG	OBP
Osorio, Luis	B-R	6-1	155	4-5-91	.232	.333	.222	32	69	13	16	2	0	0	8	15	5	2	0	10	3	1	.261	.404
Penaloza, Carmelo	R-R	6-0	165	3-1-87	.000	—	.000	4	2	1	0	0	0	0	0	1	0	0	0	1	0	0	.000	.333
Rodriguez, Jose	R-R	6-1	160	12-19-88	.192	.154	.231	21	26	3	5	0	0	0	4	6	1	0	1	9	0	0	.192	.353
Rojas, Kelvin	R-R	6-2	188	8-7-89	.216	.444	.174	51	171	22	37	4	3	2	21	11	2	1	2	43	10	1	.310	.269
Santana, Lovesquis	L-L	5-10	180	10-21-87	.224	.500	.215	34	67	7	15	3	2	0	8	13	3	1	1	14	5	1	.328	.369
Sena, Alan	R-R	6-0	180	9-24-90	.242	.214	.247	42	91	20	22	5	1	0	7	13	5	0	0	30	1	3	.319	.367
Sosa, Wilfredo	R-R	6-2	175	10-24-88	.129	.154	.122	19	62	13	8	6	0	0	5	10	3	0	1	15	2	1	.226	.276
Soto, Ramon	R-R	6-2	190	11-3-87	.286	.500	.200	4	7	1	2	0	0	1	2	0	0	0	1	0	0	.286	.375
Trinidad, Victor	R-R	6-0	173	12-23-90	.244	.278	.239	49	131	18	32	9	1	0	12	27	2	2	1	28	7	5	.328	.379

Pitching	B-T	HT	WT	DOB	W	L	ERA	G	GS	CG	SV	IP	H	R	ER	HR	BB	SO	AVG	vLH	vRH	K/9	BB/9
Adames, Joselito	R-R	6-3	190	10-26-88	0	0	0.00	1	1	0	0	4	2	0	0	0	2	5	.154	—	.154	11.25	4.50
Astacio, Andres	R-R	6-3	180	8-20-90	5	3	3.38	12	12	1	0	51	45	22	19	0	23	21	.236	.344	.214	3.73	4.09
Bautista, William	L-L	6-4	173	8-20-91	0	0	7.24	8	0	0	0	14	18	14	11	2	11	3	.327	.333	.327	1.98	7.24
Brujan, Mauricio	R-R	6-2	184	9-22-89	4	0	2.68	13	0	0	1	40	33	17	12	1	18	20	.226	.192	.233	4.46	4.02
Diaz, Victor	R-R	6-1	220	10-26-89	1	3	8.53	11	1	0	0	19	20	20	18	3	18	14	.263	.250	.267	6.63	8.53
Ferreras, Ronald	R-R	6-1	180	2-8-87	1	0	6.75	2	0	0	0	4	4	3	3	1	1	3	.267	.000	.286	6.75	2.25
Francisco, Joanel	L-L	6-3	178	11-3-88	0	0	4.05	4	0	0	0	7	2	3	3	0	5	6	.105	—	.105	8.10	6.75
German, Juan	R-R	6-1	160	12-29-88	2	1	2.73	11	0	0	0	30	26	14	9	1	12	25	.232	.176	.242	7.58	3.64
Jimenez, Deivi	R-R	6-3	205	12-30-89	1	4	3.81	13	12	0	0	50	48	30	21	3	21	32	.249	.340	.214	5.80	3.81
Jose, Luis	R-R	6-4	195	9-26-87	3	5	3.71	14	11	0	0	53	58	32	22	2	25	38	.290	.313	.283	6.41	4.22
Juma, Alexis	R-R	6-1	180	5-23-88	0	2	4.95	7	0	0	0	20	24	17	11	2	8	6	.289	.125	.328	2.70	3.60
Mota, Israel	R-R	6-1	190	12-9-90	0	0	10.80	1	1	0	0	2	2	2	2	0	3	0	.333	.000	.333	0.00	16.20
Paez, Argenis	R-R	6-3	180	10-20-90	1	6	3.57	12	12	0	0	45	45	32	18	0	27	30	.251	.200	.262	5.96	5.36
Peralta, Eyffer	R-R	6-3	186	5-30-88	1	1	2.43	12	1	0	2	30	28	11	8	0	15	17	.255	.136	.284	5.16	4.55
Perez, Wilfredo	R-R	6-0	180	7-27-88	3	2	3.16	17	0	0	1	43	46	20	15	2	13	20	.280	.393	.257	4.22	2.74
Quinonez, Jose	R-R	6-1	186	3-12-88	0	0	6.00	1	1	0	0	3	2	2	2	0	2	0	.200	.333	.143	0.00	6.00
Ramirez, Anvioris	L-L	6-1	165	3-10-88	1	0	1.13	2	2	0	0	8	3	1	1	0	0	10	.111	.000	.120	11.25	0.00
Ramos, Julio	L-L	6-1	158	2-13-88	0	1	1.50	2	1	0	0	6	6	2	1	0	2	7	.240	.000	.240	10.50	3.00
Rey, Jose	R-R	6-1	176	3-17-90	1	3	5.32	14	0	0	0	22	29	20	13	3	9	23	.302	.391	.274	9.41	3.68
Reynoso, Samuel	R-R	6-2	205	7-13-89	1	2	5.56	6	1	0	1	11	8	8	7	0	8	11	.200	.308	.148	8.74	6.35
Samuel, David	R-R	6-1	174	3-8-87	0	0	3.00	1	0	0	1	3	3	1	1	0	1	0	.273	.250	.286	0.00	3.00
Sentime, Carlos	R-R	6-2	195	12-6-87	2	1	3.34	13	3	0	4	32	31	13	12	1	10	22	.258	.174	.278	6.12	2.78
Silva, Albert	L-L	5-11	150	9-9-90	0	1	2.73	8	4	0	0	26	18	9	8	1	9	18	.198	.250	.195	6.15	3.08
Suero, Marinel	R-R	6-5	230	8-29-88	0	1	3.38	3	0	0	0	3	4	4	1	0	1	1	.364	1.000	.300	3.38	3.38

Fielding

Catcher	PCT	G	PO	A	E	DP	PB
Cruzado	.984	28	108	14	2	3	5
De Leon	.919	16	67	12	7	0	1
Ledezma	.932	6	35	6	3	0	2
Marte	.959	21	83	11	4	1	9
Millan	1.000	1	2	0	0	0	0
Penaloza	1.000	2	2	0	0	0	0
Rodriguez	1.000	20	57	8	0	0	3
Soto	1.000	4	12	0	0	0	0

First Base	PCT	G	PO	A	E	DP
Chevalier	.990	58	492	26	5	42
De La Cruz	1.000	3	9	1	0	0
Millan	1.000	1	1	0	0	0
Osorio	.988	11	77	5	1	2

Second Base	PCT	G	PO	A	E	DP
Contreras	.850	3	9	8	3	1
De La Cruz	1.000	7	8	16	0	2
Garabito	.886	10	19	12	4	4
Lendor	.935	14	22	21	3	3
Millan	.889	8	6	10	2	2
Osorio	1.000	12	17	23	0	6
Sosa	.968	7	19	11	4	6
Trinidad	1.000	24	45	35	0	6

Third Base	PCT	G	PO	A	E	DP
De La Cruz	.878	34	40	89	18	14
Garabito	.600	6	2	1	2	0
Mota	.912	35	30	74	10	5
Sosa	.800	1	2	2	1	1
Trinidad	1.000	2	0	3	0	1

Shortstop	PCT	G	PO	A	E	DP
Contreras	.911	45	55	109	16	16
De La Cruz	.946	17	22	48	4	5
Mota	1.000	1	0	2	0	0
Osorio	.895	4	6	11	2	0
Sosa	.850	8	14	20	6	1
Trinidad	.000	1	0	0	1	0

Outfield	PCT	G	PO	A	E	DP
Brazoban	.959	42	66	4	3	0
Crisostomo	1.000	3	3	1	0	1
De La Cruz	—	2	0	0	0	0
De Leon	.951	40	52	6	3	2
Garabito	.909	8	8	2	1	0
Lendor	—	2	0	0	0	0
Millan	—	1	0	0	0	0
Mota	.000	1	0	0	1	0
Rojas	.968	49	89	3	3	1
Santana	.900	31	25	2	3	1
Sena	.982	39	52	4	1	1
Trinidad	.909	15	19	1	2	0

DSL ATHLETICS 2 — ROOKIE

DOMINICAN SUMMER LEAGUE

Batting	B-T	HT	WT	DOB	AVG	vLH	vRH	G	AB	R	H	2B	3B	HR	RBI	BB	HBP	SH	SF	SO	SB	CS	SLG	OBP
Almonte, Edward	R-R	6-2	176	1-12-90	.231	.308	.211	43	121	15	28	4	3	0	11	15	3	1	0	25	7	5	.314	.331
Baez, Luis	R-R	6-3	165	5-24-91	.196	.148	.212	40	112	13	22	3	0	0	7	5	4	0	0	27	4	2	.223	.244
Blanco, Charli	R-R	6-0	155	2-23-91	.205	.300	.155	43	88	9	18	1	0	0	8	6	2	4	1	24	5	2	.216	.268
Castillo, Alexander	L-L	6-2	215	9-24-87	.233	.095	.256	48	150	17	35	7	3	1	20	22	2	2	2	36	6	1	.340	.335
Castillo, Gernaldo	R-R	5-11	145	7-17-89	.197	.333	.167	45	142	23	29	6	0	0	15	22	5	1	2	13	6	5	.238	.318
Clime, Neudy	R-R	5-11	185	2-1-89	.275	.229	.292	48	131	22	36	5	2	1	14	31	3	5	0	14	9	9	.366	.424
De Jesus, Mario	R-R	6-2	180	9-22-88	.205	.171	.217	47	127	12	26	1	2	0	13	9	1	0	4	26	7	4	.244	.255
De Los Santos, Robinson	R-R	6-3	170	2-21-90	.228	.318	.200	31	92	11	21	5	1	0	7	11	0	0	0	21	0	1	.304	.311
Garcia, Elvis	R-R	6-2	178	11-8-89	.273	.333	.254	57	187	23	51	9	0	0	17	10	6	5	3	16	12	3	.321	.325
Garcia, Martire	R-R	6-0	180	11-22-86	.207	.000	.250	24	58	5	12	2	0	1	12	5	0	0	2	10	4	3	.293	.262
Landaeta, Douglas	R-R	6-1	170	11-25-88	.267	.277	.264	51	176	30	47	9	3	0	16	12	0	2	2	23	5	5	.352	.311
Lopez, Diomes	R-R	6-2	195	1-30-89	.245	.217	.254	40	94	10	23	11	0	0	11	5	3	0	0	28	2	0	.362	.304
Made, Alcibiades	R-R	6-0	169	4-5-89	.400	1.000	.375	7	25	5	10	1	2	0	2	0	0	1	0	4	2	2	.600	.400
Mateo, Kelvin	R-R	6-1	170	8-7-89	.273	.286	.268	25	55	5	15	1	1	0	5	6	1	1	0	7	0	0	.327	.355
Narvaez, Angel	L-R	6-0	165	9-15-89	.200	.125	.235	17	25	2	5	0	0	0	1	4	1	0	0	7	0	0	.200	.333

Name	B-T	HT	WT	DOB	AVG	vLH	vRH	G	AB	R	H	2B	3B	HR	RBI	BB	HBP	SH	SF	SO	SB	CS	OBP	SLG
Peralta, Jensi	R-R	6-2	180	7-2-91	.156	.273	.118	32	90	9	14	3	0	0	6	14	1	0	1	25	5	1	.189	.274
Rodriguez, Keyter	R-R	6-1	175	2-7-86	.250	.000	.333	1	4	1	1	0	0	0	0	0	0	0	0	1	0	0	.250	.250
Rosario, Jose	R-R	6-5	219	9-2-90	.144	.111	.156	42	104	10	15	2	1	0	8	16	0	1	1	22	3	0	.183	.256
Rosario, Robin	R-R	6-2	170	11-28-90	.281	.321	.270	42	128	17	36	5	6	0	10	11	2	2	0	25	4	5	.414	.348
Toussaint, Franklin	R-R	6-1	174	9-16-89	.274	.346	.246	39	95	15	26	2	0	0	4	18	7	1	0	12	9	2	.295	.425

Pitching	B-T	HT	WT	DOB	W	L	ERA	G	GS	CG	SV	IP	H	R	ER	HR	BB	SO	AVG	vLH	vRH	K/9	BB/9
Acevedo, Rony	R-R	6-2	165	9-18-88	1	2	4.67	14	8	0	1	44	40	25	23	2	27	49	.233	.208	.236	9.95	5.48
Azor, Jose	R-R	6-2	185	10-12-88	0	2	5.60	14	0	0	1	18	17	19	11	0	21	11	.254	.429	.233	5.60	10.70
Brito, Jose	R-R	6-0	180	10-28-87	4	6	3.09	13	10	1	0	64	49	22	22	1	15	33	.211	.184	.219	4.64	2.11
Castro, Mario	R-R	6-3	150	9-3-87	2	1	3.71	15	0	0	0	34	35	25	14	1	20	20	.269	.348	.252	5.29	5.29
Delgado, Richard	R-R	6-1	177	5-15-86	1	1	3.00	4	0	0	2	6	7	2	2	0	1	4	.333	.167	.400	6.00	1.50
Duran, Omar	L-L	6-3	209	2-26-90	1	4	5.71	11	9	0	0	35	29	24	22	0	34	37	.230	.500	.221	9.61	8.83
Fortuna, Anderson	R-R	6-4	200	10-20-89	2	0	3.24	12	0	0	0	25	13	11	9	0	18	20	.160	.200	.155	7.20	6.48
German, Johan	R-R	6-5	190	12-20-88	1	0	3.86	2	0	0	0	5	5	2	2	0	2	4	.278	.200	.308	7.71	3.86
Joseph, Jonathan	R-R	6-1	180	5-17-88	1	1	4.50	3	2	0	0	10	9	6	5	0	4	13	.231	.667	.194	11.70	3.60
Merestil, Rene	L-L	6-3	185	12-30-86	1	4	6.69	17	7	0	1	38	30	34	28	0	41	33	.229	.400	.222	7.88	9.80
Oliveros, Jose	R-R	6-0	170	9-29-89	0	0	3.60	1	1	0	0	5	3	2	2	0	2	4	.176	.000	.214	7.20	3.60
Pena, Jorge	R-R	6-6	226	12-31-88	4	1	1.90	13	10	0	0	52	33	14	11	0	31	41	.191	.194	.190	7.10	5.37
Penalba, Ricardo	R-R	5-11	170	1-6-89	0	0	3.00	2	2	0	0	6	2	3	2	0	4	6	.105	.250	.067	9.00	6.00
Ramirez, Benito	R-R	6-5	180	9-23-88	0	1	5.11	9	1	0	0	12	9	12	7	0	17	12	.209	.111	.235	8.76	12.41
Reyes, Luis	R-R	6-2	160	2-4-88	5	2	0.62	17	0	0	3	43	23	6	3	0	20	36	.161	.143	.165	7.48	4.15
Sanchez, Jose	R-R	6-2	170	10-24-89	4	3	3.30	12	10	0	1	44	34	23	16	0	24	43	.222	.160	.234	8.86	4.95
Santana, Pedro	L-L	6-4	170	8-4-88	0	0	4.67	11	0	0	0	17	13	11	9	1	20	16	.206	.667	.183	8.31	10.38
Vargas, Carlos	R-R	6-1	170	8-17-88	3	1	1.37	15	2	0	1	46	27	11	7	0	13	23	.178	.238	.168	4.50	2.54
Vidal, Pedro	R-R	6-3	194	7-31-87	0	1	1.80	3	2	0	0	15	8	4	3	1	4	11	.157	.000	.170	6.60	2.40
Zapata, Roberto	R-R	6-4	171	6-28-89	0	0	18.00	3	0	0	0	2	4	4	4	0	7	0	.500	.667	.400	0.00	31.50

Fielding

Catcher	PCT	G	PO	A	E	DP	PB
Almonte	—	1	0	0	0	0	0
M. Garcia	.981	18	82	19	2	1	5
Lopez	.970	37	222	33	8	2	3
Mateo	.953	25	116	27	7	1	3
Narvaez	.976	10	35	6	1	0	5
Toussaint	1.000	1	1	1	0	0	0

First Base	PCT	G	PO	A	E	DP
A. Castillo	.975	33	223	8	6	22
De Jesus	1.000	1	1	0	0	0
M. Garcia	1.000	1	2	1	0	0
Landaeta	1.000	1	4	1	0	0
Made	1.000	1	5	0	0	0
J. Rosario	.978	41	258	15	6	14
R. Rosario	—	1	0	0	0	0
Toussaint	1.000	5	22	1	0	1

Second Base	PCT	G	PO	A	E	DP
Baez	1.000	4	9	12	0	4
G. Castillo	.991	29	51	56	1	9
Clime	.935	34	69	60	9	15
Peralta	1.000	1	1	0	0	0
Toussaint	.905	8	14	5	2	1

Third Base	PCT	G	PO	A	E	DP
G. Castillo	1.000	1	0	2	0	0
Clime	.833	5	2	13	3	2
De Jesus	.915	36	33	64	9	3
De Los Santos	.943	26	26	57	5	1
Landaeta	.750	1	0	3	1	1
Made	.842	5	4	12	3	2
Peralta		1	0	0	0	0

Shortstop	PCT	G	PO	A	E	DP
Baez	.902	35	52	86	15	16
G. Castillo	1.000	4	2	1	0	0
Clime	1.000	2	0	1	0	0
De Los Santos	1.000	5	4	8	0	1
Peralta	.907	29	37	70	11	8

Outfield	PCT	G	PO	A	E	DP
Almonte	.980	38	47	2	1	1
Blanco	.983	40	52	5	1	2
A. Castillo	—	1	0	0	0	0
E. Garcia	.990	57	97	3	1	1
Landaeta	.987	46	69	6	1	0
Lopez	1.000	1	2	0	0	0
Rodriguez	1.000	1	1	0	0	0
J. Rosario	.500	1	1	0	1	0
R. Rosario	.947	33	50	4	3	2
Toussaint	1.000	8	11	1	0	0

Philadelphia Phillies

BY JIM SALISBURY

When Charlie Manuel was hired as Phillies manager in November 2004, fans in sports-mad, championship-starved Philadelphia howled in protest. Manuel was viewed as a country bumpkin, a good ol' boy not worthy of such an important job in such a tough and demanding city.

Four years after his widely criticized hiring, Manuel earned his own World Series ring and the fans who once rejected him stood time and time again in Citizens Bank Park and chanted, "Char-lie, Char-lie, Char-lie." The man had become a legitimate folk hero, joining one-time critic Dallas Green as the only managers to win the World Series in the franchise's 126-year history.

Philadelphia's first major pro sports title in 25 years was followed by a spectacular parade down Broad Street, with National League Championship Series and World Series MVP Cole Hamels leading the way. He was 4-0, 1.80 in five postseason starts—all Phillies wins.

The 2008 World Series title actually started in 2007, after the Phillies were swept by the Rockies in the division series, their first postseason in 14 years. After rallying from 3½ games behind the Mets to win their second straight NL East title with a 13-3 finish, the Phils approached the post-season with resolve, going 11-3 in defeating the Brewers, Dodgers and Rays.

The Phils had the top bullpen in the NL during the regular season (3.22 ERA) and it allowed just eight runs in 40 innings (1.78). Closer Brad Lidge ran his string of perfection to 48 straight saves after going 41 for 41 during the regular season.

Lidge, acquired in a Nov. 2007 trade with the Astros, proved to be general manager Pat Gillick's best acquisition in a three-year run that ended with his retirement. The Phillies, however, featured a largely homegrown nucleus that dated to Ed Wade's time as GM, and Mike Arbuckle's tenure overseeing scouting and player development. Arbuckle resigned from his assistant GM post after Ruben Amaro Jr. was named as Gillick's successor.

The homegrown nucleus featured starting pitchers Hamels and Brett Myers, valuable reliever Ryan Madson, shortstop Jimmy Rollins, second baseman Chase Utley, first baseman Ryan Howard, leftfielder Pat Burrell and catcher Carlos Ruiz. Shane Victorino, a former Rule 5 pick, also came

up through the system to join the nucleus.

After an excruciatingly slow start, Howard rebounded to lead the majors in homers (48) and RBIs (146). Burrell, a free agent at season's end, finished his ninth, and possibly final, year with the club with a double that led to the winning run in Game Five of the World Series.

2008 PERFORMANCE

General Manager: Pat Gillick. **Farm Director:** Steve Noworyta. **Scouting Director:** Marti Wolever.

Class	Team	League	W	L	PCT	Finish*	Manager	Affiliate Since
Majors	Philadelphia	National	92	70	.568	^2nd (16)	Charlie Manuel	—
Triple-A	Lehigh Valley Iron Pigs	International	55	89	.382	14th (14)	Dave Huppert	2008
Double-A	Reading Phillies	Eastern	53	89	.373	12th (12)	P.J. Forbes	1967
High A	Clearwater Threshers	Florida State	64	76	.457	9th (12)	Razor Shines	1985
Low A	Lakewood BlueClaws	South Atlantic	80	60	.571	4th (16)	Steve Roadcap	2001
Short-season	Williamsport Crosscutters	New York-Penn	38	37	.507	8th (14)	Dusty Wathan	2007
Rookie	GCL Phillies	Gulf Coast	33	25	.569	^4th (16)	Rolando de Armas	1999
Overall 2008 Minor League Record			323	376	.462	24th		

* Finish in overall standings (No. of teams in league). ^League champion.

ORGANIZATION STATISTICS

PHILADELPHIA PHILLIES

NATIONAL LEAGUE

Batting	B-T	HT	WT	DOB	AVG	vLH	vRH	G	AB	R	H	2B	3B	HR	RBI	BB	HBP	SH	SF	SO	SB	CS	SLG	OBP
Bohn, T.J.	R-R	6-5	200	1-17-80	.400	1.000	.250	14	5	1	2	1	0	0	3	0	0	0	0	1	0	0	.600	.400
Bruntlett, Eric	R-R	6-0	190	3-29-78	.217	.254	.199	120	212	37	46	9	1	2	15	21	3	2	0	35	9	2	.297	.297
Burrell, Pat	R-R	6-4	235	10-10-76	.250	.279	.238	157	536	74	134	33	3	33	86	102	1	0	6	136	0	0	.507	.367
Cervenak, Mike	R-R	5-11	195	8-17-76	.154	.200	.125	10	13	0	2	0	0	0	0	0	0	0	0	5	0	0	.154	.154
Coste, Chris	R-R	6-1	215	2-4-73	.263	.296	.249	98	274	28	72	17	0	9	36	16	10	3	2	51	0	1	.423	.325
Dobbs, Greg	L-R	6-1	205	7-2-78	.301	.111	.309	128	226	30	68	14	1	9	40	11	1	0	2	40	3	1	.491	.333
Feliz, Pedro	R-R	6-1	210	4-27-75	.249	.288	.231	133	425	43	106	19	2	14	58	33	0	3	2	54	0	0	.402	.302
Golson, Greg	R-R	6-0	190	9-17-85	.000	.000	.000	6	6	2	0	0	0	0	0	0	0	0	0	4	1	0	.000	.000
Harman, Brad	R-R	6-1	195	11-19-85	.100	.167	.000	6	10	1	1	0	0	0	1	1	0	0	1	0	0	0	.200	.182
Howard, Ryan	L-L	6-4	255	11-19-79	.251	.224	.268	162	610	105	153	26	4	48	146	81	3	0	6	199	1	1	.543	.339
Iguchi, Tadahito	R-R	5-10	185	12-4-74	.286	.500	.000	4	7	0	2	1	0	0	0	0	0	0	0	0	0	0	.429	.286
2-team total (81 San Diego)					.232	—		85	310	29	72	15	1	2	24	26	0	1	0	75	8	1	.306	.292
Jenkins, Geoff	L-R	6-1	215	7-21-74	.246	.130	.256	115	293	27	72	16	0	9	29	24	1	0	4	68	1	1	.392	.301
Marson, Lou	R-R	6-1	200	6-26-86	.500	.500	.500	1	4	2	2	0	0	1	2	0	0	0	0	2	0	0	1.250	.500
Rollins, Jimmy	B-R	5-8	175	11-27-78	.277	.288	.272	137	556	76	154	38	9	11	59	58	5	3	3	55	47	3	.437	.349
Ruiz, Carlos	R-R	5-10	200	1-22-79	.219	.212	.220	117	320	47	70	14	0	4	31	44	4	4	1	38	1	2	.300	.320
Snelling, Chris	L-L	5-10	205	12-3-81	.500	—	.500	4	4	1	2	1	0	1	1	0	0	0	0	0	0	0	1.500	.500
Stairs, Matt	L-R	5-9	210	2-27-68	.294	.000	.313	16	17	4	5	1	0	2	5	1	0	0	1	3	0	0	.706	.316
Taguchi, So	R-R	5-10	170	7-2-69	.220	.184	.262	88	91	18	20	5	1	0	9	8	0	4	0	14	3	0	.297	.283
Tracy, Andy	L-R	6-3	220	12-11-73	.000		.000	4	2	0	0	0	0	0	1	0	0	1	0	1	0	0	.000	.250
Utley, Chase	L-R	6-1	200	12-17-78	.292	.277	.301	159	607	113	177	41	4	33	104	64	27	1	8	104	14	2	.535	.380
Victorino, Shane	B-R	5-9	180	11-30-80	.293	.282	.298	146	570	102	167	30	8	14	58	45	7	5	0	69	36	11	.447	.352
Werth, Jayson	R-R	6-5	225	5-20-79	.273	.303	.255	134	418	73	114	16	3	24	67	57	4	0	3	119	20	1	.498	.363

Pitching	B-T	HT	WT	DOB	W	L	ERA	G	GS	CG	SV	IP	H	R	ER	HR	BB	SO	AVG	vLH	vRH	K/9	BB/9
Blanton, Joe	R-R	6-3	255	12-11-80	4	0	4.20	13	13	0	0	71	66	36	33	10	31	49	.246	.278	.222	6.24	3.95
Carpenter, Andrew	R-R	6-3	225	5-18-85	0	0	0.00	1	0	0	1	1	0	0	0	1	1	1	.333	.500	.000	9.00	9.00
Condrey, Clay	R-R	6-3	215	11-19-75	3	4	3.26	56	0	0	1	69	66	26	25	6	19	34	.302	.320	.288	4.43	2.48
Durbin, Chad	R-R	6-2	200	12-3-77	5	4	2.87	71	0	0	1	88	81	33	28	5	35	63	.254	.311	.214	6.47	3.59
Eaton, Adam	R-R	6-2	200	11-23-77	4	8	5.80	21	19	0	0	107	131	71	69	15	44	57	.310	.318	.300	4.79	3.70
Eyre, Scott	L-L	6-1	220	5-30-72	3	0	1.88	19	0	0	0	14	8	3	3	1	3	18	.163	.174	.154	11.30	1.88
2-team total (19 Chicago)					5	0	4.21	38	0	0	0	26	23	12	12	2	7	32	—			11.22	2.45
Gordon, Tom	R-R	5-10	200	11-18-67	5	4	5.16	34	0	0	2	30	31	19	17	3	17	26	.256	.246	.266	7.89	5.16
Hamels, Cole	L-L	6-3	190	12-27-83	14	10	3.09	33	33	2	0	227	193	89	78	28	53	196	.227	.262	.215	7.76	2.10
Happ, J.A.	L-L	6-6	200	10-19-82	1	0	3.69	8	4	0	0	32	28	13	13	3	14	26	.233	.209	.247	7.39	3.98
Kendrick, Kyle	R-R	6-3	190	8-26-84	11	9	5.49	31	30	0	0	156	194	103	95	23	57	68	.304	.334	.271	3.93	3.30
Lidge, Brad	R-R	6-5	210	12-23-76	2	0	1.95	72	0	0	41	69	50	17	15	2	35	92	.198	.273	.105	11.94	4.54
Madson, Ryan	L-R	6-6	200	8-28-80	4	2	3.05	76	0	0	1	83	79	29	28	6	23	67	.254	.268	.243	7.29	2.50
Moyer, Jamie	L-L	6-0	185	11-18-62	16	7	3.71	33	33	0	0	196	199	85	81	20	62	123	.262	.240	.270	5.64	2.84
Myers, Brett	R-R	6-4	240	8-17-80	10	13	4.55	30	30	2	0	190	197	103	96	29	65	163	.267	.235	.293	7.72	3.08
Romero, J.C.	B-L	5-11	205	6-4-76	4	4	2.75	81	0	0	1	59	41	18	18	5	36	52	.197	.102	.282	7.93	5.80
Seanez, Rudy	R-R	6-1	225	10-20-68	5	4	3.53	42	0	0	0	43	38	24	17	2	25	30	.239	.247	.232	6.23	5.19
Swindle, R.J.	L-L	6-3	190	7-7-83	0	0	7.71	3	0	0	0	5	9	4	4	2	2	4	.409	.333	.462	7.71	3.86
Walrond, Les	L-L	6-3	205	11-7-76	1	1	6.10	6	0	0	0	10	13	7	7	0	9	12	.342	.154	.440	10.45	7.84

Fielding

Catcher	PCT	G	PO	A	E	DP	PB
Coste	.994	78	488	23	3	6	1
Marson	1.000	1	9	1	0	0	0
Ruiz	.993	110	623	58	5	2	4

	PCT	G	PO	A	E	DP
Coste	1.000	1	7	1	0	0
Dobbs	1.000	2	6	2	0	1
Howard	.988	159	1408	101	19	128
Utley	1.000	2	16	2	0	1

	PCT	G	PO	A	E	DP
Harman	1.000	3	2	3	0	0
Iguchi	1.000	1	1	2	0	0
Utley	.984	159	340	463	13	102

First Base	PCT	G	PO	A	E	DP
Bruntlett	1.000	2	18	1	0	2

Second Base	PCT	G	PO	A	E	DP
Bruntlett	.929	5	5	8	1	1

Third Base	PCT	G	PO	A	E	DP
Bruntlett	.955	27	16	26	2	1
Cervenak	—	2	0	0	0	0

	PCT	G	PO	A	E	DP
Dobbs	.971	52	34	67	3	7
Feliz	.974	129	73	223	8	19
Harman	—	1	0	0	0	0
Ruiz	—	1	0	0	0	0
Shortstop	**PCT**	**G**	**PO**	**A**	**E**	**DP**
Bruntlett	.970	35	39	92	4	16

	PCT	G	PO	A	E	DP
Feliz	1.000	1	1	0	0	0
Rollins	.988	132	193	393	7	71
Outfield	**PCT**	**G**	**PO**	**A**	**E**	**DP**
Bohn Jr.	.875	12	6	1	1	0
Bruntlett	1.000	36	14	0	0	0
Burrell	.991	155	202	12	2	1

	PCT	G	PO	A	E	DP
Dobbs	1.000	7	5	0	0	0
Golson	.667	3	2	0	1	0
Jenkins	.967	90	140	7	5	1
Stairs	1.000	4	5	0	0	0
Taguchi	.943	48	33	0	2	0
Victorino	.994	143	328	7	2	2
Werth	.992	125	231	9	2	2

LEHIGH VALLEY IRONPIGS

INTERNATIONAL LEAGUE

TRIPLE-A

Batting	B-T	HT	WT	DOB	AVG	vLH	vRH	G	AB	R	H	2B	3B	HR	RBI	BB	HBP	SH	SF	SO	SB	CS	SLG	OBP
Bohn, T.J.	R-R	6-5	200	1-17-80	.215	.184	.230	97	316	30	68	19	2	4	27	25	4	2	1	85	4	2	.326	.280
Cervenak, Mike	R-R	5-11	195	8-17-76	.311	.318	.309	115	456	64	142	30	2	10	66	13	7	0	6	64	5	4	.452	.336
Dawkins, Gookie	R-R	6-1	180	5-12-79	.214	1.000	.083	6	14	1	3	2	0	0	2	2	0	0	0	6	1	0	.357	.313
2-team total (12 Charlotte)					.123	—		18	57	1	7	4	0	0	4	4	0	0	0	23	2	0	.193	.180
Gradoville, Tim	R-R	6-3	195	1-30-80	.000	.000	.000	2	7	0	0	0	0	0	0	0	0	0	0	3	0	0	.000	.000
Guevara, Orlando	B-R	6-1	175	9-13-83	.091	.167	.000	4	11	1	1	0	0	0	0	0	0	0	0	4	0	0	.091	.091
Hammond, Joey	R-R	6-1	190	10-27-77	.237	.283	.215	45	139	13	33	4	1	0	5	16	1	0	2	32	1	1	.281	.316
Jaramillo, Jason	B-R	6-0	200	10-9-82	.266	.224	.288	115	421	48	112	20	0	8	39	42	6	2	2	82	1	1	.371	.340
King, Brennan	R-R	6-3	220	1-20-81	.237	.210	.248	99	342	30	81	13	0	5	34	14	5	0	4	69	0	0	.319	.274
Knott, Jon	R-R	6-3	225	8-4-78	.260	.350	.231	111	407	54	106	28	2	19	65	43	7	1	2	96	2	1	.479	.340
2-team total (17 Rochester)					.251	—		128	462	61	116	30	2	20	68	52	7	1	2	111	2	1	.455	.335
Laforest, Pete	L-R	6-2	210	1-27-78	.067	.000	.083	5	15	0	1	1	0	0	0	2	0	0	0	8	0	0	.133	.176
Moran, Javon	R-R	5-10	170	9-30-82	.303	.077	.450	13	33	7	10	3	0	1	5	3	1	1	1	7	3	0	.485	.368
Pascucci, Valentino	R-R	6-6	260	11-17-78	.232	.172	.264	25	82	4	19	2	0	1	7	18	0	0	0	25	0	1	.293	.370
Robles, Oscar	L-R	5-10	185	4-9-76	.256	.237	.260	93	309	27	79	10	0	3	38	35	0	1	1	37	0	0	.317	.330
Rouse, Mike	L-R	6-0	190	4-25-80	.250	.233	.257	89	316	30	79	17	0	2	29	14	2	11	1	67	5	3	.323	.285
2-team total (24 Charlotte)					.247	—		113	393	42	97	18	0	5	38	19	5	12	2	85	7	3	.331	.289
Smith, Casey	R-R	6-2	200	3-18-79	.170	.170	.170	96	300	21	51	7	0	3	20	16	1	2	3	64	3	1	.223	.213
Snelling, Chris	L-L	5-10	205	12-3-81	.229	.292	.208	35	96	14	22	1	0	1	8	19	3	0	2	23	1	0	.271	.367
Spidale, Mike	R-R	6-1	190	3-12-82	.176	.182	.172	12	51	6	9	3	0	0	1	1	1	0	0	8	3	0	.235	.208
Suomi, John	L-R	5-11	199	10-5-80	.244	.200	.247	24	86	6	21	8	0	1	9	2	0	0	1	13	0	0	.372	.261
Thompson, Rich	L-R	6-3	185	4-23-79	.264	.195	.287	97	352	41	93	18	5	4	42	39	4	7	3	72	25	2	.378	.342
Tracy, Andy	L-R	6-3	220	12-11-73	.288	.306	.281	124	430	71	124	34	0	22	85	65	4	2	6	96	5	0	.521	.382
Victorino, Shane	B-R	5-9	180	11-30-80	.375	.333	.500	2	8	0	3	0	0	0	0	0	0	0	0	0	0	0	.375	.375
Watson, Brandon	L-R	6-1	170	9-30-81	.305	.283	.315	126	518	78	158	21	2	6	40	26	3	10	2	53	11	9	.388	.341
Woodward, Chris	R-R	6-0	190	6-27-76	.206	.227	.195	19	63	4	13	2	0	0	1	6	1	1	0	14	0	0	.238	.286

Pitching	B-T	HT	WT	DOB	W	L	ERA	G	GS	CG	SV	IP	H	R	ER	HR	BB	SO	AVG	vLH	vRH	K/9	BB/9
Anderson, Jason	L-R	6-0	190	6-9-79	3	2	3.89	30	0	0	1	44	56	21	19	3	14	34	.313	.341	.286	6.95	2.86
Beirne, Kevin	L-R	6-4	210	1-1-74	0	3	6.86	12	2	0	0	21	25	17	16	4	9	14	.301	.325	.279	6.00	3.86
Benson, Kris	R-R	6-4	205	11-7-74	1	4	5.52	11	11	0	0	60	85	46	37	7	14	33	.344	.333	.355	4.92	2.09
Bisenius, Joe	R-R	6-3	205	9-18-82	0	1	7.06	15	0	0	0	22	24	18	17	1	18	21	.296	.222	.356	8.72	7.48
Blackley, Travis	L-L	6-3	190	11-4-82	5	10	5.41	28	21	0	0	123	132	75	74	15	59	87	.275	.193	.318	6.37	4.32
Carpenter, Andrew	R-R	6-3	225	5-18-85	0	1	2.57	1	1	0	0	7	6	2	2	1	3	5	.240	.333	.100	6.43	3.86
Carrasco, Carlos	R-R	6-3	215	3-21-87	2	2	1.72	6	6	0	0	37	37	15	7	1	13	46	.250	.215	.290	11.29	3.19
Castro, Fabio	L-L	5-7	185	1-20-85	0	2	8.10	3	2	0	0	10	14	10	9	1	6	10	.333	.400	.313	9.00	5.40
Chiavacci, Ron	R-R	6-0	240	9-5-77	1	7	5.90	11	11	0	0	58	74	39	38	9	19	50	.320	.288	.364	7.76	2.95
Childers, Matt	R-R	6-5	190	12-3-78	3	5	3.78	53	0	0	20	67	74	33	28	7	18	68	.279	.336	.226	9.18	2.43
Darensbourg, Vic	L-L	5-8	175	11-13-70	0	2	6.52	9	0	0	0	10	13	9	7	1	4	6	.317	.500	.143	5.59	3.72
Durbin, J.D.	R-R	6-0	210	2-24-82	0	1	9.75	15	6	0	0	36	58	40	39	8	19	29	.354	.378	.329	7.25	4.75
Eaton, Adam	R-R	6-2	200	11-23-77	0	1	3.00	1	1	0	0	3	5	3	1	0	1	2	.417	.375	.500	6.00	3.00
Ennis, John	R-R	6-5	220	10-17-79	4	3	3.67	40	0	0	0	54	56	26	22	5	17	59	.268	.252	.284	9.83	2.83
Green, Steve	R-R	6-2	200	1-26-78	5	1	3.09	35	1	0	0	67	56	27	23	4	29	71	.227	.215	.236	9.54	3.90
Happ, J.A.	L-L	6-6	200	10-19-82	8	7	3.60	24	23	0	0	135	116	58	54	14	48	151	.234	.245	.229	10.07	3.20
Kline, Steve	R-L	6-1	225	8-22-72	0	2	5.16	20	0	0	1	23	28	13	13	3	8	16	.298	.341	.260	6.35	3.18
Knotts, Gary	R-R	6-4	215	2-12-77	2	5	5.32	35	10	0	0	91	109	60	54	12	49	97	.303	.350	.256	8.47	4.34
2-team total (4 Norfolk)					2	7	5.08	39	11	0	0	103	117	65	58	12	52	98	—			8.59	4.56
Mazone, Brian	L-L	6-4	200	7-26-76	9	12	4.10	28	28	1	0	165	176	81	75	20	36	116	.279	.319	.260	6.34	1.97
Minix, Travis	R-R	6-1	190	8-8-77	0	1	10.57	2	2	0	0	8	8	9	9	1	2	7	.258	.176	.357	8.22	2.35
Myers, Brett	R-R	6-4	240	8-17-80	1	1	3.65	2	2	0	0	12	12	6	5	0	4	12	.255	.235	.267	8.76	2.92
Randolph, Stephen	L-L	6-3	205	5-1-74	3	2	2.66	35	0	0	4	47	29	15	14	2	31	75	.176	.102	.217	14.26	5.89
Seanez, Rudy	R-R	6-1	225	10-20-68	1	0	0.00	1	0	0	0	1	0	0	0	0	0	1	.000	.000	—	9.00	0.00
Swindle, R.J.	L-L	6-3	190	7-7-83	2	1	1.98	27	0	0	1	36	33	9	8	1	7	51	.241	.145	.305	12.63	1.73
Walrond, Les	L-L	6-3	205	11-7-76	5	8	3.32	21	17	2	0	111	106	47	41	4	42	105	.257	.286	.243	8.51	3.41

Fielding

Catcher	PCT	G	PO	A	E	DP	PB
Gradoville	1.000	2	13	1	0	0	0
Guevara	1.000	4	21	1	0	0	1
Jaramillo	.984	113	916	76	16	9	9
Laforest	1.000	4	35	3	0	0	1
Suomi	.985	23	182	10	3	2	3

First Base	PCT	G	PO	A	E	DP
Cervenak	.994	23	159	11	1	7
Hammond	1.000	2	5	1	0	1
Knott	1.000	17	107	9	0	13
Pascucci	.964	5	24	3	1	2
Robles	1.000	1	3	0	0	0

	PCT	G	PO	A	E	DP
Tracy	.997	104	795	72	3	81
Second Base	**PCT**	**G**	**PO**	**A**	**E**	**DP**
Dawkins	1.000	4	1	4	0	1
Hammond	1.000	2	1	6	0	1
Robles	.982	59	95	126	4	33
Smith	.981	88	121	233	7	51

ORGANIZATION STATISTICS

Third Base	PCT	G	PO	A	E	DP
Woodward	1.000	2	5	10	0	1
Cervenak	.916	37	20	56	7	4
Hammond	.971	18	10	23	1	1
King	.967	92	59	118	6	15
Robles	.875	8	3	11	2	1
Smith	1.000	4	1	0	0	0
Woodward	.000	1	0	0	1	0

Shortstop	PCT	G	PO	A	E	DP
Dawkins	1.000	2	1	2	0	1
Hammond	.952	23	30	50	4	8
Robles	.966	19	26	30	2	8
Rouse	.949	89	122	212	18	53
Woodward	.924	16	26	47	6	9

Outfield	PCT	G	PO	A	E	DP
Bohn Jr.	.983	94	210	15	4	2
Cervenak	1.000	12	13	0	0	0
Hammond	1.000	2	6	0	0	0
Knott	.981	80	147	6	3	1
Moran	1.000	12	15	0	0	0
Pascucci	1.000	18	29	4	0	1
Snelling	.917	8	11	0	1	0
Spidale	.970	12	31	1	1	1
Thompson	.988	94	240	6	3	1
Victorino	1.000	2	1	0	0	0
Watson	.965	119	187	7	7	3

READING PHILLIES

DOUBLE-A

EASTERN LEAGUE

Batting	B-T	HT	WT	DOB	AVG	vLH	vRH	G	AB	R	H	2B	3B	HR	RBI	BB	HBP	SH	SF	SO	SB	CS	SLG	OBP
Appert, Luke	L-R	5-10	200	7-14-80	.254	.135	.279	108	299	39	76	17	0	7	34	41	1	4	2	59	1	1	.381	.344
Blalock, Jake	R-R	6-4	205	8-6-83	.235	.378	.176	58	153	13	36	6	0	2	16	14	0	0	2	38	0	0	.314	.296
Dawkins, Gookie	R-R	6-1	180	5-12-79	.224	.222	.224	19	67	8	15	4	0	1	4	8	1	0	0	13	1	2	.328	.316
Donald, Jason	R-R	6-1	190	9-4-84	.307	.321	.302	92	362	57	111	19	4	14	54	47	4	0	1	86	11	2	.497	.391
Eylward, Mike	R-R	6-2	210	9-28-79	.225	.213	.229	72	231	25	52	13	0	5	30	20	7	0	1	52	0	1	.346	.305
Feliz, Pedro	R-R	6-1	210	4-27-75	.500	1.000	.429	2	8	2	4	0	0	2	2	0	0	0	0	2	0	0	1.250	.500
Golson, Greg	R-R	6-0	190	9-17-85	.282	.276	.284	106	426	64	120	18	4	13	60	34	1	4	5	130	23	5	.434	.333
Guevara, Orlando	B-R	6-1	175	9-13-83	.091	.100	.087	10	33	2	3	1	0	0	2	4	0	1	0	10	0	0	.121	.189
Hammond, Joey	R-R	6-1	190	10-27-77	.280	.313	.270	81	289	42	81	16	2	4	33	44	1	3	0	44	2	2	.391	.377
Harman, Brad	R-R	6-1	195	11-19-85	.210	.210	.210	117	443	49	93	16	1	17	56	43	2	2	4	138	3	1	.366	.280
Harris, Clay	R-R	6-4	220	8-25-82	.244	.346	.216	41	123	17	30	5	0	4	10	20	3	0	0	20	0	0	.382	.363
Leon, Carlos	B-R	5-10	181	8-31-79	.095	.250	.000	6	21	0	2	0	0	0	0	3	0	0	0	4	0	0	.095	.208
Mansolino, Tony	R-R	6-1	190	9-28-82	.174	.000	.190	7	23	5	4	1	0	0	3	1	0	0	0	5	0	0	.217	.240
Marson, Lou	R-R	6-1	200	6-26-86	.314	.313	.314	94	322	55	101	18	0	5	46	68	2	0	3	70	3	3	.416	.433
Moran, Javon	R-R	5-10	170	9-30-82	.252	.273	.246	83	330	46	83	17	2	1	17	30	4	4	1	52	21	2	.324	.321
Nelson, Kevin	R-R	6-3	215	4-8-81	.210	.278	.182	23	62	6	13	3	0	2	7	5	0	1	0	21	0	0	.355	.269
Sellers, Neil	R-R	6-0	195	4-3-82	.275	.256	.282	134	483	64	133	31	1	19	78	46	3	2	5	81	3	6	.462	.339
Slayden, Jeremy	L-R	6-0	185	7-28-82	.298	.344	.282	131	483	72	144	33	2	17	81	54	10	0	4	105	2	6	.480	.377
Spidale, Mike	R-R	6-1	190	3-12-82	.282	.287	.280	89	308	49	87	11	4	8	36	22	5	2	5	34	18	1	.422	.335
Suomi, John	L-R	5-11	199	10-5-80	.236	.286	.224	32	106	14	25	5	1	3	13	9	2	0	1	12	0	0	.387	.305
Tejeda, Juan	R-R	6-2	195	1-26-82	.211	.316	.183	28	90	7	19	6	0	1	5	10	0	1	0	14	0	0	.311	.290
Thomas, Scott	L-R	5-11	202	3-21-85	.000	—	.000	1	3	0	0	0	0	0	0	0	0	0	0	1	0	0	.000	.000
Thompson, Rich	L-R	6-3	185	4-23-79	.300	1.000	.125	3	10	1	3	0	1	0	1	0	0	0	1	2	0	0	.500	.273
Urick, John	L-L	6-2	210	2-22-82	.222	.000	.400	4	9	2	2	0	0	0	1	1	0	0	1	2	0	0	.222	.273
Victorino, Shane	B-R	5-9	180	11-30-80	.333	—	.333	1	3	0	1	0	0	0	0	0	0	0	0	0	0	0	.333	.333

Pitching	B-T	HT	WT	DOB	W	L	ERA	G	GS	CG	SV	IP	H	R	ER	HR	BB	SO	AVG	vLH	vRH	K/9	BB/9
Anderson, Jason	L-R	6-0	190	6-9-79	0	1	6.20	17	0	0	0	20	25	14	14	2	12	14	.309	.333	.286	6.20	5.31
Bastardo, Antonio	L-L	5-11	168	9-21-85	2	5	3.76	14	14	0	0	67	56	35	28	13	37	62	.223	.200	.229	8.33	4.97
Bisenius, Joe	R-R	6-4	205	9-18-82	3	3	3.43	28	0	0	0	42	33	18	16	5	24	33	.228	.218	.233	7.07	5.14
Bouknight, Kip	R-R	6-0	190	11-16-78	3	8	6.95	16	16	0	0	79	105	65	61	13	34	39	.318	.338	.301	4.44	3.87
Brummett, Tyson	R-R	6-0	150	8-15-84	2	9	7.28	14	14	0	0	80	105	68	65	10	46	47	.319	.305	.331	5.27	5.15
Carpenter, Andrew	R-R	6-3	225	5-18-85	6	8	5.67	16	16	0	0	94	114	68	59	13	30	69	.305	.267	.335	6.63	2.88
Carrasco, Carlos	R-R	6-3	215	3-21-87	7	7	4.32	20	19	1	0	115	109	58	55	13	45	109	.254	.258	.251	8.56	3.53
Castro, Fabio	L-L	5-7	185	1-20-85	8	2	4.40	27	16	1	0	110	109	56	54	14	46	95	.257	.261	.256	7.75	3.75
Durbin, J.D.	R-R	6-0	210	2-24-82	5	7	4.31	19	15	0	0	94	96	54	45	7	40	61	.264	.246	.281	5.84	3.83
Eaton, Adam	R-R	6-2	200	11-23-77	0	3	7.09	5	5	0	0	27	34	24	21	8	4	23	.293	.242	.352	7.76	1.35
Escalona, Sergio	L-L	6-0	178	8-3-84	0	1	2.22	15	0	0	0	24	27	12	6	3	14	29	.281	.324	.258	10.73	5.18
Garcia, Edgar	R-R	6-2	190	9-20-87	1	1	8.22	11	11	0	0	58	70	56	53	10	29	34	.299	.295	.302	5.28	4.50
Harker, Brett	R-R	6-3	185	7-9-84	0	0	7.29	11	1	0	0	21	30	17	17	4	11	10	.333	.400	.280	4.29	4.71
Hill, Ronald	R-R	6-3	225	11-29-82	1	1	6.94	10	0	0	0	12	13	10	9	3	9	9	.277	.182	.360	6.94	6.94
Johnson, Nathan	R-R	6-1	210	1-13-82	0	0	9.00	1	0	0	0	1	2	1	1	0	0	6	.500	1.000	0.00	0.00	0.00
Kershner, Jason	L-L	6-2	190	12-19-76	2	1	5.02	19	0	0	1	29	30	16	16	4	9	22	.268	.206	.295	6.91	2.83
Mackintosh, Jason	R-L	6-0	205	7-2-80	0	0	2.76	11	0	0	0	16	14	8	5	2	7	15	.219	.150	.250	8.27	3.86
Minix, Travis	R-R	6-1	190	8-8-77	3	6	3.86	22	6	0	0	56	55	31	24	4	22	42	.249	.280	.227	6.75	3.54
Myers, Brett	R-R	6-4	240	8-17-80	0	1	2.25	1	1	0	0	8	5	3	2	1	2	10	.161	.077	.222	11.25	2.25
Outman, Josh	L-L	6-1	185	9-14-84	5	4	3.20	33	5	0	1	70	68	27	25	3	37	66	.257	.202	.282	8.45	4.73
Overholt, Pat	R-R	6-2	190	2-8-84	3	8	5.86	49	1	0	10	78	76	59	51	10	49	73	.245	.287	.215	8.39	5.63
Pope, Justin	B-R	6-0	190	11-8-79	1	1	2.23	36	0	0	10	40	27	10	10	5	16	24	.188	.220	.170	5.36	3.57
Savage, William	R-R	6-4	210	8-25-84	0	1	8.31	6	0	0	0	9	13	10	8	1	3	5	.361	.273	.400	5.19	3.12
Segovia, Zack	R-R	6-2	245	4-11-83	0	1	14.40	4	1	0	0	5	7	9	8	1	6	1	.333	.375	.308	1.80	10.80
2-team total (8 Harrisburg)					4		7.38	12	7	0	0	43	57	38	35	6	20	25	—	—	—	5.27	4.22
Swindle, R.J.	L-L	6-3	190	7-7-83	1	0	0.54	11	0	0	0	17	8	1	1	0	1	16	.143	.100	.167	8.64	0.54
Valentine, Joe	R-R	6-2	210	12-24-79	0	0	10.64	4	0	0	0	11	18	14	13	1	6	7	.353	.393	.304	5.73	4.91
Walls, Samuel	R-R	5-11	195	10-31-83	0	2	7.09	23	0	0	4	27	38	30	21	3	27	18	.336	.300	.356	6.07	9.11
Youman, Shane	L-L	6-4	220	10-11-79	0	1	11.28	14	1	0	0	22	33	34	28	3	21	15	.330	.351	.317	6.04	8.46

Fielding

Catcher	PCT	G	PO	A	E	DP	PB
Blalock	1.000	1	7	0	0	0	0
Guevara	1.000	10	66	5	0	0	1
Marson	.985	88	559	43	9	3	6
Nelson	.992	21	111	6	1	2	1
Suomi	.996	29	227	8	1	3	3
Thomas	1.000	1	8	1	0	0	0

First Base	PCT	G	PO	A	E	DP
Appert	1.000	1	8	1	0	1

	B-T	HT	WT	DOB	W	L	ERA	G	GS	CG	SV	IP	H	R	ER	HR	BB	SO	AVG	vLH	vRH	K/9	BB/9
Naylor, Drew	R-R	6-4	210	5-31-86	5	3	2.99	14	14	2	0	87	69	32	29	8	21	97	.214	.194	.232	10.00	2.16
Pfinsgraff, Ben	R-R	6-0	180	11-13-83	2	3	3.41	18	0	0	2	37	28	15	14	3	6	37	.207	.207	.208	9.00	1.46
Rocchio, Joe	R-R	6-4	200	10-15-84	4	6	3.86	26	0	0	1	42	35	19	18	2	18	33	.220	.258	.194	7.07	3.86
Sampson, Julian	R-R	6-5	210	1-21-89	11	4	4.33	25	25	0	0	135	152	73	65	5	52	69	.285	.303	.270	4.60	3.47
Seanez, Rudy	R-R	6-1	225	10-20-68	1	0	0.00	1	0	0	0	1	2	2	0	0	0	1	.333	.333	.333	9.00	0.00
Simon, Jared	R-R	6-1	185	8-15-84	6	3	3.56	55	0	0	30	61	58	29	24	3	9	52	.248	.287	.221	7.71	1.34
Sterner, Zack	R-R	6-2	170	11-7-85	10	2	1.48	29	0	0	0	61	44	14	10	0	27	49	.205	.160	.243	7.27	4.01
Stutes, Mike	R-R	6-1	185	9-4-86	5	1	1.48	7	7	0	0	43	20	8	7	1	18	53	.139	.149	.129	11.18	3.80
Tejeda, Walter	L-L	6-3	187	9-28-85	4	7	4.60	25	14	0	0	86	98	54	44	2	45	65	.286	.280	.288	6.80	4.71
Worley, Vance	R-R	6-2	205	9-25-87	3	2	2.66	11	11	0	0	61	58	25	18	4	7	53	.247	.248	.246	7.82	1.03

Fielding

Catcher	PCT	G	PO	A	E	DP	PB
Arzeno	.979	4	41	5	1	0	2
D'Arnaud	.971	16	123	10	4	1	5
Kennelly	1.000	10	72	9	0	0	4
Naughton	.991	86	595	83	6	5	7
Sanchez	.991	34	197	33	2	1	6

First Base	PCT	G	PO	A	E	DP
Bolt	.996	26	203	28	1	14
Durant	.977	61	554	51	14	58
Kennelly	1.000	1	13	0	0	1
Rizzotti	.986	56	524	48	8	38

Second Base	PCT	G	PO	A	E	DP
Cambero	.950	8	10	9	1	2
Demmink	1.000	6	9	11	0	3
Mitchell	.937	106	193	301	33	54
Winn	.986	36	53	86	2	18

Third Base	PCT	G	PO	A	E	DP
Demmink	1.000	6	1	10	0	1
Mattair	.927	129	81	249	26	26
Winn	.895	13	6	28	4	2

Shortstop	PCT	G	PO	A	E	DP
Cambero	.944	6	6	11	1	2
Galvis	.968	127	224	407	21	81
Winn	.979	10	14	32	1	5

Outfield	PCT	G	PO	A	E	DP
Bolt	.960	47	69	3	3	0
Brown	.957	113	208	12	10	4
Cambero	.923	14	10	2	1	0
Demmink	.946	24	34	1	2	0
Kennelly	1.000	36	53	3	0	0
Miller	.981	35	51	1	1	0
Myers	.980	64	92	4	2	2
Susdorf	1.000	5	6	1	0	0
Taylor	.971	58	92	8	3	2
Warren	.979	66	91	3	2	0

WILLIAMSPORT CROSSCUTTERS

SHORT-SEASON

NEW YORK-PENN LEAGUE

Batting	B-T	HT	WT	DOB	AVG	vLH	vRH	G	AB	R	H	2B	3B	HR	RBI	BB	HBP	SH	SF	SO	SB	CS	SLG	OBP
Arzeno, Luis Ramon	R-R	5-11	190	8-9-84	.080	.000	.118	10	25	1	2	0	0	0	0	1	0	0	0	9	0	0	.080	.115
Binkoski, Tim	L-L	6-1	195	2-2-84	.270	.261	.272	33	115	14	31	8	0	0	10	7	0	0	0	29	1	1	.339	.311
Blackburn, Joe	R-R	6-4	215	9-4-85	.212	.188	.222	19	52	9	11	1	2	0	5	5	0	0	0	13	0	0	.308	.281
Cambero, Alberto	B-R	5-9	152	4-23-86	.500	.500	.500	1	4	1	2	0	0	0	1	0	0	0	0	1	3	0	.500	.500
D'Arnaud, Travis	R-R	6-2	195	2-10-89	.309	.353	.290	48	175	21	54	13	1	4	25	18	1	0	3	29	1	2	.463	.371
Frew, Bryan	R-L	6-1	195	3-10-86	.241	.256	.237	55	170	34	41	9	3	1	14	29	1	4	2	46	7	3	.347	.351
Haislet, Brandon	R-R	6-2	205	8-26-85	.240	.206	.255	62	225	34	54	6	0	2	21	21	9	2	1	70	12	2	.293	.323
Hamilton, Jeremy	L-L	6-1	180	11-11-86	.202	.128	.233	39	129	16	26	9	0	2	9	25	0	1	0	36	1	0	.318	.331
Hanzawa, Troy	R-R	5-9	155	9-12-85	.297	.271	.306	75	263	36	78	19	0	3	31	18	9	0	3	51	6	3	.403	.358
Hargrave, Daniel	R-R	6-0	178	12-13-85	.179	.094	.217	50	173	15	31	7	0	4	13	7	2	4	2	54	1	0	.289	.217
McDonald, Darin	R-R	6-3	195	11-3-87	.175	.333	.080	11	40	4	7	1	0	1	2	0	0	1	0	15	0	2	.275	.175
Morales, Douglas	L-L	6-0	180	6-22-86	.225	.077	.259	29	71	9	16	4	0	1	7	5	0	0	1	19	2	0	.324	.273
Murphy, Jim	R-R	6-4	240	9-16-85	.220	.100	.247	31	109	15	24	5	1	3	13	12	6	0	1	32	0	0	.367	.328
Myers, D'Arby	R-R	6-3	175	12-9-88	.266	.245	.274	50	199	29	53	13	2	1	15	14	2	2	0	28	7	4	.367	.321
Overbeck, Cody	R-R	6-1	201	6-5-86	.272	.282	.269	75	290	37	79	18	0	12	57	12	4	0	5	65	1	1	.459	.305
Quiroz, Arlon	R-R	6-0	170	11-13-86	.255	.189	.280	47	137	28	35	4	1	0	12	12	2	2	4	35	15	4	.299	.316
Susdorf, Steve	L-L	6-1	195	3-28-86	.305	.359	.289	48	167	20	51	13	0	5	35	15	1	0	3	25	0	2	.473	.360
Thomas, Scott	L-L	5-11	202	3-21-85	.235	.118	.259	30	102	7	24	8	0	0	10	3	1	1	1	33	0	1	.314	.262
Villegas Andino, Jesus	R-R	5-10	175	9-21-86	.100	.000	.143	6	20	2	2	0	0	0	2	1	0	1	0	5	0	1	.100	.143
Zaccardo, Mike	L-R	5-11	220	4-8-85	.000	.000	—	1	2	0	0	0	0	0	0	0	0	0	0	1	0	0	.000	.000

Pitching	B-T	HT	WT	DOB	W	L	ERA	G	GS	CG	SV	IP	H	R	ER	HR	BB	SO	AVG	vLH	vRH	K/9	BB/9
Arroyo, Spencer	L-L	6-3	160	8-9-88	0	2	9.28	4	2	0	1	11	12	13	11	2	9	4	.261	.200	.278	3.38	7.59
Austin, Rick	R-R	6-3	210	1-16-85	0	1	13.50	3	0	0	0	5	8	8	8	2	3	5	.333	.364	.308	8.44	5.06
Ballestas, Freddy	R-R	6-3	170	10-4-86	4	5	6.18	13	13	0	0	60	72	46	41	3	24	64	.300	.302	.299	9.65	3.62
Cisco, Mike	R-R	5-11	190	5-23-87	1	0	1.86	9	1	0	0	19	18	5	4	1	5	22	.240	.200	.260	10.24	2.33
Cloyd, Tyler	R-R	6-2	190	5-16-87	5	4	4.57	12	12	0	0	65	76	35	33	8	21	58	.298	.236	.331	8.03	2.91
De Fratus, Justin	B-R	6-4	215	10-21-87	6	5	3.67	14	14	1	0	83	87	39	34	1	25	74	.260	.268	.255	7.99	2.70
Diekman, Jacob	L-L	6-4	190	1-21-87	1	4	4.40	8	8	1	0	45	41	24	22	4	25	43	.246	.353	.233	8.60	5.00
Drabek, Kyle	R-R	6-0	185	12-8-87	1	2	2.21	4	4	0	0	20	11	6	5	1	6	10	.159	.231	.116	4.43	2.66
Ellis, Jordan	R-R	6-2	198	9-11-85	3	0	3.00	13	1	0	3	30	21	13	10	0	10	35	.196	.205	.191	10.50	3.00
Grieve, Sean	L-L	6-1	195	12-13-84	3	0	2.35	15	0	0	1	23	20	8	6	0	17	24	.235	.192	.254	9.39	6.65
Lin, Yen-Feng	R-R	6-1	205	5-22-85	0	1	7.15	14	0	0	0	23	31	20	18	4	10	17	.316	.353	.297	6.75	3.97
Matos, Miguel	R-R	6-4	178	10-26-87	0	2	4.41	6	1	0	1	16	16	10	8	2	4	18	.246	.250	.244	9.92	2.20
McConnell, Eryk	R-R	6-1	185	7-29-85	0	1	4.50	9	0	0	1	14	15	10	7	2	5	20	.263	.261	.265	12.86	3.21
Noles, Korey	L-L	5-11	185	7-18-85	1	1	2.30	10	0	0	1	16	13	4	4	1	3	13	.228	.200	.243	7.47	1.72
Oster, Jesse	R-R	5-11	200	10-12-85	1	1	7.79	10	1	0	0	17	23	15	15	2	14	7	.324	.238	.363	3.63	7.27
Pena, Riquy	R-R	6-2	162	6-17-85	0	1	12.60	4	0	0	0	5	9	10	7	1	6	7	.391	.500	.308	12.60	10.80
Rosenberg, B.J.	R-R	6-2	200	9-17-85	3	1	1.00	21	0	0	10	36	26	9	4	2	15	52	.205	.222	.198	13.00	3.75
Roth, Robert	R-R	6-1	195	8-5-88	7	2	3.39	10	10	0	0	58	47	24	22	2	21	23	.215	.176	.232	3.55	3.24
Schwimer, Michael	R-R	6-8	240	2-19-86	0	2	1.96	22	0	0	8	41	33	12	9	0	6	52	.217	.180	.235	13.50	1.32
Stutes, Mike	R-R	6-1	185	9-4-86	0	1	1.33	6	6	0	0	27	16	5	4	2	11	31	.172	.091	.217	10.33	3.67
Vartanian, Charles	R-R	6-7	265	9-17-85	0	1	6.06	11	0	0	1	16	27	19	11	1	7	13	.351	.400	.327	7.16	3.86
Worley, Vance	R-R	6-2	205	9-25-87	0	1	1.13	2	2	0	0	8	3	1	1	0	1	8	.120	1.000	.083	9.00	1.13

Fielding

Catcher	PCT	G	PO	A	E	DP	PB
Arzeno	.944	9	46	5	3	0	2
Blackburn	.976	14	117	4	3	3	3
D'Arnaud	.984	42	330	31	6	0	11
Thomas	.983	15	104	9	2	0	3
Zaccardo	1.000	1	3	0	0	0	0

First Base	PCT	G	PO	A	E	DP
Hamilton	.984	39	282	23	5	21
Morales	1.000	9	53	3	0	6
Murphy	.991	24	195	18	2	20
Susdorf	1.000	6	44	2	0	4

Second Base	PCT	G	PO	A	E	DP
Cambero	1.000	1	2	1	0	0
Frew	.947	26	40	50	5	8
Hargrave	.966	49	78	123	7	29
Villegas Andino	1.000	2	2	4	0	1

Third Base	PCT	G	PO	A	E	DP
Frew	1.000	3	0	2	0	0
Overbeck	.899	73	41	111	17	12
Villegas Andino	1.000	1	0	4	0	0

Shortstop	PCT	G	PO	A	E	DP
Frew	1.000	3	2	4	0	1

	PCT	G	PO	A	E	DP
Hanzawa	.965	75	123	235	13	44
Villegas Andino	.500	1	1	0	1	0

Outfield	PCT	G	PO	A	E	DP
Binkoski	1.000	16	24	1	0	0
Frew	.978	24	41	4	1	0
Haislet	.973	56	106	2	3	0
McDonald	.941	7	16	0	1	0
Morales	1.000	16	22	1	0	0
Myers	.976	49	81	1	2	0
Quiroz	.963	37	78	0	3	0
Susdorf	1.000	27	42	0	0	0

GCL PHILLIES   ROOKIE

GULF COAST LEAGUE

Batting	B-T	HT	WT	DOB	AVG	vLH	vRH	G	AB	R	H	2B	3B	HR	RBI	BB	HBP	SH	SF	SO	SB	CS	SLG	OBP
Antoniato, P.J.	R-R	5-9	185	7-2-83	.286	.000	.400	2	7	0	2	0	0	0	1	0	0	0	0	0	0	0	.286	.286
Arzeno, Luis Ramon	R-R	5-11	190	8-9-84	.190	.167	.200	11	42	3	8	0	1	7	0	1	0	0	9	0	0	.286	.209
Binkoski, Tim	L-L	6-1	195	2-2-84	.333	.500	.000	1	3	0	1	0	0	0	0	0	0	0	1	1	0	.333	.333
Castillo, Lendy	R-R	6-1	170	4-8-89	.212	.146	.238	45	170	23	36	8	1	3	19	7	0	2	0	36	7	0	.324	.243
Castro, Leandro	R-R	5-11	175	6-15-89	.298	.364	.264	44	161	25	48	9	1	3	19	4	1	1	1	25	9	4	.422	.317
Collier, Zach	L-L	6-2	185	9-8-90	.271	.333	.247	37	129	15	35	9	1	0	19	17	0	0	4	28	5	0	.357	.347
De Los Santos, Vladimir	R-R	6-1	176	8-6-86	.251	.204	.271	51	187	32	47	11	1	10	45	9	0	2	2	41	1	1	.481	.290
Garcia, Harold	B-R	5-11	164	10-25-86	.299	.208	.339	50	174	35	52	12	5	5	21	20	12	1	3	32	17	2	.511	.402
Gomez, Ferrel	R-R	5-11	170	10-17-86	.239	.182	.265	26	71	6	17	4	0	0	10	3	0	0	2	16	1	1	.296	.263
Gose, Anthony	L-L	6-1	190	8-10-90	.256	.222	.286	11	39	4	10	2	1	0	3	1	0	0	12	3	1	.359	.293
Hamilton, Jeremy	L-L	6-1	180	11-11-86	.327	.313	.333	16	49	5	16	2	0	0	7	4	0	1	1	16	1	0	.367	.370
Hewitt, Anthony	R-R	6-1	195	4-27-89	.197	.150	.221	33	117	14	23	7	1	1	9	7	3	0	2	55	2	0	.299	.256
Kennelly, Timothy	R-R	6-0	180	12-5-86	.400	.333	.429	4	10	0	4	1	0	0	1	2	1	0	0	2	0	0	.500	.538
King, Brennan	R-R	6-3	220	1-20-81	.200	.000	.286	5	10	1	2	0	0	0	0	3	1	0	0	3	1	0	.200	.429
Murakami, Fabio	R-R	6-1	194	3-4-88	.287	.421	.253	29	94	14	27	5	0	1	10	6	1	1	0	17	1	1	.372	.337
Murphy, Jim	R-R	6-4	240	9-16-85	.355	.429	.323	28	93	16	33	6	1	2	17	11	2	0	3	20	0	0	.505	.422
Quiroz, Arlon	R-R	6-0	170	11-13-86	.190	.250	.176	6	21	2	4	0	0	0	2	1	0	0	1	5	1	0	.190	.217
Rio-Nunez, Ruddy	R-R	6-1	190	2-16-90	.000	.000	.000	4	7	0	0	0	0	0	0	0	0	0	0	3	0	0	.000	.000
Rizzotti, Matt	L-L	6-5	235	12-24-85	.538	.333	.600	4	13	1	7	1	0	0	6	4	0	0	1	3	0	0	.769	.611
Rodriguez, Jean Carlos	R-R	5-10	204	3-27-89	.176	.091	.200	17	51	8	9	2	0	0	4	9	2	0	0	20	0	0	.216	.300
Rodriguez, Yonderman	R-R	5-11	160	2-17-87	.302	.333	.314	43	129	27	39	8	0	0	13	27	1	0	2	24	6	0	.364	.421
Saunderson, Damarii	L-L	6-3	185	11-27-89	.103	.250	.048	13	29	4	3	1	1	0	2	8	2	0	0	15	0	2	.207	.333
Schoenberger, Alan	B-R	5-10	160	1-19-89	.191	.212	.180	32	94	7	18	6	1	0	1	14	0	1	0	25	2	1	.277	.296
Valle, Sebastian	R-L	6-1	168	7-24-90	.281	.241	.303	48	167	27	47	15	0	2	18	12	4	0	2	31	0	0	.407	.341
Watson, Rob	R-R	5-10	185	12-31-79	.500	1.000	.000	1	2	0	1	1	0	0	0	0	0	0	0	1	0	0	1.000	.500

Pitching	B-T	HT	WT	DOB	W	L	ERA	G	GS	CG	SV	IP	H	R	ER	HR	BB	SO	AVG	vLH	vRH	K/9	BB/9
Arroyo, Spencer	L-L	6-3	160	8-9-88	0	2	4.26	9	4	0	0	32	37	16	15	0	5	25	.296	.297	.295	7.11	1.42
Bergh, Ryan	R-R	6-4	220	4-25-85	3	1	0.64	20	0	0	9	28	25	5	2	0	4	26	.225	.250	.211	8.26	1.27
Bolsenbroek, Mike	R-R	6-8	210	3-11-87	0	1	1.42	5	0	0	0	6	8	3	1	0	5	5	.308	.111	.412	7.11	7.11
Cloyd, Tyler	R-R	6-2	190	5-16-87	2	0	0.00	2	1	0	0	11	5	0	0	1	11	.139	.200	.063	9.00	0.82
Drabek, Kyle	R-R	6-0	185	12-8-87	0	1	2.25	4	4	0	0	12	6	3	3	0	6	6	.150	.118	.174	4.50	4.50
Eachues, Josh	B-R	6-2	200	3-20-85	0	0	0.00	1	0	0	0	1	1	0	0	0	0	.250	.000	.250	0.00	9.00
Ellis, Jordan	R-R	6-2	198	9-11-85	1	0	1.29	8	0	0	3	14	6	2	2	1	3	14	.128	.118	.133	9.00	1.93
Fike, Nate	L-L	6-1	165	1-23-88	1	7	7.20	5	0	0	0	10	15	11	8	2	5	9	.333	.300	.333	8.10	4.50
Flande, Yohan	L-L	6-2	170	1-27-86	4	1	2.19	10	9	0	0	53	41	19	13	5	11	39	.200	.178	.206	6.58	1.86
Grieve, Sean	L-L	6-1	195	12-13-84	0	0	3.68	6	0	0	1	7	8	3	3	0	3	7	.308	.500	.250	8.59	3.68
Jimenez, Esmelvin	L-L	5-10	180	2-5-87	1	1	2.49	15	0	0	1	25	20	11	7	1	7	26	.211	.111	.250	9.24	2.49
Knapp, Jason	R-R	6-5	215	8-31-90	3	1	2.61	7	6	0	0	31	26	10	9	1	12	38	.228	.167	.250	11.03	3.48
Lugo, Ebelin	R-R	6-2		4-23-90	3	1	3.82	13	3	0	0	33	37	17	14	5	11	32	.285	.297	.280	8.73	3.00
Mata, Cristobal	R-R	5-11	155	6-19-86	1	0	6.00	5	0	0	0	9	10	9	6	2	1	7	.256	.364	.214	7.00	1.00
Matos, Miguel	R-R	6-4	178	10-26-87	4	3	3.30	7	6	0	0	30	23	12	11	2	11	26	.211	.151	.268	7.80	3.30
May, Trevor	R-R	6-5	215	9-23-89	1	1	3.75	5	2	0	0	12	11	7	5	0	7	11	.256	.308	.233	8.25	5.25
Oster, Jesse	R-R	5-11	200	10-12-85	1	2	6.75	9	0	0	0	12	13	10	9	3	4	15	.283	.222	.321	11.25	3.00
Pettibone, Jon	L-R	6-5	200	7-19-90	0	1	0.00	1	1	0	0	3	2	0	0	1	0	.600	.500	.667	0.00	9.00
Poe, Chad	R-R	6-2	185	11-14-87	0	1	9.00	7	2	0	0	11	18	11	11	0	9	13	.383	.429	.364	10.64	7.36
Rocchio, Joe	R-R	6-4	200	10-15-84	0	0	0.00	2	0	0	0	3	3	0	0	0	0	2	.273	.333	.250	5.40	0.00
Rodriguez, Julio	R-R	6-4	195	8-29-90	0	1	12.19	7	0	0	0	10	18	15	14	3	6	8	.383	.387	.387	6.97	5.23
Romero, Mauricio	R-R	6-3	202	6-16-86	3	0	0.29	14	0	0	1	31	19	2	1	0	3	24	.179	.320	.136	6.89	0.86
Simon, Reginal	R-R	6-3	177	12-28-89	4	4	5.07	11	11	0	0	50	58	30	28	4	15	34	.293	.279	.300	6.16	2.72
Slate, Kyle	R-R	6-5	200	4-23-89	1	2	4.55	7	5	0	0	28	28	18	14	3	2	29	.255	.326	.209	9.43	0.65
Smith, Matt	L-L	6-4	215	6-15-79	0	0	3.60	4	4	0	0	5	3	2	2	0	1	6	.167	.000	.214	10.80	1.80
Vartanian, Charles	R-R	6-7	265	9-17-85	0	0	4.00	5	0	0	1	9	10	6	4	1	2	15	.263	.188	.318	15.00	2.00

Fielding

Catcher	PCT	G	PO	A	E	DP	PB
Arzeno	.900	1	6	3	1	0	0
Gomez	.962	22	114	11	5	0	2
J. Rodriguez	.981	13	100	3	2	1	5
Valle	.987	29	202	21	3	0	4

First Base	PCT	G	PO	A	E	DP
Arzeno	.974	5	37	1	1	4
Binkoski	1.000	1	10	1	0	2
De Los Santos	.952	7	36	4	2	5
Hamilton	.964	15	103	4	4	12
Murphy	1.000	25	210	9	0	12
Rizzotti	1.000	2	19	1	0	2
Y. Rodriguez	.976	6	40	1	1	2

Second Base	PCT	G	PO	A	E	DP
Garcia	.957	44	73	106	8	21
Y. Rodriguez	.889	2	4	4	1	1
Schoenberger	.973	15	34	39	2	1
Watson	1.000	1	1	1	0	0

Third Base	PCT	G	PO	A	E	DP
Antoniato	1.000	2	3	4	0	2
Garcia	1.000	4	2	4	0	0
Hewitt	.848	20	15	24	7	1
Kennelly	1.000	3	1	2	0	0
King	.500	2	0	1	1	0
Y. Rodriguez	.913	32	13	60	7	3
Schoenberger	—	1	0	0	0	0

Shortstop	PCT	G	PO	A	E	DP
Castillo	.952	45	51	128	9	22
Schoenberger	.891	14	24	33	7	8

Outfield	PCT	G	PO	A	E	DP
Castro	.990	44	97	5	1	0
Collier	.983	37	55	2	1	0
De Los Santos	.955	41	60	3	3	2
Gose	1.000	10	20	1	0	1
Murakami	.950	29	36	2	2	0
Quiroz	1.000	6	22	1	0	0
Rio-Nunez	.500	4	1	0	1	0
Saunderson	1.000	11	12	0	0	0
Schoenberger	1.000	2	5	0	0	0

DSL PHILLIES

ROOKIE

DOMINICAN SUMMER LEAGUE

Batting	B-T	HT	WT	DOB	AVG	vLH	vRH	G	AB	R	H	2B	3B	HR	RBI	BB	HBP	SH	SF	SO	SB	CS	SLG	OBP
Aguilar, Pedro	R-R	5-10	190	5-20-89	.221	.250	.213	56	199	21	44	8	0	1	24	21	6	1	2	23	4	5	.276	.311
Alvarez, Miguel	R-R	6-1	172	8-27-89	.288	.373	.264	63	229	31	66	8	0	2	26	15	5	2	0	32	32	13	.349	.345
Balentien, Rudney	R-R	6-0	160	11-3-89	.214	.282	.199	62	210	35	45	9	4	1	21	29	1	2	2	51	14	10	.310	.310
Best, Carlos	R-R	6-2	170	1-13-91	.167	.125	.174	25	54	6	9	0	0	0	2	1	1	0	25	3	0		.167	.328
Checo, Emmanuel	R-R	6-0	190	12-18-87	.234	.385	.198	51	137	17	32	7	1	1	17	19	3	1	5	32	4	1	.321	.329
Martinez, Eduard	L-L	6-1	175	5-28-87	.224	.318	.204	50	125	23	28	4	1	1	14	32	5	2	2	27	4	5	.296	.396
Mendez, Geancarlo	R-R	6-2	170	11-17-89	.269	.209	.284	64	219	43	59	5	1	2	28	29	15	2	4	24	17	5	.329	.386
Moscat, Anderson	R-R	6-2	188	5-31-89	.200	.238	.188	34	85	9	17	2	0	0	4	11	2	1	0	31	2	3	.224	.306
Paulino, Luis	R-R	6-2	185	6-16-89	.281	.182	.315	49	171	18	48	7	4	0	34	13	4	0	4	42	9	1	.368	.339
Tejada, Cesar	R-R	6-1	170	11-11-88	.252	.333	.237	42	115	17	29	4	2	0	7	35	3	2	0	20	13	2	.322	.438
Trinidad, Jose	R-R	6-2	175	6-13-91	.179	.125	.200	32	84	6	15	1	0	0	9	2	4	0	1	40	4	2	.190	.231
Valenzuela, Carlos	R-R	5-11	170	9-18-90	.200	.304	.172	60	215	30	43	5	0	2	22	25	9	0	3	70	18	6	.251	.306
Ventura, Nelson	R-R	5-11	174	5-14-90	.160	.250	.143	15	25	2	4	1	0	0	1	4	2	0	0	13	0	0	.200	.323
Villan, Jonathan	B-R	6-1	180	5-2-91	.271	.314	.258	62	214	37	58	6	3	1	21	30	4	4	3	56	27	8	.341	.367

Pitching	B-T	HT	WT	DOB	W	L	ERA	G	GS	CG	SV	IP	H	R	ER	HR	BB	SO	AVG	vLH	vRH	K/9	BB/9
Alvarez, Dario	L-L	6-1	170	1-17-91	4	2	3.23	18	5	0	2	53	44	21	19	1	24	51	.223	.143	.230	8.66	4.08
Alvarez, Daurius	R-R	6-2	185	9-10-87	1	0	0.00	2	1	0	0	7	4	1	0	0	1	7	.174	.000	.211	9.00	1.29
Arias, Gabirel	R-R	6-2	185	12-6-89	3	3	2.63	17	0	0	6	41	28	12	12	2	16	30	.192	.200	.196	6.59	3.51
Basil, Alvaro	R-R	6-3	170	10-28-90	2	0	0.90	10	0	0	3	20	9	4	2	1	5	21	.136	.182	.127	9.45	2.25
Bernabel, Edwin	R-R	6-2	170	2-4-86	0	3	3.63	11	0	0	2	17	13	8	7	0	14	20	.220	.417	.170	10.38	7.27
Brazoban, Domingo	R-R	6-2	175	8-8-89	1	2	7.41	12	1	0	0	17	24	16	14	3	16	12	.353	.286	.361	6.35	8.47
Carpio, Pedro	R-R	6-2	185	6-18-88	7	4	2.27	15	14	1	0	91	57	28	23	1	27	82	.178	.128	.188	8.11	2.67
Cespedes, Felix	R-R	6-3	180	4-30-91	1	2	5.11	8	7	0	0	25	27	20	14	0	9	17	.284	.333	.273	6.20	3.28
Charles, Francique	R-R	6-0	178	2-28-89	1	0	0.00	5	0	0	0	6	1	0	0	0	6	7	.056	.000	.059	11.12	9.53
Coca, Marcos	R-R	6-3	156	1-19-90	0	3	2.72	13	4	0	1	46	34	20	14	1	27	45	.200	.103	.220	8.74	5.24
De La Cruz, Daniel	R-R	6-3	175	8-10-90	5	2	2.25	13	7	0	1	56	39	22	14	1	30	51	.194	.139	.206	8.20	4.82
Estevez, Eduardo	R-R	6-1	180	2-4-88	0	0	—	1	0	0	0	0	0	0	0	0	0	0	.000	—	.000	—	—
Florentino, Antonio	R-R	6-4	180	6-5-87	0	3	5.64	8	2	0	0	22	26	22	14	1	16	15	.280	.278	.280	6.04	6.45
Gracia, Kevin	R-R	6-5	225	6-1-90	0	0	23.63	4	0	0	0	3	6	9	7	0	9	3	.429	.400	.444	10.13	30.38
Martinez, Joel	R-R	6-4	190	6-20-85	0	0	8.10	4	0	0	0	7	9	8	6	0	4	6	.321	.200	.348	8.10	5.40
Mendez, Sergio	R-R	6-2	160	8-21-91	1	1	5.40	7	4	0	0	17	17	17	10	1	14	13	.270	.263	.273	7.02	7.56
Pascual, Rey	R-R	6-1	175	4-1-87	0	0	36.00	1	0	0	0	1	4	4	4	0	2	0	.571	.500	.600	0.00	18.00
Paulino, Richy	R-R	6-3	187	8-4-90	0	1	1.35	6	0	0	0	7	3	1	1	0	4	7	.136	.500	.100	9.45	5.40
Sandoval, Raudy	R-R	6-5	205	5-4-85	1	0	2.45	7	0	0	1	11	7	7	3	1	9	7	.184	.333	.156	5.73	7.36
Sepulveda, Juan	R-R	6-5	190	1-26-89	1	0	4.91	3	0	0	0	4	1	2	2	0	5	7	.083	.000	.125	17.18	12.27
Sosa, Juan	R-R	6-2	165	10-11-89	4	1	1.37	13	12	3	1	59	48	16	9	1	25	60	.230	.292	.211	9.15	3.81

Fielding

Catcher	PCT	G	PO	A	E	DP	PB
Aguilar	.979	23	163	27	4	0	5
Checo	.985	46	294	45	5	1	8
Ventura	.981	13	46	7	1	0	2

First Base	PCT	G	PO	A	E	DP
Martinez	.917	2	11	0	1	2
Mendez	.986	48	388	37	6	31
Moscat	.995	21	171	12	1	11
Paulino	1.000	4	20	1	0	1
Tejada	1.000	1	6	0	0	0
Villan	1.000	1	3	0	0	0

Second Base	PCT	G	PO	A	E	DP
Mendez	.934	17	22	35	4	8
Tejada	.979	22	44	48	2	12
Valenzuela	.957	13	17	28	2	6
Villan	.937	18	37	37	5	5

Third Base	PCT	G	PO	A	E	DP
Martinez	1.000	1	2	3	0	0
Mendez	.833	4	3	7	2	0
Moscat	.857	8	4	14	3	2
Paulino	.889	40	30	82	14	4
Paulino	1.000	1	0	2	0	0
Tejada	1.000	1	0	2	0	0
Valenzuela	.800	16	18	26	11	5
Villan	1.000	2	3	5	0	0

Shortstop	PCT	G	PO	A	E	DP
Tejada	1.000	2	2	4	0	2
Valenzuela	.885	30	44	64	14	17
Villan	.912	40	53	102	15	16

Outfield	PCT	G	PO	A	E	DP
Alvarez	.982	62	107	4	2	1
Balentien	.958	61	66	3	3	0
Best	.900	23	16	2	2	0
Martinez	.973	47	69	3	2	2
Paulino	1.000	1	3	0	0	0
Tejada	1.000	1	1	0	0	0
Trinidad	.875	32	21	0	3	0
Villan	1.000	1	4	0	0	0

VENEZUELAN SUMMER LEAGUE

Batting	B-T	HT	WT	DOB	AVG	vLH	vRH	G	AB	R	H	2B	3B	HR	RBI	BB	HBP	SH	SF	SO	SB	CS	SLG	OBP
Alvarez, Anderson	R-R	5-11	193	1-28-88	.266	.167	.287	53	173	26	46	15	1	3	21	16	5	1	3	37	2	2	.416	.340
Bogle, Vernal	R-R	6-0	167	11-21-89	.278	.407	.242	49	126	21	35	5	2	2	12	12	7	1	0	36	10	7	.397	.372
Diaz, Francisco	B-R	5-10	158	3-21-90	.289	.250	.298	58	187	27	54	9	3	0	23	22	3	3	2	22	8	7	.369	.369
Duran, Edgar	R-R	5-11	154	2-10-91	.228	.219	.230	53	167	14	38	5	0	0	10	7	2	6	1	23	4	6	.257	.266
Granado, Jesus	R-R	6-2	163	8-7-88	.140	.182	.128	18	50	4	7	2	0	1	4	2	0	0	0	13	1	1	.240	.173
Guerra, Jorge	R-R	6-1	170	9-12-87	.283	.217	.299	60	223	27	63	16	2	2	41	19	4	0	2	30	5	0	.399	.347
Hernandez, Cesar	B-R	5-10	166	5-23-90	.315	.238	.335	60	197	31	62	7	6	1	24	33	1	1	2	22	19	7	.426	.412
Lezcano, Norberto	B-R	6-3	166	12-5-88	.187	.333	.167	33	75	4	14	3	0	0	8	3	2	2	0	21	0	0	.227	.238
Martinez, Luis	R-R	6-5	183	12-22-89	.269	.250	.274	59	208	35	56	9	3	1	24	11	6	1	2	38	8	4	.356	.322
Perdomo, Carlos	R-R	5-10	168	4-25-90	.241	.343	.218	59	191	23	46	5	4	1	22	10	6	4	1	16	9	3	.325	.298
Rossi, Levi	R-R	6-1	182	2-11-87	.300	.370	.282	60	227	40	68	13	1	3	16	14	12	3	1	48	9	4	.405	.370
Sosa, Nelson	R-R	5-11	148	9-30-89	.224	.333	.205	36	98	10	22	2	1	0	10	14	4	2	0	15	1	2	.265	.345
Tolo, Eduards	R-R	5-9	140	10-7-90	.288	.313	.281	49	153	20	44	8	0	0	14	17	2	0	3	21	6	3	.340	.360
Torres, Winder	R-R	5-11	160	8-2-90	.238	.091	.269	25	63	10	15	3	0	0	7	5	7	2	1	16	3	5	.286	.355
Unda, Luis	L-L	6-1	155	1-28-90	.239	.238	.239	47	134	14	32	2	1	0	17	13	1	0	0	14	3	6	.269	.311

Pitching	B-T	HT	WT	DOB	W	L	ERA	G	GS	CG	SV	IP	H	R	ER	HR	BB	SO	AVG	vLH	vRH	K/9	BB/9
Bastidas, Leonel	R-R	6-3	184	6-26-89	3	2	3.97	12	5	0	0	34	46	25	15	0	15	22	.329	.250	.352	5.82	3.97
Campo, Kirlian	B-L	6-0	180	5-17-90	0	0	2.61	7	0	0	0	10	4	3	3	0	4	6	.111	.000	.118	5.23	3.48
Castillo, Luis	R-R	5-11	181	1-5-89	2	0	5.33	13	0	0	1	25	37	18	15	4	3	15	.346	.269	.370	5.33	1.07
Colmenarez, Juan	L-L	6-1	165	10-22-86	6	4	2.13	14	12	0	2	72	70	23	17	2	8	48	.256	.143	.259	6.00	1.00
Espinoza, Berman	R-R	6-3	170	11-4-87	1	4	3.38	22	0	0	10	35	39	14	13	0	6	39	.289	.500	.248	10.13	1.56
Garces, Orlando	L-L	5-11	181	8-24-90	1	2	4.22	13	2	0	1	21	25	12	10	1	11	16	.309	.286	.311	6.75	4.64
Gomez, Juary	R-R	6-2	200	5-23-90	1	2	5.24	14	0	0	0	22	30	18	13	2	10	13	.326	.417	.313	5.24	4.03
Guevara, Rafael	R-R	5-11	166	11-19-90	0	0	19.29	4	0	0	0	2	4	5	5	0	6	0	.364	.286	.500	0.00	23.14
Guzman, Jorge	R-R	6-1	201	8-14-91	0	1	5.48	11	1	0	1	21	27	16	13	1	13	13	.318	.217	.355	5.48	5.48
Hernandez, Jose	R-R	6-1	201	1-21-88	4	3	3.34	13	12	0	0	65	77	30	24	3	12	42	.295	.200	.307	5.85	1.67
Izurriaga, Ely	L-L	5-11	188	6-29-90	2	2	3.54	10	1	0	3	20	27	14	8	1	9	24	.318	.500	.313	10.62	3.98
Landaeta, Manuel	R-R	6-3	162	6-14-88	2	4	3.56	11	10	0	0	43	37	22	17	2	29	27	.243	.176	.252	5.65	6.07
Lara, Daniel	R-R	6-1	178	3-8-88	1	1	4.67	16	2	0	3	35	29	27	18	0	18	17	.220	.167	.235	4.41	4.67
Leon, Luis	R-R	6-2	166	11-24-89	0	0	2.42	14	0	0	1	22	19	13	6	1	12	17	.232	.263	.222	6.85	4.84
Lopez, Jean	R-R	6-2	175	3-31-88	5	3	6.82	12	5	0	0	32	34	26	24	2	11	19	.279	.182	.315	5.40	3.13
Monzon, Yosber	R-R	6-0	176	11-4-89	0	0	5.73	14	0	0	0	22	20	16	14	0	16	21	.253	.667	.200	8.59	6.55
Pirela, Jesus	R-R	6-0	152	3-13-89	1	4	3.88	12	11	0	1	51	45	25	22	3	22	35	.246	.459	.192	6.18	3.88
Rodriguez, Ricciard	L-L	6-0	170	1-21-88	2	1	2.96	15	7	0	1	49	47	21	16	2	14	28	.253	.000	.258	5.18	2.59
Suarez, Jesus	R-R	6-3	200	12-5-88	1	0	5.40	6	0	0	0	12	9	8	7	1	6	8	.209	.333	.189	6.17	4.63

Fielding

Catcher	PCT	G	PO	A	E	DP	PB
Alvarez	.950	16	74	21	5	2	4
Diaz	.986	37	230	45	4	2	2
Guerra	.985	22	111	18	2	2	5

First Base	PCT	G	PO	A	E	DP
Alvarez	.983	28	226	12	4	24
Diaz	1.000	11	72	9	0	8
Guerra	.991	35	310	9	3	19
Unda	.971	4	31	2	1	2

Second Base	PCT	G	PO	A	E	DP
Duran	1.000	1	2	0	0	0

	PCT	G	PO	A	E	DP
Hernandez	.971	51	122	115	7	23
Perdomo	.971	14	36	31	2	9
Sosa	.967	8	17	12	1	3
Tolo	1.000	7	6	6	0	0

Third Base	PCT	G	PO	A	E	DP
Perdomo	.885	38	29	87	15	8
Tolo	.930	36	38	95	10	16

Shortstop	PCT	G	PO	A	E	DP
Duran	.931	51	79	151	17	20
Hernandez	.800	2	2	2	1	0
Sosa	.902	25	30	71	11	11

Outfield	PCT	G	PO	A	E	DP
Bogle	.964	42	52	1	2	0
Granado	.944	17	16	1	1	0
Lezcano	1.000	17	11	2	0	0
Martinez	.979	51	86	7	2	1
Rossi	.975	58	109	7	3	2
Torres	.976	24	38	2	1	1
Unda	.968	29	29	1	1	0

Pittsburgh Pirates

BY JOHN PERROTTO

The culture may have changed but the record did not.

John Russell's primary objective in his first season as the Pirates manager was to change the culture of losing that has pervaded the franchise for nearly a generation.

Russell did make an impact. The Pirates played hard right through the end of the season after quitting on manager Jim Tracy in the previous two seasons.

However, effort did not pay off in more wins.

The Pirates finished the season 67-95 and in last place in the National League Central, one game worse than their 68-94 finish of the previous season.

The Pirates wound up with a 16th consecutive sub-.500 season, tying the 1933-48 Phillies for futility that is not only a major league record but a record for all major American professional sports. The Pirates also had their fourth straight season with at least 94 losses and their third last-place finish in four seasons.

The Pirates actually seemed on their way to at least breaking the string of 90-loss seasons, if not losing seasons, as they were 50-57 on July 31 and third in the NL in runs scored.

However, rookie general manager Neal Huntington traded left fielder Jason Bay to Boston that day in a three-team deal that also saw the Red Sox send Manny Ramirez to the Dodgers. That deal, coupled with the trade of right fielder Xavier Nady to the New York Yankees five days earlier, ripped the heart out of the Pirates' lineup, and they went just 17-38 the rest of the way, finishing ninth in the NL in runs.

The Pirates acquired eight young players of various experience levels in the two trades in an effort to build up the talent base that was left all but barren by former GM Dave Littlefield. The Pirates acquired five players who were given opportunities at the major league level in righthanded starters Jeff Karstens and Ross Ohlendorf from the Yankees, reliever Craig Hansen from Boston, third baseman Andy LaRoche from the Dodgers and outfielder Brandon Moss from the Red Sox.

The others who came in the trades—lefthander Bryan Morris from the Dodgers and righthander Daniel McCutchen and outfielder Jose Tabata from the Yankees—are already among the best prospects in the farm system.

ORGANIZATION STATISTICS

PLAYERS OF THE YEAR

MAJOR LEAGUE: NATE McCLOUTH, OF

McClouth, who kept the NL's hopes alive by throwing out Dioner Navarro in the 11th inning of the All-Star Game, hit .276/.356/.497 with 26 homers and 94 RBIs, both team highs. He also shared with Lance Berkman the NL lead in doubles (46).

MINOR LEAGUE: ANDREW McCUTCHEN, OF

Since being drafted in the first round in 2005, McCutchen has done nothing but hit and further bolstered his standing in 2008. He hit .283/.372/.398 at Triple-A Indianapolis. His line included nine home runs, 26 doubles, 50 RBIs and 34 steals.

ORGANIZATION LEADERS

BATTING		*Minimum 250 at-bats
*AVG	Negrych, Jim, Lynchburg/Altoona	.359
R	Negrych, Jim, Lynchburg/Altoona	87
H	Negrych, Jim, Lynchburg/Altoona	170
TB	Durham, Miles, Hickory/Lynchburg	243
2B	Negrych, Jim, Lynchburg/Altoona	41
3B	Ford, Shelby, Altoona	10
HR	Romak, Jamie, Lynchburg/Altoona	25
RBI	Keel, Jared, Lynchburg	81
RBI	Durham, Miles, Hickory/Lynchburg	81
BB	Delaney, Jason, Altoona/Indianapolis	85
SO	Romak, Jamie, Lynchburg/Altoona	127
SB	Morgan, Nyjer, Indianapolis	44
*OBP	Negrych, Jim, Lynchburg/Altoona	.438
*SLG	Romak, Jamie, Lynchburg/Altoona	.517

PITCHING		†Minimum 75 innings
W	Crotta, Michael, Lynchburg	9
	Hamman, Corey, Altoona/Indianapolis	9
L	Welker, Duke, Hickory	13
†ERA	Herrera, Yoslan, Indianapolis/Altoona	3.41
G	Chavez, Jesse, Indianapolis	51
GS	Watson, Anthony, Lynchburg	28
	Crotta, Michael, Lynchburg	28
SV	Chavez, Jesse, Indianapolis	14
IP	Watson, Anthony, Lynchburg	152
BB	Felix, Michael, Hickory	71
SO	Barthmaier, Jimmy, Altoona/Indianapolis	111
†AVG	Barthmaier, Jimmy, Altoona/Indianapolis	.237

However, the most important newcomer to come into the system was Vanderbilt third baseman Pedro Alvarez, the Pirates' first-round draft pick and the No. 2 overall selection. However, Alvarez did not join the Pirates until after protracted and contentious contract negotiations.

2008 PERFORMANCE

General Manager: Neal Huntington. **Farm Director:** Kyle Stark. **Scouting Director:** Greg Smith.

Class	Team	League	W	L	PCT	Finish*	Manager	Affiliate Since
Majors	Pittsburgh	National	67	95	.414	14th (16)	John Russell	—
Triple-A	Indianapolis Indians	International	68	76	.472	9th (14)	Trent Jewett	2005
Double-A	Altoona Curve	Eastern	65	77	.458	9th (12)	Tim Leiper	1999
High A	Lynchburg Hillcats	Carolina	58	80	.420	7th (8)	Jeff Branson	1995
Low A	Hickory Crawdads	South Atlantic	52	87	.374	15th (16)	Gary Green	1999
Short-season	State College Spikes	New York-Penn	18	56	.243	14th (14)	Brad Fischer	1999
Rookie	GCL Pirates	Gulf Coast	37	19	.661	1st (16)	Tom Prince	1967

Overall 2008 Minor League Record   298   395   .430   28th

*Finish in overall standings (No. of teams in league). ^League champion.

ORGANIZATION STATISTICS

PITTSBURGH PIRATES

NATIONAL LEAGUE

Batting	B-T	HT	WT	DOB	AVG	vLH	vRH	G	AB	R	H	2B	3B	HR	RBI	BB	HBP	SH	SF	SO	SB	CS	SLG	OBP
Bautista, Jose	R-R	6-0	195	10-19-80	.242	.253	.238	107	314	38	76	15	0	12	44	38	2	6	3	77	1	1	.404	.325
Bay, Jason	R-R	6-2	205	9-20-78	.282	.190	.307	106	393	72	111	23	2	22	64	59	2	0	5	86	7	0	.519	.375
Bixler, Brian	R-R	6-1	200	10-22-82	.157	.182	.151	50	108	16	17	2	1	0	2	6	4	2	0	36	1	0	.194	.229
Chavez, Raul	R-R	5-11	210	3-18-73	.259	.240	.264	42	116	12	30	4	0	1	10	4	1	0	1	14	0	0	.319	.287
Cruz, Luis	R-R	6-1	180	2-10-84	.224	.000	.259	22	67	6	15	3	0	0	3	3	2	2	0	2	1	1	.269	.278
Diaz, Robinzon	R-R	6-0	225	9-19-83	.500	1.000	.000	2	6	0	3	0	0	0	1	0	0	0	0	1	1	0	.500	.500
Doumit, Ryan	B-R	6-1	210	4-3-81	.318	.330	.314	116	431	71	137	34	0	15	69	23	6	0	5	55	2	2	.501	.357
Gomez, Chris	R-R	6-1	190	6-16-71	.273	.226	.298	90	183	26	50	8	0	1	20	13	1	1	2	30	0	0	.333	.322
LaRoche, Adam	L-L	6-3	200	11-6-79	.270	.241	.282	136	492	66	133	32	3	25	85	54	2	0	6	122	1	1	.500	.341
LaRoche, Andy	R-R	6-1	225	9-13-83	.152	.103	.163	49	164	11	25	4	0	3	12	14	2	2	1	30	2	0	.232	.227
2-team total (27 Los Angeles)					.166	—	—	76	223	17	37	5	0	5	18	24	2	2	1	37	2	0	.256	.252
McLouth, Nate	L-R	5-11	180	10-28-81	.276	.261	.282	152	597	113	165	46	4	26	94	65	12	5	6	93	23	3	.497	.356
Michaels, Jason	R-R	6-0	205	5-4-76	.228	.209	.236	102	228	25	52	9	1	8	44	23	1	1	1	52	1	0	.382	.300
Mientkiewicz, Doug	L-R	6-2	205	6-19-74	.277	.250	.283	125	285	37	79	19	2	2	30	44	2	0	3	28	0	0	.379	.374
Morgan, Nyjer	L-L	6-0	175	7-2-80	.294	.240	.304	58	160	26	47	13	0	0	7	10	3	1	1	32	9	5	.375	.345
Moss, Brandon	L-R	6-0	205	9-16-83	.222	.268	.205	45	158	12	35	10	2	6	23	15	1	0	3	45	0	1	.424	.288
Nady, Xavier	R-R	6-2	215	11-14-78	.330	.313	.335	89	327	50	108	26	1	13	57	25	5	0	3	55	1	0	.535	.383
Paulino, Ronny	R-R	6-2	240	4-21-81	.212	.235	.202	40	118	8	25	5	0	2	18	11	0	0	1	24	0	0	.305	.277
Pearce, Steve	R-R	5-11	205	4-13-83	.248	.321	.222	37	109	6	27	7	0	4	15	5	3	0	2	22	2	0	.422	.294
Rivas, Luis	R-R	5-11	190	8-30-79	.218	.288	.195	79	206	25	45	6	2	3	20	13	1	2	1	27	3	2	.311	.267
Sanchez, Freddy	R-R	5-10	190	12-21-77	.271	.289	.266	145	569	75	154	26	2	9	52	21	4	8	6	63	0	1	.371	.298
Wilson, Jack	R-R	6-0	195	12-29-77	.272	.228	.282	87	305	24	83	18	1	1	22	13	5	6	1	27	2	2	.348	.312

Pitching	B-T	HT	WT	DOB	W	L	ERA	G	GS	CG	SV	IP	H	R	ER	HR	BB	SO	AVG	vLH	vRH	K/9	BB/9
Barthmaier, Jimmy	R-R	6-5	240	1-6-84	0	2	10.45	3	3	0	0	10	16	12	12	3	8	6	.364	.357	.375	5.23	6.97
Bautista, Denny	R-R	6-5	190	8-23-80	4	3	6.10	35	0	0	0	41	46	28	28	5	28	34	.295	.340	.275	7.40	6.10
Beam, T.J.	R-R	6-7	210	8-28-80	2	2	4.14	32	0	0	1	46	43	21	21	6	20	24	.251	.310	.210	4.73	3.94
Burnett, Sean	L-L	6-1	190	9-17-82	1	1	4.76	58	0	0	0	57	57	31	30	7	34	42	.271	.171	.328	6.67	5.40
Capps, Matt	R-R	6-2	255	9-3-83	2	3	3.02	49	0	0	21	54	47	20	18	5	5	39	.234	.222	.245	6.54	0.84
Chavez, Jesse	R-R	6-2	175	8-21-83	0	1	6.60	15	0	0	0	15	20	11	11	2	9	16	.328	.217	.395	9.60	5.40
Davis, Jason	R-R	6-6	225	5-8-80	2	4	5.29	14	4	0	0	34	38	24	20	2	17	13	.299	.342	.241	3.44	4.50
Duke, Zach	L-L	6-2	220	4-19-83	5	14	4.82	31	31	1	0	185	230	111	99	19	47	87	.304	.279	.308	4.23	2.29
Dumatrait, Phil	R-L	6-2	195	7-12-81	3	4	5.26	21	11	0	0	79	82	48	46	7	42	52	.271	.206	.288	5.95	4.81
Gorzelanny, Tom	L-L	6-2	220	7-12-82	6	9	6.66	21	21	0	0	105	120	79	78	20	70	67	.293	.261	.299	5.72	5.98
Grabow, John	L-L	6-2	205	11-4-78	6	3	2.84	74	0	0	4	76	60	25	24	9	37	62	.215	.239	.207	7.34	4.38
Hansen, Craig	R-R	6-6	230	11-15-83	1	4	7.47	16	0	0	1	16	11	14	13	1	20	7	.200	.154	.241	4.02	11.49
Herrera, Yoslan	R-R	6-2	200	4-28-81	1	1	9.82	5	5	0	0	18	35	20	20	1	12	10	.427	.474	.386	4.91	5.89
Karstens, Jeff	R-R	6-3	185	9-24-82	2	6	4.03	9	9	1	0	51	56	32	23	7	13	23	.279	.265	.293	4.03	2.28
Maholm, Paul	L-L	6-2	220	6-25-82	9	9	3.71	31	31	1	0	206	201	89	85	21	63	139	.263	.183	.279	6.06	2.75
Marte, Damaso	L-L	6-2	215	2-14-75	4	0	3.47	47	0	0	5	47	38	18	18	4	16	47	.217	.255	.200	9.06	3.09
Meek, Evan	R-R	6-0	205	5-12-83	0	1	6.92	9	0	0	0	13	11	11	10	3	12	7	.239	.160	.333	4.85	8.31
Morris, Matt	R-R	6-5	215	8-9-74	0	4	9.67	5	5	0	0	22	41	31	24	6	7	9	.390	.422	.367	3.63	2.82
Ohlendorf, Ross	R-R	6-4	235	8-8-82	0	3	6.35	5	5	0	0	23	36	18	16	3	12	13	.364	.404	.319	5.16	4.76
Osoria, Franquelis	R-R	6-0	200	9-12-81	4	3	6.08	43	0	0	0	61	87	43	41	10	12	31	.336	.373	.312	4.60	1.78
Salas, Marino	R-R	6-0	195	10-2-81	1	0	8.47	13	0	0	0	17	25	16	16	4	14	9	.357	.519	.256	4.76	7.41
Sanchez, Romulo	R-R	6-5	260	4-28-84	0	0	4.05	10	0	0	1	13	14	6	6	0	5	3	.292	.294	.290	2.03	4.05
Snell, Ian	R-R	5-11	200	10-30-81	7	12	5.42	31	31	0	0	164	201	107	99	18	89	135	.304	.314	.295	7.39	4.87
Taubenheim, Ty	R-R	6-5	255	11-17-82	0	0	3.00	1	1	0	0	6	7	2	2	0	3	4	.304	.286	.333	6.00	4.50
Van Benschoten, John	R-R	6-4	230	4-14-80	1	3	10.48	9	5	0	0	22	37	28	26	7	20	21	.366	.418	.304	8.46	8.06
Yates, Tyler	R-R	6-4	240	8-7-77	6	3	4.66	72	0	0	1	73	72	39	38	6	41	63	.254	.303	.224	7.73	5.03

Fielding

Catcher	PCT	G	PO	A	E	DP	PB
Chavez	.995	35	188	23	1	2	3
Diaz	1.000	1	5	1	0	1	0
Doumit	.988	106	596	59	8	8	9
Paulino	.991	32	198	16	2	3	1

First Base	PCT	G	PO	A	E	DP
Doumit	1.000	1	0	0	0	0
Gomez	1.000	5	39	4	0	6
Adam LaRoche	.993	129	1130	81	8	121
Mientkiewicz	1.000	37	290	19	0	34

Second Base	PCT	G	PO	A	E	DP
Cruz	1.000	2	6	5	0	2

	PCT	G	PO	A	E	DP
Gomez	.964	18	33	20	2	4
Rivas	.992	29	51	68	1	22
Sanchez	.989	131	291	355	7	104

Third Base	PCT	G	PO	A	E	DP
Bautista	.956	91	45	196	11	16
Gomez	.957	20	5	17	1	1
Andy LaRoche	.935	45	19	110	9	19
Mientkiewicz	.918	33	24	54	7	5
Rivas	—	1	0	0	0	0

Shortstop	PCT	G	PO	A	E	DP
Bixler	.956	39	53	121	8	28
Cruz	.989	20	32	61	1	14

	PCT	G	PO	A	E	DP
Gomez	.943	13	16	34	3	7
Rivas	.947	31	37	70	6	24
Wilson	.987	80	115	278	5	52

Outfield	PCT	G	PO	A	E	DP
Bay	.984	105	178	3	3	0
McLouth	.997	151	384	5	1	1
Michaels	.977	61	124	1	3	0
Mientkiewicz	1.000	10	20	1	0	0
Morgan	.988	44	85	0	1	0
Moss	.989	42	82	6	1	2
Nady	.990	82	189	10	2	5
Pearce	.962	29	50	1	2	0

INDIANAPOLIS INDIANS

TRIPLE-A

INTERNATIONAL LEAGUE

Batting	B-T	HT	WT	DOB	AVG	vLH	vRH	G	AB	R	H	2B	3B	HR	RBI	BB	HBP	SH	SF	SO	SB	CS	SLG	OBP
Bautista, Jose	R-R	6-0	195	10-19-80	.300	.333	.294	5	20	6	6	2	0	2	8	3	0	0	0	6	1	0	.700	.391
Bixler, Brian	R-R	6-1	200	10-22-82	.280	.311	.266	86	321	44	90	8	5	7	36	27	7	6	3	107	23	7	.402	.346
Boeve, Adam	R-R	6-2	213	6-20-80	.251	.299	.235	84	263	37	66	16	3	12	46	24	2	3	2	89	13	4	.471	.316
Bowers, Jason	R-R	5-10	183	1-27-78	.322	.294	.333	23	59	7	19	4	0	1	3	7	0	0	1	3	2	0	.441	.388
Chavez, Raul	R-R	5-11	210	3-18-73	.306	.367	.273	26	85	9	26	5	1	3	13	4	2	0	0	11	0	0	.494	.352
Cortes, Jorge	L-L	6-0	180	10-17-80	.169	.167	.169	41	83	10	14	1	0	1	5	11	2	1	1	18	1	1	.217	.278
Cruz, Luis	R-R	6-1	180	2-10-84	.325	.424	.287	32	120	19	39	10	0	3	15	3	1	3	0	14	2	4	.483	.347
Delaney, Jason	R-R	6-3	215	11-9-82	.255	.280	.247	30	98	18	25	6	1	0	8	17	1	1	2	25	0	1	.337	.364
Diaz, Robinzon	R-R	6-0	225	9-19-83	.357	.429	.286	5	14	0	5	1	0	3	0	0	0	0	0	1	2	.500	.357
2-team total (36 Syracuse)					.255	—	—	41	145	7	37	7	2	1	16	5	0	2	3	10	1	3	.352	.275
Duffy, Chris	L-L	5-9	185	4-20-80	.275	.429	.167	12	51	4	14	3	0	1	6	4	1	0	0	12	5	2	.392	.339
Hernandez, Michel	R-R	6-0	215	8-12-78	.266	.243	.275	76	252	29	67	14	2	3	17	17	2	0	0	35	0	2	.373	.317
Kata, Matt	B-R	6-1	185	3-14-78	.245	.216	.256	118	396	50	97	18	6	8	45	22	5	4	6	65	18	6	.381	.289
Maldonado, Carlos	R-R	6-1	255	1-3-79	.248	.286	.233	46	125	9	31	9	0	3	16	12	0	4	1	23	0	1	.392	.312
McCutchen, Andrew	R-R	5-11	175	10-10-86	.283	.303	.275	135	512	75	145	26	3	9	50	68	6	1	3	87	34	19	.398	.372
Morgan, Nyjer	L-L	6-0	175	7-2-80	.298	.217	.326	82	322	54	96	13	4	1	33	18	7	5	0	47	44	8	.373	.349
Mulhern, Ryan	R-R	6-2	205	11-29-80	.207	.212	.205	35	116	15	24	4	0	6	16	10	4	0	0	33	0	1	.397	.292
2-team total (58 Buffalo)					.234	—	—	93	316	45	74	15	0	13	42	36	4	0	1	96	0	1	.405	.319
Ordaz, Luis	R-R	5-11	170	8-12-75	.311	.452	.267	41	132	10	41	10	0	3	17	6	3	2	3	18	1	0	.455	.345
Paulino, Ronny	R-R	6-2	240	4-21-81	.306	.296	.310	30	111	16	34	13	1	4	18	13	0	0	2	31	0	2	.550	.373
Pearce, Steve	R-R	5-11	205	4-13-83	.251	.239	.256	103	386	47	97	26	1	12	60	32	5	4	6	75	10	4	.417	.312
Thompson, Kevin	R-R	5-10	195	9-18-79	.282	.429	.212	63	195	35	55	11	1	4	18	20	3	4	0	36	19	3	.410	.358
Walker, Neil	B-R	6-3	217	9-10-85	.242	.255	.236	133	505	69	122	25	7	16	80	29	2	4	10	102	10	6	.414	.280
Wilson, Josh	R-R	6-1	170	3-26-81	.276	.309	.260	97	293	28	81	18	1	5	32	24	9	8	3	48	11	5	.396	.347
2-team total (27 Pawtucket)					.262	—	—	124	405	44	106	24	1	7	42	29	14	8	3	71	13	5	.378	.330
Wilson, Craig	R-R	6-2	225	11-30-76	.230	.194	.247	71	217	27	50	6	0	10	27	21	10	3	0	60	3	2	.396	.327
Wilson, Jack	R-R	6-0	195	12-29-77	.333	.200	.429	4	12	2	4	1	0	0	2	0	0	0	0	1	0	0	.417	.333

Pitching	B-T	HT	WT	DOB	W	L	ERA	G	GS	CG	SV	IP	H	R	ER	HR	BB	SO	AVG	vLH	vRH	K/9	BB/9
Barthmaier, Jimmy	R-R	6-5	240	1-6-84	3	1	3.53	16	16	0	0	79	69	34	31	5	27	71	.235	.250	.222	8.09	3.08
Bayliss, Jonah	R-R	6-2	205	8-13-80	0	3	6.00	28	0	0	3	33	45	24	22	3	13	25	.326	.347	.303	6.82	3.55
2-team total (26 Syracuse)					3	5	4.58	54	0	0	5	73	81	42	37	8	25	54	—	—	—	6.69	3.10
Beam, T.J.	R-R	6-7	210	8-28-80	2	1	3.09	30	0	0	5	44	36	15	15	2	14	41	.222	.153	.278	8.45	2.89
Bernero, Adam	R-R	6-4	220	11-28-76	0	0	3.24	4	4	0	0	17	18	7	6	0	4	6	.269	.259	.275	3.24	2.16
Bullington, Bryan	R-R	6-4	220	9-30-80	4	6	5.52	15	15	0	0	75	90	54	46	8	25	60	.298	.290	.308	7.20	3.00
2-team total (10 Buffalo)					5	9	5.20	25	23	0	1	128	155	88	74	15	38	107	—	—	—	7.52	2.67
Burnett, Sean	L-L	6-1	190	9-17-82	1	1	1.04	12	0	0	3	17	9	2	2	1	8	15	.153	.192	.121	7.79	4.15
Capps, Matt	R-R	6-2	255	9-3-83	0	0	0.00	1	0	0	0	2	0	0	0	0	3	1	.000	.000	.000	5.40	16.20
Chavez, Jesse	R-R	6-2	175	8-21-83	2	6	3.80	51	0	0	14	69	58	30	29	8	22	70	.225	.282	.177	9.17	2.88
Davis, Jason	R-R	6-6	225	5-8-80	6	9	4.41	21	20	0	0	116	113	62	57	4	47	68	.261	.263	.259	5.26	3.64
Drese, Ryan	R-R	6-3	220	4-5-76	0	1	15.75	1	1	0	0	4	9	7	7	0	2	3	.450	.400	.500	6.75	4.50
German, Franklyn	R-R	6-7	260	1-20-80	1	1	3.58	24	0	0	0	28	24	12	11	3	17	22	.231	.222	.237	7.16	5.53
2-team total (5 Charlotte)					2	2	3.71	29	0	0	0	34	30	19	14	4	23	31	—	—	—	8.21	6.09
Gorzelanny, Tom	L-L	6-2	220	7-12-82	3	1	2.06	7	7	0	0	35	28	11	8	1	4	33	.215	.220	.213	8.49	1.03
Hamman, Corey	L-L	6-2	198	4-12-80	4	3	5.03	12	12	0	0	63	75	37	35	4	24	34	.301	.354	.276	4.88	3.45
Hansen, Craig	R-R	6-6	230	11-15-83	0	0	9.00	2	0	0	0	2	4	2	2	0	1	2	.500	.250	.750	9.00	4.50
2-team total (11 Pawtucket)					1	0	2.41	13	0	0	0	19	10	6	5	0	5	19	—	—	—	9.16	2.89
Hernandez, Chris	R-R	6-0	189	8-3-80	1	1	6.75	13	0	0	0	19	33	18	14	2	3	17	.388	.325	.444	8.20	1.45
Herrera, Yoslan	R-R	6-2	200	4-28-81	1	0	2.57	1	1	0	0	7	7	2	2	1	1	6	.269	.364	.200	7.71	1.29
McCutchen, Dan	R-R	6-2	190	9-26-82	3	3	4.69	8	8	0	0	48	49	25	25	12	14	41	.261	.276	.244	7.69	1.31
2-team total (11 Scranton/W-B)					7	7	4.03	19	19	2	0	118	122	57	53	22	18	99	—	—	—	7.53	1.37
Meek, Evan	R-R	6-0	220	5-12-83	0	2	2.40	23	0	0	2	41	30	12	11	2	14	34	.196	.192	.200	7.40	3.05
Miller, Matt	R-R	6-3	215	11-23-71	4	7	5.82	33	0	0	8	43	44	31	28	3	23	47	.256	.313	.207	9.76	4.78

Munoz, Luis	R-R	6-2	195	1-10-82	3	3	5.45	13	12	0	0	69	78	43	42	13	26	42	.284	.333	.231	5.45	3.38
Ohlendorf, Ross	R-R	6-4	235	8-8-82	4	3	3.47	7	7	0	0	47	46	18	18	7	8	40	.261	.267	.253	7.71	1.54
2-team total (5 Scranton/W-B)					5	4	3.65	12	12	0	0	69	74	29	28	7	13	65	—	—	—	8.48	1.70
Osoria, Franquelis	R-R	6-0	200	9-12-81	2	1	3.55	10	0	0	1	13	13	5	5	1	3	14	.265	.316	.233	9.95	2.13
Perez, Juan	R-L	6-0	180	9-3-78	2	2	3.57	20	0	0	1	23	17	10	9	3	12	35	.207	.229	.176	13.90	4.76
Reichert, Dan	R-R	6-3	175	7-12-76	0	1	4.50	1	1	0	0	4	5	5	2	0	2	2	.278	.200	.375	4.50	4.50
2-team total (8 Buffalo)					1	4	4.40	9	9	0	0	47	57	30	23	3	17	31	—	—	—	5.94	3.26
Rogers, Brian	R-R	6-4	190	7-17-82	0	1	1.26	10	0	0	0	14	14	7	2	1	4	13	.241	.235	.250	8.16	2.51
2-team total (16 Toledo)					0	2	4.98	26	0	0	0	34	42	27	19	4	16	38	—	—	—	9.96	4.19
Salas, Marino	R-R	6-0	195	10-2-81	4	3	3.47	40	0	0	4	57	40	23	22	6	30	54	.195	.239	.146	8.53	4.74
Sanchez, Romulo	R-R	6-5	260	4-28-84	5	1	3.46	33	0	0	4	55	50	27	21	5	19	32	.248	.261	.236	5.27	3.13
Taubenheim, Ty	R-R	6-5	255	11-17-82	4	9	5.60	19	19	0	0	98	102	66	61	12	39	66	.276	.305	.247	6.06	3.58
Thompson, Mike	R-R	6-4	210	11-6-80	3	3	4.25	22	8	0	0	59	72	32	28	5	22	27	.305	.317	.296	4.10	3.34
Van Benschoten, John	R-R	6-4	230	4-14-80	7	4	3.92	22	13	0	0	80	70	36	35	3	32	62	.242	.275	.207	6.95	3.59

Fielding

Catcher	PCT	G	PO	A	E	DP	PB
Chavez	1.000	23	141	20	0	2	2
Diaz	1.000	3	35	6	0	2	1
Hernandez	.998	66	392	37	1	4	4
Maldonado	.993	37	258	19	2	1	3
Paulino	.995	23	184	16	1	3	5
C. Wilson	1.000	2	3	0	0	0	0

First Base	PCT	G	PO	A	E	DP
Boeve	.985	46	363	27	6	29
Chavez	1.000	2	18	0	0	2
Delaney	.992	28	222	20	2	12
Kata	1.000	6	28	4	0	1
Mulhern	.990	13	98	5	1	8
Pearce	.985	32	230	25	4	17
C. Wilson	.986	36	258	14	4	22

Second Base	PCT	G	PO	A	E	DP
Bautista	1.000	1	1	2	0	1
Bixler	1.000	10	14	20	0	6

	PCT	G	PO	A	E	DP
Bowers	.981	11	23	30	1	5
Cruz	.967	14	29	30	2	1
Kata	.983	52	97	138	4	29
Ordaz	1.000	31	36	73	0	12
Josh Wilson	.974	38	63	87	4	18
C. Wilson	1.000	1	1	0	0	0

Third Base	PCT	G	PO	A	E	DP
Bowers	.952	7	5	15	1	1
Chavez	1.000	2	2	3	0	0
Kata	1.000	11	7	27	0	2
Ordaz	1.000	1	2	2	0	0
Walker	.947	128	107	232	19	20
Josh Wilson	1.000	3	0	4	0	0

Shortstop	PCT	G	PO	A	E	DP
Bixler	.978	74	99	219	7	37
Bowers	.938	6	4	11	1	3
Cruz	.945	16	25	27	3	7
Kata	.500	1	0	1	1	0

	PCT	G	PO	A	E	DP
Jack Wilson	1.000	4	3	4	0	1
Josh Wilson	.965	51	76	117	7	21

Outfield	PCT	G	PO	A	E	DP
Bautista	1.000	3	5	1	0	0
Boeve	1.000	15	10	0	0	0
Cortes	1.000	34	51	2	0	1
Cruz	1.000	2	4	0	0	0
Duffy	1.000	12	19	0	0	0
Kata	.990	49	93	3	1	0
McCutchen	.990	129	288	4	3	1
Morgan	.994	79	172	2	1	0
Mulhern	1.000	10	17	0	0	0
Pearce	.963	69	100	4	4	0
Thompson	.979	53	88	6	2	1
C. Wilson	.944	16	16	1	1	0
Josh Wilson	1.000	1	1	0	0	0

ALTOONA CURVE DOUBLE-A

EASTERN LEAGUE

Batting	B-T	HT	WT	DOB	AVG	vLH	vRH	G	AB	R	H	2B	3B	HR	RBI	BB	HBP	SH	SF	SO	SB	CS	SLG	OBP
Alvarez, Victor	B-R	5-11	185	6-17-83	.100	.074	.121	23	60	7	6	2	0	0	0	10	0	1	0	11	1		.133	.229
Boone, James	B-R	6-2	195	3-16-83	.219	.176	.243	96	329	36	72	12	2	10	40	39	5	3	5	107	2	3	.359	.307
Bowers, Jason	R-R	5-10	183	1-27-78	.239	.215	.250	97	309	40	74	20	2	5	40	21	3	3	4	59	12	3	.366	.291
Chang, Ray	R-R	6-0	204	8-24-83	.333	1.000	.200	5	6	1	2	1	0	0	2	0	0	0	2	0	0		.500	.500
Corley, Brad	R-R	6-2	198	12-28-83	.262	.250	.270	134	500	59	131	25	3	11	49	25	10	1	3	106	5	9	.390	.309
Cruz, Luis	R-R	6-1	180	2-10-84	.264	.320	.245	105	375	41	99	24	1	6	46	19	4	4	4	34	3	3	.381	.303
Delaney, Jason	R-R	6-3	215	11-9-82	.292	.284	.298	109	367	42	107	21	3	7	43	68	4	0	5	77	7	2	.422	.403
Dorta, Melvin	R-R	5-11	160	1-15-82	.285	.185	.332	116	403	44	115	17	5	7	43	31	4	13	2	43	18	14	.404	.341
Doumit, Ryan	B-R	6-1	210	4-3-81	.429	.333	.500	3	7	0	3	0	0	0	0	0	0	0	0	2	0	0	.429	.429
Duffy, Chris	L-L	5-9	185	4-20-80	.259	.400	.250	18	58	7	15	5	1	1	4	7	0	0	1	10	1	1	.431	.333
Finegan, Brian	R-R	6-0	190	12-15-81	.207	.154	.232	31	82	8	17	3	0	2	3	3	0	1	1	16	3	1	.317	.233
Ford, Shelby	B-R	6-3	190	12-15-84	.285	.267	.288	81	319	43	91	23	10	4	32	20	6	3	1	49	19	5	.458	.338
Gonzalez, Angel	L-R	5-11	165	12-28-85	.278	.348	.257	29	97	10	27	5	1	1	8	1	1	3	0	23	2	2	.381	.293
Lerud, Steve	L-R	6-1	210	10-13-84	.233	.250	.224	47	146	17	34	7	0	4	18	14	1	1	1	42	1	0	.363	.302
Negrych, Jim	L-R	5-10	180	3-2-85	.310	.333	.302	25	87	10	27	5	0	0	10	11	1	3	0	14	5	1	.368	.394
Pacheco, Jonel	R-R	5-9	170	10-3-82	.288	.295	.285	116	416	64	120	17	0	12	52	42	4	1	2	82	11	4	.416	.358
Perez, Miguel	R-R	6-3	200	9-25-83	.281	.318	.268	57	171	14	48	4	0	2	22	9	4	2	1	32	1	1	.339	.330
Powell, Pedro	B-R	5-7	145	5-20-84	.148	.226	.100	45	61	6	12	0	0	0	4	7	1	2	2	15	6	1	.148	.220
Reyes, Milver	R-R	5-11	200	9-3-82	.187	.200	.168	53	150	10	28	4	0	1	7	7	0	4	0	31	0	0	.233	.223
Romak, Jamie	R-R	6-2	220	9-30-85	.208	.162	.229	33	120	15	25	6	0	7	23	17	1	0	0	32	0	0	.433	.312
Tabata, Jose	R-R	5-11	160	8-12-88	.348	.250	.404	22	89	16	31	6	2	3	13	8	0	0	0	18	8	0	.562	.402
2-team total (79 Trenton)					.272	—	—	101	383	56	104	15	2	6	49	34	7	1	4	67	18	2	.368	.339
Watts, Kris	L-R	6-1	209	7-15-84	.160	.188	.147	17	50	2	8	1	0	0	3	5	0	0	0	7	1	0	.180	.236
Webster, Anthony	L-R	6-0	197	4-10-83	.229	.190	.250	91	292	41	67	11	5	5	35	23	2	4	2	21	10	6	.353	.288
Wilson, Jack	R-R	6-0	195	12-29-77	.316	.375	.273	7	19	1	6	0	0	0	0	4	1	1	0	2	1	0	.316	.458

Pitching	B-T	HT	WT	DOB	W	L	ERA	G	GS	CG	SV	IP	H	R	ER	HR	BB	SO	AVG	vLH	vRH	K/9	BB/9
Antelo, Derek	R-R	6-1	205	11-30-82	0	0	10.80	9	1	0	0	10	15	15	12	2	12	5	.349	.263	.364	4.50	10.80
Barthmaier, Jimmy	R-R	6-5	240	1-6-84	2	4	4.86	10	10	0	0	46	42	27	25	3	21	40	.240	.338	.189	7.77	4.08
Belisario, Ronald	R-R	6-2	240	12-31-82	4	4	4.74	38	0	0	9	57	63	31	30	5	25	36	.286	.263	.300	5.68	3.95
Bloom, Kyle	R-L	6-3	185	2-21-83	5	8	4.19	28	22	1	0	110	103	57	51	9	55	93	.244	.219	.252	7.63	4.51
Bresnehan, Patrick	R-R	6-1	211	4-25-83	0	0	4.29	38	0	0	6	50	44	32	24	1	50	40	.234	.194	.256	7.15	8.94
Capps, Matt	R-R	6-2	255	9-3-83	0	0	0.00	3	0	0	3	3	0	0	0	0	1	5	.000	.000	.000	15.00	3.00
Castorri, Christian	R-R	6-3	215	12-17-83	1	3	6.66	23	5	0	2	51	70	39	38	7	22	23	.323	.330	.317	4.03	3.86
Davidson, Dave	L-L	6-1	195	4-23-84	4	2	3.34	35	0	0	0	65	58	27	24	3	36	51	.248	.242	.250	7.10	5.01
Guerrero, Emilis	R-R	6-2	162	12-26-85	0	0	6.75	1	0	0	0	1	2	1	1	0	1	1	.333	.500	.000	6.75	6.75

Name	B-T	HT	WT	DOB	W	L	ERA	G	GS	CG	SV	IP	H	R	ER	HR	BB	SO	AVG	vLH	vRH	K/9	BB/9
Hamman, Corey	L-L	6-2	198	4-12-80	5	6	3.18	16	13	0	0	71	69	30	25	7	19	44	.261	.161	.288	5.60	2.42
Hankins, Derek	R-R	6-4	192	7-1-83	2	11	4.54	24	23	0	0	119	135	68	60	14	26	89	.285	.250	.311	6.73	1.97
Hernandez, Chris	R-R	6-0	189	8-3-80	4	0	2.61	14	0	0	4	21	15	6	6	1	3	23	.195	.133	.234	10.02	1.31
Herrera, Yoslan	R-R	6-2	200	4-28-81	6	9	3.46	21	21	0	0	114	114	51	44	9	36	69	.264	.251	.272	5.43	2.83
Hill, Josh	R-R	6-3	225	3-27-83	4	11	4.53	22	21	0	0	111	119	68	56	12	48	65	.278	.299	.261	5.25	3.88
Holliday, Brian	L-L	6-2	202	6-1-84	1	1	6.91	3	3	1	0	14	24	13	11	2	4	8	.381	.615	.320	5.02	2.51
Hughes, Jared	R-R	6-7	220	7-4-85	2	2	4.94	6	6	0	0	31	35	19	17	4	16	18	.278	.381	.226	5.23	4.65
Johnson, Blair	R-R	6-4	218	3-25-84	1	0	10.00	7	0	0	0	9	16	10	10	3	4	3	.400	.357	.423	3.00	4.00
Mateo, Juan	R-R	6-2	220	12-17-82	7	1	2.12	32	0	0	5	68	50	22	16	5	17	58	.202	.245	.170	7.68	2.25
Meek, Evan	R-R	6-0	220	5-12-83	1	1	2.81	9	0	0	2	16	14	5	5	0	3	17	.237	.167	.286	9.56	1.69
Munoz, Luis	R-R	6-2	195	1-10-82	1	4	7.34	7	7	0	0	31	41	25	25	4	16	14	.339	.389	.299	4.11	4.70
Pearson, Kyle	R-R	6-1	200	10-8-84	0	0	7.00	5	0	0	0	9	14	7	7	2	4	4	.368	.500	.292	4.00	4.00
Reichert, Dan	R-R	6-3	175	7-12-76	3	4	4.65	9	9	0	0	50	48	28	26	5	25	31	.251	.333	.187	5.54	4.47
Roberts, Kevin	R-R	6-0	185	5-15-84	1	1	7.56	13	0	0	0	17	14	16	14	2	15	9	.222	.269	.189	4.86	8.10
Robles, Moises	R-R	6-2	170	4-17-84	1	1	6.27	13	0	0	0	19	28	16	13	2	5	10	.359	.414	.327	4.82	2.41
Rogers, Brian	R-R	6-4	190	7-17-82	2	0	0.60	7	0	0	0	15	9	1	1	0	3	13	.173	.125	.194	7.80	1.80
2-team total (4 Binghamton)					2	0	0.47	11	0	0	1	19	12	1	1	0	5	15	—	—	—	6.98	2.33
Shortslef, Josh	R-L	6-4	250	2-1-82	5	2	3.47	29	1	0	3	62	59	29	24	3	25	51	.249	.267	.241	7.36	3.61
Sues, Jeff	R-R	6-4	228	6-8-83	3	1	3.77	24	0	0	1	43	35	19	18	3	20	55	.219	.213	.224	11.51	4.19

Fielding

Catcher	PCT	G	PO	A	E	DP	PB
Doumit	1.000	2	5	0	0	0	1
Lerud	.974	45	232	31	7	0	2
Perez	.985	49	290	31	5	3	5
Reyes	.993	47	267	23	2	6	10
Watts	.990	16	90	11	1	1	2

First Base	PCT	G	PO	A	E	DP
Delaney	.992	109	980	65	8	92
Finegan	—	1	0	0	0	0
Romak	.989	33	259	19	3	29

Second Base	PCT	G	PO	A	E	DP
Alvarez	1.000	2	4	2	0	1
Bowers	1.000	1	2	3	0	0
Cruz	.947	4	6	12	1	1
Dorta	.983	57	137	148	5	38
Finegan	1.000	10	14	23	0	5

	PCT	G	PO	A	E	DP
Ford	.972	74	171	207	11	55
Gonzalez	.947	7	16	20	2	9
Webster	1.000	1	0	1	0	1

Third Base	PCT	G	PO	A	E	DP
Alvarez	.907	22	4	35	4	1
Bowers	.962	76	46	132	7	11
Cruz	1.000	2	0	3	0	0
Dorta	.943	22	10	40	3	1
Finegan	.781	18	9	16	7	3
Ford	—	1	0	0	0	0
Gonzalez	1.000	1	1	0	0	0
Negrych	.902	19	15	40	6	6
Perez	1.000	1	0	1	0	0
Reyes	1.000	2	1	3	0	0

Shortstop	PCT	G	PO	A	E	DP
Bowers	.951	9	12	27	2	7

	PCT	G	PO	A	E	DP
Chang	.857	2	2	4	1	2
Cruz	.959	102	144	326	20	71
Dorta	.960	8	10	14	1	2
Finegan	1.000	6	8	9	0	4
Gonzalez	.938	21	33	58	6	12
Wilson	.938	6	8	22	2	2

Outfield	PCT	G	PO	A	E	DP
Boone	.983	83	174	3	3	0
Corley	.965	112	186	5	7	0
Dorta	1.000	16	28	1	0	0
Duffy	1.000	16	29	0	0	0
Pacheco	.983	109	161	8	3	1
Powell	.892	30	33	0	4	0
Tabata	1.000	22	47	0	0	0
Webster	.979	70	139	2	3	0

LYNCHBURG HILLCATS

HIGH CLASS A

CAROLINA LEAGUE

Batting	B-T	HT	WT	DOB	AVG	vLH	vRH	G	AB	R	H	2B	3B	HR	RBI	BB	HBP	SH	SF	SO	SB	CS	SLG	OBP
Alvarez, Victor	B-R	5-11	185	6-17-83	.227	.250	.214	10	22	3	5	1	0	0	3	4	0	0	0	4	2	0	.273	.346
Barksdale, James	L-L	5-10	175	5-7-85	.236	.298	.212	52	165	22	39	5	4	0	15	9	1	3	3	46	12	11	.315	.275
Bombach, Daniel	B-R	5-11	185	9-5-84	.250	.200	.275	22	76	7	19	3	0	2	12	6	2	0	0	11	1	2	.368	.321
Canal, Yonelvy	R-R	6-2	175	12-9-84	.125	.333	.000	4	8	0	1	0	0	0	1	0	0	0	0	5	0	0	.125	.222
Cavagnaro, Matt	B-R	5-11	177	8-11-85	.353	.273	.391	10	34	3	12	4	1	0	6	2	0	1	0	4	0	0	.529	.389
De Los Santos, Jose	L-R	5-11	160	2-17-85	.233	.208	.241	56	210	27	49	5	3	0	13	17	1	10	1	39	14	10	.286	.293
Durham, Miles	R-R	6-4	205	3-21-83	.220	.184	.231	57	218	29	48	6	0	4	24	15	2	0	1	49	11	4	.344	.275
Friday, Brian	R-R	5-11	180	12-16-85	.287	.250	.299	85	341	59	98	20	4	2	29	34	8	7	1	56	16	11	.387	.365
Goetz, Mike	L-R	5-10	180	7-22-84	.206	.400	.125	12	34	2	7	0	0	0	2	2	1	1	0	5	1	2	.206	.270
Gonzalez, Angel	L-R	5-11	165	12-28-85	.251	.213	.262	91	371	50	93	19	2	3	34	15	1	14	1	73	19	13	.337	.281
Jones, Christopher	R-R	6-0	205	2-27-83	.253	.310	.227	34	95	9	24	8	0	2	12	7	0	1	1	22	0	0	.400	.301
Keel, Jared	R-R	6-1	190	8-3-84	.237	.248	.233	123	410	76	97	24	2	20	81	65	15	2	4	89	16	5	.451	.358
Laboy, Albert	R-R	6-0	175	12-1-86	.182	.269	.155	33	110	10	20	2	0	1	6	9	2	5	1	20	0	0	.227	.254
Lerud, Steve	L-R	6-1	210	10-13-84	.256	.214	.270	67	234	36	60	14	0	8	40	26	8	0	5	65	1	1	.419	.344
Mansolino, Tony	R-R	6-1	190	9-28-82	.164	.154	.167	43	159	12	26	6	0	1	15	6	0	1	1	33	2	0	.220	.193
Negrych, Jim	L-R	5-10	180	3-2-85	.370	.331	.389	104	386	77	143	36	1	5	62	55	4	0	6	55	7	6	.508	.448
Picart, Greg	B-R	5-11	175	9-25-85	.148	.179	.132	25	81	4	12	4	0	0	6	1	1	1	1	12	0	0	.198	.167
Prasch, Eddie	L-R	6-0	189	1-25-86	.271	.205	.291	112	365	42	99	22	1	3	48	50	5	1	6	72	8	2	.362	.362
Presley, Alex	L-L	5-9	180	7-25-85	.258	.222	.270	82	287	39	74	15	1	6	35	29	1	5	3	50	13	6	.380	.325
Romak, Jamie	R-R	6-2	220	9-30-85	.279	.295	.275	77	290	58	81	25	0	18	57	32	6	0	3	95	0	1	.552	.360
Sakamoto, Kent	R-R	6-0	215	11-3-83	.259	.298	.247	128	482	74	125	35	3	10	66	50	4	0	9	124	5	1	.407	.328
Watts, Kris	L-R	6-1	209	7-15-84	.285	.234	.300	63	207	29	59	16	0	4	34	30	2	4	2	25	0	4	.420	.378

Pitching	B-T	HT	WT	DOB	W	L	ERA	G	GS	CG	SV	IP	H	R	ER	HR	BB	SO	AVG	vLH	vRH	K/9	BB/9
Aguirre, Rodolfo	R-R	6-1	198	7-26-85	0	0	11.37	7	0	0	0	13	26	17	16	3	6	11	.413	.458	.385	7.82	4.26
Antelo, Derek	R-R	6-1	205	11-30-82	3	2	6.34	17	2	0	0	38	51	35	27	6	9	33	.319	.283	.336	7.75	2.11
Benoit, Charles	L-L	6-2	215	9-24-84	0	4	14.66	14	0	0	0	23	49	42	38	4	13	19	.422	.563	.400	7.33	5.01
Boleska, Tom	R-R	6-0	190	7-30-86	1	0	0.00	1	0	0	0	3	0	0	0	0	0	1	.000	—	.000	3.00	0.00
Castorri, Christian	R-R	6-3	215	12-17-83	1	2	2.28	10	0	0	0	24	22	11	6	0	10	16	.234	.069	.308	6.08	3.80
Crotta, Mike	R-R	6-6	210	9-24-84	9	10	4.67	28	28	0	0	146	171	94	76	8	25	97	.284	.310	.265	5.97	1.54
Cuffman, Jake	R-R	6-4	200	3-3-85	1	2	5.23	49	0	0	1	53	51	36	31	3	47	41	.246	.313	.214	6.92	7.93
Guerrero, Emilis	R-R	6-2	162	12-26-85	1	0	0.00	1	0	0	0	3	2	0	0	0	2	2	.200	.333	.143	5.40	5.40
Holliday, Brian	L-L	6-2	202	6-1-84	6	10	5.47	27	24	0	0	125	156	87	76	13	44	70	.305	.295	.307	5.04	3.17

	B-T	HT	WT	DOB	W	L	ERA	G	GS	CG	SV	IP	H	R	ER	HR	BB	SO	AVG	vLH	vRH	K/9	BB/9
Hughes, Jared	R-R	6-7	220	7-4-85	3	9	4.60	21	21	0	0	106	108	73	54	7	50	54	.269	.308	.239	4.60	4.26
Johnson, Blair	R-R	6-4	218	3-25-84	3	2	4.06	27	1	0	0	64	69	37	29	5	17	40	.274	.250	.287	5.60	2.38
Krebs, Eric	R-R	6-3	210	5-16-85	4	2	4.11	31	0	0	3	57	48	29	26	5	29	60	.232	.214	.241	9.47	4.58
Lincoln, Brad	L-R	6-0	215	5-25-85	1	5	4.75	8	8	1	0	42	42	24	22	5	11	29	.259	.313	.224	6.26	2.38
McSwain, Matt	R-R	6-2	185	8-15-85	2	2	5.02	11	5	0	1	38	45	22	21	4	9	23	.300	.290	.309	5.50	2.15
Molleken, Dustin	L-R	6-4	228	8-21-84	3	2	6.67	16	0	0	2	28	38	23	21	2	14	26	.328	.476	.243	8.26	4.45
Moskos, Daniel	R-L	6-1	210	4-28-86	7	7	5.95	29	20	0	0	110	124	83	73	8	43	78	.284	.224	.297	6.36	3.51
Pearson, Kyle	R-R	6-1	200	10-8-84	1	1	6.75	11	0	0	4	13	12	10	10	1	12	11	.235	.250	.229	7.43	8.10
Roberts, Kevin	R-R	6-0	185	5-15-84	0	5	3.95	34	0	0	9	57	59	30	25	6	23	45	.262	.224	.286	7.11	3.63
Robles, Moises	R-R	6-2	170	4-17-84	1	1	3.80	18	0	0	6	21	31	15	9	3	3	8	.333	.405	.286	3.38	1.27
Simon, Adam	R-R	5-10	193	1-26-84	1	1	6.69	17	1	0	3	35	37	27	26	3	15	25	.272	.182	.315	6.43	3.86
Sues, Jeff	R-R	6-4	228	6-8-83	1	1	2.11	13	0	0	2	21	11	6	5	3	6	17	.153	.148	.156	7.17	2.53
Uviedo, Ronald	R-R	6-2	150	10-7-86	0	0	2.25	7	0	0	0	16	5	4	4	1	5	12	.094	.115	.074	6.75	2.81
Watson, Tony	L-L	6-4	223	5-30-85	8	12	3.56	28	28	0	0	152	149	70	60	16	36	104	.259	.214	.268	6.17	2.14

Fielding

Catcher	PCT	G	PO	A	E	DP	PB
Jones	.983	28	165	5	3	1	6
Lerud	.992	57	324	42	3	3	16
Watts	.992	54	345	38	3	3	11

First Base	PCT	G	PO	A	E	DP
Durham	.981	10	95	6	2	13
Mansolino	.986	13	135	5	2	16
Romak	.987	7	73	2	1	3
Sakamoto	.988	109	1034	67	13	90

Second Base	PCT	G	PO	A	E	DP
Alvarez	1.000	4	5	13	0	1
Bomback	1.000	5	11	12	0	3
Cavagnaro	.938	6	7	23	2	7
De Los Santos	.958	19	42	49	4	11

	PCT	G	PO	A	E	DP
Gonzalez	.959	81	181	238	18	57
Mansolino	1.000	4	4	12	0	3
Negrych	.953	17	36	46	4	7
Picart	.966	7	15	13	1	5

Third Base	PCT	G	PO	A	E	DP
Alvarez	1.000	1	1	2	0	0
Bomback	.794	11	7	20	7	1
Mansolino	.914	10	7	25	3	1
Negrych	.912	76	40	178	21	16
Prasch	.944	42	31	104	8	7

Shortstop	PCT	G	PO	A	E	DP
Alvarez	1.000	3	4	7	0	1
De Los Santos	.970	33	48	116	5	22
Friday	.962	80	120	288	16	54

	PCT	G	PO	A	E	DP
Gonzalez	.922	10	14	33	4	3
Picart	.904	17	21	45	7	10

Outfield	PCT	G	PO	A	E	DP
Barksdale	.978	47	87	1	2	1
Canal	.750	3	5	1	2	0
Durham	.974	42	71	4	2	1
Goetz	1.000	8	14	0	0	0
Keel	.962	120	168	10	7	2
Laboy	.969	33	61	2	2	0
Mansolino	1.000	8	14	1	0	0
Prasch	.956	37	65	0	3	0
Presley	.985	81	194	8	3	3
Romak	1.000	45	69	1	0	0

HICKORY CRAWDADS — LOW CLASS A

SOUTH ATLANTIC LEAGUE

Batting	B-T	HT	WT	DOB	AVG	vLH	vRH	G	AB	R	H	2B	3B	HR	RBI	BB	HBP	SH	SF	SO	SB	CS	SLG	OBP
Alvarez, Victor	B-R	5-11	185	6-17-83	.152	.111	.162	15	46	5	7	0	0	0	5	6	0	1	0	12	0	0	.152	.250
Bomback, Daniel	B-R	5-11	185	9-5-84	.247	.222	.257	59	194	22	48	12	0	1	25	22	1	3	6	36	2	0	.325	.318
Cavagnaro, Matt	B-R	5-11	177	8-11-85	.244	.288	.232	81	266	29	65	11	3	2	25	21	1	11	2	42	2	0	.331	.300
Davis, Marcus	R-R	6-3	200	11-11-84	.229	.163	.250	49	175	28	40	10	1	8	26	12	5	0	2	58	5	1	.434	.294
De Los Santos, Jose L.	R-R	5-11	160	2-17-85	.270	.262	.273	58	244	38	66	5	1	0	20	26	0	1	0	50	14	10	.299	.341
Durham, Miles	R-R	6-4	205	3-21-83	.348	.299	.364	72	287	53	100	24	1	14	57	17	7	0	4	63	7	1	.585	.394
Fields, Caleb	R-R	6-3	185	7-15-85	.073	.000	.107	15	41	1	3	0	0	0	2	1	2	0	1	13	0	0	.073	.133
Hagan, Thomas	L-R	6-2	195	9-22-83	.269	.219	.285	87	312	49	84	16	2	7	45	28	5	1	1	71	2	0	.401	.338
Hague, Matt	R-R	6-3	225	8-20-85	.321	.263	.342	57	215	25	69	14	0	6	29	20	4	0	3	28	1	0	.470	.384
Huber, Erik	R-R	6-6	230	3-6-85	.259	.226	.270	127	483	78	125	29	5	12	60	36	9	2	4	73	2	2	.414	.320
Jones, Christopher	R-R	6-0	205	2-27-83	.267	1.000	.214	4	15	1	4	2	0	0	1	0	0	0	4	0	0	.400	.313	
Laboy, Albert	R-R	6-0	175	12-1-86	.243	.263	.234	64	251	29	61	13	1	6	23	29	3	2	4	62	6	5	.375	.324
LaRoche, Adam	L-L	6-3	200	11-6-79	.600	.000	.600	3	10	2	6	1	0	1	4	2	0	0	1	0	0	1.000	.667	
Macia, Wanell	L-L	5-11	202	7-20-82	.000	.000	—	1	1	0	0	0	0	0	0	0	0	0	0	0	0	0	.000	.000
McClune, Austin	R-R	6-2	175	11-15-87	.207	.229	.199	112	425	49	88	12	4	4	40	36	5	14	5	87	10	11	.282	.274
McQueary, Aeden	R-R	5-11	180	9-19-84	.194	.318	.133	21	67	7	13	2	0	0	3	9	0	0	0	22	0	1	.224	.289
Mercer, Jordy	R-R	6-3	192	8-27-86	.250	.149	.283	50	192	21	48	7	0	4	18	12	2	1	1	44	4	3	.349	.300
Munoz, Joe	R-R	6-1	155	12-26-85	.195	.107	.241	23	82	8	16	3	0	0	10	2	3	0	0	17	2	0	.232	.241
Pena, Ronald	R-R	5-9	175	2-28-87	.248	.226	.254	84	290	26	72	16	5	2	31	25	3	0	3	85	1	3	.359	.312
Pena, Silvio	R-R	6-0	175	8-9-87	.265	.241	.273	36	117	12	31	4	1	0	9	4	1	2	1	32	5	0	.316	.293
Picart, Greg	B-R	5-11	175	9-25-85	.253	.283	.240	52	178	21	45	10	0	2	14	12	4	6	1	31	4	4	.343	.313
Simon, Keanon	L-L	5-10	170	12-6-84	.242	.191	.255	97	343	47	83	16	2	3	36	30	4	3	1	72	14	5	.327	.310
Spain, Bobby	L-R	6-4	215	5-2-85	.312	.329	.306	67	250	32	78	22	0	5	43	15	0	2	4	40	0	1	.460	.346
Walker, Andrew	R-R	6-0	210	1-22-86	.256	.246	.259	56	219	31	56	7	0	7	29	9	1	0	3	50	0	0	.384	.284

Pitching	B-T	HT	WT	DOB	W	L	ERA	G	GS	CG	SV	IP	H	R	ER	HR	BB	SO	AVG	vLH	vRH	K/9	BB/9
Aguirre, Rodolfo	R-R	6-1	198	7-26-85	2	3	4.39	6	5	0	0	27	27	13	13	6	9	16	.265	.368	.203	5.40	3.04
Amaro, Carlos	R-R	6-0	170	11-6-84	3	2	5.75	12	0	0	0	20	35	16	13	2	6	15	.385	.485	.328	6.64	2.66
Amato, Gary	R-R	6-0	210	2-5-86	0	1	13.50	1	0	0	0	2	5	4	3	1	1	1	.455	1.000	.333	4.50	4.50
Benoit, Charles	L-L	6-2	215	9-24-84	0	3	7.88	22	2	0	1	40	57	37	35	11	17	22	.333	.302	.347	4.95	3.83
Bishop, Harrison	R-R	6-3	210	8-17-84	5	2	3.23	29	0	0	1	56	40	24	20	2	20	60	.203	.239	.183	9.70	3.23
Boleska, Tom	R-R	6-0	190	7-30-86	3	3	2.36	23	0	0	5	42	28	13	11	3	11	45	.188	.254	.128	9.64	2.36
Charry, Jorge	R-R	6-1	185	12-10-86	0	0	9.95	3	0	0	0	6	13	8	7	2	2	5	.394	.286	.474	7.11	2.84
Clapp, Brad	R-R	6-1	215	5-19-86	3	3	3.32	16	16	0	0	76	87	41	28	3	20	41	.288	.239	.327	4.86	2.37
De Los Santos, Rafael	R-R	6-3	210	12-10-86	3	10	5.77	26	26	0	0	117	121	87	75	20	70	88	.269	.211	.307	6.77	5.38
Diaz, Jose	R-R	6-1	164	3-20-87	1	0	0.00	2	2	0	0	11	7	1	0	0	0	8	.189	.214	.174	6.55	0.00
Felix, Mike	L-L	5-11	206	8-13-85	4	7	5.50	35	11	0	2	87	71	59	53	5	71	62	.231	.282	.214	6.44	7.37
Foust, Matt	R-R	6-2	225	10-8-84	0	2	15.43	2	1	0	0	5	6	8	8	0	8	2	.333	.400	.308	3.86	15.43
Guerrero, Emilis	R-R	6-2	162	12-26-85	2	3	5.85	8	7	0	0	40	57	31	26	7	7	23	.337	.369	.317	5.18	1.58
Linares, Serguey	R-R	6-4	225	2-1-83	0	2	9.00	15	0	0	1	26	34	30	26	2	23	13	.324	.372	.290	4.50	7.96

Lincoln, Brad	L-R	6-0	215	5-25-85	5	5	4.65	11	11	0	0	62	72	34	32	8	6	46	.288	.266	.311	6.68	0.87
McSwain, Matt	R-R	6-2	185	8-15-85	4	5	2.17	32	7	0	4	71	62	22	17	5	13	50	.237	.283	.197	6.37	1.66
Molleken, Dustin	L-R	6-4	228	8-21-84	5	4	6.30	16	16	0	0	80	98	61	56	21	20	55	.297	.345	.259	6.19	2.25
Morris, Bryan	L-R	6-3	200	3-28-87	0	2	5.02	3	3	0	0	14	17	9	8	2	12	11	.288	.235	.360	6.91	7.53
Oliver, Zac	L-L	6-2	205	1-29-87	1	1	5.21	4	4	0	0	19	15	11	11	1	7	12	.214	.294	.189	5.68	3.32
Ortiz, Francisco	R-R	6-3	213	3-7-87	0	0	12.91	10	0	0	0	15	26	22	22	6	9	11	.371	.333	.385	6.46	5.28
Ortiz, Wilson	R-R	5-11	181	11-6-85	0	1	13.50	5	0	0	0	5	8	10	8	0	7	8	.348	.333	.357	13.50	11.81
Robles, Moises	R-R	6-2	170	4-17-84	1	1	2.00	19	0	0	6	27	23	7	6	2	1	19	.228	.273	.193	6.33	0.33
Rodriguez, Dionis	R-R	6-2	181	2-8-86	1	0	2.25	5	4	0	0	20	17	5	5	3	5	15	.230	.208	.240	6.75	2.25
Simon, Adam	R-R	5-10	193	1-26-84	1	4	6.00	26	0	0	2	42	54	31	28	6	12	35	.309	.311	.307	7.50	2.57
Uviedo, Ronald	R-R	6-2	150	10-7-86	3	1	3.01	33	0	0	5	72	70	31	24	8	15	76	.248	.273	.230	9.54	1.88
Welker, Duke	L-R	6-7	220	2-10-86	4	13	5.51	24	24	0	0	116	142	81	71	7	48	72	.307	.310	.304	5.59	3.72

Fielding

Catcher	PCT	G	PO	A	E	DP	PB
Jones	1.000	4	31	0	0	0	0
McQueary	.991	21	111	3	1	0	0
R. Pena	.986	66	394	28	6	1	12
Walker	.994	50	320	34	2	2	7

First Base	PCT	G	PO	A	E	DP
Durham	.991	64	600	35	6	59
Hagan	.986	55	466	32	7	56
Hague	.986	8	58	11	1	6
Huber	.993	14	121	12	1	10
LaRoche	1.000	2	17	1	0	1

Second Base	PCT	G	PO	A	E	DP
Alvarez	1.000	1	0	5	0	1
Bomback	.922	12	23	48	6	11
Cavagnaro	.968	78	138	227	12	53

Fields	1.000	1	2	4	0	1
S. Pena	.930	8	19	21	3	7
Picart	.981	44	84	126	4	38

Third Base	PCT	G	PO	A	E	DP
Bomback	.873	26	8	40	7	2
Hague	.891	43	33	81	14	4
S. Pena	.897	10	8	18	3	3
Picart	1.000	4	3	4	0	0
Spain	.901	62	38	107	16	9

Shortstop	PCT	G	PO	A	E	DP
Alvarez	.983	12	27	30	1	7
Bomback	—	1	0	0	0	0
De Los Santos	.940	58	93	207	19	43
Mercer	.959	48	83	149	10	40
S. Pena	.939	21	32	60	6	12

Picart	.968	5	9	21	1	4

Outfield	PCT	G	PO	A	E	DP
Bomback	—	1	0	0	0	0
Davis	.978	47	86	2	2	0
Durham	1.000	4	6	0	0	0
Fields	1.000	8	15	0	0	0
Hagan	—	2	0	0	0	0
Huber	.971	99	159	9	5	1
Laboy	.972	59	99	4	3	1
Macia	1.000	1	1	0	0	0
McClune	.983	112	270	18	5	5
Munoz	.889	14	22	2	3	0
Simon	.968	81	141	9	5	1

STATE COLLEGE SPIKES   SHORT-SEASON

NEW YORK-PENN LEAGUE

Batting	B-T	HT	WT	DOB	AVG	vLH	vRH	G	AB	R	H	2B	3B	HR	RBI	BB	HBP	SH	SF	SO	SB	CS	SLG	OBP
Anderson, Calvin	R-R	6-7	240	5-8-87	.265	.167	.303	45	170	23	45	10	2	6	28	17	2	0	1	57	1	0	.453	.337
Biela, Butch	R-R	5-11	195	12-26-88	.249	.340	.217	57	205	19	51	4	0	1	28	26	4	5	2	42	6	4	.283	.342
Carver, Mark	R-R	6-2	195	4-1-85	.217	.115	.247	34	115	10	25	4	0	1	8	10	2	1	1	37	1	1	.278	.289
Chourio, Adenson	B-R	5-9	160	7-22-86	.188	.000	.214	5	16	3	3	0	0	0	1	1	0	0	0	5	3	1	.188	.235
D'Arnaud, Chase	R-R	6-1	175	1-21-87	.286	.324	.276	43	168	26	48	10	5	1	21	11	2	0	2	30	14	2	.423	.333
Farrell, Jeremy	R-R	6-3	200	11-11-86	.287	.362	.265	52	202	23	58	12	2	1	23	20	2	1	4	56	2	2	.381	.351
Garcia, Edward	B-R	6-1	152	8-21-87	.300	.000	.333	3	10	0	3	0	0	0	1	0	0	0	1	1	0	1	.300	.273
Hague, Matt	R-R	6-3	225	8-20-85	.333	.600	.273	7	27	6	9	3	0	0	3	3	0	0	0	5	0	0	.444	.400
Latimore, Quincy	R-R	5-10	175	2-3-89	.244	.321	.218	59	221	25	54	14	5	3	20	13	0	1	1	53	6	4	.394	.285
Mendez, Miguel	R-L	6-1	170	1-8-88	.205	.182	.209	22	78	6	16	4	0	0	6	4	1	1	0	26	0	0	.256	.253
Mercer, Jordy	R-R	6-3	192	8-27-86	.250	.333	.222	6	24	5	6	1	1	1	2	1	0	0	0	3	1	0	.500	.280
Morgan, Kyle	L-L	6-1	215	8-8-86	.235	.316	.220	33	119	16	28	9	1	3	15	12	3	0	1	37	0	0	.403	.319
Payne, Matt	R-R	6-1	200	3-18-86	.278	.302	.268	50	176	20	49	7	1	0	12	29	4	2	3	49	3	4	.330	.387
Peley, Josue	R-R	6-0	177	12-24-87	.191	.206	.185	33	115	7	22	4	0	0	7	11	0	1	0	19	1	0	.226	.244
Pena, Silvio	R-R	6-0	175	8-9-87	.281	.235	.300	19	57	8	16	3	1	0	4	5	1	3	0	10	6	2	.368	.349
Rice, Chad	R-R	5-11	180	1-17-85	.212	.205	.215	48	151	19	32	5	1	1	14	18	0	5	1	37	3	2	.278	.294
Rosero, Ciro	R-R	6-1	160	7-25-86	.266	.122	.301	55	214	22	57	11	0	2	23	8	4	4	3	40	8	3	.346	.301
Rubinstein, David	R-R	6-2	190	5-18-87	.249	.205	.262	47	169	24	42	7	3	1	14	21	3	0	0	41	5	5	.343	.342
Simmons, Chris	R-R	6-1	210	4-6-86	.257	.214	.286	9	35	3	9	1	0	0	4	0	0	0	1	12	0	0	.286	.250
Vasquez, Andy	R-R	6-1	168	10-8-87	.235	.171	.256	46	166	26	39	6	2	5	23	11	4	3	0	51	6	2	.386	.298
White, Cole	R-R	6-4	205	4-3-85	.338	.296	.360	21	77	12	26	6	0	1	9	9	1	1	2	13	2	0	.455	.404

Pitching	B-T	HT	WT	DOB	W	L	ERA	G	GS	CG	SV	IP	H	R	ER	HR	BB	SO	AVG	vLH	vRH	K/9	BB/9
Alvarado, Gabriel	R-R	6-2	175	5-19-87	0	1	11.57	2	1	0	0	2	4	5	3	1	3	1	.364	.333	.375	3.86	11.57
Amaro, Carlos	R-R	6-0	170	11-6-84	1	1	1.99	9	6	0	0	32	30	12	7	1	5	12	.246	.226	.263	3.41	1.42
Amato, Gary	R-R	6-0	210	2-5-86	1	2	8.22	12	0	0	1	23	31	21	21	2	10	18	.326	.382	.295	7.04	3.91
Bankston, Maurice	R-R	6-4	205	6-17-87	0	5	6.69	9	7	0	0	35	41	29	26	2	12	19	.287	.246	.314	4.89	3.09
Brolsma, Owen	R-R	6-2	210	10-6-84	0	3	10.01	21	0	0	2	30	52	36	33	5	17	21	.382	.386	.380	6.37	5.16
Charry, Jorge	R-R	6-1	185	12-10-86	1	0	4.32	9	0	0	0	17	20	10	8	2	7	15	.299	.227	.333	8.10	3.78
Colla, Mike	R-R	6-2	220	12-23-86	0	1	24.30	4	0	0	0	3	7	11	9	0	10	5	.438	.429	.444	13.50	27.00
Cox, Tyler	R-L	6-3	200	4-9-87	0	1	13.50	1	0	0	0	2	5	3	3	0	1	3	.500	.667	.429	13.50	4.50
Foust, Matt	R-R	6-2	225	10-8-84	0	1	3.38	3	0	0	0	5	4	2	2	0	5	4	.273	.375	.214	6.75	8.44
Guerrero, Emilis	R-R	6-2	162	12-26-85	1	5	7.40	9	9	0	0	41	61	42	34	7	7	28	.330	.368	.296	6.10	1.52
Kelly, William	R-R	6-2	170	10-30-87	0	2	6.75	8	6	0	1	24	26	19	18	2	16	18	.277	.243	.298	6.75	6.00
Klinger, Brent	R-R	6-4	185	7-21-88	0	0	0.00	2	0	0	0	2	1	4	0	0	1	3	.143	.000	.200	5.40	5.40
Knotts, Alan	R-R	6-4	210	2-28-85	3	2	4.09	21	0	0	1	44	51	25	20	0	9	51	.282	.305	.270	10.43	1.84
Leach, Brian	R-R	6-3	195	4-14-86	1	3	3.98	16	8	0	0	54	54	30	24	4	20	36	.266	.269	.264	5.96	3.31
Martinez, Yoffri	R-R	6-4	210	12-17-85	2	5	3.67	25	0	0	0	49	43	24	20	1	31	44	.239	.242	.238	8.08	5.69
McPherson, Kyle	B-R	6-3	205	11-11-87	1	3	4.37	15	7	0	1	56	52	29	27	10	5	41	.240	.182	.271	6.63	0.81
Ortiz, Wilson	R-R	5-11	181	11-6-85	0	2	4.70	15	7	0	0	44	58	27	23	2	24	39	.326	.288	.352	7.98	4.91
Owens, Rudy	L-L	6-3	215	12-18-87	3	6	4.97	15	13	0	0	58	63	37	32	2	13	45	.269	.196	.290	6.98	2.02

Ponder, Allen	R-R	6-6	230	9-27-83	1	2	4.22	23	0	0	2	43	53	23	20	3	9	40	.305	.339	.286	8.44	1.90
Vasquez, Samuel	R-R	6-4	175	12-21-84	1	10	6.75	15	10	0	0	49	64	47	37	3	22	35	.308	.295	.317	6.39	4.01
Vasquez, Malvin	R-R	6-3	165	5-10-86	0	0	12.27	4	0	0	0	4	7	5	5	0	3	3	.412	.167	.545	7.36	7.36
Williams, Mike	L-L	6-5	235	8-11-86	2	2	4.67	17	0	0	0	27	29	18	14	2	11	30	.266	.273	.263	10.00	3.67

Fielding

Catcher	PCT	G	PO	A	E	DP	PB
Carver	.983	17	104	9	2	1	7
Mendez	.980	22	138	6	3	1	6
Peley	.989	33	231	27	3	1	14
Simmons	.957	7	39	5	2	1	1

First Base	PCT	G	PO	A	E	DP
Anderson	.990	36	288	18	3	26
Carver	.984	16	122	5	2	9
Farrell	.977	23	153	19	4	15
Hague	.941	2	15	1	1	0

Second Base	PCT	G	PO	A	E	DP
Chourio	1.000	4	7	17	0	0

	PCT	G	PO	A	E	DP
Pena	.889	9	19	29	6	7
Rice	.970	45	95	129	7	29
Vasquez	.987	18	30	48	1	7
Third Base	**PCT**	**G**	**PO**	**A**	**E**	**DP**
D'Arnaud	.952	5	6	14	1	2
Farrell	.878	29	21	44	9	3
Hague	.667	4	1	3	2	1
Payne	.847	38	26	57	15	5
Vasquez	.800	2	2	2	1	0
Shortstop	**PCT**	**G**	**PO**	**A**	**E**	**DP**
D'Arnaud	.921	38	51	88	12	17
Mercer	1.000	5	10	16	0	6

	PCT	G	PO	A	E	DP
Pena	1.000	9	8	16	0	1
Rice	.800	1	2	2	1	1
Vasquez	.953	28	41	60	5	12
Outfield	**PCT**	**G**	**PO**	**A**	**E**	**DP**
Biela	.991	50	103	5	1	1
Garcia	.800	3	4	0	1	0
Latimore	.949	51	106	5	6	1
Morgan	.963	15	26	0	1	0
Payne	.929	6	13	0	1	0
Rosero	.962	53	120	8	5	2
Rubinstein	.959	45	90	3	4	1
White	1.000	4	10	0	0	0

GCL PIRATES   ROOKIE

GULF COAST LEAGUE

Batting	B-T	HT	WT	DOB	AVG	vLH	vRH	G	AB	R	H	2B	3B	HR	RBI	BB	HBP	SH	SF	SO	SB	CS	SLG	OBP
Acevedo, Andury	R-R	6-4	200	8-23-90	.216	.255	.198	45	153	18	33	3	2	0	11	10	6	2	2	42	9	2	.261	.287
Aguilera, Jesus	R-R	6-1	190	8-9-87	.292	.238	.314	25	72	8	21	2	1	0	8	5	0	0	0	21	0	0	.347	.338
Chourio, Adenson	B-R	5-9	160	7-22-86	.335	.328	.339	49	185	35	62	3	0	0	13	22	3	8	2	30	30	8	.351	.410
Cunningham, Jarek	R-R	6-1	185	12-25-89	.318	.385	.294	43	148	20	47	11	1	5	22	14	6	0	6	26	2	1	.507	.385
Freeman, Wes	R-R	6-4	215	1-29-90	.182	.200	.176	6	22	1	4	1	0	0	2	1	1	0	0	4	0	1	.227	.250
Friday, Brian	R-R	5-11	180	12-16-85	.182	.000	.250	7	22	2	4	0	1	0	3	2	0	0	0	3	0	0	.273	.280
Garcia, Edward	B-R	6-1	152	8-21-87	.209	.244	.195	45	163	18	34	5	3	2	18	15	1	0	1	47	15	0	.313	.278
Garcia, Juan	R-R	5-11	185	9-6-88	.189	.143	.205	17	53	6	10	3	1	1	5	0	0	2	1	11	3	1	.340	.185
Gonzalez, Benji	R-R	5-11	160	1-16-90	.207	.231	.195	37	121	17	25	2	0	0	14	22	1	5	1	28	8	1	.223	.331
Grossman, Robbie	B-L	6-1	190	9-16-89	.188	.000	.231	5	16	3	3	1	0	0	1	4	1	0	0	7	1	0	.250	.381
Mendez, Miguel	R-L	6-1	170	1-8-88	.407	.381	.424	15	54	13	22	3	0	5	14	6	3	1	1	12	1	0	.741	.484
Morgan, Kyle	L-L	6-1	215	8-8-86	.148	.250	.105	6	27	0	4	0	1	0	2	0	0	0	1	5	0	0	.222	.143
Munoz, Joe	R-R	6-1	155	12-26-85	.300	.250	.320	20	70	10	21	3	0	0	9	3	2	0	1	12	3	1	.343	.342
Parry, Craig	R-L	6-2	195	5-21-86	.274	.208	.316	19	62	4	17	6	1	0	14	8	2	0	0	8	1	1	.403	.375
Paulino, Ronny	R-R	6-2	240	4-21-81	.286	.214	.357	8	28	3	8	1	0	1	6	2	0	0	0	3	0	0	.429	.333
Pedron, Freizer	L-R	5-11	160	9-9-86	.254	.067	.318	17	59	13	15	3	0	0	6	12	2	4	0	15	2	4	.305	.397
Roman, Edwin	R-R	5-10	160	4-8-90	.221	.244	.211	42	131	22	29	5	1	2	13	15	3	3	0	36	12	7	.321	.315
Sanchez, Victor	L-L	5-10	160	10-25-86	.284	.214	.311	34	102	14	29	2	2	0	10	13	2	5	0	14	7	7	.343	.376
Saukko, Kyle	L-R	5-11	175	12-21-88	.212	.182	.227	23	66	10	14	0	0	0	5	13	2	2	0	25	2	1	.212	.358
Silva, Carlos	R-R	6-2	165	5-31-87	.329	.235	.357	22	73	12	24	8	0	1	12	7	3	1	0	10	4	0	.479	.410
Tabata, Jose	R-R	5-11	160	8-12-88	.455	.400	.500	4	11	5	5	1	0	0	2	2	0	0	0	0	0	0	.1.091	.538
Vargas, Alex	L-L	6-2	202	6-5-86	.285	.250	.300	39	144	15	41	8	1	1	15	12	0	1	2	13	4	1	.375	.335

Pitching	B-T	HT	WT	DOB	W	L	ERA	G	GS	CG	SV	IP	H	R	ER	HR	BB	SO	AVG	vLH	vRH	K/9	BB/9
Alvarado, Gabriel	R-R	6-2	175	5-19-87	4	2	3.04	13	11	0	0	50	47	21	17	6	12	23	.249	.276	.225	4.11	2.15
Amato, Gary	R-R	6-0	210	2-5-86	2	0	0.00	8	0	0	3	13	9	0	0	0	2	19	.191	.200	.182	13.15	1.38
Aure, Chris	L-L	6-0	180	10-13-89	3	2	3.90	11	3	0	2	28	27	14	12	0	12	16	.257	.280	.250	5.20	3.90
Capps, Matt	R-R	6-2	255	9-3-83	0	0	0.00	2	2	0	0	2	2	1	0	0	0	2	.222	.200	.250	9.00	0.00
Charry, Jorge	R-R	6-1	185	12-10-86	2	1	1.17	9	0	0	3	15	11	2	2	0	3	21	.193	.227	.171	12.33	1.76
Cox, Tyler	R-L	6-3	200	4-19-86	2	3	1.79	13	7	0	0	45	35	14	9	0	11	42	.217	.212	.219	8.34	2.18
Devora, Meoli	R-R	6-2	157	11-27-87	0	0	18.00	2	0	0	0	3	7	6	6	2	0	1	.412	.286	.500	3.00	0.00
Drese, Ryan	R-R	6-3	220	4-5-76	0	0	6.00	2	2	0	0	3	2	2	2	0	2	4	.167	.000	.286	12.00	6.00
Fagan, Albert	R-R	6-7	205	11-14-86	3	4	2.88	10	4	0	1	25	17	13	8	1	6	17	.189	.086	.255	6.12	2.16
Foster, Zach	R-R	6-6	220	5-24-87	2	1	3.99	14	8	0	0	38	44	22	17	2	18	32	.291	.333	.251	7.51	4.23
Foust, Matt	R-R	6-2	225	10-8-84	2	0	3.68	17	0	0	4	29	31	17	12	0	16	16	.267	.176	.338	4.91	4.91
Garcia, Diomedes	R-R			8-13-85	1	0	1.80	4	0	0	0	5	4	1	1	0	3	4	.250	.375	.125	7.20	5.40
Guerrero, Emilis	R-R	6-2	162	12-26-85	1	0	1.13	2	1	0	0	8	8	1	1	0	1	8	.276	.294	.250	9.00	1.13
Holden, Brandon	R-R	6-4	185	1-1-88	1	3	3.90	10	3	0	0	30	28	14	13	1	5	15	.248	.212	.279	4.50	1.50
Klinger, Brent	R-R	6-4	185	7-21-88	0	0	0.66	7	0	0	0	14	7	2	1	0	3	12	.140	.200	.080	7.90	1.98
Krebs, Eric	R-R	6-3	210	5-16-85	0	0	0.00	1	0	0	0	1	1	0	0	0	0	3	.250	.000	.500	27.00	0.00
Linares, Serguey	R-R	6-4	225	2-1-83	0	0	2.57	4	2	0	0	7	5	2	2	1	3	4	.200	.300	.133	5.14	3.86
Ortiz, Francisco	R-R	6-3	213	3-7-87	1	1	2.33	11	0	0	1	19	12	5	5	0	6	15	.179	.172	.184	6.98	2.79
Paulino, Ricardo	R-R	6-1	182	8-8-86	0	2	3.34	7	6	0	0	30	32	15	11	2	3	32	.269	.235	.294	9.71	0.91
Pereira, Nelson	L-L	5-11	180	2-12-89	6	2	1.62	13	6	0	0	50	41	20	9	3	10	46	.219	.205	.223	8.28	1.80
Perez, Juan	R-L	6-0	180	9-3-78	1	0	0.00	4	0	0	0	6	2	1	0	0	2	8	.091	.000	.100	12.00	3.00
Rusova, Ivan	R-R	6-1	180	11-5-86	1	0	3.00	7	0	0	0	9	7	3	3	1	7	5	.226	.333	.125	5.00	7.00
Teller, Carlos	L-L	5-11	180	10-3-86	4	0	4.37	13	0	0	2	23	23	13	11	0	11	20	.261	.333	.239	7.94	4.37
Thompson, Mike	R-R	6-4	210	11-6-80	0	0	0.00	1	1	0	0	2	0	0	0	0	1	1	.000	.000	.000	4.50	4.50
Vasquez, Malvin	R-R	6-3	165	5-10-86	1	0	1.50	8	0	0	3	12	6	2	2	1	6	8	.150	.222	.091	6.00	4.50

Fielding

Catcher	PCT	G	PO	A	E	DP	PB
Aguilera	1.000	25	140	14	0	2	9
J. Garcia	.966	17	99	14	4	1	3
Mendez	.982	14	99	8	2	0	4
Parry	1.000	1	5	1	0	0	0
Paulino	1.000	6	37	3	0	0	1

First Base	PCT	G	PO	A	E	DP
Silva	.981	18	148	10	3	17
Vargas	.983	38	323	14	6	34

Second Base	PCT	G	PO	A	E	DP
Chourio	.956	46	109	131	11	27

	PCT	G	PO	A	E	DP
Gonzalez	1.000	3	6	6	0	1
Pedron	1.000	7	14	33	0	9
Third Base	**PCT**	**G**	**PO**	**A**	**E**	**DP**
Acevedo	.786	22	15	29	12	3
Cunningham	.893	26	19	48	8	5
Pedron	1.000	6	11	13	0	2
Silva	.833	3	2	8	2	0
Shortstop	**PCT**	**G**	**PO**	**A**	**E**	**DP**
Acevedo	.872	15	34	34	10	13
Cunningham	.947	11	21	33	3	9
Friday	.765	5	4	9	4	2

	PCT	G	PO	A	E	DP
Gonzalez	.939	29	33	90	8	18
Outfield	**PCT**	**G**	**PO**	**A**	**E**	**DP**
Freeman	.900	5	9	0	1	0
E. Garcia	1.000	43	72	4	0	3
Grossman	1.000	4	5	0	0	0
Morgan	1.000	4	5	0	0	0
Munoz	.951	17	39	0	2	0
Parry	1.000	10	14	0	0	0
Roman	.987	41	75	1	1	1
Sanchez	.972	30	30	5	1	1
Saukko	1.000	22	37	1	0	0
Tabata	1.000	3	5	0	0	0

DSL PIRATES   ROOKIE

DOMINICAN SUMMER LEAGUE

Batting	B-T	HT	WT	DOB	AVG	vLH	vRH	G	AB	R	H	2B	3B	HR	RBI	BB	HBP	SH	SF	SO	SB	CS	SLG	OBP
Arias, Julio	R-R	6-5	230	11-16-89	.167	.063	.189	33	90	3	15	1	0	2	10	7	2	1	0	47	0	1	.244	.242
Avila, Eric	R-R	6-1	165	6-9-90	.262	.200	.271	67	256	43	67	10	0	2	26	14	6	5	3	19	5	0	.324	.312
Belen, Ricardo	R-R	6-2	220	4-22-89	.000	.000	.000	4	8	0	0	0	0	0	0	0	0	0	0	2	0	0	.000	.000
Campusano, Luis	R-R	6-0	165	3-6-86	.146	.200	.139	29	41	4	6	0	0	0	2	7	0	3	0	4	1	1	.146	.271
Charles, Melvin	B-R	6-2	160	12-9-90	.097	.250	.074	20	31	4	3	0	0	0	1	4	0	0	0	14	1	1	.097	.200
Chavez, Pedro	R-R	6-0	195	5-1-88	.247	.306	.237	67	247	25	61	18	0	4	47	30	4	1	6	55	8	4	.368	.331
De La Cruz, Melvin	R-R	5-11	180	3-5-90	.255	.364	.224	27	98	22	25	0	0	0	5	12	2	2	1	33	9	2	.255	.345
Estanislao, Victor	R-R	5-11	170	3-6-87	.216	.214	.216	52	176	27	38	7	0	3	21	20	4	1	2	44	8	0	.307	.307
Feliz, Aneudy	R-R	6-2	225	7-20-87	.067	.143	.000	7	15	0	1	1	0	0	0	2	0	0	0	7	0	0	.133	.176
Fortuna, Maxel	R-R	6-2	185	8-3-88	.213	.231	.209	32	80	10	17	2	0	1	7	7	1	3	0	25	5	2	.275	.284
Goris, Diego	R-R	6-2	165	12-8-90	.245	.194	.259	44	143	16	35	2	2	0	11	5	2	1	0	21	2	3	.287	.280
Guzman, Dagoberto	R-R	6-0	165	5-15-88	.254	.182	.261	36	122	18	31	7	2	1	10	8	3	2	1	35	1	0	.369	.313
Juan, Daniel	R-R	6-0	160	9-8-87	.260	.357	.237	37	73	21	19	5	0	0	7	19	2	3	1	17	7	7	.329	.421
Lopez, Juan	R-R	5-11	180	4-20-90	.053	.333	.000	12	19	1	1	0	0	0	0	2	0	0	0	12	0	0	.053	.143
Marte, Starling	R-R	6-1	170	10-9-88	.296	.257	.302	65	257	53	76	10	2	9	44	16	14	4	2	53	20	8	.455	.367
Moreta, Jose	L-L	6-3	185	10-6-88	.252	.214	.257	49	127	20	32	4	0	1	16	18	4	0	0	28	2	2	.307	.362
Rodriguez, Chris	R-R	5-11	185	1-22-90	.215	.211	.216	57	135	11	29	3	0	1	6	9	8	0	0	36	2	3	.259	.303
Rodriguez, Gerlis	B-R	6-2	185	5-29-88	.291	.367	.279	68	234	32	68	16	1	1	28	27	2	5	1	28	15	6	.380	.367
Rojas, Ariel	R-R	6-2	185	4-6-88	.210	.192	.213	62	181	19	38	9	2	2	22	16	3	2	74	3	2	.315	.293

Pitching	B-T	HT	WT	DOB	W	L	ERA	G	GS	CG	SV	IP	H	R	ER	HR	BB	SO	AVG	vLH	vRH	K/9	BB/9
Campos, Fraylin	R-R	5-11	170	1-3-90	1	0	3.71	12	0	0	0	17	19	13	7	0	11	17	.257	.333	.232	9.00	5.82
Cedano, Rikelvin	R-R	5-10	155	10-22-89	6	3	2.19	14	13	0	0	66	60	25	16	1	22	64	.248	.250	.247	8.77	3.02
De Leon, Emmanuel	B-R	6-1	175	12-25-90	0	0	4.00	8	0	0	0	9	9	8	4	0	13		.273	.250	.280	8.00	8.00
Espinosa, Octavio	L-L	5-10	175	9-22-90	3	2	2.06	13	0	0	0	35	26	8	8	0	16	43	.206	.105	.224	11.06	4.11
Figuereo, Freddy	R-R	6-1	190	10-11-87	1	6	4.68	14	14	0	0	75	103	53	39	6	3	50	.315	.268	.335	6.00	0.36
Garcia, Wilbin	R-R	6-4	175	3-15-89	1	4	5.12	14	10	0	0	39	31	29	22	1	23	31	.221	.231	.218	7.22	5.35
Guzman, Oliberto	R-R	5-10	170	8-5-90	1	2	2.59	11	2	0	0	24	23	9	7	0	9	31	.242	.278	.220	11.47	3.33
Juan, Papiro	R-R	5-10	190	5-13-88	3	2	2.84	13	13	0	0	63	44	24	20	0	37	59	.206	.260	.177	8.38	5.26
Laureano, Melkin	R-R	6-3	205	8-26-85	4	1	2.27	20	0	0	7	44	38	14	11	3	12	50	.235	.222	.238	10.31	2.47
Lopez, Porfirio	L-L	5-10	160	3-24-90	0	1	5.50	10	0	0	0	18	20	12	11	0	8	12	.286	.200	.292	6.00	4.00
Mata, Jonathan	L-L	6-2	192	7-12-90	2	0	7.27	8	0	0	1	9	11	8	7	2	6	9	.297	.333	.294	9.35	6.23
Montero, Cristian	R-R	6-0	165	11-6-90	3	0	3.60	8	0	0	1	10	9	5	4	0	8	5	.273	.083	.381	4.50	7.20
Navarro, Eliecer	L-L	5-9	177	10-26-87	4	3	1.42	15	15	0	0	76	50	16	12	1	8	108	.185	.179	.186	12.79	0.95
Rodriguez, Rafael	L-L	5-9	165	7-13-90	4	0	3.94	14	0	0	0	30	25	18	13	5	14	29	.221	.182	.225	8.80	4.25
Sanchez, Daniel	R-R	5-11	145	4-27-86	2	4	4.50	12	0	0	1	16	20	14	8	0	10	12	.323	.280	.351	6.75	5.63
Septimo, Sandobal	R-R	6-0	175	11-24-89	3	2	3.17	16	3	0	3	54	57	31	19	4	8	28	.263	.304	.243	4.67	1.33
Taveras, Yerfi	R-R	6-2	160	11-7-88	0	0	5.56	9	0	0	2	11	13	10	7	0	6	6	.277	.250	.286	4.76	6.35
Vargas, Plasido	R-R	6-4	185	10-5-88	2	0	3.86	13	0	0	2	19	22	11	8	0	11	15	.289	.227	.315	7.23	5.30

Fielding

Catcher	PCT	G	PO	A	E	DP	PB
Arias	1.000	1	1	0	0	0	0
Belen	1.000	4	18	1	0	0	1
Campusano	.962	27	109	18	5	1	5
Charles	1.000	1	1	0	0	0	1
Feliz	1.000	6	38	1	0	0	2
Guzman	1.000	1	2	0	0	0	0
Lopez	1.000	12	47	9	0	0	3
C. Rodriguez	.973	57	369	35	11	3	14

First Base	PCT	G	PO	A	E	DP
Arias	.900	1	8	1	1	0
Fortuna	1.000	1	2	0	0	1
Juan	1.000	3	5	0	0	0
Moreta	.958	14	86	6	4	7
G. Rodriguez	.986	59	479	23	7	32

Second Base	PCT	G	PO	A	E	DP
Avila	.941	46	93	98	12	22
Charles	.875	4	2	5	1	0
Chavez	.833	1	4	1	1	0
Goris	.912	11	14	17	3	3
Guzman	.889	2	4	4	1	0
Juan	.929	17	41	38	6	7

Third Base	PCT	G	PO	A	E	DP
Avila	.946	10	12	23	2	4
Chavez	.891	62	57	140	24	11
Juan	1.000	2	0	1	0	0

Shortstop	PCT	G	PO	A	E	DP
Avila	.884	8	17	21	5	4
Charles	.800	9	7	13	5	1
Goris	.919	32	32	81	10	10

	PCT	G	PO	A	E	DP
Guzman	.906	31	47	78	13	10
Juan	—	2	0	0	0	0
Outfield	**PCT**	**G**	**PO**	**A**	**E**	**DP**
Arias	1.000	14	16	1	0	0
Campusano	1.000	2	2	1	0	0
De La Cruz	.943	26	46	4	3	2
Estanislao	.917	38	39	5	4	1
Feliz	—	1	0	0	0	0
Fortuna	.971	26	32	1	1	0
Juan	.867	6	11	2	2	1
Marte	.945	64	110	11	7	5
Moreta	—	1	0	0	0	0
Rojas	.913	57	77	7	8	0

VSL PIRATES
VENEZUELAN SUMMER LEAGUE

ROOKIE

Batting	B-T	HT	WT	DOB	AVG	vLH	vRH	G	AB	R	H	2B	3B	HR	RBI	BB	HBP	SH	SF	SO	SB	CS	SLG	OBP
Alvarez, Emilio	B-R	6-1	169	5-3-89	.250	.294	.239	34	84	12	21	2	0	2	12	15	1	1	0	20	4	2	.345	.370
Apomte, Carlos	B-R	5-11	135	2-9-91	.237	.226	.240	49	135	21	32	2	1	1	9	18	3	4	0	24	6	2	.289	.340
Aponte, Kelly	L-R	6-5	220	6-4-91	.135	.000	.208	16	37	2	5	0	0	0	2	4	0	0	0	19	0	0	.135	.220
Cabrera, Eduardo	B-R	5-11	170	4-24-88	.138	.400	.083	16	29	6	4	0	0	0	2	5	0	0	0	4	0	0	.138	.265
Cabrera, Ramon	B-R	5-7	202	11-5-89	.264	.255	.268	56	178	24	47	16	0	3	22	28	2	0	2	27	5	0	.404	.367
Cardona, Luis	B-R	5-10	152	7-29-88	.375	.500	.313	8	24	5	9	2	0	0	1	3	0	0	0	3	2	2	.458	.444
Gonzalez, Elevys	B-R	5-11	175	10-23-89	.311	.270	.325	44	151	20	47	6	1	1	23	11	3	0	1	28	3	1	.384	.367
Gonzalez, Gemmy	R-R	6-0	189	6-22-88	.224	.192	.233	66	241	26	54	12	1	8	42	17	4	0	1	39	9	9	.382	.285
Henry, Henry	R-R	5-9	164	5-29-87	.341	.340	.342	67	249	58	85	12	4	2	30	31	8	4	0	21	37	14	.446	.431
Leal, Carlos	R-R	5-10	170	2-10-90	.244	.289	.230	52	160	29	39	9	0	1	17	27	4	3	3	35	10	6	.319	.361
Lotito, Jose	B-R	6-2	175	5-22-88	.200	.308	.170	17	60	8	12	5	1	0	2	4	0	0	1	15	1	0	.317	.246
Lozada, Jonathan	R-R	5-10	150	12-17-88	.244	.188	.262	47	135	24	33	2	1	0	15	16	4	3	1	11	4	4	.274	.340
Marquez, Jairo	R-R	6-0	170	4-7-88	.247	.216	.255	57	174	28	43	9	0	3	26	22	4	0	1	14	4	3	.351	.343
Mavares, Dixon	R-R	5-11	165	7-8-86	.311	.325	.306	52	164	31	51	10	1	1	15	26	6	5	1	21	8	6	.402	.421
Noris, Rogelios	R-R	6-2	192	3-12-89	.272	.189	.299	63	217	31	59	14	2	7	35	27	7	0	3	48	3	3	.452	.366
Pino, David	R-R	5-11	150	4-28-91	.179	.200	.167	13	28	5	5	2	0	0	1	5	0	0	0	8	0	0	.250	.303
Sosa, Junior	L-L	5-10	139	10-3-90	.249	.268	.243	53	181	25	45	7	0	1	14	23	2	6	1	36	16	12	.304	.338

Pitching	B-T	HT	WT	DOB	W	L	ERA	G	GS	CG	SV	IP	H	R	ER	HR	BB	SO	AVG	vLH	vRH	K/9	BB/9
Baez, Manuel	R-R	6-0	209	5-20-88	2	1	2.64	15	5	0	0	48	41	15	14	1	14	23	.230	.241	.228	4.34	2.64
Bandres, Berdis	R-R	5-9	150	6-10-89	4	1	2.56	18	0	0	4	32	22	12	9	1	7	28	.198	.190	.200	7.96	1.99
Barrios, Edison	R-R	6-1	152	10-11-88	7	1	1.67	13	13	1	0	70	65	17	13	2	6	31	.245	.217	.251	3.99	0.77
Bermudez, Elbis	R-R	6-1	179	11-11-88	0	0	4.00	3	3	0	0	9	10	4	4	0	0	4	.263	.125	.300	4.00	0.00
Bueno, Luis	L-L	6-1	160	11-17-87	3	0	1.88	17	0	0	1	38	31	12	8	1	6	27	.221	.000	.226	6.34	1.41
Canones, Gabriel	R-R	6-0	245	3-12-87	0	5	10.35	16	0	0	0	20	21	26	23	4	18	11	.269	.222	.283	4.95	8.10
Carrasco, Roman	R-R	6-2	213	3-18-88	7	1	2.82	12	12	0	0	61	63	25	19	3	9	38	.267	.286	.264	5.64	1.34
Figuera, Luis	R-R	6-1	178	11-11-90	6	2	3.09	14	4	0	0	47	49	25	16	2	10	37	.268	.238	.272	7.14	1.93
Goatache, Deivis	L-L	6-0	139	6-23-88	1	2	2.88	11	0	0	1	25	24	9	8	4	12	13	.264	.273	4.68	4.32
Gutierrez, Edgar	R-R	6-0	170	4-16-88	4	1	2.35	35	0	0	12	46	39	15	12	1	12	35	.227	.258	.220	6.85	2.35
Gutierrez, Jorge	R-R	6-1	174	12-2-87	0	0	16.20	2	0	0	0	2	2	3	3	0	0	1	.286	.500	.200	5.40	0.00
Joves, Julio	R-R	6-2	190	4-7-91	0	0	1.04	4	1	0	0	9	5	1	1	0	6	6	.172	.000	.192	6.23	6.23
Moreno, Diego	R-R	6-1	177	7-21-86	3	1	0.87	7	6	0	0	31	21	6	3	0	4	21	.186	.250	.175	6.10	1.16
Pacheco, Yomar	R-R	6-3	200	10-4-89	1	0	0.71	6	0	0	0	13	5	2	1	0	9	9	.119	.000	.139	6.39	6.39
Paez, Ronald	R-R	6-0	167	12-18-88	0	1	9.00	6	0	0	0	6	9	11	6	0	6	6	.310	.400	.292	9.00	9.00
Ramos, Jhonatan	L-L	5-8	156	8-7-89	5	3	2.69	14	14	0	0	60	61	27	18	3	12	47	.257	.500	.251	7.01	1.79
Ruiz, Raul	L-L	5-10	158	12-4-90	1	3	4.08	16	7	0	1	53	60	26	24	3	11	29	.293	.333	.292	4.92	1.87
Verdugo, Oscar	R-R	6-1	172	1-21-90	0	0	1.77	9	2	0	0	20	20	5	4	0	8	11	.260	.385	.234	4.87	3.54
Vilchez, Francisco	R-R	6-0	183	12-28-90	2	0	1.00	6	2	0	0	18	15	5	2	1	6	19	.224	.125	.237	9.50	3.00

Fielding

Catcher	PCT	G	PO	A	E	DP	PB
E. Cabrera	1.000	15	48	8	0	0	0
R. Cabrera	.978	38	204	20	5	0	8
Marquez	.989	29	160	21	2	0	5

First Base	PCT	G	PO	A	E	DP
Alvarez	.978	31	210	10	5	15
Aponte	1.000	12	82	7	0	12
R. Cabrera	.960	9	70	2	3	5
Gonzalez	.900	3	8	1	1	3
Lotito	.985	14	128	4	2	10
Marquez	.994	18	155	6	1	13
Mavares	1.000	1	2	0	0	0
Noris	1.000	1	3	0	0	1

Second Base	PCT	G	PO	A	E	DP
Apomte	.969	38	67	88	5	18
Gonzalez	.909	3	5	5	1	3

	PCT	G	PO	A	E	DP
Henry	.967	6	15	14	1	5
Leal	.889	3	4	4	1	1
Lozada	.833	3	4	6	2	0
Mavares	.986	25	69	68	2	15

Third Base	PCT	G	PO	A	E	DP
Alvarez	.923	3	2	10	1	2
R. Cabrera	1.000	1	0	1	0	0
Gonzalez	.874	37	27	77	15	6
Henry	.917	17	14	52	6	3
Leal	1.000	5	2	10	0	1
Lozada	1.000	1	1	1	0	1
Mavares	.909	10	10	20	3	1
Pino	.880	8	7	15	3	1

Shortstop	PCT	G	PO	A	E	DP
Apomte	.833	4	3	7	2	2
Gonzalez	.853	7	10	19	5	3

	PCT	G	PO	A	E	DP
Leal	.950	48	65	165	12	22
Mavares	.966	22	21	64	3	7
Pino	1.000	1	0	1	0	0

Outfield	PCT	G	PO	A	E	DP
Alvarez	—	2	0	0	0	0
Cardona	.857	7	12	0	2	0
Gonzalez	.979	66	135	5	3	0
Lozada	.983	42	54	5	1	0
Mavares	—	1	0	0	0	0
Noris	.978	58	84	7	2	1
Pino	1.000	2	1	0	0	0
Sosa	.991	52	103	11	1	3

St. Louis Cardinals

BY DERRICK GOOLD

The Cardinals initially shrank from calling the 2008 season a "transition" year, one meant to bridge the franchise from the generation that brought a 10th World Series championship to a pipeline of younger, Cardinal-cultivated prospects. As they reached September bruised by injuries and absences, the Cardinals came to embrace a different description: Overachievers.

Both labels fit, snugly.

For the first time since 1999, the Cardinals missed the postseason in consecutive years, but  with an 86-76 record they avoided what would have been the first back-to-back losing seasons in 50 years. The Cardinals led the wild card race in July before injury and inconsistency eroded their chances to contend, and they finished fourth in a rapidly improving National League Central. They finished the season with about $30 million in aging contracts coming off the payroll and 10 rookies having made their debuts, a handful of whom left a favorable impression for an inevitable transition. "We were a good club this year," manager Tony La Russa said. "Well, good is not good enough. So how do you get better?"

It starts by staying healthier. First-year general manager John Mozeliak, who replaced longtime architect Walt Jocketty on Halloween 2007, conceded after the season that the Cardinals leveraged too much of 2008 on health. The Cardinals banked on contributions from pitchers coming off surgeries: Chris Carpenter (elbow), Mark Mulder (shoulder) and Matt Clement (shoulder). Combined they made four starts and pitched 17 innings, 15⅓ of which was by Carpenter before he went back on the disabled list. Carpenter, the only one of the three still under contract, reaches 2009 having elected to have surgery to repair a nerve near his surgically repaired right elbow.

Mozeliak's moves to reshape the offensive identity of the Cardinals proved more fruitful. He swapped disgruntled third baseman Scott Rolen for Troy Glaus and got 99 RBIs and superb defense from Glaus. Ryan Ludwick, a minor league free agent signed by Mozeliak before 2007, blossomed, becoming an NL all-star before he was an everyday player. Ludwick hit .299/.375/.591 with 37 home runs and 113 RBIs. Ludwick's .591 slugging ended up second in the league to hitter he became protec-

tion for: Albert Pujols.

Despite playing in some discomfort because an elbow nerve issue that required October surgery, Pujols hit .357/.462/.653. A leading contender for the NL MVP, Pujols fashioned his eighth consecutive 100-RBI, .300-average, 30-homer season.

ORGANIZATION STATISTICS

PLAYERS OF THE YEAR

MAJOR LEAGUE: ALBERT PUJOLS, 1B

Pujols shouldered a greater leadership role for the transitioning and overachieving Cardinals as he led the NL in slugging (.653), finished second to Chipper Jones in both average (.317) and on-base percentage (.462) and was fourth in RBIs (116).

MINOR LEAGUE: DARYL JONES, OF

Jones, one of the best athletes in the organization since being drafted in 2005, broke through in 2008 with high Class A Palm Beach and Double-A Springfield. He hit .311/.402/.474 with 12 home runs, 17 doubles, 45 RBIs and 23 steals.

MORRIS FOSTOFF

ORGANIZATION LEADERS

BATTING		*Minimum 250 at-bats
*AVG	Stavinoha, Nick, Memphis	.337
R	Phelps, Josh, Memphis	90
H	Craig, Allen, Springfield	154
TB	Phelps, Josh, Memphis	262
2B	Brown, Andrew, Quad Cities/Palm Beach/Spring.	32
3B	Yarbrough, Brandon, Springfield	8
	Jones, Daryl, Palm Beach/Springfield	8
HR	Phelps, Josh, Memphis	31
RBI	Phelps, Josh, Memphis	97
BB	Brown, Andrew, Quad Cities/Palm Beach/Spring.	58
SO	Pham, Thomas, Palm Beach/Quad Cities	156
SB	Jones, Daryl, Palm Beach/Springfield	24
*OBP	Jones, Daryl, Palm Beach/Springfield	.407
*SLG	Phelps, Josh, Memphis	.568

PITCHING		†Minimum 75 innings
W	Additon, Nicholas, Quad Cities/Palm Beach	11
L	Mortensen, Clayton, Springfield/Memphis	10
	Dickson, Brandon, Palm Beach/Springfield	10
†ERA	Additon, Nicholas, Quad Cities/Palm Beach	2.23
G	Motte, Jason, Memphis	63
GS	Walters, P.J., Springfield/Memphis	29
SV	Samuel, Francisco, Quad Cities/Palm Beach	30
IP	Walters, P.J., Springfield/Memphis	158
BB	King, Blake, Quad Cities/Palm Beach	82
SO	Walters, P.J., Springfield/Memphis	156
†AVG	Additon, Nicholas, Quad Cities/Palm Beach	.208

2008 PERFORMANCE

General Manager: John Mozeliak. **Farm/Scouting Director:** Jeff Luhnow.

Class	Team	League	W	L	PCT	Finish*	Manager	Affiliate Since
Majors	St. Louis	National	86	76	.531	6th (16)	Tony LaRussa	—
Triple-A	Memphis Redbirds	Pacific Coast	75	67	.528	5th (16)	Chris Maloney	1998
Double-A	Springfield Cardinals	Texas	76	64	.543	2nd (8)	Ron Warner	2005
High A	Palm Beach Cardinals	Florida State	75	62	.547	4th (12)	Gaylen Pitts	2003
Low A	Quad Cities River Bandits	Midwest	68	66	.507	9th (14)	Steve Dillard	2005
Short-season	Batavia Muckdogs	New York-Penn	46	28	.662	^2nd (14)	Mark DeJohn	2007
Rookie	Johnson City Cardinals	Appalachian	36	30	.545	3rd (10)	Joe Almaraz	1974
Rookie	GCL Cardinals	Gulf Coast	17	38	.309	15th (16)	Enrique Brito	2007
Overall 2008 Minor League Record			393	355	.525	7th		

* Finish in overall standings (No. of teams in league). ^League champion.

ORGANIZATION STATISTICS

ST. LOUIS CARDINALS

NATIONAL LEAGUE

Batting	B-T	HT	WT	DOB	AVG	vLH	vRH	G	AB	R	H	2B	3B	HR	RBI	BB	HBP	SH	SF	SO	SB	CS	SLG	OBP
Ankiel, Rick	L-L	6-1	210	7-19-79	.264	.224	.279	120	413	65	109	21	2	25	71	42	5	0	3	100	2	1	.506	.337
Barden, Brian	R-R	5-11	185	4-2-81	.222	.200	.250	9	9	0	2	0	0	0	1	0	0	1	0	4	0	0	.222	.222
Barton, Brian	R-R	6-3	190	4-25-82	.268	.258	.281	82	153	23	41	9	2	2	13	19	2	4	1	39	3	1	.392	.354
Duncan, Chris	L-R	6-5	230	5-5-81	.248	.147	.266	76	222	26	55	8	0	6	27	34	0	0	1	52	2	1	.365	.346
Glaus, Troy	R-R	6-5	240	8-3-76	.270	.221	.290	151	544	69	147	33	1	27	99	87	3	0	3	104	0	1	.483	.372
Izturis, Cesar	B-R	5-9	190	2-10-80	.263	.304	.237	135	414	50	109	10	3	1	24	29	6	3	2	26	24	6	.309	.319
Johnson, Mark	L-R	6-0	200	9-12-75	.294	1.000	.250	10	17	1	5	0	0	0	2	1	0	0	0	2	0	0	.294	.333
Kennedy, Adam	L-R	6-1	195	1-10-76	.280	.270	.283	115	339	42	95	17	4	2	36	21	1	0	4	43	7	1	.372	.321
LaRue, Jason	R-R	5-11	205	3-19-74	.213	.196	.220	61	164	17	35	8	1	4	21	15	5	3	2	20	0	0	.348	.296
Lopez, Felipe	B-R	6-0	195	5-12-80	.385	.412	.371	43	156	30	60	8	2	4	21	11	1	0	1	28	4	3	.538	.426
2-team total (100 Washington)					.283	—	—	143	481	64	136	28	2	6	46	43	3	2	3	82	8	8	.387	.343
Ludwick, Ryan	R-L	6-3	220	7-13-78	.299	.266	.316	152	538	104	161	40	3	37	113	62	8	1	8	146	4	4	.591	.375
Mather, Joe	R-R	6-4	195	7-23-82	.241	.219	.261	54	133	20	32	7	0	8	18	12	1	0	1	32	1	0	.474	.306
Miles, Aaron	B-R	5-8	185	12-15-76	.317	.315	.317	134	379	49	120	15	2	4	31	23	0	5	1	37	3	3	.398	.355
Molina, Yadier	R-R	5-11	220	7-13-82	.304	.323	.296	124	444	37	135	18	0	7	56	32	1	3	5	29	0	2	.392	.349
Phelps, Josh	R-R	6-3	225	5-12-78	.265	.316	.200	19	34	4	9	1	0	0	1	2	0	0	0	11	0	0	.294	.306
Pujols, Albert	R-R	6-3	230	1-16-80	.357	.411	.333	148	524	100	187	44	0	37	116	104	5	0	8	54	7	3	.653	.462
Ryan, Brendan	R-R	6-2	195	3-26-82	.244	.261	.229	80	197	30	48	9	0	0	10	16	2	3	0	31	7	2	.289	.307
Schumaker, Skip	L-R	5-10	195	2-3-80	.302	.168	.340	153	540	87	163	22	5	8	46	47	2	4	1	60	8	2	.406	.359
Stavinoha, Nick	R-R	6-2	225	5-3-82	.193	.240	.156	29	57	4	11	1	0	0	4	2	0	1	1	11	0	0	.211	.217
Washington, Rico	L-R	5-9	195	5-30-78	.158	.000	.158	14	19	2	3	2	0	0	3	3	0	0	0	6	0	0	.263	.273

Pitching	B-T	HT	WT	DOB	W	L	ERA	G	GS	CG	SV	IP	H	R	ER	HR	BB	SO	AVG	vLH	vRH	K/9	BB/9
Boggs, Mitchell	R-R	6-4	215	2-15-84	3	2	7.41	8	0	0	0	34	42	29	28	5	22	13	.304	.321	.283	3.44	5.82
Carpenter, Chris	R-R	6-6	230	4-27-75	0	1	1.76	4	3	0	0	15	16	5	3	0	4	7	.286	.158	.351	4.11	2.35
Flores, Randy	L-L	6-0	190	7-31-75	1	0	5.26	43	0	0	1	26	34	16	15	2	20	17	.315	.314	.316	5.96	7.01
Franklin, Ryan	R-R	6-3	190	3-5-73	6	6	3.55	74	0	0	17	79	86	34	31	10	30	51	.278	.268	.285	5.83	3.43
Garcia, Jaime	L-L	6-2	200	7-8-86	1	1	5.63	10	1	0	0	16	14	10	10	4	8	8	.233	.250	.227	4.50	4.50
Isringhausen, Jason	R-R	6-3	230	9-7-72	1	5	5.70	42	0	0	12	43	48	28	27	5	22	36	.279	.186	.327	7.59	4.64
Jimenez, Kelvin	R-R	6-2	195	10-27-80	0	0	5.63	15	0	0	0	24	28	15	15	5	15	11	.292	.233	.340	4.13	5.63
Kinney, Josh	R-R	6-1	215	3-31-79	0	0	0.00	7	0	0	0	7	3	0	0	0	1	8	.125	.125	.125	10.29	1.29
Lohse, Kyle	R-R	6-2	210	10-4-78	15	6	3.78	33	33	0	0	200	211	88	84	18	49	119	.272	.254	.285	5.36	2.21
Looper, Braden	R-R	6-3	235	10-28-74	12	14	4.16	33	33	1	0	199	216	101	92	25	45	108	.279	.279	.279	4.88	2.04
McClellan, Kyle	R-R	6-4	205	6-12-84	2	7	4.04	68	0	0	1	76	79	37	34	7	26	59	.269	.238	.291	7.02	3.09
Motte, Jason	R-R	6-0	195	6-22-82	0	0	0.82	12	0	0	1	11	5	2	1	0	3	16	.139	.125	.150	13.09	2.45
Mulder, Mark	L-L	6-6	215	8-5-77	0	0	10.80	3	1	0	0	2	4	2	2	0	2	2	.500	1.000	.200	10.80	10.80
Parisi, Mike	R-R	6-3	215	4-18-83	0	4	8.22	12	2	0	0	23	37	24	21	2	15	13	.363	.370	.357	5.09	5.87
Perez, Chris	R-R	6-4	225	7-1-85	3	3	3.46	41	0	0	7	42	34	18	16	5	22	42	.227	.220	.231	9.07	4.75
Pineiro, Joel	R-R	6-1	200	9-25-78	7	7	5.15	26	25	0	1	149	180	89	85	22	35	81	.301	.297	.304	4.90	2.12
Reyes, Anthony	R-R	6-2	230	10-16-81	2	1	4.91	10	0	0	1	15	16	8	8	2	3	16	.276	.192	.344	6.14	1.84
Springer, Russ	R-R	6-4	225	11-7-68	2	1	2.32	70	0	0	0	50	39	14	13	4	18	45	.212	.277	.176	8.05	3.22
Thompson, Brad	R-R	6-1	190	1-31-82	6	3	5.15	26	6	0	0	65	72	38	37	5	19	32	.293	.279	.303	4.45	2.64
Villone, Ron	L-L	6-3	245	1-16-70	1	2	4.68	74	0	0	1	50	45	27	26	4	37	50	.243	.176	.300	9.00	6.66
Wainwright, Adam	R-R	6-7	230	8-30-81	11	3	3.20	20	20	1	0	132	122	51	47	12	34	91	.245	.264	.234	6.20	2.32
Wellemeyer, Todd	R-R	6-3	205	8-30-78	13	9	3.71	32	32	0	0	192	178	84	79	25	62	134	.245	.256	.237	6.29	2.91
Worrell, Mark	R-R	6-1	215	3-8-83	0	1	7.94	4	0	0	0	6	8	5	5	1	4	4	.364	.222	.462	6.35	6.35

Fielding

Catcher	PCT	G	PO	A	E	DP	PB
Johnson	1.000	10	34	0	0	0	0
LaRue	.993	57	289	16	2	1	2
Molina	.986	119	653	70	10	7	5

First Base	PCT	G	PO	A	E	DP
Barden	—	1	0	0	0	0
Duncan	1.000	21	143	13	0	13
Glaus	1.000	4	29	2	0	5
Kennedy	.963	3	23	3	1	4

	PCT	G	PO	A	E	DP
LaRue	1.000	3	7	1	0	1
Lopez	1.000	1	2	0	0	0
Mather	1.000	4	9	1	0	1
Molina	1.000	2	13	3	0	1
Phelps	1.000	4	18	0	0	1

Pujols	.996	144	1297	135	6	119

Second Base	PCT	G	PO	A	E	DP
Barden	.833	1	1	4	1	0
Kennedy	.981	84	144	224	7	56
Lopez	.988	23	27	57	1	14
Miles	.988	85	91	165	3	47
Pujols	1.000	1	1	0	0	0
Ryan	.984	23	23	39	1	5
Washington	—	1	0	0	0	0

Third Base	PCT	G	PO	A	E	DP
Barden	1.000	4	0	2	0	0
Glaus	.982	146	99	279	7	27
Izturis	1.000	8	3	3	0	0

Lopez	.926	13	2	23	2	2
Mather	—	1	0	0	0	0
Miles	1.000	11	2	16	0	1
Ryan	.889	5	2	6	1	1
Washington	1.000	4	0	9	0	0

Shortstop	PCT	G	PO	A	E	DP
Izturis	.980	130	170	370	11	77
Lopez	1.000	5	3	7	0	1
Miles	.989	27	32	56	1	14
Ryan	.993	40	42	91	1	18

Outfield	PCT	G	PO	A	E	DP
Ankiel	.968	106	236	4	8	1
Barton	.968	45	58	2	2	0

Duncan	.975	45	77	1	2	0
Kennedy	1.000	10	15	0	0	0
Lopez	.833	9	4	1	1	0
Ludwick	.990	149	293	12	3	3
Mather	.985	44	66	1	1	0
Miles	1.000	6	6	0	0	0
Phelps	1.000	5	5	0	0	0
Ryan	1.000	3	5	0	0	0
Schumaker	.990	151	285	10	3	3
Stavinoha	1.000	18	11	0	0	0
Washington	—	2	0	0	0	0

MEMPHIS REDBIRDS

TRIPLE-A

PACIFIC COAST LEAGUE

Batting	B-T	HT	WT	DOB	AVG	vLH	vRH	G	AB	R	H	2B	3B	HR	RBI	BB	HBP	SH	SF	SO	SB	CS	SLG	OBP
Anderson, Bryan	L-R	6-1	200	12-16-86	.281	.308	.271	73	235	27	66	13	2	2	27	32	1	5	2	46	2	0	.379	.367
Barden, Brian	R-R	5-11	185	4-2-81	.285	.326	.266	103	411	60	117	21	4	9	35	38	4	0	3	72	3	3	.421	.349
Barton, Brian	R-R	6-3	190	4-25-82	.260	.167	.291	19	73	12	19	2	2	3	11	9	2	0	2	23	1	4	.466	.349
Cazana Marti, Amaury	R-R	6-1	212	9-2-74	.266	.357	.227	28	94	11	25	6	0	3	12	5	0	0	1	25	1	0	.426	.300
Duncan, Chris	L-R	6-5	230	5-5-81	.160	.286	.111	7	25	5	4	2	0	0	3	4	1	0	0	5	0	0	.240	.300
Freese, David	R-R	6-2	220	4-28-83	.306	.286	.314	131	464	83	142	29	3	26	91	39	3	0	4	111	5	2	.550	.361
Greene, Tyler	R-R	6-2	185	8-17-83	.234	.280	.221	30	111	17	26	7	0	0	7	11	4	2	0	35	6	0	.297	.325
Haerther, Cody	L-R	6-1	205	7-14-83	.250	.277	.244	100	268	26	67	17	0	3	26	23	1	2	1	56	2	3	.347	.311
Hoffpauir, Jarrett	R-R	5-9	175	6-18-83	.273	.248	.284	121	410	48	112	31	1	4	45	49	4	6	6	45	2	4	.383	.352
Jay, Jon	L-L	5-11	200	3-15-85	.345	.294	.366	16	58	8	20	4	1	1	10	6	0	0	0	11	0	1	.500	.406
Jimenez, D'Angelo	B-R	6-0	190	12-21-77	.244	.253	.241	110	303	37	74	13	1	6	36	42	0	3	4	34	6	1	.353	.332
Johnson, Gabe	R-R	6-1	205	9-21-79	.222	.300	.160	33	90	10	20	4	1	2	13	10	0	0	1	27	1	1	.356	.297
Johnson, Mark	L-R	6-0	200	9-12-75	.264	.200	.280	66	201	17	53	9	0	1	31	33	2	2	1	28	1	1	.323	.371
Mather, Joe	R-R	6-4	195	7-23-82	.303	.301	.304	59	211	45	64	14	2	17	41	32	8	1	2	36	7	2	.630	.411
Pagnozzi, Matt	R-R	6-2	205	11-10-82	.200	.333	.000	3	5	0	1	1	0	0	1	2	0	0	0	1	0	0	.400	.429
Phelps, Josh	R-R	6-3	225	5-12-78	.291	.278	.296	126	461	90	134	31	2	31	97	56	7	0	4	109	2	2	.568	.373
Rasmus, Colby	L-L	6-2	195	8-11-86	.251	.263	.246	90	331	56	83	15	0	11	36	49	1	3	3	72	15	3	.396	.346
Robinson, Shane	R-R	5-9	160	10-30-84	.220	.212	.222	42	141	10	31	4	1	1	10	5	1	2	2	24	2	3	.284	.248
Rowlett, Casey	R-R	5-8	175	2-8-83	.444	—	.444	7	9	3	4	0	0	0	1	0	0	0	0	2	1	0	.444	.444
Ryan, Brendan	R-R	6-2	195	3-26-82	.238	.176	.254	21	80	13	19	5	0	3	10	4	1	2	1	17	1	0	.413	.279
Stavinoha, Nick	R-R	6-2	225	5-3-82	.337	.363	.328	112	427	67	144	23	3	16	74	20	2	0	4	50	2	1	.518	.366
Washington, Rico	L-R	5-9	195	5-30-78	.254	.148	.283	92	252	54	64	15	0	13	40	52	7	0	3	49	0	2	.468	.392

Pitching	B-T	HT	WT	DOB	W	L	ERA	G	GS	CG	SV	IP	H	R	ER	HR	BB	SO	AVG	vLH	vRH	K/9	BB/9
Boggs, Mitchell	R-R	6-4	215	2-15-84	9	3	3.45	21	21	1	0	125	107	52	48	11	46	81	.235	.286	.189	5.82	3.30
Carpenter, Chris	R-R	6-6	230	4-27-75	0	1	3.18	1	1	0	0	6	4	2	2	0	1	5	.190	.364	.000	7.94	1.59
Castellanos, Hugo	R-R	6-4	225	6-30-80	2	1	5.61	28	4	0	0	67	78	43	42	5	36	51	.295	.289	.302	6.82	4.81
Clement, Matt	R-R	6-3	210	8-12-74	1	0	7.02	13	1	0	0	17	17	14	13	5	13	10	.266	.320	.231	5.40	7.02
Flores, Randy	L-L	6-0	190	7-31-75	0	1	2.45	15	0	0	1	18	20	6	5	2	6	14	.278	.160	.340	6.87	2.95
Flores, Ron	L-L	5-10	195	8-9-79	7	4	4.26	59	0	0	4	63	71	31	30	6	33	58	.285	.310	.273	8.24	4.69
Garcia, Jaime	L-L	6-2	200	7-8-86	4	4	4.44	13	12	0	0	71	74	41	35	6	26	59	.270	.324	.250	7.48	3.30
Hawksworth, Blake	R-R	6-3	195	3-1-83	5	7	6.09	18	16	0	0	89	111	71	60	12	38	83	.307	.331	.292	8.42	3.86
Jimenez, Kelvin	R-R	6-2	195	10-27-80	1	6	2.92	46	0	0	12	52	55	22	17	3	12	28	.278	.250	.302	4.82	2.06
Mortensen, Clayton	R-R	6-4	180	4-10-85	5	6	5.51	15	14	0	0	80	87	50	49	12	42	57	.281	.377	.179	6.41	4.73
Motte, Jason	R-R	6-0	195	6-22-82	4	3	3.24	63	0	0	9	67	64	25	24	6	26	110	.245	.269	.229	14.85	3.51
Mulder, Mark	L-L	6-6	215	8-5-77	0	3	13.50	3	3	0	0	13	28	22	20	3	5	8	.438	.333	.488	5.40	3.38
Norrick, Tyler	L-L	6-3	190	9-27-83	0	1	2.25	1	1	0	0	4	1	2	1	0	6	8	.083	.000	.250	18.00	13.50
Parisi, Mike	R-R	6-3	215	4-18-83	8	7	3.86	15	15	1	0	84	80	38	36	7	33	58	.252	.265	.241	6.21	3.54
Perez, Chris	R-R	6-4	225	7-1-85	1	1	3.20	26	0	0	11	25	18	9	9	3	12	38	.198	.182	.207	13.50	4.26
Pineiro, Joel	R-R	6-1	200	9-25-78	0	0	3.00	1	1	0	0	6	6	2	2	0	1	5	.261	.200	.308	7.50	1.50
Politte, Cliff	R-R	5-10	195	2-27-74	1	1	5.79	7	0	0	0	9	9	6	6	2	2	9	.250	.444	.185	8.68	1.93
Rauschenberger, Cory	R-R	6-1	185	7-31-84	0	0	0.00	2	0	0	0	4	5	1	0	0	3	0	.294	.333	.250	0.00	6.75
Reyes, Anthony	R-R	6-2	230	10-16-81	2	3	3.25	11	11	0	0	53	51	21	19	4	21	47	.260	.269	.250	8.03	3.59
Rogers, Joe	L-L	6-2	193	7-19-81	0	1	5.73	3	2	0	0	11	11	9	7	2	3	7	.250	.375	.222	5.73	2.45
Scherer, Matt	R-R	6-5	230	1-20-83	2	3	3.93	40	0	0	0	55	52	24	24	5	18	32	.254	.244	.261	5.24	2.93
Thompson, Brad	R-R	6-1	190	1-31-82	1	1	7.82	3	3	0	0	13	22	13	11	4	2	4	.367	.353	.385	2.84	1.42
Todd, Jess	R-R	5-11	210	4-20-86	1	1	3.97	4	4	0	0	23	19	10	10	4	11	20	.232	.182	.250	7.94	4.37
Wainwright, Adam	R-R	6-7	230	8-30-81	0	1	12.27	2	2	0	0	4	8	5	5	1	2	3	.444	.333	.500	7.36	4.91
Walters, P.J.	R-R	6-4	200	3-12-85	9	4	4.87	23	23	0	0	122	123	71	66	17	62	122	.266	.253	.277	9.00	4.57
Wasdin, John	R-R	6-2	190	8-5-72	9	6	3.51	41	8	0	3	110	102	44	43	16	20	97	.241	.278	.217	7.91	1.63
Webber, Nick	R-R	6-7	210	5-9-84	0	0	8.38	6	0	0	0	10	10	10	9	2	8	2	.263	.294	.238	1.86	7.45
Worrell, Mark	R-R	6-1	215	3-8-83	3	3	2.15	53	0	0	5	59	45	21	14	2	31	80	.210	.203	.215	12.27	4.76

Fielding

Catcher	PCT	G	PO	A	E	DP	PB												
Anderson	.986	69	514	49	8	3	8	G. Johnson	.986	18	125	14	2	2	3	Pagnozzi	1.000	2	14	2	0	0	0
								M. Johnson	.994	60	451	23	3	1	5				

First Base	PCT	G	PO	A	E	DP
Barden	1.000	6	45	4	0	5
G. Johnson	.952	3	20	0	1	1
Phelps	.993	117	989	72	7	104
Washington	.985	30	183	11	3	18

Second Base	PCT	G	PO	A	E	DP
Hoffpauir	.977	105	186	273	11	73
Jimenez	.976	46	60	105	4	22
Ryan	1.000	7	15	10	0	3
Washington	1.000	7	6	9	0	3

Third Base	PCT	G	PO	A	E	DP
Barden	.750	3	3	3	2	0

Freese	.967	120	80	216	10	26
Jimenez	.964	17	12	15	1	1
Rowlett	.800	1	0	4	1	0
Washington	.977	21	15	28	1	3

Shortstop	PCT	G	PO	A	E	DP
Barden	.967	92	139	245	13	58
Greene	.969	29	37	87	4	17
Jimenez	.970	25	35	63	3	14
Ryan	1.000	6	5	12	0	4

Outfield	PCT	G	PO	A	E	DP
Barden	—	2	0	0	0	0
Barton	1.000	18	31	1	0	0

Cazana Marti	.963	21	24	2	1	0
Duncan	1.000	7	10	1	0	0
Haerther	.973	65	71	2	2	0
Jay	1.000	16	42	1	0	0
G. Johnson	1.000	6	7	1	0	0
Mather	.971	59	91	11	3	3
Phelps	—	1	0	0	0	0
Rasmus	.981	89	204	5	4	1
Robinson	1.000	38	81	2	0	0
Ryan	1.000	10	22	2	0	0
Stavinoha	.987	102	144	5	2	0
Washington	.973	29	35	1	1	0

SPRINGFIELD CARDINALS DOUBLE-A

TEXAS LEAGUE

Batting	B-T	HT	WT	DOB	AVG	vLH	vRH	G	AB	R	H	2B	3B	HR	RBI	BB	HBP	SH	SF	SO	SB	CS	SLG	OBP
Anderson, Bryan	L-R	6-1	200	12-16-86	.388	.429	.373	19	80	12	31	5	0	2	14	4	0	1	1	12	0	0	.525	.412
Brown, Andrew	R-R	6-0	185	9-10-84	.251	.266	.246	68	247	36	62	14	0	12	38	30	4	0	1	81	1	0	.453	.340
Buckman, Brandon	L-L	6-6	205	2-14-84	.321	.263	.338	23	84	9	27	3	0	2	9	6	0	0	1	18	1	0	.429	.363
Craig, Allen	R-R	6-2	190	7-18-84	.304	.260	.316	129	506	84	154	30	0	22	85	48	10	0	4	87	2	1	.494	.373
Descalso, Daniel	L-R	5-10	190	10-19-86	.351	.500	.280	9	37	6	13	1	0	4	3	1	1	0	1	2	1	1	.432	.405
Garcia, Isaias	R-R	5-10	180	8-20-84	.284	.220	.306	71	194	24	55	7	0	5	33	5	3	1	5	31	0	1	.397	.304
Gorsett, Luke	R-R	6-1	195	5-28-85	.207	.233	.193	25	87	12	18	4	1	2	8	9	2	0	1	15	0	0	.345	.293
Greene, Tyler	R-R	6-2	185	8-17-83	.259	.275	.254	97	374	62	97	15	4	16	41	22	5	4	3	99	14	6	.449	.307
Haerther, Cody	L-R	6-1	205	7-14-83	.297	.263	.311	18	64	12	19	5	0	1	5	12	2	1	0	10	0	1	.422	.423
Hamilton, Mark	L-L	6-3	220	7-29-84	.241	.304	.222	70	245	27	59	11	0	8	29	35	1	0	0	67	0	0	.384	.338
Hill, Steven	R-R	5-11	190	3-14-85	.303	.400	.286	26	99	13	30	3	1	5	9	4	1	0	0	31	0	0	.505	.330
Jay, Jon	L-L	5-11	200	3-15-85	.306	.270	.315	96	372	57	114	17	3	11	47	39	6	7	3	46	10	7	.457	.379
Jones, Daryl	L-L	5-11	180	6-25-87	.290	.250	.304	36	124	19	36	6	1	6	14	22	3	2	0	30	6	1	.500	.409
Maestrales, Pete	B-R	5-11	190	7-4-79	.250	1.000	.143	5	8	0	2	0	0	0	1	0	0	0	1	1	0	0	.250	.222
Martinez, Jose	R-R	5-11	175	1-24-86	.253	.228	.260	127	483	50	122	20	1	8	67	20	10	10	7	44	1	4	.348	.292
Pagnozzi, Matt	R-R	6-2	205	11-10-82	.236	.250	.230	68	216	24	51	10	0	3	19	16	3	6	3	47	2	1	.324	.294
Rapoport, James	L-L	5-11	160	6-25-85	.246	.216	.253	45	183	24	45	5	3	2	18	8	4	2	2	35	12	1	.339	.289
Robinson, Shane	R-R	5-9	160	10-30-84	.352	.309	.365	63	244	46	86	17	3	4	32	17	3	3	4	34	13	5	.496	.396
Rowlett, Casey	R-R	5-8	175	2-8-83	.242	.277	.225	86	207	31	50	8	3	5	27	22	2	9	2	41	7	7	.382	.318
Ryan, Brendan	R-R	6-2	195	3-26-82	.368	.200	.429	4	19	5	7	3	0	1	3	1	1	0	0	6	1	0	.684	.429
Shorey, Mark	L-L	6-0	230	8-13-84	.304	.222	.320	114	388	49	118	28	2	11	66	29	5	2	8	110	1	0	.472	.353
Solano, Donovan	R-R	5-10	165	12-17-87	.264	.214	.282	26	106	11	28	5	0	1	11	5	4	4	1	22	2	1	.340	.319
Van Slyke, A.J.	L-R	6-2	210	11-19-83	.244	.200	.257	18	45	8	11	4	1	0	1	8	1	1	0	12	2	0	.378	.370
Wallace, Brett	L-R	6-1	245	8-26-86	.367	.438	.333	19	49	13	18	5	0	3	11	2	6	0	0	7	0	0	.653	.456
Yarbrough, Brandon	L-R	6-2	180	11-9-84	.242	.241	.242	94	306	39	74	14	8	3	37	45	4	1	3	100	2	1	.369	.344

Pitching	B-T	HT	WT	DOB	W	L	ERA	G	GS	CG	SV	IP	H	R	ER	HR	BB	SO	AVG	vLH	vRH	K/9	BB/9
Carpenter, Chris	R-R	6-6	230	4-27-75	0	0	0.00	1	1	0	0	4	1	0	0	0	4	1	.077	.000	.111	9.00	9.00
Clement, Matt	R-R	6-3	210	8-12-74	1	0	5.40	2	2	0	0	10	12	9	6	1	3	5	.286	.333	.259	4.50	2.70
Daniels, Adam	L-L	6-2	190	8-16-82	1	4	5.82	17	9	0	0	56	71	40	36	6	35	38	.314	.406	.299	6.14	5.66
Dew, Josh	R-R	6-5	225	1-15-85	1	2	4.50	38	0	0	2	50	57	34	25	3	23	54	.286	.365	.240	9.72	4.14
Dickson, Brandon	R-R	6-5	190	11-3-84	3	2	6.75	6	6	0	0	29	42	23	22	3	16	21	.347	.389	.313	6.44	4.91
Fiske, Justin	L-L	5-11	185	9-3-84	4	0	2.97	26	10	0	0	70	62	23	23	4	30	74	.242	.208	.251	9.56	3.88
Furnish, Brad	B-L	6-1	185	1-19-85	1	1	1.64	4	4	0	0	22	17	10	4	1	12	15	.221	.333	.206	6.14	4.91
Garcia, Jaime	L-L	6-2	200	7-8-86	3	2	2.06	6	6	1	0	35	26	10	8	0	16	41	.206	.286	.196	10.54	4.11
Gonzalez, Marco	R-R	6-2	205	5-28-84	7	0	3.59	47	0	0	2	58	47	27	23	4	22	35	.225	.205	.235	5.46	3.43
Gregerson, Luke	R-R	6-3	190	5-14-84	7	6	3.35	57	0	0	10	75	62	32	28	6	26	78	.221	.268	.202	9.32	3.11
Herron, Ty	R-R	6-3	190	8-5-86	5	5	5.20	15	15	0	0	81	101	50	47	9	29	59	.304	.343	.275	6.53	3.21
Honel, Kris	R-R	6-5	190	11-7-82	0	0	18.00	3	0	0	0	3	5	6	6	1	2	6	.385	.250	.444	18.00	6.00
Isringhausen, Jason	R-R	6-3	230	9-7-72	0	0	0.00	1	1	0	0	2	1	0	0	0	0	2	.167	.250	.000	10.80	0.00
Kinney, Josh	R-R	6-1	215	3-31-79	0	1	7.36	4	0	0	0	4	4	3	3	0	0	5	.286	.000	.444	12.27	0.00
McCormick, Mark	R-R	6-2	195	10-15-83	0	2	6.08	6	6	0	0	24	22	17	16	5	18	16	.253	.348	.219	6.08	6.85
Mikrut, Jon	R-R	6-4	195	11-22-82	4	3	4.25	44	0	0	0	66	63	36	31	13	20	46	.252	.300	.229	6.30	2.74
Mortensen, Clayton	R-R	6-4	180	4-10-85	4	4	4.22	11	11	0	0	60	59	31	28	6	22	48	.257	.310	.226	7.24	3.32
Mulder, Mark	L-L	6-6	215	8-5-77	3	0	2.25	3	3	0	0	16	14	4	4	1	7	9	.241	.000	.250	5.06	3.94
Mura, Kyle	R-R	6-4	215	11-24-84	3	5	2.74	11	10	0	0	62	71	24	19	6	10	25	.291	.269	.305	3.61	1.44
Ottavino, Adam	R-R	6-5	215	11-22-85	3	7	5.23	24	24	1	0	115	133	75	67	16	52	96	.291	.277	.297	7.49	4.06
Perdomo, Luis	R-R	6-0	170	4-27-84	2	2	4.50	15	0	0	1	18	18	12	9	2	6	22	.247	.310	.205	11.00	3.00
Rauschenberger, Cory	R-R	6-1	185	7-31-84	1	3	6.94	3	0	0	1	23	30	21	18	3	10	21	.309	.421	.237	8.10	3.86
Sadlowski, Kyle	R-R	6-3	190	6-19-84	2	1	5.02	15	5	0	0	38	42	22	21	3	21	10	.292	.277	.299	2.39	5.02
Salas, Fernando	R-R	6-2	200	5-30-85	7	3	3.65	60	0	0	25	74	65	31	30	12	16	100	.236	.226	.240	12.16	1.95
Scherer, Matt	R-R	6-5	230	1-20-83	0	0	2.08	5	0	0	0	4	4	1	1	1	0	5	.235	.400	.167	10.38	0.00
Todd, Jess	R-R	5-11	210	4-20-86	4	5	2.97	17	16	0	0	103	79	37	34	12	24	81	.216	.252	.196	7.08	2.10
Vander Weg, Scott	R-R	6-3	215	12-14-82	1	1	4.10	19	0	0	1	26	25	12	12	4	7	21	.260	.278	.250	7.18	2.39
Wainwright, Adam	R-R	6-7	230	8-30-81	0	0	0.00	1	1	0	0	5	4	0	0	0	0	7	.222	.167	.250	13.50	0.00
Walters, P.J.	R-R	6-4	200	3-12-85	1	2	3.25	6	6	0	0	36	35	17	13	5	8	34	.252	.378	.206	8.50	2.00
Webber, Nick	R-R	6-7	210	5-9-84	1	4	4.36	19	1	0	0	33	34	20	16	3	23	7	.262	.333	.240	1.91	6.27

Zimmermann, Rob	R-R	6-5	245	11-17-81	3	1	5.53	20	0	0	0	28	33	20	17	6	14	22	.303	.333	.288	7.16	4.55
Zuercher, Zach	L-L	6-2	215	4-10-84	1	1	5.34	29	0	0	0	30	36	20	18	7	18	23	.298	.304	.296	6.82	5.34

Fielding

Catcher	PCT	G	PO	A	E	DP	PB
Anderson	.987	16	131	20	2	0	2
Hill	1.000	4	20	3	0	0	0
Pagnozzi	.996	59	405	41	2	7	3
Yarbrough	.976	69	486	43	13	4	9

First Base	PCT	G	PO	A	E	DP
Brown	.987	43	376	14	5	45
Buckman	.983	20	157	13	3	13
Craig	1.000	2	9	0	0	1
Hamilton	.997	63	530	41	2	48
Hill	.967	12	109	8	4	7
Pagnozzi	1.000	1	4	0	0	1
Van Slyke	1.000	7	44	3	0	2

Second Base	PCT	G	PO	A	E	DP
Descalso	.962	9	17	34	2	6

	PCT	G	PO	A	E	DP
Garcia	.927	7	18	20	3	8
Maestrales	.909	2	4	6	1	0
Martinez	.986	96	205	278	7	67
Rowlett	.968	35	50	72	4	12
Ryan	1.000	1	1	0	0	0
Solano	.968	7	15	15	1	2

Third Base	PCT	G	PO	A	E	DP
Craig	.941	108	56	217	17	17
Garcia	.906	22	16	32	5	5
Greene	.875	4	1	6	1	1
Rowlett	.833	4	1	4	1	1
Ryan	1.000	2	3	4	0	0
Wallace	.964	11	7	20	1	2

Shortstop	PCT	G	PO	A	E	DP
Greene	.955	91	119	266	18	61

	PCT	G	PO	A	E	DP
Martinez	.957	33	39	96	6	15
Ryan	1.000	1	0	3	0	0
Solano	.967	20	34	55	3	10

Outfield	PCT	G	PO	A	E	DP
Brown	1.000	14	23	1	0	0
Craig	1.000	17	20	0	0	0
Gorsett	.971	19	33	0	1	0
Haerther	1.000	16	33	2	0	1
Hill	.909	9	10	0	1	0
Jay	1.000	93	247	3	0	1
Jones	1.000	34	66	4	0	0
Rapoport	.981	44	97	8	2	2
Robinson	.982	61	96	12	2	2
Rowlett	.983	45	57	1	1	0
Shorey	.978	96	167	7	4	3
Van Slyke	.833	6	4	1	1	0

PALM BEACH CARDINALS

HIGH CLASS A

FLORIDA STATE LEAGUE

Batting	B-T	HT	WT	DOB	AVG	vLH	vRH	G	AB	R	H	2B	3B	HR	RBI	BB	HBP	SH	SF	SO	SB	CS	SLG	OBP
Arburr, Matt	R-R	6-4	260	3-21-86	.208	.152	.243	47	173	32	36	7	0	9	27	26	1	0	1	68	5	0	.405	.313
Brown, Andrew	R-R	6-0	185	9-10-84	.330	.391	.308	24	88	14	29	8	0	4	15	11	1	0	0	25	0	0	.557	.410
Buckman, Brandon	L-L	6-6	205	2-14-84	.260	.212	.282	74	273	30	71	11	0	4	33	31	3	0	7	56	1	1	.344	.334
Cardona, Ismael	R-R	5-10	175	4-22-89	.000	.000	.000	1	3	0	0	0	0	0	0	0	0	0	0	0	1	0	.000	.000
Carpenter, David	R-R	6-2	200	7-15-85	.175	.222	.161	12	40	4	7	3	0	1	3	1	0	0	1	12	0	0	.325	.190
Cartie, Bryan	R-R	6-0	190	4-2-85	.264	.293	.247	77	258	24	68	19	0	3	35	31	3	5	5	41	2	1	.372	.343
Cruz, Arnoldi	R-R	5-11	205	8-18-86	.279	.245	.294	89	351	41	98	22	3	8	58	19	2	1	5	50	3	0	.427	.316
DeJesus, Antone	L-L	5-11	185	1-25-86	.278	.325	.257	85	255	41	71	4	4	0	11	45	9	6	0	52	8	6	.325	.405
Derba, Nick	R-R	5-10	190	9-9-85	.166	.213	.144	66	193	15	32	8	0	2	22	30	5	3	3	60	1	2	.238	.290
Descalso, Daniel	L-R	5-10	190	10-19-86	.243	.226	.250	115	403	57	98	24	2	8	50	33	10	5	5	53	7	7	.372	.313
Folli, Ateo	R-R	5-10	175	7-17-85	.153	.176	.147	32	85	9	13	1	1	0	6	4	1	1	1	10	1	1	.188	.198
Garcia, Isaias	R-R	5-10	180	8-20-84	.310	.267	.333	23	84	11	26	8	1	0	15	9	2	0	1	10	2	0	.429	.385
Gorsett, Luke	R-R	6-1	195	5-28-85	.229	.216	.235	75	258	28	59	13	1	5	30	24	8	1	1	57	2	4	.345	.313
Henley, Tyler	L-L	5-10	200	6-10-85	.280	.291	.274	84	329	47	92	26	4	6	40	27	6	2	4	51	7	6	.438	.342
Hill, Steven	R-R	5-11	190	3-14-85	.285	.340	.261	46	172	28	49	11	2	9	34	15	0	2	0	42	0	0	.529	.339
Jones, Daryl	L-L	5-11	180	6-25-87	.326	.340	.319	87	307	43	100	11	7	3	35	33	9	2	1	67	18	5	.476	.406
Kingrey, Charlie	L-L	6-2	210	1-19-85	.256	.302	.234	44	160	23	41	4	1	5	19	16	0	0	0	39	0	1	.388	.324
Kozma, Pete	R-R	6-0	170	4-11-88	.130	.103	.146	24	77	4	10	4	0	0	10	10	1	3	3	27	0	1	.182	.231
Luna, Aaron	R-R	5-11	200	3-28-87	.080	.125	.059	13	25	4	2	0	0	0	3	5	0	0	0	8	0	0	.080	.303
Marmol, Oliver	R-R	5-10	165	7-2-86	.180	.151	.203	44	122	16	22	5	1	1	14	8	3	2	0	29	10	0	.262	.248
Mulligan, Casey	R-R	6-2	190	10-5-87	.000	.000	.000	5	13	1	0	0	0	0	0	1	1	0	0	7	0	0	.000	.133
Nelson, Dan	B-R	5-11	180	2-12-84	.185	.200	.182	20	54	4	10	3	0	0	11	10	0	0	1	11	1	0	.241	.308
2-team total (10 Jupiter)					.165	—	—	30	85	9	14	5	0	0	15	13	0	0	2	18	2	0	.224	.270
Pham, Tommy	R-R	6-1	175	3-8-88	.146	.333	.069	27	82	9	12	3	0	1	7	7	1	2	0	30	1	1	.220	.222
Rapoport, James	L-L	5-11	160	6-25-85	.321	.375	.303	31	131	24	42	3	1	1	13	10	0	2	1	18	11	3	.382	.366
Rasmus, Colby	L-L	6-2	195	8-11-86	.000	.000	.000	3	9	1	0	0	0	0	0	1	1	0	0	3	0	0	.000	.182
Ryan, Brendan	R-R	6-2	195	3-26-82	.250	.750	.000	3	12	1	3	1	0	0	1	0	0	0	0	1	1	1	.333	.308
Solano, Donovan	R-R	5-10	165	12-17-87	.286	.301	.279	107	402	56	115	15	4	1	31	37	2	4	0	63	1	2	.351	.349
Southard, Nathan	R-R	5-10	185	10-27-83	.169	.103	.222	24	65	9	11	3	0	0	3	9	2	1	0	16	1	0	.215	.289
Van Slyke, A.J.	L-R	6-2	210	11-19-83	.111	.000	.125	4	9	2	1	0	0	0	1	2	0	0	0	2	0	0	.111	.273
Vasquez, Paul	R-R	5-10	160	3-7-85	.226	.294	.200	17	62	8	14	2	0	0	4	2	0	0	0	9	1	1	.258	.258

Pitching	B-T	HT	WT	DOB	W	L	ERA	G	GS	CG	SV	IP	H	R	ER	HR	BB	SO	AVG	vLH	vRH	K/9	BB/9
Additon, Nicholas	L-L	6-3	170	12-16-87	2	0	0.50	3	3	1	0	18	11	2	1	1	5	13	.167	.182	.159	6.50	2.50
Bilardello, Davis	L-L	6-3	190	12-3-84	6	1	4.25	33	0	0	2	42	58	23	20	2	15	27	.339	.235	.408	5.74	3.19
Castillo, Richard	R-R	5-11	165	10-11-89	1	0	1.13	6	2	0	0	16	12	3	2	0	8	19	.222	.158	.257	10.69	4.50
Clement, Matt	R-R	6-3	210	8-12-74	1	0	0.00	1	1	0	0	6	1	0	0	0	5	.056	.000	.083	7.50	0.00
Daley, Gary	R-R	6-3	200	11-1-85	0	0	6.75	4	0	0	0	3	1	2	2	0	4	1	.143	.250	.000	3.38	13.50
Daman, Wayne	R-R	6-2	195	10-1-84	0	1	5.06	13	0	0	0	21	17	12	12	3	13	17	.224	.185	.245	7.17	5.48
Daniels, Adam	L-L	6-2	190	8-16-82	1	0	0.00	2	0	0	2	2	0	0	0	0	1	1	.000	.000	.000	4.50	4.50
Degerman, Eddie	R-R	6-4	205	9-14-83	3	1	5.96	24	5	0	0	54	56	42	36	5	35	50	.267	.240	.281	8.28	5.80
Dew, Josh	R-R	6-2	225	1-15-85	3	1	1.73	21	0	0	5	26	17	5	5	0	9	33	.193	.333	.141	11.42	3.12
Diapoules, Mark	R-R	6-2	200	5-31-88	3	3	4.29	11	10	0	0	57	61	34	27	4	29	43	.280	.283	.278	6.83	4.61
Dickson, Brandon	R-R	6-5	190	11-3-84	7	8	3.51	23	17	1	1	115	119	49	45	7	37	66	.269	.276	.264	5.15	2.89
Fiske, Justin	L-L	5-11	185	9-3-84	0	0	2.08	3	0	0	0	4	1	1	1	0	2	6	.067	.333	.000	12.46	4.15
Freeman, Sam	L-L	5-11	170	6-24-87	0	0	0.00	1	0	0	0	1	0	0	0	0	1	4	.000	.000	.000	18.00	4.50
Furnish, Brad	B-L	6-1	185	1-19-85	8	8	5.17	25	20	1	0	115	108	69	66	14	51	74	.247	.279	.234	5.79	3.99
Garceau, Shaun	B-R	6-1	185	8-28-87	8	4	3.42	18	17	0	0	97	69	38	37	5	55	56	.201	.206	.198	5.18	5.09
Garner, Brandon	R-R	6-0	165	8-27-86	0	1	5.28	19	0	0	0	31	35	22	18	3	18	16	.307	.333	.290	4.70	5.28

Gonzalez, Marco	R-R	6-2	205	5-28-84	2	1	1.23	11	0	0	0	15	12	6	2	0	4	5	.231	.353	.171	3.07	2.45
Hernandez, Elvis	R-R	6-3	180	4-27-85	5	2	5.04	27	6	0	0	61	61	38	34	7	32	62	.265	.248	.279	9.20	4.75
Herron, Ty	R-R	6-3	190	8-5-86	2	2	2.70	12	9	0	1	57	49	18	17	5	11	43	.234	.207	.252	6.83	1.75
Isringhausen, Jason	R-R	6-3	230	9-7-72	0	0	0.00	1	1	0	0	2	1	0	0	0	0	1	.143	.250	.000	4.50	0.00
King, Blake	R-R	6-1	195	4-11-87	1	3	4.64	15	7	0	0	43	32	27	22	1	33	45	.218	.300	.161	9.49	6.96
Kopp, David	R-R	6-3	205	10-22-85	1	3	3.76	10	6	0	1	38	38	21	16	1	15	30	.262	.163	.304	7.04	3.52
Maiques, Kenny	R-R	6-1	185	6-25-85	1	3	6.33	27	0	0	3	27	21	22	19	0	33	23	.210	.324	.152	7.67	11.00
Mateo, Jose	R-R	6-2	180	8-31-86	0	1	7.50	1	1	1	0	6	7	6	5	1	3	2	.304	.000	.318	3.00	4.50
McCormick, Mark	R-R	6-2	195	10-15-83	0	1	3.34	11	6	0	0	35	31	19	13	2	24	34	.231	.213	.241	8.74	6.17
Mikrut, Jon	R-R	6-4	195	11-22-82	1	1	0.55	14	0	0	5	16	9	2	1	0	4	15	.158	.176	.150	8.27	2.20
Mulder, Mark	L-L	6-6	215	8-5-77	0	0	1.80	1	1	0	0	5	6	2	1	0	1	0	.300	.143	.385	1.80	0.00
Mura, Kyle	R-R	6-4	215	11-24-84	5	4	4.21	16	11	0	0	73	81	39	34	2	9	54	.282	.318	.261	6.69	1.11
Norrick, Tyler	L-L	6-3	190	9-27-83	1	2	6.87	5	5	0	0	18	19	14	14	2	11	32	.271	.111	.327	10.80	5.40
Parise, Pete	R-R	6-1	185	12-5-84	2	1	2.25	11	0	0	0	16	13	4	4	2	7	12	.232	.278	.211	6.75	3.94
Sadlowski, Kyle	R-R	6-3	190	6-19-84	3	1	3.89	11	5	0	2	42	41	18	18	2	12	34	.259	.352	.212	7.34	2.59
Samuel, Francisco	R-R	6-1	150	12-20-86	4	6	3.04	54	0	0	29	56	39	20	19	3	48	85	.196	.215	.183	13.58	7.67
Todd, Jess	R-R	5-11	210	4-20-86	3	0	1.65	7	4	0	1	27	18	7	5	0	7	35	.184	.206	.172	11.52	2.30
Tucker, Cardoza	R-R	6-2	180	11-11-84	0	2	4.22	10	0	0	1	11	18	10	5	0	11	8	.360	.375	.346	6.75	9.28

Fielding

Catcher	PCT	G	PO	A	E	DP	PB
Cardona	1.000	1	9	0	0	0	0
Carpenter	1.000	10	89	7	0	2	2
Cruz	.982	43	302	30	6	5	7
Derba	.992	65	443	49	4	6	5
Hill	1.000	5	36	1	0	0	1
Mulligan	1.000	4	17	3	0	0	0
Vasquez	.964	16	98	9	4	1	2

First Base	PCT	G	PO	A	E	DP
Arburr	.992	42	328	30	3	40
Brown	.975	18	146	11	4	14
Buckman	.980	48	406	26	9	48
Cruz	.986	9	61	4	1	10
Hill	.968	18	143	10	5	15
Nelson	1.000	4	22	2	0	2
Van Slyke	1.000	3	22	1	0	1

Second Base	PCT	G	PO	A	E	DP
Descalso	.976	101	214	271	12	76

	PCT	G	PO	A	E	DP
Folli	.924	14	31	30	5	10
Marmol	.978	11	17	28	1	5
Solano	.974	14	23	53	2	11

Third Base	PCT	G	PO	A	E	DP
Cartie	.948	65	42	105	8	12
Cruz	.933	32	17	53	5	3
Descalso	.667	2	0	2	1	0
Folli	.875	10	5	9	2	1
Garcia	.923	5	5	7	1	2
Hill	1.000	1	0	1	0	0
Mulligan	1.000	1	1	1	0	1
Nelson	.962	15	5	20	1	1
Solano	1.000	19	14	28	0	5

Shortstop	PCT	G	PO	A	E	DP
Descalso	.878	12	17	26	6	7
Folli	.846	5	3	8	2	1
Kozma	.962	24	35	65	4	14
Marmol	.925	28	35	89	10	25

	PCT	G	PO	A	E	DP
Ryan	.947	3	5	13	1	0
Solano	.958	73	119	219	15	50

Outfield	PCT	G	PO	A	E	DP
DeJesus	.995	82	180	10	1	3
Gorsett	.967	51	86	2	3	1
Henley	.971	78	124	8	4	0
Hill	1.000	8	10	0	0	0
Jones	.981	86	152	6	3	1
Kingrey	.973	34	71	1	2	0
Luna	1.000	7	8	1	0	0
Marmol	—	1	0	0	0	0
Pham	1.000	26	43	2	0	1
Rapoport	.964	30	76	4	3	0
Rasmus	1.000	3	8	1	0	0
Solano	1.000	1	1	0	0	0
Southard	1.000	21	32	0	0	0

QUAD CITIES RIVER BANDITS   LOW CLASS A

MIDWEST LEAGUE

Batting	B-T	HT	WT	DOB	AVG	vLH	vRH	G	AB	R	H	2B	3B	HR	RBI	BB	HBP	SH	SF	SO	SB	CS	SLG	OBP
Arburr, Matt	R-R	6-4	260	3-21-86	.245	.250	.243	59	208	28	51	6	0	13	33	18	1	1	0	82	0	0	.462	.308
Bolivar, Domnit	R-R	5-11	165	5-12-89	.257	.276	.250	91	343	28	88	16	5	7	36	17	0	0	1	89	6	5	.394	.291
Brown, Andrew	R-R	6-0	185	9-10-84	.274	.320	.261	34	117	18	32	10	0	5	23	17	1	0	1	30	0	1	.487	.368
Cardona, Ismael	R-R	5-10	175	4-22-89	.333	.333	.333	5	15	1	5	0	0	3	2	0	0	0	0	4	0	0	.400	.412
Carpenter, David	R-R	6-2	200	7-15-85	.280	.167	.316	8	25	3	7	1	1	0	5	5	0	1	0	6	0	0	.400	.400
Chambers, Adron	L-L	5-10	185	10-8-86	.238	.170	.249	95	336	56	80	13	7	3	25	33	10	2	3	66	13	8	.345	.322
De La Cruz, Luis	R-R	5-10	164	5-6-89	.167	.083	.188	34	120	11	20	3	0	1	7	3	0	1	1	17	0	0	.217	.185
Edwards, Jonathan	R-R	6-5	230	1-8-88	.269	.500	.219	22	78	7	21	3	0	4	13	9	0	0	2	21	2	1	.462	.337
Espinoza, Roberto	R-R	5-10	165	3-8-89	.204	.125	.239	34	103	11	21	6	0	1	14	14	2	1	1	36	0	2	.291	.308
Folli, Ateo	B-R	5-10	175	7-17-85	.264	.200	.278	45	140	22	37	8	2	2	14	12	1	2	2	20	5	2	.393	.335
Garcia, Jose	R-R	5-11	170	2-11-88	.175	.226	.160	44	137	21	24	6	1	0	5	14	2	1	0	22	3	2	.234	.261
Ingram, D'Marcus	R-R	5-9	190	3-30-88	.235	.243	.232	76	255	37	60	5	1	4	16	24	2	0	2	47	7	8	.310	.314
Kingrey, Charlie	L-L	6-2	210	1-19-85	.289	.395	.267	68	249	33	72	18	1	6	40	23	3	0	1	60	4	2	.442	.355
Kozma, Pete	R-R	6-0	170	4-11-88	.284	.323	.271	99	377	58	107	20	4	5	40	45	5	1	6	69	12	5	.398	.363
Luna, Aaron	R-R	5-11	200	3-28-87	.234	.231	.237	21	64	11	15	2	1	6	12	13	5	0	0	19	1	0	.578	.402
Marmol, Oliver	R-R	5-10	165	7-2-86	.195	.234	.178	47	154	19	30	7	1	0	12	10	6	3	0	40	12	3	.253	.271
Morales, Osvaldo	R-R	6-2	217	7-4-87	.194	.267	.159	27	93	5	18	3	1	2	6	5	1	0	1	45	0	0	.312	.240
Murphy, Blake	R-R	6-2	215	5-19-85	.210	.071	.250	21	62	5	13	1	0	2	7	10	4	0	1	22	0	0	.323	.351
Oeder, Ross	R-R	5-8	165	4-19-86	.183	.212	.171	32	109	12	20	3	0	5	15	8	2	2	0	27	1	2	.349	.252
Pelt, Charlie	L-R	6-0	203	12-28-84	.152	.000	.172	10	33	3	5	1	0	1	5	2	0	0	0	10	0	0	.273	.200
Peoples, Nicholas	R-R	5-11	190	8-10-84	.183	.158	.195	50	180	21	33	7	0	3	17	17	5	2	2	46	2	2	.272	.270
Pham, Tommy	R-R	6-1	175	3-8-88	.218	.215	.219	86	312	51	68	11	4	17	49	27	3	2	2	126	17	4	.442	.285
Pupo, Carlos	R-R	6-4	240	8-29-85	.184	.190	.182	38	141	12	26	7	0	4	17	5	2	1	0	42	0	0	.319	.223
Riportella, Beau	R-R	6-3	200	8-20-88	.094	.125	.083	11	32	2	3	1	0	0	1	4	0	0	0	5	0	0	.125	.194
Rivera, Francisco	L-L	5-11	170	12-3-88	.291	.256	.298	71	247	21	72	20	0	1	34	23	2	1	6	37	3	5	.385	.349
Roberson, Justin	R-R	5-11	170	9-16-84	.197	.190	.200	20	71	14	14	3	0	0	6	8	1	0	1	20	7	0	.239	.284
Smith, Curt	R-R	6-0	205	9-9-86	.244	.400	.225	11	45	6	11	4	0	0	10	0	1	0	1	11	0	0	.333	.255
Vasquez, Niko	R-R	5-11	175	2-26-89	.128	.167	.121	11	39	6	5	1	0	0	3	4	0	1	1	17	0	0	.154	.205
Vasquez, Paul	R-R	5-10	160	3-7-85	.331	.371	.318	40	142	18	47	13	2	4	25	5	9	2	1	20	0	1	.535	.389
Wallace, Brett	L-R	6-1	245	8-26-86	.327	.370	.308	41	153	28	50	8	1	5	25	17	7	0	0	32	0	0	.490	.418

Pitching

Pitching	B-T	HT	WT	DOB	W	L	ERA	G	GS	CG	SV	IP	H	R	ER	HR	BB	SO	AVG	vLH	vRH	K/9	BB/9
Additon, Nicholas	L-L	6-3	170	12-16-87	9	5	2.50	25	19	0	1	119	92	41	33	12	35	108	.214	.214	.215	8.17	2.65
Bradford, Jared	R-R	6-1	177	4-3-86	2	3	3.20	17	3	0	1	39	42	18	14	2	7	28	.273	.260	.286	6.41	1.60
Broderick, Brian	R-R	6-6	205	9-1-86	3	6	4.67	19	12	0	3	81	98	45	42	5	12	38	.300	.321	.278	4.22	1.33
Castillo, Richard	R-R	5-11	165	10-11-89	8	4	2.62	13	13	0	0	79	64	26	23	11	20	69	.227	.246	.211	7.86	2.28
Daman, Wayne	R-R	6-2	195	10-1-84	5	2	2.49	27	0	0	2	47	41	16	13	4	11	40	.246	.284	.220	7.66	2.11
Diapoules, Mark	R-R	6-2	200	5-31-88	5	1	3.56	13	8	0	2	56	48	27	22	3	21	52	.229	.284	.176	8.41	3.40
Eager, Thomas	R-R	6-2	200	8-12-85	2	2	5.92	15	9	0	0	52	56	39	34	5	27	30	.277	.190	.371	5.23	4.70
Fick, Chuck	R-R	6-5	187	11-20-85	6	5	3.17	20	13	0	0	94	97	50	33	6	15	67	.264	.292	.240	6.44	1.44
Fiske, Justin	L-L	5-11	185	9-3-84	0	0	5.40	11	0	0	1	12	16	7	7	1	3	16	.327	.167	.419	12.34	2.31
Frevert, Matt	R-R	6-1	190	11-16-86	0	0	0.00	3	0	0	0	4	4	0	0	0	3	0	.267	.143	.375	0.00	6.75
Garceau, Shaun	B-R	6-1	185	8-28-87	0	2	2.08	7	5	0	0	26	27	9	6	0	6	22	.262	.242	.293	7.62	2.08
Garner, Brandon	R-R	6-0	165	8-27-86	0	1	4.80	15	0	0	0	15	22	11	8	1	8	11	.328	.364	.294	6.60	4.80
Gonzalez, Dylan	R-R	6-3	175	3-7-85	1	3	5.31	26	0	0	1	42	57	30	25	7	15	41	.328	.389	.284	8.72	3.19
Hooker, Deryk	R-R	6-4	185	6-21-90	0	1	1.61	4	4	0	0	22	20	5	4	2	6	18	.241	.233	.250	7.25	2.42
King, Blake	R-R	6-2	195	4-11-87	2	5	4.41	16	8	0	0	51	47	29	25	2	49	60	.251	.236	.265	10.59	8.65
Kulik, Ryan	L-L	5-11	205	12-3-85	5	5	5.53	12	12	0	0	57	86	53	35	4	10	38	.352	.431	.328	6.00	1.58
Lynn, Lance	R-R	6-5	250	5-12-87	0	1	2.25	2	2	0	0	8	8	2	2	2	2	7	.258	.294	.214	7.88	2.25
Maiques, Kenny	R-R	6-1	185	6-25-85	1	1	5.63	8	0	0	0	8	7	6	5	0	10	7	.241	.500	.105	7.88	11.25
Maj, Jameson	R-R	6-4	225	10-22-85	0	3	5.31	5	3	0	1	20	23	12	12	2	4	17	.288	.225	.350	7.52	1.77
McGregor, Scott	R-R	6-2	193	12-19-86	0	0	2.84	3	0	0	0	6	9	3	2	0	1	2	.321	.294	.364	2.84	1.42
Parise, Pete	R-R	6-1	185	12-5-84	3	1	2.23	36	0	0	13	48	42	16	12	5	7	50	.225	.221	.228	9.31	1.30
Rondon, Jorge	R-R	6-1	175	9-16-88	1	0	3.24	8	0	0	0	8	11	4	3	0	3	5	.367	.333	.389	5.40	3.24
Rosales, Andres	R-R	6-0	140	6-13-88	0	1	3.21	4	2	0	1	14	12	5	5	2	8	8	.235	.217	.250	5.14	5.14
Samuel, Francisco	R-R	6-1	150	12-20-86	2	0	1.23	5	0	0	1	7	4	3	1	0	5	9	.154	.333	.000	11.05	6.14
Sanchez, Eduardo	R-R	5-11	155	2-16-89	5	1	2.86	24	5	0	1	57	40	23	18	1	25	55	.209	.218	.198	8.74	3.97
Spade, Matt	L-L	5-11	180	4-26-87	2	2	3.61	47	0	0	1	52	44	25	21	4	24	48	.230	.177	.256	8.25	4.13
Stambaugh, J.D.	L-L	6-2	200	10-25-84	2	5	6.43	15	4	0	1	35	47	33	25	2	7	27	.324	.354	.309	6.94	1.80
Tucker, Cardoza	R-R	6-2	180	11-11-84	3	2	8.14	15	1	0	4	24	28	24	22	3	14	31	.275	.288	.260	11.47	5.18
Wilson, Joshua	R-R	5-11	180	9-6-86	1	5	4.21	15	11	0	1	68	76	37	32	7	18	41	.284	.323	.248	5.40	2.37

Fielding

Catcher	PCT	G	PO	A	E	DP	PB
Cardona	.971	5	33	1	1	0	3
Carpenter	1.000	8	69	11	0	0	2
De La Cruz	.989	33	231	32	3	3	7
Espinoza	.988	34	227	24	3	1	7
Murphy	.994	19	146	16	1	2	1
P. Vasquez	.978	38	239	33	6	6	7

First Base	PCT	G	PO	A	E	DP
Arburr	.982	14	107	4	2	5
Brown	.988	31	234	14	3	28
Morales	.978	11	84	4	2	8
Pelt	.947	5	34	2	2	1
Pupo	.993	31	259	22	2	26
Rivera	.987	47	377	14	5	38
Smith	.941	4	29	3	2	4

Second Base	PCT	G	PO	A	E	DP
Bolivar	.981	10	22	30	1	5

	PCT	G	PO	A	E	DP
Folli	.962	43	91	109	8	30
Garcia	.961	24	36	62	4	11
Marmol	.949	29	52	78	7	16
Oeder	.967	23	56	63	4	22
Peoples	.979	9	25	21	1	5

Third Base	PCT	G	PO	A	E	DP
Bolivar	.883	74	46	128	23	13
Brown	.933	6	4	10	1	0
Folli	—	1	0	0	0	0
Garcia	.846	11	4	18	4	1
Kozma	1.000	2	2	4	0	0
Oeder	.889	7	3	13	2	1
Wallace	.949	36	31	62	5	10

Shortstop	PCT	G	PO	A	E	DP
Bolivar	.897	7	8	18	3	4
Garcia	.972	7	15	20	1	7
Kozma	.956	90	129	264	18	55

	PCT	G	PO	A	E	DP
Marmol	.909	18	27	43	7	12
Oeder	1.000	2	2	5	0	0
N. Vasquez	.949	11	12	25	2	8

Outfield	PCT	G	PO	A	E	DP
Arburr	1.000	25	33	2	0	0
Chambers	.972	89	165	8	5	1
Edwards	.946	21	34	1	2	0
Ingram	.933	74	155	11	12	3
Kingrey	.990	56	100	3	1	2
Luna	1.000	14	20	2	0	0
Peoples	.935	20	40	3	3	1
Pham	.990	83	180	11	2	5
Riportella	.882	10	15	0	2	0
Rivera	1.000	2	3	0	0	0
Roberson	.906	17	29	0	3	0

BATAVIA MUCKDOGS   SHORT-SEASON

NEW YORK-PENN LEAGUE

Batting	B-T	HT	WT	DOB	AVG	vLH	vRH	G	AB	R	H	2B	3B	HR	RBI	BB	HBP	SH	SF	SO	SB	CS	SLG	OBP
Bolivar, Domnit	R-R	5-11	165	5-12-89	.258	.231	.268	26	97	12	25	5	2	1	10	3	0	1	1	18	5	2	.381	.277
Cardona, Ismael	R-R	5-10	175	4-22-89	.143	.000	.200	3	7	0	1	0	0	0	0	0	0	0	0	1	0	0	.143	.143
Castellanos, Alex	R-R	5-11	180	8-4-86	.269	.091	.400	10	26	6	7	2	2	0	4	2	1	0	0	7	0	1	.500	.345
Curtis, Jermaine	R-R	5-11	190	7-10-87	.305	.462	.256	43	164	25	50	14	1	2	20	17	5	0	2	24	4	1	.439	.383
Cutler, Charlie	L-R	6-0	200	7-29-86	.303	.333	.295	40	142	24	43	4	1	3	18	10	4	1	0	17	0	0	.408	.365
Edwards, Jonathan	R-R	6-5	230	1-8-88	.304	.257	.328	31	102	18	31	6	1	6	16	19	3	0	0	40	0	0	.559	.427
Garcia, Jose	R-R	5-11	170	2-11-88	.240	.238	.241	70	271	48	65	13	1	1	22	25	4	3	2	53	26	3	.306	.311
Gomez, Edwin	R-R	5-11	170	3-10-88	.256	.245	.261	48	164	23	42	9	5	1	19	17	2	0	1	54	1	4	.390	.332
Lilley, Brett	L-R	5-8	170	7-30-85	.296	.211	.343	19	54	5	16	3	0	0	6	7	2	2	1	8	0	1	.352	.391
Martinez, Jairo	R-R	6-1	180	5-27-87	.107	.000	.214	13	28	2	3	1	0	0	2	0	0	0	0	14	0	0	.143	.107
Morales, Osvaldo	R-R	6-2	217	7-4-87	.067	.111	.000	6	15	3	1	1	0	0	1	1	1	0	0	6	0	0	.133	.176
Murphy, Blake	R-R	6-2	215	5-19-85	.242	.346	.200	24	91	11	22	8	1	3	13	10	2	0	0	34	0	0	.451	.330
Parejo, Frederick	R-R	6-0	165	7-5-90	.278	.268	.281	55	209	24	58	8	0	1	21	14	3	0	3	35	4	2	.330	.328
Peterson, Shane	L-L	6-0	195	2-11-88	.291	.242	.311	65	230	35	67	20	2	1	39	39	4	0	2	65	3	2	.409	.400
Riportella, Beau	R-R	6-3	200	8-20-88	.220	.211	.225	40	127	17	28	8	0	0	8	3	0	3	2	32	5	5	.283	.235
Rosa, Christian	R-R	5-8	175	9-3-86	.286	.233	.323	32	105	17	30	4	1	2	12	13	1	1	2	26	4	1	.400	.364
Scruggs, Xavier	R-R	6-1	210	9-23-87	.219	.164	.243	61	215	23	47	17	0	6	33	19	5	0	2	68	0	1	.381	.295
Sedbrook, Colt	R-R	5-11	180	7-28-85	.305	.291	.311	71	275	38	84	9	5	2	33	24	17	2	1	44	13	8	.396	.394
Swauger, Chris	L-L	6-0	195	8-11-86	.291	.304	.286	50	179	28	52	9	1	7	34	12	5	1	2	42	0	0	.469	.348
Vera, Nick	R-R	6-1	185	8-13-85	.167	.000	.250	2	6	0	1	0	0	0	0	1	0	0	0	1	0	0	.167	.286

Pitching	B-T	HT	WT	DOB	W	L	ERA	G	GS	CG	SV	IP	H	R	ER	HR	BB	SO	AVG	vLH	vRH	K/9	BB/9
Brown, George	L-L	6-1	195	6-18-86	0	3	3.42	17	6	0	3	47	51	20	18	3	8	47	.276	.243	.284	8.94	1.52
Buursma, Jason	R-R	6-3	200	9-9-85	1	3	2.35	25	0	0	3	23	24	10	6	1	9	18	.282	.276	.286	7.04	3.52
Cardenas, Hector	L-L	6-3	180	12-14-86	5	0	1.83	15	2	0	0	34	27	10	7	0	13	27	.229	.344	.186	7.08	3.41
Delgado, Ramon	R-R	6-3	195	9-3-86	6	1	2.96	15	7	0	0	55	55	20	18	1	13	46	.257	.333	.211	7.57	2.14
Eager, Thomas	R-R	6-2	200	8-12-85	6	3	1.76	14	9	0	0	56	37	12	11	1	27	40	.193	.162	.210	6.39	4.31
Gorgen, Scott	R-R	5-10	190	1-27-87	5	2	2.32	14	6	0	0	54	37	14	14	3	17	60	.186	.158	.203	9.94	2.82
Hester, Josh	R-R	6-1	185	9-3-85	2	2	4.31	14	7	0	0	48	64	31	23	3	9	47	.312	.338	.296	8.81	1.69
Kulik, Ryan	L-L	5-11	205	12-3-85	0	0	0.00	2	0	0	0	6	3	1	0	0	0	5	.150	.286	.077	7.50	0.00
Lugo, Rigoberto	R-R	5-11	196	3-7-89	0	1	7.40	21	0	0	1	21	24	19	17	2	15	21	.286	.444	.211	9.15	6.53
Lynn, Lance	R-R	6-5	250	5-12-87	1	0	0.96	6	4	0	0	19	12	5	2	0	4	22	.179	.167	.189	10.61	1.93
Maj, Jameson	R-R	6-4	225	10-22-85	2	2	3.63	9	5	0	1	40	39	19	16	2	4	37	.260	.263	.258	8.39	0.91
Mayes, LaCurtis	R-R	5-11	185	8-2-88	4	0	3.29	13	0	0	0	14	12	8	5	2	6	20	.231	.348	.138	13.17	3.95
Nieto, Arquimedes	R-R	6-0	175	4-28-89	6	1	2.95	15	9	0	0	58	53	24	19	3	18	42	.241	.216	.263	6.52	2.79
Pitts, Zach	R-R	6-3	190	3-30-86	1	5	3.31	14	7	0	0	52	47	28	19	2	15	38	.232	.247	.219	6.62	2.61
Reifer, Adam	R-R	6-2	195	6-3-86	2	1	2.97	32	0	0	22	30	18	14	10	2	15	41	.162	.086	.197	12.16	4.45
Richardson, Dan	R-R	6-2	195	3-21-85	0	1	7.85	19	0	0	0	18	17	16	16	2	18	9	.250	.346	.190	4.42	8.84
Tapia, Angel	R-R	6-1	198	2-6-88	4	2	3.86	15	9	0	0	54	59	28	23	4	28	36	.288	.244	.315	6.04	4.70
Veres, Adam	R-R	6-4	230	3-19-88	1	1	4.35	6	3	0	0	21	26	11	10	2	7	26	.313	.333	.304	11.32	3.05

Fielding

Catcher	PCT	G	PO	A	E	DP	PB
Cardona	1.000	3	20	3	0	0	0
Cutler	.990	37	273	17	3	1	7
Murphy	.974	19	141	9	4	1	2
Rosa	.981	19	153	5	3	2	2

First Base	PCT	G	PO	A	E	DP
Morales	1.000	4	16	1	0	4
Peterson	1.000	13	118	6	0	9
Scruggs	.978	61	491	32	12	66
Swauger	1.000	1	9	0	0	1

Second Base	PCT	G	PO	A	E	DP
Castellanos	.933	8	9	19	2	5
Garcia	.992	29	55	69	1	20
Lilley	.968	17	25	36	2	9
Sedbrook	.978	29	57	76	3	26

Third Base	PCT	G	PO	A	E	DP
Castellanos	—	2	0	0	0	0
Curtis	.958	39	32	81	5	7
Garcia	.960	38	22	74	4	13
Vera	.778	2	2	5	2	1

Shortstop	PCT	G	PO	A	E	DP
Bolivar	.911	25	24	78	10	19
Garcia	.880	9	17	27	6	9
Sedbrook	.906	43	59	114	18	26

Outfield	PCT	G	PO	A	E	DP
Edwards	.922	27	44	3	4	1
Gomez	.926	39	61	2	5	1
Martinez	1.000	10	7	0	0	0
Parejo	.939	53	105	3	7	0
Peterson	.988	50	77	5	1	2
Riportella	.973	35	73	0	2	0
Swauger	.927	25	37	1	3	0

JOHNSON CITY CARDINALS ROOKIE
APPALACHIAN LEAGUE

Batting	B-T	HT	WT	DOB	AVG	vLH	vRH	G	AB	R	H	2B	3B	HR	RBI	BB	HBP	SH	SF	SO	SB	CS	SLG	OBP
Bogany, Jarred	R-R	6-3	200	1-4-87	.260	.250	.263	40	123	18	32	10	1	1	15	13	1	0	1	42	5	4	.382	.333
Castellanos, Alex	R-R	5-11	180	8-4-86	.298	.270	.306	49	181	42	54	14	4	7	31	8	8	1	1	45	20	2	.536	.354
Castillo, Yunier	B-R	6-0	160	5-15-89	.130	.000	.150	6	23	3	3	0	0	0	2	0	0	1	1	7	0	0	.130	.125
Castro, Ivan	R-R	6-0	185	11-17-87	.237	.125	.261	39	139	10	33	8	0	3	21	12	0	0	1	25	0	0	.360	.296
Cawley, Jack	R-R	6-2	205	3-2-86	.330	.471	.304	33	109	24	36	7	1	0	18	18	1	1	1	20	5	3	.413	.426
Cruz, Paul	L-L	6-0	190	9-20-85	.183	.000	.194	44	131	18	24	5	1	1	9	19	0	1	1	20	4	3	.260	.285
Hage, Joey	R-R	6-0	180	2-17-89	.272	.290	.268	37	158	19	43	5	0	1	17	5	1	3	0	27	4	6	.323	.299
Lara, Edgar	R-R	6-3	210	3-2-89	.267	.212	.281	45	161	21	43	11	0	5	21	15	3	0	2	60	2	2	.429	.337
Lilley, Brett	L-R	5-8	170	7-30-85	.319	.286	.324	32	119	17	38	4	2	0	12	16	11	0	0	14	1	4	.387	.445
Martinez, Jairo	R-R	6-1	180	5-27-87	.247	.412	.206	30	85	11	21	2	0	4	17	14	3	0	1	30	1	1	.412	.369
Mateo, Luis	R-R	6-0	160	5-23-90	.284	.500	.243	20	88	12	25	0	1	1	6	3	1	0	1	17	8	2	.341	.312
Mitchell, Travis	R-R	6-3	185	9-27-87	.202	.143	.214	54	168	24	34	7	2	3	18	12	1	3	1	65	13	2	.321	.258
Morales, Osvaldo	R-R	6-2	217	7-4-87	.250	.200	.260	47	152	30	38	12	1	12	28	18	5	0	2	65	1	0	.579	.345
Noland, Rickey	R-R	6-0	215	11-4-85	.231	.083	.296	20	39	5	9	2	0	1	4	4	4	1	1	6	0	0	.359	.354
Rigoli, Matt	R-R	5-11	210	11-19-85	.205	.154	.214	32	83	10	17	5	0	2	9	12	6	1	1	28	0	0	.337	.343
Rodriguez, Ryde	B-R	6-3	232	2-2-88	.333	.500	.308	5	15	1	5	1	0	0	1	1	1	0	0	1	0	0	.400	.412
Smith, Curt	R-R	6-0	205	9-9-86	.378	.324	.391	47	193	34	73	14	1	8	49	11	3	0	1	36	3	4	.585	.418
Toribio, Guillermo	B-R	6-0	160	3-3-87	.212	.172	.222	42	146	20	31	2	0	0	5	22	0	2	1	43	11	4	.226	.314
Vasquez, Niko	R-R	5-11	175	2-26-89	.317	.325	.315	55	208	42	66	16	1	4	25	29	6	3	0	52	8	2	.462	.416

Pitching	B-T	HT	WT	DOB	W	L	ERA	G	GS	CG	SV	IP	H	R	ER	HR	BB	SO	AVG	vLH	vRH	K/9	BB/9
Blazek, Michael	R-R	6-0	180	3-16-89	1	4	5.05	13	9	0	0	46	49	33	26	4	16	47	.263	.333	.225	9.13	3.11
Bravo, Jonny	L-L	5-7	175	8-23-86	1	3	3.34	10	3	0	1	35	35	17	13	2	10	48	.254	.192	.268	12.34	2.57
Flores, Miguel	R-R	6-0	178	1-2-88	1	0	0.00	2	1	0	0	7	6	1	0	0	2	4	.231	.067	.455	4.91	2.45
Fornataro, Eric	R-R	6-1	195	1-2-88	0	1	2.57	2	1	0	1	7	5	4	2	0	3	6	.172	.214	.133	7.71	3.86
Freeman, Sam	R-L	5-11	170	6-24-87	4	1	3.70	20	0	0	2	24	23	15	10	2	12	34	.250	.087	.304	12.58	4.44
Frevert, Matt	R-R	6-1	190	11-16-86	4	0	3.26	21	0	0	1	19	18	7	7	2	6	23	.257	.296	.233	10.71	2.79
Gonzalez, Carlos	R-R	6-3	145	8-31-88	0	2	10.92	14	3	0	0	30	47	39	36	7	15	41	.348	.373	.333	12.44	4.55
Gonzalez, Reynier	R-R	6-3	180	11-5-88	2	3	4.36	14	9	0	1	54	47	27	26	1	31	53	.239	.218	.252	8.89	5.20
Hooker, Deryk	R-R	6-4	185	6-21-89	1	1	3.38	11	8	0	1	43	38	20	16	1	14	55	.239	.238	.240	11.60	2.95
Maertz, Santo	R-R	6-2	220	5-9-86	4	0	3.15	17	0	0	0	20	19	8	7	0	13	25	.260	.276	.250	11.25	5.85
Mateo, Jose	R-R	6-2	180	8-31-86	3	1	3.63	20	1	0	2	35	38	16	14	0	7	29	.275	.250	.297	7.53	1.82
Mayes, LaCurtis	R-R	5-11	185	8-2-88	0	0	2.45	4	0	0	1	4	2	1	1	0	3	5	.143	.250	.100	7.36	7.36
McGregor, Scott	R-R	6-2	193	12-19-86	4	0	0.33	7	3	0	0	27	17	3	1	0	3	20	.172	.205	.150	6.67	1.00
North, Matthew	R-R	6-5	170	5-23-88	3	1	3.83	10	7	0	0	42	42	21	18	5	12	42	.261	.234	.278	8.93	2.55
Pichardo, Joel	R-R	5-11	160	2-20-88	0	3	4.91	20	0	0	1	26	33	18	14	2	8	22	.311	.300	.318	7.71	2.81
Rondon, Jorge	R-R	6-1	175	9-16-88	2	2	4.03	21	0	0	6	22	28	12	10	1	8	21	.308	.242	.345	8.46	3.22

Name	B-T	HT	WT	DOB	W	L	ERA	G	GS	CG	SV	IP	H	R	ER	HR	BB	SO	AVG	vLH	vRH	K/9	BB/9
Rosales, Andres	R-R	6-0	140	6-13-88	0	0	3.00	4	1	0	0	12	10	5	4	2	2	12	.213	.182	.240	9.00	1.50
Santos, Randy	R-R	6-2	190	8-21-88	1	3	4.08	13	8	0	0	46	35	27	21	4	21	51	.211	.156	.245	9.91	4.08
Thomas, Kevin	R-R	6-3	215	7-8-86	2	1	2.65	10	4	0	0	34	34	15	10	1	8	27	.243	.210	.269	7.15	2.12
Veres, Adam	R-R	6-4	230	3-19-88	2	2	2.38	8	3	0	0	23	22	13	6	3	7	32	.242	.400	.164	12.71	2.78
Zawacki, Brett	R-R	6-1	190	5-2-89	1	2	7.86	10	5	0	0	34	44	31	30	4	14	36	.314	.358	.287	9.44	3.67

Fielding

Catcher	PCT	G	PO	A	E	DP	PB
Castro	.994	38	311	43	2	1	16
Cawley	.972	26	224	21	7	2	13
Noland	.955	13	74	11	4	0	4

First Base	PCT	G	PO	A	E	DP
Lara	.975	4	38	1	1	5
Martinez	1.000	1	1	1	0	0
Morales	.980	29	216	26	5	24
Rigoli	.956	9	40	3	2	3
Smith	.982	31	260	15	5	16

Second Base	PCT	G	PO	A	E	DP
Castellanos	1.000	4	13	10	0	5

	PCT	G	PO	A	E	DP
Castillo	.833	1	0	5	1	0
Lilley	.964	32	48	86	5	14
Mateo	.953	16	31	50	4	12
Toribio	.984	17	25	35	1	6

Third Base	PCT	G	PO	A	E	DP
Castellanos	.877	43	30	70	14	5
Mateo	.667	1	1	1	1	1
Rigoli	.647	11	2	9	6	1
Toribio	.892	16	8	25	4	3

Shortstop	PCT	G	PO	A	E	DP
Castellanos	.500	1	0	2	2	0
Castillo	.875	6	11	17	4	4

	PCT	G	PO	A	E	DP
Mateo	.889	4	3	5	1	1
Rodriguez	1.000	1	1	4	0	1
Toribio	.931	8	12	15	2	3
Vasquez	.964	52	81	157	9	34

Outfield	PCT	G	PO	A	E	DP
Bogany	.959	34	43	4	2	1
Castillo	.000	1	0	0	1	0
Cruz	.967	39	53	6	2	1
Hage	.926	36	63	0	5	0
Lara	.982	39	52	4	1	1
Martinez	1.000	17	21	1	0	0
Mitchell	.938	53	75	1	5	0
Rodriguez	1.000	4	5	0	0	0

GCL CARDINALS

GULF COAST LEAGUE

ROOKIE

Batting	B-T	HT	WT	DOB	AVG	vLH	vRH	G	AB	R	H	2B	3B	HR	RBI	BB	HBP	SH	SF	SO	SB	CS	SLG	OBP
Babrick, Joe	R-R	6-6	215	12-7-89	.143	.000	.169	34	77	5	11	4	0	0	2	6	4	0	1	45	0	0	.195	.239
Buck, Brian	R-R	6-1	190	2-3-86	.667	1.000	.500	5	6	2	4	0	0	0	2	1	2	0	0	0	0	0	.667	.778
Cardona, Ismael	R-R	5-10	175	4-22-89	.205	.250	.185	13	39	4	8	0	2	0	7	2	0	0	0	8	0	0	.308	.244
Castillo, Juan	R-R	5-11	160	12-13-89	.293	.308	.290	27	75	9	22	3	1	1	5	6	5	1	0	13	0	2	.400	.384
Castillo, Yunier	B-R	6-0	160	5-15-89	.256	.259	.255	40	129	16	33	3	1	1	12	6	0	0	2	29	5	3	.318	.285
Dumont, Cristofher	R-R	6-3	172	1-7-87	.118	.333	.097	13	34	4	4	1	0	0	1	3	1	0	0	10	0	0	.147	.211
Hage, Joey	R-R	6-0	180	2-17-89	.200	—	.200	1	5	0	1	0	0	0	0	0	0	0	0	1	0	0	.200	.200
Henley, Tyler	L-L	5-10	200	6-10-85	.368	—	.368	5	19	6	7	3	1	1	2	1	1	0	0	2	0	0	.789	.429
Hill, Steven	R-R	5-11	190	3-14-85	.313	.200	.364	4	16	4	5	1	0	3	5	0	0	0	0	7	0	0	.938	.313
Hiraldo, Braulio	B-R	5-11	179	7-18-88	.254	.310	.237	41	126	12	32	8	3	2	13	12	1	0	2	34	3	4	.413	.319
Mateo, Luis	R-R	6-0	160	5-23-90	.274	.188	.287	33	124	19	34	3	1	2	21	13	0	0	2	30	7	1	.363	.338
Medina, David	L-L	6-3	162	1-1-89	.193	.115	.210	51	150	24	29	8	2	3	16	18	3	1	3	53	3	1	.333	.287
Moscatel, Kevin	R-R	6-1	175	5-16-91	.136	.143	.136	26	66	5	9	1	0	0	2	4	4	1	0	21	0	2	.152	.230
Mosquera, Juan	B-R	5-10	154	1-23-88	.162	.176	.158	24	74	9	12	0	0	0	2	13	1	1	1	17	3	4	.162	.292
Obregon, Ted	R-R	5-11	170	5-4-90	.135	.143	.134	46	126	9	17	2	0	1	17	23	1	5	1	34	5	3	.175	.272
Perez, Audris	R-R	5-9	180	12-23-88	.273	.000	.333	4	11	0	3	0	0	0	2	0	1	1	0	0	0	0	.273	.308
Pupo, Carlos	R-R	6-4	240	8-29-85	.294	.000	.294	10	34	4	10	3	1	3	13	5	0	0	0	14	1	0	.706	.385
Rasmus, Colby	L-L	6-2	195	8-11-86	.556	1.000	.500	3	9	1	5	1	0	1	2	3	0	0	0	2	0	0	1.000	.667
Rodriguez, Ryde	B-R	6-3	232	2-2-88	.329	.375	.319	41	143	19	47	9	0	0	28	8	3	0	1	32	7	4	.392	.374
Rosario, Rainel	R-R	6-0	188	3-29-89	.243	.333	.225	51	169	34	41	12	2	5	20	26	5	0	1	50	9	7	.426	.358
Shepherd, Devin	R-R	6-3	225	9-9-87	.272	.444	.240	34	114	16	31	6	0	0	12	10	3	0	0	33	2	1	.325	.346
Swinson, Michael	L-R	6-2	185	9-24-89	.192	.100	.202	29	99	11	19	4	1	0	5	11	2	0	0	30	6	2	.253	.286
Teran, Kleininger	L-R	6-1	175	7-23-89	.232	.400	.216	26	56	9	13	0	0	0	3	12	1	1	0	7	0	0	.232	.377

Pitching	B-T	HT	WT	DOB	W	L	ERA	G	GS	CG	SV	IP	H	R	ER	HR	BB	SO	AVG	vLH	vRH	K/9	BB/9
Calero, Jose	R-R	6-3	185	3-7-90	0	5	4.81	12	2	1	0	34	44	22	18	6	12	22	.328	.340	.321	5.88	3.21
Concepcion, Christian	R-R	6-4	198	3-27-90	1	1	21.13	8	0	0	0	8	11	18	18	1	17	6	.344	.417	.300	7.04	19.96
Cruz, Angel	R-R	6-4	200	4-25-88	0	1	11.05	3	1	0	0	7	12	10	9	0	5	7	.387	.462	.333	8.59	6.14
Daley, Gary	R-R	6-3	200	11-1-85	0	5	24.39	17	11	0	0	10	15	34	28	0	32	5	.313	.300	.316	4.35	27.87
Diaz, Omar	R-R	6-0	170	1-7-88	0	4	5.14	12	6	0	0	35	32	21	20	1	26	26	.250	.313	.213	6.69	6.69
Ferrara, Anthony	R-L	6-1	175	9-2-89	2	1	4.50	10	2	0	0	30	27	19	15	3	14	36	.239	.042	.292	10.80	4.20
Flores, Miguel	R-R	6-0	178	1-2-88	1	2	3.19	12	3	0	0	37	35	20	13	2	8	26	.246	.208	.266	6.38	1.96
Fornataro, Eric	R-R	6-1	195	1-2-88	2	2	1.74	9	3	0	0	31	27	10	6	1	6	19	.227	.182	.237	5.52	1.74
Hawksworth, Blake	R-R	6-3	195	3-1-83	0	0	0.00	2	2	0	0	7	2	0	0	0	2	6	.091	.125	.071	7.71	2.57
Javier, Omar	R-R	6-3	165	10-4-87	0	2	7.00	5	3	0	0	18	23	18	14	0	9	10	.307	.341	.258	5.00	4.50
Kopp, David	R-R	6-3	205	10-22-85	0	0	4.91	2	2	0	0	4	2	2	2	0	0	2	.154	.500	.000	4.91	0.00
McCormick, Mark	R-R	6-2	195	10-15-83	0	0	2.25	2	2	0	0	4	3	1	1	1	2	8	.214	.200	.222	18.00	4.50
McGregor, Scott	R-R	6-2	193	12-19-86	0	0	6.75	2	0	0	0	4	7	5	3	1	1	6	.350	.000	.389	2.25	2.25
Munoz, Orlando	R-R	6-1	165	2-22-90	1	0	6.27	18	0	0	0	19	26	15	13	2	7	16	.329	.321	.333	7.71	3.38
Notti, Chris	R-R	6-5	210	9-3-88	2	4	3.20	13	6	0	0	45	40	27	16	4	17	33	.230	.239	.224	6.60	3.40
Ortiz, Pablo	R-R	6-4	175	6-11-88	2	3	6.86	11	2	0	0	21	27	22	16	0	13	14	.318	.308	.326	6.00	5.57
Penaloza, Jose	R-R	6-4	220	6-28-88	2	1	11.03	18	0	0	0	24	42	32	29	2	17	13	.396	.357	.422	4.94	6.46
Prange, Adam	R-R	6-6	215	12-5-87	1	2	6.92	15	0	0	3	13	16	14	10	1	13	9	.291	.278	.297	6.23	9.00
Rada, Jose	R-R	6-1	180	4-13-88	0	4	5.80	13	6	1	0	45	71	37	29	4	4	37	.360	.444	.329	7.40	0.80
Rosales, Andres	R-R	6-0	140	6-13-88	1	0	0.00	4	1	0	0	4	0	0	0	0	0	4	.000	.000	.000	4.50	0.00
Russell, Ronald	R-R	6-2	185	7-27-89	0	1	7.43	13	1	0	0	13	13	12	11	0	21	10	.283	.273	.292	6.75	14.18
Siegrist, Kevin	L-L	6-5	190	7-20-89	0	0	1.38	7	2	0	0	13	3	3	2	0	3	11	.070	.000	.094	7.62	2.08
Stambaugh, J.D.	L-L	6-2	200	10-25-84	0	0	0.00	3	1	0	0	4	2	0	0	0	0	2	.143	1.000	.077	4.50	0.00
Zuercher, Zach	L-L	6-2	215	4-10-84	1	0	0.00	5	0	0	0	6	3	1	0	0	1	7	.150	.000	.200	10.50	1.50

Fielding

Catcher	PCT	G	PO	A	E	DP	PB
Cardona	.986	12	62	8	1	0	5
J. Castillo	.963	23	134	22	6	1	9
Moscatel	.974	25	135	17	4	0	1
Perez	1.000	4	26	6	0	2	0

First Base	PCT	G	PO	A	E	DP
Cardona	1.000	1	2	1	0	1
Hill	1.000	2	11	1	0	2
Hiraldo	1.000	4	16	0	0	3
Medina	.976	45	341	22	9	27
Pupo	1.000	7	52	4	0	8
Teran	1.000	3	27	2	0	1

Second Base	PCT	G	PO	A	E	DP
Hiraldo	1.000	1	1	0	0	0
Mateo	.972	9	13	22	1	2
Mosquera	.957	7	12	10	1	2

	.892	43	74	92	20	21
Obregon						

Third Base	PCT	G	PO	A	E	DP
J. Castillo	.000	1	0	0	1	0
Hiraldo	.806	13	6	19	6	0
Mateo	.952	17	9	31	2	6
Medina	1.000	1	1	4	0	0
Mosquera	.867	10	12	14	4	2
Teran	.889	20	10	22	4	2

Shortstop	PCT	G	PO	A	E	DP
J. Castillo	1.000	1	1	2	0	0
Y. Castillo	.894	38	67	118	22	21
Mateo	.971	7	11	23	1	5
Mosquera	.826	7	7	12	4	2
Obregon	.875	3	2	12	2	2

Outfield	PCT	G	PO	A	E	DP
Babrick	1.000	31	38	1	0	0
Buck	1.000	1	2	0	0	0
Dumont	.955	10	20	1	1	0
Hage	1.000	1	4	0	0	0
Henley	1.000	2	2	0	0	0
Hill	—	1	0	0	0	0
Hiraldo	.833	6	5	0	1	0
Medina	1.000	3	1	0	0	0
Mosquera	1.000	1	0	1	0	0
Rasmus	1.000	3	7	1	0	1
Rodriguez	.961	39	66	7	3	2
Rosario	.970	49	92	4	3	0
Shepherd	.909	14	10	0	1	0
Swinson	.940	25	44	3	3	0
Teran	—	1	0	0	0	0

DSL CARDINALS   ROOKIE

DOMINICAN SUMMER LEAGUE

Batting	B-T	HT	WT	DOB	AVG	vLH	vRH	G	AB	R	H	2B	3B	HR	RBI	BB	HBP	SH	SF	SO	SB	CS	SLG	OBP
Avila, Michael	R-R	6-0	160	9-7-89	.219	.294	.203	37	96	21	21	5	1	3	11	16	4	1	1	38	12	3	.385	.350
Beras, Andres	R-R	6-2	175	11-30-90	.133	.286	.105	16	45	1	6	1	0	0	3	3	0	0	0	13	1	1	.156	.188
Cabrera, Juan B	R-R	6-1	151	6-22-88	.258	.250	.259	57	190	34	49	8	2	3	26	26	3	2	1	33	12	4	.368	.355
Castellano, Alexander	B-R	6-1	160	11-19-88	.237	.100	.265	52	177	23	42	4	5	0	10	19	5	2	0	48	11	3	.316	.328
Ferreira, Victor	R-R	5-11	180	2-1-91	.235	.143	.254	29	85	7	20	4	1	1	16	8	4	1	1	25	0	2	.341	.327
Lopez, Jorge	R-R	5-11	175	10-28-90	.218	.150	.233	36	110	8	24	4	0	0	10	10	1	0	1	24	2	3	.255	.287
Martina, Hayrich	R-R	6-0	170	8-3-90	.158	.222	.143	32	95	9	15	1	0	0	5	10	4	1	0	23	2	3	.168	.266
Martines, Tharick	R-R	6-2	185	11-19-90	.119	.059	.140	23	67	5	8	2	0	1	3	5	2	0	0	34	3	2	.194	.203
Martinez, Marcos	R-R	6-5	195	3-3-89	.194	.235	.187	46	124	13	24	5	0	3	9	14	4	0	1	61	1	1	.306	.294
Perez, Audris	R-R	5-9	180	12-23-88	.322	.364	.316	46	177	29	57	15	0	7	40	5	1	0	1	16	3	2	.525	.342
Perez, Wader	B-R	5-10	170	6-12-90	.247	.229	.250	62	231	41	57	13	3	0	20	35	7	1	1	27	17	11	.329	.361
Pimentel, Luis	R-R	6-1	180	12-30-88	.239	.243	.238	64	218	24	52	10	0	1	25	26	2	0	3	28	4	1	.298	.321
Polanco, Jeudis	R-R	6-1	190	6-16-90	.233	.105	.258	40	116	17	27	6	0	0	19	25	5	2	2	25	0	0	.284	.385
Reyes, Roberto	L-L	6-0	185	5-10-89	.174	.188	.172	50	161	15	28	3	5	0	16	22	5	0	1	50	6	2	.255	.291
Sandoval, Santo	R-R	6-1	180	4-20-89	.208	.154	.218	56	173	33	36	9	2	2	17	35	6	2	0	58	16	5	.318	.360
Villar, Bernardo	R-R	6-0	188	11-9-90	.148	.250	.130	17	54	5	8	1	0	0	5	12	2	0	0	16	2	1	.167	.324

Pitching	B-T	HT	WT	DOB	W	L	ERA	G	GS	CG	SV	IP	H	R	ER	HR	BB	SO	AVG	vLH	vRH	K/9	BB/9
Beltre, Braulin	L-L	6-4	180	9-1-91	0	0	12.46	4	0	0	0	4	7	6	6	0	9	4	.438	.000	.438	8.31	18.69
Castillo, Amaury	R-R	6-5	210	11-9-90	1	1	5.83	16	0	0	0	29	23	22	19	1	28	38	.232	.182	.239	11.66	8.59
Concepcion, Christian	R-R	6-4	198	3-27-90	0	0	—	1	0	0	0	2	3	3	1	2	0	1.000	1.000	1.000	—	—
Cruz, Angel	R-R	6-4	200	4-25-88	4	2	1.62	9	9	1	0	50	33	14	9	1	9	47	.185	.111	.199	8.46	1.62
De Jesus, Angel	R-R	6-6	188	2-3-89	2	4	1.75	17	5	0	0	46	38	18	9	0	19	40	.224	.148	.238	7.77	3.69
Estalis, Eduard	R-R	6-1	172	12-19-88	5	3	2.31	24	0	0	10	35	27	11	9	0	17	40	.213	.190	.217	10.29	4.37
Herrera, Keury	L-L	6-1	180	5-22-91	2	5	4.75	12	11	0	0	42	40	35	22	1	34	34	.252	.100	.262	7.34	7.34
Jaquez, Juan	R-R	6-0	172	11-7-86	0	2	6.75	12	4	0	0	23	22	20	17	2	20	16	.253	.188	.268	6.35	7.94
Jimenez, Charllan	R-R	6-1	180	11-29-90	0	2	2.92	7	3	0	0	25	20	8	8	0	7	13	.233	.273	.227	4.74	2.55
Mejia, Carlos	R-R	6-2	180	11-28-88	3	1	2.10	13	1	0	0	34	27	11	8	0	12	25	.225	.400	.200	6.55	3.15
Mercedes, Juan	L-L	6-5	205	6-1-89	0	0	7.84	4	0	0	0	10	7	10	9	0	20	11	.194	.000	.206	9.58	17.42
Pena, Pedro	L-L	6-1	189	2-22-91	2	5	3.97	18	3	0	0	48	41	24	21	1	23	49	.234	.143	.238	9.25	4.34
Pena, Yedilson	L-L	6-1	165	7-22-91	0	0	4.15	5	0	0	0	4	5	3	2	0	5	5	.167	.000	.182	10.38	16.62
Pinales, Alejandro	R-R	6-4	228	9-21-88	3	2	3.40	19	2	0	1	53	41	25	20	2	11	40	.216	.231	.213	6.79	1.87
Rivera, Eddy	R-R	5-11	185	12-18-88	0	0	3.12	12	2	0	0	17	11	8	6	1	18	23	.186	.143	.192	11.94	9.35
Santos, Ramy	L-L	6-5	175	4-22-91	0	1	4.43	12	2	0	1	22	26	14	11	0	21	14	.306	.000	.317	5.64	8.46
Santos, Walter	L-L	5-11	150	10-28-89	1	1	5.40	13	1	0	0	20	27	18	12	0	6	12	.321	.000	.338	9.00	2.70
Urena, Ramon	R-R	6-0	170	2-25-90	1	6	3.42	13	11	0	0	53	51	28	20	0	22	38	.259	.367	.240	6.49	3.76

Fielding

Catcher	PCT	G	PO	A	E	DP	PB
Ferreira	.951	8	35	4	2	0	4
A. Perez	.980	38	295	53	7	4	9
Polanco	.958	30	201	29	10	1	11

First Base	PCT	G	PO	A	E	DP
Martina	1.000	4	13	0	0	2
Martinez	.971	36	251	16	8	20
A. Perez	1.000	9	43	2	0	3
Pimentel	.978	19	123	8	3	11
Polanco	1.000	14	63	4	0	6

Second Base	PCT	G	PO	A	E	DP
Avila	.977	14	22	21	1	2

	PCT	G	PO	A	E	DP
Cabrera	1.000	8	15	17	0	4
Lopez	.989	21	46	43	1	11
W. Perez	.962	29	61	64	5	13

Third Base	PCT	G	PO	A	E	DP
Avila	1.000	1	1	0	0	0
Martina	.825	20	14	38	11	7
W. Perez	.908	28	26	63	9	7
Pimentel	.887	18	18	37	7	1
Villar	.767	8	9	14	7	2

Shortstop	PCT	G	PO	A	E	DP
Avila	.791	10	13	21	9	3
Cabrera	.932	44	84	94	13	24

	.913	10	15	27	4	2
Lopez						
W. Perez	.909	3	4	6	1	2

Outfield	PCT	G	PO	A	E	DP
Avila	1.000	6	7	1	0	1
Beras	.950	13	18	1	1	0
Cabrera	—	1	0	0	0	0
Castellano	.966	48	80	4	3	0
Ferreira	.967	15	28	1	1	1
Martines	.973	21	33	3	1	0
Martinez	1.000	9	4	1	0	0
Pimentel	1.000	8	16	0	0	0
Reyes	.966	44	81	5	3	3
Sandoval	.959	53	66	4	3	0

VSL CARDINALS   ROOKIE

VENEZUELAN SUMMER LEAGUE

Batting	B-T	HT	WT	DOB	AVG	vLH	vRH	G	AB	R	H	2B	3B	HR	RBI	BB	HBP	SH	SF	SO	SB	CS	SLG	OBP
Alcala, Yorbel	B-R	6-0	160	1-17-90	.244	.233	.248	49	156	8	38	5	1	1	9	5	6	1	1	28	0	1	.308	.292
Bolivar, Billy	R-R	5-11	170	2-18-88	.214	.263	.200	54	173	26	37	4	0	3	21	20	5	5	0	32	5	3	.289	.313
Cortez, Jose	R-R	6-0	165	1-29-89	.251	.366	.216	51	175	23	44	10	1	3	13	13	1	0	0	28	7	3	.371	.307
Dumont, Cristofher	R-R	6-3	172	1-7-87	.198	.269	.169	25	91	13	18	1	0	3	12	8	1	0	2	27	3	1	.308	.265
Fonseca, Anthony	R-R	6-1	175	2-8-89	.265	.359	.240	56	185	28	49	4	2	0	18	20	15	2	1	30	11	3	.308	.380
Garcia, Hector	R-R	6-1	185	5-16-90	.282	.222	.303	59	206	18	58	9	0	2	23	24	0	1	1	37	2	2	.354	.355
Guzman, Francisco	R-R	6-0	180	2-20-88	.240	.333	.227	13	25	5	6	0	0	0	4	4	0	0	0	4	0	0	.240	.345
Inojoza, Kaizer	R-R	6-0	175	10-7-90	.189	.167	.194	23	37	3	7	0	0	0	2	5	1	0	0	12	1	3	.189	.302
Jaspe, Peter	B-R	6-2	162	2-27-90	.203	.250	.186	30	59	4	12	1	1	0	4	2	0	2	0	18	0	0	.254	.230
Mannbel, Gerardo	R-R	5-11	165	5-16-90	.302	.345	.289	67	235	33	71	14	1	4	29	28	12	2	2	20	9	5	.421	.401
Marquez, Moises	R-R	5-9	165	7-16-90	.111	—	.111	15	18	2	2	0	0	0	0	3	1	0	0	4	0	0	.111	.273
Medina, Osmir	R-R	6-2	170	11-27-90	.269	.385	.224	36	93	16	25	5	1	0	11	7	1	3	1	30	3	2	.344	.324
Montero, Jesus	R-R	5-11	180	6-21-91	.190	.176	.194	37	79	8	15	0	0	1	10	9	5	3	0	18	1	1	.228	.312
Perez, Roberto	R-R	6-0	185	8-31-88	.196	.262	.172	54	158	17	31	5	0	3	16	18	3	0	0	39	0	1	.285	.291
Perez, Wilson	R-R	6-2	180	5-30-89	.275	.182	.300	22	51	5	14	6	1	1	4	8	2	0	0	18	0	2	.490	.393
Rivas, Limbert	R-R	6-1	185	2-21-90	.224	.294	.200	31	67	9	15	1	0	0	6	8	0	1	0	21	0	0	.239	.307
Rivero, Alberto	L-L	5-10	155	4-30-89	.309	.264	.322	66	236	32	73	10	3	2	33	26	1	8	3	30	5	6	.403	.376
Vargas, Ildemaro	R-R	6-0	170	7-16-91	.231	.143	.263	12	26	5	6	0	0	0	2	3	0	1	0	3	1	0	.231	.310
Viloria, Omar	R-R	6-2	176	2-12-91	.171	.200	.167	20	35	4	6	2	0	0	2	4	2	0	0	8	0	0	.229	.293
Vivas, Wilfred	R-R	5-11	160	11-8-89	.158	.208	.144	51	114	17	18	1	1	0	8	10	4	3	0	27	3	2	.184	.250
Yegues, Carlos	R-R	5-11	175	10-20-90	.213	.429	.185	39	61	10	13	3	0	0	4	2	1	2	0	20	3	1	.262	.250

Pitching	B-T	HT	WT	DOB	W	L	ERA	G	GS	CG	SV	IP	H	R	ER	HR	BB	SO	AVG	vLH	vRH	K/9	BB/9
Alvarado, Ruben	L-L	6-1	170	7-19-91	0	1	9.37	10	0	0	1	16	22	20	17	1	12	12	.314	.667	.299	6.61	6.61
Avendano, Javier	R-R	6-3	180	9-6-90	1	1	2.34	12	10	0	1	42	35	12	11	1	18	33	.232	.160	.246	7.02	3.83
Bier, Deimer	R-R	6-2	174	1-6-91	3	1	2.80	14	13	0	0	61	51	24	19	3	13	37	.222	.225	.221	5.46	1.92
Brito, David	R-R	6-1	175	11-12-88	4	1	0.30	18	0	0	3	30	21	2	1	0	6	13	.204	.250	.193	3.86	1.78
Cedeno, Fernando	R-R	6-1	186	11-15-89	3	8	5.13	27	0	0	0	47	63	38	27	0	23	14	.330	.344	.327	2.66	4.37
Colorado, Moises	L-L	6-3	170	12-8-89	0	3	3.12	16	8	0	0	43	34	20	15	0	24	62	.211	.500	.208	12.88	4.98
Corpas, Hector	R-R	6-0	170	1-5-90	4	8	4.92	14	9	0	0	53	59	33	29	3	22	26	.286	.200	.307	4.42	3.74
Gonzalez, Yonathan	R-R	6-1	170	10-13-87	4	2	3.93	31	2	1	9	53	53	27	23	0	9	43	.260	.306	.245	7.35	1.54
Lopez, Miguel	L-L	6-1	175	8-23-89	0	1	3.44	20	0	0	0	37	30	23	14	0	21	24	.231	.250	.230	5.89	5.15
Marquez, Fabian	R-R	6-1	178	8-18-91	2	0	2.97	18	1	0	0	36	30	18	12	3	16	32	.219	.333	.202	7.93	3.96
Noguera, Carlos	R-R	6-0	175	4-21-89	2	3	2.57	15	13	0	0	63	73	25	18	2	11	29	.292	.299	.290	4.14	1.57
Oraa, Carlos	R-R	6-3	170	10-5-89	3	2	2.31	19	0	0	0	35	38	13	9	1	14	24	.290	.323	.280	6.17	3.60
Ramos, Gregorio	R-R	5-11	170	9-27-89	0	0	4.82	9	0	0	0	9	9	7	5	0	15	8	.265	.250	.269	7.71	14.46
Rios, Geney	R-R	5-11	175	2-12-88	4	3	2.49	15	13	0	0	69	43	30	19	1	26	57	.173	.217	.163	7.47	3.41
Solarte, Jackson	R-R	6-0	171	6-14-90	1	0	13.00	7	0	0	0	9	17	14	13	0	4	6	.386	.267	.448	6.00	4.00

Fielding

Catcher	PCT	G	PO	A	E	DP	PB
Alcala	.974	31	156	29	5	2	9
Guzman	.957	5	19	3	1	1	2
Montero	.970	29	139	21	5	2	5
Rivas	.992	23	100	18	1	3	4
Viloria	.927	9	36	2	3	0	1

First Base	PCT	G	PO	A	E	DP
Alcala	.989	12	88	2	1	9
Bolivar	1.000	5	47	3	0	3
Cortez	1.000	1	2	0	0	0
Garcia	1.000	2	14	0	0	0
Guzman	.952	5	18	2	1	1
Mannbel	1.000	1	1	0	0	0
Montero	1.000	3	10	1	0	1
R. Perez	.987	51	366	23	5	26
Rivas	.889	2	7	1	1	1

Viloria	1.000	6	35	1	0	3
Yegues	.933	6	14	0	1	2

Second Base	PCT	G	PO	A	E	DP
Bolivar	.955	7	11	10	1	5
Mannbel	.983	16	24	35	1	11
Marquez	1.000	10	13	19	0	3
Vargas	.929	9	21	18	3	3
Vivas	.944	43	84	69	9	16
Yegues	1.000	6	7	13	0	2

Third Base	PCT	G	PO	A	E	DP
Bolivar	.688	6	3	8	5	0
Garcia	.873	54	36	102	20	11
Mannbel	1.000	10	6	14	0	0
Viloria	—	1	0	0	0	0
Yegues	.897	17	4	22	3	1

Shortstop	PCT	G	PO	A	E	DP
Bolivar	1.000	3	3	7	0	2
Mannbel	.924	43	79	140	18	24
Marquez	—	3	0	0	0	0
Medina	.899	31	51	100	17	14
Vargas	.500	3	0	1	1	0

Outfield	PCT	G	PO	A	E	DP
Bolivar	1.000	28	46	4	0	0
Cortez	.961	43	68	5	3	1
Dumont	.895	13	17	0	2	0
Fonseca	.991	55	99	6	1	2
Inojoza	.889	11	8	0	1	0
Jaspe	.875	14	7	0	1	0
W. Perez	.955	13	21	0	1	0
Rivero	.973	65	135	8	4	4

San Diego Padres

BY JOHN MAFFEI

In a season gone horribly wrong, a season in which his team lost 99 games, Padres manager Bud Black searched for positives.

"The best thing to come out of this is that we got a six-week jump on spring training," Black said. "We called up a lot of kids, claimed a bunch of guys, and got a good look at all of them."

The Padres found that rookie outfielders Chase Headley and Will Venable can play. And that Jody Gerut, who missed the better part of three seasons with leg injuries after back-to-back solid seasons with the Indians, is 100 percent recovered.

They found a tough, heady, durable catcher in rookie Nick Hundley.

They discovered that infielder Luis Rodriguez may be more than a journeyman and that career minor league infielder Edgar Gonzalez can hit major league pitching.

They learned Mike Adams can be a durable middle-inning or even seventh-inning man. That Cha Seung Baek, claimed off waivers from Seattle, might just fit in as a No. 4 or 5 starter. And rookie righthander Josh Geer, a third-round draft pick out of Rice in 2005 who got five starts in September, might just have the stuff to fit into the back end of the rotation (though he had injury questions after the season).

On the opposite end, Black and the Padres discovered Callix Crabbe, Brian Myrow, Justin Huber, Craig Stansberry and Colt Morton were lacking. And second baseman Matt Antonelli, one of the organization's shining stars, isn't ready for the big leagues.

On the mound, general manager Kevin Towers employed his "throw-enough-stuff-against-the-wall-and-something-will-stick" theory. Not much stuck.

Josh Banks, Bryan Corey, Joe Thatcher, Brian Falkenborg, Chad Reineke, Dirk Hayhurst, Carlos Guevara, Kevin Cameron, Sean Henn, Charlie Haeger, Scott Patterson, Jared Wells and Enrique Gonzalez never really stuck.

On the mound, starters Jake Peavy, Chris Young and Shawn Estes missed more than 40 combined starts with injuries. And Mark Prior, signed as a $1 million free agent gamble, never threw a pitch. But Heath Bell had another solid season as the eighth-inning man and closer Trevor Hoffman saved 30 games.

MAJOR LEAGUE: ADRIAN GONZALEZ, 1B

Gonzalez cemented his reputation as one of the game's most productive hitters by posting .279/.361/.510 numbers with 36 home runs and 119 RBIs, both team highs. He also delivered 32 doubles and his usual stellar defense at first base.

MINOR LEAGUE: KYLE BLANKS, 1B

The former draft-and-follow who signed in 2005 tore through Double-A San Antonio by hitting .325/.404/.514 with 20 home runs, 23 doubles and 107 RBIs. He finished fourth in the Texas League in batting, second in RBIs and second in hits (160).

JOHN SPEAR

BATTING	*Minimum 250 at-bats	
*AVG	Durango, Luis, Fort Wayne/Lake Elsinore	.328
R	Hunter, Cedric, Lake Elsinore	98
H	Hunter, Cedric, Lake Elsinore	186
TB	Hunter, Cedric, Lake Elsinore	258
2B	Sogard, Eric, Lake Elsinore	42
3B	Ambres, Chip, Portland	7
HR	Ambres, Chip, Portland	22
	Kulbacki, Kellen, Fort Wayne/Lake Elsinore	22
RBI	Blanks, Kyle, San Antonio	107
BB	Macias, Drew, San Antonio	83
SO	Carrasco, Felix, Fort Wayne	162
SB	Zawadzki, Lance, Fort Wayne/San Antonio	28
	Diaz, Javis, Lake Elsinore/Portland	28
*OBP	Myrow, Brian, Portland	.451
*SLG	Kulbacki, Kellen, Fort Wayne/Lake Elsinore	.540

PITCHING	†Minimum 75 innings	
W	Culp, Nathan, Lake Elsinore	14
L	Ramos, Cesar, Portland	11
†ERA	Buschmann, Matthew, San Antonio	2.98
G	Moreno, Edwin, San Antonio/Portland	60
	DeHoyos, Gabe, San Antonio	60
	Ellis, Jonathan, Portland/San Antonio	60
GS	Inman, William, San Antonio	28
SV	Quezada, Jackson, Fort Wayne	27
IP	Geer, Josh, Portland	167
BB	Inman, William, San Antonio	71
SO	McBryde, Jeremy, Fort Wayne	158
†AVG	Hefner, Jeremy, Fort Wayne/Lake Elsinore	.226

First baseman Adrian Gonzalez remains the cornerstone of the franchise and third baseman Kevin Kouzmanoff had a second straight solid season. The loss of shortstop Khalil Greene to a hand injury around midseason was a major loss, too.

General Manager: Kevin Towers. **Farm Director:** Grady Fuson. **Scouting Director:** Bill Gayton.

Class	Team	League	W	L	PCT	Finish*	Manager	Affiliate Since
Majors	San Diego	National	63	99	.389	15th (16)	Bud Black	—
Triple-A	Portland Beavers	Pacific Coast	70	74	.486	9th (16)	Randy Ready	2001
Double-A	San Antonio Missions	Texas	75	65	.536	5th (8)	Bill Masse	2007
High A	Lake Elsinore Storm	California	71	69	.507	4th (10)	Carlos Lezcano	2001
Low A	Fort Wayne Wizards	Midwest	71	69	.507	10th (14)	Doug Dascenzo	1999
Short-season	Eugene Emeralds	Northwest	40	36	.526	3rd (8)	Greg Riddoch	2001
Rookie	AZL Padres	Arizona	33	23	.589	4th (9)	Jose Flores	2004
Overall 2008 Minor League Record			360	336	.517	10th		

* Finish in overall standings (No. of teams in league). ^League champion.

SAN DIEGO PADRES

NATIONAL LEAGUE

Batting	B-T	HT	WT	DOB	AVG	vLH	vRH	G	AB	R	H	2B	3B	HR	RBI	BB	HBP	SH	SF	SO	SB	CS	SLG	OBP
Ambres, Chip	R-R	6-1	230	12-19-79	.195	.160	.250	24	41	3	8	1	0	0	7	0	0	0	15	1	0	.220	.313
Antonelli, Matt	R-R	6-0	200	4-8-85	.193	.083	.222	21	57	6	11	2	0	1	3	5	3	0	0	11	0	0	.281	.292
Bard, Josh	B-R	6-3	225	3-30-78	.202	.135	.230	57	178	11	36	9	0	1	16	18	1	1	0	25	0	0	.270	.279
Barrett, Michael	R-R	6-3	215	10-22-76	.202	.296	.164	30	94	9	19	3	0	2	9	9	1	1	2	16	0	0	.298	.274
Carlin, Luke	B-R	5-11	180	12-20-80	.149	.167	.145	36	94	12	14	3	1	1	6	10	1	0	0	34	0	0	.234	.238
Clark, Tony	B-R	6-7	245	6-15-72	.239	.250	.233	70	88	5	21	3	0	1	11	19	0	0	0	32	0	0	.307	.374
2-team total (38 Arizona)					.225	—	—	108	151	12	34	5	0	3	24	31	1	0	1	55	0	0	.318	.359
Crabbe, Callix	B-R	5-7	185	2-14-83	.176	.250	.136	21	34	4	6	1	0	0	2	4	1	0	0	6	1	0	.206	.282
Edmonds, Jim	L-L	6-1	210	6-27-70	.178	.118	.192	26	90	6	16	2	0	1	6	10	1	1	1	24	2	1	.233	.265
2-team total (85 Chicago)					.235	—	—	111	340	53	80	19	2	20	55	55	2	1	3	82	2	2	.479	.343
Gerut, Jody	L-L	6-0	210	9-18-77	.296	.308	.293	100	328	46	97	15	4	14	43	28	0	0	0	52	6	4	.494	.351
Giles, Brian	L-L	5-10	205	1-20-71	.306	.301	.309	147	559	81	171	40	4	12	63	87	2	0	5	52	2	2	.456	.398
Gonzalez, Edgar	R-R	6-0	180	6-14-78	.274	.283	.268	111	325	38	89	15	0	7	33	25	2	0	1	76	1	3	.385	.329
Gonzalez, Adrian	L-L	6-2	225	5-8-82	.279	.213	.320	162	616	103	172	32	1	36	119	74	7	0	3	142	0	0	.510	.361
Greene, Khalil	R-R	5-11	185	10-21-79	.213	.188	.222	105	389	30	83	15	2	10	35	22	5	0	7	100	5	1	.339	.260
Hairston, Scott	R-R	6-0	185	5-25-80	.248	.280	.224	112	326	42	81	18	3	17	31	28	3	3	2	84	3	1	.479	.312
Headley, Chase	B-R	6-2	230	5-9-84	.269	.276	.265	91	331	34	89	19	2	9	38	30	5	0	2	104	4	1	.420	.337
Huber, Justin	R-R	6-2	205	7-1-82	.246	.250	.235	33	61	5	15	3	0	2	8	3	2	1	0	19	0	0	.393	.303
Hundley, Nick	R-R	6-1	210	9-8-83	.237	.224	.243	60	198	21	47	7	1	5	24	11	2	0	5	52	0	0	.359	.278
Iguchi, Tadahito	R-R	5-10	185	12-4-74	.231	.173	.250	81	303	29	70	14	1	2	24	26	0	1	0	75	8	1	.304	.292
2-team total (4 Philadelphia)					.232	—	—	85	310	29	72	15	1	2	24	26	0	1	0	75	8	1	.306	.292
Kazmar, Sean	R-R	5-9	160	8-5-84	.205	.095	.333	19	39	2	8	1	0	0	2	6	0	5	0	1	14	0	0	.231	.289
Kouzmanoff, Kevin	R-R	6-1	210	7-25-81	.260	.237	.269	154	624	71	162	31	4	23	84	23	15	0	6	139	0	0	.433	.299
Macias, Drew	L-L	6-3	205	3-7-83	.200	.333	.176	17	20	2	4	0	0	2	5	2	0	1	2	4	0	0	.500	.250
McAnulty, Paul	L-R	5-10	220	2-24-81	.207	.000	.215	66	135	9	28	7	1	3	13	26	2	0	1	41	0	0	.341	.341
Morton, Colt	R-R	6-5	230	4-10-82	.067	.200	.000	9	15	2	1	0	0	0	1	2	0	0	1	5	0	0	.067	.167
Myrow, Brian	L-R	5-11	210	9-4-76	.143	.000	.167	21	21	1	3	0	0	1	3	2	0	0	1	5	0	0	.286	.208
Rodriguez, Luis	B-R	5-9	190	6-27-80	.287	.238	.309	64	202	22	58	11	1	0	12	13	0	7	3	13	1	1	.351	.326
Stansberry, Craig	R-R	6-0	185	6-4-82	.375	.143	.556	12	16	4	6	1	0	0	2	2	0	0	0	3	0	0	.438	.444
Venable, Will	L-L	6-2	205	10-29-82	.264	.324	.237	28	110	16	29	4	2	2	10	13	0	0	1	21	1	1	.391	.339

Pitching	B-T	HT	WT	DOB	W	L	ERA	G	GS	CG	SV	IP	H	R	ER	HR	BB	SO	AVG	vLH	vRH	K/9	BB/9
Adams, Mike	R-R	6-5	190	7-29-78	2	3	2.48	54	0	0	0	65	49	18	18	7	19	74	.209	.228	.190	10.19	2.62
Baek, Cha Seung	R-R	6-4	225	5-29-80	6	9	4.62	22	20	0	0	111	118	60	57	12	30	77	.273	.301	.244	6.24	2.43
Banks, Josh	R-R	6-3	210	7-18-82	3	6	4.75	17	14	1	0	85	94	47	45	12	32	43	.289	.293	.287	4.54	3.38
Bell, Heath	R-R	6-3	240	9-29-77	6	6	3.58	74	0	0	0	78	66	31	31	5	28	71	.229	.207	.254	8.19	3.23
Cameron, Kevin	R-R	6-1	190	12-15-79	0	0	3.60	10	0	0	0	10	10	9	4	0	6	5	.263	.286	.250	4.50	5.40
Corey, Bryan	R-R	6-0	175	10-21-73	1	3	6.23	39	0	0	0	39	42	27	27	7	9	18	.273	.278	.268	4.15	2.08
Ekstrom, Mike	R-R	6-0	185	8-30-83	0	2	7.45	8	0	0	0	10	14	8	8	2	7	6	.350	.357	.346	5.59	6.52
Estes, Shawn	R-L	6-2	200	2-18-73	2	3	4.74	9	8	0	0	44	50	26	23	6	18	19	.284	.195	.311	3.92	3.71
Falkenborg, Brian	R-R	6-7	235	1-18-78	0	1	4.22	9	0	0	0	11	15	5	5	2	8	10	.341	.300	.375	8.44	6.75
2-team total (16 Los Angeles)					2	3	5.24	25	0	0	0	22	26	13	13	4	12	19	—	—	—	7.66	4.84
Geer, Josh	R-R	6-3	190	6-2-83	2	1	2.67	5	5	0	0	27	29	8	8	2	9	16	.269	.146	.367	5.33	3.00
Germano, Justin	R-R	6-3	205	8-6-82	0	3	5.98	12	6	0	0	44	54	31	29	8	13	17	.305	.268	.330	3.50	2.68
Gonzalez, Enrique	R-R	5-10	210	7-14-82	1	0	10.80	4	0	0	0	3	4	4	4	0	2	1	.308	.333	.286	2.70	5.40
Guevara, Carlos	R-R	5-11	190	3-18-82	1	0	5.84	10	0	0	0	12	13	9	8	2	9	11	.265	.190	.321	8.03	6.57
Haeger, Charlie	R-R	6-1	220	9-19-83	0	0	16.62	4	0	0	0	4	8	10	8	2	5	4	.381	.333	.417	8.31	10.38
Hampson, Justin	L-L	6-1	205	5-24-80	2	1	2.93	35	0	0	0	31	31	11	10	1	10	19	.279	.250	.302	5.58	2.93
Hayhurst, Dirk	L-R	6-3	200	3-24-81	0	2	9.72	10	3	0	0	17	27	18	18	2	10	14	.365	.394	.341	7.56	5.40
Henn, Sean	R-L	6-4	225	4-23-81	0	0	7.71	4	0	0	0	9	11	8	8	1	9	9	.297	.100	.370	8.68	8.68
Hensley, Clay	R-R	5-11	185	8-31-79	1	2	5.31	32	1	0	0	39	36	27	23	2	25	26	.252	.288	.221	6.00	5.77
Hoffman, Trevor	R-R	6-0	220	10-13-67	3	6	3.77	48	0	0	30	45	38	19	19	8	9	46	.224	.291	.165	9.13	1.79

	B-T	HT	WT	DOB	W	L	ERA	G	GS	CG	SV	IP	H	R	ER	HR	BB	SO	AVG	vLH	vRH	K/9	BB/9
LeBlanc, Wade	L-L	6-3	200	8-7-84	1	3	8.02	5	4	0	0	21	29	19	19	7	15	14	.330	.318	.333	5.91	6.33
Ledezma, Wil	L-L	6-4	210	1-21-81	0	2	4.47	25	6	0	0	54	49	29	27	4	38	49	.245	.240	.247	8.12	6.29
2-team total (3 Arizona)					0	2	4.17	28	6	0	0	58	51	29	27	4	41	51	—	—	—	8.18	6.33
Maddux, Greg	R-R	6-0	195	4-14-66	6	9	3.99	26	26	0	0	153	161	80	68	16	26	80	.271	.260	.279	4.70	1.53
2-team total (7 Los Angeles)					8	13	4.22	33	33	0	0	194	204	105	91	21	30	98	—	—	—	4.55	1.39
Meredith, Cla	R-R	6-0	190	6-4-83	0	3	4.09	73	0	0	0	70	79	34	32	6	24	49	.290	.351	.258	6.27	3.07
Patterson, Scott	R-R	6-6	230	6-20-79	0	0	0.00	3	0	0	0	3	1	0	0	0	4	5	.091	.167	.000	13.50	10.80
Peavy, Jake	R-R	6-1	195	5-31-81	10	11	2.85	27	27	1	0	174	146	57	55	17	59	166	.226	.263	.194	8.60	3.06
Reineke, Chad	R-R	6-6	210	4-9-82	2	1	5.00	4	3	0	0	18	14	10	10	1	12	13	.219	.267	.176	6.50	6.00
Rusch, Glendon	L-L	6-1	225	11-7-74	1	2	6.41	12	0	0	0	20	22	15	14	2	11	12	.278	.310	.260	5.49	5.03
2-team total (23 Colorado)					5	5	5.16	35	9	0	0	84	94	50	48	10	25	55	—	—	—	5.92	2.69
Thatcher, Joe	L-L	6-2	225	10-4-81	0	4	8.42	25	0	0	0	26	42	25	24	4	13	17	.382	.414	.370	5.96	4.56
Tomko, Brett	R-R	6-4	220	4-7-73	0	0	1.93	6	0	0	0	9	3	2	2	0	5	9	.097	.000	.167	8.68	4.82
Wells, Jared	R-R	6-4	200	10-31-81	0	0	6.00	2	0	0	0	3	4	2	2	0	1	2	.333	.250	.375	6.00	3.00
Wolf, Randy	L-L	5-10	200	8-22-76	6	10	4.74	21	21	0	0	120	123	69	63	14	47	105	.268	.302	.259	7.90	3.53
2-team total (12 Houston)					12	12	4.30	33	33	1	0	190	191	100	91	21	71	162	—	—	—	7.66	3.36
Young, Chris	R-R	6-10	280	5-25-79	7	6	3.96	18	18	1	0	102	84	46	45	13	48	93	.221	.259	.189	8.18	4.22

Fielding

Catcher	PCT	G	PO	A	E	DP	PB
Bard	.991	49	329	20	3	1	1
Barrett	.991	30	205	16	2	0	3
Carlin	.987	36	206	14	3	2	3
Hundley	.990	59	366	32	4	4	4
Morton	1.000	7	26	5	0	0	0

First Base	PCT	G	PO	A	E	DP
Clark	1.000	1	17	1	0	4
A. Gonzalez	.996	161	1306	130	6	129
Myrow	1.000	2	9	0	0	1
Rodriguez	1.000	2	3	2	0	0

Second Base	PCT	G	PO	A	E	DP
Antonelli	.973	18	38	34	2	7
Crabbe	.786	5	4	7	3	1
E. Gonzalez	.986	72	92	189	4	35

	PCT	G	PO	A	E	DP
Hairston	1.000	1	1	1	0	0
Iguchi	.997	77	142	204	1	54
Kazmar	1.000	2	2	2	0	1
Rodriguez	1.000	7	11	10	0	4
Stansberry	.778	4	4	3	2	0

Third Base	PCT	G	PO	A	E	DP
E. Gonzalez	.800	4	1	3	1	0
Headley	.923	7	3	9	1	0
Kouzmanoff	.974	154	128	277	11	34
Rodriguez	1.000	1	1	1	0	0

Shortstop	PCT	G	PO	A	E	DP
Crabbe	1.000	3	3	4	0	1
E. Gonzalez	1.000	3	1	11	0	0
Greene	.982	105	146	289	8	66
Kazmar	.980	15	26	24	1	5

	PCT	G	PO	A	E	DP
Rodriguez	.985	52	79	121	3	33

Outfield	PCT	G	PO	A	E	DP
Ambres	.950	10	19	0	1	0
Crabbe	1.000	3	3	0	0	0
Edmonds	.985	26	63	1	1	1
Gerut	.990	87	206	2	2	1
Giles	.976	144	276	3	7	1
E. Gonzalez	1.000	5	7	1	0	1
Hairston	.989	88	184	4	2	0
Headley	.969	82	156	2	5	0
Huber	.964	22	27	0	1	0
Macias	1.000	7	11	0	0	0
McAnulty	1.000	48	66	1	0	0
Venable	1.000	27	84	1	0	0

PORTLAND BEAVERS

TRIPLE-A

PACIFIC COAST LEAGUE

Batting	B-T	HT	WT	DOB	AVG	vLH	vRH	G	AB	R	H	2B	3B	HR	RBI	BB	HBP	SH	SF	SO	SB	CS	SLG	OBP
Ambres, Chip	R-R	6-1	230	12-19-79	.279	.255	.287	112	412	82	115	27	7	22	77	56	4	0	4	89	8	3	.539	.368
Antonelli, Matt	R-R	6-0	200	4-8-85	.215	.155	.229	128	451	62	97	19	4	7	39	76	8	0	5	86	6	4	.322	.335
Bard, Josh	B-R	6-3	225	3-30-78	.133	.167	.111	6	15	2	2	0	0	1	1	2	0	0	0	3	0	0	.333	.235
Barrett, Michael	R-R	6-3	215	10-22-76	.714	.500	.800	3	7	2	5	2	0	0	4	0	0	0	0	0	0	0	1.000	.714
Carlin, Luke	B-R	5-11	180	12-20-80	.261	.133	.288	31	88	12	23	3	0	4	19	19	2	0	2	27	0	0	.432	.396
Chang, Ray	R-R	6-0	204	8-24-83	.100	.000	.100	8	10	1	1	0	0	0	0	2	1	0	0	4	0	0	.100	.308
Ciofrone, Peter	L-R	5-10	201	9-28-83	.314	.344	.304	97	370	70	116	16	3	18	53	38	9	2	2	65	1	0	.519	.389
Closser, J.D.	B-R	5-10	200	1-15-80	.130	.000	.146	17	46	3	6	1	0	1	5	7	0	2	0	13	0	0	.217	.245
2-team total (5 Iowa)					.172	—	—	22	58	4	10	2	0	1	5	7	0	2	0	17	0	0	.259	.262
Diaz, Javis	L-R	5-10	165	6-25-84	.222	1.000	.125	3	9	2	2	0	1	0	0	1	1	0	0	4	0	0	.444	.300
Dowdy, Brett	R-R	6-0	190	2-22-82	.280	.349	.257	91	343	52	96	22	3	10	35	30	5	2	2	63	7	3	.449	.345
Gerut, Jody	L-L	6-0	210	9-18-77	.308	.250	.319	27	107	22	33	9	2	5	18	13	1	0	2	11	4	1	.570	.382
Gonzalez, Edgar	R-R	6-0	180	6-14-78	.293	.267	.299	27	82	10	24	1	0	4	12	12	2	0	1	12	0	4	.451	.392
Headley, Chase	B-R	6-2	230	5-9-84	.305	.258	.321	65	259	49	79	24	1	13	40	31	3	0	2	65	0	0	.556	.383
Huber, Justin	R-R	6-2	205	7-1-82	.246	.317	.216	61	199	17	49	12	0	3	27	18	4	0	2	51	0	1	.352	.318
Hundley, Nick	R-R	6-1	210	9-8-83	.232	.120	.264	58	224	33	52	13	0	12	39	17	0	1	1	44	0	0	.451	.285
King, Tom	R-R	5-11	170	8-3-84	.200	.208	.197	76	175	16	35	7	0	2	10	19	1	4	1	29	0	0	.274	.281
McAnulty, Paul	L-R	5-10	220	2-24-81	.343	.286	.364	53	181	34	62	14	1	13	50	35	2	0	7	38	0	0	.646	.440
McDougall, Marshall	R-R	6-0	200	12-19-78	.266	.308	.255	21	64	6	17	8	0	1	10	4	0	0	1	10	0	0	.438	.304
Morton, Colt	R-R	6-5	230	4-10-82	.170	.267	.132	17	53	6	9	1	1	2	6	6	0	0	0	15	0	0	.340	.254
Myrow, Brian	L-R	5-11	210	9-4-76	.314	.284	.324	97	328	60	103	23	1	12	59	81	4	0	4	72	0	1	.500	.451
Naylor, Clinton	L-R	5-11	200	8-3-88	.000	.000	.000	2	4	0	0	0	0	0	0	1	0	0	0	3	0	0	.000	.200
Robles, Oscar	L-R	5-10	185	4-9-76	.208	.250	.200	14	53	7	11	3	0	1	10	5	0	0	1	6	0	0	.321	.271
Rodriguez, Luis	B-R	5-9	190	6-27-80	.302	.316	.299	31	96	10	29	5	1	1	8	10	0	1	0	3	0	0	.406	.368
Sinisi, Vince	L-L	6-0	195	11-7-81	.283	.258	.290	80	279	22	79	12	1	4	34	17	2	1	6	45	0	1	.376	.322
Stansberry, Craig	R-R	6-2	185	2-8-82	.249	.230	.255	75	273	44	68	13	3	7	27	45	1	1	5	55	5	6	.396	.356
Venable, Will	L-L	6-2	205	10-29-82	.292	.258	.304	120	442	70	129	26	4	14	58	44	5	3	2	103	7	3	.464	.361
Wooten, Shawn	R-R	5-10	230	7-24-72	.206	.162	.223	42	131	10	27	5	0	2	14	15	1	0	0	30	0	0	.290	.293
2-team total (16 New Orleans)					.195	—	—	58	164	14	32	6	0	3	17	16	1	0	0	37	0	0	.287	.283

Pitching	B-T	HT	WT	DOB	W	L	ERA	G	GS	CG	SV	IP	H	R	ER	HR	BB	SO	AVG	vLH	vRH	K/9	BB/9
Abraham, Paul	R-R	6-1	225	1-10-80	0	5	5.52	20	0	0	0	29	35	24	18	5	19	21	.302	.356	.246	6.44	5.83
Adams, Mike	R-R	6-5	190	7-29-78	3	1	5.52	12	0	0	0	15	21	12	9	0	9	16	.339	.333	.344	9.82	5.52
Ayala, Manny	R-R	6-3	237	11-6-84	1	0	2.25	2	1	1	0	8	4	2	2	1	4	3	.148	.083	.200	3.38	4.50
Banks, Josh	R-R	6-3	210	7-18-82	1	5	5.93	9	4	0	0	30	39	20	20	3	8	22	.310	.258	.359	6.53	2.37

Pitching	B-T	HT	WT	DOB	W	L	ERA	G	GS	CG	SV	IP	H	R	ER	HR	BB	SO	AVG	vLH	vRH	K/9	BB/9
Bass, Adam	R-R	6-6	210	7-31-81	2	2	8.06	50	0	0	1	64	86	59	57	9	38	56	.322	.304	.333	7.92	5.37
Cameron, Kevin	R-R	6-1	190	12-15-79	1	0	1.93	15	0	0	1	19	13	5	4	0	7	9	.200	.276	.139	4.34	3.38
Corey, Bryan	R-R	6-0	175	10-21-73	0	0	1.35	5	0	0	0	7	9	1	1	0	1	4	.346	.222	.412	5.40	1.35
Davis, Tyler	R-R	6-3	195	5-15-85	1	0	14.54	4	0	0	0	4	9	7	7	1	3	2	.450	.556	.364	4.15	6.23
Ellis, Jonathan	R-R	6-0	190	10-3-82	1	1	4.50	3	0	0	0	4	4	2	2	1	2	1	.250	.500	.100	2.25	4.50
Estes, Shawn	R-L	6-2	200	2-18-73	5	2	3.63	8	8	0	0	45	45	20	18	3	10	29	.260	.200	.281	5.84	2.01
Frieri, Ernesto	R-R	6-2	190	7-19-85	1	0	1.50	1	1	0	0	6	2	1	1	0	2	7	.100	.083	.125	10.50	3.00
Geer, Josh	R-R	6-3	190	6-2-83	8	9	4.54	28	27	0	0	167	187	95	84	22	45	107	.285	.326	.244	5.78	2.43
Germano, Justin	R-R	6-3	205	8-6-82	2	9	5.51	17	16	1	0	98	119	67	60	12	25	67	.300	.338	.274	6.15	2.30
Gonzalez, Enrique	R-R	5-10	210	7-14-82	7	5	4.44	35	13	0	0	99	106	58	49	10	50	82	.272	.267	.276	7.43	4.53
Guevara, Carlos	R-R	5-11	190	3-18-82	0	3	6.50	16	0	0	2	18	16	13	13	1	9	20	.232	.192	.256	10.00	4.50
Hampson, Justin	L-L	6-1	205	5-24-80	1	2	3.48	10	0	0	0	10	11	5	4	1	3	16	.256	.227	.286	13.94	2.61
Hayhurst, Dirk	L-R	6-3	200	3-24-81	2	3	3.75	46	2	0	2	84	84	36	35	7	28	98	.259	.267	.254	10.50	3.00
Henn, Sean	R-L	6-4	225	4-23-81	0	0	14.21	0	0	0	0	6	10	10	10	1	10	3	.385	.333	.429	4.26	14.21
Hensley, Clay	R-R	5-11	185	8-31-79	1	1	3.94	16	10	0	0	48	46	23	21	7	16	34	.249	.287	.202	6.38	3.00
LeBlanc, Wade	L-L	6-3	200	8-7-84	11	9	5.32	26	25	0	0	139	136	85	82	21	42	139	.259	.280	.251	9.02	2.73
Ledezma, Wil	L-L	6-4	210	1-21-81	1	0	4.41	11	0	0	1	16	14	8	8	1	4	20	.233	.238	.231	11.02	2.20
Lopez, Arturo	L-L	5-10	165	2-22-83	0	3	13.14	3	3	0	0	12	18	18	18	4	11	7	.346	.455	.317	5.11	8.03
Lopez, Wilton	R-R	6-0	190	7-19-83	0	0	9.00	1	0	0	0	1	1	1	1	0	2	1	.250	.500	.000	9.00	18.00
Madden, John	R-R	6-4	229	12-2-82	0	0	3.38	2	0	0	0	3	2	1	1	1	0	1	.200	.333	.143	3.38	0.00
Megrew, Mike	L-L	6-6	225	1-29-84	0	0	9.35	5	0	0	0	9	16	9	9	0	8	8	.400	.455	.379	8.31	8.31
Meredith, Cla	R-R	6-0	190	6-4-83	0	0	2.70	6	0	0	0	7	6	2	2	0	3	4	.231	.111	.294	5.40	4.05
Moreno, Edwin	R-R	6-1	195	7-30-80	5	6	4.35	45	0	0	18	50	37	29	24	8	26	47	.201	.180	.221	8.52	4.71
Ramos, Cesar	L-L	6-2	190	6-22-84	9	11	5.29	28	27	0	0	150	183	108	88	17	57	105	.306	.292	.311	6.31	3.43
Reineke, Chad	R-R	6-6	210	4-9-82	0	1	4.15	3	3	0	0	17	17	8	8	5	6	13	.258	.188	.324	6.75	3.12
2-team total (20 Round Rock)					5	10	4.37	23	22	1	0	130	129	70	63	20	41	113	—	—		7.84	2.85
Thatcher, Joe	L-L	6-2	225	10-4-81	5	2	2.77	37	0	0	3	39	38	17	12	2	11	44	.248	.308	.218	10.15	2.54
Tomko, Brett	R-R	6-4	220	4-7-73	0	0	9.00	5	2	0	0	5	4	5	5	1	3	6	.211	.200	.214	10.80	5.40
Vincent, Nick	R-R	6-0	175	7-12-86	0	1	5.40	1	1	0	0	5	2	4	3	1	1	4	.118	.000	.167	7.20	1.80
Wells, Jared	R-R	6-4	200	10-31-81	1	1	5.85	19	0	0	9	20	19	13	13	1	12	14	.253	.333	.179	6.30	5.40
2-team total (33 Tacoma)					1	5	6.23	52	0	0	20	61	63	43	42	7	35	56	—	—		8.31	5.19
Woodard, Robert	R-R	6-1	205	1-10-85	0	1	27.00	1	1	0	0	3	9	10	10	2	1	4	.500	.667	.417	10.80	2.70
Zarate, Mauro	R-R	6-1	180	2-8-83	1	0	5.26	18	0	0	0	26	33	16	15	5	9	22	.320	.341	.306	7.71	3.16

Fielding

Catcher	PCT	G	PO	A	E	DP	PB
Bard	1.000	4	21	2	0	1	0
Barrett	1.000	2	8	0	0	0	0
Carlin	.985	28	188	13	3	2	3
Closser	1.000	9	59	8	0	0	1
Hundley	.990	57	450	35	5	4	3
Morton	1.000	14	95	9	0	1	1
Naylor	1.000	2	5	0	0	0	0
Wooten	.996	38	238	20	1	4	5

First Base	PCT	G	PO	A	E	DP
Ciofrone	1.000	3	13	1	0	2
Closser	.500	1	1	0	1	1
Gonzalez	1.000	1	12	0	0	0
Huber	.996	28	230	12	1	25
McAnulty	1.000	2	9	0	0	2
McDougall	1.000	1	9	0	0	0
Myrow	.988	92	675	65	9	79
Sinisi	.986	24	200	18	3	14

Second Base	PCT	G	PO	A	E	DP
Antonelli	.977	125	243	313	13	81

	PCT	G	PO	A	E	DP
Chang	1.000	1	1	3	0	1
Dowdy	1.000	5	8	6	0	2
Gonzalez	1.000	1	4	1	0	1
King	.984	18	32	31	1	8
McDougall	1.000	2	5	3	0	2
Robles	1.000	2	3	7	0	1

Third Base	PCT	G	PO	A	E	DP
Chang	1.000	2	1	0	0	0
Ciofrone	.935	63	47	110	11	7
Dowdy	.971	15	8	26	1	2
Gonzalez	.933	5	2	12	1	2
Headley	.929	8	10	16	2	6
Huber	.842	6	2	14	3	0
King	.928	29	19	45	5	3
McDougall	1.000	7	2	12	0	1
Robles	1.000	3	3	4	0	1
Stansberry	.913	19	9	33	4	3

Shortstop	PCT	G	PO	A	E	DP
Chang	1.000	2	5	9	0	3
Dowdy	.934	56	79	149	16	38

	PCT	G	PO	A	E	DP
King	1.000	3	3	6	0	2
McDougall	.889	7	8	8	2	1
Robles	.960	7	10	14	1	5
Rodriguez	.961	28	39	59	4	14
Stansberry	.957	52	98	123	10	32

Outfield	PCT	G	PO	A	E	DP
Ambres	.987	108	226	4	3	0
Ciofrone	.974	25	37	1	1	0
Diaz	1.000	3	5	0	0	0
Dowdy	1.000	13	23	0	0	0
Geer	—	1	0	0	0	0
Gerut	1.000	22	52	1	0	0
Gonzalez	1.000	12	26	0	0	0
Headley	.990	56	93	3	1	0
Huber	.957	14	21	1	1	0
King	1.000	1	1	0	0	0
McAnulty	1.000	49	84	2	0	0
Sinisi	.959	44	90	3	4	1
Venable	.981	100	202	3	4	0

SAN ANTONIO MISSIONS

DOUBLE-A

TEXAS LEAGUE

Batting	B-T	HT	WT	DOB	AVG	vLH	vRH	G	AB	R	H	2B	3B	HR	RBI	BB	HBP	SH	SF	SO	SB	CS	SLG	OBP
Alley, Josh	L-L	5-8	180	9-6-83	.282	.281	.283	108	287	38	81	15	3	4	30	56	0	3	2	42	7	3	.397	.397
Baxter, Mike	L-R	6-0	190	12-7-84	.272	.209	.281	100	324	41	88	18	4	8	48	39	2	2	3	41	2	2	.426	.351
Blanks, Kyle	R-R	6-6	270	9-11-86	.325	.238	.348	132	492	75	160	23	5	20	107	51	17	0	5	90	5	4	.514	.404
Chang, Ray	R-R	6-0	204	8-24-83	.262	.308	.250	22	65	8	17	10	0	0	4	8	2	1	0	8	0	0	.415	.360
Ciofrone, Peter	L-R	5-10	201	9-28-83	.254	.455	.214	19	67	9	17	6	1	0	11	8	2	2	0	6	1	0	.373	.351
Cooper, Craig	R-L	6-1	220	10-27-84	.282	.266	.287	121	408	46	115	24	3	7	55	42	6	1	4	87	5	3	.407	.354
Dowdy, Brett	R-R	6-0	190	2-22-82	.316	.263	.325	33	136	32	43	4	1	3	15	9	3	0	1	21	6	2	.426	.369
DuBarry, B.J.	R-R	6-2	185	9-24-82	.000	—	.000	1	1	0	0	0	0	0	0	0	0	0	0	0	0	0	.000	.000
Huffman, Chad	R-R	6-1	200	4-29-85	.284	.376	.261	119	437	68	124	30	1	9	58	67	7	0	6	83	1	1	.419	.383
Johnston, Seth	R-R	6-3	204	3-12-83	.250	.262	.247	127	460	67	115	25	0	16	60	40	4	2	11	91	4	2	.409	.309
Kazmar, Sean	R-R	5-9	160	8-5-84	.264	.304	.256	111	382	53	101	21	3	3	39	38	3	6	4	66	7	4	.359	.333
Lobaton, Jose	B-R	6-0	170	10-21-84	.259	.224	.265	92	294	35	76	21	0	9	45	39	0	2	7	75	1	1	.422	.338
Lopez, Jesus	R-R	5-11	165	9-12-87	.356	.357	.356	18	59	6	21	2	1	0	10	9	0	1	0	6	0	0	.424	.441
Lopez, Gabe	R-R	5-8	170	3-11-80	.245	.301	.230	87	351	49	86	15	2	3	24	38	4	6	2	31	1	5	.325	.324

	B-T	HT	WT	DOB	AVG	vLH	vRH	G	AB	R	H	2B	3B	HR	RBI	BB	HBP	SH	SF	SO	SB	CS	SLG	OBP
Macias, Drew	L-L	6-3	205	3-7-83	.288	.277	.290	136	504	92	145	27	4	11	66	83	8	3	5	81	18	6	.423	.393
McDougall, Marshall	R-R	6-1	200	12-19-78	.256	.000	.297	10	43	5	11	4	0	0	4	2	0	0	0	6	1	0	.349	.289
Morton, Colt	R-R	6-5	230	4-10-82	.188	.220	.177	49	165	18	31	8	0	3	18	11	1	0	0	55	1	0	.291	.243
Parrish, David	R-R	6-3	220	6-13-79	.120	.125	.118	12	25	2	3	1	0	1	1	11	1	0	0	5	0	0	.280	.405
2-team total (9 Tulsa)					.172	—	—	21	58	6	10	2	0	2	3	12	1	1	0	9	0	0	.310	.324
Schemmel, Jon	R-R	5-11	190	1-27-83	.169	.200	.156	37	89	9	15	3	0	0	6	13	1	2	0	22	0	0	.202	.282
Snyder, Brian	R-R	5-10	200	3-17-82	.147	.091	.174	14	34	4	5	3	0	1	6	7	0	0	0	15	1	0	.324	.293
2-team total (61 Midland)					.234	—	—	75	252	27	59	16	1	3	35	43	1	1	0	62	2	1	.341	.348
Stocco, Matt	R-R	6-1	210	8-16-83	.212	.333	.200	10	33	4	7	1	0	1	2	3	1	0	0	8	0	0	.333	.297
Weems, Beamer	B-R	5-10	175	7-28-87	.294	.500	.231	5	17	1	5	2	0	0	2	2	0	0	0	3	0	0	.412	.368
Zawadzki, Lance	B-R	5-11	185	5-26-85	.333	.333	.000	2	3	1	1	0	0	0	0	0	0	0	0	2	0	0	.333	.333

Pitching	B-T	HT	WT	DOB	W	L	ERA	G	GS	CG	SV	IP	H	R	ER	HR	BB	SO	AVG	vLH	vRH	K/9	BB/9
Abraham, Paul	R-R	6-1	225	1-10-80	1	1	2.19	10	0	0	0	12	10	3	3	0	5	17	.213	.375	.179	12.41	3.65
Ayala, Manny	R-R	6-3	237	11-6-84	6	4	5.23	19	16	0	0	83	79	52	48	12	38	65	.255	.258	.253	7.08	4.14
Barzilla, Phil	L-L	6-0	180	1-25-79	2	2	3.78	34	1	0	0	50	46	24	21	5	21	57	.238	.284	.214	10.26	3.78
Burke, Greg	R-R	6-4	204	9-21-82	2	7	2.24	59	1	0	23	84	76	26	21	7	17	92	.238	.314	.203	9.82	1.81
Buschmann, Matt	R-R	6-3	209	2-13-84	10	6	2.98	27	27	1	0	148	137	60	49	13	58	118	.250	.323	.212	7.18	3.53
DeHoyos, Gabe	R-R	5-11	226	4-14-80	6	4	2.69	60	0	0	4	84	71	27	25	2	33	110	.228	.221	.232	11.83	3.55
DeMark, Mike	R-R	6-0	198	5-20-83	0	0	0.76	12	0	0	0	24	17	2	2	0	5	24	.205	.281	.157	9.13	1.90
Ekstrom, Mike	R-R	6-0	185	8-30-83	11	8	4.58	41	15	0	1	108	137	68	55	14	34	101	.305	.346	.283	8.42	2.83
Ellis, Jonathan	R-R	6-0	190	10-3-82	9	6	3.19	57	0	0	1	73	73	32	26	9	31	70	.260	.370	.206	8.59	3.80
Faris, Stephen	R-R	6-1	190	6-30-84	8	5	3.85	26	26	0	0	138	145	66	59	9	39	102	.277	.246	.294	6.65	2.54
Frieri, Ernesto	R-R	6-2	190	7-19-85	1	0	4.09	2	2	0	0	11	7	5	5	3	2	10	.184	.111	.207	8.18	1.64
Garrison, Steve	B-L	6-1	185	9-12-86	7	7	3.82	24	24	0	0	130	123	59	55	13	37	108	.249	.189	.260	7.50	2.57
Gwaltney, Lee	R-R	6-6	210	5-6-80	0	1	11.25	2	0	0	0	4	8	5	5	2	3	4	.364	.333	.368	6.75	4.50
Inman, Will	R-R	6-0	200	2-6-87	9	8	3.52	28	28	2	0	135	119	67	53	10	71	140	.234	.246	.228	9.31	4.72
Isenberg, Kurt	R-L	6-0	190	1-15-82	0	0	9.41	11	0	0	0	22	36	27	23	2	11	24	.364	.250	.408	9.82	4.50
Jamison, Neil	R-R	6-3	185	8-4-83	1	2	2.55	29	0	0	2	35	32	10	10	5	3	21	.232	.171	.258	6.62	2.55
Lopez, Wilton	R-R	6-0	190	7-19-83	0	2	4.93	27	0	0	0	38	41	21	21	2	9	24	.272	.375	.223	5.63	2.11
Moreno, Edwin	R-R	6-1	195	7-30-80	0	2	2.95	15	0	0	8	21	16	8	7	1	6	19	.219	.227	.216	8.02	2.53
Zarate, Mauro	R-R	6-1	180	2-8-83	2	0	1.77	28	0	0	0	46	38	12	9	3	9	41	.228	.214	.237	8.08	1.77

Fielding

Catcher	PCT	G	PO	A	E	DP	PB
Lobaton	.995	86	697	61	4	7	0
Morton	.992	46	359	20	3	3	4
Parrish	.986	11	68	3	1	0	0
Stocco	.982	10	53	3	1	0	3

First Base	PCT	G	PO	A	E	DP
Baxter	1.000	13	98	13	0	13
Blanks	.993	126	1042	67	8	77
Cooper	.978	5	42	3	1	1
Parrish	1.000	1	2	0	0	1

Second Base	PCT	G	PO	A	E	DP
Chang	1.000	12	20	15	0	3
Dowdy	.992	31	55	71	1	20

	PCT	G	PO	A	E	DP
G. Lopez	.990	85	149	231	4	40
McDougall	1.000	9	13	26	0	5
Schemmel	.897	9	11	15	3	0
Snyder	1.000	2	1	3	0	1

Third Base	PCT	G	PO	A	E	DP
Chang	—	1	0	0	0	0
Dowdy	1.000	2	1	3	0	1
Johnston	.909	123	69	200	27	12
McDougall	1.000	1	0	2	0	1
Schemmel	1.000	11	3	14	0	0
Snyder	.938	6	8	7	1	1
Weems	1.000	2	6	4	0	1
Zawadzki	.500	1	0	1	1	0

Shortstop	PCT	G	PO	A	E	DP
Chang	1.000	7	10	19	0	5
Kazmar	.964	110	146	331	18	60
J. Lopez	.989	18	34	55	1	7
Schemmel	.952	8	8	12	1	1
Weems	1.000	3	5	11	0	3

Outfield	PCT	G	PO	A	E	DP
Alley	.974	46	72	3	2	1
Baxter	.958	55	90	2	4	1
Ciofrone	.875	6	7	0	1	0
Cooper	.979	106	180	8	4	2
Huffman	.988	102	154	11	2	3
Macias	.979	128	265	12	6	3
Snyder	1.000	1	1	0	0	0

LAKE ELSINORE STORM　　　　HIGH CLASS A

CALIFORNIA LEAGUE

Batting	B-T	HT	WT	DOB	AVG	vLH	vRH	G	AB	R	H	2B	3B	HR	RBI	BB	HBP	SH	SF	SO	SB	CS	SLG	OBP
Bard, Josh	B-R	6-3	225	3-30-78	.111	.167	.000	3	9	0	1	0	0	0	2	0	0	0	0	0	0	0	.111	.273
Barrett, Michael	B-R	6-3	215	10-22-76	.667	1.000	.500	1	3	0	2	0	0	0	1	0	0	0	1	0	0	.667	.750
Baxter, Mike	L-R	6-0	190	12-7-84	.239	.235	.240	24	92	13	22	4	1	1	17	10	2	0	1	12	3	0	.337	.324
Blauer, Robbie	L-L	5-11	210	9-8-85	.219	.000	.333	11	32	6	7	3	0	2	5	0	0	1	6	0	0	.500	.278
Canham, Mitch	L-R	6-2	215	9-25-84	.285	.318	.277	113	417	65	119	28	5	8	81	66	1	1	3	73	13	1	.434	.382
Carter, Sam	R-R	6-4	210	6-5-83	.282	.320	.271	127	476	79	134	37	2	14	82	64	5	2	1	119	4	2	.456	.372
Contreras, Rayner	R-R	6-0	150	9-21-86	.309	.382	.294	54	194	22	60	10	4	0	27	21	7	1	0	36	10	5	.402	.396
Diaz, Javis	L-L	5-10	165	6-25-84	.253	.241	.256	104	367	69	93	11	3	4	37	31	4	2	4	86	28	7	.332	.315
Durango, Luis	B-R	5-10	145	4-23-86	.431	.524	.392	17	72	20	31	4	1	0	10	13	0	0	2	7	1	1	.514	.506
Dykstra, Allan	L-R	6-5	215	5-21-87	.292	.600	.211	7	24	5	7	1	0	1	10	7	1	0	0	7	0	0	.458	.469
Edmonds, Jim	L-L	6-1	210	6-27-70	.333	—	.333	2	6	2	2	0	0	0	0	0	0	0	1	0	0	.333	.333
Gunther, Barry	B-R	6-0	190	3-18-82	.220	.250	.206	15	50	11	11	4	0	0	3	4	0	0	1	7	0	0	.300	.273
Hunt, Jeremy	R-R	6-2	210	12-22-83	.266	.286	.261	101	350	45	93	22	2	11	52	41	9	0	5	63	1	2	.434	.353
Hunter, Cedric	L-L	6-0	185	3-10-88	.318	.340	.312	134	584	98	186	33	3	11	84	42	4	0	11	47	12	6	.442	.364
Iguchi, Tadahito	R-R	5-10	185	12-4-74	.400	.286	.667	3	10	4	4	0	0	0	1	1	0	0	0	1	0	0	1.000	.455
Joynt, Brian	R-R	6-4	205	3-14-85	.304	.273	.316	76	283	63	86	28	1	13	67	35	3	0	4	61	5	1	.548	.382
King, Tom	R-R	5-11	170	8-3-84	.158	.188	.150	19	76	8	12	2	0	0	4	5	0	0	0	15	0	1	.184	.210
Kulbacki, Kellen	L-L	5-11	185	11-21-85	.332	.382	.316	84	310	56	103	18	0	20	66	47	7	0	4	52	1	2	.589	.428
Lopez, Jesus	R-R	5-11	165	9-12-87	.248	.229	.253	99	339	44	84	13	0	2	38	28	3	6	4	41	2	2	.304	.307
McQueary, Aeden	R-R	5-11	180	9-19-84	.108	.176	.083	24	65	9	7	0	0	0	5	19	1	0	0	23	0	0	.108	.318
Perry, Robert	L-L	5-10	185	10-3-84	.165	.167	.165	38	115	14	19	5	1	0	11	23	5	1	2	17	3	2	.226	.324
Rivera, Jodam	B-R	5-10	180	2-4-86	.218	.259	.204	79	225	39	49	6	1	1	16	39	2	3	3	39	4	2	.267	.335

	B-T	HT	WT	DOB	AVG	vLH	vRH	G	AB	R	H	2B	3B	HR	RBI	BB	HBP	SH	SF	SO	SB	CS	SLG	OBP
Ruth, Keoni	R-R	5-11	200	3-21-85	.246	.301	.228	82	301	38	74	12	0	5	35	13	3	1	1	31	2	0	.336	.283
Schemmel, Jon	R-R	5-11	190	1-27-83	.323	.200	.381	12	31	7	10	2	0	1	3	5	0	0	0	6	1	0	.484	.417
Sogard, Eric	L-R	5-10	180	5-22-86	.308	.316	.306	133	536	97	165	42	3	10	87	79	1	0	6	62	16	7	.453	.394
Stocco, Matt	R-R	6-1	210	8-16-83	.250	—	.250	1	4	1	1	0	0	0	1	0	0	0	0	1	0	0	.500	.250

Pitching	B-T	HT	WT	DOB	W	L	ERA	G	GS	CG	SV	IP	H	R	ER	HR	BB	SO	AVG	vLH	vRH	K/9	BB/9
Axelrod, Dylan	R-R	6-0	195	7-30-85	2	1	5.29	32	0	0	0	49	51	36	29	4	19	55	.258	.303	.212	10.03	3.47
Carrillo, Cesar	R-R	6-3	175	4-29-84	3	5	5.97	15	14	0	0	57	69	43	38	6	33	32	.301	.264	.333	5.02	5.18
Culp, Nathan	L-L	6-2	180	10-9-84	14	8	3.83	27	26	0	0	157	189	83	67	10	23	74	.296	.292	.298	4.23	1.32
Daigle, Richie	R-R	6-0	197	9-9-82	3	6	5.09	30	0	0	0	41	49	28	23	3	16	16	.299	.351	.253	3.54	3.54
DeMark, Mike	R-R	6-0	198	5-20-83	1	2	2.17	42	0	0	0	50	35	14	12	4	19	53	.196	.247	.153	9.60	3.44
Dunn, Brooks	L-L	6-2	205	5-6-84	2	3	7.53	16	8	0	0	43	66	39	36	2	25	25	.365	.404	.349	5.23	5.23
Estes, Shawn	R-L	6-2	200	2-18-73	0	1	4.76	2	2	0	0	6	6	3	3	1	5	5	.273	.200	.294	7.94	4.76
Frieri, Ernesto	R-R	6-2	190	7-19-85	8	6	4.00	33	18	0	0	124	125	61	55	14	32	108	.262	.260	.264	7.86	2.33
Gomes, Brandon	R-R	5-11	175	7-15-84	2	1	2.89	22	0	0	0	28	27	13	9	3	6	36	.241	.250	.234	11.57	1.93
Hampson, Justin	L-L	6-1	205	5-24-80	0	0	0.00	5	0	0	0	6	1	0	0	0	1	4	.056	.000	.083	6.00	1.50
Hefner, Jeremy	R-R	6-4	215	3-11-86	0	0	3.60	1	1	0	0	5	3	2	2	0	2	6	.167	.286	.091	10.80	3.60
Hensley, Clay	R-R	5-11	185	8-31-79	1	0	0.00	1	1	0	0	1	0	0	0	0	0	1	.250	.500	.000	9.00	0.00
Kluber, Corey	R-R	6-4	215	4-10-86	2	5	6.01	19	16	0	0	85	93	62	57	9	34	75	.288	.344	.221	7.91	3.59
Lopez, Wilton	R-R	6-0	190	7-19-83	2	1	2.64	30	0	0	12	31	34	10	9	0	4	26	.283	.316	.254	7.63	1.17
Luebke, Cory	L-L	6-4	200	3-4-85	3	6	6.84	17	15	0	0	72	97	61	55	8	23	60	.323	.291	.336	7.47	2.86
Madden, John	R-R	6-4	229	12-2-82	2	3	3.88	52	0	0	1	72	73	34	31	2	24	45	.263	.277	.250	5.63	3.00
McDaid, Derek	R-R	6-3	200	9-27-83	0	1	5.29	21	0	0	0	32	42	23	19	1	7	18	.318	.328	.309	5.01	1.95
Miller, Drew	R-R	6-4	190	2-24-86	10	7	6.10	27	26	0	0	134	172	103	91	19	46	100	.313	.313	.313	6.70	3.08
Pelzer, Wynn	R-R	6-1	200	6-23-86	0	0	27.00	1	0	0	0	1	3	4	3	0	1	0	.500	.000	.600	0.00	9.00
Rodriguez, R.J.	R-R	6-0	175	7-5-84	6	3	4.92	58	0	0	12	75	88	44	41	5	23	53	.298	.259	.331	6.36	2.76
Scribner, Evan	R-R	6-3	190	7-19-85	2	1	2.70	20	0	0	1	23	14	7	7	3	3	31	.167	.194	.146	11.96	1.16
2-team total (5 Visalia)					2	2	2.45	25	0	0	2	33	19	9	9	4	5	41	—	—	—	11.18	1.36
Shaver, Chris	L-L	6-7	250	8-21-81	0	3	6.14	19	0	0	0	22	33	16	15	0	4	14	.351	.297	.386	5.73	1.64
Tomko, Brett	R-R	6-4	220	4-7-73	0	0	0.00	1	0	0	0	1	0	0	0	0	0	1	.000	.000	.000	9.00	0.00
Valdez, Rolando	R-R	6-1	191	1-8-86	8	5	4.00	46	11	0	4	99	90	46	44	12	24	79	.239	.197	.276	7.18	2.18
Woodard, Robert	R-R	6-1	205	1-10-85	0	0	2.43	15	1	0	0	30	19	12	8	5	9	25	.179	.245	.123	7.58	2.73
Young, Chris	R-R	6-10	280	5-25-79	0	1	3.12	2	2	0	0	9	5	3	3	3	1	7	.161	.111	.231	7.27	1.04

Fielding

Catcher	PCT	G	PO	A	E	DP	PB
Bard	1.000	2	8	0	0	0	0
Barrett	1.000	1	12	1	0	0	0
Canham	.988	107	708	52	9	5	21
Gunther	.991	14	103	6	1	0	0
McQueary	.980	24	136	13	3	0	3
Stocco	1.000	1	7	2	0	0	0

First Base	PCT	G	PO	A	E	DP
Baxter	1.000	10	78	10	0	6
Blauer	1.000	8	61	0	0	3
Carter	.986	34	252	23	4	15
Dykstra	1.000	2	19	0	0	2
Hunt	.986	82	676	43	10	60
Joynt	.923	3	12	0	1	2
Ruth	.989	22	170	12	2	10

Second Base	PCT	G	PO	A	E	DP
Iguchi	1.000	2	1	7	0	1
King	.974	7	13	25	1	6
Rivera	.966	8	12	16	1	3
Ruth	.976	20	32	50	2	6
Schemmel	—	1	0	0	0	0
Sogard	.973	110	200	348	15	58

Third Base	PCT	G	PO	A	E	DP
Contreras	.930	52	34	73	8	3
Joynt	.869	41	26	60	13	4
King	.722	10	2	11	5	0
Rivera	.942	22	14	35	3	4
Ruth	.970	22	23	41	2	6
Schemmel	.750	3	0	6	2	0
Sogard	—	1	0	0	0	0

Shortstop	PCT	G	PO	A	E	DP
Lopez	.975	99	161	300	12	56
Rivera	.978	49	61	116	4	15
Schemmel	.875	8	8	13	3	1

Outfield	PCT	G	PO	A	E	DP
Baxter	1.000	12	20	2	0	0
Blauer	1.000	2	3	0	0	0
Carter	.985	83	118	10	2	1
Diaz	.932	78	134	4	10	1
Durango	.950	14	18	1	1	0
Edmonds	—	2	0	0	0	0
Hunter	.985	126	319	9	5	3
Joynt	.944	20	30	4	2	0
Kulbacki	.963	70	148	6	6	2
Perry	.966	33	55	2	2	1
Ruth	—	1	0	0	0	0

FORT WAYNE WIZARDS

LOW CLASS A

MIDWEST LEAGUE

Batting	B-T	HT	WT	DOB	AVG	vLH	vRH	G	AB	R	H	2B	3B	HR	RBI	BB	HBP	SH	SF	SO	SB	CS	SLG	OBP
Baum, Justin	R-R	6-1	195	10-6-85	.264	.277	.255	119	440	76	116	23	5	9	70	49	5	1	5	111	3	2	.400	.341
Brown, Zach	L-L	6-0	200	3-13-85	.224	.188	.233	50	152	17	34	5	0	3	22	21	1	0	2	26	1	3	.316	.318
Buschini, Shane	L-L	6-4	220	4-24-85	.261	.080	.301	42	138	19	36	17	1	2	24	13	2	0	1	40	1	0	.442	.331
Carrasco, Felix	B-R	6-1	220	2-14-87	.237	.150	.290	117	388	56	92	16	0	16	64	59	1	1	1	162	1	1	.402	.339
Carroll, Sawyer	L-R	6-4	215	5-9-86	.219	.231	.200	18	64	5	14	3	0	0	8	6	1	1	0	19	0	0	.266	.296
Carvajal, Yefri	R-R	5-11	190	1-22-89	.268	.247	.280	121	456	54	122	27	1	4	55	25	1	2	4	100	4	2	.357	.305
Chalk, Brad	L-L	6-1	180	1-20-86	.275	.232	.296	104	385	39	106	19	3	0	43	46	2	4	2	55	19	2	.340	.354
Contreras, Anthony	L-R	5-11	185	9-26-83	.304	.241	.323	36	125	20	38	7	1	1	15	9	0	1	1	22	1	3	.400	.348
Cumberland, Drew	L-R	5-10	175	1-13-89	.286	.200	.318	53	206	29	59	8	1	1	17	17	3	1	0	24	16	4	.350	.348
DuBarry, B.J.	R-R	6-2	185	9-24-82	.095	.083	.111	8	21	0	2	0	0	0	1	4	0	0	0	8	0	0	.095	.240
Durango, Luis	B-R	5-10	145	4-26-86	.305	.227	.344	93	334	56	102	11	3	1	25	49	1	4	1	43	14	7	.365	.395
Hansen, Kevin	R-R	5-10	170	11-5-85	.000	—	.000	1	3	0	0	0	0	0	0	0	0	0	0	2	0	0	.000	.000
Hill, Ryan	L-L	6-0	190	4-5-85	.333	.000	.333	4	12	2	4	1	0	0	1	2	0	0	0	1	0	0	.417	.429
Joynt, Brian	R-R	6-4	205	3-4-85	.250	.000	.333	3	4	0	1	0	0	0	1	2	0	0	1	0	0	0	.500	.500
Kulbacki, Kellen	L-L	5-11	185	11-21-85	.164	.385	.104	18	61	9	10	2	0	2	9	9	0	0	3	19	0	2	.295	.260
Martinez, Luis	R-R	6-0	210	4-3-85	.223	.299	.176	94	305	30	68	12	1	3	19	51	2	6	0	66	3	1	.298	.338
Mercado, Angel	R-R	6-0	205	8-19-85	.235	.241	.232	42	136	19	32	5	2	4	21	12	4	0	2	36	2	0	.390	.312
Parrino, Andy	B-R	6-0	185	10-31-85	.252	.232	.262	120	405	67	102	20	0	7	43	71	4	4	3	127	8	5	.353	.366
Payne, Danny	L-L	5-10	185	9-8-85	.172	.176	.170	39	128	12	22	4	0	1	10	32	1	0	0	39	2	2	.227	.342

	B-T	HT	WT	DOB	AVG	vLH	vRH	G	AB	R	H	2B	3B	HR	RBI	BB	HBP	SH	SF	SO	SB	CS	SLG	OBP
Perry, Robert	L-L	5-10	185	10-3-84	.251	.236	.259	72	259	38	65	12	2	3	34	27	12	0	1	40	13	6	.347	.348
Solis, Ali	R-R	6-0	176	9-29-87	.159	.258	.122	35	113	10	18	6	0	2	16	14	0	2	1	40	0	0	.265	.250
Stokes, Ray	R-R	5-10	160	10-30-85	.357	.500	.250	6	14	2	5	0	0	0	1	5	1	0	0	1	0	1	.357	.550
Zawadzki, Lance	B-R	5-11	185	5-26-85	.273	.220	.304	119	454	66	124	26	5	7	58	54	4	1	5	101	28	3	.399	.352
Zornes, Adam	R-R	6-0	215	4-2-86	.261	.273	.250	13	46	5	12	3	0	0	4	4	0	0	0	14	0	0	.326	.320

Pitching	B-T	HT	WT	DOB	W	L	ERA	G	GS	CG	SV	IP	H	R	ER	HR	BB	SO	AVG	vLH	vRH	K/9	BB/9
Axelrod, Dylan	R-R	6-0	195	7-30-85	1	1	3.62	23	0	0	0	27	26	12	11	2	7	25	.245	.256	.238	8.23	2.30
Breit, Aaron	R-R	6-4	205	4-19-86	3	7	5.57	27	5	0	0	52	61	38	32	2	24	46	.293	.284	.302	8.01	4.18
Davis, Tyler	R-R	6-3	195	5-15-85	1	4	4.18	22	0	0	2	24	29	14	11	3	9	18	.302	.267	.333	6.85	3.42
Delabar, Steve	R-R	6-5	220	7-17-83	2	1	5.27	11	0	0	0	14	17	8	8	0	5	12	.321	.389	.286	7.90	3.29
Gomes, Brandon	R-R	5-11	175	7-15-84	4	2	3.49	29	2	0	0	57	63	24	22	5	19	45	.294	.361	.239	7.15	3.02
Gutierrez, Omar	R-R	6-1	215	4-10-85	1	1	6.99	25	0	0	0	28	30	24	22	2	20	38	.263	.270	.260	12.07	6.35
Harrington, Allen	L-L	5-11	185	7-3-84	3	2	3.59	13	8	0	3	58	55	24	23	3	10	53	.255	.262	.252	8.27	1.56
Hefner, Jeremy	R-R	6-4	215	3-11-86	10	5	3.33	29	24	0	0	140	117	53	52	12	41	144	.288	.202	.252	9.24	2.63
Hynes, Colt	L-L	5-11	200	6-28-85	0	2	4.60	32	0	0	0	45	60	26	23	2	11	38	.324	.306	.331	7.60	2.20
Kluber, Corey	R-R	6-4	215	4-10-86	4	3	3.21	10	10	0	0	56	49	25	20	8	13	72	.229	.266	.190	11.57	2.09
Lara, Alexis	R-R	6-0	150	3-23-87	0	0	0.00	2	0	0	0	2	1	0	0	0	2	2	.000	.333	.000	9.00	9.00
Latos, Mat	R-R	6-5	210	12-9-87	0	3	3.28	7	5	0	0	25	24	12	9	3	8	23	.250	.292	.208	8.39	2.92
Luebke, Cory	R-L	6-4	200	3-4-85	3	3	2.89	10	10	0	0	56	52	19	18	6	9	40	.265	.288	.257	6.43	1.45
McBryde, Jeremy	R-R	6-2	195	5-1-87	8	9	4.28	30	26	0	1	137	151	78	65	11	24	158	.281	.290	.273	10.40	1.58
McDaid, Derek	R-R	6-3	220	9-27-83	3	2	3.89	33	0	0	2	37	41	19	16	2	11	24	.268	.359	.173	5.84	2.68
Oland, Bryan	R-R	6-3	230	6-5-85	4	1	0.88	44	1	0	1	51	33	7	5	0	8	64	.179	.205	.158	11.29	1.41
Pelzer, Wynn	R-R	6-1	200	6-23-86	9	9	3.19	29	23	0	0	118	114	64	42	9	32	100	.248	.298	.200	7.61	2.43
Quezada, Jackson	R-R	6-4	170	8-9-86	2	4	2.12	59	0	0	27	64	42	19	15	1	19	79	.180	.257	.117	11.17	2.69
Teague, Matt	R-L	6-3	210	12-14-84	7	8	4.75	39	16	0	0	108	130	65	57	12	30	62	.300	.271	.313	5.17	2.50
Vandel, Geoff	L-L	6-1	190	6-9-87	3	1	6.40	16	5	0	1	45	52	34	32	7	11	33	.287	.259	.299	6.60	2.20
Woodard, Robert	R-R	6-1	205	1-10-85	3	4	3.25	27	5	0	2	72	61	31	26	7	14	58	.231	.230	.232	7.25	1.75

Fielding

Catcher	PCT	G	PO	A	E	DP	PB
DuBarry	.982	8	53	1	1	0	0
Martinez	.990	92	694	67	8	6	6
Solis	.977	35	287	46	8	5	6
Zornes	1.000						

First Base	PCT	G	PO	A	E	DP
Brown	.994	42	311	27	2	27
Carrasco	.985	103	819	53	13	71
Mercado	1.000	4	28	2	0	5

Second Base	PCT	G	PO	A	E	DP
Baum	.933	3	4	10	1	0
Contreras	.975	9	17	22	1	3
Cumberland	.957	8	20	24	2	5

	PCT	G	PO	A	E	DP
Hansen	1.000	1	0	4	0	0
Parrino	.967	89	166	275	15	56
Stokes	1.000	4	8	11	0	1
Zawadzki	.965	32	52	86	5	19

Third Base	PCT	G	PO	A	E	DP
Baum	.893	111	74	169	29	18
Carrasco	.500	3	1	1	2	0
Contreras	.959	15	12	35	2	4
Parrino	.879	15	9	20	4	3

Shortstop	PCT	G	PO	A	E	DP
Contreras	1.000	9	11	27	0	3
Cumberland	.922	43	86	116	17	31
Parrino	.952	13	22	18	2	3

Zawadzki	.920	79	117	193	27	44

Outfield	PCT	G	PO	A	E	DP
Buschini	.981	35	44	7	1	1
Carroll	.960	16	24	0	1	0
Carvajal	.947	110	155	7	9	1
Chalk	.979	98	179	10	4	2
Durango	.959	51	86	7	4	1
Hill	1.000	4	8	0	0	0
Joynt	1.000	3	3	0	0	0
Kulbacki	.947	15	17	1	1	0
Mercado	.955	19	20	1	1	1
Payne	.970	29	60	4	2	0
Perry	.990	59	97	2	1	0

EUGENE EMERALDS   SHORT-SEASON

NORTHWEST LEAGUE

Batting	B-T	HT	WT	DOB	AVG	vLH	vRH	G	AB	R	H	2B	3B	HR	RBI	BB	HBP	SH	SF	SO	SB	CS	SLG	OBP
Anna, Dean	L-R	5-11	180	11-24-86	.224	.240	.220	30	107	21	24	2	0	4	15	20	5	1	2	23	10	1	.355	.366
Blauer, Robbie	L-L	5-11	210	9-8-85	.255	.182	.275	42	153	19	39	7	0	2	27	25	5	1	3	21	2	2	.340	.371
Buschini, Shane	L-L	6-4	220	4-24-85	.188	.400	.148	9	32	4	6	0	0	0	5	4	0	0	0	8	0	0	.188	.278
Carroll, Sawyer	L-R	6-4	215	5-9-86	.299	.340	.282	46	177	41	53	14	3	8	39	32	0	0	2	48	5	2	.548	.403
Clark, Matt	L-R	6-5	215	12-10-86	.279	.316	.265	38	140	18	39	8	0	5	32	23	4	0	5	38	0	0	.443	.384
Darnell, James	R-R	6-2	195	1-19-87	.373	.235	.420	16	67	9	25	6	1	2	15	11	0	0	0	12	1	1	.582	.462
Decker, Jaff	L-L	5-10	190	2-23-90	.200	.000	.222	3	10	2	2	0	0	0	2	0	0	0	0	5	0	0	.200	.333
Figueroa, Cole	L-R	5-10	180	6-30-87	.289	.083	.344	32	114	23	33	6	0	5	16	24	0	1	1	16	7	2	.474	.410
Forsythe, Logan	R-R	6-1	195	1-14-87	.333	.500	.286	3	9	1	3	0	0	1	0	0	1	0	0	3	0	0	.444	.455
Gelbrich, Logan	R-R	6-3	205	12-1-85	.240	.250	.234	33	100	14	24	5	1	0	10	18	1	0	1	35	0	0	.310	.358
Hill, Ryan	L-L	6-0	190	4-5-85	.243	.297	.224	41	144	17	35	10	2	5	24	19	0	3	2	31	2	2	.444	.327
Mercado, Angel	R-R	6-0	205	8-19-85	.276	.306	.263	58	214	31	59	9	0	7	24	21	6	0	2	48	9	2	.416	.354
Naylor, Clinton	L-R	5-11	200	8-3-88	.222	.000	.267	9	18	2	4	2	0	0	3	5	0	0	0	11	0	0	.333	.391
Quiles, Emmanuel	R-R	5-11	186	10-26-89	.211	.262	.190	42	147	15	31	4	0	1	11	14	2	1	0	34	0	1	.259	.288
Railey, Joey	L-R	5-7	180	12-9-85	.219	.273	.196	21	73	16	16	2	0	0	4	8	1	1	0	10	2	1	.247	.305
Robertson, Dan	R-R	5-8	175	9-30-85	.377	.390	.373	73	302	59	114	21	3	3	45	34	5	3	4	34	20	7	.497	.443
Shunk, Derek	R-R	6-1	178	10-31-85	.222	.244	.213	41	135	22	30	7	0	3	17	23	3	2	1	36	0	1	.341	.346
Solis, Ali	R-R	6-0	176	9-29-87	.323	.385	.278	8	31	6	10	2	0	1	4	2	0	0	0	7	0	0	.484	.432
Tekotte, Blake	R-R	6-0	166	5-24-87	.285	.288	.284	47	193	43	55	15	0	6	29	27	4	1	3	45	7	4	.456	.379
Valdez, Jeudy	R-R	5-11	155	5-5-89	.227	.194	.242	59	216	35	49	10	2	5	22	18	3	2	6	64	3	4	.361	.293
Verbick, Bobby	R-R	5-11	205	1-5-85	.257	.275	.247	42	144	25	37	10	0	5	25	33	4	1	3	30	5	5	.431	.402
Weems, Beamer	B-R	5-10	175	7-28-87	.186	.083	.207	25	70	15	13	6	0	0	9	18	1	2	2	17	0	0	.271	.352

Pitching	B-T	HT	WT	DOB	W	L	ERA	G	GS	CG	SV	IP	H	R	ER	HR	BB	SO	AVG	vLH	vRH	K/9	BB/9
Bagley, Tyson	R-R	6-8	250	10-20-85	1	0	3.57	22	6	0	0	40	31	22	16	3	27	50	.203	.183	.215	11.16	6.02
Bass, Anthony	R-R	6-2	190	11-1-87	2	2	2.10	25	0	0	7	34	25	12	8	3	14	41	.197	.232	.169	10.75	3.67
Brannan, Cooper	R-R	6-4	235	11-7-84	1	0	6.33	17	0	0	0	21	28	20	15	1	10	6	.329	.379	.304	2.53	4.22
Castro, Simon	R-R	6-5	203	4-9-88	2	3	3.99	15	15	0	0	65	54	35	29	3	29	64	.223	.189	.245	8.82	3.99
Davis, Tyler	R-R	6-3	195	5-15-85	3	3	2.42	22	0	0	1	26	22	12	7	2	12	19	.222	.262	.193	6.58	4.15

	B-T	HT	WT	DOB																			
Davis, Erik	R-R	6-4	200	10-8-86	2	0	2.70	14	5	0	0	27	19	8	8	2	7	39	.200	.158	.228	13.16	2.36
Davis, Tom	R-R	6-2	215	6-3-86	0	4	8.59	11	5	0	0	29	47	30	28	8	12	26	.359	.239	.424	7.98	3.68
Garramone, Robert	R-R	6-2	175	8-22-87	1	1	7.20	8	4	0	0	25	27	22	20	1	17	18	.287	.273	.300	6.48	6.12
Gutierrez, Omar	R-R	6-1	215	4-10-85	0	0	0.00	3	0	0	1	6	5	0	0	0	1	9	.227	.333	.154	13.50	1.50
Herr, Zach	L-L	5-9	185	12-1-86	1	1	3.12	9	0	0	0	17	14	8	6	1	10	12	.219	.273	.190	6.23	5.19
Heyne, Kyle	R-R	6-5	220	8-17-84	3	4	4.19	23	0	0	1	39	37	19	18	1	14	25	.248	.250	.247	5.82	3.26
Juan, Pascual	L-L	6-2	163	2-14-85	1	2	12.71	6	0	0	0	6	7	8	8	0	5	7	.304	.222	.357	11.12	7.94
Lara, Alexis	R-R	6-0	150	3-23-87	1	0	2.79	20	0	0	0	29	18	14	9	0	28	27	.180	.231	.148	8.38	8.69
Latos, Mat	R-R	6-5	210	12-9-87	2	0	1.04	3	3	0	0	17	13	3	2	1	3	23	.197	.167	.250	11.94	1.56
Means, Matt	L-L	6-1	210	8-2-85	0	3	17.47	7	0	0	0	6	12	19	11	1	11	3	.414	.545	.333	4.76	17.47
Menchaca, Pablo	R-R	6-4	225	11-28-87	5	4	3.76	15	13	0	0	65	71	32	27	4	18	38	.282	.296	.271	5.29	2.51
Musgrave, Rob	L-L	6-1	205	9-26-85	6	1	3.21	27	0	0	0	42	34	19	15	2	11	66	.217	.320	.168	14.14	2.36
Poynter, Gary	R-R	6-2	190	6-12-87	1	0	4.10	16	2	0	0	26	31	15	12	1	18	15	.301	.311	.293	5.13	6.15
Schumacher, Nick	R-R	6-4	210	7-24-85	2	2	4.15	20	0	0	1	30	29	15	14	3	8	29	.254	.317	.219	8.60	2.37
Vandel, Geoff	L-L	6-1	190	6-9-87	3	3	3.42	15	15	0	0	74	73	32	28	3	26	51	.258	.403	.209	6.23	3.18
Vincent, Nick	R-R	6-0	175	7-12-86	3	3	5.40	16	8	0	2	43	42	32	26	6	20	38	.259	.215	.289	7.89	4.15

Fielding

Catcher	PCT	G	PO	A	E	DP	PB
Gelbrich	.974	29	204	19	6	4	13
Naylor	1.000	8	39	5	0	1	2
Quiles	.989	42	327	36	4	4	19
Solis	.977	6	36	6	1	0	1

First Base	PCT	G	PO	A	E	DP
Blauer	.981	36	301	13	6	26
Buschini	.818	1	9	0	2	3
Clark	.969	35	289	27	10	30
Mercado	.952	6	38	2	2	5

Second Base	PCT	G	PO	A	E	DP
Anna	1.000	14	25	41	0	12
Figueroa	.938	12	16	29	3	7
Railey	.968	20	34	56	3	12

Shunk	.939	8	7	24	2	3
Valdez	.967	20	27	60	3	11
Weems	1.000	4	9	13	0	3

Third Base	PCT	G	PO	A	E	DP
Anna	.842	8	5	11	3	0
Carroll	—	1	0	0	0	0
Darnell	.972	16	10	25	1	4
Forsythe	.750	3	1	2	1	0
Mercado	.860	21	19	24	7	4
Shunk	.864	28	19	38	9	2
Weems	1.000	5	3	9	0	2

Shortstop	PCT	G	PO	A	E	DP
Anna	.956	9	20	23	2	7
Figueroa	.963	17	26	52	3	11

Valdez	.952	38	57	101	8	27
Weems	.950	15	24	33	3	9

Outfield	PCT	G	PO	A	E	DP
Blauer	—	1	0	0	0	0
Buschini	1.000	5	9	1	0	0
Carroll	.977	42	80	6	2	2
Decker	1.000	3	3	0	0	0
Hill	.951	28	57	1	3	0
Mercado	.824	13	14	0	3	0
Robertson	.965	70	127	12	5	2
Tekotte	.967	46	86	1	3	1
Verbick	.974	25	37	1	1	1

AZL PADRES

ARIZONA LEAGUE

ROOKIE

Batting	B-T	HT	WT	DOB	AVG	vLH	vRH	G	AB	R	H	2B	3B	HR	RBI	BB	HBP	SH	SF	SO	SB	CS	SLG	OBP
Acosta, Kevin	R-R	5-9	150	4-15-89	.344	1.000	.300	18	32	9	11	1	0	0	2	3	1	1	0	8	3	1	.375	.417
Anna, Dean	L-R	5-11	180	11-24-86	.250	.500	.194	13	44	9	11	1	0	1	9	1	0	1	0	8	1	0	.341	.267
Atherton, Tim	R-R	6-2	196	11-7-89	.212	.083	.250	21	52	4	11	1	0	0	6	2	0	0	0	21	0	1	.231	.241
Bard, Josh	B-R	6-3	225	3-30-78	.000	—	.000	1	3	0	0	0	0	0	0	0	0	0	0	1	0	0	.000	.000
Codiroli, Jason	L-L	5-10	175	1-20-87	.309	.381	.288	51	181	39	56	5	3	1	14	31	5	1	1	33	15	7	.387	.422
Cumberland, Drew	L-R	5-10	175	1-13-89	.500	.000	.556	3	10	3	5	1	2	0	2	0	0	0	0	1	0	0	1.000	.500
Decker, Jaff	L-L	5-10	190	2-23-90	.352	.310	.362	49	159	51	56	11	2	5	34	55	2	0	0	36	9	1	.541	.523
Forsythe, Logan	R-R	6-1	195	1-14-87	.231	.000	.261	9	26	2	6	0	0	0	5	6	0	0	0	8	0	0	.231	.429
Garzon, Edgar	R-R	6-0	178	8-24-86	.275	.267	.277	34	109	10	30	7	0	1	19	8	5	0	2	21	0	2	.367	.347
Gaski, Matt	L-R	5-10	185	5-12-86	.216	.182	.221	31	88	14	19	1	0	1	11	20	1	1	1	16	1	0	.261	.364
Hansen, Kevin	R-R	5-10	170	11-5-85	.287	.278	.289	48	178	33	51	8	2	0	22	23	2	2	4	16	7	3	.354	.367
Hardin, Chris	L-L	6-2	200	12-17-85	.287	.412	.257	53	178	43	51	12	2	1	29	38	1	0	1	49	11	2	.393	.413
Lara, Robert	R-R	6-2	190	11-25-86	.344	.429	.326	49	157	29	54	13	0	3	34	37	8	1	0	30	0	2	.484	.490
Marte, Keisy	R-R	5-10	169	12-14-88	.209	.208	.295	42	136	23	38	8	0	1	13	17	0	8	2	29	8	3	.360	.355
Murphree, Aaron	L-R	6-5	235	7-10-84	.250	.120	.278	42	140	20	35	6	3	4	38	26	6	0	6	35	1	0	.421	.376
Naylor, Clinton	L-R	5-11	200	8-3-88	.167	.167	.167	6	18	3	3	0	1	0	2	5	0	0	1	9	0	0	.278	.333
Payne, Danny	L-L	5-10	185	9-8-85	.333	.500	.308	4	15	2	5	1	0	0	4	3	0	0	1	6	1	0	.400	.421
Polanco, Wary	R-R	6-2	171	3-1-88	.188	.400	.148	16	32	2	6	1	0	0	3	3	1	0	0	8	0	1	.219	.278
Railey, Joey	L-R	5-7	180	12-9-85	.255	.167	.268	18	47	7	12	3	0	0	8	7	1	1	0	10	0	0	.319	.364
Rincon, Edinson	R-R	6-1	185	8-11-90	.308	.333	.304	23	65	8	20	1	1	0	19	14	1	3	18	0	0	.354	.429
Shaughnessy, Billy	R-R	5-11	185	12-11-85	.222	.250	.220	18	45	7	10	2	0	0	3	5	0	0	1	14	2	0	.267	.294
Williams, Chase	R-R	6-3	195	2-9-85	.169	.091	.185	41	130	21	22	7	1	0	18	22	1	0	0	30	3	0	.238	.294
Zornes, Adam	R-R	6-0	215	4-2-86	.133	.000	.222	4	15	1	2	0	0	0	2	1	0	0	3	0	0	.133	.278

Pitching	B-T	HT	WT	DOB	W	L	ERA	G	GS	CG	SV	IP	H	R	ER	HR	BB	SO	AVG	vLH	vRH	K/9	BB/9
Albers, Andrew	R-L	6-1	195	10-6-85	1	0	0.00	5	2	0	0	7	3	1	0	0	3	7	.136	.143	.133	9.00	3.86
Angelucci, Alessio	R-R	6-2	190	7-28-88	1	1	5.13	14	6	0	0	33	29	25	19	1	23	29	.238	.216	.247	7.83	6.21
Boyd, Stephen	R-L	6-2	200	11-3-87	0	0	7.11	12	0	0	0	13	10	11	10	1	18	8	.227	.250	.222	5.68	12.79
Brach, Brad	R-R	6-6	210	4-12-86	1	1	2.01	17	0	0	4	22	21	5	5	0	5	33	.250	.125	.300	13.30	2.01
Cameron, Kevin	R-R	6-1	190	12-15-79	0	0	0.00	2	1	0	0	2	0	0	0	0	1	.000	.000	.000	4.50	0.00
De Paula, Jose	L-L	6-2	165	3-4-90	4	3	3.57	13	13	0	0	53	61	30	21	2	9	56	.288	.238	.300	9.51	1.53
Goins, Steve	R-R			8-29-86	2	1	4.40	16	0	0	0	31	30	17	15	2	11	30	.250	.270	.241	8.80	3.23
Gonzalez, Eric	R-R	6-5	190	9-5-86	2	0	1.19	13	0	0	2	23	17	7	3	0	5	34	.195	.222	.183	13.50	1.99
Heyne, Kyle	R-R	6-5	220	8-17-84	0	0	0.00	3	0	0	0	3	2	0	0	0	0	3	.182	.200	.167	9.00	0.00
Hudgins, John	R-R	6-2	195	8-31-81	0	1	4.50	2	0	0	0	2	1	1	1	0	2	2	.250	.000	.286	9.00	9.00
Juan, Pascual	L-L	6-2	163	2-14-85	0	0	5.54	11	0	0	0	13	15	8	8	0	4	11	.319	.222	.342	7.62	2.77
Latos, Mat	R-R	6-5	210	12-9-87	1	0	3.21	5	3	0	0	14	12	5	5	0	2	23	.231	.133	.270	14.79	1.29
Lynch, Colin	R-R	6-0	185	8-30-85	0	4	4.78	22	0	0	5	32	37	22	17	1	9	38	.289	.250	.300	10.69	2.53
Means, Matt	L-L	6-1	210	8-2-85	0	0	7.84	8	0	0	0	10	12	9	9	3	4	13	.286	.167	.306	11.32	3.48
Osuna, Stiven	R-R	6-3	170	5-5-87	7	3	2.18	14	14	0	0	70	62	26	17	0	11	57	.241	.273	.228	7.29	1.41
Poynter, Gary	R-R	6-2	190	6-12-87	0	0	4.50	6	0	0	0	6	6	3	3	0	3	7	.273	.125	.357	10.50	4.50

Schumacher, Nick	R-R	6-4	210	7-24-85	2	0	3.60	5	0	0	0	10	10	4	4	1	0	9	.244	.111	.281	8.10	0.00
Tabachnik, Mauricio	R-R	6-2	198	11-8-89	2	4	4.91	17	1	0	0	29	43	32	16	2	7	16	.321	.389	.296	4.91	2.15
Veras, Junior	R-R	6-1	215	1-16-87	3	3	7.04	12	6	0	0	31	38	32	24	2	12	20	.295	.313	.289	5.87	3.52
Wilkes, Chris	R-R	6-4	235	9-26-89	7	1	3.21	15	10	0	0	62	64	26	22	1	5	45	.269	.261	.272	6.57	0.73

Fielding

Catcher	PCT	G	PO	A	E	DP	PB
Bard	1.000	1	5	0	0	0	0
Lara	.995	44	327	43	2	2	8
Naylor	1.000	5	28	8	0	2	1
Polanco	1.000	16	60	9	0	0	1
Zornes	1.000	2	26	2	0	0	1

First Base	PCT	G	PO	A	E	DP
Garzon	.983	14	113	5	2	11
Gaski	1.000	1	1	0	0	0
Hardin	.979	48	387	29	9	36
Murphree	.975	3	37	2	1	2

Second Base	PCT	G	PO	A	E	DP
Acosta	.947	12	20	34	3	5
Anna	.981	10	22	30	1	12

Gaski	1.000	3	6	10	0	2
Hansen	.989	23	37	49	1	9
Marte	.857	1	3	3	1	1
Railey	.985	16	26	40	1	11
Shaughnessy	.862	5	7	18	4	1

Third Base	PCT	G	PO	A	E	DP
Forsythe	.929	7	4	9	1	3
Garzon	.875	18	14	28	6	4
Gaski	.839	23	11	41	10	4
Hansen	.905	8	4	15	2	0
Marte	—	1	0	0	0	0
Rincon	.680	12	4	13	8	0

Shortstop	PCT	G	PO	A	E	DP
Anna	1.000	2	2	3	0	0

Cumberland	.909	3	2	8	1	2
Hansen	.946	17	22	48	4	12
Marte	.941	38	49	110	10	23
Shaughnessy	.900	9	7	20	3	2

Outfield	PCT	G	PO	A	E	DP
Atherton	.818	15	9	0	2	0
Codiroli	.947	47	50	4	3	1
Decker	.955	45	61	2	3	1
Garzon	—	1	0	0	0	0
Hansen	1.000	6	2	0	0	0
Hardin	1.000	9	1	0	0	0
Murphree	.974	32	32	5	1	1
Payne	1.000	3	5	0	0	0
Shaughnessy	1.000	2	3	0	0	0
Williams	.961	36	45	4	2	0

DSL PADRES ROOKIE

DOMINICAN SUMMER LEAGUE

Batting	B-T	HT	WT	DOB	AVG	vLH	vRH	G	AB	R	H	2B	3B	HR	RBI	BB	HBP	SH	SF	SO	SB	CS	SLG	OBP
Andrade, Angel	R-R	6-2	205	1-6-90	.118	.000	.143	5	17	3	2	1	0	0	1	1	0	0	10	0	0	.176	.211
Armstrong, Joel	R-R	6-2	185	11-2-88	.191	.250	.179	17	47	6	9	3	0	1	9	9	4	0	1	16	1	1	.319	.361
Carrillo, Rosario	R-R	6-4	183	9-8-88	.245	.320	.228	49	139	21	34	8	2	0	11	10	4	1	0	49	6	2	.331	.314
Galvez, Jonathan	R-R	6-2	175	1-18-91	.272	.219	.285	54	162	31	44	5	1	3	31	47	6	0	1	40	8	1	.370	.449
Garce, Daniel	R-R	6-1	166	6-6-89	.193	.143	.203	58	181	22	35	6	0	0	7	17	7	1	0	61	3	2	.227	.288
Garcia, Carlos	R-R	6-3	165	3-29-89	.267	.370	.248	62	180	23	48	7	4	2	24	18	4	0	3	55	8	6	.383	.341
Gonzalez, Edisson	R-R	5-10	180	6-15-88	.225	.222	.226	18	40	6	9	0	0	0	4	8	4	0	0	11	0	1	.225	.404
Liriano, Rymer	R-R	6-0	211	6-20-91	.198	.122	.215	67	232	34	46	13	1	9	37	28	5	0	2	106	9	5	.379	.296
Lopez, Jose	R-R	5-10	175	11-10-89	.112	.000	.138	37	98	9	11	1	0	1	10	12	4	1	1	28	3	3	.153	.235
Minyeti, Jorge	B-R	5-10	180	11-7-90	.288	.324	.281	64	205	38	59	13	3	0	10	61	4	4	0	36	17	13	.380	.459
Nuno, Manuel	R-R	6-6	264	1-11-89	.183	.194	.180	59	186	19	34	8	0	5	26	31	6	2	1	65	2	0	.306	.317
Paulino, Jose	R-R	6-0	182	11-13-88	.222	.235	.218	46	144	26	32	6	0	1	15	18	3	1	1	39	7	1	.285	.319
Pozo, Jhonaldo	R-R	6-3	183	3-28-89	.235	.290	.223	62	179	22	42	10	1	5	35	32	2	0	1	68	3	3	.385	.355
Rojas, Maykor	R-R	5-11	172	11-21-89	.292	.417	.264	36	65	16	19	1	0	0	3	6	1	0	0	24	0	0	.308	.387
Sosa, Cesar	R-R	6-4	175	11-25-88	.175	.333	.146	22	57	7	10	3	0	0	7	12	1	0	0	24	0	0	.228	.329
Tiburcio, Miguel	R-R	6-3	200	1-29-91	.154	.161	.152	51	143	15	22	4	1	2	11	17	3	1	0	75	2	2	.238	.258
Tortosa, Juan	R-R	6-2	170	9-6-90	.200	.167	.208	25	60	6	12	0	1	0	5	5	4	0	0	14	2	1	.233	.304
Wilson, Hans	B-R	5-11	185	9-8-90	.243	.182	.254	47	140	17	34	5	0	1	19	21	4	0	1	47	1	2	.300	.355

Pitching	B-T	HT	WT	DOB	W	L	ERA	G	GS	CG	SV	IP	H	R	ER	HR	BB	SO	AVG	vLH	vRH	K/9	BB/9
Arias, Rafeal	R-R	6-0	165	1-3-89	0	1	3.26	19	0	0	0	19	15	12	7	0	16	14	.227	.286	.200	6.52	7.45
Chavez, Juan	R-R	6-0	200	12-25-89	3	3	4.45	15	7	0	0	61	46	33	30	8	13	52	.198	.195	.200	7.71	1.93
De La Cruz, Luis	R-R	6-6	195	6-15-89	1	4	3.64	14	9	0	1	47	38	30	19	2	30	30	.216	.217	.215	5.74	5.74
Diaz, Javer	R-R	5-10	206	2-16-90	2	1	3.45	23	0	0	2	29	33	13	11	1	4	18	.287	.317	.270	5.65	1.26
Henrique, Freddys	R-R	6-3	218	5-28-90	1	0	1.56	6	2	0	0	17	6	3	3	0	6	17	.113	.111	.114	8.83	3.12
Hernandez, Pedro	L-L	5-10	200	4-12-89	7	2	1.42	14	8	0	0	63	50	21	10	2	6	74	.216	.185	.220	10.52	0.85
Herrera, Juan	R-R	6-0	179	8-21-91	0	3	5.93	12	7	0	0	30	25	22	20	1	31	28	.223	.074	.271	8.31	9.20
Javier, Esteban	L-L	6-1	155	4-2-89	2	1	3.18	21	0	0	1	28	28	11	10	0	21	26	.248	.385	.230	8.26	6.67
Martinez, Pedro	L-L	6-3	251	9-6-90	2	4	5.11	15	8	1	0	49	39	39	28	0	41	57	.219	.063	.253	10.40	7.48
Mozo, Harlen	R-R	6-2	210	8-12-89	1	5	4.89	11	6	0	0	35	37	33	19	0	24	25	.262	.196	.295	6.43	6.17
Ojeda, Erick	R-R	6-5	260	9-18-89	1	2	1.21	13	4	0	1	37	24	12	5	0	17	21	.185	.190	.182	5.06	4.10
Oramas, Juan	L-L	5-10	215	5-11-90	3	2	1.02	19	5	0	3	53	23	12	6	0	24	70	.125	.313	.107	11.89	4.08
Rodriguez, Guillermo	R-R	6-3	200	9-13-88	1	0	6.32	13	0	0	0	16	20	16	11	2	6	18	.290	.211	.320	10.34	3.45
Rosario, Juan	R-R	6-1	178	12-12-89	1	3	4.20	11	6	0	0	41	42	26	19	3	12	24	.276	.300	.265	5.31	2.66
Sanchez, Deiber	R-R	5-10	170	3-27-89	4	5	4.65	17	2	0	4	31	24	19	16	1	13	43	.212	.219	.210	12.48	3.77
Valdez, Stalyn	R-R	6-3	185	11-14-89	1	6	4.30	13	8	0	0	59	61	39	28	3	16	44	.262	.288	.253	6.75	2.45

Fielding

Catcher	PCT	G	PO	A	E	DP	PB
Nuno	1.000	2	6	0	0	0	0
Pozo	.980	47	314	27	7	1	18
Rojas	1.000	4	14	1	0	0	0
Wilson	.963	33	224	34	10	3	11

First Base	PCT	G	PO	A	E	DP
Armstrong	.973	14	135	7	4	10
Nuno	.982	57	516	33	10	33
Paulino	1.000	6	22	1	0	1
Pozo	1.000	1	2	0	0	0

Second Base	PCT	G	PO	A	E	DP
Galvez	1.000	1	0	1	0	0

Garce	1.000	6	9	8	0	1
Gonzalez	1.000	1	0	1	0	0
Lopez	1.000	5	4	7	0	2
Minyeti	.984	62	111	143	4	26
Paulino	.800	4	7	5	3	1

Third Base	PCT	G	PO	A	E	DP
Garce	.821	9	2	21	5	1
Gonzalez	.773	7	3	14	5	0
Lopez	.901	32	21	61	9	1
Minyeti	1.000	1	0	1	0	0
Paulino	.868	38	21	84	16	9
Pozo	.500	1	0	1	1	0
Wilson	.850	7	2	15	3	0

Shortstop	PCT	G	PO	A	E	DP
Chavez	1.000	1	1	0	0	0
Galvez	.957	33	46	89	6	12
Garce	.929	41	50	107	12	16
Lopez	.818	3	3	6	2	2

Outfield	PCT	G	PO	A	E	DP
Armstrong	1.000	2	1	0	0	0
Carrillo	.915	45	48	6	5	3
Garcia	.982	52	52	3	1	0
Liriano	.975	67	113	3	3	2
Sosa	1.000	21	18	1	0	0
Tiburcio	.917	48	51	4	5	0
Tortosa	.850	19	16	1	3	0

San Francisco Giants

BY ANDY BAGGARLY

The Giants' rebuilding effort didn't appear to make much progress in 2008. They posted a fourth consecutive losing season—a trough they hadn't hit since 1974-77—and their 72-90 record represented just a one-game improvement over the previous year.

But there was Tim Lincecum's ascendance among the leagues elite pitchers. There was switch-hitting infielder Pablo Sandoval's smashing debut. There was closer Brian Wilson's breakout season. And there was a productive draft that added four quality collegiate bats to a quickly healing minor league system.

There were reasons to believe in brighter days, even though the Giants aren't primed for a World Series run in the short term. Managing partner Bill Neukom acknowledged as much in October when he took the reins from retiring owner Peter Magowan.

"Our job is to . . . have an improved performance on the field in 2009, and that means we intend to be competitive," Neukom said. "And after we are competitive, we intend to be contending. We want to be contending as soon as possible. We want to be the sort of franchise that puts a contending team on the field game in and game out, and affords its community and fan base a contending team year in and year out.

"And how we're going to do that is by emphasizing and investing even more in homegrown talent."

Some of that talent was rushed through the thin upper levels of the minor league system in 2008, with mixed results. Players like Sandoval and shortstop Emmanuel Burriss had success against major league pitching despite limited exposure above Class A. Others, like first baseman John Bowker, were exposed after a fast start.

General manager Brian Sabean said he has Sandoval penciled in as the first baseman next season, and Burriss played well enough to convince management he could be the everyday shortstop.

And Sabean showed enough to convince Neukom that the longtime GM should be allowed to complete the final year of his contract. Under new scouting director John Barr, the Giants drafted Florida State catcher and Golden Spikes winner Buster Posey with the fifth overall pick, and added two more promising hitters in Wichita State infielder Conor Gillaspie and Texas Tech outfielder

Roger Kieschnick.

The Giants also committed another chunk of money on the international front, signing 16-year-old Dominican outfielder Rafael Rodriguez for $2.55 million. The bonus broke all franchise records—before Posey shattered it with his $6 million bonus.

2008 PERFORMANCE

General Manager: Brian Sabean. **Farm Director:** Fred Stanley. **Scouting Director:** Doug Mapson.

Class	Team	League	W	L	PCT	Finish*	Manager	Affiliate Since
Majors	San Francisco	National	72	90	.444	13th (16)	Bruce Bochy	—
Triple-A	Fresno Grizzlies	Pacific Coast	67	76	.469	11th (16)	Dan Rohn	1998
Double-A	Connecticut Defenders	Eastern	68	73	.482	7th (12)	Bien Figueroa	2003
High A	San Jose Giants	California	85	55	.607	1st (10)	Steve Decker	1988
Low A	Augusta Green Jackets	South Atlantic	88	50	.638	^1st (16)	Andy Skeels	2005
Short-season	Salem-Keizer Volcanoes	Northwest	40	36	.526	4th (8)	Tom Trebelhorn	1997
Rookie	AZL Giants	Arizona	36	20	.643	^2nd (9)	Bert Hunter	2000

Overall 2008 Minor League Record 384 310 .553 3rd

* Finish in overall standings (No. of teams in league). ^League champion.

ORGANIZATION STATISTICS

SAN FRANCISCO GIANTS

NATIONAL LEAGUE

Batting	B-T	HT	WT	DOB	AVG	vLH	vRH	G	AB	R	H	2B	3B	HR	RBI	BB	HBP	SH	SF	SO	SB	CS	SLG	OBP
Alfonzo, Eliezer	R-R	5-11	220	2-7-79	.091	.000	.111	5	11	0	1	0	0	0	1	0	0	0	0	4	0	0	.091	.091
Aurilia, Rich	R-R	6-1	200	9-2-71	.283	.321	.263	140	407	33	115	21	1	10	52	30	1	0	2	56	1	1	.413	.332
Bocock, Brian	R-R	5-11	185	3-9-85	.143	.000	.167	32	7	4	1	1	0	0	2	12	0	4	0	29	4	2	.156	.258
Bowker, John	L-L	6-2	200	7-8-83	.255	.152	.266	111	326	31	83	14	3	10	43	19	3	0	2	74	1	1	.408	.300
Burriss, Manny	B-R	6-0	190	1-17-85	.283	.292	.278	95	240	37	68	6	1	1	18	23	5	5	1	24	13	5	.329	.357
Castillo, Jose	R-R	6-1	220	3-19-81	.244	.233	.248	112	394	42	96	28	4	6	35	25	1	0	0	71	2	2	.381	.290
2-team total (15 Houston)					.246	—	—	127	426	46	105	29	4	6	37	27	1	0	1	81	2	2	.376	.292
Davis, Rajai	R-R	5-11	195	10-19-80	.056	.000	.083	12	18	2	1	0	0	0	0	1	0	0	0	6	4	0	.056	.105
Denker, Travis	R-R	5-9	205	8-5-85	.243	.267	.227	24	37	6	9	4	1	1	3	5	0	0	0	10	0	0	.486	.333
Durham, Ray	B-R	5-8	205	11-30-71	.293	.221	.318	87	263	43	77	23	0	3	32	38	2	0	1	49	6	2	.414	.385
2-team total (41 Milwaukee)					.289	—	—	128	370	64	107	35	0	6	45	53	2	0	1	72	8	4	.432	.380
Frandsen, Kevin	R-R	6-0	185	5-24-82	.000	—	.000	1	1	0	0	0	0	0	0	0	0	0	0	0	0	0	.000	.000
Gillaspie, Conor	L-R	6-1	200	7-18-87	.200	.000	.200	8	5	1	1	0	0	0	0	2	0	0	0	0	0	0	.200	.429
Holm, Steve	R-R	6-0	210	10-21-79	.262	.235	.269	49	84	10	22	9	0	1	6	10	3	0	1	16	0	1	.405	.357
Horwitz, Brian	R-R	6-1	185	11-7-82	.222	.235	.211	21	36	5	8	0	0	0	2	4	5	0	0	1	0	0	.389	.310
Ishikawa, Travis	L-L	6-3	225	9-24-83	.274	.000	.280	33	95	12	26	6	0	3	15	9	0	0	0	27	1	0	.432	.337
Lewis, Fred	L-R	6-2	200	12-9-80	.282	.270	.285	133	468	81	132	25	11	9	40	51	0	0	2	124	21	7	.440	.351
McClain, Scott	R-R	6-4	230	5-19-72	.273	.167	.333	14	33	7	9	1	0	2	7	5	0	0	0	8	0	1	.485	.368
Molina, Bengie	R-R	5-11	225	7-20-74	.292	.297	.291	145	530	46	155	33	0	16	95	19	9	0	11	38	0	0	.445	.322
Ochoa, Ivan	R-R	5-9	175	12-16-82	.200	.244	.173	47	120	7	24	8	0	0	3	4	3	7	0	28	0	1	.267	.244
Ortmeier, Dan	B-L	6-4	230	5-11-81	.219	.238	.182	38	64	4	14	6	0	0	5	7	2	0	0	18	2	2	.313	.315
Roberts, Dave	L-L	5-10	180	5-31-72	.224	.000	.229	52	107	18	24	2	2	0	9	20	0	1	2	18	5	3	.280	.341
Rohlinger, Ryan	R-R	6-1	195	10-7-83	.094	.250	.042	21	32	2	3	1	1	0	2	1	0	0	0	8	0	1	.188	.121
Rowand, Aaron	R-R	6-0	220	8-29-77	.271	.286	.266	152	549	57	149	37	0	13	70	44	14	0	4	126	2	4	.410	.339
Sandoval, Pablo	B-R	5-11	245	8-11-86	.345	.237	.383	41	145	24	50	10	1	3	24	4	1	0	4	14	0	0	.490	.357
Schierholtz, Nate	L-R	6-2	215	2-15-84	.320	.333	.315	19	75	12	24	8	1	1	5	3	3	0	0	8	0	1	.493	.370
Snow, J.T.	L-L	6-2	210	2-26-68	.000	—	—	1	0	0	0	0	0	0	0	0	0	0	0	0	0	0	.000	.000
Timpner, Clay	L-L	6-2	195	5-13-83	.000	—	.000	2	1	0	0	0	0	0	0	0	0	0	0	0	0	0	.000	.000
Velez, Eugenio	B-R	6-1	160	5-16-82	.262	.235	.268	98	275	32	72	16	7	1	30	14	1	1	1	40	15	6	.382	.299
Vizquel, Omar	B-R	5-9	175	4-24-67	.222	.121	.250	92	266	24	59	10	1	0	23	24	0	7	3	29	5	4	.267	.283
Winn, Randy	B-R	6-2	195	6-9-74	.306	.289	.313	155	598	84	183	38	2	10	64	59	0	1	9	88	25	2	.426	.363

Pitching	B-T	HT	WT	DOB	W	L	ERA	G	GS	CG	SV	IP	H	R	ER	HR	BB	SO	AVG	vLH	vRH	K/9	BB/9
Cain, Matt	R-R	6-3	245	10-1-84	8	14	3.76	34	34	1	0	218	206	95	91	19	91	186	.251	.268	.235	7.69	3.76
Chulk, Vinnie	R-R	6-2	195	12-19-78	0	3	4.83	27	0	0	0	32	33	18	17	6	8	16	.260	.233	.274	4.55	2.27
Correia, Kevin	R-R	6-3	200	8-24-80	3	8	6.05	25	19	0	0	110	141	80	74	15	47	66	.310	.307	.312	5.40	3.85
Espineli, Geno	L-L	6-4	195	9-8-82	2	0	5.06	15	0	0	0	16	17	10	9	5	8	8	.258	.188	.333	4.50	4.50
Hennessey, Brad	R-R	6-2	195	2-7-80	1	2	7.81	17	4	1	0	40	63	35	35	8	15	21	.358	.333	.375	4.69	3.35
Hinshaw, Alex	L-L	6-4	190	10-31-82	2	1	3.40	48	0	0	0	40	31	16	15	5	29	47	.220	.205	.235	10.66	6.58
Lincecum, Tim	L-R	5-11	170	6-15-84	18	5	2.62	34	33	2	0	227	182	72	66	11	84	265	.221	.221	.221	10.51	3.33
Matos, Osiris	R-R	6-1	200	8-6-84	1	2	4.79	20	0	0	0	21	26	17	11	3	9	16	.302	.296	.316	6.97	3.92
Misch, Pat	R-L	6-2	195	8-18-81	0	3	5.68	15	7	0	0	52	56	34	33	11	15	38	.273	.281	.270	6.54	2.58
Palmer, Matt	R-R	6-2	200	3-21-79	0	2	8.53	3	3	0	0	13	17	13	12	1	13	3	.333	.333	.333	2.13	9.24
Romo, Sergio	R-R	5-11	190	3-4-83	3	1	2.12	29	0	0	0	34	16	13	8	3	8	33	.138	.083	.176	8.74	2.12
Sadler, Billy	R-R	6-0	195	9-21-81	0	1	4.06	33	0	0	0	44	34	21	20	6	27	42	.215	.193	.228	8.53	5.48
Sanchez, Jonathan	L-L	6-2	190	11-19-82	9	12	5.01	29	29	0	0	158	154	90	88	14	75	157	.257	.235	.263	8.94	4.27
Taschner, Jack	L-L	6-3	205	4-21-78	3	2	4.88	67	0	0	0	48	57	27	26	5	24	39	.292	.279	.308	7.31	4.50
Threets, Erick	L-L	6-5	240	11-4-81	0	1	3.60	7	0	0	0	10	11	4	4	1	6	9	.297	.400	.280	5.40	8.10
Valdez, Merkin	R-R	6-5	230	11-10-81	1	0	1.69	17	1	0	0	16	14	5	3	1	7	13	.237	.346	.152	7.31	3.94
Walker, Tyler	R-R	6-3	275	5-15-76	5	8	4.56	65	0	0	0	53	47	29	27	7	21	49	.234	.319	.186	8.27	3.54
Wilson, Brian	R-R	6-1	195	3-16-82	3	2	4.62	63	0	0	41	62	62	32	32	7	28	67	.263	.202	.320	9.67	4.04
Yabu, Keiichi	R-R	6-1	230	9-28-68	3	6	3.57	60	0	0	0	68	63	33	27	3	32	48	.243	.355	.181	6.35	4.24
Zito, Barry	L-L	6-4	205	5-13-78	10	17	5.15	32	32	0	0	180	186	115	103	16	102	120	.270	.213	.285	6.00	5.10

Fielding

Catcher	PCT	G	PO	A	E	DP	PB
Alfonzo	.917	2	10	1	1	0	0
Holm	1.000	42	190	5	0	0	1
Molina	.995	136	987	71	5	6	5
Sandoval	1.000	11	76	6	0	1	2

First Base	PCT	G	PO	A	E	DP
Aurilia	.990	82	384	26	4	52
Bowker	.988	71	448	39	6	43
Ishikawa	.984	29	161	20	3	14
McClain	1.000	4	26	2	0	1
Ortmeier	1.000	13	41	6	0	3
Sandoval	.991	17	100	12	1	7

Second Base	PCT	G	PO	A	E	DP
Aurilia	—	1	0	0	0	0
Burriss	.973	41	66	80	4	14
Castillo	.958	9	8	15	1	1

	PCT	G	PO	A	E	DP
Denker	.972	13	19	16	1	3
Durham	.989	70	130	129	3	38
Ochoa	.957	8	8	14	1	2
Rohlinger	—	1	0	0	0	0
Velez	.967	69	102	104	7	26

Third Base	PCT	G	PO	A	E	DP
Aurilia	.951	63	31	67	5	4
Castillo	.934	103	47	166	15	14
Denker	—	1	0	0	0	0
Gillaspie	1.000	2	1	0	0	0
McClain	1.000	4	3	8	0	0
Rohlinger	.864	14	7	12	3	1
Sandoval	1.000	12	3	14	0	0

Shortstop	PCT	G	PO	A	E	DP
Bocock	.966	29	39	73	4	23
Burriss	.966	47	50	93	5	11

	PCT	G	PO	A	E	DP
Castillo	1.000	4	1	1	0	0
Ochoa	.975	35	45	71	3	20
Vizquel	.993	84	108	179	2	43

Outfield	PCT	G	PO	A	E	DP
Bowker	1.000	19	27	0	0	0
Burriss	—	1	0	0	0	0
Davis	1.000	8	9	0	0	0
Horwitz	1.000	10	26	0	0	0
Lewis	.972	123	199	11	6	1
Ortmeier	1.000	15	14	1	0	0
Roberts	1.000	32	54	3	0	2
Rowand	.991	149	412	6	4	0
Schierholtz	1.000	19	40	1	0	0
Timpner	—	1	0	0	0	0
Velez	.944	17	16	1	1	0
Winn	.992	150	357	7	3	2

FRESNO GRIZZLIES — TRIPLE-A
PACIFIC COAST LEAGUE

Batting	B-T	HT	WT	DOB	AVG	vLH	vRH	G	AB	R	H	2B	3B	HR	RBI	BB	HBP	SH	SF	SO	SB	CS	SLG	OBP
Adrianza, Ehire	R-B	6-1	155	8-21-89	.500	—	.500	2	6	2	3	1	0	0	0	2	0	0	0	1	0	0	.667	.625
Alfonzo, Eliezer	R-R	5-11	220	2-7-79	.310	.286	.321	32	116	17	36	10	1	5	24	7	1	0	1	30	1	0	.543	.352
Bocock, Brian	R-R	5-11	185	3-9-85	.163	.135	.174	35	123	14	20	3	0	0	3	14	1	3	0	39	7	3	.187	.254
Bond, Casey	R-R	6-3	205	10-5-84	.000	.000	—	1	1	0	0	0	0	0	0	0	0	0	0	0	0	0	.000	.000
Bowker, John	L-L	6-2	200	7-8-83	.237	.238	.235	23	93	13	22	3	1	2	9	7	2	0	0	23	2	0	.355	.304
Buller, Dayton	R-R	6-0	190	6-22-81	.235	.308	.211	20	51	6	12	3	0	2	8	3	1	1	1	14	0	0	.412	.286
Burriss, Manny	R-R	6-0	190	1-17-85	.258	.200	.313	14	62	6	16	1	1	0	6	2	0	0	6	2	2	.306	.281
Copeland, Ben	L-L	6-1	190	12-17-83	.341	.263	.364	22	85	16	29	4	0	0	4	11	0	0	9	3	2	.388	.417
Cordido, Julio	R-R	6-1	185	7-30-80	.250	.241	.255	84	224	26	56	6	1	0	20	16	1	1	0	49	3	3	.286	.303
Denker, Travis	R-R	5-9	205	8-5-85	.282	.300	.275	62	220	42	62	20	0	7	30	31	1	1	0	46	2	0	.468	.373
Downs, Matt	R-R	6-2	190	3-19-84	.244	.208	.258	22	86	10	21	5	0	3	7	4	3	0	1	10	1	0	.407	.298
Gunther, Barry	B-R	6-0	190	3-18-82	.143	.000	.167	2	7	0	1	0	0	0	1	0	0	1	0	2	0	0	.143	.143
Harper, Brett	L-R	6-4	245	7-31-81	.315	.238	.338	123	352	48	111	32	0	20	59	13	1	0	4	57	0	1	.577	.338
Holm, Steve	R-R	6-0	210	10-21-79	.273	.267	.275	22	66	7	18	4	0	0	11	10	1	0	2	12	0	0	.333	.367
Horwitz, Brian	R-R	6-1	185	11-7-82	.277	.337	.249	86	264	40	73	11	1	7	29	31	2	2	3	42	1	1	.405	.353
Ishikawa, Travis	L-L	6-3	225	9-24-83	.310	.244	.333	48	171	35	53	19	3	16	46	14	4	0	3	36	0	1	.737	.370
Jennings, Todd	R-R	6-0	190	12-10-81	.270	.143	.300	12	37	4	10	2	0	0	4	5	1	0	0	3	1	0	.324	.372
Leone, Justin	R-R	6-1	200	3-9-77	.251	.303	.232	105	358	63	90	22	1	17	64	66	1	0	8	96	16	6	.461	.363
McClain, Scott	R-R	6-4	230	5-19-72	.300	.301	.299	134	477	87	143	32	1	29	108	72	1	0	6	98	5	2	.553	.388
Mooney, Mike	R-R	6-1	205	6-8-83	.236	.219	.250	20	72	8	17	4	0	4	6	3	2	0	0	20	2	1	.458	.286
Ochoa, Ivan	R-R	5-9	175	12-16-82	.318	.309	.322	84	292	54	93	11	4	6	32	34	7	2	3	62	20	11	.445	.399
Ortmeier, Dan	B-L	6-4	230	5-11-81	.206	.241	.191	28	97	12	20	4	0	1	9	5	0	1	0	21	4	1	.278	.245
Roberts, Dave	L-L	5-10	180	5-31-72	.387	.500	.360	11	31	4	12	4	1	2	5	6	0	0	0	6	0	2	.774	.486
Rodriguez, Guillermo	R-R	5-11	230	5-15-78	.266	.214	.288	33	94	9	25	2	0	2	12	12	0	0	0	14	0	1	.351	.349
Schierholtz, Nate	L-R	6-2	215	2-15-84	.320	.344	.311	93	350	62	112	22	10	18	73	21	4	0	2	51	9	3	.594	.363
Timpner, Clay	L-L	6-2	195	5-13-83	.245	.198	.261	119	436	64	107	19	3	3	46	33	3	5	3	61	13	6	.323	.301
Velez, Eugenio	R-B	6-1	160	5-16-82	.310	.220	.357	42	171	25	53	11	4	5	15	17	0	0	0	32	13	9	.509	.372
Vizquel, Omar	B-R	5-9	175	4-24-67	.200	.333	.000	2	5	0	1	0	0	0	0	0	0	0	0	0	0	0	.200	.200
Wald, Jake	R-R	6-2	180	2-8-81	.234	.294	.212	59	197	30	46	13	2	3	24	30	2	2	1	63	6	1	.365	.339
Whiteside, Eli	R-R	6-2	215	10-22-79	.238	.179	.259	49	151	13	36	7	0	2	22	12	1	1	4	27	2	0	.325	.292

Pitching	B-T	HT	WT	DOB	W	L	ERA	G	GS	CG	SV	IP	H	R	ER	HR	BB	SO	AVG	vLH	vRH	K/9	BB/9
Chulk, Vinnie	R-R	6-2	195	12-19-78	0	1	3.65	22	2	0	2	25	25	10	10	3	13	21	.272	.316	.241	7.66	4.74
Correia, Kevin	R-R	6-3	200	8-24-80	1	0	1.50	2	2	0	0	12	8	2	2	1	0	15	.186	.130	.250	11.25	0.00
Espineli, Geno	L-L	6-4	195	9-8-82	1	1	2.66	38	0	0	1	61	56	22	18	2	11	48	.246	.234	.252	7.08	1.62
Foppert, Jesse	R-R	6-6	220	7-10-80	2	1	7.62	24	2	0	1	41	45	37	35	9	43	28	.278	.317	.238	6.10	9.36
Fortunato, Bartolome	R-R	6-1	210	8-24-74	3	2	7.89	22	0	0	0	22	25	24	19	4	21	18	.287	.333	.238	7.48	8.72
Griffin, Daniel	R-R	6-7	245	9-29-84	0	1	18.00	1	0	0	0	1	1	2	2	0	1	1	.250	1.000	.000	9.00	9.00
Gryboski, Kevin	R-R	6-5	230	11-15-73	2	6	6.54	52	0	0	10	54	66	47	39	10	25	32	.300	.366	.252	5.37	4.19
Hammond, Steve	R-L	6-2	205	4-30-82	5	3	5.62	9	8	0	0	50	62	32	31	7	17	34	.308	.262	.321	6.16	3.08
2-team total (4 Nashville)					5	7	6.07	13	12	0	0	67	86	46	45	13	22	54	—	—	—	7.29	2.97
Hennessey, Brad	R-R	6-2	195	2-7-80	7	10	4.83	21	21	3	0	132	157	78	71	22	37	69	.303	.346	.265	4.69	2.52
Hinshaw, Alex	L-L	6-4	190	10-31-82	0	0	0.57	13	0	0	7	16	5	1	1	0	4	21	.098	.167	.061	12.06	2.30
Mateo, Julio	R-R	6-0	220	8-2-77	3	4	5.69	25	6	0	4	62	81	43	39	9	11	39	.320	.331	.310	5.69	1.61
Matos, Osiris	R-R	6-1	200	8-6-84	1	0	0.00	5	0	0	1	10	5	0	0	2	0	13	.147	.083	.182	12.10	1.86
McNiven, Brooks	R-R	6-5	180	6-19-81	0	2	11.12	8	3	0	0	17	27	22	21	5	7	8	.360	.367	.356	4.24	3.71
Messenger, Randy	R-R	6-6	270	8-13-81	3	4	4.83	29	0	0	3	41	47	24	22	4	12	30	.297	.300	.295	6.59	2.63
2-team total (12 Tacoma)					9	3	3.96	41	0	0	4	64	66	31	28	6	23	46	—	—	—	6.50	3.25
Misch, Pat	R-L	6-2	195	8-18-81	6	5	5.38	20	13	0	0	87	101	58	52	15	17	56	.296	.248	.320	5.79	2.79
Munter, Scott	R-R	6-6	260	3-7-80	2	0	2.29	30	0	0	0	35	39	10	9	3	10	16	.277	.259	.287	4.08	2.55
Novoa, Roberto	R-R	6-5	200	8-15-79	0	0	11.57	7	0	0	0	7	13	12	9	3	4	6	.371	.529	.222	7.71	5.14
Palazzolo, Steve	R-R	6-10	260	3-31-82	0	1	9.39	6	0	0	0	8	10	8	8	0	10	4	.345	.417	.294	4.70	11.74

Name	B-T	HT	WT	DOB	W	L	ERA	G	GS	CG	SV	IP	H	R	ER	HR	BB	SO	AVG	vLH	vRH	K/9	BB/9
Palmer, Matt	R-R	6-2	200	3-21-79	6	10	4.18	26	25	1	0	142	138	71	66	11	72	143	.259	.286	.231	9.06	4.56
Pereira, Nick	R-R	6-0	190	9-22-82	7	8	5.70	19	19	0	0	101	116	71	64	12	47	86	.289	.313	.265	7.66	4.19
Romo, Sergio	R-R	5-11	190	3-4-83	0	0	0.00	3	0	0	0	6	3	0	0	0	2	7	.150	.111	.182	10.50	3.00
Sadler, Billy	R-R	6-0	195	9-21-81	1	0	1.09	22	0	0	1	33	19	7	4	0	21	41	.165	.183	.145	11.18	5.73
Sadowski, Ryan	R-R	6-4	185	10-4-82	8	4	4.80	31	11	0	0	81	93	47	43	7	33	72	.291	.245	.326	8.03	3.68
Santos, Victor	R-R	6-2	205	10-2-76	5	8	6.38	29	27	1	0	140	163	114	99	28	70	107	.297	.264	.325	6.89	4.51
Threets, Erick	L-L	6-5	240	11-4-81	4	5	3.39	37	4	0	0	66	53	30	25	5	36	46	.216	.262	.193	6.24	4.88
Yabu, Keiichi	R-R	6-1	230	9-28-68	0	0	1.80	3	0	0	0	5	4	1	1	0	6	7	.222	.167	.250	12.60	10.80

Fielding

Catcher	PCT	G	PO	A	E	DP	PB
Alfonzo	.986	29	197	16	3	0	4
Buller	.992	14	118	12	1	2	1
Gunther	.952	2	20	0	1	0	1
Holm	.992	20	116	13	1	1	0
Jennings	.992	12	101	16	1	5	2
Rodriguez	.990	28	170	20	2	0	2
Whiteside	.986	43	270	18	4	1	4

First Base	PCT	G	PO	A	E	DP
Bowker	.992	13	117	8	1	18
Harper	.988	37	300	16	4	33
Ishikawa	.998	44	392	36	1	46
McClain	.998	55	457	34	1	39

Second Base	PCT	G	PO	A	E	DP
Burriss	.963	10	19	33	2	8
Cordido	1.000	6	6	13	0	4
Denker	.973	56	118	170	8	43

	PCT	G	PO	A	E	DP	PB
Downs	.964	12	26	27	2	9	
Leone	.973	14	24	47	2	10	
Ochoa	.963	28	44	87	5	18	
Velez	.988	19	44	39	1	17	
Wald	1.000	8	14	22	0	5	

Third Base	PCT	G	PO	A	E	DP
Cordido	.944	54	40	96	8	13
Denker	1.000	3	2	8	0	0
Leone	.972	25	20	49	2	9
McClain	.960	64	49	121	7	18
Wald	1.000	4	3	6	0	1

Shortstop	PCT	G	PO	A	E	DP
Adrianza	1.000	2	2	5	0	0
Bocock	.966	34	51	119	6	20
Burriss	1.000	4	6	9	0	2
Downs	1.000	3	8	6	0	3
Leone	.984	11	23	39	1	12

	PCT	G	PO	A	E	DP
Ochoa	.960	51	95	142	10	36
Vizquel	1.000	2	1	2	0	0
Wald	.985	43	55	138	3	32

Outfield	PCT	G	PO	A	E	DP
Bowker	.952	10	19	1	1	0
Copeland	.982	22	51	4	1	0
Downs	1.000	10	12	0	0	0
Harper	1.000	8	8	0	0	0
Horwitz	.973	74	101	8	3	3
Leone	.978	55	83	5	2	1
Mooney	.964	19	51	2	2	0
Ortmeier	.956	23	42	1	2	0
Roberts	1.000	10	12	1	0	0
Schierholtz	.993	89	140	10	1	1
Timpner	.987	114	218	6	3	1
Velez	.972	26	34	1	1	0
Whiteside	—	1	0	0	0	0

CONNECTICUT DEFENDERS   DOUBLE-A

EASTERN LEAGUE

Batting	B-T	HT	WT	DOB	AVG	vLH	vRH	G	AB	R	H	2B	3B	HR	RBI	BB	HBP	SH	SF	SO	SB	CS	SLG	OBP
Alfonzo, Eliezer	R-R	5-11	220	2-7-79	.363	.438	.344	19	80	8	29	7	0	2	15	2	2	0	0	18	0	0	.525	.393
Boyer, Brad	L-R	6-0	185	10-4-83	.240	.571	.186	12	50	6	12	3	0	0	5	3	0	0	2	9	0	1	.300	.283
Buller, Dayton	R-R	6-0	190	6-22-81	.207	.154	.250	11	29	5	6	2	0	1	3	1	0	0	0	12	0	0	.379	.233
Copeland, Ben	L-L	6-1	190	12-17-83	.261	.262	.263	103	372	54	97	17	13	5	42	39	3	7	2	64	21	5	.417	.334
Cordido, Julio	R-R	6-1	185	7-30-80	.116	.133	.107	13	43	4	5	0	0	0	2	0	1	0	9	0	0	.116	.156
Denker, Travis	R-R	5-9	205	8-5-85	.184	.200	.176	25	76	4	14	4	1	0	6	14	0	0	1	25	1	1	.263	.308
Haines, Kyle	B-R	6-1	170	7-28-82	.261	.240	.265	105	348	48	91	15	4	0	43	55	3	2	1	58	1	4	.328	.366
Ishikawa, Travis	L-L	6-3	225	9-24-83	.291	.172	.328	64	234	34	68	16	0	8	48	35	2	2	4	45	10	4	.462	.382
Klink, Simon	R-R	6-1	215	12-21-81	.226	.200	.229	108	349	34	79	19	1	3	35	34	4	1	0	104	2	0	.312	.302
Maroul, David	R-R	6-2	215	2-15-83	.230	.238	.225	108	366	46	84	26	0	10	35	21	2	2	1	110	2	4	.383	.274
Martinez-Esteve, Eddy	R-R	6-2	215	7-14-83	.298	.323	.289	115	396	42	118	15	0	6	42	54	4	0	1	37	2	1	.381	.387
Mooney, Mike	R-R	6-1	205	6-8-83	.167	.227	.136	20	66	7	11	3	0	4	15	1	0	0	2	15	1	1	.394	.174
Richardson, Antoan	B-R	5-8	165	10-8-83	.241	.237	.243	123	365	63	88	5	6	5	31	55	12	10	3	82	33	6	.329	.356
Rohlinger, Ryan	R-R	6-1	195	10-7-83	.296	.383	.259	44	159	27	47	12	1	6	19	13	3	3	1	20	1	1	.497	.358
Rojas, Nestor	R-R	6-0	200	11-18-83	.130	.188	.067	16	46	5	6	0	0	3	1	0	0	0	6	0	0	.130	.149
Rosario, Olmo	R-R	6-1	180	8-24-80	.298	.312	.289	124	420	58	125	31	4	11	51	20	4	2	4	67	13	5	.469	.333
Sandoval, Pablo	B-R	5-11	245	8-11-86	.337	.283	.365	44	175	29	59	13	0	8	37	8	0	0	1	20	0	1	.549	.364
Sosa, Carlos	L-R	6-1	195	5-19-83	.253	.200	.274	122	411	55	104	25	1	10	53	46	1	1	5	101	2	2	.392	.326
Wald, Jake	R-R	6-2	180	2-8-81	.262	.321	.241	52	168	26	44	10	2	2	15	13	3	3	0	44	2	0	.381	.326
Webb, Trey	R-R	6-0	170	2-11-82	.050	.143	.000	10	20	1	1	0	0	0	0	0	0	0	0	9	0	1	.050	.050
Witter, Adam	L-R	6-1	175	2-17-83	.238	.202	.251	118	400	56	95	17	2	20	77	64	3	1	3	102	1	5	.443	.345

Pitching	B-T	HT	WT	DOB	W	L	ERA	G	GS	CG	SV	IP	H	R	ER	HR	BB	SO	AVG	vLH	vRH	K/9	BB/9
Broshuis, Garrett	R-R	6-2	185	12-18-81	13	9	3.78	28	28	1	0	157	178	82	66	16	35	99	.286	.285	.286	5.68	2.01
Bump, Nate	R-R	6-2	195	7-24-76	4	3	2.64	17	10	0	0	58	47	19	17	2	22	28	.229	.192	.250	4.34	3.41
Cowart, Adam	R-R	6-2	190	8-18-83	8	7	3.76	32	23	0	0	139	170	69	58	7	29	73	.306	.324	.295	4.74	1.88
Hedrick, Justin	R-R	6-3	225	6-8-82	2	3	1.37	43	0	0	9	66	41	12	10	4	74	74	.176	.210	.150	10.14	2.88
Maday, Daryl	R-R	6-2	225	8-12-85	1	1	8.35	4	3	0	0	18	31	17	17	2	8	11	.383	.444	.333	5.40	3.93
Martinez, Joey	L-R	6-3	185	2-26-83	10	10	2.49	27	27	0	0	148	131	58	41	6	37	112	.236	.287	.196	6.81	2.25
Matos, Osiris	R-R	6-1	200	8-6-84	0	0	1.23	27	0	0	8	37	25	5	5	1	11	37	.191	.211	.176	9.08	2.70
McKae, Dave	R-R	6-2	190	11-24-81	8	9	4.57	28	22	0	0	124	139	78	63	10	35	74	.284	.301	.268	5.37	2.54
McNiven, Brooks	R-R	6-5	180	6-19-81	2	2	1.84	18	8	0	0	59	42	15	12	0	14	22	.203	.215	.193	3.38	2.15
Oseguera, Paul	L-L	6-0	180	1-6-84	3	2	4.58	19	8	0	0	57	54	33	29	4	29	45	.255	.316	.232	7.11	4.58
Palazzolo, Steve	R-R	6-10	260	3-31-82	5	5	3.56	23	0	0	1	43	30	19	17	1	29	40	.204	.193	.211	8.37	6.07
Pichardo, Kelvin	R-R	6-0	215	10-13-85	2	4	2.48	46	0	0	7	62	49	18	17	4	33	62	.214	.200	.235	9.05	4.82
Ray, Ronnie	R-R	6-3	190	5-11-84	6	4	3.10	46	0	0	1	73	80	29	25	3	24	47	.283	.349	.241	5.82	2.97
Romo, Sergio	R-R	5-11	190	3-4-83	1	1	4.00	24	0	0	11	27	22	15	12	1	7	30	.229	.242	.233	10.00	2.33
Sadowski, Ryan	R-R	6-4	185	10-4-82	1	0	3.27	9	0	0	0	11	13	5	4	0	9	9	.317	.222	.391	7.36	7.36
Sharpless, Josh	R-R	6-5	240	1-26-81	1	1	3.51	24	0	0	0	33	23	17	13	3	29	30	.193	.293	.141	8.10	7.83
Snyder, Ben	L-L	6-2	224	7-20-85	1	6	5.98	13	12	0	0	62	77	42	41	9	23	44	.308	.261	.326	6.42	3.36
Waddell, Jason	R-L	6-2	206	6-11-81	0	3	3.38	44	0	0	2	64	47	27	24	6	36	70	.209	.216	.204	9.84	5.06

Fielding

Catcher	PCT	G	PO	A	E	DP	PB
Alfonzo	.989	13	87	7	1	0	2
Buller	.971	11	64	3	2	2	3
Rojas	1.000	13	65	5	0	1	3
Sandoval	.987	30	200	23	3	2	2
Witter	.991	79	498	39	5	2	14

First Base	PCT	G	PO	A	E	DP
Alfonzo	1.000	3	24	3	0	4
Ishikawa	.993	59	520	58	4	60
Klink	.988	51	393	25	5	43
Maroul	.988	10	79	6	1	9
Sandoval	1.000	8	65	6	0	9
Witter	.974	17	131	20	4	23

Second Base	PCT	G	PO	A	E	DP
Boyer	.979	10	18	29	1	6

	PCT	G	PO	A	E	DP
Cordido	.960	5	9	15	1	4
Denker	.956	21	47	62	5	19
Haines	.980	33	61	85	3	22
Maroul	.969	19	31	63	3	16
Rosario	.960	59	128	161	12	31
Webb	1.000	2	3	5	0	2

Third Base	PCT	G	PO	A	E	DP
Boyer	.750	1	0	3	1	0
Cordido	.875	4	0	7	1	0
Denker	—	1	0	0	0	0
Klink	.944	28	22	46	4	2
Maroul	.913	67	40	148	18	13
Rohlinger	.959	44	35	83	5	8
Rosario	.667	1	2	0	1	0

Shortstop	PCT	G	PO	A	E	DP
Cordido	.889	2	3	5	1	1
Haines	.965	60	71	152	8	40
Maroul	.692	3	4	5	4	1
Rosario	.942	29	41	72	7	24
Wald	.961	52	84	165	10	38
Webb	.958	5	8	15	1	4

Outfield	PCT	G	PO	A	E	DP
Copeland	.984	100	237	10	4	8
Martinez-Esteve	.975	82	108	8	3	0
Mooney	.967	17	27	2	1	0
Richardson	.975	117	265	4	7	0
Rosario	.931	23	26	1	2	1
Sosa	.991	114	213	6	2	1
Webb	—		1	0	0	0	0

SAN JOSE GIANTS

HIGH CLASS A

CALIFORNIA LEAGUE

Batting	B-T	HT	WT	DOB	AVG	vLH	vRH	G	AB	R	H	2B	3B	HR	RBI	BB	HBP	SH	SF	SO	SB	CS	SLG	OBP
Bond, Brock	B-R	5-10	195	9-11-85	.297	.238	.306	45	155	26	46	6	0	0	19	20	5	3	0	31	9	3	.335	.394
Boyer, Brad	L-R	6-0	185	10-4-83	.348	.276	.369	75	264	42	92	12	5	7	45	36	6	6	1	53	15	5	.511	.436
Buller, Dayton	R-R	6-0	190	6-22-81	.265	.364	.083	9	34	9	9	3	0	1	5	3	1	1	0	12	2	1	.441	.342
Ciriaco, Juan	R-R	6-0	160	8-15-83	.172	.185	.167	41	87	5	15	2	0	0	7	0	3	2	1	17	1	1	.195	.229
D'Alessio, Andy	L-R	6-4	227	9-23-84	.261	.282	.255	121	459	56	120	33	1	15	78	32	0	2	1	133	5	4	.436	.309
Denker, Travis	R-R	5-9	205	8-5-85	.222	.000	.250	5	18	3	4	0	0	1	4	3	1	0	0	2	0	0	.389	.364
Downs, Matt	R-R	6-2	190	3-19-84	.304	.320	.298	109	437	74	133	30	1	17	75	34	5	7	6	57	24	13	.494	.357
Duggan, Dom	R-R	5-9	185	2-8-85	.247	.282	.217	46	85	20	21	9	0	0	12	4	2	1	1	27	5	2	.353	.293
Felmy, Robert	L-L	5-10	194	4-29-84	.283	.309	.274	126	481	62	136	25	3	6	58	35	8	5	3	79	18	7	.385	.340
Ford, Darren	R-R	5-11	195	10-1-85	.219	.267	.204	38	128	21	28	4	1	0	7	23	2	2	0	42	14	1	.266	.346
Graham, Tyler	R-R	6-0	180	1-25-84	.264	.289	.255	84	303	51	80	10	2	2	29	21	7	9	2	54	47	14	.330	.324
La Torre, Tyler	L-R	6-0	219	4-22-83	.253	.308	.244	45	99	9	25	3	0	2	8	19	0	3	0	29	1	2	.343	.373
McBryde, Mike	R-R	6-1	195	3-22-85	.295	.280	.300	125	420	73	124	10	6	5	46	37	12	10	1	84	31	10	.383	.368
Mooney, Mike	R-R	6-1	205	6-8-83	.272	.321	.250	51	173	30	47	15	1	10	25	14	5	1	1	48	11	3	.543	.342
Ortmeier, Dan	B-L	6-4	230	5-11-81	.138	.400	.083	8	29	1	4	0	0	1	1	5	1	0	0	15	1	0	.241	.286
Pill, Brett	R-R	6-4	211	9-9-84	.266	.282	.260	131	458	73	122	32	0	9	65	33	8	0	9	85	5	2	.395	.321
Rohlinger, Ryan	R-R	6-1	195	10-7-83	.285	.410	.236	73	277	45	79	16	0	7	46	34	5	1	5	50	5	1	.419	.368
Sandoval, Pablo	B-R	5-11	245	8-11-86	.359	.243	.402	68	273	61	98	25	2	12	59	23	3	0	2	39	2	1	.597	.412
Sarmiento, Elio	R-R	5-11	202	6-20-86	.250	.421	.184	26	68	7	17	4	0	1	7	4	3	1	1	13	0	0	.353	.316
Schoop, Sharlon	R-R	6-2	191	4-15-87	.246	.248	.246	125	398	54	98	18	1	7	52	35	2	8	7	88	7	3	.349	.305
Shriner, Jesse	R-R	6-1	195	2-24-85	.000	—	.000	1	1	0	0	0	0	0	0	0	0	0	0	1	0	0	.000	.000
Vizquel, Omar	B-R	5-9	175	4-24-67	.375	.333	.400	3	8	3	3	0	0	0	1	2	0	0	0	0	0	0	.375	.500
Williams, Jackson	R-R	6-1	200	5-14-86	.231	.222	.233	50	156	19	36	5	0	3	16	15	3	1	3	40	2	3	.321	.309

Pitching	B-T	HT	WT	DOB	W	L	ERA	G	GS	CG	SV	IP	H	R	ER	HR	BB	SO	AVG	vLH	vRH	K/9	BB/9
Alderson, Tim	R-R	6-6	217	11-3-88	13	4	2.79	26	26	0	0	145	125	48	45	4	34	124	.235	.265	.201	7.68	2.11
Begg, Chris	R-R	6-4	195	9-12-79	1	1	6.43	3	3	0	0	14	20	11	10	2	2	10	.351	.269	.419	6.43	1.29
Correia, Kevin	R-R	6-3	200	8-24-80	0	0	0.00	1	1	0	0	3	1	0	0	0	1	1	.091	.250	.000	2.70	2.70
Edlefsen, Steven	B-R	6-2	180	6-27-85	8	5	3.36	40	0	0	0	78	71	34	29	5	38	77	.250	.252	.248	8.92	4.40
English, Jesse	L-L	6-3	220	9-13-84	13	7	3.19	26	26	0	0	135	121	57	48	12	51	135	.240	.237	.241	8.98	3.39
Griffin, Daniel	R-R	6-7	245	9-29-84	3	5	3.28	33	0	0	4	60	53	25	22	4	25	51	.240	.267	.221	7.61	3.73
Joaquin, Waldis	R-R	6-2	190	12-25-86	0	1	4.66	9	4	0	0	19	20	13	10	2	11	23	.274	.355	.214	10.71	5.12
Maday, Daryl	R-R	6-2	225	8-12-85	3	0	2.05	4	4	0	0	22	20	6	5	1	5	27	.235	.238	.233	11.05	2.05
Musgrave, Mike	R-R	6-2	199	4-10-84	2	1	3.17	34	0	0	2	54	49	21	19	6	18	42	.243	.290	.202	7.00	3.00
Otero, Danny	R-R	6-3	205	2-19-85	1	1	3.67	27	0	0	16	27	34	14	11	1	3	23	.296	.348	.261	7.67	1.00
Paterson, Joe	R-L	6-1	210	5-19-86	3	2	3.11	34	0	0	7	38	28	22	13	1	15	41	.200	.108	.303	9.80	3.58
Paul, Ryan	L-L	6-6	225	8-10-84	0	2	2.76	15	0	0	0	16	15	5	5	0	12	16	.259	.250	.263	8.82	6.61
Pereira, Nick	R-R	6-0	190	9-22-82	2	0	1.46	2	2	0	0	12	8	4	2	0	4	12	.178	.263	.115	8.76	2.92
Pucetas, Kevin	R-R	6-4	225	11-27-84	10	7	3.02	24	24	0	0	125	115	46	42	6	27	102	.247	.236	.258	7.32	1.94
Rodriguez, Wilmin	L-L	6-2	211	5-13-85	1	1	5.64	19	0	0	0	22	32	17	14	0	19	21	.337	.396	.277	8.46	7.66
Shaver, Jason	R-R	6-5	197	12-17-84	0	4	4.50	8	0	0	0	14	13	9	7	1	2	12	.228	.281	.160	7.71	1.29
Snyder, Ben	L-L	6-2	224	7-20-85	8	3	2.00	15	14	0	0	86	79	23	19	8	18	73	.243	.189	.269	7.67	1.89
Sosa, Henry	R-R	6-2	185	7-28-85	3	4	4.31	12	12	0	0	56	62	28	27	6	18	58	.283	.342	.219	9.27	2.88
Tanner, Clayton	L-R	6-1	202	12-5-87	10	8	3.69	24	24	0	0	117	124	61	48	1	39	84	.274	.240	.291	6.46	3.00
Trinidad, Juan	R-R	6-3	220	11-6-85	1	1	1.53	43	0	0	5	59	51	11	10	5	20	49	.232	.221	.239	7.47	3.05
Turpen, Daniel	R-R	6-4	215	8-17-86	0	0	4.91	6	0	0	0	11	11	7	6	0	6	11	.262	.316	.217	9.00	4.91
Valdez, Merkin	R-R	6-5	230	11-10-81	0	0	0.00	1	0	0	1	0	0	0	0	0	0	3	.250	.000	.333	27.00	0.00
Whitaker, Craig	R-R	6-4	210	11-19-84	2	3	4.88	42	0	0	1	59	46	40	32	6	46	59	.213	.257	.174	9.00	7.02
Wilding, Taylor	R-R	6-1	190	10-22-84	1	6	3.39	46	0	0	11	72	72	29	27	5	19	74	.262	.246	.275	9.29	2.39

Fielding

Catcher	PCT	G	PO	A	E	DP	PB
Buller	1.000	6	50	6	0	1	1
La Torre	.982	26	151	12	3	1	3
Sandoval	.986	53	390	38	6	2	4
Sarmiento	.995	25	175	12	1	1	4
Shriner	1.000	1	2	0	0	0	0
Williams	.975	49	377	47	11	6	1	1

First Base	PCT	G	PO	A	E	DP
D'Alessio	.989	45	350	22	4	35
Downs	1.000	3	5	0	0	0
Ortmeier	.909	1	9	1	1	2
Pill	.993	100	757	47	6	64
Sandoval	1.000	11	81	11	0	7

Second Base	PCT	G	PO	A	E	DP
Bond	.973	36	53	90	4	14

	PCT	G	PO	A	E	DP
Boyer	.963	39	75	106	7	26
Ciriaco	.980	15	24	26	1	6
Denker	.950	4	6	13	1	3
Downs	.983	63	111	172	5	34

Third Base	PCT	G	PO	A	E	DP
Boyer	.928	34	17	47	5	2
Ciriaco	.833	9	4	1	1	0
Denker	1.000	1	3	2	0	1
Downs	.948	33	19	54	4	6
La Torre	.714	3	1	4	2	3
Pill	1.000	3	2	3	0	0
Rohlinger	.948	72	45	118	9	4

Shortstop	PCT	G	PO	A	E	DP
Ciriaco	.931	17	26	41	5	6
Downs	.955	10	13	29	2	4

	PCT	G	PO	A	E	DP
Schoop	.963	125	190	361	21	71
Vizquel	1.000	3	8	6	0	1

Outfield	PCT	G	PO	A	E	DP
Ciriaco	—	1	0	0	0	0
Downs	1.000	10	11	1	0	0
Duggan	.955	35	40	2	2	0
Felmy	.995	123	171	12	1	0
Ford	.963	36	76	2	3	0
Graham	.977	74	117	8	3	1
La Torre	1.000	4	4	0	0	0
McBryde	.959	123	238	20	11	4
Mooney	.900	43	69	3	8	0
Ortmeier	1.000	7	14	1	0	0
Sarmiento	—	1	0	0	0	0

AUGUSTA GREENJACKETS

SOUTH ATLANTIC LEAGUE

LOW CLASS A

Batting	B-T	HT	WT	DOB	AVG	vLH	vRH	G	AB	R	H	2B	3B	HR	RBI	BB	HBP	SH	SF	SO	SB	CS	SLG	OBP
Alfonzo, Eliezer	R-R	5-11	220	2-7-79	.188	.000	.200	5	16	1	3	1	0	1	6	1	0	0	1	5	0	0	.438	.222
Baker, Garrett	R-R	6-3	220	11-16-83	.264	.295	.255	119	435	60	115	24	7	9	63	33	11	2	4	89	11	5	.414	.329
Bond, Brock	B-R	5-10	195	9-11-85	.333	.364	.325	42	150	28	50	6	0	1	24	13	4	0	0	20	6	3	.393	.401
Buller, Dayton	R-R	6-0	190	6-22-81	.281	.250	.286	26	96	20	27	6	1	5	17	14	0	0	2	23	2	0	.521	.373
Ciriaco, Juan	R-R	6-0	160	8-15-83	.283	.208	.298	36	138	28	39	3	1	5	26	13	0	1	2	21	7	3	.428	.340
Corona, Ramon	R-R	5-11	190	8-10-85	.207	.250	.196	34	116	17	24	2	2	4	16	8	4	3	4	21	7	1	.362	.273
Creswell, Tayler	R-R	6-0	170	2-11-87	.200	.300	.167	13	40	5	8	1	0	0	3	4	1	0	0	14	3	1	.225	.289
Culberson, Charlie	R-R	6-1	185	4-10-89	.234	.333	.202	81	282	31	66	11	2	3	27	18	6	3	4	57	6	6	.319	.290
Davis, Andrew	B-R	5-11	195	2-11-84	.253	.267	.249	121	439	44	111	28	3	3	56	33	1	2	6	77	4	2	.351	.303
Duggan, Dom	R-R	5-9	185	2-8-85	.282	.294	.279	25	85	12	24	2	2	0	8	8	0	1	0	21	4	0	.353	.344
Jordan, Shane	L-L	5-7	170	11-26-84	.253	.314	.234	123	438	76	111	14	3	0	29	65	8	13	8	60	35	12	.299	.355
Klimas, Matt	R-R	5-11	185	7-3-87	.237	.364	.200	29	97	3	23	5	0	0	12	8	1	0	0	28	3	1	.289	.302
Neal, Thomas	R-R	6-1	205	8-17-87	.276	.222	.292	117	428	69	118	25	1	15	81	48	12	1	8	103	3	4	.444	.359
Noonan, Nick	L-R	6-0	180	5-4-89	.279	.269	.282	119	499	79	139	27	7	9	68	23	5	2	3	98	29	4	.415	.315
Peguero, Francisco	R-R	6-0	175	6-1-88	.261	.313	.242	50	180	23	47	2	4	2	15	12	1	0	1	43	15	1	.350	.309
Rojas, Nestor	R-R	6-0	200	11-18-83	.156	.172	.151	36	122	10	19	5	0	0	7	5	1	5	1	24	0	0	.197	.194
Sarmiento, Elio	R-R	5-11	202	6-20-86	.175	.077	.200	20	63	4	11	2	0	0	4	5	1	0	0	16	0	0	.206	.246
Simmons, James	R-R	6-3	190	9-3-85	.232	.132	.259	107	354	49	82	12	3	5	37	22	1	7	2	132	25	10	.325	.277
Stromsmoe, Skyler	B-R	5-10	175	3-30-84	.200	.200	.200	19	55	6	11	0	0	0	5	1	1	0	0	9	2	1	.200	.333
Villalona, Angel	R-R	6-3	200	8-13-90	.263	.316	.245	123	464	64	122	29	9	17	64	18	16	0	2	118	1	2	.435	.312
Williams, Jackson	R-R	5-11	200	5-14-86	.179	.150	.190	47	156	23	28	7	0	2	13	15	6	2	1	37	0	0	.263	.275

Pitching	B-T	HT	WT	DOB	W	L	ERA	G	GS	CG	SV	IP	H	R	ER	HR	BB	SO	AVG	vLH	vRH	K/9	BB/9
Barnes, Scott	L-L	6-3	175	9-5-87	3	2	1.38	6	6	0	0	33	15	6	5	0	7	41	.133	.179	.118	11.30	1.93
Brewer, T.J.	R-R	6-2	200	8-30-84	10	4	2.95	23	21	0	0	113	105	53	37	7	27	72	.244	.247	.241	5.73	2.15
Bumgarner, Madison	R-L	6-4	215	8-1-89	15	3	1.46	24	24	1	0	142	111	28	23	3	21	164	.216	.195	.222	10.42	1.33
Calicutt, Steven	L-L	6-2	190	2-7-84	2	3	4.25	10	8	0	0	42	46	22	20	2	14	32	.279	.239	.294	6.80	2.98
Clark, Craig	L-L	6-2	200	7-9-84	8	4	3.51	23	21	0	0	115	96	51	45	5	23	111	.224	.212	.229	8.66	1.79
Corgan, Chance	R-R	6-2	175	4-25-86	4	5	2.93	13	12	0	0	68	75	27	22	3	16	45	.281	.324	.250	5.99	2.13
De La Garza, Andy	L-L	6-4	200	10-20-84	6	2	3.33	53	0	0	9	78	63	35	29	4	14	79	.217	.211	.221	9.08	1.61
Hobson, Gib	R-R	6-3	195	1-13-85	0	0	6.14	2	2	0	0	7	10	5	5	2	1	4	.313	.286	.364	4.91	1.23
Joaquin, Waldis	R-R	6-2	190	12-25-86	1	2	4.33	27	3	0	2	52	49	32	25	1	20	49	.247	.216	.266	8.48	3.46
Lively, Mitch	R-R	6-5	230	9-7-85	1	0	1.42	10	0	0	0	13	11	5	2	0	6	18	.229	.313	.188	12.79	4.26
Lussier, Paul	R-R	6-2	220	11-7-85	0	1	4.57	17	1	0	0	22	29	11	11	5	6	17	.322	.395	.269	7.06	2.49
Maday, Daryl	R-R	6-2	225	8-12-85	9	4	1.55	21	13	0	0	105	74	20	18	3	23	92	.197	.203	.194	7.91	1.98
Mixon, David	R-R	6-3	190	9-10-84	2	1	1.55	24	0	0	5	29	28	13	5	2	10	30	.241	.283	.214	9.31	3.10
Odle, Oliver	R-R	6-0	229	7-11-85	10	7	3.77	24	22	0	0	136	153	60	57	13	9	95	.284	.284	.284	6.29	0.60
Otero, Danny	R-R	6-3	205	2-19-85	0	0	0.33	25	0	0	18	27	22	2	1	0	4	26	.214	.171	.235	8.67	1.33
Paterson, Joe	R-L	6-1	210	5-19-86	5	1	2.30	20	0	0	1	31	23	11	8	2	13	37	.204	.135	.237	10.63	3.73
Paul, Ryan	L-L	6-6	225	8-10-84	5	2	2.61	28	0	0	4	41	20	12	12	1	24	60	.147	.130	.159	13.06	5.23
Pendley, Nathan	L-L	6-4	220	9-5-81	0	0	9.64	7	0	0	0	5	7	5	5	0	4	1	.368	.429	.333	1.93	7.71
Rodriguez, Wilmin	L-L	6-2	211	5-13-85	2	1	2.45	18	0	0	1	29	20	8	8	1	25	24	.198	.265	.164	7.36	5.22
Runzler, Dan	L-L	6-4	215	3-30-85	1	0	5.47	20	0	0	0	25	25	18	15	2	19	26	.269	.323	.242	9.49	6.93
Sosa, Henry	R-R	6-2	185	7-28-85	0	0	0.00	2	0	0	0	1	1	1	0	0	2	0	.250	.000	.250	0.00	13.50
Turpen, Daniel	R-R	6-4	215	8-17-86	5	4	3.45	40	0	0	5	63	67	26	24	2	13	48	.266	.256	.272	6.89	1.87
Yntema, Orlando	R-R	6-3	180	2-21-86	0	2	5.59	14	5	0	0	39	44	25	24	1	14	28	.278	.286	.273	6.52	3.26

Fielding

Catcher	PCT	G	PO	A	E	DP	PB
Alfonzo	1.000	2	8	3	0	0	0
Buller	1.000	26	233	22	0	1	1
Klimas	.977	29	198	14	5	3	5
Rojas	.974	32	242	24	7	1	2
Sarmiento	1.000	8	50	7	0	1	2

	PCT	G	PO	A	E	DP	PB
Williams	.988	47	366	49	5	3	8

First Base	PCT	G	PO	A	E	DP
Corona	1.000	1	1	0	0	0
Klimas	1.000	1	1	0	0	0
Neal	.980	38	367	21	8	36
Rojas	1.000	4	26	1	0	2

	PCT	G	PO	A	E	DP
Villalona	.985	98	889	66	15	72

Second Base	PCT	G	PO	A	E	DP
Bond	.954	13	23	39	3	11
Ciriaco	1.000	1	3	3	0	1
Corona	.714	1	1	4	2	2
Noonan	.969	116	215	339	18	70

Sarmiento	.917	3	4 7 1 4		
Stromsmoe	1.000	6	9 15 0 0		

Third Base	PCT	G	PO	A	E	DP
Bond	.962	11	10	15	1	3
Ciriaco	1.000	1	2	4	0	1
Corona	.667	3	1	3	2	0
Davis	.945	120	56	219	16	23
Sarmiento	.889	4	3	5	1	0

Stromsmoe	.818	5	2 7 2 1		

Shortstop	PCT	G	PO	A	E	DP
Ciriaco	.928	31	36	80	9	17
Corona	.923	22	43	65	9	16
Culberson	.901	79	100	219	35	35
Stromsmoe	.975	9	9	30	1	2

Outfield	PCT	G	PO	A	E	DP
Baker	.955	103	147	2	7	1

	PCT	G	PO	A	E	DP
Bond	1.000	3	3	0	0	0
Ciriaco	1.000	2	4	1	0	0
Corona	1.000	8	6	1	0	0
Creswell	.880	12	21	1	3	0
Duggan	1.000	23	30	2	0	0
Jordan	.975	122	230	2	6	1
Peguero	.965	49	81	2	3	0
Sarmiento	1.000	4	6	0	0	0
Simmons	.985	104	198	4	3	2

SALEM-KEIZER VOLCANOES

SHORT-SEASON

NORTHWEST LEAGUE

Batting	B-T	HT	WT	DOB	AVG	vLH	vRH	G	AB	R	H	2B	3B	HR	RBI	BB	HBP	SH	SF	SO	SB	CS	SLG	OBP
Adrianza, Ehire	B-R	6-1	155	8-21-89	.400	—	.400	1	5	3	2	0	0	0	0	0	0	0	0	1	0	0	.400	.400
Ambort, Michael	B-R	6-1	215	4-23-85	.328	.316	.333	34	116	19	38	8	2	9	34	13	0	0	0	22	1	0	.664	.395
Bond, Casey	R-R	6-3	205	10-5-84	.246	.239	.249	68	240	42	59	16	1	0	21	21	10	3	2	70	15	7	.321	.330
Cook, Dan	B-R	6-3	185	6-15-86	.258	.300	.250	25	66	8	17	1	0	0	3	11	0	1	1	11	1	0	.273	.359
Crawford, Brandon	L-R	6-2	200	1-21-87	.000	—	.000	1	2	0	0	0	0	0	0	0	0	0	0	0	0	0	.000	.000
Curry, Caleb	R-R	6-0	175	4-23-86	.270	.270	.270	68	248	31	67	7	1	1	23	27	3	4	0	55	13	10	.319	.349
Flores, Jose	B-R	5-11	175	8-17-87	.300	.338	.286	73	263	40	79	13	1	1	32	40	1	4	0	60	3	3	.369	.395
Frias, Vladimir	B-R	6-2	170	9-6-86	.228	.213	.234	53	202	26	46	5	1	0	10	8	6	7	3	41	11	6	.262	.274
Gillaspie, Conor	L-R	6-1	200	7-18-87	.268	.389	.226	18	71	4	19	4	0	0	8	9	0	0	0	13	2	0	.324	.350
Kline, Trent	B-R	5-10	170	7-22-84	.209	.185	.219	29	91	11	19	2	1	2	18	12	0	1	1	19	1	4	.319	.298
Lindsley, Brooks	R-R	6-0	185	10-25-86	.254	.250	.255	26	71	12	18	4	0	0	7	12	3	1	0	14	4	1	.310	.384
Loberg, Mike	L-R	6-4	225	3-24-85	.292	.406	.255	74	281	53	82	15	4	8	49	27	5	0	4	80	6	1	.459	.360
Lormand, Ryan	R-R	6-0	165	10-30-85	.235	.274	.222	70	247	40	58	12	2	2	29	26	5	5	3	33	12	2	.324	.317
Luster, Jeremiah	R-R	5-10	175	8-31-86	.182	.250	.167	14	44	4	8	2	0	0	3	8	1	0	1	11	2	0	.227	.315
Mantle, Ryan	R-R	6-3	210	7-12-86	.000	—	.000	1	4	0	0	0	0	0	0	1	0	0	0	3	0	0	.000	.200
Monell, Johnny	L-R	5-11	205	3-27-86	.267	.262	.269	43	161	21	43	17	0	5	25	11	4	0	0	36	1	2	.466	.330
Peguero, Francisco	R-R	6-0	175	6-1-88	.307	.176	.373	50	202	33	62	11	4	2	28	9	5	2	2	43	10	3	.431	.349
Posey, Buster	R-R	6-2	195	3-27-87	.273	.000	.375	3	11	2	3	2	0	0	2	3	0	0	0	0	0	0	.455	.429
Quintana, Carlos	R-R	6-3	180	6-14-87	.071	.250	.000	5	14	1	1	0	0	0	1	3	0	0	0	7	0	0	.071	.235
Stromsmoe, Skyler	B-R	5-10	175	3-30-84	.250	.267	.241	12	44	6	11	0	0	0	5	1	1	0	6	3	1		.250	.340
Wright, Damon	R-R	6-3	205	10-28-85	.270	.300	.259	44	148	19	40	8	4	0	22	20	2	0	0	23	9	4	.378	.365
Zambrano, Eliezer	B-R	5-11	175	9-16-86	.174	.143	.182	22	69	4	12	3	0	0	11	3	0	3	1	16	0	0	.217	.205

Pitching	B-T	HT	WT	DOB	W	L	ERA	G	GS	CG	SV	IP	H	R	ER	HR	BB	SO	AVG	vLH	vRH	K/9	BB/9
Barnes, Scott	L-L	6-3	175	9-5-87	0	0	4.76	2	1	0	0	6	6	3	3	0	1	11	.250	.300	.214	17.47	1.59
Begg, Chris	R-R	6-4	195	9-12-79	0	0	4.50	2	2	0	0	12	15	6	6	1	0	8	.300	.250	.316	6.00	0.00
Bowlin, Drew	R-R	6-1	190	12-28-86	0	3	5.74	5	5	0	0	16	19	11	10	1	10	10	.302	.412	.261	5.74	5.74
Brinson, Morgan	R-R	6-3	181	12-11-86	0	0	0.00	2	0	0	0	4	4	0	0	0	4	7	.000	.000	.000	—	—
Bucardo, Wilber	R-R	6-2	175	11-20-87	6	7	4.57	16	15	0	0	67	87	47	34	4	21	40	.325	.370	.298	5.37	2.82
Casilla, Jose	R-R	6-1	190	5-21-89	0	0	2.70	2	0	0	0	3	4	1	1	0	1	4	.308	.667	.200	10.80	2.70
Edens, Joseph	R-R	5-10	193	9-26-84	1	3	3.38	24	0	0	2	35	28	14	13	3	8	41	.228	.170	.263	10.64	2.08
Eifel, Mike	R-R	6-4	232	8-13-85	1	1	3.94	18	0	0	0	30	25	16	13	3	17	28	.231	.243	.225	8.49	5.16
Fitzgerald, Justin	R-R	6-5	225	3-3-86	1	0	4.76	14	0	0	5	17	20	9	9	1	6	13	.313	.394	.226	6.88	3.18
Hobson, Gib	R-R	6-3	195	1-13-85	0	2	5.23	3	3	0	0	10	15	9	6	1	5	6	.326	.235	.379	4.35	1.74
Irving, Brian	R-R	6-2	205	4-24-86	2	1	7.14	19	1	0	1	29	40	27	23	1	18	36	.315	.273	.347	11.17	5.59
Jarvis, Jason	R-R	6-2	190	10-1-87	1	0	13.50	2	0	0	0	2	4	3	3	1	3	1	.500	1.000	.429	4.50	13.50
Kaufman, Shane	R-R	6-0	185	12-11-85	1	3	7.71	16	0	0	0	21	25	19	18	3	12	16	.298	.536	.179	6.86	5.14
King, Aaron	L-L	6-4	205	4-27-89	1	0	5.40	2	0	0	0	2	1	1	1	0	4	4	.200	.000	.333	21.60	21.60
Loree, Mike	R-R	6-6	226	9-14-86	4	3	2.44	15	15	0	0	81	63	24	22	2	7	75	.211	.193	.227	8.33	0.78
Macfarland, Steve	R-R	6-2	185	11-17-85	0	0	11.05	6	0	0	0	7	12	9	9	1	6	7	.353	.300	.375	8.59	7.36
Marte, Kelvin	R-R	6-0	180	11-24-87	0	0	6.14	8	0	0	0	7	8	5	5	0	4	10	.308	.167	.429	12.27	4.91
Neitz, Jason	L-L	6-0	170	4-24-84	5	0	1.82	25	0	0	0	30	28	7	6	1	12	19	.262	.227	.286	5.76	3.64
Pannell, J.J.	R-R	6-1	180	9-22-85	0	0	9.82	16	0	0	1	26	35	36	28	4	17	33	.318	.333	.308	11.57	5.96
Quirarte, Edwin	R-R	6-2	185	12-20-86	3	3	2.12	26	0	0	14	30	23	9	7	0	9	33	.213	.282	.174	10.01	2.73
Reichard, Andrew	R-R	6-4	235	12-4-84	3	2	2.87	15	11	0	0	63	61	25	20	4	17	63	.258	.219	.290	9.05	2.44
Ronick, Ari	L-L	6-4	205	3-25-86	4	1	4.05	16	0	0	0	60	55	32	27	5	21	60	.248	.302	.226	9.00	3.15
Runzler, Dan	L-L	6-4	215	3-30-85	0	1	2.10	27	0	0	0	30	19	8	7	1	21	43	.184	.220	.151	12.90	6.30
Stolp, Eric	R-R	6-3	182	8-18-84	3	1	2.68	19	0	0	1	40	31	15	12	0	15	22	.218	.255	.198	4.91	3.35
Surkamp, Eric	L-L	6-4	190	7-16-87	0	2	6.43	5	4	0	0	14	20	10	10	1	5	16	.351	.304	.382	10.29	3.21
Verdugo, Ryan	L-L	6-0	195	4-10-87	0	0	4.50	1	0	0	0	2	1	1	1	1	1	3	.167	.000	.200	13.50	4.50
Wilson, Chris	R-R	6-2	205	11-27-86	0	0	18.00	1	0	0	0	1	6	2	2	0	2	0	.333	.000	.333	0.00	18.00
Yntema, Orlando	R-R	6-3	180	2-21-86	5	3	5.03	10	6	0	0	34	45	21	19	4	15	18	.321	.319	.324	4.76	3.97

Fielding

Catcher	PCT	G	PO	A	E	DP	PB
Ambort	1.000	4	38	0	0	0	1
Kline	.995	23	163	21	1	2	1
Monell	.989	30	236	41	3	1	9
Posey	.960	2	22	2	1	0	0
Zambrano	1.000	22	159	12	0	2	5

First Base	PCT	G	PO	A	E	DP
Ambort	1.000	4	23	2	0	4
Lindsley	1.000	1	6	0	0	0
Loberg	.990	74	640	46	7	47
Monell	1.000	1	9	0	0	1
Quintana	1.000	1	0	1	0	0

Second Base	PCT	G	PO	A	E	DP
Cook	1.000	2	3	2	0	0
Curry	—	1	0	0	0	0
Flores	.969	7	11	20	1	2
Lindsley	1.000	3	3	0	0	0
Lormand	.981	58	98	158	5	26
Stromsmoe	.978	12	17	28	1	3

Third Base	PCT	G	PO	A	E	DP
Ambort	1.000	1	0	2	0	0
Cook	1.000	3	1	1	0	0
Flores	.962	56	39	88	5	6
Gillaspie	.909	15	5	25	3	1
Lindsley	1.000	3	0	4	0	0
Loberg	1.000	1	0	1	0	0
Quintana	.900	4	3	6	1	0

Shortstop	PCT	G	PO	A	E	DP
Adrianza	1.000	1	2	3	0	1
Cook	.857	1	3	3	1	1
Crawford	.000	1	0	0	2	0
Flores	1.000	1	0	1	0	0
Frias	.969	52	92	162	8	28
Lindsley	.931	14	17	50	5	10
Lormand	.976	12	17	23	1	3

Outfield	PCT	G	PO	A	E	DP
Bond	.992	65	111	6	1	1
Cook	1.000	16	20	0	0	0
Curry	.975	65	113	5	3	1
Lindsley	—	1	0	0	0	0
Luster	1.000	11	22	2	0	0
Mantle	.667	1	1	1	1	0
Peguero	.978	47	85	4	2	0
Wright	.978	32	44	0	1	0

AZL GIANTS — ROOKIE

ARIZONA LEAGUE

Batting	B-T	HT	WT	DOB	AVG	vLH	vRH	G	AB	R	H	2B	3B	HR	RBI	BB	HBP	SH	SF	SO	SB	CS	SLG	OBP
Adrianza, Ehire	B-R	6-1	155	8-21-89	.255	.714	.188	15	55	13	14	4	0	1	6	7	1	0	0	4	0	1	.382	.349
Cook, Dan	B-R	6-3	185	6-15-86	.243	.217	.250	29	115	19	28	2	1	0	11	9	1	1	0	27	7	1	.278	.304
Crawford, Brandon	L-R	6-2	200	1-21-87	.429	.333	.455	4	14	3	6	1	1	0	3	0	0	0	0	6	3	1	.643	.429
Creswell, Tayler	R-R	6-0	170	2-11-87	.375	.000	.400	4	16	3	6	1	0	0	5	1	1	0	0	6	1	0	.438	.444
Fairley, Wendell	L-R	6-2	190	3-17-88	.259	.206	.270	52	193	39	50	5	2	2	17	26	16	1	2	37	7	3	.337	.388
Flanigan, Rob	L-R	6-4	230	8-14-87	.223	.308	.211	31	103	14	23	6	1	1	7	7	3	0	2	32	1	1	.330	.287
Frias, Vladimir	B-R	6-2	170	9-6-86	.421	.400	.429	5	19	5	8	0	1	0	5	1	1	0	2	0	1	2	.526	.435
Gillaspie, Conor	L-R	6-1	200	7-18-87	.273	.400	.235	6	22	2	6	3	0	0	7	3	0	0	0	1	0	1	.409	.360
Hornostaj, Aaron	L-R	6-1	180	5-19-83	.250	.000	.308	5	16	1	4	0	0	0	0	3	1	0	0	5	1	0	.250	.400
Leone, Justin	R-R	6-1	200	3-9-77	.111	.500	.000	3	9	3	1	0	0	0	2	1	0	0	0	3	2	0	.111	.200
Lindsley, Brooks	R-R	6-0	185	10-25-86	.349	.500	.306	20	63	11	22	6	1	0	14	6	2	2	3	14	4	1	.476	.405
Lopez, Josh	R-R	5-9	170	1-31-89	.195	.150	.204	47	128	19	25	3	3	2	11	13	1	6	2	45	5	1	.313	.271
Lowenstein, Aaron	R-R	6-2	195	6-9-85	.191	.100	.216	15	47	3	9	4	0	0	7	2	0	0	0	10	0	0	.277	.255
Mantle, Ryan	R-R	6-3	210	7-12-86	.310	.321	.307	45	155	32	48	13	3	1	29	17	4	0	6	32	9	2	.452	.379
Mazzola, Josh	R-R	6-2	195	4-10-86	.324	.500	.289	47	170	42	55	15	4	5	35	14	9	0	5	39	3	3	.547	.394
Medina, Jose	R-R	6-0	180	11-29-86	.229	.143	.250	29	70	16	16	4	0	1	16	9	1	2	1	19	1	1	.329	.349
Monell, Johnny	L-R	5-11	205	3-27-86	.405	.300	.438	11	42	13	17	7	0	1	10	4	2	0	0	5	3	0	.643	.479
Navarro, Jesus	R-R	6-0	180	1-3-88	.303	.412	.271	27	76	9	23	4	0	0	11	6	1	0	1	23	1	1	.355	.357
Posey, Buster	R-R	6-2	195	3-27-87	.385	.167	.450	7	26	8	10	3	1	1	4	5	0	0	0	4	0	0	.692	.484
Price, Ryne	L-R	5-11	190	5-27-86	.250	.313	.234	26	80	12	20	8	0	1	16	13	3	0	2	19	1	0	.388	.367
Quintana, Carlos	R-R	6-3	180	6-14-87	.333	.750	.250	21	48	10	16	3	1	0	10	7	0	0	0	7	0	1	.438	.418
Shriner, Jesse	R-R	6-1	195	2-24-85	.200	.000	.214	6	15	1	3	1	1	0	2	0	0	0	0	2	0	0	.400	.200
Valentin, Cesar	R-R	5-11	170	10-19-88	.333	.000	.500	1	3	1	1	0	0	0	0	0	0	0	0	0	0	0	.333	.333
Weeks, Joel	L-R	5-9	180	11-30-84	.248	.278	.241	33	101	16	25	4	0	0	11	11	1	3	1	17	4	2	.287	.325
Woodbury, Ben	R-R	5-10	175	2-21-86	.317	.429	.295	41	126	32	40	8	0	0	14	24	3	5	2	11	18	1	.381	.432
Ziegler, C.J.	R-R	6-4	225	11-27-85	.262	.214	.270	53	187	26	49	17	0	7	43	35	5	0	8	38	2	1	.465	.379

Pitching	B-T	HT	WT	DOB	W	L	ERA	G	GS	CG	SV	IP	H	R	ER	HR	BB	SO	AVG	vLH	vRH	K/9	BB/9
Barnes, Scott	L-L	6-3	175	9-5-87	0	1	3.38	3	0	0	0	5	3	2	2	0	4	11	.167	.000	.188	18.56	6.75
Bowlin, Drew	R-R	6-1	190	12-28-86	1	0	12.10	7	0	0	0	10	16	15	13	0	10	11	.364	.545	.303	10.24	9.31
Bucardo, Jorge	R-R	6-1	155	10-18-89	3	1	3.68	11	11	1	0	51	51	24	21	4	15	51	.259	.250	.262	8.94	2.63
Casilla, Jose	R-R	6-1	190	5-21-89	3	1	1.59	6	0	0	0	23	19	10	4	1	1	19	.216	.300	.191	7.54	0.40
De La Rosa, Carlos	L-L	6-2	190	7-15-84	1	2	5.06	7	0	0	2	11	14	9	6	0	2	9	.304	.250	.324	7.59	1.69
Fitzgerald, Justin	R-R	6-5	225	3-31-86	0	0	0.00	3	0	0	0	4	2	0	0	0	2	6	.143	.000	.167	13.50	4.50
Geronimo, Gregorio	L-L	6-3	190	12-18-86	0	0	7.88	7	0	0	0	8	10	7	7	1	9	6	.313	.000	.357	6.75	10.13
Grabham, Brandon	R-R	6-5	230	1-30-86	2	1	2.93	10	0	0	0	15	13	8	5	1	9	14	.220	.294	.190	8.22	5.28
Hernandez, Javier	R-R	6-4	180	9-27-87	5	1	4.06	11	11	0	0	51	46	25	23	3	16	44	.240	.320	.211	7.76	2.82
Jarvis, Jason	R-R	6-2	190	10-1-87	0	0	0.00	2	0	0	0	1	2	1	0	0	0	2	.333	.000	.400	13.50	0.00
Kerth, Andrew	R-R	6-4	210	5-6-85	1	0	8.44	12	0	0	0	16	27	19	15	2	5	11	.380	.385	.378	6.19	2.81
King, Aaron	L-L	6-4	205	4-27-89	4	1	2.84	11	6	0	0	32	24	10	10	1	15	41	.216	.185	.226	11.65	4.26
King, John	R-R	6-3	180	7-5-85	0	1	25.50	7	0	0	0	6	15	18	17	1	9	3	.455	.600	.391	4.50	13.50
Lively, Mitch	R-R	6-5	230	9-7-85	0	0	0.00	2	0	0	0	3	1	0	0	0	0	4	.111	.000	.125	13.50	0.00
Marte, Kelvin	R-R	6-0	180	11-24-87	2	1	1.78	8	7	0	0	35	26	12	7	0	10	31	.211	.273	.189	7.90	2.55
Martinez, Roberto	L-L	6-1	175	5-5-86	1	0	5.23	7	0	0	0	10	15	7	6	1	1	5	.341	.188	.429	4.35	0.87
Nicholson, Kyle	R-R	6-0	205	7-31-85	6	1	1.15	11	11	1	0	63	34	10	8	1	3	54	.159	.150	.164	7.76	0.43
Nova, Meroly	L-L	6-6	165	4-16-86	0	4	7.92	9	5	0	0	25	29	25	22	2	12	17	.293	.444	.259	6.12	4.32
Palazzolo, Steve	R-R	6-10	260	3-31-82	0	0	0.00	1	0	0	0	2	1	0	0	0	2	0	.167	1.000	.000	9.00	0.00
Patino, Geomar	R-R	6-3	180	1-21-87	0	1	4.82	8	0	0	0	9	9	6	5	0	5	15	.237	.667	.156	14.46	4.82
Pendley, Nathan	L-L	6-4	220	9-5-81	0	0	4.09	6	0	0	0	11	9	5	5	1	6	4	.237	.400	.212	3.27	4.91
Rodriguez, Mario	L-L	6-2	190	8-21-88	1	1	6.75	12	0	0	0	17	26	18	13	0	7	15	.338	.250	.361	7.79	3.63
Surkamp, Eric	L-L	6-4	190	7-16-87	0	0	2.70	2	0	0	0	3	3	1	1	0	0	7	.231	.000	.273	18.90	0.00
Verdugo, Ryan	L-L	6-0	190	4-10-87	1	0	2.08	8	0	0	2	13	9	3	3	0	6	19	.200	.273	.176	13.15	4.15
Wilson, Chris	R-R	6-2	205	11-27-86	5	2	2.92	18	0	0	6	25	20	9	8	0	9	21	.233	.231	.233	7.66	3.28
Woodruff, Kyle	R-R	6-6	225	5-2-86	0	0	1.55	17	0	0	0	29	28	12	5	0	8	28	.246	.125	.278	8.69	2.48

Fielding

Catcher	PCT	G	PO	A	E	DP	PB
Lowenstein	.982	15	96	14	2	0	4
Monell	.986	10	61	8	1	0	4
Navarro	1.000	27	192	11	0	1	3
Posey	1.000	4	34	2	0	0	1
Price	.967	6	27	2	1	0	1
Shriner	.933	6	39	3	3	0	1
Weeks	.933	4	14	0	1	0	2

First Base	PCT	G	PO	A	E	DP
Flanigan	.989	12	83	4	1	6
Quintana	.975	11	72	6	2	6
Ziegler	.980	40	365	27	8	41

Second Base	PCT	G	PO	A	E	DP
Cook	.950	16	31	45	4	14
Frias	.962	5	9	16	1	5

Hornostaj	1.000	3	4 11 0 2
Leone	1.000	1	2 0 0 0
Lopez	.942	32	61 85 9 19
Quintana	—	1	0 0 0 0
Weeks	1.000	4	5 7 0 1

Third Base	PCT	G	PO	A	E	DP
Cook	.844	8	6	21	5	1
Gillaspie	1.000	3	0	4	0	1
Lopez	1.000	3	1	5	0	0
Mazzola	.934	39	20	94	8	9

Quintana	.833	6	5 5 2 1
Valentin	—	1	0 0 0 0
Weeks	1.000	1	0 3 0 1

Shortstop	PCT	G	PO	A	E	DP
Adrianza	.963	15	30	49	3	9
Crawford	1.000	3	4	7	0	0
Hornostaj	1.000	2	2	10	0	2
Lindsley	.893	8	9	16	3	6
Lopez	.933	7	14	14	2	5
Weeks	.977	22	20	65	2	12

Outfield	PCT	G	PO	A	E	DP
Cook	1.000	3	2	0	0	0
Creswell	1.000	4	7	0	0	0
Fairley	.940	51	78	1	5	0
Leone	—	2	0	0	0	0
Lindsley	.800	7	4	0	1	0
Mantle	.985	42	63	2	1	0
Medina	1.000	24	13	1	0	0
Price	.947	13	16	2	1	0
Quintana	—	2	0	0	0	0
Woodbury	.980	37	49	1	1	0

DSL GIANTS
DOMINICAN SUMMER LEAGUE

ROOKIE

Batting	B-T	HT	WT	DOB	AVG	vLH	vRH	G	AB	R	H	2B	3B	HR	RBI	BB	HBP	SH	SF	SO	SB	CS	SLG	OBP
Abad, Ramon	R-R	6-1	200	9-30-86	.238	.250	.235	30	80	14	19	3	0	0	6	14	2	0	0	30	4	4	.275	.365
Almonte, Gilberto	R-R	6-3	188	7-15-88	.270	.367	.246	48	152	23	41	10	2	1	19	20	1	2	4	19	2	0	.382	.350
Bautista, Jonathan	R-R	5-10	188	3-21-85	.244	.357	.221	32	82	11	20	1	0	0	6	10	4	0	2	8	1	3	.256	.347
Castillo, Luis	R-R	6-3	198	11-21-88	.167	.000	.192	14	30	1	5	1	0	0	4	0	0	0	0	6	1	1	.200	.265
De La Cruz, Jose	R-R			4-28-91	.266	.205	.280	63	244	37	65	11	4	2	35	12	6	1	2	46	9	6	.369	.314
Duran, Rey	R-R	6-0	200	7-31-89	.179	.200	.173	21	67	9	12	4	0	2	12	5	1	0	1	15	1	0	.328	.243
Fuentes, Robedluis	R-R	6-4	180	9-13-88	.300	.238	.315	61	210	44	63	5	0	1	21	24	6	7	1	29	4	3	.338	.386
Izturis, Julio	B-R	5-11	165	8-29-89	.284	.120	.315	47	155	49	44	4	2	1	23	46	9	1	0	21	24	5	.355	.471
Medina, Jose	R-R	6-0	180	11-29-86	.286	.500	.241	9	35	7	10	2	2	2	13	4	3	0	0	8	1	0	.629	.405
Osuna, Cesar	R-R	5-11	175	1-29-90	.244	.250	.243	59	213	49	52	18	0	3	30	30	6	4	2	28	7	2	.371	.351
Sanchez, Hector	B-R	6-0	185	11-17-89	.348	.262	.370	55	207	40	72	14	3	4	63	36	8	1	2	24	5	1	.502	.458
Santana, Victor	R-R	6-1	192	11-21-88	.252	.224	.260	63	230	39	58	15	2	4	46	27	11	1	5	60	5	1	.387	.352
Villegas, Ydwin	B-R	5-10	165	9-1-90	.219	.170	.233	47	151	20	40	4	8	7	1	0	25	40	5	7	3	36	13	.260	.348
Willoughby, Carlos	R-R	5-10	170	11-12-88	.284	.219	.296	55	194	60	55	6	3	0	24	39	7	6	4	42	33	4	.345	.414
Windster, Sundrendy	R-R	6-3	185	2-23-89	.268	.286	.265	62	224	47	60	13	0	10	43	30	3	1	4	55	1	3	.460	.356

Pitching	B-T	HT	WT	DOB	W	L	ERA	G	GS	CG	SV	IP	H	R	ER	HR	BB	SO	AVG	vLH	vRH	K/9	BB/9
Azocar, Luis	L-L	5-11	180	9-6-86	3	1	4.39	20	0	0	1	27	9	14	13	1	40	35	.103	.000	.125	11.81	13.50
Concepcion, Edward	R-R	6-3	190	10-3-88	8	2	4.20	15	14	0	0	75	85	40	35	2	20	64	.284	.326	.268	7.68	2.40
De La Cruz, Diego	L-L	6-1	182	2-12-89	1	3	6.88	10	8	0	0	35	35	30	27	6	16	41	.254	.261	.252	10.44	4.08
Fernandez, Ebert	L-L	6-3	192	10-28-90	2	0	3.53	12	5	0	0	36	21	15	14	2	27	34	.174	.000	.191	8.58	6.81
Ferrer, Miguel	R-R	6-3	168	8-7-90	8	2	2.44	13	11	0	0	63	52	20	17	1	16	42	.220	.200	.226	6.03	2.30
Garcia, Bertoni	R-R	5-11	173	7-8-91	3	0	2.29	15	1	0	0	39	22	11	10	1	24	34	.167	.167	.167	7.78	5.49
Geraldo, Walin	R-R	6-3	192	7-30-88	1	2	7.89	13	3	0	0	30	39	26	26	1	17	20	.325	.484	.270	6.07	5.16
Martinez, Rafael	R-R	6-3	185	7-9-88	1	1	1.20	8	0	0	1	15	7	3	2	0	7	12	.146	.154	.143	7.20	4.20
Mendez, Alejandro	R-R	6-1	190	9-8-85	3	2	2.55	27	0	0	15	42	34	14	12	0	24	39	.241	.237	.243	8.29	5.10
Montero, Raymundo	R-R	6-2	185	9-20-89	4	3	4.88	24	0	0	2	52	59	35	28	3	31	43	.292	.429	.248	7.49	5.40
Noel, Franklin	L-L	6-1	175	12-20-88	4	2	2.28	24	1	0	4	51	50	20	13	0	22	50	.263	.235	.266	8.77	3.86
Paniagua, Armando	R-R	5-11	155	1-11-90	1	0	0.00	4	0	0	1	8	7	0	0	0	6	2	.226	.125	.261	7.56	6.48
Perez, Luiyin	R-R			4-16-89	1	0	9.88	9	0	0	0	14	19	16	15	1	12	7	.317	.286	.326	4.61	7.90
Prada, Marcos	R-R	6-0	180	8-31-90	4	0	4.60	13	13	0	0	59	62	34	30	2	29	39	.284	.362	.256	5.98	4.45
Sanchez, Argenis	R-R	5-11	190	11-18-89	6	3	3.57	14	14	0	0	71	61	33	28	1	30	61	.236	.258	.229	7.77	3.82

Fielding

Catcher	PCT	G	PO	A	E	DP	PB
Bautista	.984	30	165	15	3	2	5
Duran	1.000	12	76	8	0	1	0
Sanchez	.979	37	294	32	7	1	10

First Base	PCT	G	PO	A	E	DP
Almonte	1.000	9	58	2	0	6
Castillo	1.000	3	12	0	0	1
Duran	—	1	0	0	0	0
Sanchez	1.000	16	121	6	0	9
Santana	.985	52	452	18	7	41

Second Base	PCT	G	PO	A	E	DP
Almonte	—	1	0	0	0	0
Bautista	—	1	0	0	0	0
Izturis	.957	36	77	103	8	25
Osuna	.940	22	35	44	5	7
Willoughby	.974	19	35	41	2	9

Third Base	PCT	G	PO	A	E	DP
Almonte	.955	38	32	74	5	7
Izturis	1.000	1	1	2	0	0
Osuna	.929	39	21	84	8	9

Shortstop	PCT	G	PO	A	E	DP
Almonte	—	1	0	0	0	0
Izturis	.944	3	3	14	1	1
Villegas	.958	67	102	214	14	37

Outfield	PCT	G	PO	A	E	DP
Abad	.833	13	5	0	1	0
De La Cruz	.958	63	103	10	5	4
Fuentes	.975	61	110	8	3	0
Medina	1.000	4	1	1	0	0
Osuna	1.000	1	1	1	0	0
Willoughby	.986	41	65	5	1	1
Windster	.970	45	62	3	2	1

Seattle Mariners

BY JOHN HICKEY

Perhaps the 2008 season could have gone worse for the Seattle Mariners, but it would take a spectacular imagination to map out just how.

After going over the top to add lefthander Erik Bedard in an expensive trade and righthander Carlos Silva in an expensive free agent signing, the Mariners began the season with dreams of challenging for the American League West title but wound up competing instead for the first pick in the 2009 draft.

Along the way, both general manager Bill Bavasi and manager John McLaren were fired, replaced on an interim basis by Lee Pelekoudas and Jim Riggleman, respectively. Richie Sexson, who had been the Mariners' RBI leader in 2005 and 2006, was released after a year and a half of struggles at the plate.

Silva started the season 3-0, then won just once more en route to a 15-loss season. Bedard had a winning season at 6-4, but he made just 15 starts and spent most of the season on the disabled list. He had labrum surgery the final week of the season and his availability for 2009 was unclear.

Righthander Felix Hernandez was the only Seattle starter to begin and end the season in the rotation without major interruptions. He reached the 200-inning plateau for the first time in his career and finished among the AL leaders in strikeouts (175), ERA (3.45) despite a paltry 9-11 record. Lefthander Jarrod Washburn, however, was a virtual no-show the final month of the season because of an abdominal injury, and righthander Miguel Batista spent much of the second half of the season in the bullpen.

On the bright side, lefthander Ryan Rowland-Smith and righthander Brandon Morrow both made the switch from relief work to the rotation after spells in the minor leagues. The performances Rowland-Smith (5-3, 3.42 in 188 innings) and Morrow (75 strikeouts in 64 innings) were enough that the Mariners actually ended the season feeling optimistic about the rotation looking toward 2009 despite a 101-loss season.

Offensively, the first half of the season saw the Mariners stumble blindly through their at-bats. However, left fielder Raul Ibanez drove in 110 runs as the hitter opposing pitchers had to fear the most. A close second was leadoff hitter Ichiro

Suzuki, who had his eighth consecutive 200-hit, 100-runs season.

Second baseman Jose Lopez emerged by hitting .297/.322/.443 with 17 home runs and 89 RBIs, and third baseman Adrian Beltre had a team-best 25 homers, but he missed the final three weeks of the season with thumb and shoulder surgeries.

ORGANIZATION LEADERS

BATTING		*Minimum 250 at-bats
*AVG	Moore, Adam, West Tenn	.319
R	Redman, Prentice, West Tenn/Tacoma	97
H	Limonta, Johan, High Desert/West Tenn	145
TB	Halman, Greg, High Desert/West Tenn	260
2B	Limonta, Johan, High Desert/West Tenn	43
3B	McOwen, James, High Desert	9
HR	Halman, Greg, High Desert/West Tenn	29
RBI	Diaz, Victor, Tacoma	100
BB	Kiger, Mark, West Tenn	73
SO	Diaz, Victor, Tacoma	149
SO	Almonte, Denny, Wisconsin	149
SB	Carroll, Daniel, High Desert/Wisconsin	38
*OBP	Hubbard, Thomas, West Tenn	.407
*SLG	Wilson, Michael, West Tenn	.549

PITCHING		†Minimum 75 innings
W	Baldwin, Andrew, Tacoma	10
L	Fister, Doug, West Tenn	14
L	Renaud, Keith, High Desert/Wisconsin	14
†ERA	Pineda, Michael, Wisconsin	1.95
G	Cotter, Aaron, High Desert/West Tenn	53
GS	Paredes, Edward, Wisconsin/West Tenn	26
SV	Kelley, Shawn, Wisconsin/High Desert/West Tenn	15
IP	Baldwin, Andrew, Tacoma	148
BB	Renaud, Keith, High Desert/Wisconsin	83
SO	Pineda, Michael, Wisconsin	128
†AVG	Pineda, Michael, Wisconsin	.216

General Manager: Bill Bavasi/Lee Pelekoudas. **Farm Director:** Greg Hunter. **Scouting Director:** Bob Fontaine.

Class	Team	League	W	L	PCT	Finish*	Manager	Affiliate Since
Majors	Seattle	American	61	101	.377	14th (14)	J. McLaren/J. Riggleman	—
Triple-A	Tacoma Rainiers	Pacific Coast	80	64	.556	5th (16)	Darren Brown	1995
Double-A	West Tenn Diamond Jaxx	Southern	70	68	.507	4th (10)	Scott Steinmann	2007
High A	High Desert Mavericks	California	58	82	.414	10th (10)	Jim Horner	2007
Low A	Wisconsin Timber Rattlers	Midwest	56	80	.412	13th (14)	Terry Pollreisz	1993
Short-season	Everett AquaSox	Northwest	32	44	.421	7th (8)	Jose Moreno	1995
Rookie	Pulaski Mariners	Appalachian	40	27	.597	2nd (10)	Rob Mummau	2008
Rookie	AZL Mariners	Arizona	21	35	.375	8th (9)	Andy Bottin	2001
Overall 2008 Minor League Record			357	400	.472	21st		

* Finish in overall standings (No. of teams in league). ^League champion.

ORGANIZATION STATISTICS

SEATTLE MARINERS
AMERICAN LEAGUE

Batting	B-T	HT	WT	DOB	AVG	vLH	vRH	G	AB	R	H	2B	3B	HR	RBI	BB	HBP	SH	SF	SO	SB	CS	SLG	OBP
Balentien, Wladimir	R-R	6-2	215	7-2-84	.202	.218	.194	71	243	23	49	13	0	7	24	16	0	0	1	79	0	1	.342	.250
Beltre, Adrian	R-R	5-11	225	4-7-79	.266	.340	.239	143	556	74	148	29	1	25	77	50	2	0	4	90	8	2	.457	.327
Betancourt, Yuniesky	R-R	5-10	195	1-31-82	.279	.275	.281	153	559	66	156	36	3	7	51	17	2	6	6	42	4	4	.392	.300
Bloomquist, Willie	R-R	5-11	195	11-27-77	.279	.351	.220	71	165	32	46	1	0	0	9	25	1	1	0	29	14	3	.285	.377
Burke, Jamie	R-R	6-0	225	9-24-71	.261	.341	.196	48	92	10	24	3	0	1	8	5	1	1	1	7	0	1	.326	.303
Cairo, Miguel	R-R	6-1	210	5-4-74	.249	.270	.235	108	221	34	55	14	2	0	23	18	4	6	1	32	5	2	.330	.316
Clement, Jeff	L-R	6-1	215	8-21-83	.227	.289	.209	66	203	17	46	10	1	5	23	15	5	0	1	63	0	1	.360	.295
Hulett, Tug	L-R	5-10	185	2-28-83	.224	.000	.239	30	49	2	11	1	0	1	2	5	1	1	0	17	0	0	.306	.309
Ibanez, Raul	L-R	6-2	225	6-2-72	.293	.305	.288	162	635	85	186	43	3	23	110	64	3	0	5	110	2	4	.479	.358
Jimerson, Charlton	R-R	6-3	215	9-22-79	.000	.000	.000	2	1	1	0	0	0	0	0	0	0	0	0	0	0	0	.000	.000
Johjima, Kenji	R-R	6-0	205	6-8-76	.227	.205	.237	112	379	29	86	19	0	7	39	19	8	1	2	33	2	0	.332	.277
Johnson, Rob	R-R	6-1	210	7-22-83	.129	.091	.150	14	31	2	4	0	0	1	2	0	0	1	0	6	0	0	.226	.129
LaHair, Bryan	L-R	6-5	220	11-5-82	.250	.091	.281	45	150	15	34	4	0	3	10	13	0	1	0	40	0	1	.346	.315
Lopez, Jose	R-R	6-0	205	11-24-83	.297	.299	.296	159	644	80	191	41	1	17	89	27	1	6	9	67	6	3	.443	.322
Morse, Mike	R-R	6-4	230	3-22-82	.222	.250	.200	5	9	0	2	1	0	0	0	1	1	0	0	4	0	0	.333	.364
Norton, Greg	B-R	6-1	205	7-6-72	.438	.667	.385	6	16	2	7	2	0	0	4	2	0	0	0	4	0	0	.563	.500
Reed, Jeremy	L-L	6-0	200	6-15-81	.269	.115	.285	97	286	30	77	18	1	2	31	18	2	3	3	38	2	3	.360	.314
Sexson, Richie	R-R	6-8	240	12-29-74	.218	.344	.178	74	252	27	55	8	0	11	30	37	0	0	3	76	1	0	.381	.315
2-team total (22 New York)					.221	—	—	96	280	29	62	9	0	12	36	43	0	0	4	86	1	0	.382	.321
Suzuki, Ichiro	L-R	5-11	170	10-22-73	.310	.288	.320	162	686	103	213	20	7	6	42	51	5	3	4	65	43	4	.386	.361
Tuiasosopo, Matt	R-R	6-2	223	5-10-86	.159	.133	.172	14	44	1	7	2	1	0	2	2	1	0	0	16	0	0	.250	.213
Valbuena, Luis	L-R	5-10	200	11-30-85	.245	.429	.214	18	49	6	12	5	0	1	4	1	0	0	1	11	0	0	.347	.315
Vidro, Jose	B-R	6-0	200	8-27-74	.234	.232	.235	85	308	28	72	11	0	7	45	18	0	2	2	36	2	1	.338	.274
Wilkerson, Brad	L-L	6-0	205	6-1-77	.232	.000	.236	19	56	1	13	4	0	0	5	10	0	2	0	15	1	2	.304	.348
2-team total (85 Toronto)					.220	—	—	104	264	21	58	12	2	4	28	35	1	4	5	68	3	5	.326	.308

Pitching	B-T	HT	WT	DOB	W	L	ERA	G	GS	CG	SV	IP	H	R	ER	HR	BB	SO	AVG	vLH	vRH	K/9	BB/9
Baek, Cha Seung	R-R	6-4	225	5-29-80	0	1	5.40	10	1	0	0	30	28	18	18	6	13	15	.250	.188	.297	4.50	3.90
Batista, Miguel	R-R	6-1	200	2-19-71	4	14	6.26	44	20	0	1	115	135	89	80	19	79	73	.295	.293	.298	5.71	6.18
Bedard, Erik	L-L	6-1	190	3-6-79	6	4	3.67	15	15	0	0	81	70	38	33	9	37	72	.231	.253	.224	8.00	4.11
Corcoran, Roy	R-R	5-10	170	5-11-80	6	2	3.22	50	0	0	3	73	65	31	26	1	36	39	.239	.258	.221	4.83	4.46
Dickey, R.A.	R-R	6-3	220	10-29-74	5	8	5.21	32	14	0	0	112	124	65	65	15	51	58	.284	.259	.309	4.65	4.09
Feierabend, Ryan	L-L	6-3	230	8-22-85	1	4	7.71	8	8	0	0	40	59	34	34	7	14	26	.355	.386	.339	5.90	3.18
Green, Sean	R-R	6-6	235	4-20-79	4	5	4.67	72	0	0	1	79	80	47	41	3	36	62	.261	.299	.233	7.06	4.10
Hernandez, Felix	R-R	6-3	230	4-8-86	9	11	3.45	31	31	2	0	201	198	85	77	17	80	175	.261	.275	.242	7.85	3.59
Jimenez, Cesar	L-L	5-11	215	11-12-84	0	2	3.41	31	2	0	0	34	32	13	13	2	13	26	.258	.317	.203	6.82	3.41
Lowe, Mark	L-R	6-3	200	6-7-83	1	5	5.37	57	0	0	1	64	78	44	38	6	34	55	.301	.354	.250	7.77	4.81
Messenger, Randy	R-R	6-6	270	8-13-81	0	0	3.55	13	0	0	1	16	16	5	5	1	5	7	.314	.250	.370	4.97	3.55
Morrow, Brandon	R-R	6-3	185	7-26-84	3	4	3.34	45	5	0	10	65	40	26	24	10	34	75	.174	.198	.149	10.44	4.73
O'Flaherty, Eric	L-L	6-2	220	2-5-85	0	1	20.25	7	0	0	0	7	16	15	15	2	4	4	.457	.500	.421	5.40	5.40
Putz, J.J.	R-R	6-5	250	2-22-77	6	5	3.88	47	0	0	15	46	46	20	20	4	28	56	.256	.258	.253	10.88	5.44
Rhodes Jr., Arthur	L-L	6-2	210	10-24-69	2	1	2.86	36	0	0	1	22	17	8	7	3	6	26	.227	.195	.265	10.64	5.32
Rowland-Smith, Ryan	L-L	6-3	240	1-26-83	5	3	3.42	47	12	0	2	118	114	49	45	13	48	77	.253	.311	.224	5.86	3.65
Silva, Carlos	R-R	6-4	245	4-23-79	4	15	6.46	28	28	1	0	153	213	114	110	20	32	69	.331	.348	.312	4.05	1.88
Thomas, Justin	L-L	6-3	225	1-18-84	0	1	6.75	8	0	0	0	4	9	3	3	0	2	2	.474	.571	.200	4.50	4.50
Washburn, Jarrod	L-L	6-1	195	8-13-74	5	14	4.69	28	26	1	1	154	174	87	80	19	50	87	.287	.252	.299	5.10	2.93
Wells, Jared	R-R	6-4	200	10-31-81	0	0	10.13	6	0	0	0	5	7	6	6	2	6	3	.304	.375	.267	5.06	10.13
Woods, Jake	L-L	6-1	200	9-3-81	0	0	6.16	15	0	0	0	19	22	13	13	5	11	9	.293	.317	.265	4.26	5.21

Fielding

Catcher

Catcher	PCT	G	PO	A	E	DP	PB
Burke	.995	43	181	10	1	0	2
Clement	.995	38	195	7	1	0	5
Johjima	.988	100	632	34	8	8	7
Johnson	1.000	10	44	7	0	0	0

First Base

First Base	PCT	G	PO	A	E	DP
Burke	1.000	1	4	0	0	1
Cairo	.998	70	414	23	1	43
LaHair	.993	36	277	18	2	37
Lopez	.991	13	100	11	1	5
Norton	.889	1	7	1	1	2
Reed	.667	1	2	0	1	0
Sexson	.997	73	568	48	2	52
Vidro	.983	9	54	5	1	6

Second Base

Second Base	PCT	G	PO	A	E	DP
Bloomquist	1.000	7	8	15	0	7
Cairo	1.000	5	7	10	0	2
Hulett	1.000	4	4	9	0	2
Lopez	.984	139	259	468	12	99
Valbuena	1.000	16	21	41	0	11

Third Base

Third Base	PCT	G	PO	A	E	DP
Beltre	.964	139	100	272	14	27
Bloomquist	—	1	0	0	0	0
Burke	1.000	1	1	0	0	0
Cairo	.971	19	13	21	1	5
Hulett	—	1	0	0	0	0
Tuiasosopo	.944	13	11	23	2	4

Shortstop

Shortstop	PCT	G	PO	A	E	DP
Betancourt	.968	153	237	401	21	98

	PCT	G	PO	A	E	DP
Bloomquist	1.000	12	17	23	0	2
Cairo	1.000	1	0	1	0	0
Hulett	1.000	4	2	1	0	0
Valbuena	1.000	1	1	1	0	1

Outfield

Outfield	PCT	G	PO	A	E	DP
Balentien	.987	68	149	6	2	0
Bloomquist	.957	43	65	1	3	0
Cairo	—	3	0	0	0	0
Ibanez	.984	153	302	9	5	1
Jimerson	—	1	0	0	0	0
Morse	1.000	5	6	2	0	0
Norton	—	1	0	0	0	0
Reed	.981	77	156	2	3	0
Suzuki	.987	160	370	11	5	2
Wilkerson	1.000	19	18	1	0	0

TACOMA RAINIERS   TRIPLE-A

PACIFIC COAST LEAGUE

Batting	B-T	HT	WT	DOB	AVG	vLH	vRH	G	AB	R	H	2B	3B	HR	RBI	BB	HBP	SH	SF	SO	SB	CS	SLG	OBP
Baez, Fleming	R-R	5-11	194	6-10-81	.000	—	.000	1	1	0	0	0	0	0	0	0	0	0	0	0	0	0	.000	.000
Balentien, Wladimir	R-R	6-2	215	7-2-84	.266	.225	.275	62	233	49	62	20	0	18	55	32	3	1	6	49	3	4	.584	.354
Benitez, Deybis	R-R	6-2	170	4-23-87	.000	—	.000	1	4	0	0	0	0	0	0	0	0	0	0	0	0	0	.000	.000
Blasi, Nick	R-R	5-10	200	9-23-81	.250	.125	.333	6	20	4	5	1	0	0	1	2	1	0	0	5	0	0	.300	.348
2-team total (30 Sacramento)					.238	—	—	36	126	17	30	4	0	2	9	6	1	0	0	28	3	1	.317	.278
Chen, Yung Chi	R-R	5-11	170	7-13-83	.249	.288	.235	69	249	37	62	11	0	3	25	21	2	5	3	33	9	2	.329	.309
Clement, Jeff	L-R	6-1	215	8-21-83	.335	.370	.323	48	173	40	58	17	0	14	43	35	3	0	0	30	0	0	.676	.455
Diaz, Victor	R-R	6-0	210	12-10-81	.280	.226	.294	107	414	65	116	38	0	24	100	49	6	0	4	149	7	2	.546	.362
2-team total (22 Round Rock)					.282	—	—	129	485	69	137	40	0	25	107	61	6	1	4	168	9	3	.520	.367
Feiner, Korey	R-R	5-11	210	9-25-81	.000	.000	.000	2	4	1	0	0	0	0	0	0	0	0	0	1	0	0	.000	.333
Garrett, Shawn	B-R	6-3	220	11-2-78	.304	.327	.296	100	388	50	118	24	1	10	62	26	1	2	1	75	5	4	.448	.349
Howard, Kevin	L-R	6-2	190	6-25-81	.324	.381	.298	20	68	15	22	4	0	8	18	8	0	1	1	11	0	0	.735	.390
2-team total (60 Las Vegas)					.275	—	—	80	247	34	68	15	0	11	45	37	0	4	1	34	1	4	.470	.348
Hulett, Tug	R-R	5-10	185	2-28-83	.298	.143	.329	91	336	71	100	22	5	14	47	49	0	8	7	73	10	5	.518	.380
Jimerson, Charlton	R-R	6-3	215	9-22-79	.233	.268	.221	55	210	23	49	8	1	11	31	3	2	3	1	80	14	7	.438	.250
Johnson, Brent	R-R	6-2	190	5-21-82	.063	.111	.033	16	48	3	3	1	0	0	5	5	1	0	0	48	0	1	.083	.167
Johnson, Rob	R-R	6-1	210	7-22-83	.305	.267	.315	112	417	55	127	30	0	9	49	37	3	3	3	61	7	6	.441	.363
Kinkade, Mike	R-R	6-1	210	5-6-73	.214	.333	.191	18	56	6	12	2	0	2	8	5	4	0	0	17	0	1	.357	.323
LaHair, Bryan	L-R	6-5	220	11-5-82	.263	.183	.286	86	316	39	83	26	1	12	53	45	1	0	0	87	1	1	.465	.356
Navarro, Oswaldo	R-R	6-0	155	10-2-84	.261	.307	.242	104	357	47	93	21	1	1	31	31	4	2	1	71	2	3	.333	.326
Nelson, Jon	R-R	6-5	235	1-16-80	.271	.294	.260	29	107	18	29	6	1	3	12	1	4	0	0	30	1	0	.430	.304
Norton, Greg	B-R	6-1	205	7-6-72	.409	.143	.533	8	22	3	9	2	0	0	3	2	0	0	1	3	1	0	.500	.440
Oliveros, Luis	R-R	6-1	205	6-18-83	.250	.250	.250	24	92	8	23	5	0	1	7	1	2	2	0	14	1	0	.337	.274
Redman, Prentice	R-R	6-3	185	8-23-79	.310	.303	.312	82	319	73	99	22	2	19	51	37	5	2	2	45	7	6	.571	.388
Reed, Jeremy	L-L	6-0	200	6-15-81	.349	.405	.330	38	149	26	52	11	1	6	21	16	1	1	1	16	1	1	.557	.413
Sardinha, Bronson	L-R	6-1	220	4-6-83	.344	.400	.333	9	32	6	11	1	0	0	5	3	0	0	1	3	1	1	.438	.389
Saunders, Michael	L-R	6-4	205	11-19-86	.242	.227	.247	24	95	12	23	4	1	3	16	9	0	1	0	30	1	2	.400	.308
Savastano, Scott	R-R	6-4	190	6-12-86	.500	.500	.500	1	4	2	2	0	0	0	0	0	0	0	0	0	0	0	.500	.500
Tuiasosopo, Matt	R-R	6-2	223	5-10-86	.281	.302	.276	111	437	87	123	32	2	13	73	47	12	0	4	104	4	0	.453	.364
Valbuena, Luis	R-L	5-10	200	11-30-85	.302	.283	.307	58	212	41	64	9	0	2	20	28	0	6	0	32	10	4	.373	.383
Wilson, Craig	R-R	6-2	225	11-30-76	.287	.231	.304	46	174	30	50	11	0	12	40	23	9	0	1	51	0	0	.557	.396
Womack, Josh	L-L	6-0	194	1-5-84	.333	.500	.300	11	12	3	4	1	0	0	2	0	1	0	0	2	1	1	.583	.429

Pitching	B-T	HT	WT	DOB	W	L	ERA	G	GS	CG	SV	IP	H	R	ER	BB	SO	AVG	vLH	vRH	K/9	BB/9
Baldwin, Andy	R-R	6-5	215	10-20-82	10	5	4.75	30	22	2	0	148	171	91	78	13	41	87	.295	.344	.240	5.30	2.50
Barzilla, Philip	L-L	6-0	180	1-25-79		1	6.28	7	0	0	0	14	13	11	10	2	7	12	.232	.292	.188	7.53	4.40
Chick, Travis	R-R	6-3	215	6-10-84	3	0	1.91	5	5	1	0	33	22	7	7	3	14	29	.193	.228	.158	7.91	3.82
Corcoran, Roy	R-R	5-10	170	5-11-80	0	0	5.02	15	0	0	4	14	14	8	8	1	13	11	.269	.333	.214	6.91	8.16
Cyr, Eric	R-L	6-4	200	2-11-79	1	0	6.75	7	1	0	0	11	12	8	8	1	7	14	.300	.238	.368	11.81	5.91
2-team total (8 Las Vegas)					2	2	9.00	15	3	0	1	33	50	33	33	10	20	38	—	—	—	10.36	5.45
Dickey, R.A.	R-R	6-2	215	10-29-74	2	5	3.44	7	7	0	0	50	58	25	19	2	8	30	.297	.337	.253	5.44	1.45
Dorman, Rich	R-R	6-2	210	9-30-78	2	4	4.78	11	8	0	0	38	43	23	20	5	9	31	.276	.302	.258	7.41	2.15
Feierabend, Ryan	L-L	6-3	230	8-22-85	7	1	2.04	13	13	0	0	75	64	21	17	5	15	48	.232	.200	.244	5.76	1.80
Huber, Jon	R-R	6-2	195	7-7-81	4	3	6.40	52	0	0	6	70	95	54	50	7	21	56	.324	.380	.285	7.17	2.69
Jakubauskas, Chris	R-R	6-2	210	5-12-78	5	1	2.59	12	9	0	0	56	52	22	16	5	14	48	.243	.196	.286	7.76	2.26
Jimenez, Cesar	L-L	5-11	215	11-12-84	1	3	3.55	29	0	0	3	38	37	19	15	3	8	47	.239	.220	.248	11.13	1.89
Kershner, Jason	L-L	6-2	190	12-19-76	1	0	2.08	4	0	0	0	4	6	1	1	0	2	3	.316	.333	.308	6.23	4.15
Messenger, Randy	R-R	6-6	270	8-13-81	6	1	2.38	12	0	0	1	23	19	7	6	2	11	16	.232	.179	.259	6.35	4.37
2-team total (29 Fresno)					9	4	3.96	41	0	0	4	64	66	31	28	6	23	46	—	—	—	6.50	3.25
Morrow, Brandon	R-R	6-3	185	7-26-84	1	2	5.01	6	5	0	0	23	17	13	13	2	11	26	.200	.297	.125	10.03	4.24
O'Flaherty, Eric	L-L	6-2	220	2-5-85	1	0	4.96	14	0	0	2	16	23	9	9	1	9	19	.333	.269	.372	10.47	4.96
Putz, J.J.	R-R	6-5	250	2-22-77	0	0	0.00	1	1	0	0	2	0	0	0	0	0	1	.000	.000	.000	5.40	0.00
Renfree, Matt	R-R	6-8	220	1-16-85	0	0	9.00	2	0	0	0	3	6	3	1	0	3		.429	.500	.400	9.00	0.00

	B-T	HT	WT	DOB	W	L	ERA	G	GS	CG	SV	IP	H	R	ER	HR	BB	SO	AVG	vLH	vRH	K/9	BB/9
Rivera, Mumba	R-R	6-5	205	12-10-80	0	2	7.11	13	0	0	0	19	21	16	15	3	13	17	.280	.313	.256	8.05	6.16
Rohrbaugh, Robert	R-L	6-2	195	12-28-83	7	5	5.25	19	18	0	1	96	109	61	56	8	28	76	.279	.280	.279	7.13	2.63
Rowland-Smith, Ryan	L-L	6-3	240	1-26-83	2	0	2.89	3	3	0	0	19	12	6	6	1	7	12	.185	.214	.176	5.79	3.38
Shoemaker, Scott	R-R	6-4	210	9-21-81	3	3	6.20	32	10	0	0	90	116	63	62	17	34	59	.320	.321	.319	5.90	3.40
Sosa, Jorge	R-R	6-2	220	4-28-77	1	0	3.68	10	0	0	2	15	14	6	6	0	13	12	.259	.294	.243	7.36	7.98
2-team total (17 Round Rock)					2	2	3.96	27	0	0	4	36	34	17	16	5	21	36	—	—	—	8.92	5.20
Souza, Justin	R-R	6-1	185	10-22-85	0	0	2.08	2	0	0	0	4	4	1	1	0	0	3	.235	.000	.400	6.23	0.00
Stark, Dennis	R-R	6-2	210	10-27-74	3	0	3.00	10	0	0	0	21	23	7	7	2	4	21	.277	.267	.283	9.00	1.71
Thomas, Justin	L-L	6-3	225	1-18-84	2	1	3.71	7	1	0	1	17	15	7	7	2	9	21	.242	.136	.300	11.12	4.76
Thorpe, Tracy	R-R	6-4	265	12-15-80	2	3	9.12	19	0	0	1	26	33	26	26	9	15	28	.317	.341	.300	9.82	5.26
Venegas, Alfredo	R-R	6-1	180	5-11-86	0	1	13.50	1	1	0	0	3	6	4	4	0	3	2	.462	.600	.000	6.75	10.13
Villarreal, Oscar	L-R	6-0	215	11-22-81	1	0	4.66	5	0	0	1	10	7	7	5	2	4	11	.189	.214	.174	10.24	3.72
2-team total (3 Colorado Springs)					1	1	5.56	8	3	0	1	23	24	18	14	3	11	18	—	—	—	7.15	4.37
Wells, Jared	R-R	6-4	200	10-31-81	0	4	6.42	33	0	0	11	41	44	30	29	6	23	42	.280	.297	.265	9.30	5.09
2-team total (19 Portland)					1	5	6.23	52	0	0	20	61	63	43	42	7	35	56	—	—	—	8.31	5.19
White, Sean	R-R	6-4	210	4-25-81	6	11	5.47	22	22	0	0	125	176	85	76	12	43	52	.339	.332	.346	3.74	3.10
Williamson, Scott	R-R	6-0	195	2-17-76	0	0	3.00	3	0	0	0	3	3	1	1	0	1	0	.273	.000	.375	0.00	3.00
Woerman, Joe	R-R	6-3	225	12-12-82	2	8	7.47	21	16	0	0	88	107	79	73	11	69	54	.308	.316	.302	5.52	7.06
Woods, Jake	L-L	6-1	200	9-3-81	6	1	4.08	32	2	0	1	64	64	29	29	7	27	54	.263	.264	.263	7.59	3.80

Fielding

Catcher	PCT	G	PO	A	E	DP	PB
Clement	.991	30	206	11	2	1	3
Feiner	1.000	2	12	2	0	0	0
R. Johnson	.986	90	595	47	9	6	21
Kinkade	.875	1	7	0	1	0	0
Oliveros	.982	22	148	12	3	4	2

First Base	PCT	G	PO	A	E	DP
Garrett	.991	34	204	20	2	30
Kinkade	1.000	3	26	1	0	1
LaHair	.996	74	628	38	3	69
Norton	1.000	3	17	1	0	0
Oliveros	1.000	2	18	2	0	4
Wilson	.993	35	273	17	2	26

Second Base	PCT	G	PO	A	E	DP
Chen	.982	46	88	131	4	27
Garrett	—	1	0	0	0	0
Howard	.857	2	3	3	1	0
Hulett	.983	36	68	103	3	22
Kinkade	.833	2	2	3	1	1
Navarro	.929	3	5	8	1	0
Valbuena	.987	57	137	164	4	44

Third Base	PCT	G	PO	A	E	DP
Chen	.939	20	12	50	4	8
Garrett	1.000	1	0	3	0	0
Howard	.963	9	10	16	1	2
B. Johnson	.667	1	0	2	1	0
Kinkade	1.000	2	2	4	0	0
Navarro	1.000	4	4	5	0	2
Savastano	1.000	1	0	1	0	0
Tuiasosopo	.904	108	82	172	27	16
Valbuena	.000	1	0	1	0	0

Shortstop	PCT	G	PO	A	E	DP
Benitez	1.000	1	0	1	0	0
Howard	1.000	7	9	18	0	5
Hulett	.984	45	75	111	3	28
Navarro	.963	96	140	250	15	63

Outfield	PCT	G	PO	A	E	DP
Balentien	.986	61	138	2	2	0
Blasi	1.000	6	15	0	0	0
Diaz	.986	43	67	5	1	0
Garrett	.984	62	120	5	2	0
Howard	1.000	2	1	0	0	0
Hulett	1.000	1	1	0	0	0
Jimerson	.986	50	137	6	2	0
B. Johnson	1.000	15	21	1	0	1
R. Johnson	.938	10	13	2	1	0
Kinkade	1.000	8	13	0	0	0
LaHair	1.000	5	4	1	0	0
Nelson	.956	26	41	2	2	1
Norton	1.000	3	2	0	0	0
Redman	.980	80	191	3	4	0
Reed	.988	36	82	0	1	0
Sardinha	.857	9	12	0	2	0
Saunders	.966	23	55	2	2	0
Wilson	1.000	2	4	0	0	0
Womack	1.000	8	14	1	0	0

WEST TENN DIAMOND JAXX

DOUBLE-A

SOUTHERN LEAGUE

Batting	B-T	HT	WT	DOB	AVG	vLH	vRH	G	AB	R	H	2B	3B	HR	RBI	BB	HBP	SH	SF	SO	SB	CS	SLG	OBP
Dominguez, Jeffrey	B-R	6-2	160	7-31-86	.205	.244	.185	109	351	35	72	15	0	2	32	30	3	12	6	75	18	4	.265	.269
Feiner, Korey	R-R	5-11	210	9-25-81	.000	.000	—	2	2	0	0	0	0	0	0	0	0	0	0	1	0	0	.000	.000
Garrett, Shawn	B-R	6-3	220	11-2-78	.276	.333	.254	23	87	16	24	8	2	1	14	7	1	1	1	21	1	0	.448	.333
Hall, Noah	R-R	5-11	205	6-9-77	.302	.438	.222	15	43	6	13	5	0	1	7	7	1	2	0	10	2	1	.488	.412
2-team total (26 Birmingham)					.252			41	127	15	32	11	0	1	19	21	3	4	0	15	3	2	.362	.371
Halman, Greg	R-R	6-4	192	8-26-87	.277	.329	.253	61	235	43	65	14	2	10	30	16	4	1	1	66	8	6	.481	.332
Hubbard, Marshall	L-R	6-2	215	4-16-82	.291	.262	.302	91	309	54	90	24	3	12	52	56	8	1	5	63	2	4	.505	.407
Johnson, Brent	R-R	6-2	190	5-21-82	.282	.300	.272	82	301	45	85	20	3	7	38	34	10	2	1	32	6	5	.439	.373
Johnson, Gabe	R-R	6-1	205	9-21-79	.243	.333	.214	14	37	5	9	2	0	2	4	1	1	1	0	12	0	0	.297	.326
Kiger, Mark	R-R	5-10	195	5-30-80	.223	.237	.217	109	376	49	84	12	2	3	40	73	1	7	0	98	3	6	.290	.351
Limonta, Johan	L-L	6-0	205	8-4-83	.296	.268	.311	98	361	51	107	32	6	10	59	37	4	0	2	87	3	2	.501	.366
Mangini, Matt	L-R	6-4	220	12-21-85	.202	.192	.206	69	238	22	48	5	0	2	25	12	3	2	2	64	0	1	.248	.247
Monzon, Erick	R-R	6-0	190	11-30-81	.209	.185	.223	45	148	16	31	3	1	2	7	15	0	5	0	44	5	0	.284	.282
Moore, Adam	R-R	6-3	220	5-8-84	.319	.342	.328	119	429	60	137	34	2	14	71	40	16	3	2	77	0	1	.506	.396
Nelson, Jon	R-R	6-5	235	1-16-80	.276	.333	.247	72	268	31	74	18	2	13	46	18	3	1	4	70	2	2	.437	.317
Oliveros, Luis	R-R	6-1	205	6-18-83	.300	.200	.333	29	100	15	30	5	0	5	9	3	0	0	1	21	0	0	.350	.375
Pimentel, Manelik	R-R	6-2	185	10-19-84	.333	1.000	.000	2	3	1	1	0	0	0	0	2	0	0	0	2	0	0	.333	.333
Prettyman, Ronnie	L-R	6-2	190	8-4-81	.182	.196	.176	52	165	26	30	7	3	4	23	8	1	7	3	39	3	0	.333	.220
Redman, Prentice	R-R	6-3	185	8-23-79	.259	.278	.253	38	135	24	35	8	0	6	25	24	2	3	1	23	2	3	.452	.377
Reynolds, Kevin	L-L	6-1	185	7-1-82	.219	.444	.130	12	32	6	7	1	1	1	2	2	0	1	0	5	2	1	.406	.265
Saunders, Michael	L-R	6-4	205	11-19-86	.290	.268	.299	67	248	46	72	18	3	8	30	30	4	6	1	66	11	6	.484	.375
Valbuena, Luis	L-R	5-10	200	11-30-85	.304	.300	.306	70	240	43	73	12	2	9	40	31	0	4	2	37	8	4	.483	.381
Wilson, Michael	R-R	6-2	215	6-29-83	.276	.331	.251	119	406	76	112	26	2	27	84	62	14	1	2	117	9	0	.549	.388
Womack, Josh	L-L	6-0	194	1-5-84	.125	.000	.200	16	8	0	1	0	0	0	1	0	0	0	0	3	0	1	.125	.111
Yepez, Jose	R-R	6-0	205	6-19-81	.345	.364	.333	9	29	2	10	4	0	0	1	2	1	2	0	4	0	0	.483	.406

Pitching	B-T	HT	WT	DOB	W	L	ERA	G	GS	CG	SV	IP	H	R	ER	HR	BB	SO	AVG	vLH	vRH	K/9	BB/9
Chick, Travis	R-R	6-3	215	6-10-84	4	5	4.28	27	11	0	0	97	92	56	46	7	44	80	.257	.304	.214	7.45	4.10
Cotter, Aaron	R-R	6-4	250	1-2-84	0	0	12.60	3	0	0	0	5	8	7	7	0	4	4	.364	.300	.417	7.20	7.20
Dorman, Rich	R-R	6-2	210	9-30-78	7	2	2.62	14	14	2	0	89	69	30	26	5	29	79	.211	.248	.178	7.96	2.92

Name	B-T	HT	WT	DOB	W	L	ERA	G	GS	CG	SV	IP	H	R	ER	HR	BB	SO	AVG	vLH	vRH	K/9	BB/9
Downs, Brodie	R-R	6-4	235	7-19-79	5	2	4.10	36	9	0	2	94	98	56	43	6	43	61	.271	.340	.221	5.82	4.10
Fister, Doug	L-R	6-8	200	2-4-84	6	14	5.43	31	23	0	0	134	155	95	81	12	45	104	.289	.286	.292	6.97	3.01
Garcia, Anderson	R-R	6-2	180	3-23-81	0	1	12.86	2	2	0	0	7	14	10	10	0	2	6	.438	.625	.250	7.71	2.57
Harris, Bryan	R-R	6-2	200	9-15-83	0	0	4.50	1	0	0	0	2	2	1	1	0	0	1	.286	.333	.250	4.50	0.00
Hernandez, Gaby	R-R	6-3	215	5-21-86	1	1	5.01	6	6	0	0	32	38	19	18	3	15	23	.297	.299	.295	6.40	4.18
2-team total (4 Carolina)					4	1	4.72	10	10	0	0	55	59	30	29	6	19	40	—	—	—	6.51	3.09
Hill, Nick	L-L	6-0	190	1-30-85	0	1	10.13	9	0	0	0	8	11	10	9	2	7	7	.306	.286	.333	7.88	7.88
Jakubauskas, Chris	R-R	6-2	210	12-22-78	3	0	0.83	6	6	0	0	33	25	4	3	1	7	24	.212	.204	.219	6.61	1.93
James, Craig	R-R	6-1	175	3-10-83	1	4	6.23	28	1	0	3	39	52	41	27	3	22	38	.319	.391	.266	8.77	5.08
Kelley, Shawn	R-R	6-2	215	4-26-84	3	1	2.11	29	0	0	9	43	31	12	10	2	17	44	.205	.167	.235	9.28	3.59
Kershner, Jason	L-L	6-2	190	12-19-76	3	2	6.28	11	0	0	0	14	22	10	10	0	7	10	.349	.190	.429	6.28	4.40
Ketchner, Ryan	L-L	6-1	190	4-19-82	7	6	4.75	25	20	0	0	116	146	68	61	11	37	70	.313	.322	.309	5.45	2.88
Mackintosh, Jason	R-L	6-0	205	7-2-80	5	4	2.86	32	0	0	2	44	34	16	14	2	10	23	.219	.206	.230	4.70	2.05
Martinez, Roman	R-R	6-3	160	8-9-84	2	2	4.78	37	0	0	0	43	49	27	23	5	18	31	.287	.292	.283	6.44	3.74
Morrow, Brandon	R-R	6-3	185	7-26-84	0	0	0.00	6	0	0	0	7	3	1	0	0	6	8	.125	.111	.133	9.82	7.36
Munoz, Luis	R-R	6-2	195	1-10-82	1	2	5.83	7	5	0	0	29	38	20	19	2	15	22	.314	.323	.305	6.75	4.60
O'Flaherty, Eric	L-L	6-2	220	2-5-85	0	0	0.00	1	0	0	0	2	1	0	0	0	2	1	.143	—	.143	9.00	0.00
Paredes, Edward	L-L	6-0	175	9-30-86	1	1	7.71	2	2	0	0	9	11	8	8	1	5	10	.314	.000	.393	9.64	4.82
Payano, Nelson	L-L	6-2	180	11-13-82	1	1	4.56	14	0	0	0	24	28	14	12	2	20	29	.301	.250	.340	11.03	7.61
2-team total (27 Mississippi)					4	3	4.16	41	0	0	0	67	69	36	31	3	42	65	—	—	—	8.73	5.64
Rhodes Jr., Arthur	L-L	6-2	210	10-24-69	0	1		1	1	0	0	0	2	3	1	0	1		.667	1.000	.000	—	—
Rivera, Mumba	R-R	6-5	205	12-10-80	5	1	2.51	28	0	0	11	32	27	12	9	1	11	35	.223	.288	.174	9.74	3.06
Stark, Dennis	R-R	6-2	210	10-27-74	3	3	4.29	13	8	0	1	42	46	21	20	2	21	23	.286	.271	.297	4.93	4.50
Thomas, Justin	L-L	6-3	225	1-18-84	7	7	4.32	25	17	1	0	119	116	66	57	11	56	106	.257	.224	.273	8.04	4.25
Thorpe, Tracy	R-R	6-4	265	12-15-80	1	1	3.67	7	7	0	0	34	26	14	14	3	15	32	.213	.293	.141	8.39	3.93
Vega, Marwin	R-R	6-0	175	10-27-86	3	3	4.72	46	1	0	2	69	67	41	36	3	44	50	.263	.280	.248	6.55	5.77
Woerman, Joe	R-R	6-3	225	12-12-82	1	3	4.34	5	5	1	0	29	27	18	14	0	12	20	.243	.196	.277	6.21	3.72

Fielding

Catcher	PCT	G	PO	A	E	DP	PB
Feiner	1.000	2	6	0	0	0	0
G. Johnson	.971	11	63	4	2	2	1
Moore	.990	107	711	87	8	8	23
Oliveros	.980	18	124	24	3	2	1
Yepez	1.000	7	38	4	0	0	0

First Base	PCT	G	PO	A	E	DP
Dominguez	1.000	2	23	0	0	2
Garrett	.976	7	37	4	1	4
Hubbard	.992	70	553	61	5	65
B. Johnson	1.000	2	5	1	0	0
Limonta	.985	58	497	33	8	36
Mangini	1.000	3	24	2	0	3
Monzon	1.000	2	15	1	0	1
Pimentel	1.000	1	1	0	0	0

Second Base	PCT	G	PO	A	E	DP
Dominguez	.967	67	148	177	11	49
Kiger	1.000	9	14	17	0	3
Valbuena	.989	69	148	212	4	47

Third Base	PCT	G	PO	A	E	DP
Dominguez	.886	20	12	27	5	0
B. Johnson	1.000	4	3	3	0	0
G. Johnson	—	0	0	0	0	0
Kiger	1.000	8	2	15	0	1
Mangini	.927	65	48	117	13	10
Monzon	1.000	1	1	0	0	0
Prettyman	.950	48	44	89	7	11
Valbuena	1.000	2	1	2	0	0

Shortstop	PCT	G	PO	A	E	DP
Dominguez	.875	11	11	24	5	3

	PCT	G	PO	A	E	DP
Kiger	.948	91	135	248	21	60
Monzon	.943	41	62	102	10	26

Outfield	PCT	G	PO	A	E	DP
Dominguez	.900	10	18	0	2	0
Garrett	.933	13	14	0	1	0
Hall	1.000	12	20	0	0	0
Halman	.972	59	137	3	4	2
Hubbard	1.000	8	6	1	0	1
B. Johnson	.985	70	131	4	2	0
Limonta	.980	30	47	3	1	0
Nelson	.957	19	21	1	1	0
Redman	.969	37	61	2	2	1
Reynolds	1.000	9	16	0	0	0
Saunders	.977	59	125	1	3	1
Wilson	.969	104	173	14	6	3
Womack	1.000	14	6	0	0	0

HIGH DESERT MAVERICKS   HIGH CLASS A

CALIFORNIA LEAGUE

Batting	B-T	HT	WT	DOB	AVG	vLH	vRH	G	AB	R	H	2B	3B	HR	RBI	BB	HBP	SH	SF	SO	SB	CS	SLG	OBP
Avila, Gerardo	L-L	6-2	185	7-15-86	.303	.500	.217	9	33	5	10	0	2	1	3	2	0	0	1	9	0	0	.515	.333
Bonilla, Leury	R-R	6-3	170	2-8-85	.301	.250	.321	68	226	38	68	11	2	3	23	25	1	3	1	60	8	7	.407	.372
Carroll, Danny	R-R	6-1	175	1-6-89	.135	.067	.153	17	74	10	10	2	0	0	5	3	4	0	0	32	7	3	.162	.210
Davenport, James	R-R	6-4	190	6-1-85	.277	.375	.256	31	94	12	26	6	3	0	7	1	3	1	1	29	4	1	.404	.303
Diaz, Ogui	R-R	6-2	170	12-1-85	.245	.283	.235	80	274	37	67	10	0	3	27	6	3	0	3	57	15	4	.314	.266
Dickey, Gavin	R-L	5-11	200	9-29-83	.242	.364	.218	41	132	23	32	9	0	1	15	5	8	1	2	27	10	3	.333	.306
Encarnacion, Fernando	R-R	6-0	185	7-23-85	.255	.375	.231	17	47	4	12	5	0	1	8	1	1	0	1	9	0	0	.426	.304
Feiner, Korey	R-R	5-11	210	9-25-81	.267	.300	.250	20	60	6	16	2	0	0	8	2	6	1	0	13	0	0	.300	.353
Fuentes, Cesar	R-R	6-0	180	4-12-87	.000	—	.000	1	1	0	0	0	0	0	0	0	0	0	0	0	0	0	.000	.000
Gillies, Tyson	L-R	6-2	190	10-31-88	.233	.000	.259	11	30	4	7	0	1	0	1	1	1	0		6	1	1	.300	.281
Halman, Greg	R-R	6-4	192	8-26-87	.268	.313	.253	67	257	52	69	15	3	19	53	16	5	1	3	76	23	1	.572	.320
Limonta, Johan	L-L	6-0	205	8-4-83	.319	.359	.300	31	119	26	38	11	2	2	20	20	0	0	1	32	1	1	.496	.414
Lo, Kuo Hui	R-R	6-2	188	9-26-85	.252	.290	.242	82	317	51	80	14	5	8	53	24	4	3	5	79	20	12	.404	.309
Mangini, Matt	R-R	6-4	220	12-21-85	.265	.267	.265	52	181	28	48	12	0	6	25	23	9	1	0	52	3	1	.431	.376
McOwen, James	L-R	6-0	200	9-26-85	.263	.294	.255	126	490	76	129	24	9	7	51	44	1	8	2	103	30	13	.392	.324
Mendez, Joel	R-R	6-3	175	5-7-88	.000	—	.000	4	0	0	0	0	0	0	0	0	0	0	0	0	1	0	.000	.000
Minaker, Chris	R-R	6-0	195	3-24-84	.285	.365	.262	123	478	66	136	41	1	6	59	24	1	7	9	59	1	2	.412	.314
Monzon, Erick	R-R	6-0	190	11-30-81	.197	.222	.190	37	132	19	26	6	1	3	13	15	0	1	0	36	6	2	.326	.279
Peguero, Carlos	L-L	6-5	210	12-27-86	.299	.250	.314	92	371	47	111	25	3	12	74	10	1	0	3	96	6	4	.480	.317
Phillips, Anthony	R-R	5-9	160	4-11-90	.111	.000	.125	3	9	0	1	0	0	0	1	0	0	0	0	3	0	0	.111	.111
Prettyman, Ronnie	L-R	6-2	190	8-4-81	.301	.205	.321	57	226	37	68	13	0	9	42	13	3	0	3	48	8	0	.478	.343
Reynolds, Kevin	L-L	6-1	185	7-1-82	.252	.091	.270	23	111	12	28	3	0	0	8	5	2	0	0	17	12	0	.279	.297
Scott, Travis	L-R	6-3	225	4-24-85	.270	.183	.292	96	348	51	94	25	1	12	60	35	4	2	4	89	5	1	.451	.340
Simokaitis, Joe	R-R	6-1	200	12-27-82	.245	.136	.264	39	151	20	37	6	0	5	20	11	1	0	1	34	3	0	.384	.299
Triunfel, Carlos	R-R	5-11	175	2-27-90	.287	.298	.284	108	436	75	125	20	4	8	49	30	5	3	5	52	30	9	.406	.336

	B-T	HT	WT	DOB																				
Valentin, Geraldo	R-R	6-0	184	9-8-82	.232	.111	.255	32	112	11	26	7	0	1	15	6	2	0	1	14	4	1	.321	.281
Yepez, Jose	R-R	6-0	205	6-19-81	.269	.143	.316	39	130	20	35	5	0	4	21	12	4	1	2	18	1	0	.400	.345

Pitching	B-T	HT	WT	DOB	W	L	ERA	G	GS	CG	SV	IP	H	R	ER	HR	BB	SO	AVG	vLH	vRH	K/9	BB/9
Asher, David	R-L	6-1	195	2-18-83	3	1	6.75	28	0	0	1	23	34	17	17	1	10	19	.354	.302	.419	7.54	3.97
Averill, Erik	L-L	6-2	190	2-9-84	0	0	9.00	1	0	0	0	1	1	1	1	0	2	1	.250	.000	.333	9.00	18.00
Bibens-Dirkx, Austin	R-R	6-2	190	4-29-85	1	1	7.95	32	0	0	1	43	58	39	38	9	16	31	.324	.319	.330	6.49	3.35
Brown, Kyle	R-L	6-2	210	1-2-86	0	0	0.00	1	0	0	0	1	1	0	0	0	1	0	.250	1.000	.000	0.00	9.00
Cotter, Aaron	R-R	6-4	250	1-2-84	3	5	3.47	50	0	0	8	62	67	32	24	6	15	59	.272	.229	.313	8.52	2.17
Escalona, Jose	L-L	5-11	165	1-7-86	0	0	3.97	8	0	0	1	11	13	5	5	2	4	10	.289	.333	.238	7.94	3.18
Garcia, Anderson	R-R	6-2	180	3-23-81	1	4	6.85	9	9	0	0	24	33	20	18	2	10	15	.344	.415	.256	5.70	3.80
Harris, Bryan	R-R	6-2	200	9-15-83	1	3	7.14	41	0	0	0	52	64	44	41	13	12	33	.305	.315	.298	5.75	2.09
Hill, Nick	L-L	6-0	190	1-30-85	2	7	4.48	35	10	0	1	94	106	63	47	10	32	69	.278	.324	.250	6.58	3.05
Hume, Donnie	R-L	6-0	185	8-29-85	0	0	3.50	3	3	0	0	18	19	10	7	4	7	14	.271	.172	.341	7.00	3.50
Jimenez, Jose	L-L	6-0	180	3-23-87	1	3	8.72	5	4	0	0	22	35	21	21	3	10	18	.368	.393	.358	7.48	4.15
Kantakevich, Joe	R-R	6-2	195	5-9-84	2	2	26.04	11	0	0	0	9	30	29	27	3	11	6	.526	.469	.600	5.79	10.61
Kelley, Shawn	R-R	6-2	215	4-26-84	0	0	0.00	12	0	0	3	12	8	1	0	0	3	12	.186	.118	.231	9.00	2.25
Kirkland, Chris	R-R	6-4	220	10-6-85	0	0	0.00	1	0	0	0	1	0	0	0	0	2	0	.000	.000	.000	0.00	18.00
Mortimore, Travis	L-L	6-5	225	8-1-84	1	5	7.87	14	12	0	0	58	86	60	51	14	34	38	.336	.435	.287	5.86	5.25
Orta, Ricky	R-R	6-2	195	11-6-84	3	5	5.05	22	15	0	0	71	80	47	40	14	27	74	.279	.268	.289	9.34	3.41
Parker, Kyle	R-R	6-3	205	4-8-85	5	3	4.27	16	16	0	0	84	75	46	40	7	39	67	.233	.235	.230	7.15	4.16
Reid, Brad	R-R	6-1	185	1-18-88	0	1	14.73	6	0	0	0	7	19	16	12	3	6	5	.475	.471	.478	6.14	7.36
Renaud, Keith	R-R	6-1	215	2-7-86	3	9	7.68	15	14	0	0	73	82	70	62	12	49	40	.289	.253	.345	4.95	6.07
Richard, Steven	R-R	6-3	240	3-7-85	3	2	4.50	32	1	0	7	42	40	24	21	2	24	42	.255	.219	.286	9.00	5.14
Santiago, Julio	L-L	6-0	155	12-8-85	5	0	5.56	42	0	0	6	66	70	42	41	4	46	49	.270	.271	.270	6.65	6.24
Souza, Justin	R-R	6-1	185	10-22-85	2	1	4.31	12	5	0	0	40	46	20	19	5	13	39	.293	.325	.260	8.85	2.95
Uhlmansiek, Steve	L-L	6-3	185	2-10-83	3	4	4.68	36	3	0	0	58	64	34	30	6	32	45	.294	.311	.281	7.02	4.99
Varvaro, Anthony	R-R	6-0	180	10-31-84	3	9	7.12	30	24	0	0	123	154	105	97	22	82	113	.313	.314	.312	8.29	6.02
Venegas, Alfredo	R-R	6-1	180	5-11-86	6	5	4.97	25	16	0	0	112	132	71	62	12	32	87	.295	.259	.333	6.97	2.56
Wagner, Michael	L-L	6-4	225	3-28-85	7	5	4.79	51	1	0	2	68	95	47	36	4	22	53	.333	.336	.331	7.05	2.93
Wild, Jake	R-R	6-5	195	8-18-84	1	5	7.18	6	6	0	0	26	39	23	21	6	16	24	.328	.298	.355	8.20	5.47
Williams, Harold	L-L	6-4	190	9-23-84	2	1	5.87	10	0	0	0	15	17	12	10	1	12	13	.288	.269	.303	7.63	7.04
Zapata, Juan	R-R	6-3	180	8-6-84	0	1	14.14	4	1	0	0	7	12	17	11	4	6	6	.343	.478	.083	7.71	7.71

Fielding

Catcher	PCT	G	PO	A	E	DP	PB
Encarnacion	.988	14	75	10	1	2	1
Feiner	.988	19	142	17	2	4	0
Scott	.982	72	495	61	10	5	23
Yepez	.979	39	287	35	7	4	4

First Base	PCT	G	PO	A	E	DP
Avila	1.000	9	84	10	0	8
Bonilla	.987	17	142	8	2	8
Davenport	1.000	4	22	1	0	3
Feiner	1.000	1	7	2	0	1
Limonta	.978	30	249	13	6	19
Mangini	1.000	1	9	1	0	1
Minaker	.995	23	170	13	1	15
Monzon	.994	24	138	25	1	18
Prettyman	1.000	1	6	0	0	1
Scott	.978	17	121	14	3	12
Simokaitis	1.000	13	103	5	0	11
Valentin	.964	11	75	5	3	3

Second Base	PCT	G	PO	A	E	DP
Bonilla	1.000	7	8	17	0	4

Catcher	PCT	G	PO	A	E	DP
Diaz	.956	30	54	77	6	12
Fuentes	1.000	1	1	1	0	1
Minaker	.968	52	72	141	7	24
Monzon	.980	8	24	26	1	3
Phillips	.941	3	10	6	1	1
Prettyman	1.000	1	3	1	0	0
Simokaitis	.966	14	16	40	2	6
Triunfel	.956	31	62	90	7	16

Third Base	PCT	G	PO	A	E	DP
Bonilla	.942	28	31	50	5	5
Davenport	1.000	3	4	8	0	0
Diaz	1.000	4	4	4	0	0
Mangini	.915	50	37	70	10	4
Monzon	.750	4	3	6	3	0
Prettyman	.949	54	39	111	8	12
Simokaitis	1.000	4	3	3	0	0

Shortstop	PCT	G	PO	A	E	DP
Diaz	.926	39	76	100	14	21
Minaker	.970	23	43	53	3	16
Monzon	1.000	2	1	9	0	2

	PCT	G	PO	A	E	DP
Prettyman	1.000	1	1	5	0	1
Simokaitis	.900	4	3	6	1	2
Triunfel	.938	73	147	169	21	40

Outfield	PCT	G	PO	A	E	DP
Bonilla	.886	22	27	4	4	2
Carroll	1.000	16	36	0	0	0
Davenport	1.000	9	18	1	0	0
Dickey	.990	39	101	0	1	0
Gillies	1.000	9	16	0	0	0
Halman	.968	59	144	7	5	2
Limonta	—	1	0	0	0	0
Lo	.941	76	107	5	7	0
McOwen	.964	111	200	16	8	2
Mendez	.500	1	0	1	0	0
Peguero	.904	58	109	4	12	2
Reynolds	1.000	28	69	0	0	0
Simokaitis	1.000	2	3	1	0	1
Valentin	1.000	6	9	0	0	0

WISCONSIN TIMBER RATTLERS

MIDWEST LEAGUE

LOW CLASS A

Batting	B-T	HT	WT	DOB	AVG	vLH	vRH	G	AB	R	H	2B	3B	HR	RBI	BB	HBP	SH	SF	SO	SB	CS	SLG	OBP
Almonte, Denny	B-R	6-2	187	9-24-88	.249	.293	.233	100	374	38	93	20	7	10	51	29	1	2	2	149	14	10	.420	.303
Arias, Jonathan	R-R	6-3	190	2-8-88	.100	—	.100	3	10	1	1	0	0	0	1	1	0	0	0	0	0	0	.100	.182
Avila, Gerardo	L-L	6-2	185	7-15-86	.191	.200	.190	15	47	3	9	1	0	0	2	3	0	1	0	14	0	0	.213	.240
Beamon, Calvin	L-L	6-0	190	5-8-84	.239	.262	.232	53	184	10	44	7	5	0	21	18	2	0	3	48	4	5	.332	.309
Carroll, Danny	R-R	6-1	175	1-9-89	.248	.258	.244	60	238	36	59	7	4	1	17	16	12	3	2	64	31	9	.324	.325
Colina, Edilio	R-R	6-2	175	10-10-88	.291	.327	.278	114	423	69	123	24	1	4	50	29	10	6	3	54	8	7	.381	.348
Diaz, Juan	B-R	6-3	180	12-12-88	.233	.158	.258	122	451	38	105	16	4	3	45	28	1	9	8	86	6	5	.306	.275
Dickey, Gavin	R-R	5-11	200	9-29-83	.279	.243	.289	48	172	20	48	12	1	2	20	7	9	0	2	40	10	9	.395	.337
Dunigan, Joe	L-L	6-1	215	3-29-86	.240	.268	.231	119	437	58	105	31	3	14	58	30	8	1	3	142	28	4	.421	.299
Feiner, Korey	R-R	5-11	210	9-25-81	.143	.000	.175	18	49	6	7	1	0	2	5	9	3	0	1	15	0	0	.286	.306
Garth, Ron	R-R	5-11	165	11-5-84	.267	.221	.284	88	318	36	85	27	2	4	36	18	7	2	2	65	8	3	.403	.319
Hernandez, Eddy	L-L	6-3	170	4-5-86	.104	.071	.113	21	67	4	7	3	0	0	4	5	0	0	0	32	2	0	.149	.167
Liddi, Alex	R-R	6-4	176	8-14-88	.244	.214	.254	125	447	65	109	26	4	6	53	42	4	1	2	115	17	5	.360	.313
Mendez, Maximo	L-L	6-2	150	11-24-86	.237	.151	.263	109	393	52	93	14	5	5	28	42	5	7	0	142	25	7	.336	.318
Meneses, Alex	R-R	5-10	185	12-21-83	.229	.247	.220	79	223	27	51	8	0	1	11	33	1	8	2	51	9	3	.278	.328

	B-T	HT	WT	DOB	AVG	vLH	vRH	G	AB	R	H	2B	3B	HR	RBI	BB	HBP	SH	SF	SO	SB	CS	SLG	OBP
Nunez, Israel	R-R	6-1	200	9-1-85	.224	.226	.224	59	196	13	44	8	0	1	16	11	3	1	0	27	2	0	.281	.276
O'Donnell, Brendon	R-R	5-11	175	10-15-84	.143	.000	.250	6	14	1	2	1	0	0	1	2	0	0	0	8	0	1	.214	.250
Ochoa, Blake	R-R	6-0	180	9-5-85	.251	.319	.229	63	191	27	48	9	2	3	23	24	1	2	2	35	2	4	.366	.335
Reynolds, Kevin	L-L	6-1	185	7-1-82	.000	.000	.000	3	5	0	0	0	0	0	0	0	1	0	0	0	2	0	0	.000	.167
Robinson, Scott	L-L	6-1	195	10-14-83	.190	.158	.200	26	79	6	15	3	0	2	6	2	0	0	0	15	0	1	.304	.210
Serrano, Terry	B-R	6-1	165	2-6-87	.286	.000	.500	5	7	2	2	0	0	0	0	2	0	0	0	3	0	0	.286	.444
White, Joe	L-R	6-3	210	1-14-86	.266	.341	.239	47	154	15	41	2	0	2	19	24	3	1	1	39	2	0	.318	.374

Pitching	B-T	HT	WT	DOB	W	L	ERA	G	GS	CG	SV	IP	H	R	ER	HR	BB	SO	AVG	vLH	vRH	K/9	BB/9
Adcock, Nathan	R-R	6-5	190	2-25-88	2	5	3.72	15	14	0	0	77	81	45	32	3	29	82	.269	.270	.268	9.54	3.38
Aumont, Phillippe	L-R	6-7	220	1-7-89	4	4	2.75	15	8	0	2	56	46	22	17	4	19	50	.224	.295	.164	8.08	3.07
Dilone, Natividad	R-R	6-0	160	9-8-82	3	2	3.38	25	0	0	1	37	25	14	14	2	16	40	.194	.131	.250	9.64	3.86
Dominguez, Robbie	R-R	6-3	190	10-26-85	0	0	0.00	2	0	0	1	2	1	0	0	0	1		.143	.000	.333	4.50	0.00
DuRocher, John	R-R	6-4	215	6-21-84	0	0	2.45	5	1	0	0	7	6	2	2	0	4	5	.214	.125	.250	6.14	4.91
Escalona, Jose	L-L	5-11	165	1-7-86	3	3	3.80	36	0	0	2	47	48	21	20	6	21	50	.254	.225	.271	9.51	3.99
Hann, Cheyne	R-R	6-6	235	9-17-84	0	0	0.00	3	0	0	0	5	2	0	0	0	6		.125	.000	.143	10.80	0.00
Harmon, Rob	R-R	6-7	239	9-28-83	0	7	7.85	31	3	0	0	39	55	35	34	3	33	42	.342	.316	.365	9.69	7.62
Harris, Bryan	R-R	6-2	200	9-15-83	0	0	2.00	8	0	0	2	9	6	2	2	0	1	9	.188	.231	.158	9.00	1.00
Hume, Donnie	R-L	6-0	185	8-29-85	6	2	2.44	11	11	0	0	52	42	18	14	4	19	50	.220	.224	.218	8.71	3.31
Jimenez, Jose	L-L	6-0	180	3-23-87	0	1	9.00	9	2	0	0	14	22	18	14	3	11	12	.349	.438	.319	7.71	7.07
Kantakevich, Joe	R-R	6-2	195	5-9-84	1	3	5.66	24	0	0	1	41	57	29	26	4	14	24	.333	.416	.266	5.23	3.05
Kelley, Shawn	R-R	6-2	215	4-26-84	0	0	3.52	8	0	0	3	8	10	3	3	0	2	12	.323	.385	.278	14.09	2.35
Lorin, Brett	L-R	6-7	245	3-31-87	0	2	4.80	8	6	0	0	30	30	17	16	1	16	32	.255	.255	.296	9.60	4.80
Meyer, Keith	L-R	6-4	180	2-10-86	3	5	4.35	42	3	0	4	72	73	38	35	7	29	69	.270	.173	.331	8.59	3.61
Moorer, Ryan	R-R	6-2	205	3-2-86	1	2	4.18	44	0	0	1	65	69	36	30	3	23	47	.272	.221	.307	6.54	3.20
Mortimore, Travis	L-L	6-5	225	8-14-84	2	1	0.53	22	0	0	0	34	14	3	2	0	12	26	.131	.125	.133	6.88	3.18
Paredes, Edward	L-L	6-0	175	9-30-86	7	11	4.63	25	24	0	0	117	121	76	60	10	52	91	.265	.311	.248	7.02	4.01
Pineda, Michael	R-R	6-5	180	1-18-89	8	6	1.95	26	21	1	0	138	109	38	30	7	35	128	.216	.220	.213	8.33	2.28
Ramirez, Juan	R-R	6-3	175	8-16-88	6	9	4.14	25	22	0	0	124	112	68	57	9	38	113	.239	.265	.217	8.20	2.76
Renaud, Keith	R-R	6-1	215	2-7-86	1	5	5.14	12	11	0	0	61	64	42	35	4	34	37	.281	.299	.270	5.43	4.99
Souza, Justin	R-R	6-1	185	10-22-85	3	3	3.69	30	0	0	4	39	36	20	16	3	13	40	.247	.333	.196	9.23	3.00
Suriel, Walter	R-R	6-2	190	7-21-86	0	2	6.00	11	1	0	0	18	21	16	12	2	15	19	.284	.367	.227	9.50	7.50
Wild, Jake	R-R	6-5	195	8-18-84	5	6	3.67	24	9	0	0	74	75	34	30	4	24	70	.261	.259	.263	8.55	2.93

Fielding

Catcher	PCT	G	PO	A	E	DP	PB
Arias	.966	3	26	2	1	0	0
Feiner	.994	18	148	13	1	1	0
Nunez	.994	59	468	48	3	3	4
Ochoa	.988	61	429	64	6	4	7

First Base	PCT	G	PO	A	E	DP
Avila	.975	15	114	2	3	7
Dunigan	.978	39	338	11	8	34
Garth	.990	53	454	52	5	44
Liddi	.958	3	20	3	1	1
Meneses	1.000	4	22	0	0	3
Robinson	1.000	25	188	13	0	10
White	.986	8	66	5	1	4

Second Base	PCT	G	PO	A	E	DP
Colina	.974	98	172	246	11	53
Garth	.979	13	11	36	1	4
Meneses	.967	30	51	67	4	13

Third Base	PCT	G	PO	A	E	DP
Colina	.667	2	1	3	2	0
Garth	.868	14	12	21	5	1
Liddi	.943	116	89	211	18	22
Meneses	.846	6	4	7	2	0
Serrano	1.000	1	1	3	0	0

Shortstop	PCT	G	PO	A	E	DP
Colina	.964	10	13	14	1	2
Diaz	.954	120	169	347	25	58

	PCT	G	PO	A	E	DP
Meneses	.938	9	14	16	2	4
Serrano	.833	2	2	3	1	0

Outfield	PCT	G	PO	A	E	DP
Almonte	.952	90	125	13	7	2
Beamon	.984	42	55	6	1	0
Carroll	.965	60	100	9	4	3
Dickey	.975	43	76	1	2	0
Dunigan	.951	58	92	6	5	0
Hernandez	1.000	7	10	1	0	0
Mendez	.948	108	198	4	11	1
Meneses	.875	5	7	0	1	0
O'Donnell	—	1	0	0	0	0
Reynolds	1.000	2	3	0	0	0

EVERETT AQUASOX   SHORT-SEASON

NORTHWEST LEAGUE

Batting	B-T	HT	WT	DOB	AVG	vLH	vRH	G	AB	R	H	2B	3B	HR	RBI	BB	HBP	SH	SF	SO	SB	CS	SLG	OBP
Baez, Fleming	R-R	5-11	194	6-10-81	.191	.244	.168	38	136	14	26	5	2	1	16	11	2	1	0	38	0	1	.279	.262
Billingsley, Ben	L-R	5-11	180	10-27-86	.227	.185	.248	60	194	23	44	11	2	5	29	24	0	8	3	61	5	3	.381	.308
Contreras, Henry	R-R	5-11	208	5-5-86	.167	.143	.200	4	12	1	2	1	0	0	3	2	3	0	0	2	0	0	.250	.412
Davenport, James	R-R	6-4	190	6-1-85	.308	.250	.400	3	13	3	4	3	0	0	1	0	0	1	0	5	1	0	.538	.308
DeJesus, Jharmidy	R-R	6-3	185	8-30-89	.267	.261	.269	28	90	12	24	4	0	4	15	6	1	3	1	28	0	1	.444	.316
Dotel, Welington	R-R	6-1	180	10-2-85	.277	.266	.283	62	202	36	56	5	3	7	22	14	5	4	0	55	19	9	.436	.339
Fromm, Brandon	L-L	6-2	220	3-4-85	.234	.206	.246	58	205	17	48	10	1	3	20	12	8	3	1	67	0	2	.337	.301
Gillies, Tyson	R-R	6-2	190	10-31-88	.313	.383	.280	61	192	36	60	6	5	2	22	35	10	3	2	46	24	7	.427	.439
Howell, Travis	R-R	6-2	220	1-19-85	.288	.250	.306	51	163	24	47	12	1	2	23	25	1		2	56	1	3	.411	.395
Nunez, Luis	R-R	6-0	170	12-31-86	.279	.214	.308	63	229	28	64	10	3	1	16	7	1	13	1	46	16	7	.362	.303
Phillips, Anthony	R-R	5-9	160	4-11-90	.187	.275	.141	59	150	23	28	5	1	2	17	21	1	11	1	42	5	4	.273	.289
Pimentel, Manelik	R-R	6-2	185	10-19-84	.230	.185	.250	66	217	16	50	11	0	2	27	31	5	1	3	45	1	3	.309	.336
Raben, Dennis	L-L	6-4	200	7-31-87	.275	.393	.222	27	91	24	25	11	0	5	14	19	2	0	0	24	1	1	.560	.411
Reynolds, Kevin	L-L	6-1	185	7-1-82	.342	.415	.314	37	146	20	50	15	1	0	18	12	0	2	0	17	8	5	.459	.392
Royster, Ryan	L-L	6-1	170	10-13-85	.196	.216	.188	57	168	18	33	6	0	2	18	34	2	3	1	53	6	2	.268	.337
Savastano, Scott	R-R	6-4	190	6-12-86	.000	.000	.000	2	3	0	0	0	0	0	0	2	0	0	0	1	0	0	.000	.400
Soto, George	R-R	6-2	190	11-19-89	.175	.267	.146	17	63	5	11	1	0	2	7	2	1	0	0	11	1	1	.222	.212
Tenbrink, Nate	L-R	6-2	202	12-21-86	.198	.170	.208	61	202	43	40	9	0	5	21	38	7	1	4	51	24	7	.317	.339

Pitching	B-T	HT	WT	DOB	W	L	ERA	G	GS	CG	SV	IP	H	R	ER	HR	BB	SO	AVG	vLH	vRH	K/9	BB/9
Averill, Erik	L-L	6-2	190	2-9-84	0	0	—	1	0	0	0	0	1	0	0	0	0	1	1.000	.000	1.000	—	—
Brown, Aaron	R-R	6-6	200	5-25-86	2	4	4.62	16	12	0	0	62	55	37	32	3	45	48	.251	.230	.265	6.93	6.50

	B-T	HT	WT	DOB	W	L	ERA	G	GS	CG	SV	IP	H	R	ER	HR	BB	SO	AVG	vLH	vRH	K/9	BB/9
Dominguez, Robbie	R-R	6-3	190	10-26-85	3	1	6.10	18	0	0	0	31	31	26	21	2	21	27	.254	.217	.276	7.84	6.10
DuRocher, John	R-R	6-4	215	6-21-84	0	0	0.00	2	0	0	1	6	0	0	0	0	0	2	.000	.000	.000	3.18	0.00
Feierabend, Ryan	L-L	6-3	230	8-22-85	0	0	5.06	2	2	0	0	11	12	6	6	1	0	10	.279	.250	.286	8.44	0.00
Fernandez, Eddy	L-L	6-2	175	11-22-86	2	4	3.58	28	1	0	1	38	42	24	15	3	16	46	.276	.286	.271	10.99	3.82
Gallagher, Nolan	R-R	6-3	190	12-20-85	1	1	2.94	8	6	0	0	34	34	16	11	1	12	23	.258	.255	.260	6.15	3.21
Hann, Phil	R-R	6-2	200	1-1-84	5	4	4.50	21	0	0	0	32	44	24	16	2	11	26	.314	.357	.286	7.31	3.09
Hensley, Steven	R-R	6-3	180	12-27-86	2	1	5.22	8	6	0	0	29	28	20	17	3	9	32	.243	.122	.333	9.82	2.76
Jakubauskas, Chris	R-R	6-2	210	12-22-78	0	0	0.00	1	1	0	0	3	1	0	0	0	0	7	.111	.167	.000	23.63	0.00
Kasparek, Kenn	R-R	6-8	200	9-23-85	2	3	4.55	10	9	0	0	32	30	22	16	2	20	40	.248	.234	.257	11.37	5.68
Kirkland, Chris	R-R	6-2	195	10-6-85	0	1	3.38	8	0	0	2	11	9	6	4	2	11	12	.220	.235	.208	10.13	9.28
LaFromboise, Bobby	L-L	6-4	185	6-25-86	2	2	3.46	13	10	0	0	42	42	21	16	3	12	35	.249	.302	.230	7.56	2.59
Lorin, Brett	L-R	6-7	245	3-31-87	1	1	2.82	5	5	0	0	22	17	10	7	1	9	29	.207	.167	.239	11.69	3.63
Martinez, Javier	L-R	6-3	225	5-26-85	1	3	3.77	22	0	0	4	29	28	12	12	1	25	29	.267	.231	.288	9.10	7.85
Pettis, Marquis	R-R	6-2	180	9-9-82	2	1	2.64	20	1	0	0	31	24	13	9	0	27	31	.212	.209	.214	9.10	7.92
Reid, Brad	R-R	6-1	185	1-18-88	1	1	5.48	16	0	0	0	23	26	14	14	4	14	12	.277	.229	.305	4.70	5.48
Renfree, Matt	R-R	6-8	220	1-16-85	0	2	2.42	23	0	0	7	45	34	12	12	2	18	47	.217	.296	.175	9.47	3.63
Rohrbaugh, Robert	R-L	6-2	195	12-28-83	0	0	0.00	1	1	0	0	3	2	0	0	0	1	1	.200	.000	.222	9.00	3.00
Salinas, Doug	R-R	6-4	195	12-5-88	2	7	5.53	21	5	0	2	57	51	44	35	5	29	55	.238	.225	.248	8.68	4.58
Staehely, Christian	R-R	6-7	205	9-28-85	2	1	4.95	19	0	0	0	36	48	32	20	1	22	30	.310	.313	.307	7.43	5.45
Suda, Kenta	R-R	6-0	172	7-22-89	0	2	16.62	2	2	0	0	4	7	9	8	1	6	1	.412	.500	.400	2.08	12.46
Suriel, Walter	R-R	6-2	190	7-21-86	4	6	6.06	15	14	0	0	79	99	57	53	12	24	67	.309	.294	.320	7.67	2.75
White, Sean	R-R	6-4	210	4-25-81	0	0	9.00	1	1	0	0	2	3	2	2	1	0	1	.375	.500	.000	4.50	0.00

Fielding

Catcher	PCT	G	PO	A	E	DP	PB
Baez	.992	32	227	31	2	3	7
Contreras	1.000	2	18	3	0	0	1
Howell	.981	44	369	48	8	7	6

First Base	PCT	G	PO	A	E	DP
Baez	.857	1	6	0	1	0
Billingsley	1.000	1	1	1	0	0
Contreras	1.000	1	11	1	0	0
DeJesus	1.000	5	32	1	0	1
Fromm	1.000	31	225	15	0	17
Howell	1.000	1	2	0	0	0
Pimentel	1.000	36	252	21	0	14
Tenbrink	1.000	8	47	4	0	5

Second Base	PCT	G	PO	A	E	DP
Billingsley	.947	22	37	35	4	4
Nunez	.942	56	102	125	14	21
Phillips	1.000	2	3	6	0	3
Soto	1.000	3	8	6	0	1

Third Base	PCT	G	PO	A	E	DP
Billingsley	.900	9	5	13	2	1
Davenport	1.000	2	1	5	0	0
DeJesus	.820	22	9	32	9	1
Pimentel	.833	3	6	4	2	1
Tenbrink	.876	46	44	76	17	3

Shortstop	PCT	G	PO	A	E	DP
Billingsley	.883	15	20	33	7	8

	PCT	G	PO	A	E	DP
Nunez	.786	6	6	5	3	0
Phillips	.924	49	66	117	15	19
Savastano	1.000	2	0	3	0	0
Soto	.871	14	19	42	9	5

Outfield	PCT	G	PO	A	E	DP
Baez	—	1	0	0	0	0
Billingsley	.929	11	25	1	2	0
Dotel	.963	58	98	6	4	3
Fromm	1.000	5	6	0	0	0
Gillies	.961	56	116	8	5	2
Raben	.973	24	35	1	1	0
Reynolds	.971	36	65	1	2	0
Royster	.952	52	74	5	4	0

PULASKI MARINERS   ROOKIE

APPALACHIAN LEAGUE

Batting	B-T	HT	WT	DOB	AVG	vLH	vRH	G	AB	R	H	2B	3B	HR	RBI	BB	HBP	SH	SF	SO	SB	CS	SLG	OBP
Arias, Jonathan	R-R	6-3	190	2-8-88	.239	.286	.228	35	113	15	27	2	2	2	16	11	3	1	4	31	1	0	.345	.313
Bello, Fred	R-R	5-10	165	10-6-87	.286	.167	.333	7	21	1	6	0	0	0	2	0	1	0	0	6	0	1	.286	.286
Benitez, Deybis	R-R	6-2	170	4-23-87	.281	.316	.275	36	121	25	34	10	0	3	17	10	2	1	2	26	0	0	.438	.341
Britton, Drew	B-R	6-0	170	7-17-87	.253	.219	.259	57	198	37	50	10	3	6	25	12	6	1	2	69	7	7	.424	.312
Brock, Jermaine	L-L	6-1	180	1-29-87	.133	.000	.154	6	15	0	2	1	0	0	2	1	0	1	0	2	1	1	.200	.188
Fuentes, Juan	R-R	6-1	170	1-28-86	.337	.324	.339	59	208	28	70	18	1	2	40	28	0	0	5	30	0	1	.462	.407
Hash, Kylee	B-R	6-2	205	3-31-88	.222	—	.222	4	9	0	2	0	0	0	1	0	0	0	0	0	0	2	.222	.222
Johnson, Tommy	R-R	5-11	215	3-14-86	.345	.455	.320	36	119	15	41	8	0	1	12	6	1	3	0	23	0	0	.437	.381
Martinez, Mario	R-R	6-1	208	11-13-89	.319	.217	.341	64	251	43	80	15	3	5	32	10	3	0	6	47	2	2	.462	.344
Noriega, Gabriel	R-R	6-2	170	9-13-90	.238	.120	.262	41	151	13	36	4	2	0	18	6	0	1	4	43	6	1	.291	.266
Phillips, Anthony	R-R	5-9	160	4-11-90	.196	.167	.205	14	56	7	11	1	0	0	4	7	1	1	1	13	4	2	.214	.292
Rivero, Jose	R-R	6-2	180	1-8-90	.251	.237	.254	63	223	38	56	5	3	5	33	22	9	1	5	67	6	2	.368	.336
Sams, Kalian	R-R	6-3	220	8-25-86	.204	.095	.230	32	108	16	22	3	1	10	20	11	3	0	0	47	1	1	.528	.295
Sanchez, Kris	L-L	6-3	220	1-9-84	.336	.412	.325	45	134	26	45	12	0	11	36	19	1	0	0	33	1	0	.672	.422
Shaffer, Jake	L-L	6-1	190	8-16-87	.247	.278	.240	31	93	18	23	4	1	1	7	9	0	1	0	19	10	3	.344	.314
Soto, George	R-R	6-2	190	11-19-89	.197	.250	.189	42	142	15	28	3	0	0	6	10	2	1	0	37	1	2	.218	.260
Trinkler, Blake	R-R	6-0	220	4-19-88	.206	.318	.188	42	131	18	27	6	1	2	16	14	4	1	0	50	0	2	.313	.320
Welsh, Guy	R-R	6-3	226	5-15-85	.297	.300	.296	45	128	20	38	8	0	3	17	24	2	0	2	25	0	2	.430	.410

Pitching	B-T	HT	WT	DOB	W	L	ERA	G	GS	CG	SV	IP	H	R	ER	HR	BB	SO	AVG	vLH	vRH	K/9	BB/9
Alvis, Jordan	R-R	6-7	235	9-16-85	2	1	7.66	15	0	0	0	22	28	22	19	0	12	12	.311	.240	.338	4.84	4.84
Brown, Kyle	R-L	6-2	210	1-2-86	0	0	4.20	10	0	0	0	15	13	14	7	0	7	17	.213	.091	.240	10.20	4.20
Czyz, Nick	L-L	6-2	215	4-10-87	6	5	4.08	14	10	0	0	57	58	28	26	4	19	54	.266	.290	.262	8.48	2.98
Esquibel, Andres	R-R	6-1	215	7-13-86	1	0	2.70	16	0	0	1	33	33	12	10	2	6	20	.260	.212	.277	5.40	1.62
Gaphardt, Brent	L-L	6-5	230	6-9-84	0	1	3.70	12	0	0	0	24	23	11	10	2	9	22	.250	.308	.227	8.14	3.33
Haas, Kyle	R-R	6-5	215	8-20-87	4	5	7.04	13	13	0	0	47	56	53	37	7	28	47	.280	.296	.269	8.94	5.32
Jimenez, Jose	L-L	6-0	180	3-23-87	1	0	3.21	3	2	0	0	14	14	7	5	1	4	14	.255	.100	.289	9.00	2.57
Johannesen-Ellis, Tommy	R-R	6-4	230	2-23-88	0	0	11.51	14	0	0	0	20	38	31	26	5	9	19	.380	.353	.394	8.41	3.98
Kasparek, Kenn	R-R	6-8	200	9-23-85	1	1	3.10	5	4	0	0	20	17	9	7	3	3	25	.234	.333	.140	11.07	1.33
Lewis, Taylor	R-R	6-4	190	6-2-88	1	3	4.54	12	9	0	0	36	38	23	18	4	18	32	.271	.346	.227	8.07	4.54
Mohr, Brooks	R-R	6-3	195	1-14-89	6	4	3.27	13	13	1	0	63	65	28	23	3	28	52	.275	.286	.270	7.39	3.98
Nation, Blake	R-R	6-8	218	5-16-87	1	2	2.74	19	0	0	11	23	21	10	7	1	8	23	.236	.258	.224	9.00	3.13
Oates, Brian	R-R	6-3	205	3-6-85	0	0	0.00	1	1	0	0	5	4	0	0	0	2	5	.250	.500	.167	9.00	3.60

	B-T	HT	WT	DOB	W	L	ERA	G	GS	CG	SV	IP	H	R	ER	HR	BB	SO	AVG	vLH	vRH	K/9	BB/9
Penney, Stephen	R-R	6-7	240	8-14-86	2	0	4.60	16	0	0	0	29	38	17	15	0	4	22	.309	.243	.337	6.75	1.23
Pullen, Brandon	L-L	6-4	200	12-7-85	0	0	5.22	16	0	0	2	29	34	19	17	5	4	32	.288	.276	.292	9.82	1.23
Rios, Jose	L-L	5-10	178	3-2-90	4	2	3.06	15	4	1	0	47	42	21	16	2	15	54	.235	.222	.238	10.34	2.87
Roy, Philip	R-R	6-4	175	7-29-87	4	0	2.08	18	0	0	5	30	23	9	7	1	10	33	.204	.139	.234	9.79	2.97
Williamson, Fabian	R-L	6-2	175	10-20-88	4	3	4.10	11	11	0	0	53	57	26	24	6	27	67	.269	.269	.269	11.45	4.61

Fielding

Catcher	PCT	G	PO	A	E	DP	PB
Arias	.978	15	114	19	3	1	9
Fuentes	.984	33	278	21	5	1	8
Hash	.962	4	24	1	1	0	0
Johnson	.986	20	126	13	2	0	3
Welsh	1.000	3	15	2	0	0	0

First Base	PCT	G	PO	A	E	DP
Fuentes	1.000	9	67	3	0	8
Sanchez	.994	43	327	22	2	24
Trinkler	.947	2	18	0	1	1
Welsh	.988	21	153	16	2	16

Second Base	PCT	G	PO	A	E	DP
Bello	1.000	1	3	2	0	1

Catcher (cont.)					
Benitez	.968	15	25	35	2	4
Noriega	.971	6	14	20	1	1
Phillips	1.000	2	6	4	0	1
Soto	.969	29	57	66	4	17
Trinkler	.975	18	34	44	2	11

Third Base	PCT	G	PO	A	E	DP
Benitez	1.000	1	0	2	0	0
Martinez	.906	62	24	130	16	11
Trinkler	1.000	1	0	1	0	0
Welsh	.895	6	3	14	2	0

Shortstop	PCT	G	PO	A	E	DP
Bello	.778	4	6	8	4	1
Benitez	1.000	6	4	14	0	2

Noriega	.952	35	54	105	8	20
Phillips	.906	12	20	28	5	3
Soto	.873	13	19	36	8	7

Outfield	PCT	G	PO	A	E	DP
Arias	.826	16	18	1	4	0
Benitez	1.000	9	4	0	0	0
Britton	.970	50	93	4	3	0
Brock	1.000	2	2	0	0	0
Rivero	.957	61	104	7	5	2
Sams	.962	32	46	5	2	0
Shaffer	.979	25	45	1	1	0
Trinkler	.857	15	12	0	2	0

AZL MARINERS — ROOKIE

ARIZONA LEAGUE

Batting	B-T	HT	WT	DOB	AVG	vLH	vRH	G	AB	R	H	2B	3B	HR	RBI	BB	HBP	SH	SF	SO	SB	CS	SLG	OBP
Arias, Jonathan	R-R	6-3	190	2-8-88	.250	.400	.182	5	16	2	4	0	0	0	3	3	0	0	1	0	0		.250	.350
Bello, Fred	R-R	5-10	165	10-6-87	.283	.417	.250	22	60	11	17	1	1	0	4	8	3	1	1	14	7	1	.333	.389
Bonilla, Leury	R-R	6-3	170	2-8-85	.250	.250	.250	7	24	2	6	1	0	0	0	1	0	0	0	7	0	1	.292	.280
Burgess, Jarrett	R-R	6-2	180	8-10-90	.227	.250	.222	54	198	30	45	9	2	0	21	18	2	1	1	58	17	4	.293	.297
Carroll, Danny	R-R	6-1	175	1-6-89	.000	—	.000	2	8	0	0	0	0	0	0	0	0	0	0	5	0	0	.000	.000
Contreras, Henry	R-R	5-11	208	5-5-86	.345	.300	.359	26	84	14	29	7	0	0	13	1	1	1	0	26	2	0	.429	.360
Davenport, James	R-R	6-4	190	6-1-85	.143	—	.143	3	14	3	2	1	0	0	1	0	0	1	0	4	0	0	.214	.200
DeJesus, Jharmidy	R-R	6-3	185	8-30-89	.339	.414	.316	34	127	27	43	12	1	6	18	14	3	0	2	35	4	1	.591	.417
Encarnacion, Fernando	R-R	6-0	185	7-23-85	.286	.667	.182	4	14	1	4	2	0	0	4	1	1	0	0	1	0	0	.429	.375
Familia, Emmanuel	R-R	6-2	190	2-5-87	.212	.167	.218	34	99	7	21	2	1	0	11	5	1	1	1	25	1	3	.253	.255
Fuentes, Cesar	R-R	6-0	180	4-12-87	.266	.231	.274	52	203	28	54	4	2	4	26	13	5	8	3	37	4	4	.365	.321
Mateo, Alfredo	R-L	6-3	200	9-12-87	.239	.237	.240	53	188	29	45	4	3	1	31	24	0	3	3	37	2	0	.362	.321
Mendez, Joel	R-R	6-3	175	5-7-88	.279	.216	.295	50	183	23	51	8	1	0	21	8	1	6	1	45	13	7	.333	.311
Molina, Randy	L-R	6-3	215	8-7-86	.248	.294	.234	39	141	18	35	5	3	0	12	16	0	2	2	28	1	2	.326	.321
Noriega, Gabriel	B-R	6-2	170	9-13-90	.421	.286	.452	9	38	7	16	0	0	0	2	1	1	0	1	6	3	0	.421	.439
Rodriguez, Josh	B-R	6-0	200	2-14-88	.000	.000	.000	3	2	0	0	0	0	0	0	0	0	0	0	2	0	0	.000	.000
Rodriguez, Robert	R-R	6-4	190	7-22-90	.215	.200	.218	50	191	24	41	5	2	2	16	4	1	2	2	56	3	2	.293	.232
Savastano, Scott	R-R	6-4	190	6-12-86	.298	.214	.313	26	94	11	28	4	2	1	15	10	0	0	0	15	4	4	.415	.365
Serrano, Terry	B-R	6-1	165	2-6-87	.250	.161	.271	41	160	27	40	4	5	1	16	12	0	5	2	37	15	5	.356	.299
Whatley, Peter	R-R	5-11	190	3-13-85	.257	.667	.172	13	35	5	9	2	0	0	5	2	0	2	0	5	0	0	.314	.297
White, Joe	L-R	6-3	210	1-14-86	.286	.250	.333	3	7	1	2	0	0	0	0	0	2	0	0	1	0	0	.286	.444

Pitching	B-T	HT	WT	DOB	W	L	ERA	G	GS	CG	SV	IP	H	R	ER	HR	BB	SO	AVG	vLH	vRH	K/9	BB/9
Alcantara, Ariel	R-R	6-3	190	5-13-89	1	5	5.01	11	8	0	0	41	46	29	23	3	21	45	.284	.268	.292	9.80	4.57
Averill, Erik	L-L	6-2	190	2-9-84	0	0	9.00	1	0	0	0	1	1	1	1	0	1	0	.250	1.000	.000	0.00	9.00
Bibens-Dirkx, Austin	R-R	6-2	190	4-29-85	0	0	2.25	6	0	0	0	8	5	2	2	0	0	10	.179	.091	.235	11.25	0.00
Birosak, Dustin	L-L	6-2	195	5-5-85	0	0	4.82	8	1	0	0	9	14	7	5	0	4	3	.359	.429	.320	2.89	3.86
Brown, Kyle	R-L	6-2	210	1-2-86	1	1	7.36	5	0	0	1	7	9	6	6	0	3	5	.333	.200	.364	6.14	3.68
Buckborough, Colin	R-R	6-5	185	4-6-89	1	3	6.53	15	2	0	2	30	27	22	22	1	23	23	.243	.205	.264	6.82	6.82
Burnett, Luke	R-R	6-8	260	12-10-86	0	0	9.00	2	2	0	0	3	5	3	3	0	2	3	.357	.333	.375	9.00	6.00
Castillo, Randy	L-R	6-2	165	10-24-89	1	1	4.81	12	0	0	0	24	29	20	13	1	10	14	.305	.290	.313	5.18	3.70
Chang, Yao Wen	R-R	6-2	202	10-31-90	0	2	5.75	15	1	0	0	20	20	17	13	2	22	18	.253	.222	.269	7.97	9.74
de Haas, Jeroen	R-R	6-5		1-1-91	0	0	4.73	12	0	0	0	13	19	9	7	2	5	2	.333	.350	.324	3.38	1.35
Feierabend, Ryan	L-L	6-3	230	8-22-85	0	1	3.86	2	2	0	0	5	4	4	2	0	3	1	.250	.000	.250	1.93	5.79
Gallagher, Nolan	R-R	6-3	190	12-20-85	0	0	6.00	3	3	0	0	9	8	7	6	3	5	8	.235	.182	.261	8.00	5.00
Gaphardt, Brent	L-L	6-5	230	6-9-84	0	0	0.00	1	1	0	0	1	0	0	0	0	1	1	.000	.000	.000	9.00	0.00
Hann, Cheyne	R-R	6-6	235	9-17-84	1	0	1.64	7	0	0	0	2	11	8	2	2	0	4	20	.205	.091	.250	16.36	3.27
Kirkland, Chris	R-R	6-4	220	10-6-85	1	0	1.29	6	0	0	0	7	4	2	1	0	2	7	.174	.000	.235	9.00	2.57
Love, Nick	R-R	6-2	210	12-12-86	1	0	8.22	14	0	0	0	23	39	22	21	0	6	16	.402	.515	.344	6.26	2.35
Maurer, Brandon	R-R	6-5		7-3-90	1	2	3.09	8	5	0	0	23	20	8	8	1	8	25	.247	.375	.163	9.64	3.09
Oates, Brian	R-R	6-3	205	3-6-85	3	4	4.19	12	6	0	0	54	47	34	25	4	27	55	.232	.222	.237	9.22	4.53
Ortiz, Richard	L-L	6-2	185	11-26-87	4	2	2.92	16	0	0	2	25	17	10	8	1	11	23	.205	.091	.246	8.39	4.01
Pribanic, Aaron	R-R	6-4	200	9-1-86	1	2	15.43	3	1	0	0	5	8	8	8	0	5	5	.364	.417	.300	9.64	9.64
Putz, J.J.	R-R	6-5	250	2-22-77	0	0	0.00	2	2	0	0	3	2	0	0	0	0	4	.200	.400	.000	12.00	0.00
Reid, Brad	R-R	6-1	185	1-18-88	1	0	9.00	1	0	0	0	2	4	2	2	0	0	1	.444	.500	.429	4.50	0.00
Stanton, Taylor	R-R	6-2	200	1-15-88	1	1	2.65	11	2	0	0	17	13	5	5	0	6	20	.213	.222	.209	10.59	3.18
Suda, Kenta	R-R	6-0	172	7-22-88	2	2	3.15	12	7	0	0	54	53	24	19	3	33	40	.262	.296	.250	6.63	5.47
Tome, Jean	R-R	6-2	200	9-5-89	1	0	5.89	8	0	0	0	18	22	19	12	0	9	19	.286	.250	.298	9.33	4.42

Fielding

Catcher	PCT	G	PO	A	E	DP	PB
Arias	.939	3	26	5	2	1	4
Contreras	.993	21	132	17	1	2	5
Encarnacion	.933	4	25	3	2	0	2
Familia	.983	33	196	39	4	1	10
J. Rodriguez	1.000	3	11	0	0	0	1
Whatley	1.000	7	36	2	0	0	2

First Base	PCT	G	PO	A	E	DP
Mateo	.964	17	128	7	5	14
Molina	.976	38	343	19	9	26
White	1.000	1	8	2	0	2

Second Base	PCT	G	PO	A	E	DP
Bello	.958	16	29	40	3	11
Fuentes	.973	30	64	82	4	15

Jobe	1.000	5	4	11	0	3
Savastano	1.000	6	8	15	0	2
Serrano	.833	3	9	6	3	0

Third Base	PCT	G	PO	A	E	DP
Contreras	1.000	1	0	1	0	0
Davenport	1.000	2	2	7	0	1
DeJesus	.923	23	19	41	5	5
Fuentes	1.000	1	0	1	0	0
Mateo	.929	27	27	52	6	5
Savastano	1.000	5	5	9	0	1

Shortstop	PCT	G	PO	A	E	DP
Bello	.500	1	0	1	1	0
Fuentes	.913	23	23	71	9	10
Noriega	.905	9	16	22	4	3

Serrano	.936	27	43	74	8	14

Outfield	PCT	G	PO	A	E	DP
Arias	1.000	1	1	1	0	0
Bello	1.000	3	4	1	0	0
Bonilla	1.000	2	3	0	0	0
Burgess	1.000	43	95	3	0	0
Carroll	1.000	2	5	1	0	0
DeJesus	1.000	1	1	0	0	0
Mendez	.942	50	76	5	5	1
R. Rodriguez	.958	48	83	8	4	1
Savastano	1.000	9	6	0	0	0
Serrano	.929	13	23	3	2	1

DSL MARINERS

ROOKIE

DOMINICAN SUMMER LEAGUE

Batting	B-T	HT	WT	DOB	AVG	vLH	vRH	G	AB	R	H	2B	3B	HR	RBI	BB	HBP	SH	SF	SO	SB	CS	SLG	OBP
Beltre, Marbin	B-R	6-3	180	3-30-90	.262	.250	.264	48	149	36	39	4	1	0	5	26	4	3	2	29	16	6	.302	.381
Carvajal, Ameilis	R-R	6-2	170	3-6-89	.265	.391	.242	52	155	34	41	11	2	2	37	36	3	2	5	38	11	3	.400	.402
Flores, Mario	R-R	6-3	195	10-9-87	.260	.391	.237	51	154	17	40	7	1	4	32	36	3	1	2	33	2	1	.396	.405
Garcia, Oliver	R-R	6-1	188	12-7-90	.178	.350	.113	30	73	7	13	3	0	1	9	14	1	0	1	27	3	2	.260	.315
Jimenez, Hassiel	R-R	6-0	195	5-8-91	.282	.381	.267	54	156	25	44	11	0	1	23	24	8	4	1	35	6	6	.372	.402
Jimenez, Jose	R-R	5-11	178	1-24-90	.111	.000	.125	3	9	1	1	0	0	1	4	1	0	0	0	1	1	0	.444	.200
Lebron, Rey	R-R	6-3	185	11-26-89	.196	.294	.178	43	107	15	21	1	2	0	5	11	2	1	0	41	4	2	.243	.283
Marte, Augusto	R-R	6-2	190	8-17-89	.127	.050	.144	41	110	11	14	1	2	8	14	6	1	0	62	2	3	.209	.262
Mercedes, Hector	R-R	6-1	200	11-10-87	.297	.250	.307	47	138	32	41	6	0	6	25	23	8	0	2	25	0	0	.471	.421
Morla, Ramon	R-R	6-1	175	11-20-89	.256	.276	.252	55	164	34	42	7	1	2	17	28	11	3	0	38	7	4	.348	.399
Nunez, Efrain	B-R	6-3	190	2-17-91	.267	.231	.274	52	161	31	43	6	5	4	28	26	6	1	1	56	6	7	.441	.387
Ozuna, Victor	R-R	6-2	180	12-2-86	.221	.273	.211	25	68	5	15	2	1	0	5	7	2	1	0	22	4	4	.279	.312
Sanon, Bertin	R-R	6-3	180	7-14-89	.211	.188	.214	42	114	21	24	4	1	2	12	18	4	2	1	31	3	4	.316	.336
van Heydoorn, Rudy	R-R	6-3	180	4-17-89	.266	.278	.265	53	154	37	41	5	0	7	35	43	13	3	1	42	9	10	.435	.460
Wel, Axel	L-L	6-3	180	4-10-91	.277	.200	.287	41	130	18	36	8	1	0	21	17	2	1	2	22	0	1	.354	.364
Zapata, Angel	R-R	6-2	185	11-25-87	.230	.143	.243	52	165	16	38	2	0	6	16	10	7	8	2	36	10	7	.242	.299
Zorrilla, Janelfry	R-R	6-2	180	9-2-90	.177	.222	.170	55	130	17	23	4	1	0	9	9	3	10	1	33	8	3	.223	.245

Pitching	B-T	HT	WT	DOB	W	L	ERA	G	GS	CG	SV	IP	H	R	ER	HR	BB	SO	AVG	vLH	vRH	K/9	BB/9
Antigua, Julio	R-R	6-2	175	8-24-91	0	1	5.16	12	1	0	0	23	29	22	13	1	12	12	.322	.143	.377	4.76	4.76
Aquino, Gregorio	R-R	6-5	175	3-5-90	1	2	7.04	13	3	0	0	23	27	21	18	1	19	25	.293	.462	.266	9.78	7.43
Bautista, Felix	R-R	6-3	180	10-10-87	3	2	2.71	18	8	0	2	73	63	34	22	5	11	80	.224	.163	.237	9.86	1.36
Celestino, Miguel	R-R	6-5	170	10-10-89	5	1	2.48	15	12	0	0	58	45	24	16	0	15	47	.212	.333	.188	7.29	2.33
Fernandez, Anthony	L-L	6-4	180	6-8-90	4	3	4.93	16	6	0	0	50	42	34	22	0	27	41	.227	.125	.232	7.33	4.83
Franco, Juan	L-L	6-3	170	8-8-86	1	0	3.00	5	0	0	0	3	2	4	1	0	4	3	.182	1.000	.100	9.00	12.00
Garcia, Francisco	L-L	6-1	180	8-14-91	2	2	11.37	6	1	0	0	6	8	8	8	0	9	8	.320	.000	.321	7.11	12.79
Germocen, Nelson	R-R	6-5	200	9-16-88	2	2	1.14	19	0	0	8	32	12	6	4	0	14	49	.120	.278	.085	13.93	3.98
Hidalgo, Ambioris	R-R	6-2	196	2-4-91	2	0	4.27	18	7	0	4	40	40	27	19	4	17	39	.258	.300	.248	8.78	3.83
Mercedes, Bruno	R-R	6-3	170	10-6-88	2	2	3.86	22	6	0	3	58	57	32	25	2	21	63	.243	.319	.223	9.72	3.24
Perdomo, Jose	R-R	6-4	200	4-12-90	4	3	3.40	19	6	0	0	56	58	24	21	1	12	40	.264	.306	.255	6.47	1.94
Perez, Henry	L-L	6-3	170	10-18-89	7	2	2.25	15	11	1	0	72	64	22	18	0	26	78	.244	.250	.244	9.75	3.25
Rijo, Cristian	L-L	6-6	180	11-25-88	1	1	4.22	10	3	0	0	21	24	13	10	1	7	16	.304	.000	.316	6.75	2.95
Rosario, Enrique	R-R	6-1	180	6-23-91	6	1	2.92	15	0	0	0	37	27	19	12	0	19	43	.199	.194	.200	10.46	4.62
Vizcaino, Joan	R-R	6-6	195	4-25-89	1	1	3.32	11	2	0	0	19	20	10	7	0	9	9	.274	.167	.295	4.26	4.26
Yan, Fello	R-R	6-2	180	9-8-90	1	0	5.52	10	0	0	0	15	14	10	9	1	10	9	.259	.250	.262	5.52	6.14

Fielding

Catcher	PCT	G	PO	A	E	DP	PB
Flores	.985	20	115	16	2	0	3
H. Jimenez	.969	53	390	43	14	3	17
J. Jimenez	.875	3	18	3	3	0	0
Mercedes	.976	5	37	4	1	0	5

First Base	PCT	G	PO	A	E	DP
Flores	.938	6	44	1	3	5
B. Mercedes	1.000	1	3	0	0	0
H. Mercedes	.996	33	231	4	1	12
Rijo	1.000	2	2	0	0	0
van Heydoorn	1.000	17	140	7	0	12
Wel	.991	18	101	4	1	8
Zapata	1.000	8	23	1	0	2

Second Base	PCT	G	PO	A	E	DP
Carvajal	.969	25	35	28	2	5

Garcia	.946	10	17	18	2	6
Morla	.960	9	14	10	1	2
Sanon	.949	9	23	14	2	1
Zapata	.922	28	52	55	9	12

Third Base	PCT	G	PO	A	E	DP
Garcia	1.000	1	0	2	0	0
Morla	.859	44	27	89	19	5
Ozuna	.667	1	0	2	1	0
Sanon	1.000	2	2	5	0	0
van Heydoorn	.895	30	22	55	9	4
Zapata	1.000	3	0	4	0	0

Shortstop	PCT	G	PO	A	E	DP
Carvajal	.917	26	35	53	8	13
Garcia	.906	9	11	18	3	3
Morla	—	1	0	0	0	0

Ozuna	.900	16	24	39	7	7
Sanon	.929	29	46	72	9	5
van Heydoorn	1.000	1	0	1	0	0

Outfield	PCT	G	PO	A	E	DP
Beltre	.957	43	66	1	3	0
Garcia	—	1	0	0	0	0
Lebron	.964	41	49	5	2	2
Marte	1.000	32	49	3	0	1
Morla	—	2	0	0	0	0
Nunez	.952	43	57	3	3	0
Wel	1.000	21	18	0	0	0
Zapata	1.000	11	9	5	0	2
Zorrilla	.938	53	71	4	5	1

VENEZUELAN SUMMER LEAGUE

Batting	B-T	HT	WT	DOB	AVG	vLH	vRH	G	AB	R	H	2B	3B	HR	RBI	BB	HBP	SH	SF	SO	SB	CS	SLG	OBP
Acevedo, Michael	R-R	6-0	185	12-5-90	.248	.228	.255	65	222	22	55	10	2	1	30	19	10	1	4	32	3	1	.324	.329
Agudelo, Jorge	R-R	6-0	175	5-30-89	.281	.293	.277	56	178	24	50	6	1	0	19	19	15	3	1	33	5	1	.326	.394
Batista, Yidid	R-R	6-0	150	10-13-89	.265	.313	.251	58	219	32	58	3	3	0	15	10	6	5	0	22	10	8	.306	.315
Del Rio, Cesar	R-R	6-1	180	11-11-87	.248	.256	.246	53	157	11	39	5	2	2	21	12	5	2	1	41	0	3	.344	.320
Diaz, Franklin	B-R	6-1	170	7-20-90	.180	.125	.190	25	50	1	9	0	0	0	4	5	3	0	1	20	0	0	.200	.288
Extrano, Jetsy	B-R	6-1	175	8-13-88	.279	.302	.270	58	201	32	56	19	0	4	42	24	3	2	3	35	1	0	.433	.359
Garcia, Alejandro	R-R	6-2	190	9-16-89	.172	.250	.143	15	29	5	5	1	0	0	2	3	1	1	0	16	0	1	.207	.273
Garcia, Eduardo	R-R	6-2	190	9-16-89	.088	.125	.077	13	34	3	3	2	0	0	2	6	0	0	0	9	0	1	.147	.225
Gonzalez, Larry	R-R	5-11	170	2-1-88	.211	.314	.172	44	128	8	27	5	1	0	9	5	5	3	0	12	1	1	.266	.268
Hart, Kenny	R-R	6-3	180	3-21-90	.198	.190	.200	41	116	12	23	2	1	0	11	6	5	2	0	28	2	2	.233	.268
Lampe, Reginald	R-R	6-3	170	3-1-90	.169	.167	.170	31	59	9	10	1	0	0	3	9	0	0	0	18	2	1	.186	.279
Ramirez, Carlos	B-R	5-11	145	12-2-88	.333	.182	.376	53	150	28	50	6	2	1	14	10	7	6	4	19	5	2	.420	.392
Rangel, Rigoberto	R-R	6-1	167	6-21-89	.274	.333	.258	46	164	20	45	6	3	0	20	17	7	3	2	23	1	2	.348	.363
Torrealba, Rafael	R-R	6-2	175	9-5-89	.271	.267	.273	41	107	19	29	6	1	0	4	10	2	4	0	15	3	3	.346	.345
Velasquez, Roberto	B-R	5-11	160	2-14-90	.262	.273	.258	61	195	35	51	4	4	0	13	21	12	3	0	24	4	2	.323	.368
Yepez, Mario	B-R	6-2	160	6-15-88	.345	.397	.326	67	238	32	82	17	4	1	44	18	9	5	5	27	11	4	.462	.404

Pitching	B-T	HT	WT	DOB	W	L	ERA	G	GS	CG	SV	IP	H	R	ER	HR	BB	SO	AVG	vLH	vRH	K/9	BB/9
Acosta, Rhonny	R-R	6-3	188	12-4-88	1	0	0.00	3	0	0	0	6	0	0	0	0	1	3	.000	.000	.000	4.26	1.42
Campos, Manuel	R-R	6-2	175	1-12-90	3	3	3.90	19	0	0	4	32	32	15	14	1	9	24	.264	.276	.261	6.68	2.51
Chourio, Johalbi	R-R	6-2	158	11-24-88	0	0	3.97	11	1	0	1	23	17	12	10	0	13	8	.215	.300	.203	3.18	5.16
Diaz, Nolan	R-R	6-1	175	3-28-91	2	2	2.75	15	6	1	2	59	63	21	18	0	4	39	.283	.239	.294	5.95	0.61
Esparza, Gerardo	R-R	6-1	180	11-11-87	4	5	1.81	15	13	0	1	70	50	31	14	1	22	59	.198	.286	.187	7.62	2.84
Gonzalez, Isliexel	R-R	6-3	185	5-10-91	0	1	5.40	6	2	0	0	8	8	5	5	1	8	5	.267	.500	.231	5.40	8.64
Guaipe, Mayckol	R-R	6-3	175	8-11-90	2	1	1.86	18	1	0	3	39	26	11	8	1	19	25	.200	.286	.195	5.82	4.42
Guanire, Oberth	R-R	6-6	190	6-21-90	2	1	3.86	12	0	0	3	19	15	9	8	0	11	17	.221	.444	.186	8.20	5.30
Medina, Yoervis	R-R	6-3	210	7-27-88	4	3	1.79	17	1	0	5	40	32	12	8	1	12	36	.213	.133	.233	8.03	2.68
Montbrum, Kervin	R-L	5-11	175	6-3-88	3	3	3.79	16	2	0	1	36	31	18	15	0	24	28	.231	.000	.240	7.07	6.06
Nava, Jessie	R-R	6-3	165	9-18-87	5	0	1.60	13	12	1	0	67	50	15	12	0	16	44	.214	.243	.208	5.88	2.14
Pereira, Ricardo	B-R	6-3	150	4-18-91	0	1	6.14	8	0	0	0	7	10	5	5	0	11	3	.323	.500	.280	3.68	13.50
Raga, Angel	R-R	6-1	168	7-25-89	3	2	5.24	11	2	0	0	22	16	14	13	0	19	13	.198	.267	.182	5.24	7.66
Ramirez, Erasmo	R-R	5-11	180	5-2-90	4	1	2.86	13	11	1	0	63	67	23	20	2	9	46	.276	.224	.289	6.57	1.29
Rodriguez, Leonardo	R-R	6-2	185	4-15-88	6	0	1.27	11	9	0	0	50	37	11	7	0	18	33	.209	.217	.208	5.98	3.26
Sabala, Reynaldo	R-R	6-3	187	8-16-90	3	4	2.72	14	9	0	1	56	45	28	17	1	24	35	.218	.342	.190	5.59	3.83

Fielding

Catcher	PCT	G	PO	A	E	DP	PB
Acevedo	.943	6	29	4	2	0	2
Del Rio	.915	10	45	9	5	1	5
Diaz	.980	25	126	19	3	1	5
Gonzalez	.974	43	225	36	7	4	6
Yepez	1.000	1	2	0	0	0	0

First Base	PCT	G	PO	A	E	DP
Acevedo	.969	11	88	6	3	8
Del Rio	.979	36	271	14	6	35
A. Garcia	.985	10	61	4	1	6
E. Garcia	.921	4	33	2	3	1
Ramirez	.996	27	228	11	1	11

Second Base	PCT	G	PO	A	E	DP
Acevedo	1.000	1	0	1	0	0

(Second Base, cont.)	PCT	G	PO	A	E	DP
Agudelo	1.000	12	34	28	0	7
Batista	.953	33	81	100	9	23
Extrano	.978	16	51	37	2	12
Ramirez	.975	10	15	24	1	4
Torrealba	1.000	1	0	2	0	0
Velasquez	1.000	6	16	23	0	6

Third Base	PCT	G	PO	A	E	DP
Acevedo	.839	10	7	19	5	2
Agudelo	.886	39	20	81	13	7
Extrano	.933	18	8	34	3	5
Lampe	.600	1	2	1	2	0
Ramirez	.952	14	6	34	2	3

Shortstop	PCT	G	PO	A	E	DP
Batista	.892	7	19	39	7	4

(Shortstop, cont.)	PCT	G	PO	A	E	DP
Extrano	1.000	11	12	36	0	4
Ramirez	1.000	3	1	2	0	1
Velasquez	.961	54	85	214	12	34

Outfield	PCT	G	PO	A	E	DP
Acevedo	1.000	36	38	2	0	0
Agudelo	—	1	0	0	0	0
A. Garcia	—	1	0	0	0	0
E. Garcia	1.000	3	3	0	0	0
Gonzalez	1.000	1	3	0	0	0
Hart	.955	36	38	4	2	0
Lampe	.737	12	14	0	5	0
Rangel	.970	40	62	3	2	1
Torrealba	.946	34	34	1	2	0
Yepez	.991	65	105	10	1	3

ORGANIZATION STATISTICS

Tampa Bay Rays

BY MARC TOPKIN

The Rays changed their name and their uniforms, and then they changed history.

In their first season without the "Devil" and with blue accents, the Rays staged one of the most stunning turnarounds in baseball history, ascending from the worst record in the majors in 2007 to the World Series in 2008.

Along the way, they blew past the franchise record of 70 wins, qualified for the playoffs for the first time in team history, won the American League East with a 97-65 record, cruised past the White Sox in the division series and ousted the defending champion Red Sox in a thrilling seven-game AL Championship Series before losing the World Series to the Phillies in five games.

"This has been an incredibly magical season, one that no one ever thought could be possible," first baseman Carlos Pena said.

And in the process they helped erase their embarrassing and oft-ridiculed past and turned the Tampa Bay area—at least temporarily—into a cowbell-ringing, Mohawk-wearing baseball hotbed.

"These guys have created baseball in Tampa Bay, I believe," principal owner Stuart Sternberg said. "I know it's a large amount to bite off and chew, but I don't think the region's three million-plus people knew what baseball could mean until this year. And that's something that's going to stick now for generations."

The Rays joined the 1991 Braves as the only teams to go from the worst record one year to the World Series the next. The key to their turnaround was a stark improvement in their pitching and defense, leading to a decrease of 273 runs allowed—the third-largest such gain in history.

A common theme of their success was team effort, a steady stream of players assuming key roles on different nights. Consider they finished first in the game's toughest division without a 15-game winner or a .300-hitter, and with only one player (Carlos Pena) with as many as 30 homers and 100 RBIs.

Shortstop Jason Bartlett was voted team MVP by members of the Tampa Bay chapter of the Baseball Writers Association of America, but it was not a clear-cut choice. Pena and rookie third baseman Evan Longoria also were worthy, as were

PLAYERS OF THE YEAR

MAJOR LEAGUE: EVAN LONGORIA, 3B

It took less than two years for the 2006 first-round draft pick to reach the majors, and when he did, he was a key figure for the AL pennant winners. His 27 home runs and 85 RBIs ranked second on the team, while his .272 average was fifth.

MINOR LEAGUE: DAVID PRICE, LHP

The 2007 first-round pick reached the majors as a September callup and was dominant out of the bullpen in the playoffs. Before that, he dominated at Double-A Montgomery, finishing 7-0, 1.89 in 57 innings and going 1-1, 5.40 in 18 innings at Triple-A Durham.

STEVE MOORE

ORGANIZATION LEADERS

BATTING		*Minimum 250 at-bats
*AVG	Johnson, Dan, Durham	.307
R	Nowak, Chris, Montgomery/Durham	87
H	Nowak, Chris, Montgomery/Durham	153
TB	Richard, Chris, Durham	255
2B	Nowak, Chris, Montgomery/Durham	37
3B	Perez, Fernando, Durham	11
HR	Richard, Chris, Durham	26
RBI	Martinez, Gabriel, Montgomery	93
BB	Johnson, Dan, Durham	84
SO	Perez, Fernando, Durham	156
SB	Loyola, Maiko, Columbus	45
*OBP	Johnson, Dan, Durham	.424
*SLG	Johnson, Dan, Durham	.556

PITCHING		†Minimum 75 innings
W	Davis, Wade, Montgomery/Durham	13
	Talbot, Mitch, Durham	13
L	Mann, Brandon, Vero Beach	12
	Rollins, Heath, Vero Beach/Montgomery	12
†ERA	Hellickson, Jeremy, Vero Beach/Montgomery	2.96
G	Deago, Roger, Montgomery	59
GS	Davis, Wade, Montgomery/Durham	28
	Talbot, Mitch, Durham	28
SV	Frontz, Neal, Vero Beach/Montgomery	26
IP	Rollins, Heath, Vero Beach/Montgomery	161
BB	Davis, Wade, Montgomery/Durham	66
SO	Hellickson, Jeremy, Vero Beach/Montgomery	162
†AVG	Niemann, Jeff, Durham	.207

catcher Dioner Navarro and middle reliever J.P. Howell.

Longoria was considered the favorite for the AL rookie of the year award, and Joe Maddon the likely overwhelming choice for the AL manager of the year award.

General Manager: Andrew Friedman. **Farm Director:** Mitch Lukevics. **Scouting Director:** R.J. Harrison.

Class	Team	League	W	L	PCT	Finish*	Manager	Affiliate Since
Majors	Tampa Bay	American	97	65	.599	^2nd (14)	Joe Maddon	—
Triple-A	Durham Bulls	International	74	70	.514	5th (14)	Charlie Montoyo	1998
Double-A	Montgomery Biscuits	Southern	69	70	.496	6th (10)	Billy Gardner	2004
High A	Vero Beach Devil Rays	Florida State	54	81	.400	11th (12)	Jim Morrison	2007
Low A	Columbus Catfish	South Atlantic	67	69	.493	10th (16)	Matt Quatraro	2007
Short-season	Hudson Valley Renegades	New York-Penn	40	35	.533	6th (14)	Joe Alvarez	1996
Rookie	Princeton Devil Rays	Appalachian	24	38	.387	9th (10)	Joe Szekely	1997
Overall 2008 Minor League Record			328	363	.475	20th		

* Finish in overall standings (No. of teams in league). ^League champion.

TAMPA BAY RAYS

AMERICAN LEAGUE

Batting	B-T	HT	WT	DOB	AVG	vLH	vRH	G	AB	R	H	2B	3B	HR	RBI	BB	HBP	SH	SF	SO	SB	CS	SLG	OBP
Aybar, Willy	B-R	5-11	200	3-9-83	.253	.266	.245	95	324	33	82	17	2	10	33	32	4	1	1	44	2	2	.410	.327
Baldelli, Rocco	R-R	6-4	200	9-25-81	.263	.292	.219	28	80	12	21	5	0	4	13	7	3	0	0	25	0	0	.475	.344
Bartlett, Jason	R-R	6-0	185	10-30-79	.286	.379	.248	128	454	48	130	25	3	1	37	22	9	5	4	69	20	6	.361	.329
Brignac, Reid	L-R	6-3	180	1-16-86	.000	.000	.000	4	10	1	0	0	0	0	0	1	0	0	0	5	0	0	.000	.091
Cannizaro, Andy	R-R	5-10	170	12-19-78	.000	—	.000	1	1	0	0	0	0	0	0	0	0	0	0	0	0	0	.000	.000
Crawford, Carl	L-L	6-2	215	8-5-81	.273	.248	.285	109	443	69	121	12	10	8	57	30	2	0	5	60	25	7	.400	.319
DiFelice, Mike	R-R	6-2	205	5-28-69	.300	.600	.200	7	20	1	6	1	0	0	4	1	1	0	0	1	0	0	.350	.364
Floyd, Cliff	L-R	6-4	230	12-5-72	.268	.250	.275	80	246	32	66	13	0	11	39	28	5	0	5	58	1	0	.455	.349
Gomes, Jonny	R-R	6-1	225	11-22-80	.182	.182	.182	77	154	23	28	5	1	8	21	15	7	0	1	46	8	1	.383	.282
Gross, Gabe	L-R	6-3	220	10-21-79	.242	.191	.256	127	302	40	73	13	3	13	38	40	2	0	1	75	2	2	.434	.333
Haynes, Nathan	L-L	5-9	170	9-7-79	.227	.250	.225	20	44	3	10	0	0	0	3	3	0	0	0	12	4	1	.227	.277
Hernandez, Michel	R-R	6-0	215	8-12-78	.200	.200	.200	5	15	2	3	0	0	0	0	0	0	0	0	3	0	0	.200	.200
Hinske, Eric	L-R	6-2	235	8-5-77	.247	.143	.262	133	381	59	94	21	1	20	60	47	3	0	1	88	10	3	.465	.333
Iwamura, Akinori	L-R	5-9	175	2-9-79	.274	.260	.280	152	627	91	172	30	9	6	48	70	4	3	3	131	8	6	.380	.349
Jaso, John	L-R	6-2	205	9-19-83	.200	.500	.125	5	10	2	2	0	0	0	0	0	0	0	0	2	0	0	.200	.200
Johnson, Dan	L-R	6-2	215	8-10-79	.200	.111	.250	10	25	3	5	0	0	2	4	3	0	0	0	7	0	0	.440	.286
2-team total (1 Oakland)					.192	—		11	26	3	5	0	0	2	4	3	0	0	0	7	0	0	.423	.276
Johnson, Elliot	B-R	6-0	185	3-9-84	.158	.167	.143	7	19	0	3	0	0	0	0	0	0	0	0	7	0	1	.158	.158
Longoria, Evan	R-R	6-2	210	10-7-85	.272	.242	.284	122	448	67	122	31	2	27	85	46	6	0	8	122	7	0	.531	.343
Navarro, Dioner	B-R	5-9	205	2-9-84	.295	.257	.308	120	427	43	126	27	0	7	54	34	3	3	3	49	0	4	.407	.349
Pena, Carlos	L-L	6-2	215	5-17-78	.247	.190	.280	139	490	76	121	24	2	31	102	96	12	0	9	166	1	1	.494	.377
Perez, Fernando	B-R	6-1	195	4-23-83	.250	.292	.222	23	60	18	15	2	0	3	8	8	1	3	0	16	5	0	.433	.348
Riggans, Shawn	R-R	6-2	210	7-25-80	.222	.233	.213	44	135	21	30	7	0	6	24	12	1	2	2	30	0	0	.407	.287
Ruggiano, Justin	R-R	6-2	205	4-12-82	.197	.174	.233	45	76	9	15	4	0	2	7	4	1	0	0	27	2	0	.329	.247
Upton, B.J.	R-R	6-3	185	8-21-84	.273	.269	.275	145	531	85	145	37	2	9	67	97	2	3	7	134	44	16	.401	.383
Zobrist, Ben	B-R	6-3	200	5-26-81	.253	.269	.242	62	198	32	50	10	2	12	30	25	2	3	7	37	3	0	.505	.339

Pitching	B-T	HT	WT	DOB	W	L	ERA	G	GS	CG	SV	IP	H	R	ER	HR	BB	SO	AVG	vLH	vRH	K/9	BB/9
Balfour, Grant	R-R	6-2	190	12-30-77	6	2	1.54	51	0	0	4	58	28	10	10	3	24	82	.143	.120	.159	12.65	3.70
Birkins, Kurt	L-L	6-2	190	8-11-80	0	0	0.90	6	0	0	0	10	5	1	1	0	5	7	.161	.083	.211	6.30	4.50
Bradford, Chad	R-R	6-5	205	9-14-74	1	0	1.42	21	0	0	0	19	18	3	3	1	8	4	.261	.318	.234	1.89	3.79
2-team total (47 Baltimore)					4	3	2.12	68	0	0	0	59	59	20	14	3	15	17	—	—	—	2.58	2.28
Dohmann, Scott	R-R	6-1	200	2-13-78	2	0	6.14	12	0	0	0	15	18	10	10	2	7	12	.310	.250	.353	7.36	4.30
Garza, Matt	R-R	6-4	205	11-26-83	11	9	3.70	30	30	3	0	185	170	83	76	19	59	128	.245	.244	.245	6.24	2.88
Glover, Gary	R-R	6-5	225	12-3-76	1	2	5.82	29	0	0	0	34	42	22	22	3	18	22	.300	.317	.286	5.82	4.76
2-team total (18 Detroit)					2	3	5.30	47	0	0	0	54	64	33	32	7	22	37	—	—	—	6.13	3.64
Hammel, Jason	R-R	6-6	220	9-2-82	4	4	4.60	40	5	0	2	78	83	45	40	11	35	44	.272	.281	.265	5.06	4.02
Howell, J.P.	L-L	6-0	175	4-25-83	6	1	2.22	64	0	0	3	89	62	29	22	6	39	92	.194	.188	.197	9.27	3.93
Jackson, Edwin	R-R	6-3	190	9-9-83	14	11	4.42	32	31	0	0	183	199	91	90	23	77	108	.281	.295	.268	5.30	3.78
Kazmir, Scott	L-L	6-0	190	1-24-84	12	8	3.49	27	27	0	0	152	123	61	59	23	70	166	.220	.198	.227	9.81	4.14
Miller, Trever	R-L	6-3	200	5-29-73	2	0	4.15	68	0	0	2	43	39	21	20	2	20	44	.242	.209	.286	9.14	4.15
Niemann, Jeff	R-R	6-9	280	2-28-83	2	1	5.06	5	2	0	0	16	18	12	9	3	8	14	.277	.200	.325	7.88	4.50
Percival, Troy	R-R	6-3	240	8-9-69	2	1	4.53	50	0	0	28	46	29	26	23	9	27	38	.178	.185	.171	7.49	5.32
Price, David	L-L	6-6	225	8-26-85	0	0	1.93	5	1	0	0	14	9	4	3	1	4	12	.176	.158	.188	7.71	2.57
Reyes, Al	R-R	6-1	230	4-10-70	2	2	4.37	26	0	0	0	23	21	12	11	2	10	19	.253	.300	.226	7.54	3.97
Ryu, J.K.	R-R	6-3	225	5-30-83	0	0	0.00	1	0	0	0	1	0	0	0	0	1	1	.000	.000	.000	6.75	6.75
Salas, Juan	R-R	6-2	230	11-7-78	0	0	7.11	5	0	0	0	6	5	5	5	0	4	8	.217	.300	.154	11.37	5.68
Shields, James	R-R	6-4	215	12-20-81	14	8	3.56	33	33	3	0	215	208	94	85	24	40	160	.254	.255	.253	6.70	1.67
Sonnanstine, Andy	L-R	6-3	185	3-18-83	13	9	4.38	32	32	1	0	193	212	105	94	21	37	124	.277	.265	.289	5.77	1.72
Talbot, Mitch	R-R	6-2	200	10-17-83	0	0	11.17	3	1	0	0	10	16	12	12	3	11	5	.381	.364	.387	4.66	10.24
Wheeler, Dan	R-R	6-3	220	12-10-77	5	6	3.12	70	0	0	13	66	44	25	23	10	22	53	.183	.215	.163	7.19	2.98

Fielding

Catcher

Catcher	PCT	G	PO	A	E	DP	PB
DiFelice	1.000	7	42	3	0	1	0
Hernandez	.955	4	20	1	1	0	0
Jaso	1.000	3	11	1	0	0	0
Navarro	.994	117	837	55	5	10	6
Riggans	.982	41	268	5	5	0	4

First Base

First Base	PCT	G	PO	A	E	DP
Aybar	1.000	19	144	11	0	10
Hinske	.989	11	78	8	1	11
D. Johnson	1.000	8	39	5	0	4
Pena	.998	132	991	106	2	117

Second Base

Second Base	PCT	G	PO	A	E	DP
Aybar	1.000	10	17	19	0	4
Iwamura	.990	152	284	397	7	109

	PCT	G	PO	A	E	DP
E. Johnson	1.000	1	3	5	0	1
Zobrist	1.000	8	11	11	0	3

Third Base

Third Base	PCT	G	PO	A	E	DP
Aybar	.958	41	29	84	5	12
Hinske	1.000	8	1	6	0	0
Longoria	.963	119	86	230	12	26
Zobrist	1.000	1	0	2	0	0

Shortstop

Shortstop	PCT	G	PO	A	E	DP
Aybar	1.000	2	2	6	0	1
Bartlett	.970	125	204	309	16	69
Brignac	.846	4	4	7	2	3
Cannizaro	1.000	1	1	0	0	0
E. Johnson	.909	2	4	6	1	3
Longoria	1.000	1	0	1	0	0

Zobrist	.949	35	51	78	7	22

Outfield

Outfield	PCT	G	PO	A	E	DP
Baldelli	.857	7	6	0	1	0
Crawford	.983	108	233	2	4	0
Gomes	.974	30	38	0	1	0
Gross	.995	123	189	7	1	0
Haynes	.962	18	25	0	1	0
Hinske	.986	89	133	4	2	0
D. Johnson	1.000	1	3	0	0	0
E. Johnson	1.000	2	4	0	0	0
Perez	1.000	23	53	1	0	1
Riggans	—	1	0	0	0	0
Ruggiano	.981	42	49	2	1	1
Upton	.983	143	378	16	7	5
Zobrist	1.000	19	29	1	0	0

DURHAM BULLS

TRIPLE-A

INTERNATIONAL LEAGUE

Batting	B-T	HT	WT	DOB	AVG	vLH	vRH	G	AB	R	H	2B	3B	HR	RBI	BB	HBP	SH	SF	SO	SB	CS	SLG	OBP
Aybar, Willy	B-R	5-11	200	3-9-83	.300	.300	.300	5	20	3	6	3	0	0	3	4	0	0	0	1	0	0	.450	.417
Bannon, Jeff	R-R	6-3	180	8-21-79	.241	.286	.227	17	58	7	14	3	0	4	8	3	0	1	1	12	0	1	.500	.274
2-team total (9 Syracuse)					.258	—	—	26	89	12	23	4	0	5	17	5	1	1	2	21	0	4	.472	.299
Brignac, Reid	R-L	6-3	180	1-16-86	.250	.236	.256	97	352	43	88	26	2	9	43	25	2	1	6	93	5	2	.412	.299
Cannizaro, Andy	R-R	5-10	170	12-19-78	.240	.266	.224	51	171	16	41	8	0	1	14	17	2	5	3	18	1	0	.304	.311
2-team total (25 Buffalo)					.267	—	—	76	255	31	68	12	0	4	28	24	2	5	3	25	1	0	.361	.331
DiFelice, Mike	R-R	6-2	205	5-28-69	.217	.212	.219	68	217	19	47	13	0	3	24	15	2	0	2	53	0	0	.318	.271
Gimenez, Hector	B-R	5-10	210	9-28-82	.226	.200	.238	43	146	11	33	8	2	2	16	8	1	1	1	36	0	0	.349	.269
Gomes, Jonny	R-R	6-1	225	11-22-80	.252	.171	.292	26	107	19	27	11	0	2	14	12	3	0	1	32	0	1	.411	.341
Guzman, Joel	R-R	6-6	250	11-24-84	.248	.268	.238	116	436	52	108	23	0	20	72	19	1	0	8	103	1	2	.438	.276
Haynes, Nathan	L-L	5-9	170	9-7-79	.253	.273	.243	77	277	28	70	8	2	2	24	11	3	4	2	59	13	3	.318	.287
Jamieson, Alex	L-R	5-11	205	4-7-83	.143	.000	.174	9	28	4	4	0	0	0	0	5	0	0	0	8	0	0	.143	.273
Jaso, John	L-R	6-2	205	9-19-83	.278	.278	.278	31	108	14	30	7	0	5	24	10	0	0	0	14	1	1	.481	.339
Johnson, Dan	L-R	6-2	215	8-10-79	.307	.275	.325	113	394	85	121	23	0	25	83	84	1	0	7	75	0	1	.556	.424
Johnson, Elliot	B-R	6-0	185	3-9-84	.261	.231	.276	107	387	49	101	26	5	9	50	33	2	5	0	104	15	3	.424	.322
Johnson, Josh	R-R	6-0	205	11-3-82	.169	.227	.148	31	83	10	14	3	0	2	10	8	2	2	0	33	1	0	.277	.258
Labandeira, Josh	R-R	5-7	180	2-25-79	.206	.167	.227	25	68	11	14	1	0	1	3	15	1	4	0	24	0	1	.265	.357
Longoria, Evan	R-R	6-2	210	10-7-85	.200	.300	.133	7	25	2	5	0	0	0	4	1	0	0	0	5	0	0	.200	.333
Merrill, Ronnie	B-R	6-1	185	11-13-78	.192	.200	.186	22	73	12	14	4	0	0	1	9	1	3	0	20	1	1	.247	.289
Nowak, Chris	R-R	6-5	225	2-21-83	.315	.250	.353	14	54	7	17	2	0	4	7	0	0	0	0	12	0	1	.352	.393
Owens, Jeremy	R-R	6-1	200	12-9-76	.149	.043	.205	18	67	5	10	0	0	3	7	2	0	0	0	21	1	0	.284	.174
Perez, Fernando	R-R	6-1	195	4-23-83	.288	.301	.280	129	511	86	147	17	11	5	36	58	2	5	3	156	43	12	.393	.361
Richard, Chris	L-L	6-2	210	6-7-74	.293	.286	.298	131	467	82	137	32	4	26	88	55	10	1	6	127	5	0	.546	.375
Rodriguez, John	L-L	6-0	205	1-20-78	.259	.200	.283	26	85	12	22	3	0	6	12	10	1	0	0	26	0	1	.506	.344
Ruggiano, Justin	R-R	6-2	205	4-12-82	.315	.310	.318	66	257	49	81	18	3	11	51	22	5	0	5	77	20	3	.537	.374
Weber, Jon	L-L	5-10	190	11-24-78	.265	.297	.255	108	389	58	103	24	4	13	51	40	3	2	5	99	11	6	.447	.334
Zobrist, Ben	B-R	6-3	200	5-26-81	.366	.333	.386	20	71	15	26	3	0	4	13	15	0	1	1	16	4	1	.577	.471

Pitching	B-T	HT	WT	DOB	W	L	ERA	G	GS	CG	SV	IP	H	R	ER	HR	BB	SO	AVG	vLH	vRH	K/9	BB/9
Andrade, Steve	R-R	6-1	260	2-6-78	0	1	7.80	10	0	0	0	15	23	15	13	4	6	13	.338	.382	.294	7.80	3.60
Balfour, Grant	R-R	6-2	190	12-30-77	1	0	0.38	15	0	0	0	24	5	1	1	1	10	39	.067	.100	.029	14.83	3.80
Bean, Colter	R-R	6-6	255	1-16-77	0	0	3.86	3	0	0	0	5	4	3	2	1	4	7	.222	.375	.100	13.50	7.71
Birkins, Kurt	L-L	6-2	190	8-11-80	2	3	7.52	36	1	0	0	41	57	34	34	4	28	29	.331	.338	.326	6.42	6.20
Cummings, Jeremy	R-R	6-2	215	11-7-76	8	3	2.87	16	14	0	1	88	76	33	28	10	23	77	.230	.219	.246	7.90	2.36
Davis, Wade	R-R	6-5	220	9-7-85	4	2	2.72	9	9	0	0	53	39	16	16	5	24	55	.205	.225	.188	9.34	4.08
DeBarr, Nick	R-R	6-4	220	8-24-83	7	5	4.73	50	0	0	1	78	77	50	41	10	39	53	.262	.297	.231	6.12	4.50
Dohmann, Scott	R-R	6-1	200	2-13-78	0	2	3.46	33	0	0	20	42	35	16	16	2	12	49	.227	.241	.211	10.58	2.59
Henderson, Brian	L-L	5-11	195	5-19-82	0	1	4.87	14	0	0	0	20	25	16	11	4	11	10	.325	.222	.415	4.43	4.87
Hendrickson, Ben	R-R	6-4	205	2-4-81	10	9	4.58	29	27	0	0	149	155	88	76	12	64	81	.271	.275	.265	4.88	3.86
Kazmir, Scott	L-L	6-0	190	1-24-84	0	0	1.80	1	1	0	0	5	3	1	1	1	1	3	.167	.000	.375	5.40	1.80
Lynn, Kevin	R-R	5-11	185	11-12-78	0	2	4.34	8	2	0	0	19	18	13	9	5	15	11	.254	.200	.335	5.30	2.41
Mason, Chris	R-R	6-1	190	7-1-84	3	10	6.21	33	17	0	0	109	144	82	75	19	41	90	.333	.339	.325	7.45	3.40
Medlock, Calvin	R-R	5-10	195	11-8-82	3	3	4.57	41	0	0	0	63	67	42	32	7	32	40	.270	.217	.328	5.71	4.57
Munter, Scott	R-R	6-6	260	3-7-80	1	1	4.84	16	0	0	0	22	31	19	12	2	6	14	.320	.326	.315	5.64	2.42
Niemann, Jeff	R-R	6-9	280	2-28-83	9	5	3.59	24	24	3	0	133	101	60	53	15	50	128	.207	.242	.162	8.66	3.38
Phillips, Heath	L-L	6-3	200	3-24-82	1	1	2.86	9	3	0	0	22	23	7	7	2	11	18	.271	.286	.263	7.36	4.50
2-team total (35 Scranton/W-B)					4	5	4.75	44	7	0	0	78	90	46	41	7	33	61	—		—	7.07	3.82
Price, David	L-L	6-6	225	8-26-85	1	1	4.50	4	4	0	0	18	22	10	9		9	17	.301	.278	.309	8.50	4.50
Prochaska, Mike	L-L	6-1	210	5-23-80	3	4	6.70	11	9	0	0	46	72	38	34	9	14	22	.356	.333	.368	4.34	2.76
Ryu, J.K.	R-R	6-3	225	5-30-83	1	2	4.38	5	5	0	0	25	26	12	12	1	9	19	.280	.296	.256	6.93	3.28
Salas, Juan	R-R	6-2	210	11-21-78	4	5	2.62	28	0	0	1	45	32	13	13	2	11	55	.201	.238	.160	10.68	2.22
Talbot, Mitch	R-R	6-2	200	10-17-83	13	9	3.86	28	28	1	0	161	165	79	69	9	35	141	.263	.232	.300	7.48	1.96
Thayer, Dale	R-R	6-0	195	12-17-80	3	1	2.77	52	0	0	9	68	73	26	21	2	24	76	.268	.271	.266	10.01	3.16

Fielding

Catcher	PCT	G	PO	A	E	DP	PB
DiFelice	.978	68	500	43	12	6	9
Gimenez	.967	26	184	18	7	2	2
Jamieson	.968	9	56	4	2	0	2
Jaso	1.000	26	186	13	0	3	2
J. Johnson	.994	24	145	15	1	1	2

First Base	PCT	G	PO	A	E	DP
Aybar	1.000	1	8	0	0	1
Gimenez	1.000	1	1	0	0	0
Guzman	1.000	3	29	3	0	2
D. Johnson	.992	29	223	29	2	22
J. Johnson	1.000	1	1	0	0	0
Richard	.992	117	988	62	9	67
Weber	1.000	1	2	0	0	0

Second Base	PCT	G	PO	A	E	DP
Aybar	.882	3	2	13	2	0
Bannon	.947	8	14	22	2	5
Brignac	1.000	4	5	9	0	2
Cannizaro	.940	35	47	93	9	19

	PCT	G	PO	A	E	DP
E. Johnson	.963	81	110	200	12	36
Labandeira	.962	13	23	28	2	6
Merrill	1.000	4	6	6	0	2
Zobrist	1.000	3	4	9	0	1

Third Base	PCT	G	PO	A	E	DP
Aybar	1.000	2	0	2	0	0
Bannon	1.000	4	6	8	0	3
Cannizaro	1.000	12	8	15	0	1
Guzman	.937	90	66	141	14	9
D. Johnson	.933	10	6	22	2	2
J. Johnson	—	1	0	0	0	0
Labandeira	.867	6	7	6	2	1
Longoria	1.000	7	3	14	0	2
Nowak	1.000	13	10	23	0	3
Zobrist	1.000	6	6	12	0	0

Shortstop	PCT	G	PO	A	E	DP
Bannon	.929	3	4	9	1	1
Brignac	.970	92	137	249	12	48
Cannizaro	.750	1	1	2	1	0

	PCT	G	PO	A	E	DP
Guzman	1.000	6	6	17	0	3
E. Johnson	.976	20	32	48	2	6
Labandeira	.857	1	3	3	1	1
Merrill	.962	18	20	56	3	9
Zobrist	.964	7	7	20	1	3

Outfield	PCT	G	PO	A	E	DP
Bannon	1.000	2	4	0	0	0
Gomes	.966	15	25	3	1	1
Guzman	.500	2	2	0	2	0
Haynes	.978	75	132	3	3	0
D. Johnson	1.000	8	12	2	0	0
E. Johnson	.950	11	17	2	1	0
Nowak	1.000	1	1	2	0	1
Owens	.980	18	46	2	1	0
Perez	.980	126	280	10	6	2
Richard	1.000	8	2	0	0	0
Rodriguez	1.000	17	26	0	0	0
Ruggiano	.977	64	126	3	3	1
Weber	.972	105	161	11	5	0

MONTGOMERY BISCUITS   DOUBLE-A

SOUTHERN LEAGUE

Batting	B-T	HT	WT	DOB	AVG	vLH	vRH	G	AB	R	H	2B	3B	HR	RBI	BB	HBP	SH	SF	SO	SB	CS	SLG	OBP
Albernaz, Craig	R-R	5-8	177	10-30-82	.340	.333	.344	14	47	10	16	2	1	1	9	4	0	2	0	9	0	0	.489	.392
Andrus, Erold	B-L	6-2	170	7-16-84	.255	.254	.256	128	466	61	119	27	7	7	59	53	3	2	7	91	3	2	.388	.331
Asanovich, Josh	R-R	6-2	185	1-31-83	.230	.188	.243	95	282	38	65	11	1	4	29	58	4	4	1	49	0	4	.319	.368
Baldelli, Rocco	R-R	6-4	200	9-25-81	.297	.294	.300	13	37	6	11	1	0	3	8	6	1	0	0	7	0	1	.568	.409
Cottrell, Patrick	R-R	5-11	179	3-16-82	.223	.185	.241	59	206	29	46	6	1	4	24	14	1	1	1	34	2	1	.320	.275
Eldridge, Rashad	B-R	6-1	185	10-16-81	.290	.255	.302	118	435	70	126	19	6	5	55	64	6	8	2	88	24	10	.395	.387
Hall, J.T	L-R	6-3	210	5-19-84	.243	.220	.252	56	189	28	46	13	1	5	19	21	2	2	2	61	1	1	.402	.322
Hughes, Rhyne	L-L	6-2	175	9-9-83	.268	.165	.299	107	395	57	106	27	1	14	52	46	8	0	1	112	2	1	.448	.356
Jamieson, Alex	L-R	5-11	205	4-7-83	.000	—	.000	3	4	0	0	0	0	0	0	1	0	0	0	2	0	0	.000	.200
Jaso, John	L-R	6-2	205	9-19-83	.271	.288	.267	85	284	51	77	13	2	7	43	62	6	1	3	33	1	0	.405	.408
Martinez, Gabriel	L-R	6-2	180	5-17-83	.276	.233	.291	133	511	69	141	29	0	20	93	49	5	0	3	107	0	0	.450	.343
Merrill, Ronnie	B-R	6-1	185	11-13-78	.263	.241	.269	103	377	64	99	13	7	5	42	58	3	10	5	67	6	2	.374	.361
Nowak, Chris	R-R	6-5	225	2-21-83	.295	.257	.307	122	461	80	136	35	4	15	77	55	13	0	6	78	6	5	.486	.381
Pedroza, Sergio	L-R	6-1	180	2-23-84	.248	.172	.269	87	298	33	74	16	0	5	35	35	7	1	1	78	13	5	.352	.340
Raburn, Johnny	B-R	6-0	164	2-16-79	.235	.250	.229	101	353	41	83	7	5	0	33	31	1	4	5	47	15	5	.283	.295
Spring, Matt	R-R	6-2	215	11-7-84	.248	.284	.235	70	246	28	61	16	1	9	30	22	3	0	3	68	0	1	.431	.314
Walton, Neil	R-R	6-5	180	2-23-84	.253	.273	.245	20	75	6	19	4	0	0	8	7	1	2	1	18	1	1	.307	.321

Pitching	B-T	HT	WT	DOB	W	L	ERA	G	GS	CG	SV	IP	H	R	ER	HR	BB	SO	AVG	vLH	vRH	K/9	BB/9
Andrade, Steve	R-R	6-1	260	2-6-78	5	3	1.18	31	1	0	5	46	23	9	6	1	31	56	.150	.206	.111	11.04	6.11
Barratt, Jonathan	R-L	5-9	165	3-19-85	0	1	19.64	4	0	0	0	4	7	8	8	1	3	3	.438	.333	.500	7.36	7.36
Bean, Colter	R-R	6-6	255	1-16-77	3	5	4.07	41	1	0	11	55	53	30	25	4	24	63	.259	.261	.257	10.25	3.90
Cromer, Jason	R-L	6-4	226	12-11-80	5	3	3.96	29	0	0	0	75	92	41	33	5	24	54	.301	.294	.304	6.48	2.88
Davis, Wade	R-R	6-5	220	9-7-85	9	6	3.85	19	19	0	0	108	104	49	46	7	42	81	.261	.265	.258	6.77	3.51
De Los Santos, Richard	R-R	6-1	175	6-4-84	5	5	3.42	14	12	0	1	79	75	32	30	4	24	39	.251	.228	.267	4.44	2.73
Deago, Roger	R-L	5-10	180	6-21-77	2	5	2.95	59	0	0	4	82	78	37	27	4	38	61	.252	.230	.264	6.67	4.15
Flanagan, Jeremy	R-R	6-3	215	4-14-81	0	1	8.66	14	0	0	0	18	30	21	17	4	7	9	.366	.385	.357	4.58	3.57
Frontz, Neal	R-R	6-3	190	4-6-84	0	2	2.82	18	0	0	7	22	28	7	7	3	8	16	.308	.273	.328	6.45	3.22
Gonzalez, Jino	L-L	6-2	180	9-5-82	2	4	5.44	37	11	0	2	88	89	54	53	7	57	68	.267	.290	.257	6.98	5.85
Hellickson, Jeremy	R-R	6-1	185	4-8-87	4	4	3.94	13	13	0	0	75	84	36	33	15	15	79	.292	.347	.251	9.44	1.79
Henderson, Brian	L-L	5-11	195	5-19-82	1	2	4.20	30	0	0	1	30	37	17	14	2	12	19	.308	.236	.369	5.70	3.60
Houser, James	L-L	6-4	185	12-15-84	3	3	2.86	20	0	0	0	94	69	38	30	4	36	76	.205	.214	.201	7.25	3.82
Kamrath, Jeff	R-R	6-3	210	4-6-82	1	2	17.72	8	1	0	1	11	19	21	21	5	15	8	.388	.375	.390	6.75	12.66
Lynn, Kevin	R-R	5-11	185	11-12-78	1	0	6.75	10	2	0	0	23	25	19	17	5	11	17	.284	.250	.313	6.75	4.37
McGee, Jake	L-L	6-3	190	8-6-86	6	4	3.94	15	15	0	0	78	65	38	34	6	37	65	.230	.213	.236	7.53	4.29
Morlan, Eduardo	R-R	6-2	200	3-1-86	4	3	3.64	30	0	0	1	47	44	21	19	5	15	45	.242	.258	.233	8.62	2.87
Price, David	L-L	6-6	225	8-26-85	7	0	1.89	9	9	1	0	57	42	13	12	7	16	55	.206	.203	.207	8.68	2.53
Prochaska, Mike	L-L	6-1	210	5-23-80	4	6	5.68	16	15	0	0	90	108	64	57	9	31	43	.297	.239	.323	4.28	3.09
Reid, Ryan	L-R	5-11	215	4-24-85	5	4	4.66	31	0	0	4	46	41	34	24	1	31	53	.232	.242	.225	10.29	6.02
Rollins, Heath	R-R	6-1	190	5-25-85	1	1	2.88	4	4	0	0	25	22	9	8	2	6	23	.244	.324	.196	8.28	2.16
Till, Brock	R-R	5-10	210	7-1-80	0	1	7.43	10	0	0	0	13	18	13	11	3	4	12	.305	.308	.304	8.10	2.70
Townsend, Wade	R-R	6-4	230	2-22-83	1	3	7.66	13	2	0	0	22	22	29	19	5	17	17	.253	.250	.255	6.85	6.85
Wlodarczyk, Mike	L-L	6-5	230	12-2-82	0	4	8.90	10	6	0	0	30	56	35	30	3	20	15	.412	.421	.408	4.45	5.93

Fielding

Catcher	PCT	G	PO	A	E	DP	PB
Albernaz	1.000	14	114	17	0	3	4
Jamieson	.923	3	11	1	1	0	0
Jaso	.978	72	494	39	12	2	6
Spring	.991	56	403	38	4	7	4

First Base	PCT	G	PO	A	E	DP
Hughes	.984	86	718	39	12	78
Martinez	.988	38	323	20	4	24
Nowak	1.000	17	153	9	0	16

Second Base	PCT	G	PO	A	E	DP
Asanovich	.979	95	183	244	9	49
Cottrell	.975	18	41	38	2	13
Raburn	1.000	36	59	91	0	27

Third Base	PCT	G	PO	A	E	DP
Cottrell	.969	41	28	95	4	9
Martinez	.875	3	3	4	1	1
Nowak	.933	98	80	183	19	17
Raburn	—	1	0	0	0	0

Shortstop	PCT	G	PO	A	E	DP
Merrill	.974	102	130	281	11	49
Raburn	.957	24	33	56	4	14
Walton	.970	20	38	59	3	15

Outfield	PCT	G	PO	A	E	DP
Andrus	.977	126	237	13	6	4

	PCT	G	PO	A	E	DP
Baldelli	.750	4	3	0	1	0
Eldridge	.981	118	249	7	5	0
Hall	.976	53	79	1	2	0
Martinez	.872	25	41	0	6	0
Nowak	1.000	6	6	4	0	1
Pedroza	.951	70	129	7	7	0
Raburn	.951	38	54	4	3	0

VERO BEACH DEVIL RAYS
FLORIDA STATE LEAGUE
HIGH CLASS A

Batting	B-T	HT	WT	DOB	AVG	vLH	vRH	G	AB	R	H	2B	3B	HR	RBI	BB	HBP	SH	SF	SO	SB	CS	SLG	OBP
Albernaz, Craig	R-R	5-8	177	10-30-82	.128	.182	.111	18	47	3	6	0	0	1	7	4	1	0	0	7	0	0	.191	.212
Ashley, Nevin	R-R	6-2	210	8-14-84	.235	.212	.241	102	327	37	77	12	1	4	26	49	8	1	1	79	5	6	.315	.348
Aybar, Willy	B-R	5-11	200	3-9-83	.250	.000	.333	3	12	1	3	0	0	0	1	1	0	0	0	2	0	0	.250	.308
Baldelli, Rocco	R-R	6-4	200	9-25-81	.216	.300	.185	11	37	3	8	1	0	2	8	4	1	0	0	10	2	0	.405	.310
Brennan, Jackson	R-R	6-0	185	8-28-82	.231	.000	.257	15	39	3	9	1	0	0	2	10	1	0	0	13	1	3	.256	.400
Callender, Joey	R-R	6-0	165	11-25-83	.220	.254	.210	86	282	20	62	11	0	1	25	10	3	3	3	34	5	4	.270	.252
De La Rosa, Jairo	R-R	6-2	170	9-8-85	.253	.279	.245	88	273	27	69	9	2	6	24	14	1	4	1	68	2	4	.366	.291
Fields, Matt	R-R	6-5	235	7-8-85	.228	.167	.246	132	482	62	110	25	2	18	57	33	15	0	1	134	9	4	.400	.298
Fontaine, Chase	L-R	6-1	200	10-22-85	.217	.286	.208	38	120	11	26	4	1	0	7	16	0	1	0	34	0	3	.267	.309
Gimenez, Hector	B-R	5-10	210	9-28-82	.194	.212	.188	38	134	11	26	2	1	4	21	15	0	1	2	32	0	0	.313	.272
Groce, Garrett	R-R	6-1	190	4-24-83	.235	.235	.235	100	349	39	82	18	1	2	27	42	5	5	4	97	5	7	.309	.323
Hall, J.T	L-R	6-3	210	5-19-84	.291	.189	.311	64	220	27	64	13	3	5	28	25	8	0	0	42	3	4	.445	.383
Hall, Matt	R-R	6-0	180	3-10-87	.185	.368	.137	32	92	7	17	5	0	0	5	11	1	1	1	19	1	1	.239	.276
Jennings, Desmond	R-R	6-2	180	10-30-86	.259	.190	.281	24	85	17	22	5	1	2	6	14	0	2	1	16	5	2	.412	.360
Lopez, Christian	R-R	6-1	185	10-10-84	.224	.136	.241	44	134	8	30	6	0	2	11	4	0	1	2	23	0	1	.313	.243
Matulia, John	L-L	6-0	175	8-19-86	.282	.265	.287	82	291	36	82	12	2	2	23	24	4	12	2	52	10	8	.357	.343
Navarro, Dioner	B-R	5-9	205	2-9-84	.400	.750	.167	4	10	4	4	1	0	1	4	6	2	0	0	1	1	0	.800	.667
Paxton, Ian	R-R	6-1	210	9-4-83	.100	.000	.143	4	10	0	1	0	0	0	0	0	0	0	0	1	0	0	.100	.100
Pena, Carlos	L-L	6-2	215	5-17-78	.000	.000	.000	1	4	0	0	0	0	0	0	1	1	0	0	0	0	0	.000	.200
Powell, Pedro	B-R	5-7	145	5-20-84	.265	.243	.275	39	117	20	31	4	0	0	6	27	1	7	1	19	23	4	.299	.404
Royster, Ryan	R-R	6-2	210	7-25-86	.265	.234	.274	118	426	50	113	13	3	9	58	32	2	2	110	5	7	3	.373	.318
Stewart, Quinn	R-R	6-0	190	8-28-83	.189	.281	.160	41	132	10	25	9	0	4	18	10	5	2	1	54	4	0	.348	.270
Suarez, Cesar	R-R	5-11	170	8-17-83	.258	.198	.273	123	480	43	124	21	2	6	52	16	6	3	7	47	18	7	.348	.287
Walton, Neil	R-R	6-5	180	2-23-84	.224	.315	.202	80	272	30	61	14	1	2	22	22	1	1	0	55	5	5	.305	.285
Zobrist, Ben	B-R	6-3	200	5-26-81	.286	—	.286	4	14	1	4	1	0	0	2	0	0	0	1	2	0	0	.357	.267

Pitching	B-T	HT	WT	DOB	W	L	ERA	G	GS	CG	SV	IP	H	R	ER	HR	BB	SO	AVG	vLH	vRH	K/9	BB/9
Baker, Brian	R-R	6-5	190	1-10-83	5	5	3.49	46	0	0	1	70	60	28	27	5	17	55	.231	.298	.193	7.11	2.20
Butler, Joshua	R-R	6-5	195	12-11-84	0	2	6.35	3	3	0	0	17	18	13	12	1	5	10	.269	.233	.297	5.29	2.65
2-team total (20 Brevard County)					0	5	5.53	23	23	0	0	99	104	66	61	11	45	73	—	—	—	6.61	4.08
Downs, Darin	R-L	6-3	190	12-26-84	0	3	6.00	10	1	0	0	21	24	15	14	1	9	24	.276	.435	.219	10.29	3.86
2-team total (17 Daytona)					2	3	4.22	27	1	0	0	49	53	26	23	1	22	49	—	—	—	9.00	4.04
Frontz, Neal	R-R	6-3	190	4-6-84	0	2	1.38	37	0	0	19	52	35	8	8	1	3	41	.192	.247	.156	7.10	2.08
Garza, Matt	R-R	6-4	205	11-26-83	0	0	9.82	1	1	0	0	4	8	4	4	0	3	4	.471	.750	.385	9.82	7.36
Hellickson, Jeremy	R-R	6-1	185	4-8-87	7	1	2.00	14	14	0	0	77	64	19	17	7	5	83	.224	.254	.200	9.74	0.59
Hernandez, Carlos	B-L	5-10	200	4-22-80	2	1	1.04	6	6	0	0	26	11	3	3	0	6	25	.131	.107	.143	8.65	2.08
James, Craig	R-R	6-1	175	3-10-83	2	0	3.18	9	1	0	0	23	25	11	8	1	7	19	.281	.361	.226	7.54	2.78
Kazmir, Scott	L-L	6-0	190	1-24-84	0	1	4.70	2	2	0	0	8	8	5	4	2	0	7	.250	.154	.316	8.22	0.00
Kelly, Chris	R-R	6-3	200	7-14-82	8	4	5.67	44	0	0	1	73	75	51	46	9	44	37	.273	.255	.284	4.56	5.42
Lynn, Kevin	R-R	5-11	185	11-12-78	0	1	4.50	7	1	0	0	10	10	5	5	2	3	7	.263	.263	.263	6.30	2.70
Mann, Brandon	L-L	6-2	165	5-16-84	3	12	4.82	25	23	0	0	131	144	88	70	18	39	103	.278	.283	.276	7.09	2.69
Morse, Ryan	L-L	6-3	200	2-23-83	2	11	4.09	28	19	0	0	132	146	76	60	11	44	80	.281	.322	.264	5.45	3.00
Noel, Wilton	R-R	6-5	180	1-1-83	2	6	4.21	26	7	0	0	66	70	40	31	8	23	46	.259	.327	.219	6.24	3.12
Owen, Ryan	L-L	6-4	200	7-26-84	2	6	4.74	35	1	0	0	49	53	35	26	5	24	44	.273	.339	.246	8.03	4.38
Price, David	L-L	6-6	225	8-26-85	4	0	1.82	6	6	0	0	35	28	7	7	0	7	37	.220	.111	.250	9.61	1.82
Reid, Ryan	L-R	5-11	215	4-24-85	3	0	0.29	21	0	0	8	31	14	2	1	0	3	45	.136	.171	.113	13.06	0.87
Reyes, Al	R-R	6-1	230	4-10-70	0	1	3.00	6	6	0	0	6	4	2	2	1	0	6	.174	.000	.235	9.00	0.00
Rollins, Heath	R-R	6-1	190	5-25-85	5	1	3.30	23	21	1	0	136	118	59	50	15	27	115	.228	.257	.207	7.59	1.78
Tiffany, Chuck	L-L	6-1	195	1-25-85	1	2	3.46	21	6	0	0	42	33	19	16	5	3	33	.217	.298	.181	6.70	7.13
Townsend, Wade	R-R	6-4	230	2-22-83	0	4	5.28	15	7	0	0	44	44	26	26	5	22	39	.265	.286	.255	7.92	4.47
Walker, Matt	R-R	6-3	195	8-16-86	4	7	4.86	22	9	0	0	67	66	41	36	8	47	48	.256	.269	.247	6.48	6.35
Wlodarczyk, Mike	L-L	6-5	230	12-2-82	4	1	2.70	26	1	0	2	47	42	16	14	3	12	47	.244	.327	.208	9.06	2.31

Fielding

Catcher	PCT	G	PO	A	E	DP	PB
Albernaz	.990	15	83	17	1	1	2
Ashley	.986	82	588	63	9	2	4
Fontaine	1.000	1	8	0	0	0	1
Gimenez	.971	9	62	5	2	0	0
Lopez	.987	36	200	21	3	3	6
Navarro	1.000	2	16	1	0	0	1
Paxton	1.000	2	6	1	0	0	1

First Base	PCT	G	PO	A	E	DP
Fields	.986	131	1179	56	17	111
J. Hall	1.000	2	17	0	0	2
Paxton	1.000	1	3	0	0	0
Walton	1.000	1	7	0	0	2

Second Base	PCT	G	PO	A	E	DP
Aybar	1.000	2	5	10	0	3
Brennan	1.000	1	3	1	0	0

	PCT	G	PO	A	E	DP
Callender	.980	79	135	209	7	53
Fontaine	.912	24	36	68	10	14
Suarez	1.000	13	23	38	0	9
Walton	.932	29	48	76	9	12
Zobrist	1.000	1	2	2	0	0

Third Base	PCT	G	PO	A	E	DP
Aybar	—	1	0	0	0	0
Callender	.923	8	1	11	1	4

De La Rosa	—	1	0 0 0 0
M. Hall	.933	5	4 10 1 1
Suarez	.928	111	55 214 21 21
Walton	.962	18	7 43 2 3
Zobrist	1.000	1	0 2 0 0
Shortstop	**PCT**	**G**	**PO A E DP**
De La Rosa	.920	83	107 214 28 47
M. Hall	.967	27	46 72 4 17

Lopez	1.000	1	2 3 0 0
Walton	.961	34	47 75 5 16
Zobrist	.667	1	0 2 1 0
Outfield	**PCT**	**G**	**PO A E DP**
Albernaz	—	1	0 0 0 0
Ashley	—	1	0 0 0 0
Brennan	1.000	13	12 0 0 0
De La Rosa	1.000	4	7 1 0 0

Groce	.990	94	186	3	2	1
J. Hall	.941	22	47	1	3	0
Jennings	.986	24	70	1	1	0
Matulia	.988	79	155	3	2	1
Powell	1.000	35	72	2	0	0
Royster	.970	105	157	6	5	1
Stewart	.941	35	59	5	4	1
Walton	.900	5	8	1	1	0

COLUMBUS CATFISH   LOW CLASS A

SOUTH ATLANTIC LEAGUE

Batting	B-T	HT	WT	DOB	AVG	vLH	vRH	G	AB	R	H	2B	3B	HR	RBI	BB	HBP	SH	SF	SO	SB	CS	SLG	OBP
Brennan, Jackson	R-R	6-0	185	8-28-82	.189	.250	.178	15	53	8	10	1	0	0	2	10	2	1	0	14	1	1	.208	.338
Callender, Joey	R-R	6-0	165	11-25-83	.245	.167	.290	13	49	3	12	1	0	0	8	2	0	1	1	9	0	0	.265	.269
Cipriano, Cody	R-R	6-0	200	1-7-85	.195	.191	.196	42	149	24	29	11	2	4	19	24	4	1	1	37	7	0	.376	.320
Dhaenens, Seth	L-R	6-2	175	5-20-84	.181	.156	.188	50	144	19	26	4	0	0	13	17	1	4	2	36	2	0	.208	.268
Fontaine, Chase	L-R	6-1	200	10-22-85	.269	.279	.264	55	186	36	50	9	2	3	24	32	1	4	2	37	2	5	.387	.376
Fronk, Reid	L-R	6-1	185	7-21-86	.287	.310	.277	124	429	76	123	29	4	17	83	74	13	1	11	103	18	11	.492	.398
Loyola, Maiko	R-R	5-11	174	7-19-85	.280	.299	.273	122	471	76	132	20	3	5	44	56	5	6	3	96	45	17	.367	.361
Luna, Omar	R-R	5-11	165	12-13-86	.251	.241	.255	111	390	54	98	19	2	1	31	16	1	5	1	58	19	10	.318	.282
Mayer, James	R-R	5-11	165	3-8-84	.043	.000	.071	8	23	0	1	0	0	0	2	3	0	1	0	4	0	0	.043	.154
McCormick, Mike	R-R	6-2	200	9-6-86	.216	.178	.231	106	375	37	81	15	1	13	49	31	2	1	5	93	2	1	.365	.276
O'Malley, Shawn	R-R	5-10	155	12-28-87	.237	.233	.238	91	334	48	79	14	3	0	23	34	11	8	2	77	28	14	.296	.325
Paxton, Ian	R-R	6-1	210	9-4-83	.270	.333	.250	31	89	6	24	4	0	3	13	6	0	0	0	21	0	0	.416	.316
Salem Jr., Emeel	L-L	6-0	180	2-11-85	.301	.364	.265	38	153	24	46	4	3	0	7	14	0	2	1	18	25	5	.366	.357
Sexton, Greg	R-R	6-2	205	2-8-85	.294	.336	.278	124	490	64	144	32	3	7	87	23	6	0	6	73	3	7	.414	.330
Stewart, Quinn	R-R	6-0	190	8-28-83	.283	.305	.275	64	226	49	64	10	2	8	44	27	2	0	4	61	11	4	.451	.359
Vogt, Stephen	L-R	6-3	215	11-1-84	.291	.339	.271	113	392	57	114	22	3	6	54	47	3	2	4	48	6	1	.408	.368
Williams, Shawn	B-R	6-2	190	9-18-83	.278	.378	.232	46	144	15	40	8	0	0	10	4	2	2	0	31	0	0	.333	.307
Wrigley, Henry	R-R	6-3	180	8-9-86	.250	.198	.273	113	404	45	101	13	10	7	60	24	2	2	5	62	7	3	.384	.292

Pitching	B-T	HT	WT	DOB	W	L	ERA	G	GS	CG	SV	IP	H	R	ER	HR	BB	SO	AVG	vLH	vRH	K/9	BB/9
Baird, John	R-R	6-4	220	5-16-86	1	4	8.33	17	1	0	2	36	51	35	33	6	18	33	.338	.317	.362	8.33	4.54
Barnett, Travis	R-R	6-7	215	10-2-83	0	1	7.55	18	0	0	0	31	35	26	26	3	16	28	.285	.275	.292	8.13	4.65
Boggan, Kevin	R-R	6-2	195	5-2-85	1	4	3.10	36	0	0	5	73	70	31	25	8	16	55	.246	.328	.189	6.81	1.98
Cobb, Alex	R-R	6-1	180	10-7-87	9	7	3.29	25	25	0	0	140	113	59	51	16	35	97	.224	.206	.238	6.25	2.26
Darcy, Jesse	R-R	6-4	205	6-13-85	8	3	3.05	29	19	1	1	133	124	53	45	12	15	98	.248	.259	.240	6.63	1.02
Fessler, Chris	R-R	6-3	200	11-21-84	1	1	10.41	14	0	0	0	23	35	29	27	5	14	14	.350	.351	.349	5.40	5.40
Fines, Woods	R-R	6-4	180	8-14-85	0	3	7.32	6	4	0	0	20	23	19	16	2	8	9	.291	.385	.245	4.12	3.66
Flores, Brian	L-L	5-10	190	1-1-85	9	7	4.19	29	21	0	0	118	119	59	55	7	45	77	.263	.222	.275	5.87	3.43
Garcia, Justin	R-R	6-1	195	12-14-86	3	5	2.49	41	0	0	7	72	41	22	20	4	20	78	.162	.196	.135	9.71	2.49
Gibson, Glenn	L-L	6-4	195	9-21-87	4	8	7.44	22	12	0	0	79	104	75	65	12	41	49	.315	.370	.297	5.61	4.69
Hall, Jeremy	R-R	6-3	200	9-16-83	10	3	4.61	21	19	0	0	105	109	55	54	8	33	83	.271	.260	.281	7.09	2.82
Hinkle, Austin	R-R	6-1	200	5-24-86	3	4	2.51	33	0	0	13	47	32	15	13	2	19	67	.189	.145	.220	12.92	3.66
Johnson, Josh	R-R	6-0	180	10-6-84	4	8	5.79	28	13	0	0	87	100	61	56	9	35	59	.297	.257	.330	6.10	3.62
Mejias, Jose Angel	R-R	6-0	150	8-18-85	3	2	4.73	34	0	0	2	59	59	36	31	7	27	33	.260	.276	.250	5.03	4.12
Ragan, Jason	R-R	6-1	175	12-12-82	8	9	4.33	24	22	0	0	108	136	70	52	15	26	65	.302	.330	.281	5.42	2.17
Risser, Travis	R-R	6-2	210	1-8-85	3	0	4.08	21	0	0	6	35	37	16	16	3	11	31	.270	.305	.244	7.90	2.80

Fielding

Catcher	PCT	G	PO	A	E	DP	PB
McCormick	.985	99	642	69	11	5	15
Paxton	.981	29	139	19	3	0	3
Vogt	1.000	17	94	22	0	0	3
Williams	1.000	2	4	1	0	0	0

First Base	PCT	G	PO	A	E	DP
Dhaenens	1.000	14	105	4	0	6
Vogt	.986	16	132	13	2	10
Williams	1.000	3	4	0	0	0
Wrigley	.991	110	974	71	9	88

Second Base	PCT	G	PO	A	E	DP
Callender	1.000	7	6	16	0	3
Cipriano	.965	33	45	94	5	23
Dhaenens	.922	23	33	62	8	19

	PCT	G	PO	A	E	DP
Fontaine	.972	32	55	85	4	11
Luna	.974	38	62	90	4	20
Mayer	.944	6	7	10	1	1
Williams	1.000	1	8	4	0	1

Third Base	PCT	G	PO	A	E	DP
Callender	1.000	2	2	6	0	0
Dhaenens	.944	11	4	13	1	0
Fronk	1.000	2	2	4	0	0
Luna	.875	11	9	26	5	5
Mayer	—	1	0	0	0	0
Sexton	.940	114	89	227	20	19

Shortstop	PCT	G	PO	A	E	DP
Callender	.913	4	6	15	2	2
Dhaenens	1.000	1	1	1	0	0

	PCT	G	PO	A	E	DP
Fontaine	1.000	1	3	1	0	0
Luna	.953	61	126	200	16	33
O'Malley	.948	71	98	176	15	37

Outfield	PCT	G	PO	A	E	DP
Brennan	.970	15	30	2	1	1
Fronk	.995	111	201	10	1	3
Loyola	.960	119	257	4	11	0
Salem Jr.	1.000	36	55	1	0	0
Stewart	.966	59	110	2	4	0
Vogt	.992	67	108	10	1	0
Williams	1.000	10	12	0	0	0

HUDSON VALLEY RENEGADES   SHORT-SEASON

NEW YORK-PENN LEAGUE

Batting	B-T	HT	WT	DOB	AVG	vLH	vRH	G	AB	R	H	2B	3B	HR	RBI	BB	HBP	SH	SF	SO	SB	CS	SLG	OBP
Appel, Jason	L-L	6-1	180	6-11-86	.368	.455	.333	12	38	6	14	1	0	0	2	2	0	0	0	6	2	1	.395	.400
Beckham, Jeremy	R-R	5-10	175	6-1-86	.220	.200	.240	24	50	3	11	0	0	0	2	4	1	2	0	18	3	0	.220	.291
Beckham, Tim	R-R	6-0	188	1-27-90	.333	.500	.250	2	6	5	2	1	0	0	2	1	0	0	1	1	0	0	.500	.556
Biell, Dustin	L-R	6-0	175	3-19-89	.400	.750	.273	7	15	3	6	1	0	0	3	0	0	0	1	2	0	0	.467	.400
Carroll, Jeff	R-R	6-2	192	8-14-84	.197	.250	.168	54	147	10	29	3	0	2	20	9	1	2	1	29	3	0	.259	.247

	B-T	HT	WT	DOB	AVG	vLH	vRH	G	AB	R	H	2B	3B	HR	RBI	BB	HBP	SH	SF	SO	SB	CS	SLG	OBP
Corder, Jason	R-R	6-2	195	9-6-85	.306	.281	.317	50	206	29	63	12	2	5	36	10	3	1	3	37	1	0	.456	.342
Estrada, Robi	B-R	5-10	170	10-8-88	.242	.231	.248	63	244	42	59	7	4	1	13	31	2	3	0	51	12	4	.316	.332
Hall, Matt	R-R	6-2	180	3-10-87	.200	.250	.188	6	20	0	4	1	0	0	1	1	0	0	0	6	0	0	.250	.238
Hauschild, Tyler	R-R	6-0	210	11-24-85	.045	.167	.000	18	22	0	1	1	0	0	0	2	2	1	0	8	0	0	.091	.192
Jefferies, Jake	L-R	6-2	200	10-30-87	.315	.373	.288	66	238	32	75	16	3	2	41	21	4	0	1	22	1	1	.433	.379
Kang, Kyeong	L-L	6-2	200	2-6-88	.278	.247	.293	69	255	38	71	15	7	6	43	20	5	1	4	62	6	2	.463	.338
McKenna, Mike	R-R	6-0	195	2-13-86	.239	.211	.254	33	109	12	26	5	1	0	14	14	1	1	1	27	0	2	.303	.328
Mollicone, John	R-R	6-1	220	9-9-85	.254	.179	.297	50	185	18	47	8	1	1	20	13	0	1	2	38	1	0	.324	.300
Reynolds, Justin	R-R	6-3	195	11-13-86	.271	.240	.287	50	144	21	39	9	2	2	25	7	1	0	2	37	10	1	.403	.305
Ross, Michael	R-	5-8	180	8-11-86	.222	.243	.200	61	216	20	48	3	1	0	18	20	2	6	4	49	30	7	.245	.289
Scelfo, Anthony	L-R	5-10	195	9-19-86	.281	.275	.283	61	221	32	62	11	8	4	24	25	2	2	1	66	11	8	.457	.357
Sheridan, Mike	L-L	6-2	205	8-8-87	.321	.500	.274	31	78	14	25	5	2	0	5	4	0	0	0	12	1	0	.436	.354
Thomas, Mark	R-R	6-1	180	5-5-88	.234	.274	.200	52	158	17	37	7	2	3	12	9	1	1	1	43	1	1	.361	.278
Tweedy, Jason	L-R	6-0	170	9-29-86	.273	.235	.291	68	256	37	70	15	2	1	24	35	5	0	4	69	24	3	.359	.367

Pitching	B-T	HT	WT	DOB	W	L	ERA	G	GS	CG	SV	IP	H	R	ER	HR	BB	SO	AVG	vLH	vRH	K/9	BB/9
Andujar, Chris	R-R	6-2	180	8-24-87	3	4	5.65	15	15	0	0	65	81	48	41	2	31	57	.300	.282	.311	7.85	4.27
Bagley, Jamie	R-R	6-3	215	7-16-87	1	1	5.59	5	0	0	0	10	10	6	6	2	5	11	.263	.429	.167	10.24	4.66
Baird, John	R-R	6-4	220	5-16-86	1	3	5.48	11	3	0	2	21	24	19	13	1	11	24	.276	.342	.224	10.13	4.64
Barnese, Nick	R-R	6-2	170	1-11-89	5	3	2.45	13	13	0	0	66	52	26	18	1	24	84	.212	.200	.218	11.45	3.27
De Los Santos, Frank	L-L	6-0	165	11-17-87	4	5	5.40	11	11	0	0	57	73	40	34	2	16	44	.320	.209	.346	6.99	2.54
Della Grotta, Robert	R-R	6-2	220	9-18-84	2	2	2.97	18	0	0	0	33	28	16	11	0	19	32	.226	.167	.250	8.64	5.13
Dyer, Shane	R-R	6-3	185	3-9-88	3	4	3.68	14	14	0	0	59	62	29	24	4	19	46	.256	.307	.227	7.06	2.91
Echeverria, Diego	R-R	5-11	190	1-1-85	4	1	4.48	17	6	0	1	64	69	40	32	5	30	32	.274	.221	.306	4.48	4.20
Fleming, Marquis	R-L	6-1	181	9-11-86	1	2	3.86	16	1	0	1	35	31	18	15	6	14	33	.235	.277	.212	8.49	3.60
Gibson, Glenn	L-L	6-4	195	9-21-87	0	0	6.65	10	0	0	1	22	31	18	16	2	14	23	.337	.391	.319	9.55	5.82
Gorgen, Matt	R-R	6-0	210	1-27-87	1	1	1.96	22	0	0	13	23	7	5	5	2	5	35	.093	.107	.085	13.70	1.96
Hayes, Tyree	R-R	6-0	175	8-8-88	5	6	3.39	15	12	1	0	72	67	38	27	4	31	46	.247	.252	.244	5.78	3.89
Long, Matt	R-R	6-3	245	10-3-84	1	0	6.27	8	0	0	1	19	19	18	13	2	11	26	.250	.192	.280	12.54	5.30
Rafferty, Tommy	R-R	6-1	165	2-5-85	2	0	4.35	15	0	0	0	21	17	10	10	0	9	25	.221	.207	.229	10.89	3.92
Risser, Travis	R-R	6-2	210	1-8-85	1	1	1.45	13	0	0	2	19	19	3	3	0	8	14	.279	.250	.300	6.75	3.86
Satow, Josh	L-L	5-10	155	12-18-85	3	0	1.23	19	0	0	2	37	31	6	5	0	17	46	.235	.205	.247	11.29	4.17
Schenk, Neil	L-L	6-3	220	6-17-86	2	2	2.84	20	0	0	1	38	32	13	12	2	11	53	.229	.260	.211	12.55	2.61
Welch, Scott	R-R	6-4	180	11-8-82	1	0	13.50	5	0	0	0	5	14	9	8	1	2	5	.483	.625	.429	8.44	3.38

Fielding

Catcher	PCT	G	PO	A	E	DP	PB
Hauschild	.982	18	49	5	1	0	2
Jefferies	.990	20	193	9	2	0	3
Mollicone	.982	7	48	7	1	0	1
Thomas	.990	51	348	39	4	0	23

First Base	PCT	G	PO	A	E	DP
Carroll	1.000	24	160	14	0	11
Mollicone	.985	40	317	17	5	36
Sheridan	.995	29	184	11	1	10

Second Base	PCT	G	PO	A	E	DP
J. Beckham	.963	8	10	16	1	4
Ross	.965	58	107	139	9	30

Tweedy	.941	13	18	30	3	6

Third Base	PCT	G	PO	A	E	DP
J. Beckham	1.000	4	3	5	0	1
Carroll	.929	26	13	52	5	3
Scelfo	.917	8	5	17	2	2
Tweedy	.944	49	23	112	8	10

Shortstop	PCT	G	PO	A	E	DP
J. Beckham	1.000	1	1	1	0	0
T. Beckham	1.000	2	3	4	0	1
Carroll	1.000	1	1	1	0	1
Estrada	.938	60	88	167	17	28
Hall	.964	5	6	21	1	1

Tweedy	.907	10	9	30	4	8

Outfield	PCT	G	PO	A	E	DP
Appel	1.000	11	19	1	0	0
J. Beckham	1.000	6	5	1	0	0
Biell	1.000	5	9	0	0	0
Corder	.952	49	75	4	4	0
Kang	.973	66	106	2	3	0
McKenna	1.000	6	11	0	0	0
Reynolds	.928	46	62	2	5	0
Scelfo	.963	52	76	2	3	0

PRINCETON DEVIL RAYS — ROOKIE

APPALACHIAN LEAGUE

Batting	B-T	HT	WT	DOB	AVG	vLH	vRH	G	AB	R	H	2B	3B	HR	RBI	BB	HBP	SH	SF	SO	SB	CS	SLG	OBP
Acosta, Mayobanex	R-R	6-1	205	11-20-87	.268	.250	.273	43	168	8	45	14	2	2	33	10	0	0	2	25	1	3	.411	.306
Beckham, Jeremy	R-R	5-10	175	6-1-86	.260	.421	.161	18	50	6	13	4	0	2	7	3	0	0	7	3	0	.340	.383
Beckham, Tim	R-R	6-0	188	1-27-90	.243	.133	.265	46	177	30	43	12	0	2	14	13	2	2	3	43	5	1	.345	.297
Biell, Dustin	L-R	6-0	175	3-19-89	.152	.121	.159	48	165	16	25	5	2	0	4	12	0	2	0	74	5	2	.206	.209
Bryles, Brian	R-R	6-1	170	11-4-89	.216	.205	.220	39	148	22	32	2	2	0	6	13	3	0	0	38	8	4	.257	.293
Francisco, Tomas	R-R	6-0	210	4-4-88	.241	.150	.269	23	87	7	21	6	0	1	7	1	2	0	2	18	0	0	.345	.261
Genao, David	R-R	5-11	210	12-15-86	.268	.310	.238	20	71	7	19	4	0	0	7	9	1	0	1	17	0	0	.324	.354
Jones, D.J.	L-L	6-1	185	12-15-87	.227	.320	.208	47	150	12	34	5	3	1	9	14	0	1	0	36	6	0	.320	.293
Luis, Diogenes	R-	5-10	169	5-7-87	.218	.147	.236	46	174	30	38	2	4	0	10	23	4	2	2	47	11	4	.276	.320
Marchena, Luis	R-R	5-10	155	11-21-89	.188	.143	.200	10	32	2	6	0	0	0	0	1	1	0	0	6	0	0	.188	.235
Morrison, Ty	L-R	6-2	170	7-22-90	.265	.143	.296	10	34	2	9	0	0	0	1	2	0	0	1	12	3	1	.265	.297
Novas, Ramon	R-R	6-2	170	10-14-87	.223	.295	.200	50	179	16	40	5	2	3	18	14	1	1	1	43	3	2	.324	.282
Otero, Elias	B-R	6-2	166	12-19-87	.332	.283	.348	55	208	38	69	13	7	5	32	21	4	1	3	45	3	0	.534	.398
Reynolds, Burt	R-R	6-1	190	9-13-88	.289	.327	.279	58	232	37	67	10	4	6	36	17	4	0	3	70	7	2	.444	.344
Reynolds, Justin	R-R	6-3	195	11-13-86	.222	.125	.263	9	27	4	6	1	2	0	4	0	0	0	6	1	1	.407	.323
Sonoqui, Eli	L-L	5-11		1-20-88	.269	.381	.243	59	219	27	59	12	0	3	29	22	2	1	1	73	2	0	.365	.340

Pitching	B-T	HT	WT	DOB	W	L	ERA	G	GS	CG	SV	IP	H	R	ER	HR	BB	SO	AVG	vLH	vRH	K/9	BB/9
Amargos, Jordi	R-R	5-11	165	2-5-86	0	1	6.75	14	0	0	0	27	27	23	20	4	15	19	.255	.237	.265	6.41	5.06
Ayers, Kyle	R-R	6-4	220	9-6-89	1	3	4.50	11	0	0	0	32	46	22	16	2	3	25	.336	.367	.318	7.03	0.84
Bagley, Jamie	R-R	6-3	215	7-16-87	2	2	2.70	15	0	0	5	23	24	9	7	2	1	29	.261	.188	.300	11.19	0.39
Chapa, Angel	R-R	6-2	170	6-14-87	3	3	5.34	14	0	0	0	30	28	18	18	6	8	31	.235	.205	.250	9.20	2.37

	B-T	HT	WT	DOB	W	L	ERA	G	GS	CG	SV	IP	H	R	ER	HR	BB	SO	AVG	vLH	vRH	K/9	BB/9
Chavez, Kevin	R-R	6-3	206	6-24-89	1	7	6.22	11	11	0	0	46	54	32	32	5	18	36	.290	.288	.292	6.99	3.50
Colome, Alexander	R-R	6-2	184	12-31-88	0	5	6.80	12	11	0	0	46	50	45	35	5	26	52	.272	.300	.258	10.10	5.05
Cruz, Joe	R-R	6-4	190	7-20-88	1	3	3.17	13	13	0	0	54	61	29	19	5	14	62	.270	.253	.278	10.33	2.33
De La Cruz, Jose	L-L	5-11	173	8-16-87	0	2	7.50	6	0	0	0	6	5	5	5	0	9	10	.263	.000	.313	15.00	13.50
Dettrich, Julius	L-L	6-4	175	9-23-88	0	1	2.70	2	1	0	0	3	3	4	1	1	1	2	.214	.000	.273	2.70	2.70
Furdal, Brad	R-R	6-2	185	10-21-90	2	1	5.52	7	2	0	0	15	17	11	9	0	7	9	.293	.421	.231	5.52	4.30
Jarman, Michael	L-L	6-1	195	6-6-85	2	2	1.52	18	0	0	4	30	20	5	5	0	9	36	.190	.167	.198	10.92	2.73
Long, Matt	R-R	6-3	245	10-3-84	0	1	10.38	7	0	0	1	9	15	11	10	1	2	9	.395	.438	.364	9.35	2.08
Luck, Chris	R-R	6-3	175	7-10-89	6	0	2.25	13	0	0	1	36	30	10	9	3	8	35	.227	.250	.216	8.75	2.00
McEachern, Jason	R-R	6-2	160	10-12-90	3	0	1.44	9	2	0	0	25	17	5	4	2	8	16	.193	.240	.175	5.76	2.88
Moore, Matt	L-L	6-2	205	6-18-89	2	2	1.66	12	12	0	0	54	30	22	10	0	19	77	.154	.250	.135	12.75	3.15
Puentes, Julio	R-R	6-5	220	2-2-86	0	0	9.00	1	0	0	0	1	1	1	1	0	3	1	.250	.000	.333	9.00	27.00
Santana, Juan	R-R	6-0	180	3-5-86	0	2	5.40	13	0	0	2	28	34	24	17	6	7	23	.281	.261	.293	7.31	2.22
Shull, Trevor	R-R	6-4	180	8-7-90	0	0	9.90	7	0	0	0	10	13	11	11	1	8	6	.325	.438	.250	5.40	7.20
Smith, Shawn	R-L	6-3	180	9-9-90	1	1	7.07	8	1	0	0	14	20	12	11	0	9	12	.328	.091	.380	7.71	5.79
Southern, Mike	R-R	6-1	190	1-8-87	0	0	9.00	5	0	0	0	6	8	6	6	1	3	2	.320	.500	.235	3.00	4.50
Suarez, Albert	R-R	6-2	186	10-8-89	0	2	3.92	11	9	0	0	44	41	28	19	3	7	37	.232	.231	.232	7.63	1.44

Fielding

Catcher	PCT	G	PO	A	E	DP	PB
Acosta	.992	39	337	50	3	5	6
Francisco	.980	21	174	20	4	0	6
Genao	1.000	2	9	1	0	0	0

First Base	PCT	G	PO	A	E	DP
Genao	.946	6	31	4	2	2
Sonoqui	.977	58	527	29	13	35

Second Base	PCT	G	PO	A	E	DP
J. Beckham	.964	7	13	14	1	4
Luis	.987	16	32	45	1	9

	PCT	G	PO	A	E	DP
Marchena	.962	10	12	13	1	4
Otero	.925	31	48	88	11	10

Third Base	PCT	G	PO	A	E	DP
J. Beckham	.941	7	6	10	1	0
Genao	1.000	1	1	1	0	0
Luis	.842	5	3	13	3	0
B. Reynolds	.795	50	28	100	33	10

Shortstop	PCT	G	PO	A	E	DP
J. Beckham	1.000	3	3	8	0	0
T. Beckham	.924	37	62	96	13	15

	PCT	G	PO	A	E	DP
Luis	.939	23	34	74	7	13

Outfield	PCT	G	PO	A	E	DP
Biell	1.000	47	71	2	0	0
Bryles	.971	38	66	1	2	0
Jones	.934	44	55	2	4	1
Luis	1.000	1	1	0	0	0
Morrison	1.000	10	11	0	0	0
Novas	.937	46	54	5	4	2
J. Reynolds	1.000	7	7	0	0	0

DSL RAYS   ROOKIE

DOMINICAN SUMMER LEAGUE

Batting	B-T	HT	WT	DOB	AVG	vLH	vRH	G	AB	R	H	2B	3B	HR	RBI	BB	HBP	SH	SF	SO	SB	CS	SLG	OBP
Caminero, Leandro	R-R	6-1	185	10-24-89	.224	.207	.227	58	214	22	48	8	1	1	20	15	3	0	2	47	5	3	.285	.282
Contreras, Ruben	B-R	6-2	190	8-18-87	.259	.308	.247	55	201	27	52	11	5	2	34	40	0	0	3	38	9	2	.393	.377
Cuello, Juan	R-R	5-11	170	5-9-89	.293	.344	.285	63	232	44	68	5	5	1	28	28	3	4	2	35	15	5	.371	.374
De Castro, Raynill	R-R	6-3	175	12-11-89	.239	.125	.254	22	67	6	16	2	0	0	5	7	1	1	0	22	2	2	.269	.320
Dorville, Edward	B-R	6-1	185	11-5-88	.250	.233	.253	55	204	40	51	10	2	2	16	28	2	4	2	66	16	6	.348	.343
Echavarria, Nelson	B-R	6-0	160	9-26-88	.177	.111	.189	34	124	22	22	4	1	0	8	10	0	0	0	41	8	3	.226	.239
Elie, Alexis	R-R	6-3	206	8-21-90	.226	.294	.211	27	93	6	21	2	1	2	19	4	4	1	1	29	0	0	.333	.284
Gomez, Hector	L-L	6-2	187	2-13-88	.234	.212	.238	58	197	35	46	7	1	4	28	44	1	0	1	55	13	1	.340	.374
Gomez, Jhonatan	R-R	6-1	180	11-13-88	.179	.091	.194	25	78	11	14	1	1	0	7	12	0	0	0	14	1	2	.218	.289
Guillen, Cesar	R-R	6-1	185	3-15-89	.343	.441	.324	53	204	45	70	14	2	2	36	21	3	0	3	16	14	4	.461	.407
Guzman, Braly	R-R	6-2	188	9-29-88	.185	.130	.196	38	130	15	24	5	0	2	13	4	6	0	0	31	0	2	.269	.243
Henriquez, Victor	R-R	6-0	170	4-1-86	.269	.240	.275	46	145	25	39	4	4	0	18	30	5	3	3	24	12	5	.352	.404
Isenia, Ludson	B-R	6-1	206	11-24-89	.053	.000	.077	7	19	2	1	0	0	0	4	0	0	0	8	0	3	.053	.217
Lafontaines, Jose	B-R	5-9	185	10-6-88	.333	.667	.167	2	9	3	3	0	1	0	1	0	0	0	1	0	0	.556	.333
Olivares, Gerardo	R-R	6-0	187	8-14-88	.278	.429	.245	55	194	29	54	13	0	4	34	19	6	1	2	25	5	2	.407	.357
Santana, Arturo	R-R	6-2	200	2-1-90	.221	.214	.222	30	77	7	17	2	1	1	11	11	2	1	2	20	0	1	.312	.326
Vasquez, Cristian	R-R	6-1	155	3-9-90	.163	.190	.157	47	129	15	21	4	2	0	4	26	1	3	0	59	4	1	.225	.308

Pitching	B-T	HT	WT	DOB	W	L	ERA	G	GS	CG	SV	IP	H	R	ER	HR	BB	SO	AVG	vLH	vRH	K/9	BB/9
Almonte, Wilmer	R-R	5-11	164	8-19-89	0	3	6.38	8	8	0	0	18	33	24	13	1	1	8	.384	.423	.367	3.93	0.49
Dominguez, Ney	L-L	6-2	160	7-17-91	0	1	4.00	7	2	0	0	9	8	5	4	0	6	8	.242	.000	.242	8.00	6.00
Fermin, Jose	R-R	6-1	180	9-16-90	0	3	5.59	18	2	0	0	29	30	29	18	2	23	18	.275	.200	.298	5.59	7.14
Galan, Genaro	L-L	6-2	196	1-20-88	0	1	—	1	1	0	0	0	0	1	1	0	1	0	.000	.000	.000	—	—
Guerrero, Joan	L-L	6-2	170	1-22-91	3	4	3.47	14	4	0	0	36	37	23	14	0	25	19	.262	.438	.240	4.71	6.19
Jasco, Joselo	R-R	6-0	170	10-12-88	1	5	5.06	15	0	0	0	21	15	14	12	1	16	16	.190	.154	.197	6.75	6.75
Lara, Braulio	L-L	6-1	180	12-20-88	2	2	3.97	17	3	0	0	34	28	21	15	1	21	39	.220	.000	.243	10.32	5.56
Liriano, Nelson	R-R	6-0	170	12-6-87	2	0	0.32	27	0	0	16	28	13	2	1	1	4	34	.131	.080	.149	10.80	1.27
Martinez, Carlos	R-R	5-11	160	5-17-89	1	1	4.35	9	0	0	1	10	11	9	5	0	6	8	.282	.083	.333	6.10	5.23
Mateo, Victor	R-R	6-5	180	7-27-89	3	4	4.07	14	7	0	0	49	41	35	22	3	24	33	.229	.228	.230	6.10	4.44
Mercedes, Aneuris	R-R	6-0	180	5-1-87	1	3	4.09	17	3	0	0	44	39	22	20	1	25	35	.242	.342	.211	7.16	5.11
Molina, Jose	L-L	5-11	160	6-26-91	0	3	3.74	18	0	0	0	34	26	18	14	0	21	26	.218	.375	.207	6.95	5.61
Monegro, Jose	R-R	6-2	180	3-22-90	2	4	2.94	12	12	0	0	49	44	26	16	1	8	24	.234	.163	.259	4.41	1.47
Ozoria, Ronny	R-R	6-3	185	6-5-89	0	1	6.75	17	0	0	0	21	22	18	16	3	18	16	.265	.133	.294	6.75	7.59
Perez, Elvin	R-R	6-0	165	3-3-86	4	3	2.22	24	0	0	1	36	33	12	9	0	11	32	.241	.375	.200	8.07	2.78
Reyes, Robinson	L-L	6-4	200	11-15-88	2	3	9.77	25	5	0	0	31	25	45	34	1	52	29	.223	.500	.208	8.33	14.94
Romero, Enny	L-L	6-3	165	1-24-91	1	0	2.76	10	0	0	0	16	11	9	5	0	8	20	.175	.333	.158	11.02	4.41
Suero, Eliazer	R-R	6-4	170	6-7-89	3	5	4.06	15	12	0	0	51	50	32	23	2	17	38	.253	.234	.258	6.71	3.00
Torres, Jose	R-R	6-2	180	4-18-91	1	1	4.71	16	0	0	0	29	25	21	15	4	11	20	.227	.375	.167	6.28	3.45
Wilsino, Juan	R-R	6-3	190	3-22-89	3	1	2.04	13	11	0	0	57	44	20	13	0	11	38	.214	.262	.193	5.97	1.73

Fielding

Catcher	PCT	G	PO	A	E	DP	PB
J. Gomez	.948	15	62	11	4	1	8
Olivares	.983	40	242	41	5	0	15
Santana	.960	29	149	19	7	0	12
Vasquez	.750	1	3	0	1	0	0

First Base	PCT	G	PO	A	E	DP
Contreras	1.000	12	114	3	0	9
Dorville	1.000	1	5	0	0	1
H. Gomez	.975	33	289	17	8	28
J. Gomez	.973	4	36	0	1	3
Guillen	.987	7	74	3	1	4
Guzman	.986	18	134	3	2	12
Henriquez	1.000	3	13	0	0	3

Second Base	PCT	G	PO	A	E	DP
Cuello	.986	56	124	157	4	32
Echavarria	.900	10	8	19	3	2
Henriquez	.889	2	4	4	1	1
Lafontaines	1.000	1	0	3	0	1
Romero	.857	1	2	4	1	0
Vasquez	.944	3	4	13	1	3

Third Base	PCT	G	PO	A	E	DP
Cuello	1.000	6	1	7	0	0
De Castro	.854	21	21	55	13	6
Guzman	.810	19	9	25	8	4
Henriquez	.920	32	24	79	9	6

Shortstop	PCT	G	PO	A	E	DP
Cuello	.571	1	2	2	3	1
Echavarria	.861	24	31	56	14	12
Henriquez	1.000	6	9	27	0	1
Lafontaines	1.000	1	1	6	0	1
Vasquez	.861	41	48	132	29	20

Outfield	PCT	G	PO	A	E	DP
Caminero	.968	58	115	6	4	2
Contreras	.947	38	70	2	4	0
Dorville	.953	47	75	6	4	2
Elie	.750	9	9	3	0	
H. Gomez	.953	26	38	3	2	1
Guillen	.986	36	63	5	1	0
Isenia	.909	6	9	1	1	0

VSL RAYS

ROOKIE

VENEZUELAN SUMMER LEAGUE

Batting	B-T	HT	WT	DOB	AVG	vLH	vRH	G	AB	R	H	2B	3B	HR	RBI	BB	HBP	SH	SF	SO	SB	CS	SLG	OBP
Acosta, Ronald	R-R	5-11	170	3-16-91	.216	.375	.172	11	37	3	8	1	0	0	2	0	0	0		9	0	0	.243	.216
Cabrera, Orlando	R-R	5-11	165	10-25-89	.000	—	.000	2	5	0	0	0	0	0	0	0	0	0		1	0	0	.000	.000
Cedeno, Julio	R-R	6-2	185	8-25-89	.283	.383	.253	70	254	38	72	17	4	8	37	25	3	0	2	29	5	2	.476	.352
Cipriota, Jacinto	R-R	5-11	180	3-23-90	.308	.455	.278	18	65	8	20	2	0	2	11	4	3	1	1	8	2	0	.431	.370
Colmenares, Jose	R-R	5-11	158	3-8-90	.274	.235	.285	43	157	24	43	5	0	2	19	12	8	1	1	15	7	4	.344	.354
Fukunaga, Claudio	B-R	5-10	165	11-5-87	.224	.220	.226	48	156	15	35	6	1	1	16	9	6	2	1	23	6	5	.295	.291
Gonzalez, Felix	B-R	5-10	165	4-4-90	.183	.233	.172	47	164	25	30	4	0	0	16	9	2	2	3	32	10	3	.207	.230
Guerra, Omar	R-R	5-11	173	12-29-86	.287	.289	.287	61	202	49	58	9	1	0	17	21	35	4	0	27	15	3	.342	.442
Hernandez, Nahum	R-R	6-0	180	9-20-89	.251	.224	.259	66	243	42	61	8	3	4	31	29	7	3	3	46	3	5	.358	.344
Isenia, Ludson	B-R	6-1	206	11-24-89	.174	.143	.183	50	161	16	28	4	1	1	9	21	1	3	0	72	0	6	.230	.273
Maldonado, Darwin	R-R	6-0	160	7-10-89	.143	.300	.117	21	70	10	10	4	0	0	3	1	0	2	1	26	1	2	.200	.189
Nagahashi, Mauricio	R-R	6-1	165	4-12-90	.168	.211	.158	34	95	9	16	2	1	0	3	7	5	0	0	27	2	2	.211	.262
Quinonez, Jonathan	R-R	6-1	187	11-27-90	.263	.125	.300	59	228	33	60	10	2	9	41	5	10	1	3	29	4	2	.443	.305
Sacks, German	R-R	6-1	185	4-20-91	.198	.176	.203	33	86	10	17	4	0	3	8	15	1	1	0	41	1	0	.349	.324
Segovia, Alejandro	R-R	6-0	181	4-27-90	.270	.375	.244	48	159	19	43	6	0	4	19	14	6	3	1	17	3	1	.384	.350
Torres, Alejandro	R-R	6-1	178	9-30-88	.316	.242	.338	67	263	37	83	14	0	5	43	13	6	6	2	29	0	1	.426	.359
Ugueto, Eliecer	R-R	6-1	161	9-18-88	.150	.000	.158	8	20	1	3	0	0	0	0	0	1	0	0	9	0	0	.150	.227

Pitching	B-T	HT	WT	DOB	W	L	ERA	G	GS	CG	SV	IP	H	R	ER	HR	BB	SO	AVG	vLH	vRH	K/9	BB/9
Andrade, Francisco	L-L	5-9	150	8-9-90	2	1	7.85	16	0	0	0	29	43	27	25	2	18	23	.358	.714	.336	7.22	5.65
Bencomo, Omar	R-R	6-1	168	2-10-89	1	6	4.45	15	8	0	0	61	68	36	30	4	3	55	.274	.314	.264	8.16	0.45
Crespo, Ali	R-R	6-4	209	2-1-90	2	1	4.97	12	2	0	1	25	23	18	14	1	6	6	.240	.167	.256	2.13	2.13
Duarte, Hugo	R-R	6-1	169	1-7-90	3	2	6.18	14	2	0	0	28	27	21	19	1	18	25	.262	.250	.265	8.13	5.86
Duenas, Carlos	L-L	5-11	165	12-28-87	4	2	4.93	21	5	0	0	49	52	34	27	0	25	34	.280	.167	.283	6.20	4.56
Espana, Luis	R-R	6-4	172	3-27-89	1	1	4.87	13	2	0	0	20	26	17	11	2	11	8	.317	.227	.350	3.54	4.87
Guedez, Raul	R-R	5-10	190	9-27-84	0	3	3.86	28	0	0	5	49	49	28	21	2	12	42	.271	.200	.288	7.71	2.20
Linares, Joice	L-L	5-10	182	4-21-90	1	5	3.68	14	6	0	1	37	40	22	15	2	12	24	.290	.167	.295	5.89	2.95
Lopez, Kevin	R-R	6-2	173	10-22-88	5	2	3.65	21	0	0	0	44	32	21	18	3	25	30	.198	.300	.183	6.09	5.08
Lopez, Reinaldo	R-R	6-2	221	4-27-91	2	2	3.97	6	3	0	0	11	10	5	5	0	3	10	.256	.333	.233	7.94	
Marquez, Juan	R-R	6-1	176	2-18-91	0	2	9.77	9	0	0	0	16	13	19	17	1	21	10	.250	.500	.175	5.74	12.06
Mavares, Deivis	R-R	5-11	156	9-19-86	5	2	1.48	27	0	0	6	49	30	11	8	0	17	62	.178	.256	.154	11.47	3.14
Mujica, Juan	L-L	5-10	185	3-21-90	0	1	7.50	12	2	0	0	12	12	12	10	3	11	6	.286	.000	.308	6.00	8.25
Quinonez, Eduar	R-R	6-3	182	8-9-89	2	1	3.80	13	6	0	0	45	44	25	19	4	18	33	.256	.294	.246	6.60	3.60
Rodriguez, Wilking	R-R	6-1	160	3-2-90	0	1	3.71	10	8	0	0	27	26	11	11	3	6	29	.260	.208	.276	9.79	2.03
Sanchez, Daniel	R-R	6-2	180	5-29-89	0	0	5.49	14	6	0	0	20	16	17	12	0	33	8	.250	.385	.216	3.66	15.10
Yendis, Luis	R-R	6-3	178	7-19-89	0	2	2.65	16	12	0	0	54	47	21	16	4	19	41	.234	.268	.225	6.79	3.15

Fielding

Catcher	PCT	G	PO	A	E	DP	PB
Colmenares	.949	5	32	5	2	0	0
Segovia	.977	23	138	33	4	5	4
Torres	.984	45	308	68	6	8	3

First Base	PCT	G	PO	A	E	DP
Cabrera	1.000	1	12	3	0	3
Colmenares	.984	8	57	5	1	13
Fukunaga	1.000	1	3	0	0	0
Isenia	1.000	1	8	0	0	0
E. Quinonez	1.000	1	8	0	0	0
J. Quinonez	.975	10	74	4	2	7
Sacks	.984	15	118	4	2	10
Segovia	.989	20	171	9	2	12
Torres	.994	20	163	14	1	22
Ugueto	1.000	1	9	1	0	0

Second Base	PCT	G	PO	A	E	DP
Acosta	1.000	1	2	3	0	0
Cipriota	.932	12	33	22	4	12
Colmenares	.981	22	58	48	2	13
Fukunaga	.963	33	69	61	5	20
Gonzalez	—	1	0	0	0	0
Guerra	.950	6	12	7	1	0
E. Quinonez	1.000	1	1	1	0	1
Ugueto	.875	5	7	7	2	1

Third Base	PCT	G	PO	A	E	DP
Cedeno	.913	64	52	169	21	15
Isenia	—	1	0	0	0	0
J. Quinonez	.737	4	4	10	5	1
Torres	.947	6	6	12	1	1
Ugueto	.000	1	0	0	2	0

Shortstop	PCT	G	PO	A	E	DP
Acosta	.884	9	14	24	5	2
Cedeno	.889	9	9	23	4	2
Fukunaga	.896	12	20	40	7	8
Gonzalez	.883	45	81	146	30	30

Outfield	PCT	G	PO	A	E	DP
Fukunaga	1.000	1	2	0	0	0
Guerra	.900	37	49	5	6	1
Hernandez	.962	65	117	8	5	3
Isenia	.943	36	48	2	3	0
Maldonado	.929	16	26	0	2	0
Nagahashi	.905	19	18	1	2	0
E. Quinonez	1.000	1	2	0	0	0
J. Quinonez	.968	43	61	0	2	0
Sacks	1.000	3	4	0	0	0

Texas Rangers

BY EVAN GRANT

So much that happened to the Rangers in 2008 indicated an organization making dynamic strides forward.

Nolan Ryan arrived with Hall of Fame respectability as club president. Talent from recent drafts and trades blossomed throughout the minor league system and made impacts on the major league club. Josh Hamilton and his amazing story of redemption made the cover of Sports Illustrated, and Hamilton took the All-Star Game by storm. And the big league club rallied back from an awful April to finish in second place in the AL West—the team's best showing since 1999.

But, at the end of the year, the season seemed to be just another chapter in the same old Rangers story. Inadequate big league pitching doomed them.

The Rangers became the fifth AL team in the last 100 years to score and allow at least 900 runs in a season. They're negative run differential (-66) was the largest of the five teams.

And it was quite a wild ride getting there.

The Rangers nearly fired manager Ron Washington a month into the season after a 7-16 start, then rallied to the fringe of contention in early August before season-ending injuries to second baseman Ian Kinsler and outfielder David Murphy crippled the lineup.

That was evident in a season-turning 19-17 loss at Boston in early August. The Rangers rallied back from a 10-run deficit to take a late lead only to become the first AL team in 50 years to lose a game while scoring as many as 17 runs.

The starting rotation was the main culprit. Every member of the Opening Day rotation spent time on the disabled list. No pitcher reached 180 innings for the second consecutive season, and the Rangers (5.507) finished in a virtual tie with the Orioles (5.51) for the worst rotation ERA in the majors. Perhaps the team's most consistent starter was righthander Scott Feldman, who ended 2007 as a sidearm reliever, and began 2008 at Double-A Frisco after changing his arm angle. Feldman led the team with 13 quality starts.

The other bright spot for the rotation: lefthander Matt Harrison, acquired from Atlanta in the Mark Teixeira deal in 2007, won nine of 12 decisions after making his major league debut. Harrison finished with four consecutive wins and

PLAYERS OF THE YEAR

MAJOR LEAGUE: JOSH HAMILTON, OF

Hamilton was electrifying at the Home Run Derby at Yankee Stadium, and it was fitting. Traded from the Reds over the winter, he electrified all year in hitting .304/.371/.530 with 32 homers, 35 doubles and an American League-best 130 RBIs.

MINOR LEAGUE: DEREK HOLLAND, LHP

A draft-and-follow out of Wallace State (Ala.), Holland signed ahead of the 2007 draft and dominated all season. He finished 13-1, 2.27 with 157 strikeouts and 40 walks in almost 151 innings combined at three levels, ending with a playoff push at Double-A Frisco.

MIKE JANES

ORGANIZATION LEADERS

BATTING		*Minimum 250 at-bats
*AVG	Cruz, Nelson, Oklahoma	.342
R	Osuna, Renny, Clinton/Bakersfield	100
H	Osuna, Renny, Clinton/Bakersfield	178
TB	Cruz, Nelson, Oklahoma	266
2B	Tracy, Chad, Bakersfield/Frisco	40
3B	Three tied with	9
HR	Cruz, Nelson, Oklahoma	37
RBI	Gac, Ian, Clinton/Bakersfield	109
BB	Whittleman, John, Bakersfield/Frisco	89
SO	Gac, Ian, Clinton/Bakersfield	170
SB	Andrus, Elvis, Frisco	54
*OBP	Cruz, Nelson, Oklahoma	.429
*SLG	Cruz, Nelson, Oklahoma	.695

PITCHING		†Minimum 75 innings
W	Hunter, Tommy, Bakersfield/Frisco/Okla.	13
	Holland, Derek, Clinton/Bakersfield/Frisco	13
L	Schlact, Michael, Frisco	11
	Tatusko, Ryan, Clinton	11
†ERA	Holland, Derek, Clinton/Bakersfield/Frisco	2.27
G	White, Bill, Oklahoma/Bakersfield	51
GS	Phillips, Zachary, Bakersfield	28
SV	Madrigal, Warner, Frisco/Oklahoma	14
IP	Hunter, Tommy, Bakersfield/Frisco/Okla.	164
BB	Phillips, Zachary, Bakersfield	73
SO	Holland, Derek, Clinton/Bakersfield/Frisco	157
†AVG	Feliz, Neftali, Clinton/Frisco	.201

a 4.46 ERA over the season's final month.

The pitching woes could not, however, overshadow Hamilton. He won AL player of the month honors in April and May and stormed into the All-Star Game's starting lineup, then hit a record 28 home runs in the first round of the home run derby at Yankee Stadium.

General Manager: Jon Daniels. **Farm Director:** Scott Servais. **Scouting Director:** Ron Hopkins.

Class	Team	League	W	L	PCT	Finish*	Manager	Affiliate Since
Majors	Texas	American	79	83	.488	9th (14)	Ron Washington	—
Triple-A	Oklahoma RedHawks	Pacific Coast	76	68	.528	6th (16)	Bobby Jones	1983
Double-A	Frisco RoughRiders	Texas	84	56	.600	1st (8)	Scott Little	2003
High A	Bakersfield Blaze	California	62	78	.443	9th (10)	Damon Berryhill	2005
Low A	Clinton LumberKings	Midwest	78	59	.569	1st (14)	Mike Micucci	2003
Short-season	Spokane Indians	Northwest	51	25	.671	^1st (8)	Tim Hulett	2003
Rookie	AZL Rangers	Arizona	34	22	.607	3rd (9)	Bill Richardson	2003
Overall 2008 Minor League Record			385	308	.556	2nd		

* Finish in overall standings (No. of teams in league). ^League champion.

ORGANIZATION STATISTICS

TEXAS RANGERS

AMERICAN LEAGUE

Batting	B-T	HT	WT	DOB	AVG	vLH	vRH	G	AB	R	H	2B	3B	HR	RBI	BB	HBP	SH	SF	SO	SB	CS	SLG	OBP
Arias, Joaquin	R-R	6-1	165	9-21-84	.291	.417	.256	32	110	15	32	7	3	0	9	7	2	1	0	12	4	1	.409	.345
Blalock, Hank	L-R	6-1	200	11-21-80	.287	.277	.291	65	258	37	74	19	1	12	38	19	2	0	2	40	1	0	.508	.338
Boggs, Brandon	B-R	5-11	205	1-9-83	.226	.227	.226	101	283	30	64	17	4	8	41	44	3	1	3	93	3	2	.399	.333
Botts, Jason	B-R	6-5	250	7-26-80	.158	.231	.120	15	38	2	6	3	0	2	5	8	0	0	0	18	0	0	.395	.304
Bradley, Milton	B-R	6-0	225	4-15-78	.321	.341	.312	126	414	78	133	32	1	22	77	80	9	0	6	112	5	3	.563	.436
Broussard, Ben	L-L	6-2	230	9-24-76	.159	.125	.162	26	82	8	13	0	0	3	5	2	0	0	0	20	0	0	.268	.225
Byrd, Marlon	R-R	6-0	245	8-30-77	.298	.277	.308	122	403	70	120	28	4	10	53	46	9	2	2	62	7	2	.462	.380
Catalanotto, Frank	L-R	6-0	205	4-27-74	.274	.167	.280	88	248	28	68	23	1	2	21	20	6	3	1	29	1	1	.399	.342
Cruz, Nelson	R-R	6-3	230	7-1-80	.330	.419	.298	31	115	19	38	9	1	7	26	17	1	0	0	28	3	1	.609	.421
Davis, Chris	L-R	6-4	235	3-17-86	.285	.279	.287	80	295	51	84	23	2	17	55	20	1	0	1	88	1	2	.549	.331
Duran, German	R-R	5-10	185	8-3-84	.231	.271	.192	60	143	22	33	6	1	3	16	7	2	5	1	32	1	1	.350	.275
Ellison, Jason	R-R	5-10	180	4-4-78	.231	.333	.200	9	13	5	3	0	0	0	2	1	0	0	0	1	0	0	.231	.286
Hamilton, Josh	L-L	6-4	235	5-21-81	.304	.288	.313	156	624	98	190	35	5	32	130	64	1	0	9	126	9	1	.530	.371
Kinsler, Ian	R-R	6-0	200	6-22-82	.319	.281	.332	121	518	102	165	41	4	18	71	45	6	7	7	67	26	2	.517	.375
Laird, Gerald	R-R	6-1	225	11-13-79	.276	.245	.288	95	344	54	95	24	0	6	41	23	6	4	4	63	2	4	.398	.329
Melhuse, Adam	B-R	6-2	210	3-27-72	.200	.250	.167	8	20	1	4	0	0	1	2	0	0	0	0	11	0	0	.200	.273
Metcalf, Travis	R-R	6-3	215	8-17-82	.232	.162	.368	23	56	11	13	2	0	6	14	3	1	0	1	12	0	0	.589	.279
Murphy, David	L-L	6-4	205	10-18-81	.275	.258	.282	108	415	64	114	28	3	15	74	31	0	2	6	70	7	2	.465	.321
Ramirez, Max	R-R	5-11	175	10-11-84	.217	.071	.281	17	46	8	10	1	0	2	9	6	3	0	0	15	0	0	.370	.345
Roberts, Ryan	R-R	5-11	190	9-19-80	.000	.000	—	1	1	0	0	0	0	0	0	0	0	0	0	1	0	0	.000	.000
Saltalamacchia, Jarrod	B-R	6-4	235	5-2-85	.253	.158	.311	61	198	27	50	13	0	3	26	31	0	0	1	74	0	2	.364	.352
Shelton, Chris	R-R	6-0	215	6-26-80	.216	.184	.250	41	97	14	21	5	0	2	11	17	0	3	0	33	1	0	.330	.333
Teagarden, Taylor	R-R	6-1	200	12-21-83	.319	.091	.389	16	47	10	15	5	0	6	17	5	1	0	0	19	0	0	.809	.396
Vazquez, Ramon	L-R	5-11	195	8-21-76	.290	.188	.310	105	300	44	87	18	3	6	40	38	0	5	4	66	0	1	.430	.365
Young, Michael	R-R	6-1	200	10-19-76	.284	.305	.276	155	645	102	183	36	2	12	82	55	2	0	6	109	10	0	.402	.339

Pitching	B-T	HT	WT	DOB	W	L	ERA	G	GS	CG	SV	IP	H	R	ER	HR	BB	SO	AVG	vLH	vRH	K/9	BB/9
Benoit, Joaquin	R-R	6-3	220	7-26-77	3	2	5.00	44	0	0	1	45	40	28	25	6	35	43	.233	.184	.282	8.60	7.00
Diaz, Jose	R-R	6-0	230	4-13-80	0	0	0.00	1	0	0	0	1	1	1	0	0	1	2	.333	.000	.500	18.00	9.00
Feldman, Scott	L-R	6-5	210	2-7-83	6	8	5.29	28	25	0	0	151	161	103	89	22	56	74	.280	.291	.269	4.40	3.33
Francisco, Frank	R-R	6-3	230	9-11-79	3	5	3.13	58	0	0	5	63	47	24	22	7	26	83	.200	.193	.207	11.79	3.69
Fukumori, Kazuo	R-R	6-0	175	8-4-76	0	0	20.25	4	0	0	0	4	11	9	9	2	4	1	.500	.250	.643	2.25	9.00
Gabbard, Kason	L-L	6-3	200	4-8-82	2	3	4.82	12	12	0	0	56	64	36	30	5	39	33	.292	.233	.307	5.30	6.27
German, Franklyn	R-R	6-7	260	1-20-80	1	3	2.08	17	0	0	0	22	18	5	5	0	13	15	.243	.300	.205	6.23	5.40
Gordon, Brian	L-R	6-0	205	8-16-78	0	0	2.25	3	0	0	0	4	4	1	1	0	0	1	.250	.100	.500	2.25	0.00
Guardado, Eddie	R-L	6-0	225	10-2-70	3	3	3.65	55	0	0	4	49	38	20	20	3	17	28	.220	.167	.252	5.11	3.10
2-team total (9 Minnesota)					4	4	4.15	64	0	0	4	56	50	26	26	4	19	33	—	—	—	5.27	3.04
Harrison, Matt	L-L	6-4	225	9-16-85	9	3	5.49	15	15	1	0	84	100	57	51	12	31	42	.300	.310	.297	4.52	3.33
Hunter III, Tommy	R-R	6-3	255	7-3-86	0	2	16.36	3	3	0	0	11	23	20	20	4	3	9	.404	.393	.414	7.36	2.45
Hurley, Eric	R-R	6-4	195	9-17-85	1	2	5.47	5	5	0	0	25	26	15	15	5	9	13	.268	.269	.267	4.74	3.28
Jennings, Jason	L-R	6-2	235	7-17-78	0	5	8.56	6	6	0	0	27	35	27	26	8	18	12	.307	.333	.281	3.95	5.93
Littleton, Wes	R-R	6-3	200	9-2-82	0	0	6.00	12	0	0	0	18	18	12	12	1	8	14	.265	.241	.282	7.00	4.00
Loe, Kameron	R-R	6-7	240	9-10-81	1	0	3.23	14	0	0	0	31	36	18	11	3	8	20	.288	.400	.208	5.87	2.35
Madrigal, Warner	R-R	6-0	200	3-21-84	0	2	4.75	31	1	0	1	36	36	22	19	4	14	22	.263	.323	.208	5.50	3.50
Mathis, Doug	R-R	6-3	220	6-7-83	2	1	6.85	8	4	0	0	22	37	20	17	3	14	9	.381	.396	.364	3.63	5.64
McCarthy, Brandon	R-R	6-7	205	7-7-83	1	1	4.09	5	5	0	0	22	20	11	10	3	10	10	.244	.293	.195	4.09	3.27
Mendoza, Luis	R-R	6-3	210	10-31-83	3	8	8.67	25	11	0	1	63	97	74	61	7	25	35	.343	.336	.350	4.97	3.55
Millwood, Kevin	R-R	6-4	230	12-24-74	9	10	5.07	29	29	3	0	169	220	104	95	18	49	125	.312	.273	.354	6.67	2.61
Murray, A.J.	B-L	6-3	220	3-17-82	1	0	3.52	2	2	0	0	8	12	4	3	0	3	5	.343	.600	.300	5.87	3.52
Nippert, Dustin	R-R	6-8	225	5-6-81	3	5	6.40	20	6	0	0	72	92	52	51	10	37	55	.308	.263	.364	6.91	4.65
Padilla, Vicente	R-R	6-2	220	9-27-77	14	8	4.74	29	29	1	0	171	185	100	90	26	65	127	.275	.312	.240	6.68	3.42
Ponson, Sidney	R-R	6-1	260	11-2-76	4	1	3.88	9	9	1	0	56	71	36	24	3	16	25	.307	.312	.303	4.04	2.59
2-team total (16 New York)					8	5	5.04	25	24	1	0	136	170	89	76	14	48	58	—	—	—	3.85	3.18

	B-T	HT	WT	DOB																			
Ramirez, Elizardo	B-R	6-0	190	1-28-83	0	1	30.38	1	0	0	0	3	8	9	9	1	2	1	.500	.333	.600	3.38	6.75
Rupe, Josh	R-R	6-2	210	8-18-82	3	1	5.14	46	0	0	0	89	93	52	51	8	46	53	.284	.308	.262	5.34	4.63
Tejeda, Robinson	R-R	6-3	230	3-24-82	0	0	9.00	4	0	0	0	6	5	6	6	1	5	4	.217	.267	.125	6.00	7.50
2-team total (25 Kansas City)					2	2	3.97	29	1	0	0	45	27	23	20	4	24	45	—	—	—	8.93	4.76
White, Bill	L-L	6-3	225	11-20-78	0	0	20.25	8	0	0	0	4	7	9	9	1	11	1	.368	.200	.429	2.25	24.75
Wilson, C.J.	L-L	6-1	210	11-18-80	2	2	6.02	50	0	0	24	46	49	35	31	8	27	41	.268	.265	.269	7.96	5.24
Wright, Jamey	R-R	6-5	230	12-24-74	8	7	5.12	75	0	0	0	84	93	57	48	5	35	60	.283	.286	.280	6.40	3.74

Fielding

Catcher	PCT	G	PO	A	E	DP	PB
Laird	.986	88	523	35	8	7	6
Melhuse	1.000	6	18	2	0	0	0
Ramirez	.984	12	56	5	1	2	0
Saltalamacchia	.976	54	345	17	9	6	6
Teagarden	.961	12	67	6	3	0	1

First Base	PCT	G	PO	A	E	DP
Blalock	.996	34	262	13	1	24
Botts	.964	8	51	2	2	7
Broussard	.987	26	202	22	3	32
Catalanotto	1.000	33	215	15	0	31
Davis	.997	51	358	34	1	52
Ramirez	1.000	3	20	4	0	5
Shelton	.989	39	241	20	3	21
Vazquez	1.000	1	2	0	0	0

Second Base	PCT	G	PO	A	E	DP
Arias	.983	30	48	67	2	19
Duran	1.000	17	24	22	0	3
Kinsler	.974	121	292	390	18	123
Vazquez	1.000	11	20	15	0	6

Third Base	PCT	G	PO	A	E	DP
Blalock	.951	31	24	54	4	6
Davis	.962	32	31	44	3	5
Duran	.921	30	13	45	5	2
Laird	1.000	2	0	3	0	0
Melhuse	1.000	2	1	2	0	0
Metcalf	.971	19	15	18	1	6
Shelton	—	1	0	0	0	0
Vazquez	.936	70	30	117	10	16

Shortstop	PCT	G	PO	A	E	DP
Duran	1.000	2	2	6	0	1
Metcalf	—	1	0	0	0	0
Vazquez	.962	26	23	52	3	15
Young	.984	151	193	465	11	113

Outfield	PCT	G	PO	A	E	DP
Boggs	.980	79	138	7	3	2
Botts	1.000	4	3	0	0	0
Bradley	.940	20	43	4	3	3
Byrd	.980	118	281	7	6	0
Catalanotto	.967	26	29	0	1	0
Cruz	.973	31	72	1	2	1
Duran	1.000	7	11	0	0	0
Ellison	1.000	7	11	0	0	0
Hamilton	.983	141	345	7	6	5
Murphy	.991	106	223	4	2	1

OKLAHOMA REDHAWKS

TRIPLE-A

PACIFIC COAST LEAGUE

Batting	B-T	HT	WT	DOB	AVG	vLH	vRH	G	AB	R	H	2B	3B	HR	RBI	BB	HBP	SH	SF	SO	SB	CS	SLG	OBP
Arias, Joaquin	R-R	6-1	165	9-21-84	.296	.300	.295	104	432	59	128	15	9	7	49	19	3	4	2	53	23	5	.421	.329
Benjamin, Casey	L-R	6-2	190	8-1-80	.245	.238	.247	74	233	35	57	2	3	8	27	35	0	7	5	58	0	0	.382	.337
Blalock, Hank	R-R	6-1	200	11-21-80	.400	—	.400	2	5	1	2	0	0	0	0	1	0	0	0	1	0	0	.400	.500
Boggs, Brandon	B-R	5-11	205	1-9-83	.309	.167	.360	18	68	12	21	4	3	0	6	7	0	0	1	20	1	1	.456	.368
Botts, Jason	B-R	6-5	250	7-26-80	.242	.250	.241	18	66	13	16	6	0	4	11	9	1	0	0	25	0	0	.515	.342
Byrd, Marlon	R-R	6-0	245	8-30-77	.313	.500	.286	4	16	3	5	2	0	0	3	2	0	0	0	6	0	1	.438	.389
Cruz, Nelson	R-R	6-3	230	7-1-80	.342	.360	.337	103	383	93	131	18	3	37	99	56	5	0	4	87	24	8	.695	.429
Davis, Chris	L-R	6-4	235	3-17-86	.333	.310	.341	31	111	25	37	7	1	10	31	13	1	0	2	29	2	0	.685	.402
Duran, German	R-R	5-10	185	8-3-84	.260	.222	.271	31	177	12	35	3	2	1	6	7	0	1	1	12	0	1	.390	.318
Ellison, Jason	R-R	5-10	180	4-4-78	.239	.208	.248	120	477	65	114	21	4	2	45	63	8	4	4	77	14	10	.312	.335
Fox, Adam	R-R	5-11	200	11-23-81	.190	.273	.146	19	63	6	12	2	0	3	5	6	0	0	0	20	1	0	.365	.261
Frostad, Emerson	L-R	6-1	210	1-13-83	.143	.000	.200	2	7	1	1	0	0	1	2	1	0	0	0	4	0	0	.571	.250
Gentry, Craig	R-R	6-2	190	11-7-83	.203	.167	.220	18	59	6	12	1	0	0	1	9	0	1	0	18	1	0	.220	.309
Gold, Nate	R-R	6-3	230	6-12-80	.255	.250	.256	127	475	73	121	29	3	23	90	61	2	0	4	121	0	1	.474	.339
Harrison, Ben	R-R	6-4	203	9-18-81	.221	.231	.217	26	86	6	19	3	1	1	7	10	1	0	1	28	0	0	.314	.306
Laird, Gerald	R-R	6-1	225	11-13-79	.000	—	.000	4	12	1	0	0	0	0	1	2	0	2	0	3	0	0	.000	.176
Mayberry, John	R-R	6-6	230	12-21-83	.263	.350	.237	114	437	49	115	30	7	16	58	30	5	1	2	85	6	2	.474	.316
Mench, Kevin	R-R	6-0	215	1-7-78	.282	.412	.224	29	110	18	31	7	2	3	18	11	0	0	1	11	0	0	.464	.344
Metcalf, Travis	R-R	6-3	215	8-17-82	.253	.205	.262	71	265	36	67	14	1	5	37	18	1	1	3	59	1	0	.370	.300
Meyer, Drew	L-R	5-10	200	8-29-81	.250	.231	.254	88	284	43	71	10	5	2	24	37	0	12	4	46	10	2	.342	.332
Ramirez, Max	R-R	5-11	175	10-11-84	.243	.286	.233	10	37	5	9	1	0	2	6	3	0	0	1	13	0	0	.432	.293
Richardson, Kevin	R-R	6-3	230	9-12-80	.251	.390	.212	55	187	25	47	10	1	6	22	18	4	2	2	53	0	0	.412	.327
Roberts, Ryan	R-R	5-11	190	9-19-80	.300	.257	.314	130	453	71	136	28	8	10	66	67	2	1	6	78	15	3	.464	.388
Saltalamacchia, Jarrod	B-R	6-4	235	5-2-85	.291	.462	.238	15	55	10	16	3	1	2	13	7	2	0	0	15	0	0	.491	.391
Shelton, Chris	R-R	6-0	215	6-26-80	.340	.378	.332	67	256	38	87	22	2	11	51	31	1	0	3	54	0	0	.570	.409
Teagarden, Taylor	R-R	6-0	210	12-21-83	.225	.225	.224	57	187	26	42	5	3	7	26	18	2	1	0	59	0	1	.396	.332
Trzesniak, Nick	R-R	6-0	210	11-19-80	.222	.222	.222	10	27	6	6	1	1	2	3	0	0	0	9	0	0	.444	.300

Pitching	B-T	HT	WT	DOB	W	L	ERA	G	GS	CG	SV	IP	H	R	ER	HR	BB	SO	AVG	vLH	vRH	K/9	BB/9
Ballard, Michael	R-L	6-2	180	2-6-84	3	3	6.81	8	8	0	0	38	57	30	29	4	7	23	.343	.281	.358	5.40	1.64
Batista, Kendy	R-R	6-2	165	7-5-81	0	0	0.00	1	0	0	0	1	0	0	0	0	0	1	.000	.000	.000	9.00	0.00
Benoit, Joaquin	R-R	6-3	220	7-26-77	1	0	0.00	2	0	0	0	3	1	0	0	0	3	1	.111	.000	.250	9.00	0.00
Calero, Kiko	R-R	6-1	210	1-9-75	1	2	7.59	18	0	0	1	21	24	18	18	4	12	21	.293	.289	.295	8.86	5.06
2-team total (8 Sacramento)					2	3	6.53	26	0	0	1	30	32	22	22	5	22	31	—	—	—	9.20	6.53
Diaz, Jose	R-R	6-0	230	4-13-80	1	1	5.50	15	0	0	2	18	15	12	11	2	14	16	.238	.185	.278	8.00	7.00
2-team total (12 New Orleans)					2	6	6.32	27	7	0	2	57	46	43	40	10	47	52	—	—	—	8.21	7.42
Francisco, Frank	R-R	6-3	230	9-11-79	0	0	0.00	8	0	0	5	9	3	0	0	0	3	16	.100	.200	.000	16.00	3.00
Fukumori, Kazuo	R-R	6-0	175	8-4-76	1	6	5.48	38	4	0	2	64	79	41	39	7	18	40	.300	.252	.340	5.63	2.53
Gabbard, Kason	L-L	6-3	200	4-8-82	0	1	4.97	2	2	0	0	13	17	8	7	2	14	12	.327	.294	.343	8.53	2.84
Gordon, Brian	L-R	6-0	205	8-16-78	4	5	4.56	18	11	0	0	71	85	43	36	14	15	51	.299	.329	.264	6.46	1.90
Harrison, Matt	L-L	6-4	225	9-16-85	3	1	3.55	6	6	0	0	38	40	15	15	3	14	20	.282	.259	.287	4.74	3.32
Hunter III, Tommy	R-R	6-3	255	7-3-86	4	2	2.89	8	8	0	0	53	55	18	17	6	9	28	.264	.373	.192	4.75	1.53
Hurley, Eric	R-R	6-4	195	9-17-85	2	5	5.30	13	13	0	0	75	86	51	44	15	29	72	.285	.292	.278	8.68	3.50
Hyatt, Jared	R-R	6-5	205	5-15-84	1	0	0.96	2	1	0	0	9	4	1	1	0	4	6	.133	.125	.136	5.79	3.86
Kometani, Paul	R-R	6-4	205	12-24-82	4	5	5.55	47	0	0	2	60	65	42	37	10	26	50	.275	.306	.248	7.50	3.90

Player	B-T	HT	WT	DOB			ERA	G	GS	CG	SV															AVG				

Lee, Derek	L-L	6-3	215	8-20-74	0	3	5.06	3	3	0	0	16	25	11	9	0	4	6	.347	.360	.340	3.38	2.25
Littleton, Wes	R-R	6-3	200	9-2-82	7	1	4.01	44	0	0	6	58	55	27	26	3	25	58	.248	.230	.262	8.95	3.86
Loe, Kameron	R-R	6-7	240	9-10-81	3	5	5.59	26	4	0	1	58	70	41	36	7	20	31	.299	.293	.303	4.81	3.10
Madrigal, Warner	R-R	6-0	200	3-21-84	0	0	3.98	17	0	0	4	20	20	10	9	2	8	25	.247	.289	.209	11.07	3.54
Maeda, Yukinaga	L-L	5-10	155	8-26-70	5	3	4.55	36	0	0	1	55	57	31	28	7	11	58	.246	.205	.299	9.43	1.79
Mathis, Doug	R-R	6-3	220	6-7-83	5	1	3.35	10	10	0	0	54	51	28	20	7	14	36	.254	.344	.180	6.04	2.35
McCarthy, Brandon	R-R	6-7	205	7-7-83	1	1	3.38	5	5	0	0	27	21	10	10	2	8	23	.212	.152	.264	7.76	2.70
Mendoza, Luis	R-R	6-3	210	10-31-83	2	3	5.14	8	8	0	0	35	43	21	20	1	8	19	.301	.327	.244	4.89	2.06
Murray, A.J.	B-L	6-3	220	3-17-82	2	2	4.00	9	9	2	0	45	51	23	20	3	15	36	.280	.302	.271	7.20	3.00
Nippert, Dustin	R-R	6-8	225	5-6-81	6	2	3.98	12	10	1	0	63	65	28	28	8	16	43	.271	.281	.261	6.11	2.27
Ponson, Sidney	R-R	6-1	260	11-2-76	1	2	3.47	5	4	0	0	23	25	9	9	3	9	12	.284	.188	.339	4.63	3.47
Puffer, Brandon	R-R	6-3	190	10-5-75	0	0	8.00	7	0	0	0	9	9	8	8	0	2	7	.265	.313	.222	7.00	2.00
Ramirez, Elizardo	R-R	6-0	190	1-28-83	10	7	4.50	27	23	0	0	160	193	97	80	24	33	85	.295	.309	.281	4.78	1.86
Rowe, Steve	R-R	6-3	215	7-17-80	4	5	4.69	27	11	0	0	79	99	54	41	12	35	48	.304	.275	.326	5.49	4.00
Tejeda, Robinson	R-R	6-3	230	3-24-82	1	1	2.18	10	4	0	1	33	20	8	8	2	10	39	.172	.196	.154	10.64	2.73
White, Bill	L-L	6-3	225	11-20-78	4	1	3.54	50	1	0	6	53	45	24	21	4	30	62	.233	.215	.246	10.46	5.06

Fielding

Catcher	PCT	G	PO	A	E	DP	PB
Frostad	1.000	2	15	2	0	0	0
Laird	1.000	4	21	1	0	0	0
Ramirez	1.000	7	39	3	0	0	1
Richardson	.990	55	350	32	4	3	2
Saltalamacchia	1.000	15	107	12	0	0	0
Teagarden	.998	57	367	37	1	0	2
Trzesniak	1.000	9	43	2	0	0	1

First Base	PCT	G	PO	A	E	DP
Blalock	1.000	2	11	1	0	0
Davis	.989	28	267	14	3	27
Gold	.994	59	500	37	3	50
Mayberry	.958	4	23	0	1	3
Mench	.978	6	42	2	1	8
Shelton	.992	49	436	37	4	40

Second Base	PCT	G	PO	A	E	DP
Arias	.956	42	87	108	9	26

	PCT	G	PO	A	E	DP	PB
Benjamin	1.000	2	3	2	0	1
Duran	.989	15	38	51	1	12
Fox	1.000	4	9	11	0	2
Meyer	.987	31	63	93	2	20
Roberts	.985	58	103	167	4	39

Third Base	PCT	G	PO	A	E	DP
Benjamin	1.000	2	0	2	0	0
Duran	1.000	4	0	1	0	0
Fox	.947	15	12	24	2	0
Metcalf	.940	71	49	138	12	19
Meyer	.857	5	5	7	2	1
Roberts	.912	51	23	111	13	7
Shelton	—	1	0	0	0	0
Trzesniak	1.000	1	1	0	0	0

Shortstop	PCT	G	PO	A	E	DP
Arias	.933	44	72	124	14	28
Benjamin	.982	64	95	182	5	43

	PCT	G	PO	A	E	DP
Duran	1.000	2	1	5	0	1
Meyer	.935	28	33	82	8	16
Roberts	.945	12	18	34	3	8

Outfield	PCT	G	PO	A	E	DP
Boggs	1.000	17	30	2	0	0
Botts	1.000	5	13	1	0	0
Byrd	1.000	3	3	1	0	0
Cruz	.978	100	169	11	4	2
Ellison	.990	120	301	11	3	3
Gentry	.980	18	49	0	1	0
Harrison	.965	26	53	2	2	0
Mayberry	.980	110	187	5	4	2
Mench	.971	15	32	1	1	0
Meyer	1.000	22	40	0	0	0
Roberts	1.000	5	5	0	0	0

FRISCO ROUGHRIDERS

DOUBLE-A

TEXAS LEAGUE

Batting	B-T	HT	WT	DOB	AVG	vLH	vRH	G	AB	R	H	2B	3B	HR	RBI	BB	HBP	SH	SF	SO	SB	CS	SLG	OBP
Andrus, Elvis	R-R	6-0	185	8-26-88	.295	.258	.303	118	482	82	142	19	2	4	65	38	6	3	6	91	54	16	.367	.350
Benjamin, Casey	L-R	6-2	190	8-1-80	.263	.333	.250	22	76	12	20	2	1	2	5	8	0	2	0	16	3	1	.395	.333
Berkery, Thomas	R-R	6-1	180	9-29-82	.230	.280	.218	80	256	35	59	14	4	4	26	33	3	2	2	65	1	4	.363	.323
Blalock, Hank	L-R	6-1	200	11-21-80	.421	.000	.471	6	19	5	8	3	0	0	4	4	0	0	0	5	1	0	.579	.522
Borbon, Julio	L-L	6-1	180	2-20-86	.337	.281	.356	60	255	40	86	12	2	5	22	14	4	6	1	32	17	11	.459	.380
Davis, Chris	L-R	6-4	235	3-17-86	.333	.276	.344	46	186	43	62	14	0	13	42	13	1	0	2	44	5	1	.618	.376
Fox, Adam	R-R	5-11	200	11-23-81	.234	.324	.209	95	321	45	75	12	3	7	42	32	6	1	6	67	7	0	.355	.310
Frostad, Emerson	L-R	6-1	210	1-13-83	.260	.232	.265	93	335	50	87	25	3	6	40	36	0	0	2	78	4	3	.406	.330
Gentry, Craig	R-R	6-2	190	11-29-83	.276	.370	.255	76	301	43	83	17	0	4	33	17	11	3	4	55	16	8	.372	.333
Gradoville, Tim	R-R	6-3	195	1-30-80	.194	.154	.207	35	108	11	21	2	0	1	11	5	2	2	1	33	1	0	.241	.241
Harrigan, Hunter	R-R	6-1	210	4-17-83	.000	.000	.000	4	13	0	0	0	0	0	0	0	0	0	0	10	0	0	.000	.000
Harrison, Ben	R-R	6-4	203	9-18-81	.300	.297	.301	91	340	66	102	23	0	17	66	42	7	0	3	99	18	2	.518	.385
Majewski, Dustin	L-L	5-11	205	8-16-81	.286	.284	.287	125	430	53	123	32	4	10	72	82	4	0	3	82	8	6	.449	.403
Mayberry, John	R-R	6-6	230	12-21-83	.268	.357	.250	21	82	16	22	8	0	4	13	4	3	0	1	21	4	1	.512	.322
Murphy, Steve	L-R	6-2	210	4-22-84	.262	.235	.268	129	508	84	133	35	9	20	87	36	4	0	9	125	15	3	.484	.311
Pina, Manuel	R-R	5-11	185	6-5-87	.275	.400	.218	23	80	7	22	7	0	0	9	5	2	1	1	12	1	0	.363	.330
Ramirez, Max	R-R	5-11	175	10-11-84	.354	.406	.346	69	243	49	86	16	2	17	50	37	7	0	2	56	2	2	.646	.450
Restko, J.T.	R-R	6-5	190	12-15-84	.193	.273	.167	27	88	6	17	1	0	1	7	8	1	0	1	23	1	0	.239	.265
Teagarden, Taylor	R-R	6-1	180	12-17-83	.169	.375	.137	16	59	6	10	2	0	2	6	8	1	0	0	23	1	0	.305	.279
Tracy, Chad	R-R	6-3	205	7-4-85	.344	.143	.403	24	93	15	32	3	0	4	15	7	0	0	1	18	2	0	.505	.386
Vallejo, Jose	B-R	6-0	172	9-11-86	.297	.286	.301	64	259	34	77	15	2	2	31	15	3	4	2	45	15	1	.394	.341
Whittleman, Johnny	L-R	6-2	195	2-11-87	.258	.125	.304	9	31	6	8	2	0	1	5	8	0	0	0	9	0	0	.419	.410

Pitching	B-T	HT	WT	DOB	W	L	ERA	G	GS	CG	SV	IP	H	R	ER	HR	BB	SO	AVG	vLH	vRH	K/9	BB/9
Ballard, Michael	R-L	6-2	180	2-6-84	8	3	4.02	17	16	1	0	96	113	46	43	3	34	72	.297	.245	.304	6.73	3.18
Bannister, John	R-R	6-4	198	12-8-84	0	4	4.56	11	3	0	1	26	26	14	13	1	22	15	.274	.333	.257	5.26	7.71
Batista, Kendy	R-R	6-2	165	7-5-81	2	2	3.91	17	0	0	2	25	26	13	11	0	12	24	.265	.138	.319	8.53	4.26
Benoit, Joaquin	R-R	6-3	220	7-26-77	0	0	16.20	3	1	0	0	2	4	3	3	0	4	1	.500	.000	.571	10.80	21.60
Diamond, Thomas	R-R	6-3	230	4-6-83	3	6	6.20	12	11	0	0	54	54	39	37	3	37	47	.267	.288	.260	7.88	6.20
Diaz, Jose	R-R	6-0	230	4-13-80	1	0	3.95	8	0	0	4	14	10	6	6	1	11	13	.208	.200	.211	8.56	7.24
Diaz, J.B.	R-R	6-2	185	6-9-83	1	1	2.60	17	0	0	0	28	19	10	8	1	7	23	.192	.219	.179	7.48	2.28
Dittler, Jake	R-R	6-4	220	11-24-82	1	1	8.64	8	4	0	0	25	40	26	24	4	15	12	.370	.458	.345	4.32	5.40
Feldman, Scott	L-R	6-5	210	2-7-83	2	0	4.26	2	2	0	0	13	11	6	6	0	2	4	.229	.167	.267	2.84	1.42
Feliz, Neftali	R-R	6-3	180	5-2-88	4	3	2.98	10	10	0	0	45	34	16	15	1	23	47	.217	.167	.243	9.33	4.57
Gabbard, Kason	L-L	6-3	200	4-8-82	0	0	2.25	1	1	0	0	4	1	1	1	0	3	6	.077	.000	.077	13.50	6.75

Name	B-T	HT	WT	DOB	W	L	ERA	G	GS	CG	SV	IP	H	R	ER	HR	BB	SO	AVG	vLH	vRH	K/9	BB/9
Garr, Brennan	R-R	6-2	190	2-22-84	2	1	3.89	32	0	0	7	44	44	21	19	2	26	54	.263	.244	.270	11.05	5.32
Gonzalez, Alfredo	B-R	5-11	165	9-17-79	5	2	4.78	36	0	0	2	75	88	44	40	9	20	61	.293	.265	.304	7.29	2.39
Gordon, Brian	L-R	6-0	205	8-16-78	2	0	0.00	15	0	0	3	22	9	1	0	0	4	18	.122	.188	.103	7.36	1.64
2-team total (1 Corpus Christi)					2	0	0.38	16	0	0	3	24	11	2	1	1	5	19	—	—	—	7.13	1.88
Hamilton, Clayton	R-R	6-5	205	6-15-82	1	3	5.14	20	0	0	1	35	34	25	20	5	13	16	.250	.261	.244	4.11	3.34
Harrison, Matt	L-L	6-4	225	9-16-85	3	2	3.33	9	9	1	0	46	49	23	17	3	14	35	.263	.276	.261	6.85	2.74
Hodges, Trey	R-R	6-3	195	6-29-78	8	8	5.76	26	18	0	0	105	113	72	67	15	52	75	.280	.292	.275	6.45	4.47
Holland, Derek	B-L	6-2	185	10-9-86	3	0	0.69	4	4	0	0	26	14	4	2	0	6	29	.163	.200	.155	10.04	2.08
Hunter III, Tommy	R-R	6-3	255	7-3-86	4	2	3.78	8	8	0	0	52	52	24	22	5	17	28	.267	.229	.279	4.82	2.92
Hurley, Eric	R-R	6-4	195	9-17-85	1	0	0.00	1	1	0	0	7	4	0	0	0	1	2	.174	.286	.125	2.45	1.23
Hyatt, Jared	R-R	6-5	205	5-15-84	1	3	3.53	9	9	1	0	51	47	25	20	3	14	45	.239	.218	.246	7.94	2.47
Jones, Beau	L-L	6-1	195	8-25-86	2	1	4.02	11	0	0	0	16	11	7	7	2	9	15	.200	.200	.200	8.62	5.17
Laughter, Andrew	R-R	6-4	227	2-24-85	2	3	4.80	30	0	0	9	45	40	26	24	3	21	36	.237	.133	.274	7.20	4.20
Lee, Derek	L-L	6-3	215	8-20-74	1	3	5.40	5	5	0	0	28	32	18	17	5	8	16	.288	.278	.290	5.08	2.54
Madrigal, Warner	R-R	6-0	200	3-21-84	1	0	1.72	14	0	0	10	16	11	4	3	1	8	18	.200	.267	.175	10.34	4.60
Mendoza, Luis	R-R	6-3	210	10-31-83	0	0	6.75	1	1	0	0	1	1	2	1	0	2	1	.167	.000	.167	6.75	13.50
Michalak, Chris	L-L	6-2	195	1-4-71	1	1	5.40	16	0	0	0	20	22	15	12	3	10	8	.289	.250	.300	3.60	4.50
2-team total (10 Midland)					1	1	5.22	26	0	0	0	29	30	23	17	6	17	17	—	—	—	5.22	5.22
Millwood, Kevin	R-R	6-4	230	12-24-74	0	1	2.25	1	1	0	0	4	5	2	1	0	2	6	.313	.167	.400	13.50	4.50
Parker, Zach	R-L	6-2	205	8-19-81	3	1	3.39	27	9	0	0	74	68	32	28	2	41	58	.246	.271	.241	7.02	4.96
Puffer, Brandon	R-R	6-3	190	10-5-75	8	0	3.90	39	0	0	1	67	76	35	29	6	16	47	.289	.317	.280	6.31	2.15
Reed, Evan	R-R	6-4	225	12-31-85	1	0	0.00	1	1	0	0	5	4	0	0	0	0	3	.222	.167	.250	5.40	0.00
Schlact, Michael	R-R	6-7	205	12-9-85	7	11	5.23	26	26	0	0	150	172	95	87	12	66	71	.292	.335	.271	4.27	3.97
Touchet, Dan	R-R	6-2	220	1-12-82	2	0	6.86	16	0	0	0	20	23	19	15	3	17	19	.291	.160	.352	8.69	7.78

Fielding

Catcher	PCT	G	PO	A	E	DP	PB
Frostad	.989	38	233	28	3	1	6
Gradoville	.973	34	204	13	6	6	0
Harrigan	1.000	3	16	1	0	0	0
Pina	1.000	20	145	19	0	1	2
Ramirez	.972	44	255	24	8	4	4
Teagarden	.989	10	84	5	1	0	1

First Base	PCT	G	PO	A	E	DP
Benjamin	1.000	2	16	1	0	3
Berkery	.966	13	106	9	4	8
Blalock	1.000	5	44	1	0	6
Davis	.985	43	389	16	6	37
Frostad	1.000	20	156	8	0	21
Majewski	.977	15	119	8	3	13
Ragsdale	1.000	10	96	4	0	12

	PCT	G	PO	A	E	DP
Ramirez	1.000	9	60	6	0	6
Restko	.993	16	138	6	1	16
Tracy	.985	15	130	5	2	14

Second Base	PCT	G	PO	A	E	DP
Berkery	.987	32	62	86	2	28
Fox	1.000	16	36	38	0	8
Ragsdale	.969	36	75	83	5	25
Vallejo	.977	64	133	161	7	46

Third Base	PCT	G	PO	A	E	DP
Berkery	.927	14	6	32	3	3
Fox	.963	78	41	169	8	10
Frostad	.952	36	20	80	5	6
Ragsdale	.909	13	8	22	3	2
Whittleman	.905	8	3	16	2	1

Shortstop	PCT	G	PO	A	E	DP
Andrus	.944	109	181	361	32	79
Benjamin	.959	19	29	64	4	20
Berkery	.857	2	1	5	1	0
Ragsdale	.984	14	23	40	1	10

Outfield	PCT	G	PO	A	E	DP
Benjamin	1.000	1	1	0	0	0
Berkery	1.000	19	34	3	0	1
Borbon	.987	59	147	0	2	0
Gentry	.994	76	167	11	1	3
Harrison	.985	41	66	1	1	0
Majewski	.986	98	206	6	3	1
Mayberry	.964	20	27	0	1	0
Murphy	.963	114	203	8	8	1
Restko	1.000	2	3	0	0	0

BAKERSFIELD BLAZE

HIGH CLASS A

CALIFORNIA LEAGUE

Batting	B-T	HT	WT	DOB	AVG	vLH	vRH	G	AB	R	H	2B	3B	HR	RBI	BB	HBP	SH	SF	SO	SB	CS	SLG	OBP
Borbon, Julio	L-L	6-1	180	2-20-86	.306	.263	.321	66	291	47	89	20	0	2	36	15	4	2	2	30	36	7	.395	.346
Cobb, Adam	L-L	5-11	185	9-5-85	.206	.250	.200	11	34	0	7	1	0	0	0	0	0	0	0	9	0	1	.235	.206
Gac, Ian	R-R	6-3	240	8-10-85	.257	.362	.232	63	245	28	63	8	0	13	49	17	5	0	6	96	0	0	.449	.311
Gerrard, Grant	L-L	6-4	220	5-1-84	.280	.307	.272	108	435	59	122	33	3	11	63	28	0	3		116	4	0	.446	.322
Gomez, Mauro	R-R	6-2	190	9-7-84	.244	.219	.255	80	316	30	77	13	0	8	41	14	3	1	2	93	0	0	.361	.281
Gradoville, Chris	R-R	6-2	220	7-10-84	.309	.400	.283	71	265	32	82	20	1	4	26	7	8	1	3	41	0	1	.438	.343
Herren, K.C.	L-R	6-2	200	8-25-85	.188	.215	.181	89	292	36	55	7	2	3	27	43	3	2	4	81	7	1	.257	.295
Kaase, Jake	L-R	6-1	185	4-14-86	.290	.227	.310	25	93	11	27	1	0	1	6	3	0	1	1	17	3	1	.333	.309
Lemon, Marcus	L-R	5-11	173	6-3-88	.295	.303	.293	118	447	80	132	30	4	8	47	46	10	14	0	69	12	8	.434	.374
Mehl, Truan	L-R	6-1	195	3-20-83	.247	.185	.266	123	450	44	111	15	2	3	46	43	2	4	4	89	27	8	.309	.313
Morrison, Erik	R-R	6-0	190	10-23-85	.236	.324	.194	32	106	12	25	4	0	3	11	13	0	0	1	27	2	0	.358	.317
Osuna, Renny	R-R	6-0	172	4-24-85	.317	.351	.307	62	259	45	82	18	1	1	23	22	1	1	3	38	6	3	.405	.371
Pina, Manuel	R-R	5-11	185	6-5-87	.265	.300	.252	61	223	31	59	10	1	3	24	14	3	1	3	22	1	0	.359	.313
Puello, Alberto	R-R	6-2	180	10-20-87	.133	.000	.182	6	15	2	2	0	0	0	1	0	0	0	0	5	0	0	.133	.133
Restko, J.T.	R-R	6-5	190	12-15-84	.293	.381	.259	38	150	14	44	10	0	5	25	10	3	1	0	40	0	0	.460	.350
Rodriguez, Timothy	R-R	6-2	210	1-24-87	.081	.063	.095	12	37	0	3	0	0	0	1	0	0	1	0	0	11	0	0	.081	.105
Stoneburner, Davis	R-R	6-0	175	1-14-85	.222	.350	.173	23	72	1	16	4	0	0	6	3	0	2	0	12	1	0	.361	.273
Tracy, Chad	R-R	6-3	205	7-4-85	.286	.290	.284	106	420	67	120	37	1	13	67	40	12	0	5	98	2	1	.471	.361
Vallejo, Jose	B-R	6-0	172	9-11-86	.287	.314	.277	75	310	48	89	14	2	9	50	26	5	0	3	46	27	3	.432	.349
Whittleman, Johnny	L-R	6-2	195	2-11-87	.257	.252	.259	118	439	72	113	36	1	9	59	81	0	1	4	113	1	2	.392	.370

Pitching	B-T	HT	WT	DOB	W	L	ERA	G	GS	CG	SV	IP	H	R	ER	HR	BB	SO	AVG	vLH	vRH	K/9	BB/9
Bannister, John	R-R	6-4	198	1-20-84	4	4	4.14	19	9	0	2	63	63	34	29	5	31	65	.265	.270	.260	7.29	4.14
Dennis, Chris	L-R	6-2	205	1-3-84	0	0	17.36	3	0	0	0	5	10	10	9	1	7	5	.435	.556	.357	9.64	13.50
Diaz, J.B.	R-R	6-2	185	6-9-83	0	1	3.69	19	0	0	1	46	49	24	19	5	12	28	.269	.329	.220	5.44	2.33
Falcon, Ryan	R-L	6-0	195	8-27-84	6	2	3.69	34	1	0	3	71	67	39	29	7	18	58	.253	.241	.261	7.39	2.17
Giles, Josh	R-R	6-1	175	8-3-84	1	2	3.98	35	0	0	1	63	67	43	28	8	30	71	.270	.342	.206	10.09	4.26
Hamilton, Clayton	R-R	6-5	205	6-15-82	1	1	3.13	17	0	0	6	32	29	11	11	2	3	26	.242	.245	.239	7.39	0.85
Holland, Derek	B-L	6-2	185	10-9-86	3	1	3.19	5	5	0	0	31	20	12	11	1	5	37	.185	.185	.185	10.74	1.45

Name	B-T	HT	WT	DOB	W	L	ERA	G	GS	CG	SV	IP	H	R	ER	HR	BB	SO	AVG	vLH	vRH	K/9	BB/9
Hunter III, Tommy	R-R	6-3	255	7-3-86	5	4	3.55	9	9	0	0	58	63	26	23	6	8	50	.279	.287	.272	7.71	1.23
Hyatt, Jared	R-R	6-5	205	5-15-84	6	5	3.92	18	12	0	0	80	78	41	35	9	29	62	.251	.228	.269	6.95	3.25
Jones, Beau	L-L	6-1	195	8-25-86	1	3	2.93	17	4	0	1	43	40	22	14	1	20	45	.241	.216	.252	9.42	4.19
Kiker, Kasey	L-L	5-10	170	11-19-87	5	5	4.73	23	21	0	0	122	138	72	64	14	37	111	.292	.321	.279	8.21	2.74
Laughter, Andrew	R-R	6-4	227	2-24-85	1	0	0.00	10	0	0	3	16	13	1	0	0	2	9	.217	.250	.194	4.96	1.10
Lueke, Josh	R-R	6-5	220	12-5-84	2	6	5.03	35	0	0	1	59	65	39	33	6	16	72	.270	.248	.289	10.98	2.44
Nelo, Hector	R-R	6-1	200	11-5-86	0	0	3.60	2	1	0	0	5	2	5	2	1	7	6	.111	.000	.167	10.80	12.60
Phillips, Zach	L-L	6-1	200	9-21-86	8	9	5.54	28	28	1	0	145	161	102	89	10	73	117	.281	.317	.262	7.28	4.54
Poveda, Omar	R-R	6-4	200	9-28-87	4	4	4.47	17	17	0	0	91	82	56	45	10	40	97	.241	.254	.227	9.63	3.97
Reed, Evan	R-R	6-4	225	12-31-85	7	10	6.25	23	23	0	0	121	130	92	84	14	55	88	.273	.304	.248	6.62	4.09
Roark, Tanner	R-R	6-2	220	10-5-86	1	3	3.60	12	2	0	1	30	27	17	12	5	13	37	.237	.255	.220	11.10	3.90
Romero, Levi	R-R	6-4	180	4-12-84	0	0	3.60	1	1	0	0	5	4	3	2	1	1	5	.211	.188	.333	9.00	1.80
Sattler, Daniel	R-R	6-3	190	11-11-83	1	4	3.91	26	0	0	0	46	47	25	20	5	18	45	.261	.287	.237	8.80	3.52
Stewart, Jordan	R-R	6-1	210	8-29-83	5	7	4.88	47	0	0	11	63	71	45	34	4	27	43	.276	.361	.203	6.18	3.88
Swanson, Glenn	L-L	6-1	175	5-15-83	1	4	6.55	7	7	0	0	33	52	24	24	7	6	28	.356	.297	.402	7.64	1.64
Tufts, Tyler	R-R	6-3	195	12-5-86	0	1	1.93	7	0	0	0	14	19	11	3	1	6	3	.311	.207	.406	1.93	3.86
White, Bill	L-L	6-3	225	11-20-78	0	0	0.00	1	0	0	0	1	0	0	0	0	0	2	.000	.000	.000	18.00	0.00

Fielding

Catcher	PCT	G	PO	A	E	DP	PB
Gradoville	.997	70	550	52	2	4	10
Pina	.994	61	440	59	3	4	6
Puello	.952	6	29	11	2	0	2
Tracy	1.000	7	66	4	0	0	2

First Base	PCT	G	PO	A	E	DP
Gac	.980	51	409	22	9	33
Gomez	.989	67	611	31	7	47
Restko	.971	20	154	12	5	21
Stoneburner	1.000	1	0	0	0	0
Tracy	1.000	2	13	2	0	0

Second Base	PCT	G	PO	A	E	DP
Kaase	.966	5	12	16	1	4
Morrison	.909	1	3	7	1	1
Osuna	.960	58	124	167	12	25
Stoneburner	.889	3	3	5	1	0
Vallejo	.968	75	146	213	12	45

Third Base	PCT	G	PO	A	E	DP
Gomez	1.000	2	2	4	0	0
Kaase	1.000	6	5	7	0	1
Morrison	.875	16	12	23	5	3
Stoneburner	.941	7	4	12	1	0
Whittleman	.912	110	87	194	27	18

Shortstop	PCT	G	PO	A	E	DP
Kaase	.948	14	20	35	3	7
Lemon	.919	115	188	301	43	55
Osuna	1.000	1	2	4	0	1
Stoneburner	.944	10	15	19	2	3

Outfield	PCT	G	PO	A	E	DP
Borbon	.979	64	138	2	3	1
Cobb	.957	11	20	2	1	1
Gerrard	.952	78	107	12	6	2
Herren	.975	82	157	2	4	0
Mehl	.973	120	242	10	7	2
Morrison	1.000	13	21	1	0	1
Rodriguez	1.000	8	18	0	0	0
Tracy	.966	51	81	3	3	1

CLINTON LUMBERKINGS
LOW CLASS A

MIDWEST LEAGUE

Batting	B-T	HT	WT	DOB	AVG	vLH	vRH	G	AB	R	H	2B	3B	HR	RBI	BB	HBP	SH	SF	SO	SB	CS	SLG	OBP
Alfonzo, Miguel	R-R	6-3	190	4-21-88	.235	.272	.222	89	293	45	69	11	1	5	37	35	8	2	2	98	7	2	.331	.331
Beltre, Engel	L-L	6-1	169	11-1-89	.283	.215	.306	130	566	87	160	26	9	8	47	15	6	10	1	105	31	11	.403	.308
Dominguez, Carlos	R-R	6-1	177	6-8-86	.247	.295	.226	57	198	18	49	7	1	4	21	7	3	0	2	35	1	0	.354	.281
Felix, Jose	R-R	5-10	198	6-28-88	.262	.143	.302	88	302	30	79	10	0	1	24	15	3	3	3	38	2	2	.305	.300
Gac, Ian	R-R	6-3	240	8-10-85	.310	.296	.313	67	255	49	79	13	1	19	60	33	8	0	2	74	1	0	.592	.403
Greene, Jonathan	R-R	6-0	200	9-6-86	.239	.214	.248	130	451	71	108	25	2	21	84	43	36	0	6	134	6	2	.443	.349
James, Andres	B-R	5-9	150	11-25-87	.199	.174	.209	82	287	39	57	7	1	0	10	11	1	10	0	67	10	6	.230	.231
Kaase, Jake	L-R	6-1	185	4-14-86	.135	.000	.139	13	37	1	5	1	0	0	3	3	0	1	0	4	1	0	.162	.200
Lawson, Matt	R-R	6-0	195	11-18-85	.251	.211	.266	100	362	57	91	15	2	6	25	35	3	11	1	79	18	7	.354	.322
Moreland, Mitch	L-L	6-2	230	9-6-85	.324	.301	.332	123	466	64	151	37	4	18	99	60	2	0	5	67	2	4	.536	.400
Murphy, Kyle	R-R	6-0	184	9-6-84	.229	.212	.237	42	109	8	25	3	1	0	7	13	3	4	1	39	5	4	.275	.325
Osuna, Renny	R-R	6-0	172	4-24-85	.360	.477	.322	68	267	55	96	21	4	3	43	31	3	2	5	27	8	1	.502	.425
Paisano, David	R-R	6-1	165	11-26-87	.130	.059	.162	18	54	6	7	2	0	0	4	6	2	0	2	11	4	0	.167	.234
Pickett, Justin	R-R	6-1	205	6-16-85	.429	.333	.455	9	28	6	12	4	0	1	6	2	1	0	0	7	2	0	.679	.484
Santana, Cristian	R-R	6-0	175	6-18-86	.232	.291	.204	87	328	36	76	17	2	11	42	19	12	0	1	121	4	2	.396	.297
Smith, Tim	L-L	6-3	225	6-14-86	.300	.252	.316	121	480	67	144	25	4	13	70	33	15	3	7	81	21	9	.450	.359
Smoak, Justin	B-L	6-3	200	12-5-86	.304	.231	.326	14	56	9	17	3	0	3	8	11	0	0	1	10	0	0	.518	.355
Stoneburner, Davis	R-R	6-0	175	1-14-85	.276	.300	.270	52	181	20	50	12	3	2	18	9	5	2	2	37	7	4	.409	.325

Pitching	B-T	HT	WT	DOB	W	L	ERA	G	GS	CG	SV	IP	H	R	ER	HR	BB	SO	AVG	vLH	vRH	K/9	BB/9
Beavan, Blake	R-R	6-7	210	1-17-89	10	6	2.37	23	23	0	0	122	105	42	32	12	20	73	.234	.263	.207	5.40	1.48
Castillo, Fabio	R-R	6-1	190	2-19-89	2	5	5.28	36	7	0	4	90	88	65	53	11	47	78	.257	.317	.217	7.77	4.68
Dennis, Chris	L-R	6-2	205	1-3-84	4	4	1.97	39	0	0	4	59	52	18	13	1	17	59	.232	.253	.219	8.95	2.58
Eppley, Cody	R-R	6-5	205	10-8-85	0	0	9.00	2	0	0	0	2	2	2	2	0	0	3	.250	.250	.250	13.50	0.00
Feliz, Neftali	R-R	6-3	180	5-2-88	6	3	2.52	17	17	0	0	82	55	25	23	2	28	106	.193	.174	.213	11.63	3.07
Flores, Adalberto	R-R	6-7	227	11-4-86	5	1	4.14	48	0	0	12	63	55	36	29	5	25	72	.215	.220	.212	10.29	3.57
Gomez, Kennil	R-R	6-3	170	4-8-88	8	4	2.97	16	15	0	0	88	75	40	29	8	20	70	.232	.201	.255	7.16	2.05
Hamburger, Mark	R-R	6-4	195	2-5-87	0	0	2.25	4	0	0	3	4	5	1	1	0	2	0	.313	.400	.273	0.00	4.50
Henry, Ben	R-R	6-4	190	4-9-89	0	1	9.00	1	1	0	0	3	3	3	3	1	2	5	.273	.333	.200	15.00	6.00
Holland, Derek	B-L	6-2	185	10-9-86	7	0	2.40	17	17	0	0	94	77	30	25	2	29	91	.228	.189	.242	8.74	2.79
Kirkman, Michael	L-L	6-4	195	9-18-86	4	3	4.36	15	14	0	0	74	78	43	36	8	23	58	.269	.260	.272	7.03	2.78
Lueke, Josh	R-R	6-5	220	12-5-84	1	1	2.61	8	0	0	2	10	10	3	3	0	2	12	.244	.333	.207	10.45	1.74
Main, Michael	R-R	6-1	170	12-14-88	2	2	2.58	10	10	0	0	45	38	16	13	4	13	50	.228	.206	.242	9.93	2.58
Murphy, Tim	L-L	6-2	190	5-7-87	1	0	2.40	3	3	0	0	15	12	4	4	3	3	11	.214	.286	.190	6.60	1.80
Nelo, Hector	R-R	6-1	200	11-5-86	1	3	2.96	17	0	0	1	24	22	16	8	1	17	19	.250	.286	.233	7.03	6.29
Ortiz, Joseph	L-L	5-7	175	8-13-90	0	1	1.97	23	0	0	4	32	23	9	7	1	16	25	.204	.211	.200	7.03	4.50
Quintero, Jorge	R-R	6-1	175	4-17-87	7	6	5.93	30	10	0	1	85	114	67	56	5	36	54	.326	.344	.311	5.72	3.81
Reed, Evan	R-R	6-4	225	12-31-85	1	0	1.50	2	2	0	0	12	8	2	2	0	2	12	.190	.188	.192	9.00	1.50

	B-T	HT	WT	DOB	W	L	ERA	G	GS	CG	SV	IP	H	R	ER	HR	BB	SO	AVG	vLH	vRH	K/9	BB/9
Romero, Levi	R-R	6-4	180	4-12-84	0	1	18.00	1	1	0	0	3	5	6	6	1	5	3	.357	.000	.500	9.00	15.00
Santana, Julio	B-R	6-1	170	12-26-85	4	2	5.97	36	0	0	1	60	78	47	40	6	17	43	.315	.318	.312	6.41	2.54
Sattler, Daniel	R-R	6-3	190	11-11-83	0	0	0.90	13	0	0	3	20	14	6	2	0	10	22	.200	.276	.146	9.90	4.50
Tatusko, Ryan	R-R	6-5	200	3-27-85	3	11	4.46	32	16	0	1	113	113	70	56	9	42	96	.256	.255	.256	7.65	3.35
Turner, Ryan	R-L	6-1	175	2-8-85	6	3	2.66	38	0	0	2	68	71	29	20	0	12	52	.271	.203	.298	6.92	1.60
Ueno, Keisuke	R-R	6-4	205	3-6-86	4	3	3.33	23	1	0	0	46	45	28	17	5	11	33	.245	.194	.277	6.46	2.15

Fielding

Catcher	PCT	G	PO	A	E	DP	PB
Dominguez	.975	55	374	47	11	2	15
Felix	.983	87	645	56	12	7	12
Pickett	1.000	6	36	6	0	0	1
Santana	.917	2	11	0	1	0	0

First Base	PCT	G	PO	A	E	DP
Gac	.988	52	458	23	6	37
Greene	1.000	4	38	1	0	3
Moreland	.991	71	600	46	6	50
Smith	1.000	2	6	0	0	1
Smoak	1.000	10	92	5	0	7

Second Base	PCT	G	PO	A	E	DP
James	1.000	2	4	1	0	1

	PCT	G	PO	A	E	DP
Lawson	.961	96	167	254	17	53
Osuna	.962	33	64	88	6	15
Stoneburner	.979	12	20	26	1	5

Third Base	PCT	G	PO	A	E	DP
Felix	1.000	1	0	1	0	0
Gac	1.000	2	0	1	0	0
Greene	.911	116	91	227	31	17
Kaase	1.000	1	1	0	0	0
Osuna	.870	7	5	15	3	2
Stoneburner	.871	12	5	22	4	3

Shortstop	PCT	G	PO	A	E	DP
James	.953	78	131	194	16	39
Kaase	.982	12	21	34	1	7

	PCT	G	PO	A	E	DP
Osuna	.930	26	51	69	9	15
Stoneburner	.961	30	54	95	6	12

Outfield	PCT	G	PO	A	E	DP
Alfonzo	.944	83	109	9	7	4
Beltre	.973	128	273	12	8	3
Moreland	.933	32	52	4	4	0
Murphy	.976	40	79	4	2	1
Paisano	1.000	18	30	2	0	1
Pickett	.000	1	0	0	1	0
Santana	.974	50	74	0	2	0
Smith	.981	81	102	4	2	1

SPOKANE INDIANS   SHORT-SEASON

NORTHWEST LEAGUE

Batting	B-T	HT	WT	DOB	AVG	vLH	vRH	G	AB	R	H	2B	3B	HR	RBI	BB	HBP	SH	SF	SO	SB	CS	SLG	OBP
Bianucci, Mike	R-R	6-1	215	6-26-86	.316	.304	.319	31	114	15	36	11	1	4	21	11	2	0	0	18	7	1	.535	.386
Bolden, Jared	L-L	6-2	180	3-18-87	.263	.250	.268	61	243	48	64	13	4	3	28	36	1	1	0	65	5	2	.387	.361
Butler, Joey	R-R	6-2	210	3-12-86	.301	.317	.295	62	226	35	68	8	5	4	31	40	5	0	0	54	9	4	.434	.417
Ecker, Donnie	L-R	6-4	190	3-9-86	.286	.500	.200	2	7	2	2	1	0	0	3	1	0	0	0	0	0	0	.429	.375
Fry, Eric	L-R	5-10	190	8-9-87	.296	.300	.295	56	216	41	64	10	0	6	31	21	6	1	3	51	6	0	.426	.370
Guinn, Dennis	R-R	6-1	210	8-2-85	.253	.235	.259	55	198	27	50	11	5	5	34	29	8	0	3	49	2	3	.434	.366
Higgins, Kyle	R-R	6-1	180	6-6-86	.271	.250	.277	36	118	22	32	8	0	0	5	14	4	2	0	24	2	2	.339	.368
Hogan, Doug	R-R	6-3	210	9-29-84	.225	.150	.250	44	160	22	36	8	0	7	30	11	1	0	2	41	1	1	.406	.276
Hollander, Michael	R-R	5-9	180	10-30-85	.000	.000	.000	2	4	1	0	0	0	0	0	2	0	0	0	0	0	0	.000	.333
Kaase, Jake	L-R	6-1	185	4-14-86	.320	.379	.302	30	125	18	40	4	2	2	21	4	0	6	0	17	0	6	.432	.341
Koncel, Ed	R-R	6-3	195	7-29-88	.205	.158	.225	40	127	15	26	7	0	2	8	19	1	4	1	54	3	3	.307	.311
Martinez, Edward	R-R	5-9	160	3-28-88	.250	.500	.167	5	8	2	2	0	0	0	0	1	0	0	0	1	1	0	.250	.333
Ogata, Jason	R-R	6-1	189	10-21-86	.244	.233	.248	54	225	29	55	4	1	2	32	18	7	3	3	49	4	1	.298	.316
Ortiz, Mike	L-L	6-2	200	5-9-89	.000	.000	.000	1	3	0	0	0	0	0	0	0	0	0	0	3	0	0	.000	.250
Paisano, David	R-R	6-1	165	11-26-87	.262	.239	.269	66	275	47	72	18	1	6	44	23	7	2	2	51	9	6	.400	.332
Pickett, Justin	R-R	6-1	205	6-16-85	.252	.412	.202	35	143	19	36	8	0	4	28	8	3	0	0	37	0	0	.392	.305
Podraza, Cody	R-R	5-8	185	11-6-87	.235	.333	.214	10	34	8	8	0	0	0	4	0	1	0	0	5	0	1	.235	.257
Rodriguez, Timothy	R-R	6-2	210	1-24-87	.323	.450	.288	24	93	17	30	3	0	0	16	9	0	0	1	24	4	2	.355	.379
West, Matt	R-R	6-1	200	11-21-88	.258	.254	.260	67	240	48	62	12	0	4	30	26	17	1	3	68	1	0	.358	.367
Zaneski, Zach	R-R	6-2	205	6-27-86	.252	.286	.244	30	103	20	26	4	0	0	11	13	1	1	0	16	0	0	.291	.342

Pitching	B-T	HT	WT	DOB	W	L	ERA	G	GS	CG	SV	IP	H	R	ER	HR	BB	SO	AVG	vLH	vRH	K/9	BB/9
Bleier, Richard	L-L	6-3	195	4-16-87	4	5	4.02	14	11	0	0	63	61	41	28	4	14	44	.247	.265	.240	6.32	2.01
Boscan, Wilfredo	R-R	6-2	160	10-26-89	9	1	3.12	15	12	0	0	69	66	30	24	4	11	70	.251	.237	.265	9.09	1.43
Brader, Dustin	R-R	6-4	220	11-13-85	2	0	1.48	17	0	0	3	24	16	10	4	0	6	20	.180	.257	.130	7.40	2.22
Evans, Eric	L-L	6-1	190	12-29-85	0	0	2.25	2	0	0	0	4	2	1	1	1	5		.143	.200	.111	11.25	2.25
Gutsie, Justin	R-R	6-1	205	1-7-87	4	0	4.91	16	0	0	0	22	24	15	12	0	13	20	.267	.341	.196	8.18	5.32
Hurley, Trevor	R-R	6-3	215	7-28-87	3	1	3.29	22	0	0	3	38	28	19	14	3	28	40	.203	.275	.161	9.39	6.57
Kirkman, Michael	L-L	6-4	195	9-18-86	1	1	0.00	2	2	0	0	10	7	4	0	0	2	9	.184	.053	.316	8.10	1.80
Miller, Justin	R-R	6-3	190	6-13-87	0	0	5.06	14	0	0	2	21	20	12	12	3	12	24	.256	.233	.271	10.13	5.06
Murphy, Tim	L-L	6-2	190	5-7-87	3	1	3.03	13	1	0	2	33	17	12	11	3	15	40	.152	.111	.171	11.02	4.13
Nam, Yoon-Hee	L-L	6-2	165	8-4-87	2	0	4.20	19	1	0	0	41	41	19	19	5	15	41	.261	.255	.264	9.07	3.32
Nevarez, Matthew	R-R	6-5	220	2-26-87	4	2	4.36	16	7	0	0	43	39	26	21	3	43	50	.238	.242	.235	10.38	8.93
Peralta, Juan	R-R	5-11	180	4-26-86	2	4	5.08	23	0	0	5	34	29	20	19	3	32	32	.246	.260	.235	8.55	5.08
Perez, Martin	L-L	6-0	165	4-4-91	1	2	3.65	15	15	0	0	62	66	32	25	3	28	53	.274	.197	.306	7.74	4.09
Pimentel, Carlos	R-R	6-3	180	12-1-89	6	3	3.31	16	13	0	0	65	48	27	24	4	31	54	.204	.204	.205	7.44	4.27
Ragsdale, Corey	R-R	6-4	175	11-10-82	2	1	3.86	6	0	0	0	7	8	3	3	0	4	4	.320	.438	.111	5.14	5.14
Ramirez, Neil	R-R	6-3	185	5-25-89	1	2	2.66	13	13	0	0	44	25	15	13	5	29	52	.166	.134	.190	10.64	5.93
Schlecht, Ryan	R-R	6-4	240	7-30-85	2	1	1.48	23	0	0	5	43	26	8	7	0	17	45	.181	.185	.177	9.49	3.59
Springston, Cliff	L-L	6-3	195	11-13-86	2	1	5.09	20	0	0	1	35	46	26	20	5	7	18	.315	.333	.308	4.58	1.78
Swanson, Glenn	L-L	6-1	175	5-15-83	0	0	0.00	1	1	0	0	5	2	0	0	0	4		.133	.000	.167	7.20	0.00
Young, Corey	L-L	6-2	175	12-30-86	1	1	2.79	21	0	0	7	29	20	11	9	1	14	34	.185	.105	.229	10.55	4.34

Fielding

Catcher	PCT	G	PO	A	E	DP	PB
Hogan	.993	44	381	47	3	7	16
Pickett	.976	6	38	3	1	0	4
Zaneski	.992	29	237	25	2	1	9

First Base	PCT	G	PO	A	E	DP
Bolden	.980	22	188	12	4	14
Guinn	.984	53	466	22	8	38
Pickett	1.000	2	18	1	0	5

Second Base	PCT	G	PO	A	E	DP
Ecker	.769	2	2	8	3	1
Higgins	.986	17	29	44	1	12
Kaase	.920	4	9	14	2	4

| Martinez | 1.000 | 3 | 3 | 4 | 0 | 1 |
| Ogata | .945 | 54 | 95 | 130 | 13 | 29 |

Third Base	PCT	G	PO	A	E	DP
Higgins	1.000	3	1	3	0	1
Kaase	.929	6	4	9	1	0
Pickett	.733	5	3	8	4	0
West	.894	67	56	104	19	9

Shortstop	PCT	G	PO	A	E	DP
Higgins	.913	17	28	45	7	6
Hollander	1.000	2	3	5	0	2
Kaase	.946	21	41	47	5	17
Koncel	.941	40	62	112	11	20

Outfield	PCT	G	PO	A	E	DP
Bianucci	.927	23	35	3	3	0

Bolden	.964	31	51	2	2	1
Butler	.974	50	74	2	2	0
Fry	.970	38	62	3	2	0
Martinez	1.000	1	3	0	0	0
Paisano	.978	64	131	1	3	0
Pickett	.000	2	0	0	1	0
Podraza	.500	8	1	0	1	0
Rodriguez	.967	18	29	0	1	0

AZL RANGERS

ROOKIE

ARIZONA LEAGUE

Batting	B-T	HT	WT	DOB	AVG	vLH	vRH	G	AB	R	H	2B	3B	HR	RBI	BB	HBP	SH	SF	SO	SB	CS	SLG	OBP
Barto, Aja	R-R	6-5	225	9-26-86	.280	.304	.275	37	132	23	37	10	1	4	21	17	9	0	1	47	2	1	.462	.396
Cobb, Adam	L-L	5-11	185	9-5-85	.284	.296	.281	30	116	16	33	9	2	0	10	14	0	1	0	22	5	0	.397	.362
Cruz, Nelson	R-R	6-3	230	7-1-80	.250	—	.250	1	4	1	1	1	0	0	1	2	0	0	0	1	0	0	.500	.500
De Los Santos, Leonel	R-R	5-10	170	10-2-89	.258	.243	.262	44	159	20	41	2	4	2	25	9	2	2	4	22	5	2	.358	.299
Dove, Chris	R-R	6-2	185	4-8-86	.237	.333	.213	30	76	16	18	2	2	0	11	15	8	0	1	28	7	1	.316	.410
Garcia, Leury	B-R	5-7	153	3-18-91	.209	.208	.210	41	129	17	27	3	3	0	14	8	0	4	3	40	12	3	.279	.250
Higgins, Kyle	R-R	6-1	180	6-6-86	.091	.000	.111	4	11	2	1	0	0	0	2	1	0	0	1	2	0	0	.091	.154
Hill, Lejuan	R-R	6-0	178	11-18-83	.252	.320	.232	33	107	18	27	8	0	4	20	13	2	1	2	26	9	6	.439	.339
Hollander, Michael	R-R	5-9	180	10-30-85	.353	.500	.321	9	34	9	12	3	1	1	5	4	0	1	1	6	2	1	.588	.410
Martinez, Edward	R-R	6-2	160	3-28-88	.289	.379	.265	42	142	28	41	6	1	0	20	13	1	9	2	24	17	5	.345	.348
McGraw, Jamie	B-R	6-2	180	2-15-85	.325	.357	.317	26	77	18	25	3	0	0	9	15	1	1	0	19	7	0	.364	.441
Morrison, Erik	R-R	6-0	190	10-23-85	.318	.222	.354	17	66	8	21	9	0	2	10	7	0	1	1	11	1	3	.545	.378
Murphy, Clark	L-L	6-2	190	12-18-89	.358	.313	.367	25	95	13	34	7	3	1	21	12	1	1	0	19	1	0	.526	.435
Ortiz, Mike	L-L	6-2	200	5-2-89	.256	.125	.287	37	125	19	32	3	2	0	12	18	1	1	2	29	2	6	.312	.349
Podraza, Cody	R-R	5-8	185	11-6-87	.360	.545	.328	19	75	18	27	4	1	1	8	8	2	1	0	16	3	2	.480	.435
Puello, Alberto	R-R	6-2	180	10-20-87	.240	.158	.268	20	75	10	18	4	2	0	7	7	1	0	1	11	1	0	.347	.310
Ramirez, Max	R-R	5-11	175	10-11-84	.800	—	.800	2	5	4	4	2	0	0	1	2	0	0	0	0	1	0	1.200	.857
Selen, Alejandro	R-R	5-10	175	3-20-89	.254	.310	.239	36	138	22	35	8	1	2	18	5	3	0	0	24	5	1	.370	.295
Torres, Kevin	R-L	6-5	193	2-24-90	.283	.625	.211	27	46	7	13	0	0	0	7	2	1	1	0	10	0	1	.283	.327
Valdez, Jairo	R-R	6-2	190	11-6-88	.200	.174	.207	30	115	17	23	6	0	2	14	5	2	0	1	33	0	0	.304	.244
Yan, Johan	R-R	6-3	185	9-27-88	.233	.310	.215	43	150	22	35	11	2	1	21	14	2	1	1	56	3	1	.353	.305

Pitching	B-T	HT	WT	DOB	W	L	ERA	G	GS	CG	SV	IP	H	R	ER	HR	BB	SO	AVG	vLH	vRH	K/9	BB/9
De Los Santos, Miguel	L-L	6-1	170	7-10-88	0	2	4.67	10	10	0	0	35	28	21	18	2	18	54	.217	.259	.206	14.02	4.67
De Los Santos, Ovispo	R-R	6-1	180	11-19-87	0	0	7.56	6	0	0	0	8	12	7	7	1	5	10	.333	.455	.280	10.80	5.40
Eppley, Cody	R-R	6-5	205	10-8-85	2	2	2.10	19	0	0	0	26	19	12	6	1	5	34	.192	.258	.162	11.92	1.75
Evans, Eric	L-L	6-1	190	12-29-85	3	2	5.46	16	0	0	0	30	37	21	18	1	12	31	.322	.412	.284	9.40	3.64
Font, Wilmer	R-R	6-4	210	5-24-90	1	0	10.38	3	0	0	0	4	1	5	5	1	1	6	.071	.000	.100	12.46	2.08
Grullon, Geuris	L-L	6-5	185	12-20-89	2	0	2.66	14	1	0	0	24	19	16	7	0	17	27	.216	.182	.227	10.27	6.46
Henry, Ben	R-R	6-4	190	4-9-89	2	2	4.15	14	7	0	0	39	42	26	18	3	25	45	.280	.292	.275	10.38	5.77
King, Justin	R-R	6-5	185	10-6-86	3	1	2.61	18	0	0	2	31	14	10	9	0	26	39	.140	.129	.145	11.32	7.55
Main, Michael	R-R	6-1	170	12-14-88	1	1	3.38	3	3	0	0	13	9	8	5	1	5	15	.188	.333	.115	10.13	3.38
Mathis, Doug	R-R	6-3	220	6-7-83	0	0	4.50	1	1	0	0	2	1	1	1	0	1	2	.143	.500	.000	13.50	0.00
McCarthy, Brandon	R-R	6-7	205	7-7-83	0	0	3.60	2	2	0	0	5	7	2	2	0	1	5	.350	.286	.385	9.00	1.80
Nelo, Hector	R-R	6-1	200	11-5-86	1	4	4.04	10	8	0	0	36	40	19	16	0	19	26	.301	.319	.291	6.56	4.79
O'Campo, Kyle	R-R	6-3	195	9-9-88	3	1	3.29	16	9	0	1	52	47	24	19	3	19	56	.249	.283	.233	9.69	3.29
Ortiz, Joseph	L-L	5-7	175	8-13-90	0	0	0.00	1	0	0	0	1	1	0	0	0	0	1	.333	—	.333	9.00	0.00
Rheinecker, John	L-L	6-2	220	5-29-79	0	1	21.00	2	2	0	0	3	10	7	7	1	0	0	.556	.500	.571	0.00	0.00
Roark, Tanner	R-R	6-2	220	10-5-86	2	1	0.73	7	0	0	0	12	9	2	1	0	3	11	.209	.313	.148	8.03	2.19
Romero, Levi	R-R	6-4	180	4-12-84	0	1	1.69	3	3	0	0	11	10	3	2	0	2	13	.250	.143	.308	10.97	1.69
Stanford, Tim	R-R	6-0	191	5-7-89	2	0	7.52	15	0	0	1	20	31	20	17	1	8	21	.365	.483	.304	9.30	3.54
Swanson, Glenn	L-L	6-1	175	5-15-83	0	1	1.80	4	3	0	0	15	9	4	3	0	2	11	.188	.000	.269	6.60	1.20
Thompson, Matt	R-R	6-3	210	2-10-90	0	1	11.88	7	0	0	0	8	25	23	11	0	4	12	.481	.500	.474	12.96	4.32
Tufts, Tyler	R-R	6-3	195	12-5-86	2	1	0.98	11	0	0	1	18	12	4	2	0	1	19	.182	.261	.140	9.33	0.49
Wagner, David	L-R	6-4	215	8-9-84	3	0	3.81	15	0	0	1	26	33	14	11	2	14	21	.311	.409	.242	7.27	4.85
Wieland, Joe	R-R	6-3	175	1-21-90	5	1	1.44	13	7	0	0	44	32	8	7	2	8	41	.200	.193	.204	8.45	1.65
Wilkins, Bobby	R-R	6-4	225	8-20-89	2	0	4.63	14	0	0	0	23	22	13	12	2	9	15	.259	.467	.145	5.79	3.47

Fielding

Catcher	PCT	G	PO	A	E	DP	PB
De Los Santos	.974	44	344	61	11	7	8
Puello	.941	4	27	5	2	1	1
Ramirez	.857	2	12	0	2	0	0
Torres	.993	27	113	23	1	1	3

First Base	PCT	G	PO	A	E	DP
Murphy	.975	17	145	8	4	12
Ortiz	.973	32	268	18	8	20
Puello	.986	9	66	7	1	6
Yan	1.000	1	10	1	0	1

Second Base	PCT	G	PO	A	E	DP
Higgins	1.000	2	3	5	0	1
Martinez	.955	26	48	78	6	12

Morrison	1.000	2	5	4	0	1
Selen	.950	27	59	73	7	11

Third Base	PCT	G	PO	A	E	DP
Hollander	.600	4	1	2	2	0
McGraw	1.000	1	0	1	0	0
Morrison	.923	4	1	11	1	0
Selen	.900	6	5	13	2	1
Yan	.852	39	26	66	16	4

Shortstop	PCT	G	PO	A	E	DP
Garcia	.874	39	41	105	21	20
Higgins	1.000	2	3	3	0	1
Hollander	.929	4	5	8	1	0
Martinez	.950	16	22	35	3	8

Outfield	PCT	G	PO	A	E	DP
Barto	.972	26	32	3	1	2
Cobb	.960	29	46	2	2	0
Cruz	1.000	1	2	0	0	0
Dove	.939	28	27	4	2	0
Hill	.980	31	42	6	1	1
McGraw	1.000	23	27	1	0	0
Morrison	1.000	4	6	3	0	0
Podraza	.957	19	20	2	1	1
Valdez	1.000	13	24	0	0	0
Yan	1.000	2	2	0	0	0

DSL RANGERS 1 — ROOKIE

DOMINICAN SUMMER LEAGUE

Batting	B-T	HT	WT	DOB	AVG	vLH	vRH	G	AB	R	H	2B	3B	HR	RBI	BB	HBP	SH	SF	SO	SB	CS	SLG	OBP
Alfonzo, Edward	R-R	6-1	185	10-29-89	.173	.146	.182	54	162	27	28	3	0	2	16	33	3	3	0	66	15	6	.228	.323
Arias, Keury	R-R	5-9	175	7-27-88	.205	.143	.240	38	78	15	16	5	0	0	11	18	2	0	0	18	4	2	.269	.367
Castillo, Yefry	R-R	5-11	175	4-22-90	.269	.172	.342	23	67	18	18	2	0	0	4	13	2	1	0	4	3	0	.299	.402
Garcia, Edwin	B-R	6-0	150	3-1-91	.292	.259	.305	62	209	28	61	7	1	0	28	31	2	6	2	28	8	4	.335	.385
Gomez, Jhonny	R-R	5-11	190	12-21-89	.250	.255	.248	50	172	19	43	6	0	1	20	33	3	3	3	32	3	5	.302	.374
Gonzalez, Mervin	R-R	6-2	190	3-16-89	.235	.250	.231	23	51	15	12	2	1	1	5	12	6	0	2	17	2	1	.373	.423
Gonzalez, Alex	R-R	5-11	165	7-7-91	.276	.286	.267	11	29	7	8	0	0	0	9	2	0	0	6	7	3	.276	.475
Lara, Juvenal	R-R	6-1	200	3-19-90	.284	.318	.267	23	67	9	19	1	2	0	16	9	1	3	0	8	5	1	.358	.377
Payano, Junior	R-R	6-1	175	2-20-90	.229	.321	.191	30	96	19	22	2	4	2	15	10	1	2	1	36	4	3	.396	.306
Perez, Alison	R-R	5-11	190	9-3-89	.190	.400	.116	22	58	4	11	2	0	0	3	3	2	0	1	6	2	0	.224	.250
Pimentel, Guillermo	R-R	6-1	190	11-12-89	.311	.323	.307	30	106	19	33	5	0	2	9	13	3	0	2	16	12	4	.415	.395
Polanco, Juan	R-R	5-11	175	7-22-90	.277	.324	.258	66	231	50	64	17	0	8	30	41	4	4	0	64	12	8	.455	.395
Salas, Roan	R-R	5-11	190	9-3-89	.281	.313	.268	33	114	18	32	8	0	2	16	11	2	0	2	16	4	2	.404	.349
Selen, Alejandro	R-R	5-10	175	3-20-89	.372	.143	.483	10	43	9	16	5	0	1	7	2	1	0	0	6	0	0	.558	.413
Solis, Emmanuel	R-R	6-3	220	6-29-89	.244	.373	.193	55	209	35	51	8	1	7	30	22	2	0	3	35	8	3	.392	.318
Ventura, Ariel	L-R	6-0	200	12-4-89	.256	.169	.296	62	207	34	53	8	6	3	20	17	5	0	2	66	8	1	.396	.325
Vizcaino, Stanly	R-R	6-0	175	10-9-88	.188	.349	.126	46	154	20	29	1	1	1	16	15	3	1	1	29	5	0	.227	.272

Pitching	B-T	HT	WT	DOB	W	L	ERA	G	GS	CG	SV	IP	H	R	ER	HR	BB	SO	AVG	vLH	vRH	K/9	BB/9
Barboza, Johan	R-R	6-1	190	8-28-91	3	0	1.63	12	0	0	1	28	31	9	5	0	5	12	.274	.261	.278	3.90	1.63
Bermudez, Rainier	R-R	5-11	175	6-8-85	4	3	2.15	14	7	0	1	46	18	13	11	1	24	67	.114	.163	.092	13.11	4.70
Caraballo, Orlando	R-R	6-3	195	8-13-89	4	1	4.21	21	9	0	0	47	46	33	22	2	47	39	.256	.171	.281	7.47	9.00
De Leon, Kelvin	R-R	6-6	185	1-5-89	4	2	2.83	13	11	0	0	57	39	25	18	2	34	66	.188	.273	.166	10.36	5.34
Garcia, Ysidro	R-R	6-0	165	5-15-87	1	1	4.61	6	0	0	0	14	15	9	7	0	6	12	.278	.077	.341	7.90	3.95
Grullon, Juan	L-L	6-0	185	3-4-90	6	1	2.44	13	8	0	0	48	37	17	13	0	25	67	.202	.136	.211	12.56	4.69
Hernandez, Carlos	R-R	6-1	185	9-19-89	0	0	2.51	4	3	0	0	14	8	6	4	1	4	17	.148	.133	.154	10.67	2.51
Mendoza, Anyenil	R-R	6-2	185	12-9-89	3	1	2.33	11	6	0	1	39	36	17	10	0	12	42	.238	.216	.246	9.78	2.79
Mendoza, Francisco	R-R	6-0	175	12-7-87	2	0	1.71	8	0	0	1	21	15	8	4	1	10	24	.188	.235	.175	10.29	4.29
Munoz, Miguel	R-R	6-4	180	6-29-88	1	0	0.28	8	5	0	0	32	21	2	1	0	7	23	.181	.242	.157	6.40	1.95
Peralta, Denny	R-R	6-4	170	12-11-89	5	3	2.57	20	0	0	4	42	42	19	12	0	13	38	.261	.231	.270	8.14	2.79
Rijo, Ezequiel	R-R	6-4	190	9-12-90	4	0	1.39	15	13	0	0	71	48	18	11	2	27	41	.191	.162	.203	5.20	3.42
Rojas, Jonathan	R-R	6-2	205	3-22-88	5	1	2.02	12	3	0	1	36	24	9	8	0	18	30	.198	.265	.172	7.57	4.54
Rosario, Carlos	L-L	5-9	155	3-13-88	0	5	4.91	15	0	0	4	37	35	27	20	2	23	26	.255	.167	.264	6.38	5.65
Rosendo, Ender	R-R	6-3	220	9-15-89	3	1	1.98	19	4	0	3	41	33	16	9	0	13	27	.214	.302	.180	5.93	2.85
Sibid, Pepe	R-R	6-0	200	2-2-88	1	0	3.20	12	0	0	2	20	15	11	7	0	14	23	.203	.273	.173	10.53	6.41

Fielding

Catcher	PCT	G	PO	A	E	DP	PB
Castillo	.968	11	83	9	3	0	1
M. Gonzalez	.970	17	105	25	4	0	4
Lara	.968	8	58	3	2	0	1
Perez	.982	9	50	5	1	0	1
Telis	.974	36	257	41	8	2	12

First Base	PCT	G	PO	A	E	DP
Gomez	.990	23	192	10	2	17
M. Gonzalez	.947	4	18	0	1	1
Lara	.977	7	39	3	1	5
Perez	.981	6	48	4	1	2
Salas	1.000	3	19	0	0	2
Vizcaino	.983	31	271	20	5	14

Second Base	PCT	G	PO	A	E	DP
Arias	.935	9	26	17	3	5

	PCT	G	PO	A	E	
Garcia	.917	7	19	14	3	1
A. Gonzalez	.964	5	12	15	1	4
Payano	.947	17	29	42	4	4
Salas	.940	21	37	41	5	6
Selen	.932	9	21	20	3	3
Vizcaino	.962	6	14	11	1	3

Third Base	PCT	G	PO	A	E	DP
Arias	.889	3	1	7	1	0
A. Gonzalez	.800	1	1	3	1	0
Salas	1.000	5	2	9	0	1
Solis	.882	52	55	110	22	14
Telis	1.000	3	1	7	0	0
Vizcaino	.889	8	4	4	1	0

Shortstop	PCT	G	PO	A	E	DP
Arias	.600	4	3	3	4	0

	PCT	G	PO	A	E	DP
Garcia	.936	54	80	153	16	19
A. Gonzalez	.778	5	6	15	6	2
Payano	.750	11	13	26	13	3

Outfield	PCT	G	PO	A	E	DP
Alfonzo	.945	53	66	3	4	0
Arias	1.000	12	5	0	0	0
Caraballo	—	1	0	0	0	0
Gomez	.926	19	25	0	2	0
Lara	1.000	1	2	0	0	0
Pimentel	.956	29	42	1	2	0
Polanco	.976	63	113	10	3	3
Telis	—	1	0	0	0	0
Ventura	.964	54	78	3	3	0
Vizcaino	—	1	0	0	0	0

DSL RANGERS 2 — ROOKIE

DOMINICAN SUMMER LEAGUE

Batting	B-T	HT	WT	DOB	AVG	vLH	vRH	G	AB	R	H	2B	3B	HR	RBI	BB	HBP	SH	SF	SO	SB	CS	SLG	OBP
Cabrera, Luis	R-R	6-2	185	8-14-90	.139	.109	.151	53	165	21	23	3	0	1	16	21	5	4	0	67	3	2	.176	.257
Castillo, Yefry	R-R	5-11	175	4-22-90	.289	.375	.267	24	76	8	22	2	0	0	12	3	3	1	0	7	0	2	.316	.341
2-team total (23 Rangers 1)					.280	—	—	47	143	26	40	4	0	0	16	16	5	2	0	11	3	2	.308	.372
Ceballo, Edward	L-R	5-11	180	10-8-90	.220	.186	.230	55	191	18	42	8	3	0	26	23	5	2	0	45	6	4	.293	.320
Chalas, Alfredo	R-R	6-0	160	6-24-91	.252	.268	.247	57	222	35	56	5	4	0	24	20	8	3	1	53	13	6	.311	.335
Del Rosario, Domingo	L-R	6-1	160	3-2-89	.192	.106	.217	63	208	32	40	3	2	0	12	38	3	2	1	53	14	4	.226	.324
Gonzalez, Alex	R-R	5-11	165	7-7-91	.186	.147	.198	50	140	18	26	3	0	0	14	21	3	3	0	35	18	5	.207	.305
2-team total (11 Rangers 1)					.201	—	—	61	169	25	34	3	0	0	14	30	5	3	0	41	25	8	.219	.338
Gonzalez, Julio	R-R	6-0	175	12-27-87	.291	.231	.310	13	55	14	16	3	1	1	9	5	2	0	1	8	10	1	.436	.365
Gonzalez, Mervin	R-R	6-2	190	3-16-89	.109	.167	.096	21	64	7	7	3	0	0	4	6	9	1	0	18	1	0	.156	.278
2-team total (23 Rangers 1)					.165	—	—	44	115	22	19	5	1	1	9	18	15	1	2	35	3	1	.252	.347
Guarucano, Gilberto	B-R	5-11	165	6-9-91	.210	.121	.236	46	143	12	30	5	0	1	17	17	4	1	0	36	1	2	.266	.309
Lara, Juvenal	R-R	6-1	200	3-19-90	.194	.267	.167	33	108	12	21	2	0	0	11	18	4	4	1	16	1	2	.213	.328
2-team total (23 Rangers 1)					.229	—	—	56	175	21	40	3	2	0	27	27	5	7	1	24	6	3	.269	.346

	B-T	HT	WT	DOB	AVG	vLH	vRH	G	AB	R	H	2B	3B	HR	RBI	BB	HBP	SH	SF	SO	SB	CS	OBP	SLG
Montes De Oca, Miguel	R-R	6-0	170	8-6-90	.259	.364	.233	15	54	11	14	2	0	0	4	7	2	0	0	11	0	3	.296	.365
Moreno, Miguel	R-R	6-2	185	1-9-90	.255	.217	.265	65	208	40	53	12	0	4	36	51	7	0	3	49	3	2	.370	.413
Mota, Ramon	B-R	5-11	190	7-20-90	.196	.235	.185	65	224	38	44	7	4	3	25	37	2	2	3	70	12	3	.304	.312
Payano, Junior	B-R	6-1	175	2-20-90	.155	.158	.155	31	116	12	18	2	0	0	4	15	0	1	0	43	9	1	.172	.252
2-team total (30 Rangers 1)					.189	—	—	61	212	31	40	4	4	2	19	25	1	3	1	79	13	4	.274	.276
Perez, Alison	R-R	5-11	190	9-3-89	.195	.471	.123	21	82	8	16	3	0	1	8	4	1	2	1	6	0	1	.268	.239
2-team total (22 Rangers 1)					.193	—	—	43	140	12	27	5	0	1	11	7	3	2	2	12	1	1	.250	.243
Pimentel, Guillermo	R-R	6-1	190	11-12-89	.286	.316	.277	29	84	21	24	4	0	2	12	22	12	1	1	19	12	5	.405	.487
2-team total (30 Rangers 1)					.300	—	—	59	190	40	57	9	0	4	21	35	15	1	3	35	24	9	.411	.440
Ventura, Wilson	R-R	5-10	175	11-13-90	.191	.308	.167	50	152	10	29	1	0	0	14	4	7	1	2	29	4	2	.197	.242

Pitching	B-T	HT	WT	DOB	W	L	ERA	G	GS	CG	SV	IP	H	R	ER	HR	BB	SO	AVG	vLH	vRH	K/9	BB/9
Alvarez, Reynaldo	R-R	6-2	185	2-27-88	4	3	3.17	26	0	0	5	54	50	27	19	4	22	56	.251	.302	.237	9.33	3.67
Borjas, Kelvin	L-L	6-0	210	6-30-89	2	5	6.49	15	8	0	0	53	68	56	38	4	33	28	.309	.176	.320	4.78	5.64
Bryan, Melvin	R-R	6-5	205	9-30-86	1	8	2.96	18	14	1	0	73	52	48	24	4	48	63	.194	.268	.161	7.77	5.92
De La Cruz, Michael	R-R	6-3	180	11-28-89	2	9	6.31	20	13	0	0	51	47	41	36	7	46	60	.247	.235	.252	10.52	8.06
Marinez, Yeyser	R-R	6-3	230	11-7-84	0	2	5.13	18	1	0	0	33	14	27	19	1	42	52	.124	.129	.122	14.04	11.34
Mayora, Raul	L-L	6-3	180	1-13-87	4	3	4.34	23	13	1	0	77	74	48	37	2	45	81	.256	.353	.243	9.51	5.28
Monegro, Jose	R-R	6-3	200	9-19-89	1	1	2.59	20	0	0	4	42	25	16	12	1	11	47	.167	.194	.158	10.15	2.38
Munoz, Miguel	R-R	6-4	180	6-29-88	2	2	3.48	11	6	1	0	41	37	22	16	2	7	40	.228	.244	.222	8.71	1.52
2-team total (8 Rangers 1)					3	2	2.08	19	11	1	0	74	58	24	17	2	14	63	—	—	—	7.70	1.71
Solano, Ismael	R-R	6-0	200	6-1-90	0	1	20.25	1	0	0	0	1	1	3	3	1	1	0	.250	.000	.250	0.00	6.75
Soto, Eleno	R-R	6-3	215	12-28-87	2	2	4.97	12	7	0	0	42	51	28	23	3	16	18	.298	.408	.254	3.89	3.46
Tirado, Pedro	L-L	6-2	180	12-18-90	0	2	5.64	11	1	0	0	22	23	20	14	3	12	12	.256	.300	.250	4.84	4.84
Urbina, Jose	R-R	6-3	190	9-8-88	3	4	5.59	17	6	0	0	47	48	42	29	3	37	37	.267	.294	.260	7.14	7.14
Zapata, Cristian	R-R	6-2	175	11-23-88	0	2	7.44	20	2	0	2	52	62	60	43	6	45	29	.300	.310	.295	5.02	7.79

Fielding

Catcher	PCT	G	PO	A	E	DP	PB
Castillo	.981	11	83	18	2	2	6
M. Gonzalez	.987	17	134	16	2	1	5
Guarucano	.958	28	173	33	9	2	11
Lara	.981	18	129	22	3	0	17
Perez	1.000	3	16	3	0	0	1

First Base	PCT	G	PO	A	E	DP
Castillo	1.000	2	9	0	0	0
Del Rosario	.978	20	177	4	4	17
J. Gonzalez	.991	12	108	3	1	8
M. Gonzalez	.957	2	19	3	1	1
Guarucano	1.000	9	70	4	0	11
Lara	.966	15	131	10	5	6
Perez	.993	14	120	14	1	14

Second Base	PCT	G	PO	A	E	DP
Chalas	.963	12	32	20	2	6
Del Rosario	.962	22	50	51	4	13
A. Gonzalez	.974	15	31	43	2	8
Payano	1.000	4	6	3	0	2
Ventura	.927	28	54	61	9	18

Third Base	PCT	G	PO	A	E	DP
Del Rosario	.933	9	6	22	2	0
Moreno	.891	64	55	157	26	16
Ventura	.556	3	2	3	4	1

Shortstop	PCT	G	PO	A	E	DP
Ceballo	—	1	0	0	0	0
Chalas	.865	46	52	121	27	20
A. Gonzalez	1.000	1	3	3	0	1

Moreno	.750	1	2	1	1	0
Payano	.761	26	34	71	33	15
Ventura	.750	2	3	3	2	0

Outfield	PCT	G	PO	A	E	DP
Cabrera	.923	49	55	5	5	1
Castillo	—	1	0	0	0	0
Ceballo	.984	47	59	3	1	1
Del Rosario	—	2	0	0	0	0
A. Gonzalez	.970	25	29	3	1	0
J. Gonzalez	1.000	1	1	1	0	0
Montes De Oca	.909	11	16	4	2	1
Mota	.936	61	111	6	8	0
Pimentel	.913	28	38	4	4	0
Ventura	1.000	6	4	0	0	0

Toronto Blue Jays

BY LARRY MILLSON

During another season that would end without a postseason appearance, the Blue Jays dipped into their past in the hopes of changing that trend.

With the team struggling in last place in the American League East with a 35-39 record, the organization changed managers on June 20, with Cito Gaston replacing John Gibbons. Gaston, 64, managed the Blue Jays to their last postseason appearance in 1993, when they defeated the Phillies for the World Series championship.

Despite an 86-76 record, the team finished fourth in the AL East. Hitting, not pitching, was a problem for the Blue Jays. They had a major-league leading ERA of 3.49, second-best in franchise history. Both the starters and relievers led the majors in ERA at 3.72 and 2.94 respectively.

The pitchers set a club record with 1,184 strikeouts—second in the AL to the Red Sox—with 231 from league leader A.J. Burnett, who went 18-10, 4.07. As usual, the team's best pitcher was Roy Halladay, who went 20-11, 2.78 with 206 strikeouts.

The staff was strong despite several key injuries that will have a rollover effect into the 2009 season. Shaun Marcum, who went 9-7, 3.39, had late-season Tommy John surgery and is lost for 2009. Casey Janssen, who had a solid 2007 in the bullpen, missed the 2008 season after having surgery to repair a torn labrum. Dustin McGowan, who had been maturing into a solid starter, had shoulder surgery in July. Reliever Jeremy Accardo was limited to 16 appearances because of injury.

The Blue Jays ranked 10th in the AL in batting average and on-base percentage at .264 and .331 and were 11th in slugging at .399. Injuries hampered the offense somewhat as well. Second baseman Aaron Hill had a concussion that ended his season in late May, the result of an on-field collision with shortstop David Eckstein. Third baseman Scott Rolen battled shoulder troubles. Center fielder Vernon Wells was twice on the disabled list with a broken wrist and a hamstring injury but hit .300/.343/.496 in 108 games.

There had been speculation about the future of general manager J.P. Ricciardi, who kept his job with two years remaining on his contract. But club president Paul Godfrey, 69, decided not to return after his contract expired at the end of the year.

ORGANIZATION LEADERS

BATTING		*Minimum 250 at-bats
*AVG	Patton, Cory, Dunedin	.305
R	Snider, Travis, Dunedin/New Hamp./Syracuse	89
H	Arencibia, J.P., Dunedin/New Hampshire	152
TB	Dopirak, Brian, Dunedin/New Hampshire	273
2B	Arencibia, J.P., Dunedin/New Hampshire	36
3B	Tolisano, John, Lansing	8
HR	Dopirak, Brian, Dunedin/New Hampshire	29
RBI	Arencibia, J.P., Dunedin/New Hampshire	105
BB	Campbell, Scott, New Hampshire	66
SO	Snider, Travis, Dunedin/New Hamp./Syracuse	154
	Jackson, Justin, Lansing	154
SB	Lydon, Wayne, Syracuse	43
*OBP	Campbell, Scott, New Hampshire	.398
*SLG	Dopirak, Brian, Dunedin/New Hampshire	.550

PITCHING		†Minimum 75 innings
W	Ray, Robert, Dunedin/New Hampshire	13
	Mills, Brad, Lansing/New Hamp./Dunedin	13
L	Wideman, A.J., New Hampshire/Dunedin	13
	Magee, Brandon, New Hampshire	13
†ERA	Mills, Brad, Lansing/New Hamp./Dunedin	1.95
G	Harang, Daryl, New Hampshire	59
GS	Ray, Robert, Dunedin/New Hampshire	29
SV	Falkenbach, Connor, Dunedin	28
IP	Ray, Robert, Dunedin/New Hampshire	167
BB	Murphy, Bill, Syracuse	84
SO	Mills, Brad, Lansing/New Hamp./Dunedin	159
†AVG	Mills, Brad, Lansing/New Hamp./Dunedin	.222

The Blue Jays gave a preview of their future when their top prospect, 20-year-old outfielder Travis Snider, was called up for the final month of the season after batting a combined .275/.358/.481 in the minors. He was impressive in his major league debut, hitting .301/.338/.466 in 24 games.

2008 PERFORMANCE

General Manager: J.P. Ricciardi. **Farm Director:** Dick Scott. **Scouting Director:** John Lalonde.

Class	Team	League	W	L	PCT	Finish*	Manager	Affiliate Since
Majors	Toronto	American	86	76	.500	7th (14)	J. Gibbons/C. Gaston	—
Triple-A	Syracuse Chiefs	International	69	73	.486	8th (14)	Doug Davis	1978
Double-A	New Hampshire Fisher Cats	Eastern	61	81	.430	11th (12)	Gary Cathcart	2003
High A	Dunedin Blue Jays	Florida State	85	53	.616	1st (12)	Omar Malave	1987
Low A	Lansing Lugnuts	Midwest	76	64	.543	3rd (14)	Clayton McCullough	2005
Short-season	Auburn Doubledays	New York-Penn	38	37	.507	7th (14)	Dennis Holmberg	2001
Rookie	GCL Blue Jays	Gulf Coast	26	32	.448	13th (16)	Dave Pano	2007
Overall 2008 Minor League Record			355	340	.511	11th		

* Finish in overall standings (No. of teams in league). ^League champion.

ORGANIZATION STATISTICS

TORONTO BLUE JAYS

AMERICAN LEAGUE

Batting	B-T	HT	WT	DOB	AVG	vLH	vRH	G	AB	R	H	2B	3B	HR	RBI	BB	HBP	SH	SF	SO	SB	CS	SLG	OBP
Barajas, Rod	R-R	6-2	245	9-5-75	.249	.204	.270	104	349	44	87	23	0	11	49	17	7	0	4	61	0	0	.410	.294
Bautista, Jose	R-R	6-0	195	10-19-80	.214	.242	.174	21	56	7	12	2	0	3	10	2	0	2	1	14	0	0	.411	.237
Coats, Buck	L-R	6-3	195	6-9-82	.200	—	.200	8	5	0	1	0	0	0	1	0	0	0	0	2	1	0	.200	.333
Diaz, Robinzon	R-R	6-0	225	9-19-83	.000		.000	1	4	0	0	0	0	0	0	0	0	0	0	1	0	0	.000	.000
Eckstein, David	R-R	5-7	175	1-20-75	.277	.333	.250	76	260	27	72	18	0	1	23	24	8	9	2	27	2	1	.358	.354
Hill, Aaron	R-R	5-11	205	3-21-82	.263	.286	.258	55	205	19	54	14	0	2	20	16	3	4	1	31	4	2	.361	.324
Inglett, Joe	L-R	5-10	185	6-29-78	.297	.276	.298	109	344	45	102	16	7	3	39	28	4	8	1	43	9	2	.407	.355
Lind, Adam	L-L	6-1	205	7-17-83	.282	.253	.294	88	326	48	92	16	4	9	40	16	2	1	4	59	2	0	.439	.316
Luna, Hector	R-R	6-1	190	2-1-80	1.000	—	1.000	2	1	0	1	0	0	0	0	0	0	0	0	0	0	1	1.000	1.000
McDonald, John	R-R	5-10	175	9-24-74	.210	.250	.184	84	186	21	39	8	0	1	18	10	2	7	2	25	3	1	.269	.255
Mench, Kevin	R-R	6-0	215	1-7-78	.243	.237	.256	51	115	18	28	11	1	0	10	14	0	0	2	18	2	0	.357	.321
Overbay, Lyle	L-L	6-2	230	1-28-77	.270	.215	.290	158	544	74	147	32	2	15	69	74	3	1	5	116	1	2	.419	.358
Rios, Alex	R-R	6-5	215	2-18-81	.291	.289	.292	155	635	91	185	47	8	15	79	44	2	0	5	112	32	8	.461	.337
Rolen, Scott	R-R	6-4	250	4-4-75	.262	.250	.266	115	408	58	107	30	3	11	50	46	10	0	3	71	5	0	.431	.349
Scutaro, Marco	R-R	5-10	185	10-30-75	.267	.268	.267	145	517	76	138	23	1	7	60	57	5	6	7	65	7	2	.356	.341
Snider, Travis	L-L	5-11	245	2-2-88	.301	.286	.305	24	73	9	22	6	0	2	13	5	0	0	2	23	0	0	.466	.338
Stairs, Matt	L-R	5-9	210	2-27-68	.250	.242	.251	105	320	42	80	11	1	11	44	41	5	0	2	87	1	1	.394	.342
Stewart, Shannon	R-R	5-11	210	2-25-74	.240	.286	.222	52	175	14	42	4	2	1	14	22	1	0	2	18	3	1	.303	.325
Thigpen, Curtis	R-R	5-11	200	4-19-83	.176	.250	.111	10	17	2	3	0	0	1	1	1	1	2	0	8	0	0	.353	.263
Thomas, Frank	R-R	6-5	275	5-27-68	.167	.143	.174	16	60	7	10	1	0	3	11	11	1	0	0	13	0	0	.333	.306
2-team total (55 Oakland)					.240	—	—	71	246	27	59	7	1	8	30	39	3	0	1	57	0	0	.374	.349
Velandia, Jorge	R-R	5-9	190	1-12-75	.000	.000	—	3	7	0	0	0	0	0	0	0	0	0	0	2	0	0	.000	.000
2-team total (7 Cleveland)					.200	—	—	10	15	1	3	1	0	0	1	0	0	0	0	4	0	0	.267	.250
Wells, Vernon	R-R	6-1	235	12-8-78	.300	.333	.290	108	427	63	128	22	1	20	78	29	3	0	7	46	4	2	.496	.343
Wilkerson, Brad	L-L	6-0	205	6-1-77	.216	.220	.216	85	208	20	45	8	2	4	23	25	1	2	5	53	2	3	.332	.297
2-team total (19 Seattle)					.220	—	—	104	264	21	58	12	2	4	28	35	1	4	5	68	3	5	.326	.308
Zaun, Gregg	B-R	5-10	205	4-14-71	.237	.163	.255	86	245	29	58	12	0	6	30	38	1	3	1	38	2	1	.359	.340

Pitching	B-T	HT	WT	DOB	W	L	ERA	G	GS	CG	SV	IP	H	R	ER	HR	BB	SO	AVG	vLH	vRH	K/9	BB/9
Accardo, Jeremy	R-R	6-2	190	12-8-81	0	3	6.57	16	0	0	4	12	15	10	9	1	4	5	.300	.300	.300	3.65	2.92
Benitez, Armando	R-R	6-4	260	11-3-72	0	1	5.68	8	0	0	0	6	4	3	4	1	2	9	.167	.250	.125	12.79	2.84
Burnett, A.J.	R-R	6-5	230	1-3-77	18	10	4.07	35	34	1	0	221	211	109	100	19	86	231	.249	.262	.231	9.39	3.50
Camp, Shawn	R-R	6-0	205	11-18-75	3	1	4.12	40	0	0	0	39	40	18	18	2	11	31	.263	.356	.204	7.09	2.52
Carlson, Jesse	L-L	6-1	160	12-31-80	7	2	2.25	69	0	0	2	60	41	16	15	6	21	55	.196	.205	.186	8.25	3.15
Downs, Scott	L-L	6-2	210	3-17-76	0	3	1.78	66	0	0	5	71	54	15	14	3	27	57	.213	.194	.226	7.26	3.44
Frasor, Jason	R-R	5-10	180	8-9-77	1	2	4.18	49	0	0	0	47	36	23	22	4	32	42	.208	.266	.174	7.99	6.08
Halladay, Roy	R-R	6-6	225	5-14-77	20	11	2.78	34	33	9	0	246	220	88	76	18	39	206	.237	.243	.230	7.54	1.43
League, Brandon	R-R	6-2	200	3-16-83	1	2	2.18	31	0	0	1	33	28	9	8	2	15	23	.230	.263	.200	6.27	4.09
Litsch, Jesse	R-R	6-1	215	3-9-85	13	9	3.58	29	28	2	0	176	178	79	70	20	39	99	.261	.270	.250	5.06	1.99
Marcum, Shaun	R-R	6-0	185	12-14-81	9	7	3.39	25	25	0	0	151	126	60	57	21	50	123	.222	.244	.200	7.31	2.97
McGowan, Dustin	R-R	6-3	230	3-24-82	6	7	4.37	19	19	1	0	111	115	60	54	9	38	85	.273	.295	.252	6.87	3.07
Parrish, John	L-L	5-11	210	11-26-77	1	1	4.04	13	6	0	0	42	47	19	19	5	15	21	.288	.305	.279	4.46	3.19
Purcey, David	L-L	6-5	230	4-22-82	3	6	5.54	12	12	1	0	65	67	41	40	9	29	58	.267	.284	.261	8.03	4.02
Richmond, Scott	R-R	6-5	225	8-30-79	1	3	4.00	5	5	1	0	27	32	12	12	2	2	20	.296	.426	.128	6.67	0.67
Ryan, B.J.	L-L	6-6	260	12-28-75	2	4	2.95	60	0	0	32	58	46	21	19	4	28	58	.216	.230	.211	9.00	4.34
Tallet, Brian	L-L	6-7	215	9-21-77	1	2	2.88	51	0	0	0	56	52	19	18	4	22	47	.243	.257	.230	7.51	3.51
Wells, Randy	R-R	6-5	235	8-28-82	0	0	0.00	1	0	0	0	1	0	0	0	0	1	0	.000	.000	.000	0.00	9.00
Wolfe, Brian	R-R	6-3	230	11-29-80	0	2	2.45	20	0	0	0	22	18	6	6	2	6	14	.234	.273	.205	5.73	2.45

Fielding

Catcher	PCT	G	PO	A	E	DP	PB
Barajas	.994	98	674	47	4	5	2
Thigpen	1.000	9	36	3	0	2	0
Zaun	.987	79	515	28	7	7	4

First Base	PCT	G	PO	A	E	DP
Barajas	1.000	4	27	5	0	4
Bautista	1.000	5	29	0	0	1
Overbay	.997	156	1316	155	5	112
Scutaro	1.000	3	15	1	0	2
Thigpen	1.000	1	1	0	0	0
Wilkerson	1.000	4	22	0	0	0

Second Base	PCT	G	PO	A	E	DP
Bautista	1.000	2	2	6	0	2
Eckstein	1.000	6	7	14	0	4
Hill	.996	55	87	150	1	27

	PCT	G	PO	A	E	DP	PB
Inglett	.984	66	123	176	5	38	
McDonald	—	1	0	0	0	0	
Scutaro	.995	50	60	126	1	19	
Velandia	1.000	1	1	0	0	0	

Third Base	PCT	G	PO	A	E	DP
Bautista	1.000	8	5	11	0	1
Inglett	1.000	6	5	13	0	1
McDonald	1.000	4	0	5	0	0
Rolen	.964	115	74	217	11	14
Scutaro	.981	41	22	84	2	8

Shortstop	PCT	G	PO	A	E	DP
Eckstein	.960	57	69	146	9	33
Inglett	1.000	2	0	2	0	0
McDonald	.960	67	80	134	9	33
Scutaro	.979	56	71	165	5	30

	PCT	G	PO	A	E	DP
Velandia	1.000	2	1	1	0	0

Outfield	PCT	G	PO	A	E	DP
Coats	1.000	7	6	0	0	0
Inglett	1.000	34	30	0	0	0
Lind	1.000	71	113	2	0	1
Mench	1.000	33	50	1	0	0
Rios	.988	151	326	14	4	3
Scutaro	1.000	3	4	1	0	0
Snider	1.000	20	25	2	0	1
Stairs	1.000	15	19	0	0	0
Stewart	1.000	40	56	3	0	3
Wells	.987	100	217	5	3	1
Wilkerson	.991	74	108	3	1	0

SYRACUSE CHIEFS   TRIPLE-A

INTERNATIONAL LEAGUE

Batting	B-T	HT	WT	DOB	AVG	vLH	vRH	G	AB	R	H	2B	3B	HR	RBI	BB	HBP	SH	SF	SO	SB	CS	SLG	OBP
Adams, Russ	L-R	6-0	205	8-30-80	.259	.267	.256	127	429	63	111	19	2	15	63	54	3	1	6	91	11	2	.417	.341
Bannon, Jeff	R-R	6-3	180	8-21-79	.290	.800	.192	9	31	5	9	1	0	1	9	2	1	0	1	9	0	0	.419	.343
2-team total (17 Durham)					.258	—	—	26	89	12	23	4	0	5	17	5	1	1	2	21	0	0	.472	.299
Cabral, Marcos	R-R	6-0	180	4-4-84	.257	.143	.286	12	35	7	9	3	0	0	2	4	1	1	1	6	0	0	.343	.341
Calderone, Adam	L-R	6-2	200	3-17-84	.125	.000	.143	3	8	1	1	1	0	0	2	3	0	0	1	3	1	0	.250	.333
Cannon, Chip	L-R	6-5	215	11-30-81	.231	.254	.223	80	251	26	58	13	0	5	30	42	2	0	2	83	1	0	.343	.343
Coats, Buck	L-R	6-3	195	6-9-82	.286	.276	.290	114	447	67	128	23	5	7	44	36	4	2	4	89	14	7	.407	.342
Demons, Chris	B-R	5-10	175	2-21-84	.056	.000	.111	8	18	1	1	0	0	0	1	1	0	0	0	5	2	0	.056	.105
Diaz, Robinzon	R-R	6-0	225	9-19-83	.244	.326	.205	36	131	7	32	7	1	1	13	5	0	2	3	10	0	1	.336	.266
2-team total (5 Indianapolis)					.255	—	—	41	145	7	37	7	2	1	16	5	0	2	3	10	1	3	.352	.275
Gutierrez, Chris	R-R	5-10	170	3-12-84	.071	.000	.091	5	14	0	1	0	0	0	0	0	0	0	0	6	0	0	.071	.188
Inglett, Joe	L-R	5-10	185	6-29-78	.407	.286	.450	15	54	12	22	2	1	6	7	1	0	0	7	1	2	.574	.484
Jeroloman, Brian	L-R	6-0	200	5-10-85	.200	.222	.193	25	75	5	15	2	0	5	11	0	2	0	17	0	0	.227	.302
Kratz, Erik	R-R	6-4	245	6-15-80	.234	.261	.222	40	145	20	34	11	1	9	24	9	2	1	1	33	1	0	.510	.287
Lind, Adam	L-L	6-1	205	7-17-83	.328	.268	.353	51	189	24	62	17	2	6	50	19	3	0	2	36	1	1	.534	.394
Lopez, Pedro	R-R	5-11	205	4-28-84	.236	.245	.232	104	339	38	80	12	1	2	27	33	2	9	2	63	4	1	.295	.306
Luna, Hector	R-R	6-1	190	2-1-80	.280	.322	.263	116	429	67	120	24	1	11	43	30	5	0	2	73	6	2	.417	.333
Lydon, Wayne	B-R	6-2	210	4-17-81	.259	.229	.273	130	499	71	129	19	3	1	42	58	3	8	5	84	43	9	.315	.336
Melillo, Kevin	L-R	5-11	195	5-14-82	.257	.213	.273	68	226	21	58	16	2	9	36	26	0	1	1	58	2	1	.465	.332
Mench, Kevin	R-R	6-0	215	1-7-78	.284	.370	.234	22	74	7	21	5	0	1	12	3	0	0	0	14	0	0	.392	.312
Nelson, Kevin	R-R	6-3	215	4-8-81	.250	—	.250	2	4	0	1	0	0	0	1	0	0	0	0	2	0	0	.250	.250
Nielsen, Eric	R-R	6-0	225	11-14-81	.190	.125	.213	19	63	6	12	1	1	2	1	0	0	0	0	7	0	0	.286	.203
Quintana, Al	R-R	5-11	205	11-9-82	.125	.500	.000	3	8	1	1	0	0	0	0	0	0	0	0	3	0	0	.125	.125
Sandoval, Danny	B-R	5-11	205	4-7-79	.295	.276	.303	79	315	38	93	14	0	7	35	16	1	3	0	43	3	3	.406	.331
2-team total (43 Buffalo)					.280	—	—	122	465	53	130	20	0	8	48	30	1	7	1	64	9	4	.374	.324
Santos, Sergio	R-R	6-3	225	7-4-83	.183	.107	.215	26	93	7	17	5	0	4	5	0	0	0	3	2	1	.237	.224
2-team total (86 Rochester)					.228	—	—	112	390	51	89	29	0	5	47	21	1	0	5	72	6	2	.341	.266
Smith, David	R-R	6-1	190	1-12-81	.302	.300	.303	18	53	9	16	2	0	3	8	11	0	0	0	10	1	1	.509	.422
Snider, Travis	L-L	5-11	245	2-2-88	.344	.286	.360	18	64	9	22	5	0	2	17	4	1	0	1	16	1	0	.516	.386
Stewart, Shannon	R-R	5-11	210	2-25-74	.000	.000	.000	1	4	0	0	0	0	0	0	0	0	0	0	0	0	0	.000	.000
Thigpen, Curtis	R-R	5-11	200	4-19-83	.222	.314	.184	96	361	28	80	23	0	3	41	21	3	5	5	58	2	1	.310	.267
Velandia, Jorge	R-R	5-9	190	1-12-75	.287	.212	.328	28	94	16	27	2	1	3	12	14	1	1	0	18	0	0	.426	.385
2-team total (52 Buffalo)					.233	—	—	80	300	34	70	5	1	3	20	34	5	5	0	67	2	0	.287	.322
Watson, Matt	L-R	5-11	205	9-5-78	.290	.246	.305	76	252	37	73	18	0	5	30	46	1	0	5	47	1	0	.421	.395
Wells, Vernon	R-R	6-1	235	12-8-78	.000	.000	.000	2	6	0	0	0	0	0	0	0	0	0	0	0	0	0	.000	.143
Zaun, Gregg	B-R	5-10	205	4-14-71	.250	.667	.000	2	8	1	2	0	0	1	0	0	0	0	0	2	0	0	.625	.250

Pitching	B-T	HT	WT	DOB	W	L	ERA	G	GS	CG	SV	IP	H	R	ER	HR	BB	SO	AVG	vLH	vRH	K/9	BB/9
Accardo, Jeremy	R-R	6-2	190	12-8-81	0	0	1.93	5	0	0	0	5	4	2	1	0	3	3	.211	.125	.273	5.79	5.79
Banks, Josh	R-R	6-3	210	7-18-82	0	2	7.02	3	3	0	0	17	21	15	13	1	5	12	.313	.286	.333	6.48	2.70
Bauer, Rick	R-R	6-6	225	1-10-77	0	0	3.18	12	0	0	3	11	10	7	4	1	7	13	.233	.167	.280	10.32	5.56
2-team total (22 Buffalo)					0	2	2.08	34	0	0	18	35	27	11	8	1	17	43	—	—	—	11.16	4.41
Bayliss, Jonah	R-R	6-2	205	8-13-80	3	2	3.40	26	0	0	2	40	36	18	15	5	12	29	.242	.212	.265	6.58	2.72
2-team total (28 Indianapolis)					3	5	4.58	54	0	0	5	73	81	42	37	8	25	54	—	—	—	6.69	3.10
Benitez, Armando	R-R	6-4	260	11-3-72	0	0	0.00	1	0	0	1	0	0	0	0	0	0	0	.000	.000	.000	0.00	0.00
Camp, Shawn	R-R	6-0	205	11-18-75	1	0	0.00	7	0	0	4	10	4	0	0	0	0	13	.125	.111	.130	11.70	0.00
Carlson, Jesse	L-L	6-1	160	12-31-80	0	0	0.00	2	0	0	0	4	1	0	0	0	0	2	.091	.000	.111	4.91	0.00
Cecil, Brett	R-L	6-3	220	7-2-86	2	3	4.11	6	6	0	0	31	28	17	14	1	16	31	.237	.357	.171	9.10	4.70
Davis, Kane	R-R	6-5	225	6-25-75	6	7	4.15	16	15	0	0	87	96	42	40	4	28	61	.281	.298	.263	6.33	2.91
De Jong, Jordan	R-R	6-0	190	4-12-79	6	2	4.04	53	0	0	5	71	70	34	32	8	37	71	.261	.319	.219	8.96	4.67
Gallo, Mike	L-L	6-0	175	4-2-77	0	1	12.71	6	0	0	0	6	15	9	8	2	3	5	.500	.438	.571	7.94	4.76
George, Chris	L-L	6-2	185	9-16-79	1	2	6.55	22	2	0	0	34	45	27	25	8	15	37	.319	.281	.345	9.70	3.93
Gosling, Mike	L-L	6-2	210	9-23-80	5	6	3.67	58	0	0	7	69	78	34	28	3	22	64	.291	.279	.299	8.39	2.88

Name	B-T	HT	WT	DOB	W	L	ERA	G	GS	CG	SV	IP	H	R	ER	HR	BB	SO	AVG	vLH	vRH	K/9	BB/9
League, Brandon	R-R	6-2	200	3-16-83	2	3	3.93	20	0	0	2	34	36	19	15	2	10	32	.261	.284	.239	8.39	2.62
Litsch, Jesse	R-R	6-1	215	3-9-85	1	1	3.60	3	3	0	0	20	18	10	8	1	4	18	.237	.222	.258	8.10	1.80
MacDonald, Mike	R-R	6-0	215	10-29-81	1	4	3.47	30	10	0	2	91	96	44	35	11	20	60	.269	.301	.239	5.96	1.99
Marcum, Shaun	R-R	6-0	185	12-14-81	0	1	2.77	2	2	0	0	13	10	5	4	0	3	15	.204	.192	.217	10.38	2.08
Matumoto, Jo	L-L	5-10	180	2-5-71	0	0	3.55	21	1	0	0	33	47	14	13	3	15	30	.346	.280	.384	8.18	4.09
Murphy, Bill	L-L	5-11	215	5-9-81	8	10	5.32	32	24	0	2	142	155	91	84	14	84	152	.280	.232	.307	9.63	5.32
Nelson, Bubba	R-R	6-0	210	8-26-81	1	1	7.64	11	0	0	1	18	19	16	15	3	12	13	.279	.304	.267	6.62	6.11
Parrish, John	L-L	5-11	210	11-26-77	10	1	2.97	17	13	0	0	91	80	42	30	5	39	100	.235	.188	.254	9.89	3.86
Purcey, David	L-L	6-5	230	4-22-82	8	6	2.69	19	19	0	0	117	97	41	35	8	34	121	.227	.218	.232	9.31	2.62
Richmond, Scott	R-R	6-5	225	8-30-79	1	3	3.56	8	8	1	0	48	44	20	19	6	13	40	.244	.279	.197	7.50	2.44
Romero, Davis	L-L	5-10	160	3-30-83	5	9	3.71	25	23	0	0	107	107	46	44	10	29	88	.263	.265	.262	7.43	2.45
Romero, Ricky	R-L	6-1	200	11-6-84	3	3	3.38	7	7	1	0	43	42	17	16	3	20	38	.263	.310	.246	8.02	4.22
Stidfole, Sean	R-R	6-2	200	3-12-84	1	3	3.27	27	0	0	0	41	32	18	15	3	19	32	.218	.230	.209	6.97	4.14
Tallet, Brian	L-L	6-7	215	9-21-77	0	0	4.50	2	0	0	0	2	2	1	1	0	1	1	.286	.500	.200	4.50	4.50
Thorpe, Tracy	R-R	6-4	265	12-15-80	2	0	2.63	13	0	0	0	14	11	4	4	1	9	18	.216	.316	.156	11.85	5.93
Wolfe, Brian	R-R	6-3	230	11-29-80	2	3	3.44	17	6	0	1	37	39	17	14	2	10	29	.277	.324	.233	7.12	2.45

Fielding

Catcher	PCT	G	PO	A	E	DP	PB
Diaz	1.000	21	181	22	0	1	4
Jeroloman	.989	23	166	9	2	0	0
Kratz	.991	39	302	38	3	6	3
Nelson	1.000	1	6	0	0	0	0
Quintana	1.000	2	7	1	0	0	2
Thigpen	.996	60	459	35	2	6	6
Zaun	1.000	1	10	0	0	0	0

First Base	PCT	G	PO	A	E	DP
Adams	1.000	1	2	0	0	0
Cannon	.995	72	542	47	3	62
Kratz	.889	1	8	0	1	0
Lind	—	1	0	0	0	0
Luna	.968	19	147	4	5	16
Melillo	.966	17	126	15	5	18
Nielsen	1.000	1	2	0	0	0
Thigpen	.985	31	239	16	4	27
Watson	.952	9	58	1	3	4

Second Base	PCT	G	PO	A	E	DP
Adams	.968	42	82	131	7	32
Cabral	.978	9	20	25	1	4
Gutierrez	1.000	1	2	0	0	0

	PCT	G	PO	A	E	DP
Inglett	.969	9	15	16	1	2
Lopez	.989	20	38	51	1	16
Melillo	.981	16	20	33	1	8
Sandoval	.960	45	89	125	9	34
Thigpen	1.000	1	0	1	0	0
Velandia	1.000	10	18	39	0	14

Third Base	PCT	G	PO	A	E	DP
Adams	—	1	0	0	0	0
Bannon	1.000	1	0	3	0	1
Cabral	1.000	5	1	3	0	0
Cannon	.760	6	5	14	6	0
Diaz	.667	2	3	1	2	0
Gutierrez	.667	2	0	2	1	2
Luna	.959	68	55	130	8	18
Melillo	.930	24	13	40	4	7
Quintana	—	1	0	0	0	0
Sandoval	1.000	13	6	31	0	6
Santos	.906	25	11	37	5	6
Thigpen	1.000	4	1	3	0	1

Shortstop	PCT	G	PO	A	E	DP
Bannon	.833	5	6	9	3	4
Cannon	1.000	1	2	6	0	2

	PCT	G	PO	A	E	DP
Gutierrez	.857	2	1	5	1	1
Lopez	.982	84	138	242	7	54
Luna	.984	19	22	41	1	9
Sandoval	.958	18	26	43	3	7
Velandia	.954	17	24	38	3	6

Outfield	PCT	G	PO	A	E	DP
Adams	.965	71	128	11	5	1
Bannon	1.000	1	1	0	0	0
Calderone	.750	3	2	1	1	0
Coats	.991	108	214	9	2	2
Demons	1.000	8	14	0	0	0
Inglett	1.000	6	15	1	0	0
Lind	.982	40	54	2	1	0
Lydon	.983	124	232	6	4	3
Mench	1.000	12	16	0	0	0
Nielsen	1.000	11	12	0	0	0
Smith	.958	13	21	2	1	0
Snider	.955	17	20	1	1	1
Stewart	1.000	1	2	0	0	0
Watson	.948	27	54	1	3	0
Wells	—	1	0	0	0	0

NEW HAMPSHIRE FISHER CATS

DOUBLE-A

EASTERN LEAGUE

Batting	B-T	HT	WT	DOB	AVG	vLH	vRH	G	AB	R	H	2B	3B	HR	RBI	BB	HBP	SH	SF	SO	SB	CS	SLG	OBP
Arencibia, J.P.	R-R	6-1	215	1-5-86	.282	.357	.247	67	262	32	74	14	0	14	43	7	2	0	4	55	0	0	.496	.302
Butler, Jacob	R-R	6-1	200	2-9-83	.242	.299	.218	122	434	50	105	25	3	16	64	62	4	0	1	116	0	0	.424	.341
Cabral, Marcos	R-R	6-0	180	4-4-84	.143	.154	.133	10	28	5	4	1	0	0	0	5	0	0	0	7	1	0	.179	.273
Campbell, Scott	L-R	6-0	200	9-25-84	.302	.194	.333	112	417	70	126	21	2	9	46	66	2	0	2	63	2	6	.427	.398
Diaz, Jonathan	R-R	5-7	165	4-10-85	.200	.400	.100	24	60	11	12	1	1	0	4	18	0	2	1	15	0	0	.250	.380
Dopirak, Brian	R-R	6-4	235	12-20-83	.287	.222	.304	22	87	5	25	6	0	2	13	2	0	0	2	10	1	1	.425	.297
Gutierrez, Chris	R-R	5-10	170	3-12-84	.254	.245	.259	82	268	42	68	17	3	2	35	43	4	1	2	61	0	4	.362	.363
Hatch, Anthony	L-R	6-4	200	8-30-83	.235	.219	.241	74	255	25	60	12	0	6	28	18	2	1	2	41	0	1	.353	.289
Jeroloman, Brian	L-R	6-0	200	5-10-85	.270	.293	.262	71	226	30	61	15	0	6	31	47	3	5	4	47	0	0	.416	.396
Klosterman, Ryan	R-R	5-11	190	5-28-82	.226	.272	.205	104	318	47	72	13	2	6	39	47	3	5	5	76	11	6	.336	.327
Kratz, Erik	R-R	6-4	245	6-15-80	.245	.357	.167	33	102	15	25	5	0	7	19	13	4	0	2	26	2	0	.500	.347
Kreuzer, Josh	R-R	6-6	245	9-28-82	.164	.186	.151	34	116	11	19	3	0	0	6	10	4	1	1	28	2	0	.190	.252
Mathews, Aaron	R-R	5-10	205	5-10-82	.296	.292	.298	72	297	47	88	13	3	6	51	25	0	4	4	47	2	3	.421	.347
Nielsen, Eric	R-R		225	11-14-81	.268	.269	.267	78	280	30	75	11	0	3	17	35	6	1	4	42	0	4	.339	.357
Patterson, Ryan	R-R	5-11	205	5-23-83	.248	.321	.211	121	460	57	114	29	3	17	53	22	3	1	4	83	7	3	.435	.284
Pettway, Brian	R-R	6-0	225	7-29-83	.000	—	.000	1	0	0	0	0	0	0	0	0	0	0	0	0	0	0	.000	.000
Phillips, Kyle	L-R	6-3	215	4-3-84	.306	.227	.321	78	268	33	82	16	0	8	34	27	1	4	1	41	0	2	.455	.370
Pinckney, Andrew	L-R	6-1	205	4-7-82	.276	.297	.270	58	185	23	51	16	1	4	13	20	1	1	2	47	1	2	.438	.346
2-team total (57 Portland)					.273	—	—	115	406	50	111	28	2	9	24	22	2	2	4	95	2	3	.419	.322
Smith, David	R-R	6-1	190	1-12-81	.265	.306	.251	76	279	42	74	26	1	12	43	39	4	0	1	81	1	1	.495	.362
Snider, Travis	L-L	5-11	245	2-2-88	.262	.225	.277	98	362	65	95	21	0	17	67	52	4	0	5	116	1	1	.461	.357

Pitching	B-T	HT	WT	DOB	W	L	ERA	G	GS	CG	SV	IP	H	R	ER	HR	BB	SO	AVG	vLH	vRH	K/9	BB/9
Blackwell, Chad	R-R	6-1	145	1-7-83	0	0	9.39	5	0	0	0	8	13	8	8	2	5	2	.394	.375	.412	2.35	5.87
Burch, Jason	R-R	6-5	215	10-15-82	0	1	5.65	10	0	0	0	14	22	9	9	1	4	16	.361	.476	.300	10.05	2.51
2-team total (21 Bowie)					3	3	4.37	31	0	0	0	45	59	25	22	4	16	42	—	—		8.34	3.18
Camardese, Brandon	R-R	6-2	205	7-2-83	0	1	12.46	5	0	0	0	4	11	6	6	0	9	4	.478	.444	.500	8.31	18.69
Cecil, Brett	R-L	6-3	220	7-2-86	6	2	2.55	18	18	0	0	78	66	24	22	4	23	87	.227	.224	.228	10.08	2.67
Dials, Zach	R-R	6-2	200	7-22-85	2	3	4.91	36	0	0	0	37	45	22	20	3	14	36	.290	.179	.375	8.84	3.44

Name	T	HT	WT	DOB	W	L	ERA	G	GS	CG	SV	IP	H	R	ER	HR	BB	SO	AVG	vLH	vRH	SO/9	BB/9
Gallo, Mike	L-L	6-0	175	4-2-77	0	0	3.57	13	0	0	3	18	20	10	7	3	9	8	.278	.323	.244	4.08	4.58
Gothreaux, Jared	R-R	6-0	200	1-27-80	0	1	7.82	22	1	0	1	38	52	34	33	5	20	25	.340	.364	.322	5.92	4.74
Harang, Daryl	L-L	6-2	225	11-19-82	4	6	5.10	59	0	0	2	65	72	38	37	6	39	54	.283	.243	.317	7.44	5.37
MacDonald, Mike	R-R	6-0	215	10-29-81	0	3	7.43	9	1	0	3	13	20	11	11	1	5	9	.357	.381	.343	6.07	3.38
Machi, Jean	R-R	5-11	245	2-1-82	2	6	4.65	21	9	0	1	70	74	37	36	3	40	51	.275	.241	.309	6.59	5.17
Magee, Brandon	R-R	6-5	215	7-26-83	7	13	4.75	28	28	3	0	163	184	95	86	14	66	69	.284	.260	.312	3.81	3.64
Matumoto, Jo	L-L	5-10	180	2-5-71	2	1	3.77	21	1	0	0	31	31	14	13	6	14	20	.265	.250	.274	6.39	4.35
McLeary, Marty	R-R	6-3	225	10-26-74	0	1	4.26	5	5	0	0	25	34	15	12	2	11	21	.340	.349	.333	7.46	3.91
Mills, Brad	L-L	6-0	185	3-5-85	3	2	1.10	6	6	0	0	33	24	11	4	2	12	32	.205	.192	.209	8.82	3.31
Nelson, Bubba	R-R	6-0	210	8-26-81	0	0	—	1	0	0	0	0	4	4	4	1	1	1	.800	1.000	.667	—	—
Overbey, Seth	L-R	6-2	185	4-30-84	4	2	4.12	53	0	0	1	74	81	38	34	6	38	53	.285	.318	.264	6.42	4.60
Pinto, Julio	R-R	6-0	225	10-23-84	4	3	6.35	20	3	0	0	45	63	32	32	4	16	30	.335	.351	.319	5.96	3.18
Ray, Robert	R-R	6-4	185	1-21-84	8	6	3.18	16	16	2	0	96	108	43	34	6	27	72	.282	.270	.293	6.73	2.52
Richmond, Scott	R-R	6-5	225	8-30-79	5	8	4.92	16	16	0	0	90	89	55	49	14	30	84	.251	.257	.245	8.43	3.01
Rodriguez, Edward	R-R	6-4	190	10-6-84	0	0	0.00	2	0	0	0	2	1	0	0	0	2	1	.200	.500	.000	5.40	10.80
Rodriguez, Kenny	R-R	6-2	190	3-17-85	1	3	11.28	7	6	1	0	22	34	29	28	2	22	10	.347	.365	.326	4.03	8.87
Roman, Orlando	R-R	6-1	210	11-28-78	1	1	7.31	21	0	0	2	32	39	29	26	5	19	30	.293	.302	.288	8.44	5.34
Romero, Ricky	R-L	6-1	200	11-6-84	5	5	4.96	21	21	0	0	122	139	70	67	9	55	78	.294	.305	.290	5.77	4.07
Stidfole, Sean	R-R	6-2	200	3-12-84	1	1	4.50	23	0	0	4	28	29	15	14	2	17	23	.276	.180	.364	7.39	5.46
Vermilyea, Jamie	R-R	6-0	190	2-10-82	3	3	7.55	20	0	0	0	39	54	34	33	7	23	26	.320	.362	.290	5.95	5.26
Wideman, A.J.	R-L	5-11	190	6-8-85	3	8	6.39	13	11	0	0	63	85	59	45	10	29	25	.318	.273	.341	3.55	4.12
Yates, Kyle	R-R	5-10	190	1-8-83	0	7	7.82	7	0	0	0	13	19	13	11	2	8	11	.328	.370	.290	7.82	5.68

Fielding

Catcher	PCT	G	PO	A	E	DP	PB
Arencibia	.986	50	313	32	5	7	7
Jeroloman	.990	65	376	26	4	4	6
Kratz	.993	19	132	14	1	3	0
Phillips	.980	12	90	6	2	0	0

First Base	PCT	G	PO	A	E	DP
Butler	.994	55	468	41	3	54
Dopirak	.976	17	153	8	4	10
Hatch	1.000	1	2	0	0	0
Kratz	.976	4	39	2	1	6
Kreuzer	.986	25	206	10	3	20
Phillips	.995	45	403	20	2	42
Pinckney	1.000	4	8	0	0	0

Second Base	PCT	G	PO	A	E	DP
Cabral	.885	6	9	14	3	0
Campbell	.987	109	199	322	7	71
Diaz	1.000	1	1	0	0	0
Gutierrez	.985	25	56	74	2	18
Klosterman	1.000	7	11	30	0	5
Pinckney	1.000	2	1	0	0	0

Third Base	PCT	G	PO	A	E	DP
Cabral	.800	3	3	5	2	0
Campbell	1.000	1	1	1	0	0
Diaz	1.000	3	2	5	0	0
Gutierrez	.926	15	4	21	2	0
Hatch	.927	70	36	129	13	14
Klosterman	.929	6	2	11	1	2
Kratz	1.000	2	1	2	0	0
Pinckney	.945	56	32	89	7	12

Shortstop	PCT	G	PO	A	E	DP
Cabral	1.000	1	0	2	0	0
Campbell	1.000	1	1	1	0	1
Diaz	.946	20	29	59	5	8
Gutierrez	.967	42	78	124	7	31
Klosterman	.971	87	155	281	13	68

Outfield	PCT	G	PO	A	E	DP
Butler	.919	46	56	1	5	0
Diaz	—	1	0	0	0	0
Klosterman	—	4	0	0	0	0
Mathews	.987	71	149	5	2	1
Nielsen	.984	74	117	9	2	0
Patterson	.980	114	234	13	5	0
Smith	.978	71	130	2	3	0
Snider	.982	59	105	5	2	2

DUNEDIN BLUE JAYS

HIGH CLASS A

FLORIDA STATE LEAGUE

Batting	B-T	HT	WT	DOB	AVG	vLH	vRH	G	AB	R	H	2B	3B	HR	RBI	BB	HBP	SH	SF	SO	SB	CS	SLG	OBP
Arencibia, J.P.	R-R	6-1	215	1-5-86	.315	.216	.351	59	248	38	78	22	0	13	62	11	1	0	2	46	0	0	.560	.344
Cabral, Marcos	R-R	6-0	180	4-4-84	.251	.176	.274	64	219	34	55	10	0	5	26	31	4	2	4	34	0	0	.365	.349
Calderone, Adam	L-R	6-2	200	3-17-84	.278	.333	.261	81	302	51	84	21	7	9	37	29	3	1	1	58	4	7	.483	.346
Collins, Joel	R-R	6-1	195	4-24-86	.500	.333	1.000	1	4	2	2	0	0	0	1	0	0	0	0	0	0	0	.500	.500
Cooper, David	L-L	6-0	175	2-12-87	.304	.222	.338	24	92	10	28	9	0	1	13	10	0	0	0	16	0	0	.435	.373
Corrente, David	R-R	6-2	210	10-13-83	.236	.111	.254	20	72	9	17	5	0	5	14	2	0	0	0	25	0	0	.514	.257
Diaz, Jonathan	R-R	5-7	165	4-10-85	.171	.300	.123	44	105	9	18	2	0	1	12	25	7	2	2	23	1	6	.219	.360
Diaz, Robinzon	R-R	6-0	225	9-19-83	.320	.111	.438	6	25	3	8	1	0	1	3	0	0	0	0	3	0	0	.480	.320
Dopirak, Brian	R-R	6-4	235	12-20-83	.308	.340	.301	106	409	77	126	25	2	27	88	47	4	0	3	100	0	0	.577	.382
Eckstein, David	R-R	5-7	175	1-20-75	.143	.000	.222	5	14	4	2	1	0	0	0	2	1	0	0	1	0	0	.214	.294
Emanuele, Chris	R-R	5-11	185	2-17-84	.245	.296	.222	116	441	73	108	22	3	8	49	47	15	6	3	95	12	5	.363	.336
Emaus, Brad	R-R	5-11	200	3-28-86	.302	.281	.314	124	473	87	143	34	3	12	71	60	2	3	5	56	12	4	.463	.380
Franko, Paul	R-R	6-0	200	6-7-84	.232	.450	.111	20	56	4	13	4	0	0	5	4	0	0	0	16	0	0	.304	.302
Gonzalez, Jesus	R-R	6-2	210	7-7-84	.228	.221	.230	94	346	35	79	19	3	11	38	21	7	0	1	85	0	1	.396	.285
Hatch, Anthony	L-R	6-4	200	8-30-83	.329	.364	.321	48	167	25	55	12	1	7	27	28	5	0	1	39	2	4	.539	.438
Lane, Matt	L-L	6-2	225	5-23-84	.200	.154	.216	42	150	13	30	9	0	3	26	16	2	0	1	49	0	0	.320	.284
Liuzza, Matt	R-R	5-11	220	2-3-84	.222	.048	.275	28	90	14	20	2	0	3	14	17	1	0	2	24	0	0	.344	.345
McDonald, John	R-R	5-10	175	9-24-74	.364	.333	.375	3	11	2	4	0	0	0	1	1	0	0	0	1	0	0	.364	.417
Nelson, Kevin	R-R	6-3	215	4-8-81	.077	.000	.111	4	13	1	1	0	0	0	0	2	0	0	0	3	0	0	.077	.200
Nicolas, Bartolo	L-L	6-2	170	8-25-84	.150	.500	.111	9	20	4	3	0	0	0	0	0	0	0	0	5	0	0	.150	.150
Patton, Cory	L-L	5-9	215	6-18-82	.305	.279	.313	109	407	70	124	30	2	13	70	45	0	0	5	78	4	1	.484	.370
Quintana, Al	R-R	5-11	205	11-9-82	.329	.265	.358	44	155	23	51	2	1	2	7	8	1	0	0	27	3	2	.394	.366
Rolen, Scott	R-R	6-4	250	4-4-75	.000	.000	.000	3	8	0	0	0	0	0	0	0	0	0	0	3	0	0	.000	.000
Sanchez, Luis	B-R	5-11	175	5-27-87	.251	.278	.241	107	331	44	83	7	4	1	35	39	1	4	2	67	3	3	.305	.330
Shoffit, Sean	L-R	6-2	205	6-9-85	.247	.219	.260	97	344	47	85	19	6	8	30	39	3	3	2	102	16	9	.407	.327
Smith, David	R-R	6-1	190	1-12-81	.231	.357	.160	12	39	2	9	3	1	0	3	5	1	0	0	11	0	0	.359	.333
Snider, Travis	L-L	5-11	245	2-2-88	.279	.316	.262	17	61	15	17	5	0	4	7	5	0	0	0	22	1	0	.557	.333
Stewart, Shannon	R-R	5-11	210	2-25-74	.125	.000	.143	6	16	0	2	0	0	0	3	1	0	0	1	4	0	0	.125	.348
Wells, Vernon	R-R	6-1	235	12-8-78	.500	.500	.500	2	8	3	4	0	0	0	4	0	0	0	0	3	0	0	.500	.500
Wilkerson, Brad	L-L	6-0	205	6-1-77	.455	.500	.444	3	11	4	5	3	0	1	1	0	0	0	0	2	0	0	1.000	.500

Pitching

Pitching	B-T	HT	WT	DOB	W	L	ERA	G	GS	CG	SV	IP	H	R	ER	HR	BB	SO	AVG	vLH	vRH	K/9	BB/9
Accardo, Jeremy	R-R	6-2	190	12-8-81	0	0	5.14	7	1	0	0	7	8	4	4	2	1	3	.286	.267	.308	3.86	1.29
Benitez, Armando	R-R	6-4	260	11-3-72	1	0	3.86	7	0	0	0	7	9	3	3	0	0	9	.300	.308	.294	11.57	0.00
Blackwell, Chad	R-R	5-11	145	1-7-83	4	3	3.18	44	0	0	2	71	63	27	25	4	12	66	.234	.255	.220	8.41	1.53
Boone, Randy	R-R	6-1	200	8-6-84	5	4	4.68	12	11	0	0	67	76	36	35	7	20	44	.291	.322	.264	5.88	2.67
Camardese, Brandon	R-L	6-2	205	7-2-83	1	0	0.53	10	0	0	0	17	9	1	1	1	5	13	.164	.111	.189	6.88	2.65
Cecil, Brett	R-L	6-3	220	7-2-86	0	0	1.74	4	4	0	0	10	6	2	2	1	2	11	.167	.063	.250	9.58	1.74
Chacin, Gustavo	L-L	5-11	205	11-4-80	1	7	7.88	11	11	0	0	46	72	43	40	9	12	22	.367	.480	.329	4.34	2.36
Crowell, Cody	L-L	6-3	205	8-23-85	6	1	4.68	23	0	0	0	25	16	16	13	1	16	20	.182	.233	.155	7.20	5.76
Cuotto, Jonas	R-R	6-0	180	9-21-86	0	0	0.00	2	0	0	0	4	1	0	0	0	1	2	.077	.200	.000	4.50	2.25
Dials, Zach	R-R	6-2	200	7-22-85	0	0	1.13	8	0	0	7	8	5	1	1	0	1	10	.172	.077	.250	11.25	1.13
Falkenbach, Connor	R-R	5-11	190	2-22-82	1	3	2.78	52	0	0	28	58	53	20	18	2	13	42	.241	.214	.257	6.48	2.01
Ginley, Kyle	R-R	6-1	230	9-1-86	7	7	4.68	17	16	1	0	77	90	45	40	7	32	55	.293	.370	.239	6.43	3.74
Gonzalez, Ray	R-R	5-10	215	11-1-85	12	4	3.14	27	20	1	1	138	155	56	48	6	30	74	.287	.314	.269	4.84	1.96
Marcum, Shaun	R-R	6-0	185	12-14-81	0	0	0.00	1	1	0	0	4	0	0	0	0	0	6	.000	.000	.000	13.50	0.00
Martin, Adrian	R-R	6-0	165	9-2-84	7	2	4.56	20	13	0	0	75	95	39	38	10	12	52	.316	.366	.281	6.24	1.44
Miller, Dan	R-R	6-3	220	7-7-86	0	0	—	1	0	0	0	0	1	1	1	0	1	0	.500	1.000	.000	—	—
Mills, Brad	L-L	6-0	185	3-5-85	4	0	1.35	6	6	0	0	33	25	9	5	2	12	35	.210	.200	.214	9.45	3.24
Page, Ryan	L-L	6-3	205	9-16-85	1	0	0.82	2	2	0	0	11	8	1	1	0	1	5	.205	.182	.214	4.09	0.82
Phillips, Paul	R-R	6-0	200	1-26-84	2	0	5.02	22	0	0	0	29	28	19	16	2	19	26	.248	.216	.263	8.16	5.97
Pinto, Julio	R-R	6-0	225	10-23-84	3	0	2.48	6	2	0	0	29	30	8	8	3	7	27	.268	.304	.242	8.38	2.17
Polanco, Celson	R-R	6-5	240	8-28-84	3	2	2.17	50	0	0	5	75	58	21	18	4	26	69	.214	.252	.188	8.32	3.13
Ray, Robert	R-R	6-4	185	1-21-84	5	3	4.20	13	13	1	0	71	71	37	33	6	18	60	.257	.273	.243	7.64	2.29
Rodriguez, Edward	R-R	6-4	190	10-6-84	2	2	3.84	49	0	0	3	59	74	30	25	3	27	32	.315	.291	.333	4.91	4.14
Rodriguez, Kenny	R-R	6-2	190	3-17-85	8	8	3.14	21	21	2	0	112	105	52	39	14	24	104	.241	.236	.244	8.38	1.93
Ryan, B.J.	L-L	6-6	260	12-28-75	0	1	2.25	4	1	0	0	4	2	1	1	0	1	5	.167	.167	.167	11.25	2.25
Starner, Nathan	L-L	6-3	200	5-29-84	4	0	1.82	28	4	0	0	59	51	14	12	0	15	53	.236	.290	.211	8.34	2.28
Wideman, A.J.	R-L	5-11	190	6-8-85	7	5	4.40	14	12	0	0	74	88	39	36	4	19	39	.300	.169	.358	4.76	2.32
Wolfe, Brian	R-R	6-3	230	11-29-80	0	0	0.00	1	0	0	0	1	0	0	0	0	0	1	.000	—	.000	9.00	9.00

Fielding

Catcher	PCT	G	PO	A	E	DP	PB
Arencibia	.988	53	365	37	5	3	8
Collins	1.000	1	9	1	0	0	0
Corrente	.982	16	100	7	2	1	3
R. Diaz	1.000	5	39	2	0	0	1
Liuzza	.995	27	176	16	1	0	4
Nelson	1.000	4	21	2	0	0	0
Quintana	.978	34	202	19	5	2	1

First Base	PCT	G	PO	A	E	DP
Cooper	.977	21	191	17	5	27
Dopirak	.986	83	741	46	11	79
Franko	1.000	12	90	6	0	9
Hatch	1.000	8	76	2	0	3
Lane	.978	16	127	8	3	13
Quintana	1.000	1	11	1	0	1

Second Base	PCT	G	PO	A	E	DP
Cabral	.983	37	68	109	3	27
J. Diaz	1.000	6	9	13	0	3
Emaus	.980	96	201	294	10	78

Third Base	PCT	G	PO	A	E	DP
Cabral	.969	13	14	17	1	1
J. Diaz	1.000	2	1	4	0	0
Emaus	.915	14	11	32	4	2
Gonzalez	.933	90	72	191	19	18
Hatch	.925	12	9	28	3	3
Quintana	.870	8	7	13	3	0
Rolen	.833	2	2	3	1	1

Shortstop	PCT	G	PO	A	E	DP
J. Diaz	.979	32	51	90	3	23
Eckstein	1.000	4	1	5	0	0

Gonzalez	.889	4	4	12	2	2
McDonald	1.000	3	1	5	0	2
Sanchez	.954	106	149	325	23	77

Outfield	PCT	G	PO	A	E	DP
Calderone	.994	75	158	4	1	0
Dopirak	1.000	5	3	1	0	0
Emanuele	.977	114	160	11	4	2
Hatch	.923	15	12	0	1	0
Nicolas	1.000	6	13	0	0	0
Patton	.953	98	169	13	9	0
Shoffit	.995	97	208	13	1	2
Smith	.950	10	18	1	1	0
Stewart	1.000	5	2	0	0	0
Wells	1.000	1	3	0	0	0

LANSING LUGNUTS   LOW CLASS A
MIDWEST LEAGUE

Batting	B-T	HT	WT	DOB	AVG	vLH	vRH	G	AB	R	H	2B	3B	HR	RBI	BB	HBP	SH	SF	SO	SB	CS	SLG	OBP
Ahrens, Kevin	B-R	6-1	205	4-26-89	.259	.262	.257	122	460	54	119	25	5	5	42	45	5	0	4	135	5	1	.367	.329
Baksh, Jonathan	L-R	6-1	205	3-1-85	.298	.296	.298	43	141	21	42	5	2	2	10	10	3	0	1	25	9	4	.404	.355
Barron, Raul	B-R	5-10	180	4-4-86	.275	.329	.257	82	313	35	86	15	3	0	32	9	3	3	2	44	11	6	.342	.300
Calderone, Adam	L-R	6-2	200	3-17-84	.194	.000	.207	8	31	2	6	1	0	0	1	0	0	0	0	5	0	1	.226	.219
Chavez, Johermyn	R-R	6-3	220	1-26-89	.211	.228	.206	115	402	40	85	20	2	7	39	25	9	1	2	128	9	5	.323	.272
Collins, Joel	R-R	6-1	195	4-24-86	.083	.000	.105	9	24	1	2	0	0	1	1	2	0	0	0	7	0	0	.208	.154
Cooper, David	L-L	6-0	175	2-12-87	.354	.136	.419	24	96	15	34	10	0	2	17	10	0	0	0	14	0	0	.521	.415
Ebarb, C.J.	L-R	5-11	215	6-11-83	.231	.205	.241	45	147	12	34	10	0	1	19	11	0	0	6	48	0	1	.320	.274
Eiland, Eric	L-L	6-2	200	9-16-88	.233	.200	.245	74	249	32	58	12	2	0	22	37	3	1	4	80	23	1	.305	.334
Jackson, Justin	R-R	6-2	186	12-11-88	.238	.228	.241	121	454	74	108	26	6	7	47	62	8	4	0	154	17	8	.368	.340
Jaspe, Jonathan	B-R	5-10	200	4-11-85	.290	.297	.287	64	238	32	69	11	1	6	36	19	1	0	4	33	3	1	.420	.340
Liuzza, Matt	R-R	5-11	220	2-3-84	.286	.384	.250	72	269	27	77	20	1	6	49	30	1	0	5	81	1	1	.435	.354
Mastroianni, Darin	R-R	5-10	195	8-26-85	.228	.178	.242	95	325	51	74	19	4	3	25	31	4	8	1	77	30	1	.311	.302
McDade, Mike	B-R	6-1	270	5-8-89	.194	.185	.199	60	216	15	42	13	0	2	19	11	1	1	1	63	0	0	.282	.236
Rodriguez, Manny	L-L	6-2	220	1-6-85	.268	.158	.303	100	395	36	106	33	2	9	71	14	1	1	3	106	1	0	.430	.293
Sierra, Moises	R-R	6-0	220	9-24-88	.246	.261	.241	130	451	50	111	16	5	9	39	26	8	1	3	114	12	11	.364	.293
Stone, Wes	R-R	5-10	190	4-16-87	.231	.154	.256	18	52	8	12	3	0	0	2	5	0	0	1	18	0	0	.288	.293
Talley, Jon	L-R	6-4	220	2-18-89	.500	—	.500	1	2	0	1	0	0	0	0	1	0	0	0	0	0	0	.500	.667
Tolisano, John	B-R	5-11	190	10-7-88	.229	.219	.233	120	432	64	99	20	8	6	47	56	1	6	110	5	2	.354	.315

Pitching	B-T	HT	WT	DOB	W	L	ERA	G	GS	CG	SV	IP	H	R	ER	HR	BB	SO	AVG	vLH	vRH	K/9	BB/9
Barbara, Michael	R-R	6-3	170	4-27-85	2	4	3.12	26	0	0	0	49	46	18	17	2	15	30	.260	.243	.271	5.51	2.76
Bell, Bobby	B-R	6-4	200	8-26-85	0	0	0.00	2	0	0	0	3	0	0	0	0	4	.000	.000	.000	12.00	0.00
Boone, Randy	R-R	6-1	200	8-6-84	6	2	2.50	15	10	1	0	76	75	26	21	3	20	53	.264	.301	.219	6.30	2.38

Name	B-T	HT	WT	DOB	W	L	ERA	G	GS	CG	SV	IP	H	R	ER	HR	BB	SO	AVG	vLH	vRH	K/9	BB/9
Buckwalter, Ross	L-R	6-0	185	1-27-85	2	0	1.07	23	0	0	0	34	28	6	4	1	5	20	.224	.218	.229	5.35	1.34
Cheng, Chi-Hung	L-L	6-1	210	6-20-85	5	9	4.88	25	14	0	0	94	122	70	51	8	49	71	.318	.286	.333	6.80	4.69
Collins, Tim	L-L	5-7	155	8-29-89	4	2	1.58	39	0	0	14	68	36	13	12	3	32	98	.156	.101	.179	12.91	4.21
Crowell, Cody	L-R	6-3	205	8-23-85	1	2	1.76	28	0	0	9	41	22	9	8	1	20	65	.153	.096	.185	14.27	4.39
Cuthbertson, Brad	R-R	5-10	175	1-7-85	1	1	6.91	10	0	0	0	14	19	16	11	3	12	18	.322	.290	.357	11.30	7.53
Dougher, Jimmy	R-R	6-7	225	7-3-85	3	1	3.89	18	4	0	0	44	46	22	19	6	5	39	.269	.215	.315	7.98	1.02
Estanga, Edgar	L-L	5-9	230	10-18-85	9	3	3.00	45	0	0	9	102	92	40	34	4	22	106	.244	.237	.248	9.35	1.94
Farina, Alan	R-R	5-11	190	8-9-86	3	1	3.07	15	0	0	1	29	19	11	10	2	14	37	.179	.200	.167	11.35	4.30
Farquhar, Danny	R-R	5-11	180	2-17-87	0	0	0.00	3	0	0	0	6	0	1	0	0	2	4	.000	.000	.000	6.00	3.00
Gailey, Frank	L-L	5-11	185	11-18-85	5	0	1.26	20	0	0	1	36	19	5	5	2	8	40	.153		.157	10.09	2.02
Ginley, Kyle	R-R	6-1	230	9-1-86	0	0	1.24	6	6	0	0	36	40	10	5	1	6	36	.280	.338	.212	8.92	1.49
Koch, Ryan	R-R	6-3	200	10-16-85	1	0	1.80	3	1	0	0	10	5	3	2	0	1	10	.143	.214	.095	9.00	0.90
Letko, Brian	L-L	6-5	195	1-23-85	4	4	4.14	15	13	1	0	63	62	39	29	4	30	51	.244	.233	.249	7.29	4.29
Magnuson, Trystan	L-R	6-8	205	6-6-85	0	9	5.40	24	24	0	0	82	91	57	49	6	35	49	.282	.291	.272	5.40	3.86
Mills, Brad	L-L	6-0	185	3-5-85	6	3	2.55	15	15	0	0	81	71	30	23	3	28	92	.233	.241	.230	10.18	3.10
O'Brien, Dan	L-L	5-10	190	9-12-84	0	0	6.55	8	0	0	0	11	13	12	8	1	9	10	.283	.314	.313	8.18	7.36
Perez, Luis	L-L	6-0	205	1-20-85	5	12	3.60	28	23	0	0	137	136	68	55	4	51	137	.264	.229	.279	8.98	3.34
Rzepczynski, Marc	L-L	6-3	205	8-29-85	7	6	2.83	22	22	0	0	121	100	41	38	2	42	124	.230	.234	.229	9.22	3.12
Starner, Nathan	L-L	6-3	200	5-29-84	1	4	1.67	8	8	0	0	43	37	11	8	1	8	45	.234	.196	.255	9.42	1.67
Wice, Joe	L-L	6-6	230	9-1-85	6	1	1.78	26	0	0	1	51	32	10	10	2	9	51	.179	.190	.172	9.06	1.60

Fielding

Catcher	PCT	G	PO	A	E	DP	PB
Collins	1.000	7	37	1	0	0	1
Ebarb	.989	37	253	24	3	4	6
Jaspe	.990	45	354	35	4	4	6
Liuzza	.992	62	573	38	5	4	6

First Base	PCT	G	PO	A	E	DP
Barron	1.000	2	14	1	0	2
Cooper	.995	21	186	19	1	16
Jaspe	.976	7	38	2	1	6
McDade	.988	57	532	35	7	50
Rodriguez	.981	57	491	29	10	53

Second Base	PCT	G	PO	A	E	DP
Barron	.974	26	37	74	3	19

	PCT	G	PO	A	E	DP
Mastroianni	1.000	2	2	2	0	0
Stone	.979	8	24	22	1	7
Tolisano	.952	108	192	301	25	72

Third Base	PCT	G	PO	A	E	DP
Ahrens	.906	104	58	201	27	18
Barron	.929	30	11	80	7	9
Jaspe	.923	7	15	21	3	1
Stone	.875	5	2	5	1	0

Shortstop	PCT	G	PO	A	E	DP
Barron	.965	23	33	77	4	16
Jackson	.956	120	188	379	26	83
Stone	—	1	0	0	0	0

Outfield	PCT	G	PO	A	E	DP
Baksh	1.000	29	52	2	0	1
Barron	1.000	3	4	0	0	0
Calderone	.857	7	6	0	1	0
Chavez	.948	103	116	12	7	2
Eiland	.970	69	95	2	3	1
Mastroianni	.977	88	163	10	4	2
Sierra	.955	128	202	11	10	3

AUBURN DOUBLEDAYS — SHORT-SEASON

NEW YORK-PENN LEAGUE

Batting	B-T	HT	WT	DOB	AVG	vLH	vRH	G	AB	R	H	2B	3B	HR	RBI	BB	HBP	SH	SF	SO	SB	CS	SLG	OBP
Amar, Adam	R-R	6-4	240	11-30-85	.302	.311	.298	67	252	30	76	17	0	9	42	22	4	0	6	28	0	0	.476	.359
Baksh, Jonathan	L-R	6-1	205	3-1-85	.333	—	.333	1	3	1	1	1	0	0	1	1	0	0	0	0	1	0	.667	.500
Collins, Joel	R-R	6-1	195	4-24-86	.326	.342	.320	48	141	20	46	13	3	3	21	7	15	0	1	17	0	1	.525	.415
Condotta, Steve	R-R	5-11	175	3-18-85	.167	.100	.214	8	24	3	4	0	0	0	2	2	0	2	1	3	1	0	.167	.222
Cooper, David	L-L	6-0	175	2-12-87	.341	.412	.324	21	85	10	29	10	1	2	21	10	0	0	0	16	0	1	.553	.411
Del Campo, Jonathan	B-R	6-2	185	5-18-88	.266	.321	.244	57	188	26	50	14	3	2	16	21	0	1	0	51	3	2	.404	.340
Demons, Chris	B-R	5-10	175	2-21-84	.236	.283	.215	56	195	34	46	8	1	0	15	34	3	7	3	53	21	2	.287	.353
Hopkins, Chris	R-R	5-11	170	9-10-87	.194	.163	.207	59	165	25	32	2	1	0	11	24	4	6	2	49	11	7	.218	.308
House, Chris	L-R	5-9	170	2-3-89	.222	.083	.250	28	72	9	16	4	0	0	4	11	0	2	0	19	0	0	.278	.325
Kervin, Bryan	L-R	5-11	180	3-23-85	.224	.156	.242	50	223	21	50	7	0	0	22	29	1	4	1	55	2	5	.256	.315
McDade, Mike	B-R	6-1	270	5-8-89	.257	.245	.261	52	191	18	49	8	1	3	27	22	1	0	2	53	1	0	.356	.333
Nicolas, Bartolo	L-L	6-2	170	8-25-84	.278	.279	.278	68	241	38	67	11	1	1	24	10	1	3	1	54	9	3	.344	.308
Rivera, Luis	R-R	6-1	190	10-12-86	.182	.115	.210	42	88	11	16	3	0	0	8	9	1	1	0	32	2	1	.216	.265
Sobolewski, Mark	R-R	6-0	190	12-24-86	.256	.364	.220	35	133	18	34	5	0	1	10	4	1	1	0	32	0	0	.316	.283
Soto, Lee	R-R	6-2	220	6-13-85	.238	.231	.241	44	151	18	36	5	1	3	13	2	1	2	0	47	4	0	.344	.253
Turkamani, Karim	R-R	5-10	190	1-20-87	.196	.105	.229	21	46	1	9	1	0	0	4	1	0	0	1	22	0	0	.217	.208
Van Kirk, Brian	R-R	6-1	195	8-10-85	.282	.326	.267	59	181	28	51	12	1	4	37	34	1	0	2	54	1	0	.425	.394
Vasquez, Carlos	R-R	6-0	150	5-15-86	.202	.185	.208	43	99	14	20	3	0	0	9	10	2	5	1	33	3	2	.232	.286

Pitching	B-T	HT	WT	DOB	W	L	ERA	G	GS	CG	SV	IP	H	R	ER	HR	BB	SO	AVG	vLH	vRH	K/9	BB/9
Anderson, John	L-L	6-3	205	11-9-88	0	0	0.00	1	0	0	0	1	1	0	0	0	1	0	.200	.000	.200	0.00	6.75
Bell, Bobby	B-R	6-4	200	8-26-85	0	0	0.96	19	0	0	10	28	15	3	3	0	0	39	.153	.132	.167	12.69	0.00
Carreno, Joel	R-R	6-0	190	3-7-87	5	5	3.42	15	13	0	0	76	74	32	29	6	19	85	.255	.252	.257	10.02	2.24
Crawford, Evan	R-L	6-1	175	9-2-86	0	2	3.03	13	5	0	0	30	21	13	10	0	16	23	.193	.321	.148	6.98	4.85
Cryer, Justin	R-R	6-1	215	6-3-86	0	3	5.10	21	0	0	3	30	41	22	17	3	12	28	.320	.279	.341	8.40	3.60
Daly, Matt	R-R	5-11	185	8-14-86	2	2	1.46	23	0	0	5	25	19	6	4	0	10	28	.204	.265	.169	10.22	3.65
Dougher, Jimmy	R-R	6-7	225	7-3-85	0	0	0.00	2	0	0	0	5	2	0	0	0	1	5	.125	.143	.111	9.64	1.93
Farquhar, Danny	R-R	5-11	180	2-17-87	2	2	2.39	12	0	0	0	26	20	10	7	1	6	27	.215	.241	.203	9.23	2.05
Gailey, Frank	L-L	5-11	185	11-18-85	1	0	1.93	9	0	0	0	5	3	1	1	0	1	5	.176	.000	.214	9.64	1.93
Huggins, Chuck	L-L	6-1	185	5-6-86	2	1	2.15	19	0	0	1	29	19	7	7	4	10	49	.173	.139	.189	15.03	3.07
Leffler, Scott	R-R	6-2	210	8-7-84	2	0	4.50	5	0	0	0	8	6	4	4	0	4	7	.207	.250	.200	7.88	4.50
Letko, Brian	L-L	6-5	195	1-23-85	0	0	0.00	1	0	0	0	2	2	0	0	0	0	2	.286	.000	.400	9.00	0.00
Liebel, Andrew	R-R	6-1	180	3-22-86	1	0	3.68	7	1	0	0	15	19	6	6	2	2	19	.311	.308	.314	11.66	1.23
Mayora, Yorman	R-R	6-1	175	4-20-87	0	1	7.04	3	0	0	0	8	9	6	6	0	2	9	.290	.429	.250	10.57	2.35

Name	B-T	HT	WT	DOB			ERA/AVG	G																						

Miller, Dan	R-R	6-3	220	7-7-86	0	0	6.75	2	0	0	0	4	6	5	3	0	2	5	.353	.500	.222	11.25	4.50
Monti, Jay	R-R	6-1	210	3-15-85	4	1	5.17	21	0	0	2	38	46	22	22	1	9	32	.305	.296	.309	7.51	2.11
Moody, Hunter	L-L	6-3	200	1-31-86	1	0	2.08	9	0	0	1	17	12	8	4	4	3	17	.185	.240	.150	8.83	1.56
O'Brien, Dan	L-L	5-10	190	9-12-84	2	0	1.65	8	0	0	0	16	13	3	3	0	6	12	.241	.100	.273	6.61	3.31
Page, Ryan	L-L	6-3	205	9-16-85	1	0	0.00	4	0	0	0	6	2	0	0	0	1	3	.111	.000	.125	4.50	1.50
Perez, Castillo	R-R	6-3	185	8-20-87	4	6	3.39	15	14	0	0	69	70	32	26	4	22	68	.262	.228	.283	8.87	2.87
Potts, Jared	L-L	6-3	200	7-4-85	1	1	1.23	3	0	0	0	7	6	4	1	0	3	9	.214	.333	.200	11.05	3.68
Roenicke, Jason	R-R	6-0	200	10-25-85	0	0	2.31	9	0	0	1	12	8	4	3	0	8	9	.190	.300	.156	6.94	6.17
Walden, Marcus	R-R	6-0	195	9-13-88	2	3	4.80	14	11	0	0	60	70	38	32	4	20	51	.288	.351	.248	7.65	3.00
Walter, Kyle	R-L	6-3	195	7-16-84	3	0	2.29	8	0	0	0	20	13	7	5	0	11	22	.183	.150	.196	10.07	5.03
Wells, Josh	R-R	6-7	198	6-6-87	6	4	3.92	16	16	0	0	64	72	32	28	0	23	47	.283	.315	.265	6.58	3.22
Wright, Matt	L-L	5-10	170	5-7-87	0	3	3.58	15	15	0	0	50	53	27	20	0	22	54	.270	.302	.261	9.66	3.93

Fielding

Catcher	PCT	G	PO	A	E	DP	PB
Collins	.997	45	352	27	1	2	7
House	.995	28	197	15	1	1	8
Turkamani	1.000	21	109	8	0	0	5

First Base	PCT	G	PO	A	E	DP
Amar	.976	18	149	13	4	9
Collins	1.000	1	1	0	0	0
Cooper	1.000	16	145	13	0	16
Del Campo	1.000	1	1	0	0	0
McDade	.971	41	311	18	10	31

Second Base	PCT	G	PO	A	E	DP
Condotta	1.000	3	3	7	0	1

Del Campo	.954	52	79	106	9	27
Vasquez	.904	27	49	54	11	13

Third Base	PCT	G	PO	A	E	DP
Collins	1.000	1	0	1	0	0
Condotta	1.000	1	0	2	0	1
Del Campo	.667	1	0	2	1	0
Sobolewski	.897	34	28	68	11	4
Soto	.873	41	23	66	13	6
Vasquez	—	1	0	0	0	0

Shortstop	PCT	G	PO	A	E	DP
Condotta	1.000	4	4	8	0	1
Kervin	.961	68	96	202	12	42

Vasquez	.923	9	13	11	2	3

Outfield	PCT	G	PO	A	E	DP
Baksh	—	1	0	0	0	0
Demons	.991	56	111	2	1	1
Hopkins	.972	55	67	2	2	0
Nicolas	.946	64	98	7	6	1
Rivera	.864	30	19	0	3	0
Van Kirk	.884	56	58	3	8	1

GCL BLUE JAYS

GULF COAST LEAGUE

ROOKIE

Batting	B-T	HT	WT	DOB	AVG	vLH	vRH	G	AB	R	H	2B	3B	HR	RBI	BB	HBP	SH	SF	SO	SB	CS	SLG	OBP
Brisker, Markus	R-R	6-4	192	8-21-90	.306	.393	.275	32	108	16	33	4	0	0	6	11	0	1	0	22	13	4	.343	.370
Crouse, Michael	R-R	6-4	205	11-22-90	.133	.000	.167	7	15	2	2	0	1	0	0	3	1	1	0	7	1	1	.267	.316
Denis-Fortier, Kevin	L-R	6-3	205	9-22-87	.250	.167	.265	13	40	3	10	6	0	1	3	1	0	0	0	22	0	0	.475	.268
Diaz, Robinzon	R-R	6-0	225	9-19-83	.386	.308	.419	15	44	9	17	3	0	2	10	2	0	2	0	4	0	0	.591	.420
Fernandez, Luis	R-R	6-0	150	11-16-87	.247	.375	.221	27	93	15	23	6	0	1	7	5	5	0	1	18	5	0	.344	.317
Fuenmayor, Balbino	R-R	6-3	195	11-26-89	.307	.262	.321	50	179	25	55	14	2	3	26	11	5	0	2	48	0	3	.458	.360
Gilligan, Kyle	R-R	6-2	185	3-7-88	.282	.261	.287	35	131	15	37	7	0	1	15	6	3	1	2	23	9	1	.359	.324
Gonzalez, Arvin	R-L	6-1	160	2-25-88	.233	.250	.229	31	90	12	21	5	0	0	9	5	1	1	0	24	6	3	.289	.281
Hurtado, Luis	R-R	5-11	175	11-4-88	.125	.167	.111	16	24	3	3	1	0	0	1	3	0	1	0	4	0	0	.167	.222
Jimenez, Antonio	R-R	6-0	185	5-1-90	.191	.167	.200	19	47	5	9	2	0	0	5	3	1	1	0	16	5	2	.234	.255
McClanahan, Justin	R-R	6-2	210	8-22-85	.282	.313	.275	47	163	33	46	8	2	8	32	16	5	0	4	40	17	8	.503	.356
McElroy, Brad	L-R	5-11	192	4-24-86	.241	.125	.270	26	79	10	19	3	1	1	8	15	3	0	0	12	5	0	.342	.381
Nelson, Nate	R-R	6-5	260	9-27-84	.171	.250	.148	26	70	5	12	4	0	2	11	6	4	0	2	31	0	1	.314	.268
Pastornicky, Tyler	R-R	5-11	170	12-13-89	.263	.257	.264	50	160	32	42	6	3	1	17	21	2	0	3	21	27	5	.356	.349
Perez, Yensy	R-R	5-11	160	7-21-87	.227	.318	.200	33	97	13	22	3	0	1	13	3	4	1	1	22	13	2	.289	.276
Ramirez, Welinton	R-R	6-2	175	4-13-87	.261	.256	.263	47	176	24	46	7	2	4	25	11	2	0	1	56	4	4	.392	.311
Rodriguez, Henry	R-L	5-11	182	10-19-87	.119	.300	.063	18	42	4	5	2	0	1	2	2	3	0	0	19	0	0	.238	.213
Stewart, Shannon	R-R	5-11	210	2-25-74	.667	—	.667	2	6	1	4	1	0	0	1	1	0	0	0	1	0	0	.833	.714
Talley, Jon	L-R	6-4	220	2-18-89	.300	.313	.296	42	140	18	42	7	1	6	29	9	3	0	3	48	1	0	.493	.348
Valdez, Jonnathan	L-R	6-4	210	9-5-90	.154	.286	.125	17	39	4	6	1	0	1	1	2	0	0	0	23	0	0	.256	.195
Wilson, Kenny	R-R	6-0	165	1-30-90	.210	.176	.219	51	162	25	34	6	2	0	12	20	7	1	2	60	25	3	.272	.319

Pitching	B-T	HT	WT	DOB	W	L	ERA	G	GS	CG	SV	IP	H	R	ER	HR	BB	SO	AVG	vLH	vRH	K/9	BB/9
Accardo, Jeremy	R-R	6-2	190	12-8-81	0	0	0.00	1	1	0	0	1	1	0	0	0	0	1	.333	.000	.500	9.00	0.00
Alvarez, Henderson	R-R	6-1	175	4-18-90	1	4	5.63	12	11	0	0	46	63	41	29	3	6	34	.310	.403	.260	6.60	1.17
Anderson, John	L-L	6-3	205	11-9-88	1	3	4.32	16	0	0	2	25	29	15	12	1	8	22	.293	.381	.269	7.92	2.88
Antolin, Dustin	R-R	6-2	180	8-9-89	2	2	4.64	12	0	0	0	21	26	12	11	1	10	14	.302	.400	.250	5.91	4.22
Armstrong, Austin	R-R	6-3	210	1-17-87	0	0	9.00	2	0	0	0	2	4	2	2	0	0	1	.444	.667	.333	4.50	0.00
Bachman, Corey	R-R	6-1	190	5-24-85	0	2	6.11	14	0	0	0	18	25	18	12	4	8	12	.333	.125	.390	6.11	4.08
Castillo, Joel	L-L	6-1	170	8-22-87	1	4	4.55	13	0	0	0	32	32	22	16	2	9	25	.262	.231	.271	7.11	2.56
Cuotto, Jonas	R-R	6-0	180	9-26-86	3	2	2.61	11	9	0	0	52	41	16	15	7	7	45	.214	.198	.225	7.84	1.22
Dunbar, Cody	R-R	6-3	225	12-4-85	0	0	3.38	4	0	0	0	5	3	3	2	1	4	6	.158	.000	.176	10.13	6.75
Gracey, Scott	R-R	6-2	190	10-15-86	0	1	3.00	10	0	0	0	24	19	9	8	0	15	22	.216	.250	.203	8.25	5.63
Holguin, Chris	R-R	5-11	185	4-25-86	4	1	3.43	10	8	0	0	42	32	20	16	2	11	31	.206	.246	.184	6.64	2.36
Jennings, Nate	R-R	6-0	180	12-22-84	0	0	—	1	0	0	0	0	0	0	0	0	2	0	.000	.000	—	—	—
Kelsey, Tyler	L-L	6-5	220	7-17-85	1	1	13.50	6	0	0	0	5	10	8	7	0	1	9	.417	.250	.450	17.36	1.93
Keng, Po-Hsuan	R-R	6-1	235	10-15-84	0	0	—	1	0	0	0	0	5	2	2	1	0	1	.833	.500	1.000	—	—
Koch, Ryan	R-R	6-3	200	10-16-85	0	2	0.82	14	4	0	5	22	15	3	2	1	3	15	.190	.192	.189	6.14	1.23
Lirette, Chase	R-R	6-3	210	6-9-85	0	3	6.04	10	10	0	0	25	33	19	17	1	6	29	.314	.375	.288	10.30	2.13
Lynch, Mike	L-L	6-2	195	1-15-87	0	0	3.00	1	0	0	0	3	5	1	1	0	2	1	.500	.000	.625	3.00	6.00
Mayora, Yorman	R-R	6-1	175	4-20-87	1	1	3.57	17	0	0	2	35	38	19	14	2	5	29	.271	.324	.252	7.39	1.27
Mendez, Willi	L-L	6-2	187	8-11-86	3	3	6.04	19	0	0	1	22	21	18	15	1	16	17	.253	.222	.262	6.85	6.45
Miller, Dan	R-R	6-3	220	7-7-86	3	2	2.28	17	0	0	2	28	24	13	7	1	11	15	.238	.293	.200	4.88	3.58

Name	B-T	HT	WT	DOB	W	L	ERA	G	GS	CG	SV	IP	H	R	ER	HR	BB	SO	AVG	vLH	vRH	K/9	BB/9
Moody, Hunter	L-L	6-3	200	1-31-86	3	0	0.93	7	2	0	0	19	16	4	2	0	3	21	.225	.250	.216	9.78	1.40
Page, Ryan	L-L	6-3	205	9-16-85	2	0	1.69	8	6	0	0	32	32	7	6	1	3	18	.264	.214	.280	5.06	0.84
Potts, Jared	L-L	6-3	200	7-4-85	4	2	4.26	14	1	0	0	32	30	17	15	3	18	31	.261	.200	.282	8.81	5.12
Zarate, Robert	L-L	6-2	165	2-1-87	0	0	0.00	2	0	0	0	2	1	0	0	0	0	1	.143	.333	.000	4.50	0.00

Fielding

Catcher	PCT	G	PO	A	E	DP	PB
Diaz	.953	7	40	1	2	0	1
Hurtado	.984	16	49	12	1	2	1
Jimenez	1.000	18	103	8	0	0	9
Rodriguez	.968	18	85	5	3	0	5
Talley	.988	14	77	6	1	1	2
Valdez	1.000	7	40	2	0	0	2

First Base	PCT	G	PO	A	E	DP
Denis-Fortier	1.000	8	81	6	0	7
McClanahan	.988	28	232	15	3	15
Nelson	.958	18	114	1	5	14

	PCT	G	PO	A	E	DP
Talley	.978	11	80	8	2	10

Second Base	PCT	G	PO	A	E	DP
Fernandez	.947	3	5	13	1	4
Gilligan	.992	23	49	70	1	14
Gonzalez	.975	26	47	70	3	17
McClanahan	1.000	8	9	18	0	5

Third Base	PCT	G	PO	A	E	DP
Fuenmayor	.937	47	34	115	10	12
Gilligan	.778	3	6	8	4	1
McClanahan	.952	10	5	15	1	2

Shortstop	PCT	G	PO	A	E	DP
Fernandez	.929	21	27	51	6	13
Gilligan	1.000	1	0	2	0	1
Pastornicky	.962	38	51	101	6	17

Outfield	PCT	G	PO	A	E	DP
Brisker	.927	31	46	5	4	2
Crouse	1.000	6	9	0	0	0
McElroy	1.000	22	26	2	0	0
Perez	.985	28	61	6	1	3
Ramirez	.980	44	93	7	2	2
Wilson	.970	47	92	4	3	1

DSL BLUE JAYS 1   ROOKIE

DOMINICAN SUMMER LEAGUE

Batting	B-T	HT	WT	DOB	AVG	vLH	vRH	G	AB	R	H	2B	3B	HR	RBI	BB	HBP	SH	SF	SO	SB	CS	SLG	OBP
Bejas, Emilio	L-L	5-11	170	8-30-89	.210	.226	.206	57	167	27	35	6	1	0	12	33	4	1	1	48	11	7	.257	.351
Betegon, Adair	R-R	6-1	185	10-22-88	.208	.208	.208	41	125	16	26	7	0	2	17	14	1	0	1	37	2	1	.312	.291
Escalante, Alesone	B-R	6-4	180	8-29-88	.178	.244	.158	62	174	29	31	3	1	0	14	33	0	3	0	60	7	5	.207	.309
Falcon, Manuel	R-R	5-11	165	1-31-90	.294	.283	.297	64	231	33	68	10	0	0	35	20	4	5	2	28	11	5	.338	.358
Ferrini, Leonardo	B-R	6-0	147	4-17-89	.283	.244	.293	63	233	45	66	6	2	0	26	38	3	7	2	40	20	6	.326	.388
Gonzalez, Gonzalo	R-R	5-10	162	7-10-89	.157	.118	.167	27	89	12	14	1	0	0	6	14	1	0	1	16	1	0	.169	.276
Mata, Argenis	R-R	5-11	165	6-12-86	.211	.175	.220	60	213	26	45	10	0	1	23	35	4	2	2	45	6	3	.272	.331
Medina, Erick	R-R	6-0	178	7-15-87	.284	.154	.310	48	155	22	44	13	1	4	30	22	7	5	3	27	5	0	.458	.390
Moreta, Ruddy	R-R	5-11	190	7-28-87	.282	.333	.272	31	124	14	35	11	2	2	19	15	1	0	0	14	3	1	.452	.364
Natera, Fausto	B-R	6-1	168	8-15-88	.292	.250	.299	31	113	21	33	5	0	1	11	14	6	2	0	23	5	4	.363	.398
Ortega, Carlos	R-R	6-1	155	3-20-89	.217	.220	.217	60	221	33	48	6	1	2	19	20	7	1	0	51	10	4	.281	.302
Perez, Carlos	R-R			10-27-90	.306	.419	.285	58	196	27	60	10	2	0	29	52	6	0	3	28	7	5	.378	.459
Rodriguez, Alexys	R-R	5-10	175	11-23-88	.207	.222	.204	42	135	17	28	5	0	0	12	24	4	2	0	23	4	2	.244	.344
Suero, Edward	R-R	6-2	200	9-30-89	.233	.286	.222	34	120	10	28	8	0	1	12	17	4	1	0	22	0	1	.325	.348

Pitching	B-T	HT	WT	DOB	W	L	ERA	G	GS	CG	SV	IP	H	R	ER	HR	BB	SO	AVG	vLH	vRH	K/9	BB/9
Acosta, Eduar	R-R	6-3	188	3-8-85	5	1	1.86	24	1	0	3	39	45	17	8	0	18	47	.287	.333	.276	10.94	4.19
Belliard, Maximiliano	L-L	6-2	162	4-11-86	0	1	5.68	4	2	0	0	6	11	7	4	1	3	5	.379	.667	.304	7.11	4.26
Cardie, Jose	R-R	6-4	175	1-8-88	1	5	3.77	13	1	0	0	29	28	14	12	2	10	27	.255	.345	.222	8.48	3.14
Diaz, Grabiel	R-R	6-2	190	2-11-88	1	3	4.42	20	0	0	2	55	69	31	27	1	18	58	.307	.278	.316	9.49	2.95
Fuenmayor, Kevin	R-R	6-3	150	4-5-90	0	1	3.38	2	2	0	0	8	6	5	3	0	2	9	.194	.000	.240	10.13	2.25
German, Victor	R-R	6-0	210	5-26-89	1	1	2.08	11	0	0	1	17	17	9	4	0	13	16	.246	.211	.260	8.31	6.75
Hernandez, Juan	L-L	6-0	180	10-25-87	7	3	1.89	16	14	0	0	76	60	20	16	1	18	97	.214	.296	.206	11.44	2.12
Jimenez, Jose	R-R	6-3	200	9-22-86	1	5	6.57	25	1	0	3	38	42	32	28	1	34	31	.284	.351	.261	7.28	7.98
Medina, Samuel	R-R	6-3	190	12-29-85	6	2	2.34	18	9	0	1	69	47	24	18	2	35	87	.192	.263	.170	11.29	4.54
Moreno, Felix	R-R	6-4	174	8-18-88	2	4	4.04	7	6	0	0	36	38	17	16	2	13	17	.275	.273	.277	4.29	3.28
Paul, Dieudone	L-L	6-2	187	9-28-87	0	0	4.50	5	3	0	0	12	10	8	6	0	3	12	.233	.250	.231	13.50	9.75
Rodriguez, Carlos	L-L	6-0	175	5-24-86	3	1	2.63	21	2	0	4	48	42	17	14	0	15	59	.236	.316	.226	11.06	2.81
Rojas, Carlos	L-L	5-11	176	12-18-87	1	3	2.62	10	7	0	0	45	35	22	13	1	10	36	.205	.167	.209	7.25	2.01
Santana, Milciades	R-R			1-20-89	1	2	6.69	15	9	0	2	39	44	35	29	2	28	18	.284	.340	.257	4.15	6.46
Severino, Wascar	R-R	6-1	165	8-1-86	0	2	7.43	4	4	0	0	13	16	14	11	0	11	17	.286	.267	.293	11.48	7.43
Velazquez, Hector	R-R	6-3	180	3-30-89	4	1	4.14	12	9	1	0	46	42	22	21	0	13	49	.247	.324	.228	9.66	2.56

Fielding

Catcher	PCT	G	PO	A	E	DP	PB
Betegon	.972	8	66	4	2	0	3
Medina	1.000	1	10	1	0	0	0
Perez	.974	38	319	53	10	2	1
Rodriguez	.973	26	222	26	7	1	7

First Base	PCT	G	PO	A	E	DP
Betegon	.987	21	148	5	2	12
Escalante	.986	10	65	7	1	3
Mata	.979	47	358	16	8	23

Second Base	PCT	G	PO	A	E	DP
Falcon	.949	51	115	107	12	19

	PCT	G	PO	A	E	DP
Ferrini	.978	14	25	19	1	2
Gonzalez	1.000	4	8	5	0	1
Mata	1.000	4	6	4	0	1
Natera	.955	10	18	24	2	7

Third Base	PCT	G	PO	A	E	DP
Escalante	.912	47	29	95	12	5
Falcon	.944	13	14	20	2	1
Gonzalez	.917	7	8	14	2	0
Mata	.857	16	9	21	5	1

Shortstop	PCT	G	PO	A	E	DP
Ferrini	.905	42	52	110	17	20

	PCT	G	PO	A	E	DP
Gonzalez	.891	11	12	29	5	2
Natera	.908	19	23	56	8	5

Outfield	PCT	G	PO	A	E	DP
Bejas	.981	54	95	7	2	1
Escalante	1.000	8	9	1	0	0
Gonzalez	1.000	2	3	0	0	0
Medina	.960	43	70	2	3	1
Moreta	.968	30	29	1	1	0
Ortega	.951	58	93	5	5	2
Perez	1.000	1	1	0	0	0
Suero	.909	26	29	1	3	0

DSL BLUE JAYS 2

ROOKIE

DOMINICAN SUMMER LEAGUE

Batting	B-T	HT	WT	DOB	AVG	vLH	vRH	G	AB	R	H	2B	3B	HR	RBI	BB	HBP	SH	SF	SO	SB	CS	SLG	OBP
Acevedo, Nicolas	B-R	6-1	185	9-12-86	.198	.143	.214	42	91	14	18	1	1	0	10	24	2	2	1	48	6	4	.231	.373
Aponte, Yeico	L-L	6-2	190	12-17-88	.296	.235	.309	55	196	29	58	9	4	2	27	20	1	2	1	51	7	7	.413	.362
Arcila, Daniel	R-L	6-1	152	7-4-90	.224	.281	.210	56	170	25	38	3	2	0	16	49	2	5	1	56	18	4	.265	.401
Caraballo, Eduardo	R-R	6-0	170	6-14-87	.271	.234	.279	66	251	38	68	17	2	0	26	24	7	3	0	60	11	4	.355	.351
Chirinos, Enyer	R-R	5-11	176	9-10-88	.203	.205	.203	64	231	34	47	9	1	0	29	27	5	0	2	58	12	5	.251	.298
Delgado, John	L-R	6-3	210	9-10-90	.243	.222	.248	57	173	17	42	8	0	1	14	37	1	3	1	31	0	1	.306	.377
Dominguez, Oliver	B-R	5-9	156	4-23-89	.305	.218	.327	69	266	49	81	22	3	5	39	45	3	0	5	57	9	3	.466	.404
Gonzalez, Gonzalo	R-R	5-10	162	7-10-89	.341	.333	.341	30	91	23	31	4	0	1	11	18	2	2	1	20	11	2	.418	.455
2-team total (27 Blue Jays 1)					.250	—	—	57	180	35	45	5	0	1	17	32	3	2	2	36	12	2	.294	.369
Hernandez, Leonardo	R-R	5-11	182	2-22-90	.256	.250	.258	44	164	15	42	4	1	0	26	12	0	1	1	13	2	1	.293	.305
Molina, Nestor	R-R	6-1	179	1-9-89	.000	.000	.000	4	5	0	0	0	0	0	0	1	5	0	0	1	0	0	.000	.500
Monge, Manuel	R-R	6-1	184	2-10-90	.197	.108	.229	52	142	12	28	4	0	0	7	22	5	0	1	60	8	8	.225	.324
Moreta, Ruddy	R-R	5-11	190	7-28-87	.309	.313	.308	27	94	17	29	7	0	2	21	22	1	0	2	14	0	3	.447	.437
2-team total (31 Blue Jays 1)					.294	—	—	58	218	31	64	18	2	4	40	37	2	0	2	28	3	4	.450	.398
Natera, Fausto	B-R	6-1	168	8-15-88	.279	.200	.304	33	122	24	34	3	2	0	13	23	2	1	1	22	8	2	.336	.399
2-team total (31 Blue Jays 1)					.285	—	—	64	235	45	67	8	2	1	24	37	8	3	1	45	13	6	.349	.399
Rodriguez, Alexys	R-R	5-10	175	11-23-88	.200	.000	.250	2	5	1	1	0	0	0	0	1	0	0	0	0	0	0	.200	.333
2-team total (42 Blue Jays 1)					.207	—	—	44	140	18	29	5	0	0	12	25	4	2	0	23	4	2	.243	.343
Suero, Edward	R-R	6-2	200	9-30-89	.202	.211	.200	28	84	8	17	3	0	0	11	23	6	1	2	35	0	1	.238	.400
2-team total (34 Blue Jays 1)					.221	—	—	62	204	18	45	11	0	1	23	40	10	2	2	57	0	2	.289	.371
Vasquez, Simon	R-R	5-11	201	6-18-88	.277	.240	.286	44	137	19	38	8	1	1	14	30	5	0	1	23	2	3	.372	.422
Vega, Hermino	R-R	5-10	160	5-21-88	.227	.143	.250	23	66	7	15	2	1	1	3	8	1	1	0	10	0	0	.333	.320

Pitching	B-T	HT	WT	DOB	W	L	ERA	G	GS	CG	SV	IP	H	R	ER	BB	SO	AVG	vLH	vRH	K/9	BB/9
Avila, Jose	L-L	6-3	190	9-14-90	0	0	10.32	11	0	0	0	11	15	13	13	0	15	12	.300	.000	.326	9.53	11.91
Bello, Fernando	R-R	6-1	180	4-27-89	3	3	1.93	10	8	0	0	47	43	13	10	0	13	42	.244	.222	.252	8.10	2.51
Bustamante, Juan	R-R	6-0	170	7-13-86	5	2	2.88	21	0	0	4	59	58	23	19	1	17	71	.251	.314	.233	10.77	2.58
Diaz, Misual	R-R	6-2	180	12-20-89	1	5	6.21	13	4	0	1	38	44	33	26	1	16	32	.284	.333	.262	7.65	3.82
Mella, Leandro	L-L	6-4	190	5-5-90	3	0	2.33	18	4	0	0	46	33	13	12	0	26	47	.209	.000	.226	9.13	5.05
Mendez, Luis	R-R	6-5	225	10-14-89	0	2	13.50	12	3	0	0	17	28	27	25	2	26	6	.400	.500	.360	3.24	14.04
Moreno, Felix	R-R	6-4	174	8-18-88	1	2	3.44	7	1	0	0	18	19	8	7	1	9	19	.275	.250	.286	9.33	4.42
2-team total (7 Blue Jays 1)					3	4	3.83	14	7	0	0	54	57	25	23	3	22	36	—	—		6.00	3.67
Paul, Dieudone	L-L	6-2	187	9-28-87	2	0	4.55	11	0	0	3	28	23	16	14	0	13	30	.235	.231	.235	9.76	4.23
2-team total (5 Blue Jays 1)					2	0	4.54	16	3	0	3	40	33	24	20	0	26	48	—	—		10.89	5.90
Pina, Carlos	L-L	5-11	169	3-5-90	4	3	3.69	13	13	0	0	68	68	35	28	3	14	64	.253	.278	.249	8.43	1.71
Ramirez, Alex	R-R	6-2	188	2-11-90	2	6	6.02	14	12	1	0	64	63	44	43	4	27	35	.263	.200	.281	4.90	3.78
Rodriguez, Richard	R-R	6-1	197	8-31-88	4	3	4.57	16	9	0	1	61	67	43	31	3	30	65	.275	.300	.266	9.59	4.43
Romero, Steven	R-R	6-2	180	8-2-90	0	0	11.15	12	1	0	1	15	28	23	19	1	7	12	.389	.333	.392	7.04	4.11
Santana, Kenllie	L-L	6-0	192	7-13-89	0	1	3.21	16	3	0	1	28	14	13	10	0	40	40	.159	.222	.152	12.86	12.86
Valdez, Denny	R-R	6-3	188	5-8-90	0	2	16.50	4	2	0	0	6	9	12	11	2	11	3	.375	.455	.308	4.50	16.50
Vargas, Jose	L-L	6-0	166	7-19-90	5	4	3.23	14	10	0	0	64	53	26	23	1	17	60	.219	.067	.229	8.44	2.39

Fielding

Catcher	PCT	G	PO	A	E	DP	PB
Delgado	1.000	1	2	1	0	0	0
Hernandez	.984	43	330	40	6	0	12
Rodriguez	1.000	1	11	0	0		1
Vasquez	.967	16	98	18	4	0	4
Vega	.973	20	124	19	4	1	5

First Base	PCT	G	PO	A	E	DP
Chirinos	1.000	8	49	3	0	3
Delgado	.989	56	436	16	5	30
Molina	1.000	1	1	0	0	1
Moreta	1.000	1	4	0	0	1
Vasquez	.991	16	106	4	1	5

Second Base	PCT	G	PO	A	E	DP
Dominguez	.966	59	120	137	9	24
Gonzalez	1.000	3	14	7	0	1
Natera	.959	12	26	21	2	5

Third Base	PCT	G	PO	A	E	DP
Arcila	.970	13	12	20	1	1
Chirinos	.940	57	49	123	11	11
Gonzalez	.900	5	2	7	1	1
Molina	1.000	1	0	1	0	0
Vega	—	1	0	0	0	0

Shortstop	PCT	G	PO	A	E	DP
Acevedo	.636	3	2	5	4	0

	PCT	G	PO	A	E	DP
Arcila	.935	43	66	107	12	13
Chirinos	1.000	1	0	1	0	0
Gonzalez	.885	8	9	14	3	2
Natera	.933	23	28	56	6	8

Outfield	PCT	G	PO	A	E	DP
Acevedo	1.000	15	13	0	0	0
Aponte	.935	53	80	7	6	0
Arcila	1.000	1	1	0	0	0
Caraballo	.967	62	113	6	4	2
Gonzalez	1.000	7	6	0	0	0
Monge	.901	47	61	3	7	0
Moreta	.917	20	20	2	2	0
Suero	.968	23	27	3	1	0

Washington Nationals

BY LACY LUSK

Somewhat appropriately, the first season at Nationals Park started with a bang and ended with a washout.

On their way to going a major league-worst 59-102, the Nationals had few highlights in their first year at a new ballpark with upper-deck views of the U.S. Capitol. The most memorable came March 30 when Ryan Zimmerman belted a walk-off home run to beat the Braves in the season opener on ESPN.

"You can't really write a better script than that," Zimmerman said that night. "It turned out perfect."

Not much else did.

The Nationals hardly made a splash in a season in which they broke camp with hopes of at least breaking even. They drew more than 2.3 million fans to see a team without a hitter who drove in more than 61 runs or a pitcher with more than 10 wins. Still, the attendance figure was the lowest for a team in an inaugural year of a ballpark in the fan-friendly era that started with the Orioles' Camden Yards in 1992.

The Nationals and Marlins were rained out on the final scheduled home date of the year, temporarily keeping Washington from its 100th loss. That came on the final weekend, when the Phillies celebrated the National League East title for the second straight season at the Nationals' expense.

The injury-riddled club's best stretch came in late August and early September with a seven-game winning streak. In the homestand, the Nationals swept three games each from the Dodgers and Braves before taking two of three from the Phillies.

Center fielder Lastings Milledge led the team with 61 RBIs and his 14 home runs were tied for tops on the club with third baseman Zimmerman. Righthander Tim Redding (10-11, 4.95 in 182 innings) was the top winner, and rookie lefty John Lannan (9-15, 3.91 in 182 innings) and righthander Joel Hanrahan (6-3, 3.95 with 93 strikeouts in 84 innings and nine saves) emerged as candidates for long-term roles.

Shortstop Cristian Guzman likely would have had a 200-hit season if not for a left thumb injury, but he still managed a career-high 183 hits and signed a two-year contract extension. Guzman represented the Nationals in the All-Star Game

and was leading the NL in hits at the break.

In the minor leagues, righthander Jordan Zimmermann, who finished the year at Double-A Harrisburg and outfielder Leonard Davis, who climbed from high Class A Potomac to Triple-A Columbus, were named the system's pitcher and player of the year.

ORGANIZATION LEADERS

BATTING	*Minimum 250 at-bats	
*AVG	Bernadina, Roger, Harrisburg/Columbus	.335
R	Lyons, Daniel, Hagerstown/Potomac	83
H	Bernadina, Roger, Harrisburg/Columbus	153
TB	Davis, Leonard, Potomac/Harr./Columbus	248
2B	Rhinehart, Bill, Potomac/Potomac/Harr.	39
3B	Orr, Pete, Columbus	11
HR	Davis, Leonard, Potomac/Harr./Columbus	25
RBI	Rhinehart, Bill, Potomac/Potomac/Harr.	89
BB	Lyons, Daniel, Hagerstown/Potomac	77
SO	Burgess, Michael, Hagerstown/Potomac	162
SB	Whiting, Boomer, Hagerstown/Potomac	47
*OBP	Bernadina, Roger, Harrisburg/Columbus	.4
*SLG	Davis, Leonard, Potomac/Harr./Columbus	.566

PITCHING	†Minimum 75 innings	
W	Mandel, Jeff, Hagerstown/Potomac	10
	Arnesen, Erik, Hagerstown/Potomac	10
	Zimmermann, Jordan, Potomac/Harrisburg	10
L	Clippard, Tyler, Columbus	13
†ERA	Zimmermann, Jordan, Potomac/Harrisburg	2.89
G	Warden, Jim Ed, Harrisburg/Columbus	57
GS	Mandel, Jeff, Hagerstown/Potomac	28
SV	Carr, Adam, Potomac/Harrisburg	16
IP	Mandel, Jeff, Hagerstown/Potomac	152
BB	Kimball, Cole, Hagerstown	83
SO	Zimmermann, Jordan, Potomac/Harrisburg	134
†AVG	Zimmermann, Jordan, Potomac/Harrisburg	.215

General Manager: Jim Bowden. **Farm Director:** Bobby Williams. **Scouting Director:** Dana Brown.

Class	Team	League	W	L	PCT	Finish*	Manager	Affiliate Since
Majors	Washington	National	59	102	.366	16th (16)	Manny Acta	—
Triple-A	Columbus Clippers	International	69	73	.486	7th (14)	Tim Foli	2007
Double-A	Harrisburg Senators	Eastern	73	69	.514	6th (12)	John Stearns	1991
High A	Potomac Nationals	Carolina	79	61	.564	^2nd (8)	Randy Knorr	2005
Low A	Hagerstown Suns	South Atlantic	61	78	.439	13th (16)	Darnell Coles	2007
Short-season	Vermont Lake Monsters	New York-Penn	33	42	.440	11th (14)	Ramon Aviles	1994
Rookie	GCL Nationals	Gulf Coast	33	22	.600	3rd (16)	Bob Henley	1998
Overall 2008 Minor League Record			348	375	.481	18th		

* Finish in overall standings (No. of teams in league). ^League champion.

ORGANIZATION STATISTICS

WASHINGTON NATIONALS

NATIONAL LEAGUE

Batting	B-T	HT	WT	DOB	AVG	vLH	vRH	G	AB	R	H	2B	3B	HR	RBI	BB	HBP	SH	SF	SO	SB	CS	SLG	OBP
Belliard, Ronnie	R-R	5-10	215	4-7-75	.287	.307	.279	96	296	37	85	22	0	11	46	37	3	1	6	58	3	2	.473	.372
Bernadina, Roger	L-L	6-1	190	6-12-84	.211	.300	.197	26	76	10	16	1	1	0	2	9	0	1	0	21	4	3	.250	.294
Bonifacio, Emilio	R-R	5-10	195	4-23-85	.248	.171	.276	41	157	26	39	5	5	0	12	14	0	3	41	6	4	.344	.305
2-team total (8 Arizona)					.243	—		49	169	29	41	6	5	0	14	14	0	0	3	46	7	4	.337	.296
Boone, Aaron	R-R	6-3	205	3-9-73	.241	.275	.220	104	232	23	56	13	1	6	28	18	2	1	2	52	0	1	.384	.299
Casto, Kory	L-R	6-2	205	12-8-81	.215	.048	.239	66	163	15	35	10	0	2	16	19	0	0	0	36	1	0	.313	.297
Dukes, Elijah	R-R	6-1	240	6-26-84	.264	.231	.278	81	276	48	73	16	2	13	44	50	6	0	2	79	13	4	.478	.386
Estrada, Johnny	B-R	5-11	255	6-27-76	.170	.100	.186	23	53	0	9	0	0	0	4	1	1	0	0	4	0	0	.170	.200
Flores, Jesus	R-R	6-0	230	10-26-84	.256	.308	.238	90	301	23	77	18	1	8	59	15	4	0	4	78	0	1	.402	.296
Gonzalez, Alberto	R-R	5-11	160	4-18-83	.347	.417	.324	17	49	9	17	6	0	1	9	4	1	0	0	6	0	1	.531	.407
Guzman, Cristian	B-R	6-0	215	3-21-78	.316	.354	.299	138	579	77	183	35	5	9	55	23	5	1	4	57	6	5	.440	.345
Harris, Willie	L-R	5-9	185	6-22-78	.251	.240	.255	140	367	58	92	14	4	13	43	50	3	3	1	66	13	3	.417	.344
Hernandez, Anderson	B-R	5-9	170	10-30-82	.333	.366	.300	28	81	11	27	4	0	0	17	10	0	0	0	8	0	0	.383	.407
Johnson, Nick	L-L	6-3	235	9-19-78	.220	.167	.247	38	109	15	24	8	0	5	20	33	4	0	1	25	0	0	.431	.415
Kearns, Austin	R-R	6-3	240	5-20-80	.217	.153	.241	86	313	40	68	10	0	7	32	35	8	0	1	63	2	2	.316	.311
Langerhans, Ryan	L-L	6-3	230	2-20-80	.234	.217	.239	73	111	17	26	5	2	3	12	25	1	2	0	31	2	0	.396	.380
Lo Duca, Paul	R-R	5-9	215	4-12-72	.230	.231	.230	46	139	13	32	7	0	0	12	9	5	0	0	9	1	0	.281	.301
2-team total (21 Florida)					.243	—		67	173	16	42	9	0	0	15	15	5	0	0	11	1	0	.295	.321
Lopez, Felipe	B-R	6-0	205	5-12-80	.234	.261	.218	100	325	34	76	20	0	2	25	32	2	2	2	54	4	5	.314	.305
2-team total (43 St. Louis)					.283	—		143	481	64	136	28	2	6	46	43	3	2	3	82	8	8	.387	.343
Mackowiak, Rob	L-R	5-11	190	6-20-76	.132	.000	.137	38	53	7	7	1	0	1	4	8	1	0	1	17	0	0	.208	.254
Milledge, Lastings	R-R	6-0	205	4-5-85	.268	.258	.272	138	523	65	140	24	2	14	61	38	14	5	7	96	24	9	.402	.330
Montz, Luke	R-R	6-2	205	7-7-83	.143	.000	.188	10	21	2	3	0	0	1	3	5	0	0	0	9	0	0	.286	.308
Nieves, Wil	R-R	5-11	185	9-25-77	.261	.304	.242	68	176	15	46	9	1	1	20	13	0	5	2	29	0	1	.341	.309
Orr, Pete	L-R	5-11	195	6-8-79	.253	.286	.250	49	75	10	19	2	1	0	7	2	1	1	0	16	1	0	.307	.282
Pena, Wily Mo	R-R	6-3	270	1-23-82	.205	.241	.179	64	195	10	40	6	0	2	10	10	0	0	1	48	0	1	.267	.243
Young, Dmitri	B-R	6-2	300	10-11-73	.280	.318	.264	50	150	15	42	6	0	4	18	20	1	0	1	28	0	0	.400	.394
Zimmerman, Ryan	R-R	6-3	230	9-28-84	.283	.333	.259	106	428	51	121	24	1	14	51	31	3	0	4	71	1	1	.442	.333

Pitching	B-T	HT	WT	DOB	W	L	ERA	G	GS	CG	SV	IP	H	R	ER	HR	BB	SO	AVG	vLH	vRH	K/9	BB/9
Ayala, Luis	R-R	6-1	200	1-12-78	1	8	5.77	62	0	0	9	58	63	41	37	6	22	36	.280	.270	.288	5.62	3.43
2-team total (19 New York)					2	10	5.71	81	0	0	9	76	86	53	48	9	24	50	—	—	—	5.95	2.85
Balester, Collin	R-R	6-5	195	6-6-86	3	7	5.51	15	15	0	0	80	92	53	49	12	28	50	.288	.278	.298	5.63	3.15
Bergmann, Jason	R-R	6-4	215	9-25-81	2	11	5.09	30	22	1	0	140	153	94	79	25	47	96	.279	.309	.243	6.19	3.03
Chico, Matt	L-L	5-11	220	6-10-83	0	6	6.19	11	8	0	0	48	63	34	33	10	17	31	.323	.351	.312	5.81	3.19
Clippard, Tyler	R-R	6-3	200	2-14-85	1	1	4.35	2	2	0	0	10	12	5	5	2	7	8	.293	.333	.261	6.97	6.10
Colome, Jesus	R-R	6-2	240	12-23-77	2	2	4.31	61	0	0	0	71	61	38	34	6	39	55	.235	.226	.241	6.97	4.94
Cordero, Chad	R-R	6-0	225	3-18-82	0	0	2.08	6	0	0	4	4	6	1	1	0	3	5	.316	.250	.429	10.38	6.23
Estrada, Marco	R-R	6-0	180	7-5-83	0	0	7.82	11	0	0	0	13	17	13	11	4	5	10	.304	.348	.273	7.11	3.55
Hanrahan, Joel	R-R	6-4	250	10-6-81	6	3	3.95	69	0	0	9	84	73	40	37	9	42	93	.233	.228	.237	9.92	4.48
Hill, Shawn	R-R	6-2	225	4-28-81	1	5	5.83	12	12	0	0	63	88	47	41	5	23	39	.331	.294	.374	5.54	3.27
Hinckley, Mike	R-L	6-3	170	10-5-82	0	0	0.00	14	0	0	0	14	8	1	0	0	3	9	.178	.222	.148	5.93	1.98
King, Ray	L-L	6-0	250	1-15-74	0	0	5.68	12	0	0	0	6	9	4	4	1	4	1	.333	.235	.500	1.42	5.68
Lannan, John	L-L	6-4	225	9-27-84	9	15	3.91	31	31	0	0	182	172	89	79	23	72	117	.252	.259	.250	5.79	3.56
Manning, Charlie	L-L	6-2	185	3-31-79	1	3	5.14	57	0	0	0	42	35	25	24	8	31	37	.224	.203	.247	7.93	6.64
Martis, Shairon	R-R	6-1	175	3-30-87	1	3	5.66	5	4	0	0	21	18	14	13	5	12	23	.228	.295	.143	10.02	5.23
Mock, Garrett	R-R	6-3	240	4-25-83	3	4	4.17	26	3	0	0	41	37	20	19	4	23	46	.239	.239	.237	10.10	5.05
O'Connor, Mike	L-L	6-3	185	8-17-80	1	1	13.00	5	1	0	0	9	11	13	13	3	11	4	.324	.167	.409	4.00	11.00
Perez, Odalis	L-L	6-0	225	6-11-77	7	12	4.34	30	30	0	0	160	182	87	77	22	55	119	.287	.218	.306	6.71	3.10
Rauch, Jon	R-R	6-11	290	9-27-78	4	2	2.98	48	0	0	17	48	42	19	16	5	8	47	.232	.245	.218	8.19	1.30
2-team total (26 Arizona)					4	8	4.14	74	0	0	18	72	69	36	33	11	16	66	—	—	—	8.29	2.01
Redding, Tim	R-R	5-11	225	2-12-78	10	11	4.95	33	33	1	0	182	195	110	100	27	65	120	.275	.277	.274	5.93	3.21
Rivera, Saul	B-R	5-10	185	12-7-77	5	6	3.96	76	0	0	0	84	90	41	37	3	35	65	.277	.271	.284	6.96	3.75
Sanches, Brian	R-R	6-0	195	8-8-78	2	0	7.36	12	0	0	0	11	16	10	9	2	5	10	.340	.368	.321	8.18	4.09

Pitching	B-T	HT	WT	DOB	W	L	ERA	G	GS	CG	SV	IP	H	R	ER	HR	BB	SO	AVG	vLH	vRH	K/9	BB/9
Schroder, Chris	R-R	6-1	210	8-20-78	0	0	5.40	4	0	0	0	5	6	3	3	2	6	3	.300	.300	.300	5.40	10.80
Shell, Steven	R-R	6-4	215	3-10-83	2	2	2.16	39	0	0	2	50	34	14	12	5	20	41	.194	.253	.150	7.38	3.60
Speigner, Levale	R-R	5-11	170	9-24-80	0	1	11.25	7	0	0	0	8	13	10	10	1	6	1	.406	.300	.583	1.13	6.75

Fielding

Catcher	PCT	G	PO	A	E	DP	PB
Estrada	.977	14	78	8	2	0	0
Flores	.990	82	474	29	5	6	7
Lo Duca	1.000	20	114	6	0	0	1
Montz	.980	8	44	4	1	1	1
Nieves	.992	61	359	31	3	4	3

First Base	PCT	G	PO	A	E	DP
Belliard	.990	33	185	14	2	14
Boone	.997	54	313	17	1	32
Casto	.988	23	149	13	2	13
Johnson	1.000	35	302	14	0	21
Langerhans	1.000	2	8	0	0	1
Lo Duca	.976	16	113	8	3	16
Young	.976	38	275	15	7	32

Second Base	PCT	G	PO	A	E	DP
Belliard	.974	29	53	60	3	20
Bonifacio	.958	37	78	82	7	25
Boone	—	1	0	0	0	
Harris	.983	14	29	30	1	9
Hernandez	1.000	16	34	43	0	9
Lopez	.970	78	128	196	10	39
Orr	.947	7	8	10	1	2

Third Base	PCT	G	PO	A	E	DP
Belliard	.918	31	16	40	5	3
Boone	.963	14	3	23	1	2
Casto	1.000	13	12	23	0	1
Gonzalez	1.000	3	1	2	0	0
Harris	1.000	14	0	6	0	0
Orr	1.000	8	4	16	0	0
Zimmerman	.967	104	95	199	10	25

Shortstop	PCT	G	PO	A	E	DP
Belliard	.944	5	6	11	1	3
Gonzalez	1.000	12	13	28	0	7
Guzman	.972	136	192	394	17	75
Harris	1.000	3	3	2	0	1
Hernandez	.667	3	3	3	3	0
Lopez	1.000	8	3	21	0	4
Orr	.905	8	9	10	2	4

Outfield	PCT	G	PO	A	E	DP
Bernadina	.980	20	46	2	1	0
Casto	1.000	9	15	1	0	1
Dukes	.965	79	158	9	6	1
Harris	.985	103	191	4	3	2
Kearns	.979	85	187	3	4	0
Langerhans	1.000	36	49	2	0	1
Lo Duca	.917	5	11	0	1	0
Lopez	1.000	8	9	1	0	0
Mackowiak	1.000	14	13	0	0	0
Milledge	.986	134	348	1	5	0
Orr	1.000	2	2	0	0	0
Pena	.971	54	99	3	3	0

COLUMBUS CLIPPERS   TRIPLE-A

INTERNATIONAL LEAGUE

Batting	B-T	HT	WT	DOB	AVG	vLH	vRH	G	AB	R	H	2B	3B	HR	RBI	BB	HBP	SH	SF	SO	SB	CS	SLG	OBP
Batista, Tony	R-R	6-0	225	12-9-73	.226	.250	.211	17	62	3	14	2	0	1	6	4	0	0	0	9	0	0	.306	.273
Bergolla, William	R-R	5-10	195	2-4-83	.265	.235	.294	20	34	3	9	2	0	1	3	0	0	0	1	5	0	0	.412	.257
Bernadina, Roger	L-L	6-1	190	6-12-84	.351	.369	.341	47	191	33	67	13	3	4	16	16	1	7	0	37	15	2	.513	.404
Bonifacio, Emilio	R-R	5-10	195	4-23-85	.452	.500	.429	8	31	9	14	2	0	0	3	4	0	0	1	4	4	2	.516	.500
Boone, Aaron	R-R	6-3	205	3-9-73	.000	.000	.000	3	8	0	0	0	0	0	1	0	0	1	0	0	0	0	.000	.111
Boone, Bret	R-R	5-10	185	4-6-69	.261	.364	.229	13	46	4	12	4	0	0	8	6	0	0	3	11	1	0	.348	.327
Broadway, Larry	L-L	6-4	230	12-17-80	.266	.252	.270	130	429	56	114	29	3	9	55	58	2	0	3	105	3	8	.410	.354
Casto, Kory	L-R	6-2	205	12-8-81	.308	.325	.300	33	130	19	40	5	0	6	26	19	0	0	0	27	1	2	.485	.396
Castro, Ofilio	R-R	6-0	160	8-18-83	.256	.333	.250	14	43	7	11	3	0	0	9	4	1	0	1	3	0	0	.326	.327
Davis, Leonard	L-R	5-10	195	12-24-83	.239	.269	.227	49	180	21	43	13	3	7	29	5	2	2	1	48	1	1	.461	.266
de Caster, Yurendell	R-R	6-0	215	9-26-79	.252	.278	.241	89	310	43	78	18	1	10	47	27	7	3	1	89	5	5	.413	.325
Diaz, Frank	R-R	6-0	211	10-6-83	.291	.262	.307	38	117	18	34	6	1	0	11	6	1	2	0	19	4	2	.359	.331
Dubois, Jason	R-R	6-4	230	3-26-79	.217	.238	.200	33	92	9	20	6	0	4	18	11	1	0	3	28	3	1	.413	.299
Dukes, Elijah	R-R	6-1	240	6-26-84	.234	.158	.286	17	47	8	11	3	1	1	6	8	2	0	0	17	2	2	.404	.368
Escobar, Alex	R-R	6-1	215	9-6-78	.257	.316	.227	67	230	29	59	12	0	6	31	20	2	0	3	47	3	3	.387	.318
Estrada, Johnny	R-R	5-11	255	6-27-76	.250	.167	.300	4	16	1	4	0	0	0	1	1	0	0	1	0	0	0	.250	.294
Flores, Jesus	R-R	6-0	230	10-26-84	.153	.063	.186	17	59	8	9	3	0	1	7	8	2	0	0	20	0	0	.254	.275
Gonzalez, Alberto	R-R	5-11	160	4-18-83	.303	.333	.292	38	33	2	10	3	0	1	3	0	1	0	0	5	0	0	.485	.324
2-team total (47 Scranton/W-B)					.258	—		55	221	25	57	11	0	5	29	16	4	2	4	35	4	2	.376	.314
Guzman, Garrett	L-L	5-9	180	2-7-83	.165	.150	.169	35	97	8	16	1	2	0	9	15	0	1	0	8	4	4	.216	.274
Herrera, Javi	R-R	6-0	200	10-8-81	.260	.300	.243	37	100	10	26	4	1	2	15	14	2	0	0	29	2	1	.380	.362
Jimenez, Luis Antonio	L-L	6-4	205	5-7-82	.330	.333	.327	33	91	9	30	6	0	1	10	12	0	1	1	22	0	1	.407	.404
Kearns, Austin	R-R	6-3	240	5-20-80	.429	.750	.300	5	14	2	6	1	1	1	6	3	1	0	1	2	0	0	.857	.526
Langerhans, Ryan	L-L	6-3	230	2-20-80	.310	.369	.284	62	213	40	66	16	2	3	31	40	1	1	2	57	12	3	.446	.418
Lo Duca, Paul	R-R	5-9	215	4-12-72	.154	.250	.111	4	13	2	0	0	0	0	2	0	0	0	0	3	0	0	.154	.267
Milledge, Lastings	R-R	6-0	205	4-5-85	.077	.000	.091	3	13	0	1	0	0	0	2	0	0	0	0	4	0	0	.077	.077
Montz, Luke	R-R	6-2	205	7-7-83	.256	.250	.258	48	168	18	43	8	1	2	18	13	0	0	0	37	1	1	.351	.309
Murphy, Tommy	B-R	5-11	200	8-27-79	.286	.345	.257	70	266	49	76	15	3	2	15	32	1	6	1	71	19	6	.387	.363
Nichols, Patrick	R-R	6-2	210	9-12-84	.083	.000	.125	6	12	1	1	0	0	0	1	1	0	0	1	5	0	0	.083	.143
Nieves, Wil	R-R	5-11	185	9-25-77	.240	.667	.182	9	25	3	6	1	0	0	2	3	0	1	0	6	1	0	.280	.321
Olmedo, Ray	R-R	5-11	170	5-31-81	.252	.206	.271	108	353	38	89	15	2	4	32	19	2	8	3	39	10	11	.340	.292
Orr, Pete	L-R	5-11	195	6-8-79	.275	.182	.316	73	284	46	78	16	11	2	33	21	4	5	2	56	19	4	.430	.331
Padilla, Jorge	R-R	6-2	200	8-11-79	.312	.299	.318	81	282	38	88	11	1	4	25	26	8	5	1	39	13	9	.401	.385
Pena, Wily Mo	R-R	6-3	270	1-23-82	.000	.000	.000	1	2	0	0	0	0	0	0	0	0	0	0	2	0	0	.000	.000
Porter, Greg	L-R	6-4	225	8-15-80	.233	.042	.327	20	73	5	17	2	0	1	6	0	0	0	0	18	1	0	.301	.291
2-team total (72 Scranton/W-B)					.255	—		92	318	32	81	17	0	3	23	24	1	0	1	73	4	2	.336	.308
Reese Jr., Pokey	R-R	5-11	190	6-10-73	.169	.125	.191	23	71	3	12	3	0	0	7	2	2	2	2	18	1	0	.225	.208
Rogers, Ed	R-R	6-0	190	8-29-78	.269	.330	.240	97	297	34	80	12	0	5	23	12	6	10	2	47	15	10	.360	.309
Spearman, Jemel	R-R	6-0	190	12-27-80	.260	.158	.323	25	50	6	13	2	1	1	12	7	0	2	1	11	4	0	.400	.345
Wallace, David	R-R	6-3	230	10-17-79	.240	.267	.225	43	125	16	30	7	0	1	12	19	0	2	0	32	0	1	.368	.345
Zimmerman, Ryan	R-R	6-3	230	9-28-84	.267	.500	.111	4	15	4	4	1	0	1	3	2	0	0	0	3	0	0	.533	.353

Pitching	B-T	HT	WT	DOB	W	L	ERA	G	GS	CG	SV	IP	H	R	ER	HR	BB	SO	AVG	vLH	vRH	K/9	BB/9
Bacsik, Mike	L-L	6-2	225	11-11-77	7	5	4.68	36	3	0	1	77	91	44	40	14	21	63	.296	.252	.330	7.36	2.45
Balester, Collin	R-R	6-5	195	6-6-86	9	3	4.00	15	15	0	0	79	79	37	35	14	23	64	.263	.267	.258	7.32	2.63
Bergmann, Jason	R-R	6-4	215	9-25-81	2	2	3.72	5	5	0	0	29	26	13	12	2	11	27	.239	.200	.278	8.38	3.41
Bittner, Tim	L-L	6-2	200	6-9-80	0	1	7.15	7	0	0	0	11	14	9	9	1	7	11	.304	.231	.333	8.74	5.56
Booker, Chris	R-R	6-3	235	12-9-76	1	3	4.94	21	0	0	8	24	18	13	13	6	18	38	.205	.174	.238	14.45	6.85
Brito, Eude	L-L	6-0	170	8-19-78	0	0	10.80	5	0	0	0	7	8	9	8	1	3	11	.286	.200	.385	14.85	4.05
Brownlie, Bobby	R-R	6-2	210	10-5-80	1	3	7.86	9	4	0	0	26	40	23	23	7	10	18	.354	.431	.250	6.15	3.42

Name	B-T	HT	WT	DOB	W	L	ERA	G	GS	CG	SV	IP	H	R	ER	HR	BB	SO	AVG	vLH	vRH	K/9	BB/9
Chico, Matt	L-L	5-11	220	6-10-83	0	0	9.00	1	1	0	0	4	7	4	4	0	2	1	.412	.500	.385	2.25	4.50
Clippard, Tyler	R-R	6-3	200	2-14-85	6	13	4.66	27	27	0	0	143	129	80	74	15	66	125	.242	.218	.272	7.87	4.15
Estrada, Marco	R-R	6-0	180	7-5-83	3	3	3.58	12	12	0	0	65	73	28	26	3	21	52	.287	.340	.250	7.16	2.89
Hill, Shawn	R-R	6-2	225	4-28-81	0	1	7.50	1	1	0	0	6	9	6	5	1	0	2	.346	.294	.444	3.00	0.00
Hinckley, Mike	R-L	6-3	170	10-5-82	0	2	3.16	20	1	0	1	26	27	11	9	0	15	20	.278	.289	.269	7.01	5.26
Kown, Andrew	L-R	6-7	210	10-7-82	3	0	3.71	3	3	0	0	17	22	7	7	0	2	13	.314	.391	.277	6.88	1.06
Manning, Charlie	L-L	6-2	185	3-31-79	0	0	1.95	19	0	0	6	28	20	8	6	1	13	34	.206	.149	.260	11.06	4.23
Martinez, Carlos	R-R	6-4	177	3-30-84	0	0	5.40	1	0	0	0	2	3	1	1	0	0	0	.375	.500	.333	0.00	0.00
Martis, Shairon	R-R	6-1	175	3-30-87	1	2	3.02	7	7	0	0	42	42	17	14	2	17	42	.261	.333	.207	9.07	3.67
Mock, Garrett	R-R	6-3	240	4-25-83	6	3	3.01	19	17	0	0	105	98	41	35	9	25	96	.249	.296	.201	8.25	2.15
Munoz, Arnie	L-L	5-9	185	6-21-82	0	0	16.62	3	0	0	0	4	5	8	8	2	7	4	.294	.167	.364	8.31	14.54
Norrito, Joey	R-R	5-10	180	8-4-82	0	0	5.40	2	0	0	0	3	8	2	2	1	0	1	.471	.429	.500	2.70	0.00
O'Connor, Mike	L-L	6-3	185	8-17-80	5	3	2.17	16	16	1	0	100	83	29	24	10	17	70	.227	.212	.234	6.32	1.54
Perrault, Josh	R-R	6-3	205	6-11-82	0	0	2.08	3	0	0	0	4	2	1	1	0	3	5	.125	.125	.125	10.38	6.23
Sanches, Brian	R-R	6-0	195	8-8-78	2	1	2.41	32	0	0	13	34	24	9	9	2	9	45	.197	.231	.171	12.03	2.41
Schroder, Chris	R-R	6-1	210	8-20-78	5	4	3.97	43	0	0	8	45	48	21	20	3	26	54	.271	.319	.238	10.92	3.97
Shell, Steven	R-R	6-4	215	3-10-83	3	2	2.62	22	4	0	1	58	49	19	17	5	14	54	.231	.280	.170	8.33	2.16
Speigner, Levale	R-R	5-11	170	9-24-80	3	0	2.22	25	1	0	0	45	36	13	11	3	8	36	.222	.213	.230	7.25	1.61
Stammen, Craig	R-R	6-3	210	3-9-84	1	4	7.33	9	8	0	0	43	62	35	35	3	16	35	.354	.311	.400	7.33	3.35
Stanford, Jason	L-L	6-1	210	1-23-77	2	2	10.05	5	3	0	0	14	19	18	16	3	9	12	.311	.278	.326	7.53	5.65
2-team total (6 Buffalo)					3	5	6.00	11	8	0	0	42	53	35	28	5	20	24	—	—	—	5.14	4.29
Tankersley, Dennis	R-R	6-2	225	2-24-79	4	4	5.10	30	14	0	0	101	121	59	57	15	41	65	.308	.318	.299	5.81	3.67
Wagner, Ryan	R-R	6-3	205	7-15-82	0	3	5.68	16	0	0	1	19	26	14	12	3	12	14	.329	.286	.364	6.63	5.68
Warden, Jim Ed	R-R	6-7	210	5-7-79	2	6	3.84	46	0	0	7	63	62	27	27	1	27	50	.259	.243	.273	7.11	3.84
Zinicola, Zech	R-R	6-1	220	3-2-85	3	3	7.53	24	0	0	0	35	44	30	29	6	17	22	.321	.270	.365	5.71	4.41

Fielding

Catcher	PCT	G	PO	A	E	DP	PB
Estrada	.974	3	37	1	1	0	0
Flores	1.000	15	122	6	0	0	1
Herrera	.992	36	218	17	2	5	5
Lo Duca	.958	3	21	2	1	0	0
Montz	.992	45	329	29	3	1	5
Nichols	.943	5	30	3	2	0	1
Nieves	1.000	9	73	5	0	2	0
Wallace	.997	42	289	26	1	0	2

First Base	PCT	G	PO	A	E	DP
Batista	1.000	6	38	3	0	6
A. Boone	1.000	3	16	0	0	3
Broadway	.996	121	884	62	4	75
Casto	.960	4	23	1	1	2
de Caster	1.000	2	8	0	0	3
Dubois	1.000	5	40	1	0	2
Escobar	1.000	4	12	2	0	0
Flores	—	1	0	0	0	0
Herrera	.667	1	2	0	1	1
Jimenez	1.000	10	79	9	0	8
Langerhans	1.000	1	9	2	0	1
Lo Duca	1.000	1	8	0	0	0
Montz	1.000	1	7	0	0	0
Porter	1.000	1	4	0	0	2

Second Base	PCT	G	PO	A	E	DP
Bergolla	.960	7	11	13	1	3
Bonifacio	.967	8	11	18	1	6

Second Base (cont.)	PCT	G	PO	A	E	DP
B. Boone	.973	11	16	20	1	3
Casto	—	1	0	0	0	0
Castro	1.000	11	15	35	0	3
Davis	.957	13	17	27	2	2
Murphy	1.000	2	0	5	0	1
Olmedo	1.000	5	6	10	0	5
Orr	.982	43	67	98	3	18
Reese Jr.	.962	16	29	46	3	13
Rogers	.983	35	47	69	2	17
Spearman	.980	12	19	30	1	6

Third Base	PCT	G	PO	A	E	DP
Batista	1.000	5	5	8	0	0
Bergolla	1.000	1	2	2	0	0
Casto	—	1	0	0	0	0
Castro	1.000	3	0	4	0	0
Davis	.885	10	6	17	3	1
de Caster	.979	85	61	130	4	14
Orr	1.000	16	10	25	0	1
Porter	.905	16	6	32	4	5
Rogers	1.000	12	9	20	0	6
Spearman	1.000	4	1	3	0	0
Zimmerman	1.000	4	4	10	0	1

Shortstop	PCT	G	PO	A	E	DP
Bergolla	1.000	2	1	5	0	0
Gonzalez	1.000	7	9	12	0	4
Olmedo	.965	93	152	202	13	51
Orr	—	1	0	0	0	0
Reese Jr.	1.000	3	9	17	0	6
Rogers	.975	49	72	121	5	19
Spearman	1.000	4	2	2	0	0

Outfield	PCT	G	PO	A	E	DP
Bergolla	1.000	2	2	0	0	0
Bernadina	1.000	47	104	4	0	2
Broadway	1.000	7	7	0	0	0
Casto	.984	30	59	3	1	1
Davis	.967	30	55	3	2	1
de Caster	.833	2	5	0	1	0
Diaz	.985	36	61	5	1	1
Dubois	.946	19	35	0	2	0
Dukes	.900	14	17	1	2	0
Escobar	1.000	12	15	0	0	0
Guzman	.965	28	52	3	2	1
Jimenez	.857	4	6	0	1	0
Kearns	1.000	3	6	0	0	0
Langerhans	.984	60	123	1	2	0
Milledge	1.000	1	7	0	0	0
Murphy	.987	69	144	10	2	2
Olmedo	—	1	0	0	0	0
Orr	1.000	18	37	1	0	0
Padilla	.993	77	144	7	1	0
Pena	—	1	0	0	0	0
Porter	1.000	2	2	0	0	0
Reese Jr.	1.000	2	2	0	0	0
Spearman	.750	4	3	0	1	0

HARRISBURG SENATORS

DOUBLE-A

EASTERN LEAGUE

Batting	B-T	HT	WT	DOB	AVG	vLH	vRH	G	AB	R	H	2B	3B	HR	RBI	BB	HBP	SH	SF	SO	SB	CS	SLG	OBP
Baez, Edgardo	R-R	6-2	190	7-12-85	.246	.321	.211	56	167	22	41	9	1	2	13	15	1	2	0	50	5	3	.347	.311
Belliard, Ronnie	R-R	5-10	215	4-7-75	.000	.000	.000	3	12	0	0	0	0	0	0	0	0	0	0	4	0	0	.000	.000
Bergolla, William	R-R	5-10	195	2-4-83	.251	.179	.280	72	267	42	67	15	0	4	26	31	1	7	3	34	5	1	.352	.328
Bernadina, Roger	L-L	6-1	190	6-12-84	.323	.356	.307	73	266	47	86	11	7	5	38	31	2	4	0	64	26	9	.474	.398
Bynum, Seth	R-R	6-0	185	12-19-80	.264	.244	.272	83	273	50	72	16	2	15	49	28	1	5	3	90	1	3	.502	.331
Castro, Ofilio	R-R	6-0	160	8-18-83	.277	.290	.270	108	375	45	104	24	1	4	37	27	1	4	0	39	0	2	.379	.328
Daniel, Mike	L-R	6-0	180	8-17-84	.256	.220	.270	134	485	61	124	12	2	14	56	59	6	5	2	126	19	11	.375	.342
Davis, Leonard	L-R	5-10	195	12-24-83	.488	.333	.514	10	41	8	20	1	0	4	10	6	0	1	0	5	2	0	.805	.553
de Caster, Yurendell	R-R	6-0	215	9-26-79	.321	.318	.324	15	56	11	18	5	0	4	16	10	2	0	0	15	1	0	.625	.441
Desmond, Ian	R-R	6-2	185	9-20-85	.251	.269	.242	93	323	42	81	14	0	12	44	31	2	6	2	78	12	8	.406	.318
Estrada, Johnny	B-R	5-11	255	6-27-76	.250	.000	.278	5	20	2	5	0	0	1	3	0	0	0	0	2	0	0	.400	.250
Guzman, Garrett	L-L	5-9	180	2-7-83	.274	.264	.278	89	288	47	79	19	2	9	54	29	0	0	4	35	5	2	.448	.336
Herrera, Javi	R-R	6-0	190	10-8-81	.264	.320	.247	42	110	27	29	7	0	1	25	6	4	0	0	23	3	2	.355	.326
Ivany, Devin	R-R	6-2	185	7-27-82	.262	.234	.279	69	206	32	54	9	2	8	25	16	4	7	0	50	4	3	.442	.327
Jimenez, Luis Antonio	L-L	6-4	205	5-7-82	.260	.301	.243	77	246	35	64	8	0	14	42	35	0	0	1	44	3	0	.463	.351
Lefave, Andrew	L-L	5-10	205	4-26-84	.250	.194	.278	58	188	32	47	12	1	2	28	31	0	3	4	29	2	5	.351	.350
Lowrance, Marvin	L-L	6-0	215	7-16-84	.286	.286	.286	47	154	27	44	13	0	8	24	20	3	0	1	40	1	0	.526	.376
Maxwell, Justin	R-R	6-5	245	11-6-83	.233	.273	.209	43	146	35	34	6	3	7	28	31	1	0	2	28	13	4	.459	.367

Batting	B-T	HT	WT	DOB	AVG	vLH	vRH	G	AB	R	H	2B	3B	HR	RBI	BB	HBP	SH	SF	SO	SB	CS	SLG	OBP
Montz, Luke	R-R	6-2	205	7-7-83	.282	.280	.283	63	220	30	62	14	0	14	53	31	0	1	2	46	0	1	.536	.368
Nichols, Patrick	R-R	6-2	210	9-12-84	.091	.000	.143	9	11	0	1	0	0	0	0	1	0	1	0	4	0	0	.091	.167
Padilla, Jorge	R-R	6-2	200	8-11-79	.330	.320	.339	33	106	25	35	4	0	1	14	17	3	1	0	12	2	2	.396	.427
Rhinehart, Bill	L-L	6-0	202	11-22-84	.233	.164	.256	61	219	23	51	15	0	7	29	27	2	0	1	49	0	0	.397	.321
Rogelstad, Matt	L-R	6-3	185	9-13-82	.311	.333	.306	14	45	6	14	2	0	0	8	3	0	0	2	9	0	0	.356	.340
Rogers, Ed	R-R	6-0	190	8-29-78	.148	.167	.133	7	27	2	4	0	0	0	0	0	0	2	0	2	0	0	.148	.148
Spearman, Jemel	R-R	6-0	190	12-27-80	.242	.163	.313	33	91	10	22	5	0	2	7	8	1	0	3	15	4	0	.363	.301
Yepez, Marcos	B-R	5-10	160	12-29-81	.251	.250	.252	67	167	22	42	9	3	1	30	23	1	11	1	37	8	4	.359	.344
Young, Dmitri	B-R	6-2	300	10-11-73	.375	.333	.400	3	8	0	3	1	0	0	3	0	0	0	0	1	0	0	.500	.545

Pitching	B-T	HT	WT	DOB	W	L	ERA	G	GS	CG	SV	IP	H	R	ER	HR	BB	SO	AVG	vLH	vRH	K/9	BB/9
Alaniz, Adrian	R-R	6-2	200	3-12-84	0	5	3.93	13	13	0	0	66	61	34	29	10	30	47	.244	.220	.260	6.38	4.07
Atilano, Luis	R-R	6-3	215	5-10-85	0	1	1.50	2	1	0	0	6	6	3	1	0	2	3	.300	.250	.333	4.50	3.00
Bittner, Tim	L-L	6-2	200	6-9-80	2	5	3.96	38	1	0	5	61	48	30	27	5	41	55	.218	.247	.201	8.07	6.02
Brito, Eude	L-L	6-0	170	8-19-78	0	0	0.00	1	0	0	0	1	0	0	0	0	1	0	.000	—	.000	13.50	13.50
2-team total (27 Binghamton)					4	2	2.88	28	1	0	0	50	44	18	16	2	17	31	—			5.58	3.06
Brownlie, Bobby	R-R	6-2	210	10-5-80	8	4	3.99	21	21	0	0	124	121	61	55	22	39	84	.255	.261	.251	6.10	2.83
Carr, Adam	R-R	6-2	220	4-1-84	3	4	6.95	30	0	0	11	34	39	27	26	7	22	27	.287	.333	.256	7.22	5.88
Crawford, Tristan	R-R	6-3	213	7-22-82	2	3	5.40	12	6	0	0	35	47	21	21	2	13	29	.307	.267	.333	7.46	3.34
Estrada, Marco	R-R	6-0	180	7-5-83	6	3	2.66	13	13	1	0	74	62	27	22	5	21	67	.223	.214	.229	8.11	3.87
Hall, Josh	R-R	6-2	190	12-10-80	1	4	8.40	7	6	0	0	30	44	31	28	6	14	13	.358	.231	.417	3.90	4.20
Hinckley, Mike	R-L	6-3	170	10-5-82	5	3	5.12	23	6	0	0	65	79	40	37	6	40	53	.307	.343	.294	7.34	5.54
Jones, Justin	L-L	6-4	190	9-25-84	2	5	5.69	12	12	1	0	55	65	41	35	4	26	44	.295	.245	.310	7.16	4.23
Kown, Andrew	R-R	6-7	210	10-7-82	0	0	30.86	2	0	0	0	2	8	8	2	3	1	.571	.500	.600	3.86	11.57
2-team total (17 Erie)					5	9	6.00	19	16	1	0	96	119	70	64	18	37	43	—			4.03	3.47
Martinez, Carlos	R-R	6-4	177	3-30-84	4	1	5.60	13	0	0	0	27	35	19	17	5	8	16	.330	.459	.261	5.27	2.63
Martis, Shairon	R-R	6-1	175	3-30-87	4	4	3.98	14	14	0	0	75	73	35	33	5	28	57	.258	.239	.271	6.87	3.38
Morales, Alex	R-R	5-11	170	12-20-82	0	0	0.00	1	0	0	0	1	1	2	0	0	1	2	.333	.000	.333	27.00	13.50
Munoz, Arnie	L-L	5-9	185	6-21-82	1	0	0.00	6	0	0	1	8	4	0	0	0	5	5	.160	.000	.235	5.63	5.63
Norrito, Joey	R-R	5-10	180	8-4-82	0	1	5.40	1	1	0	0	5	6	3	3	0	4	3	.300	.286	.308	5.40	7.20
Novoa, Yunior	L-L	6-4	180	9-11-84	2	1	2.44	32	0	0	0	52	36	16	14	2	24	50	.195	.162	.216	8.71	4.18
Nunez, Jhonny	R-R	6-3	185	11-26-85	0	0	1.13	5	0	0	0	8	9	1	1	0	6	8	.300	.500	.200	9.00	6.75
2-team total (8 Trenton)					1	0	1.65	13	0	0	0	27	25	6	5	2	12	34	—			11.20	3.95
Perez, Beltran	R-R	6-2	180	10-24-81	3	5	6.41	36	3	0	2	59	76	50	42	11	30	58	.306	.365	.270	8.85	4.58
Perrault, Josh	R-R	6-3	205	6-11-82	4	2	4.48	46	0	0	1	66	74	39	33	10	17	59	.288	.295	.284	8.01	2.31
Ramirez, Ismael	R-R	6-2	200	3-3-81	0	2	7.85	5	3	0	0	18	27	18	16	2	8	7	.351	.469	.267	3.44	3.93
Schmoll, Steve	R-R	6-2	215	2-4-80	3	5	3.07	46	0	0	7	70	78	29	24	4	17	52	.287	.344	.257	6.65	2.18
Segovia, Zack	R-R	6-2	245	4-11-83	4	1	6.45	8	6	0	0	38	50	29	27	5	14	24	.327	.323	.330	5.73	3.35
2-team total (4 Reading)					4	2	7.38	12	7	0	0	43	57	38	35	6	20	25	—			5.27	4.22
Speigner, Levale	R-R	5-11	170	9-24-80	1	0	0.61	10	0	0	0	15	8	1	1	0	5	4	.160	.211	.129	2.45	3.07
Spradlin, Jack	R-L	6-2	170	9-23-84	0	1	7.11	5	0	0	0	6	9	5	5	1	3	4	.346	.273	.400	5.68	4.26
Stammen, Craig	R-R	6-3	210	3-9-84	3	1	1.64	6	6	0	0	38	22	8	7	1	11	31	.171	.189	.158	7.28	2.58
VanAllen, Cory	L-L	6-3	180	12-24-84	3	3	5.13	10	10	0	0	47	64	30	27	4	11	36	.318	.293	.329	6.85	2.09
Warden, Jim Ed	R-R	6-7	210	5-7-79	2	1	1.29	11	0	0	2	14	9	3	2	0	6	6	.196	.167	.214	5.14	3.86
Zimmermann, Jordan	R-R	6-2	200	5-23-86	7	2	3.21	20	20	0	0	107	89	42	38	9	39	103	.226	.231	.222	8.69	3.29
Zinicola, Zech	R-R	6-1	220	3-2-85	3	2	2.89	15	0	0	6	19	22	6	6	0	13	13	.306	.222	.356	6.27	6.27

Fielding

Catcher	PCT	G	PO	A	E	DP	PB
Estrada	1.000	3	19	0	0	0	0
Herrera	.990	40	279	31	3	3	2
Ivany	.986	55	378	38	6	4	2
Montz	.994	53	290	37	2	4	4
Nichols	1.000	7	27	4	0	0	1

First Base	PCT	G	PO	A	E	DP
Castro	1.000	1	10	0	0	3
Ivany	1.000	1	6	0	0	1
Jimenez	.985	52	432	30	7	40
Lefave	.981	35	238	22	5	26
Montz	1.000	3	19	1	0	5
Rhinehart	.987	59	430	37	6	44
Yepez	1.000	2	11	0	0	0
Young	.944	3	15	2	1	2

Second Base	PCT	G	PO	A	E	DP
Belliard	.929	2	6	7	1	2
Bergolla	.968	70	125	174	10	34

	PCT	G	PO	A	E	DP
Bynum	.984	39	92	98	3	28
Castro	1.000	1	3	5	0	1
Rogelstad	.909	5	10	10	2	4
Rogers	.971	6	16	17	1	6
Yepez	.943	32	58	74	8	17

Third Base	PCT	G	PO	A	E	DP
Belliard	.750	1	0	3	1	0
Castro	.965	105	69	176	9	14
Davis	.955	8	6	15	1	2
de Caster	.953	15	8	33	2	4
Ivany	.600	1	1	2	2	0
Rogelstad	.947	6	5	13	1	0
Spearman	1.000	4	1	7	0	0
Yepez	.933	15	10	18	2	4

Shortstop	PCT	G	PO	A	E	DP
Bergolla	1.000	1	0	2	0	0
Bynum	.986	44	79	128	3	38
Castro	.667	1	2	0	1	1

	PCT	G	PO	A	E	DP
Desmond	.951	93	159	269	22	63
Rogers	1.000	1	1	1	0	0
Spearman	—	1	0	0	0	0
Yepez	.971	9	14	19	1	2

Outfield	PCT	G	PO	A	E	DP
Baez	.971	53	92	7	3	0
Bernadina	.988	69	162	8	2	3
Daniel	.987	124	221	10	3	3
Davis	1.000	2	7	0	0	0
Guzman	.947	65	68	3	4	0
Ivany	—	1	0	0	0	0
Lefave	.968	24	28	2	1	0
Lowrance	.984	41	56	6	1	3
Maxwell	.966	40	80	4	3	1
Padilla	.957	25	44	1	2	0
Spearman	1.000	29	27	1	0	0
Yepez	1.000	3	1	0	0	0

POTOMAC NATIONALS

HIGH CLASS A

CAROLINA LEAGUE

Batting	B-T	HT	WT	DOB	AVG	vLH	vRH	G	AB	R	H	2B	3B	HR	RBI	BB	HBP	SH	SF	SO	SB	CS	SLG	OBP
Baez, Edgardo	R-R	6-2	190	7-12-85	.286	.360	.268	73	255	46	73	22	0	12	52	30	2	3	0	53	6	2	.514	.366
Belliard, Ronnie	R-R	5-10	215	4-7-75	.000		.000	1	3	0	0	0	0	0	0	0	0	0	0	0	0	0	.000	.000
Brown, Dee	R-R	6-0	230	10-21-82	.296	.301	.295	100	351	57	104	20	3	8	64	29	14	0	3	93	8	3	.439	.370
Burgess, Michael	L-L	5-11	195	10-20-88	.225	.136	.265	19	71	12	16	3	0	6	19	9	2	0	1	26	0	2	.521	.325
Bynum, Seth	R-R	6-0	185	12-19-80	.266	.265	.266	50	177	28	47	13	0	6	30	14	2	0	0	36	2	1	.441	.326
Castro, Ofilio	R-R	6-0	160	8-18-83	.236	.429	.171	13	55	2	13	3	0	6	1	0	0	6	1	1	0	.291	.250
Davis, Leonard	L-R	5-10	195	12-24-83	.332	.286	.341	63	217	47	72	14	2	14	37	23	3	4	0	47	7	5	.608	.403

Batting	B-T	HT	WT	DOB	AVG	vLH	vRH	G	AB	R	H	2B	3B	HR	RBI	BB	HBP	SH	SF	SO	SB	CS	SLG	OBP
Diaz, Frank	R-R	6-0	211	10-6-83	.256	.273	.250	43	164	22	42	10	1	2	18	9	1	2	0	27	5	0	.366	.299
Doetsch, Steve	R-R	6-2	195	12-2-83	.083	.000	.111	11	24	3	2	0	0	0	2	3	0	0	1	9	0	1	.083	.179
Dukes, Elijah	R-R	6-1	240	6-26-84	.176	.000	.176	6	17	1	3	1	0	0	1	4	1	0	0	5	0	1	.235	.364
Estrada, Johnny	B-R	5-11	255	6-27-76	.357	.286	.429	4	14	1	5	1	0	0	3	1	0	0	0	1	0	0	.429	.400
Finegan, Brian	R-R	6-0	190	12-15-81	.221	.269	.200	27	86	10	19	2	0	2	13	5	1	1	2	24	5	2	.314	.266
Ivany, Devin	R-R	6-2	185	7-27-82	.250	.500	.188	11	40	7	10	3	0	1	6	4	0	0	0	8	0	0	.400	.318
King, Stephen	R-R	6-2	195	10-2-87	.214	.318	.167	19	70	4	15	2	1	0	7	5	0	0	0	11	1	1	.271	.267
Lawhorn, Darryl	L-R	6-1	180	12-18-82	.203	.143	.212	16	59	6	12	4	0	0	2	4	0	0	0	16	0	1	.271	.254
Lawhorn, Trevor	R-R	6-2	180	12-18-82	.233	.250	.227	52	176	26	41	13	1	6	24	16	0	0	4	36	5	0	.420	.291
Lefave, Andrew	L-L	5-10	205	4-26-84	.269	.269	.269	54	186	44	50	13	2	3	33	43	3	0	1	35	9	1	.409	.412
Lo Duca, Paul	R-R	5-9	215	4-12-72	.143	—	.143	5	14	0	2	1	0	0	1	3	0	0	0	2	0	0	.214	.294
Lowrance, Marvin	L-L	6-0	215	7-16-84	.268	.320	.255	74	250	39	67	17	0	12	39	37	5	0	0	59	2	2	.480	.373
Lyons, Dan	R-R	5-10	185	8-21-84	.254	.263	.250	55	197	32	50	15	3	2	33	30	10	2	3	47	6	2	.391	.375
Marrero, Chris	R-R	6-3	210	7-2-88	.250	.240	.252	70	256	40	64	15	2	11	38	25	5	0	3	55	0	0	.453	.325
Martinez, Michael	B-R	5-9	145	9-16-82	.266	.245	.273	104	417	63	111	25	6	3	58	27	7	20	2	49	25	7	.376	.320
Nichols, Patrick	R-R	6-2	210	9-12-84	.217	.231	.212	13	46	3	10	4	0	0	2	1	0	0	1	14	0	0	.304	.229
Peacock, Brian	R-R	6-1	185	8-26-84	.258	.222	.271	53	163	21	42	14	0	3	26	12	1	0	1	38	5	2	.399	.311
Plasencia, Francisco	L-L	6-1	192	6-19-84	.278	.215	.297	98	345	46	96	27	1	5	45	36	3	1	3	74	6	3	.406	.349
Rhinehart, Bill	L-L	6-0	202	11-22-84	.320	.167	.368	7	25	5	8	2	0	2	4	2	0	0	0	5	1	1	.640	.393
Rogelstad, Matt	L-R	6-3	185	9-13-82	.277	.306	.270	86	329	40	91	23	3	8	44	19	7	1	1	54	4	5	.438	.329
Seuss, Aaron	R-R	6-1	195	3-5-85	.245	.228	.252	52	200	32	49	14	1	4	21	4	7	1	2	42	2	2	.385	.282
Solano, Jhonatan	R-R	6-0	180	8-21-85	.258	.426	.213	68	225	35	58	11	0	4	24	16	4	2	3	30	2	1	.360	.315
Spearman, Jemel	R-R	6-0	190	12-27-80	.254	.231	.259	18	67	14	17	5	0	0	6	9	1	1	0	12	8	2	.328	.351
Whiting, Brandon	R-R	5-10	170	11-5-83	.284	.333	.264	43	148	33	42	1	1	2	12	15	3	3	1	28	14	4	.345	.359
Zimmerman, Ryan	R-R	6-3	230	9-28-84	.300	.000	.500	2	10	1	3	2	0	0	1	0	0	0	0	1	0	0	.500	.300

Pitching	B-T	HT	WT	DOB	W	L	ERA	G	GS	CG	SV	IP	H	R	ER	HR	BB	SO	AVG	vLH	vRH	K/9	BB/9
Abreu, Edulin	R-R	6-3	160	8-8-84	1	1	13.21	11	0	0	0	16	24	24	23	1	12	11	.353	.241	.436	6.32	6.89
Alaniz, Adrian	R-R	6-2	200	3-12-84	9	0	2.62	12	12	0	0	65	50	24	19	2	25	56	.214	.214	.214	7.71	3.44
Arnesen, Erik	R-R	6-3	260	3-19-84	4	3	4.46	8	7	0	0	42	45	24	21	6	8	36	.274	.214	.306	7.65	1.70
Atilano, Luis	R-R	6-3	215	5-10-85	5	2	2.32	15	11	0	0	62	50	21	16	5	14	39	.229	.247	.218	5.66	2.03
Beno, Martin	R-R	6-0	180	8-24-86	0	1	7.50	30	0	0	7	30	16	29	25	3	51	33	.154	.195	.127	9.90	15.30
Carr, Adam	R-R	6-2	220	4-1-84	3	4	6.15	21	0	0	5	26	29	19	18	3	13	31	.284	.216	.323	10.59	4.44
Cordero, Chad	R-R	6-0	225	3-18-82	1	0	0.00	2	1	0	0	2	1	0	0	0	0	2	.143	.000	.200	9.00	0.00
Detwiler, Ross	R-L	6-5	185	3-6-86	8	8	4.86	26	26	0	0	124	140	72	67	8	57	114	.289	.295	.287	8.27	4.14
Engles, Terrence	R-R	6-4	170	11-12-85	0	5	9.47	6	5	0	0	19	28	25	20	1	15	22	.341	.258	.392	10.42	7.11
Everts, Clint	B-R	6-2	170	8-10-84	4	2	4.80	30	1	0	3	69	74	41	37	7	30	75	.269	.304	.249	9.74	3.89
Gunderson, Kyle	R-R	6-3	215	1-31-85	1	0	1.46	6	0	0	0	12	10	2	2	1	3	10	.227	.188	.250	7.30	2.19
Hill, Shawn	R-R	6-2	225	4-28-81	1	0	0.00	1	1	0	0	5	4	0	0	1	2	4	.222	—	.222	7.20	1.80
Jones, Justin	L-L	6-4	190	9-25-84	3	1	1.48	4	4	0	0	24	20	4	4	1	8	17	.230	.100	.269	6.29	2.96
Kown, Andrew	L-R	6-7	210	10-7-82	0	2	3.00	3	1	0	0	9	9	8	3	0	5	3	.257	.143	.286	3.00	5.00
Lugo, Chris	R-R	6-1	185	11-10-86	0	0	4.05	3	0	0	0	7	7	4	3	0	1	6	.292	.300	.286	0.00	1.35
Mandel, Jeff	B-R	6-3	190	4-30-85	6	6	3.68	17	17	1	0	95	103	47	39	7	26	58	.277	.307	.257	5.48	2.45
Martinez, Carlos	R-R	6-4	177	3-30-84	0	2	3.23	28	0	0	2	53	51	27	19	0	20	39	.251	.194	.282	6.62	3.40
Morales, Alex	R-R	5-11	165	12-20-82	0	0	11.57	7	0	0	0	7	6	9	3	0	4	5	.222	.286	.200	6.43	5.14
Norrito, Joey	R-R	5-10	180	8-4-82	7	2	4.20	16	6	0	0	49	56	29	23	3	12	25	.287	.296	.282	4.56	2.19
Novoa, Yunior	L-L	6-4	180	9-11-84	2	1	1.38	13	0	0	4	26	16	4	4	1	2	27	.178	.150	.186	9.35	0.69
Nunez, Jhonny	R-R	6-3	185	11-26-85	2	8	5.22	21	17	0	0	81	88	51	47	11	21	82	.276	.298	.267	9.11	2.33
Pena, Hassan	R-R	6-2	210	3-25-85	2	2	4.15	8	8	0	0	43	42	25	20	4	24	30	.266	.319	.225	6.23	4.98
Perez, Odalis	L-L	6-0	225	6-11-77	0	0	2.25	1	1	0	0	4	3	1	1	0	0	5	.200	—	.300	11.25	0.00
Rodriguez, Osvaldo	R-R	5-11	180	6-10-84	0	0	0.00	1	0	0	0	3	0	1	0	0	2	0	.000	.000	.000	12.00	6.00
Segovia, Zack	R-R	6-2	245	4-11-83	2	1	2.70	3	3	0	0	17	17	8	5	2	3	13	.279	.321	.242	7.02	1.62
Severino, Atahualpa	L-L	5-9	170	11-6-84	0	4	3.96	26	0	0	0	39	31	18	17	2	20	31	.221	.184	.235	7.22	4.66
Spradlin, Jack	L-L	6-2	170	9-23-84	5	1	3.16	41	1	0	2	68	74	28	24	3	11	57	.277	.268	.281	7.51	1.45
Stammen, Craig	R-R	6-3	210	3-9-84	4	2	2.21	15	9	0	1	69	59	24	17	6	17	62	.227	.225	.228	8.05	2.21
VanAllen, Cory	L-L	6-3	180	12-24-84	3	0	0.66	5	4	0	0	27	18	6	2	1	7	19	.186	.190	.184	6.26	2.30
Wagner, Ryan	R-R	6-3	205	7-15-82	0	0	1.23	7	1	0	1	7	5	1	1	0	5	5	.185	.100	.235	7.36	6.14
Wilkie, Josh	R-R	6-2	190	7-22-84	1	2	2.08	46	0	0	5	61	52	14	14	1	12	45	.241	.253	.233	6.68	1.78
Zimmermann, Jordan	R-R	6-2	200	5-23-86	3	1	1.65	5	4	0	1	27	15	6	5	1	8	31	.167	.158	.173	10.21	2.63
Zinicola, Zech	R-R	6-1	220	3-2-85	2	0	0.00	8	0	0	3	12	3	0	0	0	3	15	.079	.083	.077	10.95	2.19

Fielding

Catcher	PCT	G	PO	A	E	DP	PB
Estrada	1.000	2	11	1	0	0	0
Ivany	.991	11	97	11	1	1	1
Lo Duca	1.000	4	26	2	0	0	0
Nichols	1.000	12	58	7	0	0	1
Peacock	.982	52	347	42	7	3	5
Solano	.994	67	467	66	3	1	9

First Base	PCT	G	PO	A	E	DP
Finegan	1.000	2	20	4	0	6
Lawhorn	1.000	2	19	1	0	3
Lawhorn	.959	7	43	4	2	9
Lefave	.986	52	470	38	7	38
Marrero	.988	69	598	37	8	53
Rhinehart	1.000	7	54	5	0	6
Rogelstad	.974	5	35	3	1	4

	PCT	G	PO	A	E	DP
Spearman	1.000	1	5	1	0	0

Second Base	PCT	G	PO	A	E	DP
Finegan	.984	12	22	38	1	8
Lawhorn	.882	3	6	9	2	3
Lawhorn	.952	6	6	14	1	2
Lyons	1.000	10	20	27	0	5
Martinez	.976	61	115	173	7	43
Rogelstad	.967	48	88	116	7	24
Solano	—	1	0	0	0	0
Spearman	1.000	4	9	12	0	3

Third Base	PCT	G	PO	A	E	DP
Belliard	1.000	1	1	1	0	0
Castro	.971	13	7	27	1	4
Davis	.905	55	33	101	14	11

	PCT	G	PO	A	E	DP
Finegan	.895	9	3	14	2	0
King	.934	19	18	39	4	6
Lawhorn	.938	8	2	13	1	0
Lawhorn	.872	26	7	34	6	2
Rogelstad	.966	13	9	19	1	2
Spearman	.889	4	4	4	1	0

Shortstop	PCT	G	PO	A	E	DP
Bynum	.948	50	85	154	13	35
Finegan	1.000	2	2	2	0	0
Lyons	.954	45	70	139	10	34
Martinez	.949	43	70	134	11	21
Spearman	1.000	2	3	7	0	0

Outfield	PCT	G	PO	A	E	DP
Baez	.977	72	119	8	3	0

Brown	.978	62	85	2	2	0
Burgess	1.000	16	22	2	0	0
Davis	1.000	3	3	0	0	0
Diaz	1.000	43	71	2	0	0

Doetsch	1.000	11	9	0	0	0
Dukes	1.000	4	4	0	0	0
Finegan	1.000	1	5	0	0	0
Lowrance	.962	44	50	1	2	0

Plasencia	.991	92	207	8	2	1
Seuss	.974	46	73	1	2	0
Whiting	1.000	37	72	0	0	0

HAGERSTOWN SUNS

LOW CLASS A

SOUTH ATLANTIC LEAGUE

Batting	B-T	HT	WT	DOB	AVG	vLH	vRH	G	AB	R	H	2B	3B	HR	RBI	BB	HBP	SH	SF	SO	SB	CS	SLG	OBP
Bass, Garrett	L-R	6-2	225	8-27-84	.205	.237	.191	38	132	10	27	2	0	0	11	4	0	0	0	26	0	1	.220	.228
Burgess, Michael	L-L	5-11	195	10-20-88	.249	.257	.247	112	401	60	100	26	4	18	60	46	8	0	5	136	5	1	.469	.335
Englund, Stephen	R-R	6-3	190	6-6-88	.162	.150	.165	34	117	13	19	6	0	2	9	14	2	1	1	32	1	1	.265	.261
Gildea, Mark	B-R	6-2	190	1-11-86	.171	.157	.176	91	293	33	50	12	0	4	24	49	4	4	2	102	4	3	.253	.296
Heredia, Valerio	B-R	5-10	150	3-14-86	.225	.241	.219	63	209	28	47	5	0	0	10	22	1	3	1	43	28	8	.249	.300
Jacobsen, Robert	R-R	6-1	205	8-30-84	.198	.174	.214	41	116	13	23	5	1	1	9	10	1	0	1	43	1	0	.284	.266
Kearns, Austin	R-R	6-3	240	5-20-80	.333	—	.333	2	3	2	1	0	0	1	3	0	0	1	0	0	.333	.667
King, Stephen	R-R	6-2	195	10-2-87	.284	.229	.305	87	335	39	95	21	1	6	33	32	5	1	1	75	4	4	.406	.336
Lawhorn, Trevor	R-R	6-2	180	12-18-82	.244	.214	.259	28	82	8	20	4	0	2	9	6	0	0	0	27	0	0	.366	.295
Lozada, Jose	B-R	6-0	180	12-29-85	.214	.239	.203	58	224	28	48	11	2	3	21	14	2	5	2	47	2	5	.321	.264
Lyons, Dan	R-R	5-10	185	8-21-84	.285	.333	.271	76	277	51	79	15	3	5	38	47	11	11	4	49	17	7	.415	.404
Miller, Bryan	R-R	6-0	195	7-15-86	.179	.129	.203	27	95	9	17	5	0	1	4	1	2	0		28	0	2	.263	.220
Pahuta, Tim	L-R	6-4	225	5-3-83	.269	.260	.272	116	405	42	109	24	1	17	73	33	3	0	3	83	1	0	.459	.327
Plasencia, Francisco	L-L	6-1	192	6-19-84	.282	.300	.280	21	85	18	24	10	1	2	6	7	0	1	0	25	2	1	.494	.337
Reagan, Travis	R-R	6-2	205	8-31-84	.215	.265	.197	58	191	19	41	6	0	2	14	20	3	5	2	39	0	2	.277	.296
Reese Jr., Pokey	R-R	5-11	190	6-10-73	.250	.143	.333	5	16	4	4	0	0	1	1	2	0	0	1	0	0	.438	.333
Rhinehart, Bill	L-L	6-0	202	11-22-84	.295	.238	.313	65	261	39	77	22	1	9	56	21	1	0	5	36	0	0	.490	.344
Rogers, Jake	R-R	6-1	180	3-16-84	.224	.222	.225	56	165	16	37	5	1	3	16	16	1	3	0	44	1	0	.321	.297
Rooney, Sean	R-R	5-10	205	4-12-86	.314	.338	.304	74	255	25	80	14	2	1	26	16	1	3	1	40	0	2	.396	.355
Seuss, Aaron	R-R	6-1	195	3-5-85	.304	.276	.314	71	286	43	87	23	0	10	49	13	4	0	4	49	0	2	.490	.339
Smolinski, Jake	R-R	5-11	185	2-9-89	.261	.225	.271	50	184	28	48	12	1	4	22	19	3	3	1	33	1	2	.402	.338
Solano, Jhonatan	R-R	6-0	180	8-12-85	.218	.133	.250	16	55	6	12	2	0	1	5	6	1	2	1	6	1	1	.309	.302
Souza, Steven	R-R	6-3	205	4-24-89	.266	.235	.274	23	79	14	21	4	0	2	10	8	2	0	0	26	8	2	.392	.348
Stouffer, Blake	L-R	6-0	190	10-11-85	.200	.286	.167	15	50	6	10	1	0	0	1	6	3	1	0	16	1	0	.220	.322
Valdez, Jesus	R-R	6-2	170	11-2-84	.287	.286	.288	28	108	10	31	6	0	3	13	3	1	0	2	16	0	0	.426	.307
Whiting, Brandon	R-R	5-10	170	11-5-83	.261	.308	.242	58	226	44	59	8	2	2	27	37	5	5	0	36	33	12	.341	.377

Pitching	B-T	HT	WT	DOB	W	L	ERA	G	GS	CG	SV	IP	H	R	ER	BB	SO	AVG	vLH	vRH	K/9	BB/9
Abreu, Edulin	R-R	6-3	160	8-8-84	2	1	4.03	30	0	0	6	51	57	26	23	4	20	31	.279	.241	.308	5.44	3.51
Arnesen, Erik	R-R	6-3	260	3-19-84	6	4	3.97	25	7	1	0	82	88	37	36	4	21	75	.284	.315	.261	8.27	2.31
Atilano, Luis	R-R	6-3	215	5-10-85	0	0	3.16	7	3	0	1	26	29	14	9	1	7	13	.276	.313	.246	4.56	2.45
Beno, Martin	R-R	6-0	180	8-24-86	0	1	3.38	15	0	0	6	19	17	9	7	1	13	21	.233	.269	.213	10.13	6.27
Buchter, Ryan	L-L	6-3	185	2-13-87	2	2	3.26	13	0	0	0	19	18	11	7	0	13	17	.273	.263	.277	7.91	6.05
Engles, Terrence	R-R	6-4	170	11-12-85	3	5	6.16	22	12	0	1	76	93	68	52	6	22	46	.292	.328	.264	5.45	2.61
Everts, Clint	B-R	6-2	170	8-10-84	0	2	4.63	8	0	0	2	12	7	7	6	0	9	10	.163	.143	.182	7.71	6.94
Gunderson, Kyle	R-R	6-3	215	1-31-85	4	2	2.60	34	0	0	8	55	38	17	16	4	9	42	.184	.157	.205	6.83	1.46
Harrison, Ryan	R-R	6-2	190	7-12-86	4	2	6.30	32	1	0	0	66	88	55	46	5	18	37	.327	.370	.293	5.07	2.47
Jones, Justin	L-L	6-4	190	9-25-84	1	2	3.24	2	2	0	0	8	12	6	3	0	3	4	.343	.100	.440	4.32	3.24
Kelley, Chris	R-R	6-1	200	8-8-85	1	1	7.20	1	1	0	0	5	9	4	4	1	0	2	.409	.500	.389	3.60	0.00
Kimball, Cole	R-R	6-3	225	8-1-85	6	8	5.05	28	27	1	0	128	103	75	72	5	83	122	.226	.231	.223	8.56	5.82
Leatherman, Dan	R-R	6-2	210	7-12-85	1	2	2.68	26	0	0	5	50	46	16	15	3	10	62	.222	.158	.266	11.09	1.79
Lehman, Jamie	R-R	6-2	185	3-14-85	1	3	6.00	27	0	0	0	42	62	33	28	7	8	29	.337	.397	.297	6.21	1.71
Lugo, Chris	R-R	6-1	185	11-10-86	3	2	3.86	27	2	0	2	56	54	26	24	4	15	47	.257	.299	.221	7.55	2.41
Mandel, Jeff	B-R	6-2	190	4-30-85	4	5	3.21	11	11	0	0	57	73	35	33	5	16	45	.313	.325	.301	7.11	2.53
Matias, Randy	R-R	6-0	160	9-19-86	0	1	9.00	2	1	0	0	6	10	6	6	1	4	6	.400	.308	.500	6.00	4.50
Meyers, Brad	R-R	6-6	195	9-13-85	9	7	4.79	22	21	0	0	107	129	66	57	8	34	94	.299	.308	.290	7.91	2.86
Milone, Tom	L-L	6-1	205	2-16-87	0	3	2.89	7	7	0	0	37	36	16	12	0	6	27	.257	.294	.245	6.51	1.45
Peacock, Brad	R-R	6-1	175	2-2-88	0	5	9.09	8	8	0	0	34	38	38	34	8	21	23	.284	.328	.247	6.15	5.61
Pecina, Ricardo	L-L	5-11	180	7-1-87	0	1	6.14	2	1	0	0	7	11	5	5	0	4	6	.355	.250	.391	7.36	4.91
Pena, Hassan	R-R	6-2	210	3-25-85	2	2	2.08	6	6	0	0	26	24	9	6	5	6	32	.245	.262	.232	8.31	1.73
Phillabaum, Justin	R-R	6-2	180	4-18-86	1	2	5.17	27	0	0	1	47	55	32	27	6	25	53	.289	.273	.301	10.15	4.79
Rodriguez, Osvaldo	R-R	5-11	180	6-10-84	1	2	1.06	3	3	0	0	17	13	3	2	1	4	17	.210	.240	.189	9.00	2.12
Segovia, Zack	R-R	6-2	245	4-11-83	0	1	7.20	1	1	0	0	5	8	4	4	0	0	3	.364	.600	.294	5.40	0.00
Severino, Atahualpa	L-L	5-9	170	11-6-84	2	2	4.05	15	0	0	1	33	28	17	15	2	17	34	.235	.255	.221	9.18	4.59
Smoker, Josh	L-L	6-2	195	11-26-88	0	4	11.50	5	5	0	0	18	31	27	23	5	9	21	.360	.367	.357	10.50	4.50
Tuomi, Kai	L-L	6-1	190	7-26-85	1	1	5.40	5	0	0	0	10	18	9	6	1	2	7	.375	.556	.333	6.30	1.80
Willems, Colton	R-R	6-3	175	7-30-88	5	9	3.70	20	20	0	0	109	103	58	45	7	31	60	.254	.223	.280	4.94	2.55

Fielding

Catcher	PCT	G	PO	A	E	DP	PB
Jacobsen	1.000	5	21	0	0	0	1
Reagan	.983	58	417	51	8	3	7
Rooney	.992	67	420	54	4	5	14
Solano	1.000	16	128	16	0	0	2

First Base	PCT	G	PO	A	E	DP
Jacobsen	1.000	13	96	4	0	13
Pahuta	.990	66	543	35	6	42
Rhinehart	.995	65	575	48	3	51
Rogers	1.000	1	1	0	0	0

Second Base	PCT	G	PO	A	E	DP
Heredia	.968	38	54	99	5	24
Lawhorn	.957	4	13	9	1	4
Reese Jr.	1.000	5	9	6	0	1
Rogers	.973	36	56	89	4	18
Smolinski	.974	50	107	153	7	29
Stouffer	.950	15	26	31	3	5

Third Base	PCT	G	PO	A	E	DP
Heredia	1.000	12	5	27	0	2
Jacobsen	1.000	3	2	5	0	2

	PCT	G	PO	A	E	DP
King	.918	82	46	156	18	25
Lawhorn	.875	9	3	11	2	2
Pahuta	.909	13	6	14	2	2
Rogers	.963	13	5	21	1	2
Souza	.756	19	13	21	11	2

Shortstop	PCT	G	PO	A	E	DP
King	.895	5	4	13	2	2
Lozada	.939	58	79	150	15	18
Lyons	.956	75	145	200	16	41
Souza	.833	5	5	10	3	1

Outfield	PCT	G	PO	A	E	DP
Bass	1.000	5	6	0	0	0
Burgess	.967	111	177	26	7	4
Englund	.974	33	76	0	2	0
Gildea	.971	87	195	8	6	3

	PCT	G	PO	A	E	DP
Heredia	.917	11	19	3	2	2
Jacobsen	.923	12	11	1	1	0
Lawhorn	1.000	1	1	0	0	0
Miller	.938	27	59	2	4	2
Pahuta	—	1	0	0	0	0

	PCT	G	PO	A	E	DP
Plasencia	.962	15	25	0	1	0
Rooney	—	1	0	0	0	0
Seuss	.967	52	84	3	3	0
Valdez	.930	26	46	7	4	1
Whiting	.989	47	87	0	1	0

VERMONT LAKE MONSTERS   SHORT-SEASON
NEW YORK-PENN LEAGUE

Batting	B-T	HT	WT	DOB	AVG	vLH	vRH	G	AB	R	H	2B	3B	HR	RBI	BB	HBP	SH	SF	SO	SB	CS	SLG	OBP
Arata, Nick	R-R	5-10	175	10-13-86	.230	.275	.214	44	152	20	35	8	5	0	11	14	5	0	1	54	10	3	.349	.314
Arias, Dani	B-R	5-11	175	8-24-87	.221	.174	.232	40	122	13	27	2	0	0	7	12	2	3	0	35	1	1	.238	.301
Dugger, Jake	L-L	5-10	195	3-19-85	.220	.226	.218	51	164	28	36	8	4	4	24	41	3	2	1	60	10	5	.390	.383
Englund, Stephen	R-R	6-3	190	6-6-88	.213	.180	.226	53	183	25	39	5	0	2	16	26	6	0	2	64	11	2	.273	.327
Espinosa, Danny	B-R	6-0	190	4-25-87	.328	.231	.353	19	64	8	21	2	0	0	4	17	2	3	1	17	2	2	.359	.476
Guerrero, Michael	R-R	6-0	175	10-16-86	.231	.239	.228	69	273	26	63	14	0	7	41	10	5	1	2	60	4	2	.359	.269
Jacobsen, Robert	R-R	6-1	205	8-30-84	.313	.400	.273	5	16	4	5	1	0	1	3	1	0	1	0	6	3	0	.563	.353
Jones, Marcus	R-R	6-2	190	9-9-86	.333	.214	.370	14	60	11	20	2	2	0	6	5	2	2	0	17	2	1	.433	.403
Keithley, James	R-R	6-2	185	2-18-87	.165	.226	.146	39	127	15	21	3	0	2	9	15	1	0	0	39	4	0	.236	.259
Lopez, Yhonson	L-L	6-1	160	10-27-88	.143	.118	.149	32	91	6	13	0	0	0	5	12	1	2	2	30	1	2	.143	.245
Lozada, Jose	B-R	6-0	180	12-29-85	.238	.200	.259	11	42	6	10	2	0	1	5	4	0	1	1	5	4	0	.357	.298
Moore, Tyler	R-R	6-2	185	1-30-87	.200	.250	.183	71	265	17	53	10	0	6	28	13	1	0	1	66	1	1	.306	.239
Nolan, Rick	R-R	6-0	180	4-23-86	.123	.000	.157	19	65	5	8	4	0	0	2	7	0	2	0	20	0	1	.185	.208
Norris, Derek	R-R	6-0	210	2-14-89	.278	.328	.260	70	227	42	63	12	0	10	38	63	8	0	4	56	11	9	.463	.444
Pruitt, Brian	R-R	6-1	175	12-4-86	.063	.000	.091	5	16	0	1	0	0	0	0	1	0	0	0	5	0	0	.063	.118
Smolinski, Jake	R-R	5-11	185	2-9-89	.306	.526	.253	24	98	17	30	8	1	0	9	9	1	1	0	17	4	0	.408	.370
Solis, Chris	R-R	6-2	215	1-22-86	.140	.152	.132	27	86	8	12	6	0	0	3	7	1	1	0	38	0	0	.209	.213
Souza, Steven	R-R	6-3	205	4-24-89	.189	.178	.192	48	175	27	33	7	0	5	25	24	3	4	1	54	14	7	.314	.296
Stouffer, Blake	L-R	6-0	190	10-11-85	.189	.000	.230	29	106	15	20	2	1	4	9	14	2	0	0	28	2	1	.340	.295
Tejeda, Yeurys	R-R	6-1	150	2-24-88	.227	.143	.267	12	44	5	10	1	0	1	6	1	0	0	0	13	3	0	.318	.244
Valdez, Jesus	R-R	6-2	170	11-2-84	.341	.423	.305	23	85	12	29	4	1	1	16	12	0	0	1	11	1	0	.447	.418
Young, Dmitri	B-R	6-3	300	10-11-73	.333	.200	.429	5	12	0	4	2	0	0	2	0	0	0	0	0	0	0	.500	.333

Pitching	B-T	HT	WT	DOB	W	L	ERA	G	GS	CG	SV	IP	H	R	ER	HR	BB	SO	AVG	vLH	vRH	K/9	BB/9
Arnold, Patrick	R-R	6-1	190	10-31-88	1	3	4.97	6	5	0	0	29	35	22	16	2	9	26	.285	.280	.288	8.07	2.79
Atwood, Will	L-L	6-2	180	1-13-87	2	1	2.41	12	12	0	0	52	40	17	14	2	9	60	.205	.156	.215	10.32	1.55
Dean, P.J.	R-R	6-3	175	10-27-88	1	1	1.57	10	10	0	0	46	26	10	8	2	16	34	.169	.164	.173	6.65	3.13
DeLaughter, Ryan	R-R	6-3	210	12-31-86	0	0	—	1	0	0	0	0	4	6	6	1	3	0	.800	.667	1.000	—	—
Figuereo, Johan	R-R	6-2	195	3-2-86	0	3	4.30	21	0	0	0	38	33	19	18	4	15	55	.232	.189	.258	13.14	3.58
Garrett, Austin	L-L	6-0	190	3-26-87	1	2	4.50	21	0	0	3	36	32	21	18	2	17	37	.235	.275	.219	9.25	4.25
Hicks, Graham	L-L	6-5	170	2-9-90	0	1	3.00	1	1	0	0	3	3	3	1	0	2	1	.250	—	.250	3.00	6.00
Light, Kevin	L-L	6-0	190	8-27-87	2	0	1.80	19	0	0	1	40	34	14	8	0	18	42	.222	.184	.240	9.45	4.05
Matias, Randy	R-R	6-0	160	9-19-86	2	4	7.51	15	6	0	0	44	64	39	37	6	18	39	.337	.309	.352	7.92	3.65
McCoy, Patrick	L-L	6-4	200	8-3-88	1	6	5.98	13	13	0	0	59	78	52	39	8	26	43	.316	.311	.317	6.60	3.99
McGeary, Jack	L-L	6-3	195	3-19-89	0	0	4.50	1	1	0	0	4	6	2	2	0	3	5	.375	.556	.143	11.25	6.75
Milone, Tom	L-L	6-1	205	2-16-87	1	3	4.57	6	3	0	0	22	27	12	11	4	3	22	.307	.273	.318	9.14	1.25
Peacock, Brad	R-R	6-1	175	2-2-88	4	7	3.12	14	14	2	0	75	67	38	26	3	27	54	.235	.262	.215	6.48	3.24
Pecina, Ricardo	L-L	5-11	180	7-1-87	1	4	3.29	10	7	0	0	38	38	21	14	3	15	32	.252	.278	.243	7.51	3.52
Peralta, Carlos	R-R	6-1	185	7-29-85	5	0	3.62	19	0	0	0	37	25	16	15	5	21	36	.188	.224	.167	8.68	5.06
Pinales, Jose	R-R	6-2	175	9-1-85	1	1	4.76	18	2	0	0	40	27	24	21	2	39	54	.199	.283	.156	12.25	8.85
Slovak, David	R-R	6-0	170	5-20-86	4	2	2.37	24	0	0	5	38	35	12	10	0	16	33	.252	.280	.236	7.82	3.79
Stewart, Steven	R-R	6-3	215	5-18-86	3	2	3.31	20	0	0	2	35	33	14	13	1	18	28	.244	.283	.225	7.13	4.58
Urena, Jorge	R-R	5-11	190	10-3-86	0	1	1.13	2	1	0	0	8	7	3	1	0	0	5	.241	.273	.222	5.63	0.00
Whitmer, Casey	R-R	6-1	190	3-19-87	1	1	2.87	14	0	0	1	16	16	5	5	1	8	24	.267	.273	.263	13.79	4.60

Fielding

Catcher	PCT	G	PO	A	E	DP	PB
Nolan	.994	18	163	15	1	0	1
Norris	.976	47	369	43	10	2	16
Solis	.962	13	118	8	5	0	3

First Base	PCT	G	PO	A	E	DP
Jacobsen	1.000	1	9	1	0	0
Keithley	.947	3	17	1	1	3
Moore	.985	71	515	67	9	35
Nolan	1.000	1	9	0	0	1
Young	1.000	3	14	1	0	1

Second Base	PCT	G	PO	A	E	DP
Arata	.989	18	39	51	1	9

	PCT	G	PO	A	E	DP
Keithley	.979	13	23	24	1	2
Smolinski	.957	23	58	54	5	15
Stouffer	.980	24	36	64	2	11

Third Base	PCT	G	PO	A	E	DP
Arata	1.000	5	2	3	0	1
Jacobsen	—	1	0	0	0	0
Keithley	.833	17	14	26	8	1
Souza	.842	46	47	70	22	5
Tejeda	.813	12	11	15	6	0

Shortstop	PCT	G	PO	A	E	DP
Arata	.964	15	24	30	2	9
Arias	.881	35	47	72	16	10

	PCT	G	PO	A	E	DP
Espinosa	.937	16	30	44	5	6
Lozada	.947	11	27	27	3	4

Outfield	PCT	G	PO	A	E	DP
Dugger	.958	42	66	3	3	0
Englund	1.000	53	92	4	0	0
Guerrero	.984	66	115	8	2	0
Jones	.966	14	26	2	1	0
Keithley	—					
Lopez	.971	26	31	3	1	0
Pruitt	1.000	4	5	1	0	0
Valdez	.946	23	33	2	2	0

GCL NATIONALS   ROOKIE
GULF COAST LEAGUE

Batting	B-T	HT	WT	DOB	AVG	vLH	vRH	G	AB	R	H	2B	3B	HR	RBI	BB	HBP	SH	SF	SO	SB	CS	SLG	OBP
Bass, Garrett	L-R	6-2	225	8-27-84	.412	.333	.429	5	17	2	7	2	1	0	1	1	1	0	0	1	0	1	.647	.474
Blackwood, Chris	L-R	6-2	165	11-23-87	.367	.000	.407	19	30	5	11	1	0	0	7	4	0	1	0	11	4	1	.400	.441
Boone, Aaron	R-R	6-3	205	3-9-73	.667	—	.667	1	3	0	2	1	0	0	0	0	0	0	0	0	0	0	1.000	.667
Cegles, Vic	R-R	6-0	185	7-30-85	.000	—	.000	3	6	2	0	0	0	0	0	0	1	0	0	3	0	0	.000	.143
Cruz, Frank	B-R	6-0	156	1-8-89	.133	.000	.154	14	15	6	2	0	0	0	1	1	0	0	0	7	2	0	.133	.188
Curran, Chris	L-R	5-9	170	12-21-87	.311	.120	.337	55	209	55	65	8	4	1	22	28	2	4	0	36	14	3	.402	.397

Batting	B-T	HT	WT	DOB	AVG	vLH	vRH	G	AB	R	H	2B	3B	HR	RBI	BB	HBP	SH	SF	SO	SB	CS	SLG	OBP
Desmond, Ian	R-R	6-2	185	9-20-85	.385	.333	.400	3	13	1	5	1	0	0	2	0	0	0	0	2	3	0	.462	.385
Dukes, Elijah	R-R	6-1	240	6-26-84	.000	—	.000	2	5	0	0	0	0	0	0	0	0	0	0	0	0	0	.000	.000
Estrada, Johnny	B-R	5-11	255	6-27-76	.286	—	.286	3	7	1	2	0	0	0	3	0	0	0	0	1	0	0	.286	.286
Gonzalez, Esmailyn	B-R	5-11	175	9-21-89	.343	.458	.325	51	181	42	62	12	3	2	33	23	5	4	0	19	9	2	.475	.431
Hiciano, Yan Carlos	R-R	5-8	174	11-28-86	.000	—	.000	1	1	0	0	0	0	0	0	0	0	0	0	1	0	0	.000	.000
Higley, J.R.	R-R	6-3	210	6-21-88	.346	.267	.359	35	107	17	37	12	0	0	16	21	11	0	3	32	6	3	.458	.486
Hood, Destin	R-R	6-1	180	4-3-90	.256	.000	.275	25	86	18	22	6	1	0	14	8	2	2	0	19	5	2	.349	.333
Killian, Dan	L-R	6-4	195	1-14-89	.189	.125	.198	40	132	17	25	4	2	1	28	15	7	3	1	37	3	0	.273	.303
Labrie, Ronnie	R-R	6-3	205	10-22-86	.324	.357	.320	42	139	34	45	10	2	1	26	23	3	2	3	27	9	4	.446	.423
Leon, Sandy	B-R	5-11	175	3-13-89	.189	.167	.194	26	74	12	14	1	1	0	11	9	2	1	0	18	1	2	.230	.294
Lombardozzi, Steve	B-R	6-0	170	9-20-88	.283	.300	.280	48	152	23	43	4	1	0	24	21	2	6	3	32	4	1	.322	.371
Lopez, Yhonson	L-L	6-1	160	10-27-88	.206	.500	.167	11	34	4	7	2	0	0	6	8	1	1	0	12	2	2	.265	.372
Milledge, Lastings	R-R	6-0	205	4-5-85	.250	.000	.333	2	4	1	1	0	0	0	1	1	0	0	0	0	0	0	1.000	.250
Miller, Bryan	R-R	6-0	195	7-15-86	.083	—	.083	4	12	2	1	0	0	0	3	1	0	0	0	2	1	0	.083	.154
Newsome, Brett	L-L	6-2	210	8-24-86	.189	.000	.204	23	53	7	10	1	1	0	7	5	3	2	0	18	2	0	.245	.295
Nieto, Andres	B-R	6-0	200	11-12-89	.217	.500	.190	8	23	1	5	3	0	0	3	2	1	0	0	7	0	0	.348	.308
Padron, J.P.	R-R	6-1	205	2-14-86	.192	.294	.175	41	120	19	23	8	0	0	20	27	4	3	3	36	6	1	.258	.351
Pena, Wilfri	R-R	6-0	180	5-2-87	.133	.000	.143	7	15	0	2	0	0	0	0	2	0	0	0	2	0	0	.133	.235
Phillips, Derrick	R-R	6-3	220	9-21-90	.081	.200	.063	15	37	3	3	0	0	0	2	3	2	0	1	19	1	0	.081	.186
Ramirez, J.P.	L-L	5-10	185	9-29-89	.364	.000	.364	5	11	2	4	0	0	0	8	4	0	0	0	0	0	0	.364	.533
Reese Jr., Pokey	R-R	5-11	190	6-10-73	.200	.000	.222	3	10	2	2	0	0	0	2	0	0	0	1	1	0	0	.200	.182
Sellers, Brett	R-R	6-4	165	2-13-86	.217	.273	.208	29	83	15	18	4	0	0	8	14	1	1	1	25	2	0	.265	.333
Smolinski, Jake	R-R	5-11	185	2-9-89	.111	—	.111	3	9	0	1	0	0	0	2	1	0	0	0	1	0	0	.111	.200
Soriano, Francisco	B-R	5-11	169	6-16-87	.172	.250	.152	30	58	20	10	1	0	0	5	21	1	5	0	14	4	3	.190	.400
Tejeda, Yeurys	R-R	6-1	150	2-24-88	.180	.444	.122	18	50	8	9	2	0	0	9	4	1	1	2	12	0	0	.220	.246
Urbina, Eduardo	R-R	6-2	200	9-24-87	.200	—	.200	2	5	0	1	0	0	0	1	0	0	0	0	0	0	0	.200	.333

Pitching	B-T	HT	WT	DOB	W	L	ERA	G	GS	CG	SV	IP	H	R	ER	HR	BB	SO	AVG	vLH	vRH	K/9	BB/9
Aracena, Miguel	L-L	6-2	165	3-30-87	0	1	3.45	10	0	0	0	16	19	10	6	0	10	13	.297	.364	.283	7.47	5.74
Arnold, Patrick	R-R	6-1	190	10-31-88	4	0	1.80	5	3	0	0	25	22	8	5	1	5	17	.237	.279	.200	6.12	1.80
Buchter, Ryan	L-L	6-3	185	2-13-87	2	0	0.00	4	0	0	0	5	1	0	0	0	1	8	.067	.000	.077	14.40	1.80
Demny, Paul	R-R	6-2	200	8-3-89	4	0	2.50	11	6	0	0	36	29	18	10	1	14	40	.221	.143	.258	10.00	3.50
Dill, Clayton	R-L	5-11	190	1-3-86	0	1	11.81	8	0	0	2	11	17	14	14	3	9	16	.362	.625	.308	13.50	7.59
Erb, Shane	R-R	6-5	180	5-3-87	1	2	7.58	14	0	0	2	19	28	20	16	0	9	14	.346	.263	.371	6.63	4.26
Frias, Marcos	R-R	6-2	190	12-19-88	3	4	2.92	13	9	1	0	65	66	32	21	5	14	38	.265	.200	.293	5.29	1.95
Gil, Danny	R-R	6-3	195	3-28-85	2	2	2.12	12	0	0	4	17	11	7	4	0	8	18	.186	.222	.156	13.76	4.24
Hansen, Bobby	L-L	6-5	220	12-17-89	1	2	4.50	9	7	0	0	22	25	12	11	1	11	18	.284	.091	.348	7.36	4.50
Hicks, Graham	L-L	6-5	170	2-9-90	0	0	0.00	1	1	0	0	2	1	0	0	0	2	.143	—	.143	9.00	0.00
Jaime, Juan	R-R	6-1	180	8-2-87	2	1	4.74	8	2	1	0	19	16	12	10	1	18	23	.232	.300	.200	10.89	8.53
Kelley, Chris	R-R	6-1	200	8-8-85	2	2	2.73	8	4	0	0	33	34	14	10	1	7	21	.266	.270	.264	5.73	1.91
McGeary, Jack	L-L	6-3	195	3-19-89	2	4	4.07	12	12	0	0	60	61	34	27	2	13	64	.258	.214	.277	9.65	1.96
Morales, Alex	R-R	5-11	170	12-20-82	0	0	0.00	2	0	0	0	1	0	0	0	0	1	0	.000	.000	.000	0.00	9.00
O'Connor, Mike	L-L	6-3	185	8-17-80	0	0	1.69	1	0	0	0	5	4	5	1	0	1	6	.174	.167	.176	10.13	1.69
Ramirez, Ismael	R-R	6-3	200	3-3-81	0	0	0.00	1	0	0	1	0	0	0	0	0	0	0	.000	—	.000	0.00	0.00
Segovia, Zack	R-R	6-2	245	4-11-83	1	0	4.50	2	1	0	0	6	5	3	3	0	1	6	.217	.250	.211	9.00	1.50
Silva, Damian	R-R	5-11	172	11-23-86	2	1	4.58	11	0	0	1	18	19	13	9	0	11	16	.292	.261	.310	8.15	5.60
Smith, Mason	R-R	6-5	215	11-8-85	0	1	1.69	8	0	0	4	11	8	2	2	0	5	6	.205	.214	.200	5.06	4.22
Smoker, Josh	L-L	6-2	195	11-26-88	2	1	1.37	6	6	0	0	26	20	11	4	0	13	16	.213	.077	.235	5.47	4.44
Tanco, Federico	R-R	5-11	180	4-15-86	1	2	4.43	12	0	0	2	22	26	18	11	4	6	24	.286	.171	.357	9.67	2.42
Urena, Jorge	R-R	5-11	190	10-3-86	2	0	4.56	10	1	0	0	24	28	15	12	3	5	24	.280	.323	.261	9.13	1.90
VanAllen, Cory	L-L	6-3	180	12-24-84	0	0	0.00	1	1	0	0	4	3	1	0	0	2	.231	.000	.300	4.50	0.00

Fielding

Catcher	PCT	G	PO	A	E	DP	PB
Estrada	1.000	2	8	1	0	0	0
Hiciano	1.000	1	4	0	0	0	0
Killian	.990	27	184	15	2	1	7
Leon	.976	25	186	18	5	2	2
Nieto	.750	1	6	0	2	0	0
Pena	1.000	6	23	4	0	0	4

First Base	PCT	G	PO	A	E	DP
Boone	1.000	1	7	0	0	1
Newsome	.985	21	119	9	2	17
Padron	.990	38	284	20	3	26
Sellers	1.000	1	2	1	0	0
Urbina	1.000	2	6	1	0	1

Second Base	PCT	G	PO	A	E	DP
Cegles	1.000	3	1	1	0	0
Cruz	.500	1	0	2	2	0
Gonzalez	1.000	1	1	4	0	1

	PCT	G	PO	A	E	DP
Lombardozzi	.952	38	76	81	8	20
Reese Jr.	1.000	3	4	6	0	1
Smolinski	1.000	2	4	5	0	2
Soriano	1.000	18	26	33	0	9
Tejeda	—	1	0	0	0	0

Third Base	PCT	G	PO	A	E	DP
Blackwood	1.000	1	1	0	0	0
Cruz	1.000	2	1	0	0	0
Labrie	.835	41	28	63	18	0
Soriano	—	1	0	0	0	0
Tejeda	.917	15	10	23	3	0

Shortstop	PCT	G	PO	A	E	DP
Cruz	1.000	1	1	0	0	0
Desmond	.889	3	4	4	1	2
Gonzalez	.925	47	84	138	18	31
Lombardozzi	1.000	6	6	5	0	2
Lopez	1.000	1	0	4	0	0

Soriano	1.000	2	3	5	0	2

Outfield	PCT	G	PO	A	E	DP
Bass	1.000	3	2	0	0	0
Blackwood	.944	17	16	1	1	0
Curran	.984	54	114	6	2	2
Dukes	.500	2	1	0	1	0
Higley	.938	32	43	2	3	0
Hood	.923	24	22	2	2	0
Lopez	.909	10	10	0	1	0
Milledge	1.000	2	2	0	0	0
Miller	—	1	0	0	0	0
Newsome	1.000	3	1	0	0	0
Phillips	.905	15	19	0	2	0
Ramirez	1.000	3	2	0	0	0
Sellers	1.000	23	24	1	0	1
Soriano	1.000	2	2	0	0	0

DSL NATIONALS 1   ROOKIE

DOMINICAN SUMMER LEAGUE

Batting	B-T	HT	WT	DOB	AVG	vLH	vRH	G	AB	R	H	2B	3B	HR	RBI	BB	HBP	SH	SF	SO	SB	CS	SLG	OBP
Batista, Jose	R-R	6-2	223	1-6-89	.191	.167	.200	13	47	8	9	3	0	1	7	3	0	0	0	23	0	1	.319	.240
Beltre, Juan	R-R	5-11	185	12-20-85	.138	.000	.211	11	29	8	4	0	0	1	4	2	1	0	0	13	5	0	.241	.219
Bocio, Anderson	R-R	5-11	180	11-13-88	.286	.111	.315	23	63	13	18	3	2	0	9	7	2	0	0	17	0	4	.397	.375

Name	B-R	HT	WT	DOB	AVG	vLH	vRH	G	AB	R	H	2B	3B	HR	RBI	BB	HBP	SH	SF	SO	SB	CS	SLG	OBP
Carmona, Jose	B-R	6-0	160	11-20-88	.125	.333	.000	2	8	0	1	0	0	0	1	1	0	0	0	3	0	0	.125	.222
Cespedes, Starlin	B-R	6-1	164	2-15-88	.244	.265	.237	39	127	17	31	6	1	0	19	8	3	1	2	38	9	1	.307	.300
Cuevas, Justino	R-R	5-10	160	11-30-88	.269	.267	.270	44	160	19	43	5	0	0	19	23	4	3	0	27	17	6	.300	.374
Frias, Francisco	R-R	6-0	170	5-30-87	.259	.000	.350	12	27	8	7	1	0	0	4	10	0	1	1	9	0	0	.296	.447
Gomez, Samuel	R-R	6-2	160	9-26-86	.208	.200	.209	46	106	24	22	3	2	0	16	20	5	1	0	38	9	6	.274	.359
Hernandez, Deivi	R-R	6-3	180	9-3-86	.231	.273	.214	14	39	5	9	2	0	2	4	2	1	0	0	10	0	2	.436	.286
Hiciano, Yan Carlos	R-R	5-8	174	11-28-86	.226	.300	.190	20	62	8	14	4	0	0	9	6	4	0	2	11	2	0	.290	.324
Hodge, Alejandro	R-R	6-0	160	11-15-89	.167	.263	.114	19	54	11	9	0	1	0	5	11	3	1	0	24	7	1	.204	.338
Jimenez, Hendry	B-R	5-10	160	12-30-89	.300	.200	.320	20	60	11	18	1	1	0	4	14	1	1	0	5	2	2	.350	.440
Martinez, Ricardo	R-R	6-0	175	11-27-88	.265	.200	.287	39	117	23	31	9	1	7	22	18	5	2	1	26	6	1	.538	.383
Montilla, Angelberth	R-R	6-1	180	4-11-89	.274	.288	.269	71	252	39	69	13	2	2	44	21	5	4	4	41	28	7	.365	.337
Morales, Jesus	R-R	6-1	165	12-4-89	.195	.176	.200	28	77	15	15	2	0	1	8	16	4	0	0	22	7	3	.260	.361
Perez, Eury	R-R	6-0	180	5-30-90	.324	.239	.363	60	213	51	69	9	2	4	44	32	9	5	3	36	28	6	.441	.428
Romero, Alexander	R-R	6-1	180	1-3-90	.247	.200	.264	52	150	29	37	3	0	6	25	35	8	2	2	54	3	3	.407	.410
Sanchez, Adrian	B-R	6-0	160	8-16-90	.282	.210	.309	58	227	40	64	13	1	3	32	19	3	4	4	36	21	3	.388	.340
Taveras, Danny	R-R	5-9	175	8-2-86	.251	.266	.246	63	231	62	58	5	2	1	23	46	9	3	2	48	49	16	.303	.392
Urbina, Eduardo	R-R	6-2	200	9-24-87	.262	.350	.229	42	145	30	38	3	2	2	31	20	7	0	3	33	5	7	.352	.371
Urdaneta, Juan	L-L	6-4	185	5-20-89	.156	.222	.139	16	45	7	7	0	0	0	5	5	0	0	0	17	0	1	.156	.240
Willians, Ferdinand	R-R	6-2	185	3-4-87	.167	.125	.188	21	48	9	8	6	0	0	5	9	7	1	1	24	0	0	.292	.369

Pitching	B-T	HT	WT	DOB	W	L	ERA	G	GS	CG	SV	IP	H	R	ER	HR	BB	SO	AVG	vLH	vRH	K/9	BB/9
Almonte, Raudy	L-L	6-6	190	2-27-89	0	0	14.73	3	0	0	0	4	7	6	6	0	3	4	.412	.333	.429	9.82	7.36
De La Rosa, Ruben	R-R	5-9	165	4-2-87	2	1	2.08	20	0	0	10	26	19	8	6	0	8	46	.196	.118	.238	15.92	2.77
De Los Santos, Armado	R-R	6-1	167	10-29-85	5	2	3.00	14	14	0	0	72	71	35	24	2	29	69	.259	.329	.234	8.63	3.63
Eusebio, Wilson	R-R	6-0	170	8-20-88	5	3	1.64	19	0	0	4	38	23	8	7	0	21	46	.183	.194	.179	10.80	4.93
Ferrera, Xadiel	R-R	6-2	175	5-24-88	0	0	0.00	3	0	0	0	2	1	0	0	0	1	2	.143	.000	.250	9.00	4.50
Guzman, Antonio	R-R	6-1	145	12-15-87	3	2	2.23	10	6	0	0	40	41	23	10	2	11	39	.265	.311	.245	8.70	2.45
Herrera, Roberto	L-L	6-2	170	5-18-88	1	0	2.08	7	3	0	0	17	9	6	4	0	12	23	.155	.000	.167	11.94	6.23
Martinez, Juan	R-R	6-0	182	8-16-85	7	1	1.90	15	15	0	0	80	60	22	17	2	22	76	.212	.206	.214	8.51	2.46
Molina, Jonathan	R-R	5-11	125	6-6-86	2	2	2.70	25	0	0	4	43	31	19	13	4	18	56	.194	.143	.208	11.63	3.74
Molina, Santiago	R-R	6-1	195	5-23-87	0	0	6.75	2	0	0	0	3	3	2	2	0	3	1	.333	.667	.167	3.38	10.13
Mota, Victor	R-R	6-2	200	10-21-88	0	0	0.00	5	0	0	0	7	3	2	0	0	5	7	.130	.333	.059	9.45	6.75
Ortega, Luis	R-R	6-3	170	8-4-87	3	1	1.13	5	5	2	0	32	20	5	4	0	3	35	.182	.258	.152	9.84	0.84
Paez, Ironel	R-R	6-1	165	7-28-90	0	1	2.25	3	3	0	0	8	4	2	2	0	6	14	.143	.250	.100	15.75	6.75
Perez, Julio	R-R	5-11	165	10-26-87	2	1	2.29	17	1	0	0	35	22	10	9	4	25	57	.175	.244	.136	14.52	6.37
Reyes, Carmelo	R-R	6-2	165	9-9-85	1	0	2.16	3	0	0	0	8	7	2	2	1	1	10	.241	.333	.200	10.80	1.08
Reyes, Derbin	R-R	6-1	175	3-12-87	0	0	3.00	4	3	0	0	15	8	5	5	1	8	13	.167	.455	.081	7.80	4.80
Rodriguez, Osvaldo	R-R	5-11	180	6-10-84	12	0	1.01	13	13	1	0	71	48	8	8	0	27	104	.191	.167	.201	13.18	3.42
Santamaria, Joaquin	R-R	6-4	175	9-21-89	1	1	3.78	9	0	0	2	17	14	7	7	1	8	25	.222	.214	.224	13.50	4.32
Santana, Jose	L-L	6-1	165	1-18-85	5	1	2.56	18	2	0	1	53	46	21	15	3	16	42	.241	.192	.248	7.18	2.73
Taveras, Jose	L-L	6-5	190	11-10-87	5	0	2.21	16	4	0	0	37	31	14	9	2	9	28	.221	.167	.227	6.87	2.21
Vasquez, Wanel	R-R	6-3	190	1-15-87	1	1	5.59	5	3	0	0	10	9	6	6	1	11	11	.243	.200	.259	10.24	10.24

Fielding

Catcher	PCT	G	PO	A	E	DP	PB
Bocio	.986	19	122	17	2	0	5
Hiciano	.990	20	171	22	2	0	3
Martinez	.995	35	341	29	2	1	6
Taveras	.983	5	54	3	1	0	2

First Base	PCT	G	PO	A	E	DP
Batista	1.000	10	64	5	0	9
Beltre	1.000	3	18	3	0	4
Cespedes	1.000	1	4	0	0	0
Martinez	1.000	1	2	0	0	0
Urbina	.982	42	318	16	6	28
Urdaneta	.990	16	92	6	1	10
Willians	.962	9	48	2	2	0

Second Base	PCT	G	PO	A	E	DP
Cespedes	.966	7	15	13	1	3

	PCT	G	PO	A	E	DP
Frias	.969	5	14	17	1	4
Jimenez	1.000	13	19	21	0	2
Romero	1.000	1	0	1	0	0
Sanchez	.980	51	80	114	4	19

Third Base	PCT	G	PO	A	E	DP
Cespedes	.865	17	5	40	7	6
Frias	.875	3	1	6	1	1
Romero	.842	39	24	56	15	6
Sanchez	.857	8	5	13	3	0
Willians	.840	13	7	14	4	2

Shortstop	PCT	G	PO	A	E	DP
Carmona	1.000	2	3	2	0	1
Cespedes	.846	11	9	13	4	3
Cuevas	.953	44	78	105	9	23
Frias	1.000	2	4	6	0	1

	PCT	G	PO	A	E	DP
Romero	.931	17	22	32	4	3

Outfield	PCT	G	PO	A	E	DP
Beltre	1.000	5	2	0	0	0
Bocio	—	1	0	0	0	0
Cespedes	—	2	0	0	0	0
Gomez	.977	42	40	3	1	1
Hernandez	.867	13	12	1	2	0
Hodge	1.000	19	17	5	0	0
Montilla	.957	70	81	8	4	1
Morales	1.000	26	29	2	0	0
Perez	.960	60	90	7	4	3
Willians	—	1	0	0	0	0

DSL NATIONALS 2 ROOKIE

DOMINICAN SUMMER LEAGUE

Batting	B-T	HT	WT	DOB	AVG	vLH	vRH	G	AB	R	H	2B	3B	HR	RBI	BB	HBP	SH	SF	SO	SB	CS	SLG	OBP
Altuve, Jose	R-R	6-1	185	2-20-88	.226	.255	.216	59	199	19	45	6	0	0	22	15	2	0	0	40	3	1	.256	.287
Ariza, Jesus	R-R	5-11	180	7-6-90	.192	.261	.160	27	73	12	14	0	0	0	6	15	4	1	0	28	2	1	.192	.359
Batista, Jose	R-R	6-2	223	1-6-89	.257	.286	.250	10	35	5	9	2	0	1	5	2	0	0	0	8	0	0	.400	.297
2-team total (13 Nationals 1)					.220	—		23	82	13	18	5	0	2	12	5	0	0	0	31	0	1	.354	.264
Benzant, Hector	R-R	6-1	171	1-25-87	.271	.400	.231	31	85	13	23	4	0	0	7	13	3	1	0	21	4	6	.318	.386
Cabreja, Joseph	R-R	6-3	190	1-22-90	.214	.250	.200	51	159	24	34	9	0	2	21	21	6	1	2	58	5	1	.308	.324
Carmona, Jose	R-R	6-0	160	11-20-88	.000	.000	.000	4	4	0	0	0	0	0	0	1	0	0	0	0	0	1	.000	.200
2-team total (2 Nationals 1)					.083	—		6	12	0	1	0	0	0	1	2	0	0	0	3	0	1	.083	.214
Castillo, Luis	B-R	6-1	175	11-28-89	.148	.158	.145	30	81	7	12	0	0	0	2	11	8	0	0	35	1	3	.148	.310
Concepcion, Angelito	R-R	5-11	168	8-27-89	.167	.154	.172	16	42	6	7	2	0	0	3	5	0	0	0	7	2	1	.214	.255
Cuello, Elvin	B-R	6-0	160	5-18-91	.214	.111	.242	27	84	13	18	2	0	1	12	13	1	2	1	17	5	3	.274	.323

Name	B-T	HT	WT	DOB	AVG	vLH	vRH	G	AB	R	H	2B	3B	HR	RBI	BB	HBP	SH	SF	SO	SB	CS	OBP	SLG
Cuevas, Eleazar	R-R	6-0	175	4-6-87	.220	.213	.223	65	218	36	48	8	2	2	28	34	5	1	4	59	16	7	.303	.333
Dionicio, Andres	R-R	6-0	160	12-29-87	.133	.000	.167	7	15	2	2	0	0	0	0	3	0	0	0	5	0	0	.133	.278
Fernandez, Earving	L-L	6-0	175	6-9-88	.291	.300	.288	63	213	31	62	14	0	3	24	23	3	0	1	49	7	1	.399	.367
Frias, Francisco	R-R	6-0	170	5-30-87	.269	.300	.259	26	78	10	21	6	1	0	9	19	2	1	1	23	9	4	.372	.420
2-team total (12 Nationals 1)					.267	—		38	105	18	28	7	1	0	13	29	2	2	2	32	9	4	.352	.428
Garcia, Braulio	R-R	6-2	150	10-17-87	.209	.233	.200	33	115	12	24	2	0	4	16	5	1	0	0	41	0	0	.330	.248
Gomez, Samuel	R-R	6-2	160	9-26-86	.000	.000	.000	5	10	0	0	0	0	0	0	0	0	1	0	6	0	0	.000	.000
2-team total (46 Nationals 1)					.190	—		51	116	24	22	3	2	0	16	20	5	2	0	44	9	6	.250	.333
Hernandez, Weesley	L-L	6-3	192	9-21-88	.162	.094	.188	42	117	19	19	6	0	1	11	31	4	3	2	61	13	1	.239	.351
Jimenez, Hendry	B-R	5-10	160	12-30-89	.301	.200	.333	45	163	32	49	8	3	5	19	25	2	2	5	30	19	4	.442	.390
2-team total (20 Nationals 1)					.300	—		65	223	43	67	9	4	3	23	39	3	3	5	38	24	6	.417	.404
Mojica, Francisco	R-R	6-0	190	1-7-87	.500	—	.500	1	2	0	1	0	0	0	0	0	0	0	2	0	0	1	.500	.750
Montesino, Isidro	R-R	6-0	170	9-9-86	.263	.310	.242	40	95	14	25	0	1	0	7	8	3	3	2	19	14	2	.284	.333
Peralta, Manuelysis	R-R	6-3	205	4-6-87	.203	.143	.229	24	69	8	14	5	0	0	4	7	4	2	1	23	0	1	.275	.309
Ramirez, Andruth	R-R	5-11	180	3-10-89	.175	.179	.174	40	120	14	21	6	0	1	7	19	2	1	0	43	1	2	.250	.298
Rodriguez, Elvin	R-R	6-0	186	4-17-89	.189	.214	.184	32	90	9	17	1	0	3	16	14	1	2	1	25	2	5	.300	.302
Turiano, Franklin	B-R	5-11	175	1-16-89	.353	.000	.429	8	17	4	6	2	0	1	1	1	1	0	0	3	1	1	.647	.421
Urdaneta, Juan	L-L	6-4	185	5-20-89	.203	.188	.209	41	118	5	24	3	1	0	4	18	2	2	0	40	4	3	.246	.319
2-team total (16 Nationals 1)					.190	—		57	163	12	31	3	1	0	9	23	2	2	0	57	4	2	.221	.298

Pitching	B-T	HT	WT	DOB	W	L	ERA	G	GS	CG	SV	IP	H	R	ER	HR	BB	SO	AVG	vLH	vRH	K/9	BB/9
Almonte, Raudy	L-L	6-6	190	2-27-89	0	5	14.61	13	6	0	0	20	32	37	33	2	33	20	.352	.500	.345	8.85	14.61
2-team total (3 Nationals 1)					0	5	14.63	16	6	0	0	24	39	43	39	2	36	24	—	—	—	9.00	13.50
Baez, Victor	R-R	6-1	187	2-5-91	0	0	2.25	4	0	0	0	4	4	1	1	0	1	6	.235	.400	.167	13.50	2.25
Berroa, Javier	R-R	5-11	180	8-5-87	2	5	4.83	18	0	0	1	32	30	21	17	3	20	39	.250	.346	.223	11.08	5.68
Caraballo, Jesse	R-R	6-1	190	7-17-86	2	4	4.18	12	0	0	0	24	19	16	11	3	17	28	.229	.167	.246	10.65	6.46
Castillo, Rafael	R-R	6-2	165	3-8-88	1	3	3.00	21	2	0	10	42	35	22	14	1	23	37	.220	.243	.213	7.93	4.93
Javier, Ramon	R-R	6-5	200	8-17-88	0	0	15.58	7	0	0	0	9	10	21	15	1	17	10	.270	.364	.231	10.38	17.65
Jimenez, Luis	R-R	6-7	207	9-18-88	3	6	4.55	17	14	0	0	57	43	40	29	3	41	66	.213	.190	.219	10.36	6.44
Mota, Victor	R-R	6-2	200	10-21-88	0	2	4.02	11	9	0	0	40	33	21	18	1	27	56	.221	.258	.212	12.50	6.02
2-team total (5 Nationals 1)					0	2	3.45	16	9	0	0	47	36	23	18	1	32	63	—	—	—	12.06	6.13
Ortega, Luis	R-R	6-3	170	8-4-87	4	2	2.72	10	6	0	0	43	37	16	13	1	10	49	.234	.270	.223	10.26	2.09
2-team total (5 Nationals 1)					7	2	2.04	15	11	2	0	75	57	21	17	1	13	84	—	—	—	10.08	1.56
Rivera, Manuel	R-R	6-2	170	7-2-87	3	6	2.74	14	14	0	0	62	46	26	19	3	43	59	.211	.196	.215	8.52	6.21
Rodriguez, Junior	R-R	6-0	189	2-8-89	0	1	7.50	2	2	0	0	6	9	7	5	1	5	2	.346	.500	.318	3.00	7.50
Sabala, Miguel	R-R	6-4	195	10-13-86	2	1	9.87	22	0	0	0	31	36	38	34	2	35	34	.295	.423	.260	9.87	10.16
Santamaria, Joaquin	R-R	6-4	175	9-21-89	1	0	9.00	6	0	0	0	8	10	9	8	2	10	8	.303	.083	.429	9.00	11.25
2-team total (9 Nationals 1)					2	5	5.47	15	0	0	0	25	24	16	15	3	18	33	—	—	—	12.04	6.57
Santos, Gabriel	L-L	6-0	165	1-10-90	0	1	4.62	12	1	0	0	25	26	26	13	0	13	21	.257	.250	.258	7.46	4.62
Sierra, Waldy	R-R	6-2	190	8-23-86	0	1	9.28	8	0	0	0	11	13	15	11	0	10	8	.283	.300	.278	6.75	8.44
Silverio, Roddi	R-R	6-2	204	8-21-86	0	0	18.00	2	0	0	0	2	4	4	4	0	2	2	.444	.500	.429	9.00	9.00
Tejada, Derlyn	R-R	6-1	178	9-11-87	4	3	8.50	14	0	0	0	36	45	36	34	3	18	40	.300	.342	.286	10.00	4.50
Vasquez, Wanel	R-R	6-3	190	1-15-87	1	2	2.90	12	7	0	0	40	34	24	13	3	21	44	.225	.275	.207	9.82	4.69
2-team total (5 Nationals 1)					2	3	3.42	17	10	0	0	50	43	30	19	4	32	55	—	—	—	9.90	5.76
Vizcaino, Francisco	L-L	6-0	160	7-26-88	1	2	4.33	19	7	1	0	52	40	41	25	1	46	60	.215	.200	.226	10.38	7.96

Fielding

Catcher	PCT	G	PO	A	E	DP	PB
Altuve	.983	12	102	17	2	0	2
Ariza	.978	24	201	23	5	0	15
Fernandez	1.000	1	1	0	0	0	0
Ramirez	.982	40	335	52	7	2	24

First Base	PCT	G	PO	A	E	DP
Altuve	.980	27	179	13	4	16
Batista	.944	3	16	1	1	3
Garcia	.953	17	96	6	5	6
Peralta	.962	4	25	0	1	1
Urdaneta	.959	33	179	10	8	16

Second Base	PCT	G	PO	A	E	DP
Benzant	1.000	6	8	8	0	2
Carmona	.750	1	2	1	1	0
Castillo	.857	23	40	26	11	5
Concepcion	.844	11	13	14	5	5
Jimenez	.932	27	53	56	8	17
Peralta	.906	9	13	16	3	3

Third Base	PCT	G	PO	A	E	DP
Batista	.833	4	3	7	2	1
Benzant	.825	13	7	26	7	5
Carmona	—	2	0	0	0	0
Concepcion	1.000	1	0	1	0	1
Fernandez	.854	53	42	110	26	7
Garcia	.889	3	4	4	1	0
Peralta	.857	5	4	2	1	0

Shortstop	PCT	G	PO	A	E	DP
Carmona	—	1	0	0	0	0
Concepcion	1.000	1	1	3	0	1
Cuello	.863	27	36	46	13	12
Frias	.943	26	37	63	6	7
Jimenez	.892	18	40	51	11	9
Mojica	1.000	1	0	1	0	0

Outfield	PCT	G	PO	A	E	DP
Cabreja	.887	50	57	6	8	0
Cuevas	.992	65	110	7	1	1
Dionicio	—	4	0	0	0	0
Gomez	1.000	5	6	1	0	0
Hernandez	.902	39	41	5	5	0
Montesino	.938	37	43	2	3	0
Rodriguez	.972	30	34	1	1	0
Turiano	1.000	4	4	1	0	0
Urdaneta	.909	13	19	1	2	0

MINOR
LEAGUES

New faces help minors set another record

BY JOSH LEVENTHAL

Even a sinking economy couldn't slow down minor league baseball.

The sport reached a new attendance high for a fifth consecutive season, as its total of 43,263,740 topped the previous year's mark by 450,928. Though 78 of the minors' 160 teams saw an increase at the gate, the new record was largely the result of a few teams.

Cheap tickets and a family friendly atmosphere have long been at the heart of minor league teams' successful business models. But the industry has seen its biggest growth since facility standards were implemented in the early 1990s by replacing outdated diamonds with state-of-the-art ballparks, and swapping markets that no longer supported teams with ones eager to be a part of the sport.

Three new ballparks debuted at the start of the 2008 season as Lehigh Valley replaced Ottawa in the International League and Northwest Arkansas opened in place of Wichita in the Texas League. Billings (Pioneer) also opened new Dehler Park in place of 60-year-old Cobb Field.

Each team saw a significant increase in attendance from the previous year's mark, propelling the minors to yet another record. Lehigh Valley drew 602,033 fans for an increase of 475,139 on Ottawa's season total of 126,894 in 2007. Northwest Arkansas totaled 358,792, improving by 245,424 on Wichita's 2007 showing. Billings' 133,166 total bested its previous year's mark by 17,857. In all, Billings, Lehigh Valley and Northwest Arkansas were responsible for a net growth of 738,420 fans.

"When you get a new ballpark it reintroduces people who may have been fans in the past and certainly brings in new fans," said Texas League president Tom Kayser, whose league has seen six new ballparks built in seven years. "You move from one century to the next; from a 1950s mindset to a 21st century one."

High Class A Myrtle Beach and Double-A San Antonio and Midland were among several teams that saw a bump at the gate thanks to ballpark improvements. But no performance was as noteworthy as that of low Class A Quad Cities, which managed to attract 207,048 fans—an increase of 39 percent on last season's total—despite missing 10 openings and having its ballpark, quite literally, surrounded by floodwaters in June.

CARL KLINE

Jordan Schafer became the first minor leaguer to be suspended for using HGH

Shuffling The Landscape

The latest record shouldn't last long. New teams and ballparks, as well as intriguing affiliations created after this year's player-development shuffle, are set to debut in 2009 and will likely lift minor league baseball to a new high.

The minor league affiliation shuffle wound to a close in late September, and the big winners all seemed to have one thing in common: They affiliated with the hometown big league team.

Or the home-state team. Or even a team considered a regional draw. Regardless, the golden rule of player-development contracts still holds true: The best affiliation is a local one.

The Columbus Clippers (International) bid farewell to the Nationals just two years after the Yankees left town and struck it rich when they completed what had become the worst-kept secret in minor league baseball. The Clippers will unveil Huntington Park in 2009 as the home of the Indians, who play their big league games just 140 miles northeast on Interstate 71, after signing a four-year player-development contract.

"It's like the stars have aligned," Clippers presi-

MINOR LEAGUES

dent Ken Schnacke said.

Buffalo landed on its feet after seeing a 14-year affiliation with the Indians come to an end by outdueling IL-mate Syracuse for a partnership with the in-state Mets. Though Buffalo is anything but a subway ride to Queens, the Mets' fan base certainly spreads beyond the borough and should provide a spike in attendance and a wealth of marketing opportunities for the Bisons.

The deals were not limited to the big boys, as low Class A Wisconsin tossed aside 16 years with the Mariners to ink a four-year affiliation contract with the Brewers. "This is the time of year the Packers are supposed to be in the news, not the Timber Rattlers," Wisconsin president Rob Zerjav said. "But we've been on the front page."

Just as landing a local affiliate can provide a boost for a team, losing one can be devastating. The Dodgers and Triple-A Las Vegas had been together since 2001, and the relationship was the closest Vegas would get to a hometown team.

But Cashman Field became too much for the Dodgers to bear, and they left for their former longtime affiliate in Albuquerque. Once Syracuse, which competed with Buffalo to attract the Mets, aligned with Nationals, the Blue Jays and 51s were the last ones standing and a relationship that makes little geographic sense was born.

Several relocations should also provide a boost to the sport. The Braves ended its 42-year relationship with Richmond by announcing that the club will move its Triple-A affiliate to Gwinnett County, Ga., for the 2009 season. No team had been selected to replace the Braves in Richmond and the city is likely to be without baseball in 2009.

Low Class A Columbus likely lost baseball for good when it bid farewell to its second team in 10 years after new owner Art Solomon relocated the team to Bowling Green, Ky., following the 2008 campaign. And Ripken Baseball added to its portfolio after purchasing high Class A Vero Beach and shifting it across the state of Florida to Charlotte.

Caught Up In A Scandal

Not everything was so sunny in the minors in 2008. Scandals made headlines around the sport, ranging from drug suspensions to brawls.

The aftershocks from the Mitchell Report snared the Braves' top prospect when center fielder Jordan Schafer became the first minor leaguer to be suspended for using human growth hormone. Major League Baseball announced during the first week of the minor league season that he had been suspended for the next 50 games. Schafer became the most prominent prospect to be suspended for performance-enhancing drugs since MLB began

CHANGING PARTNERS		
TEAM	**OLD AFFILIATE**	**NEW AFFILIATE**
INTERNATIONAL		
Buffalo	Indians	Mets
Columbus	Nationals	Indians
Syracuse	Blue Jays	Nationals
PACIFIC COAST		
Albuquerque	Marlins	Dodgers
Las Vegas	Dodgers	Blue Jays
New Orleans	Mets	Marlins
EASTERN		
Carolina	Marlins	Reds
Chattanooga	Reds	Dodgers
Jacksonville	Dodgers	Marlins
CALIFORNIA		
Lancaster	Red Sox	Astros
CAROLINA		
Salem	Astros	Red Sox
MIDWEST		
Clinton	Rangers	Mariners
Wisconsin	Mariners	Brewers
SOUTH ATLANTIC		
Hickory	Pirates	Rangers
West Virginia	Brewers	Pirates

publicizing drug suspensions in 2005.

According to a source with knowledge of the process, Schafer was the first player to be suspended through the work of the new MLB investigations unit. The unit, led by former New York City deputy police chief Dan Mullin, is charged with looking into any allegations of illegal use or possession of performance-enhancing drugs. In the past, there has been no department within MLB whose primary responsibility was to ensure that players are not using performance enhancing substances.

Schafer returned to Double-A Mississippi on June 2 and battled through highs and lows, both on the field and off.

"I really didn't enjoy coming to the field," Schafer said several weeks after his return. "It was just stressful. I didn't want to hear anything about what happened. I just really dreaded coming to the field."

Drug suspensions also garnered headlines as 2008 marked the first season that punishments for Dominican and Venezuelan summer league players were made public. The number of Latin American summer leaguers suspended reached 39 soon after the season ended in early September.

Baseball in Latin America also garnered attention not for the prospects emerging from the countries but because of a bonus-skimming scandal that led to the dismissal of several big league executives and scouts and threatened to envelope the sport in another scandal.

It began when David Wilder, a John Schuerholz disciple who had long been on the short list of future general managers, was fired in May by the White Sox in connection with an ongoing federal investigation into the handling of money associated with signings in the Dominican Republic. Federal investigators began looking into whether executives and scouts were pocketing portions of bonuses intended to sign Latin American prospects.

Wilder, along with scout Victor Mateo and part-time scout Domingo Toribio were dismissed after a two-month inquiry by MLB's department of investigations. A close friend of general manager Ken Williams, Wilder had been with the White Sox since 2003. His most recent title was senior director of player personnel.

Federal investigators began interviewing representatives from all 30 major league clubs after Wilder's dismissal. More dismissals soon followed. The Red Sox fired Dominican scouting supervisor Pablo Lantigua and the Yankees fired director of Latin American scouting Carlos Rios and Dominican Republic scouting director Ramon Valdivia. The Orioles dismissed national cross-checker Alan Marr, who was linked to a probe into illegal gambling.

The list was expected to grow as the investigation continues.

"The FBI's going to all the organizations . . . asking players if they received or gave money," said Clay Daniel, international scouting supervisor for the Angels. "I'm sure they're looking into scouts, personnel, people like that that may have had a hand in it."

On the diamond, a late-season brawl in the low Class A Midwest League resulted in numerous suspensions and even an assault charge for one player. The benches-clearing affair between host Dayton and Peoria drew national media attention, was documented in fan-made videos on Youtube and ended with both managers and 15 players facing suspensions. Peoria pitcher Julio Castillo fired a ball, apparently intended for the Dayton dugout, into the stands that struck a fan in the head. Castillo was arrested at the scene and in October was indicted on two felony counts of felonious assault.

Record Flood Challenges Teams

Several teams in the Midwest were left scrambling to salvage their seasons after a spring full of dreadful weather culminated with the Iowa River cresting 10 feet above floodlevels, canceling games

ORGANIZATION STANDINGS

Cumulative farm club records for the 30 major organizations, with winning percentages going back five years. Most organizations have six affiliates.

		2008						
		W	L	PCT	2007	2006	2005	2004
1.	N.Y. Yankees	406	287	.586	.597	.551	.541	.514
2.	Texas	385	308	.556	.489	.495	.473	.453
3.	San Francisco	384	310	.553	.562	.557	.555	.471
4.	L.A. Angels	376	318	.542	.490	.534	.535	.502
5.	Minnesota	362	319	.532	.534	.537	.525	.540
6.	Florida	365	324	.530	.465	.537	.555	.467
7.	St. Louis	393	355	.525	.478	.483	.464	.472
8.	Oakland	361	333	.520	.492	.499	.523	.572
9.	Boston	373	347	.518	.501	.490	.489	.455
10.	San Diego	360	336	.517	.465	.519	.454	.470
11.	Toronto	355	340	.511	.523	.504	.490	.502
12.	Atlanta	345	337	.506	.486	.506	.512	.503
13.	Cleveland	351	343	.506	.535	.524	.492	.538
14.	Chi. White Sox	348	344	.503	.475	.496	.500	.501
15.	Colorado	354	356	.499	.496	.487	.501	.482
16.	Chi. Cubs	352	370	.488	.499	.525	.496	.489
17.	L.A. Dodgers	336	358	.484	.506	.530	.545	.576
18.	Washington	348	375	.481	.443	.481	.498	.458
19.	Cincinnati	348	383	.476	.519	.423	.491	.549
20.	Tampa Bay	328	363	.475	.527	.526	.429	.467
21.	Seattle	357	400	.472	.443	.474	.482	.514
22.	Milwaukee	323	365	.469	.565	.491	.519	.511
23.	Baltimore	368	419	.468	.490	.499	.492	.520
24.	Philadelphia	323	376	.462	.488	.426	.504	.504
25.	N.Y. Mets	359	434	.453	.461	.465	.501	.455
26.	Detroit	342	422	.448	.531	.513	.472	.501
27.	Kansas City	360	455	.442	.497	.477	.509	.547
28.	Pittsburgh	298	395	.430	.480	.456	.517	.508
29.	Arizona	310	417	.426	.494	.440	.438	.424
30.	Houston	278	462	.376	.441	.557	.494	.533

POSTSEASON PLAYOFFS

League	Champion	Runner-Up
International	Scranton/WB (Yankees)	Durham (Rays)
Pacific Coast	Sacramento (Athletics)	Oklahoma (Rangers)
Eastern	Trenton (Yankees)	Akron (Indians)
Southern	Mississippi (Braves)	Carolina (Marlins)
Texas	Arkansas (Angels)	Frisco (Rangers)
California	Stockton (Athletics)	Lancaster (Red Sox)
Carolina	Potomac (Nationals)	Myrtle Beach (Braves)
Florida State	Daytona (Cubs)	Fort Myers (Twins)
Midwest	Burlington (Royals)	South Bend (Dbacks)
South Atlantic	Augusta (Giants)	W. Virginia (Brewers)
New York-Penn	Batavia (Cardinals)	Jamestown (Marlins)
Northwest	Spokane (Mariners)	Salem-Keizer (Giants)
Appalachian	Elizabethton (Twins)	Pulaski (Mariners)
Pioneer	Orem (Angels)	Great Falls (White Sox)
Arizona	Giants	Angels
Gulf Coast	Phillies	Nationals

and devastating some markets to the point teams worried how they would stay afloat financially.

The teams most impacted by the floods were Triple-A Iowa and low Class A affiliates Burlington, Cedar Rapids and Quad Cities. Cedar Rapids' Veterans Memorial Stadium sits atop the tallest point in the city, which both shielded it and provided a bird's-eye of the worst flooding the area

CONTINUED ON PAGE 338

Wieters impresses in debut

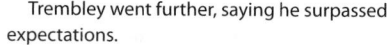

The opening salvo to Matt Wieters' pro career lit up ballparks across the East Coast this summer, as he showed his talent on and off the field, at the plate and behind it, and made himself an easy choice as the Baseball America 2008 Minor League Player of the Year.

Not only did the switch-hitter ransack the high Class A Carolina and Double-A Eastern leagues, batting a combined .355/.454/.600 with 27 home runs, but Wieters also won over coaches with a surprising feel for calling a game—which he rarely handled during his three-year stampede through Georgia Tech.

Along the way—and perhaps as significant as any of his abilities—Wieters, the Orioles first-round pick in the 2007 draft, also embraced leadership and ambassador roles within the Orioles system. Handling pitching staffs and crushing fastballs were impressive, but his generosity with fans could not go unnoticed.

As Orioles roving catching instructor Don Werner put it, "He acts like he's been around 10 years in the big leagues."

In Wieters, the Orioles appear to have a cornerstone, the kind whose presence could completely re-energize the team and its fan base. His bat is his most obvious attribute because Wieters easily bridged his production from college to the pros, with managers praising his ability to hit with power to all fields and took note of his patience at the plate. Menacing in his 6-foot-5, 230-pound, Paul Bunyan-esque frame, he walked more

Matt Wieters

RODGER WOOD

times (82) than he struck out (76).

Yet he also balanced his offensive production and strong defensive skills by proving to be a team leader.

It's no wonder president of baseball operations Andy MacPhail and Orioles manager Dave Trembley have fended off numerous questions about Wieters in the season's second half. Both spent the final week of August defusing speculation of a Wieters callup, explaining he wasn't likely to receive many at-bats. MacPhail also declined to offer specifics about Wieters' chances for a big league roster spot next season, when catcher Ramon Hernandez will be in the final year of a four-year, $27.5 million contract.

Sitting in the Orioles dugout while pondering the organization's future, MacPhail was asked what he liked of Wieters. He did not hesitate.

"Everything," MacPhail says. "He was very impressive in major league camp. It was just the right mix of confidence and yet being humble."

Trembley went further, saying he surpassed expectations.

"I think for our organization, he's a big league guy in our minor leagues," Trembley says. "And we're looking for big league players, but we're also looking for big league people. And he's at the top of the charts in all of those categories."

PREVIOUS WINNERS

1981: Mike Marshall, 1b, Albuquerque (Dodgers)
1982: Ron Kittle, of, Edmonton (White Sox)
1983: Dwight Gooden, rhp, Lynchburg (Mets)
1984: Mike Bielecki, rhp, Hawaii (Pirates)
1985: Jose Canseco, of, Huntsville/Tacoma (Athletics)
1986: Gregg Jefferies, ss, Columbia/Lynchburg/Jackson (Mets)
1987: Gregg Jefferies, ss, Jackson/Tidewater (Mets)
1988: Tom Gordon, rhp, Appleton/Memphis/Omaha (Royals)
1989: Sandy Alomar, c, Las Vegas (Padres)
1990: Frank Thomas, 1b, Birmingham (White Sox)
1991: Derek Bell, of, Syracuse (Blue Jays)
1992: Tim Salmon, of, Edmonton (Angels)
1993: Manny Ramirez, of, Canton/Charlotte (Indians)
1994: Derek Jeter, ss, Tampa/Albany/Columbus (Yankees)

1995: Andruw Jones, of, Macon (Braves)
1996: Andruw Jones, of, Durham/Greenville/Richmond (Braves)
1997: Paul Konerko, 1b, Albuquerque (Dodgers)
1998: Eric Chavez, 3b, Huntsville/Edmonton (Athletics)
1999: Rick Ankiel, lhp, Arkansas/Memphis (Cardinals)
2000: Jon Rauch, rhp, Winston-Salem/Birmingham (White Sox)
2001: Josh Beckett, rhp, Brevard County/Portland (Marlins)
2002: Rocco Baldelli, of, Bakersfield/Orlando/Durham (Devil Rays)
2003: Joe Mauer, c, Fort Myers/New Britain (Twins)
2004: Jeff Francis, lhp, Tulsa/Colorado Springs (Rockies)
2005: Delmon Young, of, Montgomery/Durham (Devil Rays)
2006: Alex Gordon, 3b, Wichita (Royals)
2007: Jay Bruce, of, Sarasota/Chattanooga/Louisville (Reds)

MINOR LEAGUES

Rochester has Silver touch

Naomi Silver will readily admit that Triple-A Rochester did not purchase short-season Batavia out of the goodness of its heart or for charitable purposes. But there is no doubting that Rochester saved baseball for its central New York neighbor when it acquired the financially floundering Muckdogs prior to the 2008 season.

Silver, the Red Wings' chief operating officer, took a first step toward making a bad situation into a winner for both Batavia and Rochester in the first year of the new working agreement. With new marketing and promotional strategies in place, there is suddenly light at the end of the tunnel and the possibility of a brighter, and long-term, future for Batavia.

"This will provide an opportunity for a lot of cross-promotion in this region that we haven't seen before in baseball teams. It seems like the perfect synergy," Silver said in April.

It is for these reasons, and years of service that have made Rochester one of the steadiest teams in the International League—as well as an active part of the local community—that

EXECUTIVE OF THE YEAR

PREVIOUS WINNERS

2002: Randy Mobley, International League
2003: Chuck Domino, Reading (Eastern)
2004: Chris Kemple, Wilmington Blue Rocks (Carolina)
2005: Jay Miller, Round Rock Express (Pacific Coast)
2006: Alan Ledford, Sacramento River Cats (Pacific Coast)
2007: Mike Moore, Minor League Baseball

Baseball America honors Silver as its 2008 Executive of the Year.

Silver's father, Morrie Silver, led a community stock drive to purchase the team and stadium in 1957 when the Cardinals announced they would no longer operate the franchise in Rochester. Naomi Silver joined the business almost 25 years ago, holds the top position in Rochester Community Baseball and has kept the team among the IL attendance leaders as well as one of the minors' top 25 merchandise selling clubs.

CONTINUED FROM PAGE 336

has experienced since 1993.

The flooding left 480 blocks of downtown Cedar Rapids underwater, displaced 35,000 people, affected 10,000 homes and covered a 10-mile radius. Cedar Rapids' ballpark served as a command center for flood relief during the crisis; the team had been out of town and did not have to postpone any games.

Yet amid so much tragedy, the Kernels opened an eight-game homestand as scheduled following the Midwest League all-star break, hoping to provide a temporary distraction for locals while doing enough business for the team to stay afloat financially.

"I think that is where the ballpark can come into play . . . We think it is a great place for people to escape for a couple of hours and take their minds off of what life has handed them," Kernels GM Jack Roeder said.

The Iowa Cubs' (Pacific Coast) Principal Park sits on the flood side of the levee built to protect Des Moines and by the first day of the flooding had taken on several feet of water spanning from the bullpen to within 20 feet of the infield.

Yet despite the conditions, Iowa GM San

Bernabe gambled that the team would be able to get in two dates of a five-game, four-day series against Nashville and turned down an offer from Memphis to host their games. The I-Cubs returned home to Des Moines from a road trip despite knowing that any games they did play would likely draw below-average attendance.

"It is a pretty fine line between revenue and expenses," Bernabe said. "Whenever you are taking dates out of a calendar, that is another opportunity lost to pay the bills."

By the next evening the water had receded out of the ballpark and the Cubs were back on the field playing a doubleheader closed to the public.

Three of the four teams took a hit at the gate. Only Quad Cities saw a significant improvement in its first full season under new management. With several ballpark enhancement in place (including improved floodwalls that kept the field dry), the River Bandits had one of the biggest increases at the gate of any team in the minors. Quad Cities welcomed a 39 percent jump over last season's total, drawing 207,048 fans despite losing 10 openings to poor weather.

Farewell To Dodgertown

Dodgertown's doors to Organized Baseball

Veteran Wheeler earns honor

Few people know more about managing in the minor leagues than Rocket Wheeler.

Wheeler piloted the Braves' high Class A Myrtle Beach club in 2008, leading a prospect-laden team to the brink of the Carolina League championship in a record-setting season. For his efforts, he is the 2008 Baseball America Minor League Manager of the Year.

The 89-51 Pelicans set a franchise record for regular season wins and nearly won the Mills Cup championship before falling to Potomac.

The Pelicans also set 14 team records and, along the way, Wheeler secured his 1,000th career victory in a 17-2 win against Kinston on Aug. 4. How sweet it was. Braves righthander Tom Glavine, down on an injury rehab assignment, pitched four innings, striking out four and yielding only one run.

For Wheeler, 2008 marked his sixth year managing in the Braves system after he had spent the prior 26 years as a player, coach or manager in the Blue Jays system. He shepherded a number of prospects through the

MANAGER OF THE YEAR

PREVIOUS WINNERS

1989: Buck Showalter, Albany (Yankees)
1990: Kevin Kennedy, Albuquerque (Dodgers)
1991: Butch Hobson, Pawtucket (Red Sox)
1992: Grady Little, Greenville (Braves)
1993: Terry Francona, Birmingham (White Sox)
1994: Tim Ireland, El Paso (Brewers)
1995: Marc Bombard, Indianapolis (Reds)
1996: Carlos Tosca, Portland (Marlins)
1997: Gary Jones, Edmonton (Athletics)
1998: Terry Kennedy, Iowa (Cubs)
1999: John Mizerock, Wichita (Royals)
2000: Joel Skinner, Buffalo (Indians)
2001: Jackie Moore, Round Rock (Astros)
2002: John Russell, Edmonton (Twins)
2003: Dave Brundage, San Antonio (Mariners)
2004: Marty Brown, Buffalo (Indians)
2005: Ken Oberkfell, Norfolk (Mets)
2006: Todd Claus, Portland (Red Sox)
2007: Matt Wallbeck, Erie (Tigers)

circuit in 2008, including six players rated among BA's Top 30 Braves prospects entering the season.

came to a close at the end of the 2008 season. First the Dodgers vacated their 61-year spring home in 2008 before shifting their base cross-country to Glendale, Ariz. Then Ripken Baseball purchased the high Class A Vero Beach Devil Rays and announced they'll move the club across the state to Charlotte for the 2009 campaign. The move ended an era in Vero, when in the fall of 1979, then-Los Angeles Dodgers owner Peter O'Malley announced he was bringing minor league baseball to town.

With a population of 16,000, Vero Beach became the smallest city in North America to host professional baseball full-time, as the Vero Beach Dodgers were born into the high Class A Florida State League.

Now, three decades later, the city is without professional baseball.

"It is really sad," said Reds farm director Terry Reynolds, who was Vero Beach's first general manager. "You never thought the Dodgers would leave, and if they did, you never thought the place would be empty."

The Vero Beach Devil Rays averaged just 761 fans in 2008, the third-lowest attendance in the Florida State League.

But for those who were connected to the team,

and for the 1,880 fans that showed up for what turned out to be the final game, the end came too soon—the scheduled finale was canceled because of poor field conditions.

"I don't know how you could duplicate the time we had there," Reynolds said. "It was a big part of our lives."

The Kids Are All Right

A handful of teenagers turned in dominant seasons around the minors.

Royals third baseman Mike Moustakas led the Midwest League with 22 home runs. The second overall pick in the draft in 2007, Moustakas played the entire season at 19 years old.

In the last 16 years, only two teenagers (ages as of July 1) have hit more home runs than Moustakas in one Midwest League season: Prince Fielder (27 HR, 2003), Wily Mo Pena (26, 2001).

Marlins outfielder Mike Stanton not only led the South Atlantic League with 39 home runs as an 18-year-old, he finished tied for second with the Athletics' Chris Carter in all of the minor leagues.

CONTINUED ON PAGE 340

TRIPLE-A

Pos	Player, Team (Organization)	AVG	OBP	SLG	AB	R	H	2B	3B	HR	RBI	BB	SO	SB	CS
C	Rob Johnson, Tacoma (Mariners)	.305	.363	.441	417	55	127	30	0	9	49	37	61	7	6
1B	Josh Whitesell, Tucson (Diamondbacks)	.328	.425	.568	475	86	156	36	0	26	110	74	136	1	2
2B	Chris Getz, Charlotte (White Sox)	.302	.366	.448	404	60	122	24	1	11	52	41	53	11	4
3B	Matt Tuiasosopo, Tacoma (Mariners)	.281	.364	.453	437	87	123	32	2	13	73	47	104	4	0
SS	Brandon Wood, Salt Lake (Angels)	.296	.375	.595	395	82	117	21	2	31	84	45	104	6	5
CF	Brett Gardner, Scranton/W-B (Yankees)	.296	.414	.422	341	68	101	12	11	3	32	70	76	37	9
OF	Chris Carter, Pawtucket (Red Sox)	.300	.356	.515	470	65	141	25	2	24	81	41	84	0	0
OF	Nate Schierholtz, Fresno (Giants)	.320	.363	.594	350	62	112	22	10	18	73	21	51	9	3
DH	David Freese, Memphis (Cardinals)	.306	.361	.550	464	83	142	29	3	26	91	39	111	5	2

Pos	Pitcher, Team (Organization)	W	L	ERA	G	GS	SV	IP	H	HR	BB	SO	G/F	WHIP	AVG
SP	Mitchell Boggs, Memphis (Cardinals)	9	3	3.45	21	21	0	125	107	11	46	81	1.67	1.22	.235
SP	J.A. Happ, Lehigh Valley (Phillies)	8	7	3.67	24	23	0	135	116	14	48	151	0.90	1.21	.234
SP	Jeff Niemann, Durham (Rays)	9	5	3.59	24	24	0	133	101	15	50	128	1.33	1.14	.207
SP	David Purcey, Syracuse (Blue Jays)	8	6	2.67	19	19	0	117	97	8	34	121	1.03	1.12	.227
RP	Jason Motte, Memphis (Cardinals)	4	3	3.67	63	0	9	67	64	6	26	110	0.67	1.35	.245

Player of the Year: Brandon Wood, ss, Salt Lake (Angels); **Manager of the Year:** Dave Miley, Scranton/Wilkes-Barre (Yankees); **Team of the Year:** Sacramento (Athletics)

DOUBLE-A

Pos	Player, Team (Organization)	AVG	OBP	SLG	AB	R	H	2B	3B	HR	RBI	BB	SO	SB	CS
C	Angel Salome, Huntsville (Brewers)	.360	.415	.559	367	67	132	30	2	13	83	33	57	3	2
1B	Kyle Blanks, San Antonio (Padres)	.325	.404	.514	492	75	160	23	5	20	107	51	90	5	4
2B	Chris Coghlan, Carolina (Marlins)	.298	.396	.429	483	83	144	32	5	7	74	67	65	34	10
3B	Mat Gamel, Huntsville (Brewers)	.329	.395	.537	508	96	167	35	7	19	96	55	111	6	7
SS	Alcides Escobar, Huntsville (Brewers)	.328	.363	.434	546	95	179	24	5	8	76	31	82	34	8
CF	Dexter Fowler, Tulsa (Rockies)	.335	.431	.515	421	92	141	31	9	9	64	65	89	20	8
OF	Matt LaPorta, Hunt./Akron (Brewers/Indians)	.279	.386	.539	362	62	101	24	2	22	74	49	75	2	1
OF	Travis Snider, New Hampshire (Blue Jays)	.262	.357	.461	362	65	95	21	0	17	67	52	116	1	1
DH	Kila Ka'aihue, Northwest Arkansas (Royals)	.314	.463	.624	287	64	90	11	0	26	79	80	41	3	2

Pos	Pitcher, Team (Organization)	W	L	ERA	G	GS	SV	IP	H	HR	BB	SO	G/F	WHIP	AVG
SP	Michael Bowden, Portland (Red Sox)	9	4	2.33	19	19	0	104	72	5	24	101	0.84	0.92	.192
SP	Vin Mazzaro, Midland (Athletics)	12	3	1.90	22	22	0	137	115	3	36	104	1.48	1.10	.229
SP	James McDonald, Jacksonville (Dodgers)	5	3	3.33	22	22	0	119	98	12	46	113	0.67	1.21	.227
SP	Chris Tillman, Bowie (Orioles)	11	4	3.33	28	28	0	136	115	10	65	154	0.82	1.33	.227
RP	Fernando Salas, Springfield (Cardinals)	7	3	3.67	60	0	25	74	65	12	16	100	0.83	1.09	.236

Player of the Year: Dexter Fowler, of, Tulsa (Rockies); **Manager of the Year:** Brad Komminsk, Bowie (Orioles); **Team of the Year:** Frisco (Rangers)

HIGH CLASS A

Pos	Player, Team (Organization)	AVG	OBP	SLG	AB	R	H	2B	3B	HR	RBI	BB	SO	SB	CS
C	Carlos Santana, I.E./Kinston (Dodgers/Indians)	.330	.435	.569	455	122	150	39	5	20	115	89	83	10	4
1B	Logan Morrison, Jupiter (Marlins)	.332	.402	.494	488	71	162	38	1	13	74	57	80	9	3
2B	Eric Sogard, Lake Elsinore (Padres)	.308	.394	.453	536	97	165	42	3	10	87	79	62	16	7
3B	Chris Carter, Stockton (Athletics)	.259	.361	.569	506	101	131	32	4	39	104	77	156	4	0
SS	Todd Frazier, Sarasota (Reds)	.281	.357	.451	366	62	103	20	3	12	54	41	84	8	4
CF	Cedric Hunter, Lake Elsinore (Padres)	.318	.362	.442	584	98	186	33	3	11	84	42	47	12	6
OF	Kellen Kulbacki, Lake Elsinore (Padres)	.332	.428	.589	304	62	101	18	0	20	66	47	52	1	2
OF	Nick Weglarz, Kinston (Indians)	.272	.396	.432	375	68	102	20	5	10	41	71	78	9	5
DH	Beau Mills, Kinston (Indians)	.293	.373	.506	482	78	141	34	3	21	90	54	105	2	3

Pos	Pitcher, Team (Organization)	W	L	ERA	G	GS	SV	IP	H	HR	BB	SO	G/F	WHIP	AVG
SP	Tim Alderson, San Jose (Giants)	13	4	2.79	26	26	0	145	125	4	34	124	1.02	1.09	.235
SP	Jake Arrieta, Frederick (Orioles)	6	5	2.87	20	20	0	113	80	7	51	120	1.33	1.16	.199
SP	Kevin Pucetas, San Jose (Giants)	10	2	3.02	24	24	0	125	115	6	27	102	1.67	1.13	.247
SP	Hector Rondon, Kinston (Indians)	11	6	3.60	27	27	0	145	130	12	42	145	0.85	1.19	.239
RP	Anthony Slama, Fort Myers (Twins)	4	1	1.01	51	0	25	71	43	0	24	110	1.67	0.94	.173

Player of the Year: Carlos Santana, c, Inland Empire/Kinston (Dodgers/Indians); **Manager of the Year:** Rocket Wheeler, Myrtle Beach (Braves); **Team of the Year:** Stockton (Athletics)

CONTINUED FROM PAGE 339

Fellow teen Madison Bumgarner dominated Sally League hitters by going 15-3 with a league-leading 1.46 ERA. The Giants 19-year-old lefthander also topped the circuit with 164 strikeouts and wins.

A FEW OTHER NOTABLES FROM 2008

■ Ben Revere doesn't qualify as a teenager, but the 20-year-old flirted with .400 for low Class A Beloit. Revere was hitting .404 as late as July 24, but a .281 August left Revere with a .379 average.

■ Triple-A Sacramento resumed a familiar place atop the Pacific Coast League by taking its second title in as many years

LOW CLASS A

Pos	Player, Team (Organization)	AVG	OBP	SLG	AB	R	H	2B	3B	HR	RBI	BB	SO	SB	CS
C	Jesus Montero, Charleston (Yankees)	.326	.376	.491	525	86	171	34	1	17	87	37	83	2	1
1B	Freddie Freeman, Rome (Braves)	.316	.378	.521	491	70	155	33	7	18	95	46	84	5	5
2B	Everth Cabrera, Asheville (Rockies)	.284	.361	.399	479	80	136	25	6	6	38	51	101	73	16
3B	Darin Holcomb, Asheville (Rockies)	.318	.400	.491	509	89	162	46	0	14	102	65	60	6	5
SS	Zach Cozart, Dayton (Reds)	.280	.330	.457	418	57	117	20	6	14	49	24	77	3	3
CF	Ben Revere, Beloit (Twins)	.379	.433	.497	340	51	129	17	10	1	43	27	31	44	13
OF	Jason Heyward, Rome (Braves)	.323	.388	.483	449	88	145	27	6	11	52	49	74	15	3
OF	Mike Stanton, Greensboro (Marlins)	.293	.381	.611	468	89	137	26	3	39	97	58	153	4	2
DH	Mike Moustakas, Burlington (Royals)	.272	.337	.468	496	77	135	25	3	22	71	43	86	8	4

Pos	Pitcher, Team (Organization)	W	L	ERA	G	GS	SV	IP	H	HR	BB	SO	G/F	WHIP	AVG
SP	Madison Bumgarner, Augusta (Giants)	15	3	1.46	24	24	0	142	111	3	21	164	0.86	0.93	.216
SP	Jhoulys Chacin, Asheville (Rockies)	10	1	1.86	16	16	0	111	82	3	30	98	2.83	1.01	.205
SP	Neftali Feliz, Clinton (Rangers)	6	3	2.52	17	17	0	82	55	2	28	106	1.67	1.01	.193
SP	Derek Holland, Clinton (Rangers)	7	0	2.40	17	0	0	94	77	2	29	91	1.30	1.13	.228
RP	Tim Collins, Lansing (Blue Jays)	4	2	1.58	39	0	14	68	36	3	32	98	1.33	1.00	.156

Player of the Year: Madison Bumgarner, lhp, Augusta (Giants); **Manager of the Year:** Joe Mikulik, Asheville (Rockies); **Team of the Year:** Augusta (Giants)

SHORT-SEASON

Pos	Player, Team (Organization)	AVG	OBP	SLG	AB	R	H	2B	3B	HR	RBI	BB	SO	SB	CS
C	Derek Norris, Vermont (Nationals)	.278	.444	.463	227	42	63	12	0	10	38	63	56	11	9
1B	Phil Disher, Tri-City (Astros)	.304	.381	.536	280	40	85	20	3	13	56	33	71	1	0
2B	Colt Sedbrook, Batavia (Cardinals)	.305	.394	.396	275	38	84	9	5	2	33	24	44	13	8
3B	Josh Vitters, Boise (Cubs)	.328	.365	.498	259	38	85	25	2	5	37	13	45	1	3
SS	Ryan Flaherty, Boise (Cubs)	.297	.369	.511	219	39	65	19	2	8	26	24	51	4	2
CF	Charlie Blackmon, Tri-City (Rockies)	.338	.390	.466	290	42	98	21	5	2	33	16	37	13	7
OF	Mitch Dening, Lowell (Red Sox)	.321	.375	.471	240	35	77	13	7	3	20	18	50	9	7
OF	Dan Robertson, Eugene (Padres)	.377	.443	.497	302	59	114	21	3	3	45	34	34	20	7
DH	Lonnie Chisenhall, Mahoning Valley (Indians)	.290	.355	.438	276	38	80	20	3	5	45	24	32	7	2

Pos	Pitcher, Team (Organization)	W	L	ERA	G	GS	SV	IP	H	HR	BB	SO	G/F	WHIP	AVG
SP	Nick Barnese, Hudson Valley (Rays)	5	3	2.45	13	13	0	66	52	1	24	84	1.32	1.15	.212
SP	Wilfredo Boscan, Spokane (Rangers)	9	1	3.12	15	12	0	69	66	4	11	70	1.50	1.11	.251
SP	Brad Holt, Brooklyn (Mets)	5	3	1.87	14	14	0	72	43	3	33	96	0.98	1.05	.171
SP	Kyle Weiland, Lowell (Red Sox)	3	3	1.50	15	10	0	60	36	1	10	68	1.64	0.77	.166
RP	Adam Reifer, Batavia (Cardinals)	2	1	2.97	32	0	22	30	18	2	15	41	1.68	1.09	.162

Player of the Year: Brad Holt, rhp, Brooklyn (Mets); **Manager of the Year:** Tim Hulett, Spokane (Rangers); **Team of the Year:** Spokane (Rangers)

ROOKIE

Pos	Player, Team (Organization)	AVG	OBP	SLG	AB	R	H	2B	3B	HR	RBI	BB	SO	SB	CS
C	Wilin Rosario, Casper (Rockies)	.316	.371	.532	263	48	83	15	3	12	49	24	57	4	3
1B	Roberto Lopez, Orem (Angels)	.400	.480	.667	270	68	108	28	1	14	72	34	23	3	2
2B	Elias Otero, Princeton (Rays)	.332	.398	.534	208	38	69	13	7	5	32	21	45	3	0
3B	Mario Martinez, Pulaski (Mariners)	.319	.344	.462	251	43	80	15	3	5	32	10	47	2	1
SS	Wilmer Flores, Kingsport (Mets)	.310	.352	.490	245	36	76	12	4	8	41	12	28	2	1
CF	Aaron Hicks, GCL Twins	.318	.409	.491	173	32	55	10	4	4	27	28	32	12	2
OF	Jaff Decker, AZL Padres	.352	.523	.541	159	51	56	11	2	5	34	55	36	9	1
OF	Angel Morales, Elizabethton (Twins)	.301	.413	.623	183	33	55	12	1	15	28	26	72	7	2
DH	Esmailyn Gonzalez, GCL Nationals	.343	.481	.475	181	42	62	12	3	2	33	23	19	9	2

Pos	Pitcher, Team (Organization)	W	L	ERA	G	GS	SV	IP	H	HR	BB	SO	G/F	WHIP	AVG
SP	Dexter Carter, Great Falls (White Sox)	6	1	2.23	15	12	0	69	44	3	25	89	1.25	1.00	.179
SP	Manuarys Correa, AZL Angels/Orem (Angels)	7	1	3.58	15	12	0	78	88	4	15	84	1.09	1.32	.282
SP	Dan Hudson, Great Falls (White Sox)	5	4	3.36	14	14	0	70	52	6	22	90	1.44	1.06	.202
SP	Matt Moore, Princeton (Rays)	2	2	1.66	12	12	0	54	30	0	19	77	2.12	0.90	.154
RP	Santos Rodriguez, GCL Braves	1	2	2.79	14	0	5	29	16	0	13	45	1.00	1.00	.155

Player of the Yearw: Wilmer Flores, ss, Kingsport (Mets); **Manager of the Year:** Rob Mummau, Pulaski (Mariners); **Team of the Year:** Great Falls (White Sox)

MINOR LEAGUES

and its fourth in the past six years. The River Cats went on to edge Scranton/Wilkes-Barre for its second straight Bricktown Showdown crown.

■ The Yankees failed to reach the postseason for the first time since 1994, but their minor league affiliates fared a bit better. The Yankees joined the 1993 Astros in having both their Double-A and Triple-A affiliates win league titles in the same season.

(Houston did it with Triple-A Tucson and Double-A Jackson.) Trenton dispatched Akron in four games to win the Eastern League, and Scranton/Wilkes-Barre won the International League's Governor's Cup by besting Durham in four games.

■ High Class A Potomac became the Nationals' first full-season affiliate to win a league title when it knocked off Myrtle Beach, three-games-to-one, to claim the Carolina League championship.

CHRIS PROCTOR

Marlins first baseman Logan Morrison
led the FSL with a .332 batting average

TONY FARLOW

Rockies 20-year-old pitcher Jhoulys
Chacin won 18 games over two levels

FIRST TEAM

Pos	Player, Levels (Organization)	AGE	AVG	OBP	SLG	G	AB	R	H	2B	3B	HR	RBI	BB	SO	SB
C	Matt Wieters, AA/HiA (Orioles)	22	.355	.454	.600	130	437	89	155	22	2	27	91	82	76	2
1B	Logan Morrison, HiA (Marlins)	21	.332	.402	.494	130	488	71	162	38	1	13	74	57	80	9
2B	Chris Coghlan, AA (Marlins)	23	.298	.396	.429	132	483	83	144	32	5	7	74	67	65	34
3B	Mat Gamel, AA/AAA (Brewers)	23	.325	.392	.531	132	529	99	172	35	7	20	99	57	121	6
SS	Alcides Escobar, AA (Brewers)	21	.328	.363	.434	131	546	95	179	24	5	8	76	31	82	34
CF	Mike Stanton, LoA (Marlins)	18	.293	.381	.611	125	468	89	137	26	3	39	97	58	153	4
OF	Jason Heyward, LoA/HiA (Braves)	19	.316	.381	.473	127	471	91	149	29	6	11	56	51	78	15
OF	Matt LaPorta, AA (Indians)	23	.279	.386	.539	101	362	62	101	24	2	22	74	49	75	2
DH	Kila Ka'aihue, AA/AAA (Royals)	24	.313	.457	.629	123	396	89	124	14	0	37	99	104	66	3

Pos	Pitcher, Levels (Organization)	AGE	W	L	ERA	G	GS	SV	IP	H	HR	BB	SO	G/F	AVG	WHIP
SP	Madison Bumgarner, LoA (Giants)	19	15	3	1.46	24	24	0	142	111	3	21	164	0.86	.216	0.93
SP	Jhoulys Chacin, LoA/HiA (Rockies)	20	18	3	2.03	28	28	0	178	143	6	42	160	2.83	.221	1.04
SP	Tommy Hanson, AA/HiA (Braves)	22	11	5	2.41	25	25	0	138	85	9	52	163	0.71	.175	0.99
SP	Derek Holland, LoA/HiA/AA (Rangers)	21	13	1	2.27	26	26	0	151	111	3	40	157	1.20	.209	1.00
RP	Daniel Bard, AA/LoA (Red Sox)	23	5	1	1.51	46	0	7	78	42	4	30	107	2.18	.158	0.93

SECOND TEAM

Pos	Player, Levels (Organization)	AGE	AVG	OBP	SLG	G	AB	R	H	2B	3B	HR	RBI	BB	SO	SB
C	Carlos Santana, HiA/AA (Indians)	22	.326	.431	.568	130	463	125	151	39	5	21	117	89	85	10
1B	Lars Anderson, HiA/AA (Red Sox)	20	.317	.417	.517	118	439	85	139	32	1	18	80	75	107	1
2B	Ivan DeJesus, AA (Dodgers)	21	.324	.419	.423	128	463	91	150	21	2	7	58	76	81	16
3B	Mike Moustakas, Low A (Royals)	19	.272	.337	.468	126	496	77	135	25	3	22	71	43	86	8
SS	Brandon Wood, AAA (Angels)	23	.296	.375	.595	103	395	82	117	21	2	31	84	45	104	6
CF	Dexter Fowler, AA (Rockies)	22	.335	.431	.515	108	421	92	141	31	9	9	64	65	89	20
OF	Michael Taylor, LoA/HiA (Phillies)	22	.346	.412	.557	132	492	76	170	39	4	19	88	50	89	15
OF	Travis Snider, AA/AAA/HiA (Blue Jays)	20	.275	.358	.481	132	484	88	133	31	0	23	91	61	153	3
DH	Pablo Sandoval, HiA/A (Giants)	22	.350	.394	.578	112	448	90	157	38	2	20	96	31	59	2

Pos	Pitcher, Levels (Organization)	AGE	W	L	ERA	G	GS	SV	IP	H	HR	BB	SO	G/F	AVG	WHIP
SP	Trevor Cahill, HiA/AA (Athletics)	20	11	5	2.61	21	19	0	124	76	5	50	136	2.43	.179	1.01
SP	Neftali Feliz, LoA/AA (Rangers)	20	10	6	2.69	27	27	0	127	89	3	51	153	1.19	.201	1.10
SP	David Price, AA/HiA/AAA (Rays)	23	12	1	2.30	19	19	0	110	92	7	32	109	1.45	.228	1.13
SP	Chris Tillman, AA (Orioles)	20	11	4	3.18	28	28	0	136	115	10	65	154	0.82	.227	1.33
RP	Rob Delaney, AA/HiA (Twins)	23	3	3	1.23	46	0	18	66	44	3	11	72	0.71	.189	0.83

Talent flows through Frisco

Elvis Andrus seemed not far from becoming a one-man army at Double-A Frisco.

The first half of the season had been full of stars and then promotions for the Rangers affiliate. One by one prospects advanced on to Triple-A Oklahoma, some on to the major leagues: Catcher Taylor Teagarden and outfielder John Mayberry departed in April. Within a three-week span just ahead of the all-star game, lefthander Matt Harrison, first baseman Chris Davis and catcher Max Ramirez followed suit.

All of 19 years old and not yet a year removed from having joined a new organization, Andrus saw his calling as he recognized the need to take on a greater role of clubhouse leader.

"I tried to tell them that there's really no difference between Double-A and A-ball," the shortstop said. "I tried to make them feel comfortable. I told them that, even if they were coming from Clinton or Bakersfield, it didn't matter. And it didn't matter if you lost a couple of games. We could still win a championship."

The Rangers supplied Frisco with an abundance of prospects all summer, and the Riders rewarded the organization with an 84-56 season that fell a victory shy of capturing the Texas League championship. The RoughRiders' all-around performance, as talent translated to success, led Baseball America to name Frisco its Minor League Team of the Year.

Six key players—Davis, Ramirez, Teagarden and pitchers Tommy Hunter, Warner Madrigal and Harrison—reached the majors well before rosters expanded Sept. 1. Promoted in late May, Davis belted 15 home runs and 47 RBIs in his first 258 at-bats.

Twelve of BA's Top 30 Rangers prospects powered the Riders to a sweep of the South

Division first- and second-half titles before Arkansas (Angels) used a seven-run sixth to win the decisive Game Five of the league championship series.

Other teams had more wins—Myrtle Beach led the minors with 89 victories, and seven others won at least 85 games. But Frisco won despite major roster turnover.

"I think when we look back on this in two or three years—and hopefully winning at the major league level—we're saying, 'Remember that club in Frisco?'" Rangers farm director Scott Servais said. "We did feel we had a special group there and we feel we have some guys right behind that group."

And then, in a nod to the scouting and player development wings of the organization, Servais added, "You're only as good as the talent that comes through your door."

Andrus, acquired in the Mark Teixeira trade in July 2007 hit .311 (91-for-292) from June 8 on after missing two weeks because of an injured finger. He committed 32 errors, but only seven after July 25, and was second in the TL with 53 steals. Just after the all-star break, Frisco received center fielder Julio Borbon and second baseman Jose Vallejo from high Class A Bakersfield. Borbon hit a combined .321/.362/.425 with seven home runs, 58 RBIs and 53 steals in his first full season after being a supplemental first-round pick out of Tennessee.

The Riders also won despite a number of changes to the rotation, with 20 pitchers making starts. The second-half boosts came from righthander Neftali Feliz (4-3, 2.98) and lefthander Derek Holland (3-0, 0.69). Both opened at low Class A Clinton.

Elvis Andrus

BILL MITCHELL

PREVIOUS WINNERS

1993: Harrisburg/Eastern (Expos)
1994: Wilmington/Carolina (Royals)
1995: Norfolk/International (Mets)
1996: Edmonton/Pacific Coast (Athletics)
1997: West Michigan/Midwest (Tigers)

1998: Mobile/Southern (Padres)
1999: Trenton/Eastern (Red Sox)
2000: Round Rock/Texas (Astros)
2001: Lake Elsinore/California (Padres)
2002: Akron/Eastern (Indians)

2003: Sacramento/Pacific Coast (Athletics)
2004: Lancaster/California (Diamondbacks)
2005: Jacksonville/Southern (Dodgers)
2006: Tucson/Pacific Coast (Diamondbacks)
2007: San Antonio/Texas (Padres)

NEW YORK

The 10th annual All-Star Futures Game revealed that the United States had some work to do before the Olympics.

The U.S. team, made up of 25 of the 60 players from whom USA Baseball picked its squad for the Beijing Olympics, got shut down by nine World pitchers at Yankee Stadium, managing just three hits in a 3-0 victory for the World.

The World's win evens the all-time Futures Game series record at five victories for both the World and the U.S., and the World win followed a pattern similar to those in most of its other victories: dominant pitching.

The U.S. team, which went on to win bronze at the Beijing Games, managed baserunners in all but two of the game's nine innings, but never mounted a serious rally until the bottom of the ninth, when Indians third baseman Wes Hodges opened the inning with a double and new Indian Matt LaPorta worked a walk to bring Rockies outfielder Dexter Fowler to the plate as the tying run.

Fowler stung a ball down the first-base line, but Giants first baseman Angel Villalona stabbed it to record the final out.

The U.S. team didn't feature every premium prospect who might otherwise have been available because it was picked by USA Baseball from a smaller player pool than the game usually has. Futures Game rosters are traditionally selected by Baseball America and Major League Baseball from all full-season minor leaguers, but USA Baseball picked this year's U.S. team to promote the Olympics and give the people picking the Olympic team a chance to see a lot of their candidates in one place.

The Olympic team was from minor leaguers who are not on 40-man rosters and who are made available by major league organizations, so the prospect pool was not quite as deep. The real story of the game was the World pitching staff, which showcased nine power arms. World pitchers gave up five walks to go with their three hits, but their nine strikeouts more than made up for it.

The hardest thrower was Athletics right-hander Henry Rodriguez, who showed his trademark wildness but also showed his overpowering velocity. He touched 100 mph several times and pitched consistently in the high 90s.

FUTURES GAME BOX SCORE

WORLD 3, U.S. 0

World

Player	AB	R	H	2B	3B	HR	RBI	BB	SO	AVG
De Jesus 2B	3	0	2	0	0	0	0	1	0	.667
Andrus, El SS	1	1	0	0	0	0	0	1	0	.000
Pena SS	1	0	0	0	0	0	0	1	1	.000
Ramirez, W LF	1	0	1	0	0	0	0	1	0	1.000
Parra RF	2	0	1	0	0	0	0	0	0	.500
Sandoval, P 1B	1	0	0	0	0	0	0	1	1	.000
Villalona 1B	2	0	0	0	0	0	0	0	1	.000
Hughes 3B	2	0	0	0	0	0	0	0	1	.000
Francisco 3B	2	0	1	0	0	0	0	0	1	.500
Campbell DH	4	1	0	0	0	0	0	0	0	.000
Martinez, F CF	2	0	1	0	0	0	0	0	0	.500
Lin, C CF	2	1	2	0	0	1	2	0	0	1.000
Castillo, W C	2	0	0	0	0	0	0	0	2	.000
Montero C	2	0	1	0	0	0	0	0	0	.500
Hernandez, G RF-LF	4	0	0	0	0	0	0	0	2	.000

BATTING: HR: Lin, C (1, 7th inning off Mattheus, 1 on, 2 out). **SB:** Andrus, El (1, 3rd base off Richard/Marson). **CS:** De Jesus (1, 2nd base by Arrieta/Teagarden), Sandoval, P (1, 2nd base by Todd/Teagarden), Ramirez, W (1, 2nd base by Anderson/Marson), Andrus, El (1, 2nd base by Anderson/Marson). **PO:** Andrus, El (1st base by Anderson), Ramirez, W (1st base by Anderson). **FIELDING: DP:** (Hughes-De Jesus-Sandoval, P).

United States

Player	AB	R	H	2B	3B	HR	RBI	BB	SO	AVG
McCutchen LF	2	0	0	0	0	0	0	0	0	.000
Golson a- PH-LF	2	0	0	0	0	0	0	0	2	.000
Pennington 2B	2	0	0	0	0	0	0	0	1	.000
Getz 2B	2	0	0	0	0	0	0	0	1	.000
Gamel 3B	0	0	0	0	0	0	0	2	0	.000
Hodges 3B	2	0	1	1	0	0	0	0	0	.500
D'Antona DH	4	0	0	0	0	0	0	0	2	.000
Schierholtz RF	4	0	0	0	0	0	0	0	1	.000
LaPorta 1B	3	0	1	0	0	0	0	1	1	.333
Fowler CF	4	0	0	0	0	0	0	0	0	.000
Marson C	1	0	0	0	0	0	0	0	0	.000
Teagarden C	0	0	0	0	0	0	0	1	0	.000
Anderson, B C	0	0	0	0	0	0	0	1	0	.000
Donald SS	2	0	1	0	0	0	0	0	0	.500
Valaika SS	1	0	0	0	0	0	0	0	1	.000

a–Struck out for McCutchen in the 5th.

BATTING: 2B: Hodges (1, Martis). **GIDP:** Fowler. **Team LOB:** 7. **FIELDING: E:** Donald (1, throw). **DP:** 3 (Teagarden-Pennington, Teagarden-Valaika, Hodges-LaPorta). **Pickoffs:** Anderson 2 (Andrus, El at 1st base, Ramirez, W at 1st base).

WORLD PITCHERS

Player	IP	H	R	ER	BB	SO	HR	ERA
Carrasco W	1.0	0	0	0	1	2	0	0.00
Trinidad	1.0	1	0	0	1	0	0	0.00
Rondon	1.0	0	0	0	0	0	0	0.00
Morlan	1.0	0	0	0	1	1	0	0.00
Pimentel	1.0	1	0	0	1	1	0	0.00
Delgado	1.0	0	0	0	0	0	0	0.00
Salas	1.0	0	0	0	0	1	0	0.00
Rodriguez H	1.0	0	0	0	1	3	0	0.00
Martis SV	1.0	1	0	0	1	0	0	0.00

U.S. PITCHERS

Player	IP	H	R	ER	BB	SO	HR	ERA
Richard L	1.0	1	1	0	1	0	0	0.00
Cahill	1.0	1	0	0	2	0	0	0.00
Anderson	1.0	1	0	0	1	0	0	0.00
Todd	1.0	0	0	0	1	1	0	0.00
Inman	1.0	0	0	0	0	1	0	0.00
Arrieta	1.0	1	0	0	0	1	0	0.00
Mattheus	1.0	2	2	2	0	0	1	18.00
Weathers	1.0	1	0	0	2	3	0	0.00
Pucetas	1.0	2	0	0	0	0	0	0.00

"Pretty impressive? That was amazing—99, 99, 100, 100? That's an amazing arm," said Twins third baseman Luke Hughes, Rodriguez's teammate on the World team.

TRIPLE-A: The Pacific Coast League scored six times in the top of the ninth inning, turning a 2-0 deficit into a 6-5 win against the International League in Louisville. All six runs were charged to Toledo righthander Blaine Neal (Tigers), who retired only one of the seven batters he faced despite touching 98 mph several times. Three consecutive singles by Tucson DH Jamie D'Antona (Diamondbacks), Salt Lake third baseman Matt Brown (Angels) and Round Rock first baseman Mark Saccomanno (Astros) plated three runs and gave the PCL its first lead of the game. The fourth PCL run scored when Richmond first baseman Barbaro Canizares (Braves) failed to field a ground-ball by Tacoma shortstop Oswaldo Navarro (Mariners). He was charged with the IL's lone error on the play.

EASTERN LEAGUE: Travis Snider was the main attraction at the Double-A Eastern League all-star game, and he didn't disappoint the hometown fans.

Travis Snider

JERRY HALE

The New Hampshire (Blue Jays) outfielder cleared the second fence in right field routinely in batting practice, then won the home run derby with 12 home runs. In the game, the North knocked off the South, 5-3, thanks to MVP Luke Hughes' sixth-inning home run. The South Division jumped out to a 1-0 lead when Reading center fielder Greg Golson hit a solo home run to left field. Golson, 22, went 2-for-5 with a home run.

SOUTHERN LEAGUE: The Northern Division was in control from start to finish in Zebulon, N.C., home of the Carolina Mudcats. Led by a solid pitching performance and home runs by Carolina second baseman Chris Coghlan (Marlins) and Tennessee right fielder Doug Deeds (Cubs), the Northerners cruised to a 6-1 victory. Coghlan broke the 2-1 game open in the fifth inning by cranking a three-run home run to right field. The one-two punch of Huntsville (Brewers) batters Michael Brantley and Alcides Escobar hit back-to-back singles, setting the stage for Coghlan's blast.

TEXAS LEAGUE: Nine innings weren't enough to settle this all-star game. Frisco outfielder Steven Murphy's (Rangers) home run in the 10th inning broke a 3-3 tie and pro-

pelled the South to a 7-3 victory. The North was three outs away from a win, but Jon Zeringue (Athletics) doubled to start the ninth and scored the tying run on an error.

CALIFORNIA-CAROLINA LEAGUE: Potomac outfielder Edgardo Baez (Nationals) was named the game's MVP after breaking a 1-1 tie in the eighth inning with a home run to right-center field, propelling the Carolina League to a 3-1 win. Frederick righthander Jake Arrieta (Orioles), who also pitched in the Futures Game, threw a scoreless first inning and was consistently 95-96 mph, earning him pitcher of the game honors.

FLORIDA STATE LEAGUE: Sarasota outfielder Drew Stubbs (Reds) took home MVP honors, hitting a two-run homer in the second to propel the West to a 9-3 win over the East. The two teams combined for 23 hits in the game at Space Coast Stadium, home of the Brevard County Manatees. Fort Myers third baseman Danny Valencia (Twins) punctuated his 2-for-5 day with a two-run triple in the West's three-run sixth.

MIDWEST LEAGUE: There was drama aplenty at Dow Diamond, home of the Great Lakes Loons, as the Western Division pulled out a thrilling 5-4, 10-inning win over the East. The score remained in a 4-4 tie after the fifth inning, until Clinton's Tim Smith (Rangers) led off the 10th with a game-winning homer, earning him MVP honors. Peoria righty Blake Parker (Cubs) struck out the side in the bottom of the frame to nail down the victory.

SOUTH ATLANTIC LEAGUE: The North cruised a 13-4 victory at Greensboro. Hagerstown's Bill Rhinehart (Nationals) went 3-for-3 with a home run and three RBIs to win MVP honors. Rome's Jason Heyward (Braves) also had a big day. Heyward hit a home run to right field on the first pitch he saw from Greensboro righthander Andrew Battisto (Marlins) to get the South on the board in the second. In the fourth, Heyward beat out an infield single after hitting a soft line drive that dropped in front of West Virginia shortstop Zelous Wheeler (Brewers). Outfielder Michael Burgess (Nationals), put on quite a display by hitting 16 home runs to win the home run derby.

(*Full-season teams only)

TEAM

WINS
Myrtle Beach (Carolina)	89
Scranton/WB (International)	88
Louisville (International)	88
Augusta (South Atlantic)	88
Trenton (Eastern)	86

LONGEST WINNING STREAK*
Salt Lake (Pacific Coast)	13
Midland (Texas)	11
Myrtle Beach (Carolina)	11
Peoria (Midwest)	11
7 teams tied	10

LOSSES
Lexington (South Atlantic)	93
Lehigh Valley (International)	89
Reading (Eastern)	89
Hickory (South Atlantic)	87
Corpus Christi (Texas)	85
Great Lakes (Midwest)	85

LONGEST LOSING STREAK*
Frederick (Carolina)	13
Columbus (South Atlantic)	12
Erie (Eastern)	12
St. Lucie (Florida State)	12
Vero Beach (Florida State)	12

BATTING AVERAGE*
Las Vegas (Pacific Coast)	.301
Tucson (Pacific Coast)	.298
Iowa (Pacific Coast	.294
Colorado Springs (Pacific Coast)	.290
Albuquerque (Pacific Coast)	.286

RUNS
Colorado Springs (Pacific Coast)	855
Las Vegas (Pacific Coast)	844
Lake Elsinore (California)	819
Iowa (Pacific Coast)	816
Albuquerque (Pacific Coast)	812

HOME RUNS
Albuquerque (Pacific Coast)	197
Tacoma (Pacific Coast)	185
Sacramento (Pacific Coast)	177
Pawtucket (International)	176
Toledo (International)	172
Omaha (Pacific Coast)	172

STOLEN BASES
Wilmington (Carolina)	258
Cedar Rapids (Midwest)	247
Asheville (South Atlantic)	227
San Jose (California)	205
Nationals (DSL)	201

EARNED RUN AVERAGE*
Augusta (South Atlantic)	2.95
Lansing (Midwest)	3.08
Trenton (Eastern)	3.13
San Jose (California)	3.26
West Michigan (Midwest)	3.29

STRIKEOUTS
Stockton (California)	1259
Lansing (Midwest)	1194
Rome (South Atlantic)	1173
Lehigh Valley (International)	1156
San Antonio (Texas)	1152

INDIVIDUAL BATTING

BATTING*
Terry Tiffee (Las Vegas)	.378
Jamie D'Antona (Tucson)	.365
Angel Salome (Huntsville)	.360
Jim Negrych (Lynchburg, Altoona)	.359
Matt Wieters (Frederick, Bowie)	.355
Pablo Sandoval (San Jose, Connecticut)	.350
Michael Taylor (Lakewood, Clearwater)	.346
Jesus Guzman (Midland, Sacramento)	.345
Nelson Cruz (Oklahoma)	.342
Daniel Nava (Lancaster)	.341
Matt Miller (Tulsa, Colorado Springs)	.341

RUNS
Carlos Santana (Inland Empire, Kinston, Akron)	125
John Raynor (Carolina)	104
Drew Sutton (Corpus Christi)	102
Christopher Carter (Stockton)	101
Freddy Guzman (Erie, Toledo)	101

HITS
Cedric Hunter (Lake Elsinore)	186
Matt Miller (Tulsa, Colorado Springs)	181
Alcides Escobar (Huntsville)	179
Renny Osuna (Clinton, Bakersfield)	178
Freddy Sandoval (Salt Lake)	176

TOP HITTING STREAKS
Quintin Berry (Clearwater)	30
Michael Jones (Greenville)	28
Josh Anderson (Richmond)	27
Peter Ciofrone (Portland)	27
John Lindsey (Las Vegas)	27
Victor Rodriguez (Tabasco)	27

MOST HITS (ONE GAME)
Luis Bolivar (Chattanooga)	6
Pedro Chourio (DSL Red Sox)	6
Ed Lucas (NW Arkansas)	6
Fernando Perez (Durham)	6
146 players tied	5

TOTAL BASES
Christopher Carter (Stockton)	288
Mark Trumbo (Rancho Cucamonga, Arkansas)	286
Michael Stanton (Greensboro)	286
Mat Gamel (Huntsville, Nashville)	281
Jake Fox (Tennessee, Iowa)	281

EXTRA-BASE HITS
Christopher Carter (Stockton)	75
Ernesto Mejia (Myrtle Beach)	73
Jake Fox (Tennessee, Iowa)	72
Joe Koshansky (Colorado Springs)	71
Mark Trumbo (Rancho Cucamonga, Arkansas)	70

DOUBLES
Ernesto Mejia (Myrtle Beach)	47
Darin Holcomb (Asheville)	46
Freddy Sandoval (Salt Lake)	45
Johan Limonta (High Desert, West Tenn)	43
Jovan Rosa (Peoria)	43

TRIPLES
Jason Pridie (Rochester)	16
Freddy Guzman (Erie, Toledo)	15
Paulo Orlando (Winston-Salem, Wilmington)	14
Tim Raines (Tucson)	13
Ben Copeland (Connecticut, Fresno)	13
Clay Fuller (Cedar Rapids)	13

HOME RUNS
Dallas McPherson (Albuquerque)	42
Christopher Carter (Stockton)	39
Michael Stanton (Greensboro)	39
Nelson Cruz (AZL Rangers, Oklahoma)	37
Kila Ka'aihue (NW Arkansas, Omaha)	37

RUNS BATTED IN
Joe Koshansky (Colorado Springs)	121
Carlos Santana (Inland Empire, Kinston, Akron)	117
Tommy Everidge (Midland)	115
Josh Whitesell (Tucson)	110
Ian Gac (Clinton, Bakersfield)	109

MOST RBIS, ONE GAME
Tommy Everidge (Midland)	10
Kyle Blanks (San Antonio)	9
Tommy Giles (Inland Empire)	9
A.J. Ellis (Las Vegas)	8
Eric Eymann (Chattanooga)	8
Lou Montanez (Bowie)	8
Agustin Murillo (Monterrey)	8
Sean Rodriguez (Salt Lake)	8

STOLEN BASES
Everth Cabrera (Asheville)	73
Freddy Guzman (Erie, Toledo)	71
Andrew Romine (Cedar Rapids)	62
Darren Ford (San Jose, Brevard County)	62
Derrick Robinson (Wilmington)	62

CAUGHT STEALING
Adrian Ortiz (Burlington, Wilmington)	20
Jose De Los Santos (Hickory, Lynchburg)	20
Andrew McCutchen (Indianapolis)	19
Erik Kanaby (Great Lakes)	19
Andrew Romine (Cedar Rapids)	18
Julio Borbon (Bakersfield, Frisco)	18
Archie Gilbert (Stockton)	18

HIT BY PITCH
Jonathan Greene (Clinton)	36
Omar Guerra (VSL TB)	35
Rather Trujillo (DSL White Sox1, DSL White Sox2)	23
Robert Stevens (Bluefield)	23
Derrick Walker (South Bend)	23

WALKS
Kila Ka'aihue (NW Arkansas, Omaha)	104
Tyler Flowers (Myrtle Beach)	98
Valentino Pascucci (Lehigh Valley, New Orleans)	95
David Cook (Charlotte, Birmingham)	93
Cliff Pennington (Midland, Sacramento)	93

STRIKEOUTS
Jeramy Laster (Lakeland)	200
Cody Johnson (Rome)	177
Ian Gac (Clinton, Bakersfield)	170
Dallas McPherson (Albuquerque)	168
Victor Diaz (Round Rock, Tacoma)	168
Corey Brown (Kane County, Stockton)	168

SACRIFICE FLIES
Tommy Everidge (Midland)	14
Wes Hodges (Akron)	12
Larry Cobb (Kane County, Stockton)	12
Sean Coughlin (South Bend)	12
6 tied with11	

SACRIFICE HITS
Nate Samson (Peoria, Iowa)	22
Michael Martinez (Potomac)	20
Nate Spears (Tennessee, Iowa)	19
Chris Cates (Beloit)	18
Michael Mitchell (Asheville)	17
Angel R. Gonzalez (Lynchburg, Altoona)	17

SLUGGING PERCENTAGE*
Nelson Cruz (Oklahoma)	.695
Kila Ka'aihue (NW Arkansas, Omaha)	.628
Dallas McPherson (Albuquerque)	.618
Michael Stanton (Greensboro)	.611
Jamie D'Antona (Tucson)	.604
Tony Blanco (Modesto, Tulsa)	.602
Mike Hessman (Toledo)	.602
Lou Montanez (Bowie)	.601
Joe Koshansky (Colorado Springs)	.600
Matt Wieters (Frederick, Bowie)	.600

ON-BASE PERCENTAGE*

Kila Ka'aihue (NW Arkansas, Omaha)	.456
James Skelton (Lakeland, Erie)	.456
Matt Wieters (Frederick, Bowie)	.454
Brian Myrow (Portland)	.451
Jim Negrych (Lynchburg, Altoona)	.438
Lou Marson (Reading)	.433
Carlos Santana (Inland Empire, Kinston, Akron)	.431
Dexter Fowler (Tulsa)	.431
Nelson Cruz (Oklahoma)	.429
Tyler Flowers (Myrtle Beach)	.427

ON BASE PLUS SLUGGING (OPS)*

Nelson Cruz (Oklahoma)	1.123
Kila Ka'aihue (NW Arkansas, Omaha)	1.085
Matt Wieters (Frederick, Bowie)	1.053
Jamie D'Antona (Tucson)	1.009
Carlos Santana (Inland Empire, Kinston, Akron)	.999
Dallas McPherson (Albuquerque)	.998
Tony Blanco (Modesto, Tulsa)	.996
Michael Stanton (Greensboro)	.993
Josh Whitesell (Tucson)	.993

BATTING AVERAGE*
BY POSITION
CATCHERS

Angel Salome (Huntsville)	.360
Matt Wieters (Frederick, Bowie)	.355
Pablo Sandoval (San Jose, Connecticut)	.350
Carlos Santana (Inland Empire, Kinston, Akron)	.326
Jesus Montero (Charleston)	.326

FIRST BASEMEN

Logan Morrison (Jupiter)	.332
Josh Whitesell (Tucson)	.328
Blake Lalli (Peoria, Dayton, Tennessee)	.326
Kyle Blanks (San Antonio)	.325
Mitchell Moreland (Clinton)	.324

SECOND BASEMEN

Jim Negrych (Lynchburg, Altoona)	.359
Renny Osuna (Clinton, Bakersfield)	.338
Bobby Scales (Iowa)	.320
Drew Sutton (Corpus Christi)	.317
Joe Thurston (Pawtucket)	.316

THIRD BASEMEN

Terry Tiffee (Las Vegas)	.378
Jamie D'Antona (Tucson)	.365
Jesus Guzman (Midland, Sacramento)	.345
Freddy Sandoval (Salt Lake)	.335
Tony Blanco (Modesto, Tulsa)	.334

SHORTSTOPS

Jesus Merchan (Tucson)	.339
Alcides Escobar (Huntsville)	.328
Ivan De Jesus (Jacksonville)	.324
Chris Valaika (Sarasota, Chattanooga)	.317
Manuel Mayorson (Carolina, Albuquerque)	.314

OUTFIELDERS

Michael Taylor (Lakewood, Clearwater)	.346
Nelson Cruz (Oklahoma)	.342
Daniel Nava (Lancaster)	.341
Matt Miller (Tulsa, Colorado Springs)	.341
Nick Stavinoha (Memphis)	.337

DESIGNATED HITTERS

Randy Ruiz (Rochester)	.320
Abel Nieves (Rancho Cucamonga)	.318
Timo Perez (Toledo)	.302
Jeff Frazier (Erie, Toledo)	.301
Barbaro Canizares (Richmond)	.300

INDIVIDUAL PITCHING

EARNED RUN AVERAGE*

Madison Bumgarner (Augusta)	1.46
Jon Kibler (West Michigan)	1.75
Chris Cody (West Virginia, Brevard County)	1.81
Michael Pineda (Wisconsin)	1.95

Brad Mills (Lansing, Dunedin, New Hampshire)	1.95
Jhoulys Chacin (Asheville, Modesto)	2.03
Zach McAllister (Charleston, Tampa)	2.09
Nicholas Additon (Quad Cities, Palm Beach)	2.23
Connor Graham (Asheville)	2.26
Derek Holland (Clinton, Bakersfield, Frisco)	2.27

WORST ERA*

Daniel Guerrero (Dayton, Sarasota)	7.67
Anthony Varvaro (High Desert)	7.12
Dustin Moseley (Rancho Cucamonga, Salt Lake)	6.73
Yorman Bazardo (Toledo)	6.72
Corey Bass (Salem)	6.70

WINS

Jhoulys Chacin (Asheville, Modesto)	18
Mitch Atkins (Tennessee, Iowa)	17
Sean O'Sullivan (Rancho Cucamonga)	16
Bradley Bergesen (Frederick, Bowie)	16
Adam Pettyjohn (Louisville)	15
Madison Bumgarner (Augusta)	15
Sam Narron (Huntsville, Nashville)	15
Vincent Mazzaro (Midland, Sacramento)	15
Levi Maxwell (Kannapolis, Winston-Salem)	15
Scott Diamond (Rome, Myrtle Beach)	15

LOSSES

Brooks Brown (Mobile)	15
Corey Bass (Salem)	15
Doug Fister (West Tenn)	14
J.D. Durbin (Reading, Lehigh Valley)	14
Robert Leonhardt (Lexington)	14
Alan Johnson (Tulsa)	14
Keith Renaud (Wisconsin, High Desert)	14

GAMES

Matt Daley (Tulsa, Colorado Springs)	63
Jason Motte (Memphis)	63
Brandon Villafuerte (Albuquerque)	62
Edwin Moreno (San Antonio, Portland)	60
Jonathan Ellis (San Antonio, Portland)	60
Gabe DeHoyos (San Antonio)	60
Fernando Salas (Springfield)	60

COMPLETE GAMES

Jose Diaz (VSL Tigers)	4
17 tied with3	

SAVES

Jon Link (Birmingham)	35
Dan Otero (Augusta, San Jose)	34
Jonathan Ortiz (Charleston)	33
Julio Manon (Bowie)	32
Randall Taylor (Asheville)	32

SHUTOUTS

Juan Sosa (DSL Phillies)	2
Michael Anton (Cedar Rapids, R. Cucamonga)	2
Bradley Bergesen (Frederick, Bowie)	2
Alfredo Figaro (West Michigan, Lakeland)	2
Daniel McCutchen (Trenton, Scranton/WB, Indianapolis)	2
Blake Wood (Wilmington, NW Arkansas)	2
Les Walrond (Iowa, Lehigh Valley)	2
Virgil Vasquez (Toledo)	2
Aneury Rodriguez (Modesto)	2
Connor Graham (Asheville)	2

INNINGS PITCHED

Keith Weiser (Modesto, Tulsa)	179.2
Charlie Haeger (Charlotte)	178.0
Jhoulys Chacin (Asheville, Modesto)	177.2
Robert Mosebach (Arkansas)	177.2
Alan Johnson (Tulsa)	175.2

WALKS

Henry Rodriguez (Stockton, Midland)	84
Bill Murphy (Syracuse)	84
Christopher Archer (Lake County)	84
Harold Garce (DSL Yankees1)	84
Connor Graham (Asheville)	83
Cole Kimball (Hagerstown)	83
Keith Renaud (Wisconsin, High Desert)	83

STRIKEOUTS

David Bromberg (Beloit)	177
David Hernandez (Bowie)	166
Madison Bumgarner (Augusta)	164
Tommy Hanson (Myrtle Beach, Mississippi)	163
Jeremy Hellickson (Vero Beach, Montgomery)	162

HITS ALLOWED

Alan Johnson (Tulsa)	217
Robert Mosebach (Arkansas)	209
Bob Keppel (Albuquerque)	208
Wes Roemer (Visalia)	199
Lucas French (Erie)	195
Rowdy Hardy (NW Arkansas)	195

STRIKEOUTS PER NINE INNINGS (STARTERS)*

David Bromberg (Beloit)	10.62
David Hernandez (Bowie)	10.60
Daniel Gutierrez (Burlington)	10.55
Dellin Betances (Charleston)	10.53
Jeremy McBryde (Fort Wayne)	10.48

STRIKEOUTS PER NINE INNINGS (RELIEVERS)*

Jason Motte (Memphis)	14.85
Corey Madden (Greensboro)	14.28
John Gaub (Lake County)	14.06
Anthony Slama (Fort Myers)	13.94

BATTING AVERAGE AGAINST (STARTERS)*

William Glen (Carolina)	.189
Connor Graham (Asheville)	.189
Jon Kibler (West Michigan)	.190

BATTING AVERAGE AGAINST (RELIEVERS)*

Tim Collins (Lansing)	.156
Julio Manon (Bowie)	.162
Justin Garcia (Columbus)	.162

MOST STRIKEOUTS, ONE GAME

Les Walrond (Lehigh Valley)	17
David Francis (Danville)	16
Scott Barnes (Augusta)	14
Edwar Cabrera (DSL Rockies)	14
Eury De La Rosa (DSL Diamondbacks)	14
Tommy Hanson (Mississippi)	14
Bradley Holt (Brooklyn)	14
Michael Pineda (Wisconsin)	14

WILD PITCHES

Maikel Cleto (Savannah, St. Lucie)	25
Henry Rodriguez (Stockton, Midland)	25
Raul Mayora (DSL Rangers2)	23
Michael Felix (Hickory)	23
6 tied with21	

BALKS

Luis Perez (Lansing)	7
Dustin Molleken (Hickory, Lynchburg)	6
Ramon Garcia (West Michigan, Lakeland)	6
Luis Noel (Delmarva)	6
Nicholas Hill (High Desert, West Tenn)	6
Moises Colorado (VSL Cardinals)	6
Jordan Norberto (South Bend)	6
Richard Brooks (Winston-Salem)	6

HIT BATTERS

Kyle Schmidt (Frederick, Bowie)	21
Rowdy Hardy (NW Arkansas)	20
David Bromberg (Beloit)	19
Julio Sanchez (DSL Cubs2)	19

INDIVIDUAL FIELDING

MOST ERRORS

Ryan Adams (Delmarva)	52
Junior Payano (DSL Rangers1, DSL Rangers2)	50
Marcus Lemon (Bakersfield)	43
Carmen Angelini (Charleston)	42
Audy Ciriaco (West Michigan)	41

	INTERNATIONAL LEAGUE	PACIFIC COAST LEAGUE	EASTERN LEAGUE	SOUTHERN LEAGUE	TEXAS LEAGUE	CALIFORNIA LEAGUE	CAROLINA LEAGUE	FLORIDA STATE LEAGUE	MIDWEST LEAGUE	SOUTH ATLANTIC LEAGUE
Best Batting Prospect	Jay Bruce, Louisville	Chase Headley, Portland	Danny Murphy, Binghamton	Mat Gamel, Huntsville	Max Ramirez, Frisco	Sean Doolittle, Stockton	Matt Wieters, Frederick	Logan Morrison, Jupiter	Ben Revere, Beloit	Jason Heyward, Rome
Best Power Prospect	Jeff Larish, Toledo	Brandon Wood, Salt Lake	Travis Snider, New Hampshire	Matt LaPorta, Huntsville	Chris Davis, Frisco	Chris Carter, Stockton	Matt Wieters, Frederick	Juan Francisco, Sarasota	Ian Gac, Clinton	Mike Stanton, Greensboro
Best Strike-Zone Judgment	Brett Gardner, Scranton/WB	Will Venable, Portland	Lou Marson, Reading	Michael Brantley, Huntsville	Kila Kaaihue, NW Arkansas	Carlos Santana, Inland Empire	Jim Negrych, Lynchburg	Logan Morrison, Jupiter	Ben Revere, Beloit	Darin Holcomb, Asheville
Best Baserunner	Brett Gardner, Scranton/WB	Ivan Ochoa, Fresno	Roger Bernadina, Harrisburg	Michael Brantley, Huntsville	Corey Wimberly, Tulsa	Peter Bourjos, Rancho Cucamonga	Derrick Robinson, Wilmington	Chris Heisey, Sarasota	Andrew Romine, Cedar Rapids	Everth Cabrera, Asheville
Fastest Baserunner	Fernando Perez, Durham	Emilio Bonifacio, Tucson	Greg Golson, Reading	John Raynor, Carolina	Ovandy Suero, NW Arkansas	Michael McBride, San Jose	Derrick Robinson, Wilmington	Darren Ford, Brevard County	Ben Revere, Beloit	Everth Cabrera, Asheville
Best Pitching Prospect	Charlie Morton, Richmond	Mitchell Boggs, Memphis	Chris Tillman, Bowie	Clayton Kershaw, Jacksonville	Vin Mazzaro, Midland	Trevor Cahill, Stockton	Tommy Hanson, Myrtle Beach	David Price, Vero Beach	Jarrod Parker, South Bend	Madison Bumgarner, Augusta
Best Fastball	David Purcey, Syracuse	Juan Morillo, Colorado Springs	Daniel Bard, Portland	Clayton Kershaw, Jacksonville	Casey Weathers, Tulsa	Henry Rodriguez, Stockton	Jake Arrieta, Frederick	Jeremy Jeffress, Brevard County	Neftali Feliz, Clinton	Maikel Cleto, Savannah
Best Breaking Pitch	Jimmy Barthmaier, Indianapolis	Gio Gonzalez, Sacramento	David Hernandez, Bowie	Clayton Kershaw, Jacksonville	Kevin Jepsen, Arkansas	Tim Alderson, San Jose	John Ely, Winston-Salem	Francisco Samuel, Palm Beach	Craig Italiano, Kane County	Drew Naylor, Lakewood
Best Changeup	Mitch Talbot, Durham	Cesar Jimenez, Tacoma	Michael Bowden, Portland	James McDonald, Jacksonville	Michael Ballard, Frisco	Jhoulys Chacin, Modesto	Hector Rondon, Kinston	Ramon Geronimo, Sarasota	Michael Anton, Cedar Rapids	Jhoulys Chacin, Asheville
Best Control	Clayton Richard, Charlotte	Wade LeBlanc, Portland	Brad Bergeson, Bowie	Jeremy Hellickson, Montgomery	Vin Mazzaro, Midland	Keith Weiser, Modesto	John Ely, Winston-Salem	Jeremy Hellickson, Vero Beach	Bryan Augenstein, South Bend	Madison Bumgarner, Augusta
Best Reliever	David Robertson, Scranton/WB	Chris Perez, Memphis	Daniel Bard, Bowie	Luis Valdez, Mississippi	Kevin Jepsen, Arkansas	Andrew Johnston, Modesto	Luis Perdomo, Kinston	Anthony Slama, Fort Myers	Jackson Quezada, Fort Wayne	Jonathan Ortiz, Charleston
Best Defensive Catcher	Ryan Hanigan, Louisville	Taylor Teagarden, Oklahoma	Drew Butera, New Britain	Cole Armstrong, Birmingham	Taylor Teagarden, Frisco	Carlos Santana, Inland Empire	Matt Wieters, Frederick	Wilson Ramos, Fort Myers	Matt Liuzza, Lansing	Joel Naughton, Lakewood
Best Defensive First Baseman	Larry Broadway, Columbus	Micah Hoffpauir, Iowa	Nick Evans, Binghamton	Gaby Sanchez, Carolina	Michael Collins, Arkansas	Sean Doolittle, Stockton	Beau Mills, Kinston	Logan Morrisson, Jupiter	Efren Navarro, Cedar Rapids	Bill Rhinehart, Hagerstown
Best Defensive Second Baseman	Eider Torres, Norfolk	Emilio Bonifacio, Tucson	Brad Harman, Reading	Luis Valbuena, West Tenn	Jose Martinez, Springfield	Jose Vallejo, Bakersfield	Travis Jones, Myrtle Beach	Bradley Emaus, Dunedin	Nate Samson, Peoria	Kris Negron, Greenville
Best Defensive Third Baseman	Neil Walker, Indianapolis	Matt Brown, Salt Lake	Ofilio Castro, Harrisburg	Van Pope, Mississippi	Mario Lisson, NW Arkansas	Larry Infante, Rancho Cucamonga	Jhon Florentino, Salem	Juan Francisco, Sarasota	Brandon Waring, Dayton	Bradley Suttle, Charleston
Best Defensive Shortstop	Reid Brignac, Durham	Brian Bocock, Fresno	Ramiro Pena, Trenton	Alcides Escobar, Huntsville	Elvis Andrus, Frisco	Jesus Lopez, Lake Elsinore	Brandon Hicks, Myrtle Beach	Cale Iorg, Lakeland	Zach Cozart, Dayton	Freddy Galvis, Lakewood
Best Infield Arm	Mike Costanzo, Norfolk	Brian Bocock, Fresno	Argenis Diaz, Portland	Alcides Escobar, Huntsville	Elvis Andrus, Frisco	Jesus Lopez, Lake Elsinore	Brandon Hicks, Myrtle Beach	Cale Iorg, Lakeland	Zach Cozart, Dayton	Freddy Galvis, Lakewood
Best Defensive Outfielder	Jason Pridie, Rochester	Yordany Ramirez, Round Rock	Austin Jackson, Trenton	Cameron Maybin, Carolina	Dexter Fowler, Tulsa	Peter Bourjos, Rancho Cucamonga	Gorkys Hernandez, Myrtle Beach	Ezequiel Carrera, St. Lucie	Evan Frey, South Bend	Che-Hsuan Lin, Greenville
Best Outfield Arm	Ryan Raburn, Toledo	Adam Jones, Tacoma	Clete Thomas, New Britain	Carlos Gonzalez, Mobile	Colby Rasmus, Springfield	Leyson Septimo, Visalia	Jordan Schafer, Myrtle Beach	Nate Southard, Palm Beach	Gerardo Parra, South Bend	Jordan Parraz, Lexington
Most Exciting Player	Andrew McCutchen, Indianapolis	Carlos Gonzalez, Sacramento	Greg Golson, Reading	Alcides Escobar, Huntsville	Dexter Fowler, Tulsa	Chad Epperson, Lancaster	Gorkys Hernandez, Myrtle Beach	Scott Cousins, Jupiter	Ben Revere, Beloit	Jason Heyward, Rome
Best Manager Prospect	Dave Brundage, Richmond	Randy Ready, Portland	Brad Komminsk, Akron	Buddy Bailey, Tennessee	Scott Little, Frisco		Jeff Branson, Lynchburg	Jeff Smith, Fort Myers	Mike Micucci, Clinton	Gary Green, Hickory

MINOR LEAGUES

Honoring excellence

Baseball America's annual Bob Freitas Awards are presented to franchises that show sustained excellence in the business of minor league baseball.

They were first presented in 1989, shortly after the death of Freitas, a longtime minor league operator, promoter and ambassador. Franchises must be in operation for at least five seasons before they're eligible to win.

Triple-A: Columbus

The Clippers have long been innovators. Their longtime home Cooper Stadium was the first minor league ballpark adorned with skyboxes and astroturf—which it replaced in the early 1990s.

Columbus' on-field success as a Yankees affiliate matched with sound business practices made it the annual top draw in the International League. The Clippers won seven league titles from 1979 to 2006 as a Yankees' affiliate, including back-to-back crowns in 1991-92, and topped the IL attendance leaderboard from 1990-92.

However the rest of the city began to catch up to the Clippers, as more and more sporting options became available around town. Attracting fans to an outdated ballpark in an out-of-the-way part of town became more of a challenge, yet the Clippers never let attendance dip below 450,000 and saw turnout grow from 480,445 in 2003 to 537,889 in 2008.

Now it may be Columbus' turn to be back on top of the International League. The Clippers will unveil a new state-of-the-art downtown ballpark in 2009, the same season they begin a relationship as the Indians top affiliate.

Fans lined up before ticket offices opened in October to purchase season tickets.

"They have been so stable and so steady," IL president Randy Mobley said. "I think they are about to get back on top again."

Double-A: Birmingham

Few teams have done as good a job of embracing a rich history while keeping pace with the ever-changing landscape of minor league baseball than Birmingham.

The Barons history dates back to the late 1800s, and the team played its games at legendary Rickwood Field from 1910 to 1988. Rickwood remains the oldest standing ballpark in the nation and the Barons return once a year for the nationally recognized Rickwood Classic. Yet the Barons remain one of the Southern League's top draws, and was only knocked out of the top two spots when new ballparks began sprouting up around the league in 2003.

Class A: Greensboro

Greensboro made the most of a tough situation in its pre-2005 era, plugging away and putting on a good show in what was considered a tough market for professional baseball. Then the Grasshoppers debuted NewBridge Bank Ballpark in '05 and have not looked back.

Baseball now booms in Greensboro, where the team has drawn well over 400,000 fans in each of the four seasons in their new home. The Grasshoppers have become so well thought of within the South Atlantic League that they hosted the all-star game in 2008.

Short-Season: Greeneville

It's no surprise that the Greeneville Astros have topped the Appalachian League in attendance in each of the past five seasons. For in 2004, the Astros teamed with local Tusculum College to build Pioneer Park—and the fans haven't stopped coming out. The Astros have drawn over 50,000 fans in each of their past three seasons—quite a feat in 34 home dates in a league known for local flavor more than packed ballparks.

PREVIOUS WINNERS

TRIPLE-A	DOUBLE-A	CLASS A	SHORT-SEASON
2000: Edmonton (Pacific Coast)	2000: Reading (Eastern)	2000: Charleston, S.C. (South Atlantic)	2000: Lowell (New York-Penn)
2001: Buffalo (International)	2001: Mobile (Southern)	2001: Delmarva (South Atlantic)	2001: Salem-Keizer (Northwest)
2002: Memphis (Pacific Coast)	2002: Chattanooga (Southern)	2002: Fort Myers (Florida State)	2002: Ogden (Pioneer)
2003: Pawtucket (International)	2003: New Britain (Eastern)	2003: Modesto (California)	2003: Spokane (Northwest)
2004: Sacramento (Pacific Coast)	2004: Round Rock (Texas)	2004: Dayton (Midwest)	2004: Burlington (Appalachian)
2005: Toledo (International)	2005: Tulsa (Texas)	2005: Lakewood (South Atlantic)	2005: Brooklyn (New York-Penn)
2006: Durham (International)	2006: Altoona (Eastern)	2006: Daytona (Florida State)	2006: Aberdeen (New York-Penn)
2007: Albuquerque (Pacific Coast)	2007: Frisco (Texas)	2007: Lake Elsinore (California)	2007: Missoula (Pioneer)

BY MATT EDDY

The Red Sox-Yankees rivalry never materialized in the American League East in 2008, but at least it was alive and well in the International League's Northern Division. The Scranton/Wilkes-Barre Yankees maintained a 2 ½-game advantage on the Pawtucket Red Sox during the regular season, and the two Triple-A powers met in the first round of the playoffs.

Paced by 29-year-old Japanese lefty Kei Igawa (14-6, 3.45 in 24 starts), Scranton's pitching staff led the league in ERA (3.67) while finishing near the top in strikeouts (1,088) as well as fewest walks (407) and home runs allowed (109). Pawtucket, though, finished a close second in ERA (3.69) and boasted a much stronger offense, leading the IL in runs (752), walks (540) and home runs (176).

By the time the playoffs rolled around, the Red Sox were without IL MVP Jeff Bailey, who had been called up by Boston. The 29-year-old first baseman/outfielder hit .301/.405/.562 with 25 home runs, 75 RBIs and a league-leading 88 runs. Pawtucket still had its three other top offensive performers in outfielders Chris Carter and Jonathan Van Every and second baseman Joe Thurston .They also had the league's most valuable pitcher: knuckleballer Charlie Zink, who went 14-6, 2.84 and narrowly missed pacing the IL in wins, ERA, innings (174) and opponent average (.223).

But in the end, Scranton needed just four games to dispatch Pawtucket and advance to the Governor's Cup finals, where it met Southern Division-winning Durham. The Bulls had eked into the playoffs with a 74-70 record that was fifth-best in the league.

The Yankees easily handled Durham, winning in four games to claim Scranton's first IL title. Led

TOP 20 PROSPECTS

1. Jay Bruce, of, Louisville (Reds)
2. Andrew McCutchen, of, Indianapolis (Pirates)
3. Wade Davis, rhp, Durham (Rays)
4. Reid Brignac, ss, Durham (Rays)
5. Jed Lowrie, ss, Pawtucket (Red Sox)
6. David Huff, lhp, Buffalo (Indians)
7. Neil Walker, 3b, Indianapolis (Pirates)
8. Denard Span, of, Rochester (Twins)
9. Charlie Morton, rhp, Richmond (Braves)
10. Homer Bailey, rhp, Louisville (Reds)
11. David Purcey, lhp, Syracuse (Blue Jays)
12. Kevin Mulvey, rhp, Rochester (Twins)
13. Matt Joyce, of, Toledo (Tigers)
14. Brandon Moss, of/1b, Pawtucket (Red Sox)
15. J.A. Happ, lhp, Lehigh Valley (Phillies)
16. Jeff Niemann, rhp, Durham (Rays)
17. Brandon Jones, of, Richmond (Braves)
18. Collin Balester, rhp, Columbus (Nationals)
19. Brett Gardner, of, Scranton/Wilkes-Barre (Yankees)
20. Chris Getz, ss/2b, Charlotte (White Sox)

by IL manager of the year Rick Sweet, Louisville established a franchise record for wins by going 88-56. The Bats fell in four games to Durham and its all-prospect rotation (Wade Davis, Jeff Niemann, David Price, Mitch Talbot) in the first round of the playoffs. In an up and down year (4-7, 4.77), Louisville righthander Homer Bailey saved his best start for last, striking out eight and walking one in six shutout innings for the Bats' lone playoff win.

Though they couldn't escape last place in the Northern Division, Lehigh Valley overcame a 3-24 start to finish at 55-89 and drew 602,033 in its first season since moving from Ottawa.

Rochester first baseman and IL rookie of the year Randy Ruiz batted .320/.366/.536 to take home league batting title. The 30-year-old, who signed as a nondrafted free agent with the Reds in 1999 out of Tallahassee (Fla.) CC, had spent just 22 games at Triple-A in the nine seasons prior to 2008.

STANDINGS

Page	Northern Division	W	L	PCT	GB	Manager	Attendance	Average	Last Penn.
214	Scranton/W-B Yankees (Yankees)	88	56	.611		Dave Miley	485,999	7,147	2008
74	Pawtucket Red Sox (Red Sox)	85	58	.594	2 ½	Ron Johnson	636,788	9,097	1984
194	Rochester Red Wings (Twins)	74	70	.514	14	Stan Cliburn	490,806	6,913	1997
314	Syracuse Chiefs (Blue Jays)	69	73	.486	18	Doug Davis	392,028	5,765	1976
113	Buffalo Bisons (Indians)	66	77	.462	21 ½	Torey Lovullo	590,386	8,812	2004
235	Lehigh Valley IronPigs (Phillies)	55	89	.382	33	Dave Huppert	602,033	8,479	1995

Page	Southern Division	W	L	PCT	GB	Manager	Attendance	Average	Last Penn.
295	Durham Bulls (Rays)	74	70	.514		Charlie Montoyo	503,636	6,995	2003
64	Norfolk Tides (Orioles)	64	78	.451	9	Gary Allenson	433,767	6,286	1985
93	Charlotte Knights (White Sox)	63	78	.447	9 ½	Marc Bombard	312,290	4,526	1999
55	Richmond Braves (Braves)	63	78	.447	9 ½	Dave Brundage	289,570	4,455	2007

Page	Western Division	W	L	PCT	GB	Manager	Attendance	Average	Last Penn.
103	Louisville Bats (Reds)	88	56	.611		Rick Sweet	631,457	9,152	2001
131	Toledo Mud Hens (Tigers)	75	69	.521	13	Larry Parrish	584,596	8,234	2006
324	Columbus Clippers (Nationals)	69	73	.486	18	Tim Foli	537,889	7,795	1996
245	Indianapolis Indians (Pirates)	68	76	.472	20	Trent Jewett	606,166	8,538	2000

PLAYOFFS—Semifinals: Scranton/Wilkes-Barre defeated Pawtucket 3-1 and Durham defeated Louisville 3-1 in best-of-five series. **Finals:** Scranton/Wilkes-Barre defeated Durham 3-1 in a best-of-five series.

CLUB BATTING

	AVG	G	AB	R	H	2B	3B	HR	RBI	BB	SO	SB	CS	OBP	SLG
Rochester	.274	144	4907	703	1345	297	47	133	656	417	1039	107	51	.333	.435
Louisville	.270	144	4944	717	1337	273	60	125	681	419	1178	110	37	.334	.426
Norfolk	.270	142	4823	635	1304	240	35	66	589	432	920	122	74	.333	.376
Pawtucket	.269	143	4821	752	1297	246	32	176	720	540	1144	64	24	.349	.443
Columbus	.264	142	4737	608	1251	246	37	83	551	451	1025	144	79	.332	.384
Durham	.264	144	4851	699	1280	266	33	153	652	491	1224	122	39	.334	.427
Charlotte	.263	141	4714	610	1238	239	20	130	556	420	999	141	56	.328	.405
Scranton/WB	.263	144	4790	680	1260	255	30	132	626	532	1014	136	50	.341	.411
Indianapolis	.262	144	4799	624	1256	249	37	114	576	401	993	198	80	.325	.400
Richmond	.262	141	4762	563	1230	248	25	89	520	392	940	153	48	.323	.381
Syracuse	.262	142	4720	593	1235	245	22	94	560	464	907	97	32	.329	.383
Lehigh Valley	.256	144	4832	552	1237	245	14	90	524	404	952	70	25	.318	.368
Toledo	.254	144	4847	690	1233	248	45	172	656	498	1206	152	46	.327	.431
Buffalo	.252	143	4749	581	1197	252	23	107	540	476	1078	59	33	.327	.382

CLUB PITCHING

	ERA	G	CG	SHO	SV	IP	H	R	ER	HR	BB	SO	AVG
Scranton/WB	3.68	144	7	14	36	1261	1171	582	514	109	407	1088	.246
Pawtucket	3.70	143	4	5	40	1252	1173	578	513	118	424	978	.249
Buffalo	3.84	143	4	10	46	1246	1272	614	532	125	403	1017	.264
Syracuse	3.88	142	2	10	33	1236	1245	611	533	101	471	1128	.263
Louisville	3.98	144	3	13	56	1292	1277	616	569	123	416	1027	.260
Rochester	4.13	144	5	7	43	1259	1300	662	578	129	449	993	.266
Charlotte	4.15	141	8	6	30	1218	1223	648	559	129	435	982	.261
Columbus	4.21	142	1	4	46	1265	1300	639	591	131	454	1089	.268
Toledo	4.24	144	6	9	39	1268	1315	662	597	130	427	1057	.269
Durham	4.25	144	4	15	40	1254	1281	682	591	130	472	1048	.265
Indianapolis	4.26	144	0	9	45	1261	1251	658	594	115	457	984	.260
Norfolk	4.36	142	2	6	31	1241	1286	704	599	110	490	1018	.269
Richmond	4.36	141	1	10	32	1232	1294	672	597	90	567	1054	.272
Lehigh Valley	4.41	144	3	6	27	1248	1332	680	612	124	465	1156	.276

CLUB FIELDING

	FPCT	PO	A	E	DP		FPCT	PO	A	E	DP
Pawtucket	.983	3755	1353	88	130	Charlotte	.976	3654	1441	123	111
Columbus	.982	3794	1341	92	121	Richmond	.976	3697	1377	123	130
Indianapolis	.981	3783	1440	99	104	Durham	.975	3762	1430	135	107
Louisville	.981	3877	1550	105	128	Syracuse	.975	3708	1453	130	143
Scranton/WB	.979	3782	1330	109	95	Norfolk	.974	3724	1387	137	121
Toledo	.979	3804	1450	113	126	Rochester	.973	3777	1430	146	139
Lehigh Valley	.977	3744	1315	117	118	Buffalo	.971	3737	1401	153	145

INDIVIDUAL BATTING LEADERS (MINIMUM 2.7 PLATE APPEARANCES PER LEAGUE GAME)

	AVG	G	AB	R	H	2B	3B	HR	RBI	BB	SO	SB
Ruiz, Randy, Rochester	.320	111	416	58	133	33	3	17	68	23	116	1
Salazar, Oscar, Norfolk	.316	112	443	73	140	42	3	13	85	42	56	8
Thurston, Joe, Pawtucket	.316	126	507	83	160	28	5	11	64	35	75	19
Anderson, Josh, Richmond	.314	121	494	77	155	25	4	4	40	30	57	42
Cervenak, Mike, Lehigh Valley	.311	115	456	64	142	30	2	10	66	13	64	5
Johnson, Dan, Durham	.307	113	394	85	121	23	0	25	83	84	75	0
Torres, Eider, Norfolk	.307	115	473	69	145	20	6	1	46	38	60	28
Watson, Brandon, Lehigh Valley	.305	126	518	78	158	21	2	6	40	26	53	11
Perez, Timo, Toledo	.302	112	427	56	129	30	2	13	63	48	43	19
Getz, Chris, Charlotte	.302	111	404	60	122	24	1	11	52	41	53	11

INDIVIDUAL PITCHING LEADERS (MINIMUM 0.8 INNINGS PITCHED PER LEAGUE GAME)

	W	L	ERA	G	GS	CG	SV	IP	H	R	BB	SO
Purcey, David, Syracuse	8	6	2.69	19	19	0	0	117	97	41	34	121
Zink, Charlie, Pawtucket	14	6	2.84	28	28	2	0	174	144	73	49	106
Liriano, Francisco, Rochester	10	2	3.28	19	19	0	0	118	102	44	31	113
Igawa, Kei, Scranton/WB	14	6	3.45	26	24	2	0	156	141	65	45	117
Lambert, Chris, Toledo	12	8	3.50	26	26	3	0	149	143	69	48	124
Pauley, David, Pawtucket	14	4	3.55	25	25	0	0	147	147	68	41	103
Niemann, Jeff, Durham	9	5	3.59	24	24	3	0	133	101	60	50	128
Happ, J.A., Lehigh Valley	8	7	3.60	24	23	0	0	135	116	58	48	151
Mulvey, Kevin, Rochester	7	9	3.77	27	27	1	0	148	152	80	48	121
Whisler, Wes, Charlotte	12	10	3.81	27	27	1	0	156	175	86	45	71

ALL-STAR TEAM

C—Ryan Hanigan, Louisville. **1B**—Oscar Salazar, Norfolk. **2B**—Joe Thurston, Pawtucket. **3B**—Mike Hessman, Toledo. **SS**—Reid Brignac, Durham. **OF**—Josh Anderson, Richmond; Jeff Bailey, Pawtucket; Chris Carter, Pawtucket. **DH**—Brad Eldred, Charlotte. **UTIL**—Chris Getz, Charlotte. **SP**—Charlie Zink, Pawtucket. **RP**—Blaine Neal, Toledo. **Most Valuable Player:** Jeff Bailey, Pawtucket. **Most Valuable Pitcher:** Charlie Zink, Pawtucket. **Rookie of the Year:** Randy Ruiz, Rochester. **Manager of the Year:** Rick Sweet, Louisville.

DEPARTMENT LEADERS

BATTING

OBP	Johnson, Dan, Durham	.424
SLG	Hessman, Mike, Toledo	.602
R	Bailey, Jeff, Pawtucket	88
H	Thurston, Joe, Pawtucket	160
TB	Richard, Chris, Durham	255
	Jones, Garrett, Rochester	255
XBH	Richard, Chris, Durham	62
2B	Salazar, Oscar, Norfolk	42
3B	Pridie, Jason, Rochester	16
HR	Eldred, Brad, Charlotte	35
RBI	Eldred, Brad, Charlotte	100
SAC	Thurston, Joe, Pawtucket	14
SF	Barker, Kevin, Louisville	10
	Walker, Neil, Louisville	10
BB	Johnson, Dan, Durham	84
IBB	Tracy, Andy, Lehigh Valley	8
	Broadway, Larry, Columbus	8
HBP	Three players tied at	14
SO	Clevlen, Brent, Toledo	166
SB	Guzman, Freddy, Toledo	56
CS	McCutchen, Andrew, Indianapolis	19
AB/SO	Perez, Timo, Toledo	9.93

PITCHING

G	Gosling, Mike, Syracuse	58
GS	Four players tied at	28
CG	Three players tied at	3
GF	Childers, Matt, Lehigh Valley	49
SV	Adkins, Jon, Louisville	30
W	Pettyjohn, Adam, Louisville	15
L	Three players tied at	13
IP	Haeger, Charlie, Charlotte	178
H	Pettyjohn, Adam, Louisville	188
R	Bazardo, Yorman, Toledo	100
ER	Bazardo, Yorman, Toledo	97
HB	Hendrickson, Ben, Durham	16
BB	Murphy, Bill, Syracuse	84
SO	Murphy, Bill, Syracuse	152
SO/9 (SP)	Happ, J.A., Lehigh Valley	9.77
SO/9 (RP)	Miller, Jim, Norfolk	10.61
BB/9	McCutchen, Daniel, Scranton/Indy	1.37
WP	Moss, Damian, Richmond	16
BK	Davis, Jason, Indianapolis	3
	Bueno, Francisley, Richmond	3
AVG	Niemann, Jeff, Durham	.207

FIELDING

C	FPCT	Santos, Omir, Norfolk	.997
	PO	Jaramillo, Jason, Lehigh Valley	916
	A	Jaramillo, Jason, Lehigh Valley	76
	E	Jaramillo, Jason, Lehigh Valley	16
	DP	Jaramillo, Jason, Lehigh Valley	9
		Colina, Alvin, Louisville	9
	PB	Phillips, Paul, Charlotte	15
1B	FPCT	Tracy, Andy, Lehigh Valley	.997
	PO	Richard, Chris, Durham	988
	A	Barker, Kevin, Louisville	80
	E	Eldred, Brad, Charlotte	10
		Ruiz, Randy, Rochester	10
	DP	Tracy, Andy, Lehigh Valley	81
2B	FPCT	Torres, Eider, Norfolk	.990
	PO	Thurston, Joe, Pawtucket	194
	A	Thurston, Joe, Pawtucket	279
	E	Three players tied at	12
	DP	Thurston, Joe, Pawtucket	76
3B	FPCT	Hessman, Mike, Toledo	.982
	PO	Walker, Neil, Indianapolis	107
	A	Walker, Neil, Indianapolis	232
	E	Walker, Neil, Indianapolis	19
	DP	Walker, Neil, Indianapolis	20
SS	FPCT	Rouse, Mike, Charlotte/LV	.956
	PO	Rouse, Mike, Charlotte/LV	154
		Janish, Paul, Louisville	154
	A	Rouse, Mike, Charlotte/LV	283
	E	Rouse, Mike, Charlotte/LV	20
	DP	Rouse, Mike, Charlotte/LV	69
OF	FPCT	Van Every, Jonathan, Pawtucket	1.000
	PO	Pridie, Jason, Rochester	337
	A	Roberson, Chris, Norfolk	22
	E	Terrero, Luis, Norfolk	13
	DP	Roberson, Chris, Norfolk	6

BY JIM SHONERD

Once again, the Sacramento River Cats could not be denied another run at a Pacific Coast League title. For the fourth time in six seasons, the River Cats emerged as the PCL's top team, and they went on to claim their second consecutive Triple-A crown by defeating the International League's Scranton/Wilkes-Barre Yankees in the Bricktown Showdown.

The River Cats (Athletics) comfortably won the Pacific Conference's Southern Division, then knocked out Salt Lake in four games in the first round of the playoffs, winning three straight games after dropping the first at home. The River Cats did much the same against Oklahoma in the PCL finals, winning again in four games.

Led by righthander Kirk Saarloos and lefthander Gio Gonzalez, the River Cats' 3.54 team ERA was the PCL's second best, behind only Memphis' 3.45. The River Cats lost Gonzalez to an August promotion, but the team received reinforcements for the playoffs from Double-A Midland in lefthander Brett Anderson and righthander Henry Rodriguez. Anderson won twice against the Redhawks. Offensively, the River Cats were paced by outfielders Carlos Gonzalez, Travis Buck and Chris Denorfia. Denorfia hit .486 during the postseason, while Gonzalez hit .406 and his three-run homer lifted Sacramento in the finale.

The Redhawks had made it to the finals by knocking out regular season champ Iowa in five games, overcoming a two-games-to-one deficit in the process. The Cubs were led by PCL manager

of the year Pat Listach, but went into the playoffs without key offensive contributors Micah Hoffpauir (promotion) and Eric Patterson (midseason trade).

Salt Lake opened the season with a 21-1 record and reached 24-2 behind a 13-game winning streak and an 11-game road winning streak. The Bees were fueled by some of the Angels' top prospects, such as shortstop Brandon Wood, second baseman Sean Rodriguez and righthanders Nick Adenhart and Jose Arredondo. All four of those players were called up at some point, leaving the Bees to slide back to the pack by the end of the year.

Albuquerque third baseman Dallas McPherson claimed the minor league home run title. McPherson had 39 home runs by the end of July, and went deep in seven straight June games.

TOP 20 PROSPECTS

1. Colby Rasmus, of, Memphis (Cardinals)
2. Chase Headley, of/3b, Portland (Padres)
3. Max Scherzer, rhp, Tucson (Diamondbacks)
4. Brandon Wood, ss/3b, Salt Lake (Angels)
5. Carlos Gonzalez, of, Sacramento (Athletics)
6. Jeff Clement, c, Tacoma (Mariners)
7. Ian Stewart, 3b, Colorado Springs (Rockies)
8. Gio Gonzalez, lhp, Sacramento (Athletics)
9. Andy LaRoche, 3b, Las Vegas (Dodgers)
10. Wladimir Balentien, of, Tacoma (Mariners)
11. Sean Rodriguez, 2b, Salt Lake (Angels)
12. Chris Perez, rhp, Memphis (Cardinals)
13. Nate Schierholtz, of, Fresno (Giants)
14. Bryan Anderson, c, Memphis (Cardinals)
15. Franklin Morales, lhp, Colorado Springs (Rockies)
16. Jaime Garcia, lhp, Memphis (Cardinals)
17. Mitchell Boggs, rhp, Memphis (Cardinals)
18. Carlos Rosa, rhp, Omaha (Royals)
19. Nick Adenhart, rhp, Salt Lake (Angels)
20. Greg Reynolds, rhp, Colorado Springs (Rockies)

STANDINGS

AMERICAN CONFERENCE

Page	Northern Division	W	L	PCT	GB	Manager	Attendance	Average	Last Penn.
83	Iowa Cubs (Cubs)	83	59	.585	—	Pat Listach	487,348	7,384	None
255	Memphis Redbirds (Cardinals)	75	67	.528	8	Chris Maloney	569,172	8,249	2000
159	Omaha Royals (Royals)	63	81	.438	21	Mike Jirschele	349,376	5,375	None
186	Nashville Sounds (Brewers)	59	81	.421	23	Frank Kremblas	354,662	5,293	2005

Page	Southern Division	W	L	PCT	GB	Manager	Attendance	Average	Last Penn.
304	Oklahoma RedHawks (Rangers)	76	68	.528	—	Bobby Jones	470,140	6,716	1965
141	Albuquerque Isotopes (Marlins)	68	75	.476	7½	Dean Treanor	593,606	8,361	1994
203	New Orleans Zephyrs (Mets)	66	75	.468	8½	K. Oberkfell/M. Scott	349,500	5,216	2001
150	Round Rock Express (Astros)	64	79	.448	11½	Dave Clark	668,623	9,286	None

PACIFIC CONFERENCE

Page	Northern Division	W	L	PCT	GB	Manager	Attendance	Average	Last Penn.
168	Salt Lake Bees (Angels)	84	60	.583	—	Bobby Mitchell	500,780	7,053	1979
284	Tacoma Rainiers (Mariners)	80	64	.556	4	Daren Brown	327,871	4,752	2001
122	Colorado Springs Sky Sox (Rockies)	71	72	.497	12½	Tom Runnells	303,048	4,392	1995
266	Portland Beavers (Padres)	70	74	.486	14	Randy Ready	392,512	5,607	1983

Page	Southern Division	W	L	PCT	GB	Manager	Attendance	Average	Last Penn.
224	Sacramento River Cats (Athletics)	83	61	.576	—	Todd Steverson	700,168	9,725	2008
177	Las Vegas 51s (Dodgers)	74	69	.517	8½	Lorenzo Bundy	374,780	5,279	1988
275	Fresno Grizzlies (Giants)	67	76	.469	15½	Dan Rohn	526,754	7,419	None
46	Tucson Sidewinders (Diamondbacks)	60	82	.423	22	Bill Plummer	245,121	3,552	2006

PLAYOFFS—Semifinals: Sacramento defeated Salt Lake 3-1 and Oklahoma defeated Iowa 3-2 in best-of-five series. **Finals:** Sacramento defeated Oklahoma 3-1 in a best-of-five series.

CLUB BATTING

	AVG	G	AB	R	H	2B	3B	HR	RBI	BB	SO	SB	CS	OBP	SLG
Las Vegas	.301	143	5047	844	1518	298	43	137	781	533	882	65	34	.373	.458
Tucson	.298	142	5033	763	1501	292	51	122	718	427	882	88	34	.355	.449
Iowa	.294	142	4797	816	1412	298	32	159	768	444	909	101	34	.357	.469
Colorado Sprgs.	.290	143	4994	855	1450	333	41	139	795	500	1033	111	39	.357	.457
Albuquerque	.286	143	4867	812	1391	272	33	197	772	516	1123	147	53	.357	.477
Salt Lake	.285	144	5012	808	1426	288	29	168	752	470	984	88	49	.351	.454
Tacoma	.283	144	4949	811	1399	329	18	185	773	519	1081	92	51	.356	.469
Memphis	.272	142	4849	710	1317	273	24	154	670	532	960	60	33	.347	.433
Oklahoma	.272	144	4868	738	1323	244	60	162	697	553	1044	97	36	.348	.446
Fresno	.271	143	4874	726	1322	281	34	154	683	486	993	114	56	.340	.438
Sacramento	.270	144	4948	786	1335	281	33	177	735	551	1136	74	34	.346	.447
Omaha	.267	144	4840	689	1294	256	35	172	651	450	980	57	26	.332	.441
Nashville	.266	140	4655	655	1236	258	31	119	606	496	986	134	46	.339	.411
Portland	.264	144	4892	714	1293	270	33	159	675	607	1013	38	27	.349	.430
New Orleans	.258	141	4681	635	1208	214	22	137	605	531	937	70	40	.337	.391
Round Rock	.258	143	4799	627	1239	245	28	151	582	406	943	79	61	.318	.415

CLUB PITCHING

	ERA	G	CG	SHO	SV	IP	H	R	ER	HR	BB	SO	AVG
Memphis	4.34	142	2	6	45	1260	1278	665	607	140	519	1096	.264
Sacramento	4.43	144	3	5	33	1273	1333	694	624	151	450	1018	.270
Oklahoma	4.47	144	3	9	31	1264	1382	709	626	152	403	947	.278
Iowa	4.55	142	2	7	36	1228	1244	690	616	143	477	1052	.264
Round Rock	4.61	143	5	5	35	1259	1365	705	644	170	418	957	.278
New Orleans	4.63	141	2	12	31	1235	1244	687	635	155	445	959	.264
Omaha	4.76	144	2	5	31	1240	1297	732	651	163	532	921	.272
Salt Lake	4.80	144	2	6	39	1270	1393	750	676	173	490	1009	.280
Tacoma	4.89	144	3	4	34	1257	1412	750	683	133	483	945	.284
Fresno	4.95	143	5	5	30	1254	1363	773	687	160	542	969	.279
Nashville	4.95	140	3	3	26	1215	1261	733	668	166	542	1010	.269
Las Vegas	5.00	143	0	3	38	1270	1456	791	705	164	541	1051	.289
Portland	5.09	144	2	7	37	1264	1382	794	713	153	485	1036	.278
Colorado Springs	5.21	143	0	4	25	1253	1393	798	724	136	592	927	.285
Tucson	5.47	142	0	3	23	1249	1422	861	759	152	559	1012	.288
Albuquerque	5.51	143	4	4	28	1242	1439	857	759	181	543	977	.293

CLUB FIELDING

	PCT	PO	A	E	DP		PCT	PO	A	E	DP
Memphis	.982	3779	1435	94	132	Salt Lake	.978	3809	1458	118	134
Fresno	.981	3762	1575	106	152	Tacoma	.978	3771	1379	114	138
Omaha	.981	3721	1492	101	173	Albuquerque	.977	3727	1593	127	161
New Orleans	.980	3705	1438	105	119	Las Vegas	.977	3809	1479	126	130
Round Rock	.979	3776	1421	112	135	Oklahoma	.977	3791	1503	122	137
Colorado Sprgs.	.978	3760	1565	118	138	Sacramento	.977	3819	1455	123	151
Iowa	.978	3684	1456	118	141	Portland	.976	3791	1376	125	137
Nashville	.978	3645	1440	117	130	Tucson	.974	3748	1410	135	140

INDIVIDUAL BATTING LEADERS (MINIMUM 2.7 PLATE APPEARANCES PER LEAGUE GAME)

	AVG	G	AB	R	H	2B	3B	HR	RBI	BB	SO	SB
Tiffee, Terry, Las Vegas	.378	93	392	73	148	39	3	9	69	27	43	1
D'Antona, Jamie, Tucson	.365	110	419	69	153	35	1	21	79	30	64	1
Cruz, Nelson, Oklahoma	.342	103	383	93	131	18	3	37	99	56	87	24
Merchan, Jesus, Tucson	.339	114	436	50	148	23	5	4	72	18	44	2
Stavinoha, Nick, Memphis	.337	112	427	67	144	23	3	16	74	20	50	2
Sandoval, Freddy, Salt Lake	.335	131	525	92	176	45	2	15	88	47	74	6
Whitesell, Josh, Tucson	.328	127	475	86	156	36	0	26	110	74	136	1
Scales, Bobby, Iowa	.320	121	387	94	124	20	2	15	59	59	90	7
Sullivan, Cory, Colorado Springs	.320	94	381	70	122	32	3	7	47	31	63	13
Brown, Matthew, Salt Lake	.320	97	400	75	128	33	4	21	67	32	80	4

INDIVIDUAL PITCHING LEADERS (MINIMUM 0.8 INNINGS PITCHED PER LEAGUE GAME)

	W	L	ERA	G	GS	CG	SV	IP	H	R	BB	SO
Boggs, Mitchell, Memphis	9	3	3.45	21	21	1	0	125	107	52	46	81
Gulin, Lindsay, Nashville	7	7	3.54	26	23	1	0	137	111	59	73	120
Stults, Eric, Las Vegas	7	7	3.82	20	20	0	0	118	118	53	35	102
Loux, Shane, Salt Lake	12	6	3.98	22	22	1	0	138	154	69	40	77
Wells, Randy, Iowa	10	4	4.02	27	19	0	0	119	127	64	34	102
Collazo, Willie, New Orleans	4	9	4.05	37	16	0	2	136	134	66	35	71
Palmer, Matt, Fresno	6	10	4.18	26	25	1	0	142	138	71	72	143
Saarloos, Kirk, Sacramento	9	4	4.22	22	22	1	0	141	150	73	36	79
Gonzalez, Gio, Sacramento	8	7	4.24	23	22	1	0	123	106	65	61	128
Alvarado, Giancarlo, Salt Lake	7	5	4.27	26	23	1	0	131	123	69	64	131

ALL-STAR TEAM

C—Rob Johnson, Tacoma. **1B**—Joe Koshansky, Colorado Springs. **2B**—Eric Patterson, Sacramento. **3B**—Matt Brown, Salt Lake/Jamie D'Antona, Tucson. **SS**—Brandon Wood, Salt Lake. **OF**—Nelson Cruz, Oklahoma; Nick Stavinoha, Memphis; Terry Tiffee, Las Vegas. **DH**—Dallas McPherson, Albuquerque. **RHP**—Shane Loux, Salt Lake. **LHP**—Gio Gonzalez, Sacramento. **RP**—Jason Bulger, Salt Lake. **Most Valuable Player:** Nelson Cruz, Oklahoma. **Pitcher of the Year:** Shane Loux, Salt Lake. **Rookie of the Year:** Josh Whitesell, Tucson. **Manager of the Year:** Pat Listach, Iowa.

DEPARTMENT LEADERS

BATTING

OBP	Myrow, Brian, Portland	.451
SLG	Cruz, Nelson, Oklahoma	.695
R	Raines, Tim, Tucson	96
H	Sandoval, Freddy, Salt Lake	176
TB	McPherson, Dallas, Abq.	277
XBH	Koshansky, Joe, Colorado Springs	71
2B	Sandoval, Freddy, Salt Lake	45
3B	Raines, Tim, Tucson	13
HR	McPherson, Dallas, Abq.	42
RBI	Koshansky, Joe, Colorado Springs	121
SAC	Meyer, Drew, Oklahoma	12
SF	Oeltjen, Trent, Tucson	11
BB	Myrow, Brian, Portland	81
IBB	Koshansky, Joe, Colorado Springs	7
HBP	Repko, Jason, Las Vegas	18
SO	McPherson, Dallas, Abq.	168
	Diaz, Victor, Round Rock, Tacoma	168
SB	Torres, Andres, Iowa	29
CS	Feliciano, Jesus, New Orleans	14
AB/SO	Figueroa, Luis, Iowa	12.33

PITCHING

G	Motte, Jason, Memphis	63
GS	Muecke, Josh, Round Rock	29
CG	Hennessey, Brad, Fresno	3
GF	Register, Steven, Colorado Springs	45
SV	Wells, Jared, Portland, Tacoma	20
W	De La Cruz, Eulogio, Albuquerque	13
L	Four players tied at	13
IP	Geer, Josh, Portland	166.2
H	Keppel, Bob, Albuquerque	208
R	Keppel, Bob, Albuquerque	120
ER	Keppel, Bob, Albuquerque	106
HB	Vasquez, Esmerling, Tucson	12
BB	Morales, Franklin, Colorado Springs	82
SO	Palmer, Matt, Fresno	143
SO/9 (SP)	Gonzalez, Gio, Sacramento	9.26
SO/9 (RP)	Motte, Jason, Memphis	14.85
BB/9	Miller, Joshua, Round Rock	1.16
WP	De La Cruz, Eulogio, Abq.	19
BK	Adenhart, Nick, Salt Lake	5
	Morales, Franklin, Colorado Springs	5
AVG	Gulin, Lindsay, Nashville	0.219

FIELDING

C	FPCT	Bellorin, Edwin, Colo. Springs	.998
	PO	Rottino, Vinny, Nashville	709
	A	Ellis, A.J., Las Vegas	54
	E	Powell, Landon, Sacramento	9
		Johnson, Rob, Tacoma	9
	DP	Hill, Koyie, Iowa	9
	PB	Johnson, Rob, Tacoma	21
1B	FPCT	Abreu, Michel, New Orleans	.996
	PO	Koshansky, Joe, Colo. Springs	1041
	A	Whitesell, Josh, Tucson	82
	E	Whitesell, Josh, Tucson	11
		Koshansky, Joe, Colo. Springs	11
	DP	Koshansky, Joe, Colo. Springs	135
2B	FPCT	Beattie, Andrew, Abq.	.978
	PO	Antonelli, Matt, Portland	243
	A	Antonelli, Matt, Portland	313
	E	Antonelli, Matt, Portland	13
	DP	Antonelli, Matt, Portland	81
3B	FPCT	Freese, David, Memphis	.967
	PO	Tuiasosopo, Matt, Tacoma	82
	A	McGehee, Casey, Iowa	222
	E	Tuiasosopo, Matt, Tacoma	27
	DP	Freese, David, Memphis	26
SS	FPCT	Hernandez, Anderson, New Orl.	.970
	PO	Merchan, Jesus, Tucson	175
	A	Merchan, Jesus, Tucson	297
	E	Blanco, Andres, Iowa	22
	DP	Merchan, Jesus, Tucson	81
OF	FPCT	Raines, Tim, Tucson	.996
	PO	Ramirez, Yordany, Round Rock	334
	A	Repko, Jason, Las Vegas	18
	E	Katin, Brendan, Nashville	10
	DP	Repko, Jason, Las Vegas	7

MINOR LEAGUES

BY CONOR GLASSEY

Trenton (Yankees) picked up in 2008 right where it left off in 2007. After the franchise won their first Eastern League title last year, the team got off to a 35-20 start over the first two months of the season on their way to putting together the best record in the league (86-54) for the second year in a row.

Six teams in the league scored more runs than Trenton, but the Thunder made up for it with solid pitching and defense. The team had the lowest ERA (3.13), allowed the fewest hits (1,064) and recorded the most strikeouts (1,122). Of the team's 12 pitchers that notched at least 40 innings, seven of them posted an ERA below 3.00. This year's pitching staff didn't have the name recognition of last year, when the team had Joba Chamberlain and Ian Kennedy for part of the season, but was anchored by righthanders George Kontos and Jason Jones and lefthander Phil Coke. The team also had solid performances from the bullpen, particularly 2006 ninth-round pick Mark Melancon, who went 6-0, 1.18.

Trenton swept the Portland (Red Sox) in the first round of the playoffs and then took three-of-four from Akron (Indians) for the league title.

Trenton's victory was painful for Bowie, who went 84-58 for the second-best record in the league. It was a bittersweet season for the Orioles' affiliate that some considered the best team in the league thanks to a plethora of talent, including the top two prospects in the league in catcher Matt Wieters and righthander Chris Tillman. The Baysox also featured outfielders Nolan Reimold and Lou Montanez and righhanders David Hernandez (who led the league in strikeouts) and Brad Bergesen (the EL pitcher of the year). Bowie's Brad Komminsk was named Eastern League manager of the year.

Taken fifth overall in the 2007 draft out of

TOP 20 PROSPECTS

1. Matt Wieters, c, Bowie (Orioles)
2. Chris Tillman, rhp, Bowie (Orioles)
3. Travis Snider, of, New Hampshire (Blue Jays)
4. Lars Anderson, 1b, Portland (Red Sox)
5. Jordan Zimmerman, rhp, Harrisburg (Nationals)
6. Carlos Carrasco, rhp, Reading (Phillies)
7. Fernando Martinez, of, Binghamton (Mets)
8. J.P. Arencibia, c, New Hampshire (Blue Jays)
9. Daniel Bard, rhp, Portland (Red Sox)
10. Austin Jackson, of, Trenton (Yankees)
11. David Huff, lhp, Akron (Indians)
12. Jose Tabata, of, Trenton (Yankees)/Altoona (Pirates)
13. Daniel Murphy, 3b/of, Binghamton (Mets)
14. Lou Marson, c, Reading (Phillies)
15. Michael Bowden, rhp, Portland (Red Sox)
16. Wes Hodges, 3b, Akron (Indians)
17. Brett Cecil, lhp, New Hampshire (Blue Jays)
18. Jon Niese, lhp, Binghamton (Mets)
19. Pablo Sandoval, c/1b, Connecticut (Giants)
20. Greg Golson, of, Reading (Phillies)

Georgia Tech, Wieters secured his spot as the best prospect in the game by hitting .355/.454/.600 with 27 home runs between high Class A Frederick (Carolina) and Bowie. Tillman, who came to the Orioles as one of the five players the Mariners gave up for Erik Bedard, was one of the youngest players in the Eastern League this year. Unfazed, he established himself as one of the best young guns in the game.

Montanez rejuvenated his career by hitting .335/.385/.601 with 26 home runs and 97 RBIs. In early August, Montanez was in the midst of a league-leading 19-game hitting streak when he was called up to the big leagues and still managed to win the EL triple crown and MVP awards.

The Baysox had to face a loaded Akron team in the first round of the playoffs. The middle of the Aeros' lineup featured one of the best prospects in the game, outfielder Matt LaPorta and Indians designated hitter Travis Hafner on a rehab assignment. Hafner played a key role in the Aeros advancing, hitting two home runs in what would be the final two games of the series.

STANDINGS

Page	Northern Division	W	L	PCT	GB	Manager	Attendance	Average	Last Penn.
215	Trenton Thunder (Yankees)	86	54	.614	—	Tony Franklin	409,131	5,762	2008
75	Portland Sea Dogs (Red Sox)	74	66	.529	12	Arnie Beyeler	412,403	6,249	2006
204	Binghamton Mets (Mets)	73	69	.514	14	Mako Oliveras	220,638	3,198	1994
276	Connecticut Defenders (Giants)	68	73	.482	18½	Bien Figueroa	202,004	3,015	2002
195	New Britain Rock Cats (Twins)	64	77	.454	22½	Bobby Cuellar	365,756	5,301	2001
315	New Hampshire Fisher Cats (Blue Jays)	61	81	.430	26	Gary Cathcart	373,227	5,332	2004

Page	Southern Division	W	L	PCT	GB	Manager	Attendance	Average	Last Penn.
65	Bowie Baysox (Orioles)	84	58	.592	—	Brad Komminsk	261,459	3,845	None
114	Akron Aeros (Indians)	80	62	.563	4	Mike Sarbaugh	342,816	5,117	2005
325	Harrisburg Senators (Nationals)	73	69	.514	11	John Stearns	164,182	2,488	1999
132	Erie SeaWolves (Tigers)	68	74	.479	16	Tom Brookens	234,955	3,405	None
246	Altoona Curve (Pirates)	65	77	.458	19	Tim Leiper	346,973	5,179	None
236	Reading Phillies (Phillies)	53	89	.373	31	P.J. Forbes	436,789	6,423	2001

PLAYOFFS—Semifinals: Trenton defeated Portland 3-0 and Akron defeated Bowie 3-1 in best-of-five series. **Finals:** Trenton defeated Akron 3-1 in a best-of-five series.

CLUB BATTING

	AVG	G	AB	R	H	2B	3B	HR	RBI	BB	SO	SB	CS	OBP	SLG
Bowie	.273	142	4749	734	1297	247	36	140	683	481	830	52	38	.343	.429
Erie	.271	142	4823	726	1309	220	47	137	684	473	1102	117	49	.341	.422
Akron	.268	142	4736	654	1269	240	41	114	597	538	895	75	31	.344	.408
Trenton	.268	140	4711	642	1262	263	32	65	592	484	853	88	39	.339	.379
Portland	.267	140	4715	704	1258	284	27	112	672	577	994	54	24	.351	.410
Binghamton	.266	142	4729	619	1258	245	25	106	569	448	961	109	44	.333	.396
New Britain	.263	141	4770	626	1255	298	33	109	599	419	997	69	45	.327	.408
Harrisburg	.262	142	4632	691	1212	233	26	138	648	546	976	117	60	.342	.413
New Hampshire	.261	142	4705	640	1230	265	19	135	606	558	1003	33	30	.343	.412
Reading	.260	142	4811	644	1253	242	22	126	595	533	1038	88	31	.338	.398
Altoona	.255	142	4640	539	1182	221	35	88	499	397	876	117	57	.318	.374
Connecticut	.255	141	4679	620	1192	244	35	101	581	490	990	92	42	.330	.387

CLUB PITCHING

	ERA	G	CG	SHO	SV	IP	H	R	ER	HR	BB	SO	AVG
Trenton	3.13	140	3	16	35	1237	1064	498	430	94	489	1122	.233
Connecticut	3.44	141	1	13	39	1236	1200	561	472	81	432	907	.256
Bowie	3.54	142	5	6	37	1235	1128	558	485	98	470	1119	.243
Akron	3.95	142	1	10	43	1224	1206	603	533	110	389	997	.257
Binghamton	4.17	142	3	13	41	1242	1273	642	575	121	471	901	.266
Portland	4.29	140	0	7	35	1213	1185	648	579	92	507	1061	.255
Harrisburg	4.30	142	2	6	35	1228	1273	661	586	128	516	965	.269
Altoona	4.35	142	2	6	32	1215	1240	666	587	110	513	876	.265
Erie	4.59	142	6	7	33	1225	1321	728	625	130	489	763	.277
New Britain	4.71	141	1	4	40	1222	1353	711	640	133	520	975	.282
New Hampshire	5.00	142	6	5	32	1225	1414	755	681	118	561	881	.290
Reading	5.23	142	2	3	28	1232	1320	808	716	156	587	948	.273

CLUB FIELDING

	PCT	PO	A	E	DP
Akron	.978	3671	1338	111	129
Bowie	.978	3704	1332	113	125
New Britain	.977	3665	1266	115	143
New Hampshire	.977	3676	1555	123	151
Trenton	.977	3712	1407	122	146
Binghamton	.976	3726	1558	132	159

	PCT	PO	A	E	DP
Altoona	.975	3645	1498	134	138
Harrisburg	.975	3684	1470	134	143
Portland	.975	3640	1282	126	116
Connecticut	.973	3709	1522	144	155
Reading	.973	3697	1349	138	118
Erie	.969	3674	1549	168	171

INDIVIDUAL BATTING LEADERS *(MINIMUM 2.7 PLATE APPEARANCES PER LEAGUE GAME)*

	AVG	G	AB	R	H	2B	3B	HR	RBI	BB	SO	SB
Montanez, Lou, Bowie	.335	116	451	90	151	32	5	26	97	36	63	4
Marson, Lou, Reading	.314	94	322	55	101	18	0	5	46	68	70	3
Murphy, Daniel, Binghamton	.308	95	357	56	110	26	1	13	67	39	46	14
Daeges, Zachary, Portland	.307	108	394	63	121	34	3	6	63	72	72	3
Donald, Jason, Reading	.307	92	362	57	111	19	4	14	54	47	86	11
Rhymes, Will, Erie	.306	131	516	76	158	21	7	3	60	44	66	17
Frazier, Jeff, Erie	.303	116	446	55	135	22	1	6	55	31	51	1
Ramirez, Wilkin, Erie	.303	110	433	74	131	24	7	19	73	43	128	46
Campbell, Scott, New Hampshire	.302	112	417	70	126	21	2	9	46	66	63	2
Tolleson, Steven, New Britain	.300	93	343	54	103	28	1	9	50	44	74	12

INDIVIDUAL PITCHING LEADERS *(MINIMUM 0.8 INNINGS PITCHED PER LEAGUE GAME)*

	W	L	ERA	G	GS	CG	SV	IP	H	R	BB	SO
Martinez, Joseph, Connecticut	10	10	2.49	27	27	0	0	148	131	58	37	112
Coke, Phil, Trenton	9	4	2.51	23	20	1	0	118	105	39	39	115
Hernandez, David, Bowie	10	4	2.68	27	27	0	0	141	112	53	71	166
Niese, Jonathon, Binghamton	6	7	3.04	22	22	2	0	124	118	53	44	112
Tillman, Chris, Bowie	11	4	3.18	28	28	0	0	136	115	53	65	154
Bergesen, Bradley, Bowie	15	6	3.22	24	23	3	0	148	143	59	27	72
Jones, Jason, Trenton	13	7	3.33	25	25	1	0	149	146	64	49	91
Herrera, Yoslan, Altoona	6	9	3.46	21	21	0	0	114	114	51	36	69
Berken, Jason, Bowie	12	4	3.58	26	25	2	0	146	141	69	38	125
Johnson, Kris, Portland	8	9	3.63	27	27	0	0	136	147	70	56	108

ALL-STAR TEAM

C—Lou Marson, Reading. **1B**—Mike Carp, Binghamton. **2B**—Scott Campbell, New Hampshire. **3B**—Wes Hodges, Akron. **SS**—Jason Donald, Reading. **OF**—Lou Montanez, Bowie; Wilkin Ramirez, Erie; Nolan Reimold, Bowie; Travis Snider, New Hampshire. **Util**—Dan Murphy, Binghamton. **RHP**—Brad Bergesen, Bowie. **LHP**—Phil Coke, Trenton. **RP**—Eddie Kunz, Binghamton. **Most Valuable Player:** Lou Montanez, Bowie. **Pitcher of the Year:** Brad Bergesen, Bowie. **Rookie of the Year:** Wes Hodges, Akron. **Manager of the Year:** Brad Komminsk, Bowie.

DEPARTMENT LEADERS

BATTING

OBP	Marson, Lou, Reading	.433
SLG	Montanez, Lou, Bowie	.601
R	Montanez, Lou, Bowie	90
H	Rhymes, Will, Erie	158
TB	Montanez, Lou, Bowie	271
XBH	Montanez, Lou, Bowie	63
2B	Lis, Erik, New Britain	36
3B	Copeland, Ben, Connecticut	13
HR	Montanez, Lou, Bowie	26
RBI	Montanez, Lou, Bowie	97
	Hodges, Wes, Akron	97
SAC	Dorta, Melvin, Altoona	13
SF	Hodges, Wes, Akron	12
BB	Carp, Mike, Binghamton	79
IBB	Curtis, Colin, Trenton	9
HBP	Bates, Aaron, Portland	18
SO	Ramirez, Wilkin, Erie	138
	Harman, Brad, Reading	138
SB	Richardson, Antoan, Connecticut	33
CS	Dorta, Melvin, Altoona	14
AB/SO	Pilittere, P.J., Trenton	11.38

PITCHING

G	Harang, Daryl, New Hampshire	59
GS	Three players tied at	28
CG	Three players tied at	3
GF	Julianel, Ben, New Hampshire	53
SV	Manon, Julio, Bowie	32
W	Bergesen, Bradley, Bowie	15
L	Magee, Brandon, New Hampshire	13
IP	French, Lucas, Erie	170
H	French, Lucas, Erie	195
R	Magee, Brandon, New Hampshire	95
ER	Magee, Brandon, New Hampshire	86
HB	Christensen, Daniel, Erie	11
	Dixon, Kevin, Akron	11
BB	Hernandez, David, Bowie	71
SO	Hernandez, David, Bowie	166
SO/9 (SP)	Hernandez, David, Bowie	10.6
SO/9 (RP)	Romero, Felix, Bowie	11.69
BB/9	Edell, Ryan, Akron	1.31
WP	Asencio, Miguel, Portland	14
BK	Rodriguez, Kenny, New Hampshire	4
AVG	Hernandez, David, Bowie	.217

FIELDING

C	FPCT	Wagner, Mark, Portland	.997
	PO	Butera, Drew, New Britain	645
	A	Wagner, Mark, Portland	60
	E	Marson, Lou, Reading	9
	DP	Wagner, Mark, Portland	8
	PB	Manriquez, Salomon, Bing.	14
		Witter, Adam, Connecticut	14
1B	FPCT	Finan, Ryan, Bowie	.993
	PO	Delaney, Jason, Altoona	980
	A	Ehlers, Cody, Trenton	69
	E	Roberson, Ryan, Erie	13
	DP	Roberson, Ryan, Erie	126
2B	FPCT	Corona, Reegie, Trenton	.994
	PO	Rhymes, Will, Erie	236
	A	Campbell, Scott, New Hamp.	322
	E	Rhymes, Will, Erie	16
	DP	Rhymes, Will, Erie	86
3B	FPCT	Castro, Ofilio, Harrisburg	.965
	PO	Sellers, Neil, Reading	90
	A	Sellers, Neil, Reading	216
	E	Hodges, Wes, Akron	28
	DP	Two players tied at	18
SS	FPCT	Davis, Blake, Bowie	.960
	PO	Coronado, Jose, Binghamton	205
	A	Coronado, Jose, Binghamton	391
	E	Coronado, Jose, Binghamton	30
	DP	Coronado, Jose, Binghamton	100
OF	FPCT	Stewart, Caleb, Binghamton	1.000
	PO	Martin, Dustin, New Britain	316
	A	Concepcion, Ambiorix, Bing.	15
		Martin, Dustin, New Britain	15
	E	Concepcion, Ambiorix, Bing.	12
	DP	Copeland, Ben, Connecticut	8

MINOR LEAGUES

BY BEN BADLER

After a slow start, key roster additions and reshuffling helped push Mississippi to the Southern League championship.

The Braves finished 30-40 in the first half, but put together a 43-26 record to win the South Division's second-half title. Mississippi improved considerably with the promotion of righthander Tommy Hanson from high Class A Myrtle Beach. Hanson, 22, had a 3.08 ERA in 98 innings after his mid-May promotion, including a nine-inning, 14-strikeout no-hitter on June 25.

The rotation got another boost when the Braves plucked righthander Kris Medlen from the bullpen and inserted him into the rotation in June. In 17 starts, Medlen had a 3.11 ERA in 90 innings with 21 walks and 90 strikeouts. The offense got help from 22-year-old center fielder Jordan Schafer, who hit .303/.387/.526 after the all-star break. He was suspended 50 games for performance-enhancing drugs in the beginning of the season.

The steady force for Mississippi all season, though, was Todd Redmond, who won the SL's most outstanding pitcher award. Redmond, 23, walked only 33 batters in 166 innings.

After Carolina swept West Tenn and Mississippi swept Birmingham in the first round of the playoffs, the Mudcats took a 2-1 series lead over the Braves. The Braves didn't cave in Game Four, which lasted 13 innings before they scored in the bottom of the inning for a 6-5 victory. Game Five went to extra innings as well, when the Braves won in the 10th after the speedy J.C. Holt scored all the way from second a wild pitch and a throwing error.

While Double-A typically features the game's best prospects, this year's Southern League crop was especially talented. The circuit boasted Jacksonville's Clayton Kershaw and Montgomery's David Price, two of baseball's best lefthanded pitching prospects. Huntsville's lineup was led by high-profile prospects Matt LaPorta, Mat Gamel, Alcides Escobar and Angel Salome. The Stars' 733 runs were 52 more than the second-highest team total in the league, as they led the SL in both on-

base percentage and slugging.

Birmingham had a league-low 3.70 ERA, while Carolina finished second at 3.86. The young Mudcats rotation featured righthanders Chris Volstad (21), Ryan Tucker (21) and Brett Sinkbeil (23) and lefthander Aaron Thompson (21). Mudcats baseman Gaby Sanchez won the league MVP after hitting .314/.404/.513 with 42 doubles.

Montgomery cycled in some of the league's youngest and better pitching prospects, including Price, righthanders Wade Davis and Jeremy Hellickson and lefty Jake McGee.

TOP 20 PROSPECTS

1. Clayton Kershaw, lhp, Jacksonville (Dodgers)
2. David Price, lhp, Montgomery (Rays)
3. Cameron Maybin, of, Carolina (Marlins)
4. Matt LaPorta, of, Huntsville (Brewers)
5. Alcides Escobar, ss, Huntsville (Brewers)
6. Chris Volstad, rhp, Carolina (Marlins)
7. Mat Gamel, 3b, Huntsville (Brewers)
8. Michael Saunders, of, West Tenn (Mariners)
9. Tommy Hanson, rhp, Mississippi (Braves)
10. Wade Davis, rhp, Montgomery (Rays)
11. Chris Coghlan, 2b, Carolina (Marlins)
12. Jeremy Hellickson, rhp, Montgomery (Rays)
13. Jordan Schafer, of, Mississippi (Braves)
14. James McDonald, rhp, Jacksonville (Dodgers)
15. Ivan DeJesus, ss, Jacksonville (Dodgers)
16. Jake McGee, lhp, Montgomery (Rays)
17. Angel Salome, c, Huntsville (Brewers)
18. Michael Brantley, cf, Huntsville (Brewers)
19. Adam Moore, c, West Tenn (Mariners)
20. Luis Valbuena, 2b, West Tenn (Mariners)

STANDINGS: SPLIT SEASON

FIRST HALF

North	W	L	PCT	GB
West Tenn	41	29	.586	—
Huntsville	41	29	.586	—
Carolina	38	32	.543	3
Chattanooga	37	33	.529	4
Tennessee	27	43	.386	14

South	W	L	PCT	GB
Birmingham	40	30	.571	—
Montgomery	34	36	.486	6
Jacksonville	33	37	.471	7
Mississippi	30	40	.429	10
Mobile	29	41	.414	11

SECOND HALF

North	W	L	PCT	GB
Carolina	42	28	.600	—
Tennessee	35	34	.507	6½
Huntsville	32	38	.457	10
Chattanooga	30	39	.435	11½
West Tenn	29	39	.426	12

South	W	L	PCT	GB
Mississippi	43	26	.623	—
Birmingham	34	33	.507	8
Montgomery	35	34	.507	8
Jacksonville	35	35	.500	8½
Mobile	29	38	.433	13

PLAYOFFS—Semifinals: Mississippi defeated Birmingham 3-0 and Carolina defeated West Tenn 3-0 in best-of-five series. **Finals:** Mississippi defeated Carolina 3-2 in a best-of-five series.

OVERALL STANDINGS

Page	Team	W	L	.PCT	GB	Manager	Attendance	Average	Last Penn.
142	Carolina Mudcats (Marlins)	80	60	.571	—	Matt Raleigh	281,012	4,073	2003
194	Birmingham Barons (White Sox)	74	63	.540	4½	Carlos Subero	302,012	4,456	2002
56	Mississippi Braves (Braves)	73	66	.525	6½	Phillip Wellman	212,107	3,166	2008
187	Huntsville Stars (Brewers)	73	67	.521	7	Don Money	160,080	2,389	2001
285	West Tenn Diamond Jaxx (Mariners)	70	68	.507	9	Scott Steinmann	140,445	2,096	2000
296	Montgomery Biscuits (Rays)	69	70	.496	10½	Billy Gardner	292,181	4,495	2007
178	Jacksonville Suns (Dodgers)	68	72	.486	12	John Shoemaker	364,365	5,438	2005
104	Chattanooga Lookouts (Reds)	67	72	.482	12½	Mike Goff	236,639	3,480	1988
84	Tennessee Smokies (Cubs)	62	77	.446	17½	Buddy Bailey	250,209	3,680	2004
47	Mobile BayBears (Diamondbacks)	58	79	.423	20½	Hector De La Cruz	232,235	3,466	2004

CLUB BATTING

	AVG	G	AB	R	H	2B	3B	HR	RBI	BB	SO	SB	CS	OBP	SLG
Huntsville	.285	140	4760	733	1358	269	36	119	669	447	933	127	43	.352	.432
Chattanooga	.269	139	4679	681	1258	273	29	115	630	469	993	88	50	.340	.413
West Tenn	.266	138	4551	671	1210	273	34	126	621	512	1028	86	47	.348	.424
Jacksonville	.265	140	4720	646	1249	239	22	94	587	541	951	128	39	.345	.384
Montgomery	.263	139	4666	671	1225	239	37	104	616	586	949	74	39	.350	.394
Tennessee	.262	139	4689	659	1228	251	34	100	603	521	968	66	38	.341	.394
Carolina	.260	140	4565	664	1188	270	35	104	603	573	1063	175	76	.348	.403
Birmingham	.259	137	4562	602	1182	230	34	110	540	427	869	111	69	.327	.397
Mississippi	.255	139	4559	628	1163	210	52	88	582	520	974	120	63	.338	.382
Mobile	.255	137	4501	557	1147	240	23	85	506	444	874	64	63	.330	.375

CLUB PITCHING

	ERA	G	CG	SHO	SV	IP	H	R	ER	HR	BB	SO	AVG
Birmingham	3.72	137	2	12	43	1209	1183	570	497	62	470	910	.260
Carolina	3.86	140	3	10	43	1221	1184	607	523	85	481	968	.257
Huntsville	3.97	140	7	9	41	1223	1189	618	539	118	519	874	.259
Mississippi	4.28	139	1	12	42	1208	1204	643	574	89	486	1032	.262
Montgomery	4.29	139	1	4	37	1219	1231	668	579	117	528	977	.264
Mobile	4.30	137	3	6	33	1181	1237	635	564	119	437	907	.272
Chattanooga	4.32	139	2	8	35	1213	1243	685	582	102	499	1063	.266
Jacksonville	4.35	140	1	6	38	1234	1227	688	596	116	554	981	.260
West Tenn	4.35	138	4	7	31	1199	1239	680	578	84	515	944	.269
Tennessee	4.65	139	0	6	30	1224	1271	718	633	153	551	946	.270

CLUB FIELDING

	PCT	PO	A	E	DP		PCT	PO	A	E	DP
Mississippi	.980	3625	1278	101	111	Carolina	.975	3662	1475	134	129
Birmingham	.978	3626	1523	114	164	Montgomery	.975	3656	1437	133	130
Mobile	.978	3542	1382	112	132	Tennessee	.974	3673	1431	134	131
Huntsville	.976	3669	1562	127	136	Chattanooga	.971	3639	1352	150	115
Jacksonville	.976	3702	1365	124	123	West Tenn	.971	3596	1428	151	132

INDIVIDUAL BATTING LEADERS (MINIMUM 2.7 PLATE APPEARANCES PER LEAGUE GAME)

	AVG	G	AB	R	H	2B	3B	HR	RBI	BB	SO	SB
Salome, Angel, Huntsville	.360	98	367	67	132	30	2	13	83	33	57	3
Gamel, Mat, Huntsville	.329	127	508	96	167	35	7	19	96	55	111	6
Escobar, Alcides, Huntsville	.328	131	546	95	179	24	5	8	76	31	82	34
Deeds, Doug, Tennessee	.325	122	416	73	135	37	3	12	58	43	100	8
De Jesus, Ivan, Jacksonville	.324	128	463	91	150	21	2	7	58	76	81	16
Moore, Adam, West Tenn	.319	119	429	60	137	34	2	14	71	40	77	0
Brantley, Michael, Huntsville	.319	106	420	80	134	17	2	4	40	50	27	28
Mayorson, Manuel, Carolina	.319	108	373	47	119	31	1	1	39	29	20	21
Sanchez, Gaby, Carolina	.314	133	478	70	150	42	1	17	92	69	70	17
Tomlin, James, Jacksonville	.313	108	383	59	120	31	2	2	35	36	47	14

INDIVIDUAL PITCHING LEADERS (MINIMUM 0.8 INNINGS PITCHED PER LEAGUE GAME)

	W	L	ERA	G	GS	CG	SV	IP	H	R	BB	SO
Cassel, Justin, Birmingham	10	4	3.11	28	28	0	0	165	171	76	57	104
McDonald, James, Jacksonville	5	3	3.19	22	22	0	0	119	98	47	46	113
Castillo, Jesus, Jacksonville	7	4	3.24	23	23	0	0	114	123	51	33	76
Lecure, Sam, Chattanooga	9	7	3.42	27	27	0	0	155	147	61	58	128
Redmond, Todd, Mississippi	13	5	3.52	28	27	0	0	166	164	72	33	133
Medlen, Kris, Mississippi	7	8	3.52	36	17	0	1	120	121	47	27	120
Wright, Brae, Huntsville	6	10	3.59	27	27	0	0	171	164	80	60	120
Jukich, Ben, Chattanooga	10	4	3.82	23	23	1	0	139	147	68	54	111
Barnette, Tony, Mobile	11	7	3.87	27	27	0	0	154	143	70	42	133
Welch, David, Huntsville	11	4	3.90	27	27	1	0	148	145	69	51	95

ALL-STAR TEAM

C—Angel Salome, Huntsville. 1B—Gaby Sanchez, Carolina. 2B—Chris Coghlan, Carolina. 3B—Mat Gamel, Huntsville. SS—Alcides Escobar, Huntsville. OF—Michael Brantley, Huntsville; Doug Deeds, Tennessee; John Raynor, Carolina. DH—Jake Fox, Tennessee. SP—David Price, Montgomery. RP—Jon Link, Birmingham. Most Valuable Player: Gaby Sanchez, Carolina. Pitcher of the Year: Todd Redmond, Mississippi. Manager of the Year: Phillip Wellman, Mississippi.

DEPARTMENT LEADERS

BATTING

OBP	De Jesus, Ivan, Jacksonville	.419
SLG	Fox, Jake, Tennessee	.580
R	Raynor, John, Carolina	104
H	Escobar, Alcides, Huntsville	179
TB	Gamel, Mat, Huntsville	273
XBH	Gamel, Mat, Huntsville	61
2B	Sanchez, Gaby, Carolina	42
3B	Young, Matt, Mississippi	11
	Colvin, Tyler, Tennessee	11
HR	Wilson, Michael, West Tenn	27
RBI	Gamel, Mat, Huntsville	96
SAC	Spears, Nate, Tennessee	19
SF	Colvin, Tyler, Tennessee	9
BB	Ka'aihue, Kala, Mississippi	88
IBB	Gamel, Mat, Huntsville	5
	Brantley, Michael, Huntsville	5
HBP	Burgess, Brandon, Mobile	18
SO	Maybin, Cameron, Carolina	124
SB	Raynor, John, Carolina	48
CS	Negron, Miguel, Birmingham	16
AB/SO	Mayorson, Manuel, Carolina	18.65

PITCHING

G	Deago, Roger, Montgomery	59
	Torres, Joseph, Birmingham	59
GS	Veal, Donald, Tennessee	29
CG	Four players tied at	2
GF	Link, Jon, Birmingham	49
SV	Link, Jon, Birmingham	35
W	Redmond, Todd, Mississippi	13
L	Brown, Brooks, Mobile	15
IP	Wright, Brae, Huntsville	170.2
H	McCulloch, Kyle, Birmingham	188
R	Fister, Doug, West Tenn	95
ER	Ambriz, Hector, Mobile	83
HB	Howard, Adam, Mobile	12
	Downs, Brodie, West Tenn	12
BB	Veal, Donald, Tennessee	81
SO	Redmond, Todd, Mississippi	133
	Barnette, Tony, Mobile	133
SO/9 (SP)	McDonald, James, Jacksonville	8.57
SO/9 (RP)	Mobley, Chris, Carolina	10.8
BB/9	Redmond, Todd, Mississippi	1.79
WP	Veal, Donald, Tennessee	18
BK	Houser, James, Montgomery	3
	Thomas, Justin, West Tenn	3
AVG	McDonald, James, Jacksonville	.227

FIELDING

F-C	FPCT	Boscan, J.C., Mississippi	.997
	PO	Moore, Adam, West Tenn	711
	A	Moore, Adam, West Tenn	87
	E	Jaso, John, Montgomery	12
	DP	Tatum, Craig, Chattanooga	11
	PB	May, Lucas, Jacksonville	24
1B	FPCT	Gutierrez, Tonys, Chattanooga	.990
	PO	Errecart, Chris, Huntsville	861
	A	Gutierrez, Tonys, Chattanooga	96
	E	Hughes, Rhyne, Montgomery	12
	DP	Byrne, Bryan, Mobile	95
2B	FPCT	Ryal, Rusty, Mobile	.984
	PO	Spears, Nate, Tennessee	238
	A	Bell, Mike, Huntsville	333
	E	Bell, Mike, Huntsville	23
	DP	Coghlan, Chris, Carolina	79
3B	FPCT	Pope, Van, Mississippi	.949
	PO	Gamel, Mat, Huntsville	89
	A	Gamel, Mat, Huntsville	245
	E	Gamel, Mat, Huntsville	30
	DP	Gamel, Mat, Huntsville	27
SS	FPCT	Merrill, Ronnie, Montgomery	.974
	PO	Escobar, Alcides, Huntsville	231
	A	Escobar, Alcides, Huntsville	429
	E	Valido, Robert, Birmingham	27
	DP	Escobar, Alcides, Huntsville	94
OF	FPCT	Tomlin, James, Jacksonville	.995
	PO	Godwin, Adam, Jacksonville	300
	A	Wilson, Michael, West Tenn	14
	E	Gartrell, Stefan, Birmingham	10
	DP	Four players tied at	4

MINOR LEAGUES

BY KARY BOOHER

When Arkansas stunned prospect-laden Frisco and won the Texas League championship in the deciding fifth and final game, the victory was more than the usual historical footnote. The Travelers finished the regular season with the lowest win total, 62-78, by a Texas League champion since Corsicana finished 50-51 in 1904. It also marked the third time this decade, second by an Arkansas club, that a TL champion had compiled a sub-.500 regular season record.

Overall, it was a snapshot of the entire Texas League season as the circuit wasn't blessed with can't-miss prospects but rather a bundle of intriguing talents fanned out across both divisions.

Tulsa center fielder Dexter Fowler was by far the most exciting player before heading off to play for Team USA in the Olympics and a late-season callup to the Rockies. Hampered by injuries the past two seasons, his potential finally connected to success as the 22-year-old switch-hitter finished among the league leaders in several offensive categories. His .431 on-base percentage second only to league MVP first baseman Kila Kaaihue.

Frisco proved to be the class of the league as it finished 84-56 and led the minors with 184 steals, 53 by 19-year-old shortstop Elvis Andrus. The Rangers affiliate sent 14 players to the majors, six that were core pieces of a team that ranked second in average, home runs and runs scored. Frisco first baseman Chris Davis was among the first-half stars as he hit 13 home runs and drove in 43 in just 186 at-bats before moving on, and the Riders fortified their lineup after the all-star break with the addition of center fielder Julio Borbon.

Springfield featured arguably the most prospects in the North Division and nearly overcame a 1-9 start and then 10-game losing streak in May before Arkansas won the first half. A big push came from righthander Jess Todd, a second-round pick from Arkansas in 2007 who struck out 81 in 103 innings. He was among a crop of young arms that once again ratcheted up the league's image as a proving ground/launching pad to the majors.

Three 21-year-old righthanders in Midland's

STANDINGS: SPLIT SEASON

FIRST HALF

North	W	L	PCT	GB
Arkansas	36	34	.514	—
Springfield	36	34	.514	—
NW Arkansas	33	37	.471	3
Tulsa	29	41	.414	7

South	W	L	PCT	GB
Frisco	43	27	.614	—
San Antonio	39	31	.557	4
Midland	34	36	.486	9
Corpus Christi	30	40	.429	13

SECOND HALF

North	W	L	PCT	GB
NW Arkansas	42	28	.600	—
Springfield	40	30	.571	2
Tulsa	29	41	.414	13
Arkansas	26	44	.371	16

South	W	L	PCT	GB
Frisco	41	29	.586	—
Midland	41	29	.586	—
San Antonio	36	34	.514	5
Corpus Christi	25	45	.357	16

PLAYOFFS—Semifinals: Frisco defeated San Antonio 3-0 and Arkansas defeated NW Arkansas 3-0 in best-of-five series.
Finals: Arkansas defeated Frisco 3-2 in a best-of-five series.

Vin Mazzaro and James Simmons and Northwest Arkansas' Dan Cortes were rated among the league's Top 20 prospects, with Mazzaro tops in ERA (1.90) and wins (12).

The Travelers finished with only the sixth-best ERA (4.50) and owned the league's worst team batting average (.259). However, the Travelers had a number of success stories. Righthander Anthony Ortega finished 9-7, 3.73, the sixth-best ERA, while righthander Dan Denham had the ninth-best ERA (4.44). The Angels affiliate was bolstered by the late additions of DH Hank Conger and first baseman Mark Trumbo, with Conger supplying 13 RBIs in the playoffs.

OVERALL STANDINGS

Page	Team	W	L	.PCT	GB	Manager	Attendance	Average	Last Penn.
305	Frisco RoughRiders (Rangers)	84	56	.600	—	Scott Little	562,166	8,147	2004
256	Springfield Cardinals (Cardinals)	76	64	.543	8	Ron Warner	461,020	6,681	1994
160	Northwest Arkansas Naturals (Royals)	75	65	.536	9	Brian Poldberg	358,792	5,200	1999
225	Midland RockHounds (Athletics)	75	65	.536	9	Webster Garrison	292,563	4,240	2005
267	San Antonio Missions (Padres)	75	65	.536	9	Bill Masse	300,267	4,352	2007
169	Arkansas Travelers (Angels)	62	78	.443	22	Bobby Magallanes	377,997	5,559	2008
123	Tulsa Drillers (Rockies)	58	82	.414	26	Stu Cole	297,409	4,439	1998
151	Corpus Christi Hooks (Astros)	55	85	.393	29	Luis Pujols	479,651	6,852	2006

CLUB BATTING

	AVG	G	AB	R	H	2B	3B	HR	RBI	BB	SO	SB	CS	OBP	SLG
Tulsa	.279	140	4899	713	1368	246	25	119	661	518	1023	158	69	.355	.413
Frisco	.277	140	4768	758	1319	274	36	129	683	480	1072	185	60	.348	.430
Midland	.275	140	4862	759	1339	260	33	127	716	556	1134	107	42	.353	.421
Springfield	.275	140	4873	681	1341	242	32	133	634	416	1022	78	38	.339	.420
Corpus Christi	.271	140	4821	659	1307	263	34	114	620	457	925	116	44	.338	.411
San Antonio	.269	140	4763	672	1283	266	28	99	622	586	866	61	33	.354	.399
NW Arkansas	.262	140	4677	640	1224	208	24	122	594	500	860	167	85	.337	.395
Arkansas	.259	140	4744	601	1227	225	28	128	556	352	896	131	73	.321	.399

CLUB PITCHING

	ERA	G	CG	SHO	SV	IP	H	R	ER	HR	BB	SO	AVG
San Antonio	3.58	140	3	20	39	1249	1212	574	497	100	439	1152	.255
NW Arkansas	4.15	140	2	11	47	1248	1270	628	576	129	396	989	.267
Springfield	4.17	140	2	7	43	1262	1276	667	585	143	494	1032	.264
Frisco	4.34	140	3	9	40	1241	1257	674	598	93	537	926	.265
Midland	4.40	140	0	9	38	1252	1300	706	611	107	574	1053	.271
Arkansas	4.50	140	4	4	33	1243	1324	706	621	103	513	912	.277
Tulsa	4.62	140	2	7	25	1251	1359	759	642	149	449	819	.280
Corpus Christi	5.12	140	0	4	21	1233	1410	769	701	147	463	915	.290

CLUB FIELDING

	PCT	PO	A	E	DP		PCT	PO	A	E	DP
NW Arkansas	.979	3744	1526	111	145	Corpus Christi	.975	3698	1486	132	164
San Antonio	.979	3746	1388	110	108	Frisco	.975	3724	1481	136	156
Arkansas	.976	3730	1597	130	150	Midland	.974	3757	1541	142	159
Springfield	.976	3785	1527	131	133	Tulsa	.969	3753	1675	176	161

INDIVIDUAL BATTING LEADERS (MINIMUM 2.7 PLATE APPEARANCES PER LEAGUE GAME)

	AVG	G	AB	R	H	2B	3B	HR	RBI	BB	SO	SB
Guzman, Jesus, Midland	.364	80	341	57	124	21	2	14	76	33	56	5
Miller, Matt, Tulsa	.344	106	407	72	140	21	0	10	87	44	45	4
Fowler, Dexter, Tulsa	.335	108	421	92	141	31	9	9	64	65	89	20
Blanks, Kyle, San Antonio	.325	132	492	75	160	23	5	20	107	51	90	5
Blanco, Tony, Tulsa	.323	103	390	59	126	34	0	23	88	31	74	6
Sutton, Drew, Corpus Christi	.317	133	520	102	165	39	4	20	69	76	98	20
Cunningham, Aaron, Midland	.317	87	347	65	110	18	6	12	52	38	92	12
Jay, Jon, Springfield	.306	96	372	57	114	17	3	11	47	39	64	9
Craig, Allen, Springfield	.304	129	506	84	154	30	0	22	85	48	87	2
Shorey, Mark, Springfield	.304	114	388	49	118	28	2	11	66	29	110	1

INDIVIDUAL PITCHING LEADERS (MINIMUM 0.8 INNINGS PITCHED PER LEAGUE GAME)

	W	L	ERA	G	GS	CG	SV	IP	H	R	BB	SO
Mazzaro, Vincent, Midland	12	3	1.90	22	22	0	0	137	115	40	36	104
Buschmann, Matthew, San Antonio	10	6	2.98	27	27	1	0	148	137	60	58	118
Simmons, James, Midland	9	6	3.51	25	25	0	0	136	150	58	32	120
Inman, William, San Antonio	9	8	3.52	28	28	2	0	135	119	67	71	140
Ortega, Anthony, Arkansas	9	7	3.73	22	22	1	0	135	124	65	49	83
Cortes, Dan, NW Arkansas	10	4	3.78	23	23	0	0	117	103	51	55	109
Garrison, Steve, San Antonio	7	7	3.82	24	24	0	0	130	123	59	37	108
Faris, Stephen, San Antonio	8	5	3.85	26	26	0	0	138	145	66	39	102
Hynick, Brandon, Tulsa	10	7	4.44	27	27	0	0	172	183	93	31	97
Denham, Dan, Arkansas	9	10	4.44	25	25	0	0	146	157	82	58	99

ALL-STAR TEAM

C—Ben Johnson, Arkansas. **1B**—Kila Ka'aihue, Northwest Arkansas. **2B**—Drew Sutton, Corpus Christi. **3B**—Allen Craig, Springfield. **SS**—Elvis Andrus, Frisco. **OF**—Aaron Cunningham, Midland; Dexter Fowler, Tulsa; Matt Miller, Tulsa. **DH**—Kyle Blanks, San Antonio; Tommy Everidge, Midland. **SP**—Matt Buschmann, San Antonio; Dan Cortes, Northwest Arkansas; Will Inman, San Antonio; Vincent Mazzaro, Midland; James Simmons, Midland; Jess Todd, Springfield. **RP**—Fernando Salas, Springfield. **Player of the Year:** Kila Ka'aihue, Northwest Arkansas . **Pitcher of the Year:** Vincent Mazzaro, Midland. **Manager of the Year:** Scott Little, Frisco.

DEPARTMENT LEADERS

BATTING

OBP	Ka'aihue, Kila, NW Arkansas	.463
SLG	Ka'aihue, Kila, NW Arkansas	.624
R	Sutton, Drew, Corpus Christi	102
H	Sutton, Drew, Corpus Christi	165
TB	Sutton, Drew, Corpus Christi	272
XBH	Murphy, Steven, Frisco	64
2B	Sutton, Drew, Corpus Christi	39
3B	Fowler, Dexter, Tulsa	9
	Murphy, Steven, Frisco	9
HR	Smith, Corey, Arkansas	26
	Ka'aihue, Kila, NW Arkansas	26
RBI	Everidge, Tommy, Midland	115
SAC	Statia, Hainley, Arkansas	12
SF	Everidge, Tommy, Midland	14
BB	Macias, Drew, San Antonio	83
IBB	Ka'aihue, Kila, NW Arkansas	7
HBP	Collins, Michael, Arkansas	21
SO	Recker, Anthony, Midland	140
SB	Wimberly, Corey, Tulsa	59
CS	Four players tied at	16
AB/SO	Falu, Irving, NW Arkansas	11.68

PITCHING

G	DeHoyos, Gabe, San Antonio	60
	Salas, Fernando, Springfield	60
GS	Mosebach, Robert, Arkansas	29
CG	Three players tied at	2
GF	Carignan, Andrew, Midland	42
SV	Salas, Fernando, Springfield	25
W	Mazzaro, Vincent, Midland	12
L	Johnson, Alan, Tulsa	14
IP	Mosebach, Robert, Arkansas	177.1
H	Johnson, Alan, Tulsa	217
R	Johnson, Alan, Tulsa	121
ER	Johnson, Alan, Tulsa	102
HB	Hardy, Rowdy, NW Arkansas	20
BB	Inman, William, San Antonio	71
SO	Inman, William, San Antonio	140
SO/9 (SP)	Inman, William, San Antonio	9.31
SO/9 (RP)	Salas, Fernando, Springfield	12.16
BB/9	Hynick, Brandon, Tulsa	1.62
WP	Three players tied at	16
BK	Inman, William, San Antonio	4
AVG	Mazzaro, Vincent, Midland	.229

FIELDING

C	FPCT	Lobaton, Jose, San Antonio	.995
	PO	Recker, Anthony, Midland	861
	A	Donachie, Adam, NW Arkansas	84
	E	Yarbrough, Brandon, Springfield	13
		Recker, Anthony, Midland	13
	DP	Donachie, Adam, NW Arkansas	9
		Johnson, Ben, Arkansas	9
	PB	Recker, Anthony, Midland	20
1B	FPCT	Blanks, Kyle, San Antonio	.993
	PO	Kindel, Jeff, Tulsa	1206
	A	Kindel, Jeff, Tulsa	87
	E	Kindel, Jeff, Tulsa	10
	DP	Kindel, Jeff, Tulsa	124
2B	FPCT	Martinez, Jose, Springfield	.986
	PO	Young, Eric, Tulsa	231
		Maddox, Marc, NW Arkansas	231
	A	Maddox, Marc, NW Arkansas	340
	E	Sutton, Drew, Corpus Christi	16
	DP	Maddox, Marc, NW Arkansas	89
3B	FPCT	Craig, Allen, Springfield	.941
	PO	Johnston, Seth, San Antonio	69
	A	Craig, Allen, Springfield	217
	E	Blanco, Tony, Tulsa	29
	DP	Smith, Corey, Arkansas	18
		Fox, Adam, Frisco	18
SS	FPCT	Kazmar, Sean, San Antonio	.964
	PO	Andrus, Elvis, Frisco	181
	A	Andrus, Elvis, Frisco	361
	E	Andrus, Elvis, Frisco	32
	DP	Andrus, Elvis, Frisco	79
OF	FPCT	Jay, Jon, Springfield	1.000
	PO	Duarte, Jose, NW Arkansas	330
	A	Duarte, Jose, NW Arkansas	18
	E	Einertson, Mitch, Corpus Christi	8
		Murphy, Steven, Frisco	8
	DP	Duarte, Jose, NW Arkansas	7

MINOR LEAGUES

BY WILL LINGO

It doesn't always (or even often) happen in the minor leagues, but in the California League in 2008, the most talented team in the league also ended up winning the league championship.

The Stockton Ports won their 11th California League title, and their first since 2002, behind a strong group of prospects from the Athletics organization. Five of those prospects ended up on the league's Top 20 Prospects list, and several others could have major league futures, such as outfielders Corey Brown and Matt Sulentic.

The team's two best prospects were pitchers Trevor Cahill and Brett Anderson, both of whom also pitched for Team USA in the Beijing Olympics and both of whom had long since moved up to Double-A by the time the Cal League playoffs rolled around.

The Ports had plenty of offense to make up for it, however. In the playoff clincher, third baseman Chris Carter hit a grand slam and a solo homer as Stockton beat Lancaster 9-3 to win the best-of-five championship series three games to one. Carter hit five home runs during the playoffs, on top of the 39 he hit during the regular season to lead the league. Carter led in several other offensive categories as well, including RBIs (104) and slugging percentage (.569).

The league's player of the year, however, was Inland Empire catcher Carlos Santana, who dominated for 99 games before getting traded from the Dodgers to the Indians. Santana batted .323/.431/.563 for the 66ers before getting traded, finishing second in the league batting race and leading the league in on-base percentage.

League ERA leader Tim Alderson, who finished with a 13-4, 2.79 mark for San Jose, was the league's pitcher of the year, establishing himself as one of the best prospects in the Giants organization in his first full professional season.

San Jose did not have as much potential major league talent as Stockton, but finished with the league's best overall record thanks to a deep pitching staff that also featured Jesse English, Clayton Tanner and Kevin Pucetas, who was selected as the league's pitcher of the year after finishing the season 10-2, 3.02.

After the season, the league saw one affiliation change, with the Red Sox leaving Lancaster and getting replaced there by the Astros.

The Visalia Oaks also will have a new look for 2009, with the team changing its name to the Rawhide. The team will also unveil significant renovations to Recreation Ballpark as well.

TOP 20 PROSPECTS

1. Trevor Cahill, rhp, Stockton (Athletics)
2. Carlos Santana, c, Inland Empire (Dodgers)
3. Lars Anderson, 1b, Lancaster (Red Sox)
4. Brett Anderson, lhp, Stockton (Athletics)
5. Jhoulys Chacin, rhp, Modesto (Rockies)
6. Tim Alderson, rhp, San Jose (Giants)
7. Pablo Sandoval, c, San Jose (Giants)
8. Josh Reddick, of, Lancaster (Red Sox)
9. Henry Rodriguez, rhp, Stockton (Athletics)
10. Cedric Hunter, of, Lake Elsinore (Padres)
11. Julio Borbon, of, Bakersfield (Rangers)
12. Jordan Walden, rhp, Rancho Cucamonga (Angels)
13. Greg Halman, of, High Desert (Mariners)
14. Chris Carter, 1b, Stockton (Athletics)
15. Carlos Triunfel, ss, High Desert (Mariners)
16. Sean Doolittle, 1b, Stockton (Athletics)
17. Peter Bourjos, of, Rancho Cucamonga (Angels)
18. Sean O'Sullivan, rhp, Rancho Cucamonga (Angels)
19. Josh Donaldson, c, Stockton (Athletics)
20. Kellen Kulbacki, of, Lake Elsinore (Padres)

STANDINGS: SPLIT SEASON

FIRST HALF

North	W	L	PCT	GB
San Jose	43	27	.614	—
Stockton	42	28	.600	1
Bakersfield	36	34	.514	7
Modesto	34	36	.486	9
Visalia	34	36	.486	9

South	W	L	PCT	GB
Lancaster	36	34	.514	—
High Desert	32	38	.457	4
Lake Elsinore	32	38	.457	4
Inland Empire	31	39	.443	5
R. Cucamonga	30	40	.429	6

SECOND HALF

North	W	L	PCT	GB
San Jose	42	28	.600	—
Modesto	36	33	.522	5½
Stockton	34	36	.486	8
Visalia	33	36	.478	8½
Bakersfield	26	44	.371	16

South	W	L	PCT	GB
Lancaster	40	30	.571	—
Lake Elsinore	39	31	.557	1
Inland Empire	38	34	.528	3
R. Cucamonga	37	35	.514	4
High Desert	26	44	.371	14

PLAYOFFS—Division Series: Lake Elsinore defeated Inland Empire 2-0 and Stockton defeated Modesto 2-1 in best-of-three series. **Semifinals:** Lancaster defeated Lake Elsinore 3-2 and Stockton defeated San Jose 3-2 in best-of-five series. **Finals:** Stockton defeated Lancaster 3-1 in a best-of-five series.

OVERALL STANDINGS

Page	Team	W	L	PCT	GB	Manager	Attendance	Average	Last Penn.
277	San Jose Giants (Giants)	85	55	.607	—	Steve Decker	183,788	2,626	2007
76	Lancaster JetHawks (Red Sox)	76	64	.543	9	Chad Epperson	124,934	1,865	None
226	Stockton Ports (Athletics)	76	64	.543	9	Darren Bush	214,080	3,058	2008
268	Lake Elsinore Storm (Padres)	71	69	.507	14	Carlos Lezcano	224,069	3,344	2001
124	Modesto Nuts (Rockies)	70	69	.504	14½	Jerry Weinstein	164,306	2,347	2004
179	Inland Empire 66ers (Dodgers)	68	73	.482	17½	John Valentin	183,845	2,589	2006
47	Visalia Oaks (Diamondbacks)	67	72	.482	17½	Mike Bell	67,045	972	1978
170	Rancho Cucamonga Quakes (Angels)	67	74	.475	18½	Ever Magallanes	286,290	4,090	1994
306	Bakersfield Blaze (Rangers)	62	78	.443	23	Damon Berryhill	67,377	963	1989
286	High Desert Mavericks (Mariners)	58	82	.414	27	Jim Horner	117,594	1,704	1997

CLUB BATTING

	AVG	G	AB	R	H	2B	3B	HR	RBI	BB	SO	SB	CS	OBP	SLG
Lancaster	.285	140	4992	796	1423	274	49	154	737	465	1107	58	21	.352	.452
Lake Elsinore	.278	140	4965	819	1380	286	27	106	744	599	815	106	41	.359	.410
San Jose	.278	140	4811	736	1337	262	23	106	665	439	999	205	76	.345	.408
R. Cucamonga	.277	141	4817	703	1332	264	55	129	647	379	1044	192	64	.333	.435
Inland Empire	.275	141	4887	777	1346	301	59	95	707	520	1087	135	70	.347	.419
Stockton	.275	140	4905	742	1349	266	38	149	681	466	1079	103	52	.343	.436
Bakersfield	.269	140	4899	668	1318	281	18	96	611	427	1058	130	36	.333	.393
High Desert	.268	140	4843	728	1299	272	37	111	661	334	1051	198	66	.321	.408
Modesto	.264	139	4762	645	1257	274	41	85	578	451	1157	146	63	.335	.392
Visalia	.259	139	4753	623	1233	232	34	72	573	430	994	118	59	.327	.368

CLUB PITCHING

	ERA	G	CG	SHO	SV	IP	H	R	ER	HR	BB	SO	AVG
San Jose	3.26	140	0	12	41	1247	1171	531	451	70	433	1128	.249
Modesto	3.96	139	3	9	36	1240	1267	633	545	90	376	968	.266
Visalia	4.14	139	2	7	36	1234	1330	654	568	125	334	1040	.274
Stockton	4.27	140	0	8	43	1254	1230	707	594	107	553	1259	.255
Bakersfield	4.49	140	1	4	30	1242	1297	755	621	123	461	1097	.268
Lancaster	4.54	140	0	6	29	1242	1391	740	627	109	331	964	.281
Lake Elsinore	4.72	140	0	1	30	1253	1385	747	656	114	382	949	.280
Rancho Cucamonga	4.89	141	3	7	36	1233	1345	767	670	100	500	929	.279
Inland Empire	4.96	141	0	10	35	1267	1375	787	698	95	565	1072	.277
High Desert	5.88	140	0	1	24	1226	1483	917	796	170	575	985	.299

CLUB FIELDING

	PCT	PO	A	E	DP		PCT	PO	A	E	DP
San Jose	.974	3741	1488	138	119	Stockton	.970	3761	1351	160	120
Inland Empire	.972	3801	1382	152	135	Visalia	.969	3703	1483	165	119
Lake Elsinore	.972	3820	1492	152	104	Bakersfield	.968	3727	1384	171	111
Modesto	.971	3717	1434	153	118	Lancaster	.968	3725	1572	177	131
R. Cucamonga	.971	3698	1567	156	131	High Desert	.964	3677	1422	193	117

INDIVIDUAL BATTING LEADERS (MINIMUM 2.7 PLATE APPEARANCES PER LEAGUE GAME)

	AVG	G	AB	R	H	2B	3B	HR	RBI	BB	SO	SB
Nava, Daniel, Lancaster	.341	85	323	54	110	27	1	10	59	43	70	4
Santana, Carlos, Inland Empire	.323	99	350	88	113	34	4	14	96	69	59	7
Hunter, Cedric, Lake Elsinore	.318	134	584	98	186	33	3	11	84	42	47	12
Nieves, Abel, Rancho Cucamonga	.318	101	336	46	107	24	2	4	54	53	74	4
Locke, Andrew, Inland Empire	.311	122	470	81	146	37	4	11	85	42	86	5
Paulk, Mike, Modesto	.310	132	510	81	158	28	3	8	66	63	79	8
Ciriaco, Pedro, Visalia	.310	124	520	85	161	26	5	5	61	18	89	40
Sulentic, Matthew, Stockton	.309	95	343	52	106	24	4	9	55	30	91	7
Sogard, Eric, Lake Elsinore	.308	133	536	97	165	42	3	10	87	79	62	16
Doolittle, Sean, Stockton	.305	86	334	64	102	25	3	18	61	46	99	7

INDIVIDUAL PITCHING LEADERS (MINIMUM 0.8 INNINGS PITCHED PER LEAGUE GAME)

	W	L	ERA	G	GS	CG	SV	IP	H	R	BB	SO
Alderson, Tim, San Jose	13	4	2.79	26	26	0	0	145	125	48	34	124
Pucetas, Kevin, San Jose	10	2	3.02	24	24	0	0	125	115	46	27	102
Weiser, Keith, Modesto	7	10	3.05	22	22	1	0	145	146	59	19	75
English, Jesse, San Jose	13	7	3.19	26	26	0	0	135	121	57	51	135
Maxwell, Blake, Lancaster	5	9	3.32	37	15	0	1	133	138	62	19	67
Tanner, Clayton, San Jose	10	8	3.69	24	24	0	0	117	124	61	39	84
Rodriguez, Aneury, Modesto	9	10	3.74	27	27	2	0	156	148	78	40	139
Culp, Nathan, Lake Elsinore	14	8	3.83	27	26	0	0	157	189	83	23	74
Rogers, Esmil, Modesto	9	7	3.95	25	25	0	0	144	146	73	45	116
Frieri, Ernesto, Lake Elsinore	8	6	4.00	33	18	0	0	124	125	61	32	108

ALL-STAR TEAM

C—Carlos Santana, Inland Empire. **1B**—Mark Trumbo, Rancho Cucamonga. **2B**—Eric Sogard, Lake Elsinore. **3B**—Jorge Jimenez, Lancaster. **SS**—Pedro Ciriaco, Inland Empire. **OF**—Cedric Hunter, Lake Elsinore; Kellen Kulbacki, Lake Elsinore; Josh Reddick, Boston. **DH**—Chris Carter, Lancaster. **UTIL**—Matt Downs, San Jose. **SP**—Kevin Pucetas, San Jose; Tim Aldeson, San Jose; Sean O'Sullivan, Rancho Cucamonga. **RP**—Andrew Johnston, Modesto. **Player of the Year:** Carlos Santana, Inland Empire. **Pitcher of the Year:** Kevin Pucetas, San Jose. **Rookie of the Year:** Chris Carter, Lancaster. **Manager of the Year:** Chad Epperson, Lancaster.

DEPARTMENT LEADERS

BATTING

OBP	Santana, Carlos, Inland Empire	.431
SLG	Carter, Chris, Stockton	.569
R	Carter, Chris, Stockton	101
H	Hunter, Cedric, Lake Elsinore	186
TB	Carter, Chris, Stockton	288
XBH	Carter, Chris, Stockton	75
2B	Sogard, Eric, Lake Elsinore	42
3B	Phillips, P.J., Rancho Cucamonga	11
HR	Carter, Chris, Stockton	39
RBI	Carter, Chris, Stockton	104
SAC	Lemon, Marcus, Bakersfield	14
SF	Ciriaco, Pedro, Visalia	11
	Hunter, Cedric, Lake Elsinore	11
BB	Whittleman, John, Bakersfield	81
IBB	Doolittle, Sean, Stockton	7
HBP	Jackson, Anthony, Modesto	15
SO	Carter, Chris, Stockton	156
SB	Bourjos, Peter, Rancho Cucamonga	50
CS	Gilbert, Archie, Stockton	18
AB/SO	Hunter, Cedric, Lake Elsinore	12.43

PITCHING

G	Rodriguez, R.J., Lake Elsinore	58
GS	Enright, Barry, Visalia	29
CG	Rodriguez, Aneury, Modesto	2
	Bell, Trevor, Rancho Cucamonga	2
GF	Demel, Sam, Stockton	35
S	tewart, Jordan, Bakersfield	35
SV	Johnston, Andrew, Modesto	24
W	O'Sullivan, Sean, Rancho Cucamonga	16
L	Four players tied at	12
IP	Enright, Barry, Visalia	164
H	Roemer, Wes, Visalia	199
R	Varvaro, Anthony, High Desert	105
	Sexton, Timothy, Inland Empire	105
ER	Varvaro, Anthony, High Desert	97
HB	Godfrey, Graham, Stockton	14
BB	Varvaro, Anthony, High Desert	82
SO	Enright, Barry, Visalia	143
SO/9 (SP)	English, Jesse, San Jose	8.98
SO/9 (RP)	Demel, Sam, Stockton	12.09
BB/9	Weiser, Keith, Modesto	1.18
WP	Pratt, Jordan, Inland Empire	21
BK	Hill, Nicholas, High Desert	6
AVG	Alderson, Tim, San Jose	.235

FIELDING

C	FPCT	Gradoville, Chris, Bakersfield	.997
	PO	Canham, Mitch, Lake Elsinore	708
	A	Easley, Ed, Visalia	74
	E	Santana, Carlos, Inland Empire	16
	DP	Santana, Carlos, Inland Empire	8
		McKenry, Michael, Modesto	8
	PB	Easley, Ed, Visalia	23
		Scott, Travis, High Desert	23
1B	FPCT	Paulk, Mike, Modesto	.995
	PO	Paulk, Mike, Modesto	1041
	A	Paulk, Mike, Modesto	74
	E	Trumbo, Mark, Rancho Cucamonga	20
	DP	Trumbo, Mark, Rancho Cucamonga	89
2B	FPCT	Sogard, Eric, Lake Elsinore	.973
	PO	Sogard, Eric, Lake Elsinore	200
	A	Sogard, Eric, Lake Elsinore	348
	E	Chiang, Chih-Hsien, Lancaster	17
	DP	Sogard, Eric, Lake Elsinore	58
3B	FPCT	Repec, Matt, Modesto	.947
	PO	Whittleman, John, Bakersfield	87
	A	Whittleman, John, Bakersfield	194
	E	Whittleman, John, Bakersfield	27
	DP	Infante, Larry, Rancho Cucamonga	20
SS	FPCT	Lopez, Jesus, Lake Elsinore	.975
	PO	Phillips, P.J., Rancho Cucamonga	216
	A	Phillips, P.J., Rancho Cucamonga	375
	E	Lemon, Marcus, Bakersfield	43
	DP	Phillips, P.J., Rancho Cucamonga	75
OF	FPCT	Felmy, Bobby, San Jose	.995
	PO	Hunter, Cedric, Lake Elsinore	319
	A	McBryde, Mike, San Jose	20
	E	Peguero, Carlos, High Desert	12
	DP	Three players tied at	4

BY JOSH LEVENTHAL

One of the few bright spots of the Nationals' dismal 2008 campaign could be found about 30 miles south of Nationals Park in Woodbridge, Va. For it was here that high Class A Potomac swept both halves of the Carolina League season before claiming the organization's first full-season championship by knocking of Myrtle Beach, three-games-to-one, to win the Mills Cup.

The big league club may have finished with the sport's worst record, but Potomac flashed hope for the Nats' future as a variety of players contributed to the championship run. Lefthander Ross Detwiler, the club's 2007 No. 1 pick, overcame a shaky regular season to lead the P-Nats with 114 strikeouts and a 4.86 ERA. Righthander Adrian Alaniz breezed through the league with a 9-0, 2.62 mark in 65 innings (12 starts) before posting a 3.93 ERA in 66 innings (13 starts) for Double-A Harrisburg, and third baseman Leonard Davis emerged with a .332/.403/.608 average. The team succeeded despite losing No. 1 prospect Chris Marrero in June to a broken ankle.

Orioles catcher Matt Wieters was the story of the league for the three months he stuck around Frederick. The 2007 fifth overall selection made a seamless transition to pro ball and terrorized pitchers for a .345/.448/.576 average (and a 1.024 on-base plus slugging percentage).

Braves prized righthander Tommy Hanson stuck around for just 40 innings and didn't give up an earned run until his fifth start of the season. He left Myrtle Beach for an early May promotion to Double-A Mississippi with a 3-1, 0.90 record and was widely considered the league's best pitcher—though he didn't qualify for our Top Prospects list.

Kinston catcher Carlos Santana was a late arrival to the Carolina League, coming to the Indians from the Dodgers as part of the deadline deal for Casey Blake. Considered by one talent evaluator to be a "mini-Wieters," Santana made a fast impression at the plate, and behind it, with a .352/.452/.590 line (he fell just a few at-bats shy of qualifying for the Top Prospects list).

Kinston and Myrtle Beach had the deepest pools of talent in the league. The Pelicans broke a franchise record for victories on the final day of the regular season and topped the club's home run record with 153, as seven players belted at least 16. Five-tool center fielder Gorkys Hernandez flashed an all-around game despite playing much of the season with an injured hamstring, and catcher Tyler Flowers and shortstop Brandon Hicks combined 36 home runs and 144 RBIs.

Kinston was fueled by the slugging duo of first baseman Beau Mills, the league MVP, and 20-year-old left field Nick Weglarz. They combined for 54 doubles and 31 home runs.

TOP 20 PROSPECTS

1. Matt Wieters, c, Frederick (Orioles)
2. Jake Arrieta, rhp, Frederick (Orioles)
3. Gorkys Hernandez, of, Myrtle Beach (Braves)
4. Nick Weglarz, of, Kinston (Indians)
5. Beau Mills, 1b, Kinston (Indians)
6. Aaron Poreda, lhp, Winston-Salem (White Sox)
7. Blake Wood, rhp, Wilmington (Royals)
8. Brandon Erbe, rhp, Frederick (Orioles)
9. Hector Rondon, rhp, Kinston (Indians)
10. Chris Marrero, 1b, Potomac (Nationals)
11. Ross Detwiler, lhp, Potomac (Nationals)
12. Tyler Flowers, c, Myrtle Beach (Braves)
13. Brandon Hicks, ss, Myrtle Beach (Braves)
14. Brandon Allen, 1b, Winston-Salem (White Sox)
15. Carlos Rivero, ss, Kinston (Indians)
16. Brandon Snyder, 1b, Frederick (Orioles)
17. John Ely, rhp, Winston-Salem (White Sox)
18. Josh Tomlin, rhp, Kinston (Indians)
19. Kanekoa Teixeira, rhp, Winston-Salem (White Sox)
20. Bill Rowell, 3b, Frederick (Orioles)

STANDINGS: SPLIT SEASON

FIRST HALF

North	W	L	PCT	GB
Potomac	42	28	.600	—
Wilmington	35	35	.500	7
Frederick	34	36	.486	8
Lynchburg	29	41	.414	13

South	W	L	PCT	GB
Myrtle Beach	45	25	.643	—
Kinston	35	34	.507	9½
Salem	30	40	.429	15
Winston-Salem	29	40	.420	15½

SECOND HALF

North	W	L	PCT	GB
Potomac	37	33	.529	—
Wilmington	34	36	.486	3
Lynchburg	29	39	.426	7
Frederick	29	40	.420	7½

South	W	L	PCT	GB
Myrtle Beach	44	26	.629	—
Winston-Salem	42	28	.600	2
Kinston	37	32	.536	6½
Salem	26	44	.371	18

PLAYOFFS—Semifinals: Potomac defeated Wilmington 3-0 and Myrtle Beach defeated Winston-Salem 3-1 in best-of-five series. **Finals:** Potomac defeated Myrtle Beach 3-1 in a best-of-five series.

OVERALL STANDINGS

Page	Team	W	L	PCT	GB	Manager	Attendance	Average	Last Penn.
57	Myrtle Beach Pelicans (Braves)	89	51	.636	—	Rocket Wheeler	242,397	3,565	2000
326	Potomac Nationals (Nationals)	79	61	.564	10	Randy Knorr	177,760	2,735	2008
115	Kinston Indians (Indians)	72	66	.522	16	Chris Tremie	130,406	1,976	2006
95	Winston-Salem Warthogs (White Sox)	71	68	.511	17½	Tim Blackwell	169,963	2,575	2003
161	Wilmington Blue Rocks (Royals)	69	71	.493	20	Darryl Kennedy	312,375	4,527	1999
66	Frederick Keys (Orioles)	63	76	.453	25½	T. Thompson/R. Hebner	295,656	4,480	2007
247	Lynchburg Hillcats (Pirates)	58	80	.420	30	Jeff Branson	162,131	2,457	2002
152	Salem Avalanche (Astros)	56	84	.400	33	Jim Pankovits	235,823	3,418	2001

CLUB BATTING

	AVG	G	AB	R	H	2B	3B	HR	RBI	BB	SO	SB	CS	OBP	SLG
Potomac	.265	140	4657	720	1234	300	27	116	670	436	943	124	52	.336	.416
Winston-Salem	.262	139	4583	625	1199	290	47	93	564	370	949	180	73	.322	.406
Lynchburg	.260	138	4585	668	1191	279	22	89	600	465	954	128	79	.333	.388
Myrtle Beach	.260	140	4678	764	1217	298	35	153	705	518	1019	109	52	.340	.437
Salem	.257	140	4752	637	1221	294	36	68	581	452	966	103	60	.327	.377
Kinston	.256	138	4632	698	1187	243	23	101	638	520	889	96	45	.337	.384
Frederick	.254	139	4524	627	1148	215	17	108	572	463	1081	123	68	.329	.380
Wilmington	.251	140	4549	591	1144	244	54	62	520	496	944	258	105	.330	.370

CLUB PITCHING

	ERA	G	CG	SHO	SV	IP	H	R	ER	HR	BB	SO	AVG
Myrtle Beach	3.49	140	4	11	51	1231	1102	596	476	88	493	1080	.239
Potomac	3.79	140	1	14	34	1208	1153	600	506	85	443	1009	.253
Wilmington	3.80	140	0	7	38	1220	1174	590	514	87	425	995	.255
Winston-Salem	4.34	139	3	7	39	1199	1195	679	578	99	479	988	.260
Frederick	4.35	139	2	9	34	1201	1147	676	580	121	523	989	.252
Kinston	4.37	138	3	7	39	1206	1179	677	586	111	444	1101	.256
Salem	4.61	140	2	6	27	1227	1271	725	628	91	482	760	.271
Lynchburg	5.02	138	1	5	31	1193	1320	787	662	108	431	823	.279

CLUB FIELDING

	PCT	PO	A	E	DP		PCT	PO	A	E	DP
Potomac	.975	3623	1498	131	128	Winston-Salem	.972	3598	1538	150	115
Wilmington	.975	3659	1464	132	139	Frederick	.971	3601	1433	153	109
Kinston	.973	3619	1400	141	102	Lynchburg	.969	3579	1583	164	131
Salem	.973	3682	1608	145	142	Myrtle Beach	.967	3694	1433	173	102

INDIVIDUAL BATTING LEADERS *(MINIMUM 2.7 PLATE APPEARANCES PER LEAGUE GAME)*

	AVG	G	AB	R	H	2B	3B	HR	RBI	BB	SO	SB
Negrych, Jim, Lynchburg	.370	104	386	77	143	36	1	5	62	55	55	7
Snyder, Brandon, Frederick	.315	116	435	70	137	33	2	13	80	29	83	3
Ori, Mark, Salem	.304	131	497	73	151	36	2	11	89	49	92	4
Brown, Dee, Potomac	.296	100	351	57	104	20	3	8	64	29	93	8
Romero, Niuman, Kinston	.296	108	395	64	117	22	1	6	53	34	55	10
Shelby, John, Winston-Salem	.295	114	447	81	132	37	7	15	80	22	98	3
Retherford, C.J., Winston-Salem	.295	130	461	66	136	28	1	16	71	37	78	11
Mills, Beau, Kinston	.293	125	482	78	141	34	3	21	90	54	105	2
Van Ostrand, James, Salem	.292	97	363	41	106	28	1	7	64	30	45	1
Cabrera, Willie, Myrtle Beach	.290	116	469	86	136	32	3	16	78	35	51	6

INDIVIDUAL PITCHING LEADERS *(MINIMUM 0.8 INNINGS PITCHED PER LEAGUE GAME)*

	W	L	ERA	G	GS	CG	SV	IP	H	R	BB	SO
Arrieta, Jake, Frederick	6	5	2.87	20	20	0	0	113	80	44	51	120
Cofield, Kyle, Myrtle Beach	8	6	3.26	24	22	0	0	116	113	54	66	80
Arguello, Douglas, Salem	10	6	3.30	27	25	2	0	142	119	59	69	90
Reynoso, Ryne, Myrtle Beach	10	6	3.36	27	26	0	0	131	121	58	37	105
Santiago, Mario, Wilmington	8	8	3.43	27	27	0	0	142	155	69	39	86
Watson, Anthony, Lynchburg	8	12	3.56	28	28	0	0	152	149	70	36	104
Kniginyzky, Matthew, Wilmington	9	8	3.57	27	27	0	0	141	133	66	51	113
Rondon, Hector, Kinston	11	6	3.60	27	27	0	0	145	130	63	42	145
Teaford, Everett, Wilmington	8	6	3.80	28	23	0	1	144	135	70	46	116
Abreu, Erick, Salem	7	6	3.98	35	19	0	1	131	141	64	33	92

ALL-STAR TEAM

C—Tyler Flowers, Myrtle Beach. **1B**—Beau Mills, Kinston. **2B**—Travis Jones, Myrle Beach; Niuman Romero, Kinston. **3B**—Jim Negrych, Lynchburg. **SS**—Brandon Hicks, Myrtle Beach. **OF**—Willie Cabrera, Myrtle Beach; John Shelby, Winston-Salem; Joe Dickerson, Wilmington; Jordan Parraz, Salem. **DH**—Ernesto Mejia, Myrtle Beach. **Util**—C.J. Retherford, Winston-Salem; Mark Ori, Salem. **SP**—Jake Arrieta, Frederick. **RP**—Luis Perdomo, Kinston. **Most Valuable Player:** Beau Mills, Kinston. **Most Valuable Pitcher:** Jake Arrieta, Frederick. **Manager of the Year:** Rocket Wheeler, Myrtle Beach.

DEPARTMENT LEADERS

BATTING

OBP	Negrych, Jim, Lynchburg	.448
SLG	Allen, Brandon, Winston-Salem	.527
R	Mejia, Ernesto, Myrtle Beach	93
H	Ori, Mark, Salem	151
TB	Mejia, Ernesto, Myrtle Beach	262
XBH	Mejia, Ernesto, Myrtle Beach	73
2B	Mejia, Ernesto, Myrtle Beach	47
3B	Orlando, Paulo, Winston-Salem, Wil.	14
HR	Mejia, Ernesto, Myrtle Beach	21
	Mills, Beau, Kinston	21
RBI	Mejia, Ernesto, Myrtle Beach	93
SAC	Martinez, Michael, Potomac	20
SF	Goedert, Jared, Kinston	9
	Sakamoto, Kent, Lynchburg	9
BB	Flowers, Tyler, Myrtle Beach	98
IBB	Wieters, Matt, Frederick	5
HBP	Keel, Jared, Lynchburg	15
SO	Tripp, Brandon, Frederick	145
SB	Robinson, Derrick, Wilmington	62
CS	Robinson, Derrick, Wilmington	17
AB/SO	Abreu, Miguel, Frederick	9.75

PITCHING

G	Diaz, Raymar, Salem	55
GS	Three players tied at	28
CG	Arguello, Douglas, Salem	2
	Erbe, Brandon, Frederick	2
GF	Chambliss, Tyler, Wilmington	43
SV	Chambliss, Tyler, Wilmington	24
W	Three players tied at	12
L	Bass, Corey, Salem	15
IP	Watson, Anthony, Lynchburg	151.2
H	Crotta, Michael, Lynchburg	171
R	Bass, Corey, Salem	110
ER	Bass, Corey, Salem	96
HB	Schmidt, Kyle, Frederick	17
BB	Arguello, Douglas, Salem	69
SO	Erbe, Brandon, Frederick	151
SO/9 (SP)	Arrieta, Jake, Frederick	9.56
SO/9 (RP)	Barrera, Henry, Wilmington	12.17
BB/9	Crotta, Michael, Lynchburg	1.54
WP	Hughes, Jared, Lynchburg	17
BK	Brooks, Richard, Winston-Salem	6
AVG	Arrieta, Jake, Frederick	.199

FIELDING

C	FPCT	Hernandez, Francisco, W-S	.993
	PO	Flowers, Tyler, Myrtle Beach	681
	A	Flowers, Tyler, Myrtle Beach	76
	E	Flowers, Tyler, Myrtle Beach	12
	DP	Morizio, Matthew, Wilmington	7
	PB	Clemens, Koby, Salem	31
1B	FPCT	Mills, Beau, Kinston	.992
	PO	Mejia, Ernesto, Myrtle Beach	1061
	A	Mejia, Ernesto, Myrtle Beach	93
	E	Mejia, Ernesto, Myrtle Beach	23
	DP	Ori, Mark, Salem	92
2B	FPCT	Buchanan, Greg, Salem	.979
	PO	Buchanan, Greg, Salem	214
	A	Abreu, Miguel, Frederick	324
	E	Jones, Travis, Myrtle Beach	19
	DP	Buchanan, Greg, Salem	77
3B	FPCT	Johnson, Josh, Wilmington	.956
	PO	Florentino, Jhon, Wilmington	84
	A	Retherford, C.J., Winston-Salem	256
	E	Retherford, C.J., Winston-Salem	24
	DP	Retherford, C.J., Winston-Salem	21
SS	FPCT	Torres, Tim, Salem	.970
	PO	Torres, Tim, Salem	180
	A	McConnell, Chris, Wilmington	371
	E	McConnell, Chris, Wilmington	28
	DP	McConnell, Chris, Wilmington	75
OF	FPCT	Rodriguez, Concepcion, M.B.	.989
	PO	Robinson, Derrick, Wilmington	279
	A	Dyson, Jarrod, Wilmington	14
	E	Orlando, Paulo, W-S/Wilm.	8
	DP	Sanchez, Salvador, Winston-Salem	7

MINOR LEAGUES

MINOR LEAGUES

BY JESSE BURKHART

Daytona's last Florida State League championship had come in 2004, when the Cubs shared the title with the Tampa Yankees after the finals were canceled because of a hurricane. In 2008, Daytona was a bit more selfish.

Following a late-season surge marked by 10 wins in its final 12 regular season games, Daytona defeated Fort Myers three-games-to-one.

Good starting pitching contributed to a league-leading 3.51 ERA, but it was exceptional relief that anchored Daytona's run. In four games against Fort Myers, the bullpen was stifling, tossing 15⅔ innings without surrendering an earned run. The collective effort was punctuated by 2008 first-round pick Andrew Cashner, who struck out four in 2⅔ innings of relief to earn the win in the clinching game.

There was no shortage of production at the plate in the FSL. Dunedin's prolific offense helped the Blue Jays finish with the best overall record at 85-53. Despite not having any hardware to show for it, their regular season-excellence was recognized in the form of five all-star selections and fifth-year skipper Omar Malave being named manager of the year. Dunedin led the league in runs, hits, doubles, home runs, RBIs, walks and slugging.

It was also a banner year for the league's first basemen. Jupiter's Logan Morrison won the MVP award after leading the league in batting (.332), on-base percentage (.402), hits (162) and doubles (38). Notably, the breakout season came while playing his home games in an extreme pitcher's park, solidifying his status as one of the league's top positional prospects. Lakeland first baseman Ryan Strieby led the league with 29 home runs—19 of which came in 39 games after July 1—despite missing the final 19 contests because of a broken hamate bone in his left wrist.

In true FSL fashion, a high-profile righthander commanded the prospect spotlight. The likes of Chad Billingsley, Justin Verlander, Yovani Gallardo and Joba Chamberlain have all passed through the FSL in the last four years on their way to majors,

and Rick Porcello could be held in the same regard in due time.

Even at age 19, the Tigers had no qualms about sending Porcello to Lakeland to make his pro debut. Commanding a mid-90s fastball and two plus breaking pitches, he led all starters in ERA (2.66) and limited opponents to a .244 average. Porcello's rare combination of youth, power and polish cemented him as the league's top prospect.

TOP 20 PROSPECTS

1. Rick Porcello, rhp, Lakeland (Tigers)
2. J.P. Arencibia, c, Dunedin (Blue Jays)
3. Logan Morrison, 1b, Jupiter (Marlins)
4. Jeremy Jeffress, rhp, Brevard County (Brewers)
5. Adrian Cardenas, 2b, Clearwater (Phillies)
6. Jeremy Hellickson, rhp, Vero Beach (Rays)
7. Sean West, lhp, Jupiter (Marlins)
8. Wilson Ramos, c, Fort Myers (Twins)
9. Scott Cousins, of, Jupiter (Marlins)
10. Michael Taylor, of, Clearwater (Phillies)
11. Todd Frazier, ss/3b, Sarasota (Reds)
12. Drew Stubbs, of, Sarasota (Reds)
13. Chris Valaika, ss, Sarasota (Reds)
14. Jose Ceda, rhp, Daytona (Cubs)
15. Juan Francisco, 3b, Sarasota (Reds)
16. Taylor Green, 3b, Brevard County (Brewers)
17. Cale Iorg, ss, Lakeland (Tigers)
18. Francisco Samuel, rhp, Palm Beach (Cardinals)
19. Jonathan Lucroy, c, Brevard County (Brewers)
20. Zach McAllister, rhp, Tampa (Yankees)

STANDINGS: SPLIT SEASON

FIRST HALF

East	W	L	PCT	GB
Palm Beach	42	28	.600	—
Brevard Co.	35	34	.507	6 ½
Daytona	35	35	.500	7
Vero Beach	34	35	.493	7 ½
Jupiter	33	36	.478	8 ½
St. Lucie	19	50	.275	22 ½

West	W	L	PCT	GB
Fort Myers	45	24	.652	—
Dunedin	37	33	.529	8 ½
Tampa	37	33	.529	8 ½
Lakeland	34	34	.507	10
Sarasota	33	37	.471	12 ½
Clearwater	32	38	.457	13 ½

SECOND HALF

East	W	L	PCT	GB
Daytona	38	24	.613	—
Jupiter	41	28	.594	½
St. Lucie	34	31	.523	5 ½
Palm Beach	33	34	.493	7 ½
Brevard Co.	31	38	.449	10 ½
Vero Beach	20	46	.303	20

West	W	L	PCT	GB
Dunedin	48	20	.706	—
Tampa	35	32	.522	12 ½
Fort Myers	32	35	.478	15 ½
Lakeland	32	36	.471	16
Clearwater	32	38	.457	17
Sarasota	27	41	.397	21

PLAYOFFS—Semifinals: Daytona defeated Palm Beach 2-1 and Fort Myers defeated Dunedin 2-0 in best-of-three series.
Finals: Daytona defeated Fort Myers 3-1 in a best-of-five series.

OVERALL STANDINGS

Page	Team	W	L	PCT	GB	Manager	Attendance	Average	Last Penn.
316	Dunedin Blue Jays (Blue Jays)	85	53	.616	—	Omar Malave	48,321	711	None
196	Fort Myers Miracle (Twins)	77	59	.566	7	Jeff Smith	124,749	1,835	1985
85	Daytona Cubs (Cubs)	73	59	.553	9	Jody Davis	164,007	2,485	2008
257	Palm Beach Cardinals (Cardinals)	75	62	.547	9 ½	Gaylen Pitts	66,073	972	2005
143	Jupiter Hammerheads (Marlins)	74	64	.536	11	Brandon Hyde	66,585	1,089	1991
216	Tampa Yankees (Yankees)	72	65	.526	12 ½	Luis Sojo	86,870	1,472	2004
133	Lakeland Flying Tigers (Tigers)	67	70	.489	17 ½	Andy Barkett	52,305	830	1992
188	Brevard County Manatees (Brewers)	66	72	.478	19	Mike Guerrero	66,256	1,035	2001
237	Clearwater Threshers (Phillies)	64	76	.457	22	Razor Shines	168,637	2,480	2007
105	Sarasota Reds (Reds)	60	78	.435	25	Joe Ayrault	43,088	643	1963
297	Vero Beach Devil Rays (Rays)	54	81	.400	29 ½	Jim Morrison	47,944	761	1990
205	St. Lucie Mets (Mets)	53	81	.396	30	Tim Teufel	93,626	1,535	2006

CLUB BATTING

	AVG	G	AB	R	H	2B	3B	HR	RBI	BB	SO	SB	CS	OBP	SLG
Daytona	.271	132	4420	617	1199	251	25	83	568	446	882	114	57	.342	.396
Dunedin	.270	138	4638	702	1254	267	33	135	646	499	993	58	42	.347	.429
Fort Myers	.266	136	4504	596	1199	209	40	81	550	442	932	83	54	.340	.384
Clearwater	.264	140	4603	592	1215	217	33	67	533	491	864	117	49	.340	.369
Sarasota	.255	138	4645	565	1183	243	34	83	528	371	973	87	28	.315	.375
Jupiter	.254	138	4558	620	1160	229	31	98	570	470	1085	127	44	.329	.383
Tampa	.253	137	4506	531	1141	234	32	70	479	389	889	130	67	.319	.366
Lakeland	.252	137	4565	622	1149	192	49	117	582	498	1139	100	76	.330	.392
Palm Beach	.252	138	4495	586	1132	219	32	75	527	456	917	85	43	.328	.365
St. Lucie	.250	134	4374	517	1095	186	30	71	459	418	879	69	58	.321	.355
Brevard Co.	.243	138	4475	534	1088	199	30	72	481	469	927	167	58	.322	.349
Vero Beach	.241	135	4389	470	1056	187	20	71	441	390	951	104	70	.310	.341

CLUB PITCHING

	ERA	G	CG	SHO	SV	IP	H	R	ER	HR	BB	SO	AVG
Daytona	3.53	132	0	7	37	1164	1017	518	454	78	479	899	.238
Fort Myers	3.53	136	4	12	43	1199	1131	545	468	65	450	1001	.249
Tampa	3.54	137	2	13	39	1191	1177	551	467	60	389	996	.260
Jupiter	3.58	138	2	7	35	1199	1126	563	474	71	420	903	.249
Dunedin	3.59	138	5	12	47	1194	1226	539	476	89	337	907	.266
Vero Beach	3.76	135	1	10	31	1169	1104	575	488	106	395	956	.248
Brevard County	3.86	138	3	11	35	1195	1168	584	513	76	506	995	.257
Palm Beach	3.88	137	4	10	51	1192	1096	588	511	74	563	980	.247
Lakeland	3.92	137	3	8	36	1207	1193	635	526	88	484	933	.259
Sarasota	4.04	138	1	10	29	1200	1217	608	538	93	465	980	.264
Clearwater	4.09	140	7	12	31	1201	1245	611	544	116	464	981	.269
St. Lucie	4.46	134	3	8	27	1143	1172	637	563	107	389	902	.266

CLUB FIELDING

	PCT	PO	A	E	DP		PCT	PO	A	E	DP
Tampa	.979	3574	1428	106	140	Jupiter	.972	3597	1485	148	124
Fort Myers	.977	3597	1400	120	111	Palm Beach	.972	3577	1407	141	147
Clearwater	.976	3601	1422	126	119	St. Lucie	.972	3420	1367	139	131
Daytona	.976	3492	1443	121	133	Brevard County	.971	3585	1450	152	126
Dunedin	.975	3582	1528	131	141	Lakeland	.970	3622	1411	153	133
Sarasota	.975	3600	1362	129	133	Vero Beach	.970	3507	1380	149	123

INDIVIDUAL BATTING LEADERS (MINIMUM 2.7 PLATE APPEARANCES PER LEAGUE GAME)

	AVG	G	AB	R	H	2B	3B	HR	RBI	BB	SO	SB
Morrison, Logan, Jupiter	.332	130	488	71	162	38	1	13	74	57	80	9
Dopirak, Brian, Dunedin	.308	106	409	77	126	25	2	27	88	47	100	0
Patton, Cory, Dunedin	.305	109	407	70	124	30	2	13	70	45	78	4
Emaus, Bradley, Dunedin	.302	124	473	87	143	34	3	12	71	60	56	12
Wright, Ty, Daytona	.300	113	426	60	128	21	1	8	72	41	71	7
Thole, Josh, St. Lucie	.300	111	347	49	104	25	2	5	56	45	38	2
Randel, Kevin, Jupiter	.298	93	326	59	97	23	4	15	62	49	84	3
Adduci, James, Daytona	.290	123	458	81	133	19	3	3	48	63	96	26
Smith, Kevin, Tampa	.290	124	445	51	129	35	1	5	62	32	93	7
Green, Taylor, Brevard County	.289	114	418	46	121	19	0	15	73	61	59	4

INDIVIDUAL PITCHING LEADERS (MINIMUM 0.8 INNINGS PITCHED PER LEAGUE GAME)

	W	L	ERA	G	GS	CG	SV	IP	H	R	BB	SO
Porcello, Rick, Lakeland	8	6	2.66	24	24	0	0	125	116	51	33	72
Carrillo, Marco, Daytona	7	6	2.88	23	17	0	0	116	82	42	33	71
Devries, Cole, Fort Myers	10	9	2.93	24	23	1	0	135	138	51	38	105
Gonzalez, Reidier, Dunedin	12	4	3.14	27	20	1	1	138	155	56	30	74
Gee, Dillon, St. Lucie	8	6	3.25	21	21	0	0	127	117	49	19	94
Rollins, Heath, Vero Beach	5	11	3.30	23	21	1	0	136	118	59	27	115
Fox, Matthew, Fort Myers	7	7	3.37	32	14	0	1	118	120	47	43	99
Owen, Dylan, St. Lucie	12	6	3.43	24	24	2	0	134	135	55	33	116
Taylor, Graham, Jupiter	11	6	3.46	23	22	1	0	140	147	59	25	95
Dickson, Brandon, Palm Beach	7	8	3.51	23	17	1	1	115	119	49	37	66

ALL-STAR TEAM

C—Wilson Ramos, Fort Myers; Josh Thole, St. Lucie. **1B**—Logan Morrison, Jupiter. **2B**—Brad Emaus, Dunedin. **3B**—Juan Francisco, Sarasota. **SS**—Cale Iorg, Lakeland. **OF**—Cory Patton, Dunedin; Quintin Berry, Clearwater; Chris Heisey, Sarasota; Jim Adduci, Dyatona. **DH**—Brian Dopirak, Dunedin. **Util**—Taylor Green. **SP**—Dylan Owen, St. Lucie; Rick Porcello, Lakeland; Graham Taylor, Jupiter. Ray Gonzalez, Dunedin. **RP**—Anthony Slama, Fort Myers, Francisco Samuel, Palm Beach. **Most Valuable Player:** Logan Morrison, Jupiter. **Pitcher of the Year:** Dylan Owen, St. Lucie. **Manager of the Year:** Omar Malave, Dunedin.

DEPARTMENT LEADERS

BATTING

OBP	Morrison, Logan, Jupiter	.402
SLG	Dopirak, Brian, Dunedin	.577
R	Emaus, Bradley, Dunedin	87
H	Morrison, Logan, Jupiter	162
TB	Francisco, Juan, Sarasota	256
XBH	Francisco, Juan, Sarasota	62
2B	Morrison, Logan, Jupiter	38
3B	Carrera, Ezequiel, St. Lucie	12
HR	Strieby, Ryan, Lakeland	29
RBI	Strieby, Ryan, Lakeland	94
SAC	Ortiz, Yancarlos, Fort Myers	13
SF	Portes, Juan, Fort Myers	11
BB	Duda, Lucas, St. Lucie	66
IBB	Bertram, Michael, Lakeland	8
HBP	Ovalle, Edward, Fort Myers	16
SO	Laster, Jeramy, Lakeland	200
SB	Berry, Quintin, Clearwater	51
CS	Berry, Quintin, Clearwater	14
AB/SO	Castro, Jose, Sarasota	11.52

PITCHING

G	Mendez, Adalberto, Jupiter	57
	Leroux, Christopher, Jupiter	57
GS	Nickerson, Jonah, Lakeland	26
	Below, Duane, Lakeland	26
CG	Four players tied at	2
GF	Mendez, Adalberto, Jupiter	53
SV	Mendez, Adalberto, Jupiter	29
	Samuel, Francisco, Palm Beach	29
W	Three players tied at	12
L	Nova, Ivan, Tampa	13
IP	Savery, Joe, Clearwater	150
H	Savery, Joe, Clearwater	171
R	Mann, Brandon, Vero Beach	88
ER	Guerra, Deolis, Fort Myers	79
HB	Gonzalez, Rafael, Sarasota	12
	Butler, Joshua, Vero Beach, Brevard Co.	12
BB	Axford, John, Brevard County	73
SO	Below, Duane, Lakeland	126
SO/9 (SP)	Below, Duane, Lakeland	8.7
SO/9 (RP)	Slama, Anthony, Fort Myers	13.94
BB/9	Gee, Dillon, St. Lucie	1.34
WP	Degerman, Eddie, Palm Beach	21
BK	Braddock, Zach, Brevard County	3
AVG	Carrillo, Marco, Daytona	0.2

FIELDING

C	FPCT	Thole, Josh, St. Lucie	.994
	PO	Gosewisch, Tuffy, Clearwater	722
	A	Gosewisch, Tuffy, Clearwater	66
	E	Rodriguez, Gabe, Sarasota	11
	DP	Purdom, John, Jupiter	7
		Thole, Josh, St. Lucie	7
	PB	Anson, Kyle, Tampa	13
1B	FPCT	Smith, Kevin, Tampa	.994
	PO	Fields, Matthew, Vero Beach	1179
	A	Urick, John, Clearwater	101
	E	Fields, Matthew, Vero Beach	17
	DP	Smith, Kevin, Tampa	114
2B	FPCT	Thomas, Tony, Daytona	.989
	PO	Thomas, Tony, Daytona	228
	A	Thomas, Tony, Daytona	320
	E	Descalso, Daniel, Palm Beach	12
		Sublett, Damon, Tampa	12
	DP	Emaus, Bradley, Dunedin	78
3B	FPCT	Hilligoss, Mitch, Tampa	.950
	PO	Francisco, Juan, Sarasota	80
	A	Suarez, Cesar, Vero Beach	214
	E	Suarez, Cesar, Vero Beach	21
	DP	Hilligoss, Mitch, Tampa	27
SS	FPCT	Barney, Darwin, Daytona	.963
	PO	Hernandez, Fidel, Clearwater	196
	A	Tejada, Ruben, St. Lucie	369
	E	Hernandez, Fidel, Clearwater	30
		Tejada, Ruben, St. Lucie	30
	DP	Tejada, Ruben, St. Lucie	83
OF	FPCT	Shoffit, Sean, Dunedin	0.995
	PO	Laster, Jeramy, Lakeland	310
	A	Milner, Gus, Clearwater	14
		Heisey, Chris, Sarasota	14
	E	Patton, Cory, Dunedin	9
	DP	Milner, Gus, Clearwater	7

MINOR LEAGUES

MINOR LEAGUES

BY CONOR GLASSEY

Burlington Bees shortstop Mike Moustakas, the second overall pick in the 2007 draft, started the season slowly, hitting just .190/.253/.226 in April. But his bat heated up with the weather, as he put the bad month behind him and hit .288/.351/.553 for the remainder of the season. With 22 home runs, Moustakas became the league's first teenage home run champion since Steve Gibralter in 1992 and was the league's top prospect.

The Bees also started the season slowly, finishing the first half of the season at the bottom of the Midwest League Western Division with a 30-39 record. Like Moustakas, the team turned things around and went 43-26 in the second half of the season, finishing in second place in the West and earning a spot in the playoffs.

From the start of August through the playoffs, the Bees went 27-9. In the first round, Burlington swept Kane County in a best-of-three series, then swept Cedar Rapids in a best-of-three series. The team then faced off against South Bend in a best-of-five finals and won the first two games before the series was canceled due to inclement weather. The Bees were named champions, giving Burlington its first title since 1999.

Beloit center fielder Ben Revere put together one of the most impressive seasons in the league. He fell 38 at-bats shy of qualifying for the batting title, but hit a robust .379/.433/.497 with 17 doubles, 10 triples and a home run. He also stole 44 bases and had nearly as many walks (27) as strikeouts (31).

The league also saw several impressive prospects on the mound. Clinton righthander Neftali Feliz and lefthander Derek Holland formed a formidable one-two punch at the top of the LumberKings rotation. Feliz started 17 games for Clinton, going 6-3, 2.52 with 106 strikeouts in 82 innings before

being promoted to Double-A Frisco. Holland also started 17 games, going 7-0, 2.40 with 91 strikeouts in 94 innings before moving on to Bakersfield and then rejoining Feliz in Frisco.

TOP 20 PROSPECTS

1. Mike Moustakas, 3b/ss, Burlington (Royals)
2. Neftali Feliz, rhp, Clinton (Rangers)
3. Jarrod Parker, rhp, South Bend (Diamondbacks)
4. Ben Revere, of, Beloit (Twins)
5. Brett Wallace, 3b, Quad Cities (Cardinals)
6. Engel Beltre, of, Clinton (Rangers)
7. Andrew Lambo, of, Great Lakes (Dodgers)
8. Philippe Aumont, rhp, Wisconsin (Mariners)
9. Derek Holland, lhp, Clinton (Rangers)
10. Neftali Soto, 3b, Dayton (Reds)
11. Danny Duffy, lhp, Burlington (Royals)
12. Craig Italiano, rhp, Kane County (Athletics)
13. Jordan Walden, rhp, Cedar Rapids (Angels)
14. Justin Jackson, ss, Lansing (Blue Jays)
15. Pete Kozma, ss, Quad Cities (Cardinals)
16. Corey Brown, of, Kane County (Athletics)
17. Juan Ramirez, rhp, Wisconsin (Mariners)
18. Danny Gutierrez, rhp, Burlington (Royals)
19. Kevin Ahrens, 3b, Lansing (Blue Jays)
20. Trevor Reckling, lhp, Cedar Rapids (Angels)

STANDINGS: SPLIT SEASON

FIRST HALF

East	W	L	PCT	GB
Lansing	39	31	.557	—
W. Michigan	37	31	.544	1
Fort Wayne	37	33	.529	2
South Bend	33	36	.478	5½
Great Lakes	30	39	.435	8½
Dayton	28	40	.412	10

West	W	L	PCT	GB
Clinton	41	26	.612	—
Kane County	39	29	.574	2½
Beloit	36	32	.529	5½
Quad Cities	33	31	.516	6½
Cedar Rapids	32	36	.471	9½
Wisconsin	31	35	.470	9½
Peoria	30	38	.441	11½
Burlington	30	39	.435	12

SECOND HALF

East	W	L	PCT	GB
South Bend	43	27	.614	—
Dayton	38	32	.543	5
Lansing	37	33	.529	6
W. Michigan	35	34	.507	7½
Fort Wayne	34	36	.486	9
Great Lakes	24	46	.343	19

West	W	L	PCT	GB
Burlington	43	26	.623	—
Cedar Rapids	40	30	.571	3½
Clinton	37	33	.529	6½
Beloit	35	35	.500	8½
Quad Cities	35	35	.500	8½
Kane County	33	37	.471	10½
Peoria	30	40	.429	13½
Wisconsin	25	45	.357	18½

PLAYOFFS—Division Series: Burlington defeated Kane County 2-0, Dayton defeated Lansing 2-0, Cedar Rapids defeated Clinton 2-0 and South Bend defeated West Michigan 2-1 in best-of-three series. **Semifinals:** Burlington defeated Cedar Rapids 2-0 and South Bend defeated Dayton 2-0 in best-of-three series. **Finals:** Burlington defeated South Bend 2-0 in a best-of-three series.

OVERALL STANDINGS

Page	Team	W	L	PCT	GB	Manager	Attendance	Average	Last Penn.
307	Clinton LumberKings (Rangers)	78	59	.569	—	Mike Micucci	114,662	1,711	1991
48	South Bend Silver Hawks (Diamondbacks)	76	63	.547	3	Mark Haley	163,479	2,404	2005
317	Lansing Lugnuts (Blue Jays)	76	64	.543	3½	Clayton McCullough	353,571	5,124	2003
161	Burlington Bees (Royals)	73	65	.529	5½	Brian Rupp	68,313	1,005	2008
134	West Michigan Whitecaps (Tigers)	72	65	.526	6	Joe DePastino	367,532	5,569	2007
171	Cedar Rapids Kernels (Angels)	72	66	.522	6½	Keith Johnson	164,568	2,456	1994
227	Kane County Cougars (Athletics)	72	66	.522	6½	Aaron Nieckula	472,596	7,161	2001
197	Beloit Snappers (Twins)	71	67	.514	7½	Nelson Prada	82,456	1,231	1995
269	Fort Wayne Wizards (Padres)	71	69	.507	8½	Doug Dascenzo	256,693	3,720	None
258	Quad Cities River Bandits (Cardinals)	68	66	.507	8½	Steve Dillard	207,048	3,451	1990
106	Dayton Dragons (Reds)	66	72	.478	12½	Donnie Scott	586,417	8,624	None
86	Peoria Chiefs (Cubs)	60	78	.435	18½	Ryne Sandberg	275,673	4,241	2002
287	Wisconsin Timber Rattlers (Mariners)	56	80	.412	21½	Terry Pollreisz	190,263	3,069	1984
180	Great Lakes Loons (Dodgers)	54	85	.388	25	Juan Bustabad	299,416	4,403	2000

CLUB BATTING

	AVG	G	AB	R	H	2B	3B	HR	RBI	BB	SO	SB	CS	OBP	SLG
Clinton	.270	137	4720	668	1275	239	35	115	606	375	1034	130	54	.336	.409
Kane County	.259	138	4628	627	1200	221	24	81	563	540	1011	149	59	.342	.370
Beloit	.258	138	4554	625	1177	181	41	63	544	434	963	179	98	.330	.358
Burlington	.258	139	4668	617	1205	223	45	112	543	401	972	156	90	.325	.397
West Michigan	.257	137	4610	581	1187	198	36	66	522	444	928	162	64	.328	.359
Dayton	.255	138	4648	595	1183	222	44	120	545	354	1161	82	50	.314	.399
Fort Wayne	.255	140	4649	631	1184	228	25	66	562	581	1097	116	44	.341	.357
Peoria	.255	139	4655	574	1187	244	24	102	519	348	948	131	74	.317	.383
South Bend	.249	139	4642	619	1155	246	22	70	558	513	974	58	42	.331	.357
Lansing	.248	140	4697	569	1165	252	41	66	518	405	1242	126	43	.312	.361
Wisconsin	.244	136	4479	527	1091	220	38	60	467	376	1146	168	73	.310	.350
Cedar Rapids	.242	138	4548	602	1101	241	48	86	534	406	1121	247	107	.314	.373
Great Lakes	.241	139	4575	504	1104	224	31	77	450	354	1044	119	64	.300	.354
Quad Cities	.241	134	4380	570	1055	208	32	101	516	396	1088	97	53	.313	.372

CLUB PITCHING

	ERA	G	CG	SHO	SV	IP	H	R	ER	HR	BB	SO	AVG
Lansing	3.08	140	2	12	36	1247	1127	524	423	59	426	1194	.242
West Michigan	3.29	137	7	10	24	1208	1072	544	442	63	459	1005	.237
South Bend	3.49	139	4	12	37	1228	1111	548	476	76	369	1018	.240
Burlington	3.50	139	1	14	37	1234	1184	569	479	93	365	1116	.254
Kane County	3.50	138	2	8	36	1220	1176	591	468	91	366	1039	.252
Clinton	3.56	137	0	7	38	1217	1146	609	478	84	400	1050	.249
Cedar Rapids	3.57	138	8	16	38	1224	1115	559	485	67	532	991	.247
Fort Wayne	3.78	140	0	9	39	1218	1217	599	512	97	328	1137	.260
Quad Cities	3.78	134	0	7	35	1153	1168	599	484	93	376	945	.264
Wisconsin	3.85	136	1	9	33	1186	1140	604	508	80	466	1068	.254
Beloit	3.86	138	5	6	30	1210	1178	614	518	93	442	1140	.255
Great Lakes	4.06	139	1	9	38	1216	1204	636	548	85	506	1120	.258
Peoria	4.07	139	1	4	38	1219	1264	662	549	115	382	923	.269
Dayton	4.21	138	1	9	40	1206	1167	651	561	89	510	983	.253

CLUB FIELDING

	PCT	PO	A	E	DP		PCT	PO	A	E	DP
South Bend	.974	3684	1389	137	113	Lansing	.968	3739	1578	175	143
Cedar Rapids	.973	3672	1545	146	139	Peoria	.968	3657	1535	173	129
Dayton	.972	3618	1354	145	102	Clinton	.966	3652	1399	179	114
Wisconsin	.971	3558	1421	150	111	Fort Wayne	.966	3653	1431	178	118
Burlington	.969	3701	1393	165	111	Kane County	.966	3660	1441	181	109
Great Lakes	.969	3648	1446	161	109	Quad Cities	.966	3459	1359	171	133
West Michigan	.969	3625	1444	162	129	Beloit	.959	3630	1358	211	111

INDIVIDUAL BATTING LEADERS *(MINIMUM 2.7 PLATE APPEARANCES PER LEAGUE GAME)*

	AVG	G	AB	R	H	2B	3B	HR	RBI	BB	SO	SB
Revere, Ben, Beloit	.379	83	340	51	129	17	10	1	43	27	31	44
Moreland, Mitchell, Clinton	.324	123	466	64	151	37	4	18	99	60	67	2
Ortiz, Adrian, Burlington	.308	100	422	50	130	10	7	3	33	15	68	29
Durango, Luis, Fort Wayne	.305	93	334	56	102	11	3	1	25	49	43	14
Smith, Timothy, Clinton	.300	121	480	67	144	25	4	13	70	33	81	21
Mee, Michael, South Bend	.299	87	318	47	95	12	1	2	38	58	39	2
Henry, Justin, West Michigan	.295	120	475	74	140	24	2	1	46	44	36	27
Rosa, Jovan, Peoria	.293	128	481	58	141	43	4	7	81	40	127	3
Samson, Nate, Peoria	.293	128	481	69	141	17	2	3	42	40	49	15
Colina, Edilio, Wisconsin	.291	114	423	69	123	24	1	4	50	29	54	8

INDIVIDUAL PITCHING LEADERS *(MINIMUM 0.8 INNINGS PITCHED PER LEAGUE GAME)*

	W	L	ERA	G	GS	CG	SV	IP	H	R	BB	SO
Kibler, Jon, West Michigan	14	5	1.75	23	23	2	0	154	103	39	32	126
Pineda, Michael, Wisconsin	8	6	1.95	26	21	1	0	138	109	38	35	128
Figaro, Alfredo, West Michigan	12	2	2.05	19	19	2	0	123	99	35	30	96
Beavan, Blake, Clinton	10	6	2.37	23	23	0	0	122	105	42	20	73
Additon, Nicholas, Quad Cities	9	5	2.50	25	19	0	1	119	92	41	35	108
Rzepczynski, Marc, Lansing	7	6	2.83	22	22	0	0	121	100	41	42	124
McCardell, Michael, Beloit	9	4	2.86	22	21	1	0	135	110	51	25	139
Caldera, Alexander, Burlington	12	6	2.89	25	25	0	0	149	141	53	36	120
Hodsdon, Scott, Kane County	5	8	2.93	25	23	0	0	120	134	60	23	86
Pelzer, Wynn, Fort Wayne	9	6	3.19	29	23	0	0	118	114	64	32	100

ALL-STAR TEAM

C—Sean Coughlin, South Bend. **1B**—Mitch Moreland, Clinton. **2B**—Larry Cobb, Kane County. **3B**—Brandon Waring, Dayton. **SS**—Zach Cozart, Dayton. **OF**—Ben Revere, Beloit; Evan Frey, South Bend; Andrew Lambo, Great Lakes. **DH**—Ian Gac, Clinton. **RHP**—Alfredo Figaro, West Michigan. **LHP**—Jon Kibler, West Michigan. **RP**—Jackson Quezada, Fort Wayne; Edgar Estanga, Lansing. **Most Valuable Player:** Ben Revere, Beloit. **Prospect of the Year:** Ben Revere, Beloit. **Manager of the Year:** Mark Haley, South Bend.

DEPARTMENT LEADERS

BATTING

OBP	Revere, Ben, Beloit	.433
SLG	Moreland, Mitchell, Clinton	.536
R	Beltre, Engel, Clinton	87
H	Beltre, Engel, Clinton	160
TB	Moreland, Mitchell, Clinton	250
XBH	Moreland, Mitchell, Clinton	59
2B	Rosa, Jovan, Peoria	43
3B	Fuller, Clay, Cedar Rapids	13
HR	Moustakas, Mike, Burlington	22
RBI	Moreland, Mitchell, Clinton	99
SAC	Samson, Nate, Peoria	22
SF	Coughlin, Sean, South Bend	12
BB	Taylor, Jason, Burlington	81
IBB	Five players tied at	4
HBP	Greene, Jonathan, Clinton	36
SO	Carrasco, Felix, Fort Wayne	162
SB	Romine, Andrew, Cedar Rapids	62
CS	Kanaby, Erik, Great Lakes	19
AB/SO	Henry, Justin, West Michigan	13.19

PITCHING

G	Quezada, Jackson, Fort Wayne	59
GS	Richmond, Jamie, Kane County	28
	Fish, Robert, Cedar Rapids	28
CG	Three players tied at	3
GF	Quezada, Jackson, Fort Wayne	49
SV	Quezada, Jackson, Fort Wayne	27
W	Kibler, Jon, West Michigan	14
L	Perez, Luis, Lansing	12
IP	Richmond, Jamie, Kane County	163.1
H	Richmond, Jamie, Kane County	175
R	Richmond, Jamie, Kane County	99
ER	Richmond, Jamie, Kane County	87
HB	Bromberg, David, Beloit	19
BB	Miller, Justin, Great Lakes	74
SO	Bromberg, David, Beloit	177
SO/9 (SP)	Bromberg, David, Beloit	10.62
SO/9 (RP)	Abreu, Juan, Burlington	12.97
BB/9	Beltre, Christian, South Bend	1.39
WP	Bromberg, David, Beloit	16
	Castillo, Fabio, Clinton	16
BK	Perez, Luis, Lansing	7
AVG	Kibler, Jon, West Michigan	.190

FIELDING

C	FPCT	Coughlin, Sean, South Bend	.990
	PO	Eigsti, Ryan, Burlington	801
	A	Eigsti, Ryan, Burlington	88
	E	Yersich, Gregory, Beloit	15
	DP	De Los Santos, Anel, Cedar Rapids	11
	PB	Dominguez, Carlos, Clinton	15
		Mesoraco, Devin, Dayton	15
1B	FPCT	Dowling, Greg, Kane County	.990
	PO	Dowling, Greg, Kane County	1074
	A	Dowling, Greg, Kane County	77
	E	Carrasco, Felix, Fort Wayne	13
		Wheeless, Chance, South Bend	13
	DP	Dowling, Greg, Kane County	86
2B	FPCT	Colina, Edilio, Wisconsin	.974
	PO	Henry, Justin, West Michigan	213
	A	Henry, Justin, West Michigan	332
	E	Tolisano, John, Lansing	25
	DP	Henry, Justin, West Michigan	78
3B	FPCT	Liddi, Alex, Wisconsin	.943
	PO	Greene, Jonathan, Clinton	91
	A	Greene, Jonathan, Clinton	227
	E	Greene, Jonathan, Clinton	31
	DP	Liddi, Alex, Wisconsin	22
SS	FPCT	Cozart, Zachary, Dayton	.978
	PO	Romine, Andrew, Cedar Rapids	200
	A	Romine, Andrew, Cedar Rapids	380
	E	Ciriaco, Audy, West Michigan	41
	DP	Jackson, Justin, Lansing	83
OF	FPCT	Reed, Justin, Dayton	.989
	PO	Beltre, Engel, Clinton	273
	A	Ortiz, Adrian, Burlington	18
	E	Ingram, D'Marcus, Quad Cities	12
	DP	Four players tied at	5

BY JIM SHONERD

Pitching wins championships, and there is no better example of that mantra in 2008 than Augusta. The GreenJackets featured the South Atlantic League's best pitching staff and their 2.95 team ERA far outpaced their nearest competition, and they rode their pitching to a 5-0 postseason record, sweeping to the franchise's first league title since 1999.

The GreenJackets had to go through two of the league's best offensive teams, Asheville and West Virginia, and did so with little difficulty. They trailed in a game only once in their five postseason wins, held Asheville to two runs in two games in the first round and then held down West Virginia to sweep the championship series as well.

Augusta's pitching staff was spearheaded by teen-age lefthander Madison Bumgarner, who won the league's pitching triple crown by going 15-3, 1.46 with 164 strikeouts. He won seven consecutive decisions to end the season, and fell just shy of a league record with 38 consecutive scoreless innings.

Augusta righthander Daryl Maday went 9-4, 1.55 before a late July callup and was replaced by lefthander Scott Barnes, who went 3-2, 1.38 down the stretch. Barnes won the clinching games in both of Augusta's playoff series.

Bumgarner was one in a superb group of talented teenagers to dominate the SAL. Greensboro outfielder Mike Stanton clubbed a franchise record 39 home runs and teammate Matt Dominguez emerged as a plus defender and advanced hitter.

In Charleston, the catching tandem of Jesus Montero and Austin Romine combined to give the RiverDogs the league's two best offensive backstops. Rome outfielder Jason Heyward finished third in the league in hitting and first baseman Freddie Freeman hitting .316 before finishing fourth in the league in RBIs. Not to be outdone by the crop of teenagers, 22-year-old Asheville third baseman Darin Holcomb took home MVP honors after hitting .318 and leading the league in doubles and RBIs.

TOP 20 PROSPECTS

1. Madison Bumgarner, lhp, Augusta (Giants)
2. Jason Heyward, of, Rome (Braves)
3. Mike Stanton, of, Greensboro (Marlins)
4. Jhoulys Chacin, rhp, Asheville (Rockies)
5. Matt Dominguez, 3b, Greensboro (Marlins)
6. Angel Villalona, 1b, Augusta (Giants)
7. Jesus Montero, c, Charleston (Yankees)
8. Austin Romine, c, Charleston (Yankees)
9. Nick Noonan, 2b, Augusta (Giants)
10. Freddie Freeman, 1b, Rome (Braves)
11. Michael Burgess, of, Hagerstown (Nationals)
12. Che-Hsuan Lin, of, Greenville (Red Sox)
13. Cole Rohrbough, lhp, Rome (Braves)
14. Jeff Locke, lhp, Rome (Braves)
15. Michael Taylor, of, Lakewood (Phillies)
16. Alex Cobb, rhp, Columbus (Rays)
17. Darin Holcomb, 3b, Asheville (Rockies)
18. Caleb Gindl, of, West Virginia (Brewers)
19. Ryan Kalish, of, Greenville (Red Sox)
20. Cody Johnson, of, Rome (Braves)

STANDINGS: SPLIT SEASON

FIRST HALF

North	W	L	PCT	GB
Lake County	41	29	.586	—
Delmarva	38	31	.551	2½
Greensboro	38	32	.543	3
Lakewood	38	32	.543	3
Hagerstown	34	35	.493	6½
West Virginia	32	37	.464	8½
Hickory	30	40	.429	11
Lexington	21	48	.304	19½

South	W	L	PCT	GB
Asheville	46	24	.657	—
Charleston	45	25	.643	1
Augusta	41	28	.594	4½
Greenville	40	30	.571	6
Savannah	33	37	.471	13
Kannapolis	31	39	.443	15
Columbus	27	43	.386	19
Rome	22	47	.319	23½

SECOND HALF

North	W	L	PCT	GB
West Virginia	45	25	.643	—
Lakewood	42	28	.600	3
Delmarva	40	30	.571	5
Lake County	34	36	.486	11
Greensboro	28	40	.412	16
Hagerstown	27	43	.386	18
Lexington	24	45	.348	20½
Hickory	22	47	.319	22½

South	W	L	PCT	GB
Augusta	47	22	.681	—
Columbus	40	26	.606	5½
Kannapolis	36	29	.554	9
Asheville	37	32	.536	10
Charleston	35	34	.507	12
Rome	34	34	.500	12½
Greenville	30	39	.435	17
Savannah	28	39	.418	18

PLAYOFFS—Semifinals: West Virginia defeated Lake County 2-1 and Augusta defeated Asheville 2-0 in best-of-three series. **Finals:** Augusta defeated West Virginia 3-0 in a best-of-five series.

OVERALL STANDINGS

Page	Team	W	L	PCT	GB	Manager	Attendance	Average	Last Penn.
278	Augusta GreenJackets (Giants)	88	50	.638	—	Andy Skeels	200,222	2,902	2008
125	Asheville Tourists (Rockies)	83	56	.597	5½	Joe Mikulik	175,892	2,625	1984
217	Charleston RiverDogs (Yankees)	80	59	.576	8½	Torre Tyson	279,606	4,173	None
238	Lakewood BlueClaws (Phillies)	80	60	.571	9	Steve Roadcap	425,166	6,346	2006
67	Delmarva Shorebirds (Orioles)	78	61	.561	10½	Ramon Sambo	226,754	3,436	2000
189	West Virginia Power (Brewers)	77	62	.554	11½	Jeff Isom	213,030	3,329	1990
116	Lake County Captains (Indians)	75	65	.536	14	Aaron Holbert	316,572	4,797	None
77	Greenville Drive (Red Sox)	70	69	.504	18½	Kevin Boles	349,116	5,060	1998
96	Kannapolis Intimidators (White Sox)	67	68	.496	19½	Chris Jones	119,668	1,899	2005
298	Columbus Catfish (Rays)	67	69	.493	20	Matt Quatraro	61,290	1,022	2007
144	Greensboro Grasshoppers (Marlins)	66	72	.478	22	Edwin Rodriguez	440,787	6,297	1982
206	Savannah Sand Gnats (Mets)	61	76	.445	26½	Donovan Mitchell	105,537	1,624	1996
328	Hagerstown Suns (Nationals)	61	78	.439	27½	Darnell Coles	137,283	2,049	None
58	Rome Braves (Braves)	56	81	.409	31½	Randy Ingle	222,168	3,366	2003
248	Hickory Crawdads (Pirates)	52	87	.374	36½	Gary Green	133,512	2,023	2004
153	Lexington Legends (Astros)	45	93	.326	43	Gregory Langbehn	370,570	5,450	2001

CLUB BATTING

	AVG	G	AB	R	H	2B	3B	HR	RBI	BB	SO	SB	CS	OBP	SLG
West Virginia	.276	139	4757	747	1312	267	36	97	668	441	1044	166	78	.343	.408
Charleston	.265	139	4737	705	1254	251	33	109	626	457	974	92	36	.334	.401
Columbus	.261	136	4501	641	1174	216	38	74	573	444	878	176	79	.331	.375
Delmarva	.261	139	4678	636	1223	265	35	91	564	426	1209	141	50	.331	.391
Greensboro	.261	138	4695	690	1224	218	18	161	631	422	1071	48	28	.330	.418
Asheville	.259	139	4676	693	1211	254	27	112	626	428	1214	227	77	.328	.397
Kannapolis	.259	135	4509	613	1169	244	26	93	549	382	1002	113	48	.323	.387
Greenville	.257	139	4738	640	1216	241	32	96	580	468	1096	121	42	.331	.382
Hickory	.257	139	4703	614	1208	236	26	84	558	375	973	81	47	.317	.372
Lakewood	.257	140	4768	651	1224	246	21	83	574	459	1009	103	42	.327	.369
Rome	.255	137	4635	571	1180	225	30	91	508	371	1045	116	58	.312	.375
Lake County	.254	140	4520	647	1146	219	31	78	577	463	991	151	62	.330	.367
Augusta	.253	138	4653	651	1178	212	36	81	576	376	1010	163	56	.317	.366
Hagerstown	.251	139	4650	608	1166	249	20	99	546	448	1060	110	56	.323	.377
Savannah	.250	137	4600	540	1152	236	34	62	483	352	1092	114	52	.308	.357
Lexington	.238	138	4582	549	1089	219	33	95	506	393	1180	151	35	.307	.362

CLUB PITCHING

	ERA	G	CG	SHO	SV	IP	H	R	ER	HR	BB	SO	AVG
Augusta	2.95	138	1	15	46	1228	1098	478	402	59	315	1118	.237
Charleston	3.42	139	1	12	45	1222	1168	588	463	68	413	1123	.249
Lake County	3.46	140	1	10	30	1203	1053	548	460	99	499	1144	.235
Lakewood	3.48	140	3	10	41	1243	1173	569	481	56	382	1029	.248
Asheville	3.54	139	8	11	43	1224	1169	582	481	99	422	1150	.250
Delmarva	3.66	139	4	8	40	1212	1083	605	493	85	442	992	.236
Savannah	3.88	137	1	11	33	1200	1145	627	517	78	438	1006	.250
Kannapolis	4.06	135	4	9	37	1169	1114	600	527	87	434	1145	.249
West Virginia	4.19	139	0	4	40	1210	1152	650	562	103	437	1078	.250
Greenville	4.30	139	0	7	42	1227	1233	687	586	110	409	1087	.261
Rome	4.32	137	3	6	25	1188	1205	667	568	64	487	1173	.261
Lexington	4.41	138	0	4	28	1212	1373	715	593	119	412	1059	.283
Columbus	4.53	136	1	6	36	1167	1192	663	585	119	380	878	.264
Greensboro	4.59	138	1	5	34	1207	1355	712	614	122	352	1019	.281
Hagerstown	4.63	139	2	6	34	1215	1300	731	622	89	428	978	.275
Hickory	5.02	139	0	4	29	1202	1313	774	670	149	455	869	.278

CLUB FIELDING

	PCT	PO	A	E	DP		PCT	PO	A	E	DP
Columbus	.973	3502	1422	136	112	Charleston	.968	3667	1471	170	116
Kannapolis	.973	3508	1348	134	112	Asheville	.967	3673	1457	173	128
Lake County	.972	3608	1435	147	126	Augusta	.967	3684	1484	174	121
Lakewood	.970	3730	1648	167	123	Hickory	.967	3607	1510	174	143
Greenville	.969	3682	1422	161	112	Savannah	.967	3600	1424	169	112
Hagerstown	.969	3645	1469	165	123	Greensboro	.965	3622	1443	185	111
Rome	.969	3563	1341	159	105	Lexington	.965	3634	1389	181	117
West Virginia	.969	3628	1474	162	111	Delmarva	.963	3638	1588	202	111

INDIVIDUAL BATTING LEADERS (MINIMUM 2.7 PLATE APPEARANCES PER LEAGUE GAME)

	AVG	G	AB	R	H	2B	3B	HR	RBI	BB	SO	SB
Fryer, Eric, West Virginia	.335	104	385	76	129	26	5	10	63	43	74	15
Montero, Jesus, Charleston	.326	132	525	86	171	34	5	17	87	37	83	2
Heyward, Jason, Rome	.323	120	449	88	145	27	6	11	52	49	74	15
Holcomb, Darin, Asheville	.318	137	509	89	162	46	0	14	102	65	60	6
Freeman, Frederick, Rome	.316	130	491	70	155	33	7	18	95	46	84	5
Brown, Matthew, Lake County	.308	122	451	64	139	26	3	8	75	35	62	3
Adams, Ryan, Delmarva	.308	119	448	68	138	26	5	11	57	36	109	12
Gindl, Caleb, West Virginia	.307	137	508	86	156	38	4	13	81	63	144	14
Mitchell, Michael, Asheville	.300	127	500	93	150	24	5	4	45	37	118	55
Romine, Austin, Charleston	.300	104	407	66	122	24	1	10	49	25	56	3

INDIVIDUAL PITCHING LEADERS (MINIMUM 0.8 INNINGS PITCHED PER LEAGUE GAME)

	W	L	ERA	G	GS	CG	SV	IP	H	R	BB	SO
Bumgarner, Madison, Augusta	15	3	1.46	24	24	1	0	142	111	28	21	164
Graham, Connor, Asheville	12	6	2.26	26	26	2	0	147	99	50	83	138
Gleason, Sean, Delmarva	12	2	2.63	30	21	2	0	151	124	54	46	108
Brewer, T.J., Augusta	10	4	2.95	23	21	0	0	113	105	53	27	72
Chapman, Chance, Lakewood	7	7	2.98	26	23	1	0	139	133	56	37	118
Darcy, Jesse, Columbus	8	3	3.05	29	19	1	1	133	124	53	15	98
Britton, Zachary, Delmarva	12	7	3.12	27	27	1	0	147	118	68	49	114
Cobb, Alexander, Columbus	9	7	3.29	25	25	0	0	140	113	59	35	97
Osuna, Edgar, Rome	10	5	3.38	30	14	2	5	125	122	53	31	135
Maxwell, Levi, Kannapolis	15	5	3.47	26	17	2	1	125	102	51	29	105

ALL-STAR TEAM

C—Jesus Montero, Charleston. **1B**—Freddie Freeman, Rome. **2B**—Everth Cabrera, Asheville. **3B**—Darin Holcomb, Asheville. **SS**—Freddy Galvis, Lakewood. **OF**—Jason Heyward, Rome; Mike Stanton, Greensboro; Caleb Gindl, West Virginia. **DH**—Eric Fryer, West Virginia. **RHP**—Jhoulys Chacin, Asheville. **LHP**—Madison Bumgarner, Augusta. **Most Valuable Player:** Darin Holcomb, Asheville. **Most Outstanding Pitcher:** Madison Bumgarner, Augusta. **Most Outstanding Prospect:** Jason Heyward, Rome. **Manager of the Year:** Joe Mikulik, Asheville.

DEPARTMENT LEADERS

BATTING

OBP	Fryer, Eric, West Virginia	.407
SLG	Stanton, Michael, Greensboro	.611
R	Mitchell, Michael, Asheville	93
H	Montero, Jesus, Charleston	171
TB	Stanton, Michael, Greensboro	286
XBH	Stanton, Michael, Greensboro	68
2B	Holcomb, Darin, Asheville	46
3B	Wrigley, Henry, Columbus	10
HR	Stanton, Michael, Greensboro	39
RBI	Holcomb, Darin, Asheville	102
SAC	Mitchell, Michael, Asheville	17
SF	Fronk, Reid, Columbus	11
BB	Fronk, Reid, Columbus	74
IBB	Stanton, Michael, Greensboro	7
HBP	Pope, Kieron, Delmarva	17
	Thompson, Mark, Lake County	17
SO	Johnson, Cody, Rome	177
SB	Cabrera, Everth, Asheville	73
CS	Loyola, Maiko, Columbus	17
	Haydel, Lee, West Virginia	17
AB/SO	Farris, Eric, West Virginia	9.08

PITCHING

G	Ortiz, Jonathan, Charleston	57
GS	Anundsen, Evan, West Virginia	28
CG	Eight players tied at	2
GF	Ortiz, Jonathan, Charleston	54
SV	Ortiz, Jonathan, Charleston	33
W	Bumgarner, Madison, Augusta	15
	Maxwell, Levi, Kannapolis	15
L	Leonhardt, Robert, Lexington	14
IP	Riordan, Cory, Asheville	168
H	Riordan, Cory, Asheville	185
R	Durand, Brett, Greensboro	102
ER	Durand, Brett, Greensboro	89
HB	Kimball, Cole, Hagerstown	17
BB	Archer, Christopher, Lake County	84
SO	Bumgarner, Madison, Augusta	164
SO/9 (SP)	Betances, Dellin, Charleston	10.53
SO/9 (RP)	Madden, Corey, Greensboro	14.28
BB/9	Odle, Oliver, Augusta	0.6
WP	Cleto, Maikel, Savannah	25
BK	Noel, Luis, Delmarva	6
AVG	Graham, Connor, Asheville	.189

FIELDING

C	FPCT	Montero, Jesus, Charleston	.993
	PO	Pena, Francisco, Savannah	685
	A	Naughton, Joel, Lakewood	83
	E	Fryer, Eric, West Virginia	12
	DP	Davis, Adam, Lake County	8
	PB	Pena, Francisco, Savannah	28
1B	FPCT	Taylor, Eric, Lexington	.992
	PO	Taylor, Eric, Lexington	1082
	A	Taylor, Eric, Lexington	76
	E	Cunningham, Jeffrey, Asheville	17
	DP	Taylor, Eric, Lexington	96
2B	FPCT	Miles, Cole, Rome	.976
	PO	Snyder, Justin, Charleston	216
	A	Snyder, Justin, Charleston	393
	E	Adams, Ryan, Delmarva	46
	DP	Snyder, Justin, Charleston	77
3B	FPCT	Davis, Andrew, Augusta	.945
	PO	Sexton, Gregory, Columbus	89
	A	Henson, Tyler, Delmarva	250
	E	Henson, Tyler, Delmarva	29
	DP	Mattair, Travis, Lakewood	26
SS	FPCT	Galvis, Freddy, Lakewood	.968
	PO	Galvis, Freddy, Lakewood	224
	A	Galvis, Freddy, Lakewood	407
	E	Angelini, Carmen, Charleston	42
	DP	Galvis, Freddy, Lakewood	81
OF	FPCT	Angle, Matthew, Delmarva	.996
	PO	McClune, Austin, Hickory	270
	A	Burgess, Michael, Hagerstown	26
	E	Loyola, Maiko, Columbus	11
	DP	Mailman, David, Greenville	6

MINOR LEAGUES

BY AARON FITT

After the city nearly lost its franchise in the offseason due to financial troubles, the Batavia Muckdogs responded to their new lease on life by winning the New York-Penn League title. Batavia swept the Jamestown Jammers in the best-of-three championship series to win the first title in the franchise's 51-year history.

In the first game of the series, the Jammers scored three runs in the bottom of the eighth to take a 3-2 lead, but Batavia third baseman Jermaine Curtis answered in the top of the ninth with his first homer in six weeks, a two-run shot that gave the Muckdogs a 4-3 win. Rain postponed the second game of the series, but the weather could not cool off Batavia's bats. Led by center fielder Frederick Parejo (4-for-4 with a double and an RBI) and right fielder Shane Peterson (2-for-5, double, two RBIs), Batavia cruised to a 9-3 win to secure the sweep. Muckdogs closer Adam Reifer picked up his second save of the postseason by striking out three over 1⅔ innings.

Reifer, who was drafted in the 11th round in 2007 out of UC Riverside, was one of the league's big stories in 2008. Finally healthy after a series of arm troubles derailed his college career, Reifer ran his fastball up to 99 mph and rated as the league's No. 3 prospect. He was just one of the league's bevy of quality prospects.

Rarely has the league seen the quality of catching it featured this summer. Tri-City's Jason Castro, a first-round pick in June out of Stanford, topped the league's prospects list, while fellow catchers Derek Norris (Vermont) and Travis d'Arnaud (Williamsport) ranked in the top five.

Jamestown's Miguel Fermin slugged a league-leading 17 homers and showed a strong arm but

TOP 20 PROSPECTS

1. Jason Castro, c, Tri-City (Astros)
2. David Cooper, 1b, Auburn (Blue Jays)
3. Adam Reifer, rhp, Batavia (Cardinals)
4. Derek Norris, c, Vermont (Nationals)
5. Travis D'Arnaud, c, Williamsport (Phillies)
6. Lonnie Chisenhall, ss, Mahoning Valley (Indians)
7. Brad Holt, rhp, Brooklyn (Mets)
8. Nick Barnese, rhp, Hudson Valley (Rays)
9. Jenrry Mejia, Brooklyn (Mets)
10. P.J. Dean, rhp, Vermont (Nationals)
11. Reese Havens, ss, Brooklyn (Mets)
12. Bryan Price, rhp, Lowell (Red Sox)
13. Brock Huntzinger, rhp, Lowell (Red Sox)
14. Danny Espinosa, ss, Vermont (Nationals)
15. Kyle Weiland, rhp, Lowell (Red Sox)
16. Tim Fedroff, of, Mahoning Valley (Indians)
17. Ike Davis, 1b, Brooklyn (Mets)
18. Chase d'Arnaud, ss, State College (Pirates)
19. Cord Phelps, 2b, Mahoning Valley (Indians)
20. Danny Farquhar, rhp, Auburn (Blue Jays)

did not crack the top 20 as a 23-year-old. Three college catchers—Hudson Valley's Jake Jefferies, Lowell's Tim Federowicz and Aberdeen's Caleb Joseph—also made strong first impressions in pro ball.

A bevy of power arms populated the league, highlighted by Reifer and second-year prep products Nick Barnese (Hudson Valley), P.J. Dean (Vermont) and Brock Huntzinger (Lowell). Then there were the oddballs: righthanders Jenrry Mejia (Brooklyn) and Danny Farquhar (Auburn) were two of the more unique prospects to pass through in recent years.

As usual, the league showcased a number of high-profile college draftees making their pro debuts, and some performed better than others. While Castro stood out and Auburn's David Cooper tore the NY-P apart, fellow first-rounder Ike Davis of Brooklyn went homerless in 215 at-bats.

STANDINGS

Page	McNamara Division	W	L	PCT	GB	Manager	Attendance	Average	Last Penn.
218	Staten Island Yankees (Yankees)	49	26	.653	—	Pat McMahon	189,876	5,274	2006
207	Brooklyn Cyclones (Mets)	45	30	.600	4	Edgar Alfonzo	265,220	7,367	2001
298	Hudson Valley Renegades (Rays)	40	35	.533	9	Joe Alvarez	150,525	4,181	1999
68	Aberdeen IronBirds (Orioles)	36	39	.480	13	Gary Kendall	247,836	6,522	1983

Page	Pinckney Division	W	L	PCT	GB	Manager	Attendance	Average	Last Penn.
259	Batavia Muckdogs (Cardinals)	46	28	.622	—	Mark Dejohn	43,167	1,199	2008
145	Jamestown Jammers (Marlins)	47	29	.618	—	Darin Everson	48,070	1,414	1991
318	Auburn Doubledays (Blue Jays)	38	37	.507	8 ½	Dennis Holmberg	64,052	1,779	2007
239	Williamsport Crosscutters (Phillies)	38	37	.507	8 ½	Dusty Wathan	64,227	1,784	2003
117	Mahoning Valley Scrappers (Indians)	31	44	.413	15 ½	Travis Fryman	123,364	3,427	2004
249	State College Spikes (Pirates)	18	56	.243	18	Brad Fischer	153,350	4,036	1994

Page	Stedler Division	W	L	PCT	GB	Manager	Attendance	Average	Last Penn.
78	Lowell Spinners (Red Sox)	40	33	.548	—	Gary DiSarcina	194,167	5,394	None
135	Oneonta Tigers (Tigers)	33	41	.446	7 ½	Ryan Newman	39,609	1,100	1998
329	Vermont Lake Monsters (Nationals)	33	52	.440	8	Ramon Aviles	91,351	2,538	1996
153	Tri-City ValleyCats (Astros)	28	45	.384	12	Pete Rancont	140,631	4,018	1997

PLAYOFFS—Semifinals: Batavia defeated Lowell 2-1 and Jamestown defeated Staten Island 2-0 in best-of-three series. **Finals:** Batavia defeated Jamestown 2-0 in a best-of-three series.

CLUB BATTING

	AVG	G	AB	R	H	2B	3B	HR	RBI	BB	SO	SB	CS	OBP	SLG
Jamestown	.282	76	2613	420	737	143	23	74	376	248	684	65	20	.350	.439
Staten Island	.269	75	2536	380	681	151	19	44	345	251	620	60	19	.339	.395
Batavia	.268	74	2507	359	673	141	23	36	311	236	590	65	31	.343	.386
Hudson Valley	.264	75	2608	339	689	121	35	27	303	229	582	109	30	.328	.368
Mahoning Valley	.257	75	2544	360	653	117	22	25	303	301	534	43	22	.340	.349
Auburn	.255	75	2478	321	632	124	13	28	287	253	618	59	24	.330	.349
State College	.254	74	2515	303	638	121	24	27	269	226	624	68	33	.321	.353
Williamsport	.252	75	2468	332	621	138	10	39	282	205	596	57	26	.316	.363
Brooklyn	.247	75	2541	284	628	127	18	45	259	230	585	28	34	.318	.364
Tri-City	.243	73	2516	322	611	113	20	52	294	225	688	42	31	.315	.366
Aberdeen	.241	75	2478	330	596	123	16	41	292	234	693	61	28	.316	.353
Oneonta	.240	74	2489	297	598	109	30	27	262	219	524	51	19	.308	.341
Lowell	.233	73	2459	312	574	127	25	38	271	259	676	89	45	.310	.352
Vermont	.224	75	2473	310	553	103	14	44	269	308	695	88	37	.318	.330

CLUB PITCHING

TEAM	ERA	G	CG	SHO	SV	IP	H	R	ER	HR	BB	SO	AVG
Brooklyn	2.78	75	0	6	32	679	551	245	208	33	263	752	.223
Staten Island	2.90	75	0	5	30	660	595	275	213	35	196	624	.240
Batavia	3.27	74	0	7	30	650	609	292	236	33	226	582	.247
Auburn	3.33	75	0	6	23	651	622	292	241	29	214	653	.249
Lowell	3.51	73	1	2	20	656	574	299	256	47	229	615	.232
Aberdeen	3.72	75	2	3	20	647	612	333	267	39	244	673	.247
Oneonta	3.75	74	0	6	22	645	641	324	269	27	245	578	.257
Vermont	3.84	75	2	3	12	665	635	352	284	46	289	632	.250
Jamestown	3.91	76	0	4	27	656	664	336	285	33	254	661	.260
Hudson Valley	3.97	75	1	5	24	665	667	362	293	38	277	636	.259
Williamsport	4.00	75	2	7	27	640	625	336	284	41	257	610	.253
Mahoning Valley	4.29	75	0	1	13	648	671	372	304	47	235	603	.261
Tri-City	4.40	73	0	1	12	646	660	390	315	50	254	581	.261
State College	5.40	74	0	3	8	644	758	461	386	49	241	509	.291

CLUB FIELDING

	PCT	PO	A	E	DP		PCT	PO	A	E	DP
Brooklyn	.978	2037	744	64	65	Auburn	.963	1954	740	103	63
Lowell	.972	1969	699	76	48	Batavia	.963	1951	755	103	87
Williamsport	.971	1919	720	80	57	Vermont	.960	1995	739	113	46
Hudson Valley	.969	1994	801	88	59	State College	.959	1931	698	111	58
Jamestown	.966	1967	764	97	67	Oneonta	.957	1935	758	122	81
Staten Island	.966	1980	794	98	65	Mahoning Valley	.955	1943	692	125	54
Aberdeen	.964	1940	729	100	52	Tri-City	.949	1939	817	147	58

INDIVIDUAL BATTING LEADERS (MINIMUM 2.7 PLATE APPEARANCES PER LEAGUE GAME)

	AVG	G	AB	R	H	2B	3B	HR	RBI	BB	SO	SB
Fermin, Miguel, Jamestown	.347	65	242	54	84	13	2	17	47	9	43	6
Baisley, Brian, Staten Island	.336	58	226	31	76	15	1	6	50	15	44	0
Lasater, Ben, Jamestown	.324	59	207	29	67	12	0	9	41	22	55	2
Gran, Paul, Jamestown	.322	70	276	52	89	14	3	6	39	23	56	13
Dening, Mitch, Lowell	.321	62	240	35	77	13	7	3	20	18	50	9
Jefferies, Jacob, Hudson Valley	.315	66	238	32	75	16	3	2	41	21	22	1
Corder, Jason, Hudson Valley	.306	50	206	29	63	12	2	5	36	10	37	1
Sedbrook, Colt, Batavia	.305	71	275	38	84	9	5	2	33	24	44	13
Wyatt, Brent, Oneonta	.305	55	197	25	60	11	3	0	14	25	41	5
Disher, Phil, Tri-City	.304	71	280	40	85	20	3	13	56	33	71	1

INDIVIDUAL PITCHING LEADERS (MINIMUM 0.8 INNINGS PITCHED PER LEAGUE GAME)

	W	L	ERA	G	GS	CG	SV	IP	H	R	BB	SO
Holt, Bradley, Brooklyn	5	3	1.87	14	14	0	0	72	43	18	33	96
Schwinden, Christopher, Brooklyn	4	1	2.01	14	8	0	0	63	53	21	12	70
Barnese, Nick, Hudson Valley	5	3	2.45	13	13	0	0	66	52	26	24	84
Phelps, David, Staten Island	8	2	2.72	15	15	0	0	73	67	28	18	52
McCurry, Cole, Aberdeen	8	3	2.76	15	15	2	0	82	67	31	22	75
Erickson, Casey, Staten Island	5	1	2.76	16	15	0	0	75	82	31	17	77
Shaw, Scott, Brooklyn	6	3	2.80	15	14	0	0	74	66	24	15	79
Zagone, Richard, Aberdeen	7	1	2.89	15	11	0	0	65	57	22	14	79
Dorn, Johnny, Jamestown	3	2	2.95	16	16	0	0	76	60	29	23	63
Peacock, Brad, Vermont	4	7	3.12	14	14	2	0	75	67	38	27	54

DEPARTMENT LEADERS

BATTING

OBP	Norris, Derek, Vermont	.444
SLG	Fermin, Miguel, Jamestown	.628
R	Fermin, Miguel, Jamestown	54
H	Gran, Paul, Jamestown	89
TB	Fermin, Miguel, Jamestown	152
XBH	Disher, Phil, Tri-City	36
2B	Synan, Jeremy, Jamestown	21
3B	Scelfo, Anthony, Hudson Valley	8
HR	Fermin, Miguel, Jamestown	17
RBI	Overbeck, Cody, Williamsport	57
SAC	Demons, Chris, Auburn	7
SF	Amar, Adam, Auburn	6
	Joseph, Caleb, Aberdeen	6
BB	Norris, Derek, Vermont	63
IBB	Norris, Derek, Vermont	4
HBP	Sedbrook, Colt, Batavia	17
SO	Dent, Ryan, Lowell	87
SB	Ross, Michael, Hudson Valley	30
CS	Norris, Derek, Vermont	9
AB/SO	Gosse, Mike, Oneonta	13.59

PITCHING

G	Reifer, Adam, Batavia	32
GS	Wells, Josh, Auburn	16
	Dorn, Johnny, Jamestown	16
CG	McCurry, Cole, Aberdeen	2
	Peacock, Brad, Vermont	2
GF	Reifer, Adam, Batavia	29
SV	Venditte, Pat, Staten Island	23
W	Shive, Andy, Staten Island	9
L	Aguero, Ramon, State College	10
IP	De Fratus, Justin, Williamsport	83.1
H	Bono, Robert, Tri-City	97
R	Noguera, Antonio, Tri-City	56
ER	Noguera, Antonio, Tri-City	45
HB	Koehler, Tom, Jamestown	10
BB	Pinales, Jose, Vermont	39
SO	Holt, Bradley, Brooklyn	96
SO/9 (SP)	Holt, Bradley, Brooklyn	11.94
SO/9 (RP)	Rulon, Brad, Staten Island	13.91
BB/9	Bono, Robert, Tri-City	1.32
WP	Holloway, Jarred, Tri-City	12
	Crawford, Skyler, Jamestown	12
BK	Eight players tied at	2
AVG	Holt, Bradley, Brooklyn	.171

FIELDING

C	FPCT	Collins, Joel, Auburn	.997
	PO	Fermin, Miguel, Jamestown	461
	A	Fermin, Miguel, Jamestown	46
	E	Norris, Derek, Vermont	10
	DP	Joseph, Caleb, Aberdeen	6
	PB	Thomas, Mark, Hudson Valley	23
1B	FPCT	Davis, Ike, Brooklyn	.998
	PO	Disher, Phil, Tri-City	556
	A	Moore, Tyler, Vermont	67
	E	Disher, Phil, Tri-City	16
	DP	Scruggs, Xavier, Batavia	66
2B	FPCT	Adams, David, Staten Island	.975
	PO	Adams, David, Staten Island	113
	A	Adams, David, Staten Island	194
	E	Gosse, Mike, Oneonta	12
	DP	Gosse, Mike, Oneonta	50
3B	FPCT	Middlebrooks, Will, Lowell	.927
	PO	Kolodny, Tyler, Aberdeen	50
	A	Kolodny, Tyler, Aberdeen	121
	E	Pounds, Bryan, Oneonta	24
	DP	Garcia, Jose, Batavia	13
		Pounds, Bryan, Oneonta	13
SS	FPCT	Hanzawa, Troy, Williamsport	.965
	PO	Hanzawa, Troy, Williamsport	123
	A	Hanzawa, Troy, Williamsport	235
	E	Staples, Joel, Jamestown	23
	DP	Hanzawa, Troy, Williamsport	44
OF	FPCT	Ratliff, Sean, Brooklyn	1.000
	PO	Bermudez, Ronald, Lowell	155
	A	Five players tied at	8
	E	Van Kirk, Brian, Auburn	8
		Mattison, Kevin, Jamestown	8
	DP	Three players tied at	3

MINOR LEAGUES

BY NATHAN RODE

Despite having only two players on the postseason all-star team, Spokane gave a glimpse of what the Rangers farm system has to offer.

The Indians dominated the Northwest League on the field and also landed five players on a deep Top 20 Prospects list.

The Indians' final record of 51-20 record was eight games better than any other club in the league, and they led the circuit in runs (436) and ERA (3.46). After dropping the first game of the championship series, they rallied with three straight wins to deny Salem-Keizer a third straight title.

Eugene outfielder Daniel Robertson was named the league's MVP after setting a record with 114 hits. He was also tops in the league in hitting (.377) and on-base percentage (.443). He went on a tear in August, batting .395/.463/.527 in 129 at-bats during the home stretch. A 33rd-round pick out of Oregon State in June, the 5-foot-8, 175-pound Robertson has a high-energy approach, good speed and terrific outfield instincts.

Salem-Keizer righthander Mike Loree flirted with perfection in three straight starts, retiring 60 of 61 batters, and finished with a NWL-best 2.44 ERA. A 50th-round pick in 2007 from Villanova, he used exceptional fastball command to breeze through the league.

While Loree seemed untouchable on the mound, Spokane righthander Wilfredo Boscan arguably had the best blend of performance and upside. He went 9-1, 3.12 in 69 innings with 70 strikeouts and 11 walks. He showed uncanny command of an 88-92 mph fastball that was complemented by a plus changeup and good, over-the-top curveball.

Boise third baseman Josh Vitters was the top prospect, not surprisingly as he was the third overall pick in the 2007 draft. He actually started the 2008 season in low Class A Peoria but developed tendinitis in his left hand and eventually settled in with the Hawks after recuperating in extended spring training. His performance did not disap-

point, as the California native hit .328/.365/.498 in 259 at-bats with five home runs and a league-best 25 doubles. He also tied a league record with a 26-game hitting streak.

Though Spokane had no problem producing runs, much of the Indians' success could be attributed to the pitching staff. Boscan led the league in wins, while lefthanders Martin Perez and Tim Murphy and righthander Neil Ramirez also made noise.

Perez, 17, led the team in starts (15) while finishing the season 1-2, 3.65 in 62 innings with 53 strikeouts and 28 walks. Murphy made 13 apperances, 12 in relief, and held opponents to a .152 average while striking out 40 in 33 innings. Ramirez had the best ERA among the regular starters at 2.66 and struck out 52 in 44 innings.

Salem-Keizer third baseman Conor Gillaspie became the first 2008 draft pick to reach the big leagues. The promotion came despite Gillaspie not playing at his best in the NWL, perhaps because of the rust he accumulated during two months of contract negotiations. Gillaspie hit just .268/.350/.324, but consistently put the barrel on the ball and should hit for gap power in the future.

TOP 20 PROSPECTS

1. Josh Vitters, 3b, Boise (Cubs)
2. Martin Perez, lhp, Spokane (Rangers)
3. Christian Friedrich, lhp, Tri-City (Rockies)
4. Neil Ramirez, rhp, Spokane (Rangers)
5. Conor Gillaspie, 3b, Salem-Keizer (Giants)
6. Wilfredo Boscan, rhp, Spokane (Rangers)
7. James Darnell, 3b, Eugene (Padres)
8. Tim Murphy, lhp, Spokane (Rangers)
9. Jharmidy DeJesus, 3b, Everett (Mariners)
10. Charlie Blackmon, of, Tri-City (Rockies)
11. Blake Tekotte, of, Eugene (Padres)
12. Ryan Flaherty, ss, Boise (Cubs)
13. Dennis Raben, of, Everett (Mariners)
14. Simon Castro, rhp, Eugene (Padres)
15. Tyson Gillies, of, Everett (Mariners)
16. Matt West, 3b, Spokane (Rangers)
17. Jason Christian, ss, Vancouver (Athletics)
18. Dusty Coleman, ss, Vancouver (Athletics)
19. Cole Figueroa, 2b/ss, Eugene (Padres)
20. Collin Cowgill, of, Yakima (Diamondbacks)

STANDINGS

Page	Eastern Division	W	L	PCT	GB	Manager	Attendance	Average	Last Penn.
308	Spokane Indians (Rangers)	51	25	.671	—	Tim Hulett	188,982	4,973	2008
87	Boise Hawks (Cubs)	43	33	.566	8	Tom Beyers	109,082	2,871	2004
126	Tri-City Dust Devils (Rockies)	36	40	.474	15	Fred Ocasio	82,021	2,158	None
49	Yakima Bears (Diamondbacks)	28	48	.368	23	Bob Didier	72,207	1,900	2000

Page	Western Division	W	L	PCT	GB	Manager	Attendance	Average	Last Penn.
279	Salem-Keizer Volcanoes (Giants)	40	36	.526	—	Tom Trebelhorn	112,425	2,959	2007
270	Eugene Emeralds (Padres)	40	36	.526	—	Greg Riddoch	130,069	3,423	1980
228	Vancouver Canadians (Athletics)	34	42	.447	6	Rick Magnante	129,073	3,585	None
288	Everett AquaSox (Mariners)	32	44	.421	8	Jose Moreno	95,294	2,508	1985

PLAYOFFS: Spokane defeated Salem-Keizer 3-1 in a best-of-five series.

CLUB BATTING

	AVG	G	AB	R	H	2B	3B	HR	RBI	BB	SO	SB	CS	OBP	SLG
Boise	.282	76	2652	417	748	189	20	43	376	301	573	75	43	.360	.417
Eugene	.270	76	2596	432	701	147	12	62	373	384	606	68	32	.370	.408
Spokane	.266	76	2662	436	709	130	19	49	377	286	627	54	32	.350	.385
Salem-Keizer	.263	76	2600	379	684	130	21	30	326	269	564	94	44	.341	.364
Tri-City	.255	76	2600	360	664	126	30	45	320	288	595	77	47	.339	.379
Everett	.247	76	2476	343	612	125	20	41	289	295	648	112	56	.338	.363
Vancouver	.234	76	2473	314	578	131	16	28	275	332	616	59	29	.334	.334
Yakima	.219	76	2473	311	542	98	24	27	245	312	609	111	46	.318	.311

CLUB PITCHING

	ERA	G	CG	SHO	SV	IP	H	R	ER	HR	BB	SO	AVG
Spokane	3.46	76	0	2	28	692	591	331	266	44	309	659	.230
Tri-City	3.70	76	0	2	16	679	643	342	279	22	274	619	.250
Eugene	4.13	76	0	5	13	668	639	377	307	46	301	606	.251
Vancouver	4.18	76	0	4	20	664	654	369	308	26	309	626	.258
Boise	4.25	76	0	2	23	678	661	381	320	46	338	602	.257
Salem-Keizer	4.26	76	0	6	24	678	695	376	321	43	268	623	.268
Everett	4.45	76	0	2	17	660	668	407	326	50	333	613	.261
Yakima	4.61	76	0	3	17	665	687	409	340	48	335	490	.267

CLUB FIELDING

	PCT	PO	A	E	DP
Salem-Keizer	.976	2035	818	71	57
Boise	.969	2034	869	94	76
Yakima	.965	1996	851	103	73
Eugene	.964	2005	790	104	76
Tri-City	.963	2037	807	109	60
Spokane	.962	2077	776	114	66
Vancouver	.962	1991	847	113	69
Everett	.957	1979	767	124	49

INDIVIDUAL BATTING LEADERS (MINIMUM 2.7 PLATE APPEARANCES PER LEAGUE GAME)

	AVG	G	AB	R	H	2B	3B	HR	RBI	BB	SO	SB
Robertson, Dan, Eugene	.377	73	302	59	114	21	3	3	45	34	34	20
Blackmon, Charles, Tri-City	.338	68	290	42	98	21	5	2	33	16	37	13
Keedy, Ryan, Boise	.333	70	252	34	84	15	1	3	40	35	58	2
Vitters, Josh, Boise	.328	61	259	38	85	25	2	5	37	13	45	1
Gillies, Tyson, Everett	.313	61	192	36	60	6	5	2	22	35	46	24
Peguero, Francisco, Salem-Keizer	.307	50	202	33	62	11	4	2	28	9	43	10
Butler, Joey, Spokane	.301	62	226	35	68	8	5	4	31	40	54	9
Flores, Jose, Salem-Keizer	.300	73	263	40	79	13	1	1	32	40	60	3
Carroll, Sawyer, Eugene	.299	46	177	41	53	14	3	8	39	32	48	5
Flaherty, Ryan, Boise	.297	56	219	39	65	19	2	8	26	24	51	4

INDIVIDUAL PITCHING LEADERS (MINIMUM 0.8 INNINGS PITCHED PER LEAGUE GAME)

	W	L	ERA	G	GS	CG	SV	IP	H	R	BB	SO
Loree, Mike, Salem-Keizer	4	3	2.44	15	15	0	0	81	63	24	7	75
Reichard, Andrew, Salem-Keizer	3	2	2.87	15	11	0	0	63	61	25	17	63
Aristil, Jonnathan, Tri-City	3	1	2.91	15	15	0	0	77	72	31	30	54
Boscan, Wilfredo, Spokane	9	1	3.12	15	12	0	0	69	66	30	11	70
Pimentel, Carlos, Spokane	6	3	3.31	16	13	0	0	65	48	27	31	54
Vandel, Geoff, Eugene	3	3	3.42	15	15	0	0	74	73	32	26	51
Perez, Martin, Spokane	1	2	3.65	15	15	0	0	62	66	32	28	53
Menchaca, Pablo, Eugene	5	4	3.76	15	13	0	0	65	71	32	18	38
Durst, Kenneth, Tri-City	4	5	3.80	15	12	0	0	64	63	34	13	61
Frazier, Parker, Tri-City	5	5	3.83	15	15	0	0	87	94	41	20	47

ALL-STAR TEAM

C—Travis Howell, Everett. **1B**—Mike Loberg, Salem-Keizer. **2B**—Josh Harrison, Boise. **3B**—Josh Vitters, Boise. **SS**—Ryan Flaherty, Boise. **OF**—Dan Robertson, Eugene; Charlie Blackmon, Tri-City; Sawyer Carroll, Eugene. **RHP**—Wilfredo Boscan, Spokane. **LHP**—Kenny Durst, Tri-City. **RP**—Jose Guzman, Vancouver; Rob Musgrave, Eugene. **Most Valuable Player:** Dan Robertson, Eugene.
Manager of the Year: Tim Hulett, Spokane.

DEPARTMENT LEADERS

BATTING

OBP	Robertson, Dan, Eugene	.443
SLG	Rundle, Andrew, Boise	.563
R	Robertson, Dan, Eugene	59
H	Robertson, Dan, Eugene	114
TB	Robertson, Dan, Eugene	150
XBH	Rundle, Andrew, Boise	33
2B	Vitters, Josh, Boise	25
3B	Six players tied at	5
HR	Cowgill, Collin, Yakima	11
RBI	Loberg, Mike, Salem-Keizer	49
SAC	Nunez, Luis, Everett	13
SF	Thomas, David, Vancouver	6
BB	Cooper, David, Yakima	66
IBB	Four players tied at	3
HBP	West, Matthew, Spokane	17
SO	Loberg, Mike, Salem-Keizer	80
SB	Gillies, Tyson, Everett	24
	Tenbrink, Nate, Everett	24
CS	Curry, Caleb, Salem-Keizer	10
AB/SO	Pacheco, Jordan, Tri-City	10.7

PITCHING

G	Guzman, Jose, Vancouver	30
GS	Morla, Ronny, Vancouver	16
CG	None	
GF	Guzman, Jose, Vancouver	26
SV	Guzman, Jose, Vancouver	15
W	Boscan, Wilfredo, Spokane	9
L	Three players tied at	7
IP	Frazier, Parker, Tri-City	87
H	Suriel, Walter, Everett	99
R	Suriel, Walter, Everett	57
ER	Suriel, Walter, Everett	53
HB	Castro, Simon, Eugene	14
BB	Taveras, Ricardo, Eugene	49
SO	Figueroa, Pedro, Vancouver	77
	Morla, Ronny, Vancouver	77
SO/9 (SP)	Figueroa, Pedro, Vancouver	10.09
SO/9 (RP)	Musgrave, Rob, Eugene	14.14
BB/9	Loree, Mike, Salem-Keizer	0.78
WP	McAtee, Bradley, Tri-City	15
BK	Figueroa, Pedro, Vancouver	4
	Ramirez, Neil, Spokane	4
AVG	Pimentel, Carlos, Spokane	.204

FIELDING

C	FPCT	Hogan, Doug, Spokane	.993
	PO	Hogan, Doug, Spokane	381
	A	Howell, Travis, Everett	48
	E	Pacheco, Jordan, Tri-City	8
		Howell, Travis, Everett	8
	DP	Three players tied at	7
	PB	Pacheco, Jordan, Tri-City	21
1B	FPCT	Loberg, Mike, Salem-Keizer	.990
	PO	Loberg, Mike, Salem-Keizer	640
	A	Napoleon, Dusty, Vancouver	51
	E	Clark, Matthew, Eugene	10
		Smith, Anthony, Yakima	10
	DP	Keedy, Ryan, Boise	55
2B	FPCT	Lormand, Ryan, Salem-Keizer	.981
	PO	Nunez, Luis, Everett	102
	A	Lormand, Ryan, Salem-Keizer	158
	E	Nunez, Luis, Everett	14
	DP	Ogata, Jason, Spokane	29
3B	FPCT	Flores, Jose, Salem-Keizer	.962
	PO	West, Matthew, Spokane	56
	A	Fie, Andrew, Yakima	164
	E	Fie, Andrew, Yakima	24
	DP	Fie, Andrew, Yakima	16
SS	FPCT	Frias, Vladimir, Salem-Keizer	.969
	PO	Frias, Vladimir, Salem-Keizer	92
	A	Frias, Vladimir, Salem-Keizer	162
	E	Christian, Jason, Vancouver	18
	DP	Christian, Jason, Vancouver	35
OF	FPCT	Bond, Casey, Salem-Keizer	.992
	PO	Paisano, David, Spokane	131
	A	Robertson, Dan, Eugene	12
	E	Four players tied at	5
	DP	Blackmon, Charles, Tri-City	4
		Burke, Kyler, Boise	4

BY MATT EDDY

It certainly wasn't surprising that Elizabethton secured its fourth Appalachian League title of the decade. No, what was surprising was that the Twins were pitted against the Pulaski Mariners, not the Danville Braves, in the finals. After all, the Twins and Braves had met in each of the past three championship series, and at least one of the two clubs has represented the league in every finals since 2000, save for 2002 when neither team made it.

Elizabethton shattered the league record for team home runs, and their 88 round-trippers were 35 more than runner-up Johnson City. The league's top two home run threats—and four of the top seven—were Twins.

Elizabethton outfielder Angel Morales batted .301/.388/.623 and led the league in slugging and with 15 home runs. The 18-year-old also ranked third in on-base percentage, extra-base hits (28) and strikeouts (72). Outfielder Evan Bigley ranked second in home runs and slugging. He hit .300/.360/.587 with 14 homers and 47 RBIs. Catcher Alex Soto and first baseman Jon Waltenbury chipped in 10 home runs apiece.

The Twins put their offensive firepower to use in the finals, outscoring Pulaski 14-4 to sweep the series in two games. Another Twin, lefthander Dan Osterbrock, won Appy League pitcher of the year honors. A seventh-round pick in 2008 from Cincinnati, the 21-year-old went 7-2, 3.00 in 13 starts, leading all pitchers in strikeouts (104) and innings (75). He issued just eight walks all year.

Pulaski, led by manager of the year Rob Mummau, halted Danville's run of four straight Eastern Division titles by going 40-27 with the league's youngest offense. Their average age was just 18.3 years. Mariners 18-year-old third baseman Mario Martinez (.319/.344/.462) and 22-year-old third-baseman-turned-catcher Juan Fuentes (.337/.407/.462), a converted third baseman, paced the offense. Shortstop Gabriel Noriega, just

17, helped shore up Pulaski's defense, though his offense was a work in progress.

Two other premium 17-year-old Latin American prospects also appeared in the Appy League during their pro debuts. Kingsport's Wilmer Flores, who signed with the Mets out of Venezuela for $700,000, batted .310/.352/.490 while leading all league shortstops in total chances, assists, putouts and double plays. Danville righthander Julio Teheran, a Colombia native who pulled down $850,000 from the Braves, pitched just 15 innings as he battled shoulder tendinitis.

Even without help from Teheran, Danville pitching led the league in ERA (3.13), strikeouts (663), and fewest home runs allowed (33). At the head of the rotation was righthander Randall Delgado (3-8, 3.13 in 14 starts), notably bolstered by a duo of righthanders: Paul Clemens (3-3, 3.39 in eight starts) and David Francis (5-3, 2.35 in eight starts).

Princeton shortstop Tim Beckham, the No. 1 overall pick in 2008 by the Rays, spent his first pro summer in the Appy League. Beckham rebounded from a poor start to hit .243/.297/.345 in 46 games.

STANDINGS

Page	Eastern Division	W	L	PCT	GB	Manager	Attendance	Average	Last Penn.
289	Pulaski Mariners	40	27	.597	—	Rob Mummau	33,679	1,021	None
59	Danville Braves	35	32	.522	5	Paul Runge	39,534	1,198	2007
69	Bluefield Orioles	29	36	.446	10	Orlando Gomez	29,867	905	2001
299	Princeton Devil Rays	24	38	.387	13 ½	Joe Szekely	24,233	932	1994
163	Burlington Royals	24	41	.369	15	Tony Tijerina	28,196	910	1993

Page	Western Division	W	L	PCT	GB	Manager	Attendance	Average	Last Penn.
198	Elizabethton Twins	41	25	.621	—	Ray Smith	28,131	907	2008
260	Johnson City Cardinals	36	30	.545	5	Joe Almaraz	21,327	688	1976
97	Bristol White Sox	34	30	.531	6	Bobby Thigpen	21,696	723	2002
208	Kingsport Mets	34	32	.515	7	N. Leyva/P. Lopez	38,589	1,169	1995
154	Greeneville Astros	30	36	.455	11	Rodney Linares	51,806	1,570	2004

PLAYOFFS: Elizabethton defeated Pulaski 2-0 in a best-of-three series.

CLUB BATTING

	AVG	G	AB	R	H	2B	3B	HR	RBI	BB	SO	SB	CS	OBP	SLG
Elizabethton	.274	66	2291	418	628	142	13	88	368	263	614	24	19	.360	.463
Bristol	.271	64	2150	343	582	107	17	38	299	138	509	87	48	.325	.389
Kingsport	.270	66	2296	351	620	127	25	48	302	183	505	36	18	.335	.410
Johnson City	.269	66	2321	362	625	125	15	53	308	232	603	84	41	.347	.405
Pulaski	.269	67	2221	333	598	110	17	51	302	204	568	40	27	.337	.403
Danville	.267	67	2277	305	608	123	20	39	271	167	524	37	22	.327	.390
Greeneville	.257	66	2239	305	575	93	23	35	265	198	570	64	37	.326	.366
Bluefield	.249	65	2130	298	531	94	13	39	260	224	561	57	35	.335	.361
Princeton	.248	62	2121	264	526	95	28	23	208	183	560	58	20	.313	.352
Burlington	.238	65	2181	266	520	82	18	25	227	172	526	48	39	.300	.327

CLUB PITCHING

	ERA	G	CG	SHO	SV	IP	H	R	ER	HR	BB	SO	AVG
Danville	3.13	67	1	6	23	586	521	267	203	33	209	663	.236
Bristol	3.58	64	1	1	19	557	539	273	222	42	182	528	.252
Greeneville	4.07	66	0	7	17	578	616	322	261	36	195	506	.270
Kingsport	4.07	66	1	4	18	566	579	329	256	49	200	528	.265
Johnson City	4.14	66	0	4	17	596	599	336	274	42	216	639	.258
Pulaski	4.29	67	2	0	22	581	606	342	275	47	215	563	.265
Bluefield	4.31	65	2	3	12	554	615	337	265	35	181	469	.278
Elizabethton	4.37	66	2	2	16	577	603	348	280	52	181	595	.266
Princeton	4.42	62	0	4	13	540	544	333	265	47	185	528	.256
Burlington	4.69	65	0	4	9	562	591	358	291	56	200	521	.269

CLUB FIELDING

	PCT	PO	A	E	DP		PCT	PO	A	E	DP
Danville	.966	1757	659	84	54	Elizabethton	.961	1730	714	98	58
Burlington	.965	1686	681	86	62	Johnson City	.958	1789	705	109	57
Kingsport	.964	1699	737	90	74	Greeneville	.956	1733	722	113	63
Pulaski	.963	1743	701	95	51	Princeton	.953	1619	655	113	44
Bristol	.962	1671	702	94	71	Bluefield	.952	1661	764	122	61

INDIVIDUAL BATTING LEADERS (MINIMUM 2.7 PLATE APPEARANCES PER LEAGUE GAME)

PLAYER, TEAM	AVG	G	AB	R	H	2B	3B	HR	RBI	BB	SO	SB
Smith, Curt, Johnson City	.378	47	193	34	73	14	1	8	49	11	36	3
Castillo, Jorge, Bristol	.365	43	167	18	61	11	2	1	25	11	43	0
Gilmore, Jon, Danville	.337	67	258	27	87	23	0	4	31	13	41	0
Fuentes, Juan, Pulaski	.337	59	208	28	70	18	1	2	40	28	30	0
Otero, Elias, Princeton	.332	55	208	38	69	13	7	5	32	21	45	3
Waltenbury, Jonathan, Elizabethton	.319	63	263	49	84	22	3	10	45	27	46	0
Kendall, Jordan, Bristol	.319	48	185	35	59	9	3	3	26	9	34	20
Martinez, Mario, Pulaski	.319	64	251	43	80	15	3	5	32	10	47	2
Vasquez, Niko, Johnson City	.317	55	208	46	66	16	1	4	25	29	52	8
Welty, Ronnie, Bluefield	.314	55	207	26	65	13	2	3	34	9	49	6

INDIVIDUAL PITCHING LEADERS (MINIMUM 0.8 INNINGS PITCHED PER LEAGUE GAME)

PITCHER, TEAM	W	L	ERA	G	GS	CG	SV	IP	H	R	BB	SO
Moore, Matthew, Princeton	2	2	1.66	12	12	0	0	54	30	22	19	77
Allen, Colin, Bluefield	3	2	2.31	14	11	0	0	62	59	25	20	64
Hodges, Casey, Danville	4	5	2.47	12	12	1	0	69	57	25	16	56
Tippett, Bradley, Elizabethton	8	3	2.55	14	14	1	0	74	70	35	9	63
Infante, Gregory, Bristol	4	3	2.66	13	12	0	0	74	63	26	19	57
Trinidad, Jose, Greeneville	3	2	2.73	10	10	0	0	56	57	23	6	40
Lanigan, Bobby, Elizabethton	6	5	2.78	13	13	0	0	74	74	33	9	65
Moreland, Kenny, Bluefield	6	4	2.93	13	13	0	0	68	70	22	6	65
Osterbrock, Daniel, Elizabethton	7	2	3.00	13	13	1	0	75	70	33	8	104
Delgado, Randall, Danville	3	8	3.13	14	14	0	0	69	63	32	30	81

ALL-STAR TEAM

C—Juan Fuentes, Pulaski. **1B**—Curt Smith, Johnson City. **2B**—Elias Otero, Princeton. **3B**—Jon Gilmore, Danville. **SS**—Wilmer Flores, Kingsport. **OF**—Evan Bigley, Elizabethton; Angel Morales, Elizabethton; Jordan Kendall, Bristol; Ronnie Welty, Bluefield. **DH**—Jonathan Waltenbury, Elizabethton. **Util**—Mario Martinez, Pulaski. **RHP**—Bradley Tippett, Elizabethton. **LHP**—Dan Osterbrock, Elizabethton. **RP**—Mark Hamburger, Elizabethton. **Player of the Year:** Curt Smith, Johnson City. **Pitcher of the Year:** Dan Osterbrock, Elizabethton. **Manager of the Year:** Rob Mummau, Pulaski.

DEPARTMENT LEADERS

BATTING

OBP	Smith, Curt, Johnson City	.418
SLG	Morales, Angel, Elizabethton	.623
R	De La Osa, Dominic, Elizabethton	50
H	Gilmore, Jon, Danville	87
TB	Waltenbury, Jonathan, Elizabethton	142
XBH	Waltenbury, Jonathan, Elizabethton	35
2B	Gilmore, Jon, Danville	23
3B	Welch, Stefan, Kingsport	8
HR	Morales, Angel, Elizabethton	15
RBI	Rodriguez, Gerardo, Danville	49
	Smith, Curt, Johnson City	49
SAC	Franco, Angel, Burlington	6
SF	Martinez, Mario, Pulaski	6
BB	De La Osa, Dominic, Elizabethton	37
IBB	Sonoqui, Eli, Princeton	3
	Smith, Curt, Johnson City	3
HBP	Stevens, Robert, Bluefield	23
SO	Biell, Dustin, Princeton	74
SB	Greene, Justin, Bristol	26
CS	Kendall, Jordan, Bristol	15
AB/SO	Flores, Wilmer, Kingsport	8.75

PITCHING

G	Hamburger, Mark, Elizabethton	27
GS	Tippett, Bradley, Elizabethton	14
	Delgado, Randall, Danville	14
CG	Nine tied at	1
GF	Hamburger, Mark, Elizabethton	25
SV	Hamburger, Mark, Elizabethton	13
W	Tippett, Bradley, Elizabethton	8
L	Delgado, Randall, Danville	8
IP	Osterbrock, Daniel, Elizabethton	75
H	Rivero, Raul, Bluefield	84
R	Haas, Kyle, Pulaski	53
ER	Berlind, Daniel, Elizabethton	48
HB	Rosenbaum, Zachary, Kingsport	12
BB	Gonzalez, Reynier, Johnson City	31
SO	Osterbrock, Daniel, Elizabethton	104
SO/9 (SP)	Moore, Matthew, Princeton	12.75
SO/9 (RP)	Rodriguez, Jacob, Burlington	12.96
BB/9	Moreland, Kenny, Bluefield	0.8
WP	Leon, Arcenio, Greeneville	18
BK	Leon, Arcenio, Greeneville	4
AVG	Moore, Matthew, Princeton	.154

FIELDING

C	FPCT	Blaquiere, Jean Luc, Kingsport	.996
	PO	Acosta, Mayobanex, Princeton	337
	A	Bernardo, Luis, Bluefield	70
	E	Bernardo, Luis, Bluefield	7
		Cawley, Jack, Johnson City	7
	DP	Santos, Orlando, Bristol	5
		Acosta, Mayobanex, Princeton	5
	PB	Castro, Ivan, Johnson City	16
1B	FPCT	Hinze, Kody, Greeneville	.986
	PO	Polanco, Elvin, Bluefield	528
	A	McNulty, Douglas, Kingsport	33
	E	Polanco, Elvin, Bluefield	14
	DP	Hinze, Kody, Greeneville	49
2B	FPCT	Garcia, Andrew, Bristol	.980
	PO	Garcia, Andrew, Bristol	113
	A	Garcia, Andrew, Bristol	178
	E	De La Osa, Dominic, Elizabethton	12
	DP	Suire, Kyle, Kingsport	46
3B	FPCT	Cruz, Fernando, Burlington	.911
	PO	Welch, Stefan, Kingsport	38
	A	Martinez, Mario, Pulaski	130
	E	Reynolds, Burt, Princeton	33
	DP	Welch, Stefan, Kingsport	15
SS	FPCT	Vasquez, Niko, Johnson City	.964
	PO	Flores, Wilmer, Kingsport	86
		Silverio, Juan, Bristol	86
	A	Flores, Wilmer, Kingsport	185
	E	Silverio, Juan, Bristol	24
	DP	Flores, Wilmer, Kingsport	46
OF	FPCT	Biell, Dustin, Princeton	1.000
	PO	Ware, L.V., Danville	122
	A	Kendall, Jordan, Bristol	11
	E	Austin, Jay, Greeneville	9
	DP	Kendall, Jordan, Bristol	4

MINOR LEAGUES

BY BEN BADLER

Former Old Dominion teammates Dan Hudson and Dexter Carter reunited in Great Falls after getting drafted in 2008, forming a dynamic one-two duo in the Voyagers rotation en route to the league title.

Carter, a 14th-round pick, led the league with a 2.23 ERA in 69 innings and ranked second in the league with 89 strikeouts. Hudson, a fifth-rounder, led the PL with 90 strikeouts in 70 innings and had a sharp 3.36 ERA.

In the championship round, Carter led Great Falls to a 4-3 victory over Orem, striking out nine and allowing just two runs to a strong Orem lineup through five innings. After Orem won the second game 3-2 in 13 innings, Hudson shut down the Owlz in the championship game, allowing one run and striking out 12 in six innings as the Voyagers emerged with an 8-5 victory.

Orem won 70 percent of its regular season games and finished with a 52-33 record.

In a league known for its offense, the Owlz led the PL with a 4.23 team ERA, tying Great Falls for the league's most strikeouts and issuing the second-fewest walks. Orem's Jayson Miller, 22, walked only seven batters in 81 innings and was the league's pitcher of the year, as the lefty's 2.33 ERA ranked second in the PL. Lefty Will Smith also showed impeccable control for the Owlz, posting a 76-to-6 strikeout-to-walk ratio in 73 innings and finishing fourth in the PL with a 3.08 ERA.

The Owlz weren't bashful at the plate, hitting .299/.369/.478 as a team to lead the league in average, on-base percentage and slugging. First baseman Roberto Lopez, a senior sign out of USC in 2008, hit .400/.480/.667 with 14 homers and 28 doubles as the league's MVP, leading the league in average, on-base percentage and slugging. Owlz third baseman Luis Jimenez hit .331/.361/.631 with a league-leading 15 home runs, while outfielder Angel Castillo's 14 home runs tied him with Lopez and Helena first baseman Brock Kjeldgaard for second.

Yet in the postseason it was the Voyagers who emerged with the league crown. Shortstop Tyler Kuhn led Great Falls with a .375/.424/.570 aver-

age, while catcher Mike Grace hit .287/.349/.491.

Casper catcher Wilin Rosario repeated the league as a 19-year-old, but his dramatic improvement in all facets of the game—particularly in the batter's box—caught the attention of league observers, and he ranked as the league's top prospect.

Ogden shortstop Devaris Gordon, who didn't qualify academically for his junior college in the spring yet was selected by the Dodgers in the fourth round, showed off premium athletic ability. Gordon hit .331/.371/.430 with 18 steals in 23 attempts. The Raptors' middle infielders provided ample offense, as second baseman Tony Delmonico batted .340/.443/.716 with 11 home runs.

TOP 20 PROSPECTS

1. Wilin Rosario, c, Casper (Rockies)
2. Cutter Dykstra, of, Helena (Brewers)
3. Will Smith, lhp, Orem (Angels)
4. Devaris Gordon, ss, Ogden (Dodgers)
5. Luis Jimenez, 3b, Orem (Angels)
6. Delta Cleary, of, Casper (Rockies)
7. Bryan Shaw, rhp, Missoula (Diamondbacks)
8. Trevor Harden, rhp, Missoula (Diamondbacks)
9. Dexter Carter, rhp, Great Falls (White Sox)
10. Kyle Russell, of, Ogden (Dodgers)
11. Pedro Baez, 3b, Ogden (Dodgers)
12. Jose Perez, rhp, Orem (Angels)
13. Efrain Nieves, lhp, Helena (Brewers)
14. Rossmel Perez, c, Missoula (Diamondbacks)
15. Angel Castillo, of, Orem (Angels)
16. Wily Peralta, rhp, Helena (Brewers)
17. Erik Komatsu, of, Helena (Brewers)
18. Dan Hudson, rhp, Great Falls (White Sox)
19. Tony Delmonico, 2b, Ogden (Dodgers)
20. Michael Kohn, rhp, Orem (Angels)

STANDINGS: SPLIT SEASON

FIRST HALF

North	W	L	PCT	GB
Billings	23	15	.605	—
Helena	20	18	.526	3
Great Falls	19	19	.500	4
Missoula	9	29	.237	14

South	W	L	PCT	GB
Orem	25	13	.658	—
Casper	23	15	.605	2
Ogden	19	19	.500	6
Idaho Falls	14	24	.368	11

SECOND HALF

North	W	L	PCT	GB
Billings	19	17	.528	—
Great Falls	20	18	.526	—
Helena	15	23	.395	5
Missoula	12	25	.324	7½

South	W	L	PCT	GB
Orem	27	10	.730	—
Ogden	23	14	.622	4
Idaho Falls	19	19	.500	8½
Casper	13	22	.371	13

PLAYOFFS—Semifinals: Orem defeated Ogden 2-1 and Great Falls defeated Billings 2-0 in best-of-three series. **Finals:** Great Falls defeated Orem 2-1 in a best-of-three series.

OVERALL STANDINGS

Page	Team	W	L	PCT	GB	Manager	Attendance	Average	Last Penn.
172	Orem Owlz (Angels)	52	23	.693	—	Tom Kotchman	108,283	2,927	2007
108	Billings Mustangs (Reds)	42	32	.568	9 ½	Julio Garcia	113,166	3,059	2001
181	Ogden Raptors (Dodgers)	42	33	.560	10	Mike Brumley	138,555	3,745	None
98	Great Falls Voyagers (White Sox)	39	37	.513	13 ½	Chris Cron	106,831	2,811	2008
126	Casper Ghosts (Rockies)	36	37	.493	15	Tony Diaz	50,580	1,445	None
190	Helena Brewers (Brewers)	35	41	.461	17 ½	Rene Gonzales	35,066	948	1984
162	Idaho Falls Chukars (Royals)	33	43	.434	19 ½	Jim Gabella	95,470	2,512	2000
50	Missoula Osprey (Diamondbacks)	21	54	.280	31	Audo Vicente	81,001	2,189	2006

CLUB BATTING

	AVG	G	AB	R	H	2B	3B	HR	RBI	BB	SO	SB	CS	OBP	SLG
Orem	.299	75	2705	521	810	178	38	76	452	255	617	73	27	.369	.478
Casper	.281	73	2495	373	701	133	29	49	334	233	575	89	48	.350	.416
Ogden	.279	75	2677	485	746	195	32	89	448	269	717	45	15	.355	.475
Billings	.276	74	2573	444	710	178	29	61	405	258	567	39	26	.351	.439
Great Falls	.273	76	2633	415	719	140	26	52	364	283	665	93	39	.353	.405
Idaho Falls	.265	76	2627	397	695	157	28	43	345	272	693	142	50	.336	.395
Helena	.262	76	2695	430	706	136	24	79	387	289	692	58	39	.340	.418
Missoula	.258	75	2612	384	675	130	33	59	336	241	632	60	36	.329	.401

CLUB PITCHING

	ERA	G	CG	SHO	SV	IP	H	R	ER	HR	BB	SO	AVG
Orem	4.25	75	0	4	19	668	662	372	314	51	223	697	.255
Great Falls	4.34	76	0	4	14	672	671	387	323	55	231	697	.256
Idaho Falls	4.70	76	0	3	15	667	700	418	348	67	323	628	.271
Billings	4.76	74	0	1	17	652	697	406	345	56	258	585	.273
Helena	4.88	76	0	4	18	694	733	446	376	65	292	655	.270
Casper	5.23	73	2	2	18	635	687	423	369	68	211	684	.271
Ogden	5.31	75	2	1	17	675	807	474	394	61	283	648	.295
Missoula	5.79	75	1	4	8	656	805	523	421	85	279	564	.302

CLUB FIELDING

	PCT	PO	A	E	DP		PCT	PO	A	E	DP
Helena	.970	2082	886	93	62	Idaho Falls	.964	2000	851	106	86
Great Falls	.966	2016	823	100	64	Casper	.962	1905	704	104	52
Billings	.965	1957	804	101	62	Ogden	.960	2024	856	119	76
Orem	.965	2003	798	103	57	Missoula	.958	1968	856	125	71

INDIVIDUAL BATTING LEADERS (MINIMUM 2.7 PLATE APPEARANCES PER LEAGUE GAME)

	AVG	G	AB	R	H	2B	3B	HR	RBI	BB	SO	SB
Lopez, Roberto, Orem	.400	67	270	68	108	28	1	14	72	34	23	3
Kuhn, Tyler, Great Falls	.375	62	256	51	96	23	9	3	46	21	35	7
Jimenez, Luis, Orem	.331	66	284	57	94	28	6	15	65	11	45	6
Gordon, Devaris, Ogden	.331	60	251	45	83	13	3	2	27	16	29	18
Sandoval, Orlando, Casper	.324	66	253	39	82	15	3	4	35	9	62	8
Komatsu, Erik, Helena	.321	68	277	61	89	19	4	11	47	30	42	8
Rosario, Wilin, Casper	.316	66	263	48	83	15	3	12	49	24	57	4
Giovanatto, Donato, Orem	.309	63	236	47	73	14	2	9	38	19	48	1
Greene, Kyle, Missoula	.302	52	212	33	64	14	0	5	26	10	59	1
Sappelt, David, Billings	.299	62	254	47	76	19	5	7	35	21	45	6

INDIVIDUAL PITCHING LEADERS (MINIMUM 0.8 INNINGS PITCHED PER LEAGUE GAME)

	W	L	ERA	G	GS	CG	SV	IP	H	R	BB	SO
Carter, Dexter, Great Falls	6	1	2.23	15	12	0	0	69	44	23	25	89
Miller, Jayson, Orem	8	2	2.33	15	13	0	0	81	75	29	7	68
Aguasviva, Geison, Ogden	3	4	2.90	13	13	0	0	71	85	39	13	60
Smith, William, Orem	8	2	3.08	16	14	0	0	73	73	28	6	76
Hodgson, Ivor, Idaho Falls	3	6	3.14	15	15	0	0	72	62	37	33	67
Casey, Bryan, Idaho Falls	3	5	3.36	16	16	0	0	72	65	31	26	66
Hudson, Daniel, Great Falls	5	4	3.36	14	14	0	0	70	52	30	22	90
Castro, Oscar, Billings	4	2	4.14	13	13	0	0	67	69	34	18	52
Houston, Dan, Casper	6	4	4.17	14	14	1	0	69	61	39	20	68
Watt, Michael, Ogden	9	4	4.35	15	15	2	0	81	91	46	21	79

ALL-STAR TEAM

C—Wilin Rosario, Casper. **1B**—Brock Jjeldgaard, Helena. **2B**—Jacob Elmore, Missoula. **3B**—Luis Jimenez, Orem. **SS**—Tyler Kuhn, Great Falls. **OF**—Angel Castillo, Orem; Kyle Russell, Ogden; Erik Komatsu, Helena. **DH**—Roberto Lopez, Orem. **P**—Jayson Miller, Orem; William Smith, Orem; Dan Houston, Casper; Dexter Carter, Great Falls; Bryan Casey, Idaho Falls; Leonardo Astorga, Billings. **Most Valuable Player:** Roberto Lopez, Orem. **Pitcher of the Year:** Jayson Miller, Orem. **Manager of the Year:** Julio Garcia, Billings.

DEPARTMENT LEADERS

BATTING

OBP	Lopez, Roberto, Orem	.480
SLG	Lopez, Roberto, Orem	.667
R	Lopez, Roberto, Orem	68
H	Lopez, Roberto, Orem	108
TB	Lopez, Roberto, Orem	180
XBH	Jimenez, Luis, Orem	49
2B	Jimenez, Luis, Orem	28
	Lopez, Roberto, Orem	28
3B	Kuhn, Tyler, Great Falls	9
HR	Jimenez, Luis, Orem	15
RBI	Lopez, Roberto, Orem	72
SAC	Perez, Darwin, Orem	8
SF	Konstanty, Michael, Billings	8
BB	Delaney, John, Helena	51
IBB	Three players tied at	2
HBP	Three players tied at	11
SO	Kjeldgaard, Brock, Helena	113
SB	Norris, Patrick, Idaho Falls	33
CS	Navarro, Reynaldo, Missoula	9
AB/SO	Lopez, Roberto, Orem	11.74

PITCHING

G	Morales, Ronald, Great Falls	28
GS	Casey, Bryan, Idaho Falls	16
CG	Watt, Michael, Ogden	2
GF	Yacko, Kurt, Casper	24
SV	Yacko, Kurt, Casper	11
W	Dutton, Jonathan, Ogden	9
	Watt, Michael, Ogden	9
	Sherrill, Garrett, Helena	9
IP	Skogley, Kevin, Great Falls	86.2
H	Reynolds, Brett, Missoula	102
R	Quezada, Rafael, Missoula	64
ER	Quezada, Rafael, Missoula	62
HB	Quezada, Rafael, Missoula	13
BB	Arneson, Jamie, Billings	42
SO	Hudson, Daniel, Great Falls	90
SO/9 (SP)	Hudson, Daniel, Great Falls	11.63
SO/9 (RP)	Albritton, Daniel, Great Falls	12.33
BB/9	Smith, William, Orem	0.74
WP	Boothe, Robert, Ogden	14
BK	Carter, Dexter, Great Falls	4
AVG	Carter, Dexter, Great Falls	.179

FIELDING

C	FPCT	Rosario, Wilin, Casper	.994
	PO	Rosario, Wilin, Casper	462
	A	Wallach, Matthew, Ogden	45
	E	Brooks, Beau, Orem	9
	DP	Perez, Rossmel, Missoula	7
		McCauley, Sean, Idaho Falls	7
	PB	Rosario, Wilin, Casper	14
1B	FPCT	White, Ryne, Missoula	.990
	PO	Kjeldgaard, Brock, Helena	744
	A	Kjeldgaard, Brock, Helena	55
	E	Three players tied at	9
	DP	Kjeldgaard, Brock, Helena	55
		Espinosa, Alberto, Idaho Falls	55
2B	FPCT	Avila, Jesus, Great Falls	.978
	PO	Contreras, Ivan, Orem	107
	A	Contreras, Ivan, Orem	166
	E	Contreras, Ivan, Orem	12
	DP	Perez, Alwin, Idaho Falls	31
3B	FPCT	Delaney, John, Helena	.929
	PO	Baez, Pedro, Ogden	47
	A	Baez, Pedro, Ogden	129
	E	Baez, Pedro, Ogden	20
	DP	Baez, Pedro, Ogden	16
SS	FPCT	Rojas, Miguel, Billings	.963
	PO	Navarro, Reynaldo, Missoula	140
	A	Navarro, Reynaldo, Missoula	228
	E	Navarro, Reynaldo, Missoula	38
	DP	Alfaro, John, Idaho Falls	43
OF	FPCT	Norris, Patrick, Idaho Falls	.993
	PO	Norris, Patrick, Idaho Falls	136
	A	Stone, Bobby, Missoula	12
	E	Brown, Tony, Billings	10
	DP	Three players tied at	3

BY JESSE BURKHART

The Angels finished atop the Arizona League standings in the first half of the season with a 21-7 record. In the second half, the Giants posted an identical 21-7 mark of their own to match up against the Angels in a one-game playoff for the league title.

The Giants went on to capture their third championship in five years by defeating the Angels 4-2. Righthander Javier Hernandez yielded just one run on five hits, striking out five and walking two in eight innings to earn the victory. First baseman C.J. Ziegler was 2-for-4 with the game's only home run, a solo shot in the fourth inning.

The title was the culmination of an all-around effort from the Giants, who finished with the third-best ERA in the league and scored the second-most runs despite not boasting a single all-star on the roster. Ziegler, San Francisco's 16th-round pick in the 2008 draft and Arizona's all-time prep home run leader, anchored the middle of the order, batting .262/.379/.465 and contributing a league-high 43 RBIs. Righthander Kyle Nicholson combined with Hernandez to stabilize the rotation, going 6-1, 1.15 and finishing the season as the league's ERA leader. Nicholson was resilient in his return from Tommy John surgery, striking out 54 and walking just three in 63 innings.

Per the norm, the league featured plenty of young Latin American talent, as organizations tend to keep their foreign-born players close to their spring training complexes as they get adjusted to the United States.

The top two prospects were supplemental first-round picks in the 2008 draft. Coming directly out of high school, Royals righthander Mike Montgomery was kept on strict pitch counts but showed an advanced feel for pitching. He also enjoyed the luxury of working closely with former Cy Young Award winner Mark Davis, one of two pitching coaches on the club. Montgomery went 2-1, 1.69 with 34 strikeouts in 43 innings.

Jaff Decker, who was tagged by the Padres six picks after Montgomery, batted .352/.523/.541 on his way to earning the league's MVP award.

He also walked 55 times in 214 plate appearances, exhibiting plate discipline well beyond that of most 18-year-olds.

But perhaps the most prodigious talent to make an appearance in the AZL was Giants catcher Buster Posey, the fifth overall pick in the 2008 draft. Posey did not qualify for the Top 20 Prospects list because he accumulated only 26 at-bats, but he hit .385 in that span.

Other offensive standouts included Cubs third baseman John Contreras (nine home runs, tied for most) and Angels outfielder Matthew Crawford (.373 batting average, 19 stolen bases), but both players were omitted from the list due to their age (22), which is old for the league.

TOP 20 PROSPECTS

1. Mike Montgomery, lhp, of, Royals
2. Jaff Decker, of, Padres
3. Jharmidy DeJesus, 3b, Mariners
4. Ehire Adrianza, ss, Giants
5. Manuarys Correa, rhp, Angels
6. Rashun Dixon, of, Athletics
7. Jake Odorizzi, rhp, Brewers
8. Tyler Sample, rhp, Royals
9. Jose Casilla, rhp, Giants
10. Yowill Espinal, ss/2b, Royals
11. Joe Wieland, rhp, Rangers
12. Tyler Chatwood, rhp, Angels
13. Jose Bonilla, c, Royals
14. Starlin Castro, ss/2b, Cubs
15. Seth Lintz, rhp, Brewers
16. Junior Lake, ss, Cubs
17. Kyle Nicholson, rhp, Giants
18. Clark Murphy, 1b, Rangers
19. Terrell Alliman, of/3b, Angels
20. Wendell Fairley, of, Giants

STANDINGS: SPLIT SEASON

FIRST HALF	W	L	PCT	GB		SECOND HALF	W	L	PCT	GB
Angels	21	7	.750	—		Giants	21	7	.750	—
Cubs	18	10	.643	3		Padres	19	9	.679	2
Rangers	17	11	.607	4		Angels	18	10	.643	3
Giants	15	13	.536	6		Rangers	17	11	.607	4
Royals	15	13	.536	6		Cubs	13	14	.481	7½
Padres	14	14	.500	7		Mariners	12	16	.429	9
Athletics	11	17	.393	10		Athletics	10	18	.357	11
Mariners	9	19	.321	12		Royals	8	20	.286	13
Brewers	6	22	.214	15		Brewers	7	20	.259	13½

PLAYOFFS: The Giants defeated the Angels in a one-game championship.

OVERALL STANDINGS

Page	Team	Complex	W	L	PCT	GB	Manager	Last Penn.
173	Angels	Tempe	39	17	.696	—	Tyrone Boykin	None
280	Giants	Scottsdale	36	20	.643	3	Bert Hunter	2008
309	Rangers	Surprise	34	22	.607	5	Bill Richardson	None
271	Padres	Peoria	33	23	.589	6	Jose Flores	2006
88	Cubs	Mesa	31	24	.564	7½	Franklin Font	2002
164	Royals	Surprise	23	33	.411	16	Julio Bruno	2003
229	Athletics	Phoenix	21	34	.375	18	Ruben Escalera	2001
290	Mariners	Peoria	21	35	.375	18	Andy Bottin	2007
190	Brewers	Phoenix	13	42	.236	25½	Tony Diggs	1990

CLUB BATTING

	AVG	G	AB	R	H	2B	3B	HR	RBI	BB	SO	SB	CS	OBP	SLG
Angels	.301	56	1874	369	564	97	38	17	309	221	377	97	41	.381	.420
Cubs	.284	55	1883	351	534	86	41	36	295	212	405	84	26	.363	.430
Giants	.276	56	1899	353	525	122	20	23	306	224	404	71	24	.365	.398
Padres	.276	56	1860	340	514	90	17	18	291	327	406	62	23	.392	.372
Rangers	.269	56	1877	308	505	101	25	20	257	191	449	84	32	.344	.381
Athletics	.261	56	1921	303	502	97	32	26	256	197	511	67	24	.340	.386
Mariners	.260	56	1898	271	493	73	24	17	219	144	437	76	34	.317	.350
Royals	.235	56	1862	240	438	77	18	24	192	151	492	85	51	.301	.335
Brewers	.213	55	1791	198	382	86	23	13	163	179	542	64	25	.297	.309

CLUB PITCHING

	ERA	G	CG	SHO	SV	IP	H	R	ER	HR	BB	SO	AVG
Angels	3.24	56	1	3	13	483	434	236	174	18	182	491	.238
Rangers	3.78	56	0	3	14	486	470	270	204	22	204	516	.256
Giants	3.90	56	2	12	10	491	465	264	213	19	171	463	.249
Padres	3.96	56	0	0	11	488	507	283	213	17	146	456	.267
Cubs	4.52	55	0	1	15	472	467	294	237	22	227	376	.259
Royals	4.77	56	0	2	15	495	554	331	261	20	213	428	.285
Athletics	4.81	56	0	1	12	491	557	348	262	31	189	413	.285
Brewers	5.07	55	0	1	8	469	483	364	264	18	261	449	.260
Mariners	5.11	56	0	2	7	488	520	343	276	27	253	431	.276

CLUB FIELDING

	PCT	PO	A	E	DP		PCT	PO	A	E	DP
Giants	.967	1474	632	71	56	Cubs	.956	1415	655	96	55
Angels	.961	1449	601	84	37	Rangers	.948	1459	633	115	47
Royals	.961	1484	630	86	59	Athletics	.946	1472	608	119	44
Padres	.960	1465	670	90	54	Brewers	.932	1407	568	145	49
Mariners	.959	1464	616	90	46						

INDIVIDUAL BATTING LEADERS *(MINIMUM 2.7 PLATE APPEARANCES PER LEAGUE GAME)*

	AVG	G	AB	R	H	2B	3B	HR	RBI	BB	SO	SB
Crawford, Matthew, Angels	.373	37	142	31	53	4	2	2	20	11	20	19
Decker, Jaff, Padres	.352	49	159	51	56	11	2	5	34	55	36	9
Lara, Robert, Padres	.344	49	157	29	54	13	0	3	34	37	30	0
Jones, Jericho, Cubs	.340	43	159	29	54	7	6	5	30	10	41	2
Alliman, Terrell, Angels	.339	45	180	36	61	17	5	1	39	12	44	8
Amarista, Alexia, Angels	.332	51	202	46	67	6	4	2	21	29	20	22
Mazzola, Josh, Giants	.324	47	170	42	55	15	4	5	35	14	39	3
Ramos, Kevin, Angels	.319	40	141	35	45	8	7	1	34	8	21	9
Woodbury, Ben, Giants	.317	41	126	32	40	8	0	0	14	24	11	18
Batista, Deivy, Royals	.317	49	161	37	51	12	2	3	21	15	32	9

INDIVIDUAL PITCHING LEADERS *(MINIMUM 0.8 INNINGS PITCHED PER LEAGUE GAME)*

	W	L	ERA	G	GS	CG	SV	IP	H	R	BB	SO
Nicholson, Kyle, Giants	6	1	1.15	11	11	1	0	63	34	10	3	54
Ramos, Julio, Athletics	3	2	1.41	14	7	0	0	51	56	17	12	36
Osuna, Stiven, Padres	7	3	2.18	14	14	0	0	70	62	26	11	57
Correa, Manuarys, Angels	5	1	2.65	10	8	0	0	58	56	23	10	67
Blanco, Joshua, Angels	4	2	2.88	14	6	0	0	50	42	21	19	52
Suda, Kenta, Mariners	2	2	3.15	12	7	0	0	54	53	24	33	40
Flores, Manuel, Angels	7	4	3.16	13	12	0	0	74	90	35	10	63
Wilkes, Chris, Padres	7	1	3.21	15	10	0	0	62	64	26	5	45
O'Campo, Kyle, Rangers	3	1	3.29	16	9	0	1	52	47	24	19	56
De Paula, Jose, Padres	4	3	3.57	13	13	0	0	53	61	30	9	56

ALL-STAR TEAM

C—Robert Lara, Padres. **1B**—Franklin Hernandez, Athletics. **2B**—Deivy Batista, Royals. **3B**—Terrell Alliman, Angels; Jharmidy De Jesus, Mariners. **SS**—Nino Leyja, Atheltics. **OF**—Jaff Decker, Padres; Jericho Jones, Cubs; Alexi Amarista, Angels. **DH**—John Contreras, Cubs. **RHSP**—Stiven Osuna, Padres. **LHSP**—Manuel Flores, Angels. **RHRP**—Cody Eppley, Rangers. **LHRP**—Julio Ramos, Athletics. **Most Valuable Player:** Jaff Decker, Padres. **Manager of the Year:** Tyrone Boykin, Angels.

DEPARTMENT LEADERS

BATTING

OBP	Decker, Jaff, Padres	.523
SLG	Perez, Nelson, Cubs	.656
R	Decker, Jaff, Padres	51
H	Hernandez, Franklin, Athletics	71
TB	Hernandez, Franklin, Athletics	110
XBH	Hernandez, Franklin, Athletics	26
	Perez, Nelson, Cubs	26
2B	Hernandez, Franklin, Athletics	17
	Alliman, Terrell, Angels	17
	Ziegler, Craig, Giants	17
3B	Perez, Nelson, Cubs	10
	Dixon, Rashun, Athletics	10
HR	Contreras, John, Cubs	9
	Perez, Nelson, Cubs	9
RBI	Ziegler, Craig, Giants	43
SAC	Martinez, Edward, Rangers	9
SF	Ziegler, Craig, Giants	8
BB	Decker, Jaff, Padres	55
IBB	10 players tied at	1
HBP	Fairley, Wendell, Giants	16
SO	Dixon, Rashun, Athletics	68
SB	Amarista, Alexia, Angels	22
SB	Campana, Tony, Cubs	22
CS	Amarista, Alexia, Angels	14
AB/SO	Woodbury, Ben, Giants	11.45

PITCHING

G	Lynch, Colin, Padres	22
GS	Osuna, Stiven, Padres	14
CG	Three players tied at	1
GF	Wilson, Christopher, Giants	15
	Eppley, Cody, Rangers	15
SV	Eppley, Cody, Rangers	7
W	Flores, Manuel, Angels	7
	Osuna, Stiven, Padres	7
	Wilkes, Chris, Padres	7
L	Martinez, Fray, Mariners	8
IP	Flores, Manuel, Angels	74
H	Flores, Manuel, Angels	90
R	Martinez, Fray, Mariners	55
ER	Martinez, Fray, Mariners	38
HB	Wilkins, Robert, Rangers	10
BB	Hellweg, John, Angels	38
SO	Correa, Manuarys, Angels	67
SO/9 (SP)	Correa, Manuarys, Angels	9.78
SO/9 (RP)	Joseph, Jonathan, Athletics	14.07
BB/9	Nicholson, Kyle, Giants	0.43
WP	Hellweg, John, Angels	19
BK	Guerrero, Luis, Brewers	5
AVG	Nicholson, Kyle, Giants	.159

FIELDING

C	FPCT	Lara, Robert, Padres	.995
	PO	De Los Santos, Leonel, Rangers	344
	A	De Los Santos, Leonel, Rangers	61
	E	De Los Santos, Leonel, Rangers	11
	DP	De Los Santos, Leonel, Rangers	7
	PB	Bonilla, Jose, Royals	16
1B	FPCT	Hernandez, Franklin, Athletics	.988
	PO	Hernandez, Franklin, Athletics	478
	A	Hernandez, Franklin, Athletics	34
	E	Three players tied at	9
	DP	Hernandez, Franklin, Athletics	43
2B	FPCT	No qualifiers	
	PO	Fuentes, Cesar, Mariners	64
	A	Ramos, Kevin, Angels	87
	E	Lopez, Josh, Giants	9
	DP	Lopez, Josh, Giants	19
3B	FPCT	Mazzola, Josh, Giants	.934
	PO	Paciorek, Joseph, Brewers	32
	A	Mazzola, Josh, Giants	94
	E	Yan, Johan, Rangers	16
	DP	Two players tied at	9
SS	FPCT	Marte, Keisy, Padres	.941
	PO	Lake, Junior, Cubs	52
	A	Lake, Junior, Cubs	114
	E	George, Carlos, Brewers	29
	DP	Espinal, Yowill, Royals	27
OF	FPCT	Burgess, Jarrett, Mariners	1.000
	PO	Burgess, Jarrett, Mariners	95
	A	Two players tied at	8
	E	Three players tied at	6
	DP	Rangel, Jose, AZL Brewers	3

The Rookie-level Gulf Coast League was loaded with first-round picks from 2008. Nowhere was that more evident than on the GCL champion Phillies. The Phillies were led by four 2008 first-rounders (third baseman Anthony Hewitt, outfielders Zach Collier and Anthony Gose and righthander Jason Knapp) along with Venezuelan catchers Sebastian Valle.

Despite the wealth of talent the Phillies managed only a 33-25 record during the regular season but turned it on for the playoffs to knock off the Nationals, two-games-to-one. The win marked the club's first title since 2002.

The Nationals finished with a similar regular season mark of 33-22 and led the league in runs scored with 319. Shortstop Esmailyn Gonzalez was named MVP after leading the league with a .343 average and finished tied for second in hits (62), second in on-base percentage (.431) and third in RBIs (33).

Beyond the Phillies contingent, the league was filled with 2008 first-rounders (led by Twins outfielder Aaron Hicks, Marlins catcher Kyle Skipworth and Red Sox shortstop/righthander Casey Kelly) and international bonus babies (headlined by Mets third baseman Jefry Marte and Red Sox third baseman Michael Almanzar).

The Pirates and Twins finished the regular season with the two best records (37-19, 35-21 respectively) but were each knocked off in the first round of the postseason. The Twins led the league in batting with a .279 average, and Hicks played a big part in that success. The 2008 14th overall pick hit .318/.409/.491 in his pro debut, ranking eighth in average.

Pitching was the Pirates key to success, amassing a league-best 2.87 ERA with 19-year-old lefthander Nelson Pereira (1.62) and 22-year-old lefthander Tyler Cox (1.79) leading the league in ERA.

The 17-year-old Marte, who signed out of the Dominican in 2007 for $550,000, hit .325/.398/.532 in his pro debut and had one of the most impressive offensive seasons in the leauge despite being one if its youngest players. Fellow Dominican Almanzar spent just half the season in the GCL before being promoted to low Class A as a 17-year-old. The $1.5 million sign hit .348/.414/.472 with four home runs in just 87 at-bats.

This season marked a dramatic shift for the league as the Dodgers, Indians, and Reds move their spring homes. The Indians and Reds are original members of the GCL, joining with six other clubs in 1968. The GCL will add the Rays for the 2009 season, and may be forced to realign their divisional format at this year's winter meetings.

TOP 20 PROSPECTS

1. Aaron Hicks, of, Twins
2. Kyle Skipworth, c, Marlins
3. Jefry Marte, 3b, Mets
4. Jason Knapp, rhp, Phillies
5. Michael Almanzar, 3b, Red Sox
6. Casey Kelly, ss/rhp, Red Sox
7. Sebastian Valle, c, Phillies
8. Zach Collier, of, Phillies
9. Jack McGeary, lhp, Nationals
10. Abner Abreu, 3b, Indians
11. Arodys Vizcaino, rhp, Yankees
12. Cesar Puello, of, Mets
13. Anthony Hewitt, 3b, Phillies
14. Esmailyn Gonzalez, ss, Nationals
15. L.J. Hoes, 2b, Orioles
16. Isaac Galloway, of, Marlins
17. Zeke Spruill, rhp, Braves
18. Destin Hood, of, Nationals
19. Derrik Gibson, 3b, Red Sox
20. Jarek Cunningham, 3b/ss, Pirates

STANDINGS

Page	Eastern Division	Complex	W	L	PCT	GB	Manager	Last Penn.
329	Nationals	Melbourne	33	22	.600	—	Bob Henley	1991
146	Marlins	Jupiter	30	24	.556	2½	Steve Watson	None
182	Dodgers	Vero Beach	30	26	.536	3½	Jeff Carter	1990
209	Mets	St. Lucie	27	27	.500	5½	Juan Lopez	None
261	Cardinals	Jupiter	17	38	.309	16	Enrique Brito	None

Page	Northern Division	Complex	W	L	PCT	GB	Manager	Last Penn.
240	Phillies	Clearwater	33	25	.569	—	Rolando de Armas	2008
219	Yankees	Tampa	31	27	.534	2	Jody Reed	2007
60	Braves	Lake Buena Vista	29	29	.500	4	Luis Ortiz	2003
118	Indians	Winter Haven	27	29	.482	5	Rouglas Odor	None
136	Tigers	Lakeland	27	31	.466	6	Basilio Cabrera	None
319	Blue Jays	Dunedin	26	32	.448	7	Dave Pano	None

Page	Southern Division	Complex	W	L	PCT	GB	Manager	Last Penn.
250	Pirates	Bradenton	26	30	.464	—	Tom Prince	None
198	Twins	Fort Myers	35	21	.625	2	Jake Mauer	None
79	Red Sox	Fort Myers	28	27	.509	8½	Dave Tomlin	2006
107	Reds	Sarasota	25	31	.446	12	Pat Kelly	None
69	Orioles	Sarasota	14	41	.255	22½	Jesus Alfaro	None

PLAYOFFS—Semifinals: Phillies defeated Pirates and Nationals defeated Twins in one-game playoffs. **Finals:** Phillies defeated Nationals 2-1 in a best-of-three series.

CLUB BATTING

	AVG	G	AB	R	H	2B	3B	HR	RBI	BB	SO	SB	CS	OBP	SLG
Twins	.279	56	1858	268	518	112	21	22	233	194	342	57	16	.356	.397
Marlins	.265	54	1715	256	454	74	27	15	225	161	349	46	33	.336	.366
Pirates	.265	56	1782	248	472	71	15	20	210	188	372	104	36	.345	.355
Mets	.264	54	1732	248	458	82	18	22	219	133	371	57	20	.331	.371
Phillies	.262	58	1869	269	489	111	15	28	234	169	440	58	13	.330	.382
Nationals	.258	55	1701	319	439	83	16	6	264	247	395	78	25	.365	.336
Orioles	.258	55	1785	212	460	75	10	13	175	140	363	46	18	.321	.333
Blue Jays	.256	58	1905	275	488	96	14	33	233	156	521	131	37	.326	.373
Braves	.254	58	1919	260	487	93	16	27	221	141	387	63	17	.322	.361
Red Sox	.249	55	1731	224	431	89	11	17	190	180	449	103	18	.326	.343
Indians	.247	56	1790	247	443	88	14	38	220	209	423	71	23	.334	.376
Reds	.246	54	1836	242	452	88	14	34	220	179	410	41	16	.321	.333
Dodgers	.242	56	1695	253	411	67	7	28	206	231	382	58	24	.346	.340
Yankees	.242	58	1799	221	435	87	11	24	182	139	380	35	14	.308	.342
Cardinals	.233	55	1701	222	397	72	15	23	187	183	472	51	34	.319	.334
Tigers	.233	58	1789	223	417	103	12	24	197	173	469	62	12	.313	.344

CLUB PITCHING

	ERA	G	CG	SHO	SV	IP	H	R	ER	HR	BB	SO	AVG
Pirates	2.87	56	0	4	19	477	422	199	152	20	147	381	.235
Twins	2.98	56	0	3	20	477	427	199	158	9	166	442	.237
Dodgers	3.23	56	3	6	10	449	402	197	161	17	163	348	.242
Braves	3.40	58	0	3	15	492	460	248	185	19	206	491	.241
Phillies	3.43	58	0	5	16	478	453	224	182	33	137	428	.248
Nationals	3.57	55	2	5	16	454	447	253	180	23	169	404	.256
Mets	3.62	54	1	6	13	447	400	247	180	12	190	440	.238
Reds	3.67	56	0	4	6	473	506	243	193	20	185	389	.274
Tigers	3.72	58	1	5	16	472	436	247	195	23	183	440	.243
Yankees	3.74	58	0	2	21	475	466	249	197	31	142	440	.253
Blue Jays	3.84	58	0	2	12	494	506	269	208	32	148	400	.264
Indians	3.91	56	0	3	14	468	438	258	202	36	171	421	.247
Red Sox	4.06	55	0	6	16	453	454	242	204	27	140	364	.260
Marlins	4.29	54	0	7	18	447	417	252	211	13	195	434	.247
Orioles	4.70	55	1	1	9	452	524	311	236	10	243	360	.290
Cardinals	5.51	55	2	0	7	447	493	349	273	29	238	343	.279

CLUB FIELDING

	PCT	PO	A	E	DP		PCT	PO	A	E	DP
Dodgers	.969	1347	541	60	37	Tigers	.961	1417	591	82	48
Blue Jays	.968	1483	623	70	52	Reds	.960	1420	568	83	44
Red Sox	.967	1358	635	68	44	Indians	.957	1403	531	87	52
Phillies	.964	1433	535	73	45	Nationals	.957	1362	512	84	49
Twins	.963	1431	556	77	46	Orioles	.956	1357	577	90	55
Marlins	.962	1341	540	75	39	Braves	.955	1477	527	94	41
Yankees	.962	1424	554	78	35	Mets	.950	1342	516	98	53
Pirates	.961	1432	569	82	59	Cardinals	.943	1342	552	114	47

INDIVIDUAL BATTING LEADERS (MINIMUM 2.7 PLATE APPEARANCES PER LEAGUE GAME)

	AVG	G	AB	R	H	2B	3B	HR	RBI	BB	SO	SB
Gonzalez, Esmailyn, Nationals	.343	51	181	42	62	12	3	2	33	23	19	9
Chourio, Adenson, Pirates	.335	49	185	35	62	3	0	0	13	22	30	30
Rosa, Garabez, Orioles	.330	49	185	24	61	8	3	4	29	1	26	4
Brooks, Robert, Braves	.329	47	155	30	51	7	5	3	20	15	27	12
Rodriguez, Ryde, Cardinals	.329	41	143	19	47	9	0	0	28	8	32	7
Marte, Jefry, Mets	.325	44	154	29	50	14	3	4	24	13	30	2
Labrie, Ronnie, Nationals	.324	42	139	34	45	10	2	1	26	23	27	9
Hicks, Aaron, Twins	.318	45	173	32	55	10	4	4	27	28	32	12
Cunningham, Jarek, Pirates	.318	43	148	20	47	11	1	5	22	14	26	2
Meyer, Edinho, Orioles	.317	42	139	17	44	9	0	3	17	12	30	0

INDIVIDUAL PITCHING LEADERS (MINIMUM 0.8 INNINGS PITCHED PER LEAGUE GAME)

	W	L	ERA	G	GS	CG	SV	IP	H	R	BB	SO
Pereira, Nelson, Pirates	6	2	1.62	13	6	0	0	50	41	20	10	46
Cox, Tyler, Pirates	2	3	1.79	13	7	0	0	45	35	14	11	42
Flande, Yohan, Phillies	4	1	2.19	10	9	0	0	53	41	19	11	39
Contreras, Edwin, Dodgers	5	0	2.30	11	9	1	0	55	44	18	12	34
Pimentel, Elisaul, Dodgers	3	6	2.41	11	10	2	0	56	43	20	13	43
Cuotto, Jonas, Blue Jays	3	2	2.61	11	9	0	0	52	41	16	7	45
Hildenbrandt, Evan, Reds	4	2	2.67	11	11	0	0	57	49	19	16	56
Familia, Jeurys, Mets	2	2	2.79	11	11	0	0	52	46	20	13	38
Kehrt, Jeremy, Red Sox	3	2	2.84	11	8	0	1	51	46	19	7	44
Salazar, Danny, Indians	4	2	2.87	11	11	0	0	53	46	19	13	43

ALL-STAR TEAM

C—Jonathan Talley, Blue Jays. 1B—Justin McClanahan, Blue Jays. 2B—Robert Brooks, Braves. 3B—Juan Sanchez, Twins. SS—Esmailyn Gonzalez, Nationals. OF—Aaron Hicks, Twins; Ryde Rodriguez, Cardinals; Chris Curran, Nationals. DH—Vladimir De Los Santos, Phillies. SP—Nelson Pereira, Pirates. RP—Ryan Bergh, Phillies. **Most Valuable Player:** Esmailyn Gonzalez, Nationals. **Manager of the Year:** Tom Prince, Pirates.

DEPARTMENT LEADERS

MINOR LEAGUES

BATTING

OBP	Carrithers, Alden, Tigers	.464
SLG	Abreu, Abner, Indians	.538
R	Curran, Chris, Nationals	55
H	Curran, Chris, Nationals	65
TB	Abreu, Abner, Indians	107
XBH	Abreu, Abner, Indians	31
2B	Abreu, Abner, Indians	16
	Maddox, Chadwick, Braves	16
3B	Manzanillo, Ernesto, Marlins	6
HR	Abreu, Abner, Indians	11
RBI	De Los Santos, Vladimir, Phillies	45
SAC	Chourio, Adenson, Pirates	8
SF	Cunningham, Jarek, Pirates	6
BB	Hoes, Jerome, Orioles	30
IBB	Fuenmayor, Balbino, Blue Jays	2
	Hicks, Aaron, Twins	2
HBP	Garcia, Harold, Phillies	12
	Brooks, Robert, Braves	12
SO	Wilson, Kenneth, Blue Jays	60
SB	Pichardo, Wilfred, Red Sox	42
CS	Pichardo, Wilfred, Red Sox	9
AB/SO	Lara, Herbert, Twins	12.17

PITCHING

G	Bergh, Ryan, Phillies	20
	Cassavechia, Nicholas, Tigers	20
GS	Tavarez, Daurin, Orioles	12
	McGeary, Jack, Nationals	12
CG	Pimentel, Elisaul, Dodgers	2
GF	Bergh, Ryan, Phillies	19
SV	Mota, Kelvin, Twins	12
W	Spruill, Ezekiel, Braves	7
L	Tavarez, Daurin, Orioles	7
IP	Frias, Marcos, Nationals	65
H	Rada, Jose, Cardinals	71
R	Alvarez, Henderson, Blue Jays	41
ER	McFarland, T.J., Indians	31
HB	Contreras, Edwin, Dodgers	10
BB	Daley, Gary, Cardinals	32
SO	McGeary, Jack, Nationals	64
SO/9 (SP)	McGeary, Jack, Nationals	9.65
SO/9 (RP)	Rodriguez, Santos, Braves	13.97
BB/9	Rada, Jose, Cardinals	0.8
WP	Daley, Gary, Cardinals	19
BK	Rada, Jose, Cardinals	4
	Jesus, Candido, Indians	4
AVG	Flande, Yohan, Phillies	.200

FIELDING

C	FPCT	Schlehuber, Braeden, Braves	.992
	PO	Schlehuber, Braeden, Braves	244
	A	Three players tied at	26
	E	Harrigan, Brandon, Tigers	10
	DP	Ricardo, Dashenko, Orioles	4
		Coddington, Kevin, Reds	4
	PB	Ricardo, Dashenko, Orioles	18
1B	FPCT	Jacobs, Chris, Dodgers	.994
	PO	Huang, Chih-Hsiang, Red Sox	372
	A	Jacobs, Chris, Dodgers	28
	E	Medina, David, Cardinals	9
	DP	Flagg, Jeffrey, Mets	40
2B	FPCT	Carrithers, Alden, Tigers	1.000
	PO	Chourio, Adenson, Pirates	109
	A	Chourio, Adenson, Pirates	131
	E	Obregon, Ted, Cardinals	20
	DP	Chourio, Adenson, Pirates	27
		Pertusati, Daniel, Marlins	27
3B	FPCT	Pfister, Frank, Reds	.963
	PO	Fuenmayor, Balbino, Blue Jays	34
	A	Fuenmayor, Balbino, Blue Jays	115
	E	Hanson, Jake, Braves	22
	DP	Abreu, Abner, Indians	13
SS	FPCT	Pastornicky, Tyler, Blue Jays	.962
	PO	Gonzalez, Esmailyn, Nationals	84
	A	Rosa, Garabez, Orioles	139
	E	Adair, Travis, Braves	24
	DP	Rosa, Garabez, Orioles	32
OF	FPCT	Garcia, Edward, Pirates	1.000
	PO	Curran, Chris, Nationals	114
	A	Sands, Jerry, Dodgers	8
	E	Pichardo, Wilfred, Red Sox	6
	DP	Four players tied at	3

BY BEN BADLER

DOMINICAN SUMMER LEAGUE

The DSL Nationals won its second consecutive title, a feat made more notable considering the league carries a whopping 37 teams. The Nationals finished 55-17, winning the regular season title before finishing off the Giants in three games to claim the championship.

Nationals Righthander Osvaldo Rodriguez, 24, led the league in ERA by going 12-0, 1.01 with 104 strikeouts (fourth in the DSL) in 71 innings. Yankees right fielder Kelvin De Leon hit .289/.399/.489 and tied for fourth in the league with nine home runs at just 17 years old. Blue Jays 17-year-old catcher Carlos Perez also stood out among young hitters, batting .306./459/.378 to tie for fifth in the league in OBP.

STANDINGS

BOCA CHICA NORTH

	W	L	PCT	GB
Twins	46	24	.657	—
Cubs 1	45	25	.643	1
Yankees 2	45	25	.643	1
White Sox 1	42	28	.600	4
Reds	40	30	.571	6
Indians	38	32	.543	8
Rockies	32	38	.457	14
Diamondbacks	25	45	.357	21
Orioles	22	48	.314	24
D'backs/Reds	15	55	.214	31

BOCA CHICA SOUTH

	W	L	PCT	GB
Giants	50	20	.714	—
Mets	44	27	.62	6½
Red Sox	43	27	.614	7
Royals	35	33	.515	14
Blue Jays1	36	34	.514	14
Blue Jays2	34	35	.493	15½
Yankees1	34	36	.486	16
Marlins	34	37	.479	16½
Cubs2	29	41	.414	21
Rays	29	41	.414	21
Dodgers	27	44	.38	23½
White Sox2	25	45	.357	25

SANTO DOMINGO NORTH

	W	L	PCT	GB
Mariners	42	24	.636	—
Phillies	35	30	.538	6½
Athletics 2	31	33	.484	10
Athletics 1	27	36	.429	13½
Cardinals	27	39	.409	15

SANTO DOMINGO WEST

	W	L	PCT	GB
Nationals 1	55	17	.764	—
Padres	30	42	.417	25
Tigers	30	42	.417	25
Nationals2	29	43	.403	26

SAN PEDRO DE MACORIS

	W	L	PCT	GB
Rangers 1	46	23	.667	—
Angels	47	24	.662	—
Pirates	40	30	.571	6½
Braves	32	38	.457	14½
Rangers 2	26	45	.366	21
Astros	20	51	.282	27

PLAYOFFS—Division Series: Angels defeated Rangers 1 2-0 and Mariners defeated Twins 2-1 in best-of-three series. **Semifinals:** Giants defeated Mariners 2-1 and Nationals 1 defeated Angels 2-1 in best-of-three series. **Finals:** Nationals 1 defeated Giants 2-1 in a best-of-three series.

INDIVIDUAL BATTING LEADERS
(MINIMUM 194 PLATE APPEARANCES)

	AVG	G	AB	R	H	2B	3B	HR	RBI	BB	SO	SB
Sanchez, Hector, Giants	.348	55	207	40	72	14	3	4	63	36	29	4
Guillen, Cesar, Rays	.343	53	204	45	70	14	2	2	36	21	16	14
Perez, Jairo, Twins	.338	48	160	38	54	16	1	4	36	20	24	8
Patino, Jeffer, White Sox 1	.327	47	168	34	55	15	2	3	28	26	23	3
Perez, Eury, Nationals 1	.324	60	213	51	69	9	2	4	44	32	36	28
Hernandez, Albert, Cubs 1	.324	56	170	33	55	12	4	1	26	19	25	6
Soto, Eduardo, Angels	.323	67	248	44	80	19	3	4	48	24	51	19
Chacoa, Miguel, Reds	.321	52	165	30	53	6	1	0	27	28	13	13
Crousset, Juan, Rockies	.320	64	259	35	83	10	5	4	42	21	40	16
Morelli, Jesus, Cubs 2	.317	56	189	39	60	11	3	5	38	34	37	13

INDIVIDUAL PITCHING LEADERS
(MINIMUM 58 INNINGS)

	W	L	ERA	G	GS	CG	SV	IP	H	R	BB	SO
Rodriguez, Osvaldo, Nationals 1	12	0	1.01	13	13	1	0	71	48	8	27	104
Mendez, Ismael, Mets	6	1	1.07	15	14	0	0	76	38	16	29	62
De Los Santos, Sammy, Dbacks	2	4	1.12	11	11	0	0	64	41	17	9	49
Castillo, Antonio, Dodgers	3	1	1.18	14	11	0	0	69	38	16	17	74
Aquino, Juan, Reds	7	2	1.27	12	11	0	0	64	49	19	10	63
Germen, Gonzalez, Mets	5	2	1.34	15	14	0	0	74	41	21	15	70
Arena, Orangel, Angels	8	1	1.36	13	13	1	0	86	52	20	25	71
Sosa, Juan, Phillies	4	1	1.37	13	12	3	1	59	48	16	25	60
Perez, Marcos, Cubs 1	6	2	1.38	13	13	0	0	65	53	17	9	52
Rijo, Ezequiel, Rangers 1	4	0	1.39	15	13	0	0	71	48	18	27	41

VENEZUELAN SUMMER LEAGUE

After finishing with the best regular season record at 46-22, the Pirates swept the Mariners in two games, culminating in a 6-2 championship game victory for a second straight VSL title.

Pirates designated hitter Henry Henry hit .341/.431/.446, ranking second in the league in on-base plus slugging percentage and first in both stolen bases (37) and caught stealing (14). Second baseman Dixon Miavares helped create runs for the Pirates, hitting .311/.421/.402 to finish fourth in OBP, while Pirates left fielder Rogelios Noris provided power by hitting .272/.366/.452 to finish fourth in slugging.

STANDINGS

	W	L	PCT	GB		W	L	PCT	GB
Pirates	46	22	.676	—	Cardinals	31	34	.477	13½
Mariners	42	26	.618	4	Rays	29	36	.446	15½
Astros	37	31	.544	9	Mets	26	42	.382	20
Phillies	32	33	.492	12½	Tigers	24	43	.358	21½

PLAYOFFS: Pirates defeated Mariners 2-0 in best-of-three championship series.

INDIVIDUAL BATTING LEADERS
(MINIMUM 194 PLATE APPEARANCES)

	AVG	G	AB	R	H	2B	3B	HR	RBI	BB	SO	SB
Yepez, Mario, Mariners	.345	67	238	32	82	17	4	1	44	18	27	11
Henry, Henry, Pirates	.341	67	249	58	85	12	4	2	30	31	21	37
Alvarez, Luis, Astros	.333	61	207	44	69	17	0	7	33	32	32	4
Martinez, Francisco, Tigers	.321	68	249	32	80	4	0	1	23	28	28	20
Torres, Alejandro, Rays	.316	67	263	37	83	14	0	5	43	13	29	0
Hernandez, Cesar, Phillies	.315	60	197	31	62	7	6	1	24	33	22	19
Mavares, Dixon, Pirates	.311	52	164	31	51	10	1	1	15	26	21	8
Rivero, Alberto, Pirates	.309	66	233	37	72	10	3	2	33	26	30	5
Mannbel, Gerardo, Cardinals	.302	67	235	33	71	14	1	4	29	28	20	9
De Los Santos, Wondy, Tigers	.301	58	186	28	56	9	3	1	15	15	20	10

INDIVIDUAL PITCHING LEADERS
(MINIMUM 58 INNINGS)

	W	L	ERA	G	GS	CG	SV	IP	H	R	BB	SO
Nava, Jessie, Mariners	5	0	1.60	13	12	1	0	67	50	15	16	44
Barrios, Edison, Pirates	7	1	1.67	13	13	1	0	70	65	17	6	31
Esparza, Gerardo, Mariners	4	5	1.81	15	13	0	1	70	50	31	22	59
Quevedo, Carlos, Astros	4	2	1.98	14	14	0	0	68	56	19	11	53
Colmenarez, Juan, Phillies	6	4	2.13	14	12	0	2	72	70	23	8	48
Diaz, Jose, Tigers	3	5	2.29	14	14	4	0	83	51	32	20	47
Rios, Geney, Cardinals	4	3	2.49	15	13	0	0	69	43	30	26	57
Noguera, Carlos, Cardinals	2	3	2.57	15	13	0	0	63	73	25	11	29
Perez, Yuri, Astros	4	4	2.68	12	11	0	0	57	43	22	19	28
Ramos, Jhonatan, Pirates	5	3	2.69	14	14	0	0	60	61	27	12	47

Surprise batterymates Matt Wieters, left, and Brian Matusz starred in the Arizona Fall League

BY KARY BOOHER

The names of the Arizona Fall League's standouts in 2008 read like a who's-who list of potential stars: Braves righthander Tommy Hanson and Orioles catcher Matt Wieters—Baseball America's Minor League Player of the Year—all the way to 18-year-old Mariners prospect Carlos Triunfel.

Put another way, never let it be said that the AFL traveled light in 2008, as the circuit celebrated its 17th season with what could become one of its best classes of prospects.

Hanson and Wieters headlined the pool of prospects, with Hanson adding to his growing reputation such that Braves general manager Frank Wren placed the "untouchable" tag on the righthander in offseason trade talks.

Just as he blew through high Class A Myrtle Beach and Double-A Mississippi during the regular season, Hanson sharpened his slider and showed an improved feel for a changeup that dominated AFL hitters. Having finished 11-5, 2.41 with 163

strikeouts in 138 innings in the regular season, his AFL performance was even better.

Hanson, a 22nd-round pick who signed as a draft-and-follow ahead of the 2006 draft, entered the AFL's final week likely to win the ERA title, as he owned a 0.76 ERA, and led with 39 strikeouts in almost 24 innings.

Many scouts agreed that Wieters was by far the most impressive position player.

The former Georgia Tech standout and 2007 Orioles first-round pick became the 2008 Minor League Player of the Year after he tore through high Class A Frederick and Double-A Bowie, hitting a ridiculous .355/.454/.600 with 27 home runs and 91 RBIs.

In the AFL, playing for the Surprise Rafters, Wieters continued on his track and earned high marks for handling the pitching staff, enhancing his game-calling and generally looking like he was ready to battle for a big league job in spring training.

Many eyes also tracked Triunfel, the youngest player in the league and its first player to have been born in the 1990s (Feb. 27, 1990).

Triunfel, signed by the Mariners out of the Dominican Republic, played for the Peoria Javelinas and showed remarkable poise as he shifted from shortstop to learn third base. He committed one error in his first nine games of playing the position, his initial exposure in a meaningful game setting.

In one game, Triunfel showed why the Mariners invested $1.3 million on his talent as the right-handed hitter shuttled a single down the right field line, completing a nine-pitch at-bat, and then made two nifty defensive plays. Among the highlights was a nice drop step on a ball hit to his left, typically troublesome for young shortstops.

A number of other young prospects were fanned out across the league, including four who were picked in the first round of the 2008 draft: Orioles righthander Brian Matusz, White Sox shortstop Gordon Beckham, Rangers first baseman Justin Smoak and Cardinals third baseman Brett Wallace.

Matusz made his pro debut in the AFL, and the lefthander didn't disappoint as he fired a scoreless and hitless three innings in his first start.

Beckham was in the top 10 in batting as he threatened .400. Wallace, who reached Double-A Springfield in late August, overcame a tough opening for the Peoria Sagauros but was hitting better than .300 entering the final week.

Smoak played three games for Surprise before transferring to the Javelinas roster as a taxi squad guy.

It was only fitting, then, that the Saguaros and Solar Sox were battling for the division crown right up to the final game.

The circuit's pleasant surprise was Mesa out-fielder Logan Morrison, a Marlins 2006 draft-and-follow out of Maple Woods Community College, the same Kansas City-area juco that was once a whistle stop for Albert Pujols.

Morrison, who starred in the AFL despite having spent all of 2008 at high Class A Jupiter, entered the final week angling for the AFL's batting and RBI titles. In his first 92 at-bats, he was hitting .424/.436/.707 with five home runs and 28 RBIs. He also was among the leaders in slugging percentage.

Morrison had hit .332/.402/.494 with 13 home runs, 38 doubles and 74 RBIs in the regular season in the Florida State League, known for its cavernous ballparks.

The Braves' Tommy Hanson dominated

BILL MITCHELL

Meanwhile, a number of other prospects made waves as well, and Mesa boasted one of the best teams because of its across-the-board talent.

Shortstop Jason Donald, a Phillies 2005 third-round pick, finished a solid season in which he starred at Double-A Reading and also helped Team USA win a bronze medal at the Beijing Games. He vied for the AFL batting title.

Tyler Flowers, the Mesa catcher and Hanson's battery mate at Myrtle Beach, by far owned the top slugging percentage (.985) with four games to go.

Peoria Saguaros outfielder Mike Baxter (Padres) owned the top on-base percentage after shedding the taxi squad label, and Scottsdale outfielder Chris Pettit (Angels) had the league's most hits.

Scottsdale infielder Drew Sutton (Astros), carrying over his breakout season at Double-A Corpus Christi, was in line to score the circuit's most runs.

On the pitching side, many scouts agreed that righthander Bud Norris was among the most impressive pitchers as he showed a 98 mph fastball. The Astros prospect shed the chains of the regular season, when he worked on extremely conservative pitch counts after he missed two mid-season months after suffering an elbow strain.

The Red Sox's Clay Buchholz, Yankees' Phil Hughes and the Diamondbacks' Max Scherzer each appeared in the AFL as well, with all pitching very well. Phoenix Desert Dogs righthander Andrew Carignan (Athletics) was the saves leader.

BY STACY KANESHIRO

The Waikiki BeachBoys' momentum from their division-clinching win carried over to their Hawaii Winter Baseball championship triumph against the West Oahu CaneFires, 5-1, on a sunny day at Les Murakami Stadium on the University of Hawaii campus.

The BeachBoys clinched the Eastern Division title the night before, after a two-out, two-run home run by Marquez Smith (Cubs) in the top of the ninth and then sweated out the bottom of the ninth when Jeremy Papelbon (Cubs) pitched into, and out of, a one-out, bases-loaded jam. Papelbon notched his league-leading seventh save in a 5-4 win against the Honolulu Sharks.

Waikiki then sealed the title behind the efforts of starter Mitsuo Yoshikawa (Nippon Ham Fighters) and reliever Steven Richard (Mariners). They combined on a five-hitter, with Yoshikawa giving up a run, four hits and two walks with six strikeouts in five innings. Richard yielded a hit in four scoreless innings of relief for his first save of the season to fend off the West champion CaneFires, who clinched their division title earlier in the week.

"Yosh has been great all year," Buster Posey (Giants) said of his batterymate. "He's a competitor. Even if he gets in a jam, he can get out of it."

And he was equally pleased with Richard.

"He did exactly what you want to do out of the bullpen," Posey said. "He came in, pounded the zone and kept pounding them. That's what you want to do with a four-run lead."

Posey then aided the pitchers' effort with his first home run of the fall, an opposite-field, three-run shot to right in the top of the seventh, that cushioned Waikiki's early 2-1 lead.

"Marquez Smith's big two-run homer kept the momentum going into today, and Buster Posey's three-run home run kind of broke it open for us," Waikiki manager Juan Bustabad said. "It's a great team effort and we fought hard and we came out on top."

It was the BeachBoys' first title in their third season in the eight-year-old league.

"They hit in the clutch situations and did what they needed to do," CaneFires manager Mike Guerrero said.

Members of the winning team each received a watch that read "2008 HWB Champions" and an HWB duffel bag. Losing team members received only the duffel bag. "It's something we can enjoy when we go home," Waikiki shortstop Todd Frazier (Reds) said.

League president Hervy Kurisu said he was

Giants 2008 first-round pick Buster Posey led Waikiki to the HWB championship

pleased with the third season of the revived HWB, which originally ran from 1993-97. "It was a gratifying season," Kurisu said. "The fans supported us. The players and coaches were tremendous and you couldn't ask for a better ending."

The league is unlikely to expand by next season because of the increased cost of flying, as well as the economy. But Kurisu said the Korea Baseball Organization might have more participants next year. The KBO's only participating team this season was the Lotte Giants.

■ As a youth growing up on Maui, Phillies Gold Glove center fielder Shane Victorino frequented Maui Stingrays games. The league had ceased operation two years after he turned pro in 1999, when he was drafted by the Dodgers out of high school. This fall he was honored by HWB at Les Murakami Stadium. A crowd of 1,609—the largest of the season and some six to eight times the usual attendance—showed up to watch him throw out the ceremonial first pitch to another champion, Pikai Winchester of the Little League World Series champion team from Waipio.

"When I got to the minor leagues, I always hoped I'd have an opportunity to play in Hawaii," Victorino said. "When I heard they were bringing it back, I was excited."

■ Yankees pitching prospect Andrew Brackman was generally pleased with his progress in Hawaii, his first extensive pitching since he was drafted in the first round in 2007 out of North Carolina State. He missed the 2008 season recovering from Tommy John surgery. The 6-foot-10 right-

BILL MITCHELL

MINOR LEAGUES

hander went 3-4, 5.56, logging 36 innings in seven starts. He struck out 36 and walked 25 for the BeachBoys.

"I just need more time, more repetitions," he said. "I'm leaving here healthy and I'll be getting ready to work out again. I need to get stronger. When the season starts up, I'll work again on what I need to work on. I can't set my expectations too high because I hadn't played in a while. I just need to be relaxed out there and keep comfortable."

Diamondbacks outfielder Cyle Hankerd drove in a HWB-best 31 runs in 2008

TOM PRIDDY

STANDINGS

EAST	W	L	PCT	GB
Waikiki BeachBoys	19	17	.528	—
Honolulu Sharks	17	18	.486	1 ½

WEST	W	L	PCT	GB
West Oahu CaneFires	19	14	.576	—
North Shore Honu	14	20	.412	5 ½

PLAYOFFS—Waikiki defeated West Oahu 5-1 in a one-game championship.
ALL-STAR TEAM: C: Jason Castro, Honu (Astros). **1B:** Yonder Alonso, BeachBoys (Reds). **2B:** Mark Hallberg, CaneFires (Diamondbacks). **3B:** Bradley Emaus, Sharks (Blue Jays). **SS:** Kyle Martin, Honu (Royals). **OF:** Dominic Brown, Sharks (Phillies); Kyle Peter, CaneFires (Tigers); Cyle Hankerd, CaneFires (Diamondbacks). **UTIL:** Buster Posey, BeachBoys (Giants). **SP:** Kyle Bloom, CaneFires (Pirates); Jeremy Bleich, BeachBoys (Yankees); Satoshi Nagai, Sharks (Rakuten Golden Eagles). **RP:** Kaimi Mead, Sharks (Indians); Jeremy Papelbon, BeachBoys (Cubs); David Pfeiffer, BeachBoys (Dodgers). **Most Valuable Player:** Mark Hallberg. **Pitcher of the Year:** Satoshi Nagai. **Offensive Player of the Year:** Cyle Hankerd. **Defensive Player of the Year:** Marquez Smith.

INDIVIDUAL BATTING LEADERS
(MINIMUM 2.0 PA/LEAGUE GAME)

PLAYER, TEAM	AVG	G	AB	R	H	HR	RBI
Brown, Dominic, Hon	.389	22	72	13	28	1	8
Peter, Kyle, WO	.370	27	92	20	34	1	12
Hallberg, Mark, WO	.362	33	116	24	42	3	21
Posey, Buster, Wai	.338	19	74	15	25	0	15
Castro, Jason, NS	.333	23	78	17	26	2	13
Emaus, Bradley, Hon	.333	26	81	18	27	2	12
Cruz, Tony, Hon	.323	26	93	9	30	0	11
Hankerd, Cyle, WO	.318	25	88	16	28	5	30
Alonso, Yonder, Wai	.308	29	104	17	32	4	17
Frazier, Todd, Wai	.295	27	95	19	28	3	22

INDIVIDUAL PITCHING LEADERS
(MINIMUM 0.4 IP/LEAGUE GAME)

PLAYER, TEAM	W	L	ERA	IP	H	BB	SO
Mead, Kaimi, Hon	0	0	1.37	20	15	8	14
Bloom, Kyle, WO	2	0	1.50	30	15	11	32
Pfeiffer, David, Wai	1	0	1.59	17	7	4	11
Kissock, Christopher, Hon	1	0	1.69	21	9	10	23
Bleich, Jeremy, Wai	3	2	1.77	36	29	12	33
Nagai, Satoshi, Hon	4	2	1.94	42	26	10	48
Yamamoto, Kazunori, Wai	3	0	1.96	18	12	4	17
Richardson, Dustin, NS	0	2	2.41	19	18	6	26
Shaw, Scott, Hon	2	2	2.51	32	12	9	35
Pratt, Jordan, Wai	0	1	2.53	21	16	14	34

HONOLULU SHARKS

BATTING	AVG	AB	R	H	2B	3B	HR	RBI	BB	SO	SB
Abruzzo, Jordan	.200	70	7	14	2	0	0	4	7	19	0
Brown, Dominic	.389	72	13	28	6	1	1	8	15	14	3
Cruz, Tony	.323	93	9	30	10	1	0	11	7	18	1
Davis, Lars	.222	63	5	14	2	0	1	7	4	19	0

Eiland, Eric	.073	41	4	3	0	0	0	5	7	17	0
Emaus, Bradley	.333	81	18	27	5	1	2	12	17	7	0
Hijirisawa, Ryo	.280	50	8	14	1	2	0	7	6	9	4
Holcomb, Darin	.163	92	9	15	4	0	1	7	11	13	0
Ka'aihue, Kala	.256	86	9	22	3	0	5	16	13	39	2
Masuda, Shintaro	.291	79	10	23	2	0	1	7	8	25	2
Mitchell, Michael	.174	86	9	15	6	1	0	5	4	24	8
Rapoport, James	.250	96	11	24	2	0	2	9	12	27	4
Taylor, Michael	.247	85	11	21	6	1	2	10	12	11	3
Tejada, Ruben	.233	86	14	20	3	1	0	10	7	14	2
Veloz, Greg	.207	87	10	18	2	0	0	7	9	27	2

PITCHING	W	L	ERA	G	GS	SV	IP	H	BB	SO
Broadway, Michael	0	2	9.82	10	1	0	15	23	16	9
Chambliss, Austin	0	1	16.71	9	0	0	7	14	6	5
Drabek, Kyle	1	2	3.05	5	2	0	21	8	4	19
Graham, Andy	2	0	1.17	8	0	3	8	5	2	7
Graham, Connor	1	1	6.62	7	7	0	18	14	20	24
Guerra, Junior	1	1	9.18	14	0	0	17	29	13	10
Herron, Tyler	0	0	0.69	7	0	0	13	14	6	11
King, Blake	0	0	4.86	13	0	0	17	14	19	16
Kissock, Christopher	1	0	1.69	12	0	0	21	9	10	23
Mead, Kaimi	0	0	1.37	15	0	2	20	15	8	14
Merritt, Roy	1	2	3.00	16	0	2	24	15	11	26
Nagai, Satoshi	4	2	1.94	8	8	0	42	26	10	48
Shaw, Scott	2	2	2.51	8	7	0	32	12	9	35
Stinson, Josh	2	2	4.50	9	5	1	22	19	13	13
Venters, Jonathan	2	3	2.90	8	7	0	31	33	8	26

NORTH SHORE HONU

BATTING	AVG	AB	R	H	2B	3B	HR	RBI	BB	SO	SB
Brown, Corey	.216	111	19	24	6	1	4	14	13	33	3
Carter, Christopher	.228	79	18	18	6	0	2	7	17	28	0
Castro, Jason	.333	78	17	26	6	0	2	13	16	22	0
Davis, Adam	.093	54	8	5	4	0	0	1	14	21	5
Hee, Jonathan	.111	9	2	1	0	0	0	0	4	4	0
Jang, Sung Woo	.208	48	5	10	1	0	0	8	12	18	0
Kalish, Ryan	.282	71	18	20	3	0	1	9	21	14	13
Martin, Kyle	.245	110	16	27	12	0	6	26	4	33	3
McBride, Matt	.285	130	18	37	11	0	3	22	15	19	1
Mertins, Kurt	.218	78	14	17	4	1	2	16	9	20	5
Moon, Kyu Hwan	.253	79	6	20	1	1	1	8	10	21	0
Navarro, Yamaico	.207	87	12	18	1	0	1	11	10	15	1
Parraz, Jordan	.213	80	8	17	1	0	1	8	9	21	3

Realini, Dustin	.171	41	5	7	2	0	0	3	9	16	0
Rivas, Ron	.216	51	6	11	1	0	0	3	3	13	1
Sato, Kenji	.242	91	9	22	4	1	0	12	8	24	2

PITCHING	W	L	ERA	G	GS	SV	IP	H	BB	SO
Capellan, Jose	0	1	4.74	7	7	0	25	33	9	22
Eguchi, Ryosuke	0	1	6.35	7	0	0	11	13	6	9
Godin, Jason	3	1	3.73	8	8	0	31	29	15	36
Ha, Jun Ho	0	1	7.80	13	0	0	15	16	15	17
Hattori, Yasutaka	3	2	5.64	8	7	0	30	34	12	25
Heo, Jun Hyeok	1	4	3.77	8	8	0	31	36	9	17
Hicks, Christopher	2	0	5.50	13	0	1	18	17	12	22
Hunter, Brett	0	1	5.59	7	0	1	10	4	6	18
Lee, Sang-Hwa	0	2	7.71	8	5	0	19	31	5	12
Meyer, Matt	3	2	5.60	15	0	1	18	20	11	22
Nemoto, Tomohisa	0	0	3.24	10	0	0	17	19	3	18
Nottingham, Shawn	1	1	4.71	13	0	0	21	21	9	26
Richardson, Dustin	0	2	2.41	12	0	0	19	18	6	26
Swaggerty, Ben	1	1	5.79	12	0	0	19	22	9	26
Taylor, Heath	0	0	2.19	4	1	0	12	14	4	9
Uchi, Tatsuya	0	0	6.00	5	0	0	6	7	2	4

WAIKIKI BEACH BOYS

BATTERS	AVG	AB	R	H	2B	3B	HR	RBI	BB	SO	SB
Alonso, Yonder	.308	104	17	32	9	0	4	21	20	23	1
Frazier, Todd	.295	95	19	28	11	2	3	22	11	20	1
Garabedian, Alex	.154	52	4	8	3	0	0	2	2	11	0
Giles, Tommy	.184	76	5	14	5	1	0	3	3	20	0
Kieschnick, Roger	.236	110	15	26	5	2	6	25	16	46	0
Limonta, Johan	.147	75	8	11	2	0	1	7	6	27	1
McOwen, James	.253	83	17	21	6	2	1	10	13	17	3
Onizaki, Yuji	.256	78	9	20	2	1	0	7	10	23	1
Posey, Buster	.338	74	15	25	4	0	0	15	7	15	0
Romine, Austin	.208	53	8	11	4	1	0	4	7	9	0
Silverio, Alfredo	.241	112	18	27	8	0	0	9	6	27	2
Smith, Marquez	.190	116	15	22	4	1	4	11	13	36	0
Sublett, Damon	.253	75	15	19	6	1	2	18	3	23	0
Thomas, Tony	.223	121	15	27	5	6	2	9	8	35	3

PITCHERS	W	L	ERA	G	GS	SV	IP	H	BB	SO
Bleich, Jeremy	3	2	1.77	7	7	0	36	29	12	33
Brackman, Andrew	3	4	5.56	8	8	0	34	31	25	36
Edlefsen, Steve	0	0	10.66	11	0	0	13	14	12	14
Guerra, Javy	0	1	4.24	11	1	1	23	20	9	28
Harmon, Rob	0	0	9.42	11	0	0	14	19	9	7
Joaquin, Waldis	2	3	5.97	8	8	0	32	35	19	20

Papelbon, Jeremy	1	0	2.45	13	0	7	15	8	9	16
Parker, Blake	1	1	6.28	11	0	0	14	18	4	16
Pfeiffer, David	1	0	1.59	11	0	3	17	7	4	11
Pratt, Jordan	0	1	2.53	10	0	1	21	16	14	34
Richard, Steven	0	0	1.93	8	0	0	14	9	6	17
Takai, Yuhei	2	2	4.05	6	6	0	27	25	15	27
Valiquette, Philippe	0	1	8.53	9	0	0	13	23	10	11
Yamamoto, Kazunori	3	0	1.96	9	0	0	18	12	4	17
Yoshikawa, Mitsuo	3	2	4.55	7	7	0	32	33	11	37

WEST OAHU CANEFIRES

BATTERS	AVG	AB	R	H	2B	3B	HR	RBI	BB	SO	SB
Burns, Gregory	.257	101	15	26	1	3	1	10	15	33	11
Crancer, Wally	.224	49	7	11	1	1	1	8	6	13	1
Durham, Miles	.273	121	24	33	8	1	3	28	12	25	1
Friday, Brian	.182	66	14	12	2	0	0	4	16	17	1
Gindl, Caleb	.281	96	13	27	6	0	3	18	12	17	1
Hallberg, Mark	.362	116	24	42	5	0	3	21	10	14	0
Hankerd, Cyle	.318	88	16	28	3	1	5	30	9	22	0
Hatcher, Chris	.283	53	9	15	2	0	3	12	4	10	0
Henson, Tyler	.266	124	28	33	13	3	1	16	25	44	3
Inouye, Matt	.250	8	0	2	0	0	0	2	0	1	0
Kurose, Haruki	.196	56	4	11	2	0	0	3	2	11	1
Loewen, Adam	.207	29	4	6	0	0	0	2	5	8	1
Negrych, Jim	.225	40	9	9	3	0	0	4	7	10	1
Peter, Kyle	.370	92	20	34	4	1	1	12	8	19	11
Schafer, Logan	.244	86	15	21	3	1	1	10	13	7	3
Skelton, James	.281	64	10	18	5	1	0	11	11	18	1

PITCHERS	W	L	ERA	G	GS	SV	IP	H	BB	SO
Bascom, Timothy	1	3	7.78	6	6	0	20	21	10	16
Bishop, Harrison	1	0	2.76	11	0	0	16	17	6	17
Bloom, Kyle	2	0	1.50	7	7	0	30	15	11	32
Cody, Chris	0	0	3.90	8	7	0	32	28	9	32
Flagello, Clifford	1	2	4.70	11	0	3	15	19	7	14
Gleason, Sean	2	2	6.08	8	4	0	24	21	13	8
Hess, Andrew	0	0	3.51	11	0	1	26	23	10	17
Kimura, Fumikazu	1	2	5.86	11	4	0	28	25	17	31
Kiyohara, Daiki	1	1	5.79	9	0	0	14	18	1	15
Krebs, Eric	0	0	5.40	3	0	0	3	5	3	3
Parker, Brian	0	0	6.75	11	0	0	17	24	9	12
Robles, Moises	1	2	3.12	14	0	5	17	19	3	15
Salberg, Chris	4	0	3.90	12	4	0	30	24	16	23
Scarpetta, Cody	2	2	8.03	4	4	0	12	13	8	18
Yokoyama, Ryunosuke	1	0	5.25	7	0	0	12	9	4	13

MINOR LEAGUES

INDEPENDENT LEAGUES

Midseason deal shows how indy ball keeps growing

BY J.J. COOPER

There's still a pretty significant gulf between affiliated baseball and the independent leagues, but every now and then, there are signs of a thaw.

The Southern Illinois Miners and the Arizona Diamondbacks teamed up for one of those little glimmers of proof that despite plenty of differences, it's all baseball.

Technically, the Diamondbacks purchased the contract of lefthander Clay Zavada from the Frontier League's Miners, and the Miners signed first baseman Brad Miller, who had just been released by the Diamondbacks. But in reality, the Diamondbacks and Miners managed to pull off a cross-league swap.

Zavada had a 1.72 ERA in 12 appearances with Southern Illinois with 22 strikeouts and four walks. It didn't take long for the Diamondbacks to see enough to know they wanted Zavada back in their organization. (They had drafted him in 2006, releasing him after the 2007 season.) But instead of simply paying the acquisition fee, farm director A.J. Hinch had a novel idea.

At the same time, Hinch was trying to find Miller a place to play. The Diamondbacks were planning on releasing the 25-year-old first baseman, but Hinch wanted to help him find a new team rather than just cutting him loose.

MLB ended up ruling that it couldn't become a straight trade, but the results were the same with Zavada joining the Diamondbacks and Miller becoming a Miner.

Getting Noticed

While the Zavada-Miller swap was a very unusual sight, Zavada was one of numerous independent leaguers to get noticed and get back to affiliated ball. At this point, there are more affiliated clubs that scout and sign players from the independent leagues than those that don't.

The relationship is somewhat symbiotic, as the independent leagues continue to succeed at moving into ballparks left available when affiliated ball moves away. Economists can debate whether trickle-down economics work, but it is clear that the independent leagues are quite happy to survive on the fringes of affiliated baseball, letting quality markets trickle into indy ball.

This year it was Wichita that made the jump

First baseman Brad Miller joined the Southern Illinois Miners in a rare deal

BILL MITCHELL

from affiliated ball to the independent leagues. With the Texas League's Wichita Wranglers moving to become the Northwest Arkansas Naturals, the American Association moved in. The newly minted Wichita Wingnuts drew more than 3,400 fans a game, up from their 1,829 average in the last year in affiliated ball.

Always Changing

It's a running joke in the independent leagues that if you're unhappy with the current alignment of leagues, just wait a couple of minutes and something will have changed. That was true again in 2008 as the South Coast League folded before the season, calling it quits after only one year. But otherwise it was a year of relative stability. The Golden Baseball League continued to grow, adding a pair of Canadian clubs as Edmonton and Calgary left the Northern League to join the Golden League. The American Association added Wichita and an expansion team in Grand Prairie.

There will be more shuffling for 2009. The United League faced an injunction from its founders to ensure it didn't merge with the Golden League or dissolve during the offseason. The Can-Am League learned that the Ottawa Rapidz were folding because of a lease dispute, and the Golden League announced plans to add a team in Tucson.

Breen finds swing on Indy stopover

Two years ago, Patrick Breen thought he was just one good season away from the big leagues. A year later, he was released.

But you won't find Breen moping or complaining about being cut loose. Breen may be the only independent leagues player who's actually happy he was in an independent league this year.

"I am a big believer that everything happens for a reason. The year I had offensively is a tribute to (Orange County hitting coach) Darrell Evans. He completely changed how I looked at hitting," Breen said. "If I had never been released by Tampa Bay, I never would have done that."

It sure worked this year. With his retooled approach, Breen broke the Golden Baseball League records for home runs (28), on-base percentage (.509), slugging percentage (.825), total bases (227) and extra-base hits (56). The center fielder also won the batting title thanks to his .396 average, and finished three RBIs short of a Triple Crown.

Patrick Breen

For his impressive season, plus his leadership role in driving Orange County to the Golden Baseball League title, Breen is the 2008 Independent Leagues Player of the Year.

It's a nice turnaround for the Rays' 2004 21st-round pick. Breen hit .302/.383/.502 in the pitcher-friendly Midwest League in 2005, and followed it up by hitting 21 home runs in only 94 games at high Class A Visalia in 2006. He got a late-season promotion to Double-A Montgomery and seemed to be establishing himself as a late-round find. As Breen saw it, he was one more good year away from getting a shot at the major leagues.

But all of that fell apart in 2007. He was beaned during a spring training game against the Yankees. In hindsight, it may have been a good idea to take a little time to recover and get over the effects of the concussion, but Breen was back on the field and in the Montgomery lineup when the season started.

He may have been in the lineup, but he had lost his stroke. Breen struggled all year, hitting only .194/.284/.344.

By the time he was told during spring training this year that he was being released, Breen was expecting it. Breen, 26, figured that his career might be over, but then he got a call from former teammate Josh Arhart, who was joining the Golden League's Orange County Flyers. The chance to play for a pair of big league stars in manager Gary Carter and hitting coach Evans helped induce Breen to give it another shot.

Within a couple of weeks, he was happy he did. Pretty quickly, Evans and Breen decided to retool his entire approach. They moved him closer to the plate, simplified his swing and got him to stand more upright. In doing so, they freed Breen up to tap into his raw power.

The results were pretty impressive. Breen started putting on shows in batting practice, launching moon shots. And since he could get around on any fastball a Golden League pitcher could throw him, it became easier to hit breaking balls and changeups as well.

The results were a season-long power binge. Breen averaged a home run every 9.8 at-bats. He had 32 multi-hit games (in 80 games played), and hit better than .400 in three of the four months of the season.

"I've never seen anyone have a better year," Evans said. "Everything he hit was a bullet."

INDEPENDENT LEAGUES

AMERICAN ASSOCIATION

For the first time in the three-year history of the reborn American Association, the Fort Worth Cats did not get to celebrate a title. The Cats were knocked out in the first-round of the playoffs by Grand Prarie, which made it to the championship series as a first-year expansion team. But the Airhogs Cinderella run ended two games short of the title, as the Sioux Falls Canaries Beau Torbert led off the 12th with a single, and a walk and bunt single loaded the bases. Patrick Reilly finished off the rally by singling through the drawn-in infield to score Torbert. Torbert's championship-clinching run was a fitting end to an impressive season. Torbert finished in the league's top five in batting average (.324), home runs (19), RBIs (71) and slugging percentage (.568) and was named the league's player of the year. The outfielder signed with the Tigers after the season ended. He'll be joined at Tigers spring training by former Canaries teammate Kris Regas. Regas was named the league's star of stars after going 1-0, 1.29 with a league-record 30 saves.

FIRST HALF

NORTH DIVISION	W	L	PCT	GB
Sioux Falls	31	17	.646	—
Wichita	26	21	.553	4.5
St. Paul	24	24	.500	7
Lincoln	21	26	.447	9.5
Sioux City	21	27	.438	10
SOUTH DIVISION	**W**	**L**	**PCT**	**GB**
Fort Worth	29	19	.604	—
Grand Prairie	27	21	.563	2
El Paso	21	27	.458	7
Pensacola	21	27	.438	8
Shreveport	17	31	.354	12

SECOND HALF

NORTH DIVISION	W	L	PCT	GB
Sioux City	31	17	.646	—
Sioux Falls	29	19	.604	2
Lincoln	29	19	.604	2
Wichita	19	29	.396	12
St. Paul	18	30	.375	13
SOUTH DIVISION	**W**	**L**	**PCT**	**GB**
Fort Worth	31	17	.646	—
Grand Prairie	29	19	.604	2
Pensacola	22	26	.458	9
El Paso	21	25	.457	9
Shreveport	9	37	.196	21

PLAYOFFS: Semifinals—Sioux Falls defeated Sioux City 3-0 and Grand Prarie defeated Fort Worth 3-1 in best-of-five series. Finals: Sioux Falls defeated Grand Prarie 3-1 in best-of-five series.
MANAGERS: El Paso—Butch Henry. Fort Worth—Chad Tredaway. Grand Prarie—Pete Incaviglia. Lincoln—Tim Johnson. Pensacola—Mac Seibert. St. Paul—George Tsamis. Shreveport—Terry Bevington/Eddie Gerald. Sioux City—Les Lancaster. Sioux Falls-Steve Shirley. Wichita—Kash Beauchamp.
ATTENDANCE: St. Paul 286,796; Fort Worth 185,175; Lincoln 182,852; El Paso 182,380; Sioux Falls 150,837; Grand Prairie 143,627; Sioux City 87,616; Pensacola 82,999; Shreveport 57,975.
ALL-STAR TEAM: C—J.B. Tucker, Grand Prarie. 1B—Brandon Sing, Pensacola. 2B—Brenan Herrera, Wichita. 3B—Grant Richardson, Sioux Falls. SS—Kevin Hooper, Wichita. OF—Bryan Fryer, Fort Worth; Brent Krause, St. Paul; Beau Torbert, Sioux Falls. DH—John Allen, Fort Worth. LHP—Joel Kirsten, Fort Worth. RHP—Nick Singleton, Sioux City. RP—Kris Regas, Sioux Falls.
Player of the Year: Beau Torbert, Sioux Falls. **Manager of the Year:** Steve Shirley, Sioux Falls.

INDIVIDUAL BATTING LEADERS

BATTER, CLUB	AVG	G	AB	R	H	HR	RBI
Hooper, Kevin, Wichita	.373	88	357	73	133	1	26
Smith, Will, Sioux Falls	.333	61	237	32	79	7	37
Fenwick, Ron, St. Paul	.328	89	335	46	110	0	40
Allen, John, Wichita	.327	96	376	61	123	20	65
Torbert, Beau, Sioux Falls	.324	90	340	65	110	19	71
Richardson, Grant, Sioux Falls	.322	96	354	88	114	16	71

Fryer, Brian, Wichita	.319	95	417	81	133	5	42
Krause, Brent, St. Paul	.317	93	353	71	112	19	56
Alvarez, Jorge, El Paso	.317	92	372	58	118	12	44
Herrera, Brenan, Wichita	.317	93	366	44	116	5	51

INDIVIDUAL PITCHING LEADERS

PITCHER, CLUB	W	L	ERA	IP	H	BB	SO
Singleton, Nick, Sioux City	8	4	2.24	113	102	32	82
Drucker, Scot, Grand Prairie	8	3	2.41	93	78	20	57
Mattison, Kieran, Grand Prairie	9	2	2.42	86	62	20	67
Gwaltney, Lee, Fort Worth	9	2	2.57	91	75	43	67
Kirsten, Joel, Fort Worth	8	3	2.69	137	134	31	89
Ford, Ryan, Sioux Falls	13	6	2.77	130	147	26	75
Villarreal, Luis, St. Paul	4	5	3.06	79	76	32	56
Grybash, Dan, Fort Worth	8	5	3.18	119	116	32	100
Gardner, Jarrett, Lincoln	11	6	3.25	130	122	17	88
Francisco, Alexander, Sioux City	12	1	3.31	101	104	28	64

EL PASO DIABLOS

BATTERS	AVG	AB	R	H	2B	3B	HR	RBI	SB
Alvarez, Jorge	.317	372	58	118	21	1	12	44	4
*Conley, Evan	.252	107	14	27	5	0	0	17	0
*Cooksey, Bryan	.268	287	38	77	16	5	1	37	7
Crespo, Ricardo	.053	19	1	1	0	0	0	0	0
Derhak, Alex	.288	271	47	78	11	0	7	34	1
Drew, Kory	.237	358	49	85	23	3	3	38	5
Garcia, Eric	.238	42	1	10	0	0	0	3	0
*Hudson, Brandon	.333	3	0	1	0	0	0	0	0
*James, Willie	.229	131	16	30	5	1	0	13	8
Keesee, David	.063	16	1	1	0	0	0	0	0
*Kent, Mat	.289	343	52	99	22	1	9	47	0
*Longmire, Marcel	.214	98	12	21	8	0	1	8	0
*Machado, Albenis	.372	86	19	32	7	0	0	9	1
*McConnell, Brandon	.294	17	2	5	1	0	1	3	0
Mejia, Roberto	.247	89	10	22	3	0	2	9	0
Neitz, Josh	.333	3	1	1	0	0	0	0	0
Olmstead, Walter	.310	184	26	57	7	7	4	36	4
*Reininger, Jarrett	.276	217	38	60	18	1	6	31	0
Smith, Bryon	.294	326	45	96	22	0	10	60	0
Smith, Stantrel	.274	237	35	65	6	7	4	33	21

PITCHERS	W	L	ERA	G	SV	IP	H	BB	SO
Bennett, Derek	1	2	5.04	13	0	25	37	13	15
Blackley, Adam	7	9	4.98	19	0	107	123	50	95
Cervera, Mike	2	0	1.13	24	13	32	29	14	39
Daniels, Isaac	0	0	0.00	2	0	1	3	0	1
Freites, Julio	0	0	22.50	3	0	2	6	2	1
Frias, Jusef	5	7	5.55	29	0	86	105	34	62
Hendricks, Donavon	1	0	11.70	9	0	10	26	4	5
Herrera, Bryan	0	0	54.00	1	0	0	2	1	0
Hintz, Beau	2	2	7.31	6	0	32	53	21	19
Holm, Jimmy	0	0	9.82	8	0	11	17	11	5
*Hudson, Brandon	2	1	4.20	23	0	30	43	7	20
*Kauten, Joshua	3	4	4.45	10	0	63	74	20	38
Knoff, Justin	1	4	7.41	13	0	51	85	19	31
Litchfield, B.J.	0	2	6.66	21	0	24	33	15	17
*Marsden, Aaron	1	0	2.25	26	2	28	31	14	15
Neitz, Josh	10	9	4.35	21	0	134	149	46	91
Nelson, Ryne	0	0	27.00	2	0	4	12	5	2
*Reininger, Jarrett	0	0	0.00	2	0	2	0	1	6
*Romero, Garvis	0	0	3.14	9	0	14	18	3	8
Schmidt, Paul	0	0	5.91	9	0	11	18	4	6
Thompson, Chris	2	1	4.05	9	3	13	14	8	15
Thurmond, Ben	0	2	6.94	3	0	12	21	3	5
Vecchio, Jason	0	1	6.26	22	3	23	27	16	23
Whigham, David	6	7	4.32	19	0	100	123	26	68

FORT WORTH CATS

BATTERS	AVG	AB	R	H	2B	3B	HR	RBI	SB
Allen, John	.327	376	61	123	23	2	20	65	3
*Bartolucci, Paul	.182	33	3	6	1	0	0	3	0
Blair, Cameron	.292	168	30	49	12	0	3	25	3

*Butler, Steve	.152	33	4	5	2	0	0	0	1
Carter, Charles	.284	356	55	101	9	5	3	39	14
Fester, Jonas	.121	58	4	7	2	0	0	3	0
Flores, Osiel	.220	118	25	26	1	1	8	19	1
Fryer, Brian	.319	417	81	133	21	4	5	42	50
Garza, Marco	.250	48	6	12	5	0	0	5	0
*Gautreau, Jake	.282	348	58	98	22	1	12	70	0
*James, Willie	.186	59	7	11	1	0	0	0	5
Lup, Ken	.260	273	28	71	10	0	0	43	3
*Montague, Ed	.257	385	50	99	26	3	6	47	20
O'Sullivan, Patrick	.262	65	15	17	7	0	3	14	1
*Riddle, Ryan	.500	2	1	1	0	0	0	0	1
Sisk, Aaron	.215	247	33	53	15	1	3	26	5
Teilon, Nilson	.311	380	73	118	20	2	17	74	14

PITCHERS	W	L	ERA	G	SV	IP	H	BB	SO
Buechner, Chris	0	0	6.35	6	0	6	5	2	7
Crow, Aaron	0	0	0.00	1	0	1	1	0	0
*Flores, Pedro	14	3	4.06	18	0	115	124	50	94
Grybash, Dan	8	5	3.18	18	0	119	116	32	100
Gwaltney, Lee	9	2	2.57	15	0	91	75	43	67
Haines, Timothy	5	6	4.93	37	0	84	86	47	69
Hedden, Wayne	1	1	4.82	6	0	9	12	7	9
Hunton, Jon	5	1	0.81	48	23	56	26	18	71
*Kirsten, Joel	8	3	2.69	20	0	137	134	31	89
*Martin, Brian	1	1	3.35	46	0	51	32	32	44
Reilly, Matthew	2	3	2.94	34	1	52	48	28	24
*Riddle, Ryan	5	4	4.28	17	0	90	106	32	57
Shearer, Kelly	0	2	8.10	4	0	7	8	11	2
Vasquez, Tim	0	0	81.00	2	0	1	4	4	0
Yates, Kyle	2	5	4.66	40	3	46	56	16	31

GRAND PRAIRIE AIRHOGS

BATTERS	AVG	AB	R	H	2B	3B	HR	RBI	SB
*Bartolucci, Paul	.250	112	9	28	2	0	0	15	1
Burgos, Victor	.333	6	1	2	0	0	0	1	0
*Carter, Brandon	.279	287	46	80	21	1	7	54	16
*Conroy, Mike	.294	228	39	67	11	5	4	34	7
Cordero, Jose	.000	3	0	0	0	0	0	0	0
Espinosa, David	.310	364	73	113	17	5	8	37	20
Garza, Aaron	.266	301	51	80	15	3	6	36	18
Heath, Demetrius	.375	8	1	3	0	0	0	0	0
Holder, Andrew	.283	339	61	96	21	1	10	47	11
Hurst, Jason	.167	18	0	3	1	0	0	0	0
Maldonado, Edwin	.281	352	51	99	17	1	11	53	6
*McConnell, Brandon	.188	16	2	3	1	0	2	3	1
McGuire, Cameron	.133	15	1	2	0	0	0	1	0
Merrell, Cody	.140	57	5	8	2	0	1	3	0
*Munoz, Billy	.268	340	38	91	16	2	9	56	2
*Nicholson, Derek	.283	307	50	87	15	4	12	55	7
Trevino, Noel	.238	105	13	25	1	0	2	15	6
Tucker, J.B.	.295	319	62	94	24	2	11	47	8

PITCHERS	W	L	ERA	G	SV	IP	H	BB	SO
Brantley, Rodney	0	1	7.40	12	0	21	18	17	15
Brockman, Ben	1	2	5.32	8	0	22	30	11	10
*Conroy, Mike	0	0	9.00	1	0	2	2	5	2
Cordero, Jose	4	4	3.49	23	0	67	72	31	34
*DeChristofaro, Vinnie	6	2	2.80	47	3	55	44	32	54
Drabek, Justin	0	1	8.59	3	0	7	7	6	4
Drucker, Scot	8	3	2.41	15	0	93	78	20	57
Furrow, Jason	0	0	4.50	2	0	2	2	1	0
Garcia, Geivy	2	1	2.60	30	2	35	23	20	40
*Garcia, Justin	8	5	4.66	23	1	87	80	42	60
Gardner, Michael	0	1	3.00	2	0	6	4	4	2
Harris, Nat	6	3	3.65	19	0	101	107	40	49
Homer, Chris	1	2	5.40	30	0	32	32	14	28
Jamnik, Jeff	1	2	3.03	7	0	30	36	4	16
*Jenkins, Aaron	3	3	3.70	28	0	49	34	33	56
MacFarland, Stephen	0	2	4.50	10	0	16	16	12	17
Mattison, Kieran	9	2	2.42	14	0	86	62	20	67
*McConnell, Brandon	0	0	9.00	1	0	1	3	1	1
Morrison, James	3	1	2.81	42	19	48	44	14	50
Nieto, Jose	0	0	18.00	1	0	1	2	1	0
Righter, Matt	2	2	7.31	9	0	28	46	13	15

Smith, Clint	0	1	40.50	2	0	1	4	1	0
Stott, Zac	2	2	3.75	5	0	24	25	10	13
*Wesley, John	0	0	0.00	6	0	6	1	2	5
Williams, Julian	0	0	36.00	1	0	1	3	1	0

LINCOLN SALTDOGS

BATTERS	AVG	AB	R	H	2B	3B	HR	RBI	SB
Adams, Skip	.327	150	28	49	10	0	4	21	7
Bramasco, Omar	.229	83	12	19	4	0	0	4	4
*Burns, Deacon	.250	72	9	18	1	0	1	7	8
Contreras, Anthony	.312	186	21	58	5	0	0	21	6
Delgado, Mario	.333	216	34	72	13	0	11	33	3
Dempsey, Joe	.229	70	7	16	6	0	0	6	1
Harrington, Corey	.188	144	18	27	6	0	0	13	11
Jose, Patrick	.282	39	7	11	0	0	1	6	1
Kaplan, Jonny	.275	255	47	70	16	4	4	26	24
*Machado, Albenis	.217	92	12	20	7	0	2	8	1
Maloney, Matt	.279	140	22	39	7	0	9	26	6
Mazur, Josh	.000	4	0	0	0	0	0	0	0
McCoy, Ross	.217	60	8	13	1	0	1	5	1
McFeely, Shea	.290	248	31	72	19	1	6	39	2
McGill, Shawn	.299	274	52	82	6	6	9	43	15
Miaso, Curt	.298	171	28	51	2	0	5	20	3
Mindick, Matt	.000	2	0	0	0	0	0	0	0
Nieblas, Luis	.189	37	4	7	1	0	0	2	0
Pellow, Kit	.344	64	16	22	3	0	6	16	1
Perez, Luis	.280	164	23	46	11	0	5	15	4
Rios, Eduardo	.275	255	26	70	16	0	6	39	1
Rodriguez, Manny	.344	64	12	22	8	0	1	7	3
Tinius, Ben	.179	84	8	15	2	0	1	11	0
*Yount, Dustin	.309	350	50	108	22	1	8	69	2
Zazueta, Amadeo	.250	8	0	2	0	0	0	0	0

PITCHERS	W	L	ERA	G	SV	IP	H	BB	SO
Alvarez, Mark	0	0	0.00	1	0	1	0	0	0
Arreola, Daryl	0	2	2.68	25	2	47	39	22	34
*Bergman, Dusty	1	0	4.71	4	0	21	21	6	17
Campbell, Brian	10	4	4.26	19	0	99	110	36	43
Cepeda, Benigno	0	1	3.68	9	2	7	4	8	8
*Clayman, Matt	0	0	8.10	4	0	3	6	4	0
*Cline, Zachary	1	1	6.35	2	0	11	10	6	4
*Daniels, Adam	2	1	1.50	10	0	6	2	3	4
*Davis, Vince	6	4	3.47	32	0	80	70	32	56
Dittfurth, Ryan	3	5	5.36	12	0	45	56	20	38
*Figueroa, Jonathan	0	1	8.31	3	0	4	4	4	4
Gardner, Jarrett	11	6	3.25	20	0	130	122	17	88
*Goodman, Mark	0	0	18.00	2	0	2	7	0	0
Hammons, Matt	0	1	4.50	6	5	6	4	5	10
Harrington, Corey	0	0	9.00	1	0	1	2	1	0
Jarvis, Jason	4	6	2.98	23	1	60	59	21	53
*Kauten, Joshua	1	3	4.04	9	0	42	46	10	22
Knox, Dan	0	0	10.13	5	0	8	12	3	8
Orozco, Alvaro	0	1	11.37	4	0	6	13	1	3
Paduch, Jim	1	1	3.12	5	1	17	14	4	10
Reekers, Jeff	0	0	2.70	2	0	3	3	2	0
Schutt, Chris	0	0	0.00	11	0	11	3	5	9
Spiehs, R.D.	3	2	4.07	24	5	60	59	15	37
Staggs, Nathan	0	0	5.40	12	4	15	14	11	12
*Stephens, Amad	0	0	2.70	2	0	3	2	2	3
Storey, Michael	1	0	4.26	7	0	6	7	4	3
Sutton, Calen	0	0	17.55	2	0	7	15	2	3
Thompson, Johnny	1	1	7.80	11	0	15	9	15	13
Trytten, Dan	5	5	3.52	17	0	102	99	44	81
*White, Adam	0	0	0.00	2	0	3	2	0	1

PENSACOLA PELICANS

BATTERS	AVG	AB	R	H	2B	3B	HR	RBI	SB
Alvarez, Rafael	.304	289	58	88	20	0	18	53	18
Aranguren, Cesar	.248	331	43	82	8	0	3	39	4
Arminio, Joe	.000	14	0	0	0	0	0	0	0
Christison, Dallas	.290	207	41	60	12	1	2	17	11
*Conley, Evan	.287	143	19	41	9	0	0	16	1
Cordova, Ricardo	.228	189	27	43	7	0	1	19	4
Cox, Billy	.289	121	18	35	7	2	4	15	4

	AVG	AB	R	H	2B	3B	HR	RBI	SB
Deleo, Adam	.154	39	7	6	1	0	0	2	0
Gamble, Sean	.149	67	6	10	2	0	0	6	0
Golliner, David	.000	5	0	0	0	0	0	0	0
Hernandez, David	.000	8	0	0	0	0	0	0	0
Joffrion, Jack	.244	135	20	33	6	0	3	18	2
*Leandro, Francisco	.305	269	43	82	22	1	4	37	14
Lewis, Will	.083	12	3	1	0	0	0	1	0
Lopez, Javier	.158	38	3	6	1	0	0	1	0
Madsen, Scott	.225	80	11	18	2	1	1	5	3
McWilliams, Arden	.172	29	2	5	0	0	0	2	1
Morgan, Josh	.200	110	15	22	3	1	1	15	6
*Pali, Matt	.269	338	50	91	22	1	7	44	8
Parzyk, Dylan	.245	233	21	57	7	0	0	23	1
Pittenger, Scott	.200	30	1	6	2	0	0	1	1
*Reynolds, Chris	.273	209	24	57	10	1	1	30	12
Sing, Brandon	.278	320	56	89	22	0	22	86	1

PITCHERS	W	L	ERA	G	SV	IP	H	BB	SO
Cameron, Dustin	3	2	1.38	34	14	39	33	8	35
*Cline, Zachary	5	8	3.97	17	0	100	110	38	51
Davis, Hunter	0	0	0.00	6	1	6	2	2	5
DeValk, Dane	5	8	5.13	22	1	102	99	37	63
*Goodman, Mark	0	1	9.26	7	0	12	21	1	8
Hendricks, T.J.	0	1	10.03	6	0	12	25	3	8
*Langdon, Donny	4	2	2.43	27	3	37	34	11	31
Marquetti, Agustin	0	0	10.80	5	0	8	10	11	8
Orgovan, Joe	1	1	9.72	2	0	8	15	6	1
Paulk, Robert	1	2	1.78	18	0	30	21	8	29
Phillips, Paul	1	1	2.77	21	1	26	28	12	29
Rafferty, Ryan	0	0	16.88	6	0	8	8	11	6
Rickey, Chris	0	0	16.62	3	0	4	7	5	2
Roque, Ulysses	1	0	3.77	9	0	14	17	4	19
Scheafer, Carl	2	2	4.77	40	0	66	89	7	25
Shanahan, Dan	0	0	12.46	5	0	9	13	8	5
*Smith, Dan	3	3	3.08	11	0	73	57	34	73
Snipes, Clegg	7	6	5.40	22	0	108	144	25	68
Tillman, Derek	2	1	6.35	17	1	23	26	16	25
Walters, Cory	0	6	7.38	8	0	39	57	10	36
Webb, John	8	9	5.29	20	0	111	116	47	88

SHREVEPORT SPORTS

BATTERS	AVG	AB	R	H	2B	3B	HR	RBI	SB
*Blue, Vince	.375	64	5	24	3	1	1	8	7
Bratton, Robert	.255	298	34	76	20	0	6	41	7
Bryant, Tommy	.244	303	38	74	18	2	6	27	0
*Burns, Deacon	.233	301	28	70	8	3	4	34	15
*Clayman, Matt	.000	2	0	0	0	0	0	0	0
Contreras, Lester	.292	24	0	7	2	0	0	4	0
*Cooksey, Bryan	.379	29	7	11	2	1	0	2	1
*Fenwick, Ron	.328	259	35	85	16	0	0	33	0
Frye, Christopher	.241	29	6	7	1	0	0	1	1
Gambill, Chad	.289	135	22	39	9	0	6	14	1
*Hale, Adam	.276	152	23	42	8	2	6	22	7
Haugen, Casey	.091	22	2	2	0	1	0	2	0
*Hudson, Brandon	.236	55	4	13	1	0	0	2	0
Humphries, Justin	.284	215	29	61	18	1	6	35	0
Lewis, Michael	.262	61	9	16	0	1	0	2	1
*Marrero, Emmanuel	.256	39	2	10	2	0	0	2	3
McClain, Terrence	.238	223	25	53	11	0	6	31	3
Miller, Adam	.207	145	13	30	2	4	0	14	1
Pilgreen, Matt	.000	1	0	0	0	0	0	0	0
*Polanco, Enohel	.218	87	15	19	2	0	0	6	1
*Quihuis-Bell, Richar	.284	261	31	84	14	2	3	38	0
*Robinson, Wade	.236	229	23	54	7	1	0	11	5
Smith, Chris	.199	196	26	39	9	0	1	12	1

PITCHERS	W	L	ERA	G	SV	IP	H	BB	SO
Ayala, Albert	0	0	6.35	5	0	11	13	8	12
Bone, Josh	1	1	3.48	27	0	44	53	10	19
*Clayman, Matt	2	8	3.67	26	0	56	57	17	40
*Cunningham, Aaron	2	2	3.53	32	1	43	43	6	30
*Hudson, Brandon	0	0	6.48	5	0	8	16	1	5
Markray, Thad	7	6	4.00	19	0	124	128	23	110
*Phillips, Justin	4	12	5.79	19	0	115	134	52	92
Pilgreen, Matt	2	8	5.52	28	0	59	73	13	52

	W	L	ERA	G	SV	IP	H	BB	SO
*Poland, Trey	0	2	2.91	22	12	22	22	10	15
Savickas, Russell	4	8	4.24	17	0	104	120	36	55
Smith, Chris	0	0	0.00	1	0	2	2	2	1
Snow, Bert	1	10	8.40	16	1	90	137	35	48
Steed, Bric	0	2	8.64	2	0	8	11	8	4
Tyson, Leo	0	0	8.79	10	0	14	16	3	13
Welch, Daniel	3	9	4.93	17	0	104	99	41	73

SIOUX CITY EXPLORERS

BATTERS	AVG	AB	R	H	2B	3B	HR	RBI	SB
Bryan, Jason	.190	42	5	8	1	0	1	4	0
Camacho, Juan	.273	344	46	94	17	0	8	59	2
Eusebio, Keith	.000	0	1	0	0	0	0	0	0
French, Anton	.238	84	14	20	3	2	1	11	2
Gabriel, Chad	.308	305	28	94	18	5	3	42	6
Gillingham, Tug	.222	63	5	14	2	0	0	3	1
Grossman, Chris	.248	310	47	77	15	0	7	39	5
Hetherington, Luke	.229	83	9	19	4	0	0	8	3
Jimerson, Charlton	.097	31	0	3	1	0	0	0	1
Jones, Dustin	.281	270	60	76	14	2	1	19	24
*Llanos, Alex	.303	337	58	102	15	2	10	60	10
McCoola, Nick	.251	346	38	87	18	0	0	35	6
Navarro, Ramon	.200	5	2	1	1	0	0	0	0
Pirman, Pete	.158	19	1	3	2	0	0	0	0
*Polanco, Enohel	.273	33	4	9	2	0	1	3	1
Rodriguez, Jorge	.139	36	2	5	0	0	0	1	1
*Schermerhorn, Derek	.264	231	30	61	14	4	1	36	16
Senreiso, Juan	.389	36	7	14	3	0	0	7	1
*Tuttle, Jason	.292	257	49	75	6	1	0	18	18
*Wagner, Geoff	.059	17	0	1	0	0	0	0	0
Walker, Sam	.206	155	13	32	11	0	0	10	4
*Young, Walter	.367	98	12	36	4	0	5	29	0

PITCHERS	W	L	ERA	G	SV	IP	H	BB	SO
*Bergman, Dusty	0	12	6.20	13	0	74	102	33	49
Cheek, Cameron	6	3	3.81	25	0	85	95	20	51
Dixon, Curt	0	0	18.00	1	0	1	2	2	0
Dumont, Alvan	7	4	3.34	26	0	89	96	25	66
Eusebio, Keith	0	0	0.00	1	0	3	0	2	2
Fagan, Robert	0	4	10.62	5	0	20	34	13	15
Fitzgerald, Kevin	0	0	11.57	2	0	2	4	3	0
Francisco, Alexander	12	1	3.31	18	0	101	104	28	64
Gibbs, Michael	0	0	6.00	4	0	6	5	1	7
Kretzschmar, Mathew	4	1	1.28	24	0	42	25	12	40
*Layden, Timothy	5	7	3.99	21	0	113	114	51	52
Marotz, Ty	3	5	3.13	40	2	69	57	26	76
McTamney, Mike	0	1	9.35	6	0	9	14	4	7
*O'Donnell, Tony	3	1	4.55	33	0	30	30	21	30
Reid, Brett	3	0	1.13	34	24	40	27	18	50
*Romero, Garvis	0	1	5.31	15	0	20	26	9	11
Russell, Steve	1	0	5.56	3	0	11	16	8	14
Singleton, Nick	8	4	2.24	17	0	113	102	32	82
Walker, Sam	0	0	0.00	1	0	1	1	0	0

SIOUX FALLS CANARIES

BATTERS	AVG	AB	R	H	2B	3B	HR	RBI	SB
Barbaro, Andrew	.258	97	11	25	7	0	1	8	0
Bardeguez, Alex	.279	86	14	24	4	0	3	12	1
*Bibbs, Kennard	.267	318	56	85	13	4	3	29	17
Grant, Ryan	.258	31	6	8	1	0	0	1	2
Hutting, Tim	.232	336	43	78	14	0	5	40	3
Mahomes, Pat	.000	1	0	0	0	0	0	0	0
*Patton, Sam	.287	356	64	102	22	0	9	52	2
*Reilly, Patrick	.287	338	54	97	21	9	13	59	12
*Reininger, Jarrett	.392	51	11	20	3	0	5	11	0
Richardson, Grant	.322	354	88	114	25	1	16	71	4
*Smith, Will	.333	237	32	79	13	0	7	37	0
Smyth, Paul	.311	318	48	99	14	2	11	60	6
Torbert, Beau	.324	340	65	110	20	3	19	71	14
Van Iderstine, Ben	.315	378	48	119	16	2	4	47	6

PITCHERS	W	L	ERA	G	SV	IP	H	BB	SO
Bays, Leonard	3	5	4.92	17	0	68	85	25	39
Casares, Kelly	3	1	5.53	30	0	41	40	22	39
*Cheppenko, Kevin	0	3	10.70	5	0	18	27	13	10

INDEPENDENT LEAGUES

	W	L	ERA	G	SV	IP	H	BB	SO
*Ford, Ryan	13	6	2.77	21	0	130	147	26	75
Garcia, Javier	1	0	0.00	4	0	7	2	1	11
Grant, Ryan	0	0	6.75	13	0	25	28	17	21
Kane, Travis	11	6	3.45	20	0	115	126	35	89
Kite, Josh	1	1	2.31	21	1	23	17	8	26
Mahomes, Pat	10	6	3.72	19	0	135	137	42	105
Moore, Benjamin	10	7	5.70	20	0	125	164	31	106
Morales, Angelo	3	0	3.44	28	0	65	61	24	53
*Regas, Kris	1	0	1.29	41	30	42	26	8	72
*Reininger, Jarrett	0	0	0.00	1	0	1	1	2	0
Roberts, Mark	4	1	1.67	31	0	32	23	14	38
Zweber, Kyle	0	0	9.82	3	0	4	5	3	3

ST. PAUL SAINTS

BATTERS	AVG	AB	R	H	2B	3B	HR	RBI	SB
Balet, Pichi	.306	209	22	64	10	1	1	23	0
Bennett, Andrew	.264	91	15	24	1	0	0	6	1
Brown, Tim	.262	282	34	74	18	0	3	39	0
*Butler, Steve	.250	64	6	16	1	0	0	5	0
Colson, Jason	.257	144	16	37	9	1	1	30	0
*Fenwick, Ron	.329	76	11	25	4	0	0	7	1
Goldberg, Zach	.167	66	2	11	0	0	0	6	0
*Hale, Adam	.219	64	8	14	3	0	4	9	0
Jordan, Scooter	.261	157	30	41	2	1	0	14	9
*Keel, Heath	.254	173	21	44	8	1	5	17	4
Krause, Brent	.317	353	71	112	25	1	19	56	15
*Longmire, Marcel	.260	177	33	46	11	0	6	36	6
Mansolino, Anthony	.389	108	14	42	4	0	3	19	1
Marshall, Andre	.000	7	1	0	0	0	0	0	0
Mojica, Jimmy	.262	61	5	16	2	0	0	3	3
Priddy, Ryan	.231	251	31	58	17	1	2	20	4
Resser, Kyle	.125	8	1	1	0	0	0	2	0
Reyes, Christian	.250	4	1	1	0	0	0	0	0
Sprout, Brian	.202	104	11	21	4	0	0	18	0
Sullivan, Kevin	.295	336	48	99	19	1	10	46	5
Thames, Julius	.283	138	23	39	5	2	0	16	8
*Thomas, Ben	.301	292	30	88	23	1	1	34	3
Womack, Josh	.181	116	16	21	2	3	1	8	5

PITCHERS	W	L	ERA	G	SV	IP	H	BB	SO
Bille, Michael	4	2	3.42	37	2	55	53	17	38
Blitstein, Jeffrey	2	3	4.99	6	0	40	47	9	20
Bolton, Dustin	4	8	5.21	25	0	93	108	24	42
*Butler, Steve	0	0	13.50	2	0	2	3	2	1
Foster, Kyle	1	1	0.00	13	1	23	15	5	19
Lord, Justin	5	9	4.04	16	0	98	110	22	54
Molldrem, Craig	0	3	2.10	23	0	34	21	10	35
Pierce, Tony	1	0	2.63	32	16	38	23	21	58
Priddy, Ryan	0	0	9.00	6	0	6	8	3	6
Regits, Josh	1	2	5.05	18	0	36	42	23	19
Robinson, Lonnie	0	1	5.57	12	0	32	31	16	25
*Romanczuk, Mark	3	4	4.34	14	0	64	71	28	39
Ruud, Charlie	12	4	3.85	19	0	112	117	26	56
Shepherd, Alec	2	4	9.26	9	0	46	70	23	24
Thames, Julius	0	0	0.00	1	0	1	0	1	2
*Villarreal, Luis	4	5	3.60	13	0	79	76	32	56
*Wesley, John	2	1	4.24	18	0	34	35	13	33
Whinnery, Brian	0	3	9.64	5	0	19	36	8	13
Wylie, Mitch	1	4	5.22	16	0	29	37	7	23

WICHITA WINGNUTS

BATTERS	AVG	AB	R	H	2B	3B	HR	RBI	SB
Amado, Jose	.238	101	11	24	2	0	0	7	1
Baker, Jimmy	.261	23	4	6	1	0	0	1	0
*Bartolucci, Paul	.235	17	2	4	0	0	0	1	0
*Bergstrom, Bub	.154	52	5	8	2	0	0	4	1
Colton, Chris	.260	339	48	88	17	4	7	40	17
*Davilla, Vic	.269	108	15	29	3	0	5	18	1
Del Rosario, Felipe	.217	157	19	34	6	1	3	14	6
Dennis, Bernie	.190	137	15	26	1	0	0	9	2
Dunham, Scott	.000	7	0	0	0	0	0	0	0
*Gailen, Blake	.266	286	40	76	19	1	3	41	8
Gates, David	.206	126	18	26	5	0	4	15	0
Herrera, Brenan	.317	366	44	116	27	5	5	51	6

	AVG	AB	R	H	2B	3B	HR	RBI	SB
Hooper, Kevin	.373	357	73	133	15	3	1	26	34
Hurn, Doug	.000	1	0	0	0	0	0	0	0
*Keel, Heath	.254	134	23	34	6	1	5	22	6
*McConnell, Brandon	.462	13	3	6	2	0	0	1	0
McQuigg, Carter	.200	5	2	1	0	0	0	1	0
Mohr, Dustan	.244	193	26	47	10	1	7	41	2
*Pearson, Steve	.263	300	31	79	16	2	5	51	5
Rider, Dave	.000	1	0	0	0	0	0	0	0
*Salazar, Richard	.000	0	1	0	0	0	0	0	0
*Schermerhorn, Derek	.186	43	6	8	2	0	0	2	2
Stevens, Jeff	.156	32	3	5	1	0	1	3	1
Thompson, Michael	.305	344	42	105	29	2	10	48	7
Ventura, Leivi	.243	37	6	9	1	0	0	3	0
*Wagner, Geoff	.000	3	0	0	0	0	0	0	0
Young, Justin	.000	1	1	0	0	0	0	0	0

PITCHERS	W	L	ERA	G	SV	IP	H	BB	SO
Ball, Ronald	2	1	3.51	8	0	26	16	26	18
Caldwell, Daniel	1	1	15.43	4	0	2	5	3	0
*Cheppenko, Kevin	3	1	3.83	23	2	42	43	31	25
Cross, David	0	0	5.21	7	0	19	18	17	13
*Davis, Bradley	8	8	3.89	18	0	111	118	27	70
Demme, Asher	0	0	29.70	4	0	3	11	7	3
Embry, Byron	3	1	3.44	38	20	37	34	8	40
Foeman, Kevin	0	0	3.86	3	0	2	4	2	4
*Gailen, Blake	1	3	4.66	13	0	37	44	15	13
Hurn, Doug	4	4	5.45	21	0	38	46	14	13
*Jenkins, Aaron	0	0	1.42	5	0	6	5	6	7
*Landeros, Leonard	7	5	4.11	17	0	96	94	49	49
Martinez, Alejandro	0	1	11.57	3	0	2	3	2	0
Mata, Gustavo	4	7	3.69	18	0	95	108	37	34
*McConnell, Brandon	0	0	0.00	1	0	0	0	0	0
Rider, Dave	0	1	5.75	10	0	20	25	9	13
Robles, Larry	1	1	4.09	4	0	22	23	13	4
*Salazar, Richard	5	7	3.57	28	0	91	81	34	62
Smith, Clint	0	0	1.80	5	0	5	4	7	3
*Stephens, Amad	2	0	1.81	35	0	50	26	25	38
*White, Adam	0	0	6.00	3	0	6	6	2	5
White, Demetri	1	3	8.87	9	0	22	20	25	24
Young, Justin	3	6	5.59	21	0	85	96	36	41

ATLANTIC LEAGUE

Whenever a new Atlantic League season begins, there's an easy way to look pretty smart. Just pick the Somerset Patriots to win the title and nearly as often as not, you'll be correct. The Patriots won their unprecedented fifth Atlantic League title by knocking off Camden in the championship round. It was the Patriots' seventh appearance in the title series. Catcher Travis Anderson provided the big blow, as he hit a walk-off home run in the bottom of the ninth in the series-clinching Game Four. He was helped by series MVP Brandon Larson, who hit .458 with three home runs in the playoffs. The Patriots also had the league's regular season player of the year as former Mets and Marlins farmhand Josh Pressley led the Atlantic League in most categories, including batting average (.354), home runs (30), hits (173), on-base percentage (.440) and slugging percentage (.605). It was a successful year for the league as a whole, as the addition of the expansion Southern Maryland Blue Crabs helped the league set an overall attendance record of 2,298,734. That broke the old record set in 2005.

FIRST HALF

LIBERTY DIVISION	W	L	PCT	GB
Camden	40	30	.571	—
Southern Maryland	36	34	.514	4
Bridgeport	33	37	.471	7
Long Island	32	38	.457	

FREEDOM DIVISION				
Somerset	40	30	.571	—
Newark	39	31	.557	1
York	30	40	.429	10
Lancaster	30	40	.429	10

SECOND HALF

LIBERTY DIVISION	W	L	PCT	GB
Long Island	39	31	.557	—
Southern Maryland	38	32	.543	1
Bridgeport	34	36	.486	5

	W	L	PCT	GB
Camden	27	43	.386	12
FREEDOM DIVISION	**W**	**L**	**PCT**	**GB**
York	41	29	.586	—
Somerset	34	36	.486	7
Lancaster	34	36	.486	7
Newark	33	37	.471	8

PLAYOFFS: Semifinals—Camden defeated Long Island 2-0 and Somerset defeated York 2-0 in best-of-three series. Finals—Somerset defeated Camden 3-1 in best-of-five series.

MANAGERS: Bridgeport—Tommy John. Camden—Joe Ferguson. Lancaster—Von Hayes. Long Island—Dave LaPoint. Newark—Wayne Krenchicki. Somerset—Sparky Lyle. Southern Maryland—Butch Hobson. York—Chris Hoiles.

ATTENDANCE—Long Island 416,752; Somerset 347,735; Lancaster 343,720; York 300,246; Camden 236,526; Southern Maryland 226,086; Newark 181,240; Bridgeport 156,429.

ALL-STAR TEAM: C—Jason Belcher, Somerset. 1B—Josh Pressley, Somerset. 2B—Henry Mateo, Bridgeport. 3B—Pat Osborn, Southern Maryland. SS—Ramon Castro, Newark. Utility—Ray Navarrette, Long Island. OF—Jason Aspito, York; Michael Woods, Lancaster; Nic Jackson, Camden, Keith Reed, Newark and Jose Herrera, Newark. DH—Carl Everett, Long Island. RHS—Joe Gannon, Southern Maryland. LHS—Randy Leek, Long Island. RP—Alec Zumwalt, Camden.

Player of the Year: Josh Pressley, Somerset. **Pitcher of the Year:** Joe Gannon, Southern Maryland. **Manager of the Year:** Butch Hobson, Southern Maryland.

INDIVIDUAL BATTING LEADERS

BATTER, CLUB	AVG	G	AB	R	H	HR	RBI
Pressley, Josh, Somerset	.354	133	489	95	173	30	101
Castro, Ramon, Newark	.352	117	480	102	169	23	84
Florence, Branden, Bridgeport	.340	106	377	61	128	8	66
Jackson, Nic, Camden	.333	107	435	90	145	16	66
Jones, Kennard, York	.333	88	360	77	120	8	49
Davenport, Ron, Camden	.332	102	404	61	134	18	93
Herrera, Jose, Newark	.331	119	478	80	158	16	93
Everett, Carl, Long Island	.327	115	419	79	137	29	100
LeCroy, Matthew, Lancaster	.326	94	380	58	124	22	83
Osborn, Pat, So. Maryland	.326	132	497	77	162	17	106

INDIVIDUAL PITCHING LEADERS

PITCHER, CLUB	W	L	ERA	IP	H	BB	SO
Gannon, Joe, So. Maryland	12	6	3.17	162	145	91	123
Leek, Randy, Long Island	12	3	3.66	177	194	36	93
Ramsey, Keith, So. Maryland	7	6	4.01	130	136	38	71
Biconda, Ryan, So. Maryland	13	8	4.26	196	240	53	129
Baez, Benito, Newark	7	5	4.51	128	146	32	93
Rakers, Aaron, York	11	8	4.52	149	173	38	130
Stanley, Pat, Newark	10	8	4.90	140	127	86	151
Adams, Brian, Somerset	11	7	4.92	135	159	37	90
Magrane, Jim, Somerset	9	11	4.97	158	189	54	108
Garcia, Jose, Newark	10	4	5.07	142	159	67	93

BRIDGEPORT BLUEFISH

BATTERS	AVG	AB	R	H	2B	3B	HR	RBI	SB
Batista, Wilson	.313	208	36	65	11	2	6	39	8
Bear, Ryan	.320	500	97	160	33	3	11	70	8
Brinkley, Darryl	.293	41	6	12	4	0	0	3	2
Caligiuri, Jay	.281	260	38	73	13	0	7	48	0
*Castillo, Carlos	.333	3	0	1	0	0	0	0	0
Darula, Bobby	.227	97	17	22	4	1	1	9	7
*Daubert, Jake	.237	97	8	23	1	0	2	15	0
*DiPietro, Ryan	.000	1	0	0	0	0	0	0	0
Doetsch, Steve	.298	94	22	28	4	0	4	18	2
*Dubose, Eric	.182	11	1	2	0	0	1	3	0
Eickhorst, Chris	.333	3	0	1	0	0	0	1	0
*Ezi, Travis	.261	272	44	71	8	6	5	25	14
Florence, Branden	.340	377	61	128	26	2	8	66	7
Greenberg, Adam	.289	45	11	13	2	2	0	5	2
Harris, Shea	.153	98	10	15	4	1	0	2	0
Hoorelbeke, Jesse	.276	497	80	137	26	2	28	106	1
Lopez, Luis	.315	511	83	161	36	2	5	77	2
Mateo, Henry	.318	535	100	170	31	6	5	52	35
*Munhall, Brian	.269	283	35	76	19	2	5	41	8

	AVG	AB	R	H	2B	3B	HR	RBI	SB
Murray, Glenn	.313	16	3	5	1	0	0	1	0
Peterson, Brian	.400	30	5	12	4	1	1	4	0
Pickering, Calvin	.265	226	32	60	14	0	8	41	2
Pike, Matthew	.000	13	3	0	0	0	0	1	0
Prieto, Alex	.269	505	77	136	27	1	12	74	5
Rodriguez, Luis	.328	128	17	42	6	0	4	24	1

PITCHERS	W	L	ERA	G	SV	IP	H	BB	SO
Bentz, Chad	1	1	5.79	14	0	19	27	12	10
Berger, Garrett	0	0	9.69	7	0	13	14	23	12
Bergstrom, Rafael	7	8	6.01	22	0	124	159	60	54
Bille, Michael	0	0	9.53	10	0	11	16	7	8
*Castillo, Carlos	0	2	7.71	5	0	19	28	10	10
*Connolly, Mike	3	4	6.81	14	0	73	83	48	46
Dicken, Randy	1	1	15.75	3	0	4	9	5	3
*DiPietro, Ryan	4	6	4.73	25	0	99	109	50	66
Doetsch, Steve	0	0	9.00	3	0	12	11	18	16
Drew, Tim	3	3	7.46	13	0	57	79	31	25
*Dubose, Eric	6	2	3.91	17	0	101	98	44	71
Eickhorst, Chris	1	1	9.35	11	0	17	21	13	4
Ellison, Derrick	1	1	1.42	22	1	25	16	16	27
Ford, Matt	1	0	10.80	4	0	8	11	9	5
Harris, Shea	0	0	0.00	1	0	1	0	1	0
Hertzler, Barry	9	10	5.47	28	0	165	206	67	83
Hesseltine, Charlie	0	0	12.75	4	0	12	27	6	6
Hoorelbeke, Jesse	0	0	4.50	2	0	2	3	1	1
Pals, Jordan	0	2	8.64	5	0	17	32	10	11
Perez, Franklin	6	3	5.25	47	0	60	67	32	53
Pike, Matthew	7	2	5.94	38	2	94	115	39	64
Ramos, Eddy	1	6	4.38	44	20	49	52	24	44
Rodriguez, Luis	1	0	0.00	1	0	1	2	0	0
*Romanczuk, Mark	0	2	11.12	5	0	17	27	18	11
Stawarz, Jarrett	0	1	8.31	1	0	4	9	4	4
*Sweeney, Matt	3	1	5.31	7	0	39	40	20	22
Tam, Jeff	3	4	3.25	46	0	44	41	9	28
Tucker, T.J.	3	3	7.39	34	2	35	59	17	19
Weimer, Andrew	5	2	4.91	20	0	33	42	13	17
*Wilkerson, Wes	1	8	8.94	39	9	48	65	31	34

CAMDEN RIVERSHARKS

BATTERS	AVG	AB	R	H	2B	3B	HR	RBI	SB
Arhart, J	.000	12	0	0	0	0	0	0	0
*Biernbaum, L.J.	.295	501	72	148	36	2	12	78	9
*Bonvechio, Brett	.227	163	28	37	8	1	7	39	1
Boyd, Shaun	.343	134	24	46	9	3	4	19	1
*Buttenfield, Nate	.000	1	0	0	0	0	0	0	0
Castillo, Alberto	.225	182	20	41	13	0	2	17	3
Cates, Gary	.286	241	41	69	14	2	0	31	12
Collet, Cody	.202	129	11	26	4	0	0	9	0
*Davenport, Ron	.332	404	61	134	28	4	18	93	1
Espinosa, David	.267	45	9	12	1	1	0	4	0
Feiner, Korey	.143	14	1	2	0	0	0	0	0
Fulse, Sheldon	.322	214	45	69	19	5	5	28	11
*Gandolfo, Rob	.261	306	32	80	10	1	0	25	1
Guerrero, Julio	.000	2	0	0	0	0	0	0	0
*Jackson, Damian	.242	62	6	15	2	0	1	4	2
*Jackson, Nic	.333	435	90	145	36	5	16	66	20
Johnson, Tim	.258	151	19	39	5	1	2	13	3
Lewis, Richard	.284	264	43	75	15	1	0	33	18
*McGarvey, Randy	.278	162	19	45	6	0	1	18	1
*Nichols, Kyle	.250	92	7	23	3	0	3	13	0
Phillips, Jason	.302	159	30	48	14	0	5	38	0
Rabe, Josh	.361	166	31	60	11	0	6	30	1
Rodriguez, Felix	.000	1	0	0	0	0	0	0	0
Sack, Darren	.000	1	1	0	0	0	0	0	0
San Pedro, Erick	.281	57	10	16	4	0	1	6	0
Suarez, Gabriel	.226	350	41	79	7	3	2	27	11
Thompson, Michael	.216	97	7	21	5	0	2	7	1
Vento, Michael	.125	8	1	1	0	0	0	0	0
*Von schell, Tyler	.288	312	34	90	11	0	10	46	0
Walker, Chris	.290	107	23	31	2	4	5	20	7
Young, Chris	.000	3	0	0	0	0	0	0	0
Zumwalt, Alec	.333	3	1	1	1	0	0	0	0

INDEPENDENT LEAGUES

PITCHERS	W	L	ERA	G	SV	IP	H	BB	SO
*Alvarez, Abe	0	0	10.80	1	0	2	4	1	2
Baez, Federico	2	4	6.06	19	0	36	36	23	32
Buttenfield, Nate	0	2	8.71	8	0	21	33	15	10
Davis, Ben	2	1	3.00	6	0	21	17	2	10
Dittfurth, Ryan	3	5	5.24	11	0	67	61	36	56
Dittler, Jake	2	6	5.37	12	0	70	86	20	42
Drese, Ryan	6	1	3.44	11	0	65	76	18	26
Flannery, Mike	5	7	5.82	44	0	68	65	47	65
Guerrero, Julio	7	2	4.04	47	0	91	95	19	58
Hernandez, Buddy	3	4	4.99	47	4	61	66	27	69
Lawrence, Brian	2	2	3.21	8	0	48	49	9	32
*Lewis, Jeremy	3	2	5.46	43	1	59	73	17	50
Lima, Jose	5	5	4.98	11	0	65	66	22	57
*Mannix, Kevin	3	10	5.42	17	0	86	101	29	54
*Nichols, Kyle	0	0	4.50	2	0	2	1	3	3
Peguero, Tony	7	3	3.95	24	0	84	94	30	55
Perkins, Vince	0	1	7.97	7	0	20	25	22	20
Rodriguez, Felix	0	0	1.09	32	4	33	25	8	25
Romero, Robert	1	0	7.84	6	0	10	7	10	12
Sack, Darren	3	5	5.83	15	0	71	70	40	68
*Thompson, Sean	1	4	6.80	12	0	42	45	23	34
Walker, Chris	1	0	0.00	1	0	3	3	0	2
*Walker, Kevin	2	2	5.53	14	0	54	65	17	51
Young, Chris	5	5	4.23	14	0	77	89	22	40
Zumwalt, Alec	4	2	2.89	50	24	56	47	20	56

LANCASTER BARNSTORMERS

BATTERS	AVG	AB	R	H	2B	3B	HR	RBI	SB
*Adamchick, David	.148	27	1	4	0	0	0	2	0
Ball, Jarred	.190	126	9	24	5	0	2	18	5
*Bladergroen, Ian	.260	334	42	87	21	1	15	51	1
Blosser, Greg	.191	47	4	9	2	0	1	7	0
Burkhart, Lance	.250	192	26	48	12	0	10	28	0
Campbell, Michael	.172	29	3	5	0	1	0	1	0
*Caruso, Mike	.316	136	21	43	4	0	0	19	2
Castillo, David	.245	151	19	37	12	0	4	21	0
*Coffie, Ivanon	.275	229	40	63	17	3	12	27	1
Evans, Joe	.222	9	1	2	1	0	0	2	0
Fenwick, Ron	.071	14	1	1	1	0	0	0	0
*Francia, Juan	.225	222	40	50	10	2	2	14	19
Gonzalez, Danny	.299	412	60	123	26	2	11	59	3
*Harris, Gary	.286	84	10	24	3	2	2	26	1
Herr, Jordan	.202	109	11	22	6	0	4	16	0
Hileman, Jutt	.236	441	53	104	23	3	13	59	5
*Kotch, Kevin	.222	72	13	16	4	1	4	8	0
LeCroy, Matthew	.326	380	58	124	16	0	22	83	1
*Mejia, Manuel	.256	266	34	68	16	1	8	45	0
*Munhall, Brian	.265	68	9	18	4	1	0	7	0
Nelson, John	.133	15	1	2	0	0	0	1	0
*Nichols, Kyle	.189	53	7	10	2	0	0	5	0
Perez, Luis	.269	52	6	14	3	0	2	7	0
Sabatella, Bryan	.323	93	16	30	6	0	3	11	3
Spanos, Vasili	.250	72	10	18	1	1	3	10	2
Stavisky, Brian	.282	110	15	31	9	0	5	20	0
*Stevenson, Ryan	.080	25	2	2	0	0	0	2	0
Tavarez, Argenis	.196	46	10	9	0	2	0	4	0
Turner, Lloyd	.300	474	80	142	19	13	13	56	13
Woods, Michael	.324	525	119	170	35	7	23	73	33

PITCHERS	W	L	ERA	G	SV	IP	H	BB	SO
*Ackerman, Eric	5	7	5.07	26	1	131	148	39	78
Alexander, Mark	0	0	0.00	2	0	1	0	3	0
Averette, Robert	0	1	8.00	7	0	11	6	6	6
Cabrera, Jose	2	1	2.79	16	6	19	17	9	20
*Cassa, Patrick	0	4	4.98	32	0	47	51	30	28
*Cullen, Ryan	7	6	2.11	49	16	64	53	13	50
Dessau, Erik	0	3	7.03	8	0	40	57	12	25
Fritz, Ben	3	1	4.39	9	0	53	63	22	48
Gomez, Ricardo	4	2	3.98	44	1	95	81	38	97
Guevara, Yamel	1	2	5.81	23	0	48	42	40	55
Hall, Josh	6	3	4.10	13	0	83	94	24	44
Hoelscher, Nate	0	2	7.11	8	0	6	9	6	4
*Kent, Steve	1	1	5.40	19	0	25	29	16	18
Mansfield, Monte	2	0	3.38	3	0	16	14	9	14

PITCHERS	W	L	ERA	G	SV	IP	H	BB	SO
Marcotte, Trevor	0	1	8.74	7	0	11	11	7	6
*Mattox, D.J.	1	3	9.00	8	0	29	41	20	14
*Mavroulis, Coby	0	0	9.00	2	0	3	5	1	2
McClaskey, Tim	2	2	6.75	6	0	29	33	9	10
Mendible, Frank	0	0	36.00	2	0	1	1	4	0
Muessig, Jeff	0	0	1.69	5	1	5	4	3	3
Nannini, Mike	1	3	5.10	6	0	30	31	22	16
Nelson, Mac	1	1	5.60	3	0	18	15	8	17
Parker, Zach	2	0	1.32	4	0	27	18	5	14
*Peeples, Ross	0	1	5.59	15	0	19	23	6	10
Renault, Nick	7	8	6.80	27	0	99	117	53	65
Rleal, Sendy	6	5	5.32	43	0	68	71	37	41
Scobie, Jason	3	6	4.46	15	0	73	75	36	49
Songster, Judd	3	2	4.12	35	2	39	44	12	32
Steinborn, Chris	1	5	8.56	6	0	27	45	10	16
Thorp, Paul	1	1	4.41	23	0	33	28	9	19
Tyler, Scott	0	1	9.00	2	0	3	5	1	3
*Wilkerson, Wes	1	0	8.78	6	0	13	13	8	3
*Youman, Shane	4	4	5.51	13	0	64	76	31	39

LONG ISLAND DUCKS

BATTERS	AVG	AB	R	H	2B	3B	HR	RBI	SB
Abernathy, Brent	.250	84	13	21	0	1	0	1	4
Alfonzo, Edgardo	.329	231	37	76	13	0	8	27	0
Ambrosini, Dominick	.191	47	5	9	2	0	0	4	1
Asahina, Jonathan	.000	1	0	0	0	0	0	0	0
Cafiero, Rob	.400	15	4	6	0	0	1	2	0
Donovan, Dennis	.242	306	41	74	15	1	2	28	1
Everett, Carl	.327	419	79	137	20	2	29	100	7
Falu, Melvin	.231	52	7	12	1	0	0	5	0
*Francia, Juan	.333	108	22	36	4	1	0	3	6
Gibbons, Jay	.280	107	11	30	9	0	5	19	0
Grezlovski, Ben	.000	1	0	0	0	0	0	0	0
Harris, Estee	.328	116	28	38	9	1	6	30	3
Haverbusch, Kevin	.289	304	51	88	20	2	14	66	6
Hidalgo, Richard	.261	111	19	29	5	1	5	16	1
*Jackson, Damian	.182	11	3	2	0	0	1	4	2
*Knippschild, Ryan	.000	1	0	0	0	0	0	0	0
*Kovatch, Billy	.316	38	9	12	0	0	0	2	1
Logan, Nook	.308	201	40	62	7	3	0	15	22
Maestrales, Pete	.221	140	18	31	6	1	1	19	2
Mendez, Donaldo	.267	146	22	39	7	3	2	14	6
Nageotte, Clint	.000	1	0	0	0	0	0	0	0
Navarrete, Ray	.307	498	105	153	36	1	27	103	7
Nelson, Bryant	.180	50	4	9	2	0	0	7	3
*Nichols, Kyle	.268	56	5	15	2	0	2	8	0
Paniagua, Jose	.000	1	0	0	0	0	0	0	0
Pogue, Jamie	.265	355	52	94	19	0	9	41	0
Rolls, Damian	.287	442	67	127	20	1	17	55	12
Rose, Mike	.156	32	2	5	2	0	0	1	0
*Rose, P.J.	.289	509	65	147	29	0	15	95	0
Sanchez, Alex	.347	147	30	51	8	3	4	13	6
*Sandora, Robert	.248	206	19	51	9	0	3	24	1
Strong, Jamal	.296	108	10	32	5	0	0	17	2

PITCHERS	W-	L	ERA	G	SV	IP	H	BB	SO
*Alvarez, Abe	7	4	4.58	31	0	75	86	30	45
Asahina, Jonathan	1	2	6.05	36	0	55	68	31	38
Cafiero, Rob	0	0	6.00	6	0	9	11	7	2
*Castillo, Carlos	1	1	3.24	3	0	17	20	3	7
*Darensbourg, Vic	4	4	4.31	26	0	40	46	14	32
*Davis, Lance	4	4	4.44	11	0	62	69	9	31
Donovan, Dennis	0	0	9.00	2	0	4	1	0	
Grezlovski, Ben	6	2	3.70	67	1	88	99	24	69
*Kent, Steve	3	3	7.51	9	0	38	46	27	22
*Knippschild, Ryan	3	4	5.30	50	1	71	80	28	55
*Leek, Randy	12	3	3.66	28	0	177	194	36	93
*Madritsch, Bobby	0	0	0.00	2	0	1	2	1	2
*Magrane, Jim	0	2	10.38	3	0	13	6	2	7
*Mannix, Kevin	0	2	10.22	5	0	12	23	14	8
Manon, Julio	1	0	2.45	5	1	7	7	2	13
Martin, Tom	1	1	3.38	6	0	5	6	2	6
Myers, Mike	1	2	9.00	8	0	21	38	12	10
Nageotte, Clint	1	5	7.53	17	0	43	64	21	25

	W	L	ERA	G	SV	IP	H	BB	SO
Osborne, Donovan	0	4	8.14	5	0	21	37	4	13
Paniagua, Jose	4	3	3.91	10	0	51	60	7	34
Pierce, Tony	1	1	3.00	6	0	6	6	8	4
Pogue, Jamie	0	0	0.00	1	0	1	1	0	0
Rice, Scott	2	2	15.68	7	0	10	23	5	11
Searles, Jon	1	2	3.86	7	0	28	31	23	16
*Shackelford, Brian	1	0	4.91	10	0	11	16	7	5
Simontacchi, Jason	0	1	6.11	7	0	18	23	7	13
Soler, Alay	4	5	6.22	16	0	88	111	27	69
Ulloa, Enmanuel	5	6	5.94	30	0	123	148	40	103
Valentine, Joe	5	3	3.32	32	13	38	29	18	34
*Wade, Travis	0	0	2.35	16	0	23	22	10	13
Weatherby, Charlie	1	1	4.34	29	9	29	31	6	20
Williams, Todd	2	2	2.68	37	8	40	35	8	22

NEWARK BEARS

BATTERS	AVG	AB	R	H	2B	3B	HR	RBI	SB
Aldridge, Cory	.365	230	43	84	17	4	7	54	0
Burgamy, Brian	.265	102	25	27	6	0	3	14	5
Castro, Ramon	.352	480	102	169	30	0	23	84	9
Gonzalez, Raul	.313	227	33	71	15	0	8	35	4
Gutierrez, Vic	.301	239	41	72	11	1	0	22	5
Haran, Gerard	.278	133	15	37	9	0	4	25	0
*Herrera, Jose	.331	478	80	158	26	7	16	93	4
Hill, Bobby	.238	362	78	86	22	1	3	35	2
Just, Mike	.276	340	71	94	15	0	2	20	21
Knazek, Scott	.219	219	27	48	9	2	1	23	0
Majewski, Val	.368	182	38	67	13	1	8	47	0
Mateo, Ruben	.298	198	35	59	14	0	16	44	2
*Mejia, Manuel	.263	118	17	31	7	0	9	25	0
Nivar, Ramon	.327	196	37	64	17	2	4	24	19
Otanez, Willis	.333	192	32	64	14	0	8	29	0
Pachot, John	.259	259	23	67	10	2	8	42	1
Reed, Keith	.295	533	90	157	36	3	26	93	13
*Simon, Randall	.321	380	45	122	21	1	11	62	0
Sweeney, Tim	.273	99	11	27	3	0	0	12	0

PITCHERS	W	L	ERA	G	SV	IP	H	BB	SO
Aldridge, Cory	0	0	0.00	1	0	2	1	2	0
Almonte, Ed	5	3	4.96	42	4	62	62	23	55
*Babula, Shaun	1	3	8.04	22	1	31	55	11	21
*Baez, Benito	7	5	4.51	20	0	128	146	32	93
Blitstein, Jeff	2	1	6.35	6	0	34	50	12	24
Bumstead, Mike	14	9	5.37	29	0	178	203	70	143
Burgamy, Brian	0	0	0.00	1	0	1	0	2	0
*Connolly, Jon	0	1	2.66	5	0	20	22	5	17
Cunnane, Will	2	0	5.82	7	0	22	31	9	16
Fields, Josh	0	1	6.23	3	0	4	3	6	3
Garcia, Jose	10	4	5.07	23	0	142	159	67	93
Giron, Roberto	2	3	5.49	13	1	41	44	9	38
Gracesqui, Frank	0	4	14.09	4	0	15	25	10	15
*Kent, Steve	0	2	4.91	15	5	15	16	8	14
Levine, Alan	0	0	1.59	11	9	11	7	5	4
Mirabal, Carlos	3	2	7.31	14	0	48	64	24	22
Nivar, Ramon	0	0	9.00	1	0	1	2	1	1
Pellegrine, David	0	2	10.50	9	0	18	25	21	9
Petrusek, Matt	0	0	0.00	4	1	6	1	2	8
Reed, Keith	0	0	0.00	1	0	1	0	3	0
Rodriguez, Frank	2	1	7.79	9	0	17	19	9	9
Scalamandre, Rich	2	1	11.23	27	0	34	49	20	23
Shibilo, Andy	2	4	3.38	25	7	32	27	24	28
*Smith, Mike	0	1	9.60	4	0	15	20	15	9
Stanley, Pat	10	8	4.90	25	0	140	127	86	151
*Sweeney, Matt	1	5	6.22	20	0	72	97	30	50
Sweeney, Tim	0	0	0.00	1	0	1	0	1	1
Trujillo, J.J.	2	6	4.01	40	8	52	57	29	43
Willey, Cory	7	2	2.96	64	1	76	77	29	71

SOMERSET PATRIOTS

BATTERS	AVG	AB	R	H	2B	3B	HR	RBI	SB
Alvarez, Gerardo	.178	275	35	49	13	1	5	31	3
Anderson, Travis	.288	240	31	69	12	3	4	20	4
Asadoorian, Rick	.300	10	2	3	0	1	0	1	1
Ayala, Elliott	.265	461	66	122	22	4	5	52	15

	AVG	AB	R	H	2B	3B	HR	RBI	SB
*Belcher, Jason	.334	299	39	100	21	0	9	53	0
Bouknight, Kip	.000	1	0	0	0	0	0	0	0
Burke, J	.174	23	3	4	1	0	1	2	2
Chiaravolloti, Vito	.234	333	58	78	22	0	17	42	0
Duncan, Jeff	.148	54	4	8	2	2	1	5	2
Granato, A	.364	33	6	12	4	0	0	6	3
Hagen, Matt	.308	428	71	132	23	4	17	71	34
Housel, David	.246	285	43	70	21	3	4	31	5
Knight, Brandon	.000	3	0	0	0	0	0	0	0
*Kotch, Kevin	.265	34	6	9	2	0	1	6	0
Larson, Brandon	.304	427	71	130	29	3	30	95	1
*Lockwood, Mike	.172	99	17	17	1	0	1	10	4
*Magrane, Jim	.000	2	0	0	0	0	0	0	0
Moore, Frank	.189	37	4	7	2	0	1	2	0
Olivares, Teuris	.297	397	55	118	31	2	9	55	10
*Pressley, Josh	.354	489	95	173	33	0	30	101	3
*Radmanovich, Ryan	.267	195	28	52	9	1	9	38	2
*Ryan, Michael	.282	238	53	67	20	1	15	44	0
Smith, Sean	.292	360	78	105	22	4	15	51	28

PITCHERS	W	L	ERA	G	SV	IP	H	BB	SO
*Adams, Brian	11	7	4.92	26	0	135	159	37	90
Alvarez, Gerardo	0	0	0.00	1	0	1	1	0	2
Asadoorian, Rick	1	0	3.42	18	0	24	27	16	28
*Batson, Byron	0	2	4.30	23	0	38	39	7	19
Bouknight, Kip	5	1	2.52	15	0	61	58	15	37
*Brey, Josh	6	5	4.98	23	0	103	120	56	50
*Brooks, Frank	5	3	4.50	43	0	54	56	13	33
Buglovsky, Chris	1	3	2.81	8	0	32	28	10	16
Cahill, Casey	6	4	4.63	56	1	70	83	29	29
Donaldson, Bo	1	1	16.20	2	0	2	1	3	1
*Fultz, Aaron	5	5	4.00	16	0	79	79	21	59
Hunton, Jon	0	0	3.68	8	1	7	6	4	8
Jacobsen, Landon	0	0	4.50	4	0	6	11	4	1
Kelly, Steve	5	11	5.47	33	0	137	148	53	102
Kirsten, J	0	0	1.29	1	0	7	3	0	6
Knight, Brandon	0	2	2.56	6	0	39	25	12	50
*Magrane, Jim	9	9	4.48	23	0	145	164	48	101
*Mattox, D.J.	0	2	7.80	4	0	15	20	11	9
Minix, Travis	0	0	1.59	13	1	17	10	6	17
Prinz, Bret	0	0	0.56	16	13	16	13	3	19
Reith, Brian	5	4	3.94	41	16	80	79	25	85
Richardson, Jason	9	2	3.69	46	0	46	33	32	59
*Till, Brock	0	2	3.98	19	1	20	22	7	14
Tollberg, Brian	2	0	4.50	5	0	18	19	3	11
*Van Hekken, Andy	3	2	4.64	7	0	43	43	13	42
Wiggins, Scott	0	1	7.52	9	0	20	26	9	20

SOUTHERN MARYLAND BLUE CRABS

BATTERS	AVG	AB	R	H	2B	3B	HR	RBI	SB
Conroy, Mike	.147	34	3	5	0	0	0	5	0
*Crozier, Eric	.265	332	55	88	19	3	13	56	10
Duplissie, Bryan	.080	25	2	2	0	0	0	0	0
Ehrnsberger, Chad	.214	206	20	44	8	1	6	25	0
Garcia, Travis	.306	72	9	22	3	2	3	20	2
*Jackson, Damian	.000	7	1	0	0	0	0	0	0
Jarosinski, Brian	.400	10	3	4	1	1	1	3	0
*Johnston, Clint	.305	429	63	131	26	4	10	54	2
Ketron, Brandon	.199	151	22	30	3	1	3	19	1
Maples, Chris	.265	393	61	104	15	3	25	77	2
McClain, Terrence	.237	59	6	14	0	0	1	2	1
*Nichols, Kyle	.245	110	14	27	2	0	5	25	1
Osborn, Pat	.326	497	77	162	39	5	17	106	8
Owens, Jeremy	.246	399	67	98	18	4	15	47	18
Perry, Anthony	.154	26	2	4	0	0	0	0	0
Polanco, Enohel	.289	83	10	24	4	1	1	5	3
*Pride, Curtis	.265	325	67	86	21	3	8	48	0
Ramistella, John	.276	508	102	140	26	4	15	67	14
*Sandel, George	.254	456	62	116	12	4	0	28	7
Shanks, James	.287	317	50	91	18	4	12	53	11
Shorsher, Adam	.238	298	32	71	16	0	13	48	2
Sullivan, Kevin	.275	51	6	14	0	0	1	8	0

PITCHERS	W	L	ERA	G	SV	IP	H	BB	SO
Almonte, Hector	1	2	6.35	9	0	6	11	2	4

	W	L	ERA	G	SV	IP	H	BB	SO
Baugh, Kenny	2	1	2.92	14	1	25	22	10	17
Bicondoa, Ryan	13	8	4.26	29	0	196	240	53	129
Blanton, Jason	4	2	3.20	55	3	65	52	24	56
*Connolly, Jonathan	3	5	5.45	13	0	66	81	29	44
Conroy, Mike	0	0	0.00	1	0	1	2	0	1
DePriest, Derrick	4	6	2.09	39	13	43	48	9	31
Farnsworth, Jeff	2	2	7.01	11	0	53	60	30	28
Gale, Chris	5	5	5.19	44	1	76	90	29	41
Gannon, Joe	12	6	3.17	23	0	162	145	91	123
Gibbs, Mike	2	1	6.23	11	0	17	18	20	13
Halama, John	4	1	1.91	8	0	57	47	8	48
Hammons, Matt	1	0	0.00	4	1	5	3	4	8
Hensley, Matt	1	1	5.68	9	0	6	9	3	10
Johnson, Adam	3	2	6.08	17	0	40	46	17	21
Jones, Greg	0	1	3.18	6	0	6	7	4	5
Mahomes, Pat	1	0	1.29	2	1	7	8	2	5
Morris, Cory	0	0	0.00	1	0	0	1	1	0
*Morse, Bryan	1	3	6.16	10	0	38	50	8	19
*Pearson, Jason	0	2	4.12	52	0	44	43	17	29
Perez, Carlos	0	1	10.38	4	0	4	6	8	4
*Ramsey, Keith	7	6	4.01	21	0	130	136	38	71
Reichert, Dan	3	1	3.40	6	0	40	38	8	38
*Schweitzer, Matt	2	3	2.90	62	7	59	60	27	61
*Shackelford, Brian	0	0	21.00	5	0	3	6	4	2
*Smith, Dan	1	1	9.24	5	2	13	13	11	7
*Till, Brock	1	1	4.74	19	0	19	28	10	6
*Wade, Travis	0	3	6.55	39	1	33	50	9	26
*Whitworth, Brad	1	2	4.50	14	0	28	31	19	19

YORK REVOLUTION

BATTERS	AVG	AB	R	H	2B	3B	HR	RBI	SB
Aracena, Sandy	.298	305	46	91	14	1	8	38	1
Ashby, Chris	.321	414	76	133	27	2	16	75	8
*Aspito, Jason	.294	469	83	138	33	2	24	105	5
Clemente, Edgard	.325	40	10	13	2	0	3	8	0
Cruz, Enrique	.285	372	64	106	18	3	6	41	14
*Daubert, Jake	.288	52	6	15	2	0	0	6	0
De Renne, Keoni	.246	492	70	121	24	2	8	56	10
Dryer, Matt	.246	362	59	89	11	0	18	58	0
Esquivel, Matt	.294	477	68	140	35	5	13	77	7
*Ezi, Travis	.186	70	9	13	6	1	1	9	3
Hillenbrand, Shea	.340	153	22	52	9	0	2	25	0
*Jones, Kennard	.333	360	77	120	18	5	8	49	17
*Kotch, Kevin	.150	40	5	6	1	0	1	3	0
McCurdy, Nick	.100	1	0	1	0	0	0	0	0
*Padgett, Matt	.303	422	59	128	31	6	9	56	1
Perez, Kenny	.289	173	27	50	13	0	3	23	2
Rosario, Sam	.250	80	10	20	0	2	1	5	3
*Sandel, George	.390	41	6	16	4	1	0	8	0
*Tanaka, Kazunori	.226	84	19	19	3	0	0	3	8
Taveras, Luis	.245	233	32	57	14	1	11	41	0
*Von Schell, Tyler	.230	165	22	38	11	0	8	29	1

PITCHERS	W	L	ERA	G	SV	IP	H	BB	SO
Ashby, Chris	0	0	0.00	2	0	2	1	0	0
Aspito, Jason	0	0	13.50	2	0	2	5	1	2
*Batson, Byron	0	0	3.38	6	0	11	14	2	5
Castillo, Frank	1	0	6.49	7	0	26	36	11	16
Foli, Daniel	7	7	4.98	40	0	98	111	48	75
*Franklin, Wayne	12	5	5.73	36	0	121	147	73	94
*Gassner, Dave	2	3	3.06	7	0	47	49	9	22
Gil, Dave	5	6	4.87	22	0	102	133	39	79
*Maust, David	0	0	0.00	1	0	1	1	0	1
McCurdy, Nick	1	2	2.04	37	8	53	46	11	60
Myette, Aaron	6	7	5.89	16	0	92	101	45	77
Nunez, Franklin	2	1	3.98	18	11	20	23	7	25
Olson, Jason	4	3	3.41	50	1	61	66	30	54
*Padgett, Matt	0	0	0.00	1	0	1	0	1	0
Padilla, Juan	1	2	5.40	23	2	28	41	7	24
Phelps, Travis	3	3	3.82	32	0	35	25	23	49
Price, Reid	0	0	6.32	11	1	16	21	5	14
Rakers, Aaron	11	8	4.52	30	0	149	173	38	130
*Rosen, Mark	0	2	3.77	14	0	14	16	15	12
Solveson, Saul	1	1	3.96	16	0	25	24	12	17

	W	L	ERA	G	SV	IP	H	BB	SO
Thurman, Corey	11	9	5.39	29	0	165	170	61	129
Totten, Heath	0	1	7.94	4	0	6	10	2	5
Trent, Matthew	0	5	4.79	46	0	62	64	32	56
Veres, Dave	1	2	2.27	35	6	36	35	8	32
*Viera, Rolando	3	2	2.98	9	0	48	38	21	46

CAN-AM LEAGUE

In 2007, the Sussex Skyhawks were the worst team in the Can-Am League and one of the worst in all of independent ball. They finished a putrid 33-60 with a roster filled with has-beens and never-will-bes. But the Skyhawks pulled off an amazing turnaround in 2008. Thanks to new manager Hal Lanier and a slew of new players brought in by Nick Belmonte, the remade Skyhawks finished the regular season 10 games above .500, then topped Worcester in the first round of the playoffs and swept Quebec for the team's first title. The Skyhawks succeeded despite not having any players in the top 10 in batting or ERA. First baseman Matthew Wetston (.299-22-60) was the team's big bat, while the Skyhawks relied heavily on an outstanding bullpen led by closer Matt Petrusek (5-2, 1.79 with 24 saves) and set-up man Michael LaLuna (2-1, 2.79 in 42 innings). Worcester's Scott Grimes was named the league's player of the year after finishing second in the league in batting (.365), third in home runs (21), second in hits (133), first in triples (6), second in on-base percentage (.442) and first in slugging percentage (.626).

FIRST HALF

	W	L	PCT	GB
Quebec	31	16	.660	—
Worcester	26	21	.553	5
Atlantic City	25	22	.532	6
New Jersey	25	22	.532	6
Sussex	25	22	.532	6
Brockton	22	25	.468	9
Nashua	21	26	.447	10
Ottawa	13	34	.277	18

SECOND HALF

	W	L	PCT	GB
Worcester	27	20	.574	—
Sussex	27	20	.574	—
Quebec	27	20	.574	—
Atlantic City	26	21	.553	1
Brockton	25	22	.532	2
Nashua	20	27	.426	7
Ottawa	18	29	.383	9
New Jersey	18	29		9

PLAYOFFS: Semifinals—Quebec defeated Atlantic City 3-1 and Sussex defeated Worcester 3-1 in best-of-five series. Finals—Sussex defeated Quebec 3-0 in best-of-five series.

MANAGERS: Atlantic City—Cecil Fielder. Brockton—Chris Miyake. Nashua—Rick Miller. New Jersey—Joe Calfapietra. Ottawa—Ed Nottle. Quebec—Michel Laplante. Sussex—Hal Lanier. Worcester—Rich Gedman.

ATTENDANCE: Quebec 140,933; Brockton 132,785; Atlantic City 124,430; New Jersey 103,817; Ottawa 101,073; Worcester 90,127; Sussex 80,500; Nashua 68,995.

ALL-STAR TEAM: C—Kyle Geiger, Ottawa. 1B—Chris Colabello, Worcester. 2B—Melvin Falu, Brockton. 3B—Pat Deschenes, Quebec. SS—Anthony Granato, Atlantic City. OF—Francisco Caraballo, Worcester; Scott Grimes, Worcester; Jud Thigpen, Brockton. DH—Jabe Bergeron, Ottawa. LHP—Tom Cochran, Worcester. RHP—Michel Simard, Quebec. RP—Jerry Dunn, Brockton.

Player of the Year: Scott Grimes, Worcester. **Manager of the Year:** Hal Lanier, Sussex.

INDIVIDUAL BATTING LEADERS

BATTER, CLUB	AVG	G	AB	R	H	HR	RBI
Falu, Melvin, Brockton	.383	93	366	62	140	10	49
Grimes, Scott, Worcester	.365	93	364	87	133	21	57
Bergeron, Jabe, Ottawa	.354	91	350	78	124	13	69
Nunez, Alex, Quebec	.339	89	330	52	112	3	47
Colabello, Chris, Worcester	.336	93	357	71	120	16	76
Abreu, Dennis, Brockton	.326	93	365	52	119	13	54
Burke, Joe, Atlantic City	.324	92	389	62	126	5	50
Allen, Luke, New Jersey	.324	81	318	56	103	9	47
Granato, Anthony, Atlantic City	.322	93	363	83	117	14	62
Geiger, Kyle, Ottawa	.319	92	357	60	114	8	48

PITCHER, CLUB	W	L	ERA	IP	H	BB	SO
Simard, Michel, Quebect	13	2	2.32	124	111	16	95
Valdez, Luis, Quebec	9	4	2.49	105	92	30	67
Kelly, John, Brockton	9	5	2.59	126	99	47	121
Cox, Adam, Atlantic City	7	3	2.62	100	86	37	112
Cochran, Tom, Worcester	13	3	2.79	119	103	40	84
Lundgren, Wayne, Brockton	11	3	3.28	137	139	25	85
Pena, Eddie, Worcester	6	5	3.42	79	79	18	44
Pavlik, Isaac, New Jersey	8	7	3.65	136	144	23	82
Serro, Ted, New Jersey	5	4	3.66	93	98	19	52
Baca, Noel, Ottawa	3	10	3.82	108	114	47	62

ATLANTIC CITY SURF

BATTERS	AVG	AB	R	H	2B	3B	HR	RBI	SB
Barrows, Derek	.333	9	1	3	2	0	0	1	0
*Burke, Joe	.324	389	62	126	23	3	5	50	17
Burrus, Josh	.263	339	59	89	21	3	10	49	26
Flores, Freddy	.250	4	1	1	0	0	0	0	0
Granato, Anthony	.322	363	83	117	28	4	14	62	31
Hogan, Billy	.234	77	9	18	5	0	1	9	1
Huguet, J.C.	.167	12	1	2	0	0	0	1	0
Hurst, Jason	.240	75	10	18	5	0	4	12	1
Keel, Heath	.314	35	4	11	5	0	0	1	0
*Keesee, David	.136	22	3	3	1	0	0	2	0
*Kim, Eddie	.306	310	40	95	15	0	4	47	4
*Kovatch, Billy	.281	121	11	34	4	1	0	19	11
Ledesma, Arturo	.172	29	6	5	0	0	0	0	1
McQuigg, Carter	.167	12	1	2	0	0	0	0	0
Plaza, William	.268	291	38	78	15	1	4	32	3
Santoro, Michael	.188	16	1	3	1	0	0	2	1
Taylor, Lucas	.280	236	46	66	8	0	2	20	19
Thoma, Brad	.280	318	57	89	17	4	8	44	3
*Williams, Clyde	.298	319	44	95	18	1	11	62	2
Zayas, Gil	.260	231	26	60	13	0	5	30	1

PITCHERS	W	L	ERA	G	SV	IP	H	BB	SO
Barrows, Derek	2	1	4.40	22	1	47	55	25	26
*Cox, Adam	7	3	2.62	18	0	100	86	37	112
Duclos, Derek	0	3	3.55	36	4	51	44	27	34
Easton, Aaron	1	3	6.75	21	2	45	58	21	37
Flores, Freddy	1	0	1.80	1	0	5	2	0	4
George, Kyle	5	2	2.09	33	6	39	25	15	30
Huguet, J.C.	9	7	4.84	24	1	134	156	39	106
Pierce, Tony	0	0	8.31	4	0	4	4	4	6
Rafferty, Ryan	1	1	8.53	5	0	6	6	5	5
Redwine, Austin	0	1	7.59	6	0	11	13	13	7
*Rodaway, Brian	10	9	3.90	22	0	141	151	37	109
Ruud, Charlie	1	1	6.11	3	0	18	27	2	13
Santoro, Michael	0	0	27.00	1	0	2	8	0	0
Shortell, Rory	11	3	4.83	27	0	119	142	40	84
Thurmond, Ben	1	1	7.50	3	0	12	20	5	5
Whitley, Walker	1	6	3.11	44	9	64	61	24	50
Wladyka, James	1	2	9.47	9	0	26	35	15	14

BROCKTON ROX

BATTERS	AVG	AB	R	H	2B	3B	HR	RBI	SB
*Abreu, Dennis	.315	168	22	53	8	2	6	28	12
*Alcantara, Ervin	.274	201	32	55	14	1	4	23	15
*Bunn, William	.000	1	0	0	0	0	0	0	0
*Colson, Jason	.273	231	22	63	8	0	9	38	1
Cox, Daniel	.000	5	0	0	0	0	0	0	0
Cuadrado, Phillip	.308	328	47	101	18	2	9	49	4
David, Derek	.231	39	6	9	1	0	0	2	1
*Davilla, Vic	.364	22	4	8	4	0	0	5	0
Dunn, Gerald	.000	1	0	0	0	0	0	0	0
Falu, Melvin	.383	366	62	140	27	2	10	49	9
Frazee, Joe	.263	38	8	10	1	0	0	7	0
Gonzalez, Tony	.172	58	4	10	3	0	1	3	0
Julien, Eugene	.239	222	33	53	11	1	1	30	6
Lebron, Francisco	.230	252	25	58	10	0	4	31	0
Maloney, Matt	.214	42	7	9	0	0	3	4	2
McGhee, Joe	.167	6	1	1	0	0	0	0	0
*Muscato, Mike	.667	3	1	2	0	0	0	1	0

	AVG	AB	R	H	2B	3B	HR	RBI	SB
Ramos, Dominic	.299	388	52	116	13	1	2	29	20
Rios, Eduardo	.413	92	19	38	5	0	5	13	1
Rubin, Lee	.236	212	25	50	11	2	1	17	1
Thigpen, Jud	.295	352	59	104	20	2	17	70	5
Torres, Mike	.224	49	1	11	2	0	0	5	0
Vander Hey, Josh	.193	109	13	21	3	0	6	14	0
*Vardaro, Nick	.286	7	2	2	0	0	0	1	0
*Womack, Josh	.217	69	12	15	3	2	2	5	7

PITCHERS	W	L	ERA	G	SV	IP	H	BB	SO
Babb, Rich	0	0	5.93	10	0	14	11	8	7
Baker, Jamie	3	5	6.29	32	2	49	60	24	32
Bergstrom, Rafael	0	0	13.50	2	0	2	8	1	1
Boker, John	0	0	18.90	2	0	3	6	2	1
*Bunn, William	2	3	6.61	11	0	33	36	27	26
Delabar, Steve	3	3	3.01	11	0	69	67	16	43
Dunn, Gerald	2	4	1.45	43	24	43	41	9	38
Frazee, Joe	0	0	18.00	1	0	1	5	0	0
Hernandez, Santos	0	1	4.29	3	0	21	23	6	13
Kelly, John	9	5	2.56	19	0	126	99	47	121
Lundgren, Wayne	11	3	3.28	20	0	137	139	25	85
McDonough, Chris	4	3	5.68	9	0	44	53	17	20
McNulty, Andy	0	0	13.50	2	0	2	4	4	2
McTamney Jr, Mike	1	4	9.31	9	0	29	50	10	12
Mercado, Rony	1	1	4.70	2	0	8	6	3	5
Noe, Keith	2	1	3.96	18	0	25	30	9	20
Pellegrine, David	0	0	2.16	5	1	8	5	4	3
*Ramos, Jacob	3	2	3.14	20	0	29	27	19	23
Smith, Mike	2	0	2.88	8	0	34	24	10	40
Thigpen, Jud	0	0	0.00	1	0	0	0	1	0
*Vardaro, Nick	0	0	9.82	4	0	4	6	4	1
Viera, Rolando	4	8	4.10	15	0	94	105	48	74
Williams, Ryan	1	2	11.74	7	0	8	12	4	5
Zachary, Matt	1	2	2.20	36	0	49	42	25	41

NASHUA PRIDE

BATTERS	AVG	AB	R	H	2B	3B	HR	RBI	SB
*Abreu, Dennis	.335	197	30	66	15	3	7	26	12
*Alcantara, Ervin	.261	142	18	37	10	0	3	16	10
Almonte, Sandy	.246	285	36	70	16	3	4	30	16
Burkett, Isaac	.000	0	1	0	0	0	0	0	0
Castro, Ismael	.300	313	37	94	19	2	2	46	4
Clemente, Edgard	.206	34	3	7	4	0	0	4	0
Duplissie, Bryan	.310	355	59	110	26	1	17	62	2
*Edmondson, Jerod	.251	243	27	61	9	2	2	19	6
Enman, Luke	.100	20	2	2	0	0	0	1	1
Ford, Greg	.000	2	1	0	0	0	0	0	0
Groff, Will	.000	10	0	0	0	0	0	0	0
Joffrion, Jack	.194	139	13	27	8	0	2	11	1
Miller, B	.000	2	0	0	0	0	0	0	0
*Pennell, Vinny	.259	332	48	86	11	2	1	25	14
Pickrel, Jeremy	.265	196	38	52	17	1	10	30	10
Rodriguez, Luis	.211	166	13	35	8	0	2	25	0
Rojas, Dorian	.243	70	7	17	5	1	0	9	1
Rosario, Sam	.263	19	4	5	1	0	0	3	2
Santos, Anthony	.125	8	2	1	0	0	0	0	0
Stancil, Hans	.222	27	3	6	0	0	0	1	0
Stevens, Lance	.000	0	1	0	0	0	0	0	0
Tavarez, Aregenis	.288	326	45	94	21	3	2	35	15
Torres, Chris	.200	85	10	17	5	0	0	8	0
Torres, Mike	.322	171	25	55	14	0	4	32	1

PITCHERS	W	L	ERA	G	SV	IP	H	BB	SO
Almonte, Sandy	0	0	3.86	1	0	2	1	1	3
*Berberian, Nate	0	0	10.80	3	0	3	9	3	2
Buckland, Ryan	0	1	21.60	3	0	3	6	5	2
Burkett, Isaac	3	6	5.49	14	0	59	59	38	38
Ford, Greg	0	0	16.20	4	0	3	8	6	3
Garces, Rich	1	0	3.71	16	0	17	14	10	11
Heimpel, Sean	1	0	3.38	5	0	5	3	2	6
*Joyce, Michael	1	1	7.08	37	0	41	46	13	32
Kosyk, Bucky	0	3	12.66	3	0	11	25	2	3
Melendez, German	1	4	6.61	11	0	33	46	14	19
Nagasaka, Hideki	8	6	5.47	19	0	109	129	46	64
O'Brien, Matt	3	1	3.12	5	0	35	29	13	15

	W	L	ERA	G	SV	IP	H	BB	SO
Palanski, Brett	3	3	3.44	19	1	34	36	8	23
Paul, Jason	4	5	4.70	24	0	98	102	40	76
Piechowski, Adam	5	0	2.51	39	5	47	39	11	64
Stawarz, Jarrett	3	4	5.82	24	0	85	106	36	38
Stevens, Lance	6	7	4.76	19	0	104	93	60	75
Suero, Nicolas	2	5	4.91	9	0	51	68	15	13
Tesseyman, John	0	2	6.19	6	1	16	23	7	8
Torres, Chris	0	0	4.63	9	0	12	13	5	2
Weimer, Andrew	0	2	4.81	23	12	24	35	11	11
Willett, Reid	0	3	7.30	3	0	12	17	9	5

NEW JERSEY JACKALS

BATTERS	AVG	AB	R	H	2B	3B	HR	RBI	SB
*Allen, Luke	.324	318	56	103	23	3	9	47	3
*Davila, Vic	.279	61	7	17	7	0	1	15	0
Gordon, Casey	.177	175	21	31	6	2	0	19	7
Kelly, Chris	.280	296	39	83	19	1	12	57	0
*Kovatch, Billy	.299	67	8	20	3	0	1	7	6
Larsen, Andrew	.258	271	27	70	12	0	1	28	3
Lauderdale, Matthew	.304	257	47	78	18	0	10	37	1
Leandro, Francisco	.242	33	7	8	2	0	0	2	0
*Maddox, Craig	.248	214	22	53	9	2	5	32	1
Murphy, Tommy	.182	55	10	10	1	0	1	5	3
Nelson, Bryant	.287	195	31	56	10	2	7	27	2
Nivar, Ramon	.221	86	13	19	4	1	3	21	7
Rodriguez, Marcos	.272	184	15	50	7	0	0	21	1
Sanders, Marcus	.302	295	58	89	13	2	2	31	17
Smithlin, Zach	.280	353	45	99	12	1	1	27	33
Tejeda, Juan	.313	329	63	103	22	2	14	63	2
Urias, David	.222	36	5	8	0	0	1	5	0
White, Scott	.206	34	5	7	1	0	1	8	0

PITCHERS	W	L	ERA	G	SV	IP	H	BB	SO
*Acosta, Jorge	1	5	5.30	8	0	36	39	15	34
Atlee, Thomas	2	4	3.99	20	1	77	104	23	54
Barnes, Justin	3	2	4.31	38	0	48	56	20	43
Cameron, Dustin	0	0	7.07	11	0	14	19	2	10
D'Alessandro, Joe	0	0	9.82	4	0	4	7	2	3
Davis, Hunter	2	4	5.23	25	0	33	41	20	25
Done, Juan	5	3	4.43	10	0	63	74	23	39
Malone, Corwin	0	1	7.04	2	0	8	9	8	7
*Martin, Brandon	2	3	5.13	29	0	40	46	27	41
*Martin, Nick	0	0	9.39	7	0	8	11	3	4
Murphy, Tommy	0	0	13.50	3	0	4	8	3	3
Pacyna, Ryan	2	2	4.64	22	0	64	70	16	33
*Pavlik, Isaac	8	7	3.65	21	0	136	144	23	82
Serro, Ted	5	4	3.66	27	0	93	98	19	52
Tressler, Aaron	3	8	5.92	16	0	87	100	32	69
*Tucker, Rusty	3	3	1.85	35	21	39	27	14	45
Vicaro, Michael	7	5	5.29	21	0	80	83	35	64

OTTAWA RAPIDZ

BATTERS	AVG	AB	R	H	2B	3B	HR	RBI	SB
Bergeron, Jabe	.354	350	78	124	29	2	13	69	0
Bouchard, Maxime	.212	33	3	7	2	0	0	2	0
Butler, Kevin	.455	11	1	5	0	0	0	1	0
*Daubert, Jake	.290	210	26	61	12	1	3	34	0
De Los Santos, Jose	.288	389	43	112	18	1	0	23	6
Dumouchel, Greg	.191	68	5	13	2	1	1	4	2
*Edwards, Dytarious	.167	42	3	7	2	0	0	1	1
Escalona, Felix	.330	100	18	33	3	0	2	13	0
Geiger, Kyle	.319	357	60	114	25	1	8	48	1
*Guanchez, Argimiro	.000	1	0	0	0	0	0	0	0
Hall, Nate	.263	152	20	40	6	1	0	22	1
Infante, Juan	.242	264	35	64	14	0	1	20	3
*Keesee, David	.000	2	0	0	0	0	0	0	0
*Lemieux, Jared	.243	272	45	66	16	2	5	31	11
*McKnight, Scott	.160	163	13	26	2	0	0	13	2
Milons, Jereme	.298	369	59	110	16	2	10	56	10
*Muscato, Mike	.103	29	3	3	0	0	2	5	0
Ndungidi, Sambu	.100	30	1	3	0	0	0	1	0
Pirman, Pete	.252	305	23	77	13	1	4	46	7
*Ramos, Jacob	.000	0	0	0	0	0	0	0	0
Salas, Jose	.226	115	10	26	3	0	1	14	2

	AVG	AB	R	H	2B	3B	HR	RBI	SB
Trainor, Nick	.000	7	0	0	0	0	0	0	0

PITCHERS	W	L	ERA	G	SV	IP	H	BB	SO
Baca, Noel	3	10	3.82	30	0	108	114	47	62
Bello, Cibney	0	0	15.00	1	0	3	8	0	1
*Bunn, William	1	2	7.01	6	0	26	22	20	18
Burrows, Angelo	3	1	2.76	40	4	49	54	18	37
Donovan, Pat	0	0	0.00	1	0	1	1	0	0
*Guanchez, Argimiro	1	3	5.35	18	0	34	34	11	33
Hawes, Adam	4	13	6.94	19	0	106	148	46	85
Infante, Juan	0	0	0.00	1	0	1	1	0	0
*Kusiewicz, Mike	3	8	4.05	18	0	113	134	32	70
Mejlholm, Karl	1	0	6.39	7	0	13	17	10	3
Pilkington, Jason	1	0	2.77	11	0	13	11	3	10
*Price, Reid	4	0	2.08	20	2	30	25	13	18
*Ramos, Jacob	1	1	5.05	10	0	36	33	23	27
*Robinson, Fraser	4	8	5.06	19	0	121	157	16	90
Strankman, Dallas	0	2	7.54	15	0	23	35	13	14
Tosoni, Matthew	1	0	2.57	4	0	7	8	3	1
*Trias, Orlando	1	4	5.52	7	0	44	52	15	25
Tucker, Cardoza	0	4	4.80	25	7	30	30	20	21
Watson, Tanner	3	7	5.24	11	0	67	80	19	48
Wilson, Joe	0	0	33.75	4	0	3	7	4	1

QUEBEC CAPITALES

BATTERS	AVG	AB	R	H	2B	3B	HR	RBI	SB
*Arellan, Felix	.417	12	1	5	0	0	0	1	0
Colafemina, Joshua	.292	233	40	68	9	0	0	28	20
Contreras, Jose	.311	264	42	82	9	3	1	29	16
D'Aoust, Patrick	.213	122	10	26	3	0	1	22	0
*Deschenes, Pat	.301	329	60	99	28	1	10	67	0
Gonzalez, Issael	.271	266	50	72	12	3	0	22	18
*Goss, Mike	.276	243	48	67	11	3	5	40	18
Lantigua, Eddie	.307	332	62	102	19	0	9	60	3
*Nunez, Alex	.339	330	52	112	16	2	3	47	20
Salvas, Jean-Michel	.259	189	27	49	8	2	2	29	6
Scalabrini, Pat	.270	359	50	97	14	1	14	57	3
Stevens, Greg	.256	289	49	74	16	1	9	44	4
*Tomlinson, Goef	.284	204	39	58	14	2	7	31	11

PITCHERS	W	L	ERA	G	SV	IP	H	BB	SO
*Arellan, Felix	1	2	4.85	33	0	43	47	35	36
Beavers, Kevin	5	4	3.99	17	0	90	114	30	40
Begg, Chris	0	2	11.32	2	0	10	22	3	5
Blanco, Ivan	2	4	4.04	29	2	42	43	18	45
Cyr, Eric	3	1	1.80	7	0	45	43	4	48
Gelinas, Karl	2	1	4.62	6	0	25	27	5	22
*Guanchez, Argimiro	0	1	18.00	2	0	2	6	4	4
James, Mark	4	3	3.02	31	1	51	50	19	45
Mondesir, James	1	0	4.50	4	0	4	6	4	1
Nadon, Erick	1	4	6.57	19	1	62	79	17	52
Neveu, JeanFrancis	0	0	9.00	1	0	3	5	0	2
Ryan, Shawn	0	0	0.00	1	0	2	1	2	1
Schutt, Jason	3	2	3.79	35	13	36	37	6	18
Simard, Michel	13	2	2.32	18	0	124	116	16	95
Stanton, T.J.	6	4	3.90	22	0	92	87	33	79
*Trias, Orlando	8	2	3.18	11	0	76	56	29	33
Valdez, Luis	9	4	2.49	19	0	105	92	30	67
*Wasylak, David	0	0	1.50	2	0	6	6	4	1

SUSSEX SKYHAWKS

BATTERS	AVG	AB	R	H	2B	3B	HR	RBI	SB
Brown, Chris	.316	342	65	108	18	2	9	43	11
Crespi, Ryan	.195	87	7	17	3	0	0	5	10
*Delgado, Mario	.239	92	10	22	7	0	2	13	0
Frazier, Alex	.305	331	55	101	22	1	12	54	5
Hackney, Matt	.129	31	1	4	0	0	0	4	0
Moreno, Jorge	.276	351	59	97	25	1	11	55	12
Panezich, Cliff	.298	47	11	14	3	0	4	9	0
Pappas, Mark	.316	19	2	6	2	0	0	5	0
*Perodin, Ron	.302	394	66	119	15	3	0	43	26
Rios, Kevin	.276	355	55	98	13	3	5	46	1
Valera, Yohanny	.252	298	35	75	19	1	5	42	0
*Vardaro, Nick	.105	19	2	2	0	0	0	0	0

	AVG	AB	R	H	2B	3B	HR	RBI	SB
*Weston, Matthew	.299	354	69	106	19	3	22	60	1
Yaconetti, Jay	.299	334	42	100	20	0	5	44	1
Young, Walter	.278	205	23	57	5	0	7	41	1

PITCHERS	W	L	ERA	G	SV	IP	H	BB	SO
Afify, Khalid	1	1	11.00	10	0	18	31	9	13
Benitez, Edisbel	0	2	9.82	5	0	18	26	21	15
*Braun, Bart	0	0	8.53	6	0	6	11	2	2
*Douglas, James	1	1	2.66	25	1	41	39	23	25
Galvez, Gary	5	5	4.70	16	0	92	96	25	71
Knoff, Justin	3	1	3.74	9	0	53	53	13	33
Laluna, Michael	2	1	2.79	26	0	42	27	26	42
Lawyer, Rich	2	3	5.58	20	1	61	88	17	20
*Lincoln, Roger	1	1	4.67	10	2	27	27	6	22
Marsden, Aaron	0	0	13.50	2	0	2	5	5	0
Michael, Mark	2	4	9.00	6	0	27	43	14	17
Petrusek, Matt	5	2	1.79	36	24	45	37	16	57
Roberts, Edward	0	3	10.89	8	0	19	29	15	12
Rogers, Michael	0	4	8.92	9	0	36	43	32	32
Ruwe, Kyle	12	5	4.67	18	0	129	163	20	72
Salvato, Matt	10	4	4.73	21	2	97	100	43	57
*Snipp, Craig	8	5	3.94	18	0	107	131	36	57
Thomas, Eric	0	0	54.00	1	0	1	1	0	0
*Vardaro, Nick	0	0	0.00	1	0	1	0	0	0

WORCESTER TORNADOES

BATTERS	AVG	AB	R	H	2B	3B	HR	RBI	SB
Caraballo, Francisco	.313	345	53	108	18	5	23	73	5
Colabello, Chris	.336	357	71	120	34	1	16	76	3
Edwards, Justin	.173	52	5	9	1	0	0	4	0
Farkes, Josh	.241	108	13	26	4	0	3	16	1
Grimes, Scott	.365	364	87	133	20	6	21	57	17
Jeroloman, Charles	.253	289	34	73	12	3	8	41	3
LaHair, Jeff	.239	205	33	49	4	1	6	27	4
MacMillan, Michael	.259	282	38	73	9	1	2	28	3
Pena, Alex	.438	16	3	7	3	0	1	2	0
Pena, Omar	.216	301	39	65	14	1	5	30	6
Santana, Rico	.194	72	5	14	1	1	0	6	0
Thaler, Brett	.167	18	6	3	0	0	0	2	0
*Trezza, Alex	.228	333	40	76	14	1	11	64	2
Weagle, Matt	.000	1	0	0	0	0	0	0	0
Weed, B.J.	.294	394	70	116	26	3	6	38	23

PITCHERS	W	L	ERA	G	SV	IP	H	BB	SO
Barnard, Chandler	1	0	4.44	11	0	26	27	8	12
Beras, Alexis	0	0	6.75	5	0	7	6	9	5
*Berberian, Nate	0	0	3.86	5	0	7	5	2	7
Birtwell, John	1	2	3.10	23	13	29	29	11	38
*Cochran, Tom	13	3	2.79	19	2	119	103	40	84
Edwards, Justin	1	0	4.37	16	0	35	38	13	25
Guerrero, Junior	7	5	5.59	19	0	106	113	42	63
Jackson, Kyle	0	1	6.88	3	0	17	14	11	10
*Lobban, Ryan	5	1	3.11	35	4	46	43	12	42
McNamara, Shaun	3	10	5.55	18	0	97	124	39	47
Mitchell, Ryan	1	1	5.27	5	1	14	13	3	12
Ociesa, Jacob	0	2	10.80	6	0	10	13	15	8
Pena, Alex	2	3	4.63	11	0	58	57	20	31
Pena, Eddie	6	5	3.42	34	9	79	79	18	44
Presutti, Shane	0	0	12.15	4	0	7	14	3	2
Sullivan, Anthony	3	1	2.57	16	0	21	17	9	22
*Wasylak, David	0	0	6.00	2	0	3	4	2	1
Weagle, Matt	10	7	4.01	20	0	123	143	23	85

CONTINENTAL LEAGUE

After finishing last in 2007, the Bay Area Toros made a very impressive turnaround in 2008. The Toros won 18 of their final 20 games, including a two-game sweep of the best-of-three championship series to claim the Continental League title. While the league remained limited to four teams, the talent level of the league made a significant step up in the league's second year. J.T. Tilghman (Astros) and Brandon Sisk (Royals) landed contracts with affiliated clubs, as Tilghman showed one of the best arms indy ball has seen in years with a 95-97 mph fastball.

	W	L	PCT	GB
Bay Area Toros	44	29	.603	—
Texarkana Gunslingers	38	34	.528	5.5

Corpus Christi Beach Dawgs	34	38	.472	9.5
McKinney Blue Thunder	29	44	.397	15

PLAYOFFS: First round: Texarkana defeated Corpus Christi, 1-0 in series truncated due to weather. Championship Round: Bay Area defeated Texarkana, 2-0 in best-of-3.

MANAGERS: Bay Area-Jim Bolt, Corpus Christi-Hector Salinas, Tarrant County-Curtis Wilkerson, Texarkana-Chris McKnight,

AWARDS: Most Valuable Player—Kyle Wells, Bay Area. Pitcher of the Year—Kevin Cooper, Bay Area. Manager of the Year—Jim Bolt, Bay Area.

INDIVIDUAL BATTING LEADERS

PLAYER, CLUB	AVG	G	AB	R	H	HR	RBI	SB
Edwards, Anthony, Texarkana	.324	70	275	51	89	2	43	15
Wells, Kyle, Bay Area	.315	60	197	25	62	2	30	6
Kmetko, Tyler, CC	.300	65	223	36	67	0	16	12
Filyaw, Gene, McKinney	.300	62	233	30	70	2	34	7
Plecki, Greg, Bay Area	.297	66	222	36	66	1	22	29
Crimoli, Gene, Texarkana	.290	66	238	31	69	1	37	7
Massie, Grant, Bay Area	.287	67	223	46	64	2	32	13
Quintana, Frank, Texarkana	.245	66	212	31	52	3	22	2
Brown, Eric, Bay Area	.240	58	196	32	47	2	26	21
Rubenstein, Brendan, Texarkana	.239	61	209	26	50	0	26	8

INDIVIDUAL PITCHING LEADERS

PLAYER, CLUB	W	L	ERA	G	SV	IP	H	BB	SO
Cooper, Kevin, Bay Area	5	3	1.71	16	0	95	56	39	83
Revere, Russell, Bay Area	8	4	1.84	18	3	108	90	29	62
Parker, Travis, CC	3	5	1.85	12	0	78	62	30	53
Leger, Ryan, McKinney	6	3	2.42	14	0	89	85	24	52
Barr, Brian, Texarkana	9	3	2.54	15	0	89	82	21	80
Kondratowiz, Ryan, CC	6	5	2.59	15	0	87	77	29	38
French, Tyler, Texarkana	3	4	2.78	15	0	87	73	37	65
Milton, John, McKinney	4	6	3.62	13	0	82	98	22	21

BAY AREA TOROS

BATTERS	AVG	AB	R	H	2B	3B	HR	RBI	SB
*Brown, Don	.232	82	11	19	4	0	1	7	7
Brown, Eric	.240	196	32	47	12	2	2	26	21
*Burum, Ben	.252	163	25	41	13	0	3	29	3
Cattell, Ryan	.243	111	12	27	5	1	3	19	4
Cox, Daniel	.208	120	13	25	5	1	0	6	1
Crossland, Brett	.405	37	4	15	3	0	1	6	2
Czekaj, Nicholas	.225	89	9	20	3	0	0	4	2
*Diaz, Jason	.290	124	22	36	0	0	0	10	26
Fernandez, Alex	.000	1	0	0	0	0	0	0	0
Frazier, Brandon	.258	31	4	8	0	0	0	4	4
Hicks, Joe	.266	139	13	37	2	2	2	26	17
Hines, Patrick	.000	13	1	0	0	0	0	0	0
Hyndsman, Mark	.250	8	0	2	0	0	0	0	0
Kottke, Ryan	.400	5	2	2	0	0	0	0	0
*Lockwood, Trent	.238	21	3	5	0	2	0	3	0
Massie, Grant	.287	223	46	64	6	3	2	32	13
Mayer, Trent	.295	61	4	18	2	0	0	6	5
Mieras, Brett	.261	46	6	12	3	0	0	4	1
Perri, Kevin	.207	58	11	12	2	1	0	4	5
Plecki, Greg	.297	222	36	66	9	1	1	22	29
Revere, Russell	.333	3	0	1	0	0	0	0	0
Roberson, Trey	.111	9	0	1	0	1	0	0	0
Rogowski, Tony	.220	109	16	24	1	0	0	8	11
Schupp, Brian	.182	33	0	6	0	0	0	4	1
Smeltzer, Will	.200	10	0	2	0	0	0	1	0
Suncar, Jose	.180	89	9	16	1	1	0	3	6
Taddia, Drew	.167	6	1	1	0	0	0	0	0
Thrush, Corey	.000	6	0	0	0	0	0	0	0
Tolan, Bobby	.188	69	4	13	1	0	1	5	1
*Wade, Kyle	.190	63	7	12	1	1	0	3	1
Wells, Kyle	.315	197	25	62	4	1	2	30	6

PITCHERS	W	L	ERA	G	SV	IP	H	BB	SO
Bartek, Michael	0	0	4.50	3	0	4	5	1	3
Beal, Zach	0	0	2.45	4	0	4	2	3	2
Brown, Ethan	0	0	0.00	1	0	1	1	2	0
Cooper, Kevin	5	3	1.71	16	0	95	56	39	83
DeFratus, Steven	0	3	2.50	12	4	40	39	6	19
Fernandez, Alex	8	0	2.68	24	0	57	48	35	42

(side tab) INDEPENDENT LEAGUES

	W	L	ERA	G	SV	IP	H	BB	SO
Kimmerling, Cody	0	0	0.00	1	0	1	1	0	0
Lauver, Loren	0	2	0.96	15	0	19	6	15	23
Laycock, Keegan	0	1	7.00	5	1	9	9	16	16
Moore, Marcus	1	0	0.00	1	0	1	0	0	0
Nelson, Ryne	2	1	0.68	16	4	26	13	15	28
Paradoski, Matthew	5	0	3.92	13	1	41	41	31	49
Rachuig, Jayson	4	2	0.96	9	1	38	25	12	31
Read, Stephen	1	3	4.04	12	0	36	31	17	30
Revere, Russell	8	4	1.84	18	3	108	90	29	62
Smeltzer, Will	1	4	3.90	15	0	28	21	17	19
Swanson, Drew	3	1	2.25	16	3	28	16	15	20
Watson, Andy	0	0	15.43	3	0	2	3	5	3
*Holder, Scott	2	1	4.38	9	1	12	7	7	8
*Luetge, Lance	0	0	5.68	8	0	6	8	6	4
*Shearer, Kelly	1	1	2.74	9	1	23	14	11	12
*Sisk, Brandon	3	3	1.65	8	0	49	36	21	59

CORPUS CHRISTI BEACH DAWGS

BATTERS	AVG	AB	R	H	2B	3B	HR	RBI	SB
Alicea, Rene	.000	1	0	0	0	0	0	0	0
Alvarez, Kyle	.000	3	0	0	0	0	0	0	0
Blanco, Luis	.330	88	6	29	4	0	1	15	0
Bond, L.	.000	1	1	0	0	0	0	0	0
Carper, Jeff	.219	73	7	16	2	1	0	5	6
Castro, Jean	.198	96	9	19	0	0	0	10	3
Catala, Pedro	.259	108	21	28	1	1	1	6	17
Chappelle, Dan	.136	44	5	6	0	0	0	4	2
Clay, Randall	.000	2	0	0	0	0	0	0	0
Coit, Johny	.100	10	0	1	0	0	0	1	0
Coleman, Brad	.288	125	9	36	2	0	0	15	4
Desnarais, Chuck	.192	78	7	15	1	0	1	10	3
Dube, Chris	.000	1	0	0	0	0	0	0	0
Elliot, Mitch	.186	86	13	16	3	0	0	4	16
Enciso, Nick	.182	33	3	6	0	0	0	3	0
Estrada, Mike	.108	102	13	11	1	0	0	4	2
Gali, Javier	.053	38	1	2	1	0	0	1	0
Guerrero, Henry	.077	26	2	2	0	0	0	3	0
Hall, Salvator	.133	15	0	2	0	0	0	0	0
Hartman, Joel	.226	62	4	14	0	0	0	5	6
Herron, Heath	.233	86	13	20	2	0	0	4	4
Hung, Carlos	.209	129	8	27	4	1	0	9	5
Jacobo, Joey	.180	100	11	18	5	2	0	9	4
King, Jeff	.154	26	3	4	1	0	0	0	1
Kmetko, Tyler	.300	223	36	67	5	1	0	16	12
Kondratowiz, Ryan	.000	1	0	0	0	0	0	0	0
Krikstan, Josh	.000	3	0	0	0	0	0	0	0
Lewis, Mark	.000	1	0	0	0	0	0	0	0
Lingren, Erik	.111	9	1	1	0	0	0	1	0
Marrero, Jonathan	.000	10	0	0	0	0	0	0	0
Martinez, Cody	.000	4	0	0	0	0	0	0	0
McCabe, Brandon	.184	103	9	19	4	1	1	13	1
Milner, Bo	.000	1	0	0	0	0	0	0	0
Molina, Bobby	.250	8	2	2	0	0	0	0	1
Morgan, Josh	.207	92	11	19	4	0	3	11	6
Parker, Travis	.000	1	1	0	0	0	0	0	0
Pello, Brandon	.100	1	0	1	0	0	0	0	0
Pfaff, Bob	.000	1	0	0	0	0	0	0	0
Roberson, Trey	.000	7	2	0	0	0	0	0	1
Rosario, Carlos	.174	23	1	4	1	0	0	2	0
Sanchez, Alejandro	.185	27	4	5	1	0	0	2	2
Sanders, Delvin	.000	2	0	0	0	0	0	0	0
Shay, Nick	.236	157	19	37	3	0	3	22	5
Sillivent, Greg	.257	74	11	19	0	0	0	6	15
White, Earl	.219	137	23	30	5	1	2	12	17

PITCHERS	W	L	ERA	G	SV	IP	H	BB	SO
Acierno, Mark	3	0	0.89	15	0	20	14	8	15
Alicea, Rene	1	1	3.14	11	7	14	10	3	17
Alzuarde, Rob	1	1	7.58	7	0	19	19	22	5
Chaffardet, Daniel	1	2	3.47	6	0	36	30	17	20
Chappelle, Dan	0	0	0.00	1	0	1	0	0	0
Dunn, Brandon	0	1	1.35	2	0	7	5	5	3
Dutka, Alex	0	4	6.44	12	0	29	36	20	12
Elliot, Mitch	0	0	0.00	1	0	1	0	1	0

	W	L	ERA	G	SV	IP	H	BB	SO
Estrada, Mike	0	1	4.29	8	0	21	23	3	6
Figueroa, Jonathan	1	0	1.50	2	0	6	1	3	4
Greanead, Matt	1	0	0.00	1	0	2	0	1	3
Jacobo, Joey	0	0	12.46	4	0	4	2	10	4
Kantz, Joe	0	1	3.00	2	0	6	6	3	4
Kondratowiz, Ryan	6	5	2.59	15	0	87	77	29	38
Krikstan, Josh	2	2	4.15	8	0	43	51	12	17
Lingren, Erik	2	0	3.65	9	0	12	12	9	8
Milner, Bo	0	0	0.00	1	0	1	1	1	2
Parker, Travis	3	5	1.85	12	0	78	62	30	53
Pello, Brandon	2	1	2.81	20	9	26	23	5	29
Pfaff, Bob	0	1	7.50	1	0	6	7	3	1
Recio, Rene	4	1	2.21	5	0	37	27	8	31
Rosario, Carlos	0	0	4.91	5	0	7	3	9	5
Savarese, Rob	0	3	7.20	8	0	25	37	11	12
Sillivent, Greg	0	0	0.00	1	0	1	0	1	1
Snider, Joe	1	2	4.40	5	0	14	13	12	13
Sosa, Miguel	2	1	1.72	10	0	37	33	18	21
Trevino, Toro	1	2	3.68	5	1	7	10	8	4
Valera, Garardo	0	3	12.91	7	0	8	10	12	5
Vasquez, Gustavo	2	0	1.93	6	0	28	23	5	15
White, Earl	0	0	6.00	2	0	3	7	3	1
Williams, Julian	0	1	18.00	2	0	2	4	2	2
Wimpee, Aaron	1	0	2.57	6	0	21	13	13	17

MCKINNEY BLUE THUNDER

BATTERS	AVG	AB	R	H	2B	3B	HR	RBI	SB
Anderson, Jonathan	.215	172	13	37	2	0	1	8	10
Betourne, Alan	.205	132	19	27	3	1	0	6	8
Bird, Nick	.134	67	4	9	1	0	2	5	0
Bourgeois, Jason	.192	120	15	23	3	0	0	6	5
Cole, Antoine	.222	45	6	10	0	0	1	5	4
Drabek, Justin	.100	2	0	2	0	0	0	0	0
Elliot, Mitch	.191	94	12	18	4	0	1	8	12
Fiallo, Adriel	.224	125	9	28	4	0	0	4	3
Filyaw, Gene	.300	233	30	70	9	4	2	34	7
Forsythe, Ryan	.254	185	22	47	2	0	0	18	9
Jackson, Jake	.237	135	20	32	7	0	1	19	1
Matos, Adam	.170	47	2	8	2	1	0	5	0
Matusik, John	.159	44	1	7	0	0	0	2	1
McCabe, Brandon	.250	76	7	19	6	0	0	11	0
Pagan, Joe	.233	210	23	49	13	0	3	27	3
Revis, Brandon	.246	171	24	42	3	2	0	7	22
Rogowski, Tony	.152	33	2	5	0	0	0	2	0
Washington, Stephen	.216	51	3	11	1	0	0	3	1
Wilkerson, Brandon	.194	196	18	38	5	0	0	13	5
Wilson, Glen	.256	195	16	50	7	0	1	22	2

PITCHERS	W	L	ERA	G	SV	IP	H	BB	SO
Betourne, Alan	0	0	0.00	1	0	1	1	0	0
Brown, Matt	1	3	1.82	1	0	40	40	13	7
Castillo, George	0	3	2.74	23	14	23	12	13	27
Cox, Mark	1	2	1.33	4	0	20	10	14	12
Dixon, Curt	0	1	1.16	7	0	23	19	10	18
Drabek, Justin	2	5	1.69	11	0	64	56	21	45
Foeman, Kevin	1	3	4.60	6	0	16	14	12	9
Frias, Hector	2	5	2.75	22	0	36	38	22	22
Furrow, Donald	2	0	1.76	7	0	41	34	16	27
Furrow, Jason	0	2	1.37	9	1	20	14	5	11
Hastings, Andrew	1	0	0.00	2	0	5	3	2	2
Hurn, Doug	0	3	6.89	3	0	16	24	8	8
Kalldin, Greg	3	1	3.11	17	0	46	46	24	20
Kelne, Andrew	0	4	5.25	14	1	36	37	20	16
Kennedy, David	2	0	0.00	6	0	6	3	3	4
Leger, Ryan	6	3	2.42	14	0	89	85	24	52
Lewis, Fielding	0	0	10.80	3	0	5	7	3	4
Markary, Marcus	3	2	2.76	7	0	42	41	10	33
Milton, John	4	6	3.62	13	0	82	98	22	21
Pagan, Joe	0	0	4.50	1	0	2	4	1	0
Russell, Jonathan	0	0	0.00	1	0	2	2	1	1
Shelton, Jeff	1	0	7.94	6	0	11	12	10	11
Watson, Andy	0	1	4.26	4	0	6	8	9	6

TEXARKANA GUNSLINGERS

BATTERS	AVG	AB	R	H	2B	3B	HR	RBI	SB
Burgess, Pat	.238	172	25	41	12	1	1	15	1
*Burke, Brian	.284	169	34	48	5	1	0	21	8
*Crimoli, Gene	.290	238	31	69	12	1	1	37	7
Doane, Josh	.278	18	2	5	1	1	0	6	1
*Edwards, Anthony	.324	275	51	89	8	7	2	43	15
*Enciso, Nick	.228	101	7	23	5	0	0	8	2
*Feller, Scott	.116	69	1	8	0	0	0	5	1
Hartman, Joel	.077	13	1	1	0	0	0	0	0
Hastings, Ray	.230	235	36	54	5	1	0	19	9
Jackel, William	.500	2	0	1	1	0	0	0	0
Jackson, Jake	.219	32	3	7	0	0	0	2	1
*Jackson, Jamaal	.312	77	9	24	3	0	0	10	0
Jennings, J.J.	.184	49	7	9	2	0	0	6	2
Lingren, Erik	.138	29	4	4	1	0	0	3	1
Marrero, Emanuel	.171	41	3	7	0	0	0	2	0
Morelli, Joey	.250	28	1	7	1	0	0	3	0
Netzel, Brad	.230	135	22	31	3	1	0	15	1
*Olsen, Mike	.169	59	5	10	2	0	0	4	0
Peavy, Dane	.176	17	4	3	0	0	0	0	0
Quintana, Frank	.245	212	31	52	10	0	3	22	2
*Reynolds, Jay	.160	50	8	8	1	0	0	9	1
Riddle, Matt	.250	12	3	3	0	0	0	0	0
Rubenstein, Brendan	.239	209	26	50	6	2	0	26	8
Sencion, Sergio	.263	99	17	26	3	0	1	19	0
Urie, Brett	.161	31	2	5	0	0	0	3	0

PITCHERS	W	L	ERA	G	SV	IP	H	BB	SO
Barr, Brian	9	3	2.54	15	0	89	82	21	80
Brown, Ethan	0	0	0.00	1	0	1	1	1	0
Buchanan, Paul	0	0	0.00	1	0	2	1	3	2
Cherry, Brad	0	0	1.74	3	0	10	15	5	8
Farren, David	0	0	0.00	1	0	4	4	1	3
Fleming, Josh	0	0	10.80	1	0	2	2	2	1
French, Tyler	3	4	2.78	15	0	87	73	37	65
Gleason, Billy	3	0	1.21	22	1	60	44	25	51
Jackel, William	3	3	3.14	30	0	49	41	21	50
Kelly, Brandon	1	4	4.66	21	1	29	27	14	23
Klassen, Trevor	0	0	0.00	1	0	1	1	0	1
Lingren, Erik	0	1	4.85	9	0	13	13	8	9
McCavitt, Jordan	7	3	3.22	25	1	45	39	12	37
Pasch, Mike	0	0	0.00	1	0	8	2	3	5
Riker, Nick	1	5	4.12	9	0	39	37	12	26
Smith, Judson	5	4	2.50	10	0	54	38	32	58
Sumter, Shaun	0	0	5.19	6	0	9	15	4	7
Tilghman, Jack	3	2	1.24	38	13	44	22	19	61
VanEs, Scott	0	1	5.40	2	0	5	5	4	7
Weitzman, Billy	0	1	3.86	4	0	16	19	3	20
Zimmerman, Ryan	0	1	5.09	3	0	18	24	3	11
*Burke, Brian	0	0	27.00	1	0	0	2	0	0
*Monte, Phil	0	1	2.62	5	0	24	17	12	17
*Wells, Brandon	1	0	2.61	7	0	10	13	5	7
*Williams, Ryan	2	1	2.76	3	0	16	13	9	17

FRONTIER LEAGUE

When the Windy City Thunderbolts promoted bench coach Mike Kashirsky in early July, there was no way for them to know that it would be the move that would ensure a second straight Frontier League title. Kashirsky was promoted when manager Brian Nelson resigned after he was suspended for six games by the league. At the time, Kashirsky, who also coaches at Robert Morris University, was told that he would be the manager through the end of the season. But under the new skipper's leadership, Windy City turned its season around. The Thunderbolts won 37 of their final 51 games to win the West Division, beat Southern Illinois in the first round of the playoffs, then waited as flooding at Kalamazoo delayed the start of the championship series for nearly a week. The league finally had to declare that all championship series games would be played at Windy City. It didn't take long for Windy City to finish off their second straight title as playoff MVP Ross Stout won game one and league MVP Phil Hawke helped the Thunderbolts to a three-game sweep.

EAST DIVISION	W	L	PCT	GB
Kalamazoo	60	36	.625	—
Traverse City	50	46	.521	10
Washington	48	48	.500	12
Florence	47	49	.490	13
Chillicothe	39	57	.406	21
Midwest	29	67	.302	31

WEST DIVISION	W	L	PCT	GB
Windy City	60	36	.625	—
Southern Illinois	58	38	.604	2
Gateway	51	45	.531	9
Rockford	48	48	.500	12
River City	47	49	.490	13
Evansville	39	57	.406	21

PLAYOFFS: Semifinals—Kalamazoo defeated Gateway 3-1 and Windy City defeated Southern Illinois 3-1 in best-of-five series. Finals: Windy City defeated Kalamazo 3-0 in best-of-five series.

MANAGERS: Chillicothe—Mark Mason. Evansville—Jason Verdugo. Florence—Jamie Keefe. Gateway—Phil Warren. Kalamazoo—Fran Riordan. Midwest—Eric Coleman. River City—Toby Rumfield. Rockford—Bob Koopman. Southern Illinois—Mike Pinto. Traverse City. Jonathan Cahill. Washington—Greg Jelks. Windy City—Brian Nelson/Mike Kashirsky.

ATTENDANCE: Southern Illinois 218,191; Traverse City 193,724; Gateway 190,892; Washington 154,444; Rockford 138,234; Evansville 119,645; Florence 106,707; Windy City 90,616; Kalamazoo 83,157; Chillicothe 67,253.

ALL-STAR TEAM: C—Charlie Lisk, Gateway; 1B—Phil Hawke, Windy City; 2B—Joe Anthonsen, Rockford; 3B—Kelly Hunt, Florence; SS—Wes Long, Windy City; OF—Jason James, Rockford; Angel Molina, Florence; Joey Metropoulos, Southern Illinois. DHs—Mike Breyman, Gateway and Jacob Dempsey, Washington. SP—Ryan Bird, Southern Illinois. RP—Brandon Pariloo, Kalamazoo.

Most Valuable Player: Phil Hawke, Windy City. **Pitcher of the Year:** Ryan Bird, Southern Illinois. **Rookie of the Year:** Brendan Murphy, Kalamazoo. **Manager of the Year:** Fran Riordan, Kalamazoo.

INDIVIDUAL BATTING LEADERS

BATTER, CLUB	AVG	G	AB	R	H	HR	RBI
Anthonsen, Joe, Rockford	.352	95	384	79	135	2	50
James, Jason, Rockford	.350	92	380	55	133	13	74
Murphy, Brendan, Kalamazoo	.332	91	331	46	110	16	77
Long, Wesley, Windy City	.331	96	369	66	122	11	71
Molina, Angel, Florence	.327	90	349	74	114	22	71
Knapp, Robbie, Rockford	.317	81	312	50	99	8	57
Sweet, Andrew, River City	.316	94	310	55	98	5	48
Metropoulos, Joey, So. Illinois	.315	93	340	74	107	20	66
Goetz, Mike, Traverse City	.314	66	245	46	77	0	22
Mochizuki, Gered, Evansville	.314	75	293	41	92	4	26

INDIVIDUAL PITCHING LEADERS

PITCHER, CLUB	W	L	ERA	IP	H	BB	SO
Nathanson, David, Traverse City	12	3	2.28	114	99	20	67
Bird, Ryan, Southern Illinois	13	3	2.48	123	97	45	152
Stout, Ross, Windy City	11	3	2.57	133	104	39	121
Gehring, Ryan, Traverse City	5	9	2.71	126	118	32	69
Little, Chris, Southern Illinois	9	4	2.90	121	106	35	94
MacFarlane, Ryan, Midwest	4	5	2.92	89	74	38	85
Bauer, Garrett, Rockford	10	6	2.98	148	114	78	151
DiPietro, Joe, Kalamazoo	7	5	3.28	107	95	40	65
Dunn, Brooks, Washington	2	6	3.32	81	82	22	58
Clark, Andy, Florence	10	2	3.36	83	60	26	79

CHILLICOTHE PAINTS

BATTERS	AVG	AB	R	H	2B	3B	HR	RBI	SB
Anderson, Sean	.197	76	9	15	0	0	0	1	3
Blackstock, Josh	.251	259	41	65	7	1	3	33	8
Brown, Joe	.000	1	0	0	0	0	0	0	0
Burgos, Richey	.178	45	5	8	0	0	0	2	1
Butler, Kevin	.238	84	9	20	3	0	0	9	3
Cantu, Adrian	.276	337	50	93	22	2	5	53	9
*Chapman, Jack	.000	3	0	0	0	0	0	0	0
*Dye, Montana	.197	122	24	24	5	0	4	20	4
Faulkner, Nathan	.273	99	11	27	1	0	2	14	1
Garcia, Bubba	.184	114	10	21	5	0	2	7	0
Garcia, Travis	.289	367	63	106	23	2	15	69	16
George, Drew	.154	39	2	6	3	0	0	0	1
Mendoza, Jaziel	.237	76	7	18	7	1	1	14	0

INDEPENDENT LEAGUES

	AVG	AB	R	H	2B	3B	HR	RBI	SBP
Miles, Jimmy	.286	21	5	6	0	0	0	0	1
Poterson, Jonathan	.215	172	20	37	6	1	5	19	3
*Rocco, Mike	.000	2	0	0	0	0	0	0	0
Rodeghero, Zach	.207	82	4	17	5	0	0	8	1
Saylor, Andrew	.276	319	45	88	17	0	3	48	5
Spiers, Joe	.215	149	18	32	4	0	0	9	11
Spragg, Stephen	.000	1	0	0	0	0	0	0	0
Storrer, Travis	.242	244	33	59	7	1	8	27	3
Thomas, J.T.	.283	53	10	15	3	0	0	6	5
Verastegui, Jerry	.295	122	8	36	8	0	0	13	0
*Vernon, Rob	.171	35	7	6	0	1	0	2	4
*Vincent, Jeff	.234	312	49	73	13	7	3	30	23
Walker, Edwin	.500	2	0	1	0	0	0	1	0
Wiesler, Marty	.000	1	0	0	0	0	0	0	0

PITCHERS	W	L	ERA	G	SV	IP	H	BB	SO
Brown, Joe	4	2	3.74	35	5	43	36	17	47
Cameron, Taylor	1	1	8.42	14	0	36	63	14	28
Farden, Luke	0	0	4.32	2	0	8.1	9	5	8
Flanigan, Ryan	1	10	6.23	27	7	74	92	30	55
Gartley, Brian	3	11	6.88	23	1	103	119	53	79
Lopez, Chris	0	1	12.00	8	0	9	13	13	9
McCormick, Andrew	5	9	4.57	20	0	100	93	66	70
*McCullough, Brian	1	3	7.25	11	0	36	41	19	17
*Michael, Jeff	0	1	6.48	14	0	25	29	9	13
Polk, Andy	8	5	4.08	22	0	132	118	38	85
*Rocco, Mike	1	5	4.73	7	0	40	41	20	25
Schmieder, Bill	0	0	9.00	1	0	1	2	0	0
Spragg, Stephen	2	1	4.48	32	0	68	63	28	48
Vrzal, Tommy	2	2	7.20	17	0	40	57	22	41
Walker, Edwin	5	3	1.79	35	6	45	25	33	51
Wiesler, Marty	6	3	4.97	38	0	67	61	33	56

EVANSVILLE OTTERS

BATTERS	AVG	AB	R	H	2B	3B	HR	RBI	SBP
Bethel, Ryan	.294	248	42	73	14	0	5	39	4
Burton, Daniel	.269	279	42	75	15	0	5	28	9
Crencenzi, C	.143	7	1	1	0	0	1	1	0
Crescenzi, Chris	.217	115	19	25	5	0	4	18	0
Fonseca, Alex	.247	170	27	42	12	0	3	19	13
Gordon, Casey	.182	88	13	16	3	3	0	10	1
Haugen, Casey	.250	4	1	1	0	0	0	1	0
Hetherington, Luke	.305	164	29	50	8	2	4	24	8
Jaros, Nick	.258	124	16	32	6	1	2	12	0
Kampsen, Adam	.143	42	4	6	2	0	0	5	0
Mochizuki, Gered	.314	293	41	92	9	1	4	26	19
Omura, Isaac	.239	314	52	75	20	0	11	46	0
Pennino, Tom	.278	216	24	60	11	0	3	33	4
Petrie, Chris	.000	5	0	0	0	0	0	0	0
Pineda, Jose	.264	288	42	76	16	0	8	42	3
*Povey, Tycen	.230	152	22	35	12	1	2	18	2
*Randall, Justin	.323	189	25	61	9	1	0	24	5
Reyes, Christian	.252	147	15	37	5	1	4	28	1
*Reynolds, Matt	.200	15	2	3	0	0	0	0	0
*Salotti, Nick	.255	137	15	35	9	1	5	23	0
*Sullivan, Mike	.242	132	21	32	6	0	1	13	6
Wille, Matt	.347	75	9	26	2	0	4	5	0

PITCHERS	W	L	ERA	G	SV	IP	H	BB	SO
Bauer, Richard	7	5	6.10	18	0	80	111	49	51
Bethel, Ryan	0	0	0.00	1	0	1	0	1	1
Blanks, Bradley	4	1	2.18	33	0	41	40	16	28
Brinkmann, Matt	0	0	9.82	4	0	4	9	1	3
Causey, Mike	0	0	13.50	2	0	2	2	4	0
Damchuk, Mike	3	6	5.23	15	0	76	95	33	59
Facer, Tristan	0	1	4.10	24	0	26	23	10	17
*Foster, Ben	1	3	4.41	16	0	35	37	21	23
Hyde, Michael	1	6	8.41	8	0	35	57	18	29
Jordan, Justin	5	5	5.40	11	0	60	76	18	37
Lewis, Jonathan	0	1	1.42	19	9	19	12	11	24
*Michael, Jeff	2	0	6.91	9	0	14	22	5	13
Nehls, Brock	0	1	9.69	5	0	13	17	11	16
*Pawelczyk, Kyle	1	0	8.10	15	0	23	31	15	20
Phillips, Billy	0	4	4.30	11	1	46	41	14	34
Renfrow, Dustin	0	4	3.73	31	0	51	51	21	65

	W	L	ERA	G	SV	IP	H	BB	SO
Rogers, Adam	8	7	4.19	20	0	127	156	23	84
Smith, Justin	1	2	3.03	32	9	33	25	23	41
Thornton, Tom	1	2	4.40	9	0	29	39	9	22
Tuomi, Kai	3	5	4.29	10	0	63	63	17	45
Utley, Nick	2	4	3.70	42	1	56	45	36	49

FLORENCE FREEDOM

BATTERS	AVG	AB	R	H	2B	3B	HR	RBI	SB
Basham, Ryan	.278	345	54	96	24	1	11	53	5
Cheney, Don	.111	9	0	1	0	0	0	0	0
Dunham, Scott	.000	5	0	0	0	0	0	0	0
Dunning, Nick	.000	1	0	0	0	0	0	0	0
*Dye, Montana	.176	51	3	9	0	0	1	5	0
Gonzalez, Eddie	.213	136	14	29	4	0	3	16	1
Grogan, Timothy	.309	178	39	55	8	1	11	33	0
Guttridge, Dan	.265	34	4	9	3	0	0	1	1
Hackney, Matt	.236	110	21	26	7	1	1	11	4
Hartle, Travis	.143	7	3	1	1	0	0	2	0
Humphrey, Benjamin	.286	7	2	2	0	0	1	0	
Hunt, Kelly	.310	294	50	91	8	2	26	73	1
Landry, Jeff	.206	165	23	34	10	0	1	15	1
Lex, Joshua	.271	188	27	51	9	0	6	28	3
Lopez, Christian	.179	28	2	5	3	0	0	0	1
McKinney, Garth	.303	370	83	112	17	4	18	65	28
Molina, Angel	.327	349	74	114	22	1	22	71	14
Mottram, William	.300	327	48	98	19	3	10	53	6
Padilla, Eric	.284	74	7	21	0	0	0	7	1
*Randall, Justin	.209	115	27	24	3	2	0	11	2
*Salotti, Nick	.338	133	22	45	7	0	7	25	1
Washington, Johnny	.186	59	12	11	1	0	1	7	1
Welch, John	.280	328	41	92	16	2	10	40	4

PITCHERS	W	L	ERA	G	SV	IP	H	BB	SO
Banks, Demetrius	0	0	4.74	9	0	19	21	16	20
Brandon, Tyler	0	0	1.04	5	0	9	8	5	6
Bruns, Josh	5	2	7.14	10	0	52	65	15	41
Canizal, Joaquin	0	1	27.00	1	0	1	2	2	0
Castle, Cody	1	3	3.71	31	14	34	32	15	31
Clark, Andy	10	2	3.36	19	1	83	60	26	79
Cross, David	0	0	5.40	2	0	3	7	0	1
Delabar, Steven	0	0	2.84	4	0	6	6	2	7
Dunning, Nick	1	1	5.50	5	0	18	11	11	13
Eberhart, Chris	0	2	6.28	24	0	29	31	12	19
Gianini, Matt	1	1	11.74	6	0	8	12	5	6
Gonzalez, Eddie	0	0	0.00	2	0	5	5	1	4
Hamlett, Brandon	0	0	1.08	9	0	17	9	11	13
Ibanez, Yosandry	3	2	2.01	36	0	45	29	17	55
Ingoglia, Christopher	6	8	4.38	29	2	125	129	39	132
*Lee, Gary	3	3	3.99	7	0	47	43	16	26
Lotito, Brent	2	0	4.38	5	0	25	24	9	11
Ludwig, James	0	0	9.00	4	0	4	6	8	0
Morrison, Ryan	0	0	0.00	1	0	0	2	2	0
*Quijano, Alain	0	1	5.40	18	0	33	42	16	29
*Rocco, Michael	0	4	7.36	8	0	22	34	8	21
Saul, Everett	7	7	5.44	19	0	81	97	28	73
Schon, Andy	0	1	5.95	5	0	20	28	11	20
Shanahan, Liam	6	7	4.52	17	0	100	113	32	53
Shao, Stephen	1	4	5.54	24	0	39	41	18	27
Stadanlick, Ryan	0	0	13.50	2	0	2	2	4	2
Villalona, Bryan	1	0	4.39	5	0	27	28	8	20

GATEWAY GRIZZLIES

BATTERS	AVG	AB	R	H	2B	3B	HR	RBI	SBP
*Alonso, John	.208	96	12	20	7	0	2	14	0
Barbato, Al	.219	32	7	7	1	1	0	0	0
Breyman, Mike	.299	338	66	101	27	3	24	86	0
Campbell, Michael	.297	290	46	86	12	1	11	59	2
*Chapman, Jack	.125	24	0	3	1	0	0	2	0
Donovan, Kyle	.000	6	1	0	0	0	0	0	0
Draper, Breck	.165	97	16	16	3	0	1	6	0
Falk, Matthew	.000	1	0	0	0	0	0	0	0
*Fultz, Travis	.220	50	10	11	3	0	3	6	1
Holdren, Stephen	.284	292	63	83	14	0	14	46	2
*House, Kevin	.133	60	5	8	1	1	1	1	2

	AVG	AB	R	H	2B	3B	HR	RBI	SBP
*Imwalle, Matt	.200	30	4	6	0	0	0	1	0
*Keene, Willie	.259	85	10	22	4	0	2	11	2
Kerins, Alex	.272	151	20	41	9	2	4	25	0
Lisk, Charlie	.313	326	63	102	12	2	24	64	6
Malone, Ryne	.296	196	39	58	12	1	9	35	4
McQuigg, Carter	.255	137	29	35	6	0	11	26	7
Minor, Robbie	.257	354	53	91	14	2	2	27	29
*Owens, Ricky	.133	15	0	2	0	0	0	0	0
*Paula, Manny	.266	177	16	47	10	1	3	29	1
Pecora, Chris	.256	164	28	42	5	3	2	14	10
Peters, Brandon	.350	20	5	7	0	0	2	9	0
*Reynolds, Matt	.158	19	3	3	1	1	0	0	1
*Rothford, Chad	.357	28	4	10	2	0	1	7	0
Saltzgaber, Ryan	.171	35	7	6	0	0	0	2	0
Scaperotta, Joseph	.209	86	13	18	7	0	4	15	1
Scott, Brandon	.200	35	3	7	0	0	0	4	0
Shelton, Kyle	.222	9	0	2	0	0	0	0	0
Thomas, Scott	.091	11	0	1	0	0	0	0	0
*Vincent, Jeff	.345	29	7	10	0	1	1	3	2
*Wilson, Josh	.154	13	1	2	0	0	0	0	0
Wright, Bobby	.300	10	0	3	0	0	0	1	0

PITCHERS	W	L	ERA	G	SV	IP	H	BB	SO
Blacksher, Derek	10	8	4.57	19	0	128	120	49	110
Boeschen, Joel	5	2	3.17	30	5	48	39	22	46
Breyman, Mike	0	0	0.00	1	0	0	0	0	1
*Castrignano, Mike	0	0	5.40	2	0	2	1	2	1
Collis, Devin	2	1	3.41	6	0	37	24	12	30
Dessau, Erik	4	5	4.65	13	0	79	93	24	43
Draper, Breck	0	0	5.40	1	0	5	4	2	3
Falk, Matthew	1	4	6.66	5	0	26	28	21	20
Fuda, Giorgio	0	0	0.00	2	0	2	1	7	1
Ganzen, Jon	0	0	21.60	3	0	3	9	0	4
Gray, Zack	0	3	1.94	31	9	42	29	26	27
Hammons, Kevin	0	2	8.10	5	0	17	20	16	12
Herman, Jason	0	1	36.00	1	0	1	3	1	0
Hertel, James	0	1	13.50	3	0	3	5	3	2
Kalb, Jon	0	0	27.00	2	0	2	6	1	1
Lilly, Justin	7	5	3.90	16	0	88	87	31	49
Mavroulis, Coby	3	0	5.18	25	0	33	21	21	20
Merricks, Alex	0	0	6.75	5	0	5	4	5	5
Revelette, Adam	2	5	4.54	19	0	79	89	36	46
Ridener, Eric	5	2	3.84	38	5	59	47	30	73
Romero, Robert	0	0	6.52	11	4	10	8	11	11
Santerre, Josh	0	0	19.64	3	0	4	7	5	3
Scott, Brandon	0	0	2.08	2	0	4	2	5	4
Seibert, Shaun	4	1	4.28	12	0	27	29	13	29
Sprouse, Shannon	1	0	4.82	7	0	9	9	3	8
White, Demetri	0	1	4.80	15	0	30	23	37	43
Williams, Brandon	7	4	3.65	17	0	89	92	33	62

KALAMAZOO KINGS

BATTERS	AVG	AB	R	H	2B	3B	HR	RBI	SBP
Achberger, Nick	.238	42	7	10	4	0	2	12	2
Anderson, Brandon	.294	282	69	83	8	3	8	32	34
Araiza, Jorge	.263	274	48	72	14	2	3	37	6
Bowling, Casey	.000	6	0	0	0	0	0	0	0
Frazee, Joseph	.117	60	8	7	1	1	1	5	2
*Fultz, Travis	.268	71	8	19	3	1	1	9	1
Grose, Jeff	.252	313	62	79	9	5	5	54	9
Hudgins, Matt	.209	196	30	41	5	0	10	34	0
Kmiecik, Kyle	.232	297	56	69	16	1	8	45	12
Makonnen, Destan	.269	145	24	39	11	0	3	18	0
Moley, Randy	.200	40	13	8	3	0	2	8	2
Murphy, Brendan	.332	331	46	110	24	1	16	77	2
*Owens, Ricky	.333	12	0	4	1	0	0	1	0
Padilla, Omar	.167	6	2	1	0	0	0	2	0
Ramos, Joseph	.281	363	67	102	19	2	10	65	45
*Rothford, Chad	.288	111	22	32	9	1	4	22	3
Russell, Mike	.285	355	67	101	21	1	19	75	1
Williams, Simon	.282	248	60	70	6	3	20	57	15
Youngblood, Cody	.107	28	5	3	0	0	1	1	5

PITCHERS	W	L	ERA	G	SV	IP	H	BB	SO
Additon, Ryan	0	0	0.00	2	0	0	1	4	0

PITCHERS	W	L	ERA	G	SV	IP	H	BB	SO
Babb, Rich	1	2	3.33	24	2	27	31	18	19
Baerlocher, Dan	7	3	3.59	36	1	43	25	18	51
Brownell, John	11	2	3.87	19	0	119	118	45	86
Carrington, Bobby	0	0	5.56	9	0	11	9	11	9
Carroll, Will	0	0	9.00	4	0	6	12	4	3
Catanese, Joe	4	3	3.16	38	1	57	50	31	58
Chad, Brian	0	0	9.64	2	0	5	4	4	2
Davis, Kevin	1	3	8.71	9	0	10	13	13	7
DiPietro, Joe	7	5	3.28	21	0	107	95	40	65
Duquette, Fred	0	0	40.50	3	0	1	1	5	1
Holm, Jimmy	1	1	6.00	10	0	18	21	9	6
Honce, Mike	0	0	30.86	3	0	2	6	5	1
Lare, Trenton	8	5	4.13	21	0	129	130	42	89
Long, Jeff	9	4	3.83	20	0	125	130	36	57
*Mann, Sam	1	1	7.89	5	0	22	33	4	6
Mongiardini, Michael	0	0	7.27	4	0	9	5	11	6
Parillo, Brandon	1	3	2.93	32	20	31	25	13	30
Pellegrine, David	1	1	5.40	3	0	8	5	13	13
Robert, Bernard	4	2	3.79	9	0	57	41	29	37
Rodgers, Dominique	0	1	12.00	5	0	6	12	4	4
Troop, Jon	2	0	3.00	17	1	27	20	14	24
Welsh, Joseph	2	0	4.64	10	0	21	23	14	11

MIDWEST SLIDERS

BATTERS	AVG	AB	R	H	2B	3B	HR	RBI	SBP
Albano, Anthony	.258	356	36	92	29	2	8	52	1
*Barrone, Ben	.210	62	8	13	2	1	3	11	0
Bertolini, Dan	.186	70	6	13	1	0	1	5	0
Colon, Angel	.133	30	0	4	0	0	0	3	0
Contreras, Lester	.248	125	17	31	6	1	2	20	1
Deluca, Sam	.250	256	31	64	12	1	5	23	4
Ferguson, Troy	.241	141	13	34	5	0	1	20	12
Graham, Jason	.190	21	2	4	1	0	0	3	0
Hightower, Cody	.128	39	5	5	1	0	0	0	0
Hine, Robbie	.204	201	24	41	5	1	0	13	3
Kidd, James	.083	12	1	1	1	0	0	0	0
Knoble, Jonnie	.257	272	43	70	11	1	1	16	26
Lombardi, Dominick	.263	194	28	51	9	6	7	36	3
Magrass, Miguel	.252	318	48	80	11	1	11	41	3
Pace, Zack	.252	314	52	79	9	2	3	30	26
Reese, Eric	.206	141	15	29	3	1	0	13	8
Shaft, Barrett	.195	82	7	16	3	0	1	6	0
Snell, Sean	.272	81	8	22	8	0	2	14	0
*Vernon, Rob	.257	74	7	19	2	0	1	5	0
Vickers, Bryan	.212	306	34	65	12	0	13	45	1
Villamar, Oscar	.053	19	0	1	0	0	0	0	0
Westman, Ryley	.184	114	12	21	7	0	0	7	1
Zaneski, Zach	.250	4	0	1	0	0	0	0	0

PITCHERS	W	L	ERA	G	SV	IP	H	BB	SO
Albury, James	2	2	6.28	28	1	53	53	36	54
Ayala, Albert	2	3	7.99	7	0	33	47	25	25
*Barrone, Ben	0	0	9.00	3	0	3	4	3	2
Bigda, Drew	0	0	8.31	18	0	17	20	20	20
Dahlin, Matt	1	4	5.54	10	0	37	53	13	26
Dandridge, Jon	0	5	4.80	38	2	54	49	40	46
Doan, Joey	1	4	7.34	8	0	34	48	17	25
*Dow, Jeremy	2	7	7.84	9	0	41	51	34	34
Fiallo, Javier	0	0	3.86	2	0	5	6	5	4
Kearcher, Kyle	7	7	4.35	19	0	114	133	24	107
MacFarlane, Ryan	4	5	2.92	19	0	89	74	38	85
Myers, Ryan	0	2	3.92	8	0	21	22	16	14
O'Hara, Patrick	1	2	6.75	10	0	27	39	10	25
Oakes, Earl	5	2	3.94	38	14	46	37	25	64
Phillips, Dale	0	1	5.40	7	0	7	10	5	4
Porter, Scott	0	0	15.00	3	0	3	3	3	2
Ravenscraft, Shawn	0	4	10.55	10	0	21	33	18	10
Rubio, Chris	1	9	5.38	27	0	74	87	46	49
Suchowiecki, Mark	2	8	8.00	21	0	75	107	53	61
Sveda, Shane	1	2	5.15	20	1	37	40	26	32
Vickers, Bryan	0	0	6.75	3	0	4	6	3	3
Whelen, Stephen	0	0	7.80	6	0	15	24	7	8

RIVER CITY RASCALS

BATTERS	AVG	AB	R	H	2B	3B	HR	RBI	SBP
Allred, Steven	.500	2	1	1	0	0	0	0	0
Baker, Jimmy	.260	50	8	13	2	0	2	8	0
Barganier, Luke	.304	372	54	113	20	5	5	55	12
Basom, Will	.312	93	10	29	10	0	0	6	0
Bettis, Andy	.143	28	1	4	0	0	0	3	1
Curry, Dale	.000	1	0	0	0	0	0	0	0
David, Derek	.000	3	0	0	0	0	0	0	0
DeBoer, Jacob	.217	161	20	35	5	1	1	19	6
Fogelson, Scott	.000	0	1	0	0	0	0	0	0
Hough, Brad	.270	356	59	96	25	1	9	60	24
Laurent, Phil	.248	335	56	83	13	2	12	47	4
Logan, Brian	.000	0	1	0	0	0	0	0	0
Marshall, Curt	.222	63	4	14	3	0	1	2	0
Maycock, Dan	.242	99	22	24	6	0	7	13	4
Miller, Jeff	.283	350	57	99	19	1	15	66	1
Mosby, Bobby	.245	139	22	34	7	0	5	21	0
Newman, Carlos	.091	11	1	1	0	0	1	2	0
Phelps, Greg	.222	9	3	2	0	0	0	0	1
Raniere, Chris	.285	221	31	63	7	0	11	36	5
*Rosa, Randy	.239	46	8	11	6	0	1	7	0
Stone, Greg	.218	243	26	53	3	1	1	24	1
Sweet, Andrew	.316	310	55	98	17	0	5	48	1
Van Slyke, A.J.	.274	106	18	29	3	1	6	17	4
Wehrle, Ryan	.267	232	39	62	14	0	8	32	4
*Wilson, Josh	.000	8	0	0	0	0	0	0	0

PITCHERS	W	L	ERA	G	SV	IP	H	BB	SO
Arnold, David	1	1	4.32	6	0	17	17	7	9
Ashner, Ryan	1	1	2.11	14	1	21	21	4	18
Benacka, Mike	3	0	0.35	22	13	26	10	17	51
Brockman, Ben	0	0	18.00	1	0	1	3	2	0
*Carrasco, Armando	2	1	14.29	9	0	6	9	6	5
*Castrignano, Mike	2	3	6.68	13	0	31	38	19	25
Clem, Chris	8	8	5.65	22	0	116	151	47	78
Corbett, Dustin	0	1	7.23	10	0	24	27	22	18
*Estrella, Luis	0	0	7.64	16	0	18	24	9	20
Evers, Patrick	2	0	1.50	5	0	12	10	4	15
Fogelson, Scott	5	10	5.33	23	0	98	108	39	79
*Jones, Desmond	0	0	1.93	5	0	5	2	6	5
Laber, Jake	4	3	4.01	11	0	67	60	39	55
*Lee, Gary	2	0	5.72	25	0	50	65	15	33
Logan, Brian	2	2	4.73	36	2	32	28	28	34
Maycock, Dan	0	0	3.38	3	0	3	3	2	0
Miller, Jonathan	3	5	3.76	31	9	91	86	37	87
Powers, Daniel	7	6	5.02	18	0	104	122	39	112
Powl, Chris	0	0	18.00	2	0	1	3	1	0
Stringer, Tim	0	0	19.06	6	0	6	11	12	6
Tollefson, Adam	3	2	4.57	23	0	45	47	19	44
Trevino, Toro	2	4	8.91	7	0	34	51	17	26
White, Adam	0	2	4.45	16	0	32	35	15	23

ROCKFORD RIVERHAWKS

BATTERS	AVG	AB	R	H	2B	3B	HR	RBI	SBP
Anthonsen, Joe	.352	384	79	135	17	3	2	50	29
Baitinger, Boe	.175	40	11	7	3	0	0	2	4
Borman, Matt	.245	94	21	23	5	0	2	15	2
Bringelson, Roy	.000	1	0	0	0	0	0	0	0
Brooks, Jonathan	.258	291	46	75	13	3	9	48	16
Burrows, Greg	.236	106	13	25	6	2	4	16	13
Cohen, Brandon	.190	137	15	26	4	0	3	12	0
Cook, Bryan	.143	28	4	4	2	0	2	4	0
Czyz, Ryan	.250	20	2	5	0	0	1	2	1
Davis, Aaron	.247	97	18	24	1	1	3	9	7
Dempsey, Joe	.245	53	12	13	2	0	0	6	2
Dulkowski, Marc	.000	1	0	0	0	0	0	0	0
Dutton, Brad	.311	341	48	106	19	1	4	49	11
Gonzalez, Tony	.312	173	23	54	12	2	5	26	5
Hulsey, Lucas	.161	31	6	5	2	0	1	3	0
James, Jason	.350	380	55	133	30	2	13	74	11
*Knapp, Robbie	.335	170	29	57	11	1	4	26	1
Kowalski, Ryan	.167	42	6	7	1	0	0	4	6

SOUTHERN ILLINOIS MINERS (continued)

BATTERS	AVG	AB	R	H	2B	3B	HR	RBI	SBP
Mazurek, Matt	.271	221	32	60	8	0	1	30	16
McArdle, Ryan	.000	10	1	0	0	0	0	2	0
Meier, Brad	.053	19	0	1	0	0	0	0	0
Pickerell, Steven	.273	33	11	9	2	0	2	9	0
*Raber, Christopher	.275	160	25	44	7	0	2	14	8
Recuenco, Rob	.000	10	0	0	0	0	0	0	0
Rivera, Carlos	.277	94	8	26	7	0	1	9	5
Rosa, Christian	.091	11	1	1	0	0	0	0	1
Sabates, Robert	.295	122	22	36	6	0	6	29	0
Santos, Nick	.190	21	1	4	0	0	0	0	0
Scripture, Mike	.204	98	8	20	1	0	1	9	1
*Stang, Corey	.210	62	11	13	3	0	1	5	2
Talbert, Scott	.238	21	4	5	1	0	1	5	0
Thamann, Jeff	.000	8	0	0	0	0	0	0	0
Thomas, Brett	.206	34	4	7	1	0	0	4	2

PITCHERS	W	L	ERA	G	SV	IP	H	BB	SO
Balteff, Shawn	2	2	2.73	27	1	26	13	21	37
Bauer, Garrett	10	6	2.98	21	0	148	114	78	151
Borman, Matt	0	0	11.57	3	0	5	12	2	2
Bringelson, Roy	1	3	5.17	37	5	47	60	20	32
Brnardic, Ryan	0	0	8.10	6	0	7	8	10	2
Cramphin, James	3	4	6.17	34	9	58	56	45	59
*Dempsey, Kyle	3	0	2.96	9	0	27	22	12	19
DiBlasi, Matt	0	0	8.10	7	1	7	9	6	3
Dulkowski, Marc	0	1	7.84	11	0	10	12	7	12
Enderle, Matt	4	2	3.48	35	0	62	64	26	22
Flattery, Tim	2	5	5.84	18	2	45	51	31	30
Himes, Drew	1	0	4.15	12	0	13	20	4	9
James, Jason	1	4	5.13	7	0	33	36	26	18
Jarman, Josh	0	0	13.50	2	0	1	4	4	2
Langlois, Chris	0	0	8.10	4	0	10	10	7	5
Marcum, Kyffin	6	1	4.78	29	1	32	21	14	33
Marksbury, Mike	0	0	10.13	4	2	3	3	2	4
*McKenzie, Marcus	0	0	2.57	5	0	7	6	7	7
McTamney, Mike	4	3	4.53	9	0	54	54	13	50
Paduch, Jim	3	6	5.07	12	0	71	76	34	59
*Pawelczyk, Kyle	0	0	12.46	4	0	4	6	5	3
Rasiarmos, George	1	0	2.08	4	0	4	3	6	6
Rucker, Peden	3	3	4.98	15	1	56	76	21	31
Schutt, Chris	2	5	6.00	15	1	69	77	35	56
Sinclair, Taylor	1	0	1.93	4	0	23	13	7	23
Wilson, Mathew	1	2	4.91	4	0	22	21	15	18

SOUTHERN ILLINOIS MINERS

BATTERS	AVG	AB	R	H	2B	3B	HR	RBI	SBP
Akashian, Brendan	.302	205	36	62	13	1	1	32	2
*Arnett, Brad	.277	47	15	13	5	1	1	9	1
Bennett, Andrew	.227	22	1	5	0	0	0	3	0
Dorn, Tim	.299	354	67	106	20	0	23	83	3
Farkes, Josh	.279	61	13	17	2	1	0	8	1
Goldsmith, Bradley	.292	65	13	19	1	1	2	14	5
Gronkowski, Grodon	.000	1	0	0	0	0	0	0	0
Guzman, Juan	.138	29	2	4	2	0	0	1	3
*House, Kevin	.316	19	6	6	0	0	1	2	6
Jones, Brandon	.276	388	56	107	24	1	18	75	2
*Keene, Willie	.287	202	34	58	7	3	12	37	5
Koski, Kevin	.285	239	46	68	7	3	3	19	16
Lairson, Tyler	.271	48	6	13	1	1	1	8	0
McMurran, Jake	.000	1	0	0	0	0	0	0	0
Metropoulos, Joey	.315	340	74	107	21	0	20	66	1
Miller, Andre	.267	60	11	16	1	1	0	5	11
Miller, Brad	.310	168	34	52	11	0	5	32	1
Milner, Beau	.154	13	4	2	0	0	0	0	0
*Paula, Manny	.232	69	8	16	3	0	3	9	0
*Rosa, Randy	.289	45	9	13	1	0	0	5	0
Roth, Tony	.290	169	38	49	7	1	5	25	6
Scanzano, Mike	.256	320	50	82	21	2	1	38	3
Smith, Jake	.289	83	8	24	5	0	1	17	0
Suttle, Eric	.285	270	45	77	8	5	4	36	9
Victor, Mike	.272	81	11	22	4	0	1	12	0

PITCHERS	W	L	ERA	G	SV	IP	H	BB	SO
Allen, Chris	6	2	3.39	13	0	61	63	20	43
Bailey, Griffin	5	5	2.79	47	6	58	58	10	44

	W	L	ERA	G	SV	IP	H	BB	SO
Biddle, George	0	0	2.89	6	0	9	12	6	6
Bird, Ryan	13	3	2.48	21	0	123	97	45	152
Cannon, Brett	0	0	2.25	5	0	4	6	3	3
*Carrasco, Armando	2	2	2.87	32	6	38	29	16	32
Dixon, Curt	0	0	15.09	7	0	11	22	6	6
Dooley, Kevin	1	0	3.00	2	0	3	1	1	4
Dorn, Tim	0	0	27.00	1	0	1	2	4	2
*Dow, Jeremy	0	3	5.40	8	1	28	31	12	23
*Estrella, Luis	0	1	8.22	3	0	8	12	8	6
Farkes, Josh	0	0	0.00	1	0	1	2	1	1
Hope, Travis	0	1	2.45	7	2	7	8	1	6
Little, Chris	9	4	2.90	20	0	121	106	35	94
Lovell, Benjamin	0	0	6.75	2	0	4	7	1	3
*McKenzie, Marcus	1	0	5.95	8	0	20	24	8	9
McMurran, Jake	4	3	2.82	46	1	73	52	35	61
Neal, Josh	0	0	4.15	3	0	4	3	3	2
Phelps, Mike	1	0	0.40	17	3	23	13	7	39
Prather, Bo	0	0	1.93	4	0	5	1	5	6
Price, Reid	2	2	4.72	7	0	34	34	13	32
Quigley, Ryan	0	0	10.29	2	0	7	9	4	5
Roark, Tanner	0	2	21.41	3	0	10	23	9	11
Roque, Ulysses	0	2	5.25	2	0	12	12	2	2
Scarpetta, Brett	9	3	3.81	15	0	87	83	30	73
Starnes, Nick	3	4	4.74	20	0	74	68	30	39
Wilburn, Brian	0	0	3.75	7	0	12	13	6	8
Zavada, Clay	2	1	1.72	12	4	16	7	4	22

TRAVERSE CITY BEACH BUMS

BATTERS	AVG	AB	R	H	2B	3B	HR	RBI	SBP
Blackburn, Joe	.241	29	3	7	1	1	1	5	0
Brown, Jeff	.211	204	27	43	10	1	2	29	1
Brummett III, John	.091	11	1	1	0	0	0	0	0
Epping, Michael	.284	341	53	97	19	3	8	53	38
Goetz, Mike	.314	245	46	77	14	1	0	22	14
*Imwalle, Matt	.194	62	7	12	2	2	0	8	1
Joseph, Alfred	.143	21	2	3	1	0	0	3	0
Kalter, Zack	.286	199	27	57	7	1	0	16	2
Kottke, Ryan	.059	17	0	1	0	0	0	0	0
Lessler, Damon	.146	41	6	6	2	0	0	5	0
Maunus, Kyle	.253	344	54	87	14	1	10	53	4
Miller, Bradley	.244	299	37	73	17	4	6	44	8
Newton, Eric	.183	142	10	26	3	0	4	16	1
Perry, Patrick	.261	299	42	78	18	0	3	37	3
*Povey, Tycen	.000	10	0	0	0	0	0	0	0
Roblin, Brad	.232	246	21	57	15	1	3	30	8
Stevens, Jeff	.333	9	2	3	0	0	0	1	0
Welker, Reed	.167	36	5	6	1	0	0	6	0
Whitesides, Jake	.256	273	40	70	15	2	8	49	10
Young, Stephen	.249	338	58	84	11	2	1	24	33
Bostelman, Brett		6	53.81	19	0	106	101	45	63

PITCHERS	W	L	ERA	G	SV	IP	H	BB	SO
Cole, Zachary	0	0	10.13	6	0	5	7	9	8
Cryer, Bryan	0	0	6.07	4	0	13	11	8	13
Curles, Weston	1	4	6.46	6	0	24	33	7	4
Dillard, Matt	1	0	6.75	5	0	7	10	2	2
Gehring, Ryan	5	9	2.71	19	0	126	118	32	69
Gjeldum, Ted	2	3	3.60	46	3	50	42	20	55
Haldis, Jon	1	3	14.90	4	0	10	16	8	3
Kalter, Zack	0	0	5.40	1	0	2	1	2	1
King, J.T.	2	5	6.75	8	0	39	55	17	13
Ledford, James	0	0	9.45	7	0	7	12	5	5
Locke, Jared	3	1	3.55	38	3	51	38	27	52
McEneaney, Peter	3	2	3.33	29	1	49	41	20	28
Nathanson, David	12	3	2.28	17	0	114	99	20	67
Pepper, Nick	2	3	2.70	41	2	40	35	15	18
Rembisz, Bryan	3	1	2.60	7	0	45	38	7	33
Roberts, Steve	3	1	2.33	14	0	58	42	26	45
Takashima, Mike	0	0	4.08	12	0	18	15	6	16
Taylor, Drew	2	1	2.77	6	0	39	30	12	30
Trausch, Matt	1	1	2.63	9	0	14	11	6	9
Williams, Jeff	3	4	3.40	39	15	42	31	18	49

WASHINGTON WILD THINGS

BATTERS	AVG	AB	R	H	2B	3B	HR	RBI	SBP
Alberts, Tim	.289	135	29	39	5	1	11	38	1
*Alonso, John	.259	27	4	7	1	0	1	5	0
*Arnett, Brad	.247	170	28	42	10	1	5	28	1
Beachum, Jeffrey	.294	51	4	15	2	0	0	8	2
Butch, Phil	.238	260	48	62	5	2	0	23	25
Butia, Michael	.174	23	2	4	2	0	0	3	0
Carrara, Christopher	.285	228	53	65	6	0	1	21	19
Dempsey, Jacob	.310	365	68	113	31	4	17	88	0
Eachues, Josh	.215	135	13	29	4	1	0	27	1
Geric, Josh	.111	18	1	2	0	1	0	1	0
Grandstrand, Brett	.295	295	48	87	17	2	4	47	13
Haran, Gerard	.224	76	8	17	4	0	4	17	0
Heffron, Adam	.195	41	5	8	1	0	0	4	0
Hoisington, Drew	.162	136	13	22	5	0	2	14	6
*Knapp, Robbie	.296	142	21	42	10	1	4	31	0
Messner, Nate	.261	295	59	77	21	5	7	47	5
O'Brien, Pat	.238	80	13	19	3	0	2	7	1
Quintana, Rene	.255	51	5	13	0	0	0	6	0
*Raber, Christopher	.272	125	28	34	9	2	1	18	10
Rochelle, Kris	.211	71	11	15	1	0	0	8	0
Sidick, Chris	.311	379	77	118	16	9	11	45	21
Sutton, Matt	.270	126	21	34	7	3	3	26	1
*Vernon, Rob	.000	9	1	0	0	0	0	0	0

PITCHERS	W	L	ERA	G	SV	IP	H	BB	SO
Austin, Rick	2	0	2.05	18	1	22	15	13	16
Bachman, Corey	1	1	2.19	7	0	12	9	4	8
Baldwin, Burke	0	1	20.65	5	0	6	14	7	5
D'Alessandro, Joe	3	2	2.52	20	4	25	21	12	26
*Dempsey, Kyle	1	1	5.02	12	0	29	25	22	24
Dunn, Brooks	2	6	3.32	14	0	81	82	22	58
Eachues, Josh	0	0	0.00	2	0	1	0	1	3
*Eisenberg, Michael	1	3	4.38	5	0	25	25	11	20
Groh, Zach	3	3	4.79	9	0	36	40	12	31
Heisel, Ian	1	1	5.82	16	4	17	20	10	16
Hollenbeck, J.J.	6	6	4.51	21	0	122	127	47	82
Horvath, Dan	4	1	3.63	38	0	45	44	16	33
Ledbetter, Aaron	9	6	5.10	21	0	138	145	33	101
Leonard, John	0	1	10.34	9	0	16	21	10	15
*Mann, Sam	2	2	5.59	18	0	29	37	8	18
Maradeo, Matthew	1	1	4.35	27	2	41	34	28	41
Reese, Kevin	0	1	12.08	10	0	13	25	8	10
Restivo, Matt	1	0	6.23	8	0	13	19	7	7
Rivera, Chris	2	3	5.49	16	1	41	47	27	21
Schellinger, Michael	9	6	3.95	21	0	114	101	29	84
Stidfole, Alan	0	2	21.86	5	0	7	21	5	3
Wladyka, James	0	1	6.17	3	0	12	18	10	8
Yurish, Matt	0	0	6.75	3	0	4	3	7	5

WINDY CITY THUNDERBOLTS

BATTERS	AVG	AB	R	H	2B	3B	HR	RBI	SBP
Amyx, Brett	.304	217	31	66	9	1	6	35	0
*Barrone, Ben	.175	103	13	18	2	0	4	13	1
Billak, Scott	.291	309	57	90	17	1	7	55	5
Brooks, Patrick	.250	12	2	3	1	0	0	1	0
Coe, Doug	.227	66	16	15	5	0	2	13	0
Coles, Mike	.302	361	68	109	26	0	12	75	25
Davis, Marcus	.133	15	3	2	0	0	0	1	0
Giblin, Ryan	.000	4	0	0	0	0	0	0	0
Grau, Philip	.071	14	2	1	0	0	0	1	0
Hawke, Phillip	.309	343	69	106	16	0	22	73	3
Hayes, LaFringe	.333	9	2	3	1	0	0	1	0
Horn, Josh	.290	366	63	106	17	2	7	43	9
Johnson, Billy	.000	3	1	0	0	0	0	0	0
Klepps, Chris	.183	60	7	11	1	0	1	5	1
Long, Wesley	.331	369	66	122	20	0	11	71	16
Lowey, Jason	.000	2	0	0	0	0	0	0	0
McBratney, Mark	.190	42	10	8	1	0	1	10	1
Mejia, Gilberto	.282	326	67	92	13	4	8	38	34
Noles, Kevin	.000	6	0	0	0	0	0	0	0
Ramon, Amos	.256	78	18	20	7	0	0	11	0

INDEPENDENT LEAGUES

	AVG	AB	R	H	2B	3B	HR	RBI	SB
Sawyer, Danny	.219	183	33	40	10	0	9	35	0
Sims, Michael	.000	7	1	0	0	0	0	0	0
*Stang, Corey	.245	106	15	26	3	2	2	17	0
*Sullivan, Mike	.363	171	40	62	12	4	3	27	8
Tellam, Justin	.284	116	22	33	5	0	5	23	0

PITCHERS	W	L	ERA	G	SV	IP	H	BB	SO
*Barrone, Ben	1	0	1.80	4	0	5	5	4	5
Dominick, Adam	4	2	5.89	19	0	44	49	14	47
*Eisenberg, Michael	0	1	4.50	4	0	20	17	17	18
Findlay, Bobby	0	0	10.38	4	0	9	10	10	3
Flake, Stephen	10	3	4.04	19	0	118	116	55	83
*Foster, Ben	0	0	18.00	2	0	2	6	2	1
Fussell, Eric	0	3	18.90	3	0	7	14	4	5
Garner, Brandon	0	0	2.57	8	1	7	2	5	5
Hess, Isaac	7	6	3.91	32	0	90	72	42	110
Hunton, Brock	0	0	11.08	3	0	13	16	10	4
Jernstad, Matt	1	0	1.29	3	0	7	3	4	6
*Jones, Desmond	2	2	6.89	16	0	16	13	24	20
Kelsey, Tyler	0	0	7.11	1	0	6	6	4	7
Lowey, Jason	3	1	4.16	33	6	63	56	25	67
Lowey, Josh	1	0	12.91	7	0	8	11	12	14
*McCullough, Brian	2	2	2.37	14	0	19	13	6	15
O'Neal, Charles	0	1	8.68	7	0	9	13	10	5
Petty, Matt	3	5	3.72	36	15	39	33	18	45
*Quijano, Alain	1	0	3.45	17	1	16	14	5	20
Ramon, Amos	5	4	4.65	19	0	101	113	24	46
Ratliff, Ted	4	1	3.44	9	0	50	46	18	22
Rebyanski, Anthony	3	2	5.89	38	0	37	34	29	41
Remenowsky, Dan	1	0	1.69	2	0	11	10	3	12
Schlecker, Derek	0	0	9.00	2	0	3	1	1	1
Sims, Dallas	1	0	6.59	4	0	14	11	10	9
Stout, Ross	11	3	2.57	19	0	133	104	39	121
Zweber, Kyle	0	0	7.71	7	1	9	10	12	6

GOLDEN LEAGUE

If you like offense, then you'll love the Golden Baseball League. If you like low-scoring games, you might want to look elsewhere. Thanks to some impressive hitters, some small ballparks and plenty of locales where the ball carries well, the Golden Baseball League made the Major League's 1930 season look like 1968. No team in the league had an ERA under 5.00, and St. George finished the season with a team ERA of 8.00 while finishing only two games under .500. Darryl Brinkley, Baseball America's 2007 Independent Leagues Player of the Year, hit .351 and finished only 10th in the batting race. It was fitting the hitter with the gaudiest of the gaudy stats, Orange County outfielder Patrick Breen, led his team to the league title. Breen led the league in batting (.396), home runs (28) was second in RBIs (97) and led the league in on-base percentage (.509) and slugging percentage (.825). He managed to help the Flyers to a league title despite being knocked out of a semifinal game when he ran full speed into an outfield wall. Breen broke a couple of ribs, but was back in the lineup as the Flyers beat Calgary for the title. Not surprisingly, Breen was named the league's most valuable player. Chico's Trevor Caughey earned the pitcher of the year honor. Caughey's 2.51 ERA was nearly a run better than anyone else in the league.

FIRST HALF

NORTH DIVISION	W	L	PCT	GB
Calgary	26	18	.591	—
Edmonton	22	22	.500	4
Reno	18	26	.409	8
Chico	15	27	.341	11
SOUTH DIVISION				
Orange County	28	15	.651	—
Yuma	24	19	.558	4
Long Beach	22	22	.500	7.5
St. George	18	26	.409	10.5

SECOND HALF

NORTH DIVISION	W	L	PCT	GB
Edmonton	29	15	.659	—
Calgary	19	24	.442	9.5
Chico	19	25	.432	10
Reno	12	32	.271	17
SOUTH DIVISION	**W**	**L**	**PCT**	**GB**
Long Beach	26	18	.591	—

	W	L	PCT	GB
St. George	25	19	.568	1
Orange County	23	20	.535	2.5
Yuma	23	21	.523	3

PLAYOFFS: Semifinals—Calgary defeated Edmonton 3-0 and Orange County defeated Long Beach 3-2 in best-of-5 series. **Finals**—Orange County defeated Calgary 3-2 in best-of-five series.

MANAGERS: Calgary—Mike Busch; Chico—Jon Macalutas; Edmonton—Brent Bowers; Long Beach—Steve Yeager; Orange County—Gary Carter; Reno—Jeffrey Leonard; St. George—Cory Snyder; Yuma—Mike Marshall.

ATTENDANCE: Chico 89,164; Long Beach 67,255; Yuma 66,899; Reno 49,367; Calgary 45,686; Edmonton 46,695; St. George 36,732; Orange County 26,604.

Most Valuable Player: Patrick Breen, Orange County. Pitcher of the Year: Trevor Caughey, Chico.

INDIVIDUAL BATTING LEADERS

BATTER, CLUB	AVG	G	AB	R	H	HR	RBI
Breen, Patrick, Orange County	.396	80	275	81	109	28	94
Jose, Felix, Calgary	.391	77	279	60	109	15	70
Lemon, Greg, St. George	.386	79	295	90	114	7	57
Arroyo, Carlos, Edmonton	.377	87	355	70	134	1	67
Acey, Jermy, Orange County	.374	85	326	84	122	21	97
Dixon, D.J., Reno	.374	59	214	43	80	10	64
Rodriguez, Jose, Yuma	.371	60	221	52	82	12	58
Bacani, David, Orange County	.369	71	274	74	101	6	45
Jova, Maikel, Yuma	.358	83	369	74	132	8	87
Brinkley, Darryl, Calgary	.351	82	308	76	108	8	60

INDIVIDUAL PITCHING LEADERS

PITCHER, CLUB	W	L	ERA	IP	H	BB	SO
Caughey, Trevor, Chico	8	5	2.51	108	98	33	81
Van Slyke, Eric, Edmonton	9	4	3.43	126	136	34	97
Rodriguez, Ricardo, Edmonton	8	2	3.84	94	112	13	69
Cramer, Bob, Orange County	7	4	3.88	93	100	16	95
Currier, Rik, Long Beach	8	5	4.64	95	103	46	100
Gruesel, Evan, Calgary	9	4	4.88	103	126	17	87
Layfield, Andrew, Long Beach	2	5	4.93	80	103	31	40
Russell, Steve, Reno	5	8	5.21	86	84	32	84
Perez, Jorge, Yuma	8	3	5.24	112	123	50	115
Bicknell, Greg, Chico	5	4	5.31	103	117	37	86

CALGARY VIPERS

BATTERS	AVG	AB	R	H	2B	3B	HR	RBI	SB
Arlis, Patrick	.273	293	51	80	24	1	7	42	0
*Ashman, Shaun	.000	6	1	0	0	0	0	0	0
Austin, R	.250	16	1	4	0	0	0	1	1
Brinkley, Darryl	.351	308	76	108	23	1	8	60	30
Castro, Nelson	.336	301	65	101	16	2	12	55	16
*Drader, Travis	.280	279	59	78	20	2	9	52	1
Duncan, Carlos	.337	196	46	66	10	1	10	51	2
Fleury, Theoren	.333	3	0	1	0	0	0	0	0
Jose, Felix	.391	279	60	109	17	0	15	70	6
Mejia, Jorge	.317	334	78	106	22	4	9	69	25
*Miller, Drew	.343	251	63	86	19	1	19	70	2
*Morban, Jose	.248	117	28	29	8	1	10	36	5
Moro, Colin	.325	252	59	82	17	2	2	40	0
O'Krane, Dillon	.100	1	0	1	0	0	0	2	0
Pellow, Kit	.136	22	2	3	0	0	0	2	0
Price, Kevin	.241	83	20	20	3	0	1	11	0
Schurman, Ryan	.000	1	1	0	0	0	0	0	0
Smith, Demond	.229	35	9	8	2	0	2	9	0
Soto, Max	.000	9	1	0	0	0	0	0	0
Tang, Jorge	.332	214	42	71	10	2	2	42	14

PITCHERS	W	L	ERA	G	SV	IP	H	BB	SO
*Alexander, Jordy	4	3	7.04	11	0	46	64	13	28
Bevis, P.J.	1	5	3.30	25	3	30	33	9	23
*Coello, Robert	1	1	5.74	12	0	16	19	7	18
*Fortunato, Bartolome	0	0	1.93	3	0	5	3	2	3
*Freeborn, Geoff	3	1	7.36	18	1	11	17	5	4
Greusel, Evan	9	4	4.88	18	0	103	126	17	87
Groeger, Jeff	0	1	4.76	6	0	23	30	7	16
Huizinga, Jon	4	3	4.60	36	4	61	75	13	44
Kramer, Sean	2	2	5.18	27	0	42	43	26	50
*Mahan, Dallas	4	3	6.75	10	0	55	70	13	39

	6	4	6.75	18	0	99	136	30	62
Melek, Nathan	6	4	6.75	18	0	99	136	30	62
Neufeld, Jordan	0	0	3.38	3	0	3	2	2	1
*Olson, Ryan	0	1	4.50	8	2	12	13	2	9
Price, Kevin	0	0	4.50	3	0	2	4	0	1
Renkert, Dane	0	2	10.38	3	0	13	23	2	4
Rivard, Reggie	4	1	6.15	24	0	41	70	17	35
Schurman, Ryan	1	4	11.37	7	0	38	67	12	20
*Sergent, Joe	4	3	6.05	13	0	55	69	18	40
*Sobkow, Phil	1	4	10.03	11	1	49	77	19	20
Suzuki, Mac	1	0	1.64	5	1	11	10	5	15

CHICO OUTLAWS

BATTERS	AVG	AB	R	H	2B	3B	HR	RBI	SB
Benavidez, Julian	.273	231	48	63	13	1	13	59	4
Boggs, Steve	.296	371	71	110	10	1	1	39	27
Ceriani, Matthew	.288	191	37	55	10	0	4	38	4
Corso, Chris	.206	34	3	7	0	1	1	9	0
Cronin, Shane	.294	160	31	47	10	0	9	30	1
Enos, Gary	.000	1	0	0	0	0	0	0	0
Garcia, Lino	.281	221	47	62	12	1	9	43	14
Garrison, Casey	.302	295	46	89	22	0	11	54	8
*Gossage, Todd	.259	197	30	51	7	2	4	28	6
Kovacs, Jesse	.248	306	64	76	20	1	5	41	9
*Luyben, Dan	.281	64	12	18	3	0	0	5	1
McCarthy, Kevin	.292	24	2	7	1	0	0	2	2
Pringle, Eric	.228	246	42	56	8	1	2	39	12
*Riley, Gabriel	.319	135	31	43	7	0	3	23	7
Silverman, Bryan	.356	146	26	52	9	2	4	35	8
*Torcato, Tony	.313	83	18	26	4	0	1	16	2
*Valdez, Jose	.313	224	55	70	15	4	8	42	6
Verastegui, Jerry	.154	39	2	6	1	0	0	3	1

PITCHERS	W	L	ERA	G	SV	IP	H	BB	SO
*Altman, Kevin	0	1	6.48	7	1	8	13	6	7
Bicknell, Greg	5	4	5.31	17	0	103	117	37	86
Casanova, Nicholas	0	3	5.45	10	0	33	30	14	15
*Caughey, Trevor	8	5	2.51	21	0	108	98	33	81
Ellis, Rob	2	5	11.87	28	0	30	54	23	20
Fasking, Berek	2	5	5.31	16	0	78	97	37	31
Gelatka, Todd	3	4	7.99	32	6	33	44	18	41
Hintz, Beau	0	2	7.82	5	0	25	36	18	15
*Landavazo, Derrick	0	0	11.25	8	0	12	17	7	10
Loop, Derrick	3	0	1.53	6	0	29	20	18	30
*Malone, Christopher	0	0	1.50	1	0	6	6	2	2
*Navarro, Scott	2	4	7.25	9	0	50	75	14	34
Oster, Jesse	0	1	6.75	1	0	1	3	2	2
*Pearson, Tyler	0	1	7.17	9	0	21	24	10	12
Quinonez, Rudolph	0	5	9.78	18	0	42	70	17	37
Richardson, Zook	1	0	0.00	2	0	3	1	1	1
*Roach, Jason	2	8	8.77	21	0	65	93	39	54
*Sheridan, Eric	3	3	6.65	12	0	46	47	28	41
Shockey, Ben	3	1	1.40	25	1	39	30	14	37
Zumbrun, Josh	0	0	54.00	1	0	0	4	0	0

EDMONTON CRACKER CATS

BATTERS	AVG	AB	R	H	2B	3B	HR	RBI	SB
*Arroyo, Carlos	.377	355	70	134	29	4	1	67	22
*Bryan, Jason	.333	6	2	2	0	0	1	1	0
Carter, Josh	.274	95	14	26	6	1	2	22	1
Castro, Jonathan	.314	277	40	87	16	2	3	45	5
Detienne, Dave	.308	13	3	4	1	0	0	1	1
House, Kevin	.267	120	20	32	6	3	3	24	11
Infante, Juan	.263	76	16	20	3	0	1	7	4
Jiannetti, Joe	.340	306	69	104	34	3	12	85	5
Lundberg, Jordan	.258	182	27	47	9	0	7	33	2
*Luyben, Dan	.319	163	37	52	9	5	6	35	2
Miller, Orlando	.319	135	29	43	10	0	2	30	0
*Morban, Jose	.335	194	41	65	10	8	13	47	5
*Nettles, Marcus	.319	339	66	108	13	7	0	32	47
Pasieka, Jon	.278	144	27	40	5	1	2	20	0
Peterson, Nicholas	.000	3	0	0	0	0	0	0	0
Touchet, Danny	.100	1	0	1	0	0	0	0	0
*Valdez, Jose	.327	49	11	16	2	0	5	17	0
*Van Rossum, Chris	.336	304	80	102	26	3	7	65	5

	.341	305	74	104	14	5	1	49	26
Yan, Ruddy	.341	305	74	104	14	5	1	49	26

PITCHERS	W	L	ERA	G	SV	IP	H	BB	SO
*Altman, Kevin	3	1	7.17	14	0	21	28	12	23
*Camardese, Brandon	1	1	13.86	9	0	12	23	11	8
*Coello, Robert	2	0	1.78	20	0	25	18	17	29
Cullen, Chris	5	1	3.20	11	0	56	59	27	24
DePaula, Jorge	2	1	3.86	6	0	40	41	10	39
Humen, David	4	4	7.67	24	0	29	42	19	25
*Malone, Christopher	0	1	4.84	4	0	22	19	15	20
*Malone, Corwin	0	0	1.93	1	0	5	5	5	5
Montero, Augustine	3	1	6.00	5	0	27	36	10	24
Mowday, Chris	1	1	9.82	3	0	11	19	4	7
Peterson, Nicholas	3	3	6.42	19	0	81	86	75	64
Rapp, Randy	1	0	9.75	8	0	12	19	7	8
Rodriguez, Ricardo	8	2	3.84	14	0	94	112	13	69
*Schmal, Joel	2	5	8.64	22	0	42	64	16	35
Sikaras, Pete	2	3	3.65	33	19	37	34	12	46
*Smyth, Steve	1	2	7.18	6	0	26	36	16	19
*Sobkow, Phil	1	1	5.68	8	0	25	32	16	19
Touchet, Danny	3	6	5.18	20	0	40	47	17	30
*Upwood, Jake	0	0	6.57	9	0	12	14	15	11
Van Slyke, Eric	9	4	3.43	24	0	126	136	34	97

LONG BEACH ARMADA

BATTERS	AVG	AB	R	H	2B	3B	HR	RBI	SB
*Bierbrodt, Nick	.000	1	0	0	0	0	0	0	0
Bramasco, Omar	.333	45	10	15	3	1	0	4	6
*Brown, Ryan	.243	37	2	9	1	0	0	5	0
*Buller, Sean	.000	1	0	0	0	0	0	0	0
Claypool, Ryan	.000	3	0	0	0	0	0	0	0
Currier, Rik	.500	2	0	1	0	0	0	0	0
Davidson, Cleatus	.258	186	40	48	12	5	1	25	5
*Flowers, Brett	.297	192	18	57	9	0	0	29	3
Glomb, Michael	.220	168	13	37	4	0	0	22	14
Gober, Dustin	.000	2	0	0	0	0	0	0	0
Guerrero, James	.188	16	2	3	1	0	0	6	0
Hutchins, Norm	.301	306	55	92	13	1	15	55	18
*Klemm, Chris	.343	201	43	69	17	3	6	32	8
Lehr, Ryan	.336	318	55	107	26	0	11	58	7
Martinez, Octavio	.294	194	34	57	13	3	4	26	6
Montero, Pedro	.149	74	7	11	0	0	0	3	2
Moss, Steve	.299	264	53	79	23	2	10	44	14
Murdy, Garrett	.000	2	0	0	0	0	0	0	0
Parrish, Dave	.344	32	11	11	2	0	3	13	0
Ramirez, David	.249	173	22	43	10	0	0	20	6
Segal, Justin	.000	1	0	0	0	0	0	0	0
*Torcato, Tony	.223	121	12	27	4	1	1	17	4
Trumble, Dan	.228	311	55	71	23	1	10	49	14
Williams, Julian	.265	223	40	59	7	4	2	17	14
*Wilson, Aaron	.316	19	3	6	2	0	0	2	0
Yoo, Stephen	.167	42	3	7	2	0	0	7	0

PITCHERS	W	L	ERA	G	SV	IP	H	BB	SO
*Bierbrodt, Nick	5	5	5.62	25	0	99	90	60	101
*Buller, Sean	2	2	4.81	28	0	39	62	18	27
Buxbaum, Danny	0	0	81.00	1	0	1	2	6	1
Cavanagh, Nick	4	1	1.47	33	15	37	32	12	34
Claypool, Ryan	7	8	7.30	17	0	86	116	55	54
Currier, Rik	8	5	4.64	16	0	95	103	46	100
Etherton, Seth	1	0	1.93	2	0	9	5	1	16
*Figueroa, Jonathan	5	1	3.51	7	0	41	34	20	45
Foltin, Wayne	2	0	0.00	13	7	14	9	3	10
Gober, Dustin	5	8	7.28	21	0	98	127	44	85
Layfield, Andrew	2	5	4.93	22	1	80	103	31	40
Martinez, Octavio	0	0	0.00	1	0	0	0	0	0
Murdy, Garrett	3	0	3.41	29	1	61	57	28	57
Segal, Justin	1	3	6.38	27	2	37	54	12	30
*Smyth, Steve	0	0	6.35	4	0	11	10	11	10
Williams, Jerome	3	2	4.95	6	0	40	48	8	28

ORANGE COUNTY FLYERS

BATTERS	AVG	AB	R	H	2B	3B	HR	RBI	SB
Acey, Jermy	.374	326	84	122	23	1	21	97	16

BATTERS	AVG	AB	R	H	2B	3B	HR	RBI	SB
Arhart, Josh	.325	212	30	69	18	0	5	35	0
Bacani, David	.369	274	74	101	19	7	6	45	13
*Breen, Patrick	.396	275	81	109	22	6	28	94	12
Crockett	.125	16	1	2	1	0	0	2	0
Guerra, Nick	.328	67	10	22	7	2	2	13	0
Jackson, Travon	.352	196	34	69	9	2	0	14	5
Jacobellis, Michael	.150	20	4	3	1	0	0	0	0
Keesee, David	.389	18	4	7	1	0	0	2	0
LaRue, Jeff	.302	318	59	96	22	1	14	69	5
Lorentz, Sean	.171	35	8	6	5	0	1	2	0
Mayorga, Gabriel	.202	104	18	21	5	0	2	12	0
Mermer, Terry	.235	51	9	12	4	0	5	15	0
Mochizuki, Gered	.000	3	0	0	0	0	0	0	0
Morales, Buddy	.252	143	27	36	10	1	4	19	1
Okano, Mark	.271	292	72	79	13	2	18	52	15
*Pacheco, Fernando	.308	286	55	88	20	2	17	62	2
Rios, Brian	.337	104	28	35	10	0	4	17	1
*Van Houten, Jeffrey	.307	163	33	50	8	1	3	30	0

PITCHERS	W	L	ERA	G	SV	IP	H	BB	SO
*Cate, Troy	1	0	1.15	3	0	16	5	1	18
Choi, Eun Chul	1	0	16.20	3	0	2	5	3	1
*Cramer, Bob	7	4	3.88	19	0	93	100	16	95
De La Rosa, Dane	2	2	4.41	32	14	35	35	13	40
Durkin, Matt	3	3	4.71	14	1	57	63	27	46
Kalter, Zack	0	1	16.71	3	0	7	18	2	6
*Mansfield, Monte	2	0	9.29	14	1	31	42	22	20
*Merricks, Charles	6	5	6.94	20	0	82	111	44	52
*Merricks, Matt	2	0	2.70	6	0	27	17	16	25
Natale, Mike	4	1	6.03	8	0	37	52	15	28
Rocco, Michael	0	0	0.00	1	0	2	1	2	1
Ruvalcaba, Ezequiel	3	2	9.84	27	3	39	52	25	33
*Sheridan, Eric	1	2	6.65	16	3	22	19	23	20
Simpson, Andre	8	5	5.80	23	2	102	136	36	88
Smith, Jesse	6	2	5.00	11	1	63	74	15	40
*Van Houten, Jeffrey	0	0	0.00	1	0	1	0	1	0
*Ward, Gabe	0	1	10.80	4	0	7	13	4	2
Zick, Jeremy	5	7	7.47	16	0	84	115	27	41

RENO SILVER SOX

BATTERS	AVG	AB	R	H	2B	3B	HR	RBI	SB
Alexander, Steven	.255	231	48	59	11	0	19	48	3
Alvarado, Andre	.274	237	44	65	12	4	3	36	18
*Alvarado, Andrew	.308	13	2	4	0	1	0	1	0
*Brown, Ryan	.331	181	37	60	11	1	11	47	3
Crespi, Ryan	.358	201	43	72	14	3	4	28	21
Dixon, D.J.	.374	214	43	80	20	2	10	64	1
*Flowers, Brett	.337	83	14	28	4	0	2	12	0
*Frederick, Kevin	.000	4	0	0	0	0	0	0	0
Geery, Adam	.218	55	8	12	5	0	0	8	0
Guilin, Gilbert	.324	34	4	11	2	0	2	6	0
Guilin, Mario	.000	7	0	0	0	0	0	0	0
*Harris, Gary	.305	328	65	100	21	2	12	41	39
Hattig, John	.339	248	46	84	23	1	12	41	1
*Henderson, Will	.250	20	6	5	0	0	1	2	0
Kavanaugh, Matthew	.258	62	4	16	2	0	0	8	1
Leslie, Reggie	.222	9	1	2	1	0	0	1	0
Madrid, Carlos	.258	248	40	64	19	1	6	34	10
Mason, Brian	.310	29	5	9	3	0	2	7	1
Mason, Bryan	.125	8	1	1	0	0	0	0	0
Mccoy, Ross	.260	231	47	60	12	6	10	38	12
Neal, Shaughn	.174	69	7	12	0	0	0	6	1
Sanders, Doug	.191	131	12	25	3	0	1	12	3
Senreiso, Juan	.309	269	55	83	21	0	14	53	13
Wharton, Ben	.184	49	9	9	0	0	0	5	1
Wright, Steven	.333	24	6	8	2	1	1	3	1

PITCHERS	W	L	ERA	G	SV	IP	H	BB	SO
Alexander, Steven	0	0	11.81	4	0	5	12	6	3
*Alvarado, Andrew	1	3	4.43	15	0	43	36	20	29
Alverez, Mark	0	1	30.38	2	0	3	13	0	1
Arnold, Mitchell	1	1	7.41	13	4	17	13	19	23
*Braun, Bart	0	2	12.33	5	0	15	25	8	6
*Brown, Ryan	0	0	12.00	2	0	3	6	1	0
Chaffardet, Daniel	0	3	9.17	4	0	18	27	16	11
Cline, Jason	0	1	18.90	5	0	10	22	8	5
Correa,	0	0	0.00	1	0	1	2	0	0
DeLaCruz, Eduardo	0	2	8.36	11	3	14	14	14	11
Fields, Chris	1	0	9.47	8	0	26	37	20	20
Flanagan, Jeremy	0	2	12.34	5	1	12	23	8	11
Frederick, Kevin	3	2	7.06	19	2	57	86	24	45
Fuda, Giorgio	0	0	9.49	6	0	12	19	16	13
Fulcher, Brian	0	0	9.00	3	0	4	4	5	3
Ginsberg, Nathan	0	1	11.20	6	0	14	18	19	13
Guilin, Mario	3	1	9.66	15	0	36	53	28	26
*Hall, Dan	0	0	18.00	1	0	1	3	1	2
Hall, Jesse	5	6	5.70	17	0	71	78	38	55
Kaiser, Marc	1	3	6.75	5	0	28	32	6	24
*Landavazo, Derrick	3	4	4.75	14	1	53	49	16	36
Ledbetter, Grant	0	0	5.28	6	0	15	17	7	13
Leslie, Reggie	1	1	6.53	9	0	30	44	26	14
*Piccirillo, Kevin	2	2	5.52	9	0	31	37	12	20
Ravenscraft, Shawn	0	0	13.50	6	0	16	34	10	8
Reeves, Mike	0	2	19.29	5	0	12	23	8	7
Russell, Steve	5	8	5.21	16	0	86	84	32	84
Sanders, Doug	0	1	6.75	10	0	19	18	15	7
Schneider, Scott	2	3	6.16	17	1	19	26	5	12
Shea, Billy	0	0	7.50	5	0	6	8	5	11
*Simon, Billy	1	2	12.94	8	0	16	25	13	20
*Simonitsch, Errol	0	4	10.24	8	0	29	46	12	24
Vasquez, Gustavo	1	1	8.44	2	0	5	4	4	6
Wilson, Paul	0	2	15.63	5	0	6	11	7	5

ST. GEORGE ROADRUNNERS

BATTERS	AVG	AB	R	H	2B	3B	HR	RBI	SB
Arias, Claudio	.418	146	36	61	14	1	13	48	3
Beltran, Juan	.250	28	5	7	2	0	0	2	1
*Brown, Ryan	.188	16	1	3	1	0	0	2	0
*Bryan, Jason	.314	51	7	16	1	0	3	8	2
Collis, Devin	.000	0	1	0	0	0	0	0	0
Dimick, Trever	.302	86	18	26	5	1	0	11	0
Done, Mike	.204	54	10	11	4	0	1	10	0
Garabito, Eddy	.339	121	22	41	13	1	9	41	2
Giron, Ysabel	.250	4	0	1	1	0	0	1	0
Gonzalez, Wiki	.350	234	61	82	20	0	13	63	4
*Harris, Gary	.300	20	2	6	0	0	0		4
*Henderson, Will	.256	43	8	11	3	0	3	11	0
*Hicks, Dustin	.273	205	44	56	10	1	7	29	3
Jacobsen, Brock	.000	5	1	0	0	0	0	0	0
*Lemon, Greg	.386	295	90	114	19	3	7	57	22
Loman, Seth	.350	220	58	77	18	2	19	60	6
Martin, Brian	.440	25	8	11	1	0	1	6	0
Melo, Juan	.286	63	15	18	3	1	1	11	1
*Nowlin, Cody	.306	288	53	88	23	2	8	61	2
Reyes, Ivan	.220	50	8	11	1	0	4	13	2
Rodriguez, Liu	.317	265	46	84	21	1	4	45	3
Sanchez, Angel	.322	115	27	37	1	2	1	12	3
Serrano, Juan	.246	211	43	52	18	1	10	40	0
*Stevenson, Ryan	.348	376	110	131	28	7	18	70	11
Taylor, Brandon	.409	127	46	52	11	0	14	46	7
Wayment, Kory	.314	35	8	11	4	0	0	8	3
Wells, Kyle	.182	11	2	2	0	0	0	0	0

PITCHERS	W	L	ERA	G	SV	IP	H	BB	SO
Abbott, Justin	5	5	6.30	13	0	74	100	30	47
Carvajal, Marcos	3	2	7.22	7	0	29	35	15	31
Collis, Devin	2	3	7.71	14	0	54	74	26	36
Cooper	0	0	9.53	2	0	6	9	5	2
De La Cruz, Maximo	0	1	13.50	4	0	11	24	5	7
Done, Mike	1	2	9.55	12	1	22	32	5	23
*Fortunato, Bartolome	0	2	4.50	12	5	14	18	5	23
Furrow, Donald	1	0	9.82	3	0	7	14	2	7
*Galva, Claudio	2	2	7.32	17	2	20	21	11	27
Giron, Ysabel	1	2	19.00	4	0	9	24	4	10
*Hall, Danny	0	0	13.50	3	0	5	14	2	3
Howerton, Jason	0	0	9.35	7	0	9	16	4	4
Hunter, Chris	1	2	12.27	9	0	22	43	12	18
Lakman, Jason	0	1	18.47	2	0	6	17	5	1
*Mansfield, Monte	6	2	5.31	13	0	59	61	21	43

	W	L	ERA	G	SV	IP	H	BB	SO
Markray, Marcus	1	0	7.27	2	0	9	14	5	8
Martinez, Gregorio	3	0	4.50	3	0	20	15	8	18
Nelson, Mac	3	0	4.66	11	0	68	68	36	62
*Norderum, Jason	1	1	3.89	32	5	37	32	24	65
Northrup, J	0	0	7.36	2	0	4	3	4	2
Ortiz, Adam	1	1	18.00	3	0	4	10	3	2
Paniagua, Jose	0	0	3.38	3	0	11	13	4	6
Pluta, Tony	1	2	7.44	34	4	42	54	28	47
Ramirez, Ismael	0	0	10.13	1	0	3	4	1	2
Romero, Garvis	0	1	9.00	3	0	9	18	5	2
Segovia, John	4	4	7.00	36	1	63	92	25	53
*Simon, Billy	4	4	11.67	17	0	39	72	18	29
Sprouse, Shannon	1	3	17.03	8	0	22	41	24	17
Tolj, Mike	0	1	22.50	1	0	4	8	6	2
Urdaneta, Lino	0	0	4.50	2	0	2	3	0	1
Williams, Harold	2	1	8.44	4	0	11	13	11	15
*Wilson, Aaron	0	3	11.09	8	0	37	68	15	30

YUMA SCORPIONS

BATTERS	AVG	AB	R	H	2B	3B	HR	RBI	SB
Almario, Yosvany	.328	244	58	80	22	2	11	57	9
Barba, Ryan	.316	275	41	87	13	2	4	47	6
*Bernal, Hector	.334	302	59	101	22	8	9	53	9
Calderon, Henry	.314	370	85	116	27	1	12	70	10
Cesar, Dionys	.288	73	17	21	6	0	3	11	0
*Chavez, Ender	.400	10	3	4	0	0	1	2	2
Cleveland, Jeremy	.335	197	48	66	12	2	7	45	4
Cummins, Phillip	.143	7	2	1	1	0	0	0	0
Diaz, Hanseld	.270	89	12	24	5	1	1	10	0
Farina, Peter	.272	217	36	59	10	0	5	42	2
Garcia, James	.000	1	0	0	0	0	0	0	0
Guillen, Jean-Carlos	.000	1	0	0	0	0	0	0	0
Hale, Darrick	.325	40	9	13	2	0	3	8	1
Hayes, Neil	.000	0	1	0	0	0	0	0	0
Irei, Toshin	.263	38	5	10	3	0	0	0	2
*Janeway, Richard	.342	342	93	117	29	4	12	58	19
Jova, Maikel	.358	369	74	132	22	2	8	87	0
Jova, Micah	.500	4	1	2	0	0	1	1	0
*Luera, Chris	.250	4	2	1	0	0	1	4	0
Marin, Limberth	.130	23	1	3	0	0	0	0	0
Martin, Mike	.000	1	0	0	0	0	0	0	0
*Megrew, Mike	.100	2	0	2	0	0	0	0	0
*Pearson, Tyler	.000	1	0	0	0	0	0	0	0
Rodriguez, Jose	.371	221	52	82	19	0	12	58	2
*Valentine, A.J.	.288	340	74	98	23	4	15	72	12
*Van Houten, Jeffrey	.273	11	3	3	1	0	0	0	0
White, Evan	.000	2	0	0	0	0	0	1	0

PITCHERS	W	L	ERA	G	SV	IP	H	BB	SO
*Alvarado, Andrew	0	0	11.05	3	0	7	16	3	2
*Brandt, Donald	1	3	9.56	5	0	16	17	13	9
Calderon, Henry	0	0	0.00	1	0	0	3	1	0
Diaz, Hanseld	0	0	0.00	1	0	1	1	0	0
Esposito, Mike	5	5	5.85	18	0	108	143	25	73
Garcia, James	2	4	6.14	32	12	44	48	24	50
Guillen, JeanCarlos	3	3	4.42	31	4	39	43	12	31
Hayes, Neil	2	1	10.66	19	3	25	43	19	19
Jensen, Jack	2	1	10.98	11	1	20	34	14	8
*Kuzniak, James	0	0	21.60	4	0	5	12	4	3
Lira, Felipe	0	0	22.50	2	0	2	6	2	1
*Luera, Chris	2	1	5.14	16	0	21	29	8	16
*Luque, Roger	5	6	7.97	17	0	87	117	33	77
Martin, Mike	4	1	4.85	19	0	26	35	14	15
McGrath, Ryan	0	2	13.15	4	0	13	27	2	8
*Megrew, Mike	0	2	9.72	4	0	17	20	14	15
*Pearson, Tyler	4	2	8.94	18	0	51	78	25	42
Perez, Jorge	8	3	5.24	20	0	112	123	50	115
Perks, Matthew	0	1	22.50	2	0	2	7	2	1
Robertson, N	0	0	7.71	2	0	5	8	2	3
Rodriguez, Jose	0	0	18.00	1	0	2	6	1	0
Romero, Anthony	0	1	9.00	11	0	25	41	7	11
Schmidt, Paul	0	0	27.00	1	0	1	4	2	1
Stringer, David	1	0	9.00	7	0	13	15	8	12
Tressler, Aaron	1	0	3.27	2	0	11	11	6	15

	W	L	ERA	G	SV	IP	H	BB	SO
White, Evan	7	4	6.10	17	0	100	138	26	81

NORTHERN LEAGUE

The Gary Railcats were making a fourth-straight appearance in the Northern League championship series, and were playing for their third title in four years. The Kansas City T-Bones had never won a league title. The Railcats had Northern League player of the year Tanner Townsend, pitcher of the year Gerald Plexico and rookie of the year Mike Rohde, while the Kansas City T-Bones had the league's second-worst team ERA and no pitchers who finished among the league's top 10 in ERA. And while Gary finished the season 14 games over .500, Kansas City had a losing record. But in the best-of-five championship series, the T-Bones pulled off the upset, beating Gary three games to one. Former Royal Ken Harvey hit four home runs in the postseason to help pace the offense while Anthony Boughner threw 6 1/3 scoreless innings in the clincher, but the T-Bones biggest star was designated hitter Jim Fasano, who hit .571 with three home runs in the championship series. Townsend earned the player of the year award after ranking second in the league in hitting (.371), first in RBIs (84) and first in slugging percentage (.623). While Kansas City proved that it's possible to turn a season around, the Schaumburg Flyers proved that it's also possible to completely fall apart. The Flyers lost their last 14 games of the season to finish 36 games below .500.

	W	L	PCT	GB
Fargo-Moorhead	62	34	.646	—
Gary	56	40	.583	6
Winnipeg	51	45	.531	11
Kansas City	46	50	.479	16
Joliet	43	53	.448	19
Schaumburg	30	66	.313	32

PLAYOFFS: Semifinals—Gary defeated Winnipeg 3-1 and Kansas City defeated Fargo-Moorhead 3-0 in best-of-five series. **Finals**—Kansas City defeated Gary 3-1 in best-of-five series.

MANAGERS: Fargo-Moorhead—Doug Simunic; Gary—Greg Tagert; Joliet—Wally Backman; Kansas City—Andy McCauley; Schamburg—Steve Maddox; Winnipeg—Rick Forney.

ATTENDANCE: Winnipeg 284,398; Kansas City 280,795; Schaumburg 202,013; Joliet 184,638; Fargo-Moorhead 117,900; Gary 159,586.

ALL-STAR TEAM: C—Alan Rick, Fargo-Moorhead. 1B—Kevin West, Winnipeg. 2B—Carlo Cota, Fargo-Moorhead. 3B—Tanner Townsend, Gary. SS—Jay Pecci, Gary. OF—Aharon Eggleston, Kansas City; Fehlandt Lentini, Winnipeg; Steve Mortimer, Fargo-Moorhead. DH—Jim Fasano, Kansas City. LHP—Jeremy Plexico, Gary. RHP—Brian Beuning, Winnipeg.

Pitcher of the Year: Jeremy Plexico, Gary. **Player of the Year:** Tanner Townsend, Gary. **Rookie Pitcher of the Year:** Billy Weitzman, Fargo-Moorhead. **Rookie Player of the Year:** Mike Rohde, Gary. **Top Defensive Player:** Joe Mathis, Fargo-Moorhead. **Manager of the Year:** Doug Simunic, Fargo-Moorhead.

INDIVIDUAL BATTING LEADERS

BATTER, CLUB	AVG	G	AB	R	H	HR	RBI
Salazar, Ruben, F-M	.378	61	254	44	96	6	53
Townsend, Tanner, Gary	.371	79	302	64	112	14	84
Metheny, Brent, Winnipeg	.357	79	300	63	107	10	57
Diaz, Juan, Joliet	.354	61	223	42	79	12	47
Watson, Rob, KC	.344	62	247	57	85	8	46
Eggleston, Aharon, KC	.332	96	379	76	126	6	62
Allensworth, Jermaine, Schaumburg	.326	85	328	52	107	4	39
Cota, Carlo, F-M	.325	96	379	80	123	8	59
McIntyre, Nick, Joliet	.323	93	371	66	120	3	52
Rohde, Nick, Gary	.319	91	348	59	111	1	55

INDIVIDUAL PITCHING LEADERS

PITCHER, CLUB	W	L	ERA	IP	H	BB	SO
Beuning, Brian, Winnipeg	6	4	1.75	82	62	30	64
Cogan, Tony, Gary	6	3	2.08	78	57	24	61
Plexico, Gerald, Gary	10	3	2.79	135	127	32	68
Koerber, Scott, F-M	10	5	2.87	78	64	36	73
Coffman, Broc, F-M	10	5	3.03	116	94	53	82
Pease, Dustin, Winnipeg	3	3	3.16	80	75	26	80
Bakker, Gary, F-M	7	3	3.46	94	76	46	69
Trolia, Aaron, Joliet	9	6	3.97	127	132	60	142
Jackson, Aaron, Winipeg	6	3	4.21	77	89	37	46
Rowe, Adam, F-M	2	4	4.22	81	106	19	42

INDEPENDENT LEAGUES

FARGO-MOORHEAD REDHAWKS

BATTERS	AVG	AB	R	H	2B	3B	HR	RBI	SB
*Berry, Boomer	.279	319	51	89	14	3	3	30	22
Castillo, David	.288	163	22	47	10	0	6	23	0
Cota, Carlo	.325	379	80	123	29	2	8	59	14
Eure, Jeffrey	.295	366	54	108	25	1	13	62	3
Hurst, Jimmy	.301	209	35	63	13	1	4	45	4
*Koerber, Scott	.440	25	9	11	5	0	0	2	0
*Mathis, Joe	.284	349	67	99	18	6	9	53	16
*Maycock, Dan	.276	76	13	21	8	0	3	15	1
Miles, Dustin	.500	2	1	1	0	0	0	0	0
*Mortimer, Steve	.295	349	66	103	28	1	19	76	30
Penprase, Zachary	.326	221	42	72	10	4	2	29	23
*Peschel, Mike	.000	1	0	0	0	0	0	0	0
Piepkorn, Jeremiah	.295	132	19	39	13	0	6	23	3
*Rick, Alan	.267	307	64	82	14	0	15	51	1
Salazar, Ruben	.378	254	44	96	22	0	6	53	1
Wayment, Kory	.146	48	9	7	2	1	1	3	1
Zimmerman, Kole	.263	160	26	42	5	0	6	27	5

PITCHERS	W	L	ERA	G	SV	IP	H	BB	SO
Bakker, Garry	7	3	3.46	16	0	94	76	46	69
Bushland, Shane	0	0	13.50	1	0	1	1	0	1
*Coffman, Broc	10	5	3.03	19	0	116	94	53	82
Cotton, Nate	1	0	1.48	30	22	30	23	11	30
George, Todd	7	1	5.01	10	0	56	56	16	32
Hetland, Nick	1	2	12.17	14	0	24	30	20	13
Humen, David	0	0	11.70	8	0	10	15	12	10
*Koerber, Scott	10	5	2.87	42	1	78	64	36	73
Laber, Jake	0	2	7.30	7	1	12	20	9	13
Lawson, Brett	7	5	5.49	19	0	95	102	71	71
*Morgan, David	1	0	5.31	39	0	61	63	31	28
*Mortimer, Steve	0	0	12.00	3	0	3	4	2	1
*Peschel, Mike	0	0	8.44	2	0	5	12	3	3
Renkert, Dane	4	4	4.91	10	0	59	66	30	44
*Rowe, Adam	2	4	4.22	32	2	81	106	19	42
Smith, Donnie	3	1	3.94	42	7	48	44	25	48
*Tomasiewicz, Kevin	1	0	3.52	7	0	8	11	4	4
Weitzman, Billy	8	2	3.03	14	0	68	60	25	44

GARY SOUTHSHORE RAILCATS

BATTERS	AVG	AB	R	H	2B	3B	HR	RBI	SB
Blakeley, Eric	.310	245	41	76	15	5	6	47	7
Esquer, Anthony	.318	129	16	41	4	0	0	18	1
Guerrero, Cristian	.312	337	69	105	15	3	16	63	15
*Haake, Steve	.278	342	64	95	23	3	9	56	20
Marconi, Rob	.290	335	71	97	20	7	8	56	10
Matsumoto, Yuki	.250	32	4	8	3	0	0	5	0
*McCarthy, John	.289	239	36	69	7	3	0	25	19
McNamee, Eric	.302	295	45	89	14	2	0	34	8
Padilla, Omar	.235	17	0	4	0	0	0	2	0
Pecci, Jay	.317	363	70	115	26	2	9	48	5
Reese, Mike	.308	263	49	81	13	2	7	39	8
*Rohde, Mike	.319	348	59	111	25	5	1	55	13
Townsend, Tanner	.371	302	64	112	26	4	14	84	11
Wallace, Brett	.274	197	29	54	16	0	1	28	3

PITCHERS	W	L	ERA	G	SV	IP	H	BB	SO
Bevis, P.J.	2	0	6.00	9	3	12	10	8	13
Boker, John	0	0	27.00	2	0	2	5	3	2
Brinkmann, Matt	0	1	6.38	21	0	24	32	12	24
*Cogan, Tony	6	3	2.08	13	0	78	57	24	61
Cook, Aaron	0	0	3.52	13	3	15	10	5	13
De la cruz, Eddie	3	1	2.70	13	0	13	7	4	7
*Dickinson, Drew	5	6	7.34	23	0	92	126	50	39
Esquer, Anthony	0	0	0.00	1	0	1	1	0	1
*Forystek, Brian	4	2	4.81	11	0	49	46	26	29
Halford, Brian	5	1	6.45	42	0	60	80	29	36
*Higelin, Brandon	3	2	4.91	50	0	44	56	17	36
*Hoelscher, Nate	1	4	4.24	22	6	23	25	12	23
Holleran, Garret	3	3	5.50	14	0	56	75	22	27
Kerber, Travis	0	0	4.82	2	0	9	13	2	7
Kobernus, Kyle	0	2	4.86	13	0	17	18	11	9
Lewis, Jon	2	1	2.33	24	0	27	23	11	20

	W	L	ERA	G	SV	IP	H	BB	SO
Misawa, Koichi	7	1	1.69	29	6	43	24	17	54
*Panozzo, Joe	0	0	4.50	6	0	6	6	6	5
Phillips, Billy	2	5	6.26	12	0	65	83	27	42
*Plexico, Gerald	10	3	2.79	21	0	135	127	32	68
Reese, Mike	0	0	36.00	1	0	1	2	5	0
*Tomasiewicz, Kevin	0	0	10.80	1	0	2	1	2	1
Tuomi, Kai	2	2	5.40	12	0	60	79	13	35

JOLIET JACKHAMMERS

BATTERS	AVG	AB	R	H	2B	3B	HR	RBI	SB
Backman, Wally	.285	256	34	73	13	4	2	37	13
Blackmon, Dennis	.269	67	15	18	7	0	1	11	0
Brooks, Doc	.307	352	69	108	21	1	16	69	12
Caruso, Mike	.270	100	18	27	1	0	0	10	4
Diaz, Juan	.354	223	42	79	10	0	12	47	0
Fillinger, Chad	.000	1	0	0	0	0	0	0	0
Fortini, Dominic	.000	0	0	0	0	0	0	0	0
Garcia, Michael	.250	36	7	9	1	0	1	8	0
Garrabrants, Steve	.304	247	46	75	24	1	5	36	6
Gomes, Joey	.303	346	60	105	18	0	14	55	6
Harris, Cory	.312	343	62	107	20	0	14	70	9
Hooft, Joseph	.268	306	53	82	16	0	2	24	10
Kinsey, Chris	.250	44	3	11	1	0	0	1	0
Launier, Andrew	.167	18	2	3	1	0	0	2	0
McIntyre, Nick	.323	371	66	120	33	0	3	52	15
*Meigs, Tyler	.000	1	0	0	0	0	0	0	0
*Mumma, Brad	.000	0	0	0	0	0	0	0	0
Prosise, Nicholas	.265	260	29	69	10	0	2	40	0
Rojas, Dorian	.267	131	31	35	10	1	2	18	4
*Scriven, Eric	.280	50	9	14	3	0	0	11	6
Sevier, Nate	.000	0	1	0	0	0	0	0	0
*Sherrer, Jason	.333	21	2	7	0	0	1	3	0
*Taylor, Dustin	.000	0	0	0	0	0	0	0	0
Thon, Freddie	.324	188	27	61	13	1	7	35	2

PITCHERS	W	L	ERA	G	SV	IP	H	BB	SO
Altman, Kevin	1	0	6.48	12	0	17	29	6	21
Backman, Wally	0	0	0.00	1	0	1	0	2	2
Buechner, Chris	0	0	8.24	17	0	20	32	13	16
Castillo, Carlos	0	1	7.48	5	0	28	49	6	9
Colacchio, Mike	0	0	16.20	4	0	5	11	3	2
Cunningham, Sam	0	2	9.56	7	0	16	19	11	3
Darley, Ned	0	2	1.80	11	4	10	10	6	8
Evoniuk, Kenny	0	0	7.56	4	0	8	16	5	5
Fillinger, Chad	4	5	3.40	30	1	48	52	16	54
*Forystek, Brian	2	4	5.44	9	0	45	52	22	37
Jernstad, Matt	0	2	11.57	5	0	9	14	5	7
Kinsey, Chris	0	3	9.60	8	0	15	25	12	7
Meigs, Tyler	2	7	3.63	53	7	72	79	26	57
*Moraga, David	8	2	5.72	15	0	79	103	29	43
*Mumma, Brad	3	0	4.32	5	0	33	33	10	19
O'Brien, Nick	0	1	12.15	4	0	7	11	2	8
Perkins, Vince	3	0	2.43	7	0	41	41	19	31
Pfautz, Craig	0	1	6.48	14	0	8	10	11	11
*Ricken, Blake	1	0	10.13	8	0	5	7	7	2
Schellinger, Mike	0	1	15.63	4	0	6	12	4	3
Sevier, Nate	4	9	5.80	22	0	127	154	43	100
Shetrone, Drew	1	1	2.93	13	6	15	12	5	18
Sutton, Jared	1	0	2.61	9	0	9	15	10	12
*Taylor, Dustin	4	2	7.21	25	1	74	102	44	59
Touchet, Danny	0	1	10.38	10	0	13	26	5	8
Trolia, Aaron	9	6	3.97	25	1	127	132	60	142
Ziegler, Dan	0	3	8.31	13	0	13	15	17	12

KANSAS CITY T-BONES

BATTERS	AVG	AB	R	H	2B	3B	HR	RBI	SB
*Brown, Neb	.283	226	39	64	15	0	7	35	10
Correll, Brad	.343	166	39	57	15	0	15	49	1
Dabbs, Chris	.167	6	1	1	0	1	0	3	0
*Eggleston, Aharon	.332	379	76	126	27	3	6	62	36
*Fasano, James	.292	367	56	107	29	0	20	84	1
*Hart, Bo	.286	126	31	36	5	1	8	30	3
Harvey, Ken	.302	222	34	67	11	3	12	45	1
Hurba, Craig	.229	192	24	44	6	0	12	43	0

	AVG	AB	R	H	2B	3B	HR	RBI	SB
*Jacobs, Greg	.384	185	41	71	18	1	11	50	3
Jaros, Nick	.188	69	13	13	3	1	1	5	3
Magness, Pat	.500	4	2	2	0	0	1	2	0
Mahar, Kevin	.297	222	40	66	13	0	9	27	15
Martin, John	.257	167	30	43	9	1	3	27	0
*McCallum, Geoff	.284	363	69	103	25	3	3	45	17
*Scriven, Eric	.249	201	32	50	3	2	3	21	8
Smith, Ryan	.179	56	7	10	1	1	2	6	0
Trout, Steven	.285	193	41	55	12	2	0	20	5
Watson, Rob	.344	247	57	85	20	1	8	46	7

PITCHERS	W	L	ERA	G	SV	IP	H	BB	SO
*Boughner, Anthony	6	7	5.14	20	0	117	138	74	69
Carrington, Bobby	1	1	9.24	8	0	13	19	12	10
*DeHart, Rick	1	0	7.71	1	0	7	8	4	3
Durost, Kenny	8	5	4.62	21	0	121	113	67	90
Garner, Adam	0	2	8.53	3	0	13	28	4	3
Haehnel, David	1	0	0.00	2	0	2	0	1	0
Hamblit, Reid	1	2	11.29	6	0	18	35	6	11
*Horner, Mark	4	0	4.22	37	0	43	56	12	36
Hummel, Rick	2	2	5.79	23	0	28	31	13	22
*Jacobs, Greg	0	0	0.00	1	0	1	1	1	0
Martinez, Brady	4	1	3.42	48	0	71	66	22	72
*Michael, Mark	1	4	6.75	5	0	23	29	14	18
*Moser, Todd	1	2	3.86	14	0	21	28	8	9
Nall, T.J.	0	0	18.00	1	0	3	5	3	2
Reese, Ty	0	1	7.71	2	0	9	12	7	2
Rhoads, Chris	4	6	5.01	31	0	101	105	36	74
Rivas, Ricardo	2	4	8.49	9	0	41	55	24	16
*Scriven, Eric	0	0	0.00	1	0	2	1	2	2
*Shaver, Chris	0	2	13.00	2	0	9	19	7	7
Shipman, Andy	1	1	2.35	10	0	15	11	5	16
Snow, Anothny	6	6	6.84	15	0	79	107	52	57
Still, Alexy	0	0	9.00	6	0	9	10	14	5
Stott, Zac	1	1	8.88	5	0	25	38	12	19
Trahan, David	2	3	5.45	35	20	35	38	18	27
*Tweddale, Payton	0	0	5.29	26	0	32	33	13	26
Watson, Rob	0	0	13.50	2	0	2	3	0	1

SCHAUMBURG FLYERS

BATTERS	AVG	AB	R	H	2B	3B	HR	RBI	SB
Allensworth, Jermain	.326	328	52	107	21	0	4	39	9
Burgos, Victor	.219	32	2	7	1	0	0	3	1
Byard, David	.000	1	1	0	0	0	0	0	0
Crowell, Kurt	.333	135	25	45	11	5	3	22	4
Fischer, Rob	.276	156	18	43	7	2	2	18	1
Gaskin, Christopher	.289	332	39	96	21	2	7	56	7
Harrison, Vince	.319	386	57	123	25	2	9	58	12
*Hart, Bo	.261	142	30	37	10	2	3	21	4
*Haske, Mark	.237	380	55	90	12	5	1	26	12
Johnson, Rontrez	.314	118	27	37	4	2	5	18	20
Joseph, Alfred	.111	9	0	1	0	0	0	0	0
Koenig, Lance	.212	312	48	66	16	3	5	27	19
*Lanto, Hank	.280	100	12	28	1	0	2	14	1
Luther, Ryan	.212	118	18	25	5	1	1	10	8
Manuel, Anthony	.000	2	0	0	0	0	0	0	0
Matos, Wilson	.262	84	9	22	3	1	1	6	0
Matthews, Dustin	.111	27	3	3	1	0	1	4	0
*Maycock, Dan	.217	69	6	15	3	1	2	11	2
McGuire, Cameron	.095	21	1	2	1	0	0	1	0
*Mumma, Brad	.000	2	0	0	0	0	0	0	0
*Pickering, Calvin	.298	131	22	39	6	0	14	38	0
Thames, Julius	.292	113	14	33	3	1	0	12	10
Weida, M	.000	0	1	0	0	0	0	0	0
Williams, Peanut	.291	333	48	97	20	1	13	64	6

PITCHERS	W	L	ERA	G	SV	IP	H	BB	SO
Brooks, Douglas	0	0	7.44	19	0	33	43	25	25
Byard, David	2	2	6.09	29	3	34	38	36	15
Demuro, B	0	0	8.59	5	0	7	6	10	5
Finch, Brian	0	7	5.76	15	0	89	120	34	40
Ford, Matt	1	1	15.75	2	0	4	7	4	2
Frega, Daniel	2	3	5.18	8	0	49	60	15	24
Goodman, Mark	1	2	10.80	17	0	28	55	13	16
Hagerty, Luke	0	0	8.10	8	0	13	15	16	14

Hansen, Bryan	0	0	11.57	2	0	2	5	1	1
Jordan, Justin	2	3	3.68	8	0	44	53	9	30
Koch, Jon	1	1	7.07	9	0	14	16	8	6
Koenig, Lance	0	0	0.00	1	0	2	0	1	2
Lanto, Hank	0	1	2.45	3	0	4	1	3	2
Luther, Ryan	0	0	9.00	1	0	1	1	3	0
*Maycock, Dan	0	0	0.00	1	0	1	0	1	0
*Moraga, David	1	2	6.86	4	0	21	32	10	13
*Mumma, Brad	6	6	5.44	15	0	96	126	18	58
Novosel, Walt	0	0	135.00	3	0	0	4	6	1
*Panozzo, Joe	0	0	15.12	5	0	8	20	8	7
Patterson, Lonnie	1	3	9.37	13	0	33	34	24	13
Popp, Jim	3	6	4.81	39	6	43	51	20	43
Robinson, Justin	0	1	5.87	6	0	8	4	3	5
Rollin, Alex	2	6	6.16	12	0	64	81	37	42
Saenz, Chris	1	1	8.42	19	0	26	31	15	18
Shelton, Brian	0	0	81.00	1	0	0	2	1	0
Shippey, Steve	5	11	7.50	20	0	114	162	63	68
Smith, John	0	0	6.00	23	6	24	21	24	31
Varner, Matthew	1	8	8.39	15	0	59	108	25	33
Weida, M	0	2	6.75	7	0	21	30	10	8

WINNIPEG WINGNUTS

BATTERS	AVG	AB	R	H	2B	3B	HR	RBI	SB
Aguilar, Trino	.265	83	13	22	7	0	3	14	2
DeSmidt, Jeff	.271	85	8	23	2	0	3	12	0
*Dixon, D.J.	.250	40	1	10	3	0	0	1	0
Ehrnsberger, Chad	.312	141	21	44	13	0	3	21	0
Everett, Brady	.150	20	3	3	1	0	0	0	0
Gray, Antoin	.269	353	36	95	23	2	7	51	3
Heath, Demetrius	.281	359	65	101	16	3	1	25	30
Hill, Jamar	.253	249	33	63	14	3	9	37	10
Lentini, Fehlandt	.298	420	71	125	27	8	9	39	37
Meadows, Tydus	.290	259	49	75	15	2	7	49	5
*Metheny, Brent	.357	300	63	107	28	1	10	57	25
*Poulin, Max	.268	306	47	82	15	3	6	32	5
Richardson, Dustin	.125	24	2	3	1	0	0	1	0
Roberson, Colin	.214	131	20	28	5	1	7	23	11
Schade, Scott	.216	51	5	11	1	0	1	3	0
*Sherrer, Jason	.179	84	8	15	1	0	0	8	0
Stillwagon, Nicholas	.188	32	2	6	0	0	0	2	0
West, Kevin	.317	347	59	110	22	1	18	74	1

PITCHERS	W	L	ERA	G	SV	IP	H	BB	SO
*Ariail, Ryan	4	2	3.88	38	0	51	54	32	58
*Baldwin, Zachary	5	7	4.70	20	0	111	138	33	55
Bay, Bear	8	7	5.28	20	0	116	131	42	102
Beuning, Brian	6	4	1.75	51	9	82	62	30	64
Blanco, Ivan	0	0	7.56	3	0	8	12	6	9
Dupas, Greg	0	0	9.00	6	0	8	9	7	6
Foltin, Wayne	1	1	10.13	17	0	16	29	12	15
Jackson, Aaron	6	3	4.21	25	0	77	89	37	46
Kalafos, Adam	0	0	17.05	7	0	6	11	8	5
Kintzler, Brandon	7	6	4.65	20	0	112	139	36	73
Mendoza, Cristian	2	4	3.80	29	11	24	25	10	27
*Michael, Mark	0	2	3.77	4	0	14	12	3	7
*Pease, Dustin	3	3	3.16	37	1	80	75	26	80
Poulin, Max	0	0	0.00	2	0	2	1	0	1
Ransom, Robert	0	2	15.12	3	0	8	16	4	5
Schade, Scott	0	0	0.00	2	0	2	1	0	1
Walker, Andrew	9	4	4.45	21	0	121	150	33	62

UNITED LEAGUE

Amarillo knocked off Alexandria in the United League championship series, but the loss on the field was only the second most painful blow for Aces fans. Because of the league's financial issues, the rules for the first round of the playoffs were tweaked during the season to ensure that the teams with superior attendance got to host the playoffs. That meant that the defending champions had to travel to San Angelo for the entire first round of the playoffs. Then in the final week of the season, the Aces learned that their final series of the season was being moved to Amarillo. Harlingen and Laredo—the two teams that didn't make the playoffs—had their seasons called early to save money. On the field, the Dillas ended the Aces bid for a three-peat as Amarillo starter Ron Lowe shut down the Aces bats while the Dillas scored four runs in the first on their way to a 7-4 win in the deciding Game Three. Alexandria ended up playing every playoff game on the road.

TEAM	W	L	PCT	GB
San Angelo	54	29	.651	—
Alexandria	50	35	.588	5
Amarillo	50	36	.581	5.5
Edinburg	41	44	.482	14
Laredo	39	48	.448	17
Harlingen	20	62	.244	33.5

PLAYOFFS: Semifinals—Alexandria defeated San Angelo 2-1 and Amarillo defeated Edinburg 2-0 in best-of-five series. Finals—Amarillo defeated Alexandria 2-1 in best-of-5 series.

MANAGERS: Alexandria—Ricky VanAsselberg. Amarillo—Brady Bogart. Edinburg—Vince Moore. Harlingen—Al Gallagher. Laredo—Dan Shwam. San Angelo—Doc Edwards.

ATTENDANCE: Amarillo 159,322; San Angelo 100,741; Edinburg 82,040; Harlingen 65,956; Alexandria 49,740; Laredo 45,542.

INDIVIDUAL BATTING LEADERS

BATTER, CLUB	AVG	G	AB	R	H	HR	RBI
Bravo, Danny, Amarillo	.372	85	328	68	122	18	90
Rodriguez, Andres, San Angelo	.368	83	353	71	130	21	107
White, Dwayne, Laredo	.357	87	345	69	123	8	61
Frichter, Bryan, San Angelo	.349	83	344	72	120	12	62
Torres, Jose, San Angelo	.345	79	278	96	96	15	50
Schneidmiller, Gary, Amarillo	.343	75	277	63	95	5	55
Sabatella, Bryan, Alexandria	.340	84	350	88	119	14	54
Cone, Aaron, San Angelo	.338	66	228	60	77	13	70
Pendergrass, Tyrone, San Angelo	.336	71	301	62	101	6	42
Reynoso, Jonathan, Amarillo	.331	85	360	102	119	16	67

INDIVIDUAL PITCHING LEADERS

PITCHER, CLUB	W	L	ERA	IP	H	BB	SO
Hernandez, Santos, Laredo	8	6	3.55	112	109	37	132
Lugo, Jorge, Harlingen	3	4	3.78	69	53	44	76
Heaston, Bryan, Edinburg	3	3	3.80	71	77	36	60
Lowe, Ronald, Amarillo	6	1	3.90	88	96	38	84
Montoya, Eric, Edinburg	10	2	3.92	106	115	35	97
Linder, Chad, Alexandria	7	3	4.15	113	125	31	110
Martinez, Gregorio, Laredo	6	5	4.17	101	103	44	116
Henschel, Brian, San Angelo	10	3	4.36	120	157	16	82
Williamson, Logan, San Angelo	12	4	4.50	104	118	44	78
Schon, Andy, Laredo	8	5	4.61	107	128	34	94

ALEXANDRIA ACES

BATTERS	AVG	AB	R	H	2B	3B	HR	RBI	SB
Bethea, Larry	.176	17	3	3	0	0	2	5	0
*Butler, Blake	.279	129	27	36	8	1	0	14	4
*Edwards, Madison	.264	239	34	63	12	0	3	30	3
Farrar, Tyler	.207	29	5	6	1	0	0	0	1
Fitzpatrick, Eddie	.208	192	30	40	9	0	1	26	1
*Gonzalez, Albert	.251	175	33	44	6	2	0	13	1
Guance, Luis	.328	320	64	105	18	0	11	61	18
Karr, Palmer	.302	252	52	76	15	1	15	51	9
*Langaigne, Selwyn	.330	297	50	98	19	1	5	50	6
Marshall, Andre	.361	169	25	61	12	1	3	32	8
*Matlock, Robert	.250	24	3	6	0	0	0	3	1
*Nichols, Brian	.385	52	12	20	2	0	4	11	0
O'Sullivan, Patrick	.355	166	34	59	15	0	13	48	2
Ovalles, Homy	.216	222	22	48	6	1	6	31	1
Ozuna, Rafael	.326	181	33	59	11	2	10	42	3
Sabatella, Bryan	.340	350	88	119	16	2	14	54	36
*Turney, Brad	.250	32	3	8	1	1	0	3	0
Umbria, Jose	.288	219	28	63	9	0	1	29	0

PITCHERS	W	L	ERA	G	SV	IP	H	BB	SO
Abriola, Derek	1	2	6.92	6	0	13	17	13	8
*Brooks, Tyler	0	0	3.09	4	0	12	9	14	7
*Cameron, Jeremy	0	0	7.94	10	0	28	55	10	10
Foster, Charlie	5	0	4.46	26	2	34	48	10	32
Garcia, Felipe	3	1	3.45	8	0	16	7	2	27
Guzman, Angel	2	4	4.45	19	0	55	56	17	62
Harris, Ryan	0	0	7.36	3	0	15	29	9	15
Hedden, Wayne	2	3	4.15	30	13	56	64	39	67
*Jimenez, Juan	0	0	8.10	5	0	10	13	6	5
*Linder, Chad	7	3	4.15	17	0	113	125	31	110

	W	L	ERA	IP	H	BB	SO		
Litchfield, B.J.	1	1	2.82	22	0	22	20	9	12
Martinez, Alejandro	5	3	6.24	13	1	49	50	32	37
Ovalles, Juan	4	4	4.02	51	11	63	59	34	95
*Portillo, Ramon	8	4	4.82	18	0	97	119	33	89
*Ramirez, Ronald	1	2	3.81	21	0	28	35	10	29
Rockholt, Ryan	0	0	9.00	6	0	9	17	8	7
*Sosa, Alexis	9	5	5.21	18	0	104	118	45	109
*Turney, Brad	0	1	13.50	2	0	5	12	1	4
*Wooley, Robert	2	2	6.23	6	0	26	35	15	23

AMARILLO DILLAS

BATTERS	AVG	AB	R	H	2B	3B	HR	RBI	SB
Ashton, Josh	.280	311	48	87	13	3	0	37	1
*Brachold, Keith	.319	339	92	108	23	9	11	75	14
Bravo, Danny	.372	328	68	122	26	1	18	90	12
Bueno, Brian	.189	95	9	18	4	1	0	8	0
*Douglas, Stephen	.290	293	47	85	13	2	3	45	16
*Gonzalez, Joel	.265	49	10	13	4	1	0	10	1
Johnson, A.J.	.278	331	61	92	17	2	19	75	5
*McLain, Sam	.282	110	15	31	7	2	1	18	1
Reynoso, Jonathan	.331	360	102	119	27	6	16	67	12
Schneidmiller, Gary	.343	277	63	95	22	0	5	55	8
Wenger, Justin	.270	233	46	63	10	1	2	24	1
Wong, Andrew	.282	301	47	85	14	5	3	45	2

PITCHERS	W	L	ERA	G	SV	IP	H	BB	SO
Allen, Taylor	8	7	5.85	17	0	108	128	44	85
Castillo, Marcos	10	6	6.17	18	0	127	162	27	79
*Jackson, Drew	3	1	3.52	14	4	15	17	3	25
Koons, David	3	0	1.86	15	3	19	21	4	17
*Lowe, Ronald	6	1	3.90	16	0	88	96	38	84
Mateo, Nathanael	1	1	3.86	25	2	30	31	16	30
*Posey, Micah	11	2	5.91	17	0	107	133	58	79
Roberts, Ralph	1	3	3.03	29	11	39	41	13	41
*Rodriguez, Jesse	2	8	6.13	19	0	72	98	37	55
*Smith, Eric	2	2	9.68	22	1	31	55	29	17
Smith, Josh	1	4	6.22	21	2	85	119	39	67
Smith, Matt	1	1	4.15	11	0	13	12	11	14
*Wooley, Robert	1	0	0.90	4	0	10	10	1	6

EDINBURG COYOTES

BATTERS	AVG	AB	R	H	2B	3B	HR	RBI	SB
Aranda, Nick	.302	96	21	29	6	0	0	11	10
Arrowood, Jason	.250	92	15	23	3	0	3	10	0
Entrekin, Alex	.307	189	41	58	14	1	4	27	6
Fermin, Angelo	.300	327	44	98	17	4	2	43	32
Garcia, Geivy	.000	1	0	0	0	0	0	0	0
Gaylord, Patrick	.287	150	22	43	5	0	1	17	1
German, Amado	.273	209	34	57	7	3	6	34	8
Gonzalez, Eric	.263	300	52	79	15	0	6	57	10
Jones, Daryl	.288	313	60	90	23	1	11	53	32
*Matlock, Robert	.295	173	29	51	6	2	2	21	1
McConnell, Brandon	.240	104	13	25	3	0	2	13	1
*Nunez, Argelis	.308	133	18	41	6	1	4	24	7
Roche, Gary	.304	250	40	76	13	0	0	41	8
Santana, Mayobanex	.274	277	46	76	16	4	3	41	5
Williams, Jermaine	.333	39	9	13	1	0	0	11	1
Wilson, Eddie	.261	88	14	23	2	0	1	10	5
Wood, Logan	.240	208	39	50	10	2	6	44	10

PITCHERS	W	L	ERA	G	SV	IP	H	BB	SO
Castro, Julio	1	4	4.36	37	9	43	34	17	53
Clay, Adam	1	3	6.62	18	0	18	27	9	8
Daniels, Isaac	0	1	7.31	12	0	16	21	23	12
Garcia, Geivy	0	3	10.50	4	0	18	31	10	24
Gaylord, Patrick	0	0	0.00	1	0	2	0	0	2
Gonzalez, Eric	0	0	4.50	2	0	2	2	0	0
Guerra, Aaron	9	3	5.38	20	0	109	123	34	95
Heaston, Bryan	3	3	3.80	36	0	71	77	36	60
*Jan, Carlos	2	4	7.43	10	0	53	74	27	47
*Martinez, Miguel	7	5	5.03	20	0	91	100	56	70
Maschino, John	3	6	8.65	24	0	60	65	50	60
McConnell, Brandon	0	0	3.86	2	0	2	4	0	3
Mondesir, James	2	2	4.50	8	0	30	24	27	23

Montoya, Eric	10	2	3.92	16	0	106	115	35	97
Prihoda, Luke	3	0	3.18	37	9	40	30	8	49
*Smith, Clint	0	1	4.50	10	0	16	17	11	7
*Steed, Bric	0	3	12.38	12	0	24	48	19	14
*Trevino, Toro	0	3	8.78	10	0	28	47	13	18
*Venas, Miliade	0	1	10.80	3	0	10	13	10	6

HARLINGEN WHITEWINGS

BATTERS	AVG	AB	R	H	2B	3B	HR	RBI	SB
*Bergstrom, Bub	.266	169	33	45	11	1	0	13	9
Cardona, Dave	.244	266	27	65	10	1	5	25	2
Fowler, David	.264	307	54	81	14	4	8	38	16
Fox, Ryan	.248	290	57	72	18	3	16	65	0
*Gonzalez, Joel	.238	126	22	30	7	0	5	19	1
Griffin, Kevin	.320	303	53	97	22	4	3	37	15
Hendricks, Trey	.218	124	8	27	4	0	1	7	0
*Johnson, Carl	.220	109	16	24	5	1	3	12	7
Kramer, Matt	.222	27	6	6	5	0	0	4	0
*Lawman, Matthew	.273	55	6	15	2	0	0	4	3
*Nichols, Brian	.291	268	33	78	9	6	9	46	4
*Nunez, Argelis	.294	197	33	58	13	0	9	40	1
Peguero, Miguel	.271	70	9	19	3	0	0	5	0
Perez, Candelario	.273	99	13	27	4	0	1	7	0
Roblez, Terry	.253	174	23	44	8	1	4	26	1
*Sillivent, Greg	.214	28	6	6	0	0	0	2	1
Slagle, Anthony	.091	44	9	4	1	0	0	4	0
Street, Chris	.000	3	0	0	0	0	0	0	0
Zazueta, Amadeo	.291	227	29	66	14	1	5	43	6

PITCHERS	W	L	ERA	G	SV	IP	H	BB	SO
Balbuena, Caleb	0	1	1.08	17	7	17	12	7	20
*Barber, Rhett	0	0	5.79	4	0	5	4	4	5
Beever, James	0	1	14.21	2	0	6	21	1	1
Bennett, Derek	1	2	6.48	18	1	25	34	20	27
Casas, Armando	0	2	15.43	4	0	14	26	12	10
Cordero, Angel	1	5	5.66	18	0	56	48	34	61
Cress, Joey	0	1	24.75	2	0	4	10	4	3
*Daly, Brian	0	3	8.82	16	0	16	31	13	13
Darling, Bobby	1	7	6.66	25	0	74	94	48	53
*DelaCruz, Maximino	0	0	0.00	1	0	1	0	0	1
Evoniuk, Kenny	0	4	6.92	8	0	40	45	35	32
Fox, Ryan	0	0	0.00	3	0	2	0	0	3
Gett, Alex	3	8	6.04	16	0	82	99	40	72
*Herrera, Bryan	0	4	7.04	6	0	31	33	34	20
*Jimenez, Juan C.	2	4	5.40	14	0	43	51	27	35
*Kling, Brandon	1	2	4.58	11	0	18	23	10	11
*Lugo, Jorge	3	4	3.78	12	0	69	53	44	76
Lutz, Todd	2	8	6.75	20	0	80	110	30	53
Nehls, Brock	1	3	6.00	5	0	30	38	17	36
*Smith, Clint	0	0	21.60	2	0	2	4	3	2
Sosa, Miguel	1	0	5.94	3	0	17	24	10	8
*Staatz, Justin	0	1	5.85	12	0	20	21	19	26
Street, Chris	1	0	6.97	11	0	10	13	10	8
*Trevino, Toro	0	1	2.08	5	0	9	6	3	6
Valentin, Daniel	2	1	4.91	5	0	22	28	6	18
*Ziegler, Dan	1	0	5.14	8	0	14	15	10	11

LAREDO BRONCOS

BATTERS	AVG	AB	R	H	2B	3B	HR	RBI	SB
*Bennett, Anthony	.263	266	52	70	12	0	2	31	9
Clemente, Edgard	.294	279	52	82	21	0	13	56	0
Day, Ben	.000	10	2	0	0	0	0	0	0
*Gamble, Sean	.266	79	15	21	2	1	1	5	3
*Gonzalez, Josue	.300	50	6	15	2	0	0	5	0
Guerrero, Santiago	.241	158	21	38	7	0	4	14	8
*Lawman, Matthew	.317	126	23	40	6	1	2	19	6
Lewis, Mark	.231	26	3	6	0	0	0	2	3
Lopez, Johnny	.288	59	9	17	2	0	1	5	0
Morrison, Joshua	.100	40	2	4	0	0	2	5	0
Padilla, Eric	.230	139	20	32	4	1	2	15	2
*Perez, Mark	.263	19	0	5	1	0	0	3	0
Ponce, Arnoldo	.316	297	51	94	23	1	8	51	1
Reyes, Ivan	.251	271	41	68	18	1	12	47	4

	.320	103	10	33	3	0	3	15	1
Salas, Jose	.320	103	10	33	3	0	3	15	1
Sanchez, Luany	.319	323	62	103	21	1	18	71	2
Tinius, Ben	.295	220	22	65	7	1	5	31	0
*White, Dwayne	.357	345	69	123	20	7	8	61	10
Wright, Steven	.241	162	32	39	10	1	5	11	7

PITCHERS	W	L	ERA	G	SV	IP	H	BB	SO
*Barber, Rhett	2	1	6.00	10	1	15	10	13	15
Bartlett, Richard	2	5	7.97	10	0	50	69	41	39
Bauman, Matt	0	0	9.75	6	0	12	16	7	12
Callaway, Mickey	2	1	3.00	7	0	18	18	8	12
Cepeda, Benigno	1	0	1.40	13	3	19	13	11	21
Cordero, Jose	0	1	23.14	1	0	2	5	4	3
Crawford, Nathan	0	2	8.87	18	1	22	29	20	16
*DelaCruz, Maximino	0	0	2.84	4	0	6	4	5	6
*Donlin, Sean	2	6	4.53	11	0	60	63	28	55
Gonzalez, Josue	0	0	9.00	1	0	1	2	0	0
Hernandez, Santos	8	6	3.55	18	0	112	109	37	132
*Jones, Rusty	1	2	4.99	39	3	49	58	23	49
Lozado, Henry	0	3	13.91	4	0	11	22	11	9
Martinez, Gregorio	6	5	4.17	17	0	101	103	44	116
Odom, John	0	1	6.10	3	0	10	13	6	6
Padilla, Eric	0	0	0.00	1	0	0	0	1	0
Sausville, Dan	3	3	5.40	33	2	55	66	39	41
Schon, Andy	8	5	4.61	17	0	107	128	34	94
Smith, John	0	2	11.17	10	2	10	11	14	13
*Staatz, Justin	0	0	7.24	9	0	14	12	17	19
Wasylak, David	3	1	3.63	26	2	35	32	26	35
Watkins, Dave	1	1	3.38	16	4	16	15	15	24
*Williams, Julian	0	3	14.19	13	0	26	52	16	26

SAN ANGELO COLTS

BATTERS	AVG	AB	R	H	2B	3B	HR	RBI	SB
*Anderson, John	.318	337	69	107	21	3	1	47	25
Beal, John	.200	45	10	9	0	1	0	7	2
Belew, Charley	.224	263	30	59	8	1	0	31	1
*Chapman, Jack	.118	17	2	2	0	0	0	3	0
*Cone, Aaron	.338	228	60	77	23	2	13	70	0
Craig, Benny	.246	142	20	35	4	0	5	21	0
Crosland, Jason	.228	145	29	33	9	1	6	20	0
*Diggs, Wyn	.301	246	43	74	9	1	4	41	1
Dunlap, Brett	.000	5	0	0	0	0	0	0	0
Frichter, Bryan	.349	344	72	120	32	3	12	62	9
*Gonzalez, Albert	.320	25	9	8	1	0	0	3	1
Landreth, Jason	.375	96	19	36	5	0	7	35	1
*McLain, Sam	.227	22	2	5	1	0	0	4	0
Mendoza, Robert	.269	26	1	7	0	0	0	1	0
Miller, Adam	.270	37	6	10	3	0	1	8	0
Mongiardo, Chris	.200	5	0	1	0	0	0	1	0
Pendergrass, Tyrone	.336	301	62	101	11	4	6	42	21
Rhomberg, Joe	.238	42	5	10	5	0	1	5	0
*Richardson, Craig	.071	14	3	1	0	0	0	0	0
Rodriguez, Andres	.368	353	71	130	27	0	21	107	1
Torres, Jose	.345	278	96	96	18	1	15	50	27

PITCHERS	W	L	ERA	G	SV	IP	H	BB	SO
*Daly, Brian	0	3	10.80	15	6	13	17	9	11
Fleming, Taylor	3	1	9.49	9	0	12	27	4	8
Freites, Julio	0	0	6.23	2	0	4	4	2	3
Greanead, Matt	0	0	6.49	16	1	26	34	18	27
Henschel, Brian	10	3	4.36	19	0	120	157	16	82
*James, Frank	7	5	5.28	19	0	106	124	42	72
*Kling, Brandon	1	0	9.00	7	0	16	23	7	11
Lively, Mitchell	0	0	2.13	11	4	13	11	0	18
Massetti, Jason	5	4	5.55	21	5	84	100	16	76
McKinney, Billy	3	4	5.98	9	0	44	52	15	27
*Merricks, Alex	4	1	5.61	14	0	26	23	21	36
Mulle, Ryan	3	2	5.45	18	1	36	47	19	29
*Robinson, Justin	1	0	1.64	12	0	11	10	4	11
Rodgers, Caleb	2	0	4.67	4	0	17	25	4	22
Romero, Robert	0	0	2.89	8	2	9	4	3	14
*Venas, Miliade	0	0	4.71	27	3	29	32	14	21
Weast, Chris	3	0	3.59	15	2	43	51	20	35
*Wilburn, Brian	0	2	2.70	4	0	10	14	4	9
*Williamson, Logan	12	4	4.50	18	0	104	118	44	78

INTERNATIONAL BASEBALL

South Korea stuns Cuba in final Olympic tourney

BY JOHN MANUEL

With the last Olympic gold medal on the line, the situation at Beijing's Wukesong Baseball Facility seemed to be exactly what Cuba wanted.

It trailed South Korea 3-2 in the last of the ninth inning, but Cuba finally had gotten to South Korea's ace starter, 21-year-old lefthander Ryu Hyun-jin. Ryu, who had given up just two runs, left with the bases loaded with one out, and Cuba's Yuliesky Gourriel came to the plate.

Gourriel in many ways is the jewel of Cuban baseball and perhaps its best-known player. His father Lourdes starred on Cuba's national teams in the 1980s, and now Gourriel has played in two Olympics and the World Baseball Classic. The 24-year-old has been regarded as Cuba's top young major league prospect for much of this decade.

Gourriel was just 8-for-34 in Beijing as he batted in the ninth, and after two solid but unspectacular seasons in Cuba's Serie Nacional, Gourriel could have used the gold-medal winning hit to burnish his reputation. A win also would re-establish Cuba's claim to international dominance, as the island nation has not won a major international tournament since Athens in the 2004 Games.

South Korean reliever Chong Tae-hyon stood in the way for both Gourriel and Cuba. The side-arming righthander pitched for South Korea in the 2000 Olympics, helping the team win its first Olympic baseball medal, a bronze, and was part of the nation's WBC club as well, a team that was undefeated through the round-robin but lost in the medal round to rival Japan in San Diego.

Chong made sure that this time, South Korea finished what it started. He got Gourriel to ground into a game-ending 6-4-3 double play to end the game. South Korea won 3-2, finished the Games undefeated to win its first Olympic gold.

Scouts and observers agreed the Koreans had the tournament's best, most complete team, and after nine straight victories, the Koreans themselves believed it. The team's most famous player, 32-year-old first baseman Lee Seung-yeop, had hit only one homer for the Yomiuri Giants in Japan this season before leaving for the Olympics. Lee then hit the two most important home runs of the event, a two-run homer to break a 2-2 tie with Japan in a 6-2 semifinal victory, then a two-run homer in the first inning of the gold-medal win.

Korean veteran Lee Seung-yeop hit the two most important homers of the Olympics

"Looking at the gold medal, I still ask myself how we pulled it off," Lee told the Korea Times when it was all over. "It's incredible. I used to think Japan was a notch above us. But that has changed after the (Olympic) competition."

Pitching Carries Korea, Cuba

South Korea took a back seat to no one because it was a team without weakness. The team had excellent starting pitching, an offense capable of winning with power, speed or situational hitting; first-rate defense; and a manager in Kim Kyung-moon who molded a group of professionals into a cohesive team. The same couldn't be said for Japan, which sent a big league roster from its pro leagues but failed to medal for the second time in the last three Olympics, and the United States, which rallied from a dispiriting loss to Cuba in the semifinal to beat Japan and win the bronze medal.

"In the past, Korea had a lot of slugging power-oriented guys, but this was a complete team," said a veteran international scout with an American League organization. "They had legit athletes, and every one of those guys had played a lot of international competition. That team was a product of Korea's player development and its international program. It's very impressive."

Another international scout with a different AL organization agreed and focused on the Koreans' pitching. Lefthanders Kim Kwang-hyun and Ryu combined to pitch 32 innings (out of the team's 82) and gave up just five runs (four earned).

"Ryu . . . would be a first-rounder in the U.S.," the second scout said. "The other lefty who beat Japan, Kim Kwang-Hyun, would be entering the draft next year. Both pitchers were first-rounders out of high school in Korea. Any college pitchers in the U.S. capable of shutting the door for eight-plus innings in a medal-round game? Korea had two."

American lefthander Mike Minor of Vanderbilt beat Cuba earlier in the summer, but that was in the Netherlands during Haarlem Honkbal Week. Those losses led to speculation that Cuba's team was in decline, but the Cubans showed that was anything but true. They led the event in scoring and beat Team USA's collegiate ace, flamethrowing righthander Stephen Strasburg (San Diego State), in the semifinal.

U.S. manager Davey Johnson had his pitching set up as he wanted, with Twins lefthander Brian Duensing and Indians righthander Jeff Stevens—both Triple-A pitchers and veterans of the 2007 gold medal-winning World Cup team—ready to relieve. But Cuba hit four homers in the 10-2 rout, including a pair of three-run shots in the eighth off Stevens and reliever Blaine Neal (Tigers), and 37-year-old righthanders Norge Vera and Pedro Luis Lazo toyed with the American lineup, allowing just six hits.

"We've beaten Cuba with regularity here lately," said USA Baseball general manager Bob Watson, "but they pitched a bit better with Vera and Lazo. They are trying to break in some new guys (in the lineup), but their experience of playing in the international game is still ther mound."

Three The Hard Way

Cuba's best shot was too good for the Americans, but Johnson rallied his players for the next day's game against Japan with a medal on the line. Scouts and Watson credited Team USA's players for coming back to earn a medal. It's the third medal for the U.S. in the five Olympics in which baseball was a medal sport, joining a bronze in 1996 and gold in 2000.

Nothing came easily for the Americans. Their two losses in the round-robin came with a walk-off 7-6 loss to South Korea in the opener, then a 5-4 loss to Cuba in a game that featured the new international tiebreaker rules. The International Baseball Federation, hoping to shorten games,

mandated prior to the Games that tie games heading into the 11th inning would begin with special speed-up rules. Teams begin the inning with runners at first and second, and managers can pick which hitter begins the inning.

The U.S.-Cuba game was the first such game, and the format didn't work for Team USA when second baseman Jayson Nix (Rockies), attempting to bunt on the inning's first pitch, fouled a ball off his face, sidelining him until the bronze-medal game. Nix's injury wasn't the only one the Americans dealt with, as they lost first baseman Matt LaPorta (Indians) for three games due to a mild concussion after he was hit by a pitch in a 9-1 victory against China.

The U.S. then had to overcome its Cuba loss in the semis, and lefthander Brett Anderson (Athletics) was shaky early as Japan led 4-1 in the third inning of the bronze-medal game. The U.S. rallied to tie in the bottom of the third on a three-run homer by Matt Brown (Angels), whose 10 RBIs were tops on the club. Anderson settled down, and the U.S. rallied for four runs in the fifth with a two-run double by catcher Taylor Teagarden (Rangers) and a two-run homer by Jason Donald (Phillies).

"After last night and coming into today, we could have folded really easily, especially when they got up 4-1," Donald said after beating Japan. "It was a great win. We would have liked to have won a gold (medal) but . . . getting out of here with a medal, that is huge."

The Olympics don't have baseball on the schedule after 2008, a factor that was the focus for much of the American media coverage of the tournament. Those who paid attention saw a gritty effort by the Americans, another shocking failure by Japan, and the panache of the Cubans. And they missed a virtuoso performance by the South Koreans.

"There's no question Korea was the better team," concluded one of the scouts. "They should've won the WBC, and they won the world juniors and the Olympics in the same month. They may not have had the best individual player, but they had the best manager, and they had the best team."

Past Olympic Games have served as springboards to big league careers for players from 11 countries other than the United States, and 119 players overall according to research by Baseball America's Jim Callis. The Beijing Games are sure to produce future big leaguers as well, as several scouts and veteran international observers considered it the strongest international tournament ever aside from the inaugural 2006 World Baseball Classic.

"The quality of play was unbelievable," said a veteran international scout. "One of the coaches from Taiwan has been to every Olympic tournament ever, and he said top to bottom it was by far the best field."

One scout credited the Chinese team with helping make the tournament as competitive as it was. China's national team program started five years ago in preparation for these Games, and the scout credited former big league manager Jim Lefebvre and his staff for getting the program from zero to competitive in that time. China won only once, but it was against Taiwan—known as Chinese Taipei internationally because China does not recognize its independence. A second scout called China's victory the biggest upset in Olympic history.

"I thought China made the whole event," the first scout said. "They were a legitimate, solid team, and they played with maximum effort out of every player."

■ Baseball comes up for a vote to return to the Olympic program in November 2009, when the International Olympic Committee picks the host city and sets the schedule for the 2016 Games. IOC president Jacques Rogge watched the bronze-medal game with IBAF president Dr. Harvey Schiller, and Rogge reiterated to media in Beijing that he wants major league players at the next Olympics. One plan the IBAF has floated to that end would have big leaguers show up for the medal round, with the current format used for the round robin. Baseball also would seem to have a better chance to get back into the Games for 2016 if the Olympics are held in Chicago or Tokyo, which are both finalists to be the host city.

One veteran observer wondered if baseball will ever fit in at the Olympics.

"You'd think they could lobby off this, with how strong this tournament was and the quality of play here," said a scout. "But then you look around the Olympics at the quality of athlete—in tennis, they had Rafael Nadal and Roger Federer and the Williams sisters, and then men's basketball had all the NBA players on all those teams. I get the sense that if it's not major league players, there won't be baseball, and I don't see major leaguers happening. Dr. Schiller is doing an amazing job, but it's a pretty uphill climb."

OLYMPIC STANDINGS

Team	W	L	R	RA	GB
*South Korea	7	0	41	22	—
*Cuba	6	1	52	23	1
*United States	5	2	40	22	2
*Japan	4	3	30	14	3
Taiwan	2	5	29	33	5
Canada	2	5	29	20	5
Netherlands	1	6	9	50	6
China	1	6	14	60	6

*Qualified for medal round

MEDAL ROUND

Aug. 22 *Semifinals*
Cuba 10, U.S. 2 | South Korea 6, Japan 2
Aug. 23 *Gold Medal Game*
South Korea 3, Cuba 2
Aug. 23 *Bronze Medal Game*
U.S. 8, Japan 4

BATTING LEADERS
(Minimum 25 Plate Appearances)

Player, Team	AVG	AB	R	H	2B	3B	HR	RBI	SB
Bell, Alexei, CUB	.500	32	10	16	3	4	2	10	0
Lee, Yong-kyu, KOR	.481	27	8	13	2	0	0	4	1
Nishioka, Tsuyoshi, JAP	.455	22	6	10	1	0	1	4	2
Weglarz, Nick, CAN	.400	25	5	10	2	0	2	5	0
Despaigne, Alfredo, CUB	.382	34	5	13	2	1	3	12	0
Hou, Feng-lian, CHN	.381	21	2	8	0	0	0	3	0
Donald, Jason, USA	.381	21	4	8	1	0	1	5	1
Kim, Hyun-soo, KOR	.370	27	3	10	2	0	0	4	2
Lee, Dae-ho, KOR	.360	25	5	9	1	0	3	10	0
Tiffee, Terry, USA	.324	37	4	12	6	0	0	5	0
Jeong, Keun-woo, KOR	.310	29	5	9	1	0	1	1	1
Peng, Cheng-min, TWN	.310	29	5	9	3	0	0	2	1
Cepeda, Frederich, CUB	.308	26	11	8	1	1	2	5	0
Sun, Ling-feng, CHN	.296	27	2	8	2	0	0	2	2
Nakajima, Hiroyuki, JAP	.296	27	2	8	4	0	0	5	1

PITCHING LEADERS
(Minimum 7 IP)

Player, Team	W	L	ERA	G	SV	IP	H	BB	SO
Naruse, Yoshihisa, JAP	1	0	0.00	4	0	12	5	3	19
Jang, Won-sam, KOR	1	0	0.00	2	0	12	6	0	11
Sanchez, Elier, CUB	1	0	0.00	2	0	9	3	3	1
Wakui, Hideaki, JAP	2	0	0.66	3	0	14	6	2	13
Begg, Chris, CAN	1	1	0.75	2	0	12	10	0	14
Sugiuchi, Toshiya, JAP	1	0	0.84	2	0	11	7	3	9
Pan, Wei-lun, TWN	0	0	0.93	2	0	10	6	2	10
Ryu, Hyun-jin, KOR	2	0	1.04	2	0	17	10	5	13
Duensing, Brian, USA	1	0	1.17	4	0	8	3	2	5
Lazo, Pedro Luis, CUB	1	0	1.26	5	2	14	9	3	14
Kim, Kwang-hyun, KOR	1	0	1.26	3	0	14	10	3	12
Strasburg, Stephen, USA	1	1	1.64	2	0	11	7	1	16
Gonzalez, Norberto, CUB	0	1	1.69	4	2	11	4	3	9
Li, Chen-hao, CHN	0	1	1.80	2	0	10	7	4	2
Vera, Norge, CUB	2	0	1.93	3	0	14	11	2	4

TEAM USA STATISTICS

Player, Pos.	AVG	G	AB	R	H	2B	3B	HR	RBI	BB	SO	SB
Jason Donald	.381	8	21	4	8	1	0	1	5	5	3	1
Terry Tiffee	.324	9	37	4	12	6	0	0	5	2	6	0
Louis Marson	.308	5	13	3	4	0	0	0	3	3	3	0
Matthew Brown	.281	9	32	4	9	3	0	2	10	6	8	2
Brian Barden	.265	8	34	8	9	3	0	1	5	4	9	1
Dexter Fowler	.250	9	28	5	7	3	1	0	2	2	4	0
John Gall	.242	8	33	5	8	4	0	1	5	2	7	0
Nate Schierholtz	.216	9	37	7	8	4	0	1	6	2	9	0
Jayson Nix	.214	3	14	3	3	1	0	1	1	1	4	0
Taylor Teagarden	.188	5	16	2	3	2	0	0	4	4	8	0
Matt LaPorta	.158	6	19	3	3	0	0	2	4	3	8	0
Mike Hessman	.091	5	22	2	2	0	0	1	1	0	11	0

Pitcher	W	L	ERA	G	GS	SV	IP	H	R	ER	BB	SO
Jake Arrieta	1	0	0.00	1	1	0	6.0	2	0	0	2	7
Kevin Jepsen	0	0	0.00	4	0	1	5.2	3	0	0	2	5
Mike Koplove	0	0	0.00	4	0	0	5.1	0	0	0	1	6
Casey Weathers	0	0	0.00	3	0	0	3.0	3	2	0	1	5
Brian Duensing	1	0	1.17	4	0	0	7.2	3	1	1	2	5
Jeremy Cummings	0	0	1.80	2	0	0	5.0	3	1	1	0	2
Trevor Cahill	0	0	2.25	2	2	0	8.0	6	2	2	5	5
Stephen Strasburg	1	1	2.45	2	2	0	11.0	7	3	3	1	16
Brett Anderson	1	0	4.97	2	2	0	12.2	13	8	7	3	10
Brandon Knight	1	0	5.91	2	2	0	10.2	13	8	7	4	7
Blaine Neal	0	0	7.36	3	0	0	3.2	5	4	3	0	2
Jeff Stevens	1	2	9.00	4	0	0	4.0	6	7	4	1	2

Red Devils take 15th crown

The Mexico Red Devils are undoubtedly the flagship franchise in the Mexican League, and they added more hardware to their trophy case in 2008 with their 15th league title, the most in league history.

Amaury Cazana Marti, on loan from the Cardinals organization, paced the offense during the regular season, and righthander Elmer Dessens led a strong pitching staff as the Red Devils showed themselves to be the league's best team from beginning to end.

Dessens, the former big league pitcher with last played with the Rockies in 2007, won the championship clincher as the Red Devils beat Monterrey four games to one in the league finals. He also went 10-4, 4.03 in 105 innings.

Marti led the offense by batting .420/.493/.617 with seven home runs in just 188 at-bats, and former big leaguer Roberto Petagine also suppled offense in a short stint with Mexico, batting

.372/.488/.605 with six home runs in 37 games.

Dessens pitched eight innings as the Red Devils won Game Five 6-1 to clinch the series. It was the Mexico City-based team's first title since 2003, and the Red Devils became the first team to win the series on the road since 1996. Lefthander Dan Serafini also had a key start in the championship series, pitching seven scoreless innings in Game Three to stake the Red Devils to a 2-1 series lead.

Jose Luis "Borrego" Sandoval was voted as the MVP for the championship series, and Red Devils manager Daniel Fernandez won his first championship as a manager, after taking seven as a player

Saltillo's Kit Pellow was the league's offensive standout, winning the triple crown by batting .385 with 34 home runs and 107 RBIs. He also posted a .459 on-base percentage and .730 slugging percentage. Saltillo won the Northern Division in the first half of the season but was eliminated in the first round of the playoffs.

STANDINGS

FIRST HALF

NORTH	W	L	PCT	GB
Saltillo	37	18	.673	—
Monclova	35	21	.625	2½
Laguna	30	26	.536	7½
Chihuahua	28	28	.500	9½
Monterrey	26	30	.464	11½
Nuevo Laredo	26	30	.464	11½
Tijuana	22	33	.400	15
Puebla	20	36	.357	17½

SOUTH	W	L	PCT	GB
Yucatan	35	20	.636	—
Mexico	31	23	.574	3½
Quintana Roo	32	24	.571	3½
Veracruz	31	25	.554	4½
Tabasco	29	26	.527	6½
Campeche	26	30	.464	9½
Minatitlan	21	35	.375	14½
Oaxaca	15	39	.278	19½

SECOND HALF

NORTH	W	L	PCT	GB
Monterrey	38	16	.704	—
Monclova	34	19	.642	3½
Saltillo	29	24	.547	8½
Chihuahua	26	25	.510	10½
Tijuana	24	28	.462	13½
Puebla	23	29	.442	14½
Laguna	22	31	.415	15½
Nuevo Laredo	13	40	.245	24½

SOUTH	W	L	PCT	GB
Mexico	35	16	.686	—
Campeche	32	19	.627	3½
Quintana Roo	33	20	.623	3½
Yucatan	29	24	.547	7½
Tabasco	26	26	.500	9½
Veracruz	26	28	.481	10½

Oaxaca	15	36	.294	20½
Minatitlan	14	38	.269	21½

PLAYOFFS—Division Series: Mexico defeated Campeche 4-0, Monterrey defeated Saltillo 4-0, Yucatan defeated Quintana Roo 4-2 and Monclova defeated Chihuahua 4-3 in best-of-five series. Semifinals: Mexico defeated Yucatan 4-2 and Monterrey defeated Monclova 4-0 in best-of-five series. Finals: Mexico defeated Monterrey 4-1 in a best-of-five series.

ATTENDANCE—Monterrey 658,492; Saltillo 350,717; Monclova 320,102; Laguna 298,759; Yucatan 261,908; Tijuana 240,615; Mexico 222,038; Quintana Roo 210,524; Chihuahua 209,986; Veracruz 205,927; Oaxaca 186,172; Nuevo Laredo 178,098; Puebla 172,527; Minatitlan 162,439; Tabasco 160,435; Campeche 149,492

INDIVIDUAL BATTING LEADERS

	AVG	G	AB	R	H	2B	3B	HR	RBI	BB	SO	SB
Pellow, Kit, Sal	.385	103	374	91	144	27	0	34	107	49	64	3
Bojorquez, Victor, Mex	.364	103	415	75	151	23	6	11	85	16	55	5
Castellano, Pedro, NL	.361	104	371	49	134	25	1	11	61	50	48	3
Quintero, Christian, Oax	.359	102	390	76	140	25	2	12	59	34	46	21
Rodriguez, Victor, Tab	.358	105	397	62	142	21	0	8	57	25	23	3
Valdes, Pedro, Oax	.357	104	359	57	128	25	0	17	78	65	31	0
White, Derrick, Tij	.356	71	264	50	94	16	0	16	66	39	40	1
Presichi, Cristhian, Sal	.351	103	382	70	134	29	1	16	74	41	39	18
Rivera, Ruben, Cam	.350	105	366	76	128	22	4	25	70	66	74	22
Arredondo, Eduardo, Mex	.349	74	289	53	101	15	2	1	27	18	19	9

INDIVIDUAL PITCHING LEADERS

	W	L	ERA	G	GS	CG	SV	IP	H	R	BB	SO
Delgadillo, Juan, Lag	10	4	2.29	21	21	0	0	130	110	45	48	78
Campos, Francisco, Cam	11	5	2.41	23	23	2	0	150	118	43	39	115
Gonzalez, Leonardo, Tab	9	8	2.53	21	20	2	0	121	110	42	35	93
Rodriguez, Nerio, Mon	17	3	2.54	20	19	0	0	124	113	38	25	98
Rivera, Oscar, Yuc	12	4	2.60	20	20	3	0	121	96	37	48	80
Ramirez, Jose, QR	11	4	2.72	26	19	0	0	103	96	34	28	42
Rivera, Francisco, NL/QR	10	7	2.77	24	19	1	1	114	112	39	26	51
Vargas, Joel, Tab	9	5	2.93	19	19	1	0	120	122	44	24	62
Rodriguez, Raul, Mon	7	6	3.04	19	18	5	0	113	103	46	22	40
Ortega, Pablo, QR	11	5	3.05	23	23	0	0	121	121	44	28	57

Seibu wins 10th Japanese crown

BY WAYNE GRACZYK

The Pacific League's Seibu Lions claimed the title of champions of Japanese baseball for 2008 after defeating the Central League's Yomiuri Giants in an exciting seven-game Japan Series.

Led by freshman manager and former Lions pitcher Hisanobu Watanabe, Seibu won its first Japan Series since 2004 and 10th since the team was bought by the Seibu Railways and moved from the city of Fukuoka to the western Tokyo suburb of Tokorozawa in the Saitama prefecture in 1979.

Lions righthander Takayuki Kishi was named Japan Series MVP after pitching 14⅔ innings of shutout ball and winning two games.

Seibu led the Pacific League throughout most of the season and qualified for the Japan Series by beating the Nippon Ham Fighters of Hokkaido in Stage Two of the Climax Series playoffs. The Fighters had finished third in the Pacific League during the regular season and defeated the second place Orix Buffaloes in Stage One of the PLCS.

The Giants, based in Tokyo and managed by Tatsunori Hara, came back from a 13-game deficit in mid-July to win the Central League pennant by two games over the Hanshin Tigers of Osaka. The Chunichi Dragons of Nagoya finished third and beat the Tigers in Stage One of the CL Climax Series. Yomiuri knocked off the Dragons in Stage Two.

A total of 67 foreigners played in Japanese baseball in 2008, including league leaders in major categories. Rick Short of the Rakuten Golden Eagles won the Pacific League batting title, edging Seibu shortstop Hiroyuki Nakajima, .332 to .331. Forty-year-old Orix slugger Tuffy Rhodes, playing his 12th season in Japan, topped the PL with 118 RBIs and hit 40 home runs while batting .277.

Yomiuri leftfielder Alex Ramirez, an eight-year Japan veteran, led the Central League with 125 RBIs while hitting .319 with 45 home runs. His teammate Seth Greisinger was the CL's leading pitcher with 17 victories, and another Giants righthander, closer Marc Kroon, led both leagues with 41 saves.

The season began with three American managers but ended with two. Marty Brown served his third year as field boss of the Carp and narrowly missed making the Central League Climax Series with a fourth-place finish. Similarly, Bobby Valentine's Chiba Lotte Marines fell a half-game shy of qualifying for the Pacific League postseason.

Brown and Valentine are expected to return to their Japanese clubs in 2009.

Terry Collins, guiding the Orix club for a second year, resigned in mid-May, leaving the Buffaloes in the hands of Japanese head coach Daijiro Oishi, who rallied the team and led Orix to a second-place finish and a berth in the Pacific League Climax Series.

Two midsummer all-star games were played, with the leagues splitting the series. The Pacific League won 5-4 at Kyocera Osaka Dome on July 31, and the Central came back with a victory by the score of 11-6 on Aug. 1 at Yokohama Stadium.

Fukuoka SoftBank Hawks manager Sadaharu Oh, the world home run king with 868 during his career and skipper of Japan's 2006 World Baseball Classic champions, retired at the end of the year, citing age (68) and health concerns.

STANDINGS

CENTRAL LEAGUE	W	L	T	Pct.	GB
Yomiuri Giants	84	57	3	.596	—
Hanshin Tigers	82	59	3	.582	2
Chunichi Dragons	71	68	5	.511	12
Hiroshima Carp	69	70	5	.496	14
Yakult Swallows	66	74	4	.471	17 ½
Yokohama BayStars	48	94	2	.338	36 ½

CLIMAX SERIES PLAYOFFS—Stage One: Chunichi defeated Hanshin 2-1 in best-of-three series. **Stage Two:** Yomiuri defeated Chunichi 3-1-1 in best-of-seven series.

INDIVIDUAL BATTING LEADERS
(MINIMUM 446 PLATE APPEARANCES)

	AVG.	AB	R	H	2B	3B	HR	RBI	SB
Uchikawa, Seiichi, BayStars	.378	500	83	189	37	1	14	67	2
Aoki, Norichika, Swallows	.347	444	85	154	29	5	14	64	31
Kurihara, Kenta, Carp	.332	557	69	185	31	1	23	103	5
Murata, Shuichi, BayStars	.323	489	89	158	25	2	46	114	0
Morino, Masahiko, Dragons	.321	358	63	115	25	1	19	59	1
Fukuchi, Kazuki, Swallows	.320	485	74	155	22	7	9	61	42
Ramirez, Alex, Giants	.319	548	84	175	28	0	45	125	1
Akahoshi, Norihiro, Tigers	.317	556	94	176	15	1	0	30	41
Higashide, Akihiro, Carp	.310	522	76	162	12	1	0	31	13
Ogasawara, Michihiro, Giants	.310	520	93	161	27	1	36	96	0
Miyamoto, Shinya, Swallows	.308	422	47	130	11	0	3	32	3
Kanemoto, Tomoaki, Tigers	.307	535	87	164	33	2	27	108	2
Arai, Takahiro, Tigers	.306	366	54	112	22	4	8	59	2
Ochoa, Alex, Carp	.306	569	74	174	29	1	15	76	3
Wada, Kazuhiro, Dragons	.302	520	60	157	34	4	16	79	1
Sekimoto, Kentaro, Tigers	.298	430	57	128	25	2	8	52	2
Iihara, Yasushi, Swallows	.291	412	64	120	18	7	9	62	28
Tanaka, Hiroyasu, Swallows	.290	510	61	148	19	1	5	50	4
Toritani, Takashi, Tigers	.281	523	66	147	17	6	13	80	4
Hatakeyama, Kazuhiro, Swallows	.279	416	43	116	22	2	9	58	2
Ibata, Hirozaku, Dragons	.277	408	51	113	16	3	5	23	8
Woods, Tyrone, Dragons	.276	490	77	135	18	0	35	77	0
Yano, Akihiro, Tigers	.275	371	20	102	17	1	4	36	0
Nakamura, Norihiro, Dragons	.274	493	56	135	20	0	24	72	0
Abe, Shinnosuke, Giants	.271	428	60	116	27	0	24	67	1
Ishihara, Yoshiyuki, Carp	.265	422	36	112	19	0	9	50	6

	AVG.	AB	R	H	2B	3B	HR	RBI	SB
Nishi, Toshihisa, BayStars	.265	476	59	126	27	1	11	50	1
Hirano, Keiichi, Tigers	.263	365	46	96	7	3	1	21	7
Yoshimura, Yuuki, BayStars	.260	530	69	138	30	4	34	91	9
Sakamoto, Hayato, Giants	.257	521	59	134	24	1	8	43	10
Lee, Byung Kyu, Dragons	.254	418	40	106	16	2	16	65	1
Kinjo, Tatsuhiko, BayStars	.247	489	44	121	16	1	9	41	0
Araki, Masahiro, Dragons	.243	538	64	131	15	2	4	28	32

Remaining U.S. and Latin Players

	AVG.	AB	R	H	2B	3B	HR	RBI	SB
Gonzalez, Luis, Giants	.307	114	15	35	7	0	2	17	0
Seabol, Scott, Carp	.273	400	25	109	18	1	15	53	0
Valdez, Wilson, Swallows	.256	78	8	20	1	0	1	8	4
Bigbie, Larry, BayStars	.255	216	25	55	12	0	8	29	1
De La Rosa, Tomas, Dragons	.243	214	20	52	12	0	7	22	0
Baldiris, Aarom, Tigers	.227	132	21	30	9	0	3	16	1
Ford, Lew, Tigers	.225	129	11	29	7	1	3	11	0
Riggs, Adam, Swallows	.202	94	9	19	3	0	3	11	0
Guiel, Aaron, Swallows	.200	225	27	45	11	0	11	35	2
Furmaniak, J.J., BayStars	.157	51	3	8	0	0	2	5	0

INDIVIDUAL PITCHING LEADERS
(MINIMUM 144 INNINGS)

	W	L	ERA	G	SV	IP	H	BB	SO
Ishikawa, Masanori, Swallows	12	10	2.68	30	0	195	180	41	112
Lewis, Colby, Carp	15	8	2.68	26	0	178	151	27	183
Utsumi, Tetsuya, Giants	12	8	2.73	29	0	184	166	68	154
Tateyama, Shohei, Swallows	12	3	2.99	24	0	153	137	31	99
Shimoyanagi, Tsuyoshi, Tigers	11	6	2.99	27	0	162	154	41	89
Greisinger, Seth, Giants	17	9	3.06	31	0	206	201	31	167
Ando, Yuya, Tigers	13	9	3.20	25	0	155	158	41	111
Iwata, Minoru, Tigers	10	10	3.28	27	0	159	168	50	101
Miura, Daisuke, BayStars	7	10	3.56	21	0	144	137	29	111
Otake, Kan, Carp	9	13	3.84	28	0	171	189	67	99

Remaining U.S., Australian and Latin Players

	W	L	ERA	G	SV	IP	H	BB	SO
Kroon, Marc, Giants	1	4	2.21	61	41	61	34	27	91
Nelson, Maximo, Dragons	0	0	3.00	6	0	6	9	4	6
Williams, Jeff, Tigers	5	4	3.09	55	5	55	54	15	65
Schultz, Mike, Carp	3	4	3.23	55	0	53	47	20	43
Burnside, Adrian, Giants	5	3	3.48	15	0	75	67	18	47
Atchison, Scott, Tigers	7	6	3.70	42	0	105	104	26	85
Douglass, Sean, Swallows	2	2	3.94	6	0	32	30	11	16
Brower, Jim, Carp	0	2	3.98	21	0	20	26	8	13
Vogelsong, Ryan, Tigers	3	4	3.99	12	0	65	65	19	50
Williams, Dave, BayStars	2	2	4.26	7	0	25	41	4	8
Gonzalez, Dicky, Swallows	1	5	4.30	8	0	44	58	9	36
White, Matt, BayStars	1	0	4.50	15	2	14	16	3	12
Wood, Mike, BayStars	3	12	4.69	26	0	136	159	45	57
Kozlowski, Ben, Carp	2	1	4.74	26	2	38	41	17	31
Hughes, Travis, Baystars	1	1	4.91	21	1	22	23	11	18
Rios, Daniel, Swallows	2	7	5.46	11	0	64	80	26	37
Resop, Chris, Tigers	0	2	6.75	8	0	21	29	7	6
Marte, Victor, Carp	0	0	13.50	1	0	2	4	1	2

PACIFIC LEAGUE	W	L	T	Pct.	GB
Saitama Seibu Lions	76	64	4	.543	—
Orix Buffaloes	75	68	1	.524	2 ½
Hokkaido Nippon Ham Fighters	73	69	2	.514	4
Chiba Lotte Marines	73	70	1	.510	4 ½
Tohoku Rakuten Golden Eagles	65	76	3	.461	11 ½
Fukuoka SoftBank Hawks	64	77	3	.454	12 ½

CLIMAX SERIES PLAYOFFS—Stage One: Nippon Ham defeated Orix 2-0 in best-of-three series. **Stage Two:** Seibu defeated Nippon Ham 4-2 in best-of-seven series.

INDIVIDUAL BATTING LEADERS
(MINIMUM 446 PLATE APPEARANCES)

	AVG.	AB	R	H	2B	3B	HR	RBI	SB
Short, Rick, Eagles	.332	491	62	163	31	2	12	71	4
Nakajima, Hiroyuki, Lions	.331	464	75	161	32	0	21	81	25
Kawasaki, Munenori, Hawks	.321	424	55	136	16	6	1	34	19
Kuriyama, Takumi, Lions	.317	527	76	167	31	3	11	72	17
Cabrera, Alex, Buffaloes	.315	504	88	159	28	2	36	104	2
Imae, Toshiaki, Marines	.309	405	57	125	37	4	12	55	3

	AVG.	AB	R	H	2B	3B	HR	RBI	SB
Sato, G.G., Lions	.302	388	62	117	30	1	21	62	1
Inaba, Atsunori, Fighters	.301	448	71	135	25	5	20	82	2
Fernandez, Jose, Eagles	.301	541	81	163	40	0	18	99	5
Nishioka, Tsuyoshi, Marines	.300	473	78	142	26	6	13	49	18
Tanaka, Kensuke, Fighters	.297	536	89	159	32	9	11	63	21
Honda, Yuichi, Hawks	.291	454	53	132	14	3	3	38	29
Matsunaka, Nobuhiko, Hawks	.290	538	79	156	28	2	25	92	3
Sledge, Terrmel, Fighters	.289	395	41	114	21	2	16	69	0
Kataoka, Yasuyuki, Lions	.287	582	85	167	25	6	4	46	50
Goto, Mitsutaka, Buffaloes	.285	410	52	117	32	0	14	57	13
Takasu, Yosuke, Eagles	.282	383	44	108	20	1	4	45	6
Matsuda, Nobuhiro, Hawks	.279	551	68	154	33	10	17	63	12
Sakaguchi, Tomotaka, Buffaloes	.278	540	68	150	15	6	2	32	13
Rhodes, Tuffy, Buffaloes	.277	499	82	138	31	1	40	118	2
Yamasaki, Takeshi, Eagles	.276	510	63	141	21	0	26	80	1
Tsuchiya, Teppei, Eagles	.270	422	52	114	29	6	5	56	5
Hidaka, Takeshi, Buffaloes	.269	447	44	112	27	1	13	47	1
Omatsu, Shoitsu, Marines	.262	447	62	117	30	2	24	91	1
Morimoto, Hichori, Fighters	.253	478	66	121	15	1	0	21	12
Watanabe, Naoto, Eagles	.251	470	79	118	11	2	0	30	34
Nakamura, Takeya, Lions	.244	524	90	128	24	4	46	101	2
Hosokawa, Toru, Lions	.238	404	42	96	20	1	16	58	0
Brazell, Craig, Lions	.234	471	59	110	19	0	27	87	0

Remaining U.S. and Latin Players

	AVG.	AB	R	H	2B	3B	HR	RBI	SB
Seguignol, Fernando, Eagles	.324	136	24	44	7	0	13	40	0
Ortiz, Jose, Eagles	.288	337	52	97	21	1	11	37	1
Agbayani, Benny, Marines	.283	279	35	79	12	3	5	42	3
Botts, Jason, Fighters	.254	142	14	36	9	0	5	16	0
Bocachica, Hiram, Lions	.251	239	43	60	13	0	20	47	3
Restovich, Michael, Hawks	.223	112	7	25	3	0	3	17	0
Zuleta, Julio, Marines	.216	241	21	52	15	1	8	33	1
LaRocca, Greg, Buffaloes	.169	89	12	15	4	0	1	9	0
Jones, Mitch, Fighters	.111	27	2	3	1	0	0	0	0

INDIVIDUAL PITCHING LEADERS
(MINIMUM 144 INNINGS)

	W	L	ERA	G	SV	IP	H	BB	SO
Iwakuma, Hisashi, Eagles	21	4	1.87	28	0	202	161	36	159
Darvish, Yu, Fighters	16	4	1.88	25	0	201	136	44	208
Komatsu, Satoshi, Buffaloes	15	3	2.51	36	0	172	134	42	151
Hoashi, Kazuyuki, Lions	11	6	2.63	27	0	175	169	38	115
Sugiuchi, Toshiya, Hawks	10	8	2.66	25	0	196	162	36	213
Otonari, Kenji, Hawks	11	8	3.12	22	0	156	122	39	138
Naruse, Yoshihisa, Marines	8	6	3.23	22	0	151	126	35	119
Yamamoto, Shogo, Buffaloes	10	6	3.38	30	0	155	166	30	90
Kishi, Takayuki, Lions	12	4	3.42	26	0	168	151	48	138
Kondo, Kazuki, Buffaloes	10	7	3.44	25	0	149	140	45	89
Sweeney, Brian, Fighters	12	5	3.48	28	0	163	139	72	90
Tanaka, Masahiro, Eagles	9	7	3.49	25	1	173	171	54	159
Wada, Tsuyoshi, Hawks	8	8	3.61	23	0	162	167	36	123
Glynn, Ryan, Fighters	7	14	3.64	26	0	163	160	61	99
Shimizu, Naoyuki, Marines	13	9	3.75	25	0	166	151	41	108
Wakui, Hideaki, Lions	10	11	3.90	25	0	173	173	51	122
Kaneko, Chihiro, Buffaloes	10	9	3.98	29	0	165	185	34	126
Watanabe, Shunsuke, Marines	13	8	4.17	26	0	173	195	29	104
Asai, Hideki, Eagles	9	11	4.38	29	0	148	165	60	122

Remaining U.S. and Latin Players

	W	L	ERA	G	SV	IP	H	BB	SO
Graman, Alex, Lions	3	3	1.42	55	31	57	47	13	42
Sikorski, Brian, Marines	5	1	2.23	54	1	48	42	10	49
Abreu, Winston, Marines	1	2	3.32	20	0	22	23	8	24
Gwyn, Marc, Eagles	1	1	3.86	19	3	19	21	7	16
Guzman, Domingo, Eagles	2	7	3.87	23	0	102	99	34	65
Guttormson, Rick, Hawks	5	7	4.05	18	0	100	104	35	51
Houlton, D.J., Hawks	4	7	4.27	28	0	84	82	31	86
Kinney, Matt, Lions	2	4	4.48	17	0	80	87	35	64
Nitkowski, C.J., Hawks	2	4	4.64	39	2	43	43	19	31
Powell, Jeremy, Marines	2	6	5.29	12	0	66	92	27	36
Ortiz, Ramon, Buffaloes	4	7	5.82	17	0	82	102	20	32
Koronka, John, Buffaloes	0	1	6.75	3	0	12	16	8	11
Junge, Eric, Buffaloes	0	1	6.97	11	0	10	16	5	14
Standridge, Jason, Hawks	0	2	7.62	3	0	13	17	6	8

Wyverns win back-to-back titles

BY THOMAS ST. JOHN

In a year when Korean baseball gained international acclaim by winning an Olympic gold medal, the SK Wyverns successfully defended their Korean Series title by defeating the Doosan Bears four games to one in the Korean Series.

When SK won its first Korea Baseball Organization title in 2007, it was considered a huge upset. But in 2008 SK jumped out to an early lead and never looked back, finishing the regular season 13 games ahead of the rest of the league with 83 wins. The team's back-to-back Korean Series victories was big news for a short time, but the biggest story of the year on the professional scene was the complete transformation of the Lotte Giants.

The Giants had been the doormat of the league and finally decided that a change was in order, hiring former major league player and manager Jerry Royster. Lotte players had been at home for every postseason since 2000, but after Royster started to turn things around in spring training, it was obvious to all that something was going to change.

Lotte won its first four games and put together no less than two 10-game winning streaks during the season. The mood was electric in the city of Busan, and Royster became a heroic figure around the city. The front office gave its full support to Royster and he did not disappoint, finishing third and making the playoffs.

The secret to his success was his "Western approach" to baseball. In Korea, the age of a player or perceived status often plays an important role in a manager's decision to play him, regardless of his ability or performance. Royster threw that out the window and made players earn their spots on the field. The result was a change in thinking and the most deserving players on the field. The most deserving player on Royster's team was import Karim Garcia who, like Royster, attained superstar status.

While the Giants completely turned things around, the Woori Heroes finished the season in seventh place and it is not known if the team will even be around for the start of the 2009 season.

After many failed attempts, the KBO found a team sponsor at the end of the 2007 season after the Hyundai Unicorns dropped sponsorship of the team. The sponsor allowed the league to begin 2008 with eight teams, as usual. However, halfway through the 2008 season, the Woori Tobacco Co. backed out of their contract and demanded that the team stop using its company name. From midway into the season, the team was known as simply the Heroes.

Of course, the biggest baseball story in the nation was Korea's national team winning the gold medal at the Beijing Olympics. For more on that story, SEE PAGE 417.

STANDINGS

	W	L	PCT	GB
SK Wyverns	83	43	.659	—
Doosan Bears	70	56	.556	13
Lotte Giants	69	57	.548	14
Samsung Lions	65	61	.516	18
Hanwha Eagles	64	62	.508	19
KIA Tigers	57	69	.452	26
Heroes	50	76	.397	33
LG Twins	46	80	.365	37

INDIVIDUAL BATTING LEADERS

	AVG	AB	R	H	2B	3B	HR	RBI	BB	SO	SB
Kim Hyun-su, Doo	.357	470	83	168	34	5	9	89	85	40	13
Hong Seung-hun, Doo	.331	423	45	140	19	2	8	63	29	35	8
Choi jung, SK	.328	406	77	133	24	1	12	61	58	58	19
Cho Seung-hwan, Lotte	.327	462	79	151	27	3	10	81	48	81	31
Kim Tae-kyun, Han	.324	410	81	133	27	1	31	92	69	67	2
Park Jae-hong, SK	.318	396	66	126	26	2	19	72	72	66	5
Lee Taek-kyun, Heroes	.317	372	59	118	19	1	12	58	52	44	18
Park Han-i, Sam	.316	370	57	117	17	2	4	41	64	37	5
Jung Keun-woo, SK	.314	491	73	154	20	4	8	58	49	53	40
Kim Joo-chan, Lotte	.313	412	75	129	16	7	1	42	32	61	32

INDIVIDUAL PITCHING LEADERS

	W	L	ERA	G	SV	SO	IP	H	ER
Yoon Seok-min, KIA	14	5	2.33	24	0	119	155	121	45
Kim Kwang-hyun, SK	16	4	2.39	27	0	150	162	127	50
Bong Jung-keun, LG	11	8	2.66	28	0	140	186	153	66
Chae Byung-yong, SK	10	2	2.70	27	0	81	137	126	43
Jang Won-seop, Heroes	12	8	2.85	27	0	126	167	145	54
Sohn Min-han, Lotte	12	4	2.97	26	0	80	179	183	66
Kenny Rayborn, SK	5	3	3.30	26	0	68	134	129	55
Ryu Hyun-jin, Han	14	7	3.31	26	0	143	166	144	66
Jung Hyun-uk, Sam	10	4	3.40	53	0	97	127	108	51
Ma Il-young, Heroes	11	11	3.49	28	0	83	173	155	77

Lions repeat as Taiwan champion

BY BEN CHEN

In a tough year marred by yet another game-fixing scandal as well as poor attendance in Taiwan, the Lions managed to defend their league title in a hard-fought seven-game series with the ever-popular Brother Elephants.

In the process, the Lions earned their sixth Chinese Professional Baseball League title, tying the Brother Elephants for most championships in league history.

The Lions won the first half of the season and earned a pass to the championship series with the best overall record on the season. The La New Bears, who had the second-best overall record and won the second half of the season, faced the No. 3 seed Brother Elephants in a best-of-five playoff series. The Elephants surprisingly swept the Bears.

The Bears featured former Dodgers player Chin-Feng Chen—who despite missing a chunk of the season due to injuries, still managed to finish in the top five in several offensive categories—and the league's first 20-game winner since 2000 in league MVP Mike Johnson, a two-time Canadian Olympian with major league experience.

The Lions boasted the league's most prolific slugger in Tilson Brito, who had 24 home runs and has now led the league the past two years, while the pitching staff was anchored by top domestic pitcher Wei-Lun Pan.

The headliner of the playoffs (and Taiwan Series) was Lions righthander Luther Hackman, a former major leaguer and midseason acquisi-

tion. Hackman won both of his starts (in games four and seven) in the Taiwan Series against the Elephants, allowing no runs in 17 innings, including a shutout in game seven. For his dominating performance he earned series MVP honors.

League attendance for the playoffs was surprisingly high, and the championship series set an all-time record for attendance: 96,825 over the seven-game series. This was unexpected, considering that it was not uncommon to see only a few hundred fans during regular season games, and a game-fixing scandal forced the league to fold one of its teams: the dmedia T-Rex (formerly known as the Macoto Cobras).

In perhaps the biggest off-field headline of the 2008 season, local authorities determined that T-Rex ownership and management, as well as players, colluded with local organized crime to throw a number of games. Three players—including former major league pitcher Cory Bailey, who was among the league leaders with a 3.07 ERA, catcher Ko-Fan Chen (a 2008 all-Star), and outfielder Yuan-Chia Chen (the all-star game MVP)—along with team coach Chao-Hui Wu were permanently expelled from the team and the CPBL.

Pending further investigation, more players from the T-Rex as well as the Chinatrust Whales are under suspicion for their role in the latest scandal that has rocked the league. In late October, the CPBL made its decision to expel the T-Rex permanently from the league. T-Rex players who aren't implicated in the scandal will be placed in a special draft for the other teams to absorb the players.

STANDINGS

FIRST HALF

	W	L	T	PCT	GB
Uni-President 7-Eleven Lions	34	16	0	.680	—
La New Bears	28	19	3	.596	4½
Brother Elephants	24	23	3	.511	8½
dmedia T-Rex	21	28	1	.429	12½
Chinatrust Whales	20	30	0	.400	14
Sinon Bulls	19	30	1	.388	14½

SECOND HALF

	W	L	T	PCT	GB
La New Bears	33	16	1	.673	—
Uni-President 7-Eleven Lions	33	17	0	.660	½
Brother Elephants	28	19	1	.596	4
Chinatrust Whales	19	31	0	.380	14½
Sinon Bulls	18	32	0	.360	15½
dmedia T-Rex	16	32	0	.333	16½

INDIVIDUAL BATTING LEADERS

	AVG	AB	R	H	2B	3B	HR	RBI	SB
Cheng-Min Peng, Elephants	.391	284	50	111	17	0	8	60	23
Kuan-Jen Chen, Elephants	.348	400	58	139	13	7	1	77	4
Wu-Hsiung Pan, Lions	.346	266	72	92	22	4	13	47	8
Tai-Shan Chang, Bulls	.344	302	46	104	17	1	11	65	6
Chih-Wei Shih, Bears	.332	397	64	132	23	3	0	46	2
Kuo-Ching Kao, Lions	.332	395	60	131	28	2	7	74	0
Ssu-Chi Chou, T-Rex	.330	336	60	111	20	7	4	34	12
Tilson Brito, Lions	.330	361	90	119	26	1	24	102	0
Chih-Sheng Lin, Bears	.318	289	52	92	12	3	11	65	11
Lien-Hung Chen, Bears	.314	309	50	97	22	0	13	65	2

INDIVIDUAL PITCHING LEADERS

	W	L	ERA	G	SV	IP	H	BB	SO
Yu-Cheng Liao, Elephants	11	3	2.31	21	0	133	114	72	102
Mike Johnson, Bears	20	2	2.45	27	1	184	175	67	107
Kobayashi Ryokan, Elephants	10	6	2.66	27	1	169	156	48	110
Wei-Lun Pan, Lions	12	2	2.78	18	0	111	113	16	87
Wen-Hsiung Hsu, Bears	10	4	2.89	23	0	134	119	49	95
Fu-Te Ni, Whales	5	12	3.34	25	0	145	170	35	132
Chih-Chiang Chang, Lions	6	5	3.48	30	1	111	115	42	61
Dan Core, Elephants	9	5	3.52	21	0	128	126	51	76
Yu-Wei Hsu, Bears	5	4	3.62	28	0	107	113	27	53
Yueh-Ping Lin, Lions	7	4	3.87	43	17	102	109	46	73

Domestic title leaves the country

BY HARVEY SAHKER

Italy's top league has often included one team that is technically outside the country. That team is San Marino, the tiny, landlocked, independent republic that is situated within Italy's borders. And in 2008, San Marino took the Italian Baseball League title out of Italy.

San Marino won its first Italian League (formerly Serie A/1) title, defeating Nettuno four games to three in the best-of-seven finals. It was a hard-fought series, with one run separating the teams in four games.

Former major league lefthander Horacio Estrada, 32, was the winning pitcher for San Marino in Game One and Game Seven. San Marino first baseman Dean Rovinelli batted only .160 (4-for-25) in the finals, but all four of his hits were home runs.

The IBL semifinals had a new format in 2008, with the top four finishers in the regular season playing one another three times each. The triple round-robin affair replaced the best-of-seven series that had been played in previous years.

Former independent leaguer Richard Austin was a one-man wrecking crew for Bologna in his first Italian campaign, leading the IBL in home runs, RBIs, total bases and slugging percentage. Austin's 10 homers marked the first time in years that an IBL player reached double digits in dingers.

Linc Mikkelsen, another ex-indy leaguer, threw a rain-shortened, six-inning no-hitter at Grosseto on Opening Day. The visitors that day were IBL newcomers Redipuglia, who were promoted from Serie A/2 after the 2007 season. Redipuglia would go on to lose 20 consecutive games before logging its first victory—then lost another 19 in a row.

STANDINGS

	W	L	PCT	GB
Unipol Banca Bologna	34	8	.809	—
Danesi Caffe Nettuno	29	13	.690	5
Montepaschi Grosseto	28	14	.666	6
T&A San Marino	25	17	.595	9
Cariparma Parma	22	20	.523	12
Telemarket Rimini	19	23	.452	15
De Angelis Rimorchi Godo	9	33	.214	25
Potocco Rangers Redipuglia	2	40	.047	32

PLAYOFFS—Semifinals: Nettuno and San Marino advanced over Bologna and Grosseto after triple round-robin among top four finishers. Finals: San Marino defeated Nettuno 4-3 in best-of-seven series.

Year of the baseball in China

In China's biggest year for baseball, the China Baseball League saw the Tianjin Lions capture their third consecutive title.

Of course, the big news in China was the baseball tournament as part of the 2008 Beijing Olympics. As the host nation, China gained an automatic entry into the field and acquitted itself well, showing the growth of the sport in China.

China went 1-6 in pool play but won its biggest game, against Taiwan. China pulled out an 8-7 victory, generating a great deal of coverage by the Chinese media and sparking a new interest in baseball.

"Everyone involved, including the players and staff, have made great sacrifices for the Beijing Olympics," said China manager Jim Lefebvre, the former major league manager who has been a key figure in baseball's development there. "The talent level of Chinese baseball players has not caught up with the world's top players, but I believe that China will definitely be able to catch up."

In the CBL, meanwhile, the Lions showed there's still a gap between them and the rest of the six-team league. The Lions led the league in batting (.340 team average) and ERA (3.52 team ERA) by comfortable margins, and lost just two games in China's 21-game schedule. Tianjin then battled through the playoffs to win the championship.

The league's second-best team was the Beijing Tigers, who advanced to the championship series for the first time in three years.

STANDINGS

SOUTHWEST	W	L	PCT	GB
Tianjin	19	2	.905	—
Beijing	12	9	.571	7
Sichuan	9	12	.429	10

SOUTHEAST	W	L	PCT	GB
Shanghai	10	11	.476	—
Guangdong	8	13	.381	2
Jiangsu	5	16	.238	5

PLAYOFFS--Semifinals: Beijing defeated Shanghai 3-0 and Tianjin defeated Guangdong 3-2 in best-of-five series. Finals: Tianjin defeated Beijing 3-0 in best-of-five series.

Records, changes highlight season

BY PETER BJARKMAN

Cuba's setbacks in international baseball, including a silver medal in the 2008 Beijing Olympics, were blows to national pride but did not signal any crisis in what Cuba considers its national sport.

Led by the headline achievements of young Santiago de Cuba slugger Alexei Bell, the "perfect season" of Habana Province veteran southpaw Yulieski González, and the milestone pitching performances of righthanders Pedro Luis Lazo and Carlos Yánes, Cuba's Serie Nacional demonstrated once again that the nation still has talent.

Santiago de Cuba easily defended its National Series title with one of the most powerful lineups of recent memory during a campaign that saw offense jump after the introduction of a new, lightweight Mizuno baseball. With Bell, first baseman José Julio Ruiz, catcher Rolando Meriño, and second baseman Héctor Olivera all ranking among the league leaders in several offensive categories, Antonio Pacheco's club swept through the postseason schedule with an overall 11-2 record.

More than 100 individual season and career marks fell in a season that celebrated some of the most significant milestones in Cuban annals. Bell became the first to blast more than 30 homers (31) and drive in more than 100 runs (111) in a season. González rang up a perfect 15-0 mark on the league's top mound staff in Habana Province. Lazo finally broke the longstanding mark for career wins in the twilight of a stellar 15-year career. And the seemingly indestructible Yánes, in his 25th season at age 44 for Isla de la Juventud, set new career milestones for total games, starts, losses and hits allowed.

STANDINGS

WEST

GROUP A	W	L	Pct.	GB
Pinar del Río	45	45	.500	—
Isla de la Juventud	40	50	.444	5
Matanzas	34	56	.378	11
Metropolitanos (Havana)	28	61	.315	16½

GROUP B	W	L	Pct.	GB
Habana Province	61	29	.678	—
Industriales (Havana)	53	35	.602	7
Sancti Spíritus	48	40	.545	12
Cienfuegos	33	57	.367	28

EAST

GROUP C	W	L	Pct.	GB
Villa Clara	55	33	.625	—
Ciego de Ávila	53	37	.589	3
Las Tunas	49	41	.544	7
Camagüey	35	55	.382	21

GROUP D	W	L	Pct.	GB
Santiago de Cuba	61	29	.678	—
Guantánamo	44	45	.494	16½
Holguín	41	49	.456	20
Granma	36	54	.400	25

PLAYOFFS—Quarterfinals: Santiago de Cuba defeated Las Tunas 3-0; Villa Clara defeated Ciego de Avila 3-2; Pinar del Río defeated Industriales 3-0; Sancti Spíritus defeated Habana Province 3-1. Semifinals: Santiago de Cuba defeated Villa Clara 4-2; Pinar del Río defeated Sancti Spíritus 4-3. Finals: Santiago de Cuba defeated Pinar del Río 4-0.

INDIVIDUAL BATTING LEADERS
(Minimum 238 Plate Appearances)

Batters	AVG	AB	R	H	2B	3B	HR	RBI
Yoandy Garlobo, Matanzas	.398	231	50	92	20	0	10	57
Leonis Martín, Villa Clara	.398	264	63	105	14	9	4	34
Yasser Gómez, Industriales	.394	231	41	91	17	2	2	54
Yoandry Urgellés, Industriales	.374	270	82	101	24	5	17	74
Kenen Bailly, Guantánamo	.367	283	74	104	19	9	14	60
Alexander Malleta, Industriales	.365	249	48	91	18	0	17	67
Osmani Urrutia, Las Tunas	.364	258	42	94	20	0	9	59
Alfredo Despaigne, Granma	.364	321	75	117	33	4	24	78
Yunier Mendoza, Sancti Spíritus	.363	325	58	118	17	0	4	40
Adalberto Ibarra, Camagüey	.363	314	57	114	25	1	8	42
Rolando Meriño, Santiago de Cuba	.361	285	77	103	29	3	9	80
Yadil Mujica, Matanzas	.358	321	60	115	19	2	9	47
Adonis Garcia, Ciego de Avila	.355	282	52	100	15	2	18	61
Isaac Martínez, Ciego de Avila	.355	327	53	116	16	2	12	54
Alexei Bell, Santiago de Cuba	.355	349	96	124	21	7	31	111
Héctor Olivera, Santiago de Cuba	.353	323	91	114	25	3	10	45
Eriel Sánchez, Sancti Spíritus	.353	312	56	110	20	0	15	67
Yordanis Samón, Granma	.351	228	29	80	17	0	5	54
Andy Zamora, Villa Clara	.350	297	65	104	16	1	5	42
Yoelvis Fiss, Ciego de Avila	.350	329	65	115	19	4	22	64
Ariel Sánchez, Matanzas	.343	356	69	122	19	12	2	52
Joan Carlos Pedroso, Las Tunas	.342	284	71	97	17	0	22	63
José Julio Ruiz, Santiago de Cuba	.341	369	83	126	21	1	11	69
Giorvis Duvergel, Guantánamo	.338	231	43	78	14	0	12	38
Yoila Cerce, Guantánamo	.337	347	69	117	11	6	12	44

INDIVIDUAL PITCHING LEADERS
(Minimum 88 Innings)

Pitchers	W	L	ERA	G	IP	BB	SO
Jonder Martínez, Habana Province	13	2	1.55	17	133.1	33	81
Yosvani Pérez, Villa Clara	11	3	2.01	17	107.1	29	46
Yulieski González, Habana Province	15	0	2.25	18	124.0	39	111
Ian Rendón, Industriales	10	2	2.37	16	102.2	45	66
Sergio Espinosa, Isla de la Juventud	5	6	2.73	35	92.1	41	88
Yadier Pedroso, Habana Province	8	3	2.73	17	105.1	35	106
Pedro Luis Lazo, Pinar del Río	10	4	2.75	20	147.1	25	92
Luis Miguel Rodríguez, Holguín	10	7	2.76	20	120.2	42	68
Norge Luis Vera, Santiago de Cuba	9	2	2.89	14	102.2	15	63
Gerardo Miranda, Habana Province	6	7	2.93	16	107.1	41	74
Yander Guevara, Ciego de Avila	8	3	3.00	17	93.0	25	37
Adiel Palma, Cienfuegos	3	8	3.22	15	89.1	36	73
Yosvani Torres, Pinar del Río	8	2	3.29	23	93.0	24	53
Yoannis Negrin, Matanzas	11	5	3.37	21	125.2	44	61
Alexander Rodríguez, Guantánamo	10	2	3.42	31	97.1	48	85
Ricardo Estevez, Camagüey	3	7	3.42	21	115.2	56	53
Yoelkis Cruz, Las Tunas	13	1	3.52	19	128.0	31	36
Maikel Folch, Ciego de Avila	9	8	3.80	19	109.0	68	51
Miguel González, Habana Province	7	5	3.83	17	101.0	35	74
Raimundo Vazquez, Isla de la Juventud	8	7	3.84	23	129.0	51	45
Carlos Yanes, Isla de la Juventud	8	7	3.88	22	123.0	47	43
Ciro Silvino Licea, Granma	2	8	3.89	17	106.1	28	56
Vicyohandri Odelín, Camagüey	6	6	3.92	20	133.1	51	47
Angel Peña, Sancti Spíritus	6	5	3.99	20	97.0	25	69
Ronald García, Isla de la Juventud	3	6	4.13	19	96.0	52	31

Jolly Roger flies high again

BY HARVEY SAHKER

The Amsterdam Pirates won their first Dutch Major League championship since 1990, sweeping defending champion Kinheim three games to none in the Holland Series to secure the title for first-year manager Rikkert Faneyte.

The former big league outfielder was the first rookie skipper to win the Holland Series since Robert Eenhoorn with Neptunus in 1999.

Amsterdam advanced to the Holland Series by defeating Neptunus in a best-of-five semifinal series that went the distance. Down by a run after eight innings in Game Five, the Pirates scored twice in the top of the ninth and hung on to win 3-2. Fausto Alvarez, Amsterdam's 47-year old Cuban DH, scored the winning run on a suicide squeeze bunt by third baseman Pavel van Zaane.

Alvarez played for 17 years in Cuba's Serie Nacional and had a .295 career batting average with 210 homers and 1096 RBIs. In 2002 he became the first Serie Nacional player to hit two home runs in an inning twice in his career. The 2008 season was his third with the Pirates. His three-run homer in the first inning of the third game of the Holland Series spurred the Pirates on to a 12-0 win.

On June 12, Neptunus pitcher Leon Boyd threw a no-hitter against the Pirates. Boyd, a 6-foot-6 Dutch-Canadian righthander, issued three walks and hit a pair of batters in a 5-2 victory. One of the runs was unearned. Less than two months later, Boyd and three relievers shared a no-hitter for the Dutch national team in a pre-Olympic exhibition game against a Korean club.

By finishing last in the Dutch Major League, ADO was forced to play a best-of-five series against the Euro Stars, champions of the First Division, for a place in the top flight in 2009. Game One of the series went 18 innings, with ADO winning 2-1. Former Can-Am Leaguer Alex Smith went seventeen innings and threw 244 pitches in the game for ADO, giving up just four hits, striking out 12 and walking seven to get the win.

Erik de Rijcke, the Euro Stars starter, went 13⅓ innings and whiffed 19 ADO batters. The next day, Game Two of the promotion-relegation series went "only" 14 innings. ADO won 9-8 and went on to win the series in five games to keep their place in the DML.

STANDINGS

	W	L	PCT	GB
Corendon Kinheim	32	10	—	
DOOR Neptunus	31	11	1	
L&D A'dam Pirates	29	13	3	
Konica Min. Pioniers	28	14	4	
Sparta/Feyenoord	21	21	.500	11
Mr. Cocker HCAW	14	28	18	
MediaMonks RCH	8	34	24	
ADO	5	37	27	

PLAYOFFS—Semifinals: Kinheim defeated Hoofddorp 3-1 and Pirates defeated Neptunus 3-2 in best-of-five series. Finals: Pirates defeated Kinheim _-_ in best-of-five series.

INDIVIDUAL BATTING LEADERS

	AVG	G	AB	R	H	HR	RBI	BB	SO	SB
Mark Duursma, Pioniers	.387	41	155	36	60	1	30	24	22	3
Sidney de Jong, Pirates	.360	40	136	38	49	6	28	35	9	4
Martijn Meeuws, Neptunus	.354	35	127	25	45	3	25	21	21	3
Glenn Romney, Pioniers	.354	33	127	30	45	1	22	23	12	1
Bas de Jong, Pirates	.333	41	156	31	52	4	42	8	18	4
Danny Rombley, Kinheim	.333	36	144	35	48	1	19	22	20	8
Dirk van 't Klooster, Kinheim	.331	34	136	23	45	0	14	12	13	1
Dè Flanegin, Pioniers	.331	35	124	23	41	3	27	20	11	0
Tjerk Smeets, Kinheim	.329	39	158	28	52	2	33	10	26	2
Eugène Kingsale, Neptunus	.326	38	138	36	45	5	23	33	14	4

INDIVIDUAL PITCHING LEADERS

	W	L	ERA	G	SV	IP	H	R	HR	BB	SO
Rob Cordemans, Sparta	9	0	0.86	15	0	94	53	11	1	16	112
David Bergman, Kinheim	8	1	1.42	13	0	76	56	21	3	27	47
Kevin Heijstek, Neptunus	7	1	1.48	13	0	55	43	11	0	19	36
Leon Boyd, Neptunus	10	2	1.64	14	0	93	70	21	0	23	86
Nick Veltkamp, Kinheim	5	2	1.99	21	0	59	44	21	2	26	37
Jan Rehacek, Pioniers	2	0	2.04	20	0	40	32	11	1	20	37
Jos de Jong, Pirates	7	0	2.18	16	0	70	54	24	1	27	65
Mihai Burlea, RCH	4	5	2.23	10	0	65	46	23	2	40	68
Kenny Berkenbosch, Pirates	10	2	2.24	16	0	76	77	25	0	21	49
Diegomar Markwell, Neptunus	9	5	2.37	15	0	91	90	28	2	32	51

CHRIS KLINE

Scouts who attended the Caribbean Series also got a look at Dominican talent of the future

Licey emerges with title as Dominicans dominate

SANTIAGO, DOMINICAN REPUBLIC

After all the horns stopped blowing, mariachi and merengue bands stopped playing and the dust cleared at Estadio Cibao, the chants of an upset were resounding through the stands: "Li-cey! Li-cey! Cam-pe-on!"

The Tigres de Licey (Licey Tigers), celebrating their 100th anniversary in the Dominican League, nearly ran the table in the 2008 Caribbean Series to win their 10th series title in a storied history.

Licey finished 5-1 in the tournament, upsetting the heavily favored and hometown Aguilas Cibaenas (Cibaenas Eagles) twice—and beating them soundly each time.

Aguilas and Licey had battled it out for the Dominican League title prior to the series, with Aguilas winning the league championship 5-3 in the nine-game series.

"There's no question how tough that series was," Licey catcher Matt Tupman (Royals) said. "It was extremely mentally draining. But we knew we'd get another shot at them with much more at stake."

The only reason Licey was even invited to the series was the lack of a representative from Puerto Rico, which canceled its season in August due to financial concerns. And no one expected the

Tigres to hang with Aguilas in the rematch, especially after the club fired manager Tim Tolman and pitching coach Mark Brewer three games into the league finals.

But the club responded to new manager Hector de la Cruz, and ripped off back-to-back wins before finally folding.

"Management decided to make a change and . . . that's all I can say about that," Tupman said. "They just won the Caribbean Series, so they obviously felt like they were doing the right thing at the time."

Licey's pitching was certainly more consistent than Aguilas, led by Ramon Ortiz. The 34-year-old righthander went 2-0, 0.00 in the series, allowing just seven hits over 12 innings.

Tupman, the lone American on the Licey club, caught every inning and wound up hitting .364.

"This is such a great rivalry, period," he said. "They killed us, just killed us in the playoffs. So to be able to come through here and win this championship, it's special. It's been a crazy winter, but it was worth it. I've never experienced anything like this at all. It just kind of hit me that in two days I have to leave for spring training. That was the furthest thing from my mind five minutes ago."

Aguilas (3-3)

Home-field advantage? Check. More big leaguers than any other team in the tournament? Check. Dominican League champions? Check. Best team in the 2008 Caribbean Series? Not even close.

Their defense was shoddy all over the diamond, the pitching was inconsistent and their bats only came alive in a series-opening 13-6 win against Mexico.

Designated hitter Miguel Tejada (Astros) hit two home runs against the Mexicans, setting a Caribbean Series all-time mark for career homers, but disappeared for the remainder of the tournament. Tejada's offensive frustration crystallized the club's inability to hit in crucial situations. He wound up hitting .208 in 24 at-bats.

Mexico (2-4)

Coming into this winter, Mexico had won just one of its last 14 games in Caribbean Series play. So after the Obregon club dropped its first four games in Santiago, Mexico appeared to be in for another disappointing showing.

But anchored by shortstop Alfredo Amezaga (Marlins) and righthander Nelson Figueroa (Mets), Mexico bounced back to knock off Licey in the biggest upset of the tournament and finished the series with a win against Venezuela.

The biggest success story was Figueroa, who went nine innings in an opening loss to Licey, but came back to pitch another two innings in the rematch and preserved a 7-4, 10-inning win.

Figueroa pitched in Mexico during the regular season before bolting to pitch for Aguilas in the Dominican League playoffs. He was a Licey killer, going 4-0, 1.45 in the postseason. But Aguilas wouldn't have their go-to bullpen arm against the Tigres in the series, as Caribbean Baseball Federation rules state that Figueroa had to play for the country during which he spent the regular winter season.

Venezuela (2-4)

For a second straight year, Triple-A Iowa manager Buddy Bailey led Aragua to the Venezuelan League title. And also for a second consecutive season, Miguel Cabrera (Tigers) decided he would not play in the Caribbean Series.

And so again, Venezuela was a light-hitting club that thrived on pitching and defense, with its biggest win coming against Aguilas and righthander Bartolo Colon in an 8-5 victory.

Outfielders Alex Nunez and Selwyn Langaigne led the offense, while third baseman Luis Maza did a decent job of filling in for Cabrera, hitting .348.

Puerto Rico Maps Out Return

When the Puerto Rican League made the stunning decision not to play its 70th season, the circuit made clear that it lacked the financial muscle to succeed in this day and age.

Look who's flexing its muscles now. The Puerto Rico Professional Baseball League received a much-needed makeover for 2008-09, even tweaking its name, and was set to launch Nov. 6 thanks to a double-barreled marketing effort that is expected to extend into TV and the Internet.

"We love baseball. But in the past we didn't have the best show. Now we have it," said Ricardo Valero, who along with his brother Carlos have worked behind the scenes with league president Jose Andreu Garcia to revive the six-team circuit.

The turning point came when the league strengthened its marketing campaign through U.S.-based SMG and Puerto Rico-based Sajo, Garcia & Partners.

Major League Baseball helped facilitate some of the marketing efforts and will provide three umpires and an intern in the league office, and has offered MLB Advanced Media to help develop a Website.

The result is that 22 games are expected to be televised, with Uno Radio Group to transmit games on seven major outlets on the island. A Website (**puertoricobaseballleague.net**) also is expected to be in place by Opening Day.

The league will feature six teams playing a 42-game schedule. Valero said Yankees catcher and Puerto Rico native Ivan Rodriguez will join the league at some point in December and play for the Caguas Creoles.

A 12-game interleague series against the Dominican Republic also is planned, with the Dominican offering Cibao Eagles, Eastern Stars and Licey Tigers for six games in Puerto Rico and the Ponce Lions, Carolina Giants and Arecibio Wolves expected to play six games in the D.R.

The Mayaguez and Aguadilla teams have merged because the Indians' stadium was demolished in order to build one ahead of the 2010 Central American and Caribbean Games. Teams have a 30-man roster limit, with no more than three Dominicans and 10 U.S. players.

The league's cancellation for the 2007-08 season was a blow to many who have participated in it during previous offseasons.

"I was sad, I was in shock," Mets catcher Raul Casanova told Baseball America last year. "That league's been there such a long time. I was very disappointed because it makes Puerto Rican players look bad."

DOMINICAN LEAGUE

REGULAR SEASON	W	L	PCT	GB
*Gigantes del Cibao	29	18	.617	—
*Tigres del Licey	29	19	.604	½
*Aguilas Cibaenas	24	24	.500	5½
*Estrellas de Oriente	23	26	.469	7
Leones del Escogido	21	28	.429	9
Azucareros del Este	19	30	.388	11

*Qualified for playoff round-robin.

PLAYOFFS	W	L	PCT	GB
Tigres del Licey	11	6	.647	—
Aguilas Cibaenas	10	7	.588	1
Estrellas de Oriente	7	10	.412	4
Gigantes del Cibao	6	11	.353	5

FINALS: Aguilas defeated Licey 5-3 in best of nine series. (Both teams advanced to Caribbean Series because Puerto Rico did not send a team.)

INDIVIDUAL BATTING LEADERS
(Minimum 2.7 PA/Team Game)

BATTER, CLUB	AVG	G	AB	R	H	HR	RBI
Melo, Juan, Esc	.318	49	176	17	56	1	23
Sinisi, Vince, Esc	.306	45	160	25	49	6	28
Bonifacio, Emilio, Lic	.300	34	140	27	42	0	12
Reyes, Argenis, Esc	.298	41	161	19	48	0	15
Morales, Kendry, Gig	.291	35	134	16	39	4	19
Gomez, Alexis, Agu	.290	35	124	23	36	3	16
Pena, Brayan, Gig	.288	41	153	19	44	3	25
Luna, Hector, Agu	.287	39	143	12	41	1	13
Lopez, Pedro, Est	.270	36	122	10	33	0	18
Martinez, Michael, Est	.268	44	142	20	38	0	7

INDIVIDUAL PITCHING LEADERS
(Minimum 0.8 IP/Team Game)

PITCHER, CLUB	W	L	ERA	IP	H	BB	SO
Beltre, Omar, Azu	4	3	2.03	44	29	13	24
Mateo, Julio, Esc	3	3	2.25	56	60	8	38
Capellan, Jose, Gig	4	2	2.61	38	38	14	33
Diaz, Joselo, Azu	4	2	2.75	56	49	19	50
Lima, Jose, Agu	3	2	2.84	51	56	14	25
Mercedes, Jose, Lic	3	2	3.04	50	56	8	31
Eckert, Harold, Lic	2	2	3.60	45	33	18	37
Lee, Derek, Agu	2	2	3.72	46	42	10	35
Heredia, Felix, Azu	0	5	4.25	49	61	17	27

MEXICAN PACIFIC LEAGUE

	W	L	PCT	PTS	GB
Obregon	39	28	.582	14	—
Mazatlan	36	30	.545	10	2½
Culiacan	35	33	.515	11.5	4½
Mochis	35	33	.515	9.5	4½
Guasave	34	33	.507	10.5	5
Navojoa	32	35	.478	10	7
Hermosillo	32	36	.471	9	7½
Mexicali	26	41	.388	7.5	13

PLAYOFFS—First Round: Culiacan defeated Navojoa 4-1, Mazatlan defeated Guasave 4-0, and Obregon defeated Mochis 4-2 in best-of-seven series. **Semifinals:** Mazatlan defeated Mochis 4-3, and Obregon defeated Culiacan 4-3 in best-of-seven series. **Finals:** Obregon defeated Mazatlan 4-1 in best-of-seven series.

INDIVIDUAL BATTING LEADERS
(Minimum 3.1 PA/Team Game)

BATTER, CLUB	AVG	G	AB	R	H	HR	RBI
Rivera, Carlos, Obr	.344	61	212	23	73	7	47
Rodriguez, Jose, Gua	.343	67	271	36	93	4	31

Presichi, Cristhian, Gua	.336	67	253	45	85	9	49
Robles, Oscar, Nav	.330	61	218	27	72	4	28
Gomez, Heber, Maz	.329	65	210	28	69	0	19
Botts, Jason, Obr	.326	64	242	41	79	9	54
Rios, Armando, Gua	.325	56	209	30	68	6	35
Cota, Jesus, Her	.323	58	195	35	63	6	24
Mendez, Francisco, Gua	.318	54	192	32	61	7	30
Padilla, Jorge, Obr	.314	66	255	45	80	7	33

INDIVIDUAL PITCHING LEADERS
(Minimum 0.8 IP/Team Game)

PITCHER, CLUB	W	L	ERA	IP	H	BB	SO
Meza, Andres, Obr	6	4	2.19	74	69	16	30
Silva, Walter, Maz	9	5	2.48	83	69	28	63
Rodriguez, Jesus, Obr	7	1	2.51	79	56	34	43
Montemayor, Humberto, Mex	5	2	2.70	73	65	18	58
Alvarez, Victor, Gua	8	2	2.78	74	58	19	46
Castillo-Betancourt, Alberto, Moc	5	1	2.82	73	65	23	63
Campos, Francisco, Her	6	4	2.83	83	78	16	76
Lehr, Justin, Obr	8	1	2.86	72	67	17	41
Ortega, Pablo, Maz	5	4	2.86	94	75	20	61
Navarro, Hector, Maz	6	3	2.90	68	60	19	46

PUERTO RICAN LEAGUE

Suspended play for 2007-2008 season.

VENEZUELAN LEAGUE

	W	L	PCT	GB
Caribes de Anzoategui	39	24	.619	—
Cardenales de Lara	34	29	.540	5
Tigres de Aragua	32	31	.508	7
Bravos de Margarita	31	32	.492	8
Tiburones de La Guaira	30	33	.476	9
Leones del Caracas	29	34	.460	10
Navegantes del Magallanes	29	34	.460	10
Aguilas del Zulia	28	35	.444	11

INDIVIDUAL BATTING LEADERS
(Minimum 2.7 PA/Team Game)

BATTER, CLUB	AVG	G	AB	R	H	HR	RBI
Castillo, Jose, Car	.384	50	203	28	78	9	41
Blanco, Gregor, LaG	.345	62	229	50	79	4	18
Alfonzo, Edgardo, Mag	.335	54	191	25	64	5	33
Callaspo, Alberto, Zul	.331	41	154	19	51	2	18
Maldonado, Carlos, Car	.327	44	156	16	51	2	22
Diaz, Frank, Mar	.323	60	232	36	75	7	31
Washington, Rico, Ori	.305	60	197	34	60	8	37
Reyes, Rene, Mar	.303	62	228	37	69	5	34
Torres, Andres, Ori	.301	52	206	40	62	5	22
Cedeno, Ronny, Ara	.300	55	207	29	62	3	16

INDIVIDUAL PITCHING LEADERS
(Minimum 0.8 IP/Team Game)

PITCHER, CLUB	W	L	ERA	IP	H	BB	SO
Carrara, Giovanni, Lara	5	1	2.30	59	54	11	37
Prieto, Ariel, Ori	5	2	2.56	53	53	6	28
Estrada, Horacio, Ara	3	3	2.58	59	60	11	37
Silva, Jesus, Mar	7	5	3.02	83	78	21	50
Bailey, Cory, Ara	2	5	3.14	66	69	21	44
Collazo, Willie, LaG	3	3	3.20	59	67	14	30
Pulido, Juan, Mag	4	4	3.84	59	72	6	29
Herrera, Alex, Ori	8	2	3.89	69	67	27	52

INTERNATIONAL BASEBALL

COLLEGE

Fresno State, the first No. 4 regional seed ever to reach Omaha, capped its run with a dog-pile

ANDREW WOOLLEY

Fresno State becomes unlikely champion

BY AARON FITT

Robert Detwiler, a construction worker from Forest Knolls, Calif., raised his son to be tough.

When Fresno State sophomore right fielder Steve Detwiler tore a ligament in his thumb on a head-first slide April 1 against Long Beach State, doctors told him he had a choice. If Detwiler had sustained just a partial tear, he would have required season-ending surgery, but since he suffered a complete tear, he could opt to play through it and have surgery after the season. He couldn't do any more damage than had already been done.

"As soon as the doctor told me I had an option, there was no doubt in my mind what I was going to do," Detwiler said. "I know if Coach (Mike) Batesole thinks I was good enough to go, I was good enough to go."

He was much more than good enough in the final game of the 2008 College World Series, making Fresno awfully glad he waited to go under the knife. Detwiler went 4-for-4 with two home runs and a double and drove in all six of Fresno State's runs, powering the Bulldogs to a 6-1 win over Georgia and their first national championship. And a wild run to the title it was for Fresno State, the lowest-seeded team ever to reach the College World Series, let alone win it.

Fresno began the season ranked No. 18 in the nation but struggled under the weight of expectations and limped to an 8-12 start. Batesole later said his team was talking too much about Omaha in March, when it should have been talking about March. But toward the end of the regular season, Fresno's eight seniors took charge of the team and got everyone on the roster to fully buy in to the selfless, team-first mentality Batesole coveted.

The Bulldogs won the Western Athletic Conference regular season and tournament crowns but entered the NCAA tournament with 27 losses and a paltry Ratings Percentage Index ranking of 89th, earning them a No. 4 seed in the Long Beach regional. Fresno set the tone for its postseason run with a 7-3 win against host Long Beach State and ace Andrew Liebel in its regional opener.

"We knew this was a good baseball team when we beat Long Beach in Long Beach and the Big West pitcher of the year in Liebel," Batesole said. "I didn't know we were going to do what we were going to do, but for me, that was satisfaction enough. I could have ended the season right there. When I knew the type of baseball team we had become, that was good enough. And maybe even before that, when these eight seniors took control of this ballclub. They decided to do things right on and off the field, all I had to do

COACHING CAROUSEL

SCHOOL	NEW COACH (PREVIOUS SCHOOL/JOB)	FORMER COACH (REASON FOR DEPARTURE)
Arkansas State	Tommy Raffo (Mississippi State assistant)	Keith Kessinger (resigned)
Arkansas-Little Rock	Scott Norwood (Ouachita Baptist, Ark., head coach)	Jim Lawler (resigned)
Auburn	John Pawlowski (College of Charleston head coach)	Tom Slater (fired)
Bradley	Elvis Dominguez (Eastern Kentucky head coach)	Dewey Kalmer (retired)
Central Florida	Terry Rooney (Louisiana State assistant)	Jay Bergman (fired)
Charleston Southern	Stuart Lake (The Citadel assistant)	Jason Murray (resigned)
College of Charleston	Monte Lee (South Carolina assistant)	John Pawlowski (Auburn head coach)
Cornell	Bill Walkenbach (Franklin & Marshall, Pa., head coach)	Tom Ford (Cornell associate head coach)
Eastern Kentucky	Jason Stein (Belmont assistant)	Elvis Dominguez (Bradley head coach)
Eastern Michigan	Jay Alexander (Wayne State, Mich., head coach)	Jake Boss (Michigan State head coach)
Evansville	Wes Carroll (Evansville assistant)	David Seifert (resigned)
Florida Atlantic	John McCormack (Florida Atlantic assistant)	Kevin Cooney (retired)
High Point	Craig Cozart (Central Florida assistant)	Sal Bando Jr. (resigned)
Hofstra	Patrick Anderson (Royals minor league instructor)	Chris Dotolo (resigned)
IPFW	Bobby Pierce (Metro State, Colo., head coach)	Billy Gernon (Michigan State assistant)
Kentucky	Gary Henderson (Kentucky assistant)	John Cohen (Mississippi State head coach)
Loyola Marymount	Jason Gill (Oregon assistant)	Frank Cruz (fired)
Michigan State	Jake Boss (Eastern Michigan head coach)	David Grewe (Louisiana State assistant)
Mississippi State	John Cohen (Kentucky head coach)	Ron Polk (retired/Alabama-Birmingham asst.)
Prairie View A&M	Waskyla Cullivan (Prairie View A&M assistant)	Michael Robertson (Texas Southern head coach)
St. Joseph's	Fritz Hamburg (Army assistant)	Lee Saverio (served as interim coach)
Stephen F. Austin	Johnny Cardenas (Stephen F. Austin assistant)	Donnie Watson (fired)
Texas-Pan American	Manny Mantrana (St. Thomas, Fla., head coach)	Willie Gawlik (fired)
Texas Southern	Michael Robertson (Prairie View A&M head coach)	Candy Robinson (resigned)
Texas Tech	Dan Spencer (Texas Tech assistant)	Larry Hays (retired)

was get out of their way."

But that was just the beginning of Fresno's grueling run to the title, which was capped with seven straight wins against national seeds. The Bulldogs won two of their next three games against San Diego to win their regional, then won two of three at the Tempe, Ariz., super-regional against Arizona State. In Omaha, Fresno State beat Rice in its CWS opener, then took two out of three from North Carolina to win the bracket.

The Bulldogs responded to adversity at each step, winning four straight elimination games heading into the best-of-three finals. That resilience loomed large against Georgia too, as Fresno blew a three-run lead in the eighth inning of Game One and overcame an early five-run deficit to win Game Two. Different players emerged as heroes along the way, from middle-of-the-lineup mainstays Steve Susdorf and Erik Wetzel to senior pitching stalwarts Clayton Allison and Brandon Burke, from unproven middle relievers Kris Tomlinson and Sean Bonesteele to bottom-of-the-order DH Jordan Ribera and, of course, Detwiler.

Early in the College World Series, Detwiler struck out swinging three times, causing his thumb to pop out of place and prompting the worst pain he's gone through since sustaining the injury.

Robert Detwiler had no sympathy. Instead, in their nightly conversations, he made fun of his son

for wincing every time he swung and missed.

"One swing of the bat makes a hero. That's what my pops told me every time I talk to him every night—just keep with it, stick with it, suck it up," Steve Detwiler said.

He entered the CWS finals batting just 4-for-39 in the NCAA tournament, but he stuck with it and sucked it up. He didn't swing and miss much in the championship series, which spared him some extra pain. He finished with championship series records for hits (eight), homers (three) and RBIs (nine).

Detwiler got the scoring started in the decisive third game with a two-run home run to right field in the second. He followed with an RBI double to left-center field in the fourth, then tacked on a mammoth three-run homer to left in the sixth, giving Fresno a 6-0 lead. Georgia got on the board on Gordon Beckham's 28th homer of the year in the eighth, but never got within sniffing distance of Fresno State.

When a reporter asked Detwiler later about being a one-man wrecking crew in the third game, he started to argue the point and spread the credit, as is the Fresno way.

"He's giving too much credit away," lefthander Justin Wilson interjected.

"Yeah, dude, we only scored six, and you knocked in all of them," closer Brandon Burke added.

Wilson should talk. He only wanted to discuss the defense, and the hitting, and the coaching, and the bullpen—forget about his own splendid evening. The junior ace was masterful on short rest, allowing just one run on five hits and a walk while striking out nine over eight innings. He finished with 129 pitches, after throwing 112 against North Carolina three days earlier.

"It was over when I saw the look in his eye in the first inning," Batesole said. "There was no doubt in my mind it was over. I knew when I saw that look in his eye that he was going to give everything he had to bring it home. And that's exactly what happened."

Wilson went 2-0, 2.21 in three CWS starts, leading all pitchers in strikeouts (20) and innings (20). But Most Outstanding Player honors went to sophomore Tommy Mendonca, who tied the single-CWS record with four home runs in Omaha and played spectacular defense at third base.

Mendonca led a Fresno State power surge that was unprecedented in the post-Gorilla Ball era. Fresno scored 62 runs in Omaha to tie a CWS record set by Southern California in 1998—year of the infamous 21-14 national championship game. (The Trojans played just five games, though, while Fresno played seven.) Fresno's 14 homers were the third-most ever by one team in Omaha, the most since both USC and Louisiana State smacked 18 homers in that same 1998 Series. Seven different players homered for Fresno in Omaha; no other team at the CWS even hit seven homers collectively.

"That impressed me most, the home runs," Georgia coach David Perno said. "They hit them every game."

The Dawgs, meanwhile, swung out of their shoes against a dominant Wilson, and they were never able to sustain any rallies.

"I think we just pushed as a group a little too hard," senior third baseman Ryan Peisel said. "Everybody tried too hard to push for the six-run home run, which we couldn't get. I don't think anybody gave up; we tried to grind it out like we have all year. We just couldn't get it done."

Getting It Done, And Not

The same could be said for the three Atlantic Coast Conference teams that made the field, as the league remains without a national title since 1955 (Wake Forest). Fresno became the only team all year to beat North Carolina twice, sending the two-time CWS runner-up home a bit earlier this year. Florida State went two-and-barbecue for the sixth time in its 19 trips to Omaha, second only to Northern Colorado in CWS his-

tory. And top-seeded Miami went just 1-2 in the event, prompting right fielder Dennis Raben to lament, "We weren't hot out here, the bats weren't swinging. We just couldn't get it done."

Sounds like Peisel and Georgia, which managed to put its first two runners on base against Clayton Allison in a last-ditch rally in the ninth in the finale, causing Fresno State to summon Burke from the bullpen. He quickly got David

COLLEGE BASEBALL

Thoms to ground into a 4-6-3 double play, then issued a walk to Peisel to bring up Matt Olson. Olson lined Burke's first pitch to right field, where it was snared by—who else?—Detwiler for the final out. Second baseman Wetzel and first

baseman Alan Ahmady mobbed Detwiler in right field, while the rest of the team buried Burke in a raucous dog-pile behind the pitcher's mound.

"I think I was directly next to Burke at the bottom of the pile, and we both after four seconds

COLLEGE WORLD SERIES CHAMPIONS: 1947—2008
Undefeated

YEAR	CHAMPION	COACH	RECORD	RUNNER-UP	MVP
1947	California*	Clint Evans	31-10	Yale	None selected
1948	Southern California	Sam Barry	40-12	Yale	None selected
1949	Texas*	Bibb Falk	23-7	Wake Forest	Charles Teague, 2b, Wake Forest
1950	Texas	Bibb Falk	27-6	Washington State	Ray VanCleef, of, Rutgers
1951	Oklahoma*	Jack Baer	19-9	Tennessee	Sid Hatfield, 1b-p, Tennessee
1952	Holy Cross	Jack Barry	21-3	Missouri	Jim O'Neill, p, Holy Cross
1953	Michigan	Ray Fisher	21-9	Texas	J.L. Smith, p, Texas
1954	Missouri	Hi Simmons	22-4	Rollins	Tom Yewcic, c, Michigan State
1955	Wake Forest	Taylor Sanford	29-7	Western Michigan	Tom Borland, p, Oklahoma State
1956	Minnesota	Dick Siebert	33-9	Arizona	Jerry Thomas, p, Minnesota
1957	California*	George Wolfman	35-10	Penn State	Cal Emery, 1b-p, Penn State
1958	Southern California	Rod Dedeaux	35-7	Missouri	Bill Thom, p, Southern California
1959	Oklahoma State	Toby Greene	27-5	Arizona	Jim Dobson, 3b, Oklahoma State
1960	Minnesota	Dick Siebert	34-7	Southern California	John Erickson, 2b, Minnesota
1961	Southern California*	Rod Dedeaux	43-9	Oklahoma State	Littleton Fowler, p, Oklahoma State
1962	Michigan	Don Lund	31-13	Santa Clara	Bob Garibaldi, p, Santa Clara
1963	Southern California	Rod Dedeaux	37-16	Arizona	Bud Hollowell, c, Southern California
1964	Minnesota	Dick Siebert	31-12	Missouri	Joe Ferris, p, Maine
1965	Arizona State	Bobby Winkles	54-8	Ohio State	Sal Bando, 3b, Arizona State
1966	Ohio State	Marty Karow	27-6	Oklahoma State	Steve Arlin, p, Ohio State
1967	Arizona State	Bobby Winkles	53-12	Houston	Ron Davini, c, Arizona State
1968	Southern California*	Rod Dedeaux	45-14	Southern Illinois	Bill Seinsoth, 1b, Southern California
1969	Arizona State	Bobby Winkles	56-11	Tulsa	John Dolinsek, of, Arizona State
1970	Southern California	Rod Dedeaux	51-13	Florida State	Gene Ammann, p, Florida State
1971	Southern California	Rod Dedeaux	53-13	Southern Illinois	Jerry Tabb, 1b, Tulsa
1972	Southern California	Rod Dedeaux	50-13	Arizona State	Russ McQueen, p, Southern California
1973	Southern California*	Rod Dedeaux	51-11	Arizona State	Dave Winfield, of-p, Minnesota
1974	Southern California	Rod Dedeaux	50-20	Miami	George Milke, p, Southern California
1975	Texas	Cliff Gustafson	56-6	South Carolina	Mickey Reichenbach, 1b, Texas
1976	Arizona	Jerry Kindall	56-17	Eastern Michigan	Steve Powers, dh-p, Arizona
1977	Arizona State	Jim Brock	57-12	South Carolina	Bob Horner, 3b, Arizona State
1978	Southern California*	Rod Dedeaux	54-9	Arizona State	Rod Boxberger, p, Southern California
1979	Cal State Fullerton	Augie Garrido	60-14	Arkansas	Tony Hudson, p, Cal State Fullerton
1980	Arizona	Jerry Kindall	45-21	Hawaii	Terry Francona, of, Arizona
1981	Arizona State	Jim Brock	55-13	Oklahoma State	Stan Holmes, of, Arizona State
1982	MiamiH	Ron Fraser	57-18	Wichita State	Dan Smith, p, Miami (Fla.)
1983	TexasH	Cliff Gustafson	66-14	Alabama	Calvin Schiraldi, p, Texas
1984	Cal State Fullerton	Augie Garrido	66-20	Texas	John Fishel, of, Cal State Fullerton
1985	Miami (Fla.)*	Ron Fraser	64-16	Texas	Greg Ellena, dh, Miami (Fla.)
1986	Arizona	Jerry Kindall	49-19	Florida State	Mike Senne, of, Arizona
1987	Stanford	Mark Marquess	53-17	Oklahoma State	Paul Carey, of, Stanford
1988	Stanford	Mark Marquess	46-23	Arizona State	Lee Plemel, p, Stanford
1989	Wichita State	Gene Stephenson	68-16	Texas	Greg Brummett, p, Wichita State
1990	Georgia	Steve Webber	52-19	Oklahoma State	Mike Rebhan, p, Georgia
1991	Louisiana State*	Skip Bertman	55-18	Wichita State	Gary Hymel, c, Louisiana State
1992	Pepperdine*	Andy Lopez	48-11	Cal State Fullerton	Phil Nevin, 3b, Cal State Fullerton
1993	Louisiana State	Skip Bertman	53-17	Wichita State	Todd Walker, 2b, Louisiana State
1994	Oklahoma*	Larry Cochell	50-17	Georgia Tech	Chip Glass, of, Oklahoma
1995	Cal State Fullerton*	Augie Garrido	57-9	Southern California	Mark Kotsay, of-p, Cal State Fullerton
1996	Louisiana State*	Skip Bertman	52-15	Miami	Pat Burrell, 3b, Miami
1997	Louisiana State*	Skip Bertman	57-13	Alabama	Brandon Larson, ss, Louisiana State
1998	Southern California	Mike Gillespie	49-17	Arizona State	Wes Rachels, 2b, Southern California
1999	Miami*	Jim Morris	50-13	Florida State	Marshall McDougall, 2b, Florida State
2000	Louisiana State*	Skip Bertman	52-17	Stanford	Trey Hodges, rhp, Louisiana State
2001	Miami*	Jim Morris	53-12	Stanford	Charlton Jimerson, of, Miami
2002	Texas*	Augie Garrido	57-15	South Carolina	Huston Street, rhp, Texas
2003	Rice	Wayne Graham	58-12	Stanford	John Hudgins, rhp, Stanford
2004	Cal State Fullerton	George Horton	47-22	Texas	Jason Windsor, rhp, Cal State Fullerton
2005	Texas*	Augie Garrido	56-16	Florida	David Maroul, 3b, Texas
2006	Oregon State	Pat Casey	50-16	North Carolina	Jonah Nickerson, rhp, Oregon State
2007	Oregon State*	Pat Casey	49-18	North Carolina	Jorge Reyes, rhp, Oregon State
2008	Fresno State	Mike Batesole	47-31	Georgia	Tommy Mendonca, 3b, Fresno State

decided it's time to get up now, or we both might never pitch again," Wilson said.

Detwiler was late to arrive at the main dog-pile after his mini-celebration in right field, but he finally joined his teammates, jumping on the top of the heap.

"He's the reason me and Wilson are hurt," Burke said.

Robert Detwiler would tell Burke to suck it up. That's what Steve did; now he gets to have surgery to remove a piece of ligament from his wrist and insert it into his thumb, followed by 12 weeks of rehab.

That's nothing for Detwiler—he's a tough kid. And besides, his thumb was the farthest thing from his mind on the field after Fresno State won the national championship, his face glistening with sweat from the jubilant celebration, his eyes aglow with amazement and incredulity.

"It's the best feeling in the world, there's no words to describe it," Detwiler said. "This is what everybody wishes for, and I've got it."

CWS NOTES

■ Under the new CWS format, play started on a Saturday instead of Friday, and the schedule was spaced out over more days, eliminating double sessions on elimination days in the first week. More days with single games meant more sessions overall, allowing the 2008 CWS to draw a record 330,099 fans, eclipsing the previous record of 310,609 set in 2006. But that figure is misleading, because average attendance was down markedly. Just 20,631 fans per session attended the 2008 Series, the lowest average since 1998. The 2007 CWS averaged 23,131 fans per session. The low point this year came in Game 11, a Saturday afternoon contest between Georgia and Stanford that drew just 15,581 fans, the fewest at a CWS game since 2004. The championship game drew just 18,932, down from 25,046 a year ago.

There was plenty of grumbling about the format change from fans, especially locals who relished the traditional Friday start. But the bigger reason for the attendance dip was likely the sluggish economy.

■ It figured to be a high-scoring College World Series thanks to a host of potent offenses and a lack of power arms, and it was just that. The 206 combined runs scored in the Series are the most since 1998, when 225 runs were scored at the apex of the "Gorilla Ball" era. This year was just the fourth time ever that the eight CWS teams combined to score more than 200 runs. The 341 combined hits set an all-time record, breaking the previous mark of 327 set in 1998, back when there was only a winner-take-all championship game. The collective batting average of .303 is the highest since 2001, marking just the fourth time ever the eight teams have combined to hit better than .300. The eight triples were the most since 1991. The combination of underwhelming pitching and fearsome hitters capable of punishing offerings left over the plate also resulted in a record

for most wild pitches in a CWS (26).

But it wasn't all grip-it-and-rip-it. There was plenty of quality defense on display at the 2008 CWS, which saw just 33 total errors—the fourth-fewest ever.

■ The West continued its recent Omaha dominance by producing another unlikely national champion. The last seven champions have come from west of the Mississippi River, including the last three (and four of the last five) from states that border the Pacific Ocean. But like Oregon State a year ago, Fresno came from out of the blue to take home the hardware. The Bulldogs

ALL-AMERICA TEAM

FIRST TEAM

POS.	NAME	YEAR	AVG	OBP	SLG	AB	R	H	HR	RBI	BB	SO	SB
C	Buster Posey, Florida State	Jr.	.460	.564	.887	248	88	114	26	92	55	27	5
1B	Justin Smoak, South Carolina	Jr.	.383	.505	.757	235	63	90	23	72	57	28	1
2B	Josh Satin, California	Sr.	.379	.500	.723	195	56	74	18	52	47	45	6
3B	Brett Wallace, Arizona State	Jr.	.410	.526	.753	239	87	98	22	83	48	33	16
SS	Gordon Beckham, Georgia	Jr.	.401	.513	.802	252	90	101	26	72	50	30	17
OF	Sawyer Carroll, Kentucky	Sr.	.419	.514	.782	234	69	98	19	83	44	33	12
OF	Blake Dean, Louisiana State	So.	.359	.439	.680	256	62	92	20	70	34	42	4
OF	Chris Shehan, Georgia Southern	Jr.	.438	.557	.835	224	84	98	22	77	53	56	22
DH	Yonder Alonso, Miami	Jr.	.367	.535	.774	199	73	73	23	71	74	23	9
UT	Ike Davis, Arizona State	Jr.	.385	.457	.742	213	64	82	16	76	31	34	6

POS.	NAME	YEAR	W	L	ERA	G	CG	SV	IP	H	BB	SO	AVG
SP	Aaron Crow, Missouri	Jr.	13	0	2.35	15	4	0	107	85	38	127	.217
SP	Brian Matusz, San Diego	Jr.	12	2	1.71	15	3	0	105	83	22	141	.211
SP	Rob Musgrave, Wichita State	Sr.	12	1	2.51	16	6	0	111	99	22	101	.241
SP	Stephen Strasburg, San Diego State	So.	8	3	1.57	13	4	0	97	61	16	133	.181
RP	Scott Bittle, Mississippi	Jr.	7	1	1.78	27	0	8	71	35	30	130	.145
UT	Ike Davis, Arizona State	Jr.	4	1	2.25	16	0	4	24	17	4	30	.193

SECOND TEAM

POS.	NAME	YEAR	AVG	OBP	SLG	AB	R	H	HR	RBI	BB	SO	SB
C	Corey Kemp, East Carolina	Sr.	.341	.444	.628	226	62	77	18	72	43	44	2
1B	David Cooper, California	Jr.	.359	.449	.682	220	55	79	19	55	37	35	0
2B	Jemile Weeks, Miami	Jr.	.367	.453	.633	226	75	83	11	59	33	37	21
3B	Conor Gillaspie, Wichita State	Jr.	.419	.500	.697	234	71	98	11	82	38	22	16
SS	Reese Havens, South Carolina	Jr.	.359	.486	.645	248	76	89	18	57	58	44	1
OF	Tim Fedroff, North Carolina	So.	.398	.464	.644	264	72	105	12	69	33	29	13
OF	Blake Tekotte, Miami	Jr.	.357	.470	.580	238	78	85	11	47	42	36	26
OF	Eric Thames, Pepperdine	Jr.	.407	.513	.769	182	58	74	13	59	35	30	11
DH	Nate Recknagel, Michigan	Sr.	.368	.465	.751	209	56	77	23	68	33	30	5
UT	Zach Putnam, Michigan	Jr.	.307	.400	.558	199	47	61	11	51	28	29	3

POS.	NAME	YEAR	W	L	ERA	G	CG	SV	IP	H	BB	SO	AVG
SP	Christian Friedrich, Eastern Kentucky	Jr.	5	1	1.43	12	0	0	82	40	33	108	.144
SP	Scott Gorgen, UC Irvine	Jr.	11	3	2.26	17	1	0	115	72	40	123	.180
SP	Chris Hernandez, Miami	Fr.	11	0	2.62	17	0	0	106	85	17	112	.218
SP	Mike Leake, Arizona State	So.	11	3	3.49	16	2	1	121	118	20	104	.254
RP	Andrew Cashner, Texas Christian	Jr.	9	4	2.32	30	0	9	54	21	27	80	.122
UT	Zach Putnam, Michigan	Jr.	9	0	2.58	12	1	0	77	62	23	78	.223

THIRD TEAM

POS.	NAME	YEAR	AVG	OBP	SLG	AB	R	H	HR	RBI	BB	SO	SB
C	Jason Castro, Stanford	Jr.	.379	.431	.617	261	64	99	13	69	24	38	5
1B	Dustin Ackley, North Carolina	So.	.408	.500	.600	255	79	104	7	50	52	25	18
2B	Johnny Giavotella, New Orleans	Jr.	.354	.470	.591	237	76	84	12	56	53	25	19
3B	Chris Dominguez, Louisville	So.	.365	.427	.687	249	68	91	21	75	23	47	11
SS	Grant Green, Southern California	So.	.390	.438	.644	205	46	80	9	46	15	35	10
OF	Collin Cowgill, Kentucky	Jr.	.361	.483	.687	223	80	84	19	60	49	52	23
OF	Jason Kipnis, Arizona State	So.	.371	.485	.667	237	76	88	14	73	51	41	24
OF	Brian Van Kirk, Oral Roberts	Sr.	.417	.511	.750	228	61	95	18	73	45	34	0
DH	Erik Komatsu, Cal State Fullerton	Jr.	.355	.459	.593	231	47	82	9	54	36	24	21
UT	Josh Romanski, San Diego	Jr.	.324	.416	.476	225	44	73	6	49	33	29	3

POS.	NAME	YEAR	W	L	ERA	G	CG	SV	IP	H	BB	SO	AVG
SP	Barry Bowden, Southern Mississippi	Sr.	8	3	2.12	12	1	0	72	49	22	78	.188
SP	Shooter Hunt, Tulane	Jr.	9	4	2.68	16	0	0	101	62	56	126	.175
SP	Chance Ruffin, Texas	Fr.	8	3	1.96	23	1	3	78	54	24	82	.191
SP	Alex White, North Carolina	So.	10	3	2.75	16	1	0	88	70	38	101	.222
RP	Joshua Fields, Georgia	Sr.	2	2	2.76	31	0	16	32	14	20	59	.125
UT	Josh Romanski, San Diego	Jr.	9	1	4.00	15	3	0	97	87	20	78	.240

were the lowest seed ever to win a championship (they were seeded fourth in the Long Beach regional), and the title was the second in school history in any sport (the other was in softball in 1998). Fresno coach Mike Batesole was the first coach to win the title in his first CWS appearance since Pepperdine's Andy Lopez did it in 1992. And the Bulldogs were the fifth straight national champion that was not a national seed.

"Obviously I think it's good, the parity in college baseball," Perno said. "It gives teams hope that they can get here, they can live a dream and make something special happen. Because (Fresno) did it, and they did it without their ace (Tanner Scheppers). And that's even a stronger message. Obviously they're around to stay. Coach Batesole does a tremendous job. I wish it hadn't happened to us, but it's great for college baseball."

■ Georgia shortstop Gordon Beckham had a magical, memorable CWS to cap his magical, memorable 2008 season. He batted .522 with two homers and five RBIs in Omaha, finishing the year with a .411 average (the highest by a Georgia player since 1981), 28 home runs (a school record and tied for the national lead with Louisiana State's Matt Clark), and 113 hits (another school record). But those remarkable accomplishments were small consolation after Georgia fell one game short of a national title.

"They played better than us tonight," said Beckham, one of the most colorful, quotable, candid players at the 2008 CWS. "Maybe we'd win the next game, who knows? But there is no next game. Tip your cap to them. I'm happy for them. Not really happy, but I'm happy for them."

OTHER TOP STORIES FROM 2008

■ Coaches from warm-weather schools got a taste of what it's like to lead a college baseball program in the North, and a number of them did not like it one bit. The uniform start date went into effect in 2008, forcing teams to play their entire 56-game schedules in 13 weeks. It was nothing new for cold-weather schools, which have traditionally started play weeks after their Sun Belt counterparts, but many warm-weather teams struggled to adapt to the compacted schedule. Teams unaccustomed to playing four or five games per week found the change a drain on their pitching and on their study time. To compensate, some conferences discussed going to four-game weekend series, and others considered eliminating their conference tournaments to have an extra week for regular-season games.

■ All those tradition-loving college baseball fans who can't imagine the College World Series without Omaha were pleased to learn in May that the NCAA and CWS of Omaha, Inc. struck an agreement to keep the event in Omaha through at least 2030. Rosenblatt Stadium's days are numbered, though, as a new downtown ballpark is scheduled to open in 2011 to accommodate the World Series.

■ Heading into the 2008 season, Paul Mainieri talked cautiously but optimistically about how nice it would be to end the Alex Box Stadium era at Louisiana State by hosting a regional. The Tigers had gotten a major talent infusion from the nation's deepest recruiting class, so Mainieri's musings were not outlandish, but the goal did seem like a longshot. As late as April 19, when LSU was 23-16 overall and 6-11 in the Southeastern Conference, it seemed like the Tigers might have a hard time just getting to a regional, nevermind hosting one.

But LSU set an SEC record by winning its final 16 games of the regular season, then swept through the conference tournament to earn a home regional and the No. 7 national seed. Then the Tigers swept through the Baton Rouge regional to extend their winning streak to a remarkable 23 games and host a superregional against UC Irvine. After dropping the opener to the Anteaters, LSU won its next two games to get back to Omaha for the first time since 2004.

■ Aside from Player of the Year Buster Posey's amazing (but failed) run at the NCAA triple crown, the most impressive

Gordon Beckham hit .522 in Omaha, though his Bulldogs fell short of the title

individual performances of 2008 belonged to pitchers. Missouri righthander Aaron Crow pitched 43 consecutive scoreless innings in March and April, believed to be the fourth-longest streak in modern Division I history. The streak, which included three shutouts in Big 12 Conference play, ended in Missouri's wild 31-12 win against Texas on April 11—a game that featured a Big 12-record four home runs by Missouri's Jacob Priday.

The other eye-popping individual effort came courtesy of San Diego State sophomore righthander Stephen Strasburg, on the very same night Crow's scoreless streak ended. In his start against Utah that night, Strasburg struck out 23 batters in a one-hit, complete-game shutout.

■ Ron Polk, the all-time winningest coach in the history of the SEC, retired after completing his 29th season at Mississippi State. Polk coached 23 of his last 34 teams to regionals, including the last five in a row before MSU's last-place finish in 2008. Eight of those teams reached Omaha, including the 2007 edition. But Polk did not go quietly into the night; when his longtime assistant Tommy Raffo was passed over as his successor in favor of another fomer Polk assistant—Kentucky head coach John Cohen—Polk lambasted Mississippi State in the media. He eventually accepted a job as a volunteer assistant under another former assistant, Alabama-Birmingham coach Brian Shoop.

Polk wasn't the only name near the top of college baseball's all-time wins list to retire in 2008. Texas Tech coach Larry Hays, whose 1,509 wins in 39 years rank fourth on the all-time list, also stepped down after the season. He was replaced by associate head coach Dan Spencer, who won two national championships as an assistant at Oregon State in 2006 and 2007.

REGIONALS

MAY 30-JUNE 2

64 teams, 16 four-team, double-elimination tournaments. Winners advance to super-regionals.

CORAL GABLES, FLA.

Host: Miami (No. 1 national seed)
Participants: No. 1 Miami (47-8), No. 2 Missouri (38-19), No. 3 Mississippi (37-24), No. 4 Bethune-Cookman (36-20).
Champion: Miami (3-0).
Runner-Up: Mississippi (2-2).
Outstanding Player: Ryan Jackson, ss, Miami.

ANN ARBOR, MICH.

Host: Michigan
Participants: Arizona (38-17), No. 2 Michigan (45-12), No. 3 Kentucky (42-17), No. 4 Eastern Michigan (25-32).
Champion: Arizona (3-0).
Runner-Up: Kentucky (2-2).
Outstanding Player: Jason Stoffel, rhp, Arizona.

CARY, N.C.

Host: North Carolina (No. 2 national seed)
Participants: No. 1 North Carolina (46-12), No. 2 UNC Wilmington (42-15), No. 3 Elon (43-16), No. 4 Mount St. Mary's (21-32).
Champion: North Carolina (3-0).
Runner-Up: UNC Wilmington (2-2).
Outstanding Player: Tim Fedroff, of, North Carolina.

CONWAY, S.C.

Host: Coastal Carolina
Participants: No. 1 Coastal Carolina (47-12), No. 2 East Carolina (40-19), No. 3 Alabama (34-26), No. 4 Columbia (22-28).
Champion: Coastal Carolina (3-0).
Runner-Up: East Carolina (2-2).
Outstanding Players: David Anderson, 1b, Coastal Carolina, Tommy Baldridge, of, Coastal Carolina.

TEMPE, ARIZ.

Host: Arizona State (No. 3 national seed)
Participants: No. 1 Arizona State (45-11), No. 2 Vanderbilt (40-20), No. 3 Oklahoma (34-24), No. 4 Stony Brook (34-24).
Champion: Arizona State (3-0).
Runner-Up: Oklahoma (2-2).
Outstanding Player: Ike Davis, 1b/lhp, Arizona State.

LONG BEACH, CALIF.

Host: Long Beach State
Participants: No. 1 Long Beach State (37-19), No. 2 San Diego (41-15), No. 3 California (33-19), No. 4 Fresno State (37-27).
Champion: Fresno State (3-1).
Runner-Up: San Diego (3-2).
Outstanding Player: Brian Matusz, lhp, San Diego.

TALLAHASSEE, FLA.

Host: Florida State (No. 4 national seed)
Participants: No. 1 Florida State (48-10), No. 2 Florida (34-22), No. 3 Tulane (37-20),

No. 4 Bucknell (29-22).
Champion: Florida State (4-1).
Runner-Up: Tulane (2-2).
Outstanding Player: Buster Posey, c, Florida State.

STILLWATER, OKLA.

Host: Oklahoma State
Participants: No. 1 Oklahoma State (42-16), No. 2 Wichita State (44-15), No. 3 Texas Christian (43-17), No. 4 Western Kentucky (33-25).
Champion: Texas Christian (3-0).
Runner-Up: Oklahoma State (2-2).
Outstanding Player: Conor Gillaspie, 3b, Wichita State.

FULLERTON, CALIF.

Host: Cal State Fullerton (No. 5 national seed)
Participants: No. 1 Cal State Fullerton (37-19), No. 2 UCLA (31-25), No. 3 Virginia (38-21), No. 4 Rider (29-26).
Champion: Cal State Fullerton (4-1).
Runner-Up: UCLA (2-2).
Outstanding Player: Brian Wilson, rhp, Cal State Fullerton.

STANFORD, CALIF.

Host: Stanford
Participants: No. 1 Stanford (33-21), No. 2 Pepperdine (36-18), No. 3 Arkansas (34-22), No. 4 UC Davis (34-22).
Champion: Stanford (4-1).
Runner-Up: Pepperdine (2-2).
Outstanding Player: Sean Ratliff, of, Stanford.

HOUSTON

Host: Rice (No. 6 national seed)
Participants: No. 1 Rice (42-13), No. 2 Texas (37-20), No. 3 St. John's (41-14), No. 4 Sam Houston State (37-23).
Champion: Rice (3-0).
Runner-Up: Texas (2-2).
Outstanding Player: Kyle Russell, of, Texas.

COLLEGE STATION, TEXAS

Host: Texas A&M
Participants: No. 1 Texas A&M (43-16), No. 2 Dallas Baptist (37-17), No. 3 Houston (39-22), No. 4 Illinois-Chicago.
Champion: Texas A&M (3-1).
Runner-Up: Houston (3-2).
Outstanding Player: Brooks Raley, lhp/of, Texas A&M.

BATON ROUGE, LA.

Host: Louisiana State (No. 7 national seed)
Participants: No. 1 Louisiana State (43-16), No. 2 Southern Mississippi (40-20), No. 3 New Orleans (42-19), No. 4 Texas Southern (16-32).
Champion: Louisiana State (3-0).
Runner-Up: Southern Mississippi (2-2).
Outstanding Player: Blake Dean, dh, Louisiana State.

LINCOLN, NEB.

Host: Nebraska
Participants: No. 1 Nebraska (40-14), No. 2 UC Irvine (38-16), No. 3 Oral Roberts (46-12), No. 4 Eastern Illinois (27-28).

Champion: UC Irvine (3-0).
Runner-Up: Oral Roberts (2-2).
Outstanding Player: Bryce Stowell, rhp, UC Irvine.

ATHENS, GA.

Host: Georgia (No. 8 national seed)
Participants: No. 1 Georgia (35-21), No. 2 Georgia Tech (39-19), No. 3 Louisville (41-19), No. 4 Lipscomb (32-28).
Champion: Georgia (4-1).
Runner-Up: Georgia Tech (2-2).
Outstanding Player: Matt Olson, of, Georgia.

RALEIGH, N.C.

Host: North Carolina State
Participants: No. 1 North Carolina State (38-20), No. 2 South Carolina (38-21), No. 3 Charlotte (43-14), No. 4 James Madison (38-17).
Champion: North Carolina State (3-0).
Runner-Up: South Carolina (2-2).
Outstanding Player: Justin Smoak, 1b, South Carolina.

SUPER-REGIONALS

JUNE 6-9

16 teams, eight best-of-three series. Winners advance to College World Series.

NORTH CAROLINA STATE AT GEORGIA

Super-Regional Site: Athens, Ga.
Georgia wins 2-1, advances to College World Series.

UC IRVINE AT LOUISIANA STATE

Super-Regional Site: Baton Rouge, La.
Louisiana State wins 2-1, advances to College World Series.

COASTAL CAROLINA AT NORTH CAROLINA

Super-Regional Site: Cary, N.C.
North Carolina wins 2-0, advances to College World Series.

ARIZONA AT MIAMI

Super-Regional Site: Coral Gables, Fla.
Miami wins 2-1, advances to College World Series.

STANFORD AT CAL STATE FULLERTON

Super-Regional Site: Fullerton, Calif.
Stanford wins 2-0, advances to College World Series.

TEXAS A&M AT RICE

Super-Regional Site: Houston.
Rice wins 2-0, advances to College World Series.

WICHITA STATE AT FLORIDA STATE

Super-Regional Site: Tallahassee, Fla.
Florida State wins 2-1, advances to College World Series.

FRESNO STATE AT ARIZONA STATE

Super-Regional Site: Tempe, Ariz.
Fresno State wins 2-1, advances to College World Series.

COLLEGE BASEBALL

Posey challenges for triple crown

BY AARON FITT

Just two years after he started as a freshman shortstop for Florida State, Buster Posey turned in one of the finest seasons ever by a college catcher in 2008, earning him Baseball America's College Player of the Year award. Posey led the nation in batting (.463), on-base percentage (566), slugging (.879), RBIs (93), hits (119) and total bases (226). He was just two behind the national leader in home runs with 26—more than triple his career total heading into the year. He even posted six saves and a 1.17 ERA in nine relief appearances on the mound. And his stellar defense and leadership behind the plate helped carry the Seminoles to the College World Series for the first time since 2001. That entire package also made Posey the No. 5 overall pick in the draft to the Giants.

Buster Posey

CLIFF WELCH

Those who have coached Posey and coached against him, as well as Posey himself, tried to put his historic season in context.

Florida State coach Mike Martin: "He is one of a kind. They just don't come along every five years like this guy. I've been here 34 years, I've never had a catcher used as a closer, never had a closer go out there and not give up a run in seven or eight appearances—and each time the game is on the line. He is one special player, and I'm proud to say student-athlete. Because that's what he is, he's a student-athlete."

Miami coach Jim Morris: "Well, he destroyed us; he was outstanding. I've heard Mike Martin say he thinks (Posey) might be the best player ever to play at Florida State, and I would have to agree with him, and I've been competing against Florida State for 25 years. Every phase of the game—he can hit, throw, receive, hit home runs—he's just outstanding in every phase."

Florida coach Kevin O'Sullivan: "I think he's certainly separated himself from the rest of the top players in the country. He's just kind of a quiet leader on that team. He's certainly handled the pitching staff very well; he makes them go. He's durable, and to be where he's at now from where he started is pretty amazing."

Tulane coach Rick Jones: "His numbers are throwback numbers, to 10 or 15 years ago—you just don't see those kind of numbers anymore, especially in that conference. Having coached Jason Varitek for three years, I see a lot of the same qualities: makeup, leadership, he's under control, he just seemed like another coach on the field. It goes past the ability. He's always under control. He's that guy in the middle of the lineup where we say, 'Oh man, I hope he comes up with nobody on.'"

Buster Posey: "I'd say probably the biggest change for me since I got to Florida State is just my maturity as a player and understanding the game better. Being able to play under Coach Martin for three years and having two years of experience in the Cape, you learn the game a lot better, and I feel like I have a better understanding of the game and how it's played, how it should be played."

PREVIOUS WINNERS

1981: Mike Sodders, 3b, Arizona State
1982: Jeff Ledbetter, of/lhp, Florida State
1983: Dave Magadan, 1b, Alabama
1984: Oddibe McDowell, of, Arizona State
1985: Pete Incaviglia, of, Oklahoma State
1986: Casey Close, of, Michigan
1987: Robin Ventura, 3b, Oklahoma State
1988: John Olerud, 1b/lhp, Washington St.
1989: Ben McDonald, rhp, Louisiana State

1990: Mike Kelly, of, Arizona State
1991: David McCarthy, 1b, Stanford
1992: Phil Nevin, 3b, Cal State Fullerton
1993: Brooks Kieschnick, dh/rhp, Texas
1994: Jason Varitek, c, Georgia Tech
1995: Todd Helton, 1b/lhp, Tennessee
1996: Kris Benson, rhp, Clemson
1997: J.D. Drew, of, Florida State
1998: Jeff Austin, rhp, Stanford

1999: Jason Jennings, rhp, Baylor
2000: Mark Teixeira, 3b, Georgia Tech
2001: Mark Prior, rhp, Southern California
2002: Khalil Greene, ss, Clemson
2003: Rickie Weeks, 2b, Southern
2004: Jered Weaver, rhp, Long Beach State
2005: Alex Gordon, 3b, Nebraska
2006: Andrew Miller, lhp, North Carolina
2007: David Price, lhp, Vanderbilt

Fox builds UNC into powerhouse

BY AARON FITT

It wasn't so long ago that the College World Series was just a pipe dream for North Carolina. Sure, the Tar Hels got close a few times. But getting close and falling short feels light years away from walking through the front gate at Rosenblatt Stadium.

"I had an email the other day from a former player who said, 'Congratulations. Back when I was playing, we were just happy to get to a super-regional. Expectations have changed,'" UNC coach Mike Fox said. "I looked at it and said, 'I guess they have.' Early on when I was here, I don't think we truly expected to do it."

The program Fox took over after the 1998 season bears little resemblance to the national powerhouse North Carolina is today. The Tar Heels broke a 17-year CWS drought in 2006 and have been back to Omaha in 2007 and 2008, finishing as national runners-up twice and in third place this year. The program doesn't even look the same on a cosmetic level; UNC will move into a sparkling new $26 million stadium at the start of 2009. For shepherding North Carolina through a dramatic transformation into a truly elite national power, Fox is BA's 2008 College Coach of the Year.

"I don't think I dreamed that we'd go to Omaha three years in a row," Fox said. "I probably had dreams that we could get there, or at least hoped that we could.

Mike Fox

SPORTS ON FILM

That's why you worked hard. If you don't dream you can do it, then you probably won't."

Perhaps Fox's greatest achievement has been selling that dream to the athletic department, administration and community, as well as to players past, present and future.

"Coach Fox has done a great job of leading the way and organizing our program from the inside out," said Chad Holbrook, who was UNC's associate head coach and recruiting coordinator before leaving for South Carolina this summer. "I mean from getting the alumni back on board to getting everybody in the university and athletic department understanding how good our program can be, instilling an attitude, a confidence level, that we weren't going to be satisfied with just being good. We wanted to be the best we could possibly be."

As much as Fox wants to cap UNC's impressive recent run with a national title, he also knows it's important to keep a sense of perspective, even after a disappointing loss to Fresno State in the CWS. Sophomore first baseman Dustin Ackley said Fox stayed positive in the locker room after the loss, emphasizing the body of work from the season and the contributions of the team's seniors. Fox, one of six men to lead his alma mater to Omaha as a player and coach, is just grateful to be where he is. As he said before the CWS began, he doesn't need a national title to validate his program or his career.

COLLEGE BASEBALL

PREVIOUS WINNERS

1981: Ron Fraser, Miami
1982: Gene Stephenson, Wichita State
1983: Barry Shollenberger, Alabama
1984: Augie Garrido, Cal State Fullerton
1985: Ron Polk, Mississippi State
1986: Skip Bertman, Louisiana State
　　　　Dave Snow, Loyola Marymount
1987: Mark Marquess, Stanford
1988: Jim Brock, Arizona State
1989: Dave Snow, Long Beach State

1990: Steve Webber, Georgia
1991: Jim Hendry, Creighton
1992: Andy Lopez, Pepperdine
1993: Gene Stephenson, Wichita State
1994: Jim Morris, Miami
1995: Pat Murphy, Arizona State
1996: Skip Bertman, Louisiana State
1997: Jim Wells, Alabama
1998: Pat Murphy, Arizona State
1999: Wayne Graham, Rice

2000: Ray Tanner, South Carolina
2001: Dave Van Horn, Nebraska
2002: Augie Garrido, Texas
2003: George Horton, Cal State Fullerton
2004: David Perno, Georgia
2005: Rick Jones, Tulane
2006: Pat Casey, Oregon State
2007: Dave Serrano, UC Irvine

Steady Hernandez has dream season

BY AARON FITT

Miami head coach Jim Morris has seen his share of mature freshmen pass through Coral Gables—the Hurricanes have produced four Freshmen of the Year during his tenure and five overall—but even he wasn't prepared for the kind of season Chris Hernandez posted. Although maybe he should have been.

"It's been unbelievable," Morris said. "You don't ever expect a freshman to do what he's done, to be honest. We thought he was going to be a very good player. (Pitching coach) J.D. Arteaga said he thought he might end up being the best lefthanded pitcher ever to pitch at Miami. Considering J.D. might be the best lefthanded pitcher ever to pitch at Miami, coming from that guy, that's saying something. And that was before season started."

"He might be the best one right now,"

CARL KLINE

Chris Hernandez

Arteaga said. "Without pitching another inning, he might be the best lefthander to ever pitch at Miami right now."

Morris and Arteaga know exactly what they're getting from Hernandez when he steps on the mound. He's going to turn in six or seven rock-solid innings, with very few walks, and he's going to give the Hurricanes a very good chance to win. As the ace of Miami's staff this spring, Hernandez used an excellent cutter, an 87-90 mph fastball, a curveball and a changeup to go 11-0, 2.72 with 117 strikeouts and 18 walks in 113 innings. For his remarkable reliability and consistency, Hernandez is Baseball America's 2008 Freshman of the Year.

"I have taken some time to look back at it a little bit, and it's been kind of a dream season," Hernandez said. "I think it's been more than a dream season. I never expected even half this stuff to happen my freshman year. It's definitely awesome."

PREVIOUS WINNERS

1982: Cory Snyder, 3b, Brigham Young
1983: Rafael Palmeiro, of, Mississippi State
1984: Greg Swindell, lhp, Texas
1985: Jack McDowell, rhp, Stanford
1986: Robin Ventura, 3b, Oklahoma State
1987: Paul Carey, of, Stanford
1988: Kirk Dressendorfer, rhp, Texas
1989: Alex Fernandez, rhp, Miami
1990: Jeffrey Hammonds, of, Stanford
1991: Brooks Kieschnick, rhp-dh, Texas
1992: Todd Walker, 2b, Louisiana State
1993: Brett Laxton, rhp, Louisiana State
1994: R.A. Dickey, rhp, Tennessee
1995: Kyle Peterson, rhp, Stanford
1996: Pat Burrell, 3b, Miami
1997: Brian Roberts, ss, North Carolina
1998: Xavier Nady, 2b, California
1999: James Jurries, 2b, Tulane
2000: Kevin Howard, 3b, Miami
2001: Michael Aubrey, of/lhp, Texas
2002: Stephen Drew, ss, Florida State
2003: Ryan Braun, ss, Miami
2004: Wade LeBlanc, lhp, Alabama
2005: Joe Savery, lhp, Rice
2006: Pedro Alvarez, 3b, Vanderbilt
2007: Dustin Ackley, 1b, North Carolina

FRESHMAN ALL-AMERICA TEAMS

FIRST TEAM

POS.	PLAYER, SCHOOL	AVG	OBP	SLG	AB	R	H	HR	RBI	SB
C	Micah Gibbs, Louisiana State	.322	.417	.448	174	31	56	2	35	2
1B	Hunter Morris, Auburn	.351	.433	.597	211	42	74	11	49	4
2B	Josh Adams, Florida	.330	.430	.536	209	42	69	8	51	11
3B	Scott Woodward, Coastal Carolina	.364	.540	.533	225	82	82	7	45	42
SS	Rick Hague, Rice	.348	.408	.549	233	40	81	8	54	4
OF	Kentrail Davis, Tennessee	.330	.435	.583	206	45	68	13	44	7
OF	Ryan Lockwood, South Florida	.415	.493	.513	193	44	80	0	37	12
OF	Brian Fletcher, Auburn	.324	.408	.611	185	42	60	10	42	6
DH	Kyle Parker, Clemson	.303	.400	.559	211	44	64	14	50	2
UT	Brett Eibner, Arkansas	.298	.405	.497	191	36	57	8	48	3

		W	L	ERA	G	SV	IP	H	BB	SO	BAA
SP	Chris Hernandez, Miami	11	0	2.72	18	0	113	92	18	117	.223
SP	Seth Maness, East Carolina	9	2	3.57	16	0	98	99	20	81	.254
SP	Shane Davis, Canisius	12	1	2.42	13	0	89	89	24	47	.264
SP	Chance Ruffin, Texas	8	3	1.96	23	3	78	54	24	82	.191
RP	Chase Dempsay, Houston	8	3	2.53	33	11	64	47	19	49	.214
UT	Brett Eibner, Arkansas	3	1	4.50	11	0	24	25	14	24	.269

SECOND TEAM

C-Rafael Neda, New Mexico (.323/.374/.530). **1B**-Jaren Matthews, Rutgers (.294/.363/.505). **2B**-Jedd Gyorko, West Virginia (.409/.450/.612). **3B**-Victor Sanchez, San Diego (.268/.346/.495). **SS**-Christian Colon, CS Fullerton (.329/.406/.444). **OF**-Ben Klafczynski, Kent State (.339/.385/.630); Gary Brown, CS Fullerton (.292/.374/.426); Michael Choice, Texas-Arlington (.376/.440/.558). **DH**-Derek Dietrich, Georgia Tech (.332/.410/.592). **UT**-Brooks Raley, Texas A&M (.259/.358/.259; 7-2, 4.76). **SP**-Matt Harvey, North Carolina (7-2, 2.79); Kyle Blair, San Diego (8-4, 3.86); Barret Loux, Texas A&M (6-2, 4.18); Thain Simon, Santa Clara (9-2, 2.59). **RP**-Kevin Rhoderick, Oregon State (0-1, 2.39, 12 SV).

Minimum 120 plate appearances, 3.0 plate appearances per game

BATTING

BATTING AVERAGE	YEAR	G	AB	H	AVG
Buster Posey, Florida State	Jr.	68	257	119	.463
Josh Phegley, Indiana	So.	61	224	98	.438
Chris Shehan, Georgia Southern	Jr.	58	224	98	.438
Jabari Graham, Alcorn State	Jr.	42	151	66	.437
Tyron Childress, Alabama A&M	Sr.	39	125	54	.432
Clay Whittemore, Jacksonville State	Sr.	57	226	96	.425
Spencer Lucian, Princeton	Sr.	42	146	62	.425
Tyler Kuhn, West Virginia	Sr.	56	238	101	.424
Ryan Keedy, Alabama-Birmingham	Sr.	60	234	99	.423
Mike Sheridan, William & Mary	Jr.	56	227	96	.423
Kyle Jensen, St. Mary's	So.	53	195	82	.421
Michael Marseco, Samford	Jr.	56	222	93	.419
Sawyer Carroll, Kentucky	Sr.	63	234	98	.419
Conor Gillaspie, Wichita State	Jr.	60	234	98	.419
Tim Park, William & Mary	Sr.	57	220	92	.418
Zach Rodeghero, Valparaiso	Sr.	56	220	92	.418
Dustin Ackley, North Carolina	So.	68	278	116	.417
Michael Higa, Hawaii-Hilo	Sr.	40	135	56	.415
Ryan Lockwood, South Florida	Fr.	47	193	80	.415
Brian Van Kirk, Oral Roberts	Sr.	62	237	98	.414
Ryan Mollica, Florida International	Jr.	55	201	83	.413
Ryan Shay, Bowling Green	Jr.	52	211	87	.412
Gordon Beckham, Georgia	Jr.	71	275	113	.411
Brett Wallace, Arizona State	Jr.	62	239	98	.410
Brett Sellers, James Madison	Sr.	55	222	91	.410
Jeremy Hamilton, Wright State	Jr.	50	183	75	.410
Cory Harrilchak, Elon	Jr.	62	205	84	.410
Nathan Ford, Cornell	Jr.	39	144	59	.410
Jedd Gyorko, West Virginia	Fr.	56	232	95	.409
Joel Del Grande, Alcorn State	Jr.	41	125	51	.408
Jerome McCullum, Arkansas-Pine Bluff	Sr.	43	157	64	.408
Eric Thames, Pepperdine	Jr.	49	182	74	.407
Randy Moley, St. Bonaventure	Sr.	53	207	84	.406
Jeremy Jones, North Carolina A&T	Sr.	59	225	91	.404
Justin Bass, Stetson	Sr.	59	240	97	.404
Jeremy Cruz, Stetson	Jr.	55	223	90	.404
Tim Fedroff, North Carolina	So.	67	285	115	.404
Curt Smith, Maine	Sr.	49	176	71	.403
Thomas Hamilton, Navy	Sr.	58	221	89	.403
Brett Nommensen, Eastern Illinois	Jr.	57	204	82	.402
Brian Hawkins, St. Mary's	Sr.	43	122	49	.402
Bryan Miller, Troy	Sr.	58	254	102	.402
Reese Wade, Furman	Fr.	49	142	57	.401
Alex Gregory, Radford	Jr.	56	207	83	.401
Justin Bour, George Mason	So.	55	221	88	.398
Ryan Lavarnway, Yale	Jr.	34	108	43	.398
Jose Lozada, Bethune-Cookman	Sr.	58	211	84	.398
Ty Wright, Georgia Southern	Jr.	50	196	78	.398
Kyle Hudson, Illinois	Jr.	53	191	76	.398

			AB	H	AVG
Brock Miller, Gardner-Webb	Jr.	51	156	62	.397
Earnest Rhone, Texas Southern	Jr.	48	151	60	.397
Damon Wright, Dartmouth	Sr.	41	151	60	.397
Jason Appel, UNC Wilmington	Sr.	62	252	100	.397
Ty Kelly, UC Davis	Fr.	58	237	94	.397
Matt Nohelty, Minnesota	Jr.	55	237	94	.397
Caleb Curry, Iowa	Sr.	55	202	80	.396
Charlie Blackmon, Georgia Tech	Sr.	62	250	99	.396
Brandon Douglas, Northern Iowa	Jr.	54	225	89	.396
Phil Cerreto, Longwood	So.	50	177	70	.395
Justin Parker, Wright State	Jr.	46	177	70	.395
Justin Toole, Iowa	Jr.	55	220	87	.395
Justin Miller, Ohio State	Jr.	53	200	79	.395
Conor Reardon, Brown	Sr.	40	157	62	.395
Mike McKenna, Florida Atlantic	Sr.	60	246	97	.394
Ben Soignier, Louisiana-Monroe	Jr.	57	236	93	.394
Frazier Hall, Southern	Fr.	38	117	46	.393
Sonny Meade, Citadel	Jr.	56	229	90	.393
Jeremie Tice, College of Charleston	Jr.	59	229	90	.393
Ryan Sontag, Arizona State	Sr.	59	168	66	.393
Jack Murphy, Princeton	So.	42	156	61	.391
Daniel Webb, Illinois	Sr.	56	192	75	.391
Jason Rodriguez, Nevada	Sr.	60	228	89	.390
Grant Green, Southern California	So.	50	205	80	.390
Chris Lewis, Western Michigan	Jr.	50	182	71	.390
Nick Santos, Dallas Baptist	Sr.	48	195	76	.390
Shane Peterson, Long Beach State	Jr.	59	213	83	.390
Ben Guez, William & Mary	Jr.	57	231	90	.390
Chris King, Tennessee Tech	Jr.	58	226	88	.389
Brandon Haislet, Hawaii	Sr.	60	229	89	.389
Kyle Higgins, Monmouth	Sr.	53	229	89	.389
Rafael Hill, Austin Peay State	Sr.	56	206	80	.388
Ben Woodbury, Missouri State	Sr.	57	237	92	.388
Andy Dirks, Wichita State	Sr.	65	250	97	.388
Nate Lape, Marshall	Jr.	59	214	83	.388
Matt Apfel, Arkansas-Little Rock	Jr.	48	186	72	.387
Jake Jefferies, UC Davis	Jr.	58	248	96	.387
Tyler Hardt, New Mexico State	Sr.	50	168	65	.387
Carlo Testa, Belmont	Jr.	58	212	82	.387
Tommy Nurre, Miami (Ohio)	Jr.	53	202	78	.386
Drew Heid, Gonzaga	So.	49	153	59	.386
Kevin Nieto, Manhattan	So.	43	153	59	.386
Thomas Belza, Oklahoma State	Fr.	50	166	64	.386
Ike Davis, Arizona State	Jr.	52	213	82	.385
Ryan Lipkin, San Francisco	So.	52	172	66	.384
Mike Kalina, Northwestern	Sr.	41	146	56	.384
Reggie Keen, Radford	So.	56	219	84	.384
Brandon Pearce, Alcorn State	Sr.	39	133	51	.383
Kyle Schultz, Butler	So.	40	120	46	.383
Justin Smoak, South Carolina	Jr.	63	235	90	.383
Cody Guymon, Utah	Jr.	54	222	85	.383

ON-BASE PERCENTAGE	YEAR	OBP
Buster Posey, Florida State	Jr.	.566
Chris Shehan, Georgia Southern	Jr.	.557
Ryan Lavarnway, Yale	Jr.	.541
Scott Woodward, Coastal Carolina	Fr.	.540
Yonder Alonso, Miami	Jr.	.534
Blake Murphy, Western Carolina	Sr.	.531
Earnest Rhone, Texas Southern	Jr.	.528
Jabari Graham, Alcorn State	Jr.	.527
Brett Wallace, Arizona State	Jr.	.526
Gordon Beckham, Georgia	Jr.	.519
Ryan Keedy, Alabama-Birmingham	Sr.	.519
Allan Dykstra, Wake Forest	Jr.	.519
Michael Stephan, Stony Brook	So.	.518
Chase Leavitt, Arkansas	Jr.	.518
Brett Nommensen, Eastern Illinois	Jr.	.518

		OBP
Jeremy Hamilton, Wright State	Jr.	.515
Sawyer Carroll, Kentucky	Sr.	.514
Eric Thames, Pepperdine	Jr.	.513
Spencer Lucian, Princeton	Sr.	.511
Matt Newman, Arizona State	Fr.	.509
Josh Phegley, Indiana	So.	.507
Tyron Childress, Alabama A&M	Sr.	.507
Shane Peterson, Long Beach State	Jr.	.506
Brian Van Kirk, Oral Roberts	Sr.	.505
Justin Smoak, South Carolina	Jr.	.505
Alex Gregory, Radford	Jr.	.504
Frazier Hall, Southern	Fr.	.503
Dustin Ackley, North Carolina	So.	.503
Ricky Orton, UNC Greensboro	Sr.	.502
Conor Gillaspie, Wichita State	Jr.	.500
Michael Higa, Hawaii-Hilo	Sr.	.500

		OBP
Jose Lozada, Bethune-Cookman	Sr.	.500
Josh Satin, California	Sr.	.500
Andy Dirks, Wichita State	Sr.	.498
Kyle Hudson, Illinois	Jr.	.498
Kyle Jensen, St. Mary's	So.	.498
Dom Lombardi, Manhattan	Fr.	.498
Curt Smith, Maine	Sr.	.498
Brock Miller, Gardner-Webb	Jr.	.497
Danny Slinkman, Texas-Arlington	Jr.	.497
Ben Soignier, Louisiana-Monroe	Jr.	.496
Preston Paramore, Arizona State	Jr.	.496
Jeremie Tice, College of Charleston	Jr.	.495
Rafael Hill, Austin Peay State	Sr.	.494
Randy Moley, St. Bonaventure	Sr.	.494
Ty Wright, Georgia Southern	Jr.	.494
Ryan Lockwood, South Florida	Fr.	.493

Jerome McCullum, Ark.-Pine Bluff	Sr.	.492
Cory Harrilchak, Elon	Jr.	.492
Kevin Reimer, Canisius	Jr.	.492
Brandon Pearce, Alcorn State	Sr.	.491
Zach Rodeghero, Valparaiso	Sr.	.490
Joel Del Grande, Alcorn State	Jr.	.490
Chris Lewis, Western Michigan	Jr.	.488
Tim Park, William & Mary	Sr.	.488
Luke Anders, Texas A&M	Jr.	.486
Reese Havens, South Carolina	Jr.	.486
Jason Kipnis, Arizona State	So.	.485
Chris Swauger, Citadel	Sr.	.485
Brad McElroy, Charlotte	Sr.	.485
Thomas Hamilton, Navy	Sr.	.485
Adrian Bowens, Alcorn State	Jr.	.484
John Allman, Kansas	Sr.	.484
Evan Wells, Gonzaga	Jr.	.484
Alden Carrithers, UCLA	Sr.	.484

SLUGGING PERCENTAGE — YEAR — SLG

Buster Posey, Florida State	Jr.	.879
Jeremie Tice, College of Charleston	Jr.	.838
Chris Shehan, Georgia Southern	Jr.	.835
Ryan Lavarnway, Yale	Jr.	.824
Gordon Beckham, Georgia	Jr.	.804
Matt Clark, Louisiana State	Jr.	.789
Sawyer Carroll, Kentucky	Sr.	.782
Ty Wright, Georgia Southern	Jr.	.781
Yonder Alonso, Miami	Jr.	.777
Greg Rohan, Kent State	Sr.	.772
Eric Thames, Pepperdine	Jr.	.769
Scott Krieger, George Mason	Jr.	.761
Justin Smoak, South Carolina	Jr.	.757
Brett Wallace, Arizona State	Jr.	.753
Nate Recknagel, Michigan	Sr.	.751
Xavier Scruggs, Nevada-Las Vegas	Jr.	.749
Brett Sellers, James Madison	Sr.	.748
Kyle Conley, Washington	Jr.	.746
Josh Phegley, Indiana	So.	.746
Chris Edmondson, Le Moyne	So.	.745
Mike Sheridan, William & Mary	Jr.	.744
Ike Davis, Arizona State	Jr.	.742
Blake Murphy, Western Carolina	Sr.	.740
Josh Vittek, Mount St. Mary's	Sr.	.736
Steven Caseres, James Madison	So.	.734
Brian Van Kirk, Oral Roberts	Sr.	.734
Tim Park, William & Mary	Sr.	.732
Mike Spina, Cincinnati	Jr.	.731
Michael Harrington, College of Charleston	Sr.	.731
Josh Satin, California	Jr.	.731
Curt Smith, Maine	Sr.	.722
Kyle Jensen, St. Mary's	Jr.	.718
Jeremy Hamilton, Wright State	Jr.	.716
Mark Carver, UNC Wilmington	Sr.	.708
Nate Lape, Marshall	Jr.	.706
Rob Lyerly, Charlotte	So.	.705
Jeremy Cruz, Stetson	Jr.	.704
Ben Soignier, Louisiana-Monroe	Jr.	.703
Jerome McCullum, Ark.-Pine Bluff	Jr.	.701
Rawley Bishop, Middle Tennessee State	Jr.	.700
Conor Gillaspie, Wichita State	Jr.	.697
Brent Smith, Grambling	Jr.	.696
Mike Lyon, Northeastern	Sr.	.693
Trent Lockwood, Texas-San Antonio	So.	.693
Nick Santomauro, Dartmouth	So.	.691
Eric Allen, Morehead State	Sr.	.690
Paul Goldschmidt, Texas State	So.	.689
Chris Dominguez, Louisville	So.	.687
Collin Cowgill, Kentucky	Sr.	.687
Anthony Russell, East Tennessee State	Sr.	.686
Bryan Miller, Troy	Sr.	.685
Damon Wright, Dartmouth	Sr.	.682
David Cooper, California	Jr.	.682
Joseph Scaperotta, New Mexico State	Sr.	.681
Angelo Songco, Loyola Marymount	So.	.681

Chad Cregar, Western Kentucky	Jr.	.680
Gabe Jacobo, Sacramento State	Jr.	.678
Cory Harrilchak, Elon	Jr.	.678
Ben Carlson, Missouri State	So.	.678
Darrion Pedro, Alabama State	Fr.	.677
Brandon Sizemore, Col. of Charleston	Jr.	.677
Brandon Douglas, Northern Iowa	Jr.	.676
Dan Black, Purdue	So.	.675
Ryan Keedy, Alabama-Birmingham	Sr.	.675
Dock Doyle, Coastal Carolina	Sr.	.675
Ricky Orton, UNC Greensboro	Sr.	.675

HOME RUNS — YEAR — HR

Gordon Beckham, Georgia	Jr.	28
Matt Clark, Louisiana State	Jr.	28
Michael Harrington, Col. of Charleston	Jr.	26
Buster Posey, Florida State	Jr.	26
Jeremie Tice, College of Charleston	Jr.	25
Yonder Alonso, Miami	Jr.	24
Nate Recknagel, Michigan	Sr.	23
Joseph Scaperotta, New Mexico State	Sr.	23
Justin Smoak, South Carolina	Jr.	23
Sean Ratliff, Stanford	Jr.	22
Chris Shehan, Georgia Southern	Jr.	22
Brett Wallace, Arizona State	Jr.	22
Mark Carver, UNC Wilmington	Sr.	21
Steven Caseres, James Madison	So.	21
Chad Cregar, Western Kentucky	Jr.	21
Chris Dominguez, Louisville	So.	21
Scott Krieger, George Mason	Jr.	21
Anthony Russell, East Tennessee State	Sr.	21
Mike Spina, Cincinnati	Jr.	21
A.J. Wirnsberger, Georgia Southern	So.	21
David Anderson, Coastal Carolina	Jr.	20
Blake Dean, Louisiana State	So.	20
Frank Pesanello, Northeastern	Jr.	20
Greg Rohan, Kent State	Sr.	20
Xavier Scruggs, Nevada-Las Vegas	Jr.	20
Brandon Sizemore, Col. of Charleston	2B	20
Josh Vittek, Mount St. Mary's	Sr.	20
C.J. Ziegler, Arizona	Sr.	20
Sawyer Carroll, Kentucky	Sr.	19
Kyle Conley, Washington	Jr.	19
David Cooper, California	Jr.	19
Collin Cowgill, Kentucky	Sr.	19
James Darnell, South Carolina	Jr.	19
Phil Disher, South Carolina	Sr.	19
Dennis Guinn, Florida State	Sr.	19
Tommy Mendonca, Fresno State	So.	19
Kyle Russell, Texas	Jr.	19
Chris Taylor, Charlotte	Sr.	19
Rawley Bishop, Middle Tennessee State	Jr.	18
Dan Black, Purdue	So.	18
Bryce Brentz, Middle Tennessee State	Fr.	18
Bennett Davis, Elon	Jr.	18
Daniel Hargrave, UNC Wilmington	Jr.	18
Reese Havens, South Carolina	Jr.	18
Corey Kemp, East Carolina	Sr.	18
Rebel Ridling, Oklahoma State	Jr.	18
David Sappelt, Coastal Carolina	Jr.	18
Josh Satin, California	Sr.	18
Matt Stiffler, Ohio	Jr.	18
Brian Van Kirk, Oral Roberts	Sr.	18
Eric Allen, Morehead State	Sr.	17
Alex Avila, Alabama	Jr.	17
Ben Carlson, Missouri State	So.	17
Paul Goldschmidt, Texas State	So.	17
Caleb Joseph, Lipscomb	Jr.	17
Roger Kieschnick, Texas Tech	Jr.	17
Nate Lape, Marshall	Jr.	17
Cody Overbeck, Mississippi	Jr.	17
Brett Sellers, James Madison	Sr.	17
Derek Wiley, Belmont	Jr.	17
Ty Wright, Georgia Southern	Jr.	17
Luke Anders, Texas A&M	Jr.	16

Franky Busani, New Mexico State	Jr.	16
Ike Davis, Arizona State	Jr.	16
Dock Doyle, Coastal Carolina	Sr.	16
Allan Dykstra, Wake Forest	Jr.	16
Nick Freitas, Southern Utah	Jr.	16
Trevor Head, Dallas Baptist	Jr.	16
Sean Hoorelbeke, Central Michigan	Sr.	16
Ryne Jernigan, South Alabama	Sr.	16
Trent Lockwood, Texas-San Antonio	So.	16
Mike McKenna, Florida Atlantic	Sr.	16
Jim Murphy, Washington State	Sr.	16
Blake Murphy, Western Carolina	Sr.	16
Tony Plagman, Georgia Tech	So.	16
Jacob Priday, Missouri	Sr.	16
Ben Soignier, Louisiana-Monroe	Jr.	16
Kyle Suire, Louisiana-Monroe	Sr.	16

RUNS BATTED IN — YEAR — RBI

Buster Posey, Florida State	Jr.	93
Alan Ahmady, Fresno State	So.	92
Steve Susdorf, Fresno State	Sr.	87
Sawyer Carroll, Kentucky	Sr.	83
Jeremie Tice, College of Charleston	Jr.	83
Brett Wallace, Arizona State	Jr.	83
Mark Carver, UNC Wilmington	Sr.	82
Chad Cregar, Western Kentucky	Jr.	82
Bennett Davis, Elon	Jr.	82
Conor Gillaspie, Wichita State	Jr.	82
Michael Harrington, Col. of Charleston	Sr.	82
Joseph Scaperotta, New Mexico State	Sr.	82
Brandon Sizemore, Col. of Charleston	Jr.	82
James Darnell, South Carolina	Jr.	81
Josh Phegley, Indiana	So.	80
Trent Lockwood, Texas-San Antonio	So.	79
Mike Spina, Cincinnati	Jr.	79
Gordon Beckham, Georgia	Jr.	77
Chris Shehan, Georgia Southern	Jr.	77
Ike Davis, Arizona State	Jr.	76
Dennis Guinn, Florida State	Sr.	76
Rob Lyerly, Charlotte	So.	76
Josh Vander Hey, New Orleans	Sr.	76
Chris Dominguez, Louisville	So.	75
Mike McKenna, Florida Atlantic	Sr.	75
Rich Poythress, Georgia	So.	75
Kyle Seager, North Carolina	So.	75
Brian Van Kirk, Oral Roberts	Sr.	74
Jason Castro, Stanford	Jr.	73
Blake Dean, Louisiana State	So.	73
Jason Kipnis, Arizona State	So.	73
A.J. Wirnsberger, Georgia Southern	So.	73
Yonder Alonso, Miami	Jr.	72
Dock Doyle, Coastal Carolina	Sr.	72
Ryne Jernigan, South Alabama	Sr.	72
Corey Kemp, East Carolina	Sr.	72
Mike Sheridan, William & Mary	Jr.	72
Justin Smoak, South Carolina	Jr.	72
Osvaldo Torres, Bethune-Cookman	Sr.	72
Dusty Coleman, Wichita State	So.	71
Tim Fedroff, North Carolina	So.	71
Sean Ratliff, Stanford	Jr.	71
Dan Black, Purdue	Sr.	70
Steven Caseres, James Madison	So.	70
Tommy Mendonca, Fresno State	So.	70
Jeremiah Parker, Georgia Southern	Sr.	70
Ben Petralli, Oral Roberts	Jr.	70
David Sappelt, Coastal Carolina	Jr.	70
Chris Taylor, Charlotte	Sr.	70
Rawley Bishop, Middle Tennessee State	Jr.	69
Darby Brown, Texas A&M	Sr.	69
Tony Delmonico, Florida State	Jr.	69
Paul Goldschmidt, Texas State	So.	69
Ryan Keedy, Alabama-Birmingham	Sr.	69
Bryce Brentz, Middle Tennessee State	Fr.	68
José Duran, Texas A&M	Jr.	68
Nate Recknagel, Michigan	Sr.	68

Michael Rockett, Texas-San Antonio	Jr.	68
Brady Shoemaker, Indiana State	Jr.	68
Ben Carlson, Missouri State	So.	67
Dexter Fontenot, Louisiana-Monroe	Sr.	67
Bryan Pounds, Houston	Sr.	67
Rebel Ridling, Oklahoma State	Sr.	67
Aaron Senne, Missouri	Sr.	67
Vince Belnome, West Virginia	So.	66
Derek Dietrich, Georgia Tech	Fr.	66
Nate Hall, UNC Wilmington	Sr.	66
Gabe Jacobo, Sacramento State	Jr.	66
Clay Whittemore, Jacksonville State	Sr.	66

DOUBLES

	YEAR	2B
Steve Susdorf, Fresno State	Sr.	33
Bryan Miller, Troy	Sr.	32
Kyle Seager, North Carolina	So.	30
Ryan Keedy, Alabama-Birmingham	Sr.	29
Jesse Hart, Wisconsin-Milwaukee	Sr.	28
Justin Bass, Stetson	Sr.	27
Ike Davis, Arizona State	Jr.	26
David Flores, Sacramento State	Sr.	26
Rob Lyerly, Charlotte	So.	26
Justin McClanahan, Louisville	Sr.	26
Mike Sheridan, William & Mary	Jr.	26
Shawn Wozniak, Wis.-Milwaukee	Jr.	26
Brandon Douglas, Northern Iowa	Jr.	25
Luke Murton, Georgia Tech	Jr.	25
Tim Park, William & Mary	Sr.	25
Michael Rockett, Texas-San Antonio	Jr.	25
David Sappelt, Coastal Carolina	Jr.	25
Todd Sebek, Sam Houston State	Sr.	25
Christopher Auten, New Mexico State	Jr.	24
Jared Clark, Cal State Fullerton	Sr.	24
Wes Dorrell, Cal Poly	Sr.	24
Wade Gaynor, Western Kentucky	So.	24
Joe McIntyre, North Carolina A&T	Sr.	24
Brandon Sizemore, Col. of Charleston	Jr.	24
Keith Stein, Sam Houston State	Sr.	24
Jake Stewart, Houston	Sr.	24
Chris Wade, Kentucky	Fr.	24
Kevin Dubler, Illinois State	Jr.	23
Mike Gosse, Oklahoma	Sr.	23
Casey Haerther, UCLA	So.	23
Chris Klepps, Siena	Sr.	23
Trent Lockwood, Texas-San Antonio	So.	23
Sean McNaughton, Brigham Young	So.	23
Ryan Mollica, Florida International	Jr.	23
Wink Nolan, Md.-Baltimore County	Jr.	23
Matt Pace, Arkansas-Pine Bluff	Fr.	23
Gordon Beckham, Georgia	Jr.	22
Sawyer Carroll, Kentucky	Sr.	22
Jordan Danks, Texas	Jr.	22
Kyle Davis, Delaware	Jr.	22
Andy Dirks, Wichita State	Sr.	22
Dock Doyle, Coastal Carolina	Sr.	22
Chris Edmondson, Le Moyne	So.	22
Tim Fedroff, North Carolina	So.	22
Andrew Giobbi, Vanderbilt	So.	22
Jake Goebbert, Northwestern	So.	22
Dan Grovatt, Virginia	Fr.	22
Brandon Haislet, Hawaii	Sr.	22
Nate Hanson, Minnesota	Jr.	22
Josh Harrison, Cincinnati	Jr.	22
Ryne Jernigan, South Alabama	Sr.	22
Tommy Nurre, Miami (Ohio)	Jr.	22
Ryan Peisel, Georgia	Sr.	22
Rich Poythress, Georgia	So.	22
Jason Rodriguez, Nevada	Sr.	22
Kevin Sandberg, Northern Colorado	Jr.	22
Justin Sanders, Lipscomb	Sr.	22
Brian Van Kirk, Oral Roberts	Sr.	22
Nick Wichser, Milwaukee	Sr.	22
Seth Williams, North Carolina	Sr.	22
Ty Wright, Georgia Southern	Jr.	22

TRIPLES

	YEAR	3B
Nathan Carter, Air Force	Fr.	10
Dane Carter, Texas A&M	Sr.	9
Tony Campana, Cincinnati	Sr.	8
Conor Gillaspie, Wichita State	Jr.	8
Jayson Langfels, Eastern Kentucky	Fr.	8
Austin Markel, West Virginia	Jr.	8
Michael Marseco, Samford	Jr.	8
Andrew Means, Indiana	Jr.	8
Justin Milo, Vermont	So.	8
Carlo Testa, Belmont	Jr.	8
Eric Thames, Pepperdine	Jr.	8
Dean Anna, Ball State	Jr.	7
Roman Batista, Coppin State	Jr.	7
Adrian Bowens, Alcorn State	Jr.	7
LaDerek Camper, Jackson State	Jr.	7
Jordan Danks, Texas	Jr.	7
José Duran, Texas A&M	Jr.	7
Thomas Field, Texas State	Jr.	7
Troy Hanzawa, San Diego State	Sr.	7
Scott Kaskie, Western Kentucky	Sr.	7
Jose Lozada, Bethune-Cookman	Sr.	7
Kyle Massie, Vermont	Sr.	7
Chris Roberts, Michigan State	So.	7
Anthony Scelfo, Tulane	Jr.	7
Ryan Schimpf, Louisiana State	So.	7
Corey Shimada, Utah	Jr.	7
Daniel Walker, Air Force	So.	7
Kent Walton, Brigham Young	Jr.	7
Joe Agreste, West Virginia	Jr.	6
Joey Butler, New Orleans	Sr.	6
Jason Christian, Michigan	Jr.	6
Carlos Del Rosario, St. John's	Jr.	6
Chris Dove, Elon	Jr.	6
Danny Espinosa, Long Beach State	Jr.	6
Shaver Hansen, Baylor	So.	6
Renaldo Hollins, Navy	Sr.	6
Jeremy Jakubowski, St. Joseph's	Sr.	6
Jarred Jimenez, Rutgers	So.	6
Jamaal Kinard, Gardner-Webb	Sr.	6
Jason Kipnis, Arizona State	So.	6
Erik Komatsu, Cal State Fullerton	Jr.	6
John Kopilchack, Wright State	Sr.	6
Tyler Kuhn, West Virginia	Sr.	6
David Mills, Notre Dame	So.	6
Kevin Nieto, Manhattan	So.	6
Corey Overholtzer, UNC Greensboro	So.	6
Henry Perkins, Columbia	Sr.	6
John Rickards, La Salle	Sr.	6
Jason Rook, Appalachian State	Jr.	6
Matt Smedberg, Seton Hall	Jr.	6
Michael Speciale, Navy	So.	6
Keith Stein, Sam Houston State	Sr.	6
Matt Stiffler, Ohio	Sr.	6
Austin Wates, Virginia Tech	Fr.	6
Clay Whittemore, Jacksonville State	Sr.	6

STOLEN BASES

	YEAR	SB	CS
Adam Yeager, Marshall	Jr.	47	9
Roly Gonzalez, Texas-Pan American	Sr.	46	9
Caleb Curry, Iowa	Sr.	45	7
Tony Campana, Cincinnati	Sr.	44	11
Scott Woodward, Coastal Carolina	Fr.	42	9
Kyle Hudson, Illinois	Jr.	40	9
Ollie Linton, UC Irvine	Jr.	40	4
Chris Dove, Elon	Jr.	38	15
Jimmy Miles, Old Dominion	Sr.	38	7
James Hayes, Rider	Jr.	37	7
Rich Goulian, Fordham	Sr.	36	10
Eric Reese, Fordham	Sr.	35	4
Brandon Scott, Campbell	Sr.	35	5
Jamel Scott, Cincinnati	So.	35	9
Cortez Cole, Jackson State	Jr.	34	3
Nick Freitas, Southern Utah	Jr.	34	4
Damian Csakai, Wagner	So.	33	2

Matt Maher, Fairleigh Dickinson	Jr.	33	4
Andrew Means, Indiana	Jr.	33	6
Brock Miller, Gardner-Webb	Jr.	33	6
Harrison Eldridge, East Carolina	Sr.	32	5
Josh Harrison, Cincinnati	Jr.	32	8
Bryce Mendonca, Pepperdine	Jr.	32	5
Randy Moley, St. Bonaventure	Sr.	32	3
Kevin Tokarski, Illinois State	Fr.	32	9
Daniel Cooke, Gardner-Webb	Jr.	31	6
Chay Derbigny, Air Force	Sr.	31	3
Ray Kruml, South Alabama	Sr.	31	6
Daniel Leach, Fordham	Sr.	31	7
Kai Kirby, Stephen F. Austin	Jr.	30	7
Greg Miclat, Virginia	Jr.	30	6
Ryan Lormand, Houston	Sr.	29	4
Nick Cox, Columbia	Fr.	28	4
A.J. Pollock, Notre Dame	So.	28	2
T.J. Steele, Arizona	Jr.	28	2
Sean Barksdale, Temple	Jr.	27	7
Willie Rueda, Texas Tech	Jr.	27	7
Blake Tekotte, Miami	Jr.	27	6
Dominic de la Osa, Vanderbilt	Sr.	27	6
Avery Barnes, Florida	Jr.	26	3
Joe Bonadonna, Illinois	Jr.	26	6
Andy Dirks, Wichita State	Sr.	26	7
J.D. Dunn, Saint Louis	So.	26	5
Justin Kelly, Grambling	Jr.	26	3
Jamaal Kinard, Gardner-Webb	Sr.	26	4
Tyler Stovall, Central Michigan	Sr.	26	3
Carlo Testa, Belmont	Jr.	26	7
Charlie Blackmon, Georgia Tech	Sr.	25	5
Gary Brown, Cal State Fullerton	Fr.	25	3
Jason DeFillipo, Siena	Jr.	25	4
Brian Gump, UC Santa Barbara	Jr.	25	7
Donny Jobe, Elon	Sr.	25	10
Todd Sebek, Sam Houston State	Sr.	25	3
Jake Stewart, Houston	Sr.	25	4
Ryan Wiser, Mississippi State	Jr.	25	4
Jeremy Beckham, Georgia Southern	Sr.	24	5
Kevin Ferreira, Jacksonville	Sr.	24	1
Brint Hardy, Alabama-Birmingham	Jr.	24	3
Cory Harrilchak, Elon	Jr.	24	1
Kyle Higgins, Monmouth	Sr.	24	6
Jason Kipnis, Arizona State	So.	24	4
Matt Nohelty, Minnesota	Jr.	24	8
Joe Oliveria, Pacific	Jr.	24	4
Joey Rodgers, Furman	Sr.	24	3
Justin Toole, Iowa	Jr.	24	7

RUNS

	YEAR	R
Erik Wetzel, Fresno State	Jr.	99
Gordon Beckham, Georgia	Jr.	97
Buster Posey, Florida State	Jr.	89
Brett Wallace, Arizona State	Jr.	87
Andy Dirks, Wichita State	Sr.	84
Chris Shehan, Georgia Southern	Jr.	84
Tyler Holt, Florida State	Fr.	83
Ben Soignier, Louisiana-Monroe	Jr.	83
Dustin Ackley, North Carolina	So.	82
Scott Woodward, Coastal Carolina	Fr.	82
Blake Tekotte, Miami	Jr.	81
Jemile Weeks, Miami	Jr.	81
Yonder Alonso, Miami	Jr.	80
Collin Cowgill, Kentucky	Sr.	80
Steve Susdorf, Fresno State	Sr.	80
Jeremie Tice, College of Charleston	Jr.	80
Tim Fedroff, North Carolina	So.	78
Ryan Peisel, Georgia	Sr.	78
T.J. Baxter, New Orleans	Sr.	77
Joey Butler, New Orleans	Sr.	77
Johnny Giavotella, New Orleans	Jr.	76
Reese Havens, South Carolina	Jr.	76
Jason Kipnis, Arizona State	So.	76
Cord Phelps, Stanford	Jr.	76
Mike Sheridan, William & Mary	Jr.	76

COLLEGE BASEBALL

Ben Guez, William & Mary	Jr.	75
Matt Stiffler, Ohio	Sr.	75
Jake Stewart, Houston	Sr.	74
Brendan Duffy, Oral Roberts	Sr.	73
James Keithley, Texas-San Antonio	Jr.	73
Andrew Means, Indiana	Jr.	72
Anthony Scelfo, Tulane	Jr.	72
William Block, Florida Atlantic	Jr.	71
Mark Carver, UNC Wilmington	Sr.	71
Conor Gillaspie, Wichita State	Jr.	71
Daniel Hargrave, UNC Wilmington	Sr.	71
Michael Harrington, Col. of Charleston	Sr.	71
Tyler Kuhn, West Virginia	Sr.	71
Jordan Danks, Texas	Jr.	70
Cory Harrilchak, Elon	Jr.	70
Ryan Jones, Wichita State	So.	70
Ryan Wood, East Carolina	Jr.	70
Sawyer Carroll, Kentucky	Sr.	69
Tony Delmonico, Florida State	Jr.	69
Ray Kruml, South Alabama	Sr.	69
Gabe Marchant, Col. of Charleston	Sr.	69
Josh Phegley, Indiana	So.	69
Brandon Sizemore, Col. of Charleston	Jr.	69
Charlie Blackmon, Georgia Tech	Sr.	68
Jason Castro, Stanford	Jr.	68
Chris Dominguez, Louisville	So.	68
Scott Kaskie, Western Kentucky	Sr.	68
Jonathan Merritt, UAB	Sr.	68
Todd Sebek, Sam Houston State	Sr.	68
Keith Stein, Sam Houston State	Sr.	68
Dane Carter, Texas A&M	Sr.	67
Kyle Colligan, Texas A&M	Jr.	67
Dennis Guinn, Florida State	Sr.	67
Mike McKenna, Florida Atlantic	Sr.	67
Tim Park, William & Mary	Sr.	67
Kyle Suire, Louisiana-Monroe	Sr.	67
Bennett Davis, Elon	Jr.	66
Greg Feltes, UNC Greensboro	Sr.	66
Thomas Field, Texas State	Jr.	66
Josh Harrison, Cincinnati	Jr.	66
Kevin Mattison, UNC Asheville	Sr.	66
Marcus Quade, New Mexico State	Sr.	66

HITS	YEAR	H
Buster Posey, Florida State	Jr.	119
Dustin Ackley, North Carolina	So.	116
Tim Fedroff, North Carolina	So.	115
Gordon Beckham, Georgia	Jr.	113
Erik Wetzel, Fresno State	Jr.	112
Alan Ahmady, Fresno State	So.	110
Ryan Peisel, Georgia	Sr.	106
Jason Castro, Stanford	Jr.	105
José Duran, Texas A&M	Jr.	103
Steve Susdorf, Fresno State	Sr.	103
Bryan Miller, Troy	Sr.	102
Tyler Kuhn, West Virginia	Sr.	101
Todd Sebek, Sam Houston State	Sr.	101
Jason Appel, UNC Wilmington	Sr.	100
Charlie Blackmon, Georgia Tech	Sr.	99
Ryan Keedy, Alabama-Birmingham	Sr.	99
Rich Poythress, Georgia	So.	99
Josh Rutledge, Alabama	Fr.	99
Sawyer Carroll, Kentucky	Sr.	98
Dane Carter, Texas A&M	Sr.	98
Conor Gillaspie, Wichita State	Jr.	98
Josh Phegley, Indiana	So.	98
Chris Shehan, Georgia Southern	Jr.	98
Brian Van Kirk, Oral Roberts	Jr.	98
Brett Wallace, Arizona State	Jr.	98
Justin Bass, Stetson	Sr.	97
Andy Dirks, Wichita State	Sr.	97
Mike McKenna, Florida Atlantic	Sr.	97
Justin Mcclanahan, Louisville	Sr.	97
Jake Jefferies, UC Davis	Jr.	96
David Macias, Vanderbilt	Sr.	96

David Sappelt, Coastal Carolina	Jr.	96
Mike Sheridan, William & Mary	Jr.	96
Clay Whittemore, Jacksonville State	Sr.	96
Zach Barrett, Middle Tennessee State	Sr.	95
Blake Dean, Louisiana State	So.	95
Tony Delmonico, Florida State	Jr.	95
Jedd Gyorko, West Virginia	Fr.	95
Troy Hanzawa, San Diego State	Sr.	95
Danny Muno, Fresno State	Fr.	95
Ty Kelly, UC Davis	Fr.	94
Matt Nohelty, Minnesota	Jr.	94
Jason Altenhof, Appalachian State	Sr.	93
Mike Gosse, Oklahoma	Sr.	93
Nick Liles, Western Carolina	So.	93
Michael Marseco, Samford	Jr.	93
Matt Olson, Georgia	Sr.	93
Kyle Seager, North Carolina	So.	93
Ben Soignier, Louisiana-Monroe	Jr.	93
Keith Stein, Sam Houston State	Sr.	93
Christopher Auten, New Mexico State	Jr.	92
Joey Butler, New Orleans	Sr.	92
Brian Dozier, Southern Mississippi	Jr.	92
Brandon May, Alabama	Sr.	92
Sean McNaughton, Brigham Young	So.	92
Tim Park, William & Mary	Sr.	92
Zach Rodeghero, Valparaiso	Sr.	92
Ben Woodbury, Missouri State	Sr.	92
Chris Dominguez, Louisville	So.	91
Jeremy Jones, North Carolina A&T	Sr.	91
Cord Phelps, Stanford	Jr.	91
Bryan Pounds, Houston	Sr.	91
Diego Seastrunk, Rice	So.	91
Brett Sellers, James Madison	Sr.	91
Matt Stiffler, Ohio	Sr.	91

TOTAL BASES	YEAR	TB
Buster Posey, Florida State	Jr.	226
Gordon Beckham, Georgia	Jr.	221
Jeremie Tice, College of Charleston	Jr.	192
Chris Shehan, Georgia Southern	Jr.	187
Sawyer Carroll, Kentucky	Sr.	183
Tim Fedroff, North Carolina	So.	183
Steve Susdorf, Fresno State	Sr.	181
Brett Wallace, Arizona State	Jr.	180
Matt Clark, Louisiana State	Jr.	179
Blake Dean, Louisiana State	So.	179
Justin Smoak, South Carolina	Jr.	178
David Sappelt, Coastal Carolina	Jr.	175
Bryan Miller, Troy	Sr.	174
Brian Van Kirk, Oral Roberts	Sr.	174
Matt Stiffler, Ohio	Sr.	172
Jason Castro, Stanford	Jr.	171
Chris Dominguez, Louisville	So.	171
Michael Harrington, Col. of Charleston	Sr.	171
Chad Cregar, Western Kentucky	Jr.	170
Xavier Scruggs, Nevada-Las Vegas	Jr.	170
Brandon Sizemore, Col. of Charleston	Jr.	170
Mike Sheridan, William & Mary	Jr.	169
Alan Ahmady, Fresno State	So.	168
Ryan Peisel, Georgia	Sr.	168
Mark Carver, UNC Wilmington	Sr.	167
Josh Phegley, Indiana	So.	167
Dustin Ackley, North Carolina	Sr.	166
Dennis Guinn, Florida State	Sr.	166
Scott Krieger, George Mason	Jr.	166
Rich Poythress, Georgia	So.	166
Brett Sellers, James Madison	Sr.	166
Ben Soignier, Louisiana-Monroe	Jr.	166
Sean McNaughton, Brigham Young	So.	165
Yonder Alonso, Miami	Jr.	164
Dock Doyle, Coastal Carolina	Sr.	164
Daniel Hargrave, UNC Wilmington	Sr.	164
David Anderson, Coastal Carolina	Jr.	163
Steven Caseres, James Madison	So.	163
Conor Gillaspie, Wichita State	Jr.	163

Justin Mcclanahan, Louisville	Sr.	163
Mike Spina, Cincinnati	Jr.	163
A.J. Wirnsberger, Georgia Southern	So.	163
Mike McKenna, Florida Atlantic	Sr.	162
Tim Park, William & Mary	Sr.	161
Collin Cowgill, Kentucky	Sr.	160
Reese Havens, South Carolina	Sr.	160
Caleb Joseph, Lipscomb	Jr.	160
Sean Ratliff, Stanford	Jr.	160
Joseph Scaperotta, New Mexico State	Sr.	160
Kyle Seager, North Carolina	So.	160
C.J. Ziegler, Arizona	Sr.	160
Justin Bass, Stetson	Sr.	159
Keith Stein, Sam Houston State	Sr.	159
Chris Taylor, Charlotte	Sr.	159
Joey Butler, New Orleans	Sr.	158
Ike Davis, Arizona State	Jr.	158
Andy Dirks, Wichita State	Sr.	158
Ryan Keedy, Alabama-Birmingham	Sr.	158
Jason Kipnis, Arizona State	So.	158
Jeremy Cruz, Stetson	Jr.	157
Paul Goldschmidt, Texas State	So.	157
Tyler Kuhn, West Virginia	Sr.	157
Cody Overbeck, Mississippi	Jr.	157
Nate Recknagel, Michigan	Sr.	157
Rawley Bishop, Middle Tennessee State	Jr.	156
Dane Carter, Texas A&M	Sr.	156
Josh Vittek, Mount St. Mary's	Sr.	156
Wade Gaynor, Western Kentucky	So.	155
Rob Lyerly, Charlotte	Sr.	155
Rebel Ridling, Oklahoma State	Sr.	155
Jake Stewart, Houston	Sr.	155
Gabe Jacobo, Sacramento State	Sr.	154
Michael Rockett, Texas-San Antonio	Jr.	154
Ben Guez, William & Mary	Jr.	153
Ty Kelly, Georgia Southern	Jr.	153

WALKS	YEAR	BB
Yonder Alonso, Miami	Jr.	76
Tyler Holt, Florida State	Fr.	64
Allan Dykstra, Wake Forest	Jr.	62
Ricky Orton, UNC Greensboro	Sr.	61
Preston Paramore, Arizona State	Jr.	60
Reese Havens, South Carolina	Jr.	58
Scott Woodward, Coastal Carolina	Fr.	58
Buster Posey, Florida State	Jr.	57
Justin Smoak, South Carolina	Jr.	57
Danny Muno, Fresno State	Fr.	55
Gordon Beckham, Georgia	Jr.	54
Anthony Scelfo, Tulane	Jr.	54
Dustin Ackley, North Carolina	So.	53
T.J. Baxter, New Orleans	Sr.	53
Johnny Giavotella, New Orleans	Jr.	53
Chris Shehan, Ga. Southern	Jr.	53
LaDerek Camper, Jackson State	Jr.	52
Jared Gayhart, Rice	Jr.	51
Jason Kipnis, Arizona State	So.	51
Blake Murphy, Western Carolina	Sr.	51
Sean O'Brien, Virginia Tech	Sr.	51
Ben Petralli, Oral Roberts	Jr.	51
Darin Ruf, Creighton	Jr.	51
Chris Swauger, Citadel	Sr.	51
Collin Cowgill, Kentucky	Sr.	49
Aaron Luna, Rice	Jr.	49
Bobby Verbick, Sam Houston State	Sr.	49
Alan Ahmady, Fresno State	So.	48
Stephen Batts, East Carolina	Jr.	48
Jordan Danks, Texas	Jr.	48
Marc Krauss, Ohio	So.	48
Marcus Quade, New Mexico State	Sr.	48
Michael Stephan, Stony Brook	So.	48
Brett Wallace, Arizona State	Jr.	48
Brett Featherston, Northern Iowa	Sr.	47
Greg Folgia, Missouri	So.	47
Zach Kayne, Davidson	Jr.	47

Miami slugger Yonder Alonso led the nation with 76 walks and blasted 24 home runs

Jack Rye, Florida State	Sr.	47
Josh Satin, California	Sr.	47
Luke Stewart, Alabama-Birmingham	So.	47
Blake Stouffer, Texas A&M	Sr.	47
Eric Allen, Morehead State	Sr.	46
Dean Anna, Ball State	Jr.	46
Logan Forsythe, Arkansas	Jr.	46
Ryan Keedy, Alabama-Birmingham	Sr.	46
Rich Poythress, Georgia	So.	46
Greg Rodgers, Saint Louis	Sr.	46
Harrison Eldridge, East Carolina	Sr.	45
Eric Reese, Fordham	Sr.	45
Corey Shimada, Utah	Jr.	45
Blake Tekotte, Miami	Jr.	45
Brian Van Kirk, Oral Roberts	Sr.	45
Ryan Wood, East Carolina	Jr.	45
Sawyer Carroll, Kentucky	Sr.	44
Nick Crawford, Alabama-Birmingham	Fr.	44
Kevin Dubler, Illinois State	Jr.	44
Packy Elkins, Belmont	So.	44
Trent Lockwood, Texas-San Antonio	So.	44
Blake McDade, Middle Tennessee State	So.	44
Nick Mullins, Pittsburgh	So.	44
Shane Peterson, Long Beach State	Jr.	44
Evan Wells, Gonzaga	Jr.	44
Erik Wetzel, Fresno State	Jr.	44
Mitch Abeita, Nebraska	Sr.	43
Andy Dirks, Wichita State	Sr.	43
J.D. Dunn, Saint Louis	So.	43
Corey Kemp, East Carolina	Sr.	43
Matt Newman, Arizona State	Fr.	43
Brian Spear, Kentucky	Sr.	43
Jason Stidham, Florida State	So.	43
Osvaldo Torres, Bethune-Cookman	Sr.	43

TOUGHEST TO STRIKE OUT	YR	AB/SO
David Mcleod, Texas-Arlington	Sr.	40.0
Vince Chiera, Akron	Sr.	35.0
Daniel Webb, Illinois	Sr.	27.4
Conor Reardon, Brown	Sr.	26.2
Ben Allen, East Tennessee State	Jr.	23.5
Jesse Hart, Wisconsin-Milwaukee	Sr.	23.4
Matt Dempsey, UC Davis	Jr.	23.3
Jason Appel, UNC Wilmington	Sr.	22.9
Chris Lewis, Western Michigan	Jr.	22.8

Jake Jefferies, UC Davis	Jr.	22.5
Manny Kumar, Grambling	Jr.	22.4
A.J. Pollock, Notre Dame	So.	21.7
Corey Valine, San Jose State	So.	21.3
Joe Romano, St. Peter's	So.	21.1
Mike Gosse, Oklahoma	Sr.	21.1
Brian Cavazos-Galvez, New Mexico	Jr.	21.0
Mike Sheridan, William & Mary	Jr.	20.6
Andrew Macdonald, Niagara	Sr.	20.3
Chad Marshall, Stony Brook	Fr.	20.0
Drew Laidig, Western Illinois	Jr.	19.2
Ryan Dew, Ohio State	So.	19.1
Curt Restko, Eastern Illinois	So.	18.4
Cooper Stewart, Western Illinois	Jr.	18.0
Sean Paino, Le Moyne	So.	17.9
Jorge Castillo, Florida International	Sr.	17.6

HIT BY PITCH	YEAR	HBP
Brett Lilley, Notre Dame	Sr.	31
Michael Stephan, Stony Brook	So.	30
Scott Woodward, Coastal Carolina	Fr.	30
Tyler Howe, Kentucky	Sr.	27
Ryan McCurdy, Duke	So.	27
Bobby Stevens, Northern Illinois	Jr.	27
Robbie Knight, Creighton	So.	24
Andy Gerhartz, Milwaukee	Jr.	23
Bennett Davis, Elon	Jr.	22
John Morgan, Samford	Sr.	22
Bubbie Spake, Gardner-Webb	Jr.	22
Luke Anders, Texas A&M	Jr.	21
Ben Carruthers, Texas Christian	Jr.	21
Mark Onorati, Manhattan	Fr.	21
John Rickards, La Salle	Sr.	21
Matt Bentley, Alabama	Sr.	20
Greg Ford, Prairie View A&M	Jr.	20
Thomas Hamilton, Navy	Sr.	20
Chris Hervey, Indiana	Jr.	20
Kevin Hoef, Iowa	Jr.	20
Jonathan Koscso, South Florida	Fr.	20
Addison Maruszak, South Florida	Jr.	20
Jim Murphy, Washington State	Sr.	20

SACRIFICE BUNTS	YEAR	SH
Robby Price, Kansas	So.	24
Whit Merrifield, South Carolina	Fr.	23
Christian Colon, Cal State Fullerton	Fr.	21

Nick Crawford, Alabama-Birmingham	Fr.	21
Chris Wade, Kentucky	Fr.	20
David Mills, Notre Dame	So.	19
Scott Elmendorf, Southern Illinois	Jr.	18
Gavin Hedstrom, Fresno State	Jr.	18
Michael Lam, Creighton	Sr.	18
Kory Morian, Charleston Southern	Jr.	17
Joe Servais, Creighton	Sr.	17
Devin Taylor, IPFW	Jr.	17
Vicente Cafaro, Creighton	Jr.	16
Billy O'Connor, Xavier	Jr.	16
Ben Orloff, UC Irvine	Jr.	16
Justin DeMarco, Cal State Northridge	Fr.	15
Drew Haynes, Louisville	Fr.	15
Josh Page, Youngstown State	Sr.	15
Hunt Woodruff, Texas Christian	Jr.	15
Eric Deragisch, UC Irvine	Jr.	14
David Hernandez, Texas	So.	14
Matt Smedberg, Seton Hall	Jr.	14

SACRIFICE FLIES	YEAR	SF
Tim Carrier, UNC Greensboro	Sr.	12
Cody Brown, Liberty	Jr.	9
Wes Dorrell, Cal Poly	So.	9
Billy Froehlich, Winthrop	Sr.	9
Josh Harrison, Cincinnati	Jr.	9
Nate Lape, Marshall	Jr.	9
Rob Lyerly, Charlotte	So.	9
Josh Phegley, Indiana	So.	9
Dan Terpak, Villanova	Sr.	9
Brandon Wikoff, Illinois	So.	9
Bucky Aona, Southern Utah	So.	8
Mike Causey, Campbell	Sr.	8
Caleb Curry, Iowa	Sr.	8
Dexter Fontenot, Louisiana-Monroe	Sr.	8
David Genao, Oral Roberts	Sr.	8
Jason Kipnis, Arizona State	So.	8
Justin Miller, Ohio State	Jr.	8
Brent Milleville, Stanford	Jr.	8
Mark Pappas, Seton Hall	Sr.	8
Kyle Seager, North Carolina	So.	8
Mike Stalowy, Illinois State	Jr.	8

COLLEGE BASEBALL

PITCHING

Minimum 50 IP, 1 IP per team game

EARNED RUN AVERAGE	YEAR	G	IP	R	ER	ERA
Matt Packer, Virginia	So.	25	71	15	9	1.14
Christian Friedrich, Eastern Kentucky	Jr.	12	82	17	13	1.43
Stephen Strasburg, San Diego State	So.	13	97	25	17	1.57
Hiram Burgos, Bethune-Cookman	Jr.	16	80	27	14	1.58
Boone Whiting, Centenary	Fr.	20	61	15	11	1.62
Brian Matusz, San Diego	Jr.	15	105	29	20	1.71
Alan DeRatt, UNC Asheville	Sr.	16	98	29	19	1.74
Scott Bittle, Mississippi	Jr.	27	71	15	14	1.78
Thomas Davis, Fordham	Sr.	13	90	31	19	1.90
Christian Bergman, UC Irvine	So.	25	60	20	13	1.94
Chance Ruffin, Texas	Fr.	23	78	23	17	1.96
Joe Testa, Wagner	Sr.	15	91	38	21	2.08
Edwin Quirarte, Cal State Northridge	Jr.	29	56	20	13	2.09
Barry Bowden, Southern Mississippi	Sr.	12	72	20	17	2.12
Kyle Thebeau, Texas A&M	Jr.	33	76	28	18	2.12
Andrew Oliver, Oklahoma State	So.	15	98	28	24	2.20
Jonathan Stephens, Samford	Jr.	12	81	25	20	2.22
Andrew Liebel, Long Beach State	Sr.	15	117	39	29	2.23
Scott Gorgen, UC Irvine	Jr.	17	116	35	29	2.26
Joey Haug, Coastal Carolina	Sr.	29	83	29	21	2.28
Mike Nihsen, Creighton	So.	15	70	29	18	2.30
Trent Appleby, Texas Christian	Fr.	24	66	21	17	2.31
Todd Roth, Pennsylvania	So.	14	62	26	16	2.32
Aaron Crow, Missouri	Jr.	15	107	33	28	2.35
Justin Marks, Louisville	So.	18	91	36	24	2.37
Shane Davis, Canisius	Fr.	13	89	31	24	2.42
Johnny Dorn, Nebraska	Sr.	15	106	34	29	2.46
Brian Booth, Jacksonville State	Sr.	29	62	27	17	2.47
Chris Fetter, Michigan	Jr.	16	95	35	26	2.47
Eric Thomas, Bethune-Cookman	Jr.	15	76	26	21	2.48
Joe Serafin, Vermont	Jr.	12	79	29	22	2.51
Rob Musgrave, Wichita State	Sr.	16	111	42	31	2.51
David Kaye, Pittsburgh	Fr.	23	54	17	15	2.51
Tim Clubb, Missouri State	Jr.	14	104	34	29	2.52
Tyler Brandon, Eastern Illinois	Sr.	26	57	29	16	2.53
Jason Buursma, Bucknell	Sr.	20	84	32	24	2.58
Zach Putnam, Michigan	Jr.	12	77	29	22	2.58
Thain Simon, Santa Clara	Fr.	20	63	27	18	2.58
Josh Rickards, Marist	Jr.	12	80	23	23	2.60
Michael Powers, Michigan	Jr.	28	62	18	18	2.60
Eddie Gamboa, UC Davis	Sr.	15	100	45	29	2.61
Shooter Hunt, Tulane	Jr.	16	101	40	30	2.68
Dan April, Mercer	Jr.	25	70	28	21	2.70
Chris Hernandez, Miami	Fr.	18	113	37	34	2.72
Joseph Gautier, Bethune-Cookman	Jr.	14	73	29	22	2.72
Matt Petiton, Tulane	So.	15	69	26	21	2.73
Tyler Lockwood, Texas Christian	So.	17	105	34	32	2.75
Ryan Page, Liberty	Sr.	16	82	33	25	2.75
Clayton Shunick, North Carolina State	Jr.	16	101	35	31	2.76
Shane Sveda, Iona	Sr.	12	85	37	26	2.76
Cody Martin, Gonzaga	Fr.	26	55	21	17	2.80
Eric Beaulac, Le Moyne	Jr.	14	92	36	29	2.83
Alex White, North Carolina	So.	20	102	43	32	2.83
McKenzie Willoughby, Eastern Kentucky	Sr.	21	60	31	19	2.84
Sheldon McDonald, Northeastern	So.	21	57	20	18	2.86
Zach Fritz, Lafayette	Fr.	10	50	18	16	2.88
John Tesseyman, Central Connecticut State	Sr.	12	94	38	30	2.88
Marquis Frink, North Carolina A&T	Sr.	29	87	42	28	2.89
Ryan Perry, Arizona	Jr.	31	75	29	24	2.89
Kevin Reese, Lafayette	Sr.	11	68	25	22	2.90
Kevin Miller, California	Fr.	21	71	28	23	2.90
George Brown, St. John's	Sr.	14	90	32	29	2.91
Brandon Knowling, IPFW	Jr.	11	68	24	22	2.91
Mike Ford, UC Santa Barbara	So.	14	94	36	31	2.96
Lucas Farden, Dayton	Sr.	22	87	33	29	2.99
Daniel Calhoun, Murray State	Jr.	13	81	38	27	3.00
Billy Gross, West Virginia	Jr.	13	75	32	25	3.01
Chris Kelley, Rice	Sr.	17	74	34	25	3.03
Cole St. Clair, Rice	Sr.	24	62	27	21	3.03
Mitch Herold, Central Florida	Jr.	14	74	29	25	3.04
Lance Harting, Longwood	So.	19	50	34	17	3.04
Mike Stangroom, Buffalo	Jr.	14	68	36	23	3.06
Justin Bristow, East Carolina	Jr.	16	94	39	32	3.07
Daniel Bibona, UC Irvine	So.	20	102	39	35	3.08
Derrick Stultz, South Florida	Fr.	12	64	28	22	3.08
Mark Serrano, Oral Roberts	Jr.	21	67	29	23	3.09
Scott Turmail, Saint Louis	Jr.	16	107	46	37	3.12
John O'Hara, Fairleigh Dickinson	Sr.	14	78	34	27	3.13
Leon Schabacker, Norfolk State	Sr.	14	83	47	29	3.13
Nick Godwin, South Carolina	Sr.	15	92	36	32	3.14
Chris Henderson, Virginia Military Institute	Jr.	12	57	26	20	3.16
Stephen Locke, Florida	Jr.	21	82	36	29	3.17
Jay Jackson, Furman	Jr.	15	99	42	35	3.17
David Gruener, Portland	Sr.	14	74	43	26	3.18
Brad McAtee, UC Davis	Jr.	15	102	45	36	3.18
Bradley Holt, UNC Wilmington	Jr.	15	93	40	33	3.18
George Lujan, San Francisco	Jr.	15	79	35	28	3.19
Jon Durket, Wright State	Jr.	19	75	31	27	3.24
Bryce Stowell, UC Irvine	So.	16	88	46	32	3.26
Hunter Moody, Louisiana-Lafayette	Sr.	14	99	38	36	3.26
Aaron Shafer, Wichita State	Jr.	16	110	52	40	3.26
Jared Alexander, Hawaii	Jr.	12	83	34	30	3.26
Zachary Groh, Binghamton	Sr.	14	85	42	31	3.27
Bobby Gagg, Coastal Carolina	Jr.	14	85	39	31	3.28
Ricardo Pecina, San Diego	Jr.	16	63	31	23	3.29
Alex MacKenzie, Canisius	Jr.	13	95	41	35	3.31
Tyler Lyons, Oklahoma State	So.	15	109	46	40	3.31
Jason Barker, Norfolk State	Jr.	19	60	33	22	3.32
Jeremy Hauer, Creighton	Jr.	18	84	35	31	3.32
Chris Rusin, Kentucky	Jr.	13	84	35	31	3.33
Brent Varnado, Southeastern Louisiana	Sr.	18	84	41	31	3.33

WINS	YEAR	W	L
Aaron Crow, Missouri	Jr.	13	0
Carlos Luna, Oral Roberts	Sr.	13	1
Alex White, North Carolina	So.	13	3
Tommy Rafferty, Arizona State	Sr.	12	0
Shane Davis, Canisius	Fr.	12	1
Rob Musgrave, Wichita State	Sr.	12	1
Bryan Cryer, New Orleans	Sr.	12	2
Matt Fairel, Florida State	So.	12	2
Tyler Lyons, Oklahoma State	So.	12	2
Brian Matusz, San Diego	Jr.	12	2
Cory Arbiso, Cal State Fullerton	Jr.	12	3
Scott Gorgen, UC Irvine	Jr.	12	3
Tim Clubb, Missouri State	Jr.	11	0
Chris Hernandez, Miami	Fr.	11	0
Bradley Holt, UNC Wilmington	Jr.	11	1
Michael Jarman, Oral Roberts	Sr.	11	3
Jeff Kaplan, Cal State Fullerton	Sr.	11	3
Mike Leake, Arizona State	So.	11	3
Aaron Shafer, Wichita State	Jr.	11	4
Ryan Strauss, Florida State	Sr.	10	1
Chris Fetter, Michigan	Jr.	10	2
Steven Hensley, Elon	Jr.	10	2
Brian Sisk, Lamar	Jr.	10	2
Ben Tootle, Jacksonville State	So.	10	2
Nick McCully, Coastal Carolina	So.	10	3
Matt Ridings, Western Kentucky	So.	10	3
Cole St. Clair, Rice	So.	10	3
Jared Bradford, Louisiana State	Sr.	10	4
Charles Williams, Jackson State	So.	10	4
Zach Putnam, Michigan	Jr.	9	0
George Brown, St. John's	Sr.	9	1
Hiram Burgos, Bethune-Cookman	Jr.	9	1
Anthony Capra, Wichita State	Jr.	9	1
Eric Erickson, Miami	So.	9	1
Josh Romanski, San Diego	Jr.	9	1
Kyle Smith, Kent State	So.	9	1
Eric Thomas, Bethune-Cookman	Jr.	9	1
Eric Beaulac, Le Moyne	Jr.	9	2
Justin Bristow, East Carolina	Jr.	9	2
Thomas Davis, Fordham	Sr.	9	2
Guido Fonseca, Northern Iowa	Sr.	9	2
Jay Jackson, Furman	Jr.	9	2
Tim Johnson, North Carolina A&T	Sr.	9	2
Seth Maness, East Carolina	Fr.	9	2
Justin Marks, Louisville	So.	9	2
Sheldon McDonald, Northeastern	So.	9	2
Hunter Moody, Louisiana-Lafayette	Sr.	9	2
Dan Osterbrock, Cincinnati	Jr.	9	2
Thain Simon, Santa Clara	Fr.	9	2
Jerry Sullivan, Oral Roberts	So.	9	2
Adam Warren, North Carolina	Jr.	9	2
Daniel Bibona, UC Irvine	So.	9	3
Steve Blevins, Marshall	Jr.	9	3
Jason Buursma, Bucknell	Sr.	9	3
Jarrett Maloy, Southern	So.	9	3
Jesse Simpson, Col. of Charleston	Jr.	9	3
Pat Venditte, Creighton	Sr.	9	3
Marquise Zachary, Jackson State	Sr.	9	3
Charles Brewer, UCLA	So.	9	4
Andrew Cashner, Texas Christian	Jr.	9	4
Bradley Chovanec, Texas-San Antonio	Sr.	9	4
Andrew Doyle, Oklahoma	So.	9	4

Dallas Gallant, Sam Houston State	Fr.	9	4
Kyle Gibson, Missouri	So.	9	4
Shooter Hunt, Tulane	Jr.	9	4
Josh Satow, Arizona State	Sr.	9	4
Zach Tritz, Texas State	Jr.	9	4
Ryan Verdugo, Louisiana State	Jr.	9	4
Justin Kraft, Centenary	Fr.	9	5
Thad Weber, Nebraska	Sr.	9	5
Justin Wilson, Fresno State	Jr.	9	5

SAVES — YEAR SV

	YEAR	SV
Tyler Conn, Southern Mississippi	Sr.	18
Joshua Fields, Georgia	Sr.	18
Eric Pettis, UC Irvine	So.	17
Justin Fitzgerald, UC Davis	Jr.	15
Nick Gaudi, Pepperdine	Sr.	15
Michael Schwimer, Virginia	Sr.	14
A.J. Griffin, San Diego	So.	14
Colin Lynch, St. John's	Jr.	13
Zach Calhoun, Texas-San Antonio	So.	13
Ryan O'Shea, New Orleans	Jr.	13
Jason Stoffel, Arizona	So.	13
Brandon Burke, Fresno State	Sr.	13
Carlos Gutierrez, Miami	Jr.	13
Kevin Rhoderick, Oregon State	Fr.	12
Josh Storm, Troy	Jr.	12
Daniel Edwards, Kansas State	Sr.	12
Josh Lindblom, Purdue	Jr.	12
Justin Esposito, Monmouth	Sr.	11
James Hayes, Rider	Jr.	11
Andrew Huebner, Wagner	Jr.	11
Greg Lane, Binghamton	Jr.	11
Drew O'Neil, Penn State	Sr.	11
Adam Jorgenson, Cal State Fullerton	Sr.	11
Tyson Bagley, Dallas Baptist	Sr.	11
Daniel Tenholder, Austin Peay State	So.	11
Matt Vaughn, Clemson	Jr.	11
Bryan Woodall, Auburn	Jr.	11
Chase Dempsay, Houston	Fr.	11
Shawn Sanford, South Florida	So.	11
Chris Kaible, Fordham	Sr.	10
Jordan Conley, Xavier	Jr.	10
Jimmy Gillheeney, North Carolina State	So.	10
Greg Johnson, South Alabama	Jr.	10
T.J. Kelly, Oral Roberts	Jr.	10
Arshwin Asjes, Temple	Jr.	10
Josh Squatrito, Towson	Jr.	10
Thomas Girdwood, Elon	Fr.	10
Pat Kantakevich, William & Mary	Sr.	10
Paul Smyth, Kansas	Jr.	10
Andy Deain, Northern Illinois	Jr.	10
Jordy Mercer, Oklahoma State	Jr.	9

STRIKEOUTS — YEAR SO

	YEAR	SO
Brian Matusz, San Diego	Jr.	141
Stephen Strasburg, San Diego State	So.	133
Scott Bittle, Mississippi	Jr.	130
Aaron Crow, Missouri	Jr.	127
Shooter Hunt, Tulane	Jr.	126
Scott Gorgen, UC Irvine	Jr.	123
Tom Koehler, Stony Brook	Sr.	123
Wade Miley, Southeastern Louisiana	Jr.	119
Chris Hernandez, Miami	Fr.	117
Clayton Shunick, North Carolina State	Jr.	114
Eric Beaulac, Le Moyne	Jr.	113
Alex White, North Carolina	So.	113

Tim Murphy, UCLA	Jr. 111
Lance Lynn, Mississippi	Jr. 110
Aaron Shafer, Wichita State	Jr. 110
Evan Fredrickson, San Francisco	Jr. 109
Christian Friedrich, Eastern Kentucky	Jr. 108
Jerry Sullivan, Oral Roberts	So. 108
Justin Wilson, Fresno State	Jr. 108
Nick Haughian, Washington	Jr. 107
Dan Hudson, Old Dominion	Jr. 107
Marquis Frink, North Carolina A&T	Sr. 106
Tim Johnson, North Carolina A&T	Sr. 106
D.J. Mitchell, Clemson	Jr. 106
Bryan Cryer, New Orleans	Sr. 104
Mike Leake, Arizona State	So. 104
Bryan Morgado, Tennessee	Fr. 104
Erik Davis, Stanford	Sr. 103
Johnny Dorn, Nebraska	Sr. 102
Mike Minor, Vanderbilt	So. 101
Rob Musgrave, Wichita State	Sr. 101
Bryce Stowell, UC Irvine	So. 101
Pat Venditte, Creighton	Sr. 101
Matt Fairel, Florida State	So. 100
Kyle Blair, San Diego	Fr. 99
Steven Hensley, Elon	Jr. 99
Carlos Luna, Oral Roberts	Sr. 99
Tommy Milone, Southern California	Jr. 98
Matt Ridings, Western Kentucky	So. 98
Daniel Bibona, UC Irvine	So. 97
Andrew Liebel, Long Beach State	Sr. 97
Rex Brothers, Lipscomb	So. 96
Guido Fonseca, Northern Iowa	Sr. 96
Kyle Gibson, Missouri	So. 96
Andrew Oliver, Oklahoma State	So. 96
Nate Solow, San Diego State	So. 96
Nick Greenwood, Rhode Island	So. 95
Bradley Holt, UNC Wilmington	Jr. 95
Michael Jarman, Oral Roberts	Sr. 95
Anthony Shawler, Old Dominion	Jr. 95
Elih Villanueva, Florida State	Jr. 95
Jay Jackson, Furman	Jr. 94
Preston Guilmet, Arizona	Jr. 93
Pat McAnaney, Virginia	Sr. 93
Jeff Kaplan, Cal State Fullerton	Sr. 92
Tyler Lyons, Oklahoma State	So. 92
John O'Hara, Fairleigh Dickinson	Sr. 92
Scott Barnes, St. John's	Jr. 90
Jared Bradford, Louisiana State	Sr. 90
Anthony Capra, Wichita State	Jr. 90
Caleb Cotham, Vanderbilt	Fr. 90
Omar Guttierrez, Texas A&M-Corpus Christi	Sr. 90

STRIKEOUTS PER NINE INNINGS — YR. K/9

	YR.	K/9
Scott Bittle, Mississippi	Jr.	16.55
Evan Fredrickson, San Francisco	Jr.	13.03
Stephen Strasburg, San Diego State	So.	12.30
Christopher Manno, Duke	So.	12.27
Brian Matusz, San Diego	Jr.	12.09
Kyle Blair, San Diego	Fr.	11.93
Christian Friedrich, Eastern Kentucky	Jr.	11.90
Bryan Morgado, Tennessee	Fr.	11.66
Sheldon McDonald, Northeastern	So.	11.43
Anthony Shawler, Old Dominion	Jr.	11.29
Shooter Hunt, Tulane	Jr.	11.26
Rashad Ford, Texas Southern	Sr.	11.21
Ricardo Pecina, San Diego	Jr.	11.14

Lance Lynn, Mississippi	Jr. 11.04
Eric Beaulac, Le Moyne	Jr. 11.02
Tom Koehler, Stony Brook	Sr. 10.93
Marquis Frink, North Carolina A&T	Sr. 10.93
Kendal Volz, Baylor	So. 10.82
James Jones, Long Island	So. 10.70
John O'Hara, Fairleigh Dickinson	Sr. 10.66
Aaron Crow, Missouri	Jr. 10.65
Anthony Capra, Wichita State	Jr. 10.62
Chris Masters, Western Carolina	So. 10.59
Pat Venditte, Creighton	Sr. 10.53
Wade Miley, Southeastern Louisiana	Jr. 10.53

HITS PER NINE INNINGS — YEAR H/9

	YEAR	H/9
Christian Friedrich, E. Kentucky	Jr.	4.41
Scott Bittle, Mississippi	Jr.	4.46
Eric Beaulac, Le Moyne	Jr.	5.46
Shooter Hunt, Tulane	Jr.	5.54
Scott Gorgen, UC Irvine	Jr.	5.60
Stephen Strasburg, San Diego State	So.	5.64
Matt Petiton, Tulane	So.	5.84
Cam Nobles, Washington	So.	6.02
Barry Bowden, Southern Miss.	Sr.	6.10
Brian Stroud, Western Michigan	So.	6.17
Chance Ruffin, Texas	Fr.	6.23
Eric Thomas, Bethune-Cookman	Jr.	6.25
Matt Packer, Virginia	So.	6.44
Chris Carpenter, Kent State	Jr.	6.54
Joseph Gautier, Bethune-Cookman	Jr.	6.56
Kevin Miller, California	Fr.	6.56
Andrew Oliver, Oklahoma State	So.	6.59
Kyle Thebeau, Texas A&M	Jr.	6.61
Sean Black, Seton Hall	So.	6.62
Alan Deratt, UNC Asheville	Sr.	6.70
Chris Fetter, Michigan	Jr.	6.75
Pat Venditte, Creighton	Sr.	6.78
Marquis Frink, North Carolina A&T	Sr.	6.80
Scott Barnes, St. John's	Jr.	6.88
Alex White, North Carolina	So.	6.90

WALKS PER NINE INNINGS — YEAR BB/9

	YEAR	BB/9
Ryan Copeland, Illinois State	So.	0.91
Dan Osterbrock, Cincinnati	Jr.	0.91
Scott Turmail, Saint Louis	Jr.	0.93
Shawn Haviland, Harvard	Sr.	0.94
Nick Hernandez, Tennessee	So.	0.97
Justin Walker, Lamar	Jr.	0.97
John Walker II, Longwood	Jr.	1.04
Vance Worley, Long Beach State	Jr.	1.05
Bobby Gagg, Coastal Carolina	Jr.	1.06
Jason Buursma, Bucknell	Sr.	1.08
Chris Henderson, VMI	Jr.	1.11
Weston Szymanski, Hartford	Jr.	1.14
George Brown, St. John's	Sr.	1.20
Eddie Gamboa, UC Davis	Sr.	1.26
Jeff Sinkiewicz, Butler	Jr.	1.27
Aaron Swenson, Youngstown State	So.	1.27
Robert Young, Dartmouth	Jr.	1.28
Phillip Hann, Cal State Northridge	Sr.	1.29
Tyler Lockwood, Texas Christian	So.	1.29
Jeff Hatcher, UNC Wilmington	Jr.	1.29
Justin Garcia, New Orleans	Sr.	1.31
Clayton Ehlert, Texas A&M	So.	1.31
Cory Arbiso, Cal State Fullerton	Jr.	1.31
John Tesseyman, Central Conn. State	Sr.	1.34
Geoff Whitaker, Columbia	Fr.	1.38

BATTING

BATTING AVERAGE	AVG
Florida State	.355
Georgia Southern	.346
William & Mary	.343
Arizona State	.342
West Virginia	.341
Indiana	.339
Illinois	.335
Sam Houston State	.335
Le Moyne	.334
College of Charleston	.334
Charlotte	.333
Alcorn State	.333
Oral Roberts	.330
Middle Tennessee State	.329
Georgia State	.329
Louisiana-Monroe	.329
Southern	.326
Oklahoma State	.326
Santa Clara	.325
Jackson State	.325
North Carolina	.324
Coastal Carolina	.324
Dallas Baptist	.323
Wright State	.323
Utah	.323

SCORING	G	R	R/G
College of Charleston	59	627	10.6
Georgia Southern	58	595	10.3
Florida State	68	663	9.8
Arizona State	62	601	9.7
New Orleans	64	581	9.1
New Mexico State	61	553	9.1
Southern	46	405	8.8
Elon	62	545	8.8
Alcorn State	45	391	8.7
Louisiana-Monroe	58	503	8.7

HOME RUNS	HR
College of Charleston	130
Georgia Southern	114
South Carolina	110
Miami	106
Florida State	103
New Mexico State	100
Louisiana State	100
Florida Atlantic	99
New Orleans	97
Georgia	96
Coastal Carolina	96

TRIPLES	3B
Jackson State	37
Air Force	32
West Virginia	30
Texas A&M	30
Oklahoma State	29
Louisiana State	28
Arizona	26
Wichita State	26
Fordham	26
Bethune-Cookman	25
New Mexico	25
Vermont	25
Texas	25
Navy	25
Sam Houston State	25

DOUBLES	2B
North Carolina	175
Florida State	163
College of Charleston	161
Wisconsin-Milwaukee	156
William & Mary	155
Liberty	155
Georgia Southern	154
Kentucky	151
New Orleans	150
Coastal Carolina	149

SLUGGING PERCENTAGE	SLG
College of Charleston	.607
Georgia Southern	.584
Florida State	.565
William & Mary	.553
Arizona State	.545
Miami	.541
Louisiana-Monroe	.538
Ball State	.534
Oklahoma State	.531
Middle Tennessee State	.528
New Orleans	.528

STOLEN BASES	SB	CS
Fordham	157	35
Elon	155	41
Houston	142	37
Iowa	138	38
Virginia	134	35
Cincinnati	133	36
Jackson State	132	32
Cal State Fullerton	126	49
Gardner-Webb	122	28
Duquesne	118	43

WALKS	BB
Florida State	435
Arizona State	400
Miami	351
New Mexico State	340
Fresno State	340
Elon	330
College of Charleston	328
UNC Wilmington	316
Tulane	307
East Carolina	307

PITCHING

EARNED RUN AVERAGE	ERA
North Carolina	2.92
Long Beach State	3.20
UC Irvine	3.27
San Diego	3.42
Texas Christian	3.63
Duke	3.71
Kentucky	3.71
North Carolina State	3.72
St. John's	3.78
Rice	3.79
Virginia	3.83
Wagner	3.85
Seton Hall	3.86
Creighton	3.88
Wichita State	3.88
Oklahoma State	3.98
Monmouth	3.99
Miami	4.00
Texas A&M	4.01
Arizona	4.04
Mississippi	4.06
Norfolk State	4.07
Bethune-Cookman	4.09

STRIKEOUTS PER NINE INNINGS	IP	SO	K/9
North Carolina	613	681	10.0
Mississippi	579	624	9.7
San Diego	534	566	9.5

	IP	H	H/9
Central Florida	512	537	9.4
Arizona	546	572	9.4
Vanderbilt	569	587	9.3
Virginia	548	551	9.0
Rice	558	552	8.9
Wichita State	566	553	8.8
Miami	575	554	8.7

HITS PER NINE INNINGS	IP	H	H/9
North Carolina	613	515	7.56
North Carolina State	567	511	8.12
St. John's	511	463	8.15
Tulane	554	505	8.20
San Diego	534	488	8.22
Seton Hall	485	450	8.35
Michigan	502	469	8.40
Washington	486	455	8.43
Wichita State	566	539	8.57
Nebraska	521	498	8.60

WALKS PER NINE	IP	BB	BB/9
Long Beach State	528	113	1.93
Cincinnati	519	143	2.48
San Diego	534	149	2.51
Virginia Military Institute	499	141	2.54
UC Riverside	475	140	2.65
Maryland-Baltimore County	417	126	2.72
Wichita State	566	177	2.81
Lafayette	397	126	2.86
Louisiana State	626	201	2.89
Cal State Fullerton	570	183	2.89
UC Davis	526	169	2.89

FIELDING

FIELDING PERCENTAGE	PCT
Duke	.978
South Carolina	.977
Creighton	.976
Western Kentucky	.976
Troy	.976
Texas Christian	.976
Pepperdine	.976
Maryland	.975
Stanford	.975
Hawaii	.975
Miami	.974
Washington	.974
Oklahoma State	.974
Kentucky	.974
Oregon State	.973
West Virginia	.973
Louisiana State	.973
New Mexico	.973
North Carolina	.972
Lamar	.972
Notre Dame	.972
Cal State Fullerton	.972
San Jose State	.972
Louisville	.972
Washington State	.972

DOUBLE PLAYS PER GAME	G	DP	DP/G
Louisiana-Monroe	58	75	1.29
Florida	58	72	1.24
Nevada	60	73	1.22
Cleveland State	53	64	1.21
Akron	49	59	1.20
Pepperdine	59	70	1.19
New Mexico	59	70	1.19
Notre Dame	55	65	1.18
Indiana	61	72	1.18
Sam Houston State	62	72	1.16
Morehead State	51	59	1.16
Sacramento State	58	67	1.16

Batters: 10 or more at-bats. **Pitchers:** 5 or more innings.

1. FRESNO STATE

Coach: Mike Batesole. **Record:** 47-31.

Player, Pos., Year	AVG	AB	R	H	2B	3B	HR	RBI	SB
Alan Ahmady, 1b, So.	.386	285	59	110	17	1	13	92	3
Erik Wetzel, 2b, Jr.	.365	307	99	112	20	1	6	41	12
Steve Susdorf, of, Sr.	.343	300	77	103	32	3	13	88	14
Danny Muno, ss, Fr.	.332	283	62	94	13	2	3	30	10
Gavin Hedstrom, of, Jr.	.305	246	51	75	10	0	7	35	5
Ryan Overland, c, Sr.	.291	158	23	46	3	0	4	24	0
Tommy Mendonca, 3b, So.	.285	291	48	83	8	1	19	70	6
Justin Wilson, dh, Jr.	.278	18	1	5	0	0	0	1	0
Steve Detwiler, of, So.	.256	238	46	61	11	0	10	53	5
Jake Johnson, c, Fr.	.232	56	4	13	3	0	1	5	0
Todd Sandell, if, Sr.	.221	77	16	17	3	0	2	7	0
Jordan Ribera, if, Fr.	.217	92	14	20	1	0	5	16	0
Trent Soares, of, Fr.	.190	105	23	20	1	0	1	12	6
Nick Hom, if, Fr.	.185	27	4	5	3	0	0	4	0
Danny Grubb, c, Jr.	.181	138	13	25	5	0	0	12	1
Blake Amador, of, Sr.	.167	12	5	2	1	0	0	0	0

Player, Pos., Year	W	L	ERA	G	SV	IP	H	BB	SO
Tanner Scheppers, rhp, Jr.	8	2	2.93	12	1	71	54	34	109
Brandon Burke, rhp, Jr.	4	6	3.33	37	13	73	65	24	43
Holden Sprague, rhp, Jr.	6	2	3.59	33	1	88	100	20	55
Clayton Allison, rhp, Sr.	4	5	3.91	19	1	97	107	22	57
Justin Wilson, lhp, Jr.	8	5	4.34	22	0	116	121	65	99
Justin Miller, rhp, Jr.	6	4	5.46	28	0	87	98	50	81
Jake Hower, rhp, Sr.	2	1	6.12	15	1	25	25	15	14
Kris Tomlinson, lhp, Jr.	2	1	6.30	26	0	20	20	9	25
Sean Bonesteele, rhp, So.	2	2	6.31	15	0	26	31	13	10
Jason Breckley, rhp, Sr.	3	2	7.66	21	2	25	31	13	28
Jake Floethe, rhp, Fr.	1	1	8.64	18	0	25	38	16	20
Gene Escat, rhp, Fr.	0	0	10.20	11	0	15	19	14	14

2. GEORGIA

Coach: David Perno. **Record:** 45-25.

Player, Pos., Year	AVG	AB	R	H	2B	3B	HR	RBI	SB
Gordon Beckham, ss, Jr.	.411	275	97	113	22	1	28	77	17
Rich Poythress, 1b, So.	.374	265	64	99	22	0	15	75	4
Ryan Peisel, 3b, Sr.	.341	311	78	106	22	2	12	56	14
Bryce Massanari, c, Jr.	.325	252	39	82	12	1	11	65	2
Jake Crane, c, Sr.	.310	29	2	9	1	0	0	3	2
Matt Olson, of, Sr.	.309	301	63	93	14	3	8	44	5
Matt Cerione, of, So.	.303	231	40	70	15	0	7	33	12
Lyle Allen, of, Fr.	.274	230	32	63	7	0	2	30	2
Joey Lewis, c/1b, So.	.264	197	23	52	7	1	6	38	0
Michael Demperio, 2b, So.	.238	172	27	41	1	2	2	16	6
David Thoms, 2b, So.	.224	67	9	15	0	0	0	4	0
Robbie O'Bryan, 1b, So.	.215	65	10	14	0	1	2	11	0
Miles Starr, 2b, Jr.	.211	38	10	8	3	0	0	5	1
Joshua Fields, dh, Jr.	.194	31	5	6	0	0	2	4	1
Adam Fuller, of, Jr.	.193	83	11	16	2	0	1	7	6

Player, Pos., Year	W	L	ERA	G	SV	IP	H	BB	SO
Joshua Fields, rhp, Sr.	3	2	3.38	36	18	37	17	22	63
Steve Esmonde, rhp, So.	2	0	3.80	14	0	24	23	3	12
Alex McRee, lhp, So.	7	1	3.98	31	0	61	57	31	65
Jason Leaver, lhp, Jr.	2	0	4.00	7	0	9	5	10	11
Dean Weaver, rhp, So.	6	1	4.24	31	1	51	52	19	47
Trevor Holder, rhp, Jr.	8	4	4.41	17	0	98	108	31	68
Stephen Dodson, rhp, Sr.	5	5	4.52	18	0	96	99	15	50
Nick Montgomery, rhp, Jr.	4	2	4.86	26	0	63	60	19	59
Will Harvil, rhp, Jr.	2	1	4.88	15	0	31	34	7	21
Nathan Moreau, lhp, Jr.	4	4	5.11	18	0	76	76	36	60
Justin Earls, lhp, So.	2	1	6.21	27	0	38	53	20	30
Stephen Ochs, lhp, So.	0	2	9.35	6	0	9	13	3	8
Justin Grimm, rhp, Fr.	0	1	10.91	19	0	31	40	24	27
Stephen Brock, rhp, So.	0	1	11.57	8	0	7	11	7	5

SPORTS ON FILM

Dustin Ackley led UNC back to Omaha

3. NORTH CAROLINA

Coach: Mike Fox. **Record:** 54-14.

Player, Pos., Year	AVG	AB	R	H	2B	3B	HR	RBI	SB
Dustin Ackley, 1b, So.	.417	278	82	116	21	4	7	51	19
Tim Fedroff, of, So.	.404	285	78	115	22	5	12	71	14
Greg Holt, 1b, Fr.	.357	28	2	10	0	0	0	4	0
Kyle Seager, 2b, So.	.347	268	62	93	30	5	9	75	5
Kyle Shelton, of, Sr.	.326	218	49	71	14	5	4	40	4
Brett Thomas, 1b, Fr.	.318	22	2	7	1	0	0	2	0
Seth Williams, of, Sr.	.315	235	43	74	22	1	8	45	3
Tim Federowicz, c, Jr.	.303	264	46	80	21	1	5	48	2
Chad Flack, 3b, Sr.	.277	274	50	76	18	1	7	49	13
Mark Fleury, c, So.	.275	149	20	41	8	0	3	25	1
Garrett Gore, ss, Jr.	.275	233	39	64	8	2	2	38	5
Ryan Graepel, ss, Jr.	.253	99	23	25	6	0	0	7	1
Ben Bunting, of, Fr.	.227	75	13	17	2	0	1	11	2
Zeke Blanton, of, Fr.	.200	20	1	4	1	0	0	2	0

Player, Pos., Year	W	L	ERA	G	SV	IP	H	BB	SO
Bryant Gaines, rhp, Fr.	0	0	0.00	7	0	7	4	2	9
Ryan Leach, rhp, Fr.	1	0	1.74	13	0	10	3	12	12
Rob Wooten, rhp, Sr.	6	2	1.87	44	5	63	43	33	73
Nate Striz, rhp, Fr.	1	0	2.00	25	2	27	22	16	30
Tyler Trice, rhp, Sr.	0	0	2.04	20	1	18	12	9	21
Brian Moran, lhp, So.	1	2	2.76	40	2	49	45	17	72
Colin Bates, rhp, Fr.	6	1	2.78	27	0	55	44	20	57
Matt Harvey, rhp, Fr.	7	2	2.79	19	0	68	52	47	80
Alex White, rhp, So.	13	3	2.83	20	0	102	78	42	113
Logan Munson, lhp, Fr.	0	0	3.00	15	0	15	13	4	12
Rob Catapano, lhp, Jr.	4	0	3.03	19	0	39	39	14	40
Patrick Johnson, rhp, Fr.	4	1	4.14	14	0	41	41	22	42
Adam Warren, rhp, Jr.	9	2	4.23	18	0	83	86	46	73
Mike Facchinei, rhp, Sr.	2	0	4.32	7	0	25	20	10	27
Tim Federowicz, rhp, Jr.	0	1	4.70	9	1	8	10	4	13

4. MIAMI

Coach: Jim Morris. **Record:** 53-11.

Player, Pos., Year	AVG	AB	R	H	2B	3B	HR	RBI	SB
Yonder Alonso, 1b, Jr.	.370	284	78	105	12	1	24	72	9
Jemile Weeks, 2b, Jr.	.363	237	81	86	17	5	13	62	22
Ryan Jackson, ss, So.	.360	242	49	87	19	1	4	50	10
Blake Tekotte, of, Jr.	.353	249	81	88	12	4	13	50	27
Adan Severino, of, Jr.	.325	160	28	52	7	2	4	22	2
Mark Sobolewski, 3b, So.	.311	257	44	80	16	1	8	62	6

COLLEGE BASEBALL

Player, Pos., Year	AVG	AB	R	H	2B	3B	HR	RBI	SB
Dave DiNatale, of, Jr.	.295	200	53	59	12	5	9	43	12
Joey Terdoslavich, of/if, Fr.	.293	123	22	36	7	0	5	25	2
Dennis Raben, of, Jr.	.292	192	51	56	14	0	10	51	5
Jason Hagerty, c, So.	.289	142	29	41	8	0	8	38	4
Ryan Perry, if, Jr.	.250	32	3	8	1	0	1	8	1
Iden Nazario, dh, Fr.	.250	12	2	3	1	0	0	1	0
Yasmani Grandal, c, Fr.	.234	124	25	29	6	0	7	28	0
Jonathan Weislow, of, So.	.208	24	5	5	3	0	0	5	2

Player, Pos., Year	W	L	ERA	G	SV	IP	H	BB	SO
Iden Nazario, lhp, Fr.	0	0	1.59	11	0	11	8	7	15
Kyle Bellamy, rhp, So.	6	0	1.86	43	3	63	40	13	75
Jason Santana, rhp, Jr.	3	0	2.29	5	1	20	14	6	13
Chris Hernandez, lhp, Fr.	11	0	2.72	18	0	113	92	18	117
Anthony Nalepa, rhp, So.	2	1	3.32	15	0	19	25	10	15
Rene Guerra, rhp, Jr.	1	0	3.60	9	0	10	7	5	10
Carlos Gutierrez, rhp, Jr.	5	4	3.81	39	13	50	43	20	72
Eric Erickson, lhp, So.	9	1	4.15	14	0	78	84	18	68
David Gutierrez, rhp, So.	5	0	4.75	17	1	53	53	18	40
Enrique Garcia, rhp, Sr.	7	3	4.85	17	0	85	97	36	66
Alex Koronis, rhp, So.	1	1	6.88	9	0	17	19	7	24
John Housey, rhp, So.	3	1	7.06	8	0	29	41	10	13
Michael Rudman, rhp, So.	0	0	7.53	8	0	14	16	7	16
P.J. Fisher, lhp, Jr.	0	0	9.00	17	0	13	23	12	10

5. STANFORD

Coach: Mark Marquess. **Record:** 41-24.

Player, Pos., Year	AVG	AB	R	H	2B	3B	HR	RBI	SB
Jason Castro, c, Jr.	.376	279	68	105	18	3	14	73	5
Cord Phelps, 2b, Jr.	.351	259	76	91	16	3	13	58	6
Austin Yount, 3b, Jr.	.333	69	11	23	8	1	0	15	0
Randy Molina, 1b, Sr.	.329	213	43	70	16	0	5	42	0
Colin Walsh, if, Fr.	.323	65	18	21	4	0	0	8	1
Joey August, of, Jr.	.323	186	35	60	12	1	1	23	1
Ben Clowe, c/of, Fr.	.300	50	9	15	4	0	3	9	0
Sean Ratliff, of, Jr.	.294	248	52	73	13	4	22	71	8
Brent Milleville, 1b, Jr.	.289	187	33	54	9	0	11	57	3
Jeff Whitlow, of, Jr.	.279	111	25	31	5	4	1	14	3
Brendan Domaracki, of, Sr.	.257	152	28	39	8	3	1	19	2
Zach Jones, 3b, So.	.249	209	36	52	13	2	3	33	11
Toby Gerhart, of, So.	.240	121	28	29	8	1	7	21	2
Jake Schlander, ss, Fr.	.232	211	32	49	5	0	0	26	3
Adam Gaylord, if, So.	.067	15	1	1	0	0	0	1	0

Player, Pos., Year	W	L	ERA	G	SV	IP	H	BB	SO
Jeremy Bleich, lhp, Jr.	3	3	2.09	11	1	47	40	27	42
Danny Sandbrink, rhp, Fr.	2	1	2.81	20	1	58	56	21	30
Austin Yount, rhp, Jr.	6	4	3.48	17	1	67	66	20	40
Drew Storen, rhp, Fr.	5	3	3.51	31	8	56	53	15	50
Blake Hancock, lhp, Jr.	1	3	4.12	20	1	24	24	9	17
Jeffrey Inman, rhp, So.	7	2	4.27	16	0	72	86	29	45
Brandt Walker, rhp, So.	0	0	4.50	6	0	6	5	7	4
Erik Davis, rhp, Sr.	8	3	4.70	18	0	103	102	40	103
David Stringer, rhp, Sr.	3	1	5.23	19	2	43	55	23	28
Max Fearnow, rhp, Jr.	2	1	6.09	17	1	44	50	24	30
Michael Marshall, rhp, Fr.	1	1	6.10	16	1	21	22	8	9
Alex Pracher, rhp, Fr.	1	1	7.42	22	1	30	41	11	24
Michael De Groot, lhp, Fr.	0	0	7.50	6	0	6	7	2	3
Cory Bannister, rhp, So.	0	0	8.22	7	0	8	14	6	3
Tom Stilson, lhp, Jr.	0	0	10.80	10	0	7	13	4	6

6. LOUISIANA STATE

Coach: Paul Mainieri. **Record:** 49-19.

Player, Pos., Year	AVG	AB	R	H	2B	3B	HR	RBI	SB
Buzzy Haydel, if, Jr.	.375	16	5	6	2	0	1	3	0
Blake Dean, of, So.	.353	269	62	95	18	3	20	73	4
Matt Clark, 1b, Jr.	.344	227	57	78	17	0	28	64	1
D.J. LeMahieu, ss, Fr.	.337	258	56	87	11	1	6	44	10
Micah Gibbs, c, Fr.	.322	174	31	56	16	0	2	35	2
Ryan Schimpf, 2b, So.	.320	250	57	80	18	7	12	54	16
Chris McGhee, if/of, Jr.	.310	29	14	9	3	0	0	3	5
Jared Mitchell, of, So.	.297	175	44	52	10	1	6	29	16
Michael Hollander, 3b, Sr.	.297	246	56	73	14	4	6	45	9
Derek Helenihi, if, Jr.	.295	241	42	71	10	4	3	43	12
Sean Ochinko, c, So.	.272	136	19	37	6	0	4	21	0
Leon Landry, of, Fr.	.271	214	38	58	10	5	5	26	12
Matt Gaudet, if, Fr.	.270	63	11	17	5	0	2	15	0
Taylor Davis, if, Jr.	.250	28	6	7	0	1	2	10	0
Johnny Dishon, of/c, Fr.	.240	50	20	12	3	2	2	12	4
Nicholas Pontiff, of, Jr.	.239	71	15	17	4	0	1	8	1
Rene Escobar, if/of, Jr.	.174	23	3	4	0	0	0	3	2
Chad Jones, of, Fr.	.154	13	2	2	1	0	0	0	1

Player, Pos., Year	W	L	ERA	G	SV	IP	H	BB	SO
Anthony Ranaudo, rhp, Fr.	1	0	0.00	8	0	12	5	6	13
Louis Coleman, rhp, Jr.	8	1	1.95	23	2	55	45	10	62
Nolan Cain, rhp, Jr.	0	0	2.37	19	0	19	10	11	11
Austin Ross, rhp, Jr.	3	1	2.58	21	3	52	51	9	37
Paul Bertuccini, rhp, So.	2	0	2.63	28	2	27	18	12	30
Ryan Verdugo, lhp, Jr.	9	4	4.12	20	0	96	95	37	85
Daniel Bradshaw, rhp, Fr.	4	5	4.12	26	4	55	51	13	52
Jordan Nicholson, rhp, Fr.	0	0	4.26	12	0	13	13	2	8
Jared Bradford, rhp, Sr.	10	4	4.48	27	5	98	115	24	90
Blake Martin, lhp, Jr.	5	3	5.08	20	0	89	86	37	81
Jordan Brown, rhp, Jr.	5	0	5.40	20	0	67	88	28	59
Shane Ardoin, lhp, So.	0	0	6.75	12	0	7	7	3	3
Ben Alsup, rhp, Fr.	0	0	6.75	5	0	5	7	1	6
Ryan Byrd, lhp, Jr.	2	1	6.82	13	0	30	46	8	17

7. FLORIDA STATE

Coach: Mike Martin. **Record:** 54-14.

Player, Pos., Year	AVG	AB	R	H	2B	3B	HR	RBI	SB
Buster Posey, c, Jr.	.463	257	89	119	21	4	26	93	5
Nick Vickerson, if, Fr.	.400	15	4	6	0	0	0	3	0
Stephen Cardullo, if, So.	.387	62	17	24	5	0	3	17	2
Stuart Tapley, 3b, Fr.	.383	196	54	75	15	1	8	40	1
Tony Delmonico, ss, Jr.	.374	254	69	95	19	2	8	69	14
Jack Rye, of, So.	.371	232	48	86	15	0	7	52	12
Tommy Oravetz, if, Jr.	.361	169	37	61	14	3	4	32	1
Mike McGee, of, Fr.	.344	160	35	55	8	3	6	36	3
Luke Smierciak, of, Fr.	.340	47	18	16	3	1	0	11	6
Dennis Guinn, 1b, Fr.	.332	259	67	86	19	2	19	76	2
Tyler Holt, of, Fr.	.324	250	83	81	10	2	3	41	15
Jason Stidham, 2b, So.	.322	255	63	82	13	2	11	63	6
Ruairi O'Connor, of, Fr.	.300	50	19	15	3	0	2	8	0
Ohmed Danesh, of, So.	.284	134	31	38	11	2	3	29	1
Jack Posey, c, Fr.	.281	64	16	18	4	0	2	17	0
Parker Brunelle, c, Fr.	.226	31	10	7	1	0	1	13	0

Player, Pos., Year	W	L	ERA	G	SV	IP	H	BB	SO
Buster Posey, rhp, Jr.	0	0	1.17	9	6	8	5	3	10
John Gast, lhp, Fr.	0	1	2.70	14	0	13	15	11	14
Bo O'Dell, rhp, Jr.	5	1	3.60	21	0	55	61	20	37
Jimmy Marshall, rhp, Jr.	6	2	3.69	38	2	46	41	31	54
Matt Fairel, lhp, So.	12	2	3.79	18	0	112	107	40	100
Elih Villanueva, rhp, Jr.	7	4	4.01	17	0	101	89	42	95
Mike McGee, rhp, Fr.	7	1	4.04	12	0	56	50	24	33
Ryan Strauss, rhp, Sr.	10	1	4.31	24	4	86	74	33	68
Geoff Parker, rhp, Fr.	6	2	4.50	14	0	60	66	20	56
Tyler Everett, rhp, Fr.	0	0	5.64	17	3	30	30	16	16
Ben Francis, rhp, So.	1	0	8.53	18	0	19	28	14	12
Ryan Vigue, lhp, Fr.	0	0	9.72	10	0	8	7	8	8

8. RICE

Coach: Wayne Graham. **Record:** 47-15.

Player, Pos., Year	AVG	AB	R	H	2B	3B	HR	RBI	SB
Diego Seastrunk, 3b, So.	.353	258	58	91	19	1	6	61	1
J.P. Padron, 1b, Sr.	.349	238	48	83	13	0	5	41	7
Rick Hague, ss, Fr.	.348	233	40	81	19	2	8	54	4
Aaron Luna, of, Jr.	.314	220	61	69	13	0	10	53	12
Jared Gayhart, of, So.	.310	239	55	74	15	4	6	47	10
Adam Zornes, c, Jr.	.301	219	42	66	10	1	12	55	2
Chad Mozingo, of, Fr.	.301	219	44	66	7	3	2	30	4
Jimmy Comerota, 2b, So.	.291	196	45	57	6	1	0	28	12
Jess Buenger, 2b, Jr.	.258	62	8	16	2	0	1	8	1
Doug Simmons, of/1b, Fr.	.237	38	6	9	3	0	1	7	1
John Hale, c, Fr.	.235	17	3	4	0	0	0	1	0
Derek Myers, if, Sr.	.234	77	22	18	3	1	3	16	2
Jordan Dodson, of, Sr.	.206	107	20	22	9	1	0	19	2
Abe Gonzales, 1b, Fr.	.176	17	2	3	1	0	0	2	0

Player, Pos., Year	W	L	ERA	G	SV	IP	H	BB	SO
Bobby Bell, rhp, Jr.	1	0	1.31	14	3	21	10	8	28
Jared Gayhart, rhp, Jr.	2	0	1.59	4	0	6	1	3	6
Jonathan Runnels, lhp, Sr.	0	0	2.63	7	0	14	19	4	12
Matt Evers, lhp, Fr.	4	1	3.00	29	0	42	35	23	54
Chris Kelley, rhp, Sr.	5	1	3.03	17	0	74	91	22	61
Cole St.Clair, lhp, Sr.	10	3	3.03	24	5	62	54	16	67
Mark Haynes, rhp, So.	0	0	3.46	9	1	13	11	5	5
Ryan Berry, rhp, So.	8	5	3.63	17	0	104	103	31	86
Bryan Price, rhp, Jr.	4	4	3.72	30	2	48	38	27	54
Matt Langwell, rhp, Jr.	5	1	4.52	17	0	74	78	29	64
Mike Ojala, rhp, So.	5	0	4.97	14	0	54	61	20	64
Lucas Luetge, lhp, Jr.	1	0	6.16	17	1	31	35	11	38
Jordan Rogers, rhp, Jr.	1	0	8.44	4	0	5	7	5	5
Will McDaniel, rhp, Sr.	1	0	9.95	5	0	6	10	6	4

9. ARIZONA STATE

Coach: Pat Murphy. **Record:** 49-13.

Player, Pos., Year	AVG	AB	R	H	2B	3B	HR	RBI	SB
Brett Wallace, 3b, Jr.	.410	239	87	98	12	2	22	83	16
Ryan Sontag, of, Sr.	.393	168	48	66	3	3	6	42	6
Ike Davis, 1b, Jr.	.385	213	64	82	26	1	16	76	6
Jason Kipnis, of, So.	.371	237	76	88	16	6	14	73	24
Marcel Champagnie, ss, Jr.	.371	151	32	56	9	3	3	37	8
Petey Paramore, c, Jr.	.355	214	64	76	10	0	7	52	4
Raoul Torrez, if, So.	.341	182	49	62	13	3	2	35	12
Mike Leake, dh, So.	.340	47	16	16	3	1	2	11	2
Kiel Roling, c, So.	.340	197	48	67	16	1	8	51	5
Matt Newman, of, Fr.	.322	115	33	37	3	2	3	28	2
Greg Bordes, c, Jr.	.304	92	22	28	6	1	0	21	1
Andy Workman, of, Fr.	.250	28	5	7	1	0	0	2	0
Mike Murphy, of, Jr.	.235	34	6	8	1	1	0	3	0
Rocky Laguna, of/1b, Sr.	.228	79	17	18	1	0	2	10	0
Mike Jones, of, Jr.	.172	58	17	10	1	0	2	8	3
Jake Elmore, 2b, Jr.	.111	45	11	5	0	0	0	3	3
Jason Jarvis, of, So.	.111	18	1	2	1	0	0	4	0

Player, Pos., Year	W	L	ERA	G	SV	IP	H	BB	SO
Ike Davis, lhp, Jr.	4	1	2.25	16	4	24	17	4	30
Mike Leake, rhp, So.	11	3	3.49	19	1	121	118	20	104
Tommy Rafferty, rhp, Sr.	12	0	3.65	35	4	74	63	18	71
Dustin Brader, rhp, Jr.	1	0	4.26	20	2	25	20	11	17
Stephen Sauer, rhp, Jr.	4	1	4.56	25	1	51	45	29	56
Josh Satow, lhp, Sr.	9	4	4.98	18	0	94	90	47	74
Reyes Dorado, rhp, Jr.	3	1	5.60	24	1	35	36	25	52
Matt Newman, lhp, Fr.	1	0	5.60	6	0	18	21	5	8
Jason Franzblau, rhp, Jr.	0	1	5.62	15	1	32	35	16	29
Kyle Brule, rhp, Fr.	0	0	6.39	11	1	13	17	3	13
Seth Blair, rhp, Fr.	4	4	6.96	19	1	54	79	22	34

10. CAL STATE FULLERTON

Coach: Dave Serrano. **Record:** 41-22.

Player, Pos., Year	AVG	AB	R	H	2B	3B	HR	RBI	SB
Eric Komatsu, of, Jr.	.355	231	47	82	16	6	9	54	21
Josh Fellhauer, of, So.	.335	269	62	90	20	4	7	40	17
Christian Colon, ss, Fr.	.329	243	59	80	12	2	4	39	13
Joel Weeks, 3b, Sr.	.322	227	37	73	13	1	2	38	4
Brian Wilson, c, Jr.	.313	80	17	25	4	1	3	18	2
Jon Wilhite, if, Sr.	.310	42	8	13	3	1	0	16	1
Billy Marcoe, c, So.	.306	49	9	15	0	0	0	1	5
Corey Jones, if, So.	.302	149	25	45	4	3	1	33	4
Jared Clark, 1b, Sr.	.294	214	39	63	24	0	9	53	6
Gary Brown, of/if, Fr.	.292	195	46	57	7	2	5	27	25
Joe Scott, 2b, Sr.	.289	83	12	24	5	1	0	11	1
Jeff Newman, of, Jr.	.277	65	15	18	0	1	0	12	7
Khris Davis, of, So.	.269	93	27	25	4	1	4	19	11
Dustin Garneau, c, Jr.	.246	138	28	34	9	0	4	24	6
Matthew Fahey, of, Jr.	.235	17	1	4	1	0	0	4	0
Chris Jones, of, Jr.	.176	34	2	6	1	0	0	2	2
Shevis Shima, if, Jr.	.043	23	7	1	1	0	0	1	1

Player, Pos., Year	W	L	ERA	G	SV	IP	H	BB	SO
Ryan Ackland, rhp, So.	1	1	2.10	23	2	26	28	5	14
Daniel Renken, rhp, Fr.	5	5	4.11	16	0	81	97	22	80
Michael Morrison, rhp, So.	2	2	4.14	27	0	54	54	24	55

Player, Pos., Year	W	L	ERA	G	SV	IP	H	BB	SO
Brian Wilson, c, Jr.	3	2	4.17	21	1	37	32	16	35
Jeff Kaplan, rhp, Sr.	11	3	4.43	18	1	112	120	36	92
Cory Arbiso, rhp, Jr.	12	3	4.46	16	0	103	119	15	72
Adam Jorgenson, rhp, Sr.	2	1	5.01	27	11	50	47	14	60
Jason Dovel, lhp, Fr.	3	4	5.32	31	0	47	41	18	45
Kevin Rath, lhp, Fr.	1	0	6.48	7	0	17	20	14	13
Travis Kelly, rhp, Sr.	1	1	6.53	19	1	41	52	19	24

11. UC IRVINE

Coach: Mike Gillespie. **Record:** 42-18.

Player, Pos., Year	AVG	AB	R	H	2B	3B	HR	RBI	SB
Jeff Cusick, 1b, Sr.	.363	157	28	57	16	2	0	29	4
Ben Orloff, ss, Jr.	.344	227	50	78	17	0	0	23	19
Sean Madigan, of, So.	.328	122	19	40	5	4	2	24	6
Dillon Bell, of, Jr.	.326	144	28	47	7	1	5	30	2
Ollie Linton, of, Jr.	.324	244	59	79	8	1	4	36	40
Francis Larson, c, So.	.314	204	31	64	13	1	7	40	5
Tony Asaro, of, Jr.	.314	102	24	32	9	1	4	21	0
Casey Stevenson, 2b, So.	.300	130	26	39	3	0	3	14	1
Sammy Donabedian, c, Jr.	.300	10	2	3	1	0	0	0	1
Eric Deragisch, 3b/of, Jr.	.299	147	20	44	4	2	1	16	6
Ryan Fisher, if/of, Fr.	.299	137	23	41	6	3	3	37	7
Josh Tavelli, if/of, Sr.	.293	99	16	29	7	1	3	19	2
Brock Bardeen, of, Jr.	.280	100	15	28	6	1	6	26	2
Tyler Hoechlin, if/of, Fr.	.250	44	12	11	1	1	1	8	2
Aaron Lowenstein, c, Sr.	.199	146	19	29	7	1	1	22	2

Player, Pos., Year	W	L	ERA	G	SV	IP	H	BB	SO
Christian Bergman, rhp, So.	5	2	1.94	25	0	60	59	16	37
Scott Gorgen, rhp, Jr.	12	3	2.26	17	0	116	72	40	123
Chris Lopez, rhp, Sr.	0	0	2.35	8	0	8	7	2	7
Eric Pettis, rhp, So.	4	3	2.62	31	17	45	37	20	50
Daniel Bibona, rhp, So.	9	3	3.08	20	0	102	97	21	97
Bryce Stowell, rhp, So.	8	3	3.26	16	0	88	82	36	101
Matt Dufour, rhp, Jr.	1	2	3.73	22	0	31	31	15	23
Crosby Slaught, rhp, Fr.	1	1	4.37	17	0	23	32	13	15
Tom Calahan, lhp, Sr.	0	1	5.62	30	0	24	35	9	23
Noel Avison, lhp, Jr.	1	0	6.23	11	0	13	17	5	8
Kyle Necke, rhp, So.	1	0	7.58	22	0	19	37	5	15

12. TEXAS A&M

Coach: Rob Childress. **Record:** 46-19.

Player, Pos., Year	AVG	AB	R	H	2B	3B	HR	RBI	SB
Jose Duran, ss, Jr.	.372	277	65	103	15	7	6	68	14
Dane Carter, 3b, Jr.	.371	264	67	98	16	9	8	64	15
Luke Anders, 1b, Jr.	.349	215	57	75	13	3	16	58	4
Darby Brown, 1b/of, Sr.	.339	230	43	78	15	1	12	69	2
Keith McInnerney, of, So.	.333	21	4	7	1	0	0	1	1
Kyle Colligan, of, Jr.	.317	243	67	77	19	0	14	39	12
Brian Ruggiano, c/if, Jr.	.315	241	53	76	13	4	9	45	3
Brodie Greene, if/of, So.	.290	145	34	42	7	3	4	27	7
Kevin Gonzalez, c, Fr.	.261	153	22	40	6	0	3	29	2
Daman Aaron, if, So.	.261	23	5	6	1	0	1	4	0
Brooks Raley, of, Fr.	.259	58	12	15	0	0	0	9	4
Blake Stouffer, 2b, Sr.	.258	233	55	60	13	0	5	38	17
Nick Fleece, if, Fr.	.231	52	10	12	3	0	0	6	1
Caleb Shofner, if, Fr.	.214	14	3	3	0	0	1	4	0
Ben Feltner, of, Sr.	.214	103	17	22	2	3	0	11	10

Player, Pos., Year	W	L	ERA	G	SV	IP	H	BB	SO
Kyle Thebeau, rhp, Jr.	6	5	2.12	33	3	76	56	37	79
Blake Rampy, rhp, Sr.	0	0	2.25	7	0	8	4	4	4
Kevin Cravey, rhp, Fr.	1	0	3.00	11	0	12	15	6	10
Shane Minks, rhp, So.	4	1	3.27	11	0	33	32	16	31
Clayton Ehlert, rhp, So.	6	2	3.41	16	0	69	78	10	48
Travis Starling, rhp, So.	8	2	3.70	28	9	49	49	16	40
Hank Robertson, rhp, Jr.	1	0	3.75	16	1	24	16	7	26
Barret Loux, rhp, Fr.	6	2	4.18	16	0	90	76	35	81
Scott Migl, rhp, So.	3	3	4.26	15	0	61	72	20	45
Brooks Raley, lhp, Fr.	7	2	4.76	18	0	93	98	27	68
Michael Heard, rhp, So.	0	1	5.40	8	0	8	4	4	10
Carson Middleton, rhp, So.	4	0	5.70	13	0	30	33	11	24
Evan Gerald, rhp, Jr.	0	0	7.94	6	0	6	9	4	7
Kirkland Rivers, lhp, Sr.	0	1	8.37	13	0	24	36	13	24

13. WICHITA STATE
Coach: Gene Stephenson. **Record:** 48-17.

Player, Pos., Year	AVG	AB	R	H	2B	3B	HR	RBI	SB
Conor Gillaspie, 3b, Jr.	.419	234	71	98	16	8	11	82	16
Andy Dirks, of, Sr.	.388	250	84	97	22	3	11	62	26
Clinton McKeever, 1b, So.	.328	177	34	58	14	0	5	39	2
Ryan Jones, of, So.	.326	261	70	85	11	5	2	43	16
Kevin Hall, of, Fr.	.320	50	21	16	4	0	0	11	4
Josh Workman, 2b, Jr.	.318	176	49	56	11	1	4	33	10
Ken Williams Jr., of, Jr.	.317	161	41	51	11	2	2	25	9
Dusty Coleman, ss, So.	.314	239	53	75	19	2	8	71	13
Tyler Weber, c, Sr.	.277	235	37	65	11	1	8	55	0
Mitch Caster, of, Fr.	.267	45	6	12	1	0	1	5	1
Tyler Hill, 1b, Sr.	.257	171	26	44	11	1	0	21	1
Bret Bascue, of, So.	.231	52	6	12	3	0	1	13	2
Taylor Brown, if, Fr.	.227	22	5	5	1	0	0	2	2
Cody Lassley, c, So.	.209	67	6	14	4	2	0	10	1
Ryan Engrav, dh, Fr.	.167	30	3	5	2	0	0	2	1
Kyle Sisney, ss/2b, Fr.	.135	37	5	5	1	1	0	4	1
Grant Muncrief, 3b, Fr.	.118	17	3	2	1	0	0	0	0

Player, Pos., Year	W	L	ERA	G	SV	IP	H	BB	SO
Khol Nanney, rhp, Sr.	5	1	1.80	22	4	35	25	11	38
Clinton McKeever, rhp, So.	0	0	1.86	7	0	10	5	4	10
Rob Musgrave, lhp, Jr.	12	1	2.51	16	0	111	99	22	101
Aaron Shafer, rhp, Jr.	11	4	3.26	16	0	110	104	28	110
Anthony Capra, lhp, Jr.	9	1	3.54	15	1	76	61	33	90
Tyler Fleming, rhp, Jr.	3	1	4.00	20	5	45	46	12	32
Tim Kelley, rhp, Fr.	4	4	4.85	12	0	52	59	9	34
Logan Hoch, lhp, Jr.	2	1	5.16	24	2	45	47	14	52
Clint Maune, rhp, Fr.	2	0	5.56	4	0	11	22	4	13
Andy Womack, rhp, Jr.	0	1	5.82	14	1	17	20	13	22
Matt Smith, rhp, Jr.	0	0	6.11	12	0	18	19	5	16
Justin Kemp, rhp, Fr.	0	2	6.89	8	0	16	15	7	17
Grant Muncrief, rhp, Fr.	0	0	7.36	10	0	15	12	13	14
Dusty Coleman, rhp, So.	0	1	10.80	6	1	5	5	2	4

14. ARIZONA
Coach: Andy Lopez. **Record:** 42-19.

Player, Pos., Year	AVG	AB	R	H	2B	3B	HR	RBI	SB
C.J. Ziegler, 1b, Sr.	.338	240	52	81	17	1	20	60	0
Mike Weldon, if, So.	.329	70	13	23	3	3	1	23	1
Bryce Ortega, ss, Fr.	.326	184	34	60	9	2	2	26	13
Colt Sedbrook, 2b, Sr.	.321	193	35	62	8	1	3	32	10
Dillon Baird, 3b, So.	.318	198	36	63	11	1	7	36	2
T.J. Steele, of, Jr.	.315	222	49	70	15	4	11	39	28
Jon Gaston, of, Jr.	.312	237	55	74	13	3	13	49	16
Brad Glenn, 3b/of, Jr.	.302	222	53	67	13	2	14	54	1
Diallo Fon, of, So.	.287	115	29	33	10	3	3	16	2
Bobby Coyle, of, Fr.	.277	101	18	28	2	1	1	13	3
Daniel Butler, c, So.	.268	56	9	15	2	2	0	12	1
Robert Abel, if, So.	.267	45	12	12	1	1	1	6	9
Rafael Valenzuela, if, So.	.259	58	8	15	5	1	0	13	1
Matt Presley, of, Fr.	.200	10	1	2	0	0	0	0	0
Dwight Childs, c, So.	.193	119	19	23	1	1	1	15	1
Hunter Pace, of, Jr.	.143	21	7	3	0	0	0	0	3

Player, Pos., Year	W	L	ERA	G	SV	IP	H	BB	SO
Daniel Schlereth, lhp, Jr.	2	0	1.81	34	1	55	30	20	76
Ryan Perry, rhp, Jr.	6	3	2.89	31	1	75	60	22	72
Jason Stoffel, rhp, Fr.	4	2	3.00	34	13	48	34	15	79
David Coulon, lhp, Sr.	8	4	4.15	16	0	85	88	36	80
Eric Berger, lhp, Jr.	8	4	4.34	18	0	75	70	34	67
Preston Guilmet, rhp, Jr.	6	4	4.38	16	0	97	104	22	93
Cory Burns, rhp, Jr.	3	0	4.98	15	0	22	26	12	23
Mike Colla, rhp, Jr.	4	2	5.16	20	0	59	71	32	53
Grayson Adams, rhp, Jr.	0	0	7.02	10	0	17	25	11	12
Matt Chaffee, lhp, Fr.	1	0	7.07	14	0	14	18	7	16

15. NORTH CAROLINA STATE
Coach: Elliott Avent. **Record:** 42-22.

Player, Pos., Year	AVG	AB	R	H	2B	3B	HR	RBI	SB
Ryan Pond, 1b/of, Sr.	.330	227	54	75	16	1	9	48	5
Matt Payne, of, Sr.	.322	227	44	73	6	2	9	50	6
Pat Ferguson, 1b/of, Jr.	.320	175	37	56	11	0	9	41	2
Marcus Jones, of, Jr.	.318	233	45	74	13	3	7	49	12
Jeremy Synan, of, Jr.	.314	210	44	66	11	1	8	45	6
Nick Stanley, c, Jr.	.305	131	29	40	8	2	2	22	1
Chris Schaeffer, c, Fr.	.298	121	25	36	3	0	3	19	0
Russell Wilson, if, Fr.	.296	71	9	21	2	1	2	8	6
Tommy Foschi, ss, Jr.	.287	195	44	56	19	1	1	28	5
Dallas Poulk, 2b, So.	.286	231	37	66	11	1	8	33	6
Devon Cartwright, of, Jr.	.275	102	22	28	12	1	4	20	2
Domonique Rodgers, of, Jr.	.256	39	9	10	2	0	0	8	1
Drew Martin, 3b, Jr.	.255	153	26	39	7	0	4	29	2
Wade Moore, of, So.	.250	16	6	4	1	0	0	1	0
Kyle Prewitt, if, Jr.	.235	17	2	4	2	0	0	0	0
Nate Cockman, c, So.	.188	16	2	3	0	0	0	0	0

Player, Pos., Year	W	L	ERA	G	SV	IP	H	BB	SO
Jimmy Gillheeney, lhp, So.	2	0	1.12	21	10	32	24	12	42
Jason Zinser, rhp, Jr.	0	1	1.26	11	1	14	7	13	17
Joey Cutler, rhp, Jr.	5	0	2.74	26	1	46	38	8	48
Clayton Shunick, rhp, Jr.	7	6	2.76	16	0	101	85	26	114
Jake Buchanan, rhp, Fr.	3	2	3.28	20	3	60	43	14	39
Sam Brown, rhp, So.	4	1	3.74	16	0	43	37	16	31
Alex Sogard, lhp, So.	4	2	4.35	23	1	52	46	28	36
Kyle Rutter, rhp, Jr.	3	1	4.50	20	2	22	20	8	18
Drew Taylor, lhp, Jr.	3	3	4.79	24	0	36	38	14	30
Eryk McConnell, rhp, Sr.	4	2	4.85	15	1	52	60	20	26
Eric Surkamp, lhp, Jr.	5	3	4.89	16	0	74	76	40	86
Jeff Stallings, rhp, Sr.	1	0	5.40	14	0	25	27	17	26
Travis High, rhp, Jr.	1	1	6.00	7	0	9	9	7	4

16. COASTAL CAROLINA
Coach: Gary Gilmore. **Record:** 50-14.

Player, Pos., Year	AVG	AB	R	H	2B	3B	HR	RBI	SB
Dock Doyle, c, Jr.	.370	243	64	90	22	2	16	72	4
Scott Woodward, 3b, Fr.	.364	225	82	82	15	1	7	45	42
Dustin King, of, Fr.	.353	17	4	6	3	0	0	5	0
Tommy Baldridge, of, Sr.	.349	232	57	81	17	0	10	44	2
David Sappelt, of, Jr.	.349	275	64	96	25	0	18	70	7
Tyler Bortnick, ss, Jr.	.345	223	56	77	15	0	6	40	8
Adam Rice, of/if, So.	.344	224	47	77	12	0	8	45	13
David Anderson, 1b, Jr.	.333	252	52	84	17	1	20	59	1
Derek Martin, if, Sr.	.300	90	12	27	4	0	1	17	0
Jose Iglesias, c, So.	.263	76	9	20	3	0	2	16	0
Rich Witten, if, Fr.	.250	24	7	6	0	0	1	7	0
Rico Noel, of, Fr.	.240	167	30	40	5	2	2	26	16
Evan Noell, c, Fr.	.235	34	6	8	4	0	0	3	0
Chance Gilmore, of, So.	.214	131	30	28	7	1	5	26	10

Player, Pos., Year	W	L	ERA	G	SV	IP	H	BB	SO
Joey Haug, rhp, Jr.	7	0	2.28	29	4	83	66	27	67
Bobby Gagg, rhp, Jr.	6	3	3.28	14	0	85	92	10	54
Nick McCully, rhp, So.	10	3	3.63	24	3	89	84	27	72
Kent Altman, rhp, Jr.	3	1	3.65	16	0	25	29	6	15
Pete Andrelczyk, rhp, Jr.	6	1	3.75	30	9	48	46	12	60
Austin Fleet, rhp, So.	5	3	4.43	16	0	61	70	29	29
David Anderson, rhp, Jr.	6	2	4.47	14	1	52	62	19	19
Cody Wheeler, lhp, Fr.	6	0	5.62	21	0	66	64	46	65
Matt Rein, lhp, Fr.	0	0	6.23	21	1	17	15	10	23
Rich Witten, rhp, Fr.	0	1	6.52	4	0	10	14	3	3
Dan Lombardozzi, rhp, So.	1	0	7.47	10	0	16	17	9	11
Jeremiah Meiners, lhp, So.	0	0	7.84	16	0	14	19	6	13
Jeff Richard, rhp, Jr.	0	0	10.54	14	0	14	17	15	11

17. OKLAHOMA STATE
Coach: Frank Anderson. **Record:** 44-18.

Player, Pos., Year	AVG	AB	R	H	2B	3B	HR	RBI	SB
Davis Duren, if, Fr.	.452	42	13	19	3	2	0	9	0
Thomas Belza, 2b, Fr.	.386	166	31	64	12	2	2	34	1
Donnie Webb, of, Jr.	.361	208	61	75	19	5	6	43	18
Matt Hague, of, Sr.	.360	250	59	90	18	2	12	57	1
Neil Medchill, of, So.	.349	172	42	60	9	3	11	41	2
Toby Davis, if, Jr.	.343	35	9	12	2	1	1	12	1
Jordy Mercer, ss, Jr.	.330	273	56	90	12	2	14	60	5
Rebel Ridling, 1b, Sr.	.321	249	60	80	17	2	18	67	0
Dean Green, 1b, Fr.	.319	144	27	46	4	1	5	24	2

Player, Pos., Year	AVG	AB	R	H	2B	3B	HR	RBI	SB
Luis Flores, c, Jr.	.298	188	44	56	11	1	5	31	0
Michael Dabbs, of, Jr.	.291	127	23	37	4	4	3	28	3
Dylan Brown, of, So.	.286	70	14	20	4	2	4	12	3
Tyrone Hambly, 3b, Jr.	.277	177	35	49	6	2	6	34	3
Ryan Pittman, c, So.	.192	26	7	5	0	0	1	7	0
Dusty Harvard, of, So.	.176	17	3	3	0	0	0	3	1
Rafael Thomas, of, Fr.	.167	42	17	7	2	0	1	7	2

Player, Pos., Year	W	L	ERA	G	SV	IP	H	BB	SO
Jared Starks, rhp, Jr.	0	0	0.00	6	1	9	7	4	6
Josh Neal, lhp, Jr.	2	0	2.12	11	0	17	13	5	9
Andrew Oliver, lhp, So.	7	2	2.20	15	0	98	72	36	96
Matt Peck, rhp, Jr.	2	1	2.83	25	5	48	38	17	24
Matt Willis, rhp, So.	1	0	3.12	8	1	26	34	4	13
Tyler Lyons, lhp, So.	12	3	3.31	15	0	109	111	19	92
Robbie Weinhardt, rhp, Sr.	6	0	3.89	25	4	44	41	20	70
Matt Gardner, rhp, Sr.	5	3	5.13	13	0	60	71	13	39
Brett Davis, lhp, Jr.	2	2	5.74	14	0	16	20	10	14
Jordy Mercer, rhp, Jr.	0	2	5.82	16	9	17	24	5	21
Jeff Breedlove, rhp, Jr.	2	0	5.94	9	0	17	21	1	12
Tyler Blandford, rhp, So.	4	6	6.23	13	1	61	66	31	51
Luis Flores, rhp, Jr.	0	0	6.75	3	0	8	10	1	7
Matt Hague, rhp, Sr.	1	0	6.97	6	0	10	12	4	8

18. SAN DIEGO
Coach: Rich Hill. Record: 44-17.

Player, Pos., Year	AVG	AB	R	H	2B	3B	HR	RBI	SB
James Meador, of, So.	.374	214	38	80	16	3	6	57	5
Kevin Hansen, 2b, Sr.	.338	216	29	73	17	1	1	40	4
Jose Valerio, 3b/1b, Jr.	.336	149	28	50	9	0	5	26	0
Michael Lugo, if/of, Jr.	.333	12	0	4	0	0	0	2	1
Kevin Muno, of, So.	.326	242	62	79	12	3	4	29	21
Josh Romanski, of, So.	.324	225	44	73	14	1	6	49	3
Sean Nicol, ss, Jr.	.313	230	56	72	13	1	0	27	9
Tony Strazzara, if/of, Fr.	.278	79	13	22	4	0	0	15	1
Logan Gelbrich, c, Sr.	.271	199	35	54	17	0	8	34	3
Victor Sanchez, 3b, Fr.	.268	220	47	59	12	1	12	47	5
Zach Walters, if, Fr.	.265	68	7	18	4	0	1	13	0
Ryan Davis, of, Sr.	.230	74	13	17	2	1	1	8	3
Nick McCoy, c, So.	.224	98	20	22	5	0	0	12	1
Steve Kaupang, 1b, Fr.	.125	24	0	3	0	0	0	1	0

Player, Pos., Year	W	L	ERA	G	SV	IP	H	BB	SO
Brian Matusz, lhp, Jr.	12	2	1.71	15	0	105	83	22	141
A.J. Griffin, rhp, So.	1	1	1.96	29	14	46	33	12	49
Scott DeNault, rhp, Jr.	0	0	3.18	7	0	6	5	2	9
Ricardo Pecina, lhp, Jr.	6	4	3.29	16	0	63	61	21	78
Sammy Solis, lhp, Fr.	3	1	3.83	17	0	49	52	12	42
Kyle Blair, rhp, Fr.	8	4	3.86	16	0	75	62	34	99
Matt Thomson, rhp, So.	2	1	3.86	16	2	33	34	11	21
Josh Romanski, lhp, So.	9	1	4.00	15	0	97	87	20	78
Darrin Campbell, rhp, Fr.	1	0	4.01	14	1	25	28	4	18
Luke Roniger, lhp, So.	0	1	5.40	12	0	10	9	3	7
Matt Couch, rhp, Sr.	2	1	6.23	5	0	22	27	6	20

19. MISSOURI
Coach: Tim Jamieson. Record: 39-21.

Player, Pos., Year	AVG	AB	R	H	2B	3B	HR	RBI	SB
T.J. Schieber, if, Fr.	.364	22	3	8	1	0	0	3	0
Rex Meyr, if/of, Fr.	.364	11	4	4	1	0	0	5	1
Aaron Senne, of, Jr.	.347	216	51	75	14	0	13	67	0
Ryan Lollis, of, Jr.	.339	227	48	77	17	0	1	42	8
Jacob Priday, of, Sr.	.332	211	47	70	15	1	16	65	7
Andrew Thigpen, if, Fr.	.324	108	15	35	5	0	1	17	0
Steve Gray, 1b, Sr.	.317	167	29	53	10	0	10	36	0
Kurt Calvert, of, Sr.	.302	159	40	48	4	3	3	25	10
Trevor Coleman, c, So.	.295	190	39	56	9	1	4	35	0
Greg Folgia, 2b, So.	.293	225	63	66	16	4	5	40	6
Dan Pietroburgo, c/if, Jr.	.267	105	13	28	3	0	1	12	0
Kyle Mach, 3b, Jr.	.259	185	37	48	12	1	2	28	0
Jonah Schmidt, if, Jr.	.238	63	13	15	3	0	3	15	0
Lee Fischer, ss, Jr.	.217	83	21	18	5	1	0	10	7
Austin Holt, if/of, Jr.	.209	43	13	9	1	0	0	5	2

Player, Pos., Year	W	L	ERA	G	SV	IP	H	BB	SO
Aaron Crow, rhp, Jr.	13	0	2.35	15	0	107	85	38	127
Ryan Allen, rhp, So.	2	1	3.60	22	1	30	31	11	32
Kyle Gibson, rhp, So.	9	4	3.84	19	2	87	86	23	96
Ian Berger, rhp, Jr.	4	5	4.54	16	0	85	85	20	68
Scooter Hicks, lhp, Jr.	3	2	4.60	24	5	29	41	5	21
Nick Tepesch, rhp, Fr.	1	3	4.85	22	4	30	33	12	17
Rick Zagone, lhp, Jr.	2	3	5.25	19	3	70	75	23	56
Brad Buehler, rhp, Fr.	1	0	5.52	11	0	15	19	11	10
Ryan Gargano, lhp, Jr.	1	0	6.04	12	1	22	23	11	18
Kelly Fick, lhp, Fr.	1	0	7.32	13	1	20	37	4	13
Greg Folgia, rhp, So.	1	1	9.28	5	0	11	22	4	13
Tyler Clark, rhp, Fr.	1	1	15.30	11	0	10	24	8	15

20. NEBRASKA
Coach: Mike Anderson. Record: 41-16.

Player, Pos., Year	AVG	AB	R	H	2B	3B	HR	RBI	SB
Jake Opitz, 2b, Sr.	.339	227	51	77	15	2	11	50	13
Mitch Abeita, c, Sr.	.337	187	45	63	7	0	10	49	7
Nick Sullivan, of, Jr.	.296	142	31	42	9	0	3	31	6
Bryce Nimmo, of, Sr.	.289	218	46	63	5	2	1	28	9
David Stewart, of, Fr.	.286	56	7	16	4	0	2	11	0
Tyler Farst, 1b/of, So.	.280	82	10	23	2	0	2	15	2
Craig Corriston, of/if, Sr.	.277	155	29	43	13	0	5	33	5
Jake Mort, 3b, Jr.	.262	210	48	55	15	3	1	13	10
Dan Johnston, if, Fr.	.260	50	10	13	3	0	0	11	2
Ben Kline, ss, Sr.	.253	170	19	43	10	0	0	23	5
D.J. Belfonte, of, So.	.241	220	47	53	15	3	1	37	14
Cody Neer, c, Jr.	.234	145	14	34	8	1	1	22	3
Andy Cotton, if, Fr.	.200	35	3	7	0	1	0	2	0
Tyler Rank, rhp, Fr.	.192	26	4	5	1	0	0	5	1
Jeff Tezak, if, Sr.	.190	21	5	4	2	0	1	2	0
Brett Sowers, if, Fr.	.148	27	1	4	0	0	0	1	0

Player, Pos., Year	W	L	ERA	G	SV	IP	H	BB	SO
Johnny Dorn, rhp, Sr.	6	2	2.45	15	0	106	82	29	102
Dan Jennings, lhp, Jr.	6	3	3.39	23	4	77	63	32	75
Mike Nesseth, rhp, Fr.	4	1	3.58	27	4	38	28	14	53
Erik Bird, rhp, Jr.	5	1	4.05	17	0	47	46	16	27
Erik Anderson, rhp, So.	1	0	4.11	15	3	15	15	7	20
Zach Herr, lhp, Jr.	3	0	4.24	28	5	34	34	13	49
Casey Hauptman, rhp, Fr.	1	0	4.34	10	1	19	16	6	16
Matt Freeman, rhp, Fr.	0	0	4.66	9	0	10	11	4	12
Aaron Pribanic, rhp, Jr.	3	4	4.72	17	0	74	78	32	59
Thad Weber, rhp, Sr.	9	5	6.15	15	0	79	97	28	72
Michael Mariot, rhp, Fr.	2	0	6.75	8	0	13	16	5	5
Joe Hatasaki, lhp, Fr.	1	0	8.00	8	0	9	12	6	1

21. TEXAS
Coach: Augie Garrido. Record: 39-22.

Player, Pos., Year	AVG	AB	R	H	2B	3B	HR	RBI	SB
Tant Shepherd, 3b/of, Fr.	.357	56	17	20	4	0	2	18	0
Russ Moldenhauer, of, So.	.355	166	35	59	16	1	1	39	1
Michael Torres, 2b, Jr.	.354	240	56	85	12	3	4	46	16
Kevin Keyes, of, Fr.	.339	59	13	20	2	1	4	10	2
Jordan Danks, of, Jr.	.321	234	70	75	22	7	7	46	14
Brandon Belt, 1b, So.	.319	238	41	76	20	2	6	65	2
Cameron Rupp, c, Fr.	.309	194	34	60	17	2	4	32	0
Kyle Lusson, of, Jr.	.306	36	7	11	1	0	0	7	1
Kyle Russell, of, Jr.	.296	203	54	60	10	3	19	56	3
David Hernandez, ss, So.	.291	213	30	62	4	1	4	38	4
Preston Clark, c, Jr.	.263	179	45	47	11	2	8	43	5
Travis Tucker, 3b, Jr.	.247	223	57	55	8	3	1	25	22
Kawika Emsley-Pai, c, Fr.	.154	13	4	2	0	0	0	1	0
Pat McCrory, ss, Jr.	.118	17	2	2	1	0	0	1	0

Player, Pos., Year	W	L	ERA	G	SV	IP	H	BB	SO
Chance Ruffin, rhp, Fr.	8	3	1.96	23	3	78	54	24	82
Hunter Harris, rhp, So.	1	0	3.60	6	1	10	8	2	8
Kenn Kasparek, rhp, Jr.	4	3	3.76	15	0	77	59	27	76
Stayton Thomas, rhp, Fr.	2	0	3.82	27	3	35	24	21	30
Casey Whitmer, rhp, So.	1	0	3.86	11	0	23	21	13	26
Marcus Tackett, rhp, So.	0	1	3.86	9	0	9	11	3	4
Brandon Belt, lhp, So.	1	0	4.08	16	2	18	17	5	16
Austin Wood, lhp, Jr.	7	3	4.43	17	0	85	84	19	42
Brandon Workman, rhp, Fr.	5	2	5.06	21	1	53	58	20	49
Cole Green, rhp, Fr.	3	7	5.28	24	3	58	67	24	44

COLLEGE BASEBALL

Player, Pos., Year		AVG	AB	R	H	2B	3B	HR	RBI	SB
Pat McCrory, ss, Jr.		0	1	5.40	13	2	13	12	5	15
Riley Boening, lhp, So.		3	1	6.34	13	0	44	55	15	25
Kyle Walker, lhp, Jr.		1	0	6.62	16	0	18	21	19	26
Keith Shinaberry, lhp, Jr.		2	1	7.15	18	0	11	16	2	2

22. MICHIGAN

Coach: Rich Maloney. **Record:** 46-14.

Player, Pos., Year	AVG	AB	R	H	2B	3B	HR	RBI	SB
Nate Recknagel, 1b/c, Jr.	.368	209	56	77	9	1	23	68	5
Adam Abraham, 3b, Jr.	.352	233	44	82	14	3	7	54	2
Kevin Cislo, of, Jr.	.348	178	41	62	5	2	1	28	18
Kenny Fellows, of, Jr.	.333	36	17	12	1	0	0	7	5
Jason Christian, ss, Jr.	.330	194	56	64	13	6	7	48	16
Mike Dufek, 1b, So.	.324	108	21	35	6	0	3	25	2
Zach Putnam, dh, Jr.	.307	199	47	61	13	2	11	51	3
Ryan LaMarre, of, Fr.	.305	141	27	43	5	0	3	23	8
Leif Mahler, 2b, Sr.	.305	233	51	71	17	0	3	42	5
Derek VanBuskirk, lf, Sr.	.294	221	53	65	10	1	10	44	11
Alan Oaks, of, So.	.250	128	18	32	5	0	6	19	2
Chris Berset, c, So.	.242	120	24	29	3	0	1	18	1
Tim Kalczynski, c/if, Jr.	.214	14	3	3	0	0	0	2	0
Mike Urban, of/2b, So.	.167	12	2	2	0	0	0	1	0

Player, Pos., Year	W	L	ERA	G	SV	IP	H	BB	SO
Chris Fetter, rhp, Jr.	10	2	2.47	16	0	95	71	28	82
Zach Putnam, rhp, Jr.	9	0	2.58	12	0	77	62	23	78
Michael Powers, rhp, Jr.	6	4	2.60	28	8	62	62	20	62
Eric Katzman, lhp, So.	2	1	3.52	17	0	38	34	28	33
Travis Smith, rhp, Fr.	5	1	4.40	15	1	43	46	20	28
Adam Abraham, rhp, Jr.	0	0	4.76	5	1	6	8	3	5
Jeff DeCarlo, lhp, So.	2	1	4.80	8	0	15	10	18	18
Tyler Burgoon, rhp, Fr.	2	0	4.86	19	5	37	40	13	29
Kolby Wood, rhp, Fr.	2	0	4.91	9	0	22	20	9	9
Matt Miller, rhp, Fr.	0	1	4.91	9	0	11	11	6	6
Mike Dufek, rhp, So.	1	0	5.84	8	1	12	13	8	10
Ben Jenzen, rhp, Jr.	4	0	7.61	14	0	37	37	19	34
Matt Gerbe, rhp, Fr.	1	0	7.82	9	0	13	14	10	13
Mike Wilson, lhp, Jr.	2	4	9.00	15	0	34	40	32	36

23. TEXAS CHRISTIAN

Coach: Jim Schlossnagle. **Record:** 45-19.

Player, Pos., Year	AVG	AB	R	H	2B	3B	HR	RBI	SB
Clint Arnold, of, Sr.	.378	238	57	90	19	0	2	36	16
Steve Ellington, of, Sr.	.348	184	32	64	7	2	2	29	0
Chris Ellington, of, Jr.	.344	183	34	63	21	2	6	55	2
Bryan Holaday, c, So.	.311	219	34	68	12	2	1	41	1
Ben Carruthers, 2b, Jr.	.308	266	65	82	12	4	2	33	15
Bryan Kervin, ss, Sr.	.288	250	36	72	12	0	3	40	2
Eric Givens, of, Fr.	.286	14	10	4	0	0	0	1	1
Matt Carpenter, 3b, Sr.	.283	226	48	64	15	3	11	46	8
Matt Vern, 1b, Sr.	.275	189	41	52	15	3	6	44	9
Hunt Woodruff, c, Jr.	.263	133	19	35	10	0	1	24	1
Brett Medlin, c, So.	.245	49	14	12	1	1	0	3	1
Jimmie Pharr, c, Fr.	.228	79	8	18	5	0	2	15	2
Aaron Schultz, if/of, Fr.	.205	44	6	9	3	0	0	2	0
Corey Steglich, if, Jr.	.167	66	9	11	1	0	1	6	2

Player, Pos., Year	W	L	ERA	G	SV	IP	H	BB	SO
Taylor Cragin, rhp, Jr.	1	0	1.61	14	2	22	20	3	14
Trent Appleby, rhp, Fr.	6	1	2.31	24	0	66	63	13	32
Andrew Cashner, rhp, Jr.	9	4	2.32	30	9	54	21	27	80
Steven Maxwell, rhp, So.	1	0	2.50	3	0	18	14	5	12
Tyler Lockwood, rhp, Jr.	7	2	2.75	17	0	105	97	15	71
Dillon Farish, rhp, Sr.	1	1	4.15	14	0	13	15	3	11
Seth Garrison, rhp, Jr.	2	3	4.41	17	1	69	75	27	44
Greg Holle, rhp, Fr.	1	2	4.50	14	0	60	71	30	32
Derek VerHagen, lhp, So.	1	0	4.50	13	0	12	13	12	8
Chris Anagnostou, rhp, Fr.	1	0	4.85	7	0	13	20	6	10
Eric Marshall, rhp, So.	3	0	4.91	16	1	26	28	13	17
Sean Hoelscher, rhp, Sr.	7	3	5.02	16	0	66	62	26	53
Paul Gerrish, rhp, So.	4	3	5.35	13	0	37	43	14	31

24. KENTUCKY

Coach: John Cohen. **Record:** 44-19.

Player, Pos., Year	AVG	AB	R	H	2B	3B	HR	RBI	SB
Sawyer Carroll, of, Sr.	.419	234	69	98	22	3	19	83	12
Ryan Wilkes, 2b, Sr.	.374	214	53	80	11	1	9	36	2
Collin Cowgill, of, Jr.	.361	233	80	84	15	2	19	60	23
Chris McClendon, 3b, Jr.	.346	179	33	62	11	1	3	33	7
Keenan Wiley, of, So.	.327	254	49	83	13	2	2	38	7
Spencer Korus, if/of, Jr.	.310	42	10	13	6	0	0	7	0
Chris Wade, ss, Fr.	.296	226	35	67	24	0	5	51	6
Tyler Howe, c, Sr.	.290	131	31	38	9	0	4	24	1
Bryan Rose, c, Jr.	.290	100	25	29	7	2	4	21	5
Brian Spear, 1b, Fr.	.283	237	51	67	19	1	10	57	3
Troy Frazier, of, So.	.256	90	23	23	5	0	3	26	2
Marcus Nidiffer, c, So.	.216	116	20	25	5	1	5	17	2
Brian Suerdick, c, Fr.	.182	11	2	2	1	0	0	1	1
Neiko Johnson, if, Fr.	.176	17	8	3	1	0	0	2	1
Chris Bisson, if, Fr.	.157	51	9	8	3	0	0	4	3
Kevin Bishop, of, Fr.	.091	11	4	1	0	0	0	0	1

Player, Pos., Year	W	L	ERA	G	SV	IP	H	BB	SO
Mike Kaczmarek, lhp, Fr.	1	0	2.13	15	0	25	25	10	23
Andrew Albers, lhp, Sr.	7	4	2.40	31	5	56	45	16	64
James Paxton, lhp, So.	4	2	2.92	17	1	52	46	25	43
Brock Baber, rhp, So.	1	3	3.03	28	1	36	34	11	27
Chris Rusin, lhp, Jr.	6	3	3.33	13	0	84	89	19	65
Tommy Warner, lhp, Sr.	3	1	3.38	12	0	24	25	7	19
Logan Darnell, lhp, Fr.	0	0	4.08	15	0	18	11	14	12
Greg Dombrowski, rhp, Sr.	6	1	4.10	16	0	79	106	13	58
Aaron Lovett, rhp, Sr.	5	1	4.31	22	1	56	56	21	42
Clint Tilford, rhp, So.	3	0	4.61	16	0	41	42	27	29
Scott Green, rhp, Jr.	6	4	4.76	20	2	57	58	16	64
Tyler Henry, rhp, So.	2	0	6.20	11	0	25	32	8	20

25. LONG BEACH STATE

Coach: Mike Weathers. **Record:** 38-21.

Player, Pos., Year	AVG	AB	R	H	2B	3B	HR	RBI	SB
Shane Peterson, 1b, Jr.	.390	213	52	83	16	2	7	50	10
Jonathan Jones, of, Fr.	.343	169	38	58	9	1	0	18	6
Danny Espinosa, ss, Jr.	.309	230	48	71	13	6	4	37	9
Jason Tweedy, 2b, Sr.	.306	121	21	37	3	3	2	21	2
Jordan Casas, of, Sr.	.302	53	8	16	1	0	0	4	1
Jason Corder, of, Sr.	.301	186	40	56	16	0	13	54	1
John Hill, c, Fr.	.296	54	7	16	2	1	0	10	0
Steve Tinoco, of, Jr.	.291	151	19	44	7	0	1	24	2
Brandon Godfrey, 3b, Sr.	.270	141	19	38	8	2	1	25	1
Rylan Sandoval, if/of, Jr.	.263	76	18	20	7	0	2	6	5
Travis Howell, c, Jr.	.253	150	19	38	8	1	0	10	2
Devin Lohman, if, Fr.	.253	87	6	22	1	1	0	8	1
Kip Masuda, c, Fr.	.250	36	3	9	0	1	0	1	0
Robert Burk, dh, So.	.241	29	2	7	0	0	1	5	0
Taylor Krick, c/3b, So.	.241	83	13	20	5	0	1	9	1
T.J. Mittelstaedt, of, So.	.219	128	19	28	5	3	0	17	2
Zach Barger, of, Jr.	.189	53	4	10	1	0	1	8	0
Chris Nelson, c, Fr.	.163	43	2	7	0	0	0	5	0
Ted Lemasters, c, Fr.	.148	27	5	4	2	0	0	3	0

Player, Pos., Year	W	L	ERA	G	SV	IP	H	BB	SO
David Brown, rhp, So.	1	0	0.00	11	0	7	4	7	6
Jason Markovitz, lhp, Fr.	2	0	1.08	11	0	8	3	0	4
Adam Wilk, lhp, So.	0	0	1.26	15	0	14	15	2	15
Nick Vincent, rhp, Jr.	4	0	1.76	26	2	31	19	5	33
Bryan Shaw, rhp, Jr.	2	1	1.84	27	8	29	25	6	35
Dustin Rasco, rhp, Jr.	2	0	2.14	23	0	21	18	6	25
Andrew Liebel, rhp, Sr.	8	4	2.22	15	0	117	104	19	97
Brett Lorin, rhp, Jr.	5	3	2.61	15	0	48	38	14	31
David Roberts, rhp, Jr.	3	1	3.58	26	1	28	27	5	26
Tyler Topp, rhp, Jr.	2	2	3.65	12	0	37	38	9	34
Vance Worley, rhp, Jr.	7	4	4.27	15	0	103	126	12	70
Jake Thompson, rhp, Fr.	2	5	4.95	13	0	67	90	21	42
David Born, lhp, Jr.	0	0	7.11	10	0	6	6	2	5

*Won automatic bid
Boldface: NCAA regional participant/conference department leader
#Conference department leader who is a non-qualifier

AMERICA EAST CONFERENCE

	Conference		Overall	
	W	**L**	**W**	**L**
Binghamton	15	8	29	27
*Stony Brook	14	10	34	26
Maryland-Baltimore County	13	11	21	29
Vermont	12	11	27	24
Hartford	10	13	18	31
Albany	10	14	17	37
Maine	8	15	20	28

ALL-CONFERENCE TEAM: C—Myckie Lugbauer, So., Maine. **1B**—Curt Smith, Sr., Maine. **2B**—Ryan James, Sr., Binghamton. **3B**—Bill Perry, Sr., Hartford. **SS**—Kyle Klee, Jr., Binghamton. **OF**—Joe Fowler, Sr., UMBC; Brendan Rowland, So., Albany; Brian Witkowski, Jr., Stony Brook. **DH**—Will Delawter, Sr., UMBC. **SP**—Zach Groh, Sr., Binghamton; Joe Serafin, Jr., Vermont. **RP**—Greg Lane, Jr., Binghamton.
Player of the Year: Curt Smith, Maine. **Pitcher of the Year:** Joe Serafin, Vermont. **Rookie of the Year:** Peter Bregartner, Binghamton. **Coach of the Year:** Joe Jancuska, UMBC.

INDIVIDUAL BATTING LEADERS
(Minimum 125 At-Bats)

	AVG	AB	R	H	2B	3B	HR	RBI	SB
Smith, Curt, Maine	.403	176	60	71	17	3	11	37	12
Delawter, Will, UMBC	.376	181	36	68	19	0	9	48	0
Fowler, Joe, UMBC	.369	198	52	73	16	1	11	54	4
Mazzurco, Steven, Stony Brook	.368	190	36	70	16	1	2	33	6
Peddicord, Scott, UMBC	.361	155	36	56	16	0	6	34	3
Witkowski, Brian, Stony Brook	.345	194	56	67	15	3	9	33	12
Lugbauer, Myckie, Maine	.343	181	36	62	19	2	5	43	1
Rowland, Brendan, Albany	.332	223	50	74	16	1	10	46	7
Amendola, Mike, Hartford	.331	163	27	54	14	2	4	31	0
Wink, Nolan, UMBC	.328	198	44	65	23	4	2	21	6
Cather, Billy, Maine	.328	195	35	64	7	0	3	25	15
Milo, Justin, Vermont	.328	192	50	63	13	8	6	40	9
Retz, Shawn, UMBC	.322	149	25	48	16	0	2	35	0
Paquette, Ethan, Vermont	.321	190	25	61	9	1	1	33	2
Lukas, Jarrett, Maine	.319	138	22	44	8	2	4	28	1
Bregartner, Peter, Binghamton	.319	204	41	65	9	0	5	29	11
Duffy, Matt, Vermont	.308	198	34	61	18	1	3	33	2
Russo, Steve, UMBC	.307	127	20	39	8	0	3	19	3
Sobocinski, Ben, Hartford	.306	186	33	57	12	3	3	19	14
Tansey, Michael, Stony Brook	.306	160	32	49	14	1	5	28	5
Stephan, Michael, Stony Brook	.305	174	49	53	10	0	11	37	0
James, Ryan, Binghamton	.303	211	54	64	9	1	3	26	21
Klee, Kyle, Binghamton	.303	208	35	63	14	3	4	41	10
McAvoy, Kevin, Maine	.301	143	24	43	8	3	2	25	4
Ivan, Brian, Binghamton	.301	163	25	49	6	0	4	32	0
Charron, Joe, Binghamton	.300	210	43	63	18	0	8	43	6
Meaney, Tom, UMBC	.299	154	30	46	10	1	3	29	1
Bowser, Adam, Hartford	.298	161	26	48	12	1	6	30	16
Dyer, Robert, Stony Brook	.298	188	29	56	13	2	7	45	2
Gugel, Ryan, Albany	.297	195	28	58	12	1	4	39	13
#Konstanty, Mike, Albany	.295	193	45	57	18	0	13	47	8

INDIVIDUAL PITCHING LEADERS
(Minimum 50 Innings)

	W	L	ERA	G	SV	IP	H	BB	SO
#Lane, Greg, Binghamton	3	2	1.97	24	11	32	25	13	23
Serafin, Joe, Vermont	6	5	2.51	12	1	79	62	30	58
Groh, Zach, Binghamton	6	3	3.27	14	0	85	87	29	79
Thompson, Eric, Vermont	7	1	3.45	13	0	70	68	39	42
Greiner, Chris, Hartford	6	1	3.65	9	0	57	54	27	56
Scanlan, Kevin, Maine	2	5	3.74	11	0	67	66	32	72
Albert, Justin, Vermont	5	5	3.76	13	0	81	86	25	62
Kubiak, David, Albany	5	0	3.92	13	0	60	55	24	33
Miller, Joe, Maine	5	2	3.93	9	0	55	48	26	46

Dennis, Jeff, Binghamton	4	5	3.97	14	0	82	68	27	62
#Purington, Jordan, Stony Brook	3	3	4.03	29	7	45	47	18	31
Smith, Murphy, Binghamton	6	4	4.09	13	0	81	85	26	61
Koehler, Tom, Stony Brook	6	5	4.15	14	0	93	88	45	111
Novakowski, Gary, Stony Brook	7	5	4.52	14	0	84	99	19	54
Jebb, Matt, Maine	2	5	4.57	14	1	65	74	30	64
Nowak, Jeremy, Stony Brook	7	2	4.62	20	7	60	68	26	51
Szymanski, Weston, Hartford	4	5	4.79	13	0	71	82	9	50
Bach, Ed, UMBC	3	6	5.11	14	0	79	94	16	35
Yannuzzi, Gio, Binghampton	2	5	5.16	13	1	52	62	18	35
Errigo, Mike, Stony Brook	4	5	5.22	14	0	71	87	39	65

ATLANTIC COAST CONFERENCE

	Conference		Overall	
ATLANTIC	**W**	**L**	**W**	**L**
Florida State	24	6	49	13
North Carolina State	18	11	42	22
Wake Forest	13	16	25	31
Clemson	11	18	31	27
Maryland	9	21	30	26
Boston College	9	21	26	27
COASTAL	**W**	**L**	**W**	**L**
*Miami	23	5	53	11
North Carolina	22	7	54	14
Georgia Tech	16	14	39	23
Virginia	15	15	39	23
Duke	10	18	37	18
Virginia Tech	6	24	23	32

ALL-CONFERENCE TEAM: C—Buster Posey, Jr., Florida State. **1B**—Yonder Alonso, Jr., Miami. **2B**—Jemile Weeks, Jr., Miami. **3B**—Mark Sobolewski, So., Miami. **SS**—Ryan Jackson, So., Miami; Greg Miclat, Jr., Virginia. **OF**—Tim Fedroff, So., North Carolina; Jack Rye, Sr., Florida State; Blake Tekotte, Jr., Miami. **DH**—Kyle Parker, Fr., Clemson. **SP**—Chris Hernandez, Fr., Miami; D.J. Mitchell, Jr., Clemson; Clayton Shunick, Jr., North Carolina State; Elih Villanueva, Jr., Florida State; Alex White, So., North Carolina. **RP**—Jimmy Gillheeney, So., North Carolina State.
Player of the Year: Buster Posey, Florida State. **Pitcher of the Year:** Alex White, North Carolina. **Freshman of the Year:** Chris Hernandez, Miami. **Coach of the Year:** Jim Morris, Miami.

INDIVIDUAL BATTING LEADERS
(Minimum 125 At-Bats)

	AVG	AB	R	H	2B	3B	HR	RBI	SB
Posey, Buster, Florida State	.463	257	89	119	21	4	26	93	5
Ackley, Dustin, North Carolina	.417	278	82	116	21	4	7	51	19
Fedroff, Tim, North Carolina	.404	285	78	115	22	5	12	71	14
Blackmon, Charlie, Georgia Tech	.396	250	68	99	12	3	8	45	25
Tapley, Stuart, Florida State	.383	196	54	75	15	1	8	40	1
Delmonico, Tony, Florida State	.374	254	69	95	19	2	8	69	14
Rye, Jack, Florida State	.371	232	48	86	15	0	7	52	12
Alonso, Yonder, Miami	.370	211	80	78	12	1	24	72	9
Weeks, Jemile, Miami	.363	237	81	86	17	5	13	62	23
Jackson, Ryan, Miami	.360	242	49	87	19	1	4	50	10
Tekotte, Blake, Miami	.353	249	81	88	12	4	13	50	27
Hassan, Alex, Duke	.353	218	62	77	17	0	4	33	14
Gould, Jeremy, Duke	.349	215	33	75	12	1	4	39	5
Seager, Kyle, North Carolina	.347	268	62	93	30	5	9	75	5
Rowland, Jeff, Georgia Tech	.335	209	47	70	8	1	4	26	22
Guinn, Dennis, Florida State	.332	259	67	86	19	2	19	76	2
Dietrich, Derek, Georgia Tech	.332	238	53	79	16	2	14	66	3
Murton, Luke, Georgia Tech	.332	211	41	70	25	0	12	51	3
Sean O'Brien, Virginia Tech	.332	202	45	67	18	1	8	40	5
Freeman, Mike, Clemson	.332	199	46	66	8	0	1	19	3
Pond, Ryan, North Carolina State	.330	227	54	75	16	1	9	48	5
Williams, Matt, Duke	.330	203	39	67	16	0	0	29	1
Shelton, Kyle, North Carolina	.326	218	49	71	14	5	4	40	4
Severino, Adan, Miami	.325	160	28	52	7	2	4	22	2
Wates, Austin, Virginia Tech	.324	216	35	70	10	6	2	33	15
Holt, Tyler, Florida State	.324	250	83	81	10	2	3	41	15

Grovatt, Dan, Virginia	.324	210	41	68	22	1	3	46	10
Nicolla, Jonathan, Duke	.324	170	29	55	13	1	5	35	1
Dykstra, Allan, Wake Forest	.323	186	51	60	12	0	16	50	7
Pupa, Jensen, Maryland	.322	199	40	64	16	0	3	24	0
#Miclat, Greg, Virginia	.320	241	52	77	11	2	0	35	**30**

INDIVIDUAL PITCHING LEADERS
(Minimum 50 Innings)

	W	L	ERA	G	SV	IP	H	BB	SO
Packer, Matt, Virginia	6	3	**1.14**	25	2	71	51	15	58
Bellamy, Kyle, Miami	6	0	1.86	43	3	63	40	13	75
#Schwimer, Michael, Virginia	3	1	1.72	26	**14**	31	19	10	36
#Wooten, Rob, North Carolina	6	2	1.87	**44**	5	63	43	33	73
Hernandez, Chris, Miami	11	0	2.72	18	0	**113**	92	18	**117**
Shunick, Clayton, N.C. State	6	6	2.76	16	0	101	84	26	114
Bates, Colin, North Carolina	6	1	2.78	27	0	55	44	20	57
Harvey, Matt, North Carolina	7	2	2.79	19	0	68	52	47	80
White, Alex, North Carolina	**13**	3	2.83	20	0	102	78	42	113
Foreman, Jonathan, Duke	2	1	2.87	12	1	53	43	26	31
Buchanan, Jake, North Carolina State	3	2	3.28	20	3	60	43	14	39
Manno, Christopher, Duke	6	2	3.38	12	0	59	50	19	80
McGuire, Deck, Georgia Tech	8	1	3.46	17	0	78	70	32	70
Mitchell, D.J., Clemson	6	5	3.47	20	0	99	97	40	106
O'Dell, Bo, Florida State	5	1	3.60	21	0	55	61	20	37
Wolcott, Andrew, Duke	3	4	3.75	12	0	70	71	23	42
Fairel, Matt, Florida State	12	2	3.79	17	0	112	107	40	100
Gutierrez, Carlos, Miami	5	4	3.81	39	13	50	43	20	72
McAnaney, Pat, Virginia	4	6	3.89	14	0	83	73	28	93
Currier, Will, Duke	6	5	3.90	13	0	58	54	20	31

ATLANTIC SUN CONFERENCE

	Conference		Overall	
	W	L	W	L
Florida Gulf Coast	25	8	38	15
Kennesaw State	21	12	30	26
*Lipscomb	19	14	33	30
North Florida	18	15	29	26
South Carolina-Upstate	17	16	25	29
Mercer	17	16	24	33
Belmont	16	17	25	33
Gardner-Webb	15	18	29	30
Stetson	15	18	26	33
Jacksonville	13	20	27	29
Campbell	13	20	21	37
East Tennessee State	9	24	18	38

ALL-CONFERENCE TEAM: C—Caleb Joseph, Jr., Lipscomb. **1B**—Jason Peacock, Sr., Florida Gulf Coast. **2B**—Jacob Robbins, Jr., Kennesaw State. **3B**—Anthony Russell, Sr., East Tennessee State. **SS**—Casey Frawley, So., Stetson. **OF**—Justin Bass, Sr., Stetson; Ozzie Borrell, Sr., Florida Gulf Coast; Carlo Testa, Jr., Belmont. **DH**—Travis Martin, Sr., North Florida. **SP**—Richard Bleier, Jr., Florida Gulf Coast; Brandon McClurg, Jr., Lipscomb; Carlo Testa, Jr., Belmont. **RP**—J.J. Crumbley, Sr., Florida Gulf Coast.
Player of the Year: Jason Peacock, Florida Gulf Coast. **Pitcher of the Year:** Richard Bleier, Florida Gulf Coast. **Freshman of the Year:** Robert Crews, Stetson. **Coach of the Year:** Dave Tollet, Florida Gulf Coast.

INDIVIDUAL BATTING LEADERS
(Minimum 125 At-Bats)

	AVG	AB	R	H	2B	3B	HR	RBI	SB
Peacock, Jason, Fla. Gulf Coast	**.434**	196	43	85	12	0	9	53	0
Bass, Justin, Stetson	.404	240	62	**97**	**27**	1	11	46	18
Cruz, Jeremy, Stetson	.404	223	57	90	18	2	15	57	0
Testa, Carlo, Belmont	.387	212	45	82	17	**8**	3	48	26
Gillan, Jeremy, Jacksonville	.377	220	38	83	10	0	9	60	3
Runion, Andrew, S.C.-Upstate	.375	216	44	81	10	2	9	39	1
Loyd, Justin, Gardner-Webb	.370	219	39	81	15	0	7	55	0
Knight, Chad, North Florida	.367	224	47	84	14	1	1	34	3
Robbins, Jacob, Kennesaw State	.362	210	57	76	6	4	0	21	17
Crews, Robert, Stetson	.361	191	39	69	12	3	7	38	10
Hannon, Andrew, North Florida	.359	184	34	66	13	0	2	44	3
Hoilman, Paul, E. Tenn. State	.353	184	48	65	18	0	9	47	3
Borrell, Ozzie, Florida Gulf Coast	.353	224	39	79	25	2	7	54	1
Frawley, Casey, Stetson	.352	253	59	89	13	4	7	37	6

Martin, Travis, North Florida	.351	202	38	71	16	0	8	48	0
Hale, Preston, North Florida	.350	214	52	75	16	1	4	34	2
Morrow, Jay, Kennesaw State	.350	203	30	71	8	0	5	41	4
Hamme, Ryan, Campbell	.349	215	51	75	15	2	5	42	13
Joseph, Caleb, Lipscomb	.348	256	54	89	20	0	17	61	7
Alvarez, Mikel, Fla. Gulf Coast	.345	206	44	71	6	2	2	35	2
Crawford, Matt, Mercer	.341	211	45	72	11	3	0	22	22
Cooke, Daniel, Gardner-Webb	.339	227	53	77	7	0	2	43	31
Bolden, Allen, Lipscomb	.339	239	**64**	81	21	1	7	47	3
Dortch, John, Mercer	.335	209	41	70	10	4	6	50	11
Rassel, Stephen, Fla. Gulf Coast	.335	218	43	73	11	3	1	33	9
McCall, Brandon, Belmont	.332	232	44	77	18	3	3	43	6
Scott, Brandon, Campbell	.330	218	39	72	17	2	6	47	**35**
Upchurch, Josh, Fla. Gulf Coast	.325	228	54	74	7	0	2	23	20
Lowe, Ellis, Campbell	.324	225	25	73	8	0	0	22	11
Shaughnessy, Billy, Mercer	.324	210	33	68	11	0	3	32	10
#Russell, Anthony, E. Tenn. State	.314	220	57	69	19	0	**21**	62	2
#Wiley, Derek, Belmont	.303	201	38	61	10	2	17	**65**	3

INDIVIDUAL PITCHING LEADERS
(Minimum 50 Innings)

	W	L	ERA	G	SV	IP	H	BB	SO
#Stohr, Tyler, North Florida	3	2	1.93	22	**10**	33	22	24	46
Bleier, Richard, Florida Gulf Coast	**7**	1	**2.19**	12	0	90	80	17	76
April, Dan, Mercer	4	4	2.70	25	0	70	61	29	55
#Burns, David, Stetson	1	2	3.24	**32**	1	42	47	16	28
McClurg, Brandon, Lipscomb	6	6	3.34	17	2	92	79	39	77
Mauldin, Andy, Stetson	**7**	2	3.61	10	0	77	79	19	38
Maxa, Ryan, Gardner-Webb	4	3	3.62	22	1	50	46	20	39
Bowley, Kyle, S. Carolina-Upstate	6	2	3.66	12	0	76	89	16	65
Woods, Nate, Belmont	5	2	3.94	16	1	62	59	23	48
Jenkins, Chad, Kennesaw State	5	5	3.96	13	0	89	91	13	78
Branham, Matt, S.C.-Upstate	6	5	4.04	12	0	85	101	18	57
Pryor, Tucker, North Florida	5	3	4.10	16	0	59	63	22	37
Coleman, Casey, Fla. Gulf Coast	**7**	3	4.11	13	0	70	71	35	58
Woodworth, Pete, Florida Gulf Coast	**7**	3	4.27	15	1	78	77	27	78
Pugliese, Nick, Stetson	3	4	4.27	12	0	65	78	**11**	39
Dobbins, Matt, Jacksonville	5	6	4.35	16	1	81	87	38	44
Pryor, Ty, North Florida	6	5	4.46	18	1	69	59	31	62
Scott, Brandon, Campbell	3	5	4.47	16	3	53	53	31	37
Ford, Hunter, Campbell	1	4	4.52	27	2	70	80	27	40
Bullard, Adam, Gardner-Webb	2	5	4.53	25	2	58	60	25	44
Andrew, Carson, Jacksonville	5	3	4.61	18	1	70	78	26	60
Swinehart, Dane, Belmont	3	3	4.62	23	2	51	68	16	28
#Brothers, Rex, Lipscomb	4	5	5.57	18	1	**97**	109	53	**96**

ATLANTIC-10 CONFERENCE

	Conference		Overall	
	W	L	W	L
*Charlotte	19	8	43	16
Xavier	19	8	27	31
Duquesne	16	10	26	29
Temple	16	11	27	29
Rhode Island	15	11	31	27
St. Bonaventure	15	12	29	24
Dayton	13	14	31	25
Fordham	13	14	29	24
George Washington	11	16	26	29
La Salle	11	16	16	36
Massachusetts	11	16	18	27
Richmond	10	16	20	31
Saint Louis	9	17	24	29
Saint Joseph's	9	18	18	34

ALL-CONFERENCE TEAM: C—Derek Mechling, Sr., Duquesne; Chris Taylor, Sr., Charlotte. **1B**—Aaron Janusey, Sr., Duquesne. **2B**—John Rickards, Sr., La Salle. **3B**—Shaun Hagey, Sr., Rhode Island. **SS**—Rich Goulian, Sr., Fordham. **OF**—Charlie Kruer, Sr., George Washington; Brad McElroy, Sr., Charlotte; Randy Moley, Sr., St. Bonaventure. **DH**—Rob Lyerly, So., Charlotte. **SP**—Tom Davis, Sr., Fordham; Michael Lucas, Sr., Xavier. **RP**—Kelly McLlain, So., Charlotte.
Player of the Year: Derek Mechling, Duquesne; Chris Taylor, Charlotte. **Pitcher of the Year:** Tom Davis, Fordham. **Rookie of the Year:** Corey Shaylor, Charlotte. **Coach of the Year:** Scott Googins, Xavier.

INDIVIDUAL BATTING LEADERS
(Minimum 125 At-Bats)

	AVG	AB	R	H	2B	3B	HR	RBI	SB
Moley, Randy, St. Bonaventure	.406	207	61	84	20	1	6	56	32
McElroy, Brad, Charlotte	.381	189	55	72	16	0	7	46	19
Shaylor, Corey, Charlotte	.366	183	46	67	8	4	2	43	4
Coogan, Hank, Rhode Island	.364	217	38	79	17	3	6	40	10
Lyerly, Rob, Charlotte	.364	220	52	80	26	2	15	76	1
Reeves, Tim, George Washington	.362	196	32	71	12	0	6	50	3
Miller, Kevin, Dayton	.362	188	33	68	9	2	0	41	5
O'Brien, Taylor, Charlotte	.361	180	50	65	7	1	3	27	13
Mechling, Derek, Duquesne	.357	199	63	71	13	0	12	43	17
Zaneski, Zach, Rhode Island	.355	217	49	77	17	1	4	46	10
McKoy, Byron, Temple	.352	182	37	64	11	0	6	31	17
Goulian, Rich, Fordham	.351	205	60	72	14	3	5	41	36
Baudinet, Brian, Massachusetts	.351	174	38	61	5	0	5	23	15
Brown, Steve, Xavier	.350	206	41	72	14	0	1	29	7
Taylor, Chris, Charlotte	.349	241	61	84	18	0	19	70	5
Randich, Anthony, St. Bonaventure	.348	155	22	54	13	0	5	45	2
Rickards, John, La Salle	.348	181	44	63	13	6	8	42	15
Kruer, Charlie, George Washington	.348	210	46	73	19	1	13	56	1
Carroll, Mike, Duquesne	.347	173	45	60	14	1	7	41	7
Richard, Zac, Xavier	.343	213	29	73	15	0	6	45	1
Bray, Aaron, Charlotte	.340	253	63	86	16	2	5	47	18
Hagey, Shaun, Rhode Island	.339	168	35	57	8	1	2	15	14
Suminski, Kevin, St. Bonaventure	.338	195	59	66	11	4	3	30	16
Jakubowski, Jeremy, St. Joseph's	.337	166	36	56	7	6	4	31	15
Moody, Shayne, Charlotte	.337	261	51	88	16	2	0	38	15
Metzroth, Ryan, Rhode Island	.336	211	46	71	15	1	6	39	1
Abokhair, Andrew, George Wash.	.333	168	44	56	12	1	5	37	5
Morrison, Eric, Duquesne	.332	190	36	63	7	3	2	40	22
Dunn, J.D., Saint Louis	.326	187	47	61	15	2	5	29	26
MacDonald, Jim, Massachusetts	.326	175	29	57	12	0	3	28	6

INDIVIDUAL PITCHING LEADERS
(Minimum 50 Innings)

	W	L	ERA	G	SV	IP	H	BB	SO
#Conley, Jordan, Xavier	2	2	1.19	21	10	23	20	9	24
Davis, Tom, Fordham	9	2	1.90	13	0	90	79	28	62
Farden, Lucas, Dayton	4	8	2.99	22	2	87	76	23	73
Turmail, Scott, Saint Louis	7	6	3.12	16	2	107	99	11	62
Mongiardini, Matt, Temple	6	5	3.59	14	0	80	76	29	42
Creevy, Mike, Xavier	6	2	3.68	26	0	73	75	19	59
Greenwood, Nick, Rhode Island	6	6	3.72	15	0	92	97	24	95
Rosenbaum, Danny, Xavier	5	3	3.79	14	0	78	74	29	82
Cantrell, Eric, George Washington	5	4	4.02	11	0	72	67	17	66
Vincent, Cody, St. Bonaventure	6	6	4.06	20	3	102	113	40	58
Mongiardini, Mike, Temple	3	2	4.08	12	0	57	49	36	43
Proctor, Michael, St. Bonaventure	6	4	4.12	15	0	74	84	23	54
Lucas, Michael, Xavier	7	2	4.15	13	0	85	90	27	64
Fuqua, Kevin, La Salle	5	9	4.17	18	3	101	101	37	77
Rosenbaum, Zach, Charlotte	5	2	4.34	12	0	64	59	40	41
Hasselhorst, Quinn, Dayton	5	2	4.37	14	0	70	87	15	39
Yermal, Joe, Charlotte	8	2	4.39	16	0	84	87	20	44
Palanski, Brett, Rhode Island	7	4	4.41	14	0	84	86	33	46
Mower, Randy, St. Joseph's	7	5	4.45	16	0	85	102	23	41
Clegg, Mitchell, Massachusetts	4	5	4.56	12	0	71	71	29	42
Eilenberg, Mitchell, Massachusetts	1	2	4.56	22	7	47	50	13	27
#Thomas, Ryan, Temple	3	2	6.62	27	0	35	43	20	29

BIG EAST CONFERENCE

	Conference		Overall	
	W	L	W	L
St. John's	20	7	42	16
Cincinnati	19	8	39	20
Notre Dame	16	10	33	21
*Louisville	16	11	41	21
Seton Hall	15	11	31	25
South Florida	14	13	31	27
West Virginia	13	14	35	21
Villanova	12	15	30	28
Connecticut	11	16	27	28
Rutgers	11	16	23	29
Pittsburgh	7	19	19	34
Georgetown	7	20	18	32

ALL-CONFERENCE TEAM:
C—Derrick Alfonso, Sr., Louisville. **1B**—Joey Angelberger, Sr., South Florida. **2B**—Josh Harrison, Jr., Cincinnati. **3B**—Chris Dominguez, So., Louisville. **SS**—Tyler Kuhn, Sr., West Virginia. **OF**—Tony Campana, Sr., Cincinnati; A.J. Pollock, So., Notre Dame; Ryan Lockwood, Fr., South Florida. **DH**—David Mills, So., Notre Dame. **P**—Justin Marks, So., Louisville; Scott Barnes, Jr., St. Johns; George Brown, Sr., St. Johns; Corey Young, Jr., Seton Hall.
Players of the Year: Chris Dominguez, Louisville; Josh Harrison, Cincinnati. **Pitcher of the Year:** George Brown, St. John's. **Rookie of the Year:** Jedd Gyorko, West Virginia. **Coach of the Year:** Ed Blankmeyer, St. John's.

INDIVIDUAL BATTING LEADERS
(Minimum 125 At-Bats)

	AVG	AB	R	H	2B	3B	HR	RBI	SB
Kuhn, Tyler, West Virginia	.424	238	71	101	17	6	9	56	7
Lockwood, Ryan, South Florida	.415	193	44	80	15	2	0	37	12
Gyorko, Jedd, West Virginia	.409	232	62	95	17	3	8	63	4
Harrison, Josh, Cincinnati	.378	238	66	90	22	3	5	54	32
Parks, Justin, West Virginia	.378	209	58	79	9	3	5	43	3
Belnome, Vince, West Virginia	.377	220	58	83	19	3	3	66	7
Shunk, Derek, Villanova	.377	228	43	86	15	2	6	51	5
Spina, Mike, Cincinnati	.377	223	56	84	12	2	21	79	0
McClanahan, Justin, Louisville	.372	261	64	97	26	2	12	59	17
Agreste, Joe, West Virginia	.369	179	49	66	15	6	6	45	1
Dominguez, Chris, Louisville	.365	249	68	91	13	2	21	75	11
Satterwhite, Cameron, Cincinnati	.364	225	49	82	21	2	14	61	0
Maruszak, Addison, South Florida	.364	231	55	84	12	0	6	32	3
Dao, John, Louisville	.356	194	37	69	13	3	3	31	16
Pollock, A.J., Notre Dame	.350	217	49	76	15	3	4	42	28
Mills, David, Notre Dame	.349	166	28	58	2	6	2	27	9
Ijames, Stewart, Louisville	.349	169	39	59	11	2	8	39	4
Del Rosario, Carlos, St. John's	.347	190	38	66	14	6	5	43	7
Grantham, Jeff, St. John's	.343	140	31	48	8	0	2	30	4
LePage, Pierre, Connecticut	.341	223	55	76	14	0	0	35	19
Brezovsky, Ross, Notre Dame	.338	195	38	66	11	1	4	35	1
Campana, Tony, Cincinnati	.338	263	60	89	8	8	1	28	44
Harrigan, Matt, Georgetown	.336	143	25	48	9	1	4	24	3
Leonard, Joe, Pittsburgh	.335	203	42	68	12	0	7	37	3
Arnold, Jeff, Louisville	.333	183	39	61	14	1	2	32	12
Feliz, Luis, Rutgers	.328	174	30	57	15	2	4	33	10
Glynn, Elliot, Connecticut	.324	170	35	55	12	1	3	41	2
Angelberger, Joey, South Florida	.323	229	54	74	19	0	11	53	3
Clark, Andrew, Louisville	.323	229	45	74	13	5	5	44	8
Nemeth, Mike, Connecticut	.321	187	25	60	13	0	0	29	2

INDIVIDUAL PITCHING LEADERS
(Minimum 50 Innings)

	W	L	ERA	G	SV	IP	H	BB	SO
Tosoni, Matt, St. John's	6	2	1.87	14	0	58	51	11	31
Marks, Justin, Louisville	9	2	2.37	18	0	91	72	39	89
Kaye, David, Pittsburgh	2	4	2.52	23	1	54	44	44	36
Brown, George, St. John's	9	1	2.91	14	0	90	85	12	59
Gross, Billy, West Virginia	5	2	3.01	13	0	75	66	34	53
Stultz, Derrick, South Florida	4	3	3.08	12	0	64	62	18	53
Black, Sean, Seton Hall	3	3	3.44	17	2	65	48	30	59
Hill, Michael, Cincinnati	6	4	3.46	15	0	81	83	16	65
Young, Corey, Seton Hall	8	4	3.52	13	0	79	70	25	78
Fontanez, Randy, South Florida	5	3	3.54	13	0	81	92	27	58
Osterbrock, Dan, Cincinnati	9	2	3.55	14	0	99	108	10	74
#Lynch, Colin, St. John's	4	1	3.58	24	13	28	24	16	23
Korpi, Wade, Notre Dame	6	3	3.59	13	0	78	78	39	58
Barnes, Scott, St. John's	7	3	3.69	15	0	90	69	45	90
Revesz, Bob, Louisville	1	0	3.90	22	1	65	73	15	41
Patterson, Matt, Rutgers	3	1	3.96	31	0	50	61	20	24
Yecker, Jared, St. John's	4	2	4.02	13	0	56	46	28	46
Gaggioli, Michael, Georgetown	2	5	4.11	10	0	66	72	15	63
Morrison, Stephen, West Virginia	6	3	4.20	12	0	84	76	49	56
Thomas, Daniel, South Florida	2	4	4.21	12	0	58	66	28	55
Yurish, Matt, West Virginia	6	2	4.27	14	0	65	71	38	74
#Sanford, Shawn, South Florida	5	5	5.21	33	2	47	61	25	46

BIG SOUTH CONFERENCE

	Conference		Overall	
	W	L	W	L
*Coastal Carolina	17	3	50	14
Liberty	14	7	35	26
Virginia Military Institute	14	7	29	26
Winthrop	11	10	26	34
High Point	9	12	20	33
Radford	6	14	24	32
UNC Asheville	6	15	24	35
Charleston Southern	6	15	18	35

ALL-CONFERENCE TEAM: C—Dock Doyle, Jr., Coastal Carolina. **1B**—Alex Gregory, Jr., Radford. **2B**—Shane Geisslinger, Sr., VMI. **3B**—Scott Woodward, Fr., Coastal Carolina. **SS**—Kevin Weidenbacher, UNC Asheville. **DH**—Derek Smith, Fr., Charleston Southern. **OF**—David Sappelt, Jr., Coastal Carolina; Tommy Baldridge, Sr., Coastal Carolina; P.K. Keller, Sr., Liberty. **SP**—Alan DeRatt, Sr., UNC Asheville; Joey Haug, Sr., Coastal Carolina; Bobby Gagg, Jr., Coastal Carolina. **RP**—Pete Andrelczyk, Jr., Coastal Carolina.

Player of the Year: Dock Doyle, Coastal Carolina. **Pitcher of the Year:** Alan DeRatt, UNC Asheville. **Freshman of the Year:** Scott Woodward, Coastal Carolina. **Coach of the Year:** Gary Gilmore, Coastal Carolina.

INDIVIDUAL BATTING LEADERS
(Minimum 125 At-Bats)

	AVG	AB	R	H	2B	3B	HR	RBI	SB
Gregory, Alex, Radford	.401	207	56	83	11	1	14	51	2
Keen, Reggie, Radford	.384	219	42	84	14	5	3	41	9
Doyle, Dock, Coastal Carolina	.370	243	64	90	22	2	16	72	4
Woodward, Scott, Coastal Carolina	.364	225	82	82	15	1	7	45	42
Baldridge, Tommy, Coastal Carolina	.349	232	57	81	17	0	10	44	2
Sappelt, David, Coastal Carolina	.349	275	64	96	25	0	18	70	7
Roberts, Sam, VMI	.348	184	30	64	14	1	0	26	12
Giammaresi, David, Liberty	.347	213	43	74	19	2	6	47	2
Bortnick, Tyler, Coastal Carolina	.345	223	56	77	15	0	6	40	8
Rice, Adam, Coastal Carolina	.344	224	47	77	12	0	8	45	13
Biagini, Tanner, VMI	.343	216	41	74	10	0	10	46	2
Perry, Mark, Charleston Southern	.341	211	38	72	5	0	3	35	6
Brown, Cody, Liberty	.341	226	46	77	21	0	9	52	2
Tisdale, Eddie, Winthrop	.340	235	46	80	15	0	5	29	7
Weidenbacher, Kevin, UNC Asheville	.337	255	48	86	15	3	2	30	3
Schwartz, Randy, High Point	.335	206	35	69	16	1	9	32	1
Anderson, David, Coastal Carolina	.333	252	52	84	17	1	20	59	1
Froehlich, Billy, Winthrop	.333	213	50	71	18	1	6	40	8
Keller, P.K., Liberty	.333	204	38	68	21	0	4	43	5
Black, Taylor, Charleston Southern	.333	174	31	58	17	0	5	34	1
Schumer, Justin, UNC Asheville	.326	230	40	75	13	1	9	50	0
Toth, Ben, Radford	.322	177	37	57	10	4	2	21	8
Arrington, Elliott, UNC Asheville	.322	233	47	75	17	0	5	54	2
Sandridge, Brian, VMI	.320	194	29	62	8	0	7	39	3
Hollinger, Errol, Liberty	.319	257	60	82	19	1	8	47	1
Nolan, Kevin, Winthrop	.319	248	34	79	18	2	2	37	11
Chinners, Nick, Charleston Southern	.318	170	23	54	10	0	2	18	2
Baatz, Danny, UNC Asheville	.315	216	28	68	13	0	5	28	1
Morian, Kory, Charleston Southern	.314	194	33	61	10	0	4	26	1
Smith, Derek, Charleston Southern	.314	188	25	59	12	0	11	42	0

INDIVIDUAL PITCHING LEADERS
(Minimum 50 Innings)

	W	L	ERA	G	SV	IP	H	BB	SO
DeRatt, Alan, UNC Asheville	8	2	1.74	16	0	98	73	36	68
#Chlebnikow, R.J., High Point	1	1	2.17	32	1	29	29	17	17
Haug, Joey, Coastal Carolina	7	0	2.28	29	4	83	66	27	67
Page, Ryan, Liberty	5	5	2.76	16	0	82	87	17	63
Henderson, Chris, VMI	5	4	3.16	12	0	57	59	7	57
Gagg, Bobby, Coastal Carolina	6	3	3.28	14	0	85	92	10	54
Evans, Eric, Radford	5	4	3.34	17	0	94	88	21	76
Bowman, Michael, VMI	4	6	3.44	18	0	92	87	25	82
Mullins, Ryan, Winthrop	7	2	3.56	15	0	66	75	20	42
Stokes, David, Liberty	8	6	3.60	15	0	100	114	16	86
McCully, Nick, Coastal Carolina	10	3	3.63	24	3	89	84	27	72
Tweddale, Payton, Charleston Southern	2	4	3.70	27	6	56	64	11	40
O'Donnell, Bubba, High Point	4	4	3.71	31	8	63	50	22	58

#Andrelczyk, Pete, Coastal Carolina	6	1	3.75	30	9	48	46	12	60
Umberger, Dustin, Liberty	8	3	3.80	21	1	83	85	19	88
Barham, Trey, VMI	4	6	3.84	16	0	96	97	23	86
Evans, Stephen, Liberty	3	3	4.07	20	3	60	55	20	55
White, Andrew, Charleston Southern	4	7	4.15	15	0	87	87	28	67
Fleet, Austin, Coastal Carolina	5	3	4.43	16	0	61	70	29	29
Anderson, David, Coastal Carolina	6	2	4.47	14	1	52	62	19	19
Bogaert, Michael, UNC Asheville	6	6	4.66	18	0	83	93	50	69
Markham, Anthony, Charleston South.	4	6	4.66	17	0	64	78	25	36

BIG TEN CONFERENCE

	Conference		Overall	
	W	L	W	L
*Michigan	26	5	46	14
Purdue	21	10	32	26
Penn State	17	15	27	31
Illinois	16	15	31	25
Ohio State	15	15	30	26
Indiana	15	17	31	30
Northwestern	14	18	21	28
Michigan State	12	18	24	29
Minnesota	10	21	20	35
Iowa	10	22	22	33

ALL-CONFERENCE TEAM: C—Josh Phegley, So., Indiana. **1B**—Nate Recknagel, Sr., Michigan. **2B**—Ben Wolgamot, Sr., Purdue. **3B**—Nate Hanson, Jr., Minnesota. **SS**—Jason Christian, Jr., Michigan. **OF**—Kyle Hudson, Jr., Illinois. **OF**—Andrew Means, Jr., Indiana; Matt Nohelty, Jr., Minnesota. **DH**—Zach Putnam, Jr., Michigan. **SP**—Matt Bashore, So., Indiana; Chris Fetter, Jr., Michigan; Zach Putnam, Jr., Michigan; Matt Bischoff, Jr., Purdue. **RP**—Drew O'Neil, Jr., Penn State.

Player of the Year: Nate Recknagel, Michigan. **Pitcher of the Year:** Zach Putnam, Michigan. **Freshman of the Year:** Eric Jokisch, Northwestern. **Coach of the Year:** Rich Maloney, Michigan.

INDIVIDUAL BATTING LEADERS
(Minimum 125 At-Bats)

	AVG	AB	R	H	2B	3B	HR	RBI	SB
Phegley, Josh, Indiana	.438	224	69	98	20	2	15	80	2
Hudson, Kyle, Illinois	.398	191	61	76	11	1	1	26	40
Nohelty, Matt, Minnesota	.397	237	53	94	7	4	1	39	24
Curry, Caleb, Iowa	.396	202	49	80	15	1	7	65	45
Toole, Justin, Iowa	.395	220	63	87	15	4	0	49	24
Miller, Justin, Ohio State	.395	200	35	79	16	0	4	61	0
Webb, Daniel, Illinois	.391	192	34	75	9	0	6	46	1
Kalina, Mike, Northwestern	.384	146	35	56	11	2	2	27	1
Sabourin, Jerrud, Indiana	.383	230	33	88	14	1	5	53	4
Haveman, Brandon, Purdue	.379	219	60	83	16	5	2	24	12
Hervey, Chris, Indiana	.373	193	48	72	10	1	2	36	13
DeSmidt, Jeff, Minnesota	.371	167	26	62	9	0	9	50	0
Wikoff, Brandon, Illinois	.369	214	46	79	12	2	1	61	11
Recknagel, Nate, Michigan	.368	209	56	77	9	1	23	68	1
Wolgamot, Ben, Purdue	.368	155	44	57	7	2	1	28	7
Roberts, Chris, Michigan State	.363	179	29	65	5	7	2	32	6
Hanson, Nate, Minnesota	.359	217	47	78	22	0	6	32	3
Ernst, Brian, Penn State	.358	218	41	78	16	0	0	27	9
Means, Andrew, Indiana	.357	252	72	90	11	8	2	32	33
Hoef, Kevin, Iowa	.357	196	52	70	9	4	3	31	17
Shuck, J.B., Ohio State	.356	174	47	62	5	3	0	23	22
Bonadonna, Joe, Illinois	.356	205	4	73	12	1	1	34	26
Goebbert, Jake, Northwestern	.353	173	41	61	22	1	10	48	3
Abraham, Adam, Michigan	.352	233	44	82	14	3	7	52	2
Cislo, Kevin, Michigan	.348	178	41	62	5	2	1	28	18
Hastings, Ryan, Illinois	.346	185	46	64	10	2	5	38	4
Blackburn, Joe, Penn State	.342	187	37	64	14	3	3	43	10
Freie, Wes, Iowa	.342	158	29	54	9	2	4	28	1
Crawford, Evan, Indiana	.335	218	43	73	9	3	1	30	18
White, Ryan, Purdue	.333	210	53	70	15	0	12	48	8

INDIVIDUAL PITCHING LEADERS
(Minimum 50 Innings)

	W	L	ERA	G	SV	IP	H	BB	SO
#Loomis, Andy, Purdue	4	1	1.72	32	0	37	31	8	30
Fetter, Chris, Michigan	10	2	2.47	16	0	95	71	28	82

COLLEGE BASEBALL

	W	L	ERA	G	SV	IP	H	BB	SO
Putnam, Zach, Michigan	9	0	2.58	12	0	77	62	23	78
Powers, Michael, Michigan	6	4	2.60	28	8	62	62	20	62
#Lindblom, Josh, Purdue	1	2	3.32	30	12	41	37	9	44
Wanamaker, Mike, Penn State	6	5	3.41	14	0	87	89	32	59
Bashore, Matt, Indiana	7	3	3.59	14	0	83	73	46	**86**
Sorensen, Mark, Michigan State	3	6	3.95	12	0	55	52	26	38
Bischoff, Matt, Purdue	6	3	3.96	14	0	77	74	25	55
Wolosiansky, Dean, Ohio State	7	4	4.22	14	0	70	84	27	37
Shuck, J.B., Ohio State	5	3	4.29	11	0	65	51	34	76
Jokisch, Eric, Northwestern	8	2	4.30	12	0	73	79	39	42
Hale, Jake, Ohio State	5	3	4.50	12	1	74	88	27	45
Cook, Kyle, Purdue	5	3	4.65	13	1	50	56	17	22
DeLucia, Dan, Ohio State	3	3	4.70	11	0	52	60	18	44
Buske, Tom, Minnesota	4	6	4.92	13	0	75	94	25	50
Cullen, Chris, Michigan State	5	4	4.95	14	0	64	71	24	37
Monterey, Mike, Michigan State	3	4	5.06	12	0	75	88	25	39
Brabender, Dustin, Minnesota	4	5	5.27	13	0	68	94	26	39
Manson, Kevin, Illinois	8	2	5.42	13	0	75	88	19	41
Jansen, Matt, Purdue	4	3	5.44	16	0	51	64	24	23
Arnett, Eric, Indiana	4	5	5.45	17	0	66	82	38	37

	AVG	AB	R	H	2B	3B	HR	RBI	SB
Ridling, Rebel, Oklahoma State	.321	249	60	80	17	2	18	67	0
Danks, Jordan, Texas	.321	234	70	75	22	7	7	46	14
Hornung, Adam, Baylor	.320	222	39	71	12	1	8	43	5
Green, Dean, Oklahoma State	.319	144	27	46	4	1	5	24	2
Belt, Brandon, Texas	.319	238	41	76	20	2	6	64	2
Gray, Steve, Missouri	.317	167	29	53	10	0	10	36	0
#Russell, Kyle, Texas	.300	203	54	61	10	3	**19**	56	3

INDIVIDUAL PITCHING LEADERS
(Minimum 50 Innings)

	W	L	ERA	G	SV	IP	H	BB	SO
Ruffin, Chance, Texas	8	3	**1.96**	23	3	78	54	24	82
Thebeau, Kyle, Texas A&M	6	5	2.12	33	3	76	56	37	79
Oliver, Andrew, Oklahoma State	7	2	2.20	15	0	98	72	36	96
Crow, Aaron, Missouri	**13**	0	2.35	15	0	107	85	38	**127**
Dorn, Johnny, Nebraska	6	2	2.45	15	0	106	82	29	102
Lyons, Tyler, Oklahoma State	12	3	3.31	15	0	**109**	111	19	92
Jennings, Dan, Nebraska	6	3	3.39	23	4	77	63	32	75
Ehlert, Clayton, Texas A&M	6	2	3.41	16	0	69	78	10	48
Hutt, Brad, Kansas State	7	4	3.65	17	0	99	104	24	49
Kempf, Willie, Baylor	6	3	3.69	16	2	68	67	33	48
Smyth, Paul, Kansas	5	5	3.73	**34**	10	60	67	12	51
Kasparek, Kenn, Texas	4	3	3.76	15	0	77	59	27	76
Duke, Ryan, Oklahoma	7	5	3.77	22	0	72	74	33	54
Gibson, Kyle, Missouri	9	4	3.84	19	2	87	86	23	96
Loux, Barret, Texas A&M	6	2	4.18	16	0	90	76	35	81
Volz, Kendal, Baylor	3	6	4.20	12	0	71	75	28	85
Murray, Justin, Kansas State	3	2	4.21	13	0	73	79	21	39
Migl, Scott, Texas A&M	3	3	4.26	15	0	61	72	20	45
Wood, Austin, Texas	7	3	4.43	17	0	85	84	19	42
Doyle, Andrew, Oklahoma	9	4	4.53	16	0	99	106	42	72
#Edwards, Daniel, Kansas State	5	3	2.47	28	**12**	40	24	15	53

BIG 12 CONFERENCE

	Conference		Overall	
	W	L	W	L
Texas A&M	19	8	46	19
Oklahoma State	18	9	44	18
Nebraska	17	9	41	16
Missouri	16	11	39	21
*Texas	15	12	39	22
Baylor	11	16	32	26
Kansas State	11	16	29	29
Oklahoma	9	17	36	26
Kansas	9	18	30	27
Texas Tech	9	18	25	30

ALL-CONFERENCE TEAM: C—Mitch Abeita, Sr., Nebraska. 1B—Luke Anders, Jr., Texas A&M. 2B—Jake Opitz, Sr., Nebraska. 3B—Dane Carter, Sr., Texas A&M. SS—Jose Duran, Jr., Texas A&M. OF—Aaron Senne, So., Missouri; Neil Medchill, So., Oklahoma St.; Kyle Colligan, Jr., Texas A&M. DH—Jacob Priday, Sr., Missouri. UTIL—Jordy Mercer, Jr., Oklahoma State. SP—Aaron Crow, Jr., Missouri; Johnny Dorn, Sr., Nebraska; Andrew Oliver, So., Oklahoma State. RP—Travis Starling, So., Texas A&M.
Player of the Year: Jose Duran, Texas A&M. **Pitcher of the Year:** Aaron Crow, Missouri. **Newcomer of the Year:** Jose Duran, Texas A&M. **Freshman of the Year:** Chance Ruffin, Texas. **Coach of the Year:** Rob Childress, Texas A&M.

INDIVIDUAL BATTING LEADERS
(Minimum 125 At-Bats)

	AVG	AB	R	H	2B	3B	HR	RBI	SB
Belza, Thomas, Oklahoma State	.386	166	31	64	12	2	2	34	1
Duran, Jose, Texas A&M	.372	277	65	103	15	7	6	68	14
Carter, Dane, Texas A&M	.371	264	67	98	16	9	8	64	15
Gosse, Mike, Oklahoma	.368	253	56	93	23	2	8	52	2
Allman, John, Kansas	.365	197	53	72	17	1	6	48	4
Rueda, Willie, Texas Tech	.361	194	39	70	14	3	0	33	27
Webb, Donnie, Oklahoma State	.361	208	61	75	19	5	6	43	18
Hague, Matt, Oklahoma State	.360	250	59	90	18	2	12	57	1
Moldenhauer, Russell, Texas	.355	166	35	59	16	1	1	39	1
Torres, Michael, Texas	.354	240	56	85	12	3	4	46	16
Anders, Luke, Texas A&M	.349	215	57	75	13	3	16	58	4
Medchill, Neil, Oklahoma State	.349	172	42	60	9	3	11	41	2
Senne, Aaron, Missouri	.347	216	51	75	14	0	13	67	0
Johnson, Casey, Oklahoma	.346	136	24	47	9	1	4	24	5
Davis, Aljay, Oklahoma	.345	226	49	78	6	1	2	40	13
Johnson, Jamie, Oklahoma	.344	224	58	77	12	3	5	27	20
Lollis, Ryan, Missouri	.339	227	48	77	17	0	1	42	8
Optiz, Jake, Nebraska	.339	227	51	77	15	2	11	51	13
Brown, Darby, Texas A&M	.339	230	43	78	15	1	12	69	2
Abeita, Mitch, Nebraska	.337	187	45	63	7	0	10	49	7
Priday, Jacob, Missouri	.332	211	47	70	15	1	16	65	7
Mercer, Jordy, Oklahoma State	.330	273	56	90	12	2	14	60	5
Faunce, Nick, Kansas	.326	141	30	46	9	2	3	13	0
Hansen, Shaver, Baylor	.326	221	48	72	16	6	6	47	8

BIG WEST CONFERENCE

	Conference		Overall	
	W	L	W	L
*Long Beach State	16	8	38	21
Cal State Fullerton	16	8	41	22
UC Irvine	14	10	42	18
UC Santa Barbara	14	10	35	21
UC Riverside	14	10	21	33
UC Davis	13	11	35	24
Cal Poly	8	16	24	32
Cal State Northridge	8	16	24	32
Pacific	5	19	14	41

ALL-CONFERENCE TEAM: C—Jake Jefferies, Jr., UC Davis. 1B—Shane Peterson, Jr., Long Beach State. 2B—Drew Garcia, Jr., UC Riverside. 3B—Brent Morel, Jr., Cal Poly. SS—Ben Orloff, Jr., UC Irvine. OF—Erik Komatsu, Jr., Cal State Fullerton; Logan Schafer, Jr., Cal Poly; Mike Zuanich, Sr., UC Santa Barbara. DH—Ryan Scoma, Jr., UC Davis. UTIL—Aaron Wible, Sr., UC Riverside. SP—Scott Gorgen, Jr., UC Irvine; Jeff Kaplan, Sr., Cal State Fullerton; Andrew Liebel, Long Beach State. RP—Christian Bergman, So., UC Irvine. CP—Eric Pettis, So., UC Irvine.
Players of the Year: Jake Jefferies, UC Davis; Shane Peterson, Long Beach State. **Pitchers of the Year:** Scott Gorgen, UC Irvine; Jeff Kaplan, Cal State Fullerton; Andrew Liebel, Long Beach State. **Freshman Player of the Year:** Ryan Pineda, Cal State Northridge. **Freshman Pitcher of the Year:** Mario Hollands, UC Santa Barbara. **Coach of the Year:** Mike Weathers, Long Beach State.

INDIVIDUAL BATTING LEADERS
(Minimum 125 At-Bats)

	AVG	AB	R	H	2B	3B	HR	RBI	SB
Kelly, Ty, UC Davis	.397	237	55	94	17	1	4	39	2
Peterson, Shane, Long Beach State	.390	213	52	83	16	2	7	50	9
Jefferies, Jake, UC Davis	.387	248	47	96	20	1	4	54	5
Morel, Brent, Cal Poly	.368	239	49	88	18	5	8	**60**	7
Schafer, Logan, Cal Poly	.365	230	45	84	17	5	9	49	6
Cusick, Jeff, UC Irvine	.363	157	28	57	16	2	0	29	4
Scoma, Ryan, UC Davis	.358	215	31	77	16	2	3	52	3
Lee, Ryan, Cal Poly	.357	196	34	70	11	3	0	21	13
Rose, Patrick, UC Santa Barbara	.357	182	41	65	11	5	1	29	8
Komatsu, Erik, Cal State Fullerton	.355	231	47	82	16	**6**	9	54	21

COLLEGE BASEBALL

Name	AVG	AB	R	H	2B	3B	HR	RBI	SB
Cates, Richard, Cal State Northridge	.350	206	37	72	16	4	2	42	2
Carlson, Shane, UC Santa Barbara	.349	212	39	74	14	2	6	53	1
Parham, John, Cal State Northridge	.348	207	37	72	9	0	6	32	0
Yoder, Luke, Cal Poly	.345	174	51	60	13	2	8	33	11
Garcia, Drew, UC Riverside	.344	218	33	75	14	1	4	51	5
Orloff, Ben, UC Irvine	.344	227	50	78	17	0	0	23	19
Jones, Jonathan, Long Beach State	.343	169	38	58	9	1	0	18	6
Fox, Chris, UC Santa Barbara	.341	220	44	75	7	4	4	39	23
Royster, Ryan, UC Davis	.336	238	63	80	11	2	10	37	13
Fellhauer, Josh, Cal State Fullerton	.335	269	62	90	24	4	7	40	17
Gonzales, Joey, UC Riverside	.330	215	48	71	10	3	4	29	15
Colon, Christian, Cal State Fullerton	.329	243	59	80	12	2	4	39	13
Zuanich, Mike, UC Santa Barbara	.327	211	47	69	9	2	14	57	2
Bell, Dillon, UC Irvine	.326	144	28	47	7	1	5	30	2
Pineda, Ryan, UC Northridge	.326	191	38	62	17	2	6	32	0
Linton, Ollie, UC Irvine	.324	244	59	79	8	1	4	36	40
Longmire, Nick, Pacific	.323	198	27	64	10	3	3	31	9
Ching, Adam, Pacific	.323	223	37	72	16	2	5	27	8
Weeks, Joel, Cal State Fullerton	.322	227	37	73	13	1	2	38	4
Gump, Brian, UC Santa Barbara	.318	239	51	76	15	3	4	36	25
#Espinosa, Danny, Long Beach State	.309	230	48	71	13	6	4	37	9
#Dorrell, Wes, Cal Poly	.304	207	33	63	24	2	5	54	0
#Clark, Jared, Cal State Fullerton	.294	214	39	63	24	0	9	53	6

INDIVIDUAL PITCHING LEADERS
(Minimum 50 Innings)

Name	W	L	ERA	G	SV	IP	H	BB	SO
Bergman, Christian, UC Irvine	5	2	1.94	25	0	60	59	16	37
Quirarte, Edwin, Cal State Northridge	4	4	2.09	29	8	56	49	20	38
Liebel, Andrew, Long Beach State	8	4	2.22	15	0	117	104	19	97
Gorgen, Scott, UC Irvine	12	3	2.26	17	0	116	72	40	123
Gamboa, Eddie, UC Davis	7	3	2.61	15	0	100	96	14	66
#Pettis, Eric, UC Irvine	4	3	2.62	31	17	45	37	20	50
Ford, Mike, UC Santa Barbara	6	4	2.96	14	0	94	78	37	76
Bibona, Daniel, UC Irvine	9	3	3.08	20	0	102	97	21	97
McAtee, Brad, UC Davis	8	5	3.18	15	0	102	106	24	64
Stowell, Bryce, UC Irvine	8	3	3.26	16	0	88	82	36	101
Martin, Michael, UC Santa Barbara	6	3	3.82	22	1	78	77	24	45
Hollands, Mario, UC Santa Barbara	7	3	4.03	14	1	83	89	26	61
Hann, Phil, Cal State Northridge	4	6	4.05	14	0	91	107	13	48
Mauldin, D.J., Cal Poly	5	5	4.08	21	4	57	59	24	49
Renken, Daniel, Cal State Fullerton	5	5	4.11	16	0	81	97	22	80
Eskew, Jared, Cal Poly	5	4	4.11	17	0	70	89	20	50
Morrison, Michael, Cal State Fullerton	2	2	4.14	27	0	54	54	24	55
Worley, Vance, Long Beach State	7	4	4.27	15	0	103	126	12	70
Huggins, Chuck, UC Santa Barbara	8	3	4.40	14	0	86	81	26	77
Kaplan, Jeff, Cal State Fullerton	11	3	4.43	18	1	112	120	36	92
Arbiso, Cory, Cal State Fullerton	12	3	4.46	16	0	103	119	15	72
#Dovel, Jason, Cal State Fullerton	3	4	5.32	31	0	47	41	18	45

COLONIAL ATHLETIC ASSOCIATION

	Conference		Overall	
	W	L	W	L
UNC Wilmington	25	4	44	17
*James Madison	20	9	39	19
George Mason	18	10	30	25
William & Mary	16	13	36	21
Old Dominion	14	14	25	27
Towson	14	16	30	28
Georgia State	12	17	33	23
Northeastern	12	17	25	26
Delaware	11	17	22	31
Virginia Commonwealth	8	17	15	30
Hofstra	7	23	19	36

ALL-CONFERENCE TEAM: C—Mark Carver, Sr., UNC Wilmington. 1B—Mike Sheridan, Jr., William & Mary. 2B—Daniel Hargrave, Sr., UNC Wilmington. 3B—Nate Hall, Sr., UNC Wilmington. SS—Mike Lyon, Sr., Northeastern. OF—Jason Appel, Sr., UNC Wilmington; Brett Sellers, Jr., James Madison; Ben Guez, Jr., William & Mary. DH—Derek Simmons, Jr., Georgia State. UTIL—Mike Tamsin, Jr., Northeastern. SP—Brad Holt, Jr., UNC Wilmington; Jeff Hatcher, Sr., UNC Wilmington. RP—Sheldon McDonald, So., Northeastern.
Player of the Year: Mark Carver, UNC Wilmington. Defensive Player of the Year: Nick Natoli, Towson. Rookie of the Year: Cameron Roth, UNC Wilmington. Coaches of the Year: Mark Scalf, UNC Wilmington; Bill Brown, George Mason.

INDIVIDUAL BATTING LEADERS
(Minimum 125 At-Bats)

Name	AVG	AB	R	H	2B	3B	HR	RBI	SB
Sheridan, Mike, William & Mary	.423	227	76	96	26	1	15	72	9
Park, Tim, William & Mary	.418	220	67	92	25	1	14	62	8
Sellers, Brett, James Madison	.410	222	57	91	18	3	17	55	16
Bour, Justin, George Mason	.398	221	57	88	14	0	15	65	0
Appel, Jason, UNC Wilmington	.397	252	64	100	16	5	5	53	21
Guez, Ben, William & Mary	.390	231	75	90	18	3	13	51	15
Krieger, Scott, George Mason	.381	218	64	83	16	2	21	60	4
Tamsin, Mike, Northeastern	.380	192	31	73	12	1	2	26	0
Simmons, Derek, Georgia State	.379	182	43	69	14	1	6	32	7
Logan, Bradley, Georgia State	.376	226	61	85	21	1	11	63	12
Miles, Jimmy, Old Dominion	.366	224	57	82	13	4	3	40	38
Lyon, Mike, Northeastern	.357	199	49	71	19	3	14	46	6
Maliniak, Greg, William & Mary	.356	222	43	79	15	1	12	59	4
Rochon-Salvas, J.M., Georgia State	.356	194	45	69	7	1	2	33	14
Foltz, Alex, James Madison	.355	214	57	76	13	4	7	38	19
Bolden, Jared, VCU	.355	172	42	61	14	2	12	44	12
Conley, Brian, Towson	.352	216	50	76	16	1	12	65	5
Cuneo, Ryan, Delaware	.351	154	30	54	13	1	6	48	1
Van Horn, Matt, Georgia State	.350	143	33	50	10	3	6	35	6
Tsakonas, Adam, Delaware	.349	146	41	51	13	1	12	33	4
Natoli, Nick, Towson	.349	215	54	75	13	1	3	37	17
Hall, Nate, UNC Wilmington	.348	227	53	79	19	0	13	66	7
Carver, Mark, UNC Wilmington	.347	236	71	82	16	3	21	82	3
Caseres, Steven, James Madison	.342	222	63	76	20	2	21	70	3
Henderson, Chris, George Mason	.339	233	55	79	20	2	5	41	4
Lake, Joe, James Madison	.338	225	47	76	15	1	2	35	10
Stifler, Jason, Towson	.337	175	29	59	9	1	10	40	3
Hargrave, Daniel, UNC Wilmington	.335	260	71	87	19	2	18	62	6
Stampone, Tyler, William & Mary	.333	228	51	76	19	2	3	31	15
Williamson, James, William & Mary	.333	168	30	56	11	2	1	28	10
Nickle, Robbie, William & Mary	.331	175	34	58	13	3	10	48	13
#Hogan, Nick, Georgia State	.306	193	48	59	6	5	2	28	16

INDIVIDUAL PITCHING LEADERS
(Minimum 50 Innings)

Name	W	L	ERA	G	SV	IP	H	BB	SO
McDonald, Sheldon, Northeastern	9	2	2.86	21	1	57	48	23	72
Kantakevich, Pat, William & Mary	5	3	3.08	32	10	50	43	22	40
Holt, Brad, UNC Wilmington	11	1	3.18	15	0	93	78	36	95
Palmer, Will, Georgia State	4	3	3.57	15	0	81	75	37	50
Bergh, Ryan, Old Dominion	6	6	3.57	19	2	91	86	36	45
Salefsky, Larry, UNC Wilmington	4	3	3.66	29	4	52	52	21	38
Grieve, Sean, William & Mary	4	1	3.71	31	6	53	53	23	56
#Roth, Cameron, UNC Wilmington	5	3	3.77	33	4	45	41	16	37
Phelps, Turner, James Madison	8	0	3.87	21	1	77	62	45	86
Brecko, Ryan, George Mason	7	2	3.94	20	4	62	54	21	29
Mengle, Kris, George Mason	4	2	4.25	14	0	66	54	17	37
Polanco, Robinson, Georgia State	8	4	4.35	14	0	89	79	36	71
Hatcher, Jeff, UNC Wilmington	6	2	4.42	15	0	98	95	14	52
Kumbatovic, Rob, Hofstra	2	7	4.56	12	0	79	107	20	54
Thomas, Ian, VCU	3	3	4.60	13	0	61	76	18	45
Hudson, Dan, Old Dominion	5	6	4.70	13	0	92	88	33	107
Hurd, Austin, Towson	1	2	4.85	21	1	52	63	30	29
Houck, Kurt, James Madison	7	2	4.90	16	0	78	78	31	73
Eppley, Cody, VCU	6	5	4.91	13	0	92	99	27	63
Frankoff, Seth, UNC Wilmington	5	2	5.10	15	0	78	92	26	52
Gerjets, Dan, George Mason	6	3	5.16	13	0	68	78	21	43
#Squatrito, Josh, Towson	2	5	7.32	27	10	52	60	17	66

CONFERENCE USA

	Conference		Overall	
	W	L	W	L
Rice	21	3	47	15
Southern Mississippi	15	9	42	22
Tulane	13	9	39	22
*Houston	14	10	42	24
East Carolina	13	11	42	21

COLLEGE BASEBALL

BaseballAmerica.com

Marshall	10	13	30	30
Central Florida	8	16	31	27
Alabama-Birmingham	7	17	26	34
Memphis	5	18	17	38

ALL-CONFERENCE TEAM: C—Corey Kemp, Sr., East Carolina. **IF**—James Ewing, Jr., Southern Mississippi; Ryan Keedy, Sr., Alabama-Birmingham; Bryan Pounds, Sr., Houston; Diego Seastrunk, So., Rice. **OF**—Harrison Eldridge, Sr., East Carolina; Nate Lape, Jr., Marshall; Jake Stewart, Sr., Houston. **DH/UT**—Anthony Scelfo, Jr., Tulane. **P**—Ryan Berry, So., Rice; Barry Bowden, Sr., Southern Mississippi; Shooter Hunt, Jr., Tulane; Seth Maness, Fr., East Carolina. **RP**—Tyler Conn, Sr., Southern Mississippi.
Player of the Year: Corey Kemp, East Carolina. **Pitcher of the Year:** Shooter Hunt, Tulane. **Freshman of the Year:** Seth Maness, East Carolina. **Newcomer of the Year:** Justin Bristow, East Carolina. **Coach of the Year:** Wayne Graham, Rice.

INDIVIDUAL BATTING LEADERS
(Minimum 125 At-Bats)

	AVG	AB	R	H	2B	3B	HR	RBI	SB
Keedy, Ryan, UAB	.423	234	61	99	29	0	10	69	5
Lape, Nate, Marshall	.388	214	62	83	17	0	17	63	20
Brown, Shane, Central Florida	.367	169	39	62	14	0	9	49	2
Ewing, James, Southern Miss.	.359	198	36	71	13	2	5	46	1
Gomez, Victor, Marshall	.358	215	34	77	9	3	11	47	1
Bailey, Dwayne, Central Florida	.356	216	47	77	10	3	0	28	21
Pounds, Bryan, Houston	.354	257	58	91	18	1	10	67	7
Seastrunk, Diego , Rice	.353	258	58	91	19	1	6	61	1
Eldridge, Harrison, East Carolina	.352	247	61	87	15	3	6	39	32
Ray, Jamie, East Carolina	.350	223	38	78	10	4	7	53	12
Padron, J.P., Rice	.349	238	48	83	13	0	5	41	7
Hague, Rick, Rice	.348	233	40	81	19	2	8	54	4
Henderson, Brandon, E. Carolina	.347	245	52	85	18	0	11	52	3
Dozier, Brian, Southern Miss.	.342	269	45	92	17	2	5	46	5
Kemp, Corey, East Carolina	.341	226	62	77	11	0	18	72	2
Hardy, Brint, UAB	.338	201	42	68	6	2	5	28	24
Batts, Stephen, East Carolina	.333	240	65	80	13	1	10	45	14
Stewart, Jake, Houston	.332	256	74	85	24	2	14	53	25
Richardson, Ryan, Central Florida	.332	184	35	61	8	4	5	31	10
Lormand, Ryan, Houston	.330	270	58	89	21	2	4	59	29
Cesario, Jimmy, Houston	.326	221	54	72	15	2	9	41	11
Crawford, Nick, UAB	.326	197	50	64	5	1	0	27	7
Arnold, Collin, Central Florida	.325	231	47	75	17	0	1	37	14
Merritt, Jonathan, UAB	.324	241	68	78	14	1	9	30	15
Yeager, Adam, Marshall	.322	245	59	79	9	5	2	20	47
Segedin, Rob, Tulane	.322	233	37	75	18	1	6	59	2
Scelfo, Anthony, Tulane	.322	230	72	74	9	7	12	54	8
Harrington, Dustin, East Carolina	.320	219	35	70	8	1	4	42	5
Matesich, Chris, Southern Miss.	.319	188	27	60	8	1	7	35	2
Henry, Seth, Tulane	.319	229	40	73	18	4	7	54	13
#Kelso, Blake, Houston	.288	274	58	79	15	3	3	35	19

INDIVIDUAL PITCHING LEADERS
(Minimum 50 Innings)

	W	L	ERA	G	SV	IP	H	BB	SO
#Conn, Tyler, Southern Miss.	1	0	1.72	27	18	37	31	15	42
Bowden, Barry, Southern Miss.	8	3	2.12	12	0	72	49	22	78
Dempsay, Chase, Houston	8	3	2.53	33	11	64	47	19	49
Hunt, Shooter, Tulane	9	4	2.68	16	0	101	62	56	126
Petiton, Matt, Tulane	7	1	2.73	15	0	69	45	23	44
Kelley, Chris, Rice	5	1	3.03	17	0	74	91	22	61
St. Clair, Cole, Rice	10	3	3.03	24	5	62	54	16	67
Herold, Mitch, Central Florida	4	4	3.04	14	0	74	66	31	70
Briston, Justin, East Carolina	9	2	3.07	16	0	94	81	27	84
Ruhlman, Josh, East Carolina	4	4	3.26	36	2	58	45	28	48
Maness, Seth, East Carolina	9	2	3.57	16	0	98	99	20	81
Berry, Ryan, Rice	8	5	3.63	17	0	104	103	31	86
Weathers, Wade, Southern Miss.	4	1	3.81	32	2	57	52	15	52
Touchton, John, Houston	5	4	4.18	22	2	65	69	20	57
Straily, Dan, Marshall	5	4	4.28	16	0	82	81	32	57
Musick, Wes, Houston	8	4	4.35	18	0	97	98	41	87
Blevins, Steve, Marshall	9	3	4.41	15	0	98	98	31	78
Hose, T.J., East Carolina	7	4	4.46	17	0	81	80	39	72
Langwell, Matt, Rice	5	1	4.52	17	0	74	78	29	64
Wright, Chris, Houston	1	0	4.59	29	2	51	59	17	49

HORIZON LEAGUE

	Conference		Overall	
	W	L	W	L
*Illinois-Chicago	17	6	35	22
Wright State	16	6	30	23
Youngstown State	13	12	23	33
Cleveland State	10	13	22	31
Wisconsin-Milwaukee	11	15	25	36
Valparaiso	8	13	21	35
Butler	7	17	12	34

ALL-CONFERENCE TEAM: C—Gerald Ogrinc, So., Wright State. **1B**—Jeremy Hamilton, Jr., Wright State. **2B**—Jesse Hart, Sr., Wisconsin-Milwaukee. **3B**—Alex Kerins, Sr., Cleveland State. **SS**—Justin Parker, Jr., Wright State. **OF**—Brad Buell, Jr., Cleveland State; Zach Rodeghero, Sr., Valparaiso; Nick Wichser, Jr., Wisconsin-Milwaukee. **DH**—Jeff Mercer, Jr., Wright State. **UTIL**—Andy Gerhartz, Jr., Wisconsin-Milwaukee. **P**—Jon Durket, Jr., Wright State; Aaron Swenson, So., Youngstown State.
Player of the Year: Jeremy Hamilton, Wright State. **Pitcher of the Year:** Aaron Swenson, Youngstown State. **Relief Pitcher of the Year:** Adam Worthington, Illinois-Chicago. **Newcomer of the Year:** Derrick Miramontes, Illinois-Chicago. **Coaches of the Year:** Mike Dee, Illinois-Chicago; Rich Pasquale, Youngstown State.

INDIVIDUAL BATTING LEADERS
(Minimum 125 At-Bats)

	AVG	AB	R	H	2B	3B	HR	RBI	SB
Rodeghero, Zach, Valparaiso	.418	220	53	92	21	1	4	54	5
Hamilton, Jeremy, Wright State	.410	183	60	75	21	4	9	50	6
Parker, Justin, Wright State	.395	177	44	70	20	0	8	53	8
Schaefer, Brett, Illinois-Chicago	.382	212	51	81	15	2	10	61	6
McGuiggan, Steve, Illinois-Chicago	.370	230	49	85	10	5	3	40	14
Iacobucci, Joe, Youngstown State	.369	176	29	65	12	1	3	33	1
Wozniak, Shawn, Wis.-Milwaukee	.364	220	42	80	26	0	6	51	3
Wichser, Nick, Wis.-Milwaukee	.357	235	61	84	22	0	6	54	9
McGrew, Casey, Wright State	.346	179	36	62	14	1	4	27	4
Hart, Jesse, Wis.-Milwaukee	.346	257	58	89	28	0	7	64	8
Mercer, Jeff, Wright State	.345	203	37	70	20	1	7	53	0
Diedrich, Erich, Youngstown State	.342	161	38	55	11	1	4	33	7
DeBruin, Dan, Valparaiso	.338	222	51	75	16	5	0	23	7
Buell, Brad, Cleveland State	.332	208	55	69	17	2	2	25	23
Carr, Jake, Illinois-Chicago	.332	202	43	67	16	2	4	39	8
Kerins, Alex, Cleveland State	.330	212	50	70	19	0	11	52	16
Wegner, Shaun, Wis.-Milwaukee	.329	149	35	49	12	0	2	23	11
Porter, Anthony, Youngstown State	.323	186	18	60	13	0	1	32	0
Vagedes, Ross, Wright State	.322	199	36	64	15	3	6	39	7
Altavilla, Tony, Illinois-Chicago	.321	140	30	45	8	1	1	20	19
Bischof, Kyle, Cleveland State	.313	201	32	63	12	0	8	47	5
Wallace, Josh, Valparaiso	.313	182	33	57	6	1	11	48	1
Page, Josh, Youngstown State	.313	214	33	67	14	0	3	22	7
Ziegel, Colin, Butler	.311	151	26	47	12	4	6	30	5
Heideman, Adam, Cleveland State	.310	142	28	44	7	1	3	16	8
Ogrinc, Gerald, Wright State	.310	168	27	52	9	0	2	28	2
Lucas, Sean, Youngstown State	.309	230	40	71	15	3	2	33	12
Rubio, Ty, Illinois-Chicago	.308	182	43	56	9	0	0	24	14
Cash, Bobby, Cleveland State	.307	189	18	58	8	1	3	27	15
#Pauley, Joe, Butler	.295	173	38	51	8	0	13	42	3
#Kopilchack, John, Wright State	.281	199	32	56	11	6	11	40	1

INDIVIDUAL PITCHING LEADERS
(Minimum 50 Innings)

	W	L	ERA	G	SV	IP	H	BB	SO
Durket, Jon, Wright State	7	2	3.24	19	0	75	74	22	55
Swenson, Aaron, Youngstown State	6	3	3.55	15	0	99	97	14	65
Miramontes, Derrick, Illinois-Chicago	6	2	3.79	19	0	97	106	23	47
Schiffhauer, Chuck, Youngstown State	1	6	3.84	16	0	80	91	26	36
Long, Brian, Cleveland State	4	5	3.98	14	0	81	92	13	51
Kaminsky, Alex, Wright State	8	2	3.98	18	0	61	62	18	31
Kool, Mike, Illinois-Chicago	6	5	4.07	19	0	91	106	25	33
Lusti, Brad, Wis.-Milwaukee	4	4	4.24	17	0	98	119	25	53
Gibbs, Elliott, Valparaiso	1	5	4.94	12	0	58	75	20	43
Sinkiewicz, Jeff, Butler	1	5	4.95	13	0	64	82	9	24
Hungerman, Josh, Cleveland State	5	3	5.11	12	0	79	85	31	64
Ferrell, Adam, Wis.-Milwaukee	3	5	5.35	29	6	71	83	25	47

COLLEGE BASEBALL

	W	L	ERA	G	SV	IP	H	BB	SO
Gulbransen, Jon, Valparaiso	3	7	5.37	15	0	62	72	24	52
Phillis, Don, Illinois-Chicago	6	1	5.50	26	3	56	67	19	41
Vukovic, Corey, Youngstown State	2	3	5.59	15	0	58	79	10	29
Kalafos, Adam, Youngstown State	5	3	5.69	17	0	62	72	34	59
Kruszka, Ryan, Butler	2	3	5.70	14	0	54	60	30	34
Suitca, Sam, Cleveland State	1	6	5.95	14	0	59	83	19	26
Shafer, Bryce, Valparaiso	4	5	6.24	15	0	71	76	31	50
Hetebrueg, Andy, Wis.-Milwaukee	6	6	6.57	17	0	86	117	34	50

IVY LEAGUE

GEHRIG	Conference		Overall	
	W	L	W	L
*Columbia	15	5	22	30
Princeton	11	9	20	22
Pennsylvania	6	13	15	23
Cornell	6	14	12	27

ROLFE	W	L	W	L
Dartmouth	15	5	25	17
Yale	9	10	20	24
Brown	9	11	20	24
Harvard	8	12	10	30

ALL-CONFERENCE TEAM: C—Jack Murphy, So., Princeton. **1B**—Mike Pagliarulo, Jr., Dartmouth. **2B**—Henry Perkins, Sr., Columbia. **3B**—Spencer Lucian, Sr., Princeton. **SS**—Erik Bell, Sr., Dartmouth. **OF**—Damon Wright, Sr., Dartmouth; Josh Cox, Sr., Yale; Nick Santomauro, So., Dartmouth. **UTIL**—Nathan Ford, Jr., Cornell. **DH**—Conor Reardon, Sr., Brown; Noah Cooper, Sr., Columbia. **P**—Russell Young, Sr., Dartmouth; John Baumann, Sr., Columbia. **RP**—Steve Gilman, Sr., Yale.
Player of the Year: Henry Perkins, Columbia. **Pitcher of the Year:** Russell Young, Dartmouth. **Rookie of the Year:** Nick Cox, Columbia.

INDIVIDUAL BATTING LEADERS
(Minimum 100 At-Bats)

	AVG	AB	R	H	2B	3B	HR	RBI	SB
Lucian, Spencer, Princeton	.425	146	31	62	14	0	4	34	10
Ford, Nathan, Cornell	.410	144	24	59	**17**	2	3	28	2
Lavarnway, Ryan, Yale	.398	108	28	43	7	0	**13**	42	4
Wright, Damon, Dartmouth	.397	151	35	60	10	3	9	39	7
Reardon, Conor, Brown	.395	157	30	62	10	0	1	25	0
Murphy, Jack, Princeton	.391	156	33	61	11	1	8	40	0
Cox, Josh, Yale	.377	191	38	**72**	14	2	0	14	21
Gable, Steve, Pennsylvania	.372	148	25	55	6	0	1	33	3
Pagliarulo, Michael, Dartmouth	.370	146	38	54	8	1	6	30	0
Colantonio, Matt, Brown	.368	136	37	50	8	0	0	25	2
Santomauro, Nick, Dartmouth	.364	162	44	59	10	5	11	**45**	0
Punal, Nick, Brown	.364	143	33	52	8	0	1	35	7
Perkins, Henry, Columbia	.363	193	41	70	16	**6**	3	34	20
Onstott, Jeff, Dartmouth	.356	160	30	57	11	0	2	22	5
Cox, Nick, Columbia	.355	200	46	71	13	5	1	21	**28**
Wren, James, Dartmouth	.346	130	24	45	7	1	1	24	2
Schropp, Stefan, Yale	.345	148	23	51	9	0	0	17	10
Daniels, Steve, Brown	.341	185	42	63	4	1	1	21	19
Di Ricco, Domenic, Cornell	.324	136	31	44	7	1	1	15	8
Blydell, Jason, Dartmouth	.321	131	26	42	6	3	0	24	5
Banos, Jason, Columbia	.316	171	40	54	**17**	0	4	31	10
Gorynski, P.J., Yale	.315	143	33	45	8	0	7	27	10
Turnham, Adrian, Princeton	.306	157	25	48	5	0	3	34	0
Bell, Erik, Dartmouth	.305	167	38	51	10	0	6	34	4
Armeny, Kyle, Pennsylvania	.302	129	21	39	5	0	6	27	2
Cooper, Noah, Columbia	.299	174	25	52	8	1	2	16	10
Nuzzo, Matt, Brown	.298	181	39	54	12	1	6	40	3
Zrenda, Ryan, Brown	.298	131	26	39	5	0	2	29	1
Gordon, William, Pennsylvania	.292	130	16	38	13	2	4	19	2
Forthun, Dean, Columbia	.292	161	17	47	11	2	0	22	2
#DeGeorge, Dan, Princeton	.273	172	47	47	9	1	2	17	9

INDIVIDUAL PITCHING LEADERS
(Minimum 40 Innings)

	W	L	ERA	G	SV	IP	H	BB	SO
#Smith, Ryan, Dartmouth	2	2	2.25	19	**7**	36	35	14	28
Roth, Todd, Pennsylvania	4	5	**2.32**	14	0	62	50	17	54
Gemberling, Brad, Princeton	2	1	3.60	9	0	45	44	14	45
Irving, Brian, Yale	4	3	3.86	9	0	51	53	22	**59**

	W	L	ERA	G	SV	IP	H	BB	SO
Hill, Matt, Cornell	5	3	4.25	11	1	55	53	22	36
Unger, Brad, Harvard	2	5	4.35	10	0	52	52	20	30
Miller, Steven, Princeton	3	2	4.36	12	0	54	57	21	55
Young, Russell, Dartmouth	5	4	4.55	9	0	65	85	12	55
Staehely, Christian, Princeton	**6**	2	4.91	9	0	55	62	12	49
Warren, Max, Harvard	1	4	4.91	11	0	44	52	14	24
Weidig, Will, Brown	4	4	4.93	9	0	49	52	19	45
Hale, David, Princeton	2	4	5.04	9	0	45	50	23	47
Young, Robert, Dartmouth	4	2	5.27	10	0	56	83	8	38
Haviland, Shawn, Harvard	2	6	5.56	12	1	57	86	6	51
Carpenter, Chase, Dartmouth	5	2	5.79	9	0	56	80	18	22
Cusick, Paul, Pennsylvania	1	4	6.18	14	0	39	43	35	35
Pappel, Corey, Cornell	2	5	6.25	10	0	45	51	29	36
Purdy, Bill, Columbia	4	5	6.30	12	1	**70**	110	17	41
Whitaker, Geoff, Columbia	**6**	3	7.21	13	0	59	94	9	38
Josselyn, Brandon, Yale	2	7	7.28	12	0	47	71	9	38
Scarlata, Joe, Columbia	5	5	7.35	12	0	64	88	21	43
#Lally, Vinny, Yale	1	1	6.04	**23**	0	22	21	14	21
#Walsh, Chris, Yale	1	3	12.00	**23**	0	24	45	15	11

METRO ATLANTIC CONFERENCE

	Conference		Overall	
	W	L	W	L
Canisius	19	5	41	13
Manhattan	19	5	31	30
Siena	15	8	30	26
*Rider	13	10	29	28
Fairfield	11	13	14	36
Niagara	10	14	22	28
Marist	8	15	19	28
Saint Peter's	7	16	20	30
Iona	4	20	4	44

ALL-CONFERENCE TEAM: C—Kevin Reimer, Jr., Cansius; Domenic Lombardi, Manhattan. **1B**—Sean Olson, Sr., Rider. **2B**—Kevin Mailloux, Jr., Canisius. **3B**—Kevin Mahoney, Jr., Canisius; Jacob Willis, Sr., Siena. **SS**—Richard Curylo, Jr., Marist. **OF**—Adam Donato, Sr., Canisius; Kevin Nieto, Jr., Manhattan; Tim Alberts, Sr., Niagra. **DH**—Albie DeSimone, Sr., Fairfield. **UTIL**—Jamie Hayes, Sr., Rider. **P**—Shane Davis, Fr., Canisius; Rob Gariano, So., Fairfield; Josh Rickards, Sr., Marist.
Player of the Year: Jacob Willis, Siena. **Pitcher of the Year:** Shane Davis, Canisius. **Relief Pitcher of the Year:** Jamie Hayes, Rider. **Rookie of the Year:** Shane Davis, Canisius. **Coach of the Year:** Mike McRae, Canisius.

INDIVIDUAL BATTING LEADERS
(Minimum 125 At-Bats)

	AVG	AB	R	H	2B	3B	HR	RBI	SB
Nieto, Kevin, Manhattan	.386	153	50	59	14	**6**	2	47	21
Mailloux, Kevin, Canisius	.377	204	**56**	77	14	1	**12**	**53**	8
Reimer, Kevin, Canisius	.369	141	36	52	11	0	3	42	6
Mahoney, Kevin, Canisius	.369	179	51	66	13	2	**12**	52	8
Willis, Jacob, Siena	.367	218	47	**80**	14	0	10	36	2
Lombardi, Dom, Manhattan	.353	167	48	59	13	3	3	38	13
Donato, Adam, Canisius	.351	171	52	60	15	2	10	37	10
Alberts, Tim, Niagara	.348	181	43	63	15	2	7	36	13
Klepps, Chris, Siena	.343	207	54	71	**23**	1	4	35	4
Onorati, Mark, Manhattan	.337	187	54	63	14	1	7	31	10
Hayes, James, Rider	.336	**238**	52	**80**	12	0	1	19	**37**
Nieto, Eric, Manhattan	.335	209	54	70	12	4	1	16	16
Curylo, Richard, Marist	.333	180	27	60	8	2	3	30	11
Heyne, Mason, Rider	.332	190	32	63	18	0	6	44	1
Williams, Maurice, Rider	.330	200	35	66	9	2	5	41	2
Olson, Sean, Rider	.327	220	49	72	17	0	11	52	6
DeFilippo, Jason, Siena	.326	181	30	59	10	1	0	24	25
Nathans, Tucker, Fairfield	.326	175	23	57	9	1	4	29	5
Kallert, Kevin, Saint Peter's	.324	179	32	58	14	2	5	36	14
Cabello, Alec, Canisius	.321	184	42	59	6	1	0	35	16
Messinger, Nick, Siena	.319	163	38	52	12	4	4	34	12
Harber, Harrison, Niagara	.316	174	33	55	8	2	1	33	10
Tiagwad, Matt, Fairfield	.314	156	23	49	11	0	2	13	1
Kurnik, Frank, Niagara	.313	163	30	51	7	4	1	33	9
Joseph, Branson, Canisius	.312	199	49	62	8	0	11	43	14
Desimone, Albie, Fairfield	.310	174	27	54	5	1	2	21	4

COLLEGE BASEBALL

Alexander, Dennis, Saint Peter's	.309	162	37	50	7	2	0	23	12
Romano, Joe, Saint Peter's	.308	169	25	52	7	0	0	31	9
Rivera, Moises, Siena	.307	166	27	51	7	1	7	42	1
MacDonald, Andrew, Niagara	.306	183	29	56	11	0	2	27	11

INDIVIDUAL PITCHING LEADERS
(Minimum 50 Innings)

	W	L	ERA	G	SV	IP	H	BB	SO
Davis, Shane, Canisius	12	1	2.42	13	0	89	89	24	47
Rickards, Josh, Marist	4	6	2.60	12	0	80	70	36	54
Sveda, Shane, Iona	1	7	2.76	12	0	85	77	29	79
#Hayes, Jamie, Rider	3	2	3.16	22	11	31	26	20	41
MacKenzie, Alex, Canisius	6	3	3.30	13	0	95	99	21	56
Morari, Daniel, Niagara	6	5	3.74	12	0	67	65	20	53
Kennedy, Jimmer, Rider	7	5	4.07	14	0	84	96	13	49
Thomas, Mike, Rider	6	3	4.15	22	0	52	66	15	40
Cary, Richard, Marist	6	2	4.28	11	0	48	61	20	24
Forman, Dan, Manhattan	8	4	4.70	15	1	82	87	48	81
Gariano, Rob, Fairfield	5	5	4.71	15	0	80	84	30	85
Hartman, Zach, Siena	8	1	4.74	14	0	74	77	26	29
Kellar, Michael, Niagara	2	4	4.99	14	1	52	63	31	33
Goemans, Mike, Canisius	7	2	5.07	14	0	76	92	26	37
Petrowski, Mike, Rider	2	6	5.12	15	1	97	111	25	77
Pendergast, Brian, Manhattan	4	4	5.23	18	3	53	57	27	44
#Casino, Matthew, Iona	0	1	5.27	24	1	27	40	11	10
Spaulding, Marcus, Niagara	6	3	5.30	12	0	70	75	29	45
Costigan, Tom, Manhattan	5	2	5.34	16	0	84	99	34	58
Innis, Chris, Saint Peter's	4	4	5.53	13	0	57	69	26	54
Hassett, Will, Siena	4	3	5.64	11	0	53	61	27	26
Chaput, Craig, Siena	5	7	6.00	14	0	87	111	42	70

MID-AMERICAN CONFERENCE

	Conference		Overall	
EAST	W	L	W	L
Kent State	16	8	36	21
Bowling Green State	16	8	32	20
Ohio	14	13	29	30
Akron	8	13	25	24
Miami (Ohio)	8	19	18	36
Buffalo	7	19	14	38
WEST				
*Eastern Michigan	15	8	25	34
Northern Illinois	16	10	28	26
Ball State	12	11	28	25
Western Michigan	12	12	29	23
Central Michigan	13	13	29	27
Toledo	10	13	18	31

ALL-CONFERENCE TEAM: C—Justin Behm, Northern Illinois. **1B**—Greg Rohan, Kent State. **2B**—Josh Ivan, Eastern Michigan. **3B**—Derek Spencer, Bowling Green State. **SS**—Ryan Shay, Bowling Green State; **OF**—Wayne Bond, Ball State; Matt Stiffler, Ohio; Chris Lewis, Western Michigan. **SP**—Chris Carpenter, Kent State; Kyle Smith, Kent State; Ethan Hollingsworth, Western Michigan; Brian Stroud, Western Michigan. **RP**—Kyle Heyne, Ball State. **DH**—Kurt Davidson, Akron. **UTIL**—Marc Krauss, Ohio.
Player of the Year: Greg Rohan, Kent State. **Pitcher of the Year:** Chris Carpenter, Kent State. **Freshman of the Year:** Brian Stroud, Western Michigan. **Coach of the Year:** Jake Boss, Eastern Michigan.

INDIVIDUAL BATTING LEADERS
(Minimum 125 At-Bats)

	AVG	AB	R	H	2B	3B	HR	RBI	SB
Shay, Ryan, Bowling Green	.412	211	53	87	19	0	5	36	15
Lewis, Chris, Western Michigan	.390	182	44	71	13	0	8	49	1
Nurre, Tommy, Miami (Ohio)	.386	202	42	78	22	0	9	48	5
Bradshaw, Steve, E. Michigan	.382	225	49	86	21	2	5	56	3
Sanders, Doug, Kent State	.377	220	51	83	13	3	7	43	3
Besl, Brandon, Ohio	.369	187	35	69	20	1	9	46	0
Foster, Andrew, Bowling Green	.361	191	48	69	17	2	6	38	7
Spencer, Derek, Bowling Green	.360	186	38	67	13	2	10	54	1
Tremblay, Chris, Kent State	.359	217	54	78	20	5	4	32	4
Rohan, Greg, Kent State	.355	197	50	70	18	2	20	61	0
Stiffler, Matt, Ohio	.354	257	75	91	15	6	18	58	7

Petraitis, Jordan, Miami (Ohio)	.352	216	46	76	19	4	8	46	5
Klimko, Chris, Ohio	.351	188	32	66	9	0	3	28	0
Thomas, Jeff, Northern Illinois	.350	183	38	64	10	1	2	34	16
Leonard, Zack, Eastern Michigan	.348	227	46	79	17	1	9	51	6
Abro, Matthew, Western Michigan	.347	213	49	74	9	0	8	41	2
Haas, Kevin, Akron	.347	213	52	74	11	3	2	30	2
Kafczynski, Ben, Kent State	.339	165	37	56	11	2	11	35	2
Galvin, Mark, Bowling Green	.339	174	30	59	13	1	6	36	3
Krauss, Marc, Ohio	.332	229	62	76	20	2	10	54	5
Stovall, Tyler, Central Michigan	.332	226	45	75	15	4	6	47	26
Hangbers, Brian, Bowling Green	.331	172	49	57	11	0	13	47	4
Rogers, Justin, Ball State	.331	163	42	54	11	1	8	40	3
Fields, Nate, Ball State	.331	148	33	49	11	1	9	35	7
Rhoad, Kyle, Eastern Michigan	.331	245	61	81	14	3	8	29	19
Ivan, Josh, Eastern Michigan	.330	212	35	70	12	2	7	45	5
Meisler, Logan, Bowling Green	.327	162	27	53	7	2	3	24	6
Davis, Jeff, Eastern Michigan	.327	214	43	70	19	2	6	50	4
Bond, Wayne, Ball State	.327	211	55	69	16	1	14	55	14
#Anna, Dean, Ball State	.319	207	63	66	17	7	11	41	5

INDIVIDUAL PITCHING LEADERS
(Minimum 50 Innings)

	W	L	ERA	G	SV	IP	H	BB	SO
Stangroom, Mike, Buffalo	2	4	3.06	14	0	68	65	21	49
Hernandez, Jesse, Central Michigan	6	4	3.36	20	1	59	63	30	43
Carpenter, Chris, Kent State	6	2	3.81	13	0	76	55	33	88
Hollingsworth, Ethan, W. Michigan	5	3	3.84	13	0	84	85	26	77
Teno, Steve, Central Michigan	7	4	3.91	18	0	90	99	26	55
Elmer, Zach, Ohio	4	4	3.93	14	0	71	66	42	47
Stroud, Brian, Western Michigan	6	0	4.02	13	1	63	43	32	53
Lawrence, Eric, Central Michigan	4	6	4.30	12	0	88	79	29	65
Cantrell, Nick, Bowling Green	8	4	4.60	22	1	59	70	17	50
Turocy, Frank, Akron	6	3	4.62	13	0	78	84	33	51
Smith, Matt, Ohio	4	2	4.64	22	1	78	90	27	45
Erwood, Matt, Miami (Ohio)	3	6	4.69	13	0	79	88	14	56
Holdenrid, Adam, Northern Illinois	5	5	4.75	13	0	78	100	26	51
Berry, Frank, Bowling Green	7	1	4.76	12	0	70	85	22	24
Morrison, Billy, Western Michigan	6	2	4.76	13	0	81	85	26	43
Taylor, Dan, Central Michigan	3	5	4.81	15	0	86	108	24	66
Feeney, Trevor, Northern Illinois	6	4	4.82	13	0	93	116	25	51
#Deain, Andy, Northern Illinois	4	1	4.83	35	10	41	30	32	52
Leady, Kevin, Bowling Green	3	4	5.03	19	3	63	64	25	37
Rigo, Chris, Ohio	6	3	5.07	14	0	98	89	39	77
#Smith, Kyle, Kent State	9	1	5.76	14	0	75	79	37	65

MID-EASTERN ATHLETIC CONFERENCE

	Conference		Overall	
	W	L	W	L
*Bethune-Cookman	17	6	36	22
North Carolina A&T	11	6	29	30
Florida A&M	11	7	20	22
Delaware State	11	7	16	33
Norfolk State	7	9	25	24
Maryland-Eastern Shore	4	9	6	50
Coppin State	0	19	4	52

ALL-CONFERENCE TEAM: C—Brian Vickers, So., Coppin State. **IF**—Charlie Gamble, So., North Carolina A&T; Kevin Hill, Sr., Delaware State; Virgil Priestly, Sr., Florida A&M; Juan Serrano, So., Norfolk State. **OF**—Jeremy Jones, So., North Carolina A&T; David Hampton, Sr., Florida A&M; Nick Wenger, Sr., Coppin State. **DH**—Omar Borges, Jr., Bethune-Cookman. **SP**—Michael Hauff, Jr., North Carolina A&T; J.P. Primus, Fr., North Carolina A&T. **RP**—Jesus Melendez, Jr., Coppin State.
Player of the Year: Jose Lozada, Bethune-Cookman. **Pitcher of the Year:** Hiram Burgos, Bethune-Cookman. **Rookie of the Year:** Tim Jones, Florida A&M. **Coach of the Year:** Mervyl Melendez, Bethune-Cookman.

INDIVIDUAL BATTING LEADERS
(Minimum 125 At-Bats)

	AVG	AB	R	H	2B	3B	HR	RBI	SB
Jones, Jeremy, N.C. A&T	.404	225	65	91	13	3	13	63	14
Lozada, Jose, Bethune-Cookman	.398	211	61	84	15	7	7	57	14
Jeffries, Jared, Florida A&M	.378	164	32	62	11	2	0	23	12
Stephenson, Brad, Norfolk State	.364	143	39	52	14	3	2	33	6

Sanchez, Jose, Delaware State	.347	170	43	59	16	1	6	30	6
Beatty, Christian, N.C. A&T	.339	218	59	74	11	2	13	55	7
Jones, Tim, Florida A&M	.338	139	30	47	10	1	5	30	4
Torres, Osvaldo, Bethune-Cookman	.337	196	40	66	16	1	12	72	3
McIntyre, Joe, N.C. A&T	.332	235	58	78	24	1	7	58	7
Bittner, Justin, Delaware State	.324	173	37	56	16	0	10	51	2
Evans, Darryl, Florida A&M	.321	159	31	51	14	3	1	31	6
Caruso, Rob, Bethune-Cookman	.325	160	33	52	8	0	3	28	4
Ortiz, Jose, Bethune-Cookman	.319	188	46	60	8	0	2	35	18
Rogers, Nick, N.C. A&T	.319	226	33	72	13	1	10	58	3
Joyce, Chris, Norfolk State	.318	176	20	56	12	2	0	44	4
George, Moriba, Norfolk State	.317	161	43	51	3	2	0	11	17
#Vaughn, Phil, UMES	.271	199	41	54	4	3	1	18	23
#Batista, Roman, Coppin State	.209	139	21	29	5	7	2	19	2

INDIVIDUAL PITCHING LEADERS
(Minimum 50 Innings)

	W	L	ERA	G	SV	IP	H	BB	SO
Burgos, Hiram, Bethune-Cookman	9	1	1.58	16	1	80	64	24	69
Thomas, Eric, Bethune-Cookman	9	1	2.48	15	1	76	53	36	74
Gautier, Joseph, Bethune-Cookman	6	3	2.72	14	0	73	53	13	74
Frink, Marquise, N.C. A&T	5	4	2.89	29	5	87	66	50	106
Shabacker, Leon, Norfolk State	6	3	3.13	14	0	83	81	21	65
#Enright, Phil, Bethune-Cookman	2	2	3.18	21	8	28	26	11	30
Barker, Jason, Norfolk State	3	1	3.32	19	1	60	62	24	42
Bright, Quinn, Norfolk State	6	6	3.43	18	0	81	86	18	62
Johnson, Tim, N.C. A&T	9	2	3.58	14	0	103	98	38	106
Seal, Joey, Norfolk State	7	4	3.69	14	2	98	92	33	74
Primus, John, N.C. A&T	6	4	4.67	10	1	71	65	30	53
Eggers, Chris, N.C. A&T	5	6	4.76	29	2	79	90	37	74
Schmidt, Josh, Delaware State	7	5	5.00	13	0	72	90	27	80
Manego, Cirilo, Florida A&M	4	4	5.62	12	1	56	56	40	51
Parga, Miguel, Florida A&M	5	3	5.67	12	0	79	74	49	57
Machado, Felix, Bethune-Cookman	3	4	5.68	17	1	52	63	23	40
Espin, Anthony, Florida A&M	3	6	5.98	13	0	59	63	46	47
Howerton, Donald, N.C. A&T	2	6	6.12	17	0	60	78	41	44
Friel, James, Delaware State	3	6	6.12	17	0	73	89	28	44
McAllister, J.R., Delaware State	3	6	8.13	16	1	80	100	55	75
Arrington, Elliott, UMES	1	8	9.09	22	1	69	110	36	42

MISSOURI VALLEY CONFERENCE

	Conference		Overall	
	W	L	W	L
*Wichita State	19	5	48	17
Missouri State	18	6	40	17
Creighton	16	8	37	21
Northern Iowa	14	10	30	24
Southern Illinois	12	12	34	23
Bradley	10	14	26	28
Indiana State	9	15	18	32
Illinois State	6	18	22	30
Evansville	4	20	14	42

ALL-CONFERENCE TEAM: C—Mark Kelly, Southern Illinois. **1B**—Darin Ruf, Creighton. **2B**—Ryan Stausborger, Indiana State. **SS**—Brandon Douglas, Northern Iowa. **3B**—Conor Gillaspie, Wichita State. **OF**—Andy Dirks, Wichita State; Ben Woodbury, Missouri State; Dan Brewer, Bradley. **DH**—Ben Carlson, Missouri State. **UTIL**—Brett Douglas, Northern Iowa. **SP**—Tim Clubb, Missouri State; Rob Musgrave, Wichita State; Anthony Capra, Wichita State. **RP**—Pat Venditte, Creighton; Matt Frevert, Missouri State.
Player of the Year: Brandon Douglas, Northern Iowa. **Pitcher of the Year:** Tim Clubb, Missouri State. **Newcomer of the Year:** Jeremy Hauer, Creighton. **Freshman of the Year:** Kevin Tokarski, Illinois State.

INDIVIDUAL BATTING LEADERS
(Minimum 125 At-Bats)

	AVG	AB	R	H	2B	3B	HR	RBI	SB
Gillaspie, Conor, Wichita State	.419	234	70	98	16	8	11	82	16
Douglas, Brandon, Northern Iowa	.396	225	51	89	25	4	10	60	10
Woodbury, Ben, Missouri State	.388	237	57	92	16	5	0	47	11
Dirks, Andy, Wichita State	.388	250	84	97	22	3	11	62	26
Carlson, Ben, Missouri State	.377	215	56	81	11	1	17	67	7
Kelly, Mark, Southern Illinois	.375	224	45	84	18	1	4	46	1
Schmidt, Chris, Indiana State	.374	214	44	80	10	3	4	41	21

Luttrell, Colby, Bradley	.363	193	35	70	12	3	6	48	3
Dubler, Kevin, Illinois State	.358	190	47	68	23	3	9	56	15
Embury, Dane, Northern Illinois	.350	203	47	71	9	0	9	42	6
Keane, Nolan, Missouri State	.349	209	56	73	13	3	4	44	12
Ruf, Darin, Creighton	.347	202	43	70	17	1	7	52	2
Drake, Brayden, Missouri State	.342	240	53	82	21	4	6	61	14
Brewer, Dan, Bradley	.341	185	51	63	15	3	6	39	5
McKeever, Clinton, Wichita State	.328	177	34	58	14	0	5	39	2
Jones, Ryan, Wichita State	.326	261	70	85	11	5	2	43	16
Fritz, Matt, Bradley	.326	129	26	42	3	0	1	18	4
Cafaro, Vicente, Creighton	.324	170	39	55	13	2	5	31	6
Strausborger, Ryan, Indiana State	.322	183	43	59	8	4	2	20	8
Hills, Adam, Southern Illinois	.320	172	34	55	12	2	2	21	3
Workman, Josh, Wichita State	.318	176	4	56	11	1	4	33	10
Knight, Robbie, Creighton	.318	214	64	68	15	2	3	30	9
Maugeri, Bret, Southern Illinois	.317	145	24	46	5	0	2	16	1
Wallace, Greg, Evansville	.317	202	28	64	17	2	2	29	5
Featherston, Brett, Northern Iowa	.315	178	40	56	12	0	13	43	4
Escue, Grant, Bradley	.314	207	30	65	17	2	3	35	1
Coleman, Dusty, Wichita State	.314	239	53	75	19	2	8	71	13
Manrique, Deric, Northern Iowa	.312	138	39	43	8	1	3	22	13
Mazzola, Josh, Missouri State	.304	158	39	48	5	1	15	50	1
#Tokarski, Kevin, Illinois State	.303	201	46	61	7	2	0	16	32

INDIVIDUAL PITCHING LEADERS
(Minimum 50 Innings)

	W	L	ERA	G	SV	IP	H	BB	SO
Nihsen, Mike, Creighton	5	2	2.30	15	0	70	61	16	40
Musgrave, Rob, Wichita State	12	1	2.51	16	0	111	99	22	101
Clubb, Tim, Missouri State	11	0	2.52	14	0	104	90	32	82
Flattery, Tim, Northern Iowa	4	0	3.00	24	1	51	56	23	44
Shafer, Aaron, Wichita State	11	4	3.26	16	0	110	104	28	110
Hauer, Jeremy, Creighton	8	2	3.32	18	0	84	74	24	55
Venditte, Pat, Creighton	9	3	3.34	37	7	86	65	21	101
Capra, Anthony, Wichita State	9	1	3.54	15	1	76	61	33	90
Theisen, Eric, Illinois State	5	5	3.74	25	3	53	53	22	25
Adams, Cody, Southern Illinois	6	4	3.75	14	0	96	104	23	78
Kirk, Nick, Northern Iowa	4	7	3.84	13	0	66	62	17	61
Copeland, Ryan, Illinois State	4	7	3.93	14	1	89	99	9	72
Taylor, Zach, Evansville	2	6	4.15	18	0	65	67	28	46
Cox, Tyler, Illinois State	4	4	4.41	13	0	63	70	25	57
Sinclair, Taylor, Northern Iowa	6	3	4.62	13	1	72	83	26	52
Foley, John, Evansville	5	5	4.66	17	1	87	85	45	57
Baumann, Buddy, Missouri State	6	4	4.66	15	1	75	77	41	71
#Gonzalez, Joe, Northern Iowa	1	2	4.82	23	9	28	25	17	13
Kelley, Tim, Wichita State	4	4	4.85	12	0	52	59	9	34
Joy, Shaun, Southern Illinois	6	3	5.01	15	0	93	108	27	41
Meade, Aaron, Missouri State	4	3	5.06	16	0	59	59	32	65

MOUNTAIN WEST CONFERENCE

	Conference		Overall	
	W	L	W	L
*Texas Christian	19	5	44	19
New Mexico	16	8	34	25
San Diego State	16	8	31	28
Utah	10	14	26	28
Brigham Young	10	14	22	36
UNLV	9	15	22	37
Air Force	4	20	18	33

ALL-CONFERENCE TEAM: C—Bryan Holaday, So., TCU. **1B**—Xavier Scruggs, Jr., UNLV. **2B**—Ben Carruthers, Jr., TCU. **3B**—Nick Romero, Jr., San Diego State. **SS**—Troy Hanzawa, Sr., San Diego State. **OF**—Sean McNaughton, So., BYU; Brian Cavazos-Galvez, Jr., New Mexico; Clint Arnold, Sr., TCU. **DH**—Cody Guymon, Jr., Utah. **P**—Stephen Strasburg, So., San Diego State; Tyler Lockwood, So., TCU; Stephen Fife, Jr., Utah. **RP**—Andrew Cashner, Jr., TCU.
Player of the Year: Xavier Scruggs, UNLV. **Pitcher of the Year:** Stephen Strasburg, San Diego State. **Freshman of the Year:** Rafael Neda, New Mexico. **Coach of the Year:** Jim Schlossnagle, Texas Christian.

INDIVIDUAL BATTING LEADERS
(Minimum 125 At-Bats)

	AVG	AB	R	H	2B	3B	HR	RBI	SB
Guymon, Cody, Utah	.383	222	52	85	15	3	5	46	2

Scruggs, Xavier, UNLV	.379	227	60	86	20	2	**20**	**65**	4
Arnold, Clint, TCU	.378	238	57	90	19	0	2	36	16
Beltran, Micheal, Utah	.372	196	20	73	9	0	0	27	4
Hanzawa, Troy, San Diego State	.370	257	54	**95**	15	7	3	50	11
Cavazos-Galves, Brian, New Mexico	.367	210	51	77	17	3	11	55	7
Shriner, Jesse, Utah	.359	220	48	79	19	2	8	47	2
Brownstein, Mike, New Mexico	.350	254	53	89	12	4	2	37	20
Ellington, Steve, TCU	.348	184	32	64	7	2	2	29	0
McNaughton, Sean, BYU	.347	265	**65**	92	**23**	4	14	53	21
Blanc, Cooper, Utah	.345	177	36	61	11	1	7	34	14
Ellington, Chris, TCU	.344	183	34	63	21	2	6	55	3
Parker, Steve, BYU	.340	215	51	73	15	3	10	42	4
Ko, Kasey, BYU	.335	200	36	67	11	0	4	42	3
Romero, Nick, San Diego State	.335	239	39	80	10	2	12	61	5
Atkinson, Kevin, New Mexico	.333	240	47	80	18	4	9	51	8
Hibbitts, Matt, New Mexico	.332	238	50	79	17	0	1	46	7
Gracey, Scott, New Mexico	.332	205	35	68	12	2	0	43	4
Shimada, Corey, Utah	.329	213	**65**	70	13	7	9	29	21
Wight, Jesse, UNLV	.328	195	42	64	14	1	1	24	8
Jones, Austin, Utah	.326	215	37	70	16	0	7	51	1
Sferra, J.J., UNLV	.325	246	46	80	13	3	1	27	5
Hennis, Dustin, Utah	.325	203	39	66	11	2	5	41	4
Neda, Rafael, New Mexico	.323	198	40	64	17	3	6	45	0
Cluff, Jonathan, BYU	.321	221	46	71	18	0	1	34	19
Walker, Braden, UNLV	.318	201	32	64	11	2	5	38	3
Colwell, Pat, San Diego State	.313	201	45	63	9	2	3	25	7
#Carter, Nathan, Air Force	.312	186	51	58	16	**10**	4	30	19
#Derbigny, Chay, Air Force	.311	183	38	57	14	1	6	33	**31**
#Carruthers, Ben, TCU	.308	**266**	**65**	82	12	4	2	33	15

INDIVIDUAL PITCHING LEADERS
(Minimum 50 Innings)

	W	L	ERA	G	SV	IP	H	BB	SO
Strasburg, Stephen, San Diego State	8	3	**1.57**	13	0	97	61	16	**133**
Appleby, Trent, TCU	6	1	2.31	24	0	66	63	13	32
Cashner, Andrew, TCU	**9**	4	2.32	**30**	8	54	21	27	80
Lockwood, Tyler, TCU	7	2	2.75	17	0	**105**	97	15	71
Budrow, Brian, Utah	6	5	3.49	13	0	80	84	22	73
Fife, Stephen, Utah	7	5	3.72	14	0	92	91	29	78
LaFromboise, Bobby, New Mexico	6	3	3.98	13	0	81	89	30	63
McLaughlin, James, San Diego State	3	2	4.04	23	2	65	66	18	47
Solow, Nate, San Diego State	6	7	4.24	15	0	91	92	31	96
Garrison, Seth, TCU	2	3	4.41	17	1	69	75	27	44
Holle, Greg, TCU	1	2	4.50	14	0	60	71	30	32
Murphy, J.R., San Diego State	5	2	4.52	15	1	66	76	19	59
Smith, Stephen, New Mexico	5	2	5.01	14	0	74	94	25	58
Hoelscher, Sean, TCU	7	3	5.02	16	0	66	62	26	53
James, John, Utah	4	7	5.05	15	1	66	77	31	49
Hales, Corey, UNLV	4	3	5.14	16	0	70	82	30	38
Keer, Will, New Mexico	3	4	5.57	18	1	53	75	20	29
Torgerson, Blake, BYU	6	5	5.68	19	2	76	98	15	35
#Chimpky, Robert, Utah	0	5	6.14	25	**9**	29	35	14	27
Hutchison, Matt, UNLV	2	6	6.50	18	0	73	94	33	46
Truesdale, Alex, Air Force	3	6	6.73	21	1	98	148	21	58

NORTHEAST CONFERENCE

	Conference		Overall	
	W	L	W	L
Monmouth	20	5	37	16
Central Connecticut State	18	9	25	24
Wagner	17	11	27	28
*Mount St. Mary's	13	11	21	34
Fairleigh Dickinson	10	16	15	38
Long Island	7	15	16	31
Sacred Heart	10	18	12	41
Quinnipiac	9	19	16	36

ALL-CONFERENCE TEAM: C—Danny Etkin, Sr., Long Island. **1B**—Josh Vittek, Sr., Mount St. Mary's. **2B**—Chris Collazo, Jr., Monmouth. **3B**—John Delaney, Sr., Quinnipiac. **SS**—Kyle Higgins, Sr., Monmouth. **OF**—Jeff Vincent, Jr., Fairleigh Dickinson; Frank DiMasi, Jr., Long Island; James Jones, So., Long Island. **DH**—Nick Pulsonetti, Fr., Monmouth. **UTIL**—Ryan Lynch, Jr., Sacred Heart. **P**—Joe Testa, Sr., Wagner; Brad

Brach, Sr., Monmouth.
Player of the Year: Kyle Higgins, Monmouth. **Pitcher of the Year:** Joe Testa, Wagner. **Rookie of the Year:** Ryan Terry, Monmouth. **Coach of the Year:** Dean Ehehalt, Monmouth.

INDIVIDUAL BATTING LEADERS
(Minimum 125 At-Bats)

	AVG	AB	R	H	2B	3B	HR	RBI	SB
Higgins, Kyle, Monmouth	**.389**	229	51	89	14	**4**	2	38	24
Vittek, Josh, Mount St. Mary's	.377	212	42	80	16	0	**20**	**64**	2
Sand, Zachary, Fairleigh Dickinson	.352	142	25	50	15	0	5	40	0
Dimasi, Frank, Long Island	.346	179	39	62	15	1	6	49	15
Delaney, John, Quinnipiac	.337	196	49	66	15	2	9	40	2
Kane, Kyle, Mount St. Mary's	.331	139	13	46	8	0	0	14	0
Kummerfeldt, Pete, Quinnipiac	.330	191	33	63	13	2	8	38	0
Maher, Matt, Fairleigh Dickinson	.328	198	38	65	9	1	3	27	**33**
Terry, Ryan, Monmouth	.326	178	42	58	15	1	8	34	13
Pulsonetti, Nick, Monmouth	.323	167	42	54	10	**4**	11	48	3
Epps, Pat, Central Conn. State	.319	160	25	51	6	0	4	22	0
Etkin, Danny, Long Island	.317	142	34	45	9	0	5	30	15
Avella, Vin, Wagner	.316	193	33	61	12	0	10	35	4
Edwards, J.J., Sacred Heart	.316	171	20	54	7	0	0	26	0
Vincent, Jeff, Fairleigh Dickinson	.316	187	37	59	12	0	0	31	15
Bottigliero, Paul, Monmouth	.313	134	35	42	12	0	3	29	1
Allaire, Sean, Central Conn. State	.313	182	37	57	14	2	3	23	6
Amatucci, Anthony, Long Island	.313	128	29	40	11	1	3	24	10
Counselman, Drew, Mount St. Mary's	.311	209	44	65	**21**	3	7	29	8
Holland, Brett, Monmouth	.310	145	33	45	7	1	1	30	17
Sousa, Zach, Sacred Heart	.309	110	10	34	4	0	1	16	0
#Csakai, Damian, Wagner	.292	209	46	61	8	1	0	14	33
#Schmidt, Paul, Sacred Heart	.268	138	18	37	**4**	4	2	22	4

INDIVIDUAL PITCHING LEADERS
(Minimum 50 Innings)

	W	L	ERA	G	SV	IP	H	BB	SO
Testa, Joe, Wagner	7	5	**2.08**	15	0	91	76	27	80
#Huebner, Andrew, Wagner	1	2	2.87	22	**11**	31	37	6	24
Tesseyman, John, Central Conn. State	**8**	3	2.88	12	0	**94**	98	14	40
Rice, Jack, Wagner	5	3	3.00	11	1	54	48	17	27
O'Hara, John, Fairleigh Dickinson	5	5	3.13	14	0	78	66	32	**92**
Brach, Brad, Monmouth	**8**	2	3.36	12	0	80	94	20	70
#Esposito, Justin, Monmouth	3	1	3.52	22	**11**	31	23	8	29
Watson, Matt, Wagner	4	7	3.55	13	0	66	67	28	32
Matta, Mike, Mount St. Mary's	5	4	3.71	**24**	4	63	75	20	38
Marc-Aurele, Matt, Monmouth	3	4	3.76	11	0	55	62	17	38
Gianini, Matt, Central Conn. State	7	3	3.98	13	1	81	90	27	46
Morrison, Kyle, Wagner	5	5	3.99	12	0	68	68	25	57
Brett, Tyler, Quinnipiac	4	6	4.60	13	0	63	67	31	51
Mayer, Andy, Quinnipiac	3	3	4.68	10	0	65	70	13	34
Moore, Brett, Mount St. Mary's	4	8	4.75	16	1	66	79	22	40
Brittenham, Max, Mount St. Mary's	4	6	4.75	16	1	83	91	31	46
Roberts, Derek, Central Conn. State	0	3	4.86	11	1	50	56	18	34
Jones, James, Long Island	4	4	4.91	14	2	51	54	29	61
Gloor, Chris, Quinnipiac	2	5	5.01	13	2	59	65	24	55
Duffy, Joe, Quinnipiac	1	7	5.07	14	3	60	71	25	35
Balbach, Jared, Sacred Heart	4	8	5.13	14	1	60	79	26	39
Meadus, John, Fairleigh Dickinson	4	6	5.15	12	0	65	61	31	54
Kerski, Ken, Central Conn. State	3	6	5.82	12	0	65	83	19	48

OHIO VALLEY CONFERENCE

	Conference		Overall	
	W	L	W	L
Jacksonville State	23	4	37	21
Samford	19	7	33	23
Austin Peay State	14	12	27	29
*Eastern Illinois	13	13	27	30
Tennessee Tech	13	14	35	23
Southeast Missouri State	12	13	26	26
Murray State	12	14	21	30
Eastern Kentucky	12	15	26	27
Morehead State	8	19	18	33
Tennessee-Martin	5	20	10	41

ALL-CONFERENCE TEAM: C—Jim Klocke, Southeast Missouri State.

1B—Matt Wagner, Southeast Missouri State. 2B—Bert Smith, Jacksonville State. 3B—Tyler Farrar, Austin Peay State. SS—Michael Marseco, Samford. OF—Brent Nommensen, Eastern Illinois; Clay Whittemore, Jacksonville State; Tyrell Cummings, Southeast Missouri State. DH—Wes Cummingham, Murray State. UTIL—Steven Leach, Jacksonville State. SP—Christian Friedrich, Eastern Kentucky; Ben Tootle, Jacksonville State. RP—Alex Jones, Jacksonville State.

Players of the Year: Clay Whittemore, Jacksonville State; Michael Marseco, Samford. **Pitcher of the Year:** Christian Friedrich, Eastern Kentucky. **Rookie of the Year:** Todd Cunningham, Jacksonville State. **Coach of the Year:** Jim Case, Jacksonville State.

INDIVIDUAL BATTING LEADERS
(Minimum 150 At-Bats)

	AVG	AB	R	H	2B	3B	HR	RBI	SB
Whittemore, Clay, Jacksonville State	.425	226	44	96	19	6	8	66	2
Marseco, Michael, Samford	.419	222	52	93	12	8	5	47	9
Nommensen, Brett, Eastern Illinois	.402	204	56	82	18	4	5	36	18
King, Chris, Tennessee Tech	.389	226	50	88	16	4	4	50	13
Hill, Rafael, Austin Peay State	.388	206	58	80	13	4	2	23	23
Cunningham, Wes, Murray State	.380	163	32	62	4	3	2	30	6
Klocke, Jim, SE Missouri State	.357	185	53	66	7	1	6	40	3
Ottrando, Anthony, E. Kentucky	.354	189	35	67	9	1	4	46	10
New, Jake, Tennessee Tech	.354	229	57	81	11	5	4	45	11
Leach, Steven, Jacksonville State	.354	229	49	81	15	0	4	58	3
Piazza, Brian, Jacksonville	.351	174	30	61	16	1	7	49	1
Rutledge, Michael, Samford	.346	191	42	66	15	2	6	52	6
Mihoci, Matt, Tennessee Tech	.340	159	30	54	13	0	0	27	1
Cunningham, Todd, Jacksonville State	.340	215	65	73	16	3	1	29	6
Barrows, Aaron, Eastern Kentucky	.339	171	43	58	14	4	1	26	14
Wagner, Matt, SE Missouri State	.337	205	37	69	9	1	11	57	3
Smith, Bert, Jacksonville State	.332	208	56	69	13	1	0	39	15
Webb, Evan, Tennessee Tech	.330	197	36	65	12	0	6	41	1
Cummings, Tyrell, SE Missouri	.329	225	49	74	16	0	12	58	3
Kirby-Jones, A.J., Tenn. Tech	.326	193	30	63	15	0	5	51	2
Johnson, Michael, Samford	.325	200	48	65	10	2	0	27	8
Bottoms, Michael, Morehead State	.323	167	23	54	9	0	5	34	1
Henry, Alex, Tennessee Tech	.318	198	44	63	8	4	2	22	4
Gladstone, Scott, Tennessee-Martin	.316	196	37	62	5	0	2	19	3
Lee, Drew, Morehead State	.313	195	38	61	12	1	7	30	6
Harris, Nick, SE Missouri State	.310	184	43	57	12	4	10	41	9
#Nelson, Thomas, Tennessee Tech	.308	221	60	68	21	4	5	37	19
#Tozark, Jordan, Eastern Illinois	.299	231	53	69	16	2	4	42	5
#Allen, Eric, Morehead State	.297	155	51	46	8	1	17	41	7

INDIVIDUAL PITCHING LEADERS
(Minimum 50 Innings)

	W	L	ERA	G	SV	IP	H	BB	SO
Friedrich, Christian, Eastern Kentucky	5	1	1.43	12	0	82	40	33	108
Stephens, Jonathan, Samford	7	0	2.22	12	0	81	70	13	43
Booth, Brian, Jacksonville State	8	0	2.47	29	2	62	51	19	67
Brandon, Tyler, Jacksonville State	3	3	2.53	26	2	57	44	38	48
#Tenholder, Daniel, Austin Peay State	4	1	2.72	30	11	36	32	17	41
Willoughby, McKenzie, E. Kentucky	4	3	2.83	21	3	60	60	28	53
Jones, Alex, Jacksonville State	8	2	2.90	28	8	50	36	22	62
Calhoun, Daniel, Murray State	5	3	3.00	13	0	81	91	15	67
Huff, Stephen, Austin Peay State	5	6	3.46	17	0	94	80	41	79
Tootle, Ben, Jacksonville State	10	2	3.87	15	0	86	87	29	79
Perconte, Mike, Murray State	4	5	4.12	13	0	79	78	17	67
Mueller, Josh, Eastern Illinois	6	7	4.48	16	0	70	59	44	79
Craycraft, Chris, Murray State	5	4	4.48	13	0	86	95	21	50
Renfrow, Dustin, SE Missouri State	6	5	4.54	17	1	85	74	30	78
Alcorn, Michael, Tennessee Tech	7	5	4.64	14	0	78	89	21	58
VanFleteren, Joshua, Samford	4	4	4.72	19	0	55	67	25	33
Jarry, Michael, Samford	4	2	4.85	15	0	69	80	12	38
Sutton, Calen, Tennessee-Martin	3	4	4.92	20	1	71	84	32	38
Dobbs, Jared, Tennessee Tech	4	5	4.95	15	0	64	65	28	51
Cicini, David, Austin Peay	2	4	4.95	22	0	73	91	19	52
Kehrer, Tyler, Eastern Kentucky	1	5	5.12	16	0	63	67	46	60

PACIFIC-10 CONFERENCE

	Conference		Overall	
	W	L	W	L
Arizona State	16	8	49	13
Stanford	14	10	41	24
UCLA	13	11	33	27
Arizona	12	12	42	19
California	12	12	33	21
Washington	11	13	33	22
Oregon State	11	13	28	24
Southern California	11	13	28	28
Washington State	8	16	30	26

ALL-CONFERENCE TEAM: C—Jason Castro, Jr., Stanford; Ryan Oritz, Fr., Oregon State; Petey Paramore, Jr., Arizona State. **1B**—David Cooper, Jr., California; Ike Davis, Jr., Arizona State; Randy Molina, Sr., Stanford. **2B**—Alden Carrithers, Sr., UCLA; Cord Phelps, Jr., Stanford; Josh Satin, Sr., California. **3B**—Brett Wallace, Jr., Arizona State; Paul Gran, Sr., Washington State. **SS**—Grant Green, So., USC. **OF**—Kyle Conley, Jr., Washington; Jon Gaston, Jr., Arizona; Jason Kipnis, So., Arizona State; Sean Ratliff, Jr., Stanford. **P**—Preston Guilmet, So., Arizona; Mike Leake, So., Arizona State; Jorden Merry, Jr., Washington; Tyson Ross, Jr., California; Daniel Schlereth, So., Arizona; Drew Storen, Fr., Stanford; Jason Stoffel, So., Arizona.

Player of the Year: Brett Wallace, Arizona State. **Pitcher of the Year:** Mike Leake, Arizona State. **Defensive Player of the Year:** Paul Gran, Washington State. **Newcomer of the Year:** Jason Kipnis, Arizona State. **Coach of the Year:** Pat Murphy, Arizona State.

INDIVIDUAL BATTING LEADERS
(Minimum 125 At-Bats)

	AVG	AB	R	H	2B	3B	HR	RBI	SB
Wallace, Brett, Arizona State	.410	239	87	98	12	2	22	83	16
Sontag, Ryan, Arizona State	.393	168	48	66	3	3	6	42	6
Green, Grant, USC	.390	205	46	80	15	5	9	46	10
Davis, Ike, Arizona State	.385	213	64	82	26	1	16	76	6
Satin, Josh, California	.379	195	56	74	11	1	18	52	6
Carrithers, Alden, UCLA	.377	223	51	84	16	3	5	47	17
Castro, Jason, Stanford	.376	279	68	105	18	3	14	73	5
Kipnis, Jason, Arizona State	.371	237	76	88	16	6	14	73	24
Perren, Derek, USC	.362	213	39	77	16	1	5	51	2
Cooper, David, California	.359	220	55	79	14	0	19	55	0
Paramore, Petey, Arizona State	.355	214	64	76	10	0	7	52	4
Phelps, Cord, Stanford	.351	259	76	91	16	3	13	58	6
Ortiz, Ryan, Oregon State	.351	188	33	66	16	1	5	55	1
Torrez, Raoul, Arizona State	.341	182	49	62	13	3	2	35	12
Roling, Kiel, Oregon State	.340	197	48	67	16	1	8	51	5
Ziegler, C.J., Arizona	.338	240	52	81	17	1	20	60	0
Conley, Kyle, Washington	.337	181	49	61	13	2	19	57	6
Lopez, Roberto, USC	.335	203	36	68	17	3	7	31	8
Coulter, Travis, Washington State	.333	228	42	76	8	4	1	29	11
Molina, Randy, Stanford	.329	213	43	70	16	0	5	42	0
Suttmeier, Scott, Washington State	.317	171	35	56	7	1	1	25	2
Robertson, Daniel, Oregon State	.327	196	44	64	12	1	2	27	8
Wallace, John, Oregon State	.326	141	33	46	5	2	3	20	9
Ortega, Bryce, Arizona	.326	184	34	60	9	2	2	26	13
Murphy, Jim, Washington State	.324	207	44	67	17	3	16	61	1
Haerther, Casey, UCLA	.324	238	45	77	23	1	12	52	10
August, Joey, Stanford	.323	186	35	60	12	1	1	23	1
George, Drew, Oregon State	.322	152	36	49	8	2	3	28	7
Sedbrook, Colt, Arizona	.321	193	35	62	8	1	3	32	10
Cutler, Charlie, California	.321	162	38	52	6	0	2	17	4
#Steele, T.J., Arizona	.315	222	49	70	15	4	11	39	28

INDIVIDUAL PITCHING LEADERS
(Minimum 50 Innings)

	W	L	ERA	G	SV	IP	H	BB	SO
Schlereth, Daniel, Arizona	2	0	1.81	34	1	55	30	20	76
Sandbrink, Danny, Stanford	2	1	2.81	20	1	58	56	21	30
Perry, Ryan, Arizona	6	3	2.89	31	1	75	60	22	72
Miller, Kevin, California	6	1	2.90	21	0	71	52	37	68
#Stoffel, Jason, Arizona	4	2	3.00	34	13	48	34	15	79
Murphy, Tim, UCLA	5	6	3.34	18	1	102	83	46	111
Yount, Austin, Stanford	6	4	3.48	17	1	67	66	20	40
Leake, Mike, Arizona State	11	3	3.49	19	1	121	118	20	104

Milone, Tommy, USC	6	6	3.51	14	0	97	94	20	98
Storen, Drew, Stanford	5	3	3.51	31	8	56	53	15	30
Merry, Jorden, Washington	8	2	3.61	14	0	82	69	30	69
Rafferty, Tommy, Arizona State	12	0	3.65	35	4	74	63	18	71
Nobles, Cam, Washington	6	4	3.74	15	0	67	45	34	57
Lafferty, Brendan, UCLA	4	3	3.74	33	3	67	61	30	56
Haughian, Nick, Washington	6	5	3.76	17	1	96	80	46	107
Way, Matt, Washington State	4	4	4.01	18	2	74	72	21	68
Miller, Jayson, Washington State	8	1	4.06	15	0	100	121	17	74
Coulon, David, Arizona	8	4	4.15	16	0	85	88	36	80
Ross, Tyson, California	7	4	4.25	12	0	78	76	33	66
Couture, Kevin, USC	6	2	4.27	18	0	84	89	19	65
Inman, Jeffrey, Stanford	7	2	4.27	16	0	72	86	29	45

PATRIOT LEAGUE

	Conference		Overall	
	W	L	W	L
Army	13	7	25	25
Navy	11	9	32	25
Holy Cross	11	9	21	28
*Bucknell	10	10	30	24
Lafayette	8	12	25	23
Lehigh	7	13	23	27

ALL-CONFERENCE TEAM: C—Brendan Akashian, Sr., Holy Cross. **1B**—Thomas Hamilton, Sr., Navy. **2B**—Mike Guadagnini, Fr., Navy. **3B**—Kendall Bolt, So., Navy. **SS**—Clint Moore, Fr., Army. **OF**—Jason Buursma, Sr., Bucknell; Joe Ercolano, Sr., Lehigh; Michael Speciale, So., Navy; Cole White, Sr., Army. **DH**—John Avanzino, So., Bucknell. **SP**—Matt Fouch, So., Army; Matt Shapiro, So., Holy Cross. **RP**—J.D. Melton, So., Navy.
Player of the Year: Jason Buursma, Bucknell. **Pitcher of the Year:** Matt Shapiro, Holy Cross. **Rookie of the Year:** Clint Moore, Army. **Coach of the Year:** Greg DiCenzo, Holy Cross.

INDIVIDUAL BATTING LEADERS
(Minimum 100 At-Bats)

	AVG	AB	R	H	2B	3B	HR	RBI	SB
Hamilton, Thomas, Navy	.403	221	44	89	10	0	3	49	2
White, Cole, Army	.373	153	44	57	14	3	8	30	8
Buursma, Jason, Bucknell	.367	158	37	58	7	1	13	37	0
Speciale, Michael, Navy	.350	234	58	82	15	6	10	47	13
Moore, Clint, Army	.350	197	46	69	14	2	6	39	14
Grandizio, Dane, Bucknell	.333	198	33	66	9	2	4	35	13
Luick, Chris, Lafayette	.329	164	28	54	5	1	1	18	10
McKague, Kevin, Army	.328	195	33	64	19	0	3	50	5
Ercolando, Joe, Lehigh	.328	180	38	59	10	1	4	29	22
Oxford, Eric, Holy Cross	.325	154	16	50	13	1	0	25	4
Bierce, Daniel, Lafayette	.324	182	29	59	7	2	3	16	12
Bolt, Kendall, Navy	.324	216	35	70	16	3	4	36	5
Guadagnini, Mike, Navy	.324	170	29	55	8	0	5	24	5
Wright, Jonathan, Navy	.323	198	28	64	12	1	0	32	1
Gomez, Gil, Holy Cross	.323	155	20	50	12	1	5	30	2
Akashian, Brendan, Holy Cross	.320	153	30	49	7	0	3	32	5
Simmons, Chris, Army	.318	170	31	54	9	2	8	42	4
Angelo, Mark, Bucknell	.316	209	33	66	8	2	2	37	8
Russell, Andrew, Lehigh	.313	150	28	47	9	4	3	29	10
Allen, Ben, Bucknell	.312	202	46	63	8	0	2	24	4
Avanzino, John, Bucknell	.308	146	24	45	8	2	9	35	0
Capozzi, Tony, Army	.302	159	33	48	8	3	3	24	4
Ernesto, Andy, Army	.301	206	41	62	15	2	2	32	10
Polchinski, J.P., Army	.299	147	31	44	7	0	6	30	4
Hollins, Renaldo, Navy	.294	187	34	55	6	6	0	15	14
Ezekiel, Joe, Lafayette	.292	130	16	38	5	0	6	23	0
McGaheran, Brendan, Lehigh	.287	181	34	52	12	1	3	26	15
Perry, Matt, Holy Cross	.285	186	32	53	16	0	2	26	4
Cupelo, Billy, Holy Cross	.279	140	11	39	10	2	0	20	0
Gorman, Jake, Holy Cross	.270	148	36	40	14	3	5	17	1

INDIVIDUAL PITCHING LEADERS
(Minimum 40 Innings)

	W	L	ERA	G	SV	IP	H	BB	SO
#Melton, J.D., Navy	2	1	1.85	19	7	24	24	9	16
Buursma, Jason, Bucknell	9	3	2.58	20	0	84	72	10	78

Fritz, Zach, Lafayette	4	1	2.88	10	0	50	43	9	37
Reese, Kevin, Lafayette	4	5	2.90	11	0	68	55	18	40
Wilson, Mathew, Bucknell	6	1	3.67	10	0	69	79	16	73
Drake, Oliver, Navy	6	3	3.70	13	0	80	79	22	78
Holmes, Bobby, Holy Cross	5	4	3.84	10	0	61	68	24	41
Mihalik, Kevin, Lehigh	2	4	3.91	11	1	51	55	17	29
Thater, Mike, Holy Cross	3	5	4.06	12	1	58	67	12	25
Matteo, Joe, Lehigh	6	3	4.11	11	0	61	63	22	55
Jarrett, Eric, Bucknell	5	6	4.29	17	0	86	85	41	60
Clothier, Drew, Army	5	5	4.38	12	0	76	76	25	62
Fouch, Matt, Army	6	2	4.53	18	0	60	57	21	44
Atkins, Jeremy, Lafayette	3	4	4.70	11	0	59	64	17	29
Seeley, Dylan, Bucknell	4	4	4.77	13	0	60	77	24	25
Eckert, Yale, Navy	2	5	4.92	11	0	60	66	15	49
McCoy, Mark, Navy	6	5	4.94	13	0	78	101	22	64
Koenigsfeld, Ben, Army	6	4	5.61	13	1	69	82	21	54
George, Ryan, Holy Cross	2	4	5.66	18	2	49	57	20	43
White, Cole, Army	2	6	6.12	11	0	50	51	28	43
Seip, Dan, Holy Cross	1	5	6.17	13	0	54	68	26	35

SOUTHEASTERN CONFERENCE

	Conference		Overall	
EAST	W	L	W	L
Georgia	20	9	45	25
Florida	17	13	34	24
Kentucky	16	14	44	19
Vanderbilt	15	14	41	22
South Carolina	15	15	40	23
Tennessee	12	18	27	29
WEST				
*Louisiana State	18	11	49	19
Alabama	16	14	35	28
Mississippi	15	15	39	26
Arkansas	14	15	34	24
Auburn	11	19	28	28
Mississippi State	9	21	23	33

ALL-CONFERENCE TEAM: C—Bryce Massanari, Georgia. **1B**—Justin Smoak, South Carolina. **2B**—Josh Adams, Florida; Ryan Wilkes, Kentucky. **3B**—Pedro Alvarez, Vanderbilt; Logan Forsythe, Arkansas. **SS**—Gordon Beckham, Georgia. **OF**—Colin Cowgill, Kentucky; Sawyer Carroll, Kentucky; Matt den Dekker, Florida; Brandon May, Alabama; David Macias, Vanderbilt. **DH**—Alex Avila, Alabama. **P**—Patrick Keating, Florida; Chris Rusin, Kentucky. **RP**—Joshua Fields, Georgia.
Player of the Year: Gordon Beckham, Georgia. **Pitcher of the Year:** Joshua Fields, Georgia. **Freshman of the Year:** Hunter Morris, Auburn. **Coach of the Year:** David Perno, Georgia.

INDIVIDUAL BATTING LEADERS
(Minimum 125 At-Bats)

	AVG	AB	R	H	2B	3B	HR	RBI	SB
Carroll, Sawyer, Kentucky	.419	234	69	98	22	3	19	83	12
Beckham, Gordon, Georgia	.411	275	97	113	22	1	28	77	17
Smoak, Justin, South Carolina	.383	235	63	90	19	0	23	72	1
Wilkes, Ryan, Kentucky	.374	214	53	80	10	1	9	36	2
Poythress, Rich, Georgia	.374	265	64	99	22	0	15	75	4
Rutledge, Josh, Alabama	.369	268	62	99	9	2	0	30	16
Leavitt, Chase, Arkansas	.366	172	60	63	10	1	3	25	9
May, Brandon, Alabama	.365	252	60	92	18	0	9	50	3
Cowgill, Collin, Kentucky	.361	233	80	84	15	2	19	60	23
Barnes, Avery, Florida	.360	225	65	81	11	4	2	19	26
Havens, Reese, South Carolina	.359	248	76	89	13	2	18	57	1
Overbeck, Cody, Mississippi	.356	253	51	90	16	0	17	59	1
Macias, David, Vanderbilt	.356	270	61	96	15	1	9	40	6
Forsythe, Logan, Arkansas	.353	184	41	65	8	2	7	33	11
Dean, Blake, Louisiana State	.353	269	62	95	18	3	20	73	4
Morris, Hunter, Auburn	.351	211	42	74	15	2	11	49	4
Figueroa, Cole, Florida	.350	223	61	78	12	1	9	57	20
Sanders, Joseph, Auburn	.348	201	40	70	19	0	6	52	12
McClendon, Chris, Kentucky	.346	179	33	62	11	1	3	33	7
Clark, Matt, Louisiana State	.344	227	57	78	17	0	28	64	1
Avila, Alex, Auburn	.343	239	57	82	12	1	17	62	0
Peisel, Ryan, Georgia	.341	311	78	106	22	2	12	56	14

COLLEGE BASEBALL

	AVG	AB	R	H	2B	3B	HR	RBI	SB
LeMahieu, D.J., Louisiana State	.337	258	56	87	11	1	6	44	10
McArthur, Brandon, Florida	.337	184	27	62	12	4	2	44	3
den Dekker, Matt, Florida	.333	213	55	71	9	2	8	48	20
Giobbi, Andrew, Vanderbilt	.332	211	32	70	22	1	3	42	2
Smith, Fuller, Mississippi	.332	208	39	69	14	0	7	32	4
Adams, Josh, Florida	.330	209	42	69	17	1	8	51	11
Davis, Kentrail, Tennessee	.330	206	45	68	7	3	13	44	7
Power, Logan, Mississippi	.329	243	47	80	13	1	9	51	8
#Schimpf, Ryan, Louisiana State	.320	250	57	80	18	7	12	54	16
#de la Osa, Dominic, Vanderbilt	.297	249	65	74	14	4	10	50	27
#Wade, Chris, Kentucky	.296	226	35	67	24	0	5	51	6

INDIVIDUAL PITCHING LEADERS
(Minimum 50 Innings)

	W	L	ERA	G	SV	IP	H	BB	SO
Bittle, Scott, Mississippi	7	1	1.78	27	8	71	35	30	130
Coleman, Louis, Louisiana State	8	1	1.95	23	2	55	45	10	62
Albers, Andrew, Kentucky	7	4	2.40	31	5	56	45	16	64
Ross, Austin, Louisiana State	3	1	2.58	21	3	52	51	9	37
Paxton, James, Kentucky	4	2	2.92	17	1	52	46	25	43
Godwin, Nick, South Carolina	7	3	3.14	15	0	92	73	23	82
Locke, Stephen, Florida	5	2	3.17	21	2	82	92	13	46
Rusin, Chris, Kentucky	6	3	3.33	13	0	84	89	19	65
#Fields, Joshua, Georgia	3	2	3.38	36	18	37	17	22	63
Dayton, Grant, Auburn	7	2	3.89	18	1	81	87	13	79
Springston, Cliff, Arkansas	5	3	3.90	16	0	88	93	26	63
Cooper, Blake, South Carolina	5	6	3.94	15	0	94	101	23	59
McRee, Alex, Georgia	7	1	3.98	31	0	61	57	31	65
Stroup, Will, Alabama	5	4	4.01	25	0	58	57	34	54
Dyson, Sam, South Carolina	8	0	4.09	12	0	51	43	28	44
Dombrowski, Greg, Kentucky	6	1	4.10	16	0	79	106	13	58
Bradshaw, Daniel, Louisiana State	4	5	4.12	26	4	55	51	13	52
Verdugo, Ryan, Louisiana State	9	4	4.12	20	0	96	95	37	82
Keating, Patrick, Florida	8	1	4.16	17	1	84	104	25	52
Pomeranz, Drew, Mississippi	4	3	4.16	17	0	71	76	30	81
Weaver, Dean, Georgia	6	1	4.24	31	1	51	52	19	47
#Minor, Mike, Vanderbilt	7	3	4.28	15	0	103	99	28	101
#Bradford, Jared, Louisiana State	10	4	4.48	18	5	98	115	24	90

SOUTHERN CONFERENCE

	Conference		Overall	
	W	L	W	L
*Elon	19	8	44	18
College of Charleston	18	9	39	20
Furman	17	10	33	24
Georgia Southern	16	11	33	25
UNC Greensboro	15	12	33	27
Appalachian State	14	13	32	27
Western Carolina	14	13	29	28
The Citadel	12	15	28	28
Wofford	6	21	24	35
Davidson	4	23	12	38

ALL-CONFERENCE TEAM: C—Blake Murhpy, Sr., Western Carolina. **1B**—Michael Harrington, Sr., College of Charleston. **2B**—Brandon Sizemore, Jr., College of Charleston. **3B**—Jeremie Tice, Jr., College of Charleston. **SS**—Jason Altenhof, Sr., Appalachian State. **OF**—Chris Shehan, Jr., Georgia State; Cory Harrilchak, Fr., Elon; Chris Swauger, Sr., Citadel. **DH**—Ty Wright, Jr., Georgia State. **SP**—Steven Hensley, Jr., Elon; Jay Jackson, Jr., Furman. **RP**—Tom Girdwood, Fr., Elon.

Player of the Year: Jeremie Tice, College of Charleston. **Pitcher of the Year:** Steven Hensley, Elon. **Freshman of the Year:** Thomas Girdwood, Elon. **Coach of the Year:** Mike Kennedy, Elon.

INDIVIDUAL BATTING LEADERS
(Minimum 125 At-Bats)

	AVG	AB	R	H	2B	3B	HR	RBI	SB
Sheehan, Chris, Georgia Southern	.438	224	84	98	17	3	22	77	22
Harrilchak, Cory, Elon	.410	205	70	84	12	5	11	46	24
Wade, Reese, Furman	.401	142	25	57	9	1	1	25	1
Wright, Ty, Georgia Southern	.398	196	63	78	22	1	17	52	8
Meade, Sonny, Citadel	.393	229	49	90	16	0	5	46	3
Tice, Jeremie, Col. of Charleston	.393	229	80	90	21	3	25	83	2
Altenhof, Jason, Appalachian State	.380	245	62	93	8	1	5	42	16

	AVG	AB	R	H	2B	3B	HR	RBI	SB
Austin, Chase, Elon	.377	183	45	69	17	1	9	51	7
Shaft, Barrett, Western Carolina	.374	222	46	83	16	3	5	47	6
Porter, Phillip, Georgia Southern	.365	219	59	80	13	0	7	45	19
Gilmartin, Michael, Wofford	.364	228	50	83	21	2	9	53	8
Tarleton, Dallas, Elon	.361	166	42	60	16	0	7	50	5
Swauger, Chris, Citadel	.360	214	59	77	18	2	10	35	3
Orton, Ricky, UNC Greensboro	.359	206	56	74	20	0	15	59	3
Richardson, David, Georgia Southern	.359	170	44	61	11	1	9	46	12
Murphy, Blake, Western Carolina	.358	173	54	62	18	0	16	57	22
Rook, Jason, Appalachian State	.358	204	46	73	11	6	6	44	7
Benedict, Griffin, Georgia Southern	.355	217	60	77	17	2	12	65	3
Greer, Brent, Western Carolina	.352	193	55	68	13	1	7	38	2
Hentz, Mike, Col. of Charleston	.352	182	58	64	15	3	7	44	8
Davis, Bennett, Elon	.350	220	66	77	15	0	18	82	11
Overholtzer, Corey, UNC Greensboro	.350	223	42	78	12	6	5	44	10
Williams, Jake, Wofford	.348	181	39	63	14	2	10	37	8
Haywood, Stuart, Col. of Charleston	.347	213	55	74	11	1	7	45	16
Liles, Nick, Western Carolina	.346	269	58	93	19	1	3	28	22
Jackson, Jay, Furman	.336	137	29	46	10	2	8	41	6
Beckham, Jeremy, Georgia Southern	.333	171	41	57	6	0	1	25	24
McCord, Clay, Col. of Charleston	.333	162	46	54	10	1	4	29	14
Rubinstein, David, Appalachian State	.332	226	57	75	19	1	9	48	12
Sizemore, Brandon, Col. of Charleston	.327	251	69	82	24	2	20	82	11
#Harrington, Michael, Col. of Charleston	.316	234	71	74	15	2	26	82	0
#Dove, Chris, Elon	.310	255	62	79	12	6	5	36	38

INDIVIDUAL PITCHING LEADERS
(Minimum 50 Innings)

	W	L	ERA	G	SV	IP	H	BB	SO
Jackson, Jay, Furman	9	2	3.17	15	0	99	77	40	94
Hensley, Steven, Elon	10	2	3.59	16	0	93	82	38	99
Simpson, Jesse, Col. of Charleston	9	3	3.88	23	6	72	71	28	83
Parry, Ian, Furman	5	5	3.88	28	2	58	68	16	54
Smith, Mason, Furman	5	4	4.05	18	0	73	85	25	54
#Girdwood, Thomas, Elon	5	2	4.15	29	10	26	24	19	31
Masters, Chris, Western Carolina	8	4	4.24	28	2	68	58	36	80
Wojciechowski, Asher, Citadel	5	1	4.50	14	0	76	70	40	78
Tavernier, Mike, Western Carolina	5	4	4.65	16	1	72	76	27	64
Wrenn, Wes, Citadel	5	5	4.66	14	0	87	102	24	48
Goldberg, Jake, Col. of Charleston	4	3	4.71	17	0	78	99	20	49
Lynn, Mike, Col. of Charleston	3	0	4.71	21	3	50	48	22	43
Crim, Matt, Citadel	6	6	4.85	14	0	72	93	24	58
#White, James, UNC Greensboro	5	1	4.96	38	0	33	36	10	23
Harrilchak, Cory, Elon	7	3	5.13	15	0	67	86	20	46
Ferrer, Kenneth, Elon	5	3	5.15	23	0	65	63	47	62
Middour, Thomas, Davidson	3	4	5.29	14	0	78	91	26	49
Andress, Matt, Appalachian State	8	4	5.30	15	0	88	99	28	64
Martin, Greg, UNC Greensboro	7	4	5.40	15	0	83	105	36	47
Quate, Zach, Appalachian State	5	3	5.40	18	0	55	61	22	46
McCall, Wes, UNC Greensboro	1	8	5.51	30	1	64	77	27	35
Summers, Scott, Wofford	7	7	5.54	17	0	88	102	37	65

SOUTHLAND CONFERENCE

	Conference		Overall	
EAST	W	L	W	L
Lamar	20	10	35	23
Northwestern State	17	12	28	28
Southeastern Louisiana	15	15	32	27
Central Arkansas	13	16	27	27
McNeese State	7	23	13	42
Nicholls State	5	25	10	44
WEST				
Texas-San Antonio	22	8	39	19
Texas State	19	11	30	27
*Sam Houston State	18	12	37	25
Texas-Arlington	16	14	26	31
Texas A&M-Corpus Christi	14	15	24	33
Stephen F. Austin	12	17	25	29

ALL-CONFERENCE TEAM: C—Anthony Jones, Sr., Northwestern State. **1B**—Paul Goldschmidt, So., Texas State. **2B**—Adam Witek, Jr., Texas State. **3B**—Seth Hammock, Jr., Sam Houston State. **SS**—Thomas Field, Jr., Texas State. **OF**—Michael Rockett, Jr., Texas-San Antonio; Keith

Stein, Sr., Sam Houston State; Kevin Crabtree, Sr., Stephen F. Austin. **DH**—Bobby Verbick, Sr., Sam Houston State. **P**—Tim Erickson, Sr., Lamar; Brian Sisk, Sr., Lamar; Wade Miley, Jr., Southeastern Louisiana. **Player of the Year:** Michael Rockett, Texas-San Antonio. **Hitter of the Year:** Paul Goldschmidt, Texas State. **Pitcher of the Year:** Tim Erickson, Lamar. **Freshman of the Year:** Michael Choice, Texas-Arlington. **Newcomer of the Year:** Stephen Flora, A&M-Corpus Christi. **Coach of the Year:** Sherman Corbett, Texas-San Antonio.

INDIVIDUAL BATTING LEADERS
(Minimum 125 At-Bats)

	AVG	AB	R	H	2B	3B	HR	RBI	SB
Hammock, Seth, Sam Houston State	.380	205	49	78	17	1	12	56	2
Flora, Stephen, Texas A&M-CC	.380	192	43	73	18	1	5	22	4
Choice, Michael, Texas-Arlington	.378	196	39	74	9	3	7	51	7
McLeod, David, Texas-Arlington	.375	200	49	75	18	3	0	29	7
Gerondale, Bryan, Texas A&M-CC	.372	196	34	73	15	1	5	39	4
Freeman, Taylor, McNeese State	.372	180	30	67	20	2	8	52	1
Slinkman, Danny, Texas-Arlington	.370	146	29	54	15	2	3	47	5
Huffman, Josh, Central Arkansas	.366	175	37	64	13	1	2	25	0
Crabtree, Kevin, Stephen F. Austin	.362	207	51	75	18	4	11	49	19
Rockett, Michael, Texas-San Antonio	.360	247	60	89	**25**	5	10	68	9
Goldschmidt, Paul, Texas State	.360	228	59	82	20	2	**17**	69	4
Tucker, Steven, Lamar	.358	226	47	81	16	1	6	44	17
Keithley, James, Texas-San Antonio	.358	243	**73**	87	16	2	6	32	15
Sebek, Todd, Sam Houston State	.357	**283**	68	**101**	25	3	5	41	25
Trevino, Ryan, Sam Houston State	.356	205	38	73	11	0	2	41	1
Stein, Keith, Sam Houston State	.355	262	68	93	24	6	10	58	6
Loftin, Lance, Texas State	.354	206	50	73	14	2	12	59	0
Palincsar, Tim, Texas-San Antonio	.350	217	62	76	14	1	8	52	6
Wheaton, Chase, Texas A&M-CC	.345	220	48	76	12	5	5	42	12
Verbick, Bobby, Sam Houston State	.343	230	64	79	14	5	14	58	3
Witek, Adam, Texas State	.342	219	37	75	6	1	2	35	16
Summerlin, Ty, SE Louisiana	.342	240	57	82	20	2	8	60	10
Link, Tyler, Lamar	.341	217	46	74	13	2	4	28	11
Jones, Anthony, Northwestern State	.340	200	31	68	14	0	5	38	7
O'Neal, Justin, Northwestern State	.340	203	44	69	14	1	4	39	6
Lockwood, Trent, Texas-San Antonio	.340	212	53	72	23	2	16	**79**	2
Theriot, Ben, Texas State	.339	183	40	62	14	0	3	45	0
Hernandez, Trey, Texas A&M-CC	.339	192	37	65	16	1	10	56	3
Randell, Laurn, Texas State	.338	210	49	71	11	0	1	38	17
Field, Thomas, Texas State	.338	240	66	81	14	7	10	44	10
#Kirby, Kai, Stephen F. Austin	.301	196	42	59	6	5	2	28	**30**

INDIVIDUAL PITCHING LEADERS
(Minimum 50 Innings)

	W	L	ERA	G	SV	IP	H	BB	SO
#Calhoun, Zach, Texas-San Antonio	4	1	1.26	26	**13**	41	22	35	54
Collins, Ryan, Southeastern Louisiana	8	3	**3.11**	23	6	55	50	15	39
Cross, Reece, Central Arkansas	4	3	3.17	20	3	54	45	16	41
Varnado, Brent, SE Louisiana	3	4	3.33	18	0	84	93	15	78
Sisk, Brian, Lamar	**10**	2	3.49	16	0	**106**	98	22	66
Gutierrez, Omar, Texas A&M-CC	6	4	3.50	17	0	87	73	47	90
Duguay, Guillaume, Sam Houston State	4	2	3.52	17	1	64	70	18	43
#Sparkman, Bryant, Texas A&M-CC	3	1	3.70	**32**	2	41	48	12	15
LeBlanc, Rene, Southeastern Louisiana	3	5	3.71	17	0	61	68	16	45
Heard, Jimmy, Northwestern State	7	5	3.82	14	0	94	93	20	66
Erickson, Tim, Lamar	8	3	3.83	27	9	82	84	19	57
Hart, Mike, Texas State	7	3	3.88	15	0	102	98	42	89
Miley, Wade, SE Louisiana	7	3	3.90	17	0	102	101	41	**119**
Hennigan, Heath, Northwestern State	3	4	3.98	15	0	84	86	23	81
Black, Josh, Southeastern Louisiana	5	4	4.02	14	0	69	73	36	63
Luetge, Lance, Stephen F. Austin	6	7	4.08	17	1	88	102	35	43
Tritz, Zack, Texas State	9	4	4.22	14	0	92	111	20	42
Cooper, Clayton, Northwestern State	5	4	4.25	14	0	78	73	19	50
Otteman, Matthew, Texas-Arlington	4	3	4.35	12	1	50	48	23	36
Cloud, Jeremy, Central Arkansas	3	5	4.55	12	0	61	76	15	34
Proudfoot, Ryan, Texas State	7	3	4.61	14	0	70	67	47	46
Whitaker, Matt, Central Arkansas	5	3	4.71	16	0	78	76	54	71

SOUTHWESTERN ATHLETIC CONFERENCE

	Conference		Overall	
EAST	**W**	**L**	**W**	**L**
Jackson State	18	5	37	22
Alcorn State	15	9	29	16
Mississippi Valley State	13	10	18	26
Alabama State	8	14	13	22
Alabama A&M	4	20	7	39
WEST				
Southern	18	6	28	18
Grambling State	15	9	21	28
Prairie View A&M	14	10	25	26
*Texas Southern	7	17	16	34
Arkansas-Pine Bluff	6	18	10	33

ALL-CONFERENCE TEAM: C—Michael Thomas, So., Southern. **1B**—Myrio Richard, So., Prairie View A&M. **2B**—Enrique Quintero, Sr., Jackson State. **3B**—Romey Bracey, Jr., Southern. **SS**—LaDerek Camper, Jr., Jackson State. **OF**—Jabari Graham, Jr., Alcorn State; Jerome McCollum, Jr., Arkansas-Pine Bluff; Brent Smith, Jr., Grambling State. **DH**—Mychal Roby, So., Grambling State. **P**—Mario Jefferson, Sr., Grambling State; Charles Williams, Jr., Jackson State; Jarret Maloy, So., Southern.
Player of the Year: Myrio Richard, Prairie View A&M. **Outstanding Hitter of the Year:** Joel Del Grande, Alcorn State. **Newcomer of the Year:** Joel Del Grande, Alcorn State. **Pitcher of the Year:** Charles Williams, Jackson State.

INDIVIDUAL BATTING LEADERS
(Minimum 100 At-Bats)

	AVG	AB	R	H	2B	3B	HR	RBI	SB
Graham, Jabari, Alcorn State	.437	151	39	66	10	0	5	46	1
Childress, Tyron, Alabama A&M	.432	125	17	54	9	2	1	25	0
Del Grande, Joel, Alcorn State	.408	125	26	51	18	0	2	42	0
McCollum, Jerome, Ark.-Pine Bluff	.408	157	44	64	18	2	8	39	8
Rhone, Earnest, Texas Southern	.397	151	48	60	10	0	9	38	2
Hall, Frazier, Southern	.393	117	39	46	9	0	3	33	2
Pearce, Brandon, Alcorn State	.383	133	43	51	11	0	5	48	1
Armstrong, James, Southern	.377	114	40	43	4	4	8	31	5
Halliman, Pernell, Jackson State	.374	171	36	64	10	4	6	43	5
Quintero, Enrique, Jackson State	.370	189	45	70	8	5	3	39	11
Richard, Myrio, Prairie View	.370	173	57	64	13	0	**10**	51	15
Pace, Matt, Arkansas-Pine Bluff	.369	149	38	55	**23**	0	5	40	1
Bowens, Adrian, Alcorn State	.368	155	59	57	11	**7**	1	27	3
Siaca, Manny, Alabama A&M	.367	139	27	51	14	1	1	16	4
Washington, Turner, Alabama A&M	.367	150	21	55	1	1	1	27	3
Pedro, Darrion, Alabama State	.363	124	39	45	8	2	9	28	7
Smith, Brent, Grambling State	.359	145	33	52	8	5	**10**	43	8
Bush, Jordan, Texas Southern	.359	145	34	52	7	2	9	50	4
Williams, Brandon, Grambling State	.356	132	30	47	6	4	0	36	5
Bracey, Romey, Southern	.356	118	43	42	5	5	4	28	8
McDavid, Brad, Southern	.356	163	37	58	11	3	7	49	1
Davis, Christopher, Alabama State	.354	113	30	40	3	0	13	17	
Tyes, Jerome, Jackson State	.343	207	50	71	9	3	8	50	10
Franklin, Victor, Southern	.342	114	41	39	8	2	5	34	7
Camper, LaDerek, Jackson State	.341	**211**	**65**	**72**	13	7	4	39	15
Holloway, Justin, Texas Southern	.338	136	30	46	7	3	3	33	1
Barker, Reggie, Arkansas-Pine Bluff	.338	160	38	54	7	1	2	25	8
Kumar, Manny, Grambling State	.333	153	37	51	11	0	2	33	2
Cole, Cortez, Jackson State	.332	208	51	69	11	2	5	42	**34**
Roby, Mychal, Grambling State	.331	151	36	50	11	2	5	41	3
#Buchanan, Jesse, Alcorn State	.307	163	44	50	10	2	9	**61**	1

INDIVIDUAL PITCHING LEADERS
(Minimum 40 Innings)

	W	L	ERA	G	SV	IP	H	BB	SO
#Quintero, Enrique, Jackson State	2	1	3.55	**25**	7	46	49	17	43
Mills, Chris, Miss. Valley State	8	4	**3.83**	16	0	82	84	24	60
Johnson, Lee, Alcorn State	4	1	3.92	23	**7**	57	70	16	49
Williams, Charles, Jackson State	**10**	4	4.33	16	0	**87**	94	42	**77**
Gonzales, Tony, Alcorn State	6	3	4.76	21	4	64	70	23	48
Jefferson, Mario, Grambling State	8	4	4.84	12	0	71	66	21	48
Aceto, Charlie, Prairie View	6	2	5.05	12	0	57	57	37	46

COLLEGE BASEBALL

Richard, Chase, Southern	5	3	5.10	11	0	60	67	12	41
Brooks, Sherrard, Southern	6	1	5.14	11	0	49	63	14	50
Maloy, Jarrett, Southern	9	3	5.43	12	0	58	72	23	44
Ford, Rashad, Texas Southern	3	6	5.75	20	1	61	60	45	76
Feeheeley, Matthew, Grambling State	3	6	6.52	10	0	50	67	23	38
Jordan, Darryl, Alcorn State	5	5	6.71	13	0	56	73	33	39
Townsend, Derrick, Miss. Valley State	3	2	6.83	18	1	54	76	24	28
Marshall, Ronald, Grambling State	4	6	6.93	12	0	61	82	24	52
Zapata, Derek, Prairie View	4	4	7.16	12	0	55	59	23	38
Zachary, Marquise, Jackson State	9	3	7.18	15	0	68	89	45	51
Taylor, Wrandal, Prairie View	6	3	7.26	14	1	62	74	14	55
Collins, Kevin, Alabama A&M	3	11	7.73	18	0	80	106	59	38
Arredondo, David, Texas Southern	2	4	7.79	13	0	50	70	16	42
Hilburn, Zeb, Alabama State	5	7	7.98	13	0	77	126	21	52

SUMMIT LEAGUE

	Conference		Overall	
	W	L	W	L
*Oral Roberts	24	4	48	14
Southern Utah	16	11	31	28
Western Illinois	13	11	21	33
Centenary	13	15	30	26
South Dakota State	9	11	22	27
Oakland	7	14	15	30
IPFW	10	17	14	36
North Dakota State	7	16	15	30

ALL-CONFERENCE TEAM: C—Ben Petralli, Jr., Oral Roberts. **1B**—Michael Notaro, Jr., Oral Roberts. **2B**—Juan Martinez, Jr., Oral Roberts. **3B**—Drew Laidig, Jr., Western Illinois. **SS**—Korby Mintken, South Dakota State. **OF**—Brendan Duffy, Sr., Oral Roberts; Nick Freitas, Jr., Southern Utah; Brian Van Kirk, Sr., Oral Roberts. **DH**—Ryan Groth, Jr., Oral Roberts. **UTIL**—Craig Parry, Sr., South Dakota State. **SP**—Brandon Knowling, Jr., IPFW; Carlos Luna, Sr., Oral Roberts. **RP**—Boone Whiting, Fr., Centenary.

Player of the Year: Brian Van Kirk, Oral Roberts. **Pitcher of the Year:** Carlos Luna, Oral Roberts. **Newcomer of the Year:** Ben Petralli, Oral Roberts. **Coach of the Year:** Rob Walton, Oral Roberts.

INDIVIDUAL BATTING LEADERS
(Minimum 125 At-Bats)

	AVG	AB	R	H	2B	3B	HR	RBI	SB
Van Kirk, Brian, Oral Roberts	.414	237	62	**98**	22	0	**18**	74	0
Zablan, Keli'i, North Dakota State	.382	220	46	84	12	5	3	34	19
Martin, Tony, South Dakota State	.365	137	28	50	10	0	2	25	1
Petralli, Ben, Oral Roberts	.354	229	60	81	21	0	9	70	0
Groth, Ryan, Oral Roberts	.351	248	50	87	20	4	9	49	3
Laidig, Drew, Western Illinois	.349	192	28	67	9	1	4	41	6
Genao, David, Oral Roberts	.347	213	58	74	9	0	10	55	0
Sexton, Scott, Oakland	.342	158	25	54	14	1	2	38	1
Mintken, Korby, South Dakota State	.342	202	48	69	10	**7**	8	45	14
Penney, Cameron, Centenary	.340	206	37	70	7	2	0	40	10
Stitz, Billy, South Dakota State	.339	165	35	56	9	2	9	40	10
Duffy, Brendan, Oral Roberts	.339	**251**	**73**	85	16	1	2	25	16
Parry, Craig, South Dakota State	.338	195	42	66	20	5	10	47	1
Wilson, Justin, Oakland	.338	151	42	51	5	1	7	23	19
Aona, Bucky, Southern Utah	.333	195	33	65	13	0	4	39	3
Martinez, Juan, Oral Roberts	.329	216	49	71	16	1	9	55	5
Wilson, Chester, Southern Utah	.326	215	33	70	10	3	2	31	3
Merkle, Rob, Oakland	.325	160	35	52	13	0	3	25	2
Deering, Tim, Centenary	.323	158	29	51	9	1	0	23	7
Miles, Sebastian, North Dakota State	.320	153	22	49	7	0	1	20	3
Stafford, Andrew, Oakland	.319	144	26	46	6	0	5	34	6
Freitas, Nick, Southern Utah	.315	219	60	69	11	0	16	39	**34**
Waddell, Cole, Western Illinois	.312	157	30	49	12	2	2	26	5
Lewis, Steele, Centenary	.308	185	35	57	7	1	2	35	16
Minissale, Kelly, Oral Roberts	.307	231	52	71	13	0	1	45	4
Price, Kenny, Western Illinois	.307	192	26	59	11	3	1	22	8
Wright, Ray, Southern Utah	.306	173	36	53	10	0	1	17	9
Davis, Jared, IPFW	.306	193	34	59	16	1	7	28	7
Pendell, Brett, Western Illinois	.305	167	27	51	6	1	0	18	3
Bernsen, Ryan, Centenary	.304	184	36	56	12	0	3	30	4

INDIVIDUAL PITCHING LEADERS
(Minimum 50 Innings)

	W	L	ERA	G	SV	IP	H	BB	SO
Whiting, Boone, Centenary	2	2	**1.62**	20	5	61	51	19	45
Bushland, Shane, North Dakota State	6	4	2.77	20	3	62	65	17	41
Knowling, Brandon, IPFW	7	1	2.91	11	0	68	63	23	51
Serrano, Mark, Oral Roberts	4	1	3.09	21	2	67	56	23	52
Luna, Carlos, Oral Roberts	**13**	1	3.35	**31**	2	99	95	43	99
Kraft, Justin, Centenary	9	5	3.38	15	0	85	91	24	67
Sullivan, Jerry, Oral Roberts	9	2	3.88	18	0	**104**	109	25	**108**
Sheehan, Jeremy, Centenary	5	4	4.09	13	0	62	79	15	33
Jarman, Michael, Oral Roberts	11	3	4.24	20	0	102	106	45	95
Tolsma, Travis, Western Illinois	4	5	4.29	12	0	71	81	22	47
Takashima, Mike, Oakland	1	4	4.68	11	0	65	67	47	50
Nielsen, Chad, IPFW	2	3	4.72	13	1	53	59	21	36
Noyes, Jacob, Southern Utah	5	3	4.79	27	5	62	57	31	63
Laber, Jake, North Dakota State	3	5	5.24	13	0	81	84	41	66
Percival, Ben, Western Illinois	3	7	5.28	15	1	73	88	23	47
Melling, Kyle, Southern Utah	3	4	5.33	22	0	79	97	23	47
Wittwer, Dustin, Southern Utah	7	5	5.40	18	1	92	107	31	69
Robinson, Dakota, Centenary	5	3	5.40	15	0	72	91	17	44
Uebelhor, Cole, IPFW	0	8	5.48	11	0	64	87	14	16
DiBernardo, Mark, Western Illinois	5	7	5.49	15	0	84	108	16	66
#Kelly, T.J., Oral Roberts	2	1	4.01	24	**10**	34	37	12	31

SUN BELT CONFERENCE

	Conference		Overall	
	W	L	W	L
Louisiana-Monroe	20	10	34	24
New Orleans	18	11	43	21
Troy	18	12	32	26
Florida Atlantic	15	12	32	27
*Western Kentucky	16	14	33	27
Louisiana-Lafayette	16	14	30	29
South Alabama	15	15	32	26
Middle Tennessee State	13	16	27	29
Florida International	12	18	20	36
Arkansas-Little Rock	10	18	16	32
Arkansas State	8	21	20	34

ALL-CONFERENCE TEAM: C—Robert Taylor, Sr., Arkansas-Little Rock. **1B**—Rawley Bishop, Jr., Middle Tennessee State. **2B**—Ryan Mollica, Jr., Florida International. **3B**—Zach Barrett, Sr., Middle Tennessee State. **SS**—Ben Soignier, Jr., Louisiana-Monroe. **OF**—Mike McKenna, Sr., Florida Atlantic; Dexter Fontenot, Sr., Louisiana-Monroe; Bryan Miller, Sr., Troy. **DH**—Chad Cregar, Jr., Western Kentucky. **UTIL**—Jeff Lanning, Jr., New Orleans. **SP**—Bryan Cryer, Sr., New Orleans; Hunter Moody, Sr., Louisiana-Lafayette. **RP**—Josh Storm, Jr., Troy.

Player of the Year: Mike McKenna, Florida Atlantic. **Pitcher of the Year:** Bryan Cryer, New Orleans. **Newcomer of the Year:** Chad Cregar, Western Kentucky. **Freshman of the Year:** Bryce Brentz, Middle Tennessee State. **Coach of the Year:** Jeff Schexnaider, Louisiana-Monroe.

INDIVIDUAL BATTING LEADERS
(Minimum 125 At-Bats)

	AVG	AB	R	H	2B	3B	HR	RBI	SB
Mollica, Ryan, Florida International	.413	201	50	83	23	1	5	49	5
Miller, Bryan, Troy	.402	254	59	**102**	**32**	2	12	64	4
McKenna, Mike, Florida Atlantic	.394	246	67	97	15	1	16	46	1
Soignier, Ben, La.-Lafayette	.394	236	**83**	93	21	2	16	46	13
Apfel, Matt, Ark.-Little Rock	.387	186	40	72	15	0	5	37	4
Barrett, Zach, Middle Tennessee	.382	249	55	95	16	0	9	46	5
Bishop, Rawley, Middle Tennessee	.372	223	64	83	19	0	18	69	2
Lanning, Jeff, New Orleans	.370	216	59	80	11	0	15	55	7
Taylor, Robert, Ark.-Little Rock	.369	179	36	66	15	0	10	41	5
Suire, Kyle, La.-Monroe	.367	226	67	83	16	1	16	65	5
Castillo, Jorge, Florida International	.367	229	47	84	19	0	9	58	0
Arata, Nick, Florida Atlantic	.365	222	61	81	11	0	13	50	7
Fontenot, Dexter, La.-Monroe	.364	209	50	76	17	0	12	67	3
Cregar, Chad, Western Kentucky	.360	250	47	90	15	1	**21**	**82**	2
Vander Hey, Josh, New Orleans	.358	229	52	82	21	0	13	76	4
Giavotella, Johnny, New Orleans	.354	237	76	84	16	2	12	56	19
McDade, Blake, Middle Tennessee	.354	206	53	73	16	3	6	51	2
Kruml, Ray, South Alabama	.352	247	69	87	21	2	8	45	**31**

Collins, Matt, La.-Monroe	.348	201	39	70	14	1	7	53	2
Block, William, Florida Atlantic	.347	245	71	85	16	0	12	47	14
Dayleg, Terrence, Western Kentucky	.347	225	45	78	15	2	7	55	3
Gaynor, Wade, Western Kentucky	.346	260	56	90	24	1	13	48	11
Butler, Joey, New Orleans	.345	**267**	77	92	21	6	11	58	13
Hines, Nathan, Middle Tennessee	.344	253	52	87	18	5	11	50	5
Jernigan, Ryne, South Alabama	.344	227	50	78	22	1	16	72	8
Schwaner, Nick, New Orleans	.341	226	46	77	13	2	12	58	8
Griffiths, Jeremy, Florida Atlantic	.338	225	59	76	9	2	5	35	6
Bohanan, Ryan, South Alabama	.333	189	41	63	11	0	9	42	1
Burnett, Tyler, Middle Tennessee	.331	157	28	52	7	0	6	21	1
Doss, David, South Alabama	.329	213	51	70	13	2	10	47	1
#Kaskie, Scott, Western Kentucky	.294	245	68	72	8	7	6	45	20

INDIVIDUAL PITCHING LEADERS
(Minimum 50 Innings)

	W	L	ERA	G	SV	IP	H	BB	SO
Moody, Hunter, La.-Lafayette	9	2	3.26	14	0	99	102	23	76
Cryer, Bryan, New Orleans	**12**	3	3.48	16	0	**103**	85	23	**104**
Ware, Chase, Arkansas State	5	6	3.57	13	0	86	84	26	67
Ridings, Matt, Western Kentucky	10	3	3.88	16	1	97	99	36	98
Roberts, Kenneth, Middle Tennessee	5	5	4.56	14	0	75	76	30	43
Beliveau, Jeff, Florida Atlantic	5	4	4.58	15	0	77	63	77	79
Whalen, Stephen, New Orleans	6	5	4.64	17	0	83	87	36	58
Cook, Michael, La.-Lafayette	5	5	4.79	15	0	68	77	25	49
Stanley, Langdon, Middle Tennessee	3	3	4.87	27	4	57	65	27	38
Allen, Chris, Florida International	4	4	4.87	11	0	61	78	15	45
Farquhar, Danny, La.-Lafayette	3	8	4.95	14	1	76	77	24	83
Davis, Rye, Western Kentucky	3	5	4.99	28	4	61	65	15	63
Jennings, Jared, La.-Monroe	4	4	5.06	16	0	85	103	26	63
Klumpp, David, Arkansas-Little Rock	3	7	5.32	14	0	90	109	22	72
Wheeler, Tim, Troy	4	7	5.44	16	0	91	106	29	61
Bullington, Chris, Arkansas State	1	3	5.49	25	4	57	57	24	50
Edwards, Chad, Middle Tennessee	4	3	5.60	19	1	64	79	19	38
Horstmann, Eric, Florida International	3	2	5.71	14	0	65	79	19	38
Garcia, Justin, New Orleans	6	2	5.77	13	0	83	106	12	73
Hightower, Matt, Western Kentucky	3	5	5.79	13	0	65	76	30	47
#Teague, Evan, Western Kentucky	4	1	2.36	**33**	0	27	23	13	27
#O'Shea, Ryan, New Orleans	3	2	3.56	31	**13**	48	48	21	46

WEST COAST CONFERENCE

	Conference		Overall	
	W	L	W	L
*San Diego	16	5	44	17
Pepperdine	14	6	38	21
Santa Clara	13	8	33	22
San Francisco	12	9	31	26
Gonzaga	10	10	30	23
St. Mary's	8	13	26	26
Loyola Marymount	7	14	23	32
Portland	3	18	21	33

ALL-CONFERENCE TEAM: C—Tommy Medica, So., Santa Clara; Logan Gelbrich, Sr., San Diego. **1B**—Ryan Heroy, Jr., Pepperdine; Ryan Wheeler, So., Loyola, Marymount. **2B**—Joey Railey, Sr., San Francisco; Brady Fuerst, Jr., Santa Clara. **SS**—Riley Henricks, Fr., Portland; Jon Karcich, So., Santa Clara. **3B**—Bryce Mendonca, Jr., Pepperdine. **OF**—Kyle Jensen, So., Saint Mary's; Drew Heid, So., Gonzaga; Evan LeBlanc, Jr., Santa Clara; James Meador, So., San Diego; Kyle Morgan, Sr., San Francisco; Angelo Songco, So., Loyola Marymount; Eric Thames, Jr., Pepperdine. **P**—Nate Garcia, So., Santa Clara; Nick Gaudi, Jr., Pepperdine; A.J. Griffin, So., San Diego; Matt Lujan, Fr., San Francisco; Brian Matusz, Jr., San Diego; Nathan Newman, Jr., Pepperdine; Josh Romanski, Jr., San Diego; Thain Simon, Fr., Santa Clara.
Player of the Year: Eric Thames, Pepperdine. **Pitcher of the Year:** Brian Matusz, San Diego. **Freshman of the Year:** Thain Simon, Santa Clara. **Defensive Player of the Year:** Joey Railey, San Francisco. **Coach of the Year:** Rich Hill, San Diego.

INDIVIDUAL BATTING LEADERS
(Minimum 125 At-Bats)

	AVG	AB	R	H	2B	3B	HR	RBI	SB
Jensen, Kyle, Saint Mary's	.421	195	48	82	17	1	13	52	10
Thames, Eric, Pepperdine	.407	182	58	74	11	8	13	59	11

Heid, Drew, Gonzaga	.386	153	41	59	13	1	2	16	7
Lipkin, Ryan, San Francisco	.384	172	34	66	9	0	2	21	2
LeBlanc, Evan, Saint Mary's	.376	229	53	**86**	14	1	7	39	11
Meador, James, San Diego	.374	214	38	80	16	3	6	57	5
Wiegand, Ryan, Gonzaga	.365	222	35	81	18	2	11	**63**	0
Songco, Angelo, Loyola Marymount	.356	191	36	68	17	0	**15**	48	1
Fuglerud, Kenny, Saint Mary's	.351	168	36	59	8	1	3	25	11
Karcich, Jon, Santa Clara	.351	208	44	73	14	0	12	51	3
Bernatz, Connor, San Francisco	.347	190	28	66	10	1	2	26	3
Conan, Ryan, Santa Clara	.346	228	49	79	17	0	3	46	3
Wheeler, Ryan, Loyola Marymount	.345	203	36	70	**20**	1	6	45	5
Medica, Tommy, Santa Clara	.342	222	43	76	15	2	6	44	1
Hansen, Kevin, San Diego	.338	216	29	73	17	1	1	40	4
Wells, Evan, San Diego	.337	193	50	65	7	1	0	36	7
Valerio, Jose, San Diego	.336	149	28	50	9	0	5	26	0
Mendonca, Bryce, Pepperdine	.332	232	42	77	13	0	0	24	**32**
Fuerst, Brady, Santa Clara	.332	199	35	66	15	0	5	44	1
Mulligan, Ryan, Saint Mary's	.329	149	25	49	5	0	1	28	3
LaMonda, A.J., Loyola Marymount	.329	219	43	72	15	1	2	29	5
Miller, Cory, Saint Mary's	.327	159	38	52	7	1	0	17	12
Muno, Kevin, San Diego	.326	**242**	**62**	79	12	3	4	29	21
Railey, Joey, San Francisco	.326	239	37	78	18	0	5	39	9
Bialosky, Mitchell, San Francisco	.326	233	42	76	15	0	8	38	0
Romanski, Josh, San Diego	.324	225	44	73	14	1	6	49	3
Kveder, Grant, Gonzaga	.322	174	29	56	9	1	0	31	7
Glomb, Michael, Loyola Marymount	.321	190	35	61	7	0	2	24	4
Chatwood, Jason, Gonzaga	.321	215	44	68	4	1	4	35	4
Aidem, Matt, Pepperdine	.316	193	33	61	14	0	3	31	1
#Meier, Danny, Portland	.284	197	38	56	12	0	**15**	46	2

INDIVIDUAL PITCHING LEADERS
(Minimum 50 Innings)

	W	L	ERA	G	SV	IP	H	BB	SO
Matusz, Brian, San Diego	**12**	2	1.71	15	0	**105**	83	22	**141**
Simon, Thain, Santa Clara	9	2	2.59	20	2	63	61	24	71
#Gaudi, Nick, Pepperdine	5	1	2.68	**29**	**15**	44	43	13	36
Martin, Cody, Gonzaga	4	1	2.80	26	9	55	50	14	51
Gruener, David, Portland	2	5	3.18	14	0	74	88	17	35
Lujan, Matt, San Francisco	7	2	3.19	15	0	79	76	29	51
Pecina, Ricardo, San Diego	6	4	3.29	16	0	63	61	21	78
Newman, Nathan, Pepperdine	8	4	3.46	15	0	94	87	42	70
Garcia, Nate, Santa Clara	7	3	3.65	14	0	86	97	27	75
Blair, Kyle, San Diego	8	4	3.86	16	0	75	62	34	99
Baugh, Matt, San Francisco	5	3	4.00	15	0	101	107	21	58
Romanski, Josh, San Diego	9	1	4.00	15	0	97	87	20	78
Triolo, Mark, Portland	5	6	4.17	13	0	69	85	20	48
Bialosky, Mitchell, San Francisco	5	6	4.50	23	5	65	75	11	51
Cho, Ernie, Loyola Marymount	1	1	4.53	24	0	50	61	24	36
Fredrickson, Evan, San Francisco	5	3	4.54	15	0	75	58	61	109
Keadle, Nate, Loyola Marymount	2	5	4.63	20	0	56	64	22	38
Fields, Matt, Gonzaga	8	3	4.92	14	0	79	88	28	70
Proszek, A.J., Gonzaga	3	4	4.92	11	0	60	63	23	35
Alexander, Scott, Pepperdine	7	4	4.95	16	0	73	62	55	46
Ronick, Ari, Portland	4	7	5.03	13	0	63	73	17	46

WESTERN ATHLETIC CONFERENCE

	Conference		Overall	
	W	L	W	L
*Fresno State	21	11	47	31
Nevada	18	14	34	26
Hawaii	18	14	29	31
San Jose State	17	14	31	25
New Mexico State	15	17	28	33
Sacramento State	14	17	24	34
Louisiana Tech	7	23	23	31

ALL-CONFERENCE TEAM: C—Joe Leghorn, Sr., New Mexico State. **1B**—Alan Ahmady, So., Fresno State. **2B**—Erik Wetzel, Jr., Fresno State. **3B**—Jason Rodriguez, Sr., Nevada. **SS**—Jonathan Hee, Sr., Hawaii. **OF**—Steve Susdorf, Sr., Fresno State; Brandon Haislet, Sr., Hawaii; Joseph Scaperotta, Sr., New Mexico State; Tim Wheeler, So., Sacramento State. **SP**—Tanner Scheppers, Jr., Fresno State; Jared Alexander, Jr., Hawaii; Kyle Howe, Sr., Nevada. **RP**—Brandon Burke, Sr., Fresno State.
Player of the Year: Steve Susdorf, Fresno State. **Pitcher of the Year:**

Tanner Scheppers, Fresno State. **Freshman of the Year:** Danny Muno, Fresno State. **Coaches of the Year:** Mike Batesole, Fresno State; Sam Piraro, San Jose State.

INDIVIDUAL BATTING LEADERS
(Minimum 125 At-Bats)

	AVG	AB	R	H	2B	3B	HR	RBI	SB
Rodriguez, Jason, Nevada	.390	228	41	89	22	1	8	62	1
Haislet, Brandon, Hawaii	.389	229	52	89	22	1	7	51	12
Hardt, Tyler, New Mexico State	.387	168	46	65	15	2	8	44	2
Ahmady, Alan, Fresno State	.382	288	60	110	17	1	13	92	3
Jacobo, Gabe, Sacramento State	.379	227	49	86	17	3	15	66	7
Hee, Jonathan, Hawaii	.368	239	49	88	15	1	3	32	2
Flores, David, Sacramento State	.366	224	53	82	26	0	8	46	8
Ciaro, David, Nevada	.366	145	35	53	11	4	5	30	6
Auten, Christopher, New Mexico State	.365	252	62	92	24	0	10	56	0
Stienstra, Danny, San Jose State	.365	189	23	69	7	3	1	32	2
Jones, Jericho, Louisiana Tech	.364	198	44	72	8	1	13	46	8
Wetzel, Erik, Fresno State	.361	310	99	112	20	1	6	41	12
Bowman, Matt, Nevada	.355	217	55	77	20	1	4	36	9
Leghorn, Joe, New Mexico State	.352	165	31	58	10	1	6	39	0
Susdorf, Steve, Fresno State	.341	302	80	103	33	3	13	87	14
Stout, Richard, Nevada	.340	206	63	70	15	2	1	27	20
Sadoian, Jason, Nevada	.336	223	56	75	18	2	4	31	9
Cobb, Adam, Louisiana Tech	.332	233	44	74	11	2	8	38	11
Oberlin, Wes, Sacramento State	.332	193	37	64	9	0	12	40	3
Blair, Ryan, Sacramento State	.330	230	52	76	16	3	5	33	15
Wheeler, Tim, Sacramento State	.330	218	38	72	12	1	3	43	10
Muno, Danny, Fresno State	.330	288	62	95	13	2	3	30	10
Kort, Shaun, Nevada	.324	222	39	72	16	1	6	60	1
Busani, Franky, New Mexico State	.324	185	46	60	8	2	16	60	0
Scaperotta, Joseph, N. Mexico State	.315	235	62	74	17	0	23	82	3
Garcia, Greg, Hawaii	.312	154	29	48	7	1	2	20	7
Martin, Jason, San Jose State	.307	166	34	51	8	2	3	27	4
Grunewald, Nick, Louisiana Tech	.305	187	40	57	7	0	6	25	20
Hale, Mike, Nevada	.304	184	39	56	14	0	8	33	5
Hedstrom, Gavin, Fresno State	.303	251	51	76	10	0	7	35	5

INDIVIDUAL PITCHING LEADERS
(Minimum 50 Innings)

	W	L	ERA	G	SV	IP	H	BB	SO
Scheppers, Tanner, Fresno State	8	2	2.93	12	1	71	54	34	109
Alexander, Jared, Hawaii	7	3	3.27	12	0	83	83	15	63
Burke, Brandon, Fresno State	4	6	3.28	38	13	74	65	25	43
Sprague, Holden, Fresno State	6	2	3.59	33	1	88	100	20	55
Allison, Clayton, Fresno State	4	5	3.91	20	1	97	108	23	57
Lassere, Andrew, Louisiana Tech	2	4	3.99	20	0	56	66	19	41
Sobczak, Scott, San Jose State	4	2	4.06	15	0	84	95	19	51
Wilson, Justin, Fresno State	9	5	4.14	23	0	124	126	66	108
Howe, Kyle, Nevada	8	3	4.15	12	0	80	74	30	48
Knotts, Alan, Louisiana Tech	3	3	4.74	15	1	57	60	20	57
Goin, Heath, New Mexico State	6	3	4.85	13	0	82	97	18	45
Stassi, Brock, Nevada	4	2	4.85	17	1	59	78	18	36
Scurry, Rod, Nevada	6	7	4.87	15	1	81	69	35	66
Rhodes, Nicholas, Hawaii	5	6	4.89	16	0	81	88	26	55
York, Trevor, Sacramento State	4	6	4.97	14	0	87	115	23	39
Smith, Brian, Sacramento State	4	1	5.17	17	1	54	55	23	33
Peterson, Max, San Jose State	5	6	5.22	16	0	69	74	38	57
Schneider, Joshua, Hawaii	6	2	5.26	15	1	51	60	24	34
Ramirez, Jose, Sacramento State	4	6	5.27	14	0	70	79	32	54
Daly, Matt, Hawaii	5	5	5.31	22	2	81	70	65	80

INDEPENDENTS

	Overall	
	W	L
Dallas Baptist	37	19
LeMoyne	33	21
Longwood	23	26
Savannah State	20	25
Northern Colorado	21	33
Hawaii-Hilo	17	27
Texas-Pan American	21	35
New York Tech	19	32
Utah Valley State	17	36
Presbyterian	13	40
North Carolina Central	6	30
Chicago State	8	42
New Jersey Tech	5	47

ALL-INDEPENDENT TEAM: C—Phil St. Amant, Sr., Le Moyne. **1B**—Chad Murray, Sr., Northern Colorado. **2B**—Ryan Goins, So., Dallas Baptist. **3B**—Trevor Head, Jr., Dallas Baptist. **SS**—Matt Nandin, Jr., Le Moyne. **OF**—Scott Croshaw, Sr., Utah Valley State; Chris Edmondson, So., Le Moyne; Roly Gonzalez, Sr., Texas-Pan American. **DH/UTIL**—Kevin Sandberg, Jr., Northern Colorado. **SP**—Eric Beaulac, Jr., Le Moyne; Marcus Moore, Sr., Utah Valley State. **RP**—Tyson Bagley, Sr., Dallas Baptist. **Player of the Year:** Chris Edmondson, Le Moyne. **Pitcher of the Year:** Eric Beaulac, Le Moyne. **Newcomer of the Year:** Effrey Valdez, New York Tech. **Coach of the Year:** Dan Heefner, Dallas Baptist.

INDIVIDUAL BATTING LEADERS
(Minimum 125 At-Bats)

	AVG	AB	R	H	2B	3B	HR	RBI	SB
Higa, Michael, Hawaii-Hilo	.407	135	25	55	9	1	2	22	8
Cerreto, Phil, Longwood	.395	177	35	70	12	1	1	30	4
Santos, Nick, Dallas Baptist	.390	195	41	76	14	0	6	38	1
Murray, Chad, Northern Colorado	.370	189	52	70	19	1	5	53	0
Edmondson, Chris, Le Moyne	.367	196	51	72	22	5	14	64	3
Enos, Ryan, Dallas Baptist	.360	203	44	73	11	3	3	44	16
Carpen, Michael, Chicago State	.359	153	42	55	7	2	0	11	17
Goins, Ryan, Dallas Baptist	.357	207	44	74	14	3	10	44	6
Haynes, Chris, Le Moyne	.353	139	35	49	11	0	7	33	1
Croshaw, Scott, Utah Valley State	.351	194	39	68	14	5	4	40	2
Lyda, Cory, Presbyterian	.349	175	35	61	15	3	1	18	6
Crawford, Stephen, Le Moyne	.347	216	48	75	15	2	1	33	16
St. Amant, Phil, Le Moyne	.343	216	38	74	18	0	7	40	2
Nandin, Matt, Le Moyne	.341	223	47	76	13	0	0	34	11
Wilkerson, Kyle, Savannah State	.341	170	36	58	16	0	7	31	5
Gonzalez, Roly, Texas-Pan American	.336	226	52	76	9	3	0	30	46
Wilson, Jonathan, Chicago State	.335	158	21	53	10	0	9	26	2
Bigley, Evan, Dallas Baptist	.333	249	55	83	20	2	13	58	13
Valdez, Effrey, New York Tech	.332	202	34	67	8	2	10	44	5
Rutenbar, Jordan, Texas-Pan American	.332	199	42	66	11	1	5	42	2
Perez, Robert, Le Moyne	.331	166	45	55	12	1	8	38	7
O'Neill, Corey, Le Moyne	.330	209	46	69	15	0	11	48	3
Head, Trevor, Dallas Baptist	.329	219	51	72	16	0	16	55	2
Brinkerhoff, Jace, Utah Valley State	.328	232	42	76	21	2	8	45	2
Sandberg, Kevin, Northern Colorado	.328	201	47	66	22	0	11	58	0
Javis, Brandon, Savannah State	.326	129	36	42	14	2	5	31	5
Morales, Cory, Northern Colorado	.322	214	50	69	14	1	3	37	8
Mendoza, Jose, Texas-Pan American	.321	212	32	68	10	2	2	35	11
Jones, Ryan, Utah Valley State	.321	234	40	75	8	0	0	24	4
Bantz, Brandon, Dallas Baptist	.319	185	35	59	16	0	4	31	2
Morreim, Justin, Longwood	.319	163	31	52	13	2	3	29	3

INDIVIDUAL PITCHING LEADERS
(Minimum 50 Innings)

	W	L	ERA	G	SV	IP	H	BB	SO
Beaulac, Eric, Le Moyne	9	2	2.83	14	0	92	56	43	113
Moore, Marcus, Utah Valley State	10	5	2.86	15	0	113	106	42	97
Harting, Luke, Longwood	6	4	3.04	19	5	50	53	11	36
Nelllis, Luke, Le Moyne	5	6	3.63	22	6	69	45		69
Davis, Joe, Hawaii-Hilo	3	4	3.67	12	0	69	71	21	43
Briere, Chris, Longwood	2	3	3.67	12	0	54	65	14	43
Tardiff, Jeff, Le Moyne	4	3	3.92	21	3	60	59	22	40
Meaker, Jordan, Dallas Baptist	7	1	4.19	15	0	88	92	34	62
Guarrasi, Andrew, New York Tech	4	6	4.38	15	0	84	88	57	63
Allegretti, Michael, Savannah State	7	4	4.48	13	0	70	86	29	37
Walker II, John, Longwood	6	4	4.57	14	0	69	87	8	35
Black, Victor, Dallas Baptist	1	6	4.97	14	0	71	66	46	56
Farrell, John, Longwood	3	4	4.97	11	0	63	80	19	35
Cisper, Cody, Texas-Pan American	6	5	5.23	14	0	74	91	41	70
Reap, Chris, Northern Colorado	5	5	5.32	12	0	69	89	28	54
Wasmund, Preston, New York Tech	2	4	5.49	15	0	59	63	41	33
Ryan, Frank, New York Tech	6	5	5.68	14	0	71	70	54	59
Tunison, Daniel, Le Moyne	4	2	5.68	13	1	51	62	17	38
Klausing, Jon, Northern Colorado	3	6	5.79	14	0	70	102	51	77
Arnold, Alford, Savannah State	2	6	5.95	13	0	65	77	44	46
Smith, Bryan, Utah Valley State	2	5	6.15	15	0	60	70	33	62
#Bagley, Tyson, Dallas Baptist	4	2	2.56	28	11	39	28	23	56

COLLEGE BASEBALL

NCAA DIVISION II

Most head baseball coaches would fear for their lives—or at least their jobs—if they needed a police escort back to the stadium to keep a mob of fans away. But for Mount Olive (N.C.) skipper Carl Lancaster, it was the culmination of 22 years of work. His Trojans had just beaten Ouachita Baptist (Ark.) in the championship game of the NCAA Division II College World Series, and the welcome home party was in full swing.

Mount Olive, ranked No. 1 in the nation for most of the year and the top seed in the tournament, cruised to a perfect 4-0 mark in Sauget, Ill., and finished the season at 58-6.

Even the championship game wasn't in doubt long. The Trojans took advantage of a two-out Ouachita Baptist error in the first inning to put up five runs. They wouldn't look back from there, coasting to a 6-2 win and the title behind a gem from pitcher Casey Hodges. Hodges tossed eight innings, giving up two runs on seven hits and striking out six.

Hodges wasn't alone in pitching lights-out for the champs. Kyle Jones sent the Trojans to the title game with a complete game in the semifinals—his second of the postseason. Such clutch performances were commonplace for the Trojans, who put five players on the all-tournament team. Hodges was joined by David Cooper, Rich Racobaldo, Alex Vertcnik and Jesse Lancaster. The Trojans also had five players drafted—one more than the more-famous Trojans, Southern California.

DIVISION II WORLD SERIES

Site: Sauget, Ill.
Participants: Sonona State, Calif. (50-13), Shippensburg, Pa. (38-24), Central Missouri (45-15), Franklin Pierce, N.H. (43-13), Ouachita Baptist, Ark. (47-14), Mount Olive, N.C. (54-6), Tampa, Fla. (42-9-1), Ashland, Ohio (39-16)
Champion: Mount Olive
Runner-Up: Ouachita Baptist
Outstanding Player: Steve Smith, Ouachita Baptist
Preliminaries
Sonoma State 10, Shippensburg 1
Central Missouri 13, Franklin Pierce 12 (11 innings)
Mount Olive 6, Ouachita Baptist 5
Ashland 6, Tampa 5
Shippensburg 9, Franklin Pierce 2 (Franklin Pierce eliminated)
Ouachita Baptist 12, Tampa 10 (Tampa eliminated)
Sonoma State 6, Central Missouri 5 (19 innings)
Mount Olive 18, Ashland 7
Ouachita Baptist 12, Ashland 5 (Ashland eliminated)
Central Missouri 5, Shippensburg 1 (Shippensburg eliminated)
Semifinals
Mount Olive 5, Central Missouri 3 (Central Missouri eliminated)
Ouachita Baptist 2, Sonoma State 1
Ouachita Baptist 2, Sonoma State 1 (Sonoma State eliminated)
Championship
Mount Olive 6, Ouachita Baptist 2

NCAA DIVISION III

"I don't think anyone can beat us twice in one day," Trinity (Conn.) College first baseman Kent Graham told the Hartford Courant the day before the NCAA Division III national championship would be decided.

It was hard to argue with Graham's bold proclamation. After all, Trinity had started the season a 44-0, an unprecedented achievement in any level of college baseball. The 45th win would clinch a perfect season and the school's first national championship. Standing in the Bantams' way was Johns Hopkins (Md.), which needed to beat Trinity twice to win the double-elimination tournament.

A perfect season slipped out of Trinity's grasp almost literally, as Hopkins scored the winning run in the ninth inning on a wild pitch third strike to take the first game 4-3. But Graham was right: the Bantams weren't going to lose twice in one day. They nearly did, trailing by a run heading into the bottom of the ninth before getting back-to-back bases-loaded walks with two outs to walk off with a 5-4 win and the national championship.

Trinity finished 45-1, but its 44-0 start is the best in college baseball history. The Bantams cruised through the New England Small College Athletic Conference and showed no signs of slowing down in the New England regional, winning every game by at least four runs. They won their first three games at the World Series in Appleton, Wis., to set up the memorable showdown with Johns Hopkins.

DIVISION III WORLD SERIES

Site: Appleton, Wis.
Participants: Kean, N.J. (39-11), Chapman, Calif. (40-5), Johns Hopkins, Md. (42-8), Adrian, Mich. (36-13), Linfield, Ore. (35-13), Wisconsin-Whitewater (42-10), Trinity, Conn. (45-1), SUNY Cortland (42-5)
Champion: Trinity
Runner-Up: Johns Hopkins
Outstanding Player: Chez Angeloni, Johns Hopkins
Preliminaries
Chapman 4, Kean 2
Johns Hopkins 3, Adrian 2 (14 innings)
Linfield 5, Wisconsin-Whitewater 1
Trinity 2, SUNY Cortland 1
Adrian 7, Kean 6 (12 innings; Kean eliminated)
Wisconsin-Whitewater 10, SUNY Cortland 2 (SUNY Cortland eliminated)
Johns Hopkins 5, Chapman 4
Trinity 6, Linfield 5
Wisconsin-Whitewater 7, Chapman 4 (Chapman eliminated)
Adrian 7, Linfield 2 (Linfield eliminated)
Trinity 8, Johns Hopkins 5
Semifinals
Wisconsin-Whitewater 13, Adrian 11
Johns Hopkins 12, Wisconsin-Whitewater 11 (Wis.-Whitewater eliminated)
Championship
Johns Hopkins 4, Trinity 3
Trinity 5, Johns Hopkins 4

NAIA

In case there was any doubt about Lewis-Clark (Idaho) State's dominance in NAIA, the Warriors reminded everyone with their third straight title and seventh in the last 10 years by twice defeating top-seeded Lee (Tenn.) at the NAIA World Series.

The title is the Warriors' 16th national championship, though this one certainly was not a waltz. They faced an early exit from the double-elimination tournament—which they hosted in Lewiston, Idaho—when they lost to Lee 5-2, snapping a seven-game winning streak in the World Series. LCSC proved resilient, however, winning three straight elimination games to take the title.

NAIA WORLD SERIES

Site: Lewiston, Idaho
Participants: Bellevue, Neb. (52-17), Embry-Riddle, Fla. (44-18), Azusa Pacific, Calif. (46-12), Lee, Tenn. (63-10), Union, Ky. (48-18), Ohio Dominican (40-16), Spring Arbor, Mich. (40-9), Oklahoma City (57-12), Lewis-Clark State, Idaho (58-7), Jamestown, N.D. (32-20)
Champion: Lewis-Clark State
Runner-Up: Lee
Outstanding Player: Brian Ward, Lewis-Clark State
PRELIMINARIES
Spring Arbor 7, Jamestown 5
Bellevue 15, Ohio Dominican 3
Union 9, Azusa Pacific 8
Lewis-Clark State 19, Embry-Riddle 0
Azusa Pacific 9, Ohio Dominican 2 (Ohio Dominican eliminated)
Embry-Riddle 10, Jamestown 5 (Jamestown eliminated)
Oklahoma City 10, Spring Arbor 2
Lee 7, Bellevue 1
Spring Arbor 11, Azusa Pacific 10 (Azusa Pacific eliminated)
Embry-Riddle 6, Bellevue 1 (Bellevue eliminated)
Lee 14, Union 8
Lewis-Clark State 9, Oklahoma City 5
Spring Arbor 8, Union 7
Oklahoma City 11, Embry-Riddle 6
Lee 5, Lewis-Clark State 2
SEMIFINALS
Lewis-Clark State 9, Spring Arbor 4 (Spring Arbor eliminated)
Lee 6, Oklahoma City 5 (Oklahoma City eliminated)
CHAMPIONSHIP
Lewis-Clark State 7, Lee 6
Lewis-Clark State 8, Lee 3

JUNIOR COLLEGES

NJCAA DIVISION I

Grayson County (Texas) breezed through the Division I Junior College World Series without a loss to take its third national title, defeating Shelton State (Ala.) in the championship in Grand Junction, Colo. The title is the Vikings' first since winning back-to-back titles in 1999 and 2000.

Site: Grand Junction, Colo.
Participants: Alvin, Texas (41-18), Central Arizona (44-22), Chipola, Fla. (45-14), Connors State, Okla. (48-19), Grayson, Texas (48-16), Hagerstown, Md. (42-19-1), Iowa Western (46-22), Johnson County, Kan. (41-18), Shelton State, Ala. (49-18), Walters State, Tenn. (55-9)
Champion: Grayson
Runner-Up: Shelton State
Outstanding Player: J.D. Alfaro, Grayson

NJCAA DIVISION II

Louisiana State-Eunice ran roughshod over tournament foes in the Division II Junior College World Series, outscoring its opponents 51-24 in Millington, Tenn., and defeating Lenoir (N.C.) 17-5 in the final game to capture its third national championship in the last five years.

Site: Millington, Tenn.
Participants: Lenoir, N.C. (54-10), Western Oklahoma State (52-12), Monroe, N.Y. (41-15), Grand Rapids, Mich. (29-24), Elgin, Ill. (32-16), Longview, Mo. (36-27), Des Moines Area, Iowa (48-18), Louisiana State-Eunice (52-12)
Champion: LSU-Eunice
Runner-Up: Lenoir
Outstanding Player: Perry Smith, LSU-Eunice

NJCAA DIVISION III

A year after finishing as the national runner-up, Joliet (Ill.) defeated Gloucester County (N.J.) 9-0 to win the Division III Junior College World Series in Tyler, Texas. The Wolves secured the title in the minimum four games, going undefeated.

Site: Tyler, Texas
Participants: Hudson Valley, N.Y. (32-10), Joliet, Ill. (49-11), Richland, Texas (47-16), Montgomery Co. Germantown, Md. (35-12), Ridgewater, Minn. (36-7-1), Suffolk West, N.Y. (30-10), Gloucester, N.J. (42-13), Manchester, Conn. (29-13-2)
Champion: Joliet
Runner-Up: Gloucester
Outstanding Player: Dillon Roark, Joliet

CALIFORNIA COMMUNITY COLLEGE ATHLETIC ASSOCIATION

Sierra defeated Southwestern 6-2 in the final game of the California Community College Athletic Association tournament to win its first state title, avenging a loss to the Jaguars earlier in the day in Fresno, Calif.

Site: Fresno
Participants: Sierra (39-15), Southwestern (40-14), Riverside (34-20), West Valley (40-11)
Champion: Sierra
Runner-Up: Southwestern
Outstanding Player: Cameron Ray, Sierra

NORTHWEST ATHLETIC ASSOCIATION OF COMMUNITY COLLEGES

Edmonds (Wash.) CC bounced back from an early loss and took two consecutive wins over Lower Columbia (Wash.) to win the Northwest Athletic Association of Community Colleges championship in Longview, Wash.

Site: Longview, Wash.
Participants: Mt. Hood (32-18), Skagit Valley (29-16), Columbia Basin (38-17), Pierce (22-24), Edmonds (38-9), Linn-Benton (32-17), Lower Columbia (30-20), Wenatchee Valley (36-10)
Champion: Edmonds
Runner-Up: Lower Columbia
Outstanding Player: Dan Ninomiya, Edmonds

BY AARON FITT

When the dust settles, the 2008 USA Baseball collegiate national team might be remembered as the program's best ever. For certain, no national team has ever topped or will ever top Team USA's 1.000 winning percentage.

Team USA finished its 2008 summer tour with an undefeated record for the first time ever with a thrilling 1-0 win over Japan in 12 innings, clinching the gold medal at the FISU World Championship in the Czech Republic. Team USA finished the summer a perfect 24-0 and established a new national team record for lowest ERA (0.88, eclipsing the previous mark of 1.29 set in 2003). Remarkably, the Americans did not allow more than two earned runs in any game and threw six shutouts, capped by the 12-inning shutout of Japan.

Team USA's offense rapped out 12 hits in the game but left 10 runners on base before finally breaking through in the 12th. With two outs in the frame, Auburn's Hunter Morris delivered a pinch-hit, broken-bat single to center to easily score Louisiana State's Micah Gibbs with the winning run. Morris also delivered a walk-off homer to beat Taiwan in the final game of FISU pool play.

Baylor righthander Kendal Volz came on to pitch the bottom of the 12th and allowed the tying run to reach third base with one out. But Volz got a strikeout and a ground out to end the game, securing his eighth save in eight opportunities this summer. He finished with a 0.00 ERA, 16 strikeouts and five walks in 14 innings over 13 appearances.

Volz, Oklahoma State's Tyler Lyons and Missouri's Kyle Gibson all came up big in the later innings as they have all summer for Team USA. The trio, which pitched almost exclusively in relief, combined to allow just two earned runs in 46 innings on the summer.

"The key to this team was the pitching, and even moreso the bullpen," Team USA coach Rob Walton said. "Guys like Lyons and Gibson and Volz, who are all starters in their own programs, accepting roles in the bullpen was big. Their doing that probably was the biggest key of the summer."

The offense benefited from timely hitting all summer long, though just one regular (California's Blake Smith at .327) finished with an average above .300.

Team USA did take two losses in its trials phase, when playing in the New England Collegiate League, but once the final roster was named, the team didn't lose. Whether with its bats or its arms, Team USA simply found ways to win every time it took the field.

COLLEGE NATIONAL TEAM STATISTICS

PLAYER, POS.	YEAR	SCHOOL	AVG	AB	R	H	2B	3B	HR	RBI	SB
Kentrail Davis, of	Fr.	Tennessee	.370	27	5	10	2	0	0	5	2
Blake Smith, of	So.	California	.327	55	16	18	5	1	3	13	0
Josh Fellhauer, of	So.	Cal State Fullerton	.299	87	21	26	6	1	2	15	2
Jared Clark, 1b	Jr.	Cal State Fullerton	.279	43	12	12	3	0	4	11	0
Hunter Morris, 1b	Fr.	Auburn	.270	37	10	10	1	0	3	9	0
Micah Gibbs, c	Fr.	Louisiana State	.264	72	14	19	3	0	2	17	0
Christian Colon, ss/2b	Fr.	Cal State Fullerton	.263	99	14	26	2	0	1	14	5
Derek Dietrich, 3b	Fr.	Georgia Tech	.259	54	9	14	4	1	1	5	0
Ryan Lipkin, c	So.	San Francisco	.256	39	4	10	2	0	2	7	0
Mike Leake, util	So.	Arizona State	.236	55	8	13	2	0	1	8	1
Ryan Jackson, ss	So.	Miami	.232	69	11	16	2	1	1	13	0
Tommy Mendonca, 3b	So.	Fresno State	.231	52	7	12	3	0	2	7	0
Matt den Dekker, of	So.	Florida	.229	70	11	16	1	1	1	9	2
Scott Woodward, 3b/of	So.	Coastal Carolina	.226	31	8	7	0	0	2	5	2
PITCHER	**YEAR**	**SCHOOL**	**W**	**L**	**ERA**	**APP**	**SV**	**IP**	**H**	**BB**	**SO**
Kendal Volz, rhp	So.	Baylor	0	0	0.00	13	8	14	6	5	16
Tyler Lyons, lhp	So.	Oklahoma State	2	0	0.00	11	0	14	4	2	17
Blake Smith, rhp	So.	California	1	0	0.00	5	2	9	3	3	11
Kevin Rhoderick, rhp	Fr.	Oregon State	0	0	0.00	1	0	1	0	0	0
Mike Leake, rhp	So.	Arizona State	3	0	0.64	8	0	28	22	6	24
Mike Minor, lhp	So.	Vanderbilt	3	0	0.75	6	0	36	21	13	37
Andrew Oliver, lhp	So.	Oklahoma State	2	0	0.93	4	0	19	10	11	24
Kyle Gibson, rhp	So.	Missouri	5	0	1.02	13	0	18	8	4	25
Stephen Strasburg, rhp	So.	San Diego State	3	0	1.06	5	0	34	16	6	48
Brett Hunter, rhp	Jr.	Pepperdine	2	0	1.47	4	0	18	7	11	26
A.J. Griffin, rhp	So.	San Diego	1	0	1.62	10	0	17	10	5	18
Chris Hernandez, lhp	Fr.	Miami	2	0	1.69	5	0	16	8	6	22

"This team's record speaks for itself," national team general manager Eric Campbell said. "Every year is special, but I don't know how we'll be able to top what this team did. They finished 24-0, they beat Cuba's best team twice, they beat Japan three times, and they won two gold medals. It speaks volumes for college baseball."

Harwich Wins 1st Cape Title

The Harwich Mariners won their first Cape Cod League championship in 21 years, beating Cotuit 2-1 in the decisive third game of the championship series. Mark Fleury (North Carolina) delivered a pinch-hit, two-run single in the ninth inning against Kettleers closer Drew Storen (Stanford), turning a 1-0 deficit into a 2-1 win for Harwich.

Harwich got a strong start from Chris Manno (Duke), who struck out nine while allowing just an unearned run on five hits and a walk over 5⅔ innings. Willie Kempf (Baylor) followed with 2⅓ scoreless to pick up the win in relief.

Days earlier, Harwich returned to the Cape League championship series for the first time in 11 years in dramatic fashion. The Mariners needed 18 innings to pull out a 1-0 win over Orleans. Cotuit held off Falmouth to reach the championship series before falling to Harwich.

KEN BABBITT

Lefthander Chris Manno struck out nine to lead Harwich to its first Cape League title

SUMMER LEAGUE ROUNDUP

■ The Santa Barbara Foresters, who went 19-11 to win the California Collegiate League championship, went on to win the National Baseball Congress World Series in Wichita. Behind a complete-game shutout from righthander Mike Ford (UC Santa Barbara), the Foresters beat the Seattle Studs 2-0 in the championship game. Ford allowed just five hits and a walk while striking out nine to secure the second NBC title in three years for Santa Barbara.

■ The Thunder Bay Border Cats took home their second Northwoods League title, winning the championship series two games to one against the Madison Mallards. The final game was a nail-biter, as Madison scored three runs in the seventh and another in the eighth to take a 5-3 lead. The Border Cats battled back with three runs of their own in the bottom of the eighth and came away with a 6-5 victory. First baseman Derek Wiley (Belmont) was the star for the Border Cats' offense, going 2-for-5 with a home run and three RBIs. His infield single capped Thunder Bay's three-run eighth, as two runs scored on the play when Madison shortstop Brandon Wikoff (Illinois) threw errantly to first.

■ Thomasville became the first team to win three consecutive Coastal Plain League championships, beating Florence 7-4 in the final game of the Petitt Cup tournament championships. A pair of teammates from The Citadel combined to score the eventual game-winning run in the fifth, as Richard Jones singled home Chris McGuiness from second to break a 4-4 tie. A third Bulldog,

outfielder Sonny Meade, put the game out of reach with a two-run homer an inning later. Patrick Dean (Boston College) picked up the win for the HiToms, working 2 2/3 innings of three-hit relief.

■ The Sanford Mainers put their clutch hitting, pitching and defense on display to win their second-ever NECBL championship with a 4-1 victory against the Newport Gulls. Sanford broke a 1-1 tie with a pair of unearned runs in the fourth inning, then turned a key double play with runners on the corners and league home run leader Alex Gregory at the plate in the eighth. The Mainers last won it all in 2004, when they also defeated Newport.

■ The Anchorage Glacier Pilots were awarded the Alaska League title in a very anticlimactic fashion. Anchorage had 11 games rained out, meaning it ended up playing five fewer games than the second-place Mat-Su Miners. League officials awarded Anchorage the title before the season was over based on a mathematical tiebreaker. Strangely, they did so despite the fact that a red-hot Mat-Su team was still technically capable of winning the pennant. "My guys are dejected. They're bumming," Miners general manager Pete Christopher told the Anchorage Daily News.

■ Luray swept Covington in the championship series of the Lineweaver Cup, outscoring the Lumberjacks 17-4 in three games. It was Luray's third consecutive appearance in the championship and its second title since joining the Valley League in 2001.

Minor emerges as USA's big-game guy

BY AARON FITT

Weeks before the USA Baseball collegiate national team put the finishing touches on its perfect summer, a first-inning pickoff might have been the biggest play of the whole summer.

In the second game of pool play at Haarlem Honkbal Week in the Netherlands, Team USA was up against a Cuban national team that was the same minus one player from its 2004 Olympic gold medal team and its 2006 World Baseball Classic squad. Cuba's Glorbis Duvergel singled against USA lefthander Mike Minor to lead off the game, but Minor stopped Cuba in its tracks and gave the Americans the momentum by picking Duvergel off first.

"Minor had a big pick early in the game, and we never lost the ability to keep playing," national team general manager Eric Campbell said. "It just kind of said, 'Hey, we'll play with anybody.' For me, everything just seemed to turn at that point."

Team USA went on to a 1-0 win over Cuba behind 6⅓ shutout innings from Minor. A week later, Minor faced Cuba again and yielded just an unearned run on four hits over six innings, leading USA to a 4-1 win and a gold medal.

But Minor saved his best for last, throwing 9⅔ brilliant innings of four-hit, shutout ball against Japan in Team USA's final game of the summer, a 1-0 win in 12 innings to secure the gold medal at the FISU World Championships and clinch a 24-0 record on the summer. Minor struck out nine without issuing a walk

Mike Minor — ALYSON BOYER

in the finale, giving him 37 strikeouts and 13 walks in a team-leading 36 innings on the summer, to go along with a 3-0, 0.75 mark. But it was his performances in the biggest games, even more than his dazzling numbers, that make Minor the 2008 Baseball America Summer Player of the Year.

Not long ago, another Vanderbilt lefthander racked up strikeouts and earned the Summer Player of the Year award while excelling for Team USA. The next spring, David Price went on to lead the nation in strikeouts, capture the Player of the Year award and become the No. 1 overall draft pick. Minor was a freshman that year pitching in Vandy's Saturday starter slot, which meant he got to sit behind the plate and chart pitches during all of Price's starts. Naturally, it was quite a learning experience for the young Minor. The biggest lesson he learned from Price?

"Basically just pounding strike after strike," Minor said. "Price just went right after (hitters), made them swing the bat and put the ball in play.

"He also had an overall ability to stay calm no matter what happened. He's just a special guy. Watching him every Friday as a freshman was kind of overwhelming, thinking that next year maybe I'll be the guy."

Like Price, Minor pitched for Team USA after his freshman year, going 5-2, 1.64 with a 37-4 K-BB mark in 33 innings. A year later, he was "the guy" for Vandy, and for Team USA.

PREVIOUS WINNERS

1984: Will Clark, 1b, Team USA; Rafael Palmeiro, of, Hutchinson (Jayhawk)
1985: Jeff King, 3b, Team USA; Bob Zupcic, of, Liberal (Jayhawk)
1986: Jack Armstrong, rhp, Wareham (Cape Cod); Mike Harkey, rhp, Fairbanks (Alaska)
1987: Cris Carpenter, rhp, Team USA
1988: Robin Ventura, 3b, Team USA; Ty Griffin, 2b, Team USA
1989: John Olerud, 1b-lhp, Palouse (Alaska)
1990: Calvin Murray, of, Anchorage Bucs (Alaska)
1991: Chris Roberts, of, Team USA
1992: Jeffrey Hammonds, of, Team USA
1993: Geoff Jenkins, of, Team USA
1994: Steve Carver, 1b, Anchorage Glacier Pilots (Alaska)
1995: Travis Lee, 1b, Team USA
1996: Seth Greisinger, rhp, Team USA
1997: Pat Burrell, 3b, Team USA
1998: Bobby Kielty, of, Bourne (Cape Cod)
1999: Xavier Nady, 3b, Team USA
2000: Mark Teixeira, 3b, Team USA
2001: Bobby Brownlie, rhp, Team USA
2002: Brad Sullivan, rhp, Team USA
2003: Jered Weaver, rhp, Team USA
2004: Daniel Carte, of, Falmouth (Cape Cod)
2005: Andrew Miller, lhp, Chatham (Cape Cod)
2006: David Price, lhp, Team USA
2007: Luke Greinke, of/rhp, Winchester (Valley)

COLLEGE BASEBALL

CAPE COD LEAGUE

EAST	W	L	T	PCT	PTS
Orleans	25	17	2	.595	52
Harwich	24	20	0	.545	48
Brewster	19	21	4	.475	42
Chatham	19	25	0	.432	38
Yarmouth-Dennis	18	25	1	.419	37

WEST	W	L	T	PCT	PTS
Cotuit	24	18	2	.571	50
Falmouth	23	20	1	.535	47
Bourne	23	20	1	.535	47
Hyannis	22	22	0	.500	44
Wareham	17	26	1	.395	35

PLAYOFFS—Semifinals: Harwich defeated Orleans 2-0 and Cotuit defeated Falmouth 2-1 in best-of-three series. **Finals:** Harwich defeated Cotuit 2-0 in best-of-three series.

TOP 30 PROSPECTS: 1. Grant Green, ss, Chatham (Jr., Southern California). 2. Dustin Ackley, of, Harwich (Jr., North Carolina). 3. Matt Harvey, rhp, Chatham (So., North Carolina). 4. Ben Tootle, rhp, Falmouth (Jr., Jacksonville State). 5. Brandon Workman, rhp, Wareham (So., Texas). 6. D.J. LeMahieu, ss, Harwich (So., Louisiana State). 7. A.J. Pollock, of, Falmouth (Jr., Notre Dame). 8. Brett Jackson, of, Cotuit (Jr., California). 9. Jeff Inman, rhp, Yarmouth-Dennis (Jr., Stanford). 10. Brad Stillings, rhp, Orleans (Jr., Kent State). 11. Ben Paulsen, 1b, Hyannis (Jr., Clemson). 12. Robbie Shields, ss, Cotuit (Jr., Florida Southern). 13. Matt Thomson, rhp, Orleans (Jr., San Diego). 14. Bryce Stowell, rhp, Bourne (signed with Indians). 15. Shawn Tolleson, rhp, Yarmouth-Dennis (So., Baylor). 16. Rich Poythress, 3b, Orleans (Jr., Georgia). 17. Kevin Patterson, 1b, Cotuit (So., Auburn). 18. Craig Fritsch, rhp, Yarmouth-Dennis (So., Baylor). 19. Mike Bianucci, of, Cotuit (signed with Rangers). 20. Brad Boxberger, rhp, Chatham (Jr., Southern California). 21. Chad Bettis, rhp, Falmouth (So., Texas Tech). 22. Tim Wheeler, of, Orleans (Jr., Sacramento State). 23. Dusty Coleman, ss, Bourne (signed with Athletics). 24. Evan Danieli, rhp, Falmouth (So., Notre Dame). 25. Sean Black, rhp, Harwich (Jr., Seton Hall). 26. Nick Hernandez, lhp, Cotuit (Jr., Tennessee). 27. Marc Krauss, of, Harwich/Bourne (Jr., Ohio). 28. Matt Bashore, lhp, Wareham (Jr., Indiana). 29. Ryan Wheeler, 1b, Brewster (Jr., Loyola Marymount). 30. Chris Dominguez, 3b, Hyannis (Jr., Louisville).

INDIVIDUAL BATTING LEADERS
(MINIMUM 119 PLATE APPEARANCES)

	AVG	G	AB	R	H	HR	RBI
Cesario, Jimmy, Falmouth	.387	34	137	20	53	1	30
Pollock, A.J., Falmouth	.377	40	162	35	61	4	25
Medica, Tommy, Harwich	.352	32	105	13	37	0	16
Green, Grant, Chatham	.348	41	161	37	56	6	21
Krauss, Marc, Bourne	.344	37	128	16	44	3	34
Henry, Jordan, Harwich	.335	42	179	42	60	0	16
Ashcraft, Trent, Hyannis	.327	43	168	21	55	0	8
Sanchez, Tony, Yarmouth-Dennis	.326	34	92	9	30	3	18
Olson, Cory, Chatham	.325	29	14	23	37	0	9
Ruf, Darin, Falmouth	.305	41	41	22	43	1	24

INDIVIDUAL PITCHING LEADERS
(MINIMUM 35 INNINGS)

	W	L	ERA	IP	H	BB	SO
Hudson, Austin, Hyannis	1	2	1.50	36	25	8	25
Thomson, Matt, Orleans	4	0	1.66	49	34	12	39
Blair, Seth, Cotuit	4	1	1.72	52	38	12	32
Landry, Kevin, Bourne	4	1	1.80	45	33	7	44
Carraway, Andrew, Hyannis	4	2	1.90	47	35	11	57
Manno, Chris, Harwich	3	0	1.93	42	25	21	45
McCully, Nick, Bourne	5	0	1.98	50	30	14	44
Baumann, Buddy, Brewster	4	1	2.35	54	40	17	41
Stowell, Bryce, Bourne	3	1	2.36	46	32	9	58
Solis, Sammy, Chatham	3	2	2.41	37	37	7	32

For players who played for two teams:
1 Stats with first team
2 Stats with second team
T combined stats

BOURNE

BATTING	AVG	AB	R	H	2B	3B	HR	RBI	SB
Bantz, Brandon	.212	118	11	25	5	0	0	9	1
Batts, Stephen	.221	113	11	25	6	1	0	9	5
Bour, Justin	.192	52	5	10	3	0	0	4	0
Cannon, Tyler	.265	117	10	31	5	1	0	9	3
Coleman, Dusty	.330	100	16	33	7	1	2	17	1
Henry, Jordan	.335	179	42	60	4	0	0	16	12
Johnson, Jamie	.250	116	13	29	4	1	2	16	3
Jones, Richard	.143	14	1	2	2	0	0	0	0
Knight, Austin	.176	51	5	9	1	0	0	3	0
2 Krauss, Marc	.353	116	16	41	5	1	3	31	1
T Krauss, Marc	.344	128	16	44	6	1	3	34	1
LePage, Pierre	.233	60	6	14	2	0	0	4	2
Madigan, Sean	.167	12	2	2	0	0	0	1	0
Murray, Michael	.000	3	0	0	0	0	0	0	0
Roller, Kyle	.270	159	20	43	12	0	2	22	0
Saade, Gabriel	.053	19	2	1	0	0	0	1	0
1 Stephenson, Brad	.297	37	5	11	2	0	0	2	1
Thomas, Rafael	.222	45	4	10	0	0	0	0	4
Williamson, James	.207	29	4	6	0	0	0	1	0
Wilson, Ross	.218	147	23	32	5	1	1	13	3

PITCHING	W	L	ERA	G	SV	IP	H	BB	SO
Allen, Ryan	0	0	11.57	4	0	5	10	4	5
Baker, Nathan	1	2	5.18	8	0	24	29	10	23
Black, Victor	0	4	7.01	10	0	26	34	23	25
Blandford, Tyler	0	2	7.31	5	0	16	19	7	27
Bowen, Ricky	3	3	3.53	8	0	43	46	14	46
Costello, Matt	0	0	9.00	1	0	1	2	1	1
Erickson, David	2	2	3.09	23	1	32	24	7	33
Grimm, Justin	0	1	5.19	8	0	9	9	4	10
Kenyon, Zach	0	0	4.50	1	0	2	4	1	2
Landry, Kevin	4	1	1.80	16	0	45	33	7	44
McCully, Nick	5	0	1.98	9	0	50	30	14	44
Negus, Phil	0	0	2.45	2	0	4	2	4	2
Petiton, Matt	0	1	8.10	3	0	7	10	6	7
Pettis, Eric	2	0	2.49	19	8	25	13	5	24
Reed, Nate	1	2	3.45	9	0	31	34	16	15
Revesz, Bob	1	0	4.37	10	2	23	24	9	12
1 Stephenson, Brad	0	0	0.00	1	0	1	0	0	0
Stowell, Bryce	3	1	2.36	9	0	46	32	9	58
Walters, Jeffrey	1	1	2.00	4	0	9	5	6	12

BREWSTER

BATTING	AVG	AB	R	H	2B	3B	HR	RBI	SB
DiNatale, David	.108	37	3	4	1	0	0	2	1
Freeman, Mike	.274	168	16	46	7	1	1	22	5
Grandal, Yasmani	.279	61	8	17	1	1	1	10	0
Kelly, Ty	.276	163	19	45	4	1	0	18	9
Klocke, Jim	.189	90	11	17	7	0	0	7	1
Lape, Nate	.222	54	7	12	4	0	3	10	0
Meador, James	.280	132	18	37	6	4	2	17	4
Milleville, Brent	.276	123	18	34	7	0	6	25	2
Nappi, Jason	.268	138	28	37	7	1	0	19	5
Poppert, Derek	.277	155	28	43	6	1	1	11	11
Powers, Connor	.265	162	26	43	4	0	5	28	0
Wheeler, Ryan	.285	158	24	45	7	0	5	18	2
Yeager, Adam	.148	27	4	4	0	0	0	1	0

PITCHING	W	L	ERA	G	SV	IP	H	BB	SO
Baumann, Buddy	4	1	2.35	9	0	54	40	17	41
2 Bronson, Evan	1	2	3.19	6	0	31	31	6	17
T Bronson, Evan	2	4	3.67	10	0	49	50	13	28
Broyles, Wade	0	0	4.24	15	1	17	16	12	20
Christiani, Nick	2	4	6.44	10	2	29	36	20	30
Claypool, Garett	0	2	4.91	11	0	26	27	21	23
Clubb, Tim	4	1	1.41	5	0	32	18	15	29
Cotham, Caleb	5	1	2.54	8	0	46	34	22	51
Dail, B.J.	0	0	4.50	1	0	2	2	1	0
Gilliam, Rob	1	4	4.89	9	0	46	52	21	42
Kelly, Ty	0	0	0.00	1	0	1	0	0	0

	W	L	ERA	G	SV	IP	H	BB	SO
LaGrow, Chris	0	1	5.01	17	0	23	23	16	19
Lamm, Mark	1	2	12.64	13	1	16	13	27	20
McKean, Rory	1	2	5.01	20	5	32	37	22	28
Meador, James	0	0	4.26	5	0	6	2	6	6
Nazario, Iden	0	1	4.05	10	1	13	11	10	17
Poppert, Derek	0	0	0.00	1	0	0	4	1	0
Woolley, Ryan	0	0	0.00	1	0	1	0	0	1

CHATHAM

BATTING	AVG	AB	R	H	2B	3B	HR	RBI	SB
Bellows, Kyle	.204	152	16	31	11	0	2	19	1
Brown, Dylan	.133	45	5	6	1	0	1	2	2
Cohen, Gabe	.243	70	6	17	4	1	1	5	1
Glime, Gregg	.126	87	8	11	1	0	1	4	0
Gomes, Yan	.313	64	7	20	3	0	2	15	0
Green, Grant	.348	161	37	56	12	1	6	21	10
Hale, David	.080	25	2	2	1	0	0	1	0
Higley, J.R.	.111	27	5	3	1	0	0	1	0
Lohman, Devin	.341	41	6	14	1	1	1	12	3
McAvoy, Kevin	.111	9	1	1	0	0	0	0	0
Mercurio, Joe	.195	87	3	17	1	0	0	3	0
Miller, Aaron	.209	43	3	9	3	0	0	3	0
Ocheltree, Evan	.266	139	16	37	7	0	3	16	0
Olson, Cory	.325	114	23	37	6	1	0	9	1
Overholtzer, Corey	.147	116	12	17	2	1	0	6	2
Papenhause, Robert	.243	37	1	9	0	0	0	3	1
Sanchez, Victor	.207	150	15	31	7	0	6	25	1
Seager, Kyle	.288	118	17	34	6	0	1	16	3

PITCHING	W	L	ERA	G	SV	IP	H	BB	SO
Bellows, Kyle	0	0	0.00	1	0	1	0	0	2
Blair, Kyle	1	1	4.22	4	0	11	10	5	14
Boxberger, Brad	1	2	2.89	19	9	19	11	8	28
Brewer, Charles	1	1	5.93	3	0	14	19	7	11
Couture, Kevin	2	3	3.86	11	0	33	28	7	28
Folino, John	0	1	5.91	5	0	11	15	3	7
Giardina, Carmine	1	3	3.48	16	1	31	32	14	28
Hale, David	0	1	6.95	11	0	22	28	13	25
Harvey, Matt	1	1	0.83	9	1	22	17	11	29
Hernandez, Bobby	1	1	4.15	10	0	30	30	8	27
Lorick, Jeff	1	2	3.10	12	0	20	17	12	24
Marks, Justin	0	1	6.33	5	0	21	27	18	20
Scanlan, Kevin	0	0	4.00	3	0	9	10	6	12
Serafin, Joe	0	2	4.55	12	0	30	32	14	28
Solis, Sammy	3	2	2.41	7	0	37	37	7	32
Thompson, Jake	2	3	4.91	6	0	26	29	15	28
Warren, Adam	3	1	4.34	5	0	29	35	6	29
Zoltak, Matt	2	0	4.06	9	0	31	35	13	25

COTUIT

BATTING	AVG	AB	R	H	2B	3B	HR	RBI	SB
Bianucci, Mike	.282	78	21	22	4	1	5	19	6
Black, Dan	.143	28	8	4	1	0	0	3	0
Crawford, Evan	.246	118	20	29	5	0	0	9	11
Gilmartin, Michael	.257	109	10	28	4	0	2	11	0
Holliman, Matthew	.149	47	7	7	3	0	1	7	0
Holt, Tyler	.167	6	0	1	0	0	0	0	0
Jackson, Brett	.238	147	29	35	6	0	4	14	8
Kelliher, Brandon	.200	5	1	1	0	0	0	0	0
Kipnis, Jason	.264	140	20	37	6	0	2	15	6
Kobernus, Jeff	.263	56	13	41	9	1	1	24	6
Lewis, Joey	.246	65	9	16	3	0	2	8	0
Mollica, Ryan	.400	5	0	2	0	0	0	1	0
Patterson, Kevin	.296	152	22	45	8	2	4	27	0
Poulk, Dallas	.259	158	22	41	9	0	0	16	2
Schaus, Jeff	.255	94	9	24	3	0	2	11	0
Shields, Robbie	.349	43	10	15	3	1	2	11	1
Stock, Robert	.270	115	16	31	3	1	1	11	6

PITCHING	W	L	ERA	G	SV	IP	H	BB	SO
Applebee, Paul	0	2	3.09	8	0	44	46	10	28
Blair, Seth	4	1	1.72	7	0	52	38	12	32
Brown, Sam	0	0	3.33	13	1	24	24	5	30
Castner, Kevin	0	0	27.00	1	0	1	2	4	1
Caulfield, Clay	0	0	9.00	3	0	4	7	3	5

	W	L	ERA	G	SV	IP	H	BB	SO
Cumpton, Brandon	2	1	4.43	7	0	20	21	13	20
Fairel, Matt	1	1	5.73	2	0	11	13	5	10
Garcia, Nate	2	2	4.93	9	0	35	36	23	27
Hernandez, Nick	6	3	2.54	9	0	57	54	13	48
Hollands, Mario	0	2	2.86	9	0	28	22	12	21
Jennings, Dan	1	0	6.00	1	0	3	2	2	4
Kobernus, Jeff	0	0	18.00	1	0	1	3	0	1
Lambert, John	0	0	7.71	4	0	5	4	5	1
Meszaros, Danny	1	1	1.37	11	1	20	14	6	25
Sogard, Alex	1	1	4.26	9	0	19	26	7	13
Stock, Robert	0	0	9.00	2	0	2	1	2	3
Storen, Drew	1	2	2.76	13	5	16	12	5	15
Von Tersch, Zach	2	1	3.48	8	0	21	20	16	15
Wolford, Daniel	3	1	3.38	14	2	24	18	10	33

FALMOUTH

BATTING	AVG	AB	R	H	2B	3B	HR	RBI	SB
Cesario, Jimmy	.387	137	20	53	8	1	1	30	9
Coleman, Trevor	.244	156	25	38	7	0	1	22	5
Di Ricco, Domenic	.167	6	1	1	0	0	0	1	0
Fletcher, Brian	.153	98	12	15	6	1	1	6	0
Gustafson, David	.182	22	2	4	0	0	0	1	0
Jones, Ryan	.255	145	22	37	3	0	8	24	8
Macias, Brandon	.039	51	3	2	0	0	0	3	0
McNee, Scott	.333	3	0	1	0	0	0	0	0
Miller, Justin	.241	29	3	7	0	0	0	1	0
Nolan, Kevin	.255	149	18	38	6	1	2	17	4
Pollock, A.J.	.377	162	35	61	15	1	4	25	11
Ruf, Darin	.305	141	22	43	7	0	1	24	2
Seastrunk, Diego	.220	41	1	9	1	0	0	5	0
Segedin, Rob	.179	28	3	5	1	0	0	2	1
Thomas, Michael	.213	89	11	19	6	0	2	11	0
Wirnsberger, A.J.	.182	44	7	8	2	1	0	0	0
Wong, Joey	.256	168	27	43	5	0	0	15	6

PITCHING	W	L	ERA	G	SV	IP	H	BB	SO
Bettis, Chad	3	0	2.68	9	0	44	35	17	39
Brothers, Rex	1	4	4.25	11	0	36	37	29	48
Claiborne, Preston	2	1	2.66	20	3	24	24	13	21
Danielli, Evan	2	0	2.95	12	0	21	19	12	23
Gloor, Chris	1	0	2.59	12	0	42	34	11	36
Hall, Shaeffer	1	1	2.41	14	0	19	20	7	18
Karns, Nate	0	2	3.13	8	0	37	25	22	34
Kountis, Jonathan	2	3	4.91	12	1	22	21	6	19
Lawler, Travis	1	0	5.40	9	0	15	20	8	15
Loup, Aaron	1	1	6.07	9	0	13	13	11	12
Reyes, Jorge	3	2	4.66	8	0	37	37	16	29
Striz, Nate	2	1	5.63	7	0	8	10	3	4
Tepesch, Nick	1	1	3.71	7	0	17	14	7	18
Tootle, Ben	3	1	1.97	22	5	32	21	14	44
Wilson, Alex	0	1	4.60	10	0	29	26	15	36

HARWICH

BATTING	AVG	AB	R	H	2B	3B	HR	RBI	SB
Ackley, Dustin	.415	41	11	17	4	1	2	10	2
Belfonte, D.J.	.280	118	18	33	8	0	1	12	11
Belt, Brandon	.248	137	20	34	7	2	5	25	0
Block, William	.174	23	2	4	0	0	0	0	0
Cusick, Jeff	.183	71	10	13	2	0	1	12	0
DiCesare, Tony	.286	14	1	4	0	0	0	1	0
Fleury, Mark	.238	84	8	20	2	1	2	14	1
Giobbi, Andrew	.228	79	15	18	6	0	4	19	1
Hansen, Shaver	.273	143	20	39	4	1	1	19	11
Hilliard, Alex	.333	15	5	5	0	0	0	0	2
Kemp, Brian	.253	75	10	19	3	1	0	4	9
1 Krauss, Marc	.250	12	0	3	1	0	0	3	0
Leavitt, Chase	.223	94	15	21	5	0	0	6	6
LeMahieu, D.J.	.290	107	16	31	5	0	1	13	3
McKenna, Patrick	.400	5	1	2	0	0	0	0	0
Medica, Tommy	.352	105	13	37	3	0	0	16	0
Pesanello, Frank	.300	10	1	3	1	0	0	2	0
Sanders, Joseph	.273	165	18	45	11	0	4	17	5
Smalling, Tim	.116	43	4	5	0	0	0	2	0
Stidham, Jason	.155	103	17	16	2	0	1	8	2

COLLEGE BASEBALL

Wise, J.T. .350 40 7 14 4 1 1 10 1

PITCHING	W	L	ERA	G	SV	IP	H	BB	SO
Belt, Brandon	1	0	0.00	2	0	6	2	3	2
Black, Sean	3	2	4.09	10	1	22	22	17	26
Bullock, William	2	2	3.40	10	0	45	44	15	30
Dupra, Brian	3	1	3.40	18	0	40	42	17	33
Eidell, Josh	1	0	2.56	14	1	32	30	4	33
Hoover, J.J.	1	0	2.45	7	0	37	36	8	38
Johnson, Patrick	1	3	4.79	7	0	21	21	8	19
Kalush, Steve	2	3	2.08	12	3	26	26	10	19
Kempf, Willie	2	2	2.97	18	2	33	25	15	35
Manno, Chris	3	0	1.93	7	0	42	25	21	45
Morrison, Michael	2	1	3.58	13	2	38	30	18	46
Quigley, Ryan	3	1	3.67	9	0	34	28	22	43
Zielinski, Matt	0	5	4.28	9	0	27	22	9	20

HYANNIS

BATTING	AVG	AB	R	H	2B	3B	HR	RBI	SB
Adams, Austin	.095	21	3	2	0	0	0	1	1
Ashcraft, Trent	.327	168	21	55	7	0	0	8	11
Casali, Curt	.172	87	11	15	1	1	1	4	1
Cornstubble, Dale	.211	95	7	20	2	0	1	6	0
Daniels, Steve	.308	13	1	4	0	1	0	0	0
Dominguez, Chris	.262	168	13	44	11	1	10	31	7
Eden, Ryan	.215	135	10	29	5	0	6	8	6
Frawley, Casey	.210	138	13	29	9	1	0	8	3
Glantz, Michael	.100	30	6	3	1	0	0	3	1
Gonzales, Joey	.212	99	6	21	1	0	0	5	7
Hinson, John	.222	18	0	4	1	0	0	1	1
Jiminez, P.J.	.400	5	1	2	0	0	0	0	0
Jones, Marcus	.228	114	15	26	4	0	1	12	2
Massanari, Bryce	.065	31	0	2	0	0	0	1	0
2 Murray, Michael	.000	4	0	0	0	0	0	1	0
T Murray, Michael	.000	7	0	0	0	0	0	1	0
Murton, Luke	.204	49	7	10	3	0	1	5	2
Nuzzo, Matt	.172	99	7	17	5	0	1	7	4
Paulsen, Ben	.290	169	23	49	9	1	8	33	1

PITCHING	W	L	ERA	G	SV	IP	H	BB	SO
Adams, Austin	0	0	0.00	2	0	2	0	0	4
Andress, Matt	0	1	5.40	3	0	3	9	2	3
Bates, Colin	1	3	2.85	7	0	41	28	20	37
Brewer, Russell	1	0	2.74	18	12	23	14	14	17
Carraway, Andrew	4	2	1.90	10	0	47	35	11	57
Franzblau, Jason	0	2	2.15	9	1	29	19	11	25
Harvil, Will	3	0	5.52	10	0	15	17	10	13
Hudson, Austin	1	2	1.50	7	0	36	25	8	25
McRee, Alex	1	1	5.30	4	0	19	24	2	22
Muren, Drew	1	2	3.24	7	0	25	21	11	21
Ridings, Matt	1	3	4.78	8	1	26	21	13	28
Sharpley, Ryan	1	1	6.84	10	1	26	36	15	37
Stoneburner, Graham	2	2	2.93	7	0	31	41	12	30
Tolliver, Ashur	3	0	2.17	15	0	29	25	14	27
Weidig, Will	3	3	3.41	10	0	37	29	21	32

ORLEANS

BATTING	AVG	AB	R	H	2B	3B	HR	RBI	SB
Bowman, Matt	.277	119	15	33	6	2	1	14	3
Brown, Gary	.222	108	20	24	5	2	2	9	12
Figueroa, Cole	.232	112	13	26	3	1	2	17	8
Freiman, Nate	.253	150	18	38	4	0	5	17	2
Hassan, Alex	.208	130	17	27	4	0	0	3	4
Kort, Shaun	.187	75	6	14	3	0	3	9	0
Murphy, Mike	.233	73	8	17	2	0	1	10	0
Olt, Michael	.250	20	2	5	1	0	0	3	0
Plagman, Tony	.158	19	0	3	1	0	0	1	0
Poythress, Rich	.311	61	9	19	4	0	0	8	2
Songco, Angelo	.261	138	26	36	9	1	8	26	3
Spraker, Kyle	.210	105	14	22	2	0	3	12	2
Tartamella, Travis	.200	70	3	14	0	0	0	7	0
Tignor, Hampton	.132	68	5	9	0	0	0	3	1
Weldon, Mike	.222	9	1	2	1	0	0	0	0
Wheeler, Tim	.265	162	27	43	5	1	4	17	15

PITCHING	W	L	ERA	G	SV	IP	H	BB	SO
Earls, Justin	3	0	1.50	9	0	18	7	4	17
Erickson, Eric	1	1	3.27	4	0	22	26	3	21
Gemberling, Brad	0	2	5.81	13	0	26	26	10	15
Glynn, Elliot	2	1	3.20	15	0	20	21	10	10
Haselhorst, Quinn	0	0	4.09	12	0	22	22	9	25
Hassan, Alex	0	1	3.00	10	5	9	6	7	13
Kamppi, Kyle	1	0	0.64	12	8	14	11	4	15
Morales, Isaac	2	2	3.62	11	0	32	33	16	16
Rasmussen, Rob	4	3	4.12	9	0	39	42	23	43
Smith, Kyle	3	3	3.98	8	0	41	34	13	26
Stillings, Brad	1	1	0.82	8	0	22	21	12	14
Thomson, Matt	4	0	1.66	12	0	49	34	12	39
Viramontes, Martin	2	2	3.75	8	0	36	32	16	23
Warner, Colin	0	0	6.75	4	0	4	5	4	1
Wilk, Adam	2	1	1.69	21	0	32	26	6	36

WAREHAM

BATTING	AVG	AB	R	H	2B	3B	HR	RBI	SB
Baker, Aaron	.258	155	16	40	8	0	4	25	1
Campbell, Raynor	.303	145	23	44	9	0	3	12	2
Dean, Blake	.243	107	10	26	4	2	0	11	2
Eibner, Brett	.214	112	16	24	6	2	4	18	7
Lemmerman, Jake	.208	101	13	21	2	0	0	12	4
Leonida, Cole	.202	89	7	18	5	0	3	15	0
Liddle, Steve	.198	111	5	22	2	2	0	8	3
May, Brandon	.000	3	0	0	0	0	0	0	0
Munroe, Buddy	.179	67	6	12	3	0	1	6	0
Pineda, Ryan	.273	150	17	41	11	2	3	18	3
Rowe, Connor	.221	149	23	33	9	1	2	12	10
Schutz, Kipp	.260	123	17	32	5	1	4	11	2
Stack-Babich, Tom	.212	33	1	7	2	0	0	1	0
Vucinich, Shea	.239	92	11	22	4	0	0	3	0

PITCHING	W	L	ERA	G	SV	IP	H	BB	SO
Bashore, Matt	2	2	3.15	7	0	20	22	9	32
Brewster, Zach	2	1	4.68	16	1	25	20	18	25
Broach, Robby	2	4	3.66	9	0	52	51	26	51
Eibner, Brett	0	0	0.00	1	0	1	1	1	1
Graham, Austin	1	0	3.48	10	0	10	11	3	7
Hicks, Chris	0	1	9.00	9	2	8	14	3	7
Keuchel, Dallas	1	3	2.63	9	0	55	55	13	36
Perlman, Max	3	1	3.11	9	0	55	49	16	36
Saris, Jimmy	0	1	3.03	16	1	33	30	16	30
Seander, Mike	0	1	27.00	2	1	1	3	1	0
Slaats, Josh	1	3	6.75	15	2	17	28	9	26
Stack-Babich, Tom	0	0	0.00	1	0	0	0	0	0
Walker, Brandt	0	0	7.71	5	0	5	8	3	3
Way, Matt	2	6	4.02	12	0	47	45	29	42
Workman, Brandon	3	3	3.44	9	0	55	45	14	67

YARMOUTH-DENNIS

BATTING	AVG	AB	R	H	2B	3B	HR	RBI	SB
Belifore, Mike	.194	36	2	7	0	0	0	1	0
Belza, Tom	.239	88	7	21	1	2	0	3	4
Cather, Billy	.333	12	3	4	0	0	1	1	1
Glad, Gunner	.091	11	0	1	0	0	0	0	0
Hood, Dustin	.250	16	1	4	0	0	0	3	0
Liles, Nick	.291	151	19	44	6	0	0	22	14
Mack, DeAngelo	.273	154	20	42	9	1	1	19	8
Marmion, Tyler	.218	78	10	17	0	0	3	13	1
Merrifield, Whit	.222	99	11	22	4	0	0	6	10
Miclat, Greg	.325	40	14	13	1	0	0	4	7
Mitchell, Jared	.091	11	2	1	0	0	0	0	2
Ochinko, Sean	.197	61	5	12	1	0	2	6	0
Ortiz, Ryan	.274	124	12	34	5	1	1	18	2
Rutledge, Josh	.294	163	26	48	9	2	1	10	8
Sanchez, Tony	.326	92	9	30	6	0	3	18	1
2 Stephenson, Brad	.250	4	3	1	0	0	0	1	0
T Stephenson, Brad	.293	41	8	12	2	0	0	3	1
Tamsin, Mike	.111	9	1	1	0	0	0	0	0
Wiley, Keenan	.268	168	22	45	10	0	0	11	12
Wilkins, Andy	.271	140	16	38	10	0	5	26	1
Young, Brandon	.095	21	2	2	0	0	0	1	0

COLLEGE BASEBALL

PITCHING	W	L	ERA	G	SV	IP	H	BB	SO
Ballard, Rhett	3	0	2.08	12	0	17	11	7	20
Belfiore, Mike	0	1	3.21	12	1	14	14	4	21
1 Bronson, Evan	1	2	4.50	4	0	18	19	7	11
Burns, Eddie	4	4	5.67	8	0	40	49	16	39
Fritsch, Craig	2	3	3.43	8	0	45	29	18	44
Glad, Gunner	0	0	0.00	2	0	1	1	1	0
Hecathorn, Kyle	0	1	2.45	2	0	4	4	2	5
Inman, Jeff	1	1	3.73	6	0	31	34	10	34
Kelly, Joe	0	1	7.31	14	4	16	22	7	17
Masters, Chris	0	2	3.81	9	0	28	27	13	29
Peavey, Greg	2	3	6.83	13	2	29	36	14	18
Ranaudo, Anthony	0	2	6.63	10	0	19	22	8	22
2 Stephenson, Brad	0	0	0.00	2	0	2	3	1	2
T Stephenson, Brad	0	0	0.00	3	0	3	3	1	2
Sullivan, Jerry	3	1	4.05	6	0	33	37	11	30
Tolleson, Shawn	1	2	3.41	12	0	37	38	12	53
ValCarcel, Miguel	0	0	4.32	5	1	8	6	3	4
Waldron, Tyler	1	2	2.92	8	0	37	38	11	33
Weaver, Dean	0	0	0.00	5	1	8	5	1	9
Wiley, Keenan	0	0	0.00	1	0	1	2	0	1

ALASKA LEAGUE

	W	L	PCT	GB
Anchorage Glacier Pilots	20	10	.667	—
Mat-Su Miners	21	14	.600	1½
Kenai Peninsula Oilers	18	17	.514	4½
Anchorage Bucs	15	20	.429	7½
Alaska Goldpanners of Fairbanks	14	19	.424	7½
Fairbanks AIA Fire	12	20	.375	9

TOP 10 PROSPECTS: 1. Steve Fischback, rhp, Mat-Su (Jr., Cal Poly). 2. Garrett Richards, rhp, Mat-Su (Jr., Oklahoma). 3. Joey Terdoslavich, 1b/3b, Glacier Pilots (So., Long Beach State). 4. Kyle Jensen, of, Mat-Su (Jr., St. Mary's). 5. Antwonie Hubbard, rhp, Glacier Pilots (R-So., Oklahoma). 6. Nick Ciolli, of, Goldpanners (Jr., Indiana State). 7. Brint Hardy, of, Athletes In Action (Sr., Alabama-Birmingham). 8. Kawika Emsley-Pai, c, Oilers (So., Lewis-Clark State, Idaho). 9. Seth Harvey, rhp, Oilers (Jr., Washington State). 10. Joe Gardner, rhp, Oilers (Jr., UC Santa Barbara).

INDIVIDUAL BATTING LEADERS
(MINIMUM 3 PLATE APPEARANCES PER TEAM GAME)

	AVG	AB	R	H	2B	3B	HR	RBI	SB
Hardy, Brint, Goldpanners	.410	122	28	50	7	1	3	19	25
Terdoslavich, Joseph, Pilots	.354	96	20	34	9	0	3	19	4
Ciolli, Nick, Goldpanners	.346	130	18	45	9	0	0	9	8
Wells, Evan, Bucs	.321	106	24	34	2	1	0	6	14
Tisdale, Kyle, Oilers	.317	123	12	39	7	1	0	18	8
Goldschmidt, Paul, Bucs	.310	145	19	45	13	0	3	20	1
Gould, Jeremy, Oilers	.310	129	11	40	11	0	3	25	1
Aliotti, Jeremy, Oilers	.304	115	15	35	4	0	0	10	4
Winn, Kevin, Goldpanners	.298	94	6	28	5	1	0	11	4
Scott, Troy, Miners	.293	116	17	34	13	0	2	25	1

INDIVIDUAL PITCHING LEADERS
(MINIMUM .9 INNINGS PER TEAM GAME)

	W	L	ERA	G	SV	IP	BB	SO
Berl, Brandon, Oilers	2	1	0.82	19	0	33	13	20
Humes, Ross, Oilers	4	0	0.84	6	0	32	6	27
Gardner, Joe, Oilers	4	0	0.96	7	0	37	15	29
Bergman, Christian, Bucs	4	2	1.34	9	0	60	8	34
Quate, Zachary, Pilots	6	1	1.49	13	0	36	9	28
Bargas, Paul, Bucs	3	2	2.40	7	0	45	13	23
Dixon, Brandon, Oilers	2	3	2.55	8	0	35	6	18
Henry, Tyler, Pilots	1	2	2.58	7	0	38	1	11
Erickson, Jason, Miners	6	1	2.79	9	0	42	7	36
Teufel, Shawn, Goldpanners	0	1	3.09	8	1	43	11	20

ATLANTIC COLLEGIATE LEAGUE

WOLFF	W	L	PCT	GB
Lehigh Valley Catz	26	12	.684	—
Kutztown Rockies	24	15	.615	2½
Quakertown Blazers	21	17	.553	5

	W	L	PCT	GB
Jersey Pilots	10	30	.250	17

KAISER	W	L	PCT	GB
Metro New York Cadets	20	19	.513	—
Peekskill Robins	19	21	.475	1½
Hampton Whalers	19	21	.475	1½
Long Island Mustangs	18	22	.450	2½

PLAYOFFS—Kutztown defeated Hampton in a one-game championship.

TOP 10 PROSPECTS: 1. Darin Gorski, lhp, Kutztown (Jr., Kutztown University, Pa.). 2. Greg Folgia, 2b, Quakertown (Jr., Missouri). 3. Kyle Morrison, rhp, Lehigh Valley (Jr., Wagner). 4. Tim Morris, 1b/of, Lehigh Valley (Jr., St. John's). 5. Alex Pracher, rhp, Quakertown (So. Stanford). 6. Chris Sedon, inf, Kutztown (Jr., Pittsburgh). 7. Jimmy Tanner, c, Lehigh Valley (Jr., South Carolina-Upstate). 8. John Flanagan, rhp, Hampton (So., Fordham). 9. Andrew Guarrasi, lhp, Hampton (Jr., New York Tech). 10. Glen Johnson, ss/3b, MetroNY (So., Jacksonville).

INDIVIDUAL BATTING LEADERS
(MINIMUM 74 PLATE APPEARANCES)

	AVG	AB	R	H	2B	3B	HR	RBI	SB
Folgia, Greg, Quakertown	.388	67	16	26	9	3	3	18	4
Whiteman, Brock, Peekskill	.369	130	20	48	13	0	2	25	4
Angelo, Mark, Quakertown	.368	87	20	32	8	0	2	12	1
Amendola, Michael, Long Island	.366	101	19	37	6	2	2	21	11
Talerico, Joe, Jersey	.366	93	13	34	3	1	0	8	17
Tanner, Jimmy, Lehigh Valley	.355	93	13	33	7	0	1	12	0
Brantley, Harold, Metro NY	.354	127	34	45	7	1	3	21	27
Wychock, Chris, Quakertown	.351	94	16	33	8	1	3	18	1
Sedon, Chris, Kutztown	.346	107	21	37	8	4	0	15	8
Schultz, John, Kutztown	.339	121	21	41	6	1	3	11	8
Russell, Andy, Quakertown	.339	127	24	43	9	2	1	19	6
Zebroski, Tom, Long Island	.338	139	38	47	15	1	2	21	25

INDIVIDUAL PITCHING LEADERS
(MINIMUM 40 INNINGS)

	W	L	ERA	G	SV	IP	H	BB	SO
Klein, Phil, Hampton	5	2	1.02	7	0	44	26	11	40
Light, Tyler, Lehigh Valley	4	1	1.27	8	0	49	34	7	32
Gorski, Darren, Kutztown	7	0	1.33	10	1	61	40	15	78
Guarrasi, Andrew, Hampton	4	2	1.70	8	0	47	45	19	57
Moran, Tom, Peekskill	6	0	1.81	20	3	49	36	14	52
Lawrence, Casey, Kutztown	2	1	2.11	8	0	47	45	8	36
Wolfe, Lex, Jersey	1	3	2.37	11	1	57	48	22	53
Mower, Randall, Quakertown	6	0	2.58	9	0	45	40	6	30
Doran, Matt, Long Island	3	1	2.59	10	0	55	50	8	28
Mertz, Trent, Kutztown	4	1	2.82	13	2	44	47	15	36
Vitale, Michael, Metro NY	5	2	2.85	9	0	41	37	9	30
Smith, Matison, Peekskill	2	4	2.87	12	1	47	32	19	40

CAL RIPKEN SR. LEAGUE

	W	L	PCT	GB
Youse's Maryland Orioles	34	7	.829	—
Bethesda Big Train	29	13	.690	5½
College Park Bombers	23	18	.561	11
Herndon Braves	17	24	.415	17
Alexandria Aces	16	23	.410	17
Rockville Express	15	25	.375	18½
Silver Spring-Tacoma Thunderbolts	15	25	.375	18½
Maryland Redbirds	13	27	.325	20½

PLAYOFFS—Youse's Maryland Orioles defeated College Park in the championship of a six-team, double-elimination tournament.

TOP 10 PROSPECTS: 1. Leon Landry, of, Youse's Orioles (So., Louisiana State). 2. Quinton Miller, rhp, Youse's Orioles (SIGNED: Pirates). 3. Kevin Brady, rhp, Youse's Orioles (Fr., Clemson). 4. Tyler Massey, 1b, Youse's Orioles (SIGNED: Rockies). 4. Jeff Rowland, of, Youse's Orioles (So., Georgia Tech). 5. Reed Gragnani, 2b, Youse's Orioles (Sr., Mills Godwin HS, Richmond). 6. Scott Swinson, rhp, Youse's Orioles (Jr., Maryland). 7. Cody Allen, rhp, Bethesda (So., Central Florida). 8. T.J. O'Grady, rhp, Herndon (Jr., George Mason). 9. Patrick Long, if, Youse's Orioles (Jr., Georgia Tech). 10. Gerard Hall, ss, Youse's Orioles (Jr., Old Dominion).

INDIVIDUAL BATTING LEADERS
(MINIMUM 105 PLATE APPEARANCES)

	AVG	AB	R	H	2B	3B	HR	RBI	SB
Celenza, Mike, College Park	.412	136	20	56	13	0	5	30	3
Stienstra, Danny, Bethesda	.391	128	28	50	5	0	0	16	0
Long, Patrick, Youse's	.385	91	24	35	9	1	1	21	5
Rowland, Jeff, Youse's	.331	142	35	47	1	2	0	19	27
King, Jordan, Bethesda	.325	120	14	39	9	0	2	21	2
Sobocinski, Ben, College Park	.323	133	22	43	6	2	0	17	11
Burnette, Chase, Youse's	.322	115	14	37	7	0	1	24	6
Skonieczki, Adam, Maryland	.318	132	18	42	5	2	4	16	12
Hall, Gerard, Youse's	.317	142	42	45	3	5	0	21	30
Adkins, Luke, Bethesda	.316	136	23	43	7	1	2	16	2

INDIVIDUAL PITCHING LEADERS
(MINIMUM 30 INNINGS)

	W	L	ERA	G	SV	IP	H	BB	SO
Hiserman, Matt, Bethesda	3	0	0.00	18	10	33	17	2	37
Swinson, Scott, Youse's	5	1	1.03	7	0	43	20	11	39
Walden, Cody, Alexandria	3	1	1.51	11	0	35	22	20	28
Hurd, Austin, Rockville	2	2	1.58	7	0	40	33	19	37
Bell, Mike, College Park	4	1	1.76	7	0	41	34	13	29
Curd, Nate, College Park	4	2	1.82	9	0	34	27	15	33
O'Brien, Darren, College Park	2	2	1.88	10	0	43	25	20	41
Brady, Kevin, Youse's	4	0	1.91	8	1	37	23	4	59
Schneider, Scott, Bethesda	6	0	2.27	8	0	35	30	13	37
Amidei, Jack, College Park	4	1	2.49	9	2	47	28	28	48

CALIFORNIA COLLEGIATE LEAGUE

	W	L	PCT	GB
Santa Barbara Foresters	19	11	.633	—
Conejo Oaks	17	13	.567	2
Santa Maria Indians	17	13	.567	2
San Luis Obispo Rattlers	16	13	.552	2½
Urban Youth Academy	11	14	.440	5½
Monterey Bay Sox	5	21	.192	12

TOP 10 PROSPECTS: 1. Kevin Keyes, of, Santa Barbara (So., Texas). 2. Kevin Gelinas, lhp, Conejo (So., Central Arizona JC). 3. Chris Joyce, lhp, Santa Barbara (Fr., UC Santa Barbara). 4. Cameron Rupp, c, Santa Barbara (So., Texas). 5. Kevin Castner, rhp, Santa Barbara (Jr., Cal Poly). 6. Josh Poytress, lhp, San Luis Obispo (Fr., Fresno State). 7. Nick Akins, 2b, MLB Urban Academy (Jr., Vanguard, Calif.). 8. Mason Radeke, rhp, San Luis Obispo (Fr., Cal Poly). 9. Neil Medchill, of, Santa Barbara (Jr., Oklahoma State). 10. Ryan Cook, rhp, Santa Barbara (Sr., Southern California).

INDIVIDUAL BATTING LEADERS
(MINIMUM 80 AT-BATS)

	AVG	AB	R	H	2B	3B	HR	RBI	SB
Mozingo, Chad, Santa Barbara	.470	83	25	39	10	0	0	20	8
Goetz, Ryan, Santa Barbara	.368	106	27	39	6	1	1	27	8
Oliver, Eric, Santa Barbara	.361	108	20	39	11	1	3	28	2
Dodos, Jimmy, Santa Maria	.361	169	37	61	10	2	8	31	8
Meagher, Josh, Santa Maria	.360	172	35	62	10	1	7	38	0
Frierson, Jarred, Urban Youth	.352	128	26	45	10	1	3	17	5
Jackson, Josh, San Luis Obispo	.333	90	16	30	8	0	0	20	4
Medchill, Neil, Santa Barbara	.328	137	33	45	10	4	4	31	8
Iden, David, Conejo	.325	114	21	37	6	2	0	15	19
Bodenchuck, Matt, Santa Maria	.323	158	32	51	11	0	7	29	7

INDIVIDUAL PITCHING LEADERS
(MINIMUM 28 INNINGS PITCHED)

	W	L	ERA	SV	IP	H	BB	SO
Carson, Andrew, Santa Barbara	4	0	0.77	0	47	24	13	45
Mitchell, Jason, Santa Maria	6	0	1.47	1	43	25	18	46
Cook, Ryan, Santa Barbara	5	2	1.97	0	45	30	15	55
Shutt, Justin, Conejo	4	2	2.09	2	43	24	15	36
Clerici, Adam, San Luis Obispo	3	2	2.29	5	39	23	10	63
Lechuga, Sheldon, Santa Maria	3	2	2.42	0	44	38	13	25
Eusebio, Chris, Santa Maria	3	1	2.57	7	28	18	10	22
Radeke, Mason, San Luis Obispo	5	3	2.72	0	53	47	22	67
Butch, T.J., Santa Maria	3	2	3.17	0	39	29	29	41
Mattox, Tyler, Santa Barbara	2	3	3.32	0	40	35	24	34

CENTRAL ILLINOIS COLLEGIATE LEAGUE

	W	L	PCT	GB
Springfield Sliders	30	17	.638	—
DuPage Dragons	26	22	.542	4½
Danville Dans	24	23	.511	6
Quincy Gems	21	27	.438	9½
Dubois Bombers	17	29	.370	12½

PLAYOFFS—Springfield defeated Danville in best-of-three championship series.

TOP 10 PROSPECTS: 1. Tyler Hess, rhp, Danville (So., Pepperdine). 2. Austin Ross, rhp, Danville (So., Louisiana State). 3. Matt Bywater, lhp, Danville (So., Pepperdine). 4. Elliot Soto, ss, Springfield (So., Creighton). 5. Bryce Shafer, rhp, Springfield (So., Valparaiso). 6. Dan Kaczrowski, 2b, Danville (Sr., Hamline University, Minn.). 7. Ryan Duffy, c/1b, Dupage (Jr., Mississippi State). 8. Brian Morrell, rhp, Quincy (Sr., Eastern Illinois). 9. Greg Houston, rhp, Danville (Jr., Mississippi State). 10. Jon Myers, ss, Quincy (Jr., Saint Louis).

INDIVIDUAL BATTING LEADERS
(MINIMUM 120 PLATE APPEARANCES)

	AVG	AB	R	H	2B	3B	HR	RBI	SB
Kaczrowski, Dan, DuPage	.389	203	41	79	11	4	2	36	21
Tokarski, Kevin, DuPage	.324	105	21	34	0	3	0	9	5
Mooney, Ryan, Springfield	.316	114	14	36	4	1	2	22	5
Muller, Kurtis, Quincy	.314	156	31	49	7	0	1	24	22
Swift, Jimmy, Springfield	.309	149	20	46	7	2	1	26	5
Pollak, Andrew, Danville	.308	172	26	53	10	2	4	32	2
Soto, Elliot, Springfield	.299	177	28	53	2	0	0	9	16
Myers, Jon, Quincy	.297	185	42	55	11	1	14	39	5
Cafaro, Vicente, Springfield	.297	148	36	44	8	0	4	22	6
Behren, Matt, DuPage	.292	154	19	45	11	0	2	20	1
Vaughn, Dennis, Springfield	.292	168	30	49	13	1	5	43	5
Fink, Wes, Dubois	.292	168	20	49	9	0	2	26	6

INDIVIDUAL PITCHING LEADERS
(MINIMUM 45 INNINGS)

	W	L	ERA	G	SV	IP	H	BB	SO
Mahon, Logan, Springfield	6	1	1.74	11	2	46	40	30	39
Stroud, Brian, DuPage	3	3	1.94	10	2	51	39	12	31
Licon, Chris, Danville	4	3	2.00	12	0	45	38	13	36
Riegler, Brad, DuPage	5	2	2.04	15	2	57	52	12	43
Marcacci, Dan, Springfield	2	3	2.31	15	5	46	40	18	34
Morrell, Brian, Quincy	5	1	2.50	11	0	57	44	22	44
Bywater, Matt, Danville	4	4	2.52	13	0	53	36	30	53
Copeland, Ryan, DuPage	3	1	2.54	9	0	49	51	10	57
Butt, Bryce, Springfield	5	2	2.62	11	0	68	61	15	57
Shafer, Bryce, Springfield	6	1	2.75	12	0	59	48	26	74

CLARK C. GRIFFITH LEAGUE

	W	L	PCT	GB
Vienna Senators	42	12	.778	—
Fairfax Nationals	31	15	.674	7½
McLean Raiders	32	21	.604	9½
Carney Pirates	10	10	.500	15
Arlington Diamonds	23	24	.489	15½
Beltway Blue Caps	21	29	.420	19
D.C. Grays	18	27	.400	20½

PLAYOFFS—Beltway defeated Fairfax in the championship of a six-team, double-elimination tournament.

TOP 10 PROSPECTS: 1. Dan Tillman, rhp, McLean (So., Florida Southern). 2. Eric Cantrell, rhp, Vienna (So., George Washington). 3. Evan Scott, rhp, Carney (Fr., James Madison). 4. Shane Brown, 3b/1b/c, Beltway (Jr., Central Florida). 5. Michael Graham, lhp, Vienna (So., Virginia Commonwealth). 6. Wade Kirkland, ss, McLean (So., Florida Southern). 7. Richard Cary, rhp, Vienna (Jr., Marist). 8. A.J. Kirby-Jones, rhp/1b, Fairfax (So., Tennessee Tech). 9. Jay Joines, rhp, Beltway (Jr., Richmond). 10. Jim Duggan, rhp, Vienna (Sr., George Washington).

INDIVIDUAL BATTING LEADERS
(MINIMUM 100 AT-BATS)

	AVG	AB	R	H	2B	3B	HR	RBI	SB
Hays, Robert, Beltway	.435	108	36	47	8	0	11	39	8
Lopez, Dan, McLean	.381	126	27	48	15	1	1	18	19

Brown, Shane, Beltway	.366	145	35	53	11	3	6	31	2
Kuroczko, Nick, Vienna	.356	101	24	36	5	0	1	22	8
Mujica, Juan, D.C.	.351	148	33	52	9	2	4	16	15
Eckert, Max, Beltway	.341	132	34	45	9	1	9	32	8
Marion, Mike, D.C.	.328	125	21	41	8	0	9	31	1
Kirkland, Wade, McLean	.327	150	32	49	15	0	5	22	10
Bachman, Greg, McLean	.325	120	17	39	14	1	3	27	2
Parra, Martin, Vienna	.320	125	31	40	8	1	7	30	10

INDIVIDUAL PITCHING LEADERS
(MINIMUM 40 INNINGS PITCHED)

	W	L	ERA	G	SV	IP	H	BB	SO
Cantrell, Eric, Vienna	5	1	2.38	10	0	45	33	7	52
Hald, Kyle, Vienna	6	0	2.40	14	0	41	30	7	60
Cary, Richard, Vienna	7	2	2.79	10	0	42	38	5	36
Joines, Jay, Beltway	4	2	2.98	9	0	42	38	13	43
Tillman, Daniel, McLean	3	1	3.28	11	0	49	43	10	61
Gibbs, Thomas, D.C.	4	4	3.62	10	0	54	54	18	25
Moore, Brett, Fairfax	4	2	3.80	8	0	45	43	12	29
Land, Taylor, Beltway	4	3	4.04	8	1	49	44	29	28
McDaniel, Cassidy, McLean	3	0	4.54	9	0	41	38	16	34
Sable, Joe, D.C.	5	1	4.82	8	0	52	51	30	24

COASTAL PLAIN LEAGUE

NORTH	W	L	PCT	GB
Edenton Steamers	35	20	.636	—
Peninsula Pilots	32	24	.571	3½
Outer Banks DareDevils	27	28	.491	8
Petersburg Generals	19	36	.345	16

SOUTH	W	L	PCT	GB
Florence RedWolves	34	21	.618	—
Wilson Tobs	31	24	.564	3
Fayetteville SwampDogs	27	29	.482	7½
Wilmington Sharks	24	31	.436	10
Columbia Blowfish	22	33	.400	12

WEST	W	L	PCT	GB
Thomasville HiToms	37	19	.661	—
Forest City Owls	28	26	.519	8
Martinsville Mustangs	24	28	.462	11
Gastonia Grizzlies	23	31	.426	13½
Asheboro Copperheads	21	34	.382	15½

PLAYOFFS— Thomasville defeated Florence in the championship game of an eight-team tournament.

TOP 10 PROSPECTS: 1. Deck McGuire, rhp, Peninsula (So., Georgia Tech). 2. Kevin Mahoney, 3b, Forest City (Sr., Canisius). 3. Steve Grife, rhp, Florence (Jr., Mercyhurst College, Pa.). 4. C.J. Beatty, of, Thomasville (Jr., North Carolina A&T). 5. Parker Bangs, rhp, Fayetteville (R-So., South Carolina). 6. Brett Nommensen, of, Edenton (Sr., Eastern Illinois). 7. Chris McGuiness, 1b, Thomasville (Jr., The Citadel). 8. Justin Sarratt, rhp, Thomasville (Jr., Clemson). 9. Luke Demko, rhp, Edenton (Sr., Rhode Island). 10. Sonny Meade, of, Thomasville (Sr., The Citadel).

INDIVIDUAL BATTING LEADERS
(MINIMUM 149 PLATE APPEARANCES)

	AVG	AB	R	H	2B	3B	HR	RBI	SB
Nommensen, Brett, Edenton	.377	159	42	60	11	0	4	22	17
Kroll, Doug, Edenton	.342	146	27	50	8	1	3	25	6
Behrendt, Kyle, Gastonia	.339	171	27	58	10	0	0	26	13
Mailloux, Kevin, Forest City	.328	195	37	64	18	0	8	35	17
Meade, Sonny, Thomasville	.326	193	33	63	12	1	4	27	5
Mahoney, Kevin, Forest City	.324	204	47	66	16	0	13	46	13
Wagner, Daniel, Asheboro	.323	220	29	71	16	1	2	34	16
Ford, Daniel, Gastonia	.318	176	23	56	11	0	2	23	0
Leeper, Bobby, Wilmington	.317	186	32	59	12	6	3	22	19
Snell, Chandler, Outer Banks	.316	187	29	59	5	1	0	21	16

INDIVIDUAL PITCHING LEADERS
(MINIMUM 45 INNINGS)

	W	L	ERA	G	SV	IP	H	BB	SO
Altman, Kent, Florence	5	0	0.92	9	0	49	39	19	38
Key, Joe, Edenton	5	2	1.01	11	0	53	34	13	43
Sarratt, Justin, Thomasville	7	1	1.06	8	0	59	35	9	57

McGuire, Deck, Peninsula	7	0	1.28	11	0	56	35	28	65
Martin, Aaron, Fayetteville	5	2	1.48	11	0	60	59	20	30
Haney, Jesse, Thomasville	4	1	1.61	7	0	44	37	15	28
Grife, Steve, Florence	4	1	1.65	10	2	49	33	22	55
Brinson, Brandon, Wilson	4	1	1.70	23	4	58	48	11	33
Gaines, Bryant, Wilmington	5	2	1.70	9	0	68	47	17	38
Mantooth, Ryne, Wilson	6	3	1.71	9	0	73	62	7	49

FLORIDA COLLEGIATE SUMMER LEAGUE

	W	L	PCT	GB
Belleview Bulldogs	24	13	.649	—
Clermont Mavericks	23	14	.622	1
Leesburg Lightning	22	18	.550	3½
Winter Park Diamond Dawgs	16	20	.444	7
Orlando Suns	14	21	.400	9
Sanford River Rats	11	24	.314	12

PLAYOFFS—Clermont defeated Belleview in the championship of a six-team playoff.

TOP 10 PROSPECTS: 1. Jeff Walters, rhp, Winter Park (Jr., Georgia). 2. Scott Shuman, rhp, Orlando (Jr., Auburn). 3. Chris Heston, rhp, Sanford (Jr., East Carolina). 4. Nick DelGuidice, ss/2b, Leesburg, (So., Florida Atlantic). 5. Tony Caldwell, c, Winter Park (Jr., Auburn). 6. Roberto Perez, c, Belleview (SIGNED: Indians). 7. Bo O'Dell, rhp, Belleview (Sr., Florida State). 8. Brayan Valencia, of, Clermont (Jr., Nova Southeastern, Fla.). 9. John Michael Blake, rhp, Leesburg (So., Lake Sumter, Fla., CC). 10. Ty Pryor, rhp, Winter Park (R-Sr., North Florida).

INDIVIDUAL BATTING LEADERS
(MINIMUM 2.5 AT-BATS PER TEAM GAME)

	AVG	AB	R	H	2B	3B	HR	RBI	SB
Mee, Andy, Belleview	.333	126	23	42	6	2	1	17	9
Penate, Luis, Belleview	.322	118	21	38	5	0	5	24	9
Valencia, Brayan, Clermont	.314	140	26	44	11	0	4	34	2
Heller, Mason, Orlando	.314	121	14	38	5	0	0	16	6
DelGuidice, Nicholas, Leesburg	.309	152	20	47	8	0	0	12	4
Collier, Robert, Clermont	.305	95	20	29	7	0	1	9	8
Latorre, James, Clermont	.302	96	15	29	4	0	3	21	1
Dye, Timothy, Clermont	.300	110	16	33	2	0	0	15	10
Prano, John, Sanford	.293	92	11	27	5	0	0	6	6
Siebenaler, Josh, Orlando	.291	117	20	34	4	1	0	12	14

INDIVIDUAL PITCHING LEADERS
(MINIMUM 1 INNING PER TEAM GAME)

	W	L	ERA	G	SV	IP	H	BB	SO
Heston, Chris, Sanford	1	2	1.00	6	1	36	29	8	32
Powell, Tyler, Clermont	5	2	1.08	8	0	50	35	17	46
Munoz, Joseph, Orlando	6	0	1.33	13	4	40	20	15	34
Mullaney, Kyle, Orlando	3	1	2.04	6	0	39	34	7	33
Postill, Jason, Belleview	3	0	2.05	14	0	44	39	10	39
O'Dell, Bo, Belleview	3	2	2.08	7	0	52	37	15	67
Dobbins, Brennan, Orlando	3	3	2.13	9	0	50	34	20	51
Vigue, Ryan, Sanford	2	4	2.15	9	0	54	37	20	40
Koch, Jake, Leesburg	6	1	2.17	10	0	54	46	6	31
Hill, Beau, Belleview	7	0	2.17	11	0	37	27	20	36

GREAT LAKES LEAGUE

	W	L	T	PCT	GB
Cincinnati Steam	30	10	0	.750	—
Stark County Terriers	26	14	0	.650	4
Delaware Cows	24	15	1	.613	5½
Columbus All-Americans	20	20	0	.500	10
Lima Locos	20	20	0	.500	10
Lake Erie Monarchs	19	21	0	.475	11
Licking County Settlers	19	21	0	.475	11
Southern Ohio Copperheads	19	21	0	.475	11
Anderson Servants	15	25	0	.375	15
Grand Lake Mariners	14	26	0	.350	16
Xenia Athletes in Action	13	26	1	.338	16½

PLAYOFFS—Cincinnati defeated Columbus in the championship of a six-team, double-elimination tournament.

TOP 10 PROSPECTS: 1. Tyler Wilson, rhp, Delaware (So., Virginia). 2. Burny Mitchem, rhp, Columbus (So., Dayton). 3. Zach Hurley, of,

Cincinnati (Jr., Ohio State). 4. Collin Brennan, rhp, Licking County (Sr., Bradley). 5. Charlie Leesman, lhp, Cincinnati (Sr., Xavier). 6. Ed Rohan, of/c, Stark County (So., Winthrop). 7. David Goforth, rhp, Delaware (So., Mississippi). 8. Nick Karow, rhp, Delaware (Jr., Furman). 9. Chris Lewis, c/of, Columbus (Jr., Western Michigan). 10. Rob Scahill, rhp, Licking County (Sr., Bradley).

INDIVIDUAL BATTING LEADERS
(MINIMUM 85 PLATE APPEARANCES)

	AVG	AB	R	H	2B	3B	HR	RBI	SB
Hurley, Zach, Cincinnati	.433	127	31	55	5	2	3	30	11
Lewis, Chris, Columbus	.411	151	27	62	10	0	4	25	1
Rohan, Ed, Stark County	.403	119	23	48	6	0	7	32	0
Dager, Pedro, Lake Erie	.376	117	28	44	7	0	2	22	15
Schmid, Alex, Lima	.365	96	12	35	3	2	3	19	0
Whitmer, Jace, Lima	.364	107	18	39	9	0	0	24	1
Spitaels, Reed, Anderson	.361	97	14	35	7	2	0	13	2
Thomas, Ben, Delaware	.354	82	11	29	10	0	3	11	1
Crooks, Aaron, Lake Erie	.351	111	20	39	1	0	0	16	10
Goebbert, Jake, Southern Ohio	.350	120	24	42	8	1	1	22	8

INDIVIDUAL PITCHING LEADERS
(MINIMUM 30 INNINGS)

	W	L	ERA	G	SV	IP	H	BB	SO
Farrell, Shane, Delaware	4	1	0.88	9	0	30	27	4	28
Leady, Kevin, Lake Erie	2	3	1.81	7	0	44	44	7	33
Wilson, Tyler, Delaware	2	2	1.82	9	0	39	23	14	48
Carr, Matt, Anderson	3	1	1.95	7	0	32	33	7	20
Mitchem, Burney, Columbus	2	2	2.04	8	0	39	31	12	49
Jenkins, Chad, Lima	3	1	2.11	8	0	47	41	6	36
Brodie, Daniel, Xenia	3	2	2.23	8	0	48	33	10	40
Kruzska, Ryan, Cincinnati	2	2	2.37	10	0	38	35	9	39
O'Gara, Joey, Cincinnati	5	0	2.39	8	0	37	36	8	30
Sand, Brian, Cincinnati	4	0	2.40	7	0	30	24	9	31

JAYHAWK LEAGUE

	W	L	PCT	GB
Hays Larks	25	11	.694	—
Derby Twins	23	13	.639	2
Nevada Griffons	21	15	.583	4
Liberal BeeJays	20	16	.556	5
El Dorado Broncos	14	22	.389	11
Dodge City A's	13	23	.361	12
Joplin Slashers	10	26	.278	15

TOP 10 PROSPECTS: 1. Patrick Cooper, rhp, Hays (So., Des Moines Area CC). 2. Cameron Monger, of, Dodge City (Jr., New Mexico). 3. Preston Springer, 3b/1b, El Dorado (So., Odessa JC). 4. Nick Zaleski, 1b/of, Liberal (Sr., Sam Houston State). 5. Steven Mazur, rhp, Hays (Jr., Notre Dame). 6. Rich Michalek, 2b, Hays (Sr., Slippery Rock, Pa.). 7. Eric Roof, c, Hays (Sr., Michigan State). 8. Chase Johnson, rhp, Hays (So., Central Arizona). 9. Jeremiah Sammy, ss, Liberal (Sr., Lamar). 10. Taylor Rogers, rhp, Liberal (Jr., Tulane).

INDIVIDUAL BATTING LEADERS
(MINIMUM 85 PLATE APPEARANCES)

	AVG	AB	H	2B	3B	HR	RBI
Zaleski, Nick, Liberal	.441	93	41	9	0	2	26
Springer, Preston, El Dorado	.415	106	44	8	1	5	22
Michalek, Rich, Hays	.364	118	43	6	0	4	27
Ewing, Clint, Liberal	.360	86	31	9	0	3	18
Davis, Matt, El Dorado	.347	118	41	14	0	3	12
Pollard, Julien, Liberal	.343	108	37	4	2	4	23
Monger, Cameron, Dodge City	.333	132	44	9	4	3	16
Sammy, Jeremiah, Liberal	.330	109	36	10	1	3	20
Templeton, Louie, Derby	.326	132	43	6	1	5	17
Kersten, Chris, Liberal	.325	120	39	14	0	3	18

INDIVIDUAL PITCHING LEADERS
(MINIMUM 30 INNINGS)

	W	L	ERA	IP	H	SO
Skelton, Will, Liberal	3	0	1.65	27	25	23
Mazur, Steve, Hays	3	0	1.85	34	24	47
Griffin, Dillon, Dodge City	2	2	2.09	39	33	28
Maffei, C.J., Joplin	2	3	2.68	37	29	32
Hauptman, Casey, Hays	5	0	2.87	47	50	44

Ratigan, Michael, Nevada	4	2	3.00	48	40	47
Cooper, Patrick, Hays	5	3	3.23	53	49	42
Mauricio, Alex, El Dorado	0	2	3.27	41	41	16
Gregerson, Erik, Derby	3	2	3.29	38	37	40
Graham, Ben, Derby	4	1	3.42	50	43	43

NEW ENGLAND COLLEGIATE LEAGUE

NORTHERN	W	L	PCT	GB
Sanford Mainers	28	14	.667	—
North Shore Navigators	26	16	.619	2
Keene Swamp Bats	24	17	.585	3½
Vermont Mountaineers	23	18	.561	4½
Holyoke Blue Sox	20	22	.476	8
Lowell All-Americans	16	26	.381	12

SOUTHERN	W	L	PCT	GB
Newport Gulls	26	16	.619	—
Pittsfield Dukes	24	18	.571	2
North Adams SteepleCats	20	22	.476	6
Manchester Silkworms	16	25	.390	9½
Torrington Twisters	14	27	.341	11½
Danbury Westerners	13	29	.310	13

PLAYOFFS— Quarterfinals: Sanford defeated Vermont 2-0, Keene defeated North Shore 2-0, Newport defeated Manchester 2-0, Pittsfield defeated North Adams 2-0. **Semifinals**: Sanford defeated Keene 2-0, Newport defeated Pittsfield 2-0. **Finals:** Sanford defeated Newport 2-0 in best-of-three championship series.

TOP 10 PROSPECTS: 1. Michael Olt, ss, Danbury (So., Connecticut). 2. Dan Mahoney, rhp, Newport (So., Connecticut). 3. Neal Davis, lhp, Newport (Jr., Virginia). 4. Casey Harman, lhp, Vermont (So., Clemson). 5. Corey Jones, 2b, Holyoke (Jr., Cal State Fullerton). 6. Jack Murphy, c, Newport (Jr., Princeton). 7. Devin Harris, of, Sanford (R-So., East Carolina). 8. Pat Lehman, rhp, Sanford (Sr., George Washington). 9. James Wood, of, Holyoke (Jr., Trinity, Conn.). 10. Cody Stanley, c, North Adams (So., UNC Wilmington).

INDIVIDUAL BATTING LEADERS
(MINIMUM 3 PLATE APPEARANCES PER TEAM GAME)

	AVG	AB	R	H	2B	3B	HR	RBI	SB
Tamsin, Mike, Newport	.417	108	27	45	11	2	1	17	1
McNaughton, Sean, North Shore	.353	150	29	53	15	7	3	33	8
Stanley, Cody, North Adams	.352	108	32	38	8	2	5	24	9
Adams, Matt, Pittsfield	.351	151	31	53	16	0	7	37	3
Pecora, Nicholas, Lowell	.347	170	20	59	3	1	0	24	1
Edmondson, Chris, Pittsfield	.339	165	32	5	6	4	4	28	2
Malloy, John, North Adams	.331	157	36	52	9	1	2	12	7
Rosenbeck, Jake, Pittsfield	.329	146	17	48	9	0	1	26	1
Rivers, Kevin, Lowell	.329	146	24	48	15	0	3	25	1
Jones, Corey, Holyoke	.325	117	13	38	6	1	1	17	12
Nandin, Matthew, Sanford	.319	141	15	45	2	0	1	14	3
Hunt, Corey, Sanford	.318	110	12	35	2	0	0	15	7
Melillo, Mike, Newport	.315	130	19	41	8	0	2	29	0
Grosso, Matt, Manchester	.310	158	13	49	11	0	0	17	3

INDIVIDUAL PITCHING LEADERS
(MINIMUM 40 INNINGS)

	W	L	ERA	G	SV	IP	H	BB	SO
Harman, Casey, Vermont	4	0	0.68	9	0	40	24	12	47
Boyce, Tim, North Adams	7	1	0.95	9	0	57	37	16	65
Ness, Michael, Pittsfield	5	1	1.08	9	0	50	29	11	33
Kitchens, Wayde, North Shore	2	1	1.30	7	0	41	35	19	32
Lehman, Pat, Sanford	4	1	1.52	8	1	47	32	11	42
Vazquez, Kyle, Pittsfield	4	0	1.99	8	0	45	40	9	41
Albert, Justin, Holyoke	7	0	2.01	9	0	53	44	27	53
Bowman, Jason, Sanford	5	2	2.21	9	0	57	58	3	35
MacKenzie, Alex, Pittsfield	3	1	2.45	9	0	55	48	13	41
Syberg, Josh, Vermont	3	1	2.57	10	0	42	40	12	41
Herter, Adam, North Shore	5	2	2.72	8	0	43	50	7	20
Greenwood, Nick, Vermont	3	3	3.09	12	0	43	43	9	44

NEW YORK COLLEGIATE LEAGUE

WEST	W	L	PCT	GB
Hornell Dodgers	32	10	.762	—
Brockport Riverbats	27	15	.643	5

Geneva Red Wings	21	17	.553	9
Allegany County Nitros	21	19	.525	10
Webster Yankees	17	24	.415	14½
Elmira Pioneers	16	23	.410	14½
Niagara Power	14	26	.350	17
Bolivar A's	14	24	.333	18

EAST	W	L	PCT	GB
Glens Falls Golden Eagles	31	10	.756	—
Amsterdam Mohawks	26	14	.650	4½
Little Falls Miners	19	23	.452	12½
Watertown Wizards	17	23	.425	13½
Bennington Bombers	15	25	.375	15½
Saratoga Phillies	12	25	.324	17

PLAYOFFS—Quarterfinals: Glens Falls defeated Watertown 2-0, Amsterdam defeated Little Falls 2-0, Hornell defeated Allegany County 2-1, Brockport defeated Geneva 2-1. **Semifinals:** Glens Falls defeated Amsterdam 2-1, Brockport defeated Hornell 2-0. **Championship:** Brockport defeated Glens Falls 2-1 in best-of-three championship series.
TOP 10 PROSPECTS: 1. Logan Darnell, lhp, Amsterdam (So., Kentucky). 2. Shane Davis, lhp, Glens Falls (R-So., Canisius). 3. Matt Branham, rhp, Brockport (Jr., South Carolina-Upstate). 4. J.D. Martinez, of, Saratoga (Jr., Nova Southeastern, Fla.). 5. Mike Spina, 3B, Amsterdam (Sr., Cincinnati). 6. Dan Forman, lhp, Amsterdam (So., Manhattan). 7. Kellen St. Luce, lhp, Saratoga (So., Vanderbilt). 8. Ryan O'Rourke, lhp, Brockport (Jr., Merrimack College, Mass.). 9. Luis Feliz, cf, Glens Falls (Sr., Rutgers). 10. Ricky Breymier, rhp, Amsterdam (Sr., Pittsburgh).

INDIVIDUAL BATTING LEADERS
(MINIMUM 100 PLATE APPEARANCES)

	AVG	AB	R	H	2B	3B	HR	RBI	SB
Perry, Matt, Geneva	.427	143	22	61	13	0	1	29	2
Martinez, J.D., Saratoga	.392	97	18	38	6	1	7	19	1
Muoio, Steve, Webster	.375	128	12	48	12	0	0	20	5
Bercume, Jeff, Bennington	.373	153	21	57	11	0	3	22	9
Eggemeyer, Adam, Hornell	.359	167	32	60	6	5	2	29	7
Marshall, Derek, Watertown	.343	105	16	36	6	0	2	21	0
Tolliver, Thomas, Allegany County	.336	122	27	41	1	0	0	11	5
Bosnik, Jesse, Brockport	.333	156	32	56	16	1	2	28	16
Uphouse, Ryan, Geneva	.333	138	31	46	13	0	1	12	10
Bergman, Joey, Bennington	.333	132	23	44	8	1	5	19	15

INDIVIDUAL PITCHING LEADERS
(MINIMUM 25 INNINGS PITCHED)

	W	L	ERA	G	SV	IP	H	BB	SO
Eastham, Kyle, Geneva	2	0	0.00	11	1	29	14	11	29
Davis, Shane, Glens Falls	5	0	0.33	8	0	54	31	8	31
Breymier, Rick, Amsterdam	2	0	0.36	11	2	25	10	15	39
Maxa, Ryan, Hornell	5	0	0.58	18	1	31	26	5	27
Davis, Rye, Elmira	6	1	0.88	8	0	51	33	12	50
Schrader, Adam, Hornell	2	1	1.30	7	0	34	22	23	36
Lucas, Sean, Saratoga	2	2	1.33	14	0	27	14	8	34
Freni, Jared, Little Falls	5	2	1.37	9	1	52	37	18	59
Macklin, Jeremy, Brockport	1	0	1.37	19	2	26	16	12	28
Goodin, Josh, Hornell	1	1	1.42	22	11	25	16	14	30

NORTHWOODS LEAGUE

NORTH	W	L	PCT	GB
Thunder Bay Border Cats	42	26	.618	—
Mankato MoonDogs	41	27	.603	1
St. Cloud River Bats	37	30	.552	4½
Alexandria Beetles	35	32	.522	6½
Rochester Honkers	30	38	.441	12
Duluth Huskies	26	42	.382	16
Brainerd Blue Thunder	23	43	.348	18

SOUTH	W	L	PCT	GB
Wisconsin Woodchucks	41	27	.603	—
La Crosse Loggers	39	29	.574	2
Green Bay Bullfrogs	35	33	.515	6
Madison Mallards	34	34	.500	7
Eau Claire Express	33	35	.485	8
Waterloo Bucks	32	34	.485	8
Battle Creek Bombers	25	43	.368	16

PLAYOFFS—Semifinals: Madison defeated Wisconsin 2-0, Thunder Bay defeated Mankato 2-0. **Championship:** Thunder Bay defeated Madison 2-1 in best-of-three championship series.
TOP 10 PROSPECTS: 1. Cory Vaughn, of, La Crosse (So., San Diego State). 2. Mike Nesseth, rhp, Duluth (R-So., Nebraska). 3. James Jones, lhp, Waterloo (Jr., Long Island). 4. Carlos Ramirez, c, Mankato (Jr., Arizona State). 5. Rob Lyerly, of/1b, Madison (Jr., Charlotte). 6. Aaron Barrett, rhp, Duluth (Jr., Mississippi). 7. Derek McCallum, 2b/ss, St. Cloud (Jr., Minnesota). 8. Ryan Goins, ss, Waterloo (Jr., Dallas Baptist). 9. Andy Burns, if, Duluth (Fr., Kentucky). 10. Nick Gaudi, rhp, Alexandria (Sr., Pepperdine).

INDIVIDUAL BATTING LEADERS
(MINIMUM 184 PLATE APPEARANCES)

	AVG	AB	R	H	2B	3B	HR	RBI	SB
Lyerly, Rob, Madison	.342	228	36	78	19	1	3	48	6
Jobe, Tim, Duluth	.338	219	40	74	15	0	9	40	5
McCallum, Derek, St. Cloud	.328	247	46	81	9	2	6	42	6
Bonfe, Joe, Eau Claire	.326	193	36	63	15	1	5	42	9
Cavan, Ryan, Green Bay	.322	174	29	56	18	0	3	35	15
Gantner, Matt, Wisconsin	.316	174	27	55	9	3	1	33	3
Ramirez, Carlos, Mankato	.315	200	37	63	19	0	10	44	2
Johnson, Kevin, St. Cloud	.313	201	31	63	13	1	5	34	0
Prince, Josh, Green Bay	.312	186	37	58	8	7	1	18	20
Weaver, Brent, Wisconsin	.312	215	39	67	22	0	4	41	2
Wikoff, Brandon, Madison	.310	226	47	70	5	1	0	24	15
Satterwhite, Cameron, Green Bay	.310	155	28	48	14	2	2	27	3
Castillo, Keith, Alexandria	.309	194	26	60	12	0	6	24	6
Melton, Derek, La Crosse	.309	194	30	60	9	2	8	45	10
Goodwin, Devin, Rochester	.307	231	38	71	8	1	6	36	24
Stephens, Eric, Rochester	.307	241	33	74	19	2	7	50	16

INDIVIDUAL PITCHING LEADERS
(MINIMUM 54 INNINGS)

	W	L	ERA	G	SV	IP	H	BB	SO
Zehr, Dan, Thunder Bay	4	0	1.15	23	2	55	45	8	46
Green, Cole, La Crosse	6	1	1.49	13	1	60	37	18	56
Lange, Matt, Green Bay	6	2	1.62	19	3	61	41	20	36
Reyes, Jimmy, Mankato	4	2	1.63	11	0	61	43	14	52
Sheldon, Ryan, St. Cloud	8	2	1.77	12	0	71	58	23	47
Pritchett, Bobby, Wisconsin	7	2	2.04	11	0	71	42	22	67
Woods, Nate, Thunder Bay	5	2	2.04	12	0	66	48	23	38
Burg, Peter, Rochester	5	3	2.09	12	0	78	64	19	30
Odegaard, Chris, Eau Claire	7	1	2.14	11	0	71	55	39	71
Thibodeaux, Jordan, St. Cloud	2	3	2.29	10	0	55	46	27	30
Nobles, Cam, Waterloo	4	3	2.39	10	0	60	38	32	56
Dott, Aaron, La Crosse	5	2	2.43	12	0	74	47	34	50
Watson, Troy, La Crosse	2	2	2.47	17	2	58	38	22	63
Haig, Phil, Rochester	5	3	2.49	11	0	68	57	36	41
Robertson, Zach, Rochester	4	3	2.52	12	0	78	52	40	97
Robinson, Andrew, Alexandria	3	4	2.52	10	0	64	51	26	39

TEXAS COLLEGIATE LEAGUE

	W	L	PCT	GB
McKinney Marshals	26	20	.565	—
Coppell Copperheads	26	22	.542	1
East Texas Pump Jacks	22	26	.458	5
Brazos Valley Bombers	20	26	.435	6

PLAYOFFS—Semifinals: McKinney defeated Brazos Valley 2-1, Coppell defeated East Texas 2-0. **Championship:** McKinney defeated Coppell 2-0 in best-of-three championship series.
TOP 10 PROSPECTS: 1. Del Howell, lhp, McKinney (So., Alabama). 2. Luke Burnett, rhp, East Texas (SIGNED: Mariners). 3. Jimmy Nelson, rhp, McKinney (So., Alabama). 4. Dustin Dickerson, 1b, Brazos Valley (Jr., Baylor). 5. Todd Cunningham, of, Brazos Valley (So., Jacksonville State). 6. Myrio Richard, of, McKinney (Jr., Prairie View A&M). 7. Mike Bolsinger, rhp, McKinney (So., Arkansas). 8. Aaron Wilkerson, rhp, East Texas (So., Panola JC, Texas). 9. Riley Boening, lhp, Coppell (R-Jr., Texas). 10. Travis Sample, 3b/of/dh, Coppell (Jr., Arkansas).

INDIVIDUAL BATTING LEADERS
(MINIMUM 50 PLATE APPEARANCES)

	AVG	AB	R	H	2B	3B	HR	RBI	SB
Sample, Travis, Coppell	.367	49	7	18	6	0	3	19	1

Hernandez, Danny, Braz.Valley	.333	57	10	19	3	1	1	8	2
Dickerson, Dustin, Braz.Valley	.314	51	6	16	2	0	1	11	1
Cunningham, Todd, Braz.Valley	.310	142	28	44	7	2	0	17	2
Holt, Brock, Coppell	.309	123	23	38	3	2	2	27	2
Delagarza, Adam, East Texas	.292	168	34	49	6	0	2	22	8
Smith, Jake, McKinney	.290	124	20	36	9	0	2	24	0
Schultz, Aaron, Coppell	.283	46	4	13	2	1	0	5	1
Richard, Myrio, McKinney	.283	152	39	43	10	3	6	36	2
Curry, Matt, East Texas	.281	146	18	41	6	0	2	25	2

INDIVIDUAL PITCHING LEADERS
(MINIMUM 25 INNINGS)

	W	L	ERA	G	SV	IP	H	BB	SO
Strickland, Sam, Brazos Valley	1	5	1.81	8	0	49	33	22	33
McClary, Tyler, Coppell	1	3	1.95	15	3	27	31	14	20
Stafford, Jared, Coppell	3	0	2.10	16	1	25	23	8	27
Boening, Riley, Coppell	2	1	2.17	6	0	37	30	11	34
Howell, Del, McKinney	2	2	2.41	14	4	33	23	19	47
Neal, Zach, Coppell	3	0	2.43	8	0	37	34	8	37
Nelson, Jimmy, McKinney	3	2	2.55	11	0	49	34	23	66
Doyle, Ryan, McKinney	1	5	2.61	16	3	31	21	17	34
Bolsinger, Michael, McKinney	2	2	2.80	10	0	45	26	20	56
Shelton, Matt, East Texas	3	1	2.89	16	0	28	13	27	32

VALLEY BASEBALL LEAGUE

NORTH	W	L	PCT	GB
Luray Wranglers	30	14	.682	—
Fauquier Gators	27	17	.614	3
Winchester Royals	27	17	.614	3
Haymarket Senators	18	26	.409	12
Woodstock River Bandits	16	28	.364	14
Front Royal Cardinals	12	32	.273	18

SOUTH	W	L	PCT	GB
Waynesboro Generals	30	14	.682	—
Staunton Braves	24	20	.545	6
Covington Lumberjacks	23	21	.523	7
Harrisonburg Turks	19	25	.432	11
New Market Rebels	16	28	.364	14

PLAYOFFS—Quarterfinals: Covington defeated Fauquier 2-0, Waynesboro defeated Haymarket 2-1, Staunton defeated Winchester 2-1, Luray defeated Harrisonburg 2-1. **Semifinals:** Luray defeated Staunton 2-0, Covington defeated Waynesboro 2-0. **Championship:** Luray defeated Covington 3-0 in best-of-five championship series.
TOP 10 PROSPECTS: 1. Ryan Schimpf, 2b, Luray (Jr., Louisiana State). 2. Alex Wimmers, rhp, Luray (So., Ohio State). 3. Jake Cowan, rhp, Waynesboro (So., San Jacinto JC, Texas). 4. Adam McClain, if/of, Luray (So., Memphis). 5. Billy Morrison, rhp, Winchester (R-Jr., Western Michigan). 6. Brandon Sizemore, 2b, Waynesboro (Sr., College of Charleston). 7. Travis Smink, lhp, Luray (Jr., Virginia Military Institute). 8. Gabriel Saade, ss, Waynesboro (Jr., Duke). 9. Mickey Wiswall, 3b, Winchester (So., Boston College). 10. Tyler Townsend, 1b, Winchester (Jr., Florida International).

INDIVIDUAL BATTING LEADERS
(MINIMUM 125 PLATE APPEARANCES)

	AVG	AB	R	H	2B	3B	HR	RBI	SB
Townsend, Tyler, Winchester	.387	142	40	55	12	1	12	36	14
Sizemore, Brandon, Waynesboro	.377	122	34	46	13	1	10	34	14
Johnson, Drew, Harrisonburg	.364	154	32	56	10	1	6	23	8
Noel, Rico, Covington	.344	128	27	44	10	1	1	16	33
Most, Max, Staunton	.339	168	34	57	13	1	2	24	20
Wiswall, Mickey, Winchester	.336	140	25	47	8	1	7	36	4
Brown, Cody, Woodstock	.333	138	25	46	13	1	0	18	2
Henry, Jesse, Front Royal	.329	146	12	48	4	0	0	20	9
Gauck, Ryan, Fauquier	.326	135	20	44	8	2	2	16	3
Agreste, Joe, Winchester	.320	128	26	41	10	1	6	21	2
Izzo, Bryon, Staunton	.313	147	24	46	7	0	0	22	5
Cruz, Jeremy, Luray	.308	117	14	36	8	0	6	19	0
Jefferson, Jeff, Luray	.307	192	38	59	8	0	9	29	6

Nidiffer, Marcus, Covington	.305	131	35	40	4	1	13	31	3
Huffer, Donovan, Staunton	.305	187	31	57	5	1	2	18	6

INDIVIDUAL PITCHING LEADERS
(MINIMUM 50 INNINGS)

	W	L	ERA	G	SV	IP	H	BB	SO
Rucinski, Drew, Luray	5	1	1.13	10	1	55	37	14	59
Baxter, Lance, Staunton	6	0	1.26	8	0	50	42	14	53
Liberatore, Adam, Waynesboro	6	1	1.36	12	0	66	40	26	58
Wimmers, Alex, Luray	5	1	1.70	11	3	53	32	19	72
Smink, Travis, Luray	6	1	1.88	11	0	62	56	10	49
Hill, Taylor, Winchester	6	1	2.53	9	0	53	47	16	59
Parker, Garrett, Harrisonburg	3	4	2.86	10	0	66	66	19	52
Pryor, Tucker, Front Royal	3	5	2.96	12	0	79	73	16	70
Leonard, John, Winchester	3	5	3.05	10	0	62	60	16	59
Tomas, Eric, Harrisonburg	4	2	3.06	8	0	53	47	23	59
Collop, Justin, Winchester	5	2	3.22	9	0	58	44	17	62
Altemus, Andy, Waynesboro	7	2	3.32	11	1	65	70	16	54
Sokolis, Gerard, Staunton	4	5	3.36	12	1	59	55	13	29
Hildreth, Ben, Haymarket	5	4	3.41	11	0	68	77	27	43
Wolosiansky, Dean, Haymarket	3	4	3.46	10	0	52	54	26	35

WEST COAST COLLEGIATE LEAGUE

EAST	W	L	PCT	GB
Wenatchee AppleSox	23	19	.548	—
Kelowna Falcons	21	20	.512	1½
Spokane RiverHawks	20	21	.488	2½
Moses Lake Pirates	13	29	.310	10

WEST	W	L	PCT	GB
Corvallis Knights	31	11	.738	—
Bend Elks	23	19	.548	8
Kitsap BlueJackets	19	23	.452	12
Bellingham Bells	17	25	.405	14

TOP 10 PROSPECTS: 1. Jake Locker, of, Bellingham (Jr., Washington). 2. Josh Osich, lhp, Corvallis (So., Oregon State). 3. Taylor Starr, rhp, Corvallis (So., Oregon State). 4. A.J. Morris, rhp, Moses Lake (Jr., Kansas State). 5. Kraig Sitton, lhp, Spokane (R-So., Oregon State). 6. Drew Heid, of, Bend (Sr., Gonzaga). 7. Chris Vitus, rhp, Spokane (So., Lane, Ore., CC). 8. Eddie Orozco, rhp, Corvallis (So., UC Riverside). 9. Nick Freitas, of, Kelowna (Sr., Southern Utah). 10. Alex Burg, c, Corvallis (Sr., Washington State).

INDIVIDUAL BATTING LEADERS
(MINIMUM 1.8 AT-BATS PER TEAM GAME)

	AVG	AB	R	H	2B	3B	HR	RBI	SB
Heid, Drew, Bend	.403	159	39	64	7	2	5	28	10
Lotti, Logan, Corvallis	.353	133	30	47	12	2	4	24	3
Walsh, Colin, Kelowna	.352	88	19	31	5	0	0	8	6
Buser, Doug, Kitsap	.338	154	33	52	5	0	0	18	12
Darr, Andrew, Bend	.330	112	13	37	8	0	2	12	3
Gebbers, Hawkins, Wenatchee	.327	150	19	49	6	1	3	21	5
Hagen, Stephen, Kelowna	.323	124	20	40	6	1	1	18	1
Hennings, Danny, Bellingham	.322	115	13	37	2	0	1	11	0
Kwan, Max, Kitsap	.315	92	15	29	8	0	5	18	0
Aona, Bucky, Kitsap	.315	162	22	51	10	0	4	39	3

INDIVIDUAL PITCHING LEADERS
(MINIMUM 0.8 INNINGS PER TEAM GAME)

	W	L	ERA	G	SV	IP	H	BB	SO
Eskew, Jared, Corvallis	3	0	1.32	6	0	34	20	10	33
Braun, Jason, Bend	5	2	1.45	17	6	37	30	15	28
Osich, Josh, Corvallis	4	0	1.54	11	0	35	28	10	41
Berger, Jon, Corvallis	4	0	1.74	11	0	51	47	9	47
Orozco, Eddie, Corvallis	3	1	1.75	9	0	36	28	11	38
McCarthy, Mike, Moses Lake	4	2	2.32	8	0	54	43	13	54
Baron, Liam, Corvallis	3	1	2.61	12	0	41	31	11	32
Triolo, Steve, Kelowna	2	1	2.67	10	0	33	30	17	31
Guinn, Aaron, Spokane	1	2	2.70	11	0	36	33	11	35
Jones, Owen, Wenatchee	3	3	2.72	11	1	49	49	16	41

HIGH
SCHOOL

National title lands at American Heritage

BY NATHAN RODE

It wasn't a perfect season, but it was plenty good enough.

With a truckload of talent, American Heritage High (Plantation, Fla.) came into the 2008 season ranked No. 4 in the country, the lowest ranking the Patriots would see all year. They stormed through the regular season, taking on bigger Florida schools and schools from other states, and captured the school's first 3-A state baseball title. Then American Heritage added one more title to its resume: Baseball America Team of the Year.

The Patriots took over the top spot in the rankings in April with a 15-1 record, the lone loss coming to Stephens County (Ga.) High and righthander Ethan Martin.

"There were a couple tough games," head coach Todd Fitz-Gerald said. "The game against Stephens County was tough. It was about 40 degrees and we had to turn around and face Ethan Martin. But the way we came back and battled, I knew we had a special group."

Soon after getting to the top spot, though, American Heritage lost 4-3 to Palm Beach (Fla.) Central High, a 6-A opponent. The Patriots were back on top by the end of April, however, and held fast, riding a 14-game win streak all the way to state and national titles.

"We had talked about it at the very beginning of the season," Fitz-Gerald said. "We really wanted to shoot for that No. 1 ranking and thought it was within reach. Then they refused to talk about it until after they won state."

American Heritage blew through the playoffs, scoring 79 runs in eight games while allowing just 21. Catcher Adrian Nieto had the game of his career in the finals, and first baseman Eric Hosmer fell a home run short of the cycle as American Heritage defeated Carroll High (Fort Pierce, Fla.) by an 8-2 score.

Nieto went 2-for-3 with two home runs and five RBIs in the clincher, while Hosmer was 3-for-3 with an RBI and three runs. And the final out couldn't have been more fitting. Hosmer, who also served as the team's closer, took the ball for the final inning, striking out the side and igniting a celebration with his catcher and friend, Nieto.

"It was just a fitting end, with him making the final pitch to (Nieto) and them being the first to

PHILL SEARS

American Heritage celebrated its first state and national titles at the same time

hug each other," Fitz-Gerald said. "I was so excited I ran out there to hug someone, but I looked like I was hugging air."

Some might question the quality of American Heritage's opponents, because as a 3-A school it played a weaker conference schedule than some of the traditional powerhouse programs. But Fitz-Gerald and his team did everything they could to dispel that. In addition to taking on the strong Palm Beach Central and Stephens County teams, they also no-hit Cullman (Ala.) High 10-0, the back-to-back 5-A Alabama champions (2007-2008) and preseason No. 26 team.

After the season, the Patriots produced four picks in the 2008 draft: Hosmer (third overall, Royals), Nieto (fifth round, Nationals), righthander Juan Carlos Sulbaran (30th round, Reds) and outfielder Joey Belviso (50th round, Angels). The rest of the lineup had several Division I signees and underclassmen who could become premium draft picks or good college players. That's a team that deserves the comparisons to a junior college team, a statement echoed by several coaches and scouts throughout the season.

American Heritage High (Plantation, Fla.) finished the season 31-2 and won the Florida 3-A state championship. The staff of Baseball America and the National High School Baseball Coaches Association unanimously voted American Heritage as the final No. 1 team in the 2008 rankings. Records do not include ties.

Rank	School	Record	Season conclusion
1.	American Heritage HS, Plantation, Fla.	31-2	State 3-A champion
2.	Bishop Gorman HS, Las Vegas	41-3	State 4-A champion
3.	Plano (Texas) West HS	40-2	State 6-A champion
4.	Owasso (Okla.) HS	36-3	State 6-A champion
5.	Brookwood HS, Snellville, Ga.	34-3	State 5-A champion
6.	Don Bosco Prep, Ramsey, N.J.	33-0	State Non-Public A champion
7.	Pleasure Ridge Park HS, Louisville	33-4	State champion
8.	Farragut HS, Knoxville	43-3	State 3-A champion
9.	Malvern (Pa.) Prep	40-3	State Independent Schools runner-up
10.	Valley Christian HS, San Jose, Calif.	30-6	CIF DI Central Coast champion
11.	Washington HS, New York City	45-2	City Division A Public School champion
12.	Lutheran HS, Orange, Calif.	23-6	CIF DI Southern Section quarterfinals
13.	South Caldwell HS, Hudson, N.C.	24-2	State 4-A quarterfinals
14.	Wilson HS, Long Beach, Calif.	28-6	CIF DI Southern Section runner up
15.	Barbe HS, St. Charles, La.	35-6	State 5-A champion
16.	Lake Brantley HS Altamonte Springs, Fla.	30-4	State 6-A champion
17.	Lakota West HS, West Chester, Ohio	26-1	State Division I semifinals
18.	Plymouth (Mass.) North HS	22-0	State Division II champion
19.	Creighton Prep, Omaha	26-4	State Class A first round
20.	Bartlett HS, Memphis, Tenn.	35-5	State 3-A runner-up
21.	Tupelo (Miss.) HS	32-7	State 5-A runner-up
22.	Simi Valley (Calif.) HS	25-8	CIF DI Southern Section champion
23.	Moody HS, Corpus Christi, Texas	26-3	State 4-A second round
24.	Sunrise Mountain HS, Peoria, Ariz.	29-4	State 5-A DII runner-up
25.	Sarasota (Fla.) HS	25-3	State 6-A regional semifinals
26.	Calallen, Corpus Christi, Texas	41-1	State 4-A champion
27.	Park Vista HS, Lake Worth, Fla.	30-2	State 6-A runner-up
28.	Vista Murrieta HS, Murrieta, Calif.	23-6	CIF DII Southern Section quarterfinals
29.	La Cueva HS, Albuquerque	28-3	State 5-A champion
30.	Dunedin (Fla.) HS	26-6	State 5-A champion
31.	Seaman HS, Topeka, Kan.	24-1	Class 5-A champion
32.	Paul VI, Fairfax, Va.	27-3	State Independent Schools champion
33.	Rocky Mountain HS, Carbondale, Col.	23-4	State 5-A champion
34.	Fayetteville (Ark.) HS	30-3	Class 7-A champion
35.	Xaverian HS, Brooklyn	27-1	City Catholic School champion
36.	Nitro (W.V.) HS	31-4	State 3-A champion
37.	Ozark (Mo.) HS	24-5	State 4-A champion
38.	Boise (Idaho) HS	28-2	State 5-A champion
39.	Norco (Calif.) HS	24-4	CIF DI Southern Section semifinals
40.	Calvert Hall HS, Baltimore	26-7	MIAA champion
41.	Brookland-Cayce HS, Cayce, S.C.	30-2	State 3-A champion
42.	Ocean Springs (Miss.) HS	28-9	Class 5-A champion
43.	Harrison HS, Kennesaw, Ga.	26-3	State 5-A first round
44.	Bellaire (Texas) HS	37-7	State 5-A semifinals
45.	Opelika (Ala.) HS	42-4	State 6-A runner-up
46.	Neuqua Valley HS, Naperville, Ill.	32-6	State 4-A semifinals
47.	Penn HS, Mishawaka, Ind.	28-3	State 4-A quarterfinals
48.	Green Valley HS, Henderson, Nev.	34-7	State 4-A runner-up
49.	Patriot HS, Riverside, Calif.	27-3	CIF DII Southern Section semifinals
50.	Timpanogos HS, Orem, Utah	22-5	State 5-A champion

Ranking Roundup

The 2007 national champions and preseason No. 1 team, Wilson High (Long Beach, Calif.), lasted just one month at the top before hitting some bumps. The Bruins dropped their second game of the season to Anaheim's Katella High 3-1 and lost their No. 2 pitcher, righthander Ray Hanson, to a broken thumb. Their best player, two-way prospect Aaron Hicks, also battled a stiff back, ultimately challenging Wilson's depth.

The Bruins finished the season 28-6 and lost in the California Interscholastic Federation Division I Southern Section finals 4-1 to Simi Valley (Calif.) High. They ended up No. 14 in the country.

"I think we had a very good season in spite of a couple things," head coach Andy Hall said. "We felt we could have repeated if we got through those early tournaments. It was cool to go back to Dodger Stadium for the championship, though. Last year was such a blur. We went twice in two years. Some never get there, so we never discount that."

Plano (Texas) West High enjoyed a dominant season, starting the year outside of the rankings, only to storm to the top with a 35-game win streak and perfect regular season (28-0). Their first loss came in the Texas Region II semifinals to Cedar Park (Texas) High, a best of three series, but the Wolves salvaged the third game to advance. Georgetown (Texas) High took the first tilt of the region finals, but Plano West took the series by winning four straight games to win the 5-A championship with a 40-2 record, an incredible feat in Texas baseball.

"We're really on cloud nine," head coach Kendall Clark said. "Back in January we thought we had the best lineup, but didn't know what kind of pitching we had. This was such a focused group and these guys were determined to win. It's been a blur, but a grind at the same time. We are exhausted. The coaches are, but the kids aren't."

Tradition Pays Off

As soon as Jeff Malm squeezed his glove at first base, capturing the final out and a third straight state championship, he turned to look for his teammates rushing the field. He joined in the celebration of Bishop Gorman High's unprecedented feat, but there was something else lingering in the back of the junior's mind.

"It crossed my mind as soon as the last one was over," Malm said of the chance of being on a fourth straight title team. "It's not over yet. You always want to go out on top as a senior."

The Las Vegas prep school went from underdog champions in 2006, when Malm was just a freshman, to a state power in 2008. The Gaels have dominated local competition and even gained national recognition by taking their talent out of state, winning numerous national events.

This kind of domination isn't completely unheard of though. Bishop Gorman's run was one of several repeat titles by teams across the country that had resumés to rival one another.

Oklahoma's Owasso High has been to the 6-A state finals 12 of the last 13 years, winning the last two. And since the 6-A level was added in 1996, the state champion has come from Owasso's own Frontier Conference.

"Our conference is pretty special," Owasso head coach Larry Turner said. "The facilities these schools have are second to none. That's a big help."

Horizon High (Scottsdale) won its second straight Arizona state title, an upset over Peoria's Sunrise Mountain. Horizon was the underdog by far. The 2007 team had two dominant right-handers: Tim Alderson, who went 22nd overall

Dodger Stadium hosts Aflac game

BY MATT BLOOD

Every year the date of the Aflac All-American Game is circled by every scout and college coach as a great opportunity to see 38 of the best prospects for the next year's draft. In its sixth year, the game became even more prestigious as it was played in a major league stadium for the first time in 2008.

Hosted at Dodger Stadium in Los Angeles, the game was split into two rosters of 19, divided by East and West, and the contest was exciting and dramatic. The East prevailed with a ninth-inning rally, winning 4-2.

The first eight innings were fast-paced and dominated by pitching. The West squad was able to push across a run in the first inning on a RBI single from right fielder Slade Heathcott (Texas HS, Texarkana, Texas) and a run in the fourth inning on back-to-back doubles from Max Stassi (Yuba City, Calif., HS) and Matt Davidson (Yucaipa, Calif., HS).

West pitchers dominated the East hitters for eight innings, allowing only one hit and striking out 12, but the East had success on the mound as well and was able to keep it close, setting up a dramatic four-run explosion in the top of the ninth.

With two outs, Brian Goodwin (Rocky Mount, N.C., HS) drove in the tying and go-ahead runs with a single to left field. Richie Shaffer (Providence HS, Charlotte, N.C.) scored the winning run, and crossed the plate while letting out a scream. Shaffer pumped his fists, chest-bumped and celebrated with teammates as if they had won the seventh game of the World Series.

"Yeah, I was pretty excited," Shaffer said. "I really didn't want to lose to those guys."

Goodwin won the game's MVP award, after he had two hits, drove in two runs and scored a run. The dramatic win marked the second year in a row that the East rallied in the ninth to defeat the West. In 2007, the East scored three runs in the ninth inning to score a 5-4 win. Tim Beckham, who went on to be the No. 1 overall pick in the 2008 draft, was the MVP after he drove in the game's winning run.

Under Armour plays in the ivy

BY MATT BLOOD

With the help of a top-tier sponsor and access to a major league stadium, this felt like a whole new ballgame.

The Under Armour All-American Game debuted at Wrigley Field in August, with the Baseball Factory team defeating Team One 5-4. Formerly called the Cape Cod Classic and held in Wareham, Mass., the game made a huge jump in terms of publicity and national television exposure (ESPNU carried the game live), with 36 of the nation's best high school baseball players, but in a way consistent with the Baseball Factory philosophy of player development. The rosters included well-known standouts from the summer showcase circuit as well as players who had not been as visible but have shown elite skills in tryouts, workouts or tournaments.

"I have to give our scouts at Baseball Factory a lot of credit when it comes to the quality of players they chose to participate in this game," Baseball Factory CEO Steve Sclafani said. "They stuck their neck out on several players and these players did not disappoint."

The game included 36 total strikeouts but also 18 hits. The last out came when Canadian lefthander Jake Eliopoulos struck out the nation's top position player, Georgia outfielder Donovan Tate, on a back-door breaking ball.

A player from each squad won MVP recognition for his performance. Mychal Givens won the award for Baseball Factory as he tallied two hits and struck out two batters while pitching, while David Renfroe was honored from Team One as he struck out five in two innings and hit the game's lone home run, a three-run shot off Eliopoulos in the eighth.

"It's hard to say which was more fun, the strikeouts or hitting the home run," Renfroe said. "I enjoyed both."

Most of the players had been playing baseball since February, when their high school seasons began, and through the summer in various tournaments and showcase events. The fatigue was noticeable, and most of the pitchers flashed velocities at least two mph lower than their typical radar gun readings.

to the Giants, and Kevin Rhoderick who was an 18th-round pick but opted to attend Oregon State instead of signing and served as the Beavers' closer this spring.

The Huskies entered the tournament short-handed after they dismissed three players from the team during the season and had other suspensions dealt out as the year rolled along. Despite such obstacles, head coach Eric Kibler says winning the title is their goal every year.

"We always think we can be there," he said. "If you don't, you're not going to get there. How can I tell my team we're playing for second place? How can I establish any kind of tradition?"

Along with the others, Horizon has established a strong tradition of winning, raising questions of how to sum up their success. If high school baseball was remotely followed and analyzed like it's professional counterpart, guys like Malm and Kibler would be all over the news as the faces of their dynasties.

"The D-word is pretty scary," Kibler said, a proud winner of state titles in 1995-96, 2005, 2007 and now 2008.

But without the payrolls, free agency and trades, it may be hard for someone to fathom how this level of success is even possible. Owasso and Horizon are both public schools, an obvious obstacle in sustaining any sort of winning streak. You play with what you get, but Kibler and Turner have worked hard to overcome such obstacles. Kibler has established a desirable community while Turner prides himself on always having the best team, rather than just individual players.

"One thing we've done really well here in the big city is establish a small community," Kibler said. "We host a lot of camps and establish an attitude of how baseball should be played. It's a privilege. Young athletes are entitled to nothing. The high school guys help out so we hear stories of 9-year-olds sitting in the stands saying 'I wanna be Husky.' They want to play in front of a thousand fans every night. That's where they want to be."

Kibler takes pride in the team's success on the field while maintaining responsibility and integrity off of it, and says he is adamant about not recruiting players.

"You must be enrolled to play here," he said. "I won't talk to you until then. I'm going to take from the neighborhood."

Even though Owasso has produced individual standouts like shortstop Pete Kozma, a first-round pick in 2007, the Rams boast balanced teams as well.

"From the beginning we haven't had just the best players," Turner said. "We have the best teams.

The best thing is our players buy into what we're trying to accomplish. I don't have any big secrets."

As a private institution, Bishop Gorman has the advantage of being able to recruit. Even so, it had to start somewhere and Malm seemed to have known it.

"Three years ago, Jeff (Malm) said we had a chance to win four in a row and I looked at him like he was crazy," head coach Chris Sheff said. "I asked him if he knew how hard it was, but he's put us in a position to actually do it."

Sheff said recruiting doesn't make it much easier. They are able to pick from a larger pool of players, but the expenses add up and not everyone can afford it. Tuition alone is $11,000. Then you have to add in the program expenses, which Sheff said can double that amount. Plus, it had been over 50 years since Bishop Gorman had won a state championship before the first of the three titles in 2006.

"Those first years had a lot of long nights," Sheff added. "The talent was there but we had to find a way to get to the top."

Something clicked, as this was only Sheff's fifth season as head coach. Before, he had just one year of coaching experience after retiring from professional baseball, where he spent 10 years in the minor leagues. Now, along with the titles he has a 111-16-2 record in the last three seasons and an overall record of 153-37-2.

Whether a public or private school, a key to such success always seems to come back to longevity, in terms of kids playing together. Colby Rasmus and his brother Cory starred in the Little League World Series in 1999. Six years later, they captured a state and national title.

Eric Hosmer, Adrian Nieto and several other members of the American Heritage High squad have been playing together since they were 11 years old.

The wheels are set in motion long before the beginning of the championship season. It just may not be realized until afterward. The dynasty title is hardly planned. It's more in hindsight. Malm certainly wasn't planning on winning three championships in a row.

"It's an incredible feeling," he said. "It's hard enough to win one. My freshman year we didn't really know any better. We were a bunch of young kids that no one expected to do anything."

Malm will be back for another try in 2009 with another young squad, but he thinks they will be ready with the experience the underclassmen are gaining this summer. The same goes for the other schools. With their tradition and dedication, titles will continue to pile up.

AROUND THE NATION

■ While events like gymnastics are usually dominated by athletes in their teens, Olympic baseball is generally played by those with some professional experience and a little more age. However, two players stood out of the crowd in the Beijing games who had just recently graduated from high school.

Brett Lawrie joined Team Canada after graduating from Brookwood SS (Langley, B.C.) and being selected 16th overall by the Milwaukee Brewers. He signed for $1.7 million right before flying to Beijing. He had 11 plate appearances and didn't collect a hit, but did drive in two runs and had a putout. Lawrie will give catching a try for the Brewers but patrolled the outfield for Canada.

NATHAN RODE
Brett Lawrie

"It felt great just to be among those guys up there with so much more experience than I do in the game," Lawrie said. "They're all 26, 27 years old, and I'm coming in at 18. But I learned a lot from those guys. It was just fun to hear my name called and just going out and playing."

Righthander **Juan Carlos Sulbaran** joined the Netherlands shortly after claiming a national title with American Heritage High and signing with the Cincinnati Reds for $500,000 as a 30th-round selection. He made one start in Beijing, lasting 4⅔ and allowing five runs (two earned) on four hits. He struck out six.

■ **John Lowery Sr.,** head coach of Jefferson High (Shenandoah Junction, W.Va.) only needed the first two games of the season to eclipse the 1,000 win mark. The Cougars defeated Freedom High (South Riding, Va.) 10-0, then put on the real show, honoring their coach with a postgame ceremony. Lowery completed his 38th year of coaching this season, all of which came with Jefferson (originally Harpers Ferry High). Along with the 1,000 wins, Lowery also has nine state titles to his credit.

■ Righthander **Sonny Gray** sustained an avulsion fracture and a third-degree sprain to his right ankle running out a ground ball during a game on April 16 and missed the rest of his senior season. A potential first-round pick in the 2008 draft, Gray plummeted to the 27th round where the Cubs selected him. Already considered a tough sign, Gray decided to honor his commitment to Vanderbilt.

■ **Tyler Hibbs,** a righthander/shortstop from Arundel High (Gambrils, Md.), was arrested on Feb. 26 on charges of marijuana possession, possession with intent to distribute and two counts of possession of drug paraphernalia. Ranked No. 218 on the 2008 High School Top 300, Hibbs was committed to Florida State, but the Seminoles rescinded his scholarship. Hibbs did not participate in Arundel's 2008 season. He enrolled at Tallahassee Community College where he will pitch and play a limited role in the infield in the spring.

Epic season benefits Martin

On a cool spring night in March, righthander Ethan Martin toed the rubber for Stephens County High (Toccoa, Ga.), in an early-season tournament matchup against American Heritage High (Plantation, Fla.), the No. 3 team in the country at the time and the eventual national champions.

The temperature hovered around 40 degrees, but nothing could cool off Martin. It was that night he rocketed up draft boards as a righthander and began his path toward becoming the 2008 Baseball America High School Player of the Year.

Martin started that game as just another high school prospect who splits his time between the mound and a position. Some scouts liked him as a third baseman who had plus bat speed with plus power potential, while others liked him on the mound.

The highlight came in his showdown with Eric Hosmer, the top power hitter among the prep ranks. Martin dealt two quick strikes with 94 and 96 mph fastballs. Then Hosmer battled and fouled off a couple of pitches. With a 2-2 count, Martin delivered a backdoor slurve and froze Hosmer for strike three.

"That was probably the biggest game," Martin said. "At that point I wasn't a pitcher, really. If I did well it was great. If I didn't, it wasn't going to affect me because I was a position player."

Martin then struck out Adrian Nieto, another top prospect, for the third out. The scouts in attendance raved about the new pitching talent now clearly on display. Stephens County won the game 6-4, one of only two blemishes on American Heritage's championship season, thanks to Martin's incredible performance. He pitched the complete game, striking out 11, and his 130th pitch hit 93 on the gun.

"We came into that game under no pressure," Martin said. "It wasn't like we were supposed to win, so we went in calm and cool. It told us we could play with anybody. We got down late in playoff games, but came back because we knew we could. It helped tremendously."

After Hosmer struck out in his first at-bat, he told Martin not to throw the fastball again:a little joke between two guys who had spent plenty of time together on the baseball showcase circuit. In the next at-bat, Hosmer saw the fastball again but popped out. He reminded Martin one last time not to throw it, but Martin wouldn't budge. In a later at-bat, Martin put one of his 94 mph

PLAYER OF THE YEAR

PREVIOUS WINNERS

1992: Preston Wilson, of/rhp, Bamberg-Ehrhardt (S.C.) HS
1993: Trot Nixon, of/lhp, New Hanover HS, Wilmington, N.C.
1994: Doug Million, lhp, Sarasota (Fla.) HS
1995: Ben Davis, c, Malvern (Pa.) Prep
1996: Matt White, rhp, Waynesboro Area (Pa.) HS
1997: Darnell McDonald, of, Cherry Creek HS, Englewood, Colo.
1998: Drew Henson, 3b/rhp, Brighton (Mich.) HS
1999: Josh Hamilton, of/lhp, Athens Drive HS, Raleigh, N.C.
2000: Matt Harrington, rhp, Palmdale (Calif.) HS
2001: Joe Mauer, c, Cretin-Derham Hall HS, St. Paul, Minn.
2002: Scott Kazmir, lhp, Cypress Falls HS, Houston
2003: Jeff Allison, rhp, Veterans Memorial HS, Peabody, Mass.
2004: Homer Bailey, rhp, LaGrange (Texas) HS
2005: Justin Upton, ss, Great Bridge HS, Chesapeake, Va.
2006: Adrian Cardenas, ss/2b, Mons. Pace HS, Opa Locka, Fla.
2007: Mike Moustakas, ss, Chatsworth (Calif.) HS

heaters high and outside, an almost impossible pitch to touch, but Hosmer flicked his wrists and sent a missile off the scoreboard in left field for a home run.

"That was the hardest hit ball I've ever seen," Martin said. "As he was going around the bases he looked at me and said, 'I told you you shouldn't have thrown it.'"

From there, Martin cruised through the season, dominating the competition on both sides of the ball and helping his team make it to the Georgia 3-A state finals. He finished the season 10-2, 1.50 with two saves and 162 strikeouts in 89 innings. At the plate he hit .509 with 18 home runs and 39 RBIs. He had 55 hits, 16 of which were doubles, giving him 34 extra-base hits.

"I couldn't ask for a better senior year," Martin said. "I wanted to go out and perform at both. It was a dream season. It was a dream come true that we made it. We really overachieved."

Martin and Stephens County fell to a talented Cartersville High team in the finals, but it didn't taint a dream season for head coach Mark Gosnell and his squad.

"He was a vital part of our program," Gosnell said. "He stepped up to be our No. 1 guy on the mound. He led our team with stats, but also with communication and leadership on and off the field."

With the high school season over, the final piece fell into place for Martin when the Dodgers made him the 15th overall pick in June.

Eric Hosmer

PHIL SEARS

L.J. Hoes

LARRY GOREN

FIRST TEAM

Pos	Player, School	Class	B-T	HT	WT	AVG	AB	R	H	2B	3B	HR	RBI	SB	Drafted
C	Kyle Skipworth, Patriot HS, Riverside, Calif.	Sr.	L-R	6-3	195	.543	94	51	51	11	2	13	47	3	Marlins (1)
IF	Eric Hosmer, American Heritage HS, Plantation, Fla.	Sr.	L-L	6-4	210	.471	87	49	41	6	3	11	27	16	Royals (1)
IF	Tim Beckham, Griffin (Ga.) HS	Sr.	R-R	6-2	190	.482	110	58	53	13	0	6	41	23	Rays (1)
IF	Anthony Hewitt, Salisbury (Conn.) School	Sr.	R-R	6-1	195	.493	73	36	36	9	5	10	23	17	Phillies (1)
IF	Derrick Gibson, Seaford (Del.) HS	Sr.	R-R	6-1	170	.652	66	40	43	7	5	6	27	14	Red Sox (2)
OF	Jay Austin, North Atlanta HS	Sr.	L-L	5-11	170	.568	74	43	42	9	4	15	52	26	Astros (2)
OF	Xavier Avery, Cedar Grove HS, Ellenwood, Ga.	Sr.	L-L	5-11	180	.561	66	42	37	6	4	8	24	–	Orioles (2)
OF	Jaff Decker, Sunrise Mountain HS, Peoria, Ariz.	Sr.	L-L	5-10	190	.556	72	45	40	14	5	14	44	21	Padres (1s)
UT	Ethan Martin, Stephens County HS, Toccoa, Ga.	Sr.	R-R	6-2	195	.509	108	36	55	16	0	18	39	11	Dodgers (1)

Pos	Player, School	Class	B-T	HT	WT	W	L	ERA	G	SV	IP	H	BB	SO	Drafted
LHP	Brett DeVall, Niceville (Fla.) HS	Sr.	R-L	6-3	215	12	1	0.41	16	2	86	45	21	140	Braves (1s)
LHP	Danny Hultzen, St. Albans School, Washington, D.C.	Sr.	L-L	6-2	195	13	0	0.74	–	–	73	–	–	140	D'Backs (10)
RHP	Taylor Jungmann, Georgetown (Texas) HS	Sr.	R-R	6-6	195	14	0	0.77	16	0	90	–	22	153	Angels (24)
RHP	Jake Odorizzi, Highland (Ill.) HS	Sr.	R-R	6-2	175	14	0	0.08	15	–	–	–	6	146	Brewers (1s)
UT	Ethan Martin, Stephens County HS, Toccoa, Ga.	Sr.	R-R	6-2	195	10	2	1.50	15	2	89	39	43	162	Dodgers (1)

SECOND TEAM

Pos.	Player, School	Class	B-T	HT	WT	AVG	AB	R	H	2B	3B	HR	RBI	SB	Drafted
C	Brandon Miller, Woodward Academy, Tyrone, Ga.	Sr.	R-R	6-1	190	.426	73	–	31	6	1	10	32	–	Red Sox (33)
IF	Destin Hood, St. Paul's Espicopal School, Mobile, Ala.	Sr.	R-R	6-1	180	.485	–	–	–	–	–	8	32	–	Nationals (2)
IF	Clark Murphy, Fallbrook (Calif.) HS	Sr.	L-L	6-2	190	.455	77	32	35	5	0	12	30	14	Rangers (5)
IF	Tyler Hanover, North Davidson HS, Lexington, N.C.	Sr.	R-R	5-7	165	.475	80	34	38	8	1	12	43	16	Undrafted
IF	Steven Proscia, Don Bosco Prep, Ramsey, N.J.	Sr.	R-R	6-2	210	.545	101	56	55	12	3	9	45	17	Twins (39)
OF	L.J. Hoes, St. John's HS, Washington, D.C.	Sr.	R-R	6-1	190	.524	.84	44	44	9	2	8	29	32	Orioles (3)
OF	J.P. Ramirez, Canyon (Texas) HS	Sr.	L-L	5-10	185	.521	94	45	49	22	8	8	48	12	Nationals (15)
OF	Zach Collier, Chino Hills (Calif.) HS	Sr.	L-L	6-2	185	.450	80	31	36	10	5	7	21	12	Phillies (1s)
UT	Aaron Hicks, Wilson HS, Long Beach, Calif.	Sr.	B-R	6-2	170	.473	.93	50	44	12	5	4	23	37	Twins (1)

	Player, School	Class	B-T	HT	WT	W	L	ERA	G	SV	IP	H	BB	SO	Drafted
LHP	Ben Flora, Plano (Texas) West HS	Sr.	L-L	6-0	175	13	0	0.96	17	1	73	51	26	112	Undrafted
RHP	Gerrit Cole, Lutheran HS, Orange, Calif.	Sr.	R-R	6-3	195	8	2	0.46	18	1	75	30	18	121	Yankees (1)
RHP	Zack Von Rosenberg, Zachary (La.) HS	Jr.	R-R	6-5	205	12	1	0.49	16	4	82	56	13	119	Not Eligible
RHP	Dylan Floro, Buhach Colony HS, Atwater, Calif.	Jr.	R-R	6-2	170	12	1	0.75	17	2	94	49	21	139	Not Eligible
UT	Aaron Hicks, Wilson HS, Long Beach, Calif.	Sr.	B-R	6-2	170	8	2	1.16	14	1	72	41	31	112	Twins (1)

Team USA youths shine abroad

For the second straight year, USA Baseball's youth national teams displayed some of the top high school talent in the nation.

The 16-and-under squad captured another gold medal, this time in the Youth Pan Am Games in Veracruz, Mexico, after taking down the host country 7-3 in the championship game.

Lefthander Philip Pfeifer of Farragut High in Knoxville started the deciding game and went six innings, allowing three runs (two earned) on three hits and a walk. He also struck out 10. Shortstop Marcus Littlewood (Pineview HS, St. George, Utah) led the offense, going 1-for-5 with a bases-loaded double in the sixth that broke a 2-2 tie.

The summer was also a confirmation of Bryce Harper's (Las Vegas High) potential. An outfielder/catcher, Harper started all eight games in the tournament and hit .571/.676/1.214 (16-for-28) with six doubles, four home runs and 16 RBIs.

At the World Junior Championship in Edmonton, the 18-and-under team's summer was shaping up to be perfect, but their run came to an abrupt halt in the championship game. After beating South Korea 4-3 in the first meeting, head coach Mark Elkins and his squad looked to be in the driver's seat. But Korean ace Yung Hoon Sung took the mound after throwing nine innings just two days earlier. He showed no signs of fatigue, scattering seven hits while striking out nine in a complete game.

Lefthander Matthew Purke of Klein (Texas) High took the loss in the championship after allowing six runs on eight hits in four innings.

AMATEUR/YOUTH CHAMPIONS 2008

TEAM USA

JUNIOR TEAM (18-AND-UNDER)

Event	Site	Champion	Runner-up
Tournament of Stars	Cary, N.C.	Dixie National	NABF
IBAF World Junior Championship	Edmonton, Alberta	South Korea	United States

YOUTH TEAM (16-AND-UNDER)

Event	Site	Champion	Runner-up
USA Junior Olympics--East	Palm Beach County, Fla.	Orlando Scorpions	Orlando Reds
USA Junior Olympics--West	Peoria & Surprise, Ariz.	San Diego Show	OC Baseball

ALL-AMERICAN AMATEUR BASEBALL ASSOCIATION (AAABA): ZANESVILLE, OHIO

Event	Site	Champion	Runner-up
World Series (21-and-Under)	Johnstown, Penn.	Youse's Maryland Orioles	McLean (Va.) Raiders

AMATEUR ATHLETIC UNION (AAU): LAKE BUENA VISTA, FLA.

Event	Site	Champion	Runner-up
10-and-Under (60-foot)	Lake Buena Vista, Fla.	Chet Lemon's Juice	Tampa Titans
11-and-Under (70-foot)	Lake Buena Vista, Fla.	East Cobb Astros	VA Storm
12-and-Under (70-foot)	Richmond, Va.	Chet Lemon's Juice	Blue Springs (Mo.) Classics
13-and-Under (90-foot)	Virginia Beach, Va.	Chet Lemon's Juice	NE Firebirds
14-and-Under (90-foot)	Sarasota, Fla.	Tampa Bay Warriors	NH Timbercats
15-and-Under	Salem, Va.	Tri State Arsenal Blue	Virginia Attack
Junior Olympics/16 & U	Detroit, Mich.	MGBA Eagles	Michigan Braves Baseball Club
18/19-and-Under	Lake Buena Vista, Fla.	Chet Lemon's Juice	Brazos Valley Renegades (Texas) Maroon

AMERICAN AMATEUR BASEBALL CONGRESS (AABC): FARMINGTON, N.M.

Event	Site	Champion	Runner-up
Gil Hodges	Brooklyn, N.Y.	Wyckoff (N.J.) Raiders	Brooklyn Bonnies
Pee Wee Reese (12 & U)	Toa Baja, Puerto Rico	Puerto Rico	Gresham Park Yard Dogs
Sandy Koufax (13 & U)	Battle Creek, Mich.	Spring Renegades	South Farmington (Mich.) Blues
Sandy Koufax (14 & U)	Surprise, Ariz.	Arizona Firebirds	Weston Rattlers
Mickey Mantle (15 & U)	Owasso, Okla.	Dallas STIX	YSL Blue Devils
Mickey Mantle (16 & U)	McKinney, Texas	All American Prospects	Dallas DBAT
Connie Mack (18 & U)	Farmington, N.M.	East Cobb (Ga.) Yankees	Midland (Ohio) Redskins
Stan Musial (open)	Huntsville, Texas	Northwest Wildcats	Lombard (Ill.) Orioles

AMERICAN LEGION BASEBALL: INDIANAPOLIS

Event	Site	Champion	Runner-up
World Series (19 & U)	Shelby, N.C.	Las Vegas	Pasco (Wash.)

BABE RUTH BASEBALL: TRENTON, N.J.

Event	Site	Champion	Runner-up
Cal Ripken (10 & U)	Abbeville, La.	West Raleigh, N.C.	Buchanan, Calif.
Cal Ripken 12-year-old (60 feet)	Martin, Tenn.	Bear, Del.	Kennewick, Wash.
13-year-old	Jamestown, N.Y.	Bryant, Ark.	College Point, N.Y.
14-year-old	Quincy, Mass.	Norwalk, Conn.	Tallahassee, Fla.
13-15-year-olds	Van Buren, Ark.	Torrance, Calif.	Westbrook, Maine
16-18-year-old	Newark, Ohio	Portland, Ore.	Modesto, Calif.

CONTINENTAL AMATEUR BASEBALL ASSOCIATION (CABA): WESTERVILLE, OHIO

Event	Site	Champion	Runner-up
9-and-Under	Woodstock, Ill.	New Lenox (Ill.) Rebels	Cincinnati Flames
10-and-Under	Westfield/Carmel, Ind.	Cincinnati Flames	Cincinnati Stix
11-and-Under	Northern Illinois	IL Gravel Baseball	Cincinnati Flames
12-and-Under	Cincinnati, Ohio	Pennsylvania Revolution	Ohio Heat
13-and-Under	Westfield/Carmel, Ind.	Summit City (Ind.) Sluggers	Louisville Panthers
14-and-Under (60x90)	San Juan, Puerto Rico	South Oakland MI A's	Seattle Select
15-and-Under	Northern Illinois	East Cobb (Ga.) Astros	Schaumburg (Ill.) Seminoles
16-and-Under	Marietta, Ga.	East Cobb (Ga.) Astros	6-4-3 DP Cougars
High school age	Euclid, Ohio	Brooklyn Bergen Beach	Florida American Legion Post 43
18-and-Under (wood)	Charleston, S.C.	South Carolina Diamond Devils 17	South Carolina Diamond Devils 18
18-and-Under (aluminum)	Struthers, Ohio	Ohio Diamond Premier	Ohio Warhawks

LITTLE LEAGUE BASEBALL: WILLIAMSPORT, PA.

Event	Site	Champion	Runner-up
Little League (11-12)	Williamsport, Pa.	Waipo , Hawaii	Mexico
Junior League (13-14)	Taylor, Mich.	Willemstad, Curacao	Hilo, Hawaii
Senior League (15-16)	Bangor, Maine	Upper Deerfield, N.J.	Willemstad, Curacao
Big League (17-18)	Easley, S.C.	South Carolina	Puerto Rico

NATIONAL AMATEUR BASEBALL FEDERATION (NABF): BOWIE, MD.

Event	Site	Champion	Runner-up
Freshman (12 & U)	Hopkinsville, Ky.	Did Not Play	
Sophomore (14 & U)	Springboro, Oh.	No results available	
Junior (16 & U)	Northville, Mich.	Summit City Sluggers	Long Island Mustangs
High School (17 & U)	Northville, Mich.	Long Island Tigers	Delco Diamonds
Senior (18 & U)	Jackson, Miss.	Bayside Yankees	TNL Sports
College (22 & U)	Toledo, Ohio	Ohio Monarchs Gold	Long Island Astros
Major (open)	Louisville, Ky.	Tampa Elite	Louisville Riverrats

PERFECT GAME/BCS FINALS: CEDAR RAPIDS, IOWA

Event	Site	Champion	Runner-up
14-and-Under	Fort Myers, Fla.	Banditos Black Austin*	Carolina Tarheels*
15-and-Under	Fort Myers, Fla.	Tampa Tigers	Round Trip Baseball
16-and-Under	Fort Myers, Fla.	Orlando Scorpions Black*	Palm Beach PAL*
17-and-Under	Fort Myers, Fla.	Diamond Vision Elite	East Cobb Astros
18-and-Under	Fort Myers, Fla.	Ohio Warhawks	Syracuse Sports Zone Chiefs

PERFECT GAME/WORLD WOOD BAT ASSOC. SUMMER CHAMPIONSHIPS: CEDAR RAPIDS, IOWA

Event	Site	Champion	Runner-up
14-and-Under	Marietta, Ga.	Roswell Hornets	Tri-State Arsenal 14u
15-and-Under	Marietta, Ga.	NorCal 2011	Kentucky Baseball Club 15's
16-and-Under	Marietta, Ga.	Richmond Braves National '10	Jack Cust Diamond Jacks 16u Gold
17-and-Under	Marietta, Ga.	Diamond Devils 17's	ABD Bulldogs '09
18-and-Under	Marietta, Ga.	Florida Bombers	Illinois Sparks 18U Black

PONY BASEBALL: WASHINGTON, PA.

Event	Site	Champion	Runner-up
Mustang (9-10)	Irving, Texas	Tamiami, Fla.	Santa Clarita, Calif.
Bronco (11-12)	Monterey, Calif.	Panama City	Taiwan
Pony (13)	Chino Hills, Calif.	Riverside, Calif.	Tustin, Calif.
Pony (13-14)	Washington, Pa.	Long Beach, Calif.	Taichung City, Taiwan
Colt (15-16)	Lafayette, Ind.	McAllen, Texas	Gurabo, Puerto Rico
Palomino (17-18)	Rancho Cucamunga, Calif.	Houston, Texas	Taiwan

REVIVING BASEBALL IN INNER CITIES (RBI): NEW YORK

Event	Site	Champion	Runner-up
Junior (13-15)	Los Angeles	Detroit	Tampa
Senior (16-18)	Los Angeles	Los Angeles	Detroit

U.S. SPECIALTY SPORTS ASSOCIATION (USSSA): PETERSBURG, VA.

Event	Site	Champion	Runner-up
10-and-Under/Majors Elite	Lake Buena Vista, Fla.	Banditos Black, Texas	Tomateros de California
11-and-Under/Majors Elite	Lake Buena Vista, Fla.	Lamorinda Baseball	West Chester Sluggers
12-and-Under/Majors Elite	Lake Buena Vista, Fla.	Norwalk Stingrays	Banditos Black, Texas
13-and-Under/Majors Elite	Lake Buena Vista, Fla.	OC Hawks of Rawlings	Team Anderson
14-and-Under/Majors Elite	Lake Buena Vista, Fla.	Bases Loaded Bombers (Ala.)	Central Texas Raiders

*Championship game not played. Teams declared co-champions.

DRAFT

Alvarez intrigue overshadows Rays' selection of Beckham

BY JOHN MANUEL

The 2008 draft produced some outcomes no baseball draft ever has seen, starting with the No. 1 overall selection.

The Tampa Bay Rays drafted first overall in '07, then again in '08. It's the first time since the draft began in 1965 that the same team picked No. 1 overall in back-to-back years, and it was the fourth time in their 13 years of drafting that Tampa Bay picked first overall.

Of course, the first three times it picked first overall—selecting Josh Hamilton (1999), Delmon Young (2003) and David Price (2007)—the team was known as the Devil Rays, and this year it was just Rays. And this year's Rays were different from their predecessors. On June 5, the day they kicked off the '08 draft with the first pick, the Rays entered the day a half-game behind the Red Sox in the American League East, and eventually the Rays passed the Red Sox, beat them in the AL Championship Series—with Price closing out Game Seven out of the bullpen—and became the first team to pick first in the draft and play in the World Series in the same year.

With less pressure to go for instant gratification in the draft, the Rays stayed true to their usual form, opting for upside and raw talent over polish and experience in their top pick. After considering Florida State catcher Buster Posey (the 2008 College Player of the Year) and Vanderbilt third baseman Pedro Alvarez, as well as San Diego lefthander Brian Matusz and Florida prep first baseman Eric Hosmer, the Rays were more than satisfied taking the top-rated high school talent on the board, shortstop Tim Beckham. They also quickly signed Beckham, giving him a bonus valued at $6.15 million, which will be paid over five years due to Beckham's two-sport ability.

The 6-foot, 188-pound Beckham played at Griffin (Ga.) High, about 40 miles south of Atlanta, and he stood out to scouts and to the Rays for his combination of smooth tools, power potential and middle-of-the-diamond potential.

"You look at this ballplayer and all of a sudden, there's about five players that came to mind," scouting director R.J. Harrison said. "It was kind of a combination of the Uptons, Gary Sheffield, Orlando Hudson and Brandon Phillips.

"I think the things that separate this kid and the reasons why I think he has a chance to play in the

The Rays signed Tim Beckham two weeks after taking him No. 1 overall

DAVID STONER

middle of the infield at shortstop are two things," Harrison said. "I think he has the physical ability to do it, and I think he has the personality to play shortstop."

Moreover, he had the personality to sign quickly. Beckham's deal was done two weeks after the Rays selected him, enabling him to get a jump on his pro career. He joined his brother Jeremy, a second baseman out of Georgia Southern whom the Rays drafted in the 17th round, at Rookie-level Princeton in the Appalachian League and got 183 at-bats, including six in the short-season New York-Penn League.

Alvarez Drama Drags On

Pittsburgh followed the Rays, with a new administration including general manager Neal Huntington and scouting director Greg Smith making the selection. The Pirates began a trend in the '08 first round by taking the top talent on the board without great regard for signability, selecting third baseman Pedro Alvarez out of Vanderbilt.

On the trivia front, Alvarez narrowly missed out

on making Vanderbilt the first program to produce back-to-back No. 1 picks, just failing to join Price. The rest of the story between the Pirates and Alvarez was anything but trivial.

Alvarez's signing came down to the Aug. 15 deadline, like many others. As the deadline approached, 10 first-round picks had yet to sign as that day dawned, and many of the top picks went down to the last minute—and, apparently, beyond. Alvarez was among the last players who agreed to terms, with the Pirates, Alvarez and agent Scott Boras apparently agreeing to a $6 million bonus.

But more than a week later, Alvarez still had yet to go to Pittsburgh for a physical, or for an introductory press conference, and the reason was apparent soon enough. On Aug. 27, the Pirates released a press release in which team president Frank Coonelly—who worked in Major League Baseball's commissioner's office and was heavily involved in the draft before joining the Pirates last fall—announced the club had requested Alvarez be placed on the restricted list.

"The Pirates are confident that the contract reached with Pedro Alvarez was agreed to and submitted to Major League Baseball in a timely fashion and properly accepted by Major League Baseball," Coonelly said in a statement that blistered Boras. "In fact, the contract between the Kansas City Royals and Eric Hosmer, another Boras client, was submitted to the Office of the Commissioner after our contract with Pedro was submitted . . . Mr. Boras has been informed that if he pursues a claim that our contract with Pedro was not timely, he puts Eric Hosmer's contract with Kansas City in jeopardy.

"Regrettably, we are not surprised that Mr. Boras would attempt to raise a meritless legal claim in an effort to compel us to renegotiate Pedro's contract to one more to his liking. We are, however, disappointed that Pedro would allow his agent to pursue this claim on his behalf. Pedro showed tremendous fortitude and independent thinking when he agreed to his contract on August 15."

The MLB Players Association reacted by filing

MAJOR LEAGUE CONTRACTS: 1998-2008

Major league contracts for draftees have become much more commonplace, with at least two given to players every year since 1998. Three players received big league deals in 2008—two by the Aug. 15 deadline, and then another to Pedro Alvarez when his deal with the Pirates was renegotiated in September. Here's the list of major league contracts since 1998:

YEAR	CLUB (ROUND)	PLAYER, POS.	BONUS	GUARANTEE
1998	Phillies (1)	Pat Burrell, 1b/of	$3,150,000	$8,000,000
	Cardinals (1)	J.D. Drew, of	$3,000,000	$7,000,000
	Cardinals (2)	Chad Hutchinson, rhp	$2,300,000	$3,400,000
1999	Marlins (1)	*Josh Beckett, rhp	$3,625,000	$7,000,000
	Tigers (1)	Eric Munson, c	$3,500,000	$6,750,000
2000	Reds (1)	*David Espinosa, ss	None	$2,950,000
	Reds (2)	Dane Sardinha, c	None	$1,950,000
	Padres (2)	Xavier Nady, 3b	$1,100,000	$2,850,000
	Devil Rays (5)	Jace Brewer, ss	$450,000	$1,200,000
2001	Cubs (1)	Mark Prior, rhp	$4,000,000	$10,500,000
	Devil Rays (1)	Dewon Brazelton, rhp	$4,200,000	$4,800,000
	Rangers (1)	Mark Teixeira, 3b	$4,500,000	$9,500,000
2002	Orioles (1)	†Adam Loewen, lhp	$3,200,000	$4,020,000
	Indians (1)	Jeremy Guthrie, rhp	$3,000,000	$4,000,000
	Rockies (4)	Jeff Baker, 3b	$200,000	$2,000,000
2003	Devil Rays (1)	*Delmon Young, of	$3,700,000	$5,800,000
	Brewers (1)	Rickie Weeks, 2b	$3,600,000	$4,790,000
2004	Tigers (1)	Justin Verlander, rhp	$3,120,000	$4,500,000
	Mets (1)	Philip Humber, rhp	$3,000,000	$4,200,000
	Devil Rays (1)	Jeff Niemann, rhp	$3,200,000	$5,200,000
	Diamondbacks (1)	Stephen Drew, ss	$4,000,000	$5,500,000
2005	Mets (1)	Mike Pelfrey, rhp	$3,550,000	$5,250,000
	Red Sox (1)	Craig Hansen, rhp	$1,300,000	$4,000,000
2006	Royals (1)	Luke Hochevar, rhp	$3,500,000	$5,250,000
	Tigers (1)	Andrew Miller, lhp	$3,550,000	$5,450,000
	Diamondbacks (1)	Max Scherzer, rhp	$3,000,000	$4,300,000
2007	Devil Rays (1)	David Price, lhp	$5,600,000	$8,500,000
	Tigers (1)	Rick Porcello, rhp	$3,580,000	$7,000,000
	Yankees (1)	Andrew Brackman, rhp	$3,350,000	$4,550,000
	Rangers (1s)	Julio Borbon, of	$800,000	$1,300,000
2008	Pirates (1)	Pedro Alvarez, 3b	$6,000,000	$6,355,000
	Reds (1)	Yonder Alonso, 1b	$2,000,000	$4,550,000
	Orioles (1)	Brian Matusz, lhp	$3,200,000	$3,472,500

*High school signee. †Draft-and-follow, signed the following year.

a grievance, arguing that the Pirates had signed Alvarez after the midnight Eastern time deadline. Union general counsel Michael Weiner said in a statement, "The Players Association learned from several sources that the commissioner's office had extended the deadline for negotiating and reporting signings with drafted players."

The grievance sucked in No. 3 overall pick Hosmer, who had played three games with the Royals but then was pulled off the field due to the grievance. But as the grievance proceeded, word leaked that the Boras Corp. had ample evidence that Alvarez's contract indeed was agreed to after midnight. Pressure from MLB prompted the Pirates to agree to re-open negotiations with Alvarez and Boras Corp. The grievance was resolved Sept. 24, and a day later Alvarez signed a revised deal, a major league contract worth $6.355 million.

"I just want the fans of Pittsburgh to judge me as the professional player that I am now, to judge me on the player that I am," Alvarez said in the

HISTORICAL SIGNIFICANCE

Only one player ever had received a bonus of more than $6 million before the 2007 draft, but the last two drafts have seen five bonuses of $6 million or more, including three of the first five players drafted in 2008. Buster Posey, taken fifth overall by the Giants, led the way with a record $6.2 million bonus. For players who signed major league contracts, only the bonus is included.

PLAYER, POS.	CLUB, YEAR (ROUND)	BONUS
Buster Posey, c	Giants '08 (1)	$6,200,000
Tim Beckham, ss	Rays '08 (1)	$6,150,000
Justin Upton, ss	Diamondbacks '05 (1)	$6,100,000
*Pedro Alvarez, 3b	Pirates '08 (1)	$6,000,000
Eric Hosmer, 1b	Royals '08 (1)	$6,000,000
Matt Wieters, c	Orioles '07 (1)	$6,000,000
*David Price, lhp	Devil Rays '07 (1)	$5,600,000
Joe Borchard, of	White Sox '00 (1)	$5,300,000
Joe Mauer, c	Twins '01 (1)	$5,150,000
B.J. Upton, ss	Devil Rays '02 (1)	$4,600,000

*Received major league contract.

DRAFT ORDER 2009

The Washington Nationals draft No. 1 overall for the first time after finishing 59-102, the worst record in the major leagues in 2008. And because the Nationals failed to sign 2008 first-rounder Aaron Crow with the ninth overall pick, the Nats will be the first team in draft history with two top-10 selections. They'll have the 10th pick as compensation for failing to sign Crow. The Washington/Montreal franchise hasn't picked first overall before, with its highest previous selection coming in 1978, when the Expos took Bill Gullickson second overall.

The Mariners were still negotiating with first-rounder Joshua Fields, so that compensation pick will disappear if they sign him. Compensation choices for unsigned first-rounders only come once, so if the Nationals, Mariners and Yankees can't sign their bonus picks in 2009, they'll wind up with nothing. The following is a list of the raw draft order for 2009, but picks after the first 16 picks could change based on free-agent signings and compensation picks.

1. Washington Nationals
2. Seattle Mariners
3. San Diego Padres
4. Pittsburgh Pirates
5. Baltimore Orioles
6. San Francisco Giants
7. Atlanta Braves
8. Cincinnati Reds
9. Detroit Tigers
10. Washington Nationals (compensation for failure to sign 2008 first-rounder Aaron Crow)
11. Colorado Rockies
12. Kansas City Royals
13. Oakland Athletics
14. Texas Rangers
15. Cleveland Indians
16. Arizona Diamondbacks
17. Los Angeles Dodgers
18. Florida Marlins
19. St. Louis Cardinals
20. Toronto Blue Jays
21. Houston Astros
22. Seattle Mariners (compensation for failure to sign 2008 first-rounder Joshua Fields)
23. Minnesota Twins
24. Chicago White Sox
25. New York Mets
26. New York Yankees
27. Milwaukee Brewers
28. Philadelphia Phillies
29. Boston Red Sox
30. Tampa Bay Rays
31. New York Yankees (compensation for failure to sign 2008 first-rounder Gerrit Cole)
32. Chicago Cubs
33. Los Angeles Angels

press conference after signing. "I will work my hardest to be the best player I can be, to be a leader on and off the field in the community."

Coonelly said later that the deadline had been extended Aug. 15 because the Pirates "begged." In settling the Alvarez/Hosmer grievance, MLB changed its draft rules, and the commissioner's office no longer can unilaterally extend the deadline past 11:59 p.m. An arbitrator will have the authority to void any deals signed after the deadline. Alvarez later showed up for instructional league in less-than-ideal physical shape.

Crow, Cole Head Unsigned

Coonelly had overseen MLB's informal slotting system—an effort to establish specific bonuses for every pick in the first five rounds of the draft—since 2000 to try to hold down signing bonuses. But with the exception of 2006, the average first-round signing bonus has increased every year since 2002. The introduction of draft rules changes in 2007 that included the Aug. 15 signing deadline (and elimination of the draft-and-follow system) were an effort to exert more control than ever over signing bonuses, but it backfired and led to an 8.5 percent increase in first-round bonuses.

Clubs that adhered to the slotting system were losing out on talent to teams that were willing to take on the commissioner's office and spend for top talent, and let MLB know about it. The commissioner's office responded, and for 2008, MLB relaxed its enforcement of the slotting system, telling clubs in a pre-draft memo to take players based on ability, not signability.

First-round bonuses went up accordingly, and that's even though two first-rounders failed to sign, the first time that had happened since 2001. (A third, Mariners selection Joshua Fields of Georgia, had yet to sign. Fields' college eligibility has expired, and the Mariners retain his rights up until a week before the 2009 draft.)

Nationals righthander Aaron Crow was one of the 10 unsigned first-round picks entering the Aug. 15 deadline, and the Nats and the Missouri righthander were far apart on a potential deal. Crow, advised by the Hendricks Bros., was looking for a deal close to the $9 million range, while the Nationals were offering $2.1 million.

The difference of opinion was one problem, but the contract Matusz got from the Orioles with the No. 4 overall pick also changed things. Matusz was generally regarded as the top pitcher in the class, followed by Crow. When Matusz signed a major league deal with a $3.2 million bonus and $3,472,500 guaranteed, the Nationals made what general manager Jim Bowden termed a "take it or leave it" offer of $3 million. Over the final hour of the negotiations, the Nats came up to $3.5 million, while Crow and the Hendricks came down to $4 million. The

TEAM EXPENDITURES

Teams combined to spend $186.5 million on draft bonuses in 2008, an amount believed to be a record and up 23 percent from the $151.8 million they shelled out in 2007. The Royals ($11,148,000), Red Sox ($10,515,000), Rays ($9,921,000) and Pirates ($9,780,000) all exceeded the previous mark for a single team, $9,745,000 by the Diamondbacks in 2005.

TEAM	SIGNED	1ST	SUPP.	'08 TOTAL	'07 TOTAL
Royals	32	1	1	$11,148,000	$6,636,900
Red Sox	29	1	1	$10,515,000	$4,843,750
Rays	28	1	0	$9,921,000	$8,023,000
Pirates	32	1	0	$9,780,500	$4,451,900
Giants	31	1	1	$9,080,000	$7,424,500
Brewers	36	1	2	$8,395,800	$4,254,700
Rangers	35	1	0	$7,388,300	$6,631,000
Twins	25	2	1	$7,330,498	$2,165,500
Indians	30	1	0	$6,984,500	$3,645,300
Orioles	36	1	0	$6,916,500	$7,981,000
Phillies	36	1	1	$6,740,500	$4,215,000
Astros	32	1	1	$6,544,500	$1,584,000
Athletics	27	1	0	$6,522,000	$4,159,400
Mets	42	2	1	$6,460,000	$3,821,300
Cubs	32	1	1	$5,545,000	$6,096,250
Cardinals	42	1	1	$5,542,000	$4,641,500
Padres	37	1	2	$5,449,000	$5,897,500
Marlins	36	1	0	$5,377,000	$3,675,750
Yankees*	34	1	1	$5,122,000	$8,035,500
Braves	23	0	1	$5,091,500	$4,858,250
Reds	34	1	0	$4,801,000	$4,894,250
Nationals*	30	1	0	$4,761,500	$7,882,300
White Sox	25	1	0	$4,663,500	$2,768,850
Diamondbacks	29	1	1	$4,493,500	$5,110,000
Dodgers	28	1	0	$4,442,500	$3,626,250
Blue Jays	35	1	0	$4,359,500	$6,584,000
Rockies	31	1	0	$4,157,000	$3,669,000
Tigers	35	1	0	$3,742,000	$7,952,000
Angels	30	0	0	$2,728,500	$1,759,600
Mariners*	36	1	0	$2,545,000	$4,542,300
Totals	**968**	**30**	**16**	**$186,547,598**	**$151,830,550**

*Didn't sign first-round pick (Mariners still in negotiations).
First: First-round picks. Supp.: Supplemental first-round picks.

THE BONUS RECORD

Rick Monday, the No. 1 overall pick in baseball's first-ever draft in 1965, signed with the Athletics for $100,000—a bonus record that lasted for a decade. The mark has been broken several times since, with Giants catcher Buster Posey setting a new record this year with his $6.2 million bonus.

The figures below represent cash bonuses and don't include guaranteed money from major league contracts, college scholarship plans or incentives. They also don't factor in discount rates for bonuses spread over multiple years for two-sport athletes, such as Justin Upton. The list considers only players who signed with the clubs that drafted them and does not include the four loophole free agents from 1996. Among that group is former Devil Rays righthander Matt White, who established a bonus standard that still stands when he signed for $10.2 million.

YEAR	PLAYER, POS., CLUB (ROUND)	BONUS
1965	Rick Monday, of, Athletics (1)	$100,000
1975	Danny Goodwin, c, Angels (1)	$125,000
1978	Kirk Gibson, of, Tigers (1)	$150,000
	*Bob Horner, 3b, Braves (1)	$162,000
1979	Bill Bordley, lhp, Giants (1#)	$200,000
	Todd Demeter, 1b, Yankees (2)	$208,000
1988	Andy Benes, rhp, Padres (1)	$235,000
1989	Tyler Houston, c, Braves (1)	$241,500
	*Ben McDonald, rhp, Orioles (1)	$350,000
	*John Olerud, 1b, Blue Jays (3)	$575,000
1991	Mike Kelly, of, Braves (1)	$575,000
	Brien Taylor, lhp, Yankees (1)	$1,550,000
1994	Paul Wilson, rhp, Mets (1)	$1,550,000
	Josh Booty, 3b, Marlins (1)	$1,600,000
1996	Kris Benson, rhp, Pirates (1)	$2,000,000
1997	Rick Ankiel, lhp, Cardinals (2)	$2,500,000
	Matt Anderson, rhp, Tigers (1)	$2,505,000
1998	*J.D. Drew, of, Cardinals (1)	$3,000,000
	*Pat Burrell, 3b, Phillies (1)	$3,150,000
	Mark Mulder, lhp, Athletics (1)	$3,200,000
	Corey Patterson, of, Cubs (1)	$3,700,000
1999	Josh Hamilton, of, Devil Rays (1)	$3,960,000
2000	Joe Borchard, of, White Sox (1)	$5,300,000
2005	Justin Upton, ss, Diamondbacks (1)	$6,100,000
2008	Buster Posey, c, Giants (1)	$6,200,000

*Major league contract.

last-minute compromises weren't enough to bridge the gap, and Crow didn't get signed.

"The system doesn't work," Bowden told the Washington Post when it was all over. "To sit there and have the negotiations that took place with several clubs between 11:30 and 12, where you're talking about huge movements with lots of players . . . and deals got done at 11:59 with literally, I understand, no conversations for long periods of time . . . I'm not sure that's the best way to do business for a sport."

The Yankees' negotiations with first-rounder Gerrit Cole, a hard-throwing prep righthander from southern California, didn't come down to the last minute. After going through the summer unsigned, Cole simply warmed to the idea of going to college, and despite a hard run by the Yankees, he enrolled at UCLA. He was considered the hardest thrower in the prep '08 draft class, having reached 100 mph with his fastball. The

Yankees also didn't sign their second-round pick, Mississippi righthander Scott Bittle, who had a shoulder injury that prompted the Yankees to decide against signing him.

To compensate, the Yankees went over-slot for righthanders Brett Marshall (sixth round, $850,000) and D.J. Mitchell (10th, $400,000), catcher Kyle Higashioka (seventh, $500,000) and shortstop Garrison Lassiter (27th, $675,000), and went over-slot for seven players total. Just four teams—Blue Jays, Cardinals, Mets and Tigers—adhered completely to the slot recommendations.

THE REST OF THE STORY

■ Four of the six largest bonuses of all time were paid out. Posey went fifth overall to the Giants and signed for a $6.2 million bonus, the largest bonus ever, just edging Beckham as well as Alvarez ($6 million bonus in the major league deal) and Hosmer ($6 million). The 27 first-round picks that signed

HIGHEST BONUSES BY ROUND

ROUND	PLAYER, POS, TEAM	YEAR	BONUS
1st	Buster Posey, c, Giants	2008	$6,200,000
Supp. 1st	Michael Garciaparra, ss, Mariners	2001	$2,000,000
2nd	Jason Young, rhp, Rockies	2000	$2,750,000
3rd	Matt Tuiasosopo, ss, Mariners	2004	$2,290,000
4th	Brad Suttle, 3b, Yankees	2007	$1,300,000
5th	Ryan Westmoreland, of, Red Sox	2008	$2,000,000
6th	Jack McGeary, lhp, Nationals	2007	$1,800,000
7th	Brett Hunter, rhp, Athletics	2007	$1,100,000
8th	Dellin Betances, rhp, Yankees	2006	$1,000,000
9th	Jason Middlebrook, rhp, Padres	1996	$750,000
10th	Luis Cota, rhp, Royals*	2003	$1,050,000
11th	Chris Huseby, rhp, Cubs	2006	$1,300,000
12th	Mike Rozier, lhp, Red Sox	2004	$1,575,000
13th	Jimmy Barthmaier, rhp, Astros	2003	$750,000
14th	Dexter Fowler, of, Rockies	2004	$925,000
15th	J.P. Ramirez, of, Nationals	2008	$1,000,000
Post-15th	Sean Henn, lhp, Yankees*	2000	$1,701,000

*Signed next year as draft-and-follow.

received an average bonus of $2,484,963, more than $300,000 than ever before, and an increase of 18.4 percent from 2007, the biggest jump in the era of MLB's recommendations for bonus slots.

■ Teams also established new standards for the average bonuses in the second, fourth, fifth, seventh, eighth and 10th rounds. Clubs gave out 43 bonuses of $1 million or more, including 10 after the first and sandwich rounds, setting two more marks. And teams spent more than ever as a whole, with the Royals and Red Sox becoming the first organizations to spend more than $10 million on a draft class (see chart, PAGE 503).

■ By handing out $11,148,000 in signing bonus money, the Royals spent more on their draft than any club in history, and four teams—with Boston, Tampa Bay and Pittsburgh joining Kansas City—spent more than the previous record (see chart). Aside from the $6 million spent on Hosmer, the Royals went above the commissioner's slot recommendations for fourth-rounder Tim Melville ($1.25 million) and spent $100,000 or more on six players drafted after the ninth round.

■ The Padres and first-rounder Allan Dykstra, a first baseman out of Wake Forest, had protracted negotiations after the Padres learned Dykstra has avascular necrosis in his hip. The Padres didn't know about the condition, which is the death of bone tissue due to a lack of blood supply, even though Dykstra sustained the injury that leads to the condition as a high school player at San Diego's Rancho Bernardo High. Dykstra was cleared to play by doctors, but the Padres were concerned about his long-term health. Eventually the Padres signed him for $1.15 million.

■ Giants third baseman Conor Gillaspie became the first member of the '08 draft class to reach the major leagues, as the Giants found a creative way to pay him more without having to give him a long-term major league contract. Gillaspie, a supplemental first-round pick out of Wichita State, hit .272 in 92 minor league at-bats—none at a full-season level—after signing for a $970,000 bonus. He got just five at-bats in the major leagues

UNSIGNED PICKS

For the first time since 2001, the first round had at least two unsigned players, and two of the three highest-rated college pitchers entering the draft—righthanders Aaron Crow and Tanner Scheppers—did not sign. Both will play in independent leagues in 2009 and re-enter the draft. Righthander Joshua Fields has used up his eligibility and can continue to negotiate with the Mariners until a week before the 2009 draft.

FIRST ROUND	School
9. Nationals: Aaron Crow, rhp	None
20. Mariners: Joshua Fields, rhp	Eligibility expired
28. Yankees: Gerrit Cole, rhp	UCLA

SECOND ROUND	School
48. Pirates: Tanner Scheppers, rhp	None
75. Yankees: Scott Bittle, rhp	*Mississippi

THIRD ROUND	School
88. Astros: Chase Davidson, 1b	Georgia

THIRD ROUND SUPPLEMENTAL	School
112. Angels: Zach Cone, of	Georgia

FOURTH ROUND	School
135: Padres: Jason Kipnis, of	*Arizona State

FIFTH ROUND	School
167. Rockies: Chris Dominguez, 3b	*Louisville
169. Angels: Khiry Cooper, of	Nebraska

SEVENTH ROUND	School
205. Royals: Jason Esposito, 3b	Vanderbilt
226. Phillies: Johnny Coy, 3b	Arizona State

NINTH ROUND	School
282. Mariners: Billy Morrison, rhp	*Western Michigan
285. Padres: Kyle Thebeau, rhp	*Texas A&M

TENTH ROUND	School
294. Pirates: Drew Gagnon, rhp	Long Beach State
296. Orioles: Chris Herrmann, 3b	Miami
297. Giants: Ryan O'Sullivan, rhp	San Diego State
298. Marlins: Trevor Holder, rhp	*Georgia
303. Rangers: Kevin Castner, rhp	*Cal Poly
307. Dodgers: Chris Joyce, lhp	UC Santa Barbara
311. Cubs: Alex Wilson, rhp	*Texas A&M
312. Mariners: Nate Newman, rhp	*Pepperdine
318. Diamondbacks: Danny Hultzen, lhp	Virginia

*Returned to same school drafted from 2008.

in eight games, recording one single and walking twice.

■ The 2008 draft had the usual big league relatives involved and continued a recent trend of brothers going in the first round. Twelfth overall pick Jemile Weeks; Oakland's first-rounder is the younger brother of Brewers second baseman Rickie Weeks, who went second overall in 2003.

■ Brother combinations have become far more common in the last dozen years. In the first 30 years of the draft, three brother combinations—Isaiah (1984, Brewers) and Phil (1986, Tigers) Clark, Phil (1978, Indians) and Jody (1979, Padres) Lansford, and Andy (1988, Padres) and Alan (1993, Cardinals) Benes—were drafted in the first round. Since 1996 there have been five brother combinations drafted in the first round, as the Weeks joined the Uptons (B.J. 2002, Justin 2005), the Drews (three brothers, J.D. in 1997 and '98, Tim in '97 and Stephen in 2004), the Weavers (Jeff in 1998, Jered in 2004) and the Youngs (Dmitri in 1996, Delmon in 2003).

FIRST OVERALL PICKS

Following is a year-by-year breakdown of the first overall pick in the June regular phase and his cash bonus, and his highest level attained. If a different player earned the largest bonus in that year, that player is noted along with the order he was picked and his bonus.

CLIFF WELCH

Rays lefthander David Price reached the majors in his first full season

YEAR	NO. 1 PICK	SCHOOL	HOMETOWN	BONUS	HIGHEST LEVEL	LARGEST BONUS (PICK NUMBER)	AMOUNT
1965	Rick Monday, of, Athletics	Arizona State	Santa Monica, Calif.	$100,000	Majors	same	$80,000
1966	Steve Chilcott, c, Mets	Antelope Valley HS	Lancaster, Calif.	75,000	Triple-A	Reggie Jackson, of, Athletics (2)	75,000
1967	Ron Blomberg, 1b, Yankees	Druid Hills HS	Atlanta	65,000	Majors	#Mike Adamson, rhp, Orioles	75,000
1968	Tim Foli, ss, Mets	Notre Dame HS	Sherman Oaks, Calif.	74,000	Majors	Lloyd Allen, rhp, Angels (12)	75,000
1969	Jeff Burroughs, of, Senators	Wilson HS	Long Beach, Calif.	88,000	Majors	same	
1970	Mike Ivie, c, Padres	Walker HS	Decatur, Ga.	75,000	Majors	#Dave Kingman, 1b, Giants	80,000
1971	Danny Goodwin, c, White Sox	Central HS	Peoria, Ill.	DNS	Majors	Ed Kurpiel, 1b, Cardinals (8)	83,750
1972	Dave Roberts, 3b, Padres	Oregon	Corvallis, Ore.	70,000	Majors	Jamie Quirk, ss, Royals (18)	78,000
1973	*David Clyde, lhp, Rangers	Westchester HS	Houston	65,000	Majors	^Alan Bannister, ss, Phillies	85,000
1974	*Bill Almon, ss, Padres	Brown	Warwick, R.I.	90,000	Majors	Willie Wilson, of, Royals (18)	90,000
1975	*Danny Goodwin, c, Angels	Southern	Peoria, Ill.	125,000	Majors	same	
1976	Floyd Bannister, lhp, Astros	Arizona State	Seattle	100,000	Majors	same	
1977	Harold Baines, of, White Sox	St. Michaels HS	St. Michaels, Md.	32,000	Majors	Paul Molitor, ss, Twins (3)	77,500
1978	*Bob Horner, 3b, Braves	Arizona State	Glendale, Ariz.	162,000	Majors	same	
1979	Al Chambers, 1b, Mariners	Harris HS	Harrisburg, Pa.	60,000	Majors	Todd Demeter, 1b, Yankees (51)	208,000
1980	Darryl Strawberry, of, Mets	Crenshaw HS	Los Angeles	152,500	Majors	same	
1981	Mike Moore, rhp, Mariners	Oral Roberts	Eakly, Okla.	100,000	Majors	Terry Blocker, of, Mets (4)	127,500
1982	Shawon Dunston, ss, Cubs	Jefferson HS	New York	135,000	Majors	Kenny Williams, of, White Sox (78)	160,000
1983	Tim Belcher, rhp, Twins	Mt. Vernon Nazarene	Sparta, Ohio	DNS	Majors	Kurt Stillwell, ss, Reds (2)	135,000
1984	Shawn Abner, of, Mets	Mechanicsburg HS	Mechanicsburg, Pa.	150,500	Majors	same	
1985	B.J. Surhoff, c, Brewers	North Carolina	Rye, N.Y.	150,000	Majors	Bobby Witt, rhp, Rangers (3)	179,000
1986	Jeff King, 3b, Pirates	Arkansas	Colorado Springs	180,000	Majors	Mark Merchant, of, Pirates (2)	165,000
1987	Ken Griffey Jr., of, Mariners	Moeller HS	Cincinnati	160,000	Majors	Jack McDowell, rhp, White Sox (5)	165,000
1988	Andy Benes, rhp, Padres	Evansville	Evansville, Ind.	235,000	Double-A	same	
1989	*Ben McDonald, rhp, Orioles	Louisiana State	Denham Springs, La.	350,000	Majors	#John Olerud, 1b, Blue Jays (79)	575,000
1990	Chipper Jones, ss, Braves	The Bolles School	Jacksonville	275,000	Majors	*Todd Van Poppel, rhp, A's (14)	500,000
						Tony Clark, 1b, Tigers (2)	500,000
1991	Brien Taylor, lhp, Yankees	East Carteret HS	Beaufort, N.C.	1,550,000	Double-A	same	
1992	Phil Nevin, 3b, Astros	Cal State Fullerton	Placentia, Calif.	700,000	Majors	Jeffrey Hammonds, of, Orioles (4)	975,000
1993	*Alex Rodriguez, ss, Mariners	Westminster Christian HS	Miami	1,000,000	Majors	Darren Dreifort, rhp, Dodgers (2)	1,300,000
1994	Paul Wilson, rhp, Mets	Florida State	Orlando, Fla.	1,550,000	Majors	Josh Booty, ss, Marlins (5)	1,600,000
1995	Darin Erstad, of, Angels	Nebraska	Jamestown, N.D.	1,575,000	Majors	same	
1996	@Kris Benson, rhp, Pirates	Clemson	Kennesaw, Ga.	2,000,000	Majors	Matt White, rhp, Giants (7)	10,200,000
1997	Matt Anderson, rhp, Tigers	Rice	Louisville	2,505,000	Majors	same	
1998	*Pat Burrell, 3b, Phillies	Miami	Boulder Creek, Calif.	3,150,000	Majors	Corey Patterson, of, Cubs (3)	3,700,000
1999	Josh Hamilton, of, Devil Rays	Athens Drive HS	Raleigh, N.C.	3,960,000	Majors	same	
2000	Adrian Gonzalez, 1b, Marlins	Eastside HS	Chula Vista, Calif.	3,000,000	Majors	Joe Borchard, of, White Sox (12)	5,300,000
2001	Joe Mauer, c, Twins	Cretn-Derham Hall	St. Paul, Minn.	5,150,000	Majors	same	
2002	Bryan Bullington, rhp, Pirates	Ball State	Fishers, Ind.	4,000,000	Majors	B.J. Upton, ss, Devil Rays (2)	4,600,000
2003	*Delmon Young, of, Devil Rays	Camarillo HS	Camarillo, Calif.	3,700,000	Majors	same	
2004	Matt Bush, ss, Padres	Mission Bay HS	El Cajon, Calif.	3,150,000	Class A	Jered Weaver, rhp, Angels	4,000,000
						Stephen Drew, ss, D-backs	4,000,000
2005	Justin Upton, ss, D'backs	Great Bridge HS	Chesapeake, Va.	6,100,000	Majors	same	
2006	*Luke Hochevar, rhp, Royals	No School	Fowler, Colo.	3,500,000	Majors	Andrew Miller, lhp, Tigers	3,550,000
2007	*David Price, lhp, Devil Rays	Vanderbilt	Murfreesboro, Tenn.	5,600,000	Majors	Matt Wieters, c, Orioles	6,000,000
2008	Tim Beckham, ss, Rays	Griffin HS	Griffin, Ga.	6,150,000	Short-season	Buster Posey, c, Giants	6,200,000

* Signed major league contract; cash bonus only reported. # Selected in June secondary phase. * Selected in January draft. @ Includes four loophole free agents; White signed with Devil Rays. ^ Selected in June secondary phase.

BILL MITCHELL

Lefthander Brian Matusz was the fourth overall pick of the Orioles and should move quickly

	TEAM	PLAYER	POS.	SCHOOL	BONUS
1	Rays	Tim Beckham	SS	HS—Griffin, Ga.	$6,150,000
2	Pirates	Pedro Alvarez	3B	Vanderbilt	$6,355,000
3	Royals	Eric Hosmer	1B	HS—Plantation, Fla.	$6,000,000
4	Orioles	Brian Matusz	LHP	San Diego	$3,200,000
5	Giants	Buster Posey	C	Florida State	$6,200,000
6	Marlins	Kyle Skipworth	C	HS—Rubidoux, Calif.	$2,300,000
7	Reds	Yonder Alonso	1B	Miami	$2,000,000
8	White Sox	Gordon Beckham	SS	Georgia	$2,600,000
9	Nationals	Aaron Crow	RHP	Missouri	Did not sign
10	Astros	Jason Castro	C	Stanford	$2,070,000
11	Rangers	Justin Smoak	1B	South Carolina	$3,500,000
12	Athletics	Jemile Weeks	2B	Miami	$1,910,000
13	Cardinals	Brett Wallace	1B	Arizona State	$1,840,000
14	Twins	Aaron Hicks	OF	HS—Long Beach	$1,780,000
15	Dodgers	Ethan Martin	RHP	HS—Toccoa, Ga.	$1,730,000
16	Brewers	Brett Lawrie	3B/C	HS—Langley, B.C.	$1,700,000
17	Blue Jays	David Cooper	1B	California	$1,500,000
18	Mets	Ike Davis	1B	Arizona State	$1,575,000
19	Cubs	Andrew Cashner	RHP	Texas Christian	$1,540,000
20	Mariners	Joshua Fields	RHP	Georgia	Yet to sign
21	Tigers	Ryan Perry	RHP	Arizona	$1,480,000
22	Mets	Reese Havens	SS	South Carolina	$1,419,000
23	Padres	Allan Dykstra	1B	Wake Forest	$1,150,000
24	Phillies	Anthony Hewitt	SS	HS—Salisbury, Conn.	$1,380,000
25	Rockies	Christian Friedrich	LHP	Eastern Kentucky	$1,350,000
26	D'backs	Daniel Schlereth	LHP	Arizona	$1,330,000
27	Twins	Carlos Gutierrez	RHP	Miami	$1,226,000
28	Yankees	Gerrit Cole	RHP	HS—Orange, Calif.	Did not sign
29	Indians	Lonnie Chisenhall	SS	Pitt (N.C.) CC	$1,100,000
30	Red Sox	Casey Kelly	RHP/SS	HS—Sarasota, Fla.	$3,000,000
31	Twins	Shooter Hunt	RHP	Tulane	$1,080,000
32	Brewers	Jake Odorizzi	RHP	HS—Highland, Ill.	$1,060,000
33	Mets	Brad Holt	RHP	UNC Wilmington	$1,040,000
34	Phillies	Zach Collier	OF	HS—Chino Hills, Calif.	$1,020,000
35	Brewers	Evan Frederickson	LHP	San Francisco	$1,010,000
36	Royals	Mike Montgomery	LHP	HS—Newhall, Calif.	$988,000
37	Giants	Conor Gillaspie	3B	Wichita State	$970,000
38	Astros	Jordan Lyles	RHP	HS—Hartsville, S.C.	$930,000
39	Cardinals	Lance Lynn	RHP	Mississippi	$938,000
40	Braves	Brett DeVall	LHP	HS—Niceville, Fla.	$1,000,000
41	Cubs	Ryan Flaherty	SS	Vanderbilt	$1,500,000
42	Padres	Jaff Decker	OF	HS—Peoria, Ariz.	$1,500,000
43	D'backs	Wade Miley	LHP	Southeastern Louisiana	$877,000
44	Yankees	Jeremy Bleich	LHP	Stanford	$700,000
45	Red Sox	Bryan Price	RHP	Rice	$849,000
46	Padres	Logan Forsythe	3B	Arkansas	$835,000
47	Rays	Kyle Lobstein	LHP	HS—Flagstaff, Ariz.	$1,500,000
48	Pirates	Tanner Scheppers	RHP	Fresno State	Did not sign
49	Royals	Johnny Giavotella	2B	New Orleans	$787,000
50	Orioles	Xavier Avery	OF	HS—Ellenwood, Ga.	$900,000
51	Phillies	Anthony Gose	OF	HS—Bellflower, Calif.	$772,000
52	Marlins	Brad Hand	LHP	HS—Chaska, Minn.	$760,000
53	Brewers	Seth Lintz	RHP	HS—Lewisburg, Tenn.	$900,000
54	Brewers	Cutter Dykstra	OF	HS—Westlake Village, Calif.	$737,000
55	Nationals	Destin Hood	OF	HS—Mobile, Ala.	$1,100,000
56	Astros	Jay Austin	OF	HS—Atlanta	$715,000
57	Rangers	Robbie Ross	LHP	HS—Lexington, Ky.	$1,575,000
58	Athletics	Tyson Ross	RHP	California	$694,000
59	Cardinals	Shane Peterson	OF	Long Beach State	$683,000
60	Twins	Tyler Ladendorf	SS	Howard (Texas) JC	$673,000
61	Dodgers	Josh Lindblom	RHP	Purdue	$663,000
62	Brewers	Cody Adams	RHP	Southern Illinois	$653,000
63	Blue Jays	Kenny Wilson	OF	HS—Tampa	$644,000
64	Braves	Tyler Stovall	LHP	HS—Hokes Bluff, Ala.	$750,000
65	Cubs	Aaron Shafer	RHP	Wichita State	$625,000
66	Mariners	Dennis Raben	OF	Miami	$616,000
67	Tigers	Cody Satterwhite	RHP	Mississippi	$606,000
68	Mets	Javier Rodriguez	OF	HS—Gurabo, P.R.	$585,000
69	Padres	James Darnell	3B	South Carolina	$740,000
70	Braves	Zeke Spruill	RHP	HS—Marietta, Ga.	$600,000
71	Phillies	Jason Knapp	RHP	HS—Annandale, N.J.	$590,000
72	Rockies	Charlie Blackmon	OF	Georgia Tech	$563,000
73	D'backs	Bryan Shaw	RHP	Long Beach State	$553,000
74	Angels	Tyler Chatwood	RHP	HS—Redlands, Calif.	$547,000
75	Yankees	Scott Bittle	RHP	Mississippi	Did not sign
76	Indians	Trey Haley	RHP	HS—Nacogdoches, Texas	$1,250,000
77	Red Sox	Derrik Gibson	SS	HS—Seaford, Del.	$600,000
78	Rays	Jake Jefferies	C	UC Davis	$515,000
79	Pirates	Jordy Mercer	SS	Oklahoma State	$508,000
80	Royals	Tyler Sample	RHP	HS—Denver	$500,000
81	Orioles	L.J. Hoes	2B	HS—Washington	$490,000
82	Giants	Roger Kieschnick	OF	Texas Tech	$525,000
83	Marlins	Edgar Olmos	LHP	HS—Van Nuys, Calif.	$478,000
84	Reds	Zach Stewart	RHP	Texas Tech	$450,000
85	Red Sox	Stephen Fife	RHP	Utah	$464,000
86	White Sox	Brent Morel	3B	Cal Poly	$440,000
87	Nationals	Danny Espinosa	SS	Long Beach State	$525,000
88	Astros	Chase Davidson	1B	HS—Milton, Ga.	Did not sign
89	Rangers	Tim Murphy	LHP	UCLA	$436,000
90	Athletics	Petey Paramore	C	Arizona State	$430,000
91	Cardinals	Niko Vasquez	SS	HS—Las Vegas	$423,000
92	Twins	Bobby Lanigan	RHP	Adelphi (N.Y.)	$417,000
93	Dodgers	Kyle Russell	OF	Texas	$410,000
94	Brewers	Logan Schafer	OF	Cal Poly	$404,000
95	Blue Jays	Andrew Liebel	RHP	Long Beach State	$340,000
96	Braves	Craig Kimbrel	RHP	Wallace State (Ala.) CC	$391,000
97	Cubs	Chris Carpenter	RHP	Kent State	$385,000
98	Mariners	Aaron Pribanic	RHP	Nebraska	$390,000
99	Tigers	Scott Green	RHP	Kentucky	$373,000
100	Mets	Kirk Nieuwenhuis	OF	Azusa Pacific (Calif.)	$360,000

ARIZONA DIAMONDBACKS (26)

1. **Daniel Schlereth, lhp, Arizona**
1s. **Wade Miley, lhp, Southeastern Louisiana** (Supplemental pick—43rd overall—for loss of Type B free agent Livan Hernandez)
2. **Bryan Shaw, rhp, Long Beach State**
3. **Kevin Eichhorn, rhp, Aptos (Calif.) HS**
4. **Ryne White, of, Purdue**
5. **Collin Cowgill, of, Kentucky**
6. **Justin Parker, ss, Wright State**
7. **Miles Reagan, rhp, El Capitan HS, Lakeside, Calif.**
8. **Pat McAnaney, lhp, Virginia**
9. **Brett Moorhouse, rhp, Indian River (Fla.) CC**
10. Danny Hultzen, lhp, St. Albans HS, Washington, D.C.
11. **Kyle Greene, 3b, Lewis-Clark State (Idaho)**
12. Daniel Webb, rhp, Heath HS, Paducah, Ky.
13. **Ollie Linton, of, UC Irvine**
14. **Trevor Harden, rhp, New Mexico JC**
15. **Bobby Stone, of, Montgomery (Texas) HS**
16. Ryan Hughes, lhp, Chabot (Calif.) JC
17. **Ryan Babineau, c, UCLA**
18. Sam Brown, rhp, North Carolina State
19. **Joseph Gautier, lhp, Bethune-Cookman**
20. **Jordan Meaker, rhp, Dallas Baptist**
21. **Bryan Woodall, rhp, Auburn**
22. Justin LaTempa, rhp, Golden West (Calif.) JC
23. Matt Long, of, Santa Clara
24. **Nelson Gomez, 3b, Keystone (Pa.)**
25. Josh Spence, lhp, Central Arizona JC
26. Alex Sogard, lhp, North Carolina State
27. **Ryan Cook, rhp, Southern California**
28. Adam Smith, ss, Klein HS, Spring, Texas
29. Travis Meiners, ss, Des Moines Area (Iowa) CC
30. **Daniel Rodriguez, of, Miami-Dade CC**
31. Taylor Cole, rhp, CC of Southern Nevada
32. Riccio Torrez, 2b, Brophy Prep, Phoenix
33. Luke Murton, 1b, Georgia Tech
34. **Jake Elmore, ss, Arizona State**
35. **Chris Davis, c, Central Arkansas**
36. **T.J. Hose, rhp, East Carolina**
37. Sanders Commings, of, Westside HS, Augusta, Ga.
38. **Jesse Orosco, rhp, Grossmont (Calif.) JC**
39. Kyle Godfrey, lhp, Wabash Valley (Ill.) CC
40. Taylor Wall, lhp, Westside HS, Houston
41. **Brendan Duffy, of, Oral Roberts**
42. Erik Stewart, rhp, Chabot (Calif.) JC
43. **Clayton Suss, rhp, Miami-Dade CC**
44. **David Cooper, ss, Mount Olive (N.C.)**
45. Jeremy Rathjen, of, Memorial HS, Houston
46. **Dan Kauffman, 1b, Juniata (Pa.)**
47. Andrew Maggi, ss, Brophy Prep, Phoenix
48. Cecil Richardson, of, Sacramento JC
49. Willie Argo, of, Assumption HS, Davenport, Iowa
50. Sean Koecheler, rhp, Palm Beach (Fla.) CC

ATLANTA BRAVES (18)

1. (Pick to Mets as compensation for Type A free agent Tom Glavine)
1s. **Brett DeVall, lhp, Niceville (Fla.)** HS (Supplemental pick—40th overall—for loss of Type B free agent Ron Mahay)
2. **Tyler Stovall, lhp, Hokes Bluff (Ala.) HS**
2s. **Zeke Spruill, rhp, Kell HS, Marietta, Ga.** (Supplemental pick—70th overall—for failure to sign 2007 second-round pick Joshua Fields)
3. **Craig Kimbrel, rhp, Wallace State (Ala.) CC**
4. **Braeden Schlehuber, c, CC of Southern Nevada**
5. **Jacob Thompson, rhp, Virginia**
6. **Adam Milligan, of, Walters State (Tenn.) CC**
7. **Paul Clemens, rhp, Louisburg (N.C.) JC**
8. **Brett Oberholtzer, lhp, Seminole (Fla.) CC**
9. **Kyle Farrell, rhp, Western Nevada CC**
10. **J.J. Hoover, rhp, Calhoun (Ala.) CC**
11. **Richard Sullivan, lhp, Savannah College of Art and Design**

12. **David Francis, rhp, Walters State (Tenn.) CC**
13. **Travis Adair, ss, Cleveland State (Tenn.) CC**
14. **Jake Hanson, 3b, Sabino HS, Tucson**
15. **Layton Hiller, of, Blinn (Texas) JC**
16. Billy Burns, of, Walton HS, Marietta, Ga.
17. Mark Pope, rhp, Walton HS, Marietta, Ga.
18. Michael Palazzone, rhp, Lassiter HS, Marietta, Ga.
19. Zac Fuesser, lhp, York (S.C.) HS
20. **Robert Brooks, ss, Wallace State (Ala.) CC**
21. **Tyler Barnett, ss, Eastern Kentucky**
22. Dane Carter, 3b, Texas A&M
23. **Casey Hodges, rhp, Mount Olive (N.C.)**
24. **Shayne Moody, ss, Charlotte**
25. Nick Fuller, rhp, Walters State (Ala.) CC
26. **Calvin Culver, of, Los Angeles Pierce JC**
27. Anthony Rendon, ss, Lamar HS, Houston
28. Quentin Cate, c, Cuesta (Calif.) JC
29. Josh Moody, lhp, Western Nevada CC
30. **Chris Shehan, of, Georgia Southern**
31. Jason Stolz, ss, Kell HS, Marietta, Ga.
32. Pat Lenton, rhp, Minnesota State-Mankato
33. Justin Fowler, rhp, Texarkana (Texas) CC
34. Matthew Price, rhp, Walker School, Augusta, Ga.
35. Zack Osborne, rhp, New Mexico JC
36. Cecil Tanner, rhp, Ware County HS, Waycross, Ga.
37. Lucas Hileman, of, Anna-Jonesboro HS, Anna, Ill.
38. Jeffrey Richard, rhp, Coastal Carolina
39. Taylor Wulf, rhp, Alvin (Texas) CC
40. Jesse Wierzbicki, c, Walters State (Tenn.) CC
41. Ian Gilley, ss, Northside HS, Fort Smith, Ark.
42. Stephen Foster, lhp, Bellevue (Wash.) CC
43. **Adam Bullard, rhp, Gardner-Webb**
44. Taylor Hart, rhp, Madison County HS, Danielsville, Ga.
45. Nick Croce, c, Mission Bay (Calif.) HS
46. Matt Harrison, ss, Green Valley HS, Henderson, Nev.
47. David Walters, rhp, Francis Marion (S.C.)
48. David Holman, rhp, Andale (Kan.) HS
49. Josh Adams, rhp, Midland Valley HS, Graniteville, S.C.
50. Dylan Lightell, rhp, West Hills (Calif.) CC

BALTIMORE ORIOLES (4)

1. **Brian Matusz, lhp, San Diego**
2. **Xavier Avery, of, Cedar Grove HS, Ellenwood, Ga.**
3. **L.J. Hoes, 2b, St. John's HS, Washington**
4. **Kyle Hudson, of, Illinois**
5. **Greg Miclat, ss, Virginia**
6. **Rick Zagone, lhp, Missouri**
7. **Caleb Joseph, c, Lipscomb**
8. **Bobby Bundy, rhp, Sperry (Okla.) HS**
9. **Nick Haughian, lhp, Washington**
10. Chris Herrmann, 3b, Alvin (Texas) CC
11. **Nathan Moreau, lhp, Georgia**
12. **Jason Rook, of, Appalachian State**
13. **Corey Thomas, 3b, Middleton HS, Tampa**
14. **Jesse Beal, rhp, South County SS, Lorton, Va.**
15. **Jason Gurka, lhp, Angelina (Texas) JC**
16. **Bobby Stevens, ss, Northern Illinois**
17. **Brian Conley, of, Towson**
18. Keith Landers, lhp, St. Peter-Marian HS, Worcester, Mass.
19. Jarret Martin, lhp, Centennial HS, Bakersfield, Calif.
20. **Ronnie Welty, of, Chandler-Gilbert (Ariz.) CC**
21. **Eddie Gamboa, rhp, UC Davis**
22. **Pat Kantakevich, rhp, William & Mary**
23. **Edwin Cintron, of, Antonio Luchetti HS, Arecibo, P.R.**
24. **T.J. Baxter, of, New Orleans**
25. **Xavier Lopez, c, Isabel Flores HS, Juncos, P.R.**
26. **Jose Barajas, rhp, Western Nevada CC**
27. **Ryan O'Shea, rhp, New Orleans**
28. **Tom Edwards, 3b, Rutgers**
29. **Dennis Perez, c, University of Puerto Rico-Arecibo**
30. Jeremy Dobbs, lhp, Daviess County HS, Owensboro, Ky.

31. **Tyler Sexton, lhp, Western Carolina**
32. Brandon Loy, ss, Rowlett (Texas) HS
33. Art Charles, 1b, Ridgeview HS, Bakersfield, Calif.
34. **Travis Keating, rhp, Northern Colorado**
35. **Buck Britton, 2b, Lubbock Christian (Texas)**
36. **Dan Eastham, rhp, Nevada**
37. **Chad Durakis, c, Maryland**
38. **Thomas Phelps, rhp, Whittier (Calif.)**
39. **Lance West, of, Bossier Parish (La.) CC**
40. Kirk Singer, ss, Los Alamitos (Calif.) HS
41. Peter Birdwell, rhp, Riverside (Calif.) CC
42. **Chase Phillips, rhp, Western Oklahoma State JC**
43. **Oliver Drake, rhp, Navy**
44. Kevin Brady, rhp, Gaithersburg (Md.) HS
45. **Zach Petersime, rhp, Rend Lake (Ill.) JC**
46. Michael Mudron, lhp, King HS, Riverside, Calif.
47. Jared Eskew, lhp, Cal Poly
48. Chris Garrison, lhp, Rocklin (Calif.) HS
49. Hector Morales, of, University of Puerto Rico-Carolina
50. Wes Soto, 2b, Riverview HS, Sarasota, Fla.

BOSTON RED SOX (30)

1. **Casey Kelly, rhp/ss, Sarasota (Fla.) HS**
1s. **Bryan Price, rhp, Rice** (Supplemental pick—45th overall—for loss of Type B free agent Eric Gagne)
2. **Derrik Gibson, ss, Seaford (Del.) HS**
3. **Stephen Fife, rhp, Utah** (Supplemental pick—85th overall—for failure to sign 2007 second-round pick Hunter Morris)
3. **Kyle Weiland, rhp, Notre Dame**
4. **Pete Hissey, of, Unionville (Pa.) HS**
5. **Ryan Westmoreland, of, Portsmouth (R.I.) HS**
6. **Ryan Lavarnway, c, Yale**
7. **Tim Federowicz, c, North Carolina**
8. **Michael Lee, rhp, Oklahoma City**
9. **Christian Vazquez, c, Puerto Rico Baseball Academy, Gurabo, P.R.**
10. **Pete Ruiz, rhp, Santa Barbara (Calif.) CC**
11. **Bryan Peterson, of, West Valley HS, Spokane, Wash.**
12. **Lance McClain, lhp, Cumberland (Tenn.)**
13. **Tyler Wilson, rhp, Armuchee HS, Rome, Ga.**
14. **Tyler Yockey, of, Acadiana HS, Lafayette, La.**
15. John Lally, lhp, Santa Margarita HS, Rancho Santa Margarita, Calif.
16. **Mitch Herold, lhp, Central Florida**
17. Jordan Cooper, rhp, Shawnee Heights HS, Tecumseh, Kan.
18. Brian Flynn, lhp, Owasso (Okla.) HS
19. Brian Humphries, of, Granite Hills HS, El Cajon, Calif.
20. Alex Meyer, rhp, Greensburg (Ind.) HS
21. **Jonathan Hee, 2b, Hawaii**
22. Anthony DeSclafani, rhp, Colts Neck (N.J.) HS
23. **Seth Garrison, rhp, Texas Christian**
24. Ricky Oropesa, 1b, Etiwanda (Calif.) HS
25. Justin Parker, lhp, Jesuit HS, Carmichael, Calif.
26. Navery Moore, rhp, Battle Ground Academy, Franklin, Tenn.
27. **Hunter Cervenka, lhp, Sterling HS, Baytown, Texas**
28. Matt Marquis, of, Immaculata HS, Somerville, N.J.
29. Jake Rogers, 3b, Dunedin (Fla.) HS
30. **Alex Hale, rhp, Richmond**
31. **Andrew Frezza, of, Barry (Fla.)**
32. Travis Shaw, 3b, Washington HS, Washington Court House, Ohio
33. Brandon Miller, c, Woodward Academy, College Park, Ga.
34. Zak Sinclair, rhp, West Allegheny HS, Imperial, Pa.
35. **Carson Blair, ss, Liberty Christian HS, Argyle, Texas**
36. **Richie Wasielewski, lhp, Brunswick (Ga.) HS**
37. **Tom DiBenedetto, ss, Trinity (Conn.)**
38. Bobby Hernandez, rhp, Barry (Fla.)
39. Yan Gomes, c/inf, Tennessee
40. Sam Stafford, lhp, Klein Collins HS, Spring, Texas
41. **Dustin Mercadante, rhp, San Diego CC**
42. Caleb Brown, of, Central Kitsap HS, Silverdale, Wash.
43. John Killen, lhp, Blue Valley HS, Stilwell, Kan.
44. Ben Whitmore, lhp, Fresno (Calif.) CC
45. Jon Griffin, 1b, Manatee (Fla.) JC
46. Jeremy Heatley, rhp, North Lake (Texas) CC
47. **Jeremy Kehrt, rhp, Southern Indiana**

48. Kevin Hoef, 3b, Iowa
49. **Zach Gentile, 2b, Western Michigan**
50. **Kyle Stroup, rhp, Grant HS, Fox Lake, Ill.**

CHICAGO CUBS (19)

1. **Andrew Cashner, rhp, Texas Christian**
1s. **Ryan Flaherty, ss, Vanderbilt** (Supplemental pick—41st overall—for loss of Type B free agent Jason Kendall)
2. **Aaron Shafer, rhp, Wichita State**
3. **Chris Carpenter, rhp, Kent State**
4. **Matt Cerda, ss, Oceanside (Calif.) HS**
5. **Justin Bristow, rhp, East Carolina**
6. **Josh Harrison, 2b, Cincinnati**
7. **Luis Flores, c, Oklahoma State**
8. **James Leverton, lhp, Texas Tech**
9. **Jay Jackson, rhp, Furman**
10. Alex Wilson, rhp, Texas A&M
11. **Toby Matchulat, rhp, Wabash Valley (Ill.) CC**
12. **Jake Opitz, 2b, Nebraska**
13. **Tony Campana, of, Cincinnati**
14. **Dan McDaniel, rhp, Chabot (Calif.) JC**
15. **Joe Coleman, rhp, Florida Gulf Coast**
16. **Ryan Keedy, 1b, Alabama-Birmingham**
17. **Jon Nagel, rhp, Independence (Kan.) CC**
18. **Jeff Beliveau, lhp, Florida Atlantic**
19. **David Macias, of, Vanderbilt**
20. **Jericho Jones, of, Louisiana Tech**
21. **Logan Watkins, ss, Goddard (Kan.) HS**
22. **Tarlandas Mitchell, rhp, Alto (Texas) HS**
23. **Ryan Sontag, of, Arizona State**
24. **David Cales, rhp, St. Xavier (Ill.)**
25. **Rebel Ridling, 1b, Oklahoma State**
26. **Josh Whitlock, rhp, West Virginia**
27. Sonny Gray, rhp, Smyrna (Tenn.) HS
28. **TeWayne Willis, of, Lincoln Memorial (Tenn.)**
29. Sean Buckley, 3b, King HS, Tampa
30. Matt White, rhp, Paris (Texas) JC
31. Kyle Wilson, 3b, Hill (Texas) JC
32. **Kurt Calvert, of, Missouri**
33. **Sean Hoorelbeke, 1b, Central Michigan**
34. **Bubba O'Donnell, rhp, High Point**
35. Ross Vagedes, rhp, Wright State
36. **Michael Brenly, c, Nevada-Las Vegas**
37. **Erik Hamren, rhp, Saddleback (Calif.) CC**
38. Sean McNaughton, of, Brigham Young
39. Jordan Brown, rhp, Louisiana State
40. Jared McDonald, ss, Pima (Ariz.) CC
41. Jordan Petraitis, ss, Miami (Ohio)
42. Derek Riley, rhp, Chandler-Gilbert (Ariz.) CC
43. Jesse Ginley, rhp, Dunnellon (Fla.) HS
44. David Doss, c, South Alabama
45. Ashton Florko, lhp, British Columbia
46. Tony Zych, rhp, St. Rita of Cascia HS, Chicago
47. Chad Cregar, of, Western Kentucky
48. Dylan Moseley, rhp, Louisiana Tech
49. Hunter Scantling, rhp, Episcopal HS, Jacksonville, Fla.
50. Pete Levitt, rhp, Pitt (N.C.) CC

CHICAGO WHITE SOX (8)

1. **Gordon Beckham, ss, Georgia**
2. (Pick to Brewers as compensation for Type A free agent Scott Linebrink)
3. **Brent Morel, 3b, Cal Poly**
4. **Drew O'Neil, rhp, Penn State**
5. **Dan Hudson, rhp, Old Dominion**
6. **Kenny Williams, of, Wichita State**
7. **Jordan Danks, of, Texas**
8. **Kevin Dubler, c, Illinois State**
9. **Ryan Strauss, rhp, Florida State**
10. **Stephen Sauer, rhp, Arizona State**
11. **Charlie Leesman, lhp, Xavier**
12. **Steven Upchurch, rhp, Faith Academy, Mobile, Ala.**
13. **Dexter Carter, rhp, Old Dominion**
14. Jorden Merry, rhp, Washington

15. **Tyler Kuhn, ss, West Virginia**
16. Brett Basham, c, Mississippi
17. Jonathan Weaver, rhp, East Leyden HS, Franklin Park, Ill.
18. **Josh Billeaud, rhp, Southern Mississippi**
19. **Justin Kuehn, rhp, Santa Clara**
20. **Justin Greene, of, Francis Marion (S.C.)**
21. **Drew Garcia, 2b, UC Riverside**
22. **Jose Vargas, 3b, Ventura (Calif.) JC**
23. Kyle Long, lhp, St. Anne's-Belfield School, Charlottesville, Va.
24. **Brett Graffy, rhp, Notre Dame**
25. Taylor Thompson, rhp, Auburn
26. **Jorge Castillo, 1b, Florida International**
27. **Doug Thennis, 1b, Texas Tech**
28. **Brandon Short, of, St. John's River (Fla.) CC**
29. Randall Thorpe, of, Heritage HS, Colleyville, Texas
30. **Kevin Asselin, rhp, Sonoma State (Calif.)**
31. James McCann, c, Dos Pueblos HS, Santa Barbara, Calif.
32. Justin Marrero, 2b, Reynoldsburg (Ohio) HS
33. Eddie Young, inf, Christian HS, El Cajon, Calif.
34. Marcus Semien, ss, St. Mary's HS, Berkeley, Calif.
35. Harold Riggins, 1b, Normal (Ill.) West HS
36. Jordan Keegan, of, Silverado HS, Las Vegas
37. Terry Doyle, rhp, Boston College
38. Steve Domecus, c, Moorpark (Calif.) JC
39. Rusty Shellhorn, lhp, Central Valley HS, Spokane Valley, Wash.
40. Mark Hawkenson, rhp, Red Mountain HS, Mesa, Ariz.
41. Mason Radeke, rhp, Santa Barbara (Calif.) HS
42. Steve Sabatino, lhp, Lockport (Ill.) Township High
43. Cory Farris, c, Boone County HS, Florence, Ky.
44. C.J. Cron, c, Mountain Pointe HS, Phoenix
45. Julian Kenner, ss, Whitney Young HS, Chicago
46. **Lee Fischer, ss, Missouri**
47. Dan Hayden, c, Xavier
48. Ricardo Alvarez, 2b, San Fernando (Calif.) HS
49. Travis Otto, 1b, Wheaton (Ill.) North HS
50. Steve Florence, ss, Simeon Career Academy, Chicago

CINCINNATI REDS (7)

1. **Yonder Alonso, 1b, Miami**
2. (Pick to Brewers as compensation for Type A free agent Francisco Cordero)
3. **Zach Stewart, rhp, Texas Tech**
4. **Tyler Cline, rhp, Cass HS, Cartersville, Ga.**
5. **Clayton Shunick, rhp, North Carolina State**
6. **Alex Buchholz, 2b, Delaware**
7. **Pedro Villarreal, rhp, Howard (Texas) JC**
8. **Cody Puckett, ss, Cal State Dominguez Hills**
9. **David Sappelt, of, Coastal Carolina**
10. **Sean Conner, of, Palm Beach (Fla.) CC**
11. **Andrew Means, of, Indiana**
12. **Kyle Day, c, Michigan State**
13. **Blaine Howell, lhp, Pensacola (Fla.) JC**
14. **Lance Janke, rhp, San Diego Christian**
15. Eric Pfisterer, lhp, Don Bosco Prep, Ramsey, N.J.
16. **Carter Morrison, of, Clayton Heights SS, Surrey, B.C.**
17. **Frank Pfister, 3b, Emory (Ga.)**
18. **Chris McMurray, c, UC Santa Barbara**
19. **Mace Thurman, lhp, Baylor**
20. **Tyler Stovall, of, Central Michigan**
21. **Theodis Bowe, of, Milford (Del.) HS**
22. **Byron Wiley, of, Kansas State**
23. **Will Hudgens, rhp, Memphis**
24. **Enrique Garcia, rhp, Miami**
25. **Raul Rodriguez, rhp, Simi Valley (Calif.) HS**
26. **Michael Bohana, rhp, Kennesaw State (Ga.)**
27. **Matt Stiffler, of, Ohio**
28. Bryce Bandilla, lhp, Bella Vista HS, Fair Oaks, Calif.
29. Ben Hunter, rhp, Wake Forest
30. **Juan Carlos Sulbaran, rhp, American Heritage HS, Plantation, Fla.**
31. Joey Housey, rhp, Nova HS, Davie, Fla.
32. **Justin Freeman, rhp, Kennesaw State (Ga.)**
33. Taylor Wrenn, 2b, Lakeland (Fla.) HS
34. **Bryan Gardner, lhp, Ithaca (N.Y.)**
35. **Matt Fairel, lhp, Florida State**

36. Erik Gregersen, rhp, Stephen F. Austin State
37. **Randall Linebaugh, rhp, Baylor**
38. Ricky Bowen, rhp, Mississippi State
39. **Mike Konstanty, 1b, Albany**
40. Dave Peterson, rhp, Los Lomas HS, Walnut Creek, Calif.
41. **Justin Walker, lhp, Lamar**
42. Benson Merritt, rhp, South Lincoln HS, Smithville, Ontario
43. Bronson Gagner, rhp, Parkview HS, Lilburn, Ga.
44. **Kevin Coddington, c, Illinois-Chicago**
45. Brendan Lobban, lhp, St. Joseph Regional HS, Montvale, N.J.
46. Grant Hogue, of, Mississippi State
47. **David Torcise, lhp, South Florida**
48. Kenny Monteith, rhp, Morristown-Beard School, Morristown, N.J.
49. Patrick White, of, West Virginia
50. Kevin Leslie, of, Faulkner (Ala.)

CLEVELAND INDIANS (29)

1. **Lonnie Chisenhall, ss, Pitt (N.C.) CC**
2. **Trey Haley, rhp, Central Heights HS, Nacogdoches, Texas**
3. **Cord Phelps, 2b, Stanford**
4. **David Roberts, rhp, Long Beach State**
5. **Zach Putnam, rhp, Michigan**
6. **Jeremie Tice, 3b, College of Charleston**
7. **Tim Fedroff, of, North Carolina**
8. **Eric Berger, lhp, Arizona**
9. **Clayton Cook, rhp, Amarillo (Texas) HS**
10. **Donnie Webb, of, Oklahoma State**
11. **Matt Langwell, rhp, Rice**
12. **Guido Fonseca, rhp, Northern Iowa**
13. **Adam Abraham, 3b, Michigan**
14. **Carlos Moncrief, rhp, Chipola (Fla.) JC**
15. **Jason Rodriguez, 3b, Nevada**
16. **T.J. House, lhp, Picayune (Miss.) Memorial HS**
17. Mitch Mormann, rhp, Des Moines Area (Iowa) CC
18. **Kaimi Mead, lhp, Hawaii Pacific**
19. **Nate Recknagel, 1b, Michigan**
20. **Marty Popham, rhp, Union (Ky.)**
21. **Ryan Blair, of, Sacramento State**
22. **Bryce Stowell, rhp, UC Irvine**
23. Otto Roberts, rhp, Belleville (Ill.) West HS
24. **Kevin Fontanez, ss, Puerto Rico Baseball Academy, Gurabo, P.R.**
25. **Steve Smith, rhp, Ouachita Baptist (Ark.)**
26. **Moises Montero, c, Chipola (Fla.) JC**
27. Michael Goodnight, rhp, Westside HS, Houston
28. **Russell Young, lhp, Dartmouth**
29. Ryan McCarney, rhp, JC of the Canyons (Calif.)
30. **Jeffrey Walters, rhp, St. Petersburg (Fla.) JC**
31. Trevor Cousineau, lhp, Davison (Mich.) HS
32. Nick Christiani, rhp, Vanderbilt
33. Roberto Perez, c, Lake City (Fla.) CC
34. Collin Brennan, rhp, Bradley
35. Eagan Smith, lhp, CC of Southern Nevada
36. Adam Warren, rhp, North Carolina
37. Chad Bell, lhp, Walters State (Tenn.) CC
38. **Brian Grening, rhp, Cal Poly**
39. **Eddie Burns, rhp, Georgia Tech**
40. **Tim Palincsar, of, Texas-San Antonio**
41. Adam Matthews, of, White Knoll HS, Lexington, S.C.
42. Logan Thompson, ss, Jupiter (Fla.) HS
43. **Mike McGuire, rhp, Delaware**
44. Cory White, rhp, Rend Lake (Ill.) CC
45. Dean Lagonosky, of, Haverford (Pa.)
46. Matt Ramsey, rhp, Farragut HS, Knoxville, Tenn.
47. Randon Henika, ss, Garber HS, Essexville, Mich.
48. Troy White, 3b, Whitney Young HS, Chicago
49. Devin Jones, rhp, Eupora (Miss.) HS
50. Hector Acosta-Carillo, of, Junction City (Kan.) HS

COLORADO ROCKIES (25)

1. **Christian Friedrich, lhp, Eastern Kentucky**
2. **Charlie Blackmon, of, Georgia Tech**
3. **Aaron Weatherford, rhp, Mississippi State**
4. **Ethan Hollingsworth, rhp, Western Michigan**

5. Chris Dominguez, 3b, Louisville
6. **Kiel Roling, c, Arizona State**
7. **Dan Houston, rhp, Boston College**
8. **Kurt Yacko, rhp, Chapman (Calif.)**
9. **Craig Bennigson, lhp, California**
10. **Stephen Dodson, rhp, Georgia**
11. **Kyle Walker, lhp, Texas**
12. **Ryan Peisel, 3b, Georgia**
13. **Erik Wetzel, 2b, Fresno State**
14. **Tyler Massey, of, Baylor School, Chattanooga, Tenn.**
15. **Juan Rodriguez, rhp, Universidad del Turabo (P.R.) JC**
16. **Chad Rose, rhp, Broward (Fla.) CC**
17. **Alan Deratt, rhp, UNC Asheville**
18. **Chad Jacobsen, 1b, South Carolina-Aiken**
19. Ben Orloff, 2b, UC Irvine
20. Nate Lape, of, Marshall
21. **Tyler Trice, rhp, North Carolina**
22. **Nick Schnaitmann, rhp, Cosumnes River (Calif.) JC**
23. Sam Elam, lhp, Notre Dame
24. **Thomas Field, ss, Texas State**
25. Andy Burns, ss, Rocky Mountain HS, Fort Collins, Colo.
26. **Adam Jorgenson, rhp, Cal State Fullerton**
27. Tim Matthews, rhp, Baylor
28. **Mike Zuanich, of, UC Santa Barbara**
29. **Matt Baugh, lhp, San Francisco**
30. **Carlos Luna, rhp, Oral Roberts**
31. **Rod Scurry, rhp, Nevada**
32. Will Scott, of, Kell HS, Marietta, Ga.
33. Aaron Gates, lhp, Orange (Calif.) Lutheran HS
34. Ryan Radcliff, c, Fairview HS, Fairview Park, Ohio
35. **Maikol Gonzalez, 2b, Tusculum (Tenn.)**
36. **Patrick Rose, of, UC Santa Barbara**
37. **Delta Cleary, of, Louisiana State-Eunice JC**
38. Tyler Pill, rhp, Covina (Calif.) HS
39. Kyle Ottoson, lhp, Eaton (Colo.) HS
40. Kemer Quirk, of, Rockhurst HS, Kansas City
41. Dean Espy, ss, Red Mountain HS, Mesa, Ariz.
42. Taylor Hightower, c, Cartersville (Ga.) HS
43. **Alex Feinberg, 2b, Vanderbilt**
44. Jordan Swagerty, rhp, Prestonwood Christian Academy, Plano, Texas
45. **Brad McAtee, rhp, UC Davis**
46. **Jimmy Cesario, 2b, Houston**
47. Mark Lincoln, rhp, American River (Calif.) JC
48. Austin Nola, ss, Catholic HS, Baton Rouge, La.
49. Roy Uhl, of, UC Riverside
50. Josh Hungerman, lhp, Cleveland State

DETROIT TIGERS (21)

1. **Ryan Perry, rhp, Arizona**
2. **Cody Satterwhite, rhp, Mississippi**
3. **Scott Green, rhp, Kentucky**
4. **Brett Jacobson, rhp, Vanderbilt**
5. **Alex Avila, c, Alabama**
6. **Tyler Stohr, rhp, North Florida**
7. **Jade Todd, lhp, Shades Valley HS, Birmingham, Ala.**
8. **Andy Dirks, of, Wichita State**
9. **Anthony Shawler, rhp, Old Dominion**
10. **Robbie Weinhardt, rhp, Oklahoma State**
11. **Brandon Douglas, ss, Northern Iowa**
12. **Brett Anderson, ss, Bristol (Conn.) Eastern HS**
13. **Jared Gayhart, rhp, Rice**
14. **Tyler Conn, lhp, Southern Mississippi**
15. **Alden Carrithers, 2b, UCLA**
16. **Thad Weber, rhp, Nebraska**
17. **Robb Waite, rhp, UC Riverside**
18. Scott Weismann, rhp, Acton-Boxborough (Mass.) Regional HS
19. **Ben Guez, of, William & Mary**
20. Ryan Lollis, of, Missouri
21. **Adam Frost, ss, St. Norbert (Wis.)**
22. Zach MacPhee, ss, O'Connor HS, Phoenix
23. **Mike Gosse, 2b, Oklahoma**
24. **Carmelo Jaime, 2b, Miami-Dade CC**
25. **Billy Nowlin, c, Golden West (Calif.) JC**

26. **Brent Wyatt, ss, Lewis-Clark State (Idaho)**
27. James Young, rhp, Southridge HS, Miami
28. **David Stokes, rhp, Liberty**
29. **Keith Stein, of, Sam Houston State**
30. **Tyler Weber, c, Wichita State**
31. **Trevor Feeney, rhp, Northern Illinois**
32. **Mark Sorensen, rhp, Michigan State**
33. **Jordan Lennerton, 1b, Oregon State**
34. **Bryan Pounds, 3b, Houston**
35. **Dan DeLucia, lhp, Ohio State**
36. **Steve Gilman, rhp, Yale**
37. **Nick Cassavecchia, rhp, Baylor**
38. **Josh Workman, 2b, Wichita State**
39. Chris Gloor, lhp, Quinnipiac (Conn.)
40. Bryan Bingham, rhp, Navarro (Texas) JC
41. **Eric Broberg, rhp, Seminole (Fla.) CC**
42. Paul Hoenecke, 3b, West Bend (Wis.) East HS
43. Tyler Grimes, ss, North HS, Wichita, Kan.
44. Brian Wheeler, of, Childersburg (Ala.) HS
45. Edward Linseman, lhp, Our Lady of Lourdes HS, Guelph, Ontario
46. Eric Roof, c, Michigan State
47. Alan Avila, 2b, Archbishop McCarthy HS, Fort Lauderdale, Fla.
48. Casey Moore, c, Saint Louis
49. Matt Robertson, rhp, Barton County (Kan.) CC
50. Landon Hernandez, c, Hawaii

FLORIDA MARLINS (6)

1. **Kyle Skipworth, c, Patriot HS, Rubidoux, Calif.**
2. **Brad Hand, lhp, Chaska (Minn.) HS**
3. **Edgar Olmos, lhp, Birmingham HS, Van Nuys, Calif.**
4. **Curtis Petersen, rhp, Ryan HS, Denton, Texas**
5. **Pete Andrelczyk, rhp, Coastal Carolina**
6. **Graham Johnson, rhp, Westlake HS, Westlake Village, Calif.**
7. **Paul Gran, 3b, Washington State**
8. **Isaac Galloway, of, Los Osos HS, Rancho Cucamonga, Calif.**
9. **Dan Jennings, lhp, Nebraska**
10. Trevor Holder, rhp, Georgia
11. **Blake Brewer, rhp, Sandy Creek HS, Tyrone, Ga.**
12. **Brandon Turner, 2b, Mississippi State**
13. **Danny Pertusati, 2b, Damien HS, La Verne, Calif.**
14. **Bryan Evans, rhp, UC Davis**
15. **Johnny Dorn, rhp, Nebraska**
16. **Andy Loomis, lhp, Purdue**
17. Ben Soignier, ss, Louisiana-Monroe
18. **Tom Koehler, rhp, SUNY Stony Brook**
19. **Justin Bass, of, Stetson**
20. **Wade Korpi, lhp, Notre Dame**
21. **Lonnie Lechelt, 2b, Oregon State**
22. **Jared Yecker, rhp, St. John's**
23. **Konrad Thieme, c, Sonoma State (Calif.)**
24. **Zach Moore, c, Dundalk (Md.) CC**
25. **Robert Taylor, c, Arkansas-Little Rock**
26. **Jason Peacock, 1b, Florida Gulf Coast**
27. **Elih Villanueva, rhp, Florida State**
28. **Kevin Mattison, of, UNC Asheville**
29. **Ricky Orton, 3b, UNC Greensboro**
30. **Skyler Crawford, rhp, Hartnell (Calif.) JC**
31. Marvin Campbell, 1b, Las Vegas HS
32. **Wayman Gooch, rhp, Lewis-Clark State (Idaho)**
33. Moses Munoz, lhp, Bossier Parish (La.) CC
34. **Matt Lokken, 3b, St. Helens (Ore.) HS**
35. **Brian Schultz, of, Florida Southern**
36. **Brandon Todd, rhp, South Carolina**
37. **Drew Clothier, rhp, Army**
38. Joey DeBernardis, 3b, Lake Zurich (Ill.) HS
39. Mikie Mahtook, of, St. Thomas More HS, Lafayette, La.
40. Trent Fuller, ss, Fairfield (Calif.) HS
41. Alan Williams, of, Mangham (La.) HS
42. **Jeremy Synan, of, North Carolina State**
43. Kess Carter, of, Ravenwood HS, Brentwood, Tenn.
44. **Joel Staples, 3b, St. Mary's**
45. Fred Atkins, of, Marin (Calif.) CC
46. **Casey Fry, lhp, Los Angeles Pierce JC**

47. Jeff Urlaub, lhp, Nevada-Las Vegas
48. Barrett Serrato, ss, Community HS, West Chicago, Ill.
49. Taylor Davis, c, Jupiter (Fla.) HS
50. Colin Hoffman, of, St. Augustine HS, San Diego

HOUSTON ASTROS (10)

1. **Jason Castro, c, Stanford**
1s. **Jordan Lyles, rhp, Hartsville (S.C.) HS** (Supplemental pick—38th overall—for loss of Type B free agent Trever Miller)
2. **Jay Austin, of, North Atlanta HS, Atlanta**
3. Chase Davidson, 1b, Milton (Ga.) HS
3s. **Ross Seaton, rhp, Second Baptist HS, Houston** (Supplemental pick—109th overall—for failure to sign 2007 third-round pick Derek Dietrich)
4. **T.J. Steele, of, Arizona**
5. **David Duncan, lhp, Georgia Tech**
6. **J.B. Shuck, of, Ohio State**
7. **Jon Gaston, of, Arizona**
8. **Brad Dydalewicz, lhp, Lake Travis HS, Austin**
9. **Luis Cruz, lhp, Academia Santa Monica, San Juan, P.R.**
10. **Jarred Holloway, lhp, St. Petersburg (Fla.) JC**
11. **Jacob Priday, of, Missouri**
12. **Jeff Hulett, ss, Okaloosa-Walton (Fla.) CC**
13. **Kyle Godfrey, rhp, Hiwassee (Tenn.) JC**
14. **Chris Hicks, rhp, Georgia Tech**
15. **Phil Disher, c, South Carolina**
16. Josh Poythress, lhp, Fowler (Calif.) HS
17. **Andy Simunic, 2b, Tennessee**
18. **David Flores, 3b, Sacramento State**
19. **Ashton Mowdy, rhp, Eastern Oklahoma State JC**
20. Shea Robin, c, Vanderbilt
21. Rodarrick Jones, of, St. John HS, Plaquemine, La.
22. Terrance Jackson, lhp, North Central Texas JC
23. Chase Huchingson, lhp, Arkansas-Fort Smith JC
24. **Danny Meier, of, Portland**
25. **Mike Hacker, lhp, Cosumnes River (Calif.) CC**
26. **Shane Wolf, lhp, Ithaca (N.Y.)**
27. **Nate Pettus, rhp, Western Oklahoma State JC**
28. **Zach Grimmett, rhp, Beggs (Okla.) HS**
29. **Chris Jackson, ss, Virginia Commonwealth**
30. **Mike Diaz, 2b, Southern Connecticut State**
31. **Philip Rummel, rhp, Kutztown (Pa.)**
32. Bryan Vollmuth, ss, Biloxi (Miss.) HS
33. Shawn Armstrong, rhp, West Craven HS, Vanceboro, N.C
34. Jordan Jankowski, c, Peters Township HS, McMurray, Pa.
35. **Rene Garcia, c, Colegio Sagrada Familia HS, Corozal, P.R.**
36. Austin Wood, rhp, Niceville (Fla.) HS
37. **Kirkland Rivers, lhp, Texas A&M**
38. Kris Castellanos, rhp, Newsome HS, Lithia, Fla.
39. Tyson Van Winkle, c, Gonzaga
40. Scott Lawson, 2b, Grayson County (Texas) CC
41. Tony McClendon, of, Damien HS, La Verne, Calif.
42. Ryan Danbury, of, North Florida CC
43. Austin Green, c, Henry HS, San Diego
44. Edmond Sparks, c, Chipola (Fla.) JC
45. Grayson Garvin, lhp, Wesleyan School, Norcross, Ga.
46. Mike Modica, lhp, George Mason
47. **Nathan Metroka, of, Compton (Calif.) CC**
48. **Danny Meszaros, rhp, College of Charleston**
49. **Chase Lehr, rhp, Glendale (Ariz.) CC**
50. Jamal Austin, of, Harrison HS, Kennesaw, Ga.

KANSAS CITY ROYALS (3)

1. **Eric Hosmer, 1b, American Heritage HS, Plantation, Fla.**
1s. **Mike Montgomery, lhp, Hart HS, Newhall, Calif.** (Supplemental pick—36th overall—for loss of Type B free agent David Riske)
2. **Johnny Giavotella, 2b, New Orleans**
3. **Tyler Sample, rhp, Mullen HS, Denver**
4. **Tim Melville, rhp, Holt HS, Wentzville, Mo.**
5. **John Lamb, lhp, Laguna Hills (Calif.) HS**
6. **Alex Llanos, of, Puerto Rico Baseball Academy, Gurabo, P.R.**
7. Jason Esposito, 3b, Amity Regional HS, Woodbridge, Conn.

8. **Malcolm Culver, rhp, Palmdale (Calif.) HS**
9. **J.D. Alfaro, ss, Grayson County (Texas) CC**
10. **Mauricio Matos, c, Clinton HS, Bronx, N.Y.**
11. Malcolm Bronson, of, Jasper (Texas) HS
12. **Keven Caldwell, of, Spartanburg Methodist (S.C.) JC**
13. **John Flanagan, lhp, Southwestern Illinois JC**
14. **Chase Hentges, rhp, Shakopee (Minn.) HS**
15. **Alberto Espinosa, 1b, Broward (Fla.) CC**
16. **Derrick Saito, lhp, Cal Poly**
17. **Jake Kuebler, 3b, Lincoln (Neb.) Southeast HS**
18. **Carlo Testa, of, Belmont**
19. **Miguel Moctezuma, c, Central Oklahoma**
20. **Shawn Griffin, of, Tennessee**
21. **Jake Theis, rhp, Mountlake Terrace (Wash.) HS**
22. **Blaine Hardy, lhp, Lewis-Clark State (Idaho)**
23. **Dale De Schepper, rhp, Mount San Jacinto (Calif.) JC**
24. **Jason Morales, 3b, UNC Pembroke**
25. **Carson Bryant, rhp, Azusa Pacific (Calif.)**
26. **Ryan Morgan, rhp, Rockhurst (Mo.)**
27. **Tim Huber, lhp, Nebraska-Omaha**
28. **Greg Billo, rhp, Sandburg HS, Orland Park, Ill.**
29. Beau Brett, 1b, Ferris HS, Spokane, Wash.
30. Rick Dodridge, lhp, Ogemaw Heights HS, West Branch, Mich.
31. Ryan Curl, of, St. Francis DeSales HS, Columbus, Ohio
32. Rey Cotilla, rhp, Miami-Dade CC
33. Eric Swegman, rhp, Young Harris (Ga.) JC
34. **Brett Richardson, rhp, Wenatchee Valley (Wash.) CC**
35. Chris Balcom-Miller, rhp, West Valley (Calif.) JC
36. Nick Purdy, rhp, St. Mary's SS, Grafton, Ontario
37. Bradin Hagens, rhp, Merced (Calif.) JC
38. **James Thompson, rhp, Columbus State (Ga.)**
39. Ryan Modglin, rhp, Scott City (Mo.) HS
40. **Pernell Halliman, rhp, Jackson State**
41. Doug Joyce, c, Stanwood (Wash.) HS
42. Marc Oslund, rhp, West HS, Torrance, Calif.
43. Cory Kiefer, rhp, Valley View HS, Moreno Valley, Calif.
44. Patrick Johnson, of, Colony HS, Ontario, Calif.
45. Ray Anderson, of, Lassiter HS, Marietta, Ga.
46. William Beckwith, 1b, West Lowndes HS, Columbus, Miss.
47. **Steve Gilgenbach, lhp, Arkansas-Little Rock**
48. Terrence Buchanan, ss, Mount Carmel HS, San Diego
49. Alan Salgado, 3b, San Ysidro HS, San Diego
50. **Travis Jones, c, Sabino HS, Tucson**

LOS ANGELES ANGELS (27)

1. (Pick to Twins as compensation for Type A free agent Torii Hunter)
2. **Tyler Chatwood, rhp, Redlands (Calif.) East Valley HS**
3. **Ryan Chaffee, rhp, Chipola (Fla.) JC**
3s. Zach Cone, of, Parkview HS, Lilburn, Ga. (Supplemental pick—112th overall—for failure to sign 2007 third-round pick Matt Harvey)
4. **Buddy Boshiers, lhp, Calhoun (Ala.) CC**
5. Khiry Cooper, of, Calvary Baptist Academy, Shreveport, La.
6. **Josh Blanco, lhp, Franklin HS, El Paso**
7. **Will Smith, lhp, Gulf Coast (Fla.) CC**
8. **Chris Scholl, rhp, Green River (Wash.) CC**
9. **Nick Farnsworth, lhp, Union HS, Tulsa, Okla.**
10. **Gabe Jacobo, 3b, Sacramento State**
11. **Rolando Gomez, ss, Flanagan HS, Pembroke Pines, Fla.**
12. **Braulio Pardo, c, St. Leo (Fla.)**
13. **Michael Kohn, rhp, College of Charleston**
14. **Reyes Dorado, rhp, Arizona State**
15. **Marcel Champagnie, of, Arizona State**
16. **John Hellweg, rhp, Florida CC**
17. Jamie Mallard, 1b, Middleton HS, Tampa
18. **Adam Younger, ss, Oral Roberts**
19. Marshall Burford, c, Manor HS, Austin
20. **Beau Brooks, c, Troy**
21. **Dwayne Bailey, 2b, Central Florida**
22. **Ryan Groth, of, Oral Roberts**
23. **Matt Crawford, of, Mercer**
24. Taylor Jungmann, rhp, Georgetown (Texas) HS
25. **Roberto Lopez, of, Southern California**
26. **Kevin Nabors, rhp, South Alabama**

27. **Tim Kiely, rhp, Trinity (Conn.)**
28. **Mike Kenney, rhp, Loyola Marymount**
29. **Jeremy Thorne, rhp, Florida Southern**
30. **Jayson Miller, lhp, Washington State**
31. John Hicks, c, Goochland (Va.) HS
32. Miguel Starks, rhp, Mundy's Mill HS, Jonesboro, Ga.
33. Jose Jimenez, 1b, Tampa
34. **Drew Taylor, lhp, North Carolina State**
35. **Demetrius Washington, of, Middle Georgia JC**
36. **Kyle Hurst, rhp, South Mountain (Ariz.) CC**
37. Evan Scott, rhp, Battlefield HS, Haymarket, Va.
38. **John Rickard, c, Bishop Gorman HS, Las Vegas**
39. Kyle Hendricks, rhp, Capistrano Valley HS, Mission Viejo, Calif.
40. Donnie Roach, rhp, Bishop Gorman HS, Las Vegas
41. Josh Edmondson, rhp, Florida
42. Chandler Griffin, rhp, Central Arizona JC
43. Kevin Ferguson, lhp, Tampa
44. David Fischer, rhp, Ballston Lake HS, Burnt Hills, N.Y.
45. Jared Clark, 1b, Cal State Fullerton
46. Ryan Hege, c, Maize (Kan.) HS
47. Josh Copeland, rhp, Alabama
48. Chris Vitus, rhp, Mount Hood (Ore.) CC
49. Will Roberts, rhp, Walker Governor's School, Richmond
50. Joey Belviso, of, American Heritage HS, Plantation, Fla.

LOS ANGELES DODGERS (15)

1. **Ethan Martin, rhp, Stephens County HS, Toccoa, Ga.**
2. **Josh Lindblom, rhp, Purdue**
3. **Kyle Russell, of, Texas**
4. **Devaris Gordon, ss, Seminole (Fla.) CC**
5. **Jon Michael Redding, rhp, Florida CC-Jacksonville**
6. **Tony Delmonico, ss, Florida State**
7. **Cole St. Clair, lhp, Rice**
8. **Nick Buss, of, Southern California**
9. **Steven Caseres, 1b, James Madison**
10. Chris Joyce, lhp, Dos Pueblos HS, Goleta, Calif.
11. **Nathan Eovaldi, rhp, Alvin (Texas) HS**
12. **Austin Yount, 3b, Stanford**
13. **Lenell McGee, of, Oakton (Ill.) CC**
14. **Clay Calfee, of, Angelo State (Texas)**
15. **Albie Goulder, 1b, Louisiana Tech**
16. Kyle Conley, of, Washington
17. Danny Coulombe, lhp, Chaparral HS, Scottsdale, Ariz.
18. **Carl Webster, rhp, McMichael HS, Madison, N.C.**
19. David Rollins, lhp, First Baptist Academy, Carthage, Texas
20. Zack Cox, 3b, Pleasure Ridge Park HS, Louisville
21. Dave Sever, rhp, Saint Louis
22. **Matt Smith, rhp, Wichita State**
23. **Brian Ruggiano, 2b, Texas A&M**
24. **Roberto Feliciano, lhp, Puerto Rico Baseball Academy, Gurabo, P.R.**
25. **Jerry Sands, of, Catawba (N.C.)**
26. Cody Weiss, rhp, Parkland HS, Allentown, Pa.
27. **Clayton Allison, rhp, Fresno State**
28. **Jordan Roberts, lhp, Embry-Riddle (Fla.)**
29. **Jonathan Runnels, lhp, Rice**
30. **Garett Green, 2b, San Diego State**
31. **Matt Magill, rhp, Royal HS, Simi Valley, Calif.**
32. **Shan Sullivan, 3b, Angelo State (Texas)**
33. **Melvin Ray, of, North Florida Christian HS, Tallahassee, Fla.**
34. Andrew Darwin, of, San Jacinto (Calif.) HS
35. Adam Westmoreland, lhp, Brookland-Cayce HS, Cayce, S.C.
36. **Jake New, of, Tennessee Tech**
37. Will Clinard, rhp, East Robertson HS, Cross Plains, Tenn.
38. Tommy Nurre, 1b, Miami (Ohio)
39. Matt Murray, rhp, Roberts HS, Pottstown, Pa.
40. Jimmy Parque, of, Skyline (Calif.) JC
41. Jett Bandy, c, Thousand Oaks (Calif.) HS
42. Adam Moskowitz, 2b, Valley HS, Des Moines, Iowa
43. Greg Zebrack, of, Campbell Hall HS, North Hollywood, Calif.
44. Matt Reed, lhp, West Stanly HS, Oakboro, N.C.
45. **Ryan Arp, c, Iowa**

MILWAUKEE BREWERS (16)

1. **Brett Lawrie, 3b/c, Brookswood SS, Langley, B.C.**
1s. **Jake Odorizzi, rhp, Highland (Ill.) HS** (Supplemental pick—32nd overall—for loss of Type A free agent Francisco Cordero)
1s. **Evan Frederickson, lhp, San Francisco** (Supplemental pick—35th overall—for loss of Type A free agent Scott Linebrink)
2. **Seth Lintz, rhp, Marshall County HS, Lewisburg, Tenn.** (Pick from Reds as compensation for Cordero)
2. **Cutter Dykstra, of, Westlake HS, Westlake Village, Calif.** (Pick from White Sox as compensation for Linebrink)
2. **Cody Adams, rhp, Southern Illinois**
3. **Logan Schafer, of, Cal Poly**
4. **Josh Romanski, lhp, San Diego**
5. **Maverick Lasker, rhp, O'Connor HS, Phoenix**
6. **Jose Duran, ss, Texas A&M**
7. **Trey Watten, rhp, Abilene Christian (Texas)**
8. **Erik Komatsu, of, Cal State Fullerton**
9. **Michael Bowman, rhp, Virginia Military Institute**
10. **Gregory Miller, rhp, Seton Hall**
11. **Michael Marseco, ss, Samford**
12. **Gerritt Sherrill, rhp, Appalachian State**
13. **Rob Wooten, rhp, North Carolina**
14. **Corey Kemp, c, East Carolina**
15. **Mark Willinsky, rhp, Santa Clara**
16. **Stosh Wawrzasek, rhp, Walnut Grove SS, Langley, B.C.**
17. **Damon Krestalude, rhp, Port St. Lucie (Fla.) HS**
18. **Nick Bucci, rhp, St. Patrick's HS, Sarnia, Ontario**
19. **Blake Billings, rhp, Hillcrest HS, Tuscaloosa, Ala.**
20. **Liam Ohlmann, rhp, Manchester (Conn.) CC**
21. **Lucas Luetge, lhp, Rice**
22. **Ben Jeffers, rhp, Chipola (Fla.) JC**
23. Marcus Knecht, of, St. Michael's College School, Toronto
24. **Brandon Ritchie, lhp, Grand Rapids (Mich.) CC**
25. **John Delaney, ss, Quinnipiac (Conn.)**
26. **Derrick Alfonso, c, Louisville**
27. Austin Adams, ss, Faulkner (Ala.)
28. Brandon Garcia, c, Bishop Gorman HS, Las Vegas
29. Tommy Collier, rhp, Cypress-Fairbanks HS, Cypress, Texas
30. **Wayne Dedrick, of, Hillcrest HS, Tuscaloosa, Ala.**
31. **Brandon Rapoza, rhp, Flagler (Fla.)**
32. Colton Farrar, rhp, First Baptist Academy, Dallas
33. Michael White, rhp, Anderson County HS, Clinton, Tenn.
34. Calvin Drummond, rhp, Huntington Beach (Calif.) HS
35. **Mike Vass, of, Chapman (Calif.)**
36. Evan Bronson, lhp, Trinity (Texas)
37. Kyle Winkler, rhp, Kempner HS, Sugar Land, Texas
38. **Michael Roberts, c, Virginia Military Institute**
39. Eric Decker, of, Minnesota
40. Nicholas Fogarty, lhp, Thornlea SS, Thornhill, Ontario
41. Joe Scott, ss, Cal State Fullerton
42. **Ryan Wood, ss, East Carolina**
43. Dexter Price, rhp, Air Academy HS, Colorado Springs
44. Kaleb Herren, rhp, North Central Texas JC
45. James Kottaras, 2b, Milliken Mills HS, Markham, Ontario
46. **Carlos George, ss, Monroe HS, Bronx, N.Y.**
47. Kayvon Bahramzadeh, rhp, Catalina Foothills HS, Tucson
48. **Marcus Salmon, rhp, Miami-Dade CC**
49. **Dan Meadows, rhp, Temple (Texas) JC**
50. Sean Nolin, lhp, Seaford (N.Y.) HS

MINNESOTA TWINS (14)

1. **Aaron Hicks, of, Wilson HS, Long Beach**
1. **Carlos Gutierrez, rhp, Miami** (Pick from Angels as compensation for Type A free agent Torii Hunter)
1s. **Shooter Hunt, rhp, Tulane** (Supplemental pick—31st overall—for loss of Hunter)
2. **Tyler Ladendorf, ss, Howard (Texas) JC**
3. **Bobby Lanigan, rhp, Adelphi (N.Y.)**
4. **Danny Ortiz, of, Harrison HS, Cayey, P.R.**
5. **Nick Romero, 3b, San Diego State**
6. **B.J. Hermsen, rhp, West Delaware HS, Manchester, Iowa**
7. **Dan Osterbrock, lhp, Cincinnati**
8. **Jeff Lanning, c, New Orleans**

9. **Mike Gonzales, 1b, Diablo Valley (Calif.) JC**
10. **Evan Bigley, of, Dallas Baptist**
11. **Dominic De La Osa, 2b, Vanderbilt**
12. **Kyle Carr, lhp, Minnesota**
13. **Michael Harrington, of, College of Charleston**
14. **Blayne Weller, rhp, Key West (Fla.) HS**
15. David Coulon, lhp, Arizona
16. Kolten Wong, 2b, Kamehameha HS, Hilo, Hawaii
17. **Blake Martin, lhp, Louisiana State**
18. Matt Nohelty, of, Minnesota
19. **Bruce Pugh, rhp, Hillsborough (Fla.) CC**
20. Aaron Barrett, rhp, Wabash Valley (Ill.) CC
21. **Steve Blevins, rhp, Marshall**
22. Kyle Witten, rhp, Bakersfield (Calif.) JC
23. Chris Odegaard, rhp, Minnesota State-Mankato
24. Lionel Morrill, of, Vauxhall HS, Crows Nest Pass, Alb.
25. **Alex Curry, rhp, Cypress (Calif.) JC**
26. **Adan Severino, of, Miami**
27. Jerico Weitzel, 2b, Ridgway (Pa.) HS
28. **Nate Hanson, 3b, Minnesota**
29. Joe Loftus, 3b, Academy of Holy Angels, Richfield, Minn.
30. **Mike Tonkin, rhp, Palmdale (Calif.) HS**
31. Lee Ridenhour, rhp, Shawnee Mission (Kan.) West HS
32. Adam Conley, lhp, Olympia (Wash.) HS
33. Luke Yoder, of, Cal Poly
34. Adam Purdy, rhp, Pell City (Ala.) HS
35. Sam Ryan, c, Tartan Senior HS, Oakdale, Minn.
36. Miers Quigley, lhp, Alabama
37. **Javier Brown, ss, Grossmont (Calif.) JC**
38. Alex Mendez, lhp, Bishop Moore HS, Orlando
39. Steve Proscia, 3b, Don Bosco Prep, Ramsey, N.J.
40. Wade Kapteyn, rhp, Evansville
41. Pat Lehman, rhp, George Washington
42. Riley Boening, lhp, Texas
43. Jeff Pickering, lhp, Nitro (W.Va.) HS
44. Colby Sokol, of, Emerald Ridge HS, Puyallup, Wash.
45. Mike Spina, 3b, Cincinnati
46. Lyndon Eusea, of, Hahnville HS, Boutte, La.
47. Tom Farmer, rhp, Akron
48. George Springer, of, Avon (Conn.) Old Farms School
49. Johnny Bromberg, rhp, Los Angeles Pierce JC
50. Tyler Anderson, lhp, Valley HS, Las Vegas

NEW YORK METS (22)

1. **Ike Davis, 1b, Arizona State** (Pick from Braves as compensation for Type A free agent Tom Glavine)
1. **Reese Havens, ss, South Carolina**
1s. **Brad Holt, rhp, UNC Wilmington** (Supplemental pick—33rd overall—for loss of Glavine)
2. **Javier Rodriguez, of, Puerto Rico Baseball Academy, Gurabo, P.R.**
3. **Kirk Nieuwenhuis, of, Azusa Pacific (Calif.)**
4. **Sean Ratliff, of, Stanford**
5. **Dock Doyle, c, Coastal Carolina**
6. **Josh Satin, 2b, California**
7. **Mike Hebert, rhp, Saugus (Calif.) HS**
8. **Eric Campbell, 3b, Boston College**
9. **Eric Beaulac, rhp, Le Moyne**
10. **Brian Valenzuela, lhp, Vista Murrieta HS, Murrieta, Calif.**
11. **Jeff Kaplan, rhp, Cal State Fullerton**
12. **Mark Cohoon, lhp, North Central Texas JC**
13. **Scott Shaw, rhp, Illinois**
14. **Brandon Moore, rhp, Indiana Wesleyan**
15. Jamie Bruno, 1b, Mandeville (La.) HS
16. **Travis Babin, rhp, Sonoma State (Calif.)**
17. **Mitch Houck, lhp, Central Florida**
18. **Collin McHugh, rhp, Berry (Ga.)**
19. **Zach Rosenbaum, rhp, UNC Charlotte**
20. **Michael Moras, c, New Haven (Conn.)**
21. **Jim Fuller, lhp, Southern Connecticut State**
22. **Chris Schwinden, rhp, Fresno Pacific (Calif.)**
23. **Evan LeBlanc, of, Santa Clara**
24. **Kyle Allen, rhp, Pendleton School, Bradenton, Fla.**
25. **Erik Turgeon, rhp, Connecticut**

26. **John Servidio, of, Barry (Fla.)**
27. **Jeff Flagg, 1b, Mississippi State**
28. **Jimmy Johnson, lhp, Biola (Calif.)**
29. **Mike Giuffre, 2b, Tottenville HS, Staten Island, N.Y.**
30. **Mike Lynn, rhp, College of Charleston**
31. **Michael Powers, rhp, Michigan**
32. Mark Grbavac, rhp, Oregon State
33. Neil Medchill, of, Oklahoma State
34. **Justin Garber, of, Shippensburg (Pa.)**
35. **Kyle Suire, 2b, Louisiana-Monroe**
36. **Jake Goldberg, rhp, College of Charleston**
37. **Tim Erickson, lhp, Lamar**
38. **Chris Hilliard, rhp, Itawamba (Miss.) CC**
39. **Charlie Hinojosa, c, Don Lugo HS, Chino, Calif.**
40. **Seth Williams, of, North Carolina**
41. **Tyler Howe, c, Kentucky**
42. **Tim Smith, rhp, Catawba (N.C.)**
43. **Mark McGonigle, of, New Orleans**
44. Jean-Francois Ricard, lhp, Ahuntsic (Quebec) JC
45. David Phillips, 1b, Texarkana (Texas) CC
46. Brian Gump, of, UC Santa Barbara
47. Matt Bischoff, rhp, Purdue
48. Tyler Baisley, of, Gateway (Ariz.) CC
49. **Doug McNulty, 1b, Akron**
50. Kameron Brunty, of, Gulf Breeze (Fla.) HS

NEW YORK YANKEES (28)

1. Gerrit Cole, rhp, Orange (Calif.) Lutheran HS
1s. **Jeremy Bleich, lhp, Stanford** (Supplemental pick—44th overall—for loss of Type B free agent Luis Vizcaino)
2. Scott Bittle, rhp, Mississippi
3. **David Adams, 2b, Virginia**
4. **Corban Joseph, ss, Franklin (Tenn.) HS**
5. **Chris Smith, of, Centennial HS, Compton, Calif.**
6. **Brett Marshall, rhp, Sterling HS, Baytown, Texas**
7. **Kyle Higashioka, c, Edison HS, Huntington Beach, Calif.**
8. **Dan Brewer, of, Bradley**
9. **Mikey O'Brien, rhp, Hidden Valley HS, Roanoke, Va.**
10. **D.J. Mitchell, rhp, Clemson**
11. **Ray Kruml, of, South Alabama**
12. **Luke Greinke, rhp, Auburn**
13. **Jack Rye, of, Florida State**
14. **David Phelps, rhp, Notre Dame**
15. **Matt Richardson, rhp, Lake Mary (Fla.) HS**
16. Luke Anders, 1b, Texas A&M
17. **Addison Maruszak, ss, South Florida**
18. **Brandon Braboy, rhp, Indianapolis**
19. **Mitch Abeita, c, Nebraska**
20. **Pat Venditte, rhp/lhp, Creighton**
21. **Mitch Delaney, 1b, Western Texas JC**
22. **Cory Arbiso, rhp, Cal State Fullerton**
23. **Ryan Wilkes, ss, Kentucky**
24. **Mike Lyon, 3b, Northeastern**
25. **Jeff Nutt, c, Arkansas**
26. Blake Monar, lhp, South Spencer HS, Rockport, Ind.
27. **Garrison Lassiter, ss, West Forsyth HS, Clemmons, N.C.**
28. **Chad Gross, of, Cuesta (Calif.) JC**
29. **Mike Jones, of, Arizona State**
30. Ben McMahan, c, Bishop Moore HS, Orlando
31. **Spencer Lucian, 2b, Princeton**
32. Andy Suiter, lhp, UC Davis
33. **Tommy Baldridge, of, Coastal Carolina**
34. **Brad Rulon, rhp, Georgia Tech**
35. **Andrew Shive, rhp, Azusa Pacific (Calif.)**
36. Chris Dwyer, lhp, Salisbury (Conn.) School
37. Justin Harper, rhp, Yavapai (Ariz.) JC
38. Clay Caulfield, rhp, College of Charleston
39. **Erik Lovett, 1b, Mount Olive (N.C.)**
40. Sam Mende, ss, Clearwater (Fla.) Central Catholic HS
41. Mykal Stokes, of, Tustin (Calif.) HS
42. **Clint Preisendorfer, lhp, San Diego Christian**
43. Matt Summers, rhp, Chaparral HS, Scottsdale, Ariz.
44. Evan Ocheltree, of, Wake Forest

45. Creede Simpson, ss, Auburn (Ala.) HS
46. Matt Veltmann, rhp, San Diego CC
47. **Ryan Flannery, rhp, Fairleigh Dickinson**
48. Rob Scahill, rhp, Bradley
49. John Folino, rhp, Connecticut
50. **Nik Turley, lhp, Harvard-Westlake School, North Hollywood, Calif.**

OAKLAND ATHLETICS (12)

1. **Jemile Weeks, 2b, Miami**
2. **Tyson Ross, rhp, California**
3. **Petey Paramore, c, Arizona State**
4. **Anthony Capra, lhp, Wichita State**
5. **Jason Christian, ss, Michigan**
6. **Tyreace House, of, JC of the Canyons (Calif.)**
7. **Brett Hunter, rhp, Pepperdine**
8. **Jeremy Barfield, of, San Jacinto (Texas) JC**
9. **Mitch LeVier, c, Fullerton (Calif.) JC**
10. **Rashun Dixon, of, Terry (Miss.) HS**
11. **Chris Berroa, of, Chipola (Fla.) JC**
12. Zac Elgie, 1b, Minot (N.D.) HS
13. **Daniel Thomas, rhp, South Florida**
14. **David Thomas, of, Catawba (N.C.)**
15. **Nino Leyja, ss, Houston Christian HS**
16. **Matt Fitts, rhp, Lewis-Clark State (Idaho)**
17. Brad Glenn, 3b, Arizona
18. Rayan Gonzalez, rhp, Luchetti HS, Arecibo, P.R.
19. **Michael Hart, rhp, Texas State**
20. **Rodney Rutherford, 3b, Columbus State (Ga.)**
21. **Mathieu LeBlanc Poirier, rhp, Ahuntsic (Quebec) JC**
22. Preston Guilmet, rhp, Arizona
23. Chris Rusin, lhp, Kentucky
24. **Ken Smalley, rhp, Delta State (Miss.)**
25. **Trey Barham, lhp, Virginia Military Institute**
26. **Ryan Doolittle, rhp, Cumberland (N.J.) CC**
27. Brent Warren, of, Xavier HS, Cedar Rapids, Iowa
28. **Dusty Coleman, ss, Wichita State**
29. **Justin Murray, rhp, Kansas State**
30. **Ryne Jernigan, 2b, South Alabama**
31. **Mickey Storey, rhp, Florida Atlantic**
32. **Ben Hornbeck, lhp, Kansas State**
33. **Shawn Haviland, rhp, Harvard**
34. Riley Welch, rhp, Desert Mountain HS, Scottsdale, Ariz.
35. Virgil Hill, of, Mission (Calif.) JC
36. Jon Berti, ss, Troy (Mich.) HS
37. Ryan Doiron, rhp, Barbe HS, Lake Charles, La.
38. Bobby Crocker, of, Aptos (Calif.) HS
39. Danny Clement, rhp, Cascia Hall Prep, Tulsa, Okla.
40. Jeff Dennis, lhp, Binghamton
41. Cody Hawn, 3b, Walters State (Tenn.) CC
42. Kent Walton, 2b, Brigham Young
43. Nick Maronde, lhp, Lexington (Ky.) Catholic HS
44. Jimmy Messer, rhp, South Caldwell HS, Hudson, N.C.
45. Derek Benny, rhp, Roseville (Calif.) HS
46. J.R. Graham, rhp, Livermore (Calif.) HS
47. Coley Crank, c, Pinole Valley HS, Pinole, Calif.
48. Brett Holland, rhp, Texas-Tyler
49. Matt Bowman, 2b, Nevada
50. Derek Wiley, 1b, Belmont

PHILADELPHIA PHILLIES (24)

1. **Anthony Hewitt, ss, Salisbury (Conn.) School**
1s. **Zach Collier, of, Chino Hills (Calif.) HS** (Supplemental pick—34th overall—for loss of Type A free agent Aaron Rowand)
2. **Anthony Gose, of, Bellflower (Calif.) HS** (Pick from Giants as compensation for Rowand)
2. **Jason Knapp, rhp, North Hunterdon HS, Annandale, N.J.**
3. **Vance Worley, rhp, Long Beach State**
3s. **Jon Pettibone, rhp, Esperanza HS, Anaheim** (Supplemental pick—110th overall—for failure to sign 2007 third-round pick Brandon Workman)
4. **Trevor May, rhp, Kelso (Wash.) HS**
5. **Jeremy Hamilton, 1b, Wright State**
6. **Colby Shreve, rhp, CC of Southern Nevada**

7. Johnny Coy, 3b, Benton HS, St. Joseph, Mo.
8. **Julio Rodriguez, rhp, Puerto Rico Baseball Academy, Gurabo, P.R.**
9. **Cody Overbeck, 3b, Mississippi**
10. **Jean Carlos Rodriguez, c, Washington HS, New York**
11. **Mike Stutes, rhp, Oregon State**
12. Ryan Weber, rhp, Clearwater (Fla.) Central Catholic HS
13. **B.J. Rosenberg, rhp, Louisville**
14. **Michael Schwimer, rhp, Virginia**
15. **Damarii Saunderson, of, Northville (Mich.) HS**
16. **Troy Hanzawa, ss, San Diego State**
17. **Jim Murphy, 1b, Washington State**
18. **Tyler Cloyd, rhp, Bellevue, Neb. (no school)**
19. **Steve Susdorf, of, Fresno State**
20. **Eryk McConnell, rhp, North Carolina State**
21. **Sean Grieve, lhp, William & Mary**
22. **Daniel Hargrave, 2b, UNC Wilmington**
23. **Brandon Haislet, of, Hawaii**
24. **Korey Noles, lhp, Columbus State (Ga.)**
25. Daniel Edwards, rhp, Kansas State
26. **Ryan Bergh, rhp, Old Dominion**
27. **Chad Poe, rhp, Bossier Parish (La.) CC**
28. **Jordan Ellis, rhp, Villanova**
29. Keon Broxton, 3b, Lakeland (Fla.) HS
30. Dwayne Henderson, ss, Southeastern HS, Detroit
31. **Spencer Arroyo, lhp, Modesto (Calif.) JC**
32. **Shaun Ellis, rhp, Polk (Fla.) CC**
33. Jamie Simpson, 1b, Dowagiac (Mich.) Union HS
34. Blaine O'Brien, rhp, Scituate (Mass.) HS
35. **Ruddy Rio-Nunez, of, Eduardo Montpetit HS, Montreal**
36. **Mike Cisco, rhp, South Carolina**
37. Matt Johnson, of, North HS, Riverside, Calif.
38. **Jarred Cosart, rhp, Clear Creek HS, League City, Texas**
39. Joe Pond, rhp, Judge Memorial HS, Salt Lake City
40. Daniel Marrs, rhp, James River HS, Midlothian, Va.
41. Mike Petello, of, Scottsdale (Ariz.) CC
42. **Mike Bolsenbroek, rhp, Ageldoorn, Netherlands (no school)**
43. **Bryan Frew, of, Nebraska-Omaha**
44. Charlie Law, rhp, Mainland Regional HS, Linwood, N.J.
45. Justin Zumwalde, 1b, Sabino HS, Tucson
46. Giovany Soto, lhp, Advanced Central College HS, Carolina, P.R.
47. **Nate Fike, lhp, Potomac State (W.Va.) JC**
48. Mark Ginther, ss, Jenks (Okla.) HS
49. Michael Russo, rhp, Hun School, Princeton, N.J.
50. Josh Hake, rhp, Park (Ariz.)

PITTSBURGH PIRATES (2)

1. **Pedro Alvarez, 3b, Vanderbilt**
2. Tanner Scheppers, rhp, Fresno State
3. **Jordy Mercer, ss, Oklahoma State**
4. **Chase D'Arnaud, ss, Pepperdine**
5. **Justin Wilson, lhp, Fresno State**
6. **Robbie Grossman, of, Cypress-Fairbanks HS, Cypress, Texas**
7. **Benji Gonzalez, ss, Puerto Rico Baseball Academy, Gurabo, P.R.**
8. **Jeremy Farrell, 3b, Virginia**
9. **Matt Hague, 3b, Oklahoma State**
10. Drew Gagnon, rhp, Liberty HS, Brentwood, Calif.
11. **David Rubinstein, of, Appalachian State**
12. **Calvin Anderson, 1b, Southern**
13. Seth Gardner, of, Highland Park HS, Dallas
14. **Mike Colla, rhp, Arizona**
15. **Chris Aure, lhp, North Pole (Alaska) HS**
16. **Wes Freeman, of, All Saints Academy, Lakeland, Fla.**
17. Jaron Shepherd, of, Navarro (Texas) JC
18. **Jarek Cunningham, ss, Mount Spokane HS, Spokane, Wash.**
19. Jason Haniger, c, Georgia Tech
20. **Quinton Miller, rhp, Shawnee HS, Medford, N.J.**
21. **Brett Klinger, rhp, Glendale (Ariz.) CC**
22. Patrick Palmeiro, 3b, Heritage HS, Colleyville, Texas
23. Austin Wright, lhp, Conant HS, Hoffman Estates, Ill.
24. Brian Litwin, 3b, St. Stephens HS, Hickory, N.C.
25. **Brian Leach, rhp, Southern Mississippi**
26. Zach Wilson, 3b, Wilson HS, Long Beach
27. Edwin Roman, of, Puerto Rico Baseball Academy HS, Gurabo, P.R.

28. **Kyle Saukko, rhp, Sierra (Calif.) JC**
29. Kevin Komstadius, 1b, East Valley HS, Yakima, Wash.
30. Daniel Martin, rhp, Panola (Texas) JC
31. Ryan Hinson, lhp, Clemson
32. T.J. Forrest, rhp, Bossier Parish (La.) CC
33. **Mark Carver, 1b, UNC Wilmington**
34. **Matt Payne, 3b, North Carolina State**
35. **Tyler Cox, lhp, Illinois State**
36. **Kyle Morgan, of, San Francisco**
37. Matt Curry, 1b, Howard (Texas) JC
38. **Alan Knotts, rhp, Louisiana Tech**
39. **Albert Fagan, rhp, Yonkers, N.Y. (no school)**
40. Beau Didier, 3b, Bellarmine Prep, Tacoma, Wash.
41. **Chris Simmons, c, Army**
42. **Cole White, of, Army**
43. Johnny Gunter, rhp, Chattahoochee Valley (Ala.) CC
44. **Mike Williams, lhp, Mount Olive (N.C.)**
45. **Allen Ponder, rhp, Auburn-Montgomery**
46. Scott McGough, ss, Plum HS, Pittsburgh
47. Jordan Craft, of, Kennesaw Mountain HS, Kennesaw, Ga.
48. **Owen Brolsma, rhp, Texas Tech**
49. **Zach Foster, rhp, Pittsburgh-Bradford**
50. **Craig Parry, of, South Dakota State**

ST. LOUIS CARDINALS (13)

1. **Brett Wallace, 1b, Arizona State**
1s. **Lance Lynn, rhp, Mississippi** (Supplemental pick—39th overall—for loss of Type B free agent Troy Percival)
2. **Shane Peterson, of, Long Beach State**
3. **Niko Vasquez, ss, Durango HS, Las Vegas**
4. **Scott Gorgen, rhp, UC Irvine**
5. **Jermaine Curtis, 3b, UCLA**
6. **Eric Fornataro, rhp, Miami-Dade CC**
7. **Anthony Ferrara, lhp, Riverview HS, Sarasota, Fla.**
8. **Ryan Kulik, lhp, Rowan (N.J.)**
9. **Aaron Luna, of, Rice**
10. **Alex Castellanos, 2b, Belmont Abbey (N.C.)**
11. **Devin Shepherd, of, CC of Southern Nevada**
12. **Michael Swinson, of, Coffee County HS, Douglas, Ga.**
13. Mitch Harris, rhp, Navy
14. **Charlie Cutler, c, California**
15. **Scott McGregor, rhp, Memphis**
16. **Miguel Flores, rhp, Cerritos (Calif.) JC**
17. **Josh Hester, rhp, Freed Hardeman (Tenn.)**
18. **Jared Bradford, rhp, Louisiana State**
19. **Xavier Scruggs, 1b, Nevada-Las Vegas**
20. **Luis Mateo, ss, Jose Rojas Cortez Superior HS, Orocovis, P.R.**
21. **Matt Rigoli, 1b, Pace (N.Y.)**
22. **Colt Sedbrook, ss, Arizona**
23. **Jonny Bravo, lhp, Azusa Pacific (Calif.)**
24. **Zach Pitts, rhp, Louisville**
25. **Jason Buursma, rhp, Bucknell**
26. **Chris Swauger, of, The Citadel**
27. **George Brown, lhp, St. John's**
28. **Matt Frevert, rhp, Missouri State**
29. **Brett Lilley, 2b, Notre Dame**
30. Brett Bruening, rhp, Grayson County (Texas) CC
31. Justin Leith, lhp, Collier HS, Naples, Fla.
32. **Sam Freeman, lhp, Kansas**
33. **Kevin Thomas, rhp, Stephen F. Austin State**
34. **Jack Cawley, c, Pace (N.Y.)**
35. Shane Boras, 2b, Serra HS, San Mateo, Calif.
36. **Chris Notti, rhp, Moorpark (Calif.) JC**
37. Danny Jimenez, lhp, St. Charles (Ill.) North HS
38. **Dan Richardson, rhp, Delaware**
39. **Curt Smith, 1b, Maine**
40. **Paul Cruz, of, Tampa**
41. **Kevin Siegrist, lhp, Palm Beach (Fla.) CC**
42. **Blake Murphy, c, Western Carolina**
43. **Joe Babrick, of, King HS, Tampa**
44. **Santo Maertz, rhp, St. Peter's (N.J.)**
45. Chris Taylor, c, Charlotte
46. Brandon Sizemore, 2b, College of Charleston

47. Ray Asaro, of, UC Irvine
48. **Adam Prange, rhp, South Mountain (Ariz.) CC**
49. **Adam Veres, rhp, St. Petersburg (Fla.) JC**
50. Danny Miranda, lhp, Miami Killian HS

SAN DIEGO PADRES (23)

1. **Allan Dykstra, 1b, Wake Forest**
1s. **Jaff Decker, of, Sunrise Mountain HS, Peoria, Ariz.** (Supplemental pick—42nd overall—for loss of Type B free agent Doug Brocail)
1s. Logan Forsythe, 3b, Arkansas (Supplemental pick—46th overall—for loss of Type B free agent Mike Cameron)
2. **James Darnell, 3b, South Carolina**
3. **Blake Tekotte, of, Miami**
3s. **Sawyer Carroll, 1b, Kentucky** (Supplemental pick—111th overall—for failure to sign 2007 third-round pick Tommy Toledo)
4. **Jason Kipnis, of, Arizona State**
5. **Anthony Bass, rhp, Wayne State (Mich.)**
6. **Cole Figueroa, ss, Florida**
7. **Adam Zornes, c, Rice**
8. **Beamer Weems, ss, Baylor**
9. Kyle Thebeau, rhp, Texas A&M
10. **Andrew Albers, lhp, Kentucky**
11. **Tyson Bagley, rhp, Dallas Baptist**
12. **Matt Clark, 1b, Louisiana State**
13. **Erik Davis, rhp, Stanford**
14. **Rob Musgrave, lhp, Wichita State**
15. Brett Mooneyham, lhp, Buhach Colony HS, Atwater, Calif.
16. **Tom Davis, rhp, Fordham**
17. **Derek Shunk, ss, Villanova**
18. **Nick Vincent, rhp, Long Beach State**
19. **Robert Lara, c, Central Florida**
20. **Jason Codiroli, of, West Valley (Calif.) JC**
21. **Joey Railey, 2b, San Francisco**
22. **Chris Wilkes, rhp, Dr. Phillips HS, Orlando**
23. Nick Conaway, rhp, Walnut Cove, N.C. (no school)
24. **Eric Gonzalez, rhp, South Alabama**
25. Logan Power, of, Mississippi
26. **Dean Anna, ss, Ball State**
27. **Aaron Murphree, of, Arkansas**
28. **Nick Schumacher, rhp, Wayne State (Neb.)**
29. **Omar Gutierrez, rhp, Texas A&M-Corpus Christi**
30. **Bobby Verbick, of, Sam Houston State**
31. Sean Gilmartin, of, Crespi Carmelite HS, Encino, Calif.
32. **Kyle Heyne, rhp, Ball State**
33. **Dan Robertson, of, Oregon State**
34. **Matt Gaski, 2b, UNC Greensboro**
35. **Logan Gelbrich, c, San Diego**
36. Jake Shadle, rhp, Graham-Kapowsin HS, Graham, Wash.
37. **Matt Means, lhp, Sonoma State (Calif.)**
38. **Zach Herr, lhp, Nebraska**
39. **Gary Poynter, rhp, Lubbock Christian (Texas)**
40. **Colin Lynch, rhp, St. John's**
41. Zach Dascenzo, c, Laurel Highlands HS, Uniontown, Pa.
42. **Brad Brach, rhp, Monmouth**
43. James Tunnell, of, Oklahoma City, Okla. (no school)

SAN FRANCISCO GIANTS (5)

1. **Buster Posey, c, Florida State**
1s. **Conor Gillaspie, 3b, Wichita State** (Supplemental pick—37th overall—for loss of Type B free agent Pedro Feliz)
2. (Pick to Phillies as compensation for Type A free agent Aaron Rowand)
3. **Roger Kieschnick, of, Texas Tech**
4. **Brandon Crawford, ss, UCLA**
5. **Edwin Quirarte, rhp, Cal State Northridge**
6. **Eric Surkamp, lhp, North Carolina State**
7. **Aaron King, lhp, Surry (N.C.) CC**
8. **Scott Barnes, lhp, St. John's**
9. **Ryan Verdugo, lhp, Louisiana State**
10. Ryan O'Sullivan, rhp, Valhalla HS, El Cajon, Calif.
11. **Justin Fitzgerald, rhp, UC Davis**
12. **Ari Ronick, lhp, Portland**
13. **Juan Carlos Perez, of, Western Oklahoma State JC**
14. **Caleb Curry, of, Iowa**

15. **Dan Cook, 2b, Florida Atlantic**
16. **C.J. Ziegler, 1b, Arizona**
17. **Brian Irving, rhp, Yale**
18. **Brooks Lindsley, ss, Lower Columbia (Wash.) JC**
19. **Ryan Mantle, of, Missouri State**
20. Trey Sutton, 2b, Southern Mississippi
21. **Mike Eifel, rhp, Dominican (Ill.)**
22. Carter Bell, 3b, Vanier SS, Toronto
23. **Jason Jarvis, rhp, Lincoln Saltdogs (American Association)**
24. Wes Musick, lhp, Houston
25. **Damon Wright, of, Dartmouth**
26. **Ryan Lormand, 2b, Houston**
27. **Kyle Woodruff, rhp, Chico State (Calif.)**
28. **Shane Kaufman, rhp, San Diego State**
29. **Rob Flanigan, 1b, North Georgia College and State**
30. **Vladimir Frias, ss, Tennessee Wesleyan**
31. **Aaron Davidson, rhp, Arkansas-Fort Smith JC**
32. John Blake, rhp, Lake Sumter (Fla.) CC
33. **Ryne Price, of, Kansas**
34. Francois LaFreniere, rhp, Ahuntsic (Quebec) JC
35. Dan Black, 3b, Purdue
36. Matt Way, lhp, Washington State
37. Jeremy Penn, rhp, Western Oklahoma State JC
38. **Chris Wilson, rhp, Trinidad State (Colo.) JC**
39. Braden Kapteyn, 3b, Illiana Christian HS, Lansing, Ill.
40. Austin Stadler, 1b, James River HS, Midlothian, Va.
41. Corey Figueroa, 2b, St. Petersburg (Fla.) JC
42. Tyler Thompson, of, Jupiter (Fla.) HS
43. Zack Thornton, rhp, Ventura (Calif.) JC
44. **Aaron Lowenstein, c, UC Irvine**
45. Kenneth Villines, 2b, Riverside HS, Durham, N.C.
46. Joey Hainsfurther, ss, Highland Park HS, Dallas
47. Abe Ruiz, 3b, Pacific Grove (Calif.) HS
48. **Leo Ochoa, 2b, Saint-Amable, Quebec (no school)**
49. Dalton Hicks, 1b, Lake Brantley HS, Altamonte Springs, Fla.
50. Jeremy Ware, rhp, Arkansas State

SEATTLE MARINERS (20)

1. Joshua Fields, rhp, Georgia
2. **Dennis Raben, of, Miami**
3. **Aaron Pribanic, rhp, Nebraska**
4. **Steven Hensley, rhp, Elon**
5. **Brett Lorin, rhp, Long Beach State**
6. **Jarrett Burgess, of, Florida Christian HS, Miami**
7. **Nate Tenbrink, 3b, Kansas State**
8. **Bobby LaFromboise, lhp, New Mexico**
9. Billy Morrison, rhp, Western Michigan
10. Nate Newman, rhp, Pepperdine
11. Matt Jensen, 2b, Clovis (Calif.) East HS
12. **Kenn Kasparek, rhp, Texas**
13. **Ryan Royster, of, UC Davis**
14. **Luke Burnett, rhp, Louisiana Tech**
15. **Jake Shaffer, of, Northern Kentucky**
16. **Ben Billingsley, 2b, Lenoir (N.C.) CC**
17. Mike Dennhardt, rhp, Don Bosco Prep, Ramsey, N.J.
18. **Travis Howell, c, Long Beach State**
19. **Taylor Lewis, rhp, Yavapai (Ariz.) JC**
20. **Fred Bello, ss, Cerro Coso (Calif.) CC**
21. **Jordan Alvis, rhp, Middle Tennessee State**
22. **Blake Nation, rhp, Georgia Southern**
23. **Brandon Maurer, rhp, Orange (Calif.) Lutheran HS**
24. **Henry Contreras, c, Cal State Los Angeles**
25. Paul Robinson, 2b, Paris (Texas) JC
26. **Taylor Stanton, rhp, Diablo Valley (Calif.) JC**
27. **Tommy Johnson, c, Marshall**
28. **Scott Savastano, ss, Franklin Pierce (N.H.)**
29. **Stephen Penney, rhp, UC Riverside**
30. **Brad Reid, rhp, Bellevue (Wash.) CC**
31. **Randy Castillo, rhp, Aiea (Hawaii) HS**
32. **Nick Love, rhp, Bellevue (Neb.)**
33. **Kyle Brown, lhp, UC Santa Barbara**
34. Ty Tostenson, of, Oak Ridge HS, El Dorado Hills, Calif.
35. **Nick Czyz, lhp, Kansas**

36. **Chris Kirkland, rhp, Memphis**
37. **Brandon Pullen, lhp, San Diego State**
38. **Andres Esquibel, rhp, Kansas**
39. **Christian Staehely, rhp, Princeton**
40. Troy Channing, c, Foothill HS, Pleasanton, Calif.
41. **Henry Cotto, of, Gateway (Ariz.) CC**
42. **Randy Molina, 1b, Stanford**
43. Mike Kindel, of, Springboro (Ohio) HS
44. **Donny Jobe, 2b, Elon**
45. Andrew Kittredge, rhp, Ferris HS, Spokane, Wash.
46. Alvin Rittman, of, Germantown (Tenn.) HS
47. Rich O'Donald, rhp, Dickinson HS, Wilmington, Del.
48. D.J. Mauldin, rhp, Cal Poly
49. **Josh Rodriguez, c, South Mountain (Ariz.) CC**
50. Walker Kelly, lhp, Arlington Heights HS, Fort Worth, Texas

TAMPA BAY RAYS (1)

1. **Tim Beckham, ss, Griffin (Ga.) HS**
2. **Kyle Lobstein, lhp, Coconino HS, Flagstaff, Ariz.**
3. **Jake Jefferies, c, UC Davis**
4. **Ty Morrison, of, Tigard (Ore.) HS**
5. **Mike Sheridan, 1b, William & Mary**
6. **Shane Dyer, rhp, South Mountain (Ariz.) CC**
7. **Jason Corder, of, Long Beach State**
8. **Anthony Scelfo, 2b, Tulane**
9. **Shawn Smith, lhp, Saugus (Calif.) HS**
10. **Matt Hall, 2b, Auburn**
11. **Brad Furdal, rhp, Ancaster HS, Ancaster, Ontario**
12. **Brian Bryles, rhp/of, North Little Rock (Ark.) HS**
13. **Jason McEachern, rhp, St. Stephens HS, Hickory, N.C.**
14. **Mike McKenna, of, Florida Atlantic**
15. Brandon Meredith, 1b, Montgomery HS, San Diego
16. **Matt Gorgen, rhp, California**
17. **Jeremy Beckham, 2b, Georgia Southern**
18. **David Genao, c, Oral Roberts**
19. **Trevor Shull, rhp, Central Valley HS, Spokane, Wash.**
20. **Jason Tweedy, 2b, Long Beach State**
21. Ryan Carpenter, lhp, Cactus HS, Peoria, Ariz.
22. **Jason Appel, of, UNC Wilmington**
23. **Neil Schenk, lhp, Memphis**
24. **Marquis Fleming, rhp, Cal State Stanislaus**
25. **Josh Satow, lhp, Arizona State**
26. **Michael Jarman, lhp, Oral Roberts**
27. **Luis Marchena, ss, Otay Ranch HS, San Diego**
28. **Tommy Rafferty, rhp, Arizona State**
29. Brandon Magee, of, Centennial HS, Corona, Calif.
30. Ryan Turner, rhp, Midland (Texas) JC
31. Greg Williams, lhp, Moeller HS, Cincinnati
32. Kyle Gaedele, of, Rolling Meadows (Ill.) HS
33. Kyle Hunter, lhp, Galesburg (Ill.) HS
34. **Matt Long, rhp, Cal State San Bernardino**
35. **Jamie Bagley, rhp, San Jacinto (Texas) JC**
36. Jordan Leyland, 1b, Sam Dimas (Calif.) HS
37. Kramer Champlin, rhp, Olympia (Wash.) HS
38. Anthony Haase, rhp, Rio Rancho (N.M.) HS
39. Andrew Gans, of, Coronado HS, Henderson, Nev.
40. Sam Gaviglio, rhp, Ashland (Ore.) HS
41. Brett Parsons, of, Navarro (Texas) JC
42. Tim Clubb, rhp, Missouri State
43. Robbie Ross, lhp, Saddleback (Calif.) CC
44. Philip Pohl, c, Cooperstown (N.Y.) Central HS
45. Royce Bolinger, of, Chaparral HS, Scottsdale, Ariz.
46. Jeff Lease, lhp, American River (Calif.) JC
47. Chris Matulis, lhp, Park Vista HS, Lake Worth, Fla.
48. Lath Guyer, rhp, Mercer
49. Kash Kalkowski, rhp, Grand Island (Neb.) HS
50. Kyle Peterson, c, Hamilton HS, Chandler, Ariz.

TEXAS RANGERS (11)

1. **Justin Smoak, 1b, South Carolina**
2. **Robbie Ross, lhp, Lexington (Ky.) Christian Academy**
3. **Tim Murphy, lhp, UCLA**
4. **Joe Wieland, rhp, Bishop Manogue HS, Reno, Nev.**

5. **Clark Murphy, 1b, Fallbrook (Calif.) HS**
6. **Richard Bleier, lhp, Florida Gulf Coast**
7. **Matt Thompson, rhp, Grace Prep Academy, Arlington, Texas**
8. **Mike Bianucci, of, Auburn**
9. **Jared Bolden, of, Virginia Commonwealth**
10. Kevin Castner, rhp, Cal Poly
11. **Cliff Springston, lhp, Arkansas**
12. **Corey Young, lhp, Seton Hall**
13. **Ed Koncel, ss, Joliet (Ill.) JC**
14. **Justin Gutsie, rhp, St. John's**
15. **Joey Butler, of, New Orleans**
16. **Justin Miller, rhp, Fresno State**
17. **Dennis Guinn, 1b, Florida State**
18. **Doug Hogan, c, Clemson**
19. Harold Martinez, ss, Braddock HS, Miami
20. **Michael Hollander, ss, Louisiana State**
21. **Dustin Brader, rhp, Arizona State**
22. **Trevor Hurley, rhp, Kansas State**
23. **Eric Evans, lhp, Radford**
24. **Adam Cobb, of, Louisiana Tech**
25. **Tanner Roark, rhp, Southern Illinois Miners (Frontier)**
26. **Chris Dove, of, Elon**
27. Charlie Lowell, lhp, Winfield (Mo.) HS
28. Nate Freiman, 1b, Duke
29. Charlie Robertson, rhp, Bella Vista HS, Fair Oaks, Calif.
30. **Justin King, rhp, Jacksonville State**
31. **Kyle Higgins, ss, Monmouth**
32. **Tyler Tufts, rhp, Indiana**
33. **Ben Petralli, c, Oral Roberts**
34. **Ryan Schlecht, rhp, Mount Olive (N.C.)**
35. John Ruettiger, of, Joliet (Ill.) Catholic Academy
36. Jack Armstrong, rhp, Jupiter (Fla.) HS
37. Matt Andriese, rhp, Redlands (Calif.) East Valley HS
38. **Jason Ogata, 2b, Oregon State**
39. Brad Miller, ss, Olympia HS, Orlando
40. **Jamie McGraw, of, Corban (Ore.)**
41. Brian Feekin, lhp, Iowa Western CC
42. Stephen Pryor, rhp, Cleveland State (Tenn.) CC
43. **Cody Eppley, rhp, Virginia Commonwealth**
44. Alex Pepe, lhp, Florida Atlantic
45. **Kevin Torres, c, Puerto Rico Baseball Academy, Gurabo, P.R.**
46. **Erik Morrison, ss, Kansas**
47. **Lejuan Hill, of, Austin Peay**
48. Daniel Bowman, of, Ashby HS, Bridgewater, Va.
49. Matt Sample, rhp, Crowder (Mo.) JC
50. Josh Rosecrans, c, Santa Fe HS, Edmond, Okla.

TORONTO BLUE JAYS (17)

1. **David Cooper, 1b, California**
2. **Kenny Wilson, of, Sickles HS, Tampa**
3. **Andrew Liebel, rhp, Long Beach State**
4. **Mark Sobolewski, 3b, Miami**
5. **Tyler Pastornicky, ss, Pendleton School, Bradenton, Fla.**
6. **Markus Brisker, of, Winter Haven (Fla.) HS**
7. **Eric Thames, of, Pepperdine**
8. **Evan Crawford, lhp, Auburn**
9. **Antonio Jimenez, c, Discipulos De Cristo HS, Bayamon, P.R.**
10. **Danny Farquhar, rhp, Louisiana-Lafayette**
11. **Dustin Antolin, rhp, Mililani (Hawaii) HS**
12. **Matt Wright, lhp, Shippensburg (Pa.)**
13. **Matt Daly, rhp, Hawaii**
14. **Chris Holguin, rhp, Lubbock Christian (Texas)**
15. **Scott Gracey, rhp, New Mexico**
16. **Michael Crouse, of, Centennial SS, Coquitlam, B.C.**
17. **Jonnathan Valdez, c, Puerto Rico Baseball Academy, Gurabo, P.R.**
18. **Bobby Bell, rhp, Rice**
19. **Jason Roenicke, rhp, UC Santa Barbara**
20. **Ryan Page, lhp, Liberty**
21. **Brian Van Kirk, of, Oral Roberts**
22. **Karim Turkamani, c, Miami-Dade CC**
23. **Chuck Huggins, lhp, UC Santa Barbara**
24. **Chris Hopkins, of, Oregon State**
25. **Brad McElroy, of, UNC Charlotte**

26. Justin Dalles, c, St. Petersburg (Fla.) JC
27. **Bryan Kervin, ss, Texas Christian**
28. **John Anderson, lhp, Chabot (Calif.) JC**
29. **Justin Cryer, rhp, Mississippi**
30. **Cody Dunbar, rhp, Texas Christian**
31. Justin Betts-Robinson, lhp, New Mexico JC
32. Ryan Scott, c, Chaparral HS, Scottsdale, Ariz.
33. **Justin McClanahan, 2b, Louisville**
34. **Austin Armstrong, rhp, Palm Beach (Fla.) CC**
35. **Hunter Moody, lhp, Louisiana-Lafayette**
36. **Ryan Koch, rhp, Florida Southern**
37. Dallas Beeler, rhp, Jenks (Okla.) HS
38. Quentin Williams, of, Pittsburgh Central Catholic HS
39. Jordan Flasher, rhp, George Mason
40. **Nate Nelson, 1b, Worcester State (Mass.)**
41. Kyle Petter, lhp, West HS, Torrance, Calif.
42. Andrew Durden, of, Indian River (Fla.) CC
43. **Tyler Ybarra, lhp, Wellington (Kan.) HS**
44. George Agyapong-Mensah, of, Western Texas JC

WASHINGTON NATIONALS (9)

1. Aaron Crow, rhp, Missouri
2. **Destin Hood, of, St. Paul's Episcopal HS, Mobile, Ala.**
3. **Danny Espinosa, ss, Long Beach State**
4. **Graham Hicks, lhp, Jenkins HS, Lakeland, Fla.**
5. **Adrian Nieto, c, American Heritage HS, Plantation, Fla.**
6. **Paul Demny, rhp, Blinn (Texas) JC**
7. **Dan Killian, c, Kellogg (Mich.) CC**
8. **Ricardo Pecina, lhp, San Diego**
9. **J.R. Higley, 1b, Sacramento CC**
10. **Tom Milone, lhp, Southern California**
11. **Marcus Jones, of, North Carolina State**
12. **Will Atwood, lhp, South Carolina**
13. **Blake Stouffer, 2b, Texas A&M**
14. Louis Coleman, rhp, Louisiana State
15. **J.P. Ramirez, of, Canyon HS, New Braunfels, Texas**
16. **Tyler Moore, 1b, Mississippi State**
17. **Jose Lozada, ss, Bethune-Cookman**
18. **Bobby Hansen, lhp, Lewis-Palmer HS, Monument, Colo.**
19. **Steve Lombardozzi, ss, St. Petersburg (Fla.) JC**
20. Nick Akins, of, Riverside (Calif.) CC
21. **Michael Guerrero, of, Mississippi**
22. **Chris Curran, 2b, Miami-Dade CC**
23. **Derrick Phillips, of, Westminster Christian Academy, St. Louis**
24. **Chris Kelley, rhp, Rice**
25. **Austin Garrett, lhp, College of Charleston**
26. Cory Mazzoni, rhp, Seneca Valley HS, Harmony, Pa.
27. **Chris Solis, c, Incarnate Word (Texas)**
28. **Nick Arata, ss, Florida Atlantic**
29. Chris Heston, rhp, Seminole (Fla.) CC
30. **Casey Whitmer, rhp, Texas**
31. Bryan Harper, lhp, Las Vegas HS
32. Scott Silverstein, lhp, St. John's HS, Washington D.C.
33. **Billy Cather, of, Maine**
34. Brian Pruitt, of, Stetson
35. Clayton Dill, rhp, Missouri Baptist
36. **John Lambert, lhp, Santa Fe (Fla.) CC**
37. **Casey Selsor, lhp, Reagan HS, San Antonio**
38. Ronnie Labrie, 3b, Lynchburg (Va.)
39. James Keithley, ss, Texas-San Antonio
40. **Avery Barnes, of, Florida**
41. **Mike Rayl, lhp, Palm Beach (Fla.) CC**
42. **Naoya Washiya, of, JC of the Desert (Calif.)**
43. **Anthony Meo, rhp, Cranston (R.I.) West HS**
44. J.P. Padron, 1b, Rice
45. **Colin Rooney, ss, Saddleback (Calif.) CC**
46. **Robbie Brantly, c, Chaparral HS, Scottsdale, Ariz**
47. **Anthony Coletti, lhp, South Broward HS, Hollywood, Fla.**
48. **Alex Dickerson, of, Poway (Calif.) HS**
49. **B.J. Zimmerman, of, Osceola HS, Kissimmee, Fla.**
50. **Fernando Frias, of, Washington HS, New York**

APPENDIX

■ **Ossie Alvarez**, a second baseman who played two seasons in the major leagues as part of a 15-year pro career, died March 8 in Guadalajara, Mexico. He was 74. Alvarez reached the majors in 1958, when he was a utilityman for the Washington Senators, appearing in 87 games spread between short, second, and third and hitting .209. He started the 1959 season with the Tigers, but returned to the minors after eight games.

■ **Jim Beauchamp**, a minor league slugger who served as an outfielder for five big league teams in a 17-year pro career that spanned 1958 to 1974, died Dec. 25, 2007, in Union City, Ga. He was 68. He finished his career with .231/.288/.334 averages with 14 home runs and 90 RBIs in 661 major league at-bats.

■ **Fred Bruckbauer**, a righthander who pitched in one game for the Twins in 1961 in a four-year pro career that spanned 1959 to 1962, died Oct. 14, 2007, in Naples, Fla. He was 69.

■ **John Buzhardt**, a righthander who pitched 11 seasons in the major leagues, died June 15 in Prosperity, S.C. He was 71.

Buzhardt pitched in six games for the Cubs in September of 1958. In his first major league start on Sept. 20, he pitched a complete game against the Dodgers, winning 3-2. He went 3-0, 1.88 in 24 big league innings that year. The Cubs traded him to the Phillies before the 1960 season, but Buzhardt went through two difficult seasons in Philadelphia before being traded again.

After the 1961 season, Philadelphia dealt Buzhardt to the White Sox. He went 9-4, 2.43 in 1963, and collected a career-high 13 wins in 1965, when he went 13-8, 3.00..He finished his career after a stint with the Astros in 1968 with a record of 71-96 and a 3.66 ERA in 1,490 major league innings.

■ **Tommy Byrne**, a wild lefthander who pitched more than a decade in the majors, died Dec. 20, 2007, in Wake Forest, N.C. He was 87.

Byrne made his major league debut with the Yankees in 1943. His first season was marked by wildness, as he walked 35 batters in 32 innings. It was a sign of things to come for Byrne, who walked more batters than he struck out during all but one year of his major league career, and led his league in walks three times and hit batsmen five times.

He went 16-5, 3.15 in 1955, setting a career high for wins. Byrne finished his major league career 85-69, 4.11 in 1,362 innings with 766 strikeouts and 1,037 walks, and went 2-2, 2.53 in

21 innings in the postseason.

■ **Skip Caray**, long-time Braves broadcaster and son of Harry Caray, died Aug. 2 in Atlanta. He was 68.

■ **Don Cardwell**, a righthander who won 102 games for five big league teams in a 14-year career, died Jan. 14 in Winston-Salem, N.C. He was 72.

Cardwell had a solid rookie campaign in 1957—4-8, 4.92 with 92 strikeouts in 128 innings—splitting his time between the rotation and bullpen. After two more solid seasons, the Phillies traded him in May 1960 to the Cubs.

Cardwell pitched a no-hitter on May 15, 1960, in his first start for Chicago, and remained a rotation fixture for the Cubs until 1962. He turned in his best year in 1961, going 15-14, 3.82 with 156 strikeouts and 88 walks in 259 innings. He retired at age 34 following a 1970 season spent with the Mets and Braves. For his career, Cardwell went 102-138, 3.92 with 1,211 strikeout and 671 walks in 2,123 innings.

■ **James Carlin**, a righthander who appeared in 16 games for the Phillies in 1941, died Nov. 29, 2003, in Birmingham. He was 89. Carlin collected three hits, including a home run, in 21 at-bats with the Phillies.

■ **Jim Castiglia**, a catcher who played his lone pro season for the Philadelphia Athletics in 1942, died Dec. 26, 2007, in Rockville, Md. He was 89. Castiglia played in 16 games for the A's, batting .389 in 18 at-bats with two RBIs.

■ **Lance Clemons**, a lefthander who played parts of three seasons in the majors in the early 1970s, died Jan. 22 in Brooksville, Fla. He was 60.

Over three seasons with the Royals, Cardinals and Red Sox, Clemons went 2-1, 6.06 in 19 appearances totaling 35 2/3 innings.

■ **Billy Consolo**, a second baseman who played 10 seasons in the major leagues, died March 27 in Westlake Village, Calif. He was 71.

Consolo spent five seasons as a utilityman for the Red Sox and Washington Senators. His best offensive season at the major league level came with the Red Sox in 1957, when he hit .270 with four home runs and 19 RBIs in 68 games.

For his career, Consolo batted .221/.315/.289 in 1,178 at-bats for the Red Sox, Senators, Twins, Phillies, Angels and Kansas City A's.

■ **Jerry Crider**, a righthander who pitched for parts of two seasons in the major leagues, died April 4 in Phoenix. He was 66.

Crider reached the majors in 1969, when he

made 20 appearances out of the Twins bullpen, going 1-0, 4.66 in 29 innings. After a trade to the White Sox, he made 24 relief appearances and eight starts, going 4-7, 4.45 in 91 innings in 1970.

■ **Chuck Daniel**, a righthander who made one appearance for the 1957 Tigers, died Jan. 1 in Hot Springs, Ark. He was 74.

■ **Deacon Donahue**, a righthander who accumulated 13 innings for the Phillies in 1943 and 1944 as part of a four-year pro career, died March 6 in Glenview, Ill. He was 87.

■ **Don Eaddy**, a third baseman who played eight professional seasons and had two brief stints with the Cubs in 1959, died on July 9 in Laconia, N.H. He was 74. He appeared in 15 games for the Cubs, mostly as a pinch runner.

■ **Terry Enyart**, a lefthander who appeared in two games for the Montreal Expos in 1974, died Feb. 15, 2007, in Zephyrhillis, Fla. He was 56.

■ **Hal Erickson**, a righthander who made 18 appearances for the 1953 Tigers, died Feb. 18 in Ogden, Utah. He was 88.

As a 33-year-old rookie, Erickson made 18 appearances out of the Detroit bullpen in 1953. He went 0-1, 4.78 in 32 big league innings before being sent back to the minors in mid-July.

■ **Bob Ferguson**, a righthander who appeared in nine games for the 1944 Reds, died May 23 in Wetumpka, Ala. He was 89. Ferguson spent much of the first half of the 1944 season with the Reds, but struggled in his nine appearances, including two starts, going 0-3, 9.00 in 16 innings.

■ **Roy Foster**, an outfielder who played in three seasons for the Indians in the 1970s, died March 21 in Tulsa. He was 62.

Foster's rookie season would turn out to be his best. In semi-regular play, the 24-year-old batted .268/.357/.468 with 23 homers and 60 RBIs in 477 at-bats. Foster went on to hit .253/.336/.438 with 45 home runs and 118 RBIs in 1,016 career big league at-bats.

■ **Alex Garbowski**, a shortstop who appeared in two games for the 1952 Tigers, died June 27 in Putnam Valley, N.Y. He was 86.

■ **Russ Gibson**, a catcher who played professionally for 16, died on July 27 in Swansea, Mass. He was 69.

Over six big league seasons spent with the Red Sox and Giants, Gibson hit .228/.267/.311 with 34 doubles, four triples, eight home runs and 78 RBIs.

■ **Jim Goodwin**, a lefthander who appeared in eight games for the 1948 White Sox, died April 12 in St. Louis. He was 81.

Goodwin opened the 1948 season in Chicago and appeared in eight games, including one start, but struggled to an 8.71 ERA in 11 innings and didn't figure in any decisions.

■ **Julio Gotay**, a shortstop who played 10 seasons in the major leagues with four different teams, died July 4 in Ponce, Puerto Rico. He was 69.

Gotay got to spend a full season in the majors for the first time in 1962, when he was the Cardinals' everyday shortstop for most of the season. He hit a respectable .255 in 369 at-bats that year.

That offseason, Gotay was part of a trade that landed the Cardinals all-star shortstop Dick Groat from the Pirates, in exchange for Gotay and righthander Don Cardwell. However, Gotay never got a chance to play everyday in Pittsburgh, and moved from the Pirates to the Angels to the Astros over his last six seasons. He ended his career in 1969 with a line of .260/.309/.323 in 988 major league at-bats.

■ **Herb Hash**, a righthander who pitched two seasons for the Red Sox, died May 20 in Culpeper, Va. He was 97.

Hash made 34 apperances, including 12 starts, for the 1940 Red Sox. He went 7-7, 3.27 with three complete games. He started the 1941 season with Red Sox, but was sent back to the minor leagues after posting a 5.63 ERA in four relief apperances.

■ **Ray Hoffman**, an infielder who played three professional seasons, died May 30 in Milton, Calif. He was 90. In 1942, Hoffman breifly joined the Washington Senators. He had 19 at-bats with the big club and recorded one major league hit.

■ **Tommy Holmes**, an outfielder who played 11 seasons in the major leagues with the Boston Braves and Brooklyn Dodgers, died April 14 in Boca Raton, Fla. He was 91.

Holmes hit .278 with four home runs and 48 RBIs as a rookie in 1942, and in 1944, he began a streak of five straight seasons in which he hit over .300. He had his best season in 1945, hitting .352 and leading the National League in home runs (28), hits (224) and doubles (47). He knocked in 117 runs as well to finish second to the Cubs' Phil Cavarretta in MVP balloting.

Holmes spent parts of the 1951 and '52 seasons as a player-manager with the Braves. He signed with the Brooklyn Dodgers after being fired by the Braves in May 1952. Holmes batted .302/.366/.432 with 1,507 hits, 88 home runs and 581 RBIs in 4,992 career big league at-bats.

■ **Cal Howe**, a lefthander who made one appearance for the 1952 Cubs, died May 5 in

Grand Rapids, Mich. He was 83.

Howe's lone major league appearance came on Sept. 26, 1952, when he pitched two scoreless innings of relief against the Cardinals.

■ **Bob Howsam**, one-time general manager of the Reds and Cardinals, died Feb. 19 in Sun City, Ariz. He was 89.

Howsam spent three seasons as GM of the Cardinals, helping them win the 1964 World Series, before enjoying an 11-year run with the Reds. Howsam helped build the The Big Red Machine that won four pennants and two World Series in the 1970s.

■ **Ken Hunt**, a righthander with the 1961 Reds, died Jan. 27 in Morgan, Utah. He was 69.

Hunt appeared in 29 games for Cincinnati, going 9-10, 3.97, with four complete games.

■ **Ron Jackson**, a first baseman who played in seven big league seasons, died on July 6 in Kalamazoo, Mich. He was 74.

In 1954, Jackson made his major league debut with the White Sox and hit .280 with four home runs over 93 at-bats. Jackson never started for the White Sox, but played in parts of six seasons.

After the 1959 season when the White Sox went to the World Series, Jackson was traded to the Red Sox for lefthander Frank Baumann. Jackson was traded again in the middle of the 1960 season to the Milwaukee Braves for catcher Ray Boone, but never played for their big league club.

■ **Art Johnson**, a lefthander who pitched three seasons for the Boston Braves, died April 27 in Holden, Mass. He was 88. From 1940 through '42, Johnson went 7-16, 3.68 over 196 innings.

■ **Niles Jordan**, a lefthander who played in parts of two major league seasons, died March 15 in Sedo-Wooley, Wash. He was 81.

Jordan went 2-4, 4.19 with 13 strikeouts, 11 walks and five home runs allowed in 43 career innings for the Phillies and Reds in 1951 and '52.

■ **Joe Kennedy**, a lefthander who pitched for five big league teams in seven seasons, died Nov. 23, 2007, in Brandon, Fla. He was 28.

He went 7-8, 4.44 in 20 starts for Tampa Bay as a 22-year-old rookie. Tampa Bay shipped him to the Rockies in December 2003 as part of a three-team trade. Kennedy would enjoy his best season in 2004, going 9-7, 3.66 in 163 innings.

Kennedy struggled out of the gate in 2005, and the Rockies flipped him to the Athletics in July. The Diamondbacks then claimed him on waivers in August 2007, before releasing him two weeks later. The Blue Jays signed him shortly thereafter.

Kennedy went 43-61, 4.79 with 558 strikeouts and 335 walks in 909 innings.

■ **George Kissel**, a longtime member of the Cardinals organization and one of baseball's unsung heroes, died Oct. 7 in Tampa. He was 88.

Kissell joined the Cardinals in 1940 when he was signed to a contract by Branch Rickey after trying out in New York and then went on to serve in the Redbirds' minor league system as a manager and instructor.

Despite his age, Kissell had remained active in the Cardinals organization, not only offering tips to minor leaguers during spring training but occasionally dropping in to visit affiliates.

In 2003, Kissell was the recipient of the Roland Hemond award presented by Baseball America.

Kissell spent 10 years in the minor leagues as an infielder. From 1946 to 1968, he worked as a manager, coach, scout and minor league instructor.

He also served as a coach for the big league club from 1969 to 1975 and was a special field assistant to general manager Bing Devine in 1976.

■ **Karl Kuehl**, who once managed the Montreal Expos and went on to become one of the most respected men in baseball, died Aug. 6 in Phoenix. He was 70.

Kuehl was named winner of the Roland Hemond Award at baseball's winter meetings in 2006 for his long-term contributions to scouting and player development.

Kuehl was the second manager in Montreal Expos history but was fired in his only season managing the club as the team let him go on Sept. 4, 1976, when the Expos were 43-85. He had managed their Triple-A club in Memphis the prior season.

■ **Jack Lamabe**, who won 33 games in seven big league seasons and became a coach at Louisiana State, died Dec. 21, 2007, in Baton Rouge. He was 71.

Lamabe went 7-4, 3.15 for the Red Sox in 1963 in a remarkable 151 innings despite making all but two of his appearances out of the bullpen. Lamabe joined the White Sox in 1966, when he went 7-9, 3.93 in 121 innings. The highlight of his season came when he tossed a no-hitter against the Red Sox. He finished his major league career with the Cubs in 1968, having gone 33-41, 4.24 with 238 strikeouts in 711 2/3 innings.

■ **Dario Lodigiani**, a second and third baseman who spent parts of six seasons with the Philadelphia Athletics and White Sox during the late 1930s and '40s, died Feb. 10 in Napa, Calif.

He was 91. For his big league career, Lodigiani batted .260/.338/.358 in 405 career games.

■ **Hersh Lyons**, a righthander who made one appearance for the 1941 Cardinals, died April 8 in Inglewood, Calif. He was 93.

■ **Bob Marquis**, an outfielder who played in 40 games for the Reds in 1953, died Nov. 28, 2007, in Beaumont, Texas. He was 82.

After six years in the minors, Marquis got his crack at the big leagues in 1953, hitting .273/.333/.477 with two home runs in 44 at-bats for Cincinnati.

■ **Cuddles Marshall**, a righthander who threw 185 innings in the majors as part of an eight-year pro career, died Dec. 14, 2007, in Santa Clarita, Calif. He was 82.

In 1946, Marshall broke into the majors as a 21-year-old with the Yankees, going 3-4, 5.33 in 81 innings. Marshall returned to the majors in 1948, though only for one game. In 1949, Marshall went 3-0, 5.11 with three saves in 21 games for the Yankees.

Marshall pitched one more major league season for the St. Louis Browns in 1950, finishing 1-3, 7.83 in 28 games. He went 7-7, 5.98 with 69 strikeouts and 158 walks in 185 big league innings.

■ **John Marzano**, a catcher who spent 10 seasons in the major leagues, died April 19 in Philadelphia. He was 45.

Marzano was the Red Sox' first-round pick (14th overall) in 1984 and needed only two full seasons in the minor leagues, reaching Boston in July of 1987. Marzano hit .244 with five home runs and 24 RBIs in 168 at-bats in his rookie year.

Marzano spent parts of three seasons as Boston's backup catcher, but war released in 1993. Marzano later spent three seasons as the Mariners' primary backup catcher. He retired with .241/.289/.344 averages in 301 career big league games. After retiring, he embarked on a career in television.

■ **Walt Masterson**, a righthander who pitched 14 seasons for three teams in the major leagues, died April 5 in Durham, N.C. He was 87.

One of the AL's youngest players early in his career, Masterson found his stride in 1947, going 12-16, 3.13 in 253 innings. He set career bests in wins, strikeouts (135), innings and ERA that year and made one of two all-star appearances.

Masterson got off to another strong start the in 1949 but was traded to the Red Sox at midseason. Masterson would spent two more seasons in Boston, primarily being used out of the bullpen,

before being dealt back to the Senators in 1952. He finished his career in 1957 with a career record of 78-100, 4.15, with 815 strikeouts and 886 walks in 1,650 innings.

■ **John McHale**, a first baseman who spent parts of five seasons with the Tigers from 1943 to '48 and later served as a big league executive for 28 years, died Jan. 17 in Stuart, Fla. He was 86.

After retiring as a player, McHale returned to baseball in 1957, beginning a 28-year front office career with four major league clubs, including an 18-year run as President of the Montreal Expos from 1969 to 1986.

■ **Steve Mingori**, a lefthander who pitched 10 seasons in the major leagues for the Indians and Royals, died July 10 in Kansas City, Mo. He was 64.

After being dealt to the Royals from the Indians in June 1973, Mingori immediately became an important part of Kansas City's bullpen as the Royals dominated the AL West in the late 1970s.

As the Royals claimed the division title in 1976, Mingori enjoyed his best season with the club, going 5-5, 2.33 in 55 appearances. Mingori went 2-4, 3.09 in 43 appearances in 1977 as the Royals won the division again. He had another successful season in 1978, posting a 2.74 ERA in 69 innings, but his Royals lost the ALCS to the Yankees for the third straight year. Mingori would finish his career with a 3.03 ERA over 385 games and 584 innings.

■ **Billy Muffett**, a righthander who pitched six seasons in the major leagues, died June 15 in Monroe, La. He was 77.

He got his first crack at the major leagues in 1957, when he made 23 relief appearances for the Cardinals and went 3-2, 2.25 in 44 innings. After going 4-6, 4.93 for St. Louis in 1958, the Cardinals traded him to the Giants. But Muffett would appear in only five games for San Francisco before being traded again, this time to the Red Sox.

He spent the entire 1961 season in Boston, but posted a 3-11, 5.65 mark and then made only one appearance in 1962.

■ **Bobby Murcer**, a five-time all-star outfielder who spent 17 seasons in the big leagues, mostly with the Yankees, died July 12 in Oklahoma City after a battle with brain cancer. He was 62.

In his prime, Murcer provided the Yankees with a durable, well-rounded center fielder who made five consecutive all-star teams and finished in the top 10 of AL MVP voting in three straight years from 1971 to 1973. In the best of those peak seasons, Murcer batted .331/.427/.543 with 25 home runs, 25 doubles, 91 walks, 14 stolen bases and 94 RBIs for the 1971 Yankees.

But after a down year in 1974, the Yankees traded Murcer to the Giants for Bobby Bonds. He played well for San Francisco, and then for the Cubs from 1977 to 1979, until a trade brought him back to the Bronx in June '79. Murcer played well in his first two seasons back with the Yankees, as a part-time outfielder and DH, but faded in 1982 and '83. He spent most of the next two decades as a Yankees announcer. Murcer batted .277/.357/.445 in 6,730 career at-bats, with 252 home runs, 1,043 RBIs, 862 walks and 841 strikeouts.

■ **Don Nicholas**, who played sparingly for the White Sox and who won six minor league stolen base titles, died October 23, 2007, in Garden Grove, Calif. He was 76.

Nicholas' running prowess earned him a callup in 1952 in which he appeared in three games and went 0-for-2. He also returned to the majors in 1954, appearing in seven games.

■ **Joe Nuxhall**, a lefthander who pitched in 16 big league seasons—predominantly for the Reds—and was the youngest major leaguer of the 20th century, died Nov. 15, 2007, in Fairfield, Ohio.

The Reds accidentally discovered Nuxhall in 1944 when scouting his 34-year-old father, Orville, to fill their roster during World War II. Though he spent much of that season on the bench, Nuxhall appeared in his one game on June 10, making him the youngest player ever to debut in the big leagues at 15 years, 10 months and 11 days.

Nuxhall didn't pitch in the majors again for eight years, but he was a fixture on the Reds pitching staff from that point forward, throwing more than 100 innings in every season but one from 1953 to 1966.

Nuxhall's finest season was probably 1955, when at age 26 he went 17-12, 3.47 in 257 innings for the Reds. After his playing career ended in 1966, Nuxhall called Reds games from 1967 to 2004, working mostly with Marty Brennaman. A two-time all-star, Nuxhall went 135-117, 3.90 in 2,303 big league innings.

■ **Johnny Podres**, a lefthander who won two games against the Yankees—including the deciding Game 7—in Brooklyn's first-ever World Series championship in 1955, died Jan. 13 in Glens Falls, N.Y.

Podres went a pedestrian 9-10, 3.95 in 1955 for a juggernaut Dodgers team that won 98 games

and led the second-place Braves by 13 1/2 games. Thus, nobody could have been prepared for Podres' superhuman performance in the World Series against the rival Yankees. Podres allowed three runs in a complete-game win in Game 3, but saved his finest work for Game 7, when he pitched a shutout. He was named first-ever Series MVP for his fine work (2-0, 1.00 in 18 innings).

Podres went on to pitch 12 more seasons, making three all-star teams and winning the World Series twice more with Los Angeles-based Dodgers teams in 1959 and 1963. For his career, he went 148-116, 3.68 with 1,435 strikeouts and 743 walks in 2,265 innings over 15 seasons.

■ **Bob Purkey**, a knuckleballer who spent 13 seasons in the big leagues, died March 16 in Bethel Park, Pa. He was 78.

After debuting with the Pirates, Purkey blossomed in Cincinnati, where he went on to become a three-time all-star. Purkey went 16-12, 3.73 in 1961 as the Reds won the National League pennant and started Game 3 of the 1961 World Series against the Yankees. He pitched a complete game but took a 3-2 loss.

Purkey had his finest season the following year, when he went 23-5, 2.81 for the Reds. He made the All-Star team and finished third in Cy Young balloting. Unfortunately, Purkey was unable to repeat that success in following seasons. Purkey pitched four more years, finishing his career with a 129-115 record and a career ERA of 3.79.

■ **Bill Ramsey**, an outfielder who appeared in 78 games for the wartime Boston Braves in 1945 as part of a 13-year pro career, died Jan. 4 in Memphis. He was 86. Ramsey hit .292/.326/.372 for the Braves, but never got another shot at the big leagues.

■ **Dave Ricketts**, a catcher who played six seasons in the major leagues, died July 13 St. Louis. He was 73.

Ricketts was the Cardinals backup catcher for most of their pennant winning 1967 season, appearing in 52 games and hitting .273 in 99 at-bats. He went on to hit .249/.278/.305 over 213 career at-bats with the Cardinals and Pirates.

■ **Steve Ridzik**, a righthander who pitched for five big league teams in 12 seasons, died Jan. 8 in Bradenton, Fla.

Starting in 1952, Ridzik spent part or all of seven seasons working mostly as a reliever for the Phillies, Reds, New York Giants and Indians. His 1953 season might have been his best. Ridzik made 12 starts that year (out of 42 games), going 9-6, 3.77 in 124 innings for the Phillies. Ridzik went 39-38, 3.79 with 406 strikeouts and 351 walks in 782 2/3 big league innings.

■ **Harry "Lefty" Schaeffer**, a lefthander who pitched nine professional seasons, including a brief stint with the Yankees in 1952, died July 12 in Shillington, Pa. He was 84.

■ **Bert Shepard**, who appeared in one game for the Washington Senators in 1945 despite having lost his right leg the previous year during combat in World War II, died June 18 in Highland, Calif. He was 87.

Active professionally from 1939 to 1955, Shepard managed to pitch in eight seasons after 1944, when his right leg was amputated below the knee after his fighter plane was shot down over Germany.

Senators owner Clark Griffith hired Shepard as pitching coach in 1945, but on Aug. 4 of that year, with Washington embroiled in its fourth doubleheader in four days and with the team trailing the Red Sox 14-2 in the fourth inning, the call to the bullpen was made for Shepard. Impressively, he went 5 1/3 innings, striking out two and giving up a lone run on three hits and a walk. The Senators lost 15-4, and Shepard stayed on as pitching coach for most of 1946.

■ **Clancy Smyres**, a second baseman who appeared in five games for the 1944 Brooklyn Dodgers, died Nov. 27, 2007, in San Fernando, Calif. He was 88.

■ **Gerry Staley**, a righthander who won 134 games and saved 61 others in a 15-year big league career spent mostly with the Cardinals and White Sox, died Jan. 2 in Hazel Dell, Wash. He was 87.

Staley established himself as a reliever for the Cardinals in 1947. While bouncing between the bullpen and the rotation in 1949, he finished second in the National League with a 2.73 ERA and a 1.14 WHIP.

He moved into the rotation permanently in 1951 at age 29 where Staley served as one of the Redbirds top starters. Beginning in '51 he rattled off his three finest seasons as a starter, going 19-13, 3.81; 17-14, 3.27; and 18-9, 3.99 all in successive seasons. For his career, Staley went 134-111, 3.70 with 727 strikeouts in 1,982 innings.

■ **Chuck Stobbs**, a lefthander who pitched 15 seasons in the major leagues, died July 11 in Sarasota, Fla. He was 79.

Stobbs was the American League's youngest player at the time of his big league debut at age 18 in 1947. His best year in Boston came in 1949,

when he went 11-6, 4.03 for the Red Sox team that fell just short of winning the pennant. After the 1951 season, the Red Sox shipped Stobbs to the White Sox, and he responded with one of his best seasons in the big leagues, going 7-12, 3.13. However, his stay in Chicago was short lived, as the White Sox sent him to the Washington Senators after the season.

Stobbs would spent the bulk of the rest of his career in Washington, finishing with a career 107-130, 4.29 record over 459 appearances.

■ **Rene Valdez**, a Cuban-born righthander who appeared in five games for the Brooklyn Dodgers in 1957, died March 16 in Miami. He was 78.

■ **Porter Vaughan**, a lefthander who pitched three seasons in the majors, died July 30 in Richmond. He was 89.

Vaughan went straight to the major leagues out of college, making his debut with the Philadelphia Athletics in June 1940. He made 15 starts and went 2-9, 5.36 that summer. Perhaps most memorably, Vaughan was one of the pitchers Ted Williams faced on the final day of the 1941 season, when Williams played both games of a doubleheader and maintained his average over .400. A shoulder injury cut his baseball career short.

■ **Carlos Velazquez**, a Puerto Rico-born righthander who appeared in 18 games for the 1973 Milwaukee Brewers died March 16, 2000, in Loiza, P.R. He was 51.

Velazquez earned his first and only big league callup at the end of the 1973 season, going 2-2, 2.61 in 38 relief innings for the Brewers.

■ **Ken Wood**, an outfielder who played for the Red Sox, St. Louis Browns and Washington Senators in the late 1940s and '50s as part of a 14-year pro career, died Nov. 22, 2007, in Myrtle Beach, S.C. He was 83. Wood hit .224/.298/.393 with 34 home runs in 995 career at-bats.

■ **Floyd Wooldridge**, a righthander who pitched one season in the major leagues for the 1955 Cardinals, died May 14 in Springfield, Mo. He was 79.

Wooldridge reached the majors in 1955, when he made 18 appearances, including eight starts, for the Cardinals. Wooldridge went 2-4, 4.81 in 58 innings before being sent back to the minors.

■ **Al Yates**, an outfielder who appeared in 24 games for the 1971 Brewers, died Nov. 23, 2007, in Miami. He was 62. After seven seasons in the minors, Yates got his one and only taste of the big leagues in 1971. He hit .277 with one home run and four RBIs in 47 at-bats for Milwaukee.

APPENDIX

WISH YOU'D GOTTEN YOUR ALMANAC SOONER?

Now if you order any of Baseball America's books and choose the Premium Shipping and Handling Option, your books will be shipped to you hot off the press via USPS Priority Mail. You'll get your books **FIRST**, before they hit the stores, giving you the fantasy league advantage or insider scoop you want.

Don't miss out: Pre-order next year's book **NOW!**